Encyclopedia of Information Systems and Services

INTERNATIONAL VOLUME

Related Titles Published by Gale Research Company

Encyclopedia of Information Systems and Services - United States Volume. Describes more than 2,200 U.S.-based information organizations, systems, and services of international, national, regional, or state scope.

New Information Systems and Services. Interedition supplement to the International and United States Volumes of the **Encyclopedia of Information Systems and Services.** Consists of two issues providing descriptions of nearly 800 new organizations and services in the fast moving information industry. Also includes update listings of data bases available through major online services.

Abstracting and Indexing Services Directory. Provides detailed descriptions of more than 2,000 abstracts journals, indexes, digests, serial bibliographies, and similar information access and alerting publications in all fields of knowledge. With publications, publishers, and keyword index.

Online Database Search Services Directory. Descriptions and analysis of the online search services provided by more than 1,000 libraries and information firms. Provides organization name, address, telephone, and key personal contact; search nature and activity information, such as annual amount of online connect hours, size of search staff, online services used, specific data bases searched, and subject fields; and availability information, including clientele served, fee policy, and search request procedure. Indexes by organization and service name, online systems used, data bases searched, search personnel, geographic location, and subject fields.

Telecommunications Systems and Services Directory. Detailed guide to national and international communications systems and services for the transmission of voice, data, text, and images. Specific areas covered include long-distance telephone services, data communications networks, teleconferencing services, electronic mail, facsimile, telex and telegram, satellite services, videotex/teletext communications services, local area networks, and transactional services such as home banking. Also covers telecommunications consultants, publishers and information sources, associations, research institutes, and regulatory bodies. Includes a telecommunications glossary and master, function/service, geographic, and personal name indexes.

ISSN 0734-9068

1985-86
Encyclopedia of Information Systems and Services

SIXTH EDITION (In Two Volumes)

An International Descriptive Guide to Approximately 3,300 Organizations, Systems, and Services Involved in the Production and Distribution of Information in Electronic Form

Including Data Base Producers and Their Products, Online Host Services and Time-Sharing Companies, Videotex/Teletext Information Services, Library and Information Networks, Bibliographic Utilities, Library Management Systems, Information Retrieval Software, Fee-Based Information on Demand Services, Document Delivery Sources, Data Collection and Analysis Centers and Firms, and Related Consultants, Service Companies, Professional and Trade Associations, Publishers, and Research Activities

INTERNATIONAL VOLUME

More Than 1,100 International and National Information Organizations, Systems, and Services Located in Approximately 65 Countries, Excluding the United States

Edited by
John Schmittroth, Jr.

Amy F. Lucas and Annette Novallo,
Associate Editors

Kathleen Young Marcaccio,
Contributing Editor

Gale Research Company • Book Tower • Detroit, Michigan 48226

Z
674.3
.K78
1985-86
v.1

John Schmittroth, Jr., *Editor*
Amy F. Lucas, *Associate Editor*
Annette Novallo, *Associate Editor*
Mark Paul Meade, *Assistant Editor*
Doris Sears, *Assistant Editor*
Christine Tomassini, *Assistant Editor*
Carol A. Wierzbicki, *Assistant Editor*

Kathleen Young Marcaccio, *Contributing Editor*
John Krol, *Contributing Associate Editor*
Janice A. DeMaggio, *Contributing Assistant Editor*

Dennis G. LaBeau, *Editorial Data Systems Director*
Donald G. Dillaman, *System Design and Development*
Robert D. Aitchison, *Data Entry Programmer*
Carol Blanchard, *Production Supervisor—External*
Dorothy Kalleberg, *External Production Assistant*
Arthur Chartow, *Art Director*

Frederick G. Ruffner, *Publisher*
James M. Ethridge, *Executive Vice President/Editorial*
Dedria Bryfonski, *Editorial Director*
John Schmittroth, Jr., *Director, Directories Division*

Library of Congress Cataloging in Publication Data

Main entry under title:

Encyclopedia of information systems and services.

   At head of title: 1985-86.
   Includes indexes.
   Contents: v. 1. International volume.

   1. Information services--Directories. 2. Information storage and retrieval systems--Directories. 3. Electronic publishing--Directories. 4. Information networks--Directories. 5. Bibliographical services--Directories. 6. Electronic data processing--Directories.
I. Schmittroth, John.
Z674.3.E52   1984   025.'.04'025   82-18359
ISBN 0-8103-1537-8 (set)
ISBN 0-8103-1538-6 (v. 1)

Copyright © 1971, 1974 by Anthony T. Kruzas
Copyright © 1978, 1981, 1982, 1985 by Gale Research Company

ISSN 0734-9068

Computerized photocomposition by
Computerized Composition Corporation
Madison Heights, Michigan

INTERNATIONAL VOLUME CONTENTS

This Encyclopedia is now published in separate International and United States volumes. See the Introduction for details.

INTRODUCTION 7
QUICK GUIDE TO USING THIS BOOK 10
CONTENT OF AN ENTRY 11
INDEX NOTES 13
INFORMATION SYSTEMS AND SERVICES DESCRIPTIVE LISTINGS 19

INDEXES

MASTER INDEX 425
DATA BASES INDEX 485
PUBLICATIONS INDEX 505
SOFTWARE INDEX 521
FUNCTION/SERVICE CLASSIFICATIONS 525
    Abstracting and Indexing 527
    Associations 531
    Community Information and Referral 531
    Computerized Searching 531
    Consultants 536
    Data Base Producers and Publishers 537
    Data Collection and Analysis 544
    Document Delivery 547
    Electronic Mail Applications 549
    Information on Demand 549
    Library and Information Networks 549
    Library Management Systems 550
    Magnetic Tape Providers 550
    Micrographic Applications 552
    Online Host Services 554
    Personal Computer Oriented Services 556
    Research and Research Projects 556
    SDI/Current Awareness 557
    Software Producers 559
    Videotex/Teletext Information Services 560
PERSONAL NAME INDEX 563
GEOGRAPHIC INDEX BY COUNTRY 589
    Argentina; Australia; Austria; Bahrain; Bangladesh; Belgium; Bolivia; Brazil; Bulgaria; Canada; Chile; China, People's Republic of; Colombia; Czechoslovakia; Denmark; Egypt; England; Ethiopia; Finland; France; German Democratic Republic; Germany, Federal Republic of; Guatemala; Hong Kong; Hungary; India; Indonesia; Iran; Ireland; Ireland, Northern; Israel; Italy; Japan; Kenya; Korea, Republic of; Luxembourg; Madagascar; Malaysia; Mexico; Morocco; Netherlands; New Zealand; Norway; Pakistan; Peru; Philippines; Poland; Portugal; Qatar; Romania; Scotland; Singapore; South Africa; Spain; Sweden; Switzerland; Taiwan; Tanzania; Thailand; Trinidad and Tobago; Tunisia; Turkey; Union of Soviet Socialist Republics; Wales; Yugoslavia.
SUBJECT INDEX 627

INTRODUCTION

This Edition 35% Larger; Published in Two Volumes

Reflecting the continued proliferation of the electronic information and publishing industries, this sixth edition of the *Encyclopedia of Information Systems and Services* contains approximately 35% more entries than the preceding edition published two years ago. This increase to a book that was already 1,250 pages in length has necessitated some sort of division of the material. Consequently, this edition is published in two volumes based on the geographic location of the organizations, systems, and services listed. Each volume comprises a main section of descriptive listings arranged alphabetically by parent organization name, together with a full set of indexes for the volume. The two volumes are as follows:

International Volume. Covers more than 1,100 international and national information organizations, systems, and services located in some 65 countries, excluding the United States.

United States Volume. Covers approximately 2,200 information organizations, systems, and services of international, national, or regional scope that are located in the United States and its territories and possessions.

The decision to divide the *Encyclopedia* geographically resulted from several considerations. One was the desire to offer individual volumes that could stand on their own, which an alphabetical split would obviously prevent. A subject arrangement of the material is complicated by the fact that entries in the *Encyclopedia* typically describe an overall system, service, or organization rather than an individual data base or publication; the increasingly multidisciplinary nature of the information sources described prevents them from being easily assigned to any single subject chapter. Finally, Gale Research Company has found considerable interest in its new international directories of research centers and associations, and it was felt that an international volume of the *Encyclopedia* (which has had international coverage since the second edition) would be equally useful. Comments and suggestions from users of the *Encyclopedia* regarding the new arrangement will be appreciated by the compilers.

Other New Features

In addition to more than 800 new entries and the two-volume format, the sixth edition introduces several other features. Continuing an effort that has extended over the past few editions, the amount of information and detail provided in entries has been expanded. One area of concentration for this edition has been in the descriptions of journals, newsletters, directories, user aids, and other publications listed in the "Publications" section of the entry. These descriptions have been expanded whenever possible with details on the types of articles, citations, or entries included, arrangement, number of listings, subject coverage, intended audience, indexes, and other information. Capsule descriptions have also been added where possible for data bases listed in online host service entries, to save the reader from having to locate the data base producer entry (which could be in the other volume of the *Encyclopedia*). To handle the longer entries that have evolved over the past few editions, a paragraph break has been introduced in typesetting to allow multiple paragraphs to appear within a single subheading in the entry format.

Another innovation with this edition—in recognition of the growing use of electronic mail—is the inclusion in the entry of the address or code through which an organization can be contacted on public electronic mail networks. This information (along with toll-free telephone and telex numbers when known) is provided in the "Contact" section at the end of the entry.

There have been two major changes in indexing. Indexes 6-20 that appeared in the fifth edition have been consolidated into the "Function/Service Classifications" index, which includes the previous 15 categories along with several new classifications. In the Subject Index, the complete organization name is now provided along with the entry number under subject headings. It is hoped that this will enable the user to further refine the search before consulting the cited listings.

Preparation of This International Volume

The *Encyclopedia of Information Systems and Services* has featured international coverage since an initial expansion occurred with the second edition published in 1974. For the International Volume of the sixth edition, all non-U.S. organizations that were described in the previous edition and its supplements were given several opportunities to review and update their listings, and several hundred new organizations were queried for information. This process resulted in hundreds of new or completely revised listings appearing in these pages, and thousands of changes in address, telephone number, personal names, etc. The International Volume contains some 1,120 entries, compared to about 850 international listings in the previous edition; approximately 10 percent of the previous listings have been dropped since the organizations involved have gone out of business or have redirected their activities. In a few cases, current information could not be obtained on a previously listed organization. If the continued operation of the organization could be verified through other sources, the listing has been reprinted from the fifth edition, with a "Special Note" provided at the beginning of the text portion of the entry to alert the reader to these circumstances.

In general, the International Volume of the *Encyclopedia of Information Systems and Services* treats information organizations, systems, and services that are truly international in scope—in that they involve or cover multiple countries— as well as operations of national scope in countries with significant information activities. (Excluded from this volume is any organization located in the United States, although the international offices of major U.S.-based firms are included in selected instances.) It is hoped that the *Encyclopedia*'s new two-volume format will provide a framework for the continued broadening and deepening of its international coverage. Further systematic surveys will be carried out to identify additional national scientific and technological information centers, national statistical offices, and national members of international information networks in an effort to gather information on systems and services appropriate for inclusion in the *Encyclopedia*. The contribution of information and suggestions from users of the International Volume is welcome.

Scope of the Encyclopedia

While significant recent developments in the information industry are reflected in this sixth edition, the essential scope of the *Encyclopedia* remains unchanged from the past few editions. The *Encyclopedia* is intended to be a comprehensive international guide to organizations, systems, and services using computers and related new technologies to produce and/or provide access to information and data of all types in all subject fields. Generally speaking, the organizations, systems, and services covered may be grouped into the following categories (with some overlapping):

1. *Information providers* that produce electronically accessible information of interest beyond their own organizations. These include publishers, professional associations, libraries, commercial firms, government agencies, educational institutions, and others. Two trends in the type of information being provided are apparent in this edition. On the one hand, there is an increasing number of data bases devoted to high technology topics such as biotechnology, robotics, telecommunications, computers, software, and others. At the same time, reduced computer and communications costs have resulted in the proliferation of full-text information online, including popular-interest information on such topics as travel, leisure, and sports.

2. *Information access services* that use electronic means to facilitate access to information produced by themselves or others. Included in this category are online host services, time-sharing companies, videotex/teletext information services, fee-based information on demand firms, bibliographic utilities, demographic and marketing data companies, and others. This edition reflects several trends in information access, including a growing number of online services dedicated to a specific profession or industry, information producers operating their own online access services, online services developing their own data bases, and gateway services providing access to multiple online host computers.

3. *Information sources on the information industry,* including associations, market and academic research organizations, reference publishers, and other organizations that analyze and provide information about the electronic information and publishing industries.

4. *Support services,* including consultants, service companies, and system houses that provide services and products specifically for the information industry. Excluded are hardware and equipment manufacturers.

Arrangement and Content of Entries

The main body in each of the International and United States Volumes of the *Encyclopedia* is arranged by parent organization name in a single alphabetic sequence. Foreign-language names are listed under the English translations whenever possible, with the vernacular supplied afterward when known. Both the vernacular foreign-language and English versions and their acronyms are listed in the Master Index. Government agencies are listed under the name of the country or other jurisdiction that operates them, and are indexed under both the government name and the agency name. The content of individual entries is as detailed as permitted by the materials supplied by the responding organization. Up to 17 categories of information are provided for each entry; these are listed and explained in a separate section following this Introduction.

Indexes

This edition of the *Encyclopedia* contains 27 indexes, 20 of which are grouped within the new "Function/ Service Classifications" section. The indexes are designed to provide in-depth access to and detailed analysis of the information contained in descriptive listings in the main body of the *Encyclopedia*. The Index Notes section following this Introduction explains each of the indexes; it should be consulted to insure full utilization of the many access points available and to obtain a full understanding of this book.

Related Titles

Gale Research Company publishes several directories related to the *Encyclopedia of Information Systems and Services*. Following is a description of each of these, comparing its coverage with that of the *Encyclopedia*:

New Information Systems and Services. A supplement to the *Encyclopedia* that appears in two issues between editions. The supplement covers both international and United States systems, services, and organizations that are either newly formed or newly identified and contacted. *New Information Systems and Services* also carries update lists of data bases offered by the major online host services. The index in the second issue is cumulative.

Abstracting and Indexing Services Directory. A directory of more than 2,000 abstracts journals, indexes, and related printed publications. Provides considerable detail on the publications listed, including in-depth analyses of scope, subjects, arrangement, etc., as well as circulation, price, and ordering information. Approximately 35 percent of the titles listed in this *Directory* also appear (with less detail) in the *Encyclopedia* since they are produced from computer information systems described here.

Online Database Search Services Directory. Provides extensive information and indexing for the online retrieval services offered by more than 1,000 libraries and information firms. Approximately 85 percent of the services covered in this *Directory* do not appear in the *Encyclopedia,* since the *Encyclopedia* excludes coverage of library search operations. The remaining 15 percent of the entries are for fee-based information firms that are covered in both directories. However, *Online Database Search Services Directory* provides much more information on the retrieval services offered and includes indexes which list users of specific data bases and online services.

Telecommunications Systems and Services Directory. International descriptive guide covering systems and services for the transmission of voice, data, images, and text, ranging from long-distance telephone services to satellite communications facilities, and from teleconferencing services to local area networks. There is approximately a 10 percent overlap with the *Encyclopedia* (in the areas of videotex/teletext and data communications networks), but the telecommunications directory emphasizes the communications and technical aspects of these services while the *Encyclopedia* focuses on the information available through them.

Custom Selections and Computer Tapes Now Available

Custom computerized selections of information in the sixth edition of *Encyclopedia of Information Systems and Services* are available from Gale. Selections can be made by geographic location, subject field, function/service type, and other categories of information appearing in the standard entry format. Produced via laser printer, the selections can include the complete text of entries or selected data, such as organization name, address, telephone number, and chief executive. Computer tapes of information in the *Encyclopedia* are also available by license for internal use. Details on these services can be obtained from the editor of the *Encyclopedia*.

Acknowledgments

The cooperation of the information professionals who took the time to respond to our questionnaires and telephone requests is greatly appreciated in this time of incessant information industry surveys. The *Encyclopedia*'s editorial staff is again thanked for their outstanding dedication and talents.

QUICK GUIDE TO USING THIS BOOK

Following is a brief guide to using the *Encyclopedia of Information Systems and Services,* emphasizing typical questions that the book answers. For additional details on the nature, scope, organization, and indexes of this *Encyclopedia,* consult the Introduction, Content of an Entry, and Index Notes sections.

**This International Volume covers only organizations located
outside of the United States**

To Find Information on a Specific ORGANIZATION, COMPANY, SYSTEM, or SERVICE: Look up the name in the Master Index, the first index in the back of this book. The Master Index lists the names and many acronyms of all organizations, companies, systems, and services appearing in descriptive listings in the main section. The number appearing after names in this index is the *entry* number of a descriptive listing rather than a page number. A name may be listed more than once in this index, indicating that there is more than one entry in which the name appears. Within the cited entry, the name may appear in boldface at the beginning of the entry or anywhere within the text, so it may be necessary to read through the entire listing to locate the information sought. Former names and foreign language names are also listed in the index when they appear in entries.

To Find Information on a Specific DATA BASE, PUBLICATION, or SOFTWARE PRODUCT: Consult the Master Index as above. This Index includes the names and many acronyms of all data bases, publications, software products, projects, conferences, etc. discussed in the text of entries. Note that the name may appear anywhere within the text of the listing referred to. (This volume also contains a Data Bases Index, Publications Index, and Software Index for users requiring separate listings of such products, but all entries in the three indexes are also included in the Master Index.)

To Find a DATA BASE on a Specific SUBJECT: Use the Subject Index, the last index in the back of this book. The Subject Index is primarily an index to the information available in computer data bases. It enables the user to locate data bases on topics ranging from agricultural research to stocks and bonds, and from toxicology to art and art history. (In addition to indexing data bases, the Subject Index selectively covers service activities such as market research or consulting as they relate to concerns of the information industry, such as office automation or computerized searching.) The Index includes many "see" and "see also" references to guide the user to proper subject headings. For the first time with this edition of the *Encyclopedia,* the full organization name appears under headings in the Subject Index, enabling the user to further refine the search. The number appearing in parentheses after the organization name in the Subject Index is the entry number of a listing in the main section.

To Find Organizations, Systems, and Services Involved in a Particular TYPE OF ACTIVITY or SERVICE: Consult the Function/Service Classifications Index. This Index classifies organizations, systems, and services described in the main section by their chief functions or types of services provided, using 20 categories ranging from Abstracting and Indexing to Videotex/Teletext Information Services. Entries appear alphabetically in all applicable categories, and the categories can be cross-checked against each other to produce more specific groupings. An explanation of the categories used is provided at the beginning of the Index. (The Function/Service Classifications represents a consolidation of indexes 6 through 20 in the fifth edition of the *Encyclopedia,* with the addition of several new classifications.)

To Find Organizations Located in a Specific COUNTRY or CITY: Consult the Geographic Index in the back of this book. Countries are listed in alphabetical order, from Argentina to Yugoslavia. Within each country, entries are subarranged alphabetically by city. Listings in the Geographic Index provide full organization and system or service name, address, telephone number, director name, and the number of the entry in the main section.

To Find a PERSON: Consult the Personal Name Index. This Index lists alphabetically persons reported as directors at the beginning of entries as well as persons reported under the "Contact" section at the end of entries.

CONTENT OF AN ENTRY

Information provided in entries in the *Encyclopedia* is based on questionnaire responses and descriptive literature submitted by the respondents. Entries are as detailed as permitted by the amount of information in the response. The following categories of data are typically included in an entry, in the order listed.

1. NAME, ADDRESS, AND TELEPHONE NUMBER. All entries include the name of an organization and, as applicable, important subunits and the particular system, service, or activity being described. Entries are arranged in a single alphabetic order by the name of the institution, organization, company, or agency which directly supports, houses, or administers the program. (A sequential number precedes each entry and is used in the indexes to refer to it.) Names in languages other than English are listed under the English-language translation whenever possible, with the foreign version following immediately afterwards in parentheses. All national government agencies are grouped under the names of their respective countries. Beneath the organization or system name appear the street location and/or mailing address and the telephone number as supplied by the respondent. If provided, alternate addresses, telex numbers, and electronic mail addresses are given under the "Contact" subheading at the end of the entry.

2. FOUNDED/SERVICE ESTABLISHED. The year when the organization was founded or when the particular system or service was established.

3. HEAD OF UNIT. Name and title of the director or administrator directly in charge of the activity.

4. STAFF. Respondents were asked to provide the total number of staff and a breakdown in the following categories: information and library professional; management professional; technicians; sales and marketing; clerical and nonprofessional; and other. Additional categories, such as subject specialist, are listed separately if provided in the response.

5. RELATED ORGANIZATIONS. Name and relationship of affiliated institutions, parent companies, government agencies, or departments, as well as nonrelated organizations providing major sources of external financial support.

6. DESCRIPTION OF SYSTEM OR SERVICE. A detailed general statement describing each program and its mission, purposes, and functions. Introduces specific activities that are fully explained elsewhere in the entry.

7. SCOPE AND/OR SUBJECT MATTER. Principal areas of interest, type of activity, or subject emphasis of the specific unit being described.

8. INPUT SOURCES. Major sources of input for the information activities described, including types of literature surveyed, documents acquired, data collected, indexing and abstracting publications searched, tape services leased, and products of online access.

9. HOLDINGS AND STORAGE MEDIA. Type and quantity of stored information in all forms, including the number of items and the time period covered by machine-readable files, and other published and unpublished material, raw data, card files, and micrographic holdings. Library holdings and special files are also listed when included in response.

10. PUBLICATIONS. Title, frequency, and description of journals, newsletters, directories, user aids, and other publications issued by the facility. Conditions of availability (excluding price) are also given, as are the name and address of the supplying organization if different from that of the reporting organization. Publications listed generally fall into three categories: titles in any subject area that are derived from computer-readable data bases; user aids, technical manuals, and other documentation for data bases, online services, or software products; and newsletters, journals, and directories about the information industry.

11. MICROFORM PRODUCTS AND SERVICES. Form, size, and conditions of availability of microforms produced or distributed by reporting unit. Significant internal utilization and applications of micrographic products and equipment are also included when this information has been supplied.

12. COMPUTER-BASED PRODUCTS AND SERVICES. Applications of computer technology in all areas of information provision and access. For information providers, includes details on their computer-readable data bases, especially the means of obtaining online or other access to them. For information access organizations, lists the data bases or online systems used in providing their services and described the types of service provided, such as online access, computerized information retrieval, SDI, special tabulations, etc. Also covers software products or turnkey systems made available to other organizations for their in-house installation and use.

13. OTHER SERVICES. A listing of major services offered by the unit other than those given in items 6, 10, 11, and 12 above.

14. CLIENTELE/AVAILABILITY. Identification of user groups and clientele for whom services are provided. Also given here are the restrictions, if any, imposed on users either in terms of accessibility to the facility or its services, or limitations on reproduction, use, or application of information supplied by subscription, lease, or rental.

15. PROJECTED PUBLICATIONS AND SERVICES. New products and services which were in the process of implementation or in an advanced planning stage at the time this edition went to press.

16. REMARKS and ADDENDA. Additional information not adaptable to the standard entry format may be listed at the end of an entry. In this section may be found former names, alternate names, appropriate "see also" references, and other types of information.

17. CONTACT. Name and title (and address and telephone number if different from that given above in item 1) of the individual to be contacted for additional information on the products or services described in the entry. Also includes toll-free telephone numbers, telex numbers, and electronic mail addresses if supplied.

In addition to the above standard categories of information, a paragraph titled "Special Note:" is used at the beginning of the text portion of an entry if there are special or unusual circumstances involved (for example, if no response could be obtained for the current edition and the entry is being reprinted from the previous edition).

INDEX NOTES

A comprehensive analytical approach and a multiplicity of access points to the contents of this book are provided by 27 indexes (20 of which are grouped in the Function/Service Classifications). The nature and scope of each of the indexes are given below. The indexes refer to main section listings by entry number rather than page number.

MASTER INDEX. An all-inclusive, one-stop listing of the organizations, systems, products, and services described in this directory. Includes name and acronym entries, arranged alphabetically, for organizations and their subdivisions and for all distinctively named systems, services, data bases, publications, software products, conferences, projects, seminars, etc. (Data bases, publications, and software are also listed in separate indexes.) *Names listed here may appear in boldface at the beginning of the entry referred to or anywhere within the text of that entry.* National government agencies are listed under both the country name and the individual agency name. Foreign language names are included in this index.

DATA BASES INDEX. Machine-readable files produced by the organizations described in this book, including bibliographic, referral, full-text, numeric, statistical, online, videotex, offline, and other types of data bases. References in this index are generally made to the producing organization rather than to organizations providing online access or tape copies. In addition to actively maintained files, the index includes data bases that are no longer updated as well as those files in the process of being computerized for the first time. Data bases known by variant names and acronyms are entered under all approaches, including the names of corresponding publications if different. When there is no distinctive name for a file, it is listed under the name of the producing organization.

PUBLICATIONS INDEX. A listing of periodicals and other print and microform publications issued by the organizations described in this book. Among these are publications produced from computer-readable data bases (these are also listed in the Data Bases Index); user guides, search aids, and similar documentation; and newsletters, journals, and directories concerned with the information field.

SOFTWARE INDEX. Software produced or provided by organizations listed in this book. Generally they are for such applications as information retrieval, automatic indexing, library automation, data base management, photocomposition, statistical data base analysis, and other information work. Listed under both full name and acronym.

FUNCTION/SERVICE CLASSIFICATIONS. A consolidation of the separate indexes 6-20 in the fifth edition, with the addition of several new categories. Classifies organizations, systems, and services into 20 main categories according to their chief functions or types of services provided. Entries appear alphabetically in all applicable categories. The classifications can be cross-checked against each other or against terms in the Subject Index to produce more specific groupings. For example, firms that both produce data bases and operate online host services may be located by comparing the Data Base Producers and Publishers group against the Online Host Services category. Similarly, bibliographic data bases in the field of agriculture can be located by comparing the Abstracting and Indexing category against the appropriate subject headings in the Subject Index. Following are descriptions of the function/service classifications used. (New with this edition are Electronic Mail Applications, Magnetic Tape Providers, Personal Computer Oriented Services, and Software Producers.)

Abstracting and Indexing. Organizations whose activities include indexing, abstracting, or both. Emphasis is on organizations issuing computer-produced publications and bibliographic data bases that are publicly available.

Associations. Professional and trade associations and other membership groups with interests and programs in the information, electronic publishing, library automation, and related fields.

Community Information and Referral. Organizations using computer and micrographic technology to support the provision of referrals to human services agencies in their communities. Applications can include computer-generated microform or hardcopy directories of agencies, online searching in response to inquiries, demographic data collection and analysis, etc.

Computerized Searching. Organizations that conduct online or batch-mode current or retrospective retrieval from computer-readable data bases. Includes organizations using publicly available data bases as well as organizations providing services from their own files only.

Consultants. Organizations and services that provide consultation, and systems analysis and design in the fields of information provision and access.

Data Base Producers and Publishers. Organizations that create (or employ a contractor to create) computer-readable files of bibliographic or nonbibliographic information for internal use or public access. Data bases produced by these organizations are listed in the separate Data Bases Index.

Data Collection and Analysis. Organizations that collect, analyze, process, evaluate, and disseminate raw numeric data in such fields as social science, science and technology, economics, and medicine. Includes standard data reference centers, social science data archives, commercial demographic and marketing firms, government agencies, research institutes, and other organizations.

Document Delivery. Organizations that, on a demand basis, locate, retrieve, and deliver the full text of periodical articles, government documents, conference proceedings, patents, reports, and other materials required by the client. Includes organizations providing services only from their own collections as well as organizations using publicly available sources. In addition to the document suppliers, organizations offering electronic ordering facilities through which suppliers can be contacted are also listed here.

Electronic Mail Applications. Organizations whose information systems and services include capabilities allowing clients to electronically send and receive messages. (Organizations offering pure electronic mail services without providing information services fall outside the scope of this directory.)

Information on Demand. Organizations providing fee-based custom information services in client-specified subject areas using publicly available print and computerized information sources. Services provided usually include online searching; document delivery; literature compilations; library research; preparation of bibliographies, abstracts, or indexes; establishment of current awareness services; etc.

Library and Information Networks. Networks, consortia, and systems that represent cooperative efforts to share resources or provide information to a specific membership. Individual network members are not listed or referenced here.

Library Management Systems. Systems and software available for installation in a library or information center to support the management of circulation, acquisitions, catalog inquiry, administration, and similar library functions. Includes systems that are marketed by commercial firms as well as systems developed internally and maintained by libraries.

Magnetic Tape Providers. Organizations that make available proprietary or public information on computer tapes or diskettes for installation and use on the client's own facilities. Includes information producers that license copies of their data bases as well as service firms that package census and other public data in computer-readable form for use by clients.

Micrographic Applications. Organizations whose computerized information storage and retrieval systems include micrographic applications and products. Excluded from this directory are companies solely concerned with micropublication or the manufacture and distribution of micrographic equipment.

Online Host Services. Organizations that maintain data bases and software on their computer facilities and permit clients at multiple remote locations to retrieve needed information using online terminals. Includes commercial online search services, government systems, time-sharing companies that carry data bases, videotex/teletext information systems, online cataloging support services, and similar operations. Also listed in this index are the major international telecommunications networks through which computers and terminals communicate.

Personal Computer Oriented Services. Online services, software, library management systems, data bases, and other systems and products that are specifically designed for or actively marketed to personal computer users (often, end users).

Research and Research Projects. Institutes, libraries, centers, government units, and market research firms that conduct research in the information field on a continuing basis.

SDI/Current Awareness. Lists organizations that report selective dissemination of information (SDI) or current awareness programs, including those based on an organization's own information resources and those that cover all available sources.

Software Producers. Organizations that produce software and make it available for use on client facilities or through time-sharing. Software applications covered by this book include information storage and retrieval, cataloging and indexing, library automation, photocomposition, statistical analysis, and other information work. The individual software programs made available by organizations appearing here are separately listed in the Software Index.

Videotex/Teletext Information Services. Organizations that provide or operate videotex/teletext information systems or services, as well as other organizations involved in the field, including consulting firms, videotex data base producers, associations, research operations, etc. Organizations listed here are also entered in other categories for which they qualify; e.g., a videotex consultant appears here and in the Consultants catgory.

PERSONAL NAME INDEX. Includes persons who are directors of organizations and systems described in this book as well as persons who serve as contact points for information about the systems. Personal and organizational titles are generally not included here.

GEOGRAPHIC INDEX BY COUNTRY. Arranges organizations listed in this book according to the countries in which they are located. Countries appear in alphabetical order, with organizations arranged by city within country. Entries in this index include organization and system name, full address, phone number, and director name.

SUBJECT INDEX. An index to the general and specific subject interests reported by the organizations described in this book. Emphasis is on thorough indexing of subjects covered by computer-readable data bases and their print counterparts, although selected information industry service activities are also indexed here. Terms used are based on a modified Library of Congress subject heading list, including "see" and "see also" references. Entries in this index now include organization and service name, followed by the entry number in parentheses.

Encyclopedia of Information Systems and Services

INTERNATIONAL VOLUME

A

★1★
A.JOUR
11, rue du Marche Saint Honore   Phone: 01 2614517
F-75001 Paris, France
Francois de Valence, Director of Publications

Description of System or Service: A.JOUR (Agence de Journalistes) is a publisher of newsletters and journals in the field of new information technologies and the information industry in France, Europe, and throughout the world. It issues Infotecture France, Infotecture Europe, Videotex, and a number of other titles. A.JOUR also operates the Data Bank and Videotex Information Center/ Centre d'Information des Banques de Donnees et du Videotex (CIBDV), which gathers and disseminates information on online data bases and data banks, their producers, online host services, videotex information services, and telecommunications. CIBDV makes this information available through telephone inquiry answering services and publications; it also conducts online searches and assists clients in determining their information needs.

Scope and/or Subject Matter: Information technology, including online data bases, online vendors and host services, videotex systems, telecommunications, electronic publishing, new products and innovations, and other information-related topics.

Input Sources: Information is derived from trade literature, periodicals, books, and research studies and reports.

Publications: 1) Infotecture France (semimonthly)—covers new developments reported in the French data base industry. 2) Infotecture Europe (semimonthly)—covers the European online information industry. 3) Videotex (semimonthly)—news on videographic systems in France and throughout the world. 4) Videotex International (semimonthly)—news on the international videotex industry. 5) Innovation & Produits Nouveaux (monthly)—covers new products and innovations in information transfer technology. 6) Cable (semimonthly)—covers interactive video communication. 7) E.A.O. (semimonthly)—covers computer-assisted learning. 8) Videotex Guide/ Magazine (quarterly)—contains descriptions of videotex services in France. 9) Information Industry (daily)—provides up-to-date coverage of the international information industry, including online data bases and host services. 10) Videodisque—forthcoming publication which will cover videodisc technology and its applications. All of the publications are available by subscription.

Clientele/Availability: Products and services are available without restrictions.

Remarks: Located at the same address as A.JOUR is the Electronic Publishers Trade Association/ Syndicat Professionel des Publications Electroniques (SPPE), an organization of French publishers.

Contact: Francois de Valence, Director of Publications, A.JOUR. (Telex 214 341 F AJOUR.)

★2★
ABALL SOFTWARE INC.
2268 Osler St.   Phone: (306) 569-2180
Regina, SK, Canada S4P 1W8   Founded: 1978
A.J.S. Ball, President

Staff: 1 Management professional; 1 clerical and nonprofessional; 1 other.

Description of System or Service: ABALL SOFTWARE INC. produces the Ocelot Library System, a software package intended for use by school and special libraries. Designed for the IBM personal computer, the System provides full-service library functions, including authority control, cataloging, circulation, and purchasing. ABALL SOFTWARE also offers consultation services in the area of library automation, specializing in public and special library applications.

Scope and/or Subject Matter: Library automation systems.

Computer-Based Products and Services: The Ocelot Library System is available for IBM personal computers.

Clientele/Availability: Services are available in North America.

Contact: A.J.S. Ball, President, Aball Software Inc.

★3★
ACI COMPUTER SERVICES
P.O. Box 42   Phone: 03 5448433
Clayton, Vic. 3168, Australia   Founded: 1977

Staff: 5 Information and library professional; 20 management professional; 120 technicians; 35 clerical and nonprofessional.

Related Organizations: The parent organization of ACI Computer Services is Australian Consolidated Industries Limited.

Description of System or Service: ACI COMPUTER SERVICES operates Ausinet, the Australian online information retrieval service. Ausinet permits interactive access to approximately 12 data bases containing mainly Australian information derived from books, conference proceedings, journals, government documents, newspapers, research reports, and other published sources. In addition to Ausinet, ACI COMPUTER SERVICES offers a private file service known as Que and makes its software available for the creation of data bases and specialized output products.

Scope and/or Subject Matter: Academic research, agriculture, business, earth sciences, education, finance, industry, national publishing, public affairs, roads, science and technology, transport, urban studies, and Southeast Asia.

Input Sources: Ausinet acquires data bases from many different organizations, including Australian and foreign federal agencies, professional associations, and business organizations.

Holdings and Storage Media: ACI holds more than 10 Ausinet data bases online and provides computer storage for Que private data bases.

Computer-Based Products and Services: ACI COMPUTER SERVICES provides online access to a variety of data bases through its Ausinet service, including the following data bases: 1) Australian Business Index; 2) Australian Earth Sciences Information System; 3) Australian Education Index; 4) Australian Financial Review; 5) Australian National Bibliography; 6) Australian Public Affairs Information Service; 7) Australian Road Research Documentation; 8) Australian Transport Literature Information System; 9) Bibliographic Information on Southeast Asia; 10) Business Review Weekly; 11) Union List of Higher Degree Theses in Australian Universities; 12) WAIT Index to Newspapers. In addition to the data bases available on Ausinet, ACI COMPUTER SERVICES offers the Que private data base service, as well as specialized services such as commercial and financial systems, financial modeling, and installation and processing of the customer's software on ACI's computer.

Other Services: Additional ACI services include educational, technical, and professional support.

Clientele/Availability: Clients are equally divided among the government, business, and academic communities.

Contact: Manager, Information Retrieval Systems, ACI Computer Services. (Telex AA 33852.)

★4★
ACTON INFORMATION RESOURCES MANAGEMENT LTD.
884 Darwin Ave.   Phone: (604) 384-2444
Victoria, BC, Canada V8X 2X6   Founded: 1980
Patricia Acton, President

Staff: 3 Information and library professional; 1 management professional; 2 clerical and nonprofessional.

Description of System or Service: ACTON INFORMATION RESOURCES MANAGEMENT LTD. provides consulting services in data base establishment and development, records management, and other aspects of library and information science.

Clientele/Availability: Services are available without restrictions.

Contact: Patricia Acton, President, Acton Information Resources Management Ltd.

★5★
ADIS PRESS AUSTRALASIA PTY LTD.
ADIS DRUG INFORMATION RETRIEVAL SYSTEM (ADIRS)
P.O. Box 34-030, Birkenhead
Auckland 10, New Zealand
G.S. Avery, Managing Director

Phone: 486-125
Service Est: 1965

Staff: 3 Information and library professional; 4 clerical and nonprofessional.

Description of System or Service: The ADIS DRUG INFORMATION RETRIEVAL SYSTEM (ADIRS) is an in-house card file designed to facilitate retrieval of current prescription drug information published in the international literature. Arranged alphabetically by drug names and classes, diseases and organ systems, the ADIRS file contains more than 250,000 citations to articles on clinical pharmacology and therapeutics. ADIRS is used by the editorial staff of ADIS Press in preparing drug information service periodicals that provide analytical reviews and original research articles. The SYSTEM is also used to provide custom searches of the literature dealing with a particular drug or clinical condition, on either an ad hoc or ongoing basis. Search results are evaluated by ADIS technical editors and drug literature analysts.

Scope and/or Subject Matter: Clinical pharmacology and therapeutics.

Input Sources: Input is derived directly from 450 journals; more than 1300 additional journals are monitored through the use of published indexes to scientific and medical literature.

Holdings and Storage Media: Drug information data is stored on 800,000 file cards covering approximately 250,000 citations, increasing at a rate of 2000 citations weekly. Also maintained is a library of 750 volumes and 15,000 journal reprints.

Publications: ADIS Press publications include the following: 1) Clinical Pharmacokinetics (bimonthly with an annual index)—contains analytical reviews and original research articles on the pharmacokinetics of drugs during clinical use. 2) Drugs (monthly with an annual subject index)—comprises articles evaluating new drugs, summaries of key reports on drugs and drug treatment, and special series on such topics as drug-induced diseases. 3) Reactions (biweekly with quarterly and annual indexes)—contains articles on drug abuse, adverse drug reactions, drug poisoning, and drug interactions. 4) Inpharma (weekly with monthly, semiannual, and annual indexes)—a bulletin reporting current information on drugs and drug treatment. 5) Sports Medicine (bimonthly)—contains reviews and original articles on sports medicine. 6) Literature Monitoring and Evaluation Service (monthly, with quarterly review)—indexes and evaluates all available literature in a particular therapeutic area. All periodicals are available in more than 80 countries by subscription. ADIS also produces custom reports and has published a number of books; a catalog is available from ADIS on upon request.

Computer-Based Products and Services: It is anticipated that the ADIS Drug Information Retrieval System will be computerized.

Clientele/Availability: Chief clients are the pharmaceutical and medical communities.

Contact: Miss J. Lobb, Information Services Manager, ADIS Press Australasia Pty Ltd. (Telex 21334 NZ.) In the United States, contact ADIS Press International Inc., 401 S. State St., Newtown, PA 18940; telephone (215) 860-2000.

★6★
ADMEDIA
ADFACTS
Postbus 7902
NL-1008 AC Amsterdam, Netherlands
Ben Spaan, Head

Phone: 020 5411345
Service Est: 1981

Staff: 3 Total.

Description of System or Service: ADFACTS is a computer-readable bibliographic data base providing information on consumer markets and products in the Netherlands. It contains citations and abstracts of daily newspaper and periodical articles covering trends and developments in more than 200 consumer markets. ADFACTS is commercially available online through Control Data Corporation (CDC).

Scope and/or Subject Matter: Netherlands consumer markets and products, including clothing, food, sweets, tobacco products, cosmetics, pharmaceuticals, furniture, domestic appliances, house and garden products, games and sports, tourism, retail and wholesale trade, finance, books and magazines, service industries, conferences, office equipment, population statistics, advertising, and economics.

Input Sources: Articles and news items from approximately 70 periodicals and 8 daily newspapers and bulletins are selected for input.

Holdings and Storage Media: The computer-readable Adfacts data base holds approximately 6000 abstracts; it is updated daily with approximately 2000 items added per year. Admedia maintains a library collection of 2500 bound volumes and subscriptions to 100 periodicals.

Computer-Based Products and Services: The ADFACTS data base is searchable online through Control Data Corporation (CDC). Data elements in the file include document number, document type, article title, source publication code and date, abstract, and article length. A weekly current awareness service and SDI services are also offered.

Clientele/Availability: Services are available without restrictions. Clients include advertising agencies, publishing companies, marketing services departments, and advertisers in the Netherlands.

Contact: Annette Cox or Gisela Reinhold, Admedia.

★7★
AFRICAN TRAINING AND RESEARCH CENTRE IN ADMINISTRATION FOR DEVELOPMENT
(Centre Africain de Formation et de Recherche Administratives pour le Developpement - CAFRAD)
AFRICAN NETWORK OF ADMINISTRATIVE INFORMATION (ANAI)
P.O. Box 310
19, Abou-Al-Alae Al-Maari
Tangier, Morocco
E.S. Asiedu, Chief

Phone: 36430
Service Est: 1981

Staff: 2 Information and library professional; 2 technicians; 3 clerical and nonprofessional; 1 other.

Description of System or Service: The AFRICAN NETWORK OF ADMINISTRATIVE INFORMATION (ANAI) is an information network established to identify, collect, evaluate, and distribute specialized materials on public administration and management needed by African libraries and government agencies. The NETWORK provides library services, issues abstracting and indexing and other publications, offers microform services, and holds conferences. It plans to implement computer-based documentation services.

Scope and/or Subject Matter: Administrative sciences in an African context, including developmental plans on local government; rural and urban development; organizational development; human resources; personnel management; training; financial management; project management; and public enterprises management.

Input Sources: Input consists of 200 periodicals, African bibliographies, and government publications.

Holdings and Storage Media: The library collection includes 18,000 volumes and subscriptions to 350 periodicals.

Publications: 1) Administrative Information Sources; 2) African Administrative Abstracts; 3) special subject bibliography series.

Microform Products and Services: Microfiche and microfilm services are available to clients.

Computer-Based Products and Services: The Network plans to develop and maintain a computer-readable data base of administrative documentation.

Clientele/Availability: Services are intended for civil servants of member African Governments and administrative managers. Researchers and students are also served.

Contact: E.S. Asiedu, Chief, African Network of Administrative Information. (Telex 33664 M.)

★8★
AGRA EUROPE
16 Lonsdale Gardens
Tunbridge Wells, Kent TN1 1PD, England
V.H.P. Lynham, Managing Director
Phone: 0892 33813
Founded: 1963

Description of System or Service: AGRA EUROPE provides international information services covering developments affecting the production and trade of agricultural, fisheries, and food commodities, with an emphasis on the European Economic Community (EEC). It publishes regular bulletins, special reports, and surveys; sponsors the annual European Agricultural Outlook Conference; and makes information available through several online and videotex data bases.

Scope and/or Subject Matter: International coverage of agriculture, fisheries, and food commodities, including EEC agricultural policy news and decisions.

Input Sources: Input is derived from the European Economic Community, other Agra Europe companies, official organizations, and special correspondents throughout Europe and other selected countries.

Holdings and Storage Media: Several Agra Europe data bases are maintained in machine-readable form.

Publications: 1) Agra Europe (weekly with quarterly indexes)—covers European and world developments affecting the production and marketing of food and agricultural commodities. 2) Green Europe (monthly)—written chiefly for readers in the British Isles; provides background information on developments affecting Common Market agriculture and allied industries. 3) Preserved Milk (twelve issues each year)—covers the dairy market situation in general and the preserved milk market in particular; contains graphs and tables on European and world production, stocks, exports, imports, and prices. 4) East Europe Agriculture (monthly)—contains detailed monthly reports and tables from the USSR and other east European countries about their agricultural market. 5) Potato Markets (weekly)—contains production, price, and market information from Europe, North America, and other significant potato countries. 6) Eurofish Report (fortnightly)—reviews the European fishing industry and gives comprehensive coverage of all EEC developments affecting catching and processing; includes political commentary from Brussels and summaries of legislation, regulations, and grants. 7) C.A.P. Monitor—continuously updated loose-leaf service providing political and legal background information for the Common Agricultural Policy of the European Community and other basic information; also contains detailed information on the market organization of the EEC regulated commodities. The above publications are available by subscription. A number of special reports are also issued and are available for purchase.

Computer-Based Products and Services: AGRA EUROPE produces the following computer-readable data bases: 1) AgInfo. 2) AGINTEL—online version of the Agra Europe publication. 3) AGNEWS—Prestel file providing up-to-the-hour information from Brussels, including EEC agricultural policy news and decisions, monetary changes, and management committee reports. 4) AGINSPEC—selected information from AgInfo.

Clientele/Availability: Services are available without restrictions.

Contact: J.E. Hosking, Chief Executive, Agra Europe. (Telex 95114 AGRATW G.)

★9★
ALBERTA DEPARTMENT OF AGRICULTURE
ECONOMIC SERVICES DIVISION
AGRICULTURAL COMMODITIES DATA BASE (AGDATA)
7000 - 113 St., 3rd Floor
Edmonton, AB, Canada T6H 5T6
Lloyd Sereda, Market Intelligence Officer
Phone: (403) 427-8239
Service Est: 1978

Staff: 1 Management professional; 2 technicians.

Description of System or Service: The AGRICULTURAL COMMODITIES DATA BASE (AGDATA) is a computer-readable data base that provides information regarding agricultural commodities in Canada and the United States. It consists of time series containing price and volume information on a number of key agricultural products. The data are selected from a variety of sources on the basis of their interest to agricultural economists and statisticians. AGDATA is commercially available through time-sharing.

Scope and/or Subject Matter: Agricultural commodities in the United States and Canada, grouped into the following series: grain and oil seeds; cattle and beef products; hogs and pork products; broilers; eggs and fowl; economic indicators; special crops and miscellaneous.

Input Sources: Data sources for AGDATA include Agriculture Canada, Canadian Grain Commission, Canadian Livestock Feed Board, Chicago Mercantile Exchange, Grain Elevator Operators, Omaha Cattle Markets, Statistics Canada, the U.S. Department of Agriculture, Winnipeg Commodity Exchange, Canadian Wheat Board, and Alberta Cattle Commission.

Holdings and Storage Media: AGDATA holds daily, weekly, monthly, quarterly, and annual time-series data in machine-readable form.

Computer-Based Products and Services: Time-shared access to the Agricultural Commodities Data Base is available through I.P. Sharp Associates Limited, where it is intended to serve as a supplement to CANSIM Mini Base data.

Clientele/Availability: Services are available without charge to clients registered with the Alberta Department of Agriculture.

Contact: Lloyd Sereda, Market Intelligence Officer, Alberta Department of Agriculture. (Telex 037 2666.)

★10★
ALBERTA MUNICIPAL AFFAIRS
CENTRAL SERVICES BRANCH
ALBERTA LAND USE PLANNING DATA BANK (LANDUP)
Jarvis Bldg., 10th Floor
9925 107 St.
Edmonton, AB, Canada T5K 2H9
Delphine Langille, System Coordinator
Phone: (403) 427-0652
Service Est: 1972

Description of System or Service: The ALBERTA LAND USE PLANNING DATA BANK (LANDUP) is a machine-readable file containing primarily Canada Land Inventory data on the agricultural, recreational, forestry, wildlife, and ungulate capabilities of land in the province of Alberta. LANDUP is used to produce computer-generated maps and tables and to provide data retrieval and manipulation services for Alberta government planning officials.

Scope and/or Subject Matter: Land use planning in the province of Alberta.

Input Sources: Data are derived from Canada Land Inventory maps, some unpublished maps, and farmland assessment forms. The data are aggregated and coded at the quarter section level.

Holdings and Storage Media: The computer-readable LANDUP Data Bank holds more than 7 million records for some 657,000 quarter sections; it is updated periodically.

Computer-Based Products and Services: The ALBERTA LAND USE PLANNING DATA BANK can be searched with an information retrieval language that allows for the selection of data by quarter section and by specified legally or politically defined areas. Results from searches performed with the language can be processed with line-printer packages to produce maps and tables. Also available are data manipulation capabilities such as weighting, acreage calculation, and interfacing with SPSS.

Clientele/Availability: Access to LANDUP is limited to the planning staff of the Alberta Municipal Affairs department. Requests from other Alberta government departments are taken under consideration.

Contact: Delphine Langille, System Coordinator, Central Services Branch.

★11★
ALBERTA PUBLIC AFFAIRS BUREAU
PUBLICATION SERVICES BRANCH
11510 Kingsway Ave.
Edmonton, AB, Canada T5G 2Y5
Susan Krywolt, Manager
Phone: (403) 427-4387
Service Est: 1974

Staff: 1 Information and library professional; 1 clerical and nonprofessional.

Description of System or Service: The PUBLICATION SERVICES BRANCH collects, indexes, and catalogs publications of the Alberta government. It provides information on and copies of Alberta statutes and regulations, and supplies ordering data for other types of government publications. In support of these activities, the BRANCH maintains four computer-readable bibliographic data bases, which are used to produce hardcopy publications. Some of the information is also publicly accessible online through the SPIRES system at the University of Alberta.

Scope and/or Subject Matter: Alberta government legislation and publications.

Input Sources: Information on government publications is obtained from depository documents, library holdings information, and bibliographies.

Holdings and Storage Media: Four machine-readable data bases are maintained.

Publications: 1) Publications Catalogue (quarterly)—available by request; lists publicly available Alberta government publications alphabetically by corporate author; annual cumulations also contain information on Alberta government periodicals. 2) Table of Alberta Legislation—lists statutes and regulations available from the Branch. 3) Index to The Alberta Gazette (annual)—indexes material published in The Alberta Gazette by authority of an enabling act; arranged in alphabetical order under several major headings.

Computer-Based Products and Services: The PUBLICATION SERVICES BRANCH produces the following machine-readable data bases on Alberta government publications: 1) Government of Alberta Publications (GAP)—includes more than 18,000 bibliographic records covering availability, price, source, and library locations information for Alberta government publications from 1905 to the present. 2) Alberta Legislation Information (ALI)—includes records of all provincial statutes and records of regulations which are readily available. 3) Alberta Gazette Index (AGI)—indexes The Alberta Gazette under several major headings. 4) Periodicals Publishing Record (PPR)—covers government of Alberta periodicals. The first three data bases are searchable online through the University of Alberta Computing Services SPIRES system.

Clientele/Availability: Publications and services are available to the public.

Contact: Susan Krywolt, Manager, Publication Services Branch.

★12★
ALBERTA RESEARCH COUNCIL
ALBERTA GEOLOGICAL SURVEY
GEOSCIENCE DATA INDEX FOR ALBERTA (GEODIAL)
Terrace Plaza, 3rd Floor   Phone: (403) 438-0555
4445 Calgary Trail South   Service Est: 1980
Edmonton, AB, Canada T6H 5R7
Joseph R. MacGillivray, Information Geologist

Staff: 1 Technician; 1 other.

Related Organizations: GEODIAL is managed in cooperation with the National GEOSCAN Centre of the Geological Survey of Canada.

Description of System or Service: The GEOSCIENCE DATA INDEX FOR ALBERTA (GEODIAL) is a computer-readable data base providing references to Alberta geological information. Used by geoscientists and others involved in Alberta geology, the data base covers relevant published and unpublished materials from federal and provincial governments, professional associations, and universities. GEODIAL is publicly available online, and searches of it are available through the Geological Survey. GEODIAL is also used to supply the Alberta contribution to the national GEOSCAN data base.

Scope and/or Subject Matter: All aspects of Alberta geology, including hydrogeology, physical geography, and soil science.

Input Sources: Input for GEODIAL is derived from the following sources: Alberta Research Council published geological reports and maps, and unpublished internal geological reports and assessment reports on Crown mineral dispositions; all publications of the Canadian Society of Petroleum Geologists, the Edmonton Geological Society, and the Saskatchewan Geological Society; all relevant publications from the Geological Survey of Canada; university theses; serial literature; and reports of various local and federal government departments and agencies.

Holdings and Storage Media: GEODIAL contains more than 5000 references in computer-readable form.

Computer-Based Products and Services: GEODIAL is publicly available online through the University of Alberta Computing Services SPIRES system. The file employs a controlled vocabulary and is searchable by author, keyword, document, type, or mineral commodity; it also includes geographic controls which permit searching by locations as fine as townships and ranges. For users unable to access the data base online, searches can be obtained on request to either the Geological Survey or Information Systems of the Alberta Research Council.

Other Services: Back-up document service is provided through the Alberta Research Council.

Clientele/Availability: Services are available without restrictions. Currently there are no royalty fees charged for GEODIAL use on SPIRES. Users include private companies, government departments, libraries, and students.

Contact: Joseph R. MacGillivray, Information Geologist, Alberta Research Council. (Telex 037 2147.)

★13★
ALBERTA RESEARCH COUNCIL
ALBERTA OIL SANDS INFORMATION CENTRE
10010 - 106th St., 6th Floor   Phone: (403) 427-8382
Edmonton, AB, Canada T5J 3L8   Service Est: 1975
Helga Radvanyi, Manager

Staff: 3 Information and library professional; 2 management professional; 5 clerical and nonprofessional.

Description of System or Service: The ALBERTA OIL SANDS INFORMATION CENTRE collects and disseminates information on Alberta oil sands, heavy oil, and enhanced oil recovery. It prepares indexes to the technical literature in these fields and makes them available in hardcopy and computer-readable form. It also publishes a newsletter, provides manual and computerized search services, and acts as a referral center.

Scope and/or Subject Matter: Technical information on Alberta oil sands, heavy oil, enhanced oil recovery, and related topics.

Input Sources: Input is gathered from journals, conference proceedings, patents, and other documents.

Holdings and Storage Media: The computer-readable Alberta Oil Sands Index data base holds approximately 8100 records with abstracts, with about 1000 new records added annually. The computer-readable Heavy Oil/Enchanced Recovery Index data base holds approximately 2500 records with abstracts and is updated with about 1000 new records annually. Hardcopy collections of documents covered in both data bases are maintained.

Publications: 1) Alberta Oil Sands Index-AOSI (annual with quarterly updates)—available by subscription; indexed by personal and corporate author, patent country, publication source, and subject. 2) Heavy Oil/Enhanced Recovery Index-HERI (annual with quarterly updates)—available by subscription; indexed by personal and corporate author, patent country, publication source, and subject. 3) TAR Paper—free newsletter.

Computer-Based Products and Services: The Alberta Oil Sands Index (AOSI) and the Heavy Oil/Enhanced Recovery Index (HERI) are available online through QL Systems Limited and the University of Alberta Computing Services SPIRES system. AOSI is also accessible through CAN/OLE. The CENTRE provides customized searches of the AOSI and HERI data bases for organizations without a terminal, and it offers computerized searching of data bases available through the major online vendors accessed by the main library of the Alberta Research Council. In addition, the CENTRE maintains a numerical data base on physical properties of oil sands.

Other Services: In addition to the services described above, the Centre offers manual literature searching and referrals.

Clientele/Availability: Information is available without restrictions.

Remarks: The Centre previously produced the Oil Sands Researchers and Research Projects directory and data base which is no longer available.

Contact: Helga Radvanyi, Manager, Alberta Oil Sands Information Centre. (Telex 037 2147.)

★14★
ALBERTA RESEARCH COUNCIL
COAL TECHNOLOGY INFORMATION CENTRE (CTIC)
11315 - 87th Ave. Phone: (403) 439-5916
Edmonton, AB, Canada T6G 2C2 Service Est: 1978
Leslie Black, Coordinator

Staff: 3.5 Total.

Related Organizations: The Centre receives support from the Alberta/ Canada Energy Resources Research Fund administered by the Alberta Research Council and the Alberta Department of Energy and Natural Resources.

Description of System or Service: The COAL TECHNOLOGY INFORMATION CENTRE (CTIC) identifies, collects, indexes, stores, retrieves, and disseminates information related to the winning, mining, and subsequent processing of coal. Among the Centre's functions is the maintenance of the machine-readable bibliographic COAL-ABS data base, which covers worldwide literature dealing with all aspects of coal technology. The data base is publicly available online, and searches of it are provided by the CTIC.

Scope and/or Subject Matter: Mining technology; coal beneficiation; coal conversion; coal combustion; environmental aspects of coal mining and processing; coal reserves and resources; proximate and ultimate analyses on Alberta coals.

Input Sources: Input for the COAL-ABS data base is drawn from journal articles, books, patents, reports, dissertations, government documents, and public proceedings.

Holdings and Storage Media: The computer-readable COAL-ABS data base contains citations and abstracts for more than 14,000 documents. Full-text copies of the documents are held by the Centre.

Publications: Current acquisitions bulletin (twice per month)—lists the latest abstracts added to the data base.

Computer-Based Products and Services: The COAL TECHNOLOGY INFORMATION CENTRE maintains and provides searches from the COAL-ABS data base, which is publicly available online through the University of Alberta Computing Services SPIRES system.

Clientele/Availability: Clients include researchers, government, industry, and academia. There are no restrictions on products or services.

Contact: Leslie Black, Coordinator, Coal Technology Information Centre.

★15★
ALBERTA RESEARCH COUNCIL
INDUSTRIAL DEVELOPMENT DEPARTMENT
INDUSTRIAL INFORMATION
Terrace Plaza, 4th Floor Phone: (403) 438-1555
4445 Calgary Trail South Service Est: 1967
Edmonton, AB, Canada T6H 5R7
Mary E. Hart, Information Specialist

Staff: 1 Information and library professional; 1 management professional; 1 clerical and nonprofessional.

Description of System or Service: INDUSTRIAL INFORMATION provides online information retrieval and document ordering services for clients in Alberta industry who do not have access to them through their own organizations and for government and educational institutions. INDUSTRIAL INFORMATION also produces COIN: Computerized Information in Canada, a computer-based directory of online data bases accessible in Canada and organizations that search them.

Scope and/or Subject Matter: Engineering, petroleum research, chemistry, business, environment, agriculture, and other topics of interest to clients.

Input Sources: Input is obtained from publicly available online data bases.

Holdings and Storage Media: Industrial Information maintains the computer-readable COIN data base, holding information about approximately 630 data bases.

Publications: COIN: Computerized Information in Canada (annual)—directory of publicly available data bases in Canada and organizations that will search them; includes keyword, subject, and organization name indexes.

Computer-Based Products and Services: INDUSTRIAL INFORMATION offers computerized information retrieval and SDI services from data bases made available by DIALOG Information Services, Inc., Bibliographic Retrieval Services (BRS), System Development Corporation (SDC), U.S. National Library of Medicine, University of Alberta Computing Services SPIRES system, CAN/OLE, QL Systems Limited, International Development Research Centre (IRDC), and Info Globe (The Globe and Mail). INDUSTRIAL INFORMATION also produces the COIN data base which is available online through the University of Alberta Computing Services SPIRES system. COIN is searchable by contact, title, keyword, type, date, and classification.

Other Services: Other services offered at no cost to the client include consulting, referrals, and educational assistance.

Clientele/Availability: Services are available without restrictions to clients in industry, government, and education in the province of Alberta.

Contact: Mary E. Hart, Information Specialist, Industrial Information. (Telex 037 2147.)

★16★
ALBERTA RESEARCH COUNCIL
SOLAR AND WIND ENERGY RESEARCH PROGRAM (SWERP) INFORMATION CENTRE
Terrace Plaza, 5th Floor Phone: (403) 438-1666
4445 Calgary Trail South Service Est: 1977
Edmonton, AB, Canada T6H 5R7
Karen D. Beliveau, Coordinator

Staff: 2 Information and library professional; 2 technicians; 1 clerical and nonprofessional.

Related Organizations: The Centre receives financial support from the Alberta/ Canada Energy Resources Research Fund.

Description of System or Service: The SOLAR AND WIND ENERGY RESEARCH PROGRAM (SWERP) INFORMATION CENTRE collects, indexes, stores, retrieves, and disseminates information on solar and wind energy. It issues indexes and current awareness publications and maintains the online SWERP data base from which literature searches are provided. Additionally, the CENTRE collaborates with the Canada Institute for Scientific and Technical Information (CISTI) to maintain the Canadian Renewable Energy Database (ENERCAN).

Scope and/or Subject Matter: Solar heating and cooling; wind energy.

Input Sources: The Centre scans more than 250 journals; additional input is derived from government documents, patents, reports, conference proceedings, and secondary sources.

Holdings and Storage Media: The computer-readable SWERP data base covers 8500 documents dating from 1975 to the present. Centre library holdings consist of 2500 bound volumes; 6000 journal reprints, reports, patents, and documents; and subscriptions to 42 periodicals.

Publications: 1) Solar and Wind Energy Research Program Index (annual)—available by subscription. Comprises four volumes consisting of a cumulative list of holdings and keyword, author, and corporate author indexes. A corresponding supplement appears semiannually. 2) Current Acquisitions List (monthly)—includes tables of contents from current journals.

Computer-Based Products and Services: The SWERP data base is available online through the University of Alberta Computing Services SPIRES system. The Centre provides computerized literature searches from it.

Other Services: The Centre also offers interlibrary loans, back-up document services, and specialized information packages on solar and wind energy topics.

Clientele/Availability: Clients include members of the academic, public, industrial, commercial, and government sectors. There are no restrictions on products and services.

Contact: Karen D. Beliveau, Coordinator, Solar and Wind Energy Research Program Information Centre. (Telex 037 2147.)

★17★
ALLM BOOKS
SMALL COMPUTER PROGRAM INDEX (SCPI)
21 Beechcroft Rd., Bushey   Phone: 0923 30150
Watford, Herts. WD2 2JU, England   Service Est: 1981
Alan Pritchard, Owner

Staff: 1 Information and library professional; 1 clerical and nonprofessional.

Description of System or Service: The SMALL COMPUTER PROGRAM INDEX (SCPI) is a comprehensive source of information on computer programs that have been published in periodicals, books, and reports. The INDEX, which is available in hardcopy and machine-readable forms, indicates where program listings appear and provides advice on obtaining copies of them. SCPI covers more than 2000 printed listings each year.

Scope and/or Subject Matter: Published computer programs, in BASIC and other languages, that can be used on microcomputers and other computers for such applications as information retrieval, business, finance, science, engineering, education, and graphics.

Input Sources: Information sources scanned include approximately 150 periodicals from the U.K., the U.S., and other countries, plus books and reports. Both current and retrospective materials are indexed.

Publications: Small Computer Program Index (bimonthly)—includes an annual cumulative index; available by subscription.

Computer-Based Products and Services: The SCPI data base can be obtained in machine-readable form.

Other Services: ALLM Books also offers consulting on computer information.

Clientele/Availability: Primary clients are microcomputer users.

Contact: Alan Pritchard, Owner, ALLM Books.

★18★
ALPHA 460 TELEVISION LTD.
Scarletts, Manor Lane   Phone: 027581 3549
Abbots Leigh   Founded: 1981
Bristol BS8 3RU, England
Michael H. Davis, Managing Director

Staff: 3 Information and library professional; 2 management professional; 1 technician; 2 clerical and nonprofessional.

Description of System or Service: ALPHA 460 TELEVISION LTD. provides full services for public and private videotex systems and maintains a news and advertising data base that can be interactively accessed over the Prestel system. The data base contains approximately 3500 pages of news, sports, local information, booklists, and advertising. In addition to providing its own data base, ALPHA 460 TELEVISION LTD. offers an umbrella service to other information providers which includes page design and creation, software, data base management services, equipment, videotex training, and consulting. The firm also maintains a private videotex system and bureau.

Scope and/or Subject Matter: Public and private videotex systems and services.

Holdings and Storage Media: The Alpha 460 Prestel data base holds 3500 pages of information in machine-readable form.

Computer-Based Products and Services: The ALPHA 460 data base on Prestel provides access to news, sports, local information, booklists, advertising, and online reservations. ALPHA 460 TELEVISION LTD. also offers a variety of other computer-based information services, including a private videotex system, information retrieval services, data base management services, and a time-sharing bureau.

Clientele/Availability: Clients range from international corporations to small classified advertisers.

Projected Publications and Services: A comprehensive national and international news service, and a sports reporting service are under development.

Contact: Michael H. Davis, Managing Director, Alpha 460 Television Ltd.

★19★
ALPHATEL SYSTEMS LTD.
11430 168 St.   Phone: (403) 452-6555
Edmonton, AB, Canada T5M 3T9

Description of System or Service: ALPHATEL SYSTEMS LTD. specializes in the custom design of interactive videotex information, training, and directory systems. Its services include videotex systems analysis and design, page creation, custom software design, instructional and training systems design and courseware production, hardware acquisition and installation, and data base maintenance. Through its sister company, Alphatel Videotex Directories Limited, the firm offers the Communications and Directory Information System (CADIS), a computer-based videotex directory and information/advertising system designed for shopping malls and similar complexes. Alphatel Videotex Directories Limited also develops other public access videotex systems and data bases for shopping centers, transit information systems, community news, and tourist information.

Scope and/or Subject Matter: Public access videotex information systems providing news, community information, transit schedules, and other information.

Input Sources: Input consists of videotex pages containing news, advertisements, and community information provided by retailers, building tenants, advertisers, and other information providers.

Holdings and Storage Media: CADIS and other Alphatel videotex directory systems have the capacity to store an unlimited number of videotex pages.

Computer-Based Products and Services: ALPHATEL SYSTEMS LTD. develops interactive videotex systems on a custom basis. Through its sister company, the firm offers the Communications and Directory Information System (CADIS), an interactive computer-based directory system. CADIS is available as a single directory system controlled by a microprocessor or as a multistation configuration controlled by one or more computers in a central location. Using specific keyboard keys and preprogrammed numbers, users can interactively select general topics and specific pages of interest from the system. When not in interactive use, a CADIS system functions as an electronic billboard displaying a predetermined series of information and advertising pages. CADIS's videotex capabilities include graphic information packages, high resolution graphics with a wide color range, image overlays, animation effects, and variable text fonts.

Clientele/Availability: Products and services are available without restrictions. Clients include shopping malls and industrial firms.

Contact: Customer Services, Alphatel Systems Ltd. or Brad Dahl, Vice-President, Marketing, Alphatel Videotex Directories Limited.

★20★
ALPHATEXT, INC.
240 Catherine St.   Phone: (613) 238-5333
Ottawa, ON, Canada K2P 2G8   Founded: 1969
Cyril Eldridge, Director

Related Organizations: Alphatext is a division of Ronalds-Federated Limited.

Description of System or Service: ALPHATEXT, INC. specializes in the electronic publishing of client materials. It offers total text management services which include computerized text editing, photocomposition, graphics processing, and information storage and retrieval for structured or unstructured data bases. Text conversion, proofreading, and custom systems and programming are also available. ALPHATEXT maintains an online computer facility in Ottawa providing clients with remote terminal access to its services and systems. Conventional batch services are also offered.

Scope and/or Subject Matter: Computerized text editing and photocomposition of telephone directories, magazines, books, industrial catalogs, manuals, and similar products in all subject areas.

Input Sources: User-created data bases are processed online, or in the form of magnetic tapes, OCR materials, punch cards, or word processing media.

Holdings and Storage Media: Client data bases are maintained in machine-readable form on Alphatext computers.

Computer-Based Products and Services: ALPHATEXT provides computerized typesetting, laser printing, and associated electronic publishing services for its clients. It also offers a total package for records managers and special services for processing diskettes.

Clientele/Availability: Services are available without restrictions.

Contact: Cyril Elridge, Director, Alphatext, Inc. In the United States, contact Carol Ruscoe, Manager, 577 E. Larned St., Suite 230, Detroit, MI 48226; telephone (313) 964-4260.

★21★
ALPINE SCIENCE INFORMATION SERVICE (ASISS)
CH-3813 Saxeten, Switzerland
Dr. Robert Utzinger, Head
Phone: 036 231041
Founded: 1983

Description of System or Service: The ALPINE SCIENCE INFORMATION SERVICE (ASISS) provides computerized searching of commercially available online data bases, compilation of bibliographies, and SDI services. Other services offered include translations, assistance in editing scientific publications, and document delivery services.

Scope and/or Subject Matter: All subject areas, with emphasis on natural sciences, medicine, toxicology, pharmacology, biochemistry, and other fields of scientific knowledge.

Input Sources: Information sources include commercially available online data bases, card files, Swiss biomedical libraries, and other sources.

Computer-Based Products and Services: The ALPINE SCIENCE INFORMATION SERVICE conducts computerized searches of more than 250 data bases available through United States and European host systems.

Clientele/Availability: Services are available without restrictions. Clients include industry, government, universities, and others.

Contact: Dr. Robert Utzinger, Alpine Science Information Service.

★22★
AMERICAN COLLEGE IN PARIS
SERVICE CALVADOS
B.P. 21-07
31, ave. Bosquet
F-75007 Paris, France
Stephen Plummer, Dean of Students
Phone: 01 7050904
Service Est: 1981

Staff: 3 Information and library professional; 2 management professional; 4 technicians; 2 sales and marketing; 1 clerical and nonprofessional.

Description of System or Service: The SERVICE CALVADOS is a microcomputer information and communications network intended primarily for owners of Apple microcomputers. The network allows users throughout France to dial directly into the American College Computer Center via Transpac, the French national packet switching network. SERVICE CALVADOS offers online access to financial and other data bases, communications facilities such as electronic mail, processing in eight high-level languages, and a library of large-scale software packages. Also offered is consulting on telecommunications and private network construction.

Scope and/or Subject Matter: Online microcomputer information and communications applications, including access to Apple user materials information.

Input Sources: Data bases are acquired from Apple Computer, Inc. and commercial data base producers.

Holdings and Storage Media: Financial data, catalogs, and technical notes are held online.

Publications: Bulletin Calvados (monthly)—published in French and free on request.

Computer-Based Products and Services: SERVICE CALVADOS provides online access to French and foreign stock exchange and other financial data, including data bases produced by Telekurs and Compagnie des Agents de Change. It also makes available Apple-related data bases such as Apple computer notes (in French), catalogs of Apple and Apple-compatible hardware and software, and catalogs of CP/M software. Additionally, software, electronic mail, bulletin boards, and other processing and communications capabilities are offered.

Clientele/Availability: Primary clients include statisticians, financial analysts, engineers, and other professional users of Apple computers. Microcomputer clubs receive special rates and arrangements.

Remarks: Calvados is a French brandy made from apples.

Contact: Stephen Plummer, Dean of Students, American College in Paris. (Telex 205926 F ACPARIS.)

★23★
AMERICAN EXPRESS EUROPE LTD.
SKYGUIDE
P.O. Box 68
Amex House, Edward St.
Brighton, East Sussex BN2 2LP, England
Mr. A. Book, Director, Consumer Services
Phone: 0273 693555
Service Est: 1982

Related Organizations: SkyGuide is the business name of the American Express Flight Information Service.

Description of System or Service: SKYGUIDE is a computer-based information service providing airport flight arrival and departure information to Prestel users. The service covers flights scheduled at airports in Scotland, England, and other European countries. SKYGUIDE information is obtained directly from airport authority computers, which are updated continuously with flight information from air traffic controllers and airlines. SKYGUIDE receives the data via a packet switched network and formats the information into Prestel frames for immediate use by Prestel users. The SKYGUIDE service, which is often less expensive to consult than telephoning the airport, receives more than 100,000 accesses per month. In addition to flight data, SKYGUIDE provides additional airport information such as directions to the airport, passenger services, and shopping facilities.

Scope and/or Subject Matter: England, Scotland, and European airport flight and related information.

Input Sources: Input is obtained directly from airport authority computers.

Holdings and Storage Media: SkyGuide information is held in machine-readable form and is continuously updated.

Computer-Based Products and Services: SKYGUIDE is a computer-based flight information service available through Prestel. SKYGUIDE flight arrival and departure information is originated by air traffic controllers and airlines which transmit the information directly to the airport authority computer for display in airport lounges. SKYGUIDE obtains the information from the airport authority computer with a microprocessor-based monitor and transmits the data via British Telecommunications' packet switching network to American Express in Brighton for editing and formatting as Prestel frames. SKYGUIDE information is then transmitted to Prestel and is immediately available for access by subscribers at home or in the office.

Clientele/Availability: The service is available to Prestel users in England, Scotland, and Europe.

Remarks: SkyGuide was awarded the British Computer Society Applications Award for 1982.

Contact: Mr. A. Book, Director, Consumer Services, American Express Europe Ltd.

★24★
ANGLO-BRAZILIAN INFORMATION SERVICE (ABIS)
Rua Deputado Lacerda Franco, 333   Phone: 011 8144155
05418 Sao Paulo SP, Brazil   Founded: 1981
John Salter, Director

Staff: 5 Information and library professional; 2 clerical and nonprofessional.

Related Organizations: The parent organizations are the Sociedade Brasileira de Cultura Inglesa and the British Council.

Description of System or Service: The ANGLO-BRAZILIAN INFORMATION SERVICE (ABIS) provides information services on a nonprofit basis in Brazil using British and other international information resources. Its services include manual and computerized information retrieval, document supply, reference work, and bibliographic advice. ABIS is an agent for the British Library and utilizes the Lending Division's international photocopy service.

Scope and/or Subject Matter: Information produced in or about Britain, with emphasis on academic and industrial research and development, higher education, science, English-language teaching, and cultural exchange.

Input Sources: The Service uses British bibliographic, educational, and cultural resources as well as international online vendors.

Holdings and Storage Media: ABIS maintains a library of 2000 bound volumes and subscriptions to 100 periodicals. Machine-readable mailing lists are also maintained.

Computer-Based Products and Services: ABIS provides computerized information retrieval services from data bases made available through BLAISE (British Library Automated Information Service), DIALOG Information Services, Inc., and System Development Corporation (SDC). ABIS also maintains an in-house mailing list and contact file data base of 9000 records for the British Council in Brazil.

Other Services: Additionally, the Anglo-Brazilian Information Service provides joint sponsorship of librarianship and information science seminars.

Clientele/Availability: Services are available without restrictions to institutions and individuals in Brazil.

Contact: Flavio Rolim, Information Officer, Anglo-Brazilian Information Service. (Telex 33254 COBT BR.)

★25★
ARABIAN GULF INFORMATION CONSULTING BUREAU
P.O. Box 922   Phone: 681276
Manama, Bahrain
Jaffer Almadhi, Managing Director

Description of System or Service: The ARABIAN GULF INFORMATION CONSULTING BUREAU provides book and periodical distribution, data base services, library support services, and library consultation.

Scope and/or Subject Matter: Information and library services.

Clientele/Availability: Services are available to clients in the government, public, and private sectors.

Contact: Jaffer Almadhi, Managing Director, Arabian Gulf Information Consulting Bureau. (Telex 8202 BAHTAG BN.) Branch offices are maintained in London and Gulf Cooperative Countries.

★26★
ARCTIC INSTITUTE OF NORTH AMERICA
ARCTIC SCIENCE AND TECHNOLOGY INFORMATION SYSTEM (ASTIS)
University of Calgary   Phone: (403) 284-7515
2500 University Dr., N.W.   Service Est: 1978
Calgary, AB, Canada T2N 1N4
Ross Goodwin, Manager

Staff: 2 Information and library professional; 1 management professional; 1 clerical and nonprofessional.

Description of System or Service: The ARCTIC SCIENCE AND TECHNOLOGY INFORMATION SYSTEM (ASTIS) collects and disseminates information on arctic regions. It maintains a computer-readable data base providing abstracts, full bibliographic descriptions, and library location codes for documents relating to the north. The data base is used to produce a current awareness bulletin and an annual microfiche bibliography; it is also commercially available online. ASTIS also offers reference services and compiles special bibliographies and other publications.

Scope and/or Subject Matter: All aspects of the north, including physical, earth, biological, and social sciences, engineering and technology, and the humanities. Geographic emphasis is on the North American arctic.

Input Sources: Input is drawn from 350 periodicals as well as monographs, government and industry reports, theses, and other materials acquired by the Arctic Institute of North America Library, the University of Calgary Library, government agency libraries, and other sources.

Holdings and Storage Media: The computer-readable ASTIS data base holds records for approximately 13,300 documents, dating primarily from 1978 to the present.

Publications: ASTIS Current Awareness Bulletin (bimonthly)—each issue contains approximately 400 citations to new arctic literature; arranged by subject, with geographic and author indexes. Also issued are online user manuals and special bibliographies.

Microform Products and Services: ASTIS Bibliography (annual)—microfiche cumulation of the data base, with detailed subject, author, geographic, and title indexes.

Computer-Based Products and Services: The ASTIS data base is searchable online through QL Systems, Ltd. and the University of Alberta Computing Services SPIRES system.

Clientele/Availability: ASTIS serves researchers, engineers, managers, and the general public.

Contact: Ross Goodwin, Manager, Arctic Science and Technology Information System.

★27★
ARGENTINA
NATIONAL ATOMIC ENERGY COMMISSION
(Comision Nacional de Energia Atomica - CNEA)
DIVISION OF TECHNICAL INFORMATION
(Division de Informacion Tecnica)
Av. del Libertador 8250   Phone: 70 7711
1429 Buenos Aires, Argentina   Service Est: 1950
Tito Suter, Division Head

Staff: 11 Information and library professional; 1 management professional; 9 clerical and nonprofessional.

Description of System or Service: The DIVISION OF TECHNICAL INFORMATION provides library and information services to the National Atomic Energy Commission. Among the services offered are computerized information searching, documentation services, and photocopying. The DIVISION also publishes reports and bibliographies, and serves as the Argentine liaison for the International Nuclear Information System (INIS).

Scope and/or Subject Matter: Atomic energy, nuclear sciences, and related fields.

Input Sources: Input is obtained from Argentine publications about science and nuclear technology, including periodicals, journals, reports, government publications, and books.

Holdings and Storage Media: The library collection contains 30,000 bound volumes; 240,000 microfiche; 72,000 reports; and subscriptions to 1500 periodicals. In addition, the Division holds International Nuclear Information System (INIS) magnetic tapes.

Publications: 1) CNEA Reports (irregular); 2) Technical Notes (irregular); 3) Courses (irregular)—all of the above are generally available free and on an exchange basis. Also published are bibliographical lists which include books, serials, microfiche, and reports.

Computer-Based Products and Services: The DIVISION provides search services from INIS tapes.

Other Services: Additional services include consulting, research, data collection and analysis, manual literature searching, and referral services.

Clientele/Availability: The Library is open to professionals; documentation services are available only to CNEA personnel.

Contact: Elsa Gutierrez, Head of Library, National Atomic Energy Commission.

★28★
ARGENTINA
NATIONAL COUNCIL FOR SCIENTIFIC AND TECHNICAL RESEARCH
(Consejo Nacional de Investigaciones Cientificas y Tecnicas - CONICET)
ARGENTINE CENTER FOR SCIENTIFIC AND TECHNOLOGICAL INFORMATION
(Centro Argentino de Informacion Cientifica y Tecnologica - CAICYT)
Moreno 431 Phone: 341777
1091 Buenos Aires, Argentina Service Est: 1976

Special Note: The above name, address, and telephone number have been verified for this edition, although no questionnaire response was received. The following text is reprinted from the 5th edition.

Description of System or Service: The ARGENTINE CENTER FOR SCIENTIFIC AND TECHNOLOGICAL INFORMATION (CAICYT) provides scientists, researchers, and others in Argentina with a variety of scientific and technological information services. It conducts online searching and SDI, maintains a library, operates a national information exchange network utilizing its copying facilities, publishes a union list of serials, and provides a register of all relevant translations.

Scope and/or Subject Matter: Scientific and technological information; science policy; information science.

Input Sources: CAICYT utilizes computer-readable data bases and hardcopy resources.

Holdings and Storage Media: The Center maintains a library.

Publications: A union list of serials in Argentine scientific and technical libraries is published.

Computer-Based Products and Services: CAICYT provides online searching of data bases made available through DIALOG Information Services, Inc. and System Development Corporation (SDC).

Clientele/Availability: Clients include scientists, researchers, and others in Argentina.

Contact: Data Base Consultant, Argentine Center for Scientific and Technological Information.

★29★
ART SALES INDEX LTD.
Pond House Phone: 42678
Weybridge, Surrey KT13 8SQ, England Founded: 1968
Richard Hislop, Director

Staff: 2 Management professional; 8 clerical and nonprofessional.

Description of System or Service: ART SALES INDEX LTD. collects and indexes information on international auction sales of works of art. It presents this information in several print publications, including the annual Art Sales Index, and through the computer-readable ASI Data Bank. The Data Bank and publications provide the following information: for artists—name, dates, and nationality; for pictures—title or description; price in pounds sterling and U.S. dollars; medium, including oils, watercolors, drawings, pastels, and gouache; whether dated, signed, or inscribed; date of sale; location and auctioneer; lot number; and if illustrated in the catalog. The ASI Data Bank is accessible worldwide through the firm's ArtQuest online service.

Scope and/or Subject Matter: Prices and details of works of art of all periods, including oil paintings, watercolors, drawings, and sculptures.

Input Sources: Information is obtained from catalogs from more than 300 auctioneers worldwide.

Holdings and Storage Media: The machine-readable ASI Data Bank contains information on more than 550,000 works of art offered at approximately 12,000 international auction sales since October 1970. It is continuously updated and approximately 55,000 additional pictures are covered each year. Some 60,000 artists are represented in the data base and about 1500 new artist names are added each year.

Publications: The following publications are available for purchase: 1) Art Sales Index (annual)—two volume set containing worldwide sales results of the previous auction season. Artists are listed in alphabetical order and pictures are listed in ascending sequence of value. 2) ASI Decade Publications—presents by periods of art the results of 10,000 international art auctions from 1970 to 1980, with details on 400,000 pictures. The following editions are available: Impressionists and 20th Century Artists, covering 12,000 artists and 155,000 pictures; 19th Century Artists, covering 20,000 artists and 164,000 pictures; and Old Masters, covering 1200 artists and 79,000 pictures. 3) Auction Prices of American Artists (biennial)—covers two complete auction seasons and includes price and details of pictures by North and South American artists of all periods; the first edition covers eight auction seasons, 1970-78.

Microform Products and Services: A monthly Art Sales Index is available on microfiche.

Computer-Based Products and Services: ART SALES INDEX LTD. produces the ASI Data Bank which contains information on works of art sold at auctions. The Data Bank can be searched by name of artist, period of art, date of sale, exact or approximate size, price of picture, and individual words in title or description of picture. The file can also be used to produce statistical analyses, including year-by-year summaries of artist's sales, showing highest, lowest, and median prices. The ASI Data Bank is available online through ArtQuest, an online service accessible worldwide. ArtQuest also includes information on past and forthcoming auction sales, including title, collection or special interest, auction house and catalog details, dates, times and viewing days, and noteworthy lots.

Clientele/Availability: Products and services are available without restrictions. Clients include art collectors, researchers, appraisers, dealers, auctioneers, and galleries.

Contact: Richard Hislop, Director, Art Sales Index Ltd. (Telex 929476 APEX G.)

★30★
ASIAN INSTITUTE OF TECHNOLOGY (AIT)
REGIONAL DOCUMENTATION CENTER
ASIAN INFORMATION CENTER FOR GEOTECHNICAL ENGINEERING (AGE)
P.O. Box 2754 Phone: 523 9300
Bangkok 10501, Thailand Service Est: 1973
Dr. Jacques Valls, Director, Documentation Center

Staff: Regional Documentation Center staff comprises 11 information and library professional; 4 management professional; 8 clerical and nonprofessional; and 3 other.

Related Organizations: AGE receives support from a number of international and national agencies.

Description of System or Service: The ASIAN INFORMATION CENTER FOR GEOTECHNICAL ENGINEERING (AGE) provides geotechnical information to developing countries. Its products and services include current awareness, bibliographic publications and a data base, literature searching, and document delivery.

Scope and/or Subject Matter: Geotechnology, including soil mechanics, foundation engineering, earthquake engineering, rock mechanics, engineering geology, and similar topics.

Input Sources: Input is derived from journals, monographs, conference proceedings, research reports, theses, unpublished materials, and other documents.

Holdings and Storage Media: The computer-readable AGE data base contains approximately 30,000 references dating from 1973 to the present. The Regional Documentation Center library collection consists of 150,000 bound volumes and subscriptions to 1100 periodicals.

Publications: 1) Asian Geotechnical Engineering Abstracts (two per year). 2) AGE Digest (every two years)—computer-produced bibliography which corresponds to the AGE data base; includes author and keyword indexes. 3) AGE Current Awareness Services (six per year). 4) AGE Holdings Lists (annual)—cover research reports, journals, and conference proceedings. 5) AGE News (four per year). The above publications are available as part of the AGE annual membership fee.

Microform Products and Services: Abstracts and documents are available on microfiche.

Computer-Based Products and Services: The ASIAN INFORMATION CENTER FOR GEOTECHNICAL ENGINEERING maintains the computer-readable AGE data base under CDS/ISIS software and uses it to produce the AGE Digest and other publications and to provide current awareness and information retrieval services. Magnetic tape copies of all citations appearing in the printed AGE Digest are available. In addition, AGE data base information from 1978 to date is expected to be made available online as the Asian Geotechnology data base through ESA/IRS.

Clientele/Availability: Primary clientele is Asian industry.

Contact: Dr. Jacques Valls, Director, Regional Documentation Center. (Telex 84276 TH.)

★31★
ASIAN INSTITUTE OF TECHNOLOGY (AIT)
REGIONAL DOCUMENTATION CENTER
ENVIRONMENTAL SANITATION INFORMATION CENTER (ENSIC)
P.O. Box 2754   Phone: 523 9300
Bangkok 10501, Thailand   Service Est: 1978
Dr. Jacques Valls, Director, Documentation Center

Related Organizations: ENSIC receives financial support from the International Development Research Centre of Canada (IDRC).

Description of System or Service: The ENVIRONMENTAL SANITATION INFORMATION CENTER (ENSIC) is concerned with meeting the information requirements of developing countries in the field of environmental sanitation. ENSIC maintains a comprehensive collection of published and unpublished documents and disseminates information through several publications, a computer-readable data base, current awareness services, literature searching, and document delivery.

Scope and/or Subject Matter: Environmental sanitation, including rural water supply and sanitation, low-cost disposal and reuse options, waste deposition devices, on-site collection and treatment, sewage collection and off-site treatment, waste management, and water management.

Input Sources: Input is derived from journals and other published and unpublished materials.

Holdings and Storage Media: The computer-readable ENSIC data base contains approximately 3700 references.

Publications: 1) Environmental Sanitation Abstracts - Low Cost Options (three times per year)—each issue contains about 150 abstracts plus author, keyword, and geographic indexes. 2) Environmental Sanitation Reviews (three times per year)—each issue contains a state-of-the-art review on a different topic. 3) ENSIC Holdings Lists (occasional). 4) Enfo (quarterly)—a newsletter reporting on ongoing or recently completed research projects, news on ENSIC activities, newly received documents, opinions, and forthcoming events. The above publications are available as part of the annual ENSIC membership fee. Booklets and manuals are also published on occasion.

Microform Products and Services: ENSIC provides copies of some documents on microfiche.

Computer-Based Products and Services: The ENVIRONMENTAL SANITATION INFORMATION CENTER maintains the computer-readable ENSIC data base under CDS/ISIS software and uses it to provide information retrieval services.

Clientele/Availability: Primary clientele is Asian industry.

Contact: Dr. Jacques Valls, Director, Regional Documentation Center. (Telex 84276 TH.)

★32★
ASIAN INSTITUTE OF TECHNOLOGY (AIT)
REGIONAL DOCUMENTATION CENTER
INTERNATIONAL FERROCEMENT INFORMATION CENTER (IFIC)
P.O. Box 2754   Phone: 523 9300
Bangkok 10501, Thailand   Service Est: 1976
Dr. Jacques Valls, Director, Documentation Center

Related Organizations: IFIC works in cooperation with national societies, universities, libraries, information centers, government agencies, research organizations, and engineering and consulting firms worldwide.

Description of System or Service: The INTERNATIONAL FERROCEMENT INFORMATION CENTER (IFIC) serves as a clearinghouse for information on ferrocement and related materials. IFIC collects published and unpublished information on all forms of ferrocement applications, maintains a computer-readable bibliographic data base, issues a quarterly journal and other publications, and offers literature searching, current awareness, and document delivery services.

Scope and/or Subject Matter: Ferrocement technology and its applications, including fiber-reinforced concrete, mortar, terrestrial applications, and marine uses.

Input Sources: Input is derived from international literature, including periodicals, books, reports, and proceedings.

Holdings and Storage Media: The computer-readable IFIC data base contains approximately 1500 references.

Publications: 1) Journal of Ferrocement (quarterly)—available by subscription. Each issue includes several technical articles, bibliographic list and other current awareness sections, and news and notes. 2) FOCUS—free introductory pamphlet; available in 14 languages. Also issued are reports, proceedings, bibliographies, dictionaries, and state-of-the-art reviews.

Microform Products and Services: IFIC provides copies of some documents on microfiche and microfilm.

Computer-Based Products and Services: The INTERNATIONAL FERROCEMENT INFORMATION CENTER maintains a computer-readable bibliographic data base under CDS/ISIS software and uses it to provide information retrieval services.

Other Services: Additionally, IFIC promotes the transfer of ferrocement technology to rural areas in developing countries through workshops, seminars, and training programs.

Clientele/Availability: IFIC membership is intended primarily for Asian industry.

Contact: Dr. Jacques Valls, Director, Regional Documentation Center. (Telex 84276 TH.)

★33★
ASIAN INSTITUTE OF TECHNOLOGY (AIT)
REGIONAL DOCUMENTATION CENTER
RENEWABLE ENERGY RESOURCES INFORMATION CENTER
    (RERIC)
P.O. Box 2754   Phone: 523 9300
Bangkok 10501, Thailand   Service Est: 1978
Dr. Jacques Valls, Director, Documentation Center

Related Organizations: RERIC receives support from a number of international and national organizations.

Description of System or Service: The RENEWABLE ENERGY RESOURCES INFORMATION CENTER (RERIC) aims at answering renewable energy questions with particular regard to applications in tropical regions. RERIC gathers information on renewable energy resources, maintains a machine-readable bibliographic data base, issues publications, and provides literature searching, current awareness, and document delivery services.

Scope and/or Subject Matter: Renewable energy resources, particularly in tropical regions, including solar energy, biofuels, wind energy, and small-scale hydropower.

Input Sources: Input is derived from journals, books, research reports, theses, conference proceedings, unpublished materials, and data bases.

Holdings and Storage Media: The computer-readable RERIC data base contains approximately 2600 references.

Publications: 1) Renewable Energy Review Journal (twice per year)—a journal providing state-of-the-art reviews on renewable energy topics. 2) RERIC News (four issues per year)—newsletter providing information on RERIC activities, new publications, on-going projects, and forthcoming events. 3) RERIC Holdings List. 4) Abstracts of AIT Reports and Publications. Other miscellaneous publications and research reports are also issued. RERIC publications are available as part of an annual membership fee.

Microform Products and Services: RERIC makes copies of some documents available on microfiche.

Computer-Based Products and Services: The RENEWABLE ENERGY RESOURCES INFORMATION CENTER maintains the computer-readable RERIC data base under CDS/ISIS software and uses it to provide literature searching services.

Clientele/Availability: RERIC serves primarily organizations in the tropical countries of Asia and the Pacific and the tropical developing regions of Africa and Central and South America.

Contact: Dr. Jacques Valls, Director, Regional Documentation Center. (Telex 84276 TH.)

★34★
ASIAN NETWORK FOR INDUSTRIAL TECHNOLOGY INFORMATION AND EXTENSION (TECHNONET ASIA)
RELC International House, Rm. 803
30 Orange Grove Rd.
Singapore 1025, Republic of Singapore
Dr. Leon V. Chico, Executive Director

Phone: 7343331
Founded: 1973

Staff: 4 Management professional; 7 clerical and nonprofessional.

Related Organizations: The International Development Research Centre (IDRC) of Canada and the Canadian International Development Agency provide direct support to TECHNONET ASIA.

Description of System or Service: The ASIAN NETWORK FOR INDUSTRIAL TECHNOLOGY INFORMATION AND EXTENSION (TECHNONET ASIA) is a cooperative grouping of 14 organizations in 11 Asian-Pacific countries which provides technical information services to improve the quality and efficiency of small- and medium-scale industrial enterprises. TECHNONET ASIA answers inquiries from members, provides current awareness services, exchanges technical information with other organizations, trains extension officers for field work, and holds workshops and seminars.

Scope and/or Subject Matter: Industry in Asia and the Pacific.

Input Sources: Input is derived from contacts with approximately 160 national and international sources of technical information including the National Research Council of Canada's Technical Information Service.

Publications: 1) TECHNONET ASIA Newsletter (quarterly). 2) Technology Digest. The Network also issues occasional reports and monographs.

Computer-Based Products and Services: Online and batch-mode searches of commercially available data bases are available within the Network.

Other Services: In addition to services described above, TECHNONET ASIA provides manual literature searching and referrals.

Clientele/Availability: TECHNONET ASIA members have priority for services; others may be considered on an individual basis.

Contact: Dr. Leon V. Chico, Executive Director, or Mary F. Sim, Assistant Program Officer, Asian Network for Industrial Technology Information and Extension. The mailing address is Tanglin P.O. Box 160, Singapore 9124, Republic of Singapore. (Telex RS21076 SINIDRC.)

★35★
ASLIB, THE ASSOCIATION FOR INFORMATION MANAGEMENT
Information House
26/27 Boswell St.
London WC1N 3JZ, England
Dennis A. Lewis, Director

Phone: 01-430 2671
Founded: 1924

Description of System or Service: ASLIB, THE ASSOCIATION FOR INFORMATION MANAGEMENT promotes better management of information as a resource. Its 2000 member organizations are information users and providers in industry and commerce, research, government, education, and the professions, from the United Kingdom and 75 other countries. ASLIB offers a research and consultancy team which specializes in solving problems relating to information collection, storage, retrieval, and dissemination. Other ASLIB activities in the field of library and information science include research and development, training courses, library and information services, conferences, meetings, and publications. Its library is the principal collection on documentation and information science in the United Kingdom, and is used to provide current awareness and other information services. Additionally, ASLIB maintains an Information Centre which offers members practical advice on all aspects of information management. Answering more than 5000 inquiries annually, the Centre also keeps an index of translations and a register of specialist translators in science and technology.

Scope and/or Subject Matter: Information management and science; documentation; library science.

Holdings and Storage Media: The Aslib library holds 18,000 volumes and subscriptions to 250 periodicals.

Publications: 1) Aslib Information (monthly)—free to members; available by subscription to nonmembers. News bulletin containing a detailed calendar of activities and developments in the library and information field. 2) Current Awareness Bulletin (monthly)—free to members; available by subscription to nonmembers. Lists citations to periodical and other literature relating to information management, arranged by subject; includes book reviews. 3) Forthcoming International Scientific and Technical Conferences (quarterly)—covers approximately 1000 conferences, symposiums, and congresses in science, technology, and medicine worldwide. 4) Aslib Proceedings (monthly)—news of latest developments in the library and information field. 5) Journal of Documentation (quarterly)—provides articles on the recording, organization, and dissemination of knowledge. 6) Program: News of Computers in Libraries (quarterly). 7) Index to Theses Accepted for Higher Degrees by the Universities of Great Britain and Ireland (twice per year)—covers theses in all subject areas from more than 40 United Kingdom and Irish universities. Other publications include handbooks, directories, monographs, research reports, and bibliographies. A catalog of publications is available by request.

Computer-Based Products and Services: ASLIB conducts online computerized information searches for corporate members.

Clientele/Availability: Membership is open to information users and providers on an international basis.

Remarks: The online search unit of Aslib is expected to merge with the Online Information Centre (see separate entry) to form the Aslib Online Resources Centre.

Contact: Dennis A. Lewis, Director, or D.S. Wood, Marketing Manager, Aslib. (Telex 23667.)

★36★
ASSOCIATION FOR INFORMATION BROKERAGE AND TECHNOLOGICAL CONSULTANCY
(Gesellschaft fur Informationsvermittlung und Technologieberatung)
IRS INFO-INSTITUTE
Blumenstr. 1
D-8000 Munich 2, Fed. Rep. of Germany
Dr. Ulrich Grosse, Managing Director

Phone: 089 263060
Service Est: 1979

Staff: Approximately 3 total.

Description of System or Service: The IRS INFO-INSTITUTE is a contract and consultancy organization operated by the Association for

Information Brokerage and Technological Consultancy and engaged in the solution of problems in the fields of technical, industrial, and scientific program development, implementation, and evaluation. The INSTITUTE provides contract information research, online literature searching, document delivery, current awareness services, technology transfer and innovation consulting, and information system development and management. Online user and management training are also offered.

Scope and/or Subject Matter: Subjects of interest to clients, with emphasis on business, finance, and technology transfer.

Computer-Based Products and Services: The IRS INFO-INSTITUTE conducts online searching of approximately 1200 data bases made available through more than 20 European and North American online host services.

Clientele/Availability: Clients include national and international organizations, government agencies, commerce, and industry. Services are available on a fee basis.

Contact: Dr. Ulrich Grosse, Managing Director, IRS Info-Institute. (Telex 5 215 873 HUKU D.)

★37★
ASSOCIATION FOR LITERARY AND LINGUISTIC COMPUTING (ALLC)
University College of North Wales   Phone: 0248 351151
Department of English   Founded: 1973
Bangor, Gwynedd LL57 2DG, Wales
Dr. Thomas N. Corns, Honorary Secretary

Description of System or Service: The ASSOCIATION FOR LITERARY AND LINGUISTIC COMPUTING (ALLC) is an international association established to further literary and linguistic research by computer, and to provide a means of communication for those concerned with such research. It holds seminars and a biennial symposium, issues publications, and supports more than 25 specialist groups. It also maintains an archive and occasionally makes available data sets.

Scope and/or Subject Matter: Literary and linguistic computing; computational linguistics; programming languages for use in the humanities; hardware and software for input and output of natural language texts.

Publications: 1) ALLC Bulletin (3 issues per year)—contains informative articles, reports on work in progress, information on new publications, a bibliography, accounts of conferences and meetings, Association news, and correspondence; available by subscription. 2) ALLC Journal (2 issues per year)—includes selected papers presented at the ALLC symposium; available by subscription.

Clientele/Availability: Scholars and institutions representing more than 30 countries have membership in the Association.

Contact: Dr. Thomas N. Corns, Honorary Secretary, Association for Literary and Linguistic Computing.

★38★
ASSOCIATION FOR RESEARCH AND DEVELOPMENT OF CHEMICAL INFORMATICS
(Association pour la Recherche et le Developpement en Informatique Chimique - ARDIC)
DARC PLURIDATA SYSTEM (DPDS)
25, rue Jussieu   Phone: 01 6332370
F-75005 Paris, France
Jacques-Emile Dubois, Professor

Staff: 2 Management professional; 10 engineers.

Related Organizations: The DARC Pluridata System was designed by the Center for Automated Information and Documentation (CIDA) at the University of Paris in accordance with the policy established by the Interministerial Mission for Scientific and Technical Information (MIDIST) of France. Support is also received from the National Center of Scientific Research (CNRS).

Description of System or Service: The DARC PLURIDATA SYSTEM (DPDS) consists of a retrieval system and a number of data bases that are publicly accessible online through ARDIC, which is a Euronet DIANE host. Designed to create, maintain, and search chemical data banks, DPDS is based on DARC (Description, Acquisition, Retrieval, and Conception), a general program for chemical information retrieval. Currently available for searching under DARC are physicochemical data banks on carbon-13 nuclear magnetic resonance (C-13 NMR) spectra, mass spectra, and crystallography.

Scope and/or Subject Matter: Chemical data retrieval, including carbon-13 nuclear magnetic resonance spectra, mass spectra, and X-ray crystallographic data.

Input Sources: DPDS acquires data from a number of organizations for the Mass Spectra Data Bank, including the U.S. National Bureau of Standards, the U.S. National Institutes of Health, the U.S. Environmental Protection Agency, and the Chemical Abstracts Service. For the X-Ray Crystallography Data Bank, data are acquired from the Cambridge University Chemical Laboratory Crystallographic Data Center. For the C-13 NMR Data Bank, information is collected by CIDA from chemical literature.

Holdings and Storage Media: The C-13 NMR Data Bank contains information on 12,000 compounds and 16,000 spectra; data on 35,000 chemical compounds are held in the Mass Spectra Data Bank; and data on 22,000 compounds are maintained in the X-Ray Crystallography Data Bank.

Computer-Based Products and Services: The DARC PLURIDATA SYSTEM operates by combining an Information Data Base (IDB) containing numerical values, spectra, bibliographic data, and other information, with a Structural Data Base (SDB) which contains the storage and retrieval data relative to the chemical compounds of the data bank. The SYSTEM is capable of the following functions: automatic input and registration of chemical structure, either by direct acquisition of the structural diagram or by transcoding from CAS Connection Tables; checking and merging of structural files originating in various sources; interactive structural and substructural searching of the SDB by alphanumerical or graphical means. It also can display structural diagrams on plotter or CRT terminals; provide interactive searching of the IDB, either directly or through the SDB; and display spectra analytically or numerical arrays synthetically on CRTs. Computerized searching of the C-13 NMR Data Bank, the Mass Spectra Data Bank, and the X-Ray Crystallography Data Bank are available to the public through ARDIC over Euronet DIANE and Transpac.

Clientele/Availability: Computer searches are available to the public on a fee basis. The System is available (under negotiated conditions) to users interested in creating their own data banks.

Remarks: ARDIC also is associated with the National Center for Chemical Information/ Centre National de l'Information Chimique (CNIC), which is described in a separate entry in these pages.

Contact: Ch. Atlani, Center for Automated Information and Documentation, 1, rue Guy de la Brosse, F-75005 Paris, France; telephone 01 3362525.

★39★
ASSOCIATION FOR THE PROMOTION OF INDUSTRY-AGRICULTURE
(Association pour la Promotion Industrie-Agriculture)
INTERNATIONAL DOCUMENTATION CENTER FOR INDUSTRIES USING AGRICULTURAL PRODUCTS
(Centre de Documentation Internationale des Industries Utilisatrices de Produits Agricoles - C.D.I.U.P.A.)
Ave. des Olympiades   Phone: 6 9209738
F-91305 Massy Cedex, France   Service Est: 1967
Gisele Carra, Director

Staff: Approximately 11 total.

Related Organizations: The International Documentation Center for Industries Using Agricultural Products receives support from the French Ministry of Agriculture, and carries out the information activities of the Commission Internationale des Industries Agricoles et Alimentaires.

Description of System or Service: The INTERNATIONAL DOCUMENTATION CENTER FOR INDUSTRIES USING AGRICULTURAL PRODUCTS (C.D.I.U.P.A.) performs abstracting and indexing of the world's literature in the field of food science, technology, and economy. Abstracts produced by the CENTER are stored in its computer-readable data base, IALINE-Pascal, for retrospective searches, current awareness services, and the production of an abstracts journal.

Scope and/or Subject Matter: Food science, technology, and economy, with emphasis on industrial utilization of agricultural products and by-products.

Input Sources: Information for the data base is obtained from journals, books, monographs, proceedings, reports, and dissertations.

Holdings and Storage Media: The machine-readable IALINE-Pascal data base holds more than 183,000 records; over 1000 new records are added monthly. The Center's collection consists of 5000 bound volumes; subscriptions to 800 periodicals; and 125,000 microfiche.

Publications: Industries Agro-Alimentaires Bibliographie Internationale (monthly).

Microform Products and Services: Most documents abstracted by the Center are stored on microfiche; full-text reproduction services are offered.

Computer-Based Products and Services: IALINE-Pascal is available on magnetic tape issued monthly or online via Telesystemes Questel. The CENTER performs retrospective searches and offers a current awareness service using the data base.

Other Services: In addition to the services described above, the CENTER offers special bibliographies, manual literature searching, translations, and document delivery.

Clientele/Availability: Services are available on a fee basis.

Contact: Gisele Carra, Director, International Documentation Center for Industries Using Agricultural Products.

★40★
ASSOCIATION OF DATABASE PRODUCERS (ADP)
Geosystems   Phone: 01-222 7305
P.O. Box 1024, Westminster   Founded: 1977
London SW1P 2JL, England
Graham Lea, Chairman

Description of System or Service: The ASSOCIATION OF DATABASE PRODUCERS (ADP) is a not-for-profit trade organization established to promote and protect the interests of those who produce machine-readable bibliographic or numeric data bases. The ASSOCIATION provides members with a forum for the communication of ideas and discussion of common problems encountered in the development, dissemination, and use of computer-based information services. It also works to develop standards and guidelines for the production and use of data bases. Additional ADP activities include acting as a referral center for its members' products, organizing exhibitions and user education seminars, and maintaining contacts with other information organizations on national and international levels.

Scope and/or Subject Matter: Data base production and commercial use.

Publications: Member's Handbook—includes notes of meetings and technical notices.

Clientele/Availability: ADP membership is composed of data base producers in the United Kingdom.

Contact: Graham Lea, Chairman, Association of Database Producers.

★41★
ASSOCIATION OF EUROPEAN AIRLINES (AEA)
AEA DATA BASE
Bte. 4   Phone: 02 6403175
350, ave. Louise
B-1050 Brussels, Belgium
Mr. K-H. Neumeister, Secretary General
Staff: 19 Total.

Description of System or Service: The AEA DATA BASE is a computer-readable file containing financial and operating statistics on the 20 major European airlines that are members of the Association of European Airlines. Included are annual data covering operating revenues, costs, and traffic statistics, and monthly data covering intra-European point-to-point statistics, international scheduled traffic statistics, and punctuality statistics. Forecasts of scheduled passenger traffic are also available. The AEA DATA BASE is accessible online, and related statistical publications are issued by the AEA.

Scope and/or Subject Matter: European airline services.

Holdings and Storage Media: The computer-readable AEA Data Base contains approximately 175,000 time series; coverage varies with the series, with the earliest data from 1965.

Publications: 1) Scheduled Intra-European Passenger and Cargo Traffic of AEA Member Airlines (monthly). 2) Traffic and Operating Data of AEA Airlines (annual).

Computer-Based Products and Services: The AEA DATA BASE is accessible online through I.P. Sharp Associates; it provides financial and operating statistics of AEA member airlines as well as forecasts of scheduled passenger traffic.

Clientele/Availability: Approval by AEA is required for access to the AEA Data Base.

Contact: Mr. M. Pisters, Assistant Secretary General, or S.T. Immonen, Administration Officer, Association of European Airlines. Telex BRURBSN (SITA) 22918.

★42★
ASSOCIATION OF EUROPEAN HOST OPERATORS GROUP (EHOG)
(Association des Centres Serveurs Europeens de Banques de Donnees)
ECHO, 15 ave. de la Faiencerie   Phone: 352 20764
L-1510 Luxembourg   Founded: 1982
Marino Saksida, President

Description of System or Service: The ASSOCIATION OF EUROPEAN HOST OPERATORS GROUP (EHOG) is a trade association of more than thirty organizations that maintain data bases on their computer facilities and make them publicly accessible online via Euronet or European national networks. A primary interest of EHOG is to encourage the simplification and standardization of accessing online data bases. Other interests of the GROUP include online availability of primary documents and user aids and education.

Scope and/or Subject Matter: Promotion of online information retrieval in Europe.

Clientele/Availability: Membership is open to organizations providing online access to data bases through Euronet or a national public network.

Contact: Roland Haber, Secretary, Association of European Host Operators Group. (Telex 3511 LU.)

★43★
ASSOCIATION OF SOCIAL SCIENCES INSTITUTES
(Arbeitsgemeinschaft Sozialwissenschaftlicher Institute)
SOCIAL SCIENCES INFORMATION CENTER
(InformationsZentrum Sozialwissenschaften - IZ)
Lennestr. 30   Phone: 0228 22810
D-5300 Bonn 1, Fed. Rep. of Germany   Service Est: 1971
Dr. Karl A. Stroetmann, Director
Staff: 50 Total.

Related Organizations: The Information Center receives funding from the German Ministry for Research and Technology/Bundesministerium fur Forschung und Technologie.

Description of System or Service: As the national information and documentation center for the social sciences, the SOCIAL SCIENCES INFORMATION CENTER (IZ) collects and disseminates information on social sciences related literature and research projects. It maintains the computer-readable SOLIS (Sozialwissenschaftliches Literaturinformationssystem) and FORIS (Forschungsinformationssystem Sozialwissenschaften) data bases. SOLIS provides bibliographic information and abstracts of German-language periodical, monographic, and other published and unpublished literature on sociology and related fields. FORIS contains descriptions of more than 30,000 planned, ongoing, and completed German, Austrian, and Swiss research projects in the social sciences and includes 7000 organization names and addresses. Both data bases are commercially available online. IZ provides information retrieval and SDI services from these files and other relevant data bases, and also issues publications in its fields of interest.

Scope and/or Subject Matter: Social sciences, including sociology, political science, economics, education, psychology, leisure, criminology, mass communications, planning, and related areas.

Input Sources: Bibliographic input is derived from approximately 600 periodicals, monographs, and nonconventional literature; other information is gathered through questionnaires and from cooperating institutions.

Holdings and Storage Media: The computer-readable SOLIS data base contains more than 30,000 references dating from 1945 to the present and is updated at an annual rate of 10,000 records. The FORIS data base contains approximately 35,000 records dating from 1971 to the present and is updated at an annual rate of 5000 records.

Publications: 1) Forschungsarbeiten in den Sozialwissenschaften: Dokumentation (annual)—directory of social science reseach projects. 2) Deutsche Soziologie 1945-1977—bibliography. Other publications cover literature and current research information in specific fields of social sciences.

Computer-Based Products and Services: The SOCIAL SCIENCES INFORMATION CENTER maintains the SOLIS and FORIS data bases which are commercially available online through INKA (Informationssystem Karlsruhe). Searchable data elements for SOLIS include author, title, place of publication, publication date, bibliographic reference, document type, German-language abstract (for documents cited since 1976), and descriptors. FORIS is searchable by project title, researchers, project leader, institution, contact, contents, time period, geographic area, methodology, data collection, interpretation, publication, working paper, project type, duration of project, sponsor, financial source, IZ source, and descriptors. The CENTER provides searching from its own data bases and from SOCIAL SCISEARCH, PsycINFO, PSYNDEX, ERIC, and other external files; SDI services are also available. Search results are available on paper, magnetic tape, or microfiche.

Other Services: Referrals to other information centers in the social sciences are also provided.

Clientele/Availability: IZ serves clients in research, education, economics, government, the media, and private organizations.

Contact: Wilfried von Lossow, Social Sciences Information Center.

★44★
ATOMIC ENERGY OF CANADA, LTD. (AECL)
CHALK RIVER NUCLEAR LABORATORIES (CRNL)
TECHNICAL INFORMATION BRANCH

Chalk River, ON, Canada K0J 1J0
G.P.L. Williams, Head
Phone: (613) 687-5581
Service Est: 1946

Staff: 7 Information and library professional; 2 management professional; 19 clerical and nonprofessional.

Related Organizations: Atomic Energy of Canada, Ltd. is a federal crown corporation reporting to the Canada Department of Energy, Mines and Resources.

Description of System or Service: The TECHNICAL INFORMATION BRANCH constitutes the principal Canadian national resource for providing nuclear information and documents, particularly technical information generated by Atomic Energy of Canada, Ltd. Through its Main Library, the BRANCH offers manual and computerized literature searching, SDI, duplication services, translations, and interlibrary loans. The Library also is developing an online library management system. Additionally, the BRANCH collaborates with atomic energy organizations in other countries to facilitate the transfer of information, and it abstracts and indexes Canadian input for the International Nuclear Information System (INIS) data base.

Scope and/or Subject Matter: Nuclear science and engineering; physics; chemistry and chemical engineering; metallurgy; engineering; electronics; mathematics and computer sciences; biochemistry; biology.

Input Sources: Literature is acquired through exchange arrangements with national and international nuclear agencies. Internally generated reports and documents and computer-readable data bases also provide input.

Holdings and Storage Media: Library holdings consist of approximately 76,000 volumes, 53,500 bound periodicals, 33,000 translations, 510,000 research reports, and subscriptions to 2000 periodicals. The AECL Document data base is maintained in machine-readable form.

Publications: 1) List of Publications (semiannual, annual). 2) Technical Information and Library Services of Atomic Energy of Canada, Ltd. 3) Serial Holdings: Main Library, Atomic Energy of Canada, Ltd. 4) CRNL Library Accessions List (weekly). 5) Energy Storage—review. 6) Pulse Radiolysis—supplement to a bibliography.

Microform Products and Services: Hard copy and duplicate microfiche are provided from nuclear research reports in microform.

Computer-Based Products and Services: The TECHNICAL INFORMATION BRANCH's library is developing the Chalk River Bibliographic Data Integrated System (CHARIBDIS), a long-term modular project for automating principal library services. Special systems include periodical ordering and a holdings list; book, periodical, and research report loans; research report indexes; and a nuclear controversy subject index. Computerized searching and current awareness services are available from data bases made available by CAN/OLE, CAN/SDI, DIALOG Information Services, Inc., and System Development Corporation (SDC), as well as from the AECL Document data base held on the CRNL computer center.

Clientele/Availability: Services are available to AECL staff on a national basis at a partial cost-recovery charge, and to outside users by negotiation.

Contact: G.P.L. Williams, Head, or Harry Greenshields, Chief Librarian, Technical Information Branch. (Telex 053 34555.)

★45★
ATOMIC ENERGY OF CANADA, LTD. (AECL)
WHITESHELL NUCLEAR RESEARCH ESTABLISHMENT (WNRE)
TECHNICAL INFORMATION SERVICES

Pinawa, MB, Canada R0E 1L0
M.O. Luke, Head
Phone: (204) 753-2311
Service Est: 1963

Staff: 6 Information and library professional; 1 management professional; 12 clerical and nonprofessional.

Related Organizations: Atomic Energy of Canada, Ltd. is a federal crown corporation reporting to the Canada Department of Energy, Mines and Resources.

Description of System or Service: The TECHNICAL INFORMATION SERVICES collects, catalogs, indexes, and disseminates information in the field of nuclear science and technology to meet the needs of the Whiteshell Nuclear Research Establishment. It provides retrospective searching and current awareness services through computerized and manual methods. Additional and miscellaneous services include technical report editing and publishing, operation of a word processing center, patent liaison and administration, contracts administration, and provision of personnel to technical committees. The TECHNICAL INFORMATION SERVICES also contributes to the international nuclear science community by preparing abstracts and indexes of Canadian literature for input to the International Nuclear Information Service (INIS) maintained by the International Atomic Energy Agency.

Scope and/or Subject Matter: Nuclear science and technology; engineering, chemistry, and physics relating to nuclear science; medical biophysics; waste management; related business and management information; environmental control and other health and safety matters related to nuclear science.

Input Sources: Input consists of scientific periodicals, books, microforms, technical reports, conference papers, research reports from associated laboratories and universities, and online data bases.

Holdings and Storage Media: Collection consists of 51,000 volumes; 400,000 hardcopy and microfiche reports; and subscriptions to 740 periodicals.

Computer-Based Products and Services: Retrospective searching and SDI services are provided from data bases made available online through commercial vendors. CAN/SDI and INIS/SDI tape services are also utilized.

Other Services: In addition to services described above, interlibrary loans are offered.

Clientele/Availability: Information retrieval and editing services are available on a commercial basis. All other services are limited to Whiteshell personnel and AECL staff and contractors.

Contact: M.O. Luke, Head, Technical Information Services. (Telex 07 57553.)

★46★
AUSTRALIA
BUREAU OF TRANSPORT ECONOMICS (BTE)
BTE INFORMATION SYSTEMS
P.O. Box 501 Civic Square   Phone: 062 469616
Canberra, A.C.T. 2608, Australia   Service Est: 1981

Staff: 1 Information and library professional; 2 clerical and nonprofessional.

Description of System or Service: BTE INFORMATION SYSTEMS produces computer-based information systems of interest to the transport community in Australia. These include the Australian Transport Literature Information System (ATLIS), the Australian Transport Information Directory (ATID), and the Australian Transport Research in Progress (ATRIP). ATLIS is a bibliographic reference system which covers current literature related to all forms of Australian transport. It includes material on general transport-related tourism, fuels and energy, industrial relations, materials handling, and regional planning. To avoid duplication with the Australian Road Index (ARI) produced by the Australian Road Research Board and the Literature Analysis System of the Office of Road Safety (LASORS), ATLIS does not include specialized material dealing with road technology, road traffic management, and road safety. Available online, the ATLIS is also used to produce printed quarterly bulletins. The Australian Transport Information Directory (ATID) is a computer-generated directory to the sources of structured collections of information relevant to Australian transport. Printed annually in a bulletin format, ATID is not complementary to any other similar transport information system and therefore includes all transport modes within its coverage. Australian Transport Research in Progress (ATRIP) is an information system containing details of transport research being undertaken in Australia. Used to produce annual bulletins, ATRIP is complementary to the ARRB Australian Road Research in Progress of the ARRB. ATID and ATRIP are not currently available online.

Scope and/or Subject Matter: All modes of Australian transport, including transport policy, planning, operations, research, information sources, and analysis.

Input Sources: Contributions to ATLIS are made by various transport libraries and other bodies located in all states and territories of Australia. More than 150 periodicals are scanned. Items indexed also include books, technical papers, research reports, conference proceedings, newspapers, theses, annual reports, statistics, press releases, and speeches. Information for inclusion in ATID is provided by the various statistical collection agencies which handle transport matters, and by researchers who have undertaken specific transport studies. Information for ATRIP is provided by researchers in transport organizations, government departments, universities, and other tertiary institutions which undertake specific transport studies.

Holdings and Storage Media: The Australian Transport Literature Information System is maintained in machine-readable form and covers the period from 1981 to the present. Updated quarterly, the bibliographic data base contains approximately 4000 entries, with 300 to 500 entries added per quarter. ATID and ATRIP are also maintained in machine readable form and cover the period from 1982 to the present.

Publications: 1) ATLIS Bulletin (quarterly)—abstracting and indexing bulletin covering current periodical literature and other published material dealing with all forms of Australian transportation. Available by subscription. 2) ATID (Australian Transport Information Directory) Bulletin (annual)—each entry includes entry number, title of information collection, agency or agencies holding the information, principal contacts in the agency or agencies, description of the information collection, and other information. Issues of the Bulletin include entries previously published, with updates when necessary. Available by subscription. 3) ATRIP (Australian Transport Research in Progress) Bulletin (annual)—each ATRIP entry includes entry number, title of the research project, current status and activity level, agency or agencies responsible for the project, principal contacts, description of the research project, progress notes, and other data. Available by subscription. The above publications can be ordered from Mail Order Sales, Australian Government Publishing Service, GPO Box 84, Canberra, A.C.T. 2601, Australia.

Microform Products and Services: For each calendar year a cumulative ATLIS Bulletin Index, having the same format as that appearing in the printed quarterly Bulletin, and a corresponding Titles Index are produced in microfiche form and are available free of charge.

Computer-Based Products and Services: BTE INFORMATION SYSTEMS maintains the computer-based ATLIS, ATID, and ATRIP information systems. The ATLIS data base is available for searching through the Ausinet system. Each entry can contain up to 18 paragraphs as well as one formatted field for range retrieval. Paragraphs include the following: year of publication; ATLIS number; title and title annotations; personal and corporate authors; abstract; notes; descriptors; identifiers; source file; conference name and details; edition statement; volume number; place of publication, publisher, date published, and reference; pagination; series title and number; International Standard Book Number; International Standard Serial Number; availability statement; and location of library holdings. All paragraphs are searchable except edition, volume, and pagination. The BTE also provides information retrieval services from its data bases.

Clientele/Availability: Users include researchers, administrators, transport operators and users, scholars, and the general public. Services are available without restrictions.

Contact: Margaret Thompson, Librarian, BTE Library Service.

★47★
AUSTRALIA
COMMONWEALTH SCIENTIFIC AND INDUSTRIAL RESEARCH ORGANIZATION (CSIRO)
CENTRAL INFORMATION, LIBRARY AND EDITORIAL SECTION (CILES)
314 Albert St.   Phone: 03 4187333
P.O. Box 89   Service Est: 1926
East Melbourne, Vic. 3002, Australia
Peter J. Judge, Officer-in-Charge

Staff: 54 Information and library professional; 6 management professional; 40 technicians; 3 sales and marketing; 30 clerical and nonprofessional; 8 other.

Related Organizations: CSIRO cooperates with the Commonwealth Regional Renewable Energy Resources Information System (CRRERIS) and the Australian Mineral Foundation's Australian Earth Sciences Information System (AESIS), which are described in separate entries in these pages.

Description of System or Service: The CENTRAL INFORMATION, LIBRARY AND EDITORIAL SECTION (CILES) provides CSIRO staff and the Australian scientific and technological community with computer-based information services, library services, and publications. It indexes research literature; produces the CSIRO Index and other computer-readable data bases; and provides search and SDI services from these files and from commercially available online data bases. CILES also provides document delivery services from its library and it publishes more than a dozen primary research journals, several indexes and bibliographies, and a union list of serials.

Scope and/or Subject Matter: Science, research, and technology, excluding clinical medicine; individual data bases are maintained on the topics of agriculture, nutrition, and research centers and publications.

Input Sources: Input is derived from data bases, literature, documents, questionnaires, and numerical data.

Holdings and Storage Media: Library holdings consist of 1 million bound volumes and subscriptions to 13,500 periodicals. Cataloging information on monograph and serials acquisitions is held in computer-readable form under the cooperative SIROCAT computerized cataloging system. CILES also maintains a number of other bibliographic and factual data bases.

Publications: 1) CSIRO Index (monthly)—covers published works of CSIRO scientists. 2) CSIRO List of Publications (CLOP)—a listing of some 4000 publications issued by CSIRO. 3) Bibliography of Infant Foods and Nutrition, 1938-1977—covers the formulation, manufacture, and properties of infant foods. 4) Scientific Serials in Australian Libraries (SSAL)—a union list. 5) Scientific and Technical Research Centres in Australia (STRC)—a directory of scientific and technological research. 6) Directory of CSIRO Research Programs. CILES also publishes 16 primary research journals and various monographs and reports; catalogs are available from the Section on request.

Microform Products and Services: All CSIRO journals as well as supplements to the union list are available on microfiche.

Computer-Based Products and Services: CILES creates and maintains the following data bases: 1) Australian Bibliography of Agriculture (ABOA)—contains approximately 25,000 records covering agricultural literature published from 1975 to the present. 2) CSIRO Index—covers more than 30,000 works published by CSIRO scientists since 1969. 3) Diretory of CSIRO Research Programs—covers some 800 programs and subprograms. 4) Infant Feeding Bibliography—holds approximately 4500 records covering worldwide publications in the fields of infant foods and nutrition. 5) Scientific and Technical Research Centres in Australia (STRC)—contains information on more than 1000 research centers and scientific societies in Australia. CILES offers retrospective searches and SDI services from these data bases and from data bases accessed online through such systems as DIALOG Information Services, Inc. and System Development Corporation (SDC). Additionally, CILES makes available numeric data bases, including a thermodynamic data bank leased from the National Physical Laboratory in England, over the CSIRO computer network, CSIRONET, to provide researchers with remote terminal access. It also offers access to the Cambridge Crystallographic Data Base, NIH-EPA Mass Spectra system, and other scientific and technical data bases and systems.

Other Services: Besides services described above, CILES provides consulting services for the solution of current information problems and guidance in long-range planning for information programs. Manual literature searching and referrals are also offered.

Clientele/Availability: Chief clientele is Australian scientific and industrial personnel.

Remarks: CILES previously published the Australian Science Index (ASI) and offered a corresponding online data base. ASI was discontinued in view of the growing number of Australian data bases covering specialized areas of science.

Contact: Clyde Garrow, Manager, Central Information Service; Peter H. Dawe, Chief Librarian, Central Library; or Basil J. Walby, Editor-in-Chief, Editorial and Publications Service, Commonwealth Scientific and Industrial Research Organization. (Telex 30236 AA.)

★48★
AUSTRALIA
NATIONAL LIBRARY OF AUSTRALIA
Parkes Place   Phone: 062 621111
Canberra, A.C.T. 2600, Australia   Service Est: 1960
Harrison Bryan, Director-General

Staff: 205 Information and library professional; 54 management professional; 54 technicians; 1 sales and marketing; 269 clerical and nonprofessional.

Related Organizations: The National Library of Australia operates through three branches: a Reference Division, a Technical Services Division, and a Co-ordination and Management Division.

Description of System or Service: The NATIONAL LIBRARY OF AUSTRALIA maintains a national collection of library materials including a comprehensive collection relating to Australia and its people, and provides library and information services throughout the country from these and other resources. In the area of bibliographical services, the LIBRARY produces the national bibliography, provides central cataloging services, and maintains union catalogs, including the national union catalogs for monographs and serials. It has developed a national online bibliographic support system known as the Australian Bibliographic Network (see separate entry following this one), and it also provides cataloging records in machine-readable or card form through its Australian MARC Record Service (AMRS), which uses Australian, U.S. Library of Congress, and British Library MARC data.

Additionally, the LIBRARY issues several major publications that are accessible as online data bases, including the Australian National Bibliography (ANB), comprising Australian MARC records added to the ANB/MARC system since 1972; the Australian Public Affairs Information Service (APAIS), a multidisciplinary subject index to Australian periodical and composite literature in the social sciences and humanities; and the National Union Catalogue of Serials (NUCOS). In addition to furnishing these and other national services, the LIBRARY acts as the Australian focus for a number of international programs and systems, including the United Nations Educational, Scientific and Cultural Organization's General Information Programme, International Serials Data System (ISDS), and International Information System on Research in Documentation (ISORID), as well as the International Standard Book Number (ISBN) program.

Scope and/or Subject Matter: Australian studies, social sciences, humanities, fine arts, life sciences, area studies (with some emphasis on Asian studies), medicine, science and technology.

Input Sources: The Library acquires materials in all media and formats from domestic and foreign sources. Input for ANB is primarily taken from literature published in Australia. Material scanned for APAIS includes Australian scholarly journals, newspapers, and conference proceedings, and overseas literature relating to Australia.

Holdings and Storage Media: Library collections include more than 3.7 million volumes and microform equivalents; 108,000 newspaper and serial titles; 5700 meters of manuscripts; 12,000 sound recordings; 38,000 paintings, drawings, and prints; 411,000 photographs; 19,000 film and video titles; 222,000 maps; 74,500 music scores; and 551,000 aerial photographs. Updated monthly, the computer-readable ANB data base holds more than 100,000 items from 1972 to date with approximately 600 records added per month. The APAIS data base includes 74,000 records dating from 1978 to the present.

Publications: 1) Australian National Bibliography-ANB (fortnightly with monthly, quarterly, and annual cumulations)—lists books, reports, and pamphlets published in Australia, and items of Australian association that are published overseas. 2) Australian Public Affairs Information Service-APAIS (monthly with annual cumulations)—subject index to current Australian literature on political, social, cultural, and economic affairs. 3) Australian Government Publications (quarterly with annual cumulations). 4) Film and Video Acquisition (quarterly). 5) Australian Books: A Select List of Recent Publications and Standard Works in Print (annual). 6) Australian Maps (annual). A variety of additional publications, including user aids, bibliographies, and union catalogs, is also issued. Orders and inquiries should be addressed to the Sales and Subscriptions Section of the National Library.

Microform Products and Services: The Library makes available a number of microform products, including the following: the Australian MARC Record Service title index on microfiche, issued annually with monthly supplements; National Union Catalogue of Serials (NUCOS), issued twice yearly; the national union catalog of monographs and the national union catalog of East Asian monographs, issued on microfilm; the ANB Catalogue, issued annually with quarterly COM supplements; quarterly additions to the National Library's catalogue on microfiche; the National Union Catalogue of Library Materials for the Handicapped (NUC:H), issued quarterly in updated form; and the National Film Lending Collection Catalogue, issued annually.

Computer-Based Products and Services: The Australian National Bibliography (ANB) and Australian Public Affairs Information Service (APAIS) data bases are searchable online through the Ausinet information network of ACI Computer Services. Searchable fields in ANB include author and title, publisher, edition, imprint, price, Precis and LC subject headings, Dewey Decimal Classification number, UDC number, LC number, geographic area codes, and language. APAIS records contain accession number, input date, title, citation, and major descriptor paragraphs; other data which appear as required include author, name, and identifiers. The NATIONAL LIBRARY, in conjunction with the Australian Department of Health, also acts as the center for the Australian MEDLINE Network (see separate entry following this one). Additionally, it accesses publicly available Australian and overseas data bases made available through Ausinet and overseas vendors and contributes input to international data systems.

Other Services: In addition to the services described above, the Library provides interlibrary loans and reference services from each of its specialist areas.

Clientele/Availability: Services are available without restrictions to domestic and foreign users.

Contact: Mr. E.R. Vellacott, Library Secretariat; telephone 062 621654. (Telex 62100.)

★49★
AUSTRALIA
NATIONAL LIBRARY OF AUSTRALIA
AUSTRALIAN BIBLIOGRAPHIC NETWORK (ABN)
Parkes Place   Phone: 062 621111
Canberra, A.C.T. 2600, Australia   Service Est: 1981
Judith A. Baskin, Director

Staff: 15 Information and library professional; 35 systems/data processing.

Description of System or Service: The AUSTRALIAN BIBLIOGRAPHIC NETWORK (ABN) is an automated national bibliographic service based on a cooperative online shared cataloging facility. ABN was established to develop a comprehensive national data base of machine-readable records for all types of library materials; to provide an inquiry system which permits the widest possible access to this national data base; to provide a range of products and services based on the national data base; to accommodate a range of decentralized services with a view to promoting the fullest possible use of the data base; and to develop an Australian authorities system. The NETWORK provides online bibliographic and inquiry services as well as batch products such as magnetic tape and COM microfiche catalogs, card sets, labels, and acquisitions lists.

Scope and/or Subject Matter: Cooperative machine-readable cataloging information in all disciplines.

Input Sources: Input consists of Australian, U.S. Library of Congress, U.S. Government Printing Office, United Kingdom, and National Library of Canada MARC records, as well as original cataloging by National Library of Australia and ABN participants, including the University of Sydney Library's Bibliographic Information on Southeast Asia (BISA) service.

Holdings and Storage Media: The computer-readable ABN data base contains 3.2 million bibliographic records and 1.7 million library locations. The bibliographic data base includes Library of Congress records since 1968, British National Bibliography records since 1980, Canadiana records since 1980, New Zealand National Bibliography records since 1982, Australian National Bibliography records since 1972, U.S. Government Printing Office information since 1976, Washington Library Network records from 1973 to 1980, and ABN participants records since 1980, with some retrospective files.

Publications: 1) ABN News; 2) ABN: A Bibliography—provides citations to literature on ABN, the Washington Library Network (WLN), and developments in the field of bibliographic networking. Users manuals are also issued.

Microform Products and Services: Individual or union catalogs are produced on demand on COM microfiche.

Computer-Based Products and Services: Operating under a modified version of the Washington Library Network's software system, the AUSTRALIAN BIBLIOGRAPHIC NETWORK provides online access to the following files: the bibliographic file—contains the basic bibliographic description for each item cataloged; the vocabulary file—contains author and subject headings, cross-references, and notes relating to the heading; the holdings file—contains participants' call numbers and library identification symbols; the working file—contains bibliographic and vocabulary records which are being input or changed. Online inquiry is available for dial-up or leased-line terminals and provides online reference searches, online access to bibliographic records and holdings information, and access to alternative locations through the immediate display of holdings information. ABN provides shared online cataloging service as well as a magnetic tape distribution service.

Clientele/Availability: Network services are available to libraries in Australia. Dial-up users of the inquiry mode are not permitted to use ABN bibliographic records as a source of cataloging data.

Projected Publications and Services: An interlibrary loan request system is under consideration and provision has been made for the system to interface with other networks and computer sytems.

Contact: Judith A. Baskin, Director, or W.S. Cathro, Executive Officer, Networks Branch, National Library of Australia. (Telex 62100.)

★50★
AUSTRALIA
NATIONAL LIBRARY OF AUSTRALIA
AUSTRALIAN MEDLINE NETWORK
Parkes Place   Phone: 062 621523
Canberra, A.C.T. 2600, Australia   Service Est: 1976
Paul Hodgson, Director

Staff: 7 Information and library professional; 2 clerical and nonprofessional.

Related Organizations: The National Library of Australia and the Australian Commonwealth Department of Health are jointly responsible for management of the Australian MEDLINE Network.

Description of System or Service: The AUSTRALIAN MEDLINE NETWORK provides biomedical-related online information retrieval, SDI, and document ordering services for clients in Australia, New Zealand, and Singapore. The NETWORK supplies interactive access to a series of data bases produced by the U.S. National Library of Medicine and Australian sources. More than 200 organizations use the service, including all Australian medical schools, the majority of major metropolitan hospitals, state health agencies, universities, private firms, and other organizations.

Scope and/or Subject Matter: Health, medicine, and related biological sciences; toxicology; health planning; medical library holdings.

Input Sources: Data bases are obtained from the U.S. National Library of Medicine and Australian sources.

Holdings and Storage Media: Seven bibliographic data bases are held online under the ELHILL retrieval programs using Commonwealth Department of Health computer facilities.

Publications: Australian MEDLINER (quarterly)—technical newsletter containing information about network developments and systems charges as well as searching advice. Relevant material from the National Library of Medicine's Technical Bulletin and other newsletters is reproduced in Australian MEDLINER. Individual data base search manuals are available for purchase from the Life Sciences Section of the National Library.

Computer-Based Products and Services: The AUSTRALIAN MEDLINE NETWORK provides online access to the following data bases: MEDLINE, Health Planning and Administration, Registry of Toxic Effects of Chemical Substances (RTECS), Toxicology Data Bank, Serials Online (SERLINE), Catalog Online (CATLINE), and Health and Medical Libraries Online Catalog (HEMLOC). HEMLOC is a Department of Health sponsored union catalog which functions as an Australian supplement to CATLINE. Another data base soon to be added is the Australian Medical Index, which treats Australian articles and reports not covered by existing services. In addition to basic online retrieval, the NETWORK includes automated SDI and document ordering facilities. The SDI service uses a computer program known as NETSDI to automatically produce a list of references on the subject of the search whenever new data are added to a data base. The AUSTRALIAN MEDLINE NETWORK can be accessed with a local telephone call by participating organizations in capital cities via the Health Department's Health Communications Network; users elsewhere are able to dial in to the network through a Telecom Australia data-switching facility.

Clientele/Availability: Clients include hospitals, universities, research institutes, government departments, information brokers, and pharmaceutical companies, as well as research staffs of private organizations.

Contact: Paul Hodgson, Director, or Sandra Henderson, Head, Customer Services, Australian MEDLINE Network. (Telex 62100.)

★51★
AUSTRALIAN ATOMIC ENERGY COMMISSION
LUCAS HEIGHTS RESEARCH LABORATORIES LIBRARY
Private Mail Bag Phone: 02 5430111
Sutherland, N.S.W. 2232, Australia Service Est: 1958
Wilson H. Neale, Head Librarian

Staff: 7 Information and library professional; 6 technicians; 3 clerical and nonprofessional.

Description of System or Service: The LUCAS HEIGHTS RESEARCH LABORATORIES LIBRARY provides manual and computer-based information services to the staff of the Australian Atomic Energy Commission and those Commonwealth Scientific and Industrial Research Organization (CSIRO) units based at Lucas Heights. As the national center for the International Nuclear Information System (INIS), the LIBRARY gathers Australian nuclear science literature for inclusion in the INIS data base; provides Australian users with online access to the collected INIS data base of worldwide nuclear literature documentation; and distributes INIS publications within Australia.

Scope and/or Subject Matter: Nuclear science and its applications; power and energy; the uranium fuel cycle.

Input Sources: The Library collects monographs, periodicals, pamphlets, conference proceedings, reports, and standards from worldwide sources including INIS and the U.S. Department of Energy. Tapes from INIS are received monthly.

Holdings and Storage Media: Library currently holds approximately 25,000 monographs; 500,000 technical reports; and 700 periodical subscriptions. It also maintains a copy of the INIS data base from 1972 to date, as well as a computer-readable union list of periodicals and a list of publications issued by the Australian Atomic Energy Commission.

Publications: A printed index to Commission reports is issued irregularly.

Microform Products and Services: Microfiche copies of the Commission report series are available.

Computer-Based Products and Services: The Library makes the INIS data base available to Australian users for online searching. Retrospective literature searches and monthly SDI services are also offered.

Other Services: In addition to the services described above, the Library offers manual literature searches and referrals.

Clientele/Availability: Services are intended for the Australian Atomic Energy Commission and Lucas Heights CSIRO staff, but others may be served on request and for a fee in the case of computer searches.

Contact: Wilson H. Neale, Head Librarian, Lucas Heights Research Laboratories Library.

★52★
AUSTRALIAN BUREAU OF STATISTICS (ABS)
P.O. Box 10 Phone: 062 526627
Belconnen, A.C.T. 2616, Australia Founded: 1905
Mr. R.J. Cameron, Australian Statistician

Staff: 3400 Total, including 180 information and library professional.
Related Organizations: The Australian Bureau of Statistics is a unit of the Department of the Treasury.

Description of System or Service: The AUSTRALIAN BUREAU OF STATISTICS (ABS) is a federal government service organization which collects, compiles, and publishes statistical information needed by private enterprise, government agencies, and the general public to understand economic and social conditions and trends in Australia. ABS makes these data available in hardcopy publications, on microfiche, and in machine-readable form. The BUREAU also answers inquiries about unpublished statistics.

Scope and/or Subject Matter: Australian economic statistics including mining, retail trade, unemployment, national accounts, balance of payments, primary and manufacturing industries, local government, prices, and overseas trade. Australian social statistics including population and housing, births, deaths, marriages, health, education, and crime.

Input Sources: The central ABS office collects statistics that concern the whole of Australia, the states and territories, and its trade relations with the world; branch offices collect statistics pertinent to their state and to local government areas within their state.

Publications: Catalogue of Publications (annual)—provides details and subject index of the nearly 1500 different statistical publications released each year. These publications are issued on a monthly, quarterly, or annual basis, and range in size from single sheets to comprehensive national and state yearbooks.

Microform Products and Services: Data available on microfiche include statistics on major economic time series, population census, international trade, transport, agriculture, and social and demographic statistics.

Computer-Based Products and Services: ABS disseminates statistical information on magnetic tape and computer printout. Data regularly released on tape include economic time series, population census, input/output series, and national accounts. A number of ABS data bases are accessible online through Computer Sciences of Australia Pty. Ltd. (see separate entry).

Clientele/Availability: ABS serves private enterprise, governments, and the general public.

Contact: Mr. M.J. Sattler, Director, Information Services, Australian Bureau of Statistics. (Telex AA 62020.)

★53★
AUSTRALIAN BUSINESS INDEX
1 Leslie St. Phone: 03 8194672
Hawthorn, Vic. 3122, Australia Founded: 1981
Neil Speirs, Editor

Staff: 2 Management professional; 1 clerical and nonprofessional.

Related Organizations: The parent organization is Specialist Newsletters, located in New South Wales; it is a publisher of newsletters for specific industries.

Description of System or Service: The AUSTRALIAN BUSINESS INDEX is a guide to financial, business, and company news reported in Australian newspapers and business journals. It is available as a printed publication, on microfiche, on computer tapes or disks, and online as the ABIX data base accessible through the ACI Ausinet service.

Scope and/or Subject Matter: Australian financial, business, and company news in every major industry; overseas business news reported in the Australian press.

Input Sources: The Index covers news items, articles, editorials, analyses, comments, and tips appearing in Australian business and financial journals and four daily publications.

Holdings and Storage Media: The ABIX data base holds approximately 240,000 citations in machine-readable form and is updated monthly with approximately 5000 citations.

Publications: Australian Business Index (monthly)—contains business and financial news citations indexed under company name, country, and subject headings appearing in a single alphabetical sequence. The publication is available by subscription which includes 11 monthly issues and an annual cumulation. Order from Specialist Newsletters, Box 430, Milsons Pt., N.S.W. 2061, Australia.

Microform Products and Services: The Index is available on 48x COM microfiche in cumulative monthly issues.

Computer-Based Products and Services: The AUSTRALIAN BUSINESS INDEX is accessible online as the ABIX data base through the ACI Ausinet service. Records in the file include month of publication, topic, and reference citations including article title, journal title abbreviation, date, and page number. Searchable elements include date, title keywords, topic, journal, or a combination of elements. The complete data base is also available on disk or tape for use on in-house systems.

Other Services: Also offered are surveys and watch services for specific industries.

Clientele/Availability: Clients include public and business libraries and financial organizations.

Contact: Neil Speirs, Editor, Australian Business Index.

★54★
AUSTRALIAN COUNCIL FOR EDUCATIONAL RESEARCH
LIBRARY AND INFORMATION SERVICES UNIT
P.O. Box 210   Phone: 03 8181271
Hawthorn, Vic. 3122, Australia
Margaret A. Findlay, Head

Staff: 2 Information and library professional; 1 technician; 1 clerical and nonprofessional.

Description of System or Service: The LIBRARY AND INFORMATION SERVICES UNIT of the Australian Council for Educational Research compiles and publishes the Australian Education Index (AEI), an index to current literature relevant to Australian education, and the Bibliography of Education Theses, a list of theses in education accepted for higher degrees at Australian universities and colleges. Information from both publications is searchable online as the Australian Education Index data base which is available through Ausinet.

Scope and/or Subject Matter: All areas and levels of education in Australia.

Input Sources: Items included in the AEI data base are selected from Australian and overseas sources including monographs, research reports, conference papers, theses, periodical articles, legislation, and book and curriculum materials reviews.

Holdings and Storage Media: The computer-readable AIE data base holds citations published in the printed index since 1979 and in the bibliography of theses since 1982. Library holdings include approximately 15,000 bound volumes.

Publications: 1) Australian Education Index (quarterly, annual cumulation)—each issue contains approximately 600 citations arranged by broad subject categories; an author and institution index; a subject index; and a list of periodicals indexed. 2) Bibliography of Education Theses: A List of Theses in Education Accepted for Higher Degrees at Australian Universities and Colleges (annual)—includes entries arranged alphabetically by author, and a supplementary subject index. Descriptors are assigned from the Australian Thesaurus of Education Descriptors.

Computer-Based Products and Services: The LIBRARY AND INFORMATION SERVICES UNIT compiles the AEI Data Base, which contains citations from the Australian Education Index and the Bibliography of Education Theses. The data base is available for online searching through Ausinet.

Clientele/Availability: Services are available without restrictions.

Contact: Margaret A. Findlay, Head, Library and Information Services Unit, Australian Council for Educational Research.

★55★
AUSTRALIAN FINANCIAL REVIEW
INFO-LINE
Box 506, GPO   Phone: 02 2822822
Sydney, N.S.W. 2001, Australia   Service Est: 1974
Janet Fish, Research Manager

Staff: 8 Information and library professional; 3 management professional; 1 technician; 1 sales and marketing; 1 other.

Related Organizations: INFO-LINE is the business information research arm of the Australian Financial Review, a national daily newspaper published by John Fairfax Ltd. INFO-LINE operates in conjunction with SVP Australia (see separate entry).

Description of System or Service: INFO-LINE is an information-on-demand service providing information and retrieval services for business. These services are based mainly on the extensive news and research files maintained by John Fairfax Ltd., although INFO-LINE also conducts original research and utilizes commercially available online data bases. Nearly 50,000 inquiries per year are handled through INFO-LINE's information-on-demand services. Additionally, INFO-LINE compiles the Australian Financial Review (AFRE) data base, which indexes articles published in the newspaper, and the Business Review Weekly (BRWE) data base, an electronic index to that publication. INFO-LINE also offers document delivery services, including materials from the U.S. National Technical Information Service and other U.S. government agencies.

Scope and/or Subject Matter: Australian and Pacific Islands business, financial, and political information, and other information of interest to clients.

Input Sources: Information sources include the Australian Financial Review and libraries of John Fairfax Ltd.; international SVP resources; local and overseas newspapers; commercially available online data bases; and affiliated overseas research groups.

Holdings and Storage Media: The computer-readable Australian Financial Review data base contains more than 17,000 citations with about 500 citations added per week. The computer-readable Business Review Weekly data base contains approximately 1500 citations with about 50 citations added per week. Fairfax libraries include files of news reports covering more than 12,000 companies and 6000 subject areas.

Publications: Business Information Australia—newsletter covering INFO-LINE services.

Microform Products and Services: Copies of NTIS documents are available on microfiche.

Computer-Based Products and Services: INFO-LINE maintains the AFRE data base, which contains the headline and first paragraph of articles appearing in the Australian Financial Review, and the BRWE data base, which contains the headline and first paragraph of articles appearing in the Business Review Weekly. The data bases are available online through Ausinet and can be searched by keywords found in the remainder of the article, company references, author, date of publication, and page number. INFO-LINE also provides computerized information retrieval from data bases available online through Data-Star, DIALOG Information Services, Inc., Dow Jones News/ Retrieval, Pergamon InfoLine Ltd., I.P. Sharp Associates, System Development Corporation (SDC), and others. Additionally, INFO-LINE collects applicable Australian research information for input to the NTIS data base.

Clientele/Availability: Primary clients include merchant banks, stockbrokers, lawyers, and government agencies. Information-on-demand services are available on a fee or subscription basis.

Projected Publications and Services: INFO-LINE plans to offer additional computerized information services.

Contact: Janet Fish, Research Manager, INFO-LINE. (Telex 24851 AA.) The electronic mail address on ACIMAIL (ACI Computer Services) is FAIRFAX.

★56★
AUSTRALIAN INSTITUTE OF CRIMINOLOGY LIBRARY
COMPUTERISED INFORMATION FROM NATIONAL
  CRIMINOLOGICAL HOLDINGS (CINCH)
10-18 Colbee Court   Phone: 062 822111
Phillip, A.C.T. 2606, Australia   Service Est: 1976
John Walker, Criminologist

Staff: 1 Information and library professional; 1 management professional; 1 technician.

Description of System or Service: COMPUTERISED INFORMATION FROM NATIONAL CRIMINOLOGICAL HOLDINGS (CINCH) is a computer-readable data base that provides a comprehensive bibliography of materials relevant to criminology in Australia, New Zealand, and Papua New Guinea. Materials covered include journals, books, government documents, theses, research reports, and other items. CINCH is used to provide retrospective search services and to publish a quarterly information bulletin.

Scope and/or Subject Matter: Criminology relating to Australia, New Zealand, and Papua New Guinea.

Input Sources: Input is derived from 300 journals and from books, government and research reports, and theses. Newspaper articles, case reports, commentaries, parliamentary debates, and historical government reports are also covered.

Holdings and Storage Media: The computer-readable CINCH data base contains approximately 6000 records dating since 1975.

Publications: Information Bulletin of Australian Criminology (quarterly)—identifies ongoing research, indexes current materials to be added to the data base, and provides information about seminars. A thesaurus is currently being developed.

Computer-Based Products and Services: The computer-readable CINCH data base is used for publication purposes and to provide retrospective search services. Searches can be conducted using approximately 1000 subject terms separately or in combination; additional search elements include author, journal title, time period, and citation categories. CINCH is maintained on the computer facilities of the Australian Scientific and Industrial Research Organization (CSIRO).

Clientele/Availability: Services are available without restrictions.

Contact: Kristina Klop, Information Services Librarian, Australian Institute of Criminology Library.

★57★
AUSTRALIAN MINERAL FOUNDATION
AUSTRALIAN EARTH SCIENCES INFORMATION SYSTEM (AESIS)
P.O. Box 97　　　　　　　　　　　Phone: 08 797821
Glenside, S.A. 5065, Australia　　　Service Est: 1976
D.S. Crowe, Director

Staff: 4 Information and library professional; 1 technician; 2 clerical and nonprofessional; 3 subject specialists.

Related Organizations: The Australian Earth Sciences Information System was created through the joint efforts of the Australian Mineral Foundation, the Australian government, private companies, and the Australian Geoscience Information Association.

Description of System or Service: The AUSTRALIAN EARTH SCIENCES INFORMATION SYSTEM (AESIS) is a nationwide computer-readable data base covering published and unpublished earth sciences literature from or about Australia. AESIS information is available in hard copy, on microfiche, and in an online data base.

Scope and/or Subject Matter: Geology, geophysics, geochemistry, mining, mineral processing, extractive metallurgy and aspects of analytical chemistry, environmental science, energy, and conservation relevant to the earth sciences.

Input Sources: AESIS acquires input from journal literature, reports, papers, maps, theses, open-file reports, and unpublished material.

Holdings and Storage Media: The machine-readable AESIS data base covers Australian earth sciences literature since 1975 and relevant foreign literature since 1979.

Publications: AESIS Quarterly—available by subscription. Contains citations added to the data base during the preceding quarter; each issue has subject, locality, author, map sheet, mine/deposit/well name, stratigraphic name, and serials indexes which are cumulated annually. 2) AESIS special lists—listings from the data base on specific minerals or other topics, each with up to six supporting indexes. 3) AESIS retrospective lists—cover open-file reports and unpublished material from 1965-1975, with supporting indexes. 4) Australian Thesaurus of Earth Sciences and Related Terms—available for purchase.

Microform Products and Services: The AESIS Cumulation, a progressive cumulation issued annually on microfiche, is produced in 5-year segments.

Computer-Based Products and Services: AESIS is searchable online through Ausinet. The Australian Mineral Foundation also provides searches of the file.

Clientele/Availability: Primary clients are Australian earth scientists.

Contact: D.A. Tellis, Information Services Manager, Australian Mineral Foundation. (Telex AA87437 AMFINC.)

★58★
AUSTRALIAN NATIONAL GALLERY (ANG)
LIBRARY
G.P.O. Box 1150　　　　　　　　　Phone: 062 712530
Canberra, A.C.T. 2601, Australia　　Service Est: 1975
Margaret Shaw, Principal Librarian

Staff: 8 Information and library professional; 4 technicians; 3 clerical and nonprofessional.

Description of System or Service: The Australian National Gallery (ANG) LIBRARY was established to document the history and growth of art and culture in Australia. The LIBRARY collects materials on all aspects of Australian art to meet the research needs of ANG staff and visiting scholars. It offers reference and information services, including computerized information retrieval from commercially available data bases. Additionally, the LIBRARY produces the Australian Art Index (AARTI) data base, which is available online and on microfiche; the Australian National Gallery Library Catalogue, which is available on microfiche; and the printed Australian National Gallery Library List of Periodicals (ANGALLOP).

Scope and/or Subject Matter: Australian art, visual and decorative arts worldwide, photography, theater arts, fashion, textiles, and related areas.

Holdings and Storage Media: Library holdings consist of monographs, serials, microfiche, pamphlets, notices, clippings, sale catalogs, acquired private collections, and the AARTI data base.

Publications: The Library produces the Australian National Gallery Library Class N Expansion Tables and the Australian National Gallery Library List of Periodicals (ANGALLOP).

Microform Products and Services: The Australian National Gallery Library Catalogue, which is updated as required, is available on microfiche in two sequences: author/title or subject. Also available is the Australian Art Index microfiche which is updated monthly and cumulated every six months.

Computer-Based Products and Services: The LIBRARY maintains the computer-readable Australian Art Index (AARTI) data base holding bibliographic information on visual art in Australia and Australian art overseas, including theater design, artistic photography, and architecture from the design point of view. It covers exhibition catalogs, monographs, theses, articles, and other sources. Operating since 1982, the AARTI data base contains more than 6500 records with an additional 300 records added each month. AARTI is available online through Ausinet. The LIBRARY also offers computerized information searches of the AARTI data base, as well as information retrieval services from data bases made available through Ausinet, DIALOG Information Services, Inc., and Research Libraries Information Network (RLIN).

Clientele/Availability: Most services are intended for ANG staff and research scholars who have received permission from the ANG.

Contact: Margaret Shaw, Principal Librarian, ANG Library. (Telex AA 61500.)

★59★
AUSTRALIAN NATIONAL RADIO ASTRONOMY OBSERVATORY
PARKES CATALOGUE OF RADIO SOURCES (PKSCAT)
P.O. Box 276　　　　　　　　　　Phone: 068 633131
Parkes, N.S.W. 2870, Australia　　Service Est: 1960
Dr. Alan E. Wright, Head

Staff: 1 Management professional; 1 other.

Description of System or Service: The machine-readable PARKES CATALOGUE OF RADIO SOURCES (PKSCAT) contains radio and optical astronomical identifications and other data. Much of the CATALOGUE, which forms part of the Continuum Astronomical Data Files, is published in major astronomical journals. PKSCAT is also provided on computer tapes.

Scope and/or Subject Matter: Astronomical data, primarily for the southern hemisphere.

Input Sources: Input is derived from original work at the Australian National Radio Astronomy Observatory and other radio and optical observatories, and from astronomical journals.

Holdings and Storage Media: Holdings include printout listings and machine-readable tapes.

Computer-Based Products and Services: Magnetic tape copies of the PARKES CATALOGUE are available at cost.

Clientele/Availability: Astronomical research workers are the primary clients.

Contact: Dr. Alan E. Wright, Principal Research Scientist, Australian National Radio Astronomy Observatory.

★60★
AUSTRALIAN NATIONAL UNIVERSITY
RESEARCH SCHOOL OF SOCIAL SCIENCES
AUSTRALIAN DEMOGRAPHIC DATA BANK
G.P.O. Box 4   Phone: (not reported)
Canberra, A.C.T. 2601, Australia
Prof. J.C. Caldwell, Head

Description of System or Service: The AUSTRALIAN DEMOGRAPHIC DATA BANK is a machine-readable collection of information about births, deaths, marriages, arrivals, and departures in Australia. The data are available in hardcopy publications, on magnetic tapes, or via direct online access to the Research School of Social Sciences computer.

Scope and/or Subject Matter: Australian demographics from 1921 to date.

Input Sources: The Australian Bureau of Statistics supplies some of the current data on magnetic tape; additional input is derived from standard publications.

Holdings and Storage Media: Information is stored in machine-readable form and is progressively updated.

Publications: 1) Australian Demographic Data Bank—available for purchase in three volumes. Volume I contains recorded vital statistics and Volume II contains annual population estimates, estimated demographic rates, and selected life tables; both volumes cover the years 1921 through 1976. Volume III covers the same type of information contained in the first two volumes but for the years 1976 through 1981. 2) Technical Guide to the Australian Demographic Data Bank.

Computer-Based Products and Services: The DATA BANK comprises three main groups of demographic data: recorded vital events classified by year of age and marital status; recorded vital events classified by year of birth; and population series classified by marital status and either year of age or year of birth. Authorized users can access the DATA BANK directly on the Research School computer or they can obtain tape copies.

Clientele/Availability: Data are available for purchase.

Contact: Dr. S. Krishnamoorthy, Research Fellow, Australian Demographic Data Bank.

★61★
AUSTRALIAN NATIONAL UNIVERSITY
RESEARCH SCHOOL OF SOCIAL SCIENCES
SOCIAL SCIENCE DATA ARCHIVES (SSDA)
G.P.O. Box 4   Phone: 062 494400
Canberra, A.C.T. 2601, Australia   Service Est: 1981
Roger Jones, Head

Staff: 1 Management professional; 4 technicians; 1 clerical and nonprofessional.

Related Organizations: The Social Science Data Archives is the agent and administrative headquarters for the Australian Consortium for Social and Political Research Inc. (ACSPRI), a national organization formed to provide access to overseas data archives.

Description of System or Service: The SOCIAL SCIENCE DATA ARCHIVES (SSDA) was established to collect and preserve computer-readable data relating to social, political, and economic affairs and to make that data available for further analysis. The SSDA selects priority subject areas for information and data collection; identifies sources of data relevant to the selected areas; negotiates the acquisition of these data for its collection; produces codebooks from the cleaned and cataloged sets; and makes the data available to social science research workers. ARCHIVES staff also provide advice on survey methods, obtain data from other archives on request, prepare publications, and offer technical consulting on the effective use of survey data to researchers throughout the Australian National University.

Scope and/or Subject Matter: Australian and overseas social science and related data.

Input Sources: Data are acquired from Australian researchers and institutions as well as overseas archives such as the Inter-university Consortium for Political and Social Research (ICPSR).

Holdings and Storage Media: Magnetic tape holdings include approximately 300 ICPSR data sets, 200 Australian data sets, and Australian census data for 1966, 1971, 1976, and 1981. A reference library on data collection activities is also maintained.

Publications: 1) ACSPRI Newsletter (semiannual)—available by request; current activities bulletin of the Consortium. 2) Inventory of Australian Surveys—gives details of 760 surveys carried out since 1970 by academic staff and post-graduate students of Australian tertiary institutions. 3) Australian Social Surveys: Journal Extracts 1974-1978—records the findings of a search of 30 Australian journals for references to surveys; currently being updated. 4) SSDA Catalogue—available for purchase. Contains a description of each data set held by the archives for the purpose of secondary analysis by researchers. Abstracts, subject, and investigator indexes are included. Codebooks are available for each data set described in the Catalogue. 5) Drug Use in Australia: A Directory of Survey Research Projects—available for purchase. Results of a project to bring together computer-readable data sets of 169 surveys relating to drug use. Abstracts, subject, and investigator indexes are included.

Microform Products and Services: The Inventory of Australian Surveys is also available on microfiche.

Computer-Based Products and Services: The ARCHIVES makes available card-image data sets on magnetic tape compatible with the user's computer facilities. Accompanying codebooks, questionnaire forms, and file format descriptions are also provided. Additionally, limited data analysis services are available.

Clientele/Availability: Primary clients are Australian National University researchers, ACSPRI members, and other researchers.

Contact: Roger Jones, Head, Social Science Data Archives.

★62★
AUSTRALIAN ROAD RESEARCH BOARD (ARRB)
AUSTRALIAN ROAD RESEARCH DOCUMENTATION (ARRD)
500 Burwood Hwy.   Phone: 03 2331211
Vermont South, Vic. 3133, Australia   Service Est: 1975

Description of System or Service: AUSTRALIAN ROAD RESEARCH DOCUMENTATION (ARRD) is a computer-readable data base covering research literature and projects relevant to the design, planning, construction, and maintenance of roads in Australia. It corresponds to the printed publications Australian Road Index (ARI) and Australian Road Research in Progress (ARRIP) which are issued by the ARRB. AUSTRALIAN ROAD RESEARCH DOCUMENTATION is available online through Ausinet, and the ARRB provides information retrieval and SDI services from the data base. Additionally, the ARRB prepares the Australian national contribution to the International Road Research Documentation (IRRD) data base maintained by the Organisation for Economic Co-Operation and Development (OECD), and provides information retrieval, SDI, and current awareness services from it.

Scope and/or Subject Matter: Roads and road transport in Australia.

Input Sources: Input is derived from published and unpublished material, including journals, conference papers, books, and reports.

Holdings and Storage Media: The machine-readable ARRD data base dates from 1977 to the present, holding approximately 2000 records per year of coverage. The ARRB Library contains 14,000 bound volumes on transport studies.

Publications: 1) Australian Road Index-ARI (quarterly with annual cumulation)—contains abstracts and indexes to current literature on Australian roads, transport, and related topics; available by subscription. 2) Australian Road Research in Progress-ARRIP (annual)—provides descriptions and indexes of research projects on roads and transport undertaken or sponsored by Australian Commonwealth and state government departments and road authorities, research organizations, scientific and professional institutions, and private companies; available by subscription. 3) Roadlit (weekly)—current awareness bulletin which lists, by subject headings, all books and reports received by the ARRB Library during the previous week; includes major journal articles and forthcoming conferences; available by subscription. Other publications and reports are also issued.

Microform Products and Services: ARI and ARRIP are available on microfiche.

Computer-Based Products and Services: AUSTRALIAN ROAD RESEARCH DOCUMENTATION, which corresponds to the ARI and ARRIP publications, is publicly available online through Ausinet. Additionally, the ARRB offers information retrieval, SDI, and current awareness services from ARRD and the IRRD data base maintained by the OECD.

Clientele/Availability: Products and services are primarily intended for use by the road transport community.

Contact: Manager, Information Services, Australian Road Research Board. (Telex 33113 AA.)

★63★
AUSTRIA
FEDERAL MINISTRY OF BUILDINGS AND TECHNOLOGY
(Bundesministerium fur Bauten und Technik)
FEDERAL RESEARCH AND TESTING ESTABLISHMENT ARSENAL
(Bundesversuchs- und Forschungsanstalt Arsenal)
ROAD RESEARCH DOCUMENTATION CENTER
(Dokumentationsstelle fur Strassen- und Verkehrswesen)
Geotechnisches Institut   Phone: 0222 782531
Franz-Grill-Str. 9, P.O. Box 8   Service Est: 1975
A-1031 Vienna 3, Austria
C.H. Warmuth, Dipl.-Ing., Head

Staff: 4 Information and library professional; 1 technician.

Description of System or Service: The ROAD RESEARCH DOCUMENTATION CENTER provides computer-based documentation and information services on national highway and road transport research, and serves as the Austrian center for the International Road Research Documentation (IRRD) system and the International Co-operation in the Field of Transport Economics Documentation (ICTED) network. As a member of the IRRD, the DOCUMENTATION CENTER supplies input on Austrian highway research activity to the network, and in return receives a copy of the international IRRD Data Base. From this data file, it provides literature searching and SDI reporting to clients in Austria. As a participant in the ICTED network, the DOCUMENTATION CENTER contributes documentation concerning transport economics, administration, and operation to the network data center in Paris, where the data are stored on computer. Literature searching and SDI services from ICTED's computer-readable TRANSDOC data base are offered. The DOCUMENTATION CENTER also collects and disseminates information on data processing programs relevant to highway traffic research.

Scope and/or Subject Matter: Highway economics and administration, design of roads, materials, soils and rocks, construction and its supervision, maintenance, traffic and transport systems, accident studies, vehicles, transport economy, operation of transport systems, freight management, and logistics.

Input Sources: Input is gathered from books, monographs, research reports, proceedings, papers, scientific serials, periodicals, doctoral theses, and computer programs and data bases.

Holdings and Storage Media: The Documentation Center holds a copy of the IRRD data base covering 135,000 international documents, and the TRANSDOC data base covering over 5000 research reports. The Documentation Center also maintains data files on 156 road traffic investigations in Austria from 1970 to date, and on 174 traffic data processing programs.

Publications: Strassenforschung- Dokumentation uber Forschungsvorhaben und Wissenschaftliche Arbeiten in Osterreich (annual)—documentation on road research activities and scientific work in road building, bridge and tunnel construction, traffic engineering, and transport research carried out in Austria.

Computer-Based Products and Services: Retrospective searching and SDI services from the IRRD and TRANSDOC data bases are offered by the Documentation Center.

Other Services: In addition to the above services, the Documentation Center offers technical consulting services and referrals.

Clientele/Availability: Services are available without restrictions.

Contact: C.H. Warmuth, Dipl.-Ing., Head, Road Research Documentation Center. (Telex 136677.)

★64★
AUSTRIA
MINISTER OF FINANCE
INTERNATIONAL PATENT DOCUMENTATION CENTER (INPADOC)
(Internationales Patentdokumentations-Zentrum)
Mollwaldplatz 4   Phone: 0222 658784
A-1040 Vienna, Austria   Service Est: 1972
Dr. Otto Auracher, Director General

Staff: 45 Total.

Related Organizations: INPADOC is owned by the Austrian Government and operated in collaboration with the World Intellectual Property Organization (WIPO).

Description of System or Service: The INTERNATIONAL PATENT DOCUMENTATION CENTER (INPADOC) compiles patent documentation on a worldwide basis and makes it available in comprehensive form to patent offices, industry, and research personnel. Through an international network of cooperative agreements with patent offices and similar organizations, INPADOC receives input from 51 countries and international organizations which account for 96 percent of the world's currently published patent documents. To handle this bibliographic data, INPADOC has devised a special software package and has created the largest computer-readable patent data base in the world, the INPADOC Data Base (IDB). Publicly available online, this data base is also used to produce several microfiche information services and publications; chief among these is the INPADOC Patent Gazette, a weekly service that is equivalent to a world patent journal. INPADOC also offers computer searches and weekly magnetic tape services, as well as a copy service for patent documents based on its extensive microfilm patent collection.

Scope and/or Subject Matter: Documentation of the world's patent literature, reflecting the current state of technological development and trends.

Input Sources: About one million patent documents are added annually from 49 countries, the European Patent Office, and the Patent Cooperation Treaty. These documents include published patents, inventors' certificates, and utility certificates, as well as published applications for the same. Input is received either in machine-readable form from patent offices in accordance with a universal read-in program, or from patent journals which are then processed by INPADOC staff.

Holdings and Storage Media: INPADOC's microfilm collection of patents issued by selected countries totals more than 30,000 16mm rolls and is continuously updated with films of the latest documents issued. Its computer files cover more than 10 million patent documents.

Publications: All of INPADOC's publications are available primarily as microform products.

Microform Products and Services: 1) INPADOC Patent Gazette-IPG (weekly)—an international patent gazette published on microfiche and containing the following services: the SNS (Selected Numerical Service), the SCS (Selected Classification Service), the SAS (Selected Applicant Service), and the SIS (Selected Inventor Service). Each issue covers all patent documents whose bibliographic data were received in the preceding week, and includes available information in INPADOC's data base concerning equivalences (patent family members). The separate services are cumulated quarterly without equivalences; these cumulations constitute the following five publications: 2) Patent Applicant Service-PAS (cumulated quarterly and annually)—a microfiche service identifying patent documents of a selected number of countries as being connected by a common applicant or owner, with listings by applicant; corresponds to IPG-SAS discussed above. 3) Patent Applicant Service to Priorities (cumulated quarterly and annually). 4) Patent Classification Service-PCS (cumulated quarterly and annually)—a microfiche service listing patent documents by common International Patent Classification (IPC) symbol; corresponds to IPG-SCS. 5) Numerical Data Base Service-NDB (cumulated quarterly and annually)—a microfiche service listing patent documents by their country of publication and their document number; corresponds to IPG-SNS. 6) Patent Inventor Service-PIS (cumulated quarterly and annually)—a microfiche service listing documents of a selected number of countries according to name of inventor, with several applications per inventor grouped by IPC symbol; corresponds to IPG-SIS.

Also issued are: 7) Patent Family Service-PFS (cumulated monthly and annually)—a microfiche service listing patent documents connected by a common priority claim under the Paris Convention according to the Convention priority country, the priority date, and the priority number. As an additional service to the PFS, INPADOC offers the INPADOC Numerical List-INL, which sorts patent families by priority country and priority date within priority number. 8) Patent Register Service-PRS (monthly)—provides legal status changes such as cancellations, withdrawals, and refusals. All of the above are available by subscription in COM microfiche with a 42x reduction ratio and dimensions of 148x105mm. Concordance lists for backfile data from 1968 to 1982 are available on microfiche. INPADOC also offers 16mm microfilm copies of patents from its collection of over 30,000 film rolls.

Computer-Based Products and Services: The world's largest computer-readable patent data base, IDB covers more than 9 million patent documents in the current file dating from 1973 to the present, and 1.5 million in the retrospective file covering selected countries for 1968-1972. IDB information is accessible online through INPADOC's online service, INKA, and Pergamon-InfoLine. Bibliographic elements for each patent document include country of publication, type of document, document publication date, International Patent Classification (IPC) symbol if present, country of priority, the number of the application which is the basis for the priority, and priority date. Other data available for documents from most of the countries include inventor name, name of owner, applicant name, invention title, national classification symbol, and other legally related domestic application.

INPADOC is continually enlarging the scope of IDB with regard to both country coverage and the number of bibliographic elements stored for each document, and it provides the following services directly from the file: 1) Individual Request Search Service—provides demand searches for family members, inventor, IPC symbol, or applicant's name; requests are usually processed within two days, with delivery in either COM microfiche or paper printout formats. 2) Survey Service—provides weekly current awareness in two areas not covered by INPADOC's microfiche information services: stages of publication in the same country, and new family members. 3) Magnetic Tape Service—provides the INPADOC Family Data Tape (IFD), a weekly list of basic bibliographic data for all patents published in the previous week, plus the publication data and numbers of any patent family members in the IDB. Also available are monthly tapes of basic and expanded Patent Registry Service data, as well as additional tape services.

Other Services: In addition to its microform and computerized search services, INPADOC offers paper copies of patent documents as well as translation of Japanese documents.

Clientele/Availability: Most services are available on a subscription basis.

Remarks: Under an agreement with the World Intellectual Property Organization (WIPO), INPADOC operates a system called Computerized Administration of Patent Documents Reclassified According to the IPC (CAPRI). Designed to collect and store IPC symbols allotted to patent documents issued before 1973, CAPRI includes a central data base holding the following bibliographic data items for patents covered: publishing country, document type and number, IPC symbol and edition, reclassifying organization, and date of INPADOC processing. When completed, the CAPRI data base is expected to be used in the establishment of patent documentation centers and in the creation of a range of further INPADOC services.

Contact: Norbert Fux, Dipl.-Kfm., International Patent Documentation Center. (Telex 136337.)

★65★
AUSTRIAN DOCUMENTATION CENTRE FOR MEDIA AND COMMUNICATION RESEARCH (ADMAC)
(Osterreichisches Dokumentationszentrum fur Medien- und Kommunikationsforschung)
Universitatsstr. 7   Phone: 0222 43002640
A-1010 Vienna, Austria   Service Est: 1981
Prof. Dr. Michael Schmolke, Head

Staff: 3 Information and library professional; 5 management; 1 clerical and nonprofessional.

Related Organizations: ADMAC is organized within the framework of the United Nations Educational, Scientific and Cultural Organization's International Network for Communication Research and Policies (COMNET) system. ADMAC also receives support from the Austrian Federal Ministry of Science and Research.

Description of System or Service: The AUSTRIAN DOCUMENTATION CENTRE FOR MEDIA AND COMMUNICATION RESEARCH (ADMAC) was established to provide a survey of communication science in Austria, to offer an active information service for an interested expert public, and to help disseminate Austrian communication research results abroad. The CENTRE collects published and nonconventional literature of Austrian origin on the topics of print, electronic, and general media. It stores bibliographic data on these materials in a computer-readable data base which is used to produce the Annual Bibliography of Austrian Mass Communication Literature. ADMAC also issues other publications, offers SDI services, and acts as a mediator and offers help in instruction. All ADMAC services are planned to be available in both German and English.

Scope and/or Subject Matter: Mass media and other communications in Austria.

Input Sources: Input sources include approximately 85 journals as well as newspapers, nonconventional literature, reports, and theses.

Holdings and Storage Media: The computer-readable Annual Bibliography of Austrian Mass Communication Literature data base holds citations and brief abstracts dating from 1976 to the present.

Publications: 1) Annual Bibliography of Austrian Mass Communication Literature—available by subscription; includes data on the documentation work in German and English. 2) mediadoc (bimonthly)—available to members; provides an Austrian media chronicle. Regular features include an international research digest, Austrian research projects and dissertations, a survey of current literature, a calendar of events, and portraits and descriptions of media personnel and institutions. A list of research projects, institutions, and directories is also issued.

Computer-Based Products and Services: The Annual Bibliography of Austrian Mass Communication Literature data base is used to produce the corresponding print publication and to provide computerized SDI services.

Clientele/Availability: Clients include scientists, media workers, and students.

Contact: Prof. Dr. Michael Schmolke, Head, ADMAC, at Sigmund Haffner Gasse 18/II, A-5020 Salzburg, Austria; telephone 0662 44511646.

★66★
AUSTRIAN NATIONAL INSTITUTE FOR PUBLIC HEALTH
(Osterreichisches Bundesinstitut fur Gesundheitswesen - OBIG)
LITERATURE SERVICE IN MEDICINE
(Literaturdienst Medizin - LID)
Stubenring 6　　　　　　　　　　Phone: 0222 52966154
A-1010 Vienna, Austria　　　　　　Founded: 1973
Dr. Robert Csepan, Project Officer

Staff: Approximately 4 total.

Description of System or Service: The LITERATURE SERVICE IN MEDICINE (LID) provides information in the medical and biological sciences. Online and batch-mode literature searching and SDI services are offered using a variety of data bases in the field. Additionally, LID is the official contact in Austria for the German Institute for Medical Documentation and Information (DIMDI) and it participates in the Health Care Literature Information Network (HECLINET).

Scope and/or Subject Matter: Medicine, biology, and related fields.

Input Sources: Input is derived from publicly available data bases offered by about 12 European organizations including DIMDI. Additional input is obtained from data bases offered by System Development Corporation (SDC), DIALOG Information Services, Inc., and ESA/IRS.

Holdings and Storage Media: The Service maintains microfilm of articles which have appeared since 1974 in the publications indexed by HECLINET.

Publications: 1) Austrian National Institute for Public Health Review (quarterly). 2) LID Information Brochure (updated regularly). 3) Austrian National Institute for Public Health Yearbook.

Computer-Based Products and Services: LID provides the following computer-based services: online and batch searching of medical data bases; providing terminal connections to, and Austrian contact for, DIMDI; searching of hospital literature using the data bases of the Health Care Literature Information Network (HECLINET); and searching of data bases carried by ESA/IRS, System Development Corporation (SDC), and DIALOG Information Services, Inc.

Other Services: In addition to computerized literature searching, LID offers document location services, manual literature searching, and referral services.

Clientele/Availability: Searching of the data bases is available only to Austrian users.

Contact: Dr. Robert Csepan, Project Officer, or Mrs. Lore Lindinger, Assistant, Literature Service in Medicine.

★67★
AVCOR
512 King St. E., Suite 303　　　　Phone: (416) 864-9240
Toronto, ON, Canada M5A 1M1
Robert Baum, President

Staff: 4 Information and library professional; 6 management professional; 6 technicians; 19 sales and marketing; 6 clerical and nonprofessional.

Related Organizations: AVCOR is a division of Southam Inc. which has interests in daily newspapers and trade magazines, radio and television broadcasting, cable television, and satellite communications.

Description of System or Service: AVCOR is an audiovisual firm that provides a variety of computer graphics and videotex systems, software, and services. It has developed the AVCOR Interactive Display (AID) system, a microcomputer-based videotex information system. Mobile AID systems are used by the Canadian Department of External Affairs to provide visitors at international trade fairs with information on Canadian companies and to collect information on the visitor's opinions and business requirements. At the exhibits, information on Canadian companies can be displayed on video screens or acquired via a printout that is tailored to the visitor's specifications. AID systems provide information in a number of languages, including English, French, German, and Japanese. In addition to their use by the Department of External Affairs, AID systems are also being utilized as electronic retail store clerks by mass market retailers and for other applications. Other services provided by AVCOR include a graphics service bureau offering frame creation design and consultation for videotex, business graphics, and graphics art applications. The bureau has designed and implemented videotex data bases for a variety of applications and can also process videotex graphics into high-resolution 35mm slides. AVCOR also developed and markets videotex software for microcomputers.

Scope and/or Subject Matter: Business communications services utilizing videotex and computer graphics; videotex data bases for business, including foreign trade and the computer and automotive industries.

Computer-Based Products and Services: In conjunction with its videotex services, AVCOR has developed the following closed-user, microcomputer-based electronic directories: Computer and Business Equipment Companies; Automotive Parts Aftermarket Companies; Original Equipment Suppliers to Vehicle Manufacturers; and SOF'SPOT Microcomputer Software Directory. The firm's AID system is used by the Department of External Affairs to provide current information on Canadian business at international trade fairs. The AID system is also utilized by mass market retailers to promote, describe, and merchandise products. Customers use the system to make their product selection, then enter their order on-site. The system maintains a proprietary inventory control and communications system to provide management with data necessary to respond to daily sales activity.

Additionally, AVCOR offers JORDAN software, which includes a package that converts the Commodore 64 microcomputer into a videotex-compatible terminal. Under development are software versions for other microcomputers. JORDAN software is available as a frame creation package for the IBM personal computer in conjunction with a medium-resolution videotex terminal and is fully compatible with AVCOR's High Resolution Slide Service. Additionally, JORDAN software can convert a microcomputer into a videotex display system for single or multiuser environments, combining color graphics and data processing activities. The system provides for hardcopy output, data entry and collection, multiple languages, communications, and full reporting functions, and is designed for such applications as market research, trade fairs, mass retail environments, training, and promotion.

Other Services: AVCOR also provides other audiovisual services, including design and production of multi-image, multi-screen presentations, on-location video and film production, animation, special effects, and teleconferencing.

Clientele/Availability: Clients include mass merchandisers, government trade departments, and commercial marketing departments.

Contact: Zal Press, Vice President, Computer Services, AVCOR.

★68★
AVIATION INFORMATION SERVICES LTD. (AISL)
208 Epsom Square　　　　　　　Phone: 01-897 1066
London Heathrow Airport　　　　　Founded: 1970
Hounslow, Middlesex TW6 2BO, England
Alan E. Smith, Head

Related Organizations: The parent organization of AISL is Airclaims Group Ltd.

Description of System or Service: AVIATION INFORMATION SERVICES LTD. (AISL) provides detailed information about the composition of airline fleets and on circumstances and the frequency of air transport accidents. It maintains the computer-readable AISL Aircraft Accident Data Base, which describes all accidents involving jet and turboprop aircraft weighing 20,000 pounds or more which resulted in the aircraft becoming a total loss or unrepairable. The data base is currently being expanded to include information on business jets and small turboprops. AISL also publishes price guides, surveys, digests, and indexes dealing with aircraft and airlines.

Scope and/or Subject Matter: Aviation, including airliner, commuter, and business aircraft accidents; airline and commuter airline fleets, airliner production, and aircraft disposition.

Input Sources: Information is obtained from airlines, aircraft manufacturers, government agencies, periodicals, newspapers, and other sources.

Holdings and Storage Media: The machine-readable Aircraft Accident Data Base covers the period 1952 to date and contains details of approximately 1000 accidents. The data base is updated as accidents occur.

Publications: 1) Information Digest (weekly); 2) Major Loss Record (amended monthly); 3) High Capacity Transport Register (amended monthly); 4) Index of Articles (monthly and annually); 5) Aircraft Price Guide (twice yearly); 6) Turbine Airliner Fleet Survey (twice yearly).

Computer-Based Products and Services: The Aircraft Accident Data Base is available online through I.P. Sharp Associates. AISL is also developing an online Aircraft Histories Data Base which will provide information on owner and operator history of all 10,000 jet and turboprop aircraft built.

Other Services: AISL also offers insurance loss adjusting, aviation accident surveying, aircraft condition surveys, and general aviation consultancy.

Clientele/Availability: Primary clients are insurance companies and aircraft industry.

Contact: Paul A. Hayes, Assistant Manager, Aviation Information Services Ltd. (Telex 934679 AIRCLM G.)

★69★
AVS INTEXT LTD.
145 Oxford St. Phone: 01-434 2034
London W1R 1TB, England Founded: 1978
Malcolm G. Smith, Managing Director

Special Note: No questionnaire response was received for this entry for the 6th edition. The entry is reprinted as it appeared in the 5th edition.

Staff: 3 Information and library professional; 4 management professional; 4 technicians; 1 clerical and nonprofessional.

Description of System or Service: AVS INTEXT LTD. acts both as an electronic publisher on the Prestel system and as a viewdata consultancy and service agency. Using information either gathered internally or obtained through joint ventures with existing publishers, it provides data bases on Prestel, including files on available online data bases and viewdata services. AVS consultancy services are supplied to more than 50 clients and include market evaluation, product design and development, and editing and production. Additionally, AVS markets and develops software for the Prestel gateway facility and for private viewdata systems. The gateway facility allows ordinary public access Prestel to be linked to a mainframe computer; the Mistel software developed by AVS transforms data on the third-party mainframe into viewdata form to permit online retrieval and real-time transactions via Prestel.

Scope and/or Subject Matter: Viewdata consulting; electronic publishing in such areas as business, travel trade, market research, advertising.

Input Sources: Input consists of original material, information from joint ventures with existing publishers, and data transfer from existing mainframe computer records.

Holdings and Storage Media: AVS manages 12,000 public access frames on Prestel for clients. It also maintains its own gateway computer and data bases.

Computer-Based Products and Services: AVS INTEXT LTD. provides access to a file covering the field of viewdata services and a file on online data bases available in the United Kingdom on Prestel. The Online Databases file consists of portions of the Information Trade Directory and provides brief descriptions of available online data bases; additional promotional information on a data base will be inserted by AVS for a fee. AVS also offers umbrella Prestel services for other publishers, markets Mistel gateway software, and provides custom software development.

Other Services: Seminars and training courses are also available.

Clientele/Availability: Services are provided to corporations, businesses, and other viewdata information providers.

Contact: Services Consultant, AVS Intext Ltd. (Telex 28604.)

B

★70★

BANGLADESH NATIONAL SCIENTIFIC AND TECHNICAL DOCUMENTATION CENTRE (BANSDOC)
Science Laboratories
Dacca 5, Bangladesh
Ahsan A. Biswas, Project Director
Phone: 507196
Founded: 1963

Staff: Approximately 36 total.

Related Organizations: BANSDOC is part of the Bangladesh Council of Scientific and Industrial Research.

Description of System or Service: The BANGLADESH NATIONAL SCIENTIFIC AND TECHNICAL DOCUMENTATION CENTRE (BANSDOC) was established to provide scientific and technical researchers in Bangladesh with access to the world's literature in their fields. Its services include document procurement, bibliography compilation, translations, and inquiry answering. BANSDOC also prepares publications.

Scope and/or Subject Matter: Natural sciences, engineering, agriculture, medicine, and related fields.

Input Sources: BANSDOC acquires photocopies or microfilms of periodical articles, book sections, patents, standards, and other documents from across the world.

Holdings and Storage Media: A collection of Bangladesh periodicals and seminar proceedings is maintained.

Publications: 1) Bangladesh Science and Technology Index (annual); 2) Scientific and Technical Periodicals of Bangladesh; 3) National Catalogue of Scientific and Technical Periodicals of Bangladesh; 4) Current Scientific and Technological Research Projects in the Universities and Research Institutions of Bangladesh; 5) Directory of Scientists and Technologists of Bangladesh. All publications are available for purchase from BANSDOC.

Microform Products and Services: BANSDOC can provide 35mm microfilm copies of documents.

Clientele/Availability: Services are available without restrictions and intended primarily for use by Bangladesh researchers and scientists in the governmental, academic, and industrial sectors.

Contact: Ahsan A. Biswas, Project Director, or MD. Osman Ghani, Bangladesh National Scientific and Technical Documentation Centre.

★71★

BANK GROUP FOR AUTOMATION IN MANAGEMENT
(Groupement de la Caisse des Depots Automatisation pour le Management - G.CAM)
Tour Maine-Montparnasse
33, ave. du Maine
F-75755 Paris Cedex 15, France
Phone: 01 5381030

Related Organizations: The Bank Group for Automation in Management is a subsidiary of the State Deposit and Consignment Bank/ Caisse des Depots et Consignations (CDC), one of the world's largest financial institutions. G.CAM services are offered in conjunction with Artemis, a CDC teleprocessing subsidiary.

Description of System or Service: The BANK GROUP FOR AUTOMATION IN MANAGEMENT (G.CAM) is a computer service and consulting company offering general time-sharing services, software design and distribution, data base development and implementation, and other computer-related services to the public and private sectors in France. Its time-sharing system utilizes TROLL, STAIRS, Mistral, APL, and ROSCOE software and provides standard data management services as well as access to a variety of news, legal, financial, and economic data bases. G.CAM-developed software includes the Brigitte and Mireille office management systems, Crocus information and automatic keywording software, and GC-20, a general analytical system. G.CAM also offers such services as computer engineering, custom programming, staff recruitment and training, turnkey operations, and facilities management.

Scope and/or Subject Matter: General time-sharing, consulting, data base and software design and implementation.

Input Sources: Data bases are acquired from private organizations and government agencies.

Holdings and Storage Media: G.CAM holds more than a dozen data bases online.

Computer-Based Products and Services: G.CAM, which is a Euronet DIANE host, maintains a time-sharing system providing general data management applications and online access to more than a dozen bibliographic and nonbibliographic data bases, including the following: 1) AGORA—a series of four files providing access to the full text of Agence France-Presse (AFP) reports covering national and international general news (AGRA), economic and financial news (AECO), sports (ASPO), and news items of lasting interest (ADOC). 2) Banque de Donnees Locales (BDL)—contains statistics on more than 36,000 local French communities; compiled by the National Institute of Statistics and Economic Studies/ Institut National de la Statistique et des Etudes Economiques (INSEE). 3) BIODOC—contains biographical information on more than 40,000 notable European personalities in all fields; prepared by Servi-Tech. 4) BIRD (Base d'Information Robert Debre)—provides bibliographic citations and abstracts to international literature covering all aspects of a child's life from conception to the end of adolescence; compiled by the International Children's Center/ Centre International de l'Enfance. 5) FRANCIS—a series of four files representing a portion of the FRANCIS data base maintained by the French Documentation Center for Human Sciences/ Centre de Documentation Sciences Humaines du CNRS; provides bibliographic coverage of company management (DOGE), general economy (ECODOC), employment and training (Emploi et Formation), and health sciences (RESHUS). 6) MERL-ECO—contains abstracts and references to world literature on business and economics; produced by Societe MERLIN GERIN. 7) RAMA—covers international literature on audiovisual and video communication; compiled by Interaudiovisuel. 8) SPHINX—provides bibliographic references to French economic and social literature; compiled by INSEE. 9) TELEXPORT—a series of files containing information on import-export offers (PROMEXPORT and PROMIMPORT), foreign trade regulations for specific countries of export (DOC-EXPORT), and French importing and exporting companies (FIRMEXPORT); produced by the Paris Chamber of Commerce and Industry/ Chambre de Commerce et d'Industrie de Paris. G.CAM also provides computer system and software design, development, and implementation services.

Clientele/Availability: Services and products are available to government agencies, para-public entities, industrial and commercial companies, local communities, service companies, mutual insurance companies, and subsidiaries of CDC.

Contact: Director General, Bank Group for Automation in Management.

★72★

BANK OF ENGLAND
FINANCIAL STATISTICS DIVISION
Threadneedle St.
London EC2R 8AH, England
Mr. G.K. Willetts, Head
Phone: 01-601 4918

Description of System or Service: The FINANCIAL STATISTICS DIVISION is responsible for the collection, analysis, and dissemination of selected United Kingdom financial indicator statistics. The data are disseminated through hardcopy publications, microfiche products, magnetic tapes, and online.

Scope and/or Subject Matter: Significant financial indicators for the United Kingdom, including industry, money supply, central government borrowing, government debt, investment, stock exchange transactions, short-term money rates, foreign exchange rates, and others.

Input Sources: Input is obtained from internal data sources and other banks and financial institutions.

Holdings and Storage Media: Monthly, quarterly, and annual time series data are held in machine-readable form.

Publications: Bank of England Quarterly Bulletin—includes statistical data collected by the Division.

Microform Products and Services: Time series data and indexes to them are produced on microfiche.

Computer-Based Products and Services: The FINANCIAL STATISTICS DIVISION makes available magnetic tapes of its financial indicators time series data base, which includes data published in the Quarterly Bulletin and additional unpublished data. The DIVISION's data are also accessible online through ADP Network Services, Inc. and other time-sharing services.

Clientele/Availability: Services are available without restrictions.

Contact: Mr. K.J. Cook, Financial Statistics Division.

★73★
BANK SOCIETY
(Societe Generale de Banque - SGB)
GENERAL DOCUMENTATION
(Documentation Generale)
SGB DATA BASE
Montagne du Parc 3   Phone: 02 5136600
B-1000 Brussels, Belgium

Staff: 40 Information and library professional.

Description of System or Service: The SGB DATA BASE is a computer-readable file containing bibliographic references and abstracts for periodical and other literature relating to banking, finance, economics, and other related topics. The DATA BASE is publicly available for online searching through Data-Star.

Scope and/or Subject Matter: Banks and banking systems in industrial and Third World nations; finance; economics; industry demography and population; and regulations and activities of the European Economic Community.

Input Sources: Input to the data base is derived from journal and other literature.

Holdings and Storage Media: The machine-readable SGB Data Base contains approximately 100,000 records, about half of which include abstracts, and is updated monthly.

Publications: A selection of articles indexed is issued weekly.

Computer-Based Products and Services: The SGB Data Base is available for online searching via Data-Star. Citations between 1974 and 1979 include references and titles to documents only; citations since 1979 also include abstracts.

Other Services: In addition to producing the SGB Data Base, the General Documentation service provides a thesaurus, a descriptive overview of the data base, and, as permitted by copyright, copies of original documents.

Clientele/Availability: The SGB Data Base is intended for use by banking and financial institutions as well as other interested organizations and persons.

Remarks: The SGB is also known as Generale Bankmaatschappis (GBM).

Contact: R. Despiegeleer, Legal Representative, Bank Society; telephone 02 5763350. (Telex 24827.)

★74★
BAR-ILAN UNIVERSITY
INSTITUTE FOR INFORMATION RETRIEVAL AND
  COMPUTATIONAL LINGUISTICS
RESPONSA PROJECT
                                       Phone: 03 718410
Ramat-gan 52100, Israel   Service Est: 1967
Prof. Yaacov Choueka, Head

Staff: 1 Information and library professional; 1 management professional; 6 technicians; 1 sales and marketing; 2 clerical and nonprofessional.

Description of System or Service: The RESPONSA PROJECT is an online full-text retrieval system operational at Bar-Ilan University. The data base consists of the full text, with no indexing or abstracting, of large collections of the Hebrew Responsa Literature and other classics and modern works of Jewish scholarship. The user can access the data base online via a suitable terminal to query, retrieve, browse, display, and print needed documents, using a variety of distance and Boolean operators. A grammatical and word manipulation component automatically compensates morphological variants of the terms searched.

Scope and/or Subject Matter: Jewish studies, Jewish law, Hebrew literature, Bible, Talmud.

Input Sources: Input is derived from printed books.

Holdings and Storage Media: The online Responsa Project data base contains the text of 248 volumes (comprising 48,000 documents and 48 million words) of Rabbinical Responsa Collections spanning 1000 years and covering more than 30 countries; the Bible; 36 tractates of the Babylonian Talmud, including Rashi commentary; and eight volumes of the collected works of S. Agnon.

Microform Products and Services: Microfiche is available for all the texts in the data base.

Computer-Based Products and Services: The RESPONSA PROJECT data base includes the full text of the Hebrew Responsa Literature and other works of Jewish scholarship. The data base is accessible online, and concordances and other specially tailored products can be produced from it. More than 1500 computerized searches have been processed for inclusion in articles, books, dissertations, and court decisions.

Other Services: Additional services include the Jewish Law Service which provides source material on the stand of Jewish law on different problems.

Clientele/Availability: Clients include scholars in Jewish studies, lawyers, rabbis, and others.

Contact: Prof. Yaacov Choueka, Head, Responsa Project.

★75★
BARIC COMPUTING SERVICES LTD.
BARIC VIEWDATA
Forest Rd.   Phone: 1890 1414
Feltham, Middlesex TW13 7EJ, England
A.R. Terry, Product Manager

Related Organizations: Baric Computing Services Ltd. is a subsidiary of International Computer, Ltd. (ICL) and Barclays Bank.

Description of System or Service: BARIC VIEWDATA provides a full range of services for implementing information services on Prestel and other viewdata systems. It designs and maintains data bases; provides consultancy and advice on viewdata applications; writes software for implementing viewdata and for linking viewdata to existing mainframe computers; provides customized training; and provides specific and general standard application software for making holiday reservations, sales reporting, banking, data base inquiry, and other applications. In addition, BARIC provides a private viewdata bureau service for customers wishing to experiment with viewdata. It can also assist with facilities for Gateway, the service that links Prestel to private viewdata and other computer networks.

Scope and/or Subject Matter: Viewdata information services in all subject areas.

Computer-Based Products and Services: BARIC VIEWDATA offers systems and services to assist other organizations in making use of viewdata technology. It also provides information via Prestel.

Clientele/Availability: Most services are intended for information providers.

Remarks: The parent organization, Baric Computing Services Ltd., is a large computer services firm that also offers data preparation, local batch processing, networking, time-sharing, computer phototypesetting, facilities management, and COM services.

Contact: A.R. Terry, Product Manager, Baric Viewdata. (Telex 22971).

★76★
BAVARIAN MINISTRY FOR FOOD, AGRICULTURE AND FORESTRY
(Bayerisches Staatsministerium fur Ernahrung, Landwirtschaft und Forsten)
BAVARIAN AGRICULTURAL INFORMATION SYSTEM
(Bayerisches Landwirtschaftliches Informationssystem - BALIS)
Ludwigstr. 2 Phone: 089 21820
D-8000 Munich 22, Fed. Rep. of Germany
Dr. Hans Haimerl, Ministerialrat Founded: 1972

Staff: 5 Information and library professional; 15 management; 15 technicians; 3 clerical and nonprofessional.

Description of System or Service: The BAVARIAN AGRICULTURAL INFORMATION SYSTEM (BALIS) is an information storage and retrieval system providing online access to approximately 50 agricultural data banks. BALIS is divided into several subsystems which comprise independent data banks or parts of data banks.

Scope and/or Subject Matter: Agricultural information, including soil production, animal breeding, market prices, subsidies, and other topics.

Input Sources: Individual data for approximately 250,000 farm units are collected.

Holdings and Storage Media: BALIS consists of approximately 50 machine-readable data banks.

Computer-Based Products and Services: Accessible online, BALIS is divided into the following subsystems: 1) The Agricultural Structure/ Agricultural Planning Subsystem consists of joint primary and specialized statistics and data used to support Bavaria's agricultural guideline plan. 2) The Financial Supporting Subsystem holds information on the financial support of individual farms. 3) The Farm Management/ Auditing Subsystem provides a basic accounting entry for every farm provided with accounting statistics. 4) Consisting of several dozen data banks, the Agricultural Construction Subsystem (ISBAU) maintains such data as construction documentation, building sections and models, construction prices, and planning and construction costs. 5) The Plant Production Subsystem (ISPFLANZ) contains data derived from land surveys and includes a detailed field report and laboratory analysis of 50,000 soil samples collected yearly. 6) The Animal Production Subsystem covers various yields, such as milk yield, records of the number of animals slaughtered, and progeny tests of 1 million cows. 7) Containing administrative marketing data, the Market Structure Reports Subsystem includes data to support the market structure.

Clientele/Availability: The system is primarily used by the Bavarian Ministry for Food, Agriculture and Forestry, with restricted public access.

Contact: Dr. Hans Haimerl, Ministerialrat, Bavarian Agricultural Information System.

★77★
BAYER AG
ENGINEERING SCIENCE DIVISION
(Ingenieur-Wissenschaftliche Abteilung)
CHEMICAL AND PROCESS ENGINEERING ABSTRACTS
(Verfahrenstechnische Berichte - VtB)
Bayerwerk Phone: 0214 3071763
D-5090 Leverkusen, Fed. Rep. of Germany
Dr. Wolfgang Springe, Head Service Est: 1921

Staff: 10 Total.

Description of System or Service: CHEMICAL AND PROCESS ENGINEERING ABSTRACTS (VtB) provides comprehensive German-language abstracting and indexing of the world literature on chemical engineering and related subjects. Information from VtB is available in print, microform, and machine-readable versions.

Scope and/or Subject Matter: Chemical engineering, process engineering, and related fields, including bioengineering, engineering materials, plant engineering, and safety and fire protection.

Input Sources: Input is derived from more than 800 journals, and from dissertations, reports, and conference proceedings.

Holdings and Storage Media: The machine-readable VtB data base holds approximately 130,000 citations, dating from 1966 to the present; about 7500 are added each year.

Publications: 1) Chemical and Process Engineering Abstracts/ Verfahrenstechnische Berichte-VtB (weekly)—available in journal or card format; indexed semiannually by keyword, author, and company name. 2) Dokumentation Verfahrenstechnik—cumulated three-year indexes to VtB. Both publications can be purchased from Verlag Chemie GmbH, Postfach 1260/1280, D-6940 Weinheim, Federal Republic of Germany; or from Verlag Chemie International, Inc., 175 Fifth Ave., New York, NY 10010.

Microform Products and Services: Recent volumes of Dokumentation Verfahrenstechnik are available from Verlag Chemie on 42x COM.

Computer-Based Products and Services: VtB information is available quarterly on magnetic tape from Verlag Chemie. Data elements provided include abstract number, source citation, and descriptors.

Clientele/Availability: Products and services are available without restrictions.

Projected Publications and Services: A VtB tape service offering English-language descriptors is expected to be available online in the near future. It will provide 75,000 citations dating back to 1975.

Contact: Dr. Wolfgang Springe, Head, or Dr. Ernst O. Schmidt, Engineering Science Division. (Telex 85103 285 BY D.)

★78★
BBM BUREAU OF MEASUREMENT
1500 Don Mills Rd. Phone: (416) 445-9800
Don Mills, ON, Canada M3B 3L7 Founded: 1944

Special Note: The above name, address, and telephone number have been verified for this edition, although no questionnaire response was received. The following text is reprinted from the 5th edition.

Staff: 18 Information and library professional; 5 management professional; 2 technicians.

Description of System or Service: The BBM BUREAU OF MEASUREMENT specializes in measuring Canadian radio and television audiences. It designs and conducts audience surveys, assembles statistical and other data, and conducts market research studies. The BUREAU issues publications and maintains a machine-readable data base which is commercially available through time-sharing.

Scope and/or Subject Matter: Number, distribution, and listening, viewing, and reading habits of Canadian radio and television broadcast audiences.

Input Sources: Some data are collected through personal diaries kept by survey participants detailing their radio listening and TV viewing habits.

Publications: The Bureau issues reports, charts, and other publications.

Computer-Based Products and Services: BBM audience measurement and demographic data are retrievable online through several media-oriented time-sharing companies.

Clientele/Availability: Products and services are intended for BBM members.

Remarks: The BBM Bureau of Measurement was originally known as the Bureau of Broadcast Measurement.

Contact: BBM Bureau of Measurement.

★79★
BEILSTEIN INSTITUTE FOR LITERATURE IN ORGANIC CHEMISTRY
(Beilstein-Institut fur Literatur der Organischen Chemie)
Varrentrappstr. 40-42 Phone: 069 7917251
D-6000 Frankfurt am Main 90, Fed. Rep. of Germany
Dr. Reiner Luckenbach, Head Founded: 1951

Staff: 160 Total.

Description of System or Service: The BEILSTEIN INSTITUTE FOR LITERATURE IN ORGANIC CHEMISTRY publishes the Beilstein Handbook of Organic Chemistry, which is a collection of critically examined and exactly reproduced data on carbon compounds. Prepared by chemists and physicists, the data are derived from international scientific literature and issued in an ongoing series of printed volumes. The INSTITUTE expects to begin offering computerized retrieval services for Handbook information sometime in 1986.

Scope and/or Subject Matter: The following aspects of carbon compounds: constitution and configuration; natural occurrence and isolation from natural products; preparation, formation, and purification; structure and energy parameters of the molecule; physical properties; chemical properties; characterization and analysis; salts and additional compounds.

Input Sources: Input is derived from international scientific journals, patent literature, and selected theses and conference reports.

Publications: Beilstein Handbook of Organic Chemistry, 1881- (13-14 volumes per year)—provides evaluated data extracted from literature referring to carbon compounds; contains formula and subject indexes. Much of the information cited is supplied with cross-references and critical comments.

Computer-Based Products and Services: Computerized data retrieval services are planned, beginning in 1986.

Clientele/Availability: Users include chemists, physicists, other scientists, and students.

Contact: Dr. Reiner Luckenbach, Head, Beilstein Institute for Literature in Organic Chemistry. In the United States, contact Springer Verlag New York Inc., 175 Fifth Ave., New York, NY 10010; telephone (212) 460-1500.

★80★
BELGIUM
MINISTRY OF ECONOMIC AFFAIRS
(Ministere des Affaires Economiques)
DATA PROCESSING CENTER
(Centre de Traitement de l'Information - CTI)
BELGIAN INFORMATION AND DISSEMINATION SERVICE
  (BELINDIS)
30, rue J.A. de Mot							Phone: 02 2336737
B-1040 Brussels, Belgium					Service Est: 1980
R. van den Abeele, Director General

Staff: Approximately 127 total.

Description of System or Service: The BELGIAN INFORMATION AND DISSEMINATION SERVICE (BELINDIS) maintains central computer facilities and provides clients with remote terminal online access to Belgian and other data bases in the areas of energy, law, and economics. The data bases are maintained under AQUARIUS-STAIRS software to facilitate information retrieval; SDI profiles are also available. BELINDIS is a host on Euronet DIANE.

Scope and/or Subject Matter: Nuclear science and technology, energy resources, coal, economics, law, legislation, and other topics.

Input Sources: BELINDIS acquires data bases from Belgian and foreign sources.

Holdings and Storage Media: Thirteen major data bases are maintained online.

Computer-Based Products and Services: The BELGIAN INFORMATION AND DISSEMINATION SERVICE makes the following data bases available for online searching: 1) BJUS—provides references with abstracts to literature covering Belgian and European justice doctrine and jurisprudence; produced by the Documentary Research Center/ Centre de Recherche Documentaire (CREDOC). 2) BLEX—contains bibliographic citations to articles published in the Belgian Monitor on Belgian law and legislation; produced by CREDOC. 3) CAPA—provides data on bankruptcies and judicial disabilities in Belgium. Contains approximately 55,000 citations, including bankruptcies dating from 1976 to the present and disabilities from 1940 to the present. 4) Coal Abstracts—contains references to published materials on coal technology and related topics; produced by IEA Coal Research. 5) Coal Research Projects—covers current research projects in coal science and technology; produced by IEA Coal Research. 6) CORALIE—factual data bank on the use of food additives in the European Communities; produced by CREDOC.

7) FALI—contains citations to monographic and periodical literature relating to foreign affairs, including international relations, political science, defense, economics and finance, and social problems; produced by the Central Library of the Belgian Ministry of Foreign Affairs. 8) Fonds Quetelet—covers literature on all aspects of economics acquired by the Belgian Ministry of Economic Affairs Fonds Quetelet Library. 9) Foreign Trade Abstracts—provides abstracts and citations to international literature on applied and commercial economics; formerly known as Economics Abstracts International (EAI). Produced by the Netherlands Foreign Trade Agency. 10) International Nuclear Information System (INIS)—cites publications related to the nuclear sciences and their peaceful applications; produced by the International Atomic Energy Agency. 11) LJUS—provides approximately 2600 bibliographic citations dating from 1981 to the present, covering case law in Luxembourg. 12) NLEX—contains the full text of law, decrees, and treaties of the Netherlands; produced by Koninklijke Vermande B.V. 13) ORBI—bibliographic file covering national legal systems and international law and institutions; contains more than 80,000 citations from 1960 onwards.

Clientele/Availability: Access to BELINDIS is on a contract basis.

Contact: Jacques Lauwerys, BELINDIS. (Telex 23509 ENERGI B.)

★81★
BELGIUM
MINISTRY OF ECONOMIC AFFAIRS
(Ministere des Affaires Economiques)
FONDS QUETELET LIBRARY DATA BASE
6, rue de l'Industrie							Phone: 02 5127950
B-1040 Brussels, Belgium
G. De SaedePeer, Head

Staff: Approximately 35 total.

Description of System or Service: The FONDS QUETELET LIBRARY DATA BASE is a machine-readable file covering monographs and journals in the field of economics acquired since 1969 by the Fonds Quetelet Library, which is the central library of the Ministry of Economic Affairs. The DATA BASE is used to support internal technical processing and reference functions, and to produce COM catalogs which are distributed to a number of other libraries. FONDS QUETELET is also remotely accessible online through BELINDIS, a Euronet DIANE host.

Scope and/or Subject Matter: Library holdings in the areas of economics, social sciences, and statistics.

Input Sources: Bibliographic descriptions of books, selected periodical articles, and other acquisitions are recorded in the system.

Holdings and Storage Media: The computer-readable data base contains approximately 200,000 records. It is updated twice a month with approximately 10,000 citations added each year. Total library holdings include 600,000 bound volumes and subscriptions to 3000 periodicals.

Publications: Acquisition list (monthly).

Microform Products and Services: COM fiche cumulative catalogs are completely republished bimonthly.

Computer-Based Products and Services: The FONDS QUETELET LIBRARY DATA BASE supports such internal library functions as acquisitions, cataloging, circulation, periodicals control, and others. It is also publicly available online through the Ministry of Economic Affairs' BELINDIS service.

Clientele/Availability: Access to the Fonds Quetelet Library Data Base is available without restrictions.

Contact: G. De SaedePeer, Head, Fonds Quetelet Library.

★82★
BELGIUM
MINISTRY OF ECONOMIC AFFAIRS
(Ministere des Affaires Economiques)
NATIONAL STATISTICAL INSTITUTE
(Institut National de Statistique)
44, rue de Louvain   Phone: 02 5139650
B-1000 Brussels, Belgium
E. Rosselle, General Director

Staff: 994 Total.

Description of System or Service: The NATIONAL STATISTICAL INSTITUTE collects, processes, and publishes Belgian statistical information. The INSTITUTE maintains computer facilities and offers online data bases.

Scope and/or Subject Matter: Belgian social and economic statistics.

Input Sources: Data are collected via surveys and other sources.

Holdings and Storage Media: Three computer-readable nonbibliographic data bases are held, as is a library collection.

Publications: A catalog of Institute publications is available.

Computer-Based Products and Services: The INSTITUTE maintains three online data bases: time series data bank; manufacturer's registry; and a communal data bank. Computer facilities include an IBM 370/158 and a Siemans 7875.

Clientele/Availability: Clients include government agencies, associations, commercial firms, academic and research institutions, and others.

Contact: E. Rosselle, General Director, or Jeanne Bavin, Librarian, National Statistical Institute.

★83★
BELGIUM
MINISTRY OF HEALTH
(Ministere de la Sante Publique)
NATIONAL POISON CONTROL CENTER
(Centre National de Prevention et de Traitement des Intoxications - CNPTI)
15 rue Joseph Stallaert   Phone: 02 3441515
B-1060 Brussels, Belgium   Service Est: 1963
Dr. Monique Govaerts-Lepicard, Medical Director

Staff: 1 Information and library professional; 1 management professional; 10 technicians; 3 clerical and nonprofessional.

Description of System or Service: Operating 24 hours per day, the NATIONAL POISON CONTROL CENTER (CNPTI) provides emergency information on drug and chemical poisoning diagnosis, treatment, and prevention. It collects toxicological data and stores them in print, microform, and machine-readable files in support of its services.

Scope and/or Subject Matter: Toxicology.

Input Sources: Data are obtained from medical and trade literature.

Holdings and Storage Media: The Center's library holdings consist of 530 bound volumes, subscriptions to 18 periodicals, and a collection of reprinted journal articles.

Microform Products and Services: The Center maintains clinical calls records on microfiche.

Computer-Based Products and Services: CNPTI operates a Toxicological Data Bank covering clinical cases and reports.

Clientele/Availability: Services are available without restrictions.

Contact: Dr. Monique Govaerts-Lepicard, Medical Director, National Poison Control Center.

★84★
BELGIUM
ROYAL LIBRARY OF BELGIUM
(Bibliotheque Royale de Belgique)
NATIONAL CENTER FOR SCIENTIFIC AND TECHNICAL DOCUMENTATION
(Centre National de Documentation Scientifique et Technique - CNDST)
4, blvd. de l'Empereur   Phone: 02 5136180
B-1000 Brussels, Belgium   Service Est: 1964
Dr. A. Cockx, Director

Staff: 40 Total.

Description of System or Service: The NATIONAL CENTER FOR SCIENTIFIC AND TECHNICAL DOCUMENTATION (CNDST) functions as a national science information center for Belgian universities and industries. It provides a variety of services including: computer-based services such as literature searches, SDI, library automation, and software development; document delivery from worldwide sources and access to materials in the Royal Library of Belgium; and publication of inventories, catalogs, indexes, and directories. The CENTER also serves as a national and international referral system and as a depository for ephemeral and underground literature. Additionally, the CNDST maintains the Belgian Translations Center/Centre Belge de Traductions (CBT), which offers the following services: translation of literature in the fields of science, technology, medicine, and agriculture written in languages difficult to access, such as Russian, Japanese, and other Slavic and Asiatic languages; procurement and documentation of translated and untranslated literature; and a current awareness service informing researchers and institutions of ongoing research conducted in non-Western languages. CBT submits all documented translations to the International Translations Centre in Delft, Netherlands, for inclusion in the World Transindex data base.

Scope and/or Subject Matter: Science and technology including medicine, agriculture, pure and applied sciences, research management, technological forecasting, translations, and computer applications to information science.

Holdings and Storage Media: CNDST maintains a collection of books, periodicals, and documents in the Royal Library of Belgium; it also has access to the 3.5 million volumes and 28,000 subscriptions held by the Royal Library. CNDST also holds machine-readable files.

Publications: 1) Belgian Environmental Research Index-BERI (semiannual). 2) Inventory of Belgian Scientific Units. 3) Who is Doing What in Belgium. 4) Permanent Inventory of Belgian Scientific Publications. 5) Key to Belgian Science. 6) Inventory of Scientific Congresses. 7) Inventaire des Centres Belges de Recherche Disposant d'une Bibliotheque ou d'un Service de Documentation—available for purchase. Contains descriptions of 1090 Belgian research units; text in French and Dutch. 8) Various user needs surveys.

Microform Products and Services: The Center produces microfiche and microfilm versions of its data bases.

Computer-Based Products and Services: CNDST provides SDI and retrospective search services from a variety of commercial data bases stored on its dedicated computer. It also accesses major online systems such as DIALOG Information Services, Inc., System Development Corporation (SDC), ESA/IRS, DIMDI, BLAISE (British Library Automated Information Service), Data-Star, INKA (Informationssystem Karlsruhe), Telesystemes Questel, and others. For bibliographic processing it maintains subscriptions to U.S. Library of Congress and British National Bibliography (BNB) MARC tapes, among others. CNDST is involved in the design of software for supporting a completely integrated library system.

Other Services: Also offered are abstracting and indexing, consulting, training seminars, conferences, manual literature searches, and copying.

Clientele/Availability: Services from CNDST are available to Belgian scientists, industry and public services, and individuals with a scientific purpose. Services from the Translations Center are available without restrictions, although priority is given to Belgian academic and industrial researchers.

Contact: Dr. A. Cockx, Director, National Center for Scientific and Technical Documentation. (Telex 21157.) For information on the Belgian Translation Center, contact Mme. I. Clemens.

★85★
BEMROSE PRINTING
P.O. Box 32　　　　　　　　　　　Phone: 0332 31242
Wayzgoose Dr.　　　　　　　　　Founded: 1860
Derby, Derbyshire DE2 6XH, England
Mr. P. Brewin, Head

Staff: 1 Information and library professional; 2 management professional; 20 technicians; 7 sales and marketing; 20 clerical and nonprofessional; 8 other.

Related Organizations: The parent company of Bemrose Printing is Bemrose Corporation.

Description of System or Service: BEMROSE PRINTING offers a variety of computerized typesetting and printing services for parts catalogs, directories, bibliographies, and similar works. It supplies data base storage and information processing for publications, including electronic merging of text and graphics as well as automatic index preparation. BEMROSE also specializes in producing typographic COM microfiche using a high-quality phototypesetter.

Scope and/or Subject Matter: Computerized typesetting of catalogs, directories, and bibliographies; printing; typographic COM.

Input Sources: Input is acquired from clients in hard copy, magnetic media, or online.

Microform Products and Services: Bemrose Printing can produce typographical COM output. The microfiche are formatted with vertical columns of continuous information, enabling users to scroll up and down the columns using the fiche reader as they would a visual display unit attached to a computer system. Continuous columns and proportional spacing also increase the capacity of the fiche. For publications that are available both in hard copy and in microform, the same typesetting style can be produced from the phototypesetter for both formats.

Computer-Based Products and Services: BEMROSE PRINTING provides publication information storage and manipulation and computerized typesetting. The service will offer laser printing in the near future.

Clientele/Availability: Services are available to industrial, government, and defense organizations.

Contact: Mr. C. Harrison, Sales Director, Bemrose Printing. (Telex 37482 BEMPNT G.)

★86★
BHRA, THE FLUID ENGINEERING CENTRE
INFORMATION SERVICES
Cranfield　　　　　　　　　　　　Phone: 0234 750422
Bedford MK43 0AJ, England　　Service Est: 1947
Mr. G.A. Watts, Head, Information Group

Staff: 11 Information and library professional; 80 management professional; 20 technicians; 5 sales and marketing; 20 clerical and nonprofessional; 94 other.

Description of System or Service: The INFORMATION SERVICES collects, processes, and disseminates worldwide information relating to all aspects of fluid engineering. It issues ten abstracts journals and other publications, offers the online FLUIDEX bibliographic data base, and holds conferences and workshops. The SERVICES also supplies copies of most documents cited in its publications and data base, and it provides technical inquiry answering and manual literature searching services.

Scope and/or Subject Matter: Fluid engineering including: flow of fluids; all aspects of design, performance, operation, and application of machinery, equipment, and structures handling or associated with fluids. Particular emphasis is on industrial pumps and similar fluids machines, pipes and pipelines (including pressure surges and solids conveyance by fluids), civil and structural engineering hydraulics, industrial aerodynamics, fluid power hydraulics and pneumatics, fluidics, fluid flow measurements, jet cutting, tribology, and fluid sealing.

Input Sources: Approximately 1000 worldwide primary journals are scanned on a regular basis. Input also includes books, conference papers and proceedings, reports, bibliographies, reviews, translations, and British patent specifications.

Holdings and Storage Media: The computer-readable FLUIDEX data base contains approximately 140,000 abstracts dating from 1973 to the present; it is updated monthly with approximately 1500 items. Library holdings include approximately 50,000 accessions.

Publications: The following abstracting and indexing journals are available by subscription: 1) Civil Engineering Hydraulics Abstracts (monthly)—provides about 2800 abstracts per year. 2) Fluid Flow Measurements Abstracts (every two months)—provides approximately 750 per year. 3) Fluid Power Abstracts (every two months)—includes about 1000 abstracts per year. 4) Fluid Sealing Abstracts (every two months)—provides 750 abstracts per year. 5) Industrial Aerodynamics Abstracts (every two months)—includes 1300 abstracts per year. 6) Pipelines Abstracts (quarterly)—provides approximately 600 abstracts per year. 7) Solid-Liquid Flow Abstracts (quarterly)—includes 600 abstracts per year. 8) Pumps and Other Fluids Machinery Abstracts (every two months)—contains 900 abstracts per year. 9) Tribos: Tribology Abstracts (monthly)—includes 2000 abstracts per year. 10) World Ports and Harbours Abstracts (every two months)—contains 1200 abstracts per year. Each issue of the above publications includes personal author, corporate author, and subject indexes, with annual cumulative indexes. BHRA also publishes search aids, special bibliographies, and state-of-the-art reviews, as well as conference proceedings in some eighteen subject areas related to fluid engineering. A catalog of publications is available by request from the Centre.

Microform Products and Services: BHRA Research Reports 1948-1977 are available in microform. The series is updated annually and is available on a subscription basis; indexes are provided in hard copy and on microfiche.

Computer-Based Products and Services: The computer-readable FLUIDEX data base contains information from BHRA abstracts journals as well as considerable additional information in related fields of fluid engineering. It is available for online searching through DIALOG Information Services, Inc. and ESA/IRS. Searchable data elements include title, author, corporate source, journal, publication year, ISSN, CODEN, language, abstract, descriptors, and section heading.

Clientele/Availability: Services are primarily for BHRA members; data base and publications are generally available.

Remarks: BHRA was formerly known as the British Hydromechanics Research Association.

Contact: Mr. G.A. Watts, Head, Information Group, BHRA, The Fluid Engineering Centre. (Telex 825059.)

★87★
BIBLIOGRAPHIC PUBLISHING CO.
(Editrice Bibliografica)
Viale Vittorio Veneto 24　　　　Phone: 02 6597950
I-20124 Milan, Italy　　　　　　　Founded: 1974
Mr. Michele Costa, Head

Staff: Approximately 6 total.

Description of System or Service: The BIBLIOGRAPHIC PUBLISHING CO. collects bibliographic information from Italian publishers on books and periodicals being published and maintains the data in machine-readable files. It makes this information available in two hardcopy publications and as computer-readable data bases that are commercially accessible online to subscribers of the corresponding hardcopy forms. The printed Catalogo dei Libri in Commercio and the corresponding Archivio Libri Italiani su Calcolatore Elettronico (ALICE) data base provide information on books published in Italy, while the Catalogo dei Periodici Italiani and the corresponding Catalogo Italiano Riviste su Calcolatore Elettronico (CIRCE) data base cover Italian periodicals. BIBLIOGRAPHIC PUBLISHING also issues and distributes a number of other publications of interest to librarians and the publishing community.

Scope and/or Subject Matter: Italian bibliography and librarianship.

Input Sources: Bibliographic information for ALICE and CIRCE is supplied by publishing companies in Italy.

Holdings and Storage Media: The machine-readable ALICE data base on books holds approximately 210,000 full bibliographic records and dates from 1976 to the present; approximately 1000 items are added each month. The machine-readable CIRCE data base holds records for approximately 8000 periodicals and is updated quarterly.

Publications: 1) Catalogo dei Libri in Commercio (biannual)—Italian books currently in print. 2) Catalogo dei Periodici Italiani. 3) Giornale della Libreria (monthly)—official organ of the Associazione Italiana Editori. A number of other publications are issued or distributed; a complete catalog is available from the firm on request.

Microform Products and Services: Microfiches Novita (monthly)—updates of the Catalogo dei Libri in Commercio on 48x COM fiche.

Computer-Based Products and Services: CIRCE and ALICE data are searchable online through CILEA (Consorzio Interuniversitario Lombardo per la Elaborazione Automatica), a host on Euronet DIANE.

Clientele/Availability: Products and services are intended for librarians, booksellers, and the Italian publishing trade; the ALICE and CIRCE data bases are accessible online to anyone subscribing to the corresponding hardcopy publications.

Contact: Mr. Michele Costa, Head, Bibliographic Publishing Co.

★88★
BIOSIS, U.K. LTD.
ZOOLOGICAL RECORD (ZR)
54 Mickelgate   Phone: 0904 642816
York YO1 1L7, England
Michael N. Dadd, General Manager

Staff: Approximately 45 total.

Related Organizations: BIOSIS, U.K. Ltd. is a subsidiary of BioSciences Information Service (BIOSIS), which is described in the United States volume of this Encyclopedia. The Zoological Record is published jointly by that organization and the Zoological Society of London.

Description of System or Service: The ZOOLOGICAL RECORD (ZR) is a detailed annual index to worldwide zoological literature with emphasis on systematic and taxonomic information. ZR is available as a hardcopy publication, on magnetic tape, and as a commercially available online data base.

Scope and/or Subject Matter: Zoology, including behavior, biochemistry, communication, disease, evolution, genetics, habitat, life cycle and development, morphological variation, nomenclature, paleontology, taxonomy, and zoogeography.

Input Sources: Input is derived from approximately 6000 serial publications, as well as theses, monographs, conference reports, and other materials.

Holdings and Storage Media: The computer-readable ZR data base contains approximately 200,000 items dating from 1978 to the present; the file is updated monthly with approximately 10,000 new items.

Publications: 1) Zoological Record-ZR (annual)—published in 27 sections corresponding to taxonomic groups of animals. Includes author, subject, geographical, paleontological, and systematic indexes. Available by subscription from BioSciences Information Service, 2100 Arch St., Philadelphia, PA 19103-1399. 2) Zoological Record Search Guide. 3) ZooScene (monthly)—newsletter reporting items of iterest to zoological information users.

Microform Products and Services: Zoological Record is available in microform from University Microfilms International.

Computer-Based Products and Services: ZOOLOGICAL RECORD is searchable online through DIALOG Information Services, Inc. as Zoological Record Online and is also available on magnetic tape. Data elements present in the file include accession number, author, title of item, title of source, bibliographic reference, date, publisher, place of publication, report number, taxonomic categories, and taxa notes.

Clientele/Availability: Clients include zoologists.

Contact: Michael N. Dadd, General Manager, Zoological Record. (Telex 57900.) In the United States, contact User Services, BioSciences Information Service; telephone (215) 587-4800. (Telex 831739.)

★89★
BIRD (ANTHONY) ASSOCIATES
193 Richmond Rd.   Phone: (not reported)
Kingston, Surrey KT2 5DD, England   Founded: 1978
Tony Bird, Head

Staff: 1 Information and library professional; 1 management; 1 technician; 1 clerical and nonprofessional.

Description of System or Service: ANTHONY BIRD ASSOCIATES provides world economic forecasts concerning the environment faced by multinational companies, with emphasis on the metal producing industries. This information is made available in printed and electronic forms.

Scope and/or Subject Matter: Macroeconomic forecasts dealing with major western economies and the aluminum, steel, and copper industries.

Input Sources: Approximately 200 publications as well as a number of data bases are utilized for input.

Holdings and Storage Media: The firm maintains numerical data in machine-readable form.

Publications: 1) World Economic Prospects (quarterly); 2) Steel Analysis (quarterly); 3) Aluminum Analysis (quarterly); 4) Aluminum Annual Review; 5) Aluminum Production Costs (annual).

Computer-Based Products and Services: The firm makes summary world economic forecast data accessible via Prestel.

Other Services: The firm also offers consulting on project appraisal.

Clientele/Availability: Services are available to corporations and government and international agencies.

Contact: Tony Bird, Head, Anthony Bird Associates.

★90★
BLACKWELL TECHNICAL SERVICES LTD.
Beaver House   Phone: 0865 244944
Hythe Bridge St.   Founded: 1980
Oxford OX1 2ET, England
Dr. Philip L. Holmes, Managing Director

Staff: 3 Information and library professional; 1 management professional; 1 technician; 2 sales and marketing; 2 clerical and nonprofessional.

Description of System or Service: BLACKWELL TECHNICAL SERVICES LTD. offers the PERLINE and BOOKLINE library management systems which employ distributed processing together with standard hardware and systems software for the control of serial and monograph acquisitions. Provided as complete packages available on four different sizes of computer, the systems are fully compatible and feature networking capability within the library, to Blackwell computer facilities, and to other library utilities. BLACKWELL TECHNICAL SERVICES LTD. also maintains the BOOKFILE data base providing details on nearly 900,000 British publications and selected overseas books, including cost and availability information. BOOKFILE is accessible online to users of the PERLINE and BOOKLINE systems. Dial-up access via standard terminal is also available using Blackwell's FIBER software.

Scope and/or Subject Matter: Computerized book and periodical ordering and control.

Input Sources: Input for the BOOKFILE data base consists of weekly British National Bibliography MARC tapes as well as monthly tapes from Whitaker's Books of the Month, Books to Come, and British Books in Print. Other sources include Blackwell catalogs, stock-holding records, and local advance information from publishers' catalogs and publicity material.

Holdings and Storage Media: The computer-readable BOOKFILE data base contains more than 880,000 bibliographic entries covering most British publications since 1969, plus many earlier items;

selected overseas English and foreign-language books are also listed. Information is gathered and updated continuously, with more than 46,000 amendments made each month.

Computer-Based Products and Services: BLACKWELL TECHNICAL SERVICES provides the following computer-based products and servic s for library management:

1) PERLINE—enables libraries to create, maintain, search, display, and print a series of interrelated files giving full details of periodical and serial records, suppliers and publishers, subscription records, end users and circulation slips, binding information, claims, and others. Primary PERLINE processes include searching by ISSN, ISBN, CODEN, and local code; public inquiry; checking in; claiming; circulation; binding control; ordering, confirmation, and invoice passing; renewal; MARC interfacing, which allows data to be transferred to and from PERLINE in full MARC format; management reports; fund accounting; and message handling and networking, which allows PERLINE users to interface to Blackwell files or other network or messaging facilities.

2) BOOKLINE—enables libraries to create, maintain, search, display, and print a series of interrelated files holding full details of suppliers, orders, claims, invoices, funds, end users and circulation lists, and candidate items which the library has a potential or actual interest in acquiring. The candidate items may be entered from machine-readable sources or keyed manually and are held in storage. BOOKLINE processing involves central and local functions. Central functions require remote access to Blackwell's computers while local functions are performed by the AMBER software package running on the user's own equipment. Central functions of BOOKLINE include BOOKFILE inquiry which allows users to search nearly 900,000 bibliographic entries and process book orders; inquiry facilities, which include monitoring an order's progress through Blackwell's orders file; submitting machine-readable orders through Blackwell's and claims for overdue items; and message handling. Local functions of BOOKLINE include ordering, checking in, claiming, accruals processing, accessions maintenance, MARC interfacing (which facilitates input to cataloging systems as well as permitting capture of records into the library's files from sources other than Blackwell's), fund accounting, and management reports.

3) BOOKFILE—a computer-readable file which is part of an integrated package of programs created to assist ordering, processing, and servicing individual and institutional book requests. The data base holds book records which are accessible to libraries with PERLINE and BOOKLINE via direct dial or the British Telecom packet-switching network. Each BOOKFILE entry includes, where available, author and series, title, subtitle, volume and edition statement, binding, publisher, publication date, ISBN, currency type and price, publication status, stock status and stock location (fields currently available to Blackwell only), record entry or revision date, date of last sale, and information source code. BOOKFILE is searchable by ISBN or control number, author, title, or a combination of author and title.

4) FIBER—accessible via a teletype-compatible (TTY) terminal, modem, and telephone, FIBER permits users to query and order from BOOKFILE. Using a simple command language, subscribers can browse, search, check citations, and order books, serials, and periodicals. FIBER also offers electronic mail facilities, allowing users to transmit messages to other FIBER users and bookstores.

Clientele/Availability: Clients include special, industrial, university, college, and public libraries of all sizes.

Contact: Barry Langton, Marketing Director, or Miss G.A. Dare, Marketing Support Manager, Blackwell Technical Services Ltd. (Telex 83118.)

★91★
BLCMP (LIBRARY SERVICES) LTD.
University of Birmingham Library   Phone: 021 4711179
P.O. Box 353   Founded: 1969
Birmingham B15 2TT, England
A.R. Hall, Managing Director

Staff: 16 Information and library professional; 2 management professional; 2 technicians; 1 sales and marketing; 8 clerical and nonprofessional; 1 other.

Description of System or Service: BLCMP (LIBRARY SERVICES) LTD. provides 37 member libraries in the United Kingdom with automated acquisitions, cataloging, and circulation control systems. Shared and stand-alone online systems are operated, and a dedicated telecommunications network is maintained.

Scope and/or Subject Matter: Automated library services.

Input Sources: The BLCMP files include MARC-format records from member libraries, the U.S. Library of Congress, and the British Library.

Holdings and Storage Media: BLCMP direct access files include 3 million bibliographic records.

Publications: Library catalogs are produced in book form, printouts, and microform.

Microform Products and Services: Microfilm and microfiche are available.

Computer-Based Products and Services: BLCMP maintains a dedicated telecommunications network and provides online library management services.

Other Services: Additional services include consulting, training, and data collection.

Clientele/Availability: Services are available to subscribing libraries.

Remarks: BLCMP (Library Services) Ltd. was formerly part of the Birmingham Libraries Co-operative Mechanisation Project.

Contact: A.R. Hall, Managing Director, BLCMP (Library Services) Ltd.

★92★
**BNF METALS TECHNOLOGY CENTRE
INFORMATION DEPARTMENT**
Grove Laboratories   Phone: 023 57 2992
Denchworth Rd.
Wantage, Oxon. OX12 9BJ, England

Special Note: The above name, address, and telephone number have been verified for this edition, although no questionnaire response was received. The following text is reprinted from the 5th edition.

Staff: 10 Information and library professional; 1 management professional; 2 technicians; 4 clerical and nonprofessional.

Related Organizations: The BNF Metals Technology Centre (formerly known as the British Non-Ferrous Metals Technology Centre) is supported by an association of firms located worldwide.

Description of System or Service: The INFORMATION DEPARTMENT of the BNF Metals Technology Centre provides a variety of library and information services to support research and development at the Centre, and to meet the information needs of members. Chief among its activities is the production of BNF Abstracts, a monthly publication that is also available in computer-readable form. BNF Abstracts covers more than 400 articles per month from the technical and trade literature, and from other publications relevant to the nonferrous metals industry; British patents and books received by the library are also included.

Scope and/or Subject Matter: Nonferrous metals, including: extraction; refining; metallurgical plant development; metalworking; foundry technology; energy and furnace development; corrosion prevention; metal finishing; environmental protection; materials testing.

Input Sources: The Department utilizes journals, patents, books, conference proceedings, and internal reports.

Holdings and Storage Media: The print collection consists of more than 60,000 items, including books and conference proceedings; over 3000 reports and technical memoranda generated by BNF; and subscriptions to 400 periodicals. The BNF Abstracts data base holds 60,000 since 1961.

Publications: BNF Abstracts (monthly).

Microform Products and Services: BNF Abstracts will become available on COM in the near future.

Computer-Based Products and Services: The BNF Abstracts data base is available on magnetic tape by lease, and it is offered online through DIALOG Information Services, Inc. as the Non-Ferrous Metals Abstracts file. The Information Department uses the data base for inquiry answering on its in-house computer.

Other Services: In addition to the services described above, the Department offers manual literature searches, referrals, and document delivery via DIALOG's DIALORDER for items cited in its data base.

Clientele/Availability: There are no restrictions on services.

Contact: Head, Membership & Management Services, BNF Metals Technology Centre.

★93★
BOLIVIA
NATIONAL SCIENTIFIC AND TECHNOLOGICAL DOCUMENTATION CENTER
(Centro Nacional de Documentacion Cientifica y Tecnologica - CNDCT)
P.O. Box 3283
La Paz, Bolivia
Hugo Loaiza-Teran, Director
Phone: 359587
Service Est: 1967

Staff: 1 Information and library professional; 1 management professional; 4 technicians; 2 clerical and nonprofessional.

Related Organizations: The Documentation Center is administered by the University of San Andres/ Universidad Mayor de San Andres.

Description of System or Service: The NATIONAL SCIENTIFIC AND TECHNOLOGICAL DOCUMENTATION CENTER (CNDCT) provides scientific and technical information services on a national scale in support of research and development by individuals or industry. Specific services offered include translations, compilation of bibliographies, hardcopy and microfilm reproduction services, and publication of a journal on information science and a bibliography series. CNDCT also serves as a depository library for publications of several international organizations, and participates in the International Information System on Research in Documentation (ISORID) and the UNISIST program.

Scope and/or Subject Matter: Science and technology, health sciences, education.

Input Sources: CNDCT acquires primary and secondary bibliographic information.

Holdings and Storage Media: Library holdings consist of 1500 bound volumes; 1700 bibliographies; and subscriptions to 100 periodicals.

Publications: 1) Actualidades (quarterly)—gives national and international coverage of information sciences. 2) Serie Bibliografica—includes bibliographies and indexes of national scientific literature.

Services: The Center offers current awareness, manual literature searching, translations, reprography, bibliography compilation, consulting, and referrals.

Clientele/Availability: Services are available to persons and institutions in Bolivia and elsewhere.

Contact: Hugo Loaiza-Teran, Director, National Scientific and Technological Documentation Center.

★94★
BONNIER BUSINESS PUBLISHING GROUP
AFFARSDATA
P.O. Box 3188
S-103 63 Stockholm, Sweden
Phone: 08 7364000

Description of System or Service: AFFARSDATA, a participant in the Scannet cooperative, provides online access to Swedish business information data bases. It makes available the full text of Swedish business journals and newspapers as well as current Swedish trade, industry, stock exchange, and related statistics.

Scope and/or Subject Matter: Swedish business information and statistics.

Input Sources: Data bases are acquired from publishing companies, government agencies, and other organizations.

Holdings and Storage Media: Five data bases are held online.

Computer-Based Products and Services: AFFARSDATA provides online access to the following data bases: 1) KOMPASS EUROPE— contains company and product information for companies in more than one dozen European countries. 2) KOMPASS SWEDEN—contains information on more than 10,000 Swedish companies and approximately 25,000 different products. 3) SCB Affarsstatistik—provides access to statistics gathered by Statistics Sweden/ Statistiska Centralbyran (SCB). Includes labor cost, consumer price, producer price, export price, import price, and domestic market price indexes and the following monthly economic indicators: national and international state of the market, index code, foreign trade, trade and services, energy development, building market, prices, labor market, and credit and exchange market. 4) Tidningsdatabasen—contains the full text of the following Swedish business periodicals: Dagens Industri/ Industry Today (January 1981 to date); Datavarlden/ Computer World (October 1982 to date); DN:s Ekonomisidor (July 1983 to date); Privata Affarer/ Private Business (December 1978 to date); TH - Transport & Hantering/ Transport & Handling (January 1982 to date); Veckans Affarer/ This Week's Business (January 1981 to date). 5) Veckans Affarers Borsinformation—provides the current exchange list from the Stockholm Fond Exchange; share index by branch; data on enter prices available at the Exchange; and company reports.

Clientele/Availability: Services are available without restrictions.

Contact: Eva Sundvall, AffarsData. (Telex 17473 BONBIZ.)

★95★
BOREAL INSTITUTE FOR NORTHERN STUDIES
LIBRARY SERVICES
Rm. CW401, Biological Science Bldg.
University of Alberta
Edmonton, AB, Canada T6G 2E9
Mrs. G.A. Cooke, Librarian
Phone: (403) 432-4409
Service Est: 1960

Staff: 2 Information and library professional; 3 technicians; 1 clerical and nonprofessional; 6 other.

Description of System or Service: The LIBRARY SERVICES of the Boreal Institute for Northern Studies offers a variety of information services relating to circumpolar and other cold regions, especially northern Canada. Included among its services are the production of three online bibliographic data bases: Boreal Northern Titles (BNT), Yukon Bibliography (YKB), and the Boreal Library Catalogue. The LIBRARY also provides a microfiche newspaper clipping service, publishes indexes and bibliographies, and offers traditional library services.

Scope and/or Subject Matter: Circumpolar and cold regions, including northern Canada, Alaska, and Greenland; Arctic exploration; northern Canadian newspapers; native Canadian peoples; mid-Canada corridor development; pipelines; and related topics including relevant fiction.

Holdings and Storage Media: Library holdings consist of more than 45,000 volumes, subscriptions to 650 periodicals and newspapers, microfilm and microfiche, and several bibliographic computer files.

Publications: 1) Northern Titles KWIC Index (monthly with annual cumulation)—index of English-language titles and authors for articles in journals, government documents, and newspapers received by the Library; available by exchange or subscription. 2) Yukon Bibliography Updates—part of the Boreal Institute for Northern Studies Occasional Publications Series. 3) Library Bulletin (monthly)—acquisitions list available by subscription or exchange. 4) BINS Bibliographic Series (monthly)--each monthly bibliography covers a different topic; available by subscription or exchange.

Microform Products and Services: Boreal Institute Vertical Files on Northern Affairs is a microfiche newspaper clipping service issued monthly with a paper-copy index; it is available by subscription from Micromedia Ltd.

Computer-Based Products and Services: The LIBRARY SERVICES produces the following three online data bases: 1) Boreal Northern Titles (BNT)—provides author and title citations for nearly 100,000 periodical articles, government documents, and newspaper articles published since 1972. Used to produce the printed Northern Titles KWIC Index, BNT is also publicly available online through QL Systems Limited. 2) Yukon Bibliography (YKB)—provides abstracts of 3600 documents on the Yukon, mainly from the period 1971 through 1981;

accessible through QL Systems. 3) Boreal Library Catalogue—contains approximately 25,000 references for materials received and cataloged by the Library since 1977; updated monthly. YKB is used to produce the BINS Bibliographic Series and is accessible online through the University of Alberta Computing Services SPIRES system.

Clientele/Availability: Services and products are available to the public.

Contact: Mrs. G.A. Cooke, Librarian, or Robin Minian, Assistant Librarian, Boreal Institute for Northern Studies Library.

★96★
BORIS KIDRIC INSTITUTE OF NUCLEAR SCIENCES
(Institut za Nuklearne Nauke Boris Kidric)
LABORATORY FOR INFORMATION SYSTEMS
(Laboratorija za Informacijske Sisteme)
P.O. Box 522 Phone: 011 444961
YU-11000 Belgrade, Yugoslavia Service Est: 1974
Dr. Miodrag Petrovic, Head

Special Note: The above name, address, and telephone number have been verified for this edition, although no questionnaire response was received. The following text is reprinted from the 5th edition.

Description of System or Service: The LABORATORY FOR INFORMATION SYSTEMS of the Boris Kidric Institute of Nuclear Sciences is involved in national and international computerized information systems. It maintains a computer-readable register of scientific research projects in Yugoslavia and a data base on doctoral theses at the University of Belgrade. The LABORATORY also acts as a national focal point for participation in such international systems as the International Nuclear Information System (INIS). The LABORATORY publishes indexes and inventories from its internal files and offers computerized searching of these and externally generated data bases.

Scope and/or Subject Matter: Scientific and technical information systems.

Holdings and Storage Media: The Institute maintains machine-readable data bases and a library of 25,000 volumes.

Publications: Publications include KWIC indexes of theses and research reports as well as a register of research projects.

Computer-Based Products and Services: The LABORATORY provides computerized search and SDI services from internal data bases and such international files as INIS, AGRIS, and the International Food Information Service (IFIS).

Other Services: Technical support and consulting services are also offered.

Clientele/Availability: Services are available primarily to national government agencies.

Contact: Dr. Miodrag Petrovic, Head, Laboratory for Information Systems. (Telex YU 11563.)

★97★
BRASSEY'S PUBLISHERS LTD.
BRASSEY'S NAVAL RECORD (BNR)
Headington Hill Hall Phone: 0865 64881
Oxford OX3 0BW, England
Rear Admiral H.C.N. Goodhart

Related Organizations: Brassey's Publishers Ltd. is a subsidiary of the Pergamon Group.

Description of System or Service: BRASSEY'S NAVAL RECORD (BNR) is a computer-readable data base providing technical details on the construction, equipment, and weapons systems of all naval vessels under construction, on order, officially authorized, or projected worldwide. Designed to serve naval construction and equipment sales and marketing applications, BRASSEY'S NAVAL RECORD is available online through Pergamon InfoLine Ltd. The data base is also used by Brassey's to provide monthly printouts of new information, regular selective information profiles, ad hoc search services, and computer tape services.

Scope and/or Subject Matter: Worldwide naval construction and equipment.

Input Sources: Input is derived from government publications, market reports, technical reports, the international defense media, and contacts with some 300 shipbuilders and leading naval architects and engineers worldwide. Classified information is not included.

Holdings and Storage Media: The computer-readable BNR data base holds technical information on more than 1500 naval vessels.

Publications: BNR Monthly—available by subscription; includes a printout of the basic data base indexed by type of ship and by navy, with monthly printouts of update information and revised indexes. A data base user's manual is also produced.

Computer-Based Products and Services: BRASSEY'S NAVAL RECORD is accessible online through Pergamon InfoLine Ltd. as the Naval Record. Services provided by Brassey's from the data base include magnetic tape leasing for the production of in-house information services; ad hoc search services for any information contained in the data base; and selective information profiles, which consist of monthly printouts of information from the file in the client's specific areas of interest.

BNR contains the following categories of information for more than 1500 naval vessels: 1) identification—country ordering vessel, vessel type and class, pennant number, name, builder (including yard, town, and country); 2) dates—date ordered or projected date of order, laid down, launched, completed, commissioned; 3) materials and dimensions—hull and deck material, superstructure material, displacement (including light load, full load, perpendicular length, overall length, waterline beam, maximum beam, depth, draught light load, draught full load, draught maximum); 4) propulsion—boilers and reactors, shafts, propellers, gearing, maximum speed, cruise speed, endurance, fuel oil, diesel oil, aircraft fuel, and submarine speed, battery, capacity, and endurance; 5) auxiliary machinery—generators, alternators, supply, transverse thrust units forward and aft; 6) armaments—missiles, guns, torpedos, rockets; 7) aircraft—fixed wing and V/STOL, rotary wing, aircraft facilities; 8) systems and sensors—ATO/WCS, radar, electronic warfare, sonar, optronic, decoys.

Clientele/Availability: Services are available without restrictions.

Remarks: Founded in 1886 by Lord Thomas Brassey, Brassey's Publishers Ltd. concentrates on providing accurate information on a wide range of contemporary military and defense topics for professional military personnel, military weapons and equipment designers, administrators, decision makers in industry and politics, and interested individuals. Brassey's other products include RUSI/Brassey's Defence Yearbook, Naval Annual, Battlefield Weapons Systems and Technology, Brassey's Multi-Lingual Military Dictionary, and the British Defence Directory data base (described in a separate entry following this one). Additionally, the firm offers printing, publishing, electronic data storage, and international distribution services to professional organizations, learned societies, and defense companies.

Contact: Sue Midgley, Publishing Manager, Brassey's Publishers Ltd. In the United States contact Kevin Maxwell, Director of Publishing, Pergamon International Information Corporation, 1340 Old Chain Bridge Rd., McLean, VA 22101; the toll-free telephone number is 800-336-7575.

★98★
BRASSEY'S PUBLISHERS LTD.
BRITISH DEFENCE DIRECTORY (BDD)
Headington Hill Hall Phone: 0865 64881
Oxford OX3 0BW, England Service Est: 1982
Rear Admiral H.C.N. Goodhart

Staff: 10 Total.

Related Organizations: Brassey's Publishers Ltd. is a subsidiary of the Pergamon Group.

Description of System or Service: The BRITISH DEFENCE DIRECTORY (BDD) is a computer-based directory of service and civilian personnel in the Ministry of Defence, Royal Navy, Army, Royal Air Force, and the British component of the NATO Command. BDD lists the area of responsibility, name, rank, date of appointment, address, and telephone number of current personnel and of future appointments when already announced. The BRITISH DEFENCE DIRECTORY is available as a quarterly printed publication and as an online data base.

Scope and/or Subject Matter: British armed services and defense-related personnel.

Input Sources: Input is derived from gazetted appointments; only unclassified information sources are used.

Holdings and Storage Media: Directory information is held in machine-readable form and updated weekly.

Publications: British Defence Directory (quarterly)—available by subscription. Arranged in five parts: Ministry of Defence, Royal Navy, Army, Royal Air Force, and NATO Command (British component), with the areas of responsibility listed for each part. The Directory also includes a comprehensive name index.

Computer-Based Products and Services: The BRITISH DEFENCE DIRECTORY data base is available online through Pergamon InfoLine Ltd. The data base is searchable by individual or group name, post, or area of responsibility. Names and addresses of target personnel can be selected from the data base and used for mailing list services.

Clientele/Availability: Services are available without restrictions.

Contact: Sue Midgley, Publishing Manager, Brassey's Publishers Ltd. In the United States contact Kevin Maxwell, Director of Publishing, Pergamon International Information Corporation, 1340 Old Chain Bridge Rd., McLean, VA 22101; the toll-free telephone number is 800-336-7575.

★99★
BRAZIL
MINISTRY OF AGRICULTURE
(Ministerio da Agricultura)
NATIONAL CENTER FOR AGRICULTURAL DOCUMENTARY
  INFORMATION
(Centro Nacional de Informacao Documental Agricola - CENAGRI)
Caixa Postal 10.2432   Phone: 061 2251101
Anexo I, Bloco H, Ala Oeste
70043 Brasilia DF, Brazil
Alberto Augusto Alves Forjaz, Head

Description of System or Service: The NATIONAL CENTER FOR AGRICULTURAL DOCUMENTARY INFORMATION (CENAGRI) provides agricultural library and information services throughout Brazil. It is the central unit of the National System for Agricultural Information and Documentation/ Sistema Nacional de Informacao e Documentacao Agricola (SNIDA), which consists of centers across the country that cooperate in selecting, processing, organizing, and disseminating agricultural information. The CENTER also coordinates a national network of agricultural libraries, creates national data bases, participates in AGRIS and CARIS, issues a number of publications, and offers current awareness, retrospective searching, and document delivery services.

Scope and/or Subject Matter: Agriculture and related areas of natural science, technology, history, and legislation.

Input Sources: Input consists of legal deposit agricultural documents, documents from foreign countries, and the AGRIS data base.

Holdings and Storage Media: The Center's library holdings include approximately 45,000 volumes, 6000 serial titles, and 60,000 microfiche documents.

Publications: 1) Bibliografia Brasiliera de Agricultura—covers conventional and nonconventional materials in subject, author, corporate author, and bibliographic reference sections. 2) Levantamentos Bibliograficos—monograph series. 3) Guia Brasiliero de Instituicoes de Pesquisa em Agricultura (annual)—includes information on agricultural research institutes in Brazil. 4) Guia Brasiliero de Pesquisadores em Agricultura (annual)—includes information on agricultural researchers and their activities. 5) Estudos Sobre o Desenvolvimento Agricola—series covering socioeconomic studies. 6) Bibliografias Agricolas—separate national and international volumes provide retrospective and current references to conventional and nonconventional material on particular agricultural products; the national volume is produced by SNIDA.

Microform Products and Services: CENAGRI coordinates and executes microfilming of domestic and foreign scientific and technical documents. It also offers assistance in microfilming projects.

Computer-Based Products and Services: CENAGRI produces national agricultural information data bases.

Clientele/Availability: Services are available to Brazilian and foreign libraries, other organizations, and individual users.

Contact: Renata Nunes Pereira, Head, Technical Process Division, CENAGRI. (Telex 061 1871.)

★100★
BRAZIL
MINISTRY OF THE INTERIOR
(Ministerio do Interior - MINTER)
DOCUMENTATION COORDINATION UNIT
(Coordenadoria de Documentacao)
Esplanada dos Ministerios   Phone: 061 2257802
Bldg. A, 2nd Floor
70054 Brasilia DF, Brazil
Angela Maria Crespo Queiroz Neves, Coordinator

Description of System or Service: The DOCUMENTATION COORDINATION UNIT is responsible for the maintenance of three computerized information systems relating to Brazilian regional development: 1) The System of Documentary Reference of MINTER (INTERDOC)—bibliographic data base covering books, periodicals, and other literature relevant to Brazilian development; used to produce catalogs and bibliographies and to provide search services. 2) The System of Legislative Reference of MINTER (INTERLEGI)—online data base comprising 24,000 items of legislation produced by the Ministry of the Interior; tape distribution services and printed catalogs are provided from it. 3) Controlled Vocabulary of MINTER/ Vocabulario Controlado do MINTER (INTERVOC)—machine-readable regional development thesaurus comprising 10,000 descriptors and 29,000 identifiers within 37 subject categories; issued in printed form and on magnetic tape.

Scope and/or Subject Matter: Brazilian regional development; poverty; finance and regional investments; housing and urban affairs; civil construction; management; business; economics; agriculture; irrigation; indigenous peoples; environmental concerns; legislation; politics; industry; energy; transportation; telecommunications; informatics.

Input Sources: Input for INTERDOC is derived from books, periodicals, bibliographies, abstracts, monographs, theses, slides, films, microforms, and maps. Input for INTERLEGI is derived from normative and legislative acts published in the MINTER Service Bulletin and the Official Union Diary. Input for INTERVOC is derived from thesauri in various subject fields and from documents of the MINTER documentary network.

Holdings and Storage Media: INTERLEGI, INTERVOC, and INTERDOC information is held in machine-readable form.

Publications: 1) Bibliography of Internal Migrations. 2) Bibliography of Urban Development. 3) Vocabulario Controlado do MINTER (INTERDOC)—thesaurus comprising six volumes, including descriptors and identifiers. The Unit also utilizes INTERLEGI to produce subject-specific catalogs of MINTER legislation.

Microform Products and Services: A collective COM catalog for INTERDOC is produced.

Computer-Based Products and Services: The DOCUMENTATION COORDINATION UNIT provides current and retrospective batch-mode searching from the INTERDOC data base, with online access expected to be made available in the near future. The UNIT offers tape distribution services from the INTERDOC, INTERLEGI, and INTERVOC data bases.

Clientele/Availability: Products and services are available to regional development specialists; primary clientele are the Ministry and government.

Projected Publications and Services: The INTERVOC thesaurus is expected to be available in English, French, and Spanish-language editions in the near future.

Contact: Angela Maria Crespo Queiroz Neves, Documentation and Library Coordinator.

★101★
BRAZIL
NATIONAL CENTER FOR MICROGRAPHIC DEVELOPMENT
(Centro Nacional de Desenvolvimento Micrografico - CENADEM)
Rua Haddock Lobo, 585-5
01414 Sao Paulo SP, Brazil
Antonio Paulo A. Silva, Director
Phone: 011 2820319
Service Est: 1975

Staff: 1 Information and library professional; 5 management professional; 30 technicians.

Description of System or Service: The NATIONAL CENTER FOR MICROGRAPHIC DEVELOPMENT (CENADEM) is concerned with promoting the use of micrographics in Latin America. CENADEM holds seminars and training sessions, and offers courses in specific areas of micrographics, such as systems design and analysis, technological developments, and future trends. The CENTER also publishes a number of technical works on micrographics, and maintains a reference library to accommodate members.

Scope and/or Subject Matter: All aspects of micrographics.

Input Sources: Input sources include major microfilm institutions and associations and their members throughout the world.

Holdings and Storage Media: The Center's library consists of 400 bound volumes, 300 microfiche of technical journal articles, and subscriptions to 15 periodicals.

Publications: CENADEM has published 40 titles including The International Dictionary of Micrographics Terms/ Vocabulario Internacional de Termos Micrograficos, The International Guide to Microform Publishers/ Guia Internacional dos Micropublicadores, Microfilm in Information Systems/ Microfilme nos Sistemas de Informacao, and The Development of Advanced Micrographics Systems/ Desenvolvimento de Sistemas Micrograficos Avancados. Other titles cover the history of micrographics, its applications, and special uses of microforms. In addition, CENADEM publishes a bimonthly journal Micrographics News/ Noticiario Micrografico which provides international coverage of new developments and events occurring in the field of micrographics.

Clientele/Availability: Services are available to private companies and to governmental agencies.

Contact: Antonio Paulo A. Silva, Director, National Center for Micrographic Development.

★102★
BRAZIL
NATIONAL COMMISSION FOR NUCLEAR ENERGY
(Comissao Nacional de Energia Nuclear)
CENTER FOR NUCLEAR INFORMATION
(Centro de Informacoes Nucleares - CIN)
Rua General Severiano, 90
22294 Rio de Janeiro RJ, Brazil
Altair Carvalho de Souza, Director
Phone: 021 2958545
Service Est: 1970

Staff: 22 Information and library professional; 7 management professional; 55 technicians; 7 clerical and nonprofessional.

Related Organizations: The Center for Nuclear Information serves as the INFORCIEN regional information center for the Organization of American States Commission of Nuclear Energy.

Description of System or Service: The CENTER FOR NUCLEAR INFORMATION (CIN) provides Brazilian scientists and technicians and other national and international clients with information services on nuclear and other forms of energy. CIN acts as the Brazilian national center for the International Nuclear Information System (INIS), which is operated by the International Atomic Energy Agency (IAEA). In this capacity, CIN catalogs, indexes, and abstracts documents submitted by Brazilian universities and research institutes; issues an annual bibliography of this information; submits input in machine-readable form to IAEA for inclusion in the INIS data base; and provides information services from the INIS data base and document collection. CIN also produces the machine-readable FONTE and SIEN energy data bases. The bibliographic FONTE data base, holding approximately 2000 records, covers Brazilian literature in the fields of conventional and alternative sources of energy. SIEN supplies international factual data on geopolitical aspects, research and power reactors, uranium mining and prospecting, and other aspects relating to the nuclear fuel cycle. Utilizing internally developed information storage and retrieval software, CIN provides the following services from international and local data bases: 1) SONAR, an SDI service under which more than 2000 user profiles are stored; 2) SUPRIR, a retrospective search service; and 3) SERVIR, a document delivery service linked to SONAR and SUPRIR. In addition, the CENTER maintains an automated union catalog covering the holdings of other institutions in Brazil.

Scope and/or Subject Matter: All aspects of nuclear science and nuclear-related topics in other sciences; conventional and alternative sources of energy; physics; computing; electrical and electronics engineering.

Input Sources: Books, journal articles, theses, and reports are scanned to provide input to the INIS and FONTE data bases.

Holdings and Storage Media: CIN maintains 480,000 microfiche and the FONTE, SIEN, INIS, ENDS, and INSPEC data bases on magnetic tape.

Publications: 1) CINFORME (monthly)—distributed to CIN clients. 2) Bibliografia Brasileira de Energia Nuclear (annual)—distributed to libraries in the field of nuclear energy and related subjects. 3) Energia-Bibliografia Seletiva (annual)—distributed to libraries and universities.

Computer-Based Products and Services: The CENTER FOR NUCLEAR INFORMATION develops information management and retrieval software and maintains the bibliographic FONTE and nonbibliographic SIEN energy data bases. Search services are provided from these files and from INIS, ENDS, and INSPEC.

Clientele/Availability: INIS-based services are available to those involved in nuclear-related activities including scientists, researchers, technicians, and postgraduate students from universities, research institutes, and private companies. The services based on other data bases are open to any interested person. The SIEN data base is restricted to CNEN staff use, except by special request.

Contact: Selma Chi Barreiro, Head, Documentation Division, or Gilda Gama de Queiroz, Center for Nuclear Information. (Telex 21280 CNEN BR.)

★103★
BRAZIL
NATIONAL COUNCIL OF SCIENTIFIC AND TECHNOLOGICAL DEVELOPMENT
(Conselho Nacional de Desenvolvimento Cientifico e Tecnologico - CNPq)
BRAZILIAN INSTITUTE FOR INFORMATION IN SCIENCE AND TECHNOLOGY
(Instituto Brasileiro de Informacao em Ciencia e Tecnologia - IBICT)
Av. W-3 N, Quadra 511
Bloco A, Ed. Bittar Lote 1
70750 Brasilia, Brazil
Phone: (not reported)
Service Est: 1976

Special Note: No questionnaire response was received for this entry for the 6th edition. The entry is reprinted as it appeared in the 5th edition.

Staff: 40 Information and library professional; 7 researchers; 41 other professional; 99 clerical and nonprofessional.

Description of System or Service: The BRAZILIAN INSTITUTE FOR INFORMATION IN SCIENCE AND TECHNOLOGY (IBICT) coordinates scientific and technical information services throughout Brazil. Among IBICT's activities are the publication of several bibliographies and catalogs; the maintenance of the Brazilian Union Catalog for Scientific and Technological Serials and the Brazilian Bibliography in Science and Technology in machine-readable form; information transfer; and the development of information storage and dissemination systems.

Scope and/or Subject Matter: Library and information science; documentation; scientific and technological information policy.

Input Sources: Input is derived from books, periodicals, pamphlets, reports, and dissertations.

Holdings and Storage Media: The Brazilian Union Catalog for Scientific and Technological Serials and the Brazilian Bibliography in Science and Technology (updated quarterly) are maintained on magnetic tape. Library holdings include 21,000 bound volumes; 3815 subscriptions to periodicals; and dissertations, pamphlets, and microfiche.

Publications: 1) Bibliografias Especializadas Brasileiras/ Specialized Brazilian Bibliographies; 2) Catalogo Coletivo de Publicacoes Periodicas/ National Union Catalog of Periodical Publications; 3) Lista de Cabecalhos de Assunto/ Subject Headings List; 4) Classificacao Decimal Universal/ Universal Decimal Classification; 5) Periodicos Brasileiros de Ciencia e Tecnologia/ Scientific and Technological Brazilian Periodicals; 6) Ciencia da Informacao/ Information Science (review). IBICT also issues a number of other publications; a list is available from it on request.

Microform Products and Services: The National Union Catalog of Periodicals is available on microfiche.

Computer-Based Products and Services: Retrospective searching of the Brazilian Bibliography in Science and Technology data base is available in batch mode. IBICT also performs online searches of international data bases for researchers.

Other Services: In addition to the services described above, IBICT provides referrals, manual literature searching, courses in information science, research, and document delivery.

Clientele/Availability: Services are available without restrictions.

Contact: Chief, Divisao de Atendimento Individualizado, Brazilian Institute for Information in Science and Technology.

★104★
BRITISH BROADCASTING CORPORATION (BBC)
BBC DATA
The Langham, Room 3　　　　　　Phone: 01-580 4468
Portland Place　　　　　　　　　Service Est: 1980
London W1A 1AA, England
Richard Hewlett, General Manager

Staff: 100 Information and library professional; 10 management professional; 22 sales and marketing; 130 clerical and nonprofessional.

Description of System or Service: BBC DATA provides information services to BBC employees and to other companies and organizations. It offers a fee-based Enquiry Service, which provides public access to the extensive information resources of the BBC's dozen library and information units. Available on an ad hoc or subscription basis, services include research, quick reference, and computerized information retrieval. BBC DATA also produces two commercially available online data bases, the BBC Summary of World Broadcasts and the BBC External Services News. The Summary of World Broadcasts contains information on international events, particularly those in, or concerning, Russia, Eastern Europe, the Far East, the Middle East, Africa, and Latin America, as reported in area broadcasts and by news agencies. Reports of major speeches, meetings and visits, and published articles are included. The External Services News covers the major British and international news stories as viewed by the BBC in London and broadcast on the BBC's External Services, including the World Service.

Scope and/or Subject Matter: International news and events; current affairs; political, economic and foreign news; and technological and scientific information.

Input Sources: The Enquiry Service utilizes BBC information resources and commercial online host services. Input for the Summary of World Broadcasts is gathered from broadcasts, major speeches, meetings, visits, and published articles in 40 languages from 120 countries translated by the BBC Monitoring Service at Caversham. For the BBC External Services News data base, a composite version (including headline) of each broadcast news story is prepared.

Holdings and Storage Media: The machine-readable Summary of World Broadcasts holds data gathered from 1982 to the present; approximately 95,000 English-language words are added each day. The External Services News data base holds composite stories gathered from 1982 to the present; approximately 25,000 words are added daily. An index to BBC programs is also maintained in machine-readable form. BBC library holdings include 180,000 bound volumes;

subscriptions to 1400 periodicals and 60 newspapers, 7 million pictures, 20 million news clippings, and numerous special indexes.

Publications: The Summary of World Broadcasts in printed form is available by subscription to governments, the media, major companies, and research institutes.

Computer-Based Products and Services: BBC DATA provides computerized search services using internal and commercially available data bases. It also produces the full-text BBC Summary of World Broadcasts data base, which is available online through Mead Data Central's NEXIS system and Datasolve's World Reporter, and the BBC External Services News, which is available through the World Reporter.

Other Services: Information brokerage and consulting services are also offered.

Clientele/Availability: Primary clients are business executives, journalists, librarians, and information specialists. Services are available on a fee basis.

Contact: Kevin Johnson, BBC Data. (Telex 265781 DATAENQ.)

★105★
BRITISH BROADCASTING CORPORATION (BBC)
CEEFAX
BBC Television Centre　　　　　Phone: 01-743 8000
Wood Lane　　　　　　　　　　Service Est: 1972
London W12 7RJ, England
Graham Clayton, Editor

Description of System or Service: CEEFAX is a teletext news and information service which can be accessed on specially adapted home television receivers. Computer-processed CEEFAX information is transmitted over broadcast television signals, picked up by the user's television, and displayed by the page with the user choosing the page. CEEFAX is broadcast on the national television stations BBC1 and BBC2, which offer, respectively, a daily newspaper format with more frequent updates, and a weekly magazine format with features, games, and entertainment items. CEEFAX provides subtitles to some broadcast programs to enable the hearing-impaired to follow them. It also offers telesoftware, a service providing broadcast computer programs for school and home users.

Scope and/or Subject Matter: News, sports, finance, weather, farming, recipes, food prices, travel, and entertainment.

Input Sources: Information is entered and updated online by British Broadcasting Corporation journalists using BBC news sources such as correspondents, news agencies, and newsrooms.

Holdings and Storage Media: CEEFAX holds more than 600 pages of news and information in computer files.

Computer-Based Products and Services: Information is stored in a data base for retrieval.

Clientele/Availability: There are no charges for the CEEFAX service but television receivers must be equipped with a decoder.

Contact: Graham Clayton, Editor, CEEFAX, British Broadcasting Corporation. (Telex 26 57 81.)

★106★
BRITISH COLUMBIA MINISTRY OF INDUSTRY AND SMALL BUSINESS DEVELOPMENT
CENTRAL STATISTICS BUREAU (CSB)
1405 Douglas St.　　　　　　　Phone: (604) 387-4521
Victoria, BC, Canada V8W 3C1　Service Est: 1977
Dr. W.P. McReynolds, Provincial Statistician

Staff: 3 Information and library professional; 4 management professional; 22 other professional; 1 technician; 4 clerical and nonprofessional.

Description of System or Service: The CENTRAL STATISTICS BUREAU (CSB), the provincial statistical agency for British Columbia, collects, compiles, and projects economic and social statistics of all kinds; provides direct assistance to other provincial government agencies in meeting their individual statistical requirements; and provides data and consultation services to a variety of users in the public and private sectors. Among the services extended to government clients are the following: statistical computer models for forecasting and analysis; survey design, management, and processing; special tabulation of statistics for regions of the province; utilization of administrative records for statistical purposes; statistical bulletins and reports; extraction and derivation of statistics for specific applications; assembly and compilation of aggregate measures; and liaison with Statistics Canada.

The BUREAU consists of three branches: the Economic and Business Statistics Branch, which develops statistical information on the British Columbia economy, including its industrial, commercial, and financial structure; the Population and Social Statistics Branch, which meets the needs of government, business, and the public for data and statistical information on the population and social characteristics of British Columbia; and the Statistical Services and Integration Branch, which performs quantitative analysis and prepares forecasts in support of the British Columbia government, and develops and operates mathematical and computer models as tools for such analysis.

Scope and/or Subject Matter: Econometrics, forecasting, demography, provincial economic accounts, current economic and social conditions, and related topics in British Columbia.

Input Sources: Input is derived from surveys and federal and provincial government sources.

Holdings and Storage Media: The Bureau maintains a wide range of data in machine-readable form, microfiche, and hardcopy.

Publications: British Columbia Economic Accounts (annual)—includes annual and quarterly data on a current and constant dollar basis from 1961 to the present. The Bureau also issues a number of other statistical publications.

Computer-Based Products and Services: The CENTRAL STATISTICS BUREAU disseminates data through a variety of computerized means. Computers are used to store and access data bases; to typeset publications via a generalized composition program; to interface the internal capacities of word processors with external data banks for report generation; to build policy models of the British Columbia economy and its industrial sector; and to produce small area information for user-defined geographic regions. The BUREAU's Economic and Business Statistics Branch is implementing the computerized British Columbia Manpower Survey, which will provide an accurate picture of the current occupational structure of the provincial labor force. The BUREAU's Population and Social Statistics Branch has developed statistical systems for generating quantitative information on the many economic, administrative, political, and resource regions of the province. CSB's Statistical Services and Integration Branch has developed short-term econometric forecasting models to produce forecasts of output, employment, and inflation, and to simulate the impact of government policy on the performance of the provincial economy. Long-term models are also being developed.

Clientele/Availability: Clients include government agencies, public and private institutions, business, industry, and the general public.

Contact: Gary Weir, Chief, Data Dissemination, Central Statistics Bureau.

★107★
BRITISH COMPUTER SOCIETY (BCS)
13 Mansfield St. Phone: 01-637 0471
London W1M 0BP, England Founded: 1957
D.W. Harding, Secretary-General

Related Organizations: The Society is affiliated with a number of computer organizations including the International Federation for Information Processing (IFIP).

Description of System or Service: The BRITISH COMPUTER SOCIETY (BCS) was established to promote public understanding of data processing equipment and techniques and to further information exchange among its members. The SOCIETY sponsors 40 special interest groups, acts as a professional qualifying body, and sponsors conferences and workshops. It also issues a number of publications; provides manual and computerized information retrieval services, photocopying, and bibliographies through its library; and cooperates with computer organizations worldwide.

Scope and/or Subject Matter: All aspects of computers and electronic data processing.

Holdings and Storage Media: BCS maintains a library in association with the Institution of Electrical Engineers (IEE). The combined collection comprises 40,000 bound volumes; subscriptions to 700 periodicals; and a pamphlet collection.

Publications: 1) Computer Journal (quarterly)—contains papers on scientific, business, and commercial subjects relating to computers. 2) Computer Bulletin (quarterly)—provides a forum concerning the role and consequences of computing in modern society; includes reviews. 3) BSC Newsletter (10 per year). 4) Computing (weekly)—published by VNU Business Publications; includes a BCS feature. These publications are free of charge to members. The Society also issues proceedings of its conferences and technical handbooks.

Computer-Based Products and Services: The joint IEE/BCS library provides computerized information retrieval relating to all aspects of electrotechnology and computers.

Clientele/Availability: The Society has more than 27,000 members; membership is open to computer operators, programmers, analysts, managers, and others associated with computers.

Contact: Information on the Society can be obtained at the address given above. For further information on BCS library and information services, contact the Assistant Librarian, IEE/BCS Library, Savoy Place, London WC2R 0BL, England; telephone 01-240 1871.

★108★
**THE BRITISH COUNCIL
CENTRAL INFORMATION SERVICE (CIS)**
10 Spring Gardens Phone: 01-930 8466
London SW1A 2BN, England
T.J. Maughan, Director

Staff: 52 Information and library professional.

Related Organizations: The British Council is a government-funded body responsible for the promotion of Britain overseas through cultural, educational, and technical cooperation.

Description of System or Service: The CENTRAL INFORMATION SERVICE (CIS) provides information services in support of British Council activities. It issues a number of publications and provides an inquiry answering service on all matters relating to British education, science, technology, and language for overseas students. CIS also produces a viewdata file on the Prestel system which covers short, full-time courses currently offered in Britain.

Scope and/or Subject Matter: British education, science, technology, and language.

Input Sources: Input for the viewdata file is derived from information supplied by universities, colleges, and training institutions in Britain (usually in the form of course leaflets or prospectuses) covering every subject.

Holdings and Storage Media: The viewdata file is held in machine-readable form.

Publications: 1) A Guide to Overseas Qualifications—loose-leaf with update service. 2) Higher Education in the United Kingdom—published for the Council by Longman. 3) British Educational Reference Books (annual). All publications are available from Design Production and Publishing Department, The British Council, 65 Davies St., London W1Y 2AA, England.

Computer-Based Products and Services: The SERVICE's viewdata file is accessible through Prestel and provides interactive access to information on British educational courses.

Clientele/Availability: Services are available to the public.

Contact: Diana Hurter, Head, Editorial Section, Central Information Service. (Telex 916522.)

★109★
BRITISH MARKET RESEARCH BUREAU LTD. (BMRB)
TARGET GROUP INDEX (TGI)
Saunders House　　　　　　　　　　　Phone: 01-567 3060
53 The Mall, Ealing
London W5 3TE, England
Philip Mitchell, Senior Assoc. Director

Related Organizations: BMRB is a subsidiary of MRB International Ltd.

Description of System or Service: The TARGET GROUP INDEX (TGI) is a national British consumer survey which links usage of brands and products with newspaper and periodical readership, television viewing, and other media exposure. Based on annual interviewing of 24,000 adults, the INDEX also includes a range of demographic data by which use of brands and products can be analyzed. The INDEX is designed to serve advertisers and media executives by providing a tool for media planning and it is available in hard copy and on computer tape from the British Market Research Bureau. TGI is also available as an online data base through several time-sharing companies.

Scope and/or Subject Matter: British consumer usage of products, services, and mass media.

Input Sources: TGI is based on a random location sample of 24,000 adults per year. Respondents are personally interviewed to collect classification data, and then given a questionnaire to be completed.

Holdings and Storage Media: The Target Group Index data base stores the following data in machine-readable form: heavy-to-light usage of more than 2500 brands in 200 consumer product fields; usage in more than 150 other areas such as banks, automobiles, and vacations; readership of 140 newspapers and periodicals; television, radio, and other media usage; and demographic data such as age, sex, income, education, marital status, and other classifications.

Publications: 1) Target Group Index (annual)—published in 34 volumes; available for purchase as a set, by individual volume, or by separate product fields. 2) Plain Man's Guide to the T.G.I.—describes the survey and services provided from it and lists all product fields covered.

Computer-Based Products and Services: The TARGET GROUP INDEX data base is available online in the United States through Interactive Market Systems and in Britain through Interactive Market Systems UK and Telmar Communications. BMRB maintains its own computer terminal facilities and conducts special analyses for TGI subscribers; computer tapes are also offered.

Clientele/Availability: Primary clients are advertisers, advertising agencies, and media owners.

Contact: Philip Mitchell, Senior Associate Director, British Market Research Bureau Ltd. (Telex 935526.)

★110★
BRITISH MEDICAL ASSOCIATION
BMA PRESS CUTTINGS DATABASE (BMAP)
Tavistock Square　　　　　　　　　　Phone: 01-387 4499
London WC1H 9JP, England　　　　Service Est: 1984
Dr. J. Dawson, Under Secretary

Description of System or Service: The BMA PRESS CUTTINGS DATABASE (BMAP) comprises brief summaries of articles and information in the media concerning key medical topics. Items of interest are drawn from British broadcasting services and newspapers and entered into the DATABASE on a daily basis. BMAP is commercially available online through Data-Star.

Scope and/or Subject Matter: Medical news and related ethical and sociological issues.

Input Sources: British broadcasting services and approximately 30 newspapers are scanned for inclusion in BMAP.

Holdings and Storage Media: The machine-readable BMA Press Cuttings Database dates from January 1984 to the present, and is updated daily with the previous day's clippings.

Computer-Based Products and Services: The BMA PRESS CUTTINGS DATABASE, which provides information on current medical affairs as reported in the media, is available for online searching through Data-Star. A typical record includes identification number, source, date of publication, keyword descriptors, and summary of article or item.

Clientele/Availability: Services are available without restrictions. Primary clients are physicians, health administrators, and information professionals.

Contact: Dr. J. Dawson, Under Secretary, British Medical Association. (Telex 265 929.)

★111★
BRITISH STANDARDS INSTITUTION (BSI)
INFORMATION DEPARTMENT
Linford Wood　　　　　　　　　　　Phone: 0908 320033
Milton Keynes, Bucks. MK14 6LE,
　England　　　　　　　　　　　　Service Est: 1982
John S. Widdowson, Group Manager

Staff: 26 Information and library professional; 4 management professional; 3 technicians; 8 clerical and nonprofessional.

Related Organizations: The Information Department serves as the United Kingdom inquiry point for ISONET and GATT.

Description of System or Service: The INFORMATION DEPARTMENT was established to provide a one-stop information service on documentary questions concerning standards and technical requirements in operation in the United Kingdom, overseas, and internationally. The DEPARTMENT is composed of the following units: inquiry section, which handles all initial inquiries and telephone orders for documents; BSI library, which maintains a large collection of standards and technical requirements documents and conducts in-depth research using library resources; and data base section, which is responsible for subject inquiries and the development of manual and computer-based information systems. A primary client of the INFORMATION DEPARTMENT is the Technical Help to Exporters (THE) unit of the British Standards Institution. THE provides consultant information services designed to assist the exporting manufacturer in solving technical exporting problems. Specific services offered include inquiry answering, library services, engineering and consulting, current awareness, publications, and technical research and translations.

Scope and/or Subject Matter: Laws, regulations, standards, codes of practice, and any other technical requirement which affects the design, operation, or performance of any item of equipment or service; also systems for certification, approval, or other proof of compliance. All industrial and commercial fields are covered, but with an emphasis on engineering disciplines.

Input Sources: Input is derived from international government regulations and standards, import/ export legislation, standards bodies, periodicals, codes of practice, technical requirements, and online data bases.

Holdings and Storage Media: The library maintains a collection of more than 500,000 standards, technical regulations, and specifications; 2000 bound volumes; and subscriptions to 400 periodicals. An experimental computer-readable data base is also held.

Publications: 1) Worldwide List of Published Standards (monthly)—listing of new British and overseas standards added to the BSI Library; available to subscribing BSI members and overseas standards organizations. 2) Technical Export News (quarterly)--contains topical features and news of international exports developments. Other publications are also issued.

Computer-Based Products and Services: The INFORMATION DEPARTMENT has developed an experimental data base covering selected British standards and regulations and other similar foreign documents. It is planned to have the full data base available for public online access through a commercial host service in 1986. The data base is being implemented with the BSI ROOT Thesaurus, which is available in machine-readable form.

Other Services: Consultancy services are offered for the development of standards information systems.

Clientele/Availability: Membership in the BSI is available to companies and organizations.

Contact: John S. Widdowson, Group Manager, Information Department. (Telex 825777 BSIMK G.)

★112★
BRITISH UNIVERSITIES FILM & VIDEO COUNCIL LTD. (BUFVC)
INFORMATION SERVICE
55 Greek St.   Phone: 01-734 3687
London W1V 5LR, England
James Ballantyne, Information Officer

Staff: Approximately 2 total.

Related Organizations: The Council is supported by a grant from the British Department of Education and Science and by members' subscriptions.

Description of System or Service: The INFORMATION SERVICE of the British Universities Film & Video Council Ltd. collects and disseminates information on the availability, use, and production of audiovisual materials in higher education. It maintains a reference library, a major collection of film catalogs from the United Kingdom and overseas, and an appraisals file on audiovisual materials currently available in the U.K. The SERVICE also maintains a computer-readable catalog of audiovisual materials and uses it to publish the BUFVC Catalogue on microfiche; the Catalogue is also commercially available online. Subject lists, short bibliographies, and single-subject catalogs are also produced.

Scope and/or Subject Matter: Audiovisual media, materials, and techniques for degree-level teaching and research in higher-education institutions.

Input Sources: Input is derived from film catalogs, books, periodicals, and appraisals from subject specialists.

Holdings and Storage Media: The Information Service maintains a collection of more than 500 British and 100 foreign audiovisual-distributor catalogs; 1900 bound volumes; and 100 periodicals and newsletters. The BUFVC Catalogue data base comprises more than 5000 records in machine-readable form.

Publications: The BUFVC publishes a newsletter, research guides, directories, and other publications; a price list is available from the Council on request.

Microform Products and Services: The BUFVC Catalogue, issued annually on microfiche, contains full descriptions of approximately 5500 audiovisual materials suitable for use in degree-level teaching. Many of the items are produced in U.K. institutions of higher education; others are recommended for use in degree-level teaching. The Catalogue is available for purchase; included is an accompanying booklet listing addresses and telephone numbers of 400 U.K. distributors.

Computer-Based Products and Services: The INFORMATION SERVICE utilizes the British Library's LOCAS catalog production service to prepare the BUFVC Catalogue. The Catalogue data base is available online through BLAISE.

Other Services: BUFVC also maintains the Audio-Visual Reference Centre (AVRC), a preview and research facility for audiovisual materials produced by members and others, and the Higher Education Film and Video Library, an outlet for specialized audiovisuals that would not normally be distributed.,

Clientele/Availability: Clients include teachers in university, polytechnic, or higher education institutions.

Remarks: The BUFVC Catalogue is the result of the merger of the Audio-Visual Materials for Higher Education Catalogue and the Higher Education Learning Programmes Information Service Catalogue (HELPIS).

Contact: Mrs. Olwen Terris, Assistant Information Officer, British Universities Film & Video Council Ltd.

★113★
BROWN'S GEOLOGICAL INFORMATION SERVICE LTD.
134 Great Portland St.   Phone: 01-580 4701
London W1N 5PH, England   Founded: 1971
G.H. Brown, Director

Staff: 2 Information and library professional; 1 management professional; 2 sales and marketing.

Description of System or Service: BROWN'S GEOLOGICAL INFORMATION SERVICE LTD. provides worldwide geological information to subscribers. Services include computerized and manual literature searching, copying, map and book ordering, translation, compilation, and editing. BROWN'S also publishes a bulletin and bibliography.

Scope and/or Subject Matter: Worldwide geological information, especially geology and petroleum and mineral exploration outside North America; also offshore science, remote sensing, space, mineralogy, paleontology, geophysics, seismic surveys, topographic mapping, maps and charts, air photographs, government policy, government agency activities, intergovernmental and international activity related to geology and exploration.

Input Sources: The Service uses published and unpublished information from its own and other libraries, and from computer-readable data bases.

Publications: 1) Brown's Geological Information Bulletin (monthly)—covers research in progress, news, and new publications; privately circulated. 2) Offshore Geological Bibliography—worldwide coverage; includes abstracts.

Computer-Based Products and Services: The SERVICE provides clients with batch-mode searches of GEODE, GeoRef, and other machine-readable data bases, and it provides SDI services using the PASCAL data base.

Other Services: Additional services include consulting, data collection and analysis, and manual literature searching.

Clientele/Availability: Services are available by subscription.

Contact: G.H. Brown, Director, or Dr. R.M. Knight, Editor and Consultant, Brown's Geological Information Service Ltd.

★114★
BRUNEL UNIVERISTY
BRUNEL INSTITUTE FOR BIOENGINEERING (BIB)
INFORMATION UNIT
   Phone: 0895 71206
Uxbridge, Middlesex UB8 3PH, England   Service Est: 1965
Ann C. Rickard, Head

Staff: 3 Information and library professional; 1 management professional.

Description of System or Service: The INFORMATION UNIT of the Brunel Institute for Bioengineering (BIB) collects and indexes worldwide literature on biomedical engineering and aids for the disabled. It stores bibliographic references in the computer-readable BECAN (Biomedical Engineering Current Awareness Notification) data base, which is used to provide literature searches and to produce current awareness bulletins, bibliographies, and indexes. The UNIT also supplies microfiche copies of documents and conducts computerized and manual literature searching.

Scope and/or Subject Matter: Engineering as applied to medicine, including instrumentation and methods, medical and biological electronics, medical ultrasonics, automation and data processing, prosthetics, cardiology, compatibility of tissues and materials, aids for the disabled, and patient monitoring equipment.

Input Sources: The Unit scans 600 primary journals published worldwide, as well as books, patents, reports, conference proceedings, theses, and secondary sources.

Holdings and Storage Media: The machine-readable BECAN data base contains approximately 40,000 references to biomedical engineering literature published since 1977. The Unit's library collection includes more than 20,000 documents on microfiche.

Publications: The INFORMATION UNIT publishes the following monthly current awareness bulletins, all of which are available by subscription: 1) Biomedical Engineering Current Awareness Notification (BECAN)—covers the international literature on all aspects of biomedical engineering, with emphasis on engineering aspects of equipment design as well as new methods. Each issue contains approximately 100 references. 2) Instrumentation and Techniques for Cardiology—cites literature on instrumentation and new techniques for cardiology. Each issue contains approximately 40 citations. 3) Electrodes for Medicine and Biology—cites literature on electrode design, construction, and development for biomedical use; contains approximately 25 references per issue. 4) Biomechanics and Orthopaedics—covers technical literature on bioengineering, medical instrumentation, patient-monitoring equipment, biomechanics, orthopedics, prosthetics, implants, ergonomics, and anthropometry. Each issue contains approximately 70 citations. 5) Equipment for the Disabled Population—covers literature on equipment for the disabled and the aged, including sensory aids, communication devices, control and information systems, alarm systems, daily living aids, and others. The UNIT also issues the following annual publications: 6) European Bioengineering Research Inventory—listing of bioengineering research centers in EEC countries; published on behalf of the European Economic Community. 7) Forthcoming Bioengineering Conferences.

Microform Products and Services: Copies of most articles indexed by the Unit are available on microfiche.

Computer-Based Products and Services: The INFORMATION UNIT conducts computerized literature searching from the BECAN data base and those offered through public online systems. BECAN references are also available on floppy disks, suitable for searching on CP/M-based microcomputers.

Clientele/Availability: Services are available on a subscription or fee basis.

Remarks: The Brunel Institute for Bioengineering Information Unit has assumed the information services of Project FAIR, part of the Clinical Research Centre of Great Britain's Medical Research Council.

Contact: Ann C. Rickard, Head, Information Unit, Brunel Institute for Bioengineering.

★115★
BRUNEL UNIVERSITY
RESEARCH UNIT FOR THE BLIND
INTERNATIONAL REGISTER OF RESEARCH ON VISUAL DISABILITY
Phone: 0895 71206
Uxbridge, Middlesex UB8 3PH, England
Dr. J.M. Gill

Description of System or Service: The INTERNATIONAL REGISTER OF RESEARCH ON VISUAL DISABILITY is a computer-readable data base and corresponding annual publication that documents worldwide nonmedical research relating to blindness. The REGISTER provides names, addresses, and descriptions of current research projects as well as information on sources of information, such as periodicals and abstracting services concerning the blind. Two related directories are also issued by the Research Unit for the Blind.

Scope and/or Subject Matter: Nonmedical research and innovative practice for the blind and visually impaired.

Input Sources: Information is gathered from questionnaires and personal contacts.

Holdings and Storage Media: Files are stored on magnetic tape.

Publications: 1) International Register of Research on Visual Disability (annual)—contains information about current nonmedical research and information sources on visual disability. 2) International Survey of Aids for the Visually Disabled—describes over 300 aids from more than 120 manufacturers; entries include manufacturer's address, telephone number, brief description of the aid, and price. 3) International Directory of Agencies for the Visually Disabled—contains information about the main organizations of and for the visually disabled in 135 countries. All publications are available for purchase.

Computer-Based Products and Services: The data base is maintained for internal use.

Clientele/Availability: Publications are available for purchase.

Contact: Dr. J.M. Gill, Research Unit for the Blind, Brunel University.

★116★
BTJ
Tornavagen 9, Box 1706 Phone: 046 140480
S-221 01 Lund, Sweden Founded: 1951
Jan Gumpert, Managing Director

Staff: Approximately 300 total.

Related Organizations: BTJ is owned by the Swedish Library Association/ Sveriges Allmanna Biblioteksforening and the Swedish Union of Municipal Authorities/ Svenska Kommunforbundet.

Description of System or Service: BTJ (Bibliotekstjanst AB/Library Service Ltd.) acts as centralized service agency for Swedish public libraries by supplying books, recordings, and other media; producing printed catalog cards, indexes, and other bibliographic aids; and providing computer-based services such as the BUMS automated circulation control system, and network access to bibliographic data bases. BTJ maintains two machine-readable files: Artikel-Sok, which contains references to items of popular interest appearing in 51 Swedish daily newspapers and more than 450 Swedish journals and yearbooks; and Bok-Sok, which contains bibliographic and holdings information for books held by libraries in 58 Swedish communities. Both files are accessible online. Printed indexes and COM catalogs are also produced from the data bases.

Scope and/or Subject Matter: Products and services for Swedish public libraries.

Input Sources: Input is derived from approximately 500 journals and newspapers and from books cataloged by BTJ.

Holdings and Storage Media: The computer-readable Bok-Sok cataloging data base holds more than 800,000 records and is updated with 60,000 records per year. Artikel-Sok holds 50,000 references since 1979.

Publications: 1) Index to Swedish Periodicals/ Svenska Tidskriftsartiklar (monthly with quarterly cumulations)—indexes the contents of 450 Swedish journals and annuals. 2) Index to Swedish Newspapers/ Svenska Tidningsartiklar (monthly with annual cumulations)—index to articles in all areas of interest in 51 Swedish daily newpapers. Both are available by subscription. 3) Union Catalog of Foreign Acquisitions by Major Swedish Public Libraries/ Utlandska Nyforvarv—lists the foreign-language acquisitions of more than 30 Swedish public libraries; entries are arranged by language. 4) BUMS Manual.

Microform Products and Services: COM catalogs are produced.

Computer-Based Products and Services: Designed to meet Swedish requirements, BTJ's computerized BUMS system combines complete subsystems, circulation control, and COM cataloging. More than 25 Swedish public libraries are affiliated with BUMS. Central cataloging is provided through BTJ, with COM catalogs on microfiche and microfilm produced for the member libraries. The Artikel-Sok and Bok-Sok data bases are available for online searching through BTJ.

Clientele/Availability: Services are available to Swedish public libraries.

Contact: Ninna Widstrand, Information Scientist, R&D Department, Bibliotekstjanst.

★117★
BUILDING CENTER
(Centro Edile)
Via Rivoltana 8 Phone: 02 7530951
I-20090 Segrate/Milan, Italy Founded: 1976

Special Note: No questionnaire response was received for this entry for the 6th edition. The entry is reprinted as it appeared in the 5th edition.

Staff: 6 Information and library professional; 4 management professional; 3 technicians; 18 clerical and nonprofessional.

Related Organizations: The Building Center is a member of the International Union of Building Centres (UICB) and the International Council for Building Research Studies and Documentation (CIB).

Description of System or Service: One of the primary functions of the BUILDING CENTER is to catalog building products and provide other information services regarding the building industry in Italy. It has developed a computerized information system covering technical information on building components and semifinished materials for the industry. The system is used to produce printed catalogs and index cards that give the name of the company which manufactures a specific product, a description of the product, its technical performance, and the approvals received by the product.

Scope and/or Subject Matter: Building products and industry in Italy.

Input Sources: The Building Center collects information from producers, exhibitors, and national and international building organizations.

Holdings and Storage Media: The computer-readable Building Center data base contains technical information on 10 major categories and 130 subcategories of building products.

Publications: The Center issues printed catalogs of building products.

Computer-Based Products and Services: Search services and SDI are provided from the Building Center data base. The data base is particularly useful for composing files and print catalogs for building products in accordance with national and international technical standards.

Other Services: In addition to its information services, the Building Center maintains a permanent exhibition of products; organizes meetings, conferences, and seminars; offers technical advice on products available; and conducts practical research and marketing studies.

Clientele/Availability: Primary users of the information services are public and private organizations responsible for technical standards and the quality of products; buyers; insurance and reinsurance companies; general designers; and consumers in the building field.

Contact: Managing Director, Building Center.

★118★
BUILDING INFORMATION INSTITUTE
Lonnrotinkatu 20 B
SF-00120 Helsinki 12, Finland
Mr. Esko Lehti, Director General
Phone: 90 645615
Founded: 1972

Staff: Approximately 60 total.

Description of System or Service: The BUILDING INFORMATION INSTITUTE provides comprehensive information and research services for the Finnish building industry. It conducts applied research and collects, stores, and distributes information on available building products and related publications, research studies, standards, and terminology. In support of its services, the INSTITUTE maintains the machine-readable Building Product File.

Scope and/or Subject Matter: Finnish construction industry.

Input Sources: The Institute collects professional literature and other relevant publications on the Finnish building industry.

Publications: The Institute has founded a publishing and distribution company, Rakennuskirja Oy, to publish Institute studies and standards and to make available publications from other national and international sources.

Computer-Based Products and Services: The computer-readable Building Product File is used to collect and disseminate information on building products currently on the market and their special properties.

Clientele/Availability: Services are available without restrictions to organizations and individuals involved in the Finnish building industry.

Remarks: The Institute maintains the Helsinki Building Centre, which acts as its information service unit.

Contact: Ms. Merja Hakkinen, Secretary, Building Information Institute.

★119★
BUILDING SERVICES RESEARCH AND INFORMATION ASSOCIATION (BSRIA)
BSRIA INFORMATION CENTRE
Old Bracknell Lane West
Bracknell, Berks. RG12 4AH, England
A.R. Eaves, Information Manager
Phone: 0344 426511
Service Est: 1957

Staff: 7 Information and library professional; 1 management professional; 4 technicians; 2 clerical and nonprofessional.

Description of System or Service: The BSRIA INFORMATION CENTRE collects, stores, and disseminates technical information for staff and member organizations of the Building Services Research and Information Association. The CENTRE issues International Building Services Abstracts and other publications, produces the corresponding computer-readable IBSEDEX data base, and provides inquiry answering and document delivery services. IBSEDEX, which is a cooperative effort with REHVA (Representatives of European Heating and Ventilation Associations), is publicly available online.

Scope and/or Subject Matter: Mechanical and electrical services associated with buildings, including heating and cookery; air conditioning and ventilation; plumbing and sanitation; lighting and power; controls and instrumentation; corrosion; heat transfer and fluid control; energy management and sources; alternative energy; indoor environment; noise and vibration; thermal and sound insulation; site and office organization; fire protection.

Input Sources: Input is derived from books, journals, research reports, standards, conference papers, government publications, and unpublished communications.

Holdings and Storage Media: The computer-readable IBSEDEX data base contains 15,000 records dating from 1979 to the present; it is updated monthly and approximately 5000 records are added each year. Library holdings consist of 6000 bound volumes; 90,000 reports, standards, and other pamphlets; and subscriptions to 350 periodicals.

Publications: 1) International Building Services Abstracts (bimonthly, with annual cumulative author/ subject indexes)—available by subscription. Each issue contains approximately 350 entries reviewing international literature on new developments in building services. Also includes subject, author, and company indexes and a source list. 2) Omnibus (quarterly)—newsletter available only to members. 3) Library Bulletin (quarterly)—free to members and other libraries. 4) BSRIA Statistics Bulletin (quarterly)—statistical data published by official and commercial organizations on British building services; available free to members and by subscription to nonmembers. 5) Computer Newsletter (quarterly)—articles on the application of computers to building services. Additional publications include application guides, project reports, technical notes, and bibliographies published on an irregular basis and available for purchase.

Computer-Based Products and Services: The IBSEDEX data base is available online through the BSRIA, Pergamon InfoLine Ltd., and ESA/IRS. Tape subscription services are also offered. Searchable data elements include title, author, journal name, publisher, publication year and type, language, trade name, Universal Decimal Classification number, controlled terms, and abstract. The CENTRE conducts online searches of IBSEDEX and data bases carried by BLAISE (British Library Automated Information Service), CIBDOC, ESA/IRS, Pergamon InfoLine Ltd., and DIALOG Information Services, Inc.

Other Services: In addition to the services described above, the Centre offers consulting, research, data collection and analysis, manual literature searching, referrals, and document delivery and photocopying.

Clientele/Availability: Services are free to members; discretionary service is provided to nonmembers, usually on a fee basis. Members include engineers, contracting firms, manufacturers, educational establishments, and commercial and public bodies.

Contact: A.R. Eaves, Information Manager, BSRIA Information Centre. (Telex 848288 BSRIAC G.)

★120★
BULGARIA
MEDICAL ACADEMY
CENTER FOR SCIENTIFIC INFORMATION IN MEDICINE AND HEALTH
(Tsentar za Nauchno-Meditsinska Informatsiia - CNIMZ)
1, Georgi Sofijsky St.   Phone: 522342
Sofia 1431, Bulgaria   Service Est: 1967
Prof. Alexi Valtchev, M.D.

Staff: 43 Information and library professional; 8 management professional; 14 technicians; 1 clerical and nonprofessional.

Related Organizations: The Center for Scientific Information in Medicine and Health receives support from the Bulgarian Central Institute for Scientific and Technical Information (CISTI).

Description of System or Service: The CENTER FOR SCIENTIFIC INFORMATION IN MEDICINE AND HEALTH (CNIMZ) works with the Bulgarian Central Medical Library (CMB) to provide library and information services in the fields of medicine and public health. It abstracts and indexes medical journals and monographs to prepare bibliographic publications and to contribute to national and international computer-readable data bases. CNIMZ also maintains a number of data bases online and supplies search and SDI services from them, and it holds machine-readable files of health statistics and demographic data for Bulgaria. Additionally, CNIMZ plays an active role in the development of MEDINFORM, an international medical information system for the Socialist countries.

Scope and/or Subject Matter: Medical sciences; public health.

Input Sources: Input is obtained from approximately 800 medical journals, and from books received in and research work carried out in the Socialist countries.

Holdings and Storage Media: The Central Medical Library holdings consist of 600,000 bound volumes and subscriptions to 7147 periodicals.

Publications: The Center publishes 27 abstracting publications and two current contents publications covering various aspects of medicine and public health.

Computer-Based Products and Services: CNIMZ conducts online searches and provides SDI services from the following data bases: Bulgarian Medical Literature (BML), Chorisont, Sirena, INIS, BIOSIS, INSPEC, COMPENDEX, CIS, and VINITI.

Other Services: Additional services offered by CNIMZ include manual literature searching, translations, consulting, and referrals.

Clientele/Availability: Services are available without restrictions.

Contact: Borjana Stantcheva, M.D., Deputy Director, Center for Scientific Information in Medicine and Health.

★121★
BULGARIA
NATIONAL AGRO-INDUSTRIAL UNION
(Natsionalen Agrarno-Promishlen Suyuz)
AGRICULTURAL ACADEMY
(Selskostopanska Akademiya)
CENTER FOR SCIENTIFIC, TECHNICAL AND ECONOMIC INFORMATION
(Tsentur za Naouchno-Technicheska i Ikonomicheska Infomatsiya)
125, Lenin Blvd., Block No. 1   Phone: 74371
1113 Sofia, Bulgaria   Service Est: 1961
Prof. N. Apostolov, Director

Staff: 102 Information and library professional.

Description of System or Service: The CENTER FOR SCIENTIFIC, TECHNICAL AND ECONOMIC INFORMATION functions as a branch information agency in the areas of agriculture and food industry. It plays a coordinating role directed to the increase of scientific and technical information efficiency and the popularization of scientific and technical achievements. Its basic subdivisions include the Central Agricultural Library, the United Information Editing Department, and the United Editing Departments of the agriculture and food journals specialized for science and for practice. The CENTER's activities include; 1) investigating information requirements; 2) acquisition and library processing of reference collections; 3) building up of reference tools; 4) maintaining factographic files; 5) conducting research on the scientific and technical information within the branch; 6) exchanging of experience and training of information specialists; 7) organizing symposia, seminars, and workshops on the problems of scientific and technical information; 8) popularizing scientific and technical achievements; 9) participating in international information systems, including AGRIS, AGROINFORM, and PISCHEPROMINFORM; 10) instructing the users of scientific and technical information; and 11) recording results from scientific and technical information.

Scope and/or Subject Matter: Scientific and information activities concerning agriculture (animal husbandry, veterinary medicine, general agronomy) and the food industry.

Input Sources: Annual input consists of 8363 periodicals, including foreign and national journals; reports; about 1700 unpublished documents (dissertations, completed scientific development reports of experts on missions abroad, FAO materials, and similar materials); and about 4000 translations.

Holdings and Storage Media: Library collection includes 400,000 volumes of books, periodicals (about 4100 titles obtained through subscriptions and book exchange), translations, microfilm, photocopies, and miscellaneous material.

Publications: 1) News in the Agricultural Practice (monthly)—8 thematic series. 2) Abstracts of Bulgarian Scientific Literature: Series A. Plant Breeding (quarterly). 3) Abstracts of Bulgarian Scientific Literature: Series B. Animal Breeding and Veterinary Medicine (quarterly). Also published are critical reviews, directories, journal articles, translated materials, methodical and normative materials, and other periodicals of a scientific or practical nature.

Microform Products and Services: The Center offers microreproduction of various documents.

Computer-Based Products and Services: The CENTER FOR SCIENTIFIC, TECHNICAL AND ECONOMIC INFORMATION provides information retrieval and SDI services from commercially available data bases, including AGRIS, BIOSIS, INIS, COMPENDEX, and others; the data bases are accesed via the computer facilities of the Central Institute for Scientific and Technical Information (CISTI). Magnetic tape services are also available.

Other Services: The Center also provides reproduction and translation services; selective abstracting; international and interlibrary loans; and bibliographical reference printing services.

Clientele/Availability: Services are available to all Bulgarian government establishments but not to individuals outside the government.

Contact: Prof. N. Apostolov, Director, or Dr. M. Kolarova, Senior Research Associate, Center for Scientific, Technical and Economic Information.

★122★
BUREAU MARCEL VAN DIJK, SA (BMVD)
Ave. Louise 409   Phone: 02 6486697
Box 1   Founded: 1959
B-1050 Brussels, Belgium
Marcel van Dijk, President

Staff: 1 Information and library professional; 5 management professional; 3 other.

Description of System or Service: BUREAU MARCEL VAN DIJK, SA (BMvD) is a management consulting firm specializing in the design, implementation, marketing, and evaluation of information services for businesses, libraries, and other organizations. The Bureau's Aide-Service organizes clients' documents through indexing, abstracting, and storage in manual or computer-based systems. Its Questions-Service provides online information retrieval as well as manual reference services for the compilation of bibliographies and state of the art reports, and answers to queries. The Bureau also evaluates, creates, and installs automated library systems and computerized information systems for business management.

Scope and/or Subject Matter: Information brokerage and consultation in the areas of science and technology, business, economics, law, medicine, marketing, and others.

Computer-Based Products and Services: The Bureau maintains access to several public online information systems to provide clients with retrospective searches and SDI.

Clientele/Availability: Services are available on a fee basis.

Contact: Georges van Slype, Brussels Director, Bureau Marcel van Dijk, SA. The firm also maintains a French office at 106 bis, rue de Rennes, F-75006 Paris; telephone 5445300.

★123★
BUSINESS INFORMATION INTERNATIONAL
34, Kompagnistr.   Phone: 01 152348
DK-1208 Copenhagen, Denmark   Founded: 1979
Alex Gorski, Managing Director

Staff: 2 Information and library professional; 1 management professional.

Description of System or Service: BUSINESS INFORMATION INTERNATIONAL provides a range of information consultancy and brokerage services for clients in Scandinavia. The company supplies information on demand in the areas of science, technology, and business either on a one-time project basis or as a current awareness service. Business information can be provided on any aspect of strategic planning, market development, product planning, and management methods. BUSINESS INFORMATION INTERNATIONAL also offers computerized searching of publicly available data bases, the SCANINFO document delivery service, and consultancy in the design and implementation of in-house information systems and services.

Scope and/or Subject Matter: Business, technology, science, information storage and retrieval systems.

Input Sources: Information is obtained from online data bases, libraries, and professionals in many fields.

Holdings and Storage Media: The firm maintains a reference collection and a computer-readable data base covering internal documentation and external information sources.

Computer-Based Products and Services: Computerized searching is conducted from data bases made available through DIALOG Information Services, Inc., System Development Corporation (SDC), ESA/IRS, General Electric's MARK III system, Control Data Corporation's CYBERNET facility, I.P. Sharp Associates, Euronet DIANE hosts, and other vendors. Advice is supplied to clients on computer hardware and software systems for information storage and retrieval. The firm also operates the Scandinavian Information Retrieval Service (SCANINFO), which fills document delivery requests. SCANINFO supplies copies or photocopies of all articles, proceedings, reprints, patents, reports, books, standards, or other printed material published in Scandinavia.

Clientele/Availability: Services are available without restrictions.

Remarks: Business Information International acts as the Scandinavian representative or liaison office for a number of companies in the information business.

Contact: Alex Gorski, Managing Director, Business Information International. (Telex 15492 BUINFO DK.)

C

★124★
CALGARY PUBLIC INFORMATION DEPARTMENT
PUBLIC RELATIONS DIVISION
CIVICHANNEL
P.O. Box 2100, Station M Phone: (403) 268-4774
Calgary, AB, Canada T2P 2M5 Service Est: 1982
Rick Lyons, Division Manager

Staff: 3 Information and library professional; 1 management professional.

Description of System or Service: CIVICHANNEL, the City of Calgary Information Service, is a videotex-based municipal information broadcast channel available to local cable television subscribers via Cablesystems Alberta Ltd. and Calgary Cable TV/FM Ltd. CIVICHANNEL uses microcomputer-controlled Telidon equipment as a passive presentation medium to display civic information in pages with full color computer graphics and text. Pages are displayed continuously in a sequence which repeats approximately every 45 minutes. Information on the system is classified by departmental categories, each identified by title or with a separate title graphic. CIVICHANNEL also televises live coverage of Calgary City Council and Board of Education meetings. In addition to operating the Calgary channel, CIVICHANNEL consults with other municipalities on similar types of information programming for the public.

Scope and/or Subject Matter: Calgary civic information, such as engineering services, tax programs, recreation, transit services, crime prevention, fire prevention, water conservation, road closures, social services, and recreational and cultural activities.

Input Sources: Information is supplied by representatives of civic departments using a standard form designed to fit presentation format.

Holdings and Storage Media: Civichannel holds information in computer-readable form for broadcasting.

Computer-Based Products and Services: CIVICHANNEL is a Telidon-based system used to make Calgary civic information accessible to area cable television subscribers. The system is composed of four functional components: 1) The Information Provider System (IPS) allows the operator to quickly create Telidon information pages by using a selection menu or actually drawing using the digitizer tablet. 2) The Central System manages the library of pages, allows local updating of the text content, and controls the actual display of pages over the cable network. 3) The local decoder unit drives a television monitor used during editing and updating, which are done as needed. 4) The remote decoder unit provides a direct drive video signal needed by the cable company to transmit the signals to the home televisions.

Clientele/Availability: Services are available to all Calgary cable subscribers with a mid-band channel converter.

Contact: Bill Pringle, Senior Communications Coordinator, Calgary Public Information Department.

★125★
CAMBRIDGE UNIVERSITY
UNIVERSITY CHEMICAL LABORATORY
CAMBRIDGE CRYSTALLOGRAPHIC DATA CENTRE (CCDC)
Lensfield Rd. Phone: 0223 66499
Cambridge CB2 1EW, England Service Est: 1965
Dr. Olga Kennard, Head

Staff: 10 Scientific professional; 4 clerical and nonprofessional.

Related Organizations: The Centre receives financial support from the British Department of Education and Science, the Science and Engineering Research Council, and various foreign government agencies.

Description of System or Service: The CAMBRIDGE CRYSTALLOGRAPHIC DATA CENTRE (CCDC) is concerned with collecting, evaluating, synthesizing, and disseminating crystal and molecular structure data obtained by diffraction methods in a form readily usable by academic and industrial scientists. It maintains the computer-readable Cambridge Structural Database (CSD), which comprises three separate files of bibliographic, chemical connectivity, and numeric data for X-ray and neutron diffraction studies of organo-carbon compounds (organics, organometallics, and metal complexes). For each entry in the Database, the following data are typically provided: chemical name, synonym, formula, full bibliography, chemical classification, connections table, crystal data, atomic coordinates, and selected physicochemical and experimental data. The CENTRE distributes the Database to more than 20 national affiliated centers to serve the worldwide academic community. Computer tapes and associated retrieval, analysis, and display software are also available by lease to other interested organizations, and the Database is commercially available online. Additionally, annual bibliographic volumes are published from the Database.

Scope and/or Subject Matter: Crystal structures of organic and organometallic compounds analyzed by X-ray or neutron diffraction methods (proteins and high polymers are not included).

Input Sources: The staff scans primary journals, prepares data abstracts, and computerizes bibliographic, connectivity, and numeric information. A substantial amount of numeric data is deposited directly by journal editors and individual scientists.

Holdings and Storage Media: The CENTRE maintains computer-readable bibliographic, connectivity, and numeric data files, retrospective to 1935, with approximately 50,000 entries in each file. The files are updated on a batch basis, with about 700 new entries added every six weeks. Also held are reprints for all entries since 1960. In addition, the Centre maintains the non-U.S.A. copy of the Protein Data Bank Files, which are processed at Brookhaven National Laboratory in Upton, New York.

Publications: 1) Molecular Structures and Dimensions-MSD (annual)—produced from the CSD Database. Each issue contains chemical and bibliographic information arranged within 86 chemical classes, plus six indexes: keyword, compound name, molecular formula, permuted formula, author, and chemical diagram. Available by subscription from: D. Reidel Publishing Company, Spuiboulevard 50, NL-3311 GR Amsterdam, Netherlands. 2) Interatomic Distances 1960-1965—produced from the CSD Database.

Computer-Based Products and Services: The CRYSTALLOGRAPHIC DATA CENTRE maintains the Cambridge Structural Database, comprising the following files: BIB, which contains the literature citation of the diffraction study along with some textual chemical information; CONN, which provides a connectivity representation of the chemical structure; and DATA, which provides the numeric results. Also known as CRYST, the Database is available for online searching through NIH-EPA Chemical Information System (CIS) and other online services. The CENTRE's Database and search software are available on lease to national and regional centers, and to other interested organizations and individuals.

Other Services: The Centre also does research in chemical substructure searching, graphics, and data base management and utilization.

Clientele/Availability: Clients include chemists, physicists, crystallographers, material scientists, molecular biologists, pharmacologists, and other scientists concerned with molecular and crystal structures.

Contact: Dr. S. Bellard, Cambridge Crystallographic Data Centre. (Telex 81204 CAMSPL G.) For information on the national center in the United States, contact Dr. W. Duax, Medical Foundation of Buffalo, Inc. Research Laboratories, 73 High St., Buffalo, NY 14203-1196.

★126★
CANADA
AGRICULTURE CANADA
MARKETING AND ECONOMICS BRANCH
AGRICULTURAL MARKETING AND TRADE (M & T) DATABASE
Sir John Carling Bldg. Phone: (613) 995-9554
Ottawa, ON, Canada K1A 0C5 Service Est: 1975
A.H. Wilmot, Manager

Staff: Approximately 2 total.

Description of System or Service: The AGRICULTURAL

MARKETING AND TRADE (M & T) DATABASE is an archived file of nearly 4000 time series relating to the production, marketing, and external trade of the principal agricultural commodities of Canada. The entire DATABASE is stored on the facilities of Datacrown Inc. for use by Agriculture Canada and other Canadian agencies. Additionally, approximately 1500 time series from the DATABASE are maintained by Agriculture Canada in a separate, updated file called the Outlook Database. This file is used for the publication of statistical tables.

Scope and/or Subject Matter: Time series applying to the production, marketing, external trade, and prices of the principal Canadian farm products. Selected data from the United States are also included.

Input Sources: Sources of information include Statistics Canada, Agriculture Canada, and the U.S. Department of Agriculture.

Holdings and Storage Media: The machine-readable M & T Database contains 2297 annual time series, 1352 monthly series, and 157 other series. The series date mainly from 1960 to 1979; the only series that are updated are those in the Outlook Database.

Publications: The Outlook Database is used to produce statistical tables in the December issue of the quarterly Market Commentary magazine published by Agriculture Canada.

Computer-Based Products and Services: The complete M & T DATABASE is accessible online through Datacrown Inc., a time-sharing company in Toronto.

Clientele/Availability: The staff of Agriculture Canada and other Canadian government departments are principal users of the file, but it can be made available to others via Datacrown through agreement with Agriculture Canada.

Contact: A.H. Wilmot, Manager, Agricultural Marketing and Trade Database.

★127★
CANADA
AGRICULTURE CANADA
MARKETING AND ECONOMICS BRANCH
COOPERATIVES UNIT
COINS
Ecole des Hautes Etudes Phone: (not reported)
  Commerciales, 5525, ave. Decelles Service Est: 1976
Montreal, PQ, Canada H3T 1U6
Michelle Champagne, Librarian

Staff: Approximately 3 total.

Related Organizations: COINS is a joint project of the Cooperatives Unit and the Ecole des Hautes Etudes Commerciales.

Description of System or Service: COINS is a computer-based information retrieval system containing references to current literature dealing with all kinds of cooperatives in Canada, as well as references to literature written by Canadians about cooperatives anywhere. COINS references are compiled by Agriculture Canada and incorporated as a subfile in the U.S. Department of Agriculture's AGRICOLA data base which is accessible through several commercial online services. Additionally, the Cooperatives Unit of Agriculture Canada will conduct searches of the file for clients who do not have access to search facilities.

Scope and/or Subject Matter: Cooperative literature by Canadians or about Canadian cooperatives.

Input Sources: Input is derived from articles, books, theses, research papers, studies, guidebooks, educational materials, and conference papers.

Holdings and Storage Media: The machine-readable COINS data base holds citations and abstracts of literature dating from 1970 to the present. All literature cited is held by the Library of Agriculture Canada and, from 1983, by the Ecole des Hautes Etudes Commerciales.

Publications: COINS Bulletin (bimonthly).

Computer-Based Products and Services: COINS may be searched as the AGC subfile of the AGRICOLA data base, which is widely available online. Searches generate listings of bibliographical references, which include a brief abstract in the language of the original document. In addition, French references include English summaries, keywords, and a translated title. The Cooperatives Unit will search COINS for those without access to local search facilities.

Clientele/Availability: COINS is available without restrictions.

Contact: Michelle Champagne, Librarian, Ecole des Hautes Etudes Commerciales.

★128★
CANADA
AGRICULTURE CANADA
SCIENTIFIC INFORMATION RETRIEVAL SECTION
PESTICIDE RESEARCH INFORMATION SYSTEM (PRIS)
Central Experimental Farm Phone: (613) 995-9073
K.W. Neatby Bldg., Room 1133 Service Est: 1981
Ottawa, ON, Canada K1A 0C6
Jacques Taky, Head

Staff: 1.5 Management professional; 1 technician; 1 clerical and nonprofessional.

Description of System or Service: The computerized PESTICIDE RESEARCH INFORMATION SYSTEM (PRIS) provides information on pest management products and organisms from the time they are introduced into Canada as experimental to the time they are registered. The SYSTEM is accessible online through Agriculture Canada.

Scope and/or Subject Matter: Pesticide research and management.

Input Sources: Data are submitted by research scientists, chemical companies, and government agencies.

Holdings and Storage Media: PRIS information is held in machine-readable form; portions of the file are bibliographic.

Computer-Based Products and Services: The PESTICIDE RESEARCH INFORMATION SYSTEM contains data on pest management products and organisms and is accessible online through Agriculture Canada. Specific information provided by the SYSTEM includes a pest management research inventory, pesticide research data, experimental pesticides information, a glossary of pesticides, and maximum residue limits data. Information retrieval and report production services are available.

Clientele/Availability: Services are available without restrictions.

Projected Publications and Services: A Pesticide Use Index is expected to be published.

Contact: Jacques Taky, Head, Scientific Information Retrieval Section, Agriculture Canada.

★129★
CANADA
CONSUMER AND CORPORATE AFFAIRS CANADA
CORPORATIONS BRANCH
CORPORATE INTEGRATED INFORMATION SYSTEM (CIIS)
Place du Portage, Phase II, 4th Fl. Phone: (819) 997-1071
50 Victoria St. Service Est: 1982
Hull, PQ, Canada K1A 0C9
Henri Denolf, Deputy Director

Staff: 3 Management professional; 34 clerical and nonprofessional.

Description of System or Service: The CORPORATE INTEGRATED INFORMATION SYSTEM (CIIS) is a computerized information system covering Canadian corporation names, addresses, directors, financial statement data, and related information. It is used by the Corporations Branch for the issuance of certificates of incorporation and corporate alteration, and for the administration of programs dealing with compliance enforcement. Information from the CIIS data base is also made available on computer tapes and COM microfiche; ad-hoc retrieval services are similarly available. Additionally, CIIS data are included in publicly available online data bases.

Scope and/or Subject Matter: Canadian corporations, including past and present corporate names, registered office and mailing addresses, names and addresses of corporate directors, status codes (active or defunct), and financial statement data (if applicable).

Input Sources: Data are keyed into the System from forms filed by corporations.

Holdings and Storage Media: Machine-readable holdings include the Corporate Integrated Information System File, the Index Sequential Control File, and the Name/ Status Index Sequential File.

Publications: Canada Corporations Bulletin (monthly)—available by subscription.

Microform Products and Services: Output from the CIIS data base is produced monthly on COM microfiche which is available by subscription.

Computer-Based Products and Services: The CORPORATE INTEGRATED INFORMATION SYSTEM is used for internal record keeping and administrative purposes and to provide computer tape and retrieval services. Currently operated in a batch mode, it is expected to be converted to an online system in due course. CIIS data are included in two commercially available online data bases produced by Canada Systems Group: the Corporate Names Data Base and the Canadian Federal Corporations and Directors Data Base (see separate entries).

Other Services: Additionally, the Branch offers a telephone inquiry service for corporate searches and provides copies and certified copies services. It also maintains an incorporation and corporate alteration service.

Clientele/Availability: Services are available to the general public.

Contact: Elaine Collins, Chief, EDP Services, Corporations Branch, Consumer and Corporate Affairs Canada; telephone (819) 994-4652.

★130★
CANADA
DEPARTMENT OF COMMUNICATIONS
TELIDON PROGRAM
365 Laurier Ave. W.   Phone: (613) 995-4743
Journal Tower S., Room 1706   Service Est: 1978
Ottawa, ON, Canada K1A 0C8
Roy Marsh, Director

Staff: 2 Information and library professional; 10 management professional; 1 technician; 10 clerical and nonprofessional.

Description of System or Service: The TELIDON PROGRAM maintains and develops a videotex/ teletext system that incorporates computer graphics and telecommunications technologies. Capable of operating over telephone lines, cable TV, optical fibers, broadcast, satellite, microwave, and packet-switching networks, the basic TELIDON system consists of a keypad, TV display unit, decoder and display generator, telecommunications link, and central and third-party computers containing data bases. Subscribers use the keypad to choose pages of information which are decoded and displayed on television receivers. First introduced in 1978, TELIDON is now being used to provide information and communication services by a variety of governmental and commercial organizations in Canada, the United States, and other countries.

Scope and/or Subject Matter: Videotex information and communications services.

Computer-Based Products and Services: TELIDON equipment and software are applicable to videotex (cable or wire distribution of information), teletext (broadcast distribution of information), and audiovisual systems. The system can be used to provide information retrieval services, telesoftware transmission, terminal-to-terminal communications, audiovisual programs, and other communication and data processing applications.

Clientele/Availability: Telidon is available to governmental and commercial organizations.

Contact: Roy Marsh, Director, Telidon Program; or the local Canadian embassy or consulate.

★131★
CANADA
DEPARTMENT OF ENERGY, MINES AND RESOURCES
CANADA CENTRE FOR MINERAL AND ENERGY TECHNOLOGY
 (CANMET)
TECHNOLOGY INFORMATION DIVISION (TID)
555 Booth St.   Phone: (613) 995-4029
Ottawa, ON, Canada K1A 0G1   Service Est: 1967
Dr. James E. Kanasy, Director

Staff: 10 Information and library professional; 3 management professional; 7 technicians; 12 clerical and nonprofessional; 7 other.

Description of System or Service: The TECHNOLOGY INFORMATION DIVISION (TID) provides technical information, documentation, and advisory services to government agencies, industry, and researchers in the fields of mining, mineral processing, metallurgy, and nonrenewable energy technology. It maintains several computer-readable data bases and a library in its areas of expertise; issues abstracting and indexing publications; prepares state-of-the-art reviews and bibliographies; and cooperates with national and international organizations involved in the provision of scientific and technical information.

Scope and/or Subject Matter: Mining, mineral processing, extractive and physical metallurgy, heavy oils, oil sands, natural gas, coal and peat technology, and health and safety of miners. Emphasis is on Canadian contributions or on application to Canadian climatic, environmental, and geological conditions.

Input Sources: The Division acquires information from journals, research reports, patent literature, monographs, theses, and government documents.

Holdings and Storage Media: The Division's computer-readable holdings include more than 60,000 citations and abstracts of reports, theses, monographs, and journal articles; these are indexed using standardized keywords based on in-house thesauri. The library collection consists of 165,000 bound volumes; subscriptions to 3000 periodicals; and 30,000 microfiche sets.

Publications: 1) MINTEC: Mining Technology Abstracts (biweekly)—provides abstracts and indexes of international English-language periodical articles, books, and other published materials; includes an author index. 2) Eastern European Mineral Technolgy - Current Contents (bimonthly). 3) Canadian Contributions to Rock Mechanics (annual). 4) CANMET Review (annual). Reports and other publications are also issued; a catalog is available from CANMET on request.

Computer-Based Products and Services: The TECHNOLOGY INFORMATION DIVISION compiles and maintains the following two major data bases: 1) Mining Technology Abstracts (MINTEC)—contains 26,000 abstracts of articles, books, reports, and papers on mining technology and related topics from 1967 to the present. 2) Mineral Processing Technology (MINPROC)—contains 8000 citations to articles on processing technology covering the period 1977 to the present. Both data bases are publicly accessible online through QL Systems Limited and are used by the DIVISION in conjunction with commercially produced data bases to provide information retrieval and SDI services. The DIVISION also maintains a copy of the International Energy Agency (IEA) Coal Data Base, which holds 37,000 records on coal mining, and makes it available online through CAN/OLE.

Clientele/Availability: Services are intended primarily for researchers and decision makers in the public and private sectors in Canada, but are available without restrictions to all domestic and foreign users.

Contact: Dr. James E. Kanasy, Director, Technology Information Division.

★132★
CANADA
DEPARTMENT OF ENERGY, MINES AND RESOURCES
CANADA CENTRE FOR REMOTE SENSING
REMOTE SENSING ON-LINE RETRIEVAL SYSTEM (RESORS)
240 Bank St., 5th Floor Phone: (613) 995-5645
Ottawa, ON, Canada K1A 0Y7 Service Est: 1971
Jacques Guerette, Manager

Staff: 4 Information and library professional; 1 technician.

Description of System or Service: The REMOTE SENSING ON-LINE RETRIEVAL SYSTEM (RESORS) is an online information service providing free and rapid access to bibliographic references relating to the techniques, instrumentation, and applications of remote sensing, photogrammetry, and image analysis. Covering documents published in English or French, the data base records title, author, publication, publisher, publication date, author affiliation, and up to twenty keywords assigned from a keyword dictionary of 1800 terms. In addition to the documents data base, RESORS also maintains a searchable index to its 35mm slide collection.

Scope and/or Subject Matter: Observation from a distance of the atmosphere or earth surface environments; processing and analysis of remote sensing data.

Input Sources: Input consists of published and unpublished reports, journal articles, symposia proceedings, conference papers, technical reports, government publications, and references from secondary sources.

Holdings and Storage Media: Machine-readable RESORS files hold more than 43,000 citations; about 400 items are added per month. A collection of over 5300 35mm slides is also maintained.

Publications: The RESORS keyword dictionary is available on request.

Computer-Based Products and Services: The RESORS bibliographic data base on remote sensing is accessible online via direct dial or DATAPAC. RESORS staff will also conduct searches of the data base on request. Keywords in the data base are assigned values which reflect their specific importance within the document, permitting references to be correlated against the user's search description.

Clientele/Availability: Online access is available primarily in Canada, but other requests will be considered. RESORS staff will conduct searches for clients worldwide.

Contact: Jacques Guerette, RESORS Manager. (Telex 053377.)

★133★
CANADA
DEPARTMENT OF ENERGY, MINES AND RESOURCES
CONSERVATION AND RENEWABLE ENERGY BRANCH
CANADIAN ENERGY INFORMATION SYSTEM
580 Booth St. Phone: (613) 995-9447
Ottawa, ON, Canada K1A 0E4 Service Est: 1979
C.S.L. McNeil, Coordinator

Description of System or Service: The CANADIAN ENERGY INFORMATION SYSTEM comprises two machine-readable data bases covering various aspects of energy in Canada. The Energy Projects Data Base is an inventory of significant research, development, and demonstration projects in Canada; it includes such information as project name, location, contact person, present status, management and funding information, and keywords. The Energy Programs Data Base contains descriptions of Canadian federal and provincial government energy programs and energy-related data bases. Access to CANADIAN ENERGY INFORMATION SYSTEM data bases is available through commercial time-sharing.

Scope and/or Subject Matter: Canadian energy research, programs, and related information.

Input Sources: Information for the data bases is acquired from various Canadian federal, provincial, and private sources.

Holdings and Storage Media: The computer-readable Energy Projects Data Base contains approximately 1000 records. The energy programs file contains approximately 100 records. Both data bases are updated irregularly.

Computer-Based Products and Services: Both Canadian Energy Information System files are searchable online through QL Systems Limited.

Clientele/Availability: Services are intended for universities, provincial and federal government agencies, private industry, consultants, and others.

Contact: C.S.L. McNeil, Demonstration Coordinator, Canadian Energy Information System.

★134★
CANADA
DEPARTMENT OF ENERGY, MINES AND RESOURCES
GEOLOGICAL SURVEY OF CANADA
ECONOMIC GEOLOGY DIVISION
CANADIAN MINERAL OCCURRENCE INDEX (CANMINDEX)
601 Booth St. Phone: (not reported)
Ottawa, ON, Canada K1A 0E8
D.F. Garson, Head

Staff: 4 Geologists; 1 clerical and nonprofessional.

Description of System or Service: The CANADIAN MINERAL OCCURRENCE INDEX (CANMINDEX) is a computer-readable file containing information relating to the spatial distribution of all mineral occurrences in Canada, as well as a selected bibliography for each occurrence. Used to produce index plots and listings, the file contains the following specific data elements: name or alternate name of occurrence as well as a unique file identification number; owner or operator name; geographic location of occurrence giving latitude and longitude and cultural information; up to 10 mineral commodities and their associated status for each occurrence; up to 7 bibliographic and 2 map references for each occurrence; and general remarks on special aspects of the occurrence.

Scope and/or Subject Matter: Index-level geological data for Canadian mineral occurrences.

Input Sources: Input is derived from National Mineral Inventory Cards, geologic literature, internal commodity files, and cooperating provincial government agencies.

Publications: Canadian Mineral Occurrence Index of the Geological Survey of Canada—GSC paper; available for purchase.

Computer-Based Products and Services: The CANMINDEX file is used to produce index plots and listings.

Clientele/Availability: CANMINDEX serves geologists within the federal and provincial governments of Canada.

Contact: D.F. Garson, Head, Mineral Resource Information Services, Geological Survey of Canada.

★135★
CANADA
DEPARTMENT OF ENERGY, MINES AND RESOURCES
GEOLOGICAL SURVEY OF CANADA
NATIONAL GEOSCAN CENTRE
601 Booth St., Room 180 Phone: (613) 992-9550
Ottawa, ON, Canada K1A 0E8 Service Est: 1970
David S. Reade, Head

Staff: 4 Total.

Description of System or Service: The NATIONAL GEOSCAN CENTRE coordinates production of the computer-readable GEOSCAN Database which provides bibliographic control of Canadian-produced and Canadian-related geoscience information, particularly unpublished government reports. An outgrowth of the Canadian Index to Geoscience Data, GEOSCAN is maintained in cooperation with a network of federal and provincial agencies that provide input. These agencies also conduct searches of the Database to produce hardcopy or COM output.

Scope and/or Subject Matter: Solid-earth geosciences, with emphasis on geology and nonrenewable energy and mineral resources.

Input Sources: Four federal and eight provincial geoscience agencies contribute bibliographic information for published and unpublished reports, journal articles, theses, and other items; priority has been given to providing coverage to unpublished government documents.

Holdings and Storage Media: The computer-readable GEOSCAN Database contains bibliographic data and keywords for more than 100,000 documents from 1845 to the present. Approximately 1000 records are added each year.

Microform Products and Services: COM output from GEOSCAN is available.

Computer-Based Products and Services: Contributing agencies use the GEOSCAN Database to produce custom hardcopy and COM indexes, catalogs, thesauri, and other GEOSCAN listings. Online searches are performed for the public on a cost-recovery basis by search intermediaries at the Library of the Geological Survey of Canada. GEOSCAN is searchable for author, title, source, general classification, document type, and keywords. The National Topographic System (NTS) is used for geographic control.

Clientele/Availability: Services are available from contributing agencies and the Library of the Geological Survey of Canada.

Remarks: The National GEOSCAN Centre was formerly known as the Canada Centre for Geoscience Data (CCGD).

Contact: David S. Reade, Head, National GEOSCAN Centre.

★136★
CANADA
DEPARTMENT OF ENERGY, MINES AND RESOURCES
TOPOGRAPHICAL SURVEY DIVISION
DIGITAL MAPPING SYSTEM
615 Booth St. Phone: (613) 995-4637
Ottawa, ON, Canada K1A 0E9
M.E.H. Young, Chief, Systems Group

Staff: Approximately 38 total.

Description of System or Service: The DIGITAL MAPPING SYSTEM is responsible for the collection, storage, retrieval, and plotting of cartographic data for the 1:50,000 Topographic Mapping Program of Canada, and for the establishment and maintenance of the National Topographic Data Base. It also provides services and support for the automation of other national mapping programs.

Scope and/or Subject Matter: Topographic mapping; geographic mapping and atlases; aeronautical charts; and other supporting activities.

Input Sources: Input consists of stereo compilation of basic data from the 1:50,000 Topographic Mapping Program, and digitizing of existing sources.

Computer-Based Products and Services: The SYSTEM offers computerized mapping services and maintains the National Topographic Data Base.

Clientele/Availability: The System primarily serves national mapping programs.

Contact: M.E.H. Young, Chief, Systems Engineering Group, Topographical Survey Division.

★137★
CANADA
DEPARTMENT OF INDUSTRY, TRADE & COMMERCE
OFFICE OF TOURISM
TOURISM RESEARCH AND DATA CENTRE (TRDC)
235 Queen St., 4th Floor, E. Phone: (613) 995-2754
Ottawa, ON, Canada K1A 0H6
Rae Bradford, Head

Staff: 1 Management professional; 3 technicians; 1 clerical and nonprofessional.

Description of System or Service: Serving as the central coordinating point in Canada for tourism documentation and data, the TOURISM RESEARCH AND DATA CENTRE (TRDC) provides information to meet the needs of federal and provincial government agencies and the travel industry in general. Its services are based on a computer-readable bilingual data base containing bibliographic information relating to domestic and foreign sources of tourism documentation and data. TRDC provides online searches from this data base and also offers interlibrary loan, reference, lending, and photocopying services.

Scope and/or Subject Matter: Canadian, American, and international tourism, travel, recreation, and leisure.

Input Sources: Materials covered by the data base include research reports, surveys, legislation, journal articles, proceedings, proposals, and statistical reports.

Holdings and Storage Media: Machine-readable files hold 6000 citations to sources of tourism documentation and data. Library holdings comprise 5000 volumes; subscriptions to 200 periodicals; and 500 boxes of pamphlets.

Publications: 1) Recent Acquisitions Lists (quarterly); 2) Book Catalogue of Tourism Research Studies—bilingual.

Computer-Based Products and Services: Online searching is conducted from the TRDC data base on the following data elements, either singly or in various combinations: subject descriptor or keyword, author, sponsor, date, document type, geographic area, and international organization.

Clientele/Availability: Services are available to anyone.

Contact: Rae Bradford, Head, Tourism Research and Data Centre.

★138★
CANADA
ENVIRONMENT CANADA
CANADIAN INVENTORY OF HISTORIC BUILDING (CIHB)
Les Terrasses de la Chaudiere Phone: (819) 994-2866
Ottawa, ON, Canada K1A 1G2 Service Est: 1970
C. Cameron, Chief

Staff: 4 Management professional; 10 professional architects and historians; 15 clerical and nonprofessional.

Description of System or Service: Believed to be the first comprehensive architectural inventory in the world supported by a computerized information system, the CANADIAN INVENTORY OF HISTORIC BUILDING (CIHB) maintains a data bank containing geocodes and machine-readable records for nearly 200,000 buildings selected in a nationwide survey of early Canadian architecture. The data bank is designed to provide rapid retrieval of information in order to allow the Historic Sites and Monuments Board of Canada to judge the architectural and historical significance of buildings, and to compare buildings of similar style and architectural value. In addition to providing data on buildings, the CIHB data bank can be used by urban geographers, sociologists, and economists to extract information on settlement patterns, ethnic influences, and growth change in Canada.

Scope and/or Subject Matter: CIHB covers over 200 years of Canadian buildings, from the late 1600's to the early 1900's; it includes such details as architectural styles, structural components, and interior trim, plus selected historical aspects of the buildings such as uses, construction dates, and architects and builders.

Input Sources: Data are collected through nationwide surveys conducted by departmental employees and trained volunteers.

Holdings and Storage Media: CIHB computer files contain more than 7 million items of information pertaining to 190,000 buildings; also held are at least 5 photographs of each building.

Publications: 1) The Buildings of Canada. 2) The Evaluation of Historic Buildings. 3) Researching Heritage Buildings. 4) Exterior Recording Training Manual. All booklets are available free of charge from CIHB.

Computer-Based Products and Services: The CIHB data bank is searchable on 80 individual data elements or combinations of them. Batch-mode searching is offered; printouts from the CIHB data bank are available on paper or microfiche.

Clientele/Availability: Services are available without restrictions.

Contact: C. Cameron, Chief, Canadian Inventory of Historic Building.

★139★
CANADA
ENVIRONMENT CANADA
INLAND WATERS DIRECTORATE
NATIONAL HYDROLOGY RESEARCH INSTITUTE
PERENNIAL SNOW AND ICE SECTION
GLACIER INVENTORY OF CANADA

Ottawa, ON, Canada K1A 0E7
C. Simon L. Ommanney, Head
Phone: (819) 997-2385
Service Est: 1968

Staff: 1 Information and library professional; 2 technicians.

Related Organizations: The Glacier Inventory of Canada is part of the Global Environmental Monitoring System (GEMS) and cooperates with the World Glacier Inventory.

Description of System or Service: The GLACIER INVENTORY OF CANADA collects and disseminates data on perennial ice and snow masses on land surfaces in Canada in order to assist in the assessment of overall water resources in that country. It maintains a machine-readable file covering the physical characteristics of glaciers as well as an archive of photographs and other materials. Also held is the machine-readable ICEREF file, which provides access to published references to work done on Canadian glaciers and is used to produce a hardcopy bibliography. The INVENTORY and its related information systems are used to support research studies and to issue data reports and analyses and other publications.

Scope and/or Subject Matter: All glaciers in Canada.

Input Sources: Maps, aerial photographs, and historical records and photographs are coded and classified for the Inventory. Quantitative data are extracted from work maps using a digitizer interfaced with a minicomputer. Scientific journals are scanned for input to ICEREF.

Holdings and Storage Media: Data sheets have been compiled for about 50,000 glaciers; complete machine-readable data are available for 15,000 of these. An archive of photographs, maps, and reports is also held. The ICEREF file covers more than 3000 references.

Publications: Glacier Inventory Notes (irregular)—series includes the Bibliography of Canadian Glaciology. Report series, atlases, and other bibliographies are also issued.

Computer-Based Products and Services: The computer-readable GLACIER INVENTORY OF CANADA file is used to provide data retrieval services on an individual request basis. Programs are available for special analysis and processing of the data. The computer-readable ICEREF file may be searched by keywords relevant to glacier information; weighted factors permit the selection of articles with maps, photographs, data, or other specified elements.

Other Services: Additional services include referrals to other snow and ice specialists if the request cannot be handled by Inventory staff.

Clientele/Availability: Services are provided to international agencies involved in glacier programs, provincial and federal government mapping agencies, other government departments, and university researchers.

Contact: C. Simon L. Ommanney, Head, Perennial Snow and Ice Section. (Telex 053 3799.)

★140★
CANADA
ENVIRONMENT CANADA
INLAND WATERS DIRECTORATE
WATDOC

Ottawa, ON, Canada K1A 0E7
Evangeline Campbell, Manager
Phone: (819) 997-1238
Service Est: 1971

Staff: 3 Information and library professional; 1 technician; 4 clerical and nonprofessional.

Description of System or Service: WATDOC is Canada's major water resources information service, producing bibliographic and referral data bases on water resources and other environmental topics relating to Canada. Report literature, journal articles, and conference papers are abstracted and indexed for the bibliographic data bases, while the referral files cover relevant data collections and systems. All of WATDOC'S data bases are available for online searching through QL Systems Limited. In addition to producing its own data bases, WATDOC acquires other relevant data bases that are not generally accessible elsewhere and makes them available on QL Systems.

Scope and/or Subject Matter: Comprehensive coverage of scientific, technical, and planning aspects of management, regulation, and control pertaining to the Canadian environment. Major fields covered include: water (every aspect), wildlife, lands, fisheries, and baseline studies.

Input Sources: WATDOC monitors more than 300 Canadian and non-Canadian journals for its bibliographic data bases. It also references conference proceedings; reports and publications of Environment Canada, other Canadian governmental agencies, universities, and research institutes; unpublished material; and data collections and data systems.

Holdings and Storage Media: More than 70,000 references are contained in WATDOC-produced data bases.

Publications: 1) WATDOC Newsletter (irregular)—news and notices for the user community. 2) Database Descriptions—includes coverage, sources, descriptions, searchable elements, and examples. 3) WATDOC Brochure. All are available free of charge from WATDOC on request.

Computer-Based Products and Services: WATDOC produces four data bases: 1) Canadian Environment (CENV)—bibliographic data base dating from 1970 to the present and holding nearly 60,000 references. 2) Environnement (ENV)—bibliographic data base dating from 1978 to the present and holding approximately 11,000 references to French-language environmental literature. 3) Data Reference (DREF)—referral data base referencing Canadian environmental data collections and systems from the early 1900s to date. All references contain a citation or statement of availability, keywords, and an abstract or description of the data collection or system. 4) Canadian Hydrological Operational Multipurpose Subprogramme (CHOMS)—data base comprising nearly 300 extensive descriptions of Canadian operational and developing hydrological technology covering the period from 1980 to date; developed as a joint effort between the HOMS National Reference Centre for Canada and the World Meteorological Organization (WMO) under WATDOC sponsorship. WATDOC also supports the North American availability of the Delft Hydro (DEL) data base, produced by Delft Hydraulics Laboratory, and the Solid Waste Management (SOL) data base which consists of references to solid waste management projects undertaken in Canada since 1970, and is produced by the Environment Canada's Environmental Protection Service. All of the above data bases produced or made available by WATDOC are publicly accessible for online searching through QL Systems Limited.

Clientele/Availability: Services are intended for the Canadian water resources and environmental community.

Remarks: WATDOC was formerly known as the Water Resources Document Reference Centre.

Contact: Evangeline Campbell, Manager, WATDOC; telephone (819) 997-2324.

★141★
CANADA
ENVIRONMENT CANADA
INLAND WATERS DIRECTORATE
WATER QUALITY BRANCH
NATIONAL WATER QUALITY DATA BANK (NAQUADAT)

Place Vincent Massey
Ottawa, ON, Canada K1A 0E7
S. Whitlow, Head
Phone: (819) 997-3422
Service Est: 1969

Staff: 2 Information and library professional; 1 management professional; 2 clerical and nonprofessional.

Description of System or Service: The NATIONAL WATER QUALITY DATA BANK (NAQUADAT) is a computerized information storage and retrieval system which contains results of water quality surveys conducted across Canada. Based on field and laboratory analyses from 8500 sampling locations, NAQUADAT contains chemical, physical, bacteriological, and hydrometric data for rivers, lakes, groundwater, precipitation, and wastewater. The DATA BANK stores this information in three hierarchical levels: 1) station (sampling point)—provides station reference number, sampling location (including the province and river basin from which the sample was taken as well as the geographic coordinates), and descriptive narrative; 2) sample—includes date of sample, project and agency name, and comments about samples; and 3) parameter—includes analytical method and analytical measurement or value. NAQUADAT is accessible online and is used to produce publications, prepare overview reports, and monitor for compliance with objectives.

Scope and/or Subject Matter: Analysis of surface and groundwater in Canada.

Input Sources: Input for NAQUADAT is obtained from water quality surveys conducted at 8500 sampling locations across Canada by regional Water Quality Branch operations and other agencies.

Holdings and Storage Media: NAQUADAT stores data from samples dating from 1960 to the present on computer tape and disk.

Publications: 1) NAQUADAT Dictionary of Parameter Codes (annual)—lists more than 1400 parameters measured, including major ions, trace metals, and organic contaminants. 2) NAQUADAT Guide to Interactive Retrieval—user guide providing search instructions. Other publications are also produced from NAQUADAT.

Computer-Based Products and Services: The NATIONAL WATER QUALITY DATA BANK is operated at the Computer Science Centre in Ottawa using the System 2000 data base management system and can be accessed via remote terminals located anywhere in Canada. The Water Quality Branch will conduct searches for clients without their own terminals. Special programs have been developed to enable major retrievals from NAQUADAT according to stipulated conditions. The resulting reports provide descriptive information for specified stations and parameters. Among the reports available are the NAQUADAT Detailed Report, which lists the different measurements stored for each sampling date; various statistical reports which present data in terms of maxima and minima, averages, and percentiles; and other reports providing inventory statistics or station information. NAQUADAT also provides the ability to produce graphical presentations and to generate files of data to be used with various statistical packages.

Clientele/Availability: Primary users of NAQUADAT are scientists with the Water Quality Branch. Other users include other federal agencies and departments, provincial agencies, universities, consultants, municipalities, and industries.

Contact: S. Whitlow, Head, Data Systems Section, Monitoring and Surveys Division, Water Quality Branch.

★142★
CANADA
ENVIRONMENT CANADA
INLAND WATERS DIRECTORATE
WATER RESOURCES BRANCH
WATER SURVEY OF CANADA

Phone: (819) 997-2098

Ottawa, ON, Canada K1A 0E7
Russell G. Boals, Director

Description of System or Service: The WATER SURVEY OF CANADA collects, collates, analyzes, stores, retrieves, and makes available streamflow, water level, and sediment data. Basic and field survey data are collected and computed using national standards. These data and data contributed by other organizations are sent to the SURVEY on forms, punched cards, or magnetic tape for storage and retrieval. It disseminates the data in various formats including punched cards, photocopies, magnetic tape, microfiche, publications, and listings.

Scope and/or Subject Matter: Canadian water resources data, including water level, discharge rate, sediment suspension, temperatures, ice thickness, and velocity.

Input Sources: Input is derived from collections and computations made by personnel at the regional offices of the Water Survey of Canada. The Survey collects data at more than 2800 gauging locations across Canada.

Holdings and Storage Media: Water Survey data are held in machine-readable files.

Publications: 1) Surface Water Data Reference Index (every 2 years)—contains descriptive information, alphabetical and station indexes, and occasional maps for all gauging stations. 2) Surface Water Data (annual)—lists for each province and the territories daily discharge or daily water levels and summaries for each month and for each year. 3) Historical Streamflow Summary (every 2 years)—contains a summary of monthly and annual mean discharges, annual extremes, and total discharges for streamflow data; published for every province and the territories. 4) Historical Water Levels Summary (every 2 years)—contains a summary of monthly and annual mean water levels and annual extremes for water level data; published for every province and the territories. 5) Sediment Data Reference Index (every 2 years)—contains descriptive information and alphabetical and station number indexes for sediment stations. 6) Sediment Data for Canadian Rivers (annual)—contains daily suspended sediment concentration, suspended load, and particle size distribution data. 7) Historical Sediment Data Summary (every 2 years)—contains monthly and annual summaries of sediment load and concentration.

Microform Products and Services: All streamflow, water level, and sediment data in metric units are available on microfiche. Each fiche contains an index and data stored in station number order by region. Two master indexes give hydrometric and sediment data for all Canadian stations.

Computer-Based Products and Services: The WATER SURVEY OF CANADA stores and retrieves computer-readable data and makes them publicly available in various formats, including computer tapes. Some field data are sensed on site and transmitted via satellites and telephone lines to regional offices throughout the country for real-time access.

Clientele/Availability: Clients include federal and provincial government departments, universities, international groups, and private individuals. Data are usually distributed free of charge.

Contact: Russell G. Boals, Director, or Douglas W. Kirk, Data Review Engineer, Water Survey of Canada.

★143★
CANADA
ENVIRONMENT CANADA
LANDS DIRECTORATE
CANADA LAND DATA SYSTEMS DIVISION
CANADA GEOGRAPHIC INFORMATION SYSTEM (CGIS)

Phone: (819) 997-2510
Service Est: 1965

Ottawa, ON, Canada K1A 0E7
Ian K. Crain, Division Chief

Staff: 11 Managemet professional; 2 technicians; 12 other.

Description of System or Service: The CANADA GEOGRAPHIC INFORMATION SYSTEM (CGIS) is a computer-based system used to read, store, analyze, and manipulate thematic map data. It is designed especially to facilitate land use planning at all levels of government by providing physical, biological, social, and economic information on Canada's land resources. CGIS is based on a data bank containing two separate sets of data for each geographic area covered. The Image Data Set (IDS) holds graphic data of the boundaries of areas; each area is identified with a unique reference number. The Descriptive Data Set (DDS) contains the thematic classification of each area, its measurement in acres or hectares, the location of its centroid, and the same reference number for the area that is stored in the IDS.

Scope and/or Subject Matter: Canadian mapping data for the following themes: land use, drainage, agriculture, forestry, ungulates, recreation, waterfowl, sport fish, shoreline, sensitivity to acid rain, ecological and biophysical data (especially in Northern Canada), census enumeration areas, and administrative boundaries.

Input Sources: Input consists of thematic map sheets from a variety of sources, entered via optical drum scanner or digitizer table; all input maps are in the Universal Transverse Mercator or Lambert Conical Conformal projections.

Holdings and Storage Media: Machine-readable files of image and descriptive information for more than 10,000 maps are maintained.

Publications: A catalog listing informal technical and application reports is available by request.

Computer-Based Products and Services: CGIS provides map data input, retrieval, and data manipulation services, with output available as reports, maps, or digital data for further processing by the user. The system features a capability called Overlay, which facilitates correlation, comparison, and complex cross-tabulations by imposing one coverage (such as census area) upon another (such as land use). A network of regional terminals allows users across the country to interactively retrieve maps and statistical reports.

Other Services: Training in the use of CGIS is also provided.

Clientele/Availability: Clients include provincial and federal government departments, corporations, universities, and land survey groups.

Contact: Dr. Ian K. Crain, Chief, Canada Land Data Systems Division. (Telex 053 3799 ENV-PVM-HULL.)

★144★
CANADA
ENVIRONMENT CANADA
LIBRARY SERVICES BRANCH
ENVIRONMENT LIBRARIES AUTOMATED SYSTEM (ELIAS)

Phone: (613) 997-1767
Ottawa, ON, Canada K1A 1C7   Service Est: 1976
Mrs. A.M. Bystram, Director of Library Services

Staff: 11 Information and library professional; 1 management professional; 17 other.

Description of System or Service: The ENVIRONMENT LIBRARIES AUTOMATED SYSTEM (ELIAS) maintains a machine-readable data base covering monographs, serials, and government publications held in Environment Canada libraries. The file is accessible online in Canada through CAN/OLE.

Scope and/or Subject Matter: Environment, including conservation, forestry, natural resources, land use, wildlife, national parks, pollution control, and related topics.

Input Sources: Participating Environment Canada libraries provide holdings information to the System.

Holdings and Storage Media: ELIAS holds approximately 39,000 records in computer-readable form.

Computer-Based Products and Services: The ELIAS data base is interactively accessible over the CAN/OLE retrieval service operated by the Canada Institute for Scientific and Technical Information (CISTI).

Clientele/Availability: Services are available without restrictions to users in Canada.

Contact: Mrs. A.M. Bystram, Director, Library Services Branch.

★145★
CANADA
HEALTH AND WELFARE CANADA
POLICY, PLANNING AND INFORMATION BRANCH
A NETWORK OF SOCIAL SECURITY INFORMATION RESOURCES (ANSSIR)

Brooke-Claxton Bldg.   Phone: (613) 995-2891
Tunney's Pasture   Service Est: 1976
Ottawa, ON, Canada K1A 0K9
Elizabeth Payne, Director

Staff: 8 Information and library professional; 2 technicians; 6 sales and marketing; 6 other.

Description of System or Service: A NETWORK OF SOCIAL SECURITY INFORMATION RESOURCES (ANSSIR) is an information system of Health and Welfare Canada used for the dissemination of machine-readable microdata, time series, and cross-sectional socioeconomic data. It was established to facilitate the evaluation, management, and planning of federal, provincial, and municipal social security programs. Under ANSSIR, data acquired from social service departments throughout Canada and sophisticated software for online data searching, manipulation, and analysis are made available to Canadian government users by remote access terminals.

Scope and/or Subject Matter: Federal and provincial socioeconomic data relevant to social security programs.

Input Sources: ANSSIR is updated on a continuing basis with data from Statistics Canada, Health and Welfare Canada, Revenue Canada, and provincial social services departments.

Holdings and Storage Media: Data are kept on tapes and online.

Computer-Based Products and Services: ANSSIR data are accessed through a commercial time-sharing company. Also available are software packages for online search, retrieval, analysis, report generation, and manipulation of the data.

Clientele/Availability: ANSSIR is available only to federal, provincial, and municipal governments.

Contact: Brian Sheen, Systems Analyst, Policy, Planning and Information Branch, Health and Welfare Canada.

★146★
CANADA
NATIONAL FILM BOARD OF CANADA
FORMAT

P.O. Box 6100, Station A   Phone: (514) 333-4524
Montreal, PQ, Canada H3C 3H5   Service Est: 1980
Donald Bidd, Senior AV Librarian

Staff: 6 Information and library professional; 1 management professional; 5 technicians.

Description of System or Service: FORMAT is a national bilingual computerized information system containing data on all Canadian-made films and other audiovisual materials. FORMAT consists of a network of files held on the computer facilities of UTLAS Inc. Online access to the files is available to UTLAS subscibers and at more than 30 National Film Board of Canada libraries and institutions in North America. Batch-mode products, featuring PRECIS subject indexes, include comprehensive and selective catalogs, magnetic tapes, and microfiche.

Scope and/or Subject Matter: All Canadian-made films and multimedia productions in all subject areas.

Input Sources: Current and retrospective information is gathered throughout Canada from agencies, distributors, public and private commercial collections, film libraries, media organizations, and others.

Holdings and Storage Media: FORMAT data on several thousand Canadian films and audiovisual materials are held in machine-readable form.

Publications: Film Canadiana (biennial)—available for purchase; Canadian filmography produced by FORMAT. Entries are arranged by film title and include credits, cast, summary, and other information.

Microform Products and Services: Edit lists, the PRECIS authority file, a thesaurus, Film Canadiana, and other FORMAT products are available on microfiche.

Computer-Based Products and Services: The FORMAT online inquiry system, developed by the National Film Board, includes MARC-coded data that are reformatted to permit easy searching using any Boolean combination of 15 selection criteria including title, series, producer, director, distributor, PRECIS subject indexing and thesaurus, abstract, running time, date or date range, type of material, and others. FORMAT is accessible online to UTLAS libraries for search and cataloging applications; direct dial access for other users is negotiable. Access to the system is maintained at National Film Board offices across Canada and in Chicago and New York, and booking services are offered. Additional FORMAT products and services include English or French-language catalogs in various forms and the modification of FORMAT software to serve internal needs of contributing agencies.

Other Services: The National Film Board also offers FORMAT-related consulting, training, referrals, data collection, conferences and workshops, pilot projects, and cost studies.

Clientele/Availability: Clients include educators, librarians, film directors, film distributors, producers, film fans, and others.

Projected Publications and Services: Direct access to FORMAT via Telidon is planned. The National Film Board also plans to widen link-ups with private industry, university, and public libraries in Canada, as well as in other countries.

Contact: Donald Bidd, Senior Audiovisual Librarian, FORMAT.

★147★
CANADA
NATIONAL LIBRARY OF CANADA
395 Wellington St.
Ottawa, ON, Canada K1A 0N4
Marianne Scott, National Librarian
Phone: (613) 995-9481
Service Est: 1953

Staff: 526 Total.

Description of System or Service: The NATIONAL LIBRARY OF CANADA/ Bibliotheque Nationale du Canada discharges a variety of national responsibilities in both the French and English languages. It maintains a comprehensive Canadiana collection based on legal deposit copies received since 1950 and has an intensive acquisition policy for earlier Canadiana. It also holds general research collections in the social sciences and humanities which complement the national scientific collections of the Canada Institute for Scientific and Technical Information (CISTI). The NATIONAL LIBRARY supplements the library resources of federal government agencies and performs a coordinating function through its Federal Libraries Liaison Office. For other libraries across Canada, the NATIONAL LIBRARY is intended to serve as a supplement rather than a replacement.

Among the many services and products offered by the various branches and departments of the NATIONAL LIBRARY are the following: compilation and publication of Canadiana, the national bibliography of Canada; maintenance of machine-readable union catalog files which may be used to locate Canadian libraries holding a specific work; distribution of machine-readable MARC cataloging information on magnetic tape; collection of Canadian masters' theses and doctoral disserations and provision of copies in microform; operation of the Canadian Cataloguing-in-Publication (CIP) Program; operation of the Library Documentation Centre, a clearinghouse on Canadian library research and development; coordination of the activities of the Canadian Book Exchange Centre, a national clearinghouse into which Canadian institutions can channel unwanted library materials and from which they can obtain additional publications deposited by other contributors; and provision of such library services as reference and referral, online literature searching and SDI from commercially available data bases, interlibrary loan, and document delivery. (Several of the above services are more fully described in separate entries following this one.) In addition, the NATIONAL LIBRARY has taken the leading part in plans for network coordination on a national scale, and is particularly interested in national bibliographic networks. The NATIONAL LIBRARY also contributes to international cooperation by participating in the CONSER (Conversion of Serials) Project, and by assigning International Standard Book Numbers (ISBN) and International Standard Serial Numbers (ISSN) to Canadian materials.

Scope and/or Subject Matter: Canadiana (materials in all subject areas published in Canada or relating to Canada); humanities; social sciences.

Input Sources: Canadian publishers are required to deposit, within a week of the publication date, two copies of each book published. The National Library purchases additional materials in the areas of humanities and social sciences. Theses and dissertations are submitted by more than 30 participating Canadian institutions.

Holdings and Storage Media: Library holdings consist of more than 1 million bound volumes; 3 million microforms; subscriptions to 27,300 periodicals; plus collections of rare books, literary manuscripts, sheet music, recorded music, Canadian newspapers, pamphlets, and Canadian, foreign, and international government documents.

Publications: 1) National Library News (monthly). 2) Annual Report of the National Librarian. 3) National Library Technical News (irregular). 4) Canadian Network Papers (irregular). 5) Publications Catalogue (annual). Inquiries regarding publications should be addressed to the Public Relations Office of the National Library of Canada at the address given above.

Microform Products and Services: The Library's Newspaper Division microfilms its original holdings of ethnic group newspapers, for purposes of preservation and research. Other microform products and services are also offered.

Computer-Based Products and Services: The NATIONAL LIBRARY OF CANADA provides a number of computer-based products and services, including maintenance of publicly available online data bases by its Canadiana Editorial Division and Union Catalogue of Serials Division, and the distribution of machine-readable cataloging information through the MARC Records Distribution Service (see separate entries following this one). The LIBRARY also uses the Dortmunder Bibliothekssystem (DOBIS), in a version modified to handle bilingual information and to accommodate multiple libraries, for online searching, cataloging, and recording the holdings of other Canadian libraries. DOBIS is used as a shared system by federal government libraries. Additionally, the Reference Services of the NATIONAL LIBRARY OF CANADA provides online searching from data bases made available through approximately a dozen host services, and it offers CAN/SDI services for workers in the social sciences and humanities using the MARC, ERIC, and Social Science Cititation Index (SSCI) data bases.

Contact: Gwynneth Evans, Executive Secretary, National Library of Canada; telephone (613) 995-3904. (Telex 053 4311.) The electronic mail address on ENVOY 100 (Telecom Canada) is OONL.REF.

★148★
CANADA
NATIONAL LIBRARY OF CANADA
CATALOGUING BRANCH
CANADIANA EDITORIAL DIVISION
395 Wellington St.
Ottawa, ON, Canada K1A 0N4
Phone: (819) 977-6200

Description of System or Service: The CANADIANA EDITORIAL DIVISION identifies all publications produced in Canada, written by Canadians, or dealing with Canadian subjects; stores the bibliographic information in computer-readable form; and disseminates it through a variety of print, microfiche, and computer-readable products. Chief among these products is Canadiana, the national bibliography of Canada, which provides cataloging records for books, theses, periodicals, pamphlets, microforms, sound recordings, musical scores, educational kits, and federal and provincial government publications. Canadiana information is available as a printed publication, on microfiche, on magnetic tape (as CAN/MARC), and online (as the OONL data base). Additional titles issued by the DIVISION include Canadiana 1867-1900: Monographs, a quarterly publication which will eventually cover more than 40,000 monographs of Canadian origin; and Canadian Theses/ Theses Canadiennes, an annual bibliography of masters' theses and doctoral dissertations accepted by more than 30 participating Canadian universities. Microform copies of the dissertations are available through the Library.

Scope and/or Subject Matter: Publications produced in Canada, written by Canadians, or of special interest or significance to Canada; Canadian theses.

Input Sources: Materials covered by the Division include books, periodicals, theses, pamphlets, microforms, musical scores, sound recordings, federal and provincial government documents, and educational kits. Excluded are university calendars, performing arts programs of limited interest, most advertising materials, annual reports of nongovernmental organizations, and other nonbook materials.

Holdings and Storage Media: The Division maintains several computer-readable files, including the computer-readable Canadiana file which contains more than 215,000 references and is updated with about 2000 new records each month.

Publications: 1) Canadiana (monthly with annual cumulation)— contains catalog records for Canadian publications. Each issue covers Canadian and foreign imprints separately; entries are arranged according to Dewey Decimal Classification number. Includes five indexes: authors/ titles/ series, English subject headings, French subject headings, ISBN, and ISSN. 2) Canadiana 1867-1900:

Monographs (quarterly)—each issue contains a register of entries plus five indexes: authors/ titles, chronological, publishers/ printers, places of publication/ printing, and subjects. 3) Canadian Theses/ Theses Canadiennes (annual)—entries are arranged by subject; includes an author index. The above publications are available from the Canadian Government Publishing Centre, Supply and Services Canada, Ottawa, ON, Canada K1A 0S9. 4) Canadian Theses on Microfiche: Catalogue/ Theses Canadiennes sur Microfiches: Catalogue (irregular)—available free of charge. 5) Canadian Subject Headings.

Microform Products and Services: The DIVISION makes the following publications available for purchase on COM microfiche: 1) Canadiana—issued several weeks in advance of its printed counterpart; includes cumulative indexes. Multiyear cumulations on microfiche are also available. 2) Canadiana Authorities—a current list of all verified subject name headings used in Canadiana; includes English and French forms with cross-references and history notes. In addition, microform copies of Canadian theses and dissertations are available for purchase through the Library's Canadian Theses on Microfiche Service.

Computer-Based Products and Services: The CANADIANA EDITORIAL DIVISION maintains computer-readable files of bibliographic information on Canadian publications and uses them to produce several publications. The DIVISION makes Canadiana information available on magnetic tape as the CAN/MARC data base, which is issued through the National Library's MARC Records Distribution Service (see separate entry), and as the online OONL data base, which is publicly accessible through CAN/OLE.

Clientele/Availability: Products and services are available without restrictions.

Contact: Canadiana Editorial Division, Cataloguing Branch, National Library of Canada.

★149★
CANADA
NATIONAL LIBRARY OF CANADA
LIBRARY DOCUMENTATION CENTRE
395 Wellington St.   Phone: (613) 995-8717
Ottawa, ON, Canada K1A 0N4   Service Est: 1970
Dr. Beryl L. Anderson, Chief

Staff: 4 Information and library professional; 2 clerical and nonprofessional.

Related Organizations: The Library Documentation Centre is part of the National Library's Public Services Branch.

Description of System or Service: The LIBRARY DOCUMENTATION CENTRE collects and disseminates up-to-date information on library and information science in Canada. Particularly concerned with obtaining published and unpublished documentation relating to the activities of Canadian libraries and information centers, it maintains extensive vertical files in its areas of interest and selects relevant books and serials for addition to the National Library's collections. The DOCUMENTATION CENTRE serves the National Library staff and the Canadian library community in general by providing reference service, literature searching, and limited current awareness services. On an international level, the LIBRARY DOCUMENTATION CENTRE serves as Canada's National Information Transfer Centre for UNESCO's International Information System on Research in Documentation (ISORID); contributes Canadian information to CURRENT RESEARCH in Library and Information Science; maintains the Canadian depository for conference papers of the International Federation of Library Associations and Institutions (IFLA); and answers information requests from foreign countries.

Scope and/or Subject Matter: Library and information science, and research in these areas; library automation and networks; Canadian library community.

Input Sources: Input to the vertical files on Canadian and other library developments is derived from CAN/SDI, external clipping services, and internal indexing of more than 200 periodicals. Reports of relevant surveys, studies, and research projects are submitted by the Canadian library community. Also indexed are research reports, transactions and proceedings of library associations, annual reports of libraries, legislation, user orientation materials, technology reports, equipment catalogs, and other materials.

Holdings and Storage Media: Holdings include vertical files of information relating to Canadian libraries, library schools, library associations, and librarians; subject files on developments in library and information science; plus various indexes, directories, and reviews.

Publications: 1) Guide to Provincial Library Agencies in Canada. 2) Canadian Library/ Information Science Research Projects: A List. 3) Bibliography series—more than 25 titles have been issued. 4) National Library Recent Acquisitions in the Field of Library Science. The first three publications are available free on request to the Library Documentation Centre; the fourth has limited distribution to Canadian government libraries, library schools, and provincial library agencies in Canada.

Services: Primary services are abstracting and indexing; advisory and consulting services; manual SDI and literature searching; reference and referrals; and copying.

Clientele/Availability: Bilingual services are available to the Canadian library community and, with some limitations, to persons outside of Canada.

Contact: Dr. Beryl L. Anderson, Chief, or Carolyn Robertson, Documentalist, Library Documentation Centre.

★150★
CANADA
NATIONAL LIBRARY OF CANADA
MARC RECORDS DISTRIBUTION SERVICE (MRDS)
395 Wellington St.   Phone: (819) 997-6200
Ottawa, ON, Canada K1A 0N4   Service Est: 1976
Margaret Stewart, Senior MARC Librarian

Description of System or Service: The Canadian MARC RECORDS DISTRIBUTION SERVICE (MRDS) provides Canadian libraries with domestic and foreign machine-readable cataloging information in magnetic tape form. It includes records from the national bibliography (Canadiana) for monographs about Canada, by Canadians, or published in Canada, as originally cataloged and recorded in Canadian MARC (CAN/MARC) Communication Format by the National Library of Canada. Foreign information distributed includes U.S. Library of Congress MARC records for monographs, British UK MARC records, INTERMARC (from the Bibliotheque Nationale in Paris), and CONSER (Conversion of Serials) records, all of which are converted into the CAN/MARC format. MRDS is also developing routines to convert Australian MARC into CAN/MARC for inclusion in its service.

Scope and/or Subject Matter: Machine-readable cataloging information for Canadian and various foreign country publications.

Input Sources: Input is received in machine-readable form from foreign sources; Canadian input corresponds to records published in Canadiana, the national bibliography.

Holdings and Storage Media: The internally generated CAN/MARC data base holds more than 215,000 Canadiana records. In addition, more than 1.7 million LC MARC records, 410,000 UK MARC records, 170,000 INTERMARC records, and 205,000 CONSER records have been converted to CAN/MARC format.

Publications: The following specifications for tape formats and character sets are issued: 1) Canadian MARC Communication Format: Authorities; 2) Canadian MARC Communication Format: Monographs; 3) Canadian MARC Communication Format: Serials. Complimentary copies of the specifications are provided to tape service subscribers and Selected Records subscribers.

Microform Products and Services: CONSER Microfiche, which lists all authenticated records in the CONSER data base and is updated annually, is available from the National Library.

Computer-Based Products and Services: The MARC RECORDS DISTRIBUTION SERVICE offers machine-readable cataloging information through eight options: 1) Selected MARC Records Service—demand searches of the MRDS source file of approximately 2 million records, with output available on magnetic tapes or unit catalog cards. 2) Retrospective Cumulations—allows libraries to request complete or partial retrospective files of records on the

MRDS master files. 3) CAN/MARC Authorities Tape Service—tapes issued every two weeks containing authority records. 4) Canadiana Tape Service—tapes issued weekly contain records of Canadiana monographs. 5) LC MARC Tape Service—weekly tapes of monograph records received by the National Library from the U.S. Library of Congress and converted to the Canadian MARC communication format for monographs. 6) UK MARC Tape Service—weekly UK MARC tapes of monograph and serial records produced for the British National Bibliography and received by the National Library. 7) CONSER Tape Service—tapes issued every four weeks contain CONSER records received from OCLC in the Canadian MARC communication format for serials. 8) INTERMARC Tape Service—monthly tapes of monograph records issued by the Bibliotheque Nationale in Paris and listed in Bibliographie de la France. Options 1 and 2 are offered on a custom basis; options 3 through 8 are available by subscription.

Clientele/Availability: Services are intended primarily for Canadian libraries but some are also available to others.

Contact: Margaret Stewart, Senior MARC Librarian, National Library of Canada. (Telex 053 4311.)

★151★
CANADA
NATIONAL LIBRARY OF CANADA
PUBLIC SERVICES BRANCH
UNION CATALOGUE OF SERIALS DIVISION
395 Wellington St.   Phone: (613) 993-6128
Ottawa, ON, Canada K1A 0N4   Service Est: 1957
Myra Clowes, Chief

Staff: 3 Information and library professional; 2 technicians; 8 clerical and nonprofessional.

Description of System or Service: The UNION CATALOGUE OF SERIALS DIVISION provides bibliographic, location, and holdings information for social sciences and humanities serials held by more than 350 Canadian libraries. In support of its activities, the DIVISION maintains the Union List of Serials in the Social Sciences and Humanities Held by Canadian Libraries, which consists of a manual card catalog and a computer-readable data base that is held under the DOBIS (Dortmunder Bibliothekssystem) data base management system operated by the National Library of Canada. Hardcopy records of serials holdings are submitted by Canadian libraries and entered into the Union List file by divisional staff; other libraries participating in DOBIS add information directly into the data base. The DIVISION makes the Union List information available on COM microfiche updated semiannually and as the commercially available online CANUCS data base.

Scope and/or Subject Matter: Serials in the social sciences and humanities held by Canadian libraries, including periodicals, proceedings of regularly and frequently held meetings and conferences, monographic series, serially published official publications with distinctive titles, regularly revised monographs, law reports, serially published loose-leaf services, serially published government publications and newspapers.

Input Sources: Reports on serial accessions, withdrawals, and revisions are submitted for inclusion in the data base by Canadian libraries. Reports are received in card, printed list, report slip, printout, or microfiche format as well as through direct online input.

Holdings and Storage Media: The machine-readable Union List of Serials file provides information for approximately 35,000 serial titles. A manual card catalog, containing approximately 500,000 cards, is also maintained.

Microform Products and Services: The Union List of Serials in the Social Sciences and Humanities Held by Canadian Libraries is issued and updated semiannually on COM microfiche arranged in register/index format.

Computer-Based Products and Services: The UNION CATALOGUE OF SERIALS DIVISION maintains and provides services from the machine-readable Union List of Serials in the Social Sciences and Humanities Held by Canadian Libraries data base, which is made publicly accessible for online searching as the CANUCS data base through CAN/OLE.

Clientele/Availability: Services are available to researchers and academic, special, public, government, and other libraries in Canada and elsewhere.

Contact: Emilie Lowenberg, Union Catalogue of Serials Division, Public Services Branch, National Library of Canada.

★152★
CANADA
NATIONAL RESEARCH COUNCIL OF CANADA
CANADA INSTITUTE FOR SCIENTIFIC AND TECHNICAL
   INFORMATION (CISTI)
Montreal Rd.   Phone: (613) 993-1600
Ottawa, ON, Canada K1A 0S2   Service Est: 1974
Elmer V. Smith, Director

Staff: 60 Information and library professional; 20 management professional; 128 clerical and nonprofessional.

Description of System or Service: The CANADA INSTITUTE FOR SCIENTIFIC AND TECHNICAL INFORMATION (CISTI) is the national resource for scientific, technical, and medical information for industry, universities, and government in Canada. Its chief aim is to initiate and provide library and information services of value to Canadian research and development efforts. CISTI offers comprehensive reference services through its Customized Literature Search Service (CLSS), which consists of subject searches using the most relevant of about 250 bibliographic data bases and CISTI's collection of printed abstracting and indexing services. CISTI also compiles bibliographies, provides loans and photocopies of documents, locates items not in the CISTI library collection, and supplies document delivery services. Several computer-based information services are provided by CISTI, including CAN/OLE, a national online service for retrospective bibliographic searching; CAN/SDI, a current awareness service; and CAN/SND, an online service for scientific numeric data bases. (Separate entries describing these services follow this one.) CISTI also maintains the computer-based Union List of Scientific Serials in Canadian Libraries, the CISTI Catalogue, and other data bases.

A number of additional special programs are offered by CISTI. The Health Sciences Resource Centre (telephone 993-1604) offers national bibliographical and reference services in the health sciences and is the Canadian MEDLARS center. The Information Exchange Centre for Federally Supported Research in Canadian Universities (telephone 993-1205) collects information on university-based research projects, publishes it in an annual directory, and makes it accessible as an online data base on CAN/OLE. The Knowledge Source Index (telephone 993-3568) is an inventory of Canadian experts in science and technology in the federal government, the Ontario government, and 12 Canadian universities. The Canadian Index of Scientific and Technical Translations (telephone 993-3372) helps locate translations in Canada, the United States, the United Kingdom, and several other countries.

Scope and/or Subject Matter: Science, technology, engineering, medicine, health sciences.

Input Sources: CISTI collects all significant scientific, technical, and medical journals and conference proceedings regardless of language or country of origin; selectively acquires books, microforms, and publicly available data bases; and acquires unpublished data.

Holdings and Storage Media: The CISTI library collection includes more than 2 million documents on microfiche; 30,000 journal titles (1000 of which are held in Canada only by CISTI); conference proceedings; 400 abstracting and indexing services; unpublished scientific data; and other literature. CISTI also maintains copies of internally and externally generated computer-readable data bases.

Publications: 1) CISTI News—newsletter provides current information on CISTI's activities and services; available by request. 2) Union List of Scientific Serials in Canadian Libraries—list of titles, holdings, and locations of more than 50,000 scientific, technical, and medical journals held by 262 Canadian libraries. 3) Directory of Federally Supported Research in Universities (annual)—lists university-based research projects funded by Canadian federal agencies. 4) Publications of the National Research Council of Canada—cumulative listing of scientific and technical papers describing experimental works carried out in the Council's laboratories since 1916. 5) Science and Technology Collections in Canadian Government Libraries—a guide. 6) Scientific Policy, Research and Development in Canada—bibliography. 7) Scientific and Technical Societies of Canada—directory of national, provincial, and regional societies concerned with the study, development, and dissemination of scientific and technical knowledge. 8) Canadian Locations of Journals Indexed for MEDLINE. 9) Health Sciences Information in Canada: Libraries—directory of significant Canadian health science collections and library services. 10) User manuals. An annual report and brochures are also issued. The above publications are available from the CISTI Publications Section.

Microform Products and Services: Microfiche and hardcopy duplications are provided from documents and periodicals stored in microform.

Computer-Based Products and Services: CISTI's CAN/OLE, CAN/SDI, and CAN/SND services are described in separate entries following this one. CISTI also produces the following data bases, which are accessible through CAN/OLE: 1) Directory of Federally Supported Research in Universities (IEC)—contains 121,000 records dating from 1971 to the present; updated annually with approximately 12,500 records. 2) CISTI Catalogue (OON)—contains 211,500 records dating from 1978 to the present; updated monthly with approximately 2000 records. 3) Union List of Scientific Serials in Canadian Libraries (UNION)—contains 65,000 records; updated biweekly. In addition, CISTI collaborates with the Alberta Research Council Solar and Wind Energy Research Program (SWERP) Information Centre in the maintenance of the Canadian Renewable Energy Database (ENERCAN).

Clientele/Availability: Services are available without restrictions to Canadian researchers, technologists, and managers in industry, universities, and government. Users should first direct their requests to the nearest library or information center.

Contact: Florentia Janson, Chief, Publicity and Communications, Canada Institute for Scientific and Technical Information; telephone (613) 993-3854. (Telex 053 3115.)

★153★
CANADA
NATIONAL RESEARCH COUNCIL OF CANADA
CANADA INSTITUTE FOR SCIENTIFIC AND TECHNICAL INFORMATION (CISTI)
CANADIAN ONLINE ENQUIRY SYSTEM (CAN/OLE)
Montreal Rd. Phone: (613) 993-1210
Ottawa, ON, Canada K1A 0S2 Service Est: 1974
Bonnie Bullock, Head, Client Services

Staff: 4 Information and library professional; 2 clerical and nonprofessional.

Description of System or Service: The CANADIAN ONLINE ENQUIRY SYSTEM (CAN/OLE) is a Canadian designed and operated national online information retrieval system for the retrospective searching of bibliographic and nonbibliographic data bases in all major fields of science and technology. Searchable using either English or French-language commands, it provides access to the world's major abstracting and indexing and other data bases as well as a number of Canadian files. CAN/OLE also provides online document ordering through its CAN/DOC service, and it offers training seminars and user aids.

Scope and/or Subject Matter: Aeronautics, agriculture, aquatic sciences, biochemistry, biology, Canadiana, chemistry, coal science and technology, communications, computers, control technology, education, electronics, energy, engineering, environment, foods, geology, government documents, metallurgy, microbiology, Northern studies, nuclear science, oil sands, ongoing research, patents, petroleum, pharmaceuticals, physics, pollution, polymers, science and technology, social science research, space technology, sports, toxicology, transportation.

Input Sources: Data bases are acquired from government agencies, professional associations, and commercial sources.

Holdings and Storage Media: Approximately two dozen data bases are held online.

Publications: 1) CAN/OLE Bulletin (bimonthly)—provides information on data bases, systems improvements, network developments, and other news items of interest to users. 2) CAN/OLE User's Manual. 3) CAN/OLE Database Manual—a three-volume set providing details for searching individual data bases on the system.

Computer-Based Products and Services: CAN/OLE makes the following data bases accessible for online searching through the Datapac telecommunications network:

1) Alberta Oil Sands Index (AOSI)—contains references to literature covering all aspects of oil sands technology; produced by the Alberta Oil Sands Information Centre. 2) Aquatic Sciences and Fisheries Abstracts (ASFA)—covers all aspects of marine biology and ocean technology; compiled by the United Nations Food and Agriculture Organization. 3) BIOSIS Previews—provides abstracts and indexing for world literature covering the biological and biomedical sciences; prepared by BioSciences Information Service. 4) CA Search—contains abstracts of literature on all aspects of chemistry and chemical engineering; compiled by Chemical Abstracts Service. 5) Canadian Register of Research and Researchers in the Social Sciences (CANREG)—provides information on approximately 5000 members of the social sciences community in Canada from the government, academic, and private sectors; prepared by the Social Science Computing Laboratory at the University of Western Ontario.

6) CANUCS (Union List of Serials in the Social Sciences and Humanities Held by Canadian Libraries)--provides holdings and location information for serials in the social sciences and humanities fields held by more than 350 Canadian libraries; produced by the National Library of Canada. 7) Coal Abstracts—contains references to literature covering all aspects of coal science and technology. 8) Coal Research Projects (COALPRO)—inventory of current research projects in coal science and technology as reported by government, academic, and research organizations in most coal-producing countries. These two data bases are prepared by the IEA Coal Research Technical Information Service. 9) CODOC (Cooperative Documents Project)—contains the combined government document holdings of 11 academic libraries in Ontario; produced by the University of Guelph Library. 10) COMPENDEX—provides references to world engineering literature; prepared by Engineering Information, Inc.

11) Ei Engineering Meetings—covers more than 2000 technical conferences held each year and includes references for the individual papers given; compiled by Engineering Information, Inc. 12) ELIAS (Environmental Libraries Automated System)—corresponds to the holdings of 15 libraries participating in the Environment Canada Departmental Library Network; produced by Environment Canada. 13) GeoRef—covers world literature relating to the geosciences and earth sciences; prepared by the American Geological Institute. 14) ICAR (Inventory of Canadian Agricultural Research)—provides coverage of ongoing agricultural research and development projects in Canada at the government, university, industry, and research levels; prepared by the Canadian Agricultural Research Council. 15) IEC (Directory of Federally Supported Research in Universities)—a compilation of Canadian university research projects in all subject areas as reported to the Information Exchange Centre at CISTI.

16) INIS—provides abstracts and indexing of literature relating to the peaceful applications of atomic energy; produced by the International Atomic Energy Agency. 17) INSPEC—provides worldwide coverage of journals and other literature dealing with all aspects of physics, electrical and electronic engineering, computer and control technology, and information technology; prepared by INSPEC. 18) Microlog Index—covers publications in all disciplines issued by Canadian government agencies at all levels, research institutions, professional associations, and special interest groups; compiled by Micromedia Ltd. 19) NTIS—contains references to reports and computer-readable data files and software dealing with U.S. government-sponsored research, development, and engineering in all disciplines; produced by the U.S. National Technical Information Service. 20) OON—contains cataloging records of monographs, technical reports, and conference proceedings in science, technology, and medicine held by CISTI.

21) OONL—provides cataloging records for publications issued in Canada, written by Canadians, or of interest to Canadians; produced by the National Library of Canada. 22) OOT (Canadian Transportation

Documentation System)—covers nonrestricted Transport Canada documents, selected Canadian government, university, and association publications, and selected U.S. and foreign documents relating to transportation; compiled by the Transport Canada Library and Information Centre. 23) Sport and Recreation Index—provides references to literature on all aspects of team and individual sports, training and equipment, recreation planning and management, sports medicine, physical education, and related topics; prepared by the Coaching Association of Canada Sports Information Resource Centre. 24) Union List of Scientific Serials in Canadian Libraries—provides holdings and location information of scientific serials held by more than 250 Canadian libraries; prepared by CISTI.

CAN/OLE's document ordering facility, CAN/DOC, permits users to submit online orders for copies of documents cited in the data bases offered through CAN/OLE.

Clientele/Availability: Clients include Canadian researchers, technologists, and managers in industry, university, and government.

Contact: Bonnie Bullock, Head, Client Services, CAN/OLE. (Telex 053 3115.) The electronic mail address on ENVOY 100 (Telecom Canada) is CISTI.CLIENT.SERV; on CAN/OLE, it is OLE075.

★154★
CANADA
NATIONAL RESEARCH COUNCIL OF CANADA
CANADA INSTITUTE FOR SCIENTIFIC AND TECHNICAL
    INFORMATION (CISTI)
CANADIAN SERVICE FOR THE SELECTIVE DISSEMINATION OF
    INFORMATION (CAN/SDI)
Montreal Rd.   Phone: (613) 993-1210
Ottawa, ON, Canada K1A 0S2   Service Est: 1969
Bonnie Bullock, Head, Client Services

Staff: 4 Information and library professional; 2 clerical and nonprofessional.

Description of System or Service: The CANADIAN SERVICE FOR THE SELECTIVE DISSEMINATION OF INFORMATION (CAN/SDI) is a computer-based current awareness service which supplies subscribers with periodic custom lists of references retrieved from publicly available data bases. The service is based on interest profiles created by CAN/SDI staff and consisting of keywords, phrases, authors, and organization names that describe the client's information needs. CAN/SDI services can be obtained through the CAN/SDI center at CISTI, or through one of the following subject-specialized centers: National Library of Canada, Agriculture Canada, Geological Survey of Canada, the Canada Centre for Mineral and Energy Technology, or Atomic Energy of Canada Limited.

Scope and/or Subject Matter: Agriculture, aquatic sciences, biosciences, cancer, chemistry, computers and control, education, electrical and electronics, engineering, fisheries, food sciences, geology, medicine, metallurgy and metals, nuclear science, physics, science and technology, social sciences, toxicology, U.S. government reports.

Input Sources: The service uses data bases produced by government agencies, professional associations, and commercial sources.

Publications: CAN/SDI Profile Design Manual.

Computer-Based Products and Services: CAN/SDI is a batch current awareness service providing subscribers with abstracts and/or references to current journal articles, conference papers, technical papers, and patents. Searches are conducted and references are mailed to clients on a weekly, semimonthly, or monthly basis, depending on the data base selected. Data bases currently covered by CAN/SDI include: 1) AGRICOLA; 2) ASFA; 3) BIOSIS Previews; 4) CA Search; 5) CANCERLIT; 6) Chemical Titles; 7) COMPENDEX; 8) Ei Engineering Meetings; 9) ERIC; 10) FSTA; 11) GeoRef; 12) INIS; 13) INSPEC; 14) LC/MARC; 15) MEDLINE; 16) METADEX; 17) NTIS; 18) Science Citation Index (SCI); 19) Social Science Citation Index (SSCI); 20) TOXLINE.

Other Services: Copies of references can be used to order documents from the loan services of CAN/SDI center libraries. CISTI also offers training in profile design on a regular basis.

Clientele/Availability: Clients include Canadian researchers, technologists, and managers in industry, university, and government.

Contact: Bonnie Bullock, Head, Client Services, CAN/SDI. (Telex 053 3115.) The electronic mail address on ENVOY 100 (Telecom Canada) is CISTI.CLIENT.SERV.; on CAN/OLE, it is OLE075.

★155★
CANADA
NATIONAL RESEARCH COUNCIL OF CANADA
CANADA INSTITUTE FOR SCIENTIFIC AND TECHNICAL
    INFORMATION (CISTI)
SCIENTIFIC NUMERIC DATABASES (CAN/SND)
Montreal Rd.   Phone: (613) 993-3294
Ottawa, ON, Canada K1A 0S2   Service Est: 1980
Dr. G.H. Wood, Manager

Staff: 2 Scientific professional; 1 clerical and nonprofessional.

Description of System or Service: The SCIENTIFIC NUMERIC DATABASES (CAN/SND) program was established to promote the use in Canada of numeric data bases in the areas of science and technology. It provides custom search services from two such data bases and makes them available online or through tape leasing. CAN/SND also maintains a worldwide inventory of numeric data bases, assists Canadians in identifying and accessing files of interest, and provides consultation to organizations wishing to generate numeric data bases.

Scope and/or Subject Matter: Numeric data bases in the fields of physics, chemistry, biology, materials, metals, astronomy, energy, and engineering.

Input Sources: Data bases and software programs are acquired from other producers as needed.

Computer-Based Products and Services: The SCIENTIFIC NUMERIC DATABASES program currently provides online access to the Cambridge Crystallographic Data Base, covering approximately 40,000 organic compounds, and to the Search Program for Infrared Spectra (SPIR) system. SPIR comprises ASTM/ Sadtler data on 140,000 infrared spectra and software incorporating the FIRST-1 Infrared Search Program. These files are accessible through the National Research Council Computation Centre via the Datapac packet-switching network. CAN/SND also plans to add additional files, including the Inorganic Crystal Structure Data Base and the NRC Metals Crystallographic Data File (CRYSTMET). Other computer-based services include custom searches conducted by CISTI staff in response to written requests and tape lease services for entire data bases or portions of them.

Clientele/Availability: Primary clients are Canadian scientific professionals. Online service is currently restricted to use in Canada.

Contact: Dr. G.H. Wood, Manager, Scientific Numeric Databases. (Telex 053 3115.) The electronic mail address on ENVOY 100 (Telecom Canada) is WOOD.GH.

★156★
CANADA
NATIONAL RESEARCH COUNCIL OF CANADA
CHEMISTRY DIVISION
METALS DATA CENTRE
Montreal Rd.   Phone: (613) 993-2527
Ottawa, ON, Canada K1A 0R6   Service Est: 1980
Dr. L.D. Calvert, Head

Staff: 2 Scientific professional; 1 technician.

Description of System or Service: The METALS DATA CENTRE collects, evaluates, synthesizes, and disseminates data on crystal structures of intermetallic phases obtained by diffraction methods. It maintains the Metals Crystallographic Data File (CRYSTMET), a computer-based compilation of crystallographic and bibliographic data for metallic structures determined by diffraction methods. The CENTRE also plans to establish and maintain additional computer-based files of bibliographic and numeric data in forms readily usable by scientists. From these computer files, the CENTRE will provide current awareness services by issuing lists of new entries when the files are updated, retrospective searches, magnetic tape services, and online access.

Scope and/or Subject Matter: Crystallographic and bibliographic data on metals and metallic phases characterized by diffraction methods.

Input Sources: Input is derived from primary journals and secondary sources. All numeric data from 1975 onward are critically evaluated for self consistency by special diagnostic programs before inclusion.

Holdings and Storage Media: The computer-readable CRYSTMET File contains 5600 entries for structures determined from 1913 to the present; and 4000 entries for metals and alloys assigned to known structure types, covering the period from 1975 to the present.

Computer-Based Products and Services: The CRYSTMET data base covers diffraction studies of metals and intermetallic compounds including hydrides and selected binary oxides. The data base includes bibliographic data such as formula of phase, author name, and journal reference. Also included are primary crystallographic data such as cell dimensions and space group density; atomic coordinates; experimental data such as R-factor, number of reflections, and type of instrument and radiation used; flags for powder studies; Pearson symbol structure code; and structure type. The CENTRE plans to make CRYSTMET available online through CISTI's Scientific Numeric Databases service and to offer tape services, quarterly current awareness, and personal and specialized searches and bibliographies.

Clientele/Availability: Primary clients are scientists.

Remarks: The Centre submits powder data patterns to the Powder Diffraction File of the JCPDS International Centre for Diffraction Data; it also provides data for the Crystal Data Determinative Tables of the U.S. National Bureau of Standards.

Contact: Dr. G.H. Wood, Manager, CISTI Scientific Numeric Databases; telephone (613) 993-3294. (Telex 053 3115.) The electronic mail address on ENVOY 100 (Telecom Canada) is WOOD.GH.

★157★
CANADA
PARLIAMENT OF CANADA
LIBRARY OF PARLIAMENT
Centre Block, Parliament Bldgs.   Phone: (613) 992-3122
Ottawa, ON, Canada K1A 0A9   Service Est: 1867
E.J. Spicer, Parliamentary Librarian

Staff: 90 Information and library professional; 11 management professional; 54 technicians; 79 clerical and nonprofessional.

Description of System or Service: The LIBRARY OF PARLIAMENT provides information, research, and bibliographic services to the Parliament of Canada. Its Information and Reference Branch processes over 40,000 reference inquiries per year, as well as maintaining extensive newspaper clipping files and machine-readable indexes to Senate committee proceedings. The inquiry answering services are supported by computerized literature searching from data bases made available through several online systems. They also include manual bibliography compilation on request; QUORUM, a daily clipping service; and photocopies of relevant clippings, periodical articles, and parts of books. The Research Branch of the Library of Parliament prepares in-depth studies in which relevant facts are stated, documented, analyzed, and interpreted in accordance with the user's requirements. It also prepares background papers on a variety of subjects. Its current issues system involves the preparation of brief summaries of topical issues, updated monthly. In addition, the research officers (including lawyers, economists, scientists, and social scientists) are on call to provide oral briefings, consultations on demand, or continuing assistance to Parliamentary committees. The Technical Services Branch of the Library acquires and processes new materials for the main library and three branch libraries.

Scope and/or Subject Matter: Parliamentary history and procedure; government and politics; foreign affairs; economics and finance; law; history, social welfare and Canadiana.

Input Sources: The Library acquires published and unpublished material in all forms, including books, periodicals, newspapers, government reports and publications (hard copy and microform), manuscripts, document microfiche services, cassettes of radio and television programs, and computer-readable data bases. The newspaper clipping files are updated daily with nearly 500 clippings from about 26 Canadian newspapers.

Holdings and Storage Media: Library holdings consist of more than 700,000 volumes; more than 300,000 microforms; approximately 1300 videocassettes; and subscriptions to more than 2400 journals and approximately 700 newspapers. In addition, 6156 newspaper clipping files are maintained, 2558 of which are current. Magnetic tape holdings include internally compiled bibliographies and indexes to committee proceedings.

Publications: 1) Annual Report of the Parliamentary Librarian; 2) Periodicals and Newspapers in the Collections of the Library of Parliament (annual); 3) Selected Additions List (monthly during session); 4) Selected Periodical Articles List (weekly during session); 5) Current Issue Reviews (updated monthly during session); 6) QUORUM (daily during session)—a compilation of press clippings; 7) Background Papers; 8) Your Library (revised as required); 9) subject bibliographies (irregular).

Computer-Based Products and Services: The LIBRARY OF PARLIAMENT provides retrospective searching and SDI from data bases made available through CAN/OLE, DIALOG Information Services, Inc., System Development Corporation (SDC), Info Globe, QL Systems, CANSIM, IDRC/MINISIS, Datasolve, Dow Jones News/Retrieval, TEXTLINE (Finsbury Data Services Ltd.), Bibliographic Retrieval Services (BRS), WESTLAW (West Publishing Company), VU/TEXT Information Services, and others. The Library also utilizes a computerized cataloging system, DOBIS, through the National Library of Canada, and maintains internal files on magnetic tape.

Other Services: In addition to services described above, the Library offers interlibrary loan services.

Clientele/Availability: Services are available to the Governor General, Senators, members of the House of Commons, officers, officials, parliamentary staff, and the press. The Library is open to the public for consultation of material unavailable elsewhere.

Contact: Lloyd Heaslip, Director, Information and Reference Branch, Library of Parliament. The electronic mail address on QL Systems is 116.

★158★
CANADA
PUBLIC ARCHIVES OF CANADA
MACHINE READABLE ARCHIVES DIVISION (MRA)
395 Wellington St.   Phone: (613) 593-7772
Ottawa, ON, Canada K1A 0N3   Service Est: 1973
Harold A. Naugler, Director

Staff: 10 Information and library professional; 5 management professional; 4 clerical and nonprofessional.

Description of System or Service: In support of the Public Archives of Canada's overall mission to acquire all significant archival material relating to Canadian life and development, the MACHINE READABLE ARCHIVES DIVISION (MRA) appraises, acquires, and preserves those machine-readable files of the federal government which are of long-term value and those of the private sector which are of national significance. Particularly concerned with preventing loss of these archival data once they are acquired, the DIVISION makes two machine-readable copies of each file, stores the copies in different physical locations, and acquires as much support documentation as possible. The DIVISION is also charged with making nonrestricted files available for reference services and secondary analysis. Divisional staff also assists other archival repositories in the establishment of machine-readable archives programs. In addition, the MRA has undertaken a joint project with the Social Policy and New Services Directorate of the Canadian Department of Communications in an effort to develop a publicly available online inventory of Canadian data files and data bases and to devise policies for the management, deposit, and maintenance of publicly funded machine-readable data files of archival and research value.

Scope and/or Subject Matter: All aspects of Canadian society, including national surveys of pay data, working conditions, labor force, prices, incomes, work ethics, and job satisfaction; nonmedical use of drugs; farm marketing data; federal election studies; and other areas.

Input Sources: Data are acquired from Canadian government departments, universities, business firms, organizations, agencies, and individuals.

Holdings and Storage Media: Two copies of all files are maintained on magnetic tape.

Publications: 1) Machine Readable Archives Bulletin (quarterly)—includes Division news and new acquisitions. 2) Catalogue of Holdings (biannual)—provides descriptive information on all processed files; indexed by title, principal investigator or organization, and subject. Both publications, as well as a brochure and a general guide to the Division, are available free of charge. Pamphlets on specific themes and based on Divisional holdings and occasional technical studies are also issued.

Microform Products and Services: Documentation manuals and data codebooks are available on microfiche.

Computer-Based Products and Services: Those machine-readable files that are not restricted are provided to responsible researchers in the form of complete tape copies, machine-readable extracts, or in hardcopy printouts. A limited amount of secondary analysis is also performed. The Division also maintains a partial Automated Inventory of Canadian Machine Readable Data Files covering more than 5000 files.

Other Services: In addition to services described above, referral services are also offered.

Clientele/Availability: Services are available to researchers on a cost-recovery basis.

Contact: Harold A. Naugler, Director, Machine Readable Archives Division.

★159★
CANADA
STATISTICS CANADA
CANADIAN SOCIO-ECONOMIC INFORMATION MANAGEMENT SYSTEM (CANSIM)
R.H. Coats Bldg., 9th Floor   Phone: (613) 995-7406
Tunney's Pasture   Service Est: 1967
Ottawa, ON, Canada K1A 0T6
W.M. Podehl, Director

Staff: 25 Total.

Description of System or Service: Serving as the official Statistics Canada vehicle for primary transmittal of machine-readable data to the public, the CANADIAN SOCIO-ECONOMIC INFORMATION MANAGEMENT SYSTEM (CANSIM) is a computerized information system for socioeconomic time series and multidimensional data acquired from Statistics Canada and other governmental and private sources. CANSIM is composed of three modules: 1) The Time Series module, offered to users as the CANSIM Main Base and Mini Base, contains current and historical time series from a broad range of interrelated socioeconomic fields. The Main Base constitutes all the time series data and accompanying software, and is available for online searching through remote terminals or as a batch service. The most widely used time series in the Main Base are also accessible as the CANSIM Mini Base through a nationwide network of secondary distributors. 2) The CANSIM Cross-Classified module is an online data base supplying multidimensional statistical aggregations of particular interest to social studies researchers. The structure of the system allows data of up to nine levels of cross-classification to be entered, stored, and retrieved. It permits the cross-tabulation and analysis of census social data with data on social phenomena in the fields of education, health, welfare, justice, and others. 3) The CANSIM Summary Data System module combines a data base containing user summary tape data from the 1976 and 1981 Canadian censuses with an interactive dialogue and an access system which allows selection, retrieval, and manipulation of summary data. Additionally, CANSIM data may be accessed via CANSIM's Telichart videotex service (see separate entry following this one).

Scope and/or Subject Matter: Major blocks of data are included for national accounts, prices, labor, agriculture, manufacturing and primary industries, capital and finance, construction, health and welfare, population, merchandising, transportation, and external trade.

Input Sources: CANSIM is updated daily with data from Statistics Canada, the Quebec Bureau of Statistics, Bank of Canada, and Health and Welfare Canada. Approximately 280 publications are represented in part or in full in the Time Series module. The Cross-Classified module comprises primarily data collected by Statistics Canada, and also includes information derived from the Canadian Census. The Summary Data System module contains data from the Canadian Census.

Holdings and Storage Media: The CANSIM Main Base holds 400,000 time series and the Mini Base contains 25,000 of these. The contents of the Mini Base are revised annually.

Publications: 1) CANSIM Main Base Series Directory—detailed guide giving title, start date, source of data, security level, updates, matrix notes, and other information on each series; 2) CANSIM Mini Base Series Directory. User manuals are also issued.

Computer-Based Products and Services: CANSIM data are available under the following options: 1) The Main, Mini, Cross-Classified, and Summary Data System data bases can be accessed online via remote terminal through Datacrown Limited, which is the host service bureau. Users may also arrange for special runs to be done by Datacrown, if they do not have their own terminals. 2) The Mini Base is available online through more than a dozen CANSIM secondary distributors with Statistics Canada ensuring standard data contents and software. The secondary distributor may add supplementary series from the Main Base in addition to those series contained in the Mini Base. 3) The CANSIM staff provides retrieval services from the Main Base and the Cross-Classified module on a cost-recovery basis. Data are available on tape or printout; manipulation programs that provide reporting, regression, modeling, forecasting, and plotting facilities are also available. 4) User Advisory Services, in regional offices of Statistics Canada, provides CANSIM retrieval services.

Access to CANSIM data bases is facilitated by several special software products. Retrieval from the Time Series data bases using CIS (CANSIM Interactive System) software provides a simple conversational means for obtaining a variety of output, ranging from standard preformatted tables to user-defined analytical reports. Retrieval packages such as TAP (CANSIM Table Analysis Package) and TABL (Table Batch Retrieval System) provide conversational sessions with the Cross-Classified data base and allow statistical manipulation and the preparation of reports and tables ready to print. The Summary Data System can aggregate tables, perform calculations, and produce customized printed reports according to the user's data and geographic specifications.

Clientele/Availability: Services are generally available with restrictions on redistribution of the data.

Contact: W.M. Podehl, Director, Canadian Socio-Economic Information Management System.

★160★
CANADA
STATISTICS CANADA
CANADIAN SOCIO-ECONOMIC INFORMATION MANAGEMENT SYSTEM (CANSIM)
TELICHART
R.H. Coats Bldg., 9th Floor   Phone: (613) 995-0575
Tunney's Pasture
Ottawa, ON, Canada K1A 0T6
W.M. Podehl, CANSIM Director

Description of System or Service: TELICHART is a videotex information service which allows the user to retrieve statistics from the CANSIM data base and display them in graphic form. The service provides interactive access to key Canadian economic and social indicators which can be formatted into color line graphs, bar charts, or point or surface chart forms. TELICHART requires simple commands to produce graphs and to perform time-series functions such as moving averages and indexing. The system is accessible online via Datapac using a Telidon terminal or personal computer with a videotex package.

Scope and/or Subject Matter: Retrieval and graphic display of Canadian statistical data.

Input Sources: Data are obtained from the CANSIM time series data base.

Computer-Based Products and Services: TELICHART offers interactive access to more than 5000 time series held in CANSIM data bases. Using a Telidon terminal or personal computer with a videotex package, users may access selected economic indicators, population statistics, Gross National Product data, selected social data, and a variety of other statistics. TELICHART calculates quarterly and annual totals and averages, moving averages, changes from previous period or year, percent changes from previous period or year, algebraic operations, linear regression or projection, and indexing or rebasing. Hardcopy output of TELICHART screen images may be transferred to printers linked to Telidon terminals. TELICHART software also allows storage of charts to make Telidon hard-copy slide presentations.

Clientele/Availability: Services are available without restrictions.

Contact: W.M. Podehl, Director, Canadian Socio-Economic Information Management System.

★161★
CANADA
TRANSPORT CANADA
LIBRARY AND INFORMATION CENTRE
2nd Floor, Tower C Phone: (613) 992-4529
Place de Ville Service Est: 1925
Ottawa, ON, Canada K1A 0N5
Serge G. Campion, Chief Librarian

Staff: 5 Information and library professional; 13 technicians; 10 clerical and nonprofessional.

Description of System or Service: The LIBRARY AND INFORMATION CENTRE provides Transport Canada employees with a variety of information services, including automated information retrieval and SDI through commercial and government online systems. It is also the focal point for the Canadian Transportation Documentation System, a computer-readable file covering documents and publications acquired by the Library and Information Centre and more than a dozen other Canadian transportation libraries. The System is used for interlibrary loans among participating libraries, and it is also publicly available online in Canada.

Scope and/or Subject Matter: Air, surface, and marine transportation.

Input Sources: Input is derived from books, periodicals, internal documents, translations, serials, conference proceedings, press releases, online data bases, and other relevant materials.

Holdings and Storage Media: The Documentation System contains 120,000 citations on machine-readable tapes and is updated quarterly. Library holdings include more than 100,000 books and documents; more than 400,000 reports on microfiche; subscriptions to more than 1800 periodicals; and a complete collection of Statistics Canada reports back to 1867 on microfiche as well as hard copy.

Microform Products and Services: The Library maintains on microfiche an author, title, and subject catalog of reports produced by the Department; location of the report is also given. Duplicates of microfiche documents are available for purchase.

Computer-Based Products and Services: The Canadian Transportation Documentation System data base (also known as OOT) is available online through CAN/OLE. The data base includes the coded portion of the Transport Canada Library's collection, comprising commercially published monographs received by the Library since 1978, nonrestricted Transport Canada documents, documents from other Transport Canada libraries, selected American and foreign documents, and Canadian government, university, and association publications. The citations in the data base can be accessed by holdings, title, author, organization, number, date, subject, form, and language indexes. The LIBRARY AND INFORMATION CENTRE will provide searches of the Documentation System data base for those without access to CAN/OLE; it also conducts searches using the following online systems: CAN/OLE, QL Systems Limited, IST-Informatheque Inc., DIALOG Information Services, Inc., and System Development Corporation (SDC).

Other Services: Additional services include manual literature searching, referrals, and photocopying.

Clientele/Availability: Services are free to Transport Canada personnel; charges are made to others.

Contact: Barbara Witt, Head, Communications and Public Services, Transport Canada Library and Information Centre. (Telex 053 3130 MOTOTT.) The electronic mail address on ENVOY 100 (Telecom Canada) is A.Huot or for interlibrary loans, ILL,OOT.

★162★
CANADA LAW BOOK LTD.
240 Edward St. Phone: (416) 773-6300
Aurora, ON, Canada L4G 3S9

Related Organizations: Canada Law Book Ltd. is the parent organization of Western Legal Publications Ltd., which is described in a separate entry in this volume.

Description of System or Service: CANADA LAW BOOK LTD. issues a variety of legal publications, including law reports, summaries, bulletins, journals, directories, law lists, and textbooks. Several of its publications are searchable online through QL Systems Limited as CAN/LAW. The major publications accessible via CAN/LAW include the following: 1) All-Canada Weekly Summaries, covering all civil cases tried in the Canadian federal and provincial court systems; 2) Canadian Criminal Cases, providing headnotes from Canadian criminal cases tried in the provincial and supreme courts; 3) Dominion Law Reports, comprising headnotes from all courts-of-record decisions in the common-law provinces and Canadian federal and supreme courts; and 4) Weekly Criminal Bulletin, providing summaries of judgments in all Canadian criminal cases.

Scope and/or Subject Matter: Canadian law.

Input Sources: Input is derived from court decisions and related publications.

Holdings and Storage Media: The online All-Canada Weekly Summaries data base covers more than 30,000 civil case decisions from 1977 to date. The Canadian Criminal Cases data base provides headnotes from more than 6000 decisions from 1971 to the present and is updated twice monthly. The Dominion Law Reports data base is also updated twice monthly and contains headnotes from more than 20,000 decisions handed down from September 1955 to date. The Weekly Criminal Bulletin data base summarizes more than 8000 decisions from October 1976 to the present.

Publications: 1) Canadian Criminal Cases; 2) Canadian Patent Reporter; 3) Dominion Law Reports; 4) Labour Arbitration Cases; 5) Land Compensation Reports; 6) Ontario Municipal Board Reports; 7) Ontario Reports; 8) All-Canada Weekly Summaries; 9) Weekly Criminal Bulletin; 10) Advocates' Quarterly; 11) Canadian Business Law Journal; 12) Criminal Law Quarterly; 13) Estates and Trusts Quarterly. In addition, abridgments, encyclopedias, directories, textbooks, and a statute service are published.

Computer-Based Products and Services: Information from All-Canada Weekly Summaries, Canadian Criminal Cases, Dominion Law Reports, and Weekly Criminal Bulletin is accessible as CAN/LAW through QL Systems Limited. CAN/LAW can be searched by any word or combination of words.

Other Services: Canada Law Book also offers a photocopy service.

Clientele/Availability: Services are available without restrictions.

Contact: M. Anne Foster, Director, CAN/LAW, Canada Law Book Ltd. The electronic mail address on QL Systems Limited is Box 100.

★163★
CANADA SYSTEMS GROUP (CSG)
FEDERAL SYSTEMS DIVISION
CANADIAN FEDERAL CORPORATIONS AND DIRECTORS DATA BASE (CFCD)
Product Sales Directorate Phone: (613) 563-4444
90 Sparks St., Suite 704
Ottawa, ON, Canada K1P 5B4

Related Organizations: CFCD is one of four Canada Systems Group data bases known collectively as Insight; it is produced from information collected by the Corporations Branch of Consumer and Corporate Affairs Canada.

Description of System or Service: The CANADIAN FEDERAL CORPORATIONS AND DIRECTORS DATA BASE (CFCD) is a computer-readable file providing information on more than 135,000 Canadian federally incorporated companies. The file includes such data as corporate names and addresses, details of incorporation, names and home addresses of corporate directors, and, when available, financial data from the last two years. The DATA BASE can be used to obtain a complete corporate profile on a corporation, to identify companies incorporated after a certain date, to obtain parent and subsidiary information on companies, to identify all corporations or directors in specific geographical areas, and for similar applications. CFCD is commercially available online, and Canada Systems Group offers a mailing label service from it.

Scope and/or Subject Matter: Canadian federally incorporated companies and their directors.

Input Sources: Information is collected by the Corporations Branch from forms completed by companies.

Holdings and Storage Media: The computer-readable CFCD Data Base contains more than 135,000 records.

Publications: A user manual is available.

Computer-Based Products and Services: The CANADIAN FEDERAL CORPORATIONS AND DIRECTORS DATA BASE is made commercially available online by Canada Systems Group. Mailing labels of either corporations or directors are also available by request from CSG. Each company is represented in CFCD by a unique record which is subdivided into formatted fields and named paragraphs. Data provided in the formatted fields include the following: incorporation date; dates of the last and previous fiscal years; and assets, revenues, and earnings as of last and previous fiscal years. Named paragraphs include such information as: present and former corporation names; mailing and registered office addresses of the corporation; Corporations Branch file number; names and home addresses of all directors of the corporation; subsidiary corporations; corporate names and amalgamation relationships; parent company; incorporation date and financial data; company status (active or inactive); act under which the company was formed; minimum, maximum, and current number of directors; and latest annual general meeting.

Clientele/Availability: Products and services are intended for users in the business and financial communities.

Contact: Marketing Representative, Federal Systems Division, Canada Systems Group.

★164★
CANADA SYSTEMS GROUP (CSG)
FEDERAL SYSTEMS DIVISION
CORPORATE NAMES DATA BASE (CNAM)
Product Sales Directorate   Phone: (613) 563-4444
90 Sparks St., Suite 704
Ottawa, ON, Canada K1P 5B4

Related Organizations: CNAM is one of four Canada Systems Group data bases known collectively as Insight; it is produced from information contributed by the Corporations Branch of Consumer and Corporate Affairs Canada and the corporations branches of provincial governments.

Description of System or Service: The CORPORATE NAMES DATA BASE (CNAM) is a commercially available online file providing summary information on approximately 2 million Canadian federal and provincial incorporations and business names, including the company name, date of incorporation, and the jurisdiction in which that company has been registered. The DATA BASE can be used to identify the existence of an incorporation or business name in Canada, to compare newly planned names to existing registered names, to identify jurisdictions in which companies operate, and to determine how long companies have been in business.

Scope and/or Subject Matter: Names of Canadian federal and provincial incorporations and businesses.

Input Sources: Input is derived from data collected by the federal and provincial corporations branches.

Holdings and Storage Media: The computer-readable CNAM Data Base contains approximately 2 million records.

Publications: A user manual is available.

Computer-Based Products and Services: The CORPORATE NAMES DATA BASE is made commercially available online by Canada Systems Group. Each corporate name is represented by one unique record which is subdivided into named paragraphs which include the following information: corporation name; reference number; jurisdiction indicating federal or provincial incorporation; incorporation date; Province of residence; status as an active or inactive entity under the incorporated name; status date indicating the date the company was last updated if active or cancelled if inactive; type of company (legal status as a business name, a proposed name, or an incorporation).

Clientele/Availability: Services are intended for researchers of corporate information.

Contact: Marketing Representative, Federal Systems Division, Canada Systems Group.

★165★
CANADA SYSTEMS GROUP (CSG)
FEDERAL SYSTEMS DIVISION
INTER-CORPORATE OWNERSHIP DATA BASE (CLRA)
Product Sales Directorate   Phone: (613) 563-4444
90 Sparks St., Suite 704
Ottawa, ON, Canada K1P 5B4

Related Organizations: CLRA is one of four Canada Systems Group data bases known collectively as Insight; it is produced from information collected by Statistics Canada.

Description of System or Service: The INTER-CORPORATE OWNERSHIP DATA BASE (CLRA) is a commercially available online file providing information on the structure of Canadian corporations. CLRA supplies the names of all holding and held companies (both domestic and foreign) in Canada as well as the respective ownership percentages in a tiered format, with each succeeding level of ownership indented.

Scope and/or Subject Matter: Ownership of Canadian corporations.

Input Sources: Input is derived from data collected by Statistics Canada under the Corporations and Labour Unions Returns Act.

Holdings and Storage Media: The computer-readable CLRA Data Base contains approximately 45,000 individual corporate structures.

Publications: A user manual is available.

Computer-Based Products and Services: The INTER-CORPORATE OWNERSHIP DATA BASE is made commercially available online by Canada Systems Group. CLRA records are subdivided into named paragraphs which are common to each record and include the following information: country of control; country of residence or province of the head office in Canada; SIC code; percentage of voting rights owned; level of ownership; name of investor, parent corporation, or owned corporation; names of companies which own the enterprise parent and their respective ownership percentages; name of the enterprise parent which is being invested in and which owns a percentage of the companies beneath it; names of all ownership relationships to other corporations.

Clientele/Availability: Services are intended for corporate executives, bankers, financiers, marketing managers, investors, and researchers.

Contact: Marketing Representative, Federal Systems Division, Canada Systems Group.

★166★
CANADA SYSTEMS GROUP (CSG)
FEDERAL SYSTEMS DIVISION
TRADE MARKS DATA BASE (TMRK)
Product Sales Directorate   Phone: (613) 563-4444
90 Sparks St., Suite 704
Ottawa, ON, Canada K1P 5B4

Related Organizations: TMRK is one of four Canada Systems Group data bases known collectively as Insight; it is produced from information collected by the Trade Marks Branch of Consumer and

Corporate Affairs Canada.

Description of System or Service: The TRADE MARKS DATA BASE (TMRK) is a commercially available online file providing information on more than 200,000 registered and pending marks. It includes the full text of all registered trademarks as well as the full text of trademark applications. The DATA BASE can be used to determine the existence of a trademark application or registration, to identify products or services covered by trademarks or applications, to identify all trademarks in specific categories, to identify pending and registered marks of a particular company or handled by a particular legal representative, and to identify trademarks due for renewal.

Scope and/or Subject Matter: Registered and pending trademarks in Canada.

Input Sources: Input is derived from information collected by the Trade Marks Branch.

Holdings and Storage Media: The computer-readable TMRK Data Base contains information on more than 200,000 trade marks.

Publications: A detailed user manual is available.

Computer-Based Products and Services: The TRADE MARKS DATA BASE is made commercially available online by Canada Systems Group. Each trademark is represented in the data base by one unique record which is subdivided into formatted fields and named paragraphs. Formatted fields include wordmark, design, certification mark, distinguishing guise marks, date the trademark was first used, and filing, priority, and registration dates. Named paragraphs include the following: registration number and date; application number and date; priority date; registered owner; agent or representative; trademark name; disclaimer; products or services for which the trademark is registered; basis of claim; associated marks; and footnotes.

Clientele/Availability: Services are available to users in need of trade mark information.

Contact: Marketing Representative, Federal Systems Division, Canada Systems Group.

★167★
CANADIAN AGRICULTURAL RESEARCH COUNCIL
INVENTORY OF CANADIAN AGRICULTURAL RESEARCH (ICAR)
Central Experimental Farm   Phone: (613) 995-9073
K.W. Neatby Bldg., Room 1133   Service Est: 1975
Ottawa, ON, Canada K1A 0C6
Dr. J.C. Rennie, Chairman

Staff: 1.5 Management professional; 1 technician; 1 clerical and nonprofessional.

Related Organizations: Related organizations include Agriculture Canada.

Description of System or Service: The INVENTORY OF CANADIAN AGRICULTURAL RESEARCH (ICAR) is a computer-readable compilation of data on research in Canada on agriculture, food, and related topics. ICAR provides current and retrospective coverage of more than 4200 project titles listed by commodity, function, and keywords. It is used in determining present levels of research activity and planning new or increased research. Information retrieval and report production are offered from the data base, and a version of ICAR is available online through CAN/OLE.

Scope and/or Subject Matter: Agriculture, food, and related research in Canada, regardless of source of funding.

Input Sources: Information is gathered by regional representatives across Canada who forward data from all establishments carrying out research in agriculture and related areas.

Holdings and Storage Media: The continuously updated ICAR data base is held in machine-readable form and contains data on more than 4200 projects.

Publications: A printed form of the Inventory is produced occasionally, as are summary tables.

Computer-Based Products and Services: The INVENTORY OF CANADIAN AGRICULTURAL RESEARCH contains research project information, including name, subject matter, location, research scientist's name, number of professional and technical person-years required, funding organizations, keywords, and other data. Information retrieval and report production services are available. A version of the ICAR data base is available online through CAN/OLE.

Clientele/Availability: Services are available without charge. Clients include scientists, administrators, research station managers, funding organizations, and others concerned with research and development in agriculture.

Contact: Cameron D. Laing, Chief, Inventory and Systems Unit, Canadian Agricultural Research Council. (Telex 053 3283.)

★168★
CANADIAN ASSOCIATION FOR INFORMATION SCIENCE/
ASSOCIATION CANADIENNE DES SCIENCES DE L'INFORMATION (CAIS/ACSI)
44 Bayswater Ave., Suite 100   Phone: (613) 725-0332
Ottawa, ON, Canada K1Y 4K3   Founded: 1970
Mary Frances Laughton, President

Description of System or Service: The CANADIAN ASSOCIATION FOR INFORMATION SCIENCE/ASSOCIATION CANADIENNE DES SCIENCES DE L'INFORMATION (CAIS/ACSI) promotes the advancement of information science in Canada by sponsoring an annual conference, issuing a variety of publications, and cooperating with related organizations.

Scope and/or Subject Matter: Production, manipulation, storage, retrieval, and dissemination of information.

Publications: 1) Canadian Journal of Information Science/ Revue Canadienne des Sciences de l'Information (annual)—contains articles on the advancement of information science in Canada; free to members and available by subscription to others. 2) CAIS/ACSI Newsletter (irregular)—provides news and information on CAIS/ACSI activities; free to members. 3) Proceedings of Annual Conferences. A catalog of publications is available by request.

Clientele/Availability: CAIS/ACSI offers regular, student, and institutional memberships.

Contact: Mary Frances Laughton, President, Canadian Association for Information Science/ Association Canadienne des Sciences de l'Information.

★169★
CANADIAN BROADCASTING CORPORATION (CBC)
PROJECT IRIS
Box 8478   Phone: (613) 731-3111
Ottawa, ON, Canada K1G 3J5   Service Est: 1981
R. O'Reilly, Office of Executive Vice President

Staff: 21 Information and library professional; 11 management professional; 4 technicians; 4 clerical and nonprofessional; 5 other.

Related Organizations: Project IRIS is a joint venture of the Canadian Broadcasting Corporation and the Canadian Department of Communications.

Description of System or Service: PROJECT IRIS (Information Relayed Instantly from the Source) has conducted field trials to evaluate the potential of teletext in Canada, and it continues to develop necessary technology and equipment in support of a national teletext service. In a field trial lasting from 1982 to 1984, PROJECT IRIS teletext services broadcast one French and two English language data bases of news, advertising, and other information throughout the 18-hour broadcast day. It distributed information via traditional broadcast transmitter to homes in Toronto and Montreal, and via satellite to homes in Calgary. Over the course of the three-year field trials, PROJECT IRIS located teletext decoders in more than 400 randomly selected homes and public locations. The field trials were used to evaluate the Canadian Broadcasting Corporation's capacity to use teletext to distribute information across Canada to general, select, and targeted public groups; to evaluate teletext as a tool to provide program support to existing CBC services, such as closed captioning for the hearing impaired; to evaluate public response to information content, presentation, and access time in order to plan future national and regional data bases; and to recommend proper action for the introduction and development of full teletext service in Canada. Beginning in 1984, efforts are being devoted to further develop applications of IRIS technology and related equipment in order to support a national service in both English and French. This follow-up developmental phase of PROJECT IRIS will last three years, and it includes the national transmission of two teletext magazines.

Scope and/or Subject Matter: Canadian national, regional, and local news and information; weather; sports; finance; advertising; arts and culture; entertainment; farming; agriculture; fishing; science; technology; and other areas.

Input Sources: Input is gathered from wire services, newspapers, news agencies, magazines, periodicals, textbooks, radio and television programs, and other sources. Teletext pages are generated by eight information provider systems and can be updated continuously.

Holdings and Storage Media: Project IRIS maintains two electronic magazines holding about 300 pages each.

Computer-Based Products and Services: PROJECT IRIS provides electronic access to two data bases of news, advertising, and other information which are transmitted throughout the broadcast day. PROJECT IRIS teletext pages are generated at national, regional, and local levels by eight information provider systems and are stored in the host computer. The host computer holds pages awaiting acceptance for broadcast, retains core pages and other select pages after transmission for future updates, and maintains a file of pages ready for transmission. Teletext pages ready for transmission are sent to the two national networks, and are available through all television transmitters across the country. PROJECT IRIS teletext pages are broadcast in cycles containing up to 300 pages in each service, and can be received by any television receiver in Canada that is equipped with a teletext decoder.

Clientele/Availability: Service is currently available to any Canadian home equipped with a decoder.

Contact: Marius Morais, Director, Project IRIS; telephone (514) 285-2614.

★170★
CANADIAN EDUCATION ASSOCIATION
CANADIAN EDUCATION INDEX (CEI) DATA BASE
252 Bloor St. W., Suite 8-200   Phone: (416) 924-7721
Toronto, ON, Canada M5S 1V5   Service Est: 1965
Maureen Davis, Editor

Staff: 1 Information and library professional; 1 clerical and nonprofessional; plus volunteer indexers.

Description of System or Service: The computer-readable CANADIAN EDUCATION INDEX (CEI) DATA BASE is used to produce a hardcopy subject and author index to Canadian periodicals, reports, and monographs written in French or English and dealing with current education concerns across Canada. The CEI DATA BASE is also utilized to prepare the Directory of Education Studies in Canada, an annual publication providing abstracts and indexing of research studies completed during the academic year by graduate students and staff in Canadian education institutions. Subject indexing for both publications uses the Canadian Education Subject Headings (CanESH) list.

Scope and/or Subject Matter: All aspects of education and related research in Canada.

Input Sources: Canadian education journals and monographs are scanned and indexed for the Canadian Education Index. Approximately 130 faculties of education, school boards, provincial departments of education, teachers' associations, and education organizations are surveyed for reports on completed studies for the Directory of Education Studies in Canada.

Holdings and Storage Media: The machine-readable CEI Data Base dates from 1976 to the present and holds records from both the Index and the Directory.

Publications: 1) Canadian Education Index/ Repertoire Canadien sur l'Education-CEI/RCE (three times per year including an annual cumulation)—each issue indexes 225 Canadian education periodicals and approximately 250 reports under 2000 subject headings; also includes an author index. 2) Directory of Education Studies in Canada/ Annuaire d'Etudes en Education au Canada (annual)—contains approximately 500 abstracts of research studies completed in Canada during the academic year; includes an author index. Both publications include a list of French subject headings which refer to equivalent English headings. 3) Canadian Education Subject Headings (CanESH)—issued periodically.

Computer-Based Products and Services: The CEI Data Base is currently used only for internal production purposes; it may be made available for searching in the future.

Clientele/Availability: Publications are available by subscription to anyone interested in Canadian education.

Remarks: The Canadian Education Association is also known as Association Canadienne d'Education.

Contact: Maureen Davis, Editor, Canadian Education Index.

★171★
CANADIAN ENGINEERING PUBLICATIONS LTD.
INFORMATION SERVICES DIVISION
111 Peter St., Suite 411   Phone: (416) 596-1624
Toronto, ON, Canada M5V 2W2   Service Est: 1965
Charles F. Broad, President

Staff: 1 Information and library professional; 1 management professional; 3 sales and marketing; 2 clerical and nonprofessional.

Description of System or Service: The INFORMATION SERVICES DIVISION produces the Canadian Catalog Service, a collection of vendor catalog data on Canadian industrial equipment, supplies, components, and services. The Catalog is produced quarterly and is available on microfilm. The DIVISION is also associated as a distributor with Information Handling Services, a division of Information Technology Group (ITG).

Scope and/or Subject Matter: Products and services of Canadian industrial vendors.

Input Sources: Input is obtained directly from vendors.

Holdings and Storage Media: Data are held on microform which is updated automatically.

Microform Products and Services: Canadian Catalog Service (quarterly)—available on 16mm cartridges.

Clientele/Availability: Clients include engineering departments and units of commercial and government organizations.

Contact: Charles F. Broad, President, Canadian Engineering Publications Ltd.

★172★
CANADIAN INFORMATION INDUSTRY ASSOCIATION (CIIA)
P.O. Box 9211   Phone: (613) 741-5274
Ottawa, ON, Canada K1G 3T9   Founded: 1980
Michael A. Dagg, President

Description of System or Service: The CANADIAN INFORMATION INDUSTRY ASSOCIATION (CIIA) is an organization of business enterprises engaged in the information industry on a profit-oriented basis. CIIA serves as a forum for communication and discussion and promotes public awareness of the industry.

Scope and/or Subject Matter: Canadian information industry.

Publications: CIIA Newsletter.

Clientele/Availability: Membership is open to for-profit information enterprises on an annual subscription basis.

Contact: Michael A. Dagg, President, Canadian Information Industry Association.

★173★
CANADIAN LAW INFORMATION COUNCIL (CLIC)
161 Laurier West   Phone: (613) 236-9766
Ottawa, ON, Canada K1P 5J2   Founded: 1973
Lois Dyer, Executive Director

Special Note: The above name, address, and telephone number have been verified for this edition, although no questionnaire response was received. The following text is reprinted from the 5th edition.

Staff: 24 Total.

Related Organizations: The Council is funded by government agencies and law societies.

Description of System or Service: The CANADIAN LAW INFORMATION COUNCIL (CLIC) is a nonprofit research and development organization concerned with the production, publication, dissemination, and use of legal information in hardcopy, microform, and machine-readable forms. Specific CLIC projects include preparation of indexes to Canadian statutory materials, production of computer-readable data bases, support of legal information service centers across Canada, and maintenance of a reference collection on the subject of computers and the law.

Scope and/or Subject Matter: Canadian legal information.

Input Sources: Input for CLIC data bases is derived from Canadian court decisions and other sources. CLIC also scans North American and European periodicals covering computers and the law.

Holdings and Storage Media: Several legal data bases are held in machine-readable form. CLIC also maintains a reference collection which includes 100 bound volumes, subscriptions to 46 periodicals, and an articles file.

Publications: 1) Summaries of Cases to be Heard by the Supreme Court of Canada. 2) Notes of Recent Decisions Rendered by the Immigration Appeal Board—includes keywords, brief statement of essential facts, issues, judicial history, and other information. 3) Regulatory Reporter—contains original language summaries of selected decisions of federal and provincial telecommunications, transportation, and energy regulatory agencies; includes cumulative subject index. 4) Canadian Directory of Public Legal Education and Information—includes national volume and separate provincial volumes; produced by the federal Department of Justice. 5) Bibliography of Canadian Law—contains 11,000 bibliographic entries for Canadian legal materials, with author and subject indexes. CLIC also publishes other guides and working papers, and distributes publications produced by Parliament and the Department of Justice.

Computer-Based Products and Services: The following data bases are produced by CLIC and made available online via QL Systems Limited: 1) Western Weekly Reports (WWR)—covers the period 1968 to the present; 2) Atlantic Provinces Reports (APR)—covers the period 1968 to the present; 3) Regulatory Reporter (CRR); 4) Manitoba Statute Citator (SMC). CLIC also maintains two machine-readable thesauri for British Columbia and Ontario statutes. CLIC provides computerized legal search services through 14 affiliated service centers across Canada.

Other Services: In addition to the services described above, CLIC offers consulting, holds conferences, sponsors research in legal information, provides computer-based instruction for law school students, and makes photocopies of the full text of any decision rendered by the Supreme Court of Canada, Federal Court of Appeal, Immigration Appeal Board, or tribunal decision summarized in the Regulatory Reporter.

Clientele/Availability: Services are available without restrictions; primary clients are lawyers and legal researchers.

Contact: Director, Computers and the Law, Canadian Law Information Council.

★174★
CANADIAN LIBRARY ASSOCIATION
CANADIAN PERIODICAL INDEX (CPI)
151 Sparks St. Phone: (613) 232-9625
Ottawa, ON, Canada K1P 5E3 Service Est: 1938
Sylvia Morrison, Editor

Staff: Approximately 10 total.

Description of System or Service: The CANADIAN PERIODICAL INDEX (CPI) is a computer-produced publication providing monthly subject and author access to Canadian periodicals.

Scope and/or Subject Matter: Complete coverage of Canadian periodicals, including the areas of business, economics, fine arts, literature, popular culture, and social sciences.

Input Sources: Approximately 138 Canadian periodicals in the English and French languages are indexed.

Holdings and Storage Media: CPI information is held in computer-readable form.

Publications: Canadian Periodical Index/ Index de Periodiques Canadiens (monthly, cumulated annually)—available by subscription. Subject and author index; each entry provides article title, author, codes denoting significant features of the article, journal title abbreviation, volume and issue numbers, page numbers, and date. Includes source list with publisher addresses. Annual cumulations dating from 1960 to the present are available.

Microform Products and Services: The Index is available on microfilm for the years 1938 to 1959.

Computer-Based Products and Services: The computer-based CPI data base is used for producing the publication and is currently only available to internal users.

Clientele/Availability: Clients include libraries and information services.

Contact: Sylvia Morrison, Editor, Canadian Periodical Index.

★175★
CANADIAN MICROGRAPHIC SOCIETY (CMS)
2175 Sheppard Ave. E., Suite 309 Phone: (416) 499-6552
Willowdale, ON, Canada M2J 1W8 Founded: 1967
Mr. R.A. Richmond, President

Description of System or Service: The CANADIAN MICROGRAPHIC SOCIETY (CMS) is a professional organization of micrographics users and supplier and service companies. CMS promotes the use of micrographics in Canadian business, disseminates information on micrographics, works for the educational needs of members, and represents the industry in questions of microform standards and law. The SOCIETY holds an annual conference and exposition, and publishes a magazine.

Scope and/or Subject Matter: All areas of micrographics.

Publications: MicroNotes (quarterly)—contains technical information, case histories, standards information, Society news of national interest, and vendor advertising; distributed to members, available to others by subscription.

Microform Products and Services: Back issues of MicroNotes since 1974 are available on microfiche.

Services: CMS activities are aimed at improving micrographic products and services in Canada by supplying members with information, holding seminars and supplier exhibitions, and representing the industry.

Clientele/Availability: CMS memberships are available on professional, corporate, and trade levels.

Contact: Jack H. Robson, Executive Director, Canadian Micrographic Society.

★176★
CAPITAL PLANNING INFORMATION LTD. (CPI)
6 Castle St. Phone: 031 2264367
Edinburgh, Scotland Founded: 1976
Brenda White, Director

Staff: 4 Information and library professional; 2 clerical and nonprofessional.

Description of System or Service: CAPITAL PLANNING INFORMATION, LTD. (CPI) provides information and consultancy services which include library planning, information systems design, contract research, and training of information staff. It also does abstracting and indexing, offers current awareness services, and conducts literature searching on request. Additionally, CPI publishes guides to sources of information.

Scope and/or Subject Matter: Information services, with specialization in planning, transport, environment, and small businesses.

Publications: The company publishes guides to sources of information.

Clientele/Availability: CPI serves local and central government agencies, industry, business, associations, and others.

Contact: Brenda White or Don Kennington, Directors, Capital Planning Information, Ltd. CPI also maintains an office at Stoneleigh, 49 Main St., Empingham, Leics. LE15 8PR, England; telephone 078 086663.

★177★
CARIBBEAN INDUSTRIAL RESEARCH INSTITUTE (CARIRI)
TECHNICAL INFORMATION SERVICE (TIS)
Tunapuna Post Office
Trinidad, Rep. of Trinidad and Tobago
Barbara Gumbs, Head
Phone: 663 4171
Service Est: 1970

Staff: 8 Information and library professional; 5 clerical and nonprofessional.

Related Organizations: The Technical Information Service receives financial assistance from the Organization of American States (OAS).

Description of System or Service: The TECHNICAL INFORMATION SERVICE (TIS) provides technical information to businesses, manufacturing and processing industries, service organizations, and government agencies in the Caribbean area through the following activities: manual and computerized literature searching, SDI, current awareness, query/response service, publications, and referrals.

Scope and/or Subject Matter: Analytical chemistry; industrial chemistry; food technology; microbiology; biochemistry; materials technology; chemical, electronic, mechanical, industrial, and civil engineering; information science; patents and copyright.

Input Sources: Input is derived from the following sources: commercial online systems, indexing and abstracting services, bibliographies, directories, industry profiles, standards and specifications, technical reports, and books.

Holdings and Storage Media: Library holdings number 25,000 bound volumes and subscriptions to 144 periodicals.

Publications: 1) Construction Cost Information Bulletin—produced in conjunction with the Quantity Surveyors Society of Trinidad & Tobago and the Central Statistical Office. 2) Accessions list (bimonthly). 3) Monographs on topics of scientific and technological interest.

Computer-Based Products and Services: TIS conducts searches of data bases available through commercial online services.

Clientele/Availability: Services are available to private and public sector organizations.

Remarks: CARIRI is a member of the World Association of Industrial and Technological Research Organizations (WAITRO).

Contact: Barbara Gumbs, Head, or Nirupa Oudit, Information Specialist, Technical Information Service. (Telex 3438 WG.)

★178★
CARLETON UNIVERSITY
DEPARTMENT OF SOCIOLOGY AND ANTHROPOLOGY
SOCIAL SCIENCE DATA ARCHIVES (SSDA)
Loeb Bldg., Rooms A711 & A713
Colonel By Dr.
Ottawa, ON, Canada K1S 5B6
Hyman Burshtyn, Director
Phone: (613) 231-7426
Service Est: 1966

Staff: 1 Management professional; 1 technician.

Description of System or Service: The SOCIAL SCIENCE DATA ARCHIVES (SSDA) was established to serve as a depository for data held by social science departments at Carleton University, as a documentation and dissemination center for these data, and as a liaison between students and faculty and other data banks and archives. Its primary objective is to make available data accessible to faculty and students, thereby facilitating and encouraging research in the social sciences. ARCHIVES holdings include both machine-readable and textual material in areas of interest. In addition, it has extensive listings of data held at most data banks and archives in North America and Western Europe. The ARCHIVES attempts to assist users in obtaining documentation and access to data held by other institutions and individuals. It will also consider requests, on an individual basis, for data analysis for outside users, and will undertake to clean data sets and create SPSS or BDMP system files.

Scope and/or Subject Matter: Social science data, including special collections in the areas of Canadian Native peoples, mental illness, language use, election studies, elites, political violence and dissent, international conflict, human rights policies, economic expansion policies, and Canadian public opinion surveys.

Input Sources: Data are obtained from campus researchers, Canadian Gallup Polls, the Inter-university Consortium for Political and Social Research at the University of Michigan, other educational institutions, and from various government and private sources.

Holdings and Storage Media: Machine-readable holdings include approximately 250 Canadian Gallup Poll surveys, conducted by the Canadian Institute of Public Opinion (CIPO) from 1945 to date; and about 350 other data sets. A library of relevant documents is also maintained.

Computer-Based Products and Services: SSDA acquires and maintains machine-readable data; disseminates selected data sets; performs statistical analyses of data; searches a keyworded index to Gallup Poll survey questions; cleans data sets; and creates SPSS and/or BMDP system files.

Other Services: In addition to the primary services of data collection and analysis, the ARCHIVES provides reference, referral, and consulting services and current awareness bulletins concerning new acquisitions. It also provides some educational services such as a series of seminars on secondary data analysis.

Clientele/Availability: Services are provided to researchers at outside institutions on an individual basis.

Contact: Wendy Watkins, Data Archivist, Social Science Data Archives.

★179★
CARLETON UNIVERSITY LIBRARY
CARLETON LIBRARY SYSTEM (CLS)
Colonel By Drive
Ottawa, ON, Canada K1S 5J7
Martin Foss, Associate University Librarian
Phone: (613) 231-6350
Service Est: 1979

Staff: 4 Information and library professional; 1 management professional; 3 technicians; 1 sales and marketing.

Description of System or Service: The CARLETON LIBRARY SYSTEM (CLS) is an integrated online library management system designed to support library functions in a time-sharing computing environment. The SYSTEM consists of two modules: CATSUP (Catalogue System Update Program) which provides for the creation and maintenance of bibliographic records online, and CUBE (Carleton University Bibliographical Enquiry), an online public access catalog facilitiy. CLS software is available for installation in other libraries.

Scope and/or Subject Matter: Online cataloging of serials and monographs in all subjects.

Input Sources: Input consists of derived cataloging from the U.S. Library of Congress, National Library of Canada, and other sources, plus original cataloging.

Holdings and Storage Media: The machine-readable CUBE data base contains approximately 600,000 bibliographic records in MARC format for monographs and serials held by the University Library. Library holdings include more than one million bound volumes, 6100 periodical subscriptions, and nearly two million microforms.

Publications: User documentation for CATSUP and CUBE and system software documentation are issued.

Microform Products and Services: An annual COM catalog of the Library's holdings is produced.

Computer-Based Products and Services: The CARLETON LIBRARY SYSTEM consists of CATSUP, a bibliographic data base of serial and monograph holdings, and CUBE, an online public access module. CUBE allows for the retrieval and display of records from CATSUP. Search elements include author, title, keyword or subject phrase, LCN, ISBN, ISSN, and call number. The CARLETON LIBRARY SYSTEM is publicly accessible upon application via the iNet Gateway, Datapac, or direct dial. CLS software is also available for installation in other libraries.

Other Services: The University Library conducts a CLS training course.

Clientele/Availability: Services are available to Carleton University staff and students as well as external users.

Projected Publications and Services: A circulation module is expected to be added to CLS.

Contact: Martin Foss, Associate University Librarian, Carleton University Library.

★180★
CAWKELL INFORMATION & TECHNOLOGY SERVICES LTD. (CITECH)
P.O. Box 5, Ickenham
Uxbridge, Middlesex UB10 8AF, England
Mr. A.E. Cawkell, Director
Phone: 0895 34327
Founded: 1981

Staff: 1 Information and library professional; 1 management professional; 1 clerical and nonprofessional.

Description of System or Service: CAWKELL INFORMATION & TECHNOLOGY SERVICES LTD. (CITECH) is an information technology consulting firm. It carries out projects on a retainer basis for organizations requiring assistance in information technology, including management problems, equipment selection and testing, system implementation, technical advice, indexing, and data collection. In addition to providing consulting services, it publishes Information Technology & People, a current awareness and reference source covering rapidly changing interrelated fields in sociotechnology, including information science, data bases, online services, office systems, networks, and videotex. CITECH also maintains a data base for in-house use.

Scope and/or Subject Matter: Information processing, telecommunications, videotex systems, office automation, microcomputer systems, electronic publishing and mail, and computer-based information and library services.

Input Sources: Input for the internal data base is derived from 25 periodicals and secondary sources.

Holdings and Storage Media: The computer-readable CITECH data base covers 6000 periodical articles.

Publications: Information Technology & People (monthly)—available by subscription. Each issue contains tutorials, in-depth reviews, and equipment, book, and conference reviews.

Computer-Based Products and Services: The computer-readable CITECH data base is held on a microcomputer for in-house purposes. Examples of CITECH projects completed or in progress include: feasibility of a microcomputer/ word processing system for journal publishing; a data collection project; advice on a computer-based information system; and an investigation of communications and computers in banking.

Clientele/Availability: Services are available without restrictions; clients are mainly large companies and research units in the United Kingdom and the United States.

Contact: Mr. A.E. Cawkell, Director, Cawkell Information & Technology Services Ltd.

★181★
CELLTECH LTD.
INFORMATION AND LIBRARY SERVICE
244-250 Bath Rd.
Slough SL1 4DY, England
Dr. Anita Crafts-Lighty, Information Manager
Phone: 0753 36162
Service Est: 1981

Staff: 2 Information and library professional; 1 management professional; 2 clerical and nonprofessional.

Description of System or Service: INFORMATION AND LIBRARY SERVICE abstracts and indexes periodical and other literature on biotechnology for inclusion in the computer-based digest service, Abstracts in BioCommerce (ABC), which covers the commercial aspects of and developments in specific areas of biotechnology. The INFORMATION AND LIBRARY SERVICE also provides full library and information services to Celltech Ltd. and its associate company, Boots-Celltech Diagnostics Ltd. Services include library access, loans, and computerized searching.

Scope and/or Subject Matter: Biotechnology, with a concentration on genetic engineering, monoclonal antibodies, immunoassays, industrial microbiology, and cell culture.

Input Sources: Input is derived from approximately 100 periodicals, newspapers, press releases, and company reports.

Holdings and Storage Media: The computer-readable Abstracts in BioCommerce data base holds 6000 digests covering 20,000 articles published from 1981 to the present. Information and Library Service maintains a collection of 4000 bound volumes, subscriptions to 250 periodicals, 1500 patents, and 1000 company reports.

Publications: Abstracts in BioCommerce (twice monthly)—each issue contains more than 100 abstracts citing approximately 300 separate articles. Abstracts are classified by company, research institute, national agency, and international agency. Each issue includes an index; a bound cumulative reference edition is produced quarterly which includes all abstracts published in the six previous editions along with annotations identifying additional citations identified since original publication. Abstracts in BioCommerce is coproduced with and can be ordered from IRL Press Ltd., P.O. Box 1, Eynsham, Oxford OX8 1JJ, England. In the U.S. order from IRL Press, 1911 Jefferson Davis Hwy., Suite 907, Arlington, VA 22202.

Microform Products and Services: Abstracts in BioCommerce is available on microfiche.

Computer-Based Products and Services: INFORMATION AND LIBRARY SERVICE maintains the bibliographic Abstracts in BioCommerce data base which covers literature in biotechnology fields. It also maintains a companion file of 5500 organization names and addresses. The data base is expected to be made publicly available online.

Clientele/Availability: Most services are available only to Celltech personnel.

Remarks: Celltech and Boots-Celltech Diagnostics offer a wide range of products and services to the biotechnology industry, including immunoassays, contract cell culture, DNA synthesis, and research.

Contact: Dr. Anita Crafts-Lighty, Information Manager, Celltech Ltd.

★182★
CENTENNIAL COLLEGE
BIBLIOCENTRE
80 Cowdray Court
Scarborough, ON, Canada M1S 4N1
Doug Wentzel, Director
Phone: (416) 299-1515
Service Est: 1968

Related Organizations: The Bibliocentre (also known as College Bibliocentre) receives support from the Ontario Ministry of Colleges and Universities, Applied Arts and Technology Branch.

Description of System or Service: Using the DOBIS/LIBIS library management system, the BIBLIOCENTRE acts as the central acquisitions processing, cataloging, and circulation facility for book and nonbook materials acquired by all Ontario community college resource centers and the Ryerson Polytechnic Istitute. It provides online access to an integrated data base supplying public catalog information as well as remote acquisitions and circulation control capabilities. BIBLIOCENTRE also produces regular microfiche catalogs as well as various computer tape and printout products.

Scope and/or Subject Matter: All subject areas and materials of interest to community college resource centers.

Input Sources: Cataloging data are obtained from the National Library of Canada, the U.S. Library of Congress, British National Bibliography, and through original cataloging.

Holdings and Storage Media: Bibliocentre online cataloging data bases include 600,000 unique title records and union holding data, plus 1.5 million bibliographic records from the National Library of Canada and the Library of Congress.

Microform Products and Services: COM catalogs are produced monthly or at a library's request; they are provided in four sequences: author, title, subject, and shelf list.

Computer-Based Products and Services: Accessible in French or English, BIBLIOCENTRE provides the following online functions: 1) Acquisitions—including vendor file, automated purchase order, fund accounting, order status, and receiving. 2) Circulation—including check-in, check-out, holds, reserves, blacklists, and fines. 3) Public catalog access. 4) Searching—by author, title, subject, publisher,

ISBN, LC number, call numbers, and other items. 5) Cataloging—including cross-references, authority structure, and derived cataloging. 6) Learning package information—data on learning packages distributed by BIBLIOCENTRE. Additionally, BIBLIOCENTRE produces catalog cards, microfiche catalogs, printouts, computer tapes, spine and barcode labels, and other products for participants.

Clientele/Availability: Services are supplied to community college resource centers in Ontario and Ryerson Polytechnic Institute.

Contact: Doug Wentzel, Director, Bibliocentre. (Telex 065 26229.)

★183★
CENTER FOR HISTORICAL SOCIAL RESEARCH
(Zentrum fur Historische Sozialforschung)
Greinstr. 2
D-5000 Cologne 41, Fed. Rep. of Germany
Phone: 0221 4704404
Founded: 1978

Staff: Approximately 13 total.

Related Organizations: The Center is associated with QUANTUM/Association for Quantification and Methods in Historical Social Research.

Description of System or Service: The CENTER FOR HISTORICAL SOCIAL RESEARCH promotes quantitative historical social research and supports interdisciplinary cooperation in this field of research. It provides data services for historical social research; furnishes information and documentation, including research inventories; undertakes special projects designed to foster quantitative historical social research; and issues data handbooks and a journal.

Scope and/or Subject Matter: Historical or process-produced data in the social sciences.

Holdings and Storage Media: The Center maintains a collection of 65 computer-readable data sets and associated documentation.

Publications: 1) Historical Social Research (quarterly)—available by subscription. International and interdisciplinary journal devoted to quantitative historical social science. Includes articles, QUANTUM news, book reviews, and conferences, as well as reports on availability of machine-readable data and the development of software. 2) Historisch-Sozialwissenschaftliche Forschungen—a series of data handbooks containing the results of quantitative historical social research.

Computer-Based Products and Services: The CENTER collects and disseminates machine-readable data sets.

Other Services: Additional services include consulting and referrals.

Clientele/Availability: Services are available to persons conducting social science research and to social science data users.

Contact: Dr. Herbert Reinke, Center for Historical Social Research.

★184★
CENTER FOR INDUSTRIAL CREATION
(Centre de Creation Industrielle - CCI)
DOCUMENTATION SERVICE
(Service Documentation)
Centre Georges Pompidou
F-75191 Paris Cedex 4, France
Marie-Claire Mayer, Information Professional
Phone: 01 2771233
Service Est: 1982

Staff: 11 Information and library professional; 1 clerical and nonprofessional.

Related Organizations: The Center for Industrial Creation is a department of the Centre National d'Art et de Culture Georges Pompidou.

Description of System or Service: The DOCUMENTATION SERVICE provides library and information services relating to industrial and urban design and architecture. It acquires, scans, abstracts, and indexes periodical articles, books, and other materials to prepare a monthly abstracts bulletin and the corresponding CECILE Data Base. The SERVICE conducts online searches of its data base and offers reference services.

Scope and/or Subject Matter: Industrial design, graphic design, architecture, and urban design.

Input Sources: Input for CECILE is derived from 300 periodicals, as well as books and microfilms.

Holdings and Storage Media: The Documentation Service maintains a library collection of 10,000 bound volumes; 100 periodical subscriptions; and photographs and other audiovisual materials. The computer-readable CECILE Data Base contains more than 32,000 references dating from 1973 to the present; it is updated monthly with approximately 700 new references.

Publications: Bulletin Mensuel d'Information du Centre de Creation Industrielle CCI—available by subscription; contains literature references and abstracts, news items, and conference and meeting announcements.

Computer-Based Products and Services: The DOCUMENTATION SERVICE maintains and conducts searches of the bibliographic CECILE Data Base, which is also publicly accessible online through Telesystemes Questel. Searchable fields in the data base include subject, author, title, source document, and language.

Clientele/Availability: Services are intended for architects, urban designers, students, government agencies, and users of the Centre Georges Pompidou.

Contact: Patrick Renaud, Information Professional, CCI Documentation Service.

★185★
CENTER FOR INTERNATIONAL PROSPECTIVE STUDIES
(Centre d'Etudes Prospectives et d'Informations Internationales - CEPII)
9, rue Georges Pitard
F-75015 Paris, France
Yves Berthelot, Director
Phone: 01 8426800
Founded: 1978

Staff: 7 Information and library professional; 1 management professional; 5 technicians; 7 clerical and nonprofessional; 27 other.

Related Organizations: CEPII was created as an affiliate of the Planning Commission of the French Prime Minister. The Club d'Information et de Reflexion sur l'Economie Mondiale (CIREM) was created by CEPII in 1981 in order to provide a place for study and for comparison of analyses and experiences concerning today's major international economic problems.

Description of System or Service: The CENTER FOR INTERNATIONAL PROSPECTIVE STUDIES (CEPII) gathers information and carries out studies on the future of the world economy, international trade, and foreign economies. In support of its activities, CEPII builds economic models, publishes studies, and maintains the machine-readable Harmonized Trade and World Economy Accounts (Comptes Harmonises sur les Echanges et l'Economie Mondiale - CHELEM) data banks, a series of files containing international trade and world economic data.

Scope and/or Subject Matter: World economy, international trade, foreign economies, economic models, and related topics.

Input Sources: Input for the CHELEM data banks is derived from United Nations organizations, the Organisation for Economic Co-Operation and Development (OECD), The World Bank, and the International Monetary Fund (IMF).

Holdings and Storage Media: The CHELEM data banks hold economic data since 1960 and are updated annually.

Publications: 1) Lettre du CEPII (8 per year)—each issue presents a brief analysis of one aspect of the world economy and reports news and developments of CEPII interests. 2) Economie Prospective Internationale (quarterly)—publishes studies undertaken by CEPII and proceedings from international colloquia. CEPII also publishes selected economic studies as separate works. CEPII publications are edited and distributed by La Documentation Francaise, 29-31 quai Voltaire, F-75340 Paris Cedex 7, France.

Computer-Based Products and Services: The CENTER FOR INTERNATIONAL PROSPECTIVE STUDIES maintains the machine-readable CHELEM data banks, which include the following files: International Trade—covers 71 product categories in 32 import areas and in 32 export areas for the years 1967 to date; Balance of Payments—covers 32 geographic areas and 112 accounts; Gross National Products—provides value and volume in dollars for 166 countries since 1960; National Accounts—provides value and volume in dollars for 32 geographic areas since 1960; World Demand—covers 55 categories of manufactured products since 1970. The CHELEM International Trade file is accessible for online searching through GSI-ECO. CEPII economic models include Sachem-Energy, an instrument of macroeconomic simulation, and Sachem-West, which describes the internal dynamics of leading Western economies.

Clientele/Availability: Products and services are available without restrictions. Chief users are economists and financial advisors.

Contact: For information about CEPII in general, contact Gerard Lafay, Deputy Director, CEPII. For information about CHELEM data banks, contact Anne-Marie Boudard, Data Banks Department, CEPII.

★186★
CENTER FOR RESEARCH AND STUDIES ON MEDITERRANEAN SOCIETIES
(Centre de Recherche et d'Etudes sur les Societes Mediterraneennes - CRESM)
Maison de la Mediterranee Phone: 42 230386
5, ave. Pasteur Founded: 1958
F-13100 Aix en Provence, France

Related Organizations: The Center is associated with the French National Center for Scientific Research/ Centre National de la Recherche Scientifique (CNRS), the University of Provence, and the University of Aix-Marseille III. It also conducts joint projects with outside organizations such as GIS Mediterranee.

Description of System or Service: The CENTER FOR RESEARCH AND STUDIES ON MEDITERRANEAN SOCIETIES (CRESM) provides research, information, and documentation services relating to contemporary North Africa. CRESM acquires and scans books, periodicals, and other published and unpublished literature covering the countries of Algeria, Libya, Morocco, and Tunisia; maintains the resulting bibliographic information in a computer-readable data base known as Maghreb; and uses it to produce an annual publication and to offer information retrieval and reference services.

Scope and/or Subject Matter: Contemporary North Africa (Algeria, Libya, Morocco, and Tunisia), including social, economic, political, cultural, and geographic aspects.

Input Sources: Input to the Maghreb Data Base is derived from books, periodicals, reports, and theses.

Holdings and Storage Media: The computer-readable Maghreb Data Base covers more than 12,000 documents published since 1978. The Center's library maintains a collection of 20,000 bound volumes and subscriptions to 200 periodicals.

Publications: 1) Yearbook of North Africa/ L'Annuaire de l'Afrique du Nord—available for purchase. 2) CRESM Newsletter/ Les Nouvelles du CRESM. The Center also publishes a variety of reports and other publications.

Computer-Based Products and Services: The CENTER FOR RESEARCH AND STUDIES ON MEDITERRANEAN SOCIETIES maintains the computer-readable Maghreb Data Base and uses it to provide information retrieval and reference services. The Data Base is stored on a university computer center and may be made available online throughout France.

Clientele/Availability: Primary users are researchers and educators.

Contact: Jean-Jacques Regnier or V. Michel, Center for Research and Studies on Mediterranean Societies.

★187★
CENTER FOR SCIENTIFIC AND TECHNICAL RESEARCH FOR THE METAL MANUFACTURING INDUSTRY
(Centre de Recherches Scientifiques et Techniques de l'Industrie des Fabrications Metalliques - CRIF)
FABRIMETAL
21, rue des Drapiers Phone: 02 5112370
B-1050 Brussels, Belgium

Special Note: No questionnaire response was received for this entry for the 6th edition. The entry is reprinted as it appeared in the 5th edition.

Description of System or Service: FABRIMETAL provides information and documentation services in the fields of materials science, welding, and plastics. It indexes relevant international scientific and technical literature for input to its ATO (Apercu Technique-Technisch Overzicht) data base and preparation of a corresponding bibliographic bulletin. FABRIMETAL also offers monthly SDI services, retrospective searching of its data base, and document delivery.

Scope and/or Subject Matter: Materials science, including welding and plastics forming processes.

Input Sources: Input is derived from more than 300 journals, and from the ISMEC, CETIM, and PASCAL data bases.

Holdings and Storage Media: The computer-readable ATO data base includes 25,000 references to welding literature dating from 1969 to the present, and 70,000 references to the literature of plastics forming processes dating from 1960 to the present.

Publications: Fabrimetal—bibliographic bulletin.

Computer-Based Products and Services: Online retrospective searches of the ATO data base are conducted by title, author, source, language, and keywords. SDI is available by subscription.

Clientele/Availability: Services are available on a subscription or fee basis.

Contact: Center for Scientific and Technical Research for the Metal Manufacturing Industry.

★188★
CENTER FOR STUDY AND RESEARCH OF THE HYDRAULIC BINDERS INDUSTRY
(Centre d'Etudes et de Recherches de l'Industrie des Liants Hydrauliques - CERILH)
DOCUMENTATION CENTER
(Centre de Documentation)
INTERCIM CEMENT DATA BASE
(INTERCIM Base de Donnees Cimentieres)
23, rue de Cronstadt Phone: 01 5311810
F-75015 Paris, France Service Est: 1969
Walter Rothlauf, Chief

Staff: 5 Information and library professional; 9 management professional; 42 technicians; 19 clerical and nonprofessional.

Related Organizations: CERILH receives support from the French Ministry of Industry and Research and the French cement industries.

Description of System or Service: The INTERCIM CEMENT DATA BASE is an international bibliographic data base providing references to literature on hydraulic binders and cement. It is used by the Documentation Center to provide computerized search services and it is commercially available online. A related printed publication that also includes abstracts is produced as well.

Scope and/or Subject Matter: Hydraulic binders, cement, Beton concrete, and their methods of testing, control, and production.

Input Sources: Input is obtained from worldwide periodicals, books, conference proceedings, standards, and patents.

Holdings and Storage Media: The computer-readable INTERCIM Cement Data Base holds approximately 20,000 references from 1969 to the present and is updated monthly, with 1500 records added per year. Library holdings include 1800 bound volumes, subscriptions to more than 100 periodicals, and approximately 5500 patents, standards, and other materials.

Publications: 1) Bulletin Analytique du Centre de Documentation du CERILH (monthly)—includes French-language abstracts with author and materials indexes. 2) Thesaurus des Liants Hydrauliques—available for purchase. The Documentation Center also issues a number of technical reports and a catalog of available translations.

Computer-Based Products and Services: The INTERCIM CEMENT DATA BASE is available online through Telesystemes Questel. Retrospective searches of the data base are available from the Documentation Center. Data elements present include the following: document number; article title in English, French, and German; other title; author; source reference; language of document; and French-language descriptors. The Documentation Center also performs computerized searches of external data bases.

Other Services: Additionally, the Documentation Center provides document delivery and translation services for publications cited in the Data Base. CERILH also organizes training courses, conferences, and symposia, and acts as the official standardization office for cement.

Clientele/Availability: Services from the Documentation Center are available without restrictions.

Remarks: The INTERCIM Cement Data Base is also known as CIM.

Contact: Walter Rothlauf, Chief, Documentation Center, Center for Study and Research of the Hydraulic Binders Industry. (Telex 250302 CERILH PUBLI/BTI.)

★189★
CENTER FOR THE STUDY OF ADVERTISING SUPPORT
(Centre d'Etude des Supports de Publicite - CESP)
32, ave. Georges-Mandel
F-75116 Paris, France
J. Antoine, General Manager
Phone: 01 5532210
Founded: 1956

Staff: 8 Information and library professional; 4 technicians; 5 clerical and nonprofessional.

Description of System or Service: The CENTER FOR THE STUDY OF ADVERTISING SUPPORT (CESP) conducts general surveys of French mass media audiences as well as specific surveys of special audiences such as youth. It makes the collected data available in annual publications and in computer-readable form.

Scope and/or Subject Matter: Audience survey data for French newspapers, radio, television, and other media.

Input Sources: CESP acquires data through original surveys.

Holdings and Storage Media: Data are held in machine-readable form.

Publications: CESP issues annual volumes containing survey data for the various media.

Computer-Based Products and Services: CESP media audience data are available on magnetic tape to subscribers in France. They can also be accessed as the Media P Data Bank available online through Compagnie Internationale de Services en Informatique (CISI). Data items include the respondent's age, sex, education, occupation, locality, and housing.

Clientele/Availability: Access to CESP data is limited to member subscribers. Membership is open to advertising agencies, industrial firms, and similar organizations.

Contact: Beatrice Le Sourd, Survey Technician, Center for the Study of Advertising Support.

★190★
CENTER FOR THE STUDY ON INFORMATION SYSTEMS IN GOVERNMENT
(Centre d'Etudes des Systemes d'Information des Administrations - CESIA)
122, ave. de Hambourg
F-13008 Marseille, France
Jean Salmona, Director General
Phone: 91 739018
Founded: 1982

Staff: 120 Total.

Description of System or Service: Through its library, the CENTER FOR THE STUDY ON INFORMATION SYSTEMS IN GOVERNMENT (CESIA) collects, abstracts, and indexes various types of documents on information systems and government from France, the United States, Canada, Japan, and developing countries. It maintains this information in the computer-readable bibliographic REDOSI data base and makes it commercially available online. CESIA also provides access to the original documents abstracted.

Scope and/or Subject Matter: Information systems as they apply to the public sector; new informatics technologies; information and development.

Input Sources: Reports, periodicals, conference proceedings, guides, directories, and reference manuals are collected for input.

Holdings and Storage Media: The computer-readable REDOSI data base contains 6000 citations with abstracts, dating from 1974 to the present. It is updated twice per month, with approximately 1200 items added per year.

Computer-Based Products and Services: The REDOSI data base is accessible online via Telesystemes Questel. It contains bibliographic references plus summaries in French to documents on information systems and informatics applications in administration. Searchable data elements include French or English article title, author and affiliation, document type, language, journal or conference title, date, abstract, and others. Available with the data base is an online geographic thesaurus and a glossary which includes compounded terms to facilitate retrieval.

Clientele/Availability: Clients include government organizations and others.

Remarks: CESIA's data base was formerly maintained by the Centre d'Etudes et d'Experimentation des Systemes d'Information (CEESI).

Contact: Francois Belleudy, Librarian, Center for the Study on Information Systems in Government.

★191★
CENTER FOR TRANSLATION DOCUMENTATION
(Centre de Preparation Documentaire a la Traduction - CPDT)
16, rue Beaurepaire
F-75010 Paris, France
Gerard Pierson, President
Phone: 01 2088632
Founded: 1973

Staff: 1 Information and library professional; 3 management professional.

Description of System or Service: The CENTER FOR TRANSLATION DOCUMENTATION (CPDT) encourages the development of glossaries and similar tools to be used in translation work. In support of its goal, the CENTER maintains a machine-readable bibliographic data base covering published works on various translation and linguistic topics.

Scope and/or Subject Matter: Language, mainly scientific and technical, but also including colloquialisms, slang, and neologisms; translation; linguistics.

Holdings and Storage Media: The Center maintains a collection of several thousand volumes and a machine-readable data base.

Publications: Monographs are issued in five series.

Microform Products and Services: CPDT makes available publications in microform.

Computer-Based Products and Services: The CENTER FOR TRANSLATION DOCUMENTATION maintains CEDATAH (Collection des Etudes Documentaires Appliquees a la Traduction Automatique et Humaine), a machine-readable data base covering publications on various topics relating to translation and linguistics.

Other Services: Consulting services are also available.

Clientele/Availability: Primary clients are translators.

Contact: Gerard Pierson, President, Center for Translation Documentation.

★192★
CENTER OF EXPERIMENTAL METALLURGY
(Centro Sperimentale Metallurgico SpA)
IRON AND STEEL DOCUMENTATION SERVICE
(Reperimento Documentazione Siderurgica - RDS)
Via di Castel Romano
I-00100 Rome, Italy
Dr. Carlo Pagliucci, Head
Phone: 06 6495223
Service Est: 1965

Staff: 20 Total.

Description of System or Service: The IRON AND STEEL DOCUMENTATION SERVICE (RDS) maintains the computer-readable RDS Data Base, which contains abstracts of literature dealing with iron and steel published since 1965. The SERVICE offers computerized information retrieval services from the file.

Scope and/or Subject Matter: Iron and steel.

Input Sources: Input is derived from published literature.

Holdings and Storage Media: The computer-readable RDS Data Base holds citations and abstracts dating from 1965 to the present.

Computer-Based Products and Services: The IRON AND STEEL DOCUMENTATION SERVICE maintains and conducts searches of the bibliographic RDS Data Base.

Clientele/Availability: Clients include metallurgical professionals.

Contact: Dr. Carlo Pagliucci, Head, or Ing. Alessandro Sabatini, Iron and Steel Documentation Service.

★193★
CENTRAL AMERICAN RESEARCH INSTITUTE FOR INDUSTRY
(Instituto Centro Americano de Investigacion y Tecnologia Industrial - ICAITI)
DIVISION OF DOCUMENTATION AND INFORMATION
Apdo. Postal 1552   Phone: 310631/5
Avenida la Reforma 4-47, Zona 10   Founded: 1961
Guatemala, Guatemala
Ms. Rocio M. Marban, Head

Staff: 5 Information and library professional; 1 technician; 3 clerical and nonprofessional.

Description of System or Service: The DIVISION OF DOCUMENTATION AND INFORMATION supports the research and consulting activities of the Central American Research Institute for Industry. Services of the DIVISION include answering inquiries from the industrial community, offering courses and seminars on information services, and conducting manual and computerized literature searches. The DIVISION also coordinates the development of information services to industry under an Organization of American States (OAS) program aimed at Central American and Dominican Republic industries. Additionally, it maintains a data base of national and regional standards of Central America, develops software for a computer-based regional union list of serials, and publishes a thesaurus for industrial information.

Scope and/or Subject Matter: Information of interest and use to industry, including standards and patents.

Input Sources: The Division utilizes print, microform, and computerized sources of information.

Holdings and Storage Media: The Division maintains computer-readable files covering Central American standards and patents. Library holdings consist of 15,000 bound volumes; microforms; and subscriptions to 300 periodicals.

Publications: 1) Tesauro de Informacion Industrial - Centro America y Republica Dominicana—keyword listing of descriptors. 2) Estudio de Usarios de Informacion Industrial—study of industry users of information.

Computer-Based Products and Services: The DIVISION maintains a computer-readable data base covering national and regional standards in Central America, and is developing a data base for Central American patents. In addition, it offers online searching using data bases made available through DIALOG Information Services, Inc., System Development Corporation (SDC), and Telesystemes Questel. The DIVISION also develops software for information work.

Other Services: Additional services include consulting and referrals.

Clientele/Availability: Services are provided to ICAITI staff, entrepreneurs, government agencies, and university students; fees are charged to most outside users.

Contact: Ms. Rocio M. Marban, Head, Division of Documentation and Information.

★194★
CENTRAL ELECTRONIC NETWORK FOR DATA PROCESSING AND ANALYSIS
(Centri Elettronici Reteconnessi Valutazione Elaborazione Dati - CERVED)
Corso Stati Uniti, 14   Phone: 49 760733
I-35100 Padova, Italy

Special Note: The above name, address, and telephone number have been verified for this edition, although no questionnaire response was received. The following text is reprinted from the 5th edition.

Description of System or Service: The CENTRAL ELECTRONIC NETWORK FOR DATA PROCESSING AND ANALYSIS (CERVED) was established by Italian chambers of commerce to implement an information processing network for the management of a national register of companies operating in Italy. It is also responsible for other national and international market information systems as part of its overall goal to provide Italian business enterprises with better information about the environment in which they operate. CERVED maintains a number of computerized registers and other files, and makes these available online over the Euronet DIANE communications network.

Scope and/or Subject Matter: Business and commercial information of interest to Italian companies.

Computer-Based Products and Services: CERVED maintains and provides online access to the following data bases: 1) SANI—register of 2 million Italian industrial, commercial, trade, and agricultural companies. 2) IBIS—covers more than 150,000 manufacturing and distribution companies in about 130 countries; provides founding year, number of employees, activities, and products. 3) ITIS—economic data on nearly 100 countries, including general economic survey, statistical data, import regulations, and development plans. 4) SANP—national Italian defaulters file containing five years of credit data on companies and individuals for checking by banks and financial institutions. 5) SDOE—information on Italian import-export companies including a register of products handled. 6) SDOI—international supply and demand file containing data on goods and services including tenders, joint venture proposals, new technologies, and other information. 7) SIBB—index to Italian official acts regarding joint stock companies.

Clientele/Availability: Services are intended for Italian business enterprises.

Contact: Mr. A. Abati, Central Electronic Network for Data Processing and Analysis (CERVED).

★195★
CENTRAL ONTARIO REGIONAL LIBRARY SYSTEM (CORLS)
INTERLIBRARY LOAN AND COMMUNICATION SYSTEM (ILCS)
129 Church St., S.   Phone: (416) 884-4395
Richmond Hill, ON, Canada L4C 1W4   Service Est: 1982
Rosemary Kavanagh, Coordinator of Systems

Staff: 1 Information and library professional; 2 technicians; 2 clerical and nonprofessional.

Related Organizations: The Central Ontario Regional Library System is funded by the Province of Ontario.

Description of System or Service: The INTERLIBRARY LOAN AND COMMUNICATION SYSTEM (ILCS) is a communication network for 20 autonomous public libraries in Ontario which allows the libraries to share resources and maintain a record of their activities. ILCS provides four main functions—interlibrary loan, film booking, circulation, and electronic mail—and maintains computer-readable data bases in support of each activity. ILCS directs interlibrary loan requests entered into the SYSTEM through the network of libraries, permitting only one library at a time to select a loan request for searching. Once a request is selected, the SYSTEM receives a command to either fill the request, allow a reserve if the lending library has the requested item but it is out on loan, or release the request which continues on to the other libraries. ILCS channels outstanding requests back to the issuing library where requests may be canceled or forwarded to the Central Ontario Regional Library System for redirection to locations outside the region. ILCS facilitates loans of print and audiovisual materials which are individually owned or cooperatively and regionally owned. ILCS allows cooperatively owned materials to be automatically booked; individually owned materials require confirmation from the lending library. In addition, ILCS provides a number of reports which monitor activity and indicate the performance of each library within the network.

Scope and/or Subject Matter: Interlibrary loans and other library resource sharing applications.

Input Sources: Input consists of information on interlibrary loan requests, acquisitions, and cooperatively owned materials.

Holdings and Storage Media: The System maintains bibliographic data bases in machine-readable form.

Computer-Based Products and Services: The INTERLIBRARY LOAN AND COMMUNICATION SYSTEM is maintained on a main computer located at the Central Ontario Regional Library System. ILCS is accessed by individual libraries equipped with a video display terminal, high-speed modem, and printer. The SYSTEM can be accessed by seven libraries simultaneously via the Bell Canada Datapac Network. The SYSTEM supports the following library functions: 1) Interlibrary loan—stores and displays all interloan requests from each library in the Central Ontario Regional Library System; a data base of library requests is created daily. 2) Film booking—stores titles and record numbers for cooperatively owned films and displays a calendar for each film which is used to automatically book each title. 3) Circulation—stores all titles and record numbers for audiovisual materials held at CORLS. The circulation data base is used by libraries to determine availability of items, schedule loans of materials on the shelf, or reserve items. 4) Electronic mail—stores and directs mail messages to one or more specific locations. ILCS also generates reports which detail each library's activity on the SYSTEM and provides statistics about the type of material requested.

Clientele/Availability: Services are available to participating libraries in central Ontario.

Contact: Rosemary Kavanagh, Coordinator of Systems, Central Ontario Regional Library System.

★196★
CENTRE FOR THE STUDY OF DEVELOPING SOCIETIES
DATA UNIT
29 Rajpur Rd. Phone: 231190
Delhi 110054, India Service Est: 1963
Dr. V.B. Singh, Research Associate

Staff: 1 Information and library professional; 1 management professional; 4 clerical and nonprofessional.

Description of System or Service: The DATA UNIT is responsible for the processing of data collected through large-scale surveys conducted by the Centre for the Study of Developing Societies (CSDS), compilation of data sets from various secondary sources, and production of data source material pertaining to socioeconomic and political conditions in India.

Scope and/or Subject Matter: Socioeconomic, demographic, and attitudinal dimensions of voters, leaders, and bureaucrats, focusing primarily on social and political change in India and other selected countries.

Input Sources: Data are obtained from surveys using a variety of sampling techniques, including purposive, stratified random sample, random sample, and universe.

Holdings and Storage Media: The Data Unit maintains more than 30 data sets on computer tape and cards. It also has holdings of code books, marginals, and other semi-processed data.

Computer-Based Products and Services: The Data Unit collects, stores, and provides secondary analysis of survey data.

Other Services: Consulting services are also available.

Clientele/Availability: Clients include research scholars and students.

Projected Publications and Services: A data source book on Indian elections is planned.

Contact: Shankar Bose, Research Associate, Data Unit.

★197★
CENTRE OF INFORMATION RESOURCE & TECHNOLOGY, SINGAPORE (CIRTS)
170, Upper Bukit Timah Rd. Phone: 4684192
No. 05-08 Founded: 1982
Singapore 2158, Republic of Singapore
Ernest Kwan-Boon Tan, Director

Staff: 5 Information and library professional; 2 management professional; 1 technician; 1 sales and marketing; 2 clerical and nonprofessional.

Description of System or Service: The CENTRE OF INFORMATION RESOURCE & TECHNOLOGY, SINGAPORE (CIRTS) was established to assist small- and medium-scale enterprises in Southeast Asia to modernize. CIRTS utilizes a variety of local and international resources, including online data bases, to provide information retrieval and current awareness services. It offers industrial consulting services aimed at solving problems associated with management and technological upgrading, and assessing and choosing new technologies. CIRTS provides a number of services in the area of business development, including identifying new technologies and organizing technology exchange programs. Additionally, the CENTRE offers training and skills development services.

Scope and/or Subject Matter: Science, technology, biotechnology, engineering, medicine, business and management, law, and other topics.

Input Sources: Information is obtained from international and local data bases, research and development institutes and technology centers worldwide, and contacts with foreign counterpart consulting groups.

Holdings and Storage Media: CIRTS maintains a library of 300 bound volumes, subscriptions to 110 periodicals, and other holdings.

Computer-Based Products and Services: The CENTRE OF INFORMATION RESOURCE & TECHNOLOGY, SINGAPORE conducts online searches of more than 200 data bases and offers SDI services. The CENTRE also maintains an internal data base on the topic of biotechnology.

Clientele/Availability: Services are available without restrictions. Chief clientele includes professional groups and associations, and individuals in Southeast Asia.

Contact: Ernest Kwan-Boon Tan, Director, Centre of Information Resource & Technology, Singapore. (Telex RS 35663.)

★198★
CHARITIES AID FOUNDATION (CAF)
INFORMATION SERVICES
48 Pembury Rd. Phone: 0732 356323
Tonbridge, Kent TN9 2JD, England
John B.C. Bennett, Head

Related Organizations: Charities Aid Foundation is affiliated with the Foundation Center in New York City.

Description of System or Service: The purpose of the INFORMATION SERVICES of the Charities Aid Foundation is to encourage effective giving by making necessary information available to donors, beneficiaries, and the general public. The SERVICES collects, collates, and disseminates information on the charitable world through publications, inquiry answering, and referrals. It is currently implementing a computer-readable data base to provide rapid retrieval and selective information from its collection of information on charitable organizations.

Scope and/or Subject Matter: All aspects of charities, particularly the fiscal areas; emphasis is on United Kingdom, European, and American philanthropy.

Input Sources: The Services acquires reports and accounts information directly from charities.

Holdings and Storage Media: Directory information is held in computer-readable form. Library holdings include hundreds of bound volumes; subscriptions to 30 periodicals; 4000 charity reports; 5000 press clippings; and a register of more than 50,000 charitable purposes.

Publications: 1) Charity Statistics (annual)—contains statistics tables and commentaries on the top 200 grantmaking trusts, charities, and corporate donors. 2) Directory of Grant-Making Trusts (every 2 years)—provides classified information on grants made by approximately 2400 U.K. charitable trusts. 3) Charitable Deeds of Covenant—contains full, detailed guidance on covenants and their administration. 4) Directories of Charitable Needs—new series detailing the organizations in particular fields of charity. 5) Tax and Charities—outlines the main tax concessions for charities and for donors to charity. 6) Charity (monthly)—magazine covering matters related to charitable giving. A users manual, conference reports, explanatory literature, leaflets, and occasional papers are also published.

Computer-Based Products and Services: The INFORMATION SERVICES is implementing a computer-readable data base which will provide information on approximately 100,000 charitable organizations.

Clientele/Availability: Clients include corporate and individual donors, charities, the media, and other groups.

Contact: John B.C. Bennett, Head, Information Services, Charities Aid Foundation. The Foundation's London Information Office is located at 12 Crane Court, Fleet St., London EC4A 2JJ, England; telephone 01-583 7772.

★199★
CHEM SYSTEMS INTERNATIONAL LTD.
28 St. James's Square
London SW1Y 4JH, England
Alan D. Plaistowe, Chairman
Phone: 01-839 4652
Founded: 1964

Staff: 2 Information and library professional; 6 management professional; 18 clerical and nonprofessional; 16 other.

Related Organizations: Chem Systems Inc. of Tarrytown, New York is the parent organization of Chem Systems International Ltd.

Description of System or Service: CHEM SYSTEMS INTERNATIONAL LTD. provides chemical engineering consultancy and information services required for conceiving, planning, and implementing new projects. Its services include market research and other commercial development functions, feasibility and project planning capabilities, laboratory research and development, process engineering, computer applications, and project management. The company also compiles and publishes numerous multiclient studies. In support of its activities, CHEM SYSTEMS scans literature, searches commercially available data bases, and maintains an in-house data base.

Scope and/or Subject Matter: Chemistry, energy, chemical engineering, plastics, resins, rubber, textiles, refining.

Input Sources: Chem Systems scans periodicals, library acquisitions lists, and advertising material; collects books, press clippings, trade literature, reports, and periodicals; and accesses online data bases.

Holdings and Storage Media: A machine-readable data base is maintained. Library holdings include 1000 bound volumes; subscriptions to 100 periodicals; and internally produced reports.

Publications: Among the numerous multiclient studies issued by Chem Systems are the following: 1) Petrochemical Manufacturing and Market Trends-PMM (annual in two parts). 2) Petroleum and Petrochemical Economics in Europe-PPE (annual in two parts). 3) Process Economics Research Planning-PERP (annual). 4) Quarterly Petrochemical Business Analysis. 5) Chemical Process Economics. A complete list of studies is available by request from the firm.

Computer-Based Products and Services: Chem Systems International maintains a machine-readable data base for internal use. It also conducts searches of data bases carried by DIALOG Information Services, Inc., System Development Corporation (SDC), ESA/IRS, Data-Star, Pergamon InfoLine Ltd., and Unilever EPCA trade statistics data base. A Prestel set is also used.

Other Services: In addition to services described above, conferences and referrals are provided.

Clientele/Availability: Most services are offered worldwide to the gas, oil refining, and petrochemical industries.

Contact: Hilary Nunn, Information Officer, Chem Systems International Ltd. (Telex 916636.)

★200★
CHEMICAL AGE
CHEMICAL AGE PROJECT FILE
12 Vandy St.
London EC2 2DE, England
Stuart Slade, Editor
Phone: 01-370 4600
Service Est: 1981

Staff: Approximately 3 total.

Description of System or Service: The CHEMICAL AGE PROJECT FILE is a machine-readable listing of more than 4000 current worldwide chemical and process industry projects including plants planned, under construction, or recently completed. It is continuously updated to provide market intelligence for process plant suppliers and contractors, operating companies, and consultants. Each project is listed by country, operating company, location, products, technology supplier, capacity, contractors, estimated cost, current status, and expected completion date. The FILE is available in standard print form by subscription. Custom retrievals, including surveys of selected products or areas of the world, are also offered.

Scope and/or Subject Matter: Plants planned, under construction, or recently completed in the chemical, petrochemical, oil refining, fertilizer, gas processing, polymer, agrochemical, pharmaceutical, mineral processing, mineral extraction, synthetic fuel, food/drink, synthetic fiber, and air separation industries.

Input Sources: Information is obtained from newspapers, periodicals, annual reports, and contacts with plant operators and contractors; also used is an archive of Chemical Age magazine surveys published since the early 1970s.

Holdings and Storage Media: The machine-readable Chemical Age Project File is continuously updated and holds information on 4000 current projects; information on completed plants is archived to provide a historical record.

Publications: Chemical Age Project File—available by subscription. Each subscription includes a yearly master list of 4000 projects classified by country. Weekly, quarterly, or monthly updates are available, and maps showing project locations in selected areas of the world are included at regular intervals. Reclassification of list sections is also available to subscribers.

Computer-Based Products and Services: The CHEMICAL AGE PROJECT FILE is held in machine-readable form, and information retrieval services and special listings are offered from it.

Clientele/Availability: Clients include process plant suppliers and contractors, operating companies, and consultants. Services are available without restrictions.

Contact: Stuart Slade, Editor, Chemical Age Project File. (Telex 896238.)

★201★
CHEMICAL INFORMATION CENTER
(Fachinformationszentrum Chemie GmbH - FIZ Chemie)
2 Steinplatz
D-1000 Berlin 12, Fed. Rep. of Germany
Dr. Michael G. Helmchen, Administrative Director
Phone: 030 3190030
Founded: 1981

Staff: 59 Information and library professional; 4 management professional; 4 technicians; 6 sales and marketing; 27 clerical and nonprofessional.

Related Organizations: FIZ Chemie receives support from the German federal and state governments, the German Chemists Society/ Gesellschaft Deutscher Chemiker (GDCh), the German Society for Chemical Equipment/ Deutsche Gesellschaft fur Chemisches Apparatewesen (DECHEMA), and the Plastics Research Society/ Forschungsgesellschaft Kunststoffe.

Description of System or Service: The CHEMICAL INFORMATION CENTER (FIZ Chemie) provides scientists and industrial chemists with information on new developments in all chemical fields. It publishes Chemischer Informationsdienst (ChemInform), a weekly abstracting journal; provides computerized information retrieval from a variety of data bases; contributes data on chemical structures and reactions to the Internationale Dokumentationsgesellschaft fur Chemie (IDC) system; issues data in card sets; and produces standard profiles and SDI services. FIZ Chemie is also the authorized marketing agent for online services of Chemical Abstracts Service (CAS) in Austria, the Federal Republic of Germany, and Switzerland.

Scope and/or Subject Matter: Theoretical, physical, analytical, inorganic, organic, macromolecular, nutritional, agricultural, and environmental chemistry; biochemistry; biotechnology; chemical technology and products; and chemical economy, history, education, information, and nomenclature.

Input Sources: Approximately 250 journals are scanned for Chemischer Informationsdienst.

Holdings and Storage Media: FIZ Chemie maintains several commercially available data bases on magnetic tape: CAS files from 1967 to date; DKI-Kunststoffe Kautschuk Fasern (KKF) from 1973 to date; DECHEMA from 1975 to date; and VtB from 1966 to date.

Publications: 1) Chemischer Informationsdienst-ChemInform (weekly)—German-language abstracts journal covering approximately 20,000 papers per year in the fields of organic chemistry, physical and preparative inorganic chemistry, chemical thermodynamics, and reactions and processes; published by Verlag Chemie GmbH, Postfach 1260/1280, D-6940 Weinheim, Federal Republic of Germany. 2) Trivialnamenkartei/ Card Index of Trivial Names—supplements are issued periodically; available in either German or English alphabetical order, each card deals with only one organic compound. Available from Verlag Chemie.

Microform Products and Services: An annual author index to ChemInform is issued on microfiche.

Computer-Based Products and Services: The CHEMICAL INFORMATION CENTER provides retrospective searching and SDI services from the following data bases: CA Search, Chemical Biological Activities (CBAC), Chemical Industry Notes (CIN), Polymer Science and Technology (POST), Chemical and Process Engineering Abstracts (VtB), Chemical Engineering and Biotechnology Abstracts Data Bank (DECHEMA), and DKI-Kunststoffe Kautschuk Fasern (KKF). CA Search, CBAC, and POST are held as part of an internal retrieval system known as CRAIS (Computer Readable Abstracting and Indexing Service). The CENTER also issues magnetic tape copies of the DECHEMA, DETHERM, and KKF data bases.

Other Services: The Center also offers referral services and workshops and seminars on online information retrieval.

Clientele/Availability: Services are generally available on a subscription basis; clients include scientists and engineers interested in chemical information.

Projected Publications and Services: FIZ Chemie is in the process of converting Chemischer Informationsdienst to machine-readable form for computerized search services. The Center also plans to issue the Card Index of Trivial Names on microfiche.

Remarks: The nucleus of the Center is Chemical Information and Documentation-Berlin/ Chemie-Information und -Dokumentation Berlin (CIDB), a division of the GDCh which was responsible for the above services prior to the creation of FIZ Chemie.

Contact: Dr. Christian Weiske, Scientific Director, Chemical Information Center. (Telex 181 255 FIZC D.)

★202★
CHILE
NATIONAL COMMISSION FOR SCIENTIFIC AND TECHNOLOGICAL
    RESEARCH
(Comision Nacional de Investigacion Cientifica y Tecnologica -
    CONICYT)
DIRECTORATE FOR INFORMATION AND DOCUMENTATION
(Directorio de Informacion y Documentacion)
Casilla 297-V   Phone: 744537
Canada 308   Service Est: 1967
Santiago, Chile

Special Note: No questionnaire response was received for this entry for the 6th edition. The entry is reprinted as it appeared in the 5th edition.

Related Organizations: CONICYT is the national FID (Federation Internationale de Documentation) member.

Description of System or Service: The DIRECTORATE FOR INFORMATION AND DOCUMENTATION serves as a clearinghouse for scientific and technical information and supervises a national system of documentation. It operates a technical inquiry answering service, compiles bibliographies on request, provides hardcopy and microform copying services, prepares translations, and maintains a technical library. The DIRECTORATE also offers consulting services to libraries and documentation centers, and provides training in library and information science.

Scope and/or Subject Matter: Science and technology.

Holdings and Storage Media: Library holdings consist of approximately 5000 volumes and subscriptions to 150 periodicals.

Publications: Serie Informacion y Documentacion (irregular). Also published are bibliographies and directories.

Microform Products and Services: The Directorate will prepare microfilm copies of documents held in Chilean libraries.

Clientele/Availability: Clients include scientists, technologists, and library and documentation centers in Chile.

Contact: Directorate for Information and Documentation.

★203★
CHINA BUILDING TECHNOLOGY DEVELOPMENT CENTRE (CBTDC)
INSTITUTE OF TECHNICAL INFORMATION
19 Che Gong Zhuang St.   Phone: 8992613
Beijing, People's Republic of China   Service Est: 1980
Mr. Xu Ronglie, Director

Related Organizations: The Centre is a unit of the Ministry of Urban and Rural Construction and Environmental Protection and is a full member of the International Council for Building Research, Studies and Documentation (CIB).

Description of System or Service: The INSTITUTE OF TECHNICAL INFORMATION studies general trends of development in building science and technology in China and other countries. It is responsible for collecting and processing domestic and foreign technical information relating to the building industry and issuing several periodicals and papers on special subjects. The INSTITUTE's services include consultation, documentation retrieval, in-library reading and lending, and document reproduction and translation. It is also organizing a nationwide information exchange network in the building community and training personnel working in this area. Additionally, the INSTITUTE offers recordings, slides, and films on a loan basis.

Scope and/or Subject Matter: Building science and technology.

Input Sources: Information is gathered from foreign and domestic information sources.

Holdings and Storage Media: The Center maintains a library of 200,000 books, 800 periodicals in Chinese and other languages, and other documents.

Publications: 1) Bibliography on Foreign Literature of Science and Technology (monthly); 2) Building Structures (bimonthly); 3) Construction Technique (bimonthly); 4) Water Supply & Sewage Engineering (bimonthly); 5) Heating, Ventilating & Air Conditioning (quarterly). The above publications are issued in Chinese. 6) Building in China - Selected Papers—an English-language journal.

Computer-Based Products and Services: The INSTITUTE OF TECHNICAL INFORMATION operates a terminal for computerized documentation retrieval.

Clientele/Availability: Clients include engineers, architects, research workers, and other personnel engaged in construction, production, education, and administration.

Remarks: The Centre was formerly known as the China Building Information Center.

Contact: Mr. Xi Ruilin, Deputy Director, or Ms. Su Yuanyuan, Division of International Affairs, China Building Technology Development Centre. (Telex 22477 CSCEC CN BEIJING.)

★204★
CHISHOLM INSTITUTE OF TECHNOLOGY LIBRARY
USER EDUCATION RESOURCES DATA BASE
900 Dandenong Rd.   Phone: 03 5732523
Caulfield East, Vic. 3145, Australia   Service Est: 1979
Megan Lilly, User Coordinator

Description of System or Service: The USER EDUCATION RESOURCES DATA BASE is a computer-readable bibliographic data base covering materials produced by Australian libraries for educational and promotional purposes. The DATA BASE is used to support the collection and dissemination of samples of such materials and to publish an annual COM catalog. A newsletter is also issued in conjunction with the project.

Scope and/or Subject Matter: Materials produced by libraries for user education, bibliographic instruction, publicity, and promotion.

Input Sources: Libraries at institutions in each state and territory of Australia submit materials for cataloging in the data base.

Holdings and Storage Media: The machine-readable data base holds 1400 records.

Publications: User News (6 per year)—newsletter available to contributors and other interested parties.

Microform Products and Services: A microfiche catalog of user materials is produced annually and is available by subscription.

Computer-Based Products and Services: The User Education Resources Data Base is maintained online on an in-house computer.

Clientele/Availability: Primary clients are Australian libraries.

Remarks: The Chisholm Institute of Technology was formerly known as the Caulfield Institute of Technology.

Contact: Megan Lilly, User Coordinator, Chisholm Institute of Technology Library.

★205★
CHRISTIAN INSTITUTIONS RESEARCH AND DOCUMENTATION CENTER
(Centre de Recherches et de Documentation des Institutions Chretiennes - CERDIC)
9, Place de l'Universite
F-67084 Strasbourg Cedex, France
Phone: 88 355539
Founded: 1968
Jean Schlick, Director

Related Organizations: CERDIC is a research center of the University of the Humanities and Social Sciences of Strasbourg (Universite des Sciences Humaines de Strasbourg) and is associated with the National Center for Scientific Research (CNRS).

Description of System or Service: The CHRISTIAN INSTITUTIONS RESEARCH AND DOCUMENTATION CENTER (CERDIC) specializes in the research and documentation of religious and theological literature. It conducts research in the following five fields: institutional and juridical texts of the Christian Churches; comparative studies of Church and State relations, particularly in the European countries; historiography of the law of the Christian Churches; revision of code of the canonical law; and the development of Third World ecumenical institutions and Churches. The CENTER publishes the Bibliographical Repertory of Christian Institutions (RIC), a basic world bibliography on Christianity and religion, and maintains a corresponding computer-readable data base. It also issues a number of related publications, provides current awareness, and offers referral services.

Scope and/or Subject Matter: Christian Churches and religious institutions, including their organization, actions, legislation, ethical and theological thinking, interrelationships, and relations with society and government.

Input Sources: Annual input for RIC includes more than 7000 articles from 1400 journals, as well as 3000 books and monographs.

Holdings and Storage Media: The RIC data base is maintained in machine-readable form.

Publications: 1) Bibliographical Repertory of Christian Institutions/ Repertoire Bibliographique des Institutions Chretiennes-RIC (semiannual)—contains bibliographical references by country, an index in 5 languages, and a general index with English keywords. Includes 8 to 10 thematic supplements per year. 2) Oecumene (annual)—an international bibliography covering current ecumenical problems; consists of reproduced computer printouts of article and monograph analyses. 3) Etat et Religion, State and Religion, Staat und Religion (semiannual)—journal in French, English, and German which focuses on the relationship between nation-states and world religions. 4) Praxis Juridique et Religion (biannual)—journal covering judicial practice in religion. A number of other publications are also issued; a complete list is available upon request from CERDIC.

Computer-Based Products and Services: RIC and related files are maintained in computer-readable form for publication and internal search purposes. Tape services are also provided.

Clientele/Availability: Clients include historians, theologians, students, and professors of religion and law. Research programs are given priority.

Contact: Marie Zimmermann, Editor, Christian Institutions Research and Documentation Center.

★206★
THE CIRPA/ADISQ FOUNDATION
(La Fondation ADISQ/CIRPA)
144 Front St. W., Suite 330
Toronto, ON, Canada M5J 2L7
Phone: (416) 593-4545
Founded: 1982
Earl Rosen, Executive Director

Staff: 1 Information and library professional; 1 management professional; 1 sales and marketing; 4 clerical and nonprofessional.

Related Organizations: The Foundation was created by the Canadian Independent Record Production Association (CIRPA) and the Association du Disque et de l'Industrie du Spectacle Quebecois (ADISQ). Supporting organizations include government agencies and industry organizations.

Description of System or Service: The CIRPA/ADISQ FOUNDATION was formed to act as the research and development arm of the Canadian recording industry and to integrate new communications technology with the music industry. The FOUNDATION's major goal is to stimulate sales of Canadian records and intensify their use in the various media by supplying information services about Canadian musical artists and records. With the support of various members of the Canadian recording industry and government agencies, the FOUNDATION develops and administers the Canadian On-line Record Database (CORD); produces and markets the bilingual Canadian Record Catalogue in printed and microfiche versions; offers consultive services; and is engaged in the implementation of a long-term plan designed to serve the music industry worldwide.

Scope and/or Subject Matter: The Canadian and worldwide music industry including information about albums, songs, performers, composers, labels, and distributors.

Input Sources: Input is derived from Canadian trade and consumer music periodicals, as well as from catalogs and label copy from all labels and distributors.

Holdings and Storage Media: The machine-readable CORD data base contains 50,000 records of information on albums, songs, composers, labels, and distributors. Information is updated weekly.

Publications: Canadian Record Catalogue/ Catalogue des Disques Canadiens (quarterly)—arranged in two volumes providing 40,000 song and album listings. Volume one contains an album title index, a performer index, and a composer index; volume two contains a song title index and a label/ distributor section. The Catalogue includes some U.S. and British recordings, and is revised annually.

Microform Products and Services: The Canadian Record Catalogue is available on microfiche.

Computer-Based Products and Services: The Canadian On-line Record Database is an alphanumeric videotex data base of 50,000 documents on Canadian music, including information published in the Canadian Record Catalogue and additional data. CORD uses the BASIS data base management system, specialized Telidon videotex software to provide graphics, and a menu-driven access system. Statistical programs for sales and airplay charts and transaction handling programs that conform to international standards are under development. The Database is available online to clients with a terminal, microcomputer, or word processor. The Foundation will provide specialized reports from the Database for clients without online access.

Clientele/Availability: Clients include record retailers, broadcasters, labels, and distributors. Services are available without restrictions.

Projected Publications and Services: The Foundation is developing information services for specialized user groups such as a library service which will handle documentary tasks related to record keeping; an in-store videotex promotion service oriented to the consumer; and a radio service offering documentation oriented to radio programmers. Also under development is a program of analog music input, processing, and transmission of sound and printed music scores, and a transaction/ order entry program offering teleshopping and networking with manufacturers, distributors, wholesalers, and retailers.

Contact: Earl Rosen, Executive Director, The CIRPA/ADISQ Foundation.

★207★
CISI-WHARTON ECONOMETRIC FORECASTING ASSOCIATES LTD.
Ebury Gate
23 Lower Belgrave St.
London SW1W 0NW, England
Phone: (not reported)
Founded: 1984

Related Organizations: CISI-Wharton is a newly formed subsidiary of Compagnie Internationale de Services en Informatique (CISI). It has assumed the online host activities of its sister CISI company, SIA Computer Services, which is located at the same address.

Description of System or Service: CISI-WHARTON ECONOMETRIC FORECASTING ASSOCIATES LTD. provides online access to data bases of macroeconomic, financial, and statistical information produced by various U.K., European, North American, and international organizations. The data can be accessed in conjunction with Wharton's economic and industrial forecasting and simulation models.

Scope and/or Subject Matter: Econometric, financial, industry, and statistical information.

Input Sources: Data bases are acquired from government agencies, international organizations, and private firms.

Holdings and Storage Media: More than two dozen files are held online.

Computer-Based Products and Services: CISI-WHARTON provides online access to a variety of statistical files, including the following: Bank of England Data Bank, CITIBASE, CRONOS, COMEXT, Financial Times Currency & Share Index, International Financial Statistics (IFS), OECD Main Economic Indicators, and U.K. Central Statistical Office Macroeconomic Data Bank. Also accessible are the following files produced by Wharton Econometric Forecasting Associates, Inc. of Philadelphia: World Model Data Bank, Foreign Exchange Data Bank, International Agriculture Data Bank, U.S. Macro Databank, U.S. Industry Data Bank, U.S. Regional Data Bank, U.S. Energy Data Bank, U.S. Long Term Data Bank, New York Data Bank, Centrally Planned Economies Data Bank, Middle East Data Bank, Latin America Data Bank, and Pacific Basin Data Bank. Economic modeling and forecasting capabilities are available.

Other Services: CISI-Wharton also offers data base training services and organizes user group meetings.

Clientele/Availability: Services are primarily available without restrictions, although access to some data bases is limited.

Contact: Heather Morley, CISI-Wharton Econometric Forecasting Associates Ltd.

★208★
CITIS LTD.
2 Rosemount Terrace
Blackrock
Dublin, Ireland
Donal P. Murphy, Director
Phone: 01 885971
Founded: 1972

Staff: 3 Information and library professional; 1 management professional; 2 sales and marketing; 3 clerical and nonprofessional.

Description of System or Service: CITIS LTD. (Construction Industry Translation and Information Services) scans worldwide technical literature in civil engineering and related areas to prepare two computer-based abstracting and indexing journals. The International Civil Engineering Abstracts journal contains citations and abstracts of books, journals, articles, and reports in the field of civil and structural engineering. Software Abstracts for Engineers (SAFE) provides details on commercially available software programs for engineering applications as well as abstracts of books and articles on engineering software. CITIS plans to make both journals available as online data bases. The firm also arranges to provide copies and translations of articles cited in International Civil Engineering Abstracts.

Scope and/or Subject Matter: Civil engineering, including structural engineering, hydraulic engineering, hydrology, foundations, soil mechanics, highways, public health engineering, tunnels, dams, and hydroelectric engineering; and software for civil, structural, and related engineering applications.

Input Sources: More than 300 European and North American journals are scanned for input, as well as selected books, conference proceedings, and information received from software producers.

Holdings and Storage Media: Two bibliographic data bases corresponding to the abstracts journals are maintained in machine-readable. The firm also maintains a library of 1000 bound volumes and subscriptions to 300 periodicals.

Publications: 1) International Civil Engineering Abstracts (10 per year)—each issue contains approximately 350 abstracts and a keyword index, which is cumulated annually. Formerly published in association with the London-based Institution of Civil Engineers under the title I.C.E. Abstracts. 2) Software Abstracts for Engineers (quarterly)—contains information on commercially available computer programs for engineering applications, including names and addresses of software firms, computers supported, program summaries and prices, and keyword index. Also provides abstracts of books and papers which cover specialist programs and algorithms, programming techniques and languages, engineering applications of computer systems and graphics packages, and reviews of existing software.

Microform Products and Services: Annual editions of the journals are available on standard 98-frame microfiche.

Computer-Based Products and Services: International Civil Engineering Abstracts and Software Abstracts for Engineers are expected to be offered as online data bases through ESA/IRS.

Clientele/Availability: Clients include libraries, engineering faculties, consulting engineers, contractors, and public authorities.

Contact: Donal P. Murphy, Director, CITIS Ltd. (Telex 30259 MSCH-EI.)

★209★
CITY OF LONDON POLYTECHNIC
FAWCETT LIBRARY
BIBLIOFEM
Old Castle St.
London E1 7NT, England
David Doughan, Assistant Librarian
Phone: 01-283 1030
Service Est: 1979

Staff: 1 Information and library professional.

Related Organizations: BIBLIOFEM is cosponsored by the Equal Opportunities Commission.

Description of System or Service: A comprehensive source of information on women, BIBLIOFEM is a computer-based joint catalog of the Fawcett Library and Equal Opportunities Commission Library, together with a continually updated bibliography of items not held by either. It is produced bimonthly on COM microfiche as the two library collections are retrospectively converted to machine-readable format and as new items for the bibliography are added.

Scope and/or Subject Matter: Women and subjects related to them, including marriage and family, employment and education, and women's movements.

Input Sources: BIBLIOFEM sources include the holdings of the Fawcett Library and the Equal Opportunities Commission, the British National Bibliography, and U.S. Library of Congress MARC files.

Holdings and Storage Media: BIBLIOFEM comprises approximately 40,000 machine-readable records. The holdings of the Fawcett Library consist of 20,000 bound volumes; 20,0000 pamphlets; periodicals, photographs, letters, press clippings, and miscellaneous items with emphasis on the period from 1860 to 1930. The Equal Opportunities Commission maintains a collection of more than 5000 books and pamphlets on current legal, social, and economic concerns.

Microform Products and Services: BIBLIOFEM is issued bimonthly on 42x microfiche. Each set of microfiche is cumulative and is arranged in two sequences: alphabetically by author, title, and series;

and classified according to the Dewey Decimal classification scheme.

Computer-Based Products and Services: BIBLIOFEM is based on computer-readable files of bibliographic information on women; no direct computerized information services are currently offered from the data base.

Clientele/Availability: BIBLIOFEM is available by subscription; those wishing to use the Fawcett Library must pay an annual fee.

Remarks: The Fawcett Library was inaugurated in 1926 by the London Society for Women's Service, which is now known as the Fawcett Society. The Library was transferred to City of London Polytechnic in 1977.

Contact: David Doughan, Assistant Librarian, City of London Polytechnic.

★210★
COACHING ASSOCIATION OF CANADA
SPORT INFORMATION RESOURCE CENTRE (SIRC)
333 River Rd. Phone: (613) 746-5357
Ottawa, ON, Canada K1L 8B9 Service Est: 1973
Gilles Chiasson, Manager

Staff: 6 Information and library professional; 2 technicians; 4 clerical and nonprofessional.

Description of System or Service: The SPORT INFORMATION RESOURCE CENTRE (SIRC) is a sports documentation and information center that collects relevant worldwide literature and catalogs it in the computer-readable Sport Data Base for rapid retrieval. The Data Base holds index descriptors, classification codes reflecting reading complexity, and other bibliographic information for all accessioned books, theses, and journal articles; it also contains citations to selected additional materials held elsewhere. SIRC uses the Data Base to produce publications and provide computerized search services. The file is also commercially available online.

Scope and/or Subject Matter: Sport, physical education, fitness, and recreation, including such areas as treatment of sport injuries, drills, sport art, coaching techniques, administration of physical education programs and facilities, and leisure and recreation; excluded from the coverage are news items and information on competition results.

Input Sources: Input is derived from relevant books, journals, and theses published worldwide.

Holdings and Storage Media: The computer-readable Sport Data Base contains more than 140,000 citations, with approximately 2000 new citations added monthly. Library holdings consist of 20,000 bound volumes, 6500 microfiche, and subscriptions to 1200 periodicals.

Publications: 1) Sport Bibliography/ Bibliographie du Sport (10 volumes)—hardcopy version of SIRC data base containing references arranged by subject; available for purchase. 2) Sport and Recreation Index/ Index de la Litterature des Sports et des Loisirs (8 per year)—computer-produced index covering approximately 1200 journal articles per month, arranged according to broad topics and by sport; available by subscription. 3) Sport and Recreation for the Disabled—an index of the resource collection of 19 organizations and resource centers across Canada specializing in information on recreation for the disabled; available for purchase. 4) Sport Thesaurus—available for purchase.

Microform Products and Services: SIRC provides microfiche duplicating services.

Computer-Based Products and Services: The Sport Data Base is available online through System Development Corporation (SDC) and CAN/OLE. Additionally, the CENTRE will provide retrospective searching and SDI services from it on request. For its internal retrieval activities, the CENTRE also uses MARC, MEDLINE, ERIC, and Social Sciences Citation Index.

Other Services: Additional services include document delivery, manual literature searching, referrals, interlibrary loans, and photocopying.

Clientele/Availability: Primary clientele is the Canadian sport community, but others are welcome. SIRC serves all levels of users, from school students to national coaches and advanced researchers.

Contact: Gilles Chiasson, Manager, Sport Information Resource Centre. (Telex 053 3660.)

★211★
COLLECTIVE FOR TRAINING AND EDUCATION IN CONNECTION WITH INFORMATION PROVISION VIA NETWORKS
(Samenwerkingsverband voor Opleiding en Vorming op het Terrein van de Informatieverzorging via Netwerken - SOVIN)
St. Antoniesbreestr. 16 Phone: 020 223955
P.O. Box 16601 Service Est: 1979
NL-1001 RC Amsterdam, Netherlands
J.H. Oudshoorn, Head

Related Organizations: The parent organization of SOVIN is the Netherlands Bibliographical and Documentary Committee/ Commissie voor Bibliografie en Documentatie (COBIDOC), which is described in a separate entry.

Description of System or Service: The COLLECTIVE FOR TRAINING AND EDUCATION IN CONNECTION WITH INFORMATION PROVISION VIA NETWORKS (SOVIN) is a Dutch national training center for online searching sponsored by several library and documentation institutions, scientific libraries, online groups such as Netherlands Association of Users of Online Information Systems (VOGIN), and the Netherlands Information Combine (NIC). SOVIN'S central training facility in Utrecht provides online training seminars, access to worldwide commercially available data bases, publication of a national course agenda, and production of course materials. Other interests of SOVIN include library automation; the investigation of cost-saving methods using minicomputers and simulation techniques; development or acquisition of audiovisual material; and the promotion of instructional material in the Dutch language.

Scope and/or Subject Matter: Online information retrieval and related topics.

Computer-Based Products and Services: SOVIN maintains online access to almost every worldwide host organization including those accessible over Euronet DIANE.

Clientele/Availability: Services are available on a contract basis to anyone in or represented in the Netherlands.

Contact: P.J.C. Rosenbrand, Collective for Training and Education in Connection with Information Provision via Networks. (Telex 18766 COBD NL.)

★212★
COLOMBIAN FUND FOR SCIENTIFIC RESEARCH
(Fondo Colombiano de Investigaciones Cientificas - COLCIENCIAS)
NATIONAL INFORMATION SYSTEM
(Sistema Nacional de Informacion - SNI)
Trv 9A No. 133-28 Phone: 2740468
Apdo. Aereo 051580
Bogota, Colombia
German Escorcia Saldarriaga, Chief

Staff: 5 Information and library professional; 1 management professional; 1 technician; 4 clerical and nonprofessional; 1 other.

Related Organizations: The National Information System receives support from the United Nations Development Programme and the Organization of American States. COLCIENCIAS is administered by the National Ministry of Education/ Ministerio de Educacion Nacional.

Description of System or Service: The NATIONAL INFORMATION SYSTEM (SNI) encourages the establishment of information services, coordinates information activities at the national level, and fosters cooperation among public and private libraries, archives, data banks, and specialized information and documentation centers and services in Colombia. The SYSTEM is composed of three levels: a national focal center; eight special information subsystems; and a network of public, university, and school libraries, and other information services. SNI issues publications, conducts research, and provides referral and consulting services.

Scope and/or Subject Matter: Colombian information and library services in all subject areas, including agriculture, health, education, economics, industry, energy, environment, and marine sciences.

Publications: Informativo SNI (bimonthly). SNI also issues research reports and studies in the information field.

Clientele/Availability: Requests for services are handled by individual network members.

Contact: German Escoria Saldarriaga, Chief, National Information System.

★213★
COMMISSION OF THE EUROPEAN COMMUNITIES (CEC)
AGRICULTURAL RESEARCH PROJECTS (AGREP) DATA BASE
Batiment Jean Monnet, B.P. 1907 Phone: 352 43011
Rue Alcide de Gasperi Service Est: 1975
Kirchberg, Luxembourg
Giorgio Trevisan, Project Leader

Related Organizations: The Commission of the European Communities (CEC) is the policy-formulating and administrative unit of the European Communities.

Description of System or Service: The AGRICULTURAL RESEARCH PROJECTS (AGREP) DATA BASE is a computer-readable file of information relating to current agricultural research projects in member countries of the European Community. It is compiled through a cooperative system of national input centers, which prepare and submit information on projects in progress in their countries. This information is integrated and processed by computer at the CEC, and the resulting total data base is distributed on tape to the national centers. AGREP information is also disseminated online and through an annual hardcopy publication.

Scope and/or Subject Matter: Extant research and development projects in the areas of agriculture, food science, forestry, fisheries, land use and development, nature conservation, veterinary medicine, and rural sociology.

Input Sources: The national input centers collect data on current research projects in their countries.

Holdings and Storage Media: The data base is maintained on magnetic tape and contains information on approximately 23,000 projects; it is updated quarterly with information on approximately 125 new projects. Projects are deleted from the file when they are terminated.

Publications: AGREP-Permanent Inventory of Agricultural Research Projects in the European Communities (annual)—two volumes consisting of a main list and indexes. It may be ordered from: Commonwealth Agricultural Bureaux, Farnham House, Farnham Royal, Slough SL2 3BN, England.

Computer-Based Products and Services: The AGREP DATA BASE supplies the title of the research project in both English and the national language, the name of the research organization and country responsible for the project, names of the scientists involved, full-text descriptive phrases, and other data. The DATA BASE is available on magnetic tape to the national input centers, and is searchable online through I/S Datacentralen and DIMDI.

Clientele/Availability: Services are available to the national input centers and others.

Contact: Giorgio Trevisan, Project Leader for Information Market and Innovation, Commission of the European Communities.

★214★
COMMISSION OF THE EUROPEAN COMMUNITIES (CEC)
COURT OF JUSTICE OF THE EUROPEAN COMMUNITIES
LEGAL DATA PROCESSING GROUP
CJUS DATA BANK
B.P. 1406 Phone: 352 43031
Kirchberg, Luxembourg Service Est: 1975
Jochen Streil, Principal Administrator

Staff: 4 Information and library professional; 1 technician; 6 clerical and nonprofessional.

Related Organizations: The Commission is the policy-formulating and administrative unit of the European Communities.

Description of System or Service: The CJUS DATA BANK is a machine-readable file containing the full text and bibliographic summaries of all judgments rendered since 1954 by the Court of Justice of the European Communities, as well as related opinions of the Advocates General. The file is searchable in English, French, and German as part of the CELEX online documentation system accessible through Honeywell Bull's Euris service. In addition to CJUS, the Legal Data Processing Group produces several internal data bases for use by the Court of Justice.

Scope and/or Subject Matter: Case law relating to the activities of the European Community.

Input Sources: Input for CJUS is derived primarily from the European Court Reports; unpublished judgments and legal journals also provide input.

Holdings and Storage Media: CJUS is a machine-readable full-text data bank covering the entire case load of the European Communities' Court of Justice since its inception in 1954; the data bank is updated monthly.

Publications: Various indexes of current case law are prepared.

Computer-Based Products and Services: The CJUS DATA BANK is publicly accessible online as part of the CELEX legal documentation system. CJUS contains the full text of judgments as well as procedural and bibliographical information; summaries of unpublished judgments are also included. In addition to CJUS, the Legal Data Processing Group maintains the CAP and DECNAT data banks on an in-house Siemens computer for use by Judges and staff of the Court of Justice. The CAP Databank covers proceedings before the European Economic Community Court. DECNAT covers national judgments applying the law of the European Communities.

Clientele/Availability: Principal users of CJUS are the courts, legal practitioners, public organizations, and national documentation centers. Other data banks are restricted to use by the Court.

Contact: Jochen Streil, Principal Administrator, CJUS Data Bank.

★215★
COMMISSION OF THE EUROPEAN COMMUNITIES (CEC)
EDUCATION INFORMATION NETWORK IN THE EUROPEAN COMMUNITY (EURYDICE)
Central Unit of EURYDICE Phone: 02 2300398
17, rue Archimede Service Est: 1976
B-1040 Brussels, Belgium
J. Richardson, Head

Staff: 6 Information and library professional; 2 management professional; 6 clerical and nonprofessional.

Related Organizations: The Network receives support from the CEC's Education Service and the European Cultural Foundation, Amsterdam. The CEC is the policy-formulating and administrative unit of the European Communities.

Description of System or Service: The EDUCATION INFORMATION NETWORK IN THE EUROPEAN COMMUNITY (EURYDICE) was established to promote the rapid exchange of information between educational policymakers at the Community and member-state levels, and in certain cases, at the regional and local levels. Consisting of national information units in the member states coordinated through the Central Unit in Brussels, EURYDICE gives priority to information requests focusing on the following policy themes: transition from school to working life; teaching and learning of foreign languages; education of migrants and their families; and policies and conditions of admission of students to higher education. (Requests outside these priority themes are dealt with if they correspond to major policy trends.) To facilitate information exchange, the NETWORK is developing a computer-readable data base in which answers to requests and material from current sources covering important comparative information will be stored. Additional EURYDICE functions include organizing information seminars and meetings, and issuing topical papers aimed at providing policy information on issues currently important to EURYDICE users.

Scope and/or Subject Matter: Educational issues affecting the European Community and its member states.

Publications: 1) The Impact of Demographic Change on Education

Systems in the European Community. 2) Compulsory Schooling in the E.C. The Central Unit also issues other topical publications, bibliographies, information brochures, and bulletins.

Computer-Based Products and Services: A computer-readable data base containing EURYDICE information is under development. It is planned to be compatible with the Euronet DIANE telecommunications service. Additionally, selected national EURYDICE units are compiling files which contain answers to requests and material from other sources and plan to convert the files to computer-based formats.

Clientele/Availability: Services are provided through national EURYDICE information units in member countries.

Contact: J. Richardson or Denise Hizette, Central Unit of EURYDICE. (Telex 65398 EURYDI B).

★216★
COMMISSION OF THE EUROPEAN COMMUNITIES (CEC) ENVIRONMENTAL INFORMATION AND DOCUMENTATION CENTERS (ENDOC) DATA BASE
Batiment Jean Monnet, B.P. 1907   Phone: 352 43012875
Rue Alcide de Gasperi   Service Est: 1978
Kirchberg, Luxembourg

Related Organizations: The Commission of the European Communities (CEC) is the policy-formulating and administrative unit of the European Communities.

Description of System or Service: The ENVIRONMENTAL INFORMATION AND DOCUMENTATION CENTERS (ENDOC) DATA BASE is a computer-readable directory of organizations in the European Communities which document and disseminate information related to one or more environmental subject areas. The centers included provide such services as abstracting and indexing, current awareness, retrospective literature searching, and reference and referral. The DATA BASE is used to produce a printed publication and it is searchable online.

Scope and/or Subject Matter: Information services in environmental subject areas.

Input Sources: Data on the centers are collected from over 500 environmental information and documentation sources in member countries.

Holdings and Storage Media: The ENDOC Data Base holds more than 500 entries gathered from 1980 to the present; it is updated annually.

Publications: ENDOC Directory (annual). A data base manual is also available.

Computer-Based Products and Services: The ENDOC DATA BASE is available online through ECHO (European Commission Host Organization), a host on Euronet DIANE. It contains the following information on each center: name, address, contact person, telephone, director, type of center, aims of the center, subject areas covered, languages of information, and types of information activities offered. ENDOC uses the multilingual descriptor system (MDS) for the subject areas covered by the centers which allows searches to be conducted in six of the official European Community languages. Magnetic tapes of ENDOC are available to environmental information and documentation centers in the European Community.

Clientele/Availability: Services are available to environmental information centers and others.

Contact: Project Leader for Scientific and Technical Inventories, Commission of the European Communities.

★217★
COMMISSION OF THE EUROPEAN COMMUNITIES (CEC) ENVIRONMENTAL RESEARCH PROJECTS (ENREP) DATA BASE
Batiment Jean Monnet, B.P. 1907   Phone: 352 43012875
Rue Alcide de Gasperi   Service Est: 1978
Kirchberg, Luxembourg

Related Organizations: The Commission of the European Communities (CEC) is the policy-formulating and administrative unit of the European Communities.

Description of System or Service: The ENVIRONMENTAL RESEARCH PROJECTS (ENREP) DATA BASE contains information on current environmental research projects conducted in member countries of the European community. Data are collected from information sources in each country, processed by computer, and made available to environmental research centers on magnetic tape and in printed form. The DATA BASE is also commercially available online through ECHO (European Commission Host Organization), a host on Euronet DIANE.

Scope and/or Subject Matter: Current European Community research projects in all areas of environment.

Input Sources: Data on projects are collected from more than 2800 organizations.

Holdings and Storage Media: The computer-readable ENREP data base holds information on 17,000 research projects gathered from 1980 to the present; it is updated regularly.

Publications: A data base manual is issued in English and French and is free to users upon request.

Computer-Based Products and Services: The ENREP DATA BASE is available on magnetic tape to environmental research centers in the European Community. It is also available online through the ECHO. Data elements in the file include organization name, project status, starting date, ending date, author, title, abstract, keywords, costs, date of information, and indication of publications. Additional records which carry the author, title, and bibliographical information on articles relating to the main topic are added. ENREP uses the unique multilingual descriptor system (MDS) for indexing projects which allows searching to be conducted in six of the official Community languages.

Clientele/Availability: Services are available to environmental research centers in the European Community and others.

Contact: Project Leader for Scientific and Technical Inventories, Commission of the European Communities.

★218★
COMMISSION OF THE EUROPEAN COMMUNITIES (CEC) EURO ABSTRACTS
Batiment Jean Monnet, B.P. 1907   Phone: 352 43012948
Rue Alcide de Gasperi
Kirchberg, Luxembourg
H.L. Scherff, Chief Administrator

Staff: 1 Management professional; 1 technician; 2 clerical and nonprofessional.

Related Organizations: The Commission is the policy-formulating and administrative unit of the European Communities.

Description of System or Service: EURO ABSTRACTS is a monthly abstracts journal which covers published results of scientific and technical research projects funded by the CEC. It is issued in two parts: Section 1, providing coverage of research performed by the European Atomic Energy Community (EURATOM) and the European Economic Community (EEC); and Section 2, covering coal and steel research. The journal is available as a printed publication and online through ECHO (European Commission Host Organization) as the EABS data base.

Scope and/or Subject Matter: Scientific and technical research carried out or sponsored by CEC, including nuclear, environmental, agricultural, energy, medical and biological (mainly in connection with radiation protection), and coal and steel research.

Input Sources: Input consists of the reports, papers, journal articles, research agreements, patents, books, and proceedings pertaining to CEC scientific and technical research.

Holdings and Storage Media: The computer-readable EABS data base contains more than 34,000 records from 1962 to date. It is updated monthly with approximately 125 records.

Publications: Euro Abstracts (monthly)—Section 1: EURATOM and EEC Research, Scientific and Technical Publications and Patents (including descriptions of training courses, seminars, conferences, and symposia organized or sponsored by the CEC); Section 2: Coal and Steel, Research Agreements, Programmes and Publications (including European Coal and Steel Community research results and information on current research). Copies of papers mentioned in EURO ABSTRACTS may be obtained from: Commission of the European Communities, Directorate General XIII - Directorate A, Batiment Jean Monnet, P.O. Box 1907, B4-009 Kirchberg, Luxembourg. Reports are available from: Office for Official Publications of the European Communities, P.O. Box 1003, Luxembourg. A data base manual in English and French is also available.

Microform Products and Services: A microfiche edition of Euro Abstracts is available. All reports published by the CEC are also available on microfiche.

Computer-Based Products and Services: Bibliographic citations in EURO ABSTRACTS are accessible online as the EABS data base, which is available through ECHO, a host on Euronet DIANE. Documents cited in the data base can be ordered online from the Office for Official Publications. Computer tapes containing annual volumes of EURO ABSTRACTS are also available, as are search services. Data elements in the file include document title in English and the original language, descriptors, author, author affiliation, research contract number, and bibliographic reference. The EABS data base includes citations to conferences held in member CEC countries which are organized or sponsored by the Commission.

Clientele/Availability: There are no restrictions on services.

Contact: H.L. Scherff, Chief Administrator, Directorate for Scientific and Technical Information and Information Management. (Telex 3423 or 3476 COMEUR LU.)

★219★
COMMISSION OF THE EUROPEAN COMMUNITIES (CEC)
EUROPEAN COMMISSION HOST ORGANIZATION (ECHO)
15, ave. de la Faiencerie   Phone: 352 20764
Luxembourg   Service Est: 1980
Roland Haber, ECHO Manager

Staff: 2 Management professional; 2 clerical and nonprofessional.

Related Organizations: The Commission of the European Communities (CEC) is the policy-formulating and administrative unit of the European Communities.

Description of System or Service: The EUROPEAN COMMISSION HOST ORGANIZATION (ECHO) is an online host service on the Euronet DIANE international packet-switching network. Using the GRIPS/DIRS command language, it provides access to CEC-produced inventory and referral data bases and other files which are not available on other computer host services. ECHO was set up as a result of a decision of the Commission of the European Communities to contribute actively to and encourage and support the use of online information in Europe.

Scope and/or Subject Matter: Data base topics include Euronet DIANE services, research projects, tenders and contracts, terminals and microcomputers, and terminology.

Input Sources: Data bases are acquired from the CEC and CEC offices as well as private organizations.

Holdings and Storage Media: ECHO holds nine publicly available data bases online.

Publications: ECHO Newsletter—provides details concerning developments of the ECHO service, new data bases, staff activities, and conference or exhibition participation. ECHO also provides free user manuals in English and French for the command language GRIPS/DIRS and for each of the individual data bases.

Computer-Based Products and Services: ECHO provides online access to the following data bases: 1) DIANE-GUIDE—provides detailed descriptions of the more than 400 data bases and data banks available through Euronet DIANE hosts; produced by Learned Information Ltd. 2) DUNIS--corresponds to the printed Directory of United Nations Information Systems which covers systems, services, and data bases within the U.N. network. 3) EABS—contains bibliographic citations appearing in the printed Euro Abstracts. Covers Commission-funded research and conferences; produced by the CEC. 4) ENDOC—directory of more than 500 environmental information and documentation centers in the Community and the services they provide; produced by the CEC. 5) ENREP—inventory of current environmental research projects in Europe; produced by the CEC. 6) EURODICAUTOM—a terminological data bank containing scientific and technical terms, definitions, and abbreviations in six official languages of the CEC; produced by the Terminology Office of the CEC. 7) Tenders Electronic Daily (TED)—listing of calls for tenders of public works contracts and public supply contracts; produced by the Office for Official Publications of the CEC. 8) Terminals Guide—provides detailed information on approximately 300 Euronet-compatible terminals and microcomputers; produced by the CEC. Searches can be carried out by trademark, type of terminal, speed, name of suppliers, and name of country. With the exception of the terminology file, ECHO data bases are held under GRIPS-DIRS retrieval software, which uses the Common Command Language as the user interface.

Clientele/Availability: ECHO services are currently available free of charge except for telecommunications costs and access to the TED data base.

Contact: Roland Haber, Manager, European Commission Host Organization. (Telex 3511.)

★220★
COMMISSION OF THE EUROPEAN COMMUNITIES (CEC)
EUROPEAN ON-LINE INFORMATION NETWORK (EURONET)
DIRECT INFORMATION ACCESS NETWORK FOR EUROPE (DIANE)
Batiment Jean Monnet, B.P. 1907   Phone: 352 43012879
Rue Alcide de Gasperi   Service Est: 1975
Kirchberg, Luxembourg
Wolfgang Huber, Main Administrator

Staff: Approximately 8 professional.

Related Organizations: Euronet DIANE is operated through the cooperation of the Post, Telegraph, and Telephone (PTTs) authorities of the ten Community members, plus Switzerland and Sweden. The CEC is the policy-formulating and administrative unit of the European Communities.

Description of System or Service: Conceived, sponsored, and designed by the Commission of the European Communities, Euronet's DIRECT INFORMATION ACCESS NETWORK FOR EUROPE (DIANE) is an international packet-switching network that supports major online systems which serve the information requirements of the European community. Utilizing a Common Command Language (CCL), Euronet DIANE permits online access to approximately 500 data bases held on the computers of more than 50 hosts. The data bases cover a wide spectrum of scientific, technical, legal, social, and economic knowledge. Additional services include a central help desk for inquiries, a free online inquiry service, and training courses. Document delivery services are under development. To further improve Euronet DIANE, the Commission encourages the coordination of sales conditions between host members, and sponsors the development of common services and facilities to overcome language and distance barriers. Euronet DIANE currently serves Belgium, Denmark, France, Federal Republic of Germany, Greece, Ireland, Italy, Luxembourg, Netherlands, Sweden, Switzerland, and the United Kingdom. More than 30 other countries have access to the network through international gateways.

Scope and/or Subject Matter: Among the subjects covered by data bases carried by Euronet DIANE hosts are the following: aerospace; agriculture and veterinary science; civil, electrical, mechanical, and chemical engineering; computing and electronics; human sciences; medicine; metallurgy; patents and law; petroleum; pharmaceuticals; business; and macroeconomics.

Publications: 1) Euronet DIANE News (bimonthly)—provides general network news and notification of new DIANE services. Also covers other areas of the information industry including information brokers, the information market, microcomputer uses, telecommunications, data bases, and online vendors, providing names and addresses for companies and services described. 2) Euronet DIANE Directory of Services (annual)—available in English, French, German, Dutch, Danish, and Italian. In addition, brochures and leaflets are available in the six languages.

Computer-Based Products and Services: The Euronet DIANE network provides rapid, low-cost data transmission using packet-switching technology. The network uses five packet switching exchanges at London, Frankfurt, Paris, Rome, and Zurich, with additional connections to other countries. Access to Euronet DIANE is provided through a direct access circuit, public telephone network, or public data networks using a synchronous or asynchronous terminal with a modem. Costs for data transmission are based on connect time and volume of data transmitted. Euronet DIANE averages 30,000 calls per month.

Remarks: Euronet is being integrated with extant national public data networks, and will gradually integrate with new national networks where they emerge.

Contact: Wolfgang Huber, Main Administrator, Euronet Direct Information Access Network for Europe. (Telex 3511 DIANE LU.)

★221★
COMMISSION OF THE EUROPEAN COMMUNITIES (CEC)
JOINT RESEARCH CENTRE (JRC)
ENVIRONMENTAL CHEMICALS DATA AND INFORMATION NETWORK (ECDIN)
Ispra Establishment Phone: 0332 789880
I-21020 Ispra (Varese), Italy Service Est: 1973
Dr. M. Boni, Project Leader

Staff: 4 Information and library professional; 1 management professional; 6 technicians; 4 clerical and nonprofessional.

Related Organizations: The Commission is the policy-formulating and administrative unit of the European Communities.

Description of System or Service: The ENVIRONMENTAL CHEMICALS DATA AND INFORMATION NETWORK (ECDIN) is a computer-readable data bank on chemicals and the environment. It provides data and information on more than 60,000 substances, including commercial chemicals, toxic natural products, compounds with significant toxicity, and by-products of these. ECDIN is available online through I/S Datacentralen.

Scope and/or Subject Matter: Chemical structure, synonyms, analytical methods, producers, processes, production and trade statistics, uses, toxicology, environmental fate, legislation, occupational health.

Input Sources: Information for the ECDIN data bank is provided by network partners using published literature and private sources.

Holdings and Storage Media: ECDIN holds chemical data and information in machine-readable form.

Computer-Based Products and Services: The ENVIRONMENTAL CHEMICALS DATA AND INFORMATION NETWORK (ECDIN) data bank is accessible online through I/S Datacentralen. The data bank contains chemical substance identity information for approximately 65,000 chemicals, data on acute toxicity for 20,000 substances, and data on chemical structures for 40,000 substances. More extensive data on chemical processes, uses, occupational health and safety, threshold values, and analytical methods are included for approximately 1500 chemicals. Data are held in approximately 28 chemical data categories. Among these are synonyms, which are held in a separate Chemical Synonym File; substance; structure; producers; plants; processes; uses; consumption patterns; bibliographic references; dispersion and transformation in the environment; Standard Industrial Classification codes; occupational safety and health; carcinogenicity; mutagenicity; and teratogenicity.

Clientele/Availability: Services are available without restrictions.

Contact: Dr. M. Boni, Project Leader, Environmental Chemicals Data and Information Network. (Telex 380042 I.)

★222★
COMMISSION OF THE EUROPEAN COMMUNITIES (CEC)
JOINT RESEARCH CENTRE (JRC)
HIGH TEMPERATURE MATERIALS DATA BANK (HTM-DB)
P.O. Box 2 Phone: 02246 5208
NL-1755 ZG Petten, Netherlands Service Est: 1980
H. Krockel, Project Manager

Staff: 7 Total.

Related Organizations: The CEC is the policy-formulating and administrative unit of the European Communities. The Data Bank is part of the High Temperature Materials Programme of the CEC Joint Research Centre.

Description of System or Service: The HIGH TEMPERATURE MATERIALS DATA BANK (HTM-DB) is an experimental computer-readable data bank for high temperature material properties. Now in its pilot stage of operation, the DATA BANK is a factual file containing measured test results, corresponding test methods and conditions, actual characteristics of the tested material, specimen characteristics, and other influencing parameters.

Scope and/or Subject Matter: Mechanical property and corrosion test results for high-temperature materials.

Input Sources: Data are derived from literature, an in-house research program, and test results of other laboratories and manufacturers.

Holdings and Storage Media: The Data Bank is maintained in machine-readable form.

Computer-Based Products and Services: Currently available for in-house use only, the HIGH TEMPERATURE MATERIALS DATA BANK consists of five files of information: the test results file; the specimens file which contains characteristics of the material; the materials file which holds such information as material designation, chemical composition, melting range, and density; the test conditions and methods file; and the source of data file which includes corporate source, author names, title, journal, book name, patent number, number of data formats, nature of test, and nature of material. The DATA BANK will eventually be made accessible online through Euronet DIANE.

Clientele/Availability: At present only internal clientele and collaborators are served.

Contact: H. Krockel, Project Manager, High Temperature Materials Data Bank. (Telex 57211 REACP.)

★223★
COMMISSION OF THE EUROPEAN COMMUNITIES (CEC)
SPECIALIZED DEPARTMENT FOR TERMINOLOGY AND COMPUTER APPLICATIONS
EURODICAUTOM
Batiment Jean Monnet A2/101 Phone: 352 43012389
B.P. 1907, Rue Alcide de Gasperi Service Est: 1962
Kirchberg, Luxembourg
Mr. J. Goetschalckx, Head

Staff: Approximately 40 total.

Related Organizations: The Commission of the European Communities (CEC) is the policy-formulating and administrative unit of the European Communities.

Description of System or Service: EURODICAUTOM is a terminological data bank containing scientific and technical terms, definitions, contextual phrases, and abbreviations in most of the official languages of the CEC. The data bank is designed to serve terminologists who are looking for translations for particular terms, and translators who need up-to-date translations of scientific and technical terms which may not be available in printed form. EURODICAUTOM is publicly available online through ECHO (European Commission Host Organization).

Scope and/or Subject Matter: Terminological analysis in such fields as agriculture, coal and steel technology, medicine and occupational health, nuclear science, transport, industry, official nomenclatures, economics, Community regulations, data processing, civil engineering, and information and documentation sciences.

Input Sources: Approximately 100 periodicals are analyzed as well as current glossaries and handbooks. Input for the data bank has also been provided from sources such as the European Parliament, national terminology offices, and professional bodies.

Holdings and Storage Media: The computer-readable EURODICAUTOM data bank holds 370,000 term records and 90,000 records containing abbreviations; approximately 2000 new items are added monthly. The Specialized Department also maintains a library collection of 7500 bound volumes and subscriptions to 200 periodicals.

Publications: 1) Bulletin (two or three per year). 2) Fil d'Ariane—

inventory of glossaries produced by all Community institutions. Additionally, glossaries are produced covering iron and steel, coke oven technology, trade union terminology, and other technical fields.

Computer-Based Products and Services: The EURODICAUTOM data bank is accessible online through ECHO, a host on Euronet DIANE. The data bank is maintained on its own software with a simplified set of commands. For each technical term or expression, EURODICAUTOM contains a keyword or expression with phrases illustrating word usage; a dictionary definition, if available; a bibliographic reference to the source of the term or expression; and additional notes. Searching is carried out on the keywords and context sentences in the source language requested. In addition, specialized glossaries can be extracted from the file.

Other Services: In addition to maintaining EURODICAUTOM, the Specialized Department supports CEC translation services in the field of terminology and documentation, developing computer-based systems for these services; contributes to the development of the automatic translation systems SYSTRAN and EUROTRA; provides terminological assistance to the CEC Translation Division; produces glossaries in various technical fields; and cooperates with international terminology services and organizations.

Clientele/Availability: The data bank is publicly accessible.

Contact: Mr. J. Goetschalckx, Advisor and Head, or Peter Ammundsen, Terminologist, Specialized Department for Terminology and Computer Applications.

★224★
COMMISSION OF THE EUROPEAN COMMUNITIES (CEC)
STATISTICAL OFFICE OF THE EUROPEAN COMMUNITIES (EUROSTAT)
COMEXT DATA BANK
Batiment Jean Monnet, B.P. 1907   Phone: 352 43013530
Rue Alcide de Gasperi   Service Est: 1981
Kirchberg, Luxembourg
Mlle. Hilf, Head of Specialized Service

Staff: Approximately 4 total.

Related Organizations: The Commission is the policy-formulating and adminstrative unit of the European Communities.

Description of System or Service: The COMEXT DATA BANK is a machine-readable file of time series data covering the European Economic Community's foreign trade and the trade between its member states. The time series are derived from statistics submitted by the Community's member countries to EUROSTAT for processing and input, and are classified according to the Community's NIMEXE product classification system and the Standard International Trade Classification (SITC) of the United Nations. The DATA BANK is commercially available online; additionally, COMEXT statistics are available on magnetic tape, on microfiche, or in printed publications.

Scope and/or Subject Matter: External trade statistics for EEC members. Countries are treated individually and are also aggregated by economic area or other grouping.

Input Sources: Statistical data for COMEXT are prepared and submitted to EUROSTAT through a cooperative system of the national statistical offices of the EEC member states.

Holdings and Storage Media: The computer-readable COMEXT file contains approximately 3.5 million basic external trade records, including monthly statistics for the current year and quarterly statistics for the two previous years.

Publications: A number of EUROSTAT publications are prepared from the COMEXT Data Bank and are available from the Statistical Office.

Microform Products and Services: COMEXT data are available on 42x microfiche.

Computer-Based Products and Services: The COMEXT DATA BANK is available on magnetic tape and online through CISI and Honeywell Bull Euris. COMEXT software features complex retrieval functions and a variety of computational capabilities including the following: selection by keyword; selection by combinations of such characteristics as periods, flows, products, trading partners, and reporting countries; and tabulation, statistical calculations, and graphs from selected information. Based on the volume of data involved, output is either by direct display or printout.

Clientele/Availability: Primary users include government agencies, academic institutions, international business firms, banks, and dealers in foreign trade.

Projected Publications and Services: In parallel with the COMEXT Data Bank, EUROSTAT is developing the SIENA data bank for users within the CEC.

Contact: M. Rambaud-Chanoz, Head of Section, or M. Poliart, COMEXT Data Bank. (Telex 3423 COMEUR LU.)

★225★
COMMISSION OF THE EUROPEAN COMMUNITIES (CEC)
STATISTICAL OFFICE OF THE EUROPEAN COMMUNITIES (EUROSTAT)
CRONOS DATA BANK
Batiment Jean Monnet, B.P. 1907   Phone: 352 43011
Rue Alcide de Gasperi   Service Est: 1974
Kirchberg, Luxembourg
Mr. Nols, Head of Department

Staff: 1 Information and library professional; 2 management professional; 4 technicians; 2 sales and marketing; 2 clerical and nonprofessional.

Related Organizations: The Commission is the policy-formulating and administrative unit of the European Communities.

Description of System or Service: The CRONOS DATA BANK is a large machine-readable file of economic time series for countries in Europe as well as a number of industrialized and developing countries outside the European Economic Community. It is used to produce EUROSTAT publications and is available online. The DATA BANK is held under the CRONOS data base management system, which features a variety of data management, retrieval, and computation capabilities in batch or interactive modes.

Scope and/or Subject Matter: Statistical time series concerning the economies of European Economic Community countries, associated overseas countries, and major third-world countries. Included are general statistics; foreign trade aggregates and trade with African, Caribbean, Pacific, and associated countries; developing countries; industrial survey and sectoral information; energy; agricultural products, prices, and accounts; balance of payments; financial accounts; national accounts; and research and development.

Input Sources: Input consists of national and international statistics submitted on questionnaires, listings, publications, and magnetic tapes.

Holdings and Storage Media: The CRONOS Data Bank contains approximately 700,000 machine-readable time series. Short term indicators are updated twice monthly.

Publications: 1) EUROSTAT Review (annual)—two trilingual volumes containing time series in the principal statistical categories covered by CRONOS. 2) Basic Statistics of the Community (annual). 3) Eurostatistics (monthly)—data for short-term economic analysis. 4) Yearbook of Regional Statistics. 5) Government Financing of Research and Development (annual). 6) EUROSTAT News (quarterly). 7) CRONOS System for the Management of Time Series—information on the contents of the Data Bank. Also issued are a number of other publications in the fields of national accounts, finance, and balance of payments; population and social conditions; industry and services; agriculture, forestry, and fisheries; and foreign trade.

Microform Products and Services: Requests for microform services are considered on an individual basis.

Computer-Based Products and Services: CRONOS is accessible online through CISI, I/S Datacentralen, and other hosts. The DATA BANK is also available directly for internal (EEC) and privileged users. Time series in the file are divided into 20 major statistical categories, such as national accounts, energy, agricultural products, and external trade. Apart from the specialist time-series fields, the System contains a priority data base for economic and general information known as ICG; certain series in the specialized domains appear in the ICG, where they are automatically updated. Additional time series will be added in the future. CRONOS is indexed in German, French, and English.

Clientele/Availability: Services are available online without restrictions.

Contact: Francois De Geujer, Content and Policy Manager, CRONOS Data Bank, Statistical Office of the European Communities. (Telex 3423/3446.)

★226★
COMMISSION OF THE EUROPEAN COMMUNITIES (CEC)
SYSTEM FOR INFORMATION ON GREY LITERATURE IN EUROPE (SIGLE)
Batiment Jean Monnet, B.P. 1907   Phone: 4301 2908
Rue Alcide de Gasperi   Service Est: 1981
Kirchberg, Luxembourg
Marcel M. Maurice, Principal Administrator

Related Organizations: SIGLE is operated by a consortium of major information centers in six European Community countries. The CEC, which is the policy-formulating and administrative unit of the European Communities, provides financial support and input contribution.

Description of System or Service: The SYSTEM FOR INFORMATION ON GREY LITERATURE IN EUROPE (SIGLE) is an international network designed to improve the detection, identification, and collection of grey or nonconventional literature in member countries. Each SIGLE center collects grey literature issued in its territory, codes and catalogs the documents according to standardized rules, and supplies the data to the central data processing unit for merging into the SIGLE data base. The computer-readable data base is distributed to each SIGLE center and is also publicly accessible through INKA (Informationssystem Karlsruhe). Additionally, SIGLE centers provide document delivery and referral services and promote document cataloging and classification by producers of nonconventional literature.

Scope and/or Subject Matter: Grey or nonconventional literature in such areas as aeronautics; agriculture; plant sciences; veterinary sciences; humanities; psychology; social sciences; biological and medical sciences; chemistry; earth sciences; electronics and electrical engineering; computer science; energy; materials; mathematical sciences; mechanical, industrial, civil, and marine engineering; methods and equipment; military sciences; missile technology; navigation, communications, detection, and countermeasures; ordnance; physics; propulsion and fuels; and space technology.

Input Sources: Input consists of grey or nonconventional literature including reports, theses, conference proceedings, and translations not commercially published; official documents issued in limited numbers; and technical recommendations and rules supplied by SIGLE national centers, associated institutions in Sweden and Luxembourg, and the CEC.

Holdings and Storage Media: The computer-readable SIGLE data base holds 15,000 citations dating from 1981 to the present.

Computer-Based Products and Services: The bibliographic SIGLE data base is accessible online through INKA via Euronet DIANE. The file is organized according to subject categories and includes the following data elements: English title, original title, author, corporate entry, report/ paper number, date, page number, language, availability, and record number. The data base is searchable using subject category codes or keywords. Master tapes of SIGLE are available to each participating center.

Clientele/Availability: Services are available without restrictions.

Contact: Marcel M. Maurice, Principal Administrator, or Mr. J.M. Gibb, System for Information on Grey Literature in Europe. (Telex 3423 COMEUR LU or 2752 EURDOC LU.)

★227★
COMMISSION OF THE EUROPEAN COMMUNITIES (CEC)
TENDERS ELECTRONIC DAILY (TED)
ECHO   Phone: 352 20764
15, ave. de la Faiencerie
Luxembourg

Related Organizations: The Commission of the European Communities (CEC) is the policy-formulating and administrative unit of the European Communities. TED is produced by the Commission's Office for Official Publications.

Description of System or Service: TENDERS ELECTRONIC DAILY (TED) is a computer-readable data base which lists calls for tenders of public works contracts and public supply contracts published in the Supplement S of the Official Journal of the European Communities. The tenders, available the morning after publication in Supplement S, are searchable online through ECHO (European Commission Host Organization), a host on Euronet DIANE. Additionally, current awareness services are offered from the TED data base.

Scope and/or Subject Matter: Tenders of public works contracts and public supply contracts for products and services in the areas of mechanical and electrical engineering, printing, fuel provision, chemical products, water treatment, hospital equipment and construction, and consumer goods.

Input Sources: Input is obtained from the hardcopy Supplement S of the Official Journal.

Holdings and Storage Media: The TED data base is maintained in machine-readable form; current tenders are continuously updated.

Publications: A data base manual is issued in English and French.

Computer-Based Products and Services: The TENDERS ELECTRONIC DAILY data base is available online through ECHO. TED is searchable in English and French. Additionally, ECHO offers current awareness services from the data base. A client profile containing product area information and preferred countries for business is maintained. Using the profile, TED is searched in client-defined areas and search results are transmitted to the client via telex.

Other Services: Special services are also offered to assist users who want to retrieve, store, and reprocess specific types of documents from the file.

Clientele/Availability: The data base is accessible on an annual subscription basis.

Contact: Roland Haber, ECHO Manager, Commission of the European Communities.

★228★
COMMODITIES RESEARCH UNIT LTD. (CRU)
31 Mount Pleasant   Phone: 01-278 0414
London WC1X 0AD, England   Founded: 1969
Mr. R.B. Goldstein, Director

Staff: 1 Information and library professional; 10 management professional; 30 technicians; 7 sales and marketing; 17 clerical and nonprofessional; 1 other.

Related Organizations: CRU maintains a branch in New York City known as CRU Consultants, Inc.

Description of System or Service: COMMODITIES RESEARCH UNIT LTD. (CRU) collects and disseminates data on mining and metals and their economics. It issues regular report series covering specific metals; provides two online data bases in the areas of lead, zinc, and silver mines and mine, smelter, and refinery capacities; and offers multiclient and client specific studies.

Scope and/or Subject Matter: Copper, lead, zinc, aluminium, nickel, tin, alumina, steel; related economic data.

Input Sources: Information is derived from national income accounts, CRU field studies, and other sources.

Holdings and Storage Media: CRU maintains two nonbibliographic data banks in computer-readable form.

Publications: 1) Quarterly Reports—separate reports for aluminium, copper, lead, nickel, and zinc. The reports analyze demand, supply, stocks, and price in detail and provide forecasts for 18 months to 2 years ahead. Subscription includes semiannual or annual seminars. An annual supplement providing five-year forecasts is also available. 2) Monthly Monitors—provide up-to-date statistics and analyses of metal and energy markets. Separate Monitors are issued for copper, zinc, tin and antimony, lead, aluminium, steel, bulk ferro-alloys, crude oil and oil products, and nickel, chrome, and molybdenum. There are discounts for multiple subscriptions. 3) Copper Studies (monthly)—covers a wide range of subjects relating to the copper industry with each issue concentrating on one or two subjects. Topics include country surveys, aspects of copper contracts, and issues of trade. An annual subject index is issued. 4) Silver Trends (six per year)—provides an appraisal and analysis of current developments in the silver market. 5) Multiclient Studies—available in the fields of aluminium; copper; lead, zinc, and silver; gold, iron ore, titanium, and uranium; and general areas.

Computer-Based Products and Services: COMMODITIES RESEARCH UNIT maintains two computer-readable data bases which are available online through ADP Network Services, Inc.: 1) The Lead, Zinc, Silver Mine Cost Model is a comprehensive data bank which covers existing and planned mines. It can be used to generate worldwide and regional supply schedules for lead, zinc, or silver using historical or projected prices. Each run can use different assumptions on coproduct metal prices, treatment and refining charges, and transportation costs. 2) The Mine, Smelter, Refinery Databank holds statistics on the capacity of all mines, smelters, and refineries (already built or under construction) that produce aluminium, copper, lead, zinc, or nickel. The Databank includes capacity figures and notes with capacity forecasts for the next five years. In addition to being accessible online, CRU data banks can also be provided in machine-readable form for use on client systems.

Clientele/Availability: Products and services are available to business and government.

Contact: Mr. R.B. Goldstein, Director, Commodities Research Unit Ltd. (Telex 264008 CRULDN G.) In the United States, contact CRU Consultants Ltd., 33 W. 54th St., New York, NY 10019; telephone (212) 765-9600. (Telex 961054 CRU NYK.) In Japan, contact Overseas Data Service Co. Ltd., Shugetsu Bldg. No. 12-7, Kita-Aoyama, 3-Chome, Minato-ku, Tokyo, Japan; telephone 4007090. (Telex J26487 ODSTHINK.)

★229★
COMMONWEALTH AGRICULTURAL BUREAUX (CAB)
CAB ABSTRACTS
Farnham House, Farnham Royal
Slough SL2 3BN, England
N.G. Jones, Executive Director
Phone: 02814 2281
Service Est: 1929

Staff: Approximately 250 total.

Related Organizations: The Commonwealth Agricultural Bureaux comprises the four Commonwealth institutes of entomology, mycology, biological control, and parasitology, along with the ten Commonwealth bureaux of agricultural economics, animal breeding and genetics, animal health, dairy science and technology, forestry, horticulture and plantation crops, nutrition, pastures and field crops, plant breeding and genetics, and soils. Additionally, the Bureaux works cooperatively with the International Food Information Service, the ARC Weed Research Organization, the National Institute for Agricultural Engineering, Bioquest Ltd., the International Bee Research Association, the International Trust for Zoological Nomenclature, and John Wiley and Sons, Inc.

Description of System or Service: Constituting the world's leading information service in the agricultural sciences, CAB ABSTRACTS is the machine-readable representation of nearly 50 abstracts journals giving worldwide coverage of literature on various aspects of agriculture and related areas of applied biology, sociology, and economics. The journals are prepared by the individual units of the Commonwealth Agricultural Bureaux according to their specialties, and are subscribed to in print or microform by 40,000 users in 150 countries. The CAB ABSTRACTS data base includes information contained in most of the journals since 1973; it is available online through several international vendors or on computer tapes from CAB.

Scope and/or Subject Matter: Every branch of agricultural science, including animal sciences, dairy science and technology, agricultural economics, engineering, forestry, human nutrition, rural development and regional planning, veterinary medicine, taxonomy, horticulture, and others. Areas of applied biology, sociology, and economics are included in the coverage.

Input Sources: More than 10,000 journals in 37 languages are scanned, along with books, technical reports, theses, patents, and other materials from around the world. About 180,000 items are selected from these sources annually for inclusion in the main abstracts journals and the data base. Significant papers are abstracted, while minor works are given only citations.

Holdings and Storage Media: The computer-readable CAB ABSTRACTS data base holds approximately 1.6 million records dating from 1973 to the present and is updated monthly with more than 10,000 new records.

Publications: MAIN ABSTRACTS JOURNALS: 1) Agricultural Engineering Abstracts (monthly). 2) Animal Breeding Abstracts (monthly)—contains about 500 abstracts per issue, plus book reviews; subject and author indexes to each volume. 3) Apicultural Abstracts—available from the International Bee Research Association (see separate entry). 4) Arid Lands Development Abstracts (ceased publication)—only published from 1980 through 1982. 5) Dairy Science Abstracts (monthly)—includes full monthly subject indexes. 6) Field Crop Abstracts (monthly). 7) Food Science & Technology Abstracts (monthly). 8) Forestry Abstracts (monthly)—covers forestry in its widest sense. 9) Forest Products Abstracts (monthly)—journal for scientists and industrialists concerned with wood and other forest products. 10) Helminthological Abstracts: Series A, Animal Helminthology (monthly). 11) Helminthological Abstracts: Series B, Plant Nematology (quarterly). 12) Herbage Abstracts (monthly)—each issue includes book reviews, as well as subject and author indexes. 13) Horticultural Abstracts (monthly)—provides 10,000 abstracts per year on horticultural and plantation crops, with comprehensive monthly and annual subject indexes. 14) Index Veterinarius (monthly)—a subject and author index to veterinary literature worldwide. 15) Leisure, Recreation and Tourism Abstracts (quarterly). 16) Nutrition Abstracts and Reviews: Series A, Human and Experimental (monthly). 17) Nutrition Abstracts and Reviews: Series B, Livestock Feeds and Feeding (monthly). 18) Plant Breeding Abstracts (monthly). 19) Protozoological Abstracts (monthly)—journal on parasitic protozoa and related organisms; with cumulative author and subject indexes.

20) Review of Applied Entomology: Series A, Agricultural (monthly). 21) Review of Applied Entomology: Series B, Medical and Veterinary (monthly). 22) Review of Medical and Veterinary Mycology (quarterly). 23) Review of Plant Pathology (monthly). 24) Rural Development Abstracts (quarterly)—journal providing overview of world literature in rural development. 25) Rural Extension, Education & Training Abstracts (quarterly)—journal with annual indexes. 26) Soils and Fertilizers (monthly)—each issue contains about 600 abstracts and references to current literature. 27) Veterinary Bulletin (monthly)—includes about 550 abstracts per issue. 28) Weed Abstracts (monthly). 29) World Agricultural Economics and Rural Sociology Abstracts (monthly).

SPECIALIST ABSTRACT JOURNALS: 30) Cotton and Tropical Fibres Abstracts (monthly). 31) Crop Physiology Abstracts (monthly). 32) Faba Bean Abstracts (quarterly). 33) Irrigation and Drainage Abstracts (quarterly). 34) Lentil Abstracts (annual). 35) Maize Quality Protein Abstracts (quarterly). 36) Ornamental Horticulture (monthly). 37) Plant Growth Regulator Abstracts (monthly). 38) Potato Abstracts (monthly). 39) Poultry Abstracts (monthly). 40) Rice Abstracts (monthly). 41) Seed Abstracts (monthly). 42) Small Animal Abstracts (quarterly). 43) Sorghum and Millets Abstracts (monthly). 44) Soyabean Abstracts (monthly). 45) Tropical Oil Seeds Abstracts (monthly). 46) Wheat, Barley and Triticale Abstracts (six per year).

PRIMARY JOURNALS: 47) Bulletin of Entomological Research (quarterly)—includes papers dealing with original research. 48) Bulletin of Zoological Nomenclature (quarterly).

SERIAL PUBLICATIONS: 49) Animal Disease Occurrence (twice per year). 50) Bibliography of Systematic Mycology (twice per year). 51) Biocontrol News and Information (quarterly). 52) Index of Current Research on Pigs (annual). 53) Index of Fungi (twice per year). 54) International Biodeterioration (quarterly)—contains information formerly found in the International Biodeterioration Bulletin, Biodeterioration Research Titles, and Waste Materials Biodegradation Research Titles. 55) Pig News and Information (quarterly).

USER AIDS: 56) CAB Abstracts Online Newsletter (quarterly)—provides information and practical hints for searching, focusing on subfiles, news, workshops, and meetings; available without charge. 57) CAB ABSTRACTS Online—available for purchase; manual describing the content and format of CAB material in each field.

Contains details such as lists of abbreviations and geographic names used by CAB, as well as recommended reference works for nomenclature. Also suggests searching techniques. 58) CAB Serials Checklist—available for purchase. Lists more than 10,000 serial titles scanned and abstracted by CAB; shows which CAB units abstract each title; and provides a guide to sources of photocopies. 59) CAB Thesaurus—available for purchase. Arranges in hierarchies approximately 48,000 entries on plant sciences, animal sciences, microbiology, parasitology, economics, and other subjects treated by CAB.

Microform Products and Services: Journal subscriptions are available on microfiche, with discounts offered to those who subscribe to both fiche and hard copy.

Computer-Based Products and Services: The CAB ABSTRACTS data base includes records from most of the journals named above, dating back to 1973. Updated monthly, the data base is available online through DIALOG Information Services, Inc., ESA/IRS, and DIMDI. It is searchable by individual journal or as an integrated whole. Current and retrospective magnetic tape services are offered by CAB for selected groups of journals or the entire data base. Additionally, CAB fills document orders placed online through DIALORDER and PRIMORDIAL.

Other Services: Also offered are manual literature searching, copying service for original articles, and referrals.

Clientele/Availability: Services are available without restrictions, with discounts on some journals offered to subscribers from countries contributing to CAB.

Remarks: An additional function of CAB is its worldwide service for the taxonomic identification of insects, mites, nematodes, microfungi, and bacteria. Heavily used by developing countries, this service makes about 20,000 identifications annually.

Contact: Sales Manager or David Hunter, Promotions Assistant, Commonwealth Agricultural Bureaux. (Telex 847964.) In North America, contact Elaine Cook, CAB North American Representative, University of Arizona, College of Agriculture, Office of Arid Lands Studies, 845 N. Park Ave., Tucson, AZ 85719; telephone (602) 621-1955 or toll-free, 800-528-4841.

★230★
COMMONWEALTH REGIONAL RENEWABLE ENERGY RESOURCES INFORMATION SYSTEM (CRRERIS)
CSIRO, P.O. Box 89
314 Albert St.
East Melbourne, Vic. 3002, Australia
Susan Harvey, Manager
Phone: 03 4187333
Founded: 1980

Staff: 2 Information and library professional; 1 clerical and nonprofessional.

Related Organizations: CRRERIS is operated by the Commonwealth Scientific and Industrial Research Organization (CSIRO) under contract to the Australian Development Assistance Bureau.

Description of System or Service: The COMMONWEALTH REGIONAL RENEWABLE ENERGY RESOURCES INFORMATION SYSTEM (CRRERIS) is a network established to facilitate the transfer of renewable energy resources information among Commonwealth countries in the Asian and Pacific regions. Among its projects is the maintenance of a computer-readable bibliographic data base on relevant publications originating in member countries. A liaison center in each country identifies documents and provides a copy of each, with indexing information, to the network center for processing into the CRRERIS data base. The data base is used to produce a published index, the Commonwealth Regional Renewable Energy Resources Index (CRRERI), and to provide information retrieval services. Documents indexed in CRRERI are available to member countries from a clearinghouse operated by the System.

Scope and/or Subject Matter: All aspects of renewable energy resources, including solar, water, sea, wind, geothermal, and fuel energy.

Input Sources: Input is derived from documents collected in member countries.

Holdings and Storage Media: The bibliographic CRRERI data base is maintained in machine-readable form.

Publications: 1) Commonwealth Regional Renewable Energy Resources Index-CRRERI (quarterly)—available to CRRERIS members. Provides citations to periodical literature, books, reports, and proceedings relevant to energy. Indexed by author and subject. 2) CRRERIS Newsletter. 3) Renewable Energy Experts Directory. 4) Renewable Energy Products Directory.

Microform Products and Services: CRRERI and copies of documents indexed therein are available on microfiche to members.

Computer-Based Products and Services: The CRRERI data base is used for publication purposes and to provide information retrieval services in a variety of formats.

Clientele/Availability: Services are available to member countries.

Contact: Susan Harvey, Manager, Commonwealth Regional Renewable Energy Resources Information System.

★231★
COMMUNICATION SERVICES LTD.
VIEWDATA SERVICES
G.P.O. Box 9872
Hong Kong
Bernard J. Howells, Manager
Phone: 05 8288220
Service Est: 1980

Related Organizations: Communication Services Ltd. is a subsidiary of Hong Kong Telephone Company, Ltd.

Description of System or Service: VIEWDATA SERVICES operates an interactive videotex service which links television receivers, terminals, and microcomputers with a centralized computer data base via telephone lines. It permits pages or frames of business and consumer information to be selected from a directory through the use of a keypad or keyboard. In addition to providing up-to-date information, VIEWDATA SERVICES offers an electronic telephone directory, gateway services which link users to third-party computers, Autoview services which display programs of specialist information continuously, closed user group services, electronic mail, telesoftware for downloading to microcomputers, and Hotelview for tourists in their hotel rooms.

Scope and/or Subject Matter: Business and consumer information, including news, travel, leisure, entertainment, business news, education, finance, stock market, commodities, telephone directory, yellow pages, and information on China.

Input Sources: Input is obtained from news services, securities firms, travel companies, airlines, education institutions, specialist publications, Hong Kong General Chamber of Commerce, and other information providers.

Holdings and Storage Media: Six major files of business and consumer information are held online.

Computer-Based Products and Services: VIEWDATA SERVICES provides interactive access to a variety of business and consumer information, including the following: electronic yellow pages; an education file providing reinforcement learning using computer-assisted techniques; SHK Securities financial information including current stock prices, foreign exchange rates, and commodities; Reuters financial data; news, sports, and leisure information; and a China file provided by the South China Morning Post. Additional services include telesoftware, closed user group services, gateway links to third-party computers, Autoview services providing continuous program display, electronic mail, and Hotelview.

Other Services: Communication Services Ltd. also offers videotex consulting services, including data base design and page creation, as well as services to foreign organizations wishing to promote their goods or services in Hong Kong.

Clientele/Availability: Services are available without restrictions in Hong Kong and overseas.

Projected Publications and Services: Remote home banking services are planned.

Contact: William Chow, Communication Services Ltd.

★232★
COMMUNICATIONS INFORMATION

Special Note: COMMUNICATIONS INFORMATION, a computer-readable data base personally maintained by Professor John B. Black of the University of Guelph Library in Canada, is reported to be no longer available. The data base was described in the fifth edition of the Encyclopedia of Information Systems and Services (entry 429) as an online file providing citations to worldwide literature covering the political, social, and legal aspects of mass communications and telecommunications.

★233★
COMPANY FOR INFORMATICS
(Societe pour l'Informatique - SPI)
SPIDEL
98, blvd. Victor Hugo　　　　　　　Phone: 7311191
F-92115 Clichy, France

Special Note: The SPIDEL online host service has been discontinued. Operational from 1979 to 1983, the service provided interactive access to AFEE, BIIPAM, CETIM, MERLIN, and other data bases. The parent company, SPI, continues to offer services in various fields of industrial and computerized applications.

Contact: Dominique Bouvier, Infocentre, Company for Informatics. (Telex 610 142 F.)

★234★
COMPU-MARK
P.O. Box 61　　　　　　　　　　　Phone: 031 499840
B-2510 Mortsel, Belgium　　　　　　Founded: 1966
Florent Gevers, Director

Staff: Approximately 80 total.

Related Organizations: Compu-Mark is the parent organization of Compu-Mark (UK) Ltd. and Compu-Mark U.S.

Description of System or Service: COMPU-MARK supplies worldwide information on trademarks to the legal and trademark professions. The firm stores information in computer files and makes it available in hardcopy publications, through computerized search services, and on magnetic tapes.

Scope and/or Subject Matter: Trademark documentation.

Input Sources: Input is derived from U.S. Official Trademark Gazette, other trademark gazettes published worldwide, and official publications of new trademark applications.

Holdings and Storage Media: Machine-readable files cover more than 6 million trademarks, including new trademarks for all countries since 1970; all registrations currently on file for France, West Germany, Austria, Great Britain, Liechtenstein, Monaco, Switzerland, United States, Belgium, Netherlands, Luxembourg, and selected African countries; and International Registrations.

Publications: 1) World Trademark Journal (weekly)—published in a card format containing trademark applications. 2) Alphabetical Directory of Benelux Trademarks (updated annually). 3) Alphabetical and Phonetic Directory of International Trademarks (quarterly cumulative supplements). 4) Alphaphonetic Directory of International Trademarks - Classification by Suffix (updated annually). 5) Rechtsstands Lexicon (cumulated quarterly)—alphabetical list of trademarks in West Germany. 6) Alphabetical Directory of French Trademarks (updated annually). 7) Alphabetical List of French Applications (monthly).

Computer-Based Products and Services: Computer-based services offered by COMPU-MARK include: 1) Trademark Availability Searches—batch-mode searches to determine the availability of proposed new trademarks in Common Market and other European countries, including International Registrations. 2) World Watch Service—searches new trademark applications published anywhere in the world and reports potential conflicts with important trademarks listed by COMPU-MARK clients; available by subscription. In addition, a weekly tape subscription service is available for all new trademark applications published worldwide for selected international classes. Tapes are also available for selected classes of all trademark applications published worldwide since 1970.

Clientele/Availability: Services are available only to the legal and trademark profession.

Contact: Florent Gevers, Director, Compu-Mark. (Telex 33875 COMPU B.)

★235★
COMPU-MARK (UK) LTD.
93 Chancery Lane　　　　　　　　Phone: 01-405 1305
London WC2A 1DT, England　　　　Founded: 1980
Florent Gevers, Director

Staff: 3 Management professional; 3 clerical and nonprofessional.

Related Organizations: The parent organization of Compu-Mark (UK) Ltd. is Compu-Mark, headquartered in Mortsel, Belgium.

Description of System or Service: COMPU-MARK (UK) LTD. provides computerized searches of its machine-readable data base of British trademark registrations and applications. Through affiliates in Belgium and the United States searches are also available for most European countries, the United States, and Africa. Additionally, COMPU-MARK (UK) makes available the U.K. Trade Marks Journal on microfiche and offers a worldwide trademark watch service.

Scope and/or Subject Matter: Trademark documentation.

Input Sources: Input is derived from the Official Trade Marks Journal of England, pending applications, official trademark gazettes published worldwide, and official publications of new trademark applications.

Holdings and Storage Media: Machine-readable files cover more than 250,000 U.K. trademarks, including all active registrations and applications.

Microform Products and Services: The U.K. Trade Marks Journal is available on microfiche.

Computer-Based Products and Services: COMPU-MARK maintains and provides online searches from a machine-readable data base of U.K. trademark registrations, applications, and pending applications.

Clientele/Availability: Services are available only to the legal and trademark professions.

Contact: David Sheppard, Compu-Mark (UK) Ltd.

★236★
COMPUSEARCH MARKET AND SOCIAL RESEARCH LTD.
16 Madison Ave.　　　　　　　　Phone: (416) 967-5881
Toronto, ON, Canada M5R 2S1
Michele Sexsmith, Director of Marketing

Description of System or Service: COMPUSEARCH MARKET AND SOCIAL RESEARCH LTD. provides clients in Canada and the United States with computerized market information services based on a machine-readable collection of census statistics, current population and income updates, consumer expenditure information, and geographic data. It offers the following services, which may be used singly or in combination: 1) Market Penetration Analysis—combines census data with client customer address information to produce reports and maps giving an accurate demographic profile of customers and an estimation of market share for any Canadian urban center. 2) AreaSearch—assists clients in locating sales markets in Canada and the U.S. by producing ranked market profiles according to client-specified demographic variables and geographic levels. 3) TRADAREA—provides analysis of any trading area of any size or shape in Canada or the U.S. using a large collection of demographic, socioeconomic, and consumer expenditure statistics. 4) Precision Prospect Analysis—supports direct mail marketing by segmenting existing lists to target mail to a specific audience. A demographic profile can be developed at the postal code level. 5) SELECT MAIL—supplies direct mail marketers with key demographic information based on Canadian postal code areas. 6) Market Feasibility Studies—combines a variety of market research information to determine the feasibility of new sites. 7) Lifestyles—locates expenditure areas of 10 major lifestyle groups with 48 individual lifestyle types derived from combining demographic and consumer expenditure data. 8) DemoGRAPHICS—produces computer-generated color graphs of socioeconomic data for any area in Canada. 9) Business Activity

Report (B.A.R.)—provides a summary of businesses and their characteristics for any location in Canada using a separate data base on Canadian corporations. Also produced is a Combined Activity report which provides data on Canadian companies and also on the potential residential and working population available in a market. The studies are custom-designed for each project. COMPUSEARCH makes its market analyses available in printed reports and maps; graphics are available for summarizing reports. The firm also offers software systems for marketing applications. The COMPUSEARCH data bases may be accessed online through commercial time-sharing.

Scope and/or Subject Matter: Market research in Canada and the United States, including demographics, housing, economics, and related topics; Canadian corporations.

Input Sources: Compusearch acquires data from Canadian and U.S. federal and local government sources.

Holdings and Storage Media: The computer-readable Compusearch demographics data base holds more than 200 separate demographic, housing, and economic variables for North America; the business data base holds data on more than 500,000 Canadian businesses.

Computer-Based Products and Services: COMPUSEARCH maintains demographic and business information data bases and provides reports and data analysis services from them. The demographic data base contains more than 200 variables for North America, including the following major categories: population, age, marital status, housing, household sites, families, children, education, labor force, income (current estimates), and consumer expenditures for more than 100 products and services. The business information data base lists more than 570,000 Canadian corporations and their business characteristics. Data in the two files are integrated to produce the Combined Activity Report and other special reports. The COMPUSEARCH data bases are also accessible to clients on a time-sharing basis. Clients accessing the data bases directly can produce a variety of TRADAREA and other standardized reports. COMPUSEARCH also offers online marketing information systems which combine social, economic, demographic, and customer sales data into interactive decision support systems. It provides customized software systems designed for expanding and consolidating sales territories, monitoring sales performance, and predicting sales potential. Other computer-based services include generation of color-coded charts and maps of any demographic area or of client specified data.

Clientele/Availability: Products and services are available without restrictions.

Contact: Michele Sexsmith, Director of Marketing, Compusearch Market and Social Research Ltd.

★237★
COMPUTER SCIENCES OF AUSTRALIA PTY. LTD. (CSA)
NETWORK SERVICES DIVISION
INFOBANK
460 Pacific Hwy. Phone: 02 4390033
St. Leonards, N.S.W. 2065, Australia Service Est: 1970
Peter J. Farrell, Product Manager

Related Organizations: Computer Sciences of Australia was formed by the AMP Society, Australia's largest life and general insurance group, and Computer Sciences Corporation (CSC), a computer services company located in Los Angeles.

Description of System or Service: INFOBANK is an online information retrieval service providing access to a wide range of government and private sector data. Accessible via INFONET, Computer Sciences Corporation's international teleprocessing network, INFOBANK comprises a series of statistical, demographic, and econometric data bases as well as applications programs for sophisticated analysis. Major statistical information available includes Australian Censuses of Population and Housing data, which are generally aggregated to the following areas: 26,000 collection districts, which are the smallest areas for which detailed statistics are available and contain approximately 300 homes each; 1200 census local government areas (LGAs), which are larger geographic areas and thus afford more of a statistical overview; and Postcodes, which are numbers assigned by Australia Post to a distributing post office. Other data bases available include motor vehicle registration information, national income forecasting models, financial data on industry groups in Australia, and U.S. economic data. Users at all levels can access and process INFOBANK information via MANAGE, a proprietary data base management system available through INFONET. INFOBANK applications include market planning and research, economic analysis and forecasting, strategic location studies, business planning, and sales and production forecasting.

Scope and/or Subject Matter: Australian and selected U.S. statistical data, ranging from population statistics to motor vehicle registrations and from agricultural production to financial and economic data.

Input Sources: The principal supplier of the statistical data used by INFOBANK is the Australian Bureau of Statistics (ABS). Input is also acquired from other federal and state government departments, from universities, and from a number of sources in the business and commercial sectors.

Holdings and Storage Media: Several dozen files holding millions of records are maintained online.

Publications: User manuals and other documentation are available from CSA.

Computer-Based Products and Services: INFOBANK provides online access to the following data bases and collections: 1) Updated annually, the Australian Municipal Information System (AMIS) is a collection of six data bases (one for each Australian state) containing data for approximately 900 local government areas (LGAs). For each LGA, AMIS provides approximately 50 cross-section data items and about 80 time-series data items. The cross-section items provide a broad description of socioeconomic characteristics of the LGA, including population characteristics, dwelling characteristics, area and valuation data, and economic activity in the areas of manufacturing, retailing, and agriculture. 2) The Collection District Data Bases contain 1971, 1976, and 1981 Census of Population and Housing data aggregated to the Australian census collection district. 3) The C76 LGA File Zero Data Bases is a set of nine data bases corresponding to the nine record types of the C76 Collection District Data Bases which aggregate data from the 1976 Census to the 1200 LGAs in Australia. 4) The C81 LGA Data Base contains approximately 1200 records aggregating data from the 1981 Census to the LGA level. Census data elements in the file are identical to those in the C81 Collection District Data Bases. 5) The C76 LGA Descriptor Data Base contains information on LGAs together with significant statistics from the 1971 Census. Information includes name of each major town within each rural LGA; area in hectares as of January, 1976; the 1971 population by male, female, and overall total; occupied dwellings, 1971; and unoccupied dwellings, 1971. 6) The C81 Geographic Descriptor Data Base contains LGA name, 1976 male, female, and total population statistics, 1976 occupied dwellings, 1976 unoccupied dwellings, and the locality code for each census LGA and for each major town within each LGA.

7) The C76 Journey-To-Work (JTW) Data Bases provide data derived from the 1976 Census on people at work and their methods of travel to their places of work. 8) The C76 Postcode Data Bases is a series of nine data bases containing data from the 1976 Census aggregated to Postcode level. 9) The C81 Postcode Data Base contains data from the 1981 Census aggregated to Postcode level. The data base contains approximately 2500 records. 10) The Econometric Data Bank contains approximately 2200 time series updated monthly by the Institute of Applied Economic and Social Research of the University of Melbourne. 11) The Agricultural Data Bases comprise six data bases containing data for each annual Agricultural Census conducted by the ABS Agricultural Information Dissemination Service (AIDS). 12) The Postcode Locality Data Base (PCODES) contains a record for each Postcode in Australia displaying the associated locality names.

13) ABS Time Series is a set of more than 1600 time series made available by the Australian Bureau of Statistics. Updated quarterly, the time series provide data on agricultural production, building, new fixed capital expenditure by private enterprise, demography, workforce, other finance, housing finance to individuals, stocks owned by private enterprise, manufacturing and mining, national accounts, prices, transport, retail sales, overseas transactions, other internal trade, and

wages and salaries. 14) NIF-10S Model Data Base is a short-term national income forecasting model consisting of 265 equations which describe the relationship between 389 economic variables acting on the Australian economy. 15) CITIBASE contains more than 5000 monthly, quarterly, and annual time series describing the U.S. economy. 16) The Grouped Enterprises Data Base is produced by the Australian Bureau of Statistics and contains a wide range of financial data pertaining to the performance of various industry sectors of the Australian economy. 17) The Victorian Motor Vehicle 1982 Registrations Data Base contains 2.3 million records on motor vehicles registered in Victoria in 1982. 18) The New South Wales Motor Vehicle 1982 Registrations Data Base contains approximately 3.3 million records representing the motor vehicles registered in New South Wales in 1982.

In addition to the MANAGE data base management system, INFOBANK offers a number of applications programs for special data manipulation or extraction, including DISTAT, a statistical tool that performs time-series analysis for econometric modeling and financial forecasting; IGL, an easy-to-use language that converts statistical data to graphic display; DEPICT and LOCATE, used to produce high-quality maps of demographic data; and FLARES, a financial analysis and modeling language that enables the user to build sophisticated planning models.

Clientele/Availability: Clients include Australian government agencies and private sector organizations, particularly major banks and retailers.

Remarks: CSA is the largest supplier of computer services in Australia. In addition to INFOBANK, it offers remote time-sharing for general data processing applications in data management, engineering sciences, management sciences, and graphics; undertakes large-scale support and development projects for state and commonwealth governments and for commerce and industry, specializing in the design and programming of communications-based distributed network systems employing data base technology and in systems implementation and operations support on any kind of computer equipment; designs, engineers, and installs processor-based real time systems, including operational defense systems, industrial systems, and data communications networks and switching systems; and provides specialized computer services to the Australian mining industry through a wholly owned subsidiary, Earth Science Computer Services.

Contact: Peter J. Farrell, Product Manager, Network Services Division, Computer Sciences of Australia Pty. Ltd.

★238★
CONFERENCE BOARD OF CANADA
APPLIED ECONOMIC RESEARCH AND INFORMATION CENTRE (AERIC)
AERIC SYSTEM
25 McArthur Rd., Suite 100   Phone: (613) 746-1261
Ottawa, ON, Canada K1L 6R3   Service Est: 1974

Staff: 6 Total.

Description of System or Service: The AERIC SYSTEM is a computerized economic information and forecasting service accessed by more than 200 subscribers from almost 60 organizations across Canada. The SYSTEM provides online access to data bases developed by AERIC and other organizations, and to AERIC forecasting models, a news and economic analysis service, and analytical and statistical tools. In addition to operating the online service, AERIC provides ongoing support of a technical and economic nature, conducts research and analysis on current and emerging issues of significance to the Canadian economy, and issues quarterly forecasting and survey publications.

Scope and/or Subject Matter: Canadian economy.

Input Sources: Input for the System includes economic and statistical data collected by AERIC and other organizations.

Holdings and Storage Media: Several data bases are held in machine-readable form.

Publications: 1) AERIC Information and Documentation—user's manual. 2) Subscriber's Supplement to the Quarterly Canadian Forecast. 3) AERIC Historical Supplements. 4) Survey of Consumer Buying Intentions. The publications are available to System subscribers.

Computer-Based Products and Services: The following data bases are available online over the AERIC SYSTEM: 1) AERIC National Database—contains 900 time series providing detailed quarterly forecasts of the Canadian economy for two years. 2) AERIC Provincial Database—contains 1200 series providing quarterly forecasts for approximately 20 key economic indicators for each of the 10 provinces for up to 18 months in the future. 3) Quarterly Survey of Consumer Buying Intentions—contains 600 series. All of the above are maintained by AERIC. 4) CANSIM Mini Base. 5) CANSIM Supplementary Series. 6) Farm Bank—food and agriculture data base produced by Agriculture Canada. 7) Steel Products Database—produced by Algoma Steel Corporation Ltd. Subscribers also have online access to AERIC forecasting models and to the TROLL, APL, TABLES, and CMS statistical programs. Additionally, AERIC provides the latest Statistics Canada releases and the Conference Board's economic commentaries through its news service; the service also includes detailed tables of the Canadian economy.

Other Services: AERIC conducts training sessions and holds seminars.

Clientele/Availability: Only members of the Conference Board of Canada may subscribe to the AERIC System.

Contact: Marketing Department, Conference Board of Canada.

★239★
CONSORTIUM OF ROYAL LIBRARY AND UNIVERSITY LIBRARIES PROJECT FOR INTEGRATED CATALOGUE AUTOMATION (PICA)
Prins Willem Alexanderhof 5   Phone: 070 140460
NL-2595 BE The Hague, Netherlands Service Est: 1969
L. Costers, Director

Staff: 24 Information and library professional; 2 management professional; 4 technicians; 5 clerical and nonprofessional.

Description of System or Service: The PROJECT FOR INTEGRATED CATALOGUE AUTOMATION (PICA), a computerized cooperative cataloging project, consists of an online data base of bibliographic information which allows users to search for titles, add or change elements, and print desired information in hard copy, on microfiche, or on magnetic tape. A catalog conversion capability compares a retrospective file with the PICA data base and adds new data to the file. Currently in use by a number of academic and public libraries in the Netherlands, PICA includes such functions as interlibrary loans, online thesauri, circulation, acquisitions, interfacing with local systems, and extended searching. Additionally, PICA has developed the national Netherlands Central Catalogue/ Interlibrary Loan System (see separate entry following this one).

Scope and/or Subject Matter: Automated cataloging and related library functions.

Input Sources: Title descriptions are obtained from British National Bibliography and U.S. Library of Congress MARC tapes.

Holdings and Storage Media: The PICA data base comprises more than 2.2 million title descriptions and is updated weekly.

Computer-Based Products and Services: PICA is used to provide computerized cataloging and related capabilities for libraries.

Clientele/Availability: The PICA system is currently used by academic and public libraries in the Netherlands.

Contact: L. Costers, Director, or A. Bossers, Deputy-Director, Project for Integrated Catalogue Automation.

★240★
CONSORTIUM OF ROYAL LIBRARY AND UNIVERSITY LIBRARIES PROJECT FOR INTEGRATED CATALOGUE AUTOMATION (PICA) NETHERLANDS CENTRAL CATALOGUE/INTERLIBRARY LOAN SYSTEM
(Nederlandse Centrale Catalogus/Interbibliothecair Leenverkeer System-NCC/IBL)
Prins Willem Alexanderhof 5
NL-2595 BE The Hague, Netherlands
L. Costers, Director
Phone: 070 140460
Service Est: 1983

Staff: 4 Information and library professional; 1 technician.

Description of System or Service: The NETHERLANDS CENTRAL CATALOG/ INTERLIBRARY LOAN SYSTEM (NCC/IBL) was established to maintain a machine-readable Dutch union catalog and to handle interlibrary loans on a national scale in the Netherlands. Developed by PICA, the SYSTEM is managed by a consortium of approximately 200 libraries that participate in the National Union Catalogue, the Technical Union Catalogue, and the Agricultural Union Catalogue. The SYSTEM's data base currently holds periodicals information from the three catalogs, with monographs data expected to be added in the near future.

Scope and/or Subject Matter: Automated cataloging and interlibrary loan.

Input Sources: Periodicals information is obtained from participating library input to the three union catalogs; monographs information is obtained from the catalogs and the PICA data base.

Holdings and Storage Media: The computer-readable NCC/IBL data base currently holds approximately 500,000 holdings records for 200,000 periodicals.

Computer-Based Products and Services: The SYSTEM is used to provide computerized cataloging and interlibrary loan services.

Clientele/Availability: NCC/IBL services are available without restrictions to Dutch libraries.

Contact: L. Costers, Director, Project for Integrated Catalogue Automation.

★241★
CONSTELLATE CONSULTANTS (P) LTD. (CONCON)
505 Vishal Bhavan
95 Nehru Place
New Delhi 110019, India
Prithvi Haldea, Chief Executive
Phone: 6417015
Founded: 1975

Staff: Approximately 50 total.

Description of System or Service: CONSTELLATE CONSULTANTS (P) LTD. (CONCON) is a consulting organization made up of information specialists in the areas of manufacturing, education, library and information science, foreign trade, accounting, architecture, and other fields. Services of CONCON consist of computerized literature searching and current awareness; consulting in library and information center planning (includes library management; indexing, cataloging, and abstracting; microform reproduction, and translations); information systems design (includes computer applications, software development, and systems analysis); information service (bibliography compilation, periodical subscription arrangement, and thesaurus development); commercial information service (Indian and world export, import, and production statistics; commodity studies, trade information, market conditions, product standards); and industrial consultancy (includes project planning and scheduling, product and market planning, project preparation for rural development). CONCON also publishes a computer-based directory dealing with computer manufacturers, users, and other computer-related organizations in India. Additionally, CONCON acts as the agent in India for the U.S. National Technical Information Service (NTIS), Engineering Information (Ei), the British Standards Institution's Technical Help to Exporters (THE), and other organizations.

Scope and/or Subject Matter: Information systems and services consulting; technology transfer; Indian computer industry.

Input Sources: CONCON utilizes the resources of publicly available data bases and the expertise of professionals in relevant fields.

Holdings and Storage Media: The Computer Directory of India data base holds computer-readable information on more than 4000 organizations and is updated quarterly. The firm maintains a small library and stores information on diskettes for use on its own computer.

Publications: Computer Directory of India (annual with quarterly updates)—contains information on more than 4000 organizations, including: Indian manufacturers and foreign distributors of computer hardware, peripherals, equipment, and supplies; organizations in India with computer installations; organizations providing software, consultancy, and data processing services; teaching and training institutions; Indian information services publishing computer and electronics journals, and suppliers of foreign books and journals; and computer-related organizations such as associations, user groups, and relevant government agencies.

Microform Products and Services: Indexes to many data bases are available on microfiche from CONCON.

Computer-Based Products and Services: CONCON maintains the machine-readable Computer Directory of India data base and utilizes it for publication purposes. Computerized searches are offered from the NTIS data base, and from data bases made available through DIALOG Information Services, Inc. CONCON also uses the NTIS data base to produce CREST, a monthly current awareness service in 177 subject areas; CREST is available by subscription worldwide. Software development and distribution services are also offered.

Other Services: Additional services include manual literature searching, referrals, and data collection and analysis.

Clientele/Availability: Clientele served includes government, industry, research institutes, consultants, educational institutions, and individuals.

Contact: Prithvi Haldea, Chief Executive, Constellate Consultants (P) Ltd. (Telex 031 2566 CARE.)

★242★
CONSTRUCTION SPECIFICATIONS CANADA (CSC) NATIONAL MASTER SPECIFICATION (NMS)
1 St. Clair Ave. W., Suite 1206
Toronto, ON, Canada M4V 1K6
Phone: (416) 922-3159

Related Organizations: The National Master Specification is an adaption of the Government of Canada Master Construction Specification, designed for government construction projects and developed jointly by five Canadian federal departments involved with construction.

Description of System or Service: The NATIONAL MASTER SPECIFICATION (NMS) is an industry-reviewed, nationally oriented specification system for general, marine, and heavy civil engineering construction projects. It serves as a resource tool for writing project specifications, as a technical reference for product, construction, and contract information, and as a checklist to minimize duplication, error, and omission in project specifications. Designed for use on small, medium, or large projects, NMS covers new or renovation construction, private sector or government work, and varying tender or contract arrangements. The system is available as a loose-leaf service, on word-processor diskettes, on magnetic tape, or through commercial time-sharing, and has provisions for manual or electronic text editing, processing, and modification suited to individual project requirements. The NMS data bank is updated continuously via a central control; the updates are released semiannually.

Scope and/or Subject Matter: Canadian construction specifications, including architectural and structural, mechanical and electrical, and marine and heavy civil engineering.

Input Sources: NMS information is based on current specification practice and technical reference documents; government and industry standards; nationally recognized references; and technical information from manufacturers, suppliers, and contractors.

Holdings and Storage Media: The centrally maintained NMS data bank is held in machine-readable form and is updated continuously.

Publications: National Master Specification—consists of more than 500 specification sections in 22 loose-leaf binders. Available in French and English, NMS is sold as a complete set or as individual binders; the first section contains general requirements applicable to the whole system.

Computer-Based Products and Services: The NMS data bank of technical specifications and text is available online through commercial time-sharing or on computer tape and diskette from CSC. NMS can be accessed with word processors, permitting users to retrieve required specifications, edit them online, and generate a final project specification. The data bank is continually updated to incorporate NMS user and industry recommendations, product and construction changes, standard and code changes, and related items.

Clientele/Availability: NMS is available without restrictions. Clients include architects, engineers, general contractors, specifications consultants, trade contractors, manufacturers, suppliers, and other construction-oriented organizations.

Remarks: Construction Specifications Canada is a multidisciplinary association concerned with improving technical communication and information management within the construction industry.

Contact: Margaret Olthuis, Administrative Assistant, Construction Specifications Canada.

★243★
CONSULTEXT
Kadyk 4
NL-8463 VC Rotsterhaule, Netherlands
Raymond M.G.P.B. Bakker, Director
Phone: 05137 1530
Founded: 1971

Description of System or Service: CONSULTEXT provides consultancy, conceptualization, design, development, evaluation, and searching services for professional, popular, scientific, and technical reference publications with emphasis on the subject area of information technology. Publications covered include mono/multilingual dictionaries, glossaries, encyclopedias, handbooks, and bibliographies. CONSULTEXT also publishes an information technology bibliography and a multilingual dictionary, and it offers classification and design for information systems.

Scope and/or Subject Matter: Reference book publishing, with emphasis on information technology, including telematics, microcomputers, microelectronics, optical communications, and others.

Publications: 1) A Comprehensive Bibliography of Reference Works on Information Technology (Informations-Technologie: Bibliographie der Nachschlagewerke)—a major survey of English and German reference literature in the field of information technology. 2) Kluwer's Universeel Technisch Woordenboek—a polytechnical dictionary series covering English, German, French, and Dutch.

Other Services: CONSULTEXT also offers translation services.

Clientele/Availability: Primary clients include publishers, government agencies, libraries, translation bureaus, data base producers, providers of self-teaching and correspondence courses, and others.

Contact: Raymond M.G.P.B. Bakker, Director, CONSULTEXT.

★244★
CONSUMERS' ASSOCIATION
TELEWHICH?
14 Buckingham St.
London WC2N 6DS, England
Phone: 01-839 1222
Service Est: 1976

Special Note: The above name, address, and telephone number have been verified for this edition, although no questionnaire response was received. The following text is reprinted from the 5th edition.

Description of System or Service: The Consumers' Association TELEWHICH? service is an information provider over the British Prestel system. It offers a data base covering consumer buying advice and impartial information on such topics as money, home management, family health, consumer law, travel, car buying, wine, and recommended restaurants, pubs, and wine bars. TELEWHICH? also acts as a consultant to other Prestel information providers. In this role, it offers the following services: data base design and management; market research; seminars and consulting on videotex; and training in data base structuring, layout, inputting, and updating.

Scope and/or Subject Matter: Consumer advice and information; Prestel program planning and management.

Publications: Which?—series of consumer advice magazines published by the Consumers' Association; used to supply information for the TeleWhich? file on Prestel.

Computer-Based Products and Services: The TELEWHICH? data base can be accessed interactively through the Prestel system.

Clientele/Availability: Services are provided to Prestel users and information providers.

Contact: Head of Advisory Services, TeleWhich?.

★245★
CONTROL DATA AUSTRALIA PTY. LTD.
CYBERTEL VIDEOTEX SERVICE
493 St. Kilda Rd.
Melbourne, Vic. 3004, Australia
Brian P. Magill, CYBERTEL Manager
Phone: 03 2689500
Service Est: 1982

Staff: 2 Management professional; 4 technicians; 4 sales and marketing.

Related Organizations: Control Data Australia Pty. Ltd. is a wholly owned subsidiary of Control Data Corporation (CDC).

Description of System or Service: CYBERTEL VIDEOTEX SERVICE is a Prestel-based videotex system that is serving as a pilot for Control Data Corporation's worldwide videotex activities. The first nationwide videotex service in Australia, CYBERTEL currently is being marketed primarily to large information providers with closed user groups. Companies, government agencies, and other organizations store information in videotex page format on computer for access by their clients via CYBERTEL using specially adapted television receivers and the telephone. CYBERTEL also offers interactive gateways to the host computers of other information providers to enable users of the service to access additional large data bases and make shopping, banking, and other business and consumer transactions in real time.

Additionally, Control Data Australia is marketing CYBERTEL through joint projects. CYBERTEL videotex technology is being combined with the SEVENTEL teletext service of Brisbane TV Ltd. (BTQ-7) to provide a new information service for specialist business and consumer interests. The hybrid system will enable viewers to access SEVENTEL's teletext-type signals, which are broadcast simultaneously with a station's normal television transmission, and select pages of news, sports, leisure, financial, and general consumer information. Users will also be able to interactively access Control Data's National Computer Network via CYBERTEL and the dial-up telephone network. An example of the type of service which could be delivered via the system is a teletext livestock catalog transmitted in television time, with a subsequent electronic livestock sale which uses videotex to collect and collate remote bidders' offers. A second joint project, ROOMSERVICE, is a videotex-based national hotel and motel reservation service delivered via CYBERTEL. Developed by Control Data Australia and Bass Communications Pty. Ltd., a leading supplier of computerized ticketing services in Australia, the reservation system can also be used to book entertainment, sporting events, and leisure activity tickets.

Scope and/or Subject Matter: Information of interest to Australian businesses; banking and finance; the automobile industry; hotel, motel, and other reservations and transactions.

Input Sources: Among the current information providers accessible via CYBERTEL are General Motors-Holden's, Jetset Tours, Australia New Zealand Banking Group, Australian International Finance Corporation, Bass Communications, Shell Australia, Imperial Chemical Industries, and Northern Territory Development Corporation.

Computer-Based Products and Services: Based on the Prestel videotex protocol, CYBERTEL is used to distribute information and provide transactional services. The system utilizes AREGON IVS software and is available in North American Presentation Level Protocol Syntax (NAPLPS) format. CYBERTEL is locally accessible in all Australian capital cities; users normally require a television-style terminal fitted with a videotex adapter. An optional hardcopy printer is also available.

Clientele/Availability: CYBERTEL is primarily used by the closed user groups of large information providers. The service currently has 25 information providers and approximately 600 users. Expansion to the general consumer market is expected to begin in several years.

Contact: Brian P. Magill, CYBERTEL Manager, Control Data Australia Pty. Ltd.

★246★
COOPERATIVE AUTOMATION GROUP (CAG)
British Library Bibliographic
   Services Division, 2 Sheraton St.
London W1V 4BH, England
Lynne J. Brindley, Secretary
Phone: (not reported)
Founded: 1980

Special Note: No questionnaire response was received for this entry for the 6th edition. The entry is reprinted as it appeared in the 5th edition.

Description of System or Service: The COOPERATIVE AUTOMATION GROUP (CAG) is a forum through which the British Library and several United Kingdom cataloging cooperatives work towards the goal of establishing a national cataloging data base. In support of this goal, CAG identifies major policy, technical, and other issues affecting the planning and interactions of national library automation services; recommends actions or studies to be undertaken; and carries out or commissions work necessary to provide a foundation for future developments. The GROUP does not currently offer any systems or services other than those available through its constituent organizations.

Scope and/or Subject Matter: Cooperative library automation.

Contact: Lynne J. Brindley, Secretary, Cooperative Automation Group.

★247★
COUNCIL FOR EDUCATIONAL TECHNOLOGY (CET)
VIDEOTEX SERVICES UNIT
3 Devonshire St.
London W1N 2BA, England
Leslie Mapp, Manager
Phone: 01-580 7553

Staff: Approximately 5 total.

Related Organizations: The Council receives funding from the Departments of Education of England, Wales, Scotland, and Northern Ireland.

Description of System or Service: The VIDEOTEX SERVICES UNIT of the Council for Educational Technology offers coordinating and consulting services to education organizations wishing to disseminate information using public videotex systems. Acting as an umbrella organization, the UNIT solicits relevant information from major educations organizations, inputs and formats it to a videotex data base, and makes the data base publicly available through British Telecom's Prestel system. In addition, the UNIT conducts research on the use of videotex in education and offers advice on the development of teletext services.

Scope and/or Subject Matter: Education and training information; videotex applications in education.

Input Sources: More than 100 educational organizations supply information for the Prestel data base.

Computer-Based Products and Services: The CET Prestel Educational Umbrella Service data base provides national education and training information, ranging from preschool to higher education, for students, teachers, and advisors. Also included is a telesoftware library.

Clientele/Availability: Services are available to organizations providing education and training information.

Contact: Leslie Mapp, Manager, Videotex Services Unit, Council for Educational Technology.

★248★
COUNCIL OF EUROPE
EUROPEAN DOCUMENTATION AND INFORMATION SYSTEM FOR EDUCATION (EUDISED)
B.P. 431 R6
F-67006 Strasbourg Cedex, France
W.F. Barrett, Administrator
Phone: 88 614961
Service Est: 1968

Description of System or Service: The EUROPEAN DOCUMENTATION AND INFORMATION SYSTEM FOR EDUCATION (EUDISED), created to form a common pool of educational ideas and experience, is a computer-based network of national education agencies concerned with processing and disseminating educational information. It has developed formats and standards for computerizing data, as well as a multilingual thesaurus in nine languages. Currently the network is active mainly in the field of educational research and development (EUDISED R&D). Eighteen European countries participate in EUDISED R&D by monitoring ongoing and recently completed research projects. Project descriptions on worksheets or machine-readable tapes are passed through a central processor and added to the EUDISED R&D data base, which is made publicly available online and is used for the publication of an abstracts bulletin.

Scope and/or Subject Matter: Educational research and development projects in Western Europe.

Input Sources: Input consists of common format worksheets that are prepared by national agencies, edited by the Council's Documentation Centre for Education in Europe, and processed through a text processing service in the United Kingdom. Network members can also submit machine-readable data, which are edited by means of a provisional printout.

Holdings and Storage Media: The online EUDISED R&D data base holds more than 4000 project records dating from 1975 to the present; it is updated with information on approximately 1000 projects annually.

Publications: 1) EUDISED R&D Bulletin (quarterly with cumulated index)—each bulletin contains computer-processed descriptions of about 250 educational research projects in English, French, or German, with subject index. Available by subscription from Carfax Publishing Company, P.O. Box 25, Abingdon, Oxon. OX14 1RW, England; in the U.S., order from Carfax Publishing Company, Hopkinton Office & Research Park, 35 South St., Hopkinton, MA 01748. 2) EUDISED Multilingual Thesaurus—covers nine languages.

Computer-Based Products and Services: The EUDISED R&D data base consists of national educational research projects of general network interest and is accessible online through ESA/IRS. Tape copies of the data base are made available to member agencies.

Clientele/Availability: Primary clients are educational administrators and researchers.

Projected Publications and Services: Expansion of the EUDISED R&D data base is expected to include the complete Thesaurus, the contents of the EUDISED newsletter and other Council of Europe publications in education, and abstracts of articles appearing in educational journals.

Contact: W.F. Barrett, Administrator, Documentation Centre for Education in Europe. (Telex 870943 STRASBOURG.)

★249★
CUMULUS SYSTEMS LTD.
1 High St.
Rickmansworth, Herts. WD3 1ET,
   England
G.T. Rhodes, Managing Director
Phone: 0923 720477
Founded: 1972

Staff: 1 Information and library professional; 4 management professional; 8 technicians; 1 sales and marketing; 2 clerical and nonprofessional.

Description of System or Service: CUMULUS SYSTEMS LTD. is a time-sharing service bureau and software development company specializing in transaction processing and decision support systems for government and commercial financial markets. Among the services offered online is TAC-G GILTS, a U.K. government securities information and analysis service providing basic current and historic stock data, three-dimensional yield function analysis, stock comparisons, and other features. CUMULUS also offers the Eurobond System, a comprehensive Eurobond settlements and dealer system. Available via time-sharing or for installation on client minicomputers, the System includes a dealer display system enabling rapid interrogation of trading activity and a complete back office system supplying support to the settlement and accounting functions. As part of the Eurobond System, users have access to the Extel Statistics' EXBOND international bond data base along with regular daily updates of new issues, coupons, sinking fund changes, and other items.

Scope and/or Subject Matter: Financial transaction processing and decision support systems for financial markets, including traded options, commodities, certificates of deposit, Eurobonds, gilt-edged securities, equity dealing, and similar applications.

Input Sources: Information is derived from commercial and government sources.

Holdings and Storage Media: The machine-readable TAC-G GILTS data base contains more than 10,000 time-series.

Computer-Based Products and Services: The CUMULUS TAC-G GILTS information service is a bureau-based U.K. government stock information and analysis service available online via a print terminal or a Prestel/ Viewdata compatible terminal such as TOPIC. Information and features available include the following: 1) Basic stock data—the normal static data associated with a given stock are displayed together with the current yield data. Historic price, yield, and yield anomaly data may be printed at selected intervals or in graphic form. 2) Three-dimensional yield function analysis—the yield function incorporates a nonlinear effect of coupon value to more fully describe the yield pattern of stocks; updated daily in order to give immediate warning of anomalies and stored historically for subsequent switch analysis. 3) Stock comparisons—any pair of stocks may be compared historically and graphically by gross yields, net yields, yield anomalies, clean price ratios, net price ratios, and stabilized price ratios. 4) Switch search facilities—switch generation facilities allow the user to search the system for suitable swaps into or out of a given security. Additionally, the system searches for swaps for all stocks on a nightly basis. Switches are suggested by the system on the basis of historic data rather than current information. For certain switches the system will automatically generate some of the historic comparison graphs mentioned above. Other facilities provided by the system include comparison of yield curves by coupon; comparison of yield curves by maturity; yield calculator; equivalent inflation rate for index-linked yields; print of 18-month and "year and a day" real returns at a specified tax rate; estimated effect of interest rate changes; table of yield surface values; and graphs of movements in the yield surface over time.

Designed for use by bond traders, banks, and other financial institutions dealing with the international multicurrency bond markets, CUMULUS SYSTEMS' Eurobond System is a modular software package which can be installed on a minicomputer in the user's office or accessed online via telephone lines on the CUMULUS time-sharing service. The system provides users with the following options: transactions recording, settlement and accounting, dealer display system, direct connections to clearing houses, links to telex switches, links to other computers, direct connection to the EXBOND data base, and Bank of England returns.

Clientele/Availability: Clients include stockbrokers, dealing houses, merchant banks, and international banks.

Projected Publications and Services: Cumulus Systems plans to make the Extel Card Data Base (EXSTAT) available via Prestel/ Viewdata terminals.

Contact: Dr. G.T. Rhodes, Marketing, Cumulus Systems Ltd.

★250★
CZECHOSLOVAKIA
INSTITUTE FOR MEDICAL INFORMATION
(Ustav Vedeckych Lekarskych Informaci - UVLI)
Vitezneho unora 31   Phone: 299956
12132 Prague 2, Czechoslovakia   Service Est: 1947
Dr. Jan Peska, Director

Staff: 104 Information and library professional; 2 management professional; 5 technicians; 15 other.

Related Organizations: The Institute works in conjunction with the National Medical Library/ Statni Lekarska Knihovna.

Description of System or Service: Acting as the country's principal center of information activities in biomedicine, the INSTITUTE FOR MEDICAL INFORMATION (UVLI) maintains a large collection of books and journals; abstracts and indexes Czechoslovak biomedical literature to create a computer-readable data base; issues bibliographies and abstracts of domestic and foreign literature; operates an interlibrary loan and exchange center; and provides manual and computerized literature searching and SDI. UVLI also coordinates, promotes, and controls library and information work in the medical libraries of Czechoslovakia.

Scope and/or Subject Matter: Biomedical sciences; public health; health-related legislation.

Input Sources: Input is gathered from journals, monographs, research reports, and medical data bases.

Holdings and Storage Media: Library holdings consist of 230,000 bound volumes, subscriptions to 1560 periodicals, and a collection of microfiche. Computer-readable data bases are also held.

Publications: 1) Bibliographia Medica Cechoslovaca (monthly). 2) Referatove Vybery—a series of 23 abstracts journals covering foreign literature in the following areas of medicine: anesthesiology, surgery, infectious diseases, physiology, pediatrics, obstetrics and gynecology, endocrinology, gastroenterology, cardiology, pneumology and tuberculosis, ophthalmology, neurology, oncology, orthopedics, otorhinolaryngology, radiology, rheumatology, dermatology, gerontology and geriatrics, pathology, sports medicine, pharmacy, and health legislation; each journal is issued on either a bimonthly or quarterly basis.

Microform Products and Services: Annual of Czechoslovak Medical Literature—microfiche bibliography of Czechoslovak medical literature published in English. Includes subject and author indexes. Available free of charge.

Computer-Based Products and Services: Batch-mode searches of Excerpta Medica files and the Czechoslovak Medical Literature Data Base are conducted by the staff of the Institute for Medical Information. SDI services are also available.

Other Services: Other services provided by the Institute include referral and reprographic services.

Clientele/Availability: Services are intended primarily for use by researchers and physicians.

Contact: Dr. Jiri Drbalek, Institute for Medical Information.

D

★251★
DAFSA
125, rue Montmartre　　　　　　　　Phone: 01 2332123
F-75081 Paris Cedex 02, France

Special Note: The above name, address, and telephone number have been verified for this edition, although no questionnaire response was received. The following text is reprinted from the 5th edition.

Related Organizations: A subsidiary is DAFSA-SNEI S.A. (see separate entry).

Description of System or Service: DAFSA provides financial, economic, and securities information on French companies and some foreign firms. It offers on-demand information services, a number of publications and print information services, and several computer-based services. Computer-based services include online data bases, magnetic tape services, and software provision.

Scope and/or Subject Matter: French companies and companies operating in France; stock and securities data.

Input Sources: Information is gathered from the French Stock Exchange and over-the-counter market and from reports on French and foreign companies.

Holdings and Storage Media: A number of nonbibliographic data bases are held in machine-readable form.

Publications: 1) Informations Internationales—detailed reports in French, English, and German on 700 companies in Europe, Australia, South Africa, Japan, and North America; includes history, management, current operations, affiliations, capitalization, balance sheet, and profit or loss account. 2) Fiches Synthetiques (updated following company's annual meeting)—financial summary sheets in French on 530 French and 350 other European companies; contains five-year table of operating ratios, concise statistical tables on production, markets, affiliations, international operations, names of directors, details of share price movement and balance sheet, and other information. 3) SEF Notices—financial data sheets on companies quoted on the French Stock Exchange or over-the-counter. 4) Desfasses SEF Directory—two volumes, one lists 16,000 French companies; the other lists personnel connected with the companies. 5) Fiches Banques—index on banking and financial activities for 70 major French banks and financial companies. 6) Fiches Profils: Transformation des Matieres Plastiques (updated each year)—card collection on plastics processing companies. 7) Fiches FAN (daily)—card file on French and foreign securities. 8) Journal de Coupons (daily)—capital changes in 25,000 companies. 9) Cahiers Financiers (biweekly)—legal and press reports on national and international stock exchanges. 10) Group Surveys (annual)—report on major European groups, their structure, activities, and principal economic and financial data. 11) Industry Surveys (revised every 12 to 18 months)—analysis and description of structure and trends of some 100 industries and services in Europe. 12) Radiographie du Capital: Les Liaisons Financieres—yearbook giving the direct and indirect financial links of more than 30,000 French companies with their percentages, and listing foreign companies from more than 40 countries in alphabetic order with their French interests; available in two print volumes or on magnetic tape.

Computer-Based Products and Services: DAFSA provides or contributes to the following computer-based services and systems: 1) In conjunction with the French Stock Exchange, DAFSA distributes machine-readable data covering 5000 French share prices and 4000 international securities. 2) It maintains the Reso Data Bank on 16,000 French companies and provides research services from it. 3) It maintains the DAFSA financial liaison file on shareholders of 30,000 French companies and their shares in 20,000 foreign companies. This data base is part of a data base system called BDA (Banques de Donnees Associees), which also includes the KOMPASS data base on 68,000 French companies and the FITEK data base covering products of French companies. 4) In cooperation with SLIGOS, it maintains the SELECVAL online financial analysis data bank system. SELECVAL provides access to several financial data bases, including stock market data and information published in DAFSA's Fiches Synthetiques, along with a full complement of flexible software packages to query, study, and present financial data on a custom basis. 5) DAFSA also supplies analytical software products for client use.

Other Services: Additional DAFSA services include micrographics, manual literature searching, inquiry answering, and provision of individually commissioned research reports.

Clientele/Availability: Products and services are available on a fee or subscription basis to banks and large French and foreign companies.

Contact: Responsable Commercial, DAFSA.

★252★
DAFSA-SNEI S.A.
FITEK
16, rue de la Banque　　　　　　　　Phone: 01 2615124
F-75002 Paris, France　　　　　　　Service Est: 1980

Special Note: The above name, address, and telephone number have been verified for this edition, although no questionnaire response was received. The following text is reprinted from the 5th edition.

Staff: 6 Information and library professional; 3 management professional; 3 technicians; 12 clerical and nonprofessional.

Related Organizations: DAFSA-SNEI S.A. is a subsidiary of DAFSA and the Industrial News Publishing Company/ Societe Nouvelle d'Editions Industrielles (SNEI), which are described in separate entries.

Description of System or Service: FITEK (Fiches Techniques) is a machine-readable data base providing technical and standardized descriptions of French industrial products and their producers. Currently being constructed, the file provides data on about 1500 companies producing or distributing primarily electrical and metalworking products. When complete, FITEK will cover the products of 13,000 companies in 60 different industrial sectors. FITEK is expected to be made commercially available online in the near future.

Scope and/or Subject Matter: French industrial company and product information, currently in the following sectors: electronic components, electrical and electronic measuring instruments, handling and lifting equipment, metalworking machinery and tools, electric lamps, and electric cables and wires.

Input Sources: Information for FITEK is gathered directly from French companies.

Holdings and Storage Media: The machine-readable FITEK data base contains 15,000 records on products of 1500 French firms.

Computer-Based Products and Services: The FITEK data base provides coverage of French industry. For each company listed, FITEK includes such information as company name, address, and telephone number; professional affiliations; product code; product description; product characteristics and specifications; place of production; and additional information.

Clientele/Availability: FITEK is intended for use by French industry, engineers, and researchers.

Remarks: FITEK is part of a data base system called BDA (Banques de Donnees Associees) which also includes SNEI's KOMPASS data base, providing data on 68,000 companies, and DAFSA's financial liaison file.

Contact: Commercial Director, DAFSA-SNEI S.A.

★253★
DAGG (MICHAEL A.) ASSOCIATES
P.O. Box 9211　　　　　　　　　　Phone: (613) 741-5274
Ottawa, ON, Canada K1G 3T9　　　Founded: 1974
Michael A. Dagg, President

Description of System or Service: MICHAEL A. DAGG ASSOCIATES is an information brokerage firm which provides consultation and research services in all subject areas to businesses and to individuals. The firm offers aid in designing information systems and developing commercial applications for Telidon videotex technology, in addition to providing such services as information resource management, bibliographic and survey research, training seminars, word processing, and marketing research for government.

Scope and/or Subject Matter: All subjects of interest to clients; emphasis is placed on small business, microcomputers, and videotex systems.

Clientele/Availability: Services are available without restrictions.

Contact: Michael A. Dagg.

★254★
**DALHOUSIE UNIVERSITY
LAW SCHOOL LIBRARY
MARINE AFFAIRS BIBLIOGRAPHY**
6061 University Ave. Phone: (902) 424-2124
Halifax, NS, Canada B3H 4H9 Service Est: 1980
Christian L. Wiktor, Law Librarian

Staff: 2 Information and library professional.

Related Organizations: The Marine Affairs Bibliography is prepared under the auspices of the Dalhousie Ocean Studies Programme.

Description of System or Service: The MARINE AFFAIRS BIBLIOGRAPHY is a comprehensive computer-based index to worldwide marine law and policy literature. The Bibliography is issued as a quarterly publication with annual cumulations. Computer printouts are also available from the Bibliography data base.

Scope and/or Subject Matter: Public and private maritime law.

Input Sources: Input is derived from approximately 800 periodicals, as well as books, national catalogs, bibliographies and indexes, reports, proceedings of conferences and workshops, official documents, treaties and agreements, and other sources.

Holdings and Storage Media: The computer-readable Bibliography data base contains approximately 20,000 records.

Publications: Marine Affairs Bibliography (quarterly with annual cumulations)—available by subscription. Entries are arranged alphabetically by author under specific categories within the following sections: general works, law of the sea, and maritime transportation and communication. Each issue includes a personal author index; corporate names, series, conference index; geographical index; and table of cases.

Computer-Based Products and Services: Computer printouts are available from the Marine Affairs Bibliography data base.

Clientele/Availability: Services are available without restrictions.

Contact: Leslie A. Foster, Editor, Marine Affairs Bibliography.

★255★
**DANISH COMMITTEE FOR SCIENTIFIC AND TECHNICAL
  INFORMATION AND DOCUMENTATION (DANDOK)**
Industriradet, Teknisk afd. Phone: (not reported)
H.C. Andersens Blvd. 18 Founded: 1970
DK-1596 Copenhagen, Denmark
Hans-Erik Hansen, Chairman

Description of System or Service: The DANISH COMMITTEE FOR SCIENTIFIC AND TECHNICAL INFORMATION AND DOCUMENTATION (DANDOK) is an advisory and planning committee for the Danish authorities responsible for scientific and technical information services, including training and research in the field.

Scope and/or Subject Matter: Information and documentation.

Clientele/Availability: DANDOK serves Danish information authorities.

Contact: Hans-Erik Hansen, Chairman, Danish Committee for Scientific and Technical Information and Documentation.

★256★
DANISH DIANE CENTER
Danmarks Tekniske Hojskole Phone: 02886666
Bygning 101 Founded: 1981
DK-2800 Lyngby, Denmark

Staff: 3 Information and library professional; 1 clerical and nonprofessional.

Related Organizations: The Center was founded by the Danish Committee for Scientific and Technical Information and Documentation (DANDOK). It cooperates with the Danish Online User Group (DOUG).

Description of System or Service: The DANISH DIANE CENTER promotes the use of available online data bases by providing free consultancy regarding data bases, networks, equipment, and courses. The CENTER sponsors demonstrations of approximately 550 data bases available through 35 different hosts and also gives lectures and courses in information retrieval. Additionally, the CENTER maintains a collection of online documentation materials, publishes a newsletter and a directory of search services, and provides referrals to experienced searchers.

Scope and/or Subject Matter: Topics related to online information retrieval, including evaluation of technical equipment, methods of data base access, data base content and specific uses, document ordering and delivery, and others.

Input Sources: The Center scans approximately 25 periodicals and newsletters in the online field.

Holdings and Storage Media: The Center maintains a collection of user manuals, newsletters, brochures, data base guides, and other documentation.

Publications: 1) DISPLAY (4-6 issues per year)—distributed free of charge; Danish-language newsletter covering telecommunications, new data bases, and other information relevant for Danish users. 2) Online Information Centers in Denmark—free of charge; indexed guide to 30 information centers and libraries offering online searches to the public.

Computer-Based Products and Services: The DANISH DIANE CENTER accesses 35 online services through Euronet DIANE, Datapak, Tymnet, Telenet, UNINET, CYBERNET, and I.P. Sharp Telecommunications Network. It provides demonstrations of the available data bases.

Clientele/Availability: Services are available to Danish users of online information.

Contact: Ulla Retlev, Keld Drube, or Klaus Sondergaard, Danish DIANE Center.

★257★
**DATA BANK FOR MEDICAMENTS
(Banque d'Informations Automatisees sur les Medicaments -
  BIAM)**
156, rue de Vaugirard Phone: 01 5559280
F-75015 Paris, France Founded: 1971
Dr. H. Ducrot, President

Related Organizations: BIAM is a cooperative effort of several French medical and pharmaceutical organizations.

Description of System or Service: The DATA BANK FOR MEDICAMENTS (BIAM) is a computerized system for the storage, processing, updating, and printing of information on drugs. Designed for use by general practitioners, hospital doctors, and dispensing, hospital, and industrial chemists, the system comprises complementary data files on pharmaceutical products and the active ingredients they hold. BIAM is accessible online from remote terminals in hospitals and medical offices in France.

Scope and/or Subject Matter: Drug information, including terminology, chemical properties, prices, administration information, therapeutic or adverse effects, mechanisms of action.

Input Sources: Data for the active ingredients file are compiled from scientific literature; the drug products file contains information provided by drug manufacturers.

Holdings and Storage Media: Machine-readable BIAM files hold data on approximately 3000 active ingredients and 8000 pharmaceutical products.

Computer-Based Products and Services: Accessible online from remote terminals, BIAM includes processing programs which carry out searches according to two standard procedures. The selection program, utilizing data stored in the form of keywords, finds drugs which possess one or more features defined by the user; Boolean operators may be used. The display program provides all information in the files for the drug names given by the user. The data files include secondary comments in free-text form with the great majority of the primary items. For example, secondary information on side effects can include details on the relationship between dose and effect, degree of severity, how to handle, specific bibliographical references, and a brief summary of any publications. Data in the form of keywords can be edited, together with the secondary data accompanying them. A special drug interaction program known as INTER permits users to list drug names and retrieve information on possible interactions.

Other Services: A simplified menu-based system for access to BIAM information has been designed for general practitioners and private pharmacists. Users can obtain information from videotex terminals through the Transpac data network.

Clientele/Availability: The system is intended for use by medical practitioners, pharmacists, and pharmacologists.

Contact: Dr. H. Ducrot, President, Data Bank for Medicaments, Hopital Necker, 149, rue de Sevres, F-75730 Paris Cedex 15, France.

★258★
DATA PROCESSING SERVICES COMPANY (DPS)
DPS INFORMATION CENTRE
87, Street 9, Maadi Phone: 507475
Cairo, Egypt Service Est: 1978
Mrs. Effat El Shooky, Manager

Staff: 3 Information and library professional; 2 management professional; 1 clerical and nonprofessional.

Description of System or Service: The DPS INFORMATION CENTRE, a specialized information center in the field of information technology, provides a variety of assistance and services to meet the needs of information specialists in Egypt and the Arab world. Services include literature searches, inquiry answering, monthly current awareness, and reading room facilities. The CENTRE also offers consultancy to organizations wishing to establish or develop library and information centers, and training courses on organizing, operating, and managing library and information services.

Scope and/or Subject Matter: Information systems and services; computers and computer applications; micrographics; library and information centers; information management; office automation.

Input Sources: The Centre acquires books, periodicals, documents, microfilms, and conference proceedings.

Holdings and Storage Media: The Centre has an English and Arabic collection of 750 books and 2000 documents, and it subscribes to 67 periodicals.

Publications: 1) Information World (monthly)—current awareness publication. 2) MIS Bulletin. 3) DPS Newsletter.

Clientele/Availability: Services are available without restrictions to all Data Processing Services Company employees and to outside researchers by appointment.

Remarks: The Data Processing Services Company was founded in 1974 to design and implement information systems. It offers a variety of management consulting services, training sessions, and seminars.

Contact: Mrs. Effat El Shooky, Manager, DPS Information Centre. (Telex 92868 KADCO UN.)

★259★
DATA RESOURCES, INC. (INTERNATIONAL OFFICES)

Special Note: The United States based DATA RESOURCES, INC. provides, among other services, online access to economic forecasts, data banks, models, and software. The firm is fully described in the United States volume of this Encyclopedia. Following are the names and addresses of the DRI international offices: 1) BELGIUM—DRI Europe, Inc., Ave. Louise 221, Boite 5, B-1050 Brussels, Belgium; telephone 02 6485445. 2) CANADA—Data Resources of Canada, 80 Bloor St., W., Suite 505, NU West Centre, Toronto M5S 2V1; telephone (416) 961-9323. 3) ENGLAND—DRI Europe, Ltd., 30 Old Queen St., St. James's Park, London SW1H 9HP, England; telephone 01-222 9571. 4) FRANCE—DRI Europe, Inc., No. 7, rue Gounod, F-75017 Paris, France; telephone 01 2673641.

★260★
DATAARKIV AB
P.O. Box 12079 Phone: 08 165220
S-102 22 Stockholm, Sweden Founded: 1980
Goran Tamm, Managing Director

Staff: 4 Information and library professional; 1 management professional; 2 technicians; 2 sales and marketing.

Related Organizations: The parent organization of DataArkiv is Informationsvarden i Stockholm AB.

Description of System or Service: DATAARKIV AB is a data base producer and online service providing access to its own files and those produced by other organizations. The firm makes available primarily Swedish-language data bases containing information on Swedish companies and products, taxation and labor legislation, marketing information, and other business and general information. DATAARKIV computer facilities are accessible through the Datapak telecommunications network.

Scope and/or Subject Matter: Business, corporate, marketing, and financial information, international news, and other topics.

Input Sources: Data bases are produced by DataArkiv and affiliated firms or acquired from other data base producers.

Holdings and Storage Media: More than one million records are held in data bases accessible through DataArkiv.

Computer-Based Products and Services: DATAARKIV provides online access to the following data bases: 1) AffarsDok—contains the full text of articles from major Swedish business magazines; updates are provided daily. 2) Esselte Info—produced with Esselte Info, the data base provides current information on taxation and labor legislation. It is updated every two months. 3) Index to the Financial Times—produced by Financial Times Business Information Ltd., the data base provides citations to business and marketing information published in newspapers, annual reports, trade journals, and other sources. 4) KOMPASS—produced with Bonniers Foretagsinformation, the data base is a directory of more than 40,000 Swedish companies and 25,000 products. It includes importers, exporters, and product producers and distributors. Updates are provided annually. 5) Swedish Market Information Bank/ Marknadsbank—provides references to articles on products, companies, and subsidiaries published in more than 900 Swedish journals, newspapers, annual reports, trade journals, and other sources. 6) TT Kalendern—a calendar of coming events. 7) TT Newsbank/ Nyhetsbanken—contains the full text of all wires sent from the Tidningarnas Telegrambyra.

Clientele/Availability: Services are available without restrictions. Primary clientele is the Swedish business community.

Contact: Goran Tamm, Managing Director, DataArkiv AB; telephone 08 541420.

★261★
DATACROWN INC.
650 McNicoll Ave. Phone: (416) 499-1012
Willowdale, ON, Canada M2H 2E1 Founded: 1972
G. Lucas, V.P. & General Manager

Staff: Staff totals more than 1000.

Related Organizations: Datacrown, Inc. is a Crowntek company.

Description of System or Service: DATACROWN INC. offers a fully integrated combination of remote batch, distributed, and interactive processing services through its international communications network. It provides access to financial data bases and a variety of software for financial, econometric, statistical, engineering, and custom applications. In addition, DATACROWN provides education, programmer productivity, systems engineering, and communications support. It maintains a library of technical manuals and reference materials, and it keeps profiles of clients' technical manual requirements to notify the clients of any updates. Complete COM services are also provided.

Scope and/or Subject Matter: Shared data processing services in the areas of finance, economics, statistics, engineering, and others.

Holdings and Storage Media: Computer-readable data bases and a technical library are maintained.

Publications: Datacrown Client Letter (bimonthly)—newsletter on Datacrown's products, services, and directions. Other newsletters and reports are also issued.

Microform Products and Services: Complete COM services are offered, including automatic indexing and the acceptance of print-image computer tapes.

Computer-Based Products and Services: DATACROWN offers online and remote batch shared processing services which include financial, econometric, statistical, engineering, and custom applications. It also provides access to CANSIM and other data bases.

Clientele/Availability: Services are available in Canada and the United States to government, manufacturing, distribution, finance, and other organizations.

Contact: Richard J. Rusyn, Manager, Sales Support, Datacrown Inc. (Telex 610 492 4373.)

★262★
DATALINE INC.
175 Bedford Rd.
Toronto, ON, Canada M5R 2L2
Dr. Joseph C. Paradi, President
Phone: (416) 964-9515
Founded: 1968

Description of System or Service: DATALINE INC. is a time-sharing company providing interactive and batch-processing facilities, software packages, and online data bases for business, scientific, and governmental applications. With central computers located in Toronto, the DATALINE service operates over a telecommunications network available to users in more than 250 locations throughout North America. In addition to its time-sharing activities, DATALINE offers consulting on the application and installation of computer-based services for private industry and government, provides documentation and training courses for its clients, and installs large-scale preprogrammed packages.

Scope and/or Subject Matter: Computing services in the areas of business and administration, finance, banking, law, education, and other fields.

Computer-Based Products and Services: DATALINE's time-sharing service provides a number of software packages and data bases. Software includes the Business Accounting and Reporting Systems (BARS), Assets Management Online System (AMOS), Remote Access Financial Transaction Service (RAFTS), Statistical Package for the Social Sciences (SPSS), and the TEXT word processing and document preparation system. Data bases available online, complete with programs to use the retrieved data, include the Toronto Stock Exchange (TSE) file of securities traded in the U.S. and Canada; a data base on Western Canadian energy resources designed for use by oil, gas, and mining interests; Canadian Socio-Economic Information Management System (CANSIM); and Health and Welfare Canada's ANSSIR (A Network of Social Security Information Resources). SDI services using the ANSSIR system are available to federal and provincial governments, and selected industrial subscribers.

Other Services: Dataline also acts as a value-added dealer for IBM hardware and software.

Clientele/Availability: Services are available without restrictions; clients include private industry and government.

Remarks: Dataline Inc. was formerly Dataline Systems Limited.

Contact: Bohdan Woloshyn, Vice President, Sales, Dataline Inc.

★263★
DATASEARCH BUSINESS INFORMATION LTD.
11 Kingsmead Square
Bath, Avon BA1 2AB, England
Paul Dolan, Director
Phone: 0225 60526
Founded: 1981

Staff: 3 Information and library professional; 1 management professional; 1 clerical and nonprofessional.

Description of System or Service: DATASEARCH BUSINESS INFORMATION LTD. provides information services on companies and businesses in the United Kingdom, United States, Canada, the Far East, and most European countries. It uses U.K. company registries and libraries, a network of overseas firms and correspondents, and online searching of publicly available data bases to collect information on client-specified companies, industries, markets, and products. DATASEARCH conducts single inquiries or monitors on a regular basis any topic a client requests.

Scope and/or Subject Matter: Companies, industries, products, and markets in the U.K. and overseas.

Input Sources: Input is gathered through a network of overseas firms and correspondents, through company registries in the United Kingdom, through manual searching of documents available at major London libraries and other sources, and through online searching of publicly available data bases.

Microform Products and Services: Company files are available on microfiche.

Computer-Based Products and Services: DATASEARCH BUSINESS INFORMATION LTD. provides computerized company information retrieval using data bases carried by DIALOG Information Services, Inc., System Development Corporation (SDC), TEXTLINE, Pergamon InfoLine Ltd., Telesystemes Questel, Data-Star, ESA/IRS, Derwent-SDC Search Service, and other online services. Search services include one-time inquiries as well as continuous company name and trademark monitoring.

Other Services: Also offered are extensive desk research services and document delivery.

Clientele/Availability: Services are available without restrictions.

Contact: Paul Dolan, Director, Datasearch Business Information Ltd.

★264★
DATASOLVE LTD.
WORLD EXPORTER
99 Staines Rd. W.
Sunbury-on-Thames, Middlesex TW16 7AH, England
J.M. Ducker, Information Services Director
Phone: 09327 85566
Service Est: 1984

Related Organizations: Datasolve Ltd. is a wholly owned subsidiary of THORN EMI.

Description of System or Service: WORLD EXPORTER is an electronic trade news retrieval system providing access to country profiles, information on large scale development projects worldwide, and relevant international business news. It is designed to serve managers in international marketing and planning, particularly those in companies manufacturing or selling capital goods, in construction and engineering companies, and in firms and institutions that supply these companies with materials, services, or finance. WORLD EXPORTER offers online access to two major services, Country Profiles and Plans and Projects Monitor. Country Profiles provides brief reports on business conditions and alerts subscribers to significant developments in 50 active trading nations outside of Western Europe, with an emphasis on those in which conditions are most unfamiliar or volatile. Country Profiles also acts as an index to WORLD EXPORTER, indicating where more detailed information is available in the Plans and Projects Monitor data base. Plans and Projects Monitor covers all major development sectors and provides details of national economic plans, including new national economic plans of developing countries, sectoral plans for developed countries, and supranational plans; consultant engineers' contracts; and project announcements, including names of sponsors, sources of finance, procurement plans, and project progress reports. WORLD EXPORTER also allows subscribers to access Datasolve's World Reporter electronic news retrieval service (see separate entry).

Scope and/or Subject Matter: International business information, international news, and information on contract and project announcements in such fields as energy, mining, petrochemicals, chemicals, telecommunications, heavy engineering, highways, tourism infrastructure, oil and gas, hospitals, agriculture, public works, education, manufacturing, and harbors.

Input Sources: Input for World Exporter data bases is collected worldwide by networks of correspondents, governments, international organizations, and news and intelligence sources, including the British Broadcasting Corporation.

Holdings and Storage Media: The World Exporter Plans and Projects Monitor data base contains information collected from 1983 to the present; it is updated daily or as information becomes available. The Country Profiles data base contains information on approximately 50 countries.

Computer-Based Products and Services: WORLD EXPORTER is available online through Datasolve Ltd. using a terminal or microcomputer with communications capabilities via direct dial or telecommunications networks. The data bases are searchable by keyword or keyword combinations using English-language commands. Search results can be displayed as project headlines or as the full-text article.

Other Services: Operational training and support services are also available to subscribers.

Clientele/Availability: Services are available on a subscription basis.

Contact: J.M. Ducker, Information Services Manager, Datasolve Ltd.

★265★
DATASOLVE LTD.
WORLD REPORTER
99 Staines Rd. W. Phone: 09327 85566
Sunbury-on-Thames, Middlesex TW16
  7AH, England Service Est: 1982
J.M. Ducker, Information Services Director

Staff: 15 Management professional; 26 technicians; 6 sales and marketing; 5 clerical and nonprofessional.

Related Organizations: Datasolve Ltd. is a wholly owned subsidiary of THORN EMI. World Reporter is a joint project of Datasolve and the British Broadcasting Corporation (BBC).

Description of System or Service: The WORLD REPORTER is an online news service providing access to six files of international news intelligence. The REPORTER includes full-text information on international commercial, political, and economic affairs as reported by the BBC Summary of World Broadcasts, BBC External Services News, The Economist, The Guardian, The Washington Post, and the Associated Press world news wire service. The WORLD REPORTER is remotely accessible online through Datasolve Ltd. for daily and retrospective searching.

Scope and/or Subject Matter: International news, politics, economics, business, finance, and related topics.

Input Sources: Input is derived from newspapers and news services.

Holdings and Storage Media: The World Reporter holds more than 100 million words of online text, with approximately 200,000 words added daily. The information is retained online for at least two years.

Publications: Datasolve World Reporter Newsletter—provides current information on the online service.

Computer-Based Products and Services: The WORLD REPORTER provides online access to the following data bases: 1) BBC Summary of World Broadcasts—covers international events as reflected in radio broadcasts and news agency reports in Russia, Eastern Europe, the Far East, the Middle East, Africa, and Latin America. 2) BBC External Services News—provides information on the major British and international news stories as viewed by the BBC in London. 3) The Economist—covers politics, economics, business, finance, science, and technology worldwide, with a concentration on developments in Britain, continental Europe, and the United States. The data base holds articles since 1982 and is updated weekly with approximately 70,000 words. 4) The Guardian—includes the full text of The Guardian newspaper, including columns and weekly feature sections. It holds articles published since 1984 and is updated daily. 5) The Washington Post—contains full text of articles, features, columns, editorials, and news stories on national and international news and business published from 1984 to the present. 6) Associated Press (AP)—includes news and analyses of political situations from around the world, coverage from the United Nations and the U.S. Congress, reports and quotes from major speeches, and profiles of personalities published since 1983. WORLD REPORTER data bases are accessible through Datasolve via British Telecom, Euronet DIANE, Telenet, and other network facilities. The files can be searched by words or phrases, dates, sources, or other relevant characteristics using simple English-language commands. A variety of information displays are possible, including headline only, short passage of the article containing the search term, or complete text.

Other Services: The Datasolve staff is available to answer questions regarding the operation of the World Reporter and to provide technical back-up to the service. Also, free operational training is provided for clients of the service.

Clientele/Availability: Services are available without restrictions. Clients include decision makers, researchers, communicators, and others, primarily in government, the media, and international corporations.

Contact: J.M. Ducker, Information Services Director, Datasolve Ltd. (Telex 8811720.)

★266★
DATA-STAR
Radio Suisse Ltd. Phone: 031 659111
Schwarztorstr. 61 Founded: 1981
CH-3000 Berne 14, Switzerland
Hans R. Probst, Managing Director

Staff: 15 Management professional; 12 sales and marketing.

Related Organizations: Radio Suisse Ltd., a worldwide telecommunications company founded in 1922, offers the Data-Star service in collaboration with Information Industries Ltd.

Description of System or Service: DATA-STAR is an online data base host service for the European market. It acquires data bases in business, science, technology, and other fields from publishers, government agencies, and associations, and stores them on its computer facilities under BRS/SEARCH software. DATA-STAR makes these data bases available for remote terminal searching by libraries and other users, and it also offers a private data base service, monthly SDI, offline printing and/or processing, and an online message switching system.

Scope and/or Subject Matter: Data bases in the fields of economics, business, chemistry, biology, medicine, engineering, electronics, and other areas.

Holdings and Storage Media: Data-Star holds more than 40 data bases online for public access.

Publications: A newsletter is issued providing information on system activities, plus searching hints and aids.

Computer-Based Products and Services: Among the publicly available data bases offered online by Data-Star are the following: 1) ABI/INFORM—contains citations and abstracts of articles from U.S. and other English-language periodical literature in the areas of business, management, and administration; produced by Data Courier Inc. 2) BIOSIS—covers literature on biology, zoology, botany, and genetics, providing citations dating from 1970 to the present with abstracts since 1976; produced by BioSciences Information Services. 3) BMA Press Cuttings Database—covers current medical affairs as reported in newspapers and broadcasts; produced by the British Medical Association. 4) BUSINESS—contains information on worldwide business opportunities and contacts; produced by ONLINE GmbH. 5) Cancer Literature (CANCERLIT)—contains bibliographic citations and summaries of oncological literature dating from 1963 to the present; produced by the National Cancer Institute of the U.S. Public Health Service's National Institutes of Health.

6) Chemical Abstracts—provides citations and summaries of chemical literature dating from 1967; produced by Chemical Abstracts Service. 7) Chemical Engineering Abstracts—provides access to worldwide primary journal literature covering all aspects of chemical engineering; produced by the Royal Society of Chemistry. 8) Chemical Industry Notes—contains extracts from business-oriented publications dealing with recent events in the chemical industry; produced by Chemical Abstracts Service. 9) Chemical Nomenclature—companion file to

Chemical Abstracts identifying chemical substances by structure and name; produced by Chemical Abstracts Service. 10) COMPENDEX (Computerized Engineering Index)—covers worldwide periodical and other literature in all fields of engineering; produced by Engineering Information, Inc.

11) Computer Database—provides indexing and abstracting of current journal and other literature covering the fields of computers, electronics, and telecommunications, as well as related topics; produced by Management Contents. 12) Dokumentation Kraftfahrwesen (DKF)/ Motor Vehicle Documentation—contains references to technical literature relating to the automotive industry, including motor vehicle design, construction, and manufacturing. 13) Dow Jones News—provides news on more than 6000 companies and more than 50 industries; produced by Dow Jones & Company, Inc. 14) Ei Engineering Meetings—covers significant published proceedings of engineering and technical conferences, symposia, meetings, and colloquia; produced by Engineering Information, Inc. 15) EMBASE—contains citations and abstracts of periodical and other literature dating from 1974 to the present covering significant research and clinical findings in human medicine and related disciplines as well as biological sciences relevant to human medicine; produced by Excerpta Medica. A parallel vocabulary file provides access to the Excerpta Medica classification system, item list, master list of medical indexing terms, and journal list.

16) Financial Times Company Information—provides abstracts of all articles in the London and Frankfurt editions of the Financial Times newspaper which refer to a company. Includes approximately 50,000 summaries per year from 1981 to the present. Produced by Financial Times Business Information Ltd. and Information Industries Ltd. 17) Foreign Trade Abstracts—provides abstracts and citations to literature on applied and commercial economics; formerly known as Economic Abstracts International. Produced by the Netherlands Foreign Trade Agency. 18) Harvard Business Review/ Online—provides abstracting and indexing of all articles published in the journal Harvard Business Review, with full texts available since 1982. 19) Hoppenstedt (HOPE)—provides detailed company descriptions of all branches and business enterprises of 20,000 major companies in the Federal Republic of Germany and West Berlin. Two related files, Hoppenstedt Austria and Hoppenstedt Netherlands, provide descriptions of major companies in those countries. Produced by Verlag Hoppenstedt & Co. 20) Industry Data Sources—identifies and describes printed and computer-readable sources of marketing and financial data on 65 key industries; produced by Information Access Company.

21) INSPEC—covers literature in physics, electrical engineering, electronics, computers, and control engineering. 22) Management Contents—contains references and abstracts of English-language periodical and other literature pertaining to business and management-related topics, dating from 1974 to the present. 23) Martindale Online—contains evaluated data on 5130 drugs and anciliary substances used worldwide as well as abstracts and references taken from the scientific literature. 24) MEDLINE—contains references to worldwide biomedical journal literature dating from 1966 to the present. A companion vocabulary file, MVOC, is also available. 25) New York Times Information Bank—provides comprehensive coverage of current affairs from U.S. newspapers and periodicals.

26) NIMH Data Base—contains references and abstracts of international literature relating to mental health dating from 1969 to 1980; formerly produced by the U.S. National Institute of Mental Health. 27) NTIS—covers publications relating to U.S. research, development, and engineering projects; produced by the U.S. National Technical Information Service. 28) PAIS—covers policy-oriented international literature in the social sciences fields, including economics, political science, sociology, and demography. English-language records date from 1976 to the present; foreign-language records date from 1972 to the present. Produced by Public Affairs Information Service. 29) PRE-MED—provides access to current articles on clinical medicine which are not yet cited in other data bases; produced by Bibliographic Retrieval Services (BRS). 30) Predicasts Annual Reports Abstracts—covers annual reports and 10-K statements issued by more than 3000 publicly held U.S. and selected international companies, providing abstracts with textual, financial, and parent company information; produced by Predicasts, Inc.

31) Predicasts Defense Markets & Technology—provides access to recently published worldwide literature on the defense industry, including citations and abstracts of journal articles, major U.S. defense contracts, defense agency reports, and defense studies. 32) Predicasts F&S Indexes—contains citations to U.S. and international company, product, and industry information. 33) Predicasts Forecasts—contains citations and abstracts of U.S. and international forecasts. 34) Predicasts PROMT—contains digests of information appearing in more than 500 sources covering worldwide developments in all industries. 35) Predicasts Time Series—contains forecast time series for major countries.

36) PsycINFO—contains references and abstracts, dating from 1967 to the present, of literature in the fields of clinical and behavioral pyschology and related disciplines; produced by the American Psychological Association. 37) SGB Data Base—contains bibliographic references and abstracts for periodical and other literature on banking, finance, economics, and other related topics dating from 1979 to the present; produced by the Bank Society/ Societe Generale de Banque. 38) Sociological Abstracts—contains citations and abstracts of the world literature in sociology and related disciplines; produced by Sociological Abstracts, Inc. 39) UFORDAT (Data Bank for Environmental Research)—consists of data for 17,000 ongoing, planned, or completed environmental research and development projects in Germany and Austria; produced by the German Federal Environmental Agency/ Umweltbundesamt. 40) ULIDAT (Data Bank for Environmental Literature)—contains citations to primarily German literature on research and development in all environmental subject areas, including air, noise, water, and others; produced by the German Federal Environmental Agency. 41) LIDAS—holds citations and abstracts of professional periodical and other literature on the automobile and transportation industries and the field of automobile technology; produced by Volkswagenwerk AG.

DATA-STAR's News-File is also available online. Additionally, DATA-STAR facilities are available for loading private data bases. Other services include SDI and the Data-Mail electronic mail service, which is based on the COMET software of Computer Corporation of America. Data-Mail permits users to exchange messages via the central computer from a computer or Telex terminal over the public telecommunications networks.

Other Services: DATA-STAR also provides data collection; file design, creation, and maintenance; and user training programs.

Clientele/Availability: Data-Star is available by subscription and is accessible over public telecommunications networks or by connection to leased lines.

Projected Publications and Services: Data-Star plans to offer online access to the Great Britain Department of Health and Social Security's health administration and hospital management file and to a medical research directory of the United Kingdom.

Remarks: Radio Suisse Ltd. maintains a telecommunications network which interconnects with U.S. and Canadian networks. Called Datac (Database Access), the network provides access to more than 250 data bases and time-sharing systems connected to the Tymnet, Telenet, Datapac, and Infoswitch networks. Radio Suisse also operates the Data-Link packet switching network, which interconnects Swiss data processing systems with similar systems abroad via the public data transmission networks.

Contact: Heinz Ochsner, Head, Commercial Division, Data-Star. (Telex 32192.)

★267★
DATASTREAM INTERNATIONAL LTD.
Monmouth House
58-64 City Rd.
London EC1Y 2AL, England
A.L. Helman, Managing Director

Phone: 01-250 3000
Founded: 1964

Staff: 300 Total.

Related Organizations: DATASTREAM is an independent company owned by Dun & Bradstreet International.

Description of System or Service: DATASTREAM INTERNATIONAL LTD. provides online financial information and computation services to banks, stockbrokers, pension funds, financial institutions, and insurance companies. It maintains extensive continuously updated data banks of financial and economic statistics and makes them accessible with user friendly software tools for data retrieval and analysis. Clients can retrieve information on a broad range of interests, from portfolio valuation to investment accounting, and from equity research to coporate finance. In addition to its own online services, DATASTREAM also provides daily information to Prestel, including stock market statistics, company accounts, and share growth comparisons on the top 1000 U.K. companies, as well as current stock market reports and economic forecasts.

Scope and/or Subject Matter: International financial, economic, stock market, and company data, including equities, fixed interest securities, market performance indexes, interest and exchange rates, company accounts, financial futures and commodities, economic time series, and key economic indicators.

Input Sources: On a 24 hour basis, Datastream data analysts gather information directly from the markets, professional information providers, company accounts, specialist publications, and newspapers; direct computer to computer links are maintained with several stock exchanges. Clients are able to provide their own input through valuations and investment accounting services.

Holdings and Storage Media: Datastream holds the following data bases online: 1) Equity Stocks—provides more than 8500 series on equities for Europe, North America, Asia, South Africa, and Australia. 2) Fixed Interest Instruments—provides 3700 series for fixed interest in the United Kingdom; 13,865 series for non-U.K. domestics in 10 countries; and 5000 international and Eurobonds, including Yankees, Bulldogs, and Samurais. 3) Company Accounts—holds data on all United Kingdom-quoted companies, USM-quoted, and 500 of the largest unquoted U.K. companies and non-U.K. owned subsidiaries. Also contains more than 6600 series for company accounts in seven other countries and company account data for 10,000 of the most active unquoted companies in the United Kingdom, including U.K. private and non-U.K. owned subsidiaries. 4) Economics Series—contains approximately 10,000 series covering 26 countries, including 7300 series maintained by Datastream and 2700 main indicator series from the OECD. 5) Stockmarket Indices, Interest and Exchange Rates, and Commodities—covers 496 domestic and international interest rates, 128 international currency exchange rates, Barclays Bank International Foreign Exchange Quotes (Intraday), 217 domestic and international stock market indexes, and 49 commodities. 6) Financial Futures—covers all contracts traded on LIFFE and the major financial futures contracts traded on the IMM and CBOT in Chicago. 7) Traded Options—covers all options traded on the London Stock Exchange and all options traded on the European Options Exchange, excluding currency options.

Publications: Statistics held on the main Datastream data base are available in any printed format required by the client, including layout, paper, and corporate style. The system is also used to produce regular periodic reports. Datastream issues the Streamline newsletter covering additions and improvements to the service, and provides a full range of manuals and user aids to clients.

Computer-Based Products and Services: DATASTREAM maintains continuously updated financial and economic data bases and makes them available along with analytical software tools through the following main services:

1) Valuation Services—provides online and printed valuation services from a system holding data on more than 47,000 securities. Valuations are available for a wide range of client requirements, including smaller funds, funds of up to 500 holdings, brokers and merchant banks funds, and investment trusts and pension and insurance funds. Clients can maintain their funds online through a series of programs or have them maintained by DATASTREAM.

2) Equity Research Services—provides research on market performance (statistics and graphics), analysis of company accounts (profile and shareholdings), and search facilities, as well as programs for traded options, Z Scores, market indexes, exchange and interest rates, and commodities. Research data are stored on approximately 20,000 equities from the major Western economies, Japan, Hong Kong, Singapore, Australia, and South Africa.

3) Economics/ News Services—DATASTREAM maintains an economic statistics service complemented by financial news and other related programs, including economic and industrial data, economic models, international share indexes, exchange and interest rates, commodity prices, news and company results, foreign exchange, graphics, and others.

4) Financial Futures Service—provides a package of programs and data which combines up-to-date quotations with graphics and research facilities. The Service comprises three main components, including: futures market quotations, statistics, and analysis; graphics; and historic and research studies on cash market instruments, economic series, stock markets, and interest and exchange rates.

5) Investment Accounting—provides institutional investors with automated double-entry bookkeeping, printed statutory reports, and online management information. Investment Accounting is fully integrated with other services such as portfolio valuations so that any entry on the investment/ general ledger will automatically update the current value of the related portfolios.

6) Business Research Services—offers a selected suite of programs assembled to meet the financial information needs of clients oriented to corporate planning, credit analysis, economics, and other related disciplines. The Services includes company accounts analysis, company shareholding, share prices, search programs, sector and stock market indexes, interest and exchange rates, commodities, economic series, economic forecasting, list and expression storage and maintenance, financial news, and Z Scores.

7) Time Series Analysis—processes large and diverse amounts of data and presents them in a comparable and easily usable format. The programs can access DATASTREAM data bases plus any restricted data bases created and maintained by the client on the system and display them on the same screen.

Other Services: Datastream cooperates with the Association of International Bond Dealers (AIBD) in the production of the following printed publications: 1) AIBD International Bond Manual (annual); 2) Weekly Eurobond Guide; and 3) Daily Eurobond Prices.

Clientele/Availability: Clients include stockbrokers, institutional investors, bankers, and industrialists. Services are available without restrictions.

Contact: S.A. Herman, Marketing Director, or Graham Wallace, Deputy Marketing Manager, Datastream International Ltd. (Telex 884230.)

★268★
DELFT HYDRAULICS LABORATORY
(Waterloopkundig Laboratorium)
INFORMATION AND DOCUMENTATION SECTION
P.O. Box 177　　　　　　　　　　Phone: 015 569353
NL-2600 MH Delft, Netherlands　　Service Est: 1957
W.W. de Mes, Head

Staff: 3 Information and library professional; 1 technician; 3.5 clerical and nonprofessional.

Description of System or Service: The INFORMATION AND DOCUMENTATION SECTION collects, abstracts, and indexes world literature on hydraulic engineering, fluid mechanics, and other related subjects. The SECTION disseminates this information through the commercially available online Delft Hydro Database and the corresponding monthly journal, Delft Hydroscience Abstracts. It also maintains and provides information services from an extensive card file of references from the journal.

Scope and/or Subject Matter: Fluid mechanics; hydraulics; hydraulic modeling and experimental techniques; hydraulic, river, coastal, and offshore engineering; instruments development; systems analysis; water resources management; water quality; mathematical modeling; and other topics.

Input Sources: Input sources include more than 600 journals, as well as congress proceedings, reports, monographs, and other current literature.

Holdings and Storage Media: The machine-readable Delft Hydro Database contains approximately 42,000 bibliographic records dating from 1977 to the present; approximately 7000 records are added annually. A card catalog containing approximately 100,000 references is also maintained. Library holdings consist of 5000 bound volumes, 20,000 reprints, and subscritpions to 350 periodicals.

Publications: Delft Hydroscience Abstracts (monthly)—available by subscription; each issue contains at least 500 references arranged within 40 subject headings; includes periodic keyword and geographic indexes. The publication was formerly known as Hyrdomechanics and Hydraulic Engineering Abstracts.

Computer-Based Products and Services: The Delft Hydro Database, containing citations and abstracts of world literature on hydraulic engineering and related topics, is commercially available for online searching through QL Systems Limited. Search elements include author, title, source, publication year, language of original document, library call number, subject classification code, controlled descriptors, and abstract. The Database utilizes a structured keyword system together with the Hydraulics Documentation Code (HDC) system originally devised for the card catalog.

Other Services: Additional services include manual literature searching, current awareness, and referrals.

Clientele/Availability: Services are available without restrictions.

Contact: W.W. de Mes, Head, Information and Documentation Section, Delft Hydraulics Laboratory. (Telex 38176 HYDEL NL.)

★269★
DENMARK
MINISTRY OF CULTURAL AFFAIRS
NATIONAL ADVISORY COUNCIL FOR DANISH RESEARCH LIBRARIES
8, Christians Brygge
DK-1219 Copenhagen, Denmark
Torkil Olsen, Chairman
Phone: 01 150111
Service Est: 1970

Staff: 2 Information and library professional; 2 clerical and nonprofessional; 4 other.

Description of System or Service: The NATIONAL ADVISORY COUNCIL FOR DANISH RESEARCH LIBRARIES was established to advise the Ministry of Cultural Affairs and other official agencies on the problems encountered by national libraries, university libraries, academic libraries, and special libraries. It also promotes coordination, standardization, and cooperation among these libraries in Denmark. Special projects of the COUNCIL include the operation of an experimental center for developing automated library processes.

Scope and/or Subject Matter: Research libraries in Denmark.

Publications: Information for Research Libraries/ Information for Forskningsbiblioteker—includes minutes of Council meetings; available on request from the National Librarian. Also available are occasional publications concerning data-processing projects.

Services: Primary services are consulting, and research and development.

Clientele/Availability: Services are available to research libraries in Denmark.

Contact: Torkil Olsen, National Librarian, Chairman, or Lotte Philipson, Librarian, National Advisory Council for Danish Research Libraries. (Telex 15009.)

★270★
DENMARK
NATIONAL TECHNOLOGICAL LIBRARY OF DENMARK
(Danmarks Tekniske Bibliotek - DTB)
AUTOMATED LIBRARY INFORMATION SYSTEM (ALIS)
Anker Engelunds Vej 1
DK-2800 Lyngby, Denmark
Bent Barnholdt, Head, Processing Department
Phone: 02 883088
Service Est: 1979

Staff: Approximately 16 total.

Related Organizations: The Automated Library Information System was developed by the National Technological Library of Denmark with the aid of I/S Datacentralen.

Description of System or Service: The AUTOMATED LIBRARY INFORMATION SYSTEM (ALIS) is a computerized system which provides circulation control and catalog searches for holdings of the National Technological Library of Denmark and several other Scandinavian libraries. ALIS consists of the following files: MONO, which contains descriptions of books and conference proceedings; PERI, which provides holdings information for serials and periodicals; RAPP, which contains citations to selected U.S. government research reports acquired since 1982; INGE, which contains references to articles in the journal Ingenioren; and NTHP, which lists all periodicals and serials held by the Norwegian Institute of Technology Library. A related file EMNE contains the Library's classification scheme in Danish. ALIS files are publicly accessible online.

Scope and/or Subject Matter: Library holdings in the area of science and technology.

Input Sources: Input to ALIS consists of the catalogs and serials holdings of the National Technological Library and other technological libraries in Denmark, Finland, Norway, and Sweden.

Holdings and Storage Media: The computer-readable ALIS data base contains a total of approximately 120,000 records and is updated monthly. The National Technological Library of Denmark maintains a collection of approximately 500,000 bound volumes and 800 current periodicals.

Publications: The Library issues a subject catalog containing all monographs and dissertations in the participating technological libraries, and a serials holdings list.

Microform Products and Services: Cumulations of the subject catalog are available on COM.

Computer-Based Products and Services: ALIS provides access to descriptions of books and conference proceedings; holdings information on periodicals and serials; citations to U.S. government research reports procured by the Library since 1982; and the Library's classification scheme in Danish. The data base is searchable by author, title, keyword, language code, ISBN, ISSN, CODEN, year of publication, and UDC number. ALIS is publicly available online through I/S Datacentralen. Interlibrary loans and copies of documents covered may be ordered directly from the user terminal.

Clientele/Availability: ALIS may be used by libraries, industrial firms, research institutions, and other interested groups.

Contact: Bent Barnholdt, Head, Processing Department, National Technological Library of Denmark.

★271★
DENMARK
POSTS AND TELEGRAPHS DENMARK
CENTRAL TELECOMMUNICATIONS SERVICES
DATAPAK
Dept. TFT-MA/dt
Farvergade 17
DK-1007 Copenhagen, Denmark
Phone: 01 124844

Description of System or Service: DATAPAK is a packet-switching public data network supporting online information retrieval from remote host computers, other forms of interactive traffic, and various forms of data collection. The network permits domestic and international data transmission through asynchronous low-speed terminals, or, using a standard X.25 interface, through high-speed computers and/or more intelligent terminals connected directly to DATAPAK. Other features include closed user group capability; network design in accordance with international standards; redundancy of important network components; reverse charging; and specification of billed data calls.

Scope and/or Subject Matter: Domestic and international data transmission; information retrieval.

Computer-Based Products and Services: DATAPAK permits access to more than 1000 online data bases held on computers in Europe, North America, Singapore, and Japan.

Other Services: Post and Telegraphs Denmark also offers DATEX, a circuit-switched public data communications service; and DATEL, which provides data transmission on leased telephone lines between two terminals with the same speeds.

Clientele/Availability: An application for a subscription to the services should be made in writing to the telecommunications administration's local office within the region in which the data terminal equipment is to be installed.

Contact: Vagn D. Jensen, Central Telecommunications Services, Posts and Telegraphs Denmark. (Telex 22999 TELCOM DK.)

★272★
DENMARK TELECOMMUNICATIONS ADMINISTRATION
(Danske Teleadministrationer)
DANISH TELEDATA SYSTEM
KTAS, Norregade 21
DK-1199 Copenhagen, Denmark
Helge Mansa, Divisional Manager
Phone: 01 993008
Service Est: 1982

Staff: 2 Information and library professional; 2 management professional; 4 technicians; 6 sales and marketing; 8 clerical and nonprofessional.

Description of System or Service: The DANISH TELEDATA SYSTEM is an electronic information and communications system for home, business, and other users in Denmark. Currently undergoing a trial run, TELEDATA provides two centrally located data centers which are accessed via telephone lines by users with alphanumeric keyboards, modems, and decoder-equipped televisions. Each TELEDATA center can accommodate 44 users simultaneously, providing news, consumer, travel, and other information in the form of text and graphics. In addition to providing access to its own data centers, the DANISH TELEDATA SYSTEM offers gateway services, connecting subscribers to selected information providers data bases. TELEDATA also provides electronic mail services and the ability to order goods and make ticket reservations.

Scope and/or Subject Matter: Consumer information and services, news, public information, travel, publishing, banking and insurance, retail trade, and education.

Input Sources: Input is provided by approximately 180 companies, institutions, and other information providers in Denmark.

Holdings and Storage Media: The Teledata data centers, which are stocked with the same information, have a storage capacity of 150,000 frames apiece.

Computer-Based Products and Services: The DANISH TELEDATA SYSTEM provides interactive access to information held in centrally located data bases. In addition, the system allows subscribers to connect with computers owned by selected information providers. TELEDATA also provides subscribers with electronic mail and transactional services.

Clientele/Availability: Services are available through 800 terminals placed with private users, at public locations such as post offices, libraries, and hospitals, and at industrial companies.

Contact: Benny Dam, Senior Executive Officer, Danish Teledata System.

★273★
DERWENT PUBLICATIONS LTD.
BIOTECHNOLOGY ABSTRACTS
Rochdale House
128 Theobalds Rd.
London WC1X 8RP, England
Phone: 01-242 5823
Service Est: 1982

Related Organizations: Derwent Publications Ltd. is a subsidiary of the International Thomson Organisation.

Description of System or Service: BIOTECHNOLOGY ABSTRACTS is a current awareness journal providing abstracts and indexes of international journal and other literature dealing with all aspects of biotechnology. It is available as a semimonthly publication and as an online data base.

Scope and/or Subject Matter: Biotechnology, including microbiology, engineering, chemistry, pharmaceuticals, agriculture, food, energy, other chemicals, cell culture, biocatalysis, purification, waste disposal, and others.

Input Sources: Input is derived from approximately 1000 scientific and technical journals, plus conference proceedings and patents literature.

Holdings and Storage Media: The online Biotechnology Abstracts data base is updated monthly and holds more than 10,000 abstracts per year of coverage.

Publications: Biotechnology Abstracts (semimonthly)—available by subscription. Each issue includes a subject index, author index, and corporate affiliation index; the indexes are cumulated annually. A list of sources scanned is published and is available by request.

Computer-Based Products and Services: The BIOTECHNOLOGY ABSTRACTS data base is available for online searching through System Development Corporation (SDC) and System Development Corporation of Japan, Ltd. Search elements include classification, supplemented title, index keywords, bibliographic details, and full abstract text.

Other Services: Copies of patents abstracted are available from Derwent's Patents Supply Division.

Clientele/Availability: Biotechnology Abstracts is available by subscription. Online access to the data base is restricted to subscribers of the print publication.

Contact: Chief, Literature Division, Derwent Publications Ltd. (Telex 267487 DERWENTINF LONDON.) Derwent's United States office is located at: 6845 Elm St., Suite 500, McLean, VA 22101; telephone (703) 790-0400.

★274★
DERWENT PUBLICATIONS LTD.
CHEMICAL REACTIONS DOCUMENTATION SERVICE (CRDS)
Rochdale House
128 Theobalds Rd.
London WC1X 8RP, England
Phone: 01-242 5823
Service Est: 1975

Related Organizations: Derwent Publications Ltd. is a subsidiary of the International Thomson Organisation.

Description of System or Service: The CHEMICAL REACTIONS DOCUMENTATION SERVICE (CRDS) is an information service intended for the commercial and academic chemical community. Basically an expansion of Theilheimer's Synthetic Methods of Organic Chemistry, CRDS encompasses a monthly abstracts journal (Journal of Synthetic Methods) covering novel synthetic methods, a computer-readable data base available online or on magnetic tape, and microform products.

Scope and/or Subject Matter: New synthetic methods in organic chemistry including: known reactions effected by new reagents or improved methodology; and interesting applications and extensions of known methods.

Input Sources: Current input for the abstracts publication and data base is derived from worldwide chemical journal literature and (through Derwent's Central Patent Index service) chemical patent specifications. The CRDS data base also holds data from Volumes 1-30 of Theilheimer's Synthetic Methods.

Holdings and Storage Media: The computer-readable CRDS data base contains more than 50,000 records dating from 1942 to the present, and is updated monthly at the rate of 250 records.

Publications: Journal of Synthetic Methods (monthly)—each issue contains 250 abstracts with full citations, arranged according to reaction type and emphasizing type of product, reactant, reagent, and reaction; includes a comprehensive subject index that is cumulated annually. In addition to the 3000 full abstracts published per annum, approximately 3000 supplementary references to previously published reactions are appended biannually.

Microform Products and Services: Microfilm abstracts and the annual cumulated subject index are available in 16mm format.

Computer-Based Products and Services: CRDS data are accessible online through System Development Corporation (SDC) and System Development Corporation of Japan, Ltd. The complete data base is accessible online by codes. The online keyword file comprises data from 1975 to date and Theilheimer's Volumes 21 through 30. The coded information is also available on magnetic tapes for in-house computer searching.

Clientele/Availability: CRDS is available by subscription.

Contact: Director, Literature Division, Derwent Publications, Ltd.

(Telex 267487 DERWENTINF LONDON.) Derwent's United States office is located at: 6845 Elm St., Suite 500, McLean, VA 22101; telephone (703) 790-0400.

★275★
DERWENT PUBLICATIONS LTD.
PATENTS DOCUMENTATION SERVICES
Rochdale House   Phone: 01-242 5823
128 Theobalds Rd.
London WC1X 8RP, England

Related Organizations: Derwent Publications Ltd. is a subsidiary of the International Thomson Organisation.

Description of System or Service: Derwent's PATENTS DOCUMENTATION SERVICES abstracts, indexes, and distributes worldwide patent specification information in hardcopy, microform, and machine-readable form. Among its products are the World Patents Index (WPI), which supplies titles and bibliographic details of general, mechanical, electrical, and chemical patents; the World Patents Abstracts (WPA), which provides abstracts with drawings of patents by country and technology; the Central Patents Index (CPI), which includes 12 subject classes of chemical patents; and the Electrical Patents Index (EPI). WPI, WPA, CPI, and EPI are variously available in the form of alerting bulletins, gazettes, abstracts journals, profile booklets, abstracts in microform, print and COM indexes, manual and punched cards, and magnetic tape. Additionally, data for all patents processed by Derwent are commercially available online as the WPI data base.

Scope and/or Subject Matter: Worldwide published and unpublished patent specifications in general, mechanical, electrical, and chemical subject areas.

Input Sources: About 11,000 patent documents from approximately 30 patent-issuing authorities are processed each week.

Holdings and Storage Media: The Derwent Patents Documentation Services covers about 6 million patents giving details on more than 3 million inventions, with 300,000 added annually. Patent information is complete from 1963 for pharmaceuticals, 1965 for agricultural chemicals, 1966 for polymers and plastics, 1970 for all other areas of chemistry (CPI), 1974 for general subjects (WPI) and for electrical and electronics (EPI).

Publications: 1) World Patents Index-WPI (weekly)—a series covering all countries according to topic, patentee, and subject matter; issued in four sections: chemical, electrical, mechanical, and general. 2) World Patents Abstracts-WPA (weekly)—abstracts with drawings; available in reports classified by country, and in subject-oriented journals for nonchemical technologies. 3) Central Patents Index-CPI—offers documentation and retrieval of chemically related patents in alerting bulletins, basic abstracts journals, profile booklets, and coded cards. 4) Electrical Patents Index-EPI—offers weekly bulletins, monthly profile booklets, and other products covering the electrical and electronics industries. Descriptive brochures giving complete lists and details of publications are available from Derwent.

Microform Products and Services: Derwent offers indexes and abstracts of patent specification information in microform, including the Patents Abstracts on Microfiche (PAM) service. Additionally, Derwent films specifications from a number of countries, and through its Patents Supply Division provides hardcopy and 16mm microfilm copies of these.

Computer-Based Products and Services: The PATENTS DOCUMENTATION SERVICES offers CPI, EPI, and WPI on magnetic tapes. Search parameters include controlled vocabulary title terms, abstract, patent and accession numbers, patentees, inventors, priorities, and manual codes. The SERVICES also makes patent information searchable online as the WPI data base available through System Development Corporation (SDC), System Development Corporation of Japan, Ltd., DIALOG Information Services, Inc., and Telesystemes Questel. Custom search services and assistance with online retrieval are provided by Derwent's Online Services Division.

Other Services: In addition to services described above, document delivery is provided.

Clientele/Availability: Products and services are available by subscription.

Remarks: Derwent, Inc., the U.S. office of Derwent Publications Ltd., produces the USCLASS and U.S. Patents Files data bases (see the United States volume of this Encyclopedia for descriptions.)

Contact: Director, Patents Division, Derwent Publications Ltd. (Telex 267487 DERWENTINF LONDON.) Derwent's United States office is located at: 6845 Elm St., Suite 500, McLean, VA 22101; telephone (703) 790-0400.

★276★
DERWENT PUBLICATIONS LTD.
PEST CONTROL LITERATURE DOCUMENTATION (PESTDOC)
Rochdale House   Phone: 01-242 5823
128 Theobalds Rd.   Service Est: 1964
London WC1X 8RP, England

Related Organizations: Derwent Publications Ltd. is a subsidiary of the International Thomson Organisation.

Description of System or Service: PEST CONTROL LITERATURE DOCUMENTATION (PESTDOC) is a comprehensive information service covering relevant papers found in the world's scientific journals on pesticides and agricultural chemicals. It provides access to this information through abstracts, abstract summaries, controlled keywords, and codes. PESTDOC products include abstracts publications, indexes, magnetic tapes, microfilm, and microfiche. PESTDOC information is also accessible online.

Scope and/or Subject Matter: Pesticides and agricultural chemicals, and related areas including chemistry, toxicology, and legislation.

Input Sources: More than 800 journals are monitored for input.

Holdings and Storage Media: The computer-readable PESTDOC data base dates from 1968 to the present and contains more than 100,000 records. It is updated eight times per year at the rate of 1000 records.

Publications: PESTDOC abstracts publications contain detailed abstracts, abstract summaries, and full bibliographic information. Several formats are available, including a classified version.

Microform Products and Services: Abstracts are available on 16mm microfilm. Author indexes are available on microfilm or microfiche.

Computer-Based Products and Services: PESTDOC abstract summaries, bibliographic citations, keywords, and codes are available on magnetic tapes. The data base is accessible online through System Development Corporation (SDC) and System Development Corporation of Japan, Ltd.

Clientele/Availability: Designed to meet the requirements of manufacturers of pesticides and agricultural chemicals, PESTDOC is available by subscription.

Contact: Director, Literature Division, Derwent Publications Ltd. (Telex 267487 DERWENTINF LONDON.) Derwent's United States office is located at: 6845 Elm St., Suite 500, McLean, VA 22101; telephone (708) 790-0400.

★277★
DERWENT PUBLICATIONS LTD.
PHARMACEUTICAL LITERATURE DOCUMENTATION (RINGDOC)
Rochdale House   Phone: 01-242 5823
128 Theobalds Rd.   Service Est: 1964
London WC1X 8RP, England

Related Organizations: Derwent Publications Ltd. is a subsidiary of the International Thomson Organisation.

Description of System or Service: PHARMACEUTICAL LITERATURE DOCUMENTATION (RINGDOC) is a comprehensive information service covering relevant papers found in the world's scientific journals on pharmaceuticals. It provides access to this information through abstracts, abstract summaries, controlled keywords, and codes. RINGDOC products include abstracts publications, indexes, magnetic tapes, microfilm, microfiche, and an online data base. A companion data base to RINGDOC, the Standard Drug File (SDF), lists approximately 7500 known drugs and other commonly occuring compounds that are indexed in RINGDOC. SDF provides the full name and standard registry name, pharmacological classification of standard activities (if any), chemical ring codes, and other codes.

Scope and/or Subject Matter: Pharmaceuticals, including chemistry, biochemistry, pharmacology, therapeutics, and toxicology.

Input Sources: More than 800 journals are scanned for input.

Holdings and Storage Media: The computer-readable RINGDOC data base contains more than 750,000 records dating from 1964 to the present and is updated monthly at the rate of 4500 records. SDF covers approximately 7500 drugs.

Publications: Abstracts publications contain detailed abstracts, abstract summaries, and full bibliographic information. Several formats are available, including classified versions.

Microform Products and Services: Microfilm of abstracts is available in 16mm format. Author indexes are provided as microfilm or microfiche.

Computer-Based Products and Services: RINGDOC abstract summaries, bibliographic citations, keywords, and codes are available on magnetic tapes. RINGDOC is accessible online through System Development Corporation (SDC) and System Development Corporation of Japan, Ltd. The Standard Drug File is accessible through SDC.

Clientele/Availability: Products and services are designed to meet the requirements of pharmaceutical manufacturers.

Contact: Director, Literature Division, Derwent Publications Ltd. (Telex 267487 DERWENTINF LONDON.) Derwent's United States office is located at: 6845 Elm St., Suite 500, McLean, VA 22101; telephone (703) 790-0400.

★278★
DERWENT PUBLICATIONS LTD.
VETERINARY LITERATURE DOCUMENTATION (VETDOC)
Rochdale House   Phone: 01-242 5823
128 Theobalds Rd.   Service Est: 1964
London WC1X 8RP, England

Related Organizations: Derwent Publications Ltd. is a subsidiary of the International Thomson Organisation.

Description of System or Service: VETERINARY LITERATURE DOCUMENTATION (VETDOC) is a comprehensive information service covering relevant papers found in the world's veterinary scientific journals. It provides access to this information through abstracts, abstract summaries, controlled keywords, and codes. VETDOC products include abstracts publications, indexes, magnetic tapes, microfilm, and microfiche. VETDOC is also accessible online.

Scope and/or Subject Matter: Veterinary drugs, vaccines, growth promotants, toxicology, hormonal control of breeding, and related topics.

Input Sources: More than 800 scientific journals are scanned for input.

Holdings and Storage Media: The computer-readable VETDOC data base contains more than 60,000 machine-readable records dating from 1968 to the present. It is updated 10 times per year at the rate of 400 records.

Publications: Abstracts publications contain detailed abstracts, abstract summaries, and full bibliographic information. Several formats are available, including a classified version.

Microform Products and Services: Microfilm of abstracts is available in 16mm format. Author indexes are provided on microfilm or microfiche.

Computer-Based Products and Services: VETDOC abstract summaries, bibliographic citations, keywords, and codes are available on magnetic tapes. VETDOC is accessible online through System Development Corporation (SDC) and System Development Corporation of Japan, Ltd.

Clientele/Availability: Designed to meet the needs of manufacturers of veterinary products, VETDOC is available by subscription.

Contact: Director, Literature Division, Derwent Publications Ltd. (Telex 267487.) Derwent's United States office is located at: 6845 Elm St., Suite 500, McLean, VA 22101; telephone (703) 790-0400.

★279★
DIALOG INFORMATION SERVICES, INC. (INTERNATIONAL REPRESENTATIVES)

Special Note: DIALOG INFORMATION SERVICES, INC. is an online service organization which is described in the United States volume of this Encyclopedia. Following is a list of DIALOG's international representatives, each of which is described in a separate entry in this volume: AUSTRALIA—Insearch Ltd./ DIALOG; CANADA—Micromedia Ltd.; EUROPE—Learned Information Ltd.; JAPAN—Kinokuniya Company Ltd. and Maruzen Company, Ltd.

★280★
DIDOT-BOTTIN
BOTTIN DATA BASES
28, rue du Docteur-Finlay   Phone: 01 5786166
F-75738 Paris Cedex 15, France

Description of System or Service: The BOTTIN DATA BASES are extensive machine-readable files providing names, addresses, and other data on various categories of French companies, institutions, and individuals. They are used to produce directories and annuals and to provide mailing lists and other selective products.

Scope and/or Subject Matter: French business, industry, commerce, government, professionals, and consumers.

Holdings and Storage Media: Examples of machine-readable files held include a data base on 250,000 companies and a file on more than 50,000 local governments.

Publications: Didot-Bottin issues numerous directories, annuals, and encyclopedias.

Computer-Based Products and Services: The BOTTIN DATA BASES are used to provide selective mailing lists and other services.

Clientele/Availability: Products and services are available internationally.

Contact: Monique Le Moal, International Service, Didot-Bottin. (Telex 204286 F.)

★281★
DOBRA IRON AND STEEL RESEARCH INSTITUTE
(Vyzkumny Ustav Hutnictvi Zeleza, Dobra - VUHZ)
INFORMETAL
   Phone: 54215
73951 Dobra, Czechoslovakia
Boris Skandera, Head

Staff: Approximately 40 total.

Related Organizations: The Federal Ministry of Metallurgy and Heavy Engineering manages the Institute's information activities. Some support is received from the metallurgical industry in Czechoslovakia.

Description of System or Service: INFORMETAL acts as a clearinghouse and coordinates the transfer of information within the Czechoslovakian national metallurgical information system. In conjunction with other collaborating information centers, it collects and stores bibliographic information on metallurgy for dissemination to Czechoslovak scientists. INFORMETAL maintains a computer-readable data base of this information, and provides abstracts journals, computerized literature searching, and SDI services.

Scope and/or Subject Matter: All aspects of metallurgy, including production of steel; extraction and treatment of metals; powder metallurgy; nonferrous metals; automation in the field of metallurgy; and economics.

Input Sources: Input is obtained from international sources including serial and nonserial publications, abstracts, and technical reports.

Holdings and Storage Media: The Library of the national information system for metallurgy contains 900,000 bound volumes; 400,000 special materials; and subscriptions to 11,500 periodicals. In addition, INFORMETAL maintains a data base of 100,000 references on magnetic tape.

Publications: INFORMETAL publishes nine internal serial publications, including technical reports, abstracts journals, indexes, and research summaries.

Computer-Based Products and Services: Computerized literature searching and SDI services are offered using the INFORMETAL data base. Online access to INFORMETAL within Czechoslovakia is planned for the near future.

Other Services: Additional services include consulting, translation into Czechoslovakian, and referral services.

Clientele/Availability: Services are intended for Czechoslovak specialists in metallurgy.

Contact: Boris Skandera, Head, Informetal. (Telex 52691.)

★282★
DOCUMENTARY RESEARCH CENTER
(Centre de Recherche Documentaire - CREDOC)
P.O. Box 11   Phone: 02 5139213
Rue de la Montagne, 34   Founded: 1967
B-1000 Brussels, Belgium

Special Note: The above name, address, and telephone number have been verified for this edition, although no questionnaire response was received. The following text is reprinted from the 5th edition.

Staff: 25 Information and library professional; 2 management professional; 14 technicians; 7 clerical and nonprofessional.

Related Organizations: CREDOC receives support from the Belgium Ministry of Justice.

Description of System or Service: The DOCUMENTARY RESEARCH CENTER (CREDOC) is a nonprofit organization that provides lawyers, notaries, and judges with research and information services in the areas of law and legislation. CREDOC maintains several machine-readable data bases which are commercially available online; among these are BJUS, which provides references with abstracts to legal doctrines and jurisprudence published in Belgium since 1968; BLEX, which indexes articles appearing in the Belgian Monitor since 1980; and CORALIE, a factual data bank on the use of food additives in the European Community. In addition to maintaining these data bases, CREDOC contributes to the Commission of European Communities' CELEX files; maintains a computer-readable Register of Wills; offers registered trademark information on microfiche; and conducts computerized literature searches.

Scope and/or Subject Matter: Law and legislation, especially relating to Belgium and the Netherlands; legal research.

Input Sources: Input to the data bases is derived from legislation, periodicals, newspapers, court decisions, case law, doctrine, and practice documentation.

Holdings and Storage Media: The computer-readable BJUS data base holds more than 120,000 records for the period since 1968; it is updated monthly. BLEX contains about 4000 citations from 1980 to date; it is updated bimonthly. Also maintained in machine-readable form are CORALIE and the Register of Wills, which contains more than 110,000 items.

Publications: Data base user manuals and a thesaurus are published by CREDOC.

Microform Products and Services: CREDOC's Microbiblex department distributes registered trademark information on microfiche.

Computer-Based Products and Services: Online access to BJUS, BLEX, and CORALIE is available through BELINDIS, a Euronet DIANE host; individual searches of the data bases may be requested through CREDOC. Searchable elements of the files can include title in French or Dutch, type of document, author, source, text in French or Dutch, status of document (for legislation), descriptors, category, and statistics. CREDOC offers computerized literature searching of data bases available through Euronet DIANE, and also provides automated services to law firms.

Clientele/Availability: Primary clients are lawyers in the public and private sectors.

Contact: General Manager, CREDOC.

★283★
DOCUPRO
Microinfo, Ltd.   Phone: 0420 86848
P.O. Box 3, Newman Lane
Alton, Hamps. GU34 2PG, England

Related Organizations: Docupro is a collaborative service of Infocom and Microinfo, Ltd. (see separate entries).

Description of System or Service: DOCUPRO provides information processing services to publishers involved in the production of abstract journals and associated online data bases. Services include cataloging, abstracting, indexing, and cross-referencing of documents in any language. Abstracts can be indicative or informative, and indexing utilizes controlled language thesauri and free-text terms or identifiers. DOCUPRO also provides text information in electronic form and copies of source documents on microfiche.

Scope and/or Subject Matter: Secondary information services in scientific and technical disciplines.

Input Sources: The company processes documents from more than 100 international sources.

Microform Products and Services: Source documents can be microfiched for organizations offering document delivery services.

Computer-Based Products and Services: DOCUPRO can provide processed text information on computer tapes or disks which can then be sorted into journal sections and pages or used to supply electronic information services.

Clientele/Availability: Services are available without restrictions on a contract basis.

Contact: Dr. Gordon Wilkinson, Manager, Docupro. (Telex 858431.)

★284★
DORTMUND INSTITUTE FOR WATER RESEARCH
(Institut fur Wasserforschung GmbH Dortmund)
DATA BANK ON SUBSTANCES HARMFUL TO WATER
(Datenbank fur Wassergefahrdende Stoffe - DABAWAS)
Zum Kellerbach   Phone: 02304 107350
D-5840 Schwerte-Geisecke, Fed. Rep.
  of Germany   Service Est: 1973
Dr. KarlHeinz Schmidt, Head

Staff: 6 Information and library professional; 4 management professional; 6 technicians; 1 sales and marketing; 1 clerical and nonprofessional.

Related Organizations: The Data Bank on Substances Harmful to Water is financed by the German Federal Department of the Interior. DABAWAS is produced in cooperation with UMPLIS, the Environmental Information and Documentation System of the German Federal Environmental Agency (see separate entry).

Description of System or Service: The DATA BANK ON SUBSTANCES HARMFUL TO WATER (DABAWAS), a computer-readable data bank on harmful substances, is used by water authorities, chemical emergency services, research institutions, and others to find measures against the accidental spill of chemicals. Batch-mode retrieval of DABAWAS information is available through the Institute.

Scope and/or Subject Matter: Identification, classification, physical properties, analysis, toxicity and hazards, and behavior in the environment of chemicals; anti-pollution measures.

Input Sources: Information is collected from safety manuals, government reports, and environmental chemicals data collections.

Holdings and Storage Media: DABAWAS holds 360,000 data sets covering 55,000 chemical names and synonyms in machine-readable form.

Computer-Based Products and Services: DABAWAS is searchable for chemical, toxicological, and environmental properties. Batch-mode services are offered by the Institute.

Other Services: Additional services include consulting, literature searching, and chemical analyses.

Clientele/Availability: Services are available without restrictions; charges are made for extensive searches.

Contact: Dr. Michael Krutz, Dortmund Institute for Water Research. (Telex 8229659 DABA D.)

★285★
DRUG INFORMATION PHARMACISTS GROUP
PHARMLINE
The London Hospital
Whitechapel Rd.
London E1 1BB, England
Michael L. Rogers, Principal Pharmacist
Phone: 01-247 5454
Service Est: 1983

Related Organizations: Pharmline is supported by a grant from the Department of Health and Social Security.

Description of System or Service: PHARMLINE is a computer-based information retrieval service providing information on all aspects of modern drug use. It contains citations and abstracts of articles from major medical and pharmaceutical journals and other sources on drug use, reactions, interactions, and therapy. PHARMLINE is searchable online by information pharmacists at the National Health Service and at more than 150 Drug Information Centres located throughout England to help answer inquiries on drugs and drug-related therapeutic problems. The service is expected to be commercially available online on a wider basis in the near future. PHARMLINE also assists in the compilation of bulletins containing evaluated drug information designed to promote safe, effective, and economic drug use. Additionally, a monthly microfiche version of PHARMLINE is produced.

Scope and/or Subject Matter: All aspects of drug use, including current drug therapy, adverse drug reactions, drug use in pregnancy, drugs for nursing mothers, drug interactions, drug stability, drugs in preventative medicine, and drugs for special patient groups.

Input Sources: Approximately 90 major medical and pharmaceutical journals, as well as reports and literature produced by the Department of Health and Social Security, are scanned for input.

Holdings and Storage Media: The computer-readable PHARMLINE data base holds bibliographic citations and abstracts and is updated weekly.

Publications: News bulletins on drugs and drug use and a thesaurus of keywords are produced.

Microform Products and Services: Pharmline abstracts are published monthly on 24x COM microfiche with a keyword index.

Computer-Based Products and Services: Operated by a British computer service bureau using CAIRS (Computer Assisted Information Retrieval System) software, PHARMLINE provides online information on drug use and drug-related problems to information pharmacists in England. It is compiled from abstracts entered remotely from terminals in individual Drug Information Centres. Records in the file contain title, author, journal title, date of publication, volume number, number of pages, and abstracts.

Clientele/Availability: Services are available to pharmacists in England. Drug Information Centres with access to Pharmline accept inquiries on drug treatment.

Contact: Michael L. Rogers, Principal Pharmacist, Drug Information Pharmacists Group.

★286★
DUTCH STATE MINES
TISDATA
P.O. Box 18
NL-6160 MD Geleen, Netherlands
J.B.P. van Nuland, Senior Engineer
Phone: 04494 65393

Description of System or Service: TISDATA is an online data bank for physical properties. It includes a package of computer programs designed to permit calculation of thermophysical properties of pure components and mixtures using theoretical and empirical methods. Also available is the TISFLO software package for simulation, optimization, and balancing redundant data in process-flowsheet calculations. TISDATA and TISFLO form parts of the Technological Information System (TIS) developed by the Dutch State Mines for carrying out calculations in the chemical process industries.

Scope and/or Subject Matter: Calculation of thermophysical properties.

Input Sources: Input is obtained from the chemical literature.

Holdings and Storage Media: TISDATA contains machine-readable data on 470 components and approximately 30 properties.

Computer-Based Products and Services: TISDATA is interactively accessible online. Each component in the system is assigned an identification number. For each property of a component, a separate program allowing calculations to be made is assigned. The array of programs constitutes TISDATA, a flexible system allowing programs to be added or replaced when required.

Clientele/Availability: TISDATA is available without restrictions.

Contact: J.B.P. van Nuland, Senior Engineer, Department of Mathematics and Process Control. (Telex 36138.)

E

★287★
EASTERN COUNTIES NEWSPAPERS
EASTEL
Prospect House
Rouen Rd.
Norwich, Norfolk NR1 1RE, England
Eric Pummell, Commercial Systems Manager
Phone: 0603 28311
Service Est: 1975

Staff: 1 Management professional; 1 clerical and nonprofessional.

Description of System or Service: EASTEL is an information provider to the British Prestel system, supplying a data base covering regional and national advertising as well as general information on the East Anglia area. EASTEL also acts as a consultant to other Prestel information providers. Services consist of data base planning and program management; routing systems; editing, input, and update; graphics design; and staff training.

Scope and/or Subject Matter: Advertising and regional information; Prestel program planning and management.

Computer-Based Products and Services: The EASTEL Database can be accessed interactively through the Prestel system.

Clientele/Availability: Services are provided to Prestel users and information providers.

Contact: Sue Lincoln, Videotex Data Base Supervisor, Eastel. (Telex 975276 ECNNCH G.)

★288★
EASTERN TELECOMMUNICATIONS PHILIPPINES, INC. (ETPI)
DATABASE ACCESS SERVICE (D.B.S.)
Telecoms Plaza
316 Sen. Gil J. Puyat Ave., Makati
Manila, Philippines
Vicente Hernandez, Deputy Vice President/Marketing
Phone: 856011

Description of System or Service: The DATABASE ACCESS SERVICE (D.B.S.) is a telecommunication service which provides remote computing capabilities to clients in Manila. D.B.S. allows clients to access computerized data bases available in the United States, Canada, and Europe.

Scope and/or Subject Matter: Access to data bases in the fields of business, technology, and other areas.

Input Sources: Overseas host services provide input.

Computer-Based Products and Services: The DATABASE ACCESS SERVICE enables clients in Manila to access data bases overseas from computer terminals via a leased line or dial-up connection. The SERVICE also offers terminals to clients on a lease basis.

Clientele/Availability: Services are available without restrictions to clients in Manila.

Remarks: Eastern Telecommunications Philippines, Inc. is also known as Eastern Telecoms.

Contact: Jose E. Geronimo, Supervisor/ Private Networks, Database Access Service, Eastern Telecommunications Philippines, Inc.; telephone 8153470. (Telex 63305 ETPNET PN.)

★289★
EASY DATA SYSTEMS LTD.
EASY DATA INTEGRATED LIBRARY SYSTEM
1385 W. 8th Ave.
Vancouver, BC, Canada V6H 3V9
Phone: (604) 734-8822
Service Est: 1975

Related Organizations: Easy Data Systems Ltd. is a subsidiary of Sydney Development Corporation.

Description of System or Service: The EASY DATA INTEGRATED LIBRARY SYSTEM is an online, minicomputer-based library automation package featuring acquisitions, cataloging, inquiry, and circulation control modules. Specific capabilities of the modules include: 1) Acquisitions—permits online, preorder searching, consolidation of locally and remotely entered orders, processing of orders, online automatic fund accounting and currency conversion, and online vendor files. 2) Cataloging—displays and maintains online bibliographic data input during acquisitions or retrieved from MARC records. Searching of the in-house, online authority file facilitates the assignment of subject headings, personal and corporate authors, and series and conference headings. Printed and/or microform catalogs can be produced in a variety of formats. 3) Inquiry—a sophisticated indexing technique providing more than twenty entry points to the bibliographic data. 4) Circulation—provides online material check-out and return with all necessary interventions, reserves/ holds processing, automatic production of notices and reports, variable loan periods, tracking of items as they move from branch to branch, and inventory control. The centralized, integrated bibliographic data base is shared by all the modules, and the integrated file structure permits production of a range of management reports and statistical analyses.

Scope and/or Subject Matter: Automation of library acquisitions, cataloging, and circulation functions.

Input Sources: Bibliographic records can be added, in-house, through the acquisitions module and/or the cataloging module. MARC record requests are formatted during ordering of a new title and the accumulated requests can be transferred at weekly intervals to a bibliographic utility or other sources of MARC records. Retrieved MARC records, either by tape or online, are used to update the temporary acquisitions-created record.

Computer-Based Products and Services: The EASY DATA INTEGRATED LIBRARY SYSTEM operates on an in-house Datapoint minicomputer. The System's modular format permits the cataloging and inquiry systems to be implemented first and the other modules as time and resources permit. Two versions of the System are available: one designed for the public, regional, county, and college library, and the other for the special, corporate, and research library. The System's Inquiry module permits direct word searching of the title data, the authority headings, and the online text file, in addition to the traditional subject, author, call number, ISBN, and LCCN access. Search terms may be combined using Boolean techniques, permitting the formulation of search strategies ranging from the simple to the complex. Hardcopy bibliographies of the search results can be printed upon demand.

Other Services: Easy Data also offers complete training and support services, specialized consulting, project planning, network design and installation, and management of client facilities.

Clientele/Availability: Clients include Canadian, U.S., and European special and public libraries.

Contact: Easy Data Systems Library Divison, Sydney Development Corporation.

★290★
ECONINTEL INFORMATION SERVICES LTD.
ECONINTEL MONITOR
37 Ludgate Hill
London EC4M 7JN, England
Phone: 01-248 4958

Special Note: The above name, address, and telephone number have been verified for this edition, although no questionnaire response was received. The following text is reprinted from the 5th edition.

Description of System or Service: The ECONINTEL MONITOR is a computerized exchange rate and interest rate information service used by corporate treasurers, foreign exchange managers, and fund managers. It comprises a computer-readable data base of current and historical exchange rates and domestic and international interest rates together with a range of software programs for analyzing the data and presenting numerical and graphical reports. The system is commercially accessible through time-sharing.

Scope and/or Subject Matter: Foreign exchange and international and domestic money markets.

Input Sources: Information is collected from the London money and foreign exchange markets.

Holdings and Storage Media: The machine-readable Econintel Monitor data base holds daily closing rates for the past 300 working days and monthly averages of the daily closing rates for the previous five years for the following: spot and forward exchange rates for 25 currencies; Eurocurrency deposit rates for 25 currencies; sterling money market rates for interbank deposits, CDs, local authority deposits, Treasury Bills, and eligible bank bills; and domestic deposit rates for other major currencies.

Publications: Foreign Exchange Yearbook.

Computer-Based Products and Services: The ECONINTEL MONITOR can be accessed worldwide through the time-sharing facilities of ADP Network Services. Clients can link the data to their own data bases of assets and liabilities. Software programs include analytical, numerical, and graphical reporting facilities for cross rates, forward rates, effective exchange rates, SDR and ECU values, covered and uncovered interest rates, covered and uncovered interest rate differentials, and programs for developing quarterly exchange rate forecasts.

Other Services: In addition to the above, Econintel Information Services Ltd. provides a foreign exchange advisory service, a foreign exchange management system, and an economic research bureau data bank.

Clientele/Availability: Clients include corporations and banks. Services are offered on an annual subscription basis.

Contact: Managing Director, Econintel Monitor.

★291★
ECONOMIC AND SOCIAL RESEARCH COUNCIL (ESRC) DATA ARCHIVE
University of Essex   Phone: 0206 860570
Wivenhoe Park   Service Est: 1967
Colchester, Essex CO4 3SQ, England
Prof. Howard Newby, Director

Staff: 5 Information and library professional; 2 management professional; 6 technicians; 2 sales and marketing; 3 clerical and nonprofessional; 1 other.

Related Organizations: The Data Archive administers the British national membership in the Inter-university Consortium for Political and Social Research at the University of Michigan in the United States.

Description of System or Service: The DATA ARCHIVE is the largest national repository of machine-readable social science data in Britain, and it serves as a national lending library for these materials. It actively seeks important new data and encourages the fullest use of its resources by making data available for secondary analysis and instructional purposes. Included in the DATA ARCHIVE's collection are time-series data, major longitudinal studies, panel surveys, major cross-national studies, and government social surveys. The DATA ARCHIVE offers data-use seminars, courses on survey design and analysis, and a visiting fellowship program for researchers. It does not generally provide actual data analysis services.

Scope and/or Subject Matter: Machine-readable social science data about, or of interest to, the United Kingdom. Broad subject categories covered include: national and regional political data; welfare, housing and mobility studies; socioeconomic studies; all aspects of education and teacher training; consumer studies; recreation and leisure planning; urban planning; population studies.

Input Sources: Data sets are acquired from individual researchers, local and central governments, and from social science archives across the world.

Holdings and Storage Media: More than 2500 machine-readable data sets are maintained, as well as a computerized index to them.

Publications: 1) Data Archive Bulletin (triannual)—available by request; includes new data acquisitions, news on organizations and upcoming events, book reviews, and a software bulletin. 2) Data Catalogue—available for purchase; contains descriptive and bibliographic accounts of each data set held. Various brochures and catalogs are also published.

Computer-Based Products and Services: Data sets on magnetic tape or floppy diskette are provided, subject to depositor restrictions, for a handling charge; a comprehensive set of programs permits formatting to user requirements.

Other Services: The Archive also provides advisory and consulting services on data use.

Clientele/Availability: Primary clients are social science researchers.

Remarks: The Economic and Social Research Council was formerly known as the Social Science Research Council (SSRC).

Contact: Prof. Howard Newby, Director, or Marcia Taylor, Chief Research Officer, Data Archive.

★292★
EDIMEDIA INC.
390, rue St. Vallierest   Phone: (418) 657-3551
Quebec City, PQ, Canada G1K 7J6
Paul A. Audet, President

Staff: 6 Information and library professional; 1 management professional; 1 sales and marketing; 1 other.

Related Organizations: Edimedia Inc. is a subsidiary of Unimedia Inc. of Montreal, Canada.

Description of System or Service: EDIMEDIA INC. is a publishing firm which produces teletext pages for electronic magazines. The firm creates teletext pages of news, sports, weather, and financial reports using Telidon technology. The pages are broadcast via cable television to receivers equipped with decoders in Quebec City, Montreal, Sherbrooke, and Victoriaville.

Scope and/or Subject Matter: Consumer and business teletext information.

Input Sources: Information is derived from the Canadian Press.

Holdings and Storage Media: The Edimedia teletext data base holds 75 pages of information daily.

Computer-Based Products and Services: EDIMEDIA INC. produces teletext pages and transmits them via satellite to Videotron Communications, which broadcasts data to home televisions equipped with decoders. The 75 pages of information are transmitted continuously in 18 to 23 minute cycles. EDIMEDIA INC. also produces pages for other teletext and videotex information providers, and it maintained a data base of 2000 pages on the Vista system.

Clientele/Availability: Services are available without restrictions.

Contact: Pierre Mathieu, Director, Edimedia Inc.

★293★
EDITEC
Calle 22 N., No. 3N-20   Phone: 686359
Cali, Valle, Colombia   Founded: 1982
Alejandro Jimenez C., Manager

Staff: 1 Information and library professional; 1 management professional; 1 clerical and nonprofessional.

Description of System or Service: EDITEC offers communication and information services in all subject areas. EDITEC provides audiovisual production, message creation for printed or audiovisual media, editing, and translation services. The firm also offers computerized information retrieval and SDI services from publicly available online data bases.

Scope and/or Subject Matter: All subjects, especially scientific and technical fields.

Input Sources: Information is obtained from commercially available online data bases and other sources.

Computer-Based Products and Services: EDITEC offers computerized searching and SDI services from data bases made available online through DIALOG Information Services, Inc.

Other Services: Editec also provides referrals.

Clientele/Availability: Services are available without restrictions on a contract basis.

Contact: Alejandro Jimenez C., Manager, Editec.

★294★
EDITIONS TECHNIQUES JURIS-DATA
123, rue d'Alesia   Phone: 01 5392291
F-75678 Paris Cedex 14, France
Philippe Durieux, President

Staff: 7 Information and library professional; 9 technicians; 3 sales and marketing.

Related Organizations: JURIS-DATA receives support from La Gazette du Palais.

Description of System or Service: JURIS-DATA is a machine-readable data base providing abstracts or analyses of French Supreme Court decisions, Paris District Court of Appeals decisions, published materials dealing with doctrines and jurisprudence, and relevant unpublished legal materials. JURIS-DATA is publicly accessible online through Telesystemes Questel.

Scope and/or Subject Matter: French judicial decisions and related legal topics.

Input Sources: Input is derived from the Gazette du Palais, Juris-Classeurs, La Semaine Juridique, and other sources.

Holdings and Storage Media: The computer-readable JURIS-DATA data base covers more than 240,000 court decisions since 1960 and relevant published and unpublished materials.

Computer-Based Products and Services: JURIS-DATA is accessible online through Telesystemes Questel.

Other Services: Additional services include reference services and SDI profiles.

Clientele/Availability: JURIS-DATA is intended for use by the legal profession and the academic community.

Contact: Philippe Nectoux, Secretaire General, Editions Techniques. (Telex Editec 270737 F.)

★295★
ELECTRICITE DE FRANCE (EDF)
OFFICE OF STUDY AND RESEARCH
INFORMATION AND DOCUMENTATION SYSTEMS DEPARTMENT
EDF-DOC DATA BASE
B.P. 408
1, ave. du General de Gaulle
F-92141 Clamart Cedex, France
Phone: 01 7654321
Service Est: 1972

Description of System or Service: The EDF-DOC DATA BASE provides coverage of internal and external research, published literature, and other technical documentation on electricity and energy. It is used internally at Electricite de France to provide publications and direct search services; the data base is also publicly available online through Telesystemes and the European Space Agency.

Scope and/or Subject Matter: Electricity, electronics, telecommunications, materials, energy sources, thermal nuclear power stations and their equipment, electrical networks, pollution, energy applications (lighting, heating, air conditioning), mathematics, metrology, informatics.

Input Sources: Published and non-published literature are scanned for input.

Holdings and Storage Media: The computer-readable EDF-DOC DATA BASE holds approximately 226,000 items dating from 1972 to the present; it is updated monthly, with more than 20,000 items added per year.

Publications: 1) Bulletin de Documentation Electricite de France; 2) Liste de Revues Analysees; 3) Liste des Congres Analyses; 4) Table des Codes Sources EDF; 5) Thesaurus EDF.

Computer-Based Products and Services: Search services and SDI are provided internally at EDF, and the data base is externally available through Telesystemes Questel and ESA/IRS.

Clientele/Availability: Services are available to Electricite de France staff and others.

Contact: Chief, Information and Documentation Systems Department, Office of Study and Research. (Telex 270400 EDFERIM.)

★296★
ELSEVIER SCIENCE PUBLISHERS B.V.
BIOMEDICAL DIVISION
EXCERPTA MEDICA (EM)
P.O. Box 1527
Molenwerf 1
NL-1000 BM Amsterdam, Netherlands
Arnold A.J. Jansen, Marketing Director
Phone: 020 5803535
Service Est: 1947

Staff: Approximately 360 total.

Description of System or Service: EXCERPTA MEDICA (EM) provides medical and health professionals with access to basic research and clinical literature through a variety of information activities. These include abstracting and indexing of relevant worldwide literature, publication of numerous abstract and citation journals, and maintenance of the computer-readable EMBASE (Excerpta Medica Data Base), which is available on magnetic tape and through international online host services. Several related data bases are also maintained. In addition, EXCERPTA MEDICA produces special information services, abstracts bulletins, and bibliographies designed to cover highly specialized subject areas in biomedical fields. Sponsored by pharmaceutical companies, scientific societies, or government institutions, these services are published in several languages simultaneously and issued two to six times per year.

Scope and/or Subject Matter: Biomedicine, human medicine, and related disciplines; drugs, pharmacy, environmental health and pollution control, toxicology, cancer, forensic science, health economics and hospital management, occupational health, and public health. Excluded from coverage are veterinary medicine, nursing, dentistry, and paramedical professions such as podiatry, optometry, and chiropractic.

Input Sources: Input includes more than 3500 biomedical periodicals (20,000 issues annually); plus books, congress proceedings, symposia, and other relevant literature.

Holdings and Storage Media: The computer-readable Excerpta Medica data base holds approximately 3 million items dating from 1974 to the present. It is updated weekly with approximately 250,000 items added each year.

Publications: 1) Excerpta Medica Series (frequency varies according to individual title)—44 abstracts journals which publish a total of approximately 160,000 abstracts annually. 2) Drug Literature Index (semimonthly, with semiannual cumulated indexes)—contains about 100,000 citations annually arranged in citation number order. Each issue has author, drug classification, generic names, trade names, and new drugs indexes. 3) Adverse Reactions Titles (monthly, with annual cumulated index)—a spin-off of Drug Literature Index, contains about 5000 citations annually. Each issue has author and subject indexes. 4) Core Journals (monthly)—current awareness abstracts journals in specialty fields, usually published about 4 to 6 weeks after primary articles are published. 5) Newsletters (monthly, bimonthly)—cover specific areas of therapy, sent to selected mailing list. 6) Retrospective abstracts journals—based on retrospective computer searches of the Excerpta Medica data base in a particular field. 7) International Congress Series—about 570 volumes published to date. 8) PROFILE: The Excerpta Medica Newsletter. Various monographs, textbooks, and handbooks are also issued.

Microform Products and Services: In cooperation with the Royal Netherlands Academy of Arts and Sciences, EM microfilms the individual journals it receives cover to cover before processing. Photocopies or duplicate microfiche of articles abstracted in Excerpta Medica's journals can be obtained from the Academy's Library, Kloveniersburgwal 29, NL-1011 JV Amsterdam, Netherlands. The MALIMET thesaurus is also available on microfiche from Excerpta Medica.

Computer-Based Products and Services: EXCERPTA MEDICA maintains the following computer-readable data bases: 1) EMBASE—provides information from the 44 EM abstracts journals, Drug Literature Index, and Adverse Reactions Titles, as well as additional unpublished information. EMBASE is available online through Bibliographic Retrieval Services (BRS), Data-Star, DIALOG Information Services, Inc., DIMDI, Hoechst, and UTOPIA (University of Tsukuba Online Processing of Information). 2) EMCANCER—subfile of EMBASE on cancer; available online through DIMDI. 3)

EMDRUGS (also known as DRUGDOC)—subfile providing information from the abstracts sections on pharmacology and from Drug Literature Index and Adverse Reactions Titles; available through DIMDI and ESA/IRS. 4) EMFORENSIC—contains abstracts from the section on forensic sciences; available through DIMDI and ESA/IRS. 5) EMHEALTH—provides information from three abstracts sections covering public health and social medicine, occupational health and industrial medicine, and environmental health and pollution control; available through DIMDI and ESA/IRS. 6) EMTOX—contains information from the abstracts section on toxicology and the predecessor section that covered both pharmacology and toxicology; available through DIMDI and ESA/IRS. 7) EMPIRES (Excerpta Medica Physicians Information Retrieval and Education Service)—provides abstracts and indexing of more than 300 key journals in the clinical sciences, providing more than 200,000 records since 1981; available through the American Medical Association's AMA/NET service as the Clinical Literature Information Bases. 8) EVOC (Excerpta Medica Vocabulary)—provides access to the following EM authority files: classification terms and codes, item-index terms and codes, EM source journal codes, and the Master List of Medical Indexing Terms (MALIMET); accessible online through Data-Star.

EXCERPTA MEDICA uses its Automated Storage and Retrieval of Biomedical Information program to provide custom searches and SDI services from the above data bases. Computer tape services are also available for the entire EM data base or any individual titles, and for the MALIMET thesaurus and EMCLAS classification system. EXCERPTA MEDICA activities are supported through the internal MARK II computer system which features facilities for identifying fringe and main concept indexing, automatic indexing, a deep level of classification, and a management information system.

Other Services: In addition to services described above, Excerpta Medica offers advisory and consulting services in software applications through subsidiary companies; data collection and analysis; systems design and programming; and audiovisual and translation services.

Clientele/Availability: Clients include physicians, medical researchers, medical libraries, hospitals, medical schools, health organizations, and pharmaceutical companies.

Contact: Arnold A.J. Jansen, Marketing Director, Database Division, Excerpta Medica. (Telex 18582 ESPA NL.) In the United States, contact Steve Ifshin, Elsevier Science Publishing Co., Inc., 52 Vanderbilt Ave., New York, NY 10017; telephone (212) 867-9040. (Telex 420643 AEP UI.)

★297★
ENGLISH TOURIST BOARD
INFORMATION UNIT
TOURTEL
4 Grosvenor Gardens   Phone: 01-730 3400
London SW1W 0DU, England   Service Est: 1979

Special Note: The above name, address, and telephone number have been verified for this edition, although no questionnaire response was received. The following text is reprinted from the 5th edition.

Staff: 1 Information and library professional; 3 technicians; 2 clerical and nonprofessional.

Related Organizations: The English Tourist Board receives support from the British Department of Trade.

Description of System or Service: TOURTEL is a data base on the Prestel system that provides information on tourist attractions and accommodations in England, as well as information from United Kingdom travel companies. It is intended mainly for use by travel agents.

Scope and/or Subject Matter: Tourist information for Britain: places to visit, events, shopping, restaurants, accommodations.

Input Sources: Information is submitted by 12 Regional Tourist Boards.

Holdings and Storage Media: Tourtel information is held in machine-readable form. The English Tourist Board also maintains 10,000 pieces of print material and subscriptions to 400 periodicals.

Computer-Based Products and Services: Comprising more than 3000 pages of information, TOURTEL is interactively searchable in Great Britain through Prestel.

Clientele/Availability: Tourtel is used almost exclusively by British travel agents.

Remarks: The English Tourist Board is also establishing a network of regional distributed computers which will hold details of all tourist accommodations and attractions known to the tourist boards. Data will be used for referral functions as well as the production of publications such as the Where to Stay series of accommodations guides.

Contact: Barbara Lucas, Information Officer, Information Unit, English Tourist Board. (Telex 266975 ETB G.)

★298★
EPOCH RESEARCH CORPORATION
2-7-12-106 Nakano   Phone: 03 3821384
Nakano-ku   Founded: 1982
Tokyo 164, Japan
Masahito Miwa, President

Staff: 3 Information and library professional; 2 management professional; 3 technicians; 2 clerical and nonprofessional.

Description of System or Service: EPOCH RESEARCH CORPORATION is an information research and consulting firm. It offers computerized information retrieval, document delivery, manual literature searching, questionnaire surveying, interviewing, and report writing services. EPOCH provides information management consulting services in the areas of office information management system design, office automation, and design and development of information systems for libraries and information centers. It also conducts information service user studies and marketing research. Additionally, EPOCH offers planning services for the design of local area library networks and local government information systems and networks.

Scope and/or Subject Matter: Information research in the areas of business, new technology, and the information industry; consulting in information management and office and library automation.

Input Sources: Input sources include major online host services; newspapers, professional journals, and news releases; and company-conducted surveys and interviews.

Holdings and Storage Media: The firm's library contains 500 bound volumes and subscriptions to 15 periodicals.

Publications: Epoch News Japan (bimonthly)—available by subscription; newsletter covering information industries in Japan.

Computer-Based Products and Services: EPOCH RESEARCH CORPORATION conducts online searches of data bases made available through DIALOG Information Services, Inc., System Development Corporation (SDC), Bibliographic Retrieval Services (BRS), NEEDS-IR (Nikkei Economic Electronic Databank Service - Information Retrieval), and HINET. EPOCH also provides training in the use of bibliographic information systems and consultation on data base and information system development and library automation.

Clientele/Availability: Services are available without restrictions on a fee basis. Clients include local government bodies, marketing researchers, publishers, and construction industries.

Contact: Makiko Miwa, Vice President, Epoch Research Corporation.

★299★
ESDU INTERNATIONAL LIMITED
251/9 Regent St.   Phone: 01-437 4894
London W1R 7AD, England   Founded: 1939
John A. Castle, Managing Director

Staff: 6 Management professional; 24 technicians; 4 sales and marketing; 12 clerical and nonprofessional.

Related Organizations: International Thomson Organisation is the parent company of ESDU International. The firm is guided in its work by several technical committees, whose international membership consists of practicing engineering experts and specialists drawn from industry, research, and universities.

Description of System or Service: ESDU INTERNATIONAL LIMITED provides technical information services to practicing professional engineers in the mechanical, structural, aeronautical, and process engineering fields. It collects, correlates, and continuously validates published and unpublished design and analysis data and methods. ESDU issues this information in a series of loose-leaf volumes that are continuously amended and expanded to reflect current research and developments in technology. User support is available from the ESDU specialists who prepare the information. Additionally, ESDU provides engineering software programs for a range of computers.

Scope and/or Subject Matter: Design and analysis data and methods in acoustic fatigue, aerodynamics, dynamics, engineering structures, fatigue, fluid mechanics-internal flow, heat transfer, mechanisms, noise, performance of aircraft, physical data-chemical and mechanical engineering, stress and strength, structures, transonic aerodynamics, tribology, and wind engineering.

Input Sources: Data and methods are derived from worldwide sources of published and unpublished literature.

Publications: ESDU information is available in hard copy in more than 150 loose-leaf volumes covering 19 engineering subjects and more than 800 individual topics. Approximately 40-50 new or amended topics are added each year.

Computer-Based Products and Services: ESDU INTERNATIONAL produces engineering software for micro, mini, and mainframe computers. Approximately 40 engineering programs covering mechanical, structural, and aeronautical engineering are available for use on the IBM PC.

Other Services: Additionally, ESDU specialists are available for support and consultation on the application of ESDU information to specific design and analysis needs.

Clientele/Availability: Services are used by engineering companies, universities, and research establishments.

Remarks: ESDU International was formerly known as Engineering Sciences Data Unit Ltd.

Contact: John Duckett, Marketing Director, ESDU International Ltd. (Telex 266168 ENDASA G.) The firm also maintains an office at 1495 Chain Bridge Rd. Suite 200, McLean, VA 22101; telephone (703) 734-7970.

★300★
ESPIAL PRODUCTIONS
P.O. Box 624, Station K Phone: (416) 485-8063
Toronto, ON, Canada M4P 2H1 Founded: 1974
Harry Campbell, General Manager

Staff: 2 Information and library professional; 1 clerical and nonprofessional; 2 other.

Description of System or Service: ESPIAL PRODUCTIONS develops cultural and educational information systems to meet the needs of governmental and nongovernmental organizations in Canada and abroad, and it prepares data bases to be used by commercial and noncommercial firms. Other services include consulting on information service development, production of audiovisual training and documentary materials in the fields of education and information science, and organization of training seminars to establish national information services. Specific projects of ESPIAL include maintenance of the computer-readable Canadian Art Auction Records data base and preparation of guides to specialized data bases in Europe, North America, and the People's Republic of China.

Scope and/or Subject Matter: Information services and data bases in cultural and educational subjects including national cultural development, social sciences, literature, Canadian art, mass media, graphic art, and communications.

Input Sources: Information sources used by Espial include Canadian, European, and third world cultural statistics and publications. Art galleries, museums, and private collectors contribute information to the art auction data base.

Holdings and Storage Media: Cumulative since 1969, the machine-readable Canadian Art Auction Records data base contains bibliographical and nonbibliographical information on 6000 entries per year.

Publications: 1) Espial Data Base Directory (annual)—descriptions of Canadian material in 115 Canadian and non-Canadian computer-readable data bases; available for purchase. 2) Canadian Art Auctions: Sales and Prices 1976-1978—values of the works of more than 1200 Canadian artists as determined at auctions held in the major Canadian auction houses; includes annotations on artists. Published in Canada by General Publishing Co., Ltd., Don Mills, Ontario.

Computer-Based Products and Services: Espial Productions maintains the Canadian Art Auction Records data base and other cultural and educational files for its clients. It also provides computerized SDI services on art auction prices.

Clientele/Availability: Services are available without restrictions. Clients include international governmental and nongovernmental agencies and organizations requiring specialized information services.

Contact: Harry Campbell, General Manager, Espial Productions.

★301★
ESSELTE BUSINESS INFORMATION
Box 1391 Phone: 08 7343400
S-171 27 Solna, Sweden
Staffan Nordstrand, Marketing Director

Staff: 1 Information and library professional; 4 management professional; 1 technician; 4 sales and marketing; 1 clerical and nonprofessional.

Description of System or Service: ESSELTE BUSINESS INFORMATION offers services in the areas of electronic publishing, graphic data processing, and videotex systems for Scandinavian and international business information.

Computer-Based Products and Services: The firm offers videotex and online services.

Clientele/Availability: Services are available without restrictions.

Contact: Fredrik Romberg, Product Manager, Esselte Business Information.

★302★
ESSELTE GROUP OF BOOKSELLERS
ESSELTE DOCUMENTATION SYSTEM
P.O. Box 62 Phone: 08 237990
S-101 20 Stockholm, Sweden Service Est: 1958
Lars-Erik Eriksson, Manager

Staff: 2 Information and library professional; 3 clerical and nonprofessional.

Description of System or Service: The ESSELTE DOCUMENTATION SYSTEM is a subscription service for information on new and forthcoming scientific, technical, and scholarly books and journals published worldwide. Subscribers receive punched cards listing the book title, author or editor's name, ISBN or ISSN, number of pages, illustrations, tables, publisher's name, and price. When the information is available, the cards also list the contents or a brief summary of contents, as well as the approximate date of publication. The SYSTEM covers 141 different subject groups from which subscribers select the subjects they wish to receive.

Scope and/or Subject Matter: Advance publication information on scientific, technical, and scholarly books and journals from all over the world in the major languages.

Input Sources: The SYSTEM uses news bulletins, leaflets, and catalogs submitted by about 1100 publishers in the preparation of its card service. Approximately 12,000 titles are selected annually for inclusion.

Clientele/Availability: The Esselte Documentation System is available on a monthly subscription basis; costs vary according to the number of subjects chosen to be received.

Remarks: The System was formerly known as the A & W Documentation System of Almqvist & Wiksell Booksellers.

Contact: Lars-Erik Eriksson, Manager, Esselte Documentation System. (Telex 12430 ALMQWIK S.)

★303★
EURODATA FOUNDATION
(Stichting Eurodata)
Broad Street House
55 Old Broad St.
London EC2M 1RX, England
S.J. Valiant, Manager
Phone: 01-638 3702
Founded: 1976

Staff: 3 Technicians; 2 other.

Related Organizations: The Eurodata Foundation is an independent body supported by 18 European telecommunications authorities under the auspices of the European Conference of Posts and Telecommunications Administrations/ Conference Europeenne des Administrations des Postes et des Telecommunications (CEPT).

Description of System or Service: The EURODATA FOUNDATION was established to serve the needs of Europe's data communications market through the following activities: conducting and coordinating studies and activities on behalf of members; marketing information services; developing a European data communications data base and a commercial information service; and acting as legal instrument when members jointly enter contractual arrangements with third parties.

Scope and/or Subject Matter: Data communications and telecommunications in Europe.

Publications: 1) Eurodata Foundation Yearbook—contains information on data and text communications services offered by members of the Eurodata Foundation. 2) Guides for Managers Series—issued for each of the following areas: teletex, videotex, and facsimile. 3) Data Communications in Europe, 1983-1991.

Clientele/Availability: Membership consists of 18 national telecommunications authorities in Europe.

Remarks: The Foundation's registered office is located at Kortenaerkade 12, The Hague, Netherlands.

Contact: Linda M. Porter, Publications Manager, Eurodata Foundation; telephone 01-638 3021. (Telex 887523 BTELCG.)

★304★
EUROLINE INC.
P.O. Box 3121, Station D
Ottawa, ON, Canada K1P 6H7
Peter D. Geldart, Director
Phone: (613) 236-3434
Founded: 1982

Description of System or Service: EUROLINE INC. provides online information retrieval from worldwide data bases covering scientific and technical literature and business information and statistics. EUROLINE also provides reports and studies to determine how online information can meet the needs of an organization, identifies and describes data bases and telecommunication procedures, and advises clients on establishing direct access to these data bases.

Scope and/or Subject Matter: All subjects of interest to clients.

Input Sources: Input is gathered from online systems worldwide.

Computer-Based Products and Services: EUROLINE INC. provides information retrieval from data bases carried by European and North American online hosts.

Other Services: Euroline is the representative in Canada and provides free information and assistance for the European Space Agency-Information Retrieval Service (ESA-IRS) and I/S Datacentralen, Cronos-Eurostat.

Clientele/Availability: Clients include private companies, research organizations, and federal and provincial government agencies.

Remarks: Euroline Inc. was formerly known as Intelegence Literature Searches.

Contact: Peter D. Geldart, Director, Euroline Inc.

★305★
EUROPE DATA
Bredestr. 24
NL-6211 HC Maastricht, Netherlands
Karel Giel, Managing Director
Phone: 043 54751
Founded: 1982

Staff: 23 Total.

Related Organizations: Europe Data was formed by Elsevier-NDU Publishers and the Limburg Industrial Development Fund.

Description of System or Service: EUROPE DATA is an electronic publishing company that specializes in abstracting and indexing services for European Communities publications. Its products include the EC Index, which covers all publicly available publications of the European Communities, and ELLIS (European Legal Literature Information Service). The company also provides abstracts and indexes for inclusion in TEXTLINE, produced by Finsbury Data Services Ltd., and European Court of Justice Reporter, published by EUROPE DATA and ESC Publishing, Oxford, England. In addition, EUROPE DATA provides document delivery through Eurodocdel, a service created by the CEC, and is the European distributor for Congressional Information Service, Inc. products.

Scope and/or Subject Matter: European Communities documents and legislative regulatory proceedings having research or public interest value.

Input Sources: Input is obtained from publications and documents produced by institutions of the European Communities, including annuals, periodicals, series, and monographs.

Holdings and Storage Media: The computer-readable EC Index data base is updated annually with approximately 8,000 records.

Publications: 1) EC Index (monthly; planned quarterly and annual cumulations)—covers publications and documents in scientific and technical areas; each entry includes a summary, description, and bibliographic details on an EC publication or document. Also includes title, subject, keyword, and other indexes. 2) European Legal Literature Information Service-ELLIS (planned quarterly with annual cumulations)—published in conjunction with the European Law Centre Ltd.; abstracts and indexes legal literature dealing with the European Communities and its institutions. 3) European Court of Justice Reporter—published jointly with ESC Publishing Ltd., Oxford, England.

Computer-Based Products and Services: The EC Index and ELLIS data bases are expected to be offered online.

Other Services: Europe Data is also available as a consultant to abstracting and indexing services.

Clientele/Availability: Primary clients include library, corporate, and national government information users.

Contact: Pauline Schoenmakers, Europe Data. (Telex 56562.)

★306★
EUROPEAN ASSOCIATION FOR THE TRANSFER OF TECHNOLOGIES, INNOVATION AND INDUSTRIAL INFORMATION (TII)
7, rue Alcide de Gasperi
B.P. 1704
L-1017 Kirchberg, Luxembourg
Christian Glockner, General Secretary
Phone: 352 438096
Founded: 1984

Staff: 2 Total.

Related Organizations: The Association was formed with the assistance of the Commission of the European Communities (CEC) and Council of Europe.

Description of System or Service: The EUROPEAN ASSOCIATION FOR THE TRANSFER OF TECHNOLOGIES, INNOVATION AND INDUSTRIAL INFORMATION (TII) was established to promote the exchange of innovation and industrial information in European countries. The ASSOCIATION's goals include stimulating innovation, promoting the development and operation of small and medium size enterprises, promoting the transfer of technology from one country to another, and helping companies use the Common Market to their advantage. The ASSOCIATION provides computerized searches and other information services; it is also creating a facsimile network to facilitate crossborder contacts between agents and agencies for the transfer of industrial information.

Scope and/or Subject Matter: Promotion of innovation in the European Common Market.

Computer-Based Products and Services: Searches are provided from relevant data bases such as TRANSINOVE.

Clientele/Availability: The Association is operated on a membership basis.

Contact: Christian Glockner, Secretary General, European Association for the Transfer of Technologies, Innovation and Industrial Information.

★307★
EUROPEAN ASSOCIATION OF INFORMATION SERVICES (EUSIDIC)
P.O. Box 429
London W4 1UJ, England
Helen Henderson, Secretary
Phone: 01-546 7968
Founded: 1970

Description of System or Service: The EUROPEAN ASSOCIATION OF INFORMATION SERVICES (EUSIDIC) is an international association for data base producers, hosts, online users, and others interested in the handling, production, and dissemination of information in electronic form. Comprising some 200 organizations from 18 European countries with associate members from 9 other countries, EUSIDIC is currently engaged in preparing and issuing Codes of Practice for electronic information. The Codes will set standards for online users, hosts, and data base producers and their contractual relationships. EUSIDIC provides an electronic mail service for its members and publishes an electronic newsletter as well as the printed Eusidic Database Guide and the Newsidic newsletter. EUSIDIC also holds an annual conference and technical meetings, and it sponsors the European Scientific Information Referral (EUSIREF) network and working groups on transborder data flow, national online user groups, and other topics.

Scope and/or Subject Matter: Production, dissemination, and use of scientific, technical, commercial, and social information in electronic form.

Publications: 1) Newsidic (bimonthly)—newsletter; free to members. 2) Eusidic Database Guide—an international directory covering more than 2800 data bases available to the public, European batch mode and online operations, and online operations networked to Europe; published by Learned Information, Oxford, England. Contains an alphabetical listing of organizations producing and operating data bases and includes indexes to organizations, data bases, networks, and subjects.

Computer-Based Products and Services: EUSIDIC has established an electronic mail service for member communications. It also publishes an electronic newsletter giving current information on EUSIDIC and related activities, technical notes on topical subjects, and information on problems of the information industry as they arise.

Clientele/Availability: Services are offered on a membership basis.

Remarks: The European Association of Information Services was formerly the European Association of Scientific Information Dissemination Centers.

Contact: Helen Henderson, Secretary, European Association of Information Services. Telex 825962 (quote EUSIDIC). The electronic mail address on Data-Mail is H. Henderson; on Telecom Gold, IMA001.

★308★
EUROPEAN BUSINESS ASSOCIATES (EBA) ON-LINE
69, rue de la Petrusse
L-8084 Bertrange, Luxembourg
Mary Clark, President
Phone: 352 318884
Founded: 1982

Staff: 1 Management professional; 2 sales and marketing; 1 clerical and nonprofessional.

Description of System or Service: EUROPEAN BUSINESS ASSOCIATES (EBA) ON-LINE is an international organization offering full marketing services within the online information, computer terminal, and network information fields. Services include market surveys, strategy and planning for market development, financial advice, and specific project control and management. The firm will contact potential users in Europe and provide customer or distributor workshops. It also assists with translation, production, storage, and distribution of multilingual literature.

Scope and/or Subject Matter: Marketing services in the information industry.

Input Sources: Information is gathered from market research reports, periodicals, scientific and marketing data bases, and contacts in computer and communication fields across Europe.

Other Services: EBA also offers marketing and management training.

Clientele/Availability: Primary clients include data base producers and online vendors.

Contact: Mary Clark, President, European Business Associates On-Line. (Telex 1753 LUX.)

★309★
EUROPEAN CONFERENCE OF MINISTERS OF TRANSPORT (ECMT)
(Conference Europeenne des Ministres des Transports - CEMT)
INTERNATIONAL CO-OPERATION IN THE FIELD OF TRANSPORT ECONOMICS DOCUMENTATION (ICTED)
(Cooperation Internationale en Matiere de Documentation sur l'Economie des Transports - CIDET)
19, rue de Franqueville
F-75775 Paris Cedex 16, France
Jan C. Terlouw, Secretary General
Phone: 01 5249722
Service Est: 1972

Staff: 3 Information and library professional.

Related Organizations: The Organisation for Economic Co-Operation and Development (OECD) provides support.

Description of System or Service: INTERNATIONAL CO-OPERATION IN THE FIELD OF TRANSPORT ECONOMICS DOCUMENTATION (ICTED) is a cooperative documentation system supported by a network of national centers responsible for abstracting and indexing original documents concerning transport economics and policy. The centers prepare abstracts of periodicals and other literature and submit them to the European Conference of Ministers of Transport (ECMT) Documentation Center where they are reproduced in machine-readable form and entered into the TRANSDOC data base. TRANSDOC is publicly available online through ESA/IRS and is used to produce a microfiche bibliography; computer tapes, special printouts, and SDI services are also available. In addition to producing TRANSDOC, the ICTED maintains a data base on current research projects and uses it to issue an annual printed publication.

Scope and/or Subject Matter: Transport economics, policy, and sociology. All types and modes of transport are covered (with emphasis on land transport), including local, urban, regional, national, and international.

Input Sources: Input for TRANSDOC is derived from 300 periodicals and from books, reports, conference proceedings, theses, patent documents, and maps and plans collected from national centers in ECMT member countries. Approximately 40 percent of the input consists of nonjournal items. Input for the research file is collected through annual surveys of 400 organizations.

Holdings and Storage Media: ICTED maintains the computer-readable TRANSDOC data base holding approximately 7500 citations dating from 1970 to the present; a nonbibliographic file covering approximately 1400 research projects is also held in machine-readable form.

Publications: Research on Transport Economics (annual)—covers research in progress at approximately 400 public and private organizations; available free of charge to organizations participating in the exchange of information or by subscription to others.

Microform Products and Services: TRANSDOC is available by subscription on annually updated COM microfiche with author, corporate author, and three title indexes.

Computer-Based Products and Services: The TRANSDOC data base is accessible online through ESA/IRS. Additionally, several of the national centers offer remote terminal access to the data base via their telephone network or telecommunications systems. The TRANSDOC bibliography is also distributed quarterly on machine-readable tape to network members; batch searches are available free of charge to members.

Clientele/Availability: Services are intended for ICTED network members, but are available on a fee basis to others in the transport field.

Contact: P. Coquand, Administrator, International Co-operation in the Field of Transport Economics Documentation.

★310★
EUROPEAN CONSORTIUM FOR POLITICAL RESEARCH
DATA INFORMATION SERVICE
Hans Holmboesgate 22
N-5000 Bergen, Norway
Stein Kuhnle, Newsletter Editor
Phone: 05 212117
Service Est: 1971

Staff: 2 Information and library professional; 1 management professional; 1 clerical and nonprofessional.

Description of System or Service: The DATA INFORMATION SERVICE of the European Consortium for Political Research publishes a newsletter dealing with current projects of data generation and software development. The quarterly European Political Data Newsletter, issued jointly with the Norwegian Social Science Data Services, reviews data of all kinds being produced and stored in Western Europe. The computer section of the newsletter provides notes on the latest algorithms and methods. The data section covers existing archival services in and beyond Europe, new projects of data organizations, data sources, news of software packages, and announcements of relevant meetings, workshops, and seminars.

Scope and/or Subject Matter: Political science data and research; data generation; computer software.

Publications: European Political Data Newsletter (quarterly).

Clientele/Availability: Services are available without restrictions.

Contact: Stein Kuhnle, Newsletter Editor, European Consortium for Political Research.

★311★
EUROPEAN COORDINATION CENTRE FOR RESEARCH AND
DOCUMENTATION IN SOCIAL SCIENCES
P.O. Box 974
Grunangergasse 2
A-1011 Vienna, Austria
Dr. Oskar Vogel, Head
Phone: 524333
Founded: 1963

Staff: 2 Information and library professional; 8 management professional; 10 clerical and nonprofessional.

Related Organizations: The Centre is an autonomous unit of the International Social Science Council.

Description of System or Service: The EUROPEAN COORDINATION CENTRE FOR RESEARCH AND DOCUMENTATION IN SOCIAL SCIENCES promotes cooperation among European researchers in social science disciplines. In support of its goal, the CENTRE has developed the European Cooperation in Social Science Information and Documentation (ECSSID) program, which works with social science information and documentation centers throughout Eastern and Western Europe to promote the exchange of relevant documents and machine-readable data on bilateral or multilateral levels.

Scope and/or Subject Matter: Social science research, information, and documentation in Europe.

Publications: ECSSID Bulletin (quarterly)—provides news on developments, activities, and publications in the area of social science information and documentation; published by and available without charge from the Library of the Hungarian Academy of Sciences, P.O. Box 7, H-1361 Budapest, Hungary.

Clientele/Availability: The Centre serves European social science researchers and information and documentation centers.

Contact: Georgy Soloviev, Scientific Secretary, European Coordination Centre for Research and Documentation in Social Sciences.

★312★
EUROPEAN INFORMATION PROVIDERS ASSOCIATION (EURIPA)
Kingsmead House
250 Kings Rd.
London SW3, England
Dr. Robert Middleton, Chairman
Phone: 01-351 2776
Founded: 1980

Description of System or Service: The EUROPEAN INFORMATION PROVIDERS ASSOCIATION (EURIPA) is an association of European data base producers and operators, computer hardware and software firms, and other organizations involved in the production, storage, and delivery of electronic information products. The objectives of EURIPA include the following: to promote, protect, and represent European information providers in accordance with the principles of free enterprise; to identify new markets; to collect data on the size and shape of the European information industry; to provide a forum for the exchange of information; to influence relevant activities of governmental and nongovernmental bodies at the national and European levels; and to promote the application of new technologies in information provision.

Scope and/or Subject Matter: European electronic information industry.

Clientele/Availability: Membership is open to individuals and organizations.

Contact: D.H. Barlow, Secretary General, European Information Providers Association.

★313★
EUROPEAN INSTITUTE FOR ADVANCED STUDIES IN
  MANAGEMENT (EIASM)
DATA BANK OF EUROPEAN DOCTORAL THESES IN MANAGEMENT
  (DISSERT 1)

Special Note: The DATA BANK OF EUROPEAN DOCTORAL THESES IN MANAGEMENT (DISSERT 1), a computer-readable file maintained by the European Institute for Advanced Studies in Management of Brussels, Belgium, is reported to be no longer available. DISSERT I was described in the fifth edition of the Encyclopedia of Information Systems and Services (entry 647) as containing citations to dissertation theses in management accepted from European universities.

★314★
EUROPEAN LAW CENTRE LTD.
EUROLEX
4 Bloomsbury Square
London WC1A 2RL, England
David R. Worlock, Managing Director
Phone: 01-404 4300
Service Est: 1980

Related Organizations: The European Law Centre Ltd. is a wholly owned subsidiary of the International Thomson Organisation.

Description of System or Service: EUROLEX is a computerized full-text legal research service providing clients with online access to legal information from the United Kingdom, other European nations, and the European Communities. It permits interactive searches on any significant word appearing in the cases, statutes, digests, legislation, and other materials present. Designed for use by persons without data processing experience, EUROLEX can be accessed with a wide range of terminal equipment.

Scope and/or Subject Matter: United Kingdom and European case law, legislation, and treaties.

Input Sources: Input for the data base is derived from the full text of several dozen legal publications and documents.

Holdings and Storage Media: Online Eurolex files contain more than 300 million words of text that include 44,000 full case reports, 23,000 items of legislation, and 75,000 digest and summary reports.

Computer-Based Products and Services: EUROLEX is held on the computer facilities of Datasolve Ltd. under STATUS software. It may be accessed over the public telephone system and most public data networks. In North America, EUROLEX is accessible through WESTLAW (West Publishing Company). Within the EUROLEX data base, source data are organized into libraries of documents which are subdivided into segments such as headnotes, citations, opinions, and judgments. Users can search an entire library or any part of it. EUROLEX provides access to the full text of the following legal publications and documents: 1) Common Market Law Reports; 2) European Court Reports; 3) Fleet Street Reports; 4) Reports of Patent Cases; 5) The Weekly Law Reports; 6) The Times Law Reports; 7) HMSO Statutes in Force; 8) Commerical Laws of Europe; 9) Current Law; 10) Council of Europe Conventions and Agreements; 11) European Law Digest; 12) European Human Rights Reports; 13) Industrial Case Reports; 14) EEC Official Journal; 15) Scots Law Times; 16) Criminal Appeal Reports; 17) Criminal Appeal Office Index; 18) Road Traffic Reports; 19) Financial Times Commercial Law Reports; 20) Tax Case Materials; 21) VAT Tribunal Reports; 22) Interfisc; 23) PLANLaw (all decisions reported in the Journal of Planning Law since 1949 and Property & Compensation Reports since 1949); and 24) NEWSLaw.

Clientele/Availability: Eurolex is available in the United Kingdom and North America. The system is intended for use by lawyers in private practice, government, and industry.

Contact: Jennie Smurthwaite, Marketing Executive, European Law Centre Ltd. (Telex 21746.)

★315★
EUROPEAN PATENT OFFICE (EPO)
EDP DEPARTMENT
EPO DATA BANKS
P.B. 5818, Patentlaan 2
NL-2280 HV Rijswijk ZH, Netherlands
O. Bullens, Department Head
Phone: 070 906789
Service Est: 1979

Special Note: The above name, address, and telephone number have been verified for this edition, although no questionnaire response was received. The following text is reprinted from the 5th edition.

Description of System or Service: The EPO DATA BANKS were established to support the internal operations of the European Patent Office and to help meet its responsibility to disseminate information on published applications and patents. They comprise the European Patent Register, the European Patent Search Documentation System, and the European Patent Administrative System (EPASYS). The European Patent Register, which holds information also published in the weekly European Patent Bulletin, is a publicly accessible file covering patents and applications appearing since December, 1978. The Search Documentation System is an internal file constructed to facilitate access to approximately 14 million systematically classified patent documents held by the EPO. EPASYS is an internal system providing status and diagnostic information on European patent applications.

Scope and/or Subject Matter: European patent information.

Holdings and Storage Media: The Register currently holds approximately 40,000 bibliographic entries; it is expected to grow by about 25,000 per year. The Search Documentation System contains bibliographic data for about 10 million of the 14 million documents held by the EPO.

Publications: European Patent Bulletin (weekly).

Microform Products and Services: Patent information is currently available on microfilm, with full COM services expected to be offered in the future.

Computer-Based Products and Services: The European Patent Register is provided online by the EPO over EURONET or public telephone networks. Available on a subscription basis, the Register is searchable by publication or application number; additional search keys for international classification symbol, applicant, priority, and inventor are being added. The Search Documentation System and EPASYS are not publicly available at the present. In special cases, patent data are provided on magnetic tape.

Other Services: In addition to services described above, the EPO maintains public inquiry offices in The Hague and Munich.

Clientele/Availability: Services are available to the European patent community and others.

Contact: O. Bullens, Head, EDP Department, European Patent Office. The secretariat of the EPO is located at Erhardstr. 27, D-8000 Munich 2, Federal Republic of Germany.

★316★
EUROPEAN SPACE AGENCY (ESA)
EUROPEAN SPACE RESEARCH AND TECHNOLOGY CENTER (ESTEC)
MATERIALS DATA RETRIEVAL SYSTEM
Postbus 299
NL-8200 AG Noordwijk ZH, Netherlands
Dr. J. Dauphin, Head, Materials Section
Phone: 01719 82118

Description of System or Service: The MATERIALS DATA RETRIEVAL SYSTEM is a computer-readable index of documents which contain information on materials used in spacecraft.

Scope and/or Subject Matter: Properties of materials used in spacecraft: thermo-optical, outgassing, flammability, offgassing and odor, thermal cycling. Identification of materials: trade name and number, manufacturer's name, type of product, chemical nature.

Input Sources: Input is derived from test results from space and aeronautical research laboratories throughout the world, as well as from open scientific and technical literature.

Holdings and Storage Media: Test results are held in computer-readable form; documents are stored on microfiche.

Publications: 1) Guidelines for Space Materials Selection (occasional). 2) Description of the Data Base (Tm 206). 3) Literature of Outgassing Materials.

Computer-Based Products and Services: The MATERIALS DATA RETRIEVAL SYSTEM is an interactive indexing system which can also be used to answer questions requiring only brief answers. It is accessed by research organizations in several European countries.

Clientele/Availability: The System is primarily for the benefit of European Space Agency and research installations in its member states.

Contact: P. Jollet, Materials Data Retrieval System; telephone 01719 83905.

★317★
EUROPEAN SPACE AGENCY (ESA)
INFORMATION RETRIEVAL SERVICE (IRS)
ESRIN, Via Galileo Galilei, C.P. 64
I-00044 Frascati (Rome), Italy
Dr. T.F. Howell, Director
Phone: 39 694011
Service Est: 1965

Description of System or Service: The INFORMATION RETRIEVAL SERVICE (IRS) operates a major European online host service providing users in Europe and worldwide with interactive access to more than 60 data bases. Features of the system include current awareness searches; online document ordering; electronic mail; a personal time-series data storage and computation system; and facilities for private data base storage. In addition to operating the online service, the IRS abstracts and indexes the European aerospace literature for input to the STAR system of the U.S. National Aeronautics and Space Administration (NASA), and maintains and disseminates microform copies of reports cited in STAR. IRS also prepares the following factual data banks which it makes accessible online: LEDA, SATELDATA, and SPACECOMPS.

Scope and/or Subject Matter: Aeronautics; astronomy; agriculture; astrophysics; biology; biomedicine; chemical, physical, engineering, and food sciences; data processing; earth and the environmental sciences; education research; electronics; energy; management sciences; metallurgy; physics; remote sensing.

Input Sources: Data bases offered through ESA/IRS are acquired from European and North American organizations. Input for the IRS factual data banks is derived from original IRS data collection efforts.

Holdings and Storage Media: Approximately 65 data bases holding more than 30 million records are available online through ESA/IRS. The IRS LEDA file holds 160,000 items; SATELDATA holds 860 items; and SPACECOMPS holds 13,000 items. Additionally, the IRS maintains a collection of satellite images and a microform collection of documents cited in STAR.

Publications: 1) News and Views (bimonthly)—newsletter. 2) ESA/

IRS User Manual.

Microform Products and Services: Microfiche and papercopy reproductions of ESA and NASA technical documents are provided to users in ESA member countries.

Computer-Based Products and Services: The INFORMATION RETRIEVAL SERVICE offers online information retrieval from bibliographic and factual data bases; online document ordering through the PRIMORDIAL service; electronic mail capabilities through the Data Dissemination System (DDS); a Personal Statistical Analyses service which provides storage facilities and mathematical and statistical means to manipulate client's time-series data; an Online Data Entry (ODE) system which prepares custom computerized business and library options to be used with client data bases stored on ESA/IRS; and downloading facilities. ESA/IRS may be accessed online through the ESA data communication network, ESANET, which consists of more than 10,000 kilometers of leased lines connected to the IRS computer in Rome. The IRS is also linked to public data transmission networks such as Euronet, Tymnet, Telenet, and telex. The service is maintained under ESA-QUEST command and retrieval language which facilitates loading and maintenance of large data files and supports the Common Command Language (CCL), which can be used on all ESA/IRS data bases, and STAIRS, which is applied in the AGRIS and INIS files. ESA-QUEST also facilitates crossfile searching and term associations. Data bases offered or planned to be offered through the INFORMATION RETRIEVAL SERVICE include the following:

1) ABI/INFORM—covers international business periodical literature in such areas as finance, management, economics, business law, and marketing; produced by Data Courier Inc. 2) ACOMPLINE—provides information on urban matters, local government, traffic, building, finance, health, and population; produced by the Greater London Council. 3) Aerospace Daily—contains the full text of the Aerospace Daily Newsletter from 1982 to the present; compiled by Ziff-Davis Publishing Co. 4) AFEE—provides abstracts of published literature dealing with hydrogeology, water resources, and related topics; produced by the French Water Study Association/ Association Francaise pour l'Etude des Eaux (AFEE). 5) AGRIS—an international index covering agriculture, food production, fishing, machinery, and pollution; produced by the United Nations Food and Agriculture Organization (FAO).

6) Aluminum (World Aluminum Abstracts)—covers the world's scientific, technical, and patent literature on aluminum; produced by the Aluminum Association. 7) AMPEREDOC—provides information on the production, transport, distribution, and utilization of electrical energy; produced by the Multinational Association of Producers and Retailers of Electricity-Documentation/ Association Multinationale des Producteurs et Revendeurs d'Electricite-Documentation. 8) AQUALINE—provides abstracts to international literature on water resources; produced by the Great Britain Water Research Centre. 9) Asian Geotechnology—covers international periodicals, books, and conference proceedings related to geotechnical engineering; prepared by the Asian Information Center for Geotechnical Engineering of the Asian Institute of Technology. 10) BIIPAM-CTIF—contains abstracts of technical documents on foundry techniques and metallurgy; produced by Pont-a-Mousson Research Center/ Centre de Recherche de Pont-a-Mousson.

11) BIOSIS—provides access to worldwide literature in the fields of biological and biomedical sciences; produced by BioSciences Information Service. 12) BNF Metals—covers worldwide journals and other publications relevant to the nonferrous metals industry; produced by BNF Metals Technology Centre. 13) Business/Professional Software Database—contains descriptive citations of business software packages designed for minicomputers or personal computers; produced by Data Courier Inc and Information Sources, Ltd. 14) CAB Abstracts—provides coverage of literature published worldwide on various aspects of agriculture; produced by Commonwealth Agricultural Bureaux. 15) CETIM—contains references to literature covering the field of mechanical engineering; produced by Technical Center for Mechanical Industries/ Centre Technique des Industries Mecaniques (CETIM).

16) CHEMABS (with CHEMABS Training subfile)—Chemical Abstracts citations from 1967 to the present; produced by Chemical Abstracts Service. 17) Chemical Engineering Abstracts (CEA)—provides abstracts and indexes of international literature covering the scientific, technical, and technocommercial aspects of chemical and process engineering; produced by the Royal Society of Chemistry. 18) CISDOC—covers worldwide journals, conference reports, laws, and standards on occupational safety and health; produced by the International Labour Office's Occupational Safety and Health Information Centre. 19) COMPENDEX (with COMPENDEX Training subfile)—provides abstracts of and extensive indexes to the world's literature in engineering; produced by Engineering Information, Inc. 20) Conference Papers Index—provides information on current research findings and papers presented at conferences and meetings throughout the world in the areas of science and technology; produced by Cambridge Scientific Abstracts.

21) COSMIC—covers computer program packages for the aerospace industry; produced by the Computer Software Management and Information Center at the University of Georgia. 22) Current Biotechnology Abstracts—provides abstracts and indexes of international journal and other literature covering the scientific, technical, and technocommercial aspects of biotechnology; produced by the Royal Society of Chemistry. 23) EDF-DOC—provides coverage of research, published literature, and other technical documentation on electricity and energy; produced by the Electricite de France (EDF). 24) EDIN (Education on INIS)—a subset of the INIS data base which is used for training purposes. 25) Ei Engineering Meetings—covers conference papers dealing with engineering; produced by Engineering Information, Inc.

26) EMDRUGS—covers worldwide literature on drugs, including Excerpta Medica sections Pharmacology, Drug Literature Index, and Adverse Reactions Titles; produced by Excerpta Medica. 27) EMFORENSIC—contains abstracts of worldwide literature on forensic sciences; produced by Excerpta Medica. 28) EMHEALTH—covers abstracts journals in the areas of public health, including Excerpta Medica sections Public Health, Social Medicine and Hygiene, Occupational Health and Industrial Medicine, and Environmental Health and Pollution Control; produced by Excerpta Medica. 29) EMTOX—covers literature published worldwide on toxicology; produced by Excerpta Medica. 30) Energyline—consists of abstracts of energy information published in Environment Abstracts and Energy Information Abstracts; produced by EIC/ Intelligence, Inc.

31) Energynet—directory of energy-related organizations and experts in the field, and current state-of-the-art in U.S. energy matters; produced by EIC/ Intelligence, Inc. 32) Enviroline—provides references to journals, conferences, and other publications concerning the environmental sciences, pollution, population control, wildlife, weather control, food, and drugs; produced by EIC/ Intelligence, Inc. 33) EUDISED R&D—covers educational research and development projects; produced by the Council of Europe. 34) FLUIDEX—contains bibliographic references to publications on fluid engineering and related fields; compiled by BHRA, The Fluid Engineering Centre. 35) FSTA (Food Science and Technology Abstracts)—provides information on research and new developments in food science and technology; produced by the International Food Information Service.

36) Frost & Sullivan Market Research Reports—a bibliographic index of market research reports which analyze and forecast segments in worldwide industries such as communications, electronic and optical components, and data processing; prepared by Frost & Sullivan, Inc. 37) HSELiNE—provides references to European journals and publications on occupational health and safety received by British Health and Safety Executive (HSE) libraries since 1977. 38) INIS—covers peaceful applications of nuclear science and technology and other aspects of nuclear energy; produced by the International Nuclear Information System (INIS) of the International Atomic Energy Agency. 39) INSPEC (with subfiles INSPEC Information and INSPEC Training)—contains abstracts of the world's technical literature in the fields of physics, electrotechnology, computers, and control; produced by the Institution of Electrical Engineers. 40) International Road Research Documentation (IRRD)—contains references to journals, research projects and computer programs related to transport engineering, road design, earth mechanics, accidents, and economics; prepared by the Road Transport Research Programme of the Organization for Economic Co-Operation and Development.

41) IBSEDEX—covers international literature on new developments in building services published in International Building Services Abstracts plus additional data; produced by the Building Services Research and Information Association. 42) ISMEC (Information Service in Mechanical Engineering)—an index to international literature on mechanical engineering and related fields; produced by Cambridge Scientific Abstracts. 43) Laboratory Hazards Bulletin—covers international scientific and technical literature on safety measures, potential hazards, and new legislation affecting the well-being of employees working in laboratories in the chemical and allied industries; produced by the Royal Society of Chemistry. 44) LABORDOC—contains abstracts of worldwide journal and monographic literature in the field of labor and industrial relations; prepared by the Central Library and Documentation Branch of the International Labour Office. 45) Labour Information Database (LID)—contains abstracts and indexes of articles appearing in the Social and Labour Bulletin, which covers recent events and developments in the social and labor fields; produced by the International Labour Office's Bureau for Labour Problems Analysis.

46) LEDA (On-Line Earthnet Data Availability)—a factual data bank containing information needed to identify scenes and images remotely sensed from space satellites and acquired by a ground station; developed by the European Space Agency. 47) MATHFILE—covers worldwide mathematical literature, including book reviews; prepared by the American Mathematical Society. 48) MERLIN-TECH—provides access to worldwide literature on electricity and electronics since 1973; produced by MERLIN GERIN Company/ Societe MERLIN GERIN. 49) METADEX—contains information on metals and metalworking published in Metals Abstracts, Metals Abstracts Index, and Alloys Index; produced by Metals Information. 50) NASA—provides references to reports, journals, and other worldwide publications on the space sciences; produced by the U.S. National Aeronautics and Space Administration's Scientific and Technical Information Office.

51) NTIS—covers government reports, announcements, and research and development reports from 250 U.S. government agencies in the areas of engineering, physics, chemistry, nuclear sciences, space technology, and earth, life, and social sciences; produced by the National Technical Information Service. 52) Oceanic Abstracts—provides access to the world's technical literature in oceanography; produced by Cambridge Scientific Abstracts. 53) Packaging Science and Technology Abstracts (PSTA)—contains abstracts of international periodical and other literature dealing with packaging science and technology; prepared by the International Food Information Service and the Fraunhofer Institute for Food Technology and Packaging. 54) PASCAL (with PASCAL Training subfile)—provides access to journals, theses, and reports published worldwide on the life sciences; produced by the National Center for Scientific Research/ Centre National de la Recherche Scientifique (CNRS) of France. 55) Pollution Abstracts—contains abstracts on international technical literature on pollution; produced by Cambridge Scientific Abstracts.

56) PRICEDATA—provides information on world market prices of commodities, major currencies, and international price trends of raw materials; compiled by SLAMARK International. 57) Robomatix Reporter—contains summaries and indexes of current literature in the field of robotics; produced by EIC/ Intelligence, Inc. 58) SATELDATA—a factual data bank which contains information on systems, subsystems, and units of ESA satellites; produced by the European Space Research and Technology Center (ESTEC). 59) SPACECOMPS (Space Components)—provides information on components for spacecraft use from such sources as project parts lists, construction analysis reports, quality audits, and test reports; produced by the European Space Agency. 60) Standards & Specifications—provides access to information on government and industry standards, specifications, and related documents dealing with a specific technology; prepared by the National Standards Association, Inc.

61) Telegen—contains abstracts and indexing of the world's literature on genetic engineering and biotechnology; prepared by EIC/ Intelligence, Inc. 62) Textline/ Newsline—contains informative abstracts of newspapers, journals, press releases, and other United Kingdom, European, and Japanese sources of information on companies, industries, and related subjects; produced by Finsbury Data Services Ltd. 63) TRANSDOC—provides bibliographic information for recently published literature dealing with transport economics, policy, and sociology; produced by the European Conference of Ministers of Transport. 64) World Transindex (WTI)—an index to scientific translations in all fields; produced by International Translations Centre/ Centre International des Traductions.

Other Services: Consulting and research services are also offered.

Clientele/Availability: ESA/IRS is accessed in more than 15 European countries and worldwide.

Contact: Dr. Georges A. Proca, Head, Online Services Division, Information Retrieval Service. (Telex 610637 ESRIN I.) IRS may also be contacted through representatives in most European countries, the United States, and Australia.

★318★
EUROTEC CONSULTANTS LTD. (ECL)
LIBRARIAN
143 Hythe Hill   Phone: 0206 72538
Colchester, Essex CO1 2NF, England
Dr. A.A. Klimowicz, Managing Director

Description of System or Service: LIBRARIAN is a powerful microcomputer-based information retrieval and analysis system specifically designed to meet the demands of medium to large cataloging environments. With LIBRARIAN, an inquirer may rapidly access information by catalog number, author, ISBN number, classification, keyword, or any combination of such items. Each installation of LIBRARIAN is tailored specifically to meet the access and information requirements of a given application such as storage and retrieval of library records, client records, research papers, consultancy, reports, or audiovisual collections.

Scope and/or Subject Matter: Large-volume information retrieval in a classified/ cataloged environment.

Input Sources: Input consists of a client's own files.

Computer-Based Products and Services: Written in a version of PASCAL that runs on most popular microcomputers, LIBRARIAN is designed to store client information in client-specified formats. Three methods of storing the content of an item are available: standard and nonstandard Dewey Decimal-like classification schemes, a keyword library generated by the user, and an abstract field where any amount of text may be stored. LIBRARIAN offers four analysis and retrieval options: by selection codes with or without combinations of range parameters, by combinations of keywords, by classification schemes, or by any combination of codes, keywords, or classification schemes. Networking capabilities are being incorporated in the software.

Other Services: Other products and services include STOCKBROKER, a general portfolio management and analysis system; independent consultancy in the areas of micro and minicomputers; and design, writing, and documentation of software systems in most high-level languages.

Clientele/Availability: Services are available without restrictions.

Contact: Mr. G.W. Angel, Systems Manager, LIBRARIAN. (Telex 987316 HSQUIP.)

★319★
EXETER UNIVERSITY TEACHING SERVICES (EUTS)
THE EXETER ABSTRACT REFERENCE SYSTEM (TEARS)
Streatham Court, Rennes Dr.   Phone: 0392 77911
Exeter, Devon. EX4 4PU, England   Service Est: 1975
Dr. Donald A. Bligh, Director

Staff: Approximately 3 total.

Description of System or Service: THE EXETER ABSTRACT REFERENCE SYSTEM (TEARS) is a computer-based information service covering higher education research in the United Kingdom. It abstracts and indexes journals, books, and other forms of published research and stores this information in a computer-readable data base. The TEARS staff provides batch-mode search services from this file for teachers and researchers.

Scope and/or Subject Matter: Research on higher education.

Input Sources: TEARS input is obtained from published research literature.

Computer-Based Products and Services: Batch-mode search services are currently offered from TEARS, with remote terminal online access planned. Record elements include author, book or article title, year of publication, journal reference or other publishing detail, place where original research was done, abstract, and keywords. Full records with or without abstracts can be provided. Information on educational and cultural films available in the United Kingdom is provided through the TEARS on Film data base.

Clientele/Availability: Services are available to teachers and educational researchers in the United Kingdom on a fee basis.

Remarks: Exeter University Teaching Services Centre is also the base for CONTACT, a national telephone information and referral service for personnel working in higher education.

Contact: Dr. Donald A. Bligh, Director, Exeter University Teaching Services.

★320★
EXPERT INFORMATION SYSTEMS LTD. (EXIS)
EXIS 1
38 Tavistock St. Phone: 01-240 0837
London WC2E 7PB, England Service Est: 1983
Ken Burgess, Managing Director

Staff: 4 Information and library professional; 4 management professional; 2 sales and marketing; 10 clerical and nonprofessional.

Related Organizations: Expert Information Systems Ltd. is part of the Whessoe Group.

Description of System or Service: EXIS 1 is a computerized information retrieval system which covers the transportation, storage, and handling of hazardous cargoes and chemicals. The system provides online access to data bases containing information on hazardous materials regulations, properties, and commercial aspects. The system is designed as a series of separately accessible modules dealing with particular areas of transport, emergency response, or technical applications. EXIS modules are being released as they are completed; initially available are the IMO Module, the ICAO Regulations Module, and the Materials Information Module. The EXIS IMO Module contains the International Maritime Dangerous Goods (IMDG) Code dealing with packaged dangerous goods, related emergency schedules, and the Medical First Aid Guide for emergency planning and response. The module provides enhanced searching on the names of dangerous goods by including 10,000 more synonyms, including trade names, than are listed in the basic IMDG. The EXIS ICAO Regulations Module covers air transport regulations, and the Materials Information Module covers information on regulated substances. In the future the following modules are expected to be added: Chemdata (U.K. Chemical Emergency Response); Hazardous Cargo Contacts; U.K. Blue Book National Maritime Regulations; ADR, on European road transport; RID, on European rail transport; ADN, on European inland waterways transport; and other modules covering national and port regulations and bulk chemicals information.

Scope and/or Subject Matter: International regulations on carriage of dangerous goods by sea, air, road, and rail; national and local regulations, including ports; hazardous materials and chemicals information.

Input Sources: Input is collected from chemical manufacturers and regulatory authorities. Each module is compiled by an editor with extensive experience in the area of application, aided by a panel of consultants regularly reviewing the data and entry procedures.

Holdings and Storage Media: EXIS data bases are maintained in machine-readable form and continuously updated.

Computer-Based Products and Services: EXIS 1 is a menu-driven system that can be accessed online by computer terminals, microcomputers, or word processors over public telephone lines, the national PSS packet-switching system, or the International Packet Switching Service (IPSS) data network. The system can also be accessed using a conventional telex machine and can be loaded onto many types of client computers. The service includes evaluation of the user's requirements and help with terminal selection and connection. The system operates on a simple question and answer routine in standard English.

Other Services: EXIS also provides an assistance desk for handling system queries, supplying referrals, and providing background training in hazardous materials, and arranges demonstrations and individual training on the system.

Clientele/Availability: EXIS 1 is intended for use by chemical manufacturers and shippers, shipowners and operators, road haulers, rail operators, tank container operators, cargo brokers, stevedores, port authorities, terminal operators, emergency services, packaging manufacturers, handling equipment manufacturers, government departments, trade associations, transport consultants, and forwarders.

Remarks: Expert Information Systems also offers engineering software for the processing and energy industries.

Contact: Pauline Eldred, Customer Service Manager, Expert Information Systems Ltd.

★321★
EXTEL COMPUTING LTD.
EXSHARE
Lowndes House Phone: 01-638 5544
1-9 City Rd. Service Est: 1967
London EC1Y 1AA, England
John B. Shapcott, Sales and Marketing Director

Staff: Approximately 150 total.

Related Organizations: Extel Computing Ltd. is a member of the Extel Group. Reuters is a joint producer of EXSHARE.

Description of System or Service: EXSHARE is an international computer-readable securities data bank covering more than 50,000 international securities traded on the leading exchanges in Europe, North and South America, Australia, and the Far East. Updated daily, it contains current official closing prices worldwide, basic security details, dividends, corporate actions (capital changes), earnings where available, exchange rate, and international market indexes. EXSHARE is available on magnetic tape, microcomputer diskette, via computer-to-computer transmission, or through commercial time-sharing.

Scope and/or Subject Matter: International securities data.

Input Sources: Data are received in a variety of mechanized forms from more than 60 stock exchanges and from more than 80 print and specialist services. Among the major sources are Reuters, Standard & Poor's, London Stock Exchange, and Extel Statistical Services.

Holdings and Storage Media: Updated daily, the machine-readable EXSHARE data bank holds information on more than 50,000 securities, 2500 Eurobonds, and 60 currencies.

Publications: EXSHARE Focal Points—newsletter reporting on changes in the service. Comprehensive documentation in support of the service is also produced.

Computer-Based Products and Services: Available on a subscription basis, complete or selected EXSHARE data are supplied on customer-specified magnetic tape, diskette, or via online transmission directly into the subscriber's computer. Subscribers may receive updated data daily, weekly, monthly, or at any other frequency as required. EXSHARE is also available via a number of time-sharing companies, including Interactive Data Services, Inc. For each security in the data base, a unique SEDOL number identifier is held, together with its offical closing price, issued capital, industrial and geographical classification, earnings and dividend details (including all relevant dates and tax markers), and comprehensive capital change data (rights, bonuses, scrips, conversion, redemptions, takeover, and mergers). Additionally, a range of market indexes and exchange rates are available.

Clientele/Availability: Clients include bankers, stockbrokers, insurance companies, mutual and pension funds, and others in the financial community. Services are available by subscription.

Remarks: EXSHARE was also known as FOCUS.

Contact: John B. Shapcott, Sales and Marketing Director, EXSHARE. (Telex 884319.)

★322★
EXTEL STATISTICAL SERVICES LTD.
EXBOND
37-45 Paul St. Phone: 01-253 3400
London EC2A 4PB, England
S.J. Pinner, Sales and Marketing Director

Related Organizations: Extel Statistical Services Ltd. is a member of the Extel Group.

Description of System or Service: EXBOND is a computer-readable data base containing information on more than 5000 Eurobonds and other issues. It corresponds to data appearing in the International Bonds Service, which is issued weekly by Extel Statistical Services Ltd. EXBOND is available by subscription on magnetic tape and it is commercially available online.

Scope and/or Subject Matter: Eurobond, Yankee, and Samurai issues, including straight bonds, floating rate notes, convertible issues, issues with warrants attached, and graduated or variable rate issues.

Input Sources: Daily prices for Eurobond and other securities are received via online data transmission.

Holdings and Storage Media: The machine-readable EXBOND data base holds daily-updated data on more than 5000 bonds.

Publications: International Bonds Service (weekly)—issued in two parts. News sheets provide preliminary details of issues coming to market and also cover events affecting existing issues; individual bond sheets give details of each issue prospectus in a standard form. Also produced is EXBOND documentation, including data and computer tape specification booklets.

Computer-Based Products and Services: EXBOND data are available by subscription on magnetic tape and are incorporated in time-sharing services offered by Interactive Data Corporation and Cumulus Systems Ltd. Typical information provided includes the following: borrower; type of bond; currency of issue; nationality; industry; Euro-clear and Cedel codes; stock exchange listings; bond category; interest basis; guarantors; lead and co-managers; issue date and price; denominations; issue size and amount outstanding; coupon and coupon dates; maturity date and price; call schedules and types; redemption schedules and types; conversion terms and history; and floating rate notes interest basis, coupon details, and marker.

Clientele/Availability: Products and services are available by subscription.

Remarks: EXBOND was formerly known as the Extel International Bonds Database.

Contact: S.J. Pinner, Sales and Marketing Director, or Robert D. Humphrey, Sales Office Manager, Extel Statistical Services Ltd. (Telex 262687.)

★323★
EXTEL STATISTICAL SERVICES LTD.
EXSTAT
37-45 Paul St. Phone: 01-253 3400
London EC2A 4PB, England
S.J. Pinner, Sales and Marketing Director

Related Organizations: Extel Statistical Services Ltd. is a member of the Extel Group.

Description of System or Service: EXSTAT is a machine-readable data base providing financial information on more than 2750 United Kingdom and overseas companies. For each company covered, it contains retrospective annual balance sheet and profit and loss account items, as well as annual net asset value, earnings, and dividends data. EXSTAT is available on magnetic tape, diskette, or through commercial time-sharing services. Data in the file are compatible with that supplied in the Extel Card service, a subscription service for company information on file cards.

Scope and/or Subject Matter: Financial information on British and non-British companies.

Input Sources: Input is derived from company annual reports, returns, and accounts.

Holdings and Storage Media: Computer files hold data on 2025 British companies, 500 continental European companies, 175 Australian companies, and 50 Japanese companies; the data date from the early 1970s to the present and are updated weekly.

Publications: An index of companies covered and other printed documentation are issued.

Computer-Based Products and Services: EXSTAT data are available by weekly subscription on magnetic tape or, under the name MicroEXSTAT, on diskette. EXSTAT is also internationally accessible through such time-sharing companies as ADP Network Services, Inc., Data Resources, Inc., Finsbury Computer Services Ltd., I.P. Sharp Associates, IBM United Kingdom Ltd., and Interactive Data Corporation. It is distributed in Japan by Nihon Keizai Shimbun, Inc. EXSTAT provides up to 319 data items for British and Irish companies and up to 226 items for foreign companies, including general company and financial data as well as income statement, balance sheet, and security data. Supplementary items for British and Irish companies include such data as investment and rental income and movements in property and other fixed assets, capital, and reserves. EXSTAT data may be combined with proprietary client data or with data from other publicly available data bases (including EXSHARE) to create unique subfiles.

Clientele/Availability: Primary clients include accountants, bankers, investment advisers, management consultants, stockbrokers, multinational corporations, business schools, and universities. A variety of contractual plans is available.

Contact: S.J. Pinner, Sales and Marketing Director, or Robert D. Humphrey, Sales Office Manager, Extel Statistical Services Ltd. (Telex 262687.)

F

★324★
FAIRPLAY PUBLICATIONS LTD.
FAIRPLAY INTERNATIONAL RESEARCH SERVICES (FIRS)
52-54 Southwark St. Phone: 01-403 3437
London SE1 1UJ, England Service Est: 1967
John Prime, Head

Staff: 8 Information and library professional; 2 management professional; 3 technicians; 4 sales and marketing; 6 clerical and nonprofessional; 4 other.

Description of System or Service: FAIRPLAY INTERNATIONAL RESEARCH SERVICES (FIRS) collects and disseminates information on ships and shipping. It maintains a computer file on all commercial vessels over 1000 tons deadweight built since 1967. FIRS provides extracts from this file on magnetic tapes or printouts according to client specifications; regular updates to the extracted information are also available. Additionally, the SERVICES issues publications and offers a consultancy service through which it gathers manual information required by clients.

Scope and/or Subject Matter: All aspects of ships and shipping, including ship building, marine sales and purchases, marine chartering, ship registers, shipping analysis, and others.

Input Sources: Input is gathered from the worldwide press, worldwide company contacts, registers, trade associations, import/export councils, government departments, shipping organizations, press releases, libraries, broker reports, company reports, personal contacts, shipowner returns, shipbuilder returns, and other sources.

Holdings and Storage Media: The machine-readable FIRS data base contains up to 85 items of information on each of 25,000 ships.

Publications: 1) FIRS Weekly Newbuilding Report—lists all newbuilding contracts reported to FIRS during the previous seven days and includes editorial comment, news of tenders, cancellations, newbuilding sales, machinery, and details of orders currently under negotiation. 2) FIRS Sale and Purchase Report (monthly)—contains details of approximately 150 individual transactions in the preceding month, follows up transactions from the previous report, supplies quarterly statistics to allow trend analysis, and provides a listing of activities on the S & P market. The parent Fairplay Publications Ltd. issues a variety of publications on marine matters.

Computer-Based Products and Services: FAIRPLAY INTERNATIONAL RESEARCH SERVICES offers ship information on magnetic tape or printouts in client-specified format. FIRS stores up to 85 items of information on each ship, including owner, builder, vessel type, price, deadweight, holds, and horsepower; any or all of the items for any or all years since 1967 can be extracted from the files according to client specifications and information needs.

Clientele/Availability: Services are available without restrictions.

Contact: Paul S.J. Hubbard, FIRS Marketing, Fairplay International Research Services.

★325★
FARMODEX FOUNDATION
FARMODEX DRUG DATA BANK
Geert Grooteplein Zuid 10 Phone: 080 516887
NL-6525 GA Nijmegen, Netherlands Service Est: 1978

Special Note: No questionnaire response was received for this entry for the 6th edition. The entry is reprinted as it appeared in the 5th edition.

Staff: 2 Total.

Description of System or Service: The machine-readable FARMODEX DRUG DATA BANK provides identifying and supplementary data on pharmaceutical products and raw materials for the manufacture of drug products available on the Dutch market. FARMODEX is based on a uniform nomenclature for the description of drug products and consists of numeric codes for article, brand drug product, and generic product. Data covered by the three codes form the FARMODEX surveillance system which links brand and generic products. The DATA BANK can be used for the preparation of formularies, maintenance of inventory records, surveillance of drug prescription, production planning, drug consumption studies, interaction signaling, medication profiles, and information retrieval. FARMODEX information is available on microfiche, in hard copy, and on computer tapes.

Scope and/or Subject Matter: Brand and generic drug products and raw materials for drug manufacture sold in the Netherlands.

Holdings and Storage Media: The Data Bank is held in machine-readable form.

Publications: FARMODEX Bulletin (4 or more issues per year).

Microform Products and Services: FARMODEX is available on microfiche and is updated monthly.

Computer-Based Products and Services: The computer-readable FARMODEX DRUG DATA BANK includes these identifying elements: brand name, generic name, strength, dosage form, route of administration, smallest dispensing unit, labeler, and packaging. Supplementary data in FARMODEX include pharmaco-therapeutic classification, interaction codes, legal status, health insurance fund code, prices, ingredients (up to 12), drug registration code, updating marks, and others. Searches of the data bank are available through FARMODEX or computer service bureaus, with results available on printouts and microfiche. The Data Bank is also available on monthly computer tapes.

Other Services: Additional services include consulting and biannual user group meetings.

Clientele/Availability: FARMODEX products are available by various subscription plans. Users include pharmaceutical manufacturers, pharmacists, and drug researchers.

Contact: Pharmacist, FARMODEX Drug Data Bank.

★326★
FAXTEL INFORMATION SYSTEMS LTD.
MARKETFAX
12 Sheppard St., Suite 500 Phone: (416) 365-1899
Toronto, ON, Canada M5H 3A1
John McLauchlan, Vice President

Staff: 6 Management professional; 5 technicians; 3 sales and marketing; 1 clerical and nonprofessional.

Description of System or Service: MARKETFAX is an online financial market analysis service which provides subscribers with information on securities, Canadian options, and commodity futures together with interactive computing facilities and color graphics capabilities. The service offers financial information which can be used with analytical programs to produce price and volume charts and point and figure charts. MARKETFAX is also used for the automatic generation of various investment scenarios.

Scope and/or Subject Matter: Securities and investment information and analysis.

Input Sources: Input consists of listings from the Toronto, Vancouver, New York, and American stock exchanges; Dow Jones, Standard and Poor's, and Toronto stock indexes, Canadian options, and commodity futures from the Chicago Board of Trade.

Holdings and Storage Media: Financial data are held in machine-readable form.

Computer-Based Products and Services: The MARKETFAX financial market analysis service is accessible online through time-sharing. It currently offers access to 100 days, 100 weeks, and 100 months of prices and volumes, including high, low, and close figures for securities trading, Canadian options, and commodity futures. The MARKETFAX service includes a set of comprehensive analytical programs permitting the user to produce price and volume charts with moving average lines, on balance volume lines, relative strength lines, oscillator lines, trend lines, weighted average lines, and momentum indicators; point and figure charts with user control of box size and reversals; price-volume charts which provide an indication of accumulation and distribution; and automatic generation of various investment scenarios.

Other Services: Faxtel Information Systems also offers workshops and seminars and assists in the production of Statistics Canada's

Telichart service.

Clientele/Availability: Services are available by subscription without restrictions. Clients include stockbrokers, institutional investors, and marketing and advertising executives.

Contact: John McLauchlan, Vice President or Stanley Braithwaite, Faxtel Information Systems Ltd. (Telex 06 986766.)

★327★
FEDERAL TECHNICAL UNIVERSITY
(Eidgenossische Technische Hochschule - ETH)
TECHNICAL CHEMISTRY LABORATORY
(Technisch-Chemisches Laboratorium)
CHEMCO PHYSICAL PROPERTIES DATA BANK
ETH-Zentrum   Phone: 01 2562211
Universitatstr. 6   Service Est: 1978
CH-8092 Zurich, Switzerland
Prof. D.W.T. Rippin, Head

Related Organizations: The Data Bank is sponsored by the European Committee for Computers in Chemical Engineering Education (EURECHA).

Description of System or Service: Intended as a demonstration data bank for teaching purposes rather than a reliable source of data, the CHEMCO PHYSICAL PROPERTIES DATA BANK provides physical property information similar to that used by chemical engineers in the design of chemical processes and plants. Data for the DATA BANK were contributed from the EPIC Data Bank of the University of Liege; its software originates from the Federal Technical University and Milan Polytechnic. The entire DATA BANK system is made available on magnetic tape to other teaching institutions.

Scope and/or Subject Matter: Instruction in the use and structure of data banks in chemical engineering.

Input Sources: Data were originally obtained from the EPIC Data Bank, but they have not been critically maintained.

Holdings and Storage Media: The Data Bank holds 5000 data items in machine-readable form.

Publications: CHEMCO Physical Properties Data Bank Manual.

Computer-Based Products and Services: The CHEMCO PHYSICAL PROPERTIES DATA BANK, comprising physical properties data together with analysis software, is made available on magnetic tape to educational institutions for a small fee. The DATA BANK may be operated in batch or interactive modes.

Clientele/Availability: The Data Bank is available for instructional use only. Primary users are chemical engineering departments of universities.

Remarks: The Data Bank is also known as the EURECHA Chemical Data Bank.

Contact: Dr. L.M. Rose, CHEMCO Physical Properties Data Bank.

★328★
FINANCIAL TIMES BUSINESS INFORMATION LTD.
BUSINESS INFORMATION SERVICE (BIS)
Bracken House   Phone: 01-248 8000
10 Cannon St.   Service Est: 1971
London EC4P 4BY, England
Richard M. Soule, Director of Research Services

Staff: 36 Information and library professional; 4 management professional; 2 technicians; 10 clerical and nonprofessional.

Related Organizations: A subsidiary of Financial Times Business Information Ltd. is McCarthy Information Ltd. (see separate entry).

Description of System or Service: The BUSINESS INFORMATION SERVICE (BIS) provides current business, statistical, and financial information to financial institutions, manufacturing and service companies, advertising agencies, management consultants, and government departments. It maintains and makes available three online data bases: 1) Currency and Share Index Databank—contains a range of time series covering international money and gold markets, the London domestic sterling market, and London and overseas stock indexes. 2) Financial Times Company Information—provides citations and abstracts of all articles in the London and Frankfurt editions of the Financial Times newspaper which refer to a company. 3) Index to the Financial Times. BIS also issues the Index to the Financial Times in print, microfiche, and computer-tape formats, and it offers MIRAC, a service supplying microfiche copies of the reports and accounts of 3500 United Kingdom publicly quoted companies. Additionally, BIS provides monitoring services on a daily, weekly, or monthly basis; computerized and manual information retrieval; inquiry answering; research and reporting services; and assistance in setting up new library information systems and developing and improving existing facilities.

Scope and/or Subject Matter: All aspects of business information, including economics, statistics, marketing, corporations, and finance.

Input Sources: Input includes the Financial Times from date of first issue, company information on file in the Financial Times Library, computer-readable data bases, and other sources of corporate and industry information.

Holdings and Storage Media: The Currency and Share Index Databank, Financial Times Company Information, and the Index to the Financial Times are maintained in machine-readable form. The library collection consists of reference books; government publications; market research reports; annual reports; press cuttings on approximately 25,000 prominent people in industry, politics, and business; official documents on more than 60,000 U.K. companies and industries; and exchange rates of currency against the pound annually since 1900 and daily since 1946.

Publications: Index to the Financial Times (monthly with annual cumulation)—divided into corporate, general, and personalities sections with cross-references; available by subscription. BIS also issues newsletters and reports.

Microform Products and Services: The Microfiche of Reports and Accounts (MIRAC) service provides microfiche copies of annual reports and accounts of United Kingdom companies, including all publicly quoted companies, nationalized industries, and companies traded on the over-the-counter market. Updated continuously, the fiche are issued about one week after publication of new reports and accounts. The Index to the Financial Times is also available on microfiche.

Computer-Based Products and Services: The BUSINESS INFORMATION SERVICE makes the Currency and Share Index Databank available online through CISI-Wharton. The Financial Times Company Information data base, which holds records dating from 1981 to the present, is searchable online through Data-Star. The Index to the Financial Times data base is available online through DataArkiv AB and is offered by BIS on magnetic tape or floppy disk. Financial Times information on actuaries share indexes, shares traded on the London Stock Exchange, and the U.S. stock market are also searchable online through I.P. Sharp Associates. Additionally, BIS facilitates its research through online searches of a variety of computer-readable data bases, including the International Monetary Fund's International Financial Statistics and Balance of Payments files; the Great Britain Central Statistical Office (CSO) Macro-Economic Data Bank; the Bank of England data bank; Eurocharts Commodities data base; and OECD data. Clients are supplied with computer printouts of data in tabular or graphic form.

Clientele/Availability: Clients include financial institutions, companies, government departments, and consultants. Information research services are available on an annual or semiannual subscription basis; fees for special projects are based on the research time involved and expenses incurred.

Contact: Anthony J. Northeast, Manager, Business Information Service; or Margaret J. Fawcett, Group Marketing Executive, Financial Times Business Information Ltd. (Telex 8811506.)

★329★
FINLAND
CENTRAL MEDICAL LIBRARY
MEDIC DATA BASE
Haartmaninkatu 4 Phone: 90 418544
SF-00290 Helsinki 29, Finland Service Est: 1978
Ritva Sievanen-Allen, Librarian

Staff: 14 Information and library professional; 9 clerical and nonprofessional.

Description of System or Service: The computer-readable MEDIC DATA BASE indexes the Finnish medical literature that is not covered by available international data bases. MEDIC is accessible for online searching and is used to produce a quarterly hardcopy bibliography known as FINMED.

Scope and/or Subject Matter: Finnish medical literature.

Input Sources: Finnish medical monographs and approximately 100 journals are scanned for input to the data base.

Holdings and Storage Media: The machine-readable MEDIC file dates from 1978 to the present and holds approximately 2000 citations per year of coverage. The Central Medical Library's holdings include 300,000 bound volumes and subscriptions to 2200 periodicals.

Publications: FINMED (quarterly)—classified and indexed Finnish medical bibliography.

Computer-Based Products and Services: MEDIC is interactively searchable via the Central Medical Library over the Euronet network. Searchable items include MeSH terms, classification codes, author names, and journal titles. The Central Medical Library also provides information retrieval from MEDIC and other online biomedical data bases.

Clientele/Availability: Services and products are available without restrictions to medical libraries, schools, companies, and others.

Contact: Irja-Liisa Oberg, Deputy Librarian, Central Medical Library. (Telex 12 1498 LKK SF.)

★330★
FINLAND
TECHNICAL RESEARCH CENTRE OF FINLAND
(Valtion Teknillinen Tutkimuskeskus - VTT)
TECHNICAL INFORMATION SERVICE
(Teknillinen Informaatiopalvelulaitos - INF)
Vuorimiehentie 5 Phone: 90 4561
SF-02150 Espoo 15, Finland Service Est: 1947
Sauli Laitinen, Director

Staff: 25 Information and library professional; 1 management professional; 21 technicians; 22 clerical and nonprofessional.

Related Organizations: The Technical Research Centre is under the jurisdiction of the Finnish Ministry of Trade and Industry.

Description of System or Service: The TECHNICAL INFORMATION SERVICE (INF) is the information service unit of the Technical Research Centre and a national technical information service in Finland. It maintains online access to more than 40 international data base vendors and several European videotex services, providing information retrieval, SDI, and current awareness services from them. It also maintains and operates the computer-based Research Register of VTT covering Centre research projects. Information held in the Research Register is available through the Finnish videotex system Telset and as a monthly and annual publication. Additionally, the SERVICE offers document delivery, handles the Centre's publishing activities, provides technical assistance in the planning of research, and contributes to Scandinavian information systems such as the BYGGDOK data base.

Scope and/or Subject Matter: Science and technology, including urban development, building technology, information technology, energy technology, process technology, and manufacturing technology.

Input Sources: Input for the Research Register data base is gathered from project reports. The Service also obtains information from Scandinavian, European, and North American online services and information centers.

Holdings and Storage Media: The machine-readable Research Register data base holds records gathered from 1970 to the present; updates are added monthly. Library holdings consist of 90,000 bound volumes; subscriptions to 1800 periodicals; and 100,000 microforms.

Publications: 1) VTT Publications—a series consisting of technical and scientific research results. 2) VTT Research Reports—a series consisting of results of research and development work. 3) VTT Research Notes—includes such features as summaries of research, literature reviews, testing and research methods, and state-of-the-art reviews. 4) VTT Symposium—comprises conferecne papers from conferences arranged by the Centre. 5) Yearbook of the Research Register—contains information on public research projects in progress during the year. Includes indexes of responsible activity units, project leaders, and keywords. Most publications are issued in English, Finnish, and Swedish.

Microform Products and Services: COM versions of the Research Register and the Yearbook of the Research Register are available, as are general microreproduction services. A library catalog is also maintained on microfiche.

Computer-Based Products and Services: The TECHNICAL INFORMATION SERVICE provides information retrieval and SDI services from data bases carried by the following online systems: ALIS, BELINDIS (Belgian Information and Dissemination Service), Bibliographic Retrieval Services (BRS), BIBSYS, BLAISE (British Library Automated Information Service), CAS ONLINE, CITERE, CNEXO, DIALOG Information Services, Inc., Data-Star, DIMDI, ESA/IRS, G.CAM, Gesellschaft fur Information und Dokumentation (GID), HELECON, IDC/SDI, Info Globe (The Globe and Mail), Informationszentrum Raum und Bau (IRB), INKA (Informationssystem Karlsruhe), INPADOC, ISI Search Network, MBANK, MEDLI, MINTTU, NIH-EPA Chemical Information System (CIS), NSI/POLYDOC, OCLC Online Computer Library Center, Inc., Pergamon InfoLine Ltd., QL Systems Limited, QZ/GUTS, I.P. Sharp Associates, SIA Ltd., System Development Corporation (SDC), TECHNOTEC, Telesystemes Questel, TENTTU, TEXTLINE (Finsbury Data Services Ltd.), 3RIP, TT-Nyhetsbanks, the Finnish videotex system Telset, and the British Prestel videotex system. The TECHNICAL INFORMATION SERVICE also maintains the computer-readable Research Register of VTT. The Register is available through Telset, and the SERVICE provides special reports from it on demand. Data elements in the file include research project title, identification number, security classification code, starting and completing dates, present position of the project, names of financial sponsors, total financing, annual costs, project leader name and names of researchers, the responsible activity unit, the cooperating units inside and outside of the Centre, bibliographical information on reports published or to be published, an abstract in Finnish, from 1 to 10 keywords in English, subject classification, UNESCO classification by scientific fields, and the OECD classification by the objectives of research.

Other Services: The Service also provides manual literature searching, referrals, and consultancy and training services in information science.

Clientele/Availability: Clients include scientists, industrial and business firms, government agencies, and the public. Requests are accepted and information dispatched by mail, telephone, telex, fascimile, directly by electronic means, or personal visit.

Contact: Sauli Laitinen, Director, Technical Information Service, Technical Research Centre of Finland. (Telex 125175.)

★331★
FINNISH COUNCIL FOR SCIENTIFIC INFORMATION AND RESEARCH LIBRARIES
(Tieteellisen Informoinnin Neuvosto - TINFO)
P.O. Box 504 Phone: 90 1734233
SF-00101 Helsinki 10, Finland Service Est: 1972
J.K. Visakorpi, Chairman

Staff: 5 Total.

Description of System or Service: The FINNISH COUNCIL FOR SCIENTIFIC INFORMATION AND RESEARCH LIBRARIES (TINFO) is an advisory body of the Ministry of Education. Its functions include coordinating and promoting the provision of scientific information, and carrying out studies and making plans for the development of library and information services. Serving as the Finnish coordinator for international cooperation in the library and information service field, TINFO follows the development of scientific information provision and library activities in Finland and abroad. The COUNCIL prepares statements, takes initiatives, and makes proposals concerning its field of activity.

Scope and/or Subject Matter: Scientific information provision; research libraries.

Publications: The Council has published a report on the reorganization of the national tasks of the scientific information and research libraries in Finland, and has also published a program for developing and improving the scientific information policy.

Services: Primary services are research and planning in the area of scientific information provision.

Clientele/Availability: The Council serves government agencies.

Contact: Hellevi Yrjola, Secretary General, Finnish Council for Scientific Information and Research Libraries. (Telex 122656 TIKES SF.)

★332★
FINNISH FOREIGN TRADE ASSOCIATION
INFORMATION DEPARTMENT
REGISTER OF EXPORTERS
Arkadiankatu 4-6 B
P.O. Box 908
SF-00101 Helsinki 10, Finland
Mr. C.G. Tollet, Association Vice President
Phone: 90 6941122
Service Est: 1977

Staff: 7 Information and library professional; 4 management professional; 1 technician; 1 sales and marketing; 8 clerical and nonprofessional; 1 other.

Description of System or Service: The REGISTER OF EXPORTERS is a computer-readable register of Finnish exporters and their products. It is used to provide information services by the Finnish Foreign Trade Association.

Scope and/or Subject Matter: Finnish export trade.

Holdings and Storage Media: The machine-readable Register contains information on approximately 2400 exporters and 6000 products.

Computer-Based Products and Services: The Register of Exporters is used to provide computerized information services on Finnish exporters and products.

Clientele/Availability: Services are available in Finland and elsewhere.

Contact: Mr. Seppo Kukkola, Head of Information Department, Finnish Foreign Trade Association; telephone 90 6959319. (Telex 121696.)

★333★
FINNISH PULP AND PAPER RESEARCH INSTITUTE
(Oy Keskuslaboratorio - Centrallaboratorium Ab)
TECHNICAL INFORMATION SERVICE
P.O. Box 136
SF-00101 Helsinki 10, Finland
Birgitta Holm, Head
Phone: 90 460411
Service Est: 1937

Staff: 3 Information and library professional; 10 clerical and nonprofessional.

Description of System or Service: The TECHNICAL INFORMATION SERVICE provides a variety of information services to Institute staff, the Finnish pulp and paper industry, and others. A major activity is the preparation and publication of a weekly survey of relevant periodical articles and patents, for which it maintains a card file registering more than 10,000 articles per year. This primary current awareness service is augmented by manual literature searching of the in-house collection and online searching of data bases accessible through commercial vendors. Additional activities include a translation service and a meetings information bulletin.

Scope and/or Subject Matter: Major interests are pulp, paper, and board; packaging is a secondary interest.

Input Sources: The library acquires all available material in relevant subject areas.

Holdings and Storage Media: The Service maintains a collection of 30,000 bound volumes and 350 periodical subscriptions.

Publications: 1) Weekly Survey of Periodicals—citations include subject group number, and added title keywords when necessary. 2) List of meetings (quarterly)—covers meetings and conferences of interest to pulp and paper industry. 3) List of accessions.

Computer-Based Products and Services: Online searching is conducted from relevant data bases.

Clientele/Availability: Primary clients are the Finnish pulp and paper industry and Institute staff.

Contact: Birgitta Holm, Head, Technical Information Service. (Telex 121030 KCL SF.)

★334★
FINNISH STANDARDS ASSOCIATION
(Suomen Standardisoimisliitto - SFS)
INFORMATION SERVICE
P.O. Box 205
SF-00121 Helsinki 12, Finland
Marjatta Aarniala, Information Specialist
Phone: 0645601

Staff: 3 Information and library professional; 2 technicians; 1 clerical and nonprofessional.

Description of System or Service: The INFORMATION SERVICE functions as an information center for national, international, and foreign standards and similar documents. It maintains and provides services from a collection of more than 200,000 standards. The SERVICE also maintains the publicly available online SFS Data Base, which contains information on Finnish standards and technical regulations.

Scope and/or Subject Matter: Standards in all subject areas.

Input Sources: Standards, standard catalogs, and standard bulletins are acquired from worldwide sources.

Holdings and Storage Media: The SFS Data Base is maintained in machine-readable form and updated continuously. More than 220,000 standards and similar documents are held in hard copy.

Publications: SFS Catalogue (annual with supplements)—list of Finnish Standards Association standards. The Association produces a variety of other publications on national and international standards.

Computer-Based Products and Services: The SFS Data Base contains the following types of data on Finnish standards and technical regulations: document identifier, title in English and Finnish, issuing body, document date, and references to international, foreign, and domestic documents. The Data Base is held at the Finnish State Computer Centre and can be accessed online through the user's own terminal.

Other Services: The Information Service also functions as the Finnish inquiry point according to the General Agreement on Tariffs and Trade (GATT) on technical barriers to trade.

Clientele/Availability: Services are available without restrictions.

Contact: Marjatta Aarniala or Maarit Alenius-Santaoja, Information Specialists, Finnish Standards Association. (Telex 122303 STAND SF.)

★335★
FINSBURY DATA SERVICES LTD.
TEXTLINE
68-74 Carter Lane
London EC4V 5EA, England
J. Graham Blease, Chairman
Phone: 01-248 9828
Service Est: 1979

Description of System or Service: TEXTLINE is a business information data base maintained by and made available online through Finsbury Data Services Ltd. It contains informative abstracts prepared from newspapers, journals, press releases, and other worldwide sources of information on companies, industries, economics, public affairs, and the European Economic Community. Accessible over several packet switching networks, the data base features extensive indexing providing access by standard company mnemonics, SIC industry and product codes, broad topic codes, assigned keywords, and free-text searching with Boolean operators. Additionally, headline summaries of news articles to be included in TEXTLINE are available online on their day of issue in a separate file known as NEWSLINE.

Scope and/or Subject Matter: Company and industry coverage includes financial matters, products, markets, costs, prices, management, and labor matters for about 100,000 organizations. Economic topics include monetary policy, demand, employment, wages, external trade, and the securities and commodities markets. Public affairs coverage includes politics, Parliament, local government, and industrial, financial, and social policies and events. Coverage of the European Economic Commission includes EEC matters and directives; economic, financial, and trade policies; and agricultural, industrial, social, and community subjects.

Input Sources: Input is derived from more than 90 newspapers and journals issued in the United Kingdom, Europe, Japan, South East Asia, Australia, the Middle East, and South America, and from press releases and other sources.

Holdings and Storage Media: TEXTLINE holds more than 500,000 abstracts dating from 1980 to the present. NEWSLINE holds approximately 1400 daily headline summaries for articles which are then abstracted and indexed within five to seven days for inclusion in the TEXTLINE data base.

Computer-Based Products and Services: The TEXTLINE and NEWSLINE data bases are held on Finsbury Data Services computers and are accessible for online searching through any international packet-switching network that connects to the British IPSS service.

Clientele/Availability: Clients include financial, industrial, professional, and commercial institutions.

Remarks: Finsbury Data Services Ltd. was formed to develop activities in the field of online text retrieval.

Contact: Stephen Rayment, Marketing Manager, or Ross T. Pike, Marketing, TEXTLINE. (Telex 892520 FINDAT G.)

★336★
FLA GROUPE LA CREATIQUE
31 blvd. Lefebvre
F-75015 Paris, France
Francois Libmann, Director
Phone: 01 5436811
Founded: 1977

Staff: 3 Information and library professional; 1 management professional; 1 clerical and nonprofessional.

Description of System or Service: FLA GROUPE LA CREATIQUE is an information consulting firm specializing in the areas of technology transfer, law, and marketing. It conducts training workshops in the area of videotex, publishes a newsletter covering legal information services, and offers consulting and training for innovation and diversification. FLA also provides computerized information retrieval from commercially available data bases and is the exclusive representative in France of the CORALIE data base.

Scope and/or Subject Matter: Information services for technology transfer, law, innovation, diversification, and marketing.

Input Sources: Input is obtained from international online services.

Publications: JURINNOV (5 per year)—available by subscription; newsletter covering law data bases and information retrieval.

Computer-Based Products and Services: FLA provides computerized information retrieval from data bases made available by more than 20 vendors.

Clientele/Availability: Services are available without restrictions.

Contact: Francois Libmann, Director, FLA Groupe La Creatique.

★337★
FOUNDATION FOR SCIENCE AND POLITICS
(Stiftung Wissenschaft und Politik - SWP)
RESEARCH INSTITUTE FOR INTERNATIONAL POLITICS AND SECURITY
(Forschungsinstitut fur Internationale Politik und Sicherheit)
LIBRARY AND DOCUMENTATION SYSTEM
Haus Eggenberg
D-8026 Ebenhausen, Fed. Rep. of Germany
Dietrich Seydel, Dipl.-Pol.
Phone: 08178 701
Service Est: 1973

Staff: 17 Information and library professional; 4 management professional; 9 technicians; 1 clerical and nonprofessional.

Description of System or Service: The LIBRARY AND DOCUMENTATION SYSTEM was established to support the scientific work of the Research Institute and to serve members of the German government and researchers in international relations. It is a computerized system for acquisitions, cataloging, indexing, retrieval, thesaurus maintenance, and production of print publications. The SYSTEM covers books, pamphlets, periodical articles, and other international relations literature acquired by the Institute since 1974. It also includes nonbibliographic information on relevant persons, institutions, events, and countries. Services provided from the SYSTEM include computerized searching, remote terminal access, and a monthly tape service.

Scope and/or Subject Matter: Current international relations, including international politics, security, conflicts, cooperation, arms control and disarmament, social processes, and economics, as well as national political systems and area studies.

Input Sources: Input consists of 12,000 items per year, including books, reports, pamphlets, journals, yearbooks, and newspapers.

Holdings and Storage Media: The System's computer-readable data base holds 120,000 items. Library holdings comprise 60,000 bound volumes, 400,000 newspaper clippings, and subscriptions to 1600 periodicals.

Publications: The SWP Thesaurus is available to users.

Computer-Based Products and Services: Maintained on a minicomputer under DOMESTIC software, the LIBRARY AND DOCUMENTATION SYSTEM provides bibliographic and nonbibliographic information on international relations. Different field structures have been developed for the various types of records, which share a common descriptor system within integrated data files. Specific record types can be retrieved by linking a field indicator to the descriptor. The SYSTEM is used to offer search services for Research Institute staff and outside users. Additionally, other international research institutes access the SYSTEM via remote terminals for retrieval and update functions. The data base is also available (in the form of inverted or sequential files) by subscription under the SWP-Tape Service.

Other Services: Additional services include manual literature searching and referrals.

Clientele/Availability: Clients include Research Institute staff, other researchers, and government agencies.

Remarks: The Library and Documentation System is also known as the International Relations Information System (IRIS).

Contact: Dietrich Seydel, Dipl.-Pol., or Volker Steidle, Dipl.-Vw., Library and Documentation System.

★338★
FRANCE
ATOMIC ENERGY COMMISSION
(Commissariat a l'Energie Atomique - CEA)
PROGRAMS DEPARTMENT
(Departement des Programmes)
ELECNUC DATABANK
B.P. 510
F-75752 Paris Cedex 15, France
Phone: 01 5458418

Description of System or Service: The ELECNUC DATABANK is a computer-readable source of data relating to the construction, maintenance, and output of nuclear power reactors and stations worldwide. Data are provided for both the gross and net electrical power output for monthly, annual, and other time periods; this information can be retrieved by single reactors or groups of units, by country, or by other parameters, such as reactor type or manufacturer of the pressure vessel. Additional data available include the principal components of the power station and information on the contractor responsible for the installation. Comparisons can be made between all possible groupings of data, including national or international basis, performance levels, reactor type, or any other parameter.

Scope and/or Subject Matter: Nuclear power reactors and stations.

Input Sources: Information is gathered from newspapers and power plant constructors and operators.

Holdings and Storage Media: The computer-readable ELECNUC Databank is updated monthly and covers more than 800 nuclear-powered, electricity-generating plants worldwide.

Computer-Based Products and Services: The ELECNUC DATABANK is accessible online through Compagnie Internationale de Services en Informatique (CISI). It includes approximately 50 different items of information for each electricity-generating, nuclear-powered station; parameters can be retrieved using keywords. Output includes reports, statistical calculations, graphs, and tables.

Clientele/Availability: Clients include the world nuclear power reactor community.

Contact: Mme. Le Mottais, Programs Department, Atomic Energy Commission.

★339★
FRANCE
ATOMIC ENERGY COMMISSION
(Commissariat a l'Energie Atomique - CEA)
SACLAY NUCLEAR RESEARCH CENTER
(Centre d'Etudes Nucleaires de Saclay)
DOCUMENTATION CENTER
(Service de Documentation)
F-91191 Gif-sur-Yvette Cedex, France
Phone: 6 9082208
Service Est: 1952

Special Note: The above name, address, and telephone number have been verified for this edition, although no questionnaire response was received. The following text is reprinted from the 5th edition.

Staff: 33 Information and library professional; 5 management professional; 38 technicians; 33 clerical and nonprofessional.

Description of System or Service: The DOCUMENTATION CENTER edits and publishes documents and reports of the French Atomic Energy Commission, produces the computer-readable ENERGIRAP and Meeting Agenda data bases, and provides input for France to the International Nuclear Information System (INIS). It maintains a copy of the INIS data base from which it provides computerized searches and SDI.

Scope and/or Subject Matter: High energy physics; nuclear physics; nuclear engineering; plasma physics; chemistry and metallurgy of nuclear materials; isotope technology; nuclear safety and health physics; radiobiology; nuclear medicine; scientific and technical meetings and conferences.

Input Sources: Input consists of periodicals, reports, theses, patents, translations, books, conference papers and proceedings, and machine-readable data bases.

Holdings and Storage Media: The Center's computer-readable ENERGIRAP data base holds about 200,000 items and its Meeting Agenda data base covers approximately 5000 announcements per year. The Center also maintains the INIS file in machine-readable format, and a library cofllection of 70,000 bound periodical volumes; 44,000 books; 450,000 reports on microfiche; and subscriptions to 1800 periodicals.

Publications: 1) Bulletin Signaletique Hebdomadaire—lists scientific and technical documents acquired by the Center. 2) Congres, Colloques et Conferences. Salons et Expositions (2 per year; monthly updates)—lists about 5000 meetings annually. 3) Liste des Publications du Commissariat a l'Energie Atomique (annual)—cites publications from France and other countries; includes annual author and partial subject indexes.

Microform Products and Services: The Atomic Energy Commission reports are maintained on microfiche and are available on an exchange basis.

Computer-Based Products and Services: The CENTER's ENERGIRAP and Meeting Agenda data bases are available online through Telesystemes Questel. ENERGIRAP (also known as ENERGI) lists world reports on energy in the Center's library. Meeting Agenda announces scientific and technical meetings and exhibitions. Reports and programs listed in these data bases can be ordered online. Additionally, the Center offers computerized searching of the INIS file and other commercially available data bases; SDI services based on INIS are offered to French users.

Other Services: The Center also provides traditional library services and translations.

Clientele/Availability: Services are intended primarily for the French nuclear community.

Contact: Chief, Documentation Center.

★340★
FRANCE
BUREAU OF GEOLOGICAL AND MINING RESEARCH
(Bureau de Recherches Geologiques et Minieres - BRGM)
NATIONAL GEOLOGICAL SURVEY
(Service Geologique National - SGN)
GEOLOGICAL INFORMATION AND DOCUMENTATION
   DEPARTMENT
(Departement Documentation et Information Geologique)
B.P. 6009
Phone: 38 638001
F-45060 Orleans Cedex, France
J. Gravesteijn, Chief

Staff: 30 Information and library professional; 5 management professional; 21 technicians; 9 sales and marketing; 5 clerical and nonprofessional.

Description of System or Service: The GEOLOGICAL INFORMATION AND DOCUMENTATION DEPARTMENT collects, processes, and disseminates earth sciences information from throughout the world. It is involved in the production and management of the PASCAL-GEODE data base produced jointly with the French National Center for Scientific Research (CNRS) and several European geological surveys. PASCAL-GEODE is used to issue publications and offer retrospective search and SDI services. The DEPARTMENT also provides services from the predecessor GEODE data base and a machine-readable Geological Bibliography of France. All three data bases are available online. Additionally, the DEPARTMENT oversees the maintenance of two nonbibliographic files: the Subsoil Data Bank and the World Gravimetric Data Bank, which are described in separate entries following this one.

Scope and/or Subject Matter: Earth sciences, including mineralogy, geochemistry, extraterrestrial geology, mineral deposits, economic geology, sedimentary and crystalline petrology, marine geology, stratigraphy, paleontology, hydrogeology, geomorphology, soil sciences, and engineering geology.

Input Sources: Input is derived from 3000 periodicals, as well as from theses, treatises, conference proceedings, maps, and other documents.

Holdings and Storage Media: PASCAL-GEODE holds approximately 400,000 references dating from 1973 to the present. GEODE holds 300,000 references from 1968 to 1972. The Geological Bibliography of France, covering the period from 1700 to 1967, holds 50,000 citations. BRGM library holdings comprise 12,000 bound volumes, 25,000 maps, and subscriptions to 1500 periodicals.

Publications: A bibliographic bulletin is issued 10 times per year.

Microform Products and Services: The bibliography is also available on microfiche.

Computer-Based Products and Services: The DEPARTMENT provides batch-mode services from PASCAL-GEODE, GEODE, and the Geological Bibliography of France. The three files are also available online through Telesystemes Questel. Additionally, PASCAL-GEODE is available online through ESA/IRS. SDI services are provided by the

DEPARTMENT on standard filing cards holding bibliographic citations and abstracts.

Other Services: Manual literature searches are also available for information not covered in the data bases.

Clientele/Availability: Primary clients are geologists.

Contact: C. Nail, Geological Information and Documentation Department, National Geological Survey. (Telex 780 258 F BRGM A.)

★341★
FRANCE
BUREAU OF GEOLOGICAL AND MINING RESEARCH
(Bureau de Recherches Geologiques et Minieres - BRGM)
NATIONAL GEOLOGICAL SURVEY
(Service Geologique National - SGN)
SUBSOIL DATA BANK
(Banque des Donnees du Sous-sol)
B.P. 6009   Phone: 38 638001
F-45060 Orleans Cedex, France
Jean-Pierre Lepretre, Geologist

Staff: 3 Management professional; 10 technicians.

Related Organizations: The Subsoil Data Bank receives administrative and maintenance support from the Geological Information and Documentation Department of the French National Geological Survey.

Description of System or Service: The SUBSOIL DATA BANK is a machine-readable file providing access to French subsoil data gathered through land observations, drilling projects, and laboratory research. It is maintained to support the collection, management, and dissemination of geological information on the French subsoil. Output from the DATA BANK is available in the form of printed lists or tables, plans produced by curve plotter, or on magnetic tape.

Scope and/or Subject Matter: Geological, geotechnical, hydrological, lithological, geothermal energy, and stratigraphic aspects of the French subsoil.

Input Sources: Data for the Subsoil Data Bank are contributed by 22 French regional geologic services.

Holdings and Storage Media: The BRGM maintains a collection of nearly 400,000 subsoil logs, reports, and other documents on microfilm. Data from about 200,000 of these are held in machine-readable form as the Subsoil Data Bank. Approximately 12,000 new works are received and processed annually.

Publications: L'Interrogation de la Banque des Donnees du Sous-sol—a user manual.

Computer-Based Products and Services: The machine-readable SUBSOIL DATA BANK is utilized to provide batch information retrieval services. It is maintained under GEISHA software developed by the BRGM. Online access to the DATA BANK is expected to be available in the near future.

Clientele/Availability: Services from the Subsoil Data Bank are provided as a public service to French citizens.

Contact: Jean-Pierre Lepretre, Geologist, Geological Information and Documentation Department. (Telex 780 258 F BRGM A.)

★342★
FRANCE
BUREAU OF GEOLOGICAL AND MINING RESEARCH
(Bureau de Recherches Geologiques et Minieres - BRGM)
NATIONAL GEOLOGICAL SURVEY
(Service Geologique National - SGN)
WORLD GRAVIMETRIC DATA BANK
(Banque Mondiale des Donnees Gravimetriques)
B.P. 6009   Phone: 38 638001
F-45060 Orleans Cedex, France   Service Est: 1975
Jean-Pierre Lepretre, Geologist

Related Organizations: The World Gravimetric Data Bank is administered and maintained by the Geological Information and Documentation Department of the French National Geological Survey at the BRGM under the sponsorship of the International Gravimetric Bureau/ Bureau Gravimetrique International (BGI).

Description of System or Service: The WORLD GRAVIMETRIC DATA BANK is a machine-readable file providing access to gravimetric measurements taken at designated land, sea, and reference station points. Obtained from published and survey sources, the data are verified and corrected and then stored in machine-readable files, which are used to provide batch-mode retrieval services and to produce magnetic tape copies of data selections.

Scope and/or Subject Matter: World gravimetric data.

Input Sources: Gravimetric data are obtained from maps, published literature, and surveys.

Holdings and Storage Media: Nearly 3 million data items are held in machine-readable form.

Publications: Bureau Gravimetrique International Bulletin d'Information.

Computer-Based Products and Services: Batch-mode searches of the WORLD GRAVIMETRIC DATA BANK are available through the Department. For each designated reference point, the DATA BANK contains such data as system of reference, geographic coordinates, type of observation, altitude of the station, precision of altitude, type of altitude, observed gravity, and other variables. Data selections on magnetic tape are also available.

Clientele/Availability: Data are available without restrictions.

Contact: Jean-Pierre Lepretre, Geologist, Geological Information and Documentation Department. (Telex 780 258 F BRGM A.)

★343★
FRANCE
FRENCH SENATE
PARLIAMENTARY DOCUMENTATION AND INFORMATION PRINTING SERVICE
(Service des Impressions de la Documentation Parlementaire et de l'Informatique)
5, rue de Vaugirard   Phone: 01 3291262
F-75291 Paris Cedex 6, France
Michel Vilain, Director

Special Note: No questionnaire response was received for this entry for the 6th edition. The entry is reprinted as it appeared in the 5th edition.

Staff: 2 Information and library professional; 2 management professional; 1 technician.

Related Organizations: The Assemblee National of France provides support in the production of some of the data bases.

Description of System or Service: The PARLIAMENTARY DOCUMENTATION AND INFORMATION PRINTING SERVICE of the French Senate maintains a series of interrelated online data bases covering various aspects of the French legislature, its legislative procedures, and the persons involved. Five files compose the series: 1) SEANCE covers Senate public sessions and committee hearings and is searchable by title or subject. 2) INTERVENTIONS provides analysis of government interventions and includes such information as the name of the person involved, political affiliation, constituency, title, and date of hearing. 3) PARLEMENT provides bibliographic coverage of literature dealing with the French Parliament and other national governmental Parliamentary bodies. 4) QUESTIONS covers issues which have been presented either in written form or orally within the Senate or National Assembly. 5) TRIBUN contains public information on the deputies, senators, and other members of the French government.

Scope and/or Subject Matter: French government.

Input Sources: Input to the data bases is derived from the Journal Officiel de Debats du Senat, senate reports, works on the French Parliament, and other sources.

Holdings and Storage Media: Five data bases are maintained in machine-readable form.

Microform Products and Services: The full text of material published in the Journal Officiel and cited in the SEANCE and QUESTIONS data bases are available on microfiche.

Computer-Based Products and Services: Data bases maintained by the SERVICE are interactively accessible online.

Clientele/Availability: The data bases are available without restrictions to the public.

Contact: Administrative Officer, Parliamentary Documentation and Information Printing Service.

★344★
FRANCE
INTERMINISTERIAL MISSION FOR SCIENTIFIC AND TECHNICAL INFORMATION
(Mission Interministerielle de l'Information Scientifique et Technique - MIDIST)
9, rue Georges Pitard   Phone: 01 8426464
F-75015 Paris, France   Service Est: 1979
M. Cassen, Director

Staff: 50 Total.

Related Organizations: The Interministerial Mission for Scientific and Technical Information reports to the French Ministere de l'Industrie et de la Recherche/ Ministry of Industry and Research. The Interministerial Mission participates in the scientific and technical information programs of international organizations and initiates bilateral cooperative agreements.

Description of System or Service: The INTERMINISTERIAL MISSION FOR SCIENTIFIC AND TECHNICAL INFORMATION (MIDIST) proposes national policy to the French government concerning the dissemination of scientific and technical information to industry, the research community, and the general public, and it develops guidelines for improving and upgrading French efforts in these areas. MIDIST coordinates the separate information activities of government ministries, initiates interministry programs with the support of the different ministries involved, and promotes access by the general public to scientific and technical knowledge. Its activities include contributing to the development and use of computerized information systems; implementing regional scientific and technical information agencies; compiling state-of-the-art scientific and technical reports; assisting libraries; and referral services. MIDIST is also involved in software development and encourages use of data transmission systems. Support is provided to publishers of scientific periodicals aimed at an international readership, technical periodicals, and related collected works. Other programs administered by MIDIST include training of information specialists and development of research in the information sciences.

Scope and/or Subject Matter: Dissemination of scientific and technical information in support of French research and industry; information systems; information science.

Publications: Bulletin d'Information (quarterly)—reports developments in the information field in France with emphasis on MIDIST activities.

Computer-Based Products and Services: MIDIST encourages and supports the development of scientific and technical data bases and data banks, technical-economic and technical-legal information systems, and implementation of host computers for scientific and technical information. MIDIST also contributes to the development of software for the processing of text, graphs, and images, and it offers incentives for using data communications networks, including Euronet DIANE and TRANSPAC.

Other Services: MIDIST also promotes dissemination of scientific and technical information to the general public by sponsoring scientific events, using scientific films, developing socioeducational activities for young people, promoting scientific and technical museums, and engaging in communication techniques research.

Clientele/Availability: Financial support is provided to public and private organizations on a governmental contract basis.

Contact: Marie-France Morin, International Relations, Interministerial Mission for Scientific and Technical Information.

★345★
FRANCE
MINISTRY OF DEFENSE
GENERAL OFFICE FOR ORDNANCE
(Delegation Generale pour l'Armement)
CENTER FOR DOCUMENTATION ON ORDNANCE
(Centre de Documentation de l'Armement - CEDOCAR)
26, blvd. Victor   Phone: (not reported)
F-75996 Paris-Armees, France

Description of System or Service: The CENTER FOR DOCUMENTATION ON ORDNANCE (CEDOCAR) collects and indexes scientific and technical literature dealing with defense technology and stores the results in a computer-readable data base, which it makes available for online searching. CEDOCAR also provides online access to several other data bases.

Scope and/or Subject Matter: Defense technology and related subjects.

Input Sources: Input to the computer-readable CEDOCAR file is drawn from French and foreign literature.

Holdings and Storage Media: The computer-readable bibliographic CEDOCAR data base contains more than 100,000 records.

Publications: Current awareness bulletins are issued.

Computer-Based Products and Services: The CENTER FOR DOCUMENTATION ON ORDNANCE maintains the computer-readable CEDOCAR data base and provides online access to several data bases through the Transpac network, including CEDOCAR, COMPENDEX, Ei Engineering Meetings, INSPEC, and METADEX.

Clientele/Availability: Services are intended for researchers and scientists in the defense field.

Contact: Center for Documentation on Ordnance.

★346★
FRANCE
MINISTRY OF EDUCATION
(Ministere de l'Education)
NATIONAL CENTER FOR PEDAGOGICAL DOCUMENTATION
(Centre National de Documentation Pedagogique - CNDP)
29, rue d'Ulm   Phone: 01 3292164
F-75230 Paris Cedex 5, France
Serge Heritier, Director General

Staff: 400 Information and library professional; 300 management professional; 600 technicians; 700 clerical and nonprofessional.

Description of System or Service: The NATIONAL CENTER FOR PEDAGOGICAL DOCUMENTATION (CNDP) is the French government agency responsible for production, documentation, and training in the areas of formal and informal education. The CNDP issues a variety of printed materials, audiovisual products, and instructional software programs, and disseminates these through a network of 106 regional, departmental, and local educational centers. It also operates a teletext system for use by the network.

Scope and/or Subject Matter: All educational subjects.

Holdings and Storage Media: Each of the 106 centers in the CNDP network maintains a library of print materials, and films, videotapes, and slides.

Publications: The CNDP publishes ten periodicals and 14 series of booklets comprising 1.8 billion pages annually.

Computer-Based Products and Services: The CNDP operates a teletext system and also makes available approximately 300 instructional software programs.

Clientele/Availability: Services and products are intended for schools and educational organizations in France.

Contact: Robert Chesnais, Chief, Departement des Relations Exterieurs, Centre National de Documentation Pedagogique. In the U.S., contact Thomas Valentin, Cultural Services, French Embassy, 972 Fifth Ave., New York, NY 10021; telephone (212) 570-4400.

★347★
FRANCE
NATIONAL CENTER FOR OCEAN UTILIZATION
(Centre National pour l'Exploitation des Oceans - CNEXO)
NATIONAL BUREAU FOR OCEAN DATA
(Bureau National des Donnees Oceaniques - BNDO)
Centre Oceanologique de Bretagne   Phone: 98 458055
B.P. 337   Service Est: 1971
F-29273 Brest Cedex, France
Dr. Marthe Melguen, Head

Staff: Approximately 40 total.

Description of System or Service: The NATIONAL BUREAU FOR OCEAN DATA (BNDO) is the French national center for scientific and technical data storage, documentation, and information analysis in the field of oceanology. BNDO maintains bibliographic and numeric data bases in such areas as aquaculture, oceanography, marine biology, marine geology, and water pollution. It provides computerized search services from its data bases and operates a publicly available online service for many of them. BNDO also offers technical assistance in applying the computer to data acquisition at sea as well as to the analysis, storage, and processing of the resulting data. Additionally, it provides assistance in the creation of bibliographic data bases.

Scope and/or Subject Matter: Data and documentation in the areas of oceanography, hydrology, aquaculture, bathythermy, bathymetry, ocean currents, marine geophysics, pollution, marine biology, fisheries, sea waves and wind, continental coastlines, geology, mineral and energy resources, and navigation.

Input Sources: Data are acquired from French oceanographic surveys and research teams, and from foreign data centers. Bibliographic information is drawn from periodicals, books, theses, research reports, conference proceedings, and other materials.

Holdings and Storage Media: BNDO maintains approximately a dozen bibliographic and numeric files in computer-readable form. Also maintained is a library collection of 17,000 bound volumes; subscriptions to 1800 journals; theses and reports; atlases and maps; oceanographic cruise data; and aerial photographs.

Computer-Based Products and Services: The NATIONAL BUREAU FOR OCEAN DATA maintains the following data bases (see separate entries following this one for full descriptions): 1) AQUADOC; 2) BIOCEAN; 3) CNEXO-BNDO; 4) DOCOCEAN; 5) geoIPOD; 6) POLUMAT; and 7) ROSCOP. In addition, BNDO maintains the REVUMER data base, which contains references to serials on oceanography that are held by the BNDO library and other selected libraries in France; and a variety of numeric data files containing physical oceanography data, including classical hydrography, bathythermy, sounding measurements, temporal measurements, and current measurements data; marine geological and geophysical data, including subsurface geological and oceanic geophysical data; cartographic data; Sea Beam bathymetric data, which provide longitudinal profiles of the ocean floor; and coastal environment data. BNDO makes many of the above data bases and numeric files accessible by remote terminal access in France through Transpac and in Europe through Euronet. The CENTER also makes selected files and subfiles available on magnetic tape and in computer-generated hardcopy formats. It conducts retrospective searching and SDI services for some of its files and offers online search services from data bases made available through Telesystemes Questel and DIALOG Information Services, Inc.

Other Services: Additional services include manual literature searching, photocopying, referrals, document delivery, and interlibrary loans.

Clientele/Availability: Products and services are available without restrictions worldwide to oceanographers, marine biologists, and other interested parties.

Contact: Michel Husson, Representative, National Bureau for Ocean Data. (Telex 940627 F OCEANEX.)

★348★
FRANCE
NATIONAL CENTER FOR OCEAN UTILIZATION
(Centre National pour l'Exploitation des Oceans - CNEXO)
NATIONAL BUREAU FOR OCEAN DATA
(Bureau National des Donnees Oceaniques - BNDO)
AQUADOC
Centre Oceanologique de Bretagne   Phone: 98 458055
B.P. 337
F-29273 Brest Cedex, France

Related Organizations: AQUADOC is produced in cooperation with Societe France-Aquaculture.

Description of System or Service: AQUADOC is a computer-readable data base providing information about French aquaculture organizations and products. Searchable online through BNDO, AQUADOC consists of three files: organizations, producers, and products and services.

Scope and/or Subject Matter: French aquaculture research centers, associations, and equipment producers and suppliers.

Holdings and Storage Media: The data base covers approximately 500 organizations and about 1000 materials and products.

Computer-Based Products and Services: AQUADOC is searchable online through BNDO.

Clientele/Availability: Primary users are aquaculture specialists.

Contact: Michel Husson, Representative, National Bureau for Ocean Data. (Telex 940627 F OCEANEX.)

★349★
FRANCE
NATIONAL CENTER FOR OCEAN UTILIZATION
(Centre National pour l'Exploitation des Oceans - CNEXO)
NATIONAL BUREAU FOR OCEAN DATA
(Bureau National des Donnees Oceaniques- BNDO)
BIOCEAN
Centre Oceanologique de Bretagne   Phone: 98 458055
B.P. 337
F-29273 Brest Cedex, France

Related Organizations: BIOCEAN was created by the Centre National de Tri d'Oceanographie Biologique (CENTOB), which is a joint effort of CNEXO and the Museum National d'Histoire Naturelle. It is maintained by BNDO.

Description of System or Service: BIOCEAN is a computer-readable data base containing biological data on marine organisms collected by French researchers during oceanographic cruises. For each organism sample collected, BIOCEAN provides a full description, species information, and complete taxonomic information. It is searchable online through BNDO.

Scope and/or Subject Matter: Marine biology.

Input Sources: Input to BIOCEAN consists of data on the marine organisms collected by French researchers.

Holdings and Storage Media: BIOCEAN is maintained in computer-readable form.

Computer-Based Products and Services: The BIOCEAN data base is accessible for online searching through BNDO. Searchable data elements include cruise name, station name, geographic area, latitude, longitude, nature of the sea bottom, depth of the sample, type of sampling equipment, zoologic group, taxonomist, trawling length, sampled species, and date.

Clientele/Availability: Primary users are marine biologists.

Contact: Michel Husson, Representative, National Bureau for Ocean Data. (Telex 940627 F OCEANEX.)

★350★
FRANCE
NATIONAL CENTER FOR OCEAN UTILIZATION
(Centre National pour l'Exploitation des Oceans - CNEXO)
NATIONAL BUREAU FOR OCEAN DATA
(Bureau National des Donnees Oceaniques - BNDO)
CNEXO-BNDO DATA BASE
Centre Oceanologie de Bretagne   Phone: 98 458055
B.P. 337
F-29273 Brest Cedex, France

Description of System or Service: The CNEXO-BNDO DATA BASE is the computer-readable catalog of the library of the National Bureau for Ocean Data. It contains bibliographic information for books, monographs, and other items acquired by the library since 1970. CNEXO-BNDO includes specialized files compiled by BNDO research teams or by selected external organizations; these files cover such topics as marine corrosion, oceanic currents, the Brittany and Mediterranean coasts, Albacore tuna in the Atlantic Ocean, marine pollution, and the pathology of aquatic animals. Items in CNEXO-BNDO that pertain to oceanology are included in the DOCOCEAN data base (see separate entry following this one).

Scope and/or Subject Matter: Oceanology, including marine pollution, oceanic currents, coastal geography, and marine animals.

Input Sources: Input to CNEXO-BNDO is derived from books, monographs, theses, research reports, congress and symposia proceedings, and several specialized files.

Holdings and Storage Media: The computer-readable data base covers items acquired by the library since 1970; specialized files cover various time periods dating back as early as 1962.

Publications: 1) Thesaurus Oceanologie—in French. 2) Library serials catalogue. Both are available for purchase.

Computer-Based Products and Services: Selected information from the CNEXO-BNDO DATA BASE is searchable online as part of the DOCOCEAN data base available through BNDO.

Clientele/Availability: Primary users include oceanographers and researchers.

Contact: Michel Husson, Representative, National Bureau for Ocean Data. (Telex 940627 F OCEANEX.)

★351★
FRANCE
NATIONAL CENTER FOR OCEAN UTILIZATION
(Centre National pour l'Exploitation des Oceans - CNEXO)
NATIONAL BUREAU FOR OCEAN DATA
(Bureau National des Donnees Oceaniques - BNDO)
DOCOCEAN
Centre Oceanologique de Bretagne   Phone: 98 458055
B.P. 337
F-29273 Brest Cedex, France

Description of System or Service: DOCOCEAN is a bibliographic data base providing integrated online access to four files: Aquatic Sciences and Fisheries Abstracts (ASFA), produced by the United Nations Food and Agriculture Organization; Oceanic Abstracts, produced by Cambridge Scientific Abstracts; PASCAL-Oceanologie, produced by the French National Center for Scientific Research (CNRS); and the CNEXO-BNDO Data Base, produced by BNDO. Maintained under MISTRAL software, DOCOCEAN allows the user to access and search the four files simultaneously; it is also possible to search a single file separately. DOCOCEAN is accessible online through BNDO.

Scope and/or Subject Matter: Oceanography, including biology, physics, and earth resources; fisheries, aquaculture, and navigation; resources exploration, including oil and gas, minerals, and energy; technology, economics, and law of the sea.

Input Sources: DOCOCEAN comprises four computer-readable files, which cover a wide range of oceanographic literature.

Holdings and Storage Media: DOCOCEAN holds information from Oceanic Abstracts since 1964, CNEXO-BNDO since 1972, PASCAL-Oceanologie since 1975, and Aquatic Sciences and Fisheries Abstracts since 1978. A total of approximately 300,000 references are included.

Computer-Based Products and Services: Searchable online through BNDO, the DOCOCEAN data base allows the user to search the four files simultaneously. Duplicate citations have been eliminated, and citations from the different files are printed in the same format for ease of use. Searchable data elements include author name and affiliation, title, source, date, language, abstract, and descriptors.

Clientele/Availability: Primary users are oceanographers, marine biologists, and researchers.

Contact: Michel Husson, Representative, National Bureau for Ocean Data. (Telex 940627 F OCEANEX.)

★352★
FRANCE
NATIONAL CENTER FOR OCEAN UTILIZATION
(Centre National pour l'Exploitation des Oceans - CNEXO)
NATIONAL BUREAU FOR OCEAN DATA
(Bureau National des Donnees Oceaniques - BNDO)
GEOIPOD
Centre Oceanologique de Bretagne   Phone: 98 458055
B.P. 337
F-29273 Brest Cedex, France

Description of System or Service: GEOIPOD is a machine-readable data base containing deep ocean geological data collected by the Glomar Challenger vessel. Accessible online through BNDO, the data base covers approximately 1000 deep-sea drillings done since 1968. GEOIPOD contains such data as the Glomar Challenger shipping route dates, site summary, age profile, carbon-carbonate, sediment smear slides, physical properties and lithology of sediments, drilling descriptive guide (covering 32 main parameters of the drilling), chemistry of igneous rocks, and core depths.

Scope and/or Subject Matter: Oceanic drilling and exploration.

Input Sources: Input consists of data from drillings conducted by the Glomar Challenger vessel.

Holdings and Storage Media: geoIPOD data cover about 1000 drillings done since 1968.

Publications: A catalog describing the contents of geoIPOD is available by request.

Computer-Based Products and Services: GEOIPOD is available for online searching through BNDO. Searchable data elements include leg number, hole number, latitude, longitude, Marsden square, physiographic features, water depth in meters, crust type, penetration (cored and total) in meters, recovery, coring of igneous rocks, lithology of igneous rocks, depth at which basement was reached (in meters), situation of the oldest sediment, age of the oldest sediment, and lithology of the oldest sediment.

Clientele/Availability: Primary users are oceanographers, geologists, and researchers.

Contact: Michel Husson, Representative, National Bureau for Ocean Data. (Telex 940627 F OCEANEX.)

★353★
FRANCE
NATIONAL CENTER FOR OCEAN UTILIZATION
(Centre National pour l'Exploitation des Oceans - CNEXO)
NATIONAL BUREAU FOR OCEAN DATA
(Bureau National des Donnees Oceaniques - BNDO)
POLUMAT
Centre Oceanologie de Bretagne   Phone: 98 458055
B.P. 337
F-29273 Brest Cedex, France

Related Organizations: POLUMAT is produced in cooperation with the Centre de Documentation de Recherche et d'Experimentations sur les Pollutions Accidentelles des Eaux (CEDRE).

Description of System or Service: POLUMAT is a machine-readable data base that contains information concerning equipment and products in France which may be utilized in the cleanup of accidental spills and other pollution of the sea. It is accessible online through BNDO.

Scope and/or Subject Matter: Pollution control, with emphasis on oil spill control.

Holdings and Storage Media: POLUMAT information is maintained in machine-readable form.

Computer-Based Products and Services: POLUMAT is searchable online through BNDO.

Clientele/Availability: Primary users are environmental experts and researchers.

Contact: Michel Husson, Representative, National Bureau for Ocean Data. (Telex 940627 F OCEANEX.)

★354★
FRANCE
NATIONAL CENTER FOR OCEAN UTILIZATION
(Centre National pour l'Exploitation des Oceans - CNEXO)
NATIONAL BUREAU FOR OCEAN DATA
(Bureau National des Donnees Oceaniques - BNDO)
ROSCOP
Centre Oceanologique de Bretagne   Phone: 98 458055
B.P. 337
F-29273 Brest Cedex, France

Description of System or Service: ROSCOP is a machine-readable inventory of oceanographic measurements collected by French or foreign research vessels. The data base holds three basic types of information for each research expedition: cruise description, sponsoring organization, and research personnel involved. ROSCOP is searchable online through BNDO.

Scope and/or Subject Matter: Oceanographic exploration.

Input Sources: ROSCOP data are submitted by French and foreign research cruise expeditions.

Holdings and Storage Media: The machine-readable ROSCOP data base holds information on approximately 8000 research expeditions; descriptions of about 200 new cruises are added each year.

Computer-Based Products and Services: The ROSCOP data base is accessible for online searching through BNDO. Searchable data elements include cruise name, vessel name, radio code of the vessel, geographic area, beginning and end dates, latitude, longitude, organization name, research scientist(s) involved, country, nature of study, name and number of the measurements, bibliographic reference, and date of last update.

Clientele/Availability: Primary users are oceanographers and researchers.

Remarks: ROSCOP takes its name from the internationally recommended form for the exchange of oceanographic data: Report of Observations and Samples Collected by Oceanographic Programs.

Contact: Michel Husson, Representative, National Bureau for Ocean Data. (Telex 940627 F OCEANEX.)

★355★
FRANCE
NATIONAL CENTER FOR SCIENTIFIC RESEARCH
(Centre National de la Recherche Scientifique - CNRS)
DOCUMENTATION CENTER FOR HUMAN SCIENCES
(Centre de Documentation Sciences Humaines - CDSH)
54, blvd. Raspail   Phone: 01 5443849
F-75270 Paris Cedex 6, France   Service Est: 1970

Staff: Approximately 60 total.

Description of System or Service: The DOCUMENTATION CENTER FOR HUMAN SCIENCES (CDSH) provides a variety of information services for the social and human sciences. A major activity is the development and production of the computerized FRANCIS (French Retrieval Automated Network for Current Information in Social and Human Sciences) system, which encompasses some 22 bibliographic data bases in various specialized subject areas of the social and human sciences. Internationally available online, FRANCIS is used by CDSH to provide standard or personalized SDI services and to publish periodical bibliographies. In addition to FRANCIS, the CENTER maintains CNRSLAB, a computer-readable data base containing descriptions of current CNRS research activities. The data base is available online and as a hardcopy publication known as Annuaire CNRS. Other activities of the CDSH include providing photocopies or microfiche of documents described in its data bases; publishing a variety of books dealing with science, information, documentation, ongoing research, and other topics; and supplying initiation and training in the techniques of automated documentation and scientific information services. CDSH also is involved in forming documentary networks which associate research laboratories and centers of different natures.

Scope and/or Subject Matter: French and international social and human sciences. FRANCIS covers the following specific fields: philosophy; educational sciences; sociology; ethnology; history of sciences and technology; history and science of literature; linguistics; prehistory and protohistory; art and archaeology; history and science of religions; administrative science; geography; energy economics; employment and professional training; health science; company management; general economy; and computers and law. CNRSLAB covers CNRS-sponsored scientific research in the fields of mathematics, physics, chemistry, earth and space sciences, oceanography, biology, life sciences, social sciences, and humanities.

Input Sources: Material indexed and abstracted in FRANCIS is derived from more than 8000 periodicals, books, reports, theses, conference proceedings, and other items. CNRSLAB data are collected directly from CNRS research units.

Holdings and Storage Media: FRANCIS comprises 22 computer-readable files holding more than 850,000 bibliographical references from 1972 to the present, with approximately 92,000 references added annually; data bases are updated at varying intervals depending upon the subject area. CNRSLAB maintains approximately 1500 records for laboratories and various research units sponsored by the CNRS, and is updated annually.

Publications: 1) Reference Bulletin/ Bulletin Signaletique (quarterly)—CDSH publishes 11 sections of this multi-indexed bibliographical review. For each section, an annual volume providing author and subject indexes and a list of periodicals analyzed is also published. 2) Repertory of Art and Archaeology/ Repertoire d'Art et Archeologie (quarterly)—covers the paleo-Christian era to 1939. 3) International Geographical Bibliography/ Bibliographique Geographique Internationale (quarterly). 4) Energy Economics/ Economie de l'Energie (11 per year)—inventory of documents dealing with energy economics in French and other languages; includes abstracts and several indexes. 5) Employment and Training/ Emploi et Formation (quarterly)—information by publications concerning employment and professional training. 6) Reseau Documentaire en Sciences Humaines de la Sante/ Human Sciences of Health-RESHUS (quarterly)—health sciences review. 7) Computer Processing and Legal Sciences/ Informatique et Sciences Juridiques (semestrial)—references on the use of computers in the field of law, and political and judicial problems caused by computerization. 8) Company Management/ Gestion des Entreprises (DOGE). 9) General Economy/ Economie Generale (ECODOC). 10) Tropical Geography/ Geographie Tropicale (CEGET). 11) Annuaire CNRS—printed publication that corresponds to CNRSLAB. 12) BRISES. Additional CSDH publications include a series of guides designed to facilitate the online use of FRANCIS.

Microform Products and Services: Copies of original documents can be provided on microfiche.

Computer-Based Products and Services: CDSH produces the FRANCIS and CNRSLAB data bases and offers a variety of services from them. FRANCIS, containing bibliographic references with abstracts and keywords to social science and humanities literature, is available online through Telesystemes Questel. FRANCIS subfiles covering health sciences (RESHUS), employment and training (Emploi et Formation), company management (DOGE), and general economy (ECODOC) are also accessible online through G.CAM. CDSH offers SDI and retrospective searches from FRANCIS. CNRSLAB, containing descriptions of laboratories and research units financed by CNRS, is accessible online as part of the LABINFO data base through Questel. Search elements include name and address of laboratory, name of director, staff, research activities, serials and equipment, CNRS number, geographic location, and subject descriptors.

Clientele/Availability: Services and products are available without restrictions.

Remarks: CNRSLAB is coproduced by the Banque des Connaissances et des Techniques (BCT).

Contact: Maryse Rahard, Documentation Center for Human Sciences. (Telex 203 104 MSH F.)

★356★
FRANCE
NATIONAL CENTER FOR SCIENTIFIC RESEARCH
(Centre National de la Recherche Scientifique - CNRS)
SCIENTIFIC AND TECHNICAL DOCUMENTATION CENTER
(Centre de Documentation Scientifique et Technique - CDST)
26, rue Boyer
F-75971 Paris Cedex 20, France
M. Michel, Director
Phone: 01 3583559
Service Est: 1940

Staff: Approximately 400 total.

Related Organizations: Support is received from the French Ministry of Industry and Research/ Ministere de l'Industrie et de la Recherche.

Description of System or Service: The SCIENTIFIC AND TECHNICAL DOCUMENTATION CENTER (CDST) of the National Center for Scientific Research (CNRS) provides one of the world's major scientific and technical information services. It abstracts and indexes all relevant worldwide journal literature and stores the results in the computer-readable PASCAL M and PASCAL S data bases, which are used to produce more than 75 topical bibliographic bulletins. The PASCAL M data base is a multidisciplinary file providing comprehensive coverage of the world's scientific and technical literature. The PASCAL S data base comprises 12 specialized subject files maintained in cooperation with outside organizations and providing exhaustive coverage in the following areas: information science, energy, metallurgy, welding, building and public works, earth sciences, food industries, biotechnology, invertebrate zoology, agronomy, tropical medicine, and oncology. The DOCUMENTATION CENTER offers SDI and magnetic tape services from PASCAL data bases, and makes most of the information publicly available online through commercial time-sharing.

Scope and/or Subject Matter: Encyclopedic coverage of science and technology, including physics, chemistry, biology, medicine, psychology, earth sciences, engineering, energy, food and agriculture, zoology, metallurgy, welding, building construction, mathematics, and other areas.

Input Sources: More than 4200 journals published worldwide are scanned for input to PASCAL M; selected additional titles are abstracted for PASCAL S.

Holdings and Storage Media: Machine-readable PASCAL files contain more than 5 million citations dating from 1973 to the present. Also maintained is an extensive library, which comprises subscriptions to 13,500 periodicals plus issues for 6000 titles no longer published; 18,000 scientific reports; 72,000 French theses; 16,000 conference proceedings; and a limited collection of books. Library collections are managed using DOBIS-LIBIS software.

Publications: Beginning in 1984, the DOCUMENTATION CENTER publishes four new series of bibliographic bulletins which replace the former Bulletin Signaletique series: 1) PASCAL SIGMA—corresponds to a division of the PASCAL M data base into three large volumes. 2) PASCAL THEMA—comprises 12 bulletins corresponding to each of the PASCAL S special subject files. 3) PASCAL FOLIO—offprints of selected PASCAL SIGMA or THEMA chapters. 4) PASCAL EXPLORE—issued as the result of searching the PASCAL data bases for specific subjects. There are 64 FOLIO and EXPLORE topical bulletins.

Computer-Based Products and Services: The SCIENTIFIC AND TECHNICAL DOCUMENTATION CENTER maintains the computer-readable PASCAL data bases covering materials published in the PASCAL SIGMA, THEMA, FOLIO, and EXPLORE series since 1984 and in the predecessor Bulletin Signaletique since 1973. Updated monthly, magnetic tapes for all PASCAL files are available by subscription. PASCAL information is also available through SDI services from the CDST. Additionally, the PASCAL M data base is available for online searching through ESA/IRS and Telesystemes Questel. Several PASCAL S files are currently available online as part of the following data bases: CANCERNET, CIBDOC, DOCOCEAN, IALINE, REDOSI, and World Transindex. Searchable data elements in PASCAL data bases include title words and keywords (in original language and in French), abstract, author name, classification code, location of work, periodical title, language, and document type.

Other Services: In addition to the services described above, the Documentation Center provides document delivery, interlibrary loans, translation, consulting, and research in reprography and information dissemination techniques.

Clientele/Availability: Products and services are available without limitations to researchers, teachers, doctors, engineers, manufacturers, students, and others in France and throughout the world.

Remarks: PASCAL is an acronym for Programme Applique a la Selection et a la Compilation Automatiques de la Litterature.

Contact: D. Pelissier, Head, Diffusion and Translation Services, Scientific and Technical Documentation Center. (Telex 220 880 CNRS DOC F.)

★357★
FRANCE
NATIONAL CENTER FOR SCIENTIFIC RESEARCH
(Centre National de la Recherche Scientifique - CNRS)
SCIENTIFIC DOCUMENTATION CENTER IN ONCOLOGY
(Centre de Documentation en Cancerologie)
CANCERNET
3, rue Guy Moquet
F-94800 Villejuif, France
M. Wolff-Terroine, Director
Phone: 01 6771616
Service Est: 1968

Staff: Approximately 10 total plus a network of analysts.

Description of System or Service: CANCERNET is an international computer-readable data base used to collect and disseminate bibliographic information on cancer and related areas. It acquires input through a network of European cooperating centers that scan the relevant scientific and medical literature in their countries and provide search and SDI services from the central data base. Internationally available online, CANCERNET is also used to produce a monthly abstracts journal. Additionally, computer tapes and document delivery services are offered.

Scope and/or Subject Matter: All aspects of cancer including clinical and experimental medicine, public health, immunology, virology, biochemistry, cell biology, and radiobiology.

Input Sources: Input is obtained from approximately 1200 journals, and from books, dissertations, reports, and conference proceedings.

Holdings and Storage Media: The machine-readable CANCERNET data base holds approximately 175,000 items dating from 1968 to the present; it is updated monthly with about 15,000 items added annually. Library holdings comprise 10,000 volumes; 40,000 reprints; and subscriptions to 500 periodicals.

Publications: 1) Cancerologie/ Oncology - Bulletin Signaletique (monthly)—abstracts journal in French and English which includes all citations added to the data base each month with keyword and author indexes. 2) CANCERNET Thesaurus—published in two sections, heirarchical and alphabetical; available in French, English, German, Spanish, and Slovenian. 3) User's Manual—French and English versions available. 4) List of current journals and serials covered by CANCERNET (annual). The above publications are available for purchase or on a subscription basis.

Computer-Based Products and Services: The CANCERNET data base uses PASCAL software for input and data management. All data included are translated into French and English. Data elements include author, author's affiliation, title, citation, abstract, keywords and free terms, language of original article and of summary, and type of article and/or publication. CANCERNET is accessible online through Telesystemes Questel. The data base is also available monthly on magnetic tape on a subscription basis; SDI and batch retrieval services are provided from it by the Documentation Center and cooperating centers. Photocopies of articles cited in SDI profiles or searches of the data base are provided on a fee basis.

Other Services: Additional services include manual literature searching, referrals, and advisory and consulting services.

Clientele/Availability: Services and products are available on a subscription or purchase basis.

Remarks: CANCERNET was formerly administered by Gustave-Roussy Institute (Institut Gustave-Roussy).

Contact: M. Wolff-Terroine, Director, or Dr. L. Ghirardi, CANCERNET. (Telex 220880 CNRS DOC F.)

★358★
FRANCE
NATIONAL INSTITUTE FOR HEALTH AND MEDICAL RESEARCH
(Institut National de la Sante et de la Recherche Medicale - INSERM)
OFFICE OF SCIENTIFIC EVALUATION
(Bureau d'Evaluation Scientifique)
INSERM RESEARCH INFORMATION BANK
(Banque d'Information sur les Recherches - BIR)
101, rue de Tolbiac   Phone: 01 5841441
F-75654 Paris Cedex 13, France

Special Note: No questionnaire response was received for this entry for the 6th edition. The entry is reprinted as it appeared in the 5th edition.

Staff: 5 Information and library professional; 1 technician; 1 clerical and nonprofessional.

Description of System or Service: The INSERM RESEARCH INFORMATION BANK (BIR) is a machine-readable file covering ongoing biomedical research projects conducted or sponsored by the French National Institute for Health and Medical Research. It is used by the Office of Scientific Evaluation to facilitate assessment of the quality and quantity of research being conducted and to answer inquiries regarding researchers and projects.

Scope and/or Subject Matter: Biomedical research, especially in the areas of genetic engineering, biotechnology, immunology, pharmacology, nutrition, reproduction, clinical investigations, mental health, and public health.

Input Sources: Input to the data base is derived from research grant applications, research reports, and laboratory reports.

Holdings and Storage Media: The machine-readable BIR data base holds data on 600 to 1000 projects per year of coverage.

Computer-Based Products and Services: The INSERM RESEARCH INFORMATION BANK (BIR) is maintained and searched online by the Office of Scientific Evaluation. For each project covered, it provides 40 administrative data items and 15 scientific data items.

Clientele/Availability: Access to BIR is limited to INSERM personnel.

Contact: Research Coordinator, INSERM.

★359★
FRANCE
NATIONAL INSTITUTE FOR INDUSTRIAL PROPERTY
(Institut National de la Propriete Industrielle - INPI)
DIVISION OF PUBLICATIONS DOCUMENTATION AND INFORMATION
(Division de la Documentation des Publications et de l'Information)
INPI DATA BASES
26 bis, rue de Leningrad   Phone: 01 5225371
F-75800 Paris Cedex 8, France

Description of System or Service: The INPI DATA BASES are four machine-readable files covering French and European patents in all patentable fields. The INPI-1 data base lists French patents reported in the printed Bulletin Officiel de la Propriete Industrielle. The INPI-2 data base covers patents reported in the European Patent Office's European Patent Bulletin. The INPI-3 data base covers patent families for 30 industrial countries. The INPI-4 data base contains the 55,000 patent groups and subgroups of the International Patent Classification (IPC) scheme. All four data bases are commercially available online.

Scope and/or Subject Matter: French and European patents.

Input Sources: Input for the data bases is supplied by INPI, the European Patent Office, and other patent documentation sources.

Holdings and Storage Media: The INPI-1 data base holds more than 530,000 items since 1969 and is updated weekly; approximately 35,000 records are added annually. The INPI-2 data base comprises nearly 100,000 items since 1978 and is updated weekly; approximately 20,000 records are added annually. The INPI-3 data base contains more than 4 million records covering 11 million patent documents since 1969; the file is updated every three weeks. The INPI-4 data base contains the 55,000 patent groups and subgroups of the International Patent Classification scheme, with a thesaurus of terms and codes.

Publications: Bulletin Officiel de la Propriete Industrielle (BOPI).

Computer-Based Products and Services: The INPI DATA BASES are available online through Telesystemes Questel.

Other Services: INPI also supplies original patent documents and French translations of the original abstracts, if needed.

Clientele/Availability: Clients include researchers, inventors, and industrial concerns.

Contact: Irene Savignon, National Institute for Industrial Property.

★360★
FRANCE
NATIONAL INSTITUTE FOR INDUSTRIAL PROPERTY
(Institut National de la Propriete Industrielle - INPI)
OFFICE OF LEGAL AND TECHNICAL DOCUMENTATION
(Bureau de Documentation Juridique et Technique)
JURINPI DATA BASE
26 bis, rue de Leningrad   Phone: 01 2932120
F-75800 Paris Cedex 8, France

Description of System or Service: The machine-readable JURINPI DATA BASE contains references to and abstracts of French legal decisions concerning patents issued since 1823 and trademarks registered since 1904. The DATA BASE is used by the Office of Legal and Technical Documentation to provide computerized search services. A related publication is also issued.

Scope and/or Subject Matter: French legal decisions related to patents and trademarks.

Input Sources: Input to the data base is derived from current published and unreported legal decisions.

Holdings and Storage Media: JURINPI data are held in machine-readable form.

Publications: Propriete Industrielle Bulletin Documentaire-PIBD (bimonthly)—industrial property documentation bulletin that provides analyses and extracts of legal decisions and literature concerning industrial property.

Computer-Based Products and Services: The JURINPI DATA BASE is used by the Office of Legal and Technical Documentation to provide computerized information retrieval services on an ad hoc or subscription basis. Various subscription plans are offered, ranging from under 10 searches per year up to 75 searches annually. Records in the DATA BASE include such information as jurisdiction, date of decision, parties involved, patent number and title, abstract, precedent cases, and bibliographic reference.

Clientele/Availability: Clients include inventors, industry, lawyers, and the academic community.

Contact: Manager, Office of Legal and Technical Documentation. (Telex 290368.)

★361★
FRANCE
NATIONAL INSTITUTE FOR RESEARCH IN INFORMATICS AND AUTOMATION
(Institut National de Recherche en Informatique et en Automatique - INRIA)
INFORMATION DISSEMINATION OFFICE
(Service Information-Diffusion - SEDIS)
B.P. 105   Phone: 3 9549020
F-78153 Le Chesnay Cedex, France   Service Est: 1979
M. Bornes, Head

Staff: 18 Information and library professional.

Description of System or Service: The INFORMATION DISSEMINATION OFFICE (SEDIS) acts as the information and documenation center for the French National Institute for Research in Informatics and Automation (INRIA). As such, SEDIS maintains a library collection on computing, automation, and information processing and maintains three computer-readable data bases: BIBLINRIA, which covers books, conference proceedings, and theses; TRAP, which deals with research reports; and INFOMEDIA, which treats computer-related audiovisual materials. The data bases are used to provide information retrieval services. Additionally, SEDIS issues a current awareness bulletin and a newsletter and offers consulting and document delivery services.

Scope and/or Subject Matter: Information processing, computer science, automation, and related topics.

Input Sources: Input is drawn from books, periodicals, conference proceedings, theses, and research reports.

Holdings and Storage Media: The SEDIS library collection comprises 15,000 bound volumes, subscriptions to 470 periodicals, and 14,000 reports and theses. Three computer-readable files are also maintained.

Publications: 1) Bulletin de Liaison de la Recherche en Informatique et en Automatique (monthly). 2) INRIATHEQUE (weekly)—covers new documents received by SEDIS.

Microform Products and Services: Microfiche of research reports and theses are available for purchase.

Computer-Based Products and Services: SEDIS maintains the BIBLINRIA, TRAP, and INFOMEDIA data bases in computer-readable form and uses them to provide information retrieval services. INFOMEDIA is also publicly accessible for online searching.

Clientele/Availability: Services are available to the public without restrictions.

Remarks: INRIA conducts fundamental and applied research in various areas of computing and automation. Areas of research include models and numerical methods, systems automation, image processing and automatic control, algorithms and computation, languages, software technology, and man-machine communication. Specific research projects conducted in the area of computerization include NADIR, which concerns teleconference and satellite communications in distributed data bases, and SOL, which regroups language action around the PASCAL system to develop compilation techniques. The Institute has also developed the Modulef data base on boundary value problems and the Modulad data base on statistical processing.

Contact: M. Bornes, Head, Information Dissemination Office, National Institute for Research in Informatics and Automation.

★362★
FRANCE
NATIONAL INSTITUTE OF AGRONOMIC RESEARCH
(Institut National de la Recherche Agronomique - INRA)
SOIL SCIENCE LABORATORY
(Laboratoire de Science du Sol)
SOIL STUDIES SERVICE
(Service d'Etude des Sols)
Place Viala   Phone: 67 630013
F-34060 Montpellier, France   Service Est: 1960

Special Note: No questionnaire response was received for this entry for the 6th edition. The entry is reprinted as it appeared in the 5th edition.

Description of System or Service: Among its activities, the SOIL STUDIES SERVICE produces machine-readable soil-related data bases and creates software to facilitate soil data analysis. Data bases it compiles include the Systeme de Transfert de l'Information Pedologique et Agronomique (STIPA) data bank of soil descriptions and analyses, and a bibliographic file of existing French soil maps.

Scope and/or Subject Matter: French soil map cartography, soil patterns, pedogenesis, land management.

Input Sources: Input to the data base is derived from current published legal literature.

Holdings and Storage Media: STIPA holds data from 3700 soil analyses and descriptions in machine-readable form.

Computer-Based Products and Services: The Soil Studies Service produces the STIPA data bank, creates software for data analysis, and provides data coding and storage facilities.

Clientele/Availability: Chief clients are soil scientists and engineers interested in land management. Data are available without restrictions, but there are limitations on use of the software.

Contact: Jean Paul Legros, Research Manager, Soil Studies Service.

★363★
FRANCE
NATIONAL INSTITUTE OF STATISTICS AND ECONOMIC STUDIES
(Institut National de la Statistique et des Etudes Economiques - INSEE)
DOCUMENTATION DIVISION
(Division Documentation)
SPHINX DATA BASE
18, blvd. Adolphe Pinard   Phone: 01 5401212
F-75675 Paris Cedex 14, France   Service Est: 1977
Mr. Chevalier, Head

Staff: 2 Information and library professional; 2 management professional; 3 technicians; 1 sales and marketing; 26 clerical and nonprofessional.

Description of System or Service: The SPHINX DATA BASE is a machine-readable bibliographic file covering French economic and social literature. Compiled by a network of French organizations, the data base is available online through commercial time-sharing.

Scope and/or Subject Matter: Economic and social information, including economics, demography, business, industry, taxation, foreign trade, politics, public health, social science, employment, city planning, and tourism and culture.

Input Sources: Input for SPHINX is derived from approximately 100 periodicals as well as monographs, yearbooks, reports, and theses; it is prepared by INSEE regional economic observatories and a central service for national documents.

Holdings and Storage Media: The computer-readable SPHINX DATA BASE holds more than 33,000 bibliographic references covering the period from 1977 to date; it is updated bimonthly, with approximately 6000 citations added annually.

Publications: 1) Catalog of Periodical Titles Abstracted in SPHINX/ Catalogue des Titres de Periodiques Depouilles dans SPHINX. 2) Thesaurus de SPHINX—available for purchase.

Computer-Based Products and Services: The machine-readable SPHINX DATA BASE contains bibliographic citations and abstracts of French social and economic literature. Searchable data elements include keyword, title, abstract, author, publication date, and type of document. The DATA BASE is commercially accessible online through G.CAM. Searches of SPHINX may also be arranged through the INSEE regional economic observatories.

Clientele/Availability: Services are publicly available.

Contact: Mr. S. Saint-Maurice, Chef de Section, SPHINX Data Base; telephone 01 5400271. (Telex 204924 F INSEE.)

★364★
FRANCE
NATIONAL INSTITUTE OF STATISTICS AND ECONOMIC STUDIES
(Institut National de la Statistique et des Etudes Economiques - INSEE)
INFORMATION SYSTEM FOR THE ECONOMY
(Systeme Informatique pour la Conjoncture - SIC)
18, blvd. Adolphe Pinard   Phone: 01 5400113
F-75675 Paris Cedex 14, France   Service Est: 1970

Description of System or Service: The INFORMATION SYSTEM FOR THE ECONOMY (SIC) collects and disseminates statistical data on current French economic conditions to support banking, market studies, trade analysis, economic research, and similar applications. The data are made available in a machine-readable time series data bank that is commercially accessible online.

Scope and/or Subject Matter: French economic data in the following areas: agriculture, domestic trade, international trade, employment, finance, government spending, exchange rate, retail and wholesale prices, housing, economic surveys, and energy statistics.

Input Sources: Data are collected from French government, financial, and industrial sources.

Holdings and Storage Media: The machine-readable SIC data bank holds more than 11,000 time series.

Computer-Based Products and Services: The SIC data bank is accessible online through CISI, GSI-ECO, and Data Resources, Inc. Software provides extensive selection, retrieval, and modeling facilities for working with the data. Searches may be conducted by series name, beginning and ending dates, source organization, measurement unit, and other variables.

Clientele/Availability: SIC is publicly available without restrictions.

Contact: Head, Information System for the Economy. (Telex 204924 F INSEE.)

★365★
FRANCE
NATIONAL INSTITUTE OF STATISTICS AND ECONOMIC STUDIES
(Institut National de la Statistique et des Etudes Economiques - INSEE)
LOCAL AREA DATA BANK
(Banque de Donnees Locales - BDL)
18, blvd. Adolphe Pinard   Phone: (not reported)
F-75675 Paris Cedex 14, France

Description of System or Service: The LOCAL AREA DATA BANK (BDL) is a computer-readable file holding several thousand data items for each of approximately 36,000 French communities. It contains statistics on population, employment, revenues, health, finance, agriculture, education, and other topics. BDL data may be manipulated to produce regional studies, maps, and other graphic representations. Searches of the DATA BANK may be arranged through INSEE; it is also commercially available online.

Scope and/or Subject Matter: French demographic and related data at the local community level.

Input Sources: Input to the Data Bank is obtained from the INSEE regional economic observatories.

Holdings and Storage Media: Data for 36,000 communities are held in machine-readable form.

Computer-Based Products and Services: The LOCAL AREA DATA BANK is searchable online through G.CAM. Searches of the DATA BANK may also be arranged through any of the INSEE regional economic observatories.

Clientele/Availability: Services are available without restrictions.

Contact: Head, Local Area Data Bank. (Telex 204924 F INSEE.)

★366★
FRANCE
NATIONAL INSTITUTE OF STATISTICS AND ECONOMIC STUDIES
(Institut National de la Statistique et des Etudes Economiques - INSEE)
MACROECONOMIC DATA BANK
(Banque de Donnees Macroeconomiques - BDM)
18, blvd. Adolphe Pinard   Phone: (not reported)
F-75675 Paris Cedex 14, France

Description of System or Service: The MACROECONOMIC DATA BANK (BDM) is a computer-readable file containing several million time series covering France, selected foreign countries, and the international economic situation. Data are held for such statistics as population, employment, revenues, consumption, national accounts, and others. BDM data are compatible for use with INSEE econometric models. Searches of the DATA BANK may be arranged through INSEE; it is also accessible online through commercial time-sharing.

Scope and/or Subject Matter: Economic and related data for France and selected national and international sectors.

Input Sources: Input to BDM is obtained from the INSEE network of regional economic observatories.

Holdings and Storage Media: The Macroeconomic Data Bank holds several million time series in machine-readable form.

Computer-Based Products and Services: The MACROECONOMIC DATA BANK is searchable online through GSI-ECO. In addition, searches of BDM may be arranged through any of the INSEE regional economic observatories.

Clientele/Availability: Services are available without restrictions.

Contact: Head, Macroeconomic Data Bank. (Telex 204924 F INSEE.)

★367★
FRANCE
NATIONAL TELECOMMUNICATIONS RESEARCH CENTER
(Centre National d'Etudes des Telecommunications - CNET)
INTERMINISTERIAL DOCUMENTATION SERVICE
(Service de Documentation Interministerielle - SDI)
TELEDOC
38-40, rue du General Leclerc   Phone: 1 6384444
F-92131 Issy les Moulineaux, France
M. Truchet, Engineer

Staff: 20 Information and library professional; 7 management professional; 1 sales and marketing; 2 clerical and nonprofessional.

Related Organizations: The National Telecommunications Research Center (CNET) is an external service of the Secretariat d'Etat aux PTT/ Secretary of State for Posts and Telecommunications.

Description of System or Service: TELEDOC is a computer-readable data base covering technical literature on telecommunications and related areas. The data base is made up of the entire content of the printed Bulletin Signaletique des Telecommunications, plus additional references. TELEDOC is commercially available online and is used by CNET to provide online searching and SDI.

Scope and/or Subject Matter: Telecommunications hardware and software, including telephony, telegraphy and facsimile, data communications, office automation, information technology and telematics, microwave and satellites, radio and television broadcasting and distribution, video communication, and fiber optics; and such related areas as acoustics, automation, data and information processing, electronics, mathematics, optics, physics, documentation science, economics, law and legislation, and management.

Input Sources: Input is derived primarily from 210 journals; covered selectively are books, conference proceedings, and reports.

Holdings and Storage Media: The machine-readable TELEDOC data base holds 96,000 items dating from 1972 to the present. It is updated monthly with 8000 items added annually. Print holdings include 25,000 bound volumes and subscriptions to 900 periodicals.

Publications: Bulletin Signaletique des Telecommunications (monthly)—each issue presents 600 bibliographic references with abstracts; available by subscription. CNET also issues other publications, including Annales des Telecommunications/ Telecommunications Annals (bimonthly), which provides original papers as well as reports and information concerning telecommunications sciences.

Microform Products and Services: The Bulletin Signaletique is available on microfiche.

Computer-Based Products and Services: Online literature searching and SDI services from the TELEDOC data base are offered by the CNET. TELEDOC is also commercially available for online searching through Telesystemes Questel. Searchable data elements include title, abstract, or descriptor keyword; author; subject; source; document type; and author affiliation. Copies of documents covered by TELEDOC and held by the CNET library may be ordered online.

Other Services: Manual literature searching services are also offered.

Clientele/Availability: TELEDOC is available without restrictions.

Contact: Mlle. Guillot or M. Bisson, Interministerial Documentation Service; telephone 1 6385620. (Telex 250317 F.)

★368★
FRANKFURT CITY AND UNIVERSITY LIBRARY
(Stadt- und Universitatsbibliothek Frankfurt)
BIBLIOGRAPHY OF LINGUISTIC LITERATURE (BLL)
(Bibliographie Linguistischer Literatur)
Bockenheimer Landstr. 134-138 Phone: 069 7907235
D-6000 Frankfurt am Main, Fed. Rep. of
  Germany
Klaus-Dieter Lehmann, Director

Related Organizations: Supporting organizations include the German Research Society.

Description of System or Service: The BIBLIOGRAPHY OF LINGUISTIC LITERATURE (BLL) is a bibliography of published materials in the field of language and linguistics. It is available as a hardcopy publication and as a computer-readable data base that is accessible online.

Scope and/or Subject Matter: Linguistics and West European languages, including American English.

Input Sources: Input is derived from books, conference reports, collected works, and more than 600 periodicals.

Holdings and Storage Media: The computer-readable BLL data base holds approximately 60,000 records, with approximately 9000 new records added per year.

Publications: Bibliographie Linguistischer Literatur/ Bibliography of Linguistic Literature (annual)—available from Verlag Vittorio Klostermann.

Computer-Based Products and Services: The BLL data base is searchable online through the Gesellschaft fur Information und Dokumentation, which is a Euronet DIANE host.

Clientele/Availability: Clients include scholars in the fields of language and linguistics.

Contact: Dr. Elke Suchan, Head, Linguistics Department, Frankfurt City and University Library.

★369★
FRASER VIDEOTEX SERVICES (FVS)
43 Bridgeport Rd. E. Phone: (519) 884-0840
Waterloo, ON, Canada N2J 2J4 Founded: 1979
Niall M. Fraser, President

Staff: 3 Total.

Related Organizations: Fraser Videotex Services is a division of Waterloo Systems Specialists Ltd.

Description of System or Service: FRASER VIDEOTEX SERVICES (FVS) makes available three videotex software packages for the creation, transfer, and presentation of pages of computer graphics. FVS also provides consulting services in the areas of videotex and computer graphics and offers videotex page creation and custom software development services.

Scope and/or Subject Matter: Videotex and computer graphics software and services.

Computer-Based Products and Services: FRASER VIDEOTEX SERVICES provides the following videotex software packages for use on CP/M and MS DOS-based microcomputers: 1) Electronic Slide Presentation (ESP) System—controls the access and display of electronic pages containing the client's product or service information stored in one or more data bases; information is displayed on a color video monitor. Electronic pages can be continuously displayed in an automatic cycle, manually chosen from the cycle, or accessed using a menu format. 2) PAGEMAKER—provides editing capabilities for videotex page design; compatible with the North American Presentation Level Protocol Syntax (NAPLPS) standard. 3) PAGETAKER—captures pages received from remote data bases and stores them on floppy disks. In addition, FRASER VIDEOTEX SERVICES provides videotex page creation services and develops custom software.

Clientele/Availability: Services are available without restrictions. Clients include educational institutions and government and service industry organizations.

Contact: Romana Hilgartner, Marketing Manager, Fraser Videotex Services.

★370★
FRASER WILLIAMS (SCIENTIFIC SYSTEMS) LTD.
CROSSBOW
London House Phone: 0625 871126
London Rd. S. Service Est: 1978
Poynton, Ches. SK12 1YP, England
B.A. Chapman, General Manager

Related Organizations: The Fraser Williams Group is the parent company of Fraser Williams (Scientific Systems) Ltd.

Description of System or Service: CROSSBOW (Computer Retrieval of Organic Sub-structures Based on Wiswesser) is a software package for the storage and retrieval of chemical structures based on Wiswesser Line Notation (WLN). Intended for use by chemical and pharmaceutical companies with large files, the system validates input of structural details, allows registration of compounds, and provides a facility for substructure searching and structure printing. CROSSBOW is compatible with Fraser Williams' CHEMLIST Package, which provides the facility to produce listings ordered by chemical name, molecular formula, and WLN; it can also automatically cross-reference all synonyms listed for a particular compound. Fraser Williams also offers laboratory data handling systems, including ARTEMIS, which encompasses online data collection and a wide range of analysis programs.

Scope and/or Subject Matter: Chemical structure storage and retrieval.

Input Sources: The system can be used for in-house or commercial chemical files.

Publications: Extensive program and user documentation is provided with CROSSBOW.

Computer-Based Products and Services: Written mainly in COBOL, CROSSBOW software is available for purchase for use on IBM 370, PR1ME, DEC, VAX, and other computers. The package comprises programs for: registration of compounds; checking of WLN; production of WLN listings and permuted indexes; generation of a fragment code; search of the fragment code, WLN, molecular formula, and reference number; generation of connection tables from the WLN; search of the connection tables; structure display; and report generation.

Other Services: Additional services offered by Fraser Williams include in-house tutorials on substructure search techniques, computer consultancy services, and systems and programming support.

Clientele/Availability: Clients include pharmaceutical and chemical companies.

Contact: Dr. L. Boyle, Consultant, Fraser Williams (Scientific Systems) Ltd. (Telex 627013.)

★371★
FRASER WILLIAMS (SCIENTIFIC SYSTEMS) LTD.
DARING
London House Phone: 0625 871126
London Rd. S.
Poynton, Ches. SK12 1YP, England
B.A. Chapman, General Manager

Related Organizations: The Fraser Williams Group is the parent company of Fraser Williams (Scientific Systems) Ltd.

Description of System or Service: DARING is a software package which converts Wiswesser Line Notations into Chemical Abstracts Service type redundant connection tables, thus providing WLN users with a link to interactive chemical search systems such as the NIH-EPA Chemical Information System (CIS). The conversion is carried out directly from WLN rather than from the CROSSBOW connection table, permitting more chemical structures to be converted than CROSSBOW allows. DARING can be used in conjunction with REWARD, a software system that produces two-dimensional chemical diagrams from DARING connection tables.

Scope and/or Subject Matter: Chemical structure format

conversion, storage, and retreival.

Input Sources: The software can be used with in-house or commercial files held in WLN format.

Computer-Based Products and Services: The DARING software package provides nearly 100 percent conversion of WLNs (polymers and inorganics excepted) into Chemical Abstracts Service type redundant connection tables. Using DARING connection tables based on WLNs, REWARD software produces x and y coordinates for each atom in the molecule which can be plotted as two-dimensional diagrams on graphics terminals or graph plotters.

Other Services: Consulting services are also offered by Fraser Williams.

Clientele/Availability: Clients include scientific users, the pharmaceutical industry, chemical industry, and others.

★372★
FRASER WILLIAMS (SCIENTIFIC SYSTEMS) LTD.
FINE CHEMICALS DIRECTORY
London House
London Rd. S.
Poynton, Ches. SK12 1YP, England
Dr. L. Boyle, Consultant
Phone: 0625 871126
Service Est: 1979

Staff: Approximately 7 total.

Related Organizations: The Fraser Williams Group is the parent company of Fraser Williams (Scientific Systems) Ltd.

Description of System or Service: The FINE CHEMICALS DIRECTORY is a comprehensive index covering commercially available fine chemicals and specialty compounds described in supplier catalogs. Available in microform and machine-readable versions, the DIRECTORY is prepared by encoding compounds in Wiswesser Line Notation (WLN) to link all sources of compounds regardless of the names used in individual catalogs. In addition to a WLN index, the DIRECTORY includes chemical name and molecular formula indexes and supplier information.

Scope and/or Subject Matter: Commercially available laboratory chemicals, including organics, inorganics, biochemicals, and dyes and stains; research chemistry; chemical and biological screening.

Input Sources: Information for the Directory is derived from chemical suppliers catalogs and data files.

Holdings and Storage Media: The machine-readable Directory data base includes more than 170,000 references to about 50,000 unique compounds.

Publications: Fine Chemicals Directory Handbook—includes a detailed description of each index in the microform directory, as well as suppliers' datasheets listing names and addresses, catalogs indexed, and restrictions on purchase of chemicals. One copy of the Handbook is provided free with each microform subscription.

Microform Products and Services: Fine Chemicals Directory (annual)—provides access to compounds through chemical name, molecular formula, and WLN indexes; available by subscription on 42x microfiche and 16mm microfilm.

Computer-Based Products and Services: The FINE CHEMICALS DIRECTORY is issued annually on magnetic tape. It comprises the Chemical Search File containing WLN, molecular formula, and registry number for each compound, and the Ancillary Data File containing the names and suppliers details for each registry number as defined by a unique parent compound. The two files can be linked by the registry number. Online access to the data base is available through Pergamon InfoLine Ltd.

Clientele/Availability: Primary clients are research organizations and laboratories, the chemical industry, libraries and information centers, and toxicology units. Material from the Directory is restricted for use solely by subscribers unless a license to copy is obtained.

Remarks: The Fine Chemicals Directory developed out of the Commercially Available Organic Chemicals Index (CAOCI) Project, which was a collaborative venture by a consortium of major European pharmaceutical and agrochemical companies to create a data base of commercially available compounds.

Contact: Dr. L. Boyle, Information Systems Consultant, Fraser Williams (Scientific Systems) Ltd. (Telex 627013.)

★373★
FRAUNHOFER SOCIETY
(Fraunhofer Gesellschaft)
INFORMATION CENTER FOR BUILDING AND PHYSICAL PLANNING
(Informationszentrum Raum und Bau - IRB)
Nobelstr. 12
D-7000 Stuttgart 80, Fed. Rep. of
  Germany
Dr.-Ing. Wilhelm Wissmann, Head
Phone: 0711 6868500
Service Est: 1977

Staff: 77 Total.

Related Organizations: The IRB operates the CIBDOC system under the direction of the International Council for Building Research, Studies and Documentation/ Conseil International du Batiment pour la Recherche, l'Etude et la Documentation (CIB), which is described in a separate entry in this volume.

Description of System or Service: The INFORMATION CENTER FOR BUILDING AND PHYSICAL PLANNING (IRB) functions as a central information agency in Germany for the fields of regional planning, city planning, housing, and civil engineering. It has the responsibility of collecting and disseminating scientific and technical information in these fields for users in industry, research, and education. For the CIB, the IRB operates the CIBDOC system providing international online access in a standardized format to national data bases concerning the building sector in CIB member countries. IRB also offers the following additional services: 1) Inquiry answering—supplying addresses of producers, research institutes, experts, and other data and facts. 2) Information retrieval—manual and computerized searches using IRB data bases, card files, reference books, and literature collections, as well as those of other institutions, statistical offices, and libraries. 3) Literature compilations—regularly updated compilations of literature references in relevant fields. 4) Document delivery—assisting in the supply of technical literature as well as research reports acquired by the IRB. 5) Individual SDI profiles—new literature references in user-specified areas are delivered on a regular basis. 6) Individual Journal Information Service (INFIS)—providing annotated index cards containing references to authors and titles in journals selected by the subscriber. 7) Current awareness publications—providing literature and research summaries in a variety of relevant fields.

Scope and/or Subject Matter: Regional planning, city planning, housing, and civil engineering, including building development, spatial structure, regulations, urban renewal, conservation, economics, regional policy, civil engineering, building politics and economics, standards, architecture, horticulture and landscaping, and construction.

Input Sources: The IRB acquires data bases and literature, including journals, books, research reports, standards, nonconventional literature, and theses.

Holdings and Storage Media: Library holdings include more than 40,000 bound volumes, subscriptions to 1500 periodicals, and more than 2 million references in card files; 8 bibliographic and nonbibliographic data bases are held online as part of CIBDOC.

Publications: 1) Schrifttum Bauwesen/ Building Literature (monthly)—available by subscription; current awareness service issued in 39 subject areas covering literature in such fields as building components, architecture, and building physics. 2) Schrifttum Raumordnung Stadtebau Wohnungswesen/ Regional Planning, City Planning, Housing Literature (monthly)—current awareness service issued in 21 subject areas covering literature in the fields of urban rehabilitation and transport. 3) Neue Bauforschungsberichte/ New Building Research Reports (bimonthly)—covers new building research reports collected by the IRB. 4) Katalog der Bauforschungsberichte/ Catalog of Building Research Reports—contains references to research reports available to the IRB since 1970, as well as references to sources of supply. 5) Neue Literaturhinweise/ New Literature Compilations (bimonthly)—reports on new subject bibliographies compiled by the IRB. 6) Katalog der Literaturhinweise/ Catalog of Literature Compilations—covers subject bibliographies compiled by the IRB; includes period of compilation and number of indicated references.

Microform Products and Services: The IRB compiles documentation of relevant research projects and makes this information available on microfiche.

Computer-Based Products and Services: Under the CIBDOC system, the INFORMATION CENTER FOR BUILDING AND PHYSICAL PLANNING coordinates online access via INKA (Informationssystem Karlsruhe) to the following data bases (see separate entries following this one for full descriptions): 1) Buildings Documentation Data Base/ Bauobjektdokumentation (BODO); 2) Building Research Projects Data Base/ Bauforschungsprojekte (BAUFO); 3) Literature Compilations Data Base/ Literaturnachweise (LINA); 4) PASCALBAT Data Base; 5) Property Services Agency Information on Construction and Architecture (PICA) Data Base; 6) Regional Planning, City Planning, Housing, Building Construction Data Base/ Raumordnung, Stadtebau, Wohnungswesen, Bauwesen (RSWB); 7) ORL-Literaturinformationssystem (ORLIS); and 8) Regional Planning, City Planning, Housing Research Projects Data Base/ Forschungsprojekte Raumordnung Stadtebau Wohnungswesen (FORS). The IRB also offers magnetic tape services, computerized literature searching, and SDI.

Clientele/Availability: Services are available to the building and construction industry, government agencies, and other interested organizations and individuals.

Contact: Dr.-Ing. Wilhelm Wissmann or Mr. J. Acevedo-Alvarez, Dipl.-Ing., Information Center for Building and Physical Planning. (Telex 7255 167.)

★374★
FRAUNHOFER SOCIETY
(Fraunhofer Gesellschaft)
INFORMATION CENTER FOR BUILDING AND PHYSICAL PLANNING
(Informationszentrum Raum und Bau - IRB)
BUILDING RESEARCH PROJECTS DATA BASE
(Bauforschungsprojekte - BAUFO)
Nobelstr. 12 Phone: 0711 6868500
D-7000 Stuttgart 80, Fed. Rep. of
 Germany
Dr.-Ing. Wilhelm Wissmann, Head

Related Organizations: The BAUFO Data Base is produced by the IRB in cooperation with the Arbeitsgemeinschaft fur Bauforschung (AGB) of the German Ministry of Building.

Description of System or Service: The BUILDING RESEARCH PROJECTS DATA BASE (BAUFO) is a computer-readable file containing descriptions of ongoing and completed research projects in the fields of building, housing, and building-related aspects of urban planning in the Federal Republic of Germany and other countries. BAUFO is publicly accessible online.

Scope and/or Subject Matter: Research in the areas of building construction, housing, and civil engineering, including legislation, economics, planning, architecture, materials, and operations.

Input Sources: Input for BAUFO is derived from research reports submitted to the IRB by the Arbeitsgemeinschaft fur Bauforschung and from German and foreign research registrations collected by the IRB.

Holdings and Storage Media: The machine-readable BAUFO Data Base contains approximately 7100 items dating from 1970 to the present; the Data Base is updated at an annual increase of 1000 items.

Publications: Mitteilungsblatt der AGB—bulletin of the AGB based on the BAUFO Data Base.

Computer-Based Products and Services: BAUFO is accessible online through the IRB's CIBDOC system via INKA (Informationssystem Karlsruhe). The DATA BASE provides German-language descriptions of ongoing and completed building research projects in West Germany, Austria, Switzerland, Sweden, the United Kingdom, the United States, Canada, and Japan. The IRB issues magnetic tape copies of the DATA BASE and provides search and SDI services from it. Searchable data elements include the following: date of completion; orderer of research work; type of research work; foreign country; responsible person or organization; beginning date; supervisor; German federal state; subject field; disciplines and uncontrolled terms; promoter; size of town or city; historical or political unit; international; district; country code or postal code; natural unit; locality; locality of author; project manager; regional index; regional descriptors; region; IRB report call number; document type; joint author; author; and corporate source.

Clientele/Availability: Services are available to the building and construction industry, government agencies, and other interested organizations and individuals.

Contact: Dr.-Ing. Wilhelm Wissmann or Mr. J. Acevedo-Alvarez, Dipl.-Ing., Information Center for Building and Physical Planning. (Telex 7255 167.)

★375★
FRAUNHOFER SOCIETY
(Fraunhofer Gesellschaft)
INFORMATION CENTER FOR BUILDING AND PHYSICAL PLANNING
(Informationszentrum Raum und Bau - IRB)
BUILDINGS DOCUMENTATION DATA BASE
(Bauobjektdokumentation - BODO)
Nobelstr. 12 Phone: 0711 6868500
D-7000 Stuttgart 80, Fed. Rep. of
 Germany
Dr.-Ing. Wilhelm Wissmann, Head

Description of System or Service: The BUILDINGS DOCUMENTATION DATA BASE (BODO) is a computer-readable bibliographic file covering the planning and construction of all types of buildings. Based on published descriptions of building projects, the DATA BASE provides such information as use of the building, urban background, construction schedule, costs, participating architects and engineers, and owners. BODO is publicly accessible online and is available on magnetic tape from the IRB.

Scope and/or Subject Matter: Planning and construction of buildings worldwide, with particular emphasis on public buildings in German-speaking countries; related aspects of urban studies, planning, and design. Particular types of buildings covered include restaurants, hotels, schools and universities, recreational and sports facilities, banks, shopping centers, industrial plants, historical buildings, libraries and museums, churches, and others.

Input Sources: Input for BODO is derived from periodicals and monographs.

Holdings and Storage Media: The machine-readable BODO Data Base contains approximately 2600 records dating from 1982 to the present; the Data Base is updated monthly at an annual increase of 1000 records.

Computer-Based Products and Services: BODO is accessible online through the IRB's CIBDOC system via INKA (Informationssystem Karlsruhe). The DATA BASE provides bibliographic references and German-language abstracts of literature describing completed, under construction, and planned buildings. The IRB issues magnetic tape copies of the DATA BASE and provides search and SDI services from it. Searchable fields include the following: author; classification code; country or postal code; corporate source; controlled terms; registration date; beginning date; date of completion; documentation service; identification number; ordering number; IRB publication reference number; regional descriptors; regional index; title; localities of author and corporate source; and uncontrolled terms.

Clientele/Availability: Services are available to the building and construction industry, government agencies, and other interested organizations and individuals.

Contact: Dr.-Ing. Wilhelm Wissmann or Mr. J. Acevedo-Alvarez, Dipl.-Ing., Information Center for Building and Physical Planning. (Telex 7255 167.)

★376★
FRAUNHOFER SOCIETY
(Fraunhofer Gesellschaft)
INFORMATION CENTER FOR BUILDING AND PHYSICAL PLANNING
(Informationszentrum Raum und Bau - IRB)
LITERATURE COMPILATIONS DATA BASE
(Literaturnachweise - LINA)
Nobelstr. 12   Phone: 0711 6868500
D-7000 Stuttgart 80, Fed. Rep. of
    Germany
Dr.-Ing. Wilhelm Wissmann, Head

Description of System or Service: The LITERATURE COMPILATIONS DATA BASE (LINA) is a computer-readable file containing references to more than 2500 subject bibliographies compiled by and available from the IRB in the fields of civil engineering, urban planning, housing, and regional planning. LINA is publicly accessible online and is available on magnetic tape from the IRB.

Scope and/or Subject Matter: Bibliographies in the areas of regional planning, city planning, housing, building construction, and civil engineering.

Input Sources: Input for LINA is derived from bibliographies produced by the IRB.

Holdings and Storage Media: The machine-readable LINA Data Base holds approximately 2600 records dating from 1965 to the present; the Data Base is updated monthly with an annual increase of 200 records.

Publications: The IRB issues a catalog of available literature compilations and bimonthly lists of new compilations.

Computer-Based Products and Services: LINA is accessible online through the IRB's CIBDOC system via INKA (Informationssystem Karlsruhe). The IRB issues magnetic tape copies of the DATA BASE and provides search and SDI services from it. Records in LINA include the number of titles cited in the IRB bibliography and are searchable by bibliography title, supplementary references, subject field, disciplines and uncontrolled terms, period of compilation, ordering number, and related references.

Clientele/Availability: Services are available to the building and construction industry, government agencies, and other interested organizations and individuals.

Contact: Dr.-Ing. Wilhelm Wissmann or Mr. J. Acevedo-Alvarez, Dipl.-Ing., Information Center for Building and Physical Planning. (Telex 7255 167.)

★377★
FRAUNHOFER SOCIETY
(Fraunhofer Gesellschaft)
INFORMATION CENTER FOR BUILDING AND PHYSICAL PLANNING
(Informationszentrum Raum und Bau - IRB)
PASCALBAT DATA BASE
Nobelstr. 12   Phone: 0711 6868500
D-7000 Stuttgart 80, Fed. Rep. of
    Germany
Dr.-Ing. Wilhelm Wissmann, Head

Related Organizations: PASCALBAT (PASCAL Batiment Travaux Publics) is produced for the CIBDOC system by the Scientific and Technical Documentation Center of the French National Center for Scientific Research (CNRS).

Description of System or Service: The computer-readable PASCALBAT DATA BASE, derived from the multidisciplinary French data base system PASCAL, contains references and abstracts of worldwide published scientific and technical literature in the fields of building, urban planning, and regional planning. PASCALBAT is publicly accessible online.

Scope and/or Subject Matter: Building, urban planning, and regional planning, including project management, materials, economics and cost, construction design and strain, and civil engineering works.

Input Sources: Input for PASCALBAT is derived from primarily French and European periodicals, monographs, research reports, theses, and proceedings, as covered by PASCAL.

Holdings and Storage Media: The machine-readable PASCALBAT Data Base holds approximately 75,000 records dating from 1973 to the present; the Data Base is updated monthly with an annual increase of 7500 records.

Computer-Based Products and Services: PASCALBAT is accessible online through the IRB's CIBDOC system and via INKA (Informationssystem Karlsruhe). The IRB provides search and SDI services from the DATA BASE. PASCALBAT bibliographic information and abstracts are in French; subject headings can be searched in English for documents which have been stored since 1982. Searchable data elements include the following: affiliation; language of author's abstract; author; classification code; corporate source; controlled and uncontrolled terms; country of publication; document type; identification number; journal title; language of original document; location; report number; publisher; publication year; ISBN; ISSN; source title; title; and serial title.

Clientele/Availability: Services are available to the building and construction industry, government agencies, and other interested organizations and individuals.

Contact: Dr.-Ing. Wilhelm Wissmann or Mr. J. Acevedo-Alvarez, Dipl.-Ing., Information Center for Building and Physical Planning. (Telex 7255 167.)

★378★
FRAUNHOFER SOCIETY
(Fraunhofer Gesellschaft)
INFORMATION CENTER FOR BUILDING AND PHYSICAL PLANNING
(Informationszentrum Raum und Bau - IRB)
PROPERTY SERVICES AGENCY INFORMATION ON
    CONSTRUCTION AND ARCHITECTURE (PICA) DATA BASE
Nobelstr. 12   Phone: 0711 6868500
D-7000 Stuttgart 80, Fed. Rep. of
    Germany
Dr.-Ing. Wilhelm Wissmann, Head

Related Organizations: PICA is produced for the CIBDOC system by the Property Services Agency Library Service, Great Britain Department of the Environment, Whitgift Centre, Wellesley Rd., Croydon CR9 3LY, England.

Description of System or Service: The PROPERTY SERVICES AGENCY INFORMATION ON CONSTRUCTION AND ARCHITECTURE (PICA) DATA BASE is a machine-readable file containing references and abstracts of scientific and technical literature in the fields of construction and architecture. PICA is publicly available online and as a printed publication.

Scope and/or Subject Matter: Construction and architecture, including conservation, legislation, design, and materials.

Input Sources: Input for PICA is derived from primarily English-language periodicals, monographs, reports, and conference proceedings.

Holdings and Storage Media: The computer-readable PICA Data Base holds approximately 42,000 records dating from 1974 to the present; the Data Base is updated monthly with an annual increase of 5000 records.

Publications: Current Information in the Construction Industry (CICI)—abstracts bulletin of the Property Services Agency; corresponds to PICA.

Computer-Based Products and Services: PICA is accessible online through the IRB's CIBDOC system via INKA (Informationssystem Karlsruhe), and the IRB provides search and SDI services from it. Searchable data elements include the following: author; classification code; corporate source; country of publication; document type; identification number; journal title; language of original document; journal issue number; publisher; publication year; ISSN; title; serial title; and uncontrolled terms.

Clientele/Availability: Services are available to the building and construction industry, government agencies, and other interested organizations and individuals.

Contact: Dr.-Ing. Wilhelm Wissmann or Mr. J. Acevedo-Alvarez, Dipl.-Ing., Information Center for Building and Physical Planning. (Telex 7255 167.)

★379★
FRAUNHOFER SOCIETY
(Fraunhofer Gesellschaft)
INFORMATION CENTER FOR BUILDING AND PHYSICAL PLANNING
(Informationszentrum Raum und Bau - IRB)
REGIONAL PLANNING, CITY PLANNING, HOUSING, BUILDING CONSTRUCTION DATA BASE
(Raumordnung, Stadtebau, Wohnungswesen, Bauwesen - RSWB)
Nobelstr. 12 Phone: 0711 6868500
D-7000 Stuttgart 80, Fed. Rep. of Germany
Dr.-Ing. Wilhelm Wissmann, Head

Description of System or Service: The REGIONAL PLANNING, CITY PLANNING, HOUSING, BUILDING CONSTRUCTION DATA BASE (RSWB) is a computer-readable file containing references and abstracts of relevant German and other literature primarily since 1979. RSWB is the successor to the ORL-Literaturinformationssystem (ORLIS) data base, previously produced by the Deutsches Institut fur Urbanistik, which contains references and abstracts concerning urban and regional planning dating from 1974 to 1978. Both RSWB and ORLIS are publicly accessible online and are available on magnetic tape from the IRB.

Scope and/or Subject Matter: Regional planning, city planning, housing, building construction, and civil engineering.

Input Sources: Input is derived from German and foreign periodicals, monographs, serial publications, research reports, theses, company literature, dissertations, standards, documentation services, and nonconventional literature.

Holdings and Storage Media: The machine-readable RSWB Data Base contains more than 200,000 records dating from 1976 to the present. RSWB is updated at an annual increase of 30,000 records. The ORLIS data base contains approximately 42,300 records dating from 1974 to 1978; the data base is no longer updated.

Publications: The IRB issues current awareness services in the fields covered by RSWB.

Computer-Based Products and Services: RSWB and ORLIS are accessible online through the IRB's CIBDOC system via INKA (Informationssystem Karlsruhe). The IRB issues magnetic tape copies of the data bases and provides search and SDI services from them. References and abstracts in both RSWB and ORLIS are in German. Searchable data elements for RSWB include the following: orderer of research work; research institute; foreign country; responsible person or organization; ordering number; German federal state; subject field; disciplines and uncontrolled terms; document type; promoter; size of city or town; publisher; historical or political unit; international; volume; district; corporate source; co-worker; month; natural unit; locality; institutions; persons; project manager; author; regional descriptors; region; IRB document call number; location; and language of document. Searchable data elements for ORLIS include the following: document type, location; author; corporate source; title; language of document; publication year; additional entries; descriptors; controlled and uncontrolled terms; persons; institutions; regional descriptors; regional index; and dates of contents.

Clientele/Availability: Services are available to the building and construction industry, government agencies, and other interested organizations and individuals.

Contact: Dr.-Ing. Wilhelm Wissmann or Mr. J. Acevedo-Alvarez, Dipl.-Ing., Information Center for Building and Physical Planning. (Telex 7255 167.)

★380★
FRAUNHOFER SOCIETY
(Fraunhofer Gesellschaft)
INFORMATION CENTER FOR BUILDING AND PHYSICAL PLANNING
(Informationszentrum Raum und Bau - IRB)
REGIONAL PLANNING, CITY PLANNING, HOUSING RESEARCH PROJECTS DATA BASE
(Forschungsprojekte Raumordnung Stadtebau Wohnungswesen - FORS)
Nobelstr. 12 Phone: 0711 6868500
D-7000 Stuttgart 80, Fed. Rep. of Germany
Dr.-Ing. Wilhelm Wissmann, Head

Related Organizations: The IRB maintains and produces the FORS Data Base in cooperation with the Bundesforschungsanstalt fur Landeskunde und Raumordnung (BFLR) in Bonn.

Description of System or Service: The REGIONAL PLANNING, CITY PLANNING, HOUSING RESEARCH PROJECTS DATA BASE (FORS) is a computer-readable file containing descriptions of ongoing and completed research projects in the areas of regional and city planning and housing, with emphasis on the Federal Republic of Germany and other German-speaking countries. FORS is publicly accessible online and is available on magnetic tape from the IRB.

Scope and/or Subject Matter: Research in the areas of regional planning, city planning, and housing, including development, population, policy, legislation, administration, and economy.

Input Sources: Input for FORS is derived from research projects reported to the IRB by the researchers.

Holdings and Storage Media: The machine-readable FORS Data Base contains approximately 4300 items dating from 1978 to the present; the Data Base is totally updated annually, with a growth of 700 items.

Microform Products and Services: FORS documentation is available on microfiche from the IRB.

Computer-Based Products and Services: FORS is accessible online through the IRB's CIBDOC system via INKA (Informationssystem Karlsruhe). The DATA BASE provides German-language descriptions, including methodology and information sources, of ongoing and completed research projects. The IRB issues magnetic tape copies of the DATA BASE and provides search and SDI services from it. Searchable fields include the following: date of completion; orderer of research work; research institute; type of research work; foreign country; responsible person or organization; beginning date; supervisor; German federal state; subject field; disciplines and uncontrolled terms; promoter; author's index; size of city or town; historical or political unit; international; district; country or postal code; natural unit; locality of author; locality; project manager; regional index; regional descriptors; region; IRB report call number; controlled terms; document type; and author.

Clientele/Availability: Services are available to the building and construction industry, government agencies, and other interested organizations and individuals.

Contact: Dr.-Ing. Wilhelm Wissmann or Mr. J. Acevedo-Alvarez, Dipl.-Ing, Information Center for Building and Physical Planning. (Telex 7255 167.)

★381★
FREE UNIVERSITY OF BRUSSELS
(Vrije Universiteit Brussel - VUB)
CENTRAL LIBRARY
VUBIS
Pleinlaan 2 Phone: 02 6401260
B-1050 Brussels, Belgium Service Est: 1976
Dr. Gerrit Alewaeters, Head

Related Organizations: VUBIS was developed by the Free University of Brussels and Interactive Systems, Inc.

Description of System or Service: VUBIS is an integrated, minicomputer-based library system designed especially to provide a user-friendly public access facility. The cataloging subsystem guides the librarian through the original cataloging process using a step-by-step dialog approach. The public access module provides library patrons with the ability to search the catalog online by author, title, or subject without knowledge of either cataloging rules or data processing techniques. Additional modules under development for VUBIS include serials and series management, acquisitions, lending, and general library administration.

Scope and/or Subject Matter: Online cataloging and public access to library holdings information.

Input Sources: Input consists of bibliographic information on acquisitions.

Holdings and Storage Media: Library holdings consist of 180,000 bound volumes and subscriptions to 2000 periodicals. The online catalog data base contains approximately 110,000 bibliographical descriptions.

Microform Products and Services: A biannual author, title, and subject catalog is produced in microform.

Computer-Based Products and Services: The bibliographic records held online on VUBIS are searchable in Dutch, English, and French, by author, title, and subject. Also provided is SDI related to new acquisitions.

Clientele/Availability: VUBIS is available to the university community.

Contact: Dr. Gerrit Alewaeters, Head, System Office, Central Library, Free University of Brussels.

★382★
FRENCH ASSOCIATION FOR STANDARDIZATION
(Association Francaise de Normalisation - AFNOR)
DATA BASES SERVICE
(Service Bases de Donnees)
AUTOMATED STANDARDS AND REGULATIONS INFORMATION ONLINE
(Normes et Reglements Informations Automatisees Accessibles en Ligne - NORIANE)
Tour Europe, Cedex 7　　　　　Phone: 01 7781326
F-92080 Paris la Defense, France　　Service Est: 1972

Staff: Approximately 9 total.

Description of System or Service: AUTOMATED STANDARDS AND REGULATIONS INFORMATION ONLINE (NORIANE) is a bibliographic data base providing technical and legal information on French and international standards and regulations. Constituting the French contribution to the ISONET international standards network, NORIANE is available for online searching through Telesystemes Questel. NORIANE information is also provided on magnetic tape and in printed publications.

Scope and/or Subject Matter: Standards and specifications on administration, agriculture, building, chemistry, consumer goods, data processing, documentation, electricity, electronics, energy, environment, food science, materials, materials handling, mechanics, metallurgy, safety, textiles, transportation, and other technical areas.

Input Sources: French input comprises standards prepared by the National Standardization Institutes, technical regulations, legislative and regulatory texts, handbooks of standards, decisions of the Commission for Public Market, publications of the Union Technique de l'Electricite (UTE) and Documents Techniques Unifies (DTU), and specifications issued by professional organizations and testing laboratories; international input consists of international and foreign standards obtained from ISONET, the International Electrotechnical Commission, and other sources.

Holdings and Storage Media: Updated semimonthly, the computer-readable NORIANE file contains approximately 36,000 citations to current standards in force.

Publications: 1) Catalogue des Normes Francaises (annual); 2) Catalogue des Normes ISO; 3) Liste des Normes Francaises Traduites. User manuals are also available.

Computer-Based Products and Services: The NORIANE data base is made available online through Telesystemes Questel and is searchable in French, English, and Spanish. Each bibliographic record in the data base contains up to 28 data elements in five major categories: identification data necessary for document ordering; bibliographic data describing the document or providing information for its selection; administrative and legal data; document contents information; and data showing legal links between documents. The data base is searchable using Mistral software which allows a range of ordering and search assistance procedures. NORIANE information on French standards (indexed according to ISONET specifications) is also available on magnetic tapes for exchange with other network members.

Other Services: In addition to the services described above, AFNOR makes available the International Technical Thesaurus and original and photocopies of documents.

Contact: Service Bases de Donnees/ Data Bases Service, French Association for Standardization. (Telex AFNOR 611 974 F.)

★383★
FRENCH COMPANY FOR THE DESIGN & IMPLEMENTATION OF RADIO & TELEVISION BROADCASTING EQUIPMENT
(Societe Francaise d'Etudes et de Realisations d'Equipements de Radiodiffusion et de Television-SOFRATEV)
ANTIOPE TELETEXT SYSTEM
21-23, rue de la Vanne　　　　Phone: 331 657133
F-92120 Montrouge, France

Related Organizations: The Antiope & Telematics Corporation (ATC) cooperates with SOFRATEV in system development.

Description of System or Service: The ANTIOPE TELETEXT SYSTEM is a computer-based news and information system which utilizes specially adapted home television receivers. Computer-produced ANTIOPE information can be transmitted over broadcast television signals or over telephone lines, picked up by the user's television, and displayed by pages chosen by the user. Applications of ANTIOPE can include transmission and retrieval of news, weather reports, sports, stock market reports, employment ads, and educational information. The user can also establish interactive communication with another user.

Scope and/or Subject Matter: Information retrieval in a variety of business and consumer-oriented subject areas.

Computer-Based Products and Services: Equipment and a complete software-based system are provided for producing, editing, transmitting, and displaying pages of alphanumeric and graphic information on a television set.

Contact: Antiope Teletext System, SOFRATEV. (Telex 203861.) In North America contact Gregory Harper, President, Antiope & Telematics Corporation, 149 E. 61st St., New York, NY 10021; telephone (212) 308-7830.

★384★
FRENCH DOCUMENTATION
(Documentation Francaise)
POLITICAL AND CURRENT EVENTS INFORMATION BANK
(Banque d'Informations Politiques et d'Actualites - BIPA)
8, ave. de l'Opera　　　　　　Phone: 01 2961422
F-75001 Paris, France　　　　Service Est: 1970

Staff: 1 Information and library professional; 1 management professional.

Related Organizations: Documentation Francaise is under the direction of the French Secretariat General du Gouvernement.

Description of System or Service: The POLITICAL AND CURRENT EVENTS INFORMATION BANK (BIPA) is a computerized data bank system providing information on politics and current events in France. Several BIPA files are available for online searching through Telesystemes Questel. Document delivery services are also available.

Scope and/or Subject Matter: Politics and current events in France.

Input Sources: Input to BIPA is derived from journal articles, newspapers, government reports, speeches, communiques, and monographs.

Holdings and Storage Media: Machine-readable BIPA files cover more than 100,000 items since 1970; approximately 20,000 items are added annually. The files are updated on a weekly or monthly basis.

Publications: Catalogue des Publications de La Documentation Francaise (annual).

Microform Products and Services: Copies of documents cited in BIPA are available on microfiche on a subscription basis. Documentation Francaise publications issued since 1977 are available on 105x148 microfiche.

Computer-Based Products and Services: The POLITICAL AND CURRENT EVENTS INFORMATION BANK comprises three major data bases: 1) LOGOS—provides bibliographic and factual information in five subfiles: BIBLIOS, which covers publications issued by La Documentation Francaise since 1970 and administrative and gray literature published since 1981; CHRONOLOGIE, a full-text file providing French political chronology since 1974; CONSEILS DES MINISTRES (also known as ACROPOL), a full-text file covering Cabinet council communiques since 1974; DECLARATIONS, which covers speeches of French political officials since 1979 (ORATEUR) and speeches of the President since 1974 (SALOMON); and PAPYRUS, which covers press records from 150 publications since 1980. 2) ICONOS—a catalog of French photographic collections. 3) HELIOS—a catalog of French administrative documentation centers. The LOGOS and HELIOS data bases are available for online searching through Telesystemes Questel.

Clientele/Availability: Services are available to the French Parliament and to public and private administrators and enterprises without restrictions.

Contact: Political and Current Events Information Bank.

★385★
FRENCH FEDERATION OF DATA BASE PRODUCERS
(Groupement Francais des Producteurs de Bases et Banques de
    Donnees - GFPBBD)
103, rue de Lille   Phone: 01 5518078
F-75007 Paris, France   Founded: 1979
M. Henry, President

Staff: 2 Management professional; 2 other.

Description of System or Service: The FRENCH FEDERATION OF DATA BASE PRODUCERS (GFPBBD) was established to promote the use of the more than 200 active and planned computer-readable data bases and videotex services produced by its members. Seeking to promote usage both nationally and internationally, the FEDERATION provides a forum for cooperation and discussion among members, and supports communication between members and government information authorities, data base vendors, and end users. Composed of about 60 full members that produce data bases plus various associate members that are in the process of producing data bases, the FEDERATION issues a directory of members, offers training courses and seminars, and organizes conferences including the international INFODIAL congress and exhibition.

Scope and/or Subject Matter: Production, promotion, and commercial use of bibliographic and nonbibliographic data bases and videotex services in all subject areas.

Publications: Directory of Data Base Producers/ Annuaire de Banques de Donnees—lists members and their data bases; available in French and English. Reports are also published at irregular intervals.

Clientele/Availability: Members must be actively concerned with data base production.

Contact: N.A. Leblanc, General Secretary, French Federation of Data Base Producers.

★386★
FRENCH INSTITUTE OF ENERGY
(Institut Francais de l'Energie - IFE)
ENERGY STUDIES AND INFORMATION CENTER
3, rue Henri Heine   Phone: 01 5244614
F-75016 Paris, France
Francine Breniere, Manager

Staff: 11 Information and library professional.

Description of System or Service: The ENERGY STUDIES AND INFORMATION CENTER prepares abstracting and indexing publications and provides other information services in the area of thermal energy, including reference and referral, current awareness publications, bibliographic activities, and syntheses of information in areas of interest. Manual and computerized literature searching and photocopying are also offered.

Scope and/or Subject Matter: Thermal energy; heat pumps; recovery of heat energy; waste products; solar energy; geothermal energy; thermal industry; insulation; climate; air pollution; heating and air conditioning; energy conservation; regulation and economics of energy.

Input Sources: Input is derived from periodicals, specialized publications, catalogs of equipment suppliers, French and foreign correspondents, other associations, data bases, legislative texts, and conference proceedings.

Holdings and Storage Media: Collection includes 22,000 specialized publications; 300 periodical titles; 20 abstracts titles; card files on documents held at the Center and organizations involved in thermal energy.

Publications: 1) Revue Generale de Thermique/ General Review of Heat (monthly); 2) Actualite Combustible Energie/ Topics in Combustible Energy (monthly). The Institute also issues syntheses, bibliographies, booklets, and a compilation of air pollution standards.

Computer-Based Products and Services: The CENTER is developing computer-readable bibliographic data bases covering its collections. Computerized information retrieval services are provided.

Clientele/Availability: Services are fee-based and intended for the members of the Institute, similar associations, and French educational and research institutions.

Contact: Francine Breniere, Manager, Energy Studies and Information Center, French Institute of Energy.

★387★
FRENCH PETROLEUM INSTITUTE
(Institut Francais des Petroles - IFP)
DOCUMENTATION CENTER
(Centre de Documentation)
1-4, ave. de Bois-Preau   Phone: 01 7490214
F-92506 Rueil-Malmaison, France

Special Note: The above name, address, and telephone number have been verified for this edition, although no questionnaire response was received. The following text is reprinted from the 5th edition.

Staff: 6 Information and scientific professional; 1 management professional; 14 technicians; 8 clerical and nonprofessional.

Description of System or Service: The DOCUMENTATION CENTER provides bibliographic control of the French Petroleum Institute's publications and research reports and maintains a variety of data banks concerned with petrochemicals, thermodynamics, geochemical analysis, and exploration and production statistics. The CENTER offers bibliographic information, state-of-the-art reports, translations, and a library with lending and photocopying services; it also participates in various cooperative programs.

Scope and/or Subject Matter: Science and technology, engineering, economics relevant to the petroleum, natural gas, and petrochemical industries, both onshore and offshore; alternative energy sources; thermodynamics.

Input Sources: Input includes books, journals, pamphlets, patents, maps, machine-readable data, microcopies, and theses from worldwide sources.

Holdings and Storage Media: The Center holds original data in computer-readable form as well as tapes from the following sources: Chemical Abstracts Service, American Petroleum Institute, University of Tulsa, and IFI/Plenum Data Company. Its library collection numbers 140,000 volumes and subscriptions to 2900 periodicals.

Publications: 1) Fiches de Documentation (monthly)—available by subscription; approximately 12,000 cards are issued per year on petroleum industry operations and economics. 2) Feuille d'Information (3 issues yearly)—scientific news with restricted distribution. Various petroleum dictionaries and thesauri, as well as bibliographic and state-of-the-art reports, are available through Societe des Editions Technip, an IFP wholly owned subsidiary publishing company located at 27, rue Ginoux, F-75737 Paris Cedex 15, France.

Computer-Based Products and Services: The DOCUMENTATION CENTER maintains the following data bases: 1) The Principal Offshore Oil-Spill Accidents and Tanker Casualties Data Bank (1955-1980). 2) Geochemical Analysis Data Base—contains information on crudes, gases, rocks and oil field waters. 3) STATSID—exploration and production statistics; co-produced with Societe Nationale Elf Aquitaine and available through commercial time-sharing. 4) IFP Thermodynamique—contains bibliographic references to international literature on physico-chemical and transfer properties of pure compounds and mixtures; available online as IFP-TH through Telesystemes Questel. The CENTER also conducts online literature searches and SDI using data bases made available through System Development Corporation (SDC), DIALOG Information Services, Inc., ESA/IRS, CYBERNET, Telesystemes Questel, Pergamon InfoLine Ltd., and Mark III Service (General Electric Information Services Company).

Other Services: Additional services include: abstracting and indexing of economic documentations; advisory and consulting services at cost; data collection on crude analysis; manual literature searching without charge; research in linguistics related to computer search strategy; interlibrary loans; software licensing; information evaluation and synthesis; activities conducted under contract; and sponsorship of meetings and training sessions.

Clientele/Availability: The usual copyright restrictions apply. Contractual restrictions may be imposed by specific data base suppliers.

Contact: Chief, Documentation Center.

★388★
FRENCH PRESS AGENCY
(Agence France-Presse - AFP)
TELEMATICS DEPARTMENT
(Departement Telematique)
AGORA
11, place de la Bourse　　　　　　　Phone: 01 2334466
B.P. 20
F-75061 Paris Cedex 2, France
Dominique Pettit, Chief

Description of System or Service: AGORA is a group of data bases containing French and international news gathered by the French Press Agency (AFP). Four main files are included: 1) AGORA-GENERAL (AGRA)—contains the full text of general national and international news on all subjects (except sports) as reported during the preceding twelve months. The file is updated daily. 2) AGORA-ECONOMIE (AECO)—provides the full text of French and international economic and financial news reported during the preceding twelve months. 3) AGORA-SPORTS (ASPO)—covers sports worldwide and includes event results and descriptions for the latest twelve months. 4) AGORA-DOCUMENTAIRE (ADOC)—contains a selection of AFP news items of lasting interest, including biographical articles, chronologies of noteworthy events, government listings, financial information, and other items. AGORA data bases are commercially available for online searching.

Scope and/or Subject Matter: French and international news, including politics, economics, culture, science and technology, industry, developing nations, commerce, agriculture, transportation, energy, banking, monetary exchanges, sports.

Input Sources: AGORA information is gathered by AFP news bureaus.

Holdings and Storage Media: Four AGORA data bases are maintained in machine-readable form. AGORA-GENERAL holds more than 250,000 items. AGORA-ECONOMIE contains approximately 40,000 items.

Computer-Based Products and Services: The full-text AGORA data bases are searchable online through G.CAM using natural language commands. The data bases can be accessed using standard ASCII or Minitel videotex terminals.

Clientele/Availability: Use of the AGORA data bases is available without restrictions.

Contact: Dominique Pettit, Chief, Telematics Department. (Telex 210 064 AFPA.)

★389★
FRENCH STOCKBROKERS SOCIETY
(Compagnie des Agents de Change - CAC)
INFORMATION AND DOCUMENTATION CENTER
(Centre d'Information et de Documentation)
4, place de la Bourse　　　　　　　Phone: 01 2618590
F-75080 Paris Cedex 2, France　　　Service Est: 1965
Bruno Montier, Director

Staff: 7 Information and library professional; 7 technicians.

Description of System or Service: The INFORMATION AND DOCUMENTATION CENTER of the French Stockbrokers Society collects and disseminates information on companies whose stocks are traded on the French Stock Exchange. It also provides economic, financial, and stock information on French industries and general information on such topics as government pricing policy, foreign investment in France, public finance, taxation, and company legal status. The CENTER issues publications, distributes stock exchange statistics on magnetic tape, and provides inquiry answering and photocopying services from its files.

Scope and/or Subject Matter: French stock exchange activity, statistics, financial markets, industry surveys, and general economic activities.

Input Sources: Input is derived from journals and reviews; published financial information; special studies on companies issued by financial organizations and banks; documents; publications on forecasting issued by national and private banks; and statistical and financial organizations.

Holdings and Storage Media: Holdings include files on corporations, industry, and general economic and financial organizations.

Publications: 1) Indices de Cours de la Compagnie des Agents de Change/ French Shares Price Indexes (daily). 2) Taux de Rendement des Valeurs Francaises et des Valeurs des Autres Pays de la Zone Franc a Revenu Variable/ French Shares Yield (5 per year)—tables showing the amount of the last dividend, the date of payment, and the yield rate calculated on the last price for each stock. 3) Graphiques de la Bourse de Paris/ Paris Stock Exchange Charts (12 or 24 per year)—gives graphic representation for French shares traded and recently listed. 4) Statistiques Mensuelles de la Bourse de Paris/ Monthly Statistics on the Paris Stock Exchange—contains statistics on market activity. 5) L'Annee Boursiere/ Annual Report on the French Stock Exchange—contains an analysis of the Stock Exchange, and graphs and tables on market, sectors, and stocks performance. A catalog of economic dossiers available from the Center is also issued.

Computer-Based Products and Services: Machine-readable tapes of stock exchange statistics are available on request.

Other Services: Photocopies of some documents are available on a fee basis.

Clientele/Availability: Services are provided to stock exchange members, journalists, students, and private investors, and to others by permission of the director.

Contact: Marc Douezy, Librarian, Information and Documentation Center. (Telex 230844.)

★390★
FRENCH TEXTILE INSTITUTE
(Institut Textile de France - ITF)
TEXTILE INFORMATION TREATMENT USERS' SERVICE (TITUS)
B.P. 79　　　　　　　　　　　　　Phone: 1 8251890
35, rue des Abondances　　　　　Service Est: 1971
F-92105 Boulogne-Billancourt Cedex,
　France
Denis Marce, Director

Staff: 10 Information and library professional; 1 management professional; 4 technicians; 8 clerical and nonprofessional.

Related Organizations: TITUS is supported by cooperating organizations in countries across the world. Main partners in TITUS are the French Textile Institute and the German Textile Information and Documentation Center/ Zentralstelle fur Textildokumentation und -Information (ZTDI).

Description of System or Service: The TEXTILE INFORMATION TREATMENT USERS' SERVICE (TITUS) is a multilingual computerized information storage and retrieval system based on abstracts of the world's textile literature submitted by a network of input centers in Europe and the Western Hemisphere. Conducted in the languages of English, French, German, and Spanish, services from TITUS are available under a variety of subscription or individual search arrangements, with the input centers providing access to the system and consultation on its use. The TITUS data base is also commercially available online in Europe and North America.

Scope and/or Subject Matter: The textile industry, ranging from the production and structure of textile fibers to processes, machines, and treatment for manufactured goods.

Input Sources: Input is derived from journals, books, patents, standards, theses, symposium proceedings, and manufacturers' notifications and reports. About 1500 documents from these sources are added monthly.

Holdings and Storage Media: The computer-readable TITUS data base, which covers the period from 1968 to the present, holds nearly 200,000 items and is updated monthly. A library collection of 7500 volumes and 850 periodical subscriptions is also maintained.

Publications: Bulletin Scientifique de l'Institut Textile de France (quarterly).

Computer-Based Products and Services: The TITUS data base includes the following data for each document it covers: original title, English title, bibliographic references, evaluation parameters, and abstracts written in either English, French, German, or Spanish by textile specialists. The data base also gives grammatical relationships for about 11,000 words in the four languages used, and permits automatic indexing and output translation in any of these languages. The following services are offered from the TITUS data base: 1) retrospective searching on any textile subject, with or without specifications as to year, language, country, and type of document; 2) semimonthly SDI services based on individual profiles; 3) monthly magnetic tape service containing abstracts of all new documents acquired; 4) public online access through Telesystemes Questel. Additionally, a multilingual thesaurus can be provided on magnetic tape.

Other Services: In addition to services described above, TITUS conducts research in the area of automatic translation and offers manual literature searching services.

Clientele/Availability: Services are available without restrictions; chief clients are members of the textile industry and textile researchers.

Projected Publications and Services: A numeric textile data bank is planned.

Contact: Jean-Marie Ducrot, Documentation and EDP Manager, Textile Information Treatment Users' Service. In Germany, contact TITUS at ZTDI, Verein fur Textildokumentation und -Information, Schloss Cromford, Cromforder Allee 22, D-4030 Ratingen 1, Federal Republic of Germany.

★391★
FRENCH WATER STUDY ASSOCIATION
(Association Française pour l'Etude des Eaux - AFEE)
NATIONAL WATER INFORMATION CENTER
(Centre National de Documentation et d'Information sur l'Eau)
21, rue Madrid   Phone: 01 5221467
F-75008 Paris, France
M. Xavier Dagallier, Director

Staff: 3 Information and library professional; 4 management professional; 3 technicians; 3 sales and marketing; 4 clerical and nonprofessional.

Description of System or Service: The NATIONAL WATER INFORMATION CENTER provides documentation and information services regarding water resources and related subjects through a computer-produced abstracts bulletin, a separate subject arrangement of abstracts, a thesaurus of terms, original document delivery, and current awareness services for abstracts in selected categories. The Center's computer-readable AFEE data base is publicly available online.

Scope and/or Subject Matter: Hydrology and hydrogeology; conservation of water resources; water supply; treatment of drinking water; sewage and industrial wastewater treatment; water pollution; toxicology; and other related areas.

Input Sources: Abstracts are derived from French and foreign journals, books, theses, and government reports.

Holdings and Storage Media: The computer-readable AFEE data base contains approximately 50,000 items and is updated monthly. AFEE's library includes the original documents that are abstracted.

Publications: Information Eaux (11 per year)—classifies citations and abstracts by degree of specialization and by quality of document.

Microform Products and Services: Microforms of abstracts and original papers are available.

Computer-Based Products and Services: AFEE's data base is accessible online through ESA/IRS.

Other Services: In addition to services described above, translations and manual literature searching are offered.

Clientele/Availability: Services are available on a subscription basis to the water research community.

Contact: Mme. Vincent, Secretaire Generale, French Water Study Association, Sophia-Antipolis, F-06560 Valbonne, France; telephone 93 742223.

★392★
FRI INFORMATION SERVICES LTD.
1801 McGill College Ave., Suite 600   Phone: (514) 842-5091
Montreal, PQ, Canada H3A 2N4   Founded: 1968
Gordon K. Landon, President

Staff: 20 Management professional; 40 technicians; 30 clerical and nonprofessional.

Description of System or Service: FRI INFORMATION SERVICES LTD. is a computer services company providing investment information and software services to the Canadian financial community for investment management and financial and economic analysis purposes. The firm provides clients with interactive access to investment data bases using microcomputers.

Scope and/or Subject Matter: Stock exchange trading data, banking data, company financial data, and economic time series.

Input Sources: Data are acquired from major stock exchanges, published financial literature, and Statistics Canada.

Computer-Based Products and Services: FRI INFORMATION SERVICES LTD. provides clients with online access to financial and economic data bases, including stock prices and volumes, bonds, CANSIM, and corporate financial statements.

Clientele/Availability: Services are intended for use by financial institutions and investment managers.

Contact: Anton Gilham, Manager, Marketing Communications, FRI Information Services Ltd.

G

★393★
GEO ABSTRACTS LTD.
Regency House
34 Duke St.
Norwich NR3 3AP, England
Prof. Keith M. Clayton, Director

Phone: 0603 26327
Founded: 1960

Staff: Approximately 7 total.

Description of System or Service: GEO ABSTRACTS LTD. abstracts and indexes the world literature in geography, geology, and related fields. It stores this information in a computer-readable data base and issues a number of abstracting journals from it. Through its Geo Books division, the firm also issues monographs, technical bulletins, bibliographies, and other publications.

Scope and/or Subject Matter: Geography, geomorphology, Quaternary era, regional planning, remote sensing, sedimentology, geophysics, ecology, international development.

Input Sources: Input is derived from approximately 2000 periodicals, plus books, reports, and proceedings.

Holdings and Storage Media: The Geo Abstacts Ltd. data base is held in machine-readable form.

Publications: 1) Geo Abstracts: Part A, Landforms and the Quaternary (6 per year)—includes about 3000 abstracts annually. 2) Geo Abstracts: Part B, Climatology and Hydrology (6 per year)—3000 abstracts annually. 3) Geo Abstracts: Part C, Economic Geography (6 per year)—about 2500 abstracts annually. 4) Geo Abstracts: Part D, Social and Historical Geography (6 per year)—2500 abstracts annually. 5) Geo Abstracts: Part E, Sedimentology (6 per year)—2500 abstracts annually. 6) Geo Abstracts: Part F, Regional and Community Planning (6 per year)—3000 abstracts annually. 7) Geo Abstracts: Part G, Remote Sensing, Photogrammetry and Cartography (6 per year)—2500 abstracts annually. The above publications are available by subscription individually or as a group; the last issue of each section annually includes an author and regional index. 8) Annual Index to Geo Abstracts—provides combined permuted subject keyword and extended author indexes to all seven sections; also includes list of journals covered. 9) Ecological Abstracts (6 per year)—provides more than 9000 abstracts annually with separate author and subject indexes. 10) Geophysics and Tectonics Abstracts (6 per year)—includes about 3000 abstracts annually. 11) International Development Abstracts (6 per year)—includes about 3000 abstracts annually. The Geo Books division of Geo AbstractsLtd. publishes other serial publications, books, and occasional bibliographies; a brochure is available from it on request.

Computer-Based Products and Services: The GEO ABSTRACTS LTD. data base holds index citations and abstracts from publications listed above, plus additional bibliographic data not published in hard copy. The data base is expected to be made available online.

Clientele/Availability: Publications and services are available without restrictions.

Contact: Ian B. Woods, Manager, Geo Abstracts Ltd. (Telex 975249 CHACOM G.)

★394★
GEOSYSTEMS
P.O. Box 1024, Westminster
London SW1P 2JL, England
Graham Lea, Director

Phone: 01-222 7305
Founded: 1966

Description of System or Service: GEOSYSTEMS abstracts and indexes all geoscience literature in the public domain for input to its computer-readable GeoArchive data base. In addition to information on current literature, GeoArchive contains references dating back to the eighteenth century. The data base utilizes a sophisticated indexing system, Geosaurus, which includes subject, geographical, and stratigraphic thesauri arranged hierarchically with an alphabetic index of more than 5000 terms. Information from GeoArchive is disseminated through Geotitles Weekly and other publications, by online retrieval, through current or retrospective searches conducted by Geosystems, and on leased magnetic tapes. In addition to maintaining GeoArchive, GEOSYSTEMS has also developed the MINSYS data base containing bibliographic and nonbibliographic source information on mining resources, organizations, locations, and other items. Other services provided by GEOSYSTEMS include document delivery via DIALORDER, a literature review service, and advisory services in the design, establishment, and implementation of geoscience information systems.

Scope and/or Subject Matter: All aspects of the geosciences, including geochemistry, paleontology, geomorphology, geological maps, stratigraphy, tectonics, mineralogy, and mining.

Input Sources: More than 100,000 items are indexed annually for inclusion within GeoArchive and Geotitles Weekly. Sources include 5000 worldwide serials, books from 1000 publishers, 100,000 geologic maps and 10,000 geologic bibliographies, conference proceedings, doctoral dissertations, standards, patents, Festschriften, sborniki, and translations. Input for the MINSYS data base includes direct data from mining companies and equipment manufacturers, press releases from 2000 organizations, annual and other reports from 1500 organizations, geoscience serials, books, and the mining and business press.

Holdings and Storage Media: The GeoArchive data base contains more than 500,000 references. Also held are the MINSYS data base and a computer-readable list of more than 10,000 serials.

Publications: 1) Geotitles Weekly—a current awareness bulletin providing bibliographic references to recently published worldwide periodical and other literature on geoscience. 2) Bibliography of Economic Geology (bimonthly)—covers worldwide published literature on economic geology. 3) Geoscience Documentation (bimonthly)—a serial bibliography of periodical articles, books, reports, and other published literature relating to geoscience. For the above publications, each issue includes a main section arranged by subject plus author, subject, geographic, and stratigraphic indexes. 4) Geoprofile - Vertebrate Paleontology (monthly)—a bibliography of worldwide published literature on vertebrate paleontology. Entries are classified by subject. 5) Bibliography of Afro-Asian-Australasian Geology. 6) Bibliography of American Geology. 7) Bibliography of European Geology. Known collectively as Bibliographies of Regional Geology, the preceding three publications are a series of monthly computer-generated SDI services from GeoArchive providing references to worldwide literature on regional and general geology and stratigraphy relating to the geographic region treated. Entries in each are classified by subject. 8) Bibliography of Engineering Geology (monthly)—an SDI service providing references to worldwide literature on engineering geology and geotechnical engineering. 9) Mining, Minerals and Metals Monitor. 10) Geosources—lists serials in geoscience published worldwide. 11) Geosaurus—available for purchase. Consists of hierarchically arranged subject, geographic, and stratigraphic thesauri which include more than 5000 terms; using in indexing for GeoArchive. 12) GeoArchive Users' Guide.

Microform Products and Services: Geotitles Repertorium—COM cumulated index to Geotitles Weekly; available by subscription.

Computer-Based Products and Services: GEOSYSTEMS maintains computer-readable data bases on geoscience and mining. They include: 1) GeoArchive, used to produce most Geosystems publications. It covers current literature and retrospective material including bibliographies, geologic maps, doctoral dissertations, and complete runs of important geoscience serials. The data base can be accessed online through DIALOG Information Services, Inc.; through GeoArchive Profiles, a current and retrospective search service available from Geosystems; and through lease of magnetic tapes. 2) MINSYS, a computer-based mining data base and information system that allows retrieval of bibliographic and nonbibliographic data. 3) Geosources, a computer listing of more than 10,000 geoscience serial publications (5000 active). Geosystems uses its own OMNISYS data base management system.

Other Services: Geosystems also collects geoscience nomenclature and terminology data, and it conducts research on user requirements and models of geoscience data. Additionally, it offers the GeoData Service for special monitoring of a client-defined topic or geographic area.

Clientele/Availability: Products and services are available by subscription or other arrangement.

Contact: Graham Lea, Director, Geosystems. In the United States, contact Anthea Gotto, Geosystems, P.O. Box 573, Cambridge, MA 02139; telephone (617) 491-7190.

★395★
**GERMAN DEMOCRATIC REPUBLIC
CENTRAL INSTITUTE FOR INFORMATION AND DOCUMENTATION**
(Zentralinstitut fur Information und Dokumentation - ZIID)
Kopenicker Str. 80-82   Phone: 2391280
DDR-1020 Berlin, German Democratic
    Republic   Service Est: 1963
Mr. H. Och, Director

Description of System or Service: The CENTRAL INSTITUTE FOR INFORMATION AND DOCUMENTATION (ZIID) provides national scientific and technical information services. It maintains library and printing facilities, has developed a state scientific and technical information network, investigates automated information handling systems, and provides reproduction services. It also participates in the training and continuing education of information professionals and issues several printed publications and a translation service in microfiche.

Scope and/or Subject Matter: Science and technology; information sciences.

Input Sources: The Institute collects periodicals, monographs, company literature, data books, conference proceedings, and reports.

Holdings and Storage Media: Library holdings of the Institute include 9000 bound volumes; subscriptions to 9050 periodicals; 1000 conference proceedings; and 25,000 pieces of company literature and data books.

Publications: The following German-language publication are available from the Institute: 1) Informatik (bimonthly)—journal on theory and practice of scientific and technical information. 2) Information Dokumentation (quarterly)—annotated list of titles. 3) Leitung und Planung von Wissenschaft und Technik/ Management and Planning of Science and Technology (bimonthly)—annotated list of titles. 4) Informationsdienst Veranstaltungskalender/ Conventions Information Service (bimonthly)—provides notifications of upcoming conventions in science and technology. 5) ZIID-Schriftenreihe/ ZIID Publications Series (irregular).

Microform Products and Services: Informationsdienst Ubersetzungen/ Translations Information Service (irregular)—provides translations on microfiche of scientific and technical literature in 25 subject areas.

Computer-Based Products and Services: Computer-supported services are offered.

Other Services: The Institute also provides consulting, bibliographic and translation services, and literature searching.

Clientele/Availability: Services are available to information professionals, scientists, and others in the German Democratic Republic.

Contact: Mr. H. Och, Director, Central Institute for Information and Documentation.

★396★
GERMAN ELECTRON-SYNCHROTRON
(Deutsches Elektronen-Synchrotron - DESY)
DESY SCIENTIFIC DOCUMENTATION AND INFORMATION SERVICE
Notkestr. 85   Phone: 040 89983602
D-2000 Hamburg 52, Fed. Rep. of
    Germany   Service Est: 1962
Dipl.-Phys. Dietmar Schmidt, Head

Staff: 1 Information and library professional; 3 physicists; 2 clerical and nonprofessional.

Description of System or Service: The DESY SCIENTIFIC DOCUMENTATION AND INFORMATION SERVICE collects and indexes published and unpublished literature in the fields of particle physics, high energy technology, and quantum field theory. It prepares information for publication in the fortnightly High Energy Physics Index and maintains an equivalent computer-readable data base known as DESY-HEP. Retrospective searches, SDI, and tape services are provided from the file.

Scope and/or Subject Matter: High energy technology, quantum field theory, elementary particle physics, and related topics.

Input Sources: Input is derived from preprints, periodicals, reports, conference proceedings, monographs, and books.

Holdings and Storage Media: The computer-readable DESY-HEP data base contains 150,000 references from 1969 to date. The library collection contains approximately 26,000 volumes, subscriptions to 325 periodical titles, 34,000 preprints and reports, and standards; a machine-readable catalog of library holdings is in production.

Publications: High Energy Physics Index/ Hochenergiephysik-Index (every two weeks, with annual cumulative indexes)—each issue contains entries arranged within subject categories and includes author, affiliation, preprint and report number, and subject indexes. Available by subscription from Fachinformationszentrum Energie, Physik, Mathematik GmbH, D-7514 Eggenstein-Leopoldshafen 2, Federal Republic of Germany. A keyword list is available from DESY.

Computer-Based Products and Services: Offline computer literature searches from the DESY-HEP data base are conducted on request and fortnightly SDI services are offered by subscription. Magnetic tapes of the data base are provided by special arrangement. Online searching facilities are planned.

Clientele/Availability: Services are available free of charge to subscribers active in pure research.

Remarks: The system is also known as the German Information System for High Energy Physics.

Contact: Dipl.-Phys. Dietmar Schmidt, Head, DESY Scientific Documentation and Information Service. (Telex 215 124 DESY D.)

★397★
GERMAN FOUNDATION FOR INTERNATIONAL DEVELOPMENT
(Deutsche Stiftung fur Internationale Entwicklung)
DOCUMENTATION CENTER
(Zentrale Dokumentation)
Hans-Bockler-Str. 5   Phone: 0228 40010
D-5300 Bonn 3, Fed. Rep. of Germany Service Est: 1961
Dieter Danckwortt, Head

Staff: 15 Information and library professional; 4 management professional; 7 technicians; 2 clerical and nonprofessional; 2 other.

Related Organizations: The Documentation Center works in cooperation with regional documentation centers for Africa, the Near East, Asia, and Latin America established by the Overseas Institute at Hamburg.

Description of System or Service: The DOCUMENTATION CENTER supports the activities of development organizations and individuals by collecting, processing, and disseminating information on developing countries and the development aid policies of Germany and other nations. The CENTER offers literature searching, reference and referrals, a current awareness service for journal articles, and the compilation of indexes and bibliographies. It maintains machine-readable files in support of its activities.

Scope and/or Subject Matter: Developing countries, with emphasis on aid, development policy of national and international organizations, and socioeconomic and cultural change.

Input Sources: Input sources include books, monographs, periodicals, and data submitted by other organizations.

Holdings and Storage Media: The CENTER's library contains 32,500 bound volumes, subscriptions to 700 periodicals, and 300,000 newspaper clippings. Machine-readable files include information on literature, research projects, and institutions.

Publications: 1) Bibliography of German Research on Developing Countries/ Entwicklungslander-Studien (annual)—covers completed and current research projects. 2) Kalender (quarterly)—lists conferences, seminars, meetings, workshops, training programs, and courses. 3) German Partners of Developing Countries/ Deutsche Partner der Entwicklungslander (irregular)—descriptions of German institutions active in development policy and aid. 4) Recent

Acquisitions/ Neuerwerbungen der Bibliothek (twice a year). 5) State-of-the-Art Reports/ Themendienst (irregular)—available information (literature and data) on specific subject areas. Publications 2, 4, and 5 are free of charge. The Foundation also issues a number of directories and other publications.

Computer-Based Products and Services: The following files, stored on magnetic tape, are used by the CENTER to prepare its publications: bibliographic and indexed data on development literature, descriptions of current and completed German research projects on development, and descriptions of German institutions active in development aid.

Clientele/Availability: Services are available without restrictions.

Remarks: The regional documentation centers working in cooperation with the CENTER include the following: Institute of African Studies, Africa Documentation Center; Institute of Asian Studies, Asia Documentation Center; Institute of Ibero-American Studies, Latin America Documentation Center; and German Orient Institute, Middle East Documentation Center. The centers offer literature documentation and publication services for their specific geographical regions, including press information services. All four centers may be contacted at Neuer Jungfernstieg 21, D-2000 Hamburg 36, Federal Republic of Germany.

Contact: Dr. Beate Brodmeier, Documentation Center, German Foundation for International Development.

★398★
GERMAN IRON AND STEEL ENGINEERS ASSOCIATION
(Verein Deutscher Eisenhuttenleute - VDEh)
INFORMATION SYSTEM ON PRODUCTION PLANTS FOR IRON & STEEL
PLANTFACTS
Betriebsforschungsinst. - Inst. fur   Phone: 0211 67071
  Angewandte Forschung, Sohnstr. 65   Service Est: 1970
D-4000 Dusseldorf 1, Fed. Rep. of
  Germany
Prof. Karl Heinz Mommertz, Head

Description of System or Service: PLANTFACTS is a computer-readable data base providing comprehensive information on the construction features of primary and finished steelmaking installations. It includes detailed data on nearly 7000 worldwide installations in 24 categories such as ore preparation, blast furnace, metallurgical plants, continuous casting machines, and hot and cold rolling mills. PLANTFACTS is used to generate tables, reports, graphs, and other special retrievals. Additional information, such as relevant literature, layouts, and drawings, are stored conventionally or on microfilm and used as background information or for special inquiries.

Scope and/or Subject Matter: Worldwide steelmaking and steelrolling production plants.

Input Sources: Input is derived from technical literature, international data exchange, reference lists, company brochures, and approximately 200 periodicals.

Holdings and Storage Media: Detailed data sets on nearly 7000 installations are stored in computer-readable PLANTFACTS data base, which is updated daily.

Publications: BFI-Informationsdienst Huttenwerksanlagen.

Computer-Based Products and Services: The PLANTFACTS data base features output programs for the selection of special data for the printing of tables with selectable formats and for the graphical evaluation of different search variables. Information retrieval services are provided from PLANTFACTS on request.

Other Services: Additional activities include consulting and referrals.

Clientele/Availability: Services are available without restrictions.

Projected Publications and Services: Online service via data communications networks is expected to be available in the near future.

Remarks: The PLANTFACTS data base was formerly known as the Anlagendatenbank (ADB).

Contact: Rudolf Ewers, Information System on Production Plants for Iron & Steel; telephone 0211 6707298. (Telex 8 582512 BFI D.)

★399★
GERMAN IRON AND STEEL ENGINEERS ASSOCIATION
(Verein Deutscher Eisenhuttenleute - VDEh)
STEEL INFORMATION SYSTEM
Betriebsforschungsinst. - Inst. fur   Phone: 0211 67071
  Angewandte Forschung, Sohnstr. 65   Service Est: 1968
D-4000 Dusseldorf 1, Fed. Rep. of
  Germany
Prof. Karl Heinz Mommertz, Head

Staff: 6 Total.

Related Organizations: The development of the Steel Information System is supported by the GID (Gesellschaft fur Information und Dokumentation) with grants from the German Ministry for Research and Technology/ Bundesministerium fur Forschung und Technologie.

Description of System or Service: The STEEL INFORMATION SYSTEM produces and provides an online host service for the STEELFACTS/S and STEELFACTS/T data bases. STEELFACTS/S is a file on standard properties of iron and steel, covering all current Deutsches Institut fur Normung (DIN) and VDEh standards in addition to some ASTM and SAE standards. STEELFACTS/T provides data on test values of iron and steel found in the literature since 1978, with selective coverage back to 1957. Additionally, the SYSTEM publishes data sheets on the properties of steels as well as nomogram collections on the kf values for the hot working of those materials. The SYSTEM also acts as an intermediary and consultant in the field of information on iron and steel and as a service center and software supplier for proprietary data bases.

Scope and/or Subject Matter: Engineering properties of iron and steel materials; material standards.

Input Sources: Input is derived from periodical literature and standards.

Holdings and Storage Media: The STEELFACTS data bases are held in machine-readable form. VDEh library holdings include 100,000 bound volumes; subscriptions to 500 periodicals; and standards.

Publications: 1) Werkstoffdaten Stahl-Eisen/ Steel and Iron Materials Data (quarterly)—loose-leaf collection of 25 data sheets covering the mechanical, technological, and physical properties of particular steel grades; includes irregular special issues on fracture mechanics. 2) Formanderungsfestigkeit Stahl-Eisen/ Yield Stress of Steel and Iron—loose-leaf collection of data sheets covering the yield stress of 18 grades of steel in a uniform graphic representation.

Computer-Based Products and Services: The STEEL INFORMATION SYSTEM makes the STEELFACTS/S and STEELFACTS/T data bases accessible on its computer facilities via the Datex-P network. The SYSTEM also offers information retrieval services, software, and evaluation of proprietary data.

Other Services: Additional services include consulting and referrals.

Clientele/Availability: Services are available to materials producers, users, and traders.

Remarks: The Steel Information System was formerly known as the Material Information System (MAINS) for Iron & Steel; the STEELFACTS files were previously known as the Werkstoffdatenbank (WDB)/ Materials Data Base (MDB).

Contact: Gert Dathe, Steel Information System; telephone 0211 6707250. (Telex 8 582512 BFI D.)

★400★
GERMAN LIBRARY INSTITUTE
(Deutsches Bibliotheksinstitut - DBI)
Bundesallee 184-185   Phone: 030 85050
D-1000 Berlin 31, Fed. Rep. of Germany Founded: 1978
Prof. Gunter Beyersdorff, Head

Staff: 30 Information and library professional; 8 management professional; 22 technicians; 31 clerical and nonprofessional.

Related Organizations: The German Library Institute is funded by the federal states and federal government.

Description of System or Service: The duties of the GERMAN LIBRARY INSTITUTE are to provide supraregional services for libraries, carrying out research and development in the field of librarianship. It maintains online computer facilities and provides library management services including maintenance of three online union catalogs: the German Union Catalog of Serials, the German Union List of Conference Proceedings, and the Lower Saxonia Serials Data Base. The INSTITUTE also issues print publications and produces COM catalogs.

Scope and/or Subject Matter: Librarianship, cataloging, bibliography, statistics, serials, library public relations, special user groups, continuing education, videotex.

Input Sources: Input consists of holdings information from client libraries.

Holdings and Storage Media: The Institute maintains three computer-readable data bases holding 370,000 serials title records, 80,000 conference proceedings title records, and 197,000 Lower Saxonia serials title records. Also maintained is a library collection of 9000 bound volumes and subscriptions to 400 periodicals.

Publications: 1) DBI-Materialien; 2) Bibliotheksdienst (monthly); 3) Schulbibliothek Aktuell (quarterly); 4) Forum Musikbibliothek (quarterly). Bibliographies, directories, and leaflets are also issued.

Microform Products and Services: The Union Catalog of Machine Readable Catalog Data of German Libraries (Verbundkatalog) and the German Union Catalog of Serials are issued on microfiche.

Computer-Based Products and Services: The GERMAN LIBRARY INSTITUTE maintains three computer-readable union catalog data bases, which are accessible online. The German Union Catalog of Serials (Online-Zeitschriftendatenbank - Online-ZDB) represents 1.1 million holdings in 205 German libraries. The bibliographic German Union List of Conference Proceedings (Online-GKS) contains records on 180,000 holdings of 80 libraries. The Lower Saxonia Serials Data Base (Online-NZN) stores information on 250,000 holdings. The data bases are accessible to German libraries through the Datex-P packet-switching network.

Clientele/Availability: Services are available to German libraries; publications and microfiche products are available for purchase.

Contact: Peter Borchardt, Public Relations Officer, German Library Institute.

★401★
GERMAN PATENT INFORMATION SYSTEM
(Deutsches Patent- und Fachinformationssystem)
SRZ Berlin   Phone: 030 2621081
Lutzowstr. 105   Founded: 1984
D-1000 Berlin 30, Fed. Rep. of Germany
Hans W. Fock, President

Related Organizations: The German Patent Information System is produced by a consortium comprising the Hartmann & Heenemann Computer Composition Center/ Satz Rechen Zentrum (SRZ); the German Patent Office/ Deutschen Patentamt (DPA); the Information Center for Energy, Physics, Mathematics/ Fachinformationszentrum Energie, Physik, Mathematik GmbH; and the Society for Information and Documentation/ Gesellschaft fur Information und Dokumentation (GID). It receives financial support from the German Ministry for Research and Technology/ Bundesministerium fur Forschung und Technologie.

Description of System or Service: The goal of the GERMAN PATENT INFORMATION SYSTEM is to achieve, through data processing and the use of data communications networks, the widest possible dissemination of patent document information for the stimulation of technical innovation. Currently under development, the SYSTEM will consist of a machine-readable data base covering patent documents registered since 1973 at the German Patent Office, including bibliographic data, abstracts, major diagrams, and, for patents dating from 1984, the full text. Currently, the SYSTEM's data base contains data for patents issued from January 1984 to date; SDI, current awareness services, and magnetic tapes and diskettes are offered.

Scope and/or Subject Matter: Patents in all subject areas.

Input Sources: Patents registered at the German Patent Office.

Holdings and Storage Media: Data for patents issued from January 1984 to date are held in machine-readable form. When completed, the System's data base will also include bibliographic data for all patent documents issued since 1973; technical abstracts for patent documents issued since 1981; and important diagrams for patents issued since 1983.

Computer-Based Products and Services: The GERMAN PATENT INFORMATION SYSTEM provides standard and individual profile services which are issued at weekly, two-week, and and four-week intervals. Standard profiles may be selected by International Patent Classification (IPC) and document type; individual profiles may be formulated by the subscriber to apply to a specific interest and are reformulated by staff. Searchable fields include document type, IPC, specification, abstract, priority, and cross-references. The SYSTEM will offer the following indexes to profile service subscribers on a semiannual or annual basis: applier; inventor; representative; IPC; and specification and/or abstract keyword. Bibliographic data and abstracts from the SYSTEM are available on magnetic tape and diskette.

Clientele/Availability: Services from the System are available without restrictions.

Contact: Hans W. Fock, President, Hartmann & Heenemann Computer Composition Center. (Telex 018 1291 SRZB D.)

★402★
GERMAN PLASTICS INSTITUTE
(Deutsches Kunststoff-Institut - DKI)
INFORMATION AND DOCUMENTATION SERVICES
(Dienstleistungen Information und Dokumentation)
Schlossgartenstr. 6 R   Phone: 06151 162206
D-6100 Darmstadt, Fed. Rep. of
   Germany   Service Est: 1955
Dietrich Braun, Director

Related Organizations: The German Plastics Institute is an establishment of the Plastics Research Society/ Forschungsgesellschaft Kunststoffe and provides information services in cooperation with the Chemical Information Center/ Fachinformationszentrum Chemie GmbH of Berlin.

Description of System or Service: The INFORMATION AND DOCUMENTATION SERVICES of the German Plastics Institute (DKI) provides a variety of information services in the area of high polymers, plastics, rubbers, and fiber materials. It abstracts articles from worldwide technical journals, publishes an abstracts journal, and maintains a computer-readable data base called the DKI-Dokumentation Kunststoffe Kautschuk Fasern (KKF). The SERVICES makes the data base available online and on magnetic tape, and offers computerized and manual literature searching, SDI, and document delivery services.

Scope and/or Subject Matter: Chemistry, physics, and science and technology of polymers including plastics, rubbers, and fiber materials.

Input Sources: Approximately 200 international technical and scientific journals are scanned regularly; input is also derived from conference proceedings, selected monographs, and German standards.

Holdings and Storage Media: The machine-readable DKI data base contains approximately 125,000 bibliographic items dating from 1973 to the present; abstracts are included since 1979. It is updated monthly with about 12,000 items added annually. A manual file contains 282,000 abstracts published in the Institute's journal since 1955. Library holdings consist of 10,000 bound volumes and subscriptions to 160 periodicals.

Publications: 1) Literatur-Schnelldienst Kunststoffe Kautschuk Fasern (monthly)—available by subscription; provides approximately 1000 references per issue. 2) DKI-Thesaurus—available for purchase.

Microform Products and Services: Abstracts are issued quarterly on microfiche and are available by subscription.

Computer-Based Products and Services: The DKI data base is available for online searching through FIZ-Technik and INKA (Informationssystem Karlsruhe). It contains descriptors and classifications as search aids. Computerized search services and SDI are offered by the Institute. Monthly magnetic tape services are also available.

Other Services: Additional services of the Institute include manual retrospective literature searches covering 1955 to the present.

Clientele/Availability: There are no restrictions on services, which are generally available on a subscription basis. Members receive a discount.

Contact: Jutta Wierer, Dipl.-Chem., German Plastics Institute.

★403★
GERMAN SOCIETY FOR CHEMICAL EQUIPMENT
(Deutsche Gesellschaft fur Chemisches Apparatewesen - DECHEMA)
INFORMATION SYSTEMS AND DATA BANKS DEPARTMENT
CHEMICAL TECHNOLOGY INFORMATION SYSTEM
(Informationssystem Chemische Technik)
Theodor-Heuss-Allee 25   Phone: 069 7564244
D-6000 Frankfurt am Main 97, Fed. Rep.
 of Germany
Dr. Reiner Eckermann, Department Head

Staff: 4 Information and library professional.

Description of System or Service: The CHEMICAL TECHNOLOGY INFORMATION SYSTEM collects, screens, and abstracts published literature relating to chemical technology and biotechnology. It makes this information available through the machine-readable DECHEMA Chemical Engineering and Biotechnology Abstracts Data Bank and a hardcopy equivalent. The data base is available on magnetic tape and is searchable online through commercial sources. Other services offered include computerized literature searching and SDI.

Scope and/or Subject Matter: Chemical engineering and biotechnology, including equipment, manufacturing, plant design and construction, computer-aided design, mathematical models and methods, laboratory techniques, analytical chemistry, safety, dangerous materials, pollution control, energy and raw materials supply and conservation, chemical reaction engineering, catalysis, unit operations, process dynamics and control, measurement, instruments, construction materials, corrosion, corrosion protection, and operating materials.

Input Sources: The System scans journals, books, and dissertations.

Holdings and Storage Media: The machine-readable DECHEMA data base holds 65,000 records for literature published since 1975; approximately 10,000 records are added each year. The System also maintains a library collection of 15,000 bound volumes and subscriptions to 250 periodicals.

Publications: 1) Chemical Engineering and Biotechnology Abstracts/ Das Konzentrat. Kurzberichte Chemische Technik und Biotechnologie (monthly)—publishes 8000 abstracts yearly classified under 8 subject sections; may be obtained by individual section or its entirety. 2) DECHEMA Thesaurus fur die Chemische Technik/ DECHEMA Thesaurus of Chemical Technology—contains approximately 26,000 descriptors.

Computer-Based Products and Services: The CHEMICAL TECHNOLOGY INFORMATION SYSTEM produces the DECHEMA Chemical Engineering and Biotechnology Abstracts Data Bank from which it offers literature searching and SDI services. The data base is available on magnetic tape and is searchable through FIZ Technik and INKA (Informationssystem Karlsruhe). Data elements include title in original language and in German, German-language abstract, language of publication, controlled terms, author, and source data. The SYSTEM also conducts searches of chemical and chemical technology data bases available through commercial vendors.

Clientele/Availability: Services and products are available without restrictions.

Contact: Dr. Reiner Eckermann, Head, Information Systems and Data Banks Department. (Telex 412 490 DCHA D.)

★404★
GERMAN SOCIETY FOR CHEMICAL EQUIPMENT
(Deutsche Gesellschaft fur Chemisches Apparatewesen - DECHEMA)
INFORMATION SYSTEMS AND DATA BANKS DEPARTMENT
DECHEMA SUBSTANCE DATA SERVICE
(DECHEMA Stoffdaten Dienst - DSD)
Theodor-Heuss-Allee 25   Phone: 069 7564244
D-6000 Frankfurt am Main 97, Fed. Rep.
 of Germany   Founded: 1974
Dr. Reiner Eckermann, Department Head

Staff: 3 Information and library professional; 1 management professional; 2 scientists.

Description of System or Service: The DECHEMA SUBSTANCE DATA SERVICE (DSD) collects, screens, analyzes, retrieves, and calculates thermophysical property data of chemical compounds and mixtures commonly found in chemical engineering. The SERVICE maintains the machine-readable DECHEMA Thermophysical Property Data Bank (DETHERM), which is used to provide data retrieval, calculation, and analysis services. DETHERM is also available on magnetic tape and as an online data bank.

Scope and/or Subject Matter: Thermophysical properties of chemical compounds and mixtures for any given fluid state, including PVT, thermodynamic, phase equilibrium, transport, surface, and safety data.

Input Sources: The Service regularly scans 80 periodicals; additional input is obtained from dissertations, data collections, and machine-readable data bases maintained by universities and chemical companies.

Holdings and Storage Media: The DECHEMA Thermophysical Property Data Bank is maintained in machine-readable form. The Service also has a collection of 600 bound volumes; microfiche; and subscriptions to 80 periodicals.

Publications: DECHEMA Chemistry Data Series—available for purchase. Covers various aspects of physical and thermophysical property data in two or three volumes each year.

Computer-Based Products and Services: The DECHEMA SUBSTANCE DATA SERVICE maintains the machine-readable DECHEMA Thermophysical Property Data Bank (DETHERM), which comprises three separate systems: 1) The Data Retrieval System (DETHERM-SDR) is used to collect and retrieve chemical data published in the literature. It holds data on the thermophysical properties of 1500 important chemical compounds and mixtures as published in more than 10,000 documents. Approximately 2000 documents are added annually. 2) The Data Calculation System (DETHERM-SDC) is used to calculate and predict pure substance and mixture data for any desired fluid state. It holds basic data for 550 chemical compounds and adds data on 50 compounds annually. 3) The Data Analysis System (DETHERM-SDA) is used to analyze physical data by means of statistical and regression methods and to evaluate thermodynamically consistent data sets. The SERVICE utilizes DETHERM to provide literature searches and data retrieval and analysis services on request. The data bank is also available for purchase on magnetic tape and the DETHERM-SDR and DETHERM-SDC files are searchable online through INKA (Informationssystem Karlsruhe). In addition, DETHERM's component systems and corresponding software programs are available for purchase.

Clientele/Availability: Services and products are available without restrictions.

Contact: Dr. Reiner Eckermann, Head, Information Systems and Data Banks Department. (Telex 412 490 DCHA D.)

★405★
GERMAN SOCIETY FOR CHEMICAL EQUIPMENT
(Deutsche Gesellschaft fur Chemisches Apparatewesen - DECHEMA)
INFORMATION SYSTEMS AND DATA BANKS DEPARTMENT
MATERIALS AND CORROSION INFORMATION SYSTEM
(Informationssystem Werkstoffe und Korrosion)
Theodor-Heuss-Allee 25   Phone: 069 7564244
D-6000 Frankfurt am Main 97, Fed. Rep.
   of Germany
Dr. Reiner Eckermann, Department Head

Staff: 2 Information and library professional.

Description of System or Service: The MATERIALS AND CORROSION INFORMATION SYSTEM collects, screens, and evaluates published data relating to corrosion and the behavior of materials in industrial equipment. It maintains the DECHEMA Corrosion Data Base (DECOR), a card index which holds bibliographic data and abstracts of literature published since 1970. DECOR is used to offer literature searching, SDI, and consulting services. The SERVICE also provides recommendations for the selection of materials for specific industrial applications.

Scope and/or Subject Matter: Materials and their properties, corrosive agents, corrosive behavior, corrosion protection, materials application in all industries.

Input Sources: Information for DECOR is gathered from journals, technical bulletins, monographs, and patents.

Holdings and Storage Media: The DECOR card index covers more than 180,000 documents published since 1970; approximately 15,000 records are added annually.

Publications: 1) Corrosion Data Sheets/ DECHEMA Werkstoff Tabelle—covers properties and corrosion behavior of materials in contact with 1000 specific corrosive agents; two supplements, each containing about 100 data sheets, are issued yearly. 2) Materials and Corrosion/ Werkstoffe und Korrosion (monthly)—issued in cooperation with Verlag Chemie, Weinheim, Federal Republic of Germany.

Computer-Based Products and Services: The System expects to convert the DECHEMA Corrosion Data Base to machine-readable form and make it accessible as an online data base in the near future.

Clientele/Availability: Services and products are available without restrictions.

Contact: Herbert Puschmann, Manager, Materials and Corrosion Information System; telephone 069 7564345. (Telex 412 490 DCHA D.)

★406★
GERMAN SOCIETY FOR CHEMICAL EQUIPMENT
(Deutsche Gesellschaft fur Chemisches Apparatewesen - DECHEMA)
INFORMATION SYSTEMS AND DATA BANKS DEPARTMENT
SUPPLY SOURCES INFORMATION SYSTEM
(Informationssystem Bezugsquellen)
Theodor-Heuss-Allee 25   Phone: 069 7564244
D-6000 Frankfurt am Main 97, Fed. Rep.
   of Germany
Dr. Reiner Eckermann, Department Head

Staff: 1 Management professional; 1 technician.

Description of System or Service: The SUPPLY SOURCES INFORMATION SYSTEM gathers information on chemical equipment manufacturers and suppliers, as well as product specifications, and maintains it in a computer-readable data base known as DEQUIP (DECHEMA Chemical Equipment Suppliers Data Base). The SYSTEM conducts searches of the data base on request.

Scope and/or Subject Matter: Manufacturers and suppliers of instruments, chemical equipment, and plants for laboratories and the chemical industry.

Input Sources: Information for DEQUIP is gathered directly from equipment suppliers, and from supplier guides, advertisements, and trade literature.

Holdings and Storage Media: The computer-readable DEQUIP data base holds approximately 16,000 records.

Computer-Based Products and Services: The SUPPLY SOURCES INFORMATION SYSTEM maintains the computer-readable DEQUIP data base, which is available online. The SYSTEM conducts searches of the data base on request.

Clientele/Availability: Services are available without restrictions.

Contact: Dr. Reiner Eckermann, Head, Information Systems and Data Banks Department. (Telex 412 490 DCHA D.)

★407★
GERMAN STANDARDS INSTITUTE
(Deutsches Institut fur Normung - DIN)
GERMAN INFORMATION CENTER FOR TECHNICAL RULES
(Deutsches Informationszentrum fur Technische Regeln - DITR)
Postfach 1107   Phone: 030 2601600
Burggrafenstr. 4-10   Service Est: 1972
D-1000 Berlin 30, Fed. Rep. of Germany
Curt Mohr, Technical Director

Staff: 6 Information and library professional; 2 management professional; 8 technicians; 4 sales and marketing; 7 clerical and nonprofessional; 3 other.

Description of System or Service: The GERMAN INFORMATION CENTER FOR TECHNICAL RULES (DITR) supplies information to the public on technical rules in force or in the draft stage in the Federal Republic of Germany. DITR maintains a computer-readable data bank on such rules and uses it to answer inquiries, provide SDI services, and produce lists and catalogs on magnetic tape and in hard copy. Online access to the data bank is also available.

Scope and/or Subject Matter: Technical rules including binding regulations, voluntary DIN standards, and specifications of other organizations.

Input Sources: Input consists of official bulletins and current information from publishers of technical rules.

Holdings and Storage Media: The computer-readable DITR data bank covers 36,000 current documents as well as approximately 23,000 technical rules no longer in force.

Publications: 1) DIN Catalogue (yearly with monthly updates); 2) DIN-Anzeiger fur Technische Regeln (monthly); 3) Catalogue on English Translations of German Standards.

Microform Products and Services: All DIN standards and legal and administrative regulations of a technical nature are available on microfiche.

Computer-Based Products and Services: The DITR data bank is accessible online and is used for inquiry answering and SDI. It also is used to produce the DIN Catalogue and to supply magnetic tapes.

Clientele/Availability: Products and services are available to all users of technical rules.

Contact: Juergen Koelling, German Information Center for Technical Rules. (Telex 185 269 DITR D.)

★408★
GERMANY
CENTER FOR AGRICULTURAL DOCUMENTATION AND INFORMATION
(Zentralstelle fur Agrardokumentation und -Information - ZADI)
Villichgasse 17   Phone: 0228 357097
D-5300 Bonn 2, Fed. Rep. of Germany   Service Est: 1969
Dr. E. Muller, Head

Staff: 13 Scientists; 20 other.

Related Organizations: The parent organizations of the Center are the Ministry for Food, Agriculture and Forestry/ Bundesministerium fur Ernahrung, Landwirtschaft und Forsten and the Federal Research Center for Nature Conservation and Landscape Ecology.

Description of System or Service: The CENTER FOR AGRICULTURAL DOCUMENTATION AND INFORMATION (ZADI) coordinates the efforts of 20 agricultural information centers in the Federal Republic of Germany. Each of the centers is responsible for collecting and evaluating German literature in a specific subject field for contribution to a national agricultural data base being established by ZADI. Additionally, ZADI implements, updates, and markets several national and international agricultural data bases that are made available online through a cooperative agreement with DIMDI. ZADI also provides search instruction and prepares documentation for these data bases.

Scope and/or Subject Matter: Agricultural science including plant breeding and production, grassland management, horticulture, protection of plants and stored products; food science, cereal and potato processing; soil sciences; economics, development, and rural sociology; animal production and veterinary science; forestry and lumber industry.

Input Sources: The 20 agricultural information centers submit bibliographic data via telecommunications to ZADI for further processing.

Publications: The Center publishes an annual directory of German research projects in the areas of agronomy, animal production and veterinary science, food science, and forestry, as well as a periodic list of related German research institutions. The Center also compiles bibliographies on relevant current topics. Additionally, data base search aids are published in German and English.

Computer-Based Products and Services: ZADI is responsible for the storage and online availability of the following data bases through DIMDI: International Information System for the Agricultural Sciences and Technology (AGRIS), Aquatic Sciences and Fisheries Abstracts (ASFA), Agricultural Research Projects (AGREP), Phytomedicine Data Base, and CAB (Commonwealth Agricultural Bureaux) Abstracts pertaining to plants. The ZADI national agricultural data base is also expected to be offered through DIMDI.

Clientele/Availability: Services are available to scientists, administration, industry, education, and consulting organizations.

Contact: Dr. K.O. von Selle, Center for Agricultural Documentation and Information.

★409★
GERMANY
FEDERAL BIOLOGICAL RESEARCH CENTER FOR AGRICULTURE AND FORESTRY
(Biologische Bundesanstalt fur Land- und Forstwirtschaft)
DOCUMENTATION CENTER FOR PHYTOMEDICINE
(Dokumentationsstelle fur Phytomedizin)
Konigin Luise Str. 19   Phone: 030 8304215
D-1000 Berlin 33, Fed. Rep. of Germany   Service Est: 1964
Prof. Wolfrudolf Laux, Head

Related Organizations: The Documentation Center works cooperatively with the Federal Biological Research Center library, the Information Center for Tropical Plant Protection (INTROP), and several other agricultural documentation centers in Germany.

Description of System or Service: The DOCUMENTATION CENTER FOR PHYTOMEDICINE provides information and documentation services in the areas of plant protection and phytopathology. A chief activity is publication of the quarterly Bibliography of Plant Protection and maintenance of a corresponding Phytomedicine Data Base/Database Phytomedizin. Computer search services are provided from this file and external online data bases.

Scope and/or Subject Matter: Phytomedicine (plant protection and phytopathology) and related fields in agriculture, biology, and chemistry.

Input Sources: Input is derived from relevant literature published worldwide.

Holdings and Storage Media: The computer-readable Phytomedicine Data Base holds 265,000 references; 15,000 new references are added annually. Library holdings include 60,000 bound volumes and 1500 current periodicals.

Publications: Bibliography of Plant Protection/ Bibliographie der Pflanzenschutzliteratur (4 issues per year)—available by subscription. Provides subject and author access; all article titles include an English translation.

Computer-Based Products and Services: The Phytomedicine Data Base, covering the literature from 1965 to the present, is held under GOLEM software for batch and online retrospective searching. The Center also conducts searches of external data bases.

Clientele/Availability: Services are available to plant pathologists, scientists, and nonscientists throughout the world.

Contact: Prof. Wolfrudolf Laux, Documentation Center for Phytomedicine.

★410★
GERMANY
FEDERAL EMPLOYMENT INSTITUTE
(Bundesanstalt fur Arbeit)
INSTITUTE FOR EMPLOYMENT RESEARCH
(Institut fur Arbeitsmarkt- und Berufsforschung - IAB)
INFORMATION AND DOCUMENTATION DEPARTMENT
(Informations- und Dokumentationsstelle)
Regensburger Str. 104   Phone: 0911 173016
D-8500 Nuremberg, Fed. Rep. of
    Germany
Gerd Peters, Head

Staff: 2 Information and library professional; 4 management professional; 1 technician; 10 clerical and nonprofessional.

Description of System or Service: The INFORMATION AND DOCUMENTATION DEPARTMENT is the central West German establishment for documentation of literature and research relating to the labor market. It maintains several computer files and offers publications and computer search services.

Scope and/or Subject Matter: Labor market theory and practice; market projections; business and regional research; vocational research and sociology; statistics.

Holdings and Storage Media: Holdings include machine-readable files and a library of 26,000 volumes and subscriptions to 700 periodicals.

Publications: 1) Literaturdokumentation zur Arbeitsmarkt- und Berufsforschung/ LitDok AB (annual)—provides references to monographs, periodical articles, and research reports. 2) Forschungsdokumentation zur Arbeitsmarkt- und Berufsforschung/ FoDok AB (three times per year)—identifies completed research projects.

Computer-Based Products and Services: The DEPARTMENT maintains three data bases documenting literature, research projects, and institutions and personnel. Retrospective searches and SDI are offered.

Clientele/Availability: Clients include German government and industry.

Contact: Gerd Peters, Head, Information and Documentation Department.

★411★
GERMANY
FEDERAL ENVIRONMENTAL AGENCY
(Umweltbundesamt)
ENVIRONMENTAL INFORMATION AND DOCUMENTATION SYSTEM
(Informations- und Dokumentationssystem Umwelt - UMPLIS)
Bismarckplatz 1   Phone: 030 8903291
D-1000 Berlin 33, Fed. Rep. of Germany   Service Est: 1974
Prof. Juergen Seggelke, Director

Staff: 15 Information and library professional; 1 management professional; 24 technicians; 2 sales and marketing; 10 clerical and nonprofessional.

Description of System or Service: The ENVIRONMENTAL INFORMATION AND DOCUMENTATION SYSTEM (UMPLIS) provides public and private users with information services in environmental and related subject areas. It provides information assistance for the coordination of environment-related research and development, and offers data processing support for relevant planning and policymaking. UMPLIS maintains a number of bibliographic and factual data bases and provides searches from these and externally generated files. It also issues publications and maintains a library.

Scope and/or Subject Matter: Environment, pollution, solid wastes, chemicals and solid wastes, environmental research, and related subjects.

Input Sources: Input is obtained from questionnaires, data exchanges, journals, research reports, books, conference papers, and worldwide patents.

Holdings and Storage Media: UMPLIS holds several data bases on machine-readable tape. Library holdings number 45,000 bound volumes and 98,000 microforms.

Publications: 1) Environmental Literature Information Service—contains references from approximately 250 publications; compiled from the ULIDAT data bank. 2) Environmental Research Catalogue—biannual printout from the UFORDAT data bank. 3) Inventory of Environmental Authorities—currently lists more than 700 authorities. 4) Inventory of Computer-aided Environmental Models.

Computer-Based Products and Services: UMPLIS maintains and provides search and SDI services from the following data bases (the first two of which are available online through Data-Star): 1) Data Bank for Environmental Literature (ULIDAT)—holds 40,000 bibliographic references to literature relating to the environment, particularly air, noise, water, solid waste, and environmental chemicals, with emphasis on German literature covering R&D projects sponsored by the German Ministry of Internal Affairs and the Federal Environmental Agency. 2) Data Bank for Environmental Research (UFORDAT)—provides information on 17,000 ongoing, planned, or completed environmental research and development projects in Germany and Austria. Produced in collaboration with the Austrian Ministry for Health Care. 3) Solid Waste Management Data Bank (AWIDAT)—details types of solid waste, recycling establishments, and relevant technologies. 4) Data Bank on Substances Harmful to Water (DABAWAS)—produced in cooperation with the Dortmund Institute for Water Research (see separate entry). Several other data systems are being developed, including the Information System for Environmental Chemicals, Chemical Plants, and Accidents (INFUCHS) and the Environment-related Hydrological Data Bank (HYDABA). Access to the external data bases is facilitated through a tape exchange program.

Clientele/Availability: Significant user groups and participators in UMPLIS are federal, state, and local governments; international scientific authorities and organizations; and the interested public. Services are available to public and private users as resources permit.

Contact: Juergen Seggelke, Director and Professor, or Peter Bialas, Environmental Information and Documentation System. (Telex 173 856 UBA D.)

★412★
GERMANY
FEDERAL INSTITUTE FOR GEOSCIENCES AND NATURAL RESOURCES
(Bundesanstalt fur Geowissenschaften und Rohstoffe - BGR)
GEOSCIENCE LITERATURE INFORMATION SERVICE
(Geowissenschaftlicher Literaturinformationsdienst)
Stilleweg 2, Postfach 510 153   Phone: 0511 6430
D-3000 Hannover 51, Fed. Rep. of
  Germany   Service Est: 1970
J. Nowak, Head

Staff: Approximately 14 total.

Related Organizations: The Geoscience Literature Information Service cooperates nationally with GEOFIZ and internationally with the American Geological Institute (AGI), the French Bureau of Geological and Mining Research (BRGM), and the French National Center for Scientific Research (CNRS).

Description of System or Service: The GEOSCIENCE LITERATURE INFORMATION SERVICE maintains the computer-readable GEOLINE data base to assist German researchers and other geoscience professionals in obtaining relevant literature of national and international scope. The data base contains German-language versions of geoscience information produced by foreign cooperating organizations, as well as additional data on German geological library holdings. The data base also incorporates HYDROLINE, a file covering the areas of water economy, hydrology, and hydrochemistry. The SERVICE provides computerized retrieval services from GEOLINE, and makes it available online through INKA (Informationssystem Karlsruhe). The SERVICE also issues abstracts journals.

Scope and/or Subject Matter: All aspects of geosciences, including geology, geophysics, paleontology, mineralogy, petrography, sedimentology, and geochemistry; water economy, hydrology, and hydrochemistry.

Input Sources: Input sources include journal articles, monographs, theses, and conference papers.

Holdings and Storage Media: The computer-readable GEOLINE data base holds more than 350,000 items dating from 1971 to the present. Approximately 300,000 of the most current records are accessible via INKA (Informationssystem Karlsruhe). The HYDROLINE file contains approximately 25,000 citations, of which the most current 3000 are searchable online through INKA.

Publications: 1) Journal of Geological Science/ Zentralblatt fur Geologie—an abstracts journal covering articles on geoscience which have appeared in German and Austrian scientific periodicals; available for purchase from Schweizerbart Publishers, Stuttgart, Federal Republic of Germany. 2) Bibliography of the Mediterranean Area.

Computer-Based Products and Services: The SERVICE provides online retrospective searches and SDI services from its GEOLINE data base. Output is provided on index cards and includes the following data elements: author, title, source, language of article and abstracts, German library location, keywords, and German standard map number for areas in Germany that are mentioned. GEOLINE and HYDROLINE data are also accessible online through INKA.

Clientele/Availability: Services are available without restrictions to researchers, other geoscience professionals, and to other interested persons.

Contact: J. Nowak, Head, Geoscience Literature Information Service. (Telex 923730.)

★413★
GERMANY
FEDERAL INSTITUTE FOR GEOSCIENCES AND NATURAL RESOURCES
(Bundesanstalt fur Geowissenschaften und Rohstoffe - BGR)
MARINE INFORMATION AND DOCUMENTATION SYSTEM
Am Klagesmarkt 14-17   Phone: 0511 1064398
D-3000 Hannover 1, Fed. Rep. of
  Germany   Service Est: 1972
Andreas Billib, Head

Staff: Approximately 4 total.

Related Organizations: Affiliated organizations include GEOFIZ and the Cooperative Group for Marine Research and Marine Technology Information/ Arbeitsgemeinschaft Information Meeresforschung und Meerestechnik (AIM).

Description of System or Service: The MARINE INFORMATION AND DOCUMENTATION SYSTEM provides access to relevant German literature in the areas of marine research and technology through maintenance of a computer-readable abstracting and indexing data base.

Scope and/or Subject Matter: Marine research and technology, marine mineral resources, offshore and diving technology, desalination, marine law.

Input Sources: Journal articles, theses, conference papers, and similar works are indexed and abstracted for inclusion in the data base.

Holdings and Storage Media: The System's computer-readable bibliographic data base covers approximately 17,000 documents.

Publications: Literature Documentation of the International Law of the Sea.

Computer-Based Products and Services: The bibliographic marine research and technology data base is available online through the computer center of the Federal Institute for Geosciences and Natural Resources and through INKA (Informationssystem Karlsruhe). The System offers retrospective literature searching and SDI services from it.

Clientele/Availability: Services are intended for industrial clientele, universities, and the public.

Contact: Dipl. Geol. Andreas Billib, Head, Marine Information and Documentation System. (Telex 922739 GFIZ HA D.)

★414★
GERMANY
FEDERAL INSTITUTE FOR GEOSCIENCES AND NATURAL RESOURCES
(Bundesanstalt fur Geowissenschaften und Rohstoffe - BGR)
SEISMOLOGICAL CENTRAL OBSERVATORY GRF
(Seismologisches Zentralobservatorium GRF)
Krankenhausstr. 1-3 Phone: 09131 25900
D-8520 Erlangen, Fed. Rep. of Germany
Dr. Helmut Aichele, Head

Description of System or Service: The SEISMOLOGICAL CENTRAL OBSERVATORY GRF collects and processes digital seismic data from seismological stations in the Federal Republic of Germany. The OBSERVATORY exchanges these data with international data centers and issues publications.

Scope and/or Subject Matter: Seismic data.

Input Sources: Data are acquired through continuous seismic monitoring and international exchanges.

Holdings and Storage Media: The Observatory maintains a Digital Data File consisting of 6000 computer tapes and dating from 1976 to the present.

Publications: Data catalogs, lists, bulletins, and other publications are issued.

Computer-Based Products and Services: The Seismological Central Observatory uses a data acquisition system for the exchange and processing of digital seismic data.

Clientele/Availability: Users include governmental, university, and institutional scientific investigators in the Federal Republic of Germany.

Contact: Dr. Helmut Aichele, Head, Seismological Central Observatory GRF. (Telex 629706.)

★415★
GERMANY
FEDERAL INSTITUTE FOR MATERIALS TESTING
(Bundesanstalt fur Materialprufung - BAM)
MEASUREMENT OF MECHANICAL QUANTITIES DOCUMENTATION
(Dokumentation Messen Mechanischer Grossen)
Unter den Eichen 87 Phone: 030 81046101
D-1000 Berlin 45, Fed. Rep. of Germany Service Est: 1973
Wilfried Schulze, Dipl-Ing.

Staff: 1 Information and library professional; 1 technician; 1 sales and marketing.

Description of System or Service: The MEASUREMENT OF MECHANICAL QUANTITIES DOCUMENTATION abstracts and indexes the world's literature relating to measurements in industry. It disseminates this information through a quarterly abstracts journal, and through computerized searches of a corresponding data base. Other services include consulting, manual literature searching, referrals, and document delivery.

Scope and/or Subject Matter: Measurement of mechanical quantities in the industrial field, including such aspects as time, temperature, humidity, velocity, acceleration, force, pressure, and weight; measurement systems; instrument methods; equipment, including such aspects as electrical, mechanical, acoustical, fluidic, and optical transducers; signal processing and display.

Input Sources: Input for the abstracts journal is gathered from 120 periodicals, plus standards, patent specifications, and reports. Additional data are obtained from secondary sources including commercially available data bases.

Holdings and Storage Media: The bibliographic Measurement of Mechanical Quantities data base is maintained in machine-readable form.

Publications: Measurement of Mechanical Quantities (quarterly)—includes more than 800 abstracts annually. Each issue contains author and keyword indexes which are cumulated annually. Abstracts are in German with English subtitles.

Computer-Based Products and Services: The service conducts searches of its own data base as well as the INSPEC, DOMA, NTIS, COMPENDEX, SDIM, and other commercially available data bases.

Clientele/Availability: Services are available without restrictions.

Remarks: The service was formerly known as the Electrical Measurement of Mechanical Quantities Documentation.

Contact: Wilfried Schulze, Dipl.-Ing., Measurement of Mechanical Quantities Documentation.

★416★
GERMANY
FEDERAL INSTITUTE FOR MATERIALS TESTING
(Bundesanstalt fur Materialprufung - BAM)
NONDESTRUCTIVE TESTING DOCUMENTATION
(Dokumentation Zerstorungsfreie Prufung - ZfP)
Unter den Eichen 87 Phone: 030 81046201
D-1000 Berlin 45, Fed. Rep. of Germany Service Est: 1976
Dr. Uta Volkel, Head

Staff: 2 Information and library professional; 3 other.

Related Organizations: Nondestructive Testing Documentation is jointly produced by Bundesanstalt fur Materialprufung (BAM) and Deutsche Gesellschaft fur Zerstorungsfreie Prufung.

Description of System or Service: NONDESTRUCTIVE TESTING DOCUMENTATION (ZfP) abstracts and indexes the world's literature related to nondestructive testing problems. It disseminates this information through a bimonthly abstracts journal and through computerized searches of a corresponding data base. Other services include consulting, manual literature searching, referrals, current awareness profiles, bibliographies for special problems of nondestructive testing, and document delivery.

Scope and/or Subject Matter: Nondestructive testing, including materials evaluation and monitoring, problems concerning principles of testing, and development of new techniques, equipment, and applications. Also included are acoustic emission testing and industrial radiation protection problems.

Input Sources: Input is derived from approximately 180 periodicals, plus standards, patent specifications, and reports. Additional data are obtained from secondary sources including commercially available data bases.

Holdings and Storage Media: The computer-readable Nondestructive Testing Documentation data base holds approximately 21,000 references dating from 1956 to the present.

Publications: 1) Referateorgan Zerstorungsfreie Prufung/ Non-Destructive Testing Abstracts Journal (6 issues per year)—available by subscription. Includes more than 1200 abstracts annually. Each issue contains author and keyword indexes which are cumulated annually in the final issue. Titles are given in English and German; abstracts are primarily in German. 2) Thesaurus Zerstorungsfreie Prufung—available for purchase.

Computer-Based Products and Services: The NONDESTRUCTIVE TESTING DOCUMENTATION data base is used to produce publications and to conduct computerized literature searching. Information from the data base is also searchable as part of the System for Documentation and Information in Metallurgy (SDIM) data base, which is available online through INKA (Informationssystem Karlsruhe).

Clientele/Availability: Services are available without restrictions.

Contact: Dr. Uta Volkel, Head, Nondestructive Testing Documentation. (Telex 183 261 BAMB D.)

★417★
GERMANY
FEDERAL INSTITUTE FOR MATERIALS TESTING
(Bundesanstalt fur Materialprufung - BAM)
RHEOLOGY AND TRIBOLOGY DOCUMENTATION CENTER
(Dokumentationstelle Rheologie und Tribologie)
Unter den Eichen 87
D-1000 Berlin 45, Fed. Rep. of Germany
Phone: 030 81045201
Service Est: 1954

Staff: 6 Total.

Related Organizations: The Rheology and Tribology Documentation Center receives support from the Deutsche Rheologische Gesellschaft.

Description of System or Service: The RHEOLOGY AND TRIBOLOGY DOCUMENTATION CENTER scans, records, classifies, stores, and disseminates information on rheology, which is the science of material deformation and flow, and tribology, which deals with the design, friction, wear, and lubrication of interacting surfaces. It publishes annual bibliographies in each field and maintains corresponding computer-readable data bases from which it provides information retrieval, SDI, and special bibliographies. The data bases are also publicly available online through INKA (Informationssystem Karlsruhe) as the Rheology Data Base and Tribology Index. Additionally, the CENTER offers research services, consulting, referrals, and conferences.

Scope and/or Subject Matter: Rheology, including rheological properties and rheometry of liquids, solids, gases, and dispersed and granular systems; tribology, including general tribology, experimental methods and equipment, materials and combinations of materials, lubrication, and fields of application.

Input Sources: Information is derived from approximately 400 international journals and abstracts services, and from books, collections, encyclopedias, monographs, proceedings, reports, dissertations, bibliographies, preprints, standards, test methods, and brochures.

Holdings and Storage Media: The machine-readable Rheology Data Base holds 33,000 records since 1976; the Tribology Index data base contains 47,000 records since 1972. Approximately 5000 records are added to each file annually. Additionally, the Center maintains bibliographic card files dating from 1945 to the present and containing more than 124,000 rheology and 105,000 tribology records.

Publications: 1) Dokumentation Rheologie/ Documentation Rheology (annual)—title bibliography covering world literature on rheology. Includes subject classification, subject index, cross references, personal and corporate author indexes, conference index, standard number index, and report index. Published since 1954. 2) Documentation Tribology (annual)—title bibliography to all literature in the field; published since 1967. Relevant information in both bibliographies is provided in English. The publications are available by subscription.

Computer-Based Products and Services: The Rheology Data Base and Tribology Index are accessible online through INKA (Informationssystem Karlsruhe), a host on Euronet DIANE and Datex-P. Data elements present in the files include title, author, source citation, and descriptors. The CENTER provides information retrieval and SDI services from the data bases and utilizes them to publish annual and special bibliographies.

Clientele/Availability: Services are available without restrictions. Users include organizations and individuals involved in materials technology and chemical engineering, food technology, biology, medicine, and other fields.

Contact: Dr.-Ing. Edith Rudolph, Head, Rheology; or Dipl.-Phys. Harald Tischer, Head, Tribology. (Telex 183 261 BAMB D.)

★418★
GERMANY
FEDERAL INSTITUTE FOR MATERIALS TESTING
(Bundesanstalt fur Materialprufung - BAM)
WELDING DOCUMENTATION
(Dokumentation Schweisstechnik - DS)
Unter den Eichen 87
D-1000 Berlin 45, Fed. Rep. of Germany
Helmut Barthelmess, Graduate Engineer
Phone: 030 81046401
Service Est: 1956

Staff: 4 Scientists.

Related Organizations: Welding Documentation is jointly supported by Bundesanstalt fur Materialprufung (BAM), Deutscher Verband fur Schweisstechnik (DVS), and Dokumentation Maschinenbau und Metallbearbeitung (DOMA).

Description of System or Service: WELDING DOCUMENTATION (DS) collects, abstracts, and indexes the world's literature on welding. It maintains a computer-readable data base of this information, and provides an abstracts journal, bibliographies, standard interest profiles, and retrospective literature searching. DS also provides users with document delivery services for a fee.

Scope and/or Subject Matter: Welding, soldering and brazing, adhesive bonding, and other allied processes.

Input Sources: Input is gathered from technical books and periodicals, patent specifications, standards, and reports worldwide.

Holdings and Storage Media: The computer-readable bibliographic DS data base contains more than 77,000 citations covering literature published from 1956 to the present.

Publications: 1) Referateorgan Schweissen und Verwandte Verfahren/ Welding and Allied Processes Abstracts Journal (every 2 months)—available by subscription. Includes approximately 1500 abstracts annually, arranged in 26 subject groups. Each issue includes cumulative author and keyword indexes. 2) Standard-Profildienst Schweisstechnik/ Welding Standard Profile Service (annual)—computer-produced lists, available in 12 welding-related subject areas, containing bibliographic information from the preceding year. DS also makes available for purchase numerous retrospective subject bibliographies.

Computer-Based Products and Services: The WELDING DOCUMENTATION conducts retrospective searching of its data base. DS bibliographic information is also searchable online as part of the DOMA data base, available through FIZ Technik, and as part of the SDIM2 data base, available through INKA (Informationssystem Karlsruhe).

Other Services: Additional services include manual literature searching and referrals. DS also performs in-depth searches which include checking related subject areas and consultation with qualified scientists.

Clientele/Availability: Services are available on a fee basis to all interested persons.

Contact: Helmut Barthelmess, Graduate Engineer, Welding Documentation. (Telex 183 261 BAMB D.)

★419★
GERMANY
FEDERAL INSTITUTE FOR OCCUPATIONAL SAFETY
(Bundesanstalt fur Arbeitsschutz)
INFORMATION AND DOCUMENTATION CENTRE FOR OCCUPATIONAL SAFETY
(Informations- und Dokumentationszentrum fur Arbeitsschutz)
Vogelpothsweg 50-52
Postfach 17 02 02
D-4600 Dortmund 17 (Dorstfeld), Fed. Rep. of Germany
Phone: 0231 17631
Service Est: 1972

Staff: 10 Information and library professional; 1 management professional; 2 technicians.

Related Organizations: The Institute is supported by the Bundesministerium fur Arbeit und Sozialordnung (BMA) and serves as the national center for the International Occupational Safety and Health Information Centre/ Centre International d'Informations de Securite ed d'Hygiene du Travail (CIS).

Description of System or Service: The INFORMATION AND DOCUMENTATION CENTRE FOR OCCUPATIONAL SAFETY provides documentation and information services dealing with occupational safety and health. It abstracts and indexes current periodical and research report literature, and stores this information in the computer-readable LITDOK (Literaturdokumentation) data base, which is used to provide computerized searches and to produce publications. Document delivery services are also supplied from a microfiche file of journal articles. For older material not covered by LITDOK, the CENTRE maintains a card file of 130,000 references from which manual searches are provided.

Scope and/or Subject Matter: Occupational safety and health; humanization of work; ergonomics.

Input Sources: Input is derived from research reports and approximately 200 periodical titles.

Holdings and Storage Media: The machine-readable LITDOK data base holds approximately 10,000 records from 1973 to the present. Library holdings number 28,000 bound volumes; 13,000 items of other material; and subscriptions to 450 periodicals.

Publications: Dokumentation Arbeitsmedizin/ Documentation Occupational Health (10 per year)—produced in cooperation with the Institute for Documentation and Information in Social Medicine and Public Health/ Institut fur Dokumentation und Information uber Sozialmedizin und Offentliches Gesundheitswesen (IDIS) and the German Institute for Medical Documentation and Information/ Deutsches Institut fur Medizinische Dokumentation und Information (DIMDI). Available by subscription from IDIS (see separate entry).

Microform Products and Services: The Centre maintains a microfiche file of original articles published since 1973 and provides microfiche or paper copies from it on request.

Computer-Based Products and Services: The CENTRE conducts online retrospective searches of the LITDOK data base containing abstracts, descriptors, and other bibliographic data from research reports and relevant periodical literature.

Other Services: Additional services offered by the Centre include consulting, research, SDI, manual and computerized literature searching, referrals, and photocopying.

Clientele/Availability: Services are available to the public.

Remarks: Other data bases maintained or developed by the Institute include FODOK (Forschungsprojektdokumentation) and SIDOK (Sicherheitstechnische Dokumentation). FODOK documents approximately 2000 ongoing and completed research projects in occupational safety and health carried out by the Institute and other German institutions. SIDOK, maintained in cooperation with the German Institute for Standardization (DIN), documents laws and regulations relating to safety at work and elsewhere. More information on these files may be obtained by contacting the Institute at the address given above.

Contact: Information and Documentation Centre for Occupational Safety, Federal Institute for Occupational Safety. (Telex 822 153.)

★420★
GERMANY
FEDERAL INSTITUTE FOR SPORTS SCIENCE
(Bundesinstitut fur Sportwissenschaft)
DOCUMENTATION AND INFORMATION DIVISION
(Fachbereich Dokumentation und Information)
SPORT AND SPORTS-SCIENTIFIC INFORMATION SYSTEM
(Sport und Sportwissenschaftliche Informationssystem - SUSIS)
Hertzstr. 1   Phone: 02234 76011
D-5000 Cologne 40, Fed. Rep. of
  Germany   Service Est: 1971
Siegfried Lachenicht, Division Director

Description of System or Service: The SPORT AND SPORTS-SCIENTIFIC INFORMATION SYSTEM (SUSIS) was established to document international sports literature, data, and research projects. SUSIS maintains the Sportliteratur (SPOLIT) data base, a machine-readable file of bibliographic documentation, and provides computerized search services. The System also utilizes the data base in the compilation of documentation studies on special topics and in the publication of an abstracts journal.

Scope and/or Subject Matter: Sports and sports science, including sporting events, individual athlete performances, sports medicine, and other topics.

Input Sources: Bibliographic input is derived from 650 international journals, monographs, theses, and conference proceedings; data are gathered from sporting events records, individual athlete performance records, physical examination records, and sports injury records.

Holdings and Storage Media: The machine-readable SPOLIT data base contains 18,000 references. SUSIS also maintains a library of 10,500 bound volumes, 25,000 reprinted journal articles, and subscriptions to 650 periodicals.

Publications: Sportdokumentation: Literatur der Sportwissenschaft (every two months)—each issue contains bibliographic citations and abstracts of current literature arranged within subject categories; reviews of new publications; a table of contents section; subject index; and author index. Indexes are cumulated annually in the last issue of the year.

Computer-Based Products and Services: SUSIS offers computerized searching of its bibliographic Sportliteratur (SPOLIT) data base. Machine-readable tapes of all SUSIS data are available for purchase.

Other Services: In addition to the services described above, consulting services are offered.

Clientele/Availability: Services are provided to researchers, those involved with legislation concerning sports, trainers, teachers, students, athletes, sports officials, and sports reporters.

Contact: Siegfried Lachenicht, Director, Documentation and Information Division.

★421★
GERMANY
FEDERAL RESEARCH CENTER FOR FISHERIES
(Bundesforschungsanstalt fur Fischerei)
INFORMATION AND DOCUMENTATION CENTER
(Informations- und Dokumentationsstelle)
Palmaille 9   Phone: 040 38905113
D-2000 Hamburg 50, Fed. Rep. of
  Germany   Service Est: 1968
Dr. Wulf P. Kirchner, Head

Staff: 9 Information and library professional.

Related Organizations: The Federal Research Center for Fisheries receives support from the German Ministry for Food, Agriculture and and Forestry/ Bundesministerium fur Ernahrung, Landwirtschaft und Forsten.

Description of System or Service: The INFORMATION AND DOCUMENTATION CENTER collects, processes, and disseminates research literature and other significant documentation in support of the activities of the Federal Research Center for Fisheries. It maintains an extensive library and accesses major online data bases to provide retrospective searches and SDI services. The CENTER also prepares input from the German-language literature for the international Aquatic Sciences and Fisheries Information System (ASFIS).

Scope and/or Subject Matter: Research in the areas of fisheries, marine biology, limnology, aquaculture, ichthyology, and related sciences.

Holdings and Storage Media: Library holdings include 55,000 bound volumes.

Computer-Based Products and Services: The Center provides retrospective searching and SDI services from major online data bases. It also maintains its periodicals catalog and several bibliographies in machine-readable form for publication purposes.

Other Services: Also provided are hardcopy or microfiche duplication services.

Clientele/Availability: Services are intended for the German fisheries research community, but are available without restrictions to the public.

Contact: Dr. Wulf P. Kirchner, Head, Information and Documentation Center. (Telex 2157 16 BFAFI.)

★422★
GERMANY
GERMAN FEDERAL DIET
(Deutscher Bundestag)
DIVISION OF SCIENTIFIC DOCUMENTATION
DOCUMENTATION AND INFORMATION SYSTEM FOR PARLIAMENTARY MATERIALS (DIP)
Bundeshaus Phone: 0228 161
D-5300 Bonn, Fed. Rep. of Germany Service Est: 1973

Staff: Approximately 200 total in the Division.

Related Organizations: The Documentation and Information System for Parliamentary Materials was developed and is maintained in cooperation with the German Federal Council (Bundesrat).

Description of System or Service: The DOCUMENTATION AND INFORMATION SYSTEM FOR PARLIAMENTARY MATERIALS (DIP) is a computerized information system providing documentation of German parliamentary processes. The essential features of the System are: an administrative data base recording complete processes in addition to single documents; abstracting and indexing using descriptor terms from the Thesaurus for Parliamentary Materials (PARTHES); the automated production of printed subject and speaker registers; and the provision of information retrieval.

Scope and/or Subject Matter: Documentation of parliamentary materials and provision of information on parliamentary processes.

Input Sources: Input is obtained from parliamentary papers and minutes of debates.

Holdings and Storage Media: Approximately 15,000 parliamentary documentation units are processed and stored annually. Stored data are accumulated in files encompassing one legislative term (normally four years).

Publications: 1) Register of Parliamentary Processes in the German Federal Diet and Federal Council/ Register zu den Verhandlungen des Deutschen Bundestages und des Bundesrates (annual)—a two-volume, subject and speaker register produced in book form on the basis of data stored in DIP. Provides documentation of parliamentary processes and the activities of members of Parliament. 2) Status of Federal Legislation/ Stand der Gesetzgebung des Bundes-GESTA (updated every two weeks)—loose-leaf bulletin.

Microform Products and Services: The Thesaurus for Parliamentary Materials is issued in microform for in-house use.

Computer-Based Products and Services: The Documentation and Information System for Parliamentary Materials is used for general document processing, information retrieval, register and index card production, and other functions. Search services conducted by DIP staff are provided for Parliament members and the general public. The computer-readable Thesaurus for Parliamentary Materials (PARTHES) supplies data support to the other program functions, including register production. The thesaurus contains 18,000 items and features more than 150,000 connective links between the various items listed.

Clientele/Availability: Services are intended for use by the federal and state parliaments; they are also available to the public upon request.

Remarks: The development of the Documentation and Information System for Parliamentary Materials was assisted by the Gesellschaft fur Mathematik und Datenverarbeitung (GMD) of the Federal Republic of Germany.

Contact: Dr. H. Schepers, Division of Scientific Documentation, German Federal Diet; telephone 0228 165167.

★423★
GERMANY
GERMAN NATIONAL LIBRARY
(Deutsche Bibliothek)
BIBLIO-DATA
Zeppelinallee 4-8 Phone: 069 75661
D-6000 Frankfurt am Main 1, Fed. Rep. of Germany Service Est: 1966
Dr. Reinhard Buchbinder, Central Services

Related Organizations: BIBLIO-DATA was developed by the Deutsche Bibliothek in cooperation with the Gesellschaft fur Information und Dokumentation, Sektion fur Technik (GID-SfT), and with support of the German Ministry for Research and Technology.

Description of System or Service: BIBLIO-DATA is the national bibliographical data bank for Germany. It covers more than 1 million German or German-language books, theses, maps, periodicals, and other items issued since 1966. BIBLIO-DATA is available online for both information retrieval and cataloging applications. Information from the data base is also available in the hardcopy Deutsche Bibliographie publication series and on magnetic tape.

Scope and/or Subject Matter: Publications in all subject areas published in Germany or in the German language.

Input Sources: Input is derived from publications acquired by the Library.

Holdings and Storage Media: Machine-readable BIBLIO-DATA files cover more than 1.2 million titles; information on approximately 100,000 new titles is added annually.

Publications: Deutsche Bibliographie—the national bibliography of the Federal Republic of Germany, comprising various sections and cumulations including the following: weekly lists of new publications and editions; weekly CIP lists of forthcoming publications; semiannual and five-year cumulations; lists of periodicals, government publications, theses, phonograph records, and music scores; and miscellaneous bibliographies and other publications.

Computer-Based Products and Services: The BIBLIO-DATA data base is maintained by the Library under DIMDI's GRIPS (General Relation Based Information Processing System) software. Searchable data elements in the file include author, publisher, ISBN, subject headings, subject group, systematic number, country code, and others. BIBLIO-DATA is publicly accessible online through INKA (Informationssystem Karlsruhe). Magnetic tapes of bibliographic records are available by subscription from the Library.

Clientele/Availability: Products and services are available without restrictions.

Contact: Dr. Reinhard Buchbinder, Central Services, Deutsche Bibliothek.

★424★
GERMANY
MINISTRY FOR RESEARCH AND TECHNOLOGY
(Bundesministerium fur Forschung und Technologie - BMFT)
ONGOING RESEARCH PROJECT DATA BANK
(Datenbank fur Forderungsvorhaben - DAVOR)
Heinemannstr. 2 Phone: 0228 593375
D-5300 Bonn 2, Fed. Rep. of Germany Service Est: 1972
Hans-Peter Heinrich, Director

Description of System or Service: The ONGOING RESEARCH PROJECT DATA BANK (DAVOR) is a computer-readable file providing comprehensive data on research projects funded by the German Ministry for Research and Technology (BMFT). It is used to produce printed catalogs, to provide search services, and to perform statistical analyses.

Scope and/or Subject Matter: Research in the physical, life, and social sciences.

Holdings and Storage Media: DAVOR is maintained in machine-readable form.

Publications: BMFT Forderungskatalog (annual). Regional surveys are also prepared.

Computer-Based Products and Services: Search services from

DAVOR are provided on request. Data elements present in the file include the following: project title, general project summary, and project objects; principal investigator and coinvestigators; performing and supporting organization names and addresses; research program of which project is a part; contract, grant, or project number assigned; project start and end dates; funding; and subject descriptors or keywords.

Clientele/Availability: Services are available to national government agencies and national, foreign, and international organizations. Services are provided at no charge.

Remarks: The BMFT also maintains the DAKOR data base system, which provides information on the projects of the other Federal Ministries.

Contact: Hans-Peter Heinrich, Director, Ongoing Research Project Data Bank.

★425★
GERMANY
MINISTRY OF ECONOMICS
(Bundesministerium fur Wirtschaft)
GERMAN FOREIGN TRADE INFORMATION OFFICE
(Bundesstelle fur Aussenhandelsinformation - BfAi)
Postfach 108007   Phone: 0221 20571
Blaubach 13   Service Est: 1951
D-5000 Cologne, Fed. Rep. of Germany
Dr. Peter Bohm, Director
Staff: 150 Total.

Description of System or Service: The GERMAN FOREIGN TRADE INFORMATION OFFICE (BfAi) provides foreign market information to existing and potential exporters, importers, and investors; establishes contacts worldwide to obtain needed information; and analyzes incoming information and efficiently presents it to interested persons. BfAi works with all relevant national and international authorities, trade associations, chambers of commerce, institutes, and companies. It maintains its own network of economic correspondents worldwide, and analyzes reports sent in by official delegates of the Federal Republic of Germany. The OFFICE issues publications, answers inquiries, maintains a library, and has implemented a data base to provide computerized information retrieval.

Scope and/or Subject Matter: Economic situations and development of markets abroad; commercial activities and business possibilities of foreign markets; nontariff barriers as they influence international trade and commercial relations; business and investment laws and acts; regulations and administrative acts regarding importing; and fiscal and customs regulations and laws.

Input Sources: Input is obtained from reports from correspondents; official reports from national and international organizations; and about 2000 economic newspapers worldwide.

Holdings and Storage Media: Library collection contains 14,000 volumes; approximately 450,000 document extracts; documents on microfilm; and 2600 subscriptions to periodicals. The BfAi also maintains documentation information on magnetic tape.

Publications: 1) Foreign Trade News/ Nachrichten fur Aussenhandel-NfA (five per week)—provides articles and reports on all aspects of foreign trade, including macroeconomic trends, specific industry trends and situations, marketing, law, customs, and procedural questions. Published jointly with Vereinigte Wirtschaftsdienste (VWD). 2) Statistical Economic Documentation/ Statistische Wirtschaftsdokumentation (StaWiDoc)—an ongoing series of market reports. 3) General Documentation on Trade and Economics/ Allgemeine Wirtschaftsdokumentation- AWiDoc (fortnightly)—indexes all new documents received by BfAi. Additionally, BfAi publishes reports dealing with legal, customs, and tariff information.

Computer-Based Products and Services: BfAi expects to provide direct online access to its library and documentation files and to offer computerized SDI services by specific geographic or subject area. Additionally, BfAi publications are computer typeset.

Clientele/Availability: Services are available without restrictions; chief clients are organizations involved in international trade.

Contact: Albert Gerhards, High Councillor, German Foreign Trade Information Office. (Telex 08 882 735 BFAK D.)

★426★
GERMANY
MINISTRY OF JUSTICE
(Bundesministerium der Justiz)
JUDICIAL INFORMATION SYSTEM
(Juristisches Informationssystem - JURIS)
Heinemannstr. 6   Phone: 0228 5814715
Postfach 20 06 50
D-5300 Bonn 2, Fed. Rep. of Germany
Werner Stewen, Head
Staff: 50 Total.

Description of System or Service: The JUDICIAL INFORMATION SYSTEM (JURIS) is a computerized judicial documentation system covering German court decisions, legal literature, and laws and regulations. It is maintained online by the Ministry of Justice.

Scope and/or Subject Matter: Jurisprudence in Germany, including fiscal, social, private, and other areas.

Input Sources: Input is derived directly from German court cases and federal laws, as well as from more than 500 periodicals.

Holdings and Storage Media: JURIS information is maintained in machine-readable files.

Computer-Based Products and Services: JURIS files are held under GOLEM/ Passat software and are accessible through a dedicated network operated by the Ministry of Justice and through direct dial.

Clientele/Availability: Chief clients are courts, administration, parliaments, and legal professions.

Contact: Werner Stewen, Ministry of Justice. (Telex 8869679; Telefax 584525.)

★427★
GERMANY
MINISTRY OF POSTS AND TELECOMMUNICATIONS
(Bundesministerium fur Post- und Fernmeldewesen)
GERMAN FEDERAL POSTAL SERVICE
(Deutsche Bundespost)
BILDSCHIRMTEXT (BTX)
Referat 251   Phone: 0228 142510
Postfach 8001   Service Est: 1983
D-5300 Bonn, Fed. Rep. of Germany
Eric Danke
Staff: 10 Management professional; 100 technicians; 300 sales and marketing; 300 clerical and nonprofessional.

Description of System or Service: BILDSCHIRMTEXT (Btx) is a publicly accessible videotex information and communication service established for the following purposes: to serve as a technical basis for the provision of information services to businesses and consumers; to permit access to privately owned computers for booking, orders, home banking, data bank inquiries, and other computer applications involving the use of optical display devices; and to support communication services between subscribers. Following field trials in Berlin and Dusseldorf, BILDSCHRIMTEXT was officially opened in late 1983 for general access throughout the Federal Republic of Germany. Subscribers with a suitably equipped Btx color television receiver can access the service via their local telephone network. BILDSCHIRMTEXT provides users with hundreds of thousands of pages of information and a variety of interactive services.

Scope and/or Subject Matter: Videotex information and communications for business and consumers; among the topics covered are stock exchanges and foreign currency information, airport arrivals and departures, hotels and restaurants, travel information, advertising and product information, telephone directories, education, social statistics, and many others.

Input Sources: Approximately 2600 private and public enterprises and institutions are information providers for the Bildschirmtext system.

Holdings and Storage Media: Btx holds several hundred thousand pages for public access.

Publications: Bildschirmtext Magazin fur Teleleser (every six weeks)—provides articles and reviews of new and existing Btx services and items related to videotex; available for purchase from Neue Mediengesellschaft, Postfach 1111, D-7900 Ulm, Fed. Rep. of Germany.

Computer-Based Products and Services: BILDSCHIRMTEXT provides information retrieval and other remote data processing and communication services, including electronic mail. Using keypads and color television receivers, subscribers can access the system to retrieve information by page number or through tree-structured indexes. BILDSCHIRMTEXT offers a number of features for information providers, including: online editing, response frames for orders and messages from subscribers, and continuous compilation of page usage statistics. Additionally, information providers can make their own computer facilities remotely accessible to subscribers through BILDSCHIRMTEXT and the Datex network. Currently, 73 external computers are registered with Btx.

Other Services: Closed user group facilities are also offered.

Clientele/Availability: Bildschirmtext is publicly available in the Federal Republic of Germany.

Contact: Eric Danke, Ministry of Posts and Telecommunications. (Telex 419511.)

★428★
GERMANY
MINISTRY OF YOUTH, FAMILY AND HEALTH
(Bundesministerium fur Jugend, Familie und Gesundheit)
GERMAN INSTITUTE FOR MEDICAL DOCUMENTATION AND INFORMATION
(Deutsches Institut fur Medizinische Dokumentation und Information - DIMDI)

Weisshausstr. 27
Postfach 420580
D-5000 Cologne 41, Fed. Rep. of Germany
Dr. Rolf Fritz, President

Phone: 0221 47241
Service Est: 1969

Staff: Approximately 90 total.

Related Organizations: DIMDI provides online access to agricultural data bases in cooperation with the German Center for Agricultural Documentation and Information/ Zentralstelle fur Agrardokumentation und -Information (ZADI). ZADI is responsible for the implementation, updating, and marketing of such data bases on the DIMDI host system, as well as for the provision of data base training courses and maintenance of data base manuals.

Description of System or Service: The GERMAN INSTITUTE FOR MEDICAL DOCUMENTATION AND INFORMATION (DIMDI) was established to carry out the acquisition, evaluation, storage, and dissemination of national and international bibliographic and other information in the field of medicine and its related disciplines using electronic data processing. It maintains online computer facilities and acquires data bases from national and international sources. DIMDI makes these data bases available to the professionally interested public using its own GRIPS (General Relation Based Information Processing System) software. Features of GRIPS include the following: realization of all postulations of the Common Command Language (CCL) for Euronet DIANE; initiation and maintenance of automatic SDI and automatic backfile searching; inverted fields for direct searching, as well as string search capabilities; truncation facilities; adjacency connectors, same-sentence restriction, and field qualifiers for free-text searches; and easy crossfile searching due to the CCL standards, compatability of data bases, and ability to switch search profiles among data bases. GRIPS also offers MAILBOX electronic mail facilities between user and host and between user and selected third parties.

Scope and/or Subject Matter: Medicine, oncology, dental medicine, veterinary medicine, social medicine, psychology, sports medicine, public health, hospital administration, medical technology, biology, biochemistry, genetic engineering, pharmacology, toxicology, agricultural sciences, food sciences, and aquatic sciences.

Input Sources: DIMDI acquires data bases from many sources, including government agencies, professional associations, and commercial organizations.

Holdings and Storage Media: DIMDI holds more than 30 online data bases containing more than 25 million records of information, with 2 million new records added annually.

Publications: 1) Information uber Online-Zugriff—provides general information on advantages and benefits of services rendered by DIMDI. 2) DIMDI-News—periodic newsletter. DIMDI also issues comprehensive manuals on data bases and on the GRIPS retrieval system in German, English, and, for major subjects, also in French. They are available free of charge to online users.

Computer-Based Products and Services: DIMDI offers online access to the following data bases under GRIPS software:

1) ABDA-Arzneistoffe (ABDA-STOFF)—provides information on active ingredients of drugs, including drug delivery, regulations, administration and dosage, indications, classifications, synonyms, derivatives, preparations, molecular formula, CAS Registry Numbers, and physicochemical properties of approximately 10,000 substances covered in periodicals, pharmacopias, and other pharmaceutical literature. Corresponds to the hard-copy handbook Pharmazeutische Stoffliste. Produced by the Bundesvereinigung Deutscher Apothekerverbande. 2) ABDA-Fertigarzneimittel (ABDA-FAM)—contains approximately 400 unit records on about 10,000 German drugs, with an annual increase of 150 unit records. Input is derived from selected journals, books, and other information from the pharmaceutical industry. Record elements include drug information on regulation of delivery, administration and dosage, dosage forms, date of marketing, properties, shelf life and storage, trade names, producers, special instructions, indications, contraindications, side effects, active ingredients, trading company, and composition. Corresponds to the Novitatenkartei and Indikationenkartei card files. Produced by the Bundesvereinigung Deutscher Apothekerverbande. 3) ABDA-Interaktionen (ABDA-INTER)—covers 101 groups of drug interactions with approximately 4200 different drugs. Data elements present include mechanism of action, recommendations, mode of acting, clinical observations, and literature. Corresponds to the printed card file Interaktionskartei. Produced by the Bundesvereinigung Deutscher Apothekerverbande. 4) AGREP (Agricultural Research Projects)—provides information on current agricultural research projects pursued in EC countries. Holds approximately 22,000 references since 1975. Produced by the Commission of the European Communities. 5) AGRIS (International Information System for the Agricultural Sciences and Technology)—holds approximately 773,000 references since 1975; produced by the United Nations Food and Agriculture Organization.

6) Animal Disease Occurrence (ADO)—subfile of CAB Abstracts/ Animal containing bibliographic information on approximately 1700 documents concerning the epidemiology of animal diseases; produced by Commonwealth Agricultural Bureaux. 7) Aquatic Sciences and Fisheries Abstracts (ASFA)—contains approximately 145,000 bibliographic references and abstracts since 1978; produced by the United Nations Food and Agriculture Organization. 8) BIOSIS—contains bibliographic citations to literature in biology, including zoology, botany, and microbiology, and related fields; produced by BioSciences Information Service. 9) CAB Abstracts/ Animal—represents the animal-relevant part of the CAB reference journals. Contains approximately 700,000 citations and abstracts dating from 1972 to the present. Produced by Commonwealth Agricultural Bureaux. 10) CAB Abstracts/ Plant—represents the plant-relevant part of CAB reference journals, providing approximately 844,000 references and abstracts, dating from 1973 to the present. Produced by Commonwealth Agricultural Bureaux.

11) Cancer Literature (CANCERLIT)—contains approximately 310,000 bibliographic citations and summaries of oncological literature dating from 1963 to the present. Produced by the National Cancer Institute of the U.S. Public Health Service's National Institutes of Health. 12) Cancer Research Projects (CANCERPROJ)—holds approximately 20,000 descriptions of ongoing cancer research projects; produced by the U.S. National Cancer Institute. 13) Chemical Dictionary Online (CHEMLINE)—provides terminological information for 530,700 chemical compounds; produced by the U.S.

National Library of Medicine's Toxicology Information Program. 14) Clinical Cancer Protocols (CLINPROT)—covers approximately 3000 protocols of clinical investigations of new anticancer agents and treatment modalities; produced by the U.S. National Cancer Institute. 15) EMBASE—contains approximately 2 million bibliographic citations and abstracts, dating from 1973 to the present, appearing in the printed Excerpta Medica as well as other sources. Also searchable are the following subfiles: EMHEALTH (public health); EMDRUGS (drugs); EMFORENSIC (forensic medicine); EMTOX (toxicology); EMCANCER (oncology); and EMTRAIN (training subfile containing some 1000 representative citations). Produced by Excerpta Medica.

16) Food Science and Technology Abstracts (FSTA)—holds approximately 250,000 bibliographic citations and summaries since 1969 to literature in the fields of food science and technology; produced by the International Food Information Service. 17) GRIPS Training Database (GRIPSLEARN)—provides approximately 1000 citations for training in the use of the GRIPS information retrieval system. 18) Health Care Literature Information Network (HECLINET)—provides approximately 58,000 citations since 1969 to literature in the fields of nonclinical aspects of hospital management and health care delivery; produced by HECLINET. 19) Health Planning and Administration Data Base (HEALTH)—contains all bibliographic citations appearing in the printed publications Hospital Literature Index, Index Medicus, International Nursing Index, Index to the Dental Literature, and MAP Notes. Holds approximately 210,000 citations since 1975. Produced by the U.S. National Library of Medicine. 20) IRCS Medical Science Database (IRCS)—contains the full text of all papers published in the printed version of the IRCS Medical Science Series of journals. Holds approximately 1200 items since 1982. Reprints of the original papers, including illustrations, may be ordered online from the data base producer, IRCS Medical Science.

21) ISI/BIOMED—contains approximately 1 million bibliographic citations since 1979 appearing in the printed publication Science Citation Index relating to biomedicine; produced by Institute for Scientific Information (ISI). 22) ISI/MULTISCI—provides more than 1 million bibliographic citations since 1979 appearing in Science Citation Index relating to nonbiomedical topics, including natural, technical, and applied sciences; produced by ISI. 23) ISTP&B (Index to Scientific & Technical Proceedings & Books)—contains bibliographic citations to approximately 3100 proceedings and more than 1650 books since 1978 relating to the natural and applied sciences and biomedicine; produced by ISI. 24) Medical Technology Documentation/Dokumentation Medizinische Technik (MEDITEC)—provides citations to literature in the field of bioengineering. Holds approximately 38,000 citations and abstracts dating from 1968 to the present; produced by FIZ Technik. 25) MEDLARS—contains approximately 3.8 million references and abstracts of biomedical literature dating from 1966 to the present (citations for 1964 and 1965 are stored in a separate file); produced by the U.S. National Library of Medicine.

26) Packaging Science and Technology Abstracts (PSTA)—provides approximately 3500 references per year since 1981 to literature in the field of packaging; produced by the International Food Information Service. 27) PsycINFO—contains approximately 400,000 references and abstracts since 1967 of literature in psychology and relevant disciplines; produced by the American Psychological Association. 28) PSYNDEX—bilingual German and English-language data base containing approximately 12,000 citations and abstracts since 1977 of periodical and other literature, as well as German-language dissertations, pertinent to psychology and related behavioral and social sciences; produced by the Center for Psychological Information and Documentation at the University of Trier. 29) Registry of Toxic Effects of Chemical Substances (RTECS)—covers 53,400 chemical substances; produced by the U.S. National Library of Medicine's Toxicology Information Program. 30) SOCIAL SCISEARCH—contains all citations appearing in the printed publication Social Science Citation Index. Holds approximately 1.5 million references dating from 1973 to the present; produced by Institute for Scientific Information.

31) Telegenline—contains all citations and abstracts included in the publication Telegen Reporter, covering literature on genetic technology. Holds more than 4000 references dating from 1973 to the present. Produced by EIC/Intelligence, Inc. 32) Toxicology Data Bank (TDB)—covers approximately 3700 chemical substances; produced by the U.S. National Library of Medicine's Toxicology Information Program. 33) TOXLINE—covers literature relating to toxicology and chemical analysis of toxic substances. Derived from major secondary source data bases and special data collections, it holds approximately 1.35 million references and abstracts dating from 1965 to the present. Produced by the Toxicology Information Program.

DIMDI offers the following computer-based services: computerized searching of its data bases; offline printing of search results; downloading, where applicable; and online document ordering. It also offers an online inquiry service providing access to a newsfile on GRIPS. Intended primarily for the retrieval of information on training courses offered outside of Germany, the service also provides information on payment for the usage of data bases; cost of an actual search; list of files available; license fees; current information; list of data bases and ports; and other data. Access to DIMDI is possible via international telex networks, Euronet DIANE, Datex-P, DIMDI's DIMDINET, and national packet-switching networks. Additionally, DIMDI leases the GRIPS software system to other hosts, including INKA (Informationssystem Karlsruhe), FIZ Technik, ECHO (European Commission Host Organization), GID (Gesellschaft fur Information und Dokumentation), and others. GRIPS-Compact, designed by DIMDI especially for in-house purposes, will be available to all interested users in the near future.

Other Services: In addition to services described above, DIMDI provides training courses.

Clientele/Availability: Products and services are intended for users in the biosciences community.

Contact: Mr. H.-E. Kurzwelly, Head, EDP-Division, German Institute for Medical Documentation and Information. (Telex 8881 364.)

★429★
GLASS INSTITUTE
(Institut du Verre)
INFORMATION AND DOCUMENTATION SERVICE
(Service Information et Documentation)
34, rue Michel-Ange　　　　　　　　Phone: 01 6514568
F-75016 Paris, France　　　　　　　Service Est: 1945
Miss A. Sellin, Chief

Staff: 1 Information and library professional; 1 management professional; 4 technicians; 2 clerical and nonprofessional.

Description of System or Service: The INFORMATION AND DOCUMENTATION SERVICE of the Glass Institute works in cooperation with several similar European institutes and societies to produce a computer-readable bibliographic data base covering the world literature on glass and refractories. The data base is used to produce printed keyword indexes and to provide information retrieval and SDI services. The SERVICE also offers document delivery, translations, bibliography compilations, and library services.

Scope and/or Subject Matter: Glass and refractories and their production, properties, and uses; furnaces and heat problems connected with glassmaking.

Input Sources: Input to the data base is derived from worldwide journals, books, brochures, and patents.

Holdings and Storage Media: The computer-readable data base holds 45,000 bibliographic references dating from 1968 to the present. Library holdings include 2600 bound volumes, subscriptions to 250 periodicals, and patents.

Publications: Verres et Refractaires (six times a year)—Institute review; includes documentation section produced from the data base. Monthly and annual keyword indexes are also prepared from the data base.

Computer-Based Products and Services: The Service provides batch-mode information retrieval and SDI services from the data base.

Clientele/Availability: Services are available without restrictions on a fee basis.

Contact: Miss A. Sellin, Chief, Information and Documentation

Service.

★430★
THE GLOBE AND MAIL
INFO GLOBE
444 Front St., W. Phone: (416) 585-5250
Toronto, ON, Canada M5V 2S9 Service Est: 1979
Barbara Hyland, General Manager

Description of System or Service: INFO GLOBE is the online information division of The Globe and Mail, providing access to The Globe and Mail Online data bank and Marketscan. The Globe and Mail Online data bank contains the full text of The Globe and Mail newspaper and its Report on Business; the data bank is updated daily with that day's news. Marketscan contains daily stock quotations from major North American stock exchanges.

Scope and/or Subject Matter: News stories, columns, editorials, business reports, political analyses, financial statements, science and technology features, court reports, letters to the editor, and other nonadvertising matter from the newspaper; stock quotations from major North American exchanges.

Input Sources: Input to The Globe and Mail Online data bank consists of the nonadvertising content of the Monday through Saturday issues of The Globe and Mail. Daily stock quotations from the Toronto, Montreal, Vancouver, Alberta, New York, and American stock exchanges are input to Marketscan.

Holdings and Storage Media: The computer-readable Globe and Mail Online data bank covers more than 500,000 articles published in The Globe and Mail since November 14, 1977 and from its Report on Business since January 1, 1978; it is updated each morning with the content of that day's printed edition. Marketscan contains daily stock quotation data for the last 250 trading days.

Publications: The Globe and Mail (daily) and The Globe and Mail Report on Business. Info Globe training and user manuals are available by request.

Microform Products and Services: Microfilm copies of The Globe and Mail and its predecessor, The Globe, are available back to 1849.

Computer-Based Products and Services: INFO GLOBE is accessible online via the Datapac, Telenet, and Tymnet telecommunications networks. Custom searches and offline print facilities for The Globe and Mail Online data bank are also available. Each article in the data bank contains the following information: document number identifying the article, its date, page, and if there was an illustration; byline; class field indicating the section of the paper that the story appeared in; dateline and number of words in the story; headline; lead paragraph; full text as it appeared in the newspaper; and controlled vocabulary terms. The Marketscan data base is also accessible via the INFO GLOBE online service. It delivers daily quotations of stock exchange transactions, with volume, highs, lows, and closing prices, and allows the user to view different stocks at the same time for performance comparison. INFO GLOBE also plans to provide online access in the near future to the Canadian Financial Database containing financial statements of Canadian public companies.

Clientele/Availability: Users include marketing, sales, planning, research, public relations, and other professionals. Fees are assessed on a usage basis.

Remarks: Info Globe is the sole marketing agent in Canada for Finsbury Data Services and Canada Systems Group's Insight data bases. It also represents the Dow Jones News/Retrieval service in Canada.

Contact: Barbara Hyland, General Manager, Info Globe. (Telex 06 219629.)

★431★
GMELIN INSTITUTE FOR INORGANIC CHEMISTRY AND RELATED FIELDS
(Gmelin-Institut fur Anorganische Chemie und Grenzgebiete)
Varrentrappstr. 40/42 Phone: 069 79171
Carl-Bosch-Haus
D-6000 Frankfurt am Main 90, Fed. Rep.
  of Germany
Dr. H.C. Ekkehard Fluck, Director

Related Organizations: The Gmelin Institute is part of the Max Planck Society for the Advancement of Science, and maintains a working relationship with the Beilstein Institute for Literature in Organic Chemistry.

Description of System or Service: The GMELIN INSTITUTE FOR INORGANIC CHEMISTRY AND RELATED FIELDS publishes the Gmelin Handbook of Inorganic Chemistry, which covers the entire field of inorganic chemistry literature from the mid-18th century to the present. The Handbook assembles and systematically classifies research findings scattered throughout the world's primary scientific literature, and provides monographic treatment of up-to-date material with an extensive background bibliography.

Scope and/or Subject Matter: Inorganic, organometallic, and physical chemistry, as well as physics.

Input Sources: A permanent staff of scientists reviews and critically assesses world inorganic chemical literature for the Handbook.

Publications: Gmelin Handbook of Inorganic Chemistry—related findings and subject matter are grouped together; includes critical evaluations and references to allied concepts to permit comparative assessment of published results. More than 450 volumes of the current 8th edition have been published; all volumes since 1982 are issued in English. In the United States, ordering information can be obtained from Springer-Verlag New York Inc., 175 Fifth Ave., New York, NY 10010. In Europe, contact Springer-Verlag, Heidelberger Platz 3, D-1000 Berlin 33, Federal Republic of Germany.

Computer-Based Products and Services: The Handbook index is produced by means of a photocomposition system that is also designed to permit automated subject searching and the production of special subset indexes.

Clientele/Availability: The Handbook is available for purchase without restrictions.

Contact: Dr. Walter Lippert, Deputy Director, Gmelin Institute for Inorganic Chemistry and Related Fields. (Telex 412526 D.) In the United States, contact Prof. Dimitri R. Stein, Gmelin Institute, United States Office, 7 Woodland Ave., Larchmont, NY 10538.

★432★
GOTHARD HOUSE GROUP OF COMPANIES, LTD.
Gothard House Phone: 0491 573602
Henley-on-Thames, Oxon. RG9 1AJ,
  England Founded: 1962
Richard S. Gothard, Chairman

Description of System or Service: The GOTHARD HOUSE GROUP OF COMPANIES, LTD. serves as international booksellers, publishers, subscription agents, and information scientists. The GROUP includes the following companies and services: 1) GHG Information and Library Services Company supplies books, journals, and other documentation worldwide. 2) International Subscriptions Ltd. provides journal subscription services and processes standing orders for annuals, serials, and other British and foreign publications. 3) Information Resources Ltd. provides document delivery, custom bibliographies, alerting systems, information retrieval, clinical trials, market surveys, indexing of journal articles, and other services in the biotechnical and pharmaceutical fields. 4) Gothard House Publications publishes books on a variety of subjects.

Scope and/or Subject Matter: Technical, scientific, medical, biotechnical, pharmaceutical, and general publications.

Input Sources: Input is derived from publishers and institutional literature, British and foreign books, and journals.

Publications: Gothard House Group publications include: 1) Drug Information Sources—details on more than 500 leading professional and trade pharmaceutical organizations worldwide, including international, national, and regional sources, company codes, price lists, handbooks, and other publications dealing with prescription pharmaceuticals. 2) Information Resources Guide: Britain—selected British sources of technical, scientific, medical, and general information. 3) Words and Phrases Used in the Pharmaceutical Industry—pharmaceutical vocabulary, company codes for drugs, and a selection of pharmaceutical books and journals. 4) Russian Space Exploration—a history of the first 21 years of Russian space exploration. All publications are available for purchase.

Computer-Based Products and Services: Gothard's subscription services are supported by a computerized system covering client requirements.

Clientele/Availability: Services are available without restrictions.

Contact: Richard S. Gothard, Chairman, Gothard House Group of Companies, Ltd.

★433★
GREAT BRITAIN
ATOMIC ENERGY AUTHORITY
ATOMIC ENERGY RESEARCH ESTABLISHMENT, HARWELL
COMPUTER SCIENCE AND SYSTEMS DIVISION
STATUS
Harwell Laboratory   Phone: 0235 24141
Didcot, Oxon. OX11 0RA, England   Service Est: 1975
Derek I. Matkin, Commercial Manager

Description of System or Service: STATUS is an information storage and retrieval software system for the maintenance, updating, and searching of large files of textual and numeric information in online or batch modes. Available features include data base creation and modification, free text or controlled vocabulary searches, and report generation from files of bibliogrpahic information, technical documents, or tabular data. STATUS is designed to operate on a variety of mainframes, minicomputers, and microcomputers using plain language storage and retrieval commands. More than 150 users in the United Kingdom, Europe, United States, and Australia have implemented the system.

Scope and/or Subject Matter: Information storage and retrieval for the following applications: personnel records, products and suppliers catalogs, directories, technical reports and records, marketing research information, plant and asset registers, catalogs of books and journals, SDI, accident and incident records, safety and health regulations, building and construction standards, systems manuals, program documentation, research and development experimental data, maintenance manuals, health records, committee minutes and records, patent and legal data, engineering documentation and change control, correspondence files from word processing centers, and others.

Input Sources: Input for STATUS can originate from a variety of sources including the user's internal manual or machine-readable files and commercially available data bases.

Computer-Based Products and Services: STATUS is implemented as an integrated suite of FORTRAN modules which adapt to varied user environments. A STATUS data base can be created by the user from a computer terminal, word processor, computer typesetting system, or other external source. A STATUS data base contains two major components: a text file and concordance. The text file accommodates any kind of textual or tabular data inserted by the user as a continuous stream, using a small number of control characters to indicate the file's internal structure. All input text is structured into four levels which may be independently searched: chapter, article, paragraph, and word. The concordance is a structured list of all words in the text file together with pointers to the places in which they occur in the text. Data base searches using STATUS are conducted with a question format using single search terms, search terms linked by logical operators, or search terms linked by positional operators. Users may display search results as a list of articles, titles, or text; browse forward or backward through the data base; or display only text containing search terms. Text may be routed, sorted, or unsorted directly to a printer or other files.

Associated software available with STATUS includes the following: 1) STATUS Report Generator—enables the user to format and present reports containing all or selected information extracted from a STATUS data base. 2) STATUS Data Preparation Aid (SDPA)—allows a wide variety of article formats within a single data base and supports this by allowing free text input by the user. 3) STATUS Thesaurus—provides a controlled language facility for indexing and retrieval. STATUS is available through franchise holders appointed by the Atomic Energy Authority; it will run on a wide variety of mainframes, minicomputers, and microcomputers.

Clientele/Availability: STATUS is available without restriction.

Contact: Derek I. Matkin, Commercial Manager, Marketing and Sales Department; telephone ext. 2704. (Telex 83135 G.)

★434★
GREAT BRITAIN
ATOMIC ENERGY AUTHORITY
ATOMIC ENERGY RESEARCH ESTABLISHMENT, HARWELL
HARWELL CENTRAL INFORMATION SERVICE
Bldg. 465, Harwell Laboratory   Phone: 0235 24141
Didcot, Oxon. OX11 0RB, England   Service Est: 1947
Mr. P.J. Jones, Head

Staff: Approximately 15 total.

Description of System or Service: The HARWELL CENTRAL INFORMATION SERVICE provides library and information services to the staff of Harwell Laboratory. Among the services offered are current awareness, computerized information retrieval, manual literature searching, and publishing. In support of its services, the INFORMATION SERVICE maintains several computer-readable bibliographic data bases including: 1) BULLETIN, which covers recently received periodical articles, books, and other documents held by the Library; this file is used to produce the weekly Harwell Information Bulletin. 2) LIBCAT, the Harwell Library Catalogue. 3) RECAP, which covers publications issued by the Atomic Energy Authority. In addition, the INFORMATION SERVICE acts as the United Kingdom center for the International Nuclear Information System (INIS). In that capacity, it contributes citations for relevant U.K. literature and holds magnetic tape copies of the INIS data base for providing retrospective search and SDI services and for preparing publications.

Scope and/or Subject Matter: Nuclear research and development; chemistry; chemical technology; computer science and systems; energy; engineering; environmental and medical sciences; instrumentation; materials; heat transfer and fluid flow; nondestructive testing; industrial waste and hazardous materials; and separation processes.

Input Sources: Input consists of all forms of literature including journals, books, conference papers, reports, and patents.

Holdings and Storage Media: The Service maintains several bibliographic data bases in computer-readable form. BULLETIN contains approximately 50,000 citations covering library accessions for the preceding two years. LIBCAT contains 9000 citations dating from 1982 to date. RECAP contains 15,000 citations for the period 1979 to date. The library collection includes 35,000 bound volumes; 260,000 reports in paper copy; 350,000 reports on microfiche; and subscriptions to 1130 periodicals. INIS data are held on magnetic tape.

Publications: 1) Harwell Information Bulletin (weekly)—lists periodical articles, patents, conference proceedings, and books which are held by the library. Items included are arranged by subjects listed on the cover of each issue. 2) Information Bulletin on Radioactive Waste (semimonthly)—prepared by the Information Service for the Radioactive Waste Project; includes computer-selected bibliographic references, indexing terms, and abstract numbers of relevant items from INIS. 3) Irradiation of Medical Products Abstract Bulletin (quarterly)—prepared under contract for the United Kingdom Panel on Gamma and Electron Irradiation; includes relevant references and abstracts from INIS. A list of additional publications is available on request.

Computer-Based Products and Services: The HARWELL CENTRAL INFORMATION SERVICE conducts literature searches and offers current awareness from its in-house bibliographic data bases. It also conducts retrospective literature searching of the INIS data base and offers SDI and magnetic tape services from it.

Clientele/Availability: Services are available on request; primary users are Harwell Laboratory staff.

Contact: Mr. P.J. Jones, Head, Harwell Central Information Service.

★435★
GREAT BRITAIN
ATOMIC ENERGY AUTHORITY
ATOMIC ENERGY RESEARCH ESTABLISHMENT, HARWELL
NATIONAL CHEMICAL EMERGENCY CENTRE (NCEC)
CHEMSAFE
Bldg. 7.22, Harwell Laboratory   Phone: 0235 24141
Didcot, Oxon. OX11 0RA, England   Service Est: 1974
Robert F. Cumberland, Centre Manager

Staff: 3 Information and library professional; 1 management professional; 2 technicians; 2 clerical and nonprofessional.

Related Organizations: CHEMSAFE was established by the Chemical Industries Association in collaboration with the Chemical Emergency Centre and the Department of the Environment.

Description of System or Service: CHEMSAFE is a machine-readable file of chemical product information designed to meet the needs of police and fire services involved in emergencies with hazardous chemicals. Data consist of trade and chemical names, hazards, recommended methods for dealing with spills and fires, first aid, identifying code marks, packaging, composition, references, and other information considered pertinent by the manufacturer. CHEMSAFE is maintained online for use by National Chemical Emergency Centre personnel. Summaries of CHEMSAFE information on microcomputer diskettes together with retrieval software are made available to others by subscription under the CHEMDATA service.

Scope and/or Subject Matter: Hazardous and potentially hazardous chemical products, including emergency action information for police and fire services.

Input Sources: Input is derived from questionnaires completed by chemical manufacturers, importers, and traders and from standard reference sources.

Holdings and Storage Media: The machine-readable CHEMSAFE data bank currently holds data on more than 30,000 chemical materials.

Computer-Based Products and Services: CHEMSAFE (also known as Hazfile) is maintained for online searching by emergency duty officers. It can be searched on a free text basis using the STATUS information retrieval system. Words, groups of words, code numbers, or parts of words or code numbers can be used as search elements. The National Chemical Emergency Centre makes the summarized version of CHEMSAFE called CHEMDATA available by subscription on magnetic tape or disk for use on microcomputers. CHEMDATA is searchable by chemical name, substance identification number, and company name and is available in English, French, German, Italian, and Spanish.

Clientele/Availability: Services are available to police and fire personnel. Access to CHEMSAFE is restricted to NCEC; CHEMDATA is available to others by subscription.

Remarks: The National Chemical Emergency Centre also provides the Chemical Emergency Agency Service (CEAS). CEAS collects detailed substances information from subscribing chemical companies for direct dissemination to public emergency services. The CEAS file currently holds data on 3000 products from 65 chemical companies.

Contact: Robert F. Cumberland, Manager, National Chemical Emergency Centre. (Telex 83135.)

★436★
GREAT BRITAIN
ATOMIC ENERGY AUTHORITY
ATOMIC ENERGY RESEARCH ESTABLISHMENT, HARWELL
NONDESTRUCTIVE TESTING CENTRE (NTC)
QUALITY TECHNOLOGY INFORMATION SERVICE (QUALTIS)
Harwell Laboratory   Phone: 0235 24141
Didcot, Oxon. OX11 0RA, England   Service Est: 1968
Mr. R.S. Sharpe, Head

Description of System or Service: The QUALITY TECHNOLOGY INFORMATION SERVICE (QUALTIS) is a current awareness and inquiry service in the field of nondestructive testing. QUALTIS maintains the computer-readable bibliographic NDT-Info data base and uses it to produce a bimonthly bulletin. The SERVICE also provides computerized literature searching from the data base, distributes NTC publications, and offers library services.

Scope and/or Subject Matter: Nondestructive testing.

Input Sources: Input consists of all forms of literature including journal articles, books, reports, conference papers, standards, patents, and trade literature. Approximately 2000 items are added to the collection each year. Input is also obtained in machine-readable format, including the INIS tapes.

Holdings and Storage Media: The computer-readable NDT-Info data base holds approximately 30,000 literature references from 1970 to date. A library collection is also maintained.

Publications: 1) NDT-Info (6 per year)—a part of NDT International which is published by Butterworth Scientific Ltd., P.O. Box 63, Guildford, Surrey, England. 2) QT Handbook—also published by Butterworth. 3) QT News—published by NTC.

Computer-Based Products and Services: QUALTIS provides batch-mode information retrieval and SDI services from the NDT-Info data base.

Other Services: Additional services include manual literature searching and referral services.

Clientele/Availability: Services are available on a subscription basis without restrictions.

Contact: Mr. R.S. Sharpe, Head, Nondestructive Testing Centre.

★437★
GREAT BRITAIN
ATOMIC ENERGY AUTHORITY
ATOMIC ENERGY RESEARCH ESTABLISHMENT, HARWELL
WASTE MANAGEMENT INFORMATION BUREAU (WMIB)
Environmental Safety Group   Phone: 0235 24141
Bldg. 7.12, Harwell Laboratory   Service Est: 1973
Didcot, Oxon. OX11 0RA, England
Miss M.A. Lund, Manager

Staff: 1.5 Information and library professional; 1 management professional; 1 technician; 1 other.

Related Organizations: The Waste Management Information Bureau receives support from the Department of the Environment. It is part of Harwell's Hazardous Materials Service (HMS) and the Environmental Safety Group.

Description of System or Service: The WASTE MANAGEMENT INFORMATION BUREAU (WMIB) is the national center for collection and dissemination of information relating to the management of nonradioactive wastes. It scans journals, research reports, and other technical documents pertaining to waste management, and abstracts and indexes these for inclusion in the computer-readable WMIB Databank. Computerized searches are provided from the Databank and other relevant data bases, and a bimonthly abstracts journal is published. The BUREAU also maintains a reference collection of all cited documents, offers copying services, and provides a range of consultancy services.

Scope and/or Subject Matter: Waste management, with emphasis on handling, treatment, disposal, recycling, and environmental hazards.

Input Sources: Input is derived from more than 180 journals and other primary sources such as reports, patents, conference proceedings, and trade literature. Secondary sources yield additional input.

Holdings and Storage Media: Covering the period from 1973 to the present, with special coverage of significant items dating back to 1938, the machine-readable WMIB Databank contains more than 29,000 items; 3000 new items are added annually.

Publications: Waste Management Information Bulletin (bimonthly)—each issue contains 500 abstracts plus a section highlighting significant documents, news of recent developments, and forthcoming events; includes subject and author indexes, which are cumulated annually in a separate volume. Available by subscription from Routledge & Kegan Paul, Broadway House, Newtown Rd., Henley-on-Thames, Oxon. RG9 1EN, England.

Computer-Based Products and Services: The WASTE MANAGEMENT INFORMATION BUREAU offers computerized searches from the WMIB Databank.

Other Services: In addition to the services described above, the Bureau provides advice on matters within its scope, acts as a referral center, and offers technical assessment and other consulting services.

Clientele/Availability: Services are available without restrictions. Members of the Bureau receive four free computer searches annually; others must pay a fee.

Contact: Miss M.A. Lund, Manager, Waste Management Information Bureau. (Telex 83135.)

★438★
GREAT BRITAIN
ATOMIC ENERGY AUTHORITY
CULHAM LABORATORY
PLASMA PHYSICS LIBRARY AND INFORMATION SERVICE

Abingdon, Oxon. OX14 3DB, England
J.L. Hall, Librarian
Phone: 0235 21840
Service Est: 1962

Staff: 4 Information and library professional; 6 clerical and nonprofessional.

Description of System or Service: The PLASMA PHYSICS LIBRARY AND INFORMATION SERVICE provides current awareness and retrospective information services for the staff of the Culham Laboratory and the adjacent JET Laboratory. The SERVICE monitors incoming journals, reports, and books; converts selected information to machine-readable format; and prepares publications and SDI materials. It also provides computerized searching from its bibliographic data base, which is known as LIBRIS.

Scope and/or Subject Matter: Plasma physics and nuclear fusion research and associated scientific and technical disciplines.

Input Sources: Input is obtained from materials received by Culham Laboratory Library.

Holdings and Storage Media: The Library collection contains 14,000 bound volumes; 55,000 reports; and 500 periodical subscriptions. The machine-readable LIBRIS data base contains more than 100,000 references to plasma physics literature dating from 1974 to the present.

Publications: Culham Laboratory Library Bulletin (weekly)—available by subscription. Each issue contains about 150 references to journal articles, books, reports, and conference proceedings relating to plasma physics, fusion reactors, and related topics. Also covers publications by the staff of the Culham and JET Laboratories.

Computer-Based Products and Services: The Library maintains the LIBRIS data base covering plasma physics and related literature and provides retrospective searches and SDI services. SDI is available externally on a subscription basis.

Clientele/Availability: Services are available to outside users by subscription.

Contact: J.L. Hall, Librarian, Plasma Physics Library and Information Service. (Telex 83189 FUSION G.)

★439★
GREAT BRITAIN
BRITISH LIBRARY
BIBLIOGRAPHIC SERVICES DIVISION

2 Sheraton St.
London W1V 4BH, England
P.R. Lewis, Director General
Phone: 01-636 1544
Service Est: 1974

Staff: 94 Information and library professional; 32 management professional; 1 technician; 5 sales and marketing; 64 clerical and nonprofessional.

Description of System or Service: The BIBLIOGRAPHIC SERVICES DIVISION is the central resource of bibliographic records and services in the United Kingdom supporting the British Library and the library community as a whole. Bibliographic records are created for forthcoming publications (from advance information received under the Cataloguing-in-Publication scheme) and for items received by legal deposit at the Copyright Receipt Office. The DIVISION makes these records widely available by publishing a range of printed bibliographies, including the British National Bibliography; by maintaining corresponding computer-readable data bases, including UK MARC, which holds all records published in the National Bibliography since 1950; and by supplying UK MARC and LC MARC records on magnetic tape. Additionally, the BIBLIOGRAPHIC SERVICES DIVISION operates the BLAISE online retrieval and cataloging service providing interactive access to UK MARC, LC MARC, and a range of other data bases. BLAISE is fully described in a separate entry following this one. Other activities of the DIVISION include operation of the UK National Serials Data Centre as a participant in the International Serials Data System.

Scope and/or Subject Matter: Bibliographic coverage of all subjects with emphasis on books.

Input Sources: The Division's record creation activities are sustained through two major programs—legal deposit and the Cataloguing-in-Publication program—operated in cooperation with U.K. publishers. Under legal deposit procedures, the following materials received by the Library from U.K. publishers: books, newspapers, periodicals, government publications, pamphlets, maps, and music. About 45,000 books per year are cataloged for the British National Bibliography and the British Catalogue of Music. Materials in English acquired by the Library's Department of Printed Books through purchase, donation, or exchange are also cataloged in the Division.

Holdings and Storage Media: The computer-readable UK MARC data base holds approximately 850,000 records covering items cataloged since 1950. Several other internally produced bibliographic data bases are also held. Hardcopy materials received and cataloged by the Division are sent to the Reference Division for storage.

Publications: 1) British National Bibliography (BNB)—issued in weekly lists, interim cumulations, and annual and multiyear cumulations; corresponds to the UK MARC data base. 2) British Catalogue of Music (BCM)—issued in interim cumulations and an annual volume. The entire file has been computerized. 3) British Education Index (BEI)—three quarterly issues with an annual cumulation; indexes journal articles appearing in more than 260 periodicals published in the U.K., as well as conference proceedings, selected European journals, some government reports, and bibliographies; corresponds to the BEI data base. 4) Serials in the British Library (SBL)—four quarterly issues listing serials with start dates after 1977 held by the divisions of the British Library and 16 other libraries; annual cumulation, including earlier titles and additional locations, are issued on microfiche. 5) British Catalogue of Audiovisual Materials (BCAVM)—list of audiovisual materials currently available for purchase or hire in the United Kingdom; corresponds to the AVMARC data base. The Division also issues a newsletter, manuals for PRECIS and UK MARC, and a range of documentation to support BLAISE services.

Microform Products and Services: The BLAISE COM Service produces catalogs on either microfiche or microfilm. Books in English, a monthly cumulation listing English-language material added to the UK MARC data base or cataloged by the U.S. Library of Congress, is available in microform. Name Authority List, Subject Authority Fiche, and PRECIS Vocabulary Fiche are also available.

Computer-Based Products and Services: The BIBLIOGRAPHIC SERVICES DIVISION conducts computer-supported cataloging and maintains the UK MARC data base. Data bases corresponding to the British Education Index (BEI), Serials in the British Library (SBL), British Catalogue of Music (BCM), and British Catalogue of Audiovisual Materials (AVMARC) publications listed above are also maintained. BEI, UK MARC, AVMARC, and other data bases are available online through BLAISE-LINE (see following entry). The DIVISION also offers the Selective Record Service and MARC Exchange Tape Service utilizing the UK MARC data base and the LC MARC data base. The Selective Record Service enables libraries to submit requests for individual records from the data bases for use in building a data base tailored to the client's requirements, maintaining and updating an existing data base, conversion projects, and cataloging special collections. The records are supplied to the client online via BLAISE-LINE or on magnetic tape. The Service is available on a monthly or special arrangement basis. The MARC Exchange Tape Service allows libraries to build files of bibliographic data for in-house use, including compiling a data base, providing a potential requirements file, and updating an existing data base. The Service is available as weekly tapes of current records or as separate annual cumulation tapes. Additionally, the DIVISION provides information retrieval services, SDI, and a British National Bibliography card service.

Clientele/Availability: Clients include librarians, the book trade, and others.

Contact: Marketing Office, Bibliographic Services Division, British Library.

★440★
GREAT BRITAIN
BRITISH LIBRARY
BIBLIOGRAPHIC SERVICES DIVISION
BLAISE (BRITISH LIBRARY AUTOMATED INFORMATION SERVICE)
2 Sheraton St.   Phone: 01-636 1544
London W1V 4BH, England   Service Est: 1977
David Martin, Director of Automated Services

Staff: Approximately 60 total.

Description of System or Service: BLAISE (British Library Automated Information Service) provides and facilitates online search services through BLAISE-LINE and BLAISE-LINK. BLAISE-LINE is an international online system providing information retrieval as well as library cataloging and bibliographic verification capabilities. It supplies clients with interactive access to UK MARC, LC MARC, and a range of related data bases of interest to librarians and information workers. BLAISE-LINE includes systems for catalog record selection, editing, and catalog production. The second service, BLAISE-LINK, is offered in collaboration with the U.S. National Library of Medicine (NLM). BLAISE-LINK allows British Library clients to directly access NLM data bases through the NLM computer complex in Maryland. Other services offered by BLAISE include an Automatic Document Request Service (ADRS), computerized information retrieval, and SDI.

Scope and/or Subject Matter: Online searching of medical, educational, general cataloging, and other data bases.

Input Sources: Data bases are acquired from British and U.S. national libraries.

Holdings and Storage Media: BLAISE-LINE holds eight bibliographic data bases and two training files online.

Publications: 1) BLAISE Newsletter (6 per year)—provides information on new system developments, features, files, events, and other topics. 2) BLAISE-LINE Mini Manual (annual)—contains summaries of data base features, commands, and searching tips. 3) BLAISE-LINE User Manual. 4) BLAISE-LINK Mini Manual (annual)—contains summaries of data base features, commands, and searching tips. 5) BLAISE-LINK User Manual. 6) UKCTRAIN Workbook. 7) MEDTRAIN Workbook. 8) MeSH Workbook.

Microform Products and Services: Selected user aids are available on microfiche, including PRECIS indexing terms.

Computer-Based Products and Services: BLAISE offers two main services, BLAISE-LINE and BLAISE-LINK. Through its IBM computer at Harlow, BLAISE-LINE offers online access to the following data bases: 1) UK MARC; 2) LC MARC; 3) British Education Index (BEI); 4) Conference Proceedings Index; 5) AVMARC; 6) Eighteenth Century Short Title Catalogue (ESTC); 7) British Library Reference Division Department of Printed Books (DPB)—covers English and foreign-language books acquired by the DPB since 1975, as well as materials from the Department of Oriental Manuscripts and Printed Books and the India Office Library and Records; 8) HELPIS (Higher Education Learning Programmes Information Service). UKCTRAIN and MEDTRAIN, two practice files, are also accessible. The following data bases are expected to be offered through BLAISE-LINE: Whitaker's British Books in Print, SIGLE (System for Information on Grey Literature in Europe), and ISTC (Incunable Short Title Catalogue). BLAISE-LINE's EDITOR software program supports catalog production and bibliography compilation. The service permits the MARC files to be searched on a wide range of data elements, including publication date, country and form of publication, language, DDC number, UDC number, LC classification number, individual and corporate authors, title, words in LC Subject Headings, and PRECIS terms. BLAISE-LINE also provides a Local Catalog Service (LOCAS) offering centralized file building and catalog production facilities.

Through the BLAISE-LINK service, BLAISE arranges for its clients to access the NLM's computer in Maryland using standard telephone lines or British Telecom's PSS, the national packet-switching network; via PSS, United Kingdom subscribers are connected to the MEDLARS data bases through the International Packet Switching Service (IPSS) and either Telenet or Tymnet. BLAISE-LINK provides online access to MEDLINE, TOXLINE, AVLINE, BIOETHICSLINE, CATLINE, CANCERLIT, CANCERPROJ, CHEMLINE, CLINPROT, HEALTH, HISTLINE, MeSH, NAF, RTECS, POPLINE, and SERLINE. BLAISE-LINK clients outside the U.K. can access the NLM files through international gateways and networks. BLAISE also provides information retrieval and SDI services from the BLAISE-LINE and BLAISE-LINK data bases.

Other Services: Additionally, BLAISE conducts training courses and seminars and provides computer terminals on a rental basis.

Clientele/Availability: Services are available on a subscription basis.

Contact: Marketing Office, Bibliographic Services Division, British Library. (Telex 21462.)

★441★
GREAT BRITAIN
BRITISH LIBRARY
BIBLIOGRAPHIC SERVICES DIVISION
SUBJECT SYSTEMS OFFICE
PRESERVED CONTEXT INDEX SYSTEM (PRECIS)
2 Sheraton St.   Phone: 01-636 1544
London W1V 4BH, England   Service Est: 1979
Derek Austin

Staff: 12 Information and library professional.

Description of System or Service: The PRESERVED CONTEXT INDEX SYSTEM (PRECIS) is a precoordinated alphabetical index system designed for use with computers. The indexer prepares a string or sequence of terms which expresses in summary form the subject of the document. The string is entered together with manipulation codes which instruct the computer how to handle the terms. Multiple index entries are generated from the single input string, and cross-references are automatically selected from a machine-held thesaurus. PRECIS indexing input can be used for computer typeset or microform indexes, and the data can be used without further processing for computer searching. PRECIS is used by the British Library to produce subject indexes for the British National Bibliography, the British Education Index, the British Catalogue of Music, and the Department of British Books. It is also applied to the Australian National Bibliography and the National Film Board of Canada.

Scope and/or Subject Matter: Computer-assisted indexing.

Publications: PRECIS: A Manual of Concept Analysis and Subject Indexing.

Microform Products and Services: 1) Subject Authority Fiche (annual)—alphabetical listing of PRECIS index entries; each entry is accompanied by subject information, including classification numbers and subject headings from the major schemes. 2) PRECIS Vocabulary Fiche (annual)—alphabetical listing of all terms used as entry points in

PRECIS indexes.
Computer-Based Products and Services: PRECIS subject data are available on computer tapes.
Clientele/Availability: PRECIS users include libraries and publishers.
Contact: Derek Austin, Subject Systems Office.

★442★
**GREAT BRITAIN
BRITISH LIBRARY
LENDING DIVISION**
Boston Spa   Phone: 0937 843434
Wetherby, West Yorks. LS23 7BQ,
  England   Service Est: 1973
Dr. M.B. Line, Director General

Staff: 141 Management professional; 449 clerical and nonprofessional; 138 other.
Description of System or Service: The LENDING DIVISION provides United Kingdom organizations and libraries and worldwide researchers with lending services from an extensive collection of serials in all subject fields and languages, current English-language monographs, and selected foreign-language documents. Its services include loans, photocopies, and fulfillment of document orders placed online through the BLAISE Automatic Document Request Service (ADRS) and through DIALOG's DIALORDER service. Additionally, the DIVISION conducts searches of BLAISE data bases in response to written requests, indexes United Kingdom literature for input to the U.S. National Library of Medicine's MEDLARS system, and prepares publications, including the Index to Conference Proceedings Received. The Index is searchable online through BLAISE as the Conference Proceedings Index file.
Scope and/or Subject Matter: World literature in all subject fields and languages, particularly serials, monographs, and proceedings.
Input Sources: The Division collects books, periodicals, documents, and unclassified reports in all subjects. Input for the conference proceedings index is derived from items received by the Lending Division or requested by other libraries, as well as specialized directories.
Holdings and Storage Media: The computer-readable Conference Proceedings Index data base covers approximately 170,000 conferences dating back to the 19th century; approximately 18,000 entries are added each year. Library holdings consist of 4.5 million volumes; subscriptions to more than 56,000 periodicals; 3.5 million documents in microform; 480,000 translations; all Her Majesty's Stationery Office (HMSO) publications from 1962 to date; most British theses; publicly available report literature; and music scores.
Publications: 1) Index to Conference Proceedings Received (monthly with annual, five-year, and ten-year cumulations)—indexes published proceedings, including those appearing in journals, reports, and books. 2) Current Serials Received (annual)—lists all serials currently taken by the Lending Division. 3) Keywords in Serial Titles-KIST (quarterly)—keyword index to all serials held by the Lending Division and includes a shelfmark listing since 1981. 4) British Reports, Translations, and Theses (monthly). 5) Interlending and Document Supply: Journal of the British Library Lending Division (quarterly). 6) Journals in Translation. 7) Translated Books Available from the BLLD. 8) Handbook of Library Holdings on Commonwealth Literature. 9) European Communities Publications: a Guide to British Library Resources. 10) Edwin Gardiner Chess Collection. The Lending Division also issues a number of free publications relating to its services.
Microform Products and Services: Periodical articles and some reports can be supplied in microform or full-size copies from microforms.
Computer-Based Products and Services: The LENDING DIVISION prepares the computer-readable Conference Proceedings Index data base, conducts online information retrieval from data bases on BLAISE, and fills document orders placed online. Entries in the Conference Proceedings Index, which is accessible through BLAISE, include conference title (with preference given to English titles in the case of multilingual conferences), sponsors, venue, conference date, ISBN or ISSN if appropriate, form of the materials, and the Lending Division shelfmark; keyterms are also assigned for each document.
Other Services: In addition to the services described above, the Lending Division assists in training MEDLARS users, offers seminars and courses for librarians and information users, and sponsors cover-to-cover translation of 10 periodicals.
Clientele/Availability: Most services are available only on a prepaid basis.
Contact: Dr. M.B. Line, Director General, Lending Division. (Telex 55781.) The electronic mail address on TELECOM GOLD is BLI 501.

★443★
**GREAT BRITAIN
BRITISH LIBRARY
REFERENCE DIVISION
EIGHTEENTH CENTURY SHORT TITLE CATALOGUE (ESTC)**
Great Russell St.   Phone: 01-636 8983
London WC1B 3DG, England
R.C. Alston, Head   Service Est: 1976

Staff: Approximately 15 total.
Related Organizations: Supporting organizations include ESTC/North America and the North American Imprints Publications Project.
Description of System or Service: The EIGHTEENTH CENTURY SHORT TITLE CATALOGUE (ESTC) is an international project established to produce a machine-readable catalog of English printing in the 18th century based on the collections of the British Library and other contributing libraries worldwide. Following AACR2 and MARC standards, the ESTC is cataloging books, pamphlets, and many types of ephemeral items printed in English anywhere in the world or printed in any language in the British Isles or in territories governed by Britain at any time during the 18th century. ESTC makes available an online data base for materials currently cataloged and also issues catalogs on microfiche.
Scope and/or Subject Matter: English printing in the 18th century, including books, pamphlets, and ephemeral materials covering the subjects of literature, science, technology, art, architecture, medicine, law, social science, politics, economics, transport, religion, philosophy, and psychology.
Input Sources: Input for ESTC is obtained from the holdings of the various departments of the Reference Division, including Printed Books, Manuscripts, and Oriental Manuscripts and Printed Books, as well as relevant items held in the Lending Division, and from records of holdings contributed from more than 700 public, academic, and special libraries in the United Kingdom, Europe, North America, and Australasia.
Holdings and Storage Media: The machine-readable Eighteenth Century Short Title Catalogue data base currently holds more than 150,000 records.
Publications: 1) Bibliography, Machine-Readable Cataloguing and the ESTC—a history of the project published by the British Library. 2) Searching the Eighteenth Century—consists of papers presented at the Symposium on the Eighteenth Century Short Title Catalogue which was sponsored by the Department of Extra-Mural Studies of the University of London. 3) ESTC Cataloguing Rules. 4) Factotum—irregularly issued newsletter of the ESTC; available free of charge from the Reference Division.
Microform Products and Services: The initial ESTC microfiche product is an author-title catalog of relevant items in the British Library collections, with indexes by date of publication, place of publication (other than London), and selected genres, including advertisements, almanacs, songs, prospectuses, and directories. The microfiche catalog will eventually be expanded to cover holdings of libraries worldwide.
Computer-Based Products and Services: The ESTC data base is available online through BLAISE-LINE and the Research Libraries Information Network (RLIN). Searchable data elements include author, title, imprint, year of publication, language of publication, general notes, library of origin, and locations.
Clientele/Availability: Users include librarians, bibliographers, and scholars in all historical disciplines.

Contact: M.J. Crump, Assistant Editor, Reference Division, British Library. In the United States, contact ESTC/North America, University Library, Louisiana State University, Baton Rouge, LA 70803; telephone (504) 388-8625. The electronic mail address on Research Libraries Information Network (RLIN) is BM.ESB.

★444★
GREAT BRITAIN
BRITISH LIBRARY
RESEARCH AND DEVELOPMENT DEPARTMENT
2 Sheraton St.
London W1V 4BH, England
Mr. B.J. Perry, Head
Phone: 01-636 1544
Service Est: 1974

Staff: 16 Management professional; 12 clerical and nonprofessional.

Description of System or Service: The RESEARCH AND DEVELOPMENT DEPARTMENT of the British Library promotes and supports research and development related to library and information operations in all subject fields. Working for the benefit of the national library and information system as a whole, the DEPARTMENT awards grants and contracts to institutions wishing to undertake projects of broad or general interest that can influence the effectiveness of primary (including preliminary) publications; the informal flow of information; the classification, cataloging, indexing, storage, retrieval, and translation of information; the operation and use of libraries and other information services; or the education and training of librarians, information scientists, and end users. The DEPARTMENT disseminates research results through reports, papers, reviews, and other publications as well as seminars and workshops.

Scope and/or Subject Matter: Library and information science research, especially in Great Britain.

Publications: 1) The British Library Research and Development Newsletter (3 per year)—announces new projects, reports on significant projects, and summarizes formal reports resulting from the projects; available free of charge. 2) The British Library Research Reviews—reports on recent advances in information technology. 3) Library and Information Research Reports-LIR—a series of research project reports.

Clientele/Availability: Clients include library and information professionals, students, and others.

Contact: Director, Research and Development Department, British Library.

★445★
GREAT BRITAIN
BRITISH LIBRARY
SCIENCE REFERENCE LIBRARY
COMPUTER SEARCH SERVICE
25 Southampton Bldgs.
Chancery Lane
London WC2A 1AW, England
Derek Greenwood, Head
Phone: 01-405 8721
Service Est: 1977

Staff: Approximately 3 total.

Description of System or Service: The COMPUTER SEARCH SERVICE provides computerized search services from more than 70 data bases made available by major international online host services. Current awareness services are also offered.

Scope and/or Subject Matter: Online searches in science, technology, business, patents, and other fields.

Input Sources: Input is obtained from commercial and government online services worldwide.

Holdings and Storage Media: The holdings of the Science Reference Library consist of 750,000 bound volumes and subscriptions to 33,000 periodicals.

Computer-Based Products and Services: The Computer Search Service provides online searching and SDI services from data bases offered through major European and U.S. vendors. Searches are usually carried out by SRL staff.

Clientele/Availability: Services are available on a fee basis, with restrictions stipulated by data base vendors.

Contact: Derek Greenwood, Head, Computer Search Service. (Telex 266959.)

★446★
GREAT BRITAIN
BRITISH LIBRARY
SCIENCE REFERENCE LIBRARY
EUROPEAN BIOTECHNOLOGY INFORMATION PROGRAM (EBIP)
Aldwych Reading Room
9 Kean St.
London WC2B 4AT, England
John A. Leigh
Phone: 01-379 6488
Service Est: 1984

Staff: 4 Information and library professional; 2 clerical and nonprofessional.

Related Organizations: The EBIP is a collaborative project with organizations in Europe, initially funded in part by the Commission of the European Communities.

Description of System or Service: The aim of the EUROPEAN BIOTECHNOLOGY INFORMATION PROGRAM (EBIP) is to facilitate the provision of biotechnology information in Europe by: 1) investigating information sources and publishing guides to their availability and use; 2) investigating information needs in biotechnology in European Economic Community (EEC) countries and identifying gaps in provision; 3) offering EEC-wide information services in biotechnology; and 4) investigating the use of modern methods which have the potential to provide ready and rapid access to information in biotechnology throughout Europe to both large and small organizations. The PROGRAM currently offers a Prestel information service and is developing a computer-readable bibliographic data base covering sources of biotechnology information. It also issues a newsletter and plans to publish directories of information sources. Additionally, using the facilities of the Science Reference Library, EBIP provides inquiry answering, referrals, document delivery, and computerized information retrieval from commercially available online data bases.

Scope and/or Subject Matter: Biotechnology, including scientific and technical aspects, news and developments, business, patents, government involvement, safety and regulation, culture collections, and research in progress.

Input Sources: The primary source of input is the Science Reference Library.

Holdings and Storage Media: EBIP maintains a computer-readable bibliographic data base of approximately 2000 records.

Publications: EBIP Newsletter (monthly). EBIP is also preparing various guides to sources of biotechnology information.

Computer-Based Products and Services: The EUROPEAN BIOTECHNOLOGY INFORMATION PROGRAM maintains a computer-readable data base covering biotechnology information sources, including publications, data bases, organizations, and information centers. The data base is expected to be made publicly available through DIMDI. EBIP also offers the Biotel biotechnology information service of Prestel. Computer retrieval services from commercially available online data bases are available to EBIP clients through the Science Reference Library's Computer Search Service.

Clientele/Availability: Services are intended for use by those concerned with research and industry in biotechnology in Europe.

Remarks: EBIP is also known as the Projet Europeen d'Information sur la Biotechnologie.

Contact: John A. Leigh, European Biotechnology Information Project. (Telex 266959.)

★447★
**GREAT BRITAIN
BRITISH TELECOMMUNICATIONS
PACKET SWITCHSTREAM (PSS)**
GO7 Lutyens House
1-6 Finsbury Circus
London EC2M 7LY, England
G.V. Spencer, Head
Phone: 01-920 0661
Service Est: 1981

Staff: Approximately 20 Total.

Description of System or Service: The PACKET SWITCHSTREAM (PSS) is a public network for data communication services using packet-switching techniques. PSS can provide support to a wide range of terminal types and operating speeds and permit a diversity of data communications applications, chief of which is information retrieval. A related service, the International Packet Switching Service (IPSS), enables PSS customers to interconnect with other networks worldwide.

Scope and/or Subject Matter: Packet-switched data communication services, including data transfer, data bureau services, information retrieval, electronic mail, electronic funds transfer, inventory control, and software testing and development.

Publications: 1) PSS-The Technical Users Guide—available for purchase. Full technical statement of the service; intended for systems and software designers. 2) PSS, The Public Data Service Directory (annual)—available free of charge; guide to areas of information accessible via PSS as well as to software and hardware suppliers. 3) Packet SwitchStream, A Basic Guide and Directory—explains system fundamentals and provides directory listings. These and other publications are available from the PSS Customer Service Group on request.

Computer-Based Products and Services: PSS offers network facilities for information exchange and retrieval between its customers. Interconnection via IPSS allows intercommunication with Europe, North America, and Japan.

Clientele/Availability: Services are available on a fee basis, charged on a combination of both elapsed time and the volume of data transmitted.

Contact: Peter Gladman, PSS Customer Information Officer, Packet SwitchStream. (Telex 883040.)

★448★
**GREAT BRITAIN
BRITISH TELECOMMUNICATIONS
PRESTEL**
Telephone House
Temple Ave.
London EC4Y 0HL, England
Richard Hooper, Director
Phone: 01-583 9811
Service Est: 1978

Staff: Approximately 200 total.

Description of System or Service: PRESTEL is an interactive viewdata service linking home television receivers and microcomputers to numerous data bases and services via telephone lines. PRESTEL data bases are maintained on several computers serving regional areas in England, and on computer facilites in other countries, including the United States. The service is accessible using viewdata terminals, television receivers equipped with viewdata adaptors, or microcomputers with viewdata packages. Using a keypad linked to the television or computer, PRESTEL users retrieve information by choosing page numbers displayed on a series of progressively specific index menus to reach the desired information. Information supplied by publishers and other organizations is presented on the television or terminal screen as a page or frame. The service currently offers access to railroad and airline schedules, real estate listings, stock market data, consumer information, sports results, and many other types of information. PRESTEL also offers interactive services allowing users to book hotel rooms, reserve airline seats, send electronic mail and telex messages, use software, and shop and bank electronically. In addition to accessing central PRESTEL computer facilities, clients can use the Prestel Gateway service to access data bases and closed user group facilities maintained on third-party computers.

Scope and/or Subject Matter: Business and consumer-oriented subject areas, including agriculture, banking services, betting, books, business news and information, buying guides, charities, clubs, computers, currency rates, engineering, financial futures and statistics, fishing, weather forecasts, games, holidays, industrial safety, international information, local information, management, marketing, oil, restaurants, schools, science, shipping, sports, travel information, and universities.

Input Sources: More than 1200 publishers, government agencies, financial institutions, travel agencies, and other organizations supply information to Prestel, including DATASTREAM International Ltd., American Express, Trusthouse Forte, British Airways, British Rail, Consumers Association, Central Office of Information, Meteorological Office, Reuters, The Wall Street Journal, The Economist, Baric, Fintel, and Lloyd's of London.

Holdings and Storage Media: PRESTEL holds more than 300,000 pages of information on its own computers and has over 20 operational gateways to third-party computers.

Publications: The Prestel User—contains the official directory to Prestel services, including the Prestel Classified Directory which lists information providers and page numbers under subject headings, and the Prestel Information Providers index which lists organizations alphabetically, with short descriptions of services and page numbers. Issued as part of the Viewdata and TV User magazine.

Computer-Based Products and Services: PRESTEL provides interactive access to numerous files of business and consumer information. To facilitate searching, an alphabetical subject index and an alphabetical information provider index are offered online. The user can select an index item from the menu and progressively narrow the selection by choosing numbers corresponding to an item on each menu page until the desired level of information is reached. Pages may also be accessed directly by page number.

In addition to general business and consumer information, PRESTEL provides specialist interactive services, among which are the following: 1) Gateway—links Prestel users to more than 20 privately maintained computer data bases and facilities via British Telecom's Packet SwitchStream (PSS). Gateway permits interactive access to large data bases of information whose storage on PRESTEL would not be economical, to computer services requiring real-time calculations, to data bases using full-text search facilities, and to other real-time and personal services such as home shopping and banking. 2) Homelink—an electronic home banking and shopping service offered by the Nottingham Building Society. 3) Mailbox—an electronic mail service through which subscribers can send messages to other Prestel users. 4) Micronet 800—provides microcomputer users with online access to software application packages and permits downloading of games, business packages, and software programs. 5) Roomservice—a hotel booking service which links Prestel users to hotels throughout the world. 6) Skytrack—provides travel agents with direct access to reservation systems of participating airlines. 7) Telex Link—enables messages of up to 100 words to be sent to any telex machine in England via Prestel; the sender receives confirmation of telex delivery via the Mailbox electronic mail service.

Clientele/Availability: Prestel is available in the U.K. and 40 overseas countries; the service currently has more than 40,000 business and residential users.

Contact: Jan Shearer, Publicity Officer, Prestel. (Telex 261040.)

★449★
**GREAT BRITAIN
CENTRAL STATISTICAL OFFICE (CSO)
CSO MACRO-ECONOMIC DATA BANK**
Great George St.
London SW1P 4AQ, England
Phone: 01-233 6135

Special Note: The above name, address, and telephone number have been verified for this edition, although no questionnaire response was received. The following text is reprinted from the 5th edition.

Description of System or Service: The CSO MACRO-ECONOMIC DATA BANK is a collection of machine-readable time series dealing with United Kingdom economics and demographics. It is made up of the following six main groups of statistics: industrial production index;

national income and expenditure; balance of payments; prices; wages and earnings; and population and manpower. The DATA BANK is available for purchase from the CSO in various forms of computer output. The file is also accessible through commercial time-sharing companies.

Scope and/or Subject Matter: Economic, financial, and social time series data for the United Kingdom.

Input Sources: The original data are collected by British government agencies.

Holdings and Storage Media: The DATA BANK holds time series dating from 1948 to the present.

Publications: Central Statistical Office Macro-Economic Data Bank Index—provides detailed information on the time series held; available for purchase.

Computer-Based Products and Services: The DATA BANK may be purchased from the CSO on printouts or magnetic tapes. It is also interactively accessible through the time-sharing facilities of ADP Network Services, Inc., I.P. Sharp Associates, CISI, and other firms.

Clientele/Availability: CSO data are copyrighted; reproduction is subject to approval by the British government.

Contact: Computer Operations Supervisor, Central Statistical Office.

★450★
GREAT BRITAIN
DEPARTMENT OF INDUSTRY
INFORMATION TECHNOLOGY DIVISION
HERMES
29 Bressenden Place   Phone: 01-213 6533
London SW1E 5DT, England

Related Organizations: HERMES is a joint project with Scicon Ltd.

Description of System or Service: HERMES is a teletex demonstration project aimed at developing an electronic mail and document delivery system which would be suitable for both general use and for the specific needs of the publishing industry. (Teletex is a business communications service which permits electronic memory typewriters and communicating word processors from different manufacturers to communicate with each other.) The first phase of HERMES will include document ordering and delivery; the regular automatic delivery of prespecified documents; and electronic mail. In later phases HERMES plans to provide document searching facilities through links to existing data base search systems.

Scope and/or Subject Matter: Teletex-based transmission, reception, and manipulation of textual materials.

Computer-Based Products and Services: HERMES services will include electronic mail, document ordering and delivery, and eventually, document search facilities.

Clientele/Availability: Potential clients include publishers, librarians, information officers, and general office workers.

Contact: S. White, Information Technology Division. (Telex 8813148 DIHQ G.)

★451★
GREAT BRITAIN
DEPARTMENT OF INDUSTRY
NATIONAL PHYSICAL LABORATORY
DIVISION OF MATERIALS APPLICATIONS
METALLURGICAL AND THERMOCHEMICAL DATA SERVICE (MTDS)
Phone: 01-977 3622
Teddington, Middlesex TW11 0LW,
  England
Dr. T.I. Barry

Staff: Approximately 6 total.

Related Organizations: The National Physical Laboratory (NPL) is the United Kingdom custodian of the NPL/SGTE Databank in cooperation with the Scientific Group Thermodata Europe (SGTE).

Description of System or Service: The METALLURGICAL AND THERMOCHEMICAL DATA SERVICE (MTDS) maintains thermodynamic data banks that provide capabilities for retrieving data and calculating thermodynamic functions and multiphase multicomponent equilibria for inorganic systems. These data banks, which include NPL/SGTE and ALLOYDATA, are used to support online and consultancy services and are also available for implementation on client computers.

Scope and/or Subject Matter: Gases, pure condensed substances, alloys, molten salts, sulfides and aqueous solutions; calculation of multicomponent phase diagrams from data for binary systems.

Input Sources: Input is derived from authoritative compilations and critically assessed data appearing in published literature.

Holdings and Storage Media: Data for 2000 inorganic compounds and many binary alloy systems are stored on disks for both mainframe and microcomputers.

Computer-Based Products and Services: MTDS makes the NPL/SGTE Databank available online through Scicon Computer Services Ltd. It also offers the NPL/SGTE and ALLOYDATA data banks as packages for implementation on the client's computer.

Clientele/Availability: Clients include metallurgists and chemists.

Contact: Dr. T.I. Barry, Manager, Metallurgical and Thermochemical Data Service. (Telex 262344.)

★452★
GREAT BRITAIN
DEPARTMENT OF THE ENVIRONMENT
BUILDING RESEARCH ESTABLISHMENT
FIRE RESEARCH STATION LIBRARY
FIRE SCIENCE ABSTRACTS (FSA)
Melrose Ave.   Phone: 953 6177
Borehamwood, Herts. WD6 2BL, England   Service Est: 1981
Jill Johnston, Librarian

Staff: 2 Information and library professional; 2 clerical and nonprofessional.

Description of System or Service: FIRE SCIENCE ABSTRACTS (FSA) is a quarterly current awareness journal providing abstracts and indexes of international journal and other literature dealing with all aspects of fire safety and science. Information from the journal is included in the computer-readable Fire Research Library Automated Information Retrieval (FLAIR) data base, from which search services are offered.

Scope and/or Subject Matter: Safety of life and protection of property from fire; occurrence of fire; fire hazards and precautions; initiation and development of combustion; fire resistance; fire detection and extinction; and related topics.

Input Sources: Input is derived from 300 periodicals and from monographs and books (approximately 2000 per year).

Holdings and Storage Media: The machine-readable FLAIR data base contains approximately 14,000 records dating from 1981 to the present. Library holdings include bound volumes, 65,000 documents, and subscriptions to 200 periodicals.

Publications: Fire Science Abstracts (quarterly)—available by subscription; each issue includes author and subject indexes, which are cumulated annually.

Computer-Based Products and Services: The machine-readable FLAIR data base, holding information from Fire Science Abstracts plus additional citations, is used to provide information retrieval services as staff and time permit.

Other Services: The Fire Research Station Library will aid in securing documents cited in Fire Science Abstracts which are not available through the usual library systems.

Clientele/Availability: Chief clients are Fire Research Station staff.

Contact: Miss P.K. Mealing, Information Officer, Fire Research Station Library. (Telex 8951648.)

★453★
GREAT BRITAIN
DEPARTMENT OF THE ENVIRONMENT
BUILDING RESEARCH ESTABLISHMENT LIBRARY
BRIX

Bucknall's Lane, Garston Phone: 0923 674040
Watford, Herts. WD2 7JR, England
P.J. Elvin, Librarian

Staff: 5 Information and library professional; 5 clerical and nonprofessional; 1 other.

Description of System or Service: BRIX is a computer-readable bibliographic data base covering literature relating to building science. Consisting of virtually unstructured natural-language records, it is maintained online for in-house use at the Building Research Establishment Library.

Scope and/or Subject Matter: Building science.

Input Sources: Input to the data base consists of references with abstracts to periodical articles, research reports, and other literature.

Holdings and Storage Media: The BRIX data base is held in computer-readable form.

Computer-Based Products and Services: BRIX is searched online at the Building Research Establishment Library; it is not presently available to outside users.

Clientele/Availability: Services are for Building Research Establishment personnel only.

Contact: P.J. Elvin, Librarian, Building Research Establishment Library.

★454★
GREAT BRITAIN
DEPARTMENT OF TRADE AND INDUSTRY
BUSINESS STATISTICS OFFICE (BSO)

Government Bldgs. Phone: 0633 56111
Cardiff Rd. Service Est: 1969
Newport, Gwent NPT 1XG, Wales
Mr. R. Ash, Director

Description of System or Service: The BUSINESS STATISTICS OFFICE (BSO) is the government's main agency for the collecting and publishing of official United Kingdom statistics for manufacturing, retailing, producer prices, and current cost accounting indexes. The BSO produces the Business Monitor series of monthly, quarterly, and annual statistical publications based on information collected regularly from British firms. Selected information is also made available on computer tapes, including Price Index Numbers for Current Cost Accounting (PINCCA) and the Classified List of Manufacturing Businesses. Additionally, the OFFICE maintains a reference library and provides inquiry answering services for its own statistics and those of other government agencies.

Scope and/or Subject Matter: British business statistics, including manufacturing, retailing, producer prices, and cost accounting statistics.

Input Sources: Input is derived from questionnaires sent to companies.

Holdings and Storage Media: Nonbibliographic computer-readable data bases are maintained including PINCCA, holding more than 280 monthly time series since 1974, and the Classified List of Manufacturing Businesses. A reference library which subscribes to 500 periodicals is also maintained.

Publications: The Business Statistics Office publishes the Business Monitor series of monthly, quarterly, and annual publications on United Kingdom firms. The three main series are: 1) Production Monitors— provide detailed sales figures for individual products manufactured in more than 150 industries, and other data describing the structure of the manufacturing industry. 2) Service and Distributive Monitors— provide timely indicators of short term trends in the service and distribution sector, such as monthly index numbers of the total sales of retailers; also include a group of reports on the results of major annual or periodic inquiries. 3) Miscellaneous Monitors—cover other subjects including travel and tourism, acquisitions and mergers, price index numbers for current cost accounting, and investments. Business Monitors are available by subscription from HMSO Books, P.O. Box 276, London SW8 5DT, England.

Computer-Based Products and Services: The BUSINESS STATISTICS OFFICE provides computer tapes of PINCCA (Price Index Numbers for Current Cost Accounting) and the Classified List of Manufacturing Businesses.

Clientele/Availability: Services are available without restrictions.

Contact: I.W. Bushnell, Librarian, Business Statistics Office. (Telex 497121.)

★455★
GREAT BRITAIN
DEPARTMENTS OF THE ENVIRONMENT AND TRANSPORT
TRANSPORT AND ROAD RESEARCH LABORATORY (TRRL)
TECHNICAL INFORMATION AND LIBRARY SERVICES

Old Wokingham Rd. Phone: 03446 3131
Crowthorne, Berks. RG11 6AU, England Service Est: 1933
Mrs. B.A. Crofts, Head

Staff: 11 Information and library professional; 7 clerical and nonprofessional.

Description of System or Service: The TECHNICAL INFORMATION AND LIBRARY SERVICES provides information and documentation services for the United Kingdom transportation community by maintaining extensive library facilities and serving as the coordinating center for English-language input to the International Road Research Documentation (IRRD) data base. To support its library and IRRD-related activities, the SERVICES maintains the computer-based Transport and Road Abstracting and Cataloging System (TRACS), which facilitates library ordering and literature control, abstracting of materials for inclusion in the IRRD data base, and online literature searching and SDI services.

Scope and/or Subject Matter: Roads, their structures, design, and construction; road safety; traffic control; road research; transportation; transport planning, sociological and environmental effects; and research.

Input Sources: The Services abstracts English-language research reports, journals, monographs, theses, conference proceedings, standards, patents, summaries of ongoing research projects, and other materials for inclusion in the IRRD data base.

Holdings and Storage Media: Computer-readable information maintained under TRACS includes the collected IRRD data base, totalling some 120,000 references, and additional data on library holdings. Library collection numbers 70,000 volumes and subscriptions to 1000 periodicals, and includes much of the literature cited in IRRD.

Computer-Based Products and Services: The SERVICES has developed the computer-based TRACS system for handling library procedures and integrating them with the IRRD abstracts data base. TRACS, which is maintained on a dedicated PR1ME minicomputer under the STATUS interactive free-text retrieval software package, allows library staff to enter a bibliographic record once and use it to print orders for new materials, to catalog materials received, and to produce reminder notices. Bibliographic information entered includes title, author, accession number, shelf mark, and other elements. TRACS permits immediate access to the IRRD data base and to current information on the availability of documents at TRRL. Computerized search and SDI services are provided from the system on a fee basis.

Clientele/Availability: Services are restricted to users in the United Kingdom and are intended primarily for Laboratory personnel.

Contact: Mrs. B.A. Crofts, Head, Technical Information and Library Services.

★456★
GREAT BRITAIN
H.M. TREASURY
U.K. TREASURY MACROECONOMIC FORECASTING MODEL AND DATABANK
Treasury Chambers Phone: 01-233 3000
Parliament St.
London SW1, England

Special Note: The above name, address, and telephone number have been verified for this edition, although no questionnaire response was received. The following text is reprinted from the 5th edition.

Description of System or Service: The U.K. TREASURY MACROECONOMIC FORECASTING MODEL AND DATABANK is an econometric modeling and forecasting system consisting of a computer model and a Treasury data bank of major U.K. economic time series. The system can generate standard reports and is accessible through time-sharing.

Scope and/or Subject Matter: United Kingdom econometrics.

Input Sources: Data are collected and regularly updated by H.M. Treasury.

Holdings and Storage Media: The machine-readable U.K. Treasury Databank holds a wide range of U.K. economic time series.

Computer-Based Products and Services: The U.K. Treasury Macroeconomic Forecasting Model and Databank system is accessible through time-sharing.

Clientele/Availability: Clients include H.M. Treasury personnel and others.

Contact: Manager, U.K. Treasury Macroeconomic Forecasting Model and Databank.

★457★
GREAT BRITAIN
HEALTH AND SAFETY EXECUTIVE (HSE)
HSE LIBRARY AND INFORMATION SERVICES
Red Hill Phone: 0742 78141
Sheffield S3 7HQ, England
Sheila Pantry, Head

Staff: Approximately 30 total.

Description of System or Service: HSE LIBRARY AND INFORMATION SERVICES encompasses six major libraries that provide Health and Safety Executive staff with a range of information services on all subjects pertinent to health and safety at work. The SERVICES maintains and provides searches from the computer-readable HSELiNE data base, which covers accessions to all HSE libraries since 1977 plus journal articles of interest. The SERVICES also offers inquiry answering, reference and referral services, translations, and interlibrary loans.

Scope and/or Subject Matter: Occupational health and safety, including physical, chemical, and medical hazards.

Input Sources: Input for HSELiNE is derived from library accessions and from 300 periodicals that are regularly scanned.

Holdings and Storage Media: The computer-readable HSELiNE data base contains more than 40,000 references with abstracts, and dates from 1977 to the present. The file is updated monthly; approximately 10,000 records are added each year. The HSE also maintains six major libraries.

Computer-Based Products and Services: The HSE LIBRARY AND INFORMATION SERVICES provides searches from the HSELiNE data base, which is publicly available online through ESA/IRS and Pergamon InfoLine Ltd. Searchable fields include title, corporate source, publication source, abstract, keywords, author, Universal Decimal Classification, ISBN, language, and accession number. Additionally, the SERVICES conducts searches of other data bases as part of its reference service and operates a computerized cataloging system.

Clientele/Availability: Chief clients are HSE staff; facilities and services are available to the public by appointment.

Contact: Sheila Pantry, Head, HSE Library and Information Services. (Telex 668113.)

★458★
GREAT BRITAIN
HOME OFFICE FORENSIC SCIENCE SERVICE
CENTRAL RESEARCH ESTABLISHMENT (CRE)
OPERATIONAL SERVICES DIVISION
Aldermaston Phone: 07356 4100
Reading, Berks. RG7 4PN, England Service Est: 1967
Mr. P.G.W. Cobb, Director

Staff: 9 Information and library professional; 3 management professional; 5 clerical and nonprofessional.

Description of System or Service: The OPERATIONAL SERVICES DIVISION provides current awareness, data collection, and computerized retrieval services in the area of forensic sciences to the Metropolitan Police Laboratory and 10 operational laboratories in the United Kingdom. In support of these services, the DIVISION maintains a machine-readable bibliographic data base.

Scope and/or Subject Matter: All aspects of forensic science, including explosives, paint, glass, plastics, pathology, body fluids, fingerprints, plant materials, hairs, fibers, drugs of abuse, serology, immunology, electrophoresis, toxicology, and a wide range of analytical techniques.

Input Sources: Input is derived from published literature, abstracts, casework data, data collected externally under contract, and commercially available data bases.

Holdings and Storage Media: The Division's bibliographic data base holds more than 47,000 items collected over a ten-year period. Also maintained is a nonbibliographic file of data obtained from forensic science laboratories. The library collection consists of 2000 volumes, reports, and subscriptions to 160 periodicals.

Publications: 1) CRE Reports (monthly)—lists reports of research projects at the Central Research Establishment; 2) Technical Notes; 3) Annual Report.

Microform Products and Services: Reports are produced in microform.

Computer-Based Products and Services: The Operational Services Division maintains bibliographic and factual data bases in the area of forensic sciences, and provides searches from them for its primary clientele.

Clientele/Availability: Primary clients are the Home Office Forensic Science Service; limited service is provided to the forensic community.

Contact: Ian W. Evett, Head, Operational Services Division, Central Research Establishment.

★459★
GREAT BRITAIN
HOUSE OF COMMONS LIBRARY
PARLIAMENTARY ON-LINE INFORMATION SYSTEM (POLIS)
  Phone: 01-219 5714
London SW1A 0AA, England Service Est: 1980
Jane Wainwright, Head, Computer & Technical Services

Staff: Approximately 8 total.

Related Organizations: POLIS was developed by Scicon Ltd. under a Central Computer and Telecommunications Agency contract.

Description of System or Service: The PARLIAMENTARY ON-LINE INFORMATION SYSTEM (POLIS) contains references and indexing for Parliamentary questions, Parliamentary proceedings, Parliamentary papers, U.K. legislation, selected official government publications, selected European Community items, the House of Commons Library Collection, and other materials. POLIS is used by Library staff to provide quick research services to Members of Parliament, and it is publicly available online to authorized users through Scicon Ltd. In addition to maintaining POLIS, the Library produces a related thesaurus and a weekly bulletin and offers a telephone and postal reference service to the public.

Scope and/or Subject Matter: United Kingdom politics, government, administration, trade, and foreign relations.

Input Sources: Input is derived from the House of Commons and House of Lords Official Report (Hansard), Parliamentary papers, votes, proceedings, and various official publications. New material is indexed daily by the Library and added to the data base each night.

Holdings and Storage Media: Machine-readable POLIS files date from October 1980 to the present and cover approximately 150,000 documents. House of Commons Library holdings include 150,000 bound volumes, subscriptions to about 1500 periodicals, and various U.K., EEC, and UN official publications.

Publications: 1) House of Commons Library Thesaurus (semiannual)—contains approximately 10,000 terms. 2) House of Commons Weekly Information Bulletin—covers changes and additions to the data base on particular subjects; produced only when Parliament is in session and published by HM Stationery Office.

Computer-Based Products and Services: POLIS is held on the computer facilities of Scicon Ltd. for online searching by House of Commons Library staff and approved external users. Typical references in the data base include date of publication, the names of government departments and Members of Parliament concerned, the source reference, the title of the item, brief summary, the subject indexing terms assigned by the House of Commons Library, and the names of any associated committees or bodies, both Parliamentary and non-Parliamentary. The POLIS data base and Thesaurus are also offered on magnetic tape.

Clientele/Availability: Products and services are intended primarily for Library staff and Members of Parliament.

Contact: Jane Wainwright, Head of Computer and Technical Services Section, House of Commons Library; Michael R. Bunbury, Sales Manager, Commercial Applications, Scicon Ltd., Sanderson House, 49 Berners St., London W1Q 4AQ, England.

★460★
GREAT BRITAIN
HOUSE OF LORDS
LIBRARY & INFORMATION CENTRE

London SW1A 0PW, England
Roger Morgan, Librarian
Phone: 01-219 5242
Service Est: 1826

Staff: 17 Information and library professional.

Description of System or Service: The LIBRARY & INFORMATION CENTRE provides the House of Lords with library and information services that include maintenance of an internal computer-readable index to the LIBRARY's holdings. It provides computerized searches from this file and from data bases made available through a number of international online services. SDI services are also offered.

Scope and/or Subject Matter: British government and law.

Input Sources: Input for the Library's internal data base is derived from all publications received by the Library, including House of Lords and House of Commons papers, Command papers, and U.K. and other official papers and pamphlets.

Holdings and Storage Media: House of Lords Library holdings include 100,000 bound volumes, subscriptions to approximately 400 periodicals, and private files and press clippings in microform.

Publications: House of Lords Library Bulletin (semiannual)—not available to the public.

Computer-Based Products and Services: The LIBRARY & INFORMATION CENTRE conducts online searching of its own data base as well as those made accessible online through BLAISE (British Library Automated Information Service), ECHO (European Commission Host Organization), World Reporter, DIALOG Information Services, Inc., ESA/IRS, Telesystemes Questel, TEXTLINE (Finsbury Data Services Ltd.), NEXIS, EURIS, Euroleх, POLIS, and others. The CENTRE also offers SDI services and makes available the Prestel, CEEFAX, and ORACLE services for patron access.

Clientele/Availability: Products and services are available only to Peers, Members of the House of Commons, and officers of Parliament.

Remarks: Other computer-based services in the House of Lords include a data base of statistical and other information about Peers.

Contact: Roger Morgan, Librarian, House of Lords.

★461★
GREAT BRITAIN
INSTITUTE OF TERRESTRIAL ECOLOGY
BIOLOGICAL RECORDS CENTRE (BRC)

Monks Wood Experimental Station
Abbots Ripton
Huntingdon, Cambs. PE17 2LS, England
Paul T. Harding, Head
Phone: 04873 381
Service Est: 1964

Staff: 5 Information and library professional; 1 technician; 1 clerical and nonprofessional.

Related Organizations: Some of the work of the Centre is done on contract with the Nature Conservancy Council with headquarters at 19 Belgrave Sq., London SW1X 8PY, England.

Description of System or Service: The BIOLOGICAL RECORDS CENTRE (BRC) collects data on the occurrence of plants and animals throughout the British Isles, and makes these data available for research and conservation purposes. To this end, the CENTRE encourages national biological societies, organizations, or individuals to make surveys of particular groups of plants or animals. It supplies record cards, assists with recording schemes, processes and maintains the data, and produces distribution maps, atlases, and copies of records. Acting as a national data bank and archive, it can furnish detailed information on locality and habitat to workers concerned with a particular species. The CENTRE also collaborates with local museums and similar organizations throughout the British Isles.

Scope and/or Subject Matter: Flora and fauna in the British Isles.

Input Sources: Data are collected from field surveys, museums, herbaria, data centers throughout the British Isles, and published sources.

Holdings and Storage Media: The majority of CENTRE data consists of lists of species from particular localities; the data for each list are stored on record cards and computer disks.

Publications: 1) Atlas of the British Flora. 2) Atlas of Ferns of the British Isles. 3) Provisional Atlas of the Bryophytes of the British Isles. 4) Provisional Atlas of the Amphibians and Reptiles of the British Isles. 5) Provisional Atlas of the Mammals of the British Isles. 6) Provisional Atlas of the Insects of the British Isles—in nine parts. 7) Atlas of the Bumblebees of the British Isles. 8) Atlas of the Non-marine Mollusca of the British Isles. 9) Provisional Atlas of the Crustacea of the British Isles. 10) Provisional Atlas of the Nematodes of the British Isles—in three parts. 11) Provisional Atlas of the Arachnida of the British Isles. 12) Provisional Atlas of the Marine Dinoflagellates of the British Isles. 13) Atlas of the Lichens of the British Isles. The CENTRE also publishes overlays of environmental factors for use with BRC distribution maps.

Computer-Based Products and Services: The BRC data bank is held on a computer at the Monks Wood Experimental Station and on the computers of the Science and Engineering Research Council at the Rutherford Laboratory. It is being incorporated in a data management system which will provide information retrieval facilities as well as the production of distribution maps.

Clientele/Availability: Services are available without restrictions.

Contact: Paul T. Harding, Head, Biological Records Centre. (Telex 32416.)

★462★
GREAT BRITAIN
MANPOWER SERVICES COMMISSION
CAREERS AND OCCUPATIONAL INFORMATION CENTRE (COIC)

Moorfoot
Sheffield S1 4PQ, England
Barry Cornish, Head
Phone: 0742 704575
Service Est: 1977

Description of System or Service: The CAREERS AND OCCUPATIONAL INFORMATION CENTRE (COIC) is a research and publishing facility providing information on careers and occupations in the United Kingdom. It issues a wide variety of video films, booklets, leaflets, and other publications on careers and working conditions, and it serves as a back-up facility for career officers as well as a resource for answering inquiries from the public. Among COIC products is

Signposts, a set of annotated and indexed catalog cards providing information on 300 occupations; Signposts information is also accessible via Prestel. Additionally, the computer-based Data on Occupations Retrieval System (DOORS) is being implemented to support all COIC research needs.

Scope and/or Subject Matter: Careers, occupations, professions, training, work conditions, and related information.

Input Sources: Information sources include industrial training boards, trade institutes, publishers, and local authority careers information units; approximately 20 career periodicals are also regularly scanned.

Holdings and Storage Media: Library holdings include 2000 bound volumes, subscriptions to 35 periodicals, and a variety of leaflets. The computer-readable's DOORS data base holds 200 occupational records.

Publications: The COIC publishes the monthly Newscheck magazine and three separate series of booklets covering available careers and professions, working conditions in particular industries and fields, and work and training involved in particular jobs within an industry or general work area. Other publications are also issued; a complete list is available by request from COIC.

Computer-Based Products and Services: The Data on Occupations Retrieval System is an online research and information tool providing a range of facts about jobs and careers. It is expected to be developed from the current 200 occupational records to some 800 records, serving as a basic resource for COIC writers and the public. The completed data base will also be marketed to career offices and job centers. Additionally, the COIC provides information via Prestel, including key extracts from the Newscheck magazine as well as a computerized version of the Signposts catalog card service.

Clientele/Availability: Services are available without restrictions.

Contact: David Greensmith, Executive Officer, Careers and Occupational Information Centre.

★463★
GREAT BRITAIN
WATER RESEARCH CENTRE (WRC)
INFORMATION SERVICE ON TOXICITY AND BIODEGRADABILITY (INSTAB)

Stevenage Laboratory Phone: 0438 312444
Elder Way Service Est: 1966
Stevenage, Herts. SG1 1TH, England
Rita M. Flain

Related Organizations: The Water Research Centre is funded by the United Kingdom water industry and other subscribing members.

Description of System or Service: The INFORMATION SERVICE ON TOXICITY AND BIODEGRADABILITY (INSTAB) provides industry and government agencies with information regarding the possible damage inflicted on aquatic life and sewage treatment processes by chemical substances contained in industrial, agricultural, and domestic effluents. It maintains an index on more than 2000 chemicals and their effects, keeping it up to date with comprehensive searching of the published literature and other sources. Services offered by INSTAB include consultation and advice for specific inquiries and annotated bibliographies and literature summaries on individual chemicals.

Scope and/or Subject Matter: Biodegradability of organic compounds; effects of chemicals on sewage treatment processes, both aerobic and anaerobic; toxicity of chemicals to aquatic organisms; environmental effects of wastes disposed of in landfills. Service is primarily concerned with freshwater environment.

Input Sources: INSTAB compiles data from primary journals, abstracts journals, and original research projects; all information is critically appraised during compilation.

Computer-Based Products and Services: Computerized searching is conducted by INSTAB.

Clientele/Availability: All services are generally supplied free of charge to clientele in the United Kingdom; services are provided to others on a fee basis.

Contact: Rita M. Flain, Information Service on Toxicity and Biodegradability. (Telex 826168.)

★464★
GREAT BRITAIN
WATER RESEARCH CENTRE (WRC)
LIBRARY AND INFORMATION SERVICES

Stevenage Laboratory Phone: 0438 312444
Elder Way Service Est: 1974
Stevenage, Herts. SG1 1TH, England
Lorna E. Newman, Manager

Staff: Approximately 25 total.

Related Organizations: The Water Research Centre is funded by the United Kingdom water industry and other subscribing members.

Description of System or Service: The LIBRARY AND INFORMATION SERVICES of the Water Research Centre collects, organizes, and disseminates information relating to water resources, water treatment, and related topics. It publishes a weekly abstracts journal known as WRC Information, which covers the international literature on the subject, and maintains a corresponding computer-readable data base known as AQUALINE. The SERVICES also maintains several libraries and offers document delivery, current awareness, computerized and manual literature searching, and referral services. The journal and various information services are available by annual subscription.

Scope and/or Subject Matter: Water research and resources, including: treatment, distribution and supply, quality and health, sewage and industrial waste water treatment, sewerage, sludge disposal, pollution and fish studies, instrumentation, control and automation, and water and wastewater distribution via pipes, sewers, and water mains, including rehabilitation and replacement strategies, network analysis, and leakage control policy.

Input Sources: The Services scans conference proceedings, books, government reports, documents, and more than 600 scientific and technical journals for input to its abstracting service.

Holdings and Storage Media: The computer-readable AQUALINE data base contains 80,000 abstracts covering literature dating from 1969 to the present. Library holdings consist of 10,000 bound volumes; 40,000 pamphlets and reports; and subscriptions to 600 periodicals.

Publications: 1) WRC Information (weekly)—each issue contains about 75 abstracts of the world water research literature. 2) Technical Reports—describe work performed by WRC in its research program. 3) AQUALINE Online User Guide. Publications are available free to members and by subscription or purchase to others.

Microform Products and Services: Cumulative five-year indexes to WRC Information covering the periods 1974-1978 and 1979-1983 are available for purchase on microfiche.

Computer-Based Products and Services: The AQUALINE data base is available for online searching through DIALOG Information Services, Inc. and ESA/IRS. Searchable data elements in the file include author, title, journal, publication year, language, summary language, abstract, descriptors, and section headings. The SERVICES will search the AQUALINE data base and other commercially available data bases for subscribing members. It also offers SDI using the AQUALINE data base and fulfills document orders placed online through DIALOG's DIALORDER or ESA/IRS's PRIMORDIAL ordering services.

Other Services: In addition to the services described above, the Services offers consulting.

Clientele/Availability: Services are available to members of the Water Research Centre and to subscribers.

Contact: Lorna E. Newman, Technical Information Manager, Library and Information Services. (Telex 848632.)

★465★
GREATER LONDON COUNCIL (GLC)
INFORMATION SERVICES GROUP
Director General's Dept.
County Hall
London SE1 7PB, England
Alan Gomersall, Group Head
Phone: 01-633 7149
Service Est: 1969

Staff: 18 Information and library professional; 2 technicians; 1 sales and marketing; 12 clerical and nonprofessional.

Description of System or Service: The INFORMATION SERVICES GROUP provides documentation and information concerning London-area local government issues to officers and elected members of the Greater London Council and the London Boroughs, and to the public at large. Its major resources are the ACOMPLIS (A Computerized London Information System) data base of urban studies and social policy literature, and an extensive Research Library which also administers other civil engineering and scientific libraries. The GROUP issues several current awareness publications and makes bibliographic information publicly available online.

Scope and/or Subject Matter: Local government, including town and country planning, traffic and transportation research, social services, social planning, environment, noise, pollution, energy, public health, government finance and management, inner-city studies, architecture and building, civil engineering, housing.

Input Sources: Input consists of documentation generated by central and local governments, literature from action groups and voluntary associations, books and journals, government literature and legislation, statistics and reports of official organizations, fugitive literature, theses, and research reports from academic institutions.

Holdings and Storage Media: The computer-readable ACOMPLIS data base currently holds more than 70,000 bibliographic items in machine-readable form; it is updated monthly with more than than 1000 items. The Research Library comprises 40,000 volumes, 50,000 pamphlets and reports, 20,000 microfiche, 20,000 slides, and 2000 periodical subscriptions including more than 350 statistics serials.

Publications: 1) Daily Intelligence Bulletin—includes abstracts from newspapers, journals, and government press releases. 2) Boroughs Intelligence Newsletter (monthly)—indicates the availability of information within the GLC and of relevant publications and documents. 3) Urban Abstracts (18 issues per year)—contains abstracts incorporating major articles from journals as well as selected books, conferences, and reports. 4) European Digest (monthly)—summarizes and lists literature on current activities in the European Community of interest to London. 5) Research Document Guides—reading lists or bibliographies with abstracts or literature reviews. Produced in response to individual requests and published if the subject matter is of general interest. 6) Tech News (weekly)—selection of items and titles from newspapers and periodicals compiled for engineers, architects, surveyors, and scientists. All publications are available free to members of the GLC and to the London Boroughs; some are available for sale to the public.

Microform Products and Services: The ACOMPLIS data base KWOC index is available by subscription on COM microfiche with quarterly updates.

Computer-Based Products and Services: The INFORMATION SERVICES GROUP provides computerized searches from the ACOMPLIS data base and makes it publicly available online as the ACOMPLINE file through ESA/IRS and Scicon Ltd. Providing indexes and abstracts of documentation received in the Research Library, the data base covers all aspects of urban studies and development. Each reference typically includes article title, personal and/or corporate author, bibliographic details, list of controlled index terms, and (in most cases) an indicative abstract. ACOMPLINE can be searched by subject index term, words in the title or abstract, document type, publication date, personal author, and corporate source; it is also possible to search for the presence of statistics in an item and to locate bibliographies. In addition to ACOMPLINE, the INFORMATION SERVICES GROUP has established the bibliographic URBALINE data base covering urban and local government issues. Available through Scicon, URBALINE provides relevant references and brief abstracts drawn from the Daily Intelligence Bulletin (DIB) and Tech News publications as well as from ACOMPLINE.

Clientele/Availability: Services are available to the public by arrangement.

Contact: Alan Gomersall, Information Services Group Head, Greater London Council.

★466★
GROUP FOR THE ADVANCEMENT OF SPECTROSCOPIC METHODS AND PHYSICOCHEMICAL ANALYSIS
(Groupement pour l'Avancement des Methodes Spectroscopiques et Physico-Chimique d'Analyse - GAMS)
INFORMATION CENTER FOR SPECTROSCOPIC AND PHYSICOCHEMICAL ANALYSIS
(Centre d'Information Spectroscopique et Physico-Chimique d'Analyse - C.I.S.)
88, blvd. Malesherbes
F-75008 Paris, France
Madame D. Sandino, Adjunct Director
Phone: 01 5639304

Description of System or Service: The INFORMATION CENTER FOR SPECTROSCOPIC AND PHYSICOCHEMICAL ANALYSIS (C.I.S.) makes available spectroscopic data to the members of the Group for the Advancement of Spectroscopic Methods and Physicochemical Analysis. Infrared, ultraviolet, nuclear magnetic resonance, and mass spectra are acquired from sources such as the ASTM/Sadtler Infrared Data Program and the Coblentz Society which compile raw spectroscopic data for distribution. The CENTER performs computerized searches using this information.

Scope and/or Subject Matter: Spectroscopic data, including infrared, ultraviolet, nuclear magnetic resonance, Raman, and mass spectra.

Input Sources: The Center uses spectra data collected by other organizations, including Sadtler Research Laboratories, Inc., American Petroleum Institute, U.S. National Institutes of Health, and the Coblentz Society.

Holdings and Storage Media: The Center's collection comprises: 234,500 infrared spectra; 39,700 ultraviolet spectra; 1000 Raman spectra; 49,500 nuclear magnetic resonance spectra; and 40,500 mass spectra.

Computer-Based Products and Services: The CENTER performs online searches of ASTM data banks of infrared spectra.

Clientele/Availability: Services are available to members of the Group.

Contact: Madame D. Sandino, Adjunct Director, Information Center for Spectroscopic and Physicochemical Analysis.

★467★
GROUP FOR THE STUDY AND RESEARCH OF TROPICAL AGRONOMY
(Groupement d'Etudes et de Recherche pour le Developpement de l'Agronomie Tropicale - GERDAT)
AGRITROP
42, rue Scheffer
F-75116 Paris, France
Genevieve Hartmann
Phone: 01 7043215
Founded: 1977

Staff: 1 Information and library professional; 1 management professional; 1 technician; 1 clerical and nonprofessional.

Description of System or Service: AGRITROP is a semiannual journal providing abstracts of French-language literature dealing with tropical agriculture. Computerized information services are expected to be offered for this information.

Scope and/or Subject Matter: Tropical agriculture, with emphasis on research and production, crops, animal husbandry, forestry, fish culture, and technology.

Input Sources: Input for AGRITROP is derived from 50 French-language periodicals and from monographs, reports, notes, and theses.

Publications: AGRITROP (twice a year)—provides approximately 800 abstracts per year; each issue is published in French, English, and Spanish editions which are available by subscription.

Computer-Based Products and Services: AGRITROP is expected to become available online in the future. SDI, literature searching, and tape services will also be available from GERDAT.

Clientele/Availability: Products are available on a fee basis.

Remarks: A data base covering agricultural products is currently under development by GERDAT.

Contact: Francoise Bodard, Secretary, or Serge Veretenicoff, Documentalist, Group for the Study and Research of Tropical Agronomy.

★468★
GRUNER & JAHR AG & CO.
G&J PRESS INFORMATION BANK
(G&J-Pressedokumentation)
Warburgstr. 50
D-2000 Hamburg 36, Fed. Rep. of
  Germany
Hans-Joachim Lienau, Manager
Phone: 040 41182051
Service Est: 1974

Staff: 78 Information and library professional; 5 management professional; 5 technicians; 12 other.

Description of System or Service: The G&J PRESS INFORMATION BANK, a text and picture retrieval system, was developed to support the editorial activities of the Gruner & Jahr magazine publishing company. The system combines computer-based indexing of newspaper and magazine materials with automated retrieval of full text from microfiche and optical disks. Text is indexed using controlled vocabulary while pictures are retrieved by consulting descriptions of their contents displayed as full text, abstracts, captions, or index terms.

Scope and/or Subject Matter: Current events and other topics covered in the general press.

Input Sources: Input is derived from more than 160 German, English, and French publications, including 40 daily newspapers.

Holdings and Storage Media: Of 8 million article clippings and 5 million pictures maintained by Gruner & Jahr, 1.2 million articles and 1 million pictures are available in the data bank.

Microform Products and Services: Text is held on 24x and 42x microfiche in an automated retrieval system which produces facsimile copies on the terminal screen or on paper.

Computer-Based Products and Services: The PRESS INFORMATION BANK is used internally at G&J to answer more than 30,000 inquiries per year; with some restrictions, the data bank is also open to third party users.

Clientele/Availability: Interested persons should inquire.

Remarks: Gruner & Jahr has established a department called Info-Marketing/ Dialogsysteme for the development of new electronic information products to be delivered to a wider range of users.

Contact: Hans-Joachim Lienau, Manager, or K. Hartmann, Gruner & Jahr AG & Co. (Telex 21 952 23.)

★469★
GSI-ECO
25, blvd. de l'Amiral Bruix
F-75782 Paris Cedex 16, France
Phone: 01 5021220
Founded: 1982

Special Note: The above name, address, and telephone number have been verified for this edition, although no questionnaire response was received. The following text is reprinted from the 5th edition.

Staff: 4 Information and library professional; 4 management professional; 4 technicians; 3 clerical and nonprofessional.

Related Organizations: GSI-ECO receives support from the Banque de France and the Institut National de la Statistique et des Etudes Economiques (INSEE).

Description of System or Service: GSI-ECO is an online service providing clients with remote terminal access to worldwide economic data gathered by various international and national organizations. To access the data, GSI-ECO makes available DATAFRANCE software, which enables clients to access several data bases simultaneously, to manipulate the numeric data, to add their own data, and to make graphic representations of the desired data. DATAFRANCE is accessible via direct dial and through Transpac, Euronet DIANE, and Tymnet networks.

Scope and/or Subject Matter: Economics, finance, world trade, and business.

Input Sources: Data banks are obtained from national and international organizations.

Holdings and Storage Media: Numeric data are held in machine-readable form.

Computer-Based Products and Services: Through its DATAFRANCE service, GSI-ECO makes available for online searching the following data banks: 1) International Financial Statistics (IMF); 2) Main Economic Indicators (OCED); 3) Indicators of Industrial Activity (OECD); 4) SIC (INSEE); 5) CRONOS (CEC); 6) CHELEM (CEPII); 7) BOSP; and 8) COE.

Clientele/Availability: Services are available without restrictions. Major clientele include companies, banks, economic think tanks, and public agencies.

Contact: Didier Weitzman, Director, GSI-ECO. (Telex 613163 F.)

★470★
GUINNESS SUPERLATIVES LIMITED
VIEWDATA SERVICES

Special Note: The VIEWDATA SERVICES of Guinness Superlatives Limited of Enfield, England are no longer available. The SERVICES were described in the fifth edition of Encyclopedia of Information Systems and Services (entry 846) as consisting of a data base on Prestel providing information from the Guinness Book of Records and other Guinness publications.

★471★
GULF ORGANIZATION FOR INDUSTRIAL CONSULTING (GOIC)
INDUSTRIAL DATA BANK DEPARTMENT (IDB)
P.O. Box 5114
Doha, Qatar
Phone: 321461
Service Est: 1979

Special Note: The above name, address, and telephone number have been verified for this edition, although no questionnaire response was received. The following text is reprinted from the 5th edition.

Staff: 4 Information and library professional; 1 management professional; 14 technicians; 4 clerical and nonprofessional.

Description of System or Service: The INDUSTRIAL DATA BANK DEPARTMENT (IDB) collects, processes, and disseminates information on industrial development for members of the Gulf Organization for Industrial Consulting (GOIC), a regional organization of seven Arabian Gulf States that is responsible for industrial cooperation and coordination among members. Industrial, technological, socioeconomic, and marketing information is collected from regional, national, and international sources and stored in computer-readable files from which search and tape services are offered. A supporting technical library and a publication unit are also maintained by IDB.

Scope and/or Subject Matter: Industrial cooperation and coordination in the Arabian Gulf States.

Input Sources: Input is derived from GOIC studies; statistical and industrial publications from regional, national, and international sources; and from commercially available data bases.

Holdings and Storage Media: Holdings consist of machine-readable files and microforms; 6400 books, pamphlets, and audiovisuals; and subscriptions to 247 English and 72 Arabic periodicals.

Publications: A quarterly magazine in Arabic and various bibliographies, surveys, status reports on selected industries, and economic reviews are published.

Computer-Based Products and Services: IDB maintains four machine-readable data bases: Gulf Industries, Technology, Socio-Economic, and Marketing. Search and tape services from these files are provided for GOIC member countries. IDB also has online access to DIALOG Information Services, Inc. and other commercial vendors.

Other Services: IDB also offers consulting, research, data collection and analysis, and translations.

Clientele/Availability: Products and services are available to member countries and regional and international organizations.

Contact: Director, Industrial Data Bank Department.

H

★472★

HANDS-ON (INFORMATION) LTD.
35-37 Victoria St.   Phone: 725224
Wellington, New Zealand   Founded: 1982
John W. Schnellenberg, Managing Director

Staff: 1 Information and library professional; 2 sales and marketing; 1 other.

Description of System or Service: HANDS-ON (INFORMATION) LTD. offers sales and consulting services relating to online information, microcomputer software, systems, and hardware. The firm provides computerized information retrieval and document delivery services through its Dator Center Ltd. division.

Scope and/or Subject Matter: Information systems consulting services; information retrieval in subject areas of interest to clients.

Input Sources: Commercially available online data bases serve as input sources.

Computer-Based Products and Services: The Dator Centre Ltd. division of HANDS-ON (INFORMATION) LTD. provides computerized information retrieval from data bases made available through DIALOG Information Services, Inc.

Clientele/Availability: Services are available without restrictions.

Contact: John W. Schnellenberg, Managing Director, Hands-On (Information) Ltd.

★473★

HANOVER PRESS
VIEWDATA SERVICES
80 Highgate Rd.   Phone: 01-267 9521
London NW5, England   Service Est: 1981
Maureen A. Miller, Editor/Director

Staff: 1 Information and library professional; 3 management professional; 5 technicians; 3 sales and marketing; 2 clerical and nonprofessional.

Description of System or Service: The Hanover Press VIEWDATA SERVICES provides three travel and business advertising and information data bases on the Prestel system operated by British Telecom. These include the following: 1) American Viewdata Services, which contains travel information for the United States and Canada; 2) World Viewdata Services, which covers travel in cities and countries worldwide; and 3) Business In View, which lists trade and consumer services. Designed for the 4000 travel agents using Prestel, as well as travel departments in business firms and other clients, the travel data baes include interactive features enabling the user to order brochures and make reservations. Several publications related to the three data bases are issued by Hanover Press.

Scope and/or Subject Matter: Advertising and related information for North American and international travel and for British commercial services.

Input Sources: State and city governments and major commercial suppliers such as airlines and hotels pay an annual fee to have their information included in the data base.

Holdings and Storage Media: Information is held in three machine-readable data bases.

Publications: 1) North American Travel Market (annual)—contains articles on travel, directories of travel organizations, and an index of services covered in the Prestel data base; supplied free to managers in the England travel industry and for a fee to others. 2) Business In View (annual)—provides listings of travel and business services available through the Prestel data bases. Includes a classified index to North American and worldwide sights, travel arrangements, and services; an index to services by country; and a general trade and consumer services listing. 3) Holiday USA & Canada (annual)—contains articles and information on tourism and tourist sites.

Computer-Based Products and Services: VIEWDATA SERVICES offers three machine-readable data bases on the British Prestel system: 1) American Viewdata Services—provides travel information for the United States and Canada; includes information on airline services, bed and breakfast establishments, apartment rental, bus travel, car hire and purchasing, cruises, hotels, national parks, rail travel, regional travel associations, sea transportation, tours, and customs regulations. 2) World Viewdata Services—contains international travel information on countries and cities worldwide, including airlines, apartments, hotels, rail and road transportation, and tours. 3) Business In View—lists general trade and consumer services such as architects, builders, catering, computers, florists, hotels, office equipment, restaurants, sporting goods, and tools.

Other Services: Also offered are consultancy services for establishing and operating videotex systems.

Clientele/Availability: Services are intended for travel agents in Great Britain and commercial and news services.

Contact: Maureen A. Miller, Editor/Director, Hanover Press. (Telex 266298 HANOVER G.)

★474★

HARKER'S SPECIALIST BOOK IMPORTERS
HARKER'S INFORMATION RETRIEVAL SYSTEMS (HIRS)
74 Glebe Point Rd.   Phone: 02 6607666
Glebe, N.S.W. 2037, Australia   Service Est: 1979
James Harker-Mortlock, Chief Executive

Staff: 1 Information and library professional; 1 management professional; 2 sales and marketing; 1 clerical and nonprofessional.

Description of System or Service: HARKER'S INFORMATION RETRIEVAL SYSTEMS (HIRS) is an information brokerage and document delivery service designed to satisfy the information needs of clients located in Australia, New Zealand, and Southeast Asia, as well as overseas clients requiring information from these areas. HIRS provides computerized retrieval services from data bases carried by international online services and manual literature searching using domestic libraries and other sources. Additionally, the firm offers a document delivery service, supplying copies of articles, journals, books, patents, specifications, conference papers, and other printed material. HIRS accepts document requests from any country placed through online ordering services or by mail, telephone, or telex. HIRS also offers SDI; consulting; a general research facility; and specialized search services for book buying and patent information.

Scope and/or Subject Matter: Scientific, technical, professional, and academic information of interest to clients.

Input Sources: Information is derived from major online vendors, as well as from Australian public and private libraries and reference services.

Computer-Based Products and Services: HIRS conducts online searching of data bases offered through DIALOG Information Services, Inc., Bibliographic Retrieval Services (BRS), System Development Corporation (SDC), ESA/IRS, QL Systems Limited, AUSINET (Australian Information Network), and others. HIRS has electronic ordering facilities on DIALOG Information Services, Inc., Bibliographic Retrieval Services (BRS), and ESA/IRS.

Other Services: HIRS represents Data Courier Inc in Australia and is willing to represent other information firms.

Clientele/Availability: Clients include government and corporate libraries, businesses, and professionals in Australia and elsewhere.

Contact: James Harker-Mortlock, Chief Executive, Harker's Specialist Book Importers. (Telex AA 23976 CTS 07-013.)

★475★

HARRIS MEDIA SYSTEMS LTD.
20 Holly St., Suite 208   Phone: (416) 487-2111
Toronto, ON, Canada M4S 3B1   Founded: 1974
Robert E. Harris, President

Staff: 2 Management professional, 4 technicians; 2 sales and marketing; 3 clerical and nonprofessional.

Description of System or Service: HARRIS MEDIA SYSTEMS LTD. provides computer services to support planning, research, and administration for advertising agencies, media, and media representatives. As part of its services, HARRIS operates an online system and provides interactive access to media-related data banks.

Consulting services are also offered.

Scope and/or Subject Matter: Media planning, research, administration.

Input Sources: Data are obtained from media surveys.

Holdings and Storage Media: The firm holds several nonbibliographic data bases on its computer facilities.

Publications: Radio Guide (4 per year).

Computer-Based Products and Services: HARRIS MEDIA SYSTEMS LTD. provides online access to data bases produced by BBM Bureau of Measurement, PBM Print Measurement Bureau, and a newspaper audience data base.

Clientele/Availability: Clients include advertising agencies and media representatives.

Contact: Robert E. Harris, President, Harris Media Systems Ltd.

★476★
HARTMANN & HEENEMANN
COMPUTER COMPOSITION CENTER
(Satz Rechen Zentrum - SRZ)
Lutzowstr. 105 Phone: 030 2621081
D-1000 Berlin 30, Fed. Rep. of Germany Service Est: 1969
Hans W. Fock, President

Staff: 25 Information and library professional; 3 management professional; 6 technicians; 3 sales and marketing; 20 clerical and nonprofessional; 68 other.

Description of System or Service: The COMPUTER COMPOSITION CENTER (SRZ) provides publishers and libraries with input, proofing, processing, and photocomposition services for bibliographic and textual typesetting files. SRZ also makes client data bases available online, distributes tapes to other data base hosts, and prepares a variety of COM products from client input. More than 35 titles are handled by SRZ, including union catalogs, personnel and subject indexes, dictionaries and lexicons, industrial catalogs, registers, law texts and commentaries, mathematical texts, musical scores, and numerical tabulation and statistical works. SRZ also participates in and provides services from the German Patent Information System (see separate entry).

Scope and/or Subject Matter: Computerized file processing and photocomposition of reference works in such areas as natural science, technology, life science, archaeology, history of art.

Input Sources: Input is derived from client manuscripts and files.

Holdings and Storage Media: SRZ maintains more than 35 client-owned data bases in machine-readable form.

Microform Products and Services: The Center produces typographical-quality microfiche and microfilm.

Computer-Based Products and Services: SRZ develops its own programs and supplies computerized file processing and photocomposition services. As a host on the Euronet DIANE and Datex networks, SRZ offers online access to such data bases as the International Food Information Services (IFIS), Poldok, and many others. It also makes its data bases available via the Bildschirmtext videotex service.

Clientele/Availability: Clients include libraries, documentation services, reference book publishers, and others with typesetting needs.

Contact: Hans W. Fock, President, Computer Composition Center. (Telex 0181291 SRZB D.)

★477★
HEALTH CARE LITERATURE INFORMATION NETWORK (HECLINET)
Institut fur Krankenhausbau Phone: 030 3143905
Strasse des 17. Juni 135 Founded: 1969
D-1000 Berlin 12, Fed. Rep. of Germany
Rudiger Schneemann

Staff: 5 Information and library professional; 1 management professional; 1 technician.

Related Organizations: HECLINET is supported by the Institute of Hospital Building/ Institut fur Krankenhausbau of the Berlin Technical University/ Technische Universitat Berlin and the German Hospital Institute/ Deutsches Krankenhausinstitut; it evolved from the Hospital Care Documentation/ Dokumentation Krankenhauswesen project formerly operated by the two institutions.

Description of System or Service: The HEALTH CARE LITERATURE INFORMATION NETWORK (HECLINET) is a cooperative computer-based bibliographic system covering literature in the area of hospital care. Institutions from Austria, Denmark, the Federal Republic of Germany, Sweden, and Switzerland participate in HECLINET by scanning literature in their respective countries, by maintaining microform libraries of journal articles and other literature indexed, and by offering computerized literature searching of the collected HECLINET data base. Information is centrally processed at the Institute of Hospital Building where it is used for producing the hardcopy publication, Health Care Information Service/ Informationsdiest Krankenhauswesen, as well as for producing computer-readable tapes and a publicly available online data base.

Scope and/or Subject Matter: Hospital administration; nonclinical aspects of health services; hospital design, construction, and maintenance; health insurance and economics; health policy and planning; personnel and training; and interdisciplinary areas.

Input Sources: Input is derived from journal articles from approximately 400 health-related journals, 700 economics journals, 200 architectural journals, and 20 operations journals; other sources include monographs, conference proceedings, and fugitive literature. There are no restrictions on country or language of sources.

Holdings and Storage Media: The machine-readable HECLINET data base contains approximately 60,000 references dating from 1969 to the present, with approximately 4500 new references added annually.

Publications: Health Care Information Service/ Informationsdienst Krankenhauswesen (6 per year)—available by subscription; provides bibliographic references and indexes to hospital care literature. 2) Thesaurus Krankenhauswesen—contains 3600 terms in German, including 2500 cross-references and 1100 descriptors, as well as 100 of the most relevant English terms.

Microform Products and Services: Microfiche and microfilm copies of original documents are available through the network on request.

Computer-Based Products and Services: The HECLINET data base is publicly available online through DIMDI. Searchable data elements include title, author, source, publication year, language, geographic heading, descriptors, and abstract. Several HECLINET members receive tape copies to service their areas.

Other Services: In addition to the services described above, consulting, research, manual literature searching, and referral services are offered.

Clientele/Availability: Services are available without restrictions.

Contact: Rudiger Schneemann, Dipl.-Ing., Institute of Hospital Building; or Dr. Jurgen Seelos, German Hospital Institute, Tersteengenstr. 9, D-4000 Dusseldorf 30, Federal Republic of Germany.

★478★
HEBREW UNIVERSITY OF JERUSALEM
AUTOMATED LIBRARY EXPANDABLE PROGRAM HEBREW
  UNIVERSITY OF JERUSALEM (ALEPH)
Yissum, P.O. Box 4279 Phone: 02 584266
Jerusalem 91042, Israel Service Est: 1980
Avner Navin, Head

Staff: Approximately 12 total.

Description of System or Service: ALEPH is an online real-time library management system which was developed as an in-house system to support a network of 23 libraries with a shared catalog and collection. It has been expanded to include a national union catalog for university libraries in Israel and to support a number of individual catalogs for additional libraries. ALEPH provides cataloging, authority file control, authority file maintenance, circulation, acquisition follow-up, and catalog search functions. A user-oriented system which combines ease of search with sophisticated information retrieval capabilities, ALEPH can be accessed in either Hebrew or English through public access terminals. In addition to the online functions, ALEPH is used to generate a number of printed products.

Scope and/or Subject Matter: Online library management.

Input Sources: Input for ALEPH consists of the bibliographic holdings of individual libraries.

Holdings and Storage Media: Among the machine-readable bibliographic data currently held under ALEPH are the following: current cataloging for the Jewish National and University Library (20,000 titles per year); the Mt. Scopus Library for the Social Sciences and Humanities, retrospective conversion and current cataloging (250,000 titles); Union List of Serials in Israel Libraries (70,000 titles); retrospective conversion of the Hebrew University science libraries (70,000 titles); catalog of LC MARC records; and a number of other files.

Computer-Based Products and Services: ALEPH provides the following automated library management functions: 1) Cataloging—composed of five subfunctions: catalog a new publication; duplicate an existing record to serve as a basis for creating a new record; update catalog record; update holdings information; and delete record. 2) Authority file maintenance—updating an entry in one of the authority files (authors, titles, subject headings), automatically updates that entry in any related documents. Cross-reference building ensures authority control in the cataloging process. 3) Circulation—includes loan, return, hold, borrower update, reader inquiry, and book inquiry information. 4) Acquisition follow-up—short or full catalog information can be entered with ordering information and the record expanded and changed when the book is received. 5) Catalog search—can be conducted in Hebrew or English using guided search with prompt screens or searched directly. Accessible data elements include author, title, subject, series, words, call numbers, Library of Congress classification numbers, internal system numbers, and others. Additionally, ALEPH is used to generate printed products, including book catalogs, book lists, and notices.

Clientele/Availability: ALEPH has been implemented at a number of Israeli libraries.

Contact: Judith Levi, Systems Librarian; telephone 02 584020. (Telex 25391 HUIL. ATT: YISSUM.)

★479★
HEINZE GMBH
VISDATA
Postfach 505
Bremerweg 184
D-3100 Celle, Fed. Rep. of Germany
Phone: 05141 500

Description of System or Service: VISDATA (Vorschiften Informationssystem) maintains a computer-readable data base covering German laws, regulations, standards, and administrative decrees relating to building, construction, and urban planning. The system is operated by Heinze GmbH in conjunction with a number of other systems and services, including Deutsche Bau-Dokumentation.

Scope and/or Subject Matter: German regulations, standards and codes related to building design, equipment, building parts, materials, expenses, and contracts.

Input Sources: Input is derived from legislation, standards, government rulings, and similar sources.

Holdings and Storage Media: The computer-readable VISDATA data base contains more than 9600 bibliographic items dating from 1975 to the present and is updated half yearly.

Computer-Based Products and Services: The VISDATA data base is searchable by article title, source publication reference, author, corporate source, classification code, document type, regional descriptors, date, and other elements.

Clientele/Availability: Clients include architects, building owners, government personnel, and others.

Contact: VISDATA, Heinze GmbH.

★480★
HELSINGIN TELSET OY
TELSET
Keskuskatu 4B
SF-00101 Helsinki 10, Finland
Tapio Kallioja, Managing Director
Phone: 0171681
Service Est: 1980

Staff: 1 Management professional; 3 sales and marketing; 1 clerical and nonprofessional.

Related Organizations: Helsingin Telset Oy is a cooperative venture of Nokia Electronics, Helsinki Telephone Company, and the Sanoma Publishing Company.

Description of System or Service: Similar to the British Prestel system, TELSET is an interactive information system through which home and business television receivers can access a centralized computer data base via telephone lines. Information supplied by various organizations is displayed on the screen as a page or frame. The user retrieves information by keying appropriate keywords or page numbers for the desired information. TELSET users can presently access current news, weather, sports, and cultural events information; community information, health advice, timetables, postal and telephone service details, and recipes; and daily economic data and information on sectors of business.

Scope and/or Subject Matter: Information access in a variety of business and consumer-related subject areas.

Input Sources: Input is obtained from the Sanoma Publishing Company, City of Helsinki, Technical Research Center of Finland, Finnish Statistical Office, Gallup polls, banks, and other sources.

Holdings and Storage Media: Telset holds approximately 25,000 pages of information on its computer facilities.

Computer-Based Products and Services: Telset provides interactive access to a central computer store of information.

Clientele/Availability: Telset is available to the public on a commercial basis.

Contact: Tapio Kallioja, Managing Director, Helsingin Telset Oy.

★481★
HELSINKI SCHOOL OF ECONOMICS LIBRARY
(Helsingin Kauppakorkeakoulun Kirjasto - HKKK)
INFORMATION SERVICES
Runeberginkatu 22-24
SF-00100 Helsinki 10, Finland
Henri Broms, Chief Librarian
Phone: 90 43131
Service Est: 1975

Staff: 15 Information and library professional; 20 technicians.

Description of System or Service: The INFORMATION SERVICES acquires, scans, and indexes European business and economics literature and maintains this information in five computer-readable data bases, known collectively as Helecon:

1) The Finnish Periodicals Index in Economics and Business (FINP) data base covers business and economics articles in Finnish periodical literature.

2) The Scandinavian Periodicals Index in Economics and Business (SCANP) data base, developed in cooperation with several other economics libraries, covers articles appearing in Swedish, Danish, Norwegian, and Finnish business and economics journals.

3) The European Index of Management Periodicals (SCIMP) data base, produced in cooperation with the European Business School Librarians' Group (EBSLG) and formerly known as Selective Cooperative Indexing of Management Periodicals, indexes British, French, German, and U.S. periodical literature on management, business, and economics.

4) The Bibliographic Index of Library Documents (BILD) data base covers books, reports, and dissertations acquired by the Library; it is produced via the Library's integrated online acquisition, cataloging, and search system.

5) The THESIS (THES) data base covers all Finnish masters and doctoral theses in management, business, and economics.

The INFORMATION SERVICES makes all five data bases accessible online. The FINP, SCANP, SCIMP, and THESIS data bases are also used to produce hardcopy indexes, and FINP is additionally available as a subscription card service. In addition to the above services, the INFORMATION SERVICES conducts online searches of publicly available data bases.

Scope and/or Subject Matter: Economics, business administration, and management.

Input Sources: Input to the FINP data base is derived from 600 Finnish journals. SCANP contains references from 200 Scandinavian journals and approximately 60 university series. Input for SCIMP is drawn from 160 British, German, French, and U.S. periodicals. The BILD data base covers books, reports, dissertations, and other items acquired by the Library. Input to the THESIS data base is derived from Finnish masters and doctoral theses.

Holdings and Storage Media: The FINP data base holds 22,000 citations covering the period 1977 to date; it is updated monthly, at an annual rate of 5000 citations. Covering the period 1977 to the present, SCANP holds 16,000 references and is updated quarterly, with 2000 records added per year. The SCIMP file covers the period 1978 to date and holds 23,000 citations; it is updated 10 times per year, with an annual growth of 5000. The BILD data base holds 16,000 references and adds about 6000 citations annually. The THESIS data base holds 1000 citations and is updated quarterly, with an annual growth of 1000.

Publications: 1) European Index of Management Periodicals-SCIMP (10 per year)—available by subscription; each issue includes a permuted subject index, author index, list of firms and persons, and a source list. 2) Scandinavian Periodicals Index in Economics and Business-SCANP (quarterly with annual cumulation)—available by subscription; arranged by subject. 3) Finnish Periodicals Index in Economics and Business-FINP (card service). 4) THESIS (annual)—bibliography of theses. 5) FINP/BILD Thesaurus—available for purchase. 6) SCIMP/SCANP Thesaurus—available for purchase.

Computer-Based Products and Services: The INFORMATION SERVICES provides online access to the FINP, SCANP, SCIMP, BILD, and THESIS data bases. SCIMP is also accessible online through the London Graduate School of Business Studies. Search elements in the SCIMP and SCANP data bases include keywords, author, broad subject group, language, publication year, and journal title. Search elements in the BILD, FINP, and THESIS data bases include keywords, author, UDC classification, language, and names of firms. Documents cited in SCIMP, SCANP, and FINP may be ordered online. The INFORMATION SERVICES provides online information retrieval from these files and from data bases carried by DIALOG Information Services, Inc., System Development Corporation (SDC), ESA/IRS, and BLAISE (British Library Automated Information Service).

Other Services: Manual literature searching and SDI services are also offered.

Remarks: The address of the European Business School Librarians' Group, coproducer of SCIMP, is: Manchester Business School Library, Booth St. W., Manchester M15 6PB, England. The address of the London Graduate School of Business Studies is: Sussex Place, Regent's Park, London NW1 4SA, England; telephone 01-262 5050.

Contact: Henri Broms, Chief Librarian, Helsinki School of Economics Library. (Telex 122220 ECON SF.)

★482★
HELSINKI UNIVERSITY LIBRARY
(Helsingin Yliopiston Kirjasto)
FINNISH NATIONAL BIBLIOGRAPHY
(Suomen Kirjallisuus)
Tukholmankatu 2   Phone: 0410566
SF-00250 Helsinki 25, Finland
Marjatta Soisalon-Soininen, Editor-in-Chief

Staff: 8 Information and library professional; 2 technicians; 3 clerical and nonprofessional.

Description of System or Service: The FINNISH NATIONAL BIBLIOGRAPHY, based on legal deposit copies at the Helsinki University Library, is published in print and in microform. Information from the BIBLIOGRAPHY since 1977 is also maintained in the computer-readable KATI data base which is expected to be made publicly available online.

Scope and/or Subject Matter: Finnish monographic and serial publications.

Input Sources: Input is derived from legal deposit copies at the Library.

Holdings and Storage Media: The machine-readable KATI data base holds 53,000 records covering monographs since 1977 and serials.

Publications: Suomen Kirjallisuus (9 per year with annual volume). A five-year volume is planned.

Microform Products and Services: Fennica (9 per year)—microfiche version of the Bibliography.

Computer-Based Products and Services: The KATI data base is expected to be made accessible online via Euronet.

Clientele/Availability: Clients include Finnish librarians and others.

Contact: Dr. Thea Aulo, Head, Bibliographic Department, Helsinki University Library.

★483★
HELSINKI UNIVERSITY OF TECHNOLOGY
(Helsingin Teknillisen Korkeakoulun Kirjasto)
UNIVERSITY LIBRARY/NATIONAL LIBRARY FOR SCIENCE AND TECHNOLOGY
Otaniementie 9   Phone: 90 4512812
SF-02150 Espoo 15, Finland
Elin Tornudd, Director

Staff: 25 Information and library professional; 1 technician; 39 clerical and nonprofessional.

Description of System or Service: The UNIVERSITY LIBRARY/NATIONAL LIBRARY FOR SCIENCE AND TECHNOLOGY offers a full spectrum of scientific and technical library and information services. It participates in several international information systems, providing online input to INIS (International Nuclear Information System), the U.S. Department of Energy's Energy Data Base (EDB), and several Nordic systems. The LIBRARY also scans Finnish scientific and technical periodicals to prepare the TALI keyword index which is searchable online and published annually in hard copy, and it maintains the TENTTU online catalog of its book and serial holdings. Additionally, the LIBRARY provides online searching and SDI services from data bases accessed though European and North American online hosts.

Scope and/or Subject Matter: Electrical engineering, mechanical engineering, forest products, mining and metallurgy, civil engineering, architecture, chemistry, physics, mathematics, geology, information processing, industrial economics, energy, and information science.

Input Sources: Input consists of Finnish and foreign books, periodicals, conference proceedings, reports, online data bases, and other materials.

Holdings and Storage Media: Library collection numbers 550,000 volumes; 550,000 microfiche; and subscriptions to 7000 periodicals. Machine-readable data base holdings consist of more than 200,000 bibliographical records which include index terms and other information for each document.

Publications: 1) Tekniikan Aikakauslehti Indeksi-TALI (annual)—KWIC index of articles appearing in Finnish science and technology periodicals. 2) OTA-kirjasto—occasional papers with an annual index of masters' theses. Other publications include monthly accession lists, dissertations, and research papers.

Microform Products and Services: Microfiche cumulations of the Library's catalogs and the TALI index are available.

Computer-Based Products and Services: The LIBRARY maintains the machine-readable TALI index to Finnish scientific and technical periodicals, and the TENTTU catalog of book, serial, and report holdings. Both data bases are publicly accessible online under 3RIP software through the University's Computing Center. The LIBRARY also holds a copy of the VINITI data base on mining engineering and expects to offer it online. Additionally, the LIBRARY conducts online searches and offers SDI services from data bases made available through DIALOG Information Services, Inc., System Development Corporation (SDC), and ESA/IRS. SDI services are provided from scientific and technical data bases processed by the Royal Institute of

Technology Library and the Karolinska Institute's Medical Information Center in Sweden. Loans and copies of the original journal articles can be ordered online through the TENTTU system and copies can be delivered by means of telefacsimile.

Other Services: Additional services include advisory and consulting services, particularly for industrial and research libraries; translation assistance; manual literature searching; and interlibrary loan.

Clientele/Availability: Services are available to universities, research institutes, industrial companies in Finland, and others requiring technical information.

Contact: Elin Tornudd, Director, University Library/ National Library for Science and Technology. (Telex 12 1591.)

★484★
HENLEY CENTRE FOR FORECASTING
2 Tudor St., Blackfriars
London EC4Y 0AA, England
Hywel G. Jones, Director
Phone: 01-353 9961
Founded: 1974

Staff: 29 Management professional; 1 technician; 2 sales and marketing; 2 clerical and nonprofessional; 8 other.

Related Organizations: The Henley Centre for Forecasting is an independent organization associated with the Management College, Henley.

Description of System or Service: The HENLEY CENTRE FOR FORECASTING is a nonprofit business, economic, and social forecasting organization providing forecasts and analysis for more than 1500 clients in over 75 countries. The CENTRE has the following five principal activities: the production of regular economic and social forecast publications available on a subscription basis; regular seminars and briefing sessions for senior executives; the provision of special consultancy studies for individual companies, banks, and government departments; the publication of various studies and yearbooks on U.K. and international economic developments; and a research program designed to develop further forecasting methods and techniques. Additionally, HENLEY's International Forecasting Group offers the CENTREX computer-based subscription service for foreign currency exchange forecasting, analysis, and simulation. The firm also develops computer-based economic models.

Scope and/or Subject Matter: Economic, social, marketing, and business forecasting; foreign currency exchange rates.

Holdings and Storage Media: Henley's CENTREX service is based on a computer-readable data bank holding daily exchange rates and interest rates on 30 currencies for the past 10 years, together with quarterly economic indicators for each country and related market information such as gold prices.

Publications: 1) Planning for Social Change—includes 3 volumes of analysis and forecasts of social research and its economic implications. 2) Framework Forecasts for the UK Economy (monthly)—provides up-to-date forecasts of the UK economy for five years ahead. 3) Forecasts of Exchange Rate Movements (monthly)—forecasts and analyzes 16 major currencies against the pound sterling. 4) Currency Profiles (monthly)—forecasts and analyzes 16 currencies against the U.S. dollar; produced in association with Manufacturers Hanover Trust Company of New York. 5) Costs and Prices (quarterly)—provides commentaries and forecasts up to five years ahead for key input costs of business. 6) Foreign Exchange Outlook (quarterly)—provides exchange rate analysis and forecasts of major non-OECD currencies. 7) Investment Markets (quarterly)—forecasts of interest rates, share price, property, gold and commodity prices, savings, and flow of funds. 8) Planning Consumer Markets (quarterly)—provides data and forecasts on consumer income, spending, and savings for the UK and its regions. 9) UK Leisure Markets (quarterly)—forecasts and analyzes consumer leisure spending in the UK; backed by field surveys. 10) The Director's Guide (monthly)—ten-section digest of the latest economic developments. 11) The Director's Guide to the EEC Economies (monthly)—gives summary and forecasts of current economic developments within the EEC. 12) Framework Forecasts for the EEC Economies (monthly)—provides forecasts and reviews of key economic variables for each EEC country for five years ahead. 13) Exchange Rate Movements Yearbook—reference data on 20 currencies with analysis and forecast of developments. 14) Manufacturing and Retailing in the 80's—research report. All publications are available by subscription.

Computer-Based Products and Services: The CENTREX foreign exchange analysis and simulation system is available through the international time-sharing facilities of Comshare. The user can trace the likely effects on exchange rates of changes in inflation, interest rates, economic growth, and other elements using a ten-year historical data base. The data base includes exchange and cross rates, spot and forward rates, inflation and interest rates, and balance of payments data. CENTREX includes graphing facilities and simulation routines and provides users with the ability to interject their own assumptions and compare the resulting estimates with the CENTRE's forecast. Operation of CENTREX does not require knowledge of computer techniques. In addition, the CENTRE maintains models of the United Kingdom's economy and a wide range of specialized marketing and business sectors.

Clientele/Availability: Research services are available on a fee basis to clients in corporate management, sales, marketing, finance, administration, planning, and personnel. Orders may be placed by telex, telephone, or letter.

Contact: David A. Passey, Director and General Manager, Administration and External Relations, Henley Centre for Forecasting. (Telex 298817.)

★485★
HERTFORDSHIRE COUNTY COUNCIL
CHILTERN ADVISORY UNIT FOR COMPUTER BASED EDUCATION (AUCBE)
Endymion Rd.
Hatfield, Herts. AL10 8AU, England
Dr. W. Tagg, Director
Phone: 07072 65443
Service Est: 1968

Staff: 1 Information and library professional; 3 management professional; 1 technician; 2 sales and marketing; 8 clerical and nonprofessional.

Related Organizations: The AUCBE is part of the national Microelectronics Education Programme.

Description of System or Service: The CHILTERN ADVISORY UNIT FOR COMPUTER BASED EDUCATION (AUCBE) provides advice and training on the teaching of computer studies and on the use of computers across the educational curriculum. It also monitors computer hardware and develops systems and applications software. Additionally, the UNIT acts as a national focus for research and development on the use of microcomputer systems for information handling, public viewdata information provision, and microcomputer-based educational technology. In support of its activities, the AUCBE maintains more than 40 curriculum-related data files, about 10 information data bases in its fields of interest, and a publicly accessible Prestel file of more than 2500 pages.

Scope and/or Subject Matter: Education and computers, teacher training, computer software, control, information handling and retrieval, artificial intelligence, word processing, and related areas.

Input Sources: The Unit regularly scans 13 regional bulletins and 30 additional periodicals; it also uses data bases made available online through DIALOG Information Services, Inc., System Development Corporation (SDC), Prestel, and other services.

Holdings and Storage Media: More than 50 data bases are held in machine-readable form, and a comprehensive library is maintained.

Publications: 1) Chiltern Computing (5 times per year)—disseminates information between teachers in all disciplines. 2) Primary Computing (3 times per year)—newsletter for the primary school teacher. A number of booklets providing software documentation and other information are also issued.

Computer-Based Products and Services: The AUCBE maintains and provides copies of more than 40 curriculum-related data files for use with MicroQUERY and QUEST software. These files include selected historical census data, information about the monarchs of England, a gazetteer of Norway, the first act of "Hamlet," information on careers, the elements in the periodic table, and others. The AUCBE also maintains about 10 information data bases such as a national microcomputer software catalog and a file on current U.K. curriculum development projects. Additional computer-based services include the public Prestel file, online and microcomputer information retrieval, telesoftware (line transmission and broadcast), and gateway services.

Other Services: Also offered is national and international consultancy on educational innovation in information technology.

Clientele/Availability: Education professionals, teacher trainees, systems and applications software designers, and information technologists are primary clients.

Contact: Mike Aston, Deputy Director, Advisory Unit for Computer Based Education. (Telex 262413.) The electronic mail address on Telecom Gold is MEP016; on Prestel, 288005.

★486★
HERTFORDSHIRE TECHNICAL LIBRARY AND INFORMATION SERVICE
HERTIS INDUSTRIAL SERVICES
Hatfield Polytechnic Library
P.O. Box 110
Hatfield, Herts. AL10 9AD, England
William A. Forster, Librarian
Phone: 07072 68100
Service Est: 1961

Staff: 3 Information and library professional; 1 management professional; 1 clerical and nonprofessional.

Description of System or Service: HERTIS INDUSTRIAL SERVICES provides information and consultancy services for industry. It also maintains the computer-readable Hertfordshire Business Data Bank which provides details on companies in the region. The Data Bank is accessible through Prestel and is used to publish a printed commercial register.

Scope and/or Subject Matter: Industrial information services; Hertfordshire company information.

Input Sources: Online host services and other information sources are used.

Holdings and Storage Media: The Hertfordshire Business Data Bank is maintained in machine-readable form.

Publications: 1) HERTIS News (quarterly); 2) Hertfordshire Industrial and Commercial Register—print version of the Data Bank.

Computer-Based Products and Services: The HERTIS INDUSTRIAL SERVICES maintains the Hertfordshire Business Data Bank which holds information on companies in Hertfordshire. The Data Bank is accessible as a gateway service on the Prestel videotex system. INDUSTRIAL SERVICES also manages the Hertfordshire Business and Community Information Service which is available through Prestel. Additionally, the SERVICES provides online brokering and SDI services for subscribers.

Clientele/Availability: Services are available without restrictions.

Contact: William A. Forster, Librarian, HERTIS Industrial Services.

★487★
HOHENHEIM UNIVERSITY
(Universitat Hohenheim)
DOCUMENTATION CENTER ON ANIMAL PRODUCTION
Postfach 700562
Paracelsusstr. 2
D-7000 Stuttgart 70, Fed. Rep. of
  Germany
Dr. Harald Haendler, Director
Phone: 0711 45012110
Service Est: 1963

Staff: 5 Information and library professional; 3 technicians; 7 clerical and nonprofessional.

Related Organizations: The Documentation Center is part of the German Information System for Nutrition, Agriculture and Forestry, which is a member of the International Information System for the Agricultural Sciences and Technology (AGRIS). The Center is also a member of the International Newtork of Feed Information Centers (INFIC).

Description of System or Service: The DOCUMENTATION CENTER ON ANIMAL PRODUCTION abstracts and indexes literature on animal production to provide input to the national German agricultural data base and to prepare a monthly card service known as Informationsdienstkartei Tierische Produktion. Covering about 5000 articles per year, the service includes authors, titles, sources, and German-language abstracts and annotations for all articles listed. This information is also made available as annual cumulations on magnetic tapes. Additionally, the DOCUMENTATION CENTER gathers analytical data relating to animal feeds to create a computer-readable data bank known as Datenbank fur Futtermittel. The data bank is used in the production of feed composition tables and similar publications, as well as for internal information retrieval applications.

Scope and/or Subject Matter: Animal breeding, husbandry, and nutrition; feeds; small animals.

Input Sources: Articles are selected regularly from 280 periodicals, and occasionally from additional serials; also scanned are monographs, doctoral theses, reports, and related materials. The feed data bank receives input from these sources and from certificates of analysis.

Holdings and Storage Media: In addition to machine-readable tapes, files of secondary and original documents are maintained.

Publications: A card service, various bibliographies, and feed composition tables are published.

Computer-Based Products and Services: The DOCUMENTATION CENTER makes the Informationsdienstkartei Tierische Produktion files available for purchase as annual magnetic tapes; search services and SDI are also expected to be offered from this data base. No external services are provided from Datenbank fur Futtermittel.

Other Services: In addition to the services described above, the Documentation Center offers manual literature searching and referrals.

Clientele/Availability: Services are available to interested individuals and institutions on a fee basis.

Contact: Dr. Harald Haendler, Director, Documentation Center on Animal Production.

★488★
HONEYWELL BULL
EURIS HOST SERVICE
Square de Meeus 5
B-1040 Brussels, Belgium
Mr. J. Quenot, Commercial Manager
Phone: 02 5138238
Service Est: 1981

Description of System or Service: The EURIS HOST SERVICE is an online service which provides access to data bases of interest to the European Economic Communities. Files available through EURIS include the CELEX data base which contains documents relating to Community law (see separate entry following this one); the Statistical Office of the European Communities COMEXT data base which holds external trade statistics of the European Community; and Congressional Information Service's CIS/Index data base covering working papers and publications of the United States Congress. The EURIS HOST SERVICE is accessible through Euronet DIANE.

Scope and/or Subject Matter: Commission of the European Communities law and related documents; statistics on Community external trade and trade between member states; and United States Congressional activities and publications.

Holdings and Storage Media: Three publicly available data bases are stored online on EURIS computers.

Computer-Based Products and Services: EURIS HOST SERVICE provides access through Euronet DIANE to the CELEX, COMEXT, and CIS/Index data bases. The SERVICE uses MISTRAL information retrieval software developed by Honeywell Bull. MISTRAL offers a choice of dialogue languages in French, English, or German. The software also permits online consultation of the thesaurus of index terms to enhance retrieval possibilities and selection of customized display and output formats.

Clientele/Availability: The Service is publicly accessible.

Contact: Mr. J. Quenot, Commercial Manager, Euris Host Service.

★489★
HONEYWELL BULL
EURIS HOST SERVICE
EUROPEAN COMMUNITY LAW
(Communitatis Europeae Lex - CELEX)
Square de Meeus 5 Phone: 02 5138238
B-1040 Brussels, Belgium
Mr. J. Quenot, Commercial Manager

Related Organizations: The CELEX system was developed by the Commission of the European Communities (CEC) and is managed by Honeywell Bull, a Belgian subsidiary of the Bull Group. All Community institutions share in and are responsible for the operation of CELEX.

Description of System or Service: EUROPEAN COMMUNITY LAW (CELEX) is an interinstitutional computerized documentation system set up by the CEC to facilitate retrieval of documents relating to Community law. Accessible in three languages, CELEX comprises the following files: a legislation file covering all Community treaties or binding acts adopted since the European Communities were established and serving as the basis for the hardcopy Register of Current Community Legal Instruments; a case law file (CJUS) covering the entire case load of the European Communities Court of Justice; a Parliamentary activities file containing European Parliament resolutions and decisions, opinions of the Economic and Social Committee, and Commission proposals; and a data base covering Parliamentary questions, including written questions, Question Time, and oral questions with or without debate. CELEX is publicly accessible through the Euris Host Service on Euronet DIANE.

Scope and/or Subject Matter: Commission of the European Communities law and related documents, including basic treaties; instruments adopted; agreements with third countries; Court of Justice decisions; preparatory documents; national measures to implement Community law in member states; questions submitted by members of the European Parliament; and published works of legal authors.

Input Sources: CELEX input is derived from the Official Journal of the European Communities, special editions, reports of cases before the Court of Justice, national publications and communications, the Digest of Community Case Law, periodicals, and other sources.

Holdings and Storage Media: CELEX comprises four main computer-readable files. The legislation file covers the period 1951 to the present and is updated weekly. The CJUS file covers judgments from 1954 to the present and is updated monthly. Acts of the European Parliament file is available from 1974 to the present, with acts prior to 1974 being gradually added. The file is updated monthly. The Parliamentary questions file covers written questions from 1963, Question Time from 1975, and oral questions from 1973 to the present. Question Time and oral questions data are updated monthly, and written questions with answers are updated two weeks after publication in the Official Journal.

Publications: Register of Current Community Legal Instruments (annual)—two volumes giving references for Community legislation in force; published in all official Community languages. Subscribers can obtain updated information via the CELEX legislation file between editions. Available from the Office for Official Publications of the European Communities, B.P. 1003, Luxembourg.

Computer-Based Products and Services: Searchable in French, English, and German, CELEX can be accessed online through the Euris Host Service on the Euronet DIANE network. Documents stored in CELEX include the following searchable elements: document number; author; legal form; title; publication reference; document date; dates of notification, entry into force, and end of validity; relationships between documents such as legal bases, previous acts amended, and subsequent acts affecting the act considered; and contents, including either the full text, a summary, or keywords. Additionally, the legislation file contains about thirty specific headings for each document; the CJUS file contains summaries and the full text of judgments published in the Reports of Cases; the Parliamentary activities file records eachact title, summary of Parliament's position, and descriptors, but does not include the text of the acts; and the question file includes title and subject of question, official and bibliographical information, descriptors, and political affiliation of the member tabling the question.

Clientele/Availability: The system is available without restrictions to all Community institutions and their services and any other user.

Contact: Mr. J. Quenot, Manager, Commercial Department, Euris Host Service.

★490★
HUBRECHT LABORATORY (INTERNATIONAL EMBRYOLOGICAL INSTITUTE)
CENTRAL EMBRYOLOGICAL LIBRARY
DOCUMENTATION AND INFORMATION SYSTEM ON DEVELOPMENTAL BIOLOGY
Uppsalalaan 8 Phone: 030 510211
NL-3584 CT Utrecht, Netherlands Service Est: 1964
Dr. J. Faber, Head of Library

Staff: 2.5 Information and library professional.

Related Organizations: The System is associated with the International Society of Development Biologists.

Description of System or Service: The DOCUMENTATION AND INFORMATION SYSTEM ON DEVELOPMENTAL BIOLOGY is an extensive collection of reprints and photocopies selected from the literature on developmental biology and related subjects. Documentation prepared for these materials includes bibliographic information, keywords, and subject classifications. Periodical articles added to the collection since 1980 are computer-searchable, and retrieval services are offered. Document delivery services are also available.

Scope and/or Subject Matter: Developmental biology of animals and man; descriptive, experimental, and molecular embryology; developmental genetics; regeneration; asexual reproduction and development; and pattern formation.

Input Sources: Information is extracted from journals, symposium reports, multi-authored books, theses, research reports, and other materials.

Holdings and Storage Media: The collection consists of 140,000 reprints, 5700 bound volumes, and subscriptions to 60 periodicals; materials date from 1850 to the present.

Computer-Based Products and Services: Periodical articles added to the collection since 1980 are indexed in a computer-readable data base from which retrieval services are offered.

Clientele/Availability: Primary clients are biologists and embryologists.

Contact: Ms. O. Kruythof, Librarian, Hubrecht Laboratory.

★491★
HUNGARIAN ACADEMY OF SCIENCES
(Magyar Tudomanyos Akademia)
INSTITUTE OF ECONOMICS
(Kozgazdasagtudomanyi Intezete)
ECONOMIC INFORMATION UNIT
(Kozgazdasagi Informacios Szolgalat)
Budaorsi ut 45 Phone: 850 878
H-1112 Budapest, Hungary Service Est: 1973
Tamas Foldi, Head

Staff: 9 Economists; 2 management professional; 2 clerical and nonprofessional.

Description of System or Service: The ECONOMIC INFORMATION UNIT is an information evaluation and analysis center which provides data relevant for economic and economic research policymaking on Hungarian and foreign economic developments, economic policy trends, and results in economics. It performs research activities and organizes data flow and data exchange in order to achieve its tasks. The UNIT also issues a bibliography and various information bulletins.

Scope and/or Subject Matter: Socio-economic problems; international trade and finance; economic policies.

Input Sources: Information sources include journals, handbooks, specialized research papers, press cutting archives, and other materials; current contents and SDI services from Hungarian libraries; and the holdings of the Institute's library.

Holdings and Storage Media: The Unit maintains a collection of 500 bound volumes, 60 periodical subscriptions, book reviews file, and research papers. The Institute of Economics library includes 50,000 bound volumes and subscriptions to 800 economic journals.

Publications: 1) Selected Bibliography of Hungarian Economic Books and Articles (bimonthly)—available by request without charge. 2) Information bulletins (6-10 per year)—each bulletin deals with a separate subject; issued in two series: the first consists of papers written on the basis of a main document, usually official or semi-official papers, or presents a survey of literature on a subject; the other series presents research findings of the Unit. The bulletins are distributed to all users. 3) Occasional bulletins—available to specialists by request. The Unit also issues research reports and book reviews.

Computer-Based Products and Services: The Unit has access to computer facilities to support its services.

Clientele/Availability: Services are restricted to use by Hungarian government personnel, scientists, and other authorized persons.

Contact: Andras Tothfalusi, Scientific Secretary, or I. Fabo, Librarian, Hungarian Academy of Sciences.

★492★
HUNGARIAN ACADEMY OF SCIENCES LIBRARY
(Magyar Tudomanyos Akademia Konyvtara - MTAK)
DEPARTMENT FOR INFORMATICS AND SCIENCE ANALYSIS
Akademia u.2   Phone: 113400
H-1361 Budapest, Hungary
Prof. T. Braun, Deputy Director

Staff: 7 Information and library professional; 3 management professional; 3 technicians; 1 sales and marketing; 1 clerical and nonprofessional.

Description of System or Service: The DEPARTMENT FOR INFORMATICS AND SCIENCE ANALYSIS offers a computerized search service utilizing magnetic tapes of the Science Citation Index data base produced by the Institute for Scientific Information. The DEPARTMENT provides SDI and retrospective search services from this data base for scientists, clinical practitioners, and other professionals. It also maintains the Publication Data Bank of the Hungarian Academy of Sciences, which contains bibliographic data for books, chapters of multiauthored books, papers in conference proceedings, and journal papers produced by the scientists from the Academy. The Data Bank is intended to provide standardized institutional bibliographies, to enable the operation of a multipurpose bibliographic search system in online and offline modes, to serve as a reference source for the computerized building of scientometric indicators, and to supply data to science policy makers and research managers.

Scope and/or Subject Matter: Life sciences, clinical medicine, biology, agriculture, veterinary science, physical and chemical sciences, and engineering and technology; bibliographic data covering all fields of science.

Input Sources: Input for the Publication Data Bank is collected from publication lists of the institutes of the Hungarian Academy of Sciences.

Holdings and Storage Media: The computer-readable Publication Data Bank contains bibliographic information on approximately 15,000 publications dating from 1976 to the present. Also maintained are magnetic tape copies of Science Citation Index.

Publications: 1) Scientometrics—international journal. 2) Informatics and Scientometrics—series of monographs.

Computer-Based Products and Services: The DEPARTMENT supplies the following types of search services of the SCI data base: Personalized Current Contents, which contains computerized listings of tables of contents from the journals it covers, plus author address; surveillance of the publication activity and citation impact of individuals, institutions, and other organizations; Automatic Subject Citation Alert (ASCA), which provides individualized computer-produced SDI services on user-selected topics; and ASCATOPICS, a weekly alerting service for standard topics. The DEPARTMENT's Publication Data Base is available online through the Computer and Automation Institute of the Academy and can be searched for the following items: author, institute, year of publication, journal title, language, type of publication, place of edition, and keywords. Offline printed lists are supplied on request.

Clientele/Availability: Search services are available to the Hungarian public. The Publication Data Bank is available to scientists and research managers of the Hungarian Academy of Sciences.

Contact: Prof. T. Braun, Deputy Director, Hungarian Academy of Sciences Library.

★493★
HUNGARY
CENTRAL STATISTICAL OFFICE (CSO)
(Kozponti Statisztikai Hivatal)
Keleti Karoly utca 5   Phone: 358 530
H-1525 Budapest Pf. 51, Hungary   Service Est: 1867

Staff: 8000 Total.

Description of System or Service: The CENTRAL STATISTICAL OFFICE (CSO) of Hungary is responsible for the collection, supply, processing, analysis, dissemination, and storage of statistical data on the conditions and development of the national economy and society as well as data necessary for the planning of national economic goals. The CSO organizes the system of state statistics gathering and supplies the central and regional state organs with data and analyses. In order to meet its objectives, the CENTRAL STATISTICAL OFFICE publishes national statistics and analyses; investigates the international socioeconomic conditions through statistical data and compares national conditions with those worldwide; carries on scientific research activity in the field of statistics, demography, sociometry, econometrics, and statistical informatics; participates in international statistical activities and in the statistical work of international organizations; and maintains the Place-Name Register of Hungary. The CSO has established several institutions oriented toward the computerization of statistical information, including the Research Institute for Computing Applications, the International Computing Education and Information Center (SZAMOK), and the Computing and Organization Service Company. Additionally, the CSO Library and Documentation Service collects official statistics of statistical offices in Hungary and other countries, maintains a computer-readable bibliographic data base of library holdings, and provides search services from this and other data bases.

Scope and/or Subject Matter: Hungarian economic and social statistics; demography; data analyses and methods.

Input Sources: The CSO conducts approximately 500 data collections annually. Approximately 70 percent of the collections are of economic statistics and the remainder of social statistical character. The CSO also conducts the population census every 10 years. Input for the CSO's bibliographic library data base is derived from 425 foreign periodicals, selected foreign books, and all Hungarian periodicals and books held by the library.

Holdings and Storage Media: The majority of data held by the CSO is in computer-readable form. The Library and Documentation Service maintains a computer-readable bibliographic data base containing 50,000 records dating from 1977 to the present. Library holdings include 600,000 bound volumes, 800 foreign periodical subscriptions, 1200 Hungarian periodical subscriptions, 800 scientific manuscripts, and 10,000 maps.

Publications: CSO periodicals include the following: 1) Statisztikai Szemle (Statistical Review); 2) Demografia (Demography); 3) Teruleti Statisztika (Regional Statistics); 4) Ipari es Epitoipari Statisztikai Ertesito (Bulletin of Industry and Construction); 5) Informacio-Elektronika (Information-Electronics); and 6) Szamitastechnika (Computing Technics). Statistical yearbooks and reports are also published. The Library and Documentation Service issues the following irregular publications: 1) Statisztikai Modszerek Temadokumentacio (Statistical Methods)—surveys of literature on various subjects. 2) Kulfoldi Statisztikai Adatforrasok (Sources of Foreign Statistical Data). 3) Torteneti Statisztikai Kotetek (Historical Statistics). 4) Torteneti Statisztikai Fuzetek (Papers in Historical Statistics).

Computer-Based Products and Services: Data processing activities of the CSO encompass the primary processing of the data, correction, primary analysis, storage of the corrected data, retrieval, and secondary processing of the stored data. The CSO currently maintains more than 1500 magnetic tapes of data. Statistical data are also preserved in the CSO's Statistical Data Base System, which comprises five data bases: industrial, foreign trade, register of economic units, and investment and labor. Most of the electronic data processing activity is conducted by the computer center of the Computing and Organization Service Company. In addition to these computing operations, the CSO Library and Documentation Service maintains a bibliographic data base of library holdings which covers the following subjects: methods of statistics, applied statistics, official statistics, applied economic analysis, forecasting, econometrics, demography, and sociology. The Service also provides retrospective information retrieval and SDI, and has access to the Data Resources, Inc. (DRI) data bases.

Clientele/Availability: Information is disseminated to state and regional administrations, the general public, scientific institutions, and international organizations.

Contact: Dr. Istvan Csahok, Director, Library and Documentation Service; telephone 350 734.

★494★
HUNGARY
MINISTRY FOR BUILDING AND URBAN DEVELOPMENT
(Epitesugyi es Varosfejlesztesi Miniszterium - EVM)
INFORMATION CENTRE FOR BUILDING
(Epitesugyi Tajekoztatasi Kozpont - ETK)
P.O. Box 83　　　　　　　　　　Phone: 117 317
Harsfa u. 21　　　　　　　　　　Service Est: 1950
H-1400 Budapest VII, Hungary
Peter Hamvay, Director

Staff: 66 Information and library professional; 39 management professional; 40 technicians; 32 sales and marketing; 364 clerical and nonprofessional.

Description of System or Service: The INFORMATION CENTRE FOR BUILDING, the central information unit in Hungary for building information, collects, maintains, and disseminates information on building and construction in Hungary and foreign countries. It collects traditional and nontraditional building documents, books, periodicals, and other materials. The CENTRE maintains a library of collected materials and its own reports and books, as well as copies of computer-readable data bases. The CENTRE disseminates information through the publication of periodicals, technical books, and abstracts and reviews of Hungarian and foreign technical literature; translations of technical materials into English and Russian; exhibitions and conferences, including a permanent building exhibit; films; computerized information retrieval and SDI services; and consulting services provided to the private industry in Hungary. The CENTRE also supervises the activities of special libraries in the building industry and performs research and development work in the field of library and information science for establishing computerized and manual information services.

Scope and/or Subject Matter: Building and construction in Hungary and worldwide.

Input Sources: Annual input to the Centre's collection consists of approximately 1200 books, 950 current Hungarian and foreign periodicals, 2800 product information documents, 4000 translations, and 5000 standards and patents. The Centre also receives data in machine-readable form.

Holdings and Storage Media: Library holdings consist of 35,000 bound volumes, subscriptions to 950 periodicals, 22,420 product information documents, 20,000 translations, 18,600 study-tour reports, 5800 research reports, and 40,000 documents, standards, patents, and other materials. The Centre also holds copies of two computer-readable data bases totalling 160,000 records.

Publications: 1) Building Articles in the Hungarian Publications/ Epitesugyi Cikkek a Magyar Idoszaki Kiadvanyokban (quarterly)—lists Hungarian journal article titles. 2) Technical and Economic Information on Building/ Epitesugyi Muszaki es Gazdasagi Tajekoztato (monthly)—contains reviews of journal articles, news, and events. 3) World News about Building and Urban Development/ Epitesugyi es Varosfeilesztesi Vilaghirado (biweekly)—provides reviews of journal articles and book excerpts. 4) Hungarian Building Bulletin (quarterly)—abstracts of Hungarian books, journals, and other documents. 5) Selective Design Data Collection/ Szelektiv Tervezesi Adatgyujtemeny (8-10 annually)—covers provisions of law, specifications, and standards. Also produced are library catalogs, accession lists, and other publications.

Microform Products and Services: Building information is produced on microfilm and microfiche.

Computer-Based Products and Services: The INFORMATION CENTRE FOR BUILDING maintains copies of the KGST-CMEA and IRB data bases for online and offline access. The KGST-CMEA data base holds approximately 50,000 records gathered since 1981 on architecture, building, and the worldwide building materials industry. The IRB data base holds approximately 110,000 records gathered since 1979 covering architecture and the building industry in Germany, other German-speaking countries, Europe, U.S., and Canada. The CENTRE offers computerized information retrieval, SDI services, and current awareness on standards themes with Hungarian translations of selected titles provided. It is also developing the SZISZ-EMIMAT data base which will contain Hungarian building information and building material regulations. The CENTRE plans to make the data base available online.

Other Services: The Centre serves as the Eastern-European Vision Habitat office of the United Nations Audiovisual Information Centre on Human Settlements. In this capacity, it promotes the utilization of worldwide housing and human settlement experiences with educational films and information materials.

Clientele/Availability: Services are available by request to government officials; planning and building firms; research institutes and other organizations; architects and engineers in the building, civil engineering, and building material industry; and private builders. Selected services are only available to officials of the Hungarian Ministry of Building and Urban Development.

Contact: Mrs. Aranka Nemeth, Head, Department for International Affairs, Ministry for Building and Urban Development. (Telex 22 6564.)

★495★
HUNGARY
NATIONAL SZECHENYI LIBRARY
(Orszagos Szechenyi Konyvtar - OSzK)
CENTRE FOR LIBRARY SCIENCE AND METHODOLOGY
(Konyvtartudomanyi es Modszertani Kozpont - KMK)
Budapest VIII, Muzeum utca 3　　　　Phone: 335 590
H-1827 Budapest Pf. 486, Hungary　　Service Est: 1949
Ferenc Szente, Director

Staff: 50 Information and library professional; 1 management professional; 5 technicians; 2 other.

Related Organizations: The Centre is sponsored and supervised by the Ministry of Culture.

Description of System or Service: The CENTRE FOR LIBRARY SCIENCE AND METHODOLOGY (KMK) is the national center for the promotion of librarianship. As such, it performs the following functions: supports the state library policy; carries out research and experiments in the area of librarianship and allied fields, and registers relevant research programs; offers assistance to Hungarian libraries in raising their level of activities and services, and in planning buildings, equipment, and furniture; organizes and promotes interlibrary cooperation; offers continuing education programs for librarians; provides information services in the areas of librarianship, bibliography, and documentation; and coordinates the activities of public libraries in Hungary. The CENTRE also acts as an International Federation of Library Associations and Institutions (IFLA) clearinghouse, and participates in international library cooperative efforts.

Scope and/or Subject Matter: Library and information science.

Input Sources: Input consists of Hungarian and foreign literature about library and information science.

Holdings and Storage Media: Library holdings consist of 56,000 bound volumes; 9200 study tour reports, dissertations, translations, and prospectuses; and subscriptions to 625 periodicals. In addition, the Centre maintains special collections in the following areas: IFLA papers and publications; tools and equipment used in library and information activities; and alphabetical and classified catalogs of all documents held by the Centre.

Publications: 1) Library and Documentation Literature/ Konyvtari es Dokumentacios Szakirodalom (quarterly)—an abstracts journal. 2) Hungarian Library and Information Science Abstracts (2/year)—the Russian title is Vengherskaya Literatura po Bibliotekovedeniu i Informatike - Referativny Zhurnal; covers Hungarian periodical and other literature on library and information science, in 20 subject categories. 3) Library Review/ Konyvtari Figyelo (bimonthly). 4) Hungarian Library Literature/ Magyar Konyvtari Szakirodalom Bibliografiaja (quarterly). 5) New Books/ Uj Konyvek. Most of the Centre's publications are available on an exchange or subscription basis.

Services: The CENTRE provides such services as SDI, consulting, literature searching, reference and referrals, research, and data collection and analysis.

Clientele/Availability: Services are intended for Hungarian and foreign experts in librarianship and information science, and for students and other interested persons.

Contact: Vera Gero, Head, Information Department, Centre for Library Science and Methodology. (Telex 224 226 BIBLNATHUNG.)

★496★
HUNGARY
NATIONAL TECHNICAL INFORMATION CENTRE AND LIBRARY
(Orszagos Muszaki Informacios Kozpont es Konyvtar - OMIKK)
P.O. Box 12   Phone: 336 300
Reviczky u. 6   Service Est: 1883
H-1428 Budapest, Hungary
Mihaly Agoston, Director General

Staff: Approximately 500 total.

Related Organizations: The Hungarian State Office for Technical Development/ Orszagos Muszaki Fejlesztesi Bizottsag provides support and control.

Description of System or Service: The NATIONAL TECHNICAL INFORMATION CENTRE AND LIBRARY (OMIKK) provides centralized documentation and information services as part of the national Hungarian Information System. It plays a coordinating role regarding scientific and technical information and operates the largest technical library open to the public in the country. The CENTRE is composed of the following main units: 1) the Department of Scientific and Technical Information Services, which processes and disseminates information from scientific and technical literature, and offers computerized and manual retrieval and SDI services; 2) the National Technical Library, which collects scientific and technical literature, monographs, journals, research reports, conference proceedings, and translations, and maintains the national registry of translations and an information center for technical films; 3) the Computer Center; and 4) the Commercial Department (Technoinform), which offers translations, information and reprographic services, organization of conferences and meetings, and publication of proceedings. OMIKK maintains contacts with approximately 900 national and international centers for the purposes of information exchange. It also is a member of the International Scientific and Technical Information System (ISTIS) of the Council for Mutual Economic Assistance.

Scope and/or Subject Matter: All areas of science, technology, and applied economics.

Input Sources: Input consists of literature, data, and documents.

Holdings and Storage Media: Collection consists of 636,000 bound volumes; subscriptions to 5900 periodicals; 70,000 research reports; approximately 600,000 copies of translations; and INSPEC, INIS, and COMPENDEX magnetic tapes.

Publications: 1) Szakirodalmi Tajekoztatok/ Technical Abstracts Journal (monthly)—in 20 series; 2) Hungarian Technical Abstracts (quarterly with cumulative annual subject and author indexes)—provides English-language abstracts of periodical and other literature written by Hungarian authors and dealing with technical research in all subject areas; 3) Muszaki Gazdasagi Tajekoztato/ Technical Economic Information (monthly); 4) Tudomanyos es Muszaki Tajekoztatas/ Scientific and Technical Information (monthly); 5) Technical Film Cards (quarterly). All items are available on an exchange basis or by subscription from the Foreign Trade Company KULTURA, P.O. Box 149, H-1389 Budapest, Hungary; Technical Film Cards may be ordered from OMIKK-Technoinform. Bibliographies, reviews, reports on scientific and technical subjects, and monographs on information science are issued at irregular intervals. A list of publications is available on request to OMIKK.

Microform Products and Services: The Centre produces microfilm and microfiche copies on request.

Computer-Based Products and Services: OMIKK provides online information retrieval from data bases carried by DIALOG Information Services, Inc., System Development Corporation (SDC), Data-Star, and International Atomic Energy Agency. It also maintains computer facilities to serve library administration and information activities.

Clientele/Availability: There are no restrictions on services. Library services are available free of charge, while information services are available for a fee or upon agreement.

Remarks: OMIKK was formerly known as the Hungarian Central Technical Library and Documentation Centre/ Orszagos Muszaki Konyvtar es Dokumentacios Kozpont (OMKDK).

Contact: Mihaly Agoston, Director General, National Technical Information Centre and Library. (Telex 22 4944 OMIKK H.)

I

★497★
I/S DATACENTRALEN (DC)
Retortvej 6-8
DK-2500 Valby, Denmark
J.U. Moos, Managing Director

Phone: 1 468122
Founded: 1959

Staff: 1400 Total.

Related Organizations: I/S Datacentralen is owned by the Danish federal government and local authorities.

Description of System or Service: I/S DATACENTRALEN provides a wide range of data processing services in support of public administration and other activities. Its services include systems design and development, service bureau functions, consultancy, delivery of turnkey systems, distributed systems, facilities management, and training. Among the information systems developed by DC for the Danish government are the following: Central Population Register, Income Taxation System, Police Information System, Government Central Pay System, Import/Export Customs System, and Employment Control and Information System. As part of its services, DATACENTRALEN operates the DC Host Centre, which provides clients with online access to a number of European data bases in the areas of environment, energy, and economics. Host Centre data bases are stored under DC-INFO/BRS, a software module which supports online information retrieval.

Scope and/or Subject Matter: Data processing services, system design and development, online information retrieval, telecommunications, and related areas.

Input Sources: The DC Host Centre acquires data bases from European organizations and government agencies.

Holdings and Storage Media: Numerous data bases and programs are held on Datacentralen computer facilities.

Publications: User Manual to DC Host Centre.

Computer-Based Products and Services: Among DATACENTRALEN's services is operation of the DC Host Centre. Accessible via the Euronet DIANE telecommunications network, the Host Centre provides online information retrieval and associated services, including offline printing, SDI, document delivery, training courses, and private file services. The DC Host Centre currently carries the following data bases:

1) AGREP (Permanent Inventory of Agricultural Research Projects)—contains approximately 23,000 descriptions of ongoing research projects relevant to agriculture, forestry, fisheries, and food and carried out in the member states of the Commission of the European Communities; updated quarterly.

2) ALIS (Automated Library Information System)--provides descriptions of approximately 120,000 documents available in the National Technological Library of Denmark or in other technological libraries in Denmark; consists of four data bases: MONO, which contains descriptions of books, monographs, dissertations, single numbers of series, and conference reports; PERI, which contains holdings of periodicals and series including yearbooks and annual reports; RAPP, which contains selected U.S. government research reports obtained since 1982; and EMNE, which contains the library's classification scheme in Danish; updated monthly.

3) ECDIN (Environmental Chemicals Data and Information Network)—factual data bank containing chemical substance identity information for approximately 65,000 chemicals, data on acute toxicity for approximately 20,000 substances, and data on chemical structures for approximately 40,000 substances; provides more extensive data on chemical processes, uses, occupational health and safety, threshold values, and analytical methods for more than 1000 chemicals. Established by the Joint Research Centre of the Commission of the European Communities.

4) Nordic Energy Index (NEI)—consists of two data bases: NEIL, which contains bibliographic references to energy literature published in Nordic countries, and NEIF, which contains descriptions of research projects in progress in all areas of energy carried out in Nordic countries. Updated monthly with 3000 references added per year; maintained by the Nordic Atomic Libraries Joint Secretariat.

5) CRONOS-EUROSTAT—contains more than 700,000 time series covering general statistics, industry and services, foreign trade, agriculture, fisheries, national accounts, research and development, and other areas; updated biweekly, monthly, quarterly, semiannually, and annually depending on the various domains; produced by the Statistical Office of the European Communities.

6) NCOM (Nordic Documentation Center for Mass Communication Research)—contains approximately 7000 items covering publications dealing with all communication media and published in Denmark, Finland, Iceland, Norway, and Sweden. Updated quarterly with approximately 1000 items added per year; produced by the five Nordic national centers of NORDICOM, which is operated by the State and University Library, Universitetsparken.

7) GATT (General Agreement on Tariffs and Trade)/ Denmark—contains references to Danish standards and technical regulations related to information on technical barriers to trade and other topics; comprises three data bases: GAT1, which contains draft proposals for national standards; GAT2, which contains existing national standards in Denmark; and GAT3, which contains current technical regulations which may be considered technical barriers to trade. Updated six times per year; established by the Danish Standards Association.

8) DVJB (Danish Veterinary and Agricultural Library Catalogue)—produced from data extracted from the joint catalog data base of the Danish Research Libraries (SAMKAT), it is an experimental data base which contains part of the Library's monograph holdings from the period 1979-1982 and will include all monographs from 1983.

9) FUTU (Futures Information Service)—contains bibliographic references to literature concerning all subject areas of forecasts, trends, and ideas about the future. Updated quarterly with about 500 documents added per year; maintained by the Institute for Futures Studies.

Other Services: DC also offers assistance to a number of international organizations, including advisory services for the establishment and management of data processing centers, information analysis, education and training, data center services, and information services.

Clientele/Availability: Services are available without restrictions.

Contact: Jon Mikkelsen, Marketing Director, I/S Datacentralen. (Telex 27122 DC DK.)

★498★
IBJ DATA SERVICE CO.
3-3, 1-Chome
Marunouchi Chiyoda-ku
Tokyo 100, Japan
Katsuhiro Katoh, Manager, Systems Research & Dev. Div.

Phone: 214-1111

Related Organizations: IBJ Data Service Co. is a subsidiary of the Industrial Bank of Japan, Ltd.

Description of System or Service: The IBJ DATA SERVICE CO. is a financial information firm providing computer-readable data bases and hardcopy reports on industrial companies listed on the Japanese stock exchanges. It compiles and produces IBJDATA, a data bank containing financial information on 100 companies representative of the manufacturing industries. IBJDATA is accessible online through the Mark III Service (General Electric Information Services Company).

IBJ DATA SERVICE CO. also produces the IBJ Financial Data File containing financial information on approximately 1600 Japanese companies in the manufacturing, electric power, railway and land transportation, and marine industries. The IBJ Data File is available on magnetic tape, and hardcopy time-series and cross-section reports are produced from it.

Scope and/or Subject Matter: Financial information on companies listed on Japanese stock exchanges. Financial companies, insurance companies, and securities dealers are not included.

Input Sources: Input is obtained from company securities reports submitted to the Ministry of Finance. Data in the reports are verified manually and by computer.

Holdings and Storage Media: The computer-readable IBJDATA data bank holds financial data on 100 companies gathered from 1964 to the present; data are updated quarterly. The IBJ Financial Data File holds data on 1600 companies gathered from 1963 to the present; it is updated quarterly until it contains 20 accounting periods of data.

Publications: Time-series and cross-section data reports are produced from the IBJ Financial Data File. Time-series reports contain data on a single company, arranged in chronological order. Each time-series table lists results of six account settlement terms in raw form. Cross-section reports contain data of a specified number of companies in the same industry at the same time, displaying totals for each item of the listed companies. The data are provided in raw form and are also analyzed to produce reports on a company's actual performance. Cross-section data are used for comparison purposes and can be provided for firms in 24 specific industries.

Computer-Based Products and Services: IBJ DATA SERVICE CO. maintains the IBJDATA data bank containing financial data on 100 industrial companies and makes is available through the Mark III Service. The data bank contains 35 financial items for each company such as balance sheet figures, profit and loss data, and stock prices; the data are edited to facilitate comparisons with similar firms in the United States. The firm also maintains the IBJ Financial Data File containing time-series data on 1600 companies and makes it available on magnetic tape. The IBJ Financial Data File includes detailed financial statements for each company including the condition of company equity, details of company bonds, long-term debts, changes in capital, cash flows and deposits, reserves, depreciation funds and sales performances, and employee details. The file contains approximately 400 financial items for each manufacturing company, approximately 400 items for each electric power company, approximately 600 items for each railway and land transportation company, and approximately 350 items for each marine transport company.

Clientele/Availability: Services are available on a fee basis.

Contact: Katsuhiro Katoh, Manager, Systems Research & Development Division, IBJ Data Service Co.

★499★
ICC INFORMATION GROUP LTD.
28-42 Banner St.
London EC1Y 8QE, England
Mr. A.J. Jewitt, Group Chairman
Phone: 01-253 6131
Founded: 1969

Staff: Approximately 150 total.

Description of System or Service: ICC INFORMATION GROUP LTD. provides information on and analysis of United Kingdom and selected European and American companies and industry sectors. It makes available several series of business, financial, and marketing reports and surveys; obtains annual reports and other documents filed by U.K. companies; and maintains and provides services from two commercially available online data bases, the Directory of Companies and the Financial Data File. The Directory of Companies data base contains directory information on more than 900,000 limited liability companies in England, Scotland, and Wales. Its companion data base, the Financial Data File, provides financial and commercial data for approximately 60,000 British companies. Copies of the latest reports and accounts of any U.K. company may be ordered directly from ICC and are available through its Automatic Updating Service. The GROUP also offers credit rating reports, providing a financial assessment of any limited company in the U.K.

Scope and/or Subject Matter: Company and industry performance in the U.K., and to a limited extent, in Europe and the U.S., including employees, directors, assets, loans, stocks, holding companies, profitability, sales and exports, capital, debts, and finances.

Input Sources: The major source of data is governmental company registries.

Holdings and Storage Media: ICC maintains the Directory of Companies data base and the Financial Data File in machine-readable form. The Directory of Companies contains more than 900,000 records and is updated weekly. The Financial Data File holds approximately 60,000 records which are current for the latest four years and is updated weekly.

Publications: The Group makes available the following publications: 1) ICC Business Ratio Reports (annual)—range of ratio reports on approximately 150 key sectors of British industry and commerce published each year. Each report ranks up to 100 leading companies in a series of 25 league tables, including profitability, asset utilization, liquidity, gearing and employee rations, and others. 2) ICC Database Newsletter—provides news on developments, demonstrations, and training courses relating to the ICC data bases. 3) ICC Financial Surveys (annual)—series of approximately 180 annually updated surveys on different sectors of British industry and commerce. Each Survey contains comparative figures for two years' turnover, gross profits, total assets, and current liabilities for public and private companies. Includes a directory of addresses, principal activities, and holding company details. 4) ICC/ DIALOG User Manual—contains a DIALOG searching section, a list of all 60,000 companies and U.K. SIC codes used in the Financial Data File, as well as details of the British post code system and background information on British companies and their disclosure requirements. 5) ICC Viewdata User Manual—contains a guide to searching the ICC data bases on ICC's Viewdata service, as well as a list of companies covered and four-digit SIC codes used in the Financial Data File. 6) Industrial Performance Analysis (annual)—survey and analysis of profitability, efficiency, and growth of more than 12,000 companies in 140 industrial and commercial sectors. 7) Key Note Publications—provides key facts and statistics for approximately 100 sectors of British and European industry, including industry structure, market size, recent developments, and future prospects. Includes a listing of recent press articles and further sources of information. 8) Market Data Reports on European Industries (occasional)—provides analyzed trade statistics. All publications are available for purchase.

Microform Products and Services: Microfiche copies of U.K. company reports and accounts are available from ICC.

Computer-Based Products and Services: The ICC INFORMATION GROUP provides the Directory of Companies data base and the Financial Data File, which are accessible online through direct dial, DIALOG Information Services, Inc., and ICC Viewdata. Magnetic tapes, floppy diskettes, and retrieval services are also provided from the data bases by ICC. Data elements present in the Directory of Companies includes registered company number, company name, registered office address, accounts reference date, made-up date of annual return, date of latest accounts, and reference to detailed financial data, if available, in the Financial Data File.

The Financial Data File provides data on consolidated accounts and business ratios and includes the following data elements: company name; registered office and trading office addresses; managing and other directors; SIC codes; date of latest accounts; fixed, intangible, and intermediate assets; stocks; debtors; other and total current assets; creditors; short term loans; other and total current liabilities; net assets; shareholders funds; long term loans; other and total long term liabilities; capital employed; sales; U.K. sales; exports; profits; interest paid; number of employees; directors and employees remuneration; depreciation; nontrading income; return on capital; profitability; profit margin; asset utilization; sales/ fixed assets; stock turnover; credit period; working capital/ sales; export ratio; liquidity; quick ratio; creditors/ debtors; gearing ratios; average remuneration; profit, sales, capital, and fixed and total assets per employee; wages/ sales; and return on shareholders. Selected data from the Financial Data File are available through Prestel. ICC Viewdata's graphic facility allows color graphic comparisons of a company's performance against either the averages for its industry or the performance of other selected companies. Other ICC Viewdata search facilities include selection by SIC code, by financial criteria, or any of the ICC Business Ratios.

Other Services: In addition to the services described above, ICC offers a Name Monitoring Service designed to aid clients in the protection of their company, trade, and brand names from infringement by competitors. ICC also offers data base training courses.

Clientele/Availability: Services are available worldwide (except that U.S. information is not available through ICC to U.S. clients).

Remarks: ICC is an acronym for Inter Company Comparisons.

Contact: Caroline Smith, Information Assistant, ICC Information Group Ltd. (Telex 23678.)

★500★
ICV INFORMATION SYSTEMS LTD.
CITISERVICE
72 Chertsey Rd. Phone: 04862 27431
Woking, Surrey, England
Mr. D.A. Taylor, Director

Description of System or Service: CITISERVICE is a machine-readable data base providing up-to-the-minute information on principal financial markets, including price quotes, news, market commentary, statistics, charts, and other related financial information. CITISERVICE information is accessible via Prestel and through a printed publication.

Scope and/or Subject Matter: Financial markets news and information.

Input Sources: Information sources include stock exchanges, stock brokers, and financial periodicals.

Holdings and Storage Media: CitiService information is held in machine-readable form.

Publications: CitiService Update (quarterly).

Computer-Based Products and Services: The CITISERVICE data base is accessible via Prestel. The data base comprises the following sections: main index; stock markets and government securities; commodity and financial futures markets; foreign exchange rates; interest rates and money markets; unit trusts; economic indicators and forecasts; and news.

Other Services: ICV Information Systems also offers software.

Clientele/Availability: Services are available without restrictions. Clients include banks, government agencies, brokers, and others.

Contact: Mr. D.A. Taylor, Director, ICV Information Systems Ltd.

★501★
IFO-INSTITUTE FOR ECONOMIC RESEARCH
(IFO-Institut fur Wirtschaftsforschung)
DEPARTMENT OF ECONOMETRICS AND DATA PROCESSING
(Abteilung Oekonometrie und Datenverarbeitung)
IFO TIME SERIES DATA BANK
Poschingerstr. 5 Phone: 089 92241
D-8000 Munich 86, Fed. Rep. of
 Germany Service Est: 1976
Georg Goldrian, Department Head

Staff: Department staff numbers approximately 10.

Description of System or Service: Developed to support economic and administrative decision making and planning, the IFO TIME SERIES DATA BANK is a computerized system supplying West German and international economic time series together with software for statistical analysis and forecasting. The DATA BANK is accessible through time-sharing or batch processing.

Scope and/or Subject Matter: West German and international economic statistics.

Input Sources: Input for the Data Bank is obtained through monthly business surveys conducted by the IFO, and from other organizations.

Holdings and Storage Media: The machine-readable DATA BANK contains approximately 6000 series of business survey data and 1500 series of official, association, and industrial statistics.

Computer-Based Products and Services: Online and batch services from the IFO Time Series Data Bank are available through the IFO-Institute for Economic Research. The software permits time series transformations, computation of statistics, time series analysis, and the estimation of univariable and multivariable forecasting models. The system also includes data management routines facilitating the generation of new data files.

Clientele/Availability: Data Bank services are available to IFO members and to others.

Contact: Silvia Richter, Economist, IFO-Institute for Economic Research; telephone 089 9224204. (Telex 522 269.)

★502★
IMAGE BASE VIDEOTEX DESIGN INC.
1011 Pape Ave., Suite 2 Phone: (416) 421-1958
Toronto, ON, Canada M4K 3V9 Founded: 1982
Neil Black, President

Staff: 2 Management professional; 3 technicians; 3 sales and marketing.

Description of System or Service: IMAGE BASE VIDEOTEX DESIGN INC. provides creative and technical support to the videotex and teletext industries. The firm offers a range of Telidon/ NAPLPS (North American Presentation Level Protocol Syntax) services, including applications development, data base design and management, and page design and creation. IMAGE BASE also offers copywriting for videotex, staff training and support, and consulting services.

Scope and/or Subject Matter: Videotex and teletext content preparation and related services.

Computer-Based Products and Services: IMAGE BASE VIDEOTEX DESIGN provides services in designing, implementing, and managing videotex data bases.

Other Services: Additionally, the firm provides transfer of videotex pages to videotape or 35mm slides, equipment rental, and translation services in English and French.

Clientele/Availability: Services are available without restrictions. Primary clients are videotex and teletext industries in both the public and private sectors.

Contact: Orest Stanko, Director of Marketing, or Sandra Smith, Director of Creative Services, Image Base Videotex Design Inc.

★503★
IMPERIAL CHEMICAL INDUSTRIES LTD. (ICI)
AGRICULTURAL DIVISION
MANAGEMENT SERVICES DEPARTMENT
ASSASSIN
P.O. Box 1, Billingham Phone: 0642 553601
Cleveland TS23 1LB, England Service Est: 1969

Special Note: No questionnaire response was received for this entry for the 6th edition. The entry is reprinted as it appeared in the 5th edition.

Staff: 5 Total.

Description of System or Service: ASSASSIN is a software system for document and information storage and retrieval. Consisting of more than 70 standard programs, it can be applied to a range of document and text-handling problems, including library files, scientific and technical literature, patents, internal reports and records, minutes and memoranda, market and technical intelligence, and contract documentation. ASSASSIN includes automatic facilities for preparing lists of terms and alphabetical indexes to the subjects in an entire collection or parts of it. It can produce indexes to names, organizations, chemical compounds, sources, and other items. Indexing may vary from free text (any word not specified on a user-defined stop-word list) to fully controlled intellectual indexing. The package is offered for installation on client computer facilities and also is available through computer service bureaus.

Scope and/or Subject Matter: Information storage and retrieval in all subject areas.

Input Sources: The package is compatible with paper-tape, magnetic tape, key-to-disk, and OCR forms of input.

Holdings and Storage Media: ASSASSIN can handle small collections of a few thousand records or large collections of several hundred thousand records.

Computer-Based Products and Services: ASSASSIN is available through the computer bureau services of ICI Agricultural Division and Mars Group Services, or by lease for use with IBM, DEC, and ICL computers. A number of standard products may be produced through ASSASSIN on paper, cards, magnetic tape, or COM, including SDI profiles and printed KWOC indexes. Also available, but not included in the standard package, are programs for abstracts journal composition and transmission to typesetting facilities, production of address labels, and preparation of articulated subject indexes. Search facilities include an interactive search package offering a range of commands, such as a character string search facility on subsets defined by a keyword search. Other aids to searching include a limited display of the thesaurus around a specified term, display of synonym groups, automatic indexing of search results, and facilities for requesting a list or explanation of commands. In addition to the interactive search facility, ASSASSIN provides nested Boolean logic and weighted term batch search facilities.

Clientele/Availability: ASSASSIN is available for lease. Clients include industrial, commercial, and government organizations.

Remarks: ASSASSIN is an acronym for the Agricultural System for the Storage and Subsequent Selection of Information.

Contact: ASSASSIN Marketing and Support.

★504★
IMS A.G.
MIDAS
Gartenstr. 2
CH-6300 Zug, Switzerland
Phone: 42 215323
Service Est: 1979

Special Note: No questionnaire response was received for this entry for the 6th edition. The entry is reprinted as it appeared in the 5th edition.

Staff: 40 Total.

Description of System or Service: MIDAS is a pharmaceutical marketing information system accessible online in Europe and the United States. It includes a data bank of sales, medical, chemical, and related pharmaceutical information collected by IMS in 30 countries. Selection and manipulation of MIDAS data is accomplished through specialized software which includes a powerful report generator. Clients may also store their own data on MIDAS.

Scope and/or Subject Matter: Medical usage and sales of pharmaceuticals.

Input Sources: IMS collects data worldwide.

Holdings and Storage Media: The MIDAS Databank, updated quarterly, covers 6 years of sales data and 2 years of medical data for 30 countries. It contains more than one billion characters.

Publications: IMS A.G. issues a number of indexes and guides to the pharmaceutical and drug chemical industries, and produces customized reports.

Computer-Based Products and Services: MIDAS can be used for selective data retrieval, market analyses, management reports, statistical tables, and other applications. The data bank includes the following elements: sales data by country and quarter; medical index data on the usage, form, and strength by diagnosis of each product; chemical weight sales of pharmaceutically active chemicals; characteristics information used to retrieve and analyze data by formula, price, date of introduction, chemical family, medical usage, application form, anatomical class, corporate structure, and similar data; and international linkage of corporations, products, chemicals, currency, World Health Organization diagnoses, and related data needed for answering multi-national inquiries. All MIDAS data are available online or in batch mode.

Other Services: In addition to the services described above, IMS provides customer support services.

Clientele/Availability: Access to MIDAS is limited to customers of IMS print services.

Remarks: In addition to MIDAS, IMS also markets several other pharmaceutical data bases which contain more detailed information about specific countries, including the following: DDB, covering Germany; ADDIMS, covering France; DATIMS, covering Belgium; MAXIMS, covering the United Kingdom; AIDIMS, covering Italy; IMSPACT, covering the U.S.; and DAVID, covering the Netherlands. Monthly sales data, extensive medical usage information, and statistics on the promotion of pharmaceuticals are available in the data bases.

Contact: Vice President, IMS A.G.

★505★
INDEPENDENT CHEMICAL INFORMATION SERVICES LTD. (ICIS)
La Tour Gand House
Pollet, St. Peter Port
Guernsey, England
Mr. H. Hinshelwood, Director
Phone: (not reported)
Founded: 1980

Staff: 8 Information and library professional; 4 management professional; 2 technicians; 5 sales and marketing; 2 clerical and nonprofessional.

Related Organizations: Related organizations include L.O.R. (Guernsey) Ltd.

Description of System or Service: INDEPENDENT CHEMICAL INFORMATION SERVICES LTD. (ICIS) collects, stores, analyzes, and disseminates price and general market information on the oil and petrochemical industries in developed countries. It maintains a machine-readable data base containing textual and numeric time-series data, and makes this information available in a series of printed reports, via telex, and through commercial computer time-sharing.

Scope and/or Subject Matter: Price and general market information relating to all aspects of the oil and petrochemical industries in developed countries.

Input Sources: Input is obtained from direct contact with more than 200 major oil and petrochemical companies worldwide.

Holdings and Storage Media: ICIS maintains textual information and time-series data in machine-readable form.

Publications: 1) Chemical Group 1 (weekly); 2) Chemical Group 2 (weekly); 3) Ethylene Cracker Report (monthly); 4) European LPG Report (semiweekly); 5) LOR Newsletter (weekly); 6) U.S. and European Crudes and Products Reports (daily); 7) U.S. LPG Report (daily).

Computer-Based Products and Services: The ICIS data base, corresponding to the printed reports listed above, is available online through the I.P. Sharp Associates time-sharing network. The data can be accessed as a written report—including quantities, spot and product prices quoted for deals concluded during the previous week, and a short paragraph on market trends—or as numeric data extracted from the text. In addition to making the data base available online, ICIS provides analysis and tape distribution services.

Other Services: The firm also offers consultancy services and conferences.

Clientele/Availability: Services are available without restrictions. Chief clients are purchasing, marketing, and analysis departments of major companies.

Contact: Mr. H. Hinshelwood, Director, Independent Chemical Information Services Ltd.

★506★
INDEXING AND ABSTRACTING SOCIETY OF CANADA (IASC)
P.O. Box 744, Station F
Toronto, ON, Canada M4Y 2N6
Ann H. Schabas, President
Phone: (not reported)
Founded: 1977

Description of System or Service: The INDEXING AND ABSTRACTING SOCIETY OF CANADA (IASC) was established to encourage the production and use of indexes and abstracts, promote the recognition of indexers and abstracters, improve indexing and abstracting techniques, and provide communication among individual indexers and abstracters in Canada. In addition to conducting an annual general meeting as well as regional group meetings, the IASC holds workshops, issues publications, and maintains liaisons with similar associations and organizations in Canada and elsewhere.

Scope and/or Subject Matter: Abstracting and indexing.

Publications: IASC/SCAD Newsletter (quarterly). The proceedings of the annual IASC meetings are also issued.

Clientele/Availability: Membership is open to any person, institution, corporation, or indexing and abstracting service interested in the promotion of the Society's objectives.

Contact: Jean V. Wheeler, Secretary/Treasurer, Indexing and Abstracting Society of Canada.

★507★
INDIA
COUNCIL OF SCIENTIFIC AND INDUSTRIAL RESEARCH (CSIR)
INDIAN NATIONAL SCIENTIFIC DOCUMENTATION CENTRE (INSDOC)
14, Satsang Vihar Marg Phone: 665837
New Delhi 110067, India Service Est: 1952
T.S. Rajagopalan, Scientist-in-Charge

Staff: 138 Information and library professional; 85 management professional; 96 technicians.

Description of System or Service: The INDIAN NATIONAL SCIENTIFIC DOCUMENTATION CENTRE (INSDOC) serves scientists and technologists in industry, government, universities, and research institutes by providing a full range of documentation services, including the following: maintenance of a national science library; document procurement, in hard copy or microfiche, from international sources; organization and dissemination of scientific information published in India; translation of scientific and technical documents into English; SDI; and bibliography compilation. INSDOC offers computerized literature services from copies of commercially available data bases, and has compiled several internal data bases for use in the preparation of union catalogs and various directories and indexes. Other INSDOC publications include a journal on library science and documentation, an abstracts periodical covering Indian scientific papers, and several guides to Russian publications.

Scope and/or Subject Matter: All fields of science and technology.

Input Sources: INSDOC acquires books, periodicals, technical reports, data bases, and other materials from around the world.

Holdings and Storage Media: INSDOC library holdings include 150,000 bound volumes, 4650 periodical subscriptions, 2500 reports, and 1000 microforms. INSDOC maintains the following internal machine-readable data bases: 1) Union Catalogue—contains approximately 24,000 records of journal holdings in some 800 libraries in India; 2) Current Research Projects in CSIR Laboratories—holds approximately 4000 entries; and 3) Scientific Personnel in CSIR Laboratories—contains information on about 3000 persons working in 38 CSIR laboratories.

Publications: 1) Agricultural Sciences - Kalpataru. (quarterly). 2) Annals of Library Science and Documentation (quarterly). 3) Annotated Bibliography on Carbon Technology. 4) Contents List of Soviet Scientific Periodicals (monthly). 5) Directory of Indian Scientific Periodicals. 6) Directory of Indian Scientific & Technical Translators. 7) Indian Science Abstracts (monthly). 8) National Index of Translations (monthly). 9) Natural Resources Survey & Exploration - Vasundhra (quarterly). 10) Recent Trends in Wind Energy. 11) Russian Scientific & Technical Publications - An Accession List (bimonthly). 12) Science Information Services in India. 13) Solid Waste Management in Developing Countries. 14) Union List of Current Scientific Serials in India.

Microform Products and Services: INSDOC makes 35mm microform copies of scientific documents on request.

Computer-Based Products and Services: INSDOC maintains and provides services from its Union Catalogue data base, Current Research Projects in CSIR Laboratories data base, and Scientific Personnel in CSIR Laboratories data base. INSDOC also provides SDI services from copies of the CA Search data base; similar services from INSPEC and COMPENDEX are being developed.

Other Services: In addition to services discussed above, INSDOC offers manual literature searching and referral services.

Clientele/Availability: Services are available to scientists, technologists, government organizations, universities, and research institutes.

Projected Publications and Services: The Directory of Scientific Research Institutions in India is expected to be published.

Remarks: INSDOC also operates regional centers in Bangalore, Madras, and Calcutta.

Contact: T.S. Rajagopalan, Scientist-in-Charge, Indian National Scientific Documentation Center.

★508★
INDIA
NATIONAL INSTITUTE OF HEALTH AND FAMILY WELFARE DOCUMENTATION CENTRE
New Mehrauli Rd. Phone: 666059
Munirka Service Est: 1977
New Delhi 110067, India
Ved Bhushan Kochhar, Senior Documentation Officer

Staff: 10 Information and library professional; 4 technicians; 11 clerical and nonprofessional.

Description of System or Service: The DOCUMENTATION CENTRE serves as the national clearinghouse for information relating to health and family welfare. The CENTRE assesses the information needs of program implementation in various disciplines and provides training and research to survey and determine the potential sources of information generation. A further goal of the CENTRE is to establish the comprehensive acquisition of information both centrally and regionally. The CENTRE maintains a library, issues publications, and offers consulting, referral, data collection, and training services.

Scope and/or Subject Matter: Health and family welfare in India, including health care and administration, public health genetics, population, education and training, biomedicine, communication, environmental problems, and other related topics.

Holdings and Storage Media: Centre holdings include 30,000 bound volumes; subscriptions to 500 periodicals; 5000 reports; and microfiche and microfilm.

Publications: The Centre issues serial bibliographies, monthly current titles listings, monthly press-clippings briefs, and quarterly accessions lists.

Clientele/Availability: Services are available to faculty of the Institute and to related organizations in India.

Contact: Ved Bhushan Kochhar, Senior Documentation Officer, Documentation Centre, National Institute of Health and Family Welfare.

★509★
INDIA
NATIONAL INSTITUTE OF OCEANOGRAPHY (NIO)
INDIAN NATIONAL OCEANOGRAPHIC DATA CENTRE (INODC)
NIO Information, Publication and Phone: 3291
  Data Division Service Est: 1966
Dona Paula 403004, Goa, India
Dr. V.V.R. Varadachari, Director

Staff: 8 Information and library professional; 4 management professional; 5 technicians; 1 sales and marketing; 2 clerical and nonprofessional; 2 other.

Related Organizations: The National Institute of Oceanography is an affiliate of the Council of Scientific and Industrial Research.

Description of System or Service: The INDIAN NATIONAL OCEANOGRAPHIC DATA CENTRE (INODC) collects and disseminates data and information on oceanography, marine sciences, and related topics, and maintains a number of computer-readable data bases in these areas. The CENTRE conducts searches of its files and utilizes them to prepare directories and bibliographies.

Scope and/or Subject Matter: Physical, chemical, biological, and geological oceanography and marine sciences; ocean engineering and instrumentation; related data and information.

Input Sources: The INODC acquires input from books, journals, scientific and technical reports, the Institute's research and survey projects, World Data Centers A and B, and other oceanographic data centers.

Holdings and Storage Media: The INODC maintains data bases on magnetic tape, disks, paper tape, and punched cards. It holds data for approximately 15,000 stations in the Indian Ocean, including a few estuaries. It also has a library collection comprising 14,500 bound volumes, subscriptions to 210 periodicals, and 3700 technical reports.

Publications: 1) Indian National Directory of Marine Research Projects. 2) Indian National Directory of Marine Scientists. 3) Indian

National Directory of Training and Education in Marine Science. 4) Mahasagar (quarterly)—journal on marine sciences. 5) INODC Newsletter (annual). The INODC also issues selected bibliographies and data atlases.

Computer-Based Products and Services: The INDIAN NATIONAL OCEANOGRAPHIC DATA CENTRE maintains the Oceanographic Data Base, which contains nonbibliographic Indian Ocean data covering the period 1959 to date. The INODC also maintains the machine-readable Computer Aided Directory Information Service (CADIS) and the Computer Aided Bibliographic Information Service (CABIS), which are utilized to produce directories and bibliographies. INODC conducts searches of the machine-readable files, and magnetic tape copies of CADIS and CABIS are available.

Clientele/Availability: Chief users are marine scientists.

Contact: Mr. R.M.S. Bhargava, Scientist in Charge, Indian National Oceanographic Data Centre. (Telex 0194 216 NIO IN.)

★510★
INDIAN COUNCIL OF AGRICULTURAL RESEARCH
AGRICULTURAL RESEARCH INFORMATION CENTRE (ARIC)
ICAR Bhavan, Dr. K.S. Krishnau Rd. Phone: 587121
New Delhi 110012, India Service Est: 1967
Mr. P.C. Bose, Information Systems Officer

Staff: 1 Information and library professional; 6 technicians; 4 clerical and nonprofessional; 1 other.

Description of System or Service: The AGRICULTURAL RESEARCH INFORMATION CENTRE (ARIC) maintains computerized information systems documenting agricultural research projects and personnel in India, and disseminates information from these through search services and publications. ARIC also contributes bibliographic input from the Indian agricultural literature to the International Information System for Agricultural Sciences and Technology (AGRIS) of the United Nations Food and Agriculture Organization, and provides the Indian agricultural community with services from the AGRIS data base.

Scope and/or Subject Matter: Current research information in the field of agriculture; documentation of agricultural information in the fields of agriculture, animal sciences, fisheries, and forestry.

Input Sources: Input is obtained from research reports, unpublished documents, monographs, serials, AGRIS magnetic tapes, and conference proceedings in the field of agriculture.

Holdings and Storage Media: Computer-readable holdings include AGRIS tapes since 1975, and research project and personnel files. Subscriptions to 200 periodicals are also maintained.

Publications: 1) Directory of Agricultural Personnel in India; 2) Directory of Agricultural Research Stations in India; 3) List of Ongoing Research Projects in Agriculture and Animal Sciences; 4) List of Completed Research Projects on Agriculture and Animal Sciences.

Computer-Based Products and Services: Batch-mode searching of ARIC's Agricultural Research Project Information System and Agricultural Research Personnel Inventory File is offered. The Centre also offers computerized searching and SDI services using the AGRIS data base.

Other Services: Additional services of the Centre are consulting, network participation, and manual literature searching.

Clientele/Availability: Services are available to agricultural scientists, administrators, and research management personnel in India.

Contact: Mr. P.C. Bose, Information Systems Officer, Agricultural Research Information Centre. (Telex 031 3707 ICAR IN.)

★511★
INDIAN COUNCIL OF SOCIAL SCIENCE RESEARCH (ICSSR)
SOCIAL SCIENCE DOCUMENTATION CENTRE (SSDC)
35, Ferozshah Rd. Phone: 381571
New Delhi 110001, India Service Est: 1970
Shri S.P. Agrawal, Director

Staff: 25 Information and library professional; 4 technicians; 7 sales and marketing; 30 clerical and nonprofessional.

Description of System or Service: The SOCIAL SCIENCE DOCUMENTATION CENTRE (SSDC) serves the information needs of social scientists in India. The CENTRE provides literature search services; offers interlibrary loans; maintains a depository of periodicals and unpublished dissertations and reports for reference purposes; does photocopying; compiles short bibliographies on demand; and retrospectively indexes Indian social science journals. SSDC is also involved in union list and catalog projects, and is the Indian correspondent for ICSSID bibliographies and the International Bulletin of Bibliography on Education.

Scope and/or Subject Matter: Social science subjects: anthropology, commerce, demography, economics, education, geography, history, law, management studies, political science, psychology, sociology, and town and country planning.

Input Sources: Published and unpublished research and reference materials are gathered by the Centre.

Holdings and Storage Media: Library collection includes 15,000 books; 2000 theses; 1500 project reports and working papers; and subscriptions to 2000 serials.

Publications: The Centre's publications include: 1) Union List of Social Science Periodicals—four volumes covering periodicals available in Delhi, Bombay, Karnataka, and Andhra Pradesh libraries. 2) Union Catalogue of Social Science Serials—32 volumes giving the location of about 31,125 serials in 550 libraries, with a separate volume on National Library Calcutta. 3) Mahatma Gandhi Bibliography—compiled in English and various Indian languages. 4) Indian Education Index (1947-1970)—covers 26 journals. 5) Retrospective Cumulative Index of Indian Social Science Journals—under preparation. 6) Directory of Social Science Research Institutions. 7) Directory of Professional Organisations in India. Both directories are available on reference cards. The Centre has also published lists of monographs, periodicals, research projects, bibliographies, and reference sources.

Microform Products and Services: Theses, research reports, and several journals are available on microfilm or microfiche.

Computer-Based Products and Services: The Centre expects to add computer facilities and offer computerized information search services.

Other Services: SSDC also offers consulting, research, referrals, photocopying, and translation services.

Clientele/Availability: Products and services are available to social scientists.

Contact: Shri S.P. Agrawal, Director, Social Science Documentation Centre; telephone 385959.

★512★
INDONESIA
NATIONAL SCIENTIFIC DOCUMENTATION CENTER
(Pusat Dokumentasi Ilmiah Nasional)
Jalan Jenderal Gatot Subroto Phone: 583467
P.O. Box 3065/Jkt. Service Est: 1965
Jakarta, Indonesia
Miss Luwarsih Pringgoadisurjo, Director

Related Organizations: The Documentation Center is operated under the Indonesian Institute of Sciences.

Description of System or Service: The NATIONAL SCIENTIFIC DOCUMENTATION CENTER provides Indonesian scientists, researchers, students, librarians, and others with a variety of scientific information and documentation services. It maintains a technical library, compiles bibliographies and directories, prepares translations, abstracts and indexes the Indonesian literature, and offers hardcopy and microform reproduction services. The CENTER also functions as the focal point of a national scientific information network and as the national center for the INFOTERRA, International Serials Data System (ISDS), and other international networks.

Scope and/or Subject Matter: Science, technology, social science, humanities.

Holdings and Storage Media: Library holdings comprise approximately 70,000 bound volumes; subscriptions to 1012 periodicals; and 30,000 titles in microform.

Publications: 1) Union Catalog of Serials; 2) Directory of Special Libraries in Indonesia; 3) Index of Indonesian Learned Periodicals; 4) Index of Indonesian Survey and Research; 5) bibliographies on various technical topics.

Microform Products and Services: Microform copies are provided from the Documentation Center's collections.

Clientele/Availability: Services are available without restrictions in Indonesia.

Contact: Miss Luwarsih Pringgoadisurjo, Director, National Scientific Documentation Center. (Telex 45875 PDIN IA.)

★513★
INDUSTRIAL LIFE-TECHNICAL SERVICES INC.
(Industrielle-Services Techniques Inc. - IST)
2, complexe Desjardins
Montreal, PQ, Canada H5B 1B3
Phone: (514) 284-1111
Founded: 1974

Staff: 200 Information and library professional; 75 management professional; 130 technicians; 18 sales and marketing; 110 clerical and nonprofessional; 67 other.

Related Organizations: IST is a subsidiary of the Industrial-Life Insurance Company and the Cooperants Mutual-Life Insurance Society.

Description of System or Service: INDUSTRIAL LIFE-TECHNICAL SERVICES INC. (IST) is a computer service company offering processing services; input preparation; software and systems services; system development and maintenance; online access to the CANSIM data base and economic and statistical software packages; computer facilities management; and computer-related consulting, feasibility studies, and education services. Additional online host services are offered through IST's subsidiary, IST-Informatheque Inc. (see separate entry).

Scope and/or Subject Matter: Computer services for a range of applications.

Input Sources: Data bases and most software offered by IST have been obtained from commercial sources. IST has developed some of the programs on the system.

Holdings and Storage Media: The IST computers hold copies of the CANSIM Mini Base and a program library of system and application packages.

Computer-Based Products and Services: Services of INDUSTRIAL LIFE-TECHNICAL SERVICES INC. include online access to the Time-Shared Reactive On-Line Laboratory (TROLL) system designed for quantitative research in economics and other social sciences. TROLL offers three research capabilities: data analysis and transformation, regression, and simulation. Presently the CANSIM Mini Base is available under TROLL. Other statistical programs available through IST for data analysis and manipulation include: SAS, SPSS, BMDP, MASSAGER, SIMSYS, DATABANK, and MOSAIC. In addition, IST offers packages to support accounting and financial management, file management, report generation, project management, and engineering. IST also makes available the IMS/VS, IDMS, System 2000, INQUIRE, and EASYTRIEVE data base support systems.

Clientele/Availability: IST serves clients in transportation, manufacturing, distribution, consulting, health care services, and government.

Contact: Gerard Briere, Manager, Marketing Products, or Lise Gregoire, Marketing Analyst, Industrial Life-Technical Services Inc.

★514★
INDUSTRIAL NEWS PUBLISHING COMPANY
(Societe Nouvelle d'Editions Industrielles - SNEI)
KOMPASS-FRANCE
22, ave. F.D. Roosevelt
F-75008 Paris, France
Phone: 01 3593759

Special Note: The above name, address, and telephone number have been verified for this edition, although no questionnaire response was received. The following text is reprinted from the 5th edition.

Related Organizations: In cooperation with DAFSA, SNEI has formed a subsidiary called DAFSA-SNEI S.A. (see separate entry).

Description of System or Service: KOMPASS-FRANCE is an online inventory of industries in France. Each record includes name, address, phone numbers, persons to contact, products, services, and banks of organizations listed. To aid users of KOMPASS-FRANCE, the Industrial News Publishing Company makes available a descriptive overview of the data base and a list of 36,000 industrial products in four languages (French, English, German, and Spanish). An annual directory is also produced from the data base.

Scope and/or Subject Matter: French companies, their products and services.

Input Sources: Information for the data base is gathered directly from companies.

Holdings and Storage Media: Descriptions of 68,000 companies are held in KOMPASS-FRANCE.

Publications: An annual printed directory of French companies is issued.

Computer-Based Products and Services: The KOMPASS-FRANCE data base is searchable online via the SLIGOS information retrieval system.

Clientele/Availability: Users include manufacturers, advertisers, and marketers.

Remarks: The KOMPASS-FRANCE data base is part of a data base system called BDA (Banques de Donnees Associees) which also includes DAFSA's financial liaison file and DAFSA-SNEI's FITEK data base providing descriptions of French industrial products and their producers.

Contact: Commercial Director, DAFSA-SNEI S.A., 16, rue de la Banque, F-75002 Paris, France.

★515★
INFOCOM
P.O. Box 61
Crawley, West Sussex RH10 4FA,
   England
Phone: 0342 713296
Founded: 1980
Dr. Gordon Wilkinson, Managing Partner

Related Organizations: Related organizations include Docupro and Microinfo, Ltd. (see separate entries).

Description of System or Service: INFOCOM is an information research and consulting organization providing specialist services to manufacturers, publishers, and information companies. Its services include information research, document translation, and communication services. INFOCOM activities currently fall into the following categories: advising companies on new technological, product, and market developments relating to their business operation; evaluating and developing products, particularly for abstracting and indexing services, and designing and implementing document acquisition and processing systems; conducting computerized and manual information retrieval from scientific and technical literature and providing analytical reports; producing bibliographies and surveys; translating, editing, abstracting, and indexing technical documents, especially report literature originating in France, West Germany, Japan, and the U.S.S.R.; identifying information sources in science and technology; and negotiating with document sources for reproduction, marketing, and distribution rights.

Scope and/or Subject Matter: Information and consulting services in the area of science and technology, with emphasis on chemical and allied industries, including analytical instrumentation.

Input Sources: Input is obtained from journals, reports, and patents as well as commercially available data bases.

Holdings and Storage Media: Library holdings include 500 bound volumes, subscriptions to a number of periodicals, and reports and patents.

Publications: 1) Guide to Research and Development—available for the United Kingdom, France, and Germany; others are in preparation. 2) Analytical Instrument Industry Report—industry newsletter. 3) Middle East Markets for Medical and Analytical Laboratory Equipment—a multi-client project report prepared by Worldwide Medical Markets Ltd. and Infocom. Available for purchase from TechPub House, P.O. Box 1, Chichester, West Sussex PO20 6XR,

England.

Computer-Based Products and Services: INFOCOM conducts computerized information retrieval, and cooperates with Docupro in data base development projects.

Clientele/Availability: Primary clients include international organizations, government departments, and industrial corporations.

Contact: Dr. Gordon Wilkinson, Managing Partner, Infocom.

★516★
INFOCON INFORMATION SERVICES, LTD.
P.O. Box 774
Station G
Calgary, AB, Canada T3A 0E0
Michael Spear, President
Phone: (403) 264-9477
Founded: 1980

Description of System or Service: INFOCON INFORMATION SERVICES, LTD. offers fee-based information research and consulting services to the corporate community. It provides computerized information retrieval from commercially available online data bases and supplies copies of cited items and other documents of interest. INFOCON also offers automated library management services from its own computer facilities, including the management of orders and interlibrary loan requests for small- and medium-sized libraries. Additionally, consulting services are available for library development and establishment of computer-based information systems.

Scope and/or Subject Matter: Subjects of interest to clients, with concentration on technical, economic, and business aspects of the energy industry; library automation.

Input Sources: Information is obtained from commercially available online data bases and other sources.

Holdings and Storage Media: Infocon maintains a library and is converting its holdings information to machine-readable form.

Computer-Based Products and Services: INFOCON conducts computerized information retrieval of bibliographic, numeric, statistical, and scientific data bases made available through public online services.

Clientele/Availability: Clients are primarily from the corporate community.

Projected Publications and Services: Infocon is currently developing a fully automated computer-based online search system for general use.

Contact: Michael Spear, President, Infocon Information Services, Ltd.

★517★
INFOLEX SERVICES LTD.
Hambleton House
17B Curzon St.
London W1, England
Dr. Stephen Castell, Director
Phone: 01-499 2410
Founded: 1977

Staff: 1 Information and library professional; 1 management professional; 6 legal professional.

Related Organizations: Infolex Services Ltd. is a subsidiary of European Study Conferences Ltd.

Description of System or Service: INFOLEX SERVICES LTD. was established to provide cost-effective information retrieval and associated services for lawyers and researchers in the United Kingdom and Europe. It has developed the CLARUS (Case Law Report Updating Service) and STALUS (Statute Law Updating Service) data bases which are interactively accessible via Prestel. CLARUS provides current references to and summaries of recently published case reports and periodical articles. STALUS includes briefings on the evolving state of current legislation and a digest of the most important recent acts. Additionally, INFOLEX provides consulting and research services, and it plans to create additional files for implementation on Prestel and other computerized retrieval systems.

Scope and/or Subject Matter: United Kingdom law and legal information.

Input Sources: Infolex lawyers abstract and index law reports and articles from All England Law Reports, Weekly Law Reports, Solicitors' Journal, Times Law Reports, Fleet Street Law Reports, European Intellectual Property Review, New Law Journal, Estates Gazettes, European Court of Judicial Review, and Law Society Gazette.

Holdings and Storage Media: Updated daily, the computer-readable CLARUS data base contains 3000 abstracts from 1977 to the present and occupies 1500 pages on the Prestel system. STALUS occupies 100 pages on Prestel.

Publications: 1) CLARUS Index—contains several hundred topic headings in loose-leaf form. 2) Infolex Newsletter.

Computer-Based Products and Services: The CLARUS and STALUS data bases are accessible online via Prestel on a private basis. CLARUS is searchable under 200 major subject headings for date, case, title, report reference, and extended case note; STALUS provides current information on recent statutes. An additional INFOLEX project involves research in the use of Prestel receivers as gateway terminals allowing users to access the Eurolex online service. Eurolex information would be retrieved for display on Prestel frames.

Clientele/Availability: Infolex's Prestel files are available on a subscription basis to professional lawyers and information scientists.

Contact: Dr. Stephen Castell, Director, Infolex Services Ltd.

★518★
INFOMART
164 Merton St.
Toronto, ON, Canada M4S 3A8
Robert McConnell, President
Phone: (416) 489-6640
Founded: 1975

Staff: Approximately 220 total.

Related Organizations: Infomart is a joint information service of Southam Inc. and Torstar Corporation. It operates Videotex America with the Times Mirror Videotex Services, Inc. of California.

Description of System or Service: INFOMART is an electronic publishing firm which provides system operation, software development, and data base creation services. System operation services include the design and installation of Telidon-based videotex services. INFOMART's four operations are Grassroots, a videotex service for agribusiness (see separate entry following this one); Cantel, a Canadian government service providing government information through public-access terminals located across Canada; VISTA, a consumer videotex field trial operated on behalf of Bell Canada; and Teleguide, a commercial service that provides a comprehensive visitors' guide for Toronto and other cities using public-access terminals. INFOMART also operates a Private File Service (PFS) using BASIS software for organizations requiring storage, processing, and online access to their own data bases.

Software development services offered for electronic publishing systems include the Infomart Telidon System Software - Version Two (ITSS-V2) software, which is implemented for 10 videotex services worldwide. The software allows high transaction rate update and retrieval functions and gateway operations. INFOMART's creative services include the provision of complete services for the design and development of Telidon data bases. The firm offers consulting, videotex page creation, and data base design services using indexing and cross-referencing techniques from their Toronto, Ottawa, and Winnipeg offices. INFOMART also offers consulting services in the areas of library science, software, and data base management.

Scope and/or Subject Matter: Videotex and teletext systems operation, development, and consulting; information storage and retrieval.

Holdings and Storage Media: Data input by clients of the PFS service are maintained in machine-readable form on Infomart computer facilities.

Publications: 1) Videotex News (bimonthly)—for videotex industry observers and executives; available at no charge. 2) Teleguide News (bimonthly)—for Teleguide information providers.

Computer-Based Products and Services: INFOMART markets and operates Telidon-based systems around the world. The firm also offers the Private File Service, an online time-sharing service utilizing an in-house DEC computer and BASIS software. The Service supports such applications as records management, document control, and library cataloging.

Clientele/Availability: Services and products are available without restrictions.

Contact: Rossanne Lee, Corporate Communications Consultant, Infomart. (Telex 06 22111.)

★519★
INFOMART
GRASSROOTS
1661 Portage Ave., Suite 511 Phone: (204) 772-9453
Winnipeg, MB, Canada R3J 3T7 Service Est: 1981
Bruno Leps, General Manager

Staff: 4 Systems engineers; 9 management professional; 5 technicians; 6 sales and marketing; 2 clerical and nonprofessional; 13 other.

Related Organizations: Grassroots is operated in conjunction with the Manitoba Telephone System (MTS).

Description of System or Service: GRASSROOTS is a videotex information, communications, and management system for farmers and others involved in agribusiness. Using Telidon technology, the service provides clients with access to news and information in the areas of agriculture, lifestyle, and finance. The agriculture features include farm and business news, weather forecasts, commodities, futures, local market prices, an educational package explaining the futures markets, newsletters on market prices and trends, government reports, seed information, farm and crop management software programs, farm equipment listings, farm realty, information on chemicals and fertilizers, and crop marketing options. GRASSROOTS lifestyle features include news, classified advertising, consumer information, employment opportunities, entertainment and travel, fashion, education, games, and consumer agency listings. Finance features include articles on interest rates, stock quotes, financial news updates, and programs which calculate farm finances.

GRASSROOTS also offers electronic mail, interactive banking, and home shopping facilities. The service is available in Canada via private telephone lines using a Telidon terminal or a personal computer or television adapted to receive Telidon. GRASSROOTS was developed using knowledge gained through Project Ida, an experimental videotex service in operation in Manitoba from 1980 to 1981.

Scope and/or Subject Matter: Topics of interest to the Canadian agricultural and agribusiness communities.

Input Sources: Input is provided by more than 200 sources, including Statistics Canada, International Wheat Council, Canadian Wheat Board, Chicago and Winnipeg stock exchanges, news and business wire services, chemical companies, farm equipment manufacturers, regional and local grain companies, provincial and federal departments of agriculture, weather services, real estate firms, insurance firms, banks, businesses, and others.

Holdings and Storage Media: Grassroots maintains more than 40,000 pages of information in machine-readable form; data are continuously updated.

Publications: A newsletter is issued bimonthly to subscribers. A users manual is also available.

Computer-Based Products and Services: Using the North American Presentation Level Protocol Syntax (NAPLPS) protocol, GRASSROOTS allows videotex pages containing sophisticated graphics and colors to be displayed on a variety of terminals and personal computers. In addition to offering agricultural and agribusiness news and information, GRASSROOTS offers electronic mail facilities, games, interactive banking, home shopping, and farm management software programs such as the Fertilizer Cost Calculator and Wheat Comparative Analyzer.

Other Services: Also offered are consulting services for the development of Telidon data bases and related uses.

Clientele/Availability: Services are available to farmers, agribusiness persons, and others.

Remarks: The Infomart and The Times Mirror Company partnership called Videotex America is planning two additional agribusiness videotex services, Grassroots California and Grassroots America.

Contact: Leigh Sigurdson, International Marketing, Infomart. The toll-free telephone number is 800-665-0302. (Telex 07 55863.) At Manitoba Telephone System, contact D.H. Forsyth, Manager, Project Grassroots; telephone (204) 949-8764.

★520★
INFOQUEST
123 Lonsdale St. Phone: 03 662 3566
Melbourne, Vic. 3000, Australia Founded: 1982
June M. Anderson, Senior Information Specialist

Staff: 3 Information and library professional; 1 sales and marketing; 2 clerical and nonprofessional.

Related Organizations: The parent organization is The Myer Emporium Ltd.

Description of System or Service: INFOQUEST is an information-on-demand firm that utilizes computerized data bases and other sources to provide clients with a wide range of scientific, technical, economic, and administrative information. Services include SDI, document delivery, data analysis, and customized research. The firm also issues a number of publications on information sources and technology.

Scope and/or Subject Matter: Business, economic, scientific, and technological information.

Input Sources: Information is obtained from more than 200 commercially available data bases as well as from journals, directories, almanacs, trade publications, bibliographies, reference material, personal contacts, and other sources.

Publications: 1) In Search of a Sunrise—provides a synopsis of current government policies and schemes for assisting new industries, and a guide to sources of advice and venture capital. 2) Sunrise Update (bimonthly)—contains current state and federal information and stock exchange listings. 3) Finding Patents—provides an overview of the patent process and a guide to patent data bases. 4) Sources of Australian Economic Information—details new electronic information sources, books, journals, government organizations, and industry associations. 5) Sources of Australian Financial Information—reports on new electronic information sources, books, journals, government organizations, and industry associations. 6) Ergonomics and the Electronic Office—includes details of articles on health and video display units, references to industry standards, and names and addresses of useful organizations. 7) Food Industry Update—furnishes an overview of the Australian food industry, overseas trends, and growth areas in the Australian market. 8) Australian Federal Government Profile—contains comprehensive biographical profiles on the Hawke Government, including biographical details, lists of speeches, and selected newspaper articles. The first two publications are available by subscription; all others are available for purchase.

Computer-Based Products and Services: INFOQUEST provides information retrieval and SDI services from data bases available online through DIALOG Information Services, Inc., System Development Corporation (SDC), Bibliographic Retrieval Services (BRS), I.P. Sharp Associates, ESA/IRS, Pergamon InfoLine Ltd., Telesystemes Questel, and Ausinet. Information requests may be submitted by telephone, via telex, in writing, or in person.

Clientele/Availability: Primary clients are Australian companies.

Projected Publications and Services: Planned publications include Information Technology: Sources of Australian Information, and Sources of Australian Rural Information.

Contact: June M. Anderson, Senior Information Specialist, Infoquest. (Telex 35222 AA.)

★521★
INFORMATION CENTER FOR ENERGY, PHYSICS, MATHEMATICS
(Fachinformationszentrum Energie, Physik, Mathematik GmbH)
Phone: 07247 824500
D7514 Eggenstein-Leopoldshafen 2,
Fed. Rep. of Germany   Founded: 1977
Dr. Werner Rittberger, Scientific Director
Staff: 280 Total.
Related Organizations: The Center cooperates with the Fachinformationszentrum Technik, Fachinformationszentrum Chemie, Fachinformationszentrum Werkstoffe, GEOFIZ, Informationszentrum Raum und Bau, and Informationszentrum Sozialwissenschaften. It also participates in an international nuclear data network with several other centers.
Description of System or Service: The INFORMATION CENTER FOR ENERGY, PHYSICS, MATHEMATICS provides a wide range of information services covering scientific and technical literature and data in a variety of fields. It maintains a series of computer-readable data bases and makes them available with other files online over its Informationssystem Karlsruhe (INKA) online service. The CENTER also conducts computerized searching from internal and external data bases, offers magnetic tape services, publishes print abstracts journals, compiles data in physics and energy, and operates a telephone reference service. Additionally, the CENTER and the Chemical Abstracts Service of Columbus, Ohio, have linked their online computer information services in an international scientific and technical information network known as STN International (see separate entry in this volume).
Scope and/or Subject Matter: Energy; nuclear research and technology; astronautics, aeronautics, and space research; physics; mathematics and informatics; astronomy and astrophysics.
Input Sources: Center input sources include periodicals, monographs, reports, conference programs and proceedings, patents, dissertations, pamphlets, documentation of research projects, and energy and physics data. The Center also acquires machine-readable data bases.
Holdings and Storage Media: The Center maintains the INKA series of data bases as well as copies of a number of other data bases. More than nine million items are held in machine-readable form, with 87,000 items added per month. Library holdings include 60,000 monographs, 1.35 million reports, and subscriptions to 5286 periodicals.
Publications: 1) High Energy Physics Index/ Hochenergiephysik-Index (every two weeks, with annual cumulative index)—published in cooperation with Deutsches Elektronensynchrotron. 2) Physics Briefs/ Physikalische Berichte-PB (fortnightly, with semiannual index)—English-language abstracts journal covering periodical and other literature in all fields of physics and related topics. Includes author and subject indexes. Prepared in cooperation with the Deutsche Physikalische Gesellschaft and the American Institute of Physics. Available by subscription from Physik Verlag, Pappelallee 3, Postfach 1260/1280, D-6940 Weinheim, Federal Republic of Germany. 3) Mathematics Abstracts/ Zentralblatt fur Mathematik und Ihre Grenzgebiete-ZFM (24 issues per year, with cumulative indexes every tenth and fiftieth issue)—covers international periodical and book literature in the areas of mathematics and computer sciences. Provides approximately 2000 abstracts and citations per issue. Edited in cooperation with the Heidelberger Akademie der Wissenschaften. Available by subscription from Springer Verlag, P.O. Box 105280, D-6900 Heidelberg, Federal Republic of Germany; or Springer Verlag New York Inc., 175 Fifth Ave., New York, NY 10010. 4) International Reviews on Mathematical Education/ Zentralblatt fur Didaktik der Mathematik-ZDM (every two months, with annual index)—covers German, French, and English-language periodical and other literature dealing with mathematical education. Provides approximately 400 citations and abstracts per issue. Prepared in cooperation with the Zentrum fur Didaktik der Mathematik at the Universitat Karlsruhe. Available by subscription from Ernst Klett Verlag, Postfach 809, D-7000 Stuttgart 1, Federal Republic of Germany. 5) Reports in the Fields of Science and Technology/ Forschungsberichte aus Technik und Naturwissenschaften-FTN (quarterly, with annual cumulative indexes on microfiche)—subject index to unpublished research reports in the natural sciences, engineering, mathematics, physics, chemistry, and related fields. Includes author, report number, and institution indexes and subject guide. Compiled in cooperation with the Technische Informationsbibliothek (TIB), Hannover. Available by subscription from Physik Verlag. 6) Physics Data/ Physik Daten—available for purchase; a series of data compilations in selected fields of physics. Most of the above publications correspond to machine-readable data bases. A complete list of publications, data compilations, special bibliographies, and reports is available from the Center.

Computer-Based Products and Services: The CENTER's online information retrieval service, Informationssystem Karlsruhe (INKA), is accessible via public national and international telephone networks and via Euronet DIANE, Telenet, Tymnet, Transpac, Datex-P, Datapac, IPSS, JCAS, Radio-Austria, RETD, and other telecommunications networks for searching of the INKA series and a number of other data bases. The INKA data bases include the following:

1) CONF—contains information on 19,000 conferences, seminars, and other meetings in scientific and technical fields; information dates from 1973 to the present and the calendar of events is available up to two years in advance.

2) Corporate Authorities (CORP)—contains more than 48,000 names of research and publishing institutions in standardized form; the data base is increased by 1500 records annually.

3) Data Compilations in Physics (PHYSCOMP)—bibliographic data base covering data compilations in all fields of physics and related topics. Contains 3300 citations dating from 1976, corresponding to the hardcopy series Physics Data.

4) ECOMP—citations to energy data compilations.

5) Energy and Economic Database (ENEC)—comprises three subfiles: Energy Balances, containing important energy balances of United Nations member states; Power Reactors, containing all important data on power reactors in the member states of the International Atomic Energy Agency (IAEA); and Reserves and Resources, containing information on reserves and resources of all energy sources based on the data collection for the World Energy Conference. Produced by the CENTER in cooperation with the IAEA.

6) ENSDF-MEDLIST—contains 1600 data sets listed in tabular form on atomic and nuclear radiation emitted from most of the known radioactive isotopes. Calculation is made by the CENTER based on ENSDF (Evaluated Nuclear Structure Data File) data using the MEDLIST computer code developed by the Nuclear Data Project of the U.S. Department of Energy's Oak Ridge National Laboratory.

7) MATH—contains citations to periodical and other literature dealing with pure and applied mathematics, corresponding to the printed publication Mathematics Abstracts. Holds more than 400,000 citations dating from 1972 to the present, with an annual increase of 45,000 citations.

8) MATHDI—provides citations and abstracts of periodical, textbook, and other literature pertaining to mathematical education and education in computer science at school and university levels. Corresponding to the printed publication International Reviews on Mathematical Education, MATHDI holds 15,000 records dating from 1977 to the present, with an annual increase of 5300 records.

9) PHYS—covers literature in all fields of physics and related topics, providing approximately 500,000 citations and abstracts dating from 1979 to the present with an annual increase of 110,000 records. Corresponds to the printed publication Physics Briefs.

Other data bases held by the CENTER and available for online searching via INKA include the following:

10) BIBLIO-DATA—German national bibliographical data bank covering more than 1 million German or German-language books, theses, maps, periodicals, and other items issued since 1966; produced by the German National Library.

11) BUSINESS—contains information on worldwide business opportunities and contacts; produced by ONLINE GmbH.

12) C-13 Nuclear Magnetic Resonance (C-13 NMR)—contains 44,000 numeric values for nuclear magnetic resonance spectra of organic chemical compounds and, as far as determined, multiplicities, relaxation times, and coupling constants. Molecular and structural

formulas are given for each compound. Retrieval options available include search of reference spectra by entering lines of a measured spectrum, the name or a fragment of the name of a chemical compound, the molecular formula, search of similar spectra, search of spectra with defined structure or substructure, and estimation of chemical shifts expected on the basis of a postulated structure. Produced by Badische Anilin- und Soda-Fabrik AG (BASF).

13) **CIBDOC Data Bases**—series of data bases covering literature and research projects in the fields of housing, building, and city planning. Includes the BAUFO, BODO, FORS, LINA, ORLIS, PASCALBAT, PICA, and RSWB data bases, which are made available through INKA by the CIBDOC system on behalf of the International Council for Building Research, Studies and Documentation.

14) **Coal Abstracts**—contains 48,000 citations since 1978 to literature in the fields of coal research and technology; produced by IEA Coal Research.

15) **Coal Research Projects**—covers current research projects in coal science and technology; produced by IEA Coal Research.

16) **COMPENDEX (Computerized Engineering Index)**—covers literature in all fields of engineering, providing more than 750,000 citations dating from 1975 to date; produced by Engineering Information, Inc.

17) **DECHEMA Chemical Engineering and Biotechnology Abstracts**—contains more than 50,000 references, dating from 1976 to the present, to publications in the fields of chemical process technology, chemical equipment, and biotechnology; produced by the German Society for Chemical Equipment.

18) **DECHEMA Thermophysical Property Data Bank (DETHERM)**—contains properties for the most important materials in chemical engineering, as well as abstracts and bibliographic data for the more than 10,000 publications from which they were derived; produced by the German Society for Chemical Equipment.

19) **DIRSLEARN**—training data bases for users wishing to familiarize themselves with the DIRS3/CCL information retrieval system; produced by DIMDI.

20) **DKI-Kunststoffe Kautschuk Fasern (KKF)**—contains more than 110,000 citations to literature, dating from 1973 to the present, on production, application, and technological properties of plastics, including physical and chemical fundamentals of polymers; produced by the German Plastics Institute.

21) **DOE Energy Data Base**—contains approximately 1 million references and abstracts, dating from 1974 to the present, of literature on energy research and technology; produced by the U.S. Department of Energy.

22) **DOMA**—covers periodical and report literature in the field of mechanical engineering and related topics, containing 300,000 citations dating from 1970 to the present; produced by the Mechanical Engineering Documentation Center/ Dokumentation Maschinenbau at FIZ Technik.

23) **Energyline**—covers literature in the field of energy, containing more than 40,000 citations and abstracts dating from 1971 to the present; produced by EIC/ Intelligence, Inc.

24) **ENSDF (Evaluated Nuclear Structure Data File)**—contains data on nuclear structures and radioactive decays of all known isotopes; produced by the Nuclear Data Project of the U.S. Department of Energy's Oak Ridge National Laboratory.

25) **ENSDF-NSR (Nuclear Structure References)**—contains 86,000 references to publications since 1910 considered in establishing the ENSDF data base; produced by the Nuclear Data Project.

26) **Forschungsinformationssystem Sozialwissenschaften (FORIS)**—contains detailed information on 34,000 social sciences research projects since 1971 in the Federal Republic of Germany, Austria, and Switzerland; produced by the Social Sciences Information Center.

27) **GEOLINE**—provides 350,000 references, dating from 1973 to the present, to periodical literature in the fields of geosciences, natural resources, and water supply; produced by the German Federal Institute for Geosciences and Natural Resources.

28) **Inorganic Crystal Structure Data Base (ICSD)**—contains data on 23,000 crystal structures of inorganic compounds; produced by the Inorganic Chemistry Institute at the University of Bonn.

29) **INIS (International Nuclear Information System)**—provides approximately 750,000 references and abstracts, dating from 1970 to the present, of worldwide literature in the fields of nuclear research and technology; produced by the International Atomic Energy Agency.

30) **INSPEC**—covers physics, electrical engineering, electronics, computers, and control engineering, providing 1.7 million citations dating from 1970 to the present; produced by INSPEC.

31) **MEDITEC**—covers literature in the field of bioengineering, holding 32,000 references dating from 1968 to the present; produced by Medical Technology Documentation/ Dokumentation Medizinische Technik at FIZ Technik.

32) **METADEX**—provides access to periodical and other literature on metallurgy and metallic materials, with 500,000 references dating from 1966 to the present including abstracts since 1979; produced by Metals Information.

33) **NTIS**—covers publications about U.S. government-sponsored and nongovernment-sponsored research, development, and engineering projects, containing 560,000 citations and abstracts dating from 1975 to the present; produced by the U.S. National Technical Information Service.

34) **PATENTE**—refers to all types of patent literature issued in Austria, Switzerland, and the Federal Republic of Germany. The data base is a selected cumulation of the weekly magnetic tapes produced by the Austrian International Patent Documentation Center (INPADOC) for the INPADOC Patent Gazette; it contains 590,000 citations dating from 1978 to the present.

35) **PATSDI**—special SDI file covering all types of patent literature from the most recent six weeks, with weekly updating of 100,000 citations. The data base is produced by INPADOC and corresponds to the INPADOC Patent Gazette.

36) **PATSDI-TEST**—training data base for users wishing to become familiar with searching for patent literature in PATSDI and PATENTE.

37) **Rheology Data Base (RHEO)**—covers literature on rheology, holding 23,000 references dating from 1976 to the present; produced by the Rheology and Tribology Documentation Center at the German Federal Institute for Materials Testing.

38) **Sozialwissenschaftliches Literaturinformationssystem (SOLIS)**—contains 17,500 citations and abstracts, dating from 1976 to the present, of periodical and nonconventional literature on sociology and related subjects; produced by the Social Sciences Information Center.

39) **System for Documentation and Information in Metallurgy (SDIM)**—covers literature dealing with metallurgy and metallic materials, containing 224,000 citations dating from 1972 to the present with abstracts since 1979; produced by the Information Center for Materials.

40) **System for Information on Grey Literature in Europe (SIGLE)**—multidisciplinary data base used for tracing nonconventional literature in European Communities member states; contains 15,000 citations dating from 1981 to the present. Produced by the Commission of the European Communities.

41) **TECLEARN**—training data base containing citations from the DOMA, MEDITEC, and ZDE data bases for users wishing to familiarize themselves with the DIRS3/CCL retrieval system and with the common data base design for the bibliographic data bases on the INKA computer. Produced by FIZ Technik.

42) **Tribology Index (TRIBO)**—contains 34,000 citations, dating from 1972 to the present, to publications on tribology, with special emphasis on nonconventional literature and Eastern-language publications; produced by the Rheology and Tribology Documentation Center at the German Federal Institute for Materials Testing.

43) **ZDE**—covers periodical and other literature in the fields of electrical engineering, electronics, computers, measurement, and control. Contains 575,000 citations and abstracts dating from 1968 to the present. Produced by the Electrical Engineering Documentation Center/ Zentralstelle Dokumentation Elektrotechnik at FIZ Technik.

Magnetic tape copies of data bases to which the CENTER holds full copyrights can be supplied. The CENTER also performs retrospective searches using its own and other data bases and provides custom profile SDI services. It offers magnetic tape copies of the CCDF Data

Bank, produced by the Cambridge Crystallographic Data Centre, and performs retrospective searches of it, offering compilations of specific numerical data including supplementary analysis of the retrieval results.

Other Services: Additional services of the Center include training of documentalists and librarians; referrals; loan and copying services for nonconventional literature; consulting and special services in the fields of information and documentation systems, computer operation, and library services.

Clientele/Availability: Most of the Center's products and services are available on a fee basis, usually without restrictions.

Contact: Dr. B. Jenschke, Online and Marketing Manager, Information Center for Energy, Physics, Mathematics; telephone 07247 824566. (Telex 7826487 FIZE D.)

★522★
INFORMATION CENTER FOR MATERIALS
(Fachinformationszentrum Werkstoffe - FIZ-W)
SYSTEM FOR DOCUMENTATION AND INFORMATION IN METALLURGY
(System Dokumentation Information Metallurgie - SDIM)
Unter den Eichen 87   Phone: 030 81040051
D-1000 Berlin 45, Fed. Rep. of Germany   Service Est: 1972
Peter Buttner, Head

Staff: 4 Information and library professional; 1 management professional; 1 sales and marketing; 4 clerical and nonprofessional.

Related Organizations: The System for Documentation and Information in Metallurgy is jointly produced by FIZ-W, Verein Deutscher Eisenhuttenleute, Verein Deutscher Giessereifachleute, and the Deutsche Gesellschaft fur Metallkunde, in cooperation with the Centre National de la Recherche Scientifique (CNRS) in Paris.

Description of System or Service: The SYSTEM FOR DOCUMENTATION AND INFORMATION IN METALLURGY (SDIM) is a computerized bibliographic information system covering metallurgy, metal production, and related topics. The SYSTEM comprises two data bases, SDIM1 and SDIM2. SDIM1 contains 172,000 citations dating from 1972 to 1979, with abstracts held on microfiche. SDIM2 contains 75,000 records dating from 1979 to the present, and incorporates abstracts and contains additional search items. The SYSTEM is accessible online through the Informationssystem Karlsruhe (INKA).

Scope and/or Subject Matter: Metallurgy; metal physics; metals production; production techniques (casting, heat treatment, cutting, forming, joining); materials.

Input Sources: Approximately 1000 journals are scanned, as well as proceedings and reports.

Holdings and Storage Media: SDIM contains a total of 247,000 records in machine-readable form. The current SDIM2 is updated monthly at an annual rate of approximately 25,000 records.

Publications: Publications planned for the future include abstracts journals, bibliographic services, and a research newsletter.

Microform Products and Services: SDIM1 abstracts are maintained on microfiche.

Computer-Based Products and Services: The SYSTEM FOR DOCUMENTATION AND INFORMATION IN METALLURGY (SDIM) is accessible online in German, French, and English over the INKA system. Searchable elements include author, title, and descriptors. Additional search elements for SDIM2 include abstract, institution, raw materials structure, and other items.

Clientele/Availability: Services are available without restrictions.

Remarks: SDIM was formerly produced by the German Federal Institute for Materials Testing/ Bundesanstalt fur Materialprufung (BAM).

Contact: Wolfgang Queren, System for Documentation and Information in Metallurgy. (Telex 183 261 BAMB D.)

★523★
INFORMATION INDIA
Madhya Pradesh Bhawan   Phone: 375545
2 Kautilya Lane, Chanakyapuri   Founded: 1982
New Delhi, India
Savita Sharma, President

Staff: 1 Information and library professional; 1 management professional; 1 clerical and nonprofessional.

Description of System or Service: INFORMATION INDIA is an information-on-demand firm serving overseas clients requiring all types of information about India. Its services include custom research, analytical reports, document delivery, facsimile, computerized and manual information searching, telephone interviewing, inquiry answering, abstracting, bibliographies, translating, and market studies and surveys. INFORMATION INDIA also acts as a representative in India for SVP France, Paris; Information Clearing House Inc.'s FIND/SVP, New York; Lambert Publications Inc., Washington, D.C.; and Environment Information Center, Inc., New York.

Scope and/or Subject Matter: Information on all subjects of interest to clients.

Input Sources: Input is derived from print and computer-readable sources, as well as from personal interviews.

Computer-Based Products and Services: Information India offers computerized information retrieval from publicly available data bases.

Clientele/Availability: Services are available without restrictions.

Contact: Savita Sharma, President, Information India. (Telex 31 3157 MPRC.)

★524★
INFORMATION INDUSTRIES LTD.
Willougby Rd.   Phone: (not reported)
Bracknell, Berks., England
Peter Martin, Director

Staff: 8 Sales and marketing.

Description of System or Service: INFORMATION INDUSTRIES LTD. cooperates with Financial Times Business Information Ltd. in the production of the commercially available online data base, Financial Times Company Information. Additionally, it markets Data-Star's online service.

Contact: Peter Martin, Director, Information Industries Ltd.

★525★
INFORMATION LONDON
388 Dundas St.   Phone: (519) 432-2211
London, ON, Canada N6B 1V8   Founded: 1969
Nathan Garber, Director

Staff: 2 Information and library professional; 1 management professional; 1 clerical and nonprofessional.

Related Organizations: Information London receives support from the City of London, the Province of Ontario, and the United Way.

Description of System or Service: INFORMATION LONDON is a community information center which provides information and referrals concerning social services available in London and the surrounding area. In support of its services, INFORMATION LONDON maintains a computer-readable data base which is used to produce a number of directories. Additionally, INFORMATION LONDON offers consulting services on data base management, questionnaire design, and community services and funding.

Scope and/or Subject Matter: Local social services covering such topics as landlord/ tenant relations, consumer protection, health, welfare, legal and financial services, education, and others.

Input Sources: Information is gathered from government documents, periodicals, almanacs, directories, and other sources, as well as from periodic general surveys of the London-area community.

Holdings and Storage Media: Information London maintains a machine-readable data base covering approximately 3500 organizations and services.

Publications: Information London issues an annual directory of community services as well as periodic directories covering day care and nursery schools, summer camps, services available to the elderly, and other services. It also publishes the Subject Authority of Community Information Subject Headings.

Computer-Based Products and Services: INFORMATION LONDON maintains a machine-readable data base which contains information on community services, government programs, agencies, and clubs in the London area. INFORMATION LONDON plans to offer online access to the data base to local libraries.

Other Services: Information London also offers educational programs on community services, consumer protection, and other topics.

Clientele/Availability: Information London serves the London community and surrounding area.

Contact: Nathan Garber, Director, Information London.

★526★
INFORMATION MANAGEMENT AND CONSULTING ASSOCIATION (IMCA)
G.P.O Box 2128T
Melbourne Vic., 3001, Australia
Helen Campbell, President
Phone: 03 8198231
Founded: 1982

Related Organizations: The IMCA is a Special Interest Group of the Library Association of Australia (LAA).

Description of System or Service: The INFORMATION MANAGEMENT AND CONSULTING ASSOCIATION (IMCA) was formed to support independent information management professionals in Australia. IMCA's objectives are to provide a forum for the exchange of information, coordinate interaction and skill sharing, set a suggested standard of conduct for information professionals, and provide a communication center and a referral point to and from its members. To further these aims, the ASSOCIATION holds regular meetings, participates in conferences, and publishes a newsletter and a directory.

Scope and/or Subject Matter: All subjects of interest to independent information professionals.

Publications: 1) IMCA Newsletter (quarterly)—available to members; contains reports on Association activities and lists upcoming events. 2) Information Consultants, Freelancers and Brokers Directory (annual)—lists fee based services in the information management field in Australia.

Clientele/Availability: The IMCA currently has more than 1000 members. Members are information professionals interested in the activities of colleagues in the same or related areas in Australia.

Remarks: The IMCA was formerly known as the Information Management and Consulting Group (IMCG).

Contact: Margaret Wanklyn, Secretary, Information Management and Consulting Association.

★527★
INFORMATION MANAGEMENT & ENGINEERING LTD. (IME)
Gough House, 57 Eden St.
Kingston on Thames KT1 1DA, England
Kathleen Bivins Noerr, President/Managing Director
Phone: 01-546 7968
Founded: 1984

Staff: 2 Management professional; 6 technicians; 1 sales and marketing; 4 clerical and nonprofessional.

Related Organizations: IME was formed by the merger of Informatics Engineering Ltd. and Information Management Associates Ltd.

Description of System or Service: INFORMATION MANAGEMENT & ENGINEERING LTD. (IME) offers software development and consultancy services to clients in the information industry. IME develops software for information handling systems, microcomputer systems, and library systems. The firm also provides custom software development services and implements existing software products for microcomputer-based information systems. IME offers consultancy in the areas of microcomputers, library automation, information networks, and electronic publishing.

Scope and/or Subject Matter: Software for information handling and cataloging systems; consulting in the areas of microcomputers, library automation, electronic publishing, and information networks.

Publications: IME Newsletter (irregular)—provides information on the company's products and serves as a forum for system users.

Computer-Based Products and Services: INFORMATION MANAGEMENT & ENGINEERING LTD. offers the following software systems for use on microcomputers: 1) LIBCEPT—a local processing system that transparently communicates with an information network. 2) The Information Navigator (TIN)—a public access terminal allied to local flexible data bases. 3) CONFER—a conference information system used with TIN. 4) FIXIT—a software engineering tool to generate information processing. 5) FATES—multiprocessor designed for information processing. 6) Interceptor. IME also designs custom software for online cataloging systems, information retrieval systems, and client-specified systems.

Clientele/Availability: Products and services are available without restrictions. Clients include international organizations, government bodies, and commercial organizations.

Contact: Kathleen Bivins Noerr, President/ Managing Director, Information Management & Engineering Ltd.

★528★
INFORMATION PLUS INC.
2 Bloor St. E., Suite 2612
Toronto, ON, Canada M4W 1A8
Deborah C. Sawyer, President
Phone: (416) 968-1062
Founded: 1979

Staff: 4 Information and library professional; 1 management professional; 1 technician; 1 sales and marketing; 2 clerical and nonprofessional.

Description of System or Service: INFORMATION PLUS INC. provides broad-based information services for a wide range of clients. The company specializes in finding information, conducting research, preparing customized reports, and providing monitoring of industries, trends, and the environment. INFORMATION PLUS also organizes information, specializing in all types of indexing. Additionally, the company consults on reference and information publications.

Scope and/or Subject Matter: All topics of interest to clients.

Computer-Based Products and Services: As part of its services, Information Plus produces computer-readable data bases that are the property of the individual clients. Online search services will be available shortly.

Clientele/Availability: Clientele includes government, business, industries, and the professions.

Contact: Deborah C. Sawyer, President, Information Plus Inc.

★529★
INFORMATION PROCESSING SOCIETY OF JAPAN (IPSJ)
Kikai Shinko Bldg.
3-5-8 Shiba-Koen, Minato-ku
Tokyo 105, Japan
Masumi Sakamoto, Secretary General
Phone: 03 4312808

Related Organizations: The Information Processing Society of Japan is a member of the International Federation for Information Processing.

Description of System or Service: The INFORMATION PROCESSING SOCIETY OF JAPAN (IPSJ) was founded to advance all aspects of information processing through the exchange of information. It holds annual and other conferences, and supports 11 special interest groups which concentrate on narrower subject areas within information processing, including computer networks, microcomputers, and data base management systems.

Scope and/or Subject Matter: Information processing, computer and information science and engineering, and related areas.

Publications: 1) Joho Shori/Information Processing (monthly)—IPSJ official journal; published in Japanese. 2) Journal of Information Processing-JIP (quarterly)—published in English; contains papers on information processing and related topics. 3) Transactions of Information Processing Society of Japan. Publications are available by subscription from Japan Publications Trading Co., Ltd., P.O. Box 5030, Tokyo International, Tokyo, Japan.

Clientele/Availability: IPSJ is a membership organization; nonmembers may subscribe to IPSJ publications.

Contact: Masumi Sakamoto, Secretary General, Information Processing Society of Japan.

★530★
INFORMATION RESEARCH LTD. (IRL)
40-42 Oxford St. Phone: 01-580 3914
London W1N 9FJ, England Founded: 1967
Dr. John P. Howard, Director

Staff: 2 Information and library professional; 4 management professional; 4 other.

Description of System or Service: INFORMATION RESEARCH LTD. (IRL) was established to provide and evaluate information for management from both published and unpublished sources. It offers a variety of information-on-demand services, including state-of-the-art surveys, literature and patent searches, technical bibliographies, and assembly and analysis of company information. IRL also offers market and product research services such as market exploration and assessment, market and product planning, and marketing intelligence. The firm carries out multiclient surveys and issues a series of profiles of selected industries and markets.

Scope and/or Subject Matter: Industrial market research in high technology areas with particular emphasis on chemicals, materials, and engineering.

Input Sources: Input is derived from periodicals, government documents, company and products literature, personal contacts, and other sources.

Publications: 1) Industry Profile Series—sample titles include The European Rubber Industry and Its Likely Future, and the UK Paint Industry. 2) Marketing Research Studies—sample titles include Prospects and Opportunities in the Growing Market for Diagnostic Reagents in Western Europe, and Specific Opportunities for Suppliers of Veterinary Drugs in Future World Markets. 3) European Paint & Resin News Monthly.

Clientele/Availability: IRL serves clients in government and industry on an international basis.

Contact: Cvetka Fuller, Director, Information Research Ltd. Telex 24224 (Ref 3251).

★531★
INFORMATION RESEARCHERS, INC. (IRI)
No. 59-3, Yoyogi 4-chome Phone: 03 3704475
Shibuya-ku Founded: 1953
Tokyo 151, Japan
Akira Yashiro, President

Special Note: The above name, address, and telephone number have been verified for this edition, although no questionnaire response was received. The following text is reprinted from the 5th edition.

Staff: 4 Information and library professional; 2 management professional; 2 clerical and nonprofessional.

Description of System or Service: INFORMATION RESEARCHERS, INC. (IRI) is an information-on-demand company providing a full range of information consultancy, gathering, retrieval, and primary and secondary research services. IRI offers market research services ranging from product acquisition to full-scale business investigations of product market share, research and development activities, and management and corporate strategies. Additional services include computerized and manual literature searching, current awareness, data collection and analysis, and document delivery. IRI also represents more than 200 foreign publishers of directories and reference books.

Scope and/or Subject Matter: All subjects of interest to clients.

Input Sources: Information is gathered from experts, trade associations, commercially available data bases, publications, and through staff in key cities worldwide.

Holdings and Storage Media: IRI maintains a library of 650 trade directories, reference books, and source books from around the world.

Computer-Based Products and Services: IRI provides computerized search services and SDI from data bases made available through NEEDS-IR (Nikkei Economic Electronic Databank Service-Information Retrieval) and the Japan Information Center of Science and Technology (JICST) On-line Information Service.

Clientele/Availability: Services are available on a fee basis.

Contact: Akira Yashiro, President, Information Researchers, Inc.

★532★
INFORMATION RESOURCES
45 Inglewood Dr. Phone: (416) 486-0239
Toronto, ON, Canada M4T 1G9 Founded: 1969
Susan P. Klement, Principal

Description of System or Service: INFORMATION RESOURCES provides consulting and information services to clients in business, education, and government. Its services include literature searching, compilation of bibliographies, literature reviews, abstracting, report writing, editing, photocopying, preparation of thesauri, and consulting. In addition, the company analyzes the library and information needs of public and private organizations and, when necessary, assists its clients in finding the appropriate personnel to fill those needs.

Scope and/or Subject Matter: Library and information needs of organizations.

Computer-Based Products and Services: Information Resources has access to major data bases for computerized searching.

Other Services: The firm also arranges workshops and continuing education sessions for library personnel across Canada and the United States.

Clientele/Availability: Services are available on a fee basis. Primary clients include industry, government, and education professionals.

Contact: Susan P. Klement, Principal, Information Resources.

★533★
INFORMATION RESOURCES RESEARCH
Bibliotheque Royale/CNDST Phone: 02 5136180
4, blvd. de l'Empereur Founded: 1981
B-1000 Brussels, Belgium
Herman-Karel de Jaeger, Secretary

Description of System or Service: INFORMATION RESOURCES RESEARCH is an independent organization that performs research in the major disciplines of the information sciences. It publishes an abstracting and indexing service on microfiche that provides access to approximately 1000 publications annually.

Scope and/or Subject Matter: Information science and technology; reference in all fields.

Input Sources: The organization monitors the publications of more than 500 institutions worldwide, scans primary and secondary journals, reviews books, and accesses the resources of the Royal Library of Belgium and online vendors.

Publications: Harnessing the Information Resource—a 400-page loose-leaf syllabus.

Microform Products and Services: Information Resources Annual—available by subscription. An abstracting and indexing service in microfiche format covering information science and core reference sources in all fields.

Services: Information Resources Research conducts research in information science and offers consulting and educational activities.

Clientele/Availability: Services are available to decision-making generalists and specialists in the field of information science.

Contact: Herman-Karel de Jaeger, Secretary, Information Resources Research. (Telex 221157.)

★534★
INFORMATION SYSTEMS DESIGN
3 Greenleaf Place
Singapore 1027, Republic of Singapore
Nancy Rasmussen, President
Phone: 4689555
Founded: 1982

Description of System or Service: INFORMATION SYSTEMS DESIGN is an information consulting firm established to meet the information needs of companies in Singapore and Southeast Asia. The firm specializes in corporate information needs assessments and the establishment of in-house information centers, including data base and information retrieval system design. Services include training of information center staff and periodic review of the center's operation. INFORMATION SYSTEMS DESIGN also conducts research seminars and provides current awareness and computerized search services.

Scope and/or Subject Matter: Information management consulting and services in banking, manufacturing, and related fields.

Computer-Based Products and Services: INFORMATION SYSTEMS DESIGN offers computerized data base searching, SDI, and current awareness services. The firm also designs client in-house data bases.

Clientele/Availability: Services are available without restrictions to clients in Southeast Asia. Fees are assigned per contract.

Contact: Nancy Rasmussen, President, Information Systems Design.

★535★
INFORMATION UNLIMITED
114 Harrogate St.
Bradford, West Yorks. BD3 OLE, England
Roy J. Jenkins, Manager
Phone: 0274 638877
Founded: 1984

Staff: 2 Total.

Description of System or Service: INFORMATION UNLIMITED is an information brokerage firm which provides online information retrieval services. The firm prepares market research reports based on data collected and provides analysis of business/ economic data. INFORMATION UNLIMITED also offers document delivery, information and marketing consultancy, and translation services.

Scope and/or Subject Matter: Information services in business, scientific, technical, patents, political, and other subjects of interest to clients.

Input Sources: Input is derived from commercially available online data bases.

Publications: A subscribers' newsletter is issued.

Computer-Based Products and Services: INFORMATION UNLIMITED conducts online searches of data bases offered through DIALOG Information Services, Inc., ECHO (European Commission Host Organization), INKA (Informationssystem Karlsruhe), FIZ Technik, ESA/IRS, System Development Corporation (SDC), Pergamon InfoLine Ltd., and Data-Star.

Clientele/Availability: Services are available on a subscription or ad hoc basis. Clients include researchers, engineers, marketing experts, and others.

Contact: Roy J. Jenkins, Manager, Information Unlimited.

★536★
INFORMETRICA LIMITED
P.O. Box 828, Station B
Ottawa, ON, Canada K1P 5P9
Andrea Grimm, Marketing Manager
Phone: (613) 238-4831
Founded: 1972

Staff: 1 Information and library professional; 7 management professional; 2 sales and marketing; 5 clerical and nonprofessional; 17 other.

Description of System or Service: INFORMETRICA LIMITED is an economic research firm that combines unique Canadian data bases and models, software, and analytical capabilities to assist management in developing effective research, planning, and decision-making environments. INFORMETRICA offers several comprehensive forecasts of Canadian economic activity that provide industry and provincial detail year-by-year to the year 2000 and beyond. Among the firm's services are the National Forecast Service, Provincial Forecast Service, and the Provincial Construction Forecast Service.

The INFORMETRICA LIMITED National Forecast Service is based on The Informetrica Model (TIM), a macroeconomic model offering a consistent and up-to-date interpretation of Canadian economic conditions. Service features include semiannual reference forecasts and several alternative scenarios which describe the Canadian economic future; semiannual workshops which provide subscribers with an opportunity to review assumptions, develop a consensus, and assess special issues; access to the complete data base and forecasts in hardcopy and machine-readable form; and access to TIM for use with the client's own studies and simulations.

The INFORMETRICA LIMITED Provincial Forecast Service is based on the firm's Regional-Industrial Model (RIM) and links to TIM. The Service examines the regional implications of various economic scenarios and economic development policies; its features include the following: semiannual provincial reference forecasts which include gross domestic product in constant dollars for more than 60 industries, investment, employment, labor supply, and sectoral incomes; alternative forecasts for each province which highlight the risks and opportunities of potential shocks to the national and regional economies; semiannual regional workshops; access to RIM for development of simulations by the client; and access to the complete provincial data base and forecasts in hardcopy or machine-readable form.

The INFORMETRICA LIMITED Provincial Construction Forecast Service is designed to meet the needs of analysts and planners involved with the construction industry. Service features include semiannual reference forecasts year-by-year for the next ten years, with detail on Canadian residential construction forecasts by province, nonresidential construction activity by province and industry, measure of investment prices, and measures of national and provincial economic activity; semiannual forecasts of 30 structure types for each province year-by-year over the next ten years, consistent with the reference forecasts; semiannual major project file which provides information on Canadian investment projects valued at $100 million or more; and access to the historical data base and forecasts in hardcopy and machine-readable form.

Each of the three services also includes INFORMETRICA'S Monthly Economic Review, a publication which highlights key issues, problems, and opportunities for the Canadian economy. INFORMETRICA also offers contract economic research services, including economic impact studies, industry and corporate models, economic information systems, regional analysis, and energy analysis. Additionally, INFORMETRICA has developed and maintains software to support its own operations and those of its clients. Software programs available include MOSAIC, which performs data management, data manipulation, statistical analysis, and graphics; and SIMSYS, which simulates econometric and other models. These programs can be accessed through major Canadian service bureaus or installed on the client's own computers.

Scope and/or Subject Matter: Canadian economics, econometrics, economic forecasting, and related subjects.

Input Sources: The firm integrates economic and statistical techniques with data obtained from U.S. and Canadian publicly available data bases.

Holdings and Storage Media: TIM and RIM combine machine-readable forecast data bases with associated historical files.

Publications: 1) Monthly Economic Review (MER)—provides information on changes in the Canadian political and economic environments and changes in Canadian and international policies. MER highlights Informetrica's national, regional, and industry forecasts as they are released and provides analysis of current economic issues, including inflation, unemployment, and energy prices. 2) Major Projects File (semiannual)—comprehensive report on Canadian investment projects valued at $100 million or more. It is detailed by province and by industry, and includes information on title, owner, location, timing, value, and status of all projects now in effect or expected to be under construction within the next ten years. Reports, newsletters, and occasional studies are also available by subscription or individually.

Computer-Based Products and Services: INFORMETRICA LIMITED has developed and offers several software systems to clients, including TIM, RIM, SIMSYS, DATABANK, MASSAGER, and MOSAIC. TIM and RIM are econometric models used to prepare the Forecast Services. The systems comprise more than 4300 measures of Canadian economic activity enabling the incorporation of detailed information and the production of a wide variety of economic indicators. Access to the forecasts and associated data bases in machine-readable form is provided through major time-sharing companies; the systems can also be installed on a client's own computer. SIMSYS (Simulation System) is a modular system of computer programs designed to assist in the development and use of econometric models. INFORMETRICA also offers MOSAIC, a multi-purpose computer program which handles applications in the areas of forecasting, econometric analysis, time series analysis, and other forms of data manipulation. The firm also designs and implements fully integrated information systems. Additionally, INFORMETRICA performs computerized searching of publicly available data bases to prepare its forecasts.

Other Services: In addition to the services described above, Informetrica also offers a number of training courses in the use of its software and in econometric and other analytical techniques. The firm also provides in-house training designed to meet the specific needs of an organization.

Clientele/Availability: Services are available by subscription. Clients include industry, federal and provincial governments, and other institutions in national and international markets. Subscribers to the National Forecast Service receive special rates for other Informetrica services and publications.

Contact: Andrea Grimm, Marketing Manager, Informetrica Limited.

★537★
INFYTEC, S.A.
Apdo. Postal No. 32-0360　　　　　　Phone: (905) 535-9939
Mexico City 06470 D.F., Mexico　　　Founded: 1976
Luis Torres, Director

Staff: 1 Information and library professional; 1 management professional; 1 sales and marketing.

Description of System or Service: INFYTEC, S.A. makes available print, microform, and computer-readable information products and services produced by University Microfilms International, Information Handling Services, Bibliographic Retrieval Services (BRS), Predicasts, Inc., and other organizations. It also offers consulting in the areas of data base design, materials selection, marketing of information services, and library design.

Scope and/or Subject Matter: Information products and services in any subject area.

Publications: Infytec produces Spanish-language user aids.

Microform Products and Services: The firm distributes microfiche and microfilm.

Computer-Based Products and Services: INFYTEC markets online data bases; makes available software for mainframes, minicomputers, and microcomputers; and offers computerized searching.

Clientele/Availability: Services are available without restrictions to Mexican educational institutions and other organizations.

Contact: Luis Torres, Director, Infytec, S.A.

★538★
INSEARCH LTD./DIALOG
P.O. Box K16　　　　　　　　　　　　Phone: 02 2646344
Haymarket, N.S.W. 2000, Australia　　Founded: 1979
Jennifer L. Affleck, Training Coordinator

Staff: 2 Information and library professional; 2 management professional; 1 clerical and nonprofessional.

Related Organizations: The parent company of Insearch Ltd./DIALOG is Insearch Ltd., a research and development company which is a separate corporate entity of the New South Wales Institute of Technology.

Description of System or Service: INSEARCH LTD./DIALOG represents DIALOG Information Services, Inc. in Australia and New Zealand. It conducts training services and offers other services related to the use of the DIALOG online system.

Scope and/or Subject Matter: All subject areas covered by DIALOG data bases.

Clientele/Availability: Services are available on an annual membership basis.

Remarks: Insearch Ltd. formerly offered the DIAL (Division of Information and Library) Services, which provided clients with customized information-on-demand services.

Contact: Jennifer L. Affleck, DIALOG Training Coordinator, Insearch Ltd./DIALOG. (Telex AA 27091.)

★539★
INSTITUTE FOR DOCUMENTATION AND INFORMATION IN SOCIAL MEDICINE AND PUBLIC HEALTH
(Institut fur Dokumentation und Information uber Sozialmedizin und Offentliches Gesundheitswesen - IDIS)
Postfach 20 10 12　　　　　　　　　Phone: 0521 86033
Westerfeldstr. 15　　　　　　　　　　Service Est: 1956
D-4800 Bielefeld 1, Fed. Rep. of
　Germany
Dr. Gerhard Sassen

Staff: 26 Information and library professional.

Related Organizations: The Institute is sponsored by the State Ministry of Labour, Health and Social Affairs of North Rhine-Westphalia and cooperates with the following organizations: Bundesanstalt fur Arbeitsschutz, Deutsches Institut fur Medizinische Dokumentation und Information (DIMDI), Deutsches Jugendinstitut (DJI), and Deutsches Zentralinstitut fur Soziale Fragen (DZSF).

Description of System or Service: The INSTITUTE FOR DOCUMENTATION AND INFORMATION IN SOCIAL MEDICINE AND PUBLIC HEALTH (IDIS) collects, processes, and disseminates information on public, occupational, and environmental health. It maintains a number of computer-readable files, including a bibliographic data base covering literature on social medicine, as well as nonbibliographic files holding school health records and inventories of research projects and experts in the field. IDIS also publishes a series of abstracts journals.

Scope and/or Subject Matter: Addiction and alcoholism; drug-induced diseases; environmental health; environmental toxicology; epidemiology; health education; industrial medicine; legal medicine; medical rehabilitation; medical statistics of Germany; mental retardation; occupational health; preventive medicine; public health; social security medicine; school health; social medicine and medical sociology; traffic medicine; expert evaluation.

Input Sources: Input includes journals, books, government publications, reports, dissertations, audiovisual materials, research notices, medical statistics, and school health records.

Holdings and Storage Media: Library collection comprises 70,000 bound volumes; microfiche and audiovisual materials; and subscriptions to 812 periodicals. Computer-readable data bases are also held.

Publications: 1) Dokumentation Arbeitsmedizin/ Documentation Occupational Health (10 per year with annual index)—provides abstracts of primarily German and English-language periodical and other literature dealing with occupational health and related topics; produced in cooperation with DIMDI and the Bundesanstalt fur Arbeitsschutz on behalf of several German government agencies. 2) Dokumentation Gefahrdung durch Alkohol, Rauchen, Drogen, Arzneimittel/ Hazards of Alcohol, Smoking, Drugs, Medicine (quarterly with annual index). 3) Dokumentation Sozialmedizin, Offentlicher Gesundheitsdienst, Arbeitsmedizin (8 per year with annual index)—covers public and occupational health literature. 4) Dokumentation Medizin im Umweltschutz (quarterly)—covers literature on health as related to environmental protection. 5) Dokumentation Impfschaden-Impferfolge (annual)—covers literature dealing with vaccination. 6) Dokumentation der Forschungsvorhaben in der Okologischen Medizin in der Bundesrepublik Deutschland (annual with index)—covers German research projects in ecological health. 7)

Mediendokumentation zur Gesundheitserziehung—covers health education media. All of the above are abstracts publications. The Institute publishes several other abstracts journals, books, and annuals; a list of titles is available from it on request.

Microform Products and Services: IDIS-SOMED-A is a COM microfiche service providing more than 33,000 citations and abstracts of occupational health literature dating from 1978 to the present. Includes author and keyword indexes. Annual updates supply approximately 5000 new references. Bibliographies and indexes are also produced on COM, and microform duplication services are provided for nonconventional literature holdings.

Computer-Based Products and Services: The IDIS bibliographic data base on social medicine holds 330,000 references consisting of abstracts and titles for literature published since 1956. Batch-mode search services are currently provided from the data base, with online access expected to be available over Euronet DIANE in the near future. Other computer-readable files maintained by IDIS include the following: German school health records (2 million items, with 230,000 added yearly); research and development in social medicine in Germany; and audiovisual materials for health education. IDIS also maintains online access to medical data bases through DIMDI.

Other Services: Additional services include referrals, manual literature searching, document delivery, and interlibrary loan.

Clientele/Availability: Services are available without restrictions.

Contact: Dr. Gerhard Sassen, Information Department, Institute for Documentation and Information in Social Medicine and Public Health.

★540★
INSTITUTE FOR FUTURES STUDIES
FUTURES INFORMATION SERVICE (FUTU)
Vesterbrogade 4A
DK-1620 Copenhagen V, Denmark
Annette Blegvad
Phone: 01 117176
Service Est: 1983

Related Organizations: The Futures Information Service was established in cooperation with I/S Datacentralen and receives financial support from the Nordic Council for Scientific Information and Research Libraries (NORDINFO).

Description of System or Service: The FUTURES INFORMATION SERVICE (FUTU) is an online bibliographic data base containing references to literature concerning forecasting, trends, and ideas about the future. It provides citations and abstracts to articles covering social, economic, and technological development in futures research worldwide. Corresponding in part to the Institute's printed Survey of Futures Studies, the data base is accessible online through I/S Datacentralen.

Scope and/or Subject Matter: All topics and subject areas concerning the future.

Input Sources: Input is derived from approximately 12 journals and periodicals.

Holdings and Storage Media: The machine-readable FUTU data base contains approximately 500 references per year of coverage since 1974; it is updated quarterly.

Publications: Survey of Futures Studies (Orientering om Fremtidsforskning)—contains articles and reviews on topics concerning the future, as well as abstracts from international periodical literature. The abstracts are included in the online FUTU data base.

Computer-Based Products and Services: The bibliographic FUTURES INFORMATION SERVICE (FUTU) data base is accessible online through I/S Datacentralen. FUTU is free-text searchable using Danish, English, and original language keywords in the article title and Danish keywords in the abstract. It can also be searched by publication title, country of origin, author, subject concepts, and language.

Other Services: Photocopies of articles abstracted can be obtained from the Institute.

Clientele/Availability: Services are available on a fee basis.

Contact: Annette Blegvad, Institute for Futures Studies.

★541★
INSTITUTE FOR GERMAN LANGUAGE
(Institut fur Deutsche Sprache - IDS)
Friedrich-Karl-Str. 12
D-6800 Mannheim 1, Fed. Rep. of Germany
Phone: 0621 44011
Founded: 1964

Staff: Approximately 85 total.

Description of System or Service: The INSTITUTE FOR GERMAN LANGUAGE (IDS) provides research and documentation on contemporary German language, linguistics, and literature. Specific IDS activities include research on and description of contemporary German language; computer-based documentation of relevant research activities and university courses; preparation of a quarterly bibliography and other publications; and maintenance of machine-readable corpora of contemporary German texts and several dictionary data bases.

Scope and/or Subject Matter: Contemporary German language and literature.

Input Sources: Information on research projects and university courses is derived from special surveys, existing documentation, and information services. The corpora of contemporary German texts is compiled from fiction, nonfiction, and textbooks; newspapers; periodicals; and spoken-language recordings.

Holdings and Storage Media: Machine-readable holdings include a research projects and university courses data base containing 7500 entries; the contemporary German texts file holding about 10 million words; and various KWIC indexes, concordances, and several dictionaries. Institute library holdings include 40,000 bound volumes, subscriptions to about 200 periodicals, and 10,000 tape recordings of spoken German.

Publications: IDS issues a quarterly bibliography and a number of other publications; a list is available from the Institute on request.

Microform Products and Services: IDS plans to produce microforms in the near future.

Computer-Based Products and Services: The INSTITUTE FOR GERMAN LANGUAGE is preparing several computer-based products and services. Documentation services are presently provided from the research projects and university courses data bases. A German dictionary data base is planned and the nonbibliographic Grammatico-Lexicographical Data Base on Contemporary German is expected to be offered online.

Clientele/Availability: Primary users are institutions and scholars on German language and linguistics.

Contact: Dr. Gerhard Stickel or Dr. Rainer Wimmer, Co-Directors, Institute for German Language.

★542★
INSTITUTE FOR INFORMATION INDUSTRY (III)
116 Nanking E Rd.
Sec. 2, 10th Floor
Taipei, Republic of China
C.M. Wang, Chairman
Phone: 02 5422540
Founded: 1979

Staff: 12 Management professional; 198 technicians; 45 clerical and nonprofessional.

Description of System or Service: The INSTITUTE FOR INFORMATION INDUSTRY (III) is a nonprofit organization whose major goal is to promote the Republic of China's information industry. Its main functions include promoting the use of computers in private and industrial sectors, assisting the private sector in developing Chinese language computing systems, collaborating with the Industrial Technology Research Institute in developing integrated computer systems, and promoting the public's knowledge of information science. The INSTITUTE consists of the following five centers which assist in carrying out the organization's functions: 1) Planning and Research Center—aids private industry in collecting and distributing computer-related data, monitors domestic and international trends in the information industry, designs software engineering methodology tools for Taiwan engineers, and develops application packages for small businesses. 2) Systems Development Center—assists government agencies, public enterprises, and private industry in the planning, design, and implementation of information systems in Taiwan. 3) International Cooperation Center—jointly develops software with foreign companies and supervises the import of information technology into the country. 4) Promotion Center—acts as the III's public relations body, and sponsors public speeches, business and technical seminars, professional symposia, panel discussions, and workshops. 5) Education and Training Center—organizes various computer training programs.

Scope and/or Subject Matter: The development of computer and information technology in the Republic of China.

Publications: 1) ROC Information Industry Yearbook (annual); 2) Information and Computer (monthly)—magazine.

Computer-Based Products and Services: The INSTITUTE FOR INFORMATION INDUSTRY develops software for a number of applications, assists with computer-based information systems design, offers computer training, and provides other computer-related services.

Clientele/Availability: Services are available without restrictions to businesses and others in the Republic of China.

Contact: Jean Chang, Director of Promotion Center, Institute for Information Industry.

★543★
INSTITUTE OF AGRICULTURAL ENGINEERING
(Instituut voor Mechanisatie, Arbeid en Gebouwen - IMAG)
IMAG DATASERVICE
Mansholtlaan 10-12   Phone: 08370 19119
NL-6708 PA Wageningen, Netherlands   Service Est: 1972
A. Hagting, Director

Staff: Approximately 6 total.

Description of System or Service: The IMAG DATASERVICE is a computerized system providing access to agricultural data banks and farm management applications programs. The system is made available to farmers, extension service members, manufacturers and dealers of machinery, research workers, and schools; it is used primarily for solving farm management problems. The system is introduced to users through workshops and seminars.

Scope and/or Subject Matter: Data on agriculture, agricultural engineering, farm management, farm buildings, arable farming, cattle breeding, and horticulture.

Input Sources: The primary source of input is agricultural time series and technical data.

Holdings and Storage Media: The IMAG Dataservice comprises more than a dozen data files and 17 programs, and is stored on the computer of the Agricultural University at Wageningen. Files are updated as needed.

Computer-Based Products and Services: The system can be accessed either interactively or batch-mode depending on the program utilized.

Other Services: Training and assistance in using the system is also provided.

Clientele/Availability: Services are intended for Dutch agricultural personnel.

Remarks: The Institute also maintains the Databank for Agricultural Mechanization, consisting of 60,000 cards and 1400 dossiers on more than 40,000 types of agricultural machines. An average of 25 specifications is provided for each machine, including technical data, prices, manufacturers, and importers.

Contact: G. van de Werken, Ing., IMAG Dataservice. (Telex 45330 CTWAG.)

★544★
INSTITUTE OF INFORMATION SCIENTISTS (IIS)
Harvest House   Phone: 0734 861345
62 London Rd.   Founded: 1958
Reading, Berks. RG1 5AS, England

Special Note: The above name, address, and telephone number have been verified for this edition, although no questionnaire response was received. The following text is reprinted from the 5th edition.

Description of System or Service: The INSTITUTE OF INFORMATION SCIENTISTS (IIS) is a professional association of individuals engaged in information work. International in scope, IIS works to promote and maintain high standards in information work and to establish qualifications for those in the profession. IIS special interest groups include the United Kingdom Online User Group (see separate entry), the Patent and Trade-Mark Searchers Group, and the Word Processing and Computer Information Systems Group. IIS publishes a journal and monographs, holds an annual conference, and sponsors seminars on selected topics.

Scope and/or Subject Matter: Information work, including subject classification, indexing and abstracting, information storage and retrieval, literature searching, compilation of bibliographies, application of computer systems, translation, research, and teaching.

Publications: 1) Journal of Information Science (six per year)—free to IIS members; available to others by subscription from North-Holland Publishing Company, P.O. Box 211, NL-1000 AC Amsterdam, Netherlands. 2) IIS Monograph Series—monographs dealing with various areas of information work; ordering information can be obtained from Andre Deutsch Ltd., 105 Great Russell St., London WC1B 3LJ, England. 3) IIS Sourcefinder Series—booklets designed to aid individuals in locating key information sources on specific industries; available for purchase from the Institute. 4) INFORM (six per year)—newsletter describing current IIS events.

Clientele/Availability: Membership in the Institute of Information Scientists is open to individuals involved in the field of information; there are no geographical restrictions.

Contact: Chairman, External Liaison Committee, Institute of Information Scientists.

★545★
INSTITUTE OF NUTRITION
(Institut fur Ernahrungswissenschaft)
DOCUMENTATION DEPARTMENT
(Abteilung Dokumentation)
Goethestr. 55   Phone: 0641 7026022
D-6300 Giessen, Fed. Rep. of Germany   Service Est: 1960
Prof. Dr. Erich Menden, Head

Staff: 2 Information and library professional; 3 clerical and nonprofessional.

Description of System or Service: The DOCUMENTATION DEPARTMENT of the Institute of Nutrition provides documentation and information services in the fields of food and human nutrition to scientists, students, and the industrial community. Among its activities is maintenance of the computer-readable Human Nutrition Database covering German journal literature. The Department offers batch-mode search services from this file and from several publicly available data bases to which it has subscriptions.

Scope and/or Subject Matter: Food science and human nutrition.

Input Sources: Information is derived primarily from West German, East German, and Austrian sources, including abstracts, reviews, journal articles, reports, dissertations, and books. Publicly available data bases are also utilized.

Holdings and Storage Media: The computer-readable bibliographic Human Nutrition Database holds several hundred thousand items dating from 1953 to the present.

Computer-Based Products and Services: The DOCUMENTATION DEPARTMENT provides batch-mode retrieval services and SDI from the Human Nutrition Database. It also maintains magnetic tape copies of and provides searches and SDI from the following external data bases: Food Science and Technology Abstracts (FSTA), MEDLARS, BIOSIS, CAB Animal, CAB Plant, SOCIAL SCISEARCH, ISI BIOMED, and TOXLINE.

Other Services: In addition to the services described above, the Department provides manual literature searching and consulting.

Clientele/Availability: Services are available without restrictions.

Contact: Mrs. Ortrud Powilleit, Documentarist, Documentation Department.

★546★
INSTITUTE OF PHYSICS AND ENERGY
NUCLEAR DATA CENTER
(Center po Jadernum Dannym)
Obninsk, U.S.S.R.

Related Organizations: The Nuclear Data Center participates in a worldwide nuclear data network with the following five centers: 1) National Nuclear Data Center, Brookhaven National Laboratory, U.S. Department of Energy; 2) Nuclear Energy Agency Data Bank, Organisation for Economic Co-Operation and Development; 3) Nuclear Data Section, International Atomic Energy Agency; 4) U.S.S.R. Center for Nuclear Structure and Reaction Data; and 5) Fachinformationszentrum Energie, Physik, Mathematik GmbH.

Description of System or Service: Serving as the nuclear data network's collection and service center for the Soviet Union, the NUCLEAR DATA CENTER collects and analyzes raw neutron data and related bibliographic information from its area, exchanges this data in common format with data collected by the other network centers from the rest of the world, and provides its area with computer-based information services and various publications derived from the collected world data. Data collected and analyzed by the CENTER are entered into the various computer-readable files maintained by network participants.

Contact: Director, Nuclear Data Center.

★547★
INSTITUTE OF RESEARCH ON FRUITS AND CITRUS FRUITS
(Institut de Recherches sur les Fruits et Agrumes - IRFA)
DOCUMENTATION CENTER
(Centre de Documentation)
6, rue de General Clergerie   Phone: 01 5531692
F-75116 Paris, France
Pierre Lossois, Head

Staff: 6 Information and library professional; 1 clerical and nonprofessional.

Related Organizations: Related organizations include the Group for the Study and Research of Tropical Agronomy/ Groupement d'Etudes et de Recherches pour le Developpement de l' Agronomie Tropicale (GERDAT.)

Description of System or Service: The DOCUMENTATION CENTER collects, indexes, stores, and disseminates information of interest to researchers and technicians in the field of tropical and subtropical fruit production and utilization. By means of an information storage and retrieval system known as FABIUS (Fabrication Automatique de Bibliographies et d'Index Utilisant des Syntagmes), the CENTER maintains the computer-readable Fruits Agro-Industrie Regions Chaudes (FAIREC) data base, a bibliographic file used to provide publications and information retrieval services. FAIREC is also commercially available online.

Scope and/or Subject Matter: Tropical and subtropical fruits, and temperate fruits under tropical climate, including their culture, transport, derivative products, and economical and technological aspects.

Input Sources: Input is derived from 250 primary and secondary periodicals; also books, theses, proceedings, and booklets.

Holdings and Storage Media: The machine-readable FAIREC data base contains 72,000 citations and abstracts dating from 1970 to the present and is updated monthly with 250 records. Library holdings include 6300 bound volumes, subscriptions to 250 periodicals, and 4500 booklets.

Publications: Fruits (monthly)—journal including a bibliographic supplement with abstracts arranged by subcategory under 8 topics.

Microform Products and Services: Original documents of less than fifty pages are held on microfilm.

Computer-Based Products and Services: The CENTER's FAIREC data base is interactively accessible through Telesystemes Questel. Searchable fields include descriptors, title, abstract, author, source, language, document type, and country. The FABIUS system used with the data base employs short phrases or word strings to describe the content of each document, along with a bibliographic citation, an abstract, and precoordinated descriptors. Information retrieval services are also available.

Other Services: The Center also offers library consulting services.

Clientele/Availability: Services are available without restrictions.

Contact: Pierre Lossois, Head, Documentation Center.

★548★
INSTITUTION OF CHEMICAL ENGINEERS
PHYSICAL PROPERTY DATA SERVICE (PPDS)
George E. Davis Bldg.   Phone: 0788 78214
165-171 Railway Terrace   Service Est: 1972
Rugby, Warw. CV21 3HQ, England
Dr. Beryl Edmonds, Manager

Staff: 9 Engineering professional; 2 management professional; 2 clerical and nonprofessional.

Related Organizations: The Physical Property Data Service is sponsored by the Great Britain Department of Industry, and is offered with the cooperation of the National Engineering Laboratory.

Description of System or Service: The PHYSICAL PROPERTY DATA SERVICE (PPDS) is a modular system of software programs and data banks providing information required for the design of chemical equipment. It permits computerized retrieval and manipulation of critically evaluated physical properties of organic chemical compounds and evaluation of thermodynamic and transport properties of gases and liquids. PPDS includes the following seven software programs: Physical Properties Package, Vapour-Liquid-Equilibrium Package, Petroleum Fractions Package, Steam Package, Equation of State Package, Estimation/ Predication Package, and Regression Package. The software can be used with three PPDS data banks holding thermodynamic, transport, and interaction data, or with data input by the client. PPDS data and software are available for installation on all mainframe computers and large minicomputers. The SERVICE can also be accessed online through several commercial time-sharing services.

Scope and/or Subject Matter: Thermophysical properties of chemical compounds and mixtures in gas and liquid states.

Input Sources: Data are gathered from published sources, and by estimation; all data are critically evaluated before inclusion in the data bank.

Holdings and Storage Media: The PPDS-PPDATA physical properties data bank contains data on 17 constant and 15 variable properties of more than 820 organic compounds. Also maintained are the PPDS-VLE and AQUA data banks. PPDS has access to data collections at the National Physical Laboratory and the National Engineering Laboratory, as well as to a comprehensive library on relevant subjects.

Publications: Numerous brochures and manuals on various features of PPDS are available by request.

Computer-Based Products and Services: The PHYSICAL PROPERTY DATA SERVICE is commercially available online through several time-sharing services. It is also available by lease or purchase for use on client computer facilities. The software packages can be used with three data banks, PPDS-PPDATA, PPDS-VLE, and AQUA. The PPDS-PPDATA data bank holds information on 1250 components; it is used with the Physical Properties Package software. The PPDS-VLE data bank stores interaction parameter data; it is used with the Vapour-Liquid-Equilibrium Package. The AQUA data bank provides thermodynamic and transport properties of salt and acid solutions; it is designed for use with the Equation of State Package. Other PPDS software packages have data necessary for calculations coded in them, or require the user to input data. PPDS can be used as a stand alone system or interfaced to chemical engineering design programs and other applications software.

Other Services: In addition, PPDS offers consulting services.

Clientele/Availability: Products and services are available without restrictions. Major clients include chemical engineering consultants and contractors, organic chemical manufacturers, oil companies, and research firms.

Remarks: PPDS was merged in 1983 with the National Engineering Laboratory's Thermophysical Properties Package (NELPAC).

Contact: Dr. Beryl Edmonds, Manager, PPDS, Institution of Chemical Engineers. (Telex 311780.) At the National Engineering Laboratory, contact Dr. D.T. Jamieson, Manager, Fluids Division, East Kilbride, Glasgow G75 0QU, Scotland; telephone 03552 20222. (Telex 777888 NELEK G.)

★549★
INSTITUTION OF ELECTRICAL ENGINEERS (IEE)
INSPEC (INFORMATION SERVICES FOR THE PHYSICS AND ENGINEERING COMMUNITIES)
Station House Phone: 0462 53331
Nightingale Rd. Service Est: 1898
Hitchin, Herts. SG5 1RJ, England
T.M. Aitchison, Director

Staff: 150 Total.

Description of System or Service: INSPEC (Information Services for the Physics and Engineering Communities) abstracts and indexes the world's scientific and technical literature to provide print, microform, and computer-based products and services in the fields of physics, electrotechnology, computers, control engineering, and information technology. It maintains the computer-readable INSPEC data base holding more than 2 million items and makes it available for online searching through vendors in Europe, North America, Japan, and elsewhere. It also uses the data base to offer retrospective literature searches, SDI, and magnetic tape services. Print products issued by INSPEC include abstracts journals, current awareness periodicals, data base user aids, and other publications. The abstracts journals and cumulative indexes are also made available in microform. Additionally, INSPEC offers the Electronic Materials Information Service (EMIS), an online service covering the properties and suppliers of electronic materials (see separate entry following this one).

Scope and/or Subject Matter: Physics, electrical engineering, electronics, computer science, control engineering, information technology, office automation.

Input Sources: Annual input to the INSPEC data base covers more than 200,000 articles from 3000 scientific journals; approximately 2000 items from books, reports, and university theses; and 25,000 papers from more than 1000 conferences.

Holdings and Storage Media: More than 2 million bibliographic records are held in the computer-readable INSPEC data base. Library holdings include 40,000 bound volumes and subscriptions to 800 periodicals.

Publications: INSPEC publishes a variety of abstracts journals, current awareness publications, and online search aids: 1) Physics Abstracts (semimonthly)—contains approximately 120,000 items per year classified under 1800 subject headings. 2) Electrical and Electronics Abstracts (monthly)—contains 60,000 items per year classified under more than 450 subject headings. 3) Computer and Control Abstracts (monthly)—contains 45,000 items annually classified under 250 subject headings. Each reference in the abstracts journals includes an abstract and full bibliographic citation; each issue of the journals contains up to six indexes. 4) IT Focus (monthly with an annual index)—each issue contains approximately 300 digests of periodical and book literature pertaining to information technology and the automated office. 5) Current Papers in Physics (semimonthly)—provides more than 74,000 references annually. 6) Current Papers in Electrical and Electronics Engineering (monthly). 7) Current Papers on Computers and Control (monthly). The Current Papers current awareness bulletins provide the titles of articles and bibliographic details for the source document and are arranged by subject; indexes are not included. 8) Key Abstracts—a series of 8 monthly journals, each providing about 200 summaries of the more important journal articles and conference proceedings; available in the following subject fields: power transmission and distribution, industrial power and control systems, communication technology, solid-state devices, electronic circuits, systems theory, electrical measurement and instrumentation, and physical measurement and instrumentation.

9) INSPEC Matters (quarterly)—newsletter designed to inform INSPEC users of new products and services and of changes and improvements to existing ones; available free of charge on request.

10) INSPEC User Manual—describes in detail INSPEC subject coverage, selection policies, indexing and classification schemes, and online searching techniques. 11) INSPEC Thesaurus—provides a complete list of all headings used by INSPEC. 12) INSPEC Classification—lists the subject categories under which all abstracts are classified. 13) Alphabetical Subject Guide to the INSPEC Classification—available free of charge on request. 14) INSPEC List of Journals and Other Serial Sources. INSPEC also publishes a number of bibliographies, research reports, and special information services.

Microform Products and Services: All back copies of INSPEC abstracts journals are available on microfilm and microfiche. 1) Physics Abstracts from 1898 to date contain in excess of 2 million items. 2) Electrical and Electronics Abstracts from 1898 to date contain more than 1 million items. 3) Computer and Control Abstracts from 1966 to date consist of more than 500,000 items. Indexes for the yearly items are separate. Cumulative indexes covering four-year periods from 1950 onwards (1966 for Computer and Control Abstracts) are available on separate reels.

Computer-Based Products and Services: The INSPEC data base is accessible through a number of online services, including Bibliographic Retrieval Services (BRS), CAN/OLE, CEDOCAR, Data-Star, DIALOG Information Services, Inc., ESA/IRS, INKA (Informationssystem Karlsruhe), Japan Information Processing Service Co. Ltd., Japan Information Center of Science and Technology (JICST), System Development Corporation (SDC), and University of Tsukuba Science Information Processing Center. Searchable data elements include author name and affiliation, title, INSPEC Classification code, controlled vocabulary, author treatment code, and abstract. Magnetic tapes of the INSPEC data base are available by subscription in two formats. INSPEC-1 provides the complete document record including the abstract and is available in four separate sections which correspond to the four abstracts journals, or in any combination of sections. Designed to provide current awareness, INSPEC-2 appears in advance of those items in INSPEC-1 and includes only the bibliographic reference, classification codes, and subject indexing. INSPEC also provides custom and standard SDI services on a subscription basis and conducts retrospective searches from the data base.

Other Services: Additional services offered by INSPEC include abstracting and indexing for external organizations, advisory and consulting services related to software provision, sponsored research in information science, and workshops on the INSPEC data base.

Clientele/Availability: Clients include information scientists, libraries, government and university research institutes, industry, and other research and teaching establishments. Services are available without restrictions on a fee basis; printed services are offered on subscription.

Remarks: The predecessor of INSPEC was Science Abstracts, which began publication in 1898.

Contact: G. Mears, Marketing Manager, INSPEC. (Telex 825962 IEE G.) Orders for microforms and all inquiries from the United States, Canada, and South America should be directed to: INSPEC, IEEE Service Center, 445 Hoes Lane, Piscataway, NJ 08854; telephone (201) 981-0060. (Telex 833233 IEEE PWAY.)

★550★
INSTITUTION OF ELECTRICAL ENGINEERS (IEE)
INSPEC (INFORMATION SERVICES FOR THE PHYSICS AND ENGINEERING COMMUNITIES)
ELECTRONIC MATERIALS INFORMATION SERVICE (EMIS)
Station House Phone: 0462 53331
Nightingale Rd.
Hitchin, Herts. SG5 1RJ, England
T.M. Aitchison, Director

Description of System or Service: The ELECTRONIC MATERIALS INFORMATION SERVICE (EMIS) is an online data base covering the properties and suppliers of materials that are of fundamental importance in solid-state electronics. The properties covered include those required for the study, processing, and production of materials and those relating to the use of materials in devices. Properties data are extracted from major English-language scientific literature and evaluated by leading scientists; scientifically qualified staff enter the results of their work into the data base. EMIS also supports the direct electronic publishing of solid state research data.

Scope and/or Subject Matter: Properties and suppliers of silicon, amorphous silicon, gallium arsenide, indium phosphide, lithium niobate, quartz, and other materials important in solid-state electronics.

Input Sources: Data and information for EMIS are assessed, selected, and extracted from the latest research and development work throughout the world. Additionally, some data are published for the first time on EMIS. All material accepted by EMIS is evaluated by scientists active in the field.

Holdings and Storage Media: EMIS data are held in machine-readable form and are updated daily.

Computer-Based Products and Services: EMIS is available online through the General Electric Information Services Company (GEISCO). The EMIS data base comprises two files: the Properties File and the Suppliers File. Each record in the Properties File provides data for one property of a single material and includes such information as record title, sample and measurement details, references to other relevant research, numeric data with relevant description and discussion, author, author address, bibliographic information on the source publications, and cross-references to other records containing relevant information. Each record in the Suppliers File includes detailed descriptions of the material systems available together with contact information for each material as well as a full list of agents worldwide where appropriate.

Clientele/Availability: Services are available without restrictions on a cost basis. Clients include electronic specialists and scientists worldwide.

Contact: G. Mears, Marketing Manager, INSPEC. (Telex 825962 IEE G.) Inquiries from the United States, Canada, and South America should be directed to: INSPEC, IEEE Service Center, 445 Hoes Lane, Piscataway, NJ 08854; telephone (201) 981-0060. (Telex 833233 IEEE PWAY.)

★551★
INSTITUTION OF MINING AND METALLURGY (IMM) LIBRARY AND INFORMATION SERVICES (LIS)
44 Portland Place   Phone: 01-580 3802
London W1N 4BR, England Service Est: 1894
Michael McGarr, Head

Staff: 5 Information and library professional; 1 clerical and nonprofessional; 2 other.

Description of System or Service: The LIBRARY AND INFORMATION SERVICES (LIS) collects, organizes, and makes available information on the world minerals industry for the use of Institution of Mining and Metallurgy members, organizations within the industry, and other interested parties. It prepares IMM Abstracts and companion indexes on cards and microfiche, and makes available a corresponding online data base known as IMMAGE. Other services include literature searching, SDI, data compilations, and photocopying.

Scope and/or Subject Matter: Economic and exploration geology; mining technology and operations; processing of minerals other than coal; nonferrous extractive metallurgy; relevant aspects of economics, health and safety, environment, legislation, management, analysis, and instrumentation.

Input Sources: LIS scans 1200 periodicals and more than 500 books and conference proceedings.

Holdings and Storage Media: The computer-readable IMMAGE data base holds approximately 5000 records per year of coverage. Library holdings include books, periodicals, reports, maps, and conference proceedings. LIS also maintains subject and geographical indexes to IMM Abstracts on microfiche (1894-1949) and cards (since 1949).

Publications: IMM Abstracts, 1950- (bimonthly)—survey of world literature on mining and related topics. Typical citation includes title, author, journal title and publisher, other publication details, and abstract; available by subscription. A catalog of other publications is available on request from the Institution.

Microform Products and Services: IMM Index to Mining and Metallurgy 1894-1949—contains more than 85,000 entries providing author, title, and bibliographic details of periodical articles, reports, proceedings, and monographs received in the library; available for purchase on 26x reduction microfiche in 23 sets arranged under three main categories of commodities, technology and operations, and countries.

Computer-Based Products and Services: The LIBRARY AND INFORMATION SERVICES maintains the computer-readable IMMAGE data base which corresponds to IMM Abstracts and includes indexing. IMMAGE is accessible online by direct dial or via PSS in the United Kingdom and IPSS internationally. Tape lease and SDI services are also offered from the data base. Records in IMMAGE can be retrieved by commodity, geographic region, mine name, technology and method, equipment type, deposit type, company or organization name, and bibliographic details such as author, publication title, and date. Search results can be output in a range of formats, from bibliographic details only to the full record including informative abstract.

Clientele/Availability: Services are available to members and nonmembers; charges are made to nonmembers.

Contact: Michael McGarr, Head, Library and Information Services. (Telex 261410.)

★552★
INTELMATIQUE
98, rue de Sevres   Phone: 01 3061636
F-75007 Paris, France   Founded: 1979
Georges Nahon, Director of Marketing

Staff: 4 Management professional; 8 technicians; 9 sales and marketing; 9 clerical and nonprofessional.

Related Organizations: Intelmatique is a unit of France Cables et Radio.

Description of System or Service: INTELMATIQUE markets a number of products and services developed under the Telematique Program of the French Directorate of Telecommunications/ Direction Generale des Telecommunications, including TELETEL, Electronic Directory Service, and Smart Card telepayment systems. TELETEL, the French national videotex system, provides interactive access to news and general information and a variety of recreation, commercial, financial, education, administrative and public, and business services. Elements of the TELETEL system package include information retrieval from a local data base or access to a third-party computer, distributed gateways, execution services software, housekeeping software, documentation, training, and maintenance and support. The Electronic Directory Service/ Service Annuaire Electronique provides TELETEL users with access to the White and Yellow Pages Directories including business advertising materials. Users may search the Directory to retrieve the telephone number of a subscriber whose name and address has been entered by the user or to retrieve a list of businesses which provide services desired by the user. INTELMATIQUE is working on a variety of other related products, including a family of low-cost computer terminals for use with the Electronic Directory Service. Additionally, INTELMATIQUE functions as an international consulting firm specializing in information technology and Smart Card systems.

Scope and/or Subject Matter: Videotex systems, Smart Card systems, computer hardware and software, electronic publishing, communications.

Input Sources: French information providers supply input for the videotex service.

Computer-Based Products and Services: INTELMATIQUE makes available the TELETEL videotex service and provides access to the electronic version of the French White and Yellow Pages Directories.

Clientele/Availability: Products and services are available without restrictions to interested parties.

Contact: Georges Nahon, Director of Marketing, Intelmatique. (Telex 203185 TELEMAT F.)

★553★
INTERFACT/SVP AB
Kungsgatan 29
P.O. Box 7037
S-10386 Stockholm, Sweden
Sven Hamrefors, Managing Director
Phone: 08 145545
Founded: 1982

Staff: 3 Information and library professional; 1 management professional; 1 sales and marketing; 1 clerical and nonprofessional.

Related Organizations: The SVP (S'il Vous Plait) Network is an affiliation of independent companies worldwide that provide information-on-demand services and are interconnected by telex. Parent organizations of INTERFACT/ SVP are Svenska Dagbladet, a newspaper, and Asblorn Habberstad, a management consulting company.

Description of System or Service: INTERFACT/SVP AB is an information broker which provides quick answers to a variety of business and general questions. It also undertakes more extensive research projects, including business intelligence, surveys, and large information gathering tasks.

Scope and/or Subject Matter: Business, market, technical, legal, economic, and other information of interest to clients.

Input Sources: Information is obtained from international SVP resources, online data bases, information contacts in Nordic countries, and other sources.

Holdings and Storage Media: Library holdings include 3500 bound volumes, 150 periodical subscriptions, and Nordic government reports.

Computer-Based Products and Services: INTERFACT/ SVP conducts computerized information retrieval from more than 1000 data bases. It also offers SDI and secondary analysis services.

Other Services: INTERFACT/SVP also offers consulting services in the area of information retrieval and conducts conferences and seminars in this area.

Clientele/Availability: Services are available on a fee basis.

Remarks: Svenska Dagbladet conducts newspaper, videotex, and other publishing activities.

Contact: Sven Hamrefors, Managing Director, INTERFACT/ SVP AB. (Telex 15924.)

★554★
INTERGOVERNMENTAL BUREAU FOR INFORMATICS (IBI)
P.O. Box 10253
23, viale Civilta del Lavoro
I-00144 Rome, Italy
Prof. Fermin A. Bernasconi, Director General
Phone: 5916041
Founded: 1974

Related Organizations: IBI was founded under the auspices of the United Nations Educational, Scientific and Cultural Organization (UNESCO).

Description of System or Service: The INTERGOVERNMENTAL BUREAU FOR INFORMATICS (IBI) promotes and fosters national and international informatics structures by serving as a clearinghouse for the exchange of experiences on cultural, social, political, and economic aspects of informatics; and by assisting in formulating policies and strategies for applying computers in public administration and for regulating the procurement and manufacture of electronic data processing equipment. IBI also carries out technical assistance, training, and fellowship programs, and it organizes international meetings and conferences, such as the Strategies and Policies for Informatics (SPIN) conferences, the World Conference on Transborder Data Flow Policies, and the Special Programme of Informatics for Development (SPINDE) project. In addition, IBI maintains the Automated Informatics Documentation System (AIDS), used for storing and retrieving bibliographic information in its areas of interest.

Scope and/or Subject Matter: All aspects of informatics, including computer equipment, applications, technology, legislation, training of personnel.

Holdings and Storage Media: IBI maintains a collection of documents and the computer-readable AIDS data base.

Publications: 1) Agora, Informatics in a Changing World (quarterly)—available by subscription. 2) IBI Newsletter (bimonthly)—available by request, free. Both publications are edited in English, French, and Spanish. 3) Automated Informatics Documentation System Trilingual Dictionary—lists more than 2000 descriptors currently used in AIDS for indexing and information retrieval; in English, Spanish, French. 4) Automated Informatics Documentation System, A Thesaurus for Informatics. IBI also publishes conference reports and guidelines.

Computer-Based Products and Services: The BUREAU's AIDS data base is used for storing and retrieving bibliographic information on informatics texts produced by IBI and other organizations.

Clientele/Availability: Services are available to member states.

Contact: Andre J. Michel, Head, Information Department, Intergovernmental Bureau for Informatics. (Telex 612065 I IBINF.)

★555★
INTERMARC GROUP
61, rue de Richelieu
F-75002 Paris, France
M. Chauveinc, Secretary
Phone: 01 2618283
Founded: 1972

Description of System or Service: The INTERMARC GROUP is composed of the national bibliographic agencies of France, Belgium, Great Britain, Germany, Netherlands, Italy, Switzerland, Spain, Denmark, and Austria. The GROUP was established to encourage the exchange of bibliographic data among its members and to develop standard formats for machine-readable bibliographic data, including monographs, serials, and authority data.

Scope and/or Subject Matter: Bibliographic data in any subject field.

Publications: 1) Intermarc Information; 2) Manuel Intermarc; 3) Intermarc 5; 4) Library Systems Seminar (annual).

Contact: M. Chauveinc, Secretary, Intermarc Group.

★556★
INTERNATIONAL ASSOCIATION FOR STATISTICAL COMPUTING (IASC)
428 Prinses Beatrixlaan
NL-2270 AZ Voorburg, Netherlands
E. Lunenberg, Director
Phone: 070 694341
Founded: 1977

Related Organizations: IASC is a section of the International Statistical Institute and is affiliated with the Australian Bureau of the Census, Bell Laboratories, U.S. Bureau of Labor Statistics, and the Statistical Office of the European Communities.

Description of System or Service: The INTERNATIONAL ASSOCIATION FOR STATISTICAL COMPUTING (IASC) was established to promote the theory, methods, and practice of statistical computing. IASC exchanges technical information through international contacts and meetings among members, institutions, and governments. It also issues publications and supports working groups to study specific topics such as software and hardware evaluation, privacy, security, survey and census processing, and statistical data bases and data base systems.

Scope and/or Subject Matter: Statistical computing.

Publications: IASC publishes a newsletter, reports, pamphlets, and books.

Clientele/Availability: Services are available to member organizations.

Contact: E. Lunenberg, Director, Permanent Office, International Statistical Institute. (Telex 32260 ISI NL.)

★557★
INTERNATIONAL ASSOCIATION FOR THE EVALUATION OF EDUCATIONAL ACHIEVEMENT (IEA)
(Association Internationale pour l'Evaluation du Rendement Scolaire)
IEA DATA BANK
Inst. of International Education Phone: 08 156656
University of Stockholm
S-106 91 Stockholm, Sweden
Richard Noonan, Associate Professor

Staff: 1 Information and library professional; 1 management professional; 1 technician; 1 clerical and nonprofessional.

Description of System or Service: The IEA DATA BANK consists of information on the academic performance of students in 22 countries. The DATA BANK covers student achievement in six subjects and includes information on the students' socioeconomic backgrounds, interests, and attitudes. It also contains information on the characteristics of the teachers and schools involved in the surveys. The DATA BANK is made available to IEA national centers in countries participating in the survey, and to other researchers.

Scope and/or Subject Matter: Data from school surveys consisting of nationally representative random samples of schools, teachers, and students age 10 to 19. Subjects tested include mathematics, science, reading comprehension, literature, English and French as foreign languages, and civics.

Input Sources: Input is derived from questionnaires and tests administered to students, teachers, and school principals.

Holdings and Storage Media: The machine-readable Data Bank contains student, teacher, and school files for each of 22 countries. Also maintained are files in which school, teacher, and student data are merged.

Publications: Data Bank Bulletin (irregular)—sent to all data bank holders and users; includes information about current status of the Data Bank, new holders, and holdings.

Computer-Based Products and Services: The IEA Data Bank of educational survey data is available on machine-readable tape.

Other Services: Routine and special programming, statistical consultation, and other services are also available.

Clientele/Availability: Services are available to qualified researchers who seek permission to use the data through their national center.

Remarks: Survey instruments (tests and questionnaires) are available from Educational Resources Information Center (ERIC) of the U.S. National Institute of Education, Washington, DC 20208.

Addendum: The IEA is an independent nonprofit scientific organization formed for the purpose of conducting and promoting educational research on an international scale.

Contact: Shirley Isgaard, Secretary, IEA Data Bank. (Telex 8105199 UNIVERS.)

★558★
INTERNATIONAL ASSOCIATION OF AGRICULTURAL LIBRARIANS AND DOCUMENTALISTS (IAALD)
TDRI, College House Phone: (not reported)
Wrights Lane Founded: 1955
London W8 5SJ, England
Miss P.J. Wortley, Secretary/Treasurer

Description of System or Service: The INTERNATIONAL ASSOCIATION OF AGRICULTURAL LIBRARIANS AND DOCUMENTALISTS (IAALD) was established to promote agricultural library science and documentation on international and national levels, as well as to serve the professional interests of agricultural librarians and documentalists. Comprising approximately 700 members from 60 countries, IAALD issues publications in the field of agricultural bibliography, documentation, and librarianship. IAALD also holds annual executive committee meetings, occasional working committee meetings, and a general assembly at least once every five years.

Scope and/or Subject Matter: Agriculture in its widest sense including forestry, agricultural engineering, veterinary sciences, fisheries, food and nutrition, and food and agricultural industries.

Publications: 1) Quarterly Bulletin of IAALD—includes an annual bibliography of professional literature. 2) IAALD News (occasional). 3) Current Agricultural Serials: A World List. 4) Primer for Agricultural Libraries. 5) World Congress of Agricultural Librarians and Documentalists: Proceedings.

Clientele/Availability: Members include agricultural librarians and documentalists from around the world.

Contact: Miss P.J. Wortley, Secretary/ Treasurer, International Association of Agricultural Librarians and Documentalists.

★559★
INTERNATIONAL ATOMIC ENERGY AGENCY (IAEA)
ENERGY AND ECONOMIC DATA BANK
P.O. Box 100 Phone: 0222 2360
Wagramerstr. 5 Service Est: 1976
A-1400 Vienna, Austria
Jayme Porto Carreiro, Engineer

Staff: 3 Information and library professional; 1 management professional; 1 technician.

Description of System or Service: The ENERGY AND ECONOMIC DATA BANK provides worldwide energy production, use, and related economic data to facilitate long-term energy planning by the IAEA and member states. The computer-readable DATA BANK comprises the following six files: information on energy production, consumption, trade, and plant capacities; energy resources; nuclear reactors and fuel cycle facilities; population; national accounts; and forecasts. The DATA BANK is held under the ADABAS data base management system and is used by the IAEA to provide inquiry answering, produce statistical bulletins and booklets on current energy situations in IAEA member countries, and to prepare forecasts.

Scope and/or Subject Matter: Nuclear and other energy production, consumption, and resources in IAEA member countries.

Input Sources: Data are collected by IAEA from questionnaires, meetings, and internal studies. The following organizations also submit data on magnetic tape or through publications: the United Nations Statistical Office; Organization for Economic Co-Operation and Development; European Economic Community; the World Bank; World Energy Conference; and the Organization of Petroleum Exporting Countries.

Holdings and Storage Media: The computer-readable Data Bank holds 3 million items stored on disk.

Publications: Reference Data Series No. 1: Energy, Electricity and Nuclear Power Estimates for the Period up to 2000 (annual).

Computer-Based Products and Services: The ENERGY AND ECONOMIC DATA BANK is used to provide retrieval services, publications, and forecasts and is expected to be made available online.

Clientele/Availability: Currently restricted to IAEA internal use, services will be made available to organizations located in IAEA member countries and international organizations.

Contact: Jayme Porto Carreiro, Engineer, International Atomic Energy Agency. (Telex 1 12645.)

★560★
INTERNATIONAL ATOMIC ENERGY AGENCY (IAEA)
INTERNATIONAL NUCLEAR INFORMATION SYSTEM (INIS)
P.O. Box 100 Phone: 0222 2360
Wagramerstr. 5 Service Est: 1970
A-1400 Vienna, Austria
Arkady G. Romanenko, Head

Staff: 12 Information and library professional; 2 management professional; 6 technicians; 21 clerical and nonprofessional.

Related Organizations: Participants in the International Nuclear Information System include 70 countries and 14 international organizations.

Description of System or Service: The INTERNATIONAL NUCLEAR INFORMATION SYSTEM (INIS) is a cooperative, decentralized computerized abstracting and indexing system providing worldwide coverage of the literature on the peaceful uses of nuclear energy.

INIS processes and merges input provided by each of the member states and redistributes the collected information twice per month on magnetic tape. The data base is made available to users by the INIS liaison officer in each country and it is publicly accessible online through the IAEA and other host services. In addition to producing the data base, INIS issues the printed abstracts journal INIS Atomindex and provides copies of technical reports and other nonconventional literature on microfiche. Another function of INIS is to help member states improve their methods of information handling.

Scope and/or Subject Matter: Peaceful applications of nuclear science and technology; other aspects of nuclear energy such as economics, nuclear law, medical applications, safeguards, inspection, and nuclear documentation.

Input Sources: Input is received from participating countries and international organizations at a rate of 70,000 items per year; approximately 20 percent of the input is nonconventional literature such as technical reports, conference preprints, patents, and theses.

Holdings and Storage Media: The computer-readable INIS data base contains approximately 860,000 entries dating from 1970 to the present. Microfiche copies of approximately 160,000 reports are also held.

Publications: 1) INIS Atomindex (semimonthly with semiannual and annual cumulative indexes)—an abstracts journal containing abstracts in English as well as some in French, Russian, and Spanish. Derived from the INIS data base, each issue contains indexes to authors, report numbers, corporate names, subjects, and conferences. 2) INIS Reference Series, including INIS Thesaurus—a set of documents containing rules, standards, formats, codes, and authority lists used by the participants in the decentralized INIS program. 3) INIS Today—a general introduction to the System.

Microform Products and Services: Full-text copies of technical reports and other nonconventional literature furnished to the System are available on microfiche on a subscription or per-item basis.

Computer-Based Products and Services: The INTERNATIONAL NUCLEAR INFORMATION SYSTEM data base is accessible for online searching through the IAEA, ESA/IRS, CAN/OLE, and BELINDIS (Belgian Information and Dissemination Service). It is also available to participating members through the semimonthly INIS magnetic tape service. National INIS centers provide a variety of services from the data base. Data elements in the file include reference number, author and affiliation, corporate entry, title in English, journal title, language of published document, imprint and collation, ISBN or ISSN, conference title, place and date, report numbers, set of descriptors for subject retrieval, indication of presence of numerical data and the subject on which data are provided, and an abstract in English and often in the language of the original document.

Other Services: Through an agreement with the United Nations Food and Agriculture Organization (FAO), the IAEA also provides online access to AGRIS, a bibliographic data base dealing with food and agriculture.

Clientele/Availability: Publications and microreproduction services are generally available. Online access to the INIS data base through the IAEA in Vienna is available to clients with the permission of the appropriate national liaison officer.

Remarks: The International Nuclear Information System was preceded by the European Nuclear Documentation System (ENDS) under jurisdiction of the Commission of the European Communities (CEC).

Contact: Arkady G. Romanenko, Head, International Nuclear Information System. (Telex 1 12645.)

★561★
INTERNATIONAL ATOMIC ENERGY AGENCY (IAEA)
NUCLEAR DATA SECTION
P.O. Box 100   Phone: 0222 2360
Wagramerstr. 5   Service Est: 1964
A-1400 Vienna, Austria
Joseph J. Schmidt, Director

Staff: 14 Management professional; 10 clerical and nonprofessional.

Related Organizations: The Nuclear Data Section participates in an international nuclear data network with five other centers: 1) National Nuclear Data Center, Brookhaven National Laboratory, U.S. Department of Energy; 2) Nuclear Energy Agency Data Bank, Organisation for Economic Co-Operation and Development; 3) Nuclear Data Center, Institute of Physics and Energy; 4) U.S.S.R. Center for Nuclear Structure and Reaction Data; and 5) Fachinformationszentrum Energie, Physik, Mathematik GmbH.

Description of System or Service: The NUCLEAR DATA SECTION of the IAEA functions as a center for data assessment and research coordination, as a data processing and exchange center, as a center for the transfer of nuclear-data technology to developing countries, and as a data service center. In this last capacity, the SECTION cooperates with other national and regional centers in the systematic worldwide collection, compilation, dissemination, and exchange of nuclear reaction, structure, and decay data. Within its service area, it provides nuclear data services, including the provision of relevant numerical data in any computer medium; distributes reports on nuclear data surveys and reviews; answers inquiries on the existence and status of nuclear data activities and availability; maintains a referral service for atomic and molecular fusion data; and publicizes available numerical data. In support of its activities the SECTION develops computerized storage and retrieval systems and provides services from such data files as the Computer Index of Neutron Data (CINDA); the index to literature on atomic collision data (CIAMDA); the experimental nuclear reaction data base (EXFOR); all internationally available evaluated neutron reaction data files; the Evaluated Nuclear Structure and Decay File (ENSDF); and various special-purpose nuclear and atomic data files. Data from these files are available as listings or plottings and on magnetic tape.

Scope and/or Subject Matter: Nuclear data, including numerical and associated information pertinent to measured, deduced, or calculated parameters of nuclear reactions induced by neutrons, charged particles, and protons, as well as nuclear structure and decay data and atomic collision data.

Input Sources: Data are collected from published and unpublished sources in the Section's service area and merged with data collected by cooperating centers.

Holdings and Storage Media: More than 4 million data records of measured and calculated nuclear reaction parameters are stored in computer-readable EXFOR files; more than 7 million records of evaluated data are stored in 80 special-purpose nuclear data files.

Publications: The Section is responsible for the publication of the CINDA and CIAMDA indexes as well as the World Request List for Nuclear Data (WRENDA) and a variety of nuclear data reports.

Computer-Based Products and Services: The SECTION provides experimental and evaluated nuclear reaction and structure and decay data in any computer medium. It also offers selective retrievals from the CINDA and CIAMDA data indexes.

Clientele/Availability: Products and services are available free of charge to eligible users.

Contact: Joseph J. Schmidt, Director, or A. Lorenz, Deputy Section Head, Nuclear Data Section. (Telex 1 12645.)

★562★
INTERNATIONAL ATOMIC ENERGY AGENCY (IAEA)
VIENNA INTERNATIONAL CENTRE (VIC) LIBRARY
P.O. Box 100   Phone: 0222 2360
Wagramerstr. 5   Service Est: 1979
A-1400 Vienna, Austria
Wilson H. Neale, Head

Staff: 10 Information and library professional; 20 clerical and nonprofessional.

Related Organizations: The Library was formed by the merger of the formerly separate libraries of the IAEA and United Nations Industrial Development Organization (UNIDO).

Description of System or Service: The VIENNA INTERNATIONAL CENTRE (VIC) LIBRARY serves the information needs of the IAEA and United Nations organizations in Vienna by providing search and SDI services from publicly available and internal data bases, by issuing several publications, and by offering reference, interlibrary loan, and photocopy services. The LIBRARY maintains for in-house use the computer-readable Library Information On-line (LION) book holdings file and LISA, a serials management data base.

Scope and/or Subject Matter: Atomic energy, industrial development, social affairs, drugs.

Input Sources: Input includes books, journals, conference proceedings, reports, and UN documents.

Holdings and Storage Media: The Library's holdings include 65,000 bound volumes; subscriptions to 3000 periodicals; and numerous documents, reports, and films.

Publications: 1) Acquisitions list (once or twice weekly); 2) serials list (annual); 3) film catalog (annual). All publications are available free on request from the Library.

Microform Products and Services: COMindex (monthly)—cumulative microfiche list of library holdings by title, author, corporate author, series, and subject.

Computer-Based Products and Services: The LIBRARY maintains the LION and LISA files online. LION covers book holdings and dates since 1971; LISA covers serials holdings. The LIBRARY also offers retrospective search and SDI services from data bases made available through DIALOG Information Services, Inc. and System Development Corporation (SDC), as well as from the INIS, AGRIS, and Industrial Development Abstracts (IDA) files held in-house.

Clientele/Availability: Primary clients are the staffs of the IAEA and the various UN organizations located at the Vienna International Centre.

Contact: Wilson H. Neale, Head, Vienna International Centre Library.

★563★
INTERNATIONAL BEE RESEARCH ASSOCIATION
APICULTURAL ABSTRACTS (AA)
Hill House, Chalfont St. Peter   Phone: 0753 885011
Gerrards Cross, Bucks. SL9 0NR, England   Service Est: 1950
Margaret Adey, Director

Staff: 12 Total.

Description of System or Service: APICULTURAL ABSTRACTS (AA) indexes and abstracts the world literature covering research and technical developments relating to bees and beekeeping. Information from AA is available in a quarterly journal, on microfiche, and in a computer-readable data base that is part of the Commonwealth Agricultural Bureaux (CAB) system.

Scope and/or Subject Matter: Bees and beekeeping, including bee foraging, pollination, social behavior, breeding, and processing of hive products.

Input Sources: Input is derived from worldwide published literature and computer-readable data bases.

Holdings and Storage Media: The Association maintains a library that includes 24,000 reprints, 3500 books, 6000 volumes of periodicals and annual reports, 1600 translations, and 100,000 subject and author bibliography cards. The computer-readable AA data base contains more than 7000 items from 1972 to the present.

Publications: Apicultural Abstracts-AA (quarterly with separate annual indexes)—available by subscription.

Microform Products and Services: AA cumulative subject and author indexes since 1973 are available on 270-frame microfiche.

Computer-Based Products and Services: Apicultural Abstracts is searchable online as part of the CAB data base, which is made available by such vendors as DIALOG Information Services, Inc., System Development Corporation (SDC), ESA/IRS, and others. Tape services are also available from CAB.

Clientele/Availability: Services are available without restrictions.

Contact: David Lowe, International Bee Research Association.

★564★
INTERNATIONAL CENTER FOR HIGHER STUDIES IN MEDITERRANEAN AGRONOMY
(Centre International des Hautes Etudes Agronomiques Mediterraneennes)
SOCIOECONOMIC DATA BANK ON THE MEDITERRANEAN COUNTRIES
(Banque de Donnees Socio-economiques des Pays Mediterraneens - MEDISTAT)
Institut Agronomique Mediterraneen   Phone: 67 632880
B.P. 1239   Service Est: 1976
F-34060 Montpellier Cedex, France
Prof. M. Allaya, Director

Description of System or Service: The SOCIOECONOMIC DATA BANK ON THE MEDITERRANEAN COUNTRIES (MEDISTAT) is a computer-readable file containing nonbibliographic data on agriculture, agronomy, and the economy in the Mediterranean countries. It is utilized to produce reports on such topics as products grown in each country, production in tons, population, utilization of farmland, use of pesticides, and international trade. The data are concentrated on the countries in the Mediterranean region, although statistics on countries around the world are also gathered.

Scope and/or Subject Matter: Agriculture, agronomy, socioeconomics, demographics and population, international trade, and national accounting of production and trade.

Input Sources: Input for the Data Bank is derived from annual statistical reports of the Mediterranean countries, and from national and international organizations dealing with agriculture and economics.

Holdings and Storage Media: Held on magnetic tape, the Data Bank contains approximately six million items from 1965 to the present.

Publications: Annuaire des Pays Mediterraneens—contains annual agricultural and economic statistics of the Mediterranean countries.

Microform Products and Services: Reports on selected topics are available on microfiche.

Computer-Based Products and Services: Computer searches of MEDISTAT are currently conducted in batch mode; online searching through time-sharing is projected for the future. The Data Bank also is utilized to produce specialized reports and statistical tables concerning specific features of Mediterranean countries.

Clientele/Availability: Clients include agricultural professionals and others.

Contact: Prof. M. Allaya, Director, International Center for Higher Studies in Mediterranean Agronomy. (Telex 480783 F.)

★565★
INTERNATIONAL CENTRE FOR SCIENTIFIC AND TECHNICAL INFORMATION (ICSTI)
(Mezdunarodjyj Centr Nauchoj i Tehniceskoj Informacii)
Kuusinena 21-b   Phone: 198 7230
125252 Moscow, U.S.S.R.   Service Est: 1969
Leonid N. Sumarokov, Director

Related Organizations: ICSTI was established as the result of an agreement by the heads of committees and ministries of science and technology of the member nations of the Council for Mutual Economic Assistance (CMEA). The members of the Centre are Bulgaria, Cuba, Czechoslovakia, German Democratic Republic, Hungary, the Mongolian People's Republic, Poland, Romania, Vietnam, and the Soviet Union.

Description of System or Service: The INTERNATIONAL CENTRE FOR SCIENTIFIC AND TECHNICAL INFORMATION (ICSTI) is involved in the following activities: creation and development of information systems; provision, on the basis of modern technology, of information services to interested organizations in member countries; publication of various information materials and other forms of dissemination of scientific and technical achievements; research and development work in modern information technology; and provision to interested organizations of methodological, scientific, and technical assistance in matters of scientific and technical information. ICSTI provides information services from an international multidisciplinary data base on research and from additional subject-oriented data bases. Services include retrospective searches, SDI, and document delivery; ICSTI data bases are also remotely accessible online. Additionally, the Centre develops and distributes software for information work.

Scope and/or Subject Matter: Scientific and technical information, including research, information processing software and hardware, and information dissemination methodology.

Holdings and Storage Media: ICSTI maintains several data bases in machine-readable form. The Centre also maintains a collection of primary documents.

Publications: 1) Achievements and Perspectives—journal providing information on matters of scientific and technical cooperation of the CMEA member countries, analytical reviews, and articles concerning results of system research and development. 2) Mechanical Engineering—journal providing information on matters of multilateral scientific and technical cooperation in the field of mechanical engineering, analytical reviews, and articles on current state-of-the-art and trends of development of scientific research and manufacturing of modern types of equipment, machines, and devices, as well as on matters of introduction of progressive technological processes. 3) Problems of Economic, Scientific and Technical Cooperation of CMEA Member Countries—journal containing abstracts of selected books and articles on the theory of world Socialist economy, vital problems of economic relations among Socialist countries, and the development of Socialist integration. 4) Problems of Information Systems—journal containing information on matters of improving functioning on the theory of information systems, assuring their informational, linguistic, and technical compatibility, as well as development and practical adaptation of modern technology. 5) Methodological Materials and Documentation on Software Packages—provides detailed descriptions of software packages offered by ICSTI. ICSTI publications are available in other countries through firms and bookselling organizations which conduct business with Mezhdunarodnaya Kniga, the Soviet foreign trade association.

Computer-Based Products and Services: The INTERNATIONAL CENTRE FOR SCIENTIFIC AND TECHNICAL INFORMATION maintains an international multidisciplinary data base in the area of research and development, as well as additional subject-oriented data bases in the fields of energy, mechanical engineering, computer technology, management, and others. ICSTI provides retrospective searching and SDI services from its data bases. The CENTRE also offers remote online access to its data bases. Additionally, ICSTI carries out the elaboration and introduction of model software packages for interactive searching and other information work. ICSTI has signed more than 100 agreements concerning provision of software to organizations of CMEA member countries.

Clientele/Availability: Services are available to participating member countries on a contract or agreement of cooperation basis.

Remarks: ICSTI participates in the International Nuclear Information System (INIS) of the International Atomic Energy Agency, the International Serials Data System (ISDS) of the United Nations Educational, Scientific and Cultural Organization, and the INFOTERRA system of the United Nations Environmental Programme.

Contact: V.A. Polushkin, International Centre for Scientific and Technical Information. (Telex 411925 MCNTI.)

★566★
INTERNATIONAL CHILDREN'S CENTRE (ICC)
(Centre International de l'Enfance)
DOCUMENTATION SERVICE
ROBERT DEBRE INFORMATION BASE
(Base d'Information Robert Debre - BIRD)
Chateau de Longchamp   Phone: 01 5067992
Bois de Boulogne   Service Est: 1981
F-75016 Paris, France
Denise Parise, Head

Staff: 9 Information and library professional; 7 clerical and nonprofessional.

Description of System or Service: The ROBERT DEBRE INFORMATION BASE (BIRD) is a computer-readable data base providing bibliographic citations and abstracts to international literature covering all aspects of a child's life, from conception to the end of adolescence, with emphasis on the child's relationship with the mother and family. All citations contained in BIRD are for documents held by the ICC; photocopies of the documents are available on request. BIRD is publicly accessible online and can be searched in French, English, and Spanish.

Scope and/or Subject Matter: All aspects of childhood and adolescence, including emotional, nutritional, health, educational, social, and others.

Input Sources: Input is derived from materials received by the ICC, including approximately 850 periodicals as well as books and documents. Literature from developing countries, including unpublished material, accounts for about thirty percent of the input.

Holdings and Storage Media: The machine-readable BIRD data base contains more than 50,000 references and abstracts; it is updated monthly with approximately 1200 new records. The file dates from 1981 to the present, with selective retrospective coverage planned. The Centre's library includes approximately 500,000 older references.

Publications: A list of descriptors, a user's manual, and a catalog of periodicals are available for purchase from the ICC.

Computer-Based Products and Services: The bibliographic ROBERT DEBRE INFORMATION BASE is available online through G.CAM. Search elements include producer; reference number; subject fields; author; title, including original title, titles translated by the author, and titles translated by the ICC; bibliographic source; year; descriptors in French, English, and Spanish; summary in French, English, and Spanish; and language.

Clientele/Availability: Services are available without restrictions. Users include physicians, sociologists, psychologists, educators, demographers, economists, agronomists, and others concerned with the health and well-being of children.

Remarks: Professor Robert Debre was involved in the 1950 creation of the International Children's Centre.

Contact: Denise Parise, Head, Documentation Service, International Children's Centre. (Telex 610584F CIENFAN.)

★567★
INTERNATIONAL CIVIL AVIATION ORGANIZATION (ICAO)
AIR NAVIGATION BUREAU
ACCIDENT INVESTIGATION AND PREVENTION SECTION
AIRCRAFT ACCIDENT/INCIDENT REPORTING SYSTEM (ADREP)
1000 Sherbrooke St. W., Suite 400   Phone: (514) 285-8160
Montreal, PQ, Canada H3A 2R2   Service Est: 1977

Staff: 3 Accident investigators; 1 computer scientist; 1 clerical and nonprofessional.

Description of System or Service: Maintained to provide flight safety information services, the AIRCRAFT ACCIDENT/ INCIDENT REPORTING SYSTEM (ADREP) collects, stores, and retrieves report information submitted by ICAO member states on aircraft accidents and incidents. Several publications are produced from the computer-readable data base, and computerized search services are supplied to member governments.

Scope and/or Subject Matter: Worldwide accidents and incidents involving aircraft over 2250 kg maximum takeoff weight.

Input Sources: Input for the data base is derived from reports submitted by members.

Holdings and Storage Media: Covering the period from 1970 to the present, the machine-readable ADREP data base holds more than 10,700 records and is updated bimonthly.

Publications: 1) ICAO/ADREP Reports Summary (bimonthly)—covers occurrences reported to ICAO; issued in English, French, and Spanish. Available at no cost to contracting states. 2) Aircraft Accident Statistics (annual)—published in English, French, and Spanish.

Computer-Based Products and Services: Computerized searches are conducted on request for accident investigators of member states.

Clientele/Availability: Use of the System is restricted to ICAO members.

Contact: Reinhard Menzel, Technical Officer, Accident Investigation and Prevention Section, International Civil Aviation Organization.

★568★
INTERNATIONAL CIVIL AVIATION ORGANIZATION (ICAO)
AIR NAVIGATION BUREAU
AERODROMES SECTION
AIRPORT CHARACTERISTICS DATA BANK (ACDB)
1000 Sherbrooke St. W., Suite 400   Phone: (514) 285-8179
Montreal, PQ, Canada H3A 2R2   Service Est: 1973
Kenneth K. Wilde, Chief

Description of System or Service: The AIRPORT CHARACTERISTICS DATA BANK (ACDB) is a computer-readable file used to store, retrieve, and publish information on the physical characteristics of more than 1000 international airports. The DATA BANK was developed to encourage compatibility of new aircraft and airports, and it includes plans for future airports. The publication Airport Characteristics is based on the file and is available in hard copy and on magnetic tape.

Scope and/or Subject Matter: Airport characteristics, including runways, obstacles, taxiways, and precision approach runways equipped with ILS.

Input Sources: Information for the data bank is obtained from national aeronautical publications, notices to airmen (NOTAMs), and correspondence with ICAO member states and regional offices.

Holdings and Storage Media: The machine-readable Airport Characteristics Data Bank holds more than 25,000 records.

Publications: Airport Characteristics (annual).

Computer-Based Products and Services: The AIRPORT CHARACTERISTICS DATA BANK is used to supply data in printed and machine-readable forms. Introduction of online service is under consideration.

Clientele/Availability: Clients include ICAO member states, aircraft manufacturers, airlines, and consultants. Services are free to members and available for a fee to others.

Contact: Kenneth K. Wilde, Chief, Aerodromes Section, International Civil Aviation Organization.

★569★
INTERNATIONAL CIVIL AVIATION ORGANIZATION (ICAO)
AIR TRANSPORT BUREAU
STATISTICS SECTION
AIR TRANSPORT STATISTICAL PROGRAM
1000 Sherbrooke St. W., Suite 400   Phone: (514) 285-8064
Montreal, PQ, Canada H3A 2R2   Service Est: 1947
D.C. Singh, Chief, Statistics Section

Staff: 1 Information and library professional; 7 management professional; 12 clerical and nonprofessional.

Description of System or Service: The AIR TRANSPORT STATISTICAL PROGRAM is a statistical reporting and analysis information system. The PROGRAM makes available machine-readable and hardcopy statistical information covering civil aviation throughout the world.

Scope and/or Subject Matter: Statistics on international airport operations; air traffic (passenger, freight, mail), finances, fleet, and personnel of scheduled and nonscheduled commercial air carriers.

Input Sources: The Program utilizes statistical reports filed by such units as airlines and airports.

Holdings and Storage Media: The system holds 2 million items (dating from 1954 to the present) related to air transport operations worldwide. Approximately 3600 published reports are held as back-up literature.

Publications: 1) Civil Aviation Statistics of the World (annual)—available for purchase. Contains summarized statistics of all Program areas. 2) Digests of Statistics—series providing detailed civil aviation statistics; comprises the following titles: Air Carrier Traffic, Air Carrier Financial Data, Air Carrier Fleet and Personnel, Air Carrier Traffic Flow, Airport Traffic, Traffic by Flight Stage, Civil Aircraft on Register, and On-flight Origin and Destination. The Digests are issued annually, with the exception of the On-flight Origin and Destination Digest which is issued quarterly.

Computer-Based Products and Services: Computer tapes of the published Digests described above are available for purchase from the ICAO.

Clientele/Availability: Services are available to member states of the ICAO, ICAO staff, airlines, nonscheduled air transport operators, airports, and other interested parties.

Contact: D.C. Singh, Chief, Statistics Section, International Civil Aviation Organization. (Telex 05 24513.)

★570★
INTERNATIONAL COFFEE ORGANIZATION (ICO)
COFFEELINE
22 Berners St.   Phone: 01-580 8591
London W1P 4DD, England   Service Est: 1982
Mr. C.P.R. Dubois, Information Officer

Description of System or Service: COFFEELINE is a bibliographic data base covering all aspects of coffee, from farming of coffee plants to its production, packaging, and marketing. References are selected from a wide range of journals from all over the world; also included are references to books, patents, reports, and theses. COFFEELINE is commercially available online and corresponds closely to the printed work, ICO Library Monthly Entries.

Scope and/or Subject Matter: Information on coffee and relevant to coffee, including botany, farming methods, marketing, legislation, industrial processing, economics, physiological effects, caffeine, and brewing and recipes.

Input Sources: Material for COFFEELINE is derived from more than 5000 journals published worldwide, and from reports, books, patents, theses, and audiovisual materials.

Holdings and Storage Media: The machine-readable COFFEELINE holds about 12,000 bibliographic references dating from 1973 to the present; 80 percent of the references added after 1980 include abstracts. Approximately 400 records are added every bimonthly update. The ICO Library collection includes 12,000 bound volumes, subscriptions to 420 periodicals, and 10,000 35mm slides.

Publications: 1) International Coffee Organization Library Monthly Entries—provides approximately 100 abstracts per issue, with annual subject, author, and geographic indexes; available by subscription. 2) The COFFEELINE Thesaurus—available for purchase.

Computer-Based Products and Services: COFFEELINE is commercially available online through DIALOG Information Services, Inc. Searchable data elements include author, title, source, publication year, language, geographic location, abstract, descriptors, section heading, and other items. Information retrieval and SDI services from the file are provided by the ICO.

Clientele/Availability: Services are publicly available.

Contact: Mr. C.P.R. Dubois, Information Officer, COFFEELINE. (Telex 267659.)

★571★
INTERNATIONAL COMMITTEE FOR SOCIAL SCIENCE
INFORMATION AND DOCUMENTATION (ICSSD)
27, rue Saint-Guillaume   Phone: 01 2603960
F-75341 Paris Cedex 7, France   Founded: 1950
Jean Meyriat, Secretary General

Staff: 5 Information and library professional; 3 clerical and nonprofessional.

Related Organizations: The International Committee for Social Science Information and Documentation receives support from the United Nations Educational, Scientific and Cultural Organization (UNESCO).

Description of System or Service: The INTERNATIONAL COMMITTEE FOR SOCIAL SCIENCE INFORMATION AND DOCUMENTATION (ICSSD) was established to design overall programs for the worldwide improvement of social science information and documentation; to serve as a technical and standardizing body by promoting the international compatibility of relevant documentary products and services; and to prepare and publish bibliographic and reference works. As part of this last function, the COMMITTEE maintains a computer-readable bibliographic data base which is used to issue bibliographies and provide information retrieval services.

Scope and/or Subject Matter: Information and documentation services in sociology, economics, political science, social and cultural anthropology, and other social sciences fields.

Input Sources: ICSSD scans 3000 periodicals and all other social science publications in any language.

Holdings and Storage Media: Approximately 70,000 bibliographic citations are held in machine-readable files.

Publications: 1) International Bibliography of the Social Sciences (annual). Four separate volumes are issued in the areas of sociology, political science, economics, and social and cultural anthropology. 2) World List of Social Science Periodicals-Liste Mondiale des Periodiques Specialises dans les Sciences Sociales (irregular)—covers approximately 3200 scholarly and secondary serials in the social sciences. Includes subject and title indexes. 3) A Register of Legal Documentation in the World. 4) World Inventory of Social Science Data Services. 5) Thesaurus for Information Processing in Sociology.

Computer-Based Products and Services: The COMMITTEE's machine-readable data base is used to publish the International Bibliography of the Social Sciences and to provide information retrieval services; it is also searchable online on an experimental basis through QL Systems Limited. The data base consists of four subfiles: Sociology, which dates from 1980 to the present and holds 7000 items per year of coverage; Political Science, dating from 1981 and covering 7000 items per year; Economics, covering 1979 to date with 8000 items per year; and Anthropology, which begins in 1981 and covers 7000 items per year.

Other Services: ICSSD also provides consulting services to UNESCO and social science professional associations and sponsors conferences and round tables.

Clientele/Availability: Membership in the Committee is limited to members nominated by associations specializing in the social sciences or in documentation.

Remarks: The Committee is also known by its French name: Comite International pour l'Information et la Documentation en Sciences Sociales (CIDSS).

Contact: Jean Meyriat, Secretary General, International Committee for Social Science Information and Documentation.

★572★
INTERNATIONAL COMPANY FOR DOCUMENTATION IN CHEMISTRY
(Internationale Dokumentationsgesellschaft fur Chemie - IDC)
Hamburger Allee 26-28   Phone: 069 79171
D-6000 Frankfurt am Main 90, Fed. Rep.
 of Germany   Founded: 1967

Staff: Approximately 160 total.

Related Organizations: IDC shareholders include 11 chemical industrial firms with about 180 related companies.

Description of System or Service: The INTERNATIONAL COMPANY FOR DOCUMENTATION IN CHEMISTRY (IDC) coordinates major chemical information sources in order to provide an integrated and comprehensive information facility in the field of chemistry. IDC gathers and abstracts chemical literature and stores the information in machine-readable files, which are made accessible to member organizations. The COMPANY also procures foreign data bases through contractual agreements, and makes those data bases available for retrieval purposes. Additionally, IDC conducts online searches for members, provides programming and data processing capabilities for chemical data, and offers document delivery.

Scope and/or Subject Matter: All aspects of chemistry including patents, chemical economics, organic and inorganic chemistry, polymer chemistry, and chemical process engineering.

Input Sources: Input for IDC data bases is obtained from journal and patent literature and such secondary sources as CAS, INPADOC, and Derwent's Central Patent Index. IDC also acquires data bases from member organizations.

Holdings and Storage Media: A number of internally and externally generated data bases are maintained in machine-readable form. All abstracts held in internal data bases are also stored in microform.

Microform Products and Services: IDC provides microfilms of abstracts from its data bases. It also offers the Patent Data Bank on COM microfiche, which is issued annually with cumulative monthly supplements.

Computer-Based Products and Services: The INTERNATIONAL COMPANY FOR DOCUMENTATION IN CHEMISTRY maintains and provides search, SDI, and tape services from the following internal data bases: 1) IDC Inorganic Data Base—contains about 180,000 citations to patents since 1973 and to journal literature since 1979; updated with 27,000 references annually. Data elements include source, year, volume, abstract number, title, patent number, filing and priority dates for patents, IPC number, journal citation, chemical composition, and nonstructural information. 2) IDC Organic Chemistry File—holds approximately 800,000 citations to patents and other literature in the field of organic chemistry since 1960; updated annually with 40,000 references. Data elements include abstract number, structural information according to GREMAS codes, and nonstructural information. 3) IDC Polymer File—contains about 96,000 references to patent literature about high-molecular organic compounds since 1975; updated with 14,000 references annually; includes structural data based on GREMAS codes. 4) IDC Patent Data Bank (Patentdatenbank-PDB)—holds more than 9 million citations to literature from 50 countries. PDB is sortable by applicant name and first date; by country and patent number; and by country and patent application number. Information on approximately 100,000 nonequivalent patents is added each year. The INTERNATIONAL COMPANY FOR DOCUMENTATION IN CHEMISTRY also provides services from the Chemical and Process Engineering Abstracts/ Verfahrenstechnische Berichte (VtB) data base and Chemical Abstracts Service data bases.

Clientele/Availability: Services and products are available to associated organizations, and, in some cases, to others.

Contact: Dr. Hartel or Dr. Kolb, Directors, International Company for Documentation in Chemistry. (Telex 412 114 IDC D.)

★573★
INTERNATIONAL COUNCIL FOR BUILDING RESEARCH, STUDIES AND DOCUMENTATION
(Conseil International du Batiment pour la Recherche, l'Etude et
 la Documentation - CIB)
Weena 704   Phone: 10 110240
P.O. Box 20704   Service Est: 1953
NL-3001 JA Rotterdam, Netherlands

Description of System or Service: The INTERNATIONAL COUNCIL FOR BUILDING RESEARCH, STUDIES AND DOCUMENTATION (CIB) seeks to encourage, facilitate, and develop international cooperation in building, housing, and planning research and documentation. It studies technical, economic, social, and environmental aspects of the building, housing, and planning field. The COUNCIL supervises the maintenance of the international online bibliographic retrieval system CIBDOC which provides access to several data bases in those fields. CIB also conducts research and educational programs, promotes coordination and cooperation among national and international organizations in the field, and holds congresses.

Scope and/or Subject Matter: Research and documentation in the fields of regional, town, and local planning; housing; civil engineering; architecture.

Publications: Building Research and Practice (6 per year)—journal. CIB also publishes an information bulletin, directories, and special reports and papers.

Computer-Based Products and Services: The COUNCIL's online CIBDOC system is coordinated by the Information Center for Building and Physical Planning (IRB) of the Fraunhofer Society (see separate entry).

Clientele/Availability: CIB is composed of individuals and institutions in the building, housing, and planning research fields.

Contact: Secretary General, International Council for Building Research, Studies and Documentation.

★574★
INTERNATIONAL COUNCIL OF SCIENTIFIC UNIONS (ICSU)
(Conseil International des Unions Scientifiques)
COMMITTEE ON DATA FOR SCIENCE AND TECHNOLOGY (CODATA)
51, blvd. de Montmorency
F-75016 Paris, France
Phyllis Glaeser, Executive Secretary
Phone: 01 5250496
Service Est: 1966

Staff: 1 Management professional; 1 clerical and nonprofessional.

Description of System or Service: The COMMITTEE ON DATA FOR SCIENCE AND TECHNOLOGY (CODATA) is a voluntary professional organization established to promote and encourage, on a wordwide basis, the production and distribution of collections of reliable numerical data of importance to the field of science and technology. CODATA is especially concerned with data of interdisciplinary significance and with projects that promote international cooperation in the compilation and dissemination of scientific data. CODATA goals include the following: 1) promoting the evaluation, compilation, and dissemination of scientific and technological data and fostering international collaboration in this field; 2) seeking, on an interdisciplinary basis, to improve the reliability, processing, management, and accessibility of data; 3) compiling and encouraging compilations of key scientific data; 4) studying methodologies for improving the quality of data compilations; and 5) undertaking feasibility studies in building data bases or data centers. Major CODATA activities include presentation of key data sets, issuing guidelines to the presentation of data, supplying information on sources of reliable data, providing education and training, coordination of multinational projects, and sponsoring international interdisciplinary conferences. Additionally, CODATA cooperates with international scientific unions, the United Nations Educational, Scientific and Cultural Organization, and other international bodies.

Scope and/or Subject Matter: Scientific and technological numerical data, including: quantitative data on properties and behavior of matter; quantitative data and characteristic values of biological, geological, and astronomical systems; and other experimental and observational values.

Publications: 1) CODATA Newsletter (quarterly)—distributed without charge to interested recipients throughout the world; it is primarily in English. 2) CODATA Bulletin (irregular)—each issue usually deals with a single subject; available by subscription. 3) CODATA Directory of Data Sources for Science and Technology—provides information on where to find quantitative data on properties and behavior of matter, quantitative data and characteristic values of biological, geological, and astronomical systems, and other experimental and observational values. Each chapter will be published as an issue of the Bulletin; when all chapters are completed they will be combined into a single volume. CODATA also issues special reports, books, and proceedings of its international conferences.

Clientele/Availability: CODATA functions as an interdisciplinary committee of the ICSU. Associate Organization memberships are available to industrial firms, data and information centers, data bank operators, national and international bodies, laboratories interested in data, and other organizations that are directly engaged in the evaluation, compilation, and dissemination of data, as well as organizations which are users or publishers of data.

Contact: Phyllis Glaeser, Executive Secretary, Committee on Data for Science and Technology. (Telex 630553 F ICSU.)

★575★
INTERNATIONAL COUNCIL OF SCIENTIFIC UNIONS ABSTRACTING BOARD (ICSU AB)
(Bureau des Resumes Analytiques du Conseil International des Unions Scientifiques)
51, blvd. de Montmorency
F-75016 Paris, France
Marthe Orfus, Executive Secretary
Phone: 01 5256592
Service Est: 1952

Staff: 1 Management professional; 1 clerical and nonprofessional.

Description of System or Service: The INTERNATIONAL COUNCIL OF SCIENTIFIC UNIONS ABSTRACTING BOARD (ICSU AB) is an international nonprofit, nongovernmental organization whose members include countries, scientific unions, and abstracting and indexing services. Its main purpose is to improve the flow of information among the world's scientists and engineers by serving as an international forum for scientific and technical abstracting and indexing services. It provides for continuing dialog between the services and the member scientists, with contributions from the coequal national members which represent the information communities of their countries. It also gives the services an opportunity for comparing experiences, problems, and research and for working cooperatively through bilateral and multilateral agreements. ICSU AB activities include annual meetings, symposia, working groups, task forces, special projects, and publications.

Scope and/or Subject Matter: Abstracting and indexing in the areas of natural sciences, physical sciences, mathematics, and technology.

Publications: International Serials Catalogue (ISC)—lists title, abbreviated title, CODEN, ISSN, member service code, and other data for 28,000 scientific and technical periodicals covered by ICSU AB member services; accompanied by an Index/ Concordance which converts CODEN and ISSN listings. The ISC and its Index/ Concordance may be ordered together or separately from the ICSU AB or, in the United States and Canada, from the BIOSIS User Services Department, 2100 Arch St., Philadelphia, PA 19103-1399. The ICSU AB also publishes conference proceedings and papers, surveys, classification schemes, and other material; a list of publications is available from the Board on request.

Clientele/Availability: Members include abstracting and indexing services, scientific unions, countries, and other organizations involved in the international abstracting and indexing community.

Contact: Marthe Orfus, Executive Secretary, International Council of Scientific Unions Abstracting Board. (Telex 630553 F ICSU.)

★576★
INTERNATIONAL DEVELOPMENT RESEARCH CENTRE (IDRC) LIBRARY
P.O. Box 8500
60 Queen St.
Ottawa, ON, Canada K1G 3H9
Phone: (613) 236-6163
Service Est: 1971

Special Note: The above name, address, and telephone number have been verified for this edition, although no questionnaire response was received. The following text is reprinted from the 5th edition.

Staff: 7 Information and library professional; 11 technicians; 4 clerical and nonprofessional.

Related Organizations: The Library is part of IDRC's Information Sciences Division. The IRDC is a public corporation created and financed by the Canadian Parliament to stimulate and support research benefiting developing countries.

Description of System or Service: The International Development Research Centre LIBRARY provides library and information services on the social and economic aspects of Third World development to IDRC staff and projects, the Canadian development community, and other development communities. It maintains, provides information from, and circulates a current collection of reference materials, books, periodicals, and fugitive literature on Third World development. Access to the collection is facilitated through COM fiche indexes and the computer-readable BIBLIOL data base, which provides numerous access points including subject and institution name. In addition to offering automated searches of BIBLIOL, the LIBRARY searches the Centre's DEVSIS and SALUS data bases, magnetic tapes provided by several international organizations, and data bases carried by various online services. It is currently operating an experimental online system which makes its data bases available throughout Canada. LIBRARY administrative and information retrieval functions are supported by MINISIS, a software package developed by IDRC and manufactured and distributed in North America by Systemhouse Ltd.

Scope and/or Subject Matter: Economic and social development of the Third World, particularly rural areas.

Holdings and Storage Media: The Library maintains a collection of 35,000 bound volumes and subscriptions to 4200 periodicals. Machine-readable holdings include copies of several data bases supplied by other organizations, and the BIBLIOL (1970 to date, updated daily), SALUS (1970 to date, updated weekly), and DEVSIS data bases.

Publications: 1) Ex Libris (monthly)—accessions list containing recent additions to the BIBLIOL data base. 2) Acronyms Related to International Development. 3) Devindex (annual)—IDRC publication providing abstracts and indexes of periodical and nonperiodical literature on Third World development; corresponds to the DEVSIS data base.

Microform Products and Services: The Library produces COM fiche indexes for personal author, corporate author, title, serials title, and corporate author authority listings.

Computer-Based Products and Services: Utilizing the MINISIS data management and retrieval system, the LIBRARY conducts computerized literature searches of its holdings data base, BIBLIOL, as well as the IDRC's DEVSIS (economic and social development) and SALUS (low cost rural health care and health workforce training in developing countries) data bases. Searches are also provided from publicly available online data bases and from data bases provided by the U.N. Food and Agriculture Organization (FAO), the International Labour Office (ILO), the United Nations Educational, Scientific and Cultural Organization (UNESCO), and the United Nations Industrial Development Organization (UNIDO). Additionally, the LIBRARY provides government and nonprofit institutions in Canada with remote terminal online access to IDRC and international organization data bases through an experimental project known as Development Data Bases: Use in Canada.

Other Services: The Library also offers SDI, consultation, referrals, and interlibrary loans, and it tests technological, methodological, and bibliographical developments and standards that may be appropriate for adoption by the international development community and for implementation within IDRC projects.

Clientele/Availability: Services are available to IDRC staff and projects, the Canadian development research community, and, as resources permit, other development communities.

Contact: Deputy Librarian, IDRC Library.

★577★
INTERNATIONAL ELECTRONIC PUBLISHING RESEARCH CENTRE (IEPRC)
Pira House Phone: 0372 376161
Randalls Rd. Founded: 1981
Leatherhead, Surrey KT22 7RU, England
Brian W. Blunden, Chief Executive

Related Organizations: The IEPRC is an independent nonprofit organization located at the facilities of Pira: Research Association for the Paper and Board, Printing and Packaging Industries.

Description of System or Service: The INTERNATIONAL ELECTRONIC PUBLISHING RESEARCH CENTRE (IEPRC) researches technical, economic, behavioral, and marketing aspects of electronic publishing for publishers, printers, and suppliers to the publishing industry. The CENTRE tests new concepts and the application of new technologies in publishing; evaluates systems, software, and electronic publishing equipment; stimulates the introduction and application of new technologies in publishing; trains personnel in new techniques; and advises in the development and applications of electronic publishing.

Scope and/or Subject Matter: Research and new developments involving the applications of electronic technologies to the publishing, printing, and communications processes, including such topics as the potential application of videodisk technology, text/tone data capture merging techniques, document delivery, and evaluating Prestel/viewdata as an interactive teaching system.

Input Sources: Input is gathered from the Centre's research results, from worldwide literature on electronic publishing developments, and from member participation.

Computer-Based Products and Services: The IEPRC cooperates in producing the Electronic Publishing Abstracts (EPA) data base maintained by Pira (see separate entry).

Other Services: Additional services include an annual research conference, consultations, international study tours, and seminars.

Clientele/Availability: Services are available through an annual membership subscription.

Contact: Brian W. Blunden, Chief Executive, or John W. Birkenshaw, Research Manager, International Electronic Publishing Research Centre. (Telex 929810.) The IEPRC maintains a North American office at the facilities of Printing Industries of America, Inc., 1730 N. Lynn St., Arlington, VA 22209; telephone (703) 841-8168.

★578★
INTERNATIONAL FEDERATION FOR DOCUMENTATION
(Federation Internationale de Documentation - FID)
P.O. Box 90402 Phone: 070 606915
NL-2509 LK The Hague, Netherlands Founded: 1895
Stella Keenan, Secretary General

Staff: 3 Information and library professional; 5 clerical and nonprofessional.

Description of System or Service: The INTERNATIONAL FEDERATION FOR DOCUMENTATION (FID) is the international professional association for the information science community. Through its members in 90 countries, it promotes the study, research, organization, and practice of information science and documentation in all fields, and provides a world forum for interested organizations and individuals to exchange and coordinate their ideas and experiences. FID sponsors regional commissions, ten committees, and various working groups and subcommittees. It holds a biennial conference and congress, sponsors and is responsible for the Universal Decimal Classification (UDC), and engages in a number of professional activities, including the joint UNESCO/FID ISORID project. The FID also issues monograph and serial publications and maintains consultative status with other international organizations.

Scope and/or Subject Matter: Information science and documentation in all fields, including science, technology, social sciences, and the humanities.

Input Sources: Input consists of data contributed by members, questionnaires, primary and secondary literature, and other materials.

Publications: 1) FID News Bulletin (monthly)—news on international, regional, and national activities in the field of information science. Includes the quarterly Document Delivery and Reproduction Survey and the Newsletter on Education and Training Programmes for Information Personnel. 2) FID Directory (biennial). 3) International Forum on Information and Documentation (quarterly). 4) Extensions and Corrections to the UDC (annual). The FID also issues other monograph and serial publications and its regional commissions and committees prepare their own newsletters. A complete list of publications is available from the Secretary General.

Clientele/Availability: Services are available to members and affiliates.

Contact: Stella Keenan, Secretary General, International Federation for Documentation.

★579★
INTERNATIONAL FEDERATION FOR DOCUMENTATION
(Federation Internationale de Documentation - FID)
RESEARCH REFERRAL SERVICE (RRS)
P.O. Box 90402
NL-2509 LK The Hague, Netherlands
Stella Keenan, Secretary General
Phone: 070 606915
Service Est: 1970

Description of System or Service: The RESEARCH REFERRAL SERVICE (RRS) of the International Federation for Documentation is concerned with documenting ongoing research and development in the fields of information science, documentation, libraries, and archives management. In cooperation with UNESCO, it operates the International Information System on Research in Documentation (ISORID), which is used to systematically collect, analyze, store, and disseminate information on relevant research projects. The chief product of ISORID is the hardcopy publication R & D Projects in Documentation and Librarianship. In addition to coordinating the ISORID system, the RESEARCH REFERRAL SERVICE provides current awareness services for ongoing and projected research and development projects in these fields, maintains a manual file of information by subject and location on several thousand research projects since 1971, and provides referrals and other services to persons or organizations undertaking research in a given area.

Scope and/or Subject Matter: Research and development in documentation, librarianship, information science, archives management, and related areas.

Input Sources: RRS collects input from FID and ISORID questionnaires, and from published data.

Holdings and Storage Media: Approximately 400 research projects from more than 70 countries and international organizations are identified each year and added to the manual master file of 5000 projects.

Publications: R & D Projects in Documentation and Librarianship (bimonthly)—available by subscription. Each issue contains descriptions of recently identified research projects and includes such details as title of project, aim and scope, project dates, institution providing sponsorship or financial support, other financial support data, person and institution in charge of project, and reports and publications issued.

Clientele/Availability: Services are available without restrictions.

Contact: Stella Keenan, Secretary General, International Federation for Documentation.

★580★
INTERNATIONAL FEDERATION FOR INFORMATION PROCESSING (IFIP)
3, rue de Marche
CH-1204 Geneva, Switzerland
K. Ando, President
Phone: 022 282649
Founded: 1960

Related Organizations: IFIP was founded under the auspices of the United Nations Educational, Scientific and Cultural Organization (UNESCO), and it retains official relationships with UNESCO and the World Health Organization (WHO). IFIP also has the status of a Scientific Affiliate of the International Council of Scientific Unions. An IFIP special interest group, the International Medical Informatics Association, is described in a separate entry in this directory.

Description of System or Service: The INTERNATIONAL FEDERATION FOR INFORMATION PROCESSING (IFIP) is a multinational federation of professional-technical societies (or groups of such societies) concerned with both the theoretical and applied aspects of information processing. IFIP promotes information science and technology by: fostering international cooperation in the field of information processing; stimulating research, development, and the application of information processing in science and human activity; furthering the dissemination and exchange of information about the subject; and encouraging education in information processing. IFIP disseminates information through congresses held every three years; technical committees, working groups, and special interest groups in areas of interest to members; and publications.

Scope and/or Subject Matter: Information processing with emphasis on computer-based processing.

Publications: 1) Computers in Industry—a periodical. 2) Information Bulletin (annual). IFIP also issues books, congress and conference proceedings, and an occasional series of general articles describing its work. A complete list of IFIP publications is available by request from the Secretariat.

Clientele/Availability: Only one society is chosen from a country to become an IFIP Full Member; it must be representative of the national activities in the information processing field. A regional group of developing countries can also be admitted as a Full Member.

Contact: K. Ando, President, or G. Roberts, Administrative Manager, International Federation for Information Processing Secretariat. (Telex 428 472 IFIP CH.)

★581★
INTERNATIONAL FEDERATION OF DATA ORGANIZATIONS FOR THE SOCIAL SCIENCES (IFDO)
Steinmetz Archives
410 Herengracht
NL-1017 BX Amsterdam, Netherlands
Frederic Bon, President
Phone: 020 225061
Founded: 1977

Description of System or Service: The INTERNATIONAL FEDERATION OF DATA ORGANIZATIONS FOR THE SOCIAL SCIENCES (IFDO) promotes projects and procedures for enhancing the exchange of data and technologies among social science data organizations throughout the world. It also stimulates the development and use of these procedures and encourages new data organizations to further these objectives. Specific IFDO activities include: coordination of archiving efforts to improve comparability of regional data bases; study of digitized cartographic coordinate data bases; implementation of standards for describing the quality of data files and their documentation; software exchange and joint software development for special data management problems; technical assistance to less developed nations; and development of standard formats for codebooks, data summaries, and bibliographic citations to data sets. Additionally, IFDO hosts international meetings and seminars, offers workbooks and teaching aids, and publishes proceedings.

Scope and/or Subject Matter: Promotion of the collection, storage, and distribution of numeric social science data for use in reanalysis and secondary analysis projects.

Publications: IFDO publishes seminar proceedings, workbooks, teaching aids, and other documents.

Computer-Based Products and Services: IFDO makes available data files and offers software for preparing precis of data file contents, for developing standard codebook formats, and for constructing adequate bibliographic citations for data files.

Clientele/Availability: IFDO members are data organizations engaged in providing the social science community with computerized numeric information, data, documentation, and analysis.

Contact: Dr. Paul F.A. de Guchteneire, International Federation of Data Organizations for the Social Sciences.

★582★
INTERNATIONAL FEDERATION OF LIBRARY ASSOCIATIONS AND INSTITUTIONS (IFLA)
P.O. Box 95312
NL-2509 CH The Hague, Netherlands
Dr. Margreet Wijnstroom, Secretary General
Phone: 070 140884
Founded: 1927

Staff: 3 Information and library professional; 1.5 clerical and nonprofessional.

Related Organizations: Supporting and sponsoring organizations include the following: Council on Library Resources, Washington, DC; Canadian International Development Agency, Ottawa; UNESCO, Paris; and the Dutch Ministry of Education and Science, The Hague.

Description of System or Service: Comprising more than 1000 library associations, libraries, and library schools in 120 countries, the INTERNATIONAL FEDERATION OF LIBRARY ASSOCIATIONS AND INSTITUTIONS (IFLA) is an independent, nonprofit organization which promotes international understanding, cooperation, and discussion and fosters research and development in all fields of library activity. In pursuit of these goals IFLA operates a central secretariat, 30 professional units, and regional offices; organizes conferences and meetings; issues publications; and collaborates with other international organizations. In Great Britain, IFLA operates the International Office for Universal Bibliographic Control (UBC), which works to implement a worldwide system for the exchange of bibliographic information, and the International Office for the Universal Availability of Publications (UAP), which attempts to make available all publications issued in all countries through interlending, exchange, removal of barriers to availability, and legal deposits. IFLA will also oversee the International MARC Technical Centre (IMTC) in Frankfurt, Germany.

Scope and/or Subject Matter: All fields of library activity, including bibliography, information services, and personnel education.

Publications: 1) IFLA Journal (quarterly). 2) IFLA Annual—includes proceedings of council meetings, annual reports, and a full list of IFLA publications. 3) IFLA Directory (biennial)—contains names and addresses of members, affiliates, and officers, and additional information on IFLA and its activities. Numerous other publications are also issued.

Clientele/Availability: IFLA memberships are available in a variety of categories to interested organizations.

Contact: Dr. Margreet Wijnstroom, Secretary General, International Federation of Library Associations and Institutions. (Telex 34402 KB NL.)

★583★
INTERNATIONAL FOOD INFORMATION SERVICE (IFIS)
FOOD SCIENCE AND TECHNOLOGY ABSTRACTS (FSTA)
Lyoner Str. 44-48　　　　　　　　　　Phone: 069 6687338
D-6000 Frankfurt am Main 71, Fed. Rep.
　of Germany　　　　　　　　　　　　Service Est: 1969
Dr. Udo Schutzsack, Joint Managing Director

Related Organizations: The International Food Information Service is a nonprofit organization incorporated in Germany and managed by the Commonwealth Agricultural Bureaux, the Gesellschaft fur Information und Dokumentation, the Institute of Food Technologists, and the Centrum voor Landbouwpublikaties en Landbouwdocumentatie.

Description of System or Service: FOOD SCIENCE AND TECHNOLOGY ABSTRACTS (FSTA) provides abstracts and indexes of worldwide periodical and other literature in all areas of food science and technology. FSTA is available as a printed publication, as a commercially available online data base, and on magnetic tape. Photocopies of all items abstracted in FSTA are available from IFIS.

Scope and/or Subject Matter: Food science and technology, including all human food commodities and aspects of food processing from (but excluding) the production of raw foods to the consumption of finished foods. Included are food composition, basic food science, microbiology, hygiene, toxicology, economics, standards, legislation, engineering, processing, packaging, and additives.

Input Sources: Input consists of approximately 1800 journals from more than 90 countries, patents from 20 countries, standards, books in all languages, conference proceedings, reviews, and reports. Literature in more than 40 languages is included; about half of the source material is in English. Scanning is performed by IFIS staff and cooperating individuals or organizations.

Holdings and Storage Media: The computer-readable FSTA data base, covering the period from 1969 to the present, holds more than 250,000 records; the data base is updated monthly at a rate of approximately 1500 records.

Publications: 1) Food Science and Technology Abstracts-FSTA (monthly)—over 19,000 abstracts of the world's food science and technology literature added annually, with monthly author and subject indexes and comprehensive annual indexes. 2) FSTA Thesaurus—available for purchase; comprehensive word list of subject headings used in FSTA. 3) IFIS Newsletter. IFIS also publishes a number of Food Annotated Bibliographies (FABs) on important specialized aspects of food science and technology.

Computer-Based Products and Services: FSTA is searchable online through such vendors as DIALOG Information Services, Inc., System Development Corporation (SDC), ESA/IRS, DIMDI, and GID (Gesellschaft fur Information und Dokumentation). It is also available by subscription on magnetic tapes, which are issued two months before publication of the hard copy version. Searchable data elements include the following: index terms; index term words; title; abstract; accession number; author; organizational source; journal title; publication year; language; patent number; category code; update code; and source. IFIS also offers computerized searching of FSTA.

Other Services: Additional services offered by IFIS include translations, photocopying, retrospective searching, SDI and current awareness services covering both literature and patents, and reference service.

Clientele/Availability: Services are available on a subscription or fee basis.

Projected Publications and Services: In cooperation with the German Federal Research Institute for Grain and Potato Processing/Bundesforschungsanstalt fur Getreide- und Kartoffelverarbeitung, IFIS is developing a Cereal Data Base covering the area of cereal processing and technology.

Contact: Dr. Udo Schutzsack, Joint Managing Director, International Food Information Service. (Telex 414351 GIDFM.) In the United Kingdom, contact Ernest J. Mann, Joint Managing Director, International Food Information Service, Lane End House, Shinfield, Reading RG2 9BB, England; telephone 0734 883895. (Telex 847204 DSIFIS.)

★584★
INTERNATIONAL FOOD INFORMATION SERVICE (IFIS)
PACKAGING SCIENCE AND TECHNOLOGY ABSTRACTS (PSTA)
Lyoner Str. 44-48　　　　　　　　　　Phone: 069 6687338
D-6000 Frankfurt am Main 71, Fed. Rep.
　of Germany　　　　　　　　　　　　Service Est: 1981
Dr. Udo Schutzsack, Joint Managing Director

Related Organizations: Packaging Science and Technology Abstracts is produced by IFIS in cooperation with the Fraunhofer Institute for Food Technology and Packaging/ Fraunhofer-Institut fur Lebensmitteltechnologie und Verpackung (ILV), Schragenhofstr. 35, D-8000 Munich 50, Federal Republic of Germany; telephone 089 1411091.

Description of System or Service: PACKAGING SCIENCE AND TECHNOLOGY ABSTRACTS (PSTA) abstracts and indexes international periodical and other literature dealing with packaging science, technology, and economics. PSTA is available as a printed publication, on magnetic tape, and as a commercially available online data base. Document delivery services for cited items are provided by IFIS.

Scope and/or Subject Matter: Packaging science and technology, including packaging economy, science, and institutions; packaging material; processing and production machines; packages; packaging accessories; goods to be packed; packaging machines; packs; testing and stress loading; and transport and storage.

Input Sources: Sources scanned include approximately 400 worldwide periodicals in more than 20 languages, as well as reports, patents, proceedings, standards, books, and industrial pamphlets.

Holdings and Storage Media: The machine-readable PSTA data base dates from 1981 to the present and contains more than 8000 references with abstracts; the data base is updated at an annual increase of 3000 records.

Publications: Packaging Science and Technology Abstracts-PSTA (every two months)—successor to Referatedienst Verpackung; contains abstracts arranged within subject categories. Each issue also includes a subject index and an author index, which are cumulated annually, and a German and English-language subject classification outline. Available by subscription from the Fraunhofer Institute for Food Technology and Packaging.

Computer-Based Products and Services: The PACKAGING SCIENCE AND TECHNOLOGY ABSTRACTS data base is available for online searching through the German Institute for Medical Documentation and Information (DIMDI), ESA/IRS, FIZ Technik, and CAN/OLE. A typical PSTA record includes accession number, article title in English and in German, author, journal title, volume and issue numbers, page numbers, year of publication, language of original article, abstract in English and in German, and German-language subject descriptors. PSTA is also available on magnetic tape, and SDI, literature searching, and document delivery services are offered by IFIS.

Clientele/Availability: PSTA is available without restriction.

Contact: Dr. Udo Schutzsack, Joint Managing Director, International Food Information Service. (Telex 414351 GIDFM). In the United Kingdom, contact Ernest J. Mann, Joint Managing Director, International Food Information Service, Lane End House, Shinfield, Reading RG2 9BB, England; telephone 0734 883895. (Telex 847204 DSIFIS.)

★585★
INTERNATIONAL FOOD INFORMATION SERVICE (IFIS)
VITIS-VITICULTURE AND ENOLOGY ABSTRACTS (VITIS-VEA)
Lyoner Str. 44-48   Phone: 069 6687338
D-6000 Frankfurt am Main 71, Fed. Rep.
    of Germany   Service Est: 1969
Dr. H. Berndt, Editor

Staff: 1 Information and library professional; 1 management professional; 1 clerical and nonprofessional.

Related Organizations: VITIS-VEA is produced by the International Food Information Service in cooperation with the German Federal Research Institute for Viticulture/ Bundesforschungsanstalt fur Rebenzuchtung Geilweilerhof (BFAR), D-6741 Siebeldingen, Federal Republic of Germany.

Description of System or Service: VITIS-VITICULTURE AND ENOLOGY ABSTRACTS (VITIS-VEA) provides English-language abstracts and indexing of international periodical and other literature dealing with grape and grapevine science and technology. VITIS-VEA is available as a printed publication and on magnetic tape from IFIS, and it is expected to be made publicly available online in the near future. Document delivery, SDI, and search services are provided from the data base by IFIS.

Scope and/or Subject Matter: Grape and grapevine science and technology, including general aspects, morphology, physiology, biochemistry, viticulture, soils, breeding, plant pathology, technology and engineering, economics, enology, and microbiology of wine.

Input Sources: Input for VITIS-VEA is derived from more than 400 periodicals in approximately 25 languages, as well as books, reports, standards, specifications, and legislation.

Holdings and Storage Media: The machine-readable VITIS-VEA data base contains approximately 20,000 items dating from 1969 to the present; the data base is updated at an annual increase of 1500 items.

Publications: VITIS-Viticulture and Enology Abstracts (quarterly, with annual index)—available by subscription; provides approximately 600 abstracts per year. Abstracts and references appearing in the quarterly publication are also available as the documentation section of the journal VITIS, which is produced by and available by subscription from the BFAR.

Computer-Based Products and Services: VITIS-VEA is available quarterly on magnetic tape from IFIS and provides approximately 600 abstracts per year with an additional 900 bibliographic references not published in the printed version. The data base is expected to be made publicly available through several online hosts in the near future. SDI and search services from VITIS-VEA are offered by the BFAR.

Clientele/Availability: VITIS-VEA products and services are available without restrictions.

Contact: Dr. Udo Schutzsack, Joint Managing Director, International Food Information Service. (Telex 414351 GIDFM.) In the United Kingdom, contact Ernest J. Mann, Joint Managing Director, International Food Information Service, Lane End House, Shinfield, Reading RG2 9BB, England; telephone 0734 883895. (Telex 847204 DSIFIS.)

★586★
INTERNATIONAL GROUP OF USERS OF INFORMATION SYSTEMS (IGIS)
Enschedepad 41   Phone: 03240 31341
NL-1324 GB Almere-Stad, Netherlands   Founded: 1981
Arvid Gundersen, Executive Officer

Description of System or Service: The INTERNATIONAL GROUP OF USERS OF INFORMATION SYSTEMS (IGIS) is a nonprofit organization founded to aid information scientists in the use of computers. It issues a journal and newsletter.

Scope and/or Subject Matter: Computer and information systems use.

Publications: Information and Management (six times per year)—available from IGIS. Also published is a bimonthly newsletter.

Clientele/Availability: Primary clients are information scientists.

Contact: Arvid Gundersen, Executive Officer, International Group of Users of Information Systems.

★587★
INTERNATIONAL INFORMATION CENTER FOR TERMINOLOGY (INFOTERM)
P.O. Box 130   Phone: 0222 267535
A-1021 Vienna, Austria   Founded: 1971
Prof. Helmut Felber, Director

Staff: 4 Information and library professional; 1 management professional; 2 clerical and nonprofessional.

Related Organizations: Infoterm was established within the framework of UNISIST (part of UNESCO General Information Programme), and it receives support from the Austrian government. It is affiliated with the Austrian Standards Institute/ Osterreichisches Normungsinstitut (ON).

Description of System or Service: The INTERNATIONAL INFORMATION CENTER FOR TERMINOLOGY (INFOTERM) seeks to coordinate terminological activities on a worldwide basis, and it provides information and documentation services in this field. INFOTERM collects and analyzes terminological information, including standardized and specialized vocabularies and terminologies from all over the world, and prepares bibliographies of these materials and guides to other sources of terminological information. INFOTERM also issues other publications, offers consulting and training in terminology, and organizes conferences and meetings. Additionally, the Center has established TermNet, an international network for cooperation in terminological activities. Major goals of TermNet include recording existing and new terminologies in machine-readable form and establishing bibliographic control over all relevant literature and documents.

Scope and/or Subject Matter: Terminology of all subject fields in all languages.

Input Sources: INFOTERM collects terminological information from worldwide sources.

Holdings and Storage Media: The Center maintains a collection of standardized vocabularies and other materials, and a library of 1500 bound volumes and subscriptions to 100 periodicals. It holds bibliographies and guides on magnetic tapes.

Publications: 1) Infoterm Newsletter (quarterly)—available free of charge. 2) TermNet News—available on an exchange basis. 3) Infoterm Series—a continuing series that has included such titles as International Bibliography of Standardized Vocabularies, World Guide to Terminological Activities, and Terminological Data Banks; available for purchase from K.G. Saur Verlag, Postfach 71 10 09, Possenbacherstr. 2b, D-8000 Munich 71, Federal Republic of Germany. A list of documents is available from the Center on request.

Computer-Based Products and Services: INFOTERM maintains magnetic tapes of bibliographies and the World Guide to Terminological Activities, primarily for publication purposes.

Clientele/Availability: Services are intended for organizations and individuals active in the field of terminology.

Contact: Magdalena Krommer-Benz, International Information Center for Terminology. (Telex 115960 ONORM A.) Infoterm maintains offices at Heinestr. 38, A-1020 Vienna, Austria.

★588★
INTERNATIONAL INFORMATION SERVICE LTD. (IIS)
Reliance Manufactory Bldg., 6th Fl.   Phone: 5 520196
24 Wong Chuk Hang Rd.   Founded: 1981
Aberdeen, Hong Kong
C.N. Shum, Editor in Chief, Director

Staff: 2 Information and library professional; 2 management professional; 1 technician; 2 sales and marketing; 3 clerical and nonprofessional.

Description of System or Service: INTERNATIONAL INFORMATION SERVICE LTD. (IIS) provides information services in the area of science and technology in China. It issues two bimonthly abstracting and indexing publications, China Science & Technology Abstracts and China Medical Abstracts; provides copies, abstracts, and translations of Chinese and other countries' scientific and technical articles; and provides translations of scientific, industrial, medical, and commercial materials from English and other languages to Chinese and from Chinese to other languages. IIS also offers direct mail, advertising, typesetting, and artwork and printing services.

Scope and/or Subject Matter: Information services in the areas of mathematics, physics, astronomy, chemistry, earth sciences, energy sources, industrial technology.

Input Sources: Input is derived from more than 150 Chinese periodicals.

Holdings and Storage Media: The firm's library holdings include 300 bound volumes and 160 periodical subscriptions.

Publications: 1) China Science & Technology Abstracts (bimonthly)—available by subscription; back issues are available for purchase. Each issue provides approximately 1000 English-language abstracts drawn from Chinese scientific and technical periodicals. 2) China Medical Abstracts (bimonthly)—contains approximately 600 abstracts and indexes from Chinese medical articles.

Clientele/Availability: Services are available without restrictions. Clients include scientists, technicians, and foreign trade corporations.

Projected Publications and Services: The China Foreign Trade Information Monthly is expected to be issued.

Remarks: IIS was formerly known as the International Science & Technology Information Service.

Contact: Mr. Lee Ming, Editor, International Information Service Ltd.

★589★
INTERNATIONAL INFORMATION SERVICES COMPANY
(Compagnie Internationale de Services en Informatique - CISI)
35, blvd. Brune   Phone: 01 5458000
F-75680 Paris Cedex 14, France

Special Note: The above name, address, and telephone number have been verified for this edition, although no questionnaire response was received. The following text is reprinted from the 5th edition.

Staff: 2000 Total.

Related Organizations: CISI is a subsidiary of the Commissariat a l'Energie Atomique (CEA).

Description of System or Service: The INTERNATIONAL INFORMATION SERVICES COMPANY (CISI) is a computer service group and online vendor providing clients with remote terminal access to scientific, technical, and economic data bases. To access the data bases, CISI offers ATHESA, MISTRAL, and MILOR software as well as general data base management systems. These information retrieval tools are enhanced by such capabilities as report generation, statistical or economic calculations, graph plotting, and microfiche. CISI also provides its online users with training sessions and courses, terminal rentals, free telephone technical assistance, offline printing, and document delivery. The general computer services section of CISI offers products and specialized skills in structural analysis, turnkey systems, computer-aided design and numerical control, complete business processing services, system development, and software translation.

Scope and/or Subject Matter: Online data bases in the areas of economics, trade, transportation, building materials, technology transfer, media, and nuclear power plants.

Input Sources: Data bases are acquired from professional associations and other organizations.

Computer-Based Products and Services: The INTERNATIONAL INFORMATION SERVICES COMPANY provides online access to the following data bases: 1) ELECNUC—produced by the Commissariat a l'Energie Atomique (CEA). 2) MEDIA M—produced by the Centre d'Etude des Supports de l'Informatique Medicale (CESSIM). 3) MEDIA P—compiled by the Centre d'Etude des Supports Publicitaires (CESP). 4) TRANSINOVE—produced by TRANSINOVE International. 5) OECD Main Economic Indicators. 6) OECD Indicators of Industrial Activity. 7) CRONOS files and 8) COMEXT—compiled by the Commission of European Communities (CEC). New files are added frequently. Additionally, CISI offers a private file service under which clients can maintain proprietary data bases online for use by authorized personnel only. CISI can be accessed via its own network, as well as Transpac, Euronet DIANE, Tymnet, Telenet, Datapac, and telex.

Clientele/Availability: Services are available on a contract basis.

Contact: International Information Services Company. (Telex 260710 F.)

★590★
INTERNATIONAL INSTITUTE OF REFRIGERATION (IIR)
(Institut International du Froid)
DOCUMENTARY SERVICE
177, blvd. Malesherbes   Phone: 01 2273235
F-75017 Paris, France
Andre Gac, Director

Staff: 2 Information and library professional; 1 management professional; 1 technician.

Description of System or Service: The DOCUMENTARY SERVICE provides library and information services relating to refrigeration, cryogenic systems, and heat pumps. It acquires, scans, abstracts, and indexes relevant worldwide literature to prepare the bilingual International Institute of Refrigeration Bulletin and the machine-readable FRIGINTER Data Base. The SERVICE provides computerized search services as well as library, document delivery, and translation services.

Scope and/or Subject Matter: Refrigeration, cryogenic systems, heat pumps, and such related topics as cryology, thermodynamics, heat and mass transfer, food science and technology, freeze-drying, and cryobiology.

Input Sources: Input for FRIGINTER is derived from 300 periodicals.

Holdings and Storage Media: The Service maintains the computer-readable bibliographic FRIGINTER Data Base and a library of 4500 bound volumes and 50,000 documents.

Publications: International Institute of Refrigeration Bulletin (bimonthly with annual subject index)—available by subscription. Each issue contains approximately 400 references and abstracts of international periodical and other literature; also includes original articles, book reviews, and announcements about forthcoming congresses and meetings. Issued as a bilingual publication in English and French.

Computer-Based Products and Services: The DOCUMENTARY SERVICE conducts searches of the FRIGINTER Data Base, which is expected to be commercially available in the near future.

Clientele/Availability: Services are intended for members of the refrigeration and related industries.

Contact: Miss C. Maunier, Librarian, Documentary Service.

★591★
INTERNATIONAL LABOUR OFFICE
BUREAU FOR LABOUR PROBLEMS ANALYSIS
LABOUR INFORMATION DATABASE (LID)
4, route des Morillons Phone: 022 996759
CH-1211 Geneva 22, Switzerland Service Est: 1974
Mrs. H. Sarfati, Chief Editor

Related Organizations: The Office serves as the secretariat, operational headquarters, and publishing house for the International Labour Organisation (ILO), a specialized agency of the United Nations.

Description of System or Service: The computer-readable LABOUR INFORMATION DATABASE (LID) contains abstracts and indexes of articles appearing in the Social and Labour Bulletin, a current awareness journal providing regular coverage and updating on recent events and developments in the social and labor fields. The DATABASE also covers other major source documents such as national legislation, collective agreements, European Economic Community (EEC) directives, and policy statements of governments and organizations of employers and workers. LID is used to provide COM microfiche and computerized search services, and it is commercially available online.

Scope and/or Subject Matter: Labor legislation, impact of new technologies, labor relations, personnel management, social security, working conditions, occupational safety and health, income distribution, employment policy, migrant workers, equal opportunity, multinational corporations, and other labor-related topics.

Input Sources: Input for LID is derived from the Social and Labour Bulletin and documents from government agencies, employers' organizations, trade unions, and regional and international organizations.

Holdings and Storage Media: Updated every 4 months, the computer-readable LID data base contains approximately 5000 records dating from 1980 to the present.

Publications: 1) Social and Labour Bulletin (quarterly)—covers major national and international labor trends; published in English, French, and Spanish. A cumulative index covering the period 1974-1980, and annual subject and geographic indexes are also available. 2) New Technologies: Impact on Employment and the Working Environment—volume of major articles on the impact of microelectronics on employment; published in English and French. 3) Collective Bargaining: A Response to the Recession in Industrialised Market Economy Countries—volume summarizes more than 400 key collective agreements and gives views of leading labor economists on future scenarios for collective bargaining. 4) Roundup volumes on selected topics.

Microform Products and Services: LID is available on cumulative COM microfiche by subscription.

Computer-Based Products and Services: Searches from the LABOUR INFORMATION DATABASE are provided upon request. The file contains bibliographic descriptions, detailed or indicative English abstracts, and indexing descriptors. LID is commercially available for online searching through ESA/IRS and as part of the LABOR data base through Telesystemes Questel.

Clientele/Availability: Clients include government agencies, employers' associations, multinational corporations, trade unions, social security and occupational safety and health institutions, academic institutions, and other interested parties.

Remarks: LID was formerly known as the INFSOC data base.

Contact: Mrs. H. Sarfati, Chief Editor, Social and Labour Bulletin. (Telex 22271 BIT CH.)

★592★
INTERNATIONAL LABOUR OFFICE
BUREAU OF STATISTICS
4, route des Morillons Phone: 022 996111
CH-1211 Geneva 22, Switzerland
Dr. R. Turvey, Chief

Staff: 15 Information and library professional; 15 clerical and nonprofessional.

Related Organizations: The Office serves as the secretariat, operational headquarters, and publishing house for the International Labour Organisation (ILO), a specialized agency of the United Nations.

Description of System or Service: The BUREAU OF STATISTICS of the International Labour Office collects international labor statistics, maintains them in machine-readable files, and makes them available in hardcopy publications.

Scope and/or Subject Matter: International statistics on such topics as employment and unemployment, wages, hours worked, and consumer price indexes.

Input Sources: The Bureau gathers information through questionnaires completed by member countries and from national statistical publications.

Holdings and Storage Media: The Bureau's machine-readable files cover the years from 1969 to the present.

Publications: 1) Bulletin of Labour Statistics (quarterly); 2) Year Book of Labour Statistics; 3) Technical guide.

Computer-Based Products and Services: The Bureau of Statistics maintains statistical labor data in computer-readable form; it expects to make the data commercially available online in the future.

Clientele/Availability: Service are available without restrictions.

Contact: Dr. R. Turvey, Chief, Bureau of Statistics.

★593★
INTERNATIONAL LABOUR OFFICE
CENTRAL LIBRARY AND DOCUMENTATION BRANCH
4, route des Morillons Phone: 022 998676
CH-1211 Geneva 22, Switzerland Service Est: 1965
Kate Wild, Chief

Staff: 12 Information and library professional; 16 clerical and nonprofessional.

Related Organizations: The Office serves as the secretariat, operational headquarters, and publishing house for the International Labour Organisation (ILO), a specialized agency of the United Nations.

Description of System or Service: The CENTRAL LIBRARY AND DOCUMENTATION BRANCH provides ILO officials and users in member states with internationally based document collections and information services to support policymaking, planning, and research in labor and related fields. It abstracts and indexes worldwide journal and monographic literature in the field of labor and industrial relations to produce the computer-readable LABORDOC data base and a corresponding hardcopy publication. The LIBRARY provides search services and SDI from the file, which is also commercially available online, and offers a number of related microform products. Additionally, the LIBRARY provides services from the IGODOC data base, covering its collection of documents from international organizations, and the ILODOC file covering ILO publications and documents.

Scope and/or Subject Matter: Worldwide coverage of labor topics with emphasis on industrial relations, labor law, employment, working conditions, vocational training, and labor-related aspects of economics, social development, rural development, and technological change.

Input Sources: Input consists of books, journal articles, conference proceedings, reports, dissertations, ILO documents and publications, and a selection of publications from other international organizations.

Holdings and Storage Media: The machine-readable LABORDOC file comprises more than 120,000 references from 1965 to date; approximately 500 items are added to the data base each month. IGODOC and ILODOC are also held in machine-readable form. The Central Library maintains a collection of 350,000 bound volumes, subscriptions to 7300 periodicals, and copies of all ILO publications since 1919.

Publications: 1) International Labour Documentation (monthly)—available by subscription. An abstracting bulletin produced from the LABORDOC file. Contains bibliographic references (with English-language abstracts and descriptors) to recent acquisitions in the Central Library, including monographs, reports, and journal articles. Each issue has separate English, French, and Spanish subject indexes, and a list of new ILO publications. 2) ILO Thesaurus—available for purchase. Covers labor, employment, and training terminology; trilingual (English, French, and Spanish).

Microform Products and Services: The following are available for purchase on COM microfiche: 1) International Labour Documentation Cumulative Catalog, 1965-1977 and 1978-1983 (updated annually). 2) Register of Periodicals in the ILO Library (updated every six months). 3) Title List of ILO Publications and Documents, 1965-1983.

Computer-Based Products and Services: The CENTRAL LIBRARY AND DOCUMENTATION BRANCH provides search and SDI services from the LABORDOC data base, which it holds under MINISIS software. LABORDOC is also commercially available online through System Development Corporation (SDC) and ESA/IRS, and as part of the LABOR data base on Telesystemes Questel. Search elements include accession number, authors, organizational source, country and year of publication, document type, language, abstract, indexing terms, ISBN, and report and publication numbers. The LIBRARY also provides services from IGODOC, ILODOC, and the Labor Information Database (LID).

Clientele/Availability: Users include ILO and other institutions engaged in policymaking, planning, or research in social and labor fields.

Contact: Kate Wild, Chief, Central Library and Documentation Branch. (Telex 22271 BIT CH.)

★594★
INTERNATIONAL LABOUR OFFICE
CONDITIONS OF WORK AND WELFARE FACILITIES BRANCH
CLEARING-HOUSE ON CONDITIONS OF WORK

CH-1211 Geneva 22, Switzerland
Linda Stoddart, Information Officer
Phone: 022 997078
Service Est: 1979

Staff: 1 Information and library professional; 1 clerical and nonprofessional.

Related Organizations: The Office serves as the secretariat, operational headquarters, and publishing house for the International Labour Organisation (ILO), a specialized agency of the United Nations.

Description of System or Service: The CLEARING-HOUSE ON CONDITIONS OF WORK coordinates a network of institutions concerned with conditions of work and quality of working life which exchange information on their research projects, meetings, training activities, and publications. The CLEARING-HOUSE stores this collected information in the machine-readable QUALIS data base for the production of publications and the provision of search services.

Scope and/or Subject Matter: Conditions of work and quality of working life, including hours of work, holidays, shift work, flexible hours and other working time issues; work organization and job content; the impact of new technology on quality of working life; working conditions of women, young workers, older workers, and other special categories; work-related welfare services and facilities; and shop floor participation in the improvement of working conditions.

Input Sources: Institutions in all regions including government agencies, employers' organizations, trade unions, research institutes, and university departments forward information using standardized forms.

Holdings and Storage Media: The Clearing-house's computer-readable QUALIS data base contains 2000 bibliographic and nonbibliographic records dating from 1979 to the present.

Publications: 1) Conditions of Work and Quality of Working Life: A Directory of Institutions—contains information on staff, funding, activities, training programs, current research projects, meetings, and publications of cooperating institutions; arranged by country, with acronym and personal name indexes. 2) Conditions of Work: A Cumulative Digest (semiannual)—worldwide coverage of current research, specific topics data, meetings, and publications; available by subscription.

Computer-Based Products and Services: The CLEARING-HOUSE ON CONDITIONS OF WORK maintains the QUALIS data base under MINISIS software. The data base is used to prepare the Digest and other publications and to provide computerized retrieval services for internal and external clients. Magnetic tapes of the file are also available in ISO format to institutions participating in the Clearing-house network.

Other Services: The Clearing-house also provides answers to requests for information on the conditions of work; a referral service; and a documentation collection including information on labor legislation.

Clientele/Availability: Services are available to International Labour Office member states; other requests may be submitted.

Contact: Linda Stoddart, Information Officer, Clearing-house on Conditions of Work.

★595★
INTERNATIONAL LABOUR OFFICE
INTERNATIONAL OCCUPATIONAL SAFETY AND HEALTH INFORMATION CENTRE
(Centre International d'Informations de Securite et d'Hygiene du Travail - CIS)

CH-1211 Geneva 22, Switzerland
Herbert Siegel, Head
Phone: 022 996740
Service Est: 1959

Staff: 8 Information and library professional; 1 management professional; 3 technicians; 1 sales and marketing; 9 clerical and nonprofessional.

Related Organizations: The Office serves as the secretariat, operational headquarters, and publishing house for the International Labour Organisation (ILO), a specialized agency of the United Nations. Established in conjunction with the International Social Security Association, CIS is supported by the Commission of the European Communities (CEC) and collaborates with the World Health Organization (WHO).

Description of System or Service: The INTERNATIONAL OCCUPATIONAL SAFETY AND HEALTH INFORMATION CENTRE (CIS) provides information and documentation services aimed at improving occupational safety and health throughout the world. The CENTRE scans worldwide literature on all aspects of occupational safety and health with the help of participating national centers in 47 countries. Abstracts of the literature are prepared and stored in the machine-readable CIS data base, which is used to produce abstracting and indexing publications and to provide computerized searches. The data base is also commercially available through major online vendors.

Scope and/or Subject Matter: Occupational safety and health, including occupational medicine and physiology; industrial toxicology; environmental hygiene; accident and disease prevention; safety engineering; loss control; conditions of work; health effects of dust, noise, and vibration exposures; ergonomics and work organization; human engineering; management techniques; occupational psychology and sociology; labor administration; workers compensation; and training and education.

Input Sources: Input is selected from more than 40,000 documents annually, including books, journal articles, laws and regulations, standards and directives, guides and manuals, data sheets, research reports, dissertations, proceedings of congresses and symposia, statistical reports, films and other audiovisual materials, and translations.

Holdings and Storage Media: The computer-readable CIS data base holds approximately 21,000 items dating from 1974 to the present. CIS also maintains a collection of about 50,000 abstracted documents in hard copy or microform as well as card files of abstracts and indexes produced between 1960 and 1973.

Publications: 1) CIS Abstracts (issued at least 7 times per year)—contains 300 abstracts per issue; available in English or French (Bulletin CIS) with cumulative subject and author indexes. 2) CIS Thesaurus—contains more than 10,000 descriptors arranged systematically by letter code, and alphabetically (keywords out of context); available in English and French. 3) CIS User's Guide. 4) List of Periodicals Abstracted—includes names and addresses of publishers and the frequency of publication. Information sheets and bibliographies on subjects of topical interest are also issued.

Microform Products and Services: Microfiche duplicates from the

CIS microfiche collection are available to subscribers.

Computer-Based Products and Services: The CENTRE conducts custom searches of the CIS data base on request for subscribers and nonsubscribers; results can be obtained in English or French. The CIS data base is accessible worldwide through Telesystemes Questel and ESA/IRS via Telenet, Tymnet, Euronet DIANE, and the international telex network. The contents of the data base are searchable in English through the Swedish National Board of Occupational Safety and Health. Each record in the data base contains CIS number, title in English, title in original language, source and journal citation, language, a 100-200 word abstract, a main descriptor field which reflects the major topics of interest in the original document, and a secondary descriptor field which provides specific keywords, document type, and Chemical Abstracts Service (CAS) Registry Number if the abstract contains chemical names or types. The data base is free-text searchable in French and English, and is also searchable by keywords and editor and author names.

Other Services: Copies of most original documents abstracted and indexed in CIS Abstracts can be obtained from CIS if they are otherwise not available.

Clientele/Availability: Products and services are available on a subscription basis to interested individuals, organizations, and governmental units. Special arrangements for users in developing countries can be made.

Remarks: Italian, Russian, Serbo-Croatian, and Spanish versions of CIS Abstracts are published by the national centers in Italy, the U.S.S.R., Yugoslavia, and Spain.

Contact: Herbert Seigel, Head or Erica Scurr, User Services Supervisor, International Occupational Safety and Health Information Centre. (Telex 222 71 BIT CH.)

★596★
INTERNATIONAL LIVESTOCK CENTRE FOR AFRICA DOCUMENTATION CENTRE
P.O. Box 5689　　　　　　　　　Phone: 183215
Addis Ababa, Ethiopia　　　　　Service Est: 1977
Michael Hailu, Head of Documentation

Staff: 8 Information and library professional; 1 management professional; 4 technicians; 7 clerical and nonprofessional.

Related Organizations: The Centre receives support from the International Development Research Centre (IDRC) of Canada.

Description of System or Service: The DOCUMENTATION CENTRE provides print, microform, and computer-based information services concerning livestock production and related topics. It maintains a library of books, serials, pamphlets, microfiche, and audiovisual materials and provides reference services from it. Through its microfiche project, it collects and reproduces nonconventional documents on livestock production from all parts of tropical Africa and distributes the microfiche, along with indexes and readers, throughout the region. The DOCUMENTATION CENTRE also maintains a computer-readable bibliographic data base that provides abstracts and indexes of the library and microfiche collections; search services are available on request. Additional services of the CENTRE include publications and document delivery.

Scope and/or Subject Matter: All aspects of livestock production including forage plant production, ecology, economics, and sociology.

Input Sources: Input is derived from books, microfiche, periodicals, pamphlets, maps, and photographs. Nonconventional documents for the microfiche project are obtained through visits to African countries.

Holdings and Storage Media: The Centre's library collection contains more than 15,000 volumes; subscriptions to approximately 850 periodicals; and 25,000 microfiche items. Indexes and abstracts for items acquired since 1981 are held in computer-readable form.

Publications: 1) Country indexes (irregular)—provide bibliographic listings and subject and author indexes of microfiched documents from African countries. 2) Accessions bulletin (quarterly)—lists items acquired by the Library other than those covered in the country indexes. 3) Serial holdings (annual). 4) Selected bibliographies (irregular). 5) Photomap acquisitions (irregular)—lists slides, maps, and photographs acquired.

Microform Products and Services: The CENTRE prepares microfiche of unpublished and otherwise unobtainable livestock-related documents from across Africa. It supplies copies of the microfiche with indexes and a microfiche reader to at least one institution in each country from which documents are gathered, and to others on request.

Computer-Based Products and Services: The DOCUMENTATION CENTRE maintains a computer-readable data base providing cataloging, indexing, and indicative abstracts for conventional and nonconventional literature it acquires. The data base is maintained under MINISIS software and is used to provide searches in response to requests made via mail, telex, or in person. Searches can be made by author, title, subject descriptors, keywords, geographic location, and other elements. The CENTRE also offers monthly SDI services from computer tapes of CAB Abstracts and the AGRIS data base, and it conducts searches of these and other agricultural data bases for staff.

Clientele/Availability: Services are available free to African users and on a fee basis to other users.

Contact: Michael Hailu, Head of Documentation, Documentation Centre. (Telex 21207 ILCA ADDIS.)

★597★
INTERNATIONAL MEDICAL INFORMATICS ASSOCIATION (IMIA)
Enschedepad 41　　　　　　　　Phone: 03240 31341
NL-1324 GB Almere-Stad, Netherlands　Founded: 1979
Arvid Gundersen, Executive Officer

Related Organizations: IMIA is a special interest group of the International Federation for Information Processing (IFIP).

Description of System or Service: The INTERNATIONAL MEDICAL INFORMATICS ASSOCIATION (IMIA) is a nonprofit organization dealing with health data processing and biomedical research. IMIA organizes the international MEDINFO Congress, held every three years, and related working conferences; it also publishes conference proceedings and position papers.

Scope and/or Subject Matter: Computer and information systems for medical health care.

Publications: Proceedings of MEDINFO and working conferences are issued.

Clientele/Availability: Members include information scientists, medical specialists, hospital managers, computer industry personnel, and others.

Contact: Arvid Gundersen, Executive Officer, International Medical Informatics Association.

★598★
INTERNATIONAL MEDICAL INFORMATION CENTER (IMIC)
30, Daikyo-cho　　　　　　　　Phone: 03 3579002
Shinjuku-ku　　　　　　　　　Founded: 1972
Tokyo 160, Japan
Daizo Ushiba, M.D., Chairman of Board of Directors

Staff: 18 Information and library professional; 2 management professional; 17 technicians; 1 sales and marketing; 25 clerical and nonprofessional.

Related Organizations: The International Medical Information Center was founded by the Keio University Medical Library and Information Center. It operates under government authority and is affiliated with professional library and information organizations.

Description of System or Service: The INTERNATIONAL MEDICAL INFORMATION CENTER (IMIC) seeks to contribute to the development of medical science by serving as a specialized information center in the field of medicine in Japan and by providing comprehensive information services to researchers, research organizations, general practitioners, and paramedical staff in Japan and overseas. IMIC offers the following specific services: 1) Literature search service—provides retrospective information retrieval and SDI services from commercially available online medical data bases and secondary publications. 2) Search training service—

provides instruction for searching MEDLINE, TOXLINE, and other data bases. 3) Translation service—assists physicians and researchers in revising or rewriting manuscripts to be submited to foreign journals. 4) Photocopy service—supplies copies of original documents with the cooperation of Keio University Medical Library and Information Center; also utilizes the resources of the interlibrary loan network in Japan and overseas. 5) Research and development activities—provides systematic research of a specific subject field by combining its other services with indexing, abstracting, classifying, analyzing, and evaluating for the preparation of a bibliography or a book; most projects are based on contracts from the government, research institutions, or private enterprises. 6) Dial access service—offers current information on medical science and health care to physicians and paramedical staff by means of cassette tape recordings played over the telephone. 7) Education and training activities—conducts training courses and seminars in medical and pharmaceutical sciences and medical documentation for IMIC supporting members and medical librarians. 8) International cooperation—undertakes activities to disseminate biomedical information in Japan to international organizations and institutes. 9) Compilation and publication service—secondary and reference materials are compiled and published to meet needs in various subject fields; IMIC publications are also issued. The INTERNATIONAL MEDICAL INFORMATION CENTER also maintains the Japan Cancer Literature (JCL) Data Base and prepares input for INIS (International Nuclear Information System).

Scope and/or Subject Matter: Biomedical and health sciences in Japan.

Input Sources: Approximately 80 Japanese medical journals are scanned to prepare English-language citations for inclusion in the JCL Data Base. Approximately 350 medical journals are scanned to prepare English-language abstracts with indexing for INIS.

Holdings and Storage Media: The bibliographic JCL Data Base is held in machine-readable form. The Center also maintains a library with holdings of 3100 books, subscriptions to approximately 1200 journals, and approximately 700 cassette tape recordings.

Publications: IMIC Journal (irregular).

Computer-Based Products and Services: The INTERNATIONAL MEDICAL INFORMATION CENTER maintains and provides services from the Japan Cancer Literature (JCL) Data Base. The CENTER also provides current and retrospective information retrieval from data bases made available through DIALOG Information Services, Inc., the Japan Information Center for Science and Technology, and System Development Corporation (SDC). Additionally, IMIC contributes to the INIS data base.

Other Services: The Center also provides consultation services to medical and hospital libraries.

Clientele/Availability: The Center provides services to researchers, research organizations, general practitioners, paramedical staffers, and others in Japan ond overseas. Pharmaceutical companies, research institutions, and other organizations can become supporting members of the Center through payment of an annual membership fee.

Contact: Yoshio Amano, Head, Operation Division, International Medical Information Center. (Telex 2323141 IMICJP J.)

★599★
INTERNATIONAL ORGANIZATION FOR STANDARDIZATION (ISO)
ISO INFORMATION NETWORK (ISONET)
ISO Central Secretariat　　　　　　　　Phone: 022 341240
1, rue de Varembe　　　　　　　　　　Service Est: 1976
CH-1211 Geneva 20, Switzerland
Mr. Olle Sturen, Secretary-General

Staff: 3 Information and library professional; 3 clerical and nonprofessional.

Related Organizations: The ISO Information Network is under the authority of the ISO Committee on Information (INFCO).

Description of System or Service: The ISO INFORMATION NETWORK (ISONET) is a decentralized network created to coordinate and systematize the exchange of information on national and international standards, technical specifications, and related documents. It functions by linking more than 50 national standards information centers in ISO member countries with the ISO Central Secretariat to form a coordinated information system. The national centers act as information and referral services for inquiries within their territories, and many provide such services as publications, microforms, and computer-based services. Each national center also registers and indexes standards in its area according to the ISONET indexing manual. The Central Secretariat serves as a reference point for international standards inquiries.

Scope and/or Subject Matter: Standards, specifications, and similar documents that facilitate the international exchange of goods, services, and information in all technical and nontechnical fields (except electrical and electronic engineering).

Input Sources: Standards information is obtained from ISO national members and from correspondent members.

Publications: 1) ISO Catalogue (annual with quarterly cumulative updates)—list of all published ISO standards. 2) ISO Bibliographies—lists of ISO standards and draft standards in given fields. 3) ISO Activities Report (annual)—overall picture of activities. 4) ISO Bulletin (monthly)—standardization news, calendar of meetings, and list of newly published standards. 5) ISO Memento (annual)—describes structure and administration of all ISO standards committees. 6) ISO Standards Handbooks—collection of ISO standards in selected technical fields. 7) ISO KWIC Index of International Standards—provides keyword access to existing standards. Brochures and pamphlets are also issued.

Microform Products and Services: Microforms of ISONET information are available in a number of ISO member countries.

Computer-Based Products and Services: Some national information centers provide machine-readable tapes, computerized search services, and SDI.

Clientele/Availability: Services are generally available by request through the national center within each member country.

Remarks: Comprising the national standards bodies of 90 countries, the International Organization for Standardization (ISO) is a specialized agency which works to establish agreement on international standards in order to expand trade, improve quality, increase productivity, and lower costs.

Contact: Mr. E.J. French, Head, Information Center, International Organization for Standardization. (Telex 23 887 ISO CH.)

★600★
INTERNATIONAL RAILWAY UNION
(Union Internationale des Chemins de Fer - UIC)
DOCUMENTATION BUREAU
14-15, rue Jean Rey　　　　　　　　　Phone: 01 2730120
F-75015 Paris, France　　　　　　　　Service Est: 1922
Andre Pettelat, Director

Staff: 5 Information and library professional; 2 management professional.

Description of System or Service: The DOCUMENTATION BUREAU of the International Railway Union (UIC) collects, selects, classifies, and maintains worldwide data on railways. It makes this information available to members through publications, library services, and other information services.

Scope and/or Subject Matter: Management and administration of railways, including railway operation, commercial services and tariffs, finance and accounting, legal matters, mechanical and civil engineering, and other modes of transport that compete with railways.

Input Sources: Data are gathered from books, periodicals, and reports.

Holdings and Storage Media: Holdings consist of 3000 volumes; subscriptions to 250 periodicals; and 800 reports.

Publications: 1) Selection of International Railway Documentation (ten issues a year); 2) Rail International; 3) Statistics of Individual Railways (annual); 4) UIC Code Leaflets. Bibliographies, manuals, reports and proceedings of colloquia and symposia, and printed vocabularies of technical terms are also available. Publications are issued in English, French, and German.

Computer-Based Products and Services: A computerized system for UIC data is under development.

Other Services: Additional services offered by the Union include research and referrals.

Clientele/Availability: Services are available to members of the UIC.

Remarks: The UIC is also known by its German name: Internationaler Eisenbahnverband.

Contact: Andre Pettelat, Director, or Miss D. Choplin, Documentaliste, Documentation Bureau. (Telex 2700835 UNIONFER PARIS.)

★601★
INTERNATIONAL REFERENCE CENTER FOR COMMUNITY WATER SUPPLY AND SANITATION (IRC)
PROGRAMME ON EXCHANGE AND TRANSFER OF INFORMATION ON COMMUNITY WATER SUPPLY AND SANITATION (POETRI)
P.O. Box 5500   Phone: 070 949322
NL-2280 HM Rijswijk, Netherlands   Service Est: 1980
Mr. Toon A. van Dam, Head

Staff: 2 Information and library professional; 1 management professional; 1 clerical and nonprofessional.

Related Organizations: The IRC is an independent foundation that acts as a World Health Organization (WHO) collaborating center.

Description of System or Service: The PROGRAMME ON EXCHANGE AND TRANSFER OF INFORMATION ON COMMUNITY WATER SUPPLY AND SANITATION (POETRI) is a framework in which developing countries, international organizations, external support agencies, and nongovernmental organizations pool resources for the exchange and transfer of technological information for rural drinking water supply and sanitation. Working through some 20 national and regional focal points, POETRI promotes the exchange of information between countries and regions, provides current awareness services, handles requests for information, and supplies special compilations of information. It also publishes bibliographies, inventories of information sources, guidelines on developing information systems in the field, and other documents and reports.

Scope and/or Subject Matter: Water supply, quality, management, conservation, evaluation, and sanitation in developing countries; solid waste management; community participation; work force development and training; appropriate technology.

Publications: POETRI publishes a monthly newsletter, bibliographies, inventories of information sources, a thesaurus and glossary, reports and technical papers, and guidelines on setting up specialized community water supply and sanitation information systems in developing countries.

Services: POETRI promotes information exchange; provides general information services, workshops, and seminars; and conducts pilot and demonstration projects.

Clientele/Availability: Services are available to national and regional network participants, United Nations agencies, and other organizations involved in CWSS.

Contact: C.H. Dietvorst, Documentalist, Programme on Exchange and Transfer of Information on Community Water Supply and Sanitation. (Telex 33296 IRC NL.)

★602★
INTERNATIONAL REFUGEE INTEGRATION RESOURCE CENTRE (IRIRC)
(Centre International d'Echanges d'Informations sur l'Integration des Refugies)
5-7, ave. de la Paix   Phone: 022 310261
CH-1202, Geneva, Switzerland   Founded: 1981
Dr. Mark Braham, Coordinator

Staff: 1 Information and library professional; 1 management professional; 1 clerical and nonprofessional; 4 other.

Related Organizations: The International Refugee Integration Resource Centre is a project of the United Nations High Commissioner for Refugees.

Description of System or Service: The INTERNATIONAL REFUGEE INTEGRATION RESOURCE CENTRE (IRIRC) is an international clearinghouse designed to consolidate, store, retrieve, and disseminate information on all aspects of refugee reception, resettlement, and integration for governmental, intergovernmental, and nongovernmental refugee-assisting organizations and for individual research workers. The CENTRE gathers and abstracts national and international refugee documentation and stores the abstracts in the machine-readable REFABS data base. The most significant abstracts are published in the quarterly Refugee Abstracts journal. The CENTRE also offers computerized information retrieval services from REFABS and from data bases made commercially available online.

Scope and/or Subject Matter: International aspects of refugees, including countries of origin; causes, conditions, and experiences of exodus; conditions, needs, and opportunities in asylum and resettlement countries; international legal documentation; and other related topics.

Input Sources: Input is derived from books, journals, and other documentation from refugee-assisting organizations, as well as commercially available online data bases.

Holdings and Storage Media: The Centre maintains the computer-readable bibliographic REFABS data base as well as a library of 2000 bound volumes, subscriptions to 50 periodicals, and press clippings.

Publications: Refugee Abstracts (quarterly)—available by subscription. Each issue includes abstracts, news headlines, reviews, author index, subject index, publishers address index, and announcements. Abstracts are arranged in six subdivisions: international aspects, origins, exodus, asylum, resettlement, and repatriation.

Computer-Based Products and Services: The CENTRE maintains the REFABS data base using BASIS software and expects to make it publicly available online. The CENTRE also offers information retrieval services from REFABS and from data bases made available online through BLAISE (British Library Automated Information Service), DIALOG Information Services, Inc., QL Systems Limited, Telesystemes Questel, System Development Corporation (SDC), and G.CAM.

Other Services: The Centre also offers consulting on refugee information and online retrieval, and it supplies referrals to other agencies and to members of the International Refugee Documentation Network.

Clientele/Availability: The services of the Centre are available to refugee-assisting organizations and accredited researchers and university departments.

Projected Publications and Services: The following publications are planned by the Centre: International Directory of Refugee-Assisting Organizations, International Bibliography of Refugee Literature, and International Thesaurus of Refugee Terminology.

Remarks: The IRIRC was established as a result of the 1980 Workshop on Integration of Refugees from Indo-China in Countries of Resettlement, which was held under the auspices of the United Nations High Commissioner for Refugees.

Contact: Dr. Mark Braham, Coordinator, International Refugee Integration Resource Centre. (Telex 27492 UNHCR CH.)

★603★
INTERNATIONAL SERIALS DATA SYSTEM (ISDS)
20, rue Bachaumont   Phone: 01 2367381
F-75002 Paris, France   Founded: 1972
Mrs. M. Rosenbaum, Director

Staff: 6 Information and library professional; 1 management professional; 2 technicians; 1 sales and marketing; 3 clerical and nonprofessional.

Related Organizations: ISDS is an autonomous intergovernmental organization established within the framework of UNISIST, an integral unit of the United Nations Educational, Scientific and Cultural Organization's General Information Programme.

Description of System or Service: The INTERNATIONAL SERIALS DATA SYSTEM (ISDS) functions as a network of 46 national and regional centers through which world serial publications are registered. Each serial publication is cataloged and assigned a unique eight-digit International Standard Serial Number (ISSN) for bibliographic control, identification, and description purposes. The ISSN provides for the control of serials in both manual and automated files and facilitates the exchange of information between computer-based data files. The INTERNATIONAL SERIALS DATA SYSTEM maintains the computer-readable ISDS Register serials data base and issues microfiche registers and bulletins from it.

Scope and/or Subject Matter: Serial publications in any subject area; approximately half of the serials covered are in the field of science and technology.

Input Sources: Input consists of bibliographic data from serials cataloged by centers participating in the System.

Holdings and Storage Media: The machine-readable ISDS data base contains information on approximately 200,000 serials, most published after 1971; older serials are registered to meet the requirements of users. The data base is continuously updated with about 30,000 records added annually.

Publications: ISDS Manual—available for purchase.

Microform Products and Services: 1) ISDS Register (annual)—provides data on registered serials; includes an ISSN index and an alphabetical title index listing key titles and variant titles. 2) ISDS Bulletin (bimonthly)—updates the ISDS Register through the listing of approximately 5000 new and amended records per issue; contains ISSN and title indexes which are cumulated from issue to issue within each volume. Both the ISDS Register and ISDS Bulletin are available by subscription on 4x6 microfiche with a 48x reduction. 3) Cumulated ISDS Register/ Bulletin Indexes (annual)—forms a single ISSN index and a single alphabetic index, listing key titles and variant titles; available as part of the Register or separately. Under agreement with the International Organization for Standardization (ISO), the ISDS also publishes the International List of Periodical Title Word Abbreviations.

Computer-Based Products and Services: The INTERNATIONAL SERIALS DATA SYSTEM maintains the ISDS Register data base and makes it available for purchase on magnetic tape; updates are available by subscription. Subsets of the data base and special services from it are also available. Records in the data base include ISSN, key title, variant forms of the title, name of issuing body, imprint, date of publication, language and country codes, former and successor titles and classification. ISDS plans to offer online and SDI services from its computer-readable files.

Clientele/Availability: Clients include libraries, information centers, abstracting and indexing services, publishers, and distributors.

Contact: Ms. Elena, Editor, International Serials Data System. (Telex 680047 F SERIALS.)

★604★
INTERNATIONAL SOCIETY OF ECOLOGICAL MODELLING (ISEM) ENVIRONMENTAL DATA AND ECOLOGICAL PARAMETERS DATA BASE (EDE)
Langkaer Vaenge 9 Phone: 02 480600
DK-3500 Vaerloese, Denmark Service Est: 1978
Dr. Sven Erik Joergensen, Secretary General

Special Note: The above name, address, and telephone number have been verified for this edition, although no questionnaire response was received. The following text is reprinted from the 5th edition.

Staff: ISEM staff includes 2 management professional; 4 technicians; 2 clerical and nonprofessional.

Description of System or Service: The ENVIRONMENTAL DATA AND ECOLOGICAL PARAMETERS DATA BASE (EDE) contains information from relevant literature published since 1970 about organisms and processes in the environment. EDE provides factual information as well as bibliographic references for each item. Parts of the data base have been published as a handbook.

Scope and/or Subject Matter: Environmental science and ecology, including basic features of organisms, chemical concentration factors, formulas used in ecological models, and lists of trade and chemical names. Concentration of pollutants in specific ecosystems are not included in EDE.

Input Sources: Some 50 international scientific journals and over 500 books and reports have been scanned for input to the data base.

Holdings and Storage Media: EDE contains approximately 180,000 records and is updated and expanded by about 90,000 records per year.

Publications: 1) Handbook of Environmental Data and Ecological Parameters—published from the data base. 2) EDE System Manual. These and other publications are available for purchase from ISEM.

Computer-Based Products and Services: The EDE DATA BASE is searchable for environmental and ecological information. It includes basic features of organisms such as size and chemical composition; concentration factors for chemical compounds; formulas used in ecological models; rate constants, equilibrium constants, and temperature coefficients for environmental processes; systematic index; and lists of trade and chemical names. ISEM also offers software applicable to ecological modeling and provides assistance in creating private data bases which can be stored in the same system and searched simultaneously with the EDE Data Base.

Clientele/Availability: Users include governmental authorities, international institutes and organizations, industries, research scientists, and consulting firms.

Contact: Dr. Sven Erik Joergensen, Secretary General, International Society of Ecological Modelling; telephone 01 370850.

★605★
INTERNATIONAL TECHNICAL PUBLICATIONS LTD.
(Publicacoes Tecnicas Internacionais Ltda. - PTI)
Rua Peixoto Gomide, 209 Phone: 011 2588442
01409 Sao Paulo SP, Brazil Founded: 1972
Pierre Grossmann, Director

Staff: 3 Information and library professional; 5 management professional; 3 technicians; 10 sales and marketing; 20 clerical and nonprofessional.

Description of System or Service: INTERNATIONAL TECHNICAL PUBLICATIONS LTD. (PTI) is an information brokerage and subscription agency in Brazil for worldwide periodical and other literature. It imports and distributes a variety of scientific and technical books, trade directories, guidebooks, manuals, standards and specifications, theses, and market research reports. PTI also offers consulting services for development of documentation centers, and it provides computerized information services.

Scope and/or Subject Matter: International literature in the fields of science, technology, administration, and marketing.

Input Sources: Input sources include publishers literature and catalogs.

Holdings and Storage Media: PTI maintains a library of 2000 bound volumes, 50 periodical subscriptions, and other materials, including microfiche holdings, publishers' catalogs, and computer-readable files.

Publications: 1) Gerencia de Informacao/ Information Management (quarterly)—distributed to 20,000 Brazilian companies, government agencies, universities, and libraries. 2) BOOKALERT (monthly).

Computer-Based Products and Services: PTI provides monthly bibliographic alerting services from the computer-based SABE 2000 (Sistema de Alerta Bibliografico Especializado) system, which covers bibliographic information in more than 2000 subject areas. It also provides information retrieval services from other data bases.

Clientele/Availability: Clients include companies, industries, government agencies, and libraries.

Contact: Pierre Grossmann, Director, or Christina Galhardo, Librarian, International Technical Publications Ltd. (Telex 1135844 APTI BR.)

★606★
INTERNATIONAL TELECOMMUNICATION UNION (ITU)
Place des Nations
CH-1211 Geneva 20, Switzerland
R.E. Butler, Secretary General
Phone: 022 995511
Founded: 1949

Related Organizations: The International Telecommunication Union is a specialized agency of the United Nations.

Description of System or Service: The INTERNATIONAL TELECOMMUNICATION UNION (ITU) is an intergovernmental organization made up of telecommunications administrations in member states around the world. ITU strives to improve and increase the use of telecommunications of all kinds by promoting international technical cooperation, by holding international conferences and meetings, by issuing publications, and by providing information services through its Central Library and Documentation Section. ITU maintains several computer-readable registers of communications facilities and uses them to prepare directories and lists.

Scope and/or Subject Matter: Historical and current information on telecommunications including telegraphy, telephone, radio communications, television, space telecommunications, broadcasting, electronics, physics, mathematics, computer science and data processing, economics, legislation and regulation.

Input Sources: Input is derived from ITU notification administrations and committees, conference proceedings, laws and regulations, and basic documents of United Nations organizations.

Holdings and Storage Media: Library holdings include 20,000 bound volumes; documentation files of press clippings, articles, and photographs; films on telecommunications and electronics; and subscriptions to 750 periodicals. ITU also holds several data banks in computer-readable form.

Publications: Among ITU publications are the following: 1) Telecommunication Journal (monthly). 2) Summary of Monitoring Information Received by the IFRB (quarterly)—gives information from about 100 radio stations around the world. 3) List of Ship Stations (annual with quarterly and semimonthly supplements). 4) International Frequency List (every 2 years; quarterly supplements). 5) List of Telegraph Offices Open for International Service (every 5 years; annual supplements). The Central Library and Documentation Section issues several publications listing library acquisitions.

Computer-Based Products and Services: ITU maintains a number of computer-readable data bases, including files corresponding to its published registers and lists. Among ITU data bases are the following: 1) Monitoring Information Data Bank—provides about 190,000 items on 100 radio broadcasting stations across the world. 2) List of Ship Stations—international register of ships fitted with a radio station; includes 100,000 records. 3) International Frequency Register—contains 1.25 million items relating to radio frequency assignments, administration, and other information. 4) List of Telegraph Offices—international register containing 240,000 records providing current names and countries of all telegraph offices open for international service. 5) Coast Frequency Reference File—international register containing 28,000 coast station notifications. ITU data bases are generally restricted to telecommunication administrations and recognized operating agencies.

Other Services: In addition to the services described above, ITU makes available regulations, maps, tables, statistics, and other materials.

Clientele/Availability: Services are intended for researchers, ITU member states, and staff.

Contact: A.G. El-Zanati, Chief, ITU Central Library and Documentation Section; telephone 022995237. (Telex 421000.)

★607★
INTERNATIONAL TELECOMMUNICATIONS USERS GROUP (INTUG)
Beechy Lees Lodge, Pilgrims' Way
Otford, Kent TN14 5SA, England
E.O. Weiss, Chairman
Phone: 0959 23784
Founded: 1974

Staff: 3 Total.

Related Organizations: The International Telecommunications Users Group is an observer member of the International Telecommunication Union (ITU).

Description of System or Service: The INTERNATIONAL TELECOMMUNICATIONS USERS GROUP (INTUG) is a nonprofit association of telecommunications users. It was established to coordinate and represent the interests of its members with regard to the introduction and development of facilities, technologies, policies, and regulations. To these ends, it serves as an international forum for the exchange of information between national user groups, assisting the formation of groups in countries where there are none; serves as an international vehicle to inform users on matters affecting telecommunications; and maintains contact and cooperation with telecommunications authorities and other relevant bodies. The GROUP holds annual and other membership meetings, establishes special committees, participates in and organizes relevant studies, and publishes a newsletter.

Scope and/or Subject Matter: International telecommunications.

Publications: INTUG Newsletter (three or four issues per year).

Clientele/Availability: Membership is open to interested persons, organizations, or groups not involved in communications as consultants, carriers, or administrators.

Remarks: INTUG is officially known as Internationale Vereniging van Telecommunicatiegebruikers and is headquartered in The Hague, Netherlands.

Contact: Mr. C.L. Metcalfe, Secretary, International Telecommunications Users Group. (Telex 263536.)

★608★
INTERNATIONAL TRANSLATIONS CENTRE (ITC)
(Centre International des Traductions)
101 Doelenstr.
NL-2611 NS Delft, Netherlands
D. van Bergeijk, Director
Phone: 015 142242
Founded: 1961

Staff: 2 Information and library professional; 3 management professional; 1 sales and marketing; 8 clerical and nonprofessional.

Related Organizations: The Centre receives support from the Netherlands Ministry of Education and Sciences.

Description of System or Service: The INTERNATIONAL TRANSLATIONS CENTRE (ITC) is a nonprofit organization serving as a clearinghouse for information on existing scientific and technical translations from any source language into Western languages. Part of a network that includes national translation centers in a dozen countries, the CENTRE maintains a central reference catalog and an information bureau to facilitate identification of and access to nearly 1 million translations. It also produces the World Transindex, a hardcopy and machine-readable index to scientific translations in all fields. Additionally, the CENTRE provides reproductions and acts as a referral center in relation to the national centers and other organizations holding translations. (The CENTRE does not perform translations itself.)

Scope and/or Subject Matter: Translations in all scientific and technical fields. Language coverage includes translations from all languages into Western languages.

Input Sources: Major input is in the form of notifications of translations from cooperating national centers and more than 200 other organizations throughout the world.

Holdings and Storage Media: The Center maintains the machine-readable World Transindex data base, which holds approximately 175,000 references and covers the period from 1977 to the present. Approximately 26,000 items are added per year.

Publications: 1) World Transindex (10 issues per year with annual source and author indexes)—published jointly with the Documentation Centre of the Centre National de la Recherche Scientifique, Paris. Announces more than 26,000 translations per year (both completed and in-progress) of serial articles, patents and standards, and monographs. 2) Journals in Translation—published jointly with the British Library Lending Division, Boston Spa. A guide to nearly 1000 journals containing translations. 3) Five-Year Cumulation of the World Index of Scientific Translations (1967-1971 and 1972-1976)—contains more than 250,000 notifications of translations received by the Centre.

Computer-Based Products and Services: Produced by means of the PASCAL system, World Transindex (WTI) data base is available online through ESA/IRS. The data base provides such bibliographic data as author name, title of translation, number of pages of translation, agency name from which the translation is available, price (when known), language, and name, year, volume, and number of the original periodical. Reproductions of translations can be ordered online through the PrimorDial service of ESA/IRS.

Clientele/Availability: Services are available without restrictions. Any organization or individual with translations available may contact the Centre or the appropriate national translation center to deposit the translations and have them announced.

Contact: D. van Bergeijk, Director, or Mrs. M. Risseeuw, Assistant Director, International Translations Centre. (Telex 38104.)

★609★
INTERNATIONAL UNION OF GEOLOGICAL SCIENCES (IUGS) COMMISSION ON STORAGE, AUTOMATIC PROCESSING AND RETRIEVAL OF GEOLOGICAL DATA (COGEODATA)
IUGS Secretariat
77, rue Claude Bernard
F-75005 Paris, France
Phone: 01 7079196
Service Est: 1967

Special Note: No questionnaire response was received for this entry for the 6th edition. The entry is reprinted as it appeared in the 5th edition.

Related Organizations: The Commission's activities are sponsored by UNESCO and other international organizations.

Description of System or Service: The COMMISSION ON STORAGE, AUTOMATIC PROCESSING AND RETRIEVAL OF GEOLOGICAL DATA (COGEODATA) promotes the application of computerized techniques to data storage and retrieval in the various disciplines of geology. Its purposes are to assess computer-oriented information technology and promote its worldwide application to the management and interpretation of geological data; to facilitate the collection, compilation, and communication of computer-processible geological data; to promote general awareness of geologic data and other relevant information resources; and to provide consulting and training within its field.

Scope and/or Subject Matter: Geology, including geochemistry, petrology, paleontology, economic geology, and stratigraphy.

Input Sources: Input is provided by COGEODATA members representing more than 20 countries and all geological disciplines. Data files are prepared by government bodies, public agencies, and private industry and are submitted on questionnaires circulated by COGEODATA.

Holdings and Storage Media: Holdings consist of publications and documents produced by COGEODATA, plus input survey data.

Publications: COGEODATA Newsletter (quarterly). A number of other publications have been issued by COGEODATA members. The IUGS issues the quarterly Geological Newsletter.

Services: Services include data collection, advisory and consulting services to the geoscience community, and compilation of bibliographies and indexes.

Clientele/Availability: Services are available to the geological community on both an international and national basis.

Projected Publications and Services: An International Index to Geological Data, listing holdings of data files worldwide, will be issued when completed.

Contact: Secretary General, International Union of Geological Sciences.

★610★
INTERPROFESSIONAL TECHNICAL UNION OF THE NATIONAL FEDERATIONS OF BUILDINGS AND PUBLIC WORKS
(Union Technique Interprofessionnelle des Federations Nationales du Batiment et des Travaux Publics)
CENTER FOR TECHNICAL ASSISTANCE AND DOCUMENTATION
(Centre d'Assistance Technique et de Documentation - CATED)
ARIANE DATA BANK
9, rue La Perouse
F-75784 Paris Cedex 16, France
Mr. J. Devoge, Head
Phone: 01 7208800
Service Est: 1972

Staff: Approximately 100 total.

Related Organizations: The Information Center Applied to Construction assisted with the development of the ARIANE Data Bank.

Description of System or Service: The machine-readable ARIANE DATA BANK provides full-text information on building technology and tools, technical building regulations, construction techniques, and building products. Designed to serve the building and construction industries, the DATA BANK is accessible online through CATED and is used for publication purposes.

Scope and/or Subject Matter: Building and environmental technology.

Input Sources: Input consists of documents from manufacturers, regulation information from government ministries and administrations, and laboratory and test-center results.

Holdings and Storage Media: The machine-readable ARIANE Data Bank covers the period from 1972 to the present and contains 600 million characters. It is updated weekly.

Publications: Repertoire CATED (annual)—a photocomposed volume containing commercial and technical information related to building and construction.

Computer-Based Products and Services: The ARIANE DATA BANK contains information on building technology and tools, technical building regulations, and building products (covering 12,000 manufacturers, 100,000 trademarks, and 3600 product families). The DATA BANK is searchable online through CATED, which may be accessed through the Euronet DIANE and Transpac networks. Batch search and SDI services are also available.

Clientele/Availability: Services are available to contractors, architects, and other building industry professionals on a subscription basis.

Projected Publications and Services: Building component and other technical catalogs will be published in the future.

Remarks: ARIANE is the acronym for Arrangement Reticule des Informations en vue de l'Approche des Notions par leur Environnement.

Contact: J.M. Ravinet, Engineer, ARIANE Data Bank.

★611★
INTERUNIVERSITY DOCUMENTATION AND INFORMATION CENTER FOR THE SOCIAL SCIENCES
(Centre de Documentation et d'Information Interuniversitaire en Sciences Sociales - CENDIS)
1, Place Montesquieu
P.O. Box 18
B-1348 Louvain-la-Neuve, Belgium
Philippe Laurent, Director
Phone: 010 418181
Service Est: 1982

Staff: 1 Information and library professional; 2 management professional; 5 technicians.

Description of System or Service: The INTERUNIVERSITY DOCUMENTATION AND INFORMATION CENTER FOR THE SOCIAL SCIENCES (CENDIS) coordinates the activities of two university centers of information and documentation in the social sciences. CENDIS BASS at the Universite Catholique de Louvain manages a statistical data base on Belgium containing more than 3000 socioeconomic variables aggregated by county. CENDIS ULB at the Universite Libre de Bruxelles maintains a bibliographic data base concerning employment and professional education.

Scope and/or Subject Matter: Social sciences, including Belgian socioeconomic statistics, employment and labor, economics, economic politics, social law, and educational aspects.

Input Sources: Input is derived from statistical information produced by specialized government institutions; more than 100 Belgian and international periodicals published in Belgium; and books, nonconventional literature, and proceedings.

Holdings and Storage Media: A statistical file and a bibliographic file are held in machine-readable form.

Publications: A bibliographical bulletin covering employment is issued; it includes an index and abstracts. A thesaurus is also issued.

Computer-Based Products and Services: CENDIS maintains and provides services from SIGEDA, a statistical data base, and from a bibliographic data base, dating from 1981 to the present, which covers employment and education. Services provided include information retrieval, SDI, and cartographic output of statistical data.

Clientele/Availability: Services are available without restrictions.

Remarks: CENDIS incorporates the former Belgian Archives for the Social Sciences (BASS) of the Universite Catholique de Louvain.

Contact: Philippe Laurent, Director, Interuniversity Documentation and Information Center for the Social Sciences.

★612★
IPC INDUSTRIAL PRESS LTD.
CHEMICAL DATA SERVICES (CDS)
Quadrant House Phone: 01-661 3500
The Quadrant
Sutton, Surrey SM2 5AS, England
Peter Dean, Manager

Related Organizations: IPC Industrial Press Ltd. is a subsidiary of Business Press International Ltd.

Description of System or Service: The CHEMICAL DATA SERVICES (CDS) collects chemical industry information from worldwide primary and secondary sources and stores it in the computer-readable Chemical Plant and Product Database, which is used to produce a variety of directories, yearbooks, and individual report services and to offer information retrieval services. The Chemical Plant and Product Database provides details on more than 15,000 plants worldwide relating to some 4000 companies producing 128 chemicals; it also includes production and trade statistics for 111 chemical products manufactured in more than 70 countries. Output from the Database can be in tabular or graphic form; statistical analysis of data is also possible. The Database is available online through ADP Network Services, Inc.; a videotex option is under development.

Scope and/or Subject Matter: Chemical industry and products in Europe, North and South America, Africa, Asia, and elsewhere.

Input Sources: Information is derived from direct contact with chemical companies, company annual reports, statistical yearbooks, national trade returns, journals, reference lists, and annuals from chemical associations.

Holdings and Storage Media: The Chemical Plant and Product Database is maintained in computer-readable form.

Publications: 1) Chemical Data Services Plant and Product Data—annual service generated from the Chemical Plant and Product Database. Provides individual data sheets containing details on more than 15,000 plants worldwide plus production figures and annual trade statistics since 1972. Replacement sheets are issued for each product when new information is added to the Database. Subscriptions are available for individual products in either series: plant or product. 2) Databooks—a series of 30 titles derived from the Chemical Plant and Product Database. Each title provides up-to-date and comprehensive information on one of 30 major industrial chemicals, including description, derivation, uses and hazards, and production figures and import and export statistics. Also includes information on production plants, such as manufacturer, plant location, existing and planned capacity, process, feedstock, licensor, and contractor. 3) Chemical Industry Year Book—contains information derived from the Database and arranged by country; includes trade and production figures for the two most recent years on the 50 main industrial chemicals, plastics, fertilizers, and polymers, as well as a list of producers and their plant locations. 4) Chemfacts—available in separate volumes for Belgium, Canada, France, Federal Republic of Germany, Italy, Japan, Netherlands, Portugal, Scandinavia, Spain, United Kingdom, and countries producing PVC (Polyvinyl Chloride). Each volume contains profiles of essential chemicals and their producers within the country or region. 5) Chemical Company Profiles: Western Europe—provides information on some 1750 chemical manufactures in 19 countries. 6) Chemical Company Profiles: The Americas—provides information on some 1700 firms in 34 countries. 7) Chemical Plant Contractor Profiles—includes full profiles of 234 companies worldwide that are involved in the construction of chemical plants. 8) Worldwide Chemical Directory—provides addresses, telephone numbers, and brief descriptions of approximately 10,500 companies which make and/or distribute all kinds of chemical products; includes a full alphabetical index. 9) Chemical Industry of Eastern Europe 1975-80—reviews the performance and plans of the chemical industry in eight Eastern European countries.

Computer-Based Products and Services: The CHEMICAL DATA SERVICES maintains the computer-readable Chemical Plant and Product Database, which is used to produce a variety of publications and to offer batch-mode search services. The Database is also available online through ADP Network Services, Inc. A videotex option is under development.

Clientele/Availability: Services are available by subscription to companies and organizations needing product-by-product chemical industry information.

Remarks: The Database is also known as the CDS Chemical Database and the IPC Chemical Database.

Contact: Peter Dean, Manager, Chemical Data Services. (Telex 892084 BISPRS G.)

★613★
IRAN
MINISTRY OF CULTURE AND HIGHER EDUCATION
IRANIAN DOCUMENTATION CENTRE (IRANDOC)
1188, Enqelab Ave. Phone: 662223
P.O. Box 51-1387 Service Est: 1968
Tehran, Iran
M.N. Mahdavi, Director

Staff: Approximately 45 total.

Description of System or Service: The IRANIAN DOCUMENTATION CENTRE (IRANDOC) was established as a national documentation center to serve the research efforts of science and technology. To achieve this objective, IRANDOC is involved in the following activities: 1) collecting, processing, and disseminating scientific and technical information; 2) supplying scientists and specialists on the national level with necessary information materials and services to back their research; 3) encouraging cooperation and coordination among Iran's research and special libraries and documentation centers; 4) publishing bibliographic and reference materials useful to the scholarly world; 5) planning and coordinating the projects of national scientific and technical information networks and serving as a link to UNESCO's UNISIST (Universal System for Information in Science and Technology); and 6) offering workshops and training courses in documentation and information science.

Scope and/or Subject Matter: Science, technology, social science, and library and information science.

Input Sources: Input comprises books, periodicals, university theses, Iranian government publications, and technical reports.

Holdings and Storage Media: The IRANDOC library includes more than 32,000 books and technical reports; over 4000 periodicals and serials, with current subscriptions to 125 titles; and approximately 8000 theses and dissertations.

Publications: 1) Iranian National Union List of Serials (irregular); 2) IRANDOC Technical Bulletin (irregular); 3) IRANDOC Social Science Abstract Bulletin (irregular); 4) IRANDOC Science Abstract Bulletin (irregular); 5) Directory of Training, Research and Information-Producing Centers in Iran (irregular). IRANDOC also issues numerous other publications; a list is available on request from the Centre.

Clientele/Availability: Services are intended for researchers and professionals.

Contact: M.N. Mahdavi, Director, Iranian Documentation Centre.

★614★
IRCS MEDICAL SCIENCE
IRCS MEDICAL SCIENCE DATABASE
St. Leonard's House
St. Leonardgate
Lancaster LA1 1PF, England
M.C.S. Buckingham, Managing Director
Phone: 0524 68116
Service Est: 1983

Related Organizations: IRCS Medical Science is a member company of Elsevier Science Publishers.

Description of System or Service: The IRCS MEDICAL SCIENCE DATABASE is a machine-readable file comprising articles published in the IRCS Medical Science series of journals. It contains the full text, including tables, of research papers published in 32 monthly English-language specialist journals covering medical and biomedical science. The DATABASE is publicly available online.

Scope and/or Subject Matter: Medical and biomedical science research.

Input Sources: The data base contains the full text of 32 IRCS Medical Science journals.

Holdings and Storage Media: Updated semimonthly, the online IRCS data base contains approximately 2500 documents dating from 1981 to the present.

Publications: 1) IRCS Medical Science (monthly)—series of 32 specialist journals covering the entire spectrum of biomedical research. Manuscripts are drawn from research centers throughout the world. Available by subscription. 2) IRCS Journal of Medical Science (monthly)—publishes a selection of papers from the IRCS series. The papers are chosen on the basis of their particular merit and their immediate or potential clinical relevance. It also contains a classified list of the titles of all papers accepted for publication that month in the IRCS Medical Science series. Available by subscription. In North America, order from Journal Information Center, Elsevier Science Publishing Co., 52 Vanderbilt Ave., New York, NY 10017.

Computer-Based Products and Services: The IRCS MEDICAL SCIENCE DATABASE is currently available online through Bibliographic Retrieval Services (BRS) and DIMDI, and is also expected to be offered through ESA/IRS and Data-Star. Searchable record elements include accession number, author name, author affiliation, title, source, publisher, language, journal section classification, format of article, ISSN, publication date, introduction, description of materials and methods, results, cited references, and citation location.

Other Services: Document delivery services are available from the publisher.

Clientele/Availability: Clients are biomedical research scientists.

Contact: M.C.S. Buckingham, Managing Director, IRCS Medical Science Database. (Telex 65123.) The electronic mail address on DIALCOM (Telecom Gold) is 81: IRC001.

★615★
IRS-DIALTECH
Ebury Bridge House
2-18 Ebury Bridge Rd.
London SW1W 8QD, England
Phone: 01-730 9678

Related Organizations: Supporting organizations include the Great Britain Department of Trade and Industry.

Description of System or Service: IRS-DIALTECH is the marketing and customer support service for ESA/IRS in the United Kingdom. It facilitates access to the more than 60 data bases made available by ESA/IRS on its computers in Italy. IRS-DIALTECH also offers the TECHSEARCH service, through which information scientists conduct searches of ESA/IRS data bases.

Scope and/or Subject Matter: Online access to data bases in the areas of science and technology.

Computer-Based Products and Services: IRS-DIALTECH provides access to and conducts searches of data bases carried online by ESA/IRS.

Clientele/Availability: IRS-DIALTECH services are intended for British users.

Contact: Brian Kingsmill, IRS-DIALTECH.

★616★
ISRAEL
NATIONAL CENTER OF SCIENTIFIC AND TECHNOLOGICAL INFORMATION (COSTI)
P.O. Box 20125
84 Hachashmonaim St.
Tel-Aviv 61201, Israel
Mrs. Zeeva Levy, Director
Phone: 03 297781
Service Est: 1961

Staff: 28 Information and library professional; 3 management professional; 1 technician; 1 sales and marketing; 7 clerical and nonprofessional.

Related Organizations: COSTI is a unit of the Israeli Ministry of Energy and Infrastructure.

Description of System or Service: The NATIONAL CENTER OF SCIENTIFIC AND TECHNOLOGICAL INFORMATION (COSTI) is concerned with promoting, improving, coordinating, and disseminating scientific and technological information in Israel. COSTI also represents Israel in information activities worldwide through memberships in international organizations and is the representative in Israel for the U.S. National Technical Information Service (NTIS). COSTI acts through the following four major departments:

1) Department of Document Acquisitions—maintains COSTI's library and provides reference services, literature searches, and compilation of bibliographies with abstracts from its own and external resources. The Department also acts as a national and international clearinghouse for such materials as reports, articles, patent specifications, computer programs, and other items; over 30,000 documents are secured per year.

2) Department of Information for Industry and R&D—supplies industrial and research clients with computerized SDI services and online searches from more than 100 computer-readable data bases.

3) Department for Systems Development and Computerized Operations—processes computerized information systems handled by COSTI, develops and tests other storage and retrieval systems, and advises libraries and information centers in Israel on computer-based methods of information management and retrieval. It has developed the software for COSTI's SDI services and software for retrospective searching. Significant programs and processes developed by the Department include a registry system for current research in Israel, a data bank on population data banks, software packages for information and analysis centers, and the applications of minicomputers to special libraries and information centers.

4) Training and Publications Department—works to advance the formal and informal training of information workers by conducting courses and seminars, and by advising librarians on specific problems. It is also responsible for the production of COSTI's publications, which include two abstracting journals and a series of guides to sources of information.

Scope and/or Subject Matter: Major interests are scientific and technological information, library science, information science, and computers.

Input Sources: Input consists of books, technical reports, periodicals, and computer-readable and hardcopy abstracting and indexing services.

Holdings and Storage Media: Library holdings consist of 4000 volumes and 200 periodical subscriptions, and include directories of information resources, technical reports, multilingual technical dictionaries, thesauri, and catalogs. COSTI also maintains magnetic tape copies of commercially available data bases and a microfiche collection of NTIS documents from 1982 to the present.

Publications: 1) Desalination Abstracts (quarterly with annual cumulations)—gathers material covering the scientific, technological, and economic aspects of water desalination from a large variety of books, journals, reports, and patent specifications; each issue contains about 250 citations and several indexes. 2) Artificial Rainfall Newsletter (quarterly)—contains about 400 abstracts per year from published and unpublished literature. 3) Calendar of Forthcoming Scientific and Technological Meetings to be Held in Israel (semiannual)—includes subject and organization indexes. 4) Directory of Special Libraries in Israel—covers 380 special libraries. 5) Directory of Scientific and Technical Associations in Israel—covers 250 scientific and technical associations. 6) Directory of Research Institutes and Industrial Laboratories in Israel—covers 450 research institutes and R&D intensive industrial concerns. 7) Union List of Abstracting and Indexing Services Received in Leading Libraries. Other publications include a bibliography series; a list of all publications issued by COSTI is available by request.

Computer-Based Products and Services: The NATIONAL CENTER OF SCIENTIFIC AND TECHNOLOGICAL INFORMATION provides online information retrieval from data bases made available through Bibliographic Retrieval Services (BRS), DIALOG Information Services, Inc., and System Development Corporation (SDC). The CENTER also provides COSTI-SDI services based on magnetic tape copies of the following data bases: AGRIS, ISI, COMPENDEX, INSPEC, NTIS, BIOSIS, and CA Search. The data bases are held on a minicomputer to provide SDI services to academic researchers and industrial users in Israel; some 1000 SDI profiles are currently being processed. Additionally, COSTI has developed the DOMESTIC minicomputer system (see separate entry following this one).

Clientele/Availability: Services are available without restrictions.

Projected Publications and Services: A data base on energy-related topics is being implemented.

Contact: Mrs. G. Gilat, Editor, Department of Publications, National Center of Scientific and Technological Information; telephone 03 297827. (Telex 03 2332.)

★617★
ISRAEL
NATIONAL CENTER OF SCIENTIFIC AND TECHNOLOGICAL
    INFORMATION (COSTI)
DOMESTIC
P.O. Box 20125   Phone: 03 297781
84 Hachashmonaim St.   Service Est: 1975
Tel-Aviv 61201, Israel
Mrs. Zeeva Levy, Director

Related Organizations: COSTI is a unit of the Israeli Ministry of Energy and Infrastructure.

Description of System or Service: DOMESTIC is designed to optimize the use of minicomputers in all facets of library and information work in special libraries and information centers. It is a modular turnkey system used to create, update, search, and print information from bibliographic, full-text, and other types of data bases. DOMESTIC can also handle the acquisitions, cataloging, circulation, and statistical management needs of an information center.

Scope and/or Subject Matter: Application of minicomputers to interactive information storage and retrieval and library management.

Publications: User's manuals are available on request.

Computer-Based Products and Services: DOMESTIC is a minicomputer-based system written in FORTRAN and consisting of three major modules: 1) The DOMESTIC module is used to create and update in-house data bases, and to store externally created data bases. Full-text searches can be conducted from DOMESTIC data bases using Boolean operators and commands similar to Euronet's. 2) The DOMLIB module is used for the library management functions of an information center. It employs a Master Document File (MDF), which includes records created online when a document is ordered and completed when it is received, and a Borrower Master File containing information on individuals and institutions sharing in interlibrary loan programs. When used in conjunction with the print module, DOMLIB can produce order forms, registers of outstanding orders, registers of materials received but not cataloged, and priority lists. Additionally, DOMLIB can generate statistical, administrative, catalog, and summary documents including indexes, circulation statistics, and overdue notices. 3) The DOMPRINT module is a batch print generator which features standard print formats and the capability to create new formats with editing commands. It is used to print data base search results and other documents needed by a library.

Clientele/Availability: Primary clients are information centers.

Remarks: DOMESTIC is an acronym for Development of Minicomputers in an Environment of Scientific and Technical Information Centers. The DOMESTIC project was originally undertaken as a joint project by COSTI and KTS Information Systems of Germany (see separate entry).

Contact: Mrs. Zeeva Levy, Director, National Center of Scientific and Technological Information.

★618★
ISRAEL ATOMIC ENERGY COMMISSION
SOREQ NUCLEAR RESEARCH CENTER
LIBRARY AND TECHNICAL INFORMATION DEPARTMENT
                                     Phone: 054 84380
Yavne 70600, Israel   Service Est: 1952
Mrs. S. Weil, Head

Staff: 7 Information and library professional; 2 management professional; 1 technician; 6 clerical and nonprofessional.

Description of System or Service: The LIBRARY AND TECHNICAL INFORMATION DEPARTMENT serves the needs of the scientific staff of Soreq Nuclear Research Center. Regular services include conventional library service, SDI provided from commercially available magnetic tape services, and assistance in publishing reports and preparation of scientific papers for journals and conferences. The DEPARTMENT has exchange agreements with more than 160 foreign institutions whose fields of interest are similar, and it distributes its staff publications (usually issued as IA Reports) to 40 scientific institutions in Israel. In addition, the DEPARTMENT provides indexing of Israeli publications in the field of nuclear science for input to the International Nuclear Information System (INIS).

Scope and/or Subject Matter: Nuclear science, encompassing nuclear physics, nuclear chemistry and nuclear engineering.

Input Sources: Input is derived from books, journals, commercially available data bases, and reports received in hard copy or as microforms.

Holdings and Storage Media: The Library's collection numbers 60,000 volumes, 220,000 technical reports, and subscriptions to 280 periodicals.

Publications: 1) IA Reports (irregular)—Israel A.E.C. reports issued by the Department; 2) LS-reports (irregular); 3) accession list of new books (bimonthly); 4) accession list of new reports (fortnightly); 5) current journal subscriptions (annual); 6) annual and other series (annual).

Computer-Based Products and Services: The Department provides computer searching and SDI services based on INIS, COMPENDEX, ISI, INSPEC, and other commercially available data bases.

Other Services: Additional services include interlibrary loans and photocopying. The Department also lends scientific films, slides, and photographs.

Clientele/Availability: Services are available only to the scientific staff of Soreq Nuclear Research Center and, upon recommendation, to cooperating scientists.

Contact: Mrs. S. Weil, Head, Library and Technical Information Department. (Telex 341955.)

★619★
IST-INFORMATHEQUE INC.
2, complexe Desjardins   Phone: (514) 284-1111
Suite 1317   Founded: 1966
Montreal, PQ, Canada H5B 1B3
Gerard Briere, Head Manager

Staff: 1 Information and library professional; 2 management professional; 2 technicians; 2 sales and marketing; 3 clerical and nonprofessional.

Related Organizations: The parent company of IST-Informatheque

Inc. is Industrial Life-Technical Services Inc./ Industrielle-Services Techniques Inc. (IST).

Description of System or Service: IST-INFORMATHEQUE INC. is the Canadian representative for Telesystemes Questel, facilitating use of the approximately 50 data bases offered online by the Paris-based online host. INFORMATHEQUE also operates an online service which provides access to several Quebec-oriented bibliographic data bases under Questel software. SDI, offline printing, document ordering, and private data base management services are also available.

Scope and/or Subject Matter: Quebec and Canadian topics; Questel data bases in science and technology, humanities, social sciences, law, business and economics, and other areas.

Input Sources: Informatheque acquires Quebec data bases from commercial firms, government agencies, and universities.

Holdings and Storage Media: Several bibliographic data bases are held online.

Computer-Based Products and Services: IST-INFORMATHEQUE INC. offers online access to several Quebec files under Questel software, including the following: 1) BIBLIOCOM—contains references to communications documentation; produced by Laval University. 2) Envirodoq—provides citations and abstracts of environmental literature relating to Quebec; prepared by the Quebec Ministry of the Environment. 3) HISCABEQ—contains references to literature on Quebec and Canadian history; compiled by Microfor Inc. 4) RADAR—provides references to articles of general interest appearing in Quebec and selected Canadian and foreign periodicals. INFORMATHEQUE also represents Telesystemes Questel in Canada.

Clientele/Availability: Services are available without restrictions.

Remarks: IST-Informatheque Inc. was formerly known as Informatech.

Contact: Denis Tournesac, Director of Marketing, IST-Informatheque Inc. The electronic mail address on Telecom Canada's iNET 2000 is INFORMATECH.1.

★620★
ITALCABLE
DIRECT ACCESS TO REMOTE DATA BASES OVERSEAS (DARDO)
Via Calabria 46-48   Phone: 396 47701
I-00187 Rome, Italy

Staff: 3 Management professional; 1 technician; 1 sales and marketing; 3 clerical and nonprofessional; 1 other.

Related Organizations: ItalCable is controlled by the Societa Finanziaria Telefonica, the IRI Group holding company for the electronics and telecommunications manufacturing and service sector.

Description of System or Service: DIRECT ACCESS TO REMOTE DATA BASES OVERSEAS (DARDO) is a packet switching network providing users with access to U.S. data bases connected to Telenet and Tymnet networks, and to European data bases connected directly or indirectly to ItalCable's gateways. DARDO also allows subscribers direct access to time-sharing facilities offering data processing capabilities for scientific, mathematical, and other applications. A special application of DARDO is the Dardo Access to Travel Service (DATS), which allows travel agency operators access to a wide range of computerized reservation systems for airlines, hotels, and car rental services, and enables them to perform online operations relative to bookings, confirmations, modifications of hotel reservations, flight segments, and other activities. DATS also automatically issues flight tickets and provides accounting and billing facilities.

Scope and/or Subject Matter: Online access to U.S. and European data bases, general data processing facilities, and travel reservation systems.

Computer-Based Products and Services: DIRECT ACCESS TO REMOTE DATA BASES OVERSEAS allows access to U.S. and European data bases through ASCII-type terminals via the national telephone network or leased circuits. Dardo Access to Travel Service allows access to computerized reservation systems through a wide range of terminals via a dedicated line, public switched telephone network, or data network.

Clientele/Availability: Services are available on a fee basis.

Contact: Customer Services, ItalCable. (Telex 61146 ITC DGI.) In the United States, contact Walter J. Bernas, Director of Commercial Activities, ItalCable USA, Inc., One World Trade Center, Suite 10231, New York, NY 10048; telephone (212) 938-1046.

★621★
ITALIAN ASSOCIATION FOR THE PRODUCTION AND
  DISTRIBUTION OF ONLINE INFORMATION
(Associazione Italiana dei Fornitori e Distributori di Informazione
  Telematica - AFDIT)
via G. Trevis, 88   Phone: (not reported)
I-00147 Rome, Italy
Dr. L. Daina, General Secretary

Description of System or Service: The ITALIAN ASSOCIATION FOR THE PRODUCTION AND DISTRIBUTION OF ONLINE INFORMATION (AFDIT) is composed of for-profit information providers, data base producers, information brokers, host computer centers, time-sharing networks, and related software houses. Concerned with all aspects of information teleprocessing, AFDIT promotes the interests of its members and conducts seminars and meetings.

Scope and/or Subject Matter: Online information in any subject area.

Clientele/Availability: Members are organizations in the online information industry.

Contact: Dr. L. Daina, General Secretary, Italian Association for the Production and Distribution of Online Information.

★622★
ITALIAN SOCIETY FOR TELEPHONE USE
(Societa Italiana per l'Esercizio Telefonico - SIP)
VIDEOTEL
Via Flaminia, 189   Phone: 06 36881
I-00196 Rome, Italy   Service Est: 1982
Angelo Ferraiuolo, Project Manager

Special Note: No questionnaire response was received for this entry for the 6th edition. The entry is reprinted as it appeared in the 5th edition.

Staff: 3 Management professional; 13 technicians; 10 clerical and nonprofessional.

Description of System or Service: VIDEOTEL is a public videotex service implemented on a two-year trial basis for approximately 1000 users in Italy. Modeled on British Prestel technology, VIDEOTEL provides more than 25,000 pages of information supplied by approximately 90 information providers. Information stored in the VIDEOTEL system is accessed by private and business users with terminals via telephone lines. VIDEOTEL also provides gateway services, connecting users with external host computers. Additional services include closed user groups, frame response for transactional applications, and electronic mail. The purposes of the project are to test market reactions for both information providers and users, to acquire relevant management experience, and to encourage Italian industry to manufacture new devices.

Scope and/or Subject Matter: Travel, transport, tourism, and leisure activities; investment and financial data; retail and distribution orders by mail; pharmaceutical and medical information; education and training; government and public administration information; property and construction data; computers, communications, and office product information; and professional services.

Input Sources: Data bases are provided by approximately 90 information providers.

Holdings and Storage Media: Approximately 25,000 pages of information are currently stored online by Videotel, which has a capacity of 250,000 frames.

Computer-Based Products and Services: VIDEOTEL provides interactive access to data bases held on its own computers as well as access to eight external host computers. Other services include closed user groups, electronic mail, and transactional services.

Clientele/Availability: Clients include business and residential users.

Contact: Angelo Ferraiuolo, Project Manager, Videotel. (Telex 610467 SIPGEN.)

★623★
ITALY
NATIONAL RESEARCH COUNCIL
(Consiglio Nazionale delle Ricerche - CNR)
CNUCE INSTITUTE
Via S. Maria 36
I-56100 Pisa, Italy
Dr. Ing. Stefano Trumpy, Director
Phone: 050 593111
Service Est: 1965

Staff: 40 Information and library professional; 5 management professional; 40 technicians; 10 clerical and nonprofessional.

Description of System or Service: The CNUCE INSTITUTE conducts research in the areas of information and computer science and provides a data processing service for the purpose of furthering the research activities of the Italian National Research Council/Consiglio Nazionale delle Ricerche (CNR) and other organizations. It offers time-sharing access to applications software and data bases through a central computer facility which can be accessed via CNUCE's data transmission network. The research wing of CNUCE is involved in a variety of informatics projects including the development of satellite and OSI-compatible networks.

Scope and/or Subject Matter: Research in computers, networks, microcomputers, computer music, space flight control, data bases, image processing, and other areas; data processing services for scientific and technical applications.

Holdings and Storage Media: CNUCE library holdings include 100 bound volumes; subscriptions to 30 periodicals; and 300 internal reports.

Publications: Rapporto (every 3 months)—provides information on CNUCE technical activities. A variety of internal reports is also issued.

Computer-Based Products and Services: CNUCE offers time-sharing services via its nationwide data transmission network and through Euronet DIANE. It provides access to a variety of simulation, mathematical, statistical, and data base management software as well as to the SSVA Data Base, a bibliographic file covering worldwide literature on glass and silicates and supplied by the Stazione Sperimentale del Vetro.

Clientele/Availability: Clientele includes all institutes and departments of the CNR, universities, research institutes, and other organizations; services are available without restrictions.

Contact: Dr. Rolando Bandinelli or Elena Lofrese, CNUCE Institute. (Telex 500371.)

★624★
ITALY
NATIONAL RESEARCH COUNCIL
(Consiglio Nazionale delle Ricerche - CNR)
INSTITUTE FOR STUDY OF SCIENTIFIC RESEARCH & DOCUMENTATION
(Istituto di Studi sulla Ricerca e Documentazione Scientifica - ISRDS)
ITALIAN REFERENCE CENTER FOR EURONET DIANE
(Centro di Riferimento Italiano DIANE - CRID)
Via Cesare de Lollis 12
I-00185 Rome, Italy
Prof. Paolo Bisogno, Head
Phone: 06 4952351
Service Est: 1979

Staff: 6 Total.

Description of System or Service: The ITALIAN REFERENCE CENTER FOR EURONET DIANE (CRID) promotes and provides information about the Euronet DIANE online network and online services in general. It offers information on network operations and services; makes referrals to appropriate information and documentation centers; provides assistance and consultation for persons wishing to contract for network services; and issues a newsletter.

Scope and/or Subject Matter: Online services available over Euronet DIANE and other international networks.

Publications: Notiziario—newsletter containing information about Euronet DIANE, including data bases available, host computers, online searching, and related seminars and conferences.

Clientele/Availability: Information is provided to Euronet DIANE and other online users, as well as to other interested parties.

Contact: Maria Pia Carosella, Italian Reference Center for Euronet DIANE. (Telex 610076 CORICERC.)

★625★
ITALY
NATIONAL RESEARCH COUNCIL
(Consiglio Nazionale delle Ricerche - CNR)
RESEARCH CENTER FOR THE STRATIGRAPHY AND PETROGRAPHY OF THE CENTRAL ALPS
(Centro di Studio per la Stratigrafia e Petrografia delle Alpi Centrali)
ARCHIVE OF ITALIAN DATA OF GEOLOGY (ADIGE)
Dipartimento di Scienze della Terra
Via Mangiagalli 34
I-20135 Milan, Italy
Dr. Roberto Potenza, Head
Phone: 02 293994
Service Est: 1980

Staff: 1 Information and library professional; 2 management professional.

Description of System or Service: The ARCHIVE OF ITALIAN DATA OF GEOLOGY (ADIGE) is a series of computer-readable data bases containing information on geological formations in Italy, especially in the Alpine region. ADIGE consists of several files which identify and describe geological formations and contain bibliographic references to information on Italian geology. Services available from the files include information retrieval and secondary analysis.

Scope and/or Subject Matter: Italian earth sciences, including stratigraphy, sedimentology, petrology, and mineralogy.

Holdings and Storage Media: Machine-readable ADIGE files hold 4000 bibliographic references, names and descriptions of 1200 geological formations, and 5000 lexical terms with English and French correspondence.

Computer-Based Products and Services: The ARCHIVE OF ITALIAN DATA OF GEOLOGY includes the following computer-readable files: 1) GEOBIB—a bibliography of Italian geology. 2) ADIGE2—contains names and basic data on geological formations. 3) SERIE—contains well logs of the Po Plain region. Information retrieval and secondary analysis services are offered from the files.

Clientele/Availability: Services are available to Italian scientific geological researchers.

Contact: Dr. Roberto Potenza, Head, Archive of Italian Data of Geology.

J

★626★
JAPAN
ENVIRONMENT AGENCY
NATIONAL INSTITUTE FOR ENVIRONMENTAL STUDIES
ENVIRONMENTAL INFORMATION DIVISION
16-2 Onogawa   Phone: 0298 516111
Yatabe-machi, Tsukuba-gun   Service Est: 1981
Ibaraki 305, Japan
Dr. Shota Hirosaki, Director

Staff: 4 Information and library professional; 5 management professional; 12 technicians; 3 clerical and nonprofessional.

Description of System or Service: The ENVIRONMENTAL INFORMATION DIVISION of the National Institute for Environmental Studies is composed of the Information and Services Section, Information Systems Section, Information Processing Section, and the Computer Center. With the goal of becoming the national environmental information center of Japan, it collects a wide range of information and data and makes them available to Institute members and others. The DIVISION maintains the computer-readable Environmental Numerical Data File, covering pollution and related subjects; provides technical computation services for Institute members; and accesses externally available data bases in its areas of interest. Additional services include maintenance of a library and preparation of publications.

Scope and/or Subject Matter: All types of environmental information.

Input Sources: Information is acquired from local, national, and foreign government agencies and from publicly available online services.

Holdings and Storage Media: The computer-readable Environmental Numerical Data File consists of the Air Quality Data File, Water Quality Data File, Photochemical Smog Data File, and Natural Environment Data File. The Division's library has a collection of 17,000 bound volumes, subscriptions to 1450 periodicals, and local government reports.

Publications: 1) Annual Report of the NIES; 2) Research Report from the NIES (occasional).

Computer-Based Products and Services: The ENVIRONMENTAL INFORMATION DIVISION maintains the Environmental Numerical Data File for internal research purposes and provides information retrieval from a copy of the U.N. Environment Programme's INFOTERRA data base. It also accesses DIALOG Information Services, Inc. and the JICST Online Information Service. Additionally, data processing services are available to Institute members.

Clientele/Availability: Services are primarily intended for Institute research scientists.

Contact: Mr. Kunihiko Shirai, Chief of General Affairs, Information and Services Section.

★627★
JAPAN
JAPAN ATOMIC ENERGY RESEARCH INSTITUTE (JAERI)
DEPARTMENT OF TECHNICAL INFORMATION
2-2-2 Uchisaiwai-cho, Chiyoda-ku   Phone: 03 5036111
Tokyo 100, Japan   Service Est: 1956
Dr. Junichi Shimokawa, Director

Staff: 26 Information and library professional; 4 management professional; 5 clerical and nonprofessional.

Description of System or Service: The DEPARTMENT OF TECHNICAL INFORMATION acts as an information center for nuclear research and development in Japan. It also participates in the International Nuclear Information System (INIS) of the International Atomic Energy Agency, providing INIS with bibliographic information pertaining to nuclear science literature originating in Japan. In turn, INIS supplies the DEPARTMENT with updates to the INIS data base on magnetic tape.

Scope and/or Subject Matter: Nuclear science and technology.

Input Sources: The Department scans Japanese nuclear literature from which it provides bibliographies and abstracts to INIS on magnetic tape.

Holdings and Storage Media: Library holdings of the Department consist of 600,000 technical reports, 33,000 bound volumes, and 1200 periodical titles. The INIS data base is also maintained.

Publications: 1) Nuclear Science Information of Japan (bimonthly with annual cumulated indexes)—bibliography of nuclear literature published in Japan. 2) Technical Publications by JAERI Staff (annual)—list of journal articles, conference papers, and reports published by JAERI staff; in English. Catalogs, current contents publications, and indexes are also issued.

Computer-Based Products and Services: The Department maintains a subscription to the INIS data base from which computerized searching is offered.

Clientele/Availability: Services are intended for the use of the Japanese nuclear community.

Contact: Takeshi Fukami, Manager, Information Division, Department of Technical Information, Japan Atomic Energy Research Institute, at Tokai-mura, Naka-gun, Ibaraki-ken, Japan; telephone 02928 25026. (Telex J24596 JAERI.)

★628★
JAPAN
MARITIME SAFETY AGENCY
HYDROGRAPHIC DEPARTMENT
JAPAN OCEANOGRAPHIC DATA CENTER (JODC)
No. 3-1, Tsukiji 5-Chome   Phone: 03 5413811
Chuo-ku   Service Est: 1965
Tokyo 104, Japan
Dr. Yoshio Iwabuchi, Director

Staff: Approximately 16 total.

Description of System or Service: The JAPAN OCEANOGRAPHIC DATA CENTER (JODC) collects, processes, analyzes, stores, compiles, and publishes all oceanographic data produced for areas located in Japanese territory. As a member of the Intergovernmental Oceanographic Commission's (IOC) data exchange system, the CENTER also exchanges data and information about oceans and seas with other national oceanographic data centers. The JODC has authority for the Responsible National Oceanographic Data Center (RNODC) for the Western Pacific Ocean Cooperative Study (WESTPAC), commenced in 1979 as an IOC program. In addition to serving as a national repository for oceanographic data, JODC fills the oceanographic data and information needs of the public and those of national and international oceanographic communities.

Scope and/or Subject Matter: Serial oceanographic station data, current data, BT data, marine pollution data, and marine geological and geophysical data.

Input Sources: Input is received from approximately 130 stations and 45 foreign countries conducting oceanographic observations; data are supplied both as code sheets and publications.

Holdings and Storage Media: Holdings consist of approximately 227,000 data sets of serial observations, 162,000 bathythermographs (BT), and 137,000 current (GEK) data sets received from various Japanese organizations and preserved by JODC on punched cards and magnetic tape. Other oceanographic products and documents, about 2000 publications annually, are maintained in hard copy.

Publications: 1) WESTPAC Newsletter (biannual). 2) JODC News (biannual)—in Japanese. 3) An Outline of the JODC (in Japanese). 4) Manual on WESTPAC Data Management. 5) Guide to CSK Data. The Center also publishes a number of atlases and catalogs of oceanographic data; a complete list of publications is available upon request to JODC.

Computer-Based Products and Services: Oceanographic data are made available on magnetic tape by request.

Other Services: Consultation relating to data is also available.

Clientele/Availability: Services are available on a contract or exchange basis.

Contact: Dr. Yoshio Iwabuchi, Director, Japan Oceanographic Data Center.

★629★
JAPAN
NATIONAL DIET LIBRARY
(Kokuritsu Kokkai Toshokan)
LIBRARY AUTOMATION SYSTEM
10-1, 1-Chome
Nagato-cho, Chiyoda-ku
Tokyo 100, Japan
Mr. Koichi Imagawa, Chief
Phone: 03 5812331
Service Est: 1965

Staff: 2 Management professional; 15 system engineers; 2 clerical and nonprofessional.

Description of System or Service: The LIBRARY AUTOMATION SYSTEM operates a number of computerized information systems to support the National Diet Library in its mission to serve the Diet, government agencies, and the public. Among the systems are JAPAN/MARC and the Japanese National Bibliography, an indexing system for Japanese periodical literature, a Western book processing system, and an index to the debates of the Diet. The systems are used to produce publications and some of them are accessible online in the Library.

Scope and/or Subject Matter: Automation of library operations, including bibliographic data on monographs and periodicals, as well as information on the National Diet.

Input Sources: Input is derived from Japanese and Western books and periodicals.

Holdings and Storage Media: Over 3 million bibliographic records are stored in machine-readable form under various systems. The Library's collection includes nearly 4 million books, 65,000 periodical titles (including more than 40,000 current subscriptions), 226,000 maps, 250,000 records, and 122,000 reels of microfilm.

Publications: 1) Japanese National Bibliography (annual). 2) Japanese National Bibliography Weekly List—available by subscription. Covers books, periodicals, and other materials received by the Library. Quarterly title and author index issued separately. 3) Japanese Periodicals Index (quarterly)—published in separate volumes for two subject areas: humanities and social science, and science and technology. 4) National Diet Library Catalog of Japanese Periodicals. 5) National Diet Library Catalog of Foreign Periodicals. 6) Monthly List of Foreign Scientific and Technical Publications. 7) Science and Technology Information Service (quarterly). 8) General Index to the Debates of the National Diet—one volume per Diet session.

Computer-Based Products and Services: The LIBRARY AUTOMATION SYSTEM maintains the following computerized information systems: 1) Japanese National Bibliography—contains a data base of approximately 340,000 records used to produce catalog cards, an annual volume, holding and subject listings and statistics, and the JAPAN/MARC catalog. Magnetic tapes of JAPAN/MARC records generated since early 1979 are available by subscription. 2) Japanese Periodicals Index—holds index records for 153,000 humanities and social science periodical articles from 1862 titles annually, plus 210,000 records for science and technology articles from 1602 titles annually, including medical science and pharmacology articles from 1979 to the present; the file dates back to 1975. 3) National Diet Library Catalog of Japanese Periodicals—contains approximately 37,000 title records used to produce quarterly cumulative supplements listing Japanese serial publications. 4) Western Book Processing System—holds approximately 1.7 million titles derived from U.S. Library of Congress MARC tapes, utilized to produce selected bibliographic data in card or list form as necessary. 5) National Diet Library Catalog of Foreign Periodicals—contains more than 28,000 titles dating back to 1971. 6) Monthly List of Foreign Scientific and Technical Publications—contains approximately 168,000 titles derived from U.S. National Technical Information Service (NTIS) tapes; used to produce an acquisitions list. 7) General Index to the Debates of the National Diet—covers debates from 1972 to date. Selected data files derived from the above systems are available for online searching on terminals within the Library.

Other Services: The National Diet Library also provides photoduplication of materials held in its collection.

Clientele/Availability: The National Diet Library serves members of the Diet, Japanese government agencies, and the Japanese public.

Contact: Mr. Koichi Imagawa, Chief, Computer Applications Section, Administrative Division, National Diet Library.

★630★
JAPAN ASSOCIATION FOR INTERNATIONAL CHEMICAL INFORMATION (JAICI)
Gakkai Center Bldg.
2-4-16 Yayoi, Bunkyo-ku
Tokyo 113, Japan
Soichi Tokizane, Manager
Phone: 03 8163462
Founded: 1971

Staff: 14 Information and library professional; 2 management professional; 2 technicians; 2 sales and marketing; 4 clerical and nonprofessional.

Related Organizations: The Japan Association for International Chemical Information receives support from the Chemical Society of Japan and 26 other chemistry-oriented academic societies in Japan.

Description of System or Service: The JAPAN ASSOCIATION FOR INTERNATIONAL CHEMICAL INFORMATION (JAICI) acts as an information center in the field of chemistry. Its primary purposes are to abstract and index Japanese chemical literature and to distribute Chemical Abstracts Service (CAS) products and services throughout Japan.

Scope and/or Subject Matter: Chemistry; chemical engineering; material-oriented scientific disciplines.

Input Sources: Input is derived from Chemical Abstracts Service files, Japanese chemical literature, and other sources.

Holdings and Storage Media: The Association maintains computer-readable copies of Chemical Abstracts Service data bases and other commercially available files.

Publications: Kagaku Shoho (biweekly)—an abstracts journal covering chemistry-oriented literature appearing in 110 Japanese periodicals.

Computer-Based Products and Services: JAICI markets CAS ONLINE in Japan and offers an SDI service called CA CUSTOM from the CA abstracts and index file. JAICI also distributes other files such as the Cambridge Crystallographic Data File.

Clientele/Availability: Services are available without restrictions. Clients include the academic, industrial, and governmental communities in Japan as well as the general public.

Contact: Dr. Hideaki Chihara or Mr. Soichi Tokizane, Manager, Japan Association for International Chemical Information. (Telex 272 3805 JAICI J.)

★631★
JAPAN DATA SERVICE CO., LTD.
Shugetsu Bldg.
3-12-7 Kita-Aoyama, Minato-ku
Tokyo 107, Japan
Akihisa Yamaguchi, President
Phone: 03 4007507
Founded: 1974

Related Organizations: The parent organization of Japan Data Service is Overseas Data Service, Company, Ltd. (see separate entry.) Other cooperating organizations include the Tokyo Broadcasting System (TBS), Idea Bank, and Opinionmeter Co., Ltd.

Description of System or Service: JAPAN DATA SERVICE CO., LTD. markets the JNN Data Bank, a comprehensive semiannual survey of Japanese consumers throughout the country. The survey involves a sample of 3000 persons and includes more than 150 survey items ranging from media exposure to lifestyles to current usage of products by category and by brand. The processed and compiled results provide information on the attitude and behavior of Japanese consumers directly and indirectly related to the commerical products available in the country. In addition to marketing the JNN Data Bank, the firm also provides related consultation services for clients.

Scope and/or Subject Matter: Japanese consumer attitudes, including media exposure and product usage.

Input Sources: Input is derived from field surveys.

Publications: The JNN Data Bank is published twice per year. It includes a Brand Research File, a Consumer Research File, and an Audience Research File. Other reports and studies are also issued.

Other Services: Various cross-tabulations and analyses are available from the JNN Data Bank.

Clientele/Availability: Clients include major Japanese corporations and others.

Contact: Yukihiko Sakamoto, or Reiji Tahara, Assistant Director, Japan Data Service Co., Ltd.

★632★
JAPAN INFORMATION CENTER OF SCIENCE AND TECHNOLOGY (JICST)
5-2, Nagatacho, 2-Chome, Chiyoda-ku Phone: 03 5816411
C.P.O. Box 1478 Founded: 1957
Tokyo, Japan
Shintaro Tabata, President

Staff: Total JICST staff consists of approximately 340; the Information Division staff totals 130 specialists in various fields of science and technology.

Related Organizations: The Center is under the executive control of the Science and Technology Agency of the Prime Minister's Office of Japan.

Description of System or Service: The JAPAN INFORMATION CENTER OF SCIENCE AND TECHNOLOGY (JICST) serves as the central organization for collecting and disseminating scientific and technological information in Japan. Journals received from sources worldwide and covering nearly all areas of science and technology are abstracted and indexed for inclusion within the JICST File on Science and Technology, a machine-readable data base used to produce the Current Bibliography on Science and Technology abstracts series. JICST also compiles data bases covering current research and medicine in Japan. JICST data bases are made available online through the JICST On-line Information Service (JOIS), which also offers data bases from the U.S. National Library of Medicine, BioSciences Information Service (BIOSIS), and other organizations in the United States and Europe. Additional services offered by JISCT include SDI and retrospective literature searching of the JICST files, photocopying, translations, and manual literature and patent searching.

Scope and/or Subject Matter: Science and technology, including: mechanical engineering; electronics and electrical engineering; chemistry and chemical engineering; metallurgy; mining and earth sciences; civil engineering and architecture; pure and applied physics; atomic energy; nuclear engineering; management science and system engineering; environmental pollution; life science; medicine.

Input Sources: Input is gathered from more than 10,000 journals in all areas of science and technology; plus technical reports, conference proceedings, and patent specifications.

Holdings and Storage Media: The computer-readable JICST File on Science and Technology contains more than 1 million citations. JICST also maintains other internally produced and commercially available data bases in machine-readable form.

Publications: 1) Current Bibliography on Science and Technology (CBST)—a series of 12 abstracts journals providing Japanese-language abstracts of literature in specific areas of science and technology. Frequency of publication ranges from three times per month to monthly; an annual index is produced for each title in the series. Derived from the JICST File on Science and Technology. 2) Abstracts of Science and Technology in Japan—provides English-language abstracts of science and technological literature in Japan; currently available in two subject areas: renewable energy and agro-industries. 3) Current Science and Technology Research in Japan (biannual)—covers current research projects being conducted in public laboratories and research organizations in Japan. 4) Journal of Information Processing and Management (monthly)—contains news and articles relating to the theory and practice of information processing and management. 5) Technology Highlights (monthly)—provides information on recent developments in technology and new products worldwide; designed for use by smaller industries. 6) Foreign Chemical Patent News (weekly)—provides abstracts of chemical patents published in the United States, United Kingdom, and West Germany. 7) Proceedings of the Annual Meeting on Information Science and Technology. 8) JICST Thesaurus—contains more than 40,000 terms. JICST also publishes a variety of handbooks and other publications. All titles are available by subscription or for purchase and may be ordered from: Japan Publications Trading Co., Ltd., Tokyo International P.O. Box 5030, Tokyo, Japan.

Microform Products and Services: CBST is available on microfilm.

Computer-Based Products and Services: The JAPAN INFORMATION CENTER OF SCIENCE AND TECHNOLOGY maintains the JICST On-line Information Service (JOIS), which provides users in Japan with remote terminal access to three internal data bases: JICST File on Science and Technology, JICST File on Research in Progress in Japan, and JICST File on Medical Science in Japan, as well as the following external data bases: BIOSIS Previews, CA Search, CANCERLIT, Coal Data Base, INSPEC, MEDLINE, TOXLINE, and others. Supporting files maintained by JICST include Medical Subject Headings (MeSH), JICST Holding List, JICST Thesaurus File on Scientific and Technological Terms, and two JOIS training files. The CENTER offers retrospective searching and SDI services from its files.

Other Services: In addition to the services described above, the Center offers short-term training courses on information handling.

Clientele/Availability: Services are available without restrictions; fees vary according to services.

Contact: Service Division, Japan Information Center of Science and Technology.

★633★
JAPAN PATENT INFORMATION CENTER (JAPATIC)
Bansui Bldg. Phone: 03 5036181
1-5-16, Toranomon, Minato-ku Founded: 1971
Tokyo 105, Japan
Hideo Saito, President

Staff: Approximately 90 total.

Related Organizations: JAPATIC is subsidized by the Japan Patent Office; it works closely with the International Patent Documentation Center (INPADOC) and the Japan Institute of Invention and Innovation.

Description of System or Service: The JAPAN PATENT INFORMATION CENTER (JAPATIC) is a nonprofit organization specializing in patent information services in Japan. JAPATIC collects information on industrial property from domestic and foreign sources and stores it in the computer-readable JAPATIC data base. The CENTER disseminates patent and trademark information through the Patent On-Line Information System (PATOLIS), an online service which provides clients with interactive remote terminal access to Japanese, United States, and INPADOC data bases. JAPATIC also offers SDI and retrospective search services, generates statistical graphs and tables, and prepares abstracting and indexing publications and microforms.

Scope and/or Subject Matter: Industrial property information: patents, utility models, design, and trademarks.

Input Sources: Patent specifications, official gazettes, abstracts, and indexes are continuously collected from major countries.

Holdings and Storage Media: JAPATIC holds computer-readable data on approximately 18 million patent and trademark documents; new data are added to the file monthly. Microform and hardcopy patent collections are also held.

Publications: 1) Japanese Patent Abstracts (KOKAI-KOHO)—provides Japanese-language abstracts of published unexamined patent applications in all technical fields arranged by division and classification; approximately 220,000 abstracts are included annually with technical drawings. An English-language version is available from the Japan Institute of Invention and Innovation. 2) Japanese Patent Indexes (annual)—contains title of invention, applicant, and other bibliographic information filed according to applicant and classification symbol for patents and utility models.

Microform Products and Services: JAPATIC produces the following COM indexes: 1) Japanese Patent Index in English—provides bibliographic information on Japanese unexamined patents published from 1976 to the present arranged by applicant, classification, and publication number. 2) Japanese Overall Concordance—a listing of application number with utility model, unexamined and examined patent numbers, application number, and registration number. 3) U.S. Patent Concordance—lists patent numbers, application numbers, and application dates of U.S. patents from 1968 to the present. 4) U.S. Patent Index—contains bibliographic data on patents including International Patent Classification and U.S. Patent Classification numbers. 5) Japanese Priority Index—provides a Japanese patent or utility model number corresponding to a foreign patent based on the same priority application. 6) Japanese Non-priority Index—contains a Japanese patent or utility model publication number corresponding to a foreign patent based on the same applicant or inventor. JAPATIC also holds patent specifications from 1955 to the present from Japan, United States, United Kingdom, West Germany, France, Union of Soviet Socialist Republics, Canada, and Switzerland on 16mm or 35mm microfilm. The patent collection is available for use by the public. COM and microreproduction services are available.

Computer-Based Products and Services: JAPATIC compiles and maintains the computer-readable JAPATIC data base covering Japanese patents, utility models, designs, and trademarks, as well as patents from 49 other countries. The data base contains, for Japanese documents, such data elements as application number and date; publication number and date; registration number and date; priority country name, number, and date; International Patent Classification; Japanese Patent Classification; applicant name; inventor name; title of invention; file history; code of attorney; short summary; abstract; drawing; free keyword; fixed keyword; and JAPATIC classification. For each foreign document, the data base holds country of publication, kind of document, document number, application number and date, publication date, International Patent Classification, priority country and number, priority date, applicant name, inventor name, and title of invention.

The JAPATIC data base is used to offer the following services: 1) PATOLIS—an online information retrieval service which provides Kana and Kanji character and alphanumeric displays of Japanese patents, utility models, industrial designs, and trademarks, as well as U.S. patents and INPADOC data bases. Searches can be performed on a select number of data elements and document types at the client's location via leased lines or the public telephone network. PATOLIS also allows retrieval of all equivalent patent documents issued by different countries based on the same priority application. 2) Batch retrieval services—offered from the JAPATIC data base, services include retrospective searching, SDI, a watch service which monitors the progress of a patent application, retrieval of all patents based on the same priority application, and preparation of statistical tables and graphs. 3) Publication services—patent-related abstracting and indexing publications are issued. The JAPATIC data base is also used to prepare English versions of Japanese patent abstracts on atomic energy for inclusion in the International Nuclear Information System (INIS). Additionally, the CENTER offers data and software for client patent management systems.

Other Services: Additional services include English translations of Japanese patent abstracts.

Clientele/Availability: Services are available without restrictions.

Contact: Shigeake Oda, Assistant Manager of Liaison Department, Japan Patent Information Center. (Telex 222 4152 JAPATI J.)

★634★
JAPAN PHARMACEUTICAL INFORMATION CENTER (JAPIC)
12-15-601, Shibuya 2-Chome   Phone: 03 4061811
Shibuya-ku, Yakugakukaikan   Founded: 1972
Tokyo 150, Japan
Fuminae Kubo, Director General

Staff: 26 Information and library professional; 3 management professional; 6 clerical and nonprofessional.

Related Organizations: Related organizations include the Ministry of Health and Welfare, other government authorities, and professional medical associations.

Description of System or Service: The JAPAN PHARMACEUTICAL INFORMATION CENTER (JAPIC) is a nonprofit foundation which collects, processes, and stores information concerning drugs in order to serve medical facilities, pharmaceutical industries, and other users. JAPIC abstracts and indexes drug package inserts and domestic literature currently available in Japan, as well as foreign information, with emphasis on the regulation and safety of drugs. It disseminates this information through a number of publications and an online bibliographic data base. JAPIC also provides literature searching and utilizes networks with affiliated organizations to supply reprints of original papers. Additional services offered by JAPIC include lectures, subject training, and a telephone drug consultation service.

Scope and/or Subject Matter: All aspects of drugs, especially their regulation and safety.

Input Sources: Information is obtained from drug package inserts, approximately 350 regularly scanned domestic publications, and from foreign publications.

Holdings and Storage Media: Bibliographic information is held in the machine-readable JAPICDOC data base which is updated with approximately 10,000 items per year. JAPIC also maintains a library of approximately 30,000 drug package inserts; subscriptions to 600 periodicals; and books and microfiche.

Publications: 1) Contents (weekly)—contains contents pages from conference proceedings and domestic journals. 2) Joho (JAPIC Weekly Bulletin)—covers foreign news, regulations, side effect information, and other topics. 3) Japan Pharmaceutical Abstracts (monthly)—provides bibliographic citations and abstracts of approximately 200 domestic journals; available in journal form or on cards. 4) Drugs in Japan—provides information on ethical and over-the-counter drugs. 5) List of Adverse Reactions to Drugs Reported in Japanese Clinical Journals.

Computer-Based Products and Services: JAPIC maintains the JAPICDOC data base which corresponds to the printed Japan Pharmaceutical Abstracts journal. The data base is available online and contains bibliographic citations, abstracts, and key words. JAPIC provides information retrieval services from the data base and from commercially available data bases. A Drugs Data Base is in preparation.

Clientele/Availability: Services are available to Center members, which include manufacturers, medical facilities, universities, pharmacists associations, administrative organizations, wholesalers, and others. Services are available to nonmembers on a limited basis.

Remarks: JAPIC is also known as the Nihon Iyaku Joho Center.

Contact: Taisuke Nagayama, Director, Japan Pharmaceutical Information Center.

★635★
JAPAN PUBLICATIONS GUIDE
CPO Box 971   Phone: 03 6618373
Tokyo 100-91, Japan   Founded: 1973
Warren E. Ball, Editor

Staff: 1 Information and library professional; 3 management professional; 2 sales and marketing; 3 clerical and nonprofessional; 4 other.

Description of System or Service: JAPAN PUBLICATIONS GUIDE provides the Japan Publication Guide Service (JPGS), a series of directories and newsletters covering English-language publications and publishers in Japan. JAPAN PUBLICATIONS GUIDE also issues the Japan Directory of Professional Associations (JDPA), a guide to more than 3000 professional associations and similar organizations in Japan. Information from both the JDPA and JPGS is maintained in computer-readable form and special selections are offered from them.

Scope and/or Subject Matter: English-language publications issued in Japan; professional associations and similar organizations in Japan.

Input Sources: Information is acquired from publishers, associations, and other sources.

Holdings and Storage Media: The JPGS Database and the JDPA

Database are maintained in machine-readable form.

Publications: The following publications are available as part of the JPGS service: 1) Japan English Magazine Directory (JEMD)—provides information on 1500 periodicals available from 1000 publishers and includes all periodicals published wholly or partly in English in Japan, including newspapers, magazines, annuals, directories, and other publications that are published regularly or irregularly for sale, without cost, or limited distribution. The JEMD includes a title section, publisher section, and subject section, which lists publications under 110 categories. Information provided for each publication includes title, frequency, average number of pages, page size, weight per issue, price per year, category, language (if not English), editor, and, for about half of the titles, the ISSN. A Hong Kong section is also included. 2) Japan English Books in Print (JEBP)—lists 2900 books, monographs, and substantial booklets published wholly or partly in English in Japan by more than 450 publishers. The JEBP includes a title section, author section, editor section, translation section, and subject section, which lists publications under 100 subject categories. Information provided for each publication includes title, language (if any other than English), author, editor, translator, number of pages, page size, price, and ISBN. A publisher section is also included and contains the name, address, and telephone number of each publisher. 3) Publishers in English in Japan—lists approximately 1500 commercial publishers, government agencies, universities, corporations, and other organizations that publish books or periodicals in English in Japan; includes publisher name, address, and telephone number. 4) JPG Letter (monthly)—4-6 page newsletter. Each of the above publications can also be purchased separately.

JAPAN PUBLICATIONS GUIDE also issues the Japan Directory of Professional Associations (JDPA), a guide to 3850 associations and similar groups, with emphasis on business, technical, and academic groups. The Directory is available for purchase and includes listings by subjects (in 120 categories), Japanese name, and English name. Information provided on each association includes name, address, telephone number, chief executive, contact person, number of members, and publications. An inter-edition update service, JDPA-Update, is also available for purchase. Additionally, JAPAN PUBLICATIONS GUIDE serves as a distributor of other periodicals and publications.

Computer-Based Products and Services: The JAPAN PUBLICATIONS GUIDE maintains the JDPA Database and the JPGS Database. The data bases are used to provide customized printouts and mailing labels. Retrievals can be conducted by any of approximately 100 subject categories. The firm also maintains the Hong Kong English Periodicals and Book Publishers (HKEP&BP) data base and makes information from it available on three printouts: 1) alphabetical listing of magazines, other periodicals, and books; 2) alphabetical listing of publisher names; and 3) JPGS code-order listing of each publisher, its address, and its publications.

Clientele/Availability: Services and publications are available without restrictions.

Contact: Warren E. Ball, Editor, Japan Publications Guide. The Japan Publications Guide Service (JPGS) is distributed by Intercontinental Marketing Corporation, located at Wako 5 Bldg., 1-19-8 Kakigaracho, Nihonbashi, Chouku, Tokyo 103, Japan, and by Pacific Subscription Service, P.O. Box 811 FDR Station, New York, NY 10150.

★636★
JORDAN & SONS LTD.
JORDANS COMPANY INFORMATION
Jordan House Phone: 01-253 3030
47 Brunswick Place
London N1 6EE, England
Ralph D.S. Leake, Director

Staff: 220 Total.

Description of System or Service: JORDANS COMPANY INFORMATION collects, processes, and publishes information on thousands of United Kingdom and overseas companies. Using government files and other sources, it provides search services which include general reports on company files, full company reports, special information from company files, watch services on new accounts, and information on new companies and foreign companies registered in the U.K. The firm also publishes Jordans Surveys, a series of reference books and reports providing detailed financial analyses of major U.K. and foreign-owned companies. Additionally, JORDANS offers the online Jordan Line Services which provides information on approximately 950,000 private and public companies including financial information on 130,000 companies. Information on dissolved companies is also included. Data can be requested through electronic means or on microfiche.

Scope and/or Subject Matter: Business and financial information on privately owned, quoted, or foreign-owned companies in the United Kingdom.

Input Sources: Input is derived from the Companies Registry Office, company financial and credit reports, and from overseas sources.

Holdings and Storage Media: The computer-readable Jordan Line Services data base holds information on approximately 950,000 companies and is updated daily.

Publications: Jordans Surveys include the following publications: 1) Britain's Top 2000 Private Companies (annual)—encyclopedia of private business in the U.K. 2) Britain's Top 1000 Foreign Owned Companies (annual)—financial profiles of leading foreign-owned companies in the United Kingdom. 3) Scotland's Top 500 Companies (annual). 4) Industrial Surveys—more concentrated studies of individual industrial sectors. Publications are available by subscription; several other reports are also issued.

Microform Products and Services: Information on individual companies is available on microfiche.

Computer-Based Products and Services: The online Jordan Line Services is accessible via direct dial or IPSS using computer terminals or communicating microcomputers. Using special text and numeric handling software, the Services provides access to the following data for nearly 1 million registered U.K. companies: details of registered office, date of incorporation, date of last filed accounts, date of last filed annual return, registered number, precise name, date of name change, and other information, including additional financial data on 130,000 of the companies. Companies can be searched by full name, any word appearing in the name, and company number. The Jordan Line Services includes an electronic mail facility which can be used to order additional documents and information on companies. Company information is also available on computer tapes.

Other Services: In addition to the services described above, Jordans provides photocopies of filed accounts or other statutory documents. Name and address labels are available for all companies published in Jordans Surveys.

Clientele/Availability: Services are available through subscription or contract arrangements.

Contact: Ralph D.S. Leake, Director of Information Services, or David Bathurst, Online Services Manager, Jordans Company Information. (Telex 261010.)

K

★637★
K-KONSULT
VA-NYTT
Library
Liljeholmstorget 7
S-117 80 Stockholm, Sweden
Gunnar Dravnieks, Head

Phone: 08 7440000
Service Est: 1970

Staff: 7 Total.

Description of System or Service: VA-NYTT is an abstracts journal and online bibliographic data base providing references to environmental literature with emphasis on water supply, sewage treatment, and solid waste treatment and recovery. Documents referenced in VA-NYTT are available from the K-Konsult library through loans or copying.

Scope and/or Subject Matter: Environmental technology including: water conservation, analysis, supply, and treatment; water pollution and control; sewage systems; sewage treatment; industrial waste water; sludge handling and treatment; solid waste treatment and recovery; industrial waste; air pollution and control; noise pollution and control; the work environment.

Input Sources: Approximately 300 technical journals plus books and technical reports are abstracted for VA-NYTT.

Holdings and Storage Media: The machine-readable data base holds 34,000 references dating from 1970 to the present.

Publications: VA-NYTT (10 issues a year)—available by subscription.

Computer-Based Products and Services: The VA-NYTT data base is searchable online through K-Konsult.

Contact: Gerard Lingre, Documentalist, K-Konsult.

★638★
KENT-BARLOW PUBLICATIONS LTD. (KBP)
Kingsmead House
250 Kings Rd., Chelsea
London SW3 5UE, England
Derek H. Barlow, Partner

Phone: 01-351 2776

Description of System or Service: KENT-BARLOW PUBLICATIONS LTD. (KBP) has developed and markets a number of software products, including data base generation systems, information retrieval software, computer-assisted learning packages, online search communication aids, and integrated office/administrative information systems. KBP software is available for use with a wide range of minicomputers and microcomputers.

Scope and/or Subject Matter: Computer programs for text manipulation and retrieval.

Computer-Based Products and Services: KENT-BARLOW PUBLICATIONS LTD. offers the following software packages: 1) EAGLE—a general purpose data base generation and information retrieval system for both hard and floppy disks. Especially designed for text retrieval, EAGLE offers easy data entry and editing facilities to the records in the data base and generates inverted indexes to all terms other than those included in a stop list. EAGLE permits retrieval by term searches which can be combined with Boolean logic. A number of utility programs are also available which allow alteration of the stop word list, production of a search term frequency count, and print out of selected documents. 2) AQUILA—providing many of the same features as EAGLE, AQUILA offers a record size capability of 2000 characters per record, and entry of up to 100 fields in any one record, 20 of which can be predefined and coded for rapid retrieval. AQUILA also features the provision for entry of nonsearchable data and facilities for data base merging. 3) STRIX—designed for use with more powerful machines, STRIX offers the same basic features as AQUILA and EAGLE as well as the ability to generate data bases with records up to 32,000 characters long. The system allows for 150 separate fields in each record and fields may be searchable either word-by-word or as a whole field. STRIX is also available to operate with an Imtec Ltd. microfilm reader.

4) CORMORANT—an extension of the AQUILA programs, this system encompasses office filing systems and storage of minutes of meetings linked to a word processing system. Currently under development for the Cambridge Health Authority, CORMORANT comprises a number of data base facilities to provide multi-user capabilities. 5) PUFFIN—permits construction of training text interspersed with questions designed to test the user's comprehension as the user proceeds through the text. The user is asked to repond to a question and if the answer is incorrect, the system provides additional learning text and repeats the question. PUFFIN features a built-in scoring system which presents, at the end of the session, a total of the user's attempts, successes, and failures, and calculates a percentage. 6) SWIFT—developed by the University of Strathclyde, SWIFT is a communications aid which assists users in accessing remote data base systems. SWIFT holds separate files of the various online computer dial-up codes, passwords, and log-on procedures. Once communication has been set up with the packet switching system, single key stroke entries send the required passwords and codes to the online computer. Similar files of search logic can also be set up and transmitted automatically or by a single key stroke. A collector file permits the capture on disk of data being transmitted and received. MAGPIE, an enhanced version which will link the system to the AQUILA package, is expected to be made available.

Clientele/Availability: Clients include government, professional, and commercial organizations; services are available without restrictions.

Remarks: Kent-Barlow Information Associates (KBIA), a related organization, provides consulting services in scientific and technical information acquisition, management, and delivery, especially in the area of computer-assisted systems.

Contact: Dr. Anthony K. Kent or Derek Barlow, Partners, Kent-Barlow Publications Ltd. (Telex 268627.)

★639★
KIEL INSTITUTE FOR WORLD ECONOMICS
(Institut fur Weltwirtschaft in Kiel)
NATIONAL LIBRARY OF ECONOMICS
(Zentralbibliothek der Wirtschaftswissenschaften)
Dusternbrooker Weg 120
Postfach 4309
D-2300 Kiel 1, Fed. Rep. of Germany
Dr. Erwin Heidemann, Director

Phone: 0431 8841

Staff: 130 Total.

Description of System or Service: The NATIONAL LIBRARY OF ECONOMICS acquires, catalogs, and indexes books, journals, and other literature on economics from across the world. It provides access to this information through a published bibliography, information searches, and SDI service for catalog cards. Under the SDI service, clients can obtain cards covering all accessioned materials in specified subject areas or geographic regions; they can also obtain index cards for articles in journals of their choice.

Scope and/or Subject Matter: Worldwide coverage of economics, political economics, and related social sciences.

Input Sources: The Library acquires books, periodicals, yearbooks, newspapers, and unpublished literature in all languages; approximately 70,000 items per year are added.

Holdings and Storage Media: Holdings consist of 1.6 million bound volumes; 19,000 current periodicals; and several catalogs holding more than 8 million cards.

Publications: 1) Bibliographie der Wirtschaftswissenschaften (semiannual); 2) Kieler Schrifttumskunden zu Wirtschaft und Gesellschaft (irregular).

Computer-Based Products and Services: Operations of the National Library are in the process of being automated.

Clientele/Availability: There are no restrictions on services.

Contact: Dr. Frauke Siefkes, National Library of Economics; telephone 0431 884365.

★640★
KINOKUNIYA COMPANY LTD.
ASK INFORMATION RETRIEVAL SERVICES
Kakoh Sakuragaoka Bldg. Phone: 03 4634391
3-24, Sakuragaoka-cho, Shibuyaku Service Est: 1972
Tokyo 150, Japan
Isao Miura, General Manager

Staff: 7 Information and library professional; 4 management professional; 2 technicians; 9 sales and marketing; 12 clerical and nonprofessional.

Description of System or Service: ASK INFORMATION RETRIEVAL SERVICES offers computerized retrieval services from publicly available data bases. It also acts as the agent in Japan for DIALOG Information Services, Inc., the NIH-EPA Chemical Information System (CIS), and the ISI Search Network by providing training, consulting, and the publication of Japanese-language user aids and newsletters.

Scope and/or Subject Matter: Science and technology, with emphasis on engineering, chemistry, physics, polymer science, and electronics; social science.

Input Sources: Input consists of magnetic tapes obtained from various government agencies and private organizations and online data bases.

Publications: KINOLIE (monthly)—a newsletter which supplies technical support information to online services users.

Computer-Based Products and Services: The ASK (Alerting-Search Service from Kinokuniya) INFORMATION RETRIEVAL SERVICES provides SDI and retrospective searches from data bases made available by the Institute for Scientific Information (ISI), U.S. National Technical Information Service (NTIS), Chemical Abstracts Service (CAS), Institution of Electrical Engineers, and Engineering Information, Inc. In addition, the service conducts online searches of data bases made available through DIALOG Information Services, Inc., NIH-EPA Chemical Information System (CIS), INKA Online, NEEDS-IR, and HiNET.

Other Services: Additional services include consulting and advisory services to customers developing new libraries; design and programming of information retrieval systems; translation of documentation for online systems; and training seminars on the use of online information retrieval systems.

Clientele/Availability: Services are available by subscription.

Remarks: Kinokuniya Company Ltd. is a bookseller concerned with the sale, promotion, and distribution of Japanese and imported books and journals in hard copy and microform. The firm also offers the KINO MARC service which provides libraries with catalog cards produced from MARC tapes; the cards can be supplied in the original format, or they can be adapted to the Japanese library classification system or a specific library's system. Kinokuniya operates more than 50 outlets in Japan and maintains 3 branches in the United States, including Kinokuniya Publications Service of New York Co., Ltd., 633 Third Ave., Suite 1925, New York, NY 10017; telephone (212) 687-1524. The London office is Kinokuniya Publications Service of London Co., Radnor House 93-97, Regent St., London W1, England; telephone 01-734 3074.

Contact: Shigehisa Nishio, Manager, ASK Information Retrieval Services.

★641★
KLUWER PUBLISHING COMPANY
JURIDICAL DATABANK
(Juridische Databank)
P.O. Box 23 Phone: 05700 91180
NL-7400 GA Deventer, Netherlands Service Est: 1979
Mr. J. Sander E. Hulshoff, General Manager

Staff: 1 Information and library professional; 3 management professional; 2 technicians; 4 sales and marketing; 5 clerical and nonprofessional.

Description of System or Service: The JURIDICAL DATABANK is an online service providing full-text retrieval of Dutch case law, statutes, legal literature, and related information for Dutch law firms and government and business legal departments. The DATABANK holds files corresponding to several Kluwer publications as well as files of information from other publications and from unpublished court cases.

Scope and/or Subject Matter: Civil, penal, international, shipping, and fiscal law.

Input Sources: Input is derived from Kluwer publications, other publications, and from unpublished court cases from various courts.

Holdings and Storage Media: Files are maintained on the system in machine-readable form.

Publications: Kluwer publications accessible in the Databank include the following: 1) Nederlandse Jurisprudentie; 2) Administratiefrechtelijve Beslissingen; 3) Data Juridica; 4) Rechtspraak van de Week; 5) Kort Geding; 6) Schip & Schade; 7) Praktijkgids; 8) Beslissingen in Belastingzaken Nederlandse Belastingrechtspraak.

Computer-Based Products and Services: Accessible online, the JURIDICAL DATABANK system operates under Status software and serves more than 800 users at 200 subscriber locations. The system provides access to information from the eight publications listed above, as well as from publications of other companies and unpublished case law. A number of private files are also maintained.

Clientele/Availability: Available on a subscription basis, services are intended for law firms and government and business legal departments.

Contact: Mr. J. Sander E. Hulshoff, General Manager, Juridical Databank. (Telex 49925.)

★642★
KOMPASS INTERNATIONAL LTD.
Neuhausstr. 4 Phone: 01 478009
CH-8044 Zurich, Switzerland Founded: 1970
Max E. Neuenschwander, Chairman

Related Organizations: KOMPASS has representatives in Australia, Belgium, Brazil, Denmark, Finland, France, Great Britain, Hong Kong, India, Indonesia, Italy, Japan, Korea, Kuwait, Luxembourg, Malaysia, Morocco, Netherlands, Norway, Philippines, Spain, Singapore, Sweden, Switzerland, Taiwan, and Thailand.

Description of System or Service: Through franchises, joint ventures, and subsidiaries, KOMPASS INTERNATIONAL LTD. supplies national industrial directories for countries worldwide. KOMPASS directories are industrial reference books designed to enable small- and medium-sized companies in all areas to obtain comprehensive information on potential customers and suppliers. The directories provide company information on size, activity, products and services, and structure, with an emphasis on information regarding executive management and contact details such as telephone and telex numbers, office hours, and others. In addition to being issued in printed form, many KOMPASS directories are produced as computer-readable data bases and various computerized services are offered. KOMPASS INTERNATIONAL is also implementing a satellite computer system to be used for computerized searching and for exchanging information between subsidiaries.

Scope and/or Subject Matter: Industrial information, including economic, company, and market information, for countries worldwide.

Input Sources: Input is gathered by information officers in the various countries who regularly visit selected companies.

Holdings and Storage Media: Numerous computer-readable data bases are maintained by Kompass publishers.

Publications: Available for some 20 countries, KOMPASS country directories list firms alphabetically by geographic location and by products and services. KOMPASS also offers specific industry directories supplying thorough coverage of one industry.

Computer-Based Products and Services: KOMPASS INTERNATIONAL works in cooperation with KC Information Systems Ltd. which operates computerized direct access information systems to coordinate standardization of data for directories produced by KOMPASS subsidiaries. Additionally, computerized searches of selected KOMPASS information are conducted to produce custom lists and mailing labels.

Clientele/Availability: Clients include firms involved in national and international trade.

Contact: Anne Heidrich, Secretary, Kompass International Ltd.

★643★
KONINKLIJKE VERMANDE B.V.
Postbus 20
Platinastr. 33
NL-5200 AA Lelystad, Netherlands
W.G.A. Van der Weyden, Head
Phone: 02550 19013

Description of System or Service: KONINKLIJKE VERMANDE B.V. is a publishing and printing firm which provides legal and other information in loose-leaf, bound, machine-readable, or periodical form tailored to the specific needs of user groups. The firm also maintains the computer-readable NLEX data base, which contains the full text of Dutch legislation, and the NSUB data base, which provides information on Dutch subsidies to business. Additionally, KONINKLIJKE VERMANDE provides conversion of client files or text to printed matter or machine-readable form, and it offers photocomposition services.

Scope and/or Subject Matter: Dutch legislation and other topics.

Input Sources: Input for the NLEX data base consists of the full text of loose-leaf juridical issues.

Holdings and Storage Media: The NSUB and NLEX data bases are held in machine-readable form. NLEX contains approximately 1200 records and is updated monthly. The firm also maintains a small library.

Publications: A variety of publications, including approximately 200 loose-leaf titles in the legal field, are available on a subscription or individual order basis. A Dutch-language user's manual for the NLEX data base is also issued.

Computer-Based Products and Services: KONINKLIJKE VERMANDE B.V. produces the NLEX data base which is accessible online through BELINDIS (Belgian Information and Dissemination Service), a Euronet DIANE host. NLEX contains the full text of laws, decrees, and treaties of the Netherlands. The firm also produces the NSUB data base which contains information on Dutch subsidies for business organizations. Additionally, the firm provides conversion of client files to machine-readable form, and it furnishes other computer services including maintenance of mailing lists.

Clientele/Availability: Primary clients are lawyers in the public and private sectors.

Contact: R.M.M. Mulder, Marketing Manager, Koninklijke Vermande B.V.

★644★
KOREA ADVANCED INSTITUTE OF SCIENCE AND TECHNOLOGY (KAIST)
EXPERIENCED LIBRARIANS AND INFORMATION PERSONNEL IN THE DEVELOPING COUNTRIES OF ASIA AND OCEANIA (ELIPA)
KAIST Library
P.O. Box 131, Dong Dae Mun
Seoul 133-00, Korea
Mr. Ke Hong Park, Head Librarian
Phone: 02 9673692
Service Est: 1980

Staff: 7 Management professional; 1 technician; 1 sales and marketing; 7 other.

Related Organizations: ELIPA is jointly sponsored by KAIST, the International Development Research Centre (IDRC), the International Federation of Library Associations and Institutions (IFLA), and the Commission for Asia and Oceania, International Federation for Documentation (FID/CAO).

Description of System or Service: EXPERIENCED LIBRARIANS AND INFORMATION PERSONNEL IN THE DEVELOPING COUNTRIES OF ASIA AND OCEANIA (ELIPA) is a computer-readable register of library and information specialists available for consulting assignments, exchange programs, or employment. Currently the data base covers specialists in Hong Kong, Indonesia, Korea, Malaysia, Papua New Guinea, Philippines, Singapore, Sri Lanka, Taiwan, and Thailand; other countries may be included in the future. ELIPA is maintained online at KAIST for the provision of search services.

Scope and/or Subject Matter: Library and information science personnel in developing countries of Asia and Oceania.

Input Sources: Input is derived from questionnaires completed by eligible persons.

Holdings and Storage Media: The ELIPA data base is held online.

Computer-Based Products and Services: ELIPA is maintained online for providing interested organizations and institutions with profiles of library or information experts in the region. Each record in ELIPA includes personal name, position, address, education, experience, special training, language ability, professional interest or speciality, and the length of time the person is available for consultancy or staff position.

Clientele/Availability: Clients include international organizations, regional institutions, learned societies, and schools. Commercial use of the information is prohibited.

Contact: Mr. Ke Hong Park, Head Librarian, Korea Advanced Institute of Science and Technology Library. (Telex K27380 KISTROK.)

★645★
KOREA INSTITUTE FOR INDUSTRIAL ECONOMICS AND TECHNOLOGY (KIET)
P.O. Box 205
Cheong Ryang
Seoul 131, Korea
Hiwhoa Moon, President
Phone: 9656211
Founded: 1982

Staff: 400 Total.

Related Organizations: The Institute is under the supervision of and receives financial support from the Korean Ministry of Commerce and Industry.

Description of System or Service: The KOREAN INSTITUTE FOR INDUSTRIAL ECONOMICS AND TECHNOLOGY (KIET) is engaged in the following three major activities: 1) Economic Research. The research undertaken includes area studies, industry studies, international economic surveys, and special topic analyses. The purpose of the research is to provide pertinent information and policy alternatives for government and industry in order to assist industrial development. 2) Information Dissemination. KIET is the national center for information on industrial technology and international market environments. To facilitate the timely dissemination of information, KIET operates a computerized data bank service utilizing data bases produced at KIET, other domestic data bases, and international commercially available data bases. KIET also maintains six regional information services branches and a number of field service teams that visit industries to provide information-related advice. 3) Business Extension. Business consultation and extension services are provided to improve the productivity and competitiveness of small- and medium-sized firms in particular.

Scope and/or Subject Matter: All areas of science and technology and industrial economics.

Input Sources: The Institute collects information in computer-readable and hardcopy forms from around the world.

Holdings and Storage Media: Machine-readable holdings consist of 9 commercially available data bases totaling nearly 6 million records. Library holdings comprise 30,000 bound volumes; 6000 reports; and subscriptions to 9000 periodicals.

Publications: KIET issues several dozen periodicals, directories, and other titles, among which are the following: 1) Current Bibliographies on Science and Technology (monthly)—available in 6 subject areas. 2) Current Listing of Articles in Science and Technolgy Journals (monthly). 3) Current Listing of Articles in Social Science Journals (monthly). 4) Foreign Patents Information Bulletin (every 10 days). 5) Korean Patent Abstracts (monthly). 6) Korean Scientific Abstracts (bimonthly). 7) Korean Medical Abstracts (quarterly).

Computer-Based Products and Services: KIET provides computerized information retrieval and SDI services from the following data bases it holds in-house: AGRIS, CA Search, CIN, COMPENDEX, INSPEC, ISMEC, NTIS, WPI, and MOST (Instruments of Testing and Research in Korea). KIET also provides services from internal data bases and files produced by the Korean Information Processing System (KIPS), including the Korean Periodicals Index, Directory of On-going Research in Korea, List of Theses for the Doctor's and Master's Degree in Korea, and Directory of Researchers in Korean Studies. Additionally, KIET accesses international online host services.

Clientele/Availability: KIET serves industry research and development institutes, academic institutions, and government agencies.

Remarks: KIET was established by the merger of the Korea International Economic Institute (KIEI) and the Korea Scientific and Technological Information Center (KORSTIC).

Contact: Youn Kyun Mok, Director, Department of Information Resources, Korean Institute for Industrial Economics and Technology. (Telex K25850.)

★646★
KTS INFORMATION SYSTEMS
(KTS Informations-Systeme GmbH)
Leopoldstr. 87
D-8000 Munich 40, Fed. Rep. of
　Germany
H.E. Seelbach, Head
Phone: 089 398057
Founded: 1979

Staff: 6 Technicians.

Description of System or Service: KTS INFORMATION SYSTEMS is a systems house specializing in development, consultation, and distribution of computer-aided information systems. It makes available the DOMESTIC minicomputer turnkey system for libraries and information centers, which it developed in conjunction with the Israel National Center for Scientific and Technological Information (see separate entry). KTS INFORMATION SYSTEMS also provides other information retrieval software for minicomputers and mainframes.

Scope and/or Subject Matter: Information retrieval systems.

Computer-Based Products and Services: KTS Information Systems provides software and turnkey systems.

Clientele/Availability: Clients include libraries, information centers, and others.

Contact: H.E. Seelbach, Head, KTS Information Systems.

★647★
KUGLER PUBLICATIONS
P.O. Box 516
NL-1180 AM Amstelveen, Netherlands
Simon Kugler, Director
Phone: 020 278070
Founded: 1974

Staff: 1 Management professional; 1 sales and marketing; 1 clerical and nonprofessional.

Description of System or Service: KUGLER PUBLICATIONS is the publisher of Criminology & Penology Abstracts, Police Science Abstracts, and other journals and books on criminology, biology, and medicine. Information from the abstracts services is held in computer-readable form and retrieval services are provided.

Scope and/or Subject Matter: Criminology, penology, police science, forensic sciences, medicine, biology.

Input Sources: Articles in major worldwide publications on criminology, police science, and related fields are scanned and evaluated for input.

Holdings and Storage Media: Abstracts and citations published in the two journals since 1981 are held in machine-readable form.

Publications: 1) Criminology & Penology Abstracts (six per year)—provides more than 3000 abstracts per year which cover the etiology of crime and juvenile delinquency, the control and treatment of offenders, criminal procedure, and the administration of justice. Each issue includes a subject and author index; both are cumulated annually. 2) Police Science Abstracts (six per year)—supplies more than 1500 abstracts per year in the areas of police science, forensic sciences, and forensic medicine. Each issue includes a subject and author index; both are cumulated annually. 3) Fossilium Catalogus I: Animalia. 4) Fossilium Catalogus II: Plantae. In the United States, publications can be ordered from Kugler Publishing, P.O. Box 5794, Berkeley, CA 94705.

Computer-Based Products and Services: Kugler Publications maintains a computer-readable data base of titles, abstracts, and indexes published in its abstracts journals. Computerized search services are offered from the data base.

Clientele/Availability: Publications and services are available without restrictions.

Contact: Simon Kugler, Director, Kugler Publications.

★648★
KYUSHU UNIVERSITY
**RESEARCH INSTITUTE OF FUNDAMENTAL INFORMATION
　SCIENCE**
10-1, Hakozaki 6-Chome
Higashi-ku, Fukuoka-shi
Fukuoka City 812, Japan
Chooichiro Asano, Director
Phone: 092 6411101
Service Est: 1967

Staff: 10 Total.

Description of System or Service: The RESEARCH INSTITUTE OF FUNDAMENTAL INFORMATION SCIENCE was established to plan and promote research activities covering all areas of information science. The INSTITUTE manages three divisions to attain its objectives: Information Theory Division, Information Processing Division, and Information Experiment Division. Reports are issued and a library is maintained by the INSTITUTE.

Scope and/or Subject Matter: Information science, including cybernetics, bionics, computer science, library science, and other areas.

Holdings and Storage Media: The Institute maintains a library of 2600 bound volumes and subscriptions to 19 periodicals.

Publications: Research reports are issued irregularly.

Clientele/Availability: Chief clients are Kyushu University faculties.

Contact: Mrs. Keiko Mukaida, or Shun-ichi Takeya, Associate Professor, Research Institute of Fundamental Information Science.

L

★649★
LANGTON ELECTRONIC PUBLISHING SYSTEMS LTD.
133 Oxford St.
London W1R 1TD, England
W.X. Wilson, Managing Director
Phone: 01-434 1031
Founded: 1974

Staff: 6 Management professional; 38 technicians; 6 sales and marketing; 8 clerical and nonprofessional; 2 other.

Related Organizations: AGB Research Plc. is the parent organization.

Description of System or Service: LANGTON ELECTRONIC PUBLISHING SYSTEMS LTD. develops and markets a range of computer-based products and systems for the electronic publishing field. It offers several software products and services which use computer technology to facilitate information retrieval, processing, and dissemination, including online retrieval, text editing, word processing, and publishing on laser printers, photocomposers, microforms, videotex, and optical discs.

Scope and/or Subject Matter: Design of computer-based information retrieval, processing, and publishing systems; videotex systems.

Input Sources: Input consists of printed or machine-readable textual information supplied by clients.

Microform Products and Services: The firm can produce microfiche containing fully composed frames and incorporating advanced indexing and cross-referencing features.

Computer-Based Products and Services: LANGTON ELECTRONIC PUBLISHING SYSTEMS LTD. offers several software packages and systems: 1) PIII—videotex system for users of IBM mainframes running under CICS/VS. Fully integrated with data processing functions, it combines the simplicity of videotex with the full power of the mainframe. PIII includes a variety of communications options including the Videogate concentrator from Micro Scope Ltd. 2) PREVIEW—a software system which assists the conversion of existing computer files to videotex files and facilitates the loading and maintenance of data bases on videotex systems. 3) COMPUSET—a photocomposition software package used to typeset client materials. 4) FICHE BUILDER—composes complete publications of text and graphics in microform, builds indexes, and compiles the fiche and frame references for inclusion in indexes and cross references. 5) ARTWORK MANAGER—a graphics data base management system which operates as a stand-alone management system and interfaces with artwork creation, CAD/CAM, editing systems, and publication systems. It also maintains a randomly accessible data base from which graphics can be automatically extracted. 6) FORMAT—a software package for preparing files containing composition commands or copymarks needed by XICS composition packages. LANGTON also markets METAFORM, an interactive work station which runs on the PERQ 2 graphics minicomputer and is designed to maximize the productivity of the Xerox 9700 type laser printers. Additionally, LANGTON is involved in the development of videodisc technology and its use for electronic publishing.

Other Services: The firm also provides support services for electronic publishing clients using its software systems.

Clientele/Availability: Primary clients are the information and communications industries.

Contact: W.X. Wilson, Managing Director, or G. Stevens, Marketing Services, Langton Electronic Publishing Systems Ltd. (Telex 21766.)

★650★
LARRATT (RICHARD) AND ASSOCIATES LTD.
R.R. 1
Demorestville, ON, Canada K0K 1W0
Richard Larratt, Head
Phone: (613) 476-5309
Founded: 1973

Staff: 2 Management professional.

Description of System or Service: RICHARD LARRATT AND ASSOCIATES LTD. provides consulting and business case studies for videotex and teletext firms. The company performs technical difficulty and cross-media analyses, system integration cost estimates, and consumer acceptance studies.

Scope and/or Subject Matter: Videotex and teletext consulting.

Clientele/Availability: Primary clients are companies wishing to offer videotex or teletext services to the home market.

Contact: Kathleen Vowinckel, Media Analyst, Richard Larratt and Associates Ltd.

★651★
LATIN AMERICAN NEWSLETTERS LTD. (LAN)
Boundary House
91-93 Charterhouse St.
London BEC1M 6LN, England
Rodolfo H. Terragno, Publisher
Phone: 01-251 0012
Founded: 1967

Staff: Approximately 30 total.

Description of System or Service: LATIN AMERICAN NEWSLETTERS LTD. (LAN) publishes several newsletters covering economic, political, and social developments in Latin America and the Caribbean. Information from the publications is available online through the NEXIS system.

Scope and/or Subject Matter: Economic, political, and social developments in Latin America and the Caribbean, including Brazil, Mexico, Central America, and the Andean and Southern Cone regions.

Input Sources: Information is collected from correspondents and analysts in every Latin American country and from computer searches of the LAN data base.

Holdings and Storage Media: The computer-readable LAN data base on NEXIS holds all issues of all English-language newsletters since 1967.

Publications: 1) Latin America Weekly Report (50 issues per year). 2) Informe Latinoamericano (50 issues per year)—in Spanish. 3) Brazil Report (10 issues per year). 4) Mexico and Central America Report (10 issues per year). 5) Caribbean Report (10 issues per year). 6) Andean Group Report (10 issues per year). 7) Southern Cone Report (10 issues per year). 8) Special Reports (6 issues per year). 9) Informes Especiales (6 issues per year)—in Spanish. 10) Latin America Commodities Report (25 issues per year)—in cooperation with ALA Publishing Group. 11) Washington Letter on Latin America (25 issues per year)—in cooperation with Washington Business Information, Inc.

Computer-Based Products and Services: The full text of LAN newsletters from 1967 to date may be searched online through Mead Data Central's NEXIS system.

Clientele/Availability: Clients include a wide range of business, government, academic, and other institutions.

Contact: Christopher Farley, General Manager, Latin American Newsletters Ltd.

★652★
LAVAL UNIVERSITY LIBRARY
(Universite Laval Bibliotheque)
SDI/LAVAL & TELEREFERENCE SERVICE
Cite Universitaire
Quebec, PQ, Canada G1K 7P4
Phone: (418) 656-3969
Service Est: 1973

Staff: Reference staff totals approximately 30 information and library professional.

Description of System or Service: The SDI/LAVAL & TELEREFERENCE SERVICE is the unit within the Laval University Library responsible for providing computerized information retrieval services. It offers batch-mode and online current awareness and retrospective searching from a variety of commercially available and locally generated data bases.

Scope and/or Subject Matter: All subjects.

Input Sources: Commercially available and local internal data bases are used.

Computer-Based Products and Services: The SERVICE provides online searches from data bases available through the following external systems: DIALOG Information Services, Inc., System Development Corporation (SDC), QL Systems Limited, U.S. National

Library of Medicine, CAN/OLE, CAN/SDI, RESORS (Canadian Center for Remote Sensing), CANSIM (Statistics Canada), MINISIS (IDRC), Bibliographic Retrieval Services (BRS), IST-Informatheque Inc., Telesystemes Questel, Pergamon InfoLine Ltd., and Info Globe (The Globe and Mail). Additionally, the SERVICE uses several data bases produced partially or totally at Laval University. These include ACUL, a data base for library acquisitions; and CIRCUL, the library circulation data base.

Other Services: Services provided in support of computerized searching include design and management of user interest profiles, manual literature searching, information counseling, and traditional reference services. The SERVICE also participates in RIBLIN, a shared-cataloging system for libraries in Quebec and Ontario.

Clientele/Availability: Services are available to the Laval academic community, the Quebec community, and others.

Remarks: SDI/Laval is also known as DSI/Laval (Diffusion Selective de l'Information).

Contact: Doris Dufour, Science Library, or Helene Genest, General Library, Laval University.

★653★
LEAGUE OF ARAB STATES
LEAGUE OF ARAB STATES DOCUMENTATION AND INFORMATION CENTER (ALDOC)
37, Khereddine Pacha St. Phone: 890100
Tunis, Tunisia Service Est: 1980
Mrs. Faria Zahawi, Director

Staff: 68 Total.

Related Organizations: Related organizations include the United Nations Development Programme (UNDP) and the United Nations Educational, Scientific and Cultural Organization (UNESCO).

Description of System or Service: The LEAGUE OF ARAB STATES DOCUMENTATION AND INFORMATION CENTER (ALDOC) has the following objectives: to meet the information needs of the League and its 22 member states at every user level; to build a comprehensive documentation base for the League; to develop and coordinate the information activities of the Arab region; and to provide technical assistance to other documentation and information centers in the Arab world. ALDOC is divided into four departments, including information processing, library and information services, information technology, and the League of Arab States Information System (ALIS). Among its services, the CENTER issues publications and maintains bibliographic and nonbibliographic computer-readable data bases.

Scope and/or Subject Matter: Issues of interest to the League and its member states, including politics, economy, legal, military, social, international affairs, current news, communications, and other topics.

Input Sources: Information is gathered from League of Arab States documents, national and international documents, periodicals, reference work, books, data banks, and other sources.

Holdings and Storage Media: ALDOC holdings include more than 11,600 bound volumes; subscriptions to 1600 periodicals; and magnetic tapes and microforms.

Publications: 1) ALIF Index (quarterly); 2) accessions list (monthly); 3) periodicals bulletin.

Computer-Based Products and Services: The LEAGUE OF ARAB STATES DOCUMENTATION AND INFORMATION CENTER maintains the bibliographic ALDOC data base and a nonbibliographic data base of trade statistics. Both files are held online.

Other Services: ALDOC also offers training for documentalists and information specialists from the Arab world.

Clientele/Availability: Clients include the General Secretariat of the League of Arab States, national and international Arab organizations, and professionals from the Arab world and abroad.

Projected Publications and Services: A number of products and services are planned by ALDOC, including a thesaurus, additional data bases and publications, and SDI and current awareness services.

Contact: Mrs. Faria Zahawi, Director, League of Arab States Documentation and Information Center. (Telex 13241.)

★654★
LEARNED INFORMATION LTD.
Besselsleigh Rd. Phone: 0865 730275
Abingdon Founded: 1977
Oxford OX13 6LG, England
Roger Bilboul, Publisher

Staff: 3 Information and library professional; 3 management professional; 2 sales and marketing; 10 clerical and nonprofessional; 6 other.

Description of System or Service: LEARNED INFORMATION LTD. provides publishing, data base production and distribution, consulting, and other services in the online information field. Among its publications are the Eusidic Database Guide, Online Review, Electronic Publishing Review, The Electronic Library, and Information Today. LEARNED INFORMATION produces the DIANE Guide data base, a guide to data bases and hosts available through Euronet DIANE, and distributes the Mideast File (MEF) data base and its corresponding print journal. The firm also provides consulting services to industry and commerce. Additionally, LEARNED INFORMATION organizes the annual National Online Meeting in New York and the International Online Information Meeting in London.

Scope and/or Subject Matter: Online information retrieval, electronic publishing, videotex, library and information sciences.

Input Sources: Information for the DIANE Guide data base is obtained from data base producers and hosts which are available through Euronet DIANE.

Holdings and Storage Media: The machine-readable DIANE Guide data base contains information on approximately 500 data bases; it is updated regularly. The Mideast File data base is also held in machine-readable form.

Publications: 1) Eusidic Database Guide (every two years)—published in association with the European Association of Information Services. Covering machine-readable data bases, producers, vendors, and networks, it consists of a main section of organization listings and data base, subject, network, and geographical indexes. 2) Online Review - The International Journal of Online Information Systems (bimonthly)—available by subscription; includes news items, book reviews, calendar of events, articles from experts, and other features. 3) Electronic Publishing Review - The International Journal for the Transfer of Published Information via Videotex and Online Media (quarterly)—available by subscription; includes news items and articles. 4) Monitor (monthly)—available by subscription; provides analytical reviews of current events in the online and electronic publishing industries. 5) The Electronic Library - The International Journal for Minicomputer, Microcomputer & Software Applications in Libraries (quarterly)—available by subscription. 6) Information Today (ten per year)—available by subscription; newspaper which focuses on the electronic delivery of information with emphasis on online data base retrieval services. 7) Information Trade Directory (every two years)—directory of information products and services; published in the U.S. by R.R. Bowker Company as Information Industry Market Place. 8) Mideast File (quarterly)—available by subscription; abstracting and indexing journal covering periodical and other literature dealing with all aspects of Middle East countries. 9) Proceedings of the national and international online meetings (annual). 10) Cumulative Index Series—consists of single indexes, by author and subject, to important serials. Learned Information also issues user aids and monographs. A catalog of the firm's publications is available from it on request.

Computer-Based Products and Services: LEARNED INFORMATION produces the DIANE Guide data base under contract with the Commission of the European Communities (CEC). Commercially available online through ECHO (European Commission Host Organization), the data base provides information on data base producers, data bases and data banks, and hosts accessible through Euronet DIANE. A typical citation for a data base producer includes organization name, country, organization type, activities, services, data bases produced, and host. Citations for data bases include data base name, type, update information, language, sources, abstract, producer, and host. LEARNED INFORMATION also distributes the Mideast (MEF) data base and makes it available on magnetic tape. Additionally, LEARNED INFORMATION makes available the Connect software package. Connect is designed for use with online information retrieval and electronic mail services. It allows for the uploading and downloading of information, including log on procedures and prepared search profiles. Connect is available for use on a number of microcomputers.

Clientele/Availability: Services and products are available for purchase and/or subscription.

Contact: Roger Bilboul, Publisher, or J.A. Ozimek, Marketing Manager, Learned Information Ltd. (Telex 837704 INFORMG.) The firm's U.S. office is located at The Anderson House, Stokes Rd., Medford, NJ 08055; telephone (609) 654-6266.

★655★
LEATHERHEAD FOOD RESEARCH ASSOCIATION INFORMATION AND LIBRARY SERVICES
Randalls Rd.　　　　　　　　　　　Phone: 76761
Leatherhead, Surrey KT22 7RY, England

Special Note: The above name, address, and telephone number have been verified for this edition, although no questionnaire response was received. The following text is reprinted from the 5th edition.

Staff: 19 Information and library professional; 2 management professional; 20 clerical and nonprofessional.

Description of System or Service: The INFORMATION AND LIBRARY SERVICES provides Association members with reference services in the area of food processing and technology. It produces the Computer Assisted Information Retrieval System (CAIRS) data base which is used for preparing current awareness publications and for providing literature searches and SDI.

Scope and/or Subject Matter: Food science and technology, nutrition, analytical chemistry, microbiology.

Input Sources: Input is derived from primary and secondary journals, standards, British and foreign patents, translations, books, and conference proceedings.

Holdings and Storage Media: The machine-readable CAIRS data base holds more than 50,000 references dating from 1973 to the present. The library collection consists of 10,000 volumes and subscriptions to 650 periodicals.

Publications: 1) Food Patents (monthly)—selected references to British and foreign patents in food science and technology. 2) Food Topics (every two months)—references to latest literature grouped in subject areas of general interest. Both publications are computer-produced. The Association also publishes a monthly abstracts journal, bibliographies, guides, and legislation manuals.

Computer-Based Products and Services: CAIRS is used to provide computerized search and SDI services. Also available is an online searching service to which members can subscribe.

Other Services: Additional services offered include manual literature searching, inquiry answering, and photocopying.

Clientele/Availability: Services are available to companies who are members of the Association; nonmembers may subscribe to certain services on a fee basis.

Remarks: The Association is also known as the British Food Manufacturing Industries Research Association. The CAIRS data base was formerly called the FRANCIS (Food Research Association Computerized Information Services) data base.

Contact: Head, Information and Library Services. (Telex 929846.)

★656★
LEGAL TECHNOLOGY GROUP (LTG)
58 S. Eaton Place　　　　　　　　　Phone: 01-730 8040
London SW1W 9JJ, England　　　　Founded: 1982
Andrew J.M. Trew, Director

Staff: 1 Information and library professional; 2 management professional; 1 technician; 2 sales and marketing; 1 clerical and nonprofessional.

Related Organizations: The parent organization of the Legal Technology Group is Legal Technology Ltd. Other supporting organizations include LTG Research Ltd.; the Institute of Law and Technology, which conducts academic research and training in computer law and technology for lawyers and government; and the Videotex Industry Association Ltd., the trade association for viewdata and teletext in the United Kingdom.

Description of System or Service: The LEGAL TECHNOLOGY GROUP (LTG) is a group of lawyers and computer specialists offering legal information brokerage and a range of consultancy services on information technology. LTG provides computerized search services for lawyers, patent agents, and others using most major United Kingdom, European, and U.S. retrieval systems. The GROUP also produces two data bases and offers a videotex software package for microcomputers. Additionally, LTG is currently working in association with national and international organizations, such as the British Broadcasting Corporation (BBC), the National Physical Laboratory, and the European Law Centre, on a number of projects, including the following: 1) Software development—training, educational, and legal diagnostic software for microcomputer, minicomputer, and mainframe applications. 2) Viewdata applications—LTG is developing a wide range of videotex applications for legal information. Current projects utilize both public and private viewdata systems and will shortly extend into teletext services. The GROUP is also working on enhancing the Prestel indexes for retrieval of legal information and on design of legal data bases for local government and overseas users. 3) Systems evaluation—testing of legal computer systems and preparation of independent reports for prospective users. 4) Education and training—provision of introductory and specialist conferences, seminars, and training courses in legal technology. 5) Consultancy and research—advice to lawyers and others on systems, software, and the applications of legal technology; continuing research into appropriate technology for legal use. 6) Information retrieval—provides the Golden Retriever intermediary services from legal data bases in the U.K., U.S., and Europe.

Scope and/or Subject Matter: Interfaces between law, legal technology, and the use of legal information; data bases on trade and environmental law.

Input Sources: Input for the LTG data bases is derived from published legal references and other sources.

Holdings and Storage Media: LTG maintains two computer-readable data bases in viewdata format.

Publications: Legal Technology (monthly).

Computer-Based Products and Services: The LEGAL TECHNOLOGY GROUP provides computerized information retrieval from more than 50 European and American legal systems, including Eurolex, WESTLAW (West Publishing Company), CELEX, and LAWTEL. Clients can request a search by mail or telephone. Lawyers with experience in using the retrieval systems conduct the search and help the user formulate search strategy and select the data base. Search results are printed out and returned by post, messenger, or, if necessary, read over the telephone. LTG also maintains the computer-readable Trade Descriptions Law data base in viewdata format. The data base contains abstracts of cases and statutes. Under development is a second data base, Commonwealth Environmental Laws. Additionally, the GROUP offers LAWTERM, a terminal videotex software package which enables a BBC microcomputer to access the Eurolex retrieval service. With LAWTERM, the user can copy information from Eurolex into a disk file, which can then be edited with a word processing package, permitting parts of the search to be saved and incorporated directly into a letter, opinion, or other legal correspondence. Under development is a version that will enable the user to construct search strategy offline, and then run the search automatically when online.

Clientele/Availability: Clients include lawyers as well as local government and international company legal departments.

Contact: Andrew J.M. Trew, Director, Legal Technology Group. The LTG information service is located at 17 Fleet St., London EC4, England.

★657★
LEIGH-BELL (PETER) & ASSOCIATES LTD.
1302 Dunbar Rd.
Burlington, ON, Canada L7P 2J9
Peter Leigh-Bell, President
Phone: (416) 634-0012
Founded: 1969

Special Note: The above name, address, and telephone number have been verified for this edition, although no questionnaire response was received. The following text is reprinted from the 5th edition.

Staff: 1 Information and library professional; 3 management professional; 10 technicians.

Related Organizations: Peter Leigh-Bell & Associates Ltd. is affiliated with Art Benjamin Associates Ltd.

Description of System or Service: PETER LEIGH-BELL & ASSOCIATES LTD. is a firm of information scientists and system consultants specializing in cost-efficient electronic text retrieval and print-to-disk conversion for office systems and information vending. In support of this work, the firm has developed the Text Query System (TQS), which is available for installation on most micro, mini, or large computers or through time-sharing. The ASSOCIATES also offers seminars in information science and advanced technologies.

Scope and/or Subject Matter: Automated text storage and retrieval; conversion of print to disk.

Input Sources: Information in print or computer-readable forms is processed.

Holdings and Storage Media: Data are maintained on magnetic tape or disk, or on video disks.

Computer-Based Products and Services: The ASSOCIATES offers time-shared access to its TQS text storage and retrieval system, which is also available for installation on a variety of computers. Additionally, the firm provides information systems design or upgrading.

Clientele/Availability: Services are intended for use by office automation projects, information vendors, and libraries.

Contact: Peter Leigh-Bell, President.

★658★
LIBRARY & INFORMATION CONSULTANTS LTD. (LINC)
9747 93rd Ave.
Edmonton, AB, Canada T6E 2V8
Ilona Kennedy, President
Phone: (403) 433-4867
Founded: 1978

Staff: Approximately 5 total.

Description of System or Service: LIBRARY & INFORMATION CONSULTANTS LTD. (LINC) provides information consulting and research services for businesses, government agencies, professional organizations, and other clients. Services include designing and evaluating information systems and services, developing indexing and records systems, setting up libraries, conducting literature searches, providing document retrieval, hiring and training information personnel, and holding seminars in research and library techniques.

Scope and/or Subject Matter: Library and information systems and services in all subject areas.

Clientele/Availability: Services are available without restrictions.

Contact: Ilona Kennedy, President, Library & Information Consultants Ltd.

★659★
LIBRARY AND INFORMATION RESEARCH GROUP (LIRG)
The Library
Newcastle upon Tyne Polytechnic
Newcastle upon Tyne NE1 8ST, England
Liz McDowell, Chairman
Phone: 0632 326002
Founded: 1977

Description of System or Service: The LIBRARY AND INFORMATION RESEARCH GROUP (LIRG) is an independent association that promotes awareness of the need for research and investigation in the fields of library and information work. The GROUP is concerned with the need to bridge the gap between library research and practice, and with ensuring the application of research findings. The pursuit and development of research methodology and methods is also emphasized. LIRG holds meetings and seminars and publishes a newsletter.

Scope and/or Subject Matter: Research and its applications in the library and information fields.

Publications: Library and Information Research News-LIRN (quarterly)—newsletter which carries the official notices and meeting reports of LIRG as well as research reports, news items, letters, and reviews.

Clientele/Availability: Membership in the Library and Information Research Group is open to individuals throughout the world.

Remarks: The Group has entered into an association agreement with the Library Association.

Contact: Liz McDowell, Chairman, Library and Information Research Group.

★660★
LIBRARY ASSOCIATION PUBLISHING LTD.
BRITISH HUMANITIES INDEX (BHI)
7 Ridgmount St.
London WC1E 7AE, England
Lyn Duffus, Editor
Phone: 01-636 7543
Service Est: 1915

Staff: 4 Information and library professional.

Description of System or Service: The BRITISH HUMANITIES INDEX (BHI) is a computer-produced journal providing subject access to approximately 400 British journals. It is available as a hardcopy publication and on microfilm.

Scope and/or Subject Matter: Arts and humanities, including archeology, criminology, education, history, literature, music, psychology, sociology, television, theater, transportation, and women's studies.

Input Sources: Input is derived from British journal literature.

Publications: British Humanities Index (quarterly, annual cumulation)—subject index to journals in the arts and humanities.

Microform Products and Services: Microfilm of the INDEX may be obtained from Oxford Microform Publications, 19a Paradise St., Oxford OX1 1LD, England.

Computer-Based Products and Services: Computer assistance is employed to speed production of the journal and to assist in the systematization of the indexing; however, direct access to the data base is currently not available.

Clientele/Availability: The Index is available by subscription.

Contact: Lyn Duffus, Editor, British Humanities Index. (Telex 21897 LALDN G.)

★661★
LIBRARY ASSOCIATION PUBLISHING LTD.
CURRENT RESEARCH IN LIBRARY & INFORMATION SCIENCE
7 Ridgmount St.
London WC1E 7AE, England
Mrs. P.T. Biggs, Editor
Phone: 01-636 7543
Service Est: 1983

Staff: 1 Information and library professional; 2 clerical and nonprofessional.

Description of System or Service: CURRENT RESEARCH IN LIBRARY & INFORMATION SCIENCE is a quarterly guide to international research and development work in librarianship, information science, archives, documentation, and the information aspects of other fields. It is intended to assist workers with research and operative problems in identifying projects of use to them, and to assist researchers by publicizing their projects. The publication also facilitates the international exchange of research information through the Federation Internationale de Documentation (FID), which uses the contents of CURRENT RESEARCH to form part of the FID Research Referral Service. CURRENT RESEARCH focuses on organization, doctoral, and post-doctoral research projects, and also contains a special section listing predoctoral theses and dissertations. CURRENT RESEARCH is available as a printed publication or on magnetic tape, and is expected to be offered as an online data base through major international vendors.

Scope and/or Subject Matter: Research and development in library and information science, archives, management, publishing and printing, reading habits, telecommunications and computing, education, and reprography.

Input Sources: New research project descriptions are gathered via questionnaire from researchers in 34 countries. Published descriptions are submitted to the researchers annually for updating.

Holdings and Storage Media: Research project data are maintained in computer-readable form.

Publications: CURRENT RESEARCH in Library & Information Science (quarterly)—available by subscription. The publication includes complete project overviews with full name/ organization and subject indexes. All current research projects and those completed in the past year are cumulated in the December issue.

Computer-Based Products and Services: CURRENT RESEARCH IN LIBRARY & INFORMATION SCIENCE is available on magnetic tape for in-house use and is expected to be made commercially available online. Data elements present include research personnel, project duration, funding, references, any qualification sought, a 140-word description, and contact name.

Clientele/Availability: CURRENT RESEARCH is available without restrictions. Primary clients include researchers, practitioners, and students in librarianship, information services, and archive work.

Remarks: The publication was formerly known as RADIALS (Research and Development - Library and Information Science) Bulletin, which was published from 1974 to 1983.

Contact: Mrs. P.T. Biggs, Editor, CURRENT RESEARCH in Library & Information Science. (Telex 21897 LALDN G.)

★662★
LIBRARY ASSOCIATION PUBLISHING LTD.
CURRENT TECHNOLOGY INDEX (CTI)
7 Ridgmount St.　　　　　　　　　　Phone: 01-636 7543
London WC1E 7AE, England　　　　Service Est: 1962
Tom Edwards, Editor

Staff: Approximately 9 total.

Description of System or Service: The CURRENT TECHNOLOGY INDEX (CTI) provides subject access to more than 350 technical journals from the United Kingdom. It is available as a hardcopy publication, on microfilm, on machine-readable tape, and online through Pergamon InfoLine Ltd.

Scope and/or Subject Matter: General technology, engineering, and other areas of applied science, excluding medicine and agriculture.

Input Sources: Input for the Index is derived from British journal literature.

Publications: 1) Current Technology Index (monthly, annual cumulation)—subject index to technical journals. Typical entry contains article title and subtitle, author, journal title, volume and issue numbers, date, and page numbers; also includes author index and source list. 2) Catchword and Trade Name Index-CATNI (quarterly)—supplement to the Index; lists product names, catchwords, jargon, and organization names associated with current technology.

Microform Products and Services: Microfilm of the INDEX may be obtained from Oxford Microform Publications Ltd., Headington Hill Hall, Oxford OX3 0BW, England.

Computer-Based Products and Services: CURRENT TECHNOLOGY INDEX is searchable online through Pergamon InfoLine Ltd. Computer-readable tapes corresponding to the INDEX are also available. Each document in the data base averages four descriptors.

Clientele/Availability: CTI is available by subscription.

Remarks: The Current Technology Index was formerly known as the British Technology Index (BTI); the title was changed in 1981.

Contact: Tom Edwards, Editor, Current Technology Index. (Telex 21897 LALDN G.)

★663★
LIBRARY ASSOCIATION PUBLISHING LTD.
LIBRARY AND INFORMATION SCIENCE ABSTRACTS (LISA)
7 Ridgmount St.　　　　　　　　　　Phone: 01-636 7543
London WC1E 7AE, England　　　　Service Est: 1969
Nicholas L. Moore, Editor

Staff: 7 Information and library professional.

Description of System or Service: Covering several areas of librarianship, information science, and print and electronic publishing, the LIBRARY AND INFORMATION SCIENCE ABSTRACTS (LISA) is a computer-produced journal available in hard copy, on microfiche, and on magnetic tapes. It also is searchable online through commercial vendors.

Scope and/or Subject Matter: Librarianship, information science, micrographics, word processing, electronic publishing, viewdata and teletext, history of librarianship.

Input Sources: Input is derived from approximately 550 periodicals from 60 countries, as well as from conference proceedings and papers, multi-author works, books, and reports.

Holdings and Storage Media: The LISA machine-readable file contains more than 61,000 citations from 1969 to date, with approximately 6000 abstracts added annually. Full text of abstracts, classifications, and foreign titles have been included in the file since 1976.

Publications: Library and Information Science Abstracts (12 per year with annual cumulative indexes)—abstracting and indexing journal; available by subscription. User aids for the data base are also issued.

Microform Products and Services: The journal is available on microfiche.

Computer-Based Products and Services: LISA is available on magnetic tapes through the LISA office. It is searchable online through DIALOG Information Services, Inc. and System Development Corporation (SDC). Data elements present in the file include accession number, title, author, source, language, index terms, abstract, and others.

Clientele/Availability: LISA is available without restrictions.

Contact: Nicholas L. Moore, Editor, Library and Information Science Abstracts. (Telex 21897 LALDN G.)

★664★
LIBRARY NETWORK OF SIBIL USERS
(Reseau des Bibliotheques Utilisant SIBIL - REBUS)
University of Lausanne Libraries　　Phone: 021 228831
6, place de la Riponne　　　　　　　Founded: 1971
CH-1005 Lausanne, Switzerland
Jean-Pierre Clavel, Library Director

Staff: 6 Total.

Description of System or Service: The LIBRARY NETWORK OF SIBIL USERS (REBUS) is a group of university, government, and other libraries in Switzerland, France, and Liechtenstein that use the computerized SIBIL (Systeme Informatise pour Bibliotheques) system to manage acquisitions, cataloging, and circulation. For acquisitions, SIBIL produces files of publishers, book suppliers, and readers who have requested new materials. The online cataloging system is designed for use in a network of cooperative cataloging. COM microfiche, lists, and catalogs filed by author and subject are produced as a result of cataloging. The circulation system performs updates of the reader and transaction files, and manages issues, returns, and reserves by means of bar codes affixed to books and patrons' cards. NETWORK members exchange bibliographic data, develop SIBIL software, and plan to exchange primary documents via a system of electronic mail.

Scope and/or Subject Matter: Library automation, including cataloging and public access to catalogs.

Input Sources: Input comprises acquisitions processing, cataloging, and circulation data provided by REBUS member libraries.

Holdings and Storage Media: The machine-readable REBUS cataloging data base holds more than 500,000 bibliographic entries.

Microform Products and Services: SIBIL is used to produce alphabetical author/ title and subject catalogs on COM microfiche. Other COM products include a Swiss union catalog of biomedical periodicals.

Computer-Based Products and Services: The LIBRARY NETWORK OF SIBIL USERS maintains a central cataloging data base using the SIBIL system. The data base can be searched online via search keys—such as title, ISBN, or call number—and by tree search methods which permit browsing through the author/ title catalog or the subject catalog. Boolean logic information retrieval is also possible. REBUS members use SIBIL for automated acquisitions, circulation, and other functions, including the production of COM catalogs, shelf lists, acquisitions lists, cards, and similar products.

Clientele/Availability: Members include university and government libraries.

Remarks: SIBIL was originally developed as the Integrated System for the University of Lausanne Libraries/ Systeme Integre pour les Bibliotheques Universitaires de Lausanne.

Contact: Hubert A. Villard, Coordinator, Library Network of SIBIL Users; telephone 021 448170.

★665★
LINKOPING UNIVERSITY LIBRARY
(Linkopings Universitetsbibliotek)
NYTTFO
Phone: 13 281000
S-581 83 Linkoping, Sweden

Description of System or Service: NYTTFO is an online data base containing descriptions of research conducted by the Universities and the Institutes of Technology at Linkoping and Lund. It covers research reports and other publications, planned and ongoing projects, and related services and courses.

Scope and/or Subject Matter: Research in all subject areas.

Input Sources: Input to the data base is obtained from researchers at the Universities and Institutes of Technology at Linkoping and Lund.

Holdings and Storage Media: The computer-readable NYTTFO data base holds bibliographic and nonbibliographic information.

Computer-Based Products and Services: NYTTFO is maintained online under 3RIP software at the Linkoping University Computer Centre and may be accessed via Datapak and other networks.

Clientele/Availability: Access to the data base is available on a cost-recovery basis.

Contact: Kristian Wallin, Linkoping University Library.

★666★
LIPMAN MANAGEMENT RESOURCES, LTD.
LMR INFORMATION SYSTEMS
ADAPTIVE LIBRARY MANAGEMENT SYSTEM (ADLIB)
54-70 Moorbridge Rd.   Phone: 0628 37123
Maidenhead, Berks. SL6 8BN, England

Staff: 5 Technicians; 4 sales and marketing.

Description of System or Service: ADAPTIVE LIBRARY MANAGEMENT SYSTEM (ADLIB) is a library management system featuring catalog maintenance and retrieval, circulation control, acquisitions, periodicals, and other modules. Each module can be user defined so the resulting system is totally individual. ADLIB operates in an online environment and it produces printed reference material, including accession lists, KWOC indexes, and catalog cards.

Scope and/or Subject Matter: Library automation, including acquisitions, circulation, and cataloging, for academic, special, and public libraries.

Publications: LMR publishes a system description of ADLIB with examples of screen and print formats.

Computer-Based Products and Services: The ADAPTIVE LIBRARY MANAGEMENT SYSTEM is constructed from a basic module and a number of optional modules. The basic module includes catalog maintenance and multi-index retrieval. A catalog entry may be of any length with some fields consisting of free text; each field is given a name and a tag. Input, editing, and display normally use formatted screens, and an unlimited number of different screen formats can be designed and stored by ADLIB. Access to the multi-index retrieval can include author, title, book number, classification, and keywords. Other ADLIB modules include circulation, acquisitions, periodicals, thesaurus maintenance, and word processing using ADEPT. ADLIB is available as a turnkey system for installation in libraries; as a product program for PR1ME and other computers; and as a bureau service on LMR's own system.

Other Services: LMR Information Systems also offers the Adaptive Information Management System (ADMIN), a related system development package which provides a data base management facility invoked by a data dictionary technique.

Clientele/Availability: Clients include academic, special, and public libraries worldwide.

Contact: Mrs. J. Fowler, Marketing Administrator, Lipman Management Resources, Ltd. (Telex 847112 LMR G.)

★667★
LLOYD'S SHIPPING INFORMATION SERVICES (LSIS)
4 Lloyds Ave.   Phone: 01-709 9166
London EC3N 3ED, England   Founded: 1976
J.R. Hughes, Chief Executive

Related Organizations: Lloyd's Shipping Information Services is a joint venture of Lloyd's Register of Shipping (an independent, international ship classification society) and Lloyd's of London Press Ltd. (a wholly owned subsidiary of Lloyd's of London).

Description of System or Service: LLOYD'S SHIPPING INFORMATION SERVICES (LSIS) disseminates shipping data gathered independently by Lloyd's Register of Shipping and Lloyd's of London Press. Using several computer-readable data bases covering ship characteristics, voyage histories, new construction, owners, casualties, and similar topics, the SERVICES provides custom inquiry answering with output available on paper, magnetic tape, diskette, or microfiche. Complete files or tailored subsets are available, and information can be supplied on a recurring basis. In addition, LSIS makes its data bases remotely accessible online. LSIS also distributes publications produced by its parent organizations.

Scope and/or Subject Matter: Merchant ships' characteristics; ships under construction or on order; ship movement, casualties, and owners.

Input Sources: Information is gathered by Lloyd's agents and correspondents and Lloyd's Register surveyors worldwide. Additional input is derived from shipping publications, technical associations, governments, and other sources.

Holdings and Storage Media: Both computerized and manual files of contemporary and historical maritime information are maintained. Current computerized files are updated daily. Historical data date back to the 18th century.

Publications: 1) Lloyd's Register of Ships (annual with monthly supplements). 2) Lloyd's List (daily)—international newspaper on shipping, insurance, transportation, energy, finance, and related topics. 3) Lloyd's Shipping Index (daily)—shipping movements of over 20,000 vessels. 4) List of Shipowners, Maritime Guide and Offshore Register (annual). 5) Tanker Casualty Bulletin (quarterly with annual update)—available by subscription; lists all reported serious tanker casualties in chronological order with details of the ship(s) involved, cargo status, weather, location of incident, severity, sequence of events, loss of life, and pollution, together with a general narrative relating to each casualty. The annual bulletin includes a compilation of the year's casualties and a summary of all nonserious cases reported. 6) Lloyd's Shipping Information Services Review—available by request; newsletter about recent activities and available services. A number of other publications are also available from Lloyd's Register of Shipping and Lloyd's of London Press Ltd.

Microform Products and Services: Annual voyage histories and other data are available on microfiche per individual requirements.

Computer-Based Products and Services: LLOYD'S SHIPPING INFORMATION SERVICES maintains several computer-readable data bases and uses them to provide computer printouts, microfiche, magnetic tapes, or diskettes prepared according to customer specifications. LSIS has also made provisions for the connection of remote terminals to its computer facilities, and it makes data accessible via Prestel. Following are descriptions of the chief LSIS data bases:

1) Shipping Movements - Voyage History File—dates from 1976 to the present, and contains known voyage histories for approximately 32,000 merchant vessels currently engaged in ocean-going world trade; includes information on previous names of the vessel, flag, classification society, vessel type, indication of owner or manager, and gross, net, and deadweight tonnage.

2) Register Book File—contains information on about 76,000 vessels of 100 gross tonnage and above, including all ships classed with Lloyd's Register, and provides such information as ship's current and former names, ship type, dimensions, shipowner, propulsion, tonnages, and speed.

3) New Construction File—gives details on all known propelled sea-going merchant ships of 100 gross tonnage and above under construction or on order, including ship's name, ship type, dimensions, propulsion, tonnage, speed, and other information.

4) Casualty Files—records all casualties to tankers since 1976 and all serious casualties to dry cargo ships since 1978, as well as records of ships broken up; includes ship's name and type, date and geographic location of casualty, sequence of events, loss of lives, cargo commodity and status, and other data.

5) Shipowner and Parent Company File—gives names and addresses of registered shipowners, managers, and parent organizations; provides all the names of ships owned or managed by each company with a limited range of related ship characteristics, including ship type, deadweight, tonnage, date of build, and other information.

6) Ships Latest Position—daily updated details on the movements of some 22,000 merchant vessels; searches by port or name can be done.

Other Services: Additional services consist of data analysis and manual literature searching.

Clientele/Availability: Clients include all sections of the shipping and transportation industries as well as government agencies.

Contact: J.R. Hughes or Dr. E.A. Muller, Joint Chief Executives, or David. A. Littlejohn, Business Manager, Lloyd's Shipping Information Services. (Telex 888379 LR LON G.)

★668★
LOGICA UK LTD.
64 Newman St.   Phone: 01-637 9111
London W1A 4SE, England   Founded: 1969
Colin Rowland, Managing Director

Staff: 743 Technical professional; 260 clerical and nonprofessional.

Description of System or Service: LOGICA UK LTD. is a professional services company in the fields of computing, data communications, and management science. As both consultants and contractors, LOGICA provides clients in government and the private sector with expertise in the following areas: design and implementation of packet-switching networks such as Euronet; computer software development; custom hardware design and construction; financial, military, and scientific information systems; dedicated minicomputer systems and microprocessor development; and market research and management studies. LOGICA cooperated with the British Broadcasting Corporation (BBC) in the development of the CEEFAX teletext system, and it markets a range of related systems under the name of CONTEXT.

Scope and/or Subject Matter: Data processing, data communications, computer software, systems engineering, and management sciences.

Computer-Based Products and Services: Services are offered in the areas of software and hardware design, development, and implementation; packet-switching networks; videotex/teletext; and consulting and research in information storage and retrieval. The firm also offers the RAPPORT relational data base management system.

Clientele/Availability: Primary clientele served are banking and financial institutions; telecommunications providers; government departments; defense, space, and research establishments; and public utilities.

Contact: Valerie Exton, Manager, Marketing Services, Logica UK Ltd. (Telex 27200.) In the United States, inquiries should be directed to Peter Smith, Marketing Services, Logica Inc., 666 Third Ave., New York, NY 10017; telephone (212) 599-0828.

★669★
LOMBARD INTERUNIVERSITY CONSORTIUM FOR DATA PROCESSING
(Consorzio Interuniversitario Lombardo per l'Elaborazione Automatica - CILEA)
Via R. Sanzio 4   Phone: 02 2132541
I-20090 Segrate/Milan, Italy   Founded: 1975
Prof. Ivo De Lotto, Director

Description of System or Service: The LOMBARD INTERUNIVERSITY CONSORTIUM FOR DATA PROCESSING (CILEA) is a network of five Italian university computer centers that provides data processing and related services for educational and research institutes in Italy. CILEA also acts as a host on the Euronet DIANE network, providing online access to several data bases.

Scope and/or Subject Matter: Academic computing services.

Computer-Based Products and Services: CILEA makes available a wide variety of software products through time-sharing. It also makes the following data bases available for remote terminal online searching via Euronet DIANE: 1) ADIGE (Archive of Italian Data of Geology)—a series of three data bases providing data and bibliographic information relating to Italian geology; produced by the Research Center for the Stratigraphy and Petrography of the Central Alps. 2) ALICE (Archivio Libri Italiani su Calcolatore Elettronico)—provides full bibliographic records for Italian books currently in print; compiled by Editrice Bibliografica. 3) CIRCE (Catalogo Italiano Riviste su Calcolatore Elettronico)—contains full information for all periodicals published in Italy; compiled by Editrice Bibliografica.

Clientele/Availability: Primary clients are universities and research organizations.

Contact: Prof. Antonio Liverani, User Services, Lombard Interuniversity Consortium for Data Processing (CILEA).

★670★
LONDON AND SOUTH EASTERN LIBRARY REGION (LASER)
33/34 Alfred Place   Phone: 01-636 9537
London WC1E 7DP, England   Founded: 1928
Miss J.M. Plaister, Director

Staff: Approximately 17 total.

Description of System or Service: The LONDON AND SOUTH EASTERN LIBRARY REGION (LASER) is a cooperative library organization providing automated bibliographic and information services to public and other types of libraries in the area. LASER maintains an online minicomputer network and offers a variety of cataloging services online or in batch mode, including selective record service, card sets, full cataloging, retrospective conversion, and union catalogs. The network also provides interlibrary loan and reference services, issues publications, and serves as an umbrella organization for input of information to the Prestel viewdata system.

Scope and/or Subject Matter: Automated bibliographical and information services and interlibrary cooperation.

Input Sources: Input consists of MARC records and local data.

Holdings and Storage Media: Machine-readable holdings number 1.3 million bibliographic entries representing the 40 million volumes held by member libraries. Records include UK MARC from 1950 to date; LASER-extra MARC entries; and LC MARC entries.

Publications: 1) LASER Directory of Libraries. 2) LASER Handbook—procedures for interlibrary lending and other forms of cooperation. 3) Union Catalogue of Sets of Music Scores. 4) Union Catalogue of Periodicals. Research and annual reports are also issued.

Microform Products and Services: 1) LASER Union Catalogue—includes author/title and locations of volumes. 2) LASER ISBN & BNB Book Number and Location Finding List. Member libraries' holdings data are also available on microfiche.

Computer-Based Products and Services: LASER provides batch and online cataloging and associated services including data preparation, computer processing, and output on COM, cards, or phototypeset copy; retrospective conversion; and selective record service with output on magnetic tape for use on in-house cataloging and circulation control systems.

Other Services: In addition to services described above, LASER is involved in sponsored research into viewdata systems and applications and offers consultancy on both automated bibliographical services and systems and viewdata systems.

Clientele/Availability: LASER services are intended for member libraries.

Contact: Peter Smith, Deputy Director, London and South Eastern Library Region. (Telex 25616.)

★671★
LONDON ENTERPRISE AGENCY
SUPPLIER IDENTIFICATION SYSTEM (S.I.S.)
69 Cannon St. Phone: 01-248 9383
London EC4N 5AB, England Service Est: 1979
P. Thackwray, Project Manager

Staff: 2 Management professional; 1 technician; 1 sales and marketing; 1 clerical and nonprofessional.

Related Organizations: The Supplier Identification System receives funding from Unilever Holdings Ltd. and the National Westminster Bank.

Description of System or Service: The SUPPLIER IDENTIFICATION SYSTEM (S.I.S.) is a computerized sourcing tool for production buyers seeking engineering subcontractors with specific manufacturing capabilities. S.I.S. contains full profiles of more than 200 London-area based firms offering up to 940 engineering processes. S.I.S. staff evaluate manufacturing drawings submitted by production buyers and select the most cost-effective method of producing the product. The S.I.S. data base is then searched to provide profiles of firms best suited to meet the required technical standards. S.I.S. can also produce lists of firms which offer simple machining operations.

Scope and/or Subject Matter: Manufacturing capabilities of engineering subcontractors in metals and plastics.

Input Sources: Data are collected from each supplier site by a team of independent engineers.

Holdings and Storage Media: Profiles of 210 firms are held in machine-readable form.

Publications: A user's guide is available.

Computer-Based Products and Services: The SUPPLIER IDENTIFICATION SYSTEM is a computer-readable data base of profiles on engineering subcontractors located in the London area. Each profile includes registered and factory address, principal contacts, skill base, turnover rate and percentage exported, current quality approvals, principal customers, and bank. Computerized search services are offered from the SYSTEM.

Clientele/Availability: Services are available without charge. Chief clients are production buyers.

Contact: P. Thackwray, Project Manager, Supplier Identification System, or Dr. N.R. Tomlinson, London Enterprise Agency. (Telex 893538.)

★672★
THE LONDON INTERNATIONAL FINANCIAL FUTURES EXCHANGE LTD. (LIFFE)
Royal Exchange Phone: 01-623 0444
London EC3V 3PJ, England Founded: 1982
R.R. St. J. Barkshire, Chairman

Staff: 1 Information and library professional; 8 management professional; 23 technicians; 5 sales and marketing; 30 clerical and nonprofessional.

Related Organizations: The Exchange works in cooperation with the International Commodities Clearing House Ltd. (ICCH), which is owned by leading British banks.

Description of System or Service: THE LONDON INTERNATIONAL FINANCIAL FUTURES EXCHANGE LTD. (LIFFE) provides facilities and information services for commodity brokers, banks, stock exchange firms, individual traders, and other members dealing in financial futures. It establishes and monitors rules of trading, collects and disseminates information relative to the market and to factors affecting prices, and provides an institutional framework for arbitrating disputes that may arise in the conduct of trading. The EXCHANGE requires all transactions to be recorded by the buyer and seller on clearing slips, which are entered by EXCHANGE staff into a computerized system to identify outstanding unmatched trades. All matched slips are then registered through the computerized clearing system of the International Commodities Clearing House Ltd. Statements of all confirmed trades are published at regular intervals on the floor of the EXCHANGE.

Scope and/or Subject Matter: Financial futures trading, including three-month Eurodollar, three-month sterling, twenty-year gilt interest rate and fifteen-year U.S. Treasury Bond contracts; sterling, swiss franc, deutsche mark, and yen currency contracts; stock index futures.

Input Sources: Input is derived from clearing slips detailing the sale and purchase of financial futures.

Holdings and Storage Media: Transaction data are held in machine-readable form. A small library is also maintained.

Publications: The Exchange produces booklets, books, and slide kits on hedging and trading techniques, case studies by banks and local authorities, and user guides for the various contracts.

Computer-Based Products and Services: THE LONDON INTERNATIONAL FINANCIAL FUTURES EXCHANGE LTD. provides computerized services which match purchase and sale transactions. It is also served by the International Commodities Clearing House Ltd. which registers Exchange members' transactions on a computerized clearing system. In addition, the EXCHANGE has offered financial futures market information on several information service networks, including The Stock Exchange's TOPIC, Prestel, DATASTREAM International Ltd., and others.

Clientele/Availability: Services are available to members of the Exchange, including banks, discount houses, money brokers, commodity brokers, stock exchange firms, and experienced individual traders.

Projected Publications and Services: The Exchange plans to offer a comprehensive online bibliography on financial futures.

Contact: Bernard Reed, Manager, Education and Industrial Relations, The London International Financial Futures Exchange Ltd. (Telex 893894 LIFFE G.)

★673★
LONDON OVER THE COUNTER MARKET (LOTC)
21 Upper Brook St. Phone: 01-629 5983
London W1, England Founded: 1979
Peter Sommer

Staff: 2 Information and library professional; 1 management professional; 1 sales and marketing.

Description of System or Service: LONDON OVER THE COUNTER MARKET (LOTC) supplies prices and background information for shares quoted on the London unlisted securities market and various London over-the-counter markets. LOTC makes these data available through online and videotex systems.

Scope and/or Subject Matter: Financial market information.

Input Sources: Information is derived via direct reporting from financial markets.

Holdings and Storage Media: Financial data are held in machine-readable form.

Computer-Based Products and Services: London Over the Counter Market obtains financial data directly from financial markets and makes it electronically accessible through Prestel and Reuters.

Other Services: LOTC also provides analysis for institutions and journals.

Clientele/Availability: Services are available without restrictions.

Contact: Peter Sommer, London Over the Counter Market.

★674★
LONDON RESEARCHERS
76 Park Rd. Phone: 01-723 8530
London NW1 4SH, England Founded: 1973
Mary Ann Colyer, Manager

Staff: 2 Information and library professional; 1 sales and marketing; 1 clerical and nonprofessional.

Related Organizations: Related organizations sharing the same address are Alan Armstrong & Associates Ltd., which offers bookselling services for special libraries, and Task Force Pro Libra which is an employment agency specializing in library, information, and research staff.

Description of System or Service: LONDON RESEARCHERS is an information brokerage firm offering services to businesses, information officers, and librarians. Services include desk research, computerized information retrieval, referrals, bibliographic verification, and document supply.

Scope and/or Subject Matter: Information retrieval in all subject areas.

Input Sources: Information is obtained from commercially available online data bases and other sources.

Computer-Based Products and Services: LONDON RESEARCHERS conducts computerized searches of data bases carried by United States and European hosts.

Clientele/Availability: Services are available on a fee basis; deposit accounts are available.

Contact: Mary Ann Colyer, Manager, London Researchers. (Telex 297635 AAALTD.)

★675★
LOUGHBOROUGH UNIVERSITY OF TECHNOLOGY
CENTRE FOR LIBRARY AND INFORMATION MANAGEMENT (CLAIM)
 Phone: 0509 213176
Loughborough, Leics. LE11 3TU, England Service Est: 1969
Peter H. Mann, Director

Staff: 4 Information and library professional; 2 clerical and nonprofessional.

Related Organizations: The Centre receives support from the British Library's Research and Development Department.

Description of System or Service: The CENTRE FOR LIBRARY AND INFORMATION MANAGEMENT (CLAIM) aims to improve the effectiveness of services in the field of library and information management through the provision of investigation, information, continuing education, and consulting services. CLAIM publishes monographs, indexes, checklists, newsletters, and bibliographies to support its goal.

Scope and/or Subject Matter: Library and information management.

Publications: 1) Academic Book Price Index (semiannual). 2) Aids to Library Administration Series (ATLAS). 3) CLAIM Research Reports. The Centre also publishes a number of other reports and documents; a list is available by request from CLAIM.

Services: Consulting and research services in the area of library and information management are the chief services offered.

Clientele/Availability: Services are available without restrictions.

Contact: Peter H. Mann, Director, Centre for Library and Information Management. (Telex 34319.)

★676★
LOUGHBOROUGH UNIVERSITY OF TECHNOLOGY
CHEMICAL ENGINEERING DEPARTMENT
PARTICLE SCIENCE AND TECHNOLOGY INFORMATION SERVICE
Ashby Rd. Phone: 0509 263171
Loughborough, Leics. LE11 3TU, England Service Est: 1969
Mr. P.J. Lloyd, Managing Director

Staff: 1 Information and library professional; 1 clerical and nonprofessional.

Description of System or Service: The PARTICLE SCIENCE AND TECHNOLOGY INFORMATION SERVICE provides current and retrospective coverage of literature in the field of particle technology. It maintains a computer-readable data base for use in publishing a monthly bulletin and COM indexes. The SERVICE also supplies documents cited in the bulletin that are difficult to find elsewhere, performs manual and computerized literature searches, offers current awareness, and prepares critical reviews of the literature on a fee basis.

Scope and/or Subject Matter: All aspects of particulate science and technology, including aerosols, colloids, emulsions, filtration, powders, air pollution, and other topics.

Input Sources: Input is derived from approximately 800 current periodicals; other sources include books, theses, reports, conference proceedings, and patents.

Holdings and Storage Media: A collection of 100,000 articles is maintained, together with the computer-readable bibliographic data base.

Publications: Current Awareness in Particle Technology (monthly)—available by subscription; includes about 800 references per month.

Microform Products and Services: The computer-generated Index to Current Awareness in Particle Technology is published annually on microfiche. It includes subject and author indexes and is available by subscription as part of Current Awareness in Particle Technology.

Computer-Based Products and Services: A machine-readable data base covering particle science literature is maintained by the SERVICE for the production of its monthly publication and indexes. Computerized literature searching and individual SDI profiles are offered.

Clientele/Availability: Services are available on a fee basis to anyone.

Contact: Richard Newbold, Information Scientist, Particle Science and Technology Information Service. (Telex 34319.)

★677★
LOUGHBOROUGH UNIVERSITY OF TECHNOLOGY LIBRARY
LIBRARY INSTRUCTION MATERIALS BANK (LIMB)
Ashby Rd. Phone: 0509 263171
Loughborough, Leics. LE11 3TU, England Service Est: 1980
Ian Malley, Head

Staff: 1 Information and library professional; 2 clerical and nonprofessional.

Related Organizations: Related organizations include the Research and Development Department of the British Library.

Description of System or Service: The LIBRARY INSTRUCTION MATERIALS BANK (LIMB) is a collection of all print and nonprint materials relevant to the teaching of information skills. It also includes literature published worldwide on the teaching of information skills. Abstracts and citations to LIMB holdings are maintained in the computer-readable LIMB Index data base which is used to provide print and microfiche indexes and current awareness services.

Scope and/or Subject Matter: Library and information skills, study skills, communication skills, library promotion, user education.

Input Sources: Input is derived from teaching materials, audiovisuals, more than 1000 journals, books, reports, proceedings, and other published and nonpublished sources worldwide, with emphasis on materials from the United Kingdom.

Holdings and Storage Media: The Collection includes teaching and instructional materials as well as journal articles, monographs, research reports, and other literature. The machine-readable LIMB

Index data base contains more than 12,000 records.

Publications: The LIMB Index (3 per year)—arranged by subject; includes abstracts.

Microform Products and Services: The LIMB Index is also available on microfiche.

Computer-Based Products and Services: The LIMB Index data base covers the holdings of the Library Instruction Materials Bank and is used to provide publications and computerized current awareness services.

Other Services: Additional services include consulting, conference organization, and research.

Clientele/Availability: Clients include librarians, teachers, and information personnel.

Contact: Ian Malley, Head, Library Instruction Materials Bank.

★678★
LOUGHBOROUGH UNIVERSITY OF TECHNOLOGY LIBRARY
MINIMAL-INPUT CATALOGUING SYSTEM (MINICS)
Ashby Rd.　　　　　　　　　　　　　Phone: 0509 263171
Loughborough, Leics. LE11 3TU, England
Dr. R.A. Wall, Deputy Librarian

Staff: Approximately 10 total.

Description of System or Service: The MINIMAL-INPUT CATALOGUING SYSTEM (MINICS) is an internal computer-based cataloging system which uses primarily locally generated input, although it will also accept edited MARC subsets. MINICS supports cataloging and other functions at the Loughborough University of Technology Library.

Scope and/or Subject Matter: Cataloging for serials, monographs, analyticals, and nonprint media.

Input Sources: Input for MINICS consists of the staff-assigned cataloging data for library acquisitions.

Holdings and Storage Media: Magnetic tapes of the following data are held: accessions and cataloging master files; serials financial control subsystems; and periodicals data system.

Microform Products and Services: COM microfiche name, title, and classified catalogs are produced.

Computer-Based Products and Services: Services include maintenance of the acquisitions and cataloging master tapes for use in cataloging, and preparation of COM catalogs.

Other Services: Consulting and research are also offered.

Clientele/Availability: The System serves the University.

Contact: Prof. A.J. Evans, Librarian, Loughborough University of Technology Library. (Telex 34319.)

★679★
LYMBURNER (JAMES R.) & SONS LTD.
ECONOMIST'S STATISTICS
20 Victoria St.　　　　　　　　　　Phone: (416) 862-0595
Toronto, ON, Canada M5C 2N8　　　Service Est: 1976
Margaret Nozaki, Data Base Manager

Staff: Approximately 10 total.

Description of System or Service: ECONOMIST'S STATISTICS is a computer-readable data base providing a variety of international economic and financial time series data. The data base is divided into three parts: 1) G.N.P. Statistics comprise current and historical income and expenditure data for the United States, United Kingdom, Canada, Germany, and Japan. The series are updated quarterly. 2) Daily, Weekly, and Monthly Statistics provide current and historical data in such areas as international currencies, interest rates, stock market prices, commodity prices and indices, gold coins, strategic metals, and world and galaxy shipping data. The data are loaded continuously from major financial centers worldwide. 3) Historical Statistics consist of a specially selected series of statistics dating back to 1800. ECONOMIST'S STATISTICS provides 6 months of daily, 2 years of weekly, 5 years of monthly, and 10 years of quarterly data online, with historical statistics held offline. The online data are accessible through James R. LymBurner & Sons Ltd. as part of a computer and communications system that includes analytical programs, graphics packages, and the MAILBOX electronic mail service. ECONOMIST'S STATISTICS information can also be obtained from the firm on magnetic tape.

Scope and/or Subject Matter: International economic and financial statistics.

Input Sources: Stock market information is obtained from the London, New York, Toronto, and Tokyo exchanges. Commodity data are from Reuters, Dow Jones, and the Economist Index. Other sources of data for Economist's Statistics include the Financial Times Ltd., Samuel Montague, N.M. Rothschild & Sons Ltd., and the U.S. National Aeronautics and Space Administration.

Holdings and Storage Media: The computer-readable Economist's Statistics data base holds 750 daily series, with 7000 total series for all time parameters.

Computer-Based Products and Services: ECONOMIST'S STATISTICS data together with analytical programs, graphics capabilities, and electronic mail services are accessible online through LymBurner & Sons via Datapac, Tymnet, Telenet, or direct dial. The online service is available without CPU charges; the only fees are for data retrieval. The data base can also be obtained on magnetic tape.

Clientele/Availability: Primary clients are major financial institutions. All data and publications are for private use only and are not to be publicly quoted.

M

★680★
MACLEAN-HUNTER LTD.
FINANCIAL POST DIVISION
FINANCIAL POST INVESTMENT DATA BANK
481 University Ave.   Phone: (416) 596-5693
Toronto, ON, Canada M5W 1A7
Mr. Cuyler Bowness, Asst. General Manager

Staff: Approximately 8 total.

Description of System or Service: The FINANCIAL POST INVESTMENT DATA BANK maintains several machine-readable data bases on corporations and securities. Its Canadian Corporate Data Bank contains data from quarterly and annual reports of Canadian companies. The Securities Data Base comprises information on Canadian and United States stocks, options, earnings, and dividends. The Predecessor and Defunct Companies data base includes industry mergers, name changes, and amalgamations occurring in the last 50 years. The data bases are made available on magnetic tape and through commercial time-sharing sources.

Scope and/or Subject Matter: Canadian corporations; Canadian and U.S. securities.

Input Sources: Data are gathered from stock exchanges, corporate reports, and other sources.

Holdings and Storage Media: The Corporate Data Bank contains up to 100 facts per year since 1959 for more than 375 Canadian corporations, as well as up to 20 items of quarterly information for 100 Canadian companies and chartered banks. The Securities Data Base covers more than 5000 Canadian, New York Stock Exchange, and Amex securities. The Predecessor and Defunct Companies data base contains approximately 10,000 records; it is updated irregularly.

Computer-Based Products and Services: The Corporate Data Bank and Securities Data Base are available online through I.P. Sharp Associates, Data Resources, Inc., and FRI Information Services Ltd. The data can also be obtained on magnetic tape from the Financial Post. Securities data made available by daily or weekly subscription include Canadian stock market, Canadian options, Canadian dividends, and U.S. stock market. The Predecessor and Defunct Companies data base is available online through QL Systems Limited.

Clientele/Availability: Clients include banks, trust companies, investment houses, universities, brokers, time-sharing companies, and major corporations.

Contact: Mr. Cuyler Bowness, Assistant General Manager, Financial Post Investment Data Bank.

★681★
MADAGASCAR
MINISTRY OF FINANCE AND ECONOMY
(Ministere Aupres de la Presidence de la Republique Charge des Finances et de l'Economie)
NATIONAL INSTITUTE OF STATISTICS AND ECONOMIC RESEARCH
(Institut National de la Statistique et de la Recherche Economique - INSRE)
B.P. 485   Phone: 20081
Antananarivo, Madagascar   Service Est: 1947
Raphael Ramanana-Rahary, Ingenieur Statisticien Economiste

Staff: 13 Statisticians; 5 others.

Description of System or Service: The NATIONAL INSTITUTE OF STATISTICS AND ECONOMIC RESEARCH (INSRE) establishes, collects, and disseminates national statistics of all types and from all sources for government use. It carries out research relating to the national economy, coordinates and conducts demographic social and technical studies using poll and census statistical methods, and manages the computerized collection of statistical information.

Scope and/or Subject Matter: Statistical information on Madagascar, including demographic, social, technical, and economic data.

Input Sources: Input is derived from polls, censuses, and research carried out by the Institute.

Holdings and Storage Media: Statistical information is held in machine-readable form. INSRE library holdings include 3000 bound volumes.

Publications: 1) Commerce Exterieur (annual); 2) Situation Economique (annual); 3) monthly bulletin.

Computer-Based Products and Services: INSRE performs computerized statistical data processing.

Clientele/Availability: Services are intended for government use.

Contact: Raphael Ramanana-Rahary, Ingenieur Statisticien Economiste, National Institute of Statistics and Economic Research.

★682★
MANAGEMENT CONSULTANTS INTERNATIONAL, INC. (MCI)
56 The Esplanade, Suite 303   Phone: (416) 364-0299
Toronto, ON, Canada M5E 1A7   Founded: 1980
Michael A. Harrison, President

Staff: 1 Management professional; 1 technician; 3 other.

Description of System or Service: MANAGEMENT CONSULTANTS INTERNATIONAL, INC. (MCI) provides clients in the information industry and other fields with consulting and research studies relating to new information and communications technologies. It provides advice on corporate strategy and long-range planning, technological forecasting, government relations, management controls, mergers and acquisitions, and marketing.

Scope and/or Subject Matter: Management consulting on videotex, electronic and international banking, telecommunications, electronic publishing, point-of-sale systems, and broadcasting.

Holdings and Storage Media: MCI maintains a library of 200 bound volumes and subscriptions to 25 periodicals.

Clientele/Availability: MCI serves information industry firms, associations, banking and finance corporations, and computers/communications companies in North America, Europe, and Japan.

Contact: Michael A. Harrison, President, Management Consultants International, Inc.

★683★
MANZ INFO DATENVERMITTLUNG GMBH
MANZ DATENBANKEN
Wiedner Hauptstr. 18   Phone: 573620
A-1040 Vienna, Austria   Service Est: 1981
Dr. Kurt Bednar, General Manager

Staff: 1 Information and library professional; 2 management professional; 1 sales and marketing; 2 clerical and nonprofessional.

Related Organizations: The parent organization of MANZ Info Datenvermittlung is MANZsche Verlags- und Universitatsbuchhandlung, a publisher of legal materials.

Description of System or Service: MANZ DATENBANKEN is an information broker offering computerized information searching of more than 750 online data bases for clients in business. Additional services include consulting; conferences; translations; training; and sales and marketing representation for online hosts and data base producers, including the provision of help desks.

Scope and/or Subject Matter: Information searching in business and management, commodities, patents, technical sciences, and other subjects.

Input Sources: Commercial online data base vendors are chief input sources.

Computer-Based Products and Services: MANZ DATENBANKEN offers computerized information retrieval services using data bases made available through approximately 30 hosts.

Clientele/Availability: Services are directed towards clients in the business community and information industry.

Contact: Dr. Kurt Bednar, General Manager, MANZ Datenbanken. (Telex 11-1390 MANZDB.)

★684★
MARINE BIOLOGICAL ASSOCIATION OF THE UNITED KINGDOM
MARINE POLLUTION INFORMATION CENTRE (MARPIC)
The Laboratory, Citadel Hill
Plymouth PL1 2PB, England
David S. Moulder, Head

Phone: 0752 21761
Service Est: 1970

Staff: 2 Information and library professional; 1 clerical and nonprofessional.

Related Organizations: The Centre is supported by the Great Britain Natural Environment Research Council (NERC).

Description of System or Service: Located at the Marine Biological Association's library, the MARINE POLLUTION INFORMATION CENTRE (MARPIC) collects and indexes relevant material on all types of marine and estuarine pollution, issues publications including a monthly current awareness bulletin, and encourages inquiries from scientists and technologists working on marine pollution. The CENTRE collects original documents and maintains one of the world's most comprehensive collections of literature in its field. It has created an extensive card index for the documents, including more than 32,000 entries arranged in broad groups under the pollutant, with subdivisions under such aspects as levels of pollutants in various sections of the marine environment and effects of pollutants on organisms. Among the CENTRE's services are literature searching, bibliography compilation, data extraction, SDI, photocopying, and reference and referral services.

Scope and/or Subject Matter: Marine and estuarine pollution, including the detection, remote sensing, monitoring, and analysis of pollutants; the levels of pollutants in seawater; sediments and organisms; the biological effects, fate, control, and removal of pollutants.

Input Sources: Input is gathered from journal articles, books, conference papers, technical reports, theses (excluding publications of a journalistic or popular nature). Approximately 2500 documents are added annually.

Holdings and Storage Media: The CENTRE maintains a collection of more than 32,000 documents, backed up by the library's collection of 12,500 books, 36,000 bound periodical volumes, subscriptions to 1450 periodicals, and 50,000 pamphlets and reprints in the areas of marine biology, oceanography, and fisheries.

Publications: 1) Marine Pollution Research Titles (monthly)—available by subscription; a current awareness publication including references to the approximately 2500 papers on marine and estuarine pollution published each year, divided into 15 subject sections. 2) Bibliography on Marine and Estuarine Oil Pollution, 1971, with supplements. 3) Bibliography on Marine and Estuarine Pesticide Pollution, 1976. 4) Subject Index on Marine and Estuarine Pollution (available from G.K. Hall, 70 Lincoln St., Boston, MA 02111). Other bibliographies are also produced.

Computer-Based Products and Services: The CENTRE supplies input to the computer-based Environmental Chemicals Data and Information Network (ECDIN) of the European Economic Community and to the International Register of Potentially Toxic Chemicals (IRPTC) of the United Nations Environment Program (UNEP). It also contributes input on marine pollution for Acquatic Sciences and Fisheries Abstracts.

Clientele/Availability: Services are available without restrictions.

Contact: David S. Moulder, Head, Marine Pollution Information Centre.

★685★
MARITIME INFORMATION CENTRE/CMO
P.O. Box 21873
NL-3001 AW Rotterdam, Netherlands
G.S. Kok

Phone: 010 130960
Founded: 1973

Staff: 5 Information and library professional; 2 clerical and nonprofessional.

Related Organizations: The Centre serves as the information processing department of the National Foundation for the Coordination of Maritime Research.

Description of System or Service: The aim of the MARITIME INFORMATION CENTRE/CMO is to make bibliographic information available online for use by shipping-related companies in the Netherlands and elsewhere. It currently maintains two machine-readable data bases, MARNA and SHIPDES. MARNA is a machine-readable bibliography of maritime affairs covering journal articles as well as a variety of other publications from the world literature. Main subjects include shipping, shipbuilding, offshore industry, the fishing industry, the navy, marine pollution, and maritime laws and regulations. SHIPDES is a bibliographic data base of ship descriptions that includes such data as ship name, weight, length, speed, and other data. Both MARNA and SHIPDES are commercially available online. Additionally, the MARITIME INFORMATION CENTRE publishes an abstracts journal and maintains an extensive library. All information cited in the data bases is available at the CENTRE and photocopies can be requested.

Scope and/or Subject Matter: Maritime and nautical literature.

Input Sources: Approximately 500 periodicals, report series, proceedings, monographs, and other publications are scanned for input to the data bases.

Holdings and Storage Media: The machine-readable MARNA file holds approximately 45,000 records dating from 1974 to the present; about 100 items are added weekly. SHIPDES holds approximately 5200 records from 1969 to date; about 75 items are added weekly. The Centre maintains an extensive library of all cited literature.

Publications: 1) Marna-News (monthly)—abstracts journal containing the latest additions to MARNA and SHIPDES. 2) MARNA Manual and Thesaurus. 3) SHIPDES Manual.

Computer-Based Products and Services: MARNA and SHIPDES are available online through a host on Euronet DIANE; regular training courses on the use of the data bases are provided by the Centre.

Clientele/Availability: Services are available without restrictions on a fee basis.

Contact: G.S. Kok, Maritime Information Centre. (Telex 26585 CMO NL.)

★686★
MARKET LOCATION
17 Waterloo Place
Warwick St.
Leamington Spa, Warwicks. CV32 5LA,
  England
A.J. Sidwell, Managing Director

Phone: 0926 34235
Founded: 1974

Staff: 50 Total.

Description of System or Service: MARKET LOCATION provides access to census-type establishment data bases on British manufacturing and distributive industries. The firm compiles and continuously monitors information on more than 100,000 separate industrial establishments and more than 200,000 retail outlets. It provides information retrieval and computer tape distribution services to assist clients in targeting sales and marketing efforts. In addition, MARKET LOCATION provides software and applications consulting in sales and marketing, management of private data bases, and other related services.

Scope and/or Subject Matter: Censuses of British industries.

Input Sources: Input is obtained from direct interviews and on-site surveys.

Holdings and Storage Media: Statistical information on more than 300,000 establishments is held in machine-readable form.

Computer-Based Products and Services: MARKET LOCATION compiles data bases on British industry and provides information retrieval and tape distribution services from them. The firm also offers management of private data bases, marketing software and applications consultancy, and decision support systems. MARKET LOCATION plans to offer additional commercial data bases and is developing online services.

Other Services: The firm also provides market analysis and special research.

Clientele/Availability: Services are available without restrictions.

Contact: Mike Clark, Marketing Director, Market Location.

★687★
MARKET RESEARCH SOCIETY
MARKET RESEARCH ABSTRACTS
15 Belgrave Square Phone: 01-235 4709
London SW1X 8PF, England Service Est: 1963

Description of System or Service: MARKET RESEARCH ABSTRACTS provides abstracts of periodical and other literature covering all fields of marketing and advertising research, as well as relevant areas of statistics, psychology, and sociology. MARKET RESEARCH ABSTRACTS is currently available as a printed publication and on microfilm, and is expected to be offered online.

Scope and/or Subject Matter: Marketing and related topics, including survey techniques; statistics, models, and forecasting; attitude and behavior research; psychographics, personality, and social psychology; communications, advertising and media research; specific applications of research; industrial market research; market research and general applications; and new product development.

Input Sources: Input is derived from approximately 40 specialist English-language journals and from market research conference proceedings.

Holdings and Storage Media: Machine-readable holdings are under development.

Publications: Market Research Abstracts (twice yearly)—available by subscription. Each issue contains approximately 150 abstracts with a subject index, an author index, and a source list. The Market Research Society also produces other publications dealing with marketing, including a newsletter, conference proceedings, a yearbook, and others.

Microform Products and Services: The journal is available on microfilm from University Microfilms International.

Computer-Based Products and Services: Several volumes of MARKET RESEARCH ABSTRACTS have been converted to computer-readable form; an online data base will be offered when all back volumes have been processed. A typical entry will include accession number, article title, author, journal reference, and abstract.

Other Services: A photostat service, covering most of the abstracted material, is available.

Clientele/Availability: Clients include market researchers, advertisers, and others. Subscription prices vary for members and nonmembers.

Contact: Mona Rumble, Market Research Abstracts.

★688★
MARKETING INTELLIGENCE CORPORATION
14-11, Yato-cho 2-Chome Phone: 0424 231111
Tanashi-shi Founded: 1960
Tokyo 188, Japan
Hiroshi Hakone, President

Staff: 30 Information and library professional; 50 management professional; 465 technicians; 65 sales and marketing; 72 clerical and nonprofessional.

Description of System or Service: MARKETING INTELLIGENCE CORPORATION provides consumer and marketing information collection and processing services. It produces the SCI consumer index data base and offers time-sharing services.

Scope and/or Subject Matter: Marketing and consumer information for Japan.

Holdings and Storage Media: The machine-readable SCI data base holds factual information dating from 1960 to the present.

Computer-Based Products and Services: MARKETING INTELLIGENCE CORPORATION produces the nonbibliographic SCI data base, a nationwide consumer index, and offers time-sharing services.

Clientele/Availability: Clients include Japanese advertising and marketing professionals.

Contact: Fumio Katagiri, Chief Secretary, Marketing Intelligence Corporation.

★689★
MARUZEN COMPANY, LTD.
MARUZEN SCIENTIFIC INFORMATION SERVICE (MASIS) CENTER
P.O. Box 5335 Phone: 03 2716068
Tokyo International 100-31, Japan Service Est: 1977
Ken I. Teramura, General Manager

Description of System or Service: The MARUZEN SCIENTIFIC INFORMATION SERVICE (MASIS) CENTER is the Japanese distributor and agent for a number of international information companies including DIALOG Information Services, Inc., Telesystemes Questel, the University of Toronto Library Automation Systems (UTLAS), IFI/Plenum Data Company, Trinco, Inc., and the Information on Demand (IOD) firm. The CENTER makes the products and services provided by these companies available in Japan and Southeast Asia. This includes access to the data bases, online searching, the production of library catalogs in various formats, and document delivery. Users can access international systems through MARUNET, the Maruzen Online Network.

Scope and/or Subject Matter: Distribution of computer-based information systems, services and products in all subject areas.

Publications: MASIS NEWS (monthly). The MASIS Center also produces Japanese editions of documentation to support the services and systems for which it is an agent or distributor. Additionally, various library catalogs are issued by the Center.

Microform Products and Services: Maruzen makes available for purchase on microfiche imported publications as well as its own published material.

Computer-Based Products and Services: The MASIS CENTER provides users in Japan and Southeast Asia with access to DIALOG Information Services, Inc., Telesystemes Questel, UTLAS, and other systems through Marunet, its high-speed network for data transmission. The CENTER also offers retrospective and SDI search services and fulfills requests for documents ordered through DIALOG's DIALORDER system.

Other Services: Additionally, MASIS Center produces user aids, offers a comprehensive training curriculum, and provides consultation services in all areas of online information.

Clientele/Availability: Clients include private industry, government agencies, academic and private research institutions, and individuals; services are available without restrictions.

Remarks: The Maruzen Co., Ltd. is a diversified company that also handles foreign books, journals, and audio-visuals.

Contact: Ken I. Teramura, General Manager, MASIS Center. (Telex J26630 MARUZEN.) An American subsidiary, Maruzen International Co., Inc. (MIC), is located at 1251 Avenue of the Americas, New York, NY 10020; telephone (212) 541-9090.

★690★
MCCARTHY INFORMATION LTD.
Manor House Phone: 0985 215151
Ash Walk Founded: 1969
Warminster, Wilts. BA12 8PY, England
Anthony Garnett, General Manager

Staff: 5 Management professional; 30 clerical and nonprofessional; 3 other.

Related Organizations: The parent organization of McCarthy Information Ltd. is Financial Times Business Information Ltd. The firm is associated with Abar Business Planning Service of Akron, Ohio.

Description of System or Service: McCARTHY INFORMATION LTD. supplies news and comment articles on industries and more than 16,000 companies in the United Kingdom, Europe, North America, and the Far East to subscribers concerned with finance and investment planning and analysis. It selects articles from international newspapers and journals, reproduces the full text on paper or microfiche, and publishes them in various categories by industry or geographic area. The services, which are fully indexed, are offered on a regular update basis; specific information from them can also be provided on demand.

Scope and/or Subject Matter: News and comments on companies and industries throughout the world.

Input Sources: Approximately 50 international newspapers and journals are scanned for input.

Publications: 1) U.K. Quoted Company Service (daily)—includes information on companies quoted on the London and provincial stock exchanges. 2) U.K. Unquoted Company Service (weekly)—covers companies without an ordinary share quotation, as well as subsidiaries and other private or government-controlled organizations. 3) Australian Company Service (weekly)—covers companies with ordinary share quotations on any of the Australian Stock Exchanges. 4) European Company Service (weekly)—covers companies quoted on West European exchanges and Europe's 5000 largest companies. 5) North American Company Service (weekly)—covers companies quoted on the New York, American, Toronto, or Montreal exchanges. 6) Industry Service (weekly)—monitors more than 60 areas of industrial activity and includes a two-way comprehensive index. 7) International Banking Service (weekly)—includes articles on U.K., European, North American, and Australian banking and currency industries. 8) Property Service (weekly)—covers information on property companies. 9) Energy Service (weekly)—includes articles on U.K., European, North American, and Australian companies working in the field. 10) Selective Service (weekly)—subscriber selects and receives information on specific companies or industries.

Microform Products and Services: All company and industry services described above are available on microfiche. McCarthy can also arrange for the delivery of reader and printer equipment.

Other Services: McCarthy also offers an on-demand copy service. Copies may be sent by mail or facsimile.

Clientele/Availability: Clients include stockbrokers, banks, investment trusts, reference libraries, insurance companies, and others.

Contact: Anthony Garnett, General Manager, McCarthy Information Ltd.

★691★
MCGILL UNIVERSITY
FACULTY OF ENGINEERING
DEPARTMENT OF MINING AND METALLURGICAL ENGINEERING
FACILITY FOR THE ANALYSIS OF CHEMICAL THERMODYNAMICS
(F*A*C*T)
3480 University St. Phone: (514) 392-5426
Montreal, PQ, Canada H3A 2A7 Service Est: 1979

Staff: 1 Information and library professional; 2 management professional.

Related Organizations: The Ecole Polytechnique at Universite de Montreal cooperates in the development of F*A*C*T. All related copyrights and legal contracts are held by Thermfact Ltd./Ltee., 447 Berwick Ave., Mount-Royal, Quebec, Canada H3R 1Z8.

Description of System or Service: The FACILITY FOR THE ANALYSIS OF CHEMICAL THERMODYNAMICS (F*A*C*T) is an interactive computing system used by chemical and metallurgical companies and university research workers for classical thermochemical calculations of phase diagrams, predominance diagrams, and reactions. The system uses data automatically retrieved from an extensive internal data bank or data supplied by the user. F*A*C*T is stored at the McGill University Computing Centre and is accessible through time-sharing.

Scope and/or Subject Matter: Chemical thermodynamical calculations and data.

Input Sources: Input is derived from Thermochemical Properties of Inorganic Substances and JANAF Thermochemical Tables.

Holdings and Storage Media: The system's data bank consists of the thermodynamic properties of over 2000 stoichiometric compounds and a limited number of binary solutions.

Publications: 1) F*A*C*T User's Guide; 2) Listing of Compounds in Main Data Base (every 2 years).

Computer-Based Products and Services: Accessible online via direct dial, Datapac, or Telenet, F*A*C*T provides users with data on thermochemical properties and several programming options. The system allows users to perform common thermochemical calculations, to search the data file for all compounds that could be formed from a set of elements, to calculate property changes for any chemical reaction, to generate isothermal predominance diagrams for systems with up to 5 elements, to determine vapor pressures of any element or compound, and other specialized functions. Additionally, users can enter and store their own data on the system, and use F*A*C*T programs for making calculations.

Other Services: Additional services include consulting and a training course.

Clientele/Availability: Clients must sign a usage agreement with the McGill University Computing Centre; services are on a fee basis.

Contact: Director, Faculty of Engineering, Department of Mining and Metallurgical Engineering. (Telex 05-268510.)

★692★
MCGILL UNIVERSITY
GRADUATE SCHOOL OF LIBRARY SCIENCE
FEES DATA BASE
McLennan Library Bldg. Phone: (514) 392-5945
3459 McTavish St. Service Est: 1980
Montreal, PQ, Canada H3A 1Y1
C.D. Hurt, Assistant Professor

Description of System or Service: The FEES DATA BASE is a machine-readable file containing citations and abstracts of world literature on the advantages and disadvantages of charging for services in tax-supported libraries. Abstracts are included for English- and French-language articles, and translations are provided for all titles.

Scope and/or Subject Matter: Charging for library services in tax-supported libraries and information centers of all kinds.

Input Sources: Input for the FEES Data Base is prepared from secondary sources covering international library literature.

Holdings and Storage Media: The machine-readable FEES Data Base covers the period from 1964 to the present; it is updated annually.

Computer-Based Products and Services: The FEES Data Base is available for online searching through QL Systems Limited.

Clientele/Availability: Services are directed toward individuals or organizations with an interest in tax-supported library and information service.

Remarks: FEES is also known as the Charging for Library Services Data Base.

Contact: C.D. Hurt, Asst. Professor, Graduate School of Library Science.

★693★
MEDICAL-PHARMACEUTICAL PUBLISHING COMPANY
(Societe d'Editions Medico-Pharmaceutiques - S.E.M.P.)
26, rue Le Brun Phone: 01 3378350
F-75013 Paris, France Founded: 1941
Christian Garlot, General Manager

Staff: 6 Information and library professional; 3 management professional; 4 technicians; 11 sales and marketing; 5 clerical and nonprofessional; 11 other.

Description of System or Service: The MEDICAL-PHARMACEUTICAL PUBLISHING COMPANY (S.E.M.P.) gathers and classifies data on pharmaceutical drugs dispensed in France. S.E.M.P. holds this information in a machine-readable data bank which is used for micropublication of several drug registers.

Scope and/or Subject Matter: Pharmaceutical drugs, cosmetic products, medical aids.

Microform Products and Services: S.E.M.P. produces the following registers in microform: 1) Sempex—20,260 references to human and veterinary drugs, including French equivalents of foreign patent medicines and noncommercial products in France. 2) Accessoirex—13,000 references to toiletries, medical and hygienic aids. 3)

Parapharmex—7000 references to cosmetics, perfumery, and oral hygiene. 4) Incompatex—3000 references to drug interactions and contraindications. 5) Tarex. All of the above are published annually with regular supplements on standard COM microfiche.

Computer-Based Products and Services: The S.E.M.P. data bank is used to store, update, and edit data for micropublication; at present, no direct search services are offered from it.

Clientele/Availability: Services are available to chemists, pharmacists, and information centers of such organizations as hospitals, manufacturers, and mutual insurance centers.

Contact: Christian Garlot, General Manager, S.E.M.P. (Telex 203046 F.)

★694★
MEMORIAL UNIVERSITY OF NEWFOUNDLAND
OCEAN ENGINEERING INFORMATION CENTRE (OEIC)
Bartlett Bldg., K-122   Phone: (709) 737-8377
St. John's, NF, Canada A1B 3X5   Service Est: 1976
Ms. J.A. Whittick, Information Researcher

Staff: 1 Research professional; 2 technicians.

Related Organizations: The OEIC is sponsored by C-CORE (Centre for Cold Ocean Resources Engineering) and the Ocean Engineering Group of the Faculty of Engineering and Applied Science at the Memorial University of Newfoundland.

Description of System or Service: The OCEAN ENGINEERING INFORMATION CENTRE (OEIC) provides members of its sponsoring groups with information search services in the subject field of cold ocean engineering. The CENTRE maintains a collection of reports and publications on the subject and places special emphasis on identifying and indexing materials not readily available through computerized bibliographic data bases or commercial abstracting services. It provides access to its resource collection through a computerized KWOC index which is also available on microfiche. Additionally, the CENTRE publishes a bulletin and provides interlibrary loan and document copying services on a limited basis.

Scope and/or Subject Matter: Cold ocean engineering, including resource development in Canadian northern waters.

Input Sources: Information sources include technical report literature from university, industry, and government sources; papers from conferences, meetings, and workshops; directories, bibliographies, and atlases; annual reports; topographic maps and nautical charts; meteorological and oceanographic data in chart and tabulated format; and satellite imagery.

Holdings and Storage Media: The Centre maintains a technical documents collection supported by a computerized index.

Publications: OEIC Information Bulletin (10 per year)—identifies recent technical literature and includes information on upcoming conferences; available to groups and individuals with whom the Centre exchanges information and to others on an annual subscription basis.

Microform Products and Services: A microfiche edition of the KWOC index to the Centre's holdings is available on an annual subscription basis. A master index and two cumulative supplements are produced each year. Associates of C-CORE receive the index at no charge.

Computer-Based Products and Services: The OCEAN ENGINEERING INFORMATION CENTRE maintains and provides services from a computerized index to its holdings.

Clientele/Availability: Services are available to members of the Centre's sponsoring groups. Services are available to nonmembers under specific contract arrangement. The Centre will accept external information requests which can be dealt with expeditiously.

Contact: Ms. B. Rodden, Information Assistant, Ocean Engineering Information Centre.

★695★
MERILEES ASSOCIATES, INC.

Special Note: MERILEES ASSOCIATES, INC., of Toronto, Canada, is reported to have suspended its services. The firm was described in the 5th edition of the Encyclopedia of Information Systems and Services (entry 1260) as providing library and information retrieval systems management consulting services.

★696★
MERLIN GERIN COMPANY
(Societe MERLIN GERIN)
DOCUMENTATION DEPARTMENT
(Service Documentation)
MERL-ECO
                                      Phone: 76 579460
F-38050 Grenoble Cedex, France
Raymond Arnaud, Department Head

Description of System or Service: MERL-ECO is a machine-readable bibliographic data base containing abstracts and references to world literature on business, economics, and related topics. It is commercially available for online searching.

Scope and/or Subject Matter: Business, management, economics, finance.

Input Sources: Input for MERL-ECO is derived from French and foreign periodicals; books, yearbooks, and brochures; and trade reports and industrial overviews.

Holdings and Storage Media: The machine-readable MERL-ECO data base contains more than 22,000 references to literature published from 1973 to date. The file is updated monthly; approximately 2400 items are added each year.

Computer-Based Products and Services: MERL-ECO is commercially available online through G.CAM. Searchable elements in the data base include title in French and original language, author, language of document, source, abstract, keywords, descriptors, and date and number of document.

Clientele/Availability: Clients include the business and financial communities.

Contact: Raymond Arnaud, Head, Documentation Department. (Telex 320892 MERGER.)

★697★
MERLIN GERIN COMPANY
(Societe MERLIN GERIN)
DOCUMENTATION DEPARTMENT
(Service Documentation)
MERLIN-TECH
                                      Phone: 76 579460
F-38050 Grenoble Cedex, France
Raymond Arnaud, Department Head

Description of System or Service: MERLIN-TECH is a computer-readable file containing abstracts and references to worldwide literature dealing with electrical and electronic engineering and related sciences. MERLIN-TECH information is available in a printed abstracts journal and as a commercially available online data base.

Scope and/or Subject Matter: Electrical and electronic engineering, including electronic circuits and instrumentation, electrotechnical devices and equipment, electricity and magnetism, power systems, energy, control systems, computer systems and equipment, materials, and testing, reliability, and safety.

Input Sources: Input for the MERLIN-TECH data base is derived from literature published worldwide.

Holdings and Storage Media: The computer-readable MERLIN-TECH data base contains approximately 30,000 items dating from 1973 to the present. The file is updated monthly; about 2300 items are added annually.

Publications: Information from MERLIN-TECH is issued in a printed abstracts journal.

Computer-Based Products and Services: MERLIN-TECH is searchable online through ESA/IRS. Searchable elements in the data base include author, title in French and original language, source, document type, language of document, country, publication date, abstract, controlled vocabulary terms, and descriptors.

Clientele/Availability: Clients include the engineering community.

Contact: Raymond Arnaud, Head, Documentation Department. (Telex 320892 MERGER.)

★698★
METALS INFORMATION (LONDON)
The Metals Society Phone: 01-839 4071
1 Carlton House Terrace
London SW1Y 5DB, England
H. David Chafe, Director

Special Note: METALS INFORMATION is a joint service of The Metals Society in London and the American Society for Metals (ASM) in Metals Park, Ohio. Its chief products are the printed Metals Abstracts journal, the corresponding online METADEX (Metals Abstracts Index) data base, and the nonbibliographic Metals Datafile online data base. Full descriptions of METALS INFORMATION products and services are provided in the United States volume of this Encyclopedia.

Contact: Metals Information (London). The London telex number is 8814 813. The U.S. office for Metals Information is located at: American Society for Metals, Metals Park, OH 44073; telephone (216) 338-5151. (Telex 980 619.)

★699★
METROPOLITAN TORONTO LIBRARY BOARD
REGIONAL BIBLIOGRAPHIC PRODUCTS DEPARTMENT
789 Yonge St. Phone: (416) 928-5333
Toronto, ON, Canada M4W 2G8 Service Est: 1968
Josephine Tsui, Manager

Staff: 1 Information and library professional; 1 management professional; 7 clerical and nonprofessional.

Related Organizations: The Metropolitan Toronto Library Board is a regional organization representing the public library systems of six area municipalities while maintaining, on its own, the most extensive public library in Canada, from which it offers direct library services to the public and backup services to the other public library systems.

Description of System or Service: The REGIONAL BIBLIOGRAPHIC PRODUCTS DEPARTMENT compiles machine-readable data bases to provide centralized cataloging services for several classes of special materials held by Toronto area public libraries and, in some cases, other libraries in the province. Designed to produce printed guides to holdings, data bases are maintained for periodicals and newspapers, 16mm films, videorecordings, talking books, and books in 14 foreign languages held by the Board's Regional Multilanguage Services. Online access to the data bases is also available through the DEPARTMENT.

Scope and/or Subject Matter: Computer-supported cataloging of specialized materials in public libraries.

Input Sources: Input to the bibliographic files is derived primarily from original cataloging records.

Holdings and Storage Media: Machine-readable files hold information on 16,000 periodicals and newspapers, 15,500 16mm films, 3400 videorecordings, 4000 talking books, and 5000 foreign language books.

Publications: 1) 16mm Films Available from the Public Libraries of Metropolitan Toronto (biannual, with quarterly supplements); 2) Guide to Periodicals and Newspapers in the Public Libraries of Metropolitan Toronto (annual, with semiannual supplements); 3) Videorecordings Available in the Public Libraries of Metropolitan Toronto; 4) Talking Books Catalog (annual); 5) Multilanguage Books on Deposit in the Public Libraries of Metropolitan Toronto. All publications are available for purchase.

Computer-Based Products and Services: The REGIONAL BIBLIOGRAPHIC PRODUCTS DEPARTMENT maintains a series of machine-readable files of original cataloging data for special materials held by various libraries, and provides participating libraries with a sophisticated online inquiry module to the data bases. The data bases are also made available to eligible institutions for production of various special listings and statistical tabulations.

Clientele/Availability: Services are generally limited to public libraries in the province of Ontario.

Remarks: Online search services from data bases made available by several major vendors are also available at the Metropolitan Toronto Library through its Metroline Computerized Bibliographic Search Service.

Contact: Josephine Tsui, Manager, Regional Bibliographic Products Department. For information on the Metroline Computerized Bibliographic Search Service, contact Helen Baltais, Metroline Search Editor; telephone (416) 928-5236.

★700★
MEXICO
NATIONAL CENTER FOR HEALTH INFORMATION AND DOCUMENTATION
(Centro Nacional de Informacion y Documentacion en Salud - CENIDS)
Rio Mixcoac 36, 9 Piso Phone: (905) 534-4820
Col. del Valle Service Est: 1976
Mexico City 03100, D.F., Mexico
Dr. Cesar A. Macias-Chapula, Director

Staff: 1 Information and library professional; 6 management professional; 1 technician; 3 sales and marketing; 3 clerical and nonprofessional; 6 other.

Related Organizations: The Mexican School of Public Health/Escuela de Salud Publica de Mexico supports CENIDS.

Description of System or Service: The NATIONAL CENTER FOR HEALTH INFORMATION AND DOCUMENTATION (CENIDS) consists of a central unit located in Mexico City and 13 regional centers in Mexico that supply computer-based and manual information services to users of biomedical information. CENIDS provides online search and SDI services, distributes custom bibliographies, and offers document retrieval from national or international libraries. CENIDS also participates in the Pan American Health Organization's Latin American Cancer Research Information Project (LACRIP) by acquiring cancer-related literature and disseminating it throughout Mexico. Additionally, CENIDS serves as the U.S. National Library of Medicine's MEDLARS center for Mexico by making the system available to Mexican institutions and offering related training courses and other services.

Scope and/or Subject Matter: Biomedical sciences.

Input Sources: CENIDS uses online services and special libraries to provide biomedical information services. It collects projects and clinical protocols in cancer produced in Mexico to send to LACRIP.

Computer-Based Products and Services: CENIDS offers online searching and SDI from biomedical data bases offered by the U.S. National Library of Medicine, DIALOG Information Services, Inc., System Development Corporation (SDC), and Bibliographic Retrieval Services (BRS).

Other Services: In addition to services described above, CENIDS conducts conferences, seminars, and demonstrations in the area of online biomedical information retrieval.

Clientele/Availability: CENIDS serves medical students, doctors, nurses, and researchers in Mexico without restrictions.

Contact: Dr. Cesar A. Macias-Chapula, Director, National Center for Health Information and Documentation.

★701★
MEXICO
NATIONAL COUNCIL OF SCIENCE AND TECHNOLOGY
(Consejo Nacional de Ciencia y Tecnologia - CONACYT)
DATA BASE CONSULTATION SERVICE
(Servicio de Consulta a Bancos de Informacion - SECOBI)
Circuito Cultural Universitario Phone: 652 4000
Ciudad Universitaria Service Est: 1976
Mexico City 04515 D.F., Mexico

Special Note: The above name, address, and telephone number have been verified for this edition, although no questionnaire response was received. The following text is reprinted from the 5th edition.

Staff: 5 Information and library professional; 4 management

professional; 10 technicians; 7 clerical and nonprofessional.

Description of System or Service: The DATA BASE CONSULTATION SERVICE (SECOBI) supports the needs of Mexican researchers and students through a variety of computer-related information and consulting services. It conducts online searches through major commercial vendors, offers document delivery and translation services, and compiles information packets in specific subject areas. SECOBI is also involved in the design and creation of local data bases, and it rents terminals and trains searchers for organizations wishing to conduct their own online searches.

Scope and/or Subject Matter: All subjects covered by the data bases; emphasis is on science and technology.

Computer-Based Products and Services: SECOBI provides online searches of data bases made available by DIALOG Information Services, Inc., System Development Corporation (SDC), Data Resources, Inc., the U.S. National Library of Medicine, and Telesystemes Questel. SDI services are also available to those clients subscribing to the information packet service.

Clientele/Availability: Services are available to Mexican institutions and information centers.

Contact: Director, Data Base Consultation Service. (Telex 017-74-521.)

★702★
MEXICO
NATIONAL INSTITUTE FOR RESEARCH ON BIOLOGICAL RESOURCES
(Instituto Nacional de Investigaciones sobre Recursos Bioticos - INIREB)
INIREB LIBRARY
Km. 2.5 Antigua Carretera a
 Coatepec, Apartado Postal 63
Xalapa 91000, Veracruz, Mexico
Alma Aguilar Caceres, Head

Phone: 281 79274
Service Est: 1976

Staff: 5 Technicians; 2 clerical and nonprofessional.

Description of System or Service: The INIREB LIBRARY provides local researchers with information services that include maintaining a technical collection on biological resources, searching national and international online data bases, and preparing and using local floristic data bases.

Scope and/or Subject Matter: Ecology, botany, zoology, wood sciences, biochemistry, land use and development, and remote sensing.

Input Sources: Depending on the researcher's needs, input is derived from data bases or hard copy sources.

Holdings and Storage Media: The Library holds local floristic data bases and the Registry of Tropical and Arid Land Current Research in machine-readable form. Library holdings consist of 15,000 bound volumes and subscriptions to 300 periodicals.

Publications: 1) Indice de Proyectos en Desarrollo en Ecologia Tropical (yearly). 2) Indice de Proyectos en Desarrollo en Ecologia de Zonas Aridas (yearly). Both of the indexes are published in Spanish, English, and French. 3) Flora de Veracruz (5 per year). 4) Biotica (quarterly)—the official journal of the INIREB. A complete catalog of INIREB publications is available by request from the Institute.

Computer-Based Products and Services: Currently used only for internal purposes, the Library's data bases are searchable by keyword, title, author, administrative unit, and classification or accession number.

Clientele/Availability: Services are available to local researchers and universities, and, on application, to other users.

Contact: Maria Luisa De la Garza, Acquisitions Department, INIREB-SECOBI. (Telex 15542 INRBME.)

★703★
MEXICO
NATIONAL INSTITUTE OF NUCLEAR RESEARCH
(Instituto Nacional de Investigaciones Nucleares)
NUCLEAR INFORMATION AND DOCUMENTATION CENTER
Apdo. Postal No. 27-190
Mexico City, Mexico 18, D.F.
Prof. Pedro Zamora Rodriguez, Head Librarian

Phone: 563 7100
Service Est: 1957

Special Note: The above name, address, and telephone number have been verified for this edition, although no questionnaire response was received. The following text is reprinted from the 5th edition.

Staff: 11 Information and library professional; 2 management professional; 10 technicians; 9 clerical and nonprofessional.

Description of System or Service: The NUCLEAR INFORMATION AND DOCUMENTATION CENTER provides the staff of the National Institute of Nuclear Research with bibliographic and information services, and it disseminates the research work done by the Institute through official publications to universities and research institutions. The CENTER also acts as a national bibliographic center on science and technology and as Mexico's International Nuclear Information System (INIS) center. Additional services include consulting, network participation, manual and computerized literature searching, and referrals.

Scope and/or Subject Matter: Science and technology, energy, nuclear energy.

Input Sources: Input consists of INIS tapes, official and commercial periodical publications, and reports of national and international research centers of energy and nuclear energy.

Holdings and Storage Media: Holdings include magnetic tapes from INIS; 30,000 bound volumes; 365,000 technical reports; and subscriptions to 665 periodicals.

Computer-Based Products and Services: Batch-mode retrospective searching and SDI are offered from the INIS data base.

Clientele/Availability: Services are available to the staff of the Institute and chief researchers of other institutions.

Contact: Prof. Pedro Zamora Rodriguez, Head Librarian, Nuclear Information and Documentation Center.

★704★
MICROFOR INC.
800, place d'Youville
Bureau 1805
Quebec, PQ, Canada G1R 3P4

Phone: (418) 692-4369
Founded: 1973

Staff: Approximately 32 total.

Related Organizations: Centre d'Edition Juridique (CEJ) in Montreal is the parent company of Microfor.

Description of System or Service: MICROFOR INC. indexes and abstracts French-language newspaper and periodical articles for inclusion in hardcopy publications and bibliographic and analytical computer-readable data bases. MICROFOR also provides consulting services in the areas of abstracting, indexing, automatic information retrieval, and bibliographic data base software.

Scope and/or Subject Matter: Local, national, and international news covering political, economic, social, and cultural events; Quebec and French current affairs; Quebec and Canadian history including historical anthropology, ethnography, and history of literature, religions, social groups, economics, and the arts.

Input Sources: Input is derived mainly from French-language newspaper and periodical articles. Additional input is obtained from library catalogs.

Holdings and Storage Media: MICROFOR maintains machine-readable data bases which contain about 335,000 documents and 3.4 million records; approximately 80,000 documents are classified under 380,000 entries each year.

Publications: 1) Index Analytique du Journal "Le Monde Diplomatique" (annual)—indexes articles appearing in the French journal, Le Monde Diplomatique. A cumulative index to articles dating from 1954-1983 is available for purchase; includes an English-French glossary of selected descriptors. 2) Index de l'Actualite Vue a Travers la Presse Ecrite (monthly with annual cumulation)—abstracts and indexes three French-language Quebec newspapers. 3) Repertoire Bibliographique d'Histoire du Quebec et du Canada—indexes and abstracts articles appearing in Revue d'Histoire de l'Amerique Francaise and approximately 400 periodicals.

Microform Products and Services: Some out-of-print annual cumulations are available on 16mm and 35mm microfiche.

Computer-Based Products and Services: MICROFOR produces the following computer-readable data bases: 1) Quebec-Actualite—corresponds to the Index de l'Actualite publication. The data base holds approximately 250,000 articles and 1.9 million records with about 2300 articles added each month. 2) Canada-Histoire—corresponds to the Repertoire Bibliographique publication. The data base contains approximately 17,000 documents and 130,000 records with about 3000 documents added every three months; available for online searching through Informatech as HISCABEQ. MICROFOR also makes available, for lease or purchase, software for the production of bibliographical and analytical computer-readable data bases.

Other Services: Additional services include abstracting, indexing, and consulting.

Clientele/Availability: Services and products are available without restrictions.

Contact: Philip Grenon, Marketing Director, or Marie Claude de Billy, Marketing Department, Microfor Inc.

★705★
MICROINFO, LTD.
P.O. Box 3, Newman Lane
Alton, Hampshire GU34 2PG, England
R.B. Selwyn, Director
Phone: 0420 86848
Founded: 1970

Related Organizations: Related organizations include Docupro and Infocom (see separate entries).

Description of System or Service: MICROINFO, LTD. operates the NTIS United Kingdom Service Center, which markets and distributes publications and services of the U.S. National Technical Information Service (NTIS) in the United Kingdom, Ireland, and in other overseas areas where there is no local NTIS agent. The company also provides document delivery service for all publications offered by the U.S. Government Printing Office. Additionally, it collects information for the NTIS data base, performs computerized literature searching, and publishes two newsletters. Other services represented by MICROINFO include the World Bank, the International Monetary Fund, and the U.S. National Standards Association.

Scope and/or Subject Matter: Science, technology, engineering, energy, environment, computer and video technology, social science, economics, business, and construction.

Publications: 1) Microinfo (monthly)—micrographics news bulletin. 2) Videoinfo (monthly)—video markets and technology news bulletin.

Microform Products and Services: All NTIS report literature is available in microform. Complete collections of U.S. government and industry standards are offered in microform with full revision service.

Computer-Based Products and Services: MICROINFO conducts online searching of the NTIS data base and disseminates published searches of NTIS, Engineering Index, American Petroleum Institute, and several other technology and management-oriented files. The firm also fulfills orders for NTIS documents placed online through DIALOG Information Services, Inc., System Development Corporation (SDC), and ESA/IRS.

Clientele/Availability: Publications and services are available by subscription or on demand as required. A deposit account service is available.

Contact: R.B. Selwyn, Director, Microinfo, Ltd. (Telex 858431 MINFO G.)

★706★
MICROMEDIA LTD.
144 Front St. W.
Toronto, ON, Canada M5J 2L7
Robert Gibson, President
Phone: (416) 593-5211
Founded: 1972

Staff: 13 Information and library professional; 6 management professional; 13 technicians; 8 sales and marketing; 10 clerical and nonprofessional.

Related Organizations: Micromedia Ltd. operates the SVP Canada service (see separate entry) and is the Canadian representative for DIALOG Information Services, Inc. and several micropublishers.

Description of System or Service: MICROMEDIA LTD. is a publishing firm whose primary activity is the distribution of serials and Canadian government documents in microform. Its Microlog service is an integrated indexing and document delivery service for report literature from Canadian government agencies, universities, research institutions, and nonprofit organizations. The service comprises a monthly indexing publication, a cataloging service providing libraries with card sets or magnetic tapes of MARC records for the documents, and full-text documents on microfiche. The Microlog index is also publicly available online. Additionally, MICROMEDIA provides most documents on a single-title demand basis on paper or microfiche. It offers Canadian and U.S. corporate reports on demand through the INSIDER service, and Canadian and foreign patents through a patents service. MICROMEDIA LTD. also publishes a number of Canadian reference works including the Canadian Business Index and the Canadian News Index, which are available in printed form and online (see separate entries following this one for full descriptions).

Scope and/or Subject Matter: Report and document literature of reference value in any subject area from Canadian federal, provincial, and local governments and nonprofit institutions; company reports and patents.

Input Sources: Reports and documents are collected from more than 350 publication sources.

Holdings and Storage Media: The online Microlog Index data base holds approximately 10,000 references dating from 1979 to the present and is updated quarterly with about 1000 new references.

Publications: 1) Microlog Index (monthly with annual cumulations)—each issue cites more than 500 current titles; contains main entry, subject, and title sections and a guide to microfiche collections. 2) Directory of Associations in Canada—a comprehensive listing of approximately 9500 international, national, interprovincial, and provincial associations in Canada, along with their chapters. 3) Canadian Library Handbook/ Guide des Bibliotheques Canadiennes—a directory of Canadian libraries (classified by location, subject, and name), publishers, and archives. Micromedia also issues a number of other publications; a catalog from the firm is available by request.

Microform Products and Services: The Microlog service makes available the full text of Canadian report and document literature on microfiche in a variety of subscription packages. Micromedia also issues individual government documents series on microfiche.

Computer-Based Products and Services: The Microlog Index data base is available online through CAN/OLE.

Clientele/Availability: Services and products are intended for use by libraries, research institutions, and government agencies.

Contact: Robert Gibson, President, or Frank X. Gagne, Manager, Database Marketing & Development, Micromedia Ltd. (Telex 065 24668.)

★707★
MICROMEDIA LTD.
CANADIAN BUSINESS INDEX (CBI)
144 Front St. W.
Toronto, ON, Canada M5J 2L7
Robert Gibson, President
Phone: (416) 593-5211

Description of System or Service: The CANADIAN BUSINESS INDEX (CBI) covers articles dealing with business, economics, and industry appearing in major Canadian newspapers and business periodicals. The CANADIAN BUSINESS INDEX is commercially available online and as a monthly printed publication.

Scope and/or Subject Matter: Canadian business, economic, industry, and company news.

Input Sources: Input is obtained from 170 Canadian trade and business publications, as well as newspapers including the Financial Post, Financial Times, and Globe and Mail.

Holdings and Storage Media: The computer-readable CBI data base contains 45,000 references per year of coverage.

Publications: Canadian Business Index-CBI (monthly with annual cumulations)—includes subject, corporation name, and personal name indexes; available by subscription.

Computer-Based Products and Services: The CANADIAN BUSINESS INDEX is available online through QL Systems Limited. It is also accessible through DIALOG Information Services, Inc. as part of the Canadian Business and Current Affairs data base, which also includes records from the Canadian News Index.

Clientele/Availability: Services are available without restrictions.

Remarks: The Canadian Business Index was formerly known as the Canadian Business Periodicals Index.

Contact: Robert Gibson, President, or Frank X. Gagne, Manager, Database Marketing & Development, Micromedia Ltd. (Telex 065 24668.)

★708★
MICROMEDIA LTD.
CANADIAN NEWS INDEX (CNI)
144 Front St. W.   Phone: (416) 593-5211
Toronto, ON, Canada M5J 2L7
Robert Gibson, President

Description of System or Service: The CANADIAN NEWS INDEX (CNI) is a computer-based index to seven major Canadian daily newspapers. The file contains references to world, national, provincial, and local news; selected letters to the editor and obituaries; government activities; labor news; sports; biographies; and reviews. The CANADIAN NEWS INDEX is commercially available online and as a monthly printed publication. A companion microfiche service provides the full text of selected articles indexed.

Scope and/or Subject Matter: Canadian news.

Input Sources: CNI indexes the following newspapers: Globe and Mail, Toronto Star, Vancouver Sun, Winnipeg Free Press, Montreal Gazette, Calgary Herald, and Halifax Chronicle-Herald.

Holdings and Storage Media: The CNI data base is maintained in machine-readable form.

Publications: Canadian News Index-CNI (monthly with annual cumulations)—guide to events and people making the news in Canada. The Index is divided into two sections: the subject index, which contains all subject terms as well as government, corporation, and organization names, and the biographical index, which is arranged by individual name. Each entry cites article heading (some with added keywords), news source, title and date, and page number. Articles are displayed under each heading in chronological order to provide a narrative approach to events of the period covered. Feature articles, columns, letters, editorials, photographs, and graphic illustrations are designated by symbols. CNI is available by subscription.

Microform Products and Services: Micromedia's Canadian Press News File monthly microfiche service provides the text of every Canadian Press article appearing in every daily paper indexed in the Canadian News Index.

Computer-Based Products and Services: The CANADIAN NEWS INDEX is available online through QL Systems Limited. It is also accessible through DIALOG Information Services, Inc. as part of the Canadian Business and Current Affairs data base, which also contains citations from the Canadian Business Index.

Clientele/Availability: Services are available without restrictions.

Contact: Robert Gibson, President, or Frank X. Gagne, Manager, Database Marketing & Development, Micromedia Ltd. (Telex 065 24668.)

★709★
MIDORI BOOK STORE COMPANY
Nishi Hankyu Bldg.   Phone: 06 3715395
Shibata 2-Chome, 1-18 Kitaku   Founded: 1947
Osaka, Japan
Masayuki Niwa, Director

Description of System or Service: The MIDORI BOOK STORE COMPANY acts as an agent in Japan for foreign and international publishers of print and machine-readable information products in scientific fields. Specific services include importing of scientific publications, international periodical subscription services, reformatting of computer tapes, online scientific information services, and dissemination of information on new scientific information products of all kinds.

Scope and/or Subject Matter: Scientific information products and services.

Input Sources: Input is derived from worldwide publishers.

Computer-Based Products and Services: MIDORI makes available computer-readable data bases in scientific and technical fields.

Clientele/Availability: Services are directed toward organizations in Japan.

Contact: Masayuki Niwa, Director, MIDORI Book Store Company. The mailing address is P.O. Box 269, Osaka Central, Osaka, Japan. (Telex 64235 J.)

★710★
MIKRO-CERID
134 bis, rue du Vieux Pont   Phone: 01 6099414
  de Sevres   Founded: 1979
F-92100 Boulogne sur Seine, France
Jean Pioch, Director

Staff: Approximately 11 total.

Related Organizations: Mikros Enterprises is the parent company of Mikro-Cerid and seven other companies.

Description of System or Service: MIKRO-CERID is an information-on-demand company that searches appropriate sources and presents compiled, verified, and organized information for clients in all fields. MIKRO-CERID also offers SDI and document delivery services. Additionally, the firm conducts training seminars in the use of online data bases, provides consulting services and feasibility studies in library management, and markets and adapts software packages for bibliographic data processing and a wide variety of library products.

Scope and/or Subject Matter: Subjects of interest to clients; library automation.

Computer-Based Products and Services: MIKRO-CERID provides online searches and SDI services from data bases made available through System Development Corporation (SDC), DIALOG Information Services, Inc., ESA/IRS, and all French systems. It also offers the EUROSERV service which fills requests placed through DIALOG's DIALORDER online document delivery service. EUROSERV provides primarily U.S. government publications and reports.

Clientele/Availability: Services are available on a fee basis without restriction.

Contact: Marie Claude Auger, Assistant, Mikro-Cerid. (Telex MIKROS 203606 F.)

★711★
MINERALOGICAL SOCIETY OF GREAT BRITAIN
MINERALOGICAL ABSTRACTS
41 Queen's Gate   Phone: 01-584 7516
London SW7 5HR, England   Service Est: 1920
Professor R. A. Howie, Principal Editor

Staff: Approximately 3 total.

Related Organizations: Mineralogical Abstracts is produced jointly with the Mineralogical Society of America.

Description of System or Service: MINERALOGICAL ABSTRACTS is a guide to literature in the fields of geochemistry, mineralogy, and petrology. It is produced as a hardcopy publication and as a computer-readable data base which is expected to be made available online.

Scope and/or Subject Matter: Geochemistry, mineralogy, and petrology, including clay minerals, experimental work, geochronology, meteorites, and gemstones.

Input Sources: Input is derived from 200 periodicals, plus books, reports, and proceedings.

Holdings and Storage Media: The computer-readable Mineralogical Abstracts data base dates from 1982 to the present and holds 5000 abstracts per year of coverage.

Publications: Mineralogical Abstracts (quarterly with annual index issue)—arranged in 18 subject categories; available by subscription.

Computer-Based Products and Services: The data base is expected to be made commercially available online in the near future.

Clientele/Availability: Clients include Society members and libraries.

Contact: Professor R.A. Howie, Editor, Mineralogical Abstracts.

★712★
MITAKA
JAPANSCAN
3-5 Tavistock St. Phone: 0926 311126
Leamington Spa, Warwicks. CV32 5PJ,
  England Service Est: 1983
Clive A. Smith, Head

Staff: 12 Information and library professional; 3 management professional; 2 technicians; 1 sales and marketing; 5 clerical and nonprofessional; 3 other.

Description of System or Service: JAPANSCAN is a current awareness and document delivery service providing information on selected industries in Japan to clients in Europe and worldwide. It publishes a series of monthly bulletins providing coverage of Japanese newspapers and periodicals literature on the food, biosciences, and pharmaceuticals and toiletries industries in Japan. JAPANSCAN bulletins cover major developments in marketing, research and development, and government activities in each industry as well as industrial news. Additionally, JAPANSCAN translates Japanese-language company profiles, journal and newspaper articles, and documentation in scientific, technical, or commercial fields to English; procures articles, journals, and product samples mentioned in JAPANSCAN bulletins; and scans leading industrial and financial newspapers, journals, and technical publications for items appearing on subjects or industrial areas of interest to clients.

Scope and/or Subject Matter: Food science and the food industry, pharmaceuticals and toiletries industry, and bioscience and biotechnology in Japan.

Input Sources: Information sources include newspapers, periodicals, reports, commercial literature, annual reports, and experts in the field.

Holdings and Storage Media: Mitaka maintains a collection of approximately 1000 directories, reference works, and scientific and technical dictionaries covering Japan and subscriptions to 150 periodicals.

Publications: 1) Food Industry Bulletin (monthly)—available by subscription. The Bulletin contains news items and commentary on marketing, research and development, industrial news, and government activities reported in leading Japanese financial and industrial publications and food journals. Each issue contains a background briefing on a major company's activities in the food industry. A Datafile section contains citations and brief descriptions of articles in Japanese journals covering marketing, food products, food technology, and food science. The Bulletin also contains two indexes: the first includes products, science, technology, marketing, and law; the second includes companies, institutes, ministries, and countries.

2) Bio-Industry Bulletin (monthly)—available by subscription. The Bulletin covers research and development, industrial news, and government activity in the biosciences as reported in the daily Japanese financial and industrial press. The Datafile section contains patent applications listings as well as citations and brief descriptions of articles published in the areas of nucleic acids and genetic engineering, enzymes, cell culture, cell growth promoters and inhibitors, immunology, virology, general microbiology, proteins, glycoproteins and related substances, lipids and related substances, cytology, general biochemistry and metabolism, biomaterials, the environment, analytical techiques, and medical physics. Each issue also includes a company profile, a subject index, and an index of companies, government bodies, and universities.

3) Pharmaceuticals and Toiletries Bulletin (monthly)—available by subscription. The Bulletin covers relevant marketing, research and development, industrial news, and government activity reported in the leading daily Japanese financial and industrial press and journals. It contains a background briefing of a major firm in the pharmaceutical or toiletries field. Citations and abstracts listed in the Datafile are arranged under the journal title by subject areas. The Bulletin includes a main index covering products, science, technology, and marketing, and a company index which also includes ministries and institutions. Annual indexes are produced for each industry publication.

Computer-Based Products and Services: Mitaka is developing an online data base for JAPANSCAN information and is planning to make it commercially available.

Clientele/Availability: Services are available without restrictions worldwide. Clients include companies planning to export to Japan and Western companies in the pharmaceuticals, foods, or biosciences industries.

Projected Publications and Services: Bulletins on office automation, information technology, ceramics, and other areas are planned.

Remarks: Mitaka is a bilingual company dealing exclusively in communications with Japan. Its communications services include the following: JAPANTRANS—provides on demand specialist translation and linguistic consultancy services; JAPANSEARCH—provides retrospective information retrieval services; JAPANFILE—produces on-demand surveys, reports, and statistics by company, industry, product, and scientific field; and JAPANPRINT—offers design and typesetting of large-scale technical and promotional publications in Japanese. Mitaka also offers interpretation and facsimile services.

Contact: Miss Fumi Yano, JAPANSCAN Services. (Telex 311959.)

★713★
MONITAN INFORMATION CONSULTANTS LTD.
Berry Edge Rd. Phone: 0207 500957
Consett, Durham DH8 5EU, England
Monica Anderton, Director

Description of System or Service: MONITAN INFORMATION CONSULTANTS LTD. is an information consulting firm providing management studies, market research, and techno-economic evaluations in biotechnology, energy, and other technical fields. Services range from the provision of short replies to the compilation of major reports and include current awareness services and computerized information retrieval from commercially available online data bases.

Scope and/or Subject Matter: Biotechnology, biomedicine, health care, energy, new information systems, new technology, working practices, and other topics.

Input Sources: Information is obtained from commercially available online data bases, personal contacts, and other sources.

Computer-Based Products and Services: MONITAN INFORMATION CONSULTANTS LTD. provides computerized information retrieval services from data bases made available through Data-Star and ESA/IRS.

Other Services: Also offered are word processing services and organization of conferences and seminars.

Clientele/Availability: Services are available without restrictions. Clients include government agencies, the Commission of the European Communities, companies, and others.

Contact: Monica Anderton, Director, Monitan Information Consultants Ltd. (Telex 53622.)

★714★
MORGAN-GRAMPIAN PLC.
M-G VIDEOTEX SERVICES
30 Calderwood St.   Phone: 01-855 7777
London SE18 6QH, England   Service Est: 1977
Peter Head, General Manager

Staff: 1 Management professional; 2 sales and marketing; 3 clerical and nonprofessional.

Description of System or Service: M-G VIDEOTEX SERVICES supplies videotex information and umbrella information provider services for the travel trade. It also provides research data on the retail music, media, and video markets.

Scope and/or Subject Matter: Videotex services for the travel trade; market research.

Input Sources: Information is obtained through company-conducted research.

Publications: Morgan-Grampian is the publisher of 40 magazines and newspapers.

Computer-Based Products and Services: M-G VIDEOTEX SERVICES provides videotex information provider services.

Clientele/Availability: Clients include the travel trades, retail music and video trades, and advertising agencies.

Contact: Peter Head, General Manager, M-G Videotex Services.

★715★
MORGAN GRENFELL & CO. LTD.
INTERFISC
23 Great Winchester St.   Phone: 01-588 4545
London EC2P 2AX, England   Service Est: 1981
Brian Laurence Kieran, Senior Assistant Director

Description of System or Service: INTERFISC is a computerized information system containing comprehensive details of double taxation treaties between more than 60 countries. Prepared by experts in the field, the data base includes the following information: standardized summary descriptions of the domestic corporate tax systems of the countries; comments on the unusual features of certain taxation systems together with explanatory examples; information on the status of double taxation treaties among the countries; current withholding tax rates on dividends, interest, and royalty income under double taxation treaties; double taxation relief. INTERFISC is searchable online through Eurolex.

Scope and/or Subject Matter: Double corporate taxation treaties between countries.

Input Sources: Input is derived from double taxation treaties and other taxation data.

Holdings and Storage Media: Interfisc information is held in machine-readable form and is updated continuously.

Computer-Based Products and Services: INTERFISC is searchable online as part of the Eurolex legal research service. Data reflect the current situation, while pending changes are clearly noted. INTERFISC also contains an optimization model using the tax data to identify the most cash-efficient method by which funds are transferred from one jurisdiction to another.

Clientele/Availability: Services are intended for lawyers and accountants.

Contact: Brian Laurence Kieran, Senior Assistant Director, Morgan Grenfell & Co. Ltd.

★716★
MOTOR VEHICLE DOCUMENTATION
(Dokumentation Kraftfahrwesen - DKF)
Gronerstr. 5   Phone: 07141 44084
D-7140 Ludwigsburg, Fed. Rep. of
   Germany   Founded: 1974

Staff: 1 Management professional; 1 technician; 1 sales and marketing; 3 clerical and nonprofessional.

Description of System or Service: MOTOR VEHICLE DOCUMENTATION (DKF) is a registered society established to process technical literature related to the automotive industry. DKF selects, documents, classifies, and indexes relevant international materials and stores this information in the machine-readable DKF data base. The data base is used to provide a number of services, including the following: 1) DKF Literature Information Service—provides, approximately every three weeks, some 800 brief reports on various topics in the automotive industry and related areas. The information is supplied in printed form on paper or cards, on magnetic tape, or as microfilm. 2) Standard Information Service—regular service designed to provide users with general information on common problems. 3) Individual Information Service—provided on a regular basis, the service supplies special information about a specific problem based on requests formulated by the user. 4) Literature Research—provides information about literature relevant to individual requests formulated by users. The DKF data base is also commercially available online.

Scope and/or Subject Matter: Motor vehicle design, construction, and manufacturing.

Input Sources: Information is gathered from approximately 300 periodicals, as well as research reports, technical journals, papers from the Society of Automotive Engineers, theses, university publications, company publications, rules and regulations, and other sources of scientific and technical information about the automotive industry.

Holdings and Storage Media: The machine-readable DKF data base holds approximately 40,000 records dating from 1974 to the present; the data base is updated monthly at an annual increase of 6000 records. Library holdings include 4000 bound volumes and 200 periodical subscriptions.

Microform Products and Services: DKF information is available on microfilm.

Computer-Based Products and Services: MOTOR VEHICLE DOCUMENTATION maintains and provides information retrieval, SDI, and magnetic tape services from the DKF data base for members. The DKF data base is also publicly available online through Data-Star and FIZ Technik. Data elements present include the following: title; German-language abstract; author; corporate source/ author affiliation; country of publication; source reference; document number; classification code; controlled terms; document type; and others.

Other Services: DKF also produces the Leistungs- und Konstruktions Datenbank (LKD).

Clientele/Availability: Clients include motor vehicle manufacturers, suppliers of components and accessories, associations, university and research institutes, and others.

Contact: Erich Feldhaus or Wolfram Schurmann, Motor Vehicle Documentation.

★717★
MULTINATIONAL ASSOCIATION OF PRODUCERS AND RETAILERS OF ELECTRICITY-DOCUMENTATION
(Association Multinationale des Producteurs et Revendeurs d'Electricite-Documentation - AMPEREDOC)
Electricity Supply Board   Phone: 01 771821
Lower Fitzwilliam St.
Dublin 2, Ireland
James C. O'Reilly, Secretary

Related Organizations: AMPEREDOC receives funding and assistance from the Commission of the European Communities (CEC).

Description of System or Service: MULTINATIONAL ASSOCIATION OF PRODUCERS AND RETAILERS OF ELECTRICITY-DOCUMENTATION (AMPEREDOC) is a European information system arising from the cooperation of electric utilities in retrieving, identifying, and disseminating all relevant documents, including nonconventional literature. AMPEREDOC maintains a multilingual bibliographic data base covering literature dealing with the generation, transmission, distribution, and utilization of electrical energy, alternative sources of energy, and allied topics of interest to public utilities. The data base is compiled from magnetic tapes submitted by participating organizations to the technical processing center at

Electricite de France, where input is merged. AMPEREDOC is made publicly available online through ESA/IRS.

Scope and/or Subject Matter: Electrical energy, alternate sources of energy, and energy-related subjects of interest to public utilities.

Input Sources: Input consists of publications, documents, conference proceedings, and nonconventional literature supplied by electric utilities.

Holdings and Storage Media: The computer-readable AMPEREDOC data base contains approximately 1500 citations.

Computer-Based Products and Services: The AMPEREDOC data base is available online through ESA/IRS.

Clientele/Availability: Services are available without restrictions.

Contact: James C. O'Reilly, Secretary, Multinational Association of Producers and Retailers of Electricity-Documentation. (Telex 25313 ESB EI).

N

★718★
NASH INFORMATION SERVICES INC.
1975 Bel Air Dr.
Ottawa, ON, Canada K2C 0X1
Dr. John C. Nash, President
Phone: (613) 225-3781
Founded: 1976

Staff: 1 Information and library professional; 1 management professional; 1 technician.

Description of System or Service: NASH INFORMATION SERVICES INC. was originally established to publish specialized source materials on microfiche. Its services have been expanded to include manual and computerized information retrieval, document delivery, and software development. NASH also offers consulting and in-house assistance and training, including development or reorganization of resource centers and client-tailored staff training in the use of in-house and other information sources.

Scope and/or Subject Matter: Information research and consulting services.

Input Sources: Input is obtained from online data bases and other sources.

Microform Products and Services: Special interest materials, including theses, bibliographies, and conference proceedings, are available on microfiche.

Computer-Based Products and Services: Nash Information Services conducts computerized searches of data bases made available through DIALOG Information Services, Inc. It also develops microcomputer software for a variety of applications, including library work.

Clientele/Availability: Clients include agencies of the U.S. and Canadian governments, as well as professionals from industry and the private sector.

Contact: Mary M. Nash, Senior Consultant, Nash Information Services Inc.

★719★
NATIONAL AUTONOMOUS UNIVERSITY OF MEXICO
(Universidad Nacional Autonoma de Mexico)
CENTER FOR SCIENTIFIC AND HUMANISTIC INFORMATION
(Centro de Informacion Cientifica y Humanistica - CICH)
Apdo. Postal 70-392
Ciudad Universitaria
Mexico City 04510 D.F., Mexico
Dr. Armando M. Sandoval, Director
Phone: 5480858
Service Est: 1971

Special Note: No questionnaire response was received for this entry for the 6th edition. The entry is reprinted as it appeared in the 5th edition.

Staff: 39 Information and library professional; 7 management professional; 25 clerical and nonprofessional.

Description of System or Service: The CENTER FOR SCIENTIFIC AND HUMANISTIC INFORMATION (CICH) provides a number of information services through its three departments. The Department of Documents maintains a reference and information library, and operates a print and microform document delivery service. The Department of Subscriptions handles an automated serials acquisition service for 140 University libraries. The Department of Information prepares two computer-based current awareness indexing journals, conducts manual and computerized literature searching, and provides SDI services.

Scope and/or Subject Matter: All subjects of interest to the University community, particularly in the areas of science, social science, economics, humanities.

Input Sources: More than 850 Latin American journals are indexed for the current awareness publications.

Holdings and Storage Media: Library holdings number 2500 books and other documents and subscriptions to 1250 periodicals. CICH also maintains computer-readable files.

Publications: 1) CLASE: Citas Latinoamericanas en Sociologia, Economia y Humanidades (quarterly)—indexes 450 Latin American sociological, economic, and humanities journals. 2) Periodica: Indice de Revistas Latinoamericanas en Ciencias (quarterly)—indexes 400 Latin American scientific journals. 3) Bibliografia Latinoamericana (twice yearly)—compiles and indexes references to articles published by Latin Americans or on Latin America in more than 6000 foreign journals. 4) Subscription Catalogue (annual).

Computer-Based Products and Services: CICH offers online literature searching from data bases made available by System Development Corporation (SDC) and DIALOG Information Services, Inc. SDI services are also provided. Internally generated computerized services include the automated serials system, as well as the processing, classifying, and printing of publications. The Center also is the Latin American input center for the ASFA Data Base and journal.

Clientele/Availability: Services are intended primarily for higher education systems in Mexico and Latin America.

Contact: Dr. Armando M. Sandoval, Director, Center for Scientific and Humanistic Information. (Telex 17-74523 UNAMME.)

★720★
NATIONAL CENTER FOR CHEMICAL INFORMATION
(Centre National de l'Information Chimique - CNIC)
La Maison de la Chimie
28 ter, rue Saint Dominique
F-75007 Paris, France
Phone: (not reported)
Founded: 1972

Staff: Approximately 15 total.

Related Organizations: The Center is a cooperative effort among the following organizations: Centre National de la Recherche Scientifique (CNRS), Association Francaise de Documentation Automatique en Chimie (AFDAC), Association pour la Recherche et le Developpement en Informatique Chimique (ARDIC), and Union des Industries Chimiques (UIC).

Description of System or Service: The NATIONAL CENTER FOR CHEMICAL INFORMATION (CNIC) offers a variety of services to facilitate access to computerized sources of information in chemistry and related sciences. As the French representative for Chemical Abstracts Service (CAS), it provides computerized SDI services from CAS data bases and it prepares them for online searching through Telesystemes Questel. CNIC also offers online search services from other publicly available data bases in chemistry and metallurgy, and it provides document delivery services. Additionally, the CENTER conducts education courses in online searching and acts as a consultant in the area of scientific information services.

Scope and/or Subject Matter: Information services in chemistry and other sciences.

Input Sources: Input sources include Chemical Abstracts Service and publicly available online services.

Computer-Based Products and Services: Utilizing CAS data bases, CNIC prepares a number of online files that are accessible through Telesystemes Questel. Among the data bases offered are the following: 1) EUCAS —contains more than 6.2 million bibliographic citations. Searchable as four separate files as follows: EUCAS67, covering the years 1967-1971; EUCAS72, covering the years 1972-1976; EUCAS77, covering the years 1977-1981; and EUCAS82, covering the years 1982 to date. 2) CANOM—contains the chemical nomenclature covered in the EUCAS files. 3) EURECAS—provides chemical structure data for the chemical literature covered in EUCAS; searchable using DARC software. CNIC also offers search and SDI from CAS and other data bases.

Clientele/Availability: Services and products are intended for users of chemical information in France.

Contact: National Center for Chemical Information.

★721★
NATIONAL COMPUTING CENTRE LTD. (NCC)
INFORMATION SERVICES DIVISION
Oxford Rd. Phone: 061 2286333
Manchester M1 7ED, England Service Est: 1966

Special Note: The above name, address, and telephone number have been verified for this edition, although no questionnaire response was received. The following text is reprinted from the 5th edition.

Staff: 10 Total.

Related Organizations: The National Computing Centre is a nonprofit organization financed by industry, commerce, and government. It is composed of computer users, manufacturers, and service organizations.

Description of System or Service: The INFORMATION SERVICES DIVISION collects, verifies, abstracts, and disseminates information on all aspects of computing in the United Kingdom. It stores this information in machine-readable files and makes it available through inquiry answering services, through hardcopy and microfiche publications, and through computerized searches and tape distribution.

Scope and/or Subject Matter: All aspects of computing and data processing including computing hardware, software, services, suppliers, literature, and installations.

Input Sources: Information is collected and abstracted from brochures, manuals, press releases, and questionnaires. Computing journals are also scanned regularly.

Publications: 1) Computing Journal Abstracts (fortnightly)—contains about 100 abstracts from 400 data processing and computing journals; available by subscription. 2) Computer Hardware Record (monthly)—contains descriptions of computer equipment including the following information: supplier, manufacturer, price, rental policy, maintenance, compatibility with other equipment, standards of use, specifications of the equipment, and optional features. 3) Computer Installation Record (CIR)—consists of 10 separate volumes of information. Each volume details installed computing equipment in a major geographical region of the United Kingdom. 4) CIR Change Service (monthly)—monitors movements in computer installations and details new sites, major upgrades, changes in management, and aged machines. 5) Computer Market Statistics (quarterly)—contains statistical analyses covering hardware, software, geography, industry, age, and distributed computing areas. 6) Computing News Roundup (monthly)—provides abstracts of news items under six headings: company news, hardware, miscellaneous, personnel, services, and software. 7) Directory of Computing Hardware—published as an aid for the location, comparison, and selection of computing hardware; based on information contained in the corresponding Hardware data base. 8) Directory of Computing Software—lists information held in the corresponding Software data base; includes a full cross-reference index of software acronyms. 9) Directory of Computing Suppliers—lists company names, addresses, and telephone numbers. Additional directories are under development. Various monographs are also published; a descriptive brochure is available from NCC on request.

Microform Products and Services: Fichefacts (quarterly)—produced on 48x microfiche, each set replaces the previous quarter's. Corresponding to the Computer Installation Record, the service provides details on every computer site in the United Kingdom and the Irish Republic; available by subscription.

Computer-Based Products and Services: The INFORMATION SERVICES DIVISION maintains computing information classified into six computer-readable data bases: 1) Hardware—computer systems, peripherals, conversion equipment, storage devices, and data transmission. 2) Installations—company name, industry sector, manufacturer and model, peripherals, applications, and other related information. 3) Literature—abstracts of articles and technical papers published in computing periodicals and journals. 4) Services—software houses, consultants, computer bureaus, other computing service industry organizations. 5) Software—utility and application programs, suppliers, suitable computers, languages, availability. 6) Suppliers—names, addresses, and locations of the companies who provide computing equipment, software, and services. Computerized searches and magnetic tapes of the data bases are available. Data retrieval is accomplished through use of NCC's Filetab file handling and report generating package. The package is adaptable to various computers and is available for purchase.

Other Services: The Information Services Division also offers manual literature searching and inquiry answering. The advisory service of NCC offers fee-based consulting in the field of data processing.

Clientele/Availability: Services are available free to NCC members and their international affiliates; a fee is charged to nonmembers.

Contact: Group Manager - Information, National Computing Centre Ltd. (Telex 668962.)

★722★
NATIONAL CONSERVATORY OF ARTS AND CRAFTS
(Conservatoire National des Arts et Metiers)
NATIONAL INSTITUTE FOR DOCUMENTATION TECHNIQUES
(Institut National des Techniques de la Documentation - INTD)
292, rue Saint-Martin Phone: 01 2712414
F-75141 Paris Cedex 3, France Service Est: 1950
Bruno Delmas, Director of Studies

Staff: Regular staff includes approximately 6 total. Teaching staff comprises visiting documentation and information science professionals.

Related Organizations: The Institute receives support from the French Ministry of Education.

Description of System or Service: The NATIONAL INSTITUTE FOR DOCUMENTATION TECHNIQUES (INTD) provides education in the area of documentation science, including information research, organization, analysis, indexing, and dissemination. The INSTITUTE also issues a monthly abstracts bulletin in the field of library and information science, the contents of which are made available online as part of the machine-readable PASCAL data bases.

Scope and/or Subject Matter: Documentation techniques in all subject areas.

Input Sources: Input for the Institute's bulletin is drawn from approximately 40 international journals in the fields of information and computer sciences and from publicly available data bases.

Holdings and Storage Media: The Institute maintains a library collection of 4600 bound volumes, subscriptions to 100 periodicals, and 2000 theses written by INTD students.

Publications: Bulletin Bibliographique INTD (monthly)—contains abstracts of library and computer sciences articles.

Computer-Based Products and Services: Information appearing in the Bulletin Bibliographique INTD is available online as part of the PASCAL data bases maintained by the French National Center for Scientific Research, Scientific and Technical Documentation Center.

Clientele/Availability: Services are intended for INTD students, documentalists, and other information professionals.

Contact: Jean-Luc Gourdin, Secretary General, National Institute for Documentation Techniques.

★723★
NATIONAL ELF AQUITAINE COMPANY
(Societe Nationale Elf Aquitaine - SNEA)
DOCUMENTARY INFORMATION SERVICE
(Service d'Information Documentaire)
STATSID
7, rue Nelaton Phone: (not reported)
F-75739 Paris Cedex 15, France

Special Note: No questionnaire response was received for this entry for the 6th edition. The entry is reprinted as it appeared in the 5th edition.

Related Organizations: STATSID is compiled by SNEA in association with the French Petroleum Company/ Compagnie Francaise des Petroles (CFP) and the French Petroleum Institute/ Institut Francais des Petroles (IFP).

Description of System or Service: STATSID is a machine-readable data base of worldwide oil and gas statistics. It provides annual exploration and production data, dating back to 1945 in most cases, for more than 250 countries or regions. Among the specific data supplied for each country are the number of oil and gas wells drilled and completed, average depth of wells, number of producing wells at year's end, success ratio, volume of yearly discoveries, and crude and natural gas production and reserves. These data can be used to analyze production and exploration efforts, and they can be combined with economic data to support financial studies. STATSID is available on magnetic tape and through commercial time-sharing.

Scope and/or Subject Matter: Worldwide petroleum and natural gas exploration and production.

Input Sources: Information for the STATSID file is gathered from international oil companies and other sources.

Holdings and Storage Media: STATSID contains machine-readable time-series data that are updated annually.

Computer-Based Products and Services: STATSID is accessible online by subscription through Mark III Service (General Electric Information Services Company). The data base is also available on magnetic tape from Elf Aquitaine.

Clientele/Availability: STATSID is intended for use by international oil companies.

Contact: Documentary Information Service, National Elf Aquitaine Company.

★724★
NATIONAL FOUNDATION FOR EDUCATIONAL RESEARCH IN ENGLAND AND WALES (NFER)
INFORMATION RESEARCH AND DEVELOPMENT UNIT
The Mere   Phone: 74123
Upton Park   Service Est: 1946
Slough, Berks. SL1 2DQ, England
David R. Streatfield, Project Head

Staff: 7 Total.

Related Organizations: NFER receives support from corporate and institutional members, the Great Britain Department of Education and Science, and other public sponsors.

Description of System or Service: The INFORMATION RESEARCH AND DEVELOPMENT UNIT comprises two main sections, the Education Management Information Exchange (EMIE) and Education Policy Information Centre. The Education Management Information Exchange assists local education authorities staff to exchange information about education policy and useful practice. It collects policy documents, answers inquiries on education policy and practice, makes information available on important educational issues, issues publications, and maintains computer-readable data bases. The Education Policy Information Centre is the focal point for the European Communities' Educational Policy Information Network, EURYDICE. It also relays requests for information from British policymakers in government and local education authorities to relevant European EURYDICE units and answers requests received from the other units.

Scope and/or Subject Matter: Educational research and development in England and Wales; educational policy and practice.

Input Sources: Print literature, research reports, and experts in the field provide input.

Holdings and Storage Media: EMIE maintains two computer-readable data bases. The NFER library maintains a collection of 18,000 volumes; NFER research tests and questionnaires; and subscriptions to 575 periodicals.

Publications: The Education Management Information Exchange issues a newsletter and other publications. Also issued are the following publications: 1) Educational Research News—available from the Information Services department, as are brochures on NFER and its programs, project newsletters, research-in-progress reports, and other materials. 2) Register of Educational Research in the United Kingdom (biennial updates)—contains approximately 2200 entries covering research in progress in the U.K., with author and subject indexes; available from NFER-Nelson Publishing Company, Darville House, 2 Oxford Rd. East, Windsor, Berks. SL4 1DF, England. 3) Educational Research (3 per year)—journal covering new research studies, short reports, and book reviews; also available from NFER-Nelson Publishing Company.

Microform Products and Services: The Register of Educational Research is available on microfiche.

Computer-Based Products and Services: The Education Management Information Exchange maintains two computer-readable data bases containing document abstracts and information on local education authority institutes and programs. The files are maintained with STAIRS software and are used in support of EMIE research and activities.

Other Services: Additional services include research workshops and seminars.

Clientele/Availability: Services are intended primarily for NFER members and research staff, but are available to others as time and resources permit.

Contact: Anthony B. Gwilliam, Senior Research Officer, Library and Information Services, National Foundation of Educational Research in England and Wales.

★725★
NATIONAL REPROGRAPHIC CENTRE FOR DOCUMENTATION (NRCD)
The Hatfield Polytechnic   Phone: 0992 552341
Bayfordbury   Founded: 1967
Hertford, Herts. SG13 8LD, England
Bernard J.S. Williams, Director

Staff: 2 Information and library professional; 3 management professional; 2 technicians; 3 clerical and nonprofessional.

Related Organizations: The Centre is aided by a grant from the British Library Research and Development Department.

Description of System or Service: The NATIONAL REPROGRAPHIC CENTRE FOR DOCUMENTATION (NRCd) provides information, advice, and education on new media for documentation, including micrographics, word processing, videotex, and other electronic media. NRCd offers consulting and advisory services to subscribers; evaluates relevant information storage, retrieval, and reproduction systems; and runs a regular program of short courses and specialized seminars. Its information service includes a comprehensive series of abstracts on systems and techniques, indexed by keywords from the Centre's thesaurus and supported by a library of original texts on microfiche which is available to members on demand. The CENTRE also maintains liaison with similar organizations throughout the world, and exchanges information with numerous agencies.

Scope and/or Subject Matter: Reprographics based on optical or electronic technology, with emphasis on micrographics, word processing, and videotex.

Input Sources: About 500 primary and secondary journals are scanned; articles are abstracted, and the full-text document is stored in microfiche form.

Holdings and Storage Media: Main holdings are an organized collection of approximately 5000 microfiche items, supported by a small library of conventional material (200 volumes). The Centre has access to about 1000 periodicals through its parent institution, The Hatfield Polytechnic.

Publications: Reprographics Quarterly (RQ)—available by subscription; includes reviews of equipment, news and editorial sections, and an Information Section providing literature abstracts with a subject keyword index. The Centre also issues evaluation reports and other publications; a list is available on request from the Centre.

Microform Products and Services: All publications are available on microfiche (105x148mm); some are available in microfiche format only.

Computer-Based Products and Services: Current information from NRCd—including news of courses, seminars, publications, and the current contents of Reprographics Quarterly—is accessible via Prestel.

Other Services: In addition to the services described above, the CENTRE performs research in computer output microfilm cataloging, performs manual literature searching, and provides referral services.

Clientele/Availability: Services are available on a subscription basis.

Free access to the advisory and information services is offered with Basic Membership and Reports Membership; membership rates for U.K. and U.S. may be obtained by request.

Contact: Anne Grimshaw, Publications and Information Officer, National Reprographic Centre for Documentation.

★726★
NATIONAL SCIENCE COUNCIL
SCIENCE AND TECHNOLOGY INFORMATION CENTER (STIC)
P.O. Box 4, Nankang   Phone: 02 7822183
Taipei, Republic of China
Chung-Ling Liu, Director

Staff: 88 Total.

Related Organizations: The Center is a participant in the Science and Technology Library Network (SATLINE), Republic of China.

Description of System or Service: The SCIENCE AND TECHNOLOGY INFORMATION CENTER (STIC) provides information services in support of scientific and technological research and development in the Republic of China. It collects scientific and technological periodicals, documents, and other foreign and domestic publications; processes, analyzes, and abstracts this information; prepares several current awareness publications for use in both academic research and industrial development; and supplies a number of technical services such as translations, referrals, SDI, and reproduction. STIC also works to improve cooperation among information service organizations by establishing exchange agreements with a variety of domestic and foreign institutions. It maintains a computer-readable union list of science and technology periodicals and a union catalog of books for libraries in the Republic of China, and has developed the computerized Management Information System of Science and Technology Resources.

Scope and/or Subject Matter: Scientific and technological information.

Input Sources: STIC acquires domestic and foreign books, periodicals, documents, patents, and other materials.

Holdings and Storage Media: Library holdings include 8846 bound volumes and subscriptions to 380 Chinese and 568 foreign periodicals.

Publications: 1) Current Contents of Selected Scientific Periodicals (monthly)—lists articles in seven categories. 2) Science and Technology Briefs (monthly)—provides abstracts of articles in nine categories, oriented toward the needs of local industries. 3) On-Going Research Projects (monthly)—includes abstracts and list of titles. 4) Scientific Research Abstracts in Republic of China (annual)—contains more than 8000 abstracts of scientific research reports; published in both Chinese and English editions. 5) Union List of Scientific Periodicals in Libraries of the Republic of China (annual)—the latest edition contains 15,472 titles. 6) National Union Catalog of Scientific and Technical Books in Libraries of the Republic of China—available in ten volumes. 7) Bibliography of Scientific Research Reports Sponsored by National Science Council, Republic of China—contains more than 7300 report titles. 8) Survey of Scientists and Engineers in Republic of China. 9) Abstract of Scientific Periodicals and Monographs (quarterly)—abstracts journal covering articles in domestic scientific periodicals and monographs in the areas of science, technology, agriculture, and medicine. 10) Report of Policy Development in Science and Technology—provides updates of news in science and technology worldwide; lists references for policymaking. The Information Center also publishes occasional monographs to introduce and evaluate advanced technology for industries, and issues semiannual publications covering relevant domestic and foreign meetings.

Microform Products and Services: The Information Center maintains a collection of documents on microfilm and microfiche, including scientific research reports.

Computer-Based Products and Services: The SCIENCE AND TECHNOLOGY INFORMATION CENTER maintains the Management Information System of Science and Technology Resources, consisting of the following machine-readable data bases: 1) Science and Technology Experts in ROC; 2) Scientific Research Abstracts in ROC; 3) Scientific Meetings in ROC; 4) Science and Technology Briefs; and 5) Union Catalog of Scientific Periodicals in the Libraries of ROC. Additionally, STIC offers search and SDI services from data bases made available through commercial online vendors, including DIALOG Information Services, Inc. and System Development Corporation (SDC).

Other Services: In addition to services described above, STIC provides document delivery for articles cited in its publications.

Clientele/Availability: Services are available to the academic research and industrial communities of the Republic of China.

Contact: Chung-Ling Liu, Director, Science and Technology Information Center.

★727★
NATURAL ENVIRONMENT RESEARCH COUNCIL
BRITISH GEOLOGICAL SURVEY
MINERALS STRATEGY AND ECONOMICS RESEARCH GROUP
MINERAL INFORMATION SECTION (MIS)
                                    Phone: 06077 6111
Keyworth, Notts. NG12 5GG, England Service Est: 1916
Anne Ramsden, Head

Staff: 3 Information and library professional; 1 clerical and nonprofessional.

Related Organizations: The MIS is also sponsored by the Great Britain Department of Trade and Industry.

Description of System or Service: The MINERAL INFORMATION SECTION (MIS) provides bibliographic information services on the economics and availability of mineral resources. The SECTION monitors relevant worldwide industrial, geological, and economics literature, and abstracts and indexes items pertaining to mineral resources. Information gathered from 1916 to 1980 is maintained in a card index, while data gathered since 1981 are held in the computer-readable MinSearch data base. The SECTION provides information retrieval and SDI services from its manual and computer files, and also makes MinSearch available online through Pergamon InfoLine Ltd. To complete its information retrieval function, the SECTION provides search services from other commercially available geological and engineering data bases.

Scope and/or Subject Matter: Economic minerals, including geology, resources, exploration, case histories of mines, finance, mineral policy, mining regulations, taxation, mineral planning, economics, end uses, and mining, processing, and extractive methods.

Input Sources: Input is derived from more than 900 journals; conference proceedings; books; reports; press releases; and news items.

Holdings and Storage Media: The card index contains 400,000 references dating from 1916 to 1981. The machine-readable MinSearch data base contains more than 11,000 records dating from 1981 to the present; it is updated with approximately 500 records per month.

Publications: The Minerals Strategy and Economics Research Group issues the following publications: 1) Mineral Dossiers—evaluative reports covering 25 minerals relevant to the United Kingdom's mineral industry. 2) Mineral Briefs—reviews on developing countries. 3) World Mineral Statistics (annual). 4) UK Mineral Statistics (annual). A thesaurus and a serials list are also issued.

Computer-Based Products and Services: The MINERAL INFORMATION SECTION offers search and SDI services from the MinSearch data base, which is also commercially available online through Pergamon InfoLine Ltd. Searchable elements in the data base include accession number, year, document type, title, author, corporate source (author affiliation), journal name, year of publication, language, abstract, and index terms. The SECTION also searches other relevant online data bases.

Other Services: The Mineral Information Section also offers consulting services on the design and creation of bibliographic data bases, and on setting up information services and suitable equipment.

Clientele/Availability: Services are available on a fee basis.

Contact: Anne Ramsden, Head, Mineral Information Section. (Telex 378173 IGSKEY G.)

★728★
**NATURAL ENVIRONMENT RESEARCH COUNCIL
BRITISH GEOLOGICAL SURVEY
NATIONAL GEOCHEMICAL DATA BANK (NGDB)**
154 Clerkenwell Rd. Phone: (not reported)
London EC1R 5DU, England Service Est: 1978

Special Note: No questionnaire response was received for this entry for the 6th edition. The entry is reprinted as it appeared in the 5th edition.

Staff: 2 Technicians; 2 clerical and nonprofessional; 1 other.

Description of System or Service: The NATIONAL GEOCHEMICAL DATA BANK (NGDB) is a centralized project for archiving, retrieving, and exchanging geochemical and related locational and geological data in machine-readable form. Designed to provide an alternative to tabular data for users in government departments, mining companies, universities, and research institutes, the NGDB acquires specific project data files produced or analyzed in the United Kingdom, including data compiled in the production of NERC's Regional Geochemical Atlas series. It also has access to three international geological data bases. From these resources, the NGDB provides clients with data retrieval, data processing and reformatting, and machine-readable copies of data.

Scope and/or Subject Matter: Igneous, sedimentary, and metamorphic rocks; drainage and soil samples; geological, geochemical, and topographical data including occurrences of metalliferous mineralization, relief, land use, and vegetation.

Input Sources: Data are derived from theses, papers, and other published and unpublished materials, and verified by Survey geochemists before archiving. Data are also contributed by universities, commercial firms, government bodies, and research institutes.

Holdings and Storage Media: NGDB consists of project and sample data files; additional data sets are added to the files when new information is obtained.

Publications: Regional Geochemical Atlases of the United Kingdom—series provides systematic data on trace elements in stream sediments; produced from NGDB.

Microform Products and Services: Output from NGDB is available on microfiche and 35mm microfilm.

Computer-Based Products and Services: The DATA BANK is archived and managed using the G-EXEC data base management system. Data are retrieved by searching the project index file and sample index files. Project data describe the project by abstract, summary (contributor, file, identifier, sample type, location, bibliography, geological setting, elements analyzed), geochemical summary (analytical method, precision, accuracy, storage, collection, preparation method, date, analyst), and general comments referring to the project. Sample data include sample geochemical data (results for major and trace elements for each sample identifier), sample fields data (sample identifier, location, major and minor rock types, stratigraphy, geological locations), and related data (petrographic data, textures, grain size, normative calculations, mineralogy, SEM data, isotope data, general comments). Data can be used to produce various diagrams and plots, contour maps, three dimensional surfaces, symbol and value posting maps, gray scale and color maps, as well as all types of simple, univariate, and multivariate statistics. Products of the DATA BANK include magnetic tapes, punched cards, or printouts; online access is planned. The NGDB also can obtain machine-readable data from these international data bases: 1) CLAIRE—data base of igneous rocks; 2) PETROS—data base of hard rocks; 3) RKNFSYS (Rock Information System)—an igneous rock data base.

Other Services: In addition to the services described above, NGDB offers consulting, and referral services.

Clientele/Availability: Services are available on a cost recovery basis.

Contact: Head, National Geochemical Data Bank.

★729★
**NATURAL ENVIRONMENT RESEARCH COUNCIL
INSTITUTE FOR MARINE ENVIRONMENTAL RESEARCH
CONTINUOUS PLANKTON RECORDER SURVEY**
Prospect Place, The Hoe Phone: 0752 21371
Plymouth, Devon. PL1 3DH, England
B.L. Bayne, Director

Staff: 17 Scientific personnel.

Description of System or Service: The CONTINUOUS PLANKTON RECORDER SURVEY records data on a routine basis from the northeastern Atlantic Ocean in order to study the effects of environmental change on the abundance and distribution of plankton. The plankton data are maintained in a machine-readable file.

Scope and/or Subject Matter: Plankton, especially the ecology of open sea plankton, and the feeding and development of zooplankton.

Input Sources: Data are derived from monthly plankton samples taken in the North Atlantic waters.

Holdings and Storage Media: Plankton data covering the period from 1948 to the present are maintained in machine-readable form.

Publications: Bulletin of Marine Ecology (irregular).

Computer-Based Products and Services: Computer-readable plankton data from the SURVEY are available for use in scientific research.

Clientele/Availability: Data are available for purchase to qualified personnel.

Remarks: The Institute for Marine Environmental Research conducts research in other areas of marine science, including estuarine ecology, near-shore ecosystems, ecological stress and pollution, simulation modeling, and environmental radioactivity. The computing facilities at the Institute are also shared with the Marine Biological Association and form part of the Natural Environment Research Council network with additional access to mainframe computers of the Science and Engineering Research Council.

Contact: G.A. Robinson or Dr. P.N. Claridge, Assistant to Director, Continuous Plankton Recorder Survey.

★730★
**NATURAL ENVIRONMENT RESEARCH COUNCIL
INSTITUTE OF OCEANOGRAPHIC SCIENCES
MARINE INFORMATION AND ADVISORY SERVICE (MIAS)**
Brook Rd., Wormley Phone: 042 8794141
Godalming, Surrey GU8 5UB, England Service Est: 1976
Dr. N.C. Flemming, Head

Description of System or Service: The MARINE INFORMATION AND ADVISORY SERVICE (MIAS) provides oceanographic data and information to commercial organizations, government agencies, and research establishments. Functioning as the United Kingdom National Oceanographic Data Centre, it collects all relevant data, stores them in machine-readable and hardcopy forms, and issues inventories, summaries, and other publications. On an international basis, MIAS maintains the Responsible National Oceanographic Data Center (RNODC) for instrumentally measured wave data worldwide.

Scope and/or Subject Matter: Marine geology, geophysics, chemistry, and physics, including data on waves, currents, tides, sea level, temperature, salinity, and other oceanographic parameters.

Input Sources: Input includes instrumentally measured data and other information.

Holdings and Storage Media: The UK National Oceanographic Data Bank is held in computer-readable form; additional data are held in hard copy.

Publications: MIAS News Bulletin. MIAS also issues information sheets and such reference publications as inventories and summaries.

Computer-Based Products and Services: The computer-readable National Oceanographic Data Bank contains numerical data and is accessed by MIAS staff for its clients.

Other Services: Consultancy and referral services are also provided.

Clientele/Availability: MIAS serves primarily organizations in the United Kingdom and adjacent areas. RNODC services are available worldwide. Charges may be made for services.

Contact: Enquiries Officer, or Dr. Denise Smythe-Wright, Publications Officer, Marine Information and Advisory Service. (Telex 858833 OCEANS G.)

★731★
NETHERLANDS
MINISTRY OF AGRICULTURE AND FISHERIES
AGRICULTURAL RESEARCH DIVISION
CENTRE FOR AGRICULTURAL PUBLISHING AND DOCUMENTATION
(Centrum voor Landbouwpublikaties en Landbouwdocumentatie - Pudoc)
P.O. Box 4
Gen. Foulkesweg 19
NL-6700 AA Wageningen, Netherlands
J.M. Schippers, Director
Phone: 08370 89222
Service Est: 1957

Staff: Approximately 40 total.

Related Organizations: Pudoc shares facilities with the Library of the Agricultural University.

Description of System or Service: The CENTRE FOR AGRICULTURAL PUBLISHING AND DOCUMENTATION (PUDOC) comprises three departments concerned with documenting and publishing agricultural research results. 1) The Documentation and Information Department collects bibliographic data, publishes secondary journals, provides current awareness, and searches computer-readable data bases and manual sources of agricultural information. The Department also supplies bibliographic data on recent Dutch agricultural research for inclusion in the United Nations Food and Agriculture Organization's AGRIS system; conducts research on techniques of information handling applied to agricultural science; and controls the bibliographic data base stored in the computer of the Bibliographic Automated System (BAS), a joint project of the Agricultural University and the Agricultural Research Division. 2) The Publishing Department operates as a nonprofit scholarly press that publishes research reports, doctoral theses, books, and other items linked with government-aided agricultural research. The Department also cooperates with the Royal Netherlands Society of Agricultural Sciences in NARD (Netherlands Agricultural Report Depository), which aims to improve the accessibility of information from research reports not available through normal channels of distribution. NARD information is disseminated through a synopsis published monthly in the Netherlands Journal of Agricultural Science and as full-text documents available on microfiche or paper. 3) The Printing Office handles internal printing needs of area ministerial research institutes and the Agricultural University.

Scope and/or Subject Matter: Agriculture, including animal husbandry, horticulture, forestry, ecology, and nutrition.

Input Sources: Pudoc utilizes online data bases as well as the libraries of universities, research institutes, and government agencies.

Holdings and Storage Media: The Centre maintains a systematic index holding 240,000 cards covering literature of the past 20 years. It also maintains a small library, a source file of bibliographic data, and machine-readable tapes supplied by secondary services.

Publications: 1) Pudoc Bulletin (quarterly)—bibliography in English of recent agricultural publications; each issue also includes an author index, index of institutes and organizations, and subject index. 2) Landbouwdocumentatie/ Agricultural Documentation (weekly)— abstracts journal in Dutch; contains annotated titles of interest to agricultural scientists, extension officers, and the agricultural industry. A wide variety of other publications is also issued; a complete list is available from Pudoc.

Microform Products and Services: Copies of NARD documents are available on microfiche.

Computer-Based Products and Services: PUDOC offers current awareness services from the AGRICOLA, AGRIS, CAB, and FSTA data bases, and retrospective literature searching using over 250 commercially available data bases. It also controls the bibliographic data base stored in the computer of BAS.

Other Services: Additional services include quick reference service and compilation of bibliographies and literature reports.

Clientele/Availability: Services are available without restrictions worldwide. For personalized information services, priority is given to staff members of the Netherlands Ministry of Agriculture and Fisheries.

Remarks: Pudoc is one of 24 institutes administered by the Agricultural Research Division of the Netherlands Ministry of Agriculture and Fisheries.

Contact: J.M. Schippers, Director, Centre for Agricultural Publishing and Documentation. (Telex 45015 BLHWG NL.)

★732★
NETHERLANDS
MINISTRY OF FOREIGN AFFAIRS
(Ministerie van Buitenlandse Zaken)
TRANSLATIONS BRANCH
(Hoofdafdeling Vertalingen)
TERMINOLOGY AND DOCUMENTATION SECTION
P.O. Box 20061
Casuariestr. 16
NL-2500 EB The Hague, Netherlands
J.R. Mengarduque, Head
Phone: 070 209270
Service Est: 1970

Staff: 2 Information and library professional; 1 management professional; 1 clerical and nonprofessional; 3 other.

Description of System or Service: The TERMINOLOGY AND DOCUMENTATION SECTION supports the activities of the Translations Branch, which works for most Dutch ministries by compiling and providing services from a computer-readable terminological data bank. The data bank uses Dutch as its source language and English, French, and German as target languages, and makes use of the Eurodicautom System of the Commission of European Communities for standard input and retrieval of terminological information. Only terms whose equivalency can be expressed by corresponding definitions or in relevant contexts are added to the file; a detailed description of the source, the date the terminological unit was entered, and synonyms are added at the same time. The data bank is publicly available online. In addition to providing the data bank, the SECTION maintains an extensive document collection and a reference library.

Scope and/or Subject Matter: Terminology, especially in the following areas: law, agreements and treaties, government, finance and economics, European political cooperation, development aid, geography of the Netherlands, urban planning, Dutch museums, administration of justice, prisons, welfare, environmental protection, and education.

Input Sources: Input for the document collection includes in-house translations, articles from newspapers and specialized periodicals, samples of standard documents and forms, biographies of prominent Dutch people, and other materials.

Holdings and Storage Media: Information on approximately 30,000 terminological units is held in machine-readable form; the data bank is updated regularly. Library holdings include 10,000 documents; more than 5000 monolingual and multilingual volumes; sets of laws; and subscriptions to 60 periodicals.

Computer-Based Products and Services: The terminological data bank is available online through Euronet DIANE. Searchable data elements include specific term or such subject categories as names of government authorities and agencies, Dutch organizations, laws, decrees and ordinances, treaties, conferences and congresses, post and job designations, environmental protection, development aid, law and education.

Clientele/Availability: The Section serves the Translations Branch, Dutch government ministries, and other translation services on request.

Contact: J.R. Mengarduque, Head, Terminology and Documentation Section.

★733★
NETHERLANDS
NETHERLANDS FOREIGN TRADE AGENCY
LIBRARY AND DOCUMENTATION BRANCH
FOREIGN TRADE ABSTRACTS
Bezuidenhoutseweg 151   Phone: 070 797221
NL-2594 AH The Hague, Netherlands
J.H. Ypma, Head, Library and Documentation Branch

Staff: 5 Information and library professional; 2 management professional; 29 clerical and nonprofessional.

Description of System or Service: Formerly called Economics Abstracts International (EAI), FOREIGN TRADE ABSTRACTS is a computer-readable data base providing abstracts and citations to literature on applied and commercial economics. The data base covers source material in English, German, French, and Dutch, with titles and abstracts appearing in the original language and descriptors in English. FOREIGN TRADE ABSTRACTS is accessible worldwide through several commercial online services. Information from the file is also available on magnetic tape, through two printed journals, and on microfiche. Additionally, copies of periodical articles covered in FOREIGN TRADE ABSTRACTS can be ordered from the Library and Documentation Branch.

Scope and/or Subject Matter: Worldwide economic information, with emphasis on foreign markets, international trade, and investment climates.

Input Sources: Input is derived from 1800 periodicals and from monographs, annual company reports, trade directories, and statistical sources. Articles on pure mathematical economics, studies of primarily local interest, and short notes are not abstracted.

Holdings and Storage Media: The computer-readable Foreign Trade Abstracts data base holds 140,000 items dating from 1974 to the present; it is updated semimonthly with approximately 14,000 items added each year. Library holdings include 100,000 bound volumes and subscriptions to 1800 periodicals.

Publications: 1) Economic Titles/ Abstracts (semimonthly with annual cumulative subject index)—each issue contains approximately 600 original language abstracts from selected publications; also contains a subject index and complete bibliographical data. 2) Key to Economic Science (semimonthly with annual subject and author indexes)—contains about 120 academic-level abstracts selected from Economic Titles/Abstracts. Both of the above journals are available by subscription from Martinus Nijhoff Publishers, P.O. Box 442, The Hague, Netherlands.

Microform Products and Services: Monthly, quarterly, or annual COM microfiche versions of Economic Titles/ Abstracts are available from Martinus Nijhoff Publishers.

Computer-Based Products and Services: FOREIGN TRADE ABSTRACTS is available online through DIALOG Information Services, Inc., Data-Star, and BELINDIS (Belgian Information and Dissemination Service). Data elements present in the file include title, author, journal, language, document type, abstract, and descriptors. The data base is also available on semimonthly magnetic tapes for use on in-house computers.

Other Services: Additional services include consulting, research, data collection and analysis, manual literature searching, and referrals.

Clientele/Availability: Services are available to firms, government and other agencies, and students.

Contact: J.H. Ypma, Head, Library and Documentation Branch. (Telex 31099 ECOZA NL.)

★734★
NETHERLANDS ASSOCIATION OF USERS OF ONLINE INFORMATION SYSTEMS
(Nederlandse Vereniging van Gebruikers van Online Informatiesystemen - VOGIN)
Library KNAW   Phone: 020 222902
Kloveniersburgwal 29   Service Est: 1977
NL-1011 JV Amsterdam, Netherlands
Dr. H.M. Rietveld, Chairman

Description of System or Service: The NETHERLANDS ASSOCIATION OF USERS OF ONLINE INFORMATION SYSTEMS (VOGIN) is a professional association which serves as a national forum for the exchange of information and experience among online searchers. VOGIN conducts instructional courses, organizes working groups, performs research in online topics, holds conferences, and studies tariffs and other information policy subjects.

Scope and/or Subject Matter: Topics of interest to online data base users in the Netherlands.

Publications: LOGIN (quarterly).

Clientele/Availability: Services are available without restrictions.

Contact: Dr. Th.W.J. Pieters, Secretary, Netherlands Association of Users of Online Information Systems.

★735★
NETHERLANDS BIBLIOGRAPHICAL AND DOCUMENTARY COMMITTEE
(Commissie voor Bibliografie en Documentatie - COBIDOC)
St. Antoniesbreestr. 16   Phone: 020 223955
P.O. Box 16601   Founded: 1972
NL-1001 RC Amsterdam, Netherlands
J.H.M. Heijnen

Staff: 3 Information and library professional; 3 management professional; 7 clerical and nonprofessional.

Related Organizations: COBIDOC is in the service of the Netherlands Ministry of Education and Sciences.

Description of System or Service: The NETHERLANDS BIBLIOGRAPHICAL AND DOCUMENTARY COMMITTEE (COBIDOC) is a national center for the management of information projects in the Netherlands. It is responsible for promoting information services by creating an organizationally and financially comprehensible structure for them. COBIDOC supports information users and suppliers through activities such as helping establish active information transfer directed at specific groups; providing administrative help with regard to passwords, invoices, and complaints; and supplying data on information provision obtained from its activities. Other services include the organization of training seminars and information workshops, and coordination of the SOVIN online training center. COBIDOC is also responsible for coordinating Netherlands information work with that of foreign and international systems and networks. In this role, it acts (or designates other Netherlands organizations to act) as the national focal point for such systems as INIS, AGRIS, ESA/IRS, SDIM, FIZ-4, DIMDI, Data-Star, Telesystemes Questel, and BELINDIS (Belgian Information and Dissemination Service).

Scope and/or Subject Matter: Information services in all subject areas, particularly those of interest to the Ministry of Education and Sciences.

Remarks: COBIDOC is gradually being transformed into a new foundation, to be called the Netherlands Bureau for Information Provision.

Contact: J.E. van Dijk, Netherlands Bibliographical and Documentary Committee. (Telex 18766 COBD NL.) The electronic mail address on ESA/IRS is 992.

★736★
NETHERLANDS CENTER FOR INFORMATION POLICY
(Centrum voor Informatie Beleid - CIB)
Prinses Beatrixlaan 5   Phone: 070 476161
NL-2595 AK The Hague, Netherlands   Founded: 1979
J.K.W. van Leeuwen, President

Staff: 5 Information and library professional.

Description of System or Service: The NETHERLANDS CENTER FOR INFORMATION POLICY (CIB) acts on behalf of sponsoring trade organizations and companies in banking, insurance, retailing, publishing, and information provision, processing, and technology. Its primary purpose is to encourage a coordinated information policy within the Dutch government and among professional information organizations. Consultation in the area of information service development is also offered.

Scope and/or Subject Matter: Dutch information policy.

Publications: The Netherlands in the Information Age.

Clientele/Availability: Services are available to members only.

Contact: J.K.W. van Leeuwen, President, Netherlands Center for Information Policy. (Telex 32146.)

★737★
NETHERLANDS INFORMATION COMBINE (NIC)
(Stichting Nederlandse Informatie Combinatie)
P.O. Box 36   Phone: 015 569330
NL-2600 AA Delft, Netherlands   Founded: 1973

Related Organizations: Netherlands Information Combine cooperates with the Center for Information and Documentation (CID) of the Netherlands Organization for Applied Scientific Research (TNO).

Description of System or Service: The NETHERLANDS INFORMATION COMBINE (NIC) is a nonprofit organization composed of thirteen companies, institutes, and universities working to improve accessibility to current information on commercially available data bases. It also supports several data bases that are accessible online.

Scope and/or Subject Matter: Research in online systems with emphasis on commercially available data bases.

Computer-Based Products and Services: As one of its activities, NIC contributes to the maintenance of the CA Search file which is offered in Europe through ESA/IRS. NIC also contributes to the Carbon-13 Nuclear Magnetic Resonance Spectral Search System of the NIH-EPA Chemical Information System (CIS).

Clientele/Availability: NIC services are intended to assist online searchers.

Contact: Charles L. Citroen, Secretary, Netherlands Information Combine. The electronic mail address on ESA/IRS is no. 152; on NIH-EPA Chemical Information System (CIS), no. 705.CITROEN.

★738★
NETHERLANDS OFFICE OF POSTS, TELEGRAPHS, AND TELEPHONES
(Staatsbedrijf der Posterijen, Telegrafie, en Telefonie)
PTT CENTRAL DIRECTORATE
(PTT Centrale Directie)
VIDITEL
P.O. Box 30000   Phone: 70754074
NL-2500 GA The Hague, Netherlands   Service Est: 1981
R.C. Meijburg, Ing.

Staff: 7 Information and library professional; 2 management professional; 2 technicians; 9 sales and marketing; 7 clerical and nonprofessional.

Description of System or Service: VIDITEL is a videotex system established by the Netherlands PTT to provide the public with varied and detailed information and with an efficient communications medium. The system is accessed via the telephone lines by home or office users using a keypad and television receiver or an alphanumeric keyboard terminal to retrieve and display information. VIDITEL makes available data bases of news, financial, sales, travel, and other information provided by public and private agencies. Using a question and answer process, the user can retrieve information through an alphabetical list of keywords, through a list of information providers, by frame number, or via a systematic search method. Information providers on the system can include reply frames enabling subscribers to answer questions, place orders, and engage in other interactive operations. In addition to public access to VIDITEL data bases, the system includes a closed user group facility, a gateway capability enabling users to access other computers, and electronic mail services through which subscribers can contact each other. Intended in part to take advantage of the extremely high telephone density in the Netherlands, VIDITEL conforms to international standards in order to make the system as universally accessible as possible.

Scope and/or Subject Matter: Netherlands and other news, finance, sales, home shopping, travel, and other information; electronic mail.

Input Sources: Input is provided by companies, government agencies, private individuals, and other information providers.

Holdings and Storage Media: Viditel information frames are held in machine-readable form and updated regularly by the information providers.

Computer-Based Products and Services: The VIDITEL videotex system provides interactive access to publicly available data bases and to closed user group videotex services which supply specific information only to target groups. Additional VIDITEL services include Vidibus, Vidipoort, and Vidibord. Vidibus is an electronic mail facility that enables subscribers to compose original messages with an alphanumeric keyboard or to send any of 70 standard messages stored in the system. Messages are transmitted to other subscribers who are notified of the waiting message when logging in or out of the system. Vidipoort is a gateway function that links the computers of some information providers directly to the VIDITEL computer, permitting subscribers to both request information and use other services offered by the information providers, such as calculation of mortgages, statistics, computation of taxes, and telebanking. Vidibord is a graphics system that combines alphamosaic and alphageographic techniques to create maps, route descriptions, logos, symbols, and other applications through the use of a graphic tablet and an electronic pen.

Clientele/Availability: Services are available to subscribers in the Netherlands. Currently the system encompasses 9000 online users, 150 independent information providers, and 600 umbrella information providers.

Contact: Ir. J. Gerrese, Deputy Manager, Viditel; telephone 70753964.

★739★
NETHERLANDS ORGANIZATION FOR APPLIED SCIENTIFIC RESEARCH
(Nederlandsche Centrale Organisatie voor Toegepast-Natuurwetenschappelijk Onderzoek - TNO)
CENTER FOR INFORMATION AND DOCUMENTATION
(Centrum voor Informatie en Documentatie - CID)
P.O. Box 36   Phone: 015 569330
Schoemakerstr. 97   Founded: 1977
NL-2600 AA Delft, Netherlands
Charles L. Citroen, Deputy Head

Staff: 6 Information and library professional; 1 management professional; 4 clerical and nonprofessional.

Description of System or Service: The CENTER FOR INFORMATION AND DOCUMENTATION (CID) disseminates scientific and technical information to the TNO staff and to outside users. Among the services offered by the CENTER are current awareness, retrospective literature and patent searches, data bank searches, and training programs.

Scope and/or Subject Matter: Science and technology; patents; chemistry; toxicology; economics.

Input Sources: Input is obtained from a variety of commercially available data bases. Additional input is derived from data banks in the field of chemical compounds and recent research projects.

Holdings and Storage Media: The Center's collection includes reports, journals, patents, and books.

Computer-Based Products and Services: CID offers the following: current awareness services for science and technology, including patents; online retrospective literature and patent searching using approximately 250 data bases offered through Euronet DIANE hosts, DIALOG Information Services, Inc., and System Development Corporation (SDC); and searches of computer-readable data banks containing spectra of compounds and recent research projects.

Other Services: Additionally, the Center offers training and consultancy services in the use of online data bases.

Clientele/Availability: Services are available to the staff of TNO and to industry, government organizations, representative groups, and individuals.

Contact: Charles L. Citroen, Deputy Head, Center for Information and Documentation. (Telex 38071 ZPTNO NL.) The electronic mail address on ESA/IRS is no. 152 or no. 166; on NIH-EPA Chemical Information System (CIS), no. 705.CITROEN.

★740★
NETHERLANDS ORGANIZATION FOR APPLIED SCIENTIFIC RESEARCH
(Nederlandsche Centrale Organisatie voor Toegepast-Natuurwetenschappelijk Onderzoek - TNO)
GROUNDWATER SURVEY
(Dienst Grondwaterverkenning)
Schoemakerstr. 97
P.O. Box 285
NL-2600 AG Delft, Netherlands
Phone: 015 569330
Founded: 1970

Special Note: The above name, address, and telephone number have been verified for this edition, although no questionnaire response was received. The following text is reprinted from the 5th edition.

Staff: 2 Information and library professional; 2 management professional; 1 technician; 10 clerical and nonprofessional.

Description of System or Service: The GROUNDWATER SURVEY collects, stores, and retrieves data on groundwater levels in the Netherlands as a means of supporting geohydrological research and the management of groundwater resources within the country. Data are gathered through volunteer observation and are added to the machine-readable groundwater data base via tape, disks, and punched cards. The GROUNDWATER SURVEY offers searches of the data base.

Scope and/or Subject Matter: Groundwater resources and levels in the Netherlands.

Input Sources: Data are gathered from observations made by various institutions on a volunteer basis.

Holdings and Storage Media: The machine-readable groundwater data base consists of four files: Files 1 and 2 contain general data on deep and shallow wells, including such variables as coordinates, depths of screens, altitude of field level, reference point, and map references; Files 3 and 4 contain actual level records for the 20,000 observation points. More than 6.5 million data items are maintained, covering a period of twenty years in some cases.

Computer-Based Products and Services: Requests for groundwater data are filled by the staff of the Groundwater Survey. Online access to the groundwater data base is available subject to approval.

Clientele/Availability: Data are available to the general public with some exceptions.

Contact: Groundwater Survey.

★741★
NETHERLANDS ORGANIZATION FOR APPLIED SCIENTIFIC RESEARCH
(Nederlandsche Centrale Organisatie voor Toegepast-Natuurwetenschappelijk Onderzoek - TNO)
INSTITUTE TNO FOR MATHEMATICS, INFORMATION PROCESSING AND STATISTICS
(Institut TNO voor Wiskunde, Informatieverwerking en Statistiek - IWIS)
P.O. Box 297
Koningin Marialaan 21
NL-2501 BD The Hague, Netherlands
J. Remmelts, Director
Phone: 070 824161
Founded: 1945

Staff: Approximately 120 total.

Description of System or Service: The INSTITUTE TNO FOR MATHEMATICS, INFORMATION PROCESSING AND STATISTICS (IWIS) supplies support in mathematics and computerized information processing both within TNO and to outside agencies. It comprises the following five departments: mathematical statistics; numerical mathematics; automation; operations research; and the computing center. Noteworthy activities of the INSTITUTE in the field of information retrieval include the development by the Automation Department of a data base management system called DARIUS, and the development of an experimental retrospective search program known as FUZZIE.

Scope and/or Subject Matter: Mathematical statistics and numerical mathematics; computer science; engineering; information technology.

Computer-Based Products and Services: The Automation Department of IWIS has developed the DARIUS and FUZZIE programs. DARIUS is a software system currently being used for production of document data bases and for automation of archives. FUZZIE is an experimental program developed to investigate the application of a retrospective search strategy by means of a syntactic tracer organized tree structure. The INSTITUTE also implements internal computer applications in computerized phototypesetting and artificial intelligence.

Other Services: Additional services include data collection and analysis for government organizations; research on new retrospective search techniques; and advisory and consulting services on statistics, mathematics, computer science, and business automation.

Clientele/Availability: IWIS serves TNO, national governmental, and other agencies.

Contact: Dr. T. de Heer, Institute TNO for Mathematics, Information Processing and Statistics.

★742★
NETHERLANDS ORGANIZATION FOR APPLIED SCIENTIFIC RESEARCH
(Nederlandsche Centrale Organisatie voor Toegepast-Natuurwetenschappelijk Onderzoek - TNO)
NATIONAL COUNCIL FOR AGRICULTURAL RESEARCH TNO
(Nationale Raad voor Landbouwkundig Onderzoek TNO)
CENTRAL PROJECT ADMINISTRATION FOR CURRENT AGRICULTURAL RESEARCH IN THE NETHERLANDS
Adelheidstr. 84
P.O. Box 297
NL-2501 BD The Hague, Netherlands
A. van den Berg, Head
Phone: 070 471021
Founded: 1962

Staff: 1 Management professional; 1 technician.

Description of System or Service: The CENTRAL PROJECT ADMINISTRATION FOR CURRENT AGRICULTURAL RESEARCH IN THE NETHERLANDS is the national center for agricultural research information and a focal point for participation in the AGREP (Agricultural Research Projects) system of the Commission of the European Communities. It collects information on agricultural research projects in the Netherlands and provides the Netherlands with information services from collected AGREP products.

Scope and/or Subject Matter: Technical and management information on current agricultural research, including forestry, fisheries, and food.

Input Sources: Input consists of descriptions of research projects submitted to the Administration by research institutes and universities.

Holdings and Storage Media: The Administration maintains approximately 4000 project descriptions.

Computer-Based Products and Services: The AGREP data base is used by the Administration for retrospective searching.

Clientele/Availability: The Administration serves agricultural researchers in the Netherlands; only written requests for information are accepted.

Contact: A. van den Berg, Head, Central Project Administration for Current Agricultural Research in the Netherlands.

★743★
NETHERLANDS ORGANIZATION FOR APPLIED SCIENTIFIC RESEARCH
(Nederlandsche Centrale Organisatie voor Toegepast-Natuurwetenschappelijk Onderzoek - TNO)
TNO STUDY AND INFORMATION CENTER ON ENVIRONMENTAL RESEARCH
(Studie- en Informatiecentrum TNO voor Milieu-Onderzoek - SCMO)
ENVIRONMENTAL RESEARCH IN THE NETHERLANDS
P.O. Box 186
NL-2600 AD Delft, Netherlands
P. Winkel, Director
Phone: 015 569330
Founded: 1970

Staff: 7 Information and library professional; 9 management

professional; 4 clerical and nonprofessional.

Description of System or Service: ENVIRONMENTAL RESEARCH IN THE NETHERLANDS, maintained by the TNO Study and Information Center on Environmental Research (SCMO), is a computer-readable inventory of environmental research projects and related literature in the Netherlands. The data base, part of a larger SCMO research program, is used to provide a basis for attuning environmental research to the environmental policy of the government, for indicating fields where research is needed, and for stimulating cooperation among research institutes. Constituting the Dutch input to the ENREP (Environmental Research Projects) data base of the Commission of the European Communities, the data base is also employed for the publication of an annual register of project descriptions and to provide search services.

Scope and/or Subject Matter: Environmental research, including air, water, and soil pollution, noise, wastes, and nature protection.

Input Sources: Project descriptions are gathered from approximately 700 research institutes.

Holdings and Storage Media: The data base contains 4100 descriptions of research projects and approximately 11,000 bibliographic references.

Publications: Research on Environment and Nature in the Netherlands/ Onderzoek naar Milieu en Natuur in Nederland (every two years)—a three-part inventory. Part one contains descriptions of current research projects. Part two provides a review of literature that has been published in relation to the projects described in part one. Part three comprises institute, keyword, and geographic indexes. The inventory is available for purchase from the Study and Information Center.

Computer-Based Products and Services: The Environmental Research in the Netherlands data base is used to provide computerized search services and to produce the registers.

Clientele/Availability: Clients include government agencies and the environmental research community.

Contact: L. de Lavieter, Head of the Information Section, TNO Study and Information Center on Environmental Research. (Telex 38071 ZPTNO NL.)

★744★
NETHERLANDS ORGANIZATION FOR INFORMATION POLICY
(Stichting Nederlands Orgaan voor de Bevordering van de Informatieverzorging - NOBIN)
19 Burgemeester van Karnebeeklaan   Phone: 070 607833
NL-2585 BA The Hague, Netherlands   Founded: 1971
J.J. Kroese, Head

Staff: Approximately 9 total.

Related Organizations: The Netherlands Organization for Information Policy is supported by the Ministries of Economic Affairs and of Education and Sciences.

Description of System or Service: The NETHERLANDS ORGANIZATION FOR INFORMATION POLICY (NOBIN) coordinates and promotes scientific and technical information-handling activities in the Netherlands and contributes to a national policy for the organization of this information. NOBIN has the following goals: to create a national information network linked to networks of other countries; to encourage training in librarianship, documentation, and information work; to evaluate existing and new information-handling methods and techniques; to create new methods and facilities for quickly disseminating current information to scientists; and to evaluate and encourage the development of hardcopy, microform, and machine-readable information media.

Scope and/or Subject Matter: All aspects of scientific and technical information-handling.

Input Sources: NOBIN collects information from published literature, internal research, and professional contacts.

Holdings and Storage Media: NOBIN maintains a library of 2000 volumes and subscriptions to 100 periodicals.

Publications: Annual reports are issued in Dutch.

Computer-Based Products and Services: The Netherlands Organization for Information Policy supports research in computer applications to information handling.

Clientele/Availability: Services are available in the Netherlands.

Contact: J.J. Kroese, Head, Netherlands Organization for Information Policy.

★745★
NETHERLANDS SOCIETY FOR INFORMATICS
(Nederlands Genootschap voor Informatica - NGI)
Paulus Potterstr. 40   Phone: 020 728222
NL-1071 DB Amsterdam, Netherlands   Founded: 1958
Ms. R. Lucas, Executive Secretary

Staff: 3 Total.

Description of System or Service: The NETHERLANDS SOCIETY FOR INFORMATICS (NGI) is a professional organization dealing with automatic information processing.

Scope and/or Subject Matter: Informatics.

Publications: NGI-Nieuws (biweekly).

Clientele/Availability: Membership comprises informatics personnel in the Netherlands.

Contact: Ms. R. Lucas, Executive Secretary, Netherlands Society for Infomatics.

★746★
NETHERLANDS SOIL SURVEY INSTITUTE
(Stichting voor Bodemkartering - STIBOKA)
SOIL INFORMATION SYSTEM
P.O. Box 98   Phone: 08370 19100
Prinses Marijkeweg 11   Service Est: 1977
NL-6700 AB Wageningen, Netherlands
A.K. Bregt, Head

Staff: 1 Information and library professional; 1 management professional; 2 technicians.

Related Organizations: The Institute receives support from the Netherlands Geological Survey.

Description of System or Service: The SOIL INFORMATION SYSTEM collects data obtained from borelog samples of the Dutch subsurface and from Dutch soil maps. It maintains the data in machine-readable form and provides information services for Institute employees and the Netherlands agricultural community.

Scope and/or Subject Matter: Soil science; sedimentation.

Holdings and Storage Media: Borelog sample and map data are maintained in machine-readable form.

Computer-Based Products and Services: The SOIL INFORMATION SYSTEM contains borelog data, which are stored on computer using the relational database management system ORACLE. Map data are held on a stand-alone cartographic system. Magnetic tapes of map data are publicly available.

Clientele/Availability: Services are available to Institute employees and those in its branch offices, and to agricultural organizations in the Netherlands.

Contact: A.K. Bregt, Head, Soil Information System. (Telex 75230 VISI NL.)

★747★
NEW OPPORTUNITY PRESS LTD.
CAREERDATA
76 St. James Lane   Phone: 01-444 7281
London N10 3RD, England   Service Est: 1978
R. Begley, Chairman

Special Note: The above name, address, and telephone number have been verified for this edition, although no questionnaire response was received. The following text is reprinted from the 5th edition.

Related Organizations: Careerdata was established with assistance from AVS Intext Ltd.

Description of System or Service: CAREERDATA is a Viewdata information service provided by New Opportunity Press Ltd., publishers of career literature. Through the service, more than 100 employers provide current information on their job vacancies for use by recent graduates and those changing jobs. CAREERDATA is interactively accessible through Prestel; it was mounted on the system as the world's first commercial Viewdata service.

Scope and/or Subject Matter: Employment opportunities in the United Kingdom.

Input Sources: The data base is continuously updated with information provided by employers.

Computer-Based Products and Services: The CAREERDATA data base is accessible through Prestel.

Clientele/Availability: Primary clients are job seekers in the U.K.

Contact: Group Advertisement Manager, Careerdata.

★748★
NEW ZEALAND
DEPARTMENT OF SCIENTIFIC AND INDUSTRIAL RESEARCH (DSIR)
DSIR CENTRAL LIBRARY
P.O. Box 9741   Phone: 858939
Wellington, New Zealand   Service Est: 1947
Paul Szentirmay, Chief Librarian

Staff: 6 Information and library professional; 1 management professional; 6 technicians; 3 clerical and nonprofessional.

Description of System or Service: The DSIR CENTRAL LIBRARY, which is the focal point for more than 20 DSIR libraries, provides library and information services to the Department of Scientific and Industrial Research and technical personnel across New Zealand. The LIBRARY maintains the computer-based Department of Scientific and Industrial Research Indexing System (SIRIS). SIRIS is utilized to produce a hardcopy abstracting and indexing journal that covers New Zealand scientific literature and to provide computerized search services from a corresponding data base. The LIBRARY also supplies searches from data bases made available by commercial vendors.

Scope and/or Subject Matter: New Zealand science and technology, with emphasis on agriculture-related disciplines; energy, environment, and science policy formulation; and information science.

Input Sources: Input includes materials about New Zealand or by authors living in New Zealand, exchange materials, U.S. technical reports, and commercially available data bases.

Holdings and Storage Media: The Library's collection contains 200,000 bound volumes; 15,000 reports; and 5000 periodical subscriptions and exchanges. Machine-readable data bases are also held.

Publications: 1) New Zealand Science Abstracts (quarterly)—available by subscription; a subject and author guide to scientific and technical papers, reports, and other literature. Formerly known as the New Zealand Scientific Literature Index. 2) DSIR Documentation—a newsletter on information and library services; available only to New Zealand research libraries.

Microform Products and Services: Microfilm copies of out-of-print New Zealand scientific works are supplied to libraries.

Computer-Based Products and Services: Information retrieval services are provided from the computer-based Department of Scientific and Industrial Research Indexing System (SIRIS).

Other Services: In addition to services described above, manual literature searching and referral services are offered.

Clientele/Availability: Most services are available without restrictions.

Contact: Paul Szentirmay, Chief Librarian, DSIR Central Library.

★749★
NEW ZEALAND
DEPARTMENT OF STATISTICS
INFORMATION NETWORK FOR OFFICIAL STATISTICS (INFOS)
Private Bag   Phone: 04 729119
Wellington, New Zealand   Service Est: 1982
R.H. D'Ath, Executive Officer

Staff: Approximately 10 total.

Description of System or Service: The INFORMATION NETWORK FOR OFFICIAL STATISTICS (INFOS) is a computerized information system which provides storage and retrieval of official statistical information gathered from governmental and private sources in New Zealand. The INFOS data base, which is still under development, holds such statistics as economic indicators, economic census data, price and wage indexes, and demographic data which are accessible through a computerized index. INFOS can be searched online by all sectors in New Zealand from remote terminals.

Scope and/or Subject Matter: New Zealand national and regional statistical data, including national accounts, economic indicators, economic census data, price indexes, wage indexes, employment and unemployment, population, demographics, external trade, migration, financial indicators, balance of payments, transport, production, and energy.

Input Sources: Statistical data are gathered from government departments and private sources. Nearly all official statistics collected in New Zealand are covered in INFOS.

Holdings and Storage Media: INFOS files are held in machine-readable form and are updated as new data become publicly available.

Publications: 1) Monthly Abstract of Statistics—Department of Statistics publication; available by subscription. 2) INFOS Newsletter—contains update information on data base expansion and production and other relevant information.

Computer-Based Products and Services: The INFORMATION NETWORK FOR OFFICIAL STATISTICS (INFOS) comprises the following three major components: 1) Computerized index—covers the INFOS statistical data base and its documentation system; allows users to search for series of interest and control the range of surveys to be searched. 2) Documentation system—holds historical information on statistical collections which assists users doing analysis over a wide time-span. Also includes details of what statistics are collected, which are published, and where these can be obtained. The documentation system includes surveys not contained in INFOS. 3) Statistical data base and data analysis system—currently contains 310,000 time series, with expansion to 500,000 series planned. Permits simple manipulations within the data base itself, or complex analyses with the SAS (Statistical Analysis System) software package; output may be produced in tabular and graphic form, suitable for reports or publications. The client's own statistical series can also be stored on the system. INFOS can be accessed online by anyone in New Zealand with compatible equipment. Segments of the data are also available on magnetic tape for clients' in-house use.

Clientele/Availability: Clientele includes government agencies, private firms, and universities; there are no restrictions on availability of the service.

Contact: R.H. D'Ath, Executive Officer, Information Network for Official Statistics.

★750★
NEWFOUNDLAND DEPARTMENT OF MINES & ENERGY
MINERAL DEVELOPMENT DIVISION LIBRARY
COMPUTERIZED RETRIEVAL SERVICES
P.O. Box 4750   Phone: (709) 737-3159
St. John's, NF, Canada A1C 5T7
Rex Gibbons, Sr. Geologist, Pub. & Info. Section

Staff: 2 Information and library professional; 1 management professional; 1 sales and marketing; 1 clerical and nonprofessional.

Description of System or Service: The COMPUTERIZED RETRIEVAL SERVICES of the Mineral Development Division Library provides online information retrieval from commercially available and in-house data bases. Internal data bases maintained include an index to geological reports and articles, as well as several nonbibliographic files.

Scope and/or Subject Matter: Newfoundland and Labrador geology, mining, and mineral resources.

Input Sources: Input is derived from reports, articles, and commercially available data bases.

Holdings and Storage Media: Library holdings consist of 2000 bound volumes; subscriptions to 42 periodicals; and approximately 8000 maps and reports. Computer-readable data bases are also held.

Computer-Based Products and Services: Retrospective searching and SDI services are offered from data bases made available by major commercial vendors. Computerized searches are also provided from the in-house index to geological and related assessment reports and other articles on Newfoundland and Labrador. Computer files are being developed for mineral occurrences, mineral claims, quarry permits and leases, mineral statistics, and minerals-related diamond drilling.

Other Services: Also offered are manual literature searching and referral services.

Clientele/Availability: Services are available to mineral exploration companies, government, universities, and the public.

Contact: Rex Gibbons, Sr. Geologist, Pub. & Info. Section. (Telex 016 4724.)

★751★
NEWFOUNDLAND TELEPHONE
TOURISM NEWFOUNDLAND
Fort William Bldg.   Phone: (709) 739-2005
P.O. Box 2110
St. Johns, NF, Canada A1C 5H6
Robert A. Newell, Corporate Planning Manager

Staff: 3 Management professional; 1 technician; 1 clerical and nonprofessional.

Related Organizations: Tourism Newfoundland receives support from the Newfoundland Department of Development (Tourism Division).

Description of System or Service: TOURISM NEWFOUNDLAND is a seasonal videotex service providing tourism-related information on Newfoundland industries to terminals located in hotels and tourist chalets throughout the province. The service provides information on hotels and motels, historic sites, tours, and local attractions and events in Newfoundland.

Scope and/or Subject Matter: Newfoundland tourism-related industries and information, including hotels, restaurants, parks, history, transportation, auto tours, climate, wildlife, local events, and attractions.

Input Sources: Information sources include brochures, calendars, and research conducted by the Government of Newfoundland.

Holdings and Storage Media: The Tourism Newfoundland videotex data base holds more than 2000 pages of information.

Computer-Based Products and Services: Using Telidon technology, TOURISM NEWFOUNDLAND provides more than 2000 pages of tourism information via terminals located throughout Newfoundland. Tourists can select topics of interest from the terminals.

Clientele/Availability: The system is publicly accessible from May to September.

Contact: Robert A. Newell, Corporate Planning Manager, Newfoundland Telephone.

★752★
NICHOLS APPLIED MANAGEMENT
10180 102nd St.   Phone: (403) 424-0091
400 Bentall Bldg.   Founded: 1973
Edmonton, AB, Canada T5J 0W5
Peter Nichols, Partner

Staff: 5 Information and library professional; 4 management professional; 1 technician; 1 clerical and nonprofessional.

Related Organizations: The firm is affiliated with Nichols Advanced Technologies Inc. It was founded under the name Peter C. Nichols & Associates Ltd. and merged in 1982 with Schick Information Systems Ltd.

Description of System or Service: NICHOLS APPLIED MANAGEMENT is a management consulting and information research firm that offers economic and socioeconomic analysis, business and financial planning, market and feasibility analysis, computer technology consulting, and information and library systems development. Among its services, NICHOLS develops software for library and records management applications and assists with the design, specification, evaluation, selection, and implementation of computer systems. The firm also conducts online searches and offers document retrieval and delivery.

Scope and/or Subject Matter: Library and records management, computer technology, market analysis, business and financial planning, and economic analysis.

Computer-Based Products and Services: NICHOLS APPLIED MANAGEMENT develops software for library and records management applications, including microcomputer-based online indexing, preparation of KWIC/KWOC indexes, and information retrieval and circulation systems. The firm also offers online search services and general computer technology consulting.

Clientele/Availability: Services are available without restrictions; primary clients include business, government, and community-based organizations.

Contact: Bruce Butler, Partner, Nichols Applied Management.

★753★
NIHON KEIZAI SHIMBUN, INC. (NIKKEI)
DATABANK BUREAU
NIKKEI ECONOMIC ELECTRONIC DATABANK SYSTEM-
  INFORMATION RETRIEVAL (NEEDS-IR)
9-5, Ohtemachi, 1-Chome, Chiyoda-ku   Phone: 03 2700251
Tokyo 100, Japan   Service Est: 1975

Staff: 2 Information and library professional; 3 management professional; 2 technicians; 4 sales and marketing; 4 clerical and nonprofessional; 5 other.

Description of System or Service: NIKKEI ECONOMIC ELECTRONIC DATABANK SYSTEM-INFORMATION RETRIEVAL (NEEDS-IR) is a bibliographic information retrieval service providing access to business and economic news. It provides on-demand searches, SDI services, and some online access for the internally compiled NKS Article Information Data Bank and two other bibliographic data bases. NKS Article Information includes Japanese-language headings (up to 40 words) or abstracts (up to 400 words) for articles published in Nihon Keizai Shimbun's economic journals. Copies of the original articles are available in paper or microfiche. In addition to being used for retrieval services, NEEDS-IR is employed in the production of several abstracting and indexing journals.

Scope and/or Subject Matter: All articles on the economy, business, finance, technology, and individual corporations, as well as political and city news stories having economic implications.

Input Sources: Input for NKS Article Information is selected from the Nihon Keizai Shimbun (Japan Economic Daily), the Nikkei Sangyo Shimbun (Nikkei Industrial Daily), and the Nikkei Ryutsu Shimbun (Nikkei Marketing Journal), all published by Nihon Keizai Shimbun, Inc. Information is also drawn from several Nikkei magazines published jointly by Nihon Keizai Shimbun and McGraw-Hill, Inc.

Holdings and Storage Media: Approximately 800,000 Nikkei news items are stored in the NKS Article Information Data Bank, with a growth rate of 150,000 headings and 50,000 abstracts per year.

Publications: 1) World Energy Information (monthly)—indexes and abstracts. 2) NEEDS-IR Local Information (monthly)—index only. 3) NEEDS-IR Food Information (monthly)—abstracts and index bulletin. 4) NEEDS-IR Countries Information (monthly)—contains numerical data and indexes.

Microform Products and Services: Microfiche copies of complete Nikkei newspapers or selected articles are available in ISO standard form.

Computer-Based Products and Services: NEEDS-IR provides information retrieval and current awareness services from the following data bases: 1) NKS Article Information Data Bank. 2) JOINT Data Base—contains the titles of papers and articles appearing in about 1000 publications, with annual input of approximately 100,000 titles; produced by the Institute of Journal of Industrial Titles. 3) IEE-Energy Data Bank—holds about 20,000 summaries and 3000 abstracts of articles on energy selected from about 60 world newspapers and magazines; maintained by the Institute of Energy Economics. The Nikkei News Recall Service (NRS), a division of NEEDS-IR, provides limited online service in the Tokyo area, with nationwide access planned.

Clientele/Availability: Services are available with restrictions on reuse of materials. Users include government offices, financial companies, institutions, and international organizations.

Contact: Masakata Komatsu, Head of Information Retrieval Section, Databank Bureau; telephone 03 2703857. (Telex J22308 NIKKEI.)

★754★
NIHON KEIZAI SHIMBUN, INC. (NIKKEI)
DATABANK BUREAU
NIKKEI ECONOMIC ELECTRONIC DATABANK SYSTEM-TIME SHARING (NEEDS-TS)
9-5 Ohtemachi, 1-Chome, Chiyoda-ku   Phone: 03 2700251
Tokyo 100, Japan   Service Est: 1970
Takashi Suzuki, Director

Staff: 20 Information and library professional; 15 management professional; 10 technicians; 15 sales and marketing; 10 clerical and nonprofessional; 10 other.

Related Organizations: NEEDS-TS receives support from the Nihon Keizai Shimbun Editing Office, the Center for Econometric Data Development & Research, the Industrial Bank of Japan, Nikkei Research, Inc., and Quotation Information Center.

Description of System or Service: The NIKKEI ECONOMIC ELECTRONIC DATABANK SYSTEM-TIME SHARING (NEEDS-TS) is a computerized information system specializing in numeric economic and business data. NEEDS-TS produces its own data bases and acquires other domestic and foreign data bases for distribution through time-sharing or on magnetic tapes and computer printouts. In addition, NEEDS-TS provides consulting and analyzes data to develop research works and forecasts.

Scope and/or Subject Matter: National and international economic, financial, business, and other types of data.

Input Sources: Input is collected from government agencies, industrial associations, individual company and foreign sources such as Data Resources, Inc. and Standard & Poor's, and international organizations such as the International Monetary Fund, Organisation for Economic Co-Operation and Development, and the United Nations.

Holdings and Storage Media: More than 25 nonbibliographic data bases are held, providing millions of data series.

Publications: 1) NEEDS-TS Economy/ Macro Forecast Review (quarterly). 2) NEEDS-TS Energy Review (quarterly). 3) NEEDS-TS Report.

Computer-Based Products and Services: NEEDS-TS provides a wide range of numerical information through time-sharing and on magnetic tape. Included are millions of international, national, regional, financial, industrial company, and special-purpose data series. The following specific data bases are available:

1) Nikkei Economic Statistics—contains more than 8000 series and a wide range of macro and industry economic statistics for the Japanese economy; most start from 1965. 2) Prices Data Bank—contains wholesale, export, and import price indexes released by the Bank of Japan. 3) Household Survey—consumer expenditures and price index items for all of Japan and the Ku-area of Tokyo; monthly series from 1970. 4) Industry (Commodity)—monthly data from 1970 to date on the production, shipment, and inventory of 469 commodities; published by the Ministry of International Trade and Industry. 5) Nikkei Input/ Output Tables—contains the government's basic tables and extended tables produced by NKS. 6) Machine Industry Input/ Output Table—produced by the Economic Research Institute, Japan Society for the Promotion of Machine Industry. 7) International Trade—monthly data since 1976 on Japan's imports and exports; covers more than 6000 goods classified according to the Commodity Classification for Foreign Trade Statistics. 8) Nikkei Energy—contains about 3000 monthly energy-related time series since 1970. 9) Japan Energy Balance Table—produced by the Institute of Energy Economics (IEE). 10) Agriculture—composed of data for Agriculture, Livestock and Feed, and Forestry subfiles; most data date since 1970 and are updated quarterly.

11) Banking and Finance—contains about 4300 time series such as money supply, exchange rates, and interest rates; also contains the Nikkei Public and Corporate Bond Index and the Commodity Price Index; most series are available monthly or quarterly from 1965. 12) Construction—contains about 12,000 monthly time series detailed by prefectural level since 1970. 13) Central Regional Databank—covers population, industry, finance, housing, and other factors for about 1100 regions in Japan. 14) Area, Population & Household Databank—covers about 3400 regions in Japan. 15) Census of Commerce Databank—contains sales and other data for 3400 regions in Japan. 16) Survey of Large Scale Stores Databank—contains the results of Nikkei's survey of 3500 large stores. 17) NKS Survey Databank—contains marketing data. 18) Media Databank—includes advertisement data for newspapers, magazines, and television, including A.C. Nielsen's TV ratings. 19) Nikkei Commodity Prices—provides daily prices and weekly, monthly, and yearly high, low, and average prices for about 300 commodities. 20) Listed Companies' Databank—contains data submitted by about 1600 companies to the Ministry of Finance; includes 267 items per company; most data date back to 1964.

21) Interim Databank—provides 68 items of semiannual financial data. 22) Consolidated Databank—contains 117 items for each of 94 companies, dating from 1978. 23) Non-Listed Companies' Databank—includes 267 financial items per company for about 840 over-the-counter and nonlisted companies, and financial data based on annual reports that include about 150 items for each of 1500 companies; both types of data are since 1977. 24) Bank Financials—covers about 200 financial items of all 157 banks in Japan since 1974. 25) Earning Estimates—includes prospects and actual results for 6 years. 26) Nikkei Stock and Bond Prices Databank—covers about 1700 issues listed on the First & Second Markets of Tokyo & Osaka Stock Exchanges and about 500 bonds; weekly, monthly, and yearly prices for the past 10 years are available. 27) Capital Market Indicators—provides about 200 kinds of daily, weekly, monthly, and yearly indicators for the past 10 years. 28) NEEDS Portfolio System—allows clients to evaluate their stock portfolio and to select the combination of return maximum or risk minimum with the aid of accumulated portfolio data such as stock rate of return, market index, and alpha and beta values.

Clientele/Availability: Services are available by subscription; clients include companies, industries, economists, bankers, and others in Japan, Europe, and North America.

Contact: Shigeru Shimizu, Deputy Manager, Databank Bureau. (Telex J22308 NIKKEI.)

★755★
NIHON KEIZAI SHIMBUN, INC. (NIKKEI)
QUOTATION INFORMATION CENTER K.K. (QUICK)
828 Otemachi Bldg.   Phone: 03 2165911
1-6-1 Otemachi, Chiyoda-ku   Service Est: 1971
Tokyo 100, Japan
Mr. Kitokuro Shiba, President

Staff: 77 Information and library professional; 13 management professional; 54 technicians; 42 sales and marketing; 28 clerical and nonprofessional; 23 other.

Related Organizations: QUICK was established and is owned mainly by Nihon Keizai Shimbun, Inc. in cooperation with Reuters News Agency, Hitachi Ltd., and major securities and banking companies in Japan.

Description of System or Service: The QUOTATION INFORMATION CENTER K.K. (QUICK) is an international information service company providing quotation information services and other financial data via computers and transmission equipment on an online real-time basis. It gathers market information online from major stock exchanges and other sources worldwide, and maintains the information in the QUICK computer center and other data processing facilities. QUICK transmits market information via leased communications circuits and direct dial telephone lines to more than 10,000 computer terminals or desktop printers in Japan, Europe, and the United States. QUICK comprises a number of individual services providing stock information gathered from Japan and overseas stock exchanges, bond and money market rates including over-the-counter prices and short-term and overseas money rates, stock and commodity information from major markets worldwide, and general, financial, and commodity news.

Scope and/or Subject Matter: Real-time data on stocks, bonds, commodities, and the money market; related general and financial news.

Input Sources: Stock prices are gathered online from several stock exchanges in Japan and overseas; bond and money market information is obtained from securities companies, banks, and the Japan Securities Dealers Association; foreign exchange rates are provided by money brokers; financial and other news is supplied by Reuters News Agency and Nihon Keizai Shimbun, Inc.

Holdings and Storage Media: Market information is maintained in machine-readable form at computer centers operated by QUICK in Tokyo and Osaka.

Computer-Based Products and Services: The QUOTATION INFORMATION CENTER K.K. (QUICK) provides the following individual services:

1) QUICK Video-I is a real-time stock information system which provides individual stock information including latest price, bid and asked prices, sequential prices, closing price for the past six days, yield, business results, and margin trade positions for the preceding day. These items cover the equities, convertible bonds, and straight bonds listed on the Tokyo and Osaka Stock Exchanges, major equities listed on the Nagoya Stock Exchange, and major overseas stock exchange prices and indexes. Video-I also provides market information such as the Nikkei Dow-Jones Average, Osaka Stock Exchange Dow-Jones Average and weekly trend, the top 20 most advanced, declined, and active stocks, number of stocks with advanced and declined prices, list of price movements by industry, exchange price indexes, percentage of issues traded, total market volume, market comments, big four brokers positions, and over-the-counter price information from stock exchanges in Japan. It also provides general, political, and company news as well as market comments and foreign exchange markets and overseas quotations.

2) QUICK Video-II is a quotation information service which provides information available in Video-I and also adds such functions as multiple-screens with Chinese ideographs (kanji), simplified Japanese characters (hiragana), and graphic chart presentations. It provides a main information frame which displays price movement of 10 selected stocks on the Nikkei Dow-Jones Average which is renewed every five minutes; a subframe which provides averages, indexes, total market volume, statement of the account settlement, historical data on stocks and convertible bonds, volume (yearly, monthly, weekly, and daily), most advanced and declined stocks, top 20 most active stocks, margin trade positions for the preceding day, number of stocks with advanced prices, number of stocks with declined prices, and news headlines; an inquiry frame which provides prices of listed stocks, convertible bonds, straight bonds, and overseas stock prices and indexes; a chart frame which displays individual stocks and averages as weekly and daily trends and price movements in graphic form; and a news frame providing news and overseas stock and money market comments.

3) The NIKKEI News Recall Service (NRS) provides access to approximately 100,000 news items stored during the past year in the Nihon Keizai Shimbun Data Bank. NRS services are available through the Video-II service.

4) The QUICK Board is a wall hanging-type stock price display board designed for use by securities companies. The Board displays stock prices from the Tokyo, Osaka, and Nagoya Stock Exchanges arranged in rows across the computer screen by security, with either the latest stock price and net change or the opening price, high price, low price, latest price, and net change displayed.

5) QUICK Video-Bond Money (BM) is an online bond and money market information service providing over-the-counter bond price information, bid and asked prices information announced by the Japan Securities Dealers Association, exchange information including straight bond and convertible bond prices and comparisons, money rates including tables of overseas and short-term money rates, bond statistics, and news and market comments. The Video-BM also provides facilities for online interoffice and client communications.

6) QUICK Video-X300 displays information on money rates gathered from money brokers and banks. As the rates change, the computer screen is automatically updated. It provides inter-bank dollar rates, the client's rates inserted by each bank, historical data, foreign exchange rates, prime rate of major American banks, and the official rate of major countries. The Video-X300 also provides news and market information and includes interoffice and client communications capabilities.

7) QUICK MT-I is an online, magnetic tape price information service which transmits stock and bond prices from Japan's three major exchanges after the close of the day's session. Data are transmitted directly from QUICK's integrated securities information system via a leased communications circuit to the client's computer.

8) The QUICK Home Printer receives real-time price information and market comments directly from the stock exchange floor via telephone lines. Price information on listed issues, convertible bonds, market comments, industry-related stock prices, and a list of straight bond prices are instantaneously printed on the Home printer in paper form.

9) The QUICK News (QN) System is an information service which transmits online price information on stocks and commodities, and financial and other company news retrieved from the QUICK video system to major Japanese newspapers for typesetting. Also available from the QN System are market comments from the Tokyo Stock Exchange, commodity news, company personnel moves, and statements of corporate accounts.

10) The QUICK CB Board displays convertible bond prices from the Tokyo and Osaka Exchanges on an online real-time basis, including opening, high, low, and latest prices and net change.

11) The QUICK Index Board provides various types of real-time financial data which can be selected from approximately 700 indexes, including the Nikkei Dow-Jones Average Index, the Government Price Index, the Foreign Exchange Rate Index, and others.

12) Videomaster is an international online system providing stock and commodity information from major markets worldwide which is maintained by Reuters News Agency in London.

13) Video-Gold provides information on the world gold market. Terminals and printers designed specifically for each QUICK service are available for lease.

Clientele/Availability: Services are available without restrictions in Japan, Hong Kong, Singapore, Australia, Bahrain, Europe, and the United States. Primary clients include financial and securities companies.

Contact: Mr. N. Wakao, Manager, Corporate Planning, Quotation Information Center K.K.; telephone 03 2015915. (Telex 02226709 QUICK J.)

★756★
NIKKEI SVP CO. LTD.
Nihon Keizai Shimbun   Phone: (not reported)
1-9-5 Ohtemachi, Chiyoda-Ku
Tokyo 100, Japan

Related Organizations: The SVP (S'il Vous Plait) Network is an affiliation of independent companies worldwide that provide information-on-demand services and are interconnected by telex.

Description of System or Service: NIKKEI SVP CO. LTD. provides clients with one-stop access to information-on-demand and other research services.

Scope and/or Subject Matter: All subjects, depending on client's needs.

Input Sources: Information is obtained from international SVP resources and other sources.

Services: Information on demand is the primary service.

Contact: Nikkei SVP Co. Ltd.

★757★
NINETEENTH CENTURY SHORT TITLE CATALOGUE (NSTC) PROJECT
Avero Publications Ltd. Phone: 0632 615790
20 Great North Rd. Founded: 1983
Newcastle upon Tyne NE2 4PS, England
Dr. F.J.G. Robinson, Director

Staff: 12 Information and library professional; 2 management professional; 2 clerical and nonprofessional.

Related Organizations: Supporting and sponsoring organizations include Avero Publications Ltd. and the Bodleian Library at Oxford.

Description of System or Service: The NINETEENTH CENTURY SHORT TITLE CATALOGUE (NSTC) PROJECT was established to produce a series of bibliographies which would act as a catalog of English printed publications in the 19th century, providing access by authors, subjects, places of imprint, titles, and date of publication. Based on the collections of the British Library and other national and academic libraries, the NSTC PROJECT is cataloging all works published in the British Isles, its colonies and dependencies both past and present, all books in English wherever published, and all translations from English. The NSTC is being implemented in three phases: the first phase will cover materials published from 1801-1815; the second phase will cover 1816-1870; and the third phase will cover 1871-1918. Each phase will be initiated by a printed union catalog of relevant publications. The CATALOGUE will eventually be held in one machine-readable data base so that updating from other libraries will be possible, together with the facility for online access.

Scope and/or Subject Matter: English printing from 1801-1918, including books, newspapers, journals, chap-books, school texts, official documents, and other materials covering all subject areas.

Input Sources: Input for NTSC is obtained from the holdings of the British Library; the Bodleian Library; the National Library of Scotland; Trinity College Library, Dublin; the University Library, Cambridge; and the University Library, Newcastle.

Holdings and Storage Media: The Nineteenth Century Short Title Catalogue is held in machine-readable form.

Publications: 1) Nineteenth Century Short Title Catalogue. Phase one of NSTC, 1801-1815, will appear in five volumes. The first four volumes will contain listings by authors; each volume will also contain subject and place of imprint indexes of all books listed. The fifth volume contains the following general sections: directories, ephemerides, periodical publications, and England, Ireland, Scotland, and London. The volume will contain subject and place of imprint indexes of all books listed, and a microfiche rearrangement of the full text in alphabetical order by title. Entries in all volumes will include, when available, author's name and epithet; birth and death dates; title; up to three classification numbers; edition statement, including year and place of imprint; and location symbol, including the different segments of each participating library's catalog. The NSTC is available for purchase from Avero Publications Ltd.; in North America, from Gale Research Company, Book Tower, Detroit, MI 48226. 2) Nineteenth Century Short Title Catalogue Newsletter—provides news and information on the progress of the project; includes brief articles and notes and is open for academic queries; available by request without charge from NSTC.

Microform Products and Services: An alphabetical title listing of all materials indexed will be made available on microfiche for each phase of the NSTC project.

Computer-Based Products and Services: The machine-readable NINETEENTH CENTURY SHORT TITLE CATALOGUE data base will be made available online to facilitate both information retrieval and updating by other libraries.

Clientele/Availability: Services are available without restrictions.

Contact: Dr. F.J.G. Robinson, Director, or Dr. G.M. Miller, Project Coordinator, Nineteenth Century Short Title Catalogue Project.

★758★
NIPPON GIJUTSU BOEKI CO., LTD. (NGB)
Kasumigaseki Bldg., 32-F, No. 2-5 Phone: 03 5817711
Kasumigaseki 3-Chome, Chiyoda-ku Founded: 1959
Tokyo 100, Japan
Mr. M. Shimada, President

Staff: 19 Management professional; 39 technicians; 20 sales and marketing; 82 clerical and nonprofessional.

Related Organizations: Nippon Gijutsu Boeki Co., Ltd. is the Japanese representative for Derwent Publications Ltd.

Description of System or Service: NIPPON GIJUTSU BOEKI CO., LTD. (NGB) provides industry and patent attorneys in Japan and overseas with comprehensive patent information and management services. It offers patent and trademark searches, English-language translations of Japanese texts, abstracting of Japanese and foreign patent specifications and other technical literature, advice on licensing of patent rights, management of patent annuities, prosecution of foreign patent and trademark applications, exporting and importing of patent specifications, and various other services in the field of industrial property. It produces punched cards and microfilm of Japanese patents and utility models and makes available official gazettes of patent offices located throughout the world.

Scope and/or Subject Matter: Japanese and overseas patents and trademarks.

Microform Products and Services: All Japanese patent specifications and utility models are held on microfilm and reproduction services are offered. COM indexes are produced for U.S. patents.

Computer-Based Products and Services: The NIPPON GIJUTSU BOEKI CO. supplies computerized information retrieval and SDI services concerning patents and utility models. In addition, it prepares punched cards in all classes of Japanese patents and utility models and supplies them to Japanese industry for use with information retrieval systems. Other computerized services include a patent renewal service, which automatically pays annuities each year.

Clientele/Availability: Products and services are available without restrictions on a fee basis.

Contact: Mr. H. Koshino, Manager of Information Department, Nippon Gijutsu Boeki Co., Ltd. (Telex 222 4621 NGB J.)

★759★
NIPPON TELEGRAPH & TELEPHONE PUBLIC CORPORATION CAPTAIN
1-1-6, Uchisaiwai-cho Phone: 03 5095913
Chiyoda-ku
Tokyo 100, Japan

Special Note: No questionnaire response was received for this entry for the 6th edition. The entry is reprinted as it appeared in the 5th edition.

Description of System or Service: CAPTAIN is a videotex information and communication system which is designed to facilitate access to travel, shopping, weather, social, and other consumer-oriented information and services. Subscribers utilize a keypad to retrieve specific information for display on home television receivers which are connected to CAPTAIN information centers via public telephone circuits. Special features of CAPTAIN include the ability to display hand-drawn pictures and structurally complex characters such as Kanji (Chinese) and Katakana and Hiragana (Japanese) language characters. An experimental CAPTAIN service has been carried out in the Tokyo metropolitan area with 2000 user terminals and the capacity of 200,000 information frames. Full public service is expected to be offered.

Scope and/or Subject Matter: Videotex information and communication services.

Computer-Based Products and Services: CAPTAIN supports information retrieval and other communication applications. Users can retrieve information for home display from one of the CAPTAIN information centers via the following request methods: by index frame, by page number (chosen from an information directory), and by keyword. CAPTAIN may also be utilized to place orders for commercial goods.

Clientele/Availability: CAPTAIN is in the experimental stage in Japan.

Remarks: The acronym CAPTAIN stands for Character and Pattern Telephone Access Information Network.

Contact: Chief of CAPTAIN Project, Engineering Bureau, Nippon Telegraph & Telephone Public Corporation, Tokyo.

★760★
NOMURA RESEARCH INSTITUTE (NRI)
INFORMATION SERVICE AND DEVELOPMENT DEPARTMENT
NRI/E JAPAN ECONOMIC & BUSINESS DATA BANK
Edobashi Bldg.　　　　　　　　　　　Phone: 03 2764768
1-11-1 Nihonbashi, Chuo-ku　　　　　Service Est: 1977
Tokyo 103, Japan
Toshiaki Kamijo, Executive Vice President

Staff: 20 Information and library professional; 6 management professional; 8 technicians; 1 sales and marketing; 5 clerical and nonprofessional.

Related Organizations: Nomura Research Institute is affiliated with the Nomura Securities Co., Ltd.

Description of System or Service: The NRI/E JAPAN ECONOMIC & BUSINESS DATA BANK is a machine-readable file containing more than 4200 weekly, monthly, quarterly, and annual time series relating to Japan's economy and industry. It includes macroeconomic data on the economy in general, specific industry and product data, financial data, and forecasts and reviews prepared by the Nomura Research Institute. The DATA BANK is internationally accessible through commercial time-sharing sources for simple data retrieval or complex modeling and analyses.

Scope and/or Subject Matter: Japan economy and business, including economic outlook, national accounts, national income statistics, foreign trade and balance of payments, labor, money and banking, production and shipments by specific industries, stocks and bonds, interest rates, and general economic forecasts and reviews.

Input Sources: The DATA BANK acquires information from more than 100 data sources, primarily government agencies and trade associations, such as the Ministry of International Trade and Industry, the Ministry of Finance, the Bank of Japan, and others.

Holdings and Storage Media: NRI/E contains approximately 4200 times series, including 1700 series for the Japanese economy in general, 1200 series for the financial field, and 1300 series for industry. Data are recorded annually (covers 10-20 years); quarterly (covers years since 1951 for national income statistics and since 1965 for others); monthly (since 1965 for most); and weekly (since 1980).

Publications: NRI Quarterly Economic Review.

Computer-Based Products and Services: The NRI/E JAPAN ECONOMIC & BUSINESS DATA BANK can be accessed worldwide via the Mark III Service (General Electric Information Services Company) and Interactive Data Corporation time-sharing services, and in Japan through Kokusai Denshin Denwa Co., Ltd.'s Valuable and Efficient Network Utility Service (VENUS). Data can be retrieved in tabular or chart drawing form and as correlation, regression, macroscopic, or standard model analyses of Japanese economic and business trends. Applications can be extended by linkage with other data banks and programs, including Minryoku Database, CITIBASE, UCLA Business Forecasting Project, BI/DATA, U.S. Economic Data Base, International Monetary Fund Data Base, OECD Economic Statistics and National Accounts, and INTLINE International.

Clientele/Availability: The Data Bank is offered on a contract basis.

Contact: Yoshiaki Akeda, Database Manager, NRI/E Japan Economic & Business Data Bank. (Telex 27586 NRITKY J.) Nomura Research Institute also maintains an office in the United States at 180 Maiden Lane, Suite 3701, New York, NY 10038; telephone (212) 747-1805 (Telex 23423619 NRIT UI); and in England at 3 Gracechurch St., London EC3V 0AD, England; telephone 01-626 1086 (Telex 51888916 NOMURES G).

★761★
NORDIC ATOMIC LIBRARIES JOINT SECRETARIAT (NALJS)
NORDIC ENERGY INDEX (NEI)
Riso Library　　　　　　　　　　　　Phone: 02 371212
P.O. Box 49　　　　　　　　　　　　Service Est: 1980
DK-4000 Roskilde, Denmark
Eva Pedersen, Coordinator

Staff: 4 Information and library professional; 2 clerical and nonprofessional.

Description of System or Service: The NORDIC ENERGY INDEX (NEI) is a computer-readable data base providing abstracts and indexes of energy literature published in the Nordic countries. It covers scientific and technical literature as well as publications of a more general nature. NEI also includes descriptions of ongoing research projects in all areas of energy carried out in the Nordic countries. The INDEX is accessible online and is used to produce printed and microfiche publications.

Scope and/or Subject Matter: All aspects of energy including science, technology, economics, legislation, policy, and social aspects; biomass, coal, nuclear, wind, and other energy sources.

Input Sources: Journals, reports, patents, and books published in Denmark, Finland, Norway, and Sweden are indexed and abstracted.

Holdings and Storage Media: The computer-readable NEI data base contains approximately 6000 items and is updated monthly.

Publications: A catalog of Nordic energy research projects is published annually.

Microform Products and Services: The Nordic Energy Index is published on quarterly microfiche.

Computer-Based Products and Services: The NORDIC ENERGY INDEX is accessible online through I/S Datacentralen. Entries in the data base include title, descriptors, and abstracts, generally in English.

Other Services: Document delivery is also available.

Clientele/Availability: Services are available without restrictions.

Contact: Birgit Pedersen, or Line Nissen, Assistant Librarian, Nordic Atomic Libraries Joint Secretariat. (Telex 43116 RISOE DK.)

★762★
NORDIC COUNCIL FOR SCIENTIFIC INFORMATION AND RESEARCH LIBRARIES (NORDINFO)
Helsinki University of Technology　　Phone: 445 2633
Library, Otnasvagen 9　　　　　　　Founded: 1977
SF-02150 Espoo 15, Finland
Bjorn Thomasson, Chairman

Staff: 2 Information and library professional; 1 technician.

Related Organizations: NORDINFO receives financial support from the Nordic Council of Ministers.

Description of System or Service: The NORDIC COUNCIL FOR SCIENTIFIC INFORMATION AND RESEARCH LIBRARIES (NORDINFO) promotes Nordic cooperation in the area of scientific information and documentation and among research libraries, primarily through funding of research and development projects. Its functions also include keeping abreast of developments in the information field in the Nordic countries as well as on an international basis; promoting and coordinating the transfer of information within and among the Nordic countries and on a wider international basis; initiating and carrying out inquiries and projects concerning methods, systems development, and education; and supporting the development of information systems in the field. NORDINFO provides financial support to Scannet, the Nordic data base network, and has cooperated in the development and implementation of many of the data bases produced by Nordic organizations. NORDINFO also works to coordinate the acquisition of library materials, to support union catalog projects, to facilitate document delivery and interlibrary loan services throughout the region, and to promote the training of personnel in libraries and other information and documentation sectors.

Scope and/or Subject Matter: Scientific information and documentation, research libraries, online information services, interlibrary cooperation.

Publications: NORDINFO-NYTT (4 per year)—newsletter available in Swedish, Danish, and Norwegian; free of charge.

Computer-Based Products and Services: NORDINFO supports the Scannet data base network and works to improve system capabilities and implement new data bases.

Clientele/Availability: Nordinfo provides funds to Nordic libraries, documentation services, and similar organizations.

Contact: Teodora Oker-Blom, Head of Secretariat, Nordic Council for Scientific Information and Research Libraries. (Telex 12 1591 TKK SF.)

★763★
NORDIC DOCUMENTATION CENTER FOR MASS COMMUNICATION RESEARCH (NORDICOM)
(Nordisk Dokumentationscentral for Massekommunikationsforskning)
State and University Library
Universitetsparken
DK-8000 Aarhus C, Denmark
Claus Kragh Hansen, Secretary
Phone: 06 122022
Service Est: 1972

Staff: 5 Information and library professional; 1 clerical and nonprofessional.

Related Organizations: The Secretariat for Nordic Cultural Co-operation provides grants for NORDICOM coordination and information activities.

Description of System or Service: The NORDIC DOCUMENTATION CENTER FOR MASS COMMUNICATION RESEARCH (NORDICOM) is made up of national centers in Finland, Denmark, Norway, Iceland, and Sweden which collect published and unpublished material from their respective countries pertaining to mass media. It abstracts and indexes pertinent literature and makes these references available through its online NCOM data base and through regularly issued bibliographies. NORDICOM also exchanges documentation and information with mass communication researchers outside the Nordic countries.

Scope and/or Subject Matter: Mass media and mass communication research, including press, radio, television, film, and new communication technology.

Input Sources: Input is derived from published Nordic literature, including books, dissertations, research reports, journals, conference papers, and public documents, and from unpublished research in the field of mass media.

Holdings and Storage Media: The computer-readable bibliographic NCOM data base contains 8500 records dating from 1975 to the present and is updated quarterly at a yearly rate of approximately 1000 records.

Publications: 1) Bibliography of Nordic Mass Communication Literature (annual)—contains author, keyword, and source indexes. 2) NORDICOM Newsletter (3-4 times per year). A special newsletter in English and lists of Scandinavian mass communication researchers and their main fields of interest are published on an irregular basis.

Computer-Based Products and Services: The NCOM data base is available online through I/S Datacentralen. Searchable data elements include author, title, year of publication, language, document type, descriptors, and abstract.

Other Services: In addition to the services listed above, NORDICOM also provides advisory and consulting services and manual literature searching.

Clientele/Availability: Services are intended for researchers, teachers, students, politicians, officials, and mass media personnel.

Contact: Claus Kragh Hansen, Secretary, Nordic Documentation Center for Mass Communication Research.

★764★
NORPAK CORPORATION
10 Hearst Way
Kanata, ON, Canada K2L 2P4
Dr. J.F. Carruthers, President
Phone: (613) 592-4164
Founded: 1975

Description of System or Service: NORPAK CORPORATION develops, manufactures, and markets NAPLPS/ NABTS based videotex and teletext hardware products and systems, including delivery systems, information provider systems, captioning systems, picture creation systems, terminals, and OEM products. The firm has supplied equipment for most North American public teletext or videotex trials, as well as equipment for internal use by major corporations. NORPAK also offers training services and consulting in the areas of videotex and teletext.

Scope and/or Subject Matter: Teletext, videotex, and related communications products.

Computer-Based Products and Services: NORPAK CORPORATION offers the following videotex, teletext, and communications products: 1) MKV Interactive Videotex Terminal. 2) Information Provider System 3—a complete NAPLPS picture creation system. 3) MKV Teletext Decoder—decodes teletext and closed captioning signals; allows selection of teletext pages and has page storage capability. 4) Teletext Encoding System—used for broadcast or cable environments; conforms to the North American Basic Teletext Specification (NABTS). 5) Caption Encoding System—a system for the preparation, preview, delivery, and transmission of captioned videotape program material. 6) Caption Creation System—a complete caption creation system.

Other Services: Custom engineering and software development services are also offered.

Clientele/Availability: Products and services are available without restrictions.

Contact: Dr. J.F. Carruthers, President, or Gordon Thorgeirson, Manager, Product Sales, NORPAK Corporation.

★765★
NORTH RHINE-WESTPHALIA INSTITUTE FOR AIR POLLUTION CONTROL
(Landesanstalt fur Immissionsschutz des Landes Nordrhein-Westfalen)
LITERATURE INFORMATION SYSTEM
(Literaturinformationssystem - LISDOK)
Wallneyer Str. 6
D-4300 Essen 1, Fed. Rep. of Germany
Dietrich Plass, Head
Phone: 0201 79951
Founded: 1972

Staff: 5 Information and library professional; 1 management professional; 3 technicians.

Related Organizations: The Institute for Air Pollution Control reports to the North Rhine-Westphalia State Ministry of Labour, Health and Social Affairs.

Description of System or Service: The LITERATURE INFORMATION SYSTEM (LISDOK) is a computer-based system for collecting, indexing, and abstracting literature on air and noise pollution. Online and batch-mode retrospective searches are offered, as well as SDI.

Scope and/or Subject Matter: Air pollution—emission sources, control methods, measurement methods, atmospheric interactions, air quality measurements, effects on plants and materials; noise pollution—vibration, noise control planning.

Input Sources: Input is derived from periodicals, reports, conference papers, and serials.

Holdings and Storage Media: The LISDOK data base is held in direct access files and on machine-readable tapes. Library holdings consist of 14,000 bound volumes and subscriptions to 250 periodicals.

Computer-Based Products and Services: The machine-readable LISDOK data base is used to provide computerized searching and SDI services.

Clientele/Availability: Services are available without restrictions.

Contact: Dietrich Plass, Head, Literature Information System.

★766★
NORWAY
MINISTRY OF FINANCES AND CUSTOMS
CENTRAL BUREAU OF STATISTICS
(Statistisk Sentralbyra)
Skippergt. 15   Phone: 02 413820
P.O. Box 4131 DEP
Oslo 1, Norway
Arne Oien, Head

Staff: 20 Information and library professional; 150 management professional; 60 technicians; 630 clerical and nonprofessional.

Description of System or Service: The CENTRAL BUREAU OF STATISTICS is the official compiler of statistics in Norway. It issues more than 100 statistical publications annually and contributes data to computer-readable data bases operated by other organizations. The BUREAU also offers analysis, research, and method development services.

Scope and/or Subject Matter: Official statistics in Norway.

Input Sources: Statistics are gathered directly through census and surveys, and indirectly through other administrative bodies.

Publications: The Bureau issues approximately 100 publications each year in five major series: Norway's Official Statistics; Statistical Analyses; Social Economic Studies; Articles; and Reports from the Central Bureau of Statistics. The BUREAU also publishes a number of monthly and weekly bulletins, including the following: 1) Monthly Bulletin of Statistics—contains current monthly and quarterly statistics. 2) Monthly Bulletin of External Trade—contains detailed monthly data on imports and exports. 3) New District Figures (monthly)—includes a bulletin for each county presenting data by municipalities. 4) Economic Trends—an appraisal of current tendencies in the Norwegian and foreign economies. 5) Weekly Bulletin of Statistics—contains summary presentations of all statistics released during the past week. 6) Banking and Credit Statistics (about 40 issues per year)—contains current statistics of private and public banks. 7) Guide to Norwegian Statistics—survey of Norwegian official statistics, systematically arranged by subject.

Computer-Based Products and Services: The CENTRAL BUREAU OF STATISTICS contributes input to data bases maintained by other Norwegian organizations.

Clientele/Availability: Publications are available by subscription.

Contact: Idar Moglestue, Deputy Director General, Information Department, Central Bureau of Statistics.

★767★
NORWEGIAN CENTER FOR INFORMATICS
(Norsk Senter for Informatikk - NSI)
Forskningsveien 1   Phone: 02 452010
Oslo 3, Norway   Founded: 1944
Hans K. Krog, Managing Director

Staff: 5 Information and library professional; 3 management professional; 8 technicians; 5 sales and marketing; 12 clerical and nonprofessional; 3 other.

Description of System or Service: The NORWEGIAN CENTER FOR INFORMATICS (NSI) provides information systems and services for industrial, research, and public activities. It operates an online information retrieval service providing clients with interactive access to a number of data bases produced by NSI or in cooperation with other organizations. NSI has developed and markets the POLYDOC and MicroPOLYDOC software systems which are used for the selection, storage, retrieval, and dissemination of information for a variety of applications. The CENTER has also developed the MISTEL electronic data processing system for videotex applications and it makes available videotex data bases. Additionally, the CENTER offers consulting services to external companies, including the organization of information and documentation system, and it cooperates with Scannet and other Scandinavian and international information and documentation policy organizations.

Scope and/or Subject Matter: Natural sciences and technology; environment; solid wastes; oil industry; mining and metallurgy; industrial activities; chemistry and chemical engineering; food science and nutrition; home economics; medicine; business, economics, and management; patents; transportation; utilities; noise; city and regional planning; education; research; information science; documentation; information retrieval systems; videotex systems and services.

Input Sources: Input consists of patents, dissertations, product information, reports, journal articles, and miscellaneous literature.

Holdings and Storage Media: The Center maintains 12 machine-readable data bases online.

Publications: 1) Artikkel-Indeks/ Article Index (monthly with annual index)—abstracts some 22,000 journal articles per year from 500 international professional journals covering technical and management developments in industry. 2) FoU-Indeks/ Research and Development Index (4 issues per year)—each issue covers more than 200 reports filed by current research projects funded by the Royal Norwegian Council for Scientific and Industrial Research. The above publications are available by subscription. NSI has also published a Norwegian multidisciplinary technical thesaurus covering 25,000 professional terms.

Microform Products and Services: Some microreproduction services are offered.

Computer-Based Products and Services: The NORWEGIAN CENTER FOR INFORMATICS makes the following data bases available for online searching: 1) Artikkel-Indeks/ Article Index (AID)—corresponds to the print journal covering literature relevant to industrial activities in Scandinavia; contains about 190,000 items with 24,000 added each year; updated monthly. 2) Eksport-Indeks/ Export Index—bibliographic data base on export markets and international business; produced in cooperation with the Export Council of Norway. 3) Fast Avfall/ Solid Waste—covers environmental research and development literature from 1974 to the present; contains 400 items with approximately 100 added each year. 4) FoU-Indeks/ R&D Index—corresponds to the print journal; contains approximately 1800 items with 600 added annually; updated quarterly. 5) Indeks IoD—covers information science, particularly fugitive information and documentation; contains approximately 1000 items dating from 1974 to the present with about 200 added each year; updated quarterly. 6) Naerinfo-Indeks/ Nutrition Index—covers chemical engineering, food science, home economics, and medicine; contains about 1000 items with 400 added each year.

7) OIL—corresponds to Olje-Indeks/ Oil Index, the print journal on oil drilling and refining produced in conjunction with the Norwegian Petroleum Directorate; contains about 18,500 items dating from 1974 with 2000 added each year; updated quarterly. 8) INFOIL II—contains information on current off-shore related and petrochemical research and development projects in Norway and the United Kingdom; produced in cooperation with the Norwegian Petroleum Directorate and the Petroleum Engineering Division of the Great Britain Department of Energy. 9) Ship Abstracts—corresponds to the print journal edited by the Ship Research Institute of Norway which covers selected ship technical and management articles since 1969; contains about 25,000 items. 10) Stoy-Indeks/ Noise Index—corresponds to the print source issued by the Technical University in Trondheim; contains about 400 items with 200 added each year; updated semiannually. 11) Regio-Indeks—covers literature on city and regional planning; produced in cooperation with the Norwegian Institute for City and Regional Planning. 12) PEPSY—covers literature on teaching and education.

Machine-readable tapes of some of the data bases are available through the CENTER, as are private file facilities on NSI computers. NSI also offers retrospective literature searching of data bases made available through DIALOG Information Services, Inc., ESA/IRS, and System Development Corporation (SDC). The CENTER has developed and markets the POLYDOC information storage and retrieval system, which is used by the CENTER for data base building and by other organizations for such applications as in-house reports, market information, patents, and product information access. POLYDOC features include flexible output formatting, an online program, FORTRAN programs, and a COM output program. A version for use with microcomputers, MicroPOLYDOC, is also marketed. Additionally, the CENTER offers videotex services, including MISTEL, an electronic data processing system and information data bases for banking, finance, insurance, transport of goods, hotels and travel, and industry and trade.

Other Services: In addition to the services described above, the Center offers educational courses and training in the use of its systems and services.

Clientele/Availability: Depending on the product or service, availability is by standard licensing agreement, regular subscription, or by cost recovery payment. Consulting services are available on a contract basis.

Remarks: Founded in 1944 as a nonprofit organization, NSI became a limited company in 1982.

Contact: Hans K. Krog, Managing Director, Norwegian Center for Informatics. (Telex 72042 NSI N.)

★768★
NORWEGIAN COMPUTING CENTRE FOR THE HUMANITIES
(NAVFs EDB-Senter for Humanistisk Forskning)
Harald Harfagresgate 31   Phone: 05 320040
P.O. Box 53   Founded: 1972
N-5014 Bergen-Universitetet, Norway
Jostein H. Hauge, Director

Staff: 2 Information and library professional; 6 management professional; 1 technician; 4 clerical and nonprofessional.

Related Organizations: The Norwegian Computing Centre for the Humanities is sponsored by the Norwegian Research Council for Science and the Humanities/ Norges Almenvitenskapelige Forskningsrad (NAVF). The Centre is located at and operated in cooperation with the University of Bergen.

Description of System or Service: The aim of the NORWEGIAN COMPUTING CENTRE FOR THE HUMANITIES is to promote the use of computers in research and development work within the humanities. Its current activities include the following: 1) management of a national information system on research in progress within the humanities and social sciences; 2) computer-based documentation service on research in progress within the humanities; 3) secretariat for the International Computer Archive of Modern English (ICAME)—serves as a clearinghouse, making available ICAME machine-readable data; 4) the Ibsen project—lemmatized concordance of Henrik Ibsen's plays and poems, produced from machine-readable data base; 5) the SIFT (Searching in Free Text) software system; 6) development of inventory systems for museums and archives; and 7) development work in the fields of computational linguistics and statistical archeology.

Scope and/or Subject Matter: Humanities; literary and linguistic computing.

Input Sources: The Centre collects machine-readable data from projects it coordinates and from projects undertaken by other organizations.

Holdings and Storage Media: An archive of English text corpora and a regularly updated data base of Norwegian humanities research are held in machine-readable form. Library holdings include more than 900 bound volumes and subscriptions to 96 periodicals.

Publications: 1) Humanistiske Data (3 per year)—available free of charge; journal providing information about the Centre's activities and other computer projects in Norway and abroad, as well as articles of professional interest. 2) ICAME News—newsletter. The Centre also publishes various books, reports, and handbooks.

Microform Products and Services: The complete text and KWIC concordance of the Brown Corpus and a KWIC concordance of the LOB Corpus are available for purchase on microfiche.

Computer-Based Products and Services: The CENTRE produces a computer-readable data base containing a bibliography and information on research in progress within the humanities. It also issues magnetic tape copies of materials held by ICAME, which include the following: 1) The Brown Corpus—a revised version with upper and lower case letters and other features which reduce the need for special codes and make the materials more easily readable; includes text and KWIC index. 2) The LOB Corpus—British English counterpart of the Brown Corpus; includes text and KWIC index. 3) The London-Lund Corpus—features spoken British English in orthographic transcription with prosodic analysis.

Other Services: In addition to services described above, the Centre provides consulting, assists in obtaining data from abroad, and offers individual instruction, courses, and seminars on the use of the computer in the humanities.

Clientele/Availability: Services are available to individual researchers, educators, academic departments, archives and museums of cultural institutions, and other institutions of advanced learning related to the field of humanities.

Projected Publications and Services: The Centre plans to issue a grammatically tagged version of the LOB corpus and a printed vocabulary derived from Ibsen's plays and poems combined with lemmatized concordances on microfiche.

Contact: Jostein H. Hauge, Director, or Kristin Natvig, Information Officer, Norwegian Computing Centre for the Humanities.

★769★
NORWEGIAN PETROLEUM DIRECTORATE
(Oljedirektoratet)
INFOIL II
P.O. Box 600   Phone: 04 533160
Lagardsveien 80
N-4001 Stavanger, Norway
Grete Schanche, Documentalist

Related Organizations: INFOIL II is produced by the Norwegian Petroleum Directorate and the Petroleum Engineering Division of the Great Britain Department of Energy in cooperation with the Norwegian Center for Informatics.

Description of System or Service: INFOIL II is a computer-readable data base containing English-language information on current offshore-related and petrochemical research and development projects in Norway and the United Kingdom. The data base is publicly available online and computerized searches are provided from it.

Scope and/or Subject Matter: Research and development projects in Norway and the United Kingdom concerning offshore oil and gas exploration, geology, exploitation, production and production facilities, pipelines, transportation, supply services, petroleum economy, and environmental and social impact of petroleum activities.

Input Sources: Input is derived from research projects reported by researchers and government agencies.

Holdings and Storage Media: The machine-readable INFOIL II data base contains more than 900 records dating from 1980 to the present; it is updated semiannually at an increase of 700 records.

Computer-Based Products and Services: The INFOIL II data base is searchable online through the Norwegian Center for Informatics (NSI). Computerized searching of the data base is also offered. Searchable data elements include project title, contractor name, sponsor, date, and keywords.

Clientele/Availability: Services are available to users in the offshore and petrochemical industries.

Contact: Grete Schanche, Documentalist, Norwegian Petroleum Directorate. (Telex 33100 NOPED.)

★770★
NORWEGIAN PETROLEUM DIRECTORATE
(Oljedirektoratet)
OIL INDEX
(Olje-Indeks)
P.O. Box 600   Phone: 04 533160
Lagardsveien 80   Service Est: 1975
N-4001 Stavanger, Norway
Grete Schanche, Documentalist

Staff: Approximately 3 total.

Related Organizations: The Oil Index is produced by the Norwegian Petroleum Directorate in conjunction with the Norwegian Center for Informatics.

Description of System or Service: The OIL INDEX is a computer-readable index to Scandinavian petroleum literature published since 1974. It is available as an online data base and as two hardcopy quarterly abstracts journals: Olje-Indeks with Norwegian keywords, and Oil Index with English keywords.

Scope and/or Subject Matter: Oil and petroleum, including petroleum geology, oil and gas exploration, reservoir technique, production, offshore constructions, pipelines, petroleum law, and the social, employment, economic, and environmental effects of petroleum activities in Scandinavia.

Input Sources: Input includes research reports, government publications, journal articles, books, patents, specifications, conference papers, newspaper articles, annual reports, preprints, and pamphlets published in the Scandinavian countries; nearly a third of the documents covered are written in English.

Holdings and Storage Media: The Oil Index data base holds approximately 18,500 citations covering literature published from 1974 to date, with 2000 new citations added annually; it is updated quarterly.

Publications: 1) Olje-Indeks (quarterly)—abstracts journal covering the literature published from 1974 to date; includes a combined Norwegian keyword index and reference section providing title, author, and other bibliographic information. 2) Oil Index (quarterly)—abstracts journal covering the literature published since 1980; contains a combined English keyword index and reference section providing title, author, and other bibliographic information.

Computer-Based Products and Services: The OIL INDEX data base, maintained under the POLYDOC search system, is available for online searching through the Norwegian Center for Informatics as the OIL data base.

Other Services: Document delivery services are also offered.

Clientele/Availability: Products and services are available without restrictions.

Contact: Grete Schanche, Documentalist, Norwegian Petroleum Directorate. (Telex 33100 NOPED.)

★771★
NORWEGIAN RESEARCH COUNCIL FOR SCIENCE AND THE HUMANITIES
(Norges Almenvitenskapelige Forskningsrad - NAVF)
NORWEGIAN SOCIAL SCIENCE DATA SERVICES
(Norsk Samfunnsvitenskapelig Datatjeneste - NSD)
Hans Holmboesgate 22 Phone: 05 212117
N-5000 Bergen, Norway Service Est: 1971
Bjorn Henrichsen, Director

Staff: 12 Information and library professional; 1 management professional; 3 clerical and nonprofessional.

Description of System or Service: The NORWEGIAN SOCIAL SCIENCE DATA SERVICES (NSD) maintains machine-readable historical, survey, census, and psychological data together with an extensive collection of software packages for data manipulation. NSD encourages data use by offering lectures, courses, and teaching packages to users, and by supporting data consultants at three universities in Oslo, Trondheim, and Tromso.

Scope and/or Subject Matter: Norwegian social science data.

Input Sources: Data are submitted by organizations such as the Norwegian Gallup Institute and the Norwegian Central Bureau of Statistics.

Publications: Brukermeldinger—newsletter.

Computer-Based Products and Services: The NSD has established eight basic data systems: 1) A data bank for communes which covers statistics for all local administrative units since 1838 with the capability to plot boundary changes. 2) A cartographic service comprising coordinate matrices for all commune boundaries in Norway. 3) A census tract data bank covering the 1960 and 1970 censuses. 4) Survey data on a variety of topics. 5) Data bank on elites including biographical information on members of Parliament since 1814 and Parliamentary roll calls since the 1870s. 6) Archive of data on voluntary associations in Norway. 7) Aggregate statistics for other nations. 8) Test data for Armed Forces recruits.

Other Services: Data research and consulting services are also offered.

Clientele/Availability: Data and services are available to social science researchers.

Contact: Bjorn Henrichsen, Director, Norwegian Social Science Data Services.

★772★
NORWEGIAN STANDARDS ASSOCIATION
(Norges Standardiseringsforbund - NSF)
STANDARD
P.O. Box 7072 Homansbyen Phone: 02 466094
N-0306 Oslo 3, Norway Service Est: 1980
Mr. O.B. Ottesen, Deputy Managing Director

Staff: 28 Total.

Description of System or Service: Established to support the information work of the Norwegian Standards Association, STANDARD is a machine-readable bibliographic file covering Norwegian standards, norms, and regulations issued by the Association and the Norwegian government. The data base is the Norwegian contribution to the international standards network, ISONET, and is available for online searching.

Scope and/or Subject Matter: Norwegian standards, electrotechnical norms, and technical regulations.

Input Sources: Input for STANDARD is derived primarily from NSF documents and Norwegian laws and regulations.

Holdings and Storage Media: The data base contains computer-readable information on 2417 Norwegian standards, 282 electrotechnical norms, 610 technical regulations, and 91 draft documents; it is updated six times per year.

Publications: The NSF issues Norwegian standards as well as annual catalogs of standards and technical regulations.

Computer-Based Products and Services: STANDARD indexes standards, norms, and regulations in Norwegian and English according to ISONET specifications. The data base is available online through the NSF and is searchable for such information as author, title, language of original document, translations, availability, Norwegian and English descriptors, and references to other documents.

Clientele/Availability: Services are available to anyone.

Contact: Mr. P. Eddie, Sales Manager, Norwegian Standards Association. (Telex 19050 NSF N.)

O

★773★
OFFICE OF ECONOMIC INFORMATION AND FORECASTING
(Bureau d'Informations et de Previsions Economiques - BIPE)
122, ave. Charles de Gaulle   Phone: 01 7471166
F-92522 Neuilly, France   Founded: 1958
Jean Hauchecorne, General Director

Staff: 2 Information and library professional; 50 management professional; 27 clerical and nonprofessional.

Description of System or Service: The OFFICE OF ECONOMIC INFORMATION AND FORECASTING (BIPE) provides short and long-term economic forecasts in the industrial field, as well as technological forecasting, environmental studies, and sociological studies. BIPE disseminates this information through publications, library and information research services, and several publicly available data bases.

Scope and/or Subject Matter: Economic and technological forecasting in the areas of industry, agriculture, building construction, electronics, consumer goods, new technologies, services, trade, and transportation; social research; environmental studies.

Input Sources: Input is derived from French and foreign periodicals, other official and unofficial literature and reports, and statistics gathered directly from employers' groups and other sources.

Holdings and Storage Media: BIPE maintains four major files of numeric data in machine-readable form. Library holdings include 3000 bound volumes; subscriptions to approximately 500 periodicals; statistical publications; and official and unofficial reports.

Publications: 1) L'Economie Francaise en ... (annual)—forecast of the French economy for the next year; issued in five volumes. 2) Previsions Glissantes Detaillees—five-year rolling forecast. A number of other publications are also issued, and special reports are produced on demand.

Computer-Based Products and Services: The OFFICE OF ECONOMIC INFORMATION AND FORECASTING produces the following machine-readable data bases: PGD—1200 time series on French industrial markets; BATREGIO—50,000 time series about the construction industry in France; CME—holds numeric data on the international trade in electronics; and CONSUM—an econometric model and data base covering consumer goods in France. TROLL software is used with econometrics and modeling data bases. The OFFICE offers information retrieval services, reporting and graphic capabilities, and microcomputer software.

Clientele/Availability: Some services are available only to member companies. Special reports may be requested by any client.

Contact: Renee Saveant, Head, Information Department, Office of Economic Information and Forecasting. (Telex BIPE 610602 F.)

★774★
ONLINE GMBH
Poststr. 42   Phone: 6221 21536
D-6900 Heidelberg 1, Fed. Rep. of
   Germany   Founded: 1980
Dr. Dieter Schumacher, Director

Staff: 1 Information and library professional; 3 management professional; 1 sales and marketing; 5 clerical and nonprofessional.

Description of System or Service: ONLINE GMBH is an information brokerage firm providing computerized information retrieval and analysis services in all academic disciplines and industrial branches. The firm will also undertake specific information gathering projects and studies, including technology state-of-the-art reviews, industry overviews, market and consumer research, new products, and innovation and diversification studies. Additionally, ONLINE offers consulting services, conducts seminars, and supplies document delivery and SDI services. ONLINE GMBH also produces the computer-readable BUSINESS data base containing information on worldwide business opportunities and contacts. The data base is commercially available online.

Scope and/or Subject Matter: Information searching in all subject areas, with emphasis on industrial innovation; worldwide trade opportunities and business contacts in all industries.

Input Sources: Commercial online data base vendors are primary input sources for information research services. Input for the BUSINESS data base is derived from catalogs, directories, and primary sources.

Computer-Based Products and Services: ONLINE GMBH produces the international BUSINESS data base of business contacts and opportunities. Publicly available online through INKA (Informationssystem Karlsruhe) and Data-Star, the data base covers opportunities for manufacturing, marketing, sales, services, representation, cooperative ventures, and research and development in all industries worldwide. ONLINE GMBH also conducts computerized searches of data bases made available through Bank Group for Automation in Management (G.CAM), Control Data Corporation (CDC), Data-Star, DIALOG Information Services, Inc., DIMDI, ESA/IRS, INKA, Pergamon InfoLine Ltd., GID (Gesellschaft fur Information und Dokumentation), System Development Corporation (SDC), Telesystemes Questel, The Source (Source Telecomputing Corporation), and TRANSINOVE.

Clientele/Availability: Services are available without restrictions.

Contact: Dr. Dieter Schumacher, Director, ONLINE GmbH. (Telex 461782.)

★775★
ONLINE INFORMATION CENTRE
Information House   Phone: 01-430 2502
26/27 Boswell St.   Founded: 1979
London WC1N 3JZ, England
Jacky Deunette, Manager

Staff: 2 Information and library professional; 1 other.

Related Organizations: The Centre is financed in part by the Great Britain Department of Trade and Industry and the British Library Research and Development Department.

Description of System or Service: The ONLINE INFORMATION CENTRE was established to promote the effective use of online services in the United Kingdom. The CENTRE serves data base producers, system and network suppliers, and present or potential online users by providing inquiry services on data bases, systems, courses, meetings, search services, thesauri, and other aspects of bibliographic, factual, and other types of online retrieval. The CENTRE also offers assistance in assessing the needs for online services, selecting equipment, and contacting systems and network suppliers. Additionally, it issues publications, maintains the Databank of UK Online Users for referral services, and functions as the UK Euronet Centre.

Scope and/or Subject Matter: All aspects of online information retrieval.

Publications: 1) Online Notes (monthly)—available by subscription; newsletter covering Centre activities, new and planned data bases, hosts, forthcoming events and training courses, and books. The following publications are available for purchase: 2) UK Online Search Services—directory of 97 information brokers and intermediary services for individuals without access to a terminal. 3) Selecting Equipment for Online Information Retrieval—discusses various types of equipment and outlines the technical points to be considered; describes video display units, printers and print terminals, acoustic couplers, modems, microcomputers, and suitable software, with prices and UK supplier addresses. 4) Going Online—beginner's guide to using online data bases; includes selected bibliography. 5) 1982 Survey of UK Online Users—reports on current online usage. The Centre also makes the following data base directories available for purchase: 6) Patents Databases—covers 15 data bases or groups of files specializing in patents. 7) Medical Databases—covers 55 biomedical data bases, including those containing a proportion of medical information. 8) Law Databases—provides information on 36 data bases or groups of data bases covering law, including services giving the full text of case/ statute law, those giving references to the law, and those covering periodical and other literature; international in coverage. 9) Building/ Construction/ Architecture Databases. 10) News Databases.

Clientele/Availability: Publications are available for purchase worldwide; inquiry and referral services are normally restricted to newsletter subscribers.

Remarks: The Online Information Centre is expected to merge with the online search unit of Aslib (see separate entry) to form the Aslib Online Resources Centre.

Contact: Principal Information Officer, Online Information Centre. (Telex 23667.)

★776★
ONLINE USERS' GROUP/IRELAND
The Library
Trinity College
Dublin 2, Ireland
Trevor Peare, Chairman
Phone: 01 772941
Founded: 1979

Description of System or Service: The ONLINE USERS' GROUP/IRELAND represents Irish users of publicly available online information retrieval services in their association with the Department of Posts and Telegraphs and with various producers and suppliers in the information marketplace. The GROUP works to provide members with current information in the field through the maintenance of ties with similar organizations in other countries and through sponsorship of training seminars and workshops. It also supplies referrals and issues informal bulletins and membership lists.

Scope and/or Subject Matter: Topics of interest to online users in Ireland.

Clientele/Availability: Membership is open to interested organizations at any level.

Contact: Agnes Neligan, Secretary, Online Users' Group/Ireland, St. Patrick's College, Maynooth, Co. Kildare, Ireland; telephone 01 285222.

★777★
ONTARIO MINISTRY OF EDUCATION
RESEARCH AND INFORMATION BRANCH
INFORMATION CENTRE
ONTARIO EDUCATION RESOURCES INFORMATION SYSTEM (ONTERIS)
Mowat Block, 13th Floor
Queen's Park
Toronto, ON, Canada M7A 1L2
Anna Lau, Coordinator
Phone: (416) 965-4110
Service Est: 1974

Staff: Approximately 10 total.

Related Organizations: ONTERIS is produced by the Ministry of Education in cooperation with the Ontario Ministry of Colleges and Universities.

Description of System or Service: The ONTARIO EDUCATION RESOURCES INFORMATION SYSTEM (ONTERIS) is a computer-readable, bilingual data base covering the following sources of education information: educational research documents generated by Ontario school boards, the Ministries of Education and of Colleges and Universities, other agencies and authorities, teachers' associations, and other education organizations; curriculum guidelines and support documents produced by the Ministry of Education and by Ontario school boards; and reports and other materials related to ministry-funded commissions, reviews, and projects. ONTERIS provides bibliographic descriptions, abstracts, and descriptors and is publicly available through Bibliographic Retrieval Services (BRS).

Scope and/or Subject Matter: Education information and research relating to Ontario.

Input Sources: Input consists of educational research documents, papers and reports, and curriculum guidelines and support documents.

Holdings and Storage Media: The machine-readable ONTERIS data base contains more than 6000 records dating from 1974 to the present and is updated every other month.

Publications: Two volumes of abstracts of educational research and a cumulative bibliography with subject, author, and title indexes have been published.

Microform Products and Services: Some documents referenced in ONTERIS are available for purchase on microfiche from government sources.

Computer-Based Products and Services: ONTERIS is available for online searching through BRS. Searchable data elements include material type and status, language, title, author, corporate author, publication information, journal title, publication date, descriptors, education level, target population, abstract, special features, tests/instruments, notes, geographic source, funding source, contact person, and availability.

Clientele/Availability: Services are available without restrictions; primary users include researchers, administrators, educators, librarians, and students.

Contact: Ilze Purmalis, Supervisor, Database Production, Information Centre.

★778★
ONTARIO MINISTRY OF NATURAL RESOURCES
MINERAL RESOURCES GROUP
ONTARIO GEOLOGICAL SURVEY
GEOSCIENCE DATA CENTRE
77 Grenville St., 8th Fl.
Toronto, ON, Canada M5S 1B3
H.A. Groen, Chief
Phone: (416) 965-4641
Service Est: 1972

Staff: 2 Management professional; 6 technicians; 7 clerical and nonprofessional.

Description of System or Service: The GEOSCIENCE DATA CENTRE collects, compiles, and maintains comprehensive information on Ontario mineral deposits in computer-readable and hardcopy formats; maintains a depository of exploration reports submitted by the mining industry; maintains a computer-readable index to geoscience data in reports published by the Ontario Geological Survey and in unpublished submissions by the industry; and maintains a computer-readable file of data for Precambrian rock samples found in Ontario. The CENTRE uses its files to provide information retrieval services and to publish indexes to reports and maps.

Scope and/or Subject Matter: Data on exploration, mineral deposits, rock analyses, and other geological information.

Input Sources: Input consists of published provincial and federal geological reports and maps; assessment work reports submitted by industry; journals, papers, and books.

Holdings and Storage Media: Holdings include 7000 manual files covering mineral deposits; computer-based inventory data on 5500 mineral deposits; and 20,000 exploration reports and drill hole logs which are currently being converted to microfiche.

Publications: 1) Index to 6500 Published Reports and Maps, Mineral Resources Group, 1891-1977. Supplements covering the years 1978-1980 and 1981-1983 are available. 2) General Index—provides keyword access to geoscience reports issued by the Ontario Geological Survey. Additional titles are also issued.

Microform Products and Services: 1) Index to Geoscience Data in 8500 Exploration Reports—available on 4x6 microfiche and updated annually. Some of the reports are also available on microfiche. 2) Mineral Deposit Inventory—microfiche index to Ontario deposits listed by deposit name, NTS quadrangle, township, and commodity.

Computer-Based Products and Services: The GEOSCIENCE DATA CENTRE compiles and maintains three computer-readable data bases: 1) Mineral Deposit Inventory Database—provides data for 5500 Ontario metallic and industrial mineral deposits. The file is searchable by deposit name, location, commodity, and development status. Each record also includes map and report references. 2) Ontario Geoscience Data Index—provides bibliographic citations to 6500 reports and maps produced by the Ontario Mineral Resources Group since 1891 and 8500 exploration reports submitted by the mining industry. Searchable data elements include commodity, geological terms, type of exploration survey, township, NTS quadrangle, author, and year. 3) Rock Chemical Database (PETROCH)—contains data on some 15,000 samples of primarily Precambrian era rocks in Ontario. The file is searchable by town or claim map name, NTS quadrangle, latitude and longitude, major oxides values, trace elements values, type of material, field rock name, and geologist. The data bases are used to provide information retrieval services and to produce a variety of indexes. Magnetic tape services are also offered.

Clientele/Availability: Services are available at cost. Clientele includes provincial government agencies and the mining industry.

Contact: H.A. Groen, Chief, Geoscience Data Centre. (Telex 06 219701 MNR CCTOR.)

★779★
ORACLE TELETEXT LTD.
Craven House, 25-32 Marshall St. Phone: 01-434 3121
London W1, England Founded: 1981
Geoffrey Hughes, Chief Executive

Staff: 2 Information and library professional; 8 management professional; 4 technicians; 9 sales and marketing; 44 clerical and nonprofessional.

Related Organizations: ORACLE is organized and administered by the Independent Television Companies Association Ltd. and transmitted by the Independent Broadcasting Authority.

Description of System or Service: ORACLE TELETEXT LTD. provides the ORACLE electronic news, advertising, and information service which can be accessed on home television receivers equipped with decoders. Under the system, computer-generated information is transmitted in digital form over broadcast television signals, picked up by the user's television, and displayed by page as selected by the user. ORACLE broadcasts teletext magazines of national and regional scope to more than 1.3 million teletext-equipped televisions in Great Britain and Northern Ireland.

Scope and/or Subject Matter: National and international news, weather, sports, advertising, finance, regional information, racing results, fashion, book and record reviews, horoscopes, leisure topics, family topics, and features on fashion, health, farming, science, and engineering.

Input Sources: News and other information is compiled by the editorial staff at Independent Television News and ORACLE Teletext Ltd; daily weather forecasts are provided by the British Meteorological Office; and travel information is obtained from London Transport, Scotland Yard, British Rail, and other sources. Paid advertising is also included.

Holdings and Storage Media: Approximately 400 pages of news and information are transmitted by ORACLE, which has a potential of 800 pages. Pages of information and advertising can be updated throughout the broadcast day with breaking news updated as it occurs.

Computer-Based Products and Services: The ORACLE system develops and stores teletext pages for seven national magazines and three regional magazines. The pages are digitally encoded, broadcast with television signals of the Independent Television Companies stations, and received by television receivers equipped with teletext decoders. The signal is converted into pages and displayed on the screen using four lines of the vertical blanking interval. Using a hand-held keypad, viewers can consult an index and select pages of news and information by page number. The selected page or series of pages is held in the decoder's memory until other instructions are given. ORACLE is also used to provide television program subtitles for the deaf and hearing impaired.

Other Services: ORACLE Teletext Ltd. also offers consultancy on cabletext and on the establishment, promotion, and operation of a complete teletext service.

Clientele/Availability: ORACLE is offered free of charge as a part of the independent television system.

Remarks: ORACLE (an acronym for Optional Reception of Announcements by Coded Line Electronics) was developed in 1973 and first transmitted publicly in 1975.

Contact: Linda Golden, Promotions Executive, ORACLE Teletext Ltd. (Telex 8813039.)

★780★
ORGANISATION FOR ECONOMIC CO-OPERATION AND DEVELOPMENT (OECD)
ECONOMIC STATISTICS AND NATIONAL ACCOUNTS DIVISION
OECD MAGNETIC TAPE SUBSCRIPTION SERVICE
2, rue Andre Pascal Phone: 01 5248200
F-75775 Paris Cedex 16, France Service Est: 1975

Description of System or Service: The purpose of the OECD MAGNETIC TAPE SUBSCRIPTION SERVICE is to make national economic statistics available in a form suitable for computer processing. Based on the computer files of the OECD Statistics Service, subscription service data are available in several categories including Main Economic Indicators, Annual National Accounts, and Overall Trade by Country. The data are also available in various printed works issued by the OECD.

Scope and/or Subject Matter: Worldwide economic time series with emphasis on OECD member countries.

Input Sources: Data are gathered from OECD member countries and other national statistical agencies.

Holdings and Storage Media: Main Economic Indicators contains approximately 1750 monthly and 250 quarterly time series from 1960. Annual National Accounts holds about 12,000 series. Overall Trade by Country covers 8000 monthly and quarterly series since 1960.

Publications: 1) Main Economic Indicators (monthly); 2) Statistics of Foreign Trade, Monthly Bulletin; 3) Labour Force Statistics (quarterly); 4) Labour Force Statistics Yearbook; 5) Quarterly National Accounts Bulletin; 6) National Accounts of OECD Countries (annual); 7) Indicators of Industrial Activity (quarterly).

Microform Products and Services: Import/Export Microtables—contain detailed data on world foreign trade on microfiche.

Computer-Based Products and Services: The following magnetic tapes are available by subscription: 1) Main Economic Indicators (updated monthly)—covers the main aggregates of national accounts, industrial production, deliveries, stocks and orders, construction, retail sales, labor, wages, prices, home and foreign finance, interest rates, foreign trade, and balance of payments; the data also appear in the publication of the same name. 2) Overall Trade by Country (updated monthly)—covers recent developments in foreign trade in all OECD member countries; corresponds to the Statistics of Foreign Trade, Monthly Bulletin. 3) Quarterly National Accounts—covers selected countries. 4) Annual National Accounts (two tapes each year)—statistics for OECD member countries; corresponds to the publication National Accounts of OECD Countries. 5) Quarterly Labour Force Statistics—covers selected countries. 6) Annual Labour Force Statistics—covers all member countries; corresponds to the OECD Labour Force Statistics Yearbook. 7) Detailed Foreign Trade Statistics (updated annually when data become available)—contents vary. 8) Indicators of Industrial Activity (updated quarterly)—corresponds to Section One, Quantitative Indicators in the publication Indicators of Industrial Activity. In addition to being available on magnetic tape, some of the above data bases are accessible online through commercial time-sharing services.

Clientele/Availability: Tapes are available by annual subscription.

Contact: Data Base Management Unit, Organisation for Economic Co-Operation and Development. (Telex 620 160 OCDE.)

★781★
ORGANISATION FOR ECONOMIC CO-OPERATION AND DEVELOPMENT (OECD)
INTERNATIONAL DEVELOPMENT INFORMATION NETWORK
Development Center Phone: 01 5248200
94, rue Chardon-Lagache Service Est: 1977
F-75016 Paris, France

Special Note: No questionnaire response was received for this entry for the 6th edition. The entry is reprinted as it appeared in the 5th edition.

Staff: 2 Management professional; 2 technicians; 3 clerical and nonprofessional.

Description of System or Service: The INTERNATIONAL

DEVELOPMENT INFORMATION NETWORK was established to facilitate communication between individuals and organizations interested in economic and social development in Third World and OECD member countries. In order to quickly disseminate research information, the NETWORK has created an online information retrieval system and data bases containing descriptions of research and training efforts. Data for the information system is gathered in cooperation with five regional associations of institutes in Asia, Arab countries, Africa, Latin America, and Europe: Association of Development Research and Training Institutes of Asia and the Pacific (ADIPA), Association of Arab Institutes and Centres for Economic and Social Research (AICARDES), Council for the Development of Economic and Social Research in Africa (CODESRIA), Latin American Social Science Council/ Consejo Latinoamericano de Ciencias Sociales (CLACSO), European Association of Development Research and Training Institutes (EADI).

Scope and/or Subject Matter: Economic and social development in Third World and OECD member countries.

Input Sources: Data are collected from the regional associations described above and from institutes and individual researchers.

Holdings and Storage Media: The data base of development research and training institutes contains approximately 1300 entries while the data base on current development research contains approximately 1500 entries. The Development Center Library consists of 16,000 books and over 1000 periodicals.

Publications: 1) Liaison Bulletin—contains information on development research projects and institutes. 2) Directory of Non-Governmental Organisations in OECD Member Countries Active in Development Co-operation—contains information on 1700 organizations; includes five indexes.

Computer-Based Products and Services: Online searches of the following data bases are performed for cooperating research centers and external users by request: 1) research and training institutes located in OECD member countries and social science research and training units in Africa, Asia, and Latin America; 2) current development research projects in Africa, Asia, and Latin America; and 3) nongovernmental organizations in OECD countries. Machine-readable files in the ISIS (Integrated Scientific Information System) format can be provided.

Clientele/Availability: There are no restrictions on services.

Contact: Development Center, Organisation for Economic Co-Operation and Development.

★782★
ORGANISATION FOR ECONOMIC CO-OPERATION AND
 DEVELOPMENT (OECD)
INTERNATIONAL ENERGY AGENCY (IEA)
IEA COAL RESEARCH
TECHNICAL INFORMATION SERVICE
14/15 Lower Grosvenor Place   Phone: 01-828 4661
London SW1W 0EX, England   Service Est: 1976
Mr. A. Baker, Head

Related Organizations: IEA Coal Research is supported by 15 IEA member countries. Its projects are operated by NCB (IEA Services) Ltd., a subsidiary of the National Coal Board.

Description of System or Service: The purpose of the TECHNICAL INFORMATION SERVICE is to disseminate information related to all aspects of coal technology in order to increase awareness of the potential of coal and the coal industry in meeting future energy needs. To meet its objectives, the SERVICE has created two computer-readable data bases, which are used to produce publications and to offer information retrieval services. The Coal Data Base provides abstracts and indexes of literature on coal science and technology and related subjects published since 1978. The Coal Research Projects Data Base provides bibliographic citations to literature describing ongoing or recently completed coal-related research projects throughout the world. Both data bases are searchable online through commercial vendors. Additionally, the TECHNICAL INFORMATION SERVICE provides SDI, inquiry answering, critical literature reviews, bibliographies, and various other publications.

Scope and/or Subject Matter: Coal science and technology, including the coal industry, reserves and exploration, mining, preparation, transport and handling, properties, processing, combustion, waste management, environmental aspects, products, health and safety, economics, and policy and management.

Input Sources: Material for the Coal Data Base is extracted from books, technical journals, research reports, dissertations, and conference papers submitted by IEA member countries in hard copy or on magnetic tape; eastern European journal literature is covered by contract. Input for the Coal Research Projects Data Base is derived from published and online directories of research, annual reports, and through personal contact with research funding or performing organizations.

Holdings and Storage Media: The computer-readable Coal Data Base contains approximately 70,000 records covering materials published from 1978 to the present; about 1000 new records are added monthly. The Coal Research Projects Data Base covers more than 6000 research projects and is updated annually.

Publications: 1) Coal Abstracts (monthly)—each issue includes approximately 1000 abstracts arranged within subject categories; also contains author and keyword indexes, which are cumulated annually. 2) Coal Data Base Guide. 3) Coal Data Base Thesaurus. 4) Coal Abstracts Serial Title Abbreviations. 5) Coal Research Projects—a series of compilations, each covering research projects in a specific geographic area. 6) Coal Calendar (bimonthly)—provides details on meetings, courses, seminars, and other events of interest to the coal industry. 7) Technical Reviews (irregular)—a series of critical literature reviews with extensive bibliographies on subjects related to coal production, use, and economics. All publications are available by subscription or for purchase.

Microform Products and Services: Microfiche copies of those reports covered in Coal Abstracts which are difficult to obtain are available from the Service.

Computer-Based Products and Services: The TECHNICAL INFORMATION SERVICE maintains the Coal Data Base and the Coal Research Projects Data Base under ASSASSIN and specially written software and makes them commercially available online. The Coal Data Base is accessible through BELINDIS (Belgian Information and Dissemination Service), CAN/OLE, INKA (Informationssystem Karlsruhe), JICST (Japan Information Center of Science and Technology), and QL Systems Limited. The Coal Research Projects Data Base, also known as CLRP, COALRIP, and COALPRO, is searchable online through BELINDIS, CAN/OLE, and INKA. The SERVICE conducts retrospective searching of its data bases and other relevant commercially available online data bases.

Clientele/Availability: Services and products are available without restrictions to interested parties worldwide.

Contact: Robert M. Davidson, Coal Data Bases, Technical Information Service, IEA Coal Research. (Telex 917624 NICEBA G.)

★783★
ORGANISATION FOR ECONOMIC CO-OPERATION AND
 DEVELOPMENT (OECD)
INTERNATIONAL ENERGY AGENCY (IEA)
IEA COAL RESEARCH
WORLD COAL RESOURCES AND RESERVES DATA BANK SERVICE
14/15 Lower Grosvenor Place   Phone: 01-828 4661
London SW1W 0EX, England   Service Est: 1975

Special Note: No questionnaire response was received for this entry for the 6th edition. The entry is reprinted as it appeared in the 5th edition.

Staff: 4 Scientific professional; 2 technicians; 1 clerical and nonprofessional.

Related Organizations: IEA Coal Research projects are operated by NCB (IEA Services) Ltd., a subsidiary of the National Coal Board.

Description of System or Service: The WORLD COAL RESOURCES AND RESERVES DATA BANK SERVICE acquires, processes, and provides data on world coal resources and reserves, including quality and mining characteristics. The SERVICE's reporting activities are directed toward the identification of reserves and their potential for exploitation as a basis for IEA policy decisions and forecasts. It is currently assessing each country's coal deposits and establishing a general world inventory. Geological, chemical, and general bibliographic information on world coal resources are maintained in machine-readable files.

Scope and/or Subject Matter: Geology and mining of coal resources.

Input Sources: Input is obtained from questionnaires, geological journals and publications, and official statistics from government sources and similar organizations.

Holdings and Storage Media: A machine-readable data base is maintained.

Computer-Based Products and Services: The WORLD COAL RESOURCES AND RESERVES DATA BANK SERVICE uses the Computer Center of the United States Geological Survey at Reston, Virginia to store and process data. The London office of the Data Bank Service is linked into the system for data input and processing. Data stored include a central reference to location, and general descriptions of a country's coalfields, coal types, and geology.

Clientele/Availability: Services are available to individuals and organizations within IEA member countries, and to others by special arrangement.

Projected Publications and Services: A lexicon is being developed to provide a comprehensive record of multinational definitions and relationships relating to coal resources and reserves.

Contact: Head, World Coal Resources and Reserves Data Bank Service. (Telex 917624 NICEBA G.)

★784★
ORGANISATION FOR ECONOMIC CO-OPERATION AND DEVELOPMENT (OECD)
INTERNATIONAL ENERGY AGENCY (IEA)
INTERNATIONAL OIL MARKET INFORMATION SYSTEM
2, rue Andre Pascal Phone: 01 5249887
F-75775 Paris Cedex 16, France Service Est: 1974
Guy Caruso, Head

Staff: Approximately 8 total.

Description of System or Service: The INTERNATIONAL OIL MARKET INFORMATION SYSTEM collects, compiles, and analyzes aggregate data on crude oil import prices in order to prepare and issue reports for IEA member governments.

Scope and/or Subject Matter: Types of data collected include import prices to IEA countries of 20 selected crude oil streams as well as average total import prices; and crude oil acquisition costs on an overall IEA basis for 20 crude oil streams.

Input Sources: Data are collected from importing oil companies via IEA governments.

Services: The primary function of the System is data collection and analysis.

Clientele/Availability: Services are presently available only to IEA governments.

Contact: Guy Caruso, Head of Oil Industry Division, International Energy Agency.

★785★
ORGANISATION FOR ECONOMIC CO-OPERATION AND DEVELOPMENT (OECD)
NUCLEAR ENERGY AGENCY (NEA)
NEA DATA BANK (NEA-DB)
B.P. 9 Phone: 9084912
F-91190 Gif-sur-Yvette, France Service Est: 1978

Staff: 27 Total.

Related Organizations: The NEA Data Bank serves OECD member countries as part of a worldwide information network with five other data centers: 1) National Nuclear Data Center, Brookhaven National Laboratory, U.S. Department of Energy; 2) Nuclear Data Center, Institute of Physics and Energy; 3) Nuclear Data Section, International Atomic Energy Agency; 4) U.S.S.R. Center for Nuclear Structure and Reaction Data; and 5) Fachinformationszentrum Energie, Physik, Mathematik GmbH.

Description of System or Service: As the worldwide neutron data network's collection and service center for Western European OECD countries and Japan, the NEA DATA BANK (NEA-DB) collects and analyzes numeric neutron data and related bibliographic information from its area, exchanges this data in the EXFOR common format with data collected from the rest of the world by other network members, and provides its area with computerized information services and various publications derived from the collected world data. The computer files created as a result of these activities include the Computer Index of Neutron Data (CINDA) file, which serves as the basis of an annual publication; the World Request List for Neutron Data (WRENDA) data base; EXFOR numerical data from experiments; and evaluated nuclear structures data files. An additional activity of the DATA BANK is the collection, documentation, and exchange of important computer programs in the nuclear energy fields.

Scope and/or Subject Matter: Bibliographic, experimental, and evaluated data on nuclear reactions involving neutrons; nuclear, neutron, and reactor physics.

Input Sources: Neutron data are derived from unpublished sources, journals, reports, conference proceedings, and theses from the NEA-DB service area and, through the other centers, from the rest of the world. Computer programs are contributed by and exchanged with U.S. code centers and some 300 laboratories under NEA-DB jurisdiction.

Holdings and Storage Media: The NEA Data Bank files hold more than 4 million data measurements and 170,000 literature references. More than 8000 major tested computer programs are held for distribution.

Publications: 1) CINDA, An Index to the Literature on Microscopic Neutron Data (annual with supplements)—published by the International Atomic Energy Authority on behalf of the four compilation centers. 2) Neutron Nuclear Data Evaluation Newsletter (semiannual). 3) News from NEA Data Bank (bimonthly). 4) NEA Data Bank Newsletter (occasional).

Computer-Based Products and Services: Magnetic tape copies and retrieval, searches, and sorting are available from any of the following computer files held by the NEA DATA BANK: 1) Computer Index of Neutron Data (CINDA)—containing 170,000 keyworded and annotated references to the literature of neutron physics. 2) Numerical data from experiments in EXFOR format—consisting of 4 million measured values, plus associated bibliographic information. 3) Evaluated Nuclear Structure Data Files—holding 400,000 evaluated measurements in such files as KEDAK, UKNDL, ENDF, JENDL, and SOKRATOR. 4) World Request List for Neutron Data (WRENDA)—comprising 1600 official requests for measurements, with comments. 5) Source codes of requested computer programs.

Clientele/Availability: Services are provided free of charge to users.

Contact: NEA Data Bank, OECD Nuclear Energy Agency.

★786★
ORGANISATION FOR ECONOMIC CO-OPERATION AND DEVELOPMENT (OECD)
ROAD TRANSPORT RESEARCH PROGRAMME
INTERNATIONAL ROAD RESEARCH DOCUMENTATION (IRRD)
2, rue Andre Pascal Phone: 01 5248200
F-75775 Paris Cedex 16, France Service Est: 1965
J.P. Magnan, Chief

Description of System or Service: INTERNATIONAL ROAD RESEARCH DOCUMENTATION (IRRD) systematically collects and disseminates information of interest to the worldwide road research community through a decentralized network of institutions from 26 countries. Each IRRD member prepares common-format abstracts and indexes for its country's published and unpublished literature, ongoing research projects, and relevant computer programs, and also shares in the coverage of information from nonmember countries. Written in English, French, or German, this input is forwarded in print or machine-readable form to the appropriate IRRD language coordinating center, which checks the information and submits it on magnetic tapes to the OECD Road Transport Research Programme in

Paris. The collected information is then disseminated in the form of monthly COM microfiche or on magnetic tape, from which the individual members provide information services to their countries. The IRRD data base is also publicly available online through ESA/IRS.

Scope and/or Subject Matter: Highway financing and administration, design of roads and related structures, materials, soils and rocks, construction and its supervision, maintenance, traffic, accident studies, vehicles.

Input Sources: Input is derived from 850 journals published in 40 countries, plus reports, books, conference proceedings, standards, patents, theses, unpublished literature, and other information concerning ongoing research and road-related computer programs; it is submitted by 35 members in 26 countries.

Holdings and Storage Media: The IRRD data base, stored on communications format tape, is held by the Paris office and most member institutions. Dating from 1972 to the present, it holds approximately 100,000 references and is updated with more than 10,000 items annually.

Microform Products and Services: COM microfiche of IRRD information is issued monthly.

Computer-Based Products and Services: The INTERNATIONAL ROAD RESEARCH DOCUMENTATION data base is searchable online through ESA/IRS. Retrospective searching and SDI services from the data base are offered by member institutions under various systems; the Paris office provides tape subscriptions and standard-interest SDI.

Clientele/Availability: Services are available without restrictions. Clients include researchers, engineers, managers, educators, and others active in highway transportation.

Contact: B. Horn, Principal Administrator, Road Transport Research Programme.

★787★
ORIEL COMPUTER SERVICES LIMITED
1-5 West St. Phone: 0608 41351
Chipping Norton, Oxon. OX7 5LY, England Founded: 1982

Special Note: No questionnaire response was received for this entry for the 6th edition. The entry is reprinted as it appeared in the 5th edition.

Staff: 3 Information and library professional; 4 management professional; 12 technicians; 16 clerical and nonprofessional.

Related Organizations: Oriel Computer Services Limited is wholly owned by the Midland Marts Group.

Description of System or Service: ORIEL COMPUTER SERVICES LIMITED provides a range of computer-based services to meet the needs of libraries and information publishers of all kinds. Services include computerized typesetting, COM, file conversion, data base maintenance, library cataloging, and turnkey systems.

Scope and/or Subject Matter: Computer-based services for libraries, government publishers, and the private information industry.

Input Sources: Oriel obtains information from H.M. Stationery Office, worldwide publishers, and other sources.

Holdings and Storage Media: Oriel holds numerous machine-readable library files numbering about 1 million records. Hardcopy holdings consist of 60,000 items.

Microform Products and Services: Oriel produces various microform products for clients.

Computer-Based Products and Services: ORIEL COMPUTER SERVICES offers a variety of computer-based services in support of information publication and organization.

Clientele/Availability: Services are intended for information publishers, libraries, and others in the information industry.

Contact: Sales Manager, Oriel Computer Services Limited.

★788★
ORNA/STEVENS CONSULTANCY
55 Telegraph Lane E. Phone: 0603 611795
Norwich, Norfolk NR1 4AR, England Founded: 1979
Elizabeth Orna

Description of System or Service: ORNA/STEVENS CONSULTANCY offers information, editorial, and typographic design consultancy services. Its services include analysis of information needs; design of information storage/ retrieval systems for organizations and individuals; thesaurus compilation and design; typographical design and print production; writing, editing, and design of system and instructional manuals and other publications; training in the presentation of information; and planning of publishing systems.

Scope and/or Subject Matter: Information and editorial services in education, information science, and other areas.

Publications: The Presentation of Information—available from Aslib Publications.

Clientele/Availability: Services are available without restrictions. Clients include public and commercial organizations.

Contact: Elisabeth Orna or Graham Stevens, Orna/Stevens Consultancy.

★789★
OVERSEAS DATA SERVICE, COMPANY, LTD. (ODS)
Shugetsu Bldg. Phone: 03 4007090
3-12-7 Kita-Aoyama, Minato-Ku Founded: 1974
Tokyo 107, Japan
Yasuhide Miura, Executive Director

Related Organizations: Overseas Data Service, Company, Ltd. is the parent organization of Japan Data Service Co., Ltd. (see separate entry).

Description of System or Service: OVERSEAS DATA SERVICE, COMPANY, LTD. is a large Japanese industrial, marketing, and social research firm providing consultation services based on research data for business corporations, government agencies, associations, and other clients. It provides information on Japanese consumers, industries, economics, and politics for Japanese and foreign clients, and it provides data on foreign markets and technologies for Japanese clients in cooperation with overseas associates. The ODS Consumer Research Division conducts the Life Style Indicator (LSI), an annual study of trends in the social environment in Japan and how they affect consumer values, behavior, attitudes, and manifestations in the marketplace. Based on the methodology of Yankelovich, Skelly and White, Inc., the ODS-LSI study is produced as a series of reports accompanied by consultations and presentations at the client's request. In addition to the LSI, the Consumer Research Division offers custom survey and analysis services. The OVERSEAS DATA SERVICE Industrial Research Division provides industrial research, technology assessment, direct investment consulting, and industrial consulting in such fields as robotics, computers and software, telecommunications, the media, and other fields. It issues reports and publications and maintains data bases.

Scope and/or Subject Matter: Consumer, industrial, and marketing research.

Input Sources: Data are collected via surveys and interviews, from online data bases, and other sources.

Publications: ODS-LSI reports are issued annually and other studies and publications are issued.

Computer-Based Products and Services: Computer processing and analysis is used to prepare ODS-LSI data. The Industrial Research Division maintains data bases in the areas of office automation, telecommunications, trade, and electronics.

Clientele/Availability: Clients include major Japanese corporations and others.

Contact: Kenzo Kanda, Director, Overseas Data Service, Company, Ltd. (Telex J26487 ODSTHINK.)

★790★
OVERSEAS TELECOMMUNICATIONS COMMISSION (AUSTRALIA) MULTIMODE INTERNATIONAL DATA ACQUISITION SERVICE (MIDAS)
G.P.O. Box 7000　　　　　　　　Phone: 02 2305000
Sydney, N.S.W. 2001, Australia　　Service Est: 1979
Mr. P. Thomas, Group Marketing Manager

Description of System or Service: The MULTIMODE INTERNATIONAL DATA ACQUISITION SERVICE (MIDAS) is an international packet-switched data transmission service which connects Australian customers to overseas data communications networks. Through these international communications links, MIDAS offers access to a wide range of online data bases, remote computing services, international corporate computers, and electronic mail facilities in North America, Europe, and South East Asia. Users of overseas packet-switched networks can also access Australian data bases connected to MIDAS. Additionally, MIDAS serves as the communications link for MINERVA, the Overseas Telecommunications Commission's international electronic messaging service. Based on the Dialcom AOS system, MINERVA offers electronic messaging, conferencing, text editing, forms processing, and telephone messaging services.

Scope and/or Subject Matter: Packet-switched data communication services; electronic mail.

Publications: A MIDAS Operator's Manual is provided free to subscribers.

Computer-Based Products and Services: MIDAS connects to a number of packet-switching systems worldwide including Telenet and Tymnet, providing a communications link to overseas data bases and other remote computing resources. It also allows users located worldwide to connect to Australian data bases and services linked to MIDAS. Accessible with asynchronous and synchronous terminals, MIDAS supports terminal-to-computer and computer-to-computer communications operations. Additionally, the SERVICE links the MINERVA electronic mail service to ITT Dialcom, Telecom Gold in England, and Dialcom communications networks in Canada, Hong Kong and Singapore. Using common English-language commands, MINERVA sends and receives messages, provides a chat feature, conferencing, an executive calendar scheduling feature, word and text processing, forms procesing, and access to an electronic notice board and a world news service. Access to an international airline guide providing information on most international airline schedules is planned.

Other Services: The Overseas Telecommunications Commission staff provides basic online training in MIDAS and, where appropriate, data base operating procedures; it also offers information on resources available through MIDAS.

Clientele/Availability: MIDAS is available to Australian business agencies, academic research institutions, and others, with fees charged on a combination of elapsed time and the volume of data transmitted and received.

Contact: Mr. P. Thomas, Group Marketing Manager of Data Services or Michael Cook, Assistant Product Manager of Data Services, Overseas Telecommunications Commission. (Telex AA 20591.) The electronic mail address on Dialcom is 58:OTC005.

★791★
OXFORD MICROFORM PUBLICATIONS LTD.
Headington Hill Hall　　　　　Phone: 0865 64881
Oxford OX3 0BW, England　　Founded: 1975
Tony Sloggett, Director & Manager

Staff: 1 Management professional; 3 technicians; 1 clerical and nonprofessional.

Related Organizations: Oxford Microform Publications is a member of the Pergamon/ BPCC Group and is the United Kingdom and European arm of Pergamon's New York-based Microforms International Marketing Corporation.

Description of System or Service: OXFORD MICROFORM PUBLICATIONS LTD. provides learned institutions, libraries, museums, and international government organizations with micropublishing and related editing, indexing, copy preparation, and distribution services. OXFORD produces microforms from a variety of input, including original documents, works of art, manuscripts, photographic negatives or positives, magnetic tapes, and disks. The company also provides COM services as well as computer-generated catalogs, concordances, and selected printouts. Other services include storage of copy and microform masters, on-demand publishing, binding of printed text with microfiche, and provision of micrographics equipment.

Scope and/or Subject Matter: Micropublishing in scholarly, educational, and technical subjects.

Input Sources: Input consists of customer-supplied documents, rare books and manuscripts, original research reports, journals and periodicals, reprint collections, symposia proceedings, theses, and other types of materials in all kinds of media.

Holdings and Storage Media: Oxford stores information in hardcopy, microform, and computer-readable forms.

Publications: Indexes and other printed publications are issued in conjunction with the firm's microform products.

Microform Products and Services: Oxford Microform Publications Ltd. provides micropublication and distribution services for customers in any subject field; microforms are produced in standard archival formats. Descriptive material on the specific micropublications distributed by the company is available from it on request.

Computer-Based Products and Services: Oxford can generate COM from customer's computer-readable input. It also produces data bases and computer-generated concordances, catalogs, indexes, and selected printouts.

Other Services: Additional services include consulting and manual literature searching.

Clientele/Availability: Services are available to organizations of all types, particularly scholarly and technical.

Contact: Tony Slogget, Director & Manager, Oxford Microform Publications Ltd. (Telex 83177.)

P

★792★
PAINT RESEARCH ASSOCIATION
INFORMATION DEPARTMENT
WORLD SURFACE COATINGS ABSTRACTS (WSCA)
Waldegrave Rd. Phone: 01 977 4427
Teddington, Middlesex TW11 8LD,
  England Service Est: 1928
D. Dasgupta, Head, Information Dept.

Staff: Approximately 7 total.

Description of System or Service: The WORLD SURFACE COATINGS ABSTRACTS (WSCA) abstracts and indexes worldwide literature on the chemical, toxicological, manufacturing, and other aspects of organic coatings. It is available as a monthly hardcopy publication and as a publicly available online data base. The Paint Research Association also provides search services from the data base and issues an associated current awareness bulletin.

Scope and/or Subject Matter: Paint and surface coatings (excluding metallic): properties; components (pigments, resins, solvents, additives); analysis; testing; corrosion; fouling; hazards, including toxicity; standard specifications; legislation; and related areas such as adhesives, electrophotographic materials, and printing inks.

Input Sources: Input is gathered from primary and secondary journals, patents, specifications, books, conference and symposia proceedings.

Holdings and Storage Media: The computer-readable WSCA data base holds approximately 70,000 records dating from 1976 to the present; it is updated with 800 new records monthly.

Publications: 1) World Surface Coatings Abstracts (monthly with annual subject, author, and numerical patent indexes)—available by subscription; contains approximately 800 abstracts per issue arranged alphabetically by author in about 50 subject categories. 2) Paint Titles (weekly)—current awareness bulletin providing subject access to international English-language literature relating to paint, varnishes, and other coatings and their raw materials.

Computer-Based Products and Services: WORLD SURFACE COATINGS ABSTRACTS is searchable online through Pergamon InfoLine Ltd. Searches of the file can be conducted by title, author, journal, document type, abstract, section heading, language, geographic location, subject descriptors, and other details. The Paint Research Association offers search services and SDI from the data base.

Clientele/Availability: There are no restrictions on services.

Remarks: WSCA was also known as Surface Coatings Abstracts.

Contact: S.C. Haworth, Librarian, Paint Research Association. (Telex 928 720.)

★793★
PAKISTAN SCIENTIFIC AND TECHNOLOGICAL INFORMATION CENTRE (PASTIC)
P-13, El-Markaz Square Phone: 24161
Sector F-7/2, P.O. Box 1217 Founded: 1974
Islamabad, Pakistan
Dr. A.R. Mohajir, Director

Related Organizations: PASTIC operates under the Ministry of Science & Technology and is under the administrative control of the Pakistan Science Foundation.

Description of System or Service: The PAKISTAN SCIENTIFIC AND TECHNOLOGICAL INFORMATION CENTRE (PASTIC) is the national center for planning, organizing, managing, and promoting scientific documentation and information services in Pakistan. Among PASTIC's services are compilation of bibliographies, abstracting and indexing, technical translation, current awareness, SDI, document supply, patent information, training courses, and production of a union catalog under the NASDATA Data Base Project. It also uses the resources of the National Science Reference Library to provide reference and lending services. PASTIC is the focal point in Pakistan for the United Nations Environment Program's INFOTERRA system, and is the representative for the U.S. National Technical Information Service.

Scope and/or Subject Matter: Scientific and technological information.

Input Sources: Input consists of scientific and technical periodicals, patents, and other documents.

Holdings and Storage Media: The National Science Reference Library holds 6000 reference works and other items and subscribes to 200 periodicals.

Publications: 1) Pakistan Science Abstracts (quarterly)—includes indicative and informative abstracts together with author and keyword subject indexes; also available on microfilm. 2) Pakistan Current Contents (monthly)—lists article titles from indigenous journals and includes indexes. 3) Patent List (monthly). 4) Union Catalogue of Scientific and Technical Periodicals in Libraries of Pakistan. 5) Directory of Scientific Periodicals of Pakistan. 6) List of PASTIC Bibliographies. 7) List of PASTIC Translations.

Microform Products and Services: PASTIC offers microform reproduction services.

Computer-Based Products and Services: The CENTRE participates in the NASDATA Data Base Project for the computerized production of the union catalog.

Clientele/Availability: Services are provided through the national center and sub-centers in the provincial capitals of Karachi, Lahore, Peshawar, and Quetta.

Contact: Ghulam Hamid Khan, Senior Documentation Officer, Pakistan Scientific and Technological Information Centre.

★794★
PAN AMERICAN HEALTH ORGANIZATION (PAHO)
PAN AMERICAN CENTRE FOR SANITARY ENGINEERING & ENVIRONMENTAL SCIENCES (CEPIS)
PAN AMERICAN INFORMATION & DOCUMENTATION NETWORK ON SANITARY ENGINEERING & ENVIRONMENTAL SCIENCES (REPIDISCA)
Los Pinos 259, Camacho Phone: 35 4135
Casilla 4337 Service Est: 1979
Lima 100, Peru
Orlando Arboleda, Manager

Staff: 5 Information and library professional; 1 management professional; 3 technicians; 2 clerical and nonprofessional.

Related Organizations: REPIDISCA receives support from the International Development Research Centre (IDRC) of Canada, the United Nations Educational, Scientific and Cultural Organization (UNESCO), and the International Reference Centre for Community Water Supply and Sanitation (IRC). The Pan American Health Organization is a specialized agency of the Organization of American States (OAS) and is the World Health Organization (WHO) regional office of the Americas.

Description of System or Service: The PAN AMERICAN INFORMATION & DOCUMENTATION NETWORK ON SANITARY ENGINEERING & ENVIRONMENTAL SCIENCES (REPIDISCA) is a cooperative decentralized network of 76 Latin American and Caribbean national centers coordinated by a central unit at CEPIS. The centers prepare worksheets giving pertinent bibliographic data, subject descriptors, geographic indicators, and some abstracts for national and regional nonconventional documents dealing with sanitary engineering and environment. These are submitted to the central unit where they are merged with data on related extra-regional and international documents and entered into the computer-readable REPINDEX data base. Using this data base, REPIDISCA provides the national centers with tape copies and computerized search and SDI services. REPIDISCA also issues several publications, produces bibliographic compilations, furnishes document delivery either on microfiche or as photocopy, and offers reference and referral services. Additionally, the Network provides advisory services on the development of new centers and holds training courses and seminars for personnel.

Scope and/or Subject Matter: Sanitation, water supply, sanitary and environmental engineering.

Input Sources: Input is derived from technical reports, feasibility studies, research projects, conference proceedings, journals, unpublished literature, and bibliographic data bases.

Holdings and Storage Media: Holdings include the computer-readable REPINDEX data base and associated files, as well as a library comprising 24,000 bound volumes, subscriptions to 200 periodicals, and copies of all documents covered in the data base.

Publications: 1) REPINDEX (quarterly)—Spanish-language subject/author index produced from the data base. 2) TABCONT/ CEPIS (bimonthly)—contains the tables of contents of 60 international water and sanitation journals in the English and Spanish languages. 3) REPIDISCA Newsletter (quarterly)—serves as a communications link within the network and with other information systems. 4) MISCA Microthesaurus—acts as REPIDISCA's basic indexing tool. A union list of serials and various manuals are also published.

Microform Products and Services: Microfiche copies of all nonconventional documents furnished to REPIDISCA will be available to the centers.

Computer-Based Products and Services: REPIDISCA maintains the following data bases: 1) REPINDEX—provides coverage of about 15,000 documents from 1965 to the present, with about 2500 new documents added annually. 2) Directory of Water and Sanitation Institutions in Latin America and the Caribbean—contains 1500 entries. 3) MISCA Microthesaurus—contains 4500 descriptors in Spanish; is being expanded to include English and Portuguese terms as well. Literature searches, SDI services, tape copies, and specialized bibliographies are produced from the REPINDEX data base, which is held online under ISIS software. A data base on environmental health specialists in the region is in the developmental stage, and REPIDISCA plans to interact with IRC's POETRI (Programme on Exchange and Transfer of Information on Community Water Supply and Sanitation) and other systems to exchange information.

Clientele/Availability: Products and services are available free of charge or at cost to network members.

Remarks: REPIDISCA is the acronym for the network's Spanish title: Red Panamericana de Informacion y Documentacion en Ingenieria Sanitaria y Ciencias Ambientales. CEPIS is the acronym for Centro Panamericano de Ingenieria Sanitaria y Ciencias del Ambiente.

Contact: Orlando Arboleda, Manager, Pan American Information & Documentation Network on Sanitary Engineering & Environmental Sciences. (Telex 21052.)

★795★
PARALOG
3RIP
P.O. Box 2284
S-103 17 Stockholm, Sweden
Phone: 08 144190
Service Est: 1979

Staff: Approximately 7 total.

Description of System or Service: 3RIP is a text data base management system for data base handling and online retrieval. It encompasses an integrated file handler, a text editor, and a powerful search system. Features include free-text and keyword searching; support for private, user-controlled files; parallel and simultaneous searching in up to 30 files; utility programs for updating data bases; and a number of versatile output formats. Additionally, 3RIP utilizes the Euronet DIANE Common Command Language (CCL). The 3RIP system has been used on varied data bases, including news agency dispatches, bibliographic references, computer program descriptions, and computerized conference messages.

Scope and/or Subject Matter: Text management and retrieval.

Computer-Based Products and Services: 3RIP runs on DEC computers and is commercially available. The system is delivered on a magnetic tape with a sample data base, system manual, and user's manual. Online help features include a menu-driven description of the system, description of each individual command with examples, and diagnostic error and warning messages.

Other Services: Paralog also consults and makes studies regarding systems programming, text processing, and information organization, in addition to marketing, supporting, and further developing 3RIP and similar products.

Clientele/Availability: Services are available without restrictions; users include telecommunications firms, banks, commercial online host services, professional societies, scientific publishers, educational institutions, museums, and newspaper publishers.

Contact: Managing Director, Paralog.

★796★
PARIS CHAMBER OF COMMERCE AND INDUSTRY
(Chambre de Commerce et d'Industrie de Paris)
DEPARTMENT OF INTERNATIONAL RELATIONS
(Direction des Relations Internationales)
TELEXPORT
Bourse de Commerce
2, rue de Viarmes
F-75001 Paris, France
Mlle. LeMaitre, Head
Phone: 01 5083643
Service Est: 1979

Description of System or Service: TELEXPORT is a computer-readable data base designed to provide users with information needed for the establishment of foreign trade relations. It comprises three separate files covering customs regulations and administrative information, business opportunities and international tenders, and information on importing and exporting firms. TELEXPORT is commercially available online and it can be accessed via telex.

Scope and/or Subject Matter: Economic, commercial, technical, and legal information for international trade.

Holdings and Storage Media: TELEXPORT data are held in machine-readable form.

Computer-Based Products and Services: TELEXPORT is accessible online through G.CAM. It comprises the following files: 1) PROMEXPORT/ PROMIMPORT—holds approximately 600 import-export business offers received by the International Relations Department. 2) DOC-EXPORT—provides information on foreign trade regulations for specific countries of export. 3) FIRMEXPORT—lists French importing and exporting companies.

Clientele/Availability: Services are available to French and foreign firms.

Contact: Mlle. LeMaitre, Department of International Relations, Paris Chamber of Commerce and Industry. (Telex 230823 CRF CCIP.)

★797★
PARIS DISTRICT INFORMATICS ADMINISTRATION
(Paris District Gestion Informatique - PGI)
INFORMATICS BIBLIO SERVICE
(Biblio Service Informatique - SB-I)
8, place Salvador Allende
B.P. 98
F-94003 Creteil Cedex, France
Anne Lemaire, Documentation Research Assistant
Phone: 01 8989102
Service Est: 1970

Related Organizations: The parent organization of PGI is the Chambre de Commerce et d'Industrie de Paris. Production of the SB-I Data Base is supported by the CCIP, the Chambre de Commerce et d'Industrie de l'Oise, the Bureau de Developpement de l'Entreprise Commerciale (BDEC), the Ecole Superieure d'Ingenieurs en Electrotechnique et Electronique (ESIEE), and Expertises: Mensuel du Droit de l'Informatique.

Description of System or Service: The INFORMATICS BIBLIO SERVICE (SB-I) is a monthly journal and online computer-readable data base covering French literature on computer science and its uses and related fields. Two additional subfiles of the data base are SB-I CAS, providing detailed information on firms utilizing informatics; and SB-I Expertises, covering cases of jurisprudence relating to informatics. The SB-I Data Base is available online through commercial time-sharing.

Scope and/or Subject Matter: Computer science, its applications, and such related fields as electronics, teleinformatics, office data processing, automation, robotics, and computer law.

Input Sources: Input for SB-I is drawn from French-language and other trade publications, newspapers, books and theses, and secondary sources. Input for the SB-I Expertises subfile is derived from articles appearing in the journal, Expertises des Systemes d'Information.

Holdings and Storage Media: Approximately 3000 citations are added annually to the SB-I Data Base, which contains more than 20,000 references dating from 1978 to the present. The file is updated semimonthly.

Publications: Biblio Service Informatique - SB-I (every two weeks)—available by subscription; loose-leaf documentation service comprising four parts: a reference section, a keyword index, an annual thematic classification of keywords, and an annual list of reference source addresses.

Computer-Based Products and Services: The SB-I Data Base is available for online searching though Telesystemes Questel. Searchable data elements include author, title, source, document type, abstract, and descriptors. The SB-I CAS subfile covers literature on small- and medium-sized businesses making use of informatics and includes information on the company's activities, importance, and organization, as well as the informatics solution chosen, equipment used, and applications. The SB-I Expertises subfile covers legal cases relating to informatics and provides such information as trial location and date and the nature, litigation, and outcome of the dispute.

Clientele/Availability: Clients include individuals and organizations in the computer industry and related fields.

Contact: Anne Lemaire, Documentation Research Assistant, Biblio Service Informatique.

★798★
PARIS OFFICE OF URBANIZATION
(Atelier Parisien d'Urbanisme - APUR)
URBAN DATA BANK OF PARIS AND THE PARIS REGION
(Banque de Donnees Urbaines de Paris et de la Region d'Ile-de-France - BDU)
17, blvd. Morland
F-75004 Paris, France
Phone: 01 2712814
Service Est: 1969

Special Note: No questionnaire response was received for this entry for the 6th edition. The entry is reprinted as it appeared in the 5th edition.

Staff: 1 Management professional; 10 technicians; 7 clerical and nonprofessional.

Related Organizations: The Urban Data Bank of Paris and the Paris Region receives support from various federal, regional, and municipal agencies.

Description of System or Service: The URBAN DATA BANK OF PARIS AND THE PARIS REGION (BDU) comprises machine-readable files of data on demography, residential movement and relocation, employment, housing, recreational facilities, buildings, construction, land use, and economics for the city of Paris and the surrounding region. The DATA BANK is used to produce statistical analyses, graphic representations, architectural designs, and maps.

Scope and/or Subject Matter: Urban planning data for the city of Paris and the surrounding region.

Input Sources: Input consists of magnetic tapes supplied by Paris municipal agencies and French government agencies.

Holdings and Storage Media: Approximately 1000 magnetic tapes and disks are held.

Publications: User manuals are published.

Computer-Based Products and Services: Access to the DATA BANK is gained via remote terminals set up at various agencies, or through online and batch searching at BDU.

Clientele/Availability: Services are available through public administrative agencies in Paris.

Contact: Director, Urban Data Bank of Paris and the Paris Region.

★799★
PARPINELLI TECNON
WORLD PETROCHEMICAL INDUSTRY DATA BANK
Via Egadi 7
I-20144 Milan, Italy
John F. Wyatt, Manager
Phone: 02 4980141
Service Est: 1968

Staff: 1 Information and library professional; 3 management professional; 1 technician; 1 sales and marketing.

Related Organizations: Parpinelli TECNON, an industrial marketing and business planning consulting firm, is a member of the TECNON Consulting Group.

Description of System or Service: The WORLD PETROCHEMICAL INDUSTRY DATA BANK consists of a machine-readable data base covering the world petrochemical industry and a software library facilitating retrieval and processing of the data. An integral part of Parpinelli TECNON's World Petrochemical Industry service, the DATA BANK is designed as an aid to the analysis and understanding of developments taking place in the petrochemical industry worldwide.

Scope and/or Subject Matter: World petrochemical industry; products covered include ethylene, propylene, butadiene, benzene, and toluene, as well as such derivatives as plastics, resins, rubbers, and fibers.

Holdings and Storage Media: The Data Bank is held in machine-readable form and is composed of more than 30,000 time series ranging from 1965 to 1990.

Computer-Based Products and Services: The WORLD PETROCHEMICAL INDUSTRY DATA BANK is accessible for data retrieval and processing. Data on producers, plant location, capacity, production, raw materials requirements, total imports and exports, and consumption are retrievable. Additionally, users have access to a software library which can be used to process and manipulate the data for in-depth analyses, such as examining supply-demand situations by company, group, region, or country. Details on accessing the DATA BANK are available from Parpinelli TECNON.

Clientele/Availability: Services are available by subscription.

Remarks: The World Petrochemical Industry Data Bank was formerly known as the European Petrochemical Industry Computerized System (EPICS).

Contact: John F. Wyatt, Manager, Petrochemical Studies, Parpinelli TECNON. (Telex 335052 TECNON I.)

★800★
PEACE RESEARCH INSTITUTE-DUNDAS
PEACE RESEARCH ABSTRACTS JOURNAL
25 Dundana Ave.
Dundas, ON, Canada L9H 4E5
Dr. Alan G. Newcombe, President
Phone: (416) 628-2356
Service Est: 1964

Staff: 7 Total.

Related Organizations: Peace Research Abstracts Journal is an official publication of the International Peace Research Association. It receives financial assistance from UNESCO, Canadian Commission for UNESCO, and Canadian International Development Agency.

Description of System or Service: PEACE RESEARCH ABSTRACTS JOURNAL is a monthly journal providing peace researchers, diplomats, and international relations specialists with abstracts and indexes of the world literature relating to peace and international affairs. It is produced with the help of a computerized subject index that is used to provide search services.

Scope and/or Subject Matter: Peace, war, and international relations.

Input Sources: Volunteer abstractors prepare approximately 500 abstracts per month from papers, monographs, and more than 600 journals published worldwide; additional input is derived from secondary sources.

Holdings and Storage Media: The computer-readable subject index covers more than 155,000 abstracts published in the first 21 volumes of the Journal.

Publications: 1) Peace Research Abstracts Journal (monthly with annual subject index and monthly and annual author index)—available by subscription. 2) Peace Research Reviews (irregular)—monograph series of literature surveys based on the abstracts journal or original research; available by subscription or single issue.

Computer-Based Products and Services: Multiple concept search services are provided from a computer-readable subject index to the Peace Research Abstracts Journal. Output is in the form of abstracts reference numbers.

Other Services: Additional services include manual literature searching and research.

Clientele/Availability: Services are available without restrictions.

Contact: Dr. Alan G. Newcombe, or Dr. Hanna Newcombe, Co-Editors, Peace Research Abstracts Journal. Searches of Peace Research Abstracts Journal are available in Europe from the Kommunikationszentrum fur Zukunfts- und Friedensforschung in Hannover GmbH, which is maintained by the Gesellschaft fur Zukunftsfragen e.v. Berlin; contact Dr. Lothar Schulze, Eichenplan 1, D-3000 Hannover, Federal Republic of Germany.

★801★
PEOPLE'S REPUBLIC OF CHINA
INSTITUTE OF SCIENTIFIC AND TECHNICAL INFORMATION OF CHINA (ISTIC)
P.O. Box 640
Beijing, People's Republic of China
Lin Zixin, Director
Phone: 464746
Service Est: 1956

Staff: 1000 Total.

Description of System or Service: The INSTITUTE OF SCIENTIFIC AND TECHNICAL INFORMATION OF CHINA (ISTIC) is the national scientific and technical information center of China. It provides information collection and processing, publishes indexes and abstracts, and conducts research in information science. In addition to issuing hardcopy indexes and abstracts, ISTIC maintains the computer-readable Chinese Pharmacy Abstracts data base and operates an international search center. Other activities include reference and referral, reprographic services, reader services, audiovisual services, translation, and information analysis.

Scope and/or Subject Matter: Science and technology.

Input Sources: Input is derived from periodicals, research reports, conference proceedings, dissertations, reference collections, microform and audiovisual materials, product catalogs and samples, and other sources.

Holdings and Storage Media: The Institute maintains the Chinese Pharmacy Abstracts data base in machine-readable form. Library holdings include 19,500 subscriptions to periodicals and more than one million copies of research reports, proceedings, and other scientific and technical literature.

Publications: The Institute issues more than 50 publications, including the Bibliography of Foreign S&T Collections in ISTIC, the Bulletin of Chinese Conference Proceedings and Papers, Industrial Economy Abstracts, and Trends in Foreign Science and Technology.

Computer-Based Products and Services: The INSTITUTE maintains the Chinese Pharmacy Abstracts data base and operates the International Online Retrieval Service Center.

Clientele/Availability: Services are available to the general public nationwide.

Contact: Lin Zixin, Director; or Wang Xiaochu, Secretary for Foreign Affairs, Institute of Scientific and Technical Information of China.

★802★
PERGAMON INFOLINE LTD.
12 Vandy St.
London EC2A 2DE, England
Sarah Dunn, Marketing Manager
Phone: 01-377 4650
Founded: 1976

Staff: 5 Information and library professional; 9 management professional; 15 technicians; 4 sales and marketing; 4 clerical and nonprofessional.

Related Organizations: Pergamon InfoLine Ltd. is a wholly owned subsidiary of Pergamon Press.

Description of System or Service: PERGAMON INFOLINE LTD. is a full service online data base host providing clients with remote terminal access to a number of scientific, technical, business, and other data bases produced by Pergamon Press and other producers. The company's online services include SDI, search save capabilties, private files services, and full customer support, training, and documentation.

Scope and/or Subject Matter: Patents, chemistry, technology, earth sciences, engineering, life sciences, British corporations, legislation, business, and management.

Input Sources: Data bases are acquired from Pergamon Press companies, professional associations, businesses, and other organizations.

Holdings and Storage Media: Approximately 30 data bases are held online for public access.

Publications: 1) InfoLine User Guide—gives details of the InfoLine system and service features and describes the individual data bases available. 2) InfoLine UPDATE (monthly)—newsletter for users.

Computer-Based Products and Services: Following is a list of data bases accessible online through PERGAMON INFOLINE LTD.:

1) CA Search—contains 4 million bibliographic citations since 1972 to worldwide literature dealing with chemistry, biochemistry, chemical engineering, and related technologies; produced by the Chemical Abstracts Service of the American Chemical Society. 2) Chemical Engineering Abstracts—provides access to worldwide primary journal literature covering all aspects of chemical engineering as well as chemically-related aspects of mechanical, civil, electrical, and instrumentation engineering; produced by the Royal Society of Chemistry. 3) COMPENDEX—contains bibliographic citations to journal and other literature covering all disciplines of engineering technology and applied science; produced by Engineering Information, Inc. 4) COMPUTERPAT—provides information on patents in the field of digital computer and data processing systems; produced by Pergamon International Information Corporation. 5) Current Awareness in Biological Sciences—provides bibliographic citations to current literature in the biological sciences and related areas; produced by Pergamon Press.

6) Current Biotechnology Abstracts—coverage of scientific, technical, and technocommercial literature on biotechnology; produced by the Royal Society of Chemistry. 7) Current Technology Index—provides subject access to United Kingdom technical journals; produced by Library Association Publishing Ltd. 8) Directory of Companies—contains information on more than 750,000 companies registered in England and Wales; each record contains company name, registered address, date of registration, and date of last accounts submitted; produced by the Companies Registration Office of Great Britain. 9) Dun & Bradstreet's Key British Enterprises—provides information on the top 20,000 companies in Britain; produced by Dun & Bradstreet Ltd. 10) Electronic Publishing Abstracts—contains citations to scientific, technical, and commercial literature dealing with electronic publishing and information technology; produced by Pira: Research Association for the Paper and Board, Printing and Packaging Industries.

11) Fine Chemicals Directory—a comprehensive catalog of commercially available research chemicals; produced by Fraser Williams (Scientific Systems) Ltd. 12) Geomechanics Abstracts—covers literature on rock and soil mechanics; produced by the Rock Mechanics Information Service of the University of London. 13) HSELiNE—covers accessions to Health and Safety Executive libraries in Great Britain; produced by the Health and Safety Executive. 14) IBSEDEX—provides bibliographic citations and abstracts of literature dealing with mechanical and electrical services associated with buildings; produced by the Building Services Research and Information Association. 15) INPADOC—more than 10 million records since 1968 providing bibliographic information on patent documents issued by national and regional patent offices; produced by the International Patent Documentation Center.

16) INPANEW—contains the most current fifteen weeks' data from the INPADOC Patent Gazette; produced by the International Patent Documentation Center. 17) Laboratory Hazards Bulletin—contains bibliographic citations and abstracts of literature on hazards likely to

be encountered by the chemical and biochemical laboratory research worker; produced by the Royal Society of Chemistry. 18) Management & Marketing Abstracts—contains bibliographic citations and abstracts of literature covering worldwide developments in the theoretical and practical aspects of management and marketing practices; produced by Pira. 19) Mass Spectrometry Bulletin—contains titles and bibliographic details for relevant current literature in the field of mass spectrometry; produced by the Royal Society of Chemistry Mass Spectrometry Data Centre. 20) MinSearch—indexes and abstracts international journal and other literature pertaining to mineral resources; produced by the Mineral Information Section of the Natural Environment Research Council.

21) Naval Record—provides technical details on the construction, equipment, and weapons systems of all naval vessels under construction, on order, officially authorized, or projected; produced by Brassey's Publishers Ltd. 22) Oceanographic Literature Review—covers all subjects related to the geographical, physical, mathematical, chemical, and biological aspects of the ocean and the sea floor; produced by Deep Sea Research. 23) PAKLEGIS—provides summaries and assessments of national, international, and EEC legislation and associated regulatory documents affecting the packaging industry; produced by Pira. 24) PATLAW—provides bibliographic information on patent, trademark, copyright, and unfair competition decisions cited in the U.S. Patents Quarterly; produced by the Bureau of National Affairs, Inc. 25) PATSEARCH—contains bibliographic citations and abstracts of all utility patents issued by the U.S. Patent and Trademark Office; produced by Pergamon International Information Corporation.

26) Pira Abstracts—contains abstracts of international scientific and technical literature on all aspects of papermaking, boardmaking, packaging, and printing; produced by Pira. 27) RAPRA Abstracts—contains bibliographic citations and abstracts to literature covering all commercial and technical aspects of the rubber and plastics industries; produced by the Rubber and Plastics Research Association of Great Britain. 28) World Surface Coatings Abstracts—contains bibliographic citations and abstracts of patents, journal articles, and standards in the fields of paint and surface coating technology and related subjects; produced by the Paint Research Association. 29) World Textiles—covers the science and technology of textiles and related materials; produced by the Shirley Institute. 30) Zinc, Lead & Cadmium Abstracts (ZLC)—covers all aspects of the production, properties, uses, and environmental effects of these metals, their alloys, and compounds; produced by the Zinc Development Association/ Lead Development Association/ Cadmium Association.

Other Services: Pergamon InfoLine also offers an integrated service which formats text, stores it in computer-readable form, and produces typeset pages.

Clientele/Availability: InfoLine is accessible via national and international telecommunications networks.

Contact: Sarah Dunn, Marketing Manager, Pergamon InfoLine Ltd. (Telex 8814614.) In North America, contact Mr. P.J. Terragno, Pergamon International Information Corporation, 1340 Old Chain Bridge Rd., McLean, VA 22101; telephone (703) 442-0900, or toll-free, 800-336-7575. (Telex 901811.) In Canada, contact Pergamon Press Canada Ltd., 150 Consumers Rd., Suite 104, Willowdale, ON, Canada M2J 1P9; telephone (416) 497-8337.

★803★
PERGAMON PRESS
CURRENT AWARENESS IN BIOLOGICAL SCIENCES (CABS)
Headington Hill Hall   Phone: 0865 64881
Oxford OX3 0BW, England   Service Est: 1982
Prof. H. Smith

Staff: 7 Information and library professional; 3 management professional; 1 sales and marketing; 4 clerical and nonprofessional.

Description of System or Service: CURRENT AWARENESS IN BIOLOGICAL SCIENCES (CABS) is a computer-readable bibliographic data base used to produce a monthly journal with the same name and 11 other specialist publications. Providing full bibliographic citations with author addresses, CABS is also commercially available online. Additionally, search services, SDI, and document delivery are provided by Pergamon. CABS was developed from the format of Pergamon's Current Advances in Plant Science and Current Advances in Ecological Sciences, which have been published since 1972 and 1975 respectively.

Scope and/or Subject Matter: Biological sciences and related areas, including biochemistry, cell and developmental biology, ecological sciences, endocrinology, genetics and molecular biology, immunology, microbiology, neuroscience, pharmacology and toxicology, physiology, and plant science.

Input Sources: More than 3000 journals are regularly scanned for CABS; reports and monographs are also covered.

Holdings and Storage Media: The machine-readable CABS data base contains more than 110,000 bibliographic citations; it is updated monthly with approximately 13,000 records.

Publications: The following monthly current awareness publications are available by subscription: 1) Current Awareness in Biological Sciences—each issue contains approximately 15,000 references arranged in more than 1600 sections in biochemistry, cell biology, ecology, genetics, immunology, microbiology, plant science, physiology, and pharmacology and toxicology; the publication was formerly known as International Abstracts of Biological Sciences. 2) Current Advances in Biochemistry. 3) Current Advances in Cell & Developmental Biology—references are arranged in more than 40 subject sections, including mitochondria, ribosomes, artificial membranes, cell types, and tissue and organ formation systems. 4) Current Advances in Ecological Sciences—references are arranged in more than 40 subject sections, including community ecology, host-parasite interactions, water relations, reproduction, erosion, and wildlife management and fish farming. 5) Current Advances in Endocrinology. 6) Current Advances in Genetics & Molecular Biology—references are arranged in more than 40 subject sections, including DNA/RNA structure, radiation and chemical mutagenesis, expression of cloned genes and transformation, genetics of animal viruses, cytogenetics, and fungal and algal genetics.

7) Current Advances in Immunology—references are arranged in more than 40 subject sections, including antigens, interferon, lymphoid tissue, immune complexes, and biotechnology. 8) Current Advances in Microbiology—references are arranged in more than 40 subject sections, including carbon transport and catabolism, nitrogen fixation, protozoa, plant viruses, food microbiology, and biodeterioration. 9) Current Advances in Neuroscience. 10) Current Advances in Pharmacology & Toxicology—references are arranged in more than 40 subject sections, including drug metabolism, second messengers, behavioral pharmacology, chemotherapy of microbial diseases, and developmental toxicology. 11) Current Advances in Physiology—references are arranged in more than 40 subject sections, including supportive tissues, plasma, brain stem, cerebellum, and visual system. 12) Current Advances in Plant Science—references are arranged in more than 40 subject sections, including respiration, growth regulators, tree growth and forest management, crop protection, ecology, and algae.

Each issue of each publication includes an author index and, at the end of each section, a list of related titles indexed in other sections of the publication.

Microform Products and Services: All publications listed above are also available on microform.

Computer-Based Products and Services: The CURRENT AWARENESS IN BIOLOGICAL SCIENCES data base is available for online searching through Pergamon InfoLine Ltd. Search elements include accession number, article title, authors, journal title, volume, part, page, author affiliation, author address, author country, and keywords. SDI and customized search services are also available.

Other Services: Copies of documents cited in CABS can be obtained through the CABS-TEXT document delivery service.

Clientele/Availability: Products and services are available without restrictions.

Contact: Mrs. J. Price, or Dr. M. Brewis, Publishing Manager, Current Awareness in Biological Sciences, Pergamon Press.

★804★
PHARMA DOCUMENTATION RING
(Pharma-Dokumentationsring - PDR)
Organon International
P.O. Box 20
NL-5340 BH Oss, Netherlands
Dr. N.W. van Putte, President

Phone: 04120 62409
Founded: 1958

Description of System or Service: The PHARMA DOCUMENTATION RING (PDR) is a cooperative effort of 14 European pharmaceutical companies to provide scientific documentation of literature, patents, and research data, and to promote the exchange of ideas and experience by information managers. It maintains various computer-readable data bases for services to member organizations.

Scope and/or Subject Matter: Information and documentation in chemistry, pharmacology, and medicine.

Clientele/Availability: Services are available to members of the Pharma Documentation Ring.

Contact: Dr. N.W. van Putte, President, Pharma Documentation Ring. (Telex 37500.)

★805★
PHARMA DOCUMENTATION SERVICE
(Pharma-Dokumentations-Service - PDS)
Karlstr. 21
D-6000 Frankfurt am Main, Fed. Rep. of
  Germany
Gertraud Stanzel

Phone: 069 2556268
Founded: 1977

Staff: 1 Information and library professional.

Related Organizations: The Pharma Documentation Service is part of Chemie Wirtschaftsforderungs GmbH and receives support from the Bundesverband der Pharmazeutischen Industrie (National Association of the Pharmaceutical Industry).

Description of System or Service: The PHARMA DOCUMENTATION SERVICE (PDS) provides the German pharmaceutical industry with a full range of information and documentation services. It conducts online searches of relevant data bases made accessible through German and United States vendors; offers library brokerage services; procures original publications upon request; prepares and distributes publications under the direction of the National Association of the Pharmaceutical Industry; and provides information management consulting services free of charge.

Scope and/or Subject Matter: Pharmaceutical sciences, biological sciences, chemistry, applied sciences, and economics.

Input Sources: PDS derives input from online data bases and other sources.

Computer-Based Products and Services: The PHARMA DOCUMENTATION SERVICE conducts online searches of data bases made available through the Deutsches Institut fur Medizinische Dokumentation und Information (DIMDI), Fachinformationszentrum Energie, Physik, Mathematik (FIZ Energie, Physik, Mathematik), Fachinformationszentrum Technik (FIZ Technik), DIALOG Information Services, Inc., and System Development Corporation (SDC).

Clientele/Availability: Services are primarily intended for the German pharmaceutical industry, but are also available to other users.

Contact: Gertraud Stanzel, Pharma Documentation Service. (Telex 04 12718 BPI D.)

★806★
PHARMACEUTICAL SOCIETY OF GREAT BRITAIN
MARTINDALE ONLINE
1 Lambeth High St.
London SE1 7JN, England
J.E.F. Reynolds, Editor

Phone: 01-735 9141

Description of System or Service: Corresponding to the printed Martindale's Extra Pharmacopoeia, MARTINDALE ONLINE is a computer-readable data base which contains evaluated data on 5130 drugs and ancillary substances used throughout the world. The evaluated data is supplemented by approximately 58,000 abstracts and references taken from the scientific literature. Each drug entry in the data base reflects the monograph structure of the Extra Pharmacopoeia and has been broken down into records which can be retrieved individually. MARTINDALE ONLINE is commercially available for online searching.

Scope and/or Subject Matter: Drugs and ancillary substances.

Holdings and Storage Media: The machine-readable Martindale data base contains information on more than 5100 drugs and ancillary substances; 50,000 drug names, synonyms, codes, and preparation names; 3000 manufacturers' names and addresses; as well as 58,000 relevant abstracts and references. It will be updated at regular intervals.

Publications: 1) Extra Pharmacopoeia—provides summaries of properties, actions, and uses of drugs and medicine in clinical use throughout the world. The book is arranged in three parts: Monographs on Drugs and Ancillary Substances—contains monographs on nearly 4000 substances arranged in 105 chapters; Supplementary Drugs and Ancillary Substances—consists of a series of short monographs on approximately 1100 drugs and ancillary substances arranged in alphabetical order by main title; and Formulas of Proprietary Medicines—provides the composition of approximately 900 proprietary medicines sold over the counter in the United Kingdom. The Extra Pharmacopoeia also includes a directory of manufacturers, an index to clinical uses, an index to Martindale identity numbers, and a general index. It is available for purchase from The Pharmaceutical Press at the address given above. 2) Martindale Thesaurus—consists of two sections: a classified section and an alphabetical index. The classified section is divided into the following categories: drugs; absorption and fate; pharmacological actions and uses; organisms; anatomy; physiology; disease and symptons; medical procedures; environment and technology; and sociology. The index directs the user to the appropriate category of the classified section. 3) Martindale Online User Guide. 4) Martindale Online Newsletter.

Computer-Based Products and Services: MARTINDALE ONLINE, which contains information on the properties, actions, and uses of drugs and medicine, is commercially available online through Bibliographic Retrieval Services (BRS) and Data-Star. The data base can be searched by free-text methods, by descriptors drawn from the Martindale Thesaurus, and by qualifiers that define the function or context of the descriptors. Qualifiers include action, administration and dosage, adverse effects, description, interaction, pregnancy and the neonate, resistance, treatment of adverse effects, use, and others.

Clientele/Availability: Product and services are available without restrictions. Clients include pharmacists and medical practitioners.

Contact: J.E.F. Reynolds, Editor of Martindale.

★807★
PHILIPPINES
NATIONAL INSTITUTE OF SCIENCE AND TECHNOLOGY (NIST)
DIVISION OF INFORMATION AND DOCUMENTATION
P.O. Box 774
Manila, Philippines
Rosario B. De Castro, Scientific Documentation Officer

Phone: 503041

Special Note: No questionnaire response was received for this entry for the 6th edition. The entry is reprinted as it appeared in the 5th edition.

Staff: 6 Information and library professional; 2 management professional; 19 clerical and nonprofessional.

Description of System or Service: The DIVISION OF INFORMATION AND DOCUMENTATION is a central clearinghouse for scientific and technological information in the Philippines, serving scientists, technologists, educators, students, and the interested public. It is responsible for selection, acquisition, and classification of books, journals, and other relevant information materials, and it provides reference, circulation, interlibrary loan, and document reproduction services from its collections. The DIVISION also provides technical inquiry answering services and bibliography compilations on special request; it has completed a bibliography of published NIST research results; and it maintains a card index to 96 scientific and technical periodicals published in the Philippines. The

DIVISION's services are expected to be expanded with the introduction of SDI and abstracting and indexing programs.

Scope and/or Subject Matter: Science and technology.

Input Sources: The Division acquires books, periodicals, pamphlets, and other materials from domestic and foreign sources.

Holdings and Storage Media: Library collection numbers 25,000 bound volumes, subscriptions to 400 periodicals, and 9000 other items.

Publications: Annual reports, brochures, and technical bulletins are issued.

Services: The Division offers reference services, manual literature searching, interlibrary loans, photocopying, abstracting and indexing.

Clientele/Availability: Services are available without restrictions to scientists, technologists, educators, students, and others in the Philippines.

Contact: Supervising Librarian, Division of Information and Documentation.

★808★
PHILIPPINES
NATIONAL SCIENCE AND TECHNOLOGY AUTHORITY (NSTA)
SCIENTIFIC CLEARINGHOUSE AND DOCUMENTATION SERVICES DIVISION (SCDSD)
Bicutan, Taguig, Metro Manila　　　Phone: 8450960
P.O. Box 3596　　　Service Est: 1975
Manila, Philippines
Dr. Irene D. Amores, Chief

Staff: 21 Information and library professional; 2 technicians; 8 clerical and nonprofessional.

Description of System or Service: The SCIENTIFIC CLEARINGHOUSE AND DOCUMENTATION SERVICES DIVISION (SCDSD) collects, processes, and disseminates scientific and technological information from local and foreign sources; evaluates, abstracts, and disseminates information found in published and unpublished Philippine and Southeast Asian scientific and technical literature; assists in the development of a national scientific information system/ network; and participates in international activities involving scientific documentation and information services. The DIVISION publishes abstracts, indexes, and bibliographies; maintains a library and offers reference services; and maintains several computer-readable data bases.

Scope and/or Subject Matter: Science and technology.

Input Sources: The Division collects books, journals, technical reports, conference proceedings, and other documents.

Holdings and Storage Media: The Division's library holdings comprise 32,000 bound volumes; a total of 4025 periodical titles on subscription, exchange, or gift; and more than 4000 microforms. Several computer-readable files are also maintained.

Publications: 1) Philippine Science and Technology Abstracts (bimonthly); 2) R & D Philippines (annual); 3) Philippine Men of Science (annual); 4) Current Contents (monthly); 5) SEA Abstracts (monthly); 6) Book Catalog of NSTA and Agencies (quarterly); 7) Series of Philippine Scientific Bibliographies (irregular).

Computer-Based Products and Services: The SCIENTIFIC CLEARINGHOUSE AND DOCUMENTATION SERVICES DIVISION maintains the following computer-readable files: 1) Research and Development Project Reports; 2) Union List of Serials of NSTA Complex Libraries; 3) Research and Development Institutions; 4) Scientists' Profile; 5) Inventory of the Scientific Clearinghouse and Documentation Services Division Holdings; 6) Graduate Theses in the Philippines—indexes theses granted from 1913 to date.

Other Services: In addition to the services described above, the Division offers document delivery, current awareness services, microfiche processing, transparency making, photoduplication, and other reprographic services.

Clientele/Availability: Services are intended for use by scientists, technologists, science educators and students, industrialists, and the public.

Projected Publications and Services: The Division plans to compile a union catalog of scientific and technological publications in the Philippines and to publish Graduate Theses in the Philippines. SDI services are also planned.

Contact: Dr. Irene D. Amores, Chief, Scientific Clearinghouse and Documentation Services Division.

★809★
PHILIPS INFORMATION SYSTEMS AND AUTOMATION DIRECT
Philips International B.V.　　　Phone: 040 784034
Bldg. VN 304, Boschdijk　　　Service Est: 1975
Eindhoven, Netherlands
Drs. K. Dijkens, Manager ISR Services

Staff: Approximately 70 total.

Description of System or Service: DIRECT is a computerized information storage and retrieval system developed and used by Philips to provide online search and SDI services from more than 50 internal data bases and the INSPEC-CCA data base. DIRECT also supports the production of hardcopy and microfiche catalogs and indexes.

Scope and/or Subject Matter: DIRECT data bases cover the subjects of data processing, mathematics, cybernetics, electronics, physics, marketing, economics, law, lighting, batteries, and other topics.

Input Sources: Input to the Philips data bases is derived from books, reports, journals, newspapers, patents, and internal information.

Holdings and Storage Media: Machine-readable holdings include the INSPEC-CCA data base which covers 200,000 documents dating from 1975 to the present, and more than 50 internal DIRECT data bases covering a total of 150,000 documents.

Publications: A thesaurus is produced and about 40 catalogs and indexes are issued each year.

Microform Products and Services: COM microfiche is produced by the system.

Computer-Based Products and Services: The DIRECT system is used primarily to store and to provide online search and SDI services from more than 50 Philips data bases. The internally developed DIRECT search software features automatic indexing of natural language input and unlimited ranking of the output based on calculated relevance to the inquiry. Boolean operators can be used within the search statement and can be combined with the free-text search and ranking capabilities. DIRECT data bases and software may be made commercially available outside the Philips company.

Other Services: In addition to services described above, Philips offers tape distribution, develops information software, provides consulting, and gives seminars on online retrieval and office automation.

Clientele/Availability: Services are intended for internal Philips users, but commercial requests for the DIRECT system will be considered.

Contact: Drs. K. Dijkens, Manager ISR Services, Philips Information Systems and Automation. (Telex 35000 PHTC NL NLYEVAX.) Commercial requests can be directed to Dr. W. Hoekstra, Philips Data Systems, P.O. Box 245, NL-7300 AE Apeldoorn, Netherlands.

★810★
PHIPPARD & ASSOCIATES STRATEGIC & TECHNOLOGICAL CONSULTING, INC.
94 Knollsbrook Dr.　　　Phone: (613) 825-1893
Nepean, ON, Canada K2J 1L8　　　Founded: 1983
Gary Phippard, President

Staff: 1 Information and library professional; 2 management professional; 1 technician; 1 sales and marketing; 1 clerical and nonprofessional.

Related Organizations: Phippard and Associates is cooperatively affiliated with more than a dozen software, equipment, consulting, and creative services companies.

Description of System or Service: PHIPPARD & ASSOCIATES STRATEGIC & TECHNOLOGICAL CONSULTING, INC. provides business development, strategic planning, technology assessment, research, project management, and procurement services relating to new information technologies, particularly videotex, teletext, and business graphics. PHIPPARD & ASSOCIATES also coordinates with affiliated suppliers to provide complete system solutions, and offers WATCHDOG, a videotex and related industry tracking and client briefing service. WATCHDOG is tailored to a client's specific interests and information is supplied via telephone briefings or short written or electronic reports. Detailed analyses and full-scale formal reports can also be provided, either regularly or on request, for specific topics.

Scope and/or Subject Matter: Videotex, teletext, business graphics, and related new information technologies and their opportunities in the business market.

Input Sources: Information sources include newspapers, magazines, periodicals, research reports, and newsletters, as well as trade shows and conferences.

Holdings and Storage Media: The firm's research library contains more than 200 bound volumes, subscriptions to approximately 30 periodicals, and more than 200 research items.

Computer-Based Products and Services: WATCHDOG reports can be supplied electronically.

Other Services: Additionally, the firm conducts introductory seminars on videotex/ teletext and business graphics for technical and nontechnical audiences.

Clientele/Availability: Services are available without restrictions. Primary clients are providers of business-to-business goods and services in North America.

Contact: Karan Williams, Manager, Phippard & Associates Strategic & Technological Consulting, Inc.

★811★
PIEDMONT CONSORTIUM FOR INFORMATION SYSTEMS
(Consorzio per il Sistema Informativo Piemonte - CSI)
Corso Unione Sovietica 216   Phone: 011 33071
I-10134 Turin, Italy   Founded: 1977
Renzo Rovaris, Director

Staff: 240 Total.

Related Organizations: The Consortium is supported by Piedmont local government organizations and is associated with the University of Turin and the Polytechnic of Turin.

Description of System or Service: The PIEDMONT CONSORTIUM FOR INFORMATION SYSTEMS (CSI PIEMONTE) is a general computer services bureau established by several local governments to serve the public and private sectors in the Piedmont region. Its primary function is to offer programming, system analysis, consulting, and related computer support services. Specific activities of CSI PIEMONTE include the maintenance of a centralized computer system to provide local government agencies with assistance in data processing and storage activities; the operation of a publicly accessible regional data service; the development of an information center to provide information brokerage services in all subjects to public and private sectors in the region; and the provision of educational programs to improve computer awareness throughout the region. CSI PIEMONTE maintains connections with Euronet DIANE and other online services and is working with academic and public officials to offer online training courses throughout the region. Additionally, the CONSORTIUM is involved with the Italian National Library Service/ Servizio Biblioteca Nazionale (SBN) in the development of a automated national library network.

Scope and/or Subject Matter: General computation, data processing, systems analysis; library automation and computerized searching; regional planning.

Computer-Based Products and Services: CSI PIEMONTE provides data processing and information brokerage services, conducts online training courses, promotes computer awareness, and is involved in library automation activities.

Clientele/Availability: Services are available to all organizations in the Piedmont region.

Contact: Giuseppe Segre, Project Manager, CSI Piemonte. (Telex 212532 CSIPIE I.)

★812★
PIRA: RESEARCH ASSOCIATION FOR THE PAPER AND BOARD, PRINTING AND PACKAGING INDUSTRIES
COMPREHENSIVE INFORMATION SERVICES
Randalls Rd.   Phone: 0372 376161
Leatherhead, Surrey KT22 7RU, England   Service Est: 1975
Brian W. Blunden, Director

Staff: 6 Information and library professional.

Description of System or Service: The COMPREHENSIVE INFORMATION SERVICES supplies the papermaking, printing, publishing, and packaging industries with broad coverage of relevant worldwide literature through a variety of print and computer-based products and services. It maintains the following four bibliographic data bases: 1) Pira Abstracts—contains abstracts and references to scientific and technical literature on all aspects of paper and boardmaking, packaging, and printing, including raw materials and additives, processes, machinery, equipment, mills, printing works, pulping, and other topics. Corresponds to information published in Paper & Board Abstracts, Printing Abstracts, and International Packaging Abstracts. 2) Management & Marketing Abstracts (MMA)—provides abstracts and citations to literature on worldwide developments in the theoretical and practical areas of management and marketing. 3) Electronic Publishing Abstracts (EPA)—provides abstracts and references to literature in electronic publishing and information technology; in particular, it covers the input, transmission, storage, and retrieval of text and images as an alternative to the publication of printed documents. Produced in cooperation with the International Electronic Publishing Research Centre. 4) PAKLEGIS—provides summaries and assessments of national, international, and EEC legislation and associated documentation related to packaging. The data bases are used to produce several monthly abstracts publications and to provide SDI, computer tape subscriptions, and online access. The SERVICES also maintains a library of documents and books, and offers manual literature searching, bibliography compilation, document delivery, and translations.

Scope and/or Subject Matter: Paper and board making, printing, packaging, management, marketing, publishing, legislation.

Input Sources: Input to the data bases is derived from more than 900 current periodicals, plus reports, papers, pamphlets, conference proceedings, standards, government documents, manufacturers' catalogs, and translations. Input to the PAKLEGIS data base concentrates on United Kingdom, EEC, and European national legislation, codes of practice, standards, and test methods relevant to packaging; coverage will be extended to include legislation from France, the United States, Scandinavia, Japan, and other countries.

Holdings and Storage Media: The four PIRA data bases are held in machine-readable form. Pira Abstracts contains more than 75,000 records dating from 1975 to the present; it is updated fortnightly at an annual increase of 10,000 records. Management & Marketing Abstracts contains approximately 17,000 records dating from 1976 to the present; it is updated monthly at a rate of approximately 200 records. Electronic Publishing Abstracts contains 7000 records dating from 1975 to the present; it is updated biweekly at an annual increase of 2400 records. PAKLEGIS contains 800 records and is updated biweekly. The Services' library holds 6000 bound volumes; subscriptions to 900 periodicals; and 30,000 reports, standards, translations, pamphlets, and similar materials.

Publications: 1) Paper & Board Abstracts (monthly); 2) Printing Abstracts (monthly); 3) International Packaging Abstracts (monthly); 4) Management & Marketing Abstracts (monthly); 5) Electronic Publishing Abstracts (monthly); 6) Advanced Abstracts Service (every two weeks)—current awareness service providing computer printouts of summaries and citations prior to their publication in the corresponding abstracts journals; available by individual subscription for all of the above abstracts journals. 7) Pira Thesaurus. 8) PAKLEGIS: A Guide to Packaging Legislation—search aid providing a summary of the PAKLEGIS data base aims and services, as well as historical aspects of packaging legislation.

Computer-Based Products and Services: The Pira Abstracts, MMA, EPA, and PAKLEGIS data bases are available for online searching via Pergamon InfoLine Ltd. Data elements present in the four files include the following: title; abstract; modifications and implications (PAKLEGIS); main headings and main heading codes; geographic location and code; company name; trade name; author; accession number; journal announcement; update code; journal name; citation; ISSN; language code; document type; and publication year. Magnetic tapes of the data bases are available by subscription or lease. The COMPREHENSIVE INFORMATION SERVICES also provides retrospective computerized search services from the data bases and offers SDI services in the form of standard or individual profiles.

Other Services: Additional services include manual literature searching, consulting, research, and referrals.

Clientele/Availability: Products and services are available to members and nonmembers.

Contact: Susan M. White, Database Group Head, Pira. (Telex 929810.)

★813★
PIRA: RESEARCH ASSOCIATION FOR THE PAPER AND BOARD, PRINTING AND PACKAGING INDUSTRIES
PRINTING AND INFORMATION TECHNOLOGY (PIT) DIVISION
Randalls Rd.　　　　　　　　　　　　Phone: 0372 376161
Leatherhead, Surrey KT22 7RU, England
Brian W. Blunden, Director

Description of System or Service: The PRINTING AND INFORMATION TECHNOLOGY (PIT) DIVISION provides research and information on new technology in the areas of printing to member companies and institutions in the printing, newspaper, publishing, and related fields. The DIVISION conducts cooperative and multiclient research projects in the field of printing technology with the results made available to members. The DIVISION also provides consultancy and inquiry answering services, seminars and training, information services, and library facilities, and cooperates with other industry organizations.

Scope and/or Subject Matter: New technology and research in the printing field, including such topics as color reproduction technology, data capture and computer typesetting, electronic scanners, printing inks and papers, and computerized color matching.

Input Sources: Input is obtained from the Division's research and from Division members.

Computer-Based Products and Services: The Printing and Information Technology Division offers custom computer-based information services for its members.

Clientele/Availability: Services are available by annual subscription.

Contact: Brian W. Blunden, Director, Printing and Information Technology Division. (Telex 929810.)

★814★
PMB PRINT MEASUREMENT BUREAU
11 Yorkville Ave.　　　　　　　　Phone: (416) 961-3205
Toronto, ON, Canada M4W 1L3　　Founded: 1972
John Chaplin, President

Staff: Approximately 5 total.

Description of System or Service: The PMB PRINT MEASUREMENT BUREAU conducts surveys of Canadian consumer magazine readers to create a standardized measuring service and buying tool for use by advertisers, agencies, and the media. It measures the number of readers of approximately 50 major magazines and collects data on the readers' use of products and services in more than 700 categories. Information on the exposure of magazine readers to other media is also gathered. The BUREAU makes its survey data available in printed, microfiche, and electronic forms.

Scope and/or Subject Matter: Number, distribution, product usage, and other media habits of Canadian consumer magazine audiences.

Input Sources: Data are collected in personal interviews with a representative sample of more than 12,000 Canadians.

Holdings and Storage Media: All survey data are held in machine-readable files.

Publications: Annual reports provide the results of the most recent survey in four volumes of readership tables.

Microform Products and Services: The Bureau provides approximately 8500 product usage tables on microfiche.

Computer-Based Products and Services: PMB readership measurement and product usage data are retrievable online through such time-sharing companies as Interactive Marketing Systems (IMS), Telmar Media Systems, and Harris Media Services.

Clientele/Availability: Products and services are available only to PMB members.

Contact: Hastings Withers, Technical Director, PMB Print Measurement Bureau.

★815★
POLAND
INSTITUTE FOR SCIENTIFIC, TECHNICAL AND ECONOMIC INFORMATION
(Instytut Informacji Naukowej, Technicznej i Ekonomicznej - IINTE)
ul. Zurawia 3/5　　　　　　　　Phone: 252809
00-926 Warsaw, Poland　　　　Service Est: 1950
Prof. Dr. Jacek Bankowski, Director

Staff: 48 Information and library professional; 21 technicians; 17 clerical and nonprofessional.

Related Organizations: IINTE is supported by the Polish Ministry of Higher Education, Science and Technology.

Description of System or Service: The INSTITUTE FOR SCIENTIFIC, TECHNICAL AND ECONOMIC INFORMATION (IINTE) is responsible for the coordination, on national and international levels, of Poland's scientific, technical, and economic information services. Serving as the national information center for information sciences and related fields, IINTE designs national information networks, performs research in all areas of information science and documentation, and develops and supervises training programs for information specialists and documentalists. It also maintains a technical library, performs literature searches, compiles bibliographies, and prepares publications in its areas of interest.

Scope and/or Subject Matter: Scientific, technical, and economic information services and systems; research in information science; user needs and information problems.

Input Sources: Literature, documents on information problems, and data bases are used.

Holdings and Storage Media: Library holdings consist of approximately 63,500 bound volumes and subscription to 172 periodicals. IINTE also maintains classification and related information in computer-readable form.

Publications: 1) Przeglad Dokumentacyjny Informacji Naukowej/ Documentation Review on Information Problems (bimonthly)—provides bibliographic citations and Polish-language abstracts of international journal articles and books dealing with information science. 2) Bibliographic Bulletin of the Clearinghouse at IINTE (supplemented annually)—contains bibliographic data on the holdings of the IINTE Clearinghouse, including thesauri and descriptor lists, tools for construction of thesauri, works in progress, classification systems and schedules, and keyword and subject headings lists; indexed by language, author/editor, and subject. 3) Universal Decimal Classification - Extensions and Corrections (3 to 4 times a year). 4) Prace IINTE/ ISTEI Reports. Publications are available by subscription.

Computer-Based Products and Services: IINTE develops software for information processing for mainframe and minicomputers.

Other Services: In addition to services described above, IINTE also provides technical consulting in the areas of information science, computerization of information processing systems, and implementation of UNESCO's Computerized Documentation System/ Integrated Set of Information Systems (CDS/ISIS) in Poland.

Clientele/Availability: Services are available to users in the field of scientific, technical, and economic information.

Remarks: The Institute is coordinating the implementation of the scientific research of the National Scientific and Technical Information System (SINTO). SINTO is a nationwide program for applying computer science to information, basic research, and methodological and organization problems.

Contact: Dr. M. Muraszkiewicz, Institute for Scientific, Technical and Economic Information. (Telex 813716 PL.)

★816★
POLAND
POLISH ACADEMY OF SCIENCES
(Polska Akademia Nauk - PAN)
SCIENTIFIC INFORMATION CENTER
(Osrodek Informacji Naukowej - OIN)
Nowy Swiat 72   Phone: 268410
00-330 Warsaw, Poland
Dr. Bronislaw Lugowski, Director

Special Note: No questionnaire response was received for this entry for the 6th edition. The entry is reprinted as it appeared in the 5th edition.

Staff: 48 Information and library professional; 37 technicians; 28 scientists; 20 clerical and nonprofessional.

Description of System or Service: The SCIENTIFIC INFORMATION CENTER coordinates activities in the field of documentation and information science conducted by the institutes and research centers of the Polish Academy of Sciences. The CENTER provides information services to the Academy and related organizations; performs research in information science; organizes training courses for information and library professionals interested in scientific information; and encourages cooperation with foreign scientific information centers. The CENTER also represents Poland in the International System of Information in Social Sciences, an organization composed of academies of sciences in the socialist countries, and acts as a national focal point for European Cooperation in Social Sciences Information and Documentation, a program of the European Center for Research and Documentation in Social Sciences.

Scope and/or Subject Matter: Scientific and technical information and documentation; research in information science.

Holdings and Storage Media: The Center's collection numbers 13,000 bound volumes; approximately 6500 periodical issues; and subscriptions to 300 periodicals.

Publications: 1) Problems of Scientific Information (semiannual)—issued in Polish with English and Russian summaries. 2) Survey of the Science of Science Information (quarterly)—in Polish. 3) Catalogue of Microfilms (annual)—issued in Polish. 4) Centre's Works—issued in Polish with English and Russian summaries.

Microform Products and Services: The Reprographic Laboratory of the Center produces microreproductions of selected, current scientific periodicals in several formats.

Other Services: The Center also provides interlibrary loans and current awareness, and participates in an international exchange of scientific documents.

Clientele/Availability: Clients include members of the Polish Academy of Sciences and information scientists.

Contact: Dr. Bronislaw Lugowski, Director, Scientific Information Center. (Telex 815614 PL.)

★817★
POLISH COMMITTEE OF STANDARDIZATION, MEASURES, AND
  QUALITY
(Polski Komitet Normalizacji i Miar i Jakosci)
CENTRE FOR INFORMATION ON STANDARDIZATION AND
  METROLOGY (COINIM)
Plac Dzierzynskiego 1   Phone: 209606
00-139 Warsaw, Poland   Service Est: 1972
Danuta Planer-Gorska, Director

Staff: 48 Information and library professional; 2 management professional; 3 technicians; 1 clerical and nonprofessional.

Description of System or Service: The CENTRE FOR INFORMATION ON STANDARDIZATION AND METROLOGY (COINIM) collects, stores, and makes available national, international, and foreign standards, metrological regulations, and related documents and information. COINIM also maintains an online data base covering national standards.

Scope and/or Subject Matter: Metrology, standardization, and the quality of measures.

Input Sources: Input consists of national, international, and foreign standards, metrological regulations, documents relating to quality, and serial and periodical publications.

Holdings and Storage Media: Holdings include 13,327 bound volumes, subscriptions to 338 periodicals, and 300,000 titles of standards.

Microform Products and Services: Polish standards are available on microfiche.

Computer-Based Products and Services: The CENTRE FOR INFORMATION ON STANDARDIZATION AND METROLOGY produces the online Automatical System of Standards and Metrological Information data base which includes complete coverage of national standards. The CENTRE also provides search services for national standards information.

Clientele/Availability: Clients include scientific and research institutions, universities, project bureaus, production plants, handicraft cooperatives, and branch centers of standardization.

Contact: Danuta Planer-Gorska, Director, Polish Committee of Standardization, Measures, and Quality; telephone 200241.

★818★
POLYTECHNIC OF CENTRAL LONDON
INFORMATION TECHNOLOGY CENTRE
309 Regent St.   Phone: 01-636 2383
London W1R 8AL, England   Service Est: 1982
Neil McLean, Head

Staff: 3 Information and library professional; 1 clerical and nonprofessional.

Related Organizations: The Information Technology Centre is supported by the Research and Development Department of the British Library.

Description of System or Service: The INFORMATION TECHNOLOGY CENTRE is a demonstration center for the purpose of familiarizing librarians and information specialists with developments of computer applications in their fields, with particular emphasis on microcomputers. The CENTRE displays hardware, software, and systems for library management, online and micro-based information retrieval, videotex, electronic mail, word processing, and data base management on a local area network. An information service is available on the automation of library housekeeping processes and on microcomputer software for libraries. In addition, the CENTRE organizes seminars and conferences on topics relevant to library technology and is also involved in coordinating a project to establish an information technology information services network using TORCH microcomputers and a telephone network.

Scope and/or Subject Matter: Applications of computer and information technologies for libraries.

Holdings and Storage Media: The Centre maintains a small reference collection.

Publications: 1) Library Micromation News (quarterly)—newsletter for microcomputer users in libraries. 2) VINE (quarterly)—newsletter on library automation.

Computer-Based Products and Services: The INFORMATION TECHNOLOGY CENTRE provides exhibitions and demonstrations of a range of hardware and software, and offers opportunities for hands-on experience. The CENTRE is also carrying out a research project on the use of a microcomputer network in developing an online catalog.

Clientele/Availability: Services are available by appointment to librarians, library school students, educators, and other interested professionals.

Contact: Mary Rowbottom or Elizabeth Taylor, Information Officers, Information Technology Centre. (Telex 261074.)

★819★
POLYTECHNICAL SCHOOL OF MONTREAL
(Ecole Polytechnique de Montreal)
TELIDON TECHNOLOGY DEVELOPMENT CENTER
(Centre d'Excellence pour le Developpement de la Technologie Telidon - CDT)
C.P. 6079, Succursale A
Montreal, PQ, Canada H3C 3A7
Phone: (514) 344-4753
J.L. Houle, Head

Staff: 4 Information and library professional; 1 management professional; 1 technician; 1 sales and marketing; 1 clerical and nonprofessional; 4.5 other.

Related Organizations: The Digital Equipment Corporation and the Canadian Department of Communications provide support.

Description of System or Service: The TELIDON TECHNOLOGY DEVELOPMENT CENTER (CDT) supports a number of activities relating to the development of Telidon technology in Quebec. It maintains a Department of Communications demonstration and promotional Telidon data base in the French language on its computer facilities, and it makes the data base available online to other government and nongovernment organizations interested in developing Francophone data base content. The CENTER also provides computer resources for organizations involved in the design of new Telidon-related hardware and software systems.

Scope and/or Subject Matter: Telidon research and development, including French-language information content.

Holdings and Storage Media: The demonstration data base currently comprises approximately 8000 pages of information.

Publications: Research papers and system descriptions are produced on an irregular basis.

Computer-Based Products and Services: The Telidon Technology Development Center provides time-sharing services for research purposes. It also offers consulting regarding Telidon hardware, software, and information content development.

Clientele/Availability: Services are available to any governmental or nongovernmental agency in Canada wishing to involve itself with the Telidon technology, subject to established objectives and guidelines.

Contact: A. Janelle, Telidon Technology Development Center. (Telex 05 24146 BIBPOLYTECH.)

★820★
PONT-A-MOUSSON RESEARCH CENTER
(Centre de Recherches de Pont-a-Mousson)
INDUSTRIAL DOCUMENTATION SERVICE
(Service de Documentation Industrielle)
BIIPAM-CTIF DATA BASE
B.P. 28
F-54703 Pont-a-Mousson Cedex, France
Phone: 8 3816029
Claude Guy, Head

Staff: 2 Management professional; 8 technicians.

Related Organizations: The BIIPAM-CTIF Data Base is a joint effort of the Pont-a-Mousson Research Center and the Foundry Industries Technical Center/ Centre Technique des Industries de la Fonderie (CTIF), Service Documentation, 12, ave. Raphael, F-75016 Paris.

Description of System or Service: The BIIPAM-CTIF DATA BASE is a computer-readable file containing citations and abstracts of journal articles and other literature dealing with metallurgy, foundry working, mechanical engineering, and related subjects. BIIPAM-CTIF is commercially available for online searching and corresponds to information published in two abstracts journals.

Scope and/or Subject Matter: Metallurgy, foundry techniques, the iron industry; corrosion, coatings, materials resistance; pipes and pipelines, fittings (gas and water mains); mechanics and mechanical engineering; automation and regulation; measurements, control, and testing; engineering science and technique; engineering organization, management, and security; fluid mechanics, hydraulics, and power engineering; optimum use of resources; pollution and pollution control or prevention; buildings, building materials, and civil engineering; maintenance and handling; plastics, elastomers, and composites with fibers; refractory products; thermics and heat insulation.

Input Sources: Input for BIIPAM-CTIF is drawn mainly from periodical literature; also covered are books, reports, conference papers, theses, and standards. Patent literature is not covered. Approximately 50 percent of the source documents are in French; 40 percent are in English.

Holdings and Storage Media: The computer-readable BIIPAM-CTIF Data Base contains more than 65,000 citations and summaries dating from 1970 to the present. It is updated monthly, with about 5000 items added annually.

Publications: 1) Diffusion Hebdomadaire Systematique—abstracts bulletin produced by the Centre de Recherches de Pont-a-Mousson. 2) Bulletin Bibliographique Fonderie—abstracts journal of the CTIF. A thesaurus is also available, and a French and English user manual is in preparation.

Computer-Based Products and Services: The BIIPAM-CTIF DATA BASE is searchable online via ESA/IRS. Records in the file generally include title in original language, author, document type, industry classification, and summary in French. CTIF information in the DATA BASE (comprising approximately 5000 records) can be selected as a subfile.

Other Services: Copies of most original documents cited in BIIPAM-CTIF are available from the Industrial Documentation Service.

Clientele/Availability: Clients include metallurgists and engineers.

Remarks: The Data Base was formerly known as the Pont-a-Mousson Industrial Information Bank/ Banque de l'Information Industrielle Pont-a-Mousson (BIIPAM).

Contact: Claude Guy, Head, or Anne-Marie Mertzweiller, Engineer, Pont-a-Mousson Research Center. (Telex 961330 F CR PAM.)

★821★
PORTUGAL
NATIONAL INSTITUTE FOR SCIENTIFIC RESEARCH
(Instituto Nacional de Investigacao Cientifica)
SCIENTIFIC AND TECHNICAL DOCUMENTATION CENTER
(Centro de Documentacao Cientifica e Tecnica - CDCT)
Av. Prof. Gama Pinto 2
1699 Lisbon codex, Portugal
Phone: 11 762891
Service Est: 1936
Carlos Pulido, Director

Staff: 5 Information and library professional; 2 management professional; 3 technicians; 5 clerical and nonprofessional; 2 other.

Description of System or Service: The SCIENTIFIC AND TECHNICAL DOCUMENTATION CENTER (CDCT) provides custom information services for clients in business, industry, education, science, medicine, and other areas. Among its services are computerized searching, current awareness, bibliography compilation, document procurement, and consultation on the creation or improvement of information centers. The DOCUMENTATION CENTER also prepares and publishes the computer-based Union Catalog of Periodicals Held by Portuguese Libraries and acts as the National Center for the Registration of Serial Publications, responsible for the allocation of International Standard Serial Numbers (ISSNs).

Scope and/or Subject Matter: Science, technology, medicine, business, and industry.

Input Sources: CDCT utilizes commercially available online data bases and the printed resources of the National Institute for Scientific Research and other Portuguese libraries.

Holdings and Storage Media: The Center maintains a collection of 300 bound volumes and subscriptions to 200 periodicals on the subjects of information science and librarianship.

Publications: Union Catalog of Periodicals Held by Portuguese Libraries.

Computer-Based Products and Services: CDCT produces the computer-based union catalog of periodicals which covers approximately 300 libraries in Portugal and 15,000 titles. CDCT performs online literature searching using ESA/IRS, Bibliographic Retrieval Services (BRS), DIALOG Information Services, Inc., Pergamon InfoLine Ltd., Telesystemes Questel, and the British Library Automated Information Service (BLAISE). SDI services are also offered.

Other Services: In addition to the services described above, the Center provides consulting and referral services.

Clientele/Availability: Services are available to government agencies and private businesses.

Contact: Gabriela Lopes da Silva, Head of Information Department, Scientific and Technical Documentation Center. (Telex 18428 EDUCA P.)

★822★
PORTUGUESE RADIO MARCONI COMPANY
(Companhia Portuguesa Radio Marconi - CPRM)
DATA BANK ACCESS SERVICE
(Servico de Acesso a Bancos de Dados - SABD)
Praca Marques de Pombal, 15
1200 Lisbon, Portugal
Helena Soares, Head, Marketing
Phone: 534191
Service Est: 1980

Staff: 3 Sales and marketing; 1 clerical and nonprofessional.

Description of System or Service: The DATA BANK ACCESS SERVICE (SABD) is a packet-switched service that provides access to the host computers connected to the U.S. domestic networks. Customer use of the Lisbon node is available through the Public Switched Telephone Network (PSTN) or leased line.

Scope and/or Subject Matter: Access to remote computer resources.

Computer-Based Products and Services: SABD provides access to computer services and online data bases available through U.S. domestic networks.

Clientele/Availability: Services are available without restrictions by subscription.

Contact: Carlos Cardiga, Promotion Services, Servico de Acesso a Bancos de Dados. (Telex 12384 CPRM P.)

★823★
PRESS ASSOCIATION LTD. (PA)
NEWSFILE
85 Fleet St.
London EC4P 4BE, England
Nicholas Kester, Marketing Manager
Phone: 01-353 7440
Service Est: 1984

Staff: 3 Management professional; 3 sales and marketing; 2 clerical and nonprofessional.

Description of System or Service: NEWSFILE is a real-time viewdata news service based on the automatic conversion of Press Association wire service material into viewdata format. It can be accessed 24 hours per day with viewdata terminals or televisions equipped with viewdata adaptors over a dial-up network. Users can select, read, and print news stories from the current day as well as from the previous six days. NEWSFILE covers news throughout the British Isles, Houses of Parliament, Royal Courts of Justice, and the European Economic Community in Brussels.

Scope and/or Subject Matter: British and European news.

Input Sources: Input consists of all general news gathered by Press Association staff. Stories are available on NEWSFILE at the same time they are transmitted over the PA teleprinter network.

Holdings and Storage Media: Newsfile stores one week's news stories, totaling more than 400,000 words, online.

Computer-Based Products and Services: Mounted with a computer service bureau on two VAX computers, NEWSFILE provides interactive real-time access to news stories gathered by the Press Association. NEWSFILE users with viewdata terminals or televisions with viewdata adaptors access the service via local telephone lines. Full-text news stories held for the current day and the previous six days can be selected by day of the week and then by time of day. NEWSFILE articles can also be accessed through index pages containing catchlines (brief two or three word identifiers) and bulletins (comprising the first five lines of a story). Each catchline index page lists 16 catchlines, corresponding NEWSFILE page numbers, and the transmission times of the first and last stories on the page. Each bulletin index page lists three bulletins, corresponding NEWSFILE page numbers for the full-text articles, and time of transmission of the first and last bulletin. Catchlines and bulletins are color coded to indicate top priority stories, Houses of Parliament news, High Courts articles, and general news. News stories selected can be read on the screen or printed out in hard copy. In addition to general news, NEWSFILE contains a MEDIAFILE which is accessible only by media subscribers. MEDIAFILE contains embargoed stories, daily and weekly diaries, and memos from Press Association staff to media subscribers.

Other Services: The Press Association Ltd. offers consulting on the methods used to create Newsfile and will make available Newsfile software.

Clientele/Availability: Services are available without restrictions in England. Clients include public relations consultants, press officers, the media, and others.

Contact: Nicholas Kester, Marketing Manager, Press Association Ltd. (Telex 22330.)

★824★
PRESSURKLIPP
SWEDISH MARKET INFORMATION BANK
(Marknadsbank)
S-112 85 Stockholm, Sweden
Ingemar Larsson, Manager
Phone: 08 541420
Service Est: 1968

Description of System or Service: The machine-readable SWEDISH MARKET INFORMATION BANK provides access to newspaper and journal articles dealing with Swedish market and marketing practices information. It is compiled from the same sources that Pressurklipp uses in providing press clipping services for more than 4000 customers. The INFORMATION BANK is available online through DataArkiv AB. Articles cited in the data base, together with a file of earlier articles, are maintained on microfiche for the provision of document delivery services.

Scope and/or Subject Matter: Swedish market information.

Input Sources: Pressurklipp regularly covers 200 Swedish daily newspapers and 600 trade journals and popular magazines.

Holdings and Storage Media: More than 45,000 citations dating from 1975 to the present are maintained online in the data base. The microfiche collection covers the period from 1969 to date and holds 75,000 documents.

Microform Products and Services: Hardcopy duplication services are offered from the microfiche file.

Computer-Based Products and Services: The SWEDISH MARKET INFORMATION BANK is accessible online through DataArkiv AB. Copies of cited articles may be ordered online.

Clientele/Availability: Clientele includes market researchers and other interested individuals.

Contact: Ingemar Larsson, Manager, Swedish Market Information Bank.

★825★
PRODINFORM TECHNICAL CONSULTING CO.
P.O. Box 453
H-1372 Budapest, Hungary
Kovacs Istvan, Director
Phone: 317 960
Founded: 1956

Staff: 60 Information and library professional; 20 management professional; 20 technicians; 20 sales and marketing; 20 clerical and nonprofessional.

Description of System or Service: PRODINFORM TECHNICAL CONSULTING CO. provides technical and economic information services for the metal industry. It also offers library consulting, bibliography compilation, referrals, data collection, abstracting and indexing, and other services.

Scope and/or Subject Matter: Information services, with emphasis on the hard metal industry.

Input Sources: Information sources include 350 periodicals, trade literature, and other materials.

Holdings and Storage Media: Library holdings include 40,000 bound volumes; subscriptions to more than 300 periodicals; 100,000 trade catalogs; and 5000 conference proceedings.

Clientele/Availability: Services are available without restrictions to engineers and clients in industry.

Remarks: The firm was formerly known as KG Informatik Produktinform.

Contact: Gabriel Gyozo, Manager, Prodinform Technical Consulting Co.

★826★
**PRODUCTION ENGINEERING RESEARCH ASSOCIATION OF GREAT BRITAIN (PERA)
INFORMATION SERVICES**

Melton Mowbray, Leics., England
V.C. Watts, Head
Phone: 0664 64133
Service Est: 1946

Staff: Approximately 10 total.

Description of System or Service: The INFORMATION SERVICES provides the following: current awareness in manufacturing technology through weekly, biweekly, or monthly bulletins prepared to individual requirements; literature searches, product surveys, and data collection; staff training in information storage and retrieval methods; and development of technical libraries and information centers in companies.

Scope and/or Subject Matter: Manufacturing technology, including metal machining, metal forming, castings, inspection, materials, management, finishing, fabrication, materials handling, packaging, safety, and other topics.

Input Sources: Input is drawn from journals, reports, monographs, books, and trade catalogs.

Holdings and Storage Media: Library holdings consist of 15,000 bound volumes; 45,000 trade catalogs; and subscriptions to 600 periodicals. Internal computer-readable files are also maintained.

Publications: PERA Bulletin (5 issues a year).

Microform Products and Services: A product data microfilm system is used.

Computer-Based Products and Services: The INFORMATION SERVICES maintains an in-house computer system utilizing CAIRS software for information storage and retrieval purposes. Computerized searches are provided from data bases carried by DIALOG Information Services, Inc., System Development Corporation (SDC), ESA/IRS, BLAISE, and Pergamon InfoLine Ltd.

Other Services: In addition to current awareness and other services listed above, PERA provides a mailing list and direct mail services and referrals.

Clientele/Availability: General information services are restricted to PERA members, but special services are undertaken on a fee basis.

Contact: V.C. Watts, Head, Library and Information Services. (Telex 34684.)

★827★
**PULP AND PAPER RESEARCH INSTITUTE OF CANADA (PAPRICAN)
TECHNICAL INFORMATION SECTION**

570 St. John's Blvd.
Pointe Claire, PQ, Canada H9R 3J9
Mrs. Hella Stahl, Manager
Phone: (514) 697-4110
Service Est: 1929

Staff: 3 Information and library professional; 1 technician; 1 clerical and nonprofessional; 1 other.

Related Organizations: The Institute is supported by the Canadian pulp and paper industry.

Description of System or Service: The TECHNICAL INFORMATION SECTION serves as the central source of information on pulp and paper technology for organizations supporting the Pulp and Paper Research Institute of Canada. It maintains a library and offers a computerized search service using commercially available data bases and an internal file covering research reports of the Institute. A thesaurus of pulp and paper terms is also offered in hard copy and on magnetic tape.

Scope and/or Subject Matter: Pulp and paper technology, including peripheral interests in chemistry, chemical engineering, physics, and mathematics.

Input Sources: Periodicals, research reports, commercial data bases, and bibliographic aids are input sources.

Holdings and Storage Media: The library collection includes approximately 18,000 volumes, subscriptions to more than 350 periodicals, and educational videocassettes. The computer-readable PAPRICAN data base covers research reports issued by the Institute from 1954 to date.

Publications: 1) Thesaurus of Pulp and Paper Terms—a controlled vocabulary for use in assigning keywords. 2) List of Library Books and Periodicals. Various research report series are issued for sponsoring organizations.

Microform Products and Services: Institute reports on microfilm are available to sponsoring organizations.

Computer-Based Products and Services: The SECTION offers SDI services and retrospective searches using its internal research reports data base and relevant commercial data bases offered through System Development Corporation (SDC), DIALOG Information Services, Inc., the Canada Institute for Scientific and Technical Information (CISTI), Pergamon InfoLine Ltd., QL Systems Limited, and Info Globe. A magnetic tape of the Thesaurus of Pulp and Paper Terms is also generally available.

Other Services: The SECTION also provides manual literature searching, reference and referral services, translations, interlibrary loans, and copying services.

Clientele/Availability: Services are intended primarily for supporting institutions in the Canadian pulp and paper fields; some services are available to other Canadian organizations.

Contact: Mrs. Hella Stahl, Manager, Technical Information Section. (Telex 05821 541.)

Q

★828★
QL SYSTEMS LIMITED
797 Princess St.
Kingston, ON, Canada K7L 1G1
Hugh Lawford, President

Phone: (613) 549-4611
Founded: 1973

Description of System or Service: QL SYSTEMS LIMITED is an online information service providing access to more than 80 data bases prepared by a variety of private and government organizations. QL SYSTEMS collects machine-readable files of legal, business, scientific, and other types of information; holds these on central computer facilities; and makes them accessible online through its QL/SEARCH information retrieval system. QL SYSTEMS also offers text-editing, photocomposition, data base creation, and electronic mail services, and it makes available QL/SEARCH and other software for use on client facilities.

Scope and/or Subject Matter: Canadian Parliament, law, and government; news and current affairs; energy; mining; environment; science and technology; business; communications; and other topics.

Input Sources: Data bases are acquired from private and government organizations and from commercial abstracting and indexing services.

Holdings and Storage Media: QL Systems holds more than 80 machine-readable data bases online.

Publications: 1) QL Update—newsletter for system users. 2) QL/SEARCH User's Manual. 3) Data base description manual.

Computer-Based Products and Services: Among the data bases publicly available through QL SYSTEMS LIMITED are the following:

1) Alberta Oil Sands Index (AOSI)—contains bibliographic citations to technical literature and other materials relating to oil sands; produced by the Alberta Oil Sands Information Centre. 2) Arctic Science and Technology—provides citations and abstracts of literature concerning all aspects of the Arctic region; produced by the Arctic Institute of North America. 3) Asbestos Information—contains abstracted and keyworded references to literature on all aspects of asbestos mining and processing; produced by the Asbestos Research Program at the University of Sherbrooke. 4) Atlantic Provinces Reports—contains headnotes of judicial decisions from New Brunswick, Nova Scotia, Newfoundland, and Prince Edward Island; produced by the Canadian Law Information Council. 5) Boreal Northern Titles—holds references to literature covering the circumpolar north, Canadian peoples, mid-Canada development, and related topics; produced by the Boreal Institute for Northern Studies.

6) British Columbia Regulations—contains regulations of British Columbia prepared by the Ministry of Attorney General. 7) CAN/LAW—contains headnotes or summaries of civil and criminal case decisions by Canadian federal and provincial courts, corresponding to the following printed publications: All-Canada Weekly Summaries; Canadian Criminal Cases; Dominion Law Reports; and Weekly Criminal Bulletin. Produced by Canada Law Book Ltd. 8) Canadian Business Index (CBI)—provides references to articles appearing in approximately 150 business publications dating from 1975 to 1981; the file is expected to be brought up-to-date in the near future. Produced by Micromedia Ltd. 9) Canadian Environment (CENV)—contains abstracts and references to Canadian water resources literature and related topics; produced by WATDOC of Environment Canada. 10) Canadian Hydrological Operational Multipurpose Subprogramme (CHOMS)—contains descriptions of Canadian operational and developing hydrological technology; sponsored by WATDOC.

11) Canadian News Index (CNI)—indexes major stories appearing in Canadian newspapers dating from 1977 to 1981; the file is expected to be brought up-to-date in the near future. Produced by Micromedia Ltd. 12) Canadian Press Newstex (CPN)—provides the full text of news stories dating from 1981 to the present. A related file, Canadian Press Extra (CPX), contains news stories dating from 1974 to 1980. Produced by The Canadian Press. 13) CANPLAINS—contains an inventory of current, recently completed, and unpublished research projects in Manitoba, Saskatchewan, and Alberta; produced by the Canadian Plains Research Center of the University of Regina. 14) Coal Abstracts—contains citations to literature in the fields of coal research and technology; produced by IEA Coal Research. 15) Constitutional Acts of Canada—covers 42 acts from the Royal Proclamation Act of 1763 to the Canada Act of 1982. A corresponding French-language data base, Lois Constitutionnelles du Canada, is also available online. Prepared by the Canadian Department of Justice.

16) Data Reference—provides detailed references to collections of water resources and environmental data collected and held in Canada; produced by WATDOC of Environment Canada. 17) Delft Hydro Database--contains abstracts and citations to world literature on hydromechanics and hydraulic engineering; produced by the Delft Hydraulics Laboratory. 18) Dominion Reports Service—provides summaries of Canadian judicial decisions edited by CCH Canadian Ltd. 19) Energy Programs Data Base—contains descriptions of Canadian federal and provincial energy programs; produced by the Canadian Department of Energy, Mines and Resources. 20) Energy Projects Data Base—consists of summaries of significant energy research, development, and demonstration projects in Canada; produced by the Canadian Department of Energy, Mines and Resources.

21) Environnement (ENV)—holds references to French-language environmental literature; produced by WATDOC of Environment Canada. 22) Exchequer Reports—contains the headnotes of the Canadian Exchequer Reports from 1877 to 1971. 23) Federal Court Reports—contains headnotes of the Federal Court of Canada Reports. A corresponding French-language data base, Les Rapports de la Cour Federale du Canada, is also available online. 24) Hansard Oral Questions—covers oral questions and responses in the Canadian House of Commons; corresponds to the French-language data base, Hansard Questions Orales. 25) Hansard Written Questions—covers written questions and responses in the Canadian House of Commons; corresponds to the French-language data base, Hansard Questions Ecrites.

26) Heavy Oil/ Enhanced Recovery (HERI)—contains bibliographic citations to technical literature, patents, government reports, and other materials on heavy oil and enhanced recovery techniques; produced by the Alberta Oil Sands Information Centre. 27) International Bibliography of the Social Sciences—experimental data base of references to literature in economics and sociology; produced by the International Committee for Social Science Information and Documentation. 28) Mineral Processing Technology (MINPROC)—provides abstracts and references to literature on mineral processing and related topics; produced by the Canada Centre for Minerals and Energy Technology (CANMET) of the Canadian Department of Energy, Mines and Resources. 29) Mining Technology Abstracts (MINTEC)—contains abstracts and references to literature on mining technology and related topics; produced by CANMET. 30) National Reporter System (NRS)—series of eight data bases containing headnotes of judicial decisions of Canadian federal and provincial courts, comprising the following: Alberta Reports; Manitoba Reports; National Reporter; New Brunswick Reports; Newfoundland and Prince Edward Island Reports; Nova Scotia Reports; Ontario Appeal Cases; and Saskatchewan Reports. Produced by Maritime Law Book Ltd.

31) Predecessor and Defunct Companies—includes industrial mergers, name changes, and amalgamations occurring in the last 50 years; produced by the Financial Post Division of MacLean-Hunter Ltd. 32) Regulations of Ontario—partial data base, in progress, covering regulations current as of 1982. 33) Regulatory Reporter—contains summaries of energy, telecommunications, and transportation decisions of Canadian provincial and federal Regulatory Boards; produced by the Canadian Law Information Council. 34) Revised Statutes of Canada—consists of acts in force as of September 1983. A corresponding French-language data base, Les Statuts Revises du Canada, is also searchable online. Produced by the Canadian Department of Justice. 35) Ruling Information System-Excise (RISE)—covers more than 6100 excise and sales tax rulings from Revenue Canada. A corresponding French-language data base, Systeme de Renseignements sur les Decisions de l'Acise (SRDA), is also available online.

36) Solid Waste (SOL)—contains detailed references to solid waste management projects undertaken in Canada since 1970; produced by the Environmental Protection Service of Environment Canada. 37) Statutes of Alberta—contains the text of the revised statutes of Alberta in force as of 1984; produced by the Legislative Counsel

Office. 38) Statutes of British Columbia—covers more than 17,300 British Columbia statutes; prepared by the Ministry of the Attorney General. 39) Statutes of Manitoba—includes all statutes and proclamations as of 1981; prepared by the Manitoba Legislative Council. 40) Statutes of New Brunswick—contains complete statutes up to September 1983; prepared by the New Brunswick Office of the Attorney General.

41) Statutes of Ontario—contains the whole of the revised statutes of Ontario, 1980 and all amendments as of February 1984. 42) Statutes of Saskatchewan—provides complete coverage of Saskatchewan statutes up to April 1982; produced by the Saskatchewan Legislative Counsel Office. 43) Statutory Orders and Regulations—covers selected regulations in force as of August 1983. A corresponding French-language data base, Documents, Ordres et Reglements Statutaires, is also available online. Prepared by the Canadian Department of Justice. 44) Supreme Court Reports—contains headnotes of the Supreme Court of Canada Reports. Corresponds to the French-language data base, Les Rapports de la Cour Supreme du Canada. 45) Tax Advance Rulings—covers income tax rulings published by the Deputy Minister of National Revenue for taxation of Canada.

46) Western Legal Publications (WLP)—provides digests of Canadian federal and selected provincial civil and criminal court decisions; produced by Western Legal Publications Ltd. 47) Western Weekly Reports—contains headnotes dating from 1968 to the present; produced by the Canadian Law Information Council. 48) Yukon Bibliography—contains abstracts of documents pertaining to all aspects of the Yukon, including its literature; produced by the Boreal Institute for Northern Studies. Also available online through QL SYSTEMS is the Mortgage Amortization (MORT) program which enables users to enter the amount of mortgage, interest rate, payment and compounding frequencies, payments, and term of mortgage, and produce tables indicating the principle and interest payments for each payment period. Additional data bases are added periodically; contact QL SYSTEMS for a current list of files made available. QL SYSTEMS also makes the following software packages available for lease or purchase: QL/SEARCH, its information retrieval software; QL/TEXT, a text-editing system which can be used as a word processing system and which has electronic mail capability; and QL/NEWS, which provides facilities for storing the full text of a newspaper and for retrieving the full text of any news story. QL SYSTEMS also offers QL/MAIL, an electronic mail service for QL SYSTEMS users. A directory of QL/MAIL users is searchable online.

Other Services: In addition to the services described above, QL Systems makes the VU/TEXT online service available in Canada and acts as the Canadian representative for WESTLAW (West Publishing Company). It also provides consulting services and offers training sessions.

Clientele/Availability: Services and products are available without restrictions. Surcharges and royalties are assessed for the use of commercial data bases offered by QL Systems.

Remarks: QL Systems evolved from the QUIC/LAW Project established in 1968 at Queen's University.

Contact: Kathryn E. Addie, Customer Service Representative, QL Systems Limited. The electronic mail address on QL/MAIL is Box 24.

★829★
QUAERE LEGAL RESOURCES LTD.
1140 W. 7th Ave.
Vancouver, BC, Canada V6H 1B5
Mr. Vian Andrews, President
Phone: (604) 736-7284
Founded: 1982

Staff: 9 Total.

Description of System or Service: QUAERE LEGAL RESOURCES LTD. provides legal research, inquiry answering, legal and corporate library consultation, data base development services, and publications. It also offers a computerized research service bureau providing online information retrieval from commercial data bases for legal and business professionals.

Scope and/or Subject Matter: Law and business.

Input Sources: Information sources include primary legal materials, including case reports and statutes, and commercially available data bases.

Holdings and Storage Media: Library holdings include 400 bound volumes and subscriptions to 10 periodicals.

Publications: 1) Quaere Law Letter (monthly)—newsletter distributed to lawyers in British Columbia. 2) Motor Vehicle Insurance Case Book (updated monthly)—available for purchase. 3) Builders' and Repairers' Lien Case Book (updated monthly)—available for purchase. 4) Seat-Belt Defense Cases (updated quarterly)—available for purchase.

Computer-Based Products and Services: QUAERE LEGAL RESOURCES LTD. conducts online searches from data bases available through Info Globe (The Globe and Mail), QL Systems Limited, WESTLAW (West Publishing Company), and others. Search requests are accepted by mail or telephone. The firm is also developing computer-readable data bases.

Clientele/Availability: Services are available on a fee basis. Clients include lawyers, law librarians, judges, and corporate executives.

Contact: Joan I. Aufiero, Director of Information Services, Quaere Legal Resources Ltd.

★830★
QUEBEC
FRENCH LANGUAGE BOARD
(Office de la Langue Francaise)
TERMINOLOGY BANK OF QUEBEC
(Banque de Terminologie du Quebec - BTQ)
700, blvd. Saint-Cyrille Est
Quebec, PQ, Canada G1R 5G7
Jean-Marie Fortin, Head
Phone: (418) 643-1802
Service Est: 1973

Staff: 31 Information and library professional; 3 management professional; 12 technicians; 5 sales and marketing; 10 clerical and nonprofessional; 4 other.

Description of System or Service: The TERMINOLOGY BANK OF QUEBEC (BTQ) maintains computer-readable files containing scientific, technological, and industrial terms as well as bibliographic citations to dictionaries and similar works. Acting as the center of a terminology information network consisting of businesses, linguistic and translation services, and national and international agencies, the TERMINOLOGY BANK provides the French equivalent of English terms; defines terms and the context in which the terms can be used; compiles bibliographies of terminological works published in Quebec or France, citing the locations at which the works can be found; produces and publishes dictionaries and vocabularies; and furnishes information about services, projects, works in progress, and individuals or organizations involved in translation in Quebec or France. Computerized search services are provided, and the BTQ data bank is remotely accessible online.

Scope and/or Subject Matter: Standardization of scientific, technological, and industrial terms in Quebec and France.

Input Sources: Input for BTQ is obtained from participating individuals and organizations as well as from published literature.

Holdings and Storage Media: Machine-readable files hold approximately 1 million terms and 35,000 bibliographic citations to dictionaries and other terminological works.

Publications: Terminological publications and bibliographies are prepared from BTQ.

Computer-Based Products and Services: Computerized searches of the TERMINOLOGY BANK OF QUEBEC data bank are conducted by staff members. Approved businesses and government agencies operating in-house computer terminals can access the file online on a subscription basis. Additionally, the French Language Board performs computerized searching of data bases available through CAN/OLE, Telesystemes Questel, DIALOG Information Services, Inc., and System Development Corporation (SDC) for organizations involved in French-language conversion.

Clientele/Availability: Services are provided on a fee basis.

Remarks: The Terminology Bank of Quebec is also known as TERMINOQ.

Contact: Mireille Lacasse, Analyst, Terminology Bank of Quebec.

★831★
QUEBEC MINISTRY OF EDUCATION
(Ministere de l'Education du Quebec)
LIBRARY HEADQUARTERS
(Centrale des Bibliotheques)
POINT DE REPERE

1685, rue Fleury est
Montreal, PQ, Canada H2C 1T1
Nicole Gilbert, Librarian in Charge
Phone: (514) 382-0895
Service Est: 1984

Related Organizations: Point de Repere is published and jointly funded by the Centrale des Bibliotheques and the Quebec National Library/ Bibliotheque Nationale du Quebec.

Description of System or Service: POINT DE REPERE abstracts and indexes Quebec and foreign French-language periodicals of general interest. It represents the merger of two predecessor publications: RADAR (Repertoire Analytique d'Articles de Revues du Quebec), which covered Quebec periodicals, and PERIODEX, which covered French-language periodicals. POINT DE REPERE is available as a printed publication and as an online data base.

Scope and/or Subject Matter: Quebec and foreign French-language periodicals in all subject areas.

Input Sources: Input for Point de Repere is derived from more than 175 Quebec periodicals and 90 foreign periodicals.

Holdings and Storage Media: The computer-readable Point de Repere data base also incorporates the former RADAR file, which comprises approximately 60,000 records covering the years 1972 to 1983, and also includes approximately 9000 abstracts per year from 1984 onwards. The data base is updated semimonthly.

Publications: Point de Repere: Index Analytique d'Articles de Periodiques Quebecois et Etrangers (bimonthly with annual cumulation)—available by subscription.

Microform Products and Services: Point de Repere selections arranged by subject or author are available by subscription on microfiche.

Computer-Based Products and Services: POINT DE REPERE is available online through the Centrales des Bibliotheques. The RADAR portion of the data base is also accessible online through IST-Informatheque Inc.

Clientele/Availability: Products and services are available without restrictions.

Contact: Nicole Gilbert, Librarian in Charge, Point de Repere, Centrale des Bibliotheques.

★832★
QUEBEC MINISTRY OF THE ENVIRONMENT
(Ministere de l'Environnement du Quebec)
DOCUMENTATION CENTER
(Centre de Documentation)
ENVIRODOQ

2360, Chemin Ste-Foy
Sainte-Foy, PQ, Canada G1V 4H2
Gerard Nobrega, Coordinator
Phone: (418) 643-5363
Service Est: 1980

Staff: 9 Information and library professional.

Description of System or Service: ENVIRODOQ is an online bibliographic data base covering environmental evaluations, environmental impact statements, and related studies on the biophysical and socioeconomic aspects of the environment. It was developed to support environmental quality law and covers both completed research and research in progress in Quebec. Most documents cited in the data base are in French, although some important studies in English are included.

Scope and/or Subject Matter: Environmental information on the province of Quebec including water, air, soil, aquatic flora and fauna, quality of life, pollution, ecosystems, and natural phenomena.

Input Sources: Envirodoq covers documents from government agencies, universities, private firms, and other sources; periodical literature is excluded from the coverage.

Holdings and Storage Media: The machine-readable Envirodoq data base includes more than 3000 items dating from 1970 to the present. Documentation Center holdings comprise 20,000 bound volumes; microfiche; and subscriptions to 400 periodicals.

Microform Products and Services: Most documents cited in the data base are available for purchase on microfiche from the Editeur Officiel du Quebec.

Computer-Based Products and Services: ENVIRODOQ is accessible online through IST-Informatheque Inc., which provides a thesaurus to facilitate searching. Searchable elements include author, title, subject, year, official place name, hydrographic basin numerical code, cartographic coordinates, administrative region numerical code, Universal Transverse Mercator coordinates, and census division.

Clientele/Availability: The data base is available without restrictions for use by government organizations, private firms, universities, and the general public.

Remarks: Envirodoq is also known as the Banque Quebecoise d'Information sur l'Environnement Quebecois.

Contact: Gerard Nobrega, Coordinator, Envirodoq.

★833★
QUEBEC NATIONAL LIBRARY
(Bibliotheque Nationale du Quebec)
FMQ (FICHIER MARC QUEBECOIS)

1700, rue Saint-Denis
Montreal, PQ, Canada H2X 3K6
Marcel Fontaine, Director
Phone: (514) 873-2783
Service Est: 1968

Staff: 2 Information and library professional; 1 management professional; 1 technician; 4 clerical and nonprofessional.

Description of System or Service: FMQ (Fichier MARC Quebecois) is a machine-readable catalog using the Canadian MARC (CAN/MARC) format to record monographs, government documents, serials, and maps published in Quebec. Used to produce a printed bibliography, FMQ is available for online searching through UTLAS, Inc. and on magnetic tape by subscription.

Scope and/or Subject Matter: Literature in all subjects published in the province of Quebec.

Input Sources: Catalog records for relevant publications received at the Quebec National Library by legal deposit are added on a semimonthly basis.

Holdings and Storage Media: Machine-readable files cover publications received since 1968.

Publications: Bibliographie du Quebec/ Bibliography of Quebec (monthly)—available for purchase. A retrospective Bibliography covering 1821-1967 is also available.

Computer-Based Products and Services: FMQ magnetic tapes are available on a semimonthly subscription basis. FMQ is accessible for online searching through UTLAS, Inc.

Clientele/Availability: Services are available to libraries and other organizations.

Contact: Marcel Fontaine, Director, FMQ. (Telex 05561294.)

★834★
QUEBEC SOCIETY FOR LEGAL INFORMATION
(Societe Quebecoise d'Information Juridique - SOQUIJ)

276, rue St-Jacques, Suite 310
Montreal, PQ, Canada H2Y 1N3
J.-M. Tetrault, Head
Phone: (514) 842-8741
Founded: 1967

Staff: Approximately 60 total.

Related Organizations: The Quebec Department of Justice is the major source of financial support for SOQUIJ.

Description of System or Service: The QUEBEC SOCIETY FOR LEGAL INFORMATION (SOQUIJ) promotes the research, development, and dissemination of legal information in order to raise the quality and accessibility of such information. Toward this goal, SOQUIJ publishes a variety of publications covering Quebec law and other legal matters and provides photocopying of selected court decisions. It also maintains Quebec and Canadian federal legal information in computer-readable form.

Scope and/or Subject Matter: Quebec and Canadian federal law.

Holdings and Storage Media: Legal information is held in microform and machine-readable files.

Publications: SOQUIJ covers Quebec and Canadian federal legal decisions through a series of publications, which includes Jurisprudence Express, a weekly service summarizing more than 1000 decisions rendered by the Supreme Court of Canada and the various courts of Quebec. A complete list of SOQUIJ publications is available on request.

Microform Products and Services: 1) Microfiches Jurisprudence Express (weekly)—provides on microfiche the full text of all court decisions summarized in Jurisprudence Express. 2) Mini-Biblex—provides on microfiche the text of Canadian and Quebec legal documents including the Statutes of Canada, the laws and regulations of Quebec, and the full texts of decisions rendered by the Supreme Court of Canada, the Superior Court of Quebec, and the Quebec Court of Appeal.

Computer-Based Products and Services: SOQUIJ maintains a machine-readable data base covering reports from the Superior Court of Quebec, the Quebec Court of Appeal, and the Supreme Court of Canada. Through its Service Dossiers, it prepares computer-produced compilations of jurisprudence on specific themes. More than 125 such compilations are available and are updated annually. Additionally, SOQUIJ offers online access to courthouse records.

Clientele/Availability: Services are intended for the legal community.

Contact: Eric Steinberg, EDP/WP Manager, Quebec Society for Legal Information.

★835★
QUEEN'S UNIVERSITY OF BELFAST
DEPARTMENT OF COMPUTER SCIENCE
DATABASE ON ATOMIC AND MOLECULAR PHYSICS

Belfast BT7 1NN, Northern Ireland
Prof. F.J. Smith
Phone: 0232 245133
Service Est: 1969

Staff: 3 Information and library professional; 1 management professional; 1 other.

Description of System or Service: The DATABASE OF ATOMIC AND MOLECULAR PHYSICS is an online data base holding numeric data for electron ionization, excitation, hydrogen atom charge transfer, and interatomic potentials extracted from the scientific literature. It is operated by a system which permits data manipulation and retrieval in a number of forms, including tables, graphs, and subroutines. A curve fit representing recommended authenticated data is also available.

Scope and/or Subject Matter: Atomic and molecular physics.

Input Sources: Data are acquired from scientific literature.

Holdings and Storage Media: Computer files of numeric data are held.

Computer-Based Products and Services: Online and offline searches of the Database are available to subscribers.

Clientele/Availability: Primary clients are physicists.

Remarks: The Database was formerly called QUODAMP.

Contact: Dr. J.G. Hughes, Department of Computer Science.

★836★
QUEEN'S UNIVERSITY OF BELFAST
DEPARTMENT OF COMPUTER SCIENCE
QUEEN'S UNIVERSITY INTERROGATION OF LEGAL LITERATURE (QUILL)

Belfast BT7 1NN, Northern Ireland
Prof. F.J. Smith, Head
Phone: 0232 245133
Service Est: 1978

Staff: 5 Information and library professional; 1 management professional; 1 other.

Related Organizations: Support is received from the Royal Irish Academy, Department of Education for Northern Ireland, and the National Law Library.

Description of System or Service: The QUEEN'S UNIVERSITY INTERROGATION OF LEGAL LITERATURE (QUILL) is a software system for online storage, editing, and retrieval of legal and other documents. It includes programs for creating files, inputting documents, editing or correcting errors, indexing, merging new material with existing material, retrieving information, ascribing or changing the properties of words in the indexes, and producing lists of indexed words. QUILL permits fast retrieval through a visual display or typewriter terminal by persons with no technical experience. The system has a wide range of indexing capabilities for legal retrieval and linguistic applications; it is used at Queen's University to maintain data bases on Northern Ireland law, ancient Celtic-Latin texts, and others.

Scope and/or Subject Matter: Full-text document storage and retrieval for legal and other applications.

Input Sources: Documents may be typed into QUILL through terminals or prepared on punched cards. Input for the Queen's law data base is derived from Northern Ireland legal statutes and case notes and a legal bulletin published at the University. The Celtic-Latin text file contains input from original Latin texts dating from the 5th to the 12th century.

Holdings and Storage Media: Several full-text data bases are maintained in machine-readable form.

Computer-Based Products and Services: QUILL is an online software system with applications for several types of documents, including library references, law statutes, minutes of meetings, correspondence, and others. The system is designed for use by clerks, lawyers, engineers, scientists, doctors, and others requiring full-text document retrieval. QUILL is used at the University to provide access to the legal and text data bases and produce analyses and concordances. A microprocessor-based version of the system, called Micro-BIRD, is available for microcomputers.

Clientele/Availability: Primary users are Queen's University researchers.

Remarks: QUILL is based on experience with the previous Queen's University On-line Bibliographic Information Retrieval and Dissemination (QUOBIRD) system.

Contact: Prof. F.J. Smith, Head, Department of Computer Science.

★837★
QUOTEL INSURANCE SERVICES LTD.
83 Clerkenwell Rd.
London EC1, England
Phone: 01-242 0747
Founded: 1971

Special Note: No questionnaire response was received for this entry for the 6th edition. The entry is reprinted as it appeared in the 5th edition.

Related Organizations: QUOTEL Insurance Services Ltd. is a subsidiary of the CRC Group.

Description of System or Service: QUOTEL INSURANCE SERVICES LTD. provides computer-based quotation and data services for life and motor vehicle insurance rates in the United Kingdom. The QUOTEL life insurance system contains rates relating to more than 100 companies and societies covering all basic contract types. Similar to the life insurance system, the QUOTEL motor vehicle system was implemented to provide current information on frequently changing premium rates. Both systems are accessible online and include supplementary statistical information such as tax and mortgage interest rates. Additionally, QUOTEL supplies a quotation service over the Prestel system.

Scope and/or Subject Matter: Life and motor vehicle insurance rates in the U.K.

Input Sources: Input is derived from 107 life insurance companies and societies and 40 motor vehicle companies and Lloyd's syndicates.

Holdings and Storage Media: The life insurance quotation system contains more than 3 million individual rates and details on more than 100 contracts. Motor vehicle information from some 40 companies is held. Both machine-readable data bases are updated daily.

Computer-Based Products and Services: The QUOTEL systems are accessible online via remote communications terminal or telex. The life insurance quotation system produces quotations and information on the following contracts: whole of life, endowment, term and convertible term insurance, mortgage protection, family income benefit, mortgage, permanent health, last survivor whole life, and annuities. A quotation or quotation survey is produced in one of four forms: 1) Market Survey—evaluates company rates and ranks companies in value for money order according to the type of quotation requested; 2) Ten Best Offices—lists top ten offices from the full market survey; 3) Select Offices—produces a quotation survey made from nominated companies selected by the user; and 4) Single Company Illustration—detailed presentation of a chosen quotation in a form suitable for the client. The motor vehicle system provides rates data plus separate files giving cross-references to each company or syndicate's rating details for car models, geographical regions of the U.K., occupations, accidents, and convictions. Information can be computed either from all available companies or syndicates, or from the client's own selection of companies and syndicates.

Other Services: General purpose time-sharing services are also available through QUOTEL using computers operated by the parent CRC Group.

Clientele/Availability: Services are intended for the insurance industry and other users in the United Kingdom.

Contact: Managing Director, QUOTEL Insurance Services Ltd.

R

★838★
RENE DESCARTES UNIVERSITY
(Universite Rene Descartes)
LABORATORY OF APPLIED ANTHROPOLOGY
(Laboratoire d'Anthropologie Appliquee)
ERGODATA
45, rue des Saints-Peres　　　　　　　　Phone: 01 2603720
F-75270 Paris Cedex 06, France
Prof. A. Coblentz, Head

Staff: 2 Information and library professional; 1 management professional; 1 technician; 1 clerical and nonprofessional; 4 other.
Related Organizations: ERGODATA was developed with the support of the French government.
Description of System or Service: ERGODATA provides computer-based information services in the field of ergonomics. It maintains the International Human Biometry and Ergonomics Data Bank (Banque de Donnees Internationales de Biometrie Humaine et d'Ergonomie) of human body measurements collected from laboratories worldwide, and provides online facilities for computations, statistical calculations, and computer-aided design using the Data Bank. ERGODATA also documents relevant published literature, research reports, and studies.
Scope and/or Subject Matter: Ergonomics, anthropometrics, biometry, biostereometrics, and biomechanics, including applications in manufacturing, architecture, and engineering; design and development of systems and equipment.
Input Sources: Anthropometric data are collected from laboratories worldwide and from other organizations on magnetic tapes or punched cards for input to the Ergonomics Data Bank. Statistical data are collected from periodical literature.
Holdings and Storage Media: The ERGODATA Ergonomics Data Bank of body measurements holds more than 4 million individual data items in machine-readable form.
Computer-Based Products and Services: ERGODATA makes its Data Bank available for remote terminal access over Transpac, Euronet DIANE, Tymnet, and other telecommunications networks; also accessible is associated software for data retrieval, statistical calculations, and modeling and design.
Clientele/Availability: ERGODATA is available without restrictions; chief users are ergonomics researchers and equipment designers.
Contact: Mr. R. Steck, or Dr. G. Ignazi, Scientific Director, ERGODATA. (Telex 240540 ANTHROP.)

★839★
RESEARCH SERVICES LTD. (RSL)
PAN EUROPEAN SURVEY
Station House, Harrow Rd.　　　　　　Phone: 01-903 8511
Stonebridge Park
Wembley, Middlesex HA9 6DE, England

Special Note: The above name, address, and telephone number have been verified for this edition, although no questionnaire response was received. The following text is reprinted from the 5th edition.
Related Organizations: The Pan European Survey is sponsored by several international newspapers and magazines.
Description of System or Service: Available in hardcopy and machine-readable forms, the PAN EUROPEAN SURVEY is a marketing and readership study of male executives and professionals in twelve European countries. The SURVEY compares readership of national and international publications against ownership and use of many products and services; it also provides occupational and demographic characteristics of participants. The participants represent a universe of approximately six million men who are economically active, aged 21 or over, and have achieved high status through educational or professional qualifications.
Scope and/or Subject Matter: European readership of national and international publications, broken down by participants' country of residence, age and marital status, education, industry, job position, main responsibility, size of establishment, international communications, product ownership, purchasing involvement, use of English in business life, and other characteristics.
Input Sources: The Survey is based on data collected in approximately 6000 personal interviews.
Holdings and Storage Media: Survey data are held in machine-readable form.
Publications: Pan European Survey (published periodically)—reports results and methodology of research.
Computer-Based Products and Services: Pan European Survey data are available on computer tape and are accessible online through commercial time-sharing sources.
Clientele/Availability: Primary clients are marketers of goods and suppliers of services.
Remarks: Research Services Ltd. provides consultancy services and a full range of survey research facilities to government, industry, and business, both in the United Kingdom and abroad. Surveys are conducted in the areas of consumer, industrial, media, social, and agricultural research. Fieldwork is supported by computer-based data collection and analysis, library and information services, and participation in an international research network. Results of surveys are provided to clients in print or machine-readable forms. RSL can also design systems for client computer access to survey data.
Contact: Managing Director, Research Services Ltd. (Telex 923755.)

★840★
RESOURCES
465 Twickenham Rd.　　　　　　　　Phone: (not reported)
Isleworth, Middlesex TW7 7DZ, England　　Founded: 1981
Genevieve M. Hibbs, Head

Description of System or Service: RESOURCES publishes a quarterly bibliographic bulletin for occupational health practice, education, and research. Information from the bulletin is maintained in machine-readable form and on-demand bibliographies are prepared from it. RESOURCES also offers computerized mailing list services for employers, employers of occupational health and safety staff, and occupational health nurses in the United Kingdom.
Scope and/or Subject Matter: All aspects of occupational health and safety, including medicine, nursing, management, education, legislation, and other topics.
Input Sources: Input is derived from more than 40 periodicals, as well as from books, publishers data, and other sources.
Holdings and Storage Media: Information from the firm's publication is held in machine-readable form and updated regularly.
Publications: Resources (quarterly)—available by subscription; supplements are issued periodically and an annual cumulative index is produced. It provides sources of information for the occupational health and safety fields. Entries are arranged by subject classification and title; a typical entry contains title, author or editor, publisher, year published, number of pages, and price.
Computer-Based Products and Services: RESOURCES maintains information from its bulletin in machine-readable form. The data base is used to provide on-demand bibliographies, which are available in camera-ready form. Also available are address lists of services, suppliers, self-help groups, publishers, and others in the health and safety field.
Clientele/Availability: Services are available without restrictions. Primary clients are occupational health nurses.
Contact: Genevieve M. Hibbs, Head, Resources.

★841★
RINGIER & CO.
RINGIER DOCUMENTATION CENTER
(Ringier Dokumentationszentrum - RDZ)
Pressehaus, Dufourstr. 23　　　　　　Phone: 01 2596111
CH-8008 Zurich, Switzerland　　　　　Service Est: 1980

Special Note: No questionnaire response was received for this entry for the 6th edition. The entry is reprinted as it appeared in the 5th edition.

Staff: 30 Information and library professional; 5 management professional; 2 technicians; 3 clerical and nonprofessional.

Description of System or Service: The RINGIER DOCUMENTATION CENTER (RDZ) maintains a news data bank using microform and computer-based technologies. It scans newspapers and periodicals published by Ringier & Co. and other organizations, and reproduces articles and photographs appearing in them on microfiche. RDZ also indexes these materials for input to a computerized retrieval system to facilitate access to the microfiche collection. Services provided by RDZ include inquiry answering and document delivery.

Scope and/or Subject Matter: Current events and other topics covered in the general press.

Input Sources: More than 100 Swiss and foreign publications in four languages are scanned by RDZ.

Holdings and Storage Media: Microfiche holdings include nearly one million articles and more than five million photographs. Index records for these are held in a computer-readable data base.

Microform Products and Services: RDZ maintains an extensive microfiche press archive from which it provides document delivery services.

Computer-Based Products and Services: Maintained under DSS (Datenbank Sofort Auskunfts System) software, the RDZ data base is used to provide computerized literature searching services.

Clientele/Availability: Services are available without restrictions.

Contact: Director, Ringier Documentation Center. (Telex 56236.)

★842★
RISO NATIONAL LABORATORY
RISO LIBRARY
P.O. Box 49
DK-4000 Roskilde, Denmark
Eva Pedersen, Chief Librarian
Phone: 02 371212
Service Est: 1957

Staff: 7 Information and library professional; 1 management professional; 12 clerical and nonprofessional.

Related Organizations: The Riso Library is the technical processing center for the Nordic Energy Index (NEI) data base which is produced by the Nordic Atomic Libraries Joint Secretariat (see separate entry in this volume).

Description of System or Service: The RISO LIBRARY is the national library for nuclear research information in Denmark. It provides the Riso National Laboratory staff with scientific literature and supplies the Danish public with information in the field of atomic energy. The LIBRARY is the Danish input center to the International Nuclear Information System (INIS), and the Nordic input center for the U.S. Department of Energy's Energy Data Base (EDB) and other energy data bases. The LIBRARY also maintains exchange agreements with research institutions worldwide in an effort to gather a complete collection of nuclear literature in Denmark. Among the services provided are online search services and translations of foreign materials, especially Russian and other Slavic languages.

Scope and/or Subject Matter: Energy information, including biomass, coal, wind, geothermal, nuclear, oil, solar, uranium, and other energy resources; air pollution and other environmental issues; heating and power generation; reactors and thermal plants; and waste heat utilization.

Input Sources: Books, periodicals, reports, pamphlets, and annual reports are received. The Library also uses data bases made available through commercial and governmental organizations.

Holdings and Storage Media: The Library maintains a collection of 60,000 bound volumes; 500,000 reports, many on microfiche; and subscriptions to 1700 periodicals.

Publications: 1) Acquisitions List (2 per week); 2) Periodical Holdings (annual); 3) List of Translated Journals (biennial).

Microform Products and Services: Copies of microfiche reports are available.

Computer-Based Products and Services: The RISO LIBRARY provides input to the INIS and EDB data bases, offers online search and SDI services from the INIS data base, and conducts online searches of data bases available through ESA/IRS, DIALOG Information Services, Inc., and System Development Corporation (SDC). It also provides computer support for the production of an annual catalog of journal holdings and technical processing of the Nordic Energy Index data base.

Other Services: The Library also offers traditional library services, including manual literature searching and referral services. Reprints of journal articles and conference papers by Riso National Laboratory staff are supplied on request.

Clientele/Availability: Services are available to the public.

Contact: Eva Pedersen, Chief Librarian, Riso Library. (Telex 43116 RISOE DK.)

★843★
ROMANIA
NATIONAL COUNCIL FOR SCIENCE AND TECHNOLOGY
(Consiliul National pentru Stiinta si Tehnologie)
NATIONAL INSTITUTE FOR INFORMATION AND DOCUMENTATION
(Institutul National de Informare si Documentare - INID)
Str. Cosmonautilor, no. 27-29
Sector 1
Bucharest 70141, Romania
Mr. Anghel Gheorghe, Director
Phone: 90 134010
Service Est: 1949

Description of System or Service: The NATIONAL INSTITUTE FOR INFORMATION AND DOCUMENTATION (INID) provides national and international information services in all areas of science and technology. An active participant in several international information organizations, INID acquires specialized documents and publications through exchange agreements with more than 650 publishers in 55 countries, and from a variety of other sources across the world. It produces a computer-readable data base of bibliographic information on Romanian and foreign periodical and nonperiodical publications, and maintains extensive library collections supported by computerized retrieval systems. From these resources it offers a range of special services, including SDI, scientific and technical translations, bibliography compilations, abstracting and indexing, and hardcopy or microform reproduction. INID is also responsible for coordinating a national network of information and documentation centers and other scientific and technical information units.

Scope and/or Subject Matter: Science and technology; scientific and technological information.

Input Sources: INID acquires books, periodicals, dissertations, documents, and research reports from across the world.

Holdings and Storage Media: The INID data base is maintained in machine-readable format, and covers the period from 1972 to the present.

Publications: 1) Abstracts of Romanian Scientific and Technical Literature (twice per year)—provides abstracts and bibliographic citations for scientific and technical literature appearing in 120 Romanian periodicals. Includes author, subject, and source indexes. Available in English, French, Romanian, and Russian by exchange or by subscription. 2) Documentation and Information Problems/ Probleme de Documentare si Informare (quarterly). Various information bulletins and reviews are also published.

Microform Products and Services: Document reproductions are available on 35mm microfilm and on microfiche.

Computer-Based Products and Services: INID maintains a computer-readable bibliographic data base covering all fields of national economy and provides computerized SDI and retrospective searching. Data elements present in the file include the following: Universal Decimal Classification, document code, author, journal title, country, editing date, and descriptors. Magnetic tape copies of the data base are available by special arrangement.

Clientele/Availability: Services are available without restrictions.

Contact: Mr. Anghel Gheorghe, Director, National Institute for Information and Documentation. (Telex 11247 INID R.)

★844★
ROYAL DUTCH SOCIETY FOR ADVANCEMENT OF PHARMACY
(Koninklijke Nederlandse Maatschappij ter Bevordering der Pharmacie - KNMP)
KNMP DRUG DATABANK
P.O. Box 30460
Alexanderstr. 11
NL-2514 JL The Hague, Netherlands
K.E. Hagenaar, System Manager

Phone: 070 655922
Founded: 1981

Description of System or Service: The KNMP DRUG DATABANK is a computer-readable factual data bank containing numerical and textual information on drugs available in the Netherlands. A monthly extract from the DATABANK, called the KNMP Drug File, is available on computer tape and diskette. Print and microfiche products are also issued.

Scope and/or Subject Matter: Pharmaceutical and related products and presentations available in the Netherlands.

Input Sources: Input is derived from pharmaceutical and medical literature, data sheets, government agencies, manufacturers, and wholesalers.

Holdings and Storage Media: The computer-readable KNMP Databank contains information on approximately 10,000 pharmaceutical products and 20,000 presentations.

Publications: 1) Informatorium Medicamentorum (biannual); 2) Taxen (monthly)—price lists.

Microform Products and Services: KNMP Drugbank and Taxen information is available on microfiche.

Computer-Based Products and Services: The KNMP DRUG DATABANK is used to provide monthly extracts on computer tape or diskette through the KNMP Drug File service. The DATABANK is also expected to be made available online.

Clientele/Availability: Subscribers include Dutch pharmacists, pharmaceutical wholesalers, and others.

Contact: K.E. Hagenaar, System Manager, KNMP Databank.

★845★
ROYAL INSTITUTE OF BRITISH ARCHITECTS (RIBA)
BRITISH ARCHITECTURAL LIBRARY (BAL)
ARCHITECTURAL PERIODICALS INDEX (API)
66 Portland Place
London W1N 4AD, England
Jan van der Wateren, Director of Library

Phone: 01-580 5533
Service Est: 1972

Staff: Approximately 4 total.

Description of System or Service: Providing access to the world's literature on architecture and related fields, the ARCHITECTURAL PERIODICALS INDEX (API) is the published version of the British Architectural Library's periodicals subject index. API indexes about 400 journals and is issued quarterly with an annual cumulation. In addition to a subject index, a names index is included in every issue, and a topographical index is included in the cumulative issue. API is available in hard copy, on catalog cards, in microform, and on magnetic tape. A photocopy service is offered for all articles cited.

Scope and/or Subject Matter: Architecture and allied arts, construction technology, design and environmental studies, landscaping, and urban planning.

Input Sources: Information for API is derived from 400 architectural journals published in some 45 countries.

Holdings and Storage Media: API data since 1978 are held in machine-readable form. The Library's holdings consist of more than 100,000 bound volumes, 1200 periodical titles, 100,000 documents, 60,000 photographs, 250,000 drawings and architectural renderings, a microform collection, and an extensive vertical file.

Publications: 1) Architectural Periodicals Index-API (quarterly with an annual cumulation)—contains citations to approximately 12,000 articles per year on architecture and related fields. 2) Architectural Keywords—a list of 3000 terms used as headings in the API as well as 7000 synonyms and cross references to those terms. Both publications are available by subscription from RIBA Publications Ltd., Finsbury Mission, Moreland St., London EC1V 8VB, England. The Library also issues a quarterly accessions list which is distributed with API.

Microform Products and Services: The Index is available in microform for purchase.

Computer-Based Products and Services: The API data base, which covers the literature from 1978 to date, can be obtained on magnetic tape.

Other Services: The Library also offers an inquiry and information service, a bibliographic service, and a photographic service.

Clientele/Availability: Products and services are available without restrictions.

Contact: Jan van der Wateren, Director, British Architectural Library.

★846★
ROYAL MUSEUM OF CENTRAL AFRICA
(Musee Royal de l'Afrique Centrale)
CENTER FOR INFORMATICS APPLIED TO DEVELOPMENT AND TROPICAL AGRICULTURE
(Centre d'Informatique Appliquee au Developpement et a l'Agriculture Tropicale - CIDAT)
AGROCLIMATOLOGY DATA BANK
(Banque de Donnees Agroclimatologie)
13, chaussee de Louvain
B-1980 Tervuren, Belgium

Phone: 02 7675401
Service Est: 1970

Staff: Approximately 7 total.

Related Organizations: The Fonds de la Recherche Fondamentale et Collective (FRFC) provides support.

Description of System or Service: The AGROCLIMATOLOGY DATA BANK is a machine-readable file providing full-text coverage of documents on the relation of ecology and climate in Africa south of the Sahara, North America, Asia, and Oceania. It is maintained as part of CIDAT's efforts to collect and disseminate information facilitating the introduction of new agricultural crops and techniques in developing tropical areas.

Scope and/or Subject Matter: Tropical agricultural crops and techniques; relationship between ecology and agriculture.

Input Sources: CIDAT gathers data from meteorological documents issued by countries in the geographic areas under consideration.

Holdings and Storage Media: The machine-readable Agroclimatology Data Bank holds 50,000 records dating from 1930 to the present.

Publications: CIDAT issues a variety of publications, including a bibliography series and a thesaurus series.

Computer-Based Products and Services: The AGROCLIMATOLOGY DATA BANK holds the full text of documents covering the relation between ecology and agriculture in several geographic regions. Particular data included in the DATA BANK are average minimum and maximum monthly temperatures, absolute temperatures, monthly rainfall, and similar data. Retrospective search and SDI services are offered from the DATA BANK.

Other Services: CIDAT provides manual literature searching services and delivery of documents included in the Data Bank.

Clientele/Availability: Services and products are available to the public.

Remarks: The Royal Museum of Central Africa is also known as Koninklijk Museum voor Midden-Afrika. CIDAT is also known as the Centrum voor Informatie-Verwerking op het Gebied van Tropische Landbouw en Ontwikkeling (CITLO).

Contact: Ing. A.B. Ergo, Scientific Advisor, Agroclimatology Data Bank, Center for Informatics Applied to Development and Tropical Agriculture.

★847★
ROYAL NETHERLANDS ACADEMY OF ARTS AND SCIENCES
(Koninklijke Nederlandse Akademie van Wetenschappen)
SOCIAL SCIENCE INFORMATION AND DOCUMENTATION CENTER
(Sociaal-Wetenschappelijk Informatie- en Documentatiecentrum - SWIDOC)
410 Herengracht
NL-1017 BX Amsterdam, Netherlands
Dr. A.F. Marks, Director
Phone: 020 225061
Service Est: 1963

Staff: 11 Information and library professional; 2 management professional; 1 technician; 4 clerical and nonprofessional; 2 other.

Related Organizations: SWIDOC is one of 10 special institutes of the Royal Netherlands Academy of Arts and Sciences and, as such, is supported by the Ministry of Education and Sciences.

Description of System or Service: The SOCIAL SCIENCE INFORMATION AND DOCUMENTATION CENTER (SWIDOC) was established to document social science research in the Netherlands and to provide information services from the published social science literature. Its activities include the computer-based registration of ongoing research projects, collection and documentation of research reports and doctoral dissertations, abstracting and indexing, manual and computerized literature searching, and preparation of publications. SWIDOC also maintains a data archive section, the Steinmetz Archives, which is described in a separate entry following this one.

Scope and/or Subject Matter: Ongoing and completed research in the social sciences in the Netherlands including the following fields: sociology, political science, anthropology, public administration sciences, psychology, pedagogics, social and economic geography, town and country planning, demography, social medicine, and those aspects of law, economics, history, and librarianship which are related to the social sciences.

Input Sources: The Center collects approximately 2200 reports and information on some 1000 social science research projects annually.

Holdings and Storage Media: Holdings consist of approximately 16,000 research reports, 2500 theses, and information on 450 libraries and documentation centers. Collection also includes 500 volumes and subscriptions to 150 periodicals in social science fields. Subject indexes and subject, author, and geographical catalogs are held in card files.

Publications: 1) Titels van Sociaalwetenschappelijk Onderzoek/ Titles of Social Science Reseach (monthly)—current awareness bulletin listing project and report titles and research institutions. 2) Informatie Lopend Onderzoek Sociale Wetenschappen/ Information on Current Social Science Research (annual)—includes details about projects, a subject index, and a list of research institutions. 3) Register of Social Science Research—cumulates the publication Information on Current Social Science Research and includes information about interim and final reports and has a number of indexes. 4) Doctoral Dissertations in the Social Sciences (annual)—lists authors and titles. 5) Periodiekenparade/ Periodicals Parade (monthly)—includestables of contents and approximately 150 journals in social science and social welfare, with separate KWIC index. The Center also offers registers on specific social science topics such as gerontology or political terrorism. All of the above publications are in Dutch. A list of other periodicals is available on request from the Center.

Microform Products and Services: Doctoral Dissertations in the Social Sciences and KWIC indexes to Periodicals Parade are available on microfiche.

Computer-Based Products and Services: The Center maintains a computer-readable register of research projects and expects to offer SDI and search services from it. SWIDOC also performs searches of data bases available online through DIALOG Information Services, Inc., System Development Corporation (SDC), and Euronet DIANE.

Other Services: Additional services include: reference and referral services; advisory and consulting services on the pattern of social sciences research; and research related to the dissemination of scientific information.

Clientele/Availability: Services are available without restrictions.

Contact: Dr. A.F. Marks, Director, or Mrs. E.Z.R. Cohen, Deputy Director, Social Science Information and Documentation Center.

★848★
ROYAL NETHERLANDS ACADEMY OF ARTS AND SCIENCES
(Koninklijke Nederlandse Akademie van Wetenschappen)
SOCIAL SCIENCE INFORMATION AND DOCUMENTATION CENTER
(Sociaal-Wetenschappelijk Informatie- en Documentatiecentrum - SWIDOC)
STEINMETZ ARCHIVES
410 Herengracht
NL-1017 BX Amsterdam, Netherlands
Dr. Paul F.A. de Guchteneire, Head
Phone: 020 225061
Service Est: 1964

Staff: 6 Information and library professional; 1 clerical and nonprofessional; 1 other.

Description of System or Service: The STEINMETZ ARCHIVES collects and archives quantitative social science research data in machine-readable form in order to make them available to researchers for secondary analysis. Services offered include computerized searching for relevant studies, provision of data and documentation, advisory and training services, and some data analysis. The ARCHIVES also maintains contacts with data archives in other countries, and can obtain data sets from them.

Scope and/or Subject Matter: Social science research data, with emphasis on the Netherlands.

Input Sources: The Archives acquires raw data and documentation from researchers.

Holdings and Storage Media: Approximately 1400 studies are held, including 650 weekly opinion polls.

Publications: Steinmetz Archives Catalogue and Guide (updated regularly)—available for purchase; provides Dutch and English-language titles, keywords, themes, sampled universe, kind of data, substudies, number of cases and variables, principal investigator, depositor, accessibility, and mode of storage.

Microform Products and Services: A KWIC index to research topics in the archived materials is available on COM microfiche.

Computer-Based Products and Services: The Archives provides machine-readable studies in SPSS file format or as a card image file; complete documentation, primarily in English, is also supplied. To assist clients in locating needed data, computerized searching of study descriptions is offered through Remote Information Query System (RIQS) software. Additionally, the Archives conducts limited data analysis.

Other Services: Also offered are consulting services on questionnaire and codebook design, and on methods of conducting analyses.

Clientele/Availability: Services are available with restrictions on the use of some data.

Contact: Dr. Paul F.A. de Guchteneire, Head, Steinmetz Archives.

★849★
ROYAL NETHERLANDS ACADEMY OF ARTS AND SCIENCES LIBRARY
(Bibliotheek Koninklijke Nederlandse Akademie van Wetenschappen)
Kloveniersburgwal 29
P.O. Box 19121
NL-1000 GC Amsterdam, Netherlands
Dr. J.A.W. Brak, Director
Phone: 020 222902

Staff: 10 Information and library professional; 1 management professional; 11 technicians; 28 clerical and nonprofessional.

Description of System or Service: The ROYAL NETHERLANDS ACADEMY OF ARTS AND SCIENCES LIBRARY is the central library for natural sciences and medicine in the Netherlands. It provides a variety of library and information services, including computerized information retrieval, online document delivery, and documentation services. The LIBRARY acts as an International Nuclear Information System (INIS) clearinghouse and serves as the technical coordinator for Netherlands input to INIS. It also serves as a clearinghouse for articles referenced in Excerpta Medica abstracts journals.

Scope and/or Subject Matter: Medicine, biology, chemistry, physics, pharmacy, and astronomy.

Input Sources: Input sources include journals, books, conference proceedings, reports, microfiche, abstracts journals, bibliographies, and online data bases.

Holdings and Storage Media: Library holdings include 260,000 bound volumes; subscriptions to 10,000 periodicals; and 9 million microfiche. The Library also maintains internal machine-readable files covering periodicals, monographs, and grey literature.

Computer-Based Products and Services: The ROYAL NETHERLANDS ACADEMY OF ARTS AND SCIENCES LIBRARY provides retrospective searching and SDI services from data bases made available through major online vendors. Additionally, the LIBRARY maintains internal computer-readable bibliographic data bases.

Clientele/Availability: Services are available without restrictions.

Contact: Dr. Th. W.J. Pieters, Royal Netherlands Academy of Arts and Sciences Library.

★850★
ROYAL NORWEGIAN COUNCIL FOR SCIENTIFIC AND INDUSTRIAL RESEARCH
NORWEGIAN SEISMIC ARRAY (NORSAR)
P.O. Box 51
N-2007 Kjeller, Norway
Frode Ringdal, Project Manager
Phone: 02 716915
Service Est: 1970

Staff: 1 Management professional; 5 technicians; 3 clerical and nonprofessional; 13 other.

Related Organizations: NORSAR was established as a joint undertaking between the Norwegian and United States governments.

Description of System or Service: The primary purpose of the NORWEGIAN SEISMIC ARRAY (NORSAR) is to conduct research on seismological problems relevant to the detection and identification of earthquakes and underground nuclear explosions. One of the world's largest seismological laboratories, NORSAR is involved in array monitoring and calibration, online data acquisition, online seismological event detection, and offline processing and analysis of event data. NORSAR publishes catalogs and research reports, and it distributes data online and on magnetic tape.

Scope and/or Subject Matter: Earthquakes, underground nuclear explosions, earthquake risk analysis, applied seismology.

Input Sources: Data collected via approximately 70 seismometers arranged in subarrays over an area of about 100 kilometers in diameter are transmitted to the data center at Kjeller for subsequent analysis.

Holdings and Storage Media: NORSAR maintains a digital seismic data base and various earthquake catalogs in machine-readable form. Data on more than 50,000 earthquakes and 400 presumed underground nuclear explosions have been recorded.

Publications: A monthly summary of recorded seismic events is distributed to seismological agencies in more than 25 countries. Research results are regularly published in project reports and in international professional journals.

Computer-Based Products and Services: NORSAR data are used to produce various reports and tapes covering seismic events. A principal product is a machine-readable monthly earthquake catalog. NORSAR also transmits data directly to other organizations.

Other Services: Additional services of NORSAR include research and consulting in applied seismology, encompassing such projects as earthquake analysis for industrial installations and seismic prospecting techniques.

Clientele/Availability: Primary clients are the Norwegian and United States governments.

Contact: Hilmar Bungum, Acting Project Manager, Norwegian Seismic Array. (Telex 18147 KCIN N.)

★851★
ROYAL SOCIETY OF CHEMISTRY (RSC)
INFORMATION SERVICES
The University
Nottingham NG7 2RD, England
Robert Welham, Director
Phone: 0602 57411
Service Est: 1969

Staff: 40 Information and library professional; 20 management professional; 5 sales and marketing; 30 clerical and nonprofessional.

Related Organizations: The Royal Society of Chemistry was formed in 1980 through the unification of the Chemical Society with the Royal Institute of Chemistry.

Description of System or Service: The INFORMATION SERVICES provides print and electronic current awareness services in chemistry, biotechnology, and related fields. Among its chief services are Chemical Engineering Abstracts, Chemical Hazards in Industry, Current Biotechnology Abstracts, Laboratory Hazards Bulletin, and Mass Spectrometry Bulletin (see separate entries following this one). The INFORMATION SERVICES also represents the Chemical Abstracts Service (CAS) in the United Kingdom, making available a number of CAS print, microform, and computer-based products and services. Additionally, the INFORMATION SERVICES provides computerized information retrieval from CAS and other online data bases.

Scope and/or Subject Matter: Chemistry, biochemistry, biology, biotechnology, chemical engineering, toxicology.

Input Sources: The Information Services scans, selects, and abstracts items from published sources of information for input to CAS and internal products.

Holdings and Storage Media: The Services maintains several internal computer-readable bibliographic data bases as well as copies of CAS, BIOSIS, and NLM data bases.

Publications: The following publications are available by subscription: 1) CA Selects (biweekly)—jointly produced with CAS; computer-produced current awareness bulletin available in approximately 140 specific fields in science and technology and including abstracts and associated bibliographic information. 2) Laboratory Hazards Bulletin (monthly)—current awareness periodical which reports on safety measures, potential hazards, and new legislation affecting employees working in laboratories. 3) Chemical Engineering Abstracts (monthly)—covers scientific, technical, and technocommercial aspects of chemical and process engineering. 4) Current Biotechnology Abstracts (monthly)—reports on the latest scientific, technical, and technocommercial advances in the field of biotechnology.

5) Methods in Organic Synthesis-MOS (monthly)—provides worldwide coverage of novel and interesting reactions and reaction schemes in the field of organic synthetic chemistry. Each issue contains approximately 200 references which include bibliographic details and schematic reaction diagrams. An author index and a four-part subject index are also included in each issue and cumulated annually. 6) Chemical Hazards in Industry (monthly)—current awareness periodical covering health and safety, chemical and biological hazards, plant safety, legislation, protective equipment, and storage relating to the chemical and allied industries. 7) Analytical Abstracts (monthly)—provides more than 12,000 abstracts each year drawn from international journal literature covering the field of analytical chemistry. Each issue includes a subject index which is cumulated every six months. 8) Information Services Newsletter (monthly)—contains items of interest to users. A complete catalog of publications issued by the Royal Society of Chemistry is available by request.

Microform Products and Services: The Information Services makes available Chemical Abstracts in microform in the United Kingdom.

Computer-Based Products and Services: The INFORMATION SERVICES produces several computer-readable data bases, as described in separate entries following this one. It also provides the computer-based Individual Customer Service and the Postal Search Services. The Individual Customer Service is an enhanced current awareness reference and retrieval service in the chemical and biological sciences. Using search strategies based on client-supplied information, the Service regularly conducts computerized searches of CA Search and BIOSIS Previews. Search results include title, bibliographic details, keywords, and, if requested, abstracts; results are available on file cards or continuous computer stationery. The Postal Search Services conducts computerized searches, in response to written requests, of BIOSIS Previews, TOXLINE, NIH-EPA Chemical Information System (CIS), CA Search, and other NLM and CAS data bases.

Clientele/Availability: Services and products are available without restrictions.

Remarks: The Information Services was formerly known as the United Kingdom Chemical Information Service (UKCIS).

Contact: Cheryl Teague, Advertising Executive, Royal Society of Chemistry. (Telex 37488 RSC G.)

★852★
ROYAL SOCIETY OF CHEMISTRY (RSC)
INFORMATION SERVICES
CHEMICAL ENGINEERING ABSTRACTS (CEA)
The University
Nottingham NG7 2RD, England
F. John Taylor, Editor
Phone: 0602 57411
Service Est: 1982

Description of System or Service: CHEMICAL ENGINEERING ABSTRACTS (CEA) provides abstracts and indexes of international literature covering the scientific, technical, and technocommercial aspects of chemical and process engineering. CEA is available as a printed publication, on magnetic tape, and as a commercially available online data base.

Scope and/or Subject Matter: Plant and process chemical engineering, covering both theoretical and practical aspects and including related subjects such as mechanical, civil, electrical, and instrumentational engineering.

Input Sources: More than 100 journals are scanned for CEA.

Holdings and Storage Media: The computer-readable CEA data base dates primarily from 1982 to the present and holds approximately 5000 records with abstracts per year of coverage.

Publications: Chemical Engineering Abstracts (monthly)—available by subscription. Each issue contains approximately 400 citations and a keyword subject index; the index is cumulated annually.

Computer-Based Products and Services: The CHEMICAL ENGINEERING ABSTRACTS data base is available online through Pergamon InfoLine Ltd., Data-Star, and ESA/IRS. A typical record includes abstract number, title, author, journal reference, journal title abbreviation, volume issue, page, date, and abstract. CEA is also available for lease on magnetic tape.

Clientele/Availability: Services are available without restrictions. Clients include research and development scientists, chemical engineers, industrial engineering librarians, plant managers, technical support staff, academic engineering librarians, marketing executives, and others.

Contact: Pam Chomicz, Information Services, Royal Society of Chemistry. (Telex 37488 RSC G.)

★853★
ROYAL SOCIETY OF CHEMISTRY (RSC)
INFORMATION SERVICES
CHEMICAL HAZARDS IN INDUSTRY (CHI)
The University
Nottingham NG7 2RD, England
Sheila Templer, Editor
Phone: 0602 57411
Service Est: 1984

Description of System or Service: CHEMICAL HAZARDS IN INDUSTRY (CHI) provides abstracts and indexes of international journal and other literature covering hazards and safe working practices in the chemical and allied industries. CHI is available as a printed publication and on magnetic tape; it is expected to be made commercially available online.

Scope and/or Subject Matter: Health and safety in the chemical and allied industries, including chemical and biological hazards, toxicology, environmental health, medicine, epidemiology, accident prevention, chemical engineering, and legislation.

Input Sources: Input is derived from 200 major primary journals; peripheral and secondary sources are covered as appropriate.

Holdings and Storage Media: The computer-readable bibliographic CHI data base dates from 1984 to the present; approximately 2500 records are added each year.

Publications: Chemical Hazards in Industry (monthly)—available by subscription. Entries are arranged in four sections: chemical hazards, including fires and explosions, hazardous waste management, and storage and transportation; biological hazards, including toxic chemicals, carcinogens and mutagens, reproductive hazards, and allergy and dermatitis; new precautions and legislation, including safe practices and equipment, and legislation; and general, including health, hygiene, and monitoring; forthcoming events; and reviews, books, and other items. Each issue contains more than 200 abstracts and chemical and subject indexes. The indexes are cumulated annually and published as a separate issue.

Computer-Based Products and Services: CHEMICAL HAZARDS IN INDUSTRY is available for purchase on magnetic tape; it is expected to be made commercially available online. A typical record includes document title, author and affiliation, abbreviated journal title, date, volume, issue, page, language if not English, and abstract. Publisher information, ISBN, technical report number, and original titles of foreign books are given when applicable. CHI records also include contact addresses and order numbers for material such as legislative documents, technical reports, and audiovisual aids. The CHI data base will also include Chemical Abstracts Service (CAS) Registry Number to facilitate the location of items relating to particular chemicals.

Clientele/Availability: Services are available without restrictions.

Contact: Pam Chomicz, Information Services, Royal Society of Chemistry. (Telex 37488 RSC G.)

★854★
ROYAL SOCIETY OF CHEMISTRY (RSC)
INFORMATION SERVICES
CURRENT BIOTECHNOLOGY ABSTRACTS (CBA)
The University
Nottingham NG7 2RD, England
H. Kidd, Editor
Phone: 0602 57411
Service Est: 1983

Description of System or Service: CURRENT BIOTECHNOLOGY ABSTRACTS (CBA) provides abstracts and indexes of international journal and other literature covering the scientific, technical, and technocommercial aspects of biotechnology. CBA is available as a printed publication, on magnetic tape, and as a commercially available online data base.

Scope and/or Subject Matter: Biotechnology, including microbiology, genetics, medicine, biochemistry, immunology, pharmaceutics, fermentation, and other topics.

Input Sources: Input is derived from approximately 200 core journals and newsletters, plus patents, books, proceedings, technical reports, government reports, newspapers, magazines, and other literature, as well as from computerized searches of relevant data bases.

Holdings and Storage Media: The computer-readable CBA data base dates from 1983 to the present and holds approximately 4000 references with abstracts per year of coverage.

Publications: Current Biotechnology Abstracts (monthly)—available by subscription. Entries are arranged in four sections: techniques, including genetic engineering/ recombinant DNA, monoclonal antibodies, immobilized enzymes, single cell proteins, and fermentation technology; technocommercial, including company and business news, and law, regulations, and safety; industrial areas, including pharmaceuticals, energy production, agriculture, chemical industry, food, and others; and general, including meetings and seminars, and books, reports, and reviews. Each issue contains approximately 350 entries and also includes subject, substance, and company indexes which are cumulated annually.

Computer-Based Products and Services: The CURRENT BIOTECHNOLOGY ABSTRACTS data base is available online through Pergamon InfoLine Ltd., Data-Star, and ESA/IRS. A typical citation includes document title, author, location of work done, journal title, volume and issue numbers, date, abstract number, and abstract. CBA is also available for lease on magnetic tape.

Clientele/Availability: Services are available without restrictions.

Contact: Pam Chomicz, Information Services, Royal Society of Chemistry. (Telex 37488 RSC G.)

★855★
ROYAL SOCIETY OF CHEMISTRY (RSC)
INFORMATION SERVICES
LABORATORY HAZARDS BULLETIN (LHB)
The University
Nottingham NG7 2RD, England
Sheila Templer, Editor
Phone: 0602 57411
Service Est: 1981

Description of System or Service: LABORATORY HAZARDS BULLETIN (LHB) provides abstracts and indexes of international scientific and technical literature covering safety measures, potential hazards, and new legislation affecting the well-being of employees working in laboratories in the chemical and allied industries. LHB is available as a printed publication, on magnetic tape, and as a commercially available online data base.

Scope and/or Subject Matter: Laboratory hazards, including chemical hazards, biological hazards, and new precautions and legislation.

Input Sources: Input is derived from international scientific and technical literature, including approximately 90 journals plus monographs, technical reports, and government reports.

Holdings and Storage Media: The computer-readable LHB data base contains more than 1700 abstracts and citations dating from 1981 to the present.

Publications: Laboratory Hazards Bulletin (monthly)—available by subscription. Each issue contains approximately 50 abstracts with a subject index; the index is cumulated annually.

Computer-Based Products and Services: The LABORATORY HAZARDS BULLETIN data base is available online through Pergamon InfoLine Ltd., Data-Star, and ESA/IRS. A typical record includes document title, bibliographic citation, and concise summary. LHB is also available for lease on magnetic tape.

Clientele/Availability: Services are available without restrictions.

Contact: Pam Chomicz, Information Services, Royal Society of Chemistry.

★856★
ROYAL SOCIETY OF CHEMISTRY (RSC)
INFORMATION SERVICES
MASS SPECTROMETRY DATA CENTRE (MSDC)
The University
Nottingham NG7 2RD, England
Stephen Down, Head
Phone: 0602 57411
Service Est: 1966

Staff: 3 Information and library professional; 3 clerical and nonprofessional.

Related Organizations: The Centre is supported by the Great Britain Department of Trade and Industry as part of the British data and information program.

Description of System or Service: The MASS SPECTROMETRY DATA CENTRE (MSDC) collects and distributes mass spectra data and information on a worldwide basis. It produces the Mass Spectrometry Bulletin, which contains citations to all relevant articles in the mass spectrometry literature; the Bulletin is available as a monthly printed publication and as a commercially available online data base. The CENTRE's other products and services include distribution of mass spectral data sheets and magnetic tapes; a bound index of spectra; document delivery; and general information services. MSDC also supplies data to, and accesses online, the Mass Spectral Search System (MSSS), which is part of the NIH-EPA Chemical Information System (CIS).

Scope and/or Subject Matter: Mass spectrometry and related topics.

Input Sources: Input is derived from approximately 400 primary scientific journals, as well as abstracting publications, monographs, technical reports, government reports, patents, and conference proceedings.

Holdings and Storage Media: The machine-readable Mass Spectrometry Bulletin data base contains approximately 130,000 references dating from 1966 to the present; it is updated monthly with about 800 references. The Centre also maintains the Mass Spectra Data Base covering approximately 25,000 full mass spectra; new spectra are added regularly.

Publications: 1) Mass Spectrometry Bulletin (monthly)—contains titles and bibliographic details for relevant current literature; each issue includes about 800 entries and subject, author, elements, general, and compound classification indexes. The Bulletin is available by subscription which includes an annual cumulative issue of the indexes. Back issues of the Bulletin are also available for purchase. 2) Eight Peak Index of Mass Spectra—seven-volume publication that assists in the identification of unknown compounds by providing the eight most abundant ions in more than 60,000 mass spectra; prepared in collaboration with Imperial Chemical Industries Ltd. 3) Mass Spectral Data Sheets—7000 spectra are available on data sheets, arranged in line diagram and tabulated forms, including m/z values, relative intensities, formula, molecular weight, and source of the spectra. The Data Sheets are available for purchase as a set or individually. 4) Mass Spectrometry—series of review volumes which describe recent developments in major areas of chemistry.

Computer-Based Products and Services: The Mass Spectrometry Bulletin (MSB) data base is available for online searching through Pergamon InfoLine Ltd. Copies of documents cited in the MSB data base are available from the Centre. The Bulletin, the Eight Peak Index of Mass Spectra, and the Mass Spectra Data Base are made available on magnetic tape. In addition, the Centre contributes to and conducts searches of the NIH-EPA Chemical Information System (CIS).

Clientele/Availability: Products and services are available to mass spectrometrists worldwide.

Contact: Pam Chomicz, Information Services, Royal Society of Chemistry. (Telex 37488 RSC G.)

★857★
ROYAL TROPICAL INSTITUTE
(Koninklijk Instituut voor de Tropen)
AGRICULTURAL INFORMATION & DOCUMENTATION SECTION (AIDS)
Mauritskade 63
NL-1092 AD Amsterdam, Netherlands
Richard M. Wilson, Acting Head
Phone: 020 924949
Service Est: 1975

Staff: 3 Information and library professional; 1 management professional; 5 clerical and nonprofessional.

Description of System or Service: The AGRICULTURAL INFORMATION & DOCUMENTATION SECTION (AIDS) is involved in the collection, abstracting, indexing, and publication of information relevant to agriculture in tropical and subtropical regions. A primary activity is maintenance of the Abstracts on Tropical Agriculture (ATA) Data Base, which is used to provide SDI, a monthly journal, and magnetic tape services; the file is also commercially available online. Additionally, AIDS holds manual files of abstracts dating back to 1916, and offers retrospective bibliographies from these. Document delivery services are also offered.

Scope and/or Subject Matter: Practical aspects of agriculture in tropical and subtropical regions; emphasis is on information of interest to extension and development workers, including crop production, crop protection, soils and fertilizers, agricultural engineering, agricultural operations, crop processing and storage, agricultural economics and development, and social effects of agricultural development.

Input Sources: About 1750 periodical titles published worldwide are regularly scanned, as well as books, reports, theses, conference proceedings, monographs, and extension pamphlets. Approximately 5500 items per year are selected from these sources.

Holdings and Storage Media: Holdings include the computer-readable ATA data base covering the years 1975 to date and holding about 48,000 records. An earlier card system is also held. All items abstracted for ATA are available in the Central Library of the Royal Tropical Institute.

Publications: Abstracts on Tropical Agriculture (monthly)—available by subscription; each issue contains about 500 abstracts arranged in 19 subject categories, with subject, geographic, author, and affiliation indexes. Also produced is an annual cumulative subject and plant taxonomic name index.

Computer-Based Products and Services: The Abstracts on Tropical Agriculture (ATA) Data Base is searchable online through System Development Corporation (SDC) as the TROPAG file. AIDS uses the data base to offer the ATA-SDI service, which provides subscribers with computer-selected abstracts printed on index cards. The data base is also available on magnetic tape.

Other Services: Additional services provided by AIDS are manual literature searching, referrals, and photocopying services for any periodical article abstracted in ATA.

Clientele/Availability: Products and services are available on a fee basis.

Contact: Richard M. Wilson, Acting Head, Agricultural Information & Documentation Section. (Telex 15080 KIT NL.)

★858★
RUBBER AND PLASTICS RESEARCH ASSOCIATION OF GREAT BRITAIN (RAPRA)
RAPRA INFORMATION CENTRE
Shawbury
Shrewsbury, Shrops. SY4 4NR, England
Paul Cantrill, Head
Phone: 0939 250383
Service Est: 1919

Staff: 12 Information and library professional; 2 management professional; 2 sales and marketing; 8 clerical and nonprofessional.

Description of System or Service: The RAPRA INFORMATION CENTRE supports the work of the Rubber and Plastics Research Association of Great Britain which acts as the International Technical Centre for Rubber and Plastics. The INFORMATION CENTRE's services include abstracting and indexing of relevant world literature in order to produce RAPRA Abstracts, which is available in hard copy, on magnetic tape, and online. The INFORMATION CENTRE also maintains the Porritt and Dawson Library and offers loans and photocopying from the collection. Both the data base and library support an inquiry answering service that handles simple questions as well as major investigations.

Scope and/or Subject Matter: Technical and commercial information relating to the rubber and plastics industries worldwide, including raw materials and monomers, polymers and polymerization, compounding ingredients, intermediate and semifinished products, applications, processing and treatment, properties and tests, company news, new product information, legislation, and industrial health and safety.

Input Sources: Information for RAPRA Abstracts is abstracted from books, reports, conference proceedings, dissertations and theses, standards and patents, and more than 500 journals and periodicals.

Holdings and Storage Media: The computer-readable RAPRA Abstracts data base holds approximately 180,000 records for literature published from 1974 to date. The file is updated monthly, with approximately 25,000 new abstracts added annually. An additional 2 million references are stored in card files and on microfilm. The Porritt and Dawson Library collection includes books, trade literature, and conference proceedings published worldwide on all aspects of the polymer industry.

Publications: 1) RAPRA Abstracts (biweekly with annual indexes)—available by subscription. Each issue contains approximately 1000 abstracts arranged by subjects. 2) International Polymer Science and Technology-IPSAT (monthly)—includes abstracts from selected Russian, East European, and Japanese polymer publications; subscribers may request full translations of cited articles. 3) Annual Index to New Products. Various search aids for the RAPRA data base are also available, including an online users manual, thesauri of descriptors and trade and company names, and a classification scheme and indexes. The Association also publishes monographs, reports, proceedings, and data sheets; a list of publications is available on request.

Computer-Based Products and Services: The RAPRA Abstracts data base contains abstracts for the period 1974 to the present. Abstracts are indexed by a mixture of free-text and controlled thesaurus terms, and are classified according to a proposed code for the systematic classification of scientific, technological, and commercial information on polymers. The data base is accessible online through Pergamon InfoLine Ltd. Additionally, the Centre uses the data base to prepare RAPRA Extracts, a biweekly SDI service supplied on printouts or cards, and to provide magnetic tape leasing services for the entire data base or subsets of it. The tape and SDI services are available by subscription.

Other Services: The Information Centre also provides manual literature searching, consultancy services, and translations from most European languages and Japanese and Russian.

Clientele/Availability: Services are available to RAPRA members and nonmembers.

Contact: Paul Cantrill, Head of Information Technology and Operations, RAPRA Information Centre. (Telex 35134.)

★859★
RWK LTD.
Ave. Rio Branco 245, Gr. 1003
20040 Rio de Janeiro RJ, Brazil
Raymond W. Kahl, Jr., President
Phone: 021 2208549
Founded: 1977

Staff: 2 Information and library professional; 3 management professional; 2 technicians; 3 sales and marketing; 3 clerical and nonprofessional.

Description of System or Service: RWK LTD. provides international technical information obtained from online and other sources to Brazil government, industry, and military. The firm also offers consulting services.

Scope and/or Subject Matter: International technical information.

Input Sources: Input is derived from online data bases and other sources.

Holdings and Storage Media: Microfilm and microfiche files are maintained.

Computer-Based Products and Services: RWK Ltd. provides searches from data bases made available by U.S. online services.

Clientele/Availability: Services are available to Brazil government, industry, and military.

Contact: Raymond W. Kahl, Jr., President, RWK Ltd. (Telex 021 34657 RWKR.)

S

★860★
SABADELL COMPUTING CENTER
(Centro Calculo Sabadell - CCS)
Carretera Ripollet a Santiga
Km. 2'750, Barbera del Valles
Barcelona, Spain
J.A. Diaz, General Manager

Phone: 3 7181699
Founded: 1963

Staff: 5 Information and library professional; 20 management professional; 70 technicians; 40 sales and marketing; 30 clerical and nonprofessional; 45 other.

Related Organizations: The Computing Center is a subsidiary of Caixa d'Estalvis de Sabadell and CISI (Compagnie Internationale de Services en Informatique).

Description of System or Service: The SABADELL COMPUTING CENTER (CCS) offers a variety of data processing services, including time-sharing and remote batch applications as well as distribution of minicomputer systems for word processing and other functions. It also supplies consulting, training, and staff recruitment services.

Scope and/or Subject Matter: General computing services.

Computer-Based Products and Services: CCS time-sharing services include online access to management information systems and the CRONOS Data Bank holding European economic time series.

Clientele/Availability: Services are available without restrictions.

Contact: C. Alonso, Technical Director, Sabadell Computing Center. (Telex 53008.)

★861★
SAMSOM DATA SYSTEMS
SAMSOM DATANET
Postbus 180
Wilhelminalaan 1
NL-2400 AD Alphen aan den Rijn,
  Netherlands

Phone: 1720 66633
Service Est: 1981

Special Note: The SAMSOM DATANET online host service is reported to have ceased its activities as of June 1984. It previously provided online access to the Delft Hydro, LISA, MARNA, MATHFILE, Ship Abstracts, SHIPDES, TELECOM, and TROPAG data bases.

Contact: A.W. Kars, Samsom Data Systems. (Telex 39751.)

★862★
SASKATCHEWAN TELECOMMUNICATIONS (SASK TEL)
AGRITEX
2121 Saskatchewan Dr.
Regina, SK, Canada S4P 3Y2
Dennis Sabat, Section Manager - Business Development

Phone: (306) 347-2112
Service Est: 1983

Staff: 4 Management professional; 2 technicians; 3 sales and marketing; 4 clerical and nonprofessional.

Description of System or Service: AGRITEX is a videotex gateway service focused at meeting the information needs of the agribusiness and farming community in Saskatchewan. It provides a directory of information providers and data bases available through the system and acts as a switching center that transparently connects the user with the data base or service requested. AGRITEX currently provides access to four systems offering such information and services as farm market trends and prices, news, weather, commodities, classified advertisements, lifestyle information, electronic mail, and farm management programs. The system is accessible via telephone lines with NAPLPS terminals, standard data terminals, and personal computers. AGRITEX is based on Pathfinder, a videotex field trial operated by SASK TEL which ended in 1983. Pathfinder offered 12,000 pages of information and provided access to such services as Grassroots, a farm-related information service, and Cantel, a government information service.

Scope and/or Subject Matter: Gateway access to information and services of interest to the agriculture and agribusiness community.

Input Sources: Input for the systems accessible through AGRITEX is provided by government departments, farm equipment manufacturers, system users, and other information providers and advertisers.

Holdings and Storage Media: Machine-readable data bases are maintained on third party computers in ASCII or Telidon format.

Computer-Based Products and Services: Services offered through the AGRITEX transparent gateway are selected through a central directory which lists data bases by topic or subject and lists information providers by subjects offered. AGRITEX connects the user to the following remote systems: 1) Grassroots, a videotex system operated by the Manitoba Telephone System and Infomart, offers approximately 20,000 pages of information to the farming industry. 2) Agnet, operated by the Institute of Agriculture and Natural Resources at the University of Nebraska-Lincoln, provides programs for agricultural management, electronic conferencing, and other communications facilities. 3) An electronic mail facilities service. 4) A service providing farm accounting and management programs.

Clientele/Availability: Services are commercially available in Saskatchewan.

Contact: Dennis Sabat, Section Manager - Business Development, Agritex.

★863★
SAUR (K.G.) VERLAG
Possenbacherstr. 2b
D-8000 Munich 71, Fed. Rep. of
  Germany
Klaus G. Saur, Publisher

Phone: 089 798901
Founded: 1948

Staff: Approximately 110 total.

Description of System or Service: K.G. SAUR VERLAG publishes a variety of books in the areas of documentation and library science. Among its publications are computer-based directories of worldwide publishers, libraries, scientific and trade associations, and books in print. The firm offers custom mailing list services from its directories and is developing additional data base services.

Scope and/or Subject Matter: Reference works in such areas as library science, documentation, information science, and data processing.

Input Sources: Input is derived from questionnaire responses, periodicals, books, and other sources.

Holdings and Storage Media: The following data bases are maintained in machine-readable form: International Books in Print (IBIP); Publishers' International Directory; World Guide to Libraries; World Guide to Scientific Associations; and World Guide to Trade Associations.

Publications: Saur titles include the following: 1) International Books in Print: English Language Titles Published Outside the U.S.A. and the United Kingdom—lists more than 140,000 available titles in English from publishers in 95 countries. 2) German Books in Print—covers more than 307,000 titles from more than 3000 publishers. 3) Publishers' International Directory—provides name, address, telephone, and Telex information for 150,000 publishers worldwide. 4) World Guide to Libraries/ Internationales Bibliotheks-Handbuch—covers 42,200 libraries of all types in 167 countries. 5) World Guide to Scientific Associations/ Internationales Verzeichnis Wissenschaftlicher Verbande und Gesellschaften—covers more than 22,000 associations and societies in more than 130 countries. 6) World Guide to Trade Associations/ Internationales Verzeichnis der Wirtschaftsverbande—gives the names and addresses of more than 46,000 trade associations in all parts of the world. K.G. Saur also publishes library catalogs, bibliographies, and literature in the fields of librarianship, documentation, and information science.

Computer-Based Products and Services: K.G. SAUR VERLAG maintains several computer-readable directory files for publication purposes and to provide mailing list services. The firm plans to make select files commercially available online.

Clientele/Availability: Services are available without restrictions.

Remarks: K.G. Saur was formerly known as Verlag Dokumentation Saur KG.

Contact: Barbara Verrel, Head of Computer Projects, K.G. Saur Verlag.

★864★
SCANNET FOUNDATION
Halsingegatan 47
S-113 31 Stockholm, Sweden
Malin Edstrom, Coordinator
Phone: 08 305940
Founded: 1976

Related Organizations: Scannet was initiated by NORDFORSK (Scandinavian Council for Applied Research) and is now financed by NORDINFO (Nordic Council for Scientific Information and Research Libraries).

Description of System or Service: The SCANNET FOUNDATION facilitates and encourages more effective use of Nordic computerized information services and resources. It compiles and distributes information about Nordic data bases and their producers and provides assistance to users of information sources. The FOUNDATION aids data base producers in the design of data bases and assists host service organizations in marketing data bases and services, both within Nordic countries and externally. SCANNET also serves to coordinate the requests of users of information sources and act as an intermediary between the users and data base producers and host service organizations.

Scope and/or Subject Matter: Nordic computerized information services and resources.

Publications: Scannet Today (2-4 per year)—newsletter covering Nordic data bases and related topics; available without charge. Scannet also prepares data base user aids.

Clientele/Availability: Services are available without charge to users and providers of Nordic computerized information services.

Remarks: Scannet was originally established as a computer communication network, but the service was taken over by the Nordic PTTs.

Contact: Malin Edstrom, Coordinator, Scannet Foundation. (Telex 12563.)

★865★
SCHIMMELPFENG GMBH
Postfach 16720
Am Hauptbahnhof 6
D-6000 Frankfurt am Main 1, Fed. Rep.
of Germany
H.-K. Weckert, Co-Director
Phone: 069 26851

Staff: Approximately 1500 total.

Description of System or Service: SCHIMMELPFENG GMBH is a business information firm that compiles and disseminates credit information on West German and international companies. Utilizing an extensive data bank of more than 10 million records, the firm produces on-demand reports that serve as a source of information for new business contacts, products delivered, constant monitoring of customers and suppliers, and establishing credit limits. In addition to its standard report information, SCHIMMELPFENG offers expanded credit information reports and special report services dealing with mergers and acquisitions, joint ventures, and major credit approvals. For quick decision making, a priority service is offered, through which preliminary information is delivered via telex or telephone followed up by a written report. In addition to its credit report services, SCHIMMELPFENG offers general information brokerage services which are described in a separate entry following this one.

Scope and/or Subject Matter: Credit and business information on companies of all types in West Germany and 140 countries worldwide.

Input Sources: Information is gathered through a network of offices in West Germany and subsidiary offices in Austria, Belgium, Denmark, the Netherlands, and elsewhere.

Computer-Based Products and Services: (Details were not available.)

Clientele/Availability: Services are available without restrictions on a fee basis. Members of the Schimmelpfeng organization receive reduced rates.

Contact: Dr. Wolfgang Spannagel, Co-Director, Schimmelpfeng GmbH. (Telex 411 403.)

★866★
SCHIMMELPFENG GMBH
SCHIMMELPFENG INFORMATION BROKER SERVICE
(Schimmelpfeng Informationsbroker)
Postfach 16720
Am Hauptbahnhof 6
D-6000 Frankfurt am Main 1, Fed. Rep.
of Germany
Peter Cornelius, Information Broker
Phone: 069 2685314
Service Est: 1982

Staff: 2 Information and library professional; 1 management professional; 2 clerical and nonprofessional.

Description of System or Service: The SCHIMMELPFENG INFORMATION BROKER SERVICE provides information retrieval, current awareness, and document delivery services on a variety of topics using online and offline information sources in West Germany and overseas. The SERVICE also provides patent current awareness services and conducts research on trademarks, standards, import and export regulations, licensing regulations, and other areas. Additional services include market research tests and studies, and compilation of lists of commercial representatives and other firms.

Scope and/or Subject Matter: Information retrieval and current awareness services in the areas of science and technology, patents, trademarks, regulations, and other subject areas.

Input Sources: Input is derived from special library collections and online data bases.

Computer-Based Products and Services: SCHIMMELPFENG INFORMATION BROKER SERVICE conducts online searches of data bases made available through international online vendors.

Clientele/Availability: Services are available without restrictions on a fee basis.

Contact: Peter Cornelius, Information Broker, Schimmelpfeng Information Broker Service. (Telex 411 403.)

★867★
SCICON LTD.
Sanderson House
49 Berners St.
London W1P 4AQ, England
Phone: 01-580 5599
Founded: 1960

Special Note: The above name, address, and telephone number have been verified for this edition, although no questionnaire response was received. The following text is reprinted from the 5th edition.

Staff: 232 Total.

Related Organizations: Scicon Ltd. is a member of the British Petroleum Ltd. group of companies.

Description of System or Service: SCICON LTD. is a computer service bureau providing a broad spectrum of products and services to a wide variety of industries. Among its services are remote batch entry and time-sharing access to statistical, analysis, planning, and other applications packages, as well as to a range of data bases. In addition, Scicon develops data bases and software for third party usage. It has developed the Parliamentary On-Line Information System (POLIS) in conjunction with the Great Britain House of Commons Library (see separate entry).

Scope and/or Subject Matter: Computer services in mathematics, finance, business, structural and chemical engineering, transportation, information retrieval, and other areas.

Input Sources: Most products are developed by Scicon staff, although some software systems are obtained through license.

Computer-Based Products and Services: SCICON offers remote batch processing and interactive time-sharing services including access to the following data bases: Parliamentary On-Line Information System (POLIS), NPL/SGTE Databank, Heat Transfer & Fluid Flow Systems (HTFS), Bank of England Databank, CSO Macro-Economic Data Bank, and the U.K. Treasury Macroeconomic

Forecasting Model and Databank. Software available includes STATUS, UNIDAS, and numerous specialized programs. Software developed by Scicon are available for purchase worldwide.

Clientele/Availability: Products and services are offered to public and private organizations and companies.

Contact: Michael R. Bunbury, Scicon Ltd.

★868★
SCIENTIFIC DOCUMENTATION CENTRE LTD. (SDC)
Halbeath House Phone: 0383 23535
Dunfermline, Fife KY12 0TZ, Scotland Founded: 1963

Special Note: The above name, address, and telephone number have been verified for this edition, although no questionnaire response was received. The following text is reprinted from the 5th edition.

Staff: 20 Professional; 8 clerical and nonprofessional.

Description of System or Service: The SCIENTIFIC DOCUMENTATION CENTRE LTD. (SDC) supplies industry, universities, and government with current awareness and SDI services in more than 1400 subject areas from 17 disciplines. SDC also offers retrospective searches from its files, which cover worldwide literature sources. Output from both services is available on 3x5 file cards or on 80-column punched cards. A document delivery service for cited articles is also provided.

Scope and/or Subject Matter: Interdisciplinary coverage in science, technology, and biology.

Input Sources: SDC covers the following sources: 3250 journals; United States, United Kingdom, and South African government reports; books and monographs; theses from over 375 universities and colleges; current research and development in 150 United Kingdom universities and colleges; and a number of secondary sources.

Holdings and Storage Media: SDC maintains a file of about 2 million references dating back to 1968.

Publications: SDC Bulletin (occasional)—includes a series of classified bibliographies.

Services: In addition to the services described above, SDC also collects spectra and makes them available in microform, and it produces Euro Abstracts, Section 1 for the Commission of the European Communities.

Clientele/Availability: Services are available on a subscription or fee basis.

Contact: P.S. Davison, Scientific Documentation Centre Ltd.

★869★
SCOTLAND
NATIONAL LIBRARY OF SCOTLAND
SCOTTISH LIBRARIES CO-OPERATIVE AUTOMATION PROJECT (SCOLCAP)
George IV Bridge Phone: 031 2264531
Edinburgh EH1 1EW, Scotland Service Est: 1976
Bernard Gallivan, Director

Staff: 6 Information and library professional; 3 technicians; 6 clerical and nonprofessional.

Description of System or Service: The SCOTTISH LIBRARIES CO-OPERATIVE AUTOMATION PROJECT (SCOLCAP) consists of an online dedicated computer system in Scotland providing automated library management services to 21 Scottish and North East England public, university, college, special, and national libraries. Among the services supplied through SCOLCAP are online cataloging, acquisitions, information retrieval, management reports, interlibrary loans, and resource sharing. Cataloging output is available in a variety of forms, including COM microfiche, computer tape, catalog cards, and printed listings. Accessible via leased lines or dial-up access, SCOLCAP provides users with access to the SCOLCAP union catalog (SCOLCAT) data base; the system also contains a link to BLAISE (British Library Automated Information Service) so that searches can be automatically transferred if the record is not found in SCOLCAT.

Scope and/or Subject Matter: Library automation, machine-readable cataloging, information retrieval, and interlibrary cooperation.

Input Sources: Input is derived from UK MARC, LC MARC, and local records.

Holdings and Storage Media: The SCOLCAT data base comprises 900,000 records or 2.5 million entries.

Publications: SCOLCAP publishes an annual report and a systems specifications manual that is available for purchase.

Microform Products and Services: The SCOLCAT union catalog is available on 48x microfiche.

Computer-Based Products and Services: The SCOTTISH LIBRARIES CO-OPERATIVE AUTOMATION PROJECT provides online cataloging, acquisitions, information retrieval, and associated products and services, including an online messaging facility. Searches of the SCOLCAT union catalog data base can be made by ISBN, BNB or LC number, SCOLCAP number, author, title, corporate keyword, and other elements. The system is accessible via leased lines and the PSS public network and includes an automatic link to BLAISE (British Library Automated Information Service). Other third-party data bases can also be searched using the SCOLCAP terminal and information retrieval facility.

Clientele/Availability: The system serves primarily Scottish and Northern England libraries.

Contact: Bernard Gallivan, Director, Scottish Libraries Co-operative Automation Project. (Telex 72638 NLSEDI G.)

★870★
SERVI-TECH
BIODOC
Ave. de l'Automne 32 Phone: 02 3548249
B-1410 Waterloo, Belgium Service Est: 1976
C.A. Muylle, Managing Director

Staff: 1 Information and library professional; 1 management professional; 1 sales and marketing; 1 clerical and nonprofessional; 1 other.

Description of System or Service: BIODOC is a computer-readable data base of biographical information on more than 40,000 notable European personalities in all fields, ranging from politics and law to science and sports. Corresponding to the French-language publication Who's Who in Europe, BIODOC contains biographies on persons from 26 European countries. Each biography in the file includes (as available) personal name and address, occupation, date and place of birth, marriage, children, eminent ancestors, education, academic distinctions, career publications, important works, decorations, memberships and clubs, hobbies and interests, and business address and telephone. BIODOC is available online.

Scope and/or Subject Matter: Notable European personalities in a broad range of professions and activities including politics, law, humanities, sports, education, science, and others.

Input Sources: International dictionaries, encyclopedias, journals, media, and other sources serve as input.

Holdings and Storage Media: The data base holds information on 40,000 persons in machine-readable form and is updated three times per year.

Publications: Who's Who in Europe (every two years)—published in French; contains approximately 2600 pages.

Microform Products and Services: The complete Who's Who in Europe is available on microfiche, with an index located on each fiche.

Computer-Based Products and Services: The BIODOC data base is searchable online through G.CAM.

Clientele/Availability: Services are available without restrictions.

Projected Publications and Services: Planned publications include an English-language Who's Who in Europe, which will be available in hard copy, on microfiche, and as a machine-readable data base.

Contact: C.A. Muylle, Managing Director, Servi-Tech.

★871★
SHARP (I.P.) ASSOCIATES LIMITED
P.O. Box 418, Exchange Tower   Phone: (416) 364-5361
2 First Canadian Place, Suite 1900   Founded: 1964
Toronto, ON, Canada M5X 1E3
I.P. Sharp, President

Staff: 25 Data base professional; 100 management professional; 365 data processing professional; 60 clerical and nonprofessional.

Description of System or Service: A multinational company with more than 60 branches worldwide, I.P. SHARP ASSOCIATES LIMITED provides remote computing services, public data bases, software, and special systems services. The firm's time-sharing services are based on a computer facility reported to be the largest APL time-sharing operation in the world. SHARP ASSOCIATES also operates IPSANET, a private packet-switching network which interfaces with Telenet, Tymnet, Telepac, Datex-P, Datapac, PSS, and Transpac to provide local telephone access to the time-sharing service from more than 600 cities around the world. I.P. SHARP time-sharing clients have access to SHARP APL software and more than 100 data bases providing some 50 million time series of public data, including information related to economics, securities, banking, finance, energy, aviation, and insurance. Also accessible is an extensive library of applications software, including packages for data base management, project planning and control, financial planning and consolidation, electronic mail, forecasting, business graphics, time-series analysis and reporting, actuarial applications, econometric analysis, and survey analysis. As well as providing access to packaged application software, the firm develops customized software for its clients.

I.P. SHARP ASSOCIATES' Special Systems Division specifies and implements on-site computer systems for such applications as defense, air traffic control, nuclear reactor control, police information, stock exchange and brokerage, microfilm retrieval, and data communications. The Division also specializes in developing real-time and online systems for manufacturing, including facilities monitoring, process control, conveyor control, production and inventory planning and control, and business information systems. Additionally, I.P. SHARP offers the Global Information Centre, which utilizes SHARP's network services and software to create integrated computer technologies for mainframes and personal computers. Components of the Global Information Centre include worldwide communications capabilities; complete hardware integration; integrated end-user software products; and public data bases and related products. The client can acquire the entire system or select those components which complement the client's existing computer configuration.

Scope and/or Subject Matter: Public data bases providing a variety of time-series data for Canada, the United States, United Kingdom, Australia, Singapore, Germany, Europe, and internationally. Among the specific topics covered are economics, prices, economic forecasting, international trade, banking and finance, stocks and bonds, commodities, money market, corporations, petroleum and the energy industry, aviation, air transportation, insurance, population statistics, and others.

Input Sources: Time-sharing services are based on numeric data bases acquired from international sources.

Holdings and Storage Media: I.P. Sharp prepares more than one dozen machine-readable data bases and provides online access to more than 100 data bases.

Publications: 1) I.P. Sharp Newsletter—available by subscription. 2) Aviation Newsletter. 3) Energy Newsletter. 4) Financial and Economic Newsletter. 5) Promis Newsletter—provides news on data bases and online searching through SHARP APL. 6) Public Data Bases Catalogue. Various brochures, user guides, manuals, and technical documentation are also issued.

Computer-Based Products and Services: I.P. SHARP ASSOCIATES LIMITED offers its system software, SHARP APL, and applications programs which can be accessed via its time-sharing services or installed on a client's in-house computer. SHARP also offers data retrieval and business graphics software, including INFOMAGIC, a menu-driven system which provides access to standard preformatted reports while allowing the user to control timeframe and search criteria. For data manipulation and customized report uses, the user can retrieve and display data using the common command language MAGIC. Other software packages can be used in conjunction with MAGIC for sophisticated econometric analysis and forecasting applications. I.P. SHARP data retrieval software also allows users to access data from the public data bases and combine them with any other SHARP data base or with the user's own data.

I.P. SHARP ASSSOCIATES LIMITED provides online access to the following data bases: 1) ABSDATA (Australian Bureau of Statistics). 2) ACOMDAILY (Australian Commodities). 3) ACT (Actuarial Data Base). 4) AEA (Association of European Airlines). 5) AECC (Australian Export Statistics). 6) AES (Australian Economic Statistics). 7) AGDATA (Agricultural Commodities). 8) AGSM (Australian Graduate School of Management, Corporate Data). 9) AISL (Aircraft Accidents). 10) AMES (Australian Major Energy Statistics). 11) APIDIST (Monthly Report of Heating Oil and Middle Distillates). 12) ARATE (Australian Financial Markets). 13) ARGREP (Petroleum Argus Daily Market Report). 14) ARGUS (Petroleum Argus Prices). 15) ASE (Australian Stock Exchange Indices). 16) BIFORECAST (Business International Economic Forecasts). 17) BIHIST (Business International Historical Data). 18) BISQ (Bank for International Settlements, Quarterly). 19) BISS (Bank for International Settlements, Semi-Annual). 20) BUNDESBANK (Deutsche Bundesbank Data).

21) CANSIM (CANSIM Mini Base and Supplement). 22) CDNBOND (Canadian Bonds). 23) CDNOPT (Canadian Stock Options). 24) CDOIP (Canadian Department of Insurance Property and Casualty Insurance). 25) CENSUS81 (1981 Canadian Census). 26) CITIBASE (Citibank Economic Data). 27) CITIFORECAST (Citibank Economic Forecast). 28) COAND (Commuter Online Origin-Destination). 29) COMERT1 (Australian Financial Data Base). 30) COMERT2 (Australian Sector Cash Flow). 31) COMERT3 (Australian Funds Market). 32) COMMBOND (Commonwealth Bank Bond Index). 33) COPS (Canadian Operating Statistics). 34) CREW (Seismic Crew Count). 35) CURRENCY (Currency Exchange Rates). 36) DEWITT (DeWitt Petrochemical Newsletters). 37) DISCLOSURE (Disclosure II Corporate Information). 38) DOIDB (Canadian Department of Insurance). 39) DPFID (Duff and Phelps Fixed Income). 40) ELECTRIC (Electric Utilities Reports).

41) ER586 (ER586 Service Segment). 42) EXSTAT (EXSTAT Corporate Information). 43) FORM41 (Form 41). 44) FPCORP (Financial Post Canadian Corporate Data). 45) FPSTOCK (Financial Post Securities). 46) FRBW (Federal Reserve Board Weekly). 47) FTACT (Financial Times Actuaries Share Indices). 48) FTSTOCK (Financial Times Share Information). 49) FUNDMONITOR (Fund Monitor Unit Trusts and Insurance Bonds). 50) HEATW (Weekly Temperatures). 51) HKSTOCK (Hong Kong Stock Exchange). 52) HUGHES (Hughes Rotary Drilling Rig Report). 53) IATA (IATA North Atlantic Traffic). 54) ICAO (ICAO Traffic Statistics). 55) ICIS (Independent Chemical Information Services). 56) IFO (West German Economic Outlook Survey). 57) IFS (International Financial Statistics). 58) IMPORTS (United States Petroleum Imports). 59) INS (U.S. International Air Travel Statistics). 60) IPA (International Petroleum Annual).

61) JSCHEDULE (Canadian Chartered Banks Monthly Statement of Assets and Liabilities). 62) KENTV (Canadian Retail Gasoline Volume). 63) LPGAS (Liquified Petroleum Gas Report). 64) MBANK (Canadian Chartered Banks, Monthly). 65) MER (Monthly Energy Review). 66) MRATE (Money Market Rate). 67) NASTOCK (North American Stock Market). 68) NEELS (National Emergency Equipment Locator System). 69) NIF10 (National Income Forecasting Model of the Australian Economy). 70) NPADEMOG (National Planning Association Demographic Data). 71) NPAECO (National Planning Association Economic Data). 72) OAG (Official Airline Guide). 73) OAND (Origin-Destination). 74) OECD (Organisation for Economic Co-Operation and Development). 75) OEES (Australian Energy Consumption Statistics). 76) OEKON (Austrian Economic Outlook Poll). 77) OSCHEDULE (Canadian Chartered Banks Quarterly Income Statement). 78) PETROFLASH (Petroflash Crude and Produce Reports). 79) PIW (Petroleum Intelligence Weekly). 80) QOS (OECD Quarterly Oil Statistics).

81) QBANK (Canadian Chartered Banks, Quarterly). 82) RETAIL (Lundberg Survey Retail Price). 83) SEDS (State Energy Data System). 84) SINGCORP (Singapore Corporate Statistics). 85) SINGSTOCK

(Singapore Stock Exchange). 86) SITC (United Nations Commodity Trade Statistics). 87) SJRUNDS (S.J. Rundt World Risk Analysis Package). 88) SOM (Lundberg Survey Share of Market). 89) STATEX (Sydney Stock Exchange Statex Prices). 90) STATISBUND (West German Statistical Data). 91) SYDSTOCK (Sydney Stock Exchange Share Prices). 92) T6 (Air Charter). 93) T9S (Combined T9/Service Segment). 94) TSE300 (Toronto Stock Exchange 300 Index and Stock Statistics). 95) UKCSO (United Kingdom Central Statistical Office). 96) USBANKS (United States Banks). 97) USBOND (United States Bonds). 98) USCPI (United States Consumer Price Index). 99) USDOE (United States Department of Energy). 100) USFLOW (United States Flow of Funds, Quarterly).

101) USOPT (United States Stock Options). 102) USPPI (United States Producer Price Index). 103) USSTOCK (United States Stock Market). 104) WBANK (Bank of Canada Weekly Financial Statistics). 105) WDEBT (World Bank Debt Tables). 106) WHOLESALE (Lundberg Survey Retail Price). 107) WIIW (Eastern Bloc Countries Economic Data). 108) WSB (Weekly Statistical Bulletin). 109) YBANK (Canadian Chartered Banks, Yearly). 110) YSCHEDULE (Canadian Chartered Banks, Annual).

Clientele/Availability: Services are available without restrictions.

Contact: Rosanne Wild, Manager, Marketing Services, I.P. Sharp Associates Limited. (Telex 0622259 IP SHARP TOR.) The firm also maintains the following headquarters: 1) I.P. Sharp Associates, Inc., 1200 First Federal Plaza, Rochester, NY 14614; telephone (716) 546-7270. 2) I.P. Sharp Associates Limited, 132 Buckingham Palace Rd., London SW1W 9SA, England; telephone 01-730 4567. 3) I.P. Sharp Associates Pty. Ltd., 8th Floor, Carlton Centre, 55 Elizabeth St., Sydney, N.S.W. 2000, Australia; telephone 02 2326366. 4) I.P. Sharp Associates (S) Pte. Ltd., 77 Robinson Rd., No. 14-00, SIA Bldg., Republic of Singapore; telephone 2230211.

★872★
SHIP RESEARCH INSTITUTE OF NORWAY
(Norges Skipsforskningsinstitutt)
SHIP ABSTRACTS
P.O. Box 6099　　　　　　　　　　Phone: 02 689280
Etterstad　　　　　　　　　　　　Service Est: 1968
Oslo 6, Norway
Svein Lunde, Editor

Related Organizations: Ship Abstracts is a joint venture of several maritime institutes and associations. It is produced in conjunction with the Norwegian Center for Informatics.

Description of System or Service: SHIP ABSTRACTS is a maritime information service provided to shipowners, shipbuilders, consultants, subcontractors, and libraries worldwide. It prepares abstracts from the international literature on ship technology, ship operation, and ocean engineering, computer processes them, and makes the information available as an online data base through the Norwegian Center for Informatics, as a machine-readable tape service, and as a hardcopy publication.

Scope and/or Subject Matter: All facets of ship technology, ship operation, and ocean engineering including: management, maritime laws and regulations, structural design and construction, power plants, ventilation, navigation, marine safety, pollution control, soundproofing, surface treatment, and economics of operation.

Input Sources: Abstracts are derived from approximately 750 periodicals as well as report series, conference proceedings, and technical and economic papers from around the world.

Holdings and Storage Media: The machine-readable data base covers about 25,000 documents.

Publications: Ship Abstracts (10 per year)—about 3000 abstracts published each year. Issues contain abstracts with references to original documents, other bibliographic details, and subject, ship name, and author indexes; available by subscription. A maritime thesaurus containing more than 9000 keywords is also available.

Computer-Based Products and Services: The SHIP ABSTRACTS data base is available on monthly machine-readable tapes, or it can be searched online via the Norwegian Center for Informatics.

Other Services: Additional services include provision of copies of original documents.

Clientele/Availability: Primary clients are shipbuilders, shipowners, and ship contractors. Services are available on request.

Contact: Svein Lunde, Editor, Ship Abstracts.

★873★
SHIRLEY INSTITUTE
TEXTILE INFORMATION SERVICES
Didsbury　　　　　　　　　　　　Phone: 061 4458141
Manchester M20 8RX, England　　　Service Est: 1921
R.J.E. Cumberbirch, Head

Staff: 9 Information and library professional; 3 management professional; 5 technicians; 2 sales and marketing; 7 clerical and nonprofessional.

Related Organizations: The Shirley Institute (cotton, silk, and man-made fibers), the Hatra (hosiery and garment), and the Wira (wool and garment) research associations collaborate in the production of the Textile Information Services, which operates under the direction of Shirley Institute.

Description of System or Service: The TEXTILE INFORMATION SERVICES records, abstracts, and indexes world literature relevant to the science, technology, and technical management and economics of the textile and related industries, and to the application of fibrous materials in all industries and technologies. The SERVICES disseminates this information through print, microform, and computer-readable products. Its primary product is the hardcopy World Textile Abstracts (WTA) and the corresponding World Textiles Database available on machine-readable tape and online. The SERVICES also provides information retrieval, literature reviews, photocopying of original articles, and translation services. Additionally, information consultation is provided on the development, operation, and use of information services by client organizations.

Scope and/or Subject Matter: Synthesis, physics, and chemistry of fiber-forming polymers; science, technology, properties, products, and utilization of fibers, yarns, and fabrics; chemical and mechanical treatment of textiles; technical management and economics of production processes; production, consumption, and international trade; test methods, quality control, specifications, standards, and legislation; pollution, safety, and health hazards; utilization and performance of textiles in industrial, engineering, medical, and other applications.

Input Sources: Information is derived from approximately 600 periodicals; U.K., U.S., and European patents; U.K., U.S., and international standards; books; pamphlets; technical and conference reports; statistical publications; and other published literature.

Holdings and Storage Media: The computer-readable World Textiles Database contains 120,000 records dating from 1970 to the present; it is updated twice monthly. Library holdings consist of textile-relevant books, reports, periodicals, and other types of literature.

Publications: 1) World Textile Abstracts-WTA (twice monthly)—summarizes approximately 10,000 items of world literature annually. Annual computer-produced author, patent, and subject indexes are published in a separate volume. 2) World Textile Abstracts Printout Subject Indexes (monthly)—consists of reduced photocopy pages of computer printouts. 3) Textile Digest (monthly)—contains abstracts of world literature published in English and of interest to textile technologists and technical management. 4) Textiles (3 per year)—provides information in nontechnical language on the science and technology of textiles, their processing, products, and properties. 5) Register of Keyterms—provided free to data base subscribers; available for purchase to online searchers. 6) Online to Textile Literature—free user aid. 7) Summaries of Foreign-Language Articles-SOFA (irregular)—covers subject areas selected for their significant content of new technical or scientific information, including information presented in graphs, figures, tables, and diagrams. Shirley Institute also issues reports of Institute technical work, surveys, and papers given at Institute conferences, and collaborates with Elsevier International Bulletins in the publication of two special monthly bulletins: High-Performance Textiles and Medical Textiles.

Microform Products and Services: World Textile Abstracts and annual volumes of the publication since 1970 are available on 16mm microfilm.

Computer-Based Products and Services: The World Textiles Database is available on machine-readable tapes issued twice monthly by Shirley Institute and is accessible online via DIALOG Information Services, Inc. and Pergamon InfoLine Ltd. Searchable elements include document reference number, title, language of original, author name, publication reference and number of references cited, type of item, author affiliation, and keyterms. Abstracts are included in the Database from January 1983 to the present.

Other Services: Additional services include market surveys, evaluation of statistical information, and information and technical consulting.

Clientele/Availability: Clients include retailers, processors, producers, and buyers of fibers and textiles; management and technical staff in the textile and related industries; educators and students; and scientists and technologists worldwide.

Contact: R.J.E. Cumberbirch, Head, Textile Information Services. (Telex 668417 SHIRLY G.)

★874★
SIEMENS AG
DATA PROCESSING DIVISION
(Bereich Datenverarbeitung)
GOLEM
Otto-Hahn-Ring 6   Phone: 089 63646184
D-8000 Munich 83, Fed. Rep. of
    Germany

Description of System or Service: GOLEM is an information retrieval and data base management software system. Using Boolean operators, it develops search questions in an easy-to-use dialogue via a video display terminal and allows parallel access by several users. Data can be modified online, and the data base can be expanded any time without the user having to conduct reorganization runs. GOLEM can be used in conjunction with Siemens' PASSAT, a system for editing documents and analyzing the contents of texts. PASSAT permits the automatic selection of search words from texts by selecting characteristic keywords with the aid of a comparative thesaurus. The keywords serve as descriptors in online searching with GOLEM.

Scope and/or Subject Matter: Computer-based information retrieval and text editing and analysis.

Publications: Various user manuals and descriptive brochures are issued.

Computer-Based Products and Services: The GOLEM information retrieval and PASSAT software products are commercially available from Siemens AG. GOLEM is used at more than 100 general purpose computer installations in Europe.

Clientele/Availability: Products and services are available without restrictions.

Contact: Klaus Kotzias, Data Processing Division, Siemens AG.

★875★
SIEMENS AG
DATA PROCESSING DIVISION
(Bereich Datenverarbeitung)
LIBRARY NETWORK SYSTEM
(Bibliothek-Verbund-System - BVS)
Otto-Hahn-Ring 6   Phone: 089 6362763
D-8000 Munich 83, Fed. Rep. of
    Germany

Description of System or Service: The LIBRARY NETWORK SYSTEM (BVS) is a multi-user software system consisting of the BVS-D data management component and the BVS-R retrieval component. Used in conjunction, the two components support generalized online data capture and modification for both structured and unstructured user data with a facility to fulfill requests for information retrieval. BVS can be used in situations requiring a considerable amount of data to be captured, modified, and administered; once stored, information may be quickly and easily accessed. The system can be adapted to any application without the necessity of making program modifications. Specialized local demands can be met by defining the user's own internal format and screen masks and by connecting additional routines via standardized user interfaces. The applications of BVS may expand as user requests increase through the addition and extension of user routines without the modification of the system nucleus.

Scope and/or Subject Matter: Data management and retrieval; library automation; network management.

Input Sources: Data are input into the system by libraries and network members.

Publications: Various user manuals are available.

Computer-Based Products and Services: LIBRARY NETWORK SYSTEM (BVS) data management and information retrieval software is commercially available from Siemens AG.

Clientele/Availability: BVS is used by libraries, information centers, and others.

Contact: Klaus Kotzias, Data Processing Division, Siemens AG.

★876★
SIEMENS AG
LANGUAGE SERVICES DEPARTMENT
TERMINOLOGY EVALUATION AND ACQUISITION METHOD
(Terminologie-Erfassungs- und Auswertungs- Methode/TEAM)
Hofmannstr. 51   Phone: 089 72241373
D-8000 Munich 70, Fed. Rep. of
    Germany   Service Est: 1968
Dr. Thomas Schneider, Manager, Terminology & Linguistics
Staff: 14 Total.

Related Organizations: Cooperating partners include several international and national agencies as well as private commercial concerns.

Description of System or Service: The TERMINOLOGY EVALUATION AND ACQUISITION METHOD (TEAM) is a computerized system used for providing terminology support to the Siemens AG translation service and to cooperating organizations. TEAM consists of software programs and a multilingual technical data base used for machine-aided translation of German, English, French, Spanish, Russian, Italian, Portuguese, Dutch, and Arabic. It is also used for computerized typesetting of dictionaries, glossaries, indexes, and other texts, and for language courses.

Scope and/or Subject Matter: Technical terminology from various fields with particular emphasis on electrical and electronics engineering, telecommunications, and data processing.

Input Sources: Input is derived from technical literature, Siemens and foreign research and development reports, terminological information from national and international standards organizations, data banks, and machine-readable tapes from cooperating organizations.

Holdings and Storage Media: The TEAM data base holds approximately 2 million records comprising multilingual entries with supplementary information.

Microform Products and Services: Output from TEAM is available on standard A6 size microfiche with 42x reduction.

Computer-Based Products and Services: TEAM is available to cooperating organizations through batch-mode services and on magnetic tapes. Online retrieval is performed in-house, with dissemination via videotex planned for the future. Entries can be retrieved through direct interrogation for a single word or multiword technical term, source or target language, or compound entries. Output depends on the end use of the information; examples include a list of responses to a keyword query or edited material for the production of foreign-language product documentation. In addition to supporting dictionary products, TEAM software can be used to maintain, update, and typeset telephone books, city directories, catalogs, indexes, and similar works.

Clientele/Availability: Services are available to cooperating organizations, and to others by special arrangement.

Contact: Dr. Thomas Schneider, Manager, Terminology & Linguistics.

(Telex 2102.)

★877★
SINGAPORE INSTITUTE OF STANDARDS AND INDUSTRIAL RESEARCH
INDUSTRIAL TECHNICAL INFORMATION SERVICE (ITIS)
P.O. Box 2611
179 River Valley Rd.
Singapore 0617, Republic of Singapore
Mrs. Tan Kim Swee, Head
Phone: 3360933
Service Est: 1972

Staff: 2 Information and library professional; 1 management professional; 5 clerical and nonprofessional; 1 other.

Related Organizations: The Industrial Technical Information Service is a participating member of TECHNONET Asia.

Description of System or Service: The INDUSTRIAL TECHNICAL INFORMATION SERVICE (ITIS) provides industrial and technical information to industrialists, manufacturers, engineers, and professionals in Singapore. On an annual subscription basis, it offers an information package consisting of current awareness services from an internally compiled data base covering the world's technical periodical literature, together with document delivery, inquiry answering, literature searching, and library services. ITIS also provides online searching of publicly available data bases and issues a newsletter.

Scope and/or Subject Matter: Technical information in the following areas: electrical, mechanical, and industrial engineering; chemical products; food and beverages; building and construction industry; wood processing and furniture industry; metal processing; shipbuilding; plastics industry; and packaging.

Input Sources: Approximately 500 scientific and technical periodicals are scanned for articles to be coded for the machine-readable ITIS data base.

Holdings and Storage Media: In addition to computer files, holdings include a collection of the world's national and international standards; microform collections of technical briefs and patent information; and subscriptions to 350 periodicals.

Publications: Technocom (quarterly)—newsletter.

Computer-Based Products and Services: ITIS offers the Computerized Current Awareness Service, a monthly SDI service based on articles selected from more than 500 journals; this file is also available for individual searches. ITIS also conducts online literature searches from data bases made available through DIALOG Information Services, Inc., System Development Corporation (SDC), and Pergamon InfoLine Ltd.

Other Services: Technical surveys and studies are also offered.

Clientele/Availability: Services are primarily intended for the use of industry in Singapore, but are extended to other countries in the region.

Contact: Mrs. Tan Kim Swee, Head, Industrial Technical Information Service.

★878★
SLAMARK INTERNATIONAL
Via Ignazio Guido, 4
I-00147 Rome, Italy
Phone: 06 5140176 476
Founded: 1971

Special Note: The above name, address, and telephone number have been verified for this edition, although no questionnaire response was received. The following text is reprinted from the 5th edition.

Staff: 2 Information and library professional; 2 management professional; 15 technicians; 11 clerical and nonprofessional.

Description of System or Service: SLAMARK INTERNATIONAL produces the computer-readable Statistical Information System (SISDATA), PRICEDATA, and ENERDATA data bases. SISDATA is a series of socioeconomic data banks covering Italy. Accessible in a time-sharing environment, SISDATA permits data manipulation and retrieval in support of market research, resource and investment planning, econometric modeling, and similar applications. PRICEDATA, also known as the Raw Materials Price Index (RAMPI), provides information on international raw material prices on more than 60 products as well as quotations for the main currencies used in international trading. ENERDATA covers Italian energy consumption since 1973. In addition to producing these data bases, SLAMARK INTERNATIONAL provides clients with computer search services from data bases made available by commercial vendors.

Scope and/or Subject Matter: Socioeconomic factors of Italy, including geographical area, climate, population, construction and public works, health and social security, agriculture, industry, transport, communications, foreign and internal trade, wholesale prices, labor, and consumption; Italian energy consumption; prices of raw materials.

Input Sources: Input is derived from the Italian central statistical office, industrial and trade associations, chambers of commerce, and other government and nongovernment sources.

Holdings and Storage Media: Updated quarterly, SISDATA data banks hold approximately 3 million items dating from 1971 to the present. PRICEDATA contains time series and currency exchange data from 1973 to date; ENERDATA is updated semiannually and contains approximately 10,000 series from 1973 to date. A library consisting of 2500 bound volumes and subscriptions to 50 periodicals is also maintained.

Computer-Based Products and Services: SISDATA is accessible through ADP Network Services for data retrieval and manipulations such as comparison of statistics in time and space and across sectors. Output is in tabular and serial forms with full descriptions in English and the language of the country surveyed. An automated bilingual vocabulary aids in searching. PRICEDATA is available online through ESA/IRS; ENERDATA, containing consumption data available by source, product, and end-use categories for coal, methane gas, petroleum, hydroelectricity, geothermal electricity, nuclear electricity, urban waste, and wood, will be made accessible online in the near future. SLAMARK also offers computerized retrieval services and SDI using data bases made available through DIALOG Information Services, Inc., System Development Corporation (SDC), and Euronet DIANE. Additionally, SLAMARK designs software and special data bases for clients.

Other Services: In addition to the services described above, SLAMARK offers consulting, research, data collection and analysis, and manual literature searching.

Clientele/Availability: Services are available without restrictions.

Contact: Information Manager, SLAMARK International.

★879★
SLIGOS
91, rue Jean-Jaures
F-92807 Puteaux Cedex, France
Phone: 01 7764242

Description of System or Service: SLIGOS is an online service providing clients with interactive access to nonbibliographic data bases in the areas of finance, economics, and industry. A major feature of SLIGOS is its software systems which enable the user to retrieve and display desired data in graph form.

Scope and/or Subject Matter: French economics, finance, companies, industry, marketing, and other topics.

Input Sources: Data bases are acquired from commercial organizations or produced by SLIGOS.

Holdings and Storage Media: About a dozen major files of numeric data are held online.

Computer-Based Products and Services: SLIGOS currently provides online access to the following: 1) AXESS is a data base service which provides access to several files—KOMPASS, DAFSA, and FITEK—containing information on French companies and their products and French financial institutions. AXESS is produced by DAFSA-SNEI. 2) The MEDIAL data base contains current and historical real-time data on advertising activity and is prepared by SECODIP. 3) The MERCATIS data base provides access to real-time data dealing with French commerce and markets. MERCATIS is coproduced by SEDES and SLIGOS. 4) The NAPLES data base service provides access to business and economic information and allows special manipulation of the data. NAPLES is produced by SLIGOS. 5) SELECVAL is a real-time financial data analysis service comprising several financial data files and a full range of flexible software packages for data manipulation. SELECVAL is coproduced by SLIGOS and DAFSA. 6) The Value Line data base contains financial information and stock prices. It is used in conjunction with various software packages which allow the user to manipulate data as needed. Value Line is produced by Value Line, Inc.

Clientele/Availability: Services are available without restrictions. Primary clients include economists, financial analysts, and marketing specialists.

Contact: IAD Department, SLIGOS.

★880★
SOCIETY FOR INFORMATION AND DOCUMENTATION
(Gesellschaft fur Information und Dokumentation - GID)
GID INFORMATION CENTER FOR INFORMATION SCIENCE AND PRACTICE
(GID-Informationszentrum fur Informationswissenschaft und -Praxis - GID-IZ)
P.O. Box 710370
Lyoner Strasse 44-48
D-6000 Frankfurt am Main 71, Fed. Rep. of Germany
Dr. Peter Budinger, Head
Phone: 069 66871
Service Est: 1977

Staff: 13 Information and library professional; 1 management professional; 8 clerical and nonprofessional.

Related Organizations: GID receives funding from the Ministry for Research and Technology and federal and state governments.

Description of System or Service: The GID INFORMATION CENTER FOR INFORMATION SCIENCE AND PRACTICE (GID-IZ) is an information center combining the functions of a central information and documentation agency with those of a special library covering the subject areas of information science and information work. The CENTER provides GID sections with the information and literature needed to fulfill the GID's function of a central institution furthering research and development of specialized information and communication in the Federal Republic of Germany. GID-IZ offers the following specific services: 1) Referral services—provides general information on existing and planned specialized information services and agencies, and on national and international information networks. 2) Retrospective searches. 3) SDI—offers individual and standard SDI services in information science and related fields. 4) Online retrieval services—produces the computer-readable INFODATA data base on information science, which is publicly available online through the GID host computer. 5) Printed and microfiche information services—produces directories, bibliographies, catalogs, and other publications. 6) Library service—includes document delivery services for all literature cited in the INFODATA data base. The CENTER also serves as the national information transfer center for the UNESCO International Information System on Research in Information and Documentation (ISORID).

Scope and/or Subject Matter: Scientific and technical information and communication, including such related fields as computer science, reprography, linguistics, journalism, communications research, and technology.

Input Sources: Input is derived from books, reports, journals, serials, government publications, and standards.

Holdings and Storage Media: The computer-readable bibliographic INFODATA data base holds more than 21,000 records. Library holdings consist of 18,000 monographs, reports, and standards, and subscriptions to 360 periodicals.

Publications: GID-IZ produces the following German-language publications: 1) Verzeichnis Deutscher Informations- und Dokumentationsstellen, Bundesrepublik Deutschland und Berlin (West)/ Directory of Specialized Information Centers and Agencies in the Federal Republic of Germany and West Berlin (every three years); 2) Forschungs- und Entwicklungsprojekte in Informationswissenschaft und -Praxis/ Research and Development Projects in the Areas of Information Science and Practice (annual); 3) Internationale IuD-Gremien mit Beteiligung aus der Bundesrepublik Deutschland und Berlin (West)/ International I&D Committees with Memberships from the Federal Republic of Germany and West Berlin; 4) Verzeichnis Informationswissenschaftlicher Zeitschriften/ List of Information Science Journals (every two years)—covers information science journals held by GID-IZ; 5) Bestandsverzeichnis Thesauri/ List of Thesauri (annual)—covers thesauri held by GID-IZ; 6) IuD-Termine/ Calendar of I&D Activities. For publication in Nachrichten fur Dokumentation (which is issued by the German Association for Documentation), GID-IZ provides the following information: recent German and foreign literature in the areas of information science and practice, German research and development projects, a calendar of international I&D activities, and current contents of selected I&D journals.

Microform Products and Services: The Center produces a bibliography of project reports published by the German Ministry for Research and Technology and a selection from the GID-IZ catalog on microfiche.

Computer-Based Products and Services: The INFODATA data base on information science literature is searchable online through the GID host service. The data base is also used by GID-IZ to provide search and SDI services. It has the following subsets: Thesauri and Classification, Education in I&D, Methods and Models in Information Science, and Infometrics.

Clientele/Availability: Products and services are available without restrictions for a small charge.

Contact: Dr. Peter Budinger, Head, Society for Information and Documentation. (Telex 4 14 351.) In the United States, contact Dr. Wolfgang H. Ettel, Head, Washington Office of GID, 1990 M St., N.W., Suite 680, Washington, DC 20036; telephone (202) 466-2808. (Telex 904064.)

★881★
SOCIETY FOR THE STUDY OF ECONOMIC AND SOCIAL DEVELOPMENT
(Societe d'Etudes pour le Developpement Economique et Social - SEDES)
MERCATIS
15, rue Bleue
F-75009 Paris, France
Gerard Cancelier, Research Director
Phone: 01 7706161
Founded: 1983

Staff: 2 Information and library professional; 1 management professional; 3 technicians; 1 sales and marketing.

Related Organizations: MERCATIS is coproduced by the Society for the Study of Economic and Social Development and SLIGOS.

Description of System or Service: MERCATIS is an online data base which contains numeric data on domestic retail markets and trade in France. It is interactively accessible through SEDES and commercial online services.

Scope and/or Subject Matter: French domestic retail markets and trade, including related economic and demographic information.

Input Sources: Data for MERCATIS are obtained from the French Institut National de la Statistique et des Etudes Economiques (INSEE), from market research companies, and from economic survey organizations.

Holdings and Storage Media: MERCATIS data are held in machine-readable form.

Publications: A newsletter is produced.

Computer-Based Products and Services: MERCATIS is accessible online by remote terminal access through SEDES and through commercial services via the Transpac, Euronet, and Tymnet networks.

Other Services: Technical assistance is available to subscribers.

Clientele/Availability: MERCATIS is intended for use by marketing specialists, economists, manufacturers, and government agencies.

Projected Publications and Services: Videotex capabilities are expected to be added to MERCATIS in the near future.

Contact: Bernard de la Bruslerie, Sales Executive, MERCATIS.

★882★
SOCIETY OF METAPHYSICIANS LTD.
INFORMATION SERVICES
Archers' Court
Stonestile Lane, The Ridge
Hastings, Sussex TN35 4PG, England
Dr. John J. Williamson, President
Phone: 0424 751577
Service Est: 1944

Staff: 1 Information and library professional; 3 management professional; 2 technicians; 2 sales and marketing; 2 clerical and nonprofessional.

Description of System or Service: The INFORMATION SERVICES provides abstracts services in the areas of neometaphysics and maintains continuously updated machine-readable files on individuals, organizations, and bibliographical and research contacts. The SERVICES provides computer-based services that include SDI and computer tape distribution.

Scope and/or Subject Matter: Neometaphysics, paraphysics, parapsychology, business systems, human aura, radiation studies in terms of energic-mechanism of living and inorganic subjects, biofeedback, UV emanation and modulation analyses, electro-imaging systems, and others.

Holdings and Storage Media: Files are held in machine-readable form and generally date back to 1944 on an international basis.

Publications: Neometaphysical Digest (quarterly)—available free to Society members and for purchase to nonmembers. Various other publications are also issued.

Computer-Based Products and Services: Machine-readable files held by the Information Services include a continuously updated list of 60,000 persons with a breakdown of qualifications and activities; and a catalog of books with their availability, subject analyses, publishers, authors, and other bibliographical information. The Services offers tape and disk distribution, SDI, and software services.

Clientele/Availability: Services are intended for members of the Society.

Contact: Dr. John J. Williamson, President, Society of Metaphysicians Ltd.

★883★
SOCIOSCOPE INC.
529 Clarence St.
Ottawa, ON, Canada K1N 5S4
Michael Gurstein, President
Phone: (613) 235-7120
Founded: 1980

Staff: 4 Technicians.

Description of System or Service: SOCIOSCOPE INC. provides consulting and research services on the human aspects of such advanced technologies as microelectronics, office automation, videotex, electronic funds transfer, and others. Examples of recent projects include the development of a methodology for the evaluation of the social impact of the Telidon videotex/ teletext system and an analysis of the potential for Canadian involvement in the videodisk industry. SOCIOSCOPE also issues reports, bibliographies, and other publications and conducts systems evaluations and workshops.

Scope and/or Subject Matter: Implications and applications of advanced technologies, including human factors, consumer and social impacts, markets, industrial opportunities, training, and systems analysis.

Input Sources: Through in-house staff and associates, the firm has resources in a wide range of related fields, including economics, computer science, and psychology.

Holdings and Storage Media: Socioscope maintains a library of 200 bound volumes, 2000 other items, and subscriptions to 20 periodicals.

Publications: 1) Telidon and Its Implications. 2) Videotex: A Working Paper on the Study of Social Impact. 3) Electronic Funds Transfer: A Comprehensive Bibliography. Other publications are also issued.

Clientele/Availability: Services are available to clients in the public and private sectors on a fee basis.

Contact: Michael Gurstein, President, Socioscope Inc.

★884★
SONOPTIC COMMUNICATIONS INC.
44 Bayswater Ave., Suite 100
Ottawa, ON, Canada K1Y 4K3
Robert Leitch, President
Phone: (613) 725-0332
Founded: 1983

Staff: 3 Management professional; 1 sales and marketing; 1 clerical and nonprofessional.

Related Organizations: Sonoptic Communications Inc. is a division of Sonoptic Media & Communications Corporation.

Description of System or Service: SONOPTIC COMMUNICATIONS INC. offers a range of consulting and project management services to firms involved in producing, managing, or disseminating information. The firm has expertise in print and electronic publishing, audiovisual and education media, office automation, and corporate communications. It has been involved in the development of more than 30 videotex operations and assists with teletext service development.

Scope and/or Subject Matter: Consulting in the areas of information dissemination and technology.

Computer-Based Products and Services: The firm provides project management and consulting services for videotex and other electronic information systems.

Clientele/Availability: Services are available without restrictions. Clients include government agencies and corporations.

Contact: David Shaw, Managing Director, Sonoptic Communications Inc.

★885★
SOUTH AFRICA
COUNCIL FOR SCIENTIFIC AND INDUSTRIAL RESEARCH (CSIR)
CENTRE FOR SCIENTIFIC AND TECHNICAL INFORMATION (CSTI)
P.O. Box 395
Pretoria 0001, South Africa
Dr. Rob van Houten, Chief Director
Phone: 012 869211
Service Est: 1946

Staff: 63 Information and library professional; 8 management professional; 14 technicians; 2 sales and marketing; 61 clerical and nonprofessional; 23 other.

Description of System or Service: The CENTRE FOR SCIENTIFIC AND TECHNICAL INFORMATION (CSTI) has the following objectives: to provide information and library services, both within the CSIR and at the national level to industry; to undertake applied research in the field of information and library science; to provide training courses to information staff in industry; to assist with the establishment of national and international information and library networks; and to provide liaison between industry and the CSIR in order to promote the use of CSIR services and facilities by industry. Among the specific services provided by the CENTRE are the following: 1) National scientific and technological library service. CSTI maintains the largest specialized techno-scientific library in South Africa. Its services include micrographic reproduction, photocopying, and interlibrary loans. The library is active in international cooperative organizations and such national projects as the production of the computer-based Periodicals in Southern African Libraries (PISAL) union list. 2) Technical Information Service acts as a liaison between industry and CSIR and offers a current awareness service in the field of industrial engineering. 3) Computerized Information Services provides information retrieval and SDI services from European and North American online services and from magnetic tape copies of commercially available data bases held in-house. 4) Document Delivery Service provides copies of documents from local and foreign collections. 5) Foreign Language Service provides translations of scientific and technical texts. 6) Documentation Support Service is responsible for courses and training in information, including those of particular interest to industry, and also coordinates CSTI's research program. 7) South African Water Information Centre (see separate entry). CSTI also carries out research and development work in communications sciences related to science and technology information transfer, and it is involved in the development and application of techniques for the storage, retrieval, and dissemination of information.

Scope and/or Subject Matter: Physical sciences and engineering including physics, chemistry, chemical engineering, water research, food research, mechanical engineering, electrical engineering, roads and transportation, building research, timber research, telecommunications, wool and textiles, oceanology, astronomy, computing sciences, and personnel research; library and information science.

Input Sources: Input is obtained from primary and secondary literature, proceedings, and reports. Computerized search services use locally developed and commercially available data bases.

Holdings and Storage Media: Library holdings include approximately 150,000 bound volumes; 24,000 pamphlets; and subscriptions to 7000 periodicals. Items cataloged since 1982 are recorded in machine-readable form. CSTI also holds copies of these machine-readable data bases: South African Water Information Centre's WATERLIT file; Biological Abstracts since 1974; Chemical Abstracts since 1974; COMPENDEX since 1975; INSPEC since 1975; Government Reports Announcements; METADEX; PsycINFO since 1975; and Science Citation Index since 1973.

Publications: 1) TI-Technical Information for Industry (irregular)—features processes, equipment, and services developed by the CSIR which have industrial applications; available free in English and Afrikaans versions. 2) Review List (weekly)—current awareness service containing the titles of articles concerned with production technology; also contains short annotations and bibliographic details of indexed publications. 3) CAS Industrial Engineering Index (annual)—includes articles which appeared in the Review Lists and other articles which were selected but not included. It consists of 3 sections: a list of articles with full bibliographic details in numerical order; a list of articles in terms of their subject classification; and a listing by keywords. 4) Manufacturing Technology Reviews-MTR (weekly)—current awareness bulletin covering periodical articles on all aspects of manufacturing technology. 5) CSIR Publications (quarterly)—computer-produced list includes Foreign Language Service translations; contains KWIC and author indexes; available free of charge.

Microform Products and Services: The library catalog and the PISAL union list are available on COM microfiche. Micrographic reproduction services are also available.

Computer-Based Products and Services: CSTI provides these computer-based services: 1) South African Retrospective Information System (SARIS)—retrospective online search service using data bases made available through international online systems. 2) South African Selective Dissemination of Information (SASDI)—computerized SDI services utilizing WATERLIT and commercial data bases held in-house. Search profiles may be standard or customized. 3) PISAL—online file containing information on approximately 60,000 titles held in 360 libraries. 4) SCIDOC—computerized indexing and retrieval system used for special document collections available in the CSIR. 5) A computerized cataloging system used for maintaining records of the CSIR's book and journal collections and for producing a COM microfiche catalog.

Other Services: Additional CSTI services are inquiry answering, provision of technical digests of information on fields of general industrial interest, consulting, research, manual literature searching, referrals, document delivery, copying, and interlibrary loans.

Clientele/Availability: Services are provided for the South African industrial and scientific communities.

Remarks: CSTI is also known by its Afrikaans name: Sentrum vir Wetenskaplike en Tegniese Inligting; the CSIR is also known as the Wetenskaplike en Nywerheidnavorsingsraad (WNNR).

Contact: Dr. Rob van Houten, Chief Director, Centre for Scientific and Technical Information. (Telex 32087 SA.)

★886★
SOUTH AFRICA
NUCLEAR DEVELOPMENT CORPORATION OF SOUTH AFRICA (NUCOR)
NUCOR LIBRARY AND INFORMATION SERVICES
Private Mail Bag X256 Phone: 012 213311
Pretoria 0001, South Africa Service Est: 1957
S.P. Korkie, Head

Staff: 23 Information and library professional; 1 management professional; 15 clerical and nonprofessional.

Description of System or Service: The NUCOR LIBRARY AND INFORMATION SERVICES acts as the national center for information on nuclear science and technology. As such, the SERVICES provides bibliographic support to persons active in the field in South Africa through the development and maintenance of a specialized library collection, reference and interlibrary loan services, current awareness and SDI services, and computerized literature. In addition, it participates in the International Nuclear Information System (INIS) through its contribution of bibliographic information and indexing for all nuclear science literature published in South Africa.

Scope and/or Subject Matter: Nuclear-related physical sciences, chemistry, materials sciences, earth sciences, life sciences, isotopes, isotope and radiation applications, engineering and technology; other aspects of nuclear energy including economics, nuclear law, nuclear documentation, safeguards, waste disposal, and inspection.

Input Sources: Input is drawn from books, journals, research reports, conference proceedings, patents, standards, and INIS magnetic tapes.

Holdings and Storage Media: NUCOR Library and Information Services maintains the complete INIS machine-readable data files from 1970 to date. Library holdings include more than 600,000 books; 574,700 reports; 33,080 bound periodicals; and subscriptions to 1240 periodicals.

Computer-Based Products and Services: The Services conducts batch-mode retrospective searches and offers SDI services using the INIS data base tapes.

Other Services: In addition to the services described above, manual literature searching and referrals are provided.

Clientele/Availability: Services are available without restrictions to the South African nuclear community.

Remarks: NUCOR was formerly known as the Atomic Energy Board (AEB).

Contact: S.P. Korkie, Head, NUCOR Library and Information Services. (Telex 30253 SA.)

★887★
SOUTH AFRICA
SOUTH AFRICAN WATER INFORMATION CENTRE (SAWIC)
P.O. Box 395 Phone: 012 869211
Pretoria 0001, South Africa

Related Organizations: SAWIC is financed by the South Africa Water Research Commission and operated by the Centre for Scientific and Technical Information (CSTI).

Description of System or Service: The SOUTH AFRICAN WATER INFORMATION CENTRE (SAWIC) supplies information on water and related subjects, with emphasis on the research being conducted, periodical literature available, and the dissemination of information in southern Africa. In support of its activities, the CENTRE maintains the computer-readable WATERLIT data base providing abstracts and indexes of relevant national and international literature. WATERLIT is used to produce publications and to provide information retrieval and SDI services; the data base is also internationally accessible online through System Development Corporation (SDC).

Scope and/or Subject Matter: Water and water-related research, including such topics as hydrology, limnology, ecology, biology, chemistry, pollution, dams and aqueducts, desalination, and other topics.

Input Sources: Input for the WATERLIT data base is derived from periodicals, reports, conference proceedings, and other literature.

Holdings and Storage Media: The machine-readable WATERLIT file contains 52,000 items dating from 1976 to the present; it is updated monthly with approximately 12,000 items added each year.

Publications: 1) Selected Journals on Water-SJOW (monthly)—consists of reproductions of the table of contents pages of important international journals in the field received by SAWIC. 2) S.A. Waterabstracts—abstracting and indexing bulletin covering South African water literature; also known as South African Water Abstracts.

Computer-Based Products and Services: The SOUTH AFRICAN WATER INFORMATION CENTRE produces the WATERLIT data base and makes it publicly available online through SDC. Searchable record elements include title, author, organization, source publication, language, availability, document type, category code, and index terms. Computerized SDI services from the data base are offered by CSTI through its South African Selective Dissemination of Information (SASDI) system.

Clientele/Availability: Services are intended for the South African water resources community.

Contact: Head, South African Water Information Centre.

★888★
SOUTH AFRICAN MEDICAL RESEARCH COUNCIL
INSTITUTE FOR MEDICAL LITERATURE (IML)
P.O. Box 70
Tygerberg 7505, South Africa
Dr. Steve F. Rossouw, Director
Phone: 21 9312151
Service Est: 1976

Staff: 5 Information and library professional; 1 management professional; 1 technician; 5 clerical and nonprofessional; 4 other.

Description of System or Service: The INSTITUTE FOR MEDICAL LITERATURE (IML) provides computerized biomedical information services to the South African research community and to health professionals. It offers online access to MEDLINE and other international data bases in life sciences fields. Information retrieval services are backed up with document provision from local and international sources, a translation service, and training in online retrieval for postgraduate students.

Scope and/or Subject Matter: Medicine, biology, health care.

Publications: 1) MIDS Newsletter (irregular); 2) MRC Annual Report.

Computer-Based Products and Services: IML provides online access to the following data bases: MEDLINE, TOXLINE, BIOSIS, PsycINFO, CAB Abstracts, Excerpta Medica, and CANCERLINE. SDI services are also offered.

Other Services: IML also provides scientific and technical editing and publishing services to scientists of the Medical Research Council.

Clientele/Availability: Primary clients are medical researchers and health professionals. There are no restrictions on services.

Contact: Dr. Steve F. Rossouw, Director, Institute for Medical Literature. (Telex 57 20525 SA.)

★889★
SOUTHEAST ASIAN REGIONAL CENTER FOR GRADUATE STUDY
    AND RESEARCH IN AGRICULTURE (SEARCA)
AGRICULTURAL INFORMATION BANK FOR ASIA (AIBA)
College
Laguna 3720, Philippines
Josephine C. Sison, Project Manager
Phone: 6735007
Service Est: 1974

Staff: 3 Information and library professional; 1 management professional; 1 systems analyst; 2 technicians; 3 clerical and nonprofessional.

Related Organizations: The Agricultural Information Bank for Asia is a project of the Southeast Asian Regional Center for Graduate Study and Research in Agriculture (SEARCA), and is funded by SEARCA and the International Development Research Centre (IDRC) in Canada.

Description of System or Service: The AGRICULTURAL INFORMATION BANK FOR ASIA (AIBA) is a multinational network that provides agricultural information services in Southeast Asia, and serves as the regional input center for the United Nations Food and Agriculture Organization (FAO) International Information System for the Agricultural Sciences and Technology (AGRIS) and the Current Agricultural Research Information System (CARIS). Under the network, agricultural literature is collected by AIBA national centers in the countries of Bangladesh, Hong Kong, Indonesia, Malaysia, Singapore, Thailand, Republic of Korea, and the Philippines. It is sent to AIBA where it is analyzed, edited, structured according to international standards, and forwarded to the worldwide AGRIS and CARIS systems in Rome. AIBA also uses the collected information to produce AGRIASIA, a regional bibliography that is available as a computer-readable data base, on microfiche, and as a hardcopy publication. AGRIASIA is also used to produce the Winged Bean Data Base, which contains research information on the legume, and a corresponding printed bibliography as well as national agricultural bibliographies, specialized bibliographies, and other reference tools. In addition, AIBA provides SDI services, document delivery using its regional microfiche file, and computerized literature searching.

Scope and/or Subject Matter: Agriculture, agricultural education, extension and advisory work, economic development, rural sociology, plant production, plant protection, forestry, animal production, aquatic sciences, fisheries, agricultural engineering, food science, natural resources, home economics, pollution, soil science, veterinary science, human nutrition, and related areas of mathematics, statistics, documentation, and information science applicable within this scope.

Input Sources: Eight national centers provide AIBA with agricultural literature including monographs, serial articles, technical reports, patents, standards, dissertations and theses, maps and atlases, and conference, seminar, and workshop papers. Since 1975, AIBA has submitted 35,000 citations from these sources to the international AGRIS system.

Holdings and Storage Media: Magnetic tapes of the AGRIS data base dating from 1975 to the present, the AGRIASIA data base dating from 1977 to the present, and the Winged Bean Data Base and regional CARIS data base dating from 1982 are held.

Publications: 1) AGRIASIA (quarterly)—current bibliography of agricultural literature including extension materials not eligible for AGRIS; each issue contains about 2000 entries and includes keyword, scientific names, author, and geographical indexes plus a list of local terms and abbreviations. 2) Winged Bean Bibliography—an annotated bibliography whose main emphasis is on winged bean production. 3) Winged Bean Flyer (biannual)—newsletter. 4) Linkedit (occasional)—newsletter facilitating the exchange of current AGRIS and AIBA information. A number of materials and specialized bibliographies are also published.

Microform Products and Services: A regional microfiche file of documents cited in AGRIASIA and the Winged Bean Bibliography supports AIBA's document delivery services.

Computer-Based Products and Services: AIBA maintains the AGRIASIA data base which is used to supply input to AGRIS, CARIS, and the Winged Bean Data Base and to provide hardcopy bibliographies, a directory of ongoing agricultural research, and a variety of other publications. AIBA also offers computerized literature searching and SDI services to the region using the AGRIS, AGRIASIA, and Winged Bean data bases.

Other Services: In addition to the above services, manual literature searching, abstracting and indexing, data collection and analysis, and referral services are provided.

Clientele/Availability: Services are intended for agricultural scientists, professors, policymakers, and students.

Remarks: The Agricultural Information Society for Asia, composed of information specialists, documentalists, and librarians, was founded by AIBA.

Contact: Josephine C. Sison, Project Manager, Agricultural Information Bank for Asia. (Telex ITT 40904 SEARCA PM.)

★890★
SPAIN
HIGHER COUNCIL FOR SCIENTIFIC RESEARCH
(Consejo Superior de Investigaciones Cientificas - CSIC)
INSTITUTE FOR INFORMATION AND DOCUMENTATION IN SCIENCE AND TECHNOLOGY
(Instituto de Informacion y Documentacion en Ciencia y Tecnologia - ICYT)
Joaquin Costa, 22
Madrid 6, Spain
Rosa de la Viesca, Director
Phone: 91 2614808
Service Est: 1972

Staff: Approximately 100 total.

Description of System or Service: The INSTITUTE FOR INFORMATION AND DOCUMENTATION IN SCIENCE AND TECHNOLOGY (ICYT) maintains the ICYT Data Bank containing bibliographic references to Spanish-language scientific and technical periodical articles. The INSTITUTE uses the Data Bank to produce a hardcopy index, to provide computerized searches and SDI, and to compile special bibliographies. The ICYT also offers library services, computerized searching and SDI from international data bases, translations, and photocopying.

Scope and/or Subject Matter: Science and technology, including industrial chemistry, electrical engineering, electronics, metallurgy, farm engineering, agronomics, management, physics, Spanish patents, life sciences, pharmacology, mathematics, astronomy, and astrophysics.

Input Sources: The Institute scans approximately 250 Spanish periodicals.

Holdings and Storage Media: The bibliographic Data Bank is held in machine-readable form, with approximately 5000 items added per year. The Institute's library collection includes 18,000 volumes and subscriptions to 2000 periodicals.

Publications: 1) Indice Espanol de Ciencia y Tecnologia (semiannual)—index to scientific and technical reviews, journals, monographs, and other publications. 2) Revista Espanola de Documentacion Cientifica (trimestrial)—published in collaboration with the Sociedad Espanola de Documentacion e Informacion Cientifica (SEDIC); primary Spanish-language journal dealing with scientific documentation. 3) Boletin de Traducciones (trimestrial)—index of translations from papers in foreign languages. The above publications are available by subscription.

Computer-Based Products and Services: The INSTITUTE utilizes the ICYT Data Bank to prepare indexes, produce special publications, and provide computerized search and SDI services. The INSTITUTE also performs searches of international online data bases in its areas of interest.

Other Services: In addition to the services described above, the Institute offers research in the automation of literature search services.

Clientele/Availability: Services are available without restrictions.

Contact: Milagros Villarreal, Secretary, Institute for Information and Documentation in Science and Technology. (Telex 22 628 CIDMDE.)

★891★
SPAIN
HIGHER COUNCIL FOR SCIENTIFIC RESEARCH
(Consejo Superior de Investigaciones Cientificas - CSIC)
INSTITUTE FOR INFORMATION AND DOCUMENTATION IN THE SOCIAL SCIENCES AND HUMANITIES
(Instituto de Informacion y Documentacion en Ciencias Sociales y Humanidades - ISOC)
Vitrubio 4, 6a
Madrid 6, Spain
Aida Mendez, Director
Phone: 2627755
Service Est: 1975

Staff: 9 Management professional; 9 other.

Description of System or Service: The INSTITUTE FOR INFORMATION AND DOCUMENTATION IN THE SOCIAL SCIENCES AND HUMANITIES (ISOC) maintains a computer-readable bibliographic data base for use in the production of annual indexes to Spanish humanities and social science literature. The INSTITUTE also offers computerized search and SDI services from international online data bases, provides document reproduction and manual literature searching, and supplies consulting and training in documentation.

Scope and/or Subject Matter: Humanities, including philosophy, religion, arts, literature, music, linguistics, history, geography, and archeology; social sciences, including law and legislation, sociology, political science, economics, psychology, anthropology, and education.

Input Sources: Input is obtained from commercially available data bases and from periodicals in the fields of the humanities and social sciences.

Holdings and Storage Media: Library holdings consist of 1500 bound volumes, and subscriptions to 1180 periodicals and 121 secondary titles.

Publications: 1) Indice Espanol de Humanidades (annual); 2) Indice Espanol de Ciencias Sociales (annual). Both publications are available by subscription.

Computer-Based Products and Services: The INSTITUTE maintains information from both of its indexes in a computer-readable data base that is expected to be offered online in the near future. The INSTITUTE also offers computerized information retrieval services from data bases made available through DIALOG Information Services, Inc., System Development Corporation (SDC), Telesystemes Questel, BELINDIS (Belgian Information and Dissemination Service), CITERE, I.P. Sharp Associates, and BLAISE (British Library Automated Information Service).

Other Services: Additional services include manual literature searching and document delivery.

Clientele/Availability: Services are intended for researchers, firms, and official institutions.

Contact: Adelaida Roman, Documentalist, Institute for Information and Documentation in the Social Sciences and Humanities.

★892★
SPAIN
MINISTRY OF HEALTH AND SAFETY
(Ministerio de Sanidad y Seguridad Social)
NATIONAL INSTITUTE OF OCCUPATIONAL SAFETY AND HEALTH
(Instituto Nacional de Seguridad e Higiene en el Trabajo)
NATIONAL INFORMATION AND DOCUMENTATION CENTER
(Centro Nacional de Informacion y Documentacion)
Calle Dulcet, s/n
Barcelona 08034, Spain
Domenec Turuguet Mayol, Chief
Phone: 932044500
Service Est: 1972

Staff: 3 Information and library professional; 1 management professional; 4 technicians; 1 sales and marketing; 4 clerical and nonprofessional.

Description of System or Service: The NATIONAL INFORMATION AND DOCUMENTATION CENTER provides collection, analysis, storage, and dissemination of documents on occupational health and safety. In support of these services, the CENTER maintains the computer-readable bibliographic Seguridad e Higiene en el Trabajo (SEHIT) data base. It also issues a current awareness bulletin.

Scope and/or Subject Matter: Occupational health and safety; occupational medicine; industrial hygiene; industrial toxicology; ergonomics; safety education.

Input Sources: Input sources include 200 journals, as well as reports, books, proceedings, official publications, and other materials.

Holdings and Storage Media: The bibliographic SEHIT data base is held in machine-readable form and contains information from 1972 to the present. Library holdings consist of 11,000 bound volumes; subscriptions to 210 periodicals; and various reports, reprints, and other materials.

Publications: Boletin Bibliografico (monthly).

Computer-Based Products and Services: The NATIONAL INFORMATION AND DOCUMENTATION CENTER produces and provides services from the bibliographic Seguridad e Higiene en el Trabajo (SEHIT) data base.

Other Services: The Center also offers consulting and referral services.

Clientele/Availability: Clients include physicians, technicians, workers, employers, and students.

Contact: Domenec Turuguet Mayol, Chief, National Information and Documentation Center.

★893★
SPANISH DRUG INFORMATION CENTER
(Centro de Informacion de Medicamentos - CINIME)
SPANISH PHARMACEUTICAL SPECIALITIES DATA BANK
(Especialidades Farmaceuticas Espanolas Data Bank - ESPES)
Calle Valenzuela 5 - 2 Izqda.　　　Phone: 91 2324300
Madrid 14, Spain　　　Service Est: 1979
Antonio Garcia Inesta, Director

Staff: 4 Information and library professional; 1 clerical and nonprofessional.

Related Organizations: ESPES sponsors include the Social Security Health Care Research Fund (Fondo de Investigaciones Sanitarias de la Seguridad Social) and the Foundation for the Development of the Social Communications Function (Fundacion para el Desarrollo de la Funcion Social de las Comunicaciones).

Description of System or Service: The SPANISH PHARMACEUTICAL SPECIALITIES DATA BANK (ESPES) is an online drug information retrieval system which covers pharmaceutical products available on the Spanish market. ESPES includes registration information on the composition and manufacture of drugs and is available in Spain through time-sharing. The DATA BANK is also used to prepare reports and publications. Additionally, ESPES is used in conjunction with the Drug Consumption Data Base (ECOM), which contains Spanish demographic data along with information on pharmaceutical consumption and expenditures. ESPES and ECOM are used jointly to determine annual pricing of pharmaceutical products.

Scope and/or Subject Matter: Drug information including: composition (active principles and excipients), manufacturer, therapeutic classification, dispensing and administration information, economic data, registration facts, consumption and expenditures, and related demographic data.

Input Sources: Drug manufacturers send data on new registered drugs to CINIME for inclusion in the ESPES Data Bank. Input for the ECOM Data Base is gathered from the Social Security Services.

Holdings and Storage Media: The ESPES and ECOM data bases are held in machine-readable form. ECOM holds 15,000 items gathered from 1981 to the present.

Publications: 1) Nomenclator—list of specialities. 2) Dictionary of Active Principles and Excipients. Special studies and reports are also issued as required.

Computer-Based Products and Services: ESPES provides information on registered drugs in Spain and is accessible online through time-sharing. A specially developed retrieval system facilitates searching from multiple remote locations. ESPES is also used with the ECOM Data Base for special applications to monitor the numbers of drugs registered and pharmaceutical specialties expenditures. For these applications, ESPES provides data on pharmaceutical specialties; ECOM provides the number of units sold and cost information. ECOM also holds data on the national population of Spain and of each province protected by the Social Security Services to produce comparative indexes showing drug consumption patterns in geographic areas and nationally.

Other Services: Additional services include consulting about drugs registered in Spain, studies of costs and simulations, and automation of drug administrative services.

Clientele/Availability: Services are available to the pharmacy community, hospitals, and governmental agencies.

Projected Publications and Services: Two additional planned data bases are TRAMIT, which will contain information on pharmaceutical specialities which are in the process of authorization for marketing, and PACTI, which will include approximately 2500 active ingredients with their therapeutic groups, pharmacological groups, Chemical Abstracts number, and other indicators.

Contact: Carmen Selva, Pharmacist, Spanish Pharmaceutical Specialities Data Bank.

★894★
SPECIAL LIBRARIES CATALOGUING, INC. (SLC)
2012 Dollarton Hwy.　　　Phone: (604) 929-3966
North Vancouver, BC, Canada V7H 1A4　　　Founded: 1979
J. McRee Elrod, Director

Staff: 2 Information and library professional; 1 clerical and nonprofessional.

Description of System or Service: SPECIAL LIBRARIES CATALOGUING, INC. (SLC) provides derivative and original cataloging for all library materials using the UTLAS Inc. automated catalog support system. Libraries supply SLC with copies of title pages or descriptions of other materials to be cataloged. The bibliographic information is entered into the UTLAS data base for production of COM catalogs, catalog cards, acquisitions lists, and other products. Copies of the bibliographic records are also available on magnetic tape.

Scope and/or Subject Matter: Machine-readable cataloging of all library materials.

Input Sources: Input is derived from photocopies of title pages for current acquisitions, photocopies of shelf list cards for retrospective conversion, and other item descriptions provided by the client library.

Microform Products and Services: COM catalogs are produced and include author, title, subject, and classed listing.

Computer-Based Products and Services: SPECIAL LIBRARIES CATALOGUING, INC. provides cataloging services for all library materials through UTLAS. The information is stored in a machine-readable data base which is used to produce COM catalogs, catalog cards, shelf lists, acquisitions lists, and other materials. Information from the data base is also available on magnetic tape.

Clientele/Availability: Services are available on a fee basis to all types of libraries.

Contact: J. McRee Elrod, Director, Special Libraries Cataloguing, Inc.

★895★
SPECIALIST SOFTWARE LTD.
4 London Wall Bldgs.　　　Phone: 01-920 0522
London EC2, England　　　Founded: 1977
Edward B. Caplin, Director

Staff: Approximately 10 total.

Description of System or Service: SPECIALIST SOFTWARE LTD. develops software for the storage, transmission, and retrieval of financial securities data. Its principal products are BONDSPEC, U.S.-BONDSPEC, and MULTI-3. BONDSPEC is accessible online through Interactive Data Corporation's time-sharing facilities, where it can be used in conjunction with a number of international securities data bases, including EXBOND. U.S.-BONDSPEC is geared to analysis, research, and valuation of United States domestic bond issues. BONDSPEC permits searches or sorts of data by entire market or selected groups by any combination of more than 40 criteria. Historical price and yield comparisons, floating rate note calculations, graphs, specialized reports, and other applications are also possible. Additional BONDSPEC options are BONDBOOK, which supports private storage and transmission of dealers' prices and positions, and BONTRAN, which provides full historical transaction recording and flexible valuation and performance reports. SPECIALIST SOFTWARE's MULTI-3 is a flexible minicomputer-based securities settlement and dealer-aid system that handles multiple users simultaneously, multiple currency accounting, and multiple securities.

Scope and/or Subject Matter: Software for financial securities analysis, valuation, and accounting, including stocks, bonds, commodities, and futures.

Input Sources: Commercial securities data bases or private client files serve as input for BONDSPEC. Data are also collected directly from some users.

Computer-Based Products and Services: BONDSPEC is accessible worldwide through the time-sharing facilities of Interactive Data Corporation for use in international bond analysis, research, and valuation. MULTI-3 is a minicomputer-based securities settlement and dealer-aid system available in London and Europe.

Other Services: Specialist Software Ltd. also provides consultancy services and individually tailored systems for research in investment fields.

Clientele/Availability: Clients include brokers, banks, and fund managers.

Contact: Edward B. Caplin, Director, Specialist Software Ltd.

★896★
**SPORTS COUNCIL
INFORMATION CENTRE**
16 Upper Woburn Place
London WC1H 0QP, England
David Scarfe, Head
Phone: 01-388 1277
Service Est: 1972

Staff: 4 Information and library professional; 2.5 clerical and nonprofessional.

Description of System or Service: The INFORMATION CENTRE of the Sports Council acts as a central clearinghouse for the collection, exchange, and distribution of information in Great Britain concerning planning, building, and managing sports and physical recreation facilities. It has developed a Prestel data base and other computer-based information systems in support of its activities.

Scope and/or Subject Matter: Support and administration of sports and physical recreation in Great Britain.

Input Sources: Information sources include books, journals, and reports.

Holdings and Storage Media: The CENTRE maintains a library collection and a computer data bank covering existing sports facilities, materials used in sports buildings, films on sports, major events, and membership information from the governing bodies of sports.

Publications: The Centre issues several publications, including directories of facilities.

Computer-Based Products and Services: A pilot computer-based system covering the CENTRE's subject interests has been initiated. Information about various sports is also available in a Prestel data base developed by the Sports Council.

Clientele/Availability: There are no restrictions on services.

Contact: David Scarfe, Head, Information Centre, Sports Council.

★897★
STACS INFORMATION SYSTEMS LTD.
3651 23rd St., N.E.
Calgary, AB, Canada T2E 6T2
Michael H. Toller, President
Phone: (403) 276-8501
Founded: 1980

Staff: 1 Management professional; 1 sales and marketing; 1 clerical and nonprofessional.

Related Organizations: Stacs Information Systems Ltd. is associated with Stacs Record Centre Ltd.

Description of System or Service: STACS INFORMATION SYSTEMS LTD. develops and markets microcomputer and minicomputer software and systems for documents management, indexing, and retrieval. The firm also provides consulting services.

Scope and/or Subject Matter: Records management and computer-assisted retrieval systems for applications in archives, artwork, business records, legal files, medical records, microfilm, photographs, publications, technical information centers, and special libraries.

Computer-Based Products and Services: Among the systems offered is OLIS, an integrated hardware and software system providing a full range of document indexing and retrieval capabilities. Using the Ohio Scientific C3 microcomputer, OLIS permits the storage of up to 99 different types of documents with a maximum of 25 variable-length fields for each type. The user determines which fields are searchable, and OLIS automatically creates keywords for them. Retrieval is possible by keyword, document number, and range of document numbers. Various reports can be produced, including KWOC indexes.

Clientele/Availability: Products and services are available without restrictions on a fee basis; primary clients are records managers within the energy industries.

Contact: Michael H. Toller, President, Stacs Information Systems Ltd.

★898★
**STANDARDS COUNCIL OF CANADA
STANDARDS INFORMATION SERVICE (SIS)**
350 Sparks St., Room 1203
Ottawa, ON, Canada K1R 7S8
M. Crainey, Manager
Phone: (613) 238-3222
Service Est: 1977

Staff: 4 Information and library professional; 2 management professional; 2 clerical and nonprofessional.

Related Organizations: The Standards Information Service is a cooperative venture of the Standards Council of Canada and the accredited standards-writing organizations of the National Standards System.

Description of System or Service: The STANDARDS INFORMATION SERVICE (SIS) assists users of standards by verifying the existence of standards documents they may require, identifying the organizations responsible for publishing them, and advising where and how standards documents may be purchased or procured. In support of these services, it produces a machine-readable data base of standards published by the accredited standards-writing organizations of Canada. A wide variety of standards are covered in the data base, including such areas as construction, household appliances, fire prevention systems, industrial equipment, and others. The data base is publicly available online and is used to produce several publications.

Scope and/or Subject Matter: Canadian and international standards, technical regulations, and certification systems.

Input Sources: Input for the machine-readable data base includes standards issued by the Canadian Gas Association, the Canadian General Standards Board, the Canadian Standards Association, Underwriters' Laboratories of Canada, and the Bureau de Normalisation du Quebec.

Holdings and Storage Media: The SIS machine-readable data base contains records on more than 5000 standards and is updated weekly. Materials held by SIS include standards, specifications, and codes issued by Canadian standards-writing organizations, and standards issued by Canadian federal departments and agencies, international standards organizations, and foreign nations. SIS also holds such reference materials as directories, periodicals, reports, pamphlets, and handbooks on standardization.

Publications: Directory and Index of Standards—numerical listing and keyword index to standards published by the accredited standards-writing organizations. 2) Directory of Standards Referenced in Canadian Federal Legislation—identifies technical standards, or their equivalents, which are called up in legislation of the Canadian federal government; includes subject index. 3) Directory of Standards and Specifications Issued by Departments and Agencies of the Government of Canada—computer-produced index providing information on standards and specifications issued by some 17 departments and agencies of the Canadian government. 4)INFORMATECH—periodic publication covering notifications received under the terms of the GATT Agreement on Technical Barriers to Trade.

Computer-Based Products and Services: SIS maintains a computer-readable data base on Canadian standards which it makes available online through COMSHARE. Records provide standard title, call number, source, date of issue, and availability in English and French. Searchable elements include keywords, combined keywords, call number, source, date of issue, and number of standards issued during a given period.

Clientele/Availability: There are no restrictions on the information services of SIS.

Contact: M. Crainey, Manager, or D. Thompson, Assistant Manager, Standards Information Division, Standards Council of Canada; the toll-free telephone number for use in Canada is 800-267-8220. (Telex 053 4403.)

★899★
STATE UNIVERSITY OF UTRECHT LIBRARY
(Rijks Universiteit Utrecht Bibliotheek)
BIOMEDICAL INFORMATION DEPARTMENT
(Afdeling Biomedische Informatie)
Yalelaan 1, P.O. Box 80159 Phone: 030 534637
NL-3508 TD Utrecht, Netherlands Service Est: 1974
Dr. Christina Verheijen-Voogd

Description of System or Service: The BIOMEDICAL INFORMATION DEPARTMENT offers computerized biomedical information services, including online information retrieval and SDI services. Document delivery is also provided.

Scope and/or Subject Matter: Biomedical sciences, including veterinary medicine, medicine, dentistry, pharmacy, and toxicology.

Input Sources: Online data bases in the biomedical sciences serve as input sources.

Computer-Based Products and Services: The Biomedical Information Department conducts retrospective searches and provides SDI services.

Clientele/Availability: Services are available without restrictions. Clients include university staff and students.

Contact: Dr. Christina Verheijen-Voogd, Biomedical Information Department.

★900★
STATUS USERS GROUP
SERC, Rutherford Appleton Lab. Phone: 0235 445666
Chilton Founded: 1981
Didcot, Oxon. OX11 0QY, England
Mrs. J.O. Lay, Hon. Secretary

Description of System or Service: The STATUS USERS GROUP was formed by users of the STATUS free-text information storage and retrieval software package produced by the Computer Science and Systems Division of the Great Britain Atomic Energy Authority (see separate entry). It was established to promote the exchange of information and ideas between STATUS users, to provide a means of presenting users' ideas and opinions to the producer, and to provide a forum for discussing and disseminating matters raised by users, franchise holders appointed by the Atomic Energy Authority, or the producer. The GROUP holds two meetings per year and issues a newsletter and conference proceedings. A number of specific groups operate under the general umbrella of the STATUS USERS GROUP, including groups concerned with individual hardware types and the STATUS in Libraries Group (SLUG).

Scope and/or Subject Matter: STATUS software, including developments and applications concerning free-text information storage and retrieval and associated systems such as word processing, microfilm, and optical character recognition.

Publications: 1) STATUS Users Group Newsletter (three per year)—contains items of interest to STATUS users; available to Group members. 2) Proceedings of annual conferences.

Clientele/Availability: Membership is open to any users or prospective users of STATUS software. The Group currently has a membership of approximately 55 organizations in Europe, Africa, and Australasia.

Contact: Mrs. J.O. Lay, Hon. Secretary, STATUS Users Group.

★901★
STN INTERNATIONAL
STN-Karlsruhe Phone: 07247 824566
Postfach 2465 Founded: 1984
D-7500 Karlsruhe 1, Fed. Rep. of
 Germany

Related Organizations: STN International is offered cooperatively by the Information Center for Energy, Physics, Mathematics/Fachinformationszentrum Energie, Physik, Mathematik GmbH and the American Chemical Society's Chemical Abstracts Service (CAS).

Description of System or Service: STN INTERNATIONAL, the Scientific & Technical Information Network, is a cooperative online service based on a dedicated telecommunications link between the computers of the Chemical Abstracts Service in the United States and the computers of the Information Center for Energy, Physics, Mathematics in Germany. The network link initially makes the CAS Online data bases accessible to European users through the German node of the network and the Information Center's PHYS (Physics Briefs) data base accessible to North American users through the United States node; other data bases will be added. The two computer systems share the Messenger information retrieval system allowing the same command language to be used for searching information files at both locations. Under the network arrangement, a particular data base is loaded at only one site, eliminating duplication in file storage and updating costs. A searcher accesses the nearest host computer and is switched automatically to whichever computer in the network stores the data base to be searched. The searcher perceives the network as a single comprehensive system and is able to search any number of files in one session. Users are also provided with rapid delivery of offline prints, quick resolution of service and billing questions, and more convenient search assistance and training through STN.

Scope and/or Subject Matter: Transmission of chemical, physics, and other scientific and technical information.

Computer-Based Products and Services: STN INTERNATIONAL provides online access to the CAS Online registry and CA files in Europe and to the PHYS data base in North America. The network operates on the Messenger software system which incorporates the following search features: right-hand truncation and internal character masking for use in defining search terms; proximity, Boolean, and link operators for combining search terms; one-letter search commands for frequently used operations; an EXPAND command that retrieves adjacent index entries for a specified search term to help in developing search strategy; and extensive online help messages to assist users in the course of a session. STN supports one-file access, complete bibliographic searching, and special technical access points.

Projected Publications and Services: Mathematics Abstracts, C-13 NMR, DECHEMA, DKI, and other data bases offered through the Informations Center's INKA (Informationssystem Karlsruhe) online service are expected to be made accessible through the Columbus node of STN International in the near future.

Contact: STN International, Information Center for Energy, Physics, Mathematics. (Telex 7826487 FIZE D.) In the United States, contact STN International, Chemical Abstracts Service, 2540 Olentangy River Rd., P.O. Box 2228, Columbus, OH 43202; telephone (614) 421-3600. (Telex 6842086 CHMAB.)

★902★
THE STOCK EXCHANGE
TECHNICAL SERVICES DEPARTMENT
TOPIC
  Phone: 01-588 2355
London EC2N 1HP, England Service Est: 1980
G.A. Hayter, Director

Staff: Approximately 65 total.

Description of System or Service: TOPIC is a computerized information service using videotex and microprocessor technology to provide professional investors and their advisors with current London Stock Exchange prices and company announcements, together with essential background information from the London International Financial Futures Exchange and Currency and Commodity Exchanges. The service is accessible using the special TOPIC color television terminal which is connected to The Stock Exchange via direct wire. The terminal can also be used to access Prestel or other compatible videotex services, to provide private information services, and to produce printed output.

Scope and/or Subject Matter: Stock exchange prices, security information, investment research, company information, financial futures, commodities, and related topics.

Input Sources: Input is collected directly from The Stock Exchange, from formal company announcements and results, from brokers' research, and from other financial exchanges and information providers.

Holdings and Storage Media: Data are stored in machine-readable form and updated frequently throughout the day.

Publications: Daily Official List—record of prices and business transacted on The Stock Exchange; available by subscription or individual copy.

Microform Products and Services: The Daily Official List is also available on standard microfiche.

Computer-Based Products and Services: The TOPIC service provides subscribers with interactive access to the following types of information: market prices for all securities actively traded on The Stock Exchange (about 2300 stocks and shares), arranged according to the official sector classifications and referenced alphabetically; company announcements edited to highlight salient points and cross-referenced to the price of the relevant shares; market overview offering graphic displays of the relative price movements of the various market sectors; information on exchange rates, interest rates, and commodity prices; specialized information on the traded options and financial futures markets; and security prices from major North American exchanges. The Technical Services Department also offers direct computer-to-computer feed of real-time changes to security price information under its Computer Readable Services (CRS), and it makes software available for purchase.

Other Services: In addition, the Technical Services Department offers consulting in the securities industry.

Clientele/Availability: TOPIC users include stockbrokers, institutional investors, investment advisors, and newspaper publishers.

Projected Publications and Services: Packet-switching access to TOPIC data is expected to be made available in Europe and overseas.

Remarks: The name TOPIC was originally an acronym for Teletext Output of Price Information by Computer.

Contact: Tony Daniel, Business Manager - TOPIC, Marketing Department, The Stock Exchange.

★903★
STOCKHOLM SCHOOL OF ECONOMICS
(Handelshogskolan i Stockholm)
ECONOMICS RESEARCH INSTITUTE
(Ekonomiska Forskningsinstitutet - EFI)
FINDATA
Skeppsbron 22 Phone: 08 238230
S-111 30 Stockholm, Sweden Service Est: 1976
Erik Eklund, Head

Description of System or Service: FINDATA is a computerized system for storing, processing, and analyzing financial data from enterprises listed at the Stockholm Stock Exchange. Available online through time-sharing, it consists of a machine-readable data base and several programs which can be used to obtain profit and loss accounts, balance sheets, and key figures for different enterprises and years, as well as to perform calculations and various statistical analyses and draw charts. A related printed chart service is also produced.

Scope and/or Subject Matter: Financial analyses of large Swedish corporations, excluding banks and insurance companies.

Input Sources: Input consists of stock exchange information and annual reports.

Holdings and Storage Media: The computer-readable FINDATA data base holds data from approximately 250 enterprises dating from 1970 to the present. About 400 data items are stored per company and year.

Publications: Charts: The Stockholm Stock Market (monthly)—designed as a technical aid in connection with buying and selling decisions in the short term and as a complement to the long term, basic company analyses. Available by subscription from Aktiv Placering AB, Chart Service, S-106 40 Stockholm, Sweden.

Computer-Based Products and Services: FINDATA is accessible online on a subscription basis through the Stockholm School of Economics. Data available includes profit and loss account and balance sheet information, number of employees, export sales, and stock prices. A variety of programs are available for use with the FINDATA data base: 1) FINSTA—provides a standardized profit and loss account, balance sheet, or statement of financial position. 2) FINSUM—sums up profit and loss accounts balance sheets, and statements of financial position for a number of companies or years. 3) FINLIST—generates tables containing separate financial data from the data base and/or key financial figures for designated companies and years. 4) FINSORT—allows selective searching of the data base. Also available are the FINPLAN1 and FINPLAN2 programs which simulate growth in capital, capital structure, and return on investment. Additionally, the FINDATA system allows users to develop their own programs to determine content and design of output. Related secondary analysis and consulting services are also offered.

Clientele/Availability: There are no restrictions on services; primary clients are banks, stockbrokers, and other financial institutions.

Contact: Erik Eklund, Head, Economics Research Institute.

★904★
STOCKHOLM UNIVERSITY COMPUTING CENTER, QZ
(Stockholms Datamaskincentral)
P.O. Box 27322 Phone: 08 679280
S-102 54 Stockholm, Sweden Founded: 1968
Bengt Olsen, Head

Staff: 100 Total.

Description of System or Service: The STOCKHOLM UNIVERSITY COMPUTING CENTER, QZ is a computer service and time-sharing bureau offering online and batch information processing services for various documentation institutes and other public and private organizations in Sweden. QZ also developed and offers the COM/PortaCOM conference and mail system.

Scope and/or Subject Matter: Computer services in all subject areas.

Computer-Based Products and Services: The STOCKHOLM UNIVERSITY COMPUTING CENTER, QZ offers online access to MEDLARS and MEDLINE, and provides batch retrieval services from 20 additional data bases. The 3RIP and ISIS text management systems are utilized for data base handling and online retrieval. QZ also offers the COM/ PortaCOM electronic conferencing and message system, which is accessible online through QZ and is available for installation on a variety of computer systems.

Clientele/Availability: Primary clientele includes universities, government, and private corporations.

Contact: Jurek Wolodarski, Programming Manager, or Monica Larsson, System Programmer, Stockholm University Computing Center, QZ. (Telex 10366 FOA S.)

★905★
STRASBOURG OBSERVATORY
STELLAR DATA CENTER
(Centre de Donnees Stellaires - CDS)
11, rue de l'Universite Phone: 88 354300
F-67000 Strasbourg, France Service Est: 1972
Prof. C. Jaschek, Director

Staff: Approximately 12 total.

Related Organizations: The Stellar Data Center works in collaboration with the Observatories of Meudon, Marseille, Lausanne-Geneva, Lyon, and Heidelberg. It has data exchange agreements with the U.S. National Space Science Data Center; the Academy of Sciences of the U.S.S.R.; the Kanazawa Institute in Japan; and the Zentralinstitut fur Astrophysik, Potsdam, German Democratic Republic.

Description of System or Service: The STELLAR DATA CENTER (CDS) was created to gather data on stars, improve the information through comparison and analysis, use the data in various research projects, and distribute the results to the astronomical community. The CENTER maintains a collection of nearly 400 astrometric, photometric, spectroscopic, and other catalogs. Extracts or complete copies of the catalogs are made available to astronomers throughout the world on magnetic tape, computer printouts, or microfiche. Additionally, the CDS maintains the Catalog of Stellar Identifications

(CSI), a dictionary of the various designations that are used for stars, which provides access to the catalog collections; the Bibliographic Star Index (BSI), supplying references to journal literature on specific stars; and the Catalog of Stellar Groups (CSG), which shows which stars belong to any of 50 groups with specific spectral characteristics. Information from the CSI and BSI is available online; the BSI is also issued on microfiche.

Scope and/or Subject Matter: Stars, including positions, proper motions, magnitudes, colors, spectra, parallaxes, and other data.

Input Sources: Information sources include astronomical journals, Center-conducted research, and other astronomical data collection organizations.

Holdings and Storage Media: Center holdings include more than 370 catalogs on magnetic tape and in microform, providing data on more than 1.2 million stars. The Catalog of Stellar Identifications (CSI) is held in machine-readable form and lists up to 40 variant names for more than 550,000 stars. The machine-readable Bibliographic Star Index (BSI) contains approximately 16,000 references for 100,000 stars, as drawn from papers in selected astronomical journals since 1950. The Catalog of Stellar Groups (CSG) covers more than 30,000 stars.

Publications: Bulletin (two per year)—provides a complete list of the catalogs held by CDS and includes retrieval instructions.

Microform Products and Services: Many of the Center's catalogs are made available on microfiche. BSI is issued annually on microfiche, with various cumulations available.

Computer-Based Products and Services: The STELLAR DATA CENTER provides special computer printouts and magnetic tape copies of its catalogs to interested astronomers at cost. Information from the Bibliographic Star Index and the Catalog of Stellar Identifications is searchable online as the SIMBAD data base. SIMBAD is maintained at the CNRS computer center at Strasbourg-Cronenbourg which is accessible via TRANSPAC.

Other Services: The Center also hosts colloquia on data centers in astronomy.

Clientele/Availability: Services are available to astronomers throughout the world.

Contact: Prof. C. Jaschek, Director, Stellar Data Center. (Telex 890 506 STAROBS.)

★906★
STUDSVIK ENERGITEKNIK AB
REPORT COLLECTION INDEX (RECODEX)
Studsvik Library   Phone: 155 80000
S-611 82 Nykoping, Sweden

Description of System or Service: The REPORT COLLECTION INDEX (RECODEX) is a machine-readable data base providing information on the energy-related report holdings of libraries in Norway, Denmark, Finland, and Sweden. RECODEX is available online and in microform by subscription.

Scope and/or Subject Matter: Reports in the areas of nuclear energy, alternative energy, physics, chemistry, and material technique.

Input Sources: Primary sources include the U.S. Department of Energy's Energy Data Base and the Studsvik Library.

Holdings and Storage Media: The computer-readable RECODEX data base covers 40,000 reports dating from 1975 to the present. Library holdings consist of 700,000 reports; 80,000 bound volumes; and subscriptions to 1400 periodicals.

Microform Products and Services: RECODEX is available on COMfiche with bimonthly updates.

Computer-Based Products and Services: RECODEX is available for online searching through Studsvik. It is searchable by report number; output consists of information on the library or libraries holding the report. Loans may be ordered at the terminal by authorized users.

Clientele/Availability: Clients include users concerned with energy-related topics.

Contact: Lars Edvardson, Studsvik Energiteknik AB.

★907★
SURVEY FORCE LTD.
Algarve House   Phone: 0795 23778
140 Borden Lane   Founded: 1973
Sittingbourne, Kent ME9 8HR, England
Keith F. Lainton, President

Staff: 1 Information and library professional; 8 management professional; 130 technicians.

Description of System or Service: SURVEY FORCE LTD. provides market research reports covering some 200 world and United States markets in a wide range of fields including industry, biotechnology, and pharmaceuticals. The firm provides research and field work and conducts computer analysis of collected data. In addition, SURVEY FORCE LTD. offers computerized mailing list services for selected markets and areas as well as for client-provided lists.

Scope and/or Subject Matter: Market research in the fields of biotechnology, pharmaceuticals, health care, insecticides, industry, diagnostics, optical, and other areas.

Input Sources: Input is obtained from research and field work.

Holdings and Storage Media: Address lists are held in machine-readable form.

Publications: The firm produces the following quarterly publications: 1) Pharmaceutical New Product Listing Service; 2) Diagnostic New Product Listing Service; 3) Diagnostic Marketing Research Service.

Computer-Based Products and Services: Survey Force Ltd. conducts computerized analysis of market research data and provides machine-readable mailing lists.

Clientele/Availability: Services are available without restrictions.

Contact: Keith F. Lainton, President, Survey Force Ltd. (Telex 826717.)

★908★
SVP AUSTRALIA
Australian Financial Review   Phone: 02 2822822
Box 506, GPO   Founded: 1973
Sydney, N.S.W. 2001, Australia
John Waugh, Manager

Related Organizations: The SVP (S'il Vous Plait) Network is an affiliation of independent companies worldwide that provide information-on-demand services and are interconnected by telex. SVP Australia is a division of John Fairfax Ltd. and operates in conjunction with the Australian Financial Review's INFO-LINE service (see separate entry).

Description of System or Service: SVP AUSTRALIA is an information-on-demand service providing rapid answers to subscribers' questions in the areas of business and finance. Subscribers can telephone, mail, or telex their inquiries to SVP; responses are provided in the form of an immediate answer, a typed report, or copies of relevant articles, statistics, press releases, and other materials.

Scope and/or Subject Matter: All subjects are covered, with emphasis on business and industrial information.

Input Sources: Input is obtained from Australian newspapers and periodicals; many foreign periodicals; company statistics; official statistics; and international SVP resources.

Holdings and Storage Media: The Fairfax newspaper library, which forms the base of SVP Australia's information sources, contains 10 million press clippings and other reference material.

Clientele/Availability: Services are available on a subscription basis.

Contact: Janet Fish, Research Manager, SVP Australia. (Telex 24851 AA.) The electronic mail address on ACIMAIL (ACI Computer Services) is FAIRFAX.

★909★
SVP BENELUX
World Trade Center   Phone: 02 2194000
Bd. Emile Jacqmain, 126 - Box 12
B-1000 Brussels, Belgium
Mr. A. Vander Elst, Manager

Related Organizations: The SVP (S'il Vous Plait) Network is an affiliation of independent companies worldwide that provide information-on-demand services and are interconnected by telex.

Description of System or Service: SVP BENELUX provides one-stop access to a variety of information and research services. Its primary activity is a subscription service which offers users telephone access to the information center. SVP BENELUX provides information on demand and makes accessible all the information gathered by the SVP Network.

Scope and/or Subject Matter: All subject areas, depending on client's needs.

Input Sources: Input is derived from all types of print and nonprint sources.

Clientele/Availability: Services are available on a fee or subscription basis.

Contact: Mr. A. Vander Elst, Manager, SVP Benelux. (Telex 26766.)

★910★
SVP CANADA
Micromedia Ltd.   Phone: (416) 593-5211
144 Front St. W.   Founded: 1975
Toronto, ON, Canada M5J 2L7
Victor V. Brunka, General Manager

Staff: 2 Information and library professional; 1 management professional; 1 technician; 2 sales and marketing; 6 other.

Related Organizations: The SVP (S'il Vous Plait) Network is an affiliation of independent companies worldwide that provide information-on-demand services and are interconnected by telex. SVP Canada is a division of Micromedia Ltd.

Description of System or Service: SVP CANADA provides clients with on-demand information research and delivery services. It offers a complete information service which includes fast fact-finding, comprehensive studies, online searching, and document delivery. SVP CANADA makes available to its clients all information gathered by the SVP Network worldwide.

Scope and/or Subject Matter: All subject areas, depending on client's needs.

Input Sources: SVP Canada utilizes international SVP resources and commercially available online data bases, as well as Micromedia files which include approximately 170 monthly Canadian trade journals, newspapers, Statistics Canada reports, Canadian government documents, Canadian patents, and more than 20,000 financial reports.

Computer-Based Products and Services: SVP CANADA provides computerized information retrieval from data bases available through Canada Systems Group (CSG), COMSHARE, Inc., DIALOG Information Services, Inc., Info Globe (The Globe and Mail), I.P. Sharp Associates, and others.

Clientele/Availability: Services are available on a membership or fee basis.

Contact: Victor V. Brunka, General Manager, SVP Canada. (Telex 065 24668.)

★911★
SVP CONSEIL
Kaufhausgasse 7   Phone: 061 238470
CH-4001 Basel, Switzerland

Related Organizations: The SVP (S'il Vous Plait) Network is an affiliation of independent companies worldwide that provide information-on-demand services and are interconnected by telex.

Description of System or Service: SVP CONSEIL is an information-on-demand organization which provides services primarily to other SVP organizations in the network including coordination of inter-SVP activities.

Scope and/or Subject Matter: All subject areas.

Input Sources: Reference works of all types, both print and nonprint, are used.

Clientele/Availability: Services are presently limited to use by other SVP organizations.

Contact: Head, SVP Conseil. (Telex 62279 SPEWI CH.)

★912★
SVP ESPANA
Diagonal, 508 4a   Phone: 93 2176463
Barcelona 08006, Spain
Xavier Grau, General Manager

Related Organizations: The SVP (S'il Vous Plait) Network is an affiliation of independent companies that provide information-on-demand services and are interconnected by telex.

Description of System or Service: SVP ESPANA provides information services to clients in business. In response to subscriber inquires, which are accepted by telephone, SVP ESPANA retrieves, organizes, analyzes, and interprets information.

Scope and/or Subject Matter: Business, marketing, economics, law, public affairs, and other topics of interest to clients.

Input Sources: Information is obtained from international SVP resources, commercially available online data bases, and other sources.

Computer-Based Products and Services: SVP ESPANA provides computerized information retrieval from data bases available through DIALOG Information Services, Inc.

Clientele/Availability: Services are available by subscription.

Contact: Alfonso Bru, Marketing Manager, SVP Espana. (Telex 97671 BCME E.)

★913★
SVP FRANCE
54, rue de Monceau   Phone: 01 7871111
F-75384 Paris Cedex 8, France   Founded: 1935
Brigitte de Gastines, President

Staff: 200 Information and library professional; 15 management professional; 30 technicians; 30 sales and marketing; 25 clerical and nonprofessional.

Related Organizations: The SVP (S'il Vous Plait) Network is an affiliation of independent companies worldwide that provide information-on-demand services and are interconnected by telex.

Description of System or Service: SVP FRANCE provides a variety of information, research, and related services to its members. The primary service is a subscription service which offers its users telephone access to the information center. Translation and direct mail services are also provided. SVP FRANCE makes available to its clients all information gathered by the SVP Network.

Scope and/or Subject Matter: All subject areas, depending on client's needs.

Input Sources: Input consists of reference materials, both print and nonprint.

Clientele/Availability: Services are available on a fee basis.

Contact: Brigitte de Gastines, President, SVP France. (Telex 650453.)

★914★
SVP ITALIA
Via Piccinni 3   Phone: 02 2043451
I-20131 Milan, Italy

Related Organizations: The SVP (S'il Vous Plait) Network is an affiliation of independent companies worldwide that provide information-on-demand services and are interconnected by telex.

Description of System or Service: SVP ITALIA provides one-stop access to a variety of information and research services. It offers information-on-demand services and provides in-depth market research studies and reports. By using its various sources and its access to numerous other organizations, both in and out of the SVP Network, SVP ITALIA makes the widest possible variety of information available to its users.

Scope and/or Subject Matter: All subject areas, depending on client's needs.

Input Sources: Input consists of reference materials, both print and nonprint.

Clientele/Availability: Services are available on a fee basis.

Contact: Mr. G. Marzolo, SVP Italia. (Telex 335649 SVPMILI.)

★915★
SVP KOREA
Joongang Daily News
58-9 Seosomun-dong, Joong-ku
Seoul, Korea
In-sup Chung, Director

Phone: 02 7527741
Founded: 1980

Staff: 7 Information and library professional; 5 management professional; 3 technicians; 4 sales and marketing; 8 clerical and nonprofessional.

Related Organizations: The SVP (S'il Vous Plait) Network is an affiliation of independent companies worldwide that provide information-on-demand services and are interconnected by telex. SVP Korea is affiliated with the Joongang Daily News.

Description of System or Service: SVP KOREA is an information clearinghouse offering information and market research services to the Korean business world. It uses the resources of Joongang Daily News as well as information gathered by the SVP Network worldwide.

Scope and/or Subject Matter: All subject areas, depending on client's needs.

Input Sources: Input is derived from Korean newspapers, periodicals, bulletins, and directories, as well as international SVP resources.

Holdings and Storage Media: Joongang library holdings consist of 50,000 bound volumes and subscriptions to 350 periodicals.

Computer-Based Products and Services: The firm plans to computerize newspaper article information.

Clientele/Availability: Services are available on a fee basis.

Contact: Ki-woong Hyun, Manager, SVP Korea. (Telex 25587 K.)

★916★
SVP SIJTHOFF
Koopmansstr. 9
NL-2288 BC Rijswijk, Netherlands

Phone: (not reported)

Related Organizations: The SVP (S'il Vous Plait) Network is an affiliation of independent companies worldwide that provide information-on-demand services and are interconnected by telex.

Description of System or Service: SVP SIJTHOFF provides clients with one-stop access to information-on-demand and other research services.

Scope and/or Subject Matter: All subject areas, depending on client's needs.

Input Sources: Information is obtained from international SVP resources and other sources.

Services: Information on demand is the primary service.

Contact: SVP Sijthoff.

★917★
SVP SOUTH AFRICA LTD.
P.O. Box 92400
Norwood 2117
Johannesburg, South Africa
Michael W. Katcs, Chairman

Phone: 728 7410
Founded: 1978

Related Organizations: The SVP (S'il Vous Plait) Network is an affiliation of independent companies that provide information-on-demand services and are interconnected by a communications network.

Description of System or Service: SVP SOUTH AFRICA LTD. provides information-on-demand, current awareness, research, and document delivery services to clients in southern Africa. Its primary service is a subscription service through which it answers telephone or written inquiries. SVP SOUTH AFRICA LTD. makes available to its clients all information gathered by the SVP Network worldwide. Additionally, the firm provides consulting and market research services.

Scope and/or Subject Matter: All subject areas, depending on client's needs.

Input Sources: Input consists of reference materials, both print and nonprint, including international SVP resources.

Computer-Based Products and Services: Computerized information retrieval services are offered.

Clientele/Availability: Services are available on a fee basis.

Contact: Michael W. Katcs, Director, SVP South Africa Ltd. (Telex 42 4493 S.A.)

★918★
SVP UNITED KINGDOM
12 Argyll St.
London W1V 1AB, England
Lord McIntosh, Head

Phone: 01-734 9272
Founded: 1983

Staff: 3 Information and library professional; 1 management professional; 2 sales and marketing; 1 clerical and nonprofessional.

Related Organizations: The SVP (S'il Vous Plait) Network is an affiliation of independent companies that provide information-on-demand services and are interconnected by telex.

Description of System or Service: SVP UNITED KINGDOM offers information consultancy, analysis, and primary and secondary research services to clients in business. It offers the Quick Information Service, which provides answers to a client's questions via telephone, telex, or mail. SVP UNITED KINGDOM also conducts special research projects and provides consumer and industrial marketing research.

Scope and/or Subject Matter: All aspects of business, including markets, products, companies, and statistics.

Input Sources: SVP United Kingdom utilizes international SVP resources, more than 300 commercially available data bases, and business, general, technical, and statistical publications.

Computer-Based Products and Services: SVP UNITED KINGDOM provides online information retrieval from data bases available through Data-Star, DIALOG Information Services, Inc., Pergamon InfoLine Ltd., Telesystemes Questel, and TEXTLINE (Finsbury Data Services Ltd.).

Clientele/Availability: Services are available on a subscription basis.

Contact: Lord McIntosh, SVP United Kingdom. (Telex 28929.)

★919★
SWALCAP
14 Portland Sq.
Bristol BS2, England
Richard F.B. Hudson, Head

Phone: 0272 277603
Founded: 1969

Staff: 4 Information and library professional; 3 management professional; 7 technicians; 2 clerical and nonprofessional.

Description of System or Service: SWALCAP provides online cataloging and circulation services for 22 member academic and special libraries. It maintains computer-readable MARC and circulation records and produces COM catalogs of library holdings for member libraries.

Scope and/or Subject Matter: Automated library circulation and cataloging.

Input Sources: Input to SWALCAP consists of catalog and circulation data provided by member libraries.

Holdings and Storage Media: More than 1 million MARC records and

2 million short author-title circulation records are held in machine-readable form.

Microform Products and Services: COM catalogs are produced for member libraries.

Computer-Based Products and Services: SWALCAP provides online cataloging, circulation, and associated services for its clients. It maintains a computer-readable file of MARC records, which can be retrieved from the system by acronym and control number, and circulation records, which can be searched by name.

Clientele/Availability: Services are offered on a membership basis to academic and special libraries.

Projected Publications and Services: SWALCAP plans to offer an integrated stand-alone library system providing online acquisitions, cataloging, circulation, and serials control.

Contact: Richard F.B. Hudson, SWALCAP.

★920★
SWEDEN
GEOLOGICAL SURVEY OF SWEDEN
(Sveriges Geologiska Undersokning - SGU)
GROUNDWATER DOCUMENTATION SECTION
(Grundvattendokumentation)
Box 670　　　　　　　　　　　　Phone: 018 179000
S-751 28 Uppsala, Sweden
Tommy Olsson, Chief Hydrogeologist

Staff: 13 Management professional; 11 technicians; 1 clerical and nonprofessional.

Description of System or Service: The GROUNDWATER DOCUMENTATION SECTION collects, stores, interprets, and disseminates Swedish hydrogeological data through its well records section and its national groundwater monitoring system of 650 stations in various geological and climatological settings. Collected data are maintained online in the QHBARK and QHGRVN data bases from which the SECTION provides information retrieval and tape distribution services. Additionally, the agency offers hydrogeological mapping services, publishes articles and booklets, and provides consulting and software.

Scope and/or Subject Matter: Swedish hydrogeology.

Input Sources: The Section receives approximately 8000 well-driller reports annually; groundwater measurement, temperature, and chemical data are provided through the network of monitoring stations.

Holdings and Storage Media: The QHBARK and QHGRVN data bases are maintained in machine-readable form.

Publications: The Documentation Section issues various irregular publications.

Computer-Based Products and Services: The DOCUMENTATION SECTION provides information retrieval and tape distribution services from the QHBARK and QHGRVN data bases, which are also accessible on a time-sharing basis. The data bases contain well records, which include information about soil, bedrock, and groundwater, and groundwater time series, which include data on quantity, quality, and temperature. The groundwater time series can be used to produce specially tailored computer compilations.

Clientele/Availability: Services are available without restrictions to government organizations, consultants, and private citizens.

Contact: Dr. Gosta Persson, Chief Hydrogeologist, Geological Survey of Sweden. (Telex 76154 GEOSWED S.)

★921★
SWEDEN
KAROLINSKA INSTITUTE LIBRARY AND INFORMATION CENTER
(Karolinska Institutets Bibliotek och Informationscentral - KIBIC)
P.O. Box 60201　　　　　　　　Phone: 08 340560
1 Solnavagen
S-104 01 Stockholm, Sweden
Dr. Hans Baude, Director

Staff: 34 Information and library professional; 22 management professional; 8 technicians; 13 clerical and nonprofessional; 11 other.

Description of System or Service: The KAROLINSKA INSTITUTE LIBRARY AND INFORMATION CENTER (KIBIC) provides national and international medical information services through the following three jointly-administered departments: 1) Karolinska Institute Library (KIB)—serves as the central medical library for Sweden and offers literature searching, interlibrary loans, publications, and photocopying services. 2) Medical Information Center (MIC)—provides a variety of computer-based services in the life sciences field, including operation of an online service supplying a network of centers with remote terminal access to MEDLARS and other data bases. MIC also searches major online vendors, maintains several tape subscriptions for batch searches, and provides computer-based SDI services. 3) Toxicological Information Service (TOX-INFO)—provides toxicological information and referral services as well as publications.

Scope and/or Subject Matter: Medicine, toxicology, and allied subjects, including cancer research, teratology, biology, chemistry, environmental science, food science, dentistry, psychology, social sciences, and demography.

Input Sources: Information sources include books, journals, reports, data bases, and audiovisual materials.

Holdings and Storage Media: The Library's collection consists of 510,000 volumes, including 220,000 theses and pamphlets; subscriptions to 3200 periodicals; 3100 portraits; and 875 manuscripts. MIC maintains the U.S. National Library of Medicine's MEDLARS data bases and other files on disk, and holds BIOSIS and Psychological Abstracts on magnetic tape.

Publications: The Library issues List Bio-med: Biomedical Serials in Scandinavian Libraries (irregular) and KIBIC-rapport (irregular). The MIC publishes MIC Nytt (irregular). TOX-INFO issues Teratology Lookout (monthly) and Tox-notiser (10 issues per year).

Microform Products and Services: TOX-INFO produces an annual microfiche KWOC index to Teratology Lookout.

Computer-Based Products and Services: The KAROLINSKA INSTITUTE LIBRARY AND INFORMATION CENTER participates in LIBRIS and offers online ordering of documents. The Medical Information Center offers the Following computer-based services: 1) operation of an online service providing clients with remote terminal access to MEDLINE, CANCERLINE, DRUGLINE, SWEMED, BIOETHICS, CLINPROT, Health Planning and Administration, RTECS, and TOXLINE; 2) provision of demand online searches of data bases available through DIALOG Information Services, Inc., ESA/IRS, and System Development Corporation (SDC); 3) collaboration with the Royal Institute of Technology Library in offering SDI services from about 20 data bases; and 4) serving as a contractor for the BIOSIS and Psychological Abstracts data bases.

Clientele/Availability: Services are publicly available, particularly to those working in medicine and allied fields.

Contact: Erkki Hakulinen, Deputy Librarian, Karolinska Institute Library, telephone 08 340560; Dr. Goran Falkenberg, M.D., Head, Medical Information Center, telephone 08 232270; or Dr. Sune Larsson, O.D., Head, TOX-INFO, telephone 08 160170. (Telex 17179 KIBIL.)

★922★
SWEDEN
NATIONAL BOARD OF HEALTH AND WELFARE
DEPARTMENT OF DRUGS
SWEDISH DRUG INFORMATION SYSTEM (SWEDIS)
P.O. Box 607　　　　　　　　　Phone: 018 174600
S-751 25 Uppsala, Sweden　　　Service Est: 1976
Per Manell, Chief Pharmaceutical Officer

Staff: Approximately 4 total.

Related Organizations: The Swedish Drug Information System was developed in collaboration with Uppsala University Data Center (UDAC).

Description of System or Service: The SWEDISH DRUG INFORMATION SYSTEM (SWEDIS) is a computerized storage and retrieval system that is used to facilitate the supervisory and administrative functions of the Department of Drugs, to provide an information resource for the pharmaceutical industry and the national health service, and to disseminate information to the public. Containing comprehensive data on all drugs on the Swedish market, SWEDIS can be accessed through remote terminals located in pharmacies, the drug industry, hospitals, medical information centers, and universities. Publications produced from SWEDIS magnetic tapes are utilized to provide information to the general public and mass media.

Scope and/or Subject Matter: Drug information in Sweden.

Input Sources: Data are collected from a variety of sources, including the drug industry, pharmacies, hospitals, and academic and research institutes.

Holdings and Storage Media: SWEDIS files are maintained in machine-readable form under the MIMER data base management system developed by UDAC.

Publications: Various publications are prepared from the System.

Computer-Based Products and Services: SWEDIS is used by the Department of Drugs for inquiry answering, and it is remotely accessible online. SWEDIS data files include the following: drug register, adverse drug reactions, administrative information, chemical classification, register of drug companies, prescription statistics, clinical trials, drug ingredients, drug packs which have appeared on the market since 1971, drug sales since 1971, annual charges for pharmaceutical specialties, herbal remedies allowed for sale, international classification of disease, register of sterile disposable articles, and tablet identification. The Swedish Drug Information System is also used to provide software and storage facilities for drug research projects in Sweden.

Clientele/Availability: Access to SWEDIS is offered throughout Sweden, as well as internationally.

Contact: Per Manell, Chief Pharmaceutical Officer, Department of Drugs. (Telex 76059 WHODRUG S.)

★923★
SWEDEN
NATIONAL BOARD OF OCCUPATIONAL SAFETY AND HEALTH
(Arbetarskyddsstyrelsen)
CIS CENTRE

S-171 84 Solna, Sweden
Per Odelycke, Chemical Engineer
Phone: 08 7309585
Service Est: 1959

Staff: 1 Total.

Description of System or Service: The CIS CENTRE is the Swedish national center for cooperation with the International Occupational Safety and Health Information Centre (CIS) of the International Labour Office in Geneva. The CIS CENTRE processes Swedish literature for input to the collected CIS data base and provides services from the data base in Sweden. Among the services offered are computerized information retrieval and SDI; the CIS CENTRE also offers online access to an English-language version of the CIS data base.

Scope and/or Subject Matter: Information retrieval and SDI services on occupational safety and health topics.

Input Sources: The CIS Centre scans relevant Swedish literature for input to the CIS data base.

Holdings and Storage Media: The Centre maintains a copy of the CIS file on Stockholm University Computing Center (QZ) facilities.

Computer-Based Products and Services: The CIS CENTRE offers search and SDI services from the computer-readable CIS data base. It also makes an English-language version of CIS accessible online.

Clientele/Availability: Information retrieval and SDI services are offered to Swedish clients; online access is offered to Scandinavian research libraries, municipal libraries, and Swedish occupational safety and health institutions.

Contact: CIS Centre.

★924★
SWEDEN
NATIONAL LIBRARY FOR PSYCHOLOGY AND EDUCATION
(Statens Psykologisk-Pedagogiska Bibliotek - SPPB)
P.O. Box 50063
Frescati Hagvag 10
S-104 05 Stockholm, Sweden
Elin Ekman, Librarian
Phone: 08 151820
Service Est: 1979

Staff: 7 Information and library professional; 5 clerical and nonprofessional; 4 other.

Description of System or Service: The Swedish NATIONAL LIBRARY FOR PSYCHOLOGY AND EDUCATION (SPPB) is a special library in the fields of education and psychology providing reference services, interlibrary loans, bibliographies, photocopies, and inquiry answering. The LIBRARY also provides computerized information retrieval and SDI services from international online host services and it participates in the maintenance of two computer-readable data bases, SBS and PEPSY. SBS (Swedish Behavioural Sciences) provides references to research reports and journal articles in the field of behavioral sciences in Sweden. The material is selected and submitted by psychological and educational departments at Swedish universities and by research institutions at Swedish teacher colleges. The original materials are in the languages of Swedish or English, and all abstracts are in English; all documents referred to are available from the LIBRARY. PEPSY (Nordisk databas i Pedagogik och Psykologi) provides abstracts and indexes of educational and psychological literature in Nordic countries. It is jointly maintained by SPPB and four other Nordic institutions. Both data bases are publicly available online.

Scope and/or Subject Matter: Behavioral sciences, education, psychology, and related fields.

Input Sources: Input for the data bases is acquired from Swedish and Nordic periodicals, reports, and other sources.

Holdings and Storage Media: SPPB library holdings comprise 210,000 bound volumes and subscriptions to 825 periodicals. The computer-readable Swedish Behavioural Sciences data base holds more than 1200 references with abstracts dating from 1978 to the present; it is updated quarterly, with about 350 new records added each year. The PEPSY data base covers literature from 1980 to the present and is updated semiannually.

Publications: Swedish Behavioural Sciences Research Reports (annual)—produced from the SBS data base. The Library also issues other publications.

Computer-Based Products and Services: SWEDISH BEHAVIOURAL SCIENCES (SBS) is accessible online through MEDICINDATA. It is searchable by author, title words, index terms, subject categories, language, document type, abstract words, sponsor, and other elements. PEPSY is accessible through the Norwegian Center for Informatics. The LIBRARY provides searches and SDI services from SBS, PEPSY, and other data bases accessed through DIALOG Information Services, Inc., ESA/IRS, Telesystemes Questel, DIMDI, and other vendors.

Clientele/Availability: Primary clients are researchers, teachers, and students.

Contact: Gunilla Appelgren, Information Officer, or Marianne Jungskar, Librarian, National Library for Psychology and Education.

★925★
SWEDEN
NATIONAL ROAD AND TRAFFIC RESEARCH INSTITUTE
(Statens Vag- och Trafikinstitut - VTI)
INFORMATION AND DOCUMENTATION SECTION

S-581 01 Linkoping, Sweden
Phone: 013 115200
Service Est: 1971

Special Note: No questionnaire response was received for this entry for the 6th edition. The entry is reprinted as it appeared in the 5th edition.

Staff: 10 Information and library professional; 3 others.

Related Organizations: The Section's GEOROAD data base is maintained in association with the Swedish Geotechnical Institute and the National Swedish Road Administration.

Description of System or Service: The INFORMATION AND DOCUMENTATION SECTION provides manual and computer-based information services relating to highways and traffic. It maintains a computer-readable bibliographic data base known as GEOROAD, which documents government reports, monographs, and other relevant materials. As the Swedish documentation center in the International Road Research Documentation (IRRD) System, the SECTION also maintains a copy of the IRRD data base. The SECTION makes the GEOROAD and IRRD files available online through an international telecommunications network, offers them on magnetic tape, and provides search and SDI services from them. Data bases made available through commercial online vendors are also searched. Additionally, the SECTION maintains an extensive library and issues publications.

Scope and/or Subject Matter: Roads, traffic, vehicles, road users, safety, and related topics.

Input Sources: Input for GEOROAD is obtained from government documents, monographs, journal articles, and data bases.

Holdings and Storage Media: The Section's library holdings consist of 35,000 bound volumes and subscriptions to 650 periodicals. The Section also maintains the computer-readable GEOROAD data base, which contains 50,000 references from 1976 to the present, and a copy of the IRRD file.

Publications: 1) VTI Aktuellt/ VTI Topics (6 per year)—abstracts and short articles. 2) VTI Publikationer/ List of Publications (4 per year). 3) VTI Nyforvarv/ VTI Accessions List (25 per year). Additional publications are also issued.

Computer-Based Products and Services: The SECTION makes the GEOROAD and IRRD data bases available for remote terminal online access. It also provides retrospective searches and SDI services from both data bases, and it offers them for lease to Swedish clientele. Additionally, the SECTION conducts searches of data bases carried by ESA/IRS, DIALOG Information Services, Inc., and System Development Corporation (SDC).

Other Services: Additional services include consulting, manual literature searching, and referral services.

Clientele/Availability: Services are available without restrictions.

Contact: Chief Librarian, National Road and Traffic Research Institute.

★926★
SWEDEN
NATIONAL SWEDISH ENVIRONMENT PROTECTION BOARD
(Statens Naturvardsverk - SNV)
SWEDISH ENVIRONMENTAL RESEARCH INDEX (SERIX)
Box 1302　　　　　　　　　　　Phone: 08 981800
S-171 25 Solna, Sweden　　　　Service Est: 1975

Description of System or Service: The SWEDISH ENVIRONMENTAL RESEARCH INDEX (SERIX) is a machine-readable data base covering environmental research projects and reports in Sweden. SERIX is publicly available online.

Scope and/or Subject Matter: Environmental research in Sweden.

Input Sources: Information for SERIX is obtained from governmental authorities, universities, and other organizations.

Holdings and Storage Media: Updated 10 times per year, the computer-readable SERIX data base covers the period from 1974 to date and holds approximately 14,000 references with 1500 added yearly.

Computer-Based Products and Services: The SWEDISH ENVIRONMENTAL RESEARCH INDEX is publicly available online. Subject classification is based mainly on INFOTERRA subject categories. Search fields include title of project/ report, project leader/ author, research and funding organizations, keywords (in Swedish), subject category and geographical area code numbers, and abstract.

Clientele/Availability: Services are available without restrictions.

Remarks: SERIX was previously administered by the Swedish Council of Environmental Information.

Contact: Barbro Hellner, National Swedish Environment Protection Board. (Telex 111 31 ENVIRON S.)

★927★
SWEDEN
NATIONAL SWEDISH TELECOMMUNICATIONS ADMINISTRATION
DATAPAK
P.O. Box 7294　　　　　　　　　Phone: 08 7808750
S-103 90 Stockholm, Sweden　　Service Est: 1980
Bo Adolfsson, Head

Description of System or Service: DATAPAK is a public packet-switching service used mainly for information retrieval traffic between Sweden and other countries such as the United States, Great Britain, and the Federal Republic of Germany.

Scope and/or Subject Matter: Telecommunications services.

Computer-Based Products and Services: Datapak permits remote terminal access to data bases and time-sharing services.

Clientele/Availability: Services are available primarily in Sweden.

Remarks: Datapak was formerly known as Telepak.

Contact: Gunnel Kling, Data Communication Sales Division, National Swedish Telecommunications Administration. (Telex 12020 DATASTH S.)

★928★
SWEDEN
PATENT AND REGISTRATION OFFICE
(Patent- och Registreringsverket)
INTERPAT SWEDEN
P.O. Box 5055　　　　　　　　　Phone: 08 7822885
S-102 42 Stockholm, Sweden
Jan Averdal, Head

Description of System or Service: INTERPAT SWEDEN is an information service designed to meet the needs of industry, researchers, and inventors for technical information contained in patent documents. Its services are divided into three sections: 1) Search—administers requests with technical content to be dealt with by engineers of the Patent Department and requests concerning designs to be dealt with by the Designs section of the Office. The Search section conducts both manual and computerized patent searches and carries out searches which have no direct technical content. It also accepts requests for weekly surveillance of Swedish and foreign patents. 2) Sales—responsible for the sale of publications in the fields of patent, trademark, and design and for sales of copies of Swedish and foreign patents. 3) External Education/ Training—coordinates and develops external courses and seminars, and plans courses for trainees from other countries.

Scope and/or Subject Matter: Swedish and foreign patents.

Input Sources: The service utilizes the holdings of the Patent and Registration Office, which include more than 30 million patent documents. It also uses INPADOC files and commercially available data bases.

Computer-Based Products and Services: InterPat Sweden conducts online searches of patent-related data bases made available through DIALOG Information Services, Inc., ESA/IRS, and System Development Corporation (SDC).

Clientele/Availability: Services are available on a fee basis. Clients include inventors, researchers, designers, and others.

Contact: Jan Averdal, Head, InterPat Sweden. (Telex 17978 PATOREG S.)

★929★
SWEDEN
RESEARCH INSTITUTE OF NATIONAL DEFENSE
(Forsvarets Forskningsanstalt - FOA)
FOA INDEX GROUP
Box 27322　　　　　　　　　　Phone: 08 631500
S-102 54 Stockholm, Sweden　　Service Est: 1963
Olov Lidman, Director

Staff: 2 Information and library professional; 1 management

professional; 2 technicians; 1 clerical and nonprofessional.

Description of System or Service: The FOA INDEX GROUP within the Swedish Research Institute of National Defense is concerned with all aspects of computerized and computer-assisted documentation efforts, including extensive systems and computer program development. The GROUP is primarily a consultant organization dealing with applied research and development activities encompassing documentation and data processing, but it also provides services to users. Its activities include development of computer programs for information retrieval; computer processing of client files; and providing SDI and other search services utilizing commercially available data bases.

Scope and/or Subject Matter: Computerized documentation and administrative systems.

Input Sources: Input is derived from commercially available data bases and the U.S. National Technical Information Service (NTIS).

Holdings and Storage Media: A copy of the NTIS data base is held on machine-readable tape.

Computer-Based Products and Services: The FOA INDEX GROUP maintains and applies its own Computer Oriented Reference System for Automatic Information Retrieval (CORSAIR) program; numerous auxiliary and ancillary computer programs are also offered. The CORSAIR program will accept subroutines designed by the clients. Retrospective literature searching and SDI services are also available.

Other Services: Additional services include advisory and consulting services, and research and design of computer applications to documentary techniques.

Clientele/Availability: The CORSAIR program is available for use at the Stockholm University Computing Center; other services are available for a fee.

Contact: Olov Lidman, Director, FOA Index Group. (Telex 10366.)

★930★
SWEDEN
ROYAL INSTITUTE OF TECHNOLOGY LIBRARY
(Kungl. Tekniska Hogskolans Bibliotek - KTHB)
INFORMATION AND DOCUMENTATION CENTER (IDC)
(Informations- och Dokumentationscentralen)
S-100 44 Stockholm, Sweden
Marie Wallin, Head
Phone: 08 7878950
Service Est: 1967

Staff: 12 Information and library professional; 3 technicians; 7 clerical and nonprofessional.

Description of System or Service: The INFORMATION AND DOCUMENTATION CENTER (IDC-KTHB) provides computer-based technical information services for research, development, and production personnel in Sweden and other European countries. It maintains two computer-readable data bases, MechEn (Mechanical Engineering) and DOLDIS (Directory of On-Line Databases in Sweden). The CENTER also provides EPOS-VIRA SDI services using about 20 commercial data bases. Additionally, the CENTER conducts computerized searches through European and U.S. online vendors, carries out research in the area of information retrieval, and acts as a EUSIREF center.

Scope and/or Subject Matter: Industrial research, mechanical engineering, and other technologies.

Input Sources: Input for the MechEn data base is derived from technical notes, product announcements, and articles from more than 150 European and American journals. MechEn does not include journals covered by ISI, COMPENDEX, and ISMEC. Input for the DOLDIS data base is derived from inventory of Swedish data bases carried out by IDC-KTHB on behalf of the Swedish Delegation for Scientific and Technical Information.

Holdings and Storage Media: The computer-readable MechEn data base contains 375,000 bibliographic references dating from 1968 to the present. It is updated twice each month, with approximately 35,000 items added each year. The DOLDIS data base contains records on approximately 100 publicly available data bases in Sweden.

Computer-Based Products and Services: Magnetic tapes of the entire MechEn data base are available for purchase. The DOLDIS data base provides English-language descriptions of approximately 100 data bases available online in Sweden, with Swedish and English-language indexing; DOLDIS is expected to be available online in the near future. The CENTER's SDI service, based on EPOS-VIRO software, is also available; approximately 20 data bases are included. In addition, retrospective online searching is conducted from data bases offered by ESA/IRS, DIALOG Information Services, Inc., System Development Corporation (SDC), and Euronet DIANE host centers.

Other Services: IDC-KTHB also offers consulting services.

Clientele/Availability: Services are available without restrictions.

Contact: Marie Wallin, Head, Information and Documentation Center. (Telex 10389 KTHB S.)

★931★
SWEDEN
ROYAL LIBRARY
(Kungl. Biblioteket)
LIBRARY INFORMATION SYSTEM (LIBRIS)
P.O. Box 5039
S-102 41 Stockholm, Sweden
Mari Bud, Director
Phone: 08 241040
Service Est: 1970

Staff: 8 Total.

Description of System or Service: The LIBRARY INFORMATION SYSTEM (LIBRIS) is a computer-based information system which aims for a joint utilization of the resources of the Swedish research libraries and a reduction in time spent cataloging these resources. It provides a data communication and processing system for the searching and cataloging of book acquisitions and the production of catalog products. The Bibliotekstjanst AB and 21 academic libraries have permanent access to LIBRIS and approximately 175 other libraries have dial-up access to the system. Catalog cards, catalogs, and lists can be produced from LIBRIS on microfiche and on paper. The SYSTEM is also used to produce several major standard catalog products including the Swedish National Bibliography, based on the Royal Library's cataloging of newly published Swedish literature; the Union Catalogue of Foreign Books in Swedish Research Libraries; and the Swedish contribution to the Nordic Union Catalogue for Periodicals (NOSP).

Scope and/or Subject Matter: Bibliographic information on Swedish and foreign titles held in Swedish research libraries.

Input Sources: Input is derived from MARC and International Serials Data System (ISDS) tapes and original cataloging of Swedish and foreign literature acquired by the Royal Library and participating Swedish research libraries.

Holdings and Storage Media: The computer-readable bibliographic LIBRIS data base contains approximately 1.2 million records covering foreign literature acquired since 1968 by Swedish research libraries represented in the Union Catalogue of Foreign Books; Swedish literature published since 1976; and two years of MARC and ISDS data.

Publications: 1) Swedish National Bibliography/ Svensk Bokforteckning. 2) Union Catalogue of Foreign Books in Swedish Research Libraries/ AKB-bok. 3) LIBRIS-meddelanden—newsletter providing general information on the system. 4) Driftmeddelanden—covers system operation.

Microform Products and Services: AKB-mikro (three per year)—microfiche catalog of foreign books acquired by Swedish research libraries. Shelf lists of local library holdings are available on microfiche.

Computer-Based Products and Services: LIBRIS provides an online catalog of the resources of Swedish research libraries and is accessed by nearly 200 participating libraries. The first participating library to acquire a new publication performs the primary cataloging and records the bibliographic information in LIBRIS. Libraries which subsequently acquire the publication can then add local classification, shelf numbers, and other information to the basic record. Data on publications on order can also be entered and supplemented when the publication is received. Libraries that record catalog items may order catalogs on local book collections, lists of newly acquired books, and shelf lists on microfiche as well as on paper. LIBRIS also makes the Swedish National Bibliography available on magnetic tape as SWEMARC.

Contact: Britt Sagnert, Librarian, LIBRIS, Royal Library. (Telex 19640 KBS S.)

★932★
SWEDEN
STATISTICS SWEDEN
(Statistiska Centralbyran - SCB)
STATISTICAL DATA BASES UNIT

S-115 81 Stockholm, Sweden
Jan Eklof, Head
Phone: 08 140560
Service Est: 1983

Staff: 3 Information and library professional; 3 management professional; 10 technicians; 1 sales and marketing; 2 clerical and nonprofessional.

Description of System or Service: The STATISTICAL DATA BASES UNIT is responsible for the data bases of Statistics Sweden and for the data base management system used to handle them. The UNIT maintains the Regional Statistics Data Base (RSDB), Time Series Data Base (TSDB), and Sub-area Statistical Data Base (DSDB) which contain population, employment, economic, census, and social statistics for international, national, regional, and local areas. The data files are constructed, maintained, and searched under the Auxiliary System for Interactive Statistics (AXIS) software system, which is designed to effectively manipulate large volumes of highly detailed information. With AXIS software, users with no previous data processing experience can retrieve statistical information, perform calculations, and specify data output formats. The STATISTICAL DATA BASES UNIT files are searchable online through time-sharing and are also offered on magnetic tape.

Scope and/or Subject Matter: Swedish and international statistical information.

Input Sources: Input is acquired from SCB surveys, government agencies, and international organizations.

Holdings and Storage Media: The three computer-readable data bases hold nearly 500 million items of information.

Publications: The SCB issues Official Statistics of Sweden (SOS), a series of publications bringing together the majority of the statistics published by official authorities in Sweden. User manuals and AXIS documentation are also issued.

Computer-Based Products and Services: The STATISTICAL DATA BASES UNIT offers online access and magnetic tape services for the following three statistical data bases: 1) Regional Statistics Data Base (RSDB)—contains statistics on Swedish population, housing, households, income, employment, education, social sciences, industry, energy, and state aid. Data are classified by county, municipality, agglomeration, and sparsely populated areas. 2) Sub-area Statistical Data Base (DSDB)—contains population statistics and 1980 census data including employment, households, and dwelling units structure. Most municipalities are broken into approximately 70,000 small areas using a system for geographical coding. The DSDB is used by government agencies at all levels for planning purposes. 3) Time Series Data Base (TSDB)—contains national and international economic statistics on national accounts, industry, energy, construction, trade, public sectors, credit market, finances, prices, foreign trade, labor market, population, income, and economic indicators. UNIT data bases are maintained under AXIS software, which allows users to retrieve data through a series of menus in a numbered selection format. AXIS can be used to prepare and present tables with statistical information; carry out per mill and per cent calculations; enter, change, and delete data; manipulate text in headings and comments; and carry out authorization checks and set classification levels. Designed for IBM 370 computers, AXIS software is also available for installation on client computers.

Clientele/Availability: Products and services are available within Sweden and abroad.

Remarks: Statistics Sweden is also known as the National Central Bureau of Statistics.

Contact: Doris Persson, Statistics Sweden. (Telex 15261 S.)

★933★
SWEDEN
SWEDISH NATIONAL ROAD ADMINISTRATION
(Statens Vagverk)
TECHNICAL DIVISION
ROAD DATA BANK
(Vagdatabank)

S-781 87 Borlange, Sweden
Per Genberg, Civil Engineer
Phone: 0243 75000
Service Est: 1973

Staff: 1 Information and library professional; 2 management professional; 7 technicians; 1 sales and marketing; 2 clerical and nonprofessional; 1 other.

Description of System or Service: The ROAD DATA BANK is a computer-based information system used to collect, process, store, and disseminate data on Swedish roads, bridges, traffic, and traffic accidents. The DATA BANK can be searched online or in batch mode to produce lists, statistics, and graphic displays; output is available in print, on microfiche, or on magnetic tapes. Clients use the system to plot routes for haulage contractors, to assist operations and maintenance personnel in planning pavement work, to analyze traffic safety measures for road designers, and to provide data for other decision-making and research applications.

Scope and/or Subject Matter: Swedish highways, including road surface and structures, traffic accidents, traffic volume and variations, alignment, bridges, and map data.

Input Sources: Input is derived from special mobile road surveys, traffic accident reports prepared by the police, and regional road administration reports; some data are directly input online.

Holdings and Storage Media: The machine-readable Road Data Bank is continuously updated and contains information on approximately 100,000 kilometers of roads, 10,000 bridges, and 100,000 traffic accidents.

Microform Products and Services: Periodic lists containing the most significant data arranged in a user-oriented format are supplied on microfiche and paper.

Computer-Based Products and Services: The ROAD DATA BANK can be accessed online or in batch mode at the Swedish National Road Administration. Road-descriptive data and traffic-regulating data are stored in the Road Data File which includes information on road width, type of surface, railway crossings, speed limits, and permitted axle load. The DATA BANK includes programs for file handling, information retrieval, and map and report generation.

Clientele/Availability: The Swedish National Road Administration is the primary user of the Road Data Bank, although services are available to the public on a limited basis.

Contact: Per Genberg, Civil Engineer, Swedish National Road Administration.

★934★
SWEDISH BUILDING CENTRE
(Svensk Byggjanst)
BUILDING COMMODITY FILE
(Byggvaruregistret - BVR)

P.O. Box 7853
S-103 99 Stockholm, Sweden
Phone: 08 7305100

Description of System or Service: The BUILDING COMMODITY FILE (BVR) is a machine-readable data base providing information on products and suppliers in the Swedish building market. Begun as a card file in 1936 and converted to machine-readable form in 1975, the FILE is used to produce an annual hardcopy index and listings of products. Current BVR information is also searchable online; historical data may be retrieved manually from the card file.

Scope and/or Subject Matter: Swedish building market products and suppliers.

Input Sources: Input is derived from technical journals, newspapers, and suppliers' materials. Information is also gathered through inquiries to suppliers, contacts with other commodity files, and exhibitions and fairs.

Holdings and Storage Media: The machine-readable Building Commodity File contains information on more than 45,000 Swedish building products available since 1976 and 12,000 suppliers active since 1975.

Publications: Building Commodity Index/ Byggvaruforteckning (annual).

Computer-Based Products and Services: The computer-readable BUILDING COMMODITY FILE holds the following data elements: product trade name, short technical description, product group, and names and addresses of the general representative, manufacturer, and regional sellers of each product. The FILE is accessible online through the Centre.

Clientele/Availability: Primary users are architects and contractors.

Contact: Lars Thunqvist, Swedish Building Centre.

★935★
SWEDISH CENTER FOR WORKING LIFE
(Arbetslivscentrum)
INFORMATION AND DOCUMENTATION DEPARTMENT
(AID Enheten)
P.O. Box 5606　　　　　　　　　Phone: 08 229980
S-114 86 Stockholm, Sweden　　Service Est: 1977

Special Note: No questionnaire response was received for this entry for the 6th edition. The entry is reprinted as it appeared in the 5th edition.

Staff: 7 Information and library professional.

Description of System or Service: The INFORMATION AND DOCUMENTATION DEPARTMENT of the Swedish Center for Working Life provides information services on work research to clients in government, industry, unions, and the academic community. Chief among these services are computerized searches from the AID data base covering the literature on industrial relations and personnel administration. Formerly maintained by the Swedish Council for Personnel Administration and known as PADOC, AID has been expanded by the Department with the addition of new (especially Nordic) materials.

Scope and/or Subject Matter: Work organization, with emphasis on equality in the workplace.

Input Sources: Input is derived from magazines, reports, and other literature within the scope of the Center for Working Life.

Holdings and Storage Media: The machine-readable AID data base contains more than 25,000 bibliographic items dating from 1969 to date. The Department also subscribes to 322 periodicals.

Computer-Based Products and Services: The DEPARTMENT offers retrospective searches and SDI from the AID data base, which is searchable for such items as author, title of item in original language or translation, title of source item, bibliographic reference, publisher, type of document, and accession number. AID is also publicly accessible online.

Clientele/Availability: Services are intended for work researchers; there are no restrictions.

Contact: Head, Information and Documentation Department.

★936★
SWEDISH COUNCIL FOR INFORMATION ON ALCOHOL AND OTHER DRUGS
(Centralforbundet for Alkohol- och Narkotikaupplysning - CAN)
P.O. Box 27302　　　　　　　　Phone: (not reported)
S-102 54 Stockholm, Sweden

Description of System or Service: The SWEDISH COUNCIL FOR INFORMATION ON ALCOHOL AND OTHER DRUGS (CAN) provides library and information services in the areas of substance abuse and dependence. Among its services, CAN maintains the following three computer-readable data bases: 1) ALCONARC—contains bibliographic and holdings information for books, technical reports, conference proceedings, and theses acquired by the CAN Library. 2) NORDRUG—provides English-language references and abstracts to journal articles and essays on research on alcohol and drug dependence. 3) DALCTRAF—contains bibliographic references to English-language literature dealing with alcohol, drugs, and transportation; a joint venture between CAN and the International Committee on Alcohol, Drugs and Traffic Safety. The CAN data bases are used to produce abstracts journals and are accessible online.

Scope and/or Subject Matter: Alcohol and drug dependence and related topics, including traffic safety.

Input Sources: Input to the data bases is derived from books, periodicals, technical reports, conference proceedings, theses, and other literature.

Holdings and Storage Media: CAN maintains a library collection and three computer-readable bibliographic data bases.

Publications: 1) Drug Abuse: Research on the Treatment of Alcohol and Drug Dependence—abstracts journal produced from NORDRUG. 2) Alcohol, Drugs and Traffic Safety: Current Research Literature—printed version of DALCTRAF.

Computer-Based Products and Services: The ALCONARC, NORDRUG, and DALCTRAF data bases are accessible online through the Stockholm University Computing Center (QZ), initially on an experimental basis.

Clientele/Availability: Services and products are intended for use by researchers and educators.

Contact: Sonja Valverius, Library, Swedish Council for Information on Alcohol and Other Drugs.

★937★
SWEDISH DELEGATION FOR SCIENTIFIC AND TECHNICAL INFORMATION
(Delegationen for Vetenskaplig och Teknisk Informationsforsorjning - DFI)
P.O. Box 43033　　　　　　　　Phone: 08 7442840
Liljeholmstorget 7　　　　　　 Service Est: 1979
S-100 72 Stockholm, Sweden
Bjorn Thomasson, Director

Staff: 16 Total.

Description of System or Service: Under the direction of the Swedish ministries of education and industry, the SWEDISH DELEGATION FOR SCIENTIFIC AND TECHNICAL INFORMATION (DFI) plans and coordinates Sweden's scientific and technical information services for use in research, development, and related activities.

Scope and/or Subject Matter: Scientific and technical information services.

Remarks: DFI replaces the Swedish Council for Scientific Information and Documentation/ Statens Rad for Vetenskaplig Information och Dokumentation (SINFDOK).

Contact: Bjorn Thomasson, Director, Swedish Delegation for Scientific and Technical Information.

★938★
SWEDISH INSTITUTE OF BUILDING DOCUMENTATION
(Institutet for Byggdokumentation - BYGGDOK)
Halsingegatan 49　　　　　　　Phone: 08 340170
S-113 31 Stockholm, Sweden　　Founded: 1966
Adolf Stern, Managing Director

Staff: 13 Information and library professional; 2 management professional; 2 sales and marketing; 2 clerical and nonprofessional; 6 other.

Related Organizations: The Swedish Institute of Building Documentation is sponsored by the National Swedish Council for Building Research. Contributors to the BODIL data base include the Danish National Center for Building Deocumentation, the Technical Research Centre of Finland, and the Norwegian Building Research Institute.

Description of System or Service: The SWEDISH INSTITUTE OF

BUILDING DOCUMENTATION (BYGGDOK) is the central national body for documentation in housing, building, and related areas. The INSTITUTE maintains a library, publishes an abstracts journal and reports, produces the computer-readable bibliographic BODIL data base, and offers retrieval and analysis services in its efforts to provide information to those connected with the building industry.

Scope and/or Subject Matter: Housing, planning, building, civil engineering, environment, installation, energy saving, and related fields.

Input Sources: Input for BODIL is obtained from journals, documents, and research reports published in Scandinavia and elsewhere (approximately 20 percent of the references in the data base originate in non-Scandinavian countries).

Holdings and Storage Media: The computer-readable BODIL data base contains approximately 50,000 items. The data base is updated fortnightly, with about 7000 new items added annually. A library collection is also maintained.

Publications: Byggreferat (10/year)—an abstracts journal published jointly with affiliated organizations. The Institute also publishes a search aid, trend reports, and related publications.

Computer-Based Products and Services: Formerly known as the BYGGDOK data base, BODIL contains such data elements as title, author, abstract, document type, language, and descriptors. It is accessible online through the Swedish Institute of Building Documentation. SDI services are also offered using the data base.

Other Services: Additional services include consulting, data collection and analysis, manual literature searching, and referral services.

Clientele/Availability: Primary clients are members of the building industry. Services are available on a fee basis without restrictions.

Contact: Mr. Bergt Eresund or Mr. Magnus Ryttarson, Marketing Assistant, Swedish Institute of Building Documentation. (Telex 12563.)

★939★
SWEDISH MECHANICAL AND ELECTRICAL ENGINEERING TRADE ASSOCIATION
(Sveriges Mekanforbund)
VERA
P.O. Box 5506
S-114 85 Stockholm, Sweden
Ralph Stroemfelt, Head
Phone: 08 7838000
Service Est: 1983

Staff: 1 Management professional; 1 sales and marketing; 1 clerical and nonprofessional.

Description of System or Service: VERA is a computer-readable data base providing citations and extensive abstracts for technical and economic publications issued by the Swedish Mechanical and Electrical Engineering Trade Association. VERA is publicly available online through the TESS Search Service, and information retrieval and document delivery services are provided by the Association.

Scope and/or Subject Matter: Technical and economic topics relating to the mechanical and electrical engineering industries.

Input Sources: Input is drawn from publications produced by the Association.

Holdings and Storage Media: The bibliographic VERA data base is held in machine-readable form and contains approximately 1200 items.

Publications: The Association issues reports and other publications.

Computer-Based Products and Services: The VERA data base is available online through the TESS Search Service. The Association also provides information retrieval services from the data base.

Other Services: Additional activities of the Association include research, consulting, and conferences in technology and business economics.

Contact: Karita Thome, Swedish Mechanical and Electrical Engineering Trade Association.

★940★
SWEDISH STANDARDS INSTITUTION (SIS)
REGIS
P.O. Box 3295
S-103 66 Stockholm, Sweden
Erik Sjostrom, Head
Phone: 08 230400
Service Est: 1983

Description of System or Service: REGIS is a computer-readable data base which contains descriptions of Swedish standards and other nongovernment technical regulations. The data base is publicly accessible online, and related publications are issued by the SIS.

Scope and/or Subject Matter: Swedish standards and other nongovernmental technical regulations.

Input Sources: Input includes new and revised Swedish standards and regulations.

Holdings and Storage Media: REGIS holds approximately 7500 computer-readable records. The Institution's library holdings consist of approximately 8000 standards and technical regulations.

Publications: 1) Katalog Over Svensk Standard (annual); 2) Swedish Standards Listed in Subject Groups (annual).

Computer-Based Products and Services: REGIS provides bibliographic descriptions of all valid and selected withdrawn standards and regulations in Sweden. It is accessible through the TESS search service and the Swedish PTT. Information retrieval services are offered by the SIS.

Clientele/Availability: Services are available without restrictions.

Contact: Ulla-Britt Mittag, Assistant, Swedish Standards Institution.

★941★
SWEDISH UNIVERSITY OF AGRICULTURAL SCIENCES
(Sveriges Lantbruksuniversitet)
ULTUNA LIBRARY
(Ultunabiblioteket)
DOCUMENTATION SECTION
S-750 07 Uppsala, Sweden
Brita Rufelt, Documentalist
Phone: 018 171000
Service Est: 1969

Staff: 5 Information and library professional.

Description of System or Service: The DOCUMENTATION SECTION of Ultuna Library provides computerized searching of publicly available data bases, as well as manual literature searching and SDI services. It participates in the Agricultural Libraries Information Network (AGLINET), selects and indexes Swedish input to the International Information System for the Agricultural Sciences and Technology (AGRIS) project of the United Nations Food and Agriculture Organization (FAO), and provides input to SWEDAGRI, a national agricultural data base.

Scope and/or Subject Matter: Agriculture, forestry, horticulture, veterinary sciences, environmental sciences, biology, food science and technology.

Input Sources: The Section processes Swedish materials for input to AGRIS and SWEDAGRI.

Holdings and Storage Media: Ultuna Library holds 5000 periodical subscriptions and an extensive monograph collection.

Computer-Based Products and Services: The Documentation Section conducts searches of online data bases made available through DIALOG Information Services, Inc., Euronet DIANE, and ESA/IRS. SDI services are offered for the AGRIS data base and the U.S. National Agricultural Library's AGRICOLA data base. The Section also participates in the maintenance of the SWEDAGRI national agricultural data base.

Clientele/Availability: Services are available to scientists, researchers and students of the Swedish University of Agricultural Sciences and to other institutes and organizations in the agricultural field.

Contact: Brita Rufelt, Documentalist, Documentation Section. (Telex 76062 WLTBIBLS.)

★942★
SWETS SUBSCRIPTION SERVICE
347b Heereweg
NL-2161 CA Lisse, Netherlands
J. Roof, Associate Director
Phone: 2521 19113

Staff: 50 Information and library professional; 6 management professional; 33 technicians; 50 sales and marketing.

Related Organizations: Swets Subscription Service is a division of Swets & Zeitlinger.

Description of System or Service: The SWETS SUBSCRIPTION SERVICE acts as an intermediary between libraries and publishers for the acquisition of periodicals, serials, monograph series, and handbooks. In support of its services, SWETS maintains a machine-readable data base containing information on serial titles and publishers. SWETS offers online check-in and claim services, and can provide check-in and invoice data on magnetic tape. It also issues a serials catalog on microfiche from its data base.

Scope and/or Subject Matter: Automated subscription services for libraries, with complete subject coverage.

Input Sources: Information for the Swets data base is obtained from publishers' announcements and national and international bibliographies.

Holdings and Storage Media: The machine-readable Swets data base contains full bibliographic information on 90,000 serial titles and information on 28,000 publishers.

Publications: Swets Info Bulletin (4 per year)—covers newly published titles and bibliographic changes.

Microform Products and Services: The Swets Catalogue of Serial Titles is available on microfiche arranged alphabetically by title, by subject, and by country of publication. KWOC indexes are also occasionally produced.

Computer-Based Products and Services: The SWETS SUBSCRIPTION SERVICE maintains a machine-readable data base to facilitate subscription services and the provision of data on magnetic tape. Specific services offered from the Swets Info System include: 1) Customer Subscription Reports (CSR)—provides monthly information on order and cancellation confirmations, claim confirmations and reports on claims, bibliographical changes relating to the client's subscriptions, and new titles in specific areas of interest. 2) Checklists—provide lists of a client's subscriptions in any sequence or combination required. 3) Subject searches—provide subject/title alphabetical lists with publishers prices to assist the client in collection building. 4) Quotations—provide price information for any group of titles based on the most currently available publisher information. 5) Price analysis reports—provide price records of a client's subscriptions over the last three years. 6) FAST—an online serial check-in, control, and claiming system originally developed for, and in cooperation with, the U.S. National Library of Medicine and the U.S. National Agricultural Library. It is designed to supply any library with its North American, British, or European titles. FAST provides each customer with a monthly cumulative list summarizing issues delivered and claimed during the current year; the lists are available on microfiche and magnetic tape.

Other Services: Swets also offers SAILS (Swets Automated Independent Library System), a fully integrated software package for the online management of all library in-house operations.

Clientele/Availability: Primary clients include university, research, industrial, and governmental libraries.

Remarks: Swets & Zeitlinger was established in Amsterdam in 1901 as a bookshop selling new and antiquarian books. After World War II, the bookshop developed into an international library service group with subsidiaries in the United States, Brazil, France, and, more recently, England.

Contact: J.J. Nouwen, Technical Customer Service, Swets Subscription Service. (Telex 41325.) In North America contact Swets North America Inc., P.O. Box 517, Berwyn, PA 19312; telephone (215) 644-4944. (Telex 814342.)

★943★
SWISS ACADEMY OF MEDICAL SCIENCES DOCUMENTATION SERVICE (DOKDI)
Waldheimstr. 20
CH-3012 Berne, Switzerland
Dr. Zdenek Urbanek, Head
Phone: 031 232572
Service Est: 1971

Staff: Approximately 9 total.

Description of System or Service: The DOCUMENTATION SERVICE (DOKDI) provides clients in Switzerland with online information searches in life sciences fields using data bases carried by European and North American vendors. It also offers related consulting and referral services.

Scope and/or Subject Matter: Agriculture, biology, biochemistry, and medicine are the chief subjects searched by DOKDI.

Input Sources: Online data bases supply input for the services.

Computer-Based Products and Services: Retrospective search and SDI services are offered from the data bases made available by the following online services: U.S. National Library of Medicine, ESA/IRS, System Development Corporation (SDC), DIALOG Information Services, Inc., Bibliographic Retrieval Services (BRS), British Library, Data-Star, and others. DOKDI conducts more than 7000 searches annually.

Clientele/Availability: Services are available mainly to clients in Switzerland.

Contact: Dr. Zdenek Urbanek, Head, Documentation Service, Swiss Academy of Medical Sciences.

★944★
SWISS CENTER OF DOCUMENTATION IN MICROTECHNOLOGY (CENTREDOC)
Rue Breguet 2
CH-2000 Neuchatel 7, Switzerland
Bernard Chapuis, Manager
Phone: 038 254181
Founded: 1964

Staff: 4 Information and library professional; 2 management professional.

Related Organizations: CENTREDOC is supported by annual fees paid by Swiss horological and microtechnical companies.

Description of System or Service: The SWISS CENTER OF DOCUMENTATION IN MICROTECHNOLOGY (CENTREDOC) provides information and documentation services in microtechnology and related areas. Services include patent documentation, computerized literature searching, current awareness, market and company information, economic analysis, technology monitoring, document delivery, and data base development.

Scope and/or Subject Matter: Microtechnology, micromechanics, microelectronics, patents, and related economic and commercial information.

Input Sources: The Center utilizes its library collection and online data bases.

Holdings and Storage Media: The Center's library holdings comprise 3200 bound volumes, subscriptions to 200 periodicals, and the full text of 62,000 patent documents.

Publications: 1) CENTREDOC Bulletin (weekly)—includes tables of contents of periodicals received by the Center. 2) Revue des Inventions Horlogeres-RIH (semimonthly)—describes new patents in horological classes.

Computer-Based Products and Services: CENTREDOC conducts online searching of data bases available through ESA/IRS, System Development Corporation (SDC), DIALOG Information Services, Inc., INKA (Informationssystem Karlsruhe), Data-Star, Telesystemes Questel, and other Euronet DIANE hosts. It also offers online data base development and management services.

Other Services: Patent watch and search services in all fields are also available.

Clientele/Availability: CENTREDOC services are intended for member firms and institutions, but most services offered by the Center are available to customers worldwide.

Contact: Bernard Chapuis, Manager, or Robert Bachelin, Engineer,

CENTREDOC.

★945★

SWISS COORDINATION CENTER FOR RESEARCH IN EDUCATION
(Schweizerische Koordinationsstelle fur Bildungsforschung - SKBF)
Entfelderstr. 61
CH-5000 Aarau, Switzerland
Armin Gretler, Director
Phone: 064 211916
Founded: 1971

Staff: 2 Information and library professional; 1 management professional; 1 technician; 2 clerical and nonprofessional.

Description of System or Service: The SWISS COORDINATION CENTER FOR RESEARCH IN EDUCATION (SKBF) maintains the Information on Educational Research and Development in Switzerland (SWINFED) data base, a computer-readable file on educational research and development projects. The CENTER provides search services and publishes new material from the data base in a bimonthly newsletter. The CENTER also acts as the national clearinghouse of educational information under the European Documentation and Information System for Education (EUDISED), and it conducts online searching through commercial vendors.

Scope and/or Subject Matter: Projects of educational research and development in Switzerland.

Input Sources: Input consists of information collected directly by SKBF as well as online data bases.

Holdings and Storage Media: The SWINFED data base holds research project descriptions in machine-readable form.

Publications: Information Bildungsforschung Schweiz (bimonthly)—newsletter distributed in Switzerland and to several national documentation centers throughout Europe. The Center also publishes reports and studies; a list of publications is available by request.

Computer-Based Products and Services: The CENTER provides online information retrieval from data bases made available by DIALOG Information Services, Inc., ESA/IRS, Data-Star, INKA (Informationssystem Karlsruhe), and Telesystemes Questel. The SWINFED data base is a permanent inquiry system, and is used for publication of the newsletter and to provide information on current projects. It is expected to be incorporated as part of a file made available online via Data-Star.

Clientele/Availability: Services are available to interested organizations and individuals.

Remarks: The Center is also known as the Centre Suisse de Coordination pour la Recherche en Matiere d'Education.

Contact: Peter Knopf, Swiss Coordination Center for Research in Education.

★946★

SWISS VIEWDATA INFORMATION PROVIDERS ASSOCIATION (SVIPA)
P.O. Box 184
CH-8021 Zurich, Switzerland
Erwin A. Nigg, Head
Phone: 01 2213187
Founded: 1979

Description of System or Service: The SWISS VIEWDATA INFORMATION PROVIDERS ASSOCIATION (SVIPA) is a group of Swiss organizations concerned with the promotion and development of videotex information services. In addition to its other services, SVIPA cooperates in the maintenance of the Viewdata Documentation Service. This service provides for the electronic documentation and retrieval of videotex-related literature.

Scope and/or Subject Matter: Videotex, teletext, and related telecommunications services, specific applications, hardware, software, and social, economic, and legal issues.

Input Sources: Input for the documentation service is derived from periodicals and newspapers.

Holdings and Storage Media: A computer-readable bibliographic data base is maintained.

Publications: SVIPA issues a bimonthly newsletter.

Computer-Based Products and Services: The Viewdata Documentation Service provides computerized information retrieval services for videotex-related literature. Among the items included in a typical citation are publication source, article title, author, language code, publication type, controlled descriptors, free-text abstract, and organizations cited.

Clientele/Availability: Primary clients are SVIPA members.

Remarks: SVIPA is also known as Verband Schweizerischer Bildschirmtext-Informationslieferanten, and as Association Suisse des Fournisseurs d'Informations Viewdata.

Contact: Erwin A. Nigg, Head, Swiss Viewdata Information Providers Association.

★947★

SWISS WILDLIFE INFORMATION SERVICE (SWIS)
Strickhofstr. 39
CH-8057 Zurich, Switzerland
Rolf Anderegg, Head
Phone: 01 3627728
Founded: 1973

Staff: 4 Information and library professional; 1 management professional.

Related Organizations: The Service is supported by the Federal Forestry Office and the University of Zurich.

Description of System or Service: The SWISS WILDLIFE INFORMATION SERVICE (SWIS) collects and disseminates information on wildlife research, conservation, and management. It scans international scientific literature in these areas for input to its computer-readable Database of Wildlife Research. The Database is used to prepare an annual hardcopy keyword index and to provide computerized retrieval services on request. The SERVICE also maintains copies of approximately 90 percent of the articles cited and provides copying services.

Scope and/or Subject Matter: Wildlife information, including behavior, conservation, diseases, ecology, food, morphology, national parks, natural resources, parasitology, physiology, pollution, population, wildlife management, and zoogeography.

Input Sources: Sources scanned include approximately 500 periodical titles, as well as reports, proceedings, dissertations, bibliographies, and publication lists.

Holdings and Storage Media: The machine-readable Database of Wildlife Research holds information on 30,000 titles from 1974 to the present and is updated quarterly. Library holdings include 1000 bound volumes and subscriptions to 250 periodicals.

Publications: Key-Word-Index of Wildlife Research (annual)—arranged by keywords with author and other indexes, including a biannual species and systematic index.

Computer-Based Products and Services: The SWISS WILDLIFE INFORMATION SERVICE maintains and provides current awareness and retrospective searches from the Database of Wildlife Research. Records in the data base include author, article title, journal, year of publication, number of titles cited, author address, language, and keyword content summaries.

Clientele/Availability: Primary clients are wildlife scientists.

Contact: Rolf Anderegg, Head, Swiss Wildlife Information Service.

★948★

SWITZERLAND
SWISS INTELLECTUAL PROPERTY OFFICE (SIPO)
TECHNICAL INFORMATION ON PATENTS (TIPAT)
Einsteinstr. 2
CH-3003 Berne, Switzerland
Mr. R. Egli, Head of Department
Phone: 031 614806
Service Est: 1984

Staff: 6 Information and library professional; 1 management professional; 1 clerical and nonprofessional.

Description of System or Service: The TECHNICAL INFORMATION ON PATENTS (TIPAT) service provides Swiss and foreign researchers and industrial clients with computerized searches from patent-related and other technical data bases accessed online through European and United States vendors. It also assists in the procurement of photocopies of cited documents.

Scope and/or Subject Matter: Preliminary information on the state of the art in all fields of technology.

Input Sources: International online services are accessed.

Computer-Based Products and Services: TIPAT performs online searching of data bases and data banks made available through such vendors as DIALOG Information Services, Inc., System Development Corporation (SDC), ESA/IRS, INKA (Informationssystem Karlsruhe), FIZ Technik, DIMDI, Pergamon InfoLine Ltd., INPADOC, Telesystemes Questel, Data-Star, and others.

Clientele/Availability: Services are available on a fee basis to interested parties in Switzerland and abroad.

Remarks: Services provided by TIPAT were assumed from the now defunct Swiss Institute for Technical Information (SITI).

Contact: Mr. R. Egli, Head of Department, Technical Information on Patents. (Telex 33130 BAGE CH.)

★949★
SYDONI S.A.
1, rue du Boccador   Phone: 01 7208834
F-75008 Paris, France   Founded: 1980

Staff: Approximately 40 total.

Related Organizations: SYDONI is affiliated with Editions Francis Lefebvre.

Description of System or Service: SYDONI S.A. compiles and maintains a series of computer-readable files covering primary and secondary sources of French legal information. Files include: 1) SYD, covering family, property, real estate, rural, and commercial law since 1962; 2) SOC, which covers socioeconomic and labor law; 3) ECO, which covers economic law, including competition, consumption, distribution, and price regulations; and 4) DIF, which covers tax law. SYDONI files are available for online searching through commercial time-sharing.

Scope and/or Subject Matter: French law, including commercial, economic, socioeconomic, tax, real estate, property, rural, and family law.

Input Sources: Information for the data bases is derived from more than 200 periodicals and from unpublished material obtained from French government agencies and courts.

Holdings and Storage Media: Coverage in the four machine-readable SYDONI files totals nearly 150,000 documents, with an annual increase of 50,000 items. The files are updated weekly.

Microform Products and Services: SYDONI offers unpublished materials on microfiche.

Computer-Based Products and Services: SYDONI makes its computer-readable files accessible online as the SYDONI Data Base available through Telesystemes Questel.

Clientele/Availability: Primary clients are French lawyers, government agencies, and others concerned with French law.

Contact: Sales Manager, SYDONI S.A.

★950★
SYSTEL (SISTEMI TELEMATICI SRL)
Via Cibrario 27   Phone: 011 7492225
I-10143 Torino, Italy   Founded: 1982
Umberto Cavallaro, General Director

Staff: 1 Information and library professional; 2 management professional; 2 technicians; 2 sales and marketing; 2 clerical and nonprofessional.

Description of System or Service: SYSTEL (Sistemi Telematici srl) provides information consulting and research services for clients in business, government, and nonprofit organizations. Consulting services are offered in information management, data base production, and training for online searching. SYSTEL provides online information retrieval and SDI services using international online services. Additionally, the firm maintains the computer-readable BASELINE data base covering commercially available online data bases and publishes a corresponding printed directory.

Scope and/or Subject Matter: Information management, online data bases, and information research in business, economics, finance, marketing, management, energy, environment, and patents.

Input Sources: BASELINE information is obtained from data base producers and documentation. SYSTEL also accesses international online services.

Holdings and Storage Media: The computer-readable BASELINE data base contains information on more than 500 commercially available data bases.

Publications: Guida alle Banche Dati/Guide to Data Banks—a two-volume publication providing information on Italian data base producers and European online services and the data bases which are made available through them.

Computer-Based Products and Services: SYSTEL maintains the computer-readable BASELINE data base which provides descriptions of more than 500 commercially available data bases, including such information as subject coverage, holdings, time period covered, input sources, and number of records. SYSTEL also offers information retrieval and SDI services from data bases made available through Data-Star, DIALOG Information Services, Inc., System Development Corporation (SDC), DIMDI, ECHO, ESA/IRS, INKA (Informationssystem Karlsruhe), Pergamon InfoLine Ltd., and Telesystemes Questel.

Clientele/Availability: Clients include corporations, banks, public administrations, industrial associations, and other interested parties.

Contact: Umberto Cavallaro, General Director, SYSTEL.

★951★
SYSTEM DEVELOPMENT CORPORATION (SDC)
SDC INFORMATION SERVICES - EUROPE
Bakers Court   Phone: (not reported)
Bakers Rd.   Service Est: 1984
Uxbridge, Middlesex UB8 1RG, England
Susan Inglis, Manager

Special Note: The newly formed SDC INFORMATION SERVICES - EUROPE provides marketing and support services in Europe for the California-based SDC Information Services (which is fully described in the United States volume of this Encyclopedia). The European office provides support for SDC's online host service and markets such related products as the ORBIT Information Retrieval System and the SearchMaster Software package. SDC INFORMATION SERVICES - EUROPE takes over the services previously offered through the Derwent-SDC Search Service.

Contact: Susan Inglis, Manager, SDC Information Services - Europe, at the above address. SDC Information Services also has associates or representatives in Australia, Japan, and Brazil. In Australia, contact SDC Information Services, 30 Alfred St., P.O. Box 439, Milsons Point, N.S.W. 2061, Australia; telephone 02 9229308. (Telex 23015 BURAD AA.) SDC is represented in Japan by System Development Corporation of Japan, Ltd. (see separate entry following this one). In Brazil, contact Barroslearn, Rua 24 de Maio 62-5.0, C.P. 6182, Cep. 01000, Sao Paulo SP, Brazil; telephone 011 2236011. (Telex 01131770 PBAS BR.)

★952★
SYSTEM DEVELOPMENT CORPORATION OF JAPAN, LTD.
SEARCH/J
Nishi-Shinjuku-Showa Bldg.   Phone: 03 3498521
1-13-12 Nishi-Shinjuku, Shinjuku-ku   Service Est: 1979
Tokyo 160, Japan
Masao Namekawa, General Manager

Staff: 1 Information and library professional; 1 management professional; 3 technicians; 2 sales and marketing; 1 clerical and nonprofessional.

Related Organizations: System Development Corporation of Japan, Ltd. is a subsidiary of the California-based System Development Corporation, which is described in the United States volume of this Encyclopedia.

Description of System or Service: SEARCH/J is an online search facility operated in Japan by the System Development Corporation.

Its computers hold copies of several data bases carried by SDC on its California facilities. Users in Japan can interactively access these without having to pay overseas telecommunications charges. SEARCH/J also maintains an action desk with experts trained in the ORBIT system. They can provide information on registration procedures, pricing, data base coverage, search strategy development, access techniques, and related matters.

Scope and/or Subject Matter: Online data bases, mainly in scientific and technical fields.

Computer-Based Products and Services: SEARCH/J provides users in Japan with local online access to the following data bases: CRDS, ORBIT, PESTDOC, RINGDOC, SAE, VETDOC, and WPI. Alternately, clients can use telecommunications links to access the full line of data bases held on SDC California computers.

Clientele/Availability: Services are intended for searchers in Japan.

Contact: Masao Namekawa, General Manager, Information Service Department, Search/J. (Telex 232 2262 SDCJ J.)

★953★
SYSTEMHOUSE LTD. (SHL)
MINISIS
2827 Riverside Dr. Phone: (613) 526-0670
Ottawa, ON, Canada K1V 0C4 Service Est: 1978
Colin Townsend, Product Manager

Related Organizations: MINISIS was developed by the International Development Research Centre (IDRC) for use in bibliographic applications.

Description of System or Service: MINISIS is a generalized information management software package designed for Hewlett-Packard HP3000 minicomputers and offering applications for libraries, information centers, museums, and other organizations requiring retrieval and reporting capabilities for large volumes of text-oriented information. It allows users who are not computer experts to create and use data bases. The system is a modular package with processors for entering, modifying, and retrieving data online; for carrying out arithmetic operations; and for producing a variety of reports. A related records management system, MINISIS-RM, allows document control and tracing and may be used to produce labels, recall slips, alphabetic and numeric indexes, and customized reports.

Scope and/or Subject Matter: Information and records management and retrieval for government and industry.

Computer-Based Products and Services: Designed to run on any HP3000 series minicomputer, MINISIS permits the user to develop a complete system based upon a sophisticated relational data base without program development. It supplies full data base management capabilities including online data entry, correction, retrieval, and report generation. The MINISIS command language supports query processing with Boolean logic, keyword searching, string searching, and other features, including a multilingual thesaurus. MINISIS also offers circulation and serials control capabilities. MINISIS-RM provides records management functions including document classification, searching, circulation, and report generation.

Clientele/Availability: MINISIS is available for lease or purchase or through a participating computer service bureau.

Remarks: Systemhouse Ltd. is Canada's largest data-processing consulting firm and supplies a full range of services for planning, development, implementation, and operation of computer-based information systems. It maintains branches throughout Canada and the United States.

Contact: Colin Townsend, Product Manager, MINISIS, Systemhouse Ltd.

T

★954★
T.C. LIBRARY SERVICES LTD.
London Rd.
Sunningdale, Berks. SL5 0EP, England
Phyllis M. Cooper, Managing Director
Phone: 0990 22009
Founded: 1984

Staff: 1 Management professional; 2 sales and marketing; 5 clerical and nonprofessional.

Description of System or Service: T.C. LIBRARY SERVICES LTD. is the United Kingdom office of the U.S.-based EBSCO Subscription Services. It makes available the full range of EBSCO computer-supported serial subscription services for academic, public, government, and special libraries. (EBSCO's services are fully described in the United States volume of this Encyclopedia.)

Contact: Phyllis M. Cooper, Managing Director, T.C. Library Services Ltd.

★955★
TANZANIA
NATIONAL CENTRAL LIBRARY
TANZANIA NATIONAL DOCUMENTATION CENTRE (TANDOC)
P.O. Box 9283
Dar es Salaam, Tanzania
Mr. E.A. Mwinyimvua, Principal Librarian
Phone: 26121
Service Est: 1976

Staff: 53 Information and library professional; 4 management professional; 150 technicians; 200 clerical and nonprofessional.

Description of System or Service: The TANZANIA NATIONAL DOCUMENTATION CENTRE (TANDOC) was established to stimulate rapid growth in key sectors of the economy and to provide information services to specialists in development technologies. Using national and international publications and information resources, TANDOC provides information and document retrieval, photocopying, and document delivery services; current awareness; and referral services connecting clients to additional contacts, specialists, and institutions worldwide. TANDOC also prepares bibliographies and abstracts of literature in technical areas and in subject areas specified by clients.

Scope and/or Subject Matter: Appropriate technology, agriculture, education, public health, economic development, industry and commerce.

Input Sources: Information sources include books, journals, reports, indexes, catalogs, government agencies, and foreign and international organizations and government agencies.

Holdings and Storage Media: The National Central Library maintains a collection of 600,000 bound volumes; subscriptions to 2000 periodicals; and documents and reports.

Publications: 1) Industrial Abstracts for Tanzania (two per year); 2) Educational Abstracts for Tanzania (two per year); 3) Agricultural Abstracts for Tanzania (two per year); 4) Union List of Periodicals in Tanzania; 5) List of Practicing Librarians & Documentalists in Tanzania. TANDOC also produces subject bibliographies and is compiling a national library directory.

Other Services: TANDOC also offers consulting services to institutions wishing to start small libraries or documentation units.

Clientele/Availability: Services are free to institutions, researchers, scholars, technologists, and individuals. A fee is assessed for photocopying services.

Contact: Mr. E.E. Kaungamno, Director, Tanzania Library Service.

★956★
TAYSON INFORMATION TECHNOLOGY INC.
275 Comstock Rd.
Toronto, ON, Canada M1L 2H2
Peter Richardson, President
Phone: (416) 288-0550
Founded: 1981

Staff: 3 Management professional; 2 sales and marketing; 1 other.

Description of System or Service: TAYSON INFORMATION TECHNOLOGY INC. offers the Tayson Personal Videotex System which supports local storage, creation, manipulation, and modification of videotex pages according to NAPLPS (North American Presentation Level Protocol Syntax) standards. Adaptable to personal or microcomputers running under MS-DOS, the System emulates large host retrieval functions through hierarchical data base structure; communicates with remote service bureaus or other local videotex terminals; and allows for downloading of pages from remote hosts or external graphics creation terminals. In addition to providing the System, TAYSON INFORMATION TECHNOLOGY offers consulting services on videotex applications.

Scope and/or Subject Matter: Microcomputer videotex applications.

Computer-Based Products and Services: The Tayson Personal Videotex System data base structure emulates large host retrieval functions for videotex pages stored on personal computers or microcomputers. The System also provides networking capabilities allowing access to other microcomputers, remote hosts, and videotex service bureaus.

Clientele/Availability: Services are available without restrictions; clients include businesses, cable operators, and government agencies.

Contact: Peter Richardson, President, Tayson Information Technology Inc. The electronic mail address on ENVOY 100 (Telecom Canada) is TAYSON.

★957★
TECHNICAL CENTER FOR MECHANICAL INDUSTRIES
(Centre Technique des Industries Mecaniques - CETIM)
DOCUMENTATION CENTER FOR MECHANICS
(Centre de Documentation de la Mecanique - CDM)
P.O. Box 67
F-60304 Senlis, France
J.N. Ostermann, Head
Phone: 4 4533266
Service Est: 1966

Staff: 2 Information and library professional; 1 management professional; 8 technicians; 6 clerical and nonprofessional.

Description of System or Service: The DOCUMENTATION CENTER FOR MECHANICS (CDM) offers information services in the field of mechanical engineering. It maintains the computer-readable CETIM data base of references and abstracts of journal articles and other technical literature, and uses it to publish a monthly abstracting and indexing journal known as the Bulletin de la Construction Mecanique. The CETIM data base is also publicly available for online searching, and document delivery services are offered. Additionally, CDM maintains three special libraries in France and supplies library research services on request.

Scope and/or Subject Matter: Mechanical engineering industry, including general problems, materials, tests and measurements, control, regulation, automation, metal machining and forming, surface treatments and coatings, thermal treatments, welding, mechanical joints, adhesive bonding, friction, wear, lubrication, machine parts, plastics, and equipment.

Input Sources: Input is drawn from more than 800 technical journals as well as proceedings, theses, books, and CETIM internal reports.

Holdings and Storage Media: The machine-readable CETIM data base holds 75,000 references and abstracts dating from 1975 to the present and is updated monthly. The library maintains 5000 volumes and subscriptions to 1000 periodicals.

Publications: Bulletin de la Construction Mecanique (monthly with annual index)—each issue contains approximately 400 references and abstracts derived from more than 800 periodicals and other sources.

Computer-Based Products and Services: The CETIM data base is available online through ESA/IRS. Searchable fields include author, classification code, document type, source, journal title, language, accession number, publication date, title, abstract, and controlled vocabulary terms. CDM fulfills document orders placed online through ESA's PRIMORDIAL service.

Clientele/Availability: Services are available without limitations to the mechanical engineering community.

Contact: J.N. Ostermann, Head, Documentation Center for Mechanics. (Telex 140006 F CETIM SENLI.)

★958★
TECHNICAL INDEXES LTD.
Willoughby Rd.　　　　　　　　　　　Phone: 0344 426311
Bracknell, Berks. RG12 4DW, England　Founded: 1964
Michael Lee, Managing Director

Staff: Approximately 100 total.

Related Organizations: Technical Indexes Ltd. is a sister company of Information Handling Services (IHS).

Description of System or Service: TECHNICAL INDEXES LTD. (ti) is a micropublisher that gathers, organizes, indexes, and publishes updated descriptive technical literature on components and equipment used in many engineering disciplines. It also publishes collections of updated and amended national standards of various countries and international standards bodies. All TECHNICAL INDEXES publications are available in microform to industrial, government, and defense research and development establishments.

Scope and/or Subject Matter: Chemical, electronic, electrical, mechanical, construction, civil, and production engineering; materials handling; laboratory equipment; drawing office equipment; defense, national, and international standards.

Input Sources: Information is gathered principally from technical sales literature and standards bodies.

Publications: Printed indexes are issued in conjunction with the firm's microform products.

Microform Products and Services: The following collections are available on microfiche and microfilm: 1) British Standards (monthly)—contains all British Standards. 2) Aerospace and Aviation Documents (quarterly)—provides aerospace standards published by British and other organizations. 3) Computer and Communications Technology Documents (twice per year)—holds standards and technical reports issued by the European Computer Manufacturers Association, documents issued by committees of the International Telecommunication Union (ITU), and videotex specifications, guides, and recommendations. 4) CENELEC Electronic Components Committee-CECC (quarterly)—contains English, French, and German-language publications and specifications issued by the CECC. The following collections are available on microfilm: 5) Defence Documents (quarterly)—contains United Kingdom defense standards, specifications, and related documents.

6) Electronic Engineering Index (three per year, with monthly updates)—provides catalogs, product specifications, and related technical information from manufacturers and suppliers of electronic equipment and components. 7) Process Engineering Index (twice per year)—contains catalogs, product specifications, and related technical information from manufacturers and suppliers of components and equipment for the processing and chemical engineering industry. 8) Manufacturing and Materials Handling Index-MMHI (twice per year)—holds manufacturers' catalogs, product specifications, application data, and related information. 9) Engineering Components and Materials Index (twice per year)—contains catalogs, product specifications, and related technical information from manufacturers and suppliers of engineering components, materials, and equipment. 10) Electronic Components of Assessed Quality-ECAQ (every two months)—provides detail specifications, issued by manufacturers, which relate to particular components approved under the BS 9000 and CECC QA schemes.

11) Laboratory Equipment Index (twice per year)—contains catalogs, product specifications, and related technical information from manufacturers and suppliers of laboratory equipment, fittings, disposables, and all types of laboratory and analytical instrumentation. 12) German DIN Standards (every two months)—holds all German national standards that are officially available in their English-language translations. The following collections are available on microfiche: 13) Deutsche DIN Normen (monthly)—provides all German standards in the German language, excluding those derived from VDE specifications. 14) Construction and Civil Engineering Index (quarterly, with monthly updates for British standards)—contains catalogs, brochures, and product literature from British manufacturers and non-British manufacturers with United Kingdom agents in the fields of construction and civil engineering.

Each issue of the above microform publications is accompanied by a cumulative hardcopy index.

Clientele/Availability: Services are available without restrictions.

Contact: Philip C. Stow, Director of Sales, or Paul Stroud, Promotions Executive, Technical Indexes Ltd. (Telex 849207 TEKINF G.)

★959★
TECHNICAL INFORMATION CENTER
(Fachinformationszentrum Technik - FIZ Technik)
Postfach 600547　　　　　　　　　　Phone: 069 43081
D-6000 Frankfurt am Main 60, Fed. Rep.
　of Germany

Description of System or Service: The TECHNICAL INFORMATION CENTER (FIZ Technik) provides information and documentation services in the areas of engineering and management. Among the specific services provided are the following: 1) Production of data bases—produces the ZDE electrical engineering, DOMA mechanical engineering, and MEDITEC medical technology data bases, which are described in separate entries following this one. 2) Information service—offers abstracts journals and SDI services for engineering information. 3) Information brokering—covers engineering, patent, and business information. 4) Full-text service—delivers copies of the original documents; online ordering is offered. 5) Online service—offers direct online access to its own data bases and other related data bases produced by other organizations. 6) Software—offers the PLIDOS information retrieval software system for Commodore 8032 computers. 7) Consulting—provides information service referrals, support for online access to FIZ Technik data bases, and seminars for online users.

Scope and/or Subject Matter: Electrical engineering and electronics; mechanical and production engineering; biomedical engineering; and management and organization.

Input Sources: FIZ Technik scans periodicals and other literature and acquires data bases from private organizations in Germany.

Holdings and Storage Media: Nine machine-readable data bases are held online by FIZ Technik.

Publications: Abstracting and current awareness publications are produced from FIZ Technik data bases. User manuals are also issued.

Computer-Based Products and Services: FIZ Technik Technik operates an online host service utilizing the GRIPS/DIRS3 information retrieval system and accessible via Euronet, national packet-switching networks, and the public telephone network. The service permits Boolean-logic searching with online display or offline printing of records; online document ordering for all items cited in the data bases is also available. The following data bases are accessible through the FIZ Technik online host service: 1) DECHEMA—covers chemical engineering. 2) DKI—plastics and polymers. 3) DKF—automotive engineering. 4) DOMA—mechanical engineering. 5) EK-MRA—nonbibliographic file of manufacturers. 6) MEDITEC—biomedical engineering. 7) TECLEARN—training data base holding records from DOMA, MEDITEC, and ZDE. 8) VDI News—full-text journal data base. 9) ZDE—electrical engineering. (Additional information on these data bases and their producers can be located through the data base index in the back of this volume.) For Commodore 8032 computers, FIZ Technik offers PLIDOS, a software system which allows preparation of online searches, quick searching and downloading, and word processing for individual finishing.

Clientele/Availability: Services are available on a fee basis without restrictions.

Projected Publications and Services: FIZ Technik plans to offer online access to the following data bases: 1) Packaging Science and Technology Abstracts (PSTA); 2) BLIS, covering management sciences; and 3) BEFO, which is produced by the Center and covers management and organization.

Contact: R. Pernsteiner, Marketing-Manager, Technical Information Center. (Telex 4 189 459 FIZT D.) The Center maintains offices at Ostbahnhofstr. 13-15, D-6000 Frankfurt am Main 1.

★960★
TECHNICAL INFORMATION CENTER
(Fachinformationszentrum Technik - FIZ Technik)
ELECTRICAL ENGINEERING DOCUMENTATION CENTER
(Zentralstelle Dokumentation Elektrotechnik - ZDE)
Postfach 600547　　　　　　　　　Phone: 069 4308255
D-6000 Frankfurt am Main 60, Fed. Rep.
　of Germany　　　　　　　　　　Service Est: 1971
Mr. W. Claassen, Head

Related Organizations: The ZDE is associated with a number of German organizations, including Verband Deutscher Elektrotechniker (VDE) and Zentralverband der Elektrotechnischen Industrie (ZVEI).

Description of System or Service: The ELECTRICAL ENGINEERING DOCUMENTATION CENTER (ZDE) provides access to the world's significant technical literature in electrical engineering and related areas. It scans all relevant journals, books, reports, and similar documents, and records them in the computer-readable ZDE data base. Online searching, SDI, publications, and other products and services are provided from the data base for German industry, educational institutions, government, and professional associations.

Scope and/or Subject Matter: Electrical engineering, including: power systems and applications; communications; computers and information processing; measurement, testing, and control; components and electronic devices.

Input Sources: Approximately 800 journals are scanned for input, as well as relevant books, reports, dissertations, and conference proceedings.

Holdings and Storage Media: The machine-readable ZDE data base contains more than 600,000 abstracts and references to literature since 1968 and is updated monthly; approximately 50,000 items are added yearly.

Publications: Literaturdienst Elektrotechnik (weekly or biweekly)—abstract service divided into 36 titles. A thesaurus, classification scheme, and list of journals are also available.

Computer-Based Products and Services: The ELECTRICAL ENGINEERING DOCUMENTATION CENTER offers computerized literature searching and standard and individual SDI services from its data base. Magnetic tape copies of the ZDE data base are also available, and it is accessible online through FIZ Technik and INKA (Informationssystem Karlsruhe). Data elements present include the following: main headings; title in original language and in German; abstract in English or German; author; corporate source/ author affiliation; source title and reference; document number; classification code; controlled terms; document type; and others.

Other Services: Document procurement services are also available through ZDE.

Clientele/Availability: There are no restrictions on services.

Remarks: References to literature published from 1968 to 1973 were maintained in the predecessor Dokumentationsring Elektrotechnik (DRE) data base and have since been incorporated in the ZDE data base, which is also known as the Literaturdatenbank Elektrotechnik.

Contact: Mr. W. Claassen, Head, Electrical Engineering Documentation Center. (Telex 4 189 459 FIZT D.) The Center maintains offices at FIZ Technik, Ostbahnhofstr. 13-15, D-6000 Frankfurt am Main 1.

★961★
TECHNICAL INFORMATION CENTER
(Fachinformationszentrum Technik - FIZ Technik)
MECHANICAL ENGINEERING DOCUMENTATION
(Dokumentation Maschinenbau - DOMA)
Postfach 600547　　　　　　　　　Phone: 069 4308227
D-6000 Frankfurt am Main 60, Fed. Rep.
　of Germany　　　　　　　　　　Service Est: 1972
W. Muller, Head

Related Organizations: DOMA is associated with Verein Deutscher Maschinenbau-Anstalten (VDMA) and Verein Deutscher Ingenieure (VDI).

Description of System or Service: MECHANICAL ENGINEERING DOCUMENTATION (DOMA) provides access to the world's literature on mechanical engineering and related fields. It maintains the machine-readable DOMA data base and provides a variety of services such as online literature searching, SDI, research and reference, and document delivery; and such products as abstracts journals, reviews, and machine-readable tapes.

Scope and/or Subject Matter: Mechanical engineering, including: mechanics, stress analysis, and thermodynamics; materials and materials testing; machine components; planning, development, and design; mechanical engineering measuring and control systems; turbines, combustion engines, pumps, and compressors; tools and machine tools; production engineering and quality control; processing machines; metallurgical and foundry engineering; construction engineering, conveying, and transportation technology; heating and drying technology and air conditioning; energy, environmental, and ocean technology; management.

Input Sources: Input is derived from approximately 600 journals, as well as reports, conference papers, dissertations, and European patents.

Holdings and Storage Media: Updated monthly, the machine-readable DOMA data base holds more than 300,000 abstracts and references to literature dating from 1970 to the present; about 30,000 items are added yearly. DOMA also maintains a collection of journals and microfilm.

Publications: DOMA Referatedienst (weekly, fortnightly, or monthly)—an abstracts journal in twelve issues, each covering a different topic. Search aids are also issued.

Computer-Based Products and Services: DOMA conducts online and batch searching of its data base and provides SDI services in standard or individual profiles. Magnetic tape copies of custom selections or the file in its entirety are also available. The DOMA data base is accessible for online searching through FIZ Technik and INKA (Informationssystem Karlsruhe). Data elements present include the following: main headings; title in original language and in German; abstract; author; corporate source/ author affiliation; source reference; document number; classification codes; controlled terms; document type; and others.

Clientele/Availability: Available without restrictions.

Remarks: The DOMA data base is also known as the Literaturdatenbank Maschinenbau.

Contact: W. Muller, Head, Mechanical Engineering Documentation. (Telex 4 189 459 FIZT D.) DOMA maintains offices at FIZ Technik, Ostbahnhofstr. 13-15, Frankfurt am Main 1.

★962★
TECHNICAL INFORMATION CENTER
(Fachinformationszentrum Technik - FIZ Technik)
MEDICAL TECHNOLOGY DOCUMENTATION
(Dokumentation Medizinische Technik - MEDITEC)
Postfach 600547　　　　　　　　　Phone: 069 4308250
D-6000 Frankfurt am Main 60, Fed. Rep.
　of Germany

Description of System or Service: MEDICAL TECHNOLOGY DOCUMENTATION (MEDITEC) produces a computer-readable data base containing references and abstracts of German and international scientific and technical literature in the field of biomedical engineering. The only German-language bibliographic data base in its field, the MEDITEC file is searchable online through commercial vendors.

Scope and/or Subject Matter: Biomedical engineering, including biological sciences, biomedical measurements, medical diagnostics, medical therapeutics, artificial organs and functions, and clinical engineering.

Input Sources: Input is derived primarily from periodicals, as well as from reports and conference papers.

Holdings and Storage Media: The machine-readable MEDITEC Data Base holds approximately 40,000 records dating from 1968 to the present; the data base is updated monthly at an annual increase of 6500 records.

Publications: Search aids are available.

Computer-Based Products and Services: The MEDITEC data base is searchable online through FIZ Technik, INKA (Informationssystem Karlsruhe), and DIMDI. Data elements present include the following: main headings; original and German-language title; abstract (primarily German-language, with some in English); author; corporate source/author affiliation; source title and reference; document number; classification code; controlled terms; document type; and others. Additionally, online ordering of cited documents is offered through FIZ Technik.

Clientele/Availability: Available without restrictions.

Contact: Medical Technology Documentation. (Telex 4 189 459 FIZT D.) MEDITEC maintains offices at FIZ Technik, Ostbahnhofstr. 13-15, D-6000 Frankfurt am Main 1.

★963★
TECHNICAL INFORMATION-DOCUMENTATION CONSULTANTS LTD.
4650 St. Catherine St. W. Phone: (514) 937-0000
Montreal, PQ, Canada H3Z 1S5 Founded: 1962
Ronald A. Javitch, Technical Director

Special Note: The above name, address, and telephone number have been verified for this edition, although no questionnaire response was received. The following text is reprinted from the 5th edition.

Staff: 5 Information and library professional; 3 management professional; 10 technicians; 4 clerical and nonprofessional.

Description of System or Service: TECHNICAL INFORMATION-DOCUMENTATION CONSULTANTS LTD. conducts information research for industry and commerce, educational institutions and academic centers, government and military agencies, research laboratories, and R&D institutes. Services include information retrieval, classification, and editing in specialized fields of technology, pure and applied science, and engineering. Abstracting publications and machine-readable files are produced for internal use. The CONSULTANTS also provide consulting, data collection and analysis, machine translation of foreign texts, SDI, manual literature searching, and referral services.

Scope and/or Subject Matter: Information work in such areas as aerospace engineering, general aviation, military recognition systems, underwater technology, plasma physics and magnetohydrodynamics, high voltage engineering, transmission systems, laser communications, applied mathematics, computer science and technology, computer graphics and display engineering, low temperature physics, biomedical electronics, biophysics.

Input Sources: Input is derived from world scientific, learned, and engineering journals, and from abstracts services and computerized data bases.

Holdings and Storage Media: The CONSULTANTS holds machine-readable files of client proprietary materials. Library holdings consist of 25,600 bound volumes; microforms; and subscriptions to 5780 periodicals.

Publications: Canadian Technical and Scientific Information News Journal (biweekly); other publications are produced for internal use through weekly scanning, reviewing, and abstracting of serials and periodicals.

Computer-Based Products and Services: The firm accesses its own classified data base and two external data bases. It is also developing a computer-based information service to be available to selected clientele.

Clientele/Availability: Services are available on a contract basis.

Contact: Ronald A. Javitch, Technical Director, Technical Information-Documentation Consultants Ltd.

★964★
TECHNICAL UNIVERSITY OF AACHEN
LABORATORY OF MACHINE TOOLS AND PRODUCTION ENGINEERING
(Laboratorium fur Werkzeugmaschinen und Betriebslehre)
CUTTING DATA INFORMATION CENTER
(Informationszentrum fur Schnittwerte - INFOS)
Werkzeugmaschinenlabor, RWTH Phone: 0241 807402
Steinbachstr. 53B Service Est: 1973
D-5100 Aachen, Fed. Rep. of Germany
Wilfried Koenig, Director

Related Organizations: The Center was formed by a group of manufacturers and users of machine tools and cutting materials, associations in the field, and universities.

Description of System or Service: The CUTTING DATA INFORMATION CENTER (INFOS) collects and disseminates data on machine tool cutting in order to improve industrial production, supports research and development, and encourages standardization in the field. It collects cutting values from European industry and research institutions, checks and evaluates the data, and stores them in machine-readable form. The CENTER makes the data available to inquirers by mail, telephone, or telex, in a form suited to the user's needs. In addition to the provision of cutting data, INFOS provides software for the determination and optimization of data calculations.

Scope and/or Subject Matter: Machine tool cutting data from turning, milling, drilling, and grinding operations, including feeds and cutting speeds, cutting depth, tool life and wear, and conditions under which cutting values are determined.

Input Sources: Data are received from European industry and research institutions. Feedback is also obtained from the user whenever possible for inclusion in the data bank.

Holdings and Storage Media: The machine-readable data bank contains about 1300 data records from systematic weartime experiments for turning of approximately 150 different materials. Additionally, data records from drilling, milling, and grinding operations are held.

Publications: The Center issues data handbooks.

Computer-Based Products and Services: A machine-readable data bank of cutting data is maintained to provide industrial users with general recommended and factory-specific cutting values. In addition, the CENTER creates programming systems which determine automatically the technological data of the machining process.

Clientele/Availability: Services are available to the public. Software and data are available for purchase.

Contact: Wilfried Koenig, Director, Cutting Data Information Center; telephone 0241 807401.

★965★
TECHNICAL UNIVERSITY OF WROCLAW
(Politechnika Wroclawska)
MAIN LIBRARY AND SCIENTIFIC INFORMATION CENTER
(Biblioteka Glowna I Osrodek Informacji Naukowo-Technicznej)
SYSTEM OF COMPUTERIZED PROCESSING OF SCIENTIFIC INFORMATION (APIN)
Wybrzeze Wyspianskiego 27 Phone: 202305
50-370 Wroclaw, Poland Service Est: 1974
Stanislaw Bekisz, Director

Staff: The staff of the Main Library and Scientific Information Center includes 86 information and library professional; 16 management professional; 44 technicians; 21 other.

Related Organizations: Support is received from the Scientific, Technical and Economic Information Center (CINTE).

Description of System or Service: The SYSTEM OF COMPUTERIZED PROCESSING OF SCIENTIFIC INFORMATION (APIN) is a library and information management system which consists of the following five subsystems: 1) IDOL, an online information retrieval system in the conversational mode, designed for retrospective searching of bibliographic data bases; 2) SABI/OC used for periodicals cataloging; 3) SABI/OZ used for cataloging books; 4) SINT/NB which contains information on scientific research carried out at the Technical University of Wroclaw; and 5) SINT/SD, an SDI service utilizing commercially available data bases. APIN-MARC, a version of the U.S. Library of Congress MARC system, was developed for cataloging in accordance with Polish bibliographical and documentation standards.

Scope and/or Subject Matter: Mathematics, physics, chemistry, architecture, civil engineering, chemical engineering, electrical and electronic engineering, mechanics, biochemistry, cybernetics, materials science, earth science, systems theory.

Input Sources: Input consists of books and periodicals, scientific papers written by the Technical University's staff, and commercially available data bases.

Holdings and Storage Media: Holdings of the Main Library and Scientific Information Center include 1 million bound volumes, subscriptions to 2910 periodicals, and machine-readable data bases.

Publications: Science. Technology. Industry. (quarterly)—an abstracts publication in Polish covering the scientific papers of Technical University researchers. Scientific papers of the Main Library and Scientific Information Center are issued in Polish.

Computer-Based Products and Services: The IDOL system permits simultaneous online access for 120 users to a data base of more than 4.5 million bibliographic records. SDI services are supplied through SINT/SD from the following data bases: ASSISTENT, COMPENDEX, INIS, INSPEC, ISMEC, PASCAL, and SEBAN. The SEBAN data base is produced through SINT/NB, which is used to disseminate information by subject and author on scientific work completed at the Technical University including research topics and data for the analysis of that work.

Clientele/Availability: Services are intended for use by Polish citizens.

Contact: Lucja Talarczyk, Manager, System of Computerized Processing of Scientific Information. (Telex 0715371 PWPL.)

★966★
TECHNOLOGY INFORMATION CENTER GOTTINGEN
(Technologie-Informationszentrum Gottingen GmbH)
Postfach 3522   Phone: 0551 44982
Zindelstr. 3/5
D-3400 Gottingen, Fed. Rep. of Germany
Isolde Peinemann, Administrative Director

Staff: Approximately 6 total.

Description of System or Service: The TECHNOLOGY INFORMATION CENTER GOTTINGEN is an information broker service providing information retrieval services in all areas of economics, science, technology, and patents. It offers computerized searching of bibliographic and nonbibliographic data bases worldwide. The CENTER also provides document delivery and translation services, and information consultation and interpretation.

Scope and/or Subject Matter: Subjects of interest to clients, including economics, science, technology, and patents.

Input Sources: The firm derives input from commercially available data bases available through major online vendors.

Computer-Based Products and Services: Technical Information Center Gottingen conducts searches of more than 600 national and international data bases. In order to facilitate closer cooperation in the formulation of search strategies, it offers to perform computerized searches at the client's location.

Clientele/Availability: Services are available on a fee basis.

Contact: Isolde Peinemann, Administrative Director, Technology Information Center Gottingen. (Telex 965 215 TINFO.)

★967★
TECHNOLOGY RESOURCE CENTER (TRC)
TECHNOBANK PROGRAM
University of Life   Phone: 6735162
Bonifacio Bldg., 3rd Floor   Service Est: 1978
Pasig Metro Manila, Philippines
Aureo P. Castro, Program Manager

Staff: 1 Information and library professional; 1 management professional; 2 technicians; 1 clerical and nonprofessional.

Description of System or Service: The TECHNOBANK PROGRAM is a technical information facility of the Technology Resource Center, which was established to promote the use, application, and commercialization of technology in the Philippines. TECHNOBANK provides for the domestic dissemination of technical reports and other information from the U.S. National Technical Information Service (NTIS) and other foreign and domestic sources of information on technology, earth sciences, business, and other topics. The PROGRAM is the Philippine's connection for the United Nations Environmental Program's International Referral System for Environmental Information (INFOTERRA); it also provides local distribution of World Bank Technical Reports. Additionally, TECHNOBANK maintains the bibliographic Philippine Patents data base covering approximately 16,000 patents. The data base is searched online to produce listings of patents on alternative methods of processing and production, general technological topics, and commercialization.

Scope and/or Subject Matter: Appropriate technology, environmental information, economic development.

Input Sources: Input is obtained from the NTIS, United Nations, World Bank, and other foreign and domestic sources.

Holdings and Storage Media: The computer-readable Philippine Patents data base holds information on 16,000 patents dating from 1948 to 1982.

Microform Products and Services: The patents collection and a collection of presidential documents are also held on microfiche.

Computer-Based Products and Services: TECHNOBANK maintains and provides searches from the Philippine Patents data base. It also maintains a data base covering presidential documents issued from 1972 to 1983. TECHNOBANK plans to offer computerized information retrieval services from foreign data bases.

Other Services: Also offered is consultancy for information center development and referral services for information on world economy, trade, industrial trends, technology, and other relevant data.

Clientele/Availability: Services are available to technology developers, small and medium scale industries, urban and rural workers, entrepreneurs, industrial workers, households, community leaders, and the public.

Remarks: The Technology Resource Center also disseminates technological news, technical advice and training, management, and financing and marketing assistance for industries making use of new technologies. The Center's address is TRC Bldg., Buenida Ave., Extension Makati, Manila, Philippines.

Contact: Aureo P. Castro, Program Manager, Technobank Program. (Telex 64002 TRC PN.)

★968★
TECNOMEDIA
Via Antonio Caccia, n. 32   Phone: 0432 43341
I-33100 Udine, Italy   Founded: 1981
Paolo Cattapan, Managing Director

Description of System or Service: TECNOMEDIA provides technology and information brokerage services for clients in business, government, and nonprofit organizations. Its services include technology transfer, patent monitoring, current awareness, and computerized information retrieval from publicly available online data bases. The firm also offers innovation and development consulting services. In addition, TECNOMEDIA cooperates with international organizations working for innovation and belongs to a group of such organizations representing 24 countries.

Scope and/or Subject Matter: Technological developments in any subject area, including agriculture, chemistry, electronics, energy, medicine, and industrial automation.

Input Sources: Information is obtained from research institutes, consulting companies, private experts, universities, and commercial and government online vendors.

Computer-Based Products and Services: TECNOMEDIA provides information retrieval services from TRANSINOVE and other data bases carried by DIALOG Information Services, Inc., System Development Corporation (SDC), ESA/IRS, Data-Star, INKA (Informationssystem Karlsruhe), and Dr. Dvorkovitz and Associates.

Clientele/Availability: Tecnomedia serves industry, banks, private inventors, development agencies, associations, and others; services are available on a fee basis.

Contact: Paolo Cattapan, Managing Director, Tecnomedia.

★969★
TEIKOKU DATA BANK, LTD.
5-20, Minami-Aoyama 2-Chome Phone: 03 4044311
Minato-ku Founded: 1900
Tokyo 107, Japan
Tsuneo Ebata, Data Base Manager

Staff: 3 Information and library professional; 8 management professional; 18 technicians; 767 sales and marketing; 32 clerical and nonprofessional.

Description of System or Service: TEIKOKU DATA BANK, LTD. is the largest producer of credit, corporate, and financial data in Japan. It gathers financial and corporate information on businesses and manufacturing firms in Japan, and maintains the data in two computer-readable files, COSMOS I and COSMOS II. Compiled from corporate financial statements, COSMOS I provides financial affairs data on 130,000 small- and medium-sized companies. It can be used to ascertain the financial reliability of a company, to discover new clients, and to support management analysis through comparison with other companies in the same field. COSMOS II contains detailed corporate and chief executive data on 800,000 of the most active manufacturing and other companies in Japan. It supports campaigns for new clients, marketing research for new locations, and development of existing business. Output from COSMOS I and COSMOS II is available in a variety of machine-readable and hardcopy formats. TEIKOKU DATA BANK, LTD. also gathers information on a single-company basis through traditional information sources and onsite investigating; compiles data on real estate; and gathers marketing information in client specified areas. Additionally, the firm produces financial newspapers and publications.

Scope and/or Subject Matter: Financial, credit, corporate, and executive information on Japanese firms.

Input Sources: Input is derived from corporate financial reports, balance sheets, profit and loss statements, and from data gathered through 80 branch offices and correspondents worldwide.

Holdings and Storage Media: Machine-readable COSMOS I files contain financial data on 130,000 companies. COSMOS II files contain business, credit, and chief company executive information on 800,000 companies. Also maintained are registered corporate income files containing data on 100,000 companies, and corporate bankruptcy files with data on 115,000 companies.

Publications: 1) Teikoku Bank and Company Yearbook/ Teikoku Ginko Kaisha Nenkan (annual)—lists data on 160,000 banks and companies. 2) All-Japan Statistical Analysis of Corporate Financial Statements/ Zenkoku Kigyo Zaimu Shohyo Bunseki Tokei—covers the financial statements of 21,000 companies. 3) Teikoku Information/ Teikoku Joho (daily)—contains news on bankrupt companies, including the name of creditors and credit amount, business outlook, analysis, and registered income of corporations. 4) Monthly National Corporate Bankruptcy Report/ Zenkoku Tosan Shukei. 5) Teikoku Times (weekly)—a newspaper which includes news and commentaries about the industrial sector, registered income of corporations, regional economy, trends in company management, and other areas. 6) Registered Corporate Income Report/ Hojin Shinkoku Shotoku (monthly)—lists corporate income amounts registered at tax offices in Japan.

Computer-Based Products and Services: TEIKOKU DATA BANK, LTD. produces COSMOS I and COSMOS II data banks which hold financial and corporate data on Japanese companies. COSMOS I contains financial information gathered from corporate financial statements and is searchable by region (prefecture), industrial classification, capital, sales, number of employees, term of settlement, and other elements. Selected or complete financial information held in COSMOS I is available on magnetic tape or in hardcopy form. COSMOS II contains key business and financial data including region location, corporate code, industrial classification, telephone number, trade style, postal code, address, date of establishment, capital, annual sales, banks, dividend, term of settlement, number of employees, main suppliers, main customers, affiliation, profit, income declared for taxes, capital structure, credit rating, and chief executive name, address, telephone number, date of birth, birth place, and education. Data held in COSMOS II are available in specialized reports containing customer specified information, on marketing cards, on address tags or labels printed for direct mail, and on magnetic tape. The COSMOS files are also accessible on a time-sharing basis. TEIKOKU DATA BANK, LTD. also maintains registered corporate income files, corporate bankruptcy files, credit report files, and other data bases.

Other Services: The firm also maintains a computer-readable Who's Who Japan data base covering 500,000 persons and uses it to publish regional directories of company executives and other celebrities. The Hokkaido edition has been published, to be followed by other regional editions.

Clientele/Availability: Services are available without restrictions. Primary clients include financial institutions, insurance companies, securities firms, government organizations, and businesses.

Contact: Mikio Sasamura, Foreign Manager, Teikoku Data Bank, Ltd.

★970★
**TEL-AVIV UNIVERSITY
SHILOAH RESEARCH CENTER FOR MIDDLE EASTERN AND
  AFRICAN STUDIES
DOCUMENTATION SYSTEM
MIDEAST FILE (MEF)**
Ramat-Aviv Phone: 03 420993
Tel-Aviv, Israel Service Est: 1982
Haim Shaked, Editor in Chief

Staff: 15 Information and library professional; 2 management professional; 3 technicians; 1 clerical and nonprofessional; 2 other.

Related Organizations: The Mideast File is produced in cooperation with Learned Information Ltd.

Description of System or Service: The MIDEAST FILE (MEF) abstracts and indexes current world literature on the contemporary Middle East, covering journals published in the Middle East as well as those published in Europe and North America. MEF is available as a quarterly printed journal, on microfiche, on magnetic tape, and as a commercially available online data base.

Scope and/or Subject Matter: Contemporary events and issues in the Middle East, including anthropology, commerce, defense and military science, economics, finance, development plans, education, foreign policy, foreign trade, geography, history, Islam, law, literature, marketing, oil, politics and government, population and demography, psychology, public administration, science and technology, sociology, and statistics. Countries covered include Bahrain, Egypt, Iran, Iraq, Israel, Jordan, Kuwait, Lebanon, Libya, Oman, Qatar, Saudi Arabia, Sudan, Syria, Turkey, United Arab Emirates, and North and South Yemen.

Input Sources: Input for MEF is derived from approximately 1200 periodical titles, as well as books, reports, monographs, book reviews, documents, conference proceedings, dissertations, government announcements, official gazettes, manifestos, agreements, laws, joint communiques, interviews, speeches, and television and radio broadcasts.

Holdings and Storage Media: The machine-readable MEF data base contains approximately 35,000 records covering items published since 1979; the data base is updated monthly and approximately 12,000 records are added each year. Additionally, the Documentation System of the Shiloah Center holds a large collection of Middle East source materials, including Middle Eastern newspapers and periodicals, reference works, bibliographies, pamphlets and professional journals in Middle Eastern and European languages, newspaper and periodical clippings, broadcast monitoring reports, and dissertations.

Publications: Mideast File-MEF (quarterly)—abstracting and indexing journal covering international literature dealing with all aspects of the Middle East; each issue includes a subject index and an author index which are cumulated annually. MEF is available by subscription from Learned Information Ltd., Besselsleigh Rd., Abingdon, Oxford OX13 6LG, England; in the United States, order from Learned Information, Inc., Anderson House, Stokes Rd., Medford, NJ 08055.

Microform Products and Services: A microfiche version of Mideast File is published simultaneously with each issue of the journal.

Computer-Based Products and Services: The MIDEAST FILE is available for online searching through DIALOG Information Services, Inc. Search elements include abstract, descriptor, identifier (named company), named person, section heading, title, author, ISBN, country of publication, corporate source, document type, edition, historical period, journal name, language, publisher, publication year, reviewer name, report number, and series information. MEF includes alternate spellings of transliterated Arabic names. The FILE is also available on magnetic tape through lease arrangement with Learned Information.

Clientele/Availability: MEF is intended for academia, diplomats, economists, administrators, executives, risk analysis specialists, journalists, librarians, marketing organizations, financial corporations, commercial banks, and foreign ministries.

Remarks: The Mideast File is a by-product of the Documentation System's computerized retrieval system, which utilizes the facilities of the Tel-Aviv University Computation Center. The retrieval system covers holdings of the Shiloah Center as well as the holdings of a network of specialized libraries and information centers dealing in the various fields of Middle Eastern studies. The participants provide input on new acquisitions, journals, and reference works to the joint data base. Other activities of the network include coordinated acquisitions of periodical literature and a joint quarterly newsletter; a cooperative computer-based cataloging system is planned. SDI and query services are currently available.

Contact: Ami Salant, Director, Mideast File Database Project. (Telex 342171 VERSY IL.)

★971★
TELECOM CANADA
DATAPAC
410 Laurier Ave. W., Room 770 Phone: (613) 560-3030
Ottawa, ON, Canada K1P 6H5 Service Est: 1977
Douglas Sloane, President

Related Organizations: Telecom Canada is a consortium of Canada's nine major telecommunications carriers and Telesat Canada.

Description of System or Service: DATAPAC is a national shared data network designed to accommodate a wide variety of users, functions, and equipment. It utilizes packet switching technology which passes all information through nodal switches in the form of discrete units or packets. Transmission routes, through the use of virtual circuits and logical channels, are assigned only as and when they are required for the actual transmission of data. DATAPAC can provide support to a wide range of terminal types and operating speeds, and permits a diversity of data communications applications, including data retrieval and collection, inquiry and response, time-sharing, and bulk transfer.

Scope and/or Subject Matter: Packet-switched data communications services.

Computer-Based Products and Services: Intelligent terminals can access DATAPAC using X.25 protocol and a full-duplex, synchronous physical connection. Nonintelligent terminals can access through synchronous or asynchronous connections to a Packet Assembler/Disassembler (PAD), which converts data into X.25-specified packets. DATAPAC connects to Telenet and Tymnet in the United States and to 37 countries worldwide. DATAPAC uses some facilities of the Dataroute digital transmission system.

Clientele/Availability: Services are available on a fee basis, charged basically on the volume of information transmitted.

Remarks: Telecom Canada was formerly known as the TransCanada Telephone System.

Contact: Ruth Foster, Section Manager, Public Relations, Telecom Canada. The toll-free telephone number in Canada is 800-267-7400. (Telex 610 562 1911.) The electronic mail address on ENVOY 100 (Telecom Canada) is RD.FOSTER.

★972★
TELECOM CANADA
iNET 2000
410 Laurier Ave. W., Room 770 Phone: (613) 560-3030
Ottawa, ON, Canada K1P 6H5 Service Est: 1982
Douglas Sloane, President

Related Organizations: Telecom Canada is a consortium of Canada's nine major telecommunications carriers and Telesat Canada.

Description of System or Service: iNET 2000 is a user-oriented intelligent network designed to offer a single point of access to multiple remote computer-based information services. The network was developed to simplify the process of gathering, using, and communicating information for managers, executives, salespeople, and others requiring access to information. iNET 2000 provides access to videotex and ASCII-type data bases made available by various online information providers. The network offers such features as electronic directories of available services, automatic access to connected hosts, individual user profiles recognized by the network, and consolidated billing. The network is accessible from any location within Canada through standard alphanumeric or videotex terminals via telephone lines, private lines, or packet switching systems. iNET 2000 also connects with international packet switching networks allowing subscribers access to systems available in the United States and overseas. Additionally, full messaging services are available to users.

Scope and/or Subject Matter: Gateway access to a variety of business and consumer-oriented information services.

Computer-Based Products and Services: iNET 2000 facilitates online access to remote computer services. The user signs onto the network only once per session; access to other hosts through the service is performed automatically. iNET 2000 includes three types of directories to simplify access: 1) National directory—provides a consolidated listing of publicly available services which can be accessed through iNET. 2) Organization directory—provides a complete listing of all services available to common interest groups such as banking, real estate, or travel. 3) Personal directory—contains a listing of services which an individual iNET subscriber uses frequently. The network recognizes each individual through a user profile which defines how the user interacts with the system with respect to language, levels of expertise and authority, billing requirements, and other user-specified parameters.

Clientele/Availability: Services are available without restrictions.

Remarks: Telecom Canada was formerly known as TransCanada Telephone System.

Contact: Ruth Foster, Section Manager, Public Relations, Telecom Canada. The toll-free telephone number in Canada is 800-267-7400. (Telex 610 562 1911.) The electronic mail address on ENVOY 100 (Telecom Canada) is RD.FOSTER.

★973★
TELE-DIRECT (PUBLICATIONS) INC.
55 Town Centre Ct., 5th Floor Phone: (416) 296-4435
Scarborough, ON, Canada M1P 4X5
Eric Rand, Director of Business Development

Staff: Approximately 10 total.

Related Organizations: Tele-Direct (Publications) Inc. is a subsidiary of Bell Canada Enterprises.

Description of System or Service: TELE-DIRECT (PUBLICATIONS) INC. offers a full range of videotex-related services including consultation, training, application development, and page creation.

TELE-DIRECT also publishes Videotex Canada, a quarterly magazine which covers all aspects of the videotex industry with an emphasis on Canadian operations.

Scope and/or Subject Matter: Videotex information services.

Publications: Videotex Canada (quarterly)—contains technical articles on systems, standards information, educational opportunities, and new product and service news. Each issue contains a data base directory and a directory of files available through videotex services. It is available by subscription.

Computer-Based Products and Services: TELE-DIRECT (PUBLICATIONS) INC. develops pages for use on videotex systems and offers consultation and training services for videotex operations.

Clientele/Availability: Products and services are available without restrictions.

Contact: Eric Rand, Director of Business Development, or J. Brown-Tourigny, Managing Editor, Tele-Direct (Publications) Inc.

★974★
TELEGLOBE CANADA
NOVATEX

Special Note: NOVATEX, a service of Teleglobe Canada in Montreal, has been reported to be out of business. NOVATEX was described in the supplement to the fifth edition of Encyclopedia of Information Systems and Services (entry 2807) as an international videotex business information service, based on modified Telidon technology.

★975★
TELEKURS AG
INVESTDATA SYSTEM
Neugasse 247   Phone: 01 2752111
CH-8021 Zurich, Switzerland
Max Ruegg, Managing Director

Staff: 50 Information and library professional; 30 management professional; 80 technicians; 20 sales and marketing; 100 clerical and nonprofessional; 20 other.

Related Organizations: Telekurs AG is a service company sponsored by the Swiss financial community.

Description of System or Service: The INVESTDATA SYSTEM is a comprehensive computerized system based on information gathered on a real-time basis from all major security and commodity markets of the world. Remotely searchable online, INVESTDATA provides immediate access to the latest price quotations on securities, option contracts, and commodities, as well as key performance ratios, various indexes, and indicators of trends. Telex, computer tape, and printout services are also available from the data bank.

Scope and/or Subject Matter: Worldwide stocks, bonds, commodities, and money market information.

Input Sources: Input is obtained by online data collection from 80 stock exchanges and 18 commodity markets.

Holdings and Storage Media: The machine-readable data bank holds information on approximately 100,000 securities.

Computer-Based Products and Services: Accessible online from a terminal located in the client's place of business, INVESTDATA provides access to the following: 1) Market information, including current situation, current situation with previous day's prices, latest quotations of underlying stock together with all option series, securities selection and limit watch capabilities, market features (most active, most advanced, most declined, statistics), and money rates. 2) Basic securities data, accessible by stock symbol, securities code, or security's name in alphabetical form. 3) Capital and dividend information, including dividend payments and developments affecting capital. INVESTDATA users may communicate with each other via their terminals, and an optional printer permits hardcopy output. In addition to online access, INVESTDATA also offers several magnetic tape services, including daily tapes with price information on stocks and bonds.

Clientele/Availability: Services are designed for traders, portfolio managers, administrative managers, and similar clients.

Contact: B. Lichtensteiger, Director of Financial Information Services, Telekurs AG.

★976★
TELEMAP LTD.
MICRONET 800
Scriptor Court   Phone: 01-278 3143
155 Farringdon Rd.   Service Est: 1983
London EC1B 1PA, England
Timothy R. Schoonmaker, Managing Director

Staff: 8 Information and library professional; 4 management professional; 8 technicians; 6 sales and marketing; 8 clerical and nonprofessional.

Related Organizations: Micronet 800 is a joint project of EMAP (East Midland Allied Press) Business & Computer Publications Ltd., British Telecommunications, and Prism Microproducts.

Description of System or Service: MICRONET 800 is a networking facility on Prestel which provides microcomputer users in Great Britain with access to data base information, software packages, and communications services. The MICRONET data base contains news, business news, computer product comparisons, software reviews, dealership and price details, classified advertising, educational and utilities programs, program demonstrations, advertisements, and interactive game programs, and also offers facilities for closed user groups. MICRONET 800 also supplies access to software application packages online and permits downloading of games, business packages, and other software programs. Communication services include electronic mail, bulletin board, and telex services, and a gateway connecting MICRONET 800 users to other data bases and information services available through Prestel.

Scope and/or Subject Matter: Educational, business, and general information; software packages; electronic communications and electronic publishing.

Input Sources: Information is obtained from computer hardware and software dealers and manufacturers, education professionals, and other information providers.

Holdings and Storage Media: Micronet 800 data are maintained in machine-readable form.

Publications: A Micronet 800 newsletter is free to subscribers. A quarterly Micronet directory of available services is also produced.

Computer-Based Products and Services: MICRONET 800 is a networking facility for microcomputers using the Prestel viewdata system. It enables users to access Micronet data bases, software, and communication services and provides a gateway link to other videotex data bases available through Prestel. MICRONET 800 is accessible via telephone lines with microcomputers equipped with a direct connect modem and associated software.

Clientele/Availability: Service is available by subscription to microcomputer users.

Contact: Timothy R. Schoonmaker, Managing Director, Micronet 800.

★977★
TELESYSTEMES
QUESTEL
83-85, blvd. Vincent Auriol   Phone: 01 5826464
F-75013 Paris, France   Service Est: 1978
Michel Dancoisne, Director

Staff: 100 Total.

Related Organizations: France Cables et Radio is the parent organization of Telesystemes.

Description of System or Service: QUESTEL provides information scientists, librarians, engineers, research workers, managers, and others with remote terminal online access to more than 40 bibliographic and nonbibliographic data bases covering science, technology, business, law, and other subjects. The QUESTEL information retrieval software allows users to access data bases interactively in several different languages. In addition, customer files can be maintained on the Telesystemes computer for online retrieval, editing, and sorting by authorized personnel. QUESTEL also makes DARC (chemical structures searching) and Piaf (analysis and processing of full text) software available for system users. Full customer support services are provided.

Scope and/or Subject Matter: Science and technology; chemistry; energy; geology; agriculture; food and nutrition; textiles; computer and information sciences; telecommunications; business and industry; labor; finance; law; government; patents; standards; humanities and social sciences; architecture; urban planning; research.

Input Sources: Data bases are acquired from professional associations, government bodies, publishers, research institutes, and other organizations.

Holdings and Storage Media: More than 40 data bases are held online.

Publications: Questel makes available a system workbook and data base user manuals as well as newsletters, documentation, thesauri, and source lists provided by the data base producers.

Computer-Based Products and Services: QUESTEL provides online access to the following data bases: 1) CANCERNET—provides abstracts of cancer literature; produced by the French Centre National de la Recherche Scientifique (CNRS). 2) CANOM—contains the nomenclature of chemical compounds covered in the EUCAS files; prepared by the Centre National de l'Information Chimique (CNIC). 3) CECILE—provides abstracts of periodical and other literature relating to industrial and urban design and architecture; compiled by the Centre de Creation Industrielle. 4) CIS-ILO—covers worldwide literature on occupational safety and health; produced by the International Labour Office International Occupational Safety and Health Information Centre. 5) DEFOTEL—contains information for 1500 French and foreign companies quoted on the French Stock exchange; produced by Cote Desfosses.

6) EDF-DOC—contains references to technical publications on electricity and energy; prepared by Electricite de France. 7) ENERGIRAP—provides access to unpublished scientific and technical literature dealing with energy-related topics; compiled by Centre d'Etudes Nucleaires de Saclay. 8) ESSOR—provides administrative personnel and activities information for approximately 75,000 French companies; produced by Union Francaise des Annuaires Professionels (UFAP). 9) EUCAS—contains more than 6 million bibliographic citations to world chemical literature; prepared by the Centre National d'Information Chimique (CNIC) in conjunction with Chemical Abstracts Service (CAS). 10) EURECAS—contains data for more than 6 million chemical compound structures identifiable by CAS Registry Number and searchable using DARC software; prepared by CNIC and CAS.

11) FAIREC—covers literature on tropical and subtropical fruit production and utilization; compiled by the Institut de Recherches sur les Fruits et Agrumes (IRFA). 12) FRANCIS—covers social science and humanities literature published between 1972 to date; prepared by the Centre de Documentation Sciences Humaines du CNRS. 13) GEODE—covers worldwide geological literature; produced by the French Bureau de Recherches Geologiques et Minieres (BRGM). 14) GRAPPE--covers French industry, including its markets, products, and economic environment; produced by the Assemblee Permanente des Chambres de Commerce et d'Industrie (APCCI). 15) HELIOS—provides directory information for sources of French government information; compiled by La Documentation Francaise.

16) IALINE—provides abstracts and indexing of world literature on food science, technology, and economy; prepared by the Centre de Documentation des Industries Utilisatrices des Produits Agricoles (CDIUPA). 17) IFP-TH—contains references to international literature on physicochemical and transfer properties of pure chemical compounds and mixtures; compiled by the Institut Francaise des Petroles (IFP). 18) Index Chemicus Online—provides access to journal literature covering organic compounds reported as new in the literature since 1962; prepared by the Institute for Scientific Information. 19) INPI-1—lists French patents covered by the printed Bulletin Officiel de la Propriete Industrielle. 20) INPI-2—covers patents reported in the European Patent Bulletin issued by the European Patent Office.

21) INPI-3—covers patent families for 30 industrial countries. 22) INPI-4—contains 55,000 patent groups and subgroups covered in the International Patent Classification (IPC) scheme. The INPI Data Bases are prepared by the Institut National de la Propriete Industrielle (INPI). 23) INTERCIM—covers literature on cement and hydraulic binders; produced by the Centre d'Etudes et de Recherches de l'Industrie des Liants Hydrauliques (CERILH). 24) JURIS-DATA—provides abstracts or analyses of French Supreme Court decisions, Paris District Court of Appeals decisions, published materials dealing with doctrines and jurisprudence, and relevant unpublished materials; compiled by Editions Techniques. 25) LABINFO—covers research activities and services of French research organizations in the public and private sectors; produced by the Agence Nationale de Valorisation de la Recherche (ANVAR) in cooperation with the CNRS.

26) LABOR—comprises the LABORDOC and INFSOC files covering published literature and government documents dealing with industrial relations, labor law, and related topics; compiled by the International Labour Office. 27) LEX—contains the text of all French laws and regulations in force; prepared by the Secretariat General du Gouvernement Francais. 28) LOGOS—provides bibliographic and textual information on politics and current events in France; compiled by La Documentation Francaise. 29) Meeting Agenda—provides announcements of congresses, conferences, workshops, seminars, and exhibits dealing with energy topics; prepared by the Centre d'Etudes Nucleaires de Saclay. 30) NORIANE—contains references to technical and legal information on French and international standards; prepared by the Association Francaise de Normalisation (AFNOR).

31) PASCAL—contains more than 5 million citations providing multidisciplinary access to world literature, including such areas as physical sciences, earth sciences, life sciences, and engineering; produced by the Centre de Documentation Scientifique et Technique du CNRS. 32) QUESTA6 and QUESTA7—contains the text of the written and oral questions addressed to Cabinet Ministers by members of the French Parliament relating to legal, social, economic, and political problems in France; produced by the Assemblee Nationale. 33) REDOSI—covers literature dealing with management information systems in France and abroad; prepared by the Centre d'Etudes des Systemes d'Information des Administration (CESIA). 34) SB-I—covers primarily French literature dealing with computer science, computer applications, and related fields; compiled by Paris District Gestion Informatique (PGI). 35) SPECTRA—contains mass spectral data for 40,000 compounds; prepared by the U.S. Environmental Protection Agency.

36) SYDONI—covers sources of French law information; produced by SYDONI S.A. 37) TELEDOC—covers technical literature on telecommunications and related areas; compiled by the French Centre National d'Etudes des Telecommunications (CNET). 38) TITUS—provides references and abstracts of world textile literature; produced by the Institut Textile de France. 39) TRANSIN—contains the full text of announcements of offers of and requests for patented technologies and new products and innovations; produced by Transinove International. 40) URBAMET—covers published literature and audiovisual materials dealing with town planning, urban environment, and tranportation; compiled by Reseau URBAMET. 41) World Patents Index—provides bibliographic coverage of general, mechanical, electrical, and chemical patents applied for or issued worldwide; prepared by Derwent Publications, Ltd.

Other Services: In addition to the services described above, Questel provides training courses in several languages and customer support services including software design, consulting, and facilities management.

Clientele/Availability: Services are available without a start-up fee. Questel can be telephoned directly via the Euronet, Transpac, Datapac, Tymnet, Telenet, Uninet, and Telex networks.

Contact: Catherine Spinola, Marketing Manager, Telesystemes Questel. (Telex 204 594 F.) In the United States, contact Questel, Inc., 1625 Eye St., N.W., Suite 818, Washington, DC 20006; telephone (202) 296-1604 or toll-free 800-424-9600. Questel is represented in Canada by IST-Informatheque Inc. and in Japan by Maruzen Company, Ltd. (see separate entries in this volume).

★978★
TERNISIEN LISTING
60, Allee de la Meute
F-78110 Le Vesinet, France
Dr. Jean A. Ternisien, Compiler
Phone: 9521745
Founded: 1981

Description of System or Service: The TERNISIEN LISTING is a selective international repertory of nonferrous metallurgical products designed for the use of research departments, industrial laboratories, designers, suppliers, and others. Information from the LISTING is made available in printed form and on computer diskettes.

Scope and/or Subject Matter: Nonferrous metallurgical products.

Input Sources: Metallurgical companies submit information for the Listing.

Holdings and Storage Media: The complete Ternisien Listing data base is stored on 10 computer diskettes.

Publications: Ternisien Listing—provides information on the uses and suppliers of metallurgical products.

Computer-Based Products and Services: The complete TERNISIEN LISTING or subsets of it are available on computer diskettes.

Clientele/Availability: Services are available without restrictions.

Contact: Dr. Jean A. Ternisien, Compiler, Ternisien Listing.

★979★
TESS SEARCH SERVICE
(TESS Sokservice)
P.O. Box 3295
S-103 66 Stockholm, Sweden
Phone: 08 230400

Description of System or Service: The TESS SEARCH SERVICE is a cooperative effort of several Swedish technical organizations to produce and provide online access to technical data bases.

Scope and/or Subject Matter: Mechanical and electrical engineering, iron and steel, standards, technical terminology, and other related topics.

Input Sources: Bibliographic input is processed by the cooperating organizations.

Holdings and Storage Media: Four online data bases are maintained.

Computer-Based Products and Services: Using 3RIP software with the CCL command language, the TESS SEARCH SERVICE provides online access to the following data bases: 1) REGIS—contains references to Swedish standards and other nongovernment technical standards; produced by the Swedish Standards Institution. 2) STEELDOC—contains references to research reports covering the area of iron and steel; produced by the Swedish Ironmasters Association. 3) TERMDOK—provides definitions and translations of technical terms; produced by the Swedish Center for Technical Terminology. 4) VERA—contains approximately 1200 citations to technical and other literature for the mechanical engineering industries; produced by the Swedish Mechanical and Electrical Engineering Trade Association.

Clientele/Availability: Primary clients are Swedish technical organizations.

Contact: Ulla-Britt Mittag, TESS Search Service.

★980★
TEXTILE AND CLOTHING INFORMATION CENTRE (TCIC)
(Centre d'Information Textile Habillement - CITH)
24, rue Montoyer
B-1040 Brussels, Belgium
Mr. C. Blum, Secretary General
Phone: 02 2307629
Founded: 1980

Related Organizations: The Centre receives support from the Co-ordinating Committee for the Textile Industries in the EEC (COMITEXTIL), the Association Europeenne des Industries de l'Habillement (AEIH), and the national textile and clothing manufacturers associations in European Economic Community countries.

Description of System or Service: The TEXTILE AND CLOTHING INFORMATION CENTRE collects, integrates, and disseminates statistical data on the textile and clothing industry in European Economic Community countries. It maintains the computer-readable nonbibliographic CITH Data Bank and makes it publicly accessible online. The CENTRE also issues publications.

Scope and/or Subject Matter: Textile and clothing industry in EEC countries, including production, consumption, imports and exports, industry structure, market trends, and related economic and social information.

Input Sources: Data are obtained from official, professional, and private organizations.

Holdings and Storage Media: The nonbibliographic CITH Data Bank is maintained in machine-readable form.

Publications: CITH INFO (quarterly)—provides news on business developments in the textile and clothing industries in EEC countries. A variety of statistical reports are also available.

Computer-Based Products and Services: The TEXTILE AND CLOTHING INFORMATION CENTRE maintains the CITH Data Bank, which is available for online searching through Euronet DIANE as the CITEX data base. The CENTRE also provides searches of the Data Bank and makes it available on magnetic tape.

Clientele/Availability: Services are intended for the European textile and clothing industry.

Contact: Mr. B. Bruyere, Assistant to the Director, Textile and Clothing Information Centre. (Telex 22380 EURTEX.)

★981★
THERMODATA ASSOCIATION
THERMODATA-THERMDOC DATA BANK
Domaine Universitaire
P.O. Box 66
F-38402 St-Martin-d'Heres Cedex,
    France
Yves Deniel, Director
Phone: 76 427690
Service Est: 1974

Staff: Approximately 4 total.

Related Organizations: The French Ministry of Education, the French Ministry of Industry and Research, the Centre National de la Recherche Scientifique (CNRS), and the Direction des Recherches et Etudes Techniques provide support. Thermodata works with the Scientific Group Thermodata Europe (SGTE).

Description of System or Service: The THERMODATA-THERMDOC DATA BANK is a computer-readable collection of critically evaluated data covering inorganic and metallurgical thermodynamics, together with bibliographic references and relevant comments. The DATA BANK contains evaluated data for elements and stoichiometric compounds including standard enthalpy and entropy of formation, temperature and enthalpy of transformation, and molar specific heat, along with software to produce tables or functions such as Gibbs energies. A group of consultants is also available for solving such problems as the establishment of equilibrium conditions in multicomponent systems.

Scope and/or Subject Matter: Selected and critically assessed data for: numerical calculations in thermochemistry; process evaluation and feasibility analysis; applied physical chemistry; metallurgy and metals processing; metallurgical engineering; ceramics and refractory hard metal; geo- and mineral chemistry; industrial inorganic chemistry.

Input Sources: Data are selected from journals and are critically evaluated by scientific institutions in Europe.

Holdings and Storage Media: More than 30,000 bibliographic and nonbibliographic items are available; coverage begins with 1966.

Computer-Based Products and Services: The DATA BANK is offered online by Thermodata over the Transpac and Euronet DIANE networks. It is also used by the Association in the provision of inquiry-answering and consulting services. Additionally, the Association makes available the Hydrogene Information data base on hydrogen in minerals and plans to make available the Hydrogene dans les Metaux data base on hydrogen in metals.

Clientele/Availability: There are no restrictions on services.

Contact: Dr. Bertrand Cheynet, Engineer, Research Department, Thermodata Association. (Telex 980145 F THERMO SMHER.)

★982★
TIJL DATAPRESS
Blaloweg 20
NL-8041 AH Zwolle, Netherlands
G.B.R. Smits, Managing Director
Phone: 05200 10801
Founded: 1978

Special Note: The above name, address, and telephone number have been verified for this edition, although no questionnaire response was received. The following text is reprinted from the 5th edition.

Related Organizations: Koninklijke Tijl is the parent company of Tijl Datapress.

Description of System or Service: TIJL DATAPRESS is a data base publisher of Dutch industrial and financial information. It issues directories, a daily stock exchange newspaper, and other publications. TIJL DATAPRESS also makes information available through a commercial videotex service.

Scope and/or Subject Matter: Netherlands industrial and financial information.

Publications: Tijl Datapress issues a variety of directories and other publications.

Computer-Based Products and Services: TIJL DATAPRESS offers industrial directory information and Amsterdam stock exchange data through the Dutch videotex service. It is also involved in the transmission of financial data for newspapers.

Contact: G.B.R. Smits, Managing Director, Tijl Datapress.

★983★
TIMBER RESEARCH AND DEVELOPMENT ASSOCIATION (TRADA)
INFORMATION AND ADVISORY DEPARTMENT
TIMBER INFORMATION KEYWORD RETRIEVAL (TINKER)
Stocking Lane
Hughenden Valley
High Wycombe, Bucks. HP14 4ND,
   England
R.T. Allcorn, Head
Phone: 0240 243091
Service Est: 1974

Staff: 2 Information and library professional; 2 clerical and nonprofessional.

Description of System or Service: TIMBER INFORMATION KEYWORD RETRIEVAL (TINKER) is an online information storage and retrieval system providing references to forest products literature. TINKER is used by the Association's library to perform literature searches and prepare printed bibliographies and indexes. In addition to maintaining TINKER, the Association also coordinates information on behalf of timber interests for input to the CONTEXT (formerly CONTEL) construction industry data base on Prestel.

Scope and/or Subject Matter: Utilization of timber and wood-based products.

Input Sources: Worldwide literature received by the library is indexed for TINKER; this includes books, periodicals, reports, standards, patents, and pamphlets.

Holdings and Storage Media: The computer-readable TINKER data base contains more than 13,000 items referring to literature collected by the library since 1974. The library maintains 8000 bound volumes; subscriptions to more than 200 periodicals; and 30,000 reports, pamphlets, and standards.

Publications: Timber Pallet and Packaging Digest—available by subscription. Bibliographies on a wide range of subjects have been compiled using TINKER; a list with ordering information is available by request from TRADA.

Computer-Based Products and Services: Retrospective searches and SDI services are provided from TINKER by the library staff. Items selected for TINKER are assigned up to 12 keywords from an in-house thesaurus and are coded to include authors, complete title, full reference, language code, year of publication, filing information, and affiliation code. The CONTEXT data base on Prestel includes technical references, a subject index, cost and product information, and a directory of organizations.

Other Services: Also available from the library are manual literature searching, photocopying, and interlibrary loans.

Clientele/Availability: Services are generally available on a fee basis; Association members receive discounts.

Contact: R.T. Allcorn, Head, Information and Advisory Department. (Telex 83292.)

★984★
TOKYO SHOKO RESEARCH, LTD. (TSR)
DATA BANK SERVICE
Shinichi Bldg., 9-6, 1-Chome
Shinbashi, Minato-ku
Tokyo 105, Japan
Yo Ito, Executive Vice President
Phone: 03 574 2219
Service Est: 1978

Staff: 6 Total.

Description of System or Service: The DATA BANK SERVICE maintains computer-readable files of statistical information on more than 800,000 companies located in Japan. It makes this information available in printed form, on machine-readable tapes and diskettes, and via time-sharing. Market research services are also offered.

Scope and/or Subject Matter: Statistical information on companies located in Japan.

Input Sources: Information is gathered via credit reports from approximately 90 branch offices of Tokyo Shoko Research.

Holdings and Storage Media: TSR machine-readable files hold approximately 80 categories of statistics on approximately 800,000 companies.

Computer-Based Products and Services: The DATA BANK SERVICE makes statistical information on Japanese companies available through commercial time-sharing sources and on computer tapes and diskettes.

Clientele/Availability: Services are available without restrictions. Clients include banks, businesses, and the Japanese government.

Contact: Kazuhiko Haibara, Manager, Data Bank Service, Tokyo Shoko Research, Ltd.

★985★
TORONTO DEPARTMENT OF THE CITY CLERK
COMPUTERIZED TEXT PROCESSING AND RETRIEVAL SYSTEM
**   FOR CITY COUNCIL INFORMATION**
Toronto City Hall
100 Queen St. W.
Toronto, ON, Canada M5H 2N2
Roy V. Henderson, City Clerk
Phone: (416) 947-7020
Service Est: 1975

Staff: 1 Information and library professional; 3 management professional; 3 technicians; 16 clerical and nonprofessional; 8 other.

Related Organizations: The Toronto Department of Management Services provides computer systems support for the Computerized Text Processing and Retrieval System.

Description of System or Service: The COMPUTERIZED TEXT PROCESSING AND RETRIEVAL SYSTEM FOR CITY COUNCIL INFORMATION is a text editing, information retrieval, and photocomposition system functioning within the Toronto Department of the City Clerk. Facilities and services are provided to civic employees, officials, and department heads for entering reports and documents into the SYSTEM to support the work of the City Council. The SYSTEM maintains full-text documents and is searchable online using natural language queries.

Scope and/or Subject Matter: Public issues relevant to the City of Toronto.

Input Sources: Input is derived from documentation presented to City Council and its committees by City of Toronto departments, ratepayers' associations, outside agencies, and the general public.

Holdings and Storage Media: Data bases in the System hold full texts of 30,000 documents, including all City of Toronto by-laws enacted since January, 1977. Data bases are updated weekly; about 600 documents are added each month.

Publications: Minutes of the Council of the Corporation of the City of Toronto (biweekly)—phototypeset from the System.

Computer-Based Products and Services: Online searching for reports and by-laws is available at departmental terminals to civic employees and at the City Clerk's Department to the general public for on-site use of materials. The SYSTEM is also used for text editing, updating, and formatting in the preparation of phototypeset materials.

Other Services: Manual literature searching and training in the use of the System are also provided by the Department.

Clientele/Availability: Services are available without restrictions.

Projected Publications and Services: Online availability of general by-laws enacted prior to 1977 is planned, as well as the development of a thesaurus to assist online searching and to generate an automated index.

Contact: Sandra Ebel, Systems Coordinator, Toronto Department of the City Clerk.

★986★
TORONTO STOCK EXCHANGE DATA PRODUCTS
The Exchange Tower   Phone: (416) 947-4700
2 First Canadian Place
Toronto, ON, Canada M5X 1J2
David F. Orr, Data Products Manager

Description of System or Service: The Toronto Stock Exchange DATA PRODUCTS section makes Canadian stock market information available in machine-readable form. It provides magnetic tapes of bid, ask, last trade, net change, open, high, and low data at the close of trading. Also available from the Toronto Stock Exchange are ticker services providing trade data to subscribers.

Scope and/or Subject Matter: Canadian stocks, options, and futures.

Holdings and Storage Media: Machine-readable files of market information are maintained and updated daily.

Computer-Based Products and Services: The DATA PRODUCTS section offers market information on magnetic tapes. Two Toronto Stock Exchange data bases are also accessible online through I.P. Sharp Associates: 1) Canadian Stock Options (CDNOPT)—provides daily trading statistics for both put and call options traded in Toronto and Montreal and issued by Trans Canada Options Inc. Contains 31,200 time series, including open, high, low, and closing prices, volume and value traded, open interest and trading unit, bid and ask prices, and exercise price and price of underlying security. Updated daily and holds data for the past 200 trading days. 2) Toronto Stock Exchange 300 Index and Stock Statistics (TSE300)—contains trading statistics for 300 stocks and 62 major and minor indexes as well as stock performance data. Covers the top 300 stocks in terms of average quoted market value. For each stock and index, includes 20 time series and 4 static facts, including high, low, and closing values, base value, earnings per share, quoted market value, earnings adjusted index, volume and value traded, price-earnings ratio, relative weight on composite, dividends per share, adjusted shares (float), dividends adjusted to index, aggregate earnings pool, dividend yield, and aggregate dividend payout. Provides daily coverage from January 1976, weekly from 1971, and monthly from 1956.

Clientele/Availability: Services are intended for securities-related companies in Canada.

Contact: David F. Orr, Data Products Manager, Toronto Stock Exchange.

★987★
TRANSINOVE INTERNATIONAL
INPI   Phone: 01 2932120
26 bis, rue de Leningrad   Founded: 1974
F-75800 Paris Cedex 8, France
Olivier Arondel, Assistant Manager

Staff: 1 Management professional; 1 sales and marketing.

Related Organizations: The TRANSINOVE data bank was developed in conjunction with the Agence National de Valorisation de la Recherche (ANVAR) and Compagnie Internationale de Services en Informatique (CISI). It is sponsored by various French governmental agencies.

Description of System or Service: TRANSINOVE INTERNATIONAL gathers offers of and requests for patented technologies, new products and inventions, and innovative ideas in need of development from the private and public sectors worldwide. It indexes the information and stores it in machine-readable form to produce a monthly current awareness bulletin and the online TRANSIN data bank. TRANSINOVE services are intended to assist technology holders and users to find business ventures and to promote corporate development through investment in new technology.

Scope and/or Subject Matter: Technology transfer; patents; new products and inventions; industrial know-how.

Input Sources: The data bank covers technologies developed by research centers and laboratories, private industry, public corporations, and independent inventors. Information is submitted on standard input forms and indexed by Transinove before being entered into the data bank.

Holdings and Storage Media: Information on approximately 4000 technologies announced during the preceding three years is held in machine-readable form. The data bank is updated every two weeks, with approximately 1500 new technologies added annually.

Publications: La Lettre de Transinove (monthly)—available by subscription. Each issue contains 30 to 40 descriptions newly added to the data bank. Titles are in French and in English; descriptions are in French only.

Computer-Based Products and Services: TRANSINOVE INTERNATIONAL makes the TRANSIN data bank available for online searching through Telesystemes Questel. The data bank contains such data elements as International Patent Classification (IPC) code, type of opportunity code, development stage, descriptive title, technology level and descriptors, abstract, technical skill descriptors, agency or company source, contact person name and address, publication reference number, and file input date.

Clientele/Availability: Services are available without restrictions to corporations, investors, and others.

Contact: Olivier Arondel, Assistant Manager, Transinove International. (Telex 290368 F INPI PARIS.)

★988★
TRANSNATIONAL DATA REPORTING SERVICE, INC. (EUROPEAN OFFICE)
P.O. Box 6152   Phone: 3120 737311
NL-1005 ED Amsterdam, Netherlands

Special Note: Above is the European mailing address of Transnational Data Reporting Service, Inc., which maintains its headquarters in Springfield, Virginia, U.S.A. The firm collects and disseminates information on policies, regulations, and data protection statutes pertaining to the exchange of information across international boundries, and it publishes the Transnational Data Report. A complete description of Transnational's products and services is provided in the United States volume of this Encyclopedia. (The telex number for the European office is 12170 IBAC NL.)

★989★
TRANSPAC
33, ave. du Maine, B.P. 145   Phone: 01 5385211
F-75755 Paris Cedex 15, France   Founded: 1978
Mr. P. Fortin, Director

Staff: 126 Technicians; 24 sales and marketing; 204 other.

Related Organizations: Transpac was developed by the French Ministry of Posts and Telecommunications.

Description of System or Service: TRANSPAC is a public packet switching network facilitating general teleprocessing activities and permitting interactive access to data bases carried by French online search service companies. TRANSPAC is designed to accommodate a wide variety of applications, including conversational and time-sharing services, offline data collection with deferred transmission, remote batch processing, data exchange between subscribers' host computers, and transmission of electronic mail, messages, and facsimiles.

Scope and/or Subject Matter: Teleprocessing in all subject areas.

Publications: 1) Technical Specifications for Using the Network (updated once or twice per year)—in French; 2) List of Services Accessible through Transpac (annual)—in French.

Computer-Based Products and Services: TRANSPAC is organized around dedicated communication computers to provide concentration and switching of data. Users can be connected directly to the Transpac network with leased lines or by telephone or Telex switched connections. The network can be accessed by local telephone call throughout France and is connected to other networks in Europe and North America, including Euronet DIANE, Telenet, Tymnet, and DATEX-P. Charges are based mainly on the volume of data transmitted.

Clientele/Availability: Clientele include service bureaus, online services, industry, banking establishments, distribution corporations, and government agencies.

Contact: Bernard Simon, Chef du Service Formation/ Promotion, Direction Commerciale, Transpac. (Telex 260676.) The electronic mail address on Transpac is TPAC.

★990★
TT NEWSBANK
(TT Nyhetsbanken)
Kungsholmstorg 5
S-105 12 Stockholm, Sweden
Gun-Britt Balck, General Manager

Phone: 08 132600
Founded: 1980

Related Organizations: TT Newsbank is a subsidiary of Tidningarnas Telegrambyra (TT) and is affiliated with Informationsvarden i Stockholm AB and DataArkiv AB.

Description of System or Service: The TT NEWSBANK maintains a computer-readable data base designed to store and disseminate the archival material of the Tidningarnas Telegrambyra (TT) news wire service. Serving the Swedish press and other institutions, the data base is accessible online 24 hours per day. It contains the full text of all TT news articles; information from it is retrievable through keyword searching.

Scope and/or Subject Matter: News of all kinds, including domestic and foreign, parliamentary, ministry and government, sports, and stock exchange data.

Input Sources: The data base comprises all articles from the news wire service. Approximately 11,000 lines are transmitted daily from the editorial computer via teleprinter network to NEWSBANK. Input will be provided on magnetic tape in the near future.

Holdings and Storage Media: The computer-readable NEWSBANK file holds approximately 100,000 articles per year of coverage. The articles are stored in full for five years; indexing terms are stored for eight years.

Computer-Based Products and Services: The machine-readable NEWSBANK data base is accessible online through TT Newsbank or DataArkiv. Articles in the file are accessed through a keyword register, which is updated daily. Upon receipt of the article in the file, it is displayed on a special screen and its keywords are marked with a lightpen, which automatically updates the register. Keywords needed for retrieval but not included in the original article are fed manually into the computer. Each article in the file is indexed by more than 15 keywords.

Clientele/Availability: Primary clients are newspapers, broadcasting companies, and news agencies; services are available without restrictions.

Contact: Gun-Britt Balck, General Manager, TT Newsbank.

★991★
TURKEY
SCIENTIFIC AND TECHNICAL RESEARCH COUNCIL OF TURKEY
TURKISH SCIENTIFIC AND TECHNICAL DOCUMENTATION CENTER (TURDOK)
Ataturk Bulvari 221
Kavaklidere
Ankara, Turkey

Phone: 262770
Service Est: 1966

Staff: Approximately 30 total.

Description of System or Service: The TURKISH SCIENTIFIC AND TECHNICAL DOCUMENTATION CENTER (TURDOK) has the following objectives: to meet the information and documentation requirements of Turkish scientists, research workers, and industrialists; to publicize information and documentation activities in the country; and to contribute to the training of information specialists and documentalists by organizing short courses and providing on-the-job training facilities.

Scope and/or Subject Matter: Basic and applied sciences; agriculture; industrial management; medicine; information and library science.

Input Sources: Input consists of approximately 500 worldwide abstracting and indexing journals; bibliographies; conference proceedings; most Turkish journals; research reports; theses; doctoral dissertations; and some card services. Documents are classified and indexed by UDC and descriptors.

Holdings and Storage Media: TURDOK maintains a collection of 10,000 bound volumes and subscriptions to 728 periodicals.

Publications: 1) Current Titles in Turkish Science (monthly)—bibliography and index to literature received in the TURDOK library; available in Turkish and English versions. 2) National and International Meetings on Science and Technology (quarterly). 3) Union Catalogues of Scientific and Technical Periodicals of the Libraries in Ankara, Izmir, and Istanbul. 4) Modern Documentation and Information Practices—Turkish translation of the FID publication. 5) Turkish Dissertation Index (annual)—covers dissertations and theses in the fields of science, economics, management, and education; issued in English and Turkish. 6) Directory of Information Sources in Turkey. Reports, directories, and bibliographies are also issued as required.

Services: Services include indexing, advisory and consulting services, data collection and analysis of domestic material, manual literature searching, research, interlibrary loan, SDI, document procurement and reproduction, translation, and training in documentation.

Clientele/Availability: Services are available without restrictions; fees vary with services required.

Projected Publications and Services: TURDOK is studying the possibility of computerizing its operations.

Contact: Rezan Kockar, Library Director, Turkish Scientific and Technical Documentation Center.

U

★992★
UHDE GMBH
UHDE THERMOPHYSICAL PROPERTIES PROGRAM PACKAGE
Postfach 262   Phone: 0231 5472710
Friedrich-Uhde-Str.
D-4600 Dortmund 1, Fed. Rep. of
   Germany
Dr. Klaus Neumann

Staff: 3000 Total at Uhde GmbH.

Description of System or Service: The UHDE THERMOPHYSICAL PROPERTIES PROGRAM PACKAGE is a computerized system used by chemical engineers for calculating the thermophysical properties of pure chemical substances and mixtures. The PROGRAM PACKAGE consists of a limited basic data collection on the physical properties of 350 chemical compounds and mixtures, estimation programs for obtaining approximations for unknown basic data, and calculation programs for computing physical properties.

Scope and/or Subject Matter: Thermophysical properties of pure chemical substances and mixtures in gas, liquid, or solid states.

Input Sources: Input consists of basic thermophysical data derived from published literature.

Computer-Based Products and Services: The PROGRAM PACKAGE is available on a license basis for installation on client computers. It consists of a data bank and programs which perform the following functions: read in a thermophysical properties vector that is not complete, and calculate and estimate the missing properties of pure substances; calculate the thermodynamic properties for a given mixture at given conditions (for a given stream); and calculate tables for a certain thermodynamic property of a given mixture for given temperature/pressure array. The system can also accept additional client data for calculations and it produces computer printouts.

Other Services: In addition to offering the Thermophysical Properties Program Package, Uhde GmbH provides computer programs in the field of plant design and construction for the chemical industry.

Clientele/Availability: Primary clients are chemical manufacturers and engineering contractors. The package is available for a company's internal use only.

Contact: Dr. Klaus Neumann, Uhde Thermophysical Properties Program Package. (Telex 0822 187.)

★993★
UNILEVER COMPUTER SERVICES LTD. (UCSL)
EUROPEAN PETROCHEMICAL ASSOCIATION (EPCA) TRADE STATISTICS DATABASE
55/57 Clarendon Rd.   Phone: 0923 47911
Watford, Herts. WD1 1SA, England
Dr. Nigel Walker, Marketing Manager

Related Organizations: The European Petrochemical Association sponsors, directs, and promotes the development of the EPCA Trade Statistics Database. Unilever Computer Services Ltd. is a wholly owned subsidiary of Unilever Ltd.

Description of System or Service: The EUROPEAN PETROCHEMICAL ASSOCIATION (EPCA) TRADE STATISTICS DATABASE is an online data base containing published government import/export information on approximately 2000 chemical and allied products from Europe, Japan, and the United States. EPCA data are stored in NIMEXE (nomenclature import/export Europe), Canadian, United States, and Japanese product code classifications, and include product qualification, reporting country, month of trade, import/export indicator, country of trade, value in reporting country currency, volume in weight units, volume in alternative units of measure, cumulative values and volumes, and, for U.S. data, port of exit or entry. Information from the DATABASE can be obtained through interactive searching or regular delivery of various reports by mail or computer linkup.

Scope and/or Subject Matter: Chemical products import and export trade statistics.

Input Sources: Statistics are acquired monthly on magnetic tape from the statistics and customs offices of Belgium, Canada, France, Germany, Italy, Japan, Netherlands, United Kingdom, and United States and converted to a common format.

Holdings and Storage Media: The computer-readable EPCA data base covers some 2000 chemical products and contains more than 8 million items of discrete information. Current data covering a period of at least 12 months are held online; archived historical data are held offline.

Computer-Based Products and Services: The EPCA TRADE STATISTICS DATABASE is accessible online through Unilever Computer Services Ltd. over the UCSL Interlink, Euronet DIANE, IPSS, Telenet, and Tymnet telecommunications networks. Monthly reports produced from the DATABASE include the following: standard import/export detail—lists values and volumes of imports and exports between a reporting country and a number of trading countries, for a given product in a given month; import/export matrix—provides a comparison of values and volumes as reported by the contributing countries, for a given product in a given month or time period; deduced import/export trend—deduces trade for a nonreporting country by scanning the reverse trade with a reporting country; and other reports showing trading trend analysis over given time frames and price calculations.

Clientele/Availability: The data base primarily serves the needs of EPCA's 250 member companies that represent all the major petrochemical producers and distributors in Western Europe. Other clients include chemical manufacturers and distributors worldwide.

Contact: Dr. Nigel Walker, Marketing Manager, EPCA Trade Statistics Database. (Telex 893538.)

★994★
UNILEVER COMPUTER SERVICES LTD. (UCSL)
WORLD TRADE STATISTICS DATABASE (TRADSTAT)
55/57 Clarendon Rd.   Phone: 0923 47911
Watford, Herts. WD1 1SA, England   Service Est: 1984
Dr. Nigel Walker, Marketing Manager

Staff: 2 Management professional; 4 technicians; 2 sales and marketing; 1 clerical and nonprofessional.

Related Organizations: TRADSTAT was developed in conjunction with the EPCA (European Petrochemical Association). Unilever Computer Services Ltd. is a wholly owned subsidiary of Unilever Ltd.

Description of System or Service: The WORLD TRADE STATISTICS DATABASE (TRADSTAT) is an online data base containing published government import/export information on more than 15,000 products from Europe, Japan, Canada, and the United States. TRADSTAT comprises three data bases: the first contains monthly figures showing import and export details between France, Belgium, Netherlands, Italy, Germany, United Kingdom, Canada, United States, Japan, and the rest of the world; the second data base holds annual figures for the same countries as well as details from a selected number of other major trading nations; and the third data base is a product codes file developed using UCSL's DECO full-text information retrieval software. TRADSTAT product data are stored in NIMEXE (nomenclature import/export Europe), United States, Japanese, and Canadian customs product classifications. The data include reporting country, month of trade, import/export indicator, country of trade, volumes and prices, value, volume by weight, volume in alternative units of measure, prices, cumulative value, and, for European data, NIMEXE code national subdivisions. Information from TRADESTAT can be obtained through interactive searching or through delivery of various reports by mail or computer linkup.

Scope and/or Subject Matter: Import and export trade statistics for a variety of products.

Input Sources: Data are acquired on magnetic tape from statistics and customs offices of Belgium, Canada, France, West Germany, Italy, Japan, Netherlands, Spain, United Kingdom, and United States and are converted to a common format.

Holdings and Storage Media: The machine-readable TRADSTAT files cover more than 15,500 products. The monthly import/export file contains 30 million records; the year-end file contains 5 million records; and the product code file holds 30,000 records.

Computer-Based Products and Services: The WORLD TRADE STATISTICS DATABASE is accessible online through Unilever Computer Services Ltd. over the UCSL Interlink, IPSS, Telenet, and Tymnet telecommunications networks. Reports produced from the DATABASE include the following: import/export report—lists weight volumes and value or prices of imports or exports between a reporting country and all the trading countries of origin or destination for a product or group of products in a given month; import (or export) trend report—provides a monthly analysis of volumes, values, and prices over any 12 month timescale and shows trade between the requested reporting country and a selection, or all, of the countries of origin (or destination); deduced trend report—derives imports or exports for any other country by scanning all the reporting countries' trade with that country; and various import/export matrix reports showing a comparison of figures as reported by the contributing countries.

Clientele/Availability: Services are available on an annual subscription plus charges basis. Data users include major industrial corporations, trade associations, and government departments.

Contact: N.R. Tomlinson, Business Development Manager, Unilever Computer Services Ltd. In the United States, contact Sage Data Inc., 104 Carnegie Center, Princeton, NJ 08540; telephone (609) 924-3000.

★995★
UNION OF SOVIET SOCIALIST REPUBLICS
ACADEMY OF SCIENCES OF THE U.S.S.R.
ASTRONOMICAL COUNCIL DATA CENTER
MANAGEMENT SYSTEM FOR ASTRONOMICAL DATA IN MACHINE-READABLE FORM

Pyatnitskaya 48
109017 Moscow, U.S.S.R.
Phone: 233 1702
Service Est: 1979

Special Note: No questionnaire response was received for this entry for the 6th edition. The entry is reprinted as it appeared in the 5th edition.

Staff: 6 Information and library professional; 2 management professional; 2 technicians; 2 clerical and nonprofessional.

Related Organizations: The Astronomical Council Data Center works in collaboration with the Stellar Data Center/Centre de Donnees Stellaires (CDS), which is located at Strasbourg Observatory in France, and the Zentralinstitut fur Astrophysik, Potsdam, German Democratic Republic.

Description of System or Service: The MANAGEMENT SYSTEM FOR ASTRONOMICAL DATA IN MACHINE-READABLE FORM is a computerized system used to compile, process, and distribute astronomical data in machine-readable form. The SYSTEM maintains catalogs and tables of stars, stellar systems, and other celestial objects for distribution and exchange with Soviet observatories and the Stellar Data Center. A computerized system known as SPARTAK is also maintained to monitor request registration and response.

Scope and/or Subject Matter: Astronomical data, including position, kinematics, photometry, and spectroscopy.

Input Sources: Input consists of data received from Stellar Data Center and other foreign centers, as well as Soviet catalogs prepared in machine-readable form in collaboration with other Soviet observatories. Soviet astronomical periodicals are surveyed to systematize the data.

Holdings and Storage Media: Approximately 300 astronomical data files are maintained on magnetic tape. The Center has a library collection of 23,000 bound volumes; subscriptions to 118 periodicals; and 61 catalogs.

Computer-Based Products and Services: The SYSTEM is used to compile, process, retrieve, and copy catalog data for distribution among U.S.S.R. and other observatories.

Clientele/Availability: Services are available to Soviet observatories and other astronomical institutions.

Contact: Director, Management System for Astronomical Data in Machine-Readable Form.

★996★
UNION OF SOVIET SOCIALIST REPUBLICS
ACADEMY OF SCIENCES OF THE U.S.S.R.
INSTITUTE FOR HIGH TEMPERATURES
THERMOPHYSICAL PROPERTIES CENTER

Korovinskoje r., IVTAN
127412, Moscow I-412, U.S.S.R.
Dr. Victor F. Baibuz, Director
Phone: 4859572
Service Est: 1973

Staff: Approximately 20 total.

Description of System or Service: The THERMOPHYSICAL PROPERTIES CENTER, a scientific information center on pure substance properties, supplies information to scientific institutions, organizations, agencies, and directly to scientists and specialists. Its services include abstracting and indexing of published information on thermal and physical properties of individual substances; dissemination of numerical data tables on properties; and fulfillment of special requests for property analysis and computations. In support of its services, the CENTER maintains two computer-readable data bases: the bibliographic Documentary Information Bank and the nonbibliographic BATHEDA Thermophysical Data Bank.

Scope and/or Subject Matter: Thermal and physical properties of organic and elementary inorganic matter as well as elastic, electrical magnetic, and optical properties related to them.

Input Sources: Input for the Documentary Information Bank is derived from 500 periodicals and continuing editions, collections of scientific works, conference transactions, monographs, reports, and other materials. Input for BATHEDA consists of data recommended by international and national organizations, data evaluated by the Center staff, and experimental data.

Holdings and Storage Media: The computer-readable Documentary Information Bank contains information on approximately 40,000 documents and is updated with about 5000 new records per year. The data base covers domestic literature for the past 15 years and foreign literature for the past 10 years. The nonbibliographic BATHEDA file is also maintained in computer-readable form.

Publications: Reviews on Thermophysical Properties of Substances (6 per year).

Computer-Based Products and Services: The THERMOPHYSICAL PROPERTIES CENTER maintains and provides services from two data bases. 1) The Documentary Information Bank contains bibliographic citations and abstracts of scientific literature covering thermal and physical properties of organic and inorganic matter. The data base is used to provide information retrieval services and regular selection of abstracts from new accessions. 2) The BATHEDA Thermophysical Data Bank contains the values of physical constants and tables of thermal and linked properties of those substances. The data can be displayed on a terminal screen, transferred directly to the user's own data base, or obtained in printed form.

Clientele/Availability: Services are available to the Academy of Sciences, other scientific institutions, and interested individuals.

Contact: Dr. Michail S. Trachtenherts, Thermophysical Properties Center.

★997★
UNION OF SOVIET SOCIALIST REPUBLICS
ACADEMY OF SCIENCES OF THE U.S.S.R.
INSTITUTE FOR THEORETICAL ASTRONOMY
MINOR PLANETS, COMETS, AND SATELLITES DEPARTMENT

Naberezhnaya Kutuzova 10
191187 Leningrad, U.S.S.R.
Prof. Yu. V. Batrakov, Head
Phone: 272 9083

Staff: 2 Management professional; 20 technicians; 3 clerical and nonprofessional.

Description of System or Service: The MINOR PLANETS, COMETS, AND SATELLITES DEPARTMENT compiles data during its investigation of the motion of minor planets, comets, and natural satellites. The data are stored on magnetic tape and used to prepare an annual publication.

Scope and/or Subject Matter: Motion and orbits of minor planets, comets, and satellites.

Holdings and Storage Media: The Department maintains machine-readable files covering the orbital elements of more than 3000 permanently numbered minor planets.

Publications: Ephemerides of Minor Planets/ Ephemeridy Malykh Planet (annual)—contains orbital elements and opposition ephemerides of all numbered planets.

Computer-Based Products and Services: The Department makes its machine-readable data file available on an exchange basis.

Clientele/Availability: Clients include professional astronomers, observatories, and institutions conducting observational or computational research on minor planets.

Contact: Dr. V.A. Shor, Assistant Head, Minor Planets, Comets, and Satellites Department. (Telex 121578 ITA SU.)

★998★
UNION OF SOVIET SOCIALIST REPUBLICS
ALL-UNION INSTITUTE OF SCIENTIFIC AND TECHNICAL INFORMATION
(Vsesoyuznyy Institut Nauchnoy i Teknicheskoy Informatsii - VINITI)
Baltiyskaya Ulitsa 14   Phone: 151 5501
Moscow A-219, U.S.S.R.   Service Est: 1952

Special Note: No information from VINITI has been received since the 4th edition of the Encyclopedia.

Staff: Several thousand full-time professionals.

Related Organizations: VINITI is administered by the U.S.S.R. State Committee for Science and Technology and the Academy of Sciences of the U.S.S.R.

Description of System or Service: Functioning as an integral unit in a national Soviet information network, the ALL-UNION INSTITUTE OF SCIENTIFIC AND TECHNICAL INFORMATION (VINITI) acquires, analyzes, and processes with computer support the domestic and foreign scientific and technical literature in order to provide a comprehensive series of abstracts bulletins and various other publications and services. VINITI also conducts extensive research in all areas of information science, including research on automated systems for scientific and technical information, and provides consulting and training services to staff members of other Soviet institutions.

Scope and/or Subject Matter: All aspects of natural, engineering, and exact sciences; information science.

Input Sources: Over 1.3 million abstracts are prepared annually from about 50,000 domestic and foreign books, periodicals, patents, and other documents obtained by purchase or exchange. After processing, original materials are stored at VINITI for 5-8 years, then deposited in other Soviet libraries.

Holdings and Storage Media: VINITI's collection consists of about 125,000 volumes, 600,000 periodicals, and microforms of original documents. Machine-readable files are also maintained.

Publications: Referativnyi Zhurnal/ Abstracts Journal (monthly)—published in numerous series covering different technical topics; most series are available by subscription from V/O Mezhdunarodnaya Kniga, Moscow 121200, U.S.S.R. Bibliographies, reports, and other publications are also issued as required.

Microform Products and Services: Microform document copies are available.

Computer-Based Products and Services: Automated storage and retrieval of abstracted information is performed using an automated reference information system for science and technology. Full retrospective search and SDI services are available for some files.

Other Services: In addition to services described above, VINITI provides a reference information service for information science.

Clientele/Availability: Services are available by special arrangement.

Contact: Director, All-Union Institute of Scientific and Technical Information.

★999★
UNION OF SOVIET SOCIALIST REPUBLICS
U.S.S.R. STATE COMMITTEE ON THE UTILIZATION OF ATOMIC ENERGY
CENTER FOR NUCLEAR STRUCTURE AND REACTION DATA
(Center po Atomn. i Jadernum Dannym - CAJAD)
Kurchatov Atomic Energy Institute   Phone: 1961557
196182 Moscow, U.S.S.R.   Service Est: 1972
Dr. F.E. Chukreev, Head

Staff: Approximately 11 total.

Related Organizations: The Center for Nuclear Structure and Reaction Data participates in a worldwide nuclear data network with the following five centers: 1) Nuclear Data Section, International Atomic Energy Agency; 2) National Nuclear Data Center, Brookhaven National Laboratory, U.S. Department of Energy; 3) Nuclear Energy Agency Data Bank, Organisation for Economic Co-Operation and Development; 4) Nuclear Data Center, Institute of Physics and Energy; and 5) Fachinformationszentrum Energie, Physik, Mathematik GmbH.

Description of System or Service: The CENTER FOR NUCLEAR STRUCTURE AND REACTION DATA (CAJAD) gathers and evaluates non-neutron nuclear data for international exchange through the worldwide nuclear data network. It also maintains copies of data contributed by other network members and disseminates evaluated and experimental data and related bibliographic information on magnetic tapes and printouts.

Scope and/or Subject Matter: Nuclear structures; charged particle reactions; radioactivity decay.

Input Sources: Data are acquired from other nuclear data centers participating in the network.

Holdings and Storage Media: CAJAD maintains magnetic tapes of data in the common exchange format.

Computer-Based Products and Services: CAJAD provides numerical and bibliographical information retrieval services from such network data bases as the Evaluated Nuclear Structure Data File (ENSDF) and the EXFOR Files. Output can be supplied on printouts or tapes.

Clientele/Availability: CAJAD's main clients are scientists in the U.S.S.R. and allied countries.

Contact: Dr. F.E. Chukreev, Head, Center for Nuclear Structure and Reaction Data.

★1000★
UNITED KINGDOM ONLINE USER GROUP (UKOLUG)
Institute of Information Scientists   Phone: 0734 861345
Harvest House, 62 London Rd.   Founded: 1978
Reading, Berks. RG1 5AS, England
Chris Parker, Chairman

Description of System or Service: The UNITED KINGDOM ONLINE USER GROUP (UKOLUG) is a special interest group of the Institute of Information Scientists (IIS) concerned with online information retrieval. UKOLUG represents the interests of users engaged in library and information work, and it holds meetings, conferences, and seminars.

Scope and/or Subject Matter: All aspects of online information retrieval including international online information systems, data banks, and the Prestel system.

Clientele/Availability: UKOLUG membership is open to IIS members and nonmembers by subscription.

Contact: Chris Parker, Chairman, United Kingdom Online User Group.

★1001★
UNITED NATIONS
ADVISORY COMMITTEE FOR THE CO-ORDINATION OF INFORMATION SYSTEMS (ACCIS)
Pavillons du Petit-Saconnex   Phone: 022 346011
16, ave. Jean-Trembley   Service Est: 1983
CH-1209 Geneva, Switzerland
George Thompson, Officer in Charge

Staff: 1 Information and library professional; 2 management

professional; 2 clerical and nonprofessional.

Related Organizations: The ACCIS was established by decision of the United Nations Administrative Committee on Co-ordination.

Description of System or Service: The ADVISORY COMMITTEE FOR THE CO-ORDINATION OF INFORMATION SYSTEMS (ACCIS) provides consultancy services for organizations of the United Nations system. Its primary goals are to facilitate access by member states to UN information and to promote the improvement of the information infrastructure within the UN system. ACCIS activities help to ensure the more efficient operation of planned or existing UN information systems and services by enhancing their capacity to collect, store, retrieve, and disseminate information. It comprises all the organizations of the UN system, each of which has designated a focal point which is responsible for publicizing ACCIS activities and involving its organization in relevant ACCIS projects. ACCIS work is also carried out by technical panels comprising specialists from UN organizations possessing the appropriate expertise in the following areas: computer-based communication services; register of development activities; and access to UN data bases. ACCIS disseminates information by preparing material which provides an overview of UN information resources and by promoting its diffusion through each organization to member states and users at the national level. ACCIS produces the Directory of United Nations Information Systems, which is available in print form and as the commercially available online DUNIS data base.

Scope and/or Subject Matter: Information systems containing substantive information available within organizations of the UN system and of potential use to member states.

Input Sources: Input is obtained from United Nations agencies.

Holdings and Storage Media: The machine-readable DUNIS data base contains information on more than 230 UN information services and more than 100 computerized data bases and data banks; it is updated annually.

Publications: 1) Directory of United Nations Information Systems—provides information on information services and data bases offered or available through UN organizations and agencies; also includes information on offices, information centers, and libraries providing access to these systems. Available for purchase from United Nations Publications, Palais des Nations, CH-1211 Geneva 10, Switzerland; or United Nations Publications, New York, NY 10017, U.S.A. 2) Register of United Nations Serials Publications—consolidated listing of approximately 2000 UN serials; available for purchase. 3) ACCIS Newsletter (bimonthly)—reports on ACCIS activities, reviews recent developments in information technology, examines new and improved systems within the UN system, provides details of seminars and conferences on information topics, and reviews pertinent new publications; available by request. A DUNIS users manual, in French, English, or Spanish, is also available by request.

Computer-Based Products and Services: The ACCIS Directory of United Nations Information Systems is available online through ECHO (European Commission Host Organization) as the DUNIS data base. Search elements for information services include: name, acronym, country, address, content, type of service, status, language, sources, geographic access, availability, services provided, and others. Search elements for data bases include: name, organization, department, country, address, content, and file details, including time span, total citations, update frequency, language, sources, data, index, aids, availability, software, and others. DUNIS can also be searched via controlled terms taken from a trilingual (English, French, Spanish) vocabulary. In addition to producing DUNIS, ACCIS is studying ways of facilitating telecommunications links between UN organizations.

Other Services: Additionally, ACCIS provides an advisory service to UN organizations regarding proposals for new information systems, or the modification of existing ones.

Clientele/Availability: Services are available without restrictions.

Projected Publications and Services: ACCIS is considering developing a data base on serials produced by UN organizations, a data base on economic and social development documents published by UN organizations, and a register of technical cooperation projects financed and/or executed by UN organizations.

Remarks: ACCIS is the successor to the United Nations Inter-Organization Board for Information Systems (IOB).

Contact: George Thompson, Officer in Charge, or Elaine Kuczek, Associate Officer, Advisory Committee for the Co-ordination of Information Systems.

★1002★
UNITED NATIONS
ECONOMIC AND SOCIAL COMMISSION FOR ASIA AND THE PACIFIC (ESCAP)
ESCAP LIBRARY
ESCAP BIBLIOGRAPHIC INFORMATION SYSTEM (EBIS)
United Nations Bldg.　　　　　　　　　Phone: 282 9161
Rajadamnern Ave.
Bangkok 10200, Thailand
N. Peter Cummins, Library Chief

Staff: 10 Information and library professional; 13 other.

Description of System or Service: The ESCAP BIBLIOGRAPHIC INFORMATION SYSTEM maintains a computer-readable bibliographic data base on economic and social development and related issues. Information for the data base is contributed by a network which includes information units within ESCAP, other United Nations information centers in Bangkok, and selected national institutes in Asia and the Pacific region. The ESCAP data base is used to publish bibliographies, provide search and SDI services, and produce magnetic tapes for exchange with regional and international institutions.

Scope and/or Subject Matter: Economic and social development, economic conditions, economic cooperation, agriculture, food, industry, trade, raw materials, commodities, natural resources, mineral resources, energy, water resources, transport, shipping and ports, statistics, environment, and transnational corporations.

Input Sources: Input is derived from ESCAP and United Nations documents, serials, and general literature.

Holdings and Storage Media: EBIS holds approximately 20,000 machine-readable records from 1980 to date, increasing by about 9000 items annually. Library holdings include 100,000 bound volumes and subscriptions to 3000 periodicals.

Publications: 1) Asian Bibliography (semiannual)—contains citations to selected English-language periodical articles, books, and other literature on socioeconomic development in Asia and the Pacific. Includes author, title, and area indexes. 2) Register of Serials (biannual). 3) ESCAP Documents and Publications (annual). 4) Rural Development: A Selected Bibliography (semiannual).

Computer-Based Products and Services: The ESCAP Bibliographic Information System provides descriptions of socioeconomic documents and serials from about 40 member countries in Asia and the Pacific. Bibliographic elements present in the System include author, citation, indexing terms, and document symbols. The data base is used to provide information retrieval, SDI, and magnetic tape services. A subfile of the data base dealing with population is maintained by the ESCAP Population Division.

Clientele/Availability: Services are available to the government agencies, research institutes, and national libraries of ESCAP member countries.

Contact: N. Peter Cummins, Chief, ESCAP Library. (Telex 82392 ESCAP TH or 82315 ESCAP TH.)

★1003★
UNITED NATIONS
ECONOMIC AND SOCIAL COMMISSION FOR ASIA AND THE PACIFIC (ESCAP)
POPULATION DIVISION
POPULATION CLEARING-HOUSE AND INFORMATION SECTION
United Nations Bldg.　　　　　　　　　Phone: 282 9161
Rajadamnern Ave.　　　　　　　　　Service Est: 1969
Bangkok 10200, Thailand
Helen K. Kolbe, Section Chief

Staff: 6 Information and library professional; 3 management professional; 1 technician; 14 clerical and nonprofessional.

Related Organizations: Support is received from the United Nations Fund for Population Activities.

Description of System or Service: The POPULATION CLEARING-HOUSE AND INFORMATION SECTION provides information on population, fertility, and family planning in Asia and the Pacific for governmental and nongovernmental organizations in that region, and for other United Nations organizations. The SECTION functions as the Regional Population Information Centre and as the regional focal point for the International Population Information Network (POPIN). The SECTION offers computerized literature searches, provides reference and documentation services, and offers training and advisory services for librarians and information specialists. The SECTION also coordinates the Population Library/ Information Centre Network, a resource-sharing group of 220 population libraries. Additionally, the SECTION maintains the computer-readable ESCAP Bibliographic Information System/ Population File (EBIS/ POPFILE) data base.

Scope and/or Subject Matter: Population, demography, family planning, birth control, fertility, mortality, and related socioeconomic fields.

Input Sources: Input consists of monographs, serials, reports, dissertations, proceedings, audiovisual materials, laws and regulations, and unpublished documents.

Holdings and Storage Media: The library collection includes approximately 15,000 volumes, 450 periodical titles, and microforms.

Publications: 1) ADOPT: Asian and Worldwide Documents on Population Topics (monthly)—contains abstracts and indexes of new population literature. 2) Asian-Pacific Population Programme News (quarterly). 3) Population Headliners (monthly). 4) Directory of Regional Demographic Research and Teaching Institutions. Research papers and reports are also issued.

Microform Products and Services: Publications issued by the Population Division are available on microfiche.

Computer-Based Products and Services: The POPULATION CLEARING-HOUSE AND INFORMATION SECTION maintains the computerized ESCAP Bibliographic Information System/ Population File (EBIS/ POPFILE) data base. The SECTION conducts computerized literature searches.

Clientele/Availability: The Section serves organizations in the Asia and Pacific region and other United Nations organizations.

Projected Publications and Services: Planned activities include preparation of a newsletter for the Population Library/ Information Centre Network.

Contact: Helen K. Kolbe, Chief, Population Clearing-house and Information Section.

★1004★
UNITED NATIONS
ECONOMIC AND SOCIAL COMMISSION FOR ASIA AND THE PACIFIC (ESCAP)
STATISTICS DIVISION
UN/ESCAP STATISTICAL INFORMATION SERVICES
United Nations Bldg.   Phone: 282 9161
Rajadamnern Ave.   Service Est: 1948
Bangkok 10200, Thailand
Mr. M.A. Sahib, Chief

Staff: 3 Management professional; 11 clerical and nonprofessional.

Description of System or Service: The UN/ESCAP STATISTICAL INFORMATION SERVICES collects and publishes socioeconomic and other statistical data from ESCAP member countries. Some of these data are held in machine-readable files which are used to provide computerized information retrieval services.

Scope and/or Subject Matter: Socioeconomic data, demography, social statistics, national accounts, production, and trade.

Input Sources: ESCAP member countries and other UN agencies provide data to the Services in the form of publications, periodic questionnaires, magnetic tapes, and computer printouts.

Holdings and Storage Media: Approximately 10,000 time series of foreign trade statistics are held in machine-readable form. Library holdings include 14,000 bound volumes.

Publications: 1) ESCAP Statistical Yearbook for Asia and the Pacific; 2) Quarterly Bulletin of Statistics for Asia and the Pacific; 3) Statistical Indicators for Asia and the Pacific; 4) Handbook on Agricultural Statistics for Asia and the Pacific (annual); 5) Foreign Trade Statistics for Asia and the Pacific (annual)—issued in two series.

Computer-Based Products and Services: The SERVICES maintains machine-readable files of foreign trade statistics relating to ESCAP member countries. The files are used to produce the Foreign Trade Statistics for Asia and the Pacific publication and to provide computerized information retrieval services.

Clientele/Availability: Primary clients include the secretariat staff, publications users, research institutions, and individuals.

Contact: M.A. Sahib, Chief, Statistics Division, or R.H. Sherif, Chief, Statistical Information Section. (Telex 8239 ESCAP TH or 82315 ESCAP TH.)

★1005★
UNITED NATIONS
ECONOMIC COMMISSION FOR AFRICA (ECA)
PAN-AFRICAN DOCUMENTATION AND INFORMATION SYSTEM (PADIS)
P.O. Box 3001   Phone: 447200
Addis Ababa, Ethiopia   Service Est: 1980
Dr. J.K. Quirino-Lanhounmey, Project Director

Staff: 5 Information and library professional; 4 management professional; 13 technicians; 6 clerical and nonprofessional.

Related Organizations: PADIS support is provided by the United Nations Development Programme, the African Development Bank, and the International Development Research Centre in Canada.

Description of System or Service: The PAN-AFRICAN DOCUMENTATION AND INFORMATION SYSTEM (PADIS) is an international computer-based information and telecommunications network established to collect, process, and distribute information required by policy makers, technicians, planners, and others engaged in the economic and social development of African states. PADIS will have the following major components when completed: 1) PADIS-NET—the PADIS telecommunications network for systems interaction and information dissemination throughout Africa; will also link with existing international networks. 2) PADIS-DEV—an economic and social reference data base covering development plans of African countries as well as facts, trends, analyses, and official policies regarding development. 3) PADIS-STAT—statistical data bases for all 54 African countries covering industry, trade, finance, national accounts, distribution and transportation, and demographic and social topics. 4) PADIS-COM—a collection of other complementary files produced by regional institutions, national documentation centers, and the ECA. 5) PADIS-ADMIN—integrated administrative management system of the ECA, handling personnel, finance, general services, conference services, and the library. 6) PADIS-PROM—project management and monitoring data base. PADIS will disseminate information online and through hardcopy publications, microfiche, and magnetic tape services; develop or obtain software for a variety of applications; and provide consultancy, assistance, and training to countries for development of national data bases.

Scope and/or Subject Matter: African industry, trade, finance, agriculture, forestry, fishing, energy, mining, manufacturing, construction, national accounts, distribution, transportation, communications, tourism, demographics, sociology, education, government, environment, health, labor force, population, and data processing.

Input Sources: PADIS data are provided by ECA member states and regions.

Holdings and Storage Media: Holdings include hard copies, microfiche, and computer tapes. The PADIS-DEV data base holds 1500 machine-readable records.

Publications: Devindex Africa (quarterly)—index to literature on economic and social development in Africa. Progress reports, manuals, brochures, and other publications are also issued.

Microform Products and Services: Documents which have been analyzed by the PADIS Computerized Documentation Section are available on microfiche.

Computer-Based Products and Services: PADIS consists of African statistical and bibliographic data bases, systems software, and a telecommunications network linking PADIS members with each other and with Euronet DIANE, the United Nations Statistical Office, and other UN agencies and offices in Geneva and Vienna. It has acquired the following software: TDP, for word processing; SPSS, for statistical analysis; MINISIS, for bibliographic information storage and retrieval; INSIGHT, for data entry and retrieval; IPACS, for online planning and budget control; ISEA, for econometric analysis; and ASK, for data base interrogation and reporting.

Other Services: Additional services of PADIS include cataloging, abstracting and indexing, current awareness, document delivery, and referrals.

Clientele/Availability: Chief clients are the African governments, the Economic Commission for Africa, and other UN agencies.

Contact: Dr. J.K. Quirino-Lanhounmey, Project Director, or Kebour Ghenna, Chief, Computerzed Documentation Section, Pan-African Documentation and Information System.

★1006★
UNITED NATIONS
ECONOMIC COMMISSION FOR LATIN AMERICA
(Comision Economica para America Latina - CEPAL)
LATIN AMERICAN CENTER FOR ECONOMIC AND SOCIAL
  DOCUMENTATION
(Centro Latinoamericano de Documentacion Economica y Social -
  CLADES)
Avda. Dag Hammarskjold s/n   Phone: 485051
Casilla 179-D   Service Est: 1971
Santiago, Chile
Claudionor Evangelista, Director

Staff: 10 Information and library professional; 4 clerical and nonprofessional.

Related Organizations: CLADES maintains close contact with United Nations organizations and the International Development Research Centre (IDRC) in Canada.

Description of System or Service: The LATIN AMERICAN CENTER FOR ECONOMIC AND SOCIAL DOCUMENTATION (CLADES) was established to promote and support national documentation and information services in Latin America, and to ensure that the technologies of these services are compatible to permit transfer of bibliographic information. The Center also seeks to coordinate initiatives in these fields to avoid duplication of effort and investment in equipment and systems unsuitable for the needs of the region. CLADES issues publications and maintains several computer-readable data bases in the area of development information.

Scope and/or Subject Matter: Information science, documentation, standardization, information storage and retrieval, indexing languages, training, technical aid and cooperation, economic and social planning.

Input Sources: Input to the CLADES data bases includes monographs, serial publications, reports, conference papers, surveys, bibliographies, and directories.

Holdings and Storage Media: CLADES maintains several data bases in machine-readable form.

Publications: PLANINDEX (biannual). A number of special bibliographies, directories, lists of descriptors, methodological documents, and brochures are issued. All publications are available by exchange.

Computer-Based Products and Services: CLADES provides computerized searches of the following data bases: CLADBIB—contains documents from the Economic Commission for Latin America and Latin American Institute for Economic and Social Planning; CLIN—documents on integration; CLAPLAN—documents on planning; CLADIR—directories of Latin American development information units.

Other Services: In addition to services described above, CLADES provides referrals and manual literature searches.

Clientele/Availability: Services are available free of charge to researchers and organizations cooperating with CLADES.

Contact: Claudionor Evangelista, Director, Latin American Center for Economic and Social Documentation. (Telex UN 441054 Santiago.)

★1007★
UNITED NATIONS
ECONOMIC COMMISSION FOR LATIN AMERICA
(Comision Economica para America Latina - CEPAL)
LATIN AMERICAN DEMOGRAPHIC CENTER
(Centro Latinoamericano de Demografia - CELADE)
LATIN AMERICAN POPULATION DOCUMENTATION SYSTEM
(Sistema de Documentacion sobre Poblacion en America Latina -
  DOCPAL)
Alonso de Cordova 3107   Phone: 2283206
Casilla 91   Service Est: 1976
Santiago, Chile
Betty Johnson, Head

Staff: 1 Information and library professional; 1 technician; 1 clerical and nonprofessional.

Description of System or Service: The LATIN AMERICAN POPULATION DOCUMENTATION SYSTEM (DOCPAL) abstracts and indexes published and unpublished literature dealing with population in Latin America and the Caribbean, stores the results in a computer-readable data base, and uses it to produce a semiannual abstracts journal and to provide search services. DOCPAL also provides specialized bibliographies on demand as well as document delivery services, and supplies technical assistance to national centers in the field of population documentation.

Scope and/or Subject Matter: Population studies written in or about Latin America and the Caribbean countries since 1970.

Input Sources: Input is derived from books, journals, conference papers, reports, and other significant documents.

Holdings and Storage Media: Approximately 22,500 documents are covered in the computer-readable DOCPAL data base; about 1500 records are added each year.

Publications: 1) DOCPAL Resumenes sobre Poblacion en America Latina/ DOCPAL Latin American Population Abstracts (semiannual)—available by subscription. Each issue contains approximately 750 Spanish-language abstracts arranged within subject categories; subject, author, and geographic indexes; list of journals covered; and journal directory with addresses. 2) Multilingual population thesaurus. 3) DOCPAL procedures manual.

Computer-Based Products and Services: Computerized searches of the DOCPAL data base, which is maintained online at the United Nations Latin American Demographic Center, are conducted in response to written requests.

Clientele/Availability: Services are available to all but are intended primarily for Latin American and Caribbean countries.

Contact: Betty Johnson, Head, DOCPAL, or Dr. Arthur M. Conning, Head, Population Documentation & Demographic Data Processing Division, CELADE. (Telex ITT 441054.)

★1008★
UNITED NATIONS
FOOD AND AGRICULTURE ORGANIZATION (FAO)
AQUATIC SCIENCES AND FISHERIES INFORMATION SYSTEM
  (ASFIS)
Via delle Terme di Caracalla   Phone: 06 5797
I-00100 Rome, Italy   Service Est: 1973
E.F. Akyuz, Chief

Related Organizations: The United Nations Ocean Economics and Technology Branch and the UNESCO Intergovernmental Oceanographic Commission cooperated with FAO in the development of ASFIS. Approximately 25 institutions located throughout the world participate in ASFIS through the contribution of input.

Description of System or Service: The AQUATIC SCIENCES AND

FISHERIES INFORMATION SYSTEM (ASFIS) is an international computer-based system for the collection and dissemination of marine and freshwater environmental information. A network of input centers across the world scans, selects, abstracts, and indexes journal articles, reports, monographs, and other relevant literature. This processed information is forwarded to the coordinating center in Rome which produces a variety of products and services. Chief among these is the Aquatic Sciences and Fisheries Abstracts (ASFA) journal and an equivalent computer-readable data base. ASFIS also maintains the Computerized ASFIS Register of Experts and Institutions and uses it to produce a variety of directories.

Scope and/or Subject Matter: Science, technology, and management of marine and freshwater environment, including socioeconomic and legal aspects.

Input Sources: More than 5000 journals, plus reports, books, conference papers, theses, and atlases are indexed and abstracted for ASFA by participating institutions. Input for the Computerized ASFIS Register of Experts and Institutions is derived from questionnaire responses.

Holdings and Storage Media: The computer-readable ASFA data base holds approximately 200,000 bibliographic records dating from 1975 to the present; it is updated monthly. The ASFIS Register is also held in machine-readable form.

Publications: 1) Aquatic Sciences and Fisheries Abstracts-ASFA (monthly with annual cumulative indexes)—published in two parts: Part 1 covers biological sciences and the conservation and use of living resources. Part 2 covers ocean technology, policy, and the use and conservation of nonliving resources. Both publications include monthly corporate author, author, subject, taxonomic, and geographic indexes. 2) World List of Serial Titles in Aquatic Sciences and Fisheries. 3) ASFA Aquaculture Abstracts. 4) Freshwater and Aquaculture Contents Tables-FACT (monthly)—current awareness service reproducing the table of contents pages of international periodicals dealing with freshwater sciences and aquaculture. 5) Marine Science Contents Tables-MSCT (monthly)—current awareness service reproducing the table of contents pages of international periodicals dealing with marine science and technology. 6) International Directory of Marine Scientists. Additional directories, ASFIS user aids, and authority lists are issued by FAO.

Computer-Based Products and Services: The Aquatic Sciences and Fisheries Abstracts (ASFA) data base is searchable online through DIALOG Information Services, Inc., CAN/OLE, DIMDI, ESA/IRS, and DOCOCEAN. Magnetic tapes of ASFA information are supplied free to participating national agencies. The Computerized ASFIS Register data base is used to publish directories. Magnetic tapes of the Register are also available.

Clientele/Availability: Clients include scientists, technologists, administrators, and legislators with interests in marine and freshwater environments.

Remarks: ASFIS has absorbed the activities of the Marine and Coastal Technology Information Service (MACTIS) formerly operated by the UN Ocean Economics and Technology Branch.

Contact: E.F. Akyuz, Chief, Fisheries Information Data and Statistics Service, Food and Agriculture Organization. In the United States, contact Robert R. Freeman, U.S. National Oceanic and Atmospheric Administration, Page Bldg. 2, 3300 Whitehaven St. N.W., Washington, DC 20235; telephone (202) 634-7722.

★1009★
UNITED NATIONS
FOOD AND AGRICULTURE ORGANIZATION (FAO)
CURRENT AGRICULTURAL RESEARCH INFORMATION SYSTEM (CARIS)
CARIS Coordinating Center
Via delle Terme di Caracalla
I-00100 Rome, Italy
Phone: 06 57971
Service Est: 1972

Staff: 2 Information and library professional; 1 clerical and nonprofessional.

Description of System or Service: The CURRENT AGRICULTURAL RESEARCH INFORMATION SYSTEM (CARIS) provides a mechanism for collection, processing, storage, and dissemination of information on current agricultural research institutions, workers, and projects in developing countries. The decentralized CARIS scheme consists of regional and national centers located throughout the world which are responsible in their respective countries or regions for data collection, processing, and dissemination. A central data base composed of a mixture of national and regional files is managed by the CARIS Coordinating Center in Rome for service to the participating countries, as well as for exchange with information collected by similar systems in the developed countries. Primary products of the SYSTEM include national and regional printed directories and machine-readable files on tapes or diskettes.

Scope and/or Subject Matter: Research carried out in or on behalf of developing countries in the subject areas of agriculture, animal production, forestry, fisheries, and food.

Input Sources: Input is gathered by regional and national centers from questionnaires sent to research institutions and workers.

Holdings and Storage Media: Computerized files are maintained in ISIS/ISO format at FAO, and in ISIS or MINISIS format at the national and regional centers.

Computer-Based Products and Services: Online searches from CARIS files are conducted by the Coordinating Center on request. Searches can be made for institutions, workers, and projects according to the AGRIS/ CARIS classification scheme and the multilingual AGROVOC thesaurus.

Clientele/Availability: Services are available for FAO member countries.

Contact: E.K. Samaha, CARIS Coordinating Center. (Telex 610181 FAO I.)

★1010★
UNITED NATIONS
FOOD AND AGRICULTURE ORGANIZATION (FAO)
ECONOMIC AND SOCIAL DEPARTMENT
HUMAN RESOURCES, INSTITUTIONS AND AGRARIAN REFORM DIVISION
POPULATION DOCUMENTATION CENTER (PDC)
Via delle Terme di Caracalla
I-00100 Rome, Italy
Phone: 06 57973628
Service Est: 1974
Ms. I. Losseau, Population Programme Officer

Staff: 1 Information and library professional; 2 clerical and nonprofessional.

Related Organizations: The Population Documentation Center receives support from the United Nations Fund for Population Activities (UNFPA).

Description of System or Service: The POPULATION DOCUMENTATION CENTER (PDC) serves as the focal point within the FAO for population-related information. It uses computerized information storage and retrieval systems to support FAO population programs relating to agricultural rural development and to disseminate information on FAO population documents to interested individuals and institutions. PDC maintains the POPTIO data base which includes information on relevant non-FAO documentation available in the CENTER. It also collects FAO population documents which are listed in the Population File of the FAO Documentation data base maintained by the David Lubin Memorial Library (see separate entry). Additionally, the CENTER supports the UN's Population Information Network (POPIN) and the FAO's AGRIS system.

Scope and/or Subject Matter: Rural population, women, and families, particularly in developing countries.

Input Sources: The Center collects specialized serials, monographs, reports, and other population-related materials from the FAO and other sources.

Holdings and Storage Media: The Center maintains computer-readable data bases and a library collection of 1200 bound volumes, subscriptions to 60 periodicals, and 6200 reports and other materials.

Publications: FAO/UNFPA projects; bibliography of publications and documents; other bibliographies.

Computer-Based Products and Services: The CENTER maintains the POPTIO data base online. The data base holds approximately 3300 references on non-FAO documents related to population in the context of rural development. The Population File, holding more than 1700 references to FAO population documents, is available online as part of the FAO Documentation data base. Searches from both data bases are conducted on request. The CENTER also maintains a computerized mailing list of institutions involved in population related to rural development activities in developing countries and interested in receiving FAO population publications.

Clientele/Availability: Services are available without restrictions to FAO staff and individuals and institutions of FAO member states involved in population and rural development activities. Data base searches are conducted without charge.

Contact: Ms. I. Losseau, Population Programme Officer, Population Documentation Center. (Telex 610181 FAO I.)

★1011★
UNITED NATIONS
FOOD AND AGRICULTURE ORGANIZATION (FAO)
INFOFISH
P.O. Box 10899   Phone: 914466
Kuala Lumpur 01-02, Malaysia
Erik Hempel, Acting Project Manager

Staff: 28 Total.

Description of System or Service: The Food and Agriculture Organization's INFOFISH project is a marketing information and advisory service specializing in Asian/Pacific fisheries. It was established to promote trade in fish and fishery products from and within this region, which includes some of the largest fishing nations in the world. INFOFISH objectives are to contribute to a balanced supply of fish products in the participating countries and to make the best use of export opportunities within and outside the region; to improve the utilization of raw material and processing facilities in the fishery industry of the region; and to facilitate the transfer of fish utilization technology and its application among countries in the Asian/Pacific region. Specific services offered by INFOFISH include the following: 1) Trade Promotion Service—assists the fish trade by identifying new marketing opportunities and/or new sources of supplies for companies in the region. 2) Technical Advisory Service—provides technical information to the fish industry in the region on all post-harvest aspects of fisheries as well as basics on fish farming. 3) Marketing Information Service—provides regular information on world and regional fish markets through the INFOFISH Trade News and INFOFISH Marketing Digest publications. Information from Trade News is also available electronically through the FISHLINE service. INFOFISH also provides services from a computerized register of information on buyers, sellers, and product lines.

Scope and/or Subject Matter: All aspects of fish handling and marketing in the Asian/Pacific region.

Input Sources: INFOFISH gathers information from a number of sources in the fishing industry.

Holdings and Storage Media: INFOFISH Trade News information is held in machine-readable form and updated fortnightly. INFOFISH also maintains a computerized register of information on approximately 2000 importers of fish products worldwide and approximately 650 producers in the Asia/Pacific region.

Publications: 1) INFOFISH Trade News (fortnightly)—available by subscription. Reports on major fish commodity markets and prices; coverage includes canned, dried, salted, fresh, frozen, and live fish, with special coverage on shrimp and tuna. 2) INFOFISH Marketing Digest (bimonthly)—available by subscription. Contains feature articles by experts on a variety of topics, including product and market opportunities, import regulations, equipment choices, processing, storage, packaging, shipping, and investment. 3) Trade Data Package—consists of a series of international market studies which are available for purchase individually or as a set; studies are available on the following topics: tuna, shrimp, cephalopods, fishmeal, seaweed, dried fish, finfish, and import regulations. Additionally, INFOFISH commissions special studies.

Computer-Based Products and Services: INFOFISH's FISHLINE service provides online access to INFOFISH Trade News, which contains news on fish market trends and prices. FISHLINE is arranged in 150 sections which provide information on eight different product groups and prices on approximately 450 fish products. The FISHLINE service is remotely accessible via computer or telex facilities. INFOFISH also maintains and provides services from a computerized register of information on buyers, sellers, and product lines.

Other Services: INFOFISH also provides technical assistance on all aspects of fish handling and marketing, including advice on plant design, quality control, processing standards, and the profitable use of discards or under-utilized species.

Clientele/Availability: Services are available to producers, exporters, and importers of fish products; primary users are INFOFISH member countries.

Contact: Erik Hempel, Acting Project Manager, INFOFISH. (Telex 31560 INFISH MA.)

★1012★
UNITED NATIONS
FOOD AND AGRICULTURE ORGANIZATION (FAO)
INTERNATIONAL INFORMATION SYSTEM FOR THE
   AGRICULTURAL SCIENCES AND TECHNOLOGY (AGRIS)
AGRIS Coordinating Center   Phone: 06 5797
Via delle Terme di Caracalla   Service Est: 1975
I-00100 Rome, Italy
A. Lebowitz, Head

Description of System or Service: The INTERNATIONAL INFORMATION SYSTEM FOR THE AGRICULTURAL SCIENCES AND TECHNOLOGY (AGRIS) is designed to carry out the collection, storage, and retrieval of information related to currently produced agricultural documents. AGRIS is a decentralized system of 130 national and regional input centers throughout the world that provide bibliographic data to the AGRIS Coordinating Center in Rome for integrating and computer processing. Chief products of the system are the monthly printed publication AGRINDEX and the corresponding AGRIS online data base.

Scope and/or Subject Matter: Agriculture, food, human nutrition, environment, economics, animal science, veterinary science, fisheries, forestry, natural resources, energy, and pollution.

Input Sources: AGRIS centers input information about periodical literature, monographs, reports, patents, standards, dissertations, proceedings, trade catalogs, laws and regulations, and unpublished documents.

Holdings and Storage Media: The computer-readable AGRIS data base holds approximately one million records.

Publications: AGRINDEX (monthly)—international index published in English with original language titles of documents. Arranged in 17 subject categories with author, commodities, geographic, and other indexes.

Computer-Based Products and Services: The AGRIS data base, covering international agricultural literature, is available online through ESA/IRS, DIMDI, and the International Atomic Energy Agency. Online access and SDI services are also available through some national and regional AGRIS centers. The Coordinating Center in Rome offers the AGRIS Output Tape on a monthly subscription basis. The Center also provides advisory services and training in the use of the system.

Clientele/Availability: Services are available to all who require agricultural information, including researchers, teachers, planners, decision makers, and extension personnel. In some countries the authorization of the National AGRIS Center may be required in order to access the data base.

Contact: A. Lebowitz, Head, AGRIS Coordinating Center. (Telex 610181 FAO I.)

★1013★
UNITED NATIONS
FOOD AND AGRICULTURE ORGANIZATION (FAO)
LIBRARY AND DOCUMENTATION SYSTEMS DIVISION
DAVID LUBIN MEMORIAL LIBRARY

Via delle Terme di Caracalla
I-00100 Rome, Italy
Phone: 06 57971
Service Est: 1948

Staff: 12 Information and library professional; 4 technicians; 38 clerical and nonprofessional.

Description of System or Service: As the central library of the Food and Agriculture Organization (FAO), the DAVID LUBIN MEMORIAL LIBRARY maintains an extensive collection of FAO publications and unpublished documents as well as selected publications issued by the United Nations and its specialized agencies. It stores bibliographic and cataloging data for FAO publications in computer-readable files and uses them to provide magnetic tape and retrospective search services and to produce catalogs and current awareness publications. Data bases maintained by the LIBRARY include FAO Documentation, providing bibliographic records of FAO technical and socioeconomic documents, and the FAO Library Catalogue of Monographs, covering books and monographic series acquired since 1976. In addition, the LIBRARY offers computerized searching of external data bases.

Scope and/or Subject Matter: Agriculture, agricultural economics and statistics, fisheries, forestry, food and nutrition, and rural development.

Input Sources: Input consists of documents and publications of the FAO, material from other UN agencies, commercial publications, and publicly available data bases.

Holdings and Storage Media: The machine-readable FAO Documentation data base contains approximately 75,000 bibliographic records dating from 1967 to the present. The machine-readable FAO Library Catalogue of Monographs data base contains approximately 20,000 bibliographic records dating from 1976 to the present. Library holdings include approximately 1 million bound volumes, subscriptions to 9000 periodicals, and microfiche duplicates of approximately 90,000 documents.

Publications: 1) FAO Documentation - Current Bibliography (bimonthly, with COM indexes)—available free of charge. 2) List of Selected Articles (monthly)—restricted to FAO staff. 3) List of Serials Currently Received (irregular).

Microform Products and Services: The following are available for purchase on COM microfiche: 1) FAO Documentation—provides cumulative bibliographic record of FAO technical and socioeconomic publications and unrestricted documents indexed since 1976; includes subject, author, division, and project indexes, with geographic indexes since 1980. 2) FAO Library Catalogue of Monographs—provides cumulative bibliographic record of books and monographic series added to the Library collections since 1976; includes subject, author, series, conference, and title indexes, with geographic indexes since 1980. 3) FAO Library List of Serials—provides complete record of serials held by the Library; includes listings by title, subject category, and country. All FAO publications and documents cited in the FAO Documentation data base are available on 105x150mm microfiche by annual subscription or for purchase individually.

Computer-Based Products and Services: The LUBIN LIBRARY maintains the FAO Documentation and FAO Library Catalogue of Monographs data bases online and uses them to produce COM microfiche catalogs and offer retrospective searches. The data bases are also available on magnetic tape. Additionally, the LIBRARY provides retrospective searching of external online data bases such as AGRICOLA, AGRIS, BIOSIS, CAB, FSTA, and PASCAL, and offers a bimonthly SDI service based on AGRIS tapes.

Clientele/Availability: Services are available to FAO staff; external access may be granted to qualified research workers and government officials working in the subject fields of the FAO.

Contact: Colin I. Barnes, Chief, Documentation Processing Section, David Lubin Memorial Library. (Telex 610181 FAO I.)

★1014★
UNITED NATIONS
FOOD AND AGRICULTURE ORGANIZATION (FAO)
STATISTICS DIVISION
INTERLINKED COMPUTERIZED STORAGE AND PROCESSING SYSTEM OF FOOD AND AGRICULTURAL DATA (ICS)

Via delle Terme di Caracalla
I-00100 Rome, Italy
K. Becker, Head
Phone: 06 5797
Service Est: 1973

Staff: 1 Information and library professional; 1 management professional; 5 technicians; 30 clerical and nonprofessional.

Related Organizations: The System is a joint effort of user organizations throughout the Food and Agriculture Organization. Design and development was accomplished principally by the Statistics Division and the Management Services Division.

Description of System or Service: The INTERLINKED COMPUTERIZED STORAGE AND PROCESSING SYSTEM OF FOOD AND AGRICULTURAL DATA (ICS) is a computer-based system for the storage, retrieval, selection, processing, analysis, and dissemination of statistical data on food and agricultural commodities. The SYSTEM is primarily for use by various divisions of the Food and Agriculture Organization (FAO); however, several products are available for purchase, including yearbooks, bulletins, and magnetic tapes.

Scope and/or Subject Matter: Worldwide food, agriculture, fishery, and forestry statistics, including data on human population, crops and livestock production, livestock numbers, agricultural machinery, pesticides, fertilizers, land use, trade, fishery and forestry commodities and related commodity production.

Input Sources: Monographs, serials, reports, trade catalogs, unpublished documents, questionnaires, and FAO estimates are scanned for input.

Holdings and Storage Media: The ICS machine-readable files contain more than 200,000 statistical items dating from 1961 to the present.

Publications: 1) FAO Monthly Bulletin of Statistics—contains statistical tables on crop, livestock products for production, and trade and prices. 2) FAO Production Yearbook—production indexes and annual data on land use and irrigation, population, crops, livestock numbers, products, and means of production. 3) FAO Trade Yearbook—contains trade indexes, data on trade of agricultural products and agricultural requisites. 4) FAO Fertilizer Yearbook—contains annual data on production consumption, trade, available supply of fertilizers, consumption indicators, fertilizer prices, development, capacity, and forecast, and the state of fertilizers. 5) FAO Yearbook of Forest Products and Trade—contains annual data on forestry production. 6) Food Balance Sheets (every three years)—contains country, supply, and utilization data per capita consumption.

Computer-Based Products and Services: The ICS system consists of machine-readable data and reference files covering statistical information from more than 200 countries and territories and on approximately 800 commodities. The system is used by FAO divisions for extraction, aggregation, and calculation of series data. The files are searchable on these fields: geographic region, country, commodity, element (production, trade, utilization, and others), and year. The following machine-readable tapes are offered yearly for purchase: 1) FAO Production Yearbook—contains approximately 23,000 time series from the Crops, the Livestock Numbers and Products, and the Means of Production sections of the Production Yearbook. 2) FAO Trade Yearbook—contains about 52,000 time series reported in the Trade in Agricultural Commodities and the Trade in Agricultural Requisites sections of the Trade Yearbook. 3) FAO Yearbook of Forest Products—contains about 25,000 time series covering all production and trade series reported in the Yearbook. 4) FAO Fertilizer Yearbook—contains approximately 7000 time series on production, trade, consumption, and prices paid by farmers.

Clientele/Availability: The ICS system serves FAO member states, international organizations, and statistical institutions.

Contact: F. Pariboni, Assistant to Division Director, Statistics Division, Food and Agriculture Organization. (Telex 610181 FAO I.)

★1015★
UNITED NATIONS EDUCATIONAL, SCIENTIFIC AND CULTURAL ORGANIZATION (UNESCO)
CENTER FOR SOCIAL SCIENCE RESEARCH AND DOCUMENTATION FOR THE ARAB REGION (ARCSS)
Zamalek P.O.　　　　　　　　　　　　　　Phone: 650159
Cairo, Egypt　　　　　　　　　　　　　　Service Est: 1978
Dr. Ahmad M. Khalifa, Director General

Staff: Approximately 25 total.

Description of System or Service: The CENTER FOR SOCIAL SCIENCE RESEARCH AND DOCUMENTATION FOR THE ARAB REGION (ARCSS) promotes regional cooperation between documentation and research institutions in order to improve the contribution of the social sciences to development efforts in the Arab region. It seeks to do this by establishing a Regional Arab Information Network for Social Sciences (RAINSS); by acting as a clearinghouse for social science, development, communication, and other relevant materials generated in the Arab region and elsewhere; and by maintaining data base files and providing access to them through retrospective searches, current awareness, and SDI. The CENTER also issues publications, conducts training programs, and organizes seminars, conferences, and symposia.

Scope and/or Subject Matter: Social sciences, development, information and documentation, communication.

Input Sources: ARCSS acquires print and nonprint information from international sources.

Holdings and Storage Media: ARCSS maintains data base files and a library of 450 books and other publications and subscriptions to 109 periodicals.

Publications: 1) ARCSS Newsletter (3 per year)—published in Arabic and English; 2) Directory of Social Science Research and Documentation Institutions in the Arab Region; 3) Bibliography on Petroleum and Social Values; 4) Bibliography of Bibliographies in Social Sciences; 5) Arab Social Science Index; 6) Annotated Bibliography on the Child. Other bibliographies, indexes, abstracts, and conference proceedings are issued.

Microform Products and Services: Micrographic reproductions are produced to facilitate exchange and transfer of information within the Arab region and abroad.

Computer-Based Products and Services: Computerized documentation and information services are provided through the ARCSS Systems and Automated Applications Section.

Clientele/Availability: Services are geared towards social science institutions and centers, decision makers, and researchers in the Arab region and abroad.

Contact: Dr. Ahmad M. Khalifa, Director General, Center for Social Science Research and Documentation for the Arab Region.

★1016★
UNITED NATIONS EDUCATIONAL, SCIENTIFIC AND CULTURAL ORGANIZATION (UNESCO)
DIVISION OF SCIENCE AND TECHNOLOGY POLICIES
SCIENCE AND TECHNOLOGY POLICIES INFORMATION EXCHANGE PROGRAMME (PIPS)
7, place de Fontenoy　　　　　　　　　Phone: 01 5681000
F-75700 Paris, France
Yvan de Hemptinne, Director

Staff: 1 Information and library professional; 1 management professional; 1 technician; 2 clerical and nonprofessional.

Description of System or Service: The SCIENCE AND TECHNOLOGY POLICIES INFORMATION EXCHANGE PROGRAMME (PIPS), which supersedes the SPINES pilot program, was established to facilitate the exchange, at the national and international levels, of documents and factual data that have a direct bearing on the formulation and monitoring of national science and technology policies. PIPS contributes to the development in UNESCO member countries of compatible information services dealing with science and technology policies. It provides consulting and technical assistance to national centers which are creating both bibliographic data bases covering documents dealing with science and technology policies and factual data bases on national scientific and technology resources. In addition, PIPS is developing an international data base on institutions, specialists, courses, and research projects in the field. It is expected that the national information services will eventually be linked into an international network.

Scope and/or Subject Matter: Policymaking, management, transfer, and assessment in science and technology as it applies to UNESCO's member states.

Input Sources: For the international data base, PIPS gathers information on relevant governmental and parliamentary bodies and research projects, studies, and courses carried out by academic and nonacademic institutions in UNESCO's member states.

Publications: 1) SPINES Feasibility Study. 2) SPINES Thesaurus—issued in English and French, it will also be available in Spanish and Portuguese. 3) SPINES Subject Categories. 4) Manual for the Development of National Documentation Units and Bibliographic Data Bases for Science and Technology Policy. 5) National Scientific and Technological Potential Survey Interviewer's Guide. 6) World Directory of Research Projects, Studies and Courses in Science and Technology Policy. 7) World Directory of National Science and Technology Policy-Making Bodies.

Computer-Based Products and Services: The SCIENCE AND TECHNOLOGY POLICIES INFORMATION EXCHANGE PROGRAMME is implementing the international data base using the UNESCO CDS/ISIS software. Computer tapes containing data collected for the World Directory of Research Projects and the World Directory of Policy-Making Bodies are available. The PROGRAMME also provides technical assistance in the use of several software products for the management and analysis of factual data.

Clientele/Availability: Users are policymakers, managers, administrators, scientific researchers, teachers, and students active in the field of science and technology policies in member states.

Projected Publications and Services: The PROGRAMME is preparing a manual for surveying national scientific and technological potential and for developing the resulting data base.

Contact: Bruno de Padirac, Senior Project Officer, Science and Technology Policies Information Exchange Programme; telephone 01 5686163.

★1017★
UNITED NATIONS EDUCATIONAL, SCIENTIFIC AND CULTURAL ORGANIZATION (UNESCO)
DIVISION OF THE UNESCO LIBRARY, ARCHIVES AND DOCUMENTATION SERVICES
COMPUTERIZED DOCUMENTATION SERVICE/INTEGRATED SET OF INFORMATION SYSTEMS (CDS/ISIS)
7, Place de Fontenoy　　　　　　　　　Phone: 01 5771610
F-75700 Paris, France

Description of System or Service: The COMPUTERIZED DOCUMENTATION SERVICE/ INTEGRATED SET OF INFORMATION SYSTEMS (CDS/ISIS) is a generalized data base management system designed for handling non-numerical data bases of any size. CDS/ISIS performs three main functions: file maintenance, which includes data preparation, data entry, modification of existing records, and updating of master and inverted files; retrieval, which includes batch and online search capabilities; and sorting and printing facilities, which are used for the production of catalogs, indexes, and special types of output, and which include a photocomposition interface. CDS/ISIS is used by more than 80 national institutions or international organizations.

Scope and/or Subject Matter: Computerized information storage and retrieval for libraries, documentation centers, and other applications.

Input Sources: CDS/ISIS may be used to index and catalog reports, documents, periodical articles, monographs, and other items.

Publications: CDS/ISIS Newsletter (semiannual)—provides a forum for CDS/ISIS users. A variety of CDS/ISIS user manuals is available.

Computer-Based Products and Services: The CDS/ISIS system runs on IBM 360, 370, or 303X computers and on RIAD 1035, 1040, and 1060 computers in both batch and online modes. Features of the software include the following: user-controlled composition of each master file through field definition tables; generalized logical record structure for master records; online or batch data entry, correction, and editing; access to master records via an inverted file; inverted file initiated changes to master records; controlled or uncontrolled indexing vocabulary; online or batch information retrieval using root and proximity searching, group or field level searching, and Boolean operators; integrated thesaurus; multifile searching and indexing; printing in different formats; and standardized communications format interface.

Other Services: In addition to services described above, UNESCO provides personnel training, project setup, coordination, and administrative support.

Clientele/Availability: The CDS/ISIS package is available to organizations in member states and in the United Nations family; users agree to not use the system for commercial purposes and to participate in technical advisory group activities.

Remarks: The original version of ISIS was developed in 1964 by the International Labour Organization; it was combined with CDS in 1975. A minicomputer-based version of ISIS, MINISIS, has been developed by the International Development Research Centre in Canada.

Contact: Division of the UNESCO Library, Archives and Documentation Services.

★1018★
UNITED NATIONS EDUCATIONAL, SCIENTIFIC AND CULTURAL ORGANIZATION (UNESCO)
ENERGY INFORMATION SECTION
7, Place de Fontenoy   Phone: 01 5683903
F-75700 Paris, France   Service Est: 1981
C.M. Gottschalk, Chief

Staff: 2 Information and library professional; 2 management professional; 2 other.

Description of System or Service: The ENERGY INFORMATION SECTION seeks to improve the flow of energy information at the international, national, and regional levels by establishing regional pilot projects, identifying and developing energy information sources, and providing technical support to UNESCO member states. Especially concerned with new and renewable sources of energy and rural applications of this technology, the SECTION publishes a directory of energy research centers and information sources which is available in hardcopy and machine-readable forms.

Scope and/or Subject Matter: Development and promotion of information systems, services, and sources covering new and renewable energy.

Holdings and Storage Media: Directory data are held in machine-readable form.

Publications: International Directory of Research Centres and Information Sources, Services and Systems in New and Renewable Energies.

Computer-Based Products and Services: The International Directory is available on magnetic tape.

Other Services: In addition to the services described above, the Section sponsors and coordinates training programs, meetings, and infrastructure improvement projects to encourage the development of an international network of information systems and services relating to energy. To this end, it has established regional and sub-regional NRSE information networks for developing countries in Asia and the Pacific, Latin America, Africa, and the Arab States.

Clientele/Availability: Services are available to UNESCO member states.

Contact: C.M. Gottschalk, Chief, Energy Information Section.

★1019★
UNITED NATIONS EDUCATIONAL, SCIENTIFIC AND CULTURAL ORGANIZATION (UNESCO)
GENERAL INFORMATION PROGRAMME
7, Place de Fontenoy   Phone: 01 5771610
F-75700 Paris, France   Service Est: 1977

Special Note: The above name, address, and telephone number have been verified for this edition, although no questionnaire response was received. The following text is reprinted from the 5th edition.

Description of System or Service: The GENERAL INFORMATION PROGRAMME is concerned with the development and promotion of information systems and services in the fields of scientific and technological information, documentation, libraries, and archives at the regional, national, and international levels. Its activities fall into the following categories: formulation of information policies and plans; dissemination of methods, norms, and standards for information handling; development of information infrastructures; development of specialized information systems; and training and education of information specialists and users of information. The PROGRAMME also endeavors to strengthen UNESCO's role in the field of information within the United Nations system and to expand the Universal System for Information in Science and Technology (UNISIST) as a conceptual framework for the development of information systems and services. UNISIST is a long-term intergovernmental program designed to facilitate the flow and use of information science, technology, and other fields.

Scope and/or Subject Matter: Development and promotion of information systems and services, with particular attention to socioeconomic information and the needs of developing countries.

Publications: 1) General Information Programme: UNISIST Newsletter (four per year)—provides current information on activities in the fields of scientific and technological information and documentation, libraries, and archives; free of charge. 2) UNESCO Journal of Information Science, Librarianship and Archives Administration (four per year)—available by subscription.

Services: The Programme answers inquiries, distributes publications, and provides referrals to other sources of information.

Clientele/Availability: Chief clients are member states of UNESCO, field experts, and specialists.

Contact: Chief, Programme Promotion, Evaluation and Documentation Support Section, General Information Programme.

★1020★
UNITED NATIONS EDUCATIONAL, SCIENTIFIC AND CULTURAL ORGANIZATION (UNESCO)
INTERGOVERNMENTAL OCEANOGRAPHIC COMMISSION (IOC)
MARINE ENVIRONMENTAL DATA INFORMATION REFERRAL SYSTEM (MEDI)
7, place de Fontenoy   Phone: 01 5771610
F-75700 Paris, France   Service Est: 1976

Related Organizations: MEDI participants include a number of international organizations.

Description of System or Service: The MARINE ENVIRONMENTAL DATA INFORMATION REFERRAL SYSTEM (MEDI) provides the marine science community with information concerning the availability, location, and characteristics of interdisciplinary as well as traditional marine science data collections held by international marine-oriented organizations and centers. MEDI maintains a computer-readable data base for recording and retrieving information about existing marine environmental data files. The MEDI data base is used to produce a catalog and index providing details of marine data holdings of all participating centers. Specialized subjects indexes for broad subject areas and geographic plots of worldwide data distribution are also available.

Scope and/or Subject Matter: All aspects of marine science, including meteorology, pollution, dynamics (currents, tides, waves), physical and chemical oceanography, hydrography, biology, geology/geophysics, radioactive pollution, fishery statistics, and bathymetry.

Input Sources: Technical descriptions are submitted on MEDI input registration forms by international, regional, and national centers as part of an international network.

Holdings and Storage Media: The computer-readable data base holds several thousand data file descriptions and is continuously updated.

Publications: 1) Marine Environmental Data Information Referral Catalogue (MEDI Catalogue)—periodic publication in the IOC Manuals and Guides series; provides descriptions of all registered data holdings. 2) MEDI Index—provides a means of readily identifying data files in the Catalogue. 3) MEDI Operations Manual. A brochure describing MEDI's products and services is available in English, French, Spanish, and Russian. Special publications on specific problems of global interest are also produced.

Computer-Based Products and Services: Searches of the MEDI data base are conducted by the IOC MEDI Co-ordination Centre or MEDI contacts at participating international organizations. Search results are available in index format or as geographic plots. Records in the data base include an organizational description and information on its individual data files including file name, period of record, availability of file, type of platform, parameters, geographic location, mode of data storage, and names and addresses of data contacts.

Clientele/Availability: Information is available to national and international centers and institutions. Most searches are provided without charge as an exchange service with participating organizations.

Remarks: The MEDI Co-ordination Centre also acts as a sectoral focal point for marine sciences within INFOTERRA.

Contact: Steven J. Tibbitt, Assistant Secretary, Intergovernmental Oceanographic Commission. (Telex 204461.)

★1021★
UNITED NATIONS EDUCATIONAL, SCIENTIFIC AND CULTURAL ORGANIZATION (UNESCO)
INTERNATIONAL BUREAU OF EDUCATION (IBE)
DOCUMENTATION AND INFORMATION UNIT
P.O. Box 199　　　　　　　　　　Phone: 022 981455
CH-1211 Geneva 20, Switzerland
Aida M. Furtado, Head

Staff: 6 Information and library professional; 7 clerical and nonprofessional.

Description of System or Service: The DOCUMENTATION AND INFORMATION UNIT is responsible for the maintenance of a documentation center and the development of the International Network of Educational Information (INED) in conjunction with UNESCO regional offices and member states. It collects relevant documents and information from INED members and other sources, maintains the corresponding IBEDOC computer-readable bibliographic data base, and produces regular and ad hoc bibliographies and current awareness lists. The UNIT also maintains the computer-readable IBECENT data base covering educational information services and research institutions, and uses it to publish directories.

Scope and/or Subject Matter: Comparative education and educational policy, particularly legislation, planning, reform, and innovations.

Input Sources: UNESCO member states and other international organizations contribute monographs, serials, reports, dissertations, proceedings, and other documents to the Unit.

Holdings and Storage Media: The computer-readable IBEDOC data base holds 8000 items with approximately 1300 added per year. The IBECENT and IBETERM data bases are also held in computer-readable form. Documentation center holdings consists of 75,000 items; ERIC documents on microfiche; and IBE microfiche series.

Publications: 1) Educational Documentation and Information: the IBE Bulletin (quarterly)—contains approximately 350 bibliographical references on specific topics, most with annotations; issues include indexes and an introduction analyzing the bibliography; available by subscription. 2) IBEDOC Information (quarterly)—INED liaison bulletin reporting on INED news and activities, and events and institutions of interest to educational documentation professionals; available without charge. 3) Innovation Awareness List (quarterly)—annotated bibliography on literature relating to innovations, reform, change, and new developments in education. 4) Documentation Centre Acquisition List (two per year)—arranged in alphabetical order by title or author; includes subject index; available by request. 5) Directory of Educational Documentation and Information Services—lists about 110 institutions engaged in documentation and information work covering the whole educational field at national, regional, and international levels. 6) Directory of Documentation and Information Services in Adult Education—registers approximately 180 institutions; includes a supplemental listing of abstracting services in the field of adult education. 7) Directory of Educational Research Institutions—survey of about 500 institutions and other organizations engaged in education research around the world. Entries include official name of the institution, translation, address, year established, name of director, research objectives, and other information; arranged geographically and includes keyword indexes in English, French, and Spanish. 8) UNESCO/IBE Education Thesaurus—available in English, French, and Spanish; Arabic and Russian editions in preparation.

Microform Products and Services: The Unit issues the Series of International Reports on Education (SIRE) on microfiche. SIRE consists of UNESCO and IBE unpublished documents relevant for educational information activities.

Computer-Based Products and Services: The DOCUMENTATION AND INFORMATION UNIT maintains the computer-readable IBEDOC, IBECENT, and IBETERM data bases for producing regular publications and special printouts. IBEDOC contains records of the documentation center's acquisitions, and is available on computer tape at cost. IBECENT holds information on educational institutions and is used to produce the three directories described above. IBETERM corresponds to the UNESCO/IBE Education Thesaurus and contains 11,000 records.

Other Services: In addition to the services described above, the Unit answers requests for information by supplying bibliographies, documents, and photocopies. It also provides in-service training for personnel from member states.

Clientele/Availability: Services are available to IBE and UNESCO staff or field experts, official agencies in UNESCO member states, and other international and regional educational organizations.

Contact: Aida M. Furtado, Head, Documentation and Information Unit. (Telex 22644.)

★1022★
UNITED NATIONS EDUCATIONAL, SCIENTIFIC AND CULTURAL ORGANIZATION (UNESCO)
SOCIAL AND HUMAN SCIENCE DOCUMENTATION CENTRE
7, place de Fontenoy　　　　　　Phone: 01 5681000
F-75700 Paris, France　　　　　　Service Est: 1952

Staff: 1 Information and library professional; 4 other.

Description of System or Service: The SOCIAL AND HUMAN SCIENCE DOCUMENTATION CENTRE contributes to and supports the social and human science information and documentation programs of UNESCO by serving as a clearinghouse for relevant UNESCO documentation as well as an information service center for specialists at headquarters and in the field. Services are also provided to international governmental and nongovernmental organizations, to member states through their national UNESCO commissions, and to training, research, and documentation centers. The CENTRE issues publications and maintains computer-readable data bases in the following areas: 1) social science research and advanced training institutions; 2) social science specialists; 3) current empirical projects relevant to UNESCO programs; 4) social science periodicals; and 5) social science information, documentation, and data services.

Scope and/or Subject Matter: Social and human science information of interest to UNESCO and its member states.

Input Sources: Information is supplied by institutions and social scientists in answer to questionnaires and letters. Documents supplied by respondents and social science literature circulated from the UNESCO Library are additional sources of input.

Holdings and Storage Media: The Centre's machine-readable files contain information on 2000 active research and advanced training institutions; 1500 individual specialists; nearly 700 research in progress documents; 320 information services; and more than 2600 social science periodicals. Basic records are supported by files of documents.

Publications: 1) Social and Human Science Documentation Centre Information Note—occasional newsletter; 2) Reports and Papers in the Social Sciences; 3) World Directory of Social Science Institutions;

4) World List of Social Science Periodicals; 5) Selective Inventory of Information Services.

Computer-Based Products and Services: The CENTRE maintains a computerized storage, retrieval, and updating system known as DARE. Data are made available on magnetic tape, at the CENTRE's discretion. Online searching of the data is conducted by the CENTRE's staff. SDI services are also available.

Other Services: Additionally, the Centre offers advisory and consulting services, manual literature searching, and current awareness services.

Clientele/Availability: Services are available to UNESCO members, to international organizations, to training, research, and documentation centers, and to individual scholars in member states.

Contact: C. Bauer, Social and Human Science Documentation Centre.

★1023★
UNITED NATIONS EDUCATIONAL, SCIENTIFIC AND CULTURAL ORGANIZATION (UNESCO)
UNIVERSAL SYSTEM FOR INFORMATION IN SCIENCE AND TECHNOLOGY (UNISIST)
UNISIST INTERNATIONAL CENTRE FOR BIBLIOGRAPHIC DESCRIPTIONS (UNIBID)
7, Place de Fontenoy   Phone: (not reported)
F-75700 Paris, France   Service Est: 1976
Wolfgang Lohner, Head

Staff: 2 Information and library professional.

Related Organizations: UNIBID is operated within the framework of UNISIST, an integral part of UNESCO's General Information Programme (see separate entry).

Description of System or Service: The UNISIST INTERNATIONAL CENTRE FOR BIBLIOGRAPHIC DESCRIPTIONS (UNIBID) is concerned with the maintenance, updating, and distribution of reference manuals for machine-readable bibliographic descriptions and machine-readable descriptions of research projects and institutions. UNIBID also participates in international standardization activities. It collects information in support of these activities.

Scope and/or Subject Matter: Machine-readable bibliographic description and related subjects; international cooperation, standardization, and networking in information science and librarianship.

Input Sources: Input is collected from international standards, general guidelines, and procedural manuals of various information systems.

Publications: 1) Reference Manual for Machine-Readable Bibliographic Descriptions; 2) Reference Manual for Machine-Readable Descriptions of Research Projects and Institutions—both are available from UNIBID.

Computer-Based Products and Services: In conjunction with the Institut fur Maschinelle Dokumentation, UNIBID is developing a portable information processing package for use on micro-, mini-, and mainframe computers. The package is intended to encourage the use of international standards, especially in the area of documentation.

Other Services: In addition to collecting information in subjects of interest, UNIBID provides consulting and advisory services.

Clientele/Availability: Services are available to public or private institutions.

Contact: Wolfgang Lohner, Head, Section for the Promotion of Methods, Norms, and Standards, UNESCO.

★1024★
UNITED NATIONS ENVIRONMENT PROGRAMME (UNEP)
INDUSTRY AND ENVIRONMENT OFFICE
INDUSTRY AND ENVIRONMENT DATA BASE
17, rue Margueritte   Phone: 01 7661640
F-75017 Paris, France   Service Est: 1979

Special Note: No questionnaire response was received for this entry for the 6th edition. The entry is reprinted as it appeared in the 5th edition.

Description of System or Service: The INDUSTRY AND ENVIRONMENT DATA BASE is a computer-readable file on the environmental aspects of industrial manufacturing and production processes. It stores selected international information submitted by a network of national centers with competence in particular industrial sectors and by other United Nations organizations, particularly UNIDO. Information in the DATA BASE is organized into two parts: one contains bibliographic references while the other comprises evaluated information packaged into the following four environmental topic files: pollution abatement and control technologies (PACT) used in industrial sectors for reducing the release of pollutants; discharge standards (DIST), including references to recommended sampling and analytical procedures; ambient quality standards (QUAL) related to industrial pollutants; and a planned file on environmental technology costs (COST) for industrial pollution abatement and control. Computerized searches of the DATA BASE are conducted by the Industry and Environment Office in response to written, telephone, or telex requests.

Scope and/or Subject Matter: Environmental aspects of the following industries: pulp, paper, petroleum, aluminum, motor vehicle, agro-industry, iron, steel, chemical, and nonferrous metals.

Input Sources: Information for the data base is derived from government and industry publications, documents of international organizations, research reports, meeting papers, 12 technical journals, and about 50 newsletters.

Holdings and Storage Media: About 3000 entries are held in machine-readable form. The Office also maintains subscriptions to 155 periodicals and has a collection of conference papers.

Computer-Based Products and Services: The INDUSTRY AND ENVIRONMENT DATA BASE is held online on the UNESCO computer and searches from it are conducted by the Industry and Environment Office on request. The DATA BASE includes cross-references to UNEP's International Register of Potentially Toxic Chemicals (IRPTC) and INFOTERRA.

Clientele/Availability: Services are available free to decision makers and technical personnel in government, industry, and scientific and educational institutions.

Contact: Senior Programme Officer, Industry and Environment Office.

★1025★
UNITED NATIONS ENVIRONMENT PROGRAMME (UNEP)
INFOTERRA
P.O. Box 30552   Phone: 333930
Nairobi, Kenya   Service Est: 1973
Woyen Lee, Acting Director

Staff: 3 Information and library professional; 1 management professional; 2 technicians; 1 sales and marketing; 7 clerical and nonprofessional.

Description of System or Service: INFOTERRA, the International Referral System for Sources of Environmental Information, is a worldwide network of 120 national focal points which collect data on organizational sources of environmental information and submit it to UNEP. The data are organized, computerized, and distributed as hardcopy directories and on magnetic tapes. The focal points use the collected information to provide national and international referral services. Computerized searches of the data base are also available from UNEP. More than 500 inquiries per month are processed by the INFOTERRA network.

Scope and/or Subject Matter: Environment, including environmental aspects of atmosphere and climate; marine environment; freshwater environment; energy; disasters; natural resources; land use; food and agriculture; animal and plant wildlife; human settlements and habitat; human health and well-being; transportation; technology and industry; monitoring and assessment; management and planning; education, training, and information; pollution; wastes; environmental sciences; and others.

Input Sources: Information on environmental information sources is submitted by national focal points and United Nations agencies.

Holdings and Storage Media: The machine-readable INFOTERRA files hold data on 9500 information sources in 88 countries and 13 United Nations agencies.

Publications: 1) INFOTERRA International Directory of Sources (biennial)—published by UNEP and distributed throughout the network. The Directory lists research institutes, laboratories, institutes of higher learning, libraries, documentation centers, consulting services, and other organizations which provide information on environmental problems. It provides details on the areas of expertise and other attributes of each source; available in English, French, Russian, and Spanish. 2) INFOTERRA Bulletin (bimonthly)—provides news and information on INFOTERRA activities.

Computer-Based Products and Services: The INFOTERRA International Directory of Sources is distributed on magnetic tape to the national focal points. Computerized searches of the Directory are available through INFOTERRA's Programme Activity Centre; searches of commercially available online bibliographic data bases are also offered.

Clientele/Availability: Referral services are available free to those interested in environmental problems; access is through national focal points.

Contact: Mik Magnusson, Information Officer, INFOTERRA. (Telex 22068.)

★1026★
UNITED NATIONS ENVIRONMENT PROGRAMME (UNEP)
INTERNATIONAL REGISTER OF POTENTIALLY TOXIC CHEMICALS (IRPTC)
Palais des Nations Phone: 022 985850
CH-1211 Geneva 10, Switzerland Service Est: 1976
Jan W. Huismans, Director

Staff: 3 Information and library professional; 2 management professional; 3 technicians; 4 clerical and nonprofessional.

Description of System or Service: The INTERNATIONAL REGISTER OF POTENTIALLY TOXIC CHEMICALS (IRPTC) is used for the collection, storage, and dissemination of information supporting chemical hazards evaluation. Currently being developed, the computer-based Register covers the biological, chemical, and physical activity of chemicals hazardous to man and the environment. Workshops to instruct IRPTC national correspondents on the use of the Register are held regularly. In addition, a Bulletin is issued and a query-response service operated.

Scope and/or Subject Matter: Physical and chemical properties of chemicals; identification and control of chemical hazards; methods of sampling and analysis; national regulations on human health and the environment, including descriptions of conditions under which chemicals are safe for use.

Input Sources: Input is obtained from secondary publications submitted by national and international agencies responsible for chemical evaluation, as well as primary sources of scientific information.

Holdings and Storage Media: Holdings include machine-readable IRPTC files and the U.S. National Institute for Occupational Safety and Health's Registry of Toxic Effects of Chemical Substances (RTECS). Library holdings consist of 30,000 microfiche; monographs; and subscriptions to approximately 100 periodicals.

Publications: 1) IRPTC Bulletin (3 per year)—published in four languages. 2) International Register of Potentially Toxic Chemicals - Part A. Also issued are IRPTC data profile series, register attribute series, information series, and a legal file.

Computer-Based Products and Services: Computerization of the INTERNATIONAL REGISTER OF POTENTIALLY TOXIC CHEMICALS is being implemented; the data base covers a rapidly growing list of chemicals.

Other Services: Also offered are data collection and analysis, manual literature searching, referrals, and consulting services.

Clientele/Availability: Services are available to individuals of all nations depending upon the extent of available resources.

Contact: Jan W. Huismans, Director, or M. Gilbert, Scientific Affairs Officer, International Register of Potentially Toxic Chemicals. (Telex 28 877 UNEP CH.)

★1027★
UNITED NATIONS INDUSTRIAL DEVELOPMENT ORGANIZATION (UNIDO)
INDUSTRIAL INFORMATION SECTION
INDUSTRIAL AND TECHNOLOGICAL INFORMATION BANK (INTIB)
Vienna International Centre Phone: 0222 26310
P.O. Box 300 Service Est: 1977
A-1400 Vienna, Austria

Staff: 7 Information and library professional; 1 management professional; 16 clerical and nonprofessional.

Description of System or Service: The INDUSTRIAL AND TECHNOLOGICAL INFORMATION BANK (INTIB) provides information services in the area of industrial development for planners, policymakers, and administrators in developing countries. Its activities include: maintenance of the Industrial Development Abstracts (IDA) data base, which covers UNIDO publications and which is used to produce an abstracts journal and to provide computerized search services; operation of the UNIDO Industrial Inquiry Service, which provides technical inquiry answering services for developing countries; and sponsorship of the Technological Information Exchange System (TIES), a network with members in 32 countries that promotes the exchange of information on technology contracts.

Scope and/or Subject Matter: Technology and industry, especially as it pertains to developing countries.

Input Sources: Input is derived from the United Nations Industrial Development Organization, books, periodicals, data banks, and other worldwide information sources.

Holdings and Storage Media: INTIB's computer-readable IDA data base holds 13,000 abstracts.

Publications: 1) Industrial Development Abstracts (5 issues per year)—contains abstracts of UNIDO documents and meeting papers. 2) UNIDO Guides to Information Sources (2-4 issues per year)—each issue covers a branch of industry of concern to developing countries. Both publications are available from the United Nations Sales Section in New York City and Geneva. 3) Directory of Industrial Information Services and Systems in Developing Countries—available from UNIDO free of charge. 4) UNIDO Newsletter (monthly)—available from UNIDO free of charge. 5) TIES Newsletter (6 issues per year). 6) Development and Transfer of Technology Series (irregular).

Microform Products and Services: A microform collection of unrestricted UNIDO documents is available for distribution from the United Nations Sales Office in Geneva.

Computer-Based Products and Services: INTIB maintains the Industrial Development Abstracts data base from which literature search and SDI services are offered. Currently holding 13,000 abstracts, the data base indexes and abstracts UNIDO documents and publications.

Other Services: In addition to the services described above, INTIB offers reference and referral services; provides manual literature searching; and supplies UNIDO documents or advice on specific technical subjects.

Clientele/Availability: Computerized searching and SDI services are restricted to UNIDO staff and personnel; general advisory and information services are intended for industrial planners, managers, and engineers in developing countries.

Contact: J.R. Cote, Industrial Information Officer, Industrial Information Section. (Telex 135612.)

★1028★
UNITED NATIONS UNIVERSITY
REFERRAL SERVICE SYSTEM
Toho Seimei Bldg. Phone: 03 4992811
15-1 Shibuya, 2-Chome, Shibuya-ku Service Est: 1975
Tokyo 150, Japan
Shigeo Minowa, Chief, Academic Services

Staff: 2 Information and library professional; 3 management

professional; 2 technicians; 2 sales and marketing; 6 clerical and nonprofessional.

Related Organizations: The Referral Service System receives support from the United Nations and the United Nations Educational, Scientific and Cultural Organization (UNESCO).

Description of System or Service: The REFERRAL SERVICE SYSTEM is a computerized system for the collection and dissemination of information relative to the programs of the United Nations University (UNU). Presently the SYSTEM includes the following components: an institutions file system (covers research institutions active in UNU's priority areas); a computer-based library catalog system; a correspondents file system (covers affiliated researchers and recipients of UNU academic publications); a mailing list system for the distribution of UNU general publicity materials; and a budget control system.

Scope and/or Subject Matter: Research and information on world hunger, human and social development, utilization and management of natural resources, and knowledge and science.

Input Sources: Input to the data base is obtained from monographs, serials, reports, dissertations, proceedings, trade catalogs, questionnaires, directories, bibliographies, and unpublished documents.

Holdings and Storage Media: Computer-readable data are held on disk.

Computer-Based Products and Services: The REFERRAL SERVICE SYSTEM maintains an online data base for internal applications. Computerized information retrieval and machine-readable tape services are planned.

Other Services: Additional services of the unit are consulting, manual literature searching, referrals, and photoduplication.

Clientele/Availability: Research results are disseminated to affiliates of UNU, policymakers, universities and other educational institutions, mass media, and UN organizations.

Contact: Shigeo Minowa, Chief, Academic Services, United Nations University.

★1029★
UNIVERSAL LIBRARY SYSTEMS LTD.
205-1571 Bellevue Ave.   Phone: (604) 926-7421
West Vancouver, BC, Canada V7V 1A6   Founded: 1976
J.A. Speight, President

Staff: 10 Information and library professional; 3 management professional; 8 technicians; 2 sales and marketing; 4 clerical and nonprofessional.

Description of System or Service: UNIVERSAL LIBRARY SYSTEMS LTD. provides ULISYS, a fully online automated bibliographic retrieval and circulation control system which utilizes scanning wands to read bar-coded book labels and patron cards. Operated on a minicomputer, ULISYS can be used to perform such circulation functions as checking library materials in and out, fines management, holds management, message storage and retrieval, interlibrary loans, activity status reporting, and reserve materials management. The system permits searching by title, author, call number, item number, ISBN, LC card number, and patron name. ULISYS can also be used to maintain an online public-access catalog, which includes comprehensive instructions to assist inexperienced users.

Scope and/or Subject Matter: Bibliographic retrieval and circulation control systems.

Computer-Based Products and Services: ULISYS is an online circulation control and public access catalog system which is available with Digital PDP 11 and VAX 11 series minicomputers as a turnkey installation. ULISYS software is available for institutions that have access to Digital computers. Programs, enhancements, and maintenance are provided on an ongoing basis.

Other Services: Consulting services on the use of the system are also offered.

Clientele/Availability: Clients include academic, public, and special libraries.

Contact: J.A. Speight, President, Universal Library Systems Ltd. In the United States, contact James Taylor or Barbara Loomis, Universal Library Systems Inc., 1609A Broadway, Bellingham, WA; telephone (206) 676-4624.

★1030★
UNIVERSAL POSTAL UNION
(Union Postale Universelle - UPU)
INTERNATIONAL BUREAU
(Bureau International)
STATISTICS OF POSTAL SERVICES
(Statistique des Services Postaux)
Weltpoststr. 4   Phone: 031 432211
CH-3000 Berne 15, Switzerland   Service Est: 1974
Mohamed Ibrahim Sobhi, Bureau Director

Staff: Approximately 3 total.

Related Organizations: The Universal Postal Union is a specialized agency of the United Nations.

Description of System or Service: The Universal Postal Union's STATISTICS OF POSTAL SERVICES is a compilation of data on various aspects of postal services and operations for some 160 countries. Data are gathered through questionnaires completed annually by each country's postal service. Areas covered include number of personnel employed, number of post offices, types of postal operations, financial aspects, and delivery services. The data are maintained in machine-readable form and published annually.

Scope and/or Subject Matter: Postal services statistics worldwide.

Input Sources: Information is gathered through annual questionnaires sent to the postal services in approximately 160 countries.

Holdings and Storage Media: Postal statistics dating from 1964 to the present are maintained in machine-readable form.

Publications: 1) Statistique des Services Postaux (annual)—a country-by-country breakdown of postal services data. 2) Rapport Annuel sur la Situation des Services Postaux—provides summary data on various postal service topics. These publications may be purchased from the International Bureau of the Universal Postal Union at the above address.

Computer-Based Products and Services: Statistics of Postal Services data are maintained in machine-readable form to facilitate the production of annual survey and summary publications.

Clientele/Availability: Services are available without restrictions.

Contact: M. Goudet, Premier Secretary, International Bureau of the Universal Postal Union.

★1031★
UNIVERSITY LIBRARY OF HANNOVER AND TECHNICAL INFORMATION LIBRARY
(Universitatsbibliothek Hannover und Technische Informationsbibliothek - UB/TIB)
Welfengarten 1B   Phone: 0511 7622268
D-3000 Hannover 1, Fed. Rep. of
  Germany   Service Est: 1959
Dr. Gerhard Schlitt, Director

Staff: 75 Information and library professional; 134 clerical and nonprofessional.

Related Organizations: The University Library functions as the main library of the Universitat Hannover. The Technical Information Library is financed by the German federal and state governments.

Description of System or Service: The UNIVERSITY LIBRARY OF HANNOVER AND TECHNICAL INFORMATION LIBRARY (UB/TIB) forms one organizational unit and shares joint management, administration, book processing, and reader services. It serves as the central national library for science and engineering with the major function of supplying literature, through online document ordering, facsimile, interlibrary loan, and photocopying, to German companies, research institutions, and individuals. Other UB/TIB services include computerized searching and the maintenance of terminals for patrons wishing to conduct online searches of major bibliographic data bases in science and technology. The UB/TIB also issues current awareness publications on East European and East Asian scientific and technical literature, indexes German scientific and technical research reports, performs computerized cataloging, and issues catalogs on COM microfiche.

Scope and/or Subject Matter: Science and technology, with emphasis on physics, mathematics, and chemistry.

Input Sources: Input for the Eastern-languages current awareness service is derived from nonconventional literature, 400 journals, collections of articles, and conference proceedings.

Holdings and Storage Media: Library holdings include 2 million bound volumes and subscriptions to 20,000 periodicals.

Publications: 1) Ostsprachige Fachliteratur: Ausgabe Osteuropa (monthly)—available by subscription. Series of nine subject-specific current awareness bulletins covering scientific and technical periodicals and serial publications from Eastern Europe. Each issue contains Western-language translations of table of contents pages, new translations of technical literature, and, in some series, abstracts of nonconventional literature. 2) Ostsprachige Fachliteratur: Ausgabe Ostasien (monthly)—available by subscription. Series of subject-specific bulletins covering scientific and technical periodicals and serial publications from East Asia. Each issue provides Western-language translations of table of contents pages and new translations of technical literature. 3) Fortschrittsberichte Technik/ Naturwissenschaften—available by subscription. Card index service providing more than 1500 references annually to bibliographic reviews and progress reports appearing in scientific and technical periodicals held by the UB/TIB. Includes subject index. 4) Forschungsberichte aus Technik und Naturwissenschaften/ Reports in the Fields of Science and Technology (quarterly)—produced in cooperation with Fachinformationszentrum Energie, Physik, Mathematik GmbH; provides references to German nonconventional literature held by the UB/TIB and other libraries. 5) Ubersetzungszeitschriften—available for purchase; list of translations journals held by the UB/TIB. 6) List of UB/TIB current and retrospective periodical and serial publication holdings—available for purchase.

Microform Products and Services: The UB/TIB produces and makes available for purchase the following on COM microfiche: 1) Sowietische Wissenschaftlich-Technische Institutionen und Ihre Veroffentlichungen/ Soviet Scientific and Technical Institutions and Their Publications; 2) KWOC index of periodical and serial title holdings; 3) list of scientific periodical holdings of central technical and other libraries; and 4) lists of East European and Soviet periodical title holdings.

Computer-Based Products and Services: The UB/TIB maintains machine-readable catalogs of its holdings utilizing the computer facilities of the Library Computer Center-Lower Saxony/ Bibliotheksrechenzentrum Niedersachsen (BRZN), and uses them for publication purposes. Documents may be ordered online through the TIBORDER system which is available through DIALOG Information Services, Inc., INKA (Informationssystem Karlsruhe), and ESA/IRS; rapid delivery of requested articles is available via facsimile transmission. The UB/TIB also performs online searches of commercially available bibliographic data bases and maintains terminals for patrons to conduct their own searches.

Other Services: The UB/TIB functions as the German national translations center and provides input to the International Translations Center (ITC), Delft.

Clientele/Availability: Clientele includes corporations, companies, research institutions, and individuals in the Federal Republic of Germany. Services are available without restrictions.

Contact: Jobst Tehnzen, Deputy Librarian, University Library of Hannover and Technical Information Library. (Telex 9221 68 TIBHN D.)

★1032★
UNIVERSITY OF ABERDEEN
DEPARTMENT OF POLITICAL ECONOMY
WAGE ROUNDS DATA BANK
Phone: 0224 40241
Aberdeen AB9 2TY, Scotland
R.F. Elliott, Professor

Description of System or Service: The WAGE ROUNDS DATA BANK is a computer-readable file containing detailed records of all national wage settlements in the United Kingdom from 1950 to 1975. The DATA BANK includes information on implementation dates, settlement details, trade unions party to the negotiations, and many other supplementary details. A range of computer programs permitting access to the DATA BANK have been developed, and the file is available on magnetic tape.

Scope and/or Subject Matter: Trade union wage settlements in the United Kingdom.

Input Sources: Information is collected from U.K. Department of Employment publications and unpublished data.

Holdings and Storage Media: The Data Bank is maintained in machine-readable form and covers the period from 1950 to 1975.

Computer-Based Products and Services: The Wage Rounds Data Bank, permitting analysis of U.K. wage agreements, may be obtained on magnetic tape.

Clientele/Availability: Services are available upon application.

Contact: R.F. Elliott, Professor, Department of Political Economy, University of Aberdeen; or D. Bell, University Computing Centre, 150 Don St., Aberdeen AB2 1XQ, Scotland.

★1033★
UNIVERSITY OF ALBERTA
COMPUTING SERVICES
INFORMATION SYSTEMS GROUP
352 General Services Bldg. Phone: (403) 432-3884
Edmonton, AB, Canada T6G 2H1 Service Est: 1972
Ron Senda, Senior Information Analyst

Staff: 1 Information and library professional; 1 management professional; 3 technicians.

Related Organizations: The Information Services Division of the Alberta Research Council provides support.

Description of System or Service: Using the SPIRES data base management system, the INFORMATION SYSTEMS GROUP of the University of Alberta Computing Services provides clients with interactive access to approximately 30 publicly available data bases in diverse subject areas. The GROUP also offers contract programming, support, distribution, and training for SPIRES software.

Scope and/or Subject Matter: Data bases in the fields of energy, oil industry, education, government documents, clothing and textiles, Soviet and East European studies, home economics, languages, women in sports, and other topics.

Input Sources: Data bases are acquired from Alberta libraries, government agencies, and other organizations.

Holdings and Storage Media: Approximately 30 publicly available data bases holding from 500 to 200,000 items are held by the Computing Services, as are more than 200 private data bases.

Publications: 1) SPIRES Data Base Management. 2) SPIRES Reference to Data Library and Programlist. 3) SPIRES Searching of ERIC Data Bases.

Computer-Based Products and Services: Among the data bases offered online by the INFORMATION SYSTEMS GROUP are the following:

1) Alberta Gazette Index (AGI)—corresponds to the current year of the printed Alberta Gazette, the official organ of the Government of Alberta; entries are arranged in eight categories: advertisements, appointments, government notices, Orders in Council, proclamations, resignations, and retirements. Produced by the Publication Services Branch of the Alberta Public Affairs Bureau.

2) Alberta Legislative Information (ALI)—contains bibliographic

citations dating from 1980 to the present on legislation currently available from the Alberta Public Affairs Bureau; searchable by subject, act name, document number, and agency. Produced by the Publication Services Branch of the Alberta Public Affairs Bureau.

3) ALPFILE (Administrative Laboratory Project)—contains approximately 4000 citations dating from 1976 to the present on nonprint materials for the teaching of students in the field of educational administration; searchable by author, title, keyword, date, medium, document number, and file number. Produced by the University of Alberta Department of Educational Administration.

4) AOSI (Alberta Oil Sands Index)—provides coverage dating from 1980 to the present on documents on or related to all aspects of Alberta oil sands held by the Alberta Oil Sands Information Centre.

5) ASTIS (Arctic Science & Technology Information System)—contains more than 13,000 citations to publications relating to all aspects of the Arctic; short abstracts accompany each citation and most entries contain a library/location code which indicates where the full document may be obtained. Produced by the Arctic Institute of North America.

6) BOREAL (Boreal Library Catalogue)—contains catalog records received by the Boreal Institute for Northern Studies Library since 1977; also includes monograph and serial analytics received from the Scott Polar Research Institute of Cambridge, England. Items cataloged cover all subject areas, including fiction, as they relate to the Arctic and cold regions of the world, with emphasis on Canada's northern and boreal forest regions, Alaska, and other circumpolar countries; produced by the Boreal Institute for Northern Studies.

7) CALDOC (Calgary Public Library Government Documents)—contains approximately 4600 bibliographic citations to Canadian, Alberta, and Calgary government publications held by the Social Sciences Department of the Calgary Public Library; searchable by author, corporate author, title, and location.

8) CAMN (Canadian Directory of Completed Master's Theses in Nursing)—contains approximately 400 entries providing information on all master's theses of interest to nurses and completed in Canada since 1977; produced by the University of Alberta Faculty of Nursing.

9) CIJE (Current Index to Journals in Education)—contains abstracts from U.S. and some foreign journals relating to education; derived from the ERIC data base produced by the U.S. National Institute of Education.

10) CLTXBIB (Clothes and Textiles Bibliography)—contains bibliographic references dating from 1980 to the present on literature relating to clothes and textiles; compiled and maintained by the Faculty of Home Economics at the University of Alberta.

11) Coal Abstracts (COAL-ABS)—contains more than 14,000 bibliographic references to technical literature on coal technology; online access to the data base must be arranged through the Coal Technology Information Centre of the Alberta Research Council.

12) COIN (A Directory of Computerized Information in Canada)—contains information on approximately 630 data bases available in Canada; produced by Industrial Information of the Alberta Research Council.

13) CORN (Canadian Clearinghouse for Ongoing Research in Nursing)—contains information on all investigators currently conducting nursing research in Canada, their institutions, and the titles of their projects; produced by the University of Alberta Faculty of Nursing.

14) Data Library (Data Library Catalogue)—contains bibliographic citations to catalog records of files that are part of the Computing Services Data Library collection and other files which have been registered with the Data Library but are owned by other departments within the University; searchable by author, title, subject, series, publisher, date, and holding status.

15) DATALIB Resources (Data Library and Archives Directory)—contains information on existing North American and European data libraries and archives, including addresses, contact persons, subject area, and conditions of the use and distribution of data; equivalent to the printed Keyword-out-of-Context (KWOC) Index to Data Archives.

16) GAP (Government of Alberta Publications)—contains more than 17,000 bibliographic citations to publications of the Government of Alberta from 1905 through the present; searchable by author, corporate author, title, subject, location, and type. It is compiled and maintained by the Publication Services Branch of the Alberta Public Affairs Bureau.

17) GEODIAL (Geological Data Indexed for Alberta)—contains approximately 5000 references to reports with geological data and information; maintained by the Alberta Geological Survey of the Alberta Research Council.

18) Language Catalogue—contains 9000 bibliographic citations for items held by the Language Laboratories Materials Resource Centre.

19) Library (Index to Publications Owned by Computing Services)—contains approximately 1300 references to publications held by staff members of the Department of Computing Services.

20) PROGRAMLIST (Index of Software Supported by Computing Services)—contains information on approximately 3000 programs and subroutines supported by the Computing Services. Corresponds to the printed Keyword-out-of-Context (KWOC) Index to Computing Services Programs.

21) RIE (Resources in Education)—derived from the ERIC data base produced by the U.S. National Institute of Education.

22) SCITECH (Science & Technology Databank)—holds approximately 30,000 catalog records for acquisitions of the Alberta Departments of Agriculture and Environment and the Alberta Research Council.

23) SEED (Soviet and East European Data)—contains approximately 11,000 citations to catalog records of the University of Alberta Library holdings relating to Soviet and East European Studies; searchable by author, corporate author, title, subject, call number, category, and country.

24) SLAVICA (Slavic Philology)—contains more than 10,000 citations to catalog records of the University of Alberta Library holdings in the field of Slavic Philology; searchable by author, corporate author, title, subject, call number, category, and country.

25) SWERP (Solar and Wind Energy Research Program)—contains approximately 8500 bibliographic citations to literature on all aspects of solar and wind energy; produced by the Alberta Research Council.

26) THESIS (Theses in Home Economics)—contains approximately 600 bibliographic citations relating to theses in home economics; searchable by author, title, descriptor (keyword), university, advisor, format, level, and date.

27) WASIRS (Women And Sports Information Retrieval System)—contains approximately 1700 bibliographic citations dating from 1979 to the present on literature on women in sports; searchable by author, title, subject, journal name, source, and date. It is maintained by the Department of Physical Education and Recreation at the University of Alberta.

In addition to the SPIRES system, the Computing Services offers the PLATO educational system and the Textform computer-assisted publishing and graphics programs.

Clientele/Availability: Computer facilities are accessible via direct dial or the Datapac, Telenet, or Tymshare telecommunications networks to users with a Computing Services account.

Contact: Mrs. Yana M. Lamont, Librarian and SPIRES Consultant, Computing Services.

★1034★
UNIVERSITY OF ALBERTA
DEPARTMENT OF EDUCATIONAL ADMINISTRATION
ADMINISTRATION LABORATORY PROJECT (ALP) FILE

Edmonton, AB, Canada T6G 2H4
Aurelia C. Dacong, Administrative Officer

Phone: (403) 432-3792
Service Est: 1975

Staff: Approximately 8 total.

Description of System or Service: The computer-readable ADMINISTRATION LABORATORY PROJECT (ALP) FILE provides bibliographic coverage of the Laboratory's collection of educational administration media materials, which are designed to enhance classroom instruction and serve as student resource materials. ALPFILE search elements include file number, publisher, source, medium, author, title, cost, task, skill, process, abstract, and keywords. The Laboratory makes the ALPFILE publicly available online, and also offers searches of ERIC, hardware for media use, and consultation.

Scope and/or Subject Matter: Educational administration media materials.

Input Sources: Input is derived from media publishers and suppliers and from on-site productions.

Holdings and Storage Media: ALPFILE holds 4000 machine-readable records.

Computer-Based Products and Services: ALPFILE is available online through the University of Alberta Computing Services SPIRES system.

Clientele/Availability: Chief users are the University's graduate students in educational administration.

Contact: Aurelia C. Dacong, Administrative Officer, Department of Educational Administration.

★1035★
UNIVERSITY OF ALBERTA
DEPARTMENT OF SOCIOLOGY
POPULATION RESEARCH LABORATORY

Edmonton, AB, Canada T6G 2H4
L.W. Kennedy, Director
Phone: (403) 432-4659
Service Est: 1966

Staff: 1 Information and library professional; 3 management professional; 1 sales and marketing; 3 other.

Description of System or Service: POPULATION RESEARCH LABORATORY serves as the demographic, urban, and survey research arm of the Department of Sociology. The LABORATORY performs demographic and survey contract work, conducts an annual survey within the city of Edmonton, issues publications, and makes its collection of Canadian census data and other data sets available to researchers.

Scope and/or Subject Matter: Sociology with emphasis on demography and survey research.

Input Sources: Input consists of data sets on magnetic tape; government documents on Canada; books, documents, and manuscripts on sociology; and survey data on Alberta obtained by questionnaire.

Holdings and Storage Media: Data set holdings consist of Census of Canada summary tapes and a number of surveys done in Alberta and the Edmonton area. The joint library of the Laboratory and the Department of Sociology holds 5000 bound volumes and subscriptions to 200 periodicals.

Publications: 1) Canadian Studies in Population (annual)—available by subscription; 2) Edmonton area series; 3) discussion paper series; 4) Alberta series; 5) population reprints. All series publications are available free of charge.

Computer-Based Products and Services: The Laboratory provides batch-mode retrieval services from Census of Canada tapes and will also supply tape copies of its data sets with the permission of the Director.

Other Services: Additional services include consulting.

Clientele/Availability: Services are available without restrictions to faculty, students, and the public.

Contact: Cliff Kinzel, Research Technologist, Population Research Laboratory.

★1036★
UNIVERSITY OF ALBERTA
FACULTY OF NURSING
CANADIAN CLEARINGHOUSE FOR ONGOING RESEARCH IN NURSING (CORN)

3-103-H Clinical Sciences Bldg.
Edmonton, AB, Canada T6G 2G3
Dr. Janice Morse, Associate Professor
Phone: (403) 432-6250
Service Est: 1976

Description of System or Service: The CANADIAN CLEARINGHOUSE FOR ONGOING RESEARCH IN NURSING (CORN) maintains a bilingual computer-readable data base covering all investigators currently conducting nursing research in Canada, their institutions, and the titles of their research projects. CORN is designed to increase networking among researchers and potential researchers, and to inform others on nursing research in progress. The data base is publicly available online through the University of Alberta Computing Services.

Scope and/or Subject Matter: Canadian nursing research.

Input Sources: Input is obtained from universities and other research groups.

Holdings and Storage Media: The machine-readable CORN data base contains more than 100 active items. Entries are entered into the data base when a research proposal is approved, and removed when the project is completed.

Publications: User's Guide.

Computer-Based Products and Services: The CORN data base is interactively accessible over Datapac through the University of Alberta Computing Services SPIRES system. The data base can be searched in French or English and a typical record includes name of researcher, institution/ address of researcher, title of project, and translated title of project. If the project is a thesis, information is also provided on degree sought, anticipated date of completion, and name of advisor.

Clientele/Availability: Services are available without restrictions. Primary clients are researchers in nursing.

Remarks: CORN is also known as l'Inventaire Canadien des Recherches Presentement en Vigueur en Nursing.

Contact: Dr. Janice Morse, Associate Professor, Faculty of Nursing, University of Alberta.

★1037★
UNIVERSITY OF ALBERTA
FACULTY OF NURSING
CANADIAN DIRECTORY OF COMPLETED MASTER'S THESES IN NURSING (CAMN)

3-103-H Clinical Sciences Bldg.
Edmonton, AB, Canada T6G 2G3
Dr. Janice Morse, Associate Professor
Phone: (403) 432-6250
Service Est: 1984

Description of System or Service: The CANADIAN DIRECTORY OF COMPLETED MASTER'S THESES IN NURSING (CAMN) is a bilingual computer-readable data base which provides information on all master's theses of interest to nurses and completed in Canada since 1977. CAMN is publicly available online through the University of Alberta Computing Services' SPIRES system.

Scope and/or Subject Matter: Canadian master's theses in, or related to, nursing.

Input Sources: Input is obtained from Canadian schools of nursing and the library collection of the Canadian Nurses Association.

Holdings and Storage Media: The machine-readable CAMN data base contains more than 400 entries on master's theses completed since 1977.

Publications: User's Manual.

Computer-Based Products and Services: The CAMN data base is interactively accessible over Datapac through the University of Alberta Computing Services SPIRES system. The data base can be searched in French or English and a typical citation includes author, thesis title, year degree was awarded, institution, and name of advisor.

Clientele/Availability: Services are available without restrictions. Primary clients are researchers in nursing and health fields.

Remarks: The Directory is also known as Le Repertoire des Theses de Maitrise Completees en Nursing.

Contact: Dr. Janice Morse, Associate Professor, Faculty of Nursing, University of Alberta.

★1038★
UNIVERSITY OF ASTON
DEPARTMENT OF BIOLOGICAL SCIENCES
BIODETERIORATION CENTRE

Special Note: The BIODETERIORATION CENTRE at the University of Aston closed at the end of 1983. Its three journals—International Biodeterioration Bulletin, Biodeterioration Research Titles, and Waste Materials Biodegradation Research Titles—have been amalgamated into International Biodeterioration, which is available from the Commonwealth Agricultural Bureaux (see separate entry).

★1039★
UNIVERSITY OF BATH
CENTRE FOR CATALOGUE RESEARCH
Claverton Down
Bath BA2 7AY, England
Philip Bryant, Director
Phone: 0225 61244
Service Est: 1977

Staff: 4 Information and library professional; 1 clerical and nonprofessional.

Related Organizations: The Centre receives funding from the Research and Development Department of the British Library.

Description of System or Service: The CENTRE FOR CATALOGUE RESEARCH acts on behalf of all types of libraries in the United Kingdom as the national focal point for research, information, and education in the field of catalog research and development. It conducts research into what information should be included in bibliographic records, how the records should be acquired and created, and related topics. The CENTRE disseminates research results through publications, organizes seminars and courses, and provides answers to users' questions regarding library catalog organization, access, and automation.

Scope and/or Subject Matter: The use of bibliographic records for acquisitions, cataloging, and issue systems; keyword catalogs; online access; public access to library files; resource sharing schemes; subject access; user studies; and other related areas of study.

Publications: Centre for Catalogue Research Newsletter (semiannual)—available by request; provides news and information on Centre activities. The Centre also publishes research and other periodic reports on cataloging and related topics.

Computer-Based Products and Services: The Centre for Catalogue Research provides advice and research in the area of online catalog access, use, and design.

Other Services: The Centre also provides consultancy and referral services.

Clientele/Availability: Services are available without restrictions on a cost-recovery basis. Primary users include librarians, systems staff, and book trade staff.

Contact: Philip Bryant, Director, Centre for Catalogue Research. (Telex 449097.)

★1040★
UNIVERSITY OF BERGEN
DEPARTMENT OF SCANDINAVIAN LANGUAGES AND LITERATURE
NORWEGIAN TERM BANK
(Norsk Termbank)
Stromgaten 53
N-5000 Bergen, Norway
Kolbjorn Heggstad, Professor
Phone: 05 320040
Service Est: 1981

Staff: Approximately 3 total.

Related Organizations: Organizations supporting the Norwegian Term Bank include the Center of Technical Terminology, the Norwegian Language Council, and the Norwegian University Press.

Description of System or Service: The NORWEGIAN TERM BANK is a computer-readable file of some 150,000 Norwegian terms and their equivalents in one to eight foreign languages. Several terminological dictionaries have been published from the data base, and specialized lists can be produced from it on paper, microfiche, or magnetic tape.

Scope and/or Subject Matter: Norwegian technical terms and their foreign equivalents.

Input Sources: Dictionaries and standards provide input for Term Bank.

Holdings and Storage Media: Approximately 50,000 records covering 150,000 terms are held in machine-readable form.

Publications: Term Bank has been used to publish 11 terminological dictionaries.

Microform Products and Services: Custom output from the data base can be provided on microfiche.

Computer-Based Products and Services: The NORWEGIAN TERM BANK is used to produce standard and custom technical dictionaries.

Clientele/Availability: Clients include Norwegian scientists, engineers, linguists, and others.

Contact: Bjarne Norevik, Consultant, Norwegian Term Bank.

★1041★
UNIVERSITY OF BIRMINGHAM
DEPARTMENT OF ENGINEERING PRODUCTION
ERGONOMICS INFORMATION ANALYSIS CENTRE
P.O. Box 363
Birmingham B15 2TT, England
Prof. K.B. Haley, Director
Phone: 021 4721301
Service Est: 1968

Staff: 1 Information and library professional; 2 clerical and nonprofessional; 3 other.

Description of System or Service: The ERGONOMICS INFORMATION ANALYSIS CENTRE collects, abstracts, and disseminates information on ergonomics. It publishes an abstracts journal, prepares special bibliographies and literature reviews, and provides document delivery for cited articles. The CENTRE also offers inquiry answering and consulting services.

Scope and/or Subject Matter: Ergonomics, human factors, human engineering.

Input Sources: Input is drawn from periodicals, reports, theses, books, patents, and standard specifications.

Holdings and Storage Media: The Centre maintains a collection of more than 88,000 abstracts since 1959; also held are 7000 reports, 150 volumes, and subscriptions to 120 periodicals.

Publications: Ergonomics Abstracts (quarterly)—available by subscription. Each issue contains approximately 625 abstracts of articles and reports, a classified subject index, an index of applications to specific industries and occupations, and a book reviews section. The Centre also issues specialized bibliographies, a list of which is available on request.

Clientele/Availability: There are no restrictions on services.

Contact: Miss C. Stapleton, Manager, Ergonomics Information Analysis Centre.

★1042★
UNIVERSITY OF BONN
(Universitat Bonn)
INORGANIC CHEMISTRY INSTITUTE
(Anorganisch Chemisches Institut)
INORGANIC CRYSTAL STRUCTURE DATA BASE (ICSD)
Gerhard-Domagk-Str. 1
D-5300 Bonn 1, Fed. Rep. of Germany
Dr. G. Bergerhoff
Phone: 0228 732657
Service Est: 1977

Description of System or Service: Modelled on the Cambridge Crystallographic Data Centre's organic data base, the INORGANIC CRYSTAL STRUCTURE DATA BASE (ICSD) is a computer-readable file providing details on more than 20,000 published structures of inorganic crystals. Each entry in the ICSD contains complete descriptive data for the crystal structure together with the bibliographic and other data necessary to characterize the compound and its structure determination. The DATA BASE is commercially available online; magnetic tape and information retrieval services are also offered.

Scope and/or Subject Matter: Crystal structure data for inorganic compounds.

Input Sources: Data are collected from primary literature in the field, including more than 200 periodicals, and are critically evaluated before being input into the Data Base.

Holdings and Storage Media: The computer-readable ICSD Data Base contains data for more than 20,000 structures published in the literature since 1977; it is updated with approximately 1200 entries per year.

Publications: A detailed user manual is available in English and in German.

Computer-Based Products and Services: The INORGANIC CRYSTAL STRUCTURE DATA BASE is publicly available online through INKA (Informationssystem Karlsruhe). Searchable data elements include chemical element with oxidation state, group names of elements, mineral names, number of different elements present in the compound, standardized remarks, space group name, journal CODEN, author name, and year of publication. Search services and magnetic tape services are also available.

Clientele/Availability: Data are available to the public.

Contact: Dr. G. Bergerhoff, Inorganic Crystal Structure Data Base, Inorganic Chemistry Institute, University of Bonn. (Telex 8 86 657 UNIBO D.)

★1043★
UNIVERSITY OF BRITISH COLUMBIA
B.C. HOSPITAL PROGRAMS BRANCH
DRUG AND POISON INFORMATION CENTRE (DPIC)
St. Paul's Hospital
1081 Burrard St.
Vancouver, BC, Canada V6Z 1Y6
Mary Nelson, Program Director
Phone: (604) 682-2344
Service Est: 1975

Staff: 8 Information and library professional; 2 clerical and nonprofessional.

Description of System or Service: The DRUG AND POISON INFORMATION CENTRE (DPIC) provides hospitals and health professionals in British Columbia with continuously updated information on toxic or potentially toxic substances. Specific DPIC services include publication of the Drug Information Reference and the Poison Management Manual from machine-readable files, production of other publications, manual and computerized literature searching, and clinically oriented drug and poison information services for health professionals. DPIC also offers a poison control information service directly to the public.

Scope and/or Subject Matter: Drug and poison information, poison control, care and treatment of poisoned patients, drug abuse.

Input Sources: Input consists of reports from participating hospitals; commercial and U.S. and Canadian government sources of drug and poison information; and various print materials. DPIC regularly indexes 270 medical journals.

Holdings and Storage Media: Computer-readable DPIC files hold approximately 2000 entries. The Centre also maintains a collection of books and periodicals.

Publications: 1) Drug Information Reference-DIR (annual)—contains current profiles on 200 of the most frequently used and clinically useful drugs, with emphasis on Canadian products. 2) Poison Management Manual-PMM (annual)—contains potential toxicity and treatment recommendations for the 250 most commonly encountered and serious poisonings. 3) Drug Information Perspectives Newsletter (quarterly). 4) Poisoning Perspectives Newsletter (quarterly).

Computer-Based Products and Services: DPIC maintains computer-readable data bases corresponding to the Drug Information Reference and the Poison Management Manual. Updated annually, the data bases are used for publication purposes and to conduct occasional searches.

Clientele/Availability: Services are available to health professionals in British Columbia. Poison control service is available to the public.

Contact: Mary Nelson, Program Director, Drug and Poison Information Centre.

★1044★
UNIVERSITY OF BRITISH COLUMBIA
DATA LIBRARY
Computing Centre
2075 Wesbrook Mall
Vancouver, BC, Canada V6T 1W5
Ms. Laine Ruus, Head
Phone: (604) 228-5587
Service Est: 1972

Staff: 1 Information and library professional; 1 programmer; 1 clerical and nonprofessional.

Related Organizations: The Data Library is a joint operation of the University Library and the Computing Centre.

Description of System or Service: The DATA LIBRARY was established to centralize the acquisition, organization, storage, and servicing of machine-readable nonbibliographic data files on the campus. Its main functions are to provide data and services in support of the teaching and research activities of the university community, and to collect data files, especially those produced locally.

Scope and/or Subject Matter: Nonbibliographic data in social sciences, humanities, sciences, and other areas.

Input Sources: Data files are acquired from other archives, government agencies, and several social research consortia.

Holdings and Storage Media: The DATA LIBRARY maintains approximately 800 machine-readable files, as well as 800 bound volumes and subscriptions to 20 periodicals.

Microform Products and Services: University of British Columbia Data Library Catalogue—available on microfiche.

Computer-Based Products and Services: Depending on restrictions stipulated by depositors, data files are copied gratis onto requestor-supplied computer tapes.

Other Services: The Data Library also provides statistical and programming consultation to data file users.

Clientele/Availability: Services are available without restrictions, unless otherwise indicated by the depositor.

Contact: Ms. Laine Ruus, Head, Data Library.

★1045★
UNIVERSITY OF COLOGNE
(Universitat zu Koln)
CENTRAL ARCHIVES FOR EMPIRICAL SOCIAL RESEARCH
(Zentralarchiv fur Empirische Sozialforschung - ZA)
Bachemer Str. 40
D-5000 Cologne 41, Fed. Rep. of
  Germany
Prof. Dr. Erwin K. Scheuch, Director
Phone: 0221 444086
Service Est: 1960

Staff: 10 Information and library professional; 1 management professional; 25 clerical and nonprofessional.

Related Organizations: Support is received from the German Ministry for Research and Technology/ Bundesministerium fur Forschung und Technologie.

Description of System or Service: The CENTRAL ARCHIVES FOR EMPIRICAL SOCIAL RESEARCH (ZA) acquires, checks, converts, and stores complete primary materials of German social surveys to make the data available for further analysis, for the preparation of new surveys, and for teaching purposes. Archive holdings comprise machine-readable data, questionnaires, codebooks, and study descriptions, as well as an extensive library on the methods and results of empirical studies. The CENTRAL ARCHIVES publishes an annual inventory of empirical research projects in German-speaking countries, and compiles lists of survey archive holdings in other European countries and the United States. It conducts an annual seminar on newly developed data analysis techniques, provides counseling on data selection, survey design, and advanced analysis techniques, and hosts related research projects.

Scope and/or Subject Matter: Empirical social surveys and methodology, including population surveys on a broad range of topics; investigations of specific social groups, such as occupational groups and young people; panel studies including before and after election surveys; and cross-national studies.

Input Sources: Survey research data and documents are acquired from commercial and academic sources.

Holdings and Storage Media: Archival holdings consist of the complete primary materials for more than 1200 surveys, with all surveys and some codebooks also available in machine-readable form. The library holdings deal with the methods and results of empirical studies and include 10,000 volumes of monographs, encyclopedias, collections of tables, reports, and unpublished papers.

Publications: 1) ZA-Information (biannual)—newsletter. 2) List of Archive Holdings—gives user regulations and a description of selected surveys. 3) Empirische Sozialforschung/ Empirical Social Research (annual)—covers contents, methods, objectives, and progress of empirical research projects in German-speaking countries; about 2000 projects per year are included. Published by Verlag Dokumentation, Possenbacherstr. 2b, Postfach 711009, D-8000 Munich 70, Fed. Rep. of Germany. 4) Umfragen aus der Empirischen Sozialforschung 1945-1982: Datenbestandskatalog/ Inquiries into Empirical Social Research 1945-1982: Catalogue of Holdings. Published by Campus Verlag, Myliusstr. 15, D-6000 Frankfurt am Main, Fed. Rep. of Germany.

Computer-Based Products and Services: The CENTRAL ARCHIVES computer files contain more than 1200 surveys and codebooks for selected surveys. Copies of data are available on tape or cards according to user specifications. Retrospective searching of questions from the survey pool is offered through the Zentralarchiv Retrieval System (Z.A.R. System).

Other Services: Additionally, the Central Archives provides consulting and research services, complete documentation, manual literature searching, and referral services.

Clientele/Availability: Archive holdings are generally available for scientific use to those interested in survey research. Access to the data is governed by the User Regulations.

Contact: Franz Bauske, Dipl.-Kfm., or Ekkehard Mochmann, Manager, Central Archives for Empirical Social Research.

★1046★
UNIVERSITY OF DORTMUND
(Universitat Dortmund)
DORTMUND DATA BANK (DDB)
Lehrstuhl Technische Chemie B
P.O. Box 500500
D-4600 Dortmund 50, Fed. Rep. of
    Germany
Prof. Dr.U. Onken, Head
Phone: 0231 7552696
Service Est: 1973

Staff: 3 Information and library professional; 2 management professional; 1 technician; 6 other.

Description of System or Service: The DORTMUND DATA BANK (DDB) is a computerized compilation of vapor-liquid equilibrium data on more than 12,000 binary and multicomponent mixtures (including water) with a boiling point above zero degrees centigrade. Specific pure component properties of covered compounds are also included. Derived from the published literature, data from the DDB are available in printed or machine-readable form.

Scope and/or Subject Matter: The development of predictive methods for the calculation of vapor-liquid, liquid-liquid, and solid-liquid equilibria and heat of mixing data.

Input Sources: Input is derived from about 150 journals.

Holdings and Storage Media: DDB machine-readable holdings include 12,000 data sets in the vapor-liquid equilibrium data base; pure component properties for more than 1000 compounds; and various data management programs.

Publications: Vapor-Liquid Equilibrium Data Collection (Volume I of the DECHEMA Chemistry Data Series)—available from DECHEMA, Theodor-Heuss-Allee 25, D-6000 Frankfurt am Main 97, Germany.

Computer-Based Products and Services: The DORTMUND DATA BANK consists of compilations of vapor-liquid equilibrium and pure component properties data. The DATA BANK is available on magnetic tape together with programs for data management, correlation, consistency testing, and plotting.

Clientele/Availability: Primary clients are chemical engineers and chemists.

Contact: Prof. Dr. U. Onken, University of Dortmund. (Telex 822445 UNIDO.)

★1047★
UNIVERSITY OF DUNDEE
LAW LIBRARY
EUROPEAN DOCUMENTATION CENTRE (EDC)
Perth Rd.
Dundee DD1 4HN, Scotland
David R. Hart, Librarian
Phone: 0382 23181
Service Est: 1981

Staff: Approximately 3 total.

Description of System or Service: The EUROPEAN DOCUMENTATION CENTRE (EDC) maintains and makes available a representative collection of the official publications of the European Communities. To provide access to these documents, it also maintains EDCKEY, a computer-readable index that is available online.

Scope and/or Subject Matter: European Communities publications in all subject areas.

Input Sources: The Centre acquires general information publications and documents from major institutions of the European Communities, including COM documents, SEC documents, and European Parliament working documents.

Holdings and Storage Media: The Centre maintains a collection of documents and the EDCKEY computer-readable bibliographic data base holding more than 9000 records. Coverage for most indexed publications generally begins in 1974.

Publications: A User Guide and Reference Card are available to subscribers.

Computer-Based Products and Services: The EUROPEAN DOCUMENTATION CENTRE maintains the bibliographic EDCKEY data base online to provide access to its collection of European Communities publications. Title keywords, additional subject descriptors, and other data elements may be searched using Boolean logic.

Clientele/Availability: Clients include University staff, other European Documentation Centres, and other information units.

Contact: David R. Hart, Librarian, European Documentation Centre. (Telex 76293.)

★1048★
UNIVERSITY OF DUSSELDORF
(Universitat Dusseldorf)
RESEARCH DIVISION FOR PHILOSOPHY INFORMATION AND DOCUMENTATION
(Forschungsabteilung fur Philosophische Information und Dokumentation)
PHILOSOPHY INFORMATION SERVICE
(Philosophie Informationsdienst - PHI)
Universitatsstr. 1
D-4000 Dusseldorf 1, Fed. Rep. of
    Germany
Dr. Norbert Henrichs, Head
Phone: 0611 3112913
Service Est: 1967

Staff: 5 Information and library professional; 1 management professional; 2 technicians; 1 clerical and nonprofessional; 6 other.

Description of System or Service: The PHILOSOPHY INFORMATION SERVICE (PHI) of the Research Division for Philosophy Information and Documentation collects, processes, and disseminates information on current and historical philosophy and philosophers. It maintains several computer-readable data bases, including Philosophische Dokumentation, which abstracts and indexes relevant periodical literature, and Living Philosophers, a bio-bibliographical data base derived from questionnaire responses from philosophers. PHI provides search services from both files in response to written requests. Additionally, the Philosophische Dokumentation data base is used to produce a series of bibliographies and indexes.

Scope and/or Subject Matter: Philosophy and the philosophy of science.

Input Sources: Input is obtained from about 250 current

philosophical journals and serials, and from historical periodicals. Questionnaires sent to philosophers are an additional source of input.

Holdings and Storage Media: The Service maintains several computer-readable data bases which include Philosophische Dokumentation and Living Philosophers. Library holdings consist of 70,000 bound volumes and 150 subscriptions to periodicals.

Publications: Philosophische Dokumentation (4 new volumes per year)—a series of international cumulative indexes and bibliographies to major journals and serials. Series 1 is intended to cover all philosophic journals of the present and past. Indexes to current periodicals are published in collaboration with The Philosophers Index, Bowling Green State University, Ohio. Series 2 and 3, author and problem bibliographies, will be published when sufficient data are collected. Philosophische Dokumentation is published and distributed by Kraus-Thomson Organization Ltd., FL-9491 Nendeln, Liechtenstein.

Microform Products and Services: The PHI thesaurus is available on COM fiche.

Computer-Based Products and Services: PHI conducts online searches of the Philosophische Dokumentation and Living Philosophers data bases in response to requests from the academic community. Maintained under GRIPS/DIRS software together with an internally devised program, Philosophische Dokumentation provides access to all relevant literature published since 1970 through 60,000 keyword terms and 20,000 author names. PHI also maintains or is planning several additional data bases, including Epistolographie (1750-1850), covering published and unpublished letters of philosophers of the period.

Other Services: Also offered are SDI, manual literature searching, referrals, and consulting.

Clientele/Availability: Services are available without limitation and at no cost.

Contact: Dr. Norbert Henrichs, Head, Research Division for Philosophy Information and Documentation.

★1049★
UNIVERSITY OF GOTHENBURG
MEDICINDATA
P.O. Box 33031   Phone: 031 411110
S-400 33 Gothenburg, Sweden   Service Est: 1974

Staff: Approximately 10 total.

Description of System or Service: A member of the Scannet cooperative, MEDICINDATA is an online host service providing users in the Nordic countries with access to data bases dealing with behavioral sciences, chemistry, and information and documentation. Data bases offered online include the Swedish Behavioural Sciences (SBS) data base, two Chemical Information System (CIS) subfiles on mass spectra and crystallography, and the electronic journal EXTEMPLO.

Scope and/or Subject Matter: Chemical and technical data; crystallography; mass spectrometry; behavioral sciences; information and documentation.

Computer-Based Products and Services: MEDICINDATA makes the following data bases accessible online: 1) Swedish Behavioural Sciences (SBS)—provides references to research reports and journal literature dealing with behavioral sciences in Sweden; produced by the Swedish National Library for Psychology and Education/ Statens Psykologisk-Pedagogiska Bibliotek (SPPB). 2) CHEM—comprises two Chemical Information System (CIS) subfiles: the Mass Spectral Search System and the Cambridge Crystallographic Data Base. 3) EXTEMPLO—an electronic journal providing news on forthcoming conferences, courses, seminars, and lectures concerning information and documentation and taking place in Denmark, Finland, Norway, or Sweden.

Clientele/Availability: Services are intended mainly for Nordic clientele.

Contact: Goran Nilsson, MEDICINDATA.

★1050★
UNIVERSITY OF GUELPH LIBRARY
COOPERATIVE DOCUMENTS NETWORK PROJECT (CODOC)
Library Administration Office   Phone: (519) 824-4120
Guelph, ON, Canada N1G 2W1   Service Est: 1971
Virginia Gillham, Assistant Librarian

Description of System or Service: The COOPERATIVE DOCUMENTS NETWORK PROJECT (CODOC) produces a union catalog covering the government document collections in 11 libraries in Ontario and Quebec. The catalog is available on COM microfiche and as an online data base accessible through CAN/OLE. Custom COM catalogs can also be produced for participants. Additionally, a subsystem of CODOC called GDoc, the holdings of the University of Guelph Library document collection, is available online through QL Systems Limited.

Scope and/or Subject Matter: Government publishing at all levels, including the following jurisdictions: Canadian federal and provincial, U.S. federal and state, United Kingdom, France, Germany, Russia, Commonwealth countries, and the United Nations and its agencies.

Input Sources: Member libraries supply document coding records to CODOC.

Holdings and Storage Media: The complete CODOC data base contains more than 700,000 computer-readable records and is updated every two months.

Publications: CODOC Manual.

Microform Products and Services: Union COMfiche Catalog—includes title access master, corporate author index, and series index. Participant-specific COMfiche is available by corporate author, personal author, title, serial, series, and KWOC index.

Computer-Based Products and Services: The CODOC data base contains bibliographic records of the government document collections in member libraries. The following data are searchable: holdings (library code for each of the participating libraries); title; author (primary and up to 8 secondary authors); organization (corporate names, sponsoring bodies, series title); number; date; form; and language of publication. CODOC is available online to Canadian users via CAN/OLE. GDoc is available online to Canadian and international users via QL Systems Limited.

Clientele/Availability: Services are available without restrictions.

Contact: Virginia Gillham, Assistant Librarian, University of Guelph Library. (Telex 069 565 40.)

★1051★
UNIVERSITY OF HAIFA LIBRARY
HAIFA ON-LINE BIBLIOGRAPHIC TEXT SYSTEM (HOBITS)
Mount Carmel   Phone: 04 240288
Haifa 31999, Israel   Service Est: 1977
Elhanan Adler, Head

Staff: 6 Information and library professional; 1 clerical and nonprofessional.

Description of System or Service: The HAIFA ON-LINE BIBLIOGRAPHIC TEXT SYSTEM (HOBITS) is a software system designed for the collection and manipulation of bibliographic data. HOBITS enables library and other users to create data bases for producing catalogs and bibliographies in various formats, and for conducting searches. HOBITS comprises standard programs for input, editing, and searching, and employs a unified file and record format. Accessed via a menu format, HOBITS also includes print programs designed according to user requirements using standard routines, as well as a subsystem for thesaurus maintenance. HOBITS is used at the University of Haifa Library to maintain several data bases including the Index to Hebrew Periodicals, the Land of Israel Data Bank, the Index to 19th Century Eretz-Israel Newspapers, and other bibliographic files.

Scope and/or Subject Matter: Information storage and retrieval software used for library catalogs, periodical indexes, English-language book files, archival files, and special bibliographic projects including kibbutz studies, Holocaust, Yiddish periodicals, and others.

Input Sources: Bibliographic data are entered via coding sheets and diskettes.

Holdings and Storage Media: Various bibliographic data bases are held in machine-readable form under HOBITS. Library holdings include 430,000 bound volumes, subscriptions to 11,000 periodicals, and other materials.

Publications: Annual Index to Hebrew Periodicals. Catalogs and bibliographies are produced irregularly according to user needs.

Microform Products and Services: The Union List of Technion Recent Acquisitions, the University of Haifa Periodical Holdings, and the Cumulated Index to Hebrew Periodicals are available on microfiche.

Computer-Based Products and Services: The HAIFA ON-LINE BIBLIOGRAPHIC TEXT SYSTEM is used to maintain several data bases including the Index to Hebrew Periodicals which contains 60,000 records dating from 1977 to date; the Land of Israel Data Bank which contains 8000 retrospective records dealing with the history, geography, and archeology of the land of Israel; the Index to 19th Century Eretz-Israel Newspapers which covers more than 7000 articles; and bibliographic data bases for special projects. The contents of HOBITS data bases are accessible online. HOBITS is also used for the production of catalogs and bibliographies, and to provide an SDI service for new book information.

Clientele/Availability: Primary clients are institutions, libraries, and researchers in Israel.

Remarks: Also located at the University of Haifa Library is the MARC Israel (MARCIS) project, which produces worksheets, catalog cards, and archival files from U.S. Library of Congress MARC files.

Contact: Elhanan Adler, Assistant Director, Library, or Jody Branse, Programmer, Haifa On-line Bibliographic Text System.

★1052★
UNIVERSITY OF LEEDS
DEPARTMENT OF PHYSICAL CHEMISTRY
HIGH TEMPERATURE REACTION RATE DATA CENTRE
Leeds, Yorkshire LS2 9JT, England
Dr. D.L. Baulch, Director
Phone: 0532 31751
Service Est: 1967

Staff: Approximately 3 total.

Related Organizations: The Centre is sponsored by the Science Research Council of the British Department of Education and Science. It maintains close liaison with the U.S. National Bureau of Standards, which conducts projects of a related nature.

Description of System or Service: The HIGH TEMPERATURE REACTION RATE DATA CENTRE was established to provide scientists and engineers with reliable information on the rates of elementary chemical reactions which are important at the high temperatures encountered in a number of systems. The available data are compiled, evaluated, and issued in bound volumes. They are presented on an Arrhenius diagram and discussed critically; whenever possible, a rate constant is recommended in the form of an Arrhenius expression. Error limits are given together with appropriate thermodynamic data over a range of temperature.

Scope and/or Subject Matter: Elementary chemical reactions relevant to combustion, air pollution, and aeronomy; gas phase reactions important in high temperature systems such as rocket propulsion and gas turbine engines.

Input Sources: Input consists largely of scientific papers from a wide range of sources.

Holdings and Storage Media: Almost 10,000 papers have been indexed and stored; the majority relevant to the area of gas phase kinetics.

Publications: Evaluated Kinetic Data for High-Temperature Reactions, Volumes 1-4. Volumes 1-3 are available from the Butterworth Group, 88 Kingsway, London WC2B 6AB, England. Volume 4 is a supplement of the Journal of Physical and Chemical Reference Data.

Services: The Centre can provide advisory and consulting services on specific topics within the area of gas phase kinetics.

Clientele/Availability: Products and services are available without restrictions.

Contact: Dr. D.L. Baulch, Director, High Temperature Reaction Rate Data Centre.

★1053★
UNIVERSITY OF LEEDS
MEDICAL AND DENTAL LIBRARY
ONCOLOGY INFORMATION SERVICE
Leeds, W. Yorks. LS2 9JT, England
Daphne Roberts, Oncology Information Officer
Phone: 0532 450059
Service Est: 1974

Staff: 2 Information and library professional; 1 clerical and nonprofessional.

Related Organizations: The Oncology Information Service is funded by the Department of Health and Social Security through the Yorkshire Regional Cancer Organisation.

Description of System or Service: The ONCOLOGY INFORMATION SERVICE provides computer-based information services in the field of cancer for doctors, researchers, and other interested persons. It scans approximately 1700 periodicals and other material for input to a computer-readable data base which is used to produce 19 current awareness bulletins and provide computerized retrieval services. The SERVICE also offers an inquiry answering service which includes searches of online cancer-related data bases.

Scope and/or Subject Matter: All aspects of cancer.

Input Sources: The Information Service scans 1700 periodicals, plus books, conference proceedings, and other documents for input to its data base.

Holdings and Storage Media: A computer-readable bibliographic data base is maintained.

Publications: The ONCOLOGY INFORMATION SERVICE publishes monthly current awareness bulletins in the following 17 areas: breast cancer, brain and nervous system, gynecological neoplasms, cancer chemotherapy, genetics and cancer, digestive tract cancers, hematological neoplasms, head and neck cancers, immunological aspects, community medicine aspects, skin cancers, bone and soft tissue, pediatric cancers, cancer radiotherapy, thoracic cancers, tumor markers, and urogenital cancers. The SERVICE also publishes two bimonthly abstracts bulletins covering cancer information for nursing staff and relief of pain in cancer. The bulletins are available by subscription, and a library package providing the complete set of all 19 bulletins is offered. Also available for purchase is a biannual booklist that covers recent monographs on cancer.

Computer-Based Products and Services: The ONCOLOGY INFORMATION SERVICE data base holds references published in the current awareness bulletins and is used to provide retrospective search services. The SERVICE also conducts online searches of relevant data bases carried by Data-Star.

Clientele/Availability: Services and publications are available without restrictions to cancer professionals and others.

Contact: Daphne Roberts, Oncology Information Officer.

★1054★
UNIVERSITY OF LEICESTER
PRIMARY COMMUNICATIONS RESEARCH CENTRE
University Rd.
Leicester LE1 7RH, England
Prof. A.J. Meadows, Project Head
Phone: 0533 556223
Service Est: 1976

Staff: 6 Information and library professional; 1 technician; 2 clerical and nonprofessional.

Related Organizations: The Primary Communications Research Centre receives research funds from the British Library Research and Development Department.

Description of System or Service: The PRIMARY COMMUNICATIONS RESEARCH CENTRE conducts research on the origin, dissemination, and use of research and technical information in scientific, technical, and professional fields. It places particular emphasis on new areas of information technology, including viewdata, videotex, and videodisc publishing, and examines the implications for the communication process. Examples of current CENTRE projects include the following: a survey of the use of word processing by United Kingdom publishers; a study of the structure, finance, and control of communications activities in learned societies; a project investigating the alternatives available for phototypesetting manuscripts prepared on a computer; and a project assessing the status of teleconferencing in the field of communications now and for the future. The CENTRE produces a series of detailed research reports, offers consultancy, provides short courses, and maintains a computerized mailing list of publishers and learned societies in England.

Scope and/or Subject Matter: Primary communications, research, information science and technology, and scientific, technical, and professional information in all subject areas, including science, humanities, social science, medicine, agriculture, and technology.

Input Sources: Information sources include surveys, journals, television, radio, newspapers, learned societies, and other sources.

Holdings and Storage Media: A mailing list of learned societies and publishers is maintained in machine-readable form.

Publications: The Centre produces detailed reports on its research projects. Among the titles available are the following: 1) Information Technology in Industrial Information Services—provides a survey of available technologies and equipment found in special libraries such as word processors, computers, terminals, optical character readers, microform, videotex, and telex, and outlines current equipment uses and future plans. Includes a directory of related publications and services. 2) Learned Societies, Journals and Collaboration with Publishers—based on a survey of 500 United Kingdom learned societies; provides details on the collaboration between learned societies and commercial publishers in producing journals, including working and financial arrangements and explanations of written agreements. 3) Primary Communications: An Annotated Review of the Literature Since 1970—selective bibliography for publishers, authors, libraries, and others involved in scholarly communication. 4) Information Technology, Policy Decision Making in the U.K.—a research report and bibliography on the effect of government policy decisions in information technology including telecommunications, electronic publishing, cable and satellite tv, and others. The Centre also produces Helppacks, a series of booklets on practical aspects of scholarly communication; titles include: Running a Refereeing System; Sources of Funding for Research and Publication; and Direct Mail Marketing for Scholarly Publishers.

Computer-Based Products and Services: Computerized selections from the Center's mailing list files are available, with output provided on mailing labels.

Clientele/Availability: Services are available without restrictions. Primary clients include publishers, learned societies, and others involved in professional communication.

Projected Publications and Services: A data base on new methods and techniques for scholarly communication is planned for the future.

Contact: Prof. A.J. Meadows, Project Head, or Mary Feeney, Research Assistant, Primary Communications Research Centre.

★1055★
UNIVERSITY OF LONDON
CENTRAL INFORMATION SERVICE (CIS)
Senate House, Malet St.　　　　　　　　Phone: 01 6368000
London WC1 7HU, England　　　　　　　Service Est: 1974
Mrs. Alina Vickery, Senior Information Systems Officer

Staff: 4 Information and library professional; 1 clerical and nonprofessional.

Description of System or Service: The CENTRAL INFORMATION SERVICE (CIS) offers a range of computerized information services and related consulting services for the University of London community and external users. It provides computerized information retrieval using international online vendors and conducts training sessions in online search techniques, microcomputer applications, computer programming, and systems analysis. The SERVICE also offers consulting services in the areas of library systems and information management and undertakes funded research projects. Additionally, CIS maintains the computer-based Inventory of Abstracting and Indexing Services Produced in the U.K. and makes available a number of microcomputer software programs, including MIRABILIS, an information retrieval and data base management program, and AQUEST, a library acquisitions package.

Scope and/or Subject Matter: Information retrieval in all academic subject disciplines; computerized information and library systems and services.

Input Sources: European and North American online services are accessed.

Holdings and Storage Media: A machine-readable inventory of abstracting and indexing services is maintained.

Publications: Central Information Services News—provides information on CIS products and services. MIRABILIS and AQUEST user's manuals are also available.

Computer-Based Products and Services: The CENTRAL INFORMATION SERVICE provides information retrieval and SDI services from data bases made available through DIALOG Information Services, Inc., System Development Corporation (SDC), Pergamon InfoLine Ltd., Telesystemes Questel, Data-Star, ESA/IRS, BLAISE (British Library Automated Information Service), and other vendors. CIS also produces the computer-based Inventory of Abstracting and Indexing Services Produced in the U.K. which is available for use on microcomputer.

Additionally, the CENTRAL INFORMATION SERVICE has developed a number of software programs for use on microcomputers, including MIRABILIS and AQUEST. MIRABILIS is an information retrieval and data base management program which allows the user to create data bases suitable for storing bibliographic information such as journal citations or library catalog information. Working with this program, the user can create indexes and retrieve records by searching for individual terms, phrases, personal names, dates, classification numbers, or any elements included in the record. Additional MIRABILIS features include record sorting according to user specifications, tailored printouts, and subfiles created from the original data base. MIRABILIS also allows transfer of records between files, data base merging, and data base creation of records taken from various sources.

AQUEST is a library acquisitions system which can handle up to 5000 orders. It is built around main file records consisting of bibliographic details together with fields for supplier, order number, date of order, date of receipt, source of information, and other fields. This file can be searched by author, title, ISBN, ISSN, record number, invoice number, order number, and supplier. AQUEST also maintains a budget file which informs the user on amounts spent or committed, and it prints order forms, receipt slips, accessions lists, and other materials. Both MIRABILIS and AQUEST software packages are available for use on CP/M microcomputers. MIRABILIS can also be used with the SERVICE's data base of abstracting and indexing services. CIS also produces software programs for use on Commodore PET 32K computers, including an accounting program, a program that produces bulletins, and other programs.

Clientele/Availability: Services are available without restrictions. Primary clients are students and faculty of the University of London.

Contact: Mrs. Alina Vickery, Senior Information Systems Officer, Central Information Service, University of London.

★1056★
UNIVERSITY OF LONDON
IMPERIAL COLLEGE OF SCIENCE AND TECHNOLOGY
DEPARTMENT OF MINERAL RESOURCES ENGINEERING
ROCK MECHANICS INFORMATION SERVICE
Royal School of Mines　　　　　　　　Phone: 01-589 5111
Prince Consort Rd.　　　　　　　　　　Service Est: 1968
London SW7 2BP, England
A.M. Smith, Information Scientist

Staff: 2 Information and library professional; 1 clerical and nonprofessional.

Related Organizations: The Rock Mechanics Information Service is financed by a research grant from Pergamon Press.

Description of System or Service: The ROCK MECHANICS

INFORMATION SERVICE collects and organizes literature references to rock and soil mechanics. This information is stored in computer-readable form and used to produce the printed Geomechanics Abstracts and a corresponding commercially available online data base.

Scope and/or Subject Matter: Rock and soil mechanics; related aspects of mining, civil engineering, geophysics, geology and hydrogeology, fracture mechanics.

Input Sources: Conference proceedings, technical reports, books, theses, and more than 100 journals and secondary sources are scanned regularly for input.

Holdings and Storage Media: The computer-readable data base contains approximately 16,000 references covering the period 1969 to 1976 and approximately 10,000 references with abstracts since 1977. The file is updated every two months.

Publications: 1) Geomechanics Abstracts (every 2 months)—published as part of the International Journal of Rock Mechanics and Mining Sciences by Pergamon Press, Ltd., Headington Hill Hall, Oxford OX3 0BW, England. 2) Thesaurus of Rock and Soil Mechanics Terms—published by Pergamon Press, Ltd. 3) KWIC Index to Rock Mechanics Literature—provides nearly 25,000 references for the period from 1870 to 1976; includes full bibliographic details and subject and author indexes. Various bibliographies are also issued; a list is available from the Service.

Computer-Based Products and Services: The Geomechanics Abstracts data base from 1977 to the present is searchable online through Pergamon InfoLine Ltd. Retrospective searches of the online data base and earlier computer-readable holdings are provided by the SERVICE.

Clientele/Availability: Products and services are available without restrictions. Primary clients include geologists, rock and soil mechanics engineers, mining and exploration technologists, geophysicists, and mining and construction engineers.

Contact: A.M. Smith, Information Scientist, Rock Mechanics Information Service.

★1057★
UNIVERSITY OF MELBOURNE
DEPARTMENT OF GEOLOGY
COMPUTERISED LIBRARY OF ANALYSED IGNEOUS ROCKS (CLAIR)
Parkville, Vic. 3052, Australia
Phone: 345 1844
Service Est: 1969

Special Note: No questionnaire response was received for this entry for the 6th edition. The entry is reprinted as it appeared in the 5th edition.

Description of System or Service: The COMPUTERISED LIBRARY OF ANALYSED IGNEOUS ROCKS (CLAIR) comprises a machine-readable file of chemical analyses of igneous rocks derived from the worldwide published literature, together with an internally developed software package facilitating data manipulation and reduction. The system is used to support research at the University of Melbourne; it is also made available to others for purchase.

Scope and/or Subject Matter: Petrological data.

Input Sources: All input is obtained from published sources, including journals, books, and monographs.

Holdings and Storage Media: More than 26,000 chemical analyses and related information are held on magnetic tape; the file is continuously updated.

Computer-Based Products and Services: The CLAIR Data File provides chemical data and the following additional information (when available) for each of the 26,000 analyses covered: journal name; author; date of publication of the reference from which the analysis came; geographic code for continent and individual country; latitude and longitude; geological age of rock; field occurrence; and rock name compounded as one noun and up to three adjectives. The CLAIR Data System software includes manipulative programs for updating, editing, extracting, and formatting data, and reduction programs for analyses, recalculations, histograms, and plotting. Available in versions for several types of computers, the Data System software can be used for storage, retrieval, and processing of numeric and nonnumeric data in any type of large data file.

Clientele/Availability: The System is available for a small fee.

Contact: Head, Computerised Library of Analysed Igneous Rocks.

★1058★
UNIVERSITY OF MILAN
(Universita Degli Studi di Milano)
HIGHER INSTITUTE OF SOCIOLOGY
(Istituto Superiore di Sociologia)
DATA AND PROGRAM ARCHIVE FOR THE SOCIAL SCIENCES
(Archivio Dati e Programmi per le Scienze Sociali - ADPSS)
via G. Cantoni 4
I-20144 Milan, Italy
Stefano Draghi, Director
Phone: 02 4986187
Service Est: 1972

Staff: Approximately 5 total.

Description of System or Service: The DATA AND PROGRAM ARCHIVE FOR THE SOCIAL SCIENCES (ADPSS) maintains and develops data files concerned with the social, economic, and political structure of Italian society. ADPSS also devises computer programs for the analysis of social science data and organizes courses in social science research methodology.

Scope and/or Subject Matter: Social science, economics, political science, electoral behavior, and other data regarding Italian society.

Input Sources: Data are supplied by the Istituto Centrale di Statistica and other institutional producers. Surveys also provide input.

Holdings and Storage Media: Survey data and ecological files concerned with Italian society are held in machine-readable form.

Computer-Based Products and Services: ADPSS elaborates and archives machine-readable files, and it provides tape distribution.

Clientele/Availability: Primary clientele are universities and research institutes.

Contact: Stefano Draghi, Director, Data and Program Archive for the Social Sciences.

★1059★
UNIVERSITY OF NEW BRUNSWICK LIBRARIES
PHOENIX
Box 7500
Fredericton, NB, Canada E3B 5H5
Sheila Laidlaw, University Librarian
Phone: (506) 453-4740
Service Est: 1981

Description of System or Service: PHOENIX is a machine-readable catalog for the Harriet Irving Library, its branches, the Law Library, and the Ward Chipman Library at the Saint John campus. PHOENIX consists of MARC and UTLAS Inc. contributed records and is searchable online.

Scope and/or Subject Matter: Online library catalog covering general academic topics, including special collections on engineering and law.

Input Sources: Input consists of bibliographic records for monographs, serials, microfilms, and audiovisual materials.

Holdings and Storage Media: The machine-readable PHOENIX library catalog comprises the following data bases: 1) LIBRARY—contains more than 190,000 records of the Harriet Irving Library and its branches. 2) CLEO—covers more than 18,000 holdings on microfilm of early printed books. 3) WCL—contains more than 15,600 records of the Ward Chipman Library. 4) MMI—lists more than 500 records of materials pertaining to Native American Indians. 5) ENLIST—covers more than 150,000 records in engineering literature.

Publications: An in-house newsletter is produced.

Microform Products and Services: A COM back-up program is under development.

Computer-Based Products and Services: PHOENIX is a computer-readable catalog of MARC and UTLAS contributed records. It is accessible online to other libraries.

Clientele/Availability: The PHOENIX system was designed for use by the staff and patrons of the University Libraries.

Contact: Alan C. Burk, Head of Public Services, University of New Brunswick Libraries. (Telex 014 46186.) The electronic mail address on ENVOY 100 (Telecom Canada) is Admin/UNB.FTON.

★1060★
UNIVERSITY OF NEW SOUTH WALES
AUSTRALIAN GRADUATE SCHOOL OF MANAGEMENT
CENTRE FOR RESEARCH IN FINANCE (CRIF)
P.O. Box 1
Kensington, N.S.W. 2033, Australia
Ray J. Ball, Director
Phone: 662 0300
Service Est: 1980

Staff: 4 Management professional; 1 technician; 6 other.

Related Organizations: The Centre for Management Research and Development (CMRD) is the parent organization of the Centre for Research in Finance.

Description of System or Service: The CENTRE FOR RESEARCH IN FINANCE (CRIF) maintains and provides services from several Australian financial data bases. The data bases include current information on all securities traded on all Australian stock exchanges, an extensive microfiche annual report file, and a computer-readable annual report data file. Additionally, CRIF offers a risk measurement service providing calculation of beta factors for individual firms and by industry for the Australian equities market.

Scope and/or Subject Matter: Finance, accounting, risk measurement, corporate reporting.

Input Sources: Information in the data files includes month-end stock prices from Australian stock exchanges; company restructuring data as reported to stock exchanges; published annual reports; and other data.

Holdings and Storage Media: Several financial data files are held in machine-readable form. Published corporate annual reports are held on microfiche and in machine-readable form.

Publications: 1) Risk Measurement Service (annual)—available for purchase; provides estimates of risks as well as historical return performance on all companies listed on the stock exchange. 2) Australian Journal of Management.

Microform Products and Services: Annual reports for most listed companies are available on microfiche.

Computer-Based Products and Services: CRIF distributes the following data files on machine-readable tapes: 1) Share Price Record—contains monthly share data for all senior equity shares of all companies traded on any Australian stock exchange since 1974; covers both mining and industrial boards. 2) Annual Report Record—contains more than 120 balance sheet and income statement items per company for more than 600 companies since 1950; updated throughout the year. CRIF also produces the Risk Measurement Service, available on floppy diskette and in printed form and used for estimating any security's beta risk.

Other Services: Additional services include consulting on all areas of corporate finance.

Clientele/Availability: Clients include portfolio managers, the business community, and academics.

Projected Publications and Services: CRIF plans to produce commodities prices, futures markets, and fixed interest data bases.

Contact: Nick Frisina, Research Officer, Centre for Research in Finance; telephone 662 0254. (Telex AA 26054.)

★1061★
UNIVERSITY OF OSLO
ROYAL UNIVERSITY LIBRARY
PLANNING DEPARTMENT
Drammensvegen 42
Oslo 2, Norway
Tor Blekastad, Deputy Librarian
Phone: 02 564980

Staff: 6 Information and library professional; 1 clerical and nonprofessional; 1 other.

Description of System or Service: Major activities of the PLANNING DEPARTMENT of the Royal University Library include operation of the Norwegian MARC (NORMARC) system, and maintenance of national union lists of serials and books. NORMARC is a computer-based system implemented for the central cataloging of Norwegian imprints, including books and selected papers from some 400 Norwegian periodicals. It is used to provide a variety of products and services, including the national bibliography, catalog cards, microform products, and remote terminal online access. Implemented for handling foreign monographs, the national union catalog of books (UBO:BOK) utilizes a data base of U.S Library of Congress and British Library (UK) MARC records combined with local records. The Union Catalog for Periodicals in Norwegian Libraries (SAMKATPER) is a computer-readable file covering the serial holdings of approximately 350 libraries in Norway. Print and microform products are derived from it.

Scope and/or Subject Matter: Cataloging of books published in Norway and elsewhere; periodicals held by Norwegian libraries.

Input Sources: Input consists of holdings registered by the Royal University Library.

Holdings and Storage Media: NORMARC and union catalog data are maintained in machine-readable form. Computer tapes of LC MARC records since 1974 and UK MARC records since 1976 are also held.

Publications: 1) Norsk Bokfortegnelse (monthly; annual and five-year cumulations)—the Norwegian national bibliography. 2) Norsk Tidsskriftartikler (quarterly and annual). 3) Union Catalog for Periodicals in Norwegian Libraries-SAMKATPER (every second year)—printed in four subject groups: biology/ medicine; humanities; social sciences; natural science/ mathematics.

Microform Products and Services: Alphabetical or subject-classified NORMARC catalogs and alphabetical SAMKATPER catalogs are available on COM microfiche.

Computer-Based Products and Services: NORMARC is used for the national central cataloging of Norwegian imprints and for producing the Library's catalog cards. It also is used to produce Norwegian official book statistics and for input to Index Translationum. Retrieval lists are produced from both NORMARC and SAMKATPER; NORMARC, SAMKATPER, and UBO:BOK are also publicly available online.

Clientele/Availability: Primary clients are Norwegian libraries.

Contact: Tor Blekastad, Deputy Librarian, Royal University Library. (Telex 16078 UB N.)

★1062★
UNIVERSITY OF PARIS-NANTERRE
GROUP FOR APPLIED MACROECONOMIC ANALYSIS
(Groupe d'Analyse Macroeconomique Appliquee - GAMA)
2, rue de Rouen
F-92001 Nanterre, France
Prof. Raymond Courbis, Director
Phone: 01 7259234
Service Est: 1972

Staff: 1 Information and library professional; 8 management professional; 1 technician.

Related Organizations: The Group for Applied Macroeconomic Analysis receives support from the National Center for Scientific Research/ Centre National de la Recherche Scientifique (CNRS).

Description of System or Service: The GROUP FOR APPLIED MACROECONOMIC ANALYSIS (GAMA) is a scientific center involved with computerized modeling and forecasting. For forecasts and simulations, it has developed four models of the French economy: NOGLI, an annual macro-sectoral model for short to medium-term forecasting; PROTEC, a quarterly model; ANAIS, a highly disaggregated input-output model covering 90 industries; and REGIS, a multiregional model covering seven areas in France. ANAIS is made publicly available online in conjunction with a forecasts data bank; the other models are used for macroeconomic and sectoral forecasts and simulations of economic policies. In addition to model development, GAMA provides consulting on economic simulations or ad hoc modeling.

Scope and/or Subject Matter: Forecasts and simulations of the French economy.

Input Sources: Input is derived from government data and from information gathered directly by GAMA.

Holdings and Storage Media: The computer-readable ANAIS data base contains time-series data for 90 industries.

Publications: 1) Prevision et Analyse Economique (quarterly)—review of forecasts and economic analysis; available by subscription. 2) Forecasts for the Forecasts' Users Group.

Computer-Based Products and Services: The ANAIS model and forecasts data bank is available online through CISI.

Clientele/Availability: Clients include the French government, banks, private and public firms, and unions.

Contact: Prof. Raymond Courbis, Director, Group for Applied Macroeconomic Analysis.

★1063★
UNIVERSITY OF PARIS-SOUTH
(Universite de Paris-Sud)
GASES AND PLASMAS PHYSICS LABORATORY
(Laboratoire de Physique des Gaz et des Plasmas)
GAPHYOR
Bldg. 212　　　　　　　　　　　　Phone: 6 9417250
F-91405 Orsay Cedex, France　　Service Est: 1970
Prof. Jean-Loup Delcroix, Head

Staff: 1 Management professional; 1.5 technical, sales, and marketing; 1 clerical and nonprofessional.

Related Organizations: GAPHYOR is supported by the Centre National de la Recherche Scientifique (CNRS) of the Mission Interministeriel de la Documentation Informatique Scientifique et Technique (MIDIST), and by the Ministere de la Defense Direction des Recherches Etudes et Techniques (DRET).

Description of System or Service: GAPHYOR is a computerized retrieval system on published properties of neutral or ionized atoms, molecules, and gases. It is characterized by an identification and a fine sorting of data obtained by using a simple code for writing molecules and collision processes (and chemical reactions) instead of using keywords. The chemical systems described by GAPHYOR cannot be too complex (one to four chemical elements, molecules of less than nine atoms). Within these limits a molecule is coded by indicating the constituting elements, the chemical formula, the ionization state, and the eventual excitation. GAPHYOR is publicly available online and is used to produce a quarterly bulletin and to provide computerized retrieval services.

Scope and/or Subject Matter: Simple properties of atoms and molecules, their interaction properties, and the macroscopic properties of gases and plasmas.

Input Sources: Input is derived from journals and periodicals, books, laboratory reports, and conference proceedings.

Holdings and Storage Media: Computer-readable GAPHYOR files contain more than 150,000 entries with approximately 15,000 added annually. For those systems composed of one or two elements, the data base is relatively complete since 1970; for those with three or four elements, the file begins in 1975.

Publications: GAPHYOR Bulletin (quarterly)—available by subscription.

Computer-Based Products and Services: The GAPHYOR system is accessible online through CIRCE and uses the SYGAL (System-Gaphor-Language) conversational system. Record elements include a sketch of the physicochemical process; journal title; volume and page numbers; author; geographical location of the work; and related information such as energy, range, and identification as theoretical or experimental. Computerized searches and current awareness services from GAPHYOR are provided by the Laboratory.

Other Services: The GAPHYOR staff also provides consulting and special literature searching.

Clientele/Availability: There are no restrictions on clientele.

Remarks: GAPHYOR is an acronym for Gaz-Physique-Orsay.

Contact: Prof. Jean-Loup Delcroix, Head, or William Assal, Computer Engineer, GAPHYOR. (Telex 629 166 F FAC ORS.)

★1064★
UNIVERSITY OF QUEBEC
(Universite du Quebec)
DIRECT ACCESS DATA BANK AT THE UNIVERSITY OF QUEBEC
(Banque de Donnees a Acces Direct de l'Universite du Quebec - BADADUQ)
2875, blvd. Laurier　　　　　　Phone: (418) 657-2450
Sainte-Foy, PQ, Canada G1V 2M3　Service Est: 1971
Laval Du Breuil, Head

Special Note: No questionnaire response was received for this entry for the 6th edition. The entry is reprinted as it appeared in the 5th edition.

Description of System or Service: The DIRECT ACCESS DATA BANK AT THE UNIVERSITY OF QUEBEC (BADADUQ) is an online catalog providing holdings information for 12 libraries in the University of Quebec network. Libraries submit bibliographic data to BADADUQ in either batch or online, interactive mode. Students and faculty access the data base for information on a library's holdings; it also serves as the union catalog for the network.

Scope and/or Subject Matter: Machine-readable bibliographic data for university library collections.

Input Sources: Input for the BADADUQ data base consists of bibliographic data for documents acquired since 1972 by the Montreal campus and since 1975 for the other University campuses, and bibliographic data on serials held by the campuses.

Holdings and Storage Media: More than 650,000 records are maintained in the master file; an additional 100,000 items are added each year. Other files include index keywords, authors, title, and book class; auxiliary files comprising code dictionaries, keyword codes, keyword references, and user comments.

Publications: Teledoc (irregular)—available by request.

Microform Products and Services: Microforms of information from the data base are produced in any format at the user's request.

Computer-Based Products and Services: Information retrieval from the BADADUQ data base is available online for students and faculty on all campuses. Additionally, the University permits various educational and government units to maintain access to BADADUQ via Datapac.

Clientele/Availability: The BADADUQ system is intended for use by students, faculty, and staff of the University of Quebec campuses.

Contact: Laval Du Breuil, Head, Documentation Systems.

★1065★
UNIVERSITY OF READING LIBRARY
LOCATION REGISTER OF TWENTIETH CENTURY ENGLISH LITERARY MANUSCRIPTS AND LETTERS
Whiteknights　　　　　　　　Phone: 0734 751364
Reading RG6 2AE, England　　Service Est: 1982
Dr. David C. Sutton, Senior Research Officer

Staff: 2 Information and library professional; 1 clerical and nonprofessional.

Description of System or Service: The LOCATION REGISTER OF TWENTIETH CENTURY ENGLISH LITERARY MANUSCRIPTS AND LETTERS was established to locate and list all 20th century literary manuscripts in English which are available for consultation in the British Isles. The REGISTER is held in machine-readable form and covers all types of materials ranging from large collections in national museums and libraries to single pieces of paper. A microfiche version of the REGISTER is in preparation.

Scope and/or Subject Matter: The English literary works of any essayist, poet, novelist, or dramatist, regardless of literary merit or interest, who died after December 31, 1899.

Input Sources: Input is obtained from printed sources as well as from visits to libraries, museums, record offices, and other repositories in the British Isles.

Holdings and Storage Media: The Location Register was created and is maintained in computer-readable form.

Microform Products and Services: A microfiche version of the Register is under development.

Computer-Based Products and Services: The LOCATION REGISTER is maintained as a computer-readable data base on BLAISE-LOCAS (British Library Automated Information Service - Local Catalogue Service).

Clientele/Availability: Clients include literary researchers and others.

Contact: Dr. David C. Sutton, Senior Research Officer, Location Register of Twentieth Century English Literary Manuscripts and Letters.

★1066★
UNIVERSITY OF REGINA
CANADIAN PLAINS RESEARCH CENTER (CPRC)
INFORMATION SERVICES

Regina, SK, Canada S4S 0A2
Dr. M. Evelyn Jonescu, Director
Phone: (306) 584-4758
Service Est: 1973

Staff: 1 Information and library professional; 5 technicians.

Description of System or Service: The INFORMATION SERVICES of the Canadian Plains Research Center (CPRC) promotes research and communication in all aspects of Canadian Plains studies by compiling the computer-readable CANPLAINS inventory of current and recently completed research projects and issuing print publications. Searches of the CANPLAINS data base are available from the CPRC; the data base is also commercially available online.

Scope and/or Subject Matter: Research related to the Northern Great Plains including the humanities, fine arts, natural and social sciences, environmental research, education, human justice, native and ethnic studies, geography, North American prairies, and Western Canadian history.

Input Sources: Input is derived from published literature and from descriptions of research in progress, reports, and theses contributed by individual researchers, government agencies, and supporting organizations.

Holdings and Storage Media: The machine-readable CANPLAINS data base holds approximately 18,000 items and is updated with approximately 3000 records per year.

Publications: 1) Canadian Plains Bulletin—newsletter; 2) Prairie Forum (semiannual)—available by subscription. A monograph series on a wide variety of plains-related topics is also published.

Computer-Based Products and Services: The CPRC Information Services provides computerized search services from the CANPLAINS data base and makes the data base available online through QL Systems. It is searchable for subject, researcher/ author name and address, title of item, source of funding, geographic location, and other elements. The data base can be used to list recent research on any prairie-related topic, to produce directories of researchers, to print bibliographies, to create mailing lists, to locate funding sources, and for other applications.

Other Services: Additional services include conferences and contract research.

Clientele/Availability: Products and services are available on a fee basis; clients include online search services, researchers, government departments, and organizations.

Contact: Carol MacDonald, Coordinator of Information Services, Canadian Plains Research Center; telephone (306) 584-4015.

★1067★
UNIVERSITY OF SASKATCHEWAN LIBRARY
REFERENCE DEPARTMENT
UNIVERSITY OF SASKATCHEWAN LIBRARIES MACHINE-ASSISTED REFERENCE TELESERVICES (SMART)

Saskatoon, SK, Canada S7N 0W0
Victor G. Wiebe, Head, Reference Department
Phone: (306) 343-4295
Service Est: 1969

Staff: 5 Information and library professional; 7 clerical and nonprofessional.

Description of System or Service: The UNIVERSITY OF SASKATCHEWAN LIBRARIES MACHINE-ASSISTED REFERENCE TELESERVICES (SMART) is a service of the Reference Department which enables the Library to provide patrons with custom bibliographies, document delivery, and bibliographic verification. Online searches and SDI services from publicly available data bases are offered. In addition, training and expertise in the use of bibliographic and numeric data bases are provided.

Scope and/or Subject Matter: Science and technology, social sciences, business, and humanities.

Input Sources: Input is derived from government and commercial data bases.

Holdings and Storage Media: For direct support of SMART, the Reference Department maintains a collection of 5 serial publications, 100 data base and systems manuals, and 150 thesauri and codebooks.

Computer-Based Products and Services: SMART conducts online searching of data bases available from CAN/OLE, CAN/SDI, I.P. Sharp Associates Limited, Telcom Canada's ENVOY 100, RESORS, International Development Research Centre (IDRC), QL Systems Limited, System Development Corporation (SDC), U.S. National Library of Medicine, Info Globe, Institute for Scientific Information, DIALOG Information Services, Inc., and Bibliographic Retrieval Services (BRS). SDI services are offered from these vendors and from SELDOM, an internal system providing access to LC/MARC and CAN/MARC data. Online searches may also be performed at any of the University's five branch libraries.

Other Services: Additional services include interlibrary loans, reference, photocopying, document delivery, and user education seminars.

Clientele/Availability: Services are available without restrictions.

Contact: Robert R. Boychuk, Online Services Librarian, University of Saskatchewan Library. (Telex 0742659.) The electronic mail address on QL Systems Limited is Mail-box 118; on ENVOY 100 (Telecom Canada), ILL.SSU.

★1068★
UNIVERSITY OF SASKATCHEWAN LIBRARY
SYSTEMS AND PLANNING UNIT

Saskatoon, SK, Canada S7N 0W0
Peter Burslem, Acting Head
Phone: (306) 343-4216
Service Est: 1970

Staff: 1 Information and library professional; 1 clerical and nonprofessional.

Description of System or Service: The SYSTEMS AND PLANNING UNIT works in conjunction with the University of Saskatchewan Administrative Systems to design, implement, and operate automated systems for control of such library operations as cataloging, acquisitions, serials, and circulation. To facilitate its services, it maintains a complete copy of the LC and CAN/MARC monographs data base, current UK MARC monographs and serials data, and a Library Holdings File for University of Saskatchewan libraries.

Scope and/or Subject Matter: Automated library services.

Input Sources: Input is derived from the MARC Records Distribution Service of the National Library of Canada and from internally created records.

Holdings and Storage Media: The Library Holdings File currently contains machine-readable records for approximately 525,000 titles (out of a total of 550,000 titles housed in various campus collections); the MARC data base holds approximately 1.9 million records for monographs.

Microform Products and Services: Library catalogs are produced on COM.

Computer-Based Products and Services: The major systems operated by the UNIT include the following: 1) MARC Data Base System—based on subscription to weekly CAN/MARC format tapes for monographs. This system provides records for input to the cataloging and acquisition system; additionally, the UNIT produces catalog cards from these tapes as a service to the Vancouver Public Library. 2) SELDOM (Selective Dissemination of MARC)—weekly SDI services from MARC tapes are conducted for some 135 faculty and staff members at the University of Saskatchewan; search profiles may be structured according to subject heading, LC or Dewey Decimal classification numbers, publisher, series, keyword in title, geographic code, or date. 3) TESA-1 (Technical Services Automation - Phase 1), Acquisitions and Cataloging System—includes an In-Process File, which is regularly matched against MARC tapes, and a Library Holdings File representing titles cataloged on the system. The latter file produces catalog cards, acquisitions lists, and various other selected lists of holdings; output is available in COM microform. 4) TESA-2, Serials Control System—envisaged as a control system covering all aspects of the acquisition, cataloging, and processing of serial publications held by the campus libraries; currently a complete inventory and conversion of serial holdings is under way, and more than 20,000 titles on campus have been processed. 5) Circulation Control System—an online, minicomputer-based system utilizing light pen scanners and bar-coded identification labels; online public access to the circulation inventory file is provided by call number.

Clientele/Availability: Services are intended primarily for University of Saskatchewan libraries.

Contact: Peter Burslem, Acting Head, Systems and Planning Department, University of Saskatchewan Library. The electronic mail address on ENVOY 100 (Telecom Canada) is P.BURSLEM.

★1069★
UNIVERSITY OF SHEFFIELD
BIOMEDICAL INFORMATION SERVICE

Sheffield S10 2TN, England Phone: 0742 78555
Mr. J.K. Barkla, Director Service Est: 1966

Staff: 3 Information and library professional; 12 clerical and nonprofessional.

Description of System or Service: The BIOMEDICAL INFORMATION SERVICE provides University staff and scientists elsewhere with monthly current awareness bulletins in the areas of physiology, cell biology, and related sciences. Covering more than 150 specific topics, the bulletins are grouped into two classes and are based on journals and computer search profiles.

Scope and/or Subject Matter: Cell biology, physiology, and related biomedical topics.

Input Sources: Input is obtained from original and abstracts journals, from Index Medicus, and from computer search profiles.

Publications: 1) Express Bulletins (monthly)—a series of 58 current awareness publications, each covering a single topic; citations include author, title, reference, and author affiliation and address. 2) Economy Bulletins (monthly)—a series of more than 100 current awareness publications based on sections of Index Medicus or MEDLINE computer searches by permission of the U.S. National Library of Medicine.

Computer-Based Products and Services: The Biomedical Information Service secures computerized search services for subscribers on written request.

Other Services: In addition to the services described above, the Service conducts research, makes referrals, and offers manual literature searching.

Clientele/Availability: Services are designed primarily for scientists and researchers, but are available to others.

Contact: Mr. J.K. Barkla, Director, Biomedical Information Service. (Telex 54348 ULSHEF G.)

★1070★
UNIVERSITY OF SHEFFIELD
CENTRE FOR RESEARCH ON USER STUDIES (CRUS)
Western Bank Phone: 0742 738608
Sheffield S10 2TN, England Service Est: 1975
Colin Harris, Director

Staff: Approximately 7 total.

Related Organizations: The Centre receives funds from the Research and Development Department of the British Library.

Description of System or Service: The CENTRE FOR RESEARCH ON USER STUDIES (CRUS) investigates people's needs for information and literature of all kinds, and such problems as how people recognize information needs, how they search for information and literature using both formal and informal sources, and how and in what form they obtain and make use of it. Its activities in these areas include original research projects, advisory and consultancy services, and education and training courses aimed at encouraging the application of research and research findings to the development of more effective user service. The CENTRE maintains a collection of completed research studies, a comprehensive retrospective index to the literature, and a register of ongoing research.

Scope and/or Subject Matter: Research into the needs and problems of users of information.

Input Sources: Input to the indexes is obtained from comprehensive literature scanning in the areas of communications, social sciences, and information and library science.

Holdings and Storage Media: Collection consists of 500 bound volumes, and extensive reprint and microfiche holdings.

Publications: CRUS News (3 per year)—provides information on research projects and publications; free on application. Occasional papers are also published.

Services: Primary services are consultancy, research, referrals, and manual literature searching.

Clientele/Availability: CRUS serves the library and information science community.

Contact: Colin Harris, Director, Centre for Research on User Studies.

★1071★
UNIVERSITY OF SHERBROOKE
(Université de Sherbrooke)
ASBESTOS RESEARCH PROGRAM
(Programme de Recherche sur l'Amiante de l'Universite de Sherbrooke - PRAUS)
INFORMATION CENTER
(Informatheque)
Sherbrooke, PQ, Canada J1K 2R1 Phone: (819) 565-3616
Mrs. Asta Sokov, Director Service Est: 1977

Staff: 2 Information and library professional; 3 technicians; 2 clerical and nonprofessional.

Related Organizations: Related organizations include the Institut de Recherche et Developpement d'Amiante (IRDA) and the Canadian Asbestos Information Center.

Description of System or Service: The INFORMATION CENTER collects, stores, and disseminates information on all aspects of asbestos. It maintains an extensive documentation collection and the computer-readable ASBEST data base to provide comprehensive and current aid to bibliographic research. The CENTER also maintains several other machine-readable files including the Catalog of Patents Related to Asbestos and the Asbestos Manufacturers Catalog. The CENTER offers literature searches, current awareness, bibliography preparation, consultations, and reference services, and it makes ASBEST commercially available for online searching.

Scope and/or Subject Matter: All aspects of asbestos, including chemistry, geology, biology, physics, industrial, sanitary engineering, commercial, economics, law, medical, social, and others.

Input Sources: Information is gathered from international data bases, from U.S. and Canadian government officials and researchers, and from more than 3000 periodicals, proceedings, research reports, monographs, theses, standards, patents, laws, and other sources.

Holdings and Storage Media: The CENTER maintains a collection of approximately 500 bound volumes, 30,000 journal articles, and subscriptions to 32 periodicals. The computer-readable ASBEST data base contains approximately 7000 references. Other machine-readable files are also maintained.

Publications: A new acquisitions list is issued.

Computer-Based Products and Services: The ASBEST data base is commercially available online through QL Systems Limited Limited as the Asbestos Information file. Searchable data elements include author, title in original language, keyword phrases, and abstracts (in

English). The CENTER also maintains the following machine-readable files: 1) Catalog of Patents Related to Asbestos. 2) List of Persons and Organizations Related to Asbestos Research and Technology. 3) Catalog of Publications. 4) Asbestos Manufacturers Catalog (in progress).

Clientele/Availability: Clients include members of PRAUS, IRDA, and SNA, as well as outside customers.

Contact: Mrs. Asta Sokov, Director, Informatheque-PRAUS. The electronic mail address on ENVOY 100 (Telecom Canada) is PFB.QSHERURA.

★1072★
UNIVERSITY OF SYDNEY
SAMPLE SURVEY CENTRE (SSC)
City Rd.
Sydney, N.S.W. 2006, Australia
Dr. Terence W. Beed, Director

Phone: 02 6923624
Service Est: 1975

Staff: 1 Information and library professional; 3 management professional; 1 technician; 1 sales and marketing; 2 other.

Related Organizations: The Social Science Data Archives (SSDA) of the Australian National University (see separate entry) cooperates with the Sample Survey Centre.

Description of System or Service: The SAMPLE SURVEY CENTRE (SSC) provides an on-campus facility for staff who require advice and assistance in running sample surveys and in acquiring data drawn from survey archives. The CENTRE also conducts original surveys in a variety of fields, and maintains an ongoing research program into the political impact of public opinion polls. Results from the Centre's surveys as well as others collected on a worldwide basis are computer-readable and may be searched by outside users.

Scope and/or Subject Matter: Survey research in social sciences and related disciplines.

Input Sources: The Centre's major information sources are its clients, the press releases and computer tabulations of public opinion poll organizations, and data sets accessible through the Australian Consortium for Social and Political Research (ACSPRI) and similar European and North American organizations. It also scans major Australian daily newspapers and news magazines for news on surveys of all types.

Holdings and Storage Media: The Centre maintains 400 bound volumes, a clipping file of 3500 items, and the following Australian data bases: Australian Bureau of Statistics: Census of Population and Housing, 1981; National Educational Survey, 1977; National Survey of Post-Secondary Teaching Staff, 1977; Australian Opinion Polls User Service data base.

Publications: 1) Newsletter of the University of Sydney Sample Survey Centre (quarterly)—covers data generated by sample surveys reported in five Australian daily and weekly newspapers and six major newspapers in Sydney and Melbourne. 2) Australian Opinion Polls. Occasional papers dealing with methodological and substantive issues in survey research are also issued.

Microform Products and Services: All press releases and subscriber reports issued by Australian pollsters from 1941 to 1977 are available on microfiche.

Computer-Based Products and Services: The CENTRE offers AOPUS: Australian Opinion Polls User Service, an online listing of all question areas covered by polls in Australia from 1941 to the present, as well as an online index to survey-related news items. Also available are tapes for the Australian Census of Population and Housing 1981 sample files, National Educational Survey, and National Survey of Post-Secondary Teaching Staff. In addition, the Centre makes available the Survey Management System. SMS is used for self-completion surveys, response logging, and generation of reminder mailings to respondents.

Other Services: In addition to data collection and analysis, the Centre provides consulting, referrals, and advanced training workshops in survey methodology.

Clientele/Availability: Services are available to University of Sydney faculty and staff, other Australian and foreign universities and colleges, and government departments.

Contact: Dr. Terence W. Beed, Director, Sample Survey Centre. (Telex AA20056 FISHLIB.)

★1073★
UNIVERSITY OF SYDNEY LIBRARY
BIBLIOGRAPHIC INFORMATION ON SOUTHEAST ASIA (BISA)
Phone: 02 6923738
Sydney, N.S.W. 2006, Australia
Service Est: 1978
Helen Jarvis, Director

Staff: 4 Information and library professional; 1 technician; 2 other.

Related Organizations: BISA is funded by the Australian University International Development Plan.

Description of System or Service: BIBLIOGRAPHIC INFORMATION ON SOUTHEAST ASIA (BISA) is a machine-readable data base covering Australian library holdings, journal articles, and other information from and about Southeast Asia, particularly the countries of Indonesia, Malaysia, and Singapore. The BISA data base is commercially available online and is used to produce a catalog and bibliographies on COM.

Scope and/or Subject Matter: Published works from and about Southeast Asia in general and Indonesia, Malaysia, and Singapore in particular, covering all languages and subject areas, including economics, resources, agriculture, government, religion, literature, history and geography, and science and technology.

Input Sources: Input is derived from the Australian MARC records service and the card catalogs of the National Library of Australia, the Australian National University Library, Monash University Library, and the University of Sydney Library. BISA also indexes the Far Eastern Economic Review and other journals.

Holdings and Storage Media: The machine-readable BISA data base contains approximately 20,000 bibliographic records.

Publications: 1) A Guide to BISA. 2) An Authority System Proposal for BISA.

Microform Products and Services: The following are available for purchase on microfiche: 1) BISA Catalogue on Microfiche (semiannual)—author/ title and subject sequences appear in each issue; produced from the BISA master file. 2) Far Eastern Economic Review Index on Microfiche (cumulated quarterly). 3) HAMKA: A Bibliography of the Works of Prof. Dr. Haji Abdul Malik Karim Amrullah. 4) Twenty Years of Indonesian Fiction 1940-1960: A Bibliography Selected from the IDC Collection. 5) Singapore/ Malaysia Conferences on Health and Related Sciences—compiled from the holdings of the National University of Singapore. 6) Chinese Kungfu Stories in Indonesian: A Bibliography Selected from the IDC Collection. 7) Malaysian Serials: Non-government. 8) Asian Agricultural Research and Development: A Bibliography. 9) Philippine Ethnographic Series (The H. Otley Beyer manuscript collection): Bisayan Ethnography. 10) The Vietnamese Collection of the ANU Library.

Computer-Based Products and Services: The BISA data base is available for online searching through Ausinet and the Australian Bibliographic Network (ABN). Data base record elements for books include author, title, subject, language, publisher, date of publication, place of publication, physical description, notes, descriptors, location information, and other data. Machine-readable tapes of BISA will be available in the future.

Clientele/Availability: Services are available without restrictions.

Remarks: The BISA was originally undertaken by the University of Sydney Department of Indonesian and Malayan Studies as an attempt to provide improved access to the growing collection of Southeast Asian material in Australian libraries. A card catalog of more than 50,000 items, representing the holding of four major Australian libraries, was developed. In 1978, the University of Sydney Library joined the Department in a project to construct a machine-readable data base to this card catalog.

Contact: Helen Jarvis, Director, or Nergida Cross, Bibliographic Information on Southeast Asia. (Telex AA 20056.)

★1074★
UNIVERSITY OF TASMANIA LIBRARY
UNION LIST OF HIGHER DEGREE THESES IN AUSTRALIAN LIBRARIES
Box 252C, G.P.O. Phone: 002 202219
Hobart, Tasmania 7001, Australia Service Est: 1966
Mrs. Gillian Blain, Editor

Staff: 2 Information and library professional; 1 technician.

Description of System or Service: The UNION LIST OF HIGHER DEGREE THESES IN AUSTRALIAN LIBRARIES is a printed and computer-readable listing of theses presented for master's or doctorate degrees at Australian universities and colleges. Published in a cumulative edition to 1965 with subsequent supplements, the UNION LIST includes information on the subject and title of the thesis, author's name, degree awarded, and libraries holding copies of the thesis. The UNION LIST is available for purchase in hard copy from the University of Tasmania; information from it is also searchable online through Ausinet.

Scope and/or Subject Matter: Higher degree theses accepted by Australian universities; all subject areas are represented.

Input Sources: Records for the Union List are provided by libraries of the institutions awarding the degrees. The records are usually in the form of the contributing library's own catalog input.

Holdings and Storage Media: Union List data dating from 1969 to the present are maintained in machine-readable form.

Publications: Union List of Higher Degree Theses in Australian Libraries—available for purchase from the University's Publication Office.

Computer-Based Products and Services: UNION LIST data from 1975 to date are accessible online as the HDEG data base through Ausinet. Search elements include subject categories, title, author's name, degree awarded, date degree awarded, awarding institution, names of libraries holding a copy of the thesis, and keywords. Subject categories used are based on those employed in Dissertation Abstracts International.

Clientele/Availability: The Union List is available without restrictions.

Contact: Mrs. Gillian Blain, Editor, Union List of Higher Degree Theses in Australian Libraries. (Telex 58150.)

★1075★
UNIVERSITY OF TOKYO
COMPUTER CENTER
UNIVERSITY OF TOKYO ON-LINE INFORMATION RETRIEVAL (TOOL-IR) SYSTEM
2-11-16 Yayoi, Bunkyo-ku Phone: 03 8122111
Tokyo 113, Japan Service Est: 1973
Dr. Hiroshi Ozawa

Staff: 1 Information and library professional; 3 technicians.

Description of System or Service: The UNIVERSITY OF TOKYO ON-LINE INFORMATION RETRIEVAL (TOOL-IR) SYSTEM is an online information retrieval system permitting the Japanese academic community to interactively search a number of commercial and academic data bases. TOOL-IR also offers information system development and software for users wishing to maintain their own data bases.

Scope and/or Subject Matter: Data bases in science and technology.

Holdings and Storage Media: More than 7 data bases are held online.

Computer-Based Products and Services: Online or batch-mode access is offered for CA Search, CA Condensates, COMPENDEX, INSPEC Computer and Control Literature, Crystallographic Data Centre bibliographic and numeric files, the Union List of Scientific Periodicals (Japan), and other data bases. Computerized SDI services are available for CA Search and CA Condensates.

Other Services: In addition to the above, TOOL-IR provides research in the area of information retrieval and private file services.

Clientele/Availability: Services are available to academic personnel in Japan.

Contact: Dr. Hiroshi Ozawa, Computer Center, University of Tokyo.

★1076★
UNIVERSITY OF TOKYO
FACULTY OF ENGINEERING
DEPARTMENT OF SYNTHETIC CHEMISTRY
EROICA SYSTEM FOR BASIC PROPERTIES OF ORGANIC COMPOUNDS
7-3-1 Hongo, Bunkyo-ku Phone: 03 8122111
Tokyo 113, Japan

Special Note: No questionnaire response was received for this entry for the 6th edition. The entry is reprinted as it appeared in the 5th edition.

Staff: 3 Total.

Description of System or Service: The EROICA SYSTEM FOR BASIC PROPERTIES OF ORGANIC COMPOUNDS is a computerized system for calculating the fundamental physical properties of organic compounds. It includes both a data base and an estimation system. Covering more than 8500 compounds, the data base contains major nonspectral data on physical properties such as molecular weight, melting point, boiling point, heat of formation, latent heat, vapor heat capacity, liquid and vapor enthalpy, liquid and vapor viscosity, vapor pressure, liquid density, and second virial coefficients. In addition to numerical values, the CAS Registry Number is included for half of the substances in the system. The EROICA estimation system permits estimations for most of the compounds in the data base.

Scope and/or Subject Matter: Physical properties of compounds.

Input Sources: Data are derived from authorized tertiary documents.

Holdings and Storage Media: The EROICA data base holds machine-readable data for approximately 8500 organic compounds.

Computer-Based Products and Services: The EROICA SYSTEM is searchable online at the University of Tokyo and it will be made available for purchase in the near future. Data from it are also expected to be accessible through NIH-EPA Chemical Information System (CIS).

Remarks: In addition to the EROICA System, the Department of Synthetic Chemistry has developed and maintains the computer-based GRACE and STERIC systems. GRACE covers gas phase radical reactions for approximately 1300 compounds and STERIC handles the geometry of organic molecules and includes the coordinates of ring compounds.

Contact: Professor, Department of Synthetic Chemistry.

★1077★
UNIVERSITY OF TORONTO
FACULTY OF LIBRARY AND INFORMATION SCIENCE LIBRARY
SUBJECT ANALYSIS SYSTEMS COLLECTION (SASC)
140 St. George St. Phone: (416) 978-7060
Toronto, ON, Canada M5S 1A1 Service Est: 1924
Diane Henderson, Chief Librarian

Description of System or Service: The SUBJECT ANALYSIS SYSTEMS COLLECTION (SASC) consists of classification schemes, thesauri, and subject heading lists that provide both practical assistance for librarians selecting or designing subject schemes for their collections and a major resource for research in subject analysis and its development. Supported by computer-based author/title and subject catalogs, the COLLECTION is available to outside users for on-site reference use or through a fee-based search and loan service.

Scope and/or Subject Matter: English-language materials for the subject analysis of library collections in a broad range of subject areas, issued from the early 1900's to the present.

Holdings and Storage Media: The Collection comprises approximately 2000 titles, most of which are in monograph or typescript format, but also including pamphlets, computer printouts, and microforms. Catalog records for these are held in machine-readable form.

Publications: A printed catalog is expected to be produced from the SASC data base.

Computer-Based Products and Services: A computer-readable data base covering the Collection is maintained.

Other Services: Consultation, referrals, loans, and manual literature searching are also offered.

Clientele/Availability: Librarians are the primary users of the Collection.

Remarks: Compilers and publishers are invited to deposit copies of their English-language or bilingual (English/ Canadian French) subject classification schemes with the Collection as they are issued.

Contact: Diane Henderson, Chief Librarian, Faculty of Library and Information Science Library.

★1078★
UNIVERSITY OF TRIER
(Universitat Trier)
CENTER FOR PSYCHOLOGICAL INFORMATION AND DOCUMENTATION
(Zentralstelle fur Psychologische Information und Dokumentation - ZPID)
Postfach 3825
Schneidershof
D-5500 Trier, Fed. Rep. of Germany
Leo Montada, Head
Phone: 0651 716221
Service Est: 1972

Staff: 9 Information and library professional; 1 management professional; 1 technician; 1 sales and marketing; 4 clerical and nonprofessional.

Related Organizations: ZPID is affiliated with the German Institute for Medical Documentation and Information/ Deutsches Institut fur Medizinische Dokumentation und Information (DIMDI).

Description of System or Service: The CENTER FOR PSYCHOLOGICAL INFORMATION AND DOCUMENTATION (ZPID) is the largest psychological information and documentation center in the Federal Republic of Germany. It documents psychology literature from German-language countries and disseminates this information through abstracting and indexing and other publications and through the computer-readable PSYNDEX data base, which is commercially available online. The CENTER also provides computerized search and SDI services from international psychology-oriented data bases. Additionally, ZPID conducts ongoing research on the needs and uses of psychological information and offers consulting and referrals.

Scope and/or Subject Matter: All areas of psychology and related disciplines including psychiatry, sociology, education, physiology, criminology, linguistics, and business management.

Input Sources: Sources of input include approximately 150 German-language psychological journals as well as dissertations, technical reports, and books.

Holdings and Storage Media: The computer-readable PSYNDEX data base holds approximately 12,000 references with abstracts dating from 1977 to the present. Approximately 3500 new records are added annually.

Publications: Psychologischer Index (quarterly)—provides abstracts of psychological literature from German-language countries. 2) Bibliographie Deutschsprachiger Psychologischer Dissertationen (annual)—provides abstracts of German-language psychological dissertations.

Computer-Based Products and Services: The PSYNDEX data base, containing all information published in the Psychologischer Index and the Bibliographie, is publicly available online through DIMDI. Records in the file include bibliographic reference, classification and index terms compatible with the controlled vocabulary of PsycINFO, and a German-language abstract (with an additional English abstract for about 50 percent of the documents). ZPID provides information retrieval services from PSYNDEX, and it operates a retrieval system to provide search and SDI services from PsycINFO and Social SciSearch.

Clientele/Availability: Services are available without restrictions.

Contact: Jurgen Beling, Dipl. Psych., Center for Psychological Information and Documentation.

★1079★
UNIVERSITY OF TRONDHEIM
(Universitetet i Trondheim)
NORWEGIAN INSTITUTE OF TECHNOLOGY
(Norges Tekniske Hogskole)
UNIVERSITY LIBRARY
(Universitetsbiblioteket)
N-7034 Trondheim NTH, Norway
Knut Thalberg, Chief Librarian
Phone: 7 595110
Service Est: 1912

Staff: 38 Information and library professional; 23 clerical and nonprofessional.

Description of System or Service: In addition to serving the University community, the UNIVERSITY LIBRARY also functions as the Central Technological Library of Norway and serves Norwegian industry and the general public. Among its services are reference, referrals, loans, copying, online search and SDI services, and document delivery services, including fulfillment of requests placed through DIALOG's DIALORDER. The LIBRARY also maintains the computer-readable BIBSYS data base, which corresponds to its catalog, and a data base on trade literature known as FIRMKAT. The data bases are searched online and are used to produce microfiche products. Other functions of the LIBRARY include providing training in the utilization of scientific and technical literature; publishing bibliographies; and coordinating interlibrary work among Norwegian technological libraries.

Scope and/or Subject Matter: All aspects of the exact sciences; technology; architecture and art; trade; and other topics of interest to Norwegian industrialists.

Input Sources: Input is received in all media from numerous domestic and foreign sources.

Holdings and Storage Media: The Library consists of 840,000 bound volumes; 190,000 standards; 2.5 million patents; 25,000 items of trade literature; 240,000 reports on microfiche; and subscriptions to 9437 periodicals. Computer-readable records of Library holdings and the trade literature collection are also maintained.

Publications: 1) Scandinavian Technology Libraries' Congress Lists (4 per year); 2) Research reports (irregular); 3) Facsimilia Scientia et Technica Norwegica.

Microform Products and Services: The Library makes the following available on microfiche: 1) BIBSYS, the library catalog; 2) FIRMKAT, which covers trade literature; and 3) Periodicals in the Library of the Norwegian Institute of Technology. Microreproduction services are also available.

Computer-Based Products and Services: The UNIVERSITY LIBRARY maintains the BIBSYS catalog and FIRMKAT trade literature data bases online. It also conducts retrospective searches utilizing data bases made available by ESA/IRS, DIALOG Information Services, Inc.; System Development Corporation (SDC), Scannet, INKA (Informationssystem Karlsruhe), Telesystemes Questel, Pergamon InfoLine Ltd., and others. SDI services from data bases in technology and science are processed by the Royal Institute of Technology Library (RITL), Stockholm, Sweden, and are available to Norwegian clientele through the Library.

Other Services: In addition to services described above, the Library offers consulting, research, and manual literature searching.

Clientele/Availability: Services are generally available without restrictions.

Contact: Knut Thalberg, Chief Librarian, University Library. (Telex 55186 NTHHB N.)

★1080★
UNIVERSITY OF TSUKUBA
SCIENCE INFORMATION PROCESSING CENTER
1-1-1 Tennodai
Sakura-mura, Niihari-gun
Ibaraki-ken, Japan 305
Kazuhiko Nakayama, Managing Director
Phone: 0298 532451
Service Est: 1978

Staff: 4 Information and library professional; 1 management professional; 11 technicians; 1 sales and marketing; 9 clerical and nonprofessional.

Description of System or Service: The main functions of the SCIENTIFIC INFORMATION PROCESSING CENTER are to manage and maintain computer systems; to provide assistance and support to those using computer services for education, research, and other information processing activities; and to develop and service scientific information systems. The CENTER operates the online UTOPIA (University of Tsukuba Online Processing of Information) information retrieval system, providing remote terminal access to 26 commercially available data bases, as well as the online TULIPS (Tsukuba University Library Information Processing System) service. Additionally, the CENTER maintains a computer-readable data base covering available data bases, issues a KWIC index in microform to Japan MARC, and provides training to librarians in computerized information handling.

Scope and/or Subject Matter: Computing services and information retrieval for research, education, science, and administration.

Input Sources: Most data bases and software are obtained from commercial and government sources.

Holdings and Storage Media: The Center maintains computer files holding more than 400,000 book title records. The UTOPIA system stores 26 data bases comprising more than 20 million records.

Publications: 1) Center News; 2) UTOPIA User's Guide.

Microform Products and Services: A KWIC index to Japan MARC is produced in microform.

Computer-Based Products and Services: Using the UTOPIA data base management and retrieval software, the SCIENCE INFORMATION PROCESSING CENTER provides remote terminal online access to the following data bases: 1) Arts & Humanities Citation Index; 2) Biological Abstracts; 3) BIOSIS Previews; 4) CAB Abstracts; 5) CANCERLIT; 6) CANCERNET; 7) Cancer Research Projects (CANPROJ); 8) Comprehensive Dissertation Index; 9) CIJE; 10) Clinical Protocols (CLINPROT); 11) COMPENDEX; 12) Database of Databases (DBDB)—produced by TICIPS and holding 700 records; 13) Energyline; 14) Enviroline; 15) Excerpta Medica; 16) INSPEC; 17) International Pharmaceutical Abstracts; 18) Japan MARC; 19) LC MARC; 20) LISA; 21) Psychological Abstracts; 22) Pollution Abstracts; 23) RIE; 24) Science Citation Index: 25) Social Science Citation Index; 26) UK MARC. The TULIPS (Tsukuba University Library Information Processing System) is also accessible online through the CENTER.

Clientele/Availability: The Center serves the academic and research communities of the University of Tsukuba, including faculty, students, and staff, and researchers of other institutions.

Contact: Kazuhiko Nakayama, Managing Director, Science Information Processing Center. (Telex 3652580.)

★1081★
UNIVERSITY OF UMEA
(Umea Universitet)
DEMOGRAPHIC DATA BASE
(Demografiska Databasen)

S-901 87 Umea, Sweden
Prof. Jan Sundin, Managing Director

Phone: 090 165723
Service Est: 1973

Staff: 2 Information and library professional; 11 management professional; 10 technicians; 7 sales and marketing; 36 clerical and nonprofessional.

Description of System or Service: The DEMOGRAPHIC DATA BASE collects, registers, and computerizes historical demographic and social data on individuals listed in 19th century Swedish church records. Established for research, educational, and archival purposes, the data base is also designed to encourage scientific collaboration using the data and, where suitable, to develop methodology. Historically, church registers have been kept by Swedish priests since the 17th century to record information about all individuals in their parishes. The DEMOGRAPHIC DATA BASE presents the information as it appears in the church registers and provides a complete biography on each individual listed. The system facilitates cross-sectional studies of the whole population as well as longitudinal analyses of demographic changes. The DATA BASE is used to provide information retrieval and magnetic tape distribution services to researchers and to generate reports and other publications. It is also available online for limited use.

Scope and/or Subject Matter: Demography, history, historical geography, church history, educational history, and other subjects that use 19th century Swedish population registers as a base.

Input Sources: Input is collected from 19th century catechetical examination records and other church records, including records of migrations, births and baptisms, marriages, and deaths and burials.

Holdings and Storage Media: The machine-readable Demographic Data Base contains information on approximately 70,000 individuals in seven Swedish parishes and includes 300,000 items of information. The data base covers the time period from 1800 to 1895 continuously.

Publications: The Demographic Data Base is used to issue a variety of monographs and reports.

Computer-Based Products and Services: The DEMOGRAPHIC DATA BASE is available on magnetic tape and is accessible online on a limited basis to researchers. The DATA BASE consists of a source system and an event system as well as a number of special files. The source files consist of a file for each type of source, including a parish catechetical examination file, register of births, register of deaths, register of marriages, and register of migration. Annotations and causes of deaths are separated from other data and stored in special files. The main functions of the source files are to reconstruct the sources in their original form; to create biographies of the individuals to be found in the sources; and to make possible family reconstitution by storing links between individuals. The event file contains adapted data of individuals made on the basis of the source files. The selection of variables which are included in a complete biography represent identity data, demographic events, and the status of the individual in different respects and at different points in time. Identity information includes birth data, name(s), legitimate or illegitimate birth, and twinship. Demographic events data include date of birth, death, marriage ceremony, change of residence within parish or across parish border, and previous and later domicile. Information on status at given points of time includes trade (profession), social status, civil status, residence, and position in family or household. The file also indicates relations to other individuals (parents, spouse, children) and information on the sources.

Other Services: The University of Umea also maintains a research department supporting researchers who use the data base and provides conferencing arrangements and data collection.

Clientele/Availability: Services are available to researchers from universities in Sweden and elsewhere.

Contact: Christina Danell, Demographic Data Base; telephone 090 165957.

★1082★
UNIVERSITY OF VALENCIA
(Universidad de Valencia)
BIOMEDICAL DOCUMENTATION AND INFORMATION CENTER
(Centro de Documentacion e Informatica Biomedica)
Avda. Blasco Ibanez, 17
Valencia 10, Spain
Prof. Maria-Luz Terrada Ferrandis, Director

Phone: 96 3610373
Service Est: 1960

Staff: 20 Information and library professional; 11 technicians; 4 clerical and nonprofessional; 2 other.

Related Organizations: Organizations supporting the Center include the Caja de Ahorros de Valencia and the Consejo Superior de Investigaciones Cientificas (CSIC).

Description of System or Service: The BIOMEDICAL DOCUMENTATION AND INFORMATION CENTER provides medical information services and systems on national and international levels. A primary activity is production of the Spanish medical index, Indice Medico Espanol (IME), which is available in hardcopy and machine-readable forms. The CENTER also produces other computer-based indexes, conducts online searching of international medical data bases, trains information users, maintains a research library, and offers SDI and photocopying. Additionally, the CENTER contributes a selection of Spanish works on medicine for inclusion in the PASCAL system and collaborates with a Spanish pediatrics association in compiling and maintaining a computerized registry of pediatric cancer cases in Spain. The CENTER is also involved in the analysis of medical and scientific activities in Valencia, the study of medical terminology in relation to scientific information systems, and new applications of computers to the problems of biomedical information.

Scope and/or Subject Matter: Biomedicine, medicine, biological sciences, agronomy, and related scientific, technical, and social areas.

Input Sources: The Center scans and indexes approximately 200 Spanish journals for input to its publications and data bases. It accesses international online services for its search services.

Holdings and Storage Media: Machine-readable holdings include the Spanish medical index (IME) data base containing about 100,000 citations, the Valencian scientific index (ICV) data base, the cancer registry, and other data bases. The Center's library includes 6500 bound volumes and subscriptions to 320 periodicals.

Publications: 1) Indice Medico Espanol-IME (trimestrial)—Spanish medical index; contains title pages of medical periodicals published in Spain, with subject and author indexes. 2) Suplemento Internacional del Indice Medico Espanol—international supplement to IME; covers Spanish medical works published in foreign countries. 3) Indice Cientifico Valenciano-ICV (biennial)—Valencian science index; covers all areas of science, medicine, and technology. 4) Cuadernos de Documentacion e Informatica Biomedica—covers biomedical books. The Center also collaborates in the publication of a Spanish review of scientific documentation called the Revista Espanola de Documentacion Cientifica and issues occasional monographs.

Computer-Based Products and Services: The CENTER conducts computerized literature searches from its Spanish medical index (IME) and Valencian science (ICV) data bases, and from data bases offered by DIALOG Information Services, Inc., System Development Corporation (SDC), U.S. National Library of Medicine, and ESA/IRS. In addition to its search services, the CENTER has developed an integrated hospital information system that supports storage and analysis of clinical documents to assist hospitals in providing patient care, performing research, and teaching.

Clientele/Availability: Products and services are intended for biomedical professionals.

Contact: Prof. Maria-Luz Terrada Ferrandis, Director, Biomedical Documentation and Information Center.

★1083★
UNIVERSITY OF WARWICK LIBRARY
WARWICK STATISTICS SERVICE
Gibbet Hill Rd. Phone: 0203 418938
Coventry CV4 7AL, England Service Est: 1971
David Mort, Manager

Staff: 2 Information and library professional; 1 sales and marketing; 2 clerical and nonprofessional.

Description of System or Service: The WARWICK STATISTICS SERVICE is an information service for commercial and market statistics that is based on one of the United Kingdom's leading collections of statistics. Available on a subscription or a single-usage basis, the SERVICE includes the following components: an Enquiry Service for statistics on countries, markets, industries, companies, and other areas; Research and Analyses, including statistical analyses or prepared desk research reports; Personal Access, allowing clients to use the collection in person; Alerting Service for updating statistical series to client specifications; and a monthly newsletter. The SERVICE also maintains online access to commercially available data bases.

Scope and/or Subject Matter: Statistical information on international trade, economics, countries, production, employment, demographics, and markets; company information on U.K. and major international firms; literature on management and marketing.

Input Sources: The Service collects major international official statistics, national official statistics of 120 countries, quasi-official and trade association statistics, published market research, business press items, general international directories, and business and management indexes and abstracts.

Holdings and Storage Media: The statistics collection numbers 10,000 titles, including 3000 current statistics serials. The Service also has access to the University Library's large business and economics collection, which includes more than 4000 periodical subscriptions.

Publications: Market and Statistics News (monthly)—newsletter containing articles on business information sources, news items, and an accessions list; available free of charge to Service subscribers and to nonmembers by purchase. Occasional marketing reviews on particular countries or industries are also produced.

Computer-Based Products and Services: The Service conducts searches of data bases made available through System Development Corporation (SDC) and DIALOG Information Services, Inc.

Other Services: Additional services include consulting and referrals, manual literature searching, and photocopying.

Clientele/Availability: Services are available by subscription or by single-usage arrangement.

Contact: David Mort, Manager, Warwick Statistics Service. (Telex 31406.)

★1084★
UNIVERSITY OF WATERLOO
DEPARTMENT OF RECREATION
LEISURE STUDIES DATA BANK
2026 Administrative Services Bldg. Phone: (519) 885-1211
Waterloo, ON, Canada N2L 3G1 Service Est: 1973
Dr. E.M. Avedon, Director

Staff: 1.5 Management professional; 1 technician; 1 clerical and nonprofessional.

Related Organizations: The Leisure Studies Data Bank is affiliated with several national and international social science data organizations.

Description of System or Service: The LEISURE STUDIES DATA BANK collects and archives machine-readable data relating to leisure research and makes them available to students and researchers for reference and reanalysis purposes. In addition to providing data sets and computer facilities, the DATA BANK offers a variety of associated services, including the following: statistical analyses and review of data; cleaning, editing, and documenting of data; instrument construction; interpretation; report writing and photocopying; and research design construction.

Scope and/or Subject Matter: Data relating to leisure, tourism, sport, fitness, outdoor recreation, time use and related topics.

Input Sources: Data are acquired from researchers worldwide, and from other private and public sources.

Holdings and Storage Media: More than 100 machine-readable data sets are maintained, along with supplementary documentation.

Publications: Leisure Studies Data Bank Catalogue of Holdings—references each data file under a number of headings, including title, date of study, principal investigator, population studied, number of variables, sample size, abstract.

Computer-Based Products and Services: DATA BANK holdings can be accessed online or in a batch mode through the University of Waterloo Department of Computer Sciences and Datapac. Cleaned and edited data sets can also be supplied on magnetic tape for use on other installations. DATA BANK staff can provide a variety of interpretation and analysis services.

Clientele/Availability: Services are available without restrictions on a cost-recovery basis.

Contact: Mr. Terry Stewart, Associate Director, Leisure Studies Data Bank.

★1085★
UNIVERSITY OF WATERLOO
FACULTY OF HUMAN KINETICS AND LEISURE STUDIES
INFORMATION RETRIEVAL SYSTEM FOR THE SOCIOLOGY OF LEISURE AND SPORT (SIRLS)

Waterloo, ON, Canada N2L 3G1
Betty Smith, Database Manager
Phone: (519) 885-1211
Service Est: 1972

Staff: 1 Information and library professional; 1 technician; 1 clerical and nonprofessional.

Description of System or Service: The INFORMATION RETRIEVAL SYSTEM FOR THE SOCIOLOGY OF LEISURE AND SPORT (SIRLS) is a computerized information system and documentation center covering the relevant social science literature. It is used to produce a journal, Sociology of Leisure & Sport Abstracts, and to provide search services. It is also accessible online. Document duplication services in paper copy or microfiche are provided for most articles cited.

Scope and/or Subject Matter: Social sciences relating to sports and leisure, including sociology, psychology, social psychology, history, philosophy, economics, and anthropology.

Input Sources: Input is derived from English and foreign-language journals, conference papers, theses, government documents, unpublished papers, and secondary sources.

Holdings and Storage Media: The computer-readable SIRLS data base holds abstracted references to approximately 13,000 documents; copies of more than 10,000 of these are held in the documentation center. Approximately 1000 documents are added annually to the System.

Publications: 1) Sociology of Leisure & Sport Abstracts (3 per year)—provides a review of international social science literature pertaining to leisure activities. Abstracts are arranged by entry number and indexed by subject and author. Published by and available by subscription from Elsevier Scientific Publishing Company, P.O. Box 211, NL-1000 AE Amsterdam, Netherlands. 2) SIRLS Descriptor List & Thesaurus. 3) SIRLS User's Manual.

Microform Products and Services: Most documents contained in the SIRLS system are available on microfiche.

Computer-Based Products and Services: The SIRLS data base is accessible online with SPIRES search software through the University of Waterloo. Searches are also performed by SIRLS staff for clients without access to a terminal. Records in the SIRLS data base include the following data elements: author, title, complete bibliographic citation, abstract, descriptors, and document number.

Other Services: SIRLS also maintains a reading room that is open to the public. Photocopies of most documents covered by SIRLS are available on a fee basis.

Clientele/Availability: There are no restrictions on services.

Projected Publications and Services: SIRLS plans to offer selected full documents online in the future.

Contact: Betty Smith, Database Manager and Consultant, SIRLS. (Telex 069 55259.)

★1086★
UNIVERSITY OF WESTERN ONTARIO
SCHOOL OF LIBRARY AND INFORMATION SCIENCE
NESTED PHRASE INDEXING SYSTEM (NEPHIS)

London, ON, Canada N6G 1H1
Timothy C. Craven, Associate Professor
Phone: (519) 679-3542
Service Est: 1975

Description of System or Service: The NESTED PHRASE INDEXING SYSTEM (NEPHIS) is a software system for computer-assisted permuted subject indexing. Using NEPHIS, the indexer supplies the computer with a string of index terms and additional tags to represent a subject. The system then manipulates the string to produce a set of permuted subject entries, each of which is a complete representation of the original subject. NEPHIS is available for installation on in-house computer facilities.

Scope and/or Subject Matter: Permuted subject indexing.

Holdings and Storage Media: Under NEPHIS software, the School of Library and Information Science maintains machine-readable indexes to the Journal of the American Society for Information Science, 1974-1975, publications of the Canadian Department of Energy, Mines and Resources through April 1978, and French and English indexes to the Canadian Journal of Information Science, 1976-1980.

Publications: String Indexing: NEPHIS.

Computer-Based Products and Services: Copies of NEPHIS software are available in MACRO-10, DECsystem10 FORTRAN, Cyber73 FORTRAN, DECsystem10 BASIC, PET2001 BASIC, or DPL. Advice is supplied on problems encountered in implementing the system.

Clientele/Availability: NEPHIS is offered to interested individuals and organizations.

Contact: Timothy C. Craven, Associate Professor, School of Library and Information Science.

★1087★
UNIVERSITY OF WESTERN ONTARIO
SOCIAL SCIENCE COMPUTING LABORATORY (SSCL)
INFORMATION SYSTEMS PROGRAMME

London, ON, Canada N6A 5C2
Dr. Edward H. Hanis, Director
Phone: (519) 679-6378

Description of System or Service: The INFORMATION SYSTEMS PROGRAMME acquires, maintains, and supports the use of social science data and analysis software for research and instruction in the Social Science Computing Laboratory. It develops and maintains numeric and textual information systems including the Canadian Register of Research and Researchers in the Social Sciences, a data base covering Canadian social science research projects, investigators, and publications. Selected information from the Register is available online through CAN/OLE as the CANREGISTER data base. The PROGRAMME also maintains a data resources library containing codebooks and guides for machine-readable resources, and a data archive and program library containing specialized analysis software and research files. Additionally, the PROGRAMME provides direct access to the Canadian Socio-Economic Information Management System (CANSIM) and provides search results in printed or machine-readable form.

Scope and/or Subject Matter: Social sciences research and data.

Input Sources: The Programme acquires data through the Interuniversity Consortium for Political and Social Research (ICPSR), Canadian and U.S. governments, and other sources. Input for the research register is gathered from questionnaires completed by Canadian social scientists in government, industry, and education.

Holdings and Storage Media: The Programme maintains a data archive and program library of machine-readable research files and specialized analytical software, as well as a data resources library of printed documentation. The machine-readable research register holds information on 8000 social scientists, 5000 research projects, and 30,000 publications.

Publications: SSCL Newsletter (twice per year)—free to the University of Western Ontario community; available by request to others.

Computer-Based Products and Services: The INFORMATION SYSTEMS PROGRAMME provides data analysis and development services, searches of the CANSIM data base, and maintenance of the computer-readable Canadian Register of Research and Researchers in the Social Sciences. Covering research in all social science fields, including interdisciplinary areas such as Canadian and environmental studies, the Register provides four principal categories of information: biographical information; professional qualifications and specialization; current research, including project title, principal investigator and associates, geographic focus, and funding; and selected publications, including forthcoming publications, significant reports, and white papers not included in standard bibliographic sources. Nonproprietary information from the Register is used to compile CANREGISTER, which is commercially available online through CAN/OLE.

Other Services: The Social Science Computing Laboratory also provides instructional services, research support, research design and analysis, custom software design and programming, word processing, and data entry services.

Clientele/Availability: Services are available without restrictions.

Contact: Slavko Manojlovich, Data Resources Librarian, Social Science Computing Laboratory.

★1088★
UNIVERSITY OF WESTERN ONTARIO
SYSTEMS ANALYSIS, CONTROL AND DESIGN ACTIVITY (SACDA)
Engineering Science Bldg.
London, ON, Canada N6A 5B9
Cecil F. Shewchuk, Director
Phone: (519) 679-6570
Service Est: 1973

Special Note: The above name, address, and telephone number have been verified for this edition, although no questionnaire response was received. The following text is reprinted from the 5th edition.

Staff: 6 Technicians; 1 clerical and nonprofessional; 1 other.

Description of System or Service: The SYSTEMS ANALYSIS, CONTROL AND DESIGN ACTIVITY (SACDA) is a group of professionals specializing in the areas of engineering modeling, simulation, and analysis for the processing industries. The basis of SACDA's services are computer programs it has developed or acquired from external sources. Many of these programs are made accessible throughout the world via time-sharing networks, and on magnetic tapes, cards, or other machine-readable form. Among the programs available are the Comprehensive Industrial Materials Property Package (CIMPP) and MADCAP, both of which are supported by a data bank of more than 30 materials properties. SACDA also can provide a number of user interfaces; produce a model of the process used by an individual company which can be mounted in a computer file accessible via time-sharing; develop a custom program on a proprietary basis; and produce a program to facilitate data input.

Scope and/or Subject Matter: Physical and thermodynamic properties of materials, particularly of chemicals and petrochemicals; process engineering.

Input Sources: Data are extracted from books and handbooks on prediction and estimation of properties, and from major technical journals and periodicals.

Holdings and Storage Media: The SACDA materials properties data bank features over 300 Fortran subroutines, correlations for more than 300 species, and data for more than 30 properties.

Publications: SACDA provides complete documentation for all its programs; updates are issued as changes occur.

Computer-Based Products and Services: SACDA makes available several process engineering programs via the Datapac, Telenet, and Tymnet telecommunications networks. Programs are also supplied to clients on magnetic tapes, cards, and other forms suitable for mounting on mainframes and minicomputers. Two of SACDA's programs, CIMPP and MADCAP, use a data bank of properties data to produce physical property and thermodynamic calculations. Results obtained from calculations can be printed in tabular form, plotted, or transferred internally to other computer systems.

Other Services: In addition to services described above, SACDA offers training sessions and telephone consulting.

Clientele/Availability: Clients include the chemical, mining, petroleum, and pulp and paper industries, and consulting engineers and equipment manufacturers serving those industries.

Contact: Cecil F. Shewchuck, Director, Systems Analysis, Control and Design Activity.

★1089★
UNWIN BROTHERS LTD.
Gresham Press
Old Woking, Surrey, England
John Quinney, Head
Phone: (not reported)

Staff: 250 Total, including 12 management professional; 9 technicians; 12 sales and marketing.

Related Organizations: The parent organization is the Martins Printing Group.

Description of System or Service: UNWIN BROTHERS LTD. creates data bases for subsequent typesetting and printing. The firm also provides updating of data bases and interfacing into other electronic media.

Scope and/or Subject Matter: Electronic publishing and printing of directories and other materials.

Input Sources: Information on magnetic tape and floppy disk is converted and processed.

Computer-Based Products and Services: The firm provides data base creation, conversion, typesetting, and related services.

Clientele/Availability: Services are intended for publishers.

Contact: Mr. R. Joseph, Marketing Director, Unwin Brothers Ltd.

★1090★
UPDATE AB
P.O. Box 53120
S-400 15 Gothenburg, Sweden
Ronny Korsberg
Phone: 031 178390
Founded: 1981

Description of System or Service: UPDATE AB is an information broker providing manual and online retrieval of market information for clients in business and government in Sweden. UPDATE AB also provides market surveys, market analyses, desk research, SDI, and document delivery services. Research results are analyzed and documented in written reports.

Scope and/or Subject Matter: Business and market information.

Input Sources: Information is obtained from commercially available data bases and other sources.

Computer-Based Products and Services: UPDATE AB offers computerized information retrieval and SDI services from approximately 400 online market data bases.

Other Services: Consulting services and training in online information retrieval are also offered.

Clientele/Availability: Update AB serves major industries, advertising agencies, organizations, and government agencies in Sweden. The firm also provides assistance to foreign companies interested in Scandinavian market information and information brokers requiring a Scandinavian contact.

Contact: Ronny Korsberg or Maria Vahlgren Wall, Update AB.

★1091★
URBAMET NETWORK
(Reseau URBAMET)
IAURIF
21-23, rue Miollis
F-75732 Paris Cedex 15, France
Phone: 01 5675503

Related Organizations: Four central coordinating bodies promote URBAMET: Agence Cooperation et Amenagement, Paris; Centre d'Etudes Techniques de l'Equipement Nord-Picardie/ Docamenor, Lille; Institut d'Amenagement et d'Urbanisme de la Region d'Ile-de-France (IAURIF), Paris; and Service Technique de l'Urbanisme Centre de Documentation sur l'Urbanisme, Paris.

Description of System or Service: The URBAMET NETWORK is a collaborative documentation network of more than 40 specialized French information centers concerned with city and regional planning and related topics. The NETWORK prepares abstracts and indexes of worldwide journal literature, government and research documents, audiovisual materials, and other items. It publishes this information in a series of bibliographic bulletins and also maintains a corresponding data base that is commercially available online. Additionally, the NETWORK provides document delivery services for cited materials.

Scope and/or Subject Matter: Scientific, technical, economic, and legal information relating to: urban, regional, and land planning and management; housing and architecture; environment, ecology, and landscape; transportation and traffic; environmental protection. Geographic coverage includes France, Northwest Europe, developing countries, and large cities worldwide.

Input Sources: Input is derived from 750 periodicals and from books, reports, documents, photographs, maps, slides, and films.

Holdings and Storage Media: The computer-readable URBAMET data base contains 60,000 document citations and 19,000 audiovisual citations dating from 1976 to the present. The data base is updated monthly, with about 10,000 items added annually.

Publications: The following bibliographic bulletins are issued: 1) Reference; 2) Reference Ile de France; 3) Cahiers de Documentation; 4) Bulletin inter Villes Nouvelles.

Microform Products and Services: Index et Catalogues URBAMET is available on COM to members.

Computer-Based Products and Services: The URBAMET data base is accessible online through Telesystemes Questel. Searchable fields include title, abstract, corporate source, author, subject descriptor, publication date, document type, document location, media, citation number, and others. SDI services from the data base are available by subscription.

Other Services: Original documents are available on a fee basis from cooperating institutions.

Clientele/Availability: Clients include architects, town planners, local authorities, information officers, librarians, journalists, teachers, and others.

Remarks: URBAMET is an acronym for Urbanisme, Amenagement, Environnement et Transports.

Contact: Michel Henry, Director, Communication-Information-Documentation Division, Institute for Management and Planning in the Paris Region. (Telex 204824 F SREDESR.)

★1092★
USACO CORPORATION
13-12 Shimbashi Phone: 03 5026471
1-Chome, Minato-ku Founded: 1952
Tokyo 105, Japan
Mr. Takashi Yamakawa, President

Staff: 10 Information and library professional; 6 management professional; 6 technicians; 26 sales and marketing; 27 clerical and nonprofessional.

Description of System or Service: The USACO CORPORATION is an agent in Japan representing United States information and publishing companies. Its activities include overseas subscription sales, commercially available data bases sales, support and consultation on microfilming, and information systems design.

Scope and/or Subject Matter: Information services and publications in all subject areas.

Computer-Based Products and Services: USACO offers data bases for sale and provides search and SDI services from major scientific and technical data bases.

Clientele/Availability: Services are available to clients in Japan.

Projected Publications and Services: Planned publications include a manual of available machine-readable files and a micrographics directory.

Remarks: The USACO Corporation was formerly known as U.S.-Asiatic Co., Ltd.

Contact: Mr. Takashi Yamakawa, President, USACO Corporation.

★1093★
USERLINK SYSTEMS LTD.
Mansion House Chambers Phone: 061 4298232
22A High St. Founded: 1980
Stockport, Ches. SK1 1EG, England
Dr. Philip W. Williams, Director

Staff: 2 Management professional; 4 technicians; 2 sales and marketing; 2 clerical and nonprofessional.

Description of System or Service: USERLINK SYSTEMS LTD. is involved in the development and sale of user friendly communications programs to make online access simpler and less expensive using microcomputers. It also develops microcomputer based equipment that facilitates online access using dumb terminals. Additionally, USERLINK provides consultancy on all aspects of online access and offers customized solutions to hardware and software problems in fields relating to computerized searching.

Scope and/or Subject Matter: Microcomputer programs and equipment for online information retrieval, time-sharing systems, online data entry, electronic mail, library cataloging, online book ordering, videotex access, and related applications.

Computer-Based Products and Services: USERLINK products include a complete integrated terminal, a terminal attachment for use with existing terminals and modems, and a portable briefcase terminal. USERLINK also offers the ASSIST intelligent communication programs for use with Z80 CP/M microcomputers. ASSIST features include the following: fully automatic log-on using one command; full speed transmission of stored text using one keystroke per line; retention of text and messages for reuse; word processing facilities; direct and immediate access to the remote computer at all times; and automatic transmission of complete blocks of text to the remote computer.

Other Services: Userlink Systems Ltd. also offers consultation and educational courses.

Clientele/Availability: Clients include users of all online services.

Remarks: The firm was formerly known as Williams and Nevin.

Contact: Dr. Philip W. Williams, Director, or Helen B. Williams, Userlink Systems Ltd.

★1094★
UTLAS INC.
80 Bloor St. W., 2nd Floor Phone: (416) 923-0890
Toronto, ON, Canada M5S 2V1 Founded: 1971
Arthur D. Parker, President & Chief Executive Officer

Staff: 26 Information and library professional; 19 management professional; 64 technicians; 4 sales and marketing; 55 clerical and nonprofessional.

Related Organizations: UTLAS Inc. is a wholly owned subsidiary of the University of Toronto.

Description of System or Service: Formerly known as the University of Toronto Library Automation Systems, UTLAS INC. is a bilingual bibliographic utility supplying computer-based systems, services, and products to library clients worldwide. Services are based on the Catalogue Support System (CATSS), which provides libraries with online access to a large data base of bibliographic and authority records. Other UTLAS services include a resource-sharing data inquiry system, a fully integrated acquisitions control system, an online authority control system, an automated library acquisitions system, and service unit for catalog conversion and data base creation projects. UTLAS annually generates more than 10 million catalog cards and other products for over 1800 catalogs in some 600 libraries on six continents.

Scope and/or Subject Matter: Automated cataloging with authority control and acquisition of monographs, serials, audiovisuals, microforms, rare books, maps, music and sound recordings, manuscripts, machine-readable data files, and other library materials.

Input Sources: Input to CATSS is derived from U.S. Library of Congress (LC) MARC tapes, National Library of Canada MARC tapes, Bibliotheque Nationale du Quebec MARC tapes, British Library MARC tapes, INTERMARC tapes, the U.S. National Library of Medicine, U.S. Government Printing Office, Canadian Institute for Historical Microreproductions, plus records of client libraries.

Holdings and Storage Media: The CATSS data base contains more than 22 million records, including 5.4 million MARC records; 19.7 million records held in client files; and 2.3 million authority records. The entire data base is held online.

Publications: 1) Newsletter (monthly). 2) CATSS News (irregular)—technical newsletter. Full documentation on products and services, including coding manuals, and a system manual, are also provided.

Microform Products and Services: COM catalogs are produced for more than 100 client libraries.

Computer-Based Products and Services: UTLAS INC. offers the following networked or local computer-based systems, services, and products for libraries:

1) CATSS—provides libraries with online access to a large data base

of bibliographic and authority records and permits original, derived, or shared cataloging. Additional features include online preorder searching; ordering from vendors; monitoring of orders, claims, and cancellations; and an electronic messaging facility. Encompasses client-owned bibliographic files shared among a network of more than 275 institutions, which are searchable by bibliographic identification number or by text. Client records can be used to produce catalog cards, COM and printed catalogs, acquisitions lists, spine and book pocket labels, magnetic tapes, and printed or COM KWIC indexes.

2) REFCATSS—public service support system providing interlibrary loan search facilities to verify requests and identify locations in one search, and interlibrary loan request capabilities, allowing the client to transmit requests through the electronic message facility and check on the availability of material requested. REFCATSS can also be used as an online supplement to the client's catalog, to trace on-order items, and to search for recent additions to the collection, as well as to prepare individualized bibliographies.

3) ACCORD (Acquisitions par CATSS/ CATSS Ordering)—online acquisitions control system enabling the client to interfile flagged order records with client permanent holdings and create purchase orders, claims, and cancellations. Features include preorder searching on the CATSS data base, interface with the library's cataloging operations, facility for ordering from any publisher or vendor, and local control over printing, scheduling, quality and format of purchase orders, claims, and cancellations.

4) Online Authority Control System—fully integrated authority control facility enabling the client to create and maintain authorized forms of names, uniform titles, series, and subject headings. Allows online searching when establishing headings and automatically checks the client's bibliographic records against existing authority files at the time of input. Interacts with the CATSS bibliographic system to produce a full cross-reference structure on COM and printed book catalogs.

5) INNOVACQ—automated library acquisitions system providing a range of acquisitions functions, including those necessary to order items, maintain order records, manage fund accounting, and evaluate vendors. Available as a microcomputer-based system or fully integrated with the ACCORD ordering system and the UTLAS data base.

6) CATSSERVICES—service unit of specially trained operators who will carry out catalog conversion or data base creation projects for large or small collections. Working from shelf list cards, the CATSSERVICES staff search the UTLAS data base, make copies of records that match the shelf list cards, and add local call number and holdings information. If no match is found, the staff will create an original MARC record based on the shelf list card information. Both derived and original records become part of a data base from which catalog products such as cards, printed and microform catalogs, or a MARC-formatted tape can be generated.

Other Services: In addition to the services described above, UTLAS provides training, consulting, and specialized retrospective conversion.

Clientele/Availability: Products and services are available to any library or library services center.

Contact: Harriet Velazquez, Vice-President, Marketing, or Wyley L. Powell, Public Relations, UTLAS Inc. (Telex 065 24479.)

V

★1095★
VAN HALM (JOHAN) & ASSOCIATES
P.O. Box 688
NL-3800 AR Amersfoort, Netherlands
Johan van Halm, Director
Phone: 033 18024
Founded: 1976

Description of System or Service: JOHAN VAN HALM & ASSOCIATES provides consultancy and related services to data base producers and vendors, telecommunication services, document delivery suppliers, government information agencies, and professional associations in the field. The firm offers investigations and research projects in the area of information services and products, including data gathering and synthesizing, reporting of new developments, and determining and analyzing the information needs of various target groups. Additionally, the ASSOCIATES designs, establishes, and manages projects involving information marketing, data base and secondary information products, and business information. Other services offered include the following: organization of joint ventures and other cooperative schemes between companies and institutions; temporary representations at exhibitions and conferences; teaching and seminar management; advice on recruitment of information professionals; organization of libraries, archives, and information services; development of information policies; and literature searching and document delivery.

Scope and/or Subject Matter: Information and library systems, services, and products in all subject areas.

Computer-Based Products and Services: The firm maintains a computer-readable data base comprising names and addresses of librarians, information professionals, and information managers.

Clientele/Availability: Clients include the information industry, libraries, government agencies, associations, and end users.

Contact: Johan van Halm, Director, Johan van Halm & Associates.

★1096★
VDI-VERLAG GMBH
VDI NEWS DATA BASE
Graf-Recke-Str. 84
D-4000 Dusseldorf 1, Fed. Rep. of
   Germany
Phone: 0211 62141
Service Est: 1983

Related Organizations: VDI-Verlag GmbH is associated with the Association of German Engineers/ Verein Deutscher Ingenieure (VDI), located at the same address.

Description of System or Service: The VDI NEWS DATA BASE is the online full-text version of the weekly journal VDI-Nachrichten, which covers engineering-related economics, science, and technology.

Scope and/or Subject Matter: Economic, scientific, and technical aspects of engineering, including agricultural, automotive, electrical, mechanical, and production engineering. Also technology related to construction, design, energy, materials, plastics, propulsion, and textiles.

Input Sources: The Data Base contains the contributions of the editorial staff of VDI-Nachrichten.

Holdings and Storage Media: The online VDI News Data Base holds more than 3000 full-text articles dating from 1983 to the present; the Data Base is updated with 80 new articles weekly.

Publications: VDI-Nachrichten/ VDI News (weekly).

Computer-Based Products and Services: The VDI NEWS DATA BASE is searchable online through FIZ Technik. All text terms in the articles may be used for searching; the DATA BASE does not contain figures, tables, or advertisements. Data elements present include the article number, publication date, issue number, page number, author, article title and subtitle, and full text of article.

Clientele/Availability: Services are available on a fee basis.

Contact: VDI-Verlag GmbH. (Telex 08 586 525.)

★1097★
VEANER (ALLEN B.) ASSOCIATES
45 Inglewood Dr.
Toronto, ON, Canada M4T 1G9
Allen B. Veaner, Principal
Phone: (416) 486-0239
Founded: 1983

Description of System or Service: ALLEN B. VEANER ASSOCIATES provides public and private sector clients with consulting services in computerized library networking, word processing and microcomputers, microform applications in libraries, and in the areas of library personnel, administration, organization, and management. The firm also conducts orientation and training programs in implementing advanced technologies.

Scope and/or Subject Matter: Library and information science and technology.

Clientele/Availability: Services are available without restrictions; primary clients are in education, government, and industry.

Contact: Allen B. Veaner, Principal.

★1098★
VERLAG HOPPENSTEDT & CO.
EK-MRA DATA BASE
Havelstr. 9
D-6100 Darmstadt 1, Fed. Rep. of
   Germany
Phone: 06151 3801

Description of System or Service: The EK-MRA DATA BASE is a commercially available online version of the purchase guide Messtechnik, Regelungstechnik, Automatik issued by Verlag Hoppenstedt. It contains addresses and product specifications of manufacturers of measurement, control, and automation equipment in the Federal Republic of Germany, Austria, and Switzerland.

Scope and/or Subject Matter: Manufacturers of equipment for measurement, control, and automation.

Input Sources: Input for the Data Base is derived from the printed publication.

Holdings and Storage Media: The machine-readable EK-MRA Data Base holds addresses and product information for approximately 1900 manufacturers and is revised every two years.

Publications: Messtechnik, Regelungstechnik, Automatik/ Measurement, Control, Automation.

Computer-Based Products and Services: The EK-MRA DATA BASE is searchable online through FIZ Technik. Data elements present include document number, manufacturer name and address, product specification, subject index terms, and product classifications.

Clientele/Availability: Services are available on a fee basis.

Remarks: Verlag Hoppenstedt also publishes the Handbuch der Grossunternehmen/ Handbook of Major Companies which is available online through Data-Star. The data base provides detailed company descriptions of all branches and business enterprises of 20,000 major companies in the Federal Republic of Germany. Related files covering Austria and the Netherlands are also available.

Contact: Verlag Hoppenstedt & Co. (Telex 419 258 HOPP D.)

★1099★
VIDEOACCESS
24 Erie Ave.
London, ON, Canada N6J 1J1
Peter G. Watson, President
Phone: (519) 672-2432
Founded: 1982

Staff: 3 Information and library professional; 1 technician; 1 clerical and nonprofessional.

Related Organizations: VideoAccess is a division of Argosy Distributors, Ltd.

Description of System or Service: VIDEOACCESS is an electronic publishing firm which develops content for interactive videotex and videodisc systems. Using Telidon technology, the firm produces a variety of monthly advertising-supported electronic magazines containing information on home computing, home improvement, gardening, and other topics. VIDEOACCESS offers complete turnkey page creation services, including copywriting, editing, page documentation, graphic design, input, and updating. The firm matches information providers with advertisers and produces custom data bases for videotex, cabletex, and teletext systems, mall directory systems, point-of-purchase displays, and trade shows. Additionally, the firm offers a graphics library containing stock graphics, logos, formats, and type fonts used for page creation.

Scope and/or Subject Matter: Videotex, teletext, and cabletex page creation and data base development.

Input Sources: Input consists of national and local advertising and information content provided by VideoAccess, advertisers, or third-party information providers.

Holdings and Storage Media: Several electronic magazines are maintained.

Computer-Based Products and Services: VIDEOACCESS produces monthly magazine format data bases using Cableshare or Norpak Mark IV Telidon authoring systems and Cableshare Picture Painters for graphic design. The data bases contain approximately 250 pages of information and national advertising and are designed with a window format which allows for the insertion of local advertising pages. VIDEOACCESS data bases include the following: Home Computing Guide, Home Improvement Guide, Garden Guide, Dining Guide, Summer Fun/Winter Fun, Christmas Crafts, Service Directory, and Senior Update. The firm also offers a VideoAccess EFX Library graphics package containing more than 500 graphics files which can be used as electronic pages or in page design. The EFX Library is available for purchase on floppy disks or other computer-readable forms.

Other Services: Also offered are consulting services in the areas of data base design, account servicing, management and coordination of the videotex production process, staffing recommendations, and other system development services. Feasibility studies into videotex and teletext are also conducted.

Clientele/Availability: Products and services are available without restrictions.

Projected Publications and Services: VideoAccess plans to offer electronic magazines covering such topics as car care, music, fitness and nutrition, movies, taxes, diets, plants, travel, real estate, and book reviews.

Contact: Peter G. Watson, President, VideoAccess.

★1100★
VIDEOTEX INDUSTRY ASSOCIATION LTD.
1 Chapel Court   Phone: (not reported)
Borough High St.   Founded: 1978
London SE1 1HH, England

Staff: 1 Management professional; 1 clerical and nonprofessional.

Description of System or Service: The VIDEOTEX INDUSTRY ASSOCIATION LTD. is an organization made up of public and private viewdata/ videotex publishers. Its purposes are to promote the interests of the viewdata industry, to act as a liaison between government bodies and persons involved in the industry, and to establish relevant standards. The ASSOCIATION pursues these goals by holding conferences and debates, by making studies, and by participating in negotiations. Currently more than 90 organizations providing information on Prestel, the U.K. viewdata system, are members.

Scope and/or Subject Matter: Viewdata or videotex information provision, and related subjects.

Publications: 1) Current Affairs—newsletter; 2) Yearbook; 3) Guide to Choosing Viewdata Systems; 4) Prestel Gateway Cost Effectiveness; 5) Code of Practice.

Clientele/Availability: Membership is open to individuals and companies with an interest in the viewdata industry.

Remarks: The Videotex Industry Association Ltd. was formerly known as the Association of Viewdata Information Providers Ltd. (AVIP).

Contact: Geoff Andrew, Videotex Industry Association Ltd.

★1101★
VIDEOTEX INFORMATION SERVICE PROVIDERS ASSOCIATION OF CANADA (VISPAC)
130 Albert St., Suite 1007   Phone: (613) 236-4756
Ottawa, ON, Canada K1P 5G4   Founded: 1979

Staff: 2 Management professional.

Description of System or Service: The VIDEOTEX INFORMATION SERVICE PROVIDERS ASSOCIATION OF CANADA (VISPAC) is an association of more than 50 companies formed to promote, develop, and represent the interests of its members with regard to their involvement in the videotex industry and related systems in Canada. Specific objectives of the ASSOCIATION include the following: to provide for the exchange of information; to communicate with the government on any issue affecting the interests of its members; to promote compatibility standards for videotex systems; to encourage the unrestricted flow of electronic information; to protect the copyrights of its members; to stimulate growth in the videotex market; to maintain standards of conduct within the industry; to advance public education concerning videotex; and to propose equitable forms of contracts and other documents used in the industry.

Scope and/or Subject Matter: Videotex, viewdata, teletext.

Publications: VISPAC Newsletter (10 per year).

Clientele/Availability: Membership is open to companies providing videotex services and to companies that are interested in videotex information provision.

Contact: Leonard Levencrown, Secretary, Videotex Information Service Providers Association of Canada.

★1102★
VIEWTEL SERVICES LTD.
28 Colmore Circus   Phone: 021 2363366
Birmingham B4 6AX, England   Founded: 1975
P. McC. Montague, Technical Development Director

Staff: 8 Technicians; 4 sales and marketing; 4 clerical and nonprofessional; 4 other.

Related Organizations: Viewtel is a subsidiary of BPM Holdings Ltd., publisher of The Birmingham Post & Mail.

Description of System or Service: VIEWTEL SERVICES LTD. is the provider of Viewtel 202, a news and advertising data base that can be interactively accessed over the Prestel viewdata system. The data base provides daily coverage of national, international, business, financial, sports, weather, and travel news, as well as classified and display advertising. In addition to providing its own viewdata data base, VIEWTEL SERVICES LTD. offers an umbrella service for other information providers that includes frame rental, data base design, data input, and management of closed user groups. It also offers international viewdata consultancy and market research.

Scope and/or Subject Matter: News and advertising; viewdata consultancy.

Holdings and Storage Media: Viewtel 202 is held in machine-readable form.

Computer-Based Products and Services: Viewtel 202 is interactively accessible over Prestel for searches of local, national, and international news, travel news, advertising, and general information and entertainment. In 1983, it became the first Prestel data base to attain a total of 10 million frame accesses.

Clientele/Availability: Viewtel 202 is available without a frame charge to Prestel users. Viewtel's umbrella and consulting services are provided to advertisers and companies wishing to be information providers on Prestel.

Contact: John V. Foxton, Marketing Manager, Viewtel Services Ltd. (Telex 337552.)

★1103★
VIRTUAL CITY ASSOCIATES LTD. (VCA)
21 Upper Brook St.
London W1, England
Peter Sommer
Phone: 01-491 2775
Founded: 1981

Staff: 1 Information and library professional; 2 management professional; 2 technicians.

Description of System or Service: VIRTUAL CITY ASSOCIATES LTD. (VCA) provides consulting services in the areas of telecommunications, computer hardware and software, and radio communications. It specializes in legal and regulatory work and in evaluations for financial institutions. VCA also arranges for the custom installation of equipment.

Scope and/or Subject Matter: Communications and computer technology.

Clientele/Availability: Services are available without restrictions in the United Kingdom and the United States.

Contact: Peter Sommer, Virtual City Associates Ltd.

★1104★
VOLKSWAGENWERK AG
DOCUMENTATION SECTION
(FE-Dokumentation)
Postfach
D-3180 Wolfsburg 1, Fed. Rep. of Germany
Fritz Schael
Phone: 05361 924639
Service Est: 1971

Staff: 24 Total.

Description of System or Service: The DOCUMENTATION SECTION provides personnel of Volkswagenwerk with information and library services that include maintenance of two computer-readable data bases. These data bases consist of LIDAS, a bibliographic file of abstracts from the professional literature, and the nonbibliographic CARS Vehicle Data Bank System/ Fahrzeug-Datenbank-System, holding technical data on automobile models.

Scope and/or Subject Matter: All aspects of motor vehicles and automotive engineering, including social and economic matters related to the automotive industry.

Holdings and Storage Media: Library holdings comprise 60,000 bound volumes, subscriptions to 460 periodicals, and a card file of 150,000 abstracts. Machine-readable files are also held.

Publications: Referatedienst—contains abstracts from the current literature.

Computer-Based Products and Services: 1) The bibliographic LIDAS data base holds more than 78,000 abstracts from professional literature since 1971 and is maintained under STAIRS software to provide retrospective search and SDI services. LIDAS is also publicly available online through Data-Star. 2) The CARS Vehicle Data Bank System supplies up to 350 data elements each for 1800 current automobile models and 14,000 previous models. Derived from manufacturers' literature, repair manuals, press releases, technical periodicals, and other sources, the data bank is used for selective retrievals and trend analysis. It is held under CDC Query-Update software.

Clientele/Availability: Services are externally available with restrictions.

Contact: Fritz Schael, Documentation Section.

W

★1105★
WARREN (L.M.), INC.
2000 W. 12th Ave.
Vancouver, BC, Canada V6J 2G2
Lois M. Warren, President
Phone: (604) 734-0755
Founded: 1979

Staff: Approximately 5 total.

Description of System or Service: L.M. WARREN, INC. provides online information retrieval, analysis, and SDI services. Other services include training and consulting for library planning, automation, data base production, and intracorporate networks for information transfer.

Scope and/or Subject Matter: Patents, science, technology, engineering, marketing, finance, corporate planning, urban planning, and library science.

Input Sources: The firm uses commercially available data bases.

Computer-Based Products and Services: L.M. WARREN, INC. provides SDI and online searching of data bases available through Bibliographic Retrieval Services (BRS), Dow Jones News/Retrieval, ESA/IRS, System Development Corporation (SDC), CAN/OLE, DIALOG Information Services, Inc., ECHO, Finsbury Data Services Ltd., I.P. Sharp Associates, Info Globe, NewsNet, Inc., Pergamon InfoLine Ltd., QL Systems Limited, Samsom Data Systems, Telesystemes Questel, the Canada Centre for Remote Sensing, and the University of British Columbia Computing Centre. The compiled information can be delivered to clients via electronic mail.

Clientele/Availability: Clients include government, industry, associations, and educational institutions.

Contact: Lois M. Warren, President, L.M. Warren, Inc. (Telex 0451158.) The electronic mail address on ENVOY 100 (Telecom Canada) is L.M.WARREN.

★1106★
THE WELDING INSTITUTE (WI)
INFORMATION SERVICES
Abington Hall
Cambridge CB1 6AL, England
Rodney T. Bryant, Head
Phone: 0223 891162

Staff: 6 Management professional; 1 technician; 6 other.

Description of System or Service: The INFORMATION SERVICES abstracts and indexes world welding literature. It stores this information in the machine-readable Weldasearch data base from which it offers the following services: 1) Current awareness service—provides a monthly selection of Weldasearch abstracts which are tailored to a client's particular topic of interest; abstracts are provided in booklet format which also includes information on forthcoming events in welding technology, such as conferences and training courses. 2) Specialist reference lists—annually updated compilations of bibliographic citations and abstracts in more than 100 specific areas of welding technology. 3) Literature abstracts—a monthly service containing the complete output of abstracts which is available in hardcopy or on microfilm. 4) Magnetic tape service—the Weldasearch file is available for lease on magnetic tape which includes abstracts and index terms and a monthly updating service. 5) Online access—the Weldasearch data base is interactively searchable through DIALOG Information Services, Inc. 6) Manual information storage and retrieval system—provides all published information processed by the Institute and consists of a bulletin or microfilm of abstracts, the list of keywords added to each, and a computer-compiled dual dictionary index which is undated monthly and cumulated quarterly.

Scope and/or Subject Matter: Technology and practice of welding, including brazing, soldering, thermal cutting, weld surfacing, metal spraying, design of welded structures, fatigue of welds, brittle fracture, welding and joining equipment, corrosion, welded construction, quality control, inspection and nondestructive testing, pipelines, pressure vessels, offshore structures, and other topics.

Input Sources: Input is derived from approximately 4000 worldwide technical journals as well as from research reports, conference papers, theses, books and monographs, British patents and standards, and special publications.

Holdings and Storage Media: The machine-readable Weldasearch data base contains approximately 70,000 records dating from 1967 to the present. It is updated monthly, with nearly 6000 items processed each year.

Publications: 1) Weldasearch Abstracts are published monthly as A4 hard copy. A computer-compiled dual dictionary index to the abstracts is published separately on a monthly basis. 2) International Welding Thesaurus. 3) Metal Construction (monthly)—contains abstracts, charts, and illustrations. The above titles are available for purchase from the Institute's Publications Department.

Microform Products and Services: Weldasearch Abstracts are available on 16mm microfilm. The back-file may also be obtained on microfilm complete with its own dual dictionaries to facilitate retrospective information retrieval.

Computer-Based Products and Services: The INFORMATION SERVICES offers computerized searches, SDI, and magnetic tape services from the Weldasearch data base. The magnetic tape service includes monthly updates and can be used by the client to conduct retrospective searches, provide internal bulletins and current awareness services, and merge selected portions of the data base wih other client data. Additionally, the Weldasearch data base can be searched online through DIALOG Information Services. Data base search elements include author, journal name, language, publication year, abstract, descriptor, note, and title.

Other Services: The Information Services also provides a rapid photocopy service for most items cited in Weldasearch. Additional services available to Institute research members include advisory and consulting services and microfiche copies of all internal reports.

Clientele/Availability: Products and services are available without restrictions; Institute members are charged reduced prices.

Contact: Rodney T. Bryant, Head, Information Services, The Welding Institute. (Telex 81183.)

★1107★
WESTERN AUSTRALIAN INSTITUTE OF TECHNOLOGY (WAIT)
T.L. ROBERTSON LIBRARY
WAIT INDEX TO NEWSPAPERS
Kent St.
South Bentley, W.A. 6102, Australia
Bryan Kelman, Information Retrieval Librarian
Phone: 09 3507203
Service Est: 1980

Description of System or Service: The WAIT INDEX TO NEWSPAPERS is a computer-readable data base providing abstracting and indexing of all major items appearing in The National Times newspaper. It is available online through the ACI Ausinet service as the WEST data base.

Scope and/or Subject Matter: Australian and other news and current events.

Input Sources: The National Times is comprehensively covered by the data base.

Holdings and Storage Media: Citations and abstracts dating from 1980 to the present are held in machine-readable form.

Computer-Based Products and Services: The WAIT Index to Newspapers is a bibliographic data base accessible online through Ausinet as the WEST data base. Additionally, the T.L. Robertson Library offers Institute and industrial clients information retrieval services through Ausinet, DIALOG Information Services, Inc., System Development Corporation (SDC), Bibliographic Retrieval Services (BRS), and ESA/IRS.

Clientele/Availability: Services are available without restrictions.

Contact: Bryan Kelman, Information Retrieval Librarian, T.L. Robertson Library. (Telex AA 92983.)

★1108★
WESTERN LEGAL PUBLICATIONS LTD.
301 One Alexander St. Phone: (604) 687-5671
Vancouver, BC, Canada V6A 1B2 Founded: 1971
Phil George, Gen. Mgr.

Staff: 2 Management professional; 2 sales and marketing; 8 clerical and nonprofessional; 1 other.

Related Organizations: The parent company of Western Legal Publications Ltd. is Canada Law Book Ltd. (see separate entry).

Description of System or Service: WESTERN LEGAL PUBLICATIONS LTD. publishes digests of Canadian federal and selected provincial civil and criminal court decisions. The full text of several of its publications is commercially available online as the Western Legal Publications (WLP) data base.

Scope and/or Subject Matter: Canadian law.

Input Sources: Input is derived from court decisions and other related court publications.

Holdings and Storage Media: The machine-readable WLP data base contains approximately 25,000 digests of court decisions, including the following: British Columbia civil and criminal court and B.C. Labour Relations Board decisions dating from 1979 to the present; civil and criminal court decisions for Manitoba, Saskatchewan, and Alberta dating from 1980 to the present; Supreme Court of Canada decisions dating from 1980 to the present; and Federal Court of Appeal decisions dating from 1981 to the present.

Publications: 1) Supreme Court of Canada Decisions (issued as needed)—loose-leaf service providing digests of all Supreme Court decisions. 2) Canadian Charter of Rights Decisions (every two weeks)—provides digests of all available decisions respecting the Charter of Rights and the Bill of Rights. 3) Federal Court of Appeal Decisions (monthly)—provides digests of all current decisions of the Federal Court of Appeal. 4) Alberta Decisions, Civil and Criminal Cases (monthly)—provides digests of all available judgments of the Alberta Court of Appeal, the Court of Queen's Bench, and District Courts of Alberta. 5) Alberta/ Saskatchewan/ Manitoba Criminal Conviction Cases (monthly)—contains a digest for each criminal conviction decision made available by the Appellate and Trial Divisions of the Superior Courts and the County and District Courts of the three provinces. 6) British Columbia Decisions, Civil Cases (every two weeks)—provides access to available civil decisions of the B.C. Court of Appeal, Supreme Court, and County Courts, and selected decisions of the Provincial Courts; digests are also available monthly in individual subject-specific series.

7) British Columbia Decisions, Criminal Cases (monthly)—contains digests of available criminal decisions in British Columbia. 8) British Columbia Decisions, Labour Arbitration in B.C. (monthly)—provides summaries of all arbitration awards filed with the Ministry of Labour. 9) British Columbia Decisions, Labour Relations Board Decisions (monthly)—contains digests of all formal and letter decisions made by the B.C. Labour Relations Board. 10) Manitoba Decisions, Civil and Criminal Cases (monthly)—contains digests of the Manitoba Court of Appeal, Court of Queen's Bench, and County Courts decisions. 11) Ontario Decisions, Criminal Cases (monthly)—provides access to decisions of the Ontario Court of Appeal, High Court of Justice, County and District Courts, and Provincial Courts of Ontario, and all decisions of the Supreme Court of Canada in criminal matters emanating from Ontario. 12) Saskatchewan Decisions, Civil and Criminal Cases (monthly)—contains digests of decisions made by the Saskatchewan Court of Appeal, Court of Queen's Bench, and District Courts. Civil and criminal case decisions are published on loose-leaf pages and are mailed to subscribers to be filed by subject in a binder. Also published for each province are monthly citators which provide access to all current decisions made within a province pertaining to the interpretation and application of statutes and rules.

Computer-Based Products and Services: The Western Legal Publications (WLP) data base is available online through QL Systems Limited and can be searched by any word or combination of words.

Other Services: Photocopies of full reasons for judgment of all cases digested by Western Legal Publications are available on a fee basis.

Clientele/Availability: Publications are available by subscription; a 50 percent discount is available to students.

Contact: Nancy Cotter, Sales and Marketing, Western Legal Publications Ltd. The electronic mail address on QL Systems Limited is Box 123.

★1109★
WOLFF (RUDOLF) & CO. LTD.
WOLFF RESEARCH
Plantation House, 2nd Floor Phone: 01-626 8765
10-15 Mincing Lane
London EC3M 3DB, England
Mrs. Elli Gifford, Director of Research

Staff: 3 Information and library professional; 2 management professional; 3 technicians; 3 sales and marketing; 3 clerical and nonprofessional.

Description of System or Service: WOLFF RESEARCH collates commodity price data and maintains them in a machine-readable data base which is commercially available through time-sharing. It utilizes the data for time series analysis. The firm also publishes commodity chart services and offers a trading service.

Scope and/or Subject Matter: Commodity futures.

Input Sources: Data are collected daily from more than 50 United States and London commodities markets.

Holdings and Storage Media: The computer-readable Wolff Research data base contains daily data from 1973 to the present and monthly data from 1960 to the present.

Publications: The Wolff Charts Comprehensive Chart Service consists of the following publications: 1) Investment Timing Monitor (monthly); 2) Technical Traders Bulletin (weekly); 3) Special Reports (issued when warranted by market movements).

Computer-Based Products and Services: The Wolff Research commodities data base is available for time-shared access through I.P. Sharp Associates.

Other Services: In addition to services described above, Wolff Research offers consultancy on commodities.

Clientele/Availability: Services are available to all, subject to contract conditions which prohibit the resale of data.

Remarks: Wolff Research was formerly known as Eurocharts.

Contact: Mrs. Elli Gifford, Director of Research, Rudolf Wolff & Co. Ltd. (Telex 885034.)

★1110★
WORLD HEALTH ORGANIZATION (WHO)
DIVISION OF HEALTH STATISTICS
WORLD HEALTH STATISTICS DATA BASE (WHS)
20, ave. Appia Phone: 022 912111
CH-1211 Geneva 27, Switzerland Service Est: 1948

Related Organizations: The World Health Organization is a specialized agency of the United Nations.

Description of System or Service: The WORLD HEALTH STATISTICS DATA BASE (WHS) is a computer-readable file used to produce annual and quarterly statistical publications and to provide information services to government health organizations, health research institutions, research workers, medical schools, and public libraries.

Scope and/or Subject Matter: Health and demographic statistics, mortality, morbidity, cancer, communicable diseases, health manpower, hospitals.

Input Sources: Eighty percent of the information is derived from questionnaire returns from governments; the remainder is taken from official government reports.

Holdings and Storage Media: The WHS Data Base is maintained on magnetic tape.

Publications: 1) World Health Statistics Quarterly (WHOHPT); 2) World Health Statistics Annual (WHOANL). User documentation is also available.

Computer-Based Products and Services: The WORLD HEALTH STATISTICS DATA BASE, which is indexed using the International

Classification of Diseases (ICD), is available on magnetic tape and services from it are provided by the Division of Health Statistics.

Clientele/Availability: Services are free of charge to governments and research institutions, and are available on a cost-recovery basis to others.

Contact: Dr. H. Hansluwka, Global Epidemiological Surveillance and Health Situation Assessment, World Health Organization. (Telex 27821 OMS.)

★1111★
WORLD HEALTH ORGANIZATION (WHO)
DIVISION OF NONCOMMUNICABLE DISEASES
ORAL HEALTH UNIT
GLOBAL ORAL DATA BANK
20, ave. Appia   Phone: (not reported)
CH-1211 Geneva 27, Switzerland   Service Est: 1973

Special Note: No questionnaire response was received for this entry for the 6th edition. The entry is reprinted as it appeared in the 5th edition.

Related Organizations: The World Health Organization is a specialized agency of the United Nations.

Description of System or Service: The GLOBAL ORAL DATA BANK is a machine-readable file containing information on oral diseases, including periodontal diseases and cancer. The diseases are classified by country, type of survey, type of data, and age. Information on dental services and work force is also available for some countries. The Oral Health Unit conducts searches of the DATA BANK upon request.

Scope and/or Subject Matter: Oral diseases epidemiology, dental caries, periodontal diseases, oral cancer, dental work force.

Input Sources: Input is derived from surveys and other sources.

Holdings and Storage Media: The Oral Data Bank is maintained on computer tapes and diskettes.

Computer-Based Products and Services: Searches of the Data Bank are conducted upon request. Requests should specify ages and countries of interest.

Clientele/Availability: Services are available without restrictions.

Contact: Chief, Oral Health Unit.

★1112★
WORLD HEALTH ORGANIZATION (WHO)
EASTERN MEDITERRANEAN REGIONAL OFFICE (EMRO)
INFORMATION SERVICES
P.O. Box 1517   Phone: 30090
Alexandria, Egypt   Service Est: 1978

Staff: 2 Management professional; 2 other.

Related Organizations: The World Health Organization is a specialized agency of the United Nations.

Description of System or Service: The Eastern Mediterranean Regional Office INFORMATION SERVICES (EMRO-INF) is a public information service that provides health-related information to national health agencies in the region and to WHO field officers involved in implementing WHO programs. EMRO INFORMATION SERVICES also serves as a Regional Network for Health Science Information and provides searches of the U.S. National Library of Medicine's MEDLARS data base.

Scope and/or Subject Matter: Primary health care, health work force development, family health, disease control, disease prevention, environmental health, water supply.

Input Sources: Sources of information include the combined holdings of a number of national and international libraries.

Computer-Based Products and Services: EMRO Information Services provides searches from the MEDLARS data base on request.

Other Services: Photocopy and advisory services are also offered.

Clientele/Availability: Services are available to countries, institutions, and individual researchers in the region.

Contact: G.A. Guirguis, Librarian, Eastern Mediterranean Regional Office. (Telex 54028 WHO UN.)

★1113★
WORLD HEALTH ORGANIZATION (WHO)
INTERNATIONAL AGENCY FOR RESEARCH ON CANCER (IARC)
CLEARING-HOUSE FOR ON-GOING RESEARCH IN CANCER
  EPIDEMIOLOGY
150, cours Albert Thomas   Phone: 7 8758181
F-69372 Lyon Cedex 08, France   Service Est: 1974
Dr. C.S. Muir, Chief

Staff: 1 Information and library professional; 2 management professional; 2 technicians; 2 clerical and nonprofessional; 2 other.

Related Organizations: The Clearing-House is run jointly with the German Cancer Research Center (Deutsches Krebsforschungszentrum - DKFZ) within the framework of the International Cancer Research Data Bank (ICRDB) Program of the U.S. National Cancer Institute. The World Health Organization is one of the specialized agencies of the United Nations.

Description of System or Service: The CLEARING-HOUSE FOR ON-GOING RESEARCH IN CANCER EPIDEMIOLOGY collects summary information on current studies in the field of cancer epidemiology. This information, which is the basis of an annual directory, is stored in machine-readable form, and is supplied to the ICRDB Program for inclusion in the CANCERPROJ data base. Additionally, the Clearing-House provides special computerized searches of the information it collects.

Scope and/or Subject Matter: Ongoing studies in human cancer epidemiology. Studies dealing with diagnosis, clinical trials, and screening programs are excluded unless they include epidemiological evaluation.

Input Sources: Information is gathered through questionnaire mailings to scientists worldwide.

Publications: Directory of On-going Research in Cancer Epidemiology (annual)—contains descriptions of approximately 1300 current projects with cross-indexing. Also published by the IARC is the Information Bulletin on the Survey of Chemicals Being Tested for Carcinogenicity, which is a computer-produced listing of ongoing and recently completed long-term carcinogenicity studies on approximately 970 chemicals.

Computer-Based Products and Services: The Clearing-House conducts computerized searches of project information which has not yet been published.

Clientele/Availability: Primary clients are epidemiologists; there are no charges for computerized searches.

Remarks: The International Agency for Research on Cancer (IARC) has a broad program in epidemiology and environmental carcinogenesis. It also provides the secretariat for the International Association of Cancer Registries (IACR), a professional society that acts as a clearinghouse for information from population-based registries. The IACR organizes meetings, coordinates collaborative studies, publishes a newsletter and, with IARC, issues the Cancer Incidence in Five Continents series.

Contact: For information on the Clearing-House or the IACR, contact Dr. C.S. Muir, Chief, Unit of Descriptive Epidemiology, International Agency for Research on Cancer. (Telex 380 023.)

★1114★
WORLD HEALTH ORGANIZATION (WHO)
WHO COLLABORATING CENTRE FOR COLLECTION AND
  EVALUATION OF DATA ON COMPARATIVE VIROLOGY
Veterinarstr. 13   Phone: 089 21802155
D-8000 Munich 22, Fed. Rep. of
  Germany   Service Est: 1978
Prof. Dr. Peter A. Bachmann, Director

Related Organizations: The Centre is established at the Institute of Medical Microbiology, Infectious and Epidemic Medicine, Veterinary Faculty, Ludwig Maximilian's University. The World Health Organization is a specialized agency of the United Nations.

Description of System or Service: The WHO COLLABORATING

CENTRE FOR COLLECTION AND EVALUATION OF DATA ON COMPARATIVE VIROLOGY was created with the following objectives: 1) to establish, collate, and maintain detailed information on viruses affecting animals and man and to establish a catalog of virus data; 2) to determine from the information, and in collaboration with working teams, which viruses are important and whether reference reagents are required; 3) to identify gaps in knowledge and promising lines of research; 4) to make available technical information on viral diagnosis as well as handling, storage, and other matters concerned with virus materials; 5) to watch particularly for diseases with zoonotic potentials; and 6) to collect and distribute information on viral contamination of cell cultures and other systems used for virus propagation and diagnosis. Information and data collected by the CENTRE is stored on computer, and information retrieval services are provided. The CENTRE also serves as a meeting point for microbiologists and organizes symposia and meetings on selected topics of virology.

Scope and/or Subject Matter: Virology, including physical and chemical characteristics of viruses, biological properties, epidemiological data, natural and experimental infections, diagnostic techniques, and information sources.

Input Sources: Input is obtained from questionnaires completed by specialists and from other sources.

Holdings and Storage Media: The Centre holds virology data in 140 machine-readable files.

Microform Products and Services: Data are available on microfiche.

Computer-Based Products and Services: The WHO COLLABORATING CENTRE FOR COLLECTION AND EVALUATION OF DATA ON COMPARATIVE VIROLOGY maintains virology data and information in the computer-readable DAISY data base and provides information retrieval services from it. Complete data on a given virus can be retrieved as well as single properties. Important references with abstracts accompany all data retrieved. A computer program is used that produces links between different virus species and their properties in order to provide maximum information. Data are available in hard copy, on microfiche, or on magnetic tape.

Other Services: The Centre also offers consultation services.

Clientele/Availability: Clients include virologists, national public health and veterinary authorities, and institutions including libraries and health organizations.

Projected Publications and Services: A Vaccine Data Bank is planned.

Contact: Prof. Dr. Peter A. Bachmann, Director, WHO Collaborating Centre for Collection and Evaluation of Data on Comparative Virology.

★1115★
WORLD HEALTH ORGANIZATION (WHO)
WHO COLLABORATING CENTRE FOR INTERNATIONAL DRUG MONITORING
P.O. Box 607 Phone: 018 155880
S-751 25 Uppsala, Sweden Service Est: 1968

Related Organizations: The World Health Organization is one of the specialized agencies of the United Nations.

Description of System or Service: The WHO COLLABORATING CENTRE FOR INTERNATIONAL DRUG MONITORING collects and disseminates data on adverse reactions to drugs. Data submitted by medical professionals in 25 countries are analyzed by the CENTRE and entered in its International Drug Information System (INTDIS), a computer-readable data bank which is available for online searching. Comprising a case report register, a drug register, and a terminology file, INTDIS is used to compile listings of drugs causing adverse reactions for distribution to participants, and to provide custom search services.

Scope and/or Subject Matter: Adverse drug reactions including death, neoplasms, fetal malformations, drug dependence, and others.

Input Sources: Input consists of case reports on standard forms or magnetic tape prepared by medical and health professionals in participating countries.

Holdings and Storage Media: INTDIS currently contains data from approximately 350,000 case reports, and is growing at the rate of 70,000 per year.

Publications: Adverse Reaction Newsletter (quarterly)—reviews current drug problems in the participating countries.

Microform Products and Services: COM microfiche products include an annual compilation of reported reactions, an annual printout of the drug register, and a printout of adverse reaction terminology.

Computer-Based Products and Services: The WHO COLLABORATING CENTRE FOR INTERNATIONAL DRUG MONITORING maintains the computer-readable International Drug Information System (INTDIS) data bank, which covers adverse drug reactions and consists of a case reports register, a drug register, and a terminology section. The case report register is divided into four parts, corresponding to the structure of an adverse reaction report: 1) administrative reports—containing case identification and patient data; 2) adverse reactions reports—containing a code description of the observed reaction; 3) drugs reports—providing information about the administered drugs; and 4) medical reports—containing background information and comments by national centers. The drug register, divided into seven tables, contains proprietary and nonproprietary names of drugs and substances, including manufacturer names, chemical, pharmacological, and therapeutic classifications of each substance, and Chemical Abstracts Service (CAS) Registry Number. The terminology section contains the WHO Adverse Reaction Terminology and the International Classification of Diseases. Additional features of INTDIS include computerized error checking of incoming data against the terminology section.

The data bank is searchable online via data communications networks from terminals located at the participating national centers and is used to produce regular listings of drugs causing serious reactions in several categories, and selected additional listings. Special retrievals from the data bank are also provided on request; these are backed up with searches of the medical literature to give full documentation. Regular listings are also produced on magnetic tape.

Clientele/Availability: Services are available to countries participating in the drug reporting system.

Contact: Sten Olsson, Pharmacist, WHO Collaborating Centre for International Drug Monitoring. (Telex 76079 WHODRUG S.)

★1116★
WORLD INTELLECTUAL PROPERTY ORGANIZATION (WIPO)
(Organisation Mondiale de la Propriete Intellectuelle - OMPI)
PERMANENT COMMITTEE ON PATENT INFORMATION (PCPI)
34, chemin des Colombettes Phone: 022 999111
CH-1211 Geneva 20, Switzerland
Paul Claus, Director

Staff: 4 Information and library professional; 3 management professional; 7 clerical and nonprofessional.

Related Organizations: The Permanent Committee on Patent Information is composed of the national patent offices of 60 countries, the European Patent Office, and the Organisation Africaine de la Propriete Intellectuelle, and the English Speaking African Regional Industrial Property Organization (ESARIPO).

Description of System or Service: The PERMANENT COMMITTEE ON PATENT INFORMATION (PCPI) works to encourage and institute close cooperation, particularly among national and regional industrial property offices, in all matters concerning patent information. It is involved in the revision of the International Patent Classification (IPC), the annual publication of industrial property statistics, the elaboration of documentary standards in the field of patent documentation, and cooperation with INPADOC (International Patent Documentation Center) in the provision of a wide range of online and microfiche patent information services. The COMMITTEE also provides technical assistance to developing countries to facilitate their access to technological information contained in patent documents.

Scope and/or Subject Matter: Patents in all fields.

Input Sources: Patents, published patent applications, and related literature are acquired from member countries.

Computer-Based Products and Services: The PCPI cooperates in providing computerized patent information services from INPADOC data bases.

Other Services: The Committee is also involved in research in systems design and development, and in the preparation of standards to be used by industrial property offices.

Clientele/Availability: Services are intended for participating offices, which determine their availability to other users. Special services are provided for users in developing countries.

Contact: Paul Claus, Director, Classifications and Patent Information Division, World Intellectual Property Organization. (Telex 22376.)

★1117★
WORLD METEOROLOGICAL ORGANIZATION (WMO)
COMMISSION FOR HYDROLOGY
OPERATIONAL HYDROLOGY PROGRAMME
HYDROLOGICAL OPERATIONAL MULTIPURPOSE
  SUBPROGRAMME (HOMS)
Case Postale No. 5   Phone: 022 346400
41, avenue Giuseppe Motta   Service Est: 1981
CH-1211 Geneva 20, Switzerland
Prof. J. Nemec, Director, HWR Department

Staff: 2 Professional; 1 clerical and nonprofessional.

Description of System or Service: The HYDROLOGICAL OPERATIONAL MULTIPURPOSE SUBPROGRAMME (HOMS) assists technology transfer among more than 70 national hydrological services which have established HOMS national reference centers. The centers are responsible for submitting relevant technology transfer components such as manuals, instrument catalogs, descriptions of equipment, and computer software. These components support activities of hydrological services and are designed to satisfy various levels of complexity ranging from simple manual techniques to sophisticated computer software. Each component accepted by HOMS is described in a two-page entry in the HOMS Reference Manual, which serves as the basis for technology transfer among members. The manual is computer-produced and is also available in machine-readable form to the national reference centers.

Scope and/or Subject Matter: Hydrological networks; hydrological data collection, transmission, processing, storage and retrieval; hydrological instruments and equipment; hydrological forecasting; hydrological models.

Input Sources: National hydrological services, WMO field projects, and other international organizations involved in water matters contribute information to HOMS.

Holdings and Storage Media: The HOMS Reference Manual is held in machine-readable form.

Publications: 1) HOMS Reference Manual-HRM—contains brief descriptions of all available components and information on the entire HOMS project. 2) HOMS Newsletter (about 2 per year).

Computer-Based Products and Services: The machine-readable HOMS data base contains descriptions of more than 400 available components with indexes by number and keywords in titles; it is distributed to national reference centers on magnetic tape or diskettes.

Clientele/Availability: Services are available to national hydrological services, field projects, technical cooperation organizations, and other United Nations agencies active in hydrology.

Contact: Prof. J. Nemec, Hydrological Operational Multipurpose Subprogramme.

★1118★
WORLD METEOROLOGICAL ORGANIZATION (WMO)
WORLD CLIMATE PROGRAMME DEPARTMENT
WORLD CLIMATE DATA INFORMATION REFERRAL SERVICE
  (INFOCLIMA)
Case Postale No. 5   Phone: 022 346400
41, ave. Giuseppe Motta   Service Est: 1984
CH-1211 Geneva 20, Switzerland
Dr. Thomas D. Potter, Director

Related Organizations: Several international organizations provide support.

Description of System or Service: Under the WORLD CLIMATE DATA INFORMATION REFERRAL SERVICE (INFOCLIMA), information on the availability of climatological, oceanographic, and other geophysical data is collected centrally by the WMO Secretariat and provided to WMO member states to assist them in their data referral services.

Scope and/or Subject Matter: Sources of data used in the study of climate and climate variations.

Input Sources: Input is derived from national and international climatological data centers.

Clientele/Availability: Services are available to WMO member states.

Contact: Dr. Thomas D. Potter, Director, World Climate Programme Department.

★1119★
WORLD METEOROLOGICAL ORGANIZATION (WMO)
WORLD WEATHER WATCH (WWW)
Case Postale No. 5   Phone: 022 346400
41, ave. Giuseppe Motta   Service Est: 1968
CH-1211 Geneva 20, Switzerland

Special Note: No questionnaire response was received for this entry for the 6th edition. The entry is reprinted as it appeared in the 5th edition.

Description of System or Service: The WORLD WEATHER WATCH (WWW) is a worldwide, computer-based information service that acquires, processes, and disseminates meteorological and other environmental information via a system of world, national, and regional centers linked by a data transmission network. Nearly 20,000 stations in the Global Observing System (GOS) collect observational data using air, land, sea, and other platforms. These data are gathered and processed by centers in the Global Data-processing System (GDPS), and transmitted on a real-time basis through the WWW Global Telecommunication System (GTS). Additionally, the GDPS centers maintain and make accessible compatible data banks of meteorological and environmental data for non-real-time applications. In all, approximately 10 million characters of alphanumeric data and 2000 weather charts are exchanged daily through the WWW.

Scope and/or Subject Matter: Meteorology, oceanography, environmental sciences.

Input Sources: Participants in the WWW Global Observing System include 9000 land stations, 7000 mobile ship stations, 3000 aircraft stations, 100 background pollution monitoring stations, 50 ocean buoys, and polar-orbiting and geostationary satellites. Data from these stations are processed and stored by approximately 175 national meteorological services and other GDPS centers.

Holdings and Storage Media: The WWW maintains machine-readable registers of 9000 land stations, 9000 meteorological bulletins, and 7000 mobile ship stations. The individual centers maintain computer-readable data banks of local meteorological and related data.

Publications: The WWW system is used to produce meteorological bulletins and pictorial products such as weather analyses and forecast charts.

Microform Products and Services: Various kinds of microforms are produced by the main WWW centers.

Computer-Based Products and Services: The WORLD WEATHER

WATCH distributes alphanumeric and pictorial meteorological information on a real-time basis through its Global Telecommunication System. Information provided by the WWW system consists of basic meteorological, hydrological, oceanographic, and other environmental data for several types of applications; weather analyses, warnings, and forecasts for general purposes and special applications that include agriculture, shipping, fishing, transportation, hydrology, water management, industry, and recreation; and warnings against natural disasters caused by meteorological phenomena, particularly tropical cyclones. All information entering the WWW system can be made available at any of the participating centers. The World Weather Watch also maintains on magnetic tape international registers of meteorological land stations, mobile ship stations, and meteorological bulletins.

Other Services: In addition, advisory services are offered on WWW planning and implementation.

Clientele/Availability: Services are restricted to national meteorological services of WMO member countries and to various international programs.

Contact: Director, World Weather Watch Department.

Y

★1120★
YORK UNIVERSITY
INSTITUTE FOR BEHAVIOURAL RESEARCH (IBR)
Administrative Studies Bldg.　　　Phone: (416) 667-3026
4700 Keele St.　　　　　　　　　Service Est: 1968
Downsview, ON, Canada M3J 2R6
Prof. Gordon Darroch, Director

Staff: 1 Information and library professional; 2 management professional; 3 programmer/ analyst; 3 clerical and nonprofessional.

Description of System or Service: THE INSTITUTE FOR BEHAVIOURAL RESEARCH (IBR) provides a complete range of survey research facilities for national, provincial, and metropolitan surveys. All phases of survey research—from instrument design through data collection, analysis, and reporting—are undertaken by IBR staff; related seminars and consultation services are offered as well. The INSTITUTE also promotes social science research at York University and elsewhere by providing data analysis and bibliographic information services. It maintains one of Canada's largest collections of numeric social science data, most of which have been edited and redocumented, and makes available an extensive library of computer programs to facilitate secondary analysis. Bibliographic information services are provided through the Social Science Information System (SSIS), a computerized information retrieval system used to conduct searches from three social science-related data bases, including an in-house file covering relevant Canadian periodical literature. Additionally, the INSTITUTE offers services from several specialized files, including the Canadian Women of Note Archive of biographical information.

Scope and/or Subject Matter: Primary focus is on sociology, political science, and social psychology; secondary interest is in geography, economics, education, and health.

Input Sources: Numeric data sets are acquired from academic, government, and private institutions and individuals. The SSIS service uses the PsycINFO data base, ERIC's Current Index to Journals in Education (CIJE), and an in-house file that abstracts and indexes 39 Canadian journals.

Holdings and Storage Media: The IBR maintains approximately 300 computer-readable numeric data sets. Bibliographic files hold a total of 350,000 citations; about 50,000 citations are added annually.

Publications: Canadian Social Science Data Archive Catalogue—available for purchase; lists abstracts of data sets held, plus other IBR services. A list of other publications is available by request.

Computer-Based Products and Services: The INSTITUTE's numeric data set holdings include the following: Canadian Gallup Poll surveys, 1945 to 1975; Canadian national election surveys; bilingual/bicultural surveys; cross-national and cross-cultural data sets, including more than 100 surveys of non-Canadian populations and a comprehensive data resource on Black African nations; the Canadian Census Data Archive, which offers retrieval capability for aggregate data through the Canadian Census Data Management System; and the Educational Research Data Archive which covers studies of students and the education process. IBR supplies the data sets with codebooks for a fee and also offers a large library of computer programs for social science data analysis. The INSTITUTE's Social Science Information System is used to provide batch search services of the internally compiled Social Science Journal File/ Canadian Social Science Abstracts file, the PsycINFO data base, and the ERIC CIJE file. IBR also makes available specialized bibliographies and other files including the Canadian Women of Note Archive (CWONC), which contains biographical abstracts covering 1000 Canadian women, and is available on microfiche or magnetic tape.

Other Services: IBR also offers consulting in the areas of collection, management, and analysis of social science data and questionnaire design.

Clientele/Availability: Search services are available free to faculty and students of York University and on a fee basis to other users.

Contact: Anne Oram, Data Librarian, or John Tibert, Manager, Programming, Institute for Behavioural Research. (Telex 065 24736.)

★1121★
YUGOSLAV CENTER FOR TECHNICAL AND SCIENTIFIC DOCUMENTATION
(Jugoslovenski Centar za Tehnicku i Naucnu Dokumentaciju)
Slobodana Penezica-Krcuna 29/31　　Phone: 644184
P.O. Box 724　　　　　　　　　　　Founded: 1952
YU-11000 Belgrade, Yugoslavia
Alexsic Miodrag, Director

Special Note: The above name, address, and telephone number have been verified for this edition, although no questionnaire response was received. The following text is reprinted from the 5th edition.

Description of System or Service: The YUGOSLAV CENTER FOR TECHNICAL AND SCIENTIFIC DOCUMENTATION collects, stores, and disseminates scientific, technical, and economic information in support of national economic development and scientific research. It maintains extensive library collections and offers bibliography compilations as well as regular publication of technical abstracts bulletins in 24 subject areas. The CENTER also provides comprehensive lending and hardcopy or microfiche reproduction services, and it will procure documents from abroad through its cooperation in international documentation and information organizations and programs. Actively engaged in research on the methods, techniques, and processes of scientific information services and documentation, the CENTER regularly publishes a journal in these areas. Additional services include current awareness, translations, and consulting on information problems.

Scope and/or Subject Matter: Scientific and technical information and documentation.

Input Sources: Input consists of primary and secondary publications from domestic and foreign sources.

Holdings and Storage Media: Library holdings number more than 770,000 volumes and 1600 periodical subscriptions.

Publications: 1) Bulletin of Documentation (11 per year)—abstracts journal published in 24 technical topics; 2) Informatika (quarterly)—covers theory and practice of information science and documentation; 3) Scientific and Professional Meetings in Yugoslavia and Foreign Countries (twice per year); 4) Bibliography on Automatic Data Processing (bimonthly); 5) Microfilm Techniques (bimonthly). All publications are available by subscription or purchase.

Microform Products and Services: The Center provides microfilm copying and developing.

Other Services: In addition to services described above, the Center offers editorial and printing services.

Clientele/Availability: Most services are available without restrictions.

Contact: Alexsic Miodrag, Director, Yugoslav Center for Technical and Scientific Documentation.

Z

★1122★
ZINC DEVELOPMENT ASSOCIATION/LEAD DEVELOPMENT ASSOCIATION/CADMIUM ASSOCIATION (ZDA/LDA/CA) LIBRARY AND ABSTRACTING SERVICE
34 Berkeley Square
London W1X 6AJ, England
Dr. D.A. Temple, Director General
Phone: 01-499 6636
Service Est: 1980

Staff: 6 Information and library professional; 1 sales and marketing; 2 clerical and nonprofessional.

Description of System or Service: The LIBRARY AND ABSTRACTING SERVICE provides information on lead, zinc, and cadmium and their alloys and compounds. It abstracts and indexes current world literature on the production, properties, and uses of these metals and makes this information available in three quarterly journals and through the computer-readable Zinc, Lead & Cadmium Abstracts (ZLC) Database, which is available on magnetic tape and online. The LIBRARY AND ABSTRACTING SERVICE also offers SDI services, document delivery, referrals, manual literature searching, and computerized information retrieval services from ZLC and other commercially available online data bases.

Scope and/or Subject Matter: Lead, zinc, cadmium and their alloys, compounds, and uses, including batteries, ceramics, corrosion protection, die casting, electric vehicles, environmental aspects, galvanizing, gravity casting, paints, patents, pigments, semiconductors, standards, and other related topics.

Input Sources: The Service utilizes commercially available data bases and print sources such as journals, reports, standards, patents, and conference proceedings.

Holdings and Storage Media: The machine-readable ZLC Database holds approximately 14,000 bibliographic citations and abstracts dating from 1970 to the present; it is updated monthly. Library holdings comprise 2000 bound volumes and subscriptions to 350 periodicals.

Publications: 1) Zinc Abstracts (quarterly)—each issue includes approximately 150 abstracts of world literature on the production, properties, and uses of zinc, its alloys, and its compounds; abstracts are arranged by subject categories. 2) Lead Abstracts (quarterly)—each issue includes approximately 150 abstracts of world literature on the production, properties, and uses of lead, its alloys, and its compounds; abstracts are arranged by subject categories. 3) Cadmium Abstracts (quarterly)—each issue includes approximately 100 abstracts of world literature on the production, properties, and uses of cadmium, its alloys, and its compounds; abstracts are arranged by subject categories. Each publication also includes annual author, subject, patent, and standards indexes.

Computer-Based Products and Services: The LIBRARY AND ABSTRACTING SERVICE produces the Zinc, Lead, & Cadmium Abstracts (ZLC) Database which is available for online searching through Pergamon InfoLine Ltd. The SERVICE also provides SDI services from the data base and makes it available on magnetic tape. Additionally, the SERVICE conducts computerized information retrieval from data bases made available through BLAISE (British Library Automated Information Service), DIALOG Information Services, Inc., and ESA/IRS.

Clientele/Availability: Services are available without restrictions. Members of the LDA, ZDA, and CA can access the ZLC Database on Pergamon InfoLine Ltd. at reduced connect-hour rates.

Remarks: The ZDA, LDA, and CA are nontrading bodies supported by leading producers of metals in Europe, North America, Australia, Asia, and elsewhere.

MASTER INDEX

An all-inclusive, one-stop listing of the organizations, systems, products, and services described in this directory. Includes name and acronym entries, arranged alphabetically, for organizations and their subdivisions and for all distinctively named systems, services, data bases, publications, software products, conferences, projects, seminars, etc. (Data bases, publications, and software are also listed in separate indexes.) *Names listed here may appear in boldface at the beginning of the entry referred to or anywhere within the text of that entry.* National government agencies are listed under both the country name and the individual agency name. Foreign language names are included in this index.

The Master Index in this International Volume contains more than 9,000 listings in all.

A & W Documentation System 302
A Computerized London Information System (ACOMPLIS) Data Base 465
A.JOUR 1
A Network of Social Security Information Resources 145
AA (Apicultural Abstracts) 563
AARTI (Australian Art Index) Data Base 58
AB Pressurklipp 824
Aball Software Inc. 2
Abar Business Planning Service 690
ABC (Abstracts in BioCommerce) 181
ABDA-Arzneistoffe (ABDA-STOFF) Data Base 428
ABDA-FAM (ABDA-Fertigarzneimittel) Data Base 428
ABDA-Fertigarzneimittel (ABDA-FAM) Data Base 428
ABDA-INTER (ABDA-Interaktionen) Data Base 428
ABDA-Interaktionen (ABDA-INTER) Data Base 428
ABDA-STOFF (ABDA-Arzneistoffe) Data Base 428
ABIS (Anglo-Brazilian Information Service) 24
ABIX 53
ABN (Australian Bibliographic Network) 49
ABN: A Bibliography 49
ABN News 49
ABOA (Australian Bibliography of Agriculture) 47
ABS (Australian Bureau of Statistics) 52
ABS (Australian Bureau of Statistics) Time Series Data Base 237
ABS Catalogue of Publications 52
ABSDATA (I.P. Sharp Associates) 871
Abstract of Scientific Periodicals and Monographs 726
Abstracts in BioCommerce 181
Abstracts of AIT Reports and Publications 33
Abstracts of Bulgarian Scientific Literature: Series A. Plant Breeding 121
Abstracts of Bulgarian Scientific Literature: Series B. Animal Breeding and Veterinary Medicine 121
Abstracts of Romanian Scientific and Technical Literature 843
Abstracts of Science and Technology in Japan 632
Abstracts on Tropical Agriculture 857
Abteilung Dokumentation - Institut fur Ernahrungswissenschaft 545
Abteilung Oekonometrie und Datenverarbeitung - IFO-Institut fur Wirtschaftsforschung 501
Academic Book Price Index 675
Academy of Sciences of the U.S.S.R. 995
Academy of Sciences of the U.S.S.R. 996
Academy of Sciences of the U.S.S.R. 997
Academy of Sciences of the U.S.S.R. 998
Accessoirex 693
Accident Investigation and Prevention Section - Air Navigation Bureau - International Civil Aviation Organization 567
ACCIS (Advisory Committee for the Co-ordination of Information Systems) 1001
ACCIS Newsletter 1001
ACCORD (Acquisitions par CATSS/CATSS Ordering) 1094
ACDB (Airport Characteristics Data Bank) 568
Achievements and Perspectives 565
ACI Computer Services 3
ACOMDAILY Data Base (I.P. Sharp Associates) 871
ACOMPLINE 465
ACOMPLIS (A Computerized London Information System) Data Base 465
Acquisitions par CATSS/CATSS Ordering 1094
Acronyms Related to International Development 576
ACROPOL 384
ACSI (Association Canadienne des Sciences de l'Information) 168
ACSPRI (Australian Consortium for Social and Political Research Inc.) 61
ACSPRI Newsletter 61
ACT Data Base (I.P. Sharp Associates) 871
Acton Information Resources Management Ltd. 4
Actualidades 93
Actualite Combustible Energie 386
Actuarial Data Base (I.P. Sharp Associates) 871
ACUL 652
Adaptive Information Management System 666
Adaptive Library Management System (ADLIB) 666
ADB (Anlagendatenbank) 398
ADDIMS Data Base 504
Adfacts 6
ADIGE (Archive of Italian Data of Geology) 625
ADIGE2 625
ADIRS (ADIS Drug Information Retrieval System) 5
ADIS Drug Information Retrieval System 5
ADIS Press Australasia Pty Ltd. 5
ADISQ (Association du Disque et de l'Industrie du Spectacle Quebecois) 206
ADLIB (Adaptive Library Management System) 666
ADMAC (Austrian Documentation Centre for Media and Communication Research) 65
Admedia 6
ADMIN (Adaptive Information Management System) 666

Administratiefrechtelijve Beslissingen 641
Administration Laboratory Project (ALP) File 1034
Administrative Information Sources 7
ADO (Animal Disease Occurrence) Data Base 428
ADOC (AGORA-DOCUMENTAIRE) 388
ADOPT: Asian and Worldwide Documents on Population Topics 1003
ADP (Association of Database Producers) 40
ADP Member's Handbook 40
ADPSS (Archivio Dati e Programmi per le Scienze Sociali) - Istituto Superiore di Sociologia - Universita Degli Studi di Milano 1058
ADREP (Aircraft Accident/Incident Reporting System) 567
ADRS (Automatic Document Request Service) - British Library 440
Adverse Reaction Newsletter 1115
Adverse Reactions Titles 296
Advisory Committee for the Co-ordination of Information Systems 1001
Advocates' Quarterly 162
AEA (Association of European Airlines) 41
AEB (Atomic Energy Board) - South Africa 886
AECC Data Base (I.P. Sharp Associates) 871
AECL (Atomic Energy of Canada, Ltd.) 44
AECL (Atomic Energy of Canada, Ltd.) 45
AECL Document Data Base 44
AECO (AGORA-ECONOMIE) 388
AEI (Australian Education Index) Data Base 54
AEIH (Association Europeenne des Industries de l'Habillement) 980
AERIC (Applied Economic Research and Information Centre) - Conference Board of Canada 238
AERIC Historical Supplements 238
AERIC Information and Documentation 238
AERIC National Database 238
AERIC Provincial Database 238
AERIC System 238
Aerodromes Section - Air Navigation Bureau - International Civil Aviation Organization 568
Aerospace and Aviation Documents 958
Aerospace Daily (ESA/IRS) 317
AES Data Base (I.P. Sharp Associates) 871
AESIS (Australian Earth Sciences Information System) 57
AESIS Cumulation 57
AESIS Quarterly 57
AFDAC (Association Francaise de Documentation Automatique en Chimie) 720
Afdeling Biomedische Informatie - Rijks Universiteit Utrecht Bibliotheek 899
AFDIT (Associazione Italiana dei Fornitori e Distributori di Informazione Telematica) 621
AFEE (Association Francaise pour l'Etude des Eaux) 391
AffarsData 94
AffarsDok 260
AFNOR (Association Francaise de Normalisation) 382
AFP (Agence France-Presse) 388
AFP-AGORA Data Bases 388
AFRE (Australian Financial Review) Data Base 55
Africa Documentation Center - Institute of African Studies 397
African Administrative Abstracts 7
African Development Bank 1005
African Network of Administrative Information 7
African Training and Research Centre in Administration for Development 7
AGB Research Plc. 649
AGC File 127
AGDATA (Agricultural Commodities Data Base) 9
AGE (Asian Information Center for Geotechnical Engineering) 30
AGE Current Awareness Services 30
AGE Digest 30
AGE Holdings Lists 30
AGE News 30
Agence Cooperation et Amenagement 1091
Agence de Journalistes (A.JOUR) 1
Agence France-Presse 388
Agence National de Valorisation de la Recherche 987
AGI (Alberta Gazette Index) 11
AGI (American Geological Institute) 412
AgInfo 8
AGINSPEC 8
AGINTEL 8
AGNEWS 8
AGORA 388
AGORA-DOCUMENTAIRE (ADOC) 388
AGORA-ECONOMIE (AECO) 388
AGORA-GENERAL (AGRA) 388
Agora, Informatics in a Changing World 554
AGORA-SPORTS (ASPO) 388
AGRA (AGORA-GENERAL) 388
Agra Europe 8
AGREP (Agricultural Research Projects) Data Base 213
AGREP-Permanent Inventory of Agricultural Research Projects in the European Communities 213

AGRIASIA 889
Agricultural Abstracts for Tanzania 955
Agricultural Academy - National Agro-Industrial Union - Bulgaria 121
Agricultural Commodities Data Base 9
Agricultural Data Bank (NEEDS-TS) 754
Agricultural Data Bases (Australian Bureau of Statistics) 237
Agricultural Division - Imperial Chemical Industries Ltd. 503
Agricultural Documentation/Landbouwdocumentatie 731
Agricultural Engineering Abstracts 229
Agricultural Information & Documentation Section - Royal Tropical Institute 857
Agricultural Information Bank for Asia 889
Agricultural Information Society for Asia 889
Agricultural Marketing and Trade Database 126
Agricultural Research Division - Ministry of Agriculture and Fisheries - Netherlands 731
Agricultural Research Information Centre - Indian Council of Agricultural Research 510
Agricultural Research Personnel Inventory File 510
Agricultural Research Project Information System Data Base 510
Agricultural Research Projects (AGREP) Data Base 213
Agricultural Sciences - Kalpataru 507
Agricultural System for the Storage and Subsequent Selection of Information (ASSASSIN) 503
Agricultural Union Catalogue (Netherlands) 240
Agricultural University Library 731
Agriculture Canada 126
Agriculture Canada 127
Agriculture Canada 128
Agriculture Canada 167
AGRINDEX 1012
AGRIS (International Information System for the Agricultural Sciences and Technology) 1012
Agritex 862
AGRITROP 467
Agroclimatology Data Bank 846
AGSM Data Base (I.P. Sharp Associates) 871
AIBA (Agricultural Information Bank for Asia) 889
AIBD (Association of International Bond Dealers) 267
AIBD International Bond Manual 267
AID (Artikkel-Indeks) 767
AID (AVCOR Interactive Display) 67
AID Data Base 935
AID Enheten - Arbetslivscentrum 935
AIDIMS Data Base 504
AIDS (Agricultural Information & Documentation Section) - Royal Tropical Institute 857
AIDS (Automated Informatics Documentation System) Data Base 554
Aids to Library Administration Series 675
AIM (Arbeitsgemeinschaft Information Meeresforschung und Meerestechnik) Data Base 413
Air Charter Data Base (I.P. Sharp Associates) 871
Air Navigation Bureau - International Civil Aviation Organization 567
Air Navigation Bureau - International Civil Aviation Organization 568
Air Quality Data File 626
Air Transport Bureau - International Civil Aviation Organization 569
Air Transport Statistical Program - Statistics Section - Air Transport Bureau - International Civil Aviation Organization 569
Airclaims Group Ltd. 68
Aircraft Accident Data Base 68
Aircraft Accident/Incident Reporting System 567
Aircraft Accident Statistics 567
Aircraft Histories Data Base 68
Aircraft Price Guide 68
Airport Characteristics 568
Airport Characteristics Data Bank 568
AISL (Aviation Information Services Ltd.) 68
AISL (Aviation Information Services Ltd.) Aircraft Data Bases 68
AISL Information Digest 68
AIT (Asian Institute of Technology) 30
AIT (Asian Institute of Technology) 31
AIT (Asian Institute of Technology) 32
AIT (Asian Institute of Technology) 33
AJOUR 1
AKB-bok 931
AKB-mikro 931
Alan Armstrong & Associates Ltd. 674
Alberta/Canada Energy Resources Research Fund 14
Alberta/Canada Energy Resources Research Fund 16
Alberta Decisions, Civil and Criminal Cases 1108
Alberta Department of Agriculture 9
Alberta Department of Energy and Natural Resources 14
Alberta Gazette Index (AGI) 11
Alberta Geological Survey 12
Alberta Government Periodicals Publishing Record (PPR) Data Base 11
Alberta Government Publications Catalogue 11
Alberta Land Use Planning Data Bank 10
Alberta Legislation Information (ALI) Data Base 11
Alberta Municipal Affairs 10
Alberta Oil Sands Index 13
Alberta Oil Sands Information Centre 13
Alberta Public Affairs Bureau 11
Alberta Reports (National Reporter System) 828
Alberta Research Council 12
Alberta Research Council 13
Alberta Research Council 14
Alberta Research Council 15
Alberta Research Council 16
Alberta Research Council 1033
Alberta/Saskatchewan/Manitoba Criminal Conviction Cases 1108
Alcohol, Drugs and Traffic Safety: Current Research Literature 936
ALCONARC 936
ALDOC (League of Arab States Documentation and Information Center) 653
ALEPH (Automated Library Expandable Program Hebrew University of Jerusalem) 478
Alerting-Search Service from Kinokuniya 640
ALI (Alberta Legislation Information) Data Base 11
ALICE (Archivio Libri Italiani su Calcolatore Elettronico) 87
ALIF Index 653
ALIS (Automated Library Information System) - National Technological Library of Denmark 270
ALIS (League of Arab States Information System) 653
All-Canada Weekly Summaries 162
All-Japan Statistical Analysis of Corporate Financial Statements 969
All-Union Institute of Scientific and Technical Information - Union of Soviet Socialist Republics 998
ALLC (Association for Literary and Linguistic Computing) 37
ALLC Bulletin 37
ALLC Journal 37
Allen B. Veaner Associates 1097
Allgemeine Wirtschaftsdokumentation 425
ALLM Books 17
ALLOYDATA 451
Almqvist & Wiksell Booksellers 302
ALPFILE 1034
Alpha 460 Prestel Data Base 18
Alpha 460 Television Ltd. 18
Alphabetical and Phonetic Directory of International Trademarks 234
Alphabetical Directory of Benelux Trademarks 234
Alphabetical Directory of French Trademarks 234
Alphabetical List of French Applications 234
Alphabetical Subject Guide to the INSPEC Classification 549
Alphaphonetic Directory of International Trademarks 234
Alphatel Systems Ltd. 19
Alphatel Videotex Directories Limited 19
Alphatext, Inc. 20
Alpine Science Information Service 21
Aluminium Monitor 228
Aluminium Quarterly 228
Aluminum Analysis 89
Aluminum Annual Review 89
Aluminum Production Costs 89
American Chemical Society 901
American College in Paris 22
American Express Europe Ltd. 23
American Express Flight Information Service 23
American Geological Institute 412
American Society for Metals 698
American Viewdata Services 473
AMES Data Base (I.P. Sharp Associates) 871
AMIS (Australian Municipal Information System) 237
AMP Society 237
AMPEREDOC (Association Multinationale des Producteurs et Revendeurs d'Electricite-Documentation) 717
AMPEREDOC Data Base 717
AMRS (Australian MARC Record Service) 48
ANAI (African Network of Administrative Information) 7
ANAIS 1062
Analytical Abstracts 851
Analytical Instrument Industry Report 515
ANB (Australian National Bibliography) 48
ANB Catalogue 48
Andean Group Report 651
ANG (Australian National Gallery) 58
Anglo-Brazilian Information Service 24
Animal Breeding Abstracts 229
Animal Disease Occurrence 229
Animal Disease Occurrence (ADO) Data Base 428
Animal Production Information Card Service Data Base 487
Anlagendatenbank (ADB) 398
Annales des Telecommunications 367
Annals of Library Science and Documentation 507
Annotated Bibliography on Carbon Technology 507
Annotated Bibliography on the Child 1015
Annuaire CNRS 355
Annuaire de Banques de Donnees 385
Annuaire de l'Afrique du Nord 186

Annuaire des Pays Mediterraneens   564
Annuaire d'Etudes en Education au Canada   170
Annual Bibliography of Austrian Mass Communication Literature   65
Annual Index to Geo Abstracts   393
Annual Index to Hebrew Periodicals   1051
Annual Index to New Products (Rubber and Plastics Research Association of Great Britain   858
Annual Labour Force Statistics (OECD)   780
Annual National Accounts (OECD)   780
Annual of Czechoslovak Medical Literature   250
Annual Report of the NIES   626
Annual Report on the French Stock Exchange   389
Annual Report Record   1060
Anorganisch Chemisches Institut - Universitat Bonn   1042
ANSSIR (A Network of Social Security Information Resources)   145
Anthony Bird Associates   89
Antiope & Telematics Corporation   383
Antiope Teletext System   383
ANVAR (Agence National de Valorisation de la Recherche)   987
AOPUS (Australian Opinion Polls User Service)   1072
AOSI (Alberta Oil Sands Index)   13
AP (Associated Press) Data Base (Datasolve World Reporter)   265
APAIS (Australian Public Affairs Information Service) Data Base   48
Apercu Technique-Technisch Overzicht (ATO)   187
API (Architectural Periodicals Index)   845
Apicultural Abstracts   563
APIDIST Data Base (I.P. Sharp Associates)   871
APIN (System of Computerized Processing of Scientific Information)   965
APIN-MARC   965
Applied Economic Research and Information Centre - Conference Board of Canada   238
APR (Atlantic Provinces Reports)   173
APUR (Atelier Parisien d'Urbanisme)   798
AQUA Data Bank   548
Aquaculture Abstracts (ASFA)   1008
AQUADOC   348
AQUALINE   464
AQUALINE Online User Guide   464
AQUARIUS-STAIRS   80
Aquatic Sciences and Fisheries Abstracts   1008
Aquatic Sciences and Fisheries Information System   1008
AQUEST   1055
AQUILA   638
Arab Social Science Index   1015
Arabian Gulf Information Consulting Bureau   25
ARATE Data Base (I.P. Sharp Associates)   871
Arbeitsgemeinschaft fur Bauforschung - Germany   374
Arbeitsgemeinschaft Information Meeresforschung und Meerestechnik   413
Arbeitsgemeinschaft Sozialwissenschaftlicher Institute   43
Arbetarskyddsstyrelsen   923
Arbetslivscentrum   935
Architectural Keywords   845
Architectural Periodicals Index   845
Archive of Italian Data of Geology   625
Archivio Dati e Programmi per le Scienze Sociali - Istituto Superiore di Sociologia - Universita Degli Studi di Milano   1058
Archivio Libri Italiani su Calcolatore Elettronico (ALICE)   87
ARCSS (Center for Social Science Research and Documentation for the Arab Region)   1015
ARCSS Newsletter   1015
Arctic Institute of North America   26
Arctic Science and Technology Information System   26
ARDIC (Association pour la Recherche et le Developpement en Informatique Chimique)   38
ARDIC (Association pour la Recherche et le Developpement en Informatique Chimique)   720
Area, Population & Household Databank (NEEDS-TS)   754
AreaSearch - Compusearch Market and Social Research Ltd.   236
Argentina - National Atomic Energy Commission   27
Argentina - National Council for Scientific and Technical Research   28
Argentine Center for Scientific and Technological Information   28
Argosy Distributors, Ltd.   1099
ARGREP Data Base (I.P. Sharp Associates)   871
ARGUS Data Base (I.P. Sharp Associates)   871
ARI (Australian Road Index)   62
ARIANE (Arrangement Reticule des Informations en vue de l'Approche des Notions par leur Environnement) Data Bank   610
ARIC (Agricultural Research Information Centre) - Indian Council of Agricultural Research   510
Arid Lands Development Abstracts   229
Armstrong (Alan) & Associates Ltd.   674
Arrangement Reticule des Informations en vue de l'Approche des Notions par leur Environnement (ARIANE) Data Bank   610
ARRB (Australian Road Research Board)   62
ARRD (Australian Road Research Documentation)   62
ARRIP (Australian Road Research in Progress) Data Base   62
Art Benjamin Associates Ltd.   657

Art Sales Index   29
Art Sales Index (ASI) Data Bank   29
Art Sales Index Ltd.   29
Artemis   71
ARTEMIS   370
Article Index   767
Artificial Rainfall Newsletter   616
Artikel-Sok   116
Artikkel-Indeks   767
ArtQuest   29
ARTWORK MANAGER   649
ASBEST Data Base   1071
Asbestos Information   1071
Asbestos Manufacturers Catalog   1071
Asbestos Research Program - University of Sherbrooke   1071
Asblorn Habberstad   553
ASE Data Base (I.P. Sharp Associates)   871
ASFA (Aquatic Sciences and Fisheries Abstracts) Data Base   1008
ASFA Aquaculture Abstracts   1008
ASFIS (Aquatic Sciences and Fisheries Information System)   1008
ASFIS Register of Experts and Institutions   1008
ASI (Art Sales Index) Data Bank   29
ASI (Australian Science Index)   47
ASI Decade Publications   29
Asia Documentation Center - Institute of Asian Studies   397
Asian Agricultural Research and Development: A Bibliography   1073
Asian and Worldwide Documents on Population Topics (ADOPT)   1003
Asian Bibliography   1002
Asian Geotechnical Engineering Abstracts   30
Asian Geotechnology Data Base   30
Asian Information Center for Geotechnical Engineering   30
Asian Institute of Technology   30
Asian Institute of Technology   31
Asian Institute of Technology   32
Asian Institute of Technology   33
Asian Network for Industrial Technology Information and Extension   34
Asian-Pacific Population Programme News   1003
ASISS (Alpine Science Information Service)   21
ASK Information Retrieval Services   640
Aslib Information   35
Aslib Online Resources Centre   35
Aslib Online Resources Centre   775
Aslib Proceedings   35
Aslib, The Association for Information Management   35
ASM (American Society for Metals)   698
ASPO (AGORA-SPORTS)   388
ASSASSIN (Agricultural System for the Storage and Subsequent Selection of Information)   503
ASSIST   1093
Associated Press (AP) Data Base (Datasolve World Reporter)   265
Association Canadienne d'Education   170
Association Canadienne des Sciences de l'Information   168
Association des Centres Serveurs Europeens de Banques de Donnees   42
Association du Disque et de l'Industrie du Spectacle Quebecois   206
Association Europeenne des Industries de l'Habillement   980
Association for Information Brokerage and Technological Consultancy   36
Association for Information Management, Aslib   35
Association for Literary and Linguistic Computing   37
Association for Quantification and Methods in Historical Social Research   183
Association for Research and Development of Chemical Informatics   38
Association for Research and Development of Chemical Informatics   720
Association for the Promotion of Industry-Agriculture   39
Association Francaise de Documentation Automatique en Chimie   720
Association Francaise de Normalisation   382
Association Francaise pour l'Etude des Eaux   391
Association Internationale pour l'Evaluation du Rendement Scolaire   557
Association Multinationale des Producteurs et Revendeurs d'Electricite-Documentation   717
Association of Database Producers   40
Association of European Airlines   41
Association of European Host Operators Group   42
Association of German Engineers   961
Association of German Engineers   1096
Association of International Bond Dealers   267
Association of Social Sciences Institutes   43
Association of Viewdata Information Providers Ltd.   1100
Association pour la Promotion Industrie-Agriculture   39
Association pour la Recherche et le Developpement en Informatique Chimique   38
Association pour la Recherche et le Developpement en Informatique Chimique   720
Association Suisse des Fournisseurs d'Informations Viewdata   946
Associazione Italiana dei Fornitori e Distributori di Informazione

Telematica 621
ASTIS (Arctic Science and Technology Information System) 26
ASTIS Bibliography 26
ASTIS Current Awareness Bulletin 26
Astronomical Council Data Center - Academy of Sciences of the U.S.S.R. 995
ATA (Abstracts on Tropical Agriculture) Data Base 857
ATC (Antiope & Telematics Corporation) 383
Atelier Parisien d'Urbanisme 798
ATHESA 589
ATID (Australian Transport Information Directory) 46
ATID Bulletin 46
Atlantic Provinces Reports (APR) 173
Atlas of Ferns of the British Isles 461
Atlas of the British Flora 461
Atlas of the Bumblebees of the British Isles 461
Atlas of the Lichens of the British Isles 461
Atlas of the Non-marine Mollusca of the British Isles 461
ATLIS (Australian Transport Literature Information System) 46
ATLIS Bulletin 46
ATO (Apercu Technique-Technisch Overzicht) 187
Atomic Energy Authority - Great Britain 433
Atomic Energy Authority - Great Britain 434
Atomic Energy Authority - Great Britain 435
Atomic Energy Authority - Great Britain 436
Atomic Energy Authority - Great Britain 437
Atomic Energy Authority - Great Britain 438
Atomic Energy Board - South Africa 886
Atomic Energy Commission - France 338
Atomic Energy Commission - France 339
Atomic Energy Commission - France 589
Atomic Energy of Canada, Ltd. 44
Atomic Energy of Canada, Ltd. 45
Atomic Energy Research Establishment, Harwell 433
Atomic Energy Research Establishment, Harwell 434
Atomic Energy Research Establishment, Harwell 435
Atomic Energy Research Establishment, Harwell 436
Atomic Energy Research Establishment, Harwell 437
Atomic Energy Research Institute - Japan 627
Atomindex 560
ATRIP (Australian Transport Research in Progress) 46
ATRIP Bulletin 46
AUCBE (Chiltern Advisory Unit for Computer Based Education) 485
Auction Prices of American Artists 29
Audio-Visual Materials for Higher Education Catalogue 112
Ausinet 3
Australia - Bureau of Transport Economics 46
Australia - Commonwealth Scientific and Industrial Research Organization 47
Australia - Commonwealth Scientific and Industrial Research Organization 230
Australia - Development Assistance Bureau 230
Australia - National Library of Australia 48
Australia - National Library of Australia 49
Australia - National Library of Australia 50
Australia Overseas Telecommunications Commission 790
Australian Art Index 58
Australian Atomic Energy Commission 51
Australian Bibliographic Network 49
Australian Bibliography of Agriculture (ABOA) 47
Australian Books: A Select List of Recent Publications and Standard Works in Print 48
Australian Bureau of Statistics 52
Australian Bureau of Statistics (ABS) Time Series Data Base 237
Australian Business Index 53
Australian Commodities Data Base (I.P. Sharp Associates) 871
Australian Company Service 690
Australian Consolidated Industries Limited 3
Australian Consortium for Social and Political Research Inc. 61
Australian Council for Educational Research 54
Australian Demographic Data Bank 60
Australian Earth Sciences Information System 57
Australian Economic Statistics Data Base (I.P. Sharp Associates) 871
Australian Education Index 54
Australian Energy Consumption Statistics Data Base (I.P. Sharp Associates) 871
Australian Export Statistics Data Base (I.P. Sharp Associates) 871
Australian Federal Government Profile 520
Australian Financial Data Base (I.P. Sharp Associates) 871
Australian Financial Markets Data Base (I.P. Sharp Associates) 871
Australian Financial Review 55
Australian Funds Market Data Base (I.P. Sharp Associates) 871
Australian Government Publications 48
Australian Graduate School of Management 1060
Australian Graduate School of Management, Corporate Data Base (I.P. Sharp Associates) 871
Australian Institute of Criminology Library 56
Australian Journal of Management 1060
Australian Major Energy Statistics Data Base (I.P. Sharp Associates) 871
Australian Maps 48
Australian MARC Record Service 48
Australian Medical Index 50
Australian MEDLINE Network 50
Australian MEDLINER 50
Australian Mineral Foundation 57
Australian Municipal Information System 237
Australian National Bibliography 48
Australian National Gallery 58
Australian National Gallery Library Catalogue 58
Australian National Gallery Library Class N Expansion Tables 58
Australian National Gallery Library List of Periodicals 58
Australian National Radio Astronomy Observatory 59
Australian National University 60
Australian National University 61
Australian Opinion Polls 1072
Australian Opinion Polls User Service 1072
Australian Public Affairs Information Service 48
Australian Road Index 62
Australian Road Research Board 62
Australian Road Research Documentation (ARRD) 62
Australian Road Research in Progress 62
Australian Science Index 47
Australian Scientific and Technological Reports 48
Australian Sector Cash Flow Data Base (I.P. Sharp Associates) 871
Australian Social Surveys: Journal Extracts 1974-1978 61
Australian Stock Exchange Indices Data Base (I.P. Sharp Associates) 871
Australian Thesaurus of Earth Sciences and Related Terms 57
Australian Transport Information Directory (ATID) 46
Australian Transport Literature Information System (ATLIS) 46
Australian Transport Research in Progress (ATRIP) 46
Australian University International Development Plan 1073
Austria - Federal Ministry of Buildings and Technology 63
Austria - Federal Ministry of Science and Research 65
Austria - Federal Research and Testing Establishment Arsenal 63
Austria - Minister of Finance 64
Austrian Documentation Centre for Media and Communication Research 65
Austrian Economic Outlook Poll Data Base (I.P. Sharp Associates) 871
Austrian National Institute for Public Health 66
Austrian National Institute for Public Health Review 66
Austrian National Institute for Public Health Yearbook 66
Austrian Standards Institute 587
Authority System Proposal for BISA 1073
Automated Informatics Documentation System (AIDS) Data Base 554
Automated Informatics Documentation System, A Thesaurus for Informatics 554
Automated Informatics Documentation System Trilingual Dictionary 554
Automated Inventory of Canadian Machine Readable Data Files 158
Automated Library Expandable Program Hebrew University of Jerusalem 478
Automated Library Information System - National Technological Library of Denmark 270
Automated Standards and Regulations Information Online 382
Automated Storage and Retrieval of Biomedical Information 296
Automatic Document Request Service - British Library 440
Automatical System of Standards and Metrological Information Data Base 817
Automotive Parts Aftermarket Companies Directory 67
Autoview Services 231
Auxiliary System for Interactive Statistics (AXIS) 932
AVCOR 67
AVCOR Interactive Display 67
Avero Publications Ltd. 757
Aviation Information Services Ltd. 68
Aviation Information Services Ltd. (AISL) Aircraft Data Bases 68
Aviation Newsletter (I.P. Sharp Associates) 871
AVIP (Association of Viewdata Information Providers Ltd.) 1100
AVMARC 439
AVS Intext Ltd. 69
AVS Intext Ltd. 747
AVS Intext Prestel Data Bases 69
AWIDAT (Solid Waste Management Data Bank) 411
AXESS 879
AXIS (Auxiliary System for Interactive Statistics) 932
B.A.R. (Business Activity Report) - Compusearch Market and Social Research Ltd. 236
B.C. Hospital Programs Branch - University of British Columbia 1043
BADADUQ (Banque de Donnees a Acces Direct de l'Universite du Quebec) 1064
BAL (British Architectural Library) 845
BALIS (Bayerisches Landwirtschaftliches Informationssystem) 76
BAM (Bundesanstalt fur Materialprufung) - Germany 415
BAM (Bundesanstalt fur Materialprufung) - Germany 416
BAM (Bundesanstalt fur Materialprufung) - Germany 417
BAM (Bundesanstalt fur Materialprufung) - Germany 418

MASTER INDEX

BAM (Bundesanstalt fur Materialprufung) - Germany 522
Bangladesh National Scientific and Technical Documentation Centre 70
Bangladesh Science and Technology Index 70
Bank Financials Databank (NEEDS-TS) 754
Bank for International Settlements, Quarterly Data Base (I.P. Sharp Associates) 871
Bank for International Settlements, Semi-Annual Data Base (I.P. Sharp Associates) 871
Bank Group for Automation in Management 71
Bank of Canada Weekly Financial Statistics Data Base (I.P. Sharp Associates) 871
Bank of England 72
Bank of England Financial Statistics Data Base 72
Bank of England Quarterly Bulletin 72
Bank Society 73
Banking and Finance Data Bank (NEEDS-TS) 754
Banque de Donnees a Acces Direct de l'Universite du Quebec 1064
Banque de Donnees Agroclimatologie 846
Banque de Donnees du Service Annuaire Electronique 552
Banque de Donnees Internationales de Biometrie Humaine et d'Ergonomie 838
Banque de Donnees Locales (INSEE) 365
Banque de Donnees Macroeconomiques (INSEE) 366
Banque de Donnees Socio-economiques des Pays Mediterraneens 564
Banque de Donnees Urbaines de Paris et de la Region d'Ile-de-France 798
Banque de l'Information Industrielle Pont-a-Mousson (BIIPAM) 820
Banque de Terminologie du Quebec 830
Banque des Connaissances et des Techniques 355
Banque des Donnees du Sous-sol 341
Banque d'Information sur les Recherches INSERM (BIR) 358
Banque d'Informations Automatisees sur les Medicaments 257
Banque d'Informations Politiques et d'Actualites 384
Banque Mondiale des Donnees Gravimetriques 342
Banque Quebecoise d'Information sur l'Environnement Quebecois 832
Banques de Donnees Associees (BDA) 251
Banques de Donnees Associees (BDA) 252
Banques de Donnees Associees (BDA) 514
BANSDOC (Bangladesh National Scientific and Technical Documentation Centre) 70
BAR (Business Activity Report) - Compusearch Market and Social Research Ltd. 236
Bar-Ilan University 74
Barclays Bank 75
Baric Computing Services Ltd. 75
Baric Viewdata 75
Barroslearn 951
BAS (Bibliographic Automated System) Data Base 731
Base de Donnees Cimentieres 188
Base d'Information Robert Debre 566
BASELINE 950
Basic Statistics of the Community 225
BASS (Belgian Archives for the Social Sciences) 611
Bass Communications Pty. Ltd. 245
BATHEDA Thermophysical Data Bank 996
BATREGIO 773
Battlefield Weapons Systems and Technology 97
BAUFO (Bauforschungsprojekte) 374
Bauforschungsprojekte (BAUFO) 374
Bauobjektdokumentation (BODO) 375
Bavarian Agricultural Information System 76
Bavarian Ministry for Food, Agriculture and Forestry 76
Bayer AG 77
Bayerisches Landwirtschaftliches Informationssystem 76
Bayerisches Staatsministerium fur Ernahrung, Landwirtschaft und Forsten 76
BBC (British Broadcasting Corporation) 104
BBC (British Broadcasting Corporation) 105
BBC (British Broadcasting Corporation) 265
BBC Data 104
BBC External Services News Data Base 104
BBC Summary of World Broadcasts 104
BBM Bureau of Measurement 78
BCAVM (British Catalogue of Audiovisual Materials) Data Base 439
BCM (British Catalogue of Music) Data Base 439
BCS (British Computer Society) 107
BCT (Banque des Connaissances et des Techniques) 355
BDA (Banques de Donnees Associees) 251
BDA (Banques de Donnees Associees) 252
BDA (Banques de Donnees Associees) 514
BDD (British Defence Directory) 98
BDEC (Bureau de Developpement de l'Entreprise Commerciale) 797
BDL (Banque de Donnees Locales - INSEE) 365
BDM (Banque de Donnees Macroeconomiques - INSEE) 366
BDU (Banque de Donnees Urbaines de Paris et de la Region d'Ile-de-France) 798
BECAN (Biomedical Engineering Current Awareness Notification) 114
BEFO 959
BEI (British Education Index) 439

Beilstein Handbook of Organic Chemistry 79
Beilstein-Institut fur Literatur der Organischen Chemie 79
Beilstein Institute for Literature in Organic Chemistry 79
Belgian Archives for the Social Sciences 611
Belgian Environmental Research Index 84
Belgian Information and Dissemination Service 80
Belgian National Statistical Institute Data Bases 82
Belgian Translations Center 84
Belgium - Ministry of Economic Affairs 80
Belgium - Ministry of Economic Affairs 81
Belgium - Ministry of Health 83
Belgium - Royal Library of Belgium 84
BELINDIS (Belgian Information and Dissemination Service) 80
Bell Canada Enterprises 973
Bemrose Corporation 85
Bemrose Printing 85
Benjamin (Art) Associates Ltd. 657
Bereich Datenverarbeitung - Siemens AG 874
Bereich Datenverarbeitung - Siemens AG 875
Berlin Technical University 477
Beslissingen in Belastingzaken Nederlandse Belastingrechtspraak 641
Bestandsverzeichnis Thesauri 880
Betriebsforschungsinstitut 398
Betriebsforschungsinstitut 399
BfAi (Bundesstelle fur Aussenhandelsinformation) - Germany 425
BFAR (Bundesforschungsanstalt fur Rebenzuchtung Geilweilerhof) - Germany 585
BFI-Informationsdienst Huttenwerksanlagen 398
BFLR (Bundesforschungsanstalt fur Landeskunde und Raumordnung) - Germany 380
BGI (Bureau Gravimetrique International) 342
BGR (Bundesanstalt fur Geowissenschaften und Rohstoffe) - Germany 412
BGR (Bundesanstalt fur Geowissenschaften und Rohstoffe) - Germany 413
BGR (Bundesanstalt fur Geowissenschaften und Rohstoffe) - Germany 414
BHI (British Humanities Index) 660
BHRA FLUIDEX 86
BHRA, The Fluid Engineering Centre 86
BIAM (Banque d'Informations Automatisees sur les Medicaments) 257
BIB (Brunel Insititute for Bioengineering) 114
BIBLINRIA 361
BIBLIO-DATA 423
Biblio Service Informatique 797
Bibliocentre - Centennial College 182
BIBLIOCOM 619
BiblioFem 209
Bibliografia Brasileira de Agricultura 99
Bibliografia Brasileira de Energia Nuclear 102
Bibliografia Latinoamericana 719
Bibliografias Agricolas 99
Bibliographia Medica Cechoslovaca 250
Bibliographic Automated System (BAS) Data Base 731
Bibliographic Bulletin of the Clearinghouse at IINTE 815
Bibliographic Index of Library Documents (BILD) 481
Bibliographic Information on Southeast Asia 1073
Bibliographic Publishing Co. 87
Bibliographic Services Division - British Library 439
Bibliographic Services Division - British Library 440
Bibliographic Services Division - British Library 441
Bibliographic Star Index (BSI) 905
Bibliographical Repertory of Christian Institutions 205
Bibliographie der Pflanzenschutzliteratur 409
Bibliographie der Wirtschaftswissenschaften 639
Bibliographie Deutschsprachiger Psychologischer Dissertationen 1078
Bibliographie du Quebec 833
Bibliographie du Sport 210
Bibliographie Linguistischer Literatur 368
Bibliographies of Regional Geology 394
Bibliographique Geographique Internationale 355
Bibliography, Machine-Readable Cataloguing and the ESTC 443
Bibliography of Afro-Asian-Australasian Geology 394
Bibliography of American Geology 394
Bibliography of Bibliographies in Social Sciences 1015
Bibliography of Canadian Glaciology 139
Bibliography of Canadian Law 173
Bibliography of Economic Geology 394
Bibliography of Education Theses: A List of Theses in Education Accepted for Higher Degrees at Australian Universities and Colleges 54
Bibliography of Engineering Geology 394
Bibliography of European Geology 394
Bibliography of Foreign S&T Collections in ISTIC 801
Bibliography of German Research on Developing Countries 397
Bibliography of Infant Foods and Nutrition, 1938-1977 47
Bibliography of Internal Migrations 100
Bibliography of Linguistic Literature 368

Bibliography of Nordic Mass Communication Literature 763
Bibliography of Plant Protection 409
Bibliography of Quebec 833
Bibliography of Scientific Research Reports Sponsored by National Science Council, Republic of China 726
Bibliography of Systematic Mycology 229
Bibliography of the Mediterranean Area 412
Bibliography of Urban Development 100
Bibliography on Automatic Data Processing 1121
Bibliography on Foreign Literature of Science and Technology 203
Bibliography on Marine and Estuarine Oil Pollution 684
Bibliography on Marine and Estuarine Pesticide Pollution 684
Bibliography on Petroleum and Social Values 1015
BIBLIOL Data Base 576
BIBLIOS 384
Biblioteka Glowna I Osrodek Informacji Naukowo-Technicznej - Politechnika Wroclawska 965
Bibliotekstjanst 116
Bibliotheek Koninklijke Nederlandse Akademie van Wetenschappen 849
Bibliothek-Verbund-System 875
Bibliotheksdienst 400
Bibliotheque Nationale du Canada 147
Bibliotheque Nationale du Quebec 831
Bibliotheque Nationale du Quebec 833
Bibliotheque Royale de Belgique 84
BIBSYS Data Base 1079
BIFORECAST Data Base (I.P. Sharp Associates) 871
BIHIST Data Base (I.P. Sharp Associates) 871
BIIPAM (Banque de l'Information Industrielle Pont-a-Mousson) 820
BIIPAM-CTIF Data Base 820
BILD (Bibliographic Index of Library Documents) 481
Bildschirmtext 427
Bildschirmtext Magazin fur Teleleser 427
BINS Bibliographic Series 95
Bio-Industry Bulletin 712
BIOCEAN 349
Biocontrol News and Information 229
Biodeterioration Centre - Department of Biological Sciences - University of Aston 1038
Biodeterioration Research Titles 1038
BIODOC 870
Biological Records Centre - Institute of Terrestrial Ecology - Great Britain 461
Biologische Bundesanstalt fur Land- und Forstwirtschaft - Germany 409
Biomechanics and Orthopaedics 114
Biomedical Division - Elsevier Science Publishers B.V. 296
Biomedical Documentation and Information Center - University of Valencia 1082
Biomedical Engineering Current Awareness Notification 114
Biomedical Information Department - State University of Utrecht Library 899
Biomedical Information Service - University of Sheffield 1069
BioSciences Information Service 88
BIOSIS (BioSciences Information Service) 88
BIOSIS, U.K. Ltd. 88
Biotechnology Abstracts 273
Biotel 446
Biotica 702
BIPA (Banque d'Informations Politiques et d'Actualites) 384
BIPE (Bureau d'Informations et de Previsions Economiques) 773
BIR (Banque d'Information sur les Recherches INSERM) 358
Bird (Anthony) Associates 89
BIRD (Base d'Information Robert Debre) 566
Birmingham Libraries Co-operative Mechanisation Project 91
Birmingham Post & Mail 1102
BIS (Business Information Service) - Financial Times Business Information Ltd. 328
BISA (Bibliographic Information on Southeast Asia) 1073
BISA Catalogue on Microfiche 1073
BISQ Data Base (I.P. Sharp Associates) 871
BISS Data Base (I.P. Sharp Associates) 871
BJUS Data Base 282
Black (Prof. John B.) Communications Information Data Base 232
Blackwell BOOKFILE 90
Blackwell Technical Services Ltd. 90
BLAISE (British Library Automated Information Service) 440
BLAISE COM Service 439
BLAISE-LINE 440
BLAISE-LINE Mini Manual 440
BLAISE-LINE User Manual 440
BLAISE-LINK 440
BLAISE-LINK Mini Manual 440
BLAISE-LINK User Manaual 440
BLAISE Newsletter 440
BLCMP (Library Services) Ltd. 91
BLEX Data Base 282
BLIS 959

BLL (Bibliography of Linguistic Literature) 368
BMA (Bundesministerium fur Arbeit und Sozialordnung) - Germany 419
BMA Press Cuttings Database 110
BMAP (BMA Press Cuttings Database) 110
BMFT (Bundesministerium fur Forschung und Technologie) Data Bank 424
BMFT Forderungskatalog 424
BML (Bulgarian Medical Literature) Data Base 120
BMRB (British Market Research Bureau Ltd.) 109
BMvD (Bureau Marcel van Dijk, SA) 122
BNB (British National Bibliography) Data Base 439
BNDO (Bureau National des Donnees Oceaniques) - Centre National pour l'Exploitation des Oceans - France 347
BNDO (Bureau National des Donnees Oceaniques) - Centre National pour l'Exploitation des Oceans - France 348
BNDO (Bureau National des Donnees Oceaniques) - Centre National pour l'Exploitation des Oceans - France 349
BNDO (Bureau National des Donnees Oceaniques) - Centre National pour l'Exploitation des Oceans - France 350
BNDO (Bureau National des Donnees Oceaniques) - Centre National pour l'Exploitation des Oceans - France 351
BNDO (Bureau National des Donnees Oceaniques) - Centre National pour l'Exploitation des Oceans - France 352
BNDO (Bureau National des Donnees Oceaniques) - Centre National pour l'Exploitation des Oceans - France 353
BNDO (Bureau National des Donnees Oceaniques) - Centre National pour l'Exploitation des Oceans - France 354
BNDO (Bureau National des Donnees Oceaniques) Data Banks 347
BNF Abstracts 92
BNF Metals Technology Centre 92
BNR (Brassey's Naval Record) 97
BNR Monthly 97
BNT (Boreal Northern Titles) 95
BODIL Data Base 938
Bodleian Library 757
BODO (Bauobjektdokumentation) 375
Bok-Sok 116
Boletin Bibliografico 892
Boletin de Traducciones 890
Bolivia - National Scientific and Technological Documentation Center 93
BONDBOOK 895
BONDSPEC 895
Bonnier Business Publishing Group 94
BONTRAN 895
Book Catalog of NSTA and Agencies (Philippines) 808
Book Catalogue of Tourism Research Studies 137
BOOKALERT 605
BOOKFILE 90
BOOKLINE - Blackwell Technical Services Ltd. 90
Boots-Celltech Diagnostics Ltd. 181
Boreal Institute for Northern Studies 95
Boreal Library Catalogue 95
Boreal Northern Titles (BNT) 95
Boris Kidric Institute of Nuclear Sciences 96
Boris Kidric Laboratory for Information Systems Data Bases 96
Boroughs Intelligence Newsletter 465
Bottin Data Bases 280
BPM Holdings Ltd. 1102
Brassey's Multi-Lingual Military Dictionary 97
Brassey's Naval Record 97
Brassey's Publishers Ltd. 97
Brassey's Publishers Ltd. 98
Brazil - Ministry of Agriculture 99
Brazil - Ministry of the Interior 100
Brazil - National Center for Micrographic Development 101
Brazil - National Commission for Nuclear Energy 102
Brazil - National Council of Scientific and Technological Development 103
Brazil Ministry of the Interior Data Bases 100
Brazil Report 651
Brazilian Bibliography in Science and Technology 103
Brazilian Institute for Information in Science and Technology 103
Brazilian Union Catalog for Scientific and Technological Serials 103
BRC (Biological Records Centre) - Institute of Terrestrial Ecology - Great Britain 461
BRGM (Bureau de Recherches Geologiques et Minieres) - France 340
BRGM (Bureau de Recherches Geologiques et Minieres) - France 341
BRGM (Bureau de Recherches Geologiques et Minieres) - France 342
BRGM (Bureau de Recherches Geologiques et Minieres) - France 412
Brigitte 71
Brisbane TV Ltd. 245
BRISES 355
Britain's Top 1000 Foreign Owned Companies 636
Britain's Top 2000 Private Companies 636
British Architectural Library 845
British Broadcasting Corporation 104
British Broadcasting Corporation 105
British Broadcasting Corporation 265

British Catalogue of Audiovisual Materials 439
British Catalogue of Music 439
British Columbia Decisions, Civil Cases 1108
British Columbia Decisions, Criminal Cases 1108
British Columbia Decisions, Labour Arbitration in B.C. 1108
British Columbia Decisions, Labour Relations Board Decisions 1108
British Columbia Economic Accounts 106
British Columbia Hospital Programs Branch - University of British Columbia 1043
British Columbia Manpower Survey Data Base 106
British Columbia Ministry of Industry and Small Business Development 106
British Columbia Regulations 828
British Computer Society 107
British Council 24
British Council 108
British Council Prestel File 108
British Defence Directory 98
British Education Index 439
British Educational Reference Books 108
British Food Manufacturing Industries Research Association 655
British Geological Survey - Natural Environment Research Council 727
British Geological Survey - Natural Environment Research Council 728
British Humanities Index 660
British Hydromechanics Research Association 86
British Independent Broadcasting Authority 779
British Library 246
British Library 439
British Library 440
British Library 441
British Library 442
British Library 443
British Library 444
British Library 445
British Library 446
British Library 677
British Library 818
British Library 1039
British Library Automated Information Service 440
British Library Conference Proceedings Index 442
British Library Department of Printed Books (DPB) Data Base 440
British Library Research and Development Newsletter 444
British Library Research Reviews 444
British Market Research Bureau Ltd. 109
British Medical Association 110
British National Bibliography 439
British Non-Ferrous Metals Technology Centre 92
British Petroleum Ltd. 867
British Reports, Translations, and Theses 442
British Standards 958
British Standards Institution 111
British Technology Index 662
British Telecommunications 447
British Telecommunications 448
British Telecommunications 976
British Universities Film & Video Council Ltd. 112
BRIX - Building Research Establishment Library - Department of the Environment - Great Britain 453
BRIX Data Base 453
Brown Corpus 768
Brown's Geological Information Bulletin 113
Brown's Geological Information Service Ltd. 113
Brukermeldinger 771
Brunel Institute for Bioengineering 114
Brunel University 114
Brunel University 115
Brussels Free University 381
BRWE (Business Review Weekly) Data Base 55
BSC Newsletter 107
BSI (Bibliographic Star Index) 905
BSI (British Standards Institution) 111
BSO (Business Statistics Office) - Department of Trade and Industry - Great Britain 454
BSRIA (Building Services Research and Information Association) 119
BSRIA Statistics Bulletin 119
BTE (Bureau of Transport Economics) - Australia 46
BTE Information Systems 46
BTI (British Technology Index) 662
BTJ (Bibliotekstjanst) 116
BTQ (Banque de Terminologie du Quebec) 830
BTQ-7 (Brisbane TV Ltd.) 245
Btx (Bildschirmtext) 427
BUFVC (British Universities Film & Video Council Ltd.) 112
BUFVC Catalogue 112
Builders' and Repairers' Lien Case Book 829
Building Articles in Hungarian Publications 494
Building Center 117
Building Commodity File 934
Building Commodity Index 934

Building/Construction/Architecture Databases 775
Building in China - Selected Papers 203
Building Information Institute 118
Building Product File 118
Building Research and Practice 573
Building Research Establishment - Department of the Environment - Great Britain 452
Building Research Establishment Library - Department of the Environment - Great Britain 453
Building Research Projects Data Base 374
Building Services Research and Information Association 119
Building Structures 203
Buildings Documentation Data Base 375
Buildings of Canada 138
Bulgaria - Central Medical Library 120
Bulgaria - Medical Academy 120
Bulgaria - National Agro-Industrial Union 121
Bulgarian Medical Literature (BML) Data Base 120
Bulk Ferro-Alloys Monitor 228
BULLETIN (Harwell Central Information Service) 434
Bulletin Analytique du Centre de Documentation du CERILH 188
Bulletin Bibliographique Fonderie 820
Bulletin Bibliographique INTD 722
Bulletin Calvados 22
Bulletin CIS 595
Bulletin de Documentation Electricite de France 295
Bulletin de la Construction Mecanique 957
Bulletin de Liaison de la Recherche en Informatique et en Automatique 361
Bulletin inter Villes Nouvelles 1091
Bulletin Mensuel d'Information du Centre de Creation Industrielle CCI 184
Bulletin of Chinese Conference Proceedings and Papers 801
Bulletin of Documentation 1121
Bulletin of Entomological Research 229
Bulletin of Industry and Construction 493
Bulletin of Labour Statistics 592
Bulletin of Marine Ecology 729
Bulletin of Zoological Nomenclature 229
Bulletin Officiel de la Propriete Industrielle 359
Bulletin Scientifique de l'Institut Textile de France 390
Bulletin Signaletique 355
Bulletin Signaletique 356
Bulletin Signaletique des Telecommunications 367
Bulletin Signaletique Hebdomadaire 339
BUMS Data Base 116
BUMS Manual 116
BUMS System 116
Bundesanstalt fur Arbeit - Germany 410
Bundesanstalt fur Arbeitsschutz - Germany 419
Bundesanstalt fur Geowissenschaften und Rohstoffe - Germany 412
Bundesanstalt fur Geowissenschaften und Rohstoffe - Germany 413
Bundesanstalt fur Geowissenschaften und Rohstoffe - Germany 414
Bundesanstalt fur Materialprufung - Germany 415
Bundesanstalt fur Materialprufung - Germany 416
Bundesanstalt fur Materialprufung - Germany 417
Bundesanstalt fur Materialprufung - Germany 418
Bundesanstalt fur Materialprufung - Germany 522
BUNDESBANK Data Base (I.P. Sharp Associates) 871
Bundesforschungsanstalt fur Fischerei - Germany 421
Bundesforschungsanstalt fur Getreide- und Kartoffelverarbeitung - Germany 583
Bundesforschungsanstalt fur Landeskunde und Raumordnung - Germany 380
Bundesforschungsanstalt fur Rebenzuchtung Geilweilerhof - Germany 585
Bundesinstitut fur Sportwissenschaft - Germany 420
Bundesministerium der Justiz 426
Bundesministerium fur Arbeit und Sozialordnung - Germany 419
Bundesministerium fur Bauten und Technik - Austria 63
Bundesministerium fur Ernahrung, Landwirtschaft und Forsten - Germany 408
Bundesministerium fur Ernahrung, Landwirtschaft und Forsten - Germany 421
Bundesministerium fur Forschung und Technologie - Germany 43
Bundesministerium fur Forschung und Technologie - Germany 399
Bundesministerium fur Forschung und Technologie - Germany 401
Bundesministerium fur Forschung und Technologie - Germany 424
Bundesministerium fur Forschung und Technologie - Germany 880
Bundesministerium fur Forschung und Technologie - Germany 1045
Bundesministerium fur Jugend, Familie und Gesundheit - Germany 428
Bundesministerium fur Post- und Fernmeldewesen - Germany 427
Bundesministerium fur Wirtschaft - Germany 425
Bundesstelle fur Aussenhandelsinformation - Germany 425
Bundesverband der Pharmazeutischen Industrie 805
Bundesversuchs- und Forschungsanstalt Arsenal - Bundesministerium fur Bauten und Technik - Austria 63
Bureau de Developpement de l'Entreprise Commerciale 797
Bureau de Documentation Juridique et Technique - Institut National de la

Propriete Industrielle - France   360
Bureau de Recherches Geologiques et Minieres - France   340
Bureau de Recherches Geologiques et Minieres - France   341
Bureau de Recherches Geologiques et Minieres - France   342
Bureau de Recherches Geologiques et Minieres - France   412
Bureau des Resumes Analytiques du Conseil International des Unions Scientifiques   575
Bureau d'Evaluation Scientifique - Institut National de la Sante et de la Recherche Medicale - France   358
Bureau d'Informations et de Previsions Economiques   773
Bureau for Labour Problems Analysis - International Labour Office   591
Bureau Gravimetrique International   342
Bureau Gravimetrique International Bulletin d'Information   342
Bureau International - Union Postale Universelle   1030
Bureau Marcel van Dijk, SA   122
Bureau National des Donnees Oceaniques (BNDO) Data Banks   347
Bureau National des Donnees Oceaniques - Centre National pour l'Exploitation des Oceans - France   347
Bureau National des Donnees Oceaniques - Centre National pour l'Exploitation des Oceans - France   348
Bureau National des Donnees Oceaniques - Centre National pour l'Exploitation des Oceans - France   349
Bureau National des Donnees Oceaniques - Centre National pour l'Exploitation des Oceans - France   350
Bureau National des Donnees Oceaniques - Centre National pour l'Exploitation des Oceans - France   351
Bureau National des Donnees Oceaniques - Centre National pour l'Exploitation des Oceans - France   352
Bureau National des Donnees Oceaniques - Centre National pour l'Exploitation des Oceans - France   353
Bureau National des Donnees Oceaniques - Centre National pour l'Exploitation des Oceans - France   354
Bureau of Broadcast Measurement   78
Bureau of Geological and Mining Research - France   340
Bureau of Geological and Mining Research - France   341
Bureau of Geological and Mining Research - France   342
Bureau of Geological and Mining Research - France   412
Bureau of Statistics - International Labour Office   592
Bureau of Transport Economics - Australia   46
Business Activity Report - Compusearch Market and Social Research Ltd.   236
BUSINESS Data Base (ONLINE GmbH)   774
Business In View   473
Business Information Australia   55
Business Information International   123
Business Information Service - Financial Times Business Information Ltd.   328
Business International Economic Forecasts Data Base (I.P. Sharp Associates)   871
Business International Historical Data Base (I.P. Sharp Associates)   871
Business Monitor Series   454
Business Press International Ltd.   612
Business Review Weekly (BRWE) Data Base   55
Business Statistics Office - Department of Trade and Industry - Great Britain   454
BVR (Byggvaruregistret)   934
BVS (Bibliothek-Verbund-System)   875
BYGGDOK (Institutet for Byggdokumentation)   938
Byggreferat   938
Byggvaruforteckning   934
Byggvaruregistret   934
C-13 Nuclear Magnetic Resonance (BASF)   521
C.A.P. Monitor   8
C-CORE (Centre for Cold Ocean Research Engineering)   694
C.D.I.U.P.A. (Centre de Documentation Internationale des Industries Utilisatrices de Produits Agricoles)   39
C.I.S. (Centre d'Information Spectroscopique et Physico-Chimique d'Analyse)   466
C76 Journey-To-Work Data Bases   237
C76 LGA Descriptor Data Base   237
C76 LGA File Zero Data Bases   237
C76 Postcode Data Bases   237
C81 Geographic Descriptor Data Base   237
C81 LGA Data Base   237
C81 Postcode Data Base   237
CA (Cadmium Association)   1122
CA Selects   851
CAB (Commonwealth Agricultural Bureaux)   229
CAB (Commonwealth Agricultural Bureaux)   583
CAB Abstracts   229
CAB Abstracts/Animal (DIMDI)   428
CAB Abstracts Online Newsletter   229
CAB Abstracts/Plant (DIMDI)   428
CAB Serials Checklist   229
CAB Thesaurus   229
CABIS (Computer Aided Bibliographic Information Service) Data Base   509
Cable   1

Cablesystems Alberta Ltd.   124
CABS (Current Awareness in Biological Sciences)   803
CABS-TEXT   803
CAC (Compagnie des Agents de Change)   389
CADIS (Communications and Directory Information System)   19
CADIS (Computer Aided Directory Information Service) Data Base   509
Cadmium Abstracts   1122
Cadmium Association   1122
CAF (Charities Aid Foundation)   198
CAFRAD (Centre Africain de Formation et de Recherche Administratives pour le Developpement)   7
CAG (Cooperative Automation Group)   246
Cahiers de Documentation   1091
Cahiers Financiers   251
CAICYT (Centro Argentino de Informacion Cientifica y Tecnologica)   28
CAIRS (Computer Assisted Information Retrieval System) - Leatherhead Food Research Association   655
CAIS (Canadian Association for Information Science)   168
CAIS/ACSI Newsletter   168
Caisse des Depots et Consignations   71
Caixa d'Estalvis de Sabadell   860
Caja de Ahorros de Valencia   1082
CAJAD (Center po Atomn. i Jadernum Dannym) - U.S.S.R. State Committee on the Utilization of Atomic Energy - Union of Soviet Socialist Republics   999
CALDOC (Calgary Public Library Government Documents)   1033
Calendar of Forthcoming Scientific and Technological Meetings to be Held in Israel   616
Calendar of I&D Activities   880
Calgary Cable TV/FM Ltd.   124
Calgary Public Information Department   124
Calgary Public Library Government Documents (CALDOC)   1033
Calvados Service Data Bases   22
Cambridge Crystallographic Data Centre   125
Cambridge Structural Database (CSD)   125
Cambridge University   125
CAMN (Canadian Directory of Completed Master's Theses in Nursing)   1037
CAMN User's Manual   1037
CAN (Centralforbundet for Alkohol- och Narkotikaupplysning)   936
CAN/DOC   153
CAN/LAW   162
CAN/MARC   148
CAN/MARC   150
CAN/OLE (Canadian Online Enquiry System)   153
CAN/OLE Bulletin   153
CAN/OLE Database Manual   153
CAN/OLE User's Manual   153
CAN/SDI (Canadian Service for the Selective Dissemination of Information)   154
CAN/SDI Profile Design Manual   154
CAN/SND (Scientific Numeric Databases) - Canada Institute for Scientific and Technical Information   155
Canada - Agriculture Canada   126
Canada - Agriculture Canada   127
Canada - Agriculture Canada   128
Canada - Agriculture Canada   167
Canada - Consumer and Corporate Affairs Canada   129
Canada - Department of Communications   130
Canada - Department of Communications   819
Canada - Department of Energy, Mines and Resources   44
Canada - Department of Energy, Mines and Resources   45
Canada - Department of Energy, Mines and Resources   131
Canada - Department of Energy, Mines and Resources   132
Canada - Department of Energy, Mines and Resources   133
Canada - Department of Energy, Mines and Resources   134
Canada - Department of Energy, Mines and Resources   135
Canada - Department of Energy, Mines and Resources   136
Canada - Department of Industry, Trade & Commerce   137
Canada - Environment Canada   138
Canada - Environment Canada   139
Canada - Environment Canada   140
Canada - Environment Canada   141
Canada - Environment Canada   142
Canada - Environment Canada   143
Canada - Environment Canada   144
Canada - Health and Welfare Canada   145
Canada - National Film Board of Canada   146
Canada - National Library of Canada   147
Canada - National Library of Canada   148
Canada - National Library of Canada   149
Canada - National Library of Canada   150
Canada - National Library of Canada   151
Canada - National Research Council of Canada   152
Canada - National Research Council of Canada   153
Canada - National Research Council of Canada   154
Canada - National Research Council of Canada   155

Canada - National Research Council of Canada   156
Canada - Parliament of Canada   157
Canada - Public Archives of Canada   158
Canada - Statistics Canada   159
Canada - Statistics Canada   160
Canada - Transport Canada   161
Canada Centre for Geoscience Data   135
Canada Centre for Mineral and Energy Technology   131
Canada Centre for Remote Sensing   132
Canada Corporations Bulletin   129
Canada Geographic Information System   143
Canada-Histoire Data Base   704
Canada Institute for Scientific and Technical Information   152
Canada Institute for Scientific and Technical Information   153
Canada Institute for Scientific and Technical Information   154
Canada Institute for Scientific and Technical Information   155
Canada Land Data Systems Division - Lands Directorate - Environment Canada   143
Canada Law Book Ltd.   162
Canada Law Book Ltd.   1108
Canada Library of Parliament Data Bases   157
Canada Systems Group   163
Canada Systems Group   164
Canada Systems Group   165
Canada Systems Group   166
Canadian Agricultural Research Council   167
Canadian Art Auction Records Data Base   300
Canadian Art Auctions: Sales and Prices   300
Canadian Asbestos Information Center   1071
Canadian Association for Information Science   168
Canadian Bonds Data Base (I.P. Sharp Associates)   871
Canadian Book Exchange Centre   147
Canadian Broadcasting Corporation   169
Canadian Business and Current Affairs   707
Canadian Business and Current Affairs   708
Canadian Business Index   707
Canadian Business Law Journal   162
Canadian Business Periodicals Index   707
Canadian Catalog Service   171
Canadian Charter of Rights Decisions   1108
Canadian Chartered Banks, Annual Data Base (I.P. Sharp Associates)   871
Canadian Chartered Banks, Monthly Data Base (I.P. Sharp Associates)   871
Canadian Chartered Banks Monthly Statement of Assets and Liabilities Data Base (I.P. Sharp Associates)   871
Canadian Chartered Banks, Quarterly Data Base (I.P. Sharp Associates)   871
Canadian Chartered Banks Quarterly Income Statement Data Base (I.P. Sharp Associates)   871
Canadian Chartered Banks, Yearly Data Base (I.P. Sharp Associates)   871
Canadian Clearinghouse for Ongoing Research in Nursing   1036
Canadian Contributions to Rock Mechanics   131
Canadian Corporate Data Bank   680
Canadian Criminal Cases   162
Canadian Department of Insurance Data Base (I.P. Sharp Associates)   871
Canadian Department of Insurance Property and Casualty Insurance Data Base (I.P. Sharp Associates)   871
Canadian Directory of Completed Master's Theses in Nursing   1037
Canadian Directory of Public Legal Education and Information   173
Canadian Education Association   170
Canadian Education Index   170
Canadian Education Subject Headings   170
Canadian Energy Information System   133
Canadian Engineering Publications Ltd.   171
Canadian Environment (CENV) Data Base   140
Canadian Exchequer Reports   828
Canadian Federal Corporations and Directors Data Base   163
Canadian Financial Database   430
Canadian Geographic Information System (CGIS) Data Sets   143
Canadian Hydrological Operational Multipurpose Subprogramme (CHOMS) Data Base   140
Canadian Independent Record Production Association   206
Canadian Index of Scientific and Technical Translations   152
Canadian Index to Geoscience Data   135
Canadian Information Industry Association   172
Canadian International Development Agency   34
Canadian Inventory of Historic Building   138
Canadian Journal of Information Science   168
Canadian Law Information Council   173
Canadian Library Association   174
Canadian Library Handbook   706
Canadian Library/Information Science Research Projects: A List   149
Canadian Locations of Journals Indexed for MEDLINE   152
Canadian MARC   148
Canadian MARC   150
Canadian MARC Communication Format Specifications Series   150
Canadian Micrographic Society   175
Canadian Mineral Occurrence Index   134
Canadian Network Papers   147
Canadian News Index   708
Canadian On-line Record Database (CORD)   206
Canadian Online Enquiry System   153
Canadian Operating Statistics Data Base (I.P. Sharp Associates)   871
Canadian Patent Reporter   162
Canadian Periodical Index   174
Canadian Plains Bulletin   1066
Canadian Plains Research Center   1066
Canadian Press Extra (CPX)   828
Canadian Press NewsFile   708
Canadian Press Newstex (CPN)   828
Canadian Record Catalogue   206
Canadian Register of Research and Researchers in the Social Sciences   1087
Canadian Renewable Energy Database (ENERCAN)   16
Canadian Renewable Energy Database (ENERCAN)   152
Canadian Retail Gasoline Volume Data Base (I.P. Sharp Associates)   871
Canadian Service for the Selective Dissemination of Information   154
Canadian Social Science Abstracts   1120
Canadian Social Science Data Archive Catalogue   1120
Canadian Socio-Economic Information Management System   159
Canadian Socio-Economic Information Management System   160
Canadian Standards Information Service Data Base   898
Canadian Stock Options (CDNOPT) Data Base   986
Canadian Studies in Population   1035
Canadian Subject Headings   148
Canadian Technical and Scientific Information News Journal   963
Canadian Theses   148
Canadian Theses on Microfiche: Catalogue   148
Canadian Theses on Microfiche Service   148
Canadian Transportation Documentation System   161
Canadian Women of Note Archive (CWONC)   1120
Canadiana   148
Canadiana Editorial Division - Cataloguing Branch - National Library of Canada   148
CANCERNET   357
CANCERNET Thesaurus   357
CANCERNET User's Manual   357
Cancerologie/Oncology - Bulletin Signaletique   357
CANMET (Canada Centre for Mineral and Energy Technology)   131
CANMET Review   131
CANMINDEX (Canadian Mineral Occurrence Index)   134
CANOM   720
CANPLAINS Data Base   1066
CANREGISTER   1087
CANSIM (Canadian Socio-Economic Information Management System)   159
CANSIM (Canadian Socio-Economic Information Management System)   160
CANSIM (Canadian Socio-Economic Information Management System) Cross-Classified Base   159
CANSIM (Canadian Socio-Economic Information Management System) Main Base   159
CANSIM (Canadian Socio-Economic Information Management System) Mini Base   159
CANSIM Interactive System (CIS)   159
CANSIM Main Base Series Directory   159
CANSIM Mini Base Series Directory   159
CANSIM Summary Data System   159
CANSIM Table Analysis Package (TAP)   159
Cantel   518
CANUCS (Union List of Serials in the Social Sciences and Humanities Held by Canadian Libraries) Data Base   151
CAOCI (Commercially Available Organic Chemicals Index) Project   372
CAP Databank   214
CAPA   80
Capital Market Indicators (NEEDS-TS)   754
Capital Planning Information Ltd.   176
CAPRI (Computerized Administration of Patent Documents Reclassified According to the IPC) Data Base   64
CAPTAIN   759
Caption Creation System   764
Caption Encoding System   764
Careerdata   747
Careers and Occupational Information Centre   462
Caribbean Industrial Research Institute   177
Caribbean Report   651
CARIRI (Caribbean Industrial Research Institute)   177
CARIS (Current Agricultural Research Information System)   1009
Carleton Library System   179
Carleton University   178
Carleton University Bibliographical Enquiry   179
Carleton University Library   179
CARS Vehicle Data Bank System   1104
CAS (Chemical Abstracts Service)   901

CAS Industrial Engineering Index   885
Case Law Report Updating Service (CLARUS) Data Base   517
Catalog of Patents Related to Asbestos   1071
Catalog of Periodical Titles Abstracted in SPHINX   363
Catalog of Stellar Groups (CSG)   905
Catalog of Stellar Indentifications (CSI)   905
Catalogo Coletivo de Publicacoes Periodicas   103
Catalogo dei Libri in Commercio   87
Catalogo dei Periodici Italiani   87
Catalogo Italiano Riviste su Calcolatore Elettronico (CIRCE)   87
Catalogue des Disques Canadiens   206
Catalogue des Normes Francaises   382
Catalogue des Normes ISO   382
Catalogue des Publications de la Documentation Francaise   384
Catalogue des Titres de Periodiques Depouilles dans SPHINX   363
Catalogue on English Translations of German Standards   407
Catalogue Support System   1094
Catalogue Support System (CATSS) Data Base   1094
Catalogue System Update Program   179
Cataloguing Branch - National Library of Canada   148
Catchword and Trade Name Index   662
CATED (Centre d'Assistance Technique et de Documentation)   610
CATSS (Catalogue Support System)   1094
CATSS News   1094
CATSUP (Catalogue System Update Program)   179
Caulfield Institute of Technology Library   204
Cawkell Information & Technology Services Ltd.   180
CBA (Current Biotechnology Abstracts)   854
CBC (Canadian Broadcasting Corporation)   169
CBI (Canadian Business Index)   707
CBST (Current Bibliography on Science and Technology) Data Base   632
CBT (Centre Belge de Traductions)   84
CBTDC (China Building Technology Development Centre)   203
CCDC (Cambridge Crystallographic Data Centre)   125
CCGD (Canada Centre for Geoscience Data)   135
CCI (Centre de Creation Industrielle)   184
CCS (Centro Calculo Sabadell)   860
CDC (Caisse des Depots et Consignations)   71
CDC (Control Data Corporation)   245
CDCT (Centro de Documentacao Cientifica e Tecnica) - Instituto Nacional de Investigacao Cientifica - Portugal   821
CDIUPA (Centre de Documentation Internationale des Industries Utilisatrices de Produits Agricoles   39
CDM (Centre de Documentation de la Mecanique) - Centre Technique des Industries Mecaniques   957
CDNBOND Data Base (I.P. Sharp Associates)   871
CDNOPT (Canadian Stock Options) Data Base   986
CDOIP Data Base (I.P. Sharp Associates)   871
CDS (Centre de Donnees Stellaires) - Strasbourg Observatory   905
CDS (Centre de Donnees Stellaires) - Strasbourg Observatory   995
CDS (Chemical Data Services) - IPC Industrial Press Ltd.   612
CDS/ISIS (Computerized Documentation Service/Integrated Set of Information Systems)   1017
CDS/ISIS Newsletter   1017
CDSH (Centre de Documentation Sciences Humaines) - Centre National de la Recherche Scientifique - France   355
CDST (Centre de Documentation Scientifique et Technique) - Centre National de la Recherche Scientifique - France   356
CDT (Centre d'Excellence pour le Developpement de la Technologie Telidon)   819
CEA (Chemical Engineering Abstracts)   852
CEA (Commissariat a l'Energie Atomique) - France   338
CEA (Commissariat a l'Energie Atomique) - France   339
CEA (Commissariat a l'Energie Atomique) - France   589
CEAS (Chemical Emergency Agency Service)   435
CEC (Commission of the European Communities)   213
CEC (Commission of the European Communities)   214
CEC (Commission of the European Communities)   215
CEC (Commission of the European Communities)   216
CEC (Commission of the European Communities)   217
CEC (Commission of the European Communities)   218
CEC (Commission of the European Communities)   219
CEC (Commission of the European Communities)   220
CEC (Commission of the European Communities)   221
CEC (Commission of the European Communities)   222
CEC (Commission of the European Communities)   223
CEC (Commission of the European Communities)   224
CEC (Commission of the European Communities)   225
CEC (Commission of the European Communities)   226
CEC (Commission of the European Communities)   227
CEC (Commission of the European Communities)   306
CEC (Commission of the European Communities)   489
CEC (Commission of the European Communities)   595
CEC (Commission of the European Communities)   717
CECILE Data Base   184
CEDATAH (Collection des Etudes Documentaires Appliquees a la Traduction Automatique et Humaine) Data Base   191
CEDOCAR (Centre de Documentation de l'Armement)   345

CEDRE (Centre de Documentation de Recherche et d'Experimentations sur les Pollutions Accidentelles des Eaux)   353
CEEFAX   105
CEESI (Centre d'Etudes et d'Experimentation des Systemes d'Information)   190
CEI (Canadian Education Index) Data Base   170
CEJ (Centre d'Edition Juridique)   704
CELADE (Centro Latinoamericano de Demografia)   1007
CELEX (Communitatis Europeae Lex)   489
Celltech Ltd.   181
Cement Data Base   188
CEMT (Conference Europeenne des Ministres des Transports)   309
CENADEM (Centro Nacional de Desenvolvimento Micrografico) - Brazil   101
CENAGRI (Centro Nacional de Informacao Documental Agricola) - Ministerio da Agricultura - Brazil   99
CENDIS (Centre de Documentation et d'Information Interuniversitaire en Sciences Sociales)   611
CENELEC Electronic Components Committee   958
CENIDS (Centro Nacional de Informacion y Documentacion en Salud) - Mexico   700
Census of Commerce Databank (NEEDS-TS)   754
CENSUS81 Data Base (I.P. Sharp Associates)   871
Centennial College   182
Centennial College Bibliocentre Data Base   182
Center for Agricultural Documentation and Information - Ministry for Food, Agriculture and Forestry - Germany   408
Center for Agricultural Documentation and Information Data Base   408
Center for Automated Information and Documentation   38
Center for Documentation on Ordnance   345
Center for Econometric Data Development & Research   754
Center for Historical Social Research   183
Center for Industrial Creation   184
Center for Informatics Applied to Development and Tropical Agriculture - Royal Museum of Central Africa   846
Center for Information and Documentation - Netherlands Organization for Applied Scientific Research   739
Center for International Prospective Studies   185
Center for Nuclear Information - National Commission for Nuclear Energy - Brazil   102
Center for Nuclear Structure and Reaction Data - U.S.S.R. State Committee on the Utilization of Atomic Energy - Union of Soviet Socialist Republics   999
Center for Psychological Information and Documentation   1078
Center for Research and Studies on Mediterranean Societies   186
Center for Scientific and Humanistic Information - National Autonomous University of Mexico   719
Center for Scientific and Technical Research for the Metal Manufacturing Industry   187
Center for Scientific Information in Medicine and Health - Medical Academy - Bulgaria   120
Center for Scientific, Technical and Economic Information - Agricultural Academy - National Agro-Industrial Union - Bulgaria   121
Center for Social Science Research and Documentation for the Arab Region   1015
Center for Study and Research of the Hydraulic Binders Industry   188
Center for Technical Assistance and Documentation - Interprofessional Technical Union of the National Federations of Buildings and Public Works   610
Center for the Study of Advertising Support   189
Center for the Study on Information Systems in Government   190
Center for Translation Documentation   191
Center of Experimental Metallurgy   192
Center of Research and Documentation of Christian Institutions   205
Center of Technical Terminology   1040
Center po Atomn. i Jadernum Dannym - U.S.S.R. State Committee on the Utilization of Atomic Energy - Union of Soviet Socialist Republics   999
Center po Jadernum Dannym   546
CENTOB (Centre National de Tri d'Oceanographie Biologique)   349
Central American National and Regional Standards Data Base   193
Central American Patents Data Base   193
Central American Research Institute for Industry   193
Central Archives for Empirical Social Research - University of Cologne   1045
Central Bureau of Statistics - Ministry of Finances and Customs - Norway   766
Central Computer and Telecommunications Agency - Great Britain   459
Central Electronic Network for Data Processing and Analysis   194
Central Embryological Library - Hubrecht Laboratory   490
Central Information, Library and Editorial Section - Commonwealth Scientific and Industrial Research Organization - Australia   47
Central Information Service - The British Council   108
Central Information Service - University of London   1055
Central Information Services News (University of London)   1055
Central Institute for Information and Documentation - German Democratic Republic   395
Central Library - Free University of Brussels   381
Central Library and Documentation Branch - International Labour

Office 593
Central Medical Library - Bulgaria 120
Central Medical Library - Finland 329
Central Ontario Regional Library System 195
Central Patents Index 275
Central Project Administration for Current Agricultural Research in the Netherlands 742
Central Regional Databank (NEEDS-TS) 754
Central Research Establishment - Home Office Forensic Science Service - Great Britain 458
Central Services Branch - Alberta Municipal Affairs 10
Central Statistical Office - Great Britain 449
Central Statistical Office Macro-Economic Data Bank 449
Central Statistical Office Macro-Economic Data Bank Index 449
Central Statistics Bureau - British Columbia Ministry of Industry and Small Business Development 106
Central Technological Library of Norway 1079
Central Telecommunications Services - Posts and Telegraphs Denmark 271
Central Unit of EURYDICE 215
Centrale des Bibliotheques - Ministere de l'Education du Quebec 831
Centralforbundet for Alkohol- och Narkotikaupplysning 936
Centre Africain de Formation et de Recherche Administratives pour le Developpement 7
Centre Belge de Traductions 84
Centre d'Assistance Technique et de Documentation - Union Technique Interprofessionnelle des Federations Nationales du Batiment et des Travaux Publics 610
Centre de Creation Industrielle 184
Centre de Documentation - Centre d'Etudes et de Recherches de l'Industrie des Liants Hydrauliques 188
Centre de Documentation - Institut de Recherches sur les Fruits et Agrumes 547
Centre de Documentation - Institut Francais des Petroles 387
Centre de Documentation - Ministere de l'Environnement du Quebec 832
Centre de Documentation de la Mecanique - Centre Technique des Industries Mecaniques 957
Centre de Documentation de l'Armement 345
Centre de Documentation de Recherche et d'Experimentations sur les Pollutions Accidentelles des Eaux 353
Centre de Documentation en Cancerologie - Centre National de la Recherche Scientifique - France 357
Centre de Documentation et d'Information Interuniversitaire en Sciences Sociales 611
Centre de Documentation Internationale des Industries Utilisatrices de Produits Agricoles 39
Centre de Documentation Sciences Humaines 355
Centre de Documentation Scientifique et Technique - Centre National de la Recherche Scientifique - France 356
Centre de Documentation Scientifique et Technique - Centre National de la Recherche Scientifique - France 377
Centre de Documentation sur l'Urbanisme - Service Technique de l'Urbanisme 1091
Centre de Donnees Stellaires - Strasbourg Observatory 905
Centre de Donnees Stellaires - Strasbourg Observatory 995
Centre de Preparation Documentaire a la Traduction 191
Centre de Recherche Documentaire 282
Centre de Recherche et d'Etudes sur les Societes Mediterraneennes 186
Centre de Recherches de Pont-a-Mousson 820
Centre de Recherches et de Documentation des Institutions Chretiennes 205
Centre de Recherches Scientifiques et Techniques de l'Industrie des Fabrications Metalliques 187
Centre de Traitement de l'Information - Ministere des Affaires Economiques - Belgium 80
Centre d'Edition Juridique 704
Centre d'Etude des Supports de Publicite 189
Centre d'Etudes des Systemes d'Information des Administrations 190
Centre d'Etudes et de Recherches de l'Industrie des Liants Hydrauliques 188
Centre d'Etudes et d'Experimentation des Systemes d'Information 190
Centre d'Etudes Nucleaires de Saclay 339
Centre d'Etudes Prospectives et d'Informations Internationales 185
Centre d'Etudes Techniques de l'Equipement Nord-Picardie/Docamenor 1091
Centre d'Excellence pour le Developpement de la Technologie Telidon 819
Centre d'Information des Banques de Donnees et du Videotex 1
Centre d'Information et de Documentation - Compagnie des Agents de Change 389
Centre d'Information Spectroscopique et Physico-Chimique d'Analyse 466
Centre d'Information Textile Habillement 980
Centre d'Informatique Appliquee au Developpement et a l'Agriculture Tropicale 846
Centre d'Informatique et de Documentation Automatique 38

Centre for Agricultural Publishing and Documentation 583
Centre for Agricultural Publishing and Documentation 731
Centre for Catalogue Research - University of Bath 1039
Centre for Catalogue Research Newsletter 1039
Centre for Cold Ocean Research Engineering 694
Centre for Information on Standardization and Metrology 817
Centre for Library and Information Management - Loughborough University of Technology 675
Centre for Library Science and Methodology - National Szechenyi Library - Hungary 495
Centre for Management Research and Development - Australian Graduate School of Management 1060
Centre for Research in Finance - Australian Graduate School of Management 1060
Centre for Research on User Studies - University of Sheffield 1070
Centre for Scientific and Technical Information - Council for Scientific and Industrial Research - South Africa 885
Centre for the Study of Developing Societies 196
Centre International de l'Enfance 566
Centre International d'Echanges d'Informations sur l'Integration des Refugies 602
Centre International des Hautes Etudes Agronomiques Mediterraneennes 564
Centre International des Traductions 608
Centre International d'Informations de Securite et d'Hygiene du Travail 595
Centre National d'Art et de Culture Georges Pompidou 184
Centre National de Documentation et d'Information sur l'Eau - Association Francaise pour l'Etude des Eaux 391
Centre National de Documentation Pedagogique - France 346
Centre National de Documentation Scientifique et Technique - Bibliotheque Royale de Belgique 84
Centre National de la Recherche Scientifique - France 186
Centre National de la Recherche Scientifique - France 355
Centre National de la Recherche Scientifique - France 356
Centre National de la Recherche Scientifique - France 357
Centre National de la Recherche Scientifique - France 377
Centre National de la Recherche Scientifique - France 412
Centre National de la Recherche Scientifique - France 720
Centre National de la Recherche Scientifique - France 981
Centre National de l'Information Chimique 720
Centre National de Prevention et de Traitement des Intoxications - Ministere de la Sante Publique - Belgium 83
Centre National de Tri d'Oceanographie Biologique 349
Centre National d'Etudes des Telecommunications - France 367
Centre National pour l'Exploitation des Oceans - France 347
Centre National pour l'Exploitation des Oceans - France 348
Centre National pour l'Exploitation des Oceans - France 349
Centre National pour l'Exploitation des Oceans - France 350
Centre National pour l'Exploitation des Oceans - France 351
Centre National pour l'Exploitation des Oceans - France 352
Centre National pour l'Exploitation des Oceans - France 353
Centre National pour l'Exploitation des Oceans - France 354
Centre Oceanologique de Bretagne 347
Centre of Information Resource & Technology, Singapore 197
Centre Suisse de Coordination pour la Recherche en Matiere d'Education 945
Centre Technique des Industries de la Fonderie 820
Centre Technique des Industries Mecaniques 957
CENTREDOC (Swiss Center of Documentation in Microtechnology) 944
CENTREDOC Bulletin 944
CENTREX Data Base 484
Centri Elettronici Reteconnessi Valutazione Elaborazione Dati 194
Centro Argentino de Informacion Cientifica y Technologica 28
Centro Calculo Sabadell 860
Centro de Documentacao Cientifica e Tecnica - Instituto Nacional de Investigacao Cientifica - Portugal 821
Centro de Documentacion e Informatica Biomedica - Universidad de Valencia 1082
Centro de Informacion Cientifica y Humanistica - Universidad Nacional Autonoma de Mexico 719
Centro de Informacion de Medicamentos 893
Centro de Informacoes Nucleares - Comissao Nacional de Energia Nuclear - Brazil 102
Centro di Riferimento Italiano DIANE 624
Centro di Studio per la Stratigrafia e Petrografia delle Alpi Centrali 625
Centro Edile 117
Centro Latinoamericano de Demografia 1007
Centro Latinoamericano de Documentacion Economica y Social 1006
Centro Latinoamericano de Desenvolvimento Micrografico - Brazil 101
Centro Nacional de Documentacion Cientifica y Tecnologica - Bolivia 93
Centro Nacional de Informacao Documental Agricola - Ministerio da Agricultura - Brazil 99
Centro Nacional de Informacion y Documentacion - Instituto Nacional de Seguridad e Higiene en el Trabajo - Ministerio de Sanidad y Seguridad Social - Spain 892
Centro Nacional de Informacion y Documentacion en Salud -

Mexico 700
Centro Panamericano de Ingenieria Sanitaria y Ciencias del Ambiente 794
Centro Sperimentale Metallurgico SpA 192
Centrum voor Informatie Beleid 736
Centrum voor Informatie en Documentatie 739
Centrum voor Informatie-Verwerking op het Gebied van Tropische Landbouw en Ontwikkeling 846
Centrum voor Landbouwpublikaties en Landbouwdocumentatie 583
Centrum voor Landbouwpublikaties en Landbouwdocumentatie 731
CENV (Canadian Environment) Data Base 140
CEPAL (Comision Economica para America Latina) 1006
CEPAL (Comision Economica para America Latina) 1007
CEPII (Centre d'Etudes Prospectives et d'Informations Internationales) 185
CEPIS (Centro Panamericano de Ingenieria Sanitaria y Ciencias del Ambiente) 794
CEPT (Conference Europeenne des Administrations des Postes et des Telecommunications) 303
CERDIC (Centre de Recherches et de Documentation des Institutions Chretiennes) 205
Cereal Data Base 583
CERILH (Centre d'Etudes et de Recherches de l'Industrie des Liants Hydrauliques) 188
CERVED (Centri Elettronici Reteconnessi Valutazione Elaborazione Dati) 194
CESIA (Centre d'Etudes des Systemes d'Information des Administrations) 190
CESP (Centre d'Etude des Supports de Publicite) 189
CET (Council for Educational Technology) 247
CET Prestel Educational Umbrella Service Data Base 247
CETIM (Centre Technique des Industries Mecaniques) 957
CFCD (Canadian Federal Corporations and Directors Data Base) 163
CFP (Compagnie Francaise des Petroles) 723
CGIS (Canada Geographic Information System) 143
Chalk River Bibliographic Data Integrated System (CHARIBDIS) 44
Chalk River Nuclear Laboratories 44
Chambre de Commerce et d'Industrie de l'Oise 797
Chambre de Commerce et d'Industrie de Paris 796
Chambre de Commerce et d'Industrie de Paris 797
Character and Pattern Telephone Access Information Network (CAPTAIN) 759
Charging for Library Services Data Base 692
CHARIBDIS (Chalk River Bibliographic Data Integrated System) 44
Charitable Deeds of Covenant 198
Charities Aid Foundation 198
Charity 198
Charity Statistics 198
Charts: The Stockholm Stock Market 903
CHELEM (Comptes Harmonises sur les Echanges et l'Economie Mondiale) 185
Chem Systems Inc. 199
Chem Systems International Ltd. 199
CHEMCO Physical Properties Data Bank 327
CHEMCO Physical Properties Data Bank Manual 327
CHEMDATA 435
Chemfacts 612
Chemical Abstracts Service 901
Chemical Age 200
Chemical Age Project File 200
Chemical and Process Engineering Abstracts 77
Chemical Company Profiles: The Americas 612
Chemical Company Profiles: Western Europe 612
Chemical Data Service Databooks 612
Chemical Data Services - IPC Industrial Press Ltd. 612
Chemical Data Services Chemical Database 612
Chemical Data Services Plant and Product Data 612
Chemical Emergency Agency Service 435
Chemical Engineering Abstracts 852
Chemical Engineering and Biotechnology Abstracts 403
Chemical Engineering Department - Loughborough University of Technology 676
Chemical Equipment Suppliers Data Base (DECHEMA) 406
Chemical Group 1 505
Chemical Group 2 505
Chemical Hazards in Industry 853
Chemical Industries Association 435
Chemical Industries Union 720
Chemical Industry of Eastern Europe 1975-80 612
Chemical Industry Year Book 612
Chemical Information and Documentation-Berlin 201
Chemical Information Center 201
Chemical Information Center 402
Chemical Information System - MEDICINDATA 1049
Chemical Plant and Product Database 612
Chemical Plant Contractor Profiles 612
Chemical Process Economics 199
Chemical Reactions Documentation Service 274
Chemical Society 851

Chemical Society of Japan 630
Chemical Technology Information System 403
Chemie-Information und -Dokumentation Berlin 201
Chemie Wirtschaftsforderungs GmbH 805
ChemInform 201
Chemischer Informationsdienst 201
Chemistry Division - National Research Council of Canada 156
CHEMLIST Package 370
CHEMSAFE 435
CHI (Chemical Hazards in Industry) 853
Chile - National Commission for Scientific and Technological Research 202
Chiltern Advisory Unit for Computer Based Education 485
Chiltern Computing 485
China - Institute of Scientific and Technical Information of China 801
China - Ministry of Urban and Rural Construction and Environmental Protection 203
China Building Information Center 203
China Building Technology Development Centre 203
China Foreign Trade Information Monthly 588
China Medical Abstracts 588
China, Republic of - National Science Council 726
China Science & Tecnology Abstracts 588
Chinese Kungfu Stories in Indonesian: A Bibliography Selected from the IDC Collection 1073
Chinese Pharmacy Abstracts 801
Chisholm Institute of Technology Library 204
CHOMS (Canadian Hydrological Operational Multipurpose Subprogramme) Data Base 140
Christian Institutions Research and Documentation Center 205
Christmas Crafts 1099
CHRONOLOGIE 384
CIAMDA (Index to Literature on Atomic Collision Data) 561
CIB (Centrum voor Informatie Beleid) 736
CIB (Conseil International du Batiment pour la Recherche, l'Etude et la Documentation) 373
CIB (Conseil International du Batiment pour la Recherche, l'Etude et la Documentation) 573
CIBDOC 373
CIBDV (Centre d'Information des Banques de Donnees et du Videotex) 1
CICH (Centro de Informacion Cientifica y Humanistica) - Universidad Nacional Autonoma de Mexico 719
CID (Centrum voor Informatie en Documentatie) 739
CIDA (Centre d'Informatique et de Documentation Automatique) 38
CIDAT (Centre d'Informatique Appliquee au Developpement et a l'Agriculture Tropicale) 846
CIDB (Chemie-Information und -Dokumentation Berlin) 201
CIDET (Cooperation Internationale en Matiere de Documentation sur l'Economie des Transports) 309
CIDSS (Comite International pour l'Information et la Documentation en Sciences Sociales) 571
Ciencia da Informacao 103
CIHB (Canadian Inventory of Historic Building) 138
CIIA (Canadian Information Industry Association) 172
CIIA Newsletter 172
CIIS (Corporate Integrated Information System) 129
CILEA (Consorzio Interuniversitario Lombardo per l'Elaborazione Automatica) 669
CILES (Central Information, Library and Editorial Section) - Commonwealth Scientific and Industrial Research Organization - Australia 47
CIM Data Base 188
CIMPP (Comprehensive Industrial Materials Property Package) 1088
CIN (Centro de Informacoes Nucleares) - Comissao Nacional de Energia Nuclear - Brazil 102
CINCH (Computerised Information from National Criminological Holdings) 56
CINDA (Computer Index of Neutron Data) 785
CINDA, An Index to the Literature on Microscopic Neutron Data 785
CINFORM 102
CINIME (Centro de Informacion de Medicamentos) 893
CIRCE (Catalogo Italiano Riviste su Calcolatore Elettronico) 87
CIRCUL 652
Circulation Control System - University of Saskatchewan Library 1068
CIREM (Club d'Information et de Reflexion sur l'Economie Mondiale) 185
CIRPA (Canadian Independent Record Production Association) 206
CIRPA/ADISQ Foundation 206
CIRTS (Centre of Information Resource & Technology, Singapore) 197
CIS (CANSIM Interactive System) 159
CIS (Central Information Service) - The British Council 108
CIS (Central Information Service) - University of London 1055
CIS (Centre d'Information Spectroscopique et Physico-Chimique d'Analyse) 466
CIS (Centre International d'Informations de Securite et d'Hygiene du Travail) 595
CIS Abstracts 595

CIS Centre - National Board of Occupational Safety and Health - Sweden 923
CIS List of Periodicals Abstracted 595
CIS Thesaurus 595
CIS User's Guide 595
CISI (Compagnie Internationale de Services en Informatique) 207
CISI (Compagnie Internationale de Services en Informatique) 589
CISI (Compagnie Internationale de Services en Informatique) 860
CISI (Compagnie Internationale de Services en Informatique) 987
CISI-Wharton Econometric Forecasting Associates Ltd. 207
CISTI (Canada Institute for Scientific and Technical Information) 152
CISTI (Canada Institute for Scientific and Technical Information) 153
CISTI (Canada Institute for Scientific and Technical Information) 154
CISTI (Canada Institute for Scientific and Technical Information) 155
CISTI Catalogue 152
CISTI News 152
CITECH (Cawkell Information & Technology Services Ltd.) 180
CITEX Data Base 980
CITH (Centre d'Information Textile Habillement) 980
CITH INFO 980
Citibank Economic Data Base (I.P. Sharp Associates) 871
Citibank Economic Forecast Data Base (I.P. Sharp Associates) 871
CITIBASE Data Base (I.P. Sharp Associates) 871
CITIFORECAST Data Base (I.P. Sharp Associates) 871
CITIS Ltd. 208
CitiService 500
CitiService Update 500
CITLO (Centrum voor Informatie-Verwerking op het Gebied van Tropische Landbouw en Ontwikkeling) 846
City of Calgary Information Service 124
City of London Polytechnic 209
Civichannel - Public Relations Division - Calgary Public Information Department 124
Civil Aviation Statistics of the World 569
Civil Engineering Hydraulics Abstracts 86
CJUS (Court of Justice of the European Communities) Data Bank 214
CLADBIB Data Base 1006
CLADES (Centro Latinoamericano de Documentacion Economica y Social) 1006
CLADIR Data Base 1006
CLAIM (Centre for Library and Information Management) - Loughborough University of Technology 675
CLAIM Research Reports 675
CLAIR (Computerised Library of Analysed Igneous Rocks) 1057
CLAIR Data System 1057
CLAPLAN Data Base 1006
CLARUS (Case Law Report Updating Service) Data Base 517
CLARUS Index 517
CLASE: Citas Latinoamericanas en Sociologia, Economia y Humanidades 719
Classified List of Manufacturing Businesses Data Base 454
Clearing-House for On-going Research in Cancer Epidemiology 1113
Clearing-house on Conditions of Work 594
CLEO Data Base 1059
CLIC (Canadian Law Information Council) 173
CLIN Data Base 1006
Clinical Literature Information Bases 296
Clinical Pharmacokinetics 5
Clinical Research Centre - Medical Research Council - Great Britain 114
Clothes and Textiles Bibliography (CLTXBIB) 1033
CLRA (Inter-Corporate Ownership Data Base) 165
CLRP (Coal Research Projects) Data Base 782
CLS (Carleton Library System) 179
CLSS (Customized Literature Search Service) - Canada Institute for Scientific and Technical Information 152
CLTXBIB (Clothes and Textiles Bibliography) 1033
Club d'Information et de Reflexion sur l'Economie Mondiale 185
CMB (Central Medical Library) - Bulgaria 120
CME Data Base 773
CMEA (Council for Mutual Economic Assistance) 565
CMO Maritime Information Centre 685
CMRD (Centre for Management Research and Development) - Australian Graduate School of Management 1060
CMS (Canadian Micrographic Society) 175
CNAM (Corporate Names Data Base) 164
CNDCT (Centro Nacional de Documentacion Cientifica y Tecnologica) - Bolivia 93
CNDP (Centre National de Documentation Pedagogique) - France 346
CNDST (Centre National de Documentation Scientifique et Technique) - Bibliotheque Royale de Belgique 84
CNEA (Comision Nacional de Energia Atomica) - Argentina 27
CNEA Reports 27
CNET (Centre National d'Etudes des Telecommunications) - France 367
CNEXO (Centre National pour l'Exploitation des Oceans) - France 347
CNEXO (Centre National pour l'Exploitation des Oceans) - France 348
CNEXO (Centre National pour l'Exploitation des Oceans) - France 349
CNEXO (Centre National pour l'Exploitation des Oceans) - France 350

CNEXO (Centre National pour l'Exploitation des Oceans) - France 351
CNEXO (Centre National pour l'Exploitation des Oceans) - France 352
CNEXO (Centre National pour l'Exploitation des Oceans) - France 353
CNEXO (Centre National pour l'Exploitation des Oceans) - France 354
CNEXO-BNDO Data Base 350
CNI (Canadian News Index) 708
CNIC (Centre National de l'Information Chimique) 720
CNIMZ (Tsentar za Nauchno-Meditsinska Informatsiia) - Bulgaria 120
CNPq (Conselho Nacional de Desenvolvimento Cientifico e Tecnologico) - Brazil 103
CNPTI (Centre National de Prevention et de Traitement des Intoxications) - Ministere de la Sante Publique - Belgium 83
CNR (Consiglio Nazionale delle Ricerche) - Italy 623
CNR (Consiglio Nazionale delle Ricerche) - Italy 624
CNR (Consiglio Nazionale delle Ricerche) - Italy 625
CNRS (Centre National de la Recherche Scientifique) - France 186
CNRS (Centre National de la Recherche Scientifique) - France 355
CNRS (Centre National de la Recherche Scientifique) - France 356
CNRS (Centre National de la Recherche Scientifique) - France 357
CNRS (Centre National de la Recherche Scientifique) - France 377
CNRS (Centre National de la Recherche Scientifique) - France 412
CNRS (Centre National de la Recherche Scientifique) - France 720
CNRS (Centre National de la Recherche Scientifique) - France 981
CNRSLAB 355
CNUCE Institute - National Research Council - Italy 623
Co-ordinating Committee for the Textile Industries in the EEC 980
Coaching Association of Canada 210
COAL-ABS 14
Coal Abstracts 782
Coal Abstracts Serial Title Abbreviations 782
Coal Calendar 782
Coal Data Base 782
Coal Data Base Guide 782
Coal Data Base Thesaurus 782
Coal Research Projects Data Base 782
Coal Technology Information Centre - Alberta Research Council 14
COALPRO 782
COALRIP 782
COAND Data Base (I.P. Sharp Associates) 871
Coast Frequency Reference File 606
COBIDOC (Commissie voor Bibliografie en Documentatie) 211
COBIDOC (Commissie voor Bibliografie en Documentatie) 735
CODATA (Committee on Data for Science and Technology) 574
CODATA Bulletin 574
CODATA Directory of Data Sources for Science and Technology 574
CODATA Newsletter 574
CODOC (Cooperative Documents Network Project) 1050
CODOC Manual 1050
COFFEELINE 570
COFFEELINE Thesaurus 570
COGEODATA (Commission on Storage, Automatic Processing and Retrieval of Geological Data) 609
COGEODATA Newsletter 609
COIC (Careers and Occupational Information Centre) 462
COIN: Computerized Information in Canada 15
COINIM (Centre for Information on Standardization and Metrology) 817
COINS 127
COINS Bulletin 127
COLCIENCIAS (Fondo Colombiano de Investigaciones Cientificas) 212
Collection des Etudes Documentaires Appliquees a la Traduction Automatique et Humaine (CEDATAH) Data Base 191
Collection District Data Bases 237
Collective Bargaining: A Response to the Recession in Industrialised Market Economy Countries 591
Collective for Training and Education in Connection with Information Provision via Networks 211
College Bibliocentre 182
College of Agriculture - University of Arizona 229
Colombia - National Ministry of Education 212
Colombian Fund for Scientific Research 212
COM/PortaCOM 904
Combined T9/Service Segment Data Base (I.P. Sharp Associates) 871
COMERT1 Data Base (I.P. Sharp Associates) 871
COMERT2 Data Base (I.P. Sharp Associates) 871
COMERT3 Data Base (I.P. Sharp Associates) 871
COMEXT Data Bank 224
Comision Economica para America Latina 1006
Comision Economica para America Latina 1007
Comision Nacional de Energia Atomica - Argentina 27
Comision Nacional de Investigacion Cientifica y Tecnologica - Chile 202
Comissao Nacional de Energia Nuclear - Brazil 102
Comite International pour l'Information et la Documentation en Sciences Sociales 571
COMITEXTIL (Co-ordinating Committee for the Textile Industries in the EEC) 980
COMMBOND Data Base (I.P. Sharp Associates) 871

Commerce Exterieure 681
Commercial Laws of Europe (Eurolex) 314
Commercially Available Organic Chemicals Index Project 372
Commissariat a l'Energie Atomique - France 338
Commissariat a l'Energie Atomique - France 339
Commissariat a l'Energie Atomique - France 589
Commissie voor Bibliografie en Documentatie 211
Commissie voor Bibliografie en Documentatie 735
Commission for Asia and Oceania, International Federation for Documentation 644
Commission for Hydrology - World Meteorological Organization 1117
Commission Internationale des Industries Agricoles et Alimentaires 39
Commission of the European Communities 213
Commission of the European Communities 214
Commission of the European Communities 215
Commission of the European Communities 216
Commission of the European Communities 217
Commission of the European Communities 218
Commission of the European Communities 219
Commission of the European Communities 220
Commission of the European Communities 221
Commission of the European Communities 222
Commission of the European Communities 223
Commission of the European Communities 224
Commission of the European Communities 225
Commission of the European Communities 226
Commission of the European Communities 227
Commission of the European Communities 306
Commission of the European Communities 489
Commission of the European Communities 595
Commission of the European Communities 717
Commission on Storage, Automatic Processing and Retrieval of Geological Data 609
Committee on Data for Science and Technology 574
Commodities Data Base (Wolff Research) 1109
Commodities Research Unit Ltd. 228
Common Market Law Reports (Eurolex) 314
Commonwealth Agricultural Bureaux 229
Commonwealth Agricultural Bureaux 583
Commonwealth Agricultural Bureaux (CAB) Abstracts 229
Commonwealth Bank Bond Index Data Base (I.P. Sharp Associates) 871
Commonwealth Environmental Laws Data Base 656
Commonwealth Regional Renewable Energy Resources Index 230
Commonwealth Regional Renewable Energy Resources Information System 230
Commonwealth Scientific and Industrial Research Organization - Australia 47
Commonwealth Scientific and Industrial Research Organization - Australia 230
Commonwealth Scientific and Industrial Research Organization (CSIRO) Index 47
Communication Services Ltd. 231
Communications and Directory Information System 19
Communications Information 232
Communitatis Europeae Lex 489
Commuter Online Origin-Destination Data Base (I.P. Sharp Associates) 871
COMNET (International Network for Communication Research and Policies) 65
Compagnie des Agents de Change 389
Compagnie Francaise des Petroles 723
Compagnie Internationale de Services en Informatique 207
Compagnie Internationale de Services en Informatique 589
Compagnie Internationale de Services en Informatique 860
Compagnie Internationale de Services en Informatique 987
Companhia Portuguesa Radio Marconi 822
Companies Registration Office Directory of Companies 802
Company Accounts Data Base (Datastream) 267
Company for Informatics 233
Company Management 355
Comprehensive Bibliography of Reference Works on Information Technology 243
Comprehensive Industrial Materials Property Package 1088
Comprehensive Information Services - Pira: Research Association for the Paper and Board, Printing and Packaging Industries 812
Comptes Harmonises sur les Echanges et l'Economie Mondiale (CHELEM) 185
Compu-Mark 234
Compu-Mark 235
Compu-Mark (UK) Ltd. 235
Compulsory Schooling in the E.C. 215
Compusearch Market and Social Research Ltd. 236
COMPUSET 649
Computer Aided Bibliographic Information Service (CABIS) Data Base 509
Computer Aided Directory Information Service (CADIS) Data Base 509
Computer and Business Equipment Companies Directory 67

Computer and Communications Technology Documents 958
Computer and Control Abstracts 549
Computer Assisted Information Retrieval System - Leatherhead Food Research Association 655
Computer Bulletin 107
Computer Center - University of Tokyo 1075
Computer Composition Center - Hartmann & Heenemann 401
Computer Composition Center - Hartmann & Heenemann 476
Computer Directory of India 241
Computer Hardware Record 721
Computer Index of Neutron Data (CINDA) 785
Computer Installation Record 721
Computer Journal 107
Computer Market Statistics 721
Computer Newsletter 119
Computer Oriented Reference System for Automatic Information Retrieval (CORSAIR) 929
Computer Processing and Legal Sciences 355
Computer Readable Services - Technical Services Department - The Stock Exchange 902
Computer Retrieval of Organic Sub-structures Based on Wiswesser (CROSSBOW) 370
Computer Science and Systems Division - Atomic Energy Research Establishment, Harwell 433
Computer Sciences Corporation 237
Computer Sciences of Australia Pty. Ltd. 237
Computer Search Service - Science Reference Library - British Library 445
Computerised Information from National Criminological Holdings 56
Computerised Library of Analysed Igneous Rocks 1057
Computerized Administration of Patent Documents Reclassified According to the IPC (CAPRI) Data Base 64
Computerized ASFIS Register of Experts and Institutions 1008
Computerized Documentation Service/Integrated Set of Information Systems (CDS/ISIS) 1017
Computerized Information in Canada (COIN) Data Base 15
Computerized London Information System Data Base 465
Computerized Retrieval Services - Mineral Development Division Library - Newfoundland Department of Mines & Energy 750
Computerized Text Processing and Retrieval System for City Council Information - Toronto Department of the City Clerk 985
Computerized Text Processing and Retrieval System for Toronto City Council Information 985
COMPUTERPAT 802
Computers in Industry 580
Computing 107
Computing and Organization Service Company - Central Statistical Office - Hungary 493
Computing Centre - University of British Columbia 1044
Computing Journal Abstracts 721
Computing News Roundup 721
Computing Services - University of Alberta 1033
Computing Technics 493
CONACYT (Consejo Nacional de Ciencia y Tecnologia) - Mexico 701
CONCON (Constellate Consultants Ltd.) 241
Conditions of Work: A Cumulative Digest 594
Conditions of Work and Quality of Working Life: A Directory of Institutions 594
Conditions of Work and Welfare Facilities Branch - International Labour Office 594
CONF 521
CONFER 527
Conference Board of Canada 238
Conference Europeenne des Administrations des Postes et des Telecommunications 303
Conference Europeenne des Ministres des Transports 309
Conference Proceedings Index (British Library) 442
Congres, Colloques et Conferences, Salons et Expositions 339
CONICET (Consejo Nacional de Investigaciones Cientificas y Tecnicas) - Argentina 28
CONICYT (Comision Nacional de Investigacion Cientifica y Tecnologica) - Chile 202
Connect 654
Conseil International des Unions Scientifiques 574
Conseil International du Batiment pour la Recherche, l'Etude et la Documentation 373
Conseil International du Batiment pour la Recherche, l'Etude et la Documentation 573
CONSEILS DES MINISTRES 384
Consejo Nacional de Ciencia y Tecnologia - Mexico 701
Consejo Nacional de Investigaciones Cientificas y Tecnicas - Argentina 28
Consejo Superior de Investigaciones Cientificas - Spain 890
Consejo Superior de Investigaciones Cientificas - Spain 891
Consejo Superior de Investigaciones Cientificas - Spain 1082
Conselho Nacional de Desenvolvimento Cientifico e Tecnologico - Brazil 103
Conservation and Renewable Energy Branch - Department of Energy, Mines and Resources - Canada 133

Conservatoire National des Arts et Metiers   722
Consiglio Nazionale delle Ricerche - Italy   623
Consiglio Nazionale delle Ricerche - Italy   624
Consiglio Nazionale delle Ricerche - Italy   625
Consiliul National pentru Stiinta si Tehnologie - Romania   843
Consortium of Royal Library and University Libraries   239
Consortium of Royal Library and University Libraries   240
Consorzio Interuniversitario Lombardo per l'Elaborazione Automatica   669
Consorzio per il Sistema Informativo Piemonte   811
Constellate Consultants (P) Ltd.   241
Constitutional Acts of Canada   828
Construction and Civil Enginering Index   958
Construction Cost Information Bulletin   177
Construction Data Bank (NEEDS-TS)   754
Construction Industry Translation and Information Services   208
Construction Specifications Canada   242
Construction Technique   203
CONSULTEXT   243
CONSUM   773
Consumer and Corporate Affairs Canada   129
Consumer Research Division - Overseas Data Service, Company, Ltd.   789
Consumers' Association   244
CONTACT   319
CONTEL Data Base   983
Contents (Japan Pharmaceutical Information Center)   634
Contents List of Soviet Scientific Periodicals   507
CONTEXT   668
CONTEXT Data Base   983
Continuous Plankton Recorder Survey   729
Continuum Astronomical Data Files   59
Control Data Australia Pty. Ltd.   245
Control Data Corporation   245
Controlled Vocabulary of MINTER   100
Cooperants Mutual-Life Insurance Society   513
Cooperation Internationale en Matiere de Documentation sur l'Economie des Transports   309
Cooperative Automation Group   246
Cooperative Documents Network Project   1050
Cooperative Group for Marine Research and Marine Technology Information   413
Cooperatives Unit - Marketing and Economics Branch - Agriculture Canada   127
Coordenadoria de Documentacao - Ministerio do Interior - Brazil   100
Coordinating Committee for the Textile Industries in the EEC   980
Copper Monitor   228
Copper Quarterly   228
Copper Studies   228
COPS Data Base (I.P. Sharp Associates)   871
Copyright Receipt Office - Great Britain   439
CORALIE Data Base   282
CORD (Canadian On-line Record Database)   206
CORLS (Central Ontario Regional Library System)   195
CORMORANT   638
CORN (Canadian Clearinghouse for Ongoing Research in Nursing)   1036
CORN User's Guide   1036
CORP (Corporate Authorities)   521
Corporate Authorities (CORP)   521
Corporate Data Bank (Financial Post)   680
Corporate Integrated Information System   129
Corporate Names Data Base   164
Corporations Branch - Consumer and Corporate Affairs Canada   129
Corrosion Data Base (DECHEMA)   405
Corrosion Data Sheets   405
CORSAIR (Computer Oriented Reference System for Automatic Information Retrieval)   929
COSMOS I   969
COSMOS II   969
COSTI (National Center of Scientific and Technological Information) - Israel   616
COSTI (National Center of Scientific and Technological Information) - Israel   617
COSTI-SDI   616
Costs and Prices (Henley Centre for Forecasting)   484
Cotton and Tropical Fibres Abstracts   229
Council for Educational Technology   247
Council for Educational Technology Prestel Educational Umbrella Service Data Base   247
Council for Information on Alcohol and Other Drugs - Sweden   936
Council for Mutual Economic Assistance   565
Council for Scientific and Industrial Research - South Africa   885
Council of Europe   248
Council of Europe   306
Council of Europe Conventions and Agreements (Eurolex)   314
Council of Scientific and Industrial Research - India   507
Council of Scientific and Industrial Research - India   509
Country Profiles Data Base   264
Court of Justice of the European Communities   214

CPDT (Centre de Preparation Documentaire a la Traduction)   191
CPI (Canadian Periodical Index)   174
CPI (Capital Planning Information Ltd.)   176
CPI (Central Patents Index)   275
CPN (Canadian Press Newstex)   828
CPRC (Canadian Plains Research Center)   1066
CPRM (Companhia Portuguesa Radio Marconi)   822
CPX (Canadian Press Extra)   828
CRC Group   837
CRDS (Chemical Reactions Documentation Service)   274
CRE (Central Research Establishment) - Home Office Forensic Science Service - Great Britain   458
CRE Reports   458
CREDOC (Centre de Recherche Documentaire)   282
CRESM (Centre de Recherche et d'Etudes sur les Societes Mediterraneennes)   186
CRESM Newsletter   186
CREST   241
CREW Data Base (I.P. Sharp Associates)   871
CRID (Centro di Riferimento Italiano DIANE)   624
CRIF (Centre de Recherches Scientifiques et Techniques de l'Industrie des Fabrications Metalliques)   187
CRIF (Centre for Research in Finance) - Australian Graduate School of Management   1060
Criminal Appeal Office Index (Eurolex)   314
Criminal Appeal Reports (Eurolex)   314
Criminal Law Quarterly   162
Criminology & Penology Abstracts   647
CRNL (Chalk River Nuclear Laboratories)   44
Crocus   71
CRONOS   225
CRONOS System for the Management of Time Series   225
Crop Physiology Abstracts   229
CROSSBOW (Computer Retrieval of Organic Sub-structures Based on Wiswesser)   370
Crowntek   261
CRR (Regulatory Reporter)   173
CRRERIS (Commonwealth Regional Renewable Energy Resources Information System)   230
CRRERIS Newsletter   230
CRS (Computer Readable Services) - Technical Services Department - The Stock Exchange   902
CRU (Commodities Research Unit Ltd.)   228
CRU Consultants, Inc.   228
Crude Oil & Oil Products Monitor   228
CRUS (Centre for Research on User Studies) - University of Sheffield   1070
CRUS News   1070
CRYST Data Base   125
Crystallographic Data Centre - University Chemical Laboratory - Cambridge University   125
CRYSTMET (Metals Crystallographic) Data File   156
CSA (Computer Sciences of Australia Pty. Ltd.)   237
CSB (Central Statistics Bureau) - British Columbia Ministry of Industry and Small Business Development   106
CSC (Computer Sciences Corporation)   237
CSC (Construction Specifications Canada)   242
CSD (Cambridge Structural Database)   125
CSDS (Centre for the Study of Developing Societies)   196
CSG (Canada Systems Group)   163
CSG (Canada Systems Group)   164
CSG (Canada Systems Group)   165
CSG (Canada Systems Group)   166
CSG (Catalog of Stellar Groups)   905
CSI (Catalog of Stellar Identifications)   905
CSI Piemonte   811
CSIC (Consejo Superior de Investigaciones Cientificas) - Spain   890
CSIC (Consejo Superior de Investigaciones Cientificas) - Spain   891
CSIC (Consejo Superior de Investigaciones Cientificas) - Spain   1082
CSIR (Council for Scientific and Industrial Research) - South Africa   885
CSIR (Council of Scientific and Industrial Research) - India   507
CSIR Publications   885
CSIRO (Commonwealth Scientific and Industrial Research Organization) - Australia   47
CSIRO (Commonwealth Scientific and Industrial Research Organization) - Australia   230
CSIRO Index   47
CSIRO List of Publications   47
CSIRONET   47
CSO (Central Statistical Office) - Great Britain   449
CSO (Central Statistical Office) - Hungary   493
CSO Library and Documentation Service Data Base   493
CSO Macro-Economic Data Bank   449
CSO Statistical Data Base System   493
CSTI (Centre for Scientific and Technical Information) - Council for Scientific and Industrial Research - South Africa   885
CTI (Centre de Traitement de l'Information) - Ministere des Affaires Economiques - Belgium   80

CTI (Current Technology Index) 662
CTIC (Coal Technology Information Centre) - Alberta Research Council 14
CTIF (Centre Technique des Industries de la Fonderie) 820
CTIF-BIIPAM Data Base 820
Cuadernos de Documentacion e Informatica Biomedica 1082
CUBE (Carleton University Bibliographical Enquiry) 179
Culham Laboratory - Atomic Energy Authority - Great Britain 438
Culham Laboratory Library Bulletin 438
Culham Laboratory Library Data Base 438
Cumulated Index to Hebrew Periodicals 1051
Cumulated ISDS Register/Bulletin Indexes 603
Cumulus Systems Ltd. 249
Currency and Share Index Databank 328
Currency Exchange Rates Data Base (I.P. Sharp Associates) 871
Currency Profiles 484
Current Advances in Biochemistry 803
Current Advances in Cell & Developmental Biology 803
Current Advances in Ecological Sciences 803
Current Advances in Endocrinology 803
Current Advances in Genetics & Molecular Biology 803
Current Advances in Immunology 803
Current Advances in Microbiology 803
Current Advances in Neuroscience 803
Current Advances in Pharmacology & Toxicology 803
Current Advances in Physiology 803
Current Advances in Plant Science 803
Current Agricultural Research Information System 1009
Current Agricultural Serials: A World List 558
Current Awareness Bulletin (Aslib) 35
Current Awareness in Biological Sciences 803
Current Awareness in Particle Technology 676
Current Bibliographies on Science and Technology 645
Current Bibliography on Science and Technology 632
Current Biotechnology Abstracts 854
Current Contents (Philippines) 808
Current Contents of Selected Scientific Periodicals 726
Current Information in the Construction Industry 378
Current Law (Eurolex) 314
Current Listing of Articles in Science and Technology Journals 645
Current Listing of Articles in Social Science Journals 645
Current Papers in Electrical and Electronics Engineering 549
Current Papers in Physics 549
Current Papers on Computers and Control 549
CURRENT RESEARCH in Library & Information Science 661
Current Research Projects in CSIR Laboratories Data Base 507
Current Science and Technology Research in Japan 632
Current Scientific and Technological Research Projects in the Universities and Research Institutions of Bangladesh 70
Current Serials Received (British Library) 442
Current Technology Index 662
Current Titles in Turkish Science 991
Customized Literature Search Service - Canada Institute for Scientific and Technical Information 152
Cutting Data Information Center - Laboratory of Machine Tools and Production Engineering - Technical University of Aachen 964
CWONC (Canadian Women of Note Archive) 1120
CYBERTEL Videotex Service 245
Czechoslovak Medical Literature Data Base 250
Czechoslovakia - Federal Ministry of Metallurgy and Heavy Engineering 281
Czechoslovakia - Institute for Medical Information 250
Czechoslovakia - National Medical Library 250
D.B.S. (Database Access Service) - Eastern Telecommunications Philippines, Inc. 288
DABAWAS (Datenbank fur Wassergefahrdende Stoffe) 284
DAFSA 251
DAFSA-SNEI S.A. 252
Dagg (Michael A.) Associates 253
Daily Eurobond Prices 267
Daily Intelligence Bulletin 465
Daily Official List 902
Dairy Science Abstracts 229
DAISY Data Base 1114
DAKOR Data Base 424
DALCTRAF 936
Dalhousie Ocean Studies Programme 254
Dalhousie University 254
DANDOK (Danish Committee for Scientific and Technical Information and Documentation) 255
DANDOK (Danish Committee for Scientific and Technical Information and Documentation) 256
Danish Committee for Scientific and Technical Information and Documentation 255
Danish Committee for Scientific and Technical Information and Documentation 256
Danish DIANE Center 256
Danish National Center for Building Documentation 938
Danish Online User Group 256

Danish Teledata System 272
Danish Veterinary and Agricultural Library Catalogue (DVJB) Data Base 497
Danmarks Tekniske Bibliotek 270
Danske Teleadministrationer 272
DARC 977
DARC (Description, Acquisition, Retrieval, and Conception) 38
DARC Pluridata System 38
DARDO (Direct Access to Remote Data Bases Overseas) 620
Dardo Access to Travel Service 620
DARE Data Base 1022
DARING 371
DARIUS 741
Data and Program Archive for the Social Sciences - Higher Institute of Sociology - University of Milan 1058
Data Archive - Economic and Social Science Research Council 291
Data Archive Bulletin 291
Data Bank Access Service - Portuguese Radio Marconi Company 822
Data Bank and Videotex Information Center 1
Data Bank for Environmental Literature (ULIDAT) 411
Data Bank for Environmental Research (UFORDAT) 411
Data Bank for Medicaments 257
Data Bank of European Doctoral Theses in Management 313
Data Bank on Substances Harmful to Water 284
Data Bank Service - Tokyo Shoko Research, Ltd. 984
Data Base Consultation Service - National Council of Science and Technology - Mexico 701
Data Base on Contemporary German 541
Data Bases Service - French Association for Standardization 382
Data Communications in Europe, 1983-1991 303
Data Compilations in Physics (PHYSCOMP) 521
Data Dissemination System 317
Data Information Service - European Consortium for Political Research 310
Data Juridica 641
Data Library - University of Alberta Computing Services 1033
Data Library - University of British Columbia 1044
Data Library and Archives Directory (DATALIB Resources) 1033
Data Library Catalogue 1033
Data-Link 266
Data-Mail 266
Data on Occupations Retrieval System (DOORS) 462
Data Processing Center - Ministry of Economic Affairs - Belgium 80
Data Processing Division - Siemens AG 874
Data Processing Division - Siemens AG 875
Data Processing Services Company 258
Data Products - Toronto Stock Exchange 986
Data Reference (DREF) Data Base (WATDOC) 140
Data Resources, Inc. (International Offices) 259
Data Resources of Canada 259
Data-Star 266
Data-Star News-File 266
Data Unit - Centre for the Study of Developing Societies 196
DataArkiv AB 260
DataArkiv AB 990
DATABANK 536
Databank Bureau - Nihon Keizai Shimbun, Inc. 753
Databank Bureau - Nihon Keizai Shimbun, Inc. 754
Databank for Agricultural Mechanization 543
Database Access Service - Eastern Telecommunications Philippines, Inc. 288
Database of Databases (University of Tsukuba) 1080
Database of Wildlife Research 947
Database on Atomic and Molecular Physics 835
Database Phytomedizin 409
Databooks (Chemical Data Service) 612
Datac 266
Datacentralen (I/S) 497
Datacrown Client Letter 261
Datacrown Inc. 261
DATAFRANCE 469
DATALIB Resources (Data Library and Archives Directory) 1033
Dataline Inc. 262
Dataline Systems Limited 262
Datapac 971
DATAPAK 271
Datapak 927
Datasearch Business Information Ltd. 263
Datasolve Ltd. 264
Datasolve Ltd. 265
Datasolve World Reporter Newsletter 265
DataStar 266
Datastream International Ltd. 267
DATEL 271
Datenbank fur Forderungsvorhaben - Bundesministerium fur Forschung und Technologie - Germany 424
Datenbank fur Futtermittel 487
Datenbank fur Wassergefahrdende Stoffe (DABAWAS) 284
DATEX 271

DATIMS Data Base 504
Dator Centre Ltd. 472
DATS (Dardo Access to Travel Service) 620
DAVID Data Base 504
David Lubin Memorial Library - Library and Documentation Systems Division - Food and Agriculture Organization 1013
DAVOR (Datenbank fur Forderungsvorhaben) - Bundesministerium fur Forschung und Technologie - Germany 424
DBDB (University of Tsukuba Database of Databases) 1080
DBI (Deutsches Bibliotheksinstitut) 400
DBI-Materialien 400
DBS (Database Access Service) - Eastern Telecommunications Philippines, Inc. 288
DC (I/S Datacentralen) 497
DC Host Centre 497
DDB (Dortmund Data Bank) 1046
DDB Data Base 504
DDS (Data Dissemination System) 317
DECHEMA (Deutsche Gesellschaft fur Chemisches Apparatewesen) 403
DECHEMA (Deutsche Gesellschaft fur Chemisches Apparatewesen) 404
DECHEMA (Deutsche Gesellschaft fur Chemisches Apparatewesen) 405
DECHEMA (Deutsche Gesellschaft fur Chemisches Apparatewesen) 406
DECHEMA Chemical Engineering and Biotechnology Abstracts Data Bank 403
DECHEMA Chemical Equipment Suppliers Data Base (DEQUIP) 406
DECHEMA Chemistry Data Series 404
DECHEMA Corrosion Data Base (DECOR) 405
DECHEMA Stoffdaten Dienst 404
DECHEMA Substance Data Service 404
DECHEMA Thermophysical Property Data Bank (DETHERM) 404
DECHEMA Thesaurus fur die Chemische Technik 403
DECHEMA Werkstoff Tabelle 405
DECLARATIONS 384
DECNAT Databank 214
DECO 994
DECOR (DECHEMA Corrosion Data Base) 405
Defence Documents 958
DEFOTEL 977
Delegation Generale pour l'Armement - Ministry of Defense - France 345
Delegationen for Vetenskaplig och Teknisk Informationsforsorjning 937
Delft Hydraulics Laboratory 268
Delft Hydro Database 268
Delft Hydroscience Abstracts 268
Demografia 493
Demografiska Databasen - Umea Universitet 1081
Demographic Data Base - University of Umea 1081
DemoGRAPHICS - Compusearch Market and Social Research Ltd. 236
Demography 493
Denmark - Ministry of Cultural Affairs 269
Denmark - National Technological Library of Denmark 270
Denmark - Posts and Telegraphs 271
Denmark Telecommunications Administration 272
Departement des Programmes - Commissariat a l'Energie Atomique - France 338
Departement Documentation et Information Geologique - Service Geologique National - France 340
Department for Informatics and Science Analysis - Hungarian Academy of Sciences Library 492
Department of Biological Sciences - University of Aston 1038
Department of Communications - Canada 130
Department of Communications - Canada 819
Department of Computer Science - Queen's University of Belfast 835
Department of Computer Science - Queen's University of Belfast 836
Department of Drugs - National Board of Health and Welfare - Sweden 922
Department of Econometrics and Data Processing - IFO-Institute for Economic Research 501
Department of Education and Science - Great Britain 112
Department of Educational Administration - University of Alberta 1034
Department of Energy - Great Britain 769
Department of Energy, Mines and Resources - Canada 44
Department of Energy, Mines and Resources - Canada 45
Department of Energy, Mines and Resources - Canada 131
Department of Energy, Mines and Resources - Canada 132
Department of Energy, Mines and Resources - Canada 133
Department of Energy, Mines and Resources - Canada 134
Department of Energy, Mines and Resources - Canada 135
Department of Energy, Mines and Resources - Canada 136
Department of Engineering Production - University of Birmingham 1041
Department of Geology - University of Melbourne 1057
Department of Health and Social Security - Great Britain 285

Department of Health and Social Security - Great Britain 1053
Department of Indonesian and Malayan Studies - University of Sydney 1073
Department of Industry - Great Britain 450
Department of Industry - Great Britain 451
Department of Industry - Great Britain 548
Department of Industry, Trade & Commerce - Canada 137
Department of International Relations - Paris Chamber of Commerce and Industry 796
Department of Mineral Resources Engineering - Imperial College of Science and Technology - University of London 1056
Department of Mining and Metallurgical Engineering - Faculty of Engineering - McGill University 691
Department of Physical Chemistry - University of Leeds 1052
Department of Political Economy - University of Aberdeen 1032
Department of Printed Books Data Base 440
Department of Recreation - University of Waterloo 1084
Department of Scandinavian Languages and Literature - University of Bergen 1040
Department of Scientific and Industrial Research - New Zealand 748
Department of Scientific and Industrial Research Indexing System (SIRIS) 748
Department of Sociology - University of Alberta 1035
Department of Sociology and Anthropology - Carleton University 178
Department of Statistics - New Zealand 749
Department of Synthetic Chemistry - Faculty of Engineering - University of Tokyo 1076
Department of Technical Information - Japan Atomic Energy Research Institute 627
Department of the Environment - Great Britain 378
Department of the Environment - Great Britain 437
Department of the Environment - Great Britain 452
Department of the Environment - Great Britain 453
Department of the Environment - Great Britain 455
Department of Trade - Great Britain 297
Department of Trade and Industry - Great Britain 454
Department of Trade and Industry - Great Britain 615
Department of Trade and Industry - Great Britain 727
Department of Transport - Great Britain 455
Departments of the Environment and Transport - Great Britain 455
DEPICT 237
DEQUIP (DECHEMA Chemical Equipment Suppliers Data Base) 406
Derwent Patents Documentation Services Data Bases 275
Derwent Publications Ltd. 273
Derwent Publications Ltd. 274
Derwent Publications Ltd. 275
Derwent Publications Ltd. 276
Derwent Publications Ltd. 277
Derwent Publications Ltd. 278
Derwent-SDC Search Service 951
Desalination Abstracts 616
Description, Acquisition, Retrieval, and Conception (DARC) 38
Desenvolvimento de Sistemas Microgråficos Avancados 101
Desfasses SEF Directory 251
DESY (Deutsches Elektronen-Synchrotron) 396
DESY-HEP 396
DESY Scientific Documentation and Information Service - German Electron-Synchrotron 396
Detailed Foreign Trade Statistics (OECD) 780
DETHERM (DECHEMA Thermophysical Property Data Bank) 404
Deutsche Bau-Dokumentation 479
Deutsche Bibliographie 423
Deutsche Bibliothek 423
Deutsche Bundesbank Data Base (I.P. Sharp Associates) 871
Deutsche Bundespost - Bundesministerium fur Post- und Fernmeldewesen - Germany 427
Deutsche DIN Normen 958
Deutsche Gesellschaft fur Chemisches Apparatewesen 403
Deutsche Gesellschaft fur Chemisches Apparatewesen 404
Deutsche Gesellschaft fur Chemisches Apparatewesen 405
Deutsche Gesellschaft fur Chemisches Apparatewesen 406
Deutsche Gesellschaft fur Zerstorungsfreie Prufung 416
Deutsche Rheologische Gesellschaft 417
Deutsche Soziologie 1945-1977 43
Deutsche Stiftung fur Internationale Entwicklung 397
Deutschen Patentamt 401
Deutscher Bundesrat 422
Deutscher Bundestag 422
Deutscher Verband fur Schweisstechnik 418
Deutsches Bibliotheksinstitut 400
Deutsches Elektronen-Synchrotron 396
Deutsches Informationszentrum fur Technische Regeln 407
Deutsches Institut fur Medizinische Dokumentation und Information 428
Deutsches Institut fur Medizinische Dokumentation und Information 1078
Deutsches Institut fur Normung 407
Deutsches Institut fur Urbanistik 379
Deutsches Krankenhausinstitut 477

Deutsches Krebsforschungszentrum 1113
Deutsches Kunststoff-Institut 402
Deutsches Patent- und Fachinformationssystem 401
Development Data Bases: Use in Canada Project 576
Development of Advanced Micrographics Systems 101
Development of Minicomputers in an Environment of Scientific and Technical Information Centers (DOMESTIC) 617
Devindex 576
Devindex Africa 1005
DEVSIS Data Base 576
DeWitt Petrochemical Newsletters Data Base (I.P. Sharp Associates) 871
DFI (Delegationen for Vetenskaplig och Teknisk Informationsforsorjning) 937
Diagnostic Marketing Research Service 907
Diagnostic New Product Listing Service 907
DIAL (Division of Information and Library) Services - Insearch Ltd. 538
DIALOG Information Services, Inc. (International Representatives) 279
DIALTECH 615
DIANE (Direct Information Access Network for Europe) 220
DIANE Guide Data Base 654
DIB (Daily Intelligence Bulletin) Data Base 465
Dictionary of Active Principles and Excipients 893
Didot-Bottin 280
Dienst Grondwaterverkenning - Nederlandsche Centrale Organisatie voor Toegepast-Natuurwetenschappelijk Onderzoek 740
Dienstleistungen Information und Dokumentation - Deutsches Kunststoff-Institut 402
DIF Data Base 949
Diffusion Hebdomadaire Systematique 820
DIFU (Deutsches Institut fur Urbanistik) 379
Digital Mapping System - Topographical Survey Division - Department of Energy, Mines and Resources - Canada 136
DIMDI (Deutsches Institut fur Medizinische Dokumentation und Information) 428
DIMDI (Deutsches Institut fur Medizinische Dokumentation und Information) 1078
DIMDI-News 428
DIN (Deutsches Institut fur Normung) 407
DIN-Anzeiger fur Technische Regeln 407
DIN Catalogue 407
Dining Guide 1099
DIP (Documentation and Information System for Parliamentary Materials) - German Federal Diet 422
DIRECT 809
Direct Access Data Bank at the University of Quebec 1064
Direct Access to Remote Data Bases Overseas 620
DIRECT Data Bases 809
Direct Information Access Network for Europe 220
Direction de la Documentation Francaise 384
Direction des Recherches et Etudes Techniques 981
Direction des Relations Internationales - Chambre de Commerce et d'Industrie de Paris 796
Directorate for Information and Documentation - Chile 202
Directorate of Telecommunications - France 552
Directories of Charitable Needs 198
Directorio de Informacion y Documentacion - Chile 202
Director's Guide to the EEC Economies 484
Directory and Index of Standards 898
Directory of Agricultural Personnel in India 510
Directory of Agricultural Research Stations in India 510
Directory of Associations in Canada 706
Directory of Companies (Pergamon InfoLine Ltd.) 802
Directory of Companies Data Base (ICC Information Group Ltd.) 499
Directory of Completed Master's Theses in Nursing (Canadian) 1037
Directory of Computing Hardware 721
Directory of Computing Software 721
Directory of Computing Suppliers 721
Directory of CSIRO Research Programs 47
Directory of Data Base Producers 385
Directory of Documentation and Information Services in Adult Education 1021
Directory of Education Studies in Canada 170
Directory of Educational Documentation and Information Services 1021
Directory of Educational Research Institutions 1021
Directory of Federally Supported Research in Universities 152
Directory of Grant-Making Trusts 198
Directory of Indian Scientific & Technical Translators 507
Directory of Industrial Information Services and Systems in Developing Countries 1027
Directory of Information Sources in Turkey 991
Directory of Non-Governmental Organisations in OECD Member Countries Active in Development Co-operation 781
Directory of On-going Research in Cancer Epidemiology 1113
Directory of On-going Research in Korea 645
Directory of On-line Databases in Sweden (DOLDIS) 930

Directory of Professional Organisations in India 511
Directory of Regional Demographic Research and Teaching Institutions 1003
Directory of Research Institutes and Industrial Laboratories in Israel 616
Directory of Researchers in Korean Studies 645
Directory of Scientific and Technical Associations in Israel 616
Directory of Scientific Periodicals of Pakistan 793
Directory of Scientific Research Institutions in India 507
Directory of Scientists and Technologists of Bangladesh 70
Directory of Social Science Research and Documentation Institutions in the Arab Region 1015
Directory of Social Science Research Institutions (India) 511
Directory of Special Libraries in Indonesia 512
Directory of Special Libraries in Israel 616
Directory of Specialized Information Centers and Agencies in the Federal Republic of Germany and West Berlin 880
Directory of Standards and Specifications Issued by Departments and Agencies of the Government of Canada 898
Directory of Standards Referenced in Canadian Federal Legislation 898
Directory of Training, Research and Information-Producing Centers in Iran 613
Directory of United Nations Information Systems 1001
Directory of Water and Sanitation Institutions in Latin America and the Caribbean 794
DIRSLEARN 521
Disclosure II Corporate Information Data Base (I.P. Sharp Associates) 871
DISPLAY 256
DISSERT 1 (Data Bank of European Doctoral Theses in Management) 313
DISTAT 237
DITR (Deutsches Informationszentrum fur Technische Regeln) 407
Division de Informacion Tecnica - Comision Nacional de Energia Atomica - Argentina 27
Division Documentation - Institut National de la Statistique et des Etudes - France 363
Division of Documentation and Information - Central American Research Institute for Industry 193
Division of Health Statistics - World Health Organization 1110
Division of Information and Documentation - National Institute of Science and Technology - Philippines 807
Division of Information and Library (DIAL) Services - Insearch Ltd. 538
Division of Materials Applications - National Physical Laboratory - Great Britain 451
Division of Noncommunicable Diseases - World Health Organization 1111
Division of Science and Technology Policies - United Nations Educational, Scientific and Cultural Organization 1016
Division of Scientific Documentation - German Federal Diet 422
Division of Technical Information - National Atomic Energy Commission - Argentina 27
Division of the UNESCO Library, Archives, and Documentation Services 1017
DKF (Dokumentation Kraftfahrwesen) 716
DKFZ (Deutsches Krebsforschungszentrum) 1113
DKI (Deutsches Kunststoff-Institut) 402
DKI-Dokumentation Kunststoffe Kautschuk Fasern 402
DKI-Thesaurus 402
DOBIS (Dortmunder Bibliothekssystem) 147
Dobra Iron and Steel Research Institute 281
DOC-EXPORT 796
DOCOCEAN 351
DOCPAL (Sistema de Documentacion sobre Poblacion en America Latina) 1007
DOCPAL Latin American Population Abstracts 1007
DOCPAL Resumenes sobre Poblacion en America Latina 1007
Doctoral Dissertations in the Social Sciences 847
Documentary Information Bank 996
Documentary Information Service - National Elf Aquitaine Company 723
Documentary Research Center 282
Documentary Service - International Institute of Refrigeration 590
Documentation and Information Division - Federal Institute for Sports Science - Germany 420
Documentation and Information Problems 843
Documentation and Information System for Parliamentary Materials - German Federal Diet 422
Documentation and Information System on Developmental Biology 490
Documentation and Information Unit - International Bureau of Education 1021
Documentation Bureau - International Railway Union 600
Documentation Center - Center for Study and Research of the Hydraulic Binders Industry 188
Documentation Center - French Petroleum Institute 387
Documentation Center - German Foundation for International Development 397

Documentation Center - Institute of Research on Fruits and Citrus Fruits 547
Documentation Center - Quebec Ministry of the Environment 832
Documentation Center - Saclay Nuclear Research Center 339
Documentation Center for Human Sciences - National Center for Scientific Research - France 355
Documentation Center for Mechanics - Technical Center for Mechanical Industries 957
Documentation Center for Phytomedicine - Federal Biological Research Center for Agriculture and Forestry - Germany 409
Documentation Center on Animal Production - Hohenheim University 487
Documentation Centre - International Livestock Centre for Africa 596
Documentation Centre - National Institute of Health and Family Welfare - India 508
Documentation Centre for Education in Europe 248
Documentation Coordination Unit - Ministry of the Interior - Brazil 100
Documentation Department - Institute of Nutrition 545
Documentation Department - MERLIN GERIN Company 696
Documentation Department - MERLIN GERIN Company 697
Documentation Division - National Institute of Statistics and Economic Studies - France 363
Documentation Francaise 384
Documentation Generale - Societe Generale de Banque 73
Documentation Occupational Health 419
Documentation Occupational Health 539
Documentation Review on Information Problems 815
Documentation Rheology 417
Documentation Section - Ultuna Library 941
Documentation Section - Volkswagenwerk AG 1104
Documentation Service - Center for Industrial Creation 184
Documentation Service - International Children's Centre 566
Documentation Service - Swiss Academy of Medical Sciences 943
Documentation System - Shiloah Research Center for Middle Eastern and African Studies 970
Documentation Tribology 417
Documents, Ordres et Reglements Statutaires 828
Docupro 283
DOIDB Data Base (I.P. Sharp Associates) 871
DOKDI (Documentation Service) - Swiss Academy of Medical Sciences 943
Dokumentation Arbeitsmedizin 419
Dokumentation Arbeitsmedizin 539
Dokumentation der Forschungsvorhaben in der Okologischen Medizin in der Bundesrepublik Deutschland 539
Dokumentation Gefahrdung durch Alkohol, Rauchen, Drogen, Arzneimittel 539
Dokumentation Impfschaden-Impferfolge 539
Dokumentation Kraftfahrwesen 716
Dokumentation Krankenhauswesen 477
Dokumentation Maschinenbau 961
Dokumentation Medizin im Umweltschutz 539
Dokumentation Medizinische Technik 962
Dokumentation Messen Mechanischer Grossen 415
Dokumentation Rheologie 417
Dokumentation Schweisstechnik 418
Dokumentation Sozialmedizin, Offentlicher Gesundheitsdienst, Arbeitsmedizin 539
Dokumentation Verfahrenstechnik 77
Dokumentation Zerstorungsfreie Prufung 416
Dokumentationsring Elektrotechnik (DRE) Data Base 960
Dokumentationsstelle fur Phytomedizin - Biologische Bundesanstalt fur Land- und Forstwirtschaft - Germany 409
Dokumentationsstelle fur Strassen- und Verkehrswesen - Bundesministerium fur Bauten und Technik - Austria 63
Dokumentationsstelle Rheologie und Tribologie 417
DOLDIS (Directory of On-Line Databases in Sweden) 930
DOMA (Dokumentation Maschinenbau) 961
DOMA Referatedienst 961
DOMESTIC 617
Dominion Law Reports 162
Dominion Reports Service 828
DOMLIB 617
DOMPRINT 617
DOORS (Data on Occupations Retrieval System) 462
Dortmund Data Bank 1046
Dortmund Institute for Water Research 284
Dortmunder Bibliothekssystem (DOBIS) 147
DOUG (Danish Online User Group) 256
DPA (Deutschen Patentamt) 401
DPB (British Library Department of Printed Books) Data Base 440
DPDS (DARC Pluridata System) 38
DPFID Data Base (I.P. Sharp Associates) 871
DPIC (Drug and Poison Information Centre) - B.C. Hospital Programs Branch - University of British Columbia 1043
DPS (Data Processing Services Company) 258
DPS Information Centre 258
DPS Newsletter 258
DRE (Dokumentationsring Elektrotechnik) Data Base 960

DREF (Data Reference) Data Base (WATDOC) 140
DRI Europe 259
Driftmeddelanden 931
Drug Abuse: Research on the Treatment of Alcohol and Drug Dependence 936
Drug and Poison Information Centre - B.C. Hospital Programs Branch - University of British Columbia 1043
Drug Consumption Data Base 893
Drug Information Perspectives Newsletter 1043
Drug Information Pharmacists Group 285
Drug Information Reference 1043
Drug Information Sources 432
Drug Literature Index 296
Drug Use in Australia: A Directory of Survey Research Projects 61
DRUGDOC 296
Drugs 5
Drugs Data Base 634
Drugs in Japan 634
DS (Dokumentation Schweisstechnik) 418
DSD (DECHEMA Stoffdaten Dienst) 404
DSI/Laval - Universite Laval Bibliotheque 652
DSIR (Department of Scientific and Industrial Research) - New Zealand 748
DSIR Central Library - Department of Scientific and Industrial Research - New Zealand 748
DSIR Documentation 748
DTB (Danmarks Tekniske Bibliotek) 270
Duff and Phelps Fixed Income Data Base (I.P. Sharp Associates) 871
Dun & Bradstreet International 267
Dun & Bradstreet's Key British Enterprises 802
DUNIS (Directory of United Nations Information Systems) Data Base 1001
Dutch State Mines 286
DVJB (Danish Veterinary and Agricultural Library Catalogue) Data Base 497
DVS (Deutscher Verband fur Schweisstechnik) 418
E.A.O. 1
EABS (Euro Abstracts) Data Base 218
EAGLE 638
EAI (Economics Abstracts International) 733
Earning Estimates Data Bank (NEEDS-TS) 754
Earth Science Computer Services 237
East Europe Agriculture 8
East Midland Allied Press 976
Eastel 287
Eastern Bloc Countries Economic Data Base (I.P. Sharp Associates) 871
Eastern Counties Newspapers 287
Eastern European Mineral Technology - Current Contents 131
Eastern Mediterranean Regional Office - World Health Organization 1112
Eastern Telecommunications Philippines, Inc. 288
Eastern Telecoms 288
Easy Data Integrated Library System 289
Easy Data Systems Ltd. 289
EBA (European Business Associates) On-Line 308
EBIP (European Biotechnology Information Program) 446
EBIP Newsletter 446
EBIS (ESCAP Bibliographic Information System) 1002
EBIS/POPFILE (ESCAP Bibliographic Information System/Population File) 1003
EBSCO Subscription Services (United Kingdom Office) 954
EBSLG (European Business School Librarians' Group) 481
EC Index 305
ECA (Economic Commission for Africa) 1005
ECDIN (Environmental Chemicals Data and Information Network) 221
ECHO (European Commission Host Organization) 219
ECHO Newsletter 219
ECL (Eurotec Consultants Ltd.) 318
ECMT (European Conference of Ministers of Transport) 309
ECO Data Base 949
Ecole des Hautes Etudes Commerciales 127
Ecole Polytechnique de Montreal 691
Ecole Polytechnique de Montreal 819
Ecole Superieure d'Ingenieurs en Electrotechnique et Electronique 797
Ecological Abstracts 393
ECOM Data Base 893
ECOMP 521
Econintel Information Services Ltd. 290
Econintel Monitor 290
Econometric Data Bank (University of Melbourne) 237
Economic and Business Statistics Branch - Central Statistics Bureau - British Columbia Ministry of Industry and Small Business Development 106
Economic and Social Commission for Asia and the Pacific - United Nations 1002
Economic and Social Commission for Asia and the Pacific - United Nations 1003
Economic and Social Commission for Asia and the Pacific - United

Nations 1004
Economic and Social Commission for Asia and the Pacific Bibliographic Information System Data Base 1002
Economic and Social Department - Food and Agriculture Organization 1010
Economic and Social Research Council 291
Economic Commission for Africa 1005
Economic Commission for Latin America 1006
Economic Commission for Latin America 1007
Economic Geology Division - Geological Survey of Canada 134
Economic Information Unit - Institute of Economics - Hungarian Academy of Sciences 491
Economic Services Division - Alberta Department of Agriculture 9
Economic Statistics and National Accounts Division - Organisation for Economic Co-Operation and Development 780
Economic Titles/Abstracts 733
Economics Abstracts International (EAI) 733
Economics Research Institute - Stockholm School of Economics 903
Economics Series Data Base (Datastream) 267
Economie de l'Energie 355
Economie Generale 355
Economie Prospective Internationale 185
Economist Data Base (Datasolve World Reporter) 265
Economist's Statistics 679
Economy Bulletins (Biomedical Information Service) 1069
ECSSID (European Cooperation in Social Science Information and Documentation) 311
ECSSID Bulletin 311
EDC (European Documentation Centre) - University of Dundee 1047
EDCKEY Data Base 1047
EDE (Environmental Data and Ecological Parameters Data Base) 604
EDE System Manual 604
EDF (Electricite de France) 295
EDF-DOC Data Base 295
Edimedia Inc. 292
EDIN (Education on INIS) 317
Editec 293
Editions Francis Lefebvre 949
Editions Techniques 294
Editrice Bibliografica 87
EDP Department - European Patent Office 315
Education Information Network in the European Community 215
Education Management Information Exchange 724
Education on INIS (EDIN) 317
Education Policy Information Centre 724
Education Service - Commission of the European Communities 215
Educational Abstracts for Tanzania 955
Educational Documentation and Information: the IBE Bulletin 1021
Educational Research 724
Educational Research News 724
EEC Official Journal (Eurolex) 314
EFI (Ekonomiska Forskningsinstitutet) - Handelshogskolan i Stockholm 903
EFX Library 1099
EHOG (Association of European Host Operators Group) 42
EIASM (European Institute for Advanced Studies in Management) 313
Eidgenossische Technische Hochschule 327
Eight Peak Index of Mass Spectra 856
Eighteenth Century Short Title Catalogue 443
EK-MRA Data Base 1098
Ekonomiska Forskningsinstitutet - Handelshogskolan i Stockholm 903
Eksport Indeks 767
ELECNUC Databank 338
Electric Utilities Reports Data Base (I.P. Sharp Associates) 871
Electrical and Electronics Abstracts 549
Electrical Engineering Documentation Center 960
Electrical Measurement of Mechanical Quantities Documentation 415
Electrical Patents Index 275
Electricite de France 295
Electrodes for Medicine and Biology 114
Electronic Components of Assessed Quality 958
Electronic Directory Service 552
Electronic Engineering Index 958
Electronic Funds Transfer: A Comprehensive Bibliography 883
Electronic Library 654
Electronic Materials Information Service 550
Electronic Publishers Trade Association 1
Electronic Publishing Abstracts 812
Electronic Publishing Review 654
Electronic Slide Presentation System 369
Elf Aquitaine 723
ELIAS (Environment Libraries Automated System) 144
ELIPA (Experienced Librarians and Information Personnel in the Developing Countries of Asia and Oceania) 644
ELLIS (European Legal Literature Information Service) 305
Elsevier-NDU Publishers 305
Elsevier Science Publishers B.V. 296
Elsevier Science Publishers B.V. 614
Elsevier Science Publishing Co., Inc. 296

EM (Excerpta Medica) 296
EMAP Business & Computer Publications Ltd. 976
EMBASE (Excerpta Medica Data Base) 296
EMCANCER 296
EMCLAS Classification System 296
EMDRUGS 296
EMFORENSIC 296
EMHEALTH 296
EMIE (Education Management Information Exchange) 724
EMIS (Electronic Materials Information Service) 550
EMPIRES (Excerpta Medica Physicians Information Referral and Education Service) 296
Empirical Social Research 1045
Empirische Sozialforschung 1045
Emploi et Formation 355
Employment and Training 355
EMRO (Eastern Mediterranean Regional Office) - World Health Organization 1112
EMTOX 296
EMTRAIN (DIMDI) 428
ENDOC (Environmental Information and Documentation Centers) Data Base 216
ENDOC Directory 216
ENDS (European Nuclear Documentation System) 560
ENERCAN (Canadian Renewable Energy Database) 16
ENERCAN (Canadian Renewable Energy Database) 152
ENERDATA 878
ENERGI 339
Energia-Bibliografia Seletiva 102
ENERGIRAP 339
Energy and Economic Data Bank - International Atomic Energy Agency 559
Energy Economics 355
Energy Information Section - United Nations Educational, Scientific and Cultural Organization 1018
Energy Newsletter (I.P. Sharp Associates) 871
Energy Programs Data Base 133
Energy Projects Data Base 133
Energy Service 690
Energy Storage 44
Energy Studies and Information Center - French Institute of Energy 386
Enfo 31
Engineering Components and Materials Index 958
Engineering Science Division - Bayer AG 77
Engineering Sciences Data Unit Ltd. 299
English Tourist Board 297
Enitesugyi es Varosfeilesztesi Vilaghirado 494
ENLIST Data Base 1059
ENREP (Environmental Research Projects) Data Base 217
ENSDF-MEDLIST 521
ENSIC (Environmental Sanitation Information Center) 31
ENSIC Holdings List 31
ENV (Environnement) Data Base 140
Envirodoq 832
Environment Agency - Japan 626
Environment Canada 138
Environment Canada 139
Environment Canada 140
Environment Canada 141
Environment Canada 142
Environment Canada 143
Environment Canada 144
Environment Libraries Automated System 144
Environment-related Hydrological Data Bank (HYDABA) 411
Environmental Chemicals Data and Information Network 221
Environmental Data and Ecological Parameters Data Base 604
Environmental Information and Documentation Centers (ENDOC) Data Base 216
Environmental Information and Documentation System - Federal Environmental Agency - Germany 411
Environmental Information Division - National Institute for Environmental Studies - Environment Agency - Japan 626
Environmental Literature Information Service 411
Environmental Numerical Data File 626
Environmental Research Catalogue 411
Environmental Research in the Netherlands 743
Environmental Research Projects (ENREP) Data Base 217
Environmental Safety Group - Atomic Energy Research Establishment, Harwell 437
Environmental Sanitation Abstracts - Low Cost Options 31
Environmental Sanitation Information Center 31
Environmental Sanitation Reviews 31
Environnement (ENV) Data Base 140
EPA (Electronic Publishing Abstracts) 812
EPASYS (European Patent Administrative System) 315
EPCA (European Petrochemical Association) Trade Statistics Database 993
Ephemerides of Minor Planets 997

EPI (Electrical Patents Index) 275
EPIC (Education Policy Information Centre) 724
EPICS (European Petrochemical Industry Computerized System) 799
Epitesugyi Cikkek a Magyar Idoszaki Kiadvanyokban 494
Epitesugyi es Varosfejlesztesi Miniszterium 494
Epitesugyi Muszaki es Gazdasagi Tajekoztato 494
Epitesugyi Tajekoztatsi Kozpont - Epitesugyi es Varosfejlesztesi Miniszterium 494
EPO (European Patent Office) 315
EPO Data Banks 315
Epoch News Japan 298
Epoch Research Corporation 298
EPOS-VIRA 930
Equal Opportunities Commission - Great Britain 209
Equation of State Package 548
Equipment for the Disabled Poplation 114
Equity Stocks Data Base (Datastream) 267
ER586 Service Segment Data Base (I.P. Sharp Associates) 871
ERGODATA 838
Ergonomics Abstracts 1041
Ergonomics and the Electronic Office 520
Ergonomics Information Analysis Centre 1041
EROICA Data Base 1076
EROICA System for Basic Properties of Organic Compounds 1076
ESA (European Space Agency) 316
ESA (European Space Agency) 317
ESA/IRS 317
ESA-QUEST 317
ESANET 317
ESCAP (Economic and Social Commission for Asia and the Pacific) - United Nations 1002
ESCAP (Economic and Social Commission for Asia and the Pacific) - United Nations 1003
ESCAP (Economic and Social Commission for Asia and the Pacific) - United Nations 1004
ESCAP Bibliographic Information System 1002
ESCAP Bibliographic Information System/Population File 1003
ESCAP Documents and Publications 1002
ESCAP Library 1002
ESCAP Statistical Yearbook for Asia and the Pacific 1004
Escuela de Salud Publica de Mexico 700
ESDU International Limited 299
ESIEE (Ecole Superieure d'Ingenieurs Electrotechnique et Electronique) 797
ESP (Electronic Slide Presentation) System 369
Especialidades Farmaceuticas Espanolas Data Bank 893
ESPES (Especialidades Farmaceuticas Espanolas Data Bank) 893
Espial Data Base Directory 300
Espial Productions 300
ESRC (Economic and Social Research Council) 291
ESRIN (European Space Research Institute) 317
Esselte Business Information 301
Esselte Documentation System 302
Esselte Group of Booksellers 302
Esselte Info 260
ESSOR 977
Estates and Trusts Quarterly 162
ESTC (Eighteenth Century Short Title Catalogue) 443
ESTC Cataloguing Rules 443
ESTC/North America 443
ESTEC (European Space Research and Technology Center) 316
Estimation/Prediction Package 548
Estudio de Usarios de Informacion Industrial 193
Estudos Sobre o Desenvolvimento Agricola 99
Etat et Religion, State and Religion, Staat und Religion 205
ETH (Eidgenossische Technische Hochschule) 327
Ethylene Cracker Report 505
ETK (Epitesugyi Tajekoztatsi Kozpont) - Epitesugyi es Varosfejlesztesi Miniszterium 494
ETPI (Eastern Telecommunications Philippines, Inc.) 288
EUCAS 720
EUDISED Multilingual Thesaurus 248
EUDISED R&D Data Base 248
EUDISED R&D Bulletin 248
EURECAS 720
EURECHA (European Committee for Computers in Chemical Engineering Education) 327
EURECHA Chemical Data Bank 327
EURIPA (European Information Providers Association) 312
Euris Host Service 488
Euris Host Service 489
Euro Abstracts 218
Eurobond System 249
Eurocharts 1109
Eurodata Foundation 303
Eurodata Foundation Yearbook 303
EURODICAUTOM 223
EURODICAUTOM Bulletin 223
Eurofish Report 8

Eurolex 314
Eurolex Data Bases 314
Euroline Inc. 304
Euronet (European On-Line Information Network) 220
Euronet DIANE 220
Euronet DIANE Directory of Services 220
Euronet DIANE News 220
Europe Data 305
European Agricultural Outlook Conference 8
European Association for the Transfer of Technologies, Innovation and Industrial Information 306
European Association of Information Services 307
European Association of Scientific Information Dissemination Centers 307
European Bioengineering Research Inventory 114
European Biotechnology Information Program 446
European Business Associates On-Line 308
European Business School Librarians' Group 481
European Commission Host Organization 219
European Committee for Computers in Chemical Engineering Education 327
European Communities Publications: a Guide to British Library Resources 442
European Community Law 489
European Company Service 690
European Conference of Ministers of Transport 309
European Conference of Posts and Telecommunications Administrations 303
European Consortium for Political Research 310
European Cooperation in Social Science Information and Documentation 311
European Coordination Centre for Research and Documentation in Social Sciences 311
European Court of Justice Reporter 305
European Court Reports (Eurolex) 314
European Cultural Foundation 215
European Digest 465
European Documentation and Information System for Education 248
European Documentation Centre - University of Dundee 1047
European Human Rights Reports (Eurolex) 314
European Index of Management Periodicals 481
European Information Providers Association 312
European Institute for Advanced Studies in Management 313
European Law Centre Ltd. 314
European Law Digest (Eurolex) 314
European Legal Literature Information Service 305
European LPG Report 505
European Nuclear Documentation System 560
European On-Line Information Network 220
European Paint & Resin News Monthly 530
European Patent Administrative System (EPASYS) 315
European Patent Bulletin 315
European Patent Office 315
European Patent Register 315
European Patent Search Documentation System 315
European Petrochemical Association 993
European Petrochemical Association 994
European Petrochemical Association (EPCA) Trade Statistics Database 993
European Petrochemical Industry Computerized System 799
European Political Data Newsletter 310
European Scientific Information Referral 307
European Space Agency 316
European Space Agency 317
European Space Research and Technology Center 316
European Space Research Institute 317
European Study Conferences Ltd. 517
EUROSERV 710
EUROSTAT (Statistical Office of the European Communities) 224
EUROSTAT (Statistical Office of the European Communities) 225
EUROSTAT News 225
EUROSTAT Review 225
Eurostatistics 225
Eurotec Consultants Ltd. 318
EURYDICE (Education Information Network in the European Community) 215
Eusidic (European Association of Information Services) 307
Eusidic Database Guide 307
Eusidic Database Guide 654
EUSIREF (European Scientific Information Referral) 307
EUTS (Exeter University Teaching Services) 319
Evaluated Kinetic Data for High-Temperature Reactions 1052
Evaluation of Historic Buildings 138
EVOC (Excerpta Medica Vocabulary) Data Base 296
Ex Libris 576
EXBOND 322
Excerpta Medica 296
Excerpta Medica Core Journals 296
Excerpta Medica Data Base (EMBASE) 296

Excerpta Medica Newsletters 296
Excerpta Medica Physicians Information Referral and Education Service (EMPIRES) 296
Excerpta Medica Vocabulary (EVOC) Data Base 296
Exchange Rate Movements Yearbook 484
Exchequer Reports 828
Exeter Abstract Reference System 319
Exeter University Teaching Services 319
EXFOR Files 561
EXFOR Files 785
EXIS (Expert Information Systems Ltd.) 320
EXIS 1 320
Experienced Librarians and Information Personnel in the Developing Countries of Asia and Oceania 644
Expert Information Systems Ltd. 320
Expertises: Mensuel du Droit de l'Informatique 797
EXPLORE 356
Export Index 767
Express Bulletins (Biomedical Information Service) 1069
EXSHARE 321
EXSHARE Focal Points 321
EXSTAT 323
Extel Cards 323
Extel Computing Ltd. 321
Extel Group 321
Extel Group 322
Extel Group 323
Extel International Bonds Database 322
Extel Statistical Services Ltd. 322
Extel Statistical Services Ltd. 323
EXTEMPLO 1049
Extensions and Corrections to the UDC 578
Extra Pharmacopoeia 806
Faba Bean Abstracts 229
FABIUS (Fabrication Automatique de Bibliographies et d'Index Utilisant des Syntagmes) 547
Fabrication Automatique de Bibliographies et d'Index Utilisant des Syntagmes (FABIUS) 547
Fabrimetal 187
Fachbereich Dokumentation und Information - Bundesinstitut fur Sportwissenschaft - Germany 420
Fachinformationszentrum Chemie GmbH 201
Fachinformationszentrum Chemie GmbH 402
Fachinformationszentrum Energie, Physik, Mathematik GmbH 521
Fachinformationszentrum Energie, Physik, Mathematik GmbH 901
Fachinformationszentrum Technik 959
Fachinformationszentrum Technik 960
Fachinformationszentrum Technik 961
Fachinformationszentrum Technik 962
Fachinformationszentrum Werkstoffe 522
Facility for the Analysis of Chemical Thermodynamics 691
Facsimilia Scientia et Technica Norwegica 1079
Fact (Facility for the Analysis of Chemical Thermodynamics) 691
Fact User's Guide 691
Fact's Listing of Compounds in Main Data Base 691
Factotum 443
Faculty of Engineering - McGill University 691
Faculty of Engineering - University of Tokyo 1076
Faculty of Human Kinetics and Leisure Studies - University of Waterloo 1085
Faculty of Library and Information Science Library - University of Toronto 1077
Faculty of Nursing - University of Alberta 1036
Faculty of Nursing - University of Alberta 1037
Fahrzeug-Datenbank-System 1104
FAIR (Fast Access Information Retrieval) 114
FAIREC (Fruits Agro-Industrie Regions Chaudes) Data Base 547
Fairfax (John) Ltd. 55
Fairfax (John) Ltd. 908
Fairplay International Research Services 324
Fairplay Publications Ltd. 324
FALI 80
FAO (Food and Agriculture Organization) 1008
FAO (Food and Agriculture Organization) 1009
FAO (Food and Agriculture Organization) 1010
FAO (Food and Agriculture Organization) 1011
FAO (Food and Agriculture Organization) 1012
FAO (Food and Agriculture Organization) 1013
FAO (Food and Agriculture Organization) 1014
FAO Documentation - Current Bibliography 1013
FAO Documentation Data Base 1013
FAO Fertilizer Yearbook 1014
FAO Library Catalogue of Monographs 1013
FAO Library List of Serials 1013
FAO Monthly Bulletin of Statistics 1014
FAO Production Yearbook 1014
FAO Statistics Data Bases 1014
FAO Trade Yearbook 1014
FAO Yearbook of Forest Products and Trade 1014

Far Eastern Economic Review Index on Microfiche 1073
Farm Bank (AERIC) 238
FARMODEX Bulletin 325
FARMODEX Drug Data Bank 325
FARMODEX Foundation 325
Fast Access Information Retrieval (FAIR) 114
Fast Avfall 767
FATES 527
Fawcett Library - City of London Polytechnic 209
Faxtel Information Systems Ltd. 326
FE-Dokumentation - Volkswagenwerk AG 1104
Federal Biological Research Center for Agriculture and Forestry - Germany 409
Federal Court of Appeal Decisions 1108
Federal Court of Canada Reports 828
Federal Employment Institute - Germany 410
Federal Environmental Agency - Germany 411
Federal Institute for Geosciences and Natural Resources - Germany 412
Federal Institute for Geosciences and Natural Resources - Germany 413
Federal Institute for Geosciences and Natural Resources - Germany 414
Federal Institute for Materials Testing - Germany 415
Federal Institute for Materials Testing - Germany 416
Federal Institute for Materials Testing - Germany 417
Federal Institute for Materials Testing - Germany 418
Federal Institute for Materials Testing - Germany 522
Federal Institute for Occupational Safety - Germany 419
Federal Institute for Sports Science - Germany 420
Federal Ministry of Buildings and Technology - Austria 63
Federal Ministry of Metallurgy and Heavy Engineering - Czechoslovakia 281
Federal Ministry of Science and Research - Austria 65
Federal Research and Testing Establishment Arsenal - Federal Ministry of Buildings and Technology - Austria 63
Federal Research Center for Fisheries - Germany 421
Federal Research Center for Nature Conservation and Landscape Ecology - Germany 408
Federal Research Institute for Viticulture - Germany 585
Federal Reserve Board Weekly Data Base (I.P. Sharp Associates) 871
Federal Systems Division - Canada Systems Group 163
Federal Systems Division - Canada Systems Group 164
Federal Systems Division - Canada Systems Group 165
Federal Systems Division - Canada Systems Group 166
Federal Technical University 327
Federation Internationale de Documentation 578
Federation Internationale de Documentation 579
Feed Composition Data Bank 487
FEES Data Base 692
Fennica 482
Feuille d'Information (Institut Francais des Petroles) 387
FIBER 90
FICHE BUILDER 649
Fiches Banques 251
Fiches de Documentation (Institut Francais des Petroles) 387
Fiches FAN 251
Fiches Profils: Transformation des Matieres Plastiques 251
Fiches Synthetiques 251
Fiches Techniques (FITEK) Data Bank 252
Fichier MARC Quebecois (FMQ) 833
FID (Federation Internationale de Documentation) 578
FID (Federation Internationale de Documentation) 579
FID/CAO (Commission for Asia and Oceania, International Federation for Documentation) 644
FID Directory 578
FID News Bulletin 578
Field Crop Abstracts 229
Fil d'Ariane 223
Filetab 721
Film and Video Acquisition 48
Film Canadiana 146
Financial Data File (ICC Information Group Ltd.) 499
Financial Futures Data Base (Datastream) 267
Financial and Economic Newsletter (I.P. Sharp Associates) 871
Financial Post Canadian Corporate Data Base (I.P. Sharp Associates) 871
Financial Post Division - MacLean-Hunter Ltd. 680
Financial Post Investment Data Bank 680
Financial Post Securities Data Base (I.P. Sharp Associates) 871
Financial Statistics Division - Bank of England 72
Financial Times Actuaries Share Indices Data Base (I.P. Sharp Associates) 871
Financial Times Business Information Ltd. 328
Financial Times Business Information Ltd. 690
Financial Times Commercial Law Reports (Eurolex) 314
Financial Times Company Information 328
Financial Times Currency and Share Index Databank 328
Financial Times Index 328

MASTER INDEX

Financial Times Share Information Data Base (I.P. Sharp Associates) 871
FINDATA 903
Finding Patents 520
Fine Chemicals Directory 372
Fine Chemicals Directory Handbook 372
Finland - Central Medical Library 329
Finland - Ministry of Education 331
Finland - Ministry of Trade and Industry 330
Finland - National Library for Science and Technology 483
Finland - Technical Research Centre of Finland 330
FINLIST 903
FINMED 329
Finnish Council for Scientific Information and Research Libraries 331
Finnish Foreign Trade Association 332
Finnish National Bibliography 482
Finnish Periodicals Index in Economics and Business 481
Finnish Pulp and Paper Research Institute 333
Finnish Register of Exporters Data Base 332
Finnish Standards Association 334
FINP (Finnish Periodicals Index in Economics and Business) 481
FINP/BILD Thesaurus 481
FINPLAN 903
Finsbury Data Services Ltd. 335
FINSORT 903
FINSTA 903
FINSUM 903
Fire Research Library Automated Information Retrieval (FLAIR) Data Base 452
Fire Research Station Library - Building Research Establishment - Department of the Environment - Great Britain 452
Fire Science Abstracts 452
FIRMEXPORT 796
FIRMKAT Data Base 1079
FIRS (Fairplay International Research Services) 324
FIRS Sale and Purchase Report 324
FIRS Weekly Newbuilding Report 324
FIRST-1 Infrared Search Program 155
FISHLINE 1011
FITEK (Fiches Techniques) Data Bank 252
Fixed Interest Instruments Data Base (Datastream) 267
FIXIT 527
FIZ Chemie 201
FIZ Chemie 402
FIZ Technik 959
FIZ Technik 960
FIZ Technik 961
FIZ Technik 962
FIZ-W (Fachinformationszentrum Werkstoffe) 522
FLA Groupe La Creatique 336
FLAIR (Fire Research Library Automated Information Retrieval) Data Base 452
FLARES 237
Fleet Street Reports (Eurolex) 314
Flora de Vercruz 702
Fluid Engineering Centre, BHRA 86
Fluid Flow Measurements Abstracts 86
Fluid Power Abstracts 86
Fluid Sealing Abstracts 86
FLUIDEX 86
FMQ (Fichier MARC Quebecois) 833
FOA (Forsvarets Forskningsanstalt) - Sweden 929
FOA Index Group - Research Institute of National Defense - Sweden 929
FOCUS 321
FODOK (Forschungsprojektdokumentation) Data Base 419
FOLIO 356
Fondation ADISQ/CIRPA 206
Fondo Colombiano de Investigaciones Cientificas 212
Fonds de la Recherche Fondamentale et Collective 846
Fonds Quetelet Library Data Base 81
FONTE Data Base 102
Food and Agriculture Organization 1008
Food and Agriculture Organization 1009
Food and Agriculture Organization 1010
Food and Agriculture Organization 1011
Food and Agriculture Organization 1012
Food and Agriculture Organization 1013
Food and Agriculture Organization 1014
Food Annotated Bibliographies 583
Food Balance Sheets 1014
Food Industry Bulletin 712
Food Industry Update 520
Food Patents 655
Food Research Association Computerized Information Services 655
Food Science and Technology Abstracts 583
Food Topics 655
Forecasts for the Forecasts' Users Group 1062
Forecasts of Exchange Rate Movements 484

Foreign Chemical Patent News 632
Foreign Exchange Outlook 484
Foreign Exchange Yearbook 290
Foreign Patents Information Bulletin 645
Foreign Trade Abstracts 733
Foreign Trade News 425
Foreign Trade Statistics for Asia and the Pacific 1004
Forest Products Abstracts 229
Forestry Abstracts 229
FORIS (Forschungsinformationssystem Sozialwissenschaften) 43
Form 41 Data Base (I.P. Sharp Associates) 871
Formanderungsfestigkeit Stahl-Eisen 399
FORMAT 146
FORMAT 649
FORS (Forschungsprojekte Raumordnung Stadtebau Wohnungswesen) 380
Forschungs- und Entwicklungsprojekte in Informationswissenschaft und -Praxis 880
Forschungsabteilung fur Philosophische Information und Dokumentation - Universitat Dusseldorf 1048
Forschungsarbeiten in den Sozialwissenschaften: Dokumentation 43
Forschungsberichte aus Technik und Naturwissenschaften 521
Forschungsdokumentation zur Arbeitsmarkt- und Berufsforschung 410
Forschungsgesellschaft Kunststoffe 402
Forschungsinformationssystem Sozialwissenschaften (FORIS) 43
Forschungsinstitut fur Internationale Politik und Sicherheit 337
Forschungsprojektdokumentation (FODOK) Data Base 419
Forschungsprojekte Raumordnung Stadtebau Wohnungswesen (FORS) 380
Forsvarets Forskningsanstalt - Sweden 929
Forthcoming Bioengineering Conferences 114
Forthcoming International Scientific and Technical Conferences 35
Fortschrittsberichte Technik/Naturwissenschaften 1031
Forum Musikbibliothek 400
Fossilium Catalogus 647
FoU-Indeks 767
Foundation for Science and Politics 337
Foundry Industries Technical Center 820
FPCORP Data Base (I.P. Sharp Associates) 871
FPSTOCK Data Base (I.P. Sharp Associates) 871
Framework Forecasts for the ECC Economies 484
Framework Forecasts for the UK Economy 484
France - Atomic Energy Commission 338
France - Atomic Energy Commission 339
France - Atomic Energy Commission 589
France - Bureau of Geological and Mining Research 340
France - Bureau of Geological and Mining Research 341
France - Bureau of Geological and Mining Research 342
France - Bureau of Geological and Mining Research 412
France - Direction Generale des Telecommunications 552
France - French Senate 343
France - Interministerial Mission for Scientific and Technical Information 344
France - Ministry of Agriculture 39
France - Ministry of Defense 345
France - Ministry of Education 346
France - Ministry of Education 722
France - Ministry of Education 981
France - Ministry of Industry and Research 344
France - Ministry of Industry and Research 981
France - Ministry of Posts and Telecommunications 989
France - National Center for Chemical Information 720
France - National Center for Ocean Utilization 347
France - National Center for Ocean Utilization 348
France - National Center for Ocean Utilization 349
France - National Center for Ocean Utilization 350
France - National Center for Ocean Utilization 351
France - National Center for Ocean Utilization 352
France - National Center for Ocean Utilization 353
France - National Center for Ocean Utilization 354
France - National Center for Pedagogical Documentation 346
France - National Center for Scientific Research 186
France - National Center for Scientific Research 355
France - National Center for Scientific Research 356
France - National Center for Scientific Research 357
France - National Center for Scientific Research 377
France - National Center for Scientific Research 412
France - National Center for Scientific Research 720
France - National Geological Survey 340
France - National Geological Survey 341
France - National Geological Survey 342
France - National Institute for Health and Medical Research 358
France - National Institute for Industrial Property 359
France - National Institute for Industrial Property 360
France - National Institute for Industrial Property 987
France - National Institute for Research in Informatics and Automation 361
France - National Institute of Agronomic Research 362
France - National Institute of Statistics and Economic Studies 363

France - National Institute of Statistics and Economic Studies   364
France - National Institute of Statistics and Economic Studies   365
France - National Institute of Statistics and Economic Studies   366
France - National Telecommunications Research Center   367
France - Parliamentary Documentation and Information Printing Service   343
France - Secretary of State for Posts and Telecommunications   367
France-Aquaculture   348
France Cables et Radio   552
France Cables et Radio   977
FRANCIS (Food Research Association Computerized Information Services)   655
FRANCIS (French Retrieval Automated Network for Current Information in Social and Human Sciences) Data Bases   355
Frankfurt City and University Library   368
Fraser Videotex Services   369
Fraser Williams (Scientific Systems) Ltd.   370
Fraser Williams (Scientific Systems) Ltd.   371
Fraser Williams (Scientific Systems) Ltd.   372
Fraunhofer Gesellschaft   373
Fraunhofer Gesellschaft   374
Fraunhofer Gesellschaft   375
Fraunhofer Gesellschaft   376
Fraunhofer Gesellschaft   377
Fraunhofer Gesellschaft   378
Fraunhofer Gesellschaft   379
Fraunhofer Gesellschaft   380
Fraunhofer-Institut fur Lebensmitteltechnologie und Verpackung   584
Fraunhofer Institute for Food Technology and Packaging   584
Fraunhofer Society   373
Fraunhofer Society   374
Fraunhofer Society   375
Fraunhofer Society   376
Fraunhofer Society   377
Fraunhofer Society   378
Fraunhofer Society   379
Fraunhofer Society   380
FRBW Data Base (I.P. Sharp Associates)   871
Free University of Brussels   381
French Association for Automatic Documentation in Chemistry   720
French Association for Standardization   382
French Company for the Design & Implementation of Radio & Television Broadcasting Equipment   383
French Documentation   384
French Federation of Data Base Producers   385
French Institute of Energy   386
French Language Board - Quebec   830
French Petroleum Company   723
French Petroleum Institute   387
French Petroleum Institute   723
French Press Agency   388
French Retrieval Automated Network for Current Information in Social and Human Sciences (FRANCIS) Data Bases   355
French Senate   343
French Shares Price Indexes   389
French Shares Yield   389
French Stockbrokers Society   389
French Textile Institute   390
French Water Study Association   391
Freshwater and Aquaculture Contents Tables   1008
FRFC (Fonds de la Recherche Fondamentale et Collective)   846
FRI Information Services Ltd.   392
FRIGINTER Data Base   590
Fruits   547
Fruits Agro-Industrie Regions Chaudes (FAIREC) Data Base   547
FSA (Fire Science Abstracts)   452
FSTA (Food Science and Technology Abstracts)   583
FSTA Thesaurus   583
FT Business Information Ltd.   328
FTACT Data Base (I.P. Sharp Associates)   871
FTSTOCK Data Base (I.P. Sharp Associates)   871
Fund Monitor Unit Trusts and Insurance Bonds Data Base (I.P. Sharp Associates)   871
FUNDMONITOR Data Base (I.P. Sharp Associates)   871
FUTU (Futures Information Service)   540
Futures Information Service   540
FUZZIE   741
FVS (Fraser Videotex Services)   369
G & J (Gruner & Jahr) Press Information Bank   468
G & J-Pressedokumentation   468
G.CAM (Groupement de la Caisse des Depots Automatisation pour le Management)   71
GAMA (Groupe d'Analyse Macroeconomique Appliquee)   1062
GAMS (Groupement pour l'Avancement des Methodes Spectroscopiques et Physico-Chimique d'Analyse)   466
GAP (Government of Alberta Publications) Data Base   11
GAPHYOR (Gaz-Physique-Orsay)   1063
GAPHYOR Bulletin   1063
Garden Guide   1099

Gas Physics Orsay (GAPHYOR)   1063
Gases and Plasmas Physics Laboratory - University of Paris-South   1063
Gateway Service - Prestel   448
GATT (General Agreement on Tariffs and Trade) Data Base/Denmark   497
Gaz-Physique-Orsay (GAPHYOR)   1063
Gazette du Palais   294
GBM (Generale Bankmaatschappis)   73
GC-20   71
GDCh (Gesellschaft Deutscher Chemiker)   201
GDoc Data Base   1050
GDPS (Global Data-processing System)   1119
GEISHA   341
GEMS (Global Environmental Monitoring System)   139
General Agreement on Tariffs and Trade (GATT) Data Base/Denmark   497
General Documentation - Bank Society   73
General Documentation on Trade and Economics   425
General Economy   355
General Index to the Debates of the National Diet (Japan)   629
General Information Programme - United Nations Educational, Scientific and Cultural Organization   603
General Information Programme - United Nations Educational, Scientific and Cultural Organization   1019
General Information Programme - United Nations Educational, Scientific and Cultural Organization   1023
General Information Programme: UNISIST Newsletter   1019
General Office for Ordnance - Ministry of Defense - France   345
General Relation Based Information Processing System (GRIPS)   428
General Review of Heat   386
Generale Bankmaatschappis   73
Geo Abstracts Ltd.   393
Geo Books   393
GeoArchive   394
GeoArchive Users' Guide   394
GEOBIB   625
Geochemical Analysis Data Base   387
GeoData Service   394
GEODE   340
GEODIAL (Geoscience Data Index for Alberta)   12
GEOFIZ   412
GEOFIZ   413
Geographie Tropicale   355
geoIPOD   352
GEOLINE   412
Geological Bibliography of France   340
Geological Information and Documentation Department - National Geological Survey - France   340
Geological Newsletter   609
Geological Survey of Canada   134
Geological Survey of Canada   135
Geological Survey of Sweden   920
Geomechanics Abstracts   1056
Geophysics and Tectonics Abstracts   393
Geoprofile - Vertebrate Paleontology   394
GEOROAD Data Base   925
Geosaurus   394
GEOSCAN Database   135
Geoscience Data Centre - Ontario Geological Survey   778
Geoscience Data Index for Alberta   12
Geoscience Documentation   394
Geoscience Literature Information Service - Federal Institute for Geosciences and Natural Resources - Germany   412
Geosources   394
Geosystems   394
Geotitles Repertorium   394
Geotitles Weekly   394
Geowissenschaftlicher Literaturinformationsdienst - Bundesanstalt fur Geowissenschaften und Rohstoffe - Germany   412
Geowissenschaftlicher Literaturinformationsdienst Data Base   412
GERDAT (Groupement d'Etudes et de Recherche pour le Developpement de l'Agronomie Tropicale)   467
Gerencia de Informacao/Information Management   605
German Bibliography Data Base   423
German Books in Print   863
German Cancer Research Center   1113
German Chemists Society   201
German Democratic Republic - Central Institute for Information and Documentation   395
German DIN Standards   958
German Electron-Synchrotron   396
German Federal Council   422
German Federal Diet   422
German Federal Postal Service - Ministry of Posts and Telecommunications - Germany   427
German Foreign Trade Information Office   425
German Foundation for International Development   397
German Hospital Institute   477

German Information Center for Technical Rules   407
German Information System for High Energy Physics   396
German Information System for Nutrition, Agriculture and Forestry   487
German Institute for Medical Documentation and Information   428
German Institute for Medical Documentation and Information   1078
German Iron and Steel Engineers Association   398
German Iron and Steel Engineers Association   399
German Library Institute   400
German National Library   423
German Orient Institute   397
German Partners of Developing Countries   397
German Patent Information System   401
German Patent Office   401
German Plastics Institute   402
German Psychological Literature Data Base (PSYNDEX)   1078
German Research Society   368
German Society for Chemical Equipment   403
German Society for Chemical Equipment   404
German Society for Chemical Equipment   405
German Society for Chemical Equipment   406
German Society for Information and Documentation   880
German Standards Institute   407
German Union Catalog of Serials   400
German Union List of Conference Proceedings   400
Germany - Arbeitsgemeinschaft fur Bauforschung   374
Germany - Bundesforschungsanstalt fur Getreide- und Kartoffelverarbeitung   583
Germany - Bundesforschungsanstalt fur Landeskunde und Raumordnung   380
Germany - Bundesministerium fur Arbeit und Sozialordnung   419
Germany - Federal Biological Research Center for Agriculture and Forestry   409
Germany - Federal Employment Institute   410
Germany - Federal Environmental Agency   411
Germany - Federal Institute for Geosciences and Natural Resources   412
Germany - Federal Institute for Geosciences and Natural Resources   413
Germany - Federal Institute for Geosciences and Natural Resources   414
Germany - Federal Institute for Materials Testing   415
Germany - Federal Institute for Materials Testing   416
Germany - Federal Institute for Materials Testing   417
Germany - Federal Institute for Materials Testing   418
Germany - Federal Institute for Materials Testing   522
Germany - Federal Institute for Occupational Safety   419
Germany - Federal Institute for Sports Science   420
Germany - Federal Research Center for Nature Conservation and Landscape Ecology   408
Germany - Federal Research Institute for Viticulture   585
Germany - German National Library   423
Germany - Ministry for Food, Agriculture and Forestry   408
Germany - Ministry for Food, Agriculture and Forestry   421
Germany - Ministry for Research and Technology   43
Germany - Ministry for Research and Technology   399
Germany - Ministry for Research and Technology   401
Germany - Ministry for Research and Technology   424
Germany - Ministry for Research and Technology   880
Germany - Ministry for Research and Technology   1045
Germany - Ministry of Building   374
Germany - Ministry of Economics   425
Germany - Ministry of Justice   426
Germany - Ministry of Posts and Telecommunications   427
Germany - Ministry of Youth, Family and Health   428
Gesellschaft Deutscher Chemiker   201
Gesellschaft fur Information und Dokumentation   583
Gesellschaft fur Information und Dokumentation   880
Gesellschaft fur Informationsvermittlung und Technologieberatung   36
Gesellschaft fur Zukunftsfragen e.v. Berlin   800
Gestion des Entreprises   355
GFPBBD (Groupement Francais des Producteurs de Bases et Banques de Donnees)   385
GHG (Gothard House Group)   432
GHG Information and Library Services Company   432
GID (Gesellschaft fur Information und Dokumentation)   583
GID (Gesellschaft fur Information und Dokumentation)   880
GID Information Center for Information Science and Practice   880
GID-Informationszentrum fur Informationswissenschaft und - Praxis   880
GID-IZ (GID-Informationszentrum fur Informationswissenschaft und - Praxis)   880
Giornale della Libreria   87
GIS Mediterranee   186
Glacier Inventory Notes   139
Glacier Inventory of Canada   139
Glass Institute   429
Glass Institute Information and Documentation Data Base   429
GLC (Greater London Council)   465

Global Data-processing System   1119
Global Environmental Monitoring System   139
Global Information Center (I.P. Sharp Associates)   871
Global Observing System   1119
Global Oral Data Bank   1111
Global Telecommunication System   1119
Globe and Mail Online, The   430
Globe and Mail, The   430
Glomar Challenger   352
Gmelin Handbook of Inorganic Chemistry   431
Gmelin Handbook of Inorganic Chemistry Index   431
Gmelin-Institut fur Anorganische Chemie und Grenzgebiete   431
Gmelin Institute for Inorganic Chemistry and Related Fields   431
GOIC (Gulf Organization for Industrial Consulting)   471
Going Online   775
GOLEM   874
GOS (Global Observing System)   1119
Gothard House Group of Companies, Ltd.   432
Gothard House Publications   432
Government Financing of Research and Development (EUROSTAT)   225
Government of Alberta Publications (GAP) Data Base   11
GRACE Data Base   1076
Graduate School of Library Science - McGill University   692
Graduate Theses in the Philippines Data Base   808
Grammatico-Lexicographical Data Base on Contemporary German   541
Graphiques de la Bourse de Paris   389
GRAPPE   977
Grassroots   519
Great Britain - Atomic Energy Authority   433
Great Britain - Atomic Energy Authority   434
Great Britain - Atomic Energy Authority   435
Great Britain - Atomic Energy Authority   436
Great Britain - Atomic Energy Authority   437
Great Britain - Atomic Energy Authority   438
Great Britain - British Library   246
Great Britain - British Library   439
Great Britain - British Library   440
Great Britain - British Library   441
Great Britain - British Library   442
Great Britain - British Library   443
Great Britain - British Library   444
Great Britain - British Library   446
Great Britain - British Library   677
Great Britain - British Library   818
Great Britain - British Library   1039
Great Britain - British Telecommunications   447
Great Britain - British Telecommunications   448
Great Britain - British Telecommunications   976
Great Britain - Central Computer and Telecommunications Agency   459
Great Britain - Central Statistical Office   449
Great Britain - Department of Education and Science   112
Great Britain - Department of Energy   769
Great Britain - Department of Health and Social Security   285
Great Britain - Department of Health and Social Security   1053
Great Britain - Department of Industry   450
Great Britain - Department of Industry   451
Great Britain - Department of Industry   548
Great Britain - Department of the Environment   378
Great Britain - Department of the Environment   437
Great Britain - Department of the Environment   452
Great Britain - Department of the Environment   453
Great Britain - Department of the Environment   455
Great Britain - Department of Trade   297
Great Britain - Department of Trade and Industry   454
Great Britain - Department of Trade and Industry   615
Great Britain - Department of Trade and Industry   727
Great Britain - Department of Transport   455
Great Britain - Departments of the Environment and Transport   455
Great Britain - Equal Opportunities Commission   209
Great Britain - H.M. Treasury   456
Great Britain - Health and Safety Executive   457
Great Britain - Home Office Forensic Science Service   458
Great Britain - House of Commons Library   459
Great Britain - House of Lords   460
Great Britain - Independent Broadcasting Authority   779
Great Britain - Institute of Terrestrial Ecology   461
Great Britain - Manpower Services Commission   462
Great Britain - Medical Research Council   114
Great Britain - National Engineering Laboratory   548
Great Britain - National Physical Laboratory   451
Great Britain - National Reprographic Centre for Documentation   725
Great Britain - Water Research Centre   463
Great Britain - Water Research Centre   464
Greater London Council   465
Greater London Council Intelligence Bulletins   465
Green Europe   8
Gresham Press   1089
GRIPS (General Relation Based Information Processing System)   428

GRIPS-Compact 428
GRIPS Training Database (GRIPSLEARN) 428
GRIPSLEARN (GRIPS Training Database) 428
Groundwater Documentation Section - Geological Survey of Sweden 920
Groundwater Survey - Netherlands Organization for Applied Scientific Research 740
Group for Applied Macroeconomic Analysis 1062
Group for the Advancement of Spectroscopic Methods and Physicochemical Analysis 466
Group for the Study and Research of Tropical Agronomy 467
Group Surveys 251
Groupe d'Analyse Macroeconomique Appliquee 1062
Groupe La Creatique 336
Grouped Enterprises Data Base 237
Groupement de la Caisse des Depots Automatisation pour le Management 71
Groupement d'Etudes et de Recherche pour le Developpement de l'Agronomie Tropicale 467
Groupement Francais des Producteurs de Bases et Banques de Donnees 385
Groupement pour l'Avancement des Methodes Spectroscopiques et Physico-Chimique d'Analyse 466
Grundvattendokumentation - Sveriges Geologiska Undersokning 920
Gruner & Jahr AG & Co. 468
Gruner & Jahr Press Information Bank 468
GSI-ECO 469
GTS (Global Telecommunication System) 1119
Guardian Data Base (Datasolve World Reporter) 265
Guia Brasileiro de Instituicoes de Pesquisa em Agricultura 99
Guia Brasileiro de Pesquisadores em Agricultura 99
Guia Internacional dos Micropublicadores 101
Guida alle Banche Dati 950
Guide des Bibliotheques Canadiennes 706
Guide to BISA 1073
Guide to Choosing Viewdata Systems 1100
Guide to CSK Data 628
Guide to Data Banks 950
Guide to Norwegian Statistics 766
Guide to Overseas Qualifications 108
Guide to Periodicals and Newspapers in the Public Libraries of Metropolitan Toronto 699
Guide to Provincial Library Agencies in Canada 149
Guide to Research and Development 515
Guidelines for Space Materials Selection 316
Guides for Managers Series (Eurodata Foundation) 303
Guinness Superlatives Limited 470
Gulf Organization for Industrial Consulting 471
Gustave-Roussy Institute 357
H.M. Treasury - Great Britain 456
Haifa On-line Bibliographic Text System 1051
HAMKA: A Bibliography of the Works of Prof. Dr. Haji Abdul Malik Karim Amrullah 1073
Handbook of Environmental Data and Ecological Parameters 604
Handbook of Library Holdings on Commonwealth Literature 442
Handbook on Agricultural Statistics for Asia and the Pacific 1004
Handbuch der Grossunternehmen 1098
Handelshogskolan i Stockholm 903
Hands-On (Information) Ltd. 472
Hanover Press 473
Hansard Oral Questions 828
Hansard Written Questions 828
Harker's Information Retrieval Systems 474
Harker's Specialist Book Importers 474
Harmonized Trade and World Economy Accounts Data Banks 185
Harnessing the Information Resource 533
Harris Media Systems Ltd. 475
Hartmann & Heenemann 401
Hartmann & Heenemann 476
Harwell Central Information Service 434
Harwell Information Bulletin 434
Hatfield Polytechnic 725
Hatfield Polytechnic Library 486
Hatra (Hosiery and Allied Trade Research Association) 873
Hazardous Materials Service - Atomic Energy Research Establishment, Harwell 437
Hazards of Alcohol, Smoking, Drugs, Medicine 539
Hazfile 435
HDC (Hydraulics Documentation Code) 268
HDEG (Union List of Higher Degree Theses in Australian Libraries) 1074
Health and Medical Libraries Online Catalog (HEMLOC) 50
Health and Safety Executive - Great Britain 457
Health and Welfare Canada 145
Health Care Information Service 477
Health Care Literature Information Network 477
Health Sciences Information in Canada: Libraries 152
Health Sciences Resource Centre - Canada Institute for Scientific and Technical Information 152

Heating, Ventilating, & Air Conditioning 203
HEATW Data Base (I.P. Sharp Associates) 871
Heavy Oil/Enhanced Recovery Index 13
Hebrew University of Jerusalem 478
HECLINET (Health Care Literature Information Network) 477
Heinze GmbH 479
Helecon Data Bases 481
HELIOS 384
Helminthological Abstracts: Series A, Animal Helminthology 229
Helminthological Abstracts: Series B, Plant Nematology 229
HELPIS (Higher Education Learning Programmes Information Service Catalogue) 112
Helppacks 1054
Helsingin Kauppakorkeakoulun Kirjasto 481
Helsingin Teknillisen Korkeakoulun Kirjasto 483
Helsingin Telset Oy 480
Helsingin Yliopiston Kirjasto 482
Helsinki Building Centre 118
Helsinki School of Economics Library 481
Helsinki Telephone Company 480
Helsinki University Library 482
Helsinki University of Technology 483
HEMLOC (Health and Medical Libraries Online Catalog) 50
Henley Centre for Forecasting 484
Henley Management College 484
Henrik Ibsen Concordance 768
Herbage Abstracts 229
HERI (Heavy Oil/Enhanced Recovery Index) 13
HERMES 450
Hertfordshire Business and Community Information Service 486
Hertfordshire Business Data Bank 486
Hertfordshire County Council 485
Hertfordshire Industrial and Commercial Register 486
Hertfordshire Technical Library and Information Service 486
HERTIS Industrial Services 486
HERTIS News 486
High Capacity Transport Register 68
High Energy Physics Index 396
High-Performance Textiles 873
High Temperature Materials Data Bank 222
High Temperature Reaction Rate Data Centre 1052
Higher Council for Scientific Research - Spain 890
Higher Council for Scientific Research - Spain 891
Higher Education in the United Kingdom 108
Higher Education Learning Programmes Information Service Catalogue (HELPIS) 112
Higher Institute of Sociology - University of Milan 1058
HIRS (Harker's Information Retrieval Systems) 474
HISCABEQ 704
Historical Sediment Data Summary 142
Historical Social Research 183
Historical Statistics 493
Historical Streamflow Summary 142
Historical Water Levels Summary 142
Historisch-Sozialwissenschaftliche Forschungen 183
Hitachi Ltd. 755
HKEP&BP (Hong Kong English Periodicals and Book Publishers) Data Base 635
HKKK (Helsingin Kauppakorkeakoulun Kirjasto) 481
HKSTOCK Data Base (I.P. Sharp Associates) 871
HMS (Hazardous Materials Service) - Atomic Energy Research Establishment, Harwell 437
HMSO Statutes in Force (Eurolex) 314
HOBITS (Haifa On-line Bibliographic Text System) 1051
Hochenergiephysik-Index 396
Hohenheim University 487
Hojin Shinkoku Shotoku 969
Holiday USA & Canada 473
Home Computing Guide 1099
Home Improvement Guide 1099
Home Office Forensic Science Service - Great Britain 458
Homelink - Prestel 448
HOMS (Hydrological Operational Multipurpose Subprogramme) - Operational Hydrology Programme - Commission for Hydrology - World Meteorological Organization 1117
HOMS National Reference Centre for Canada 140
HOMS Newsletter 1117
HOMS Reference Manual 1117
Honeywell Bull 488
Honeywell Bull 489
Hong Kong English Periodicals and Book Publishers (HKEP&BP) Data Base 635
Hong Kong Stock Exchange Data Base (I.P. Sharp Associates) 871
Hong Kong Telephone Company, Ltd. 231
Hoofdafdeling Vertalingen - Ministerie van Buitenlandse Zaken 732
Hoppenstedt & Co. 1098
Horticultural Abstracts 229
Hospital Care Documentation Project 477
Hotelview Services 231

House of Commons Library - Great Britain   459
House of Commons Library Thesaurus   459
House of Commons Weekly Information Bulletin   459
House of Lords - Great Britain   460
House of Lords Library Bulletin   460
House of Lords Library Data Bases   460
HSE (Health and Safety Executive) - Great Britain   457
HSE Library and Information Services - Health and Safety Executive - Great Britain   457
HSELiNE Data Base   457
HTM-DB (High Temperature Materials Data Bank)   222
Hubrecht Laboratory (International Embryological Institute)   490
Hughes Rotary Drilling Rig Report Data Base (I.P. Sharp Associates)   871
Human Nutrition Database   545
Human Resources, Institutions and Agrarian Reform Division - Economic and Social Department - Food and Agriculture Organization   1010
Human Sciences of Health   355
Humanistiske Data   768
Hungarian Academy of Sciences   491
Hungarian Academy of Sciences Library   492
Hungarian Academy of Sciences Publication Data Bank   492
Hungarian Building Bulletin   494
Hungarian Central Technical Library and Documentation Centre   496
Hungarian Information System   496
Hungarian Library and Information Science Abstracts   495
Hungarian Library Literature   495
Hungarian Technical Abstracts   496
Hungary - Central Statistical Office   493
Hungary - Ministry for Building and Urban Development   494
Hungary - National Szechenyi Library   495
Hungary - National Technical Information Centre and Library   496
HYDABA (Environment-related Hydrological Data Bank)   411
Hydraulics Documentation Code   268
Hydrogene dans les Metaux   981
Hydrogene Information   981
Hydrographic Department - Maritime Safety Agency - Japan   628
HYDROLINE   412
Hydrological Operational Multipurpose Subprogramme - Operational Hydrology Programme - Commission for Hydrology - World Meteorological Organization   1117
Hydromechanics and Hydraulic Engineering Abstracts   268
I.C.E. Abstracts   208
I.P. Sharp Associates Limited   871
I.P. Sharp Newsletter   871
I/S Datacentralen   497
IA Reports   618
IAALD (International Association of Agricultural Librarians and Documentalists)   558
IAALD News   558
IAALD Quarterly Bulletin   558
IAB (Institut fur Arbeitsmarkt- und Berufsforschung) - Bundesanstalt fur Arbeit - Germany   410
IACR (International Association of Cancer Registries)   1113
IAEA (International Atomic Energy Agency)   559
IAEA (International Atomic Energy Agency)   560
IAEA (International Atomic Energy Agency)   561
IAEA (International Atomic Energy Agency)   562
IAEA Energy and Economic Data Bank   559
IALINE-Pascal   39
IARC (International Agency for Research on Cancer)   1113
IASC (Indexing and Abstracting Society of Canada)   506
IASC (International Association for Statistical Computing)   556
IASC Newsletter   556
IASC/SCAD Newsletter   506
IATA North Atlantic Traffic Data Base (I.P. Sharp Associates)   871
IAURIF (Institut d'Amenagement et d'Urbanisme de la Region d'Ile-de-France)   1091
IBE (International Bureau of Education)   1021
IBECENT   1021
IBEDOC (International Bureau of Education Documentation and Information Unit) Data Base   1021
IBEDOC Information   1021
IBETERM   1021
IBI (Intergovernmental Bureau for Informatics)   554
IBI Newsletter   554
IBICT (Instituto Brasileiro de Informacao em Ciencia e Tecnologia)   103
IBIP (International Books in Print) Data Base   863
IBIS Data Base   194
IBJ Data Service Co.   498
IBJ Financial Data File   498
IBJDATA   498
IBR (Institute for Behavioural Research) - York University   1120
IBSEDEX Data Base   119
Ibsen (Henrik) Concordance   768
ICAITI (Instituto Centro Americano de Investigacion y Tecnologia Industrial)   193
ICAME (International Computer Archive of Modern English)   768

ICAME News   768
ICAO (International Civil Aviation Organization)   567
ICAO (International Civil Aviation Organization)   568
ICAO (International Civil Aviation Organization)   569
ICAO/ADREP Reports Summary   567
ICAO Air Transport Statistics Data Base   569
ICAO Aircraft Accident Data Base   567
ICAO Airport Characteristics Data Bank   568
ICAO Digests of Statistics   569
ICAO Regulations Module   320
ICAO Traffic Statistics Data Base (I.P. Sharp Associates)   871
ICAR (Inventory of Canadian Agricultural Research)   167
ICC (International Children's Centre)   566
ICC Business Ratio Reports   499
ICC Database Newsletter   499
ICC/DIALOG User Manual   499
ICC Financial Surveys   499
ICC Information Group Ltd.   499
ICC Viewdata   499
ICC Viewdata User Manual   499
ICCH (International Commodities Clearing House Ltd.)   672
ICEREF   139
ICI (Imperial Chemical Industries Ltd.)   503
ICIS (Independent Chemical Information Services Ltd.)   505
ICL (International Computer, Ltd.)   75
ICO (International Coffee Organization)   570
ICONOS   384
ICS (Interlinked Computerized Storage and Processing System of Food and Agricultural Data)   1014
ICSD (Inorganic Crystal Structure Data Base)   1042
ICSSD (International Committee for Social Science Information and Documentation)   571
ICSSR (Indian Council of Social Science Research)   511
ICSTI (International Centre for Scientific and Technical Information)   565
ICSU (International Council of Scientific Unions)   574
ICSU (International Council of Scientific Unions)   575
ICSU AB (International Council of Scientific Unions Abstracting Board)   575
ICTED (International Co-operation in the Field of Transport Economics Documentation)   309
ICV (Indice Cientifico Valenciano)   1082
ICV Information Systems Ltd.   500
ICYT (Instituto de Informacion y Documentacion en Ciencia y Tecnologia)   890
IDA (Industrial Development Abstracts)   1027
Ida Project   519
IDB (Industrial Data Bank Department) - Gulf Organization for Industrial Consulting   471
IDB (INPADOC Data Base)   64
IDC (Information and Documentation Center) - Royal Institute of Technology Library - Sweden   930
IDC (Internationale Dokumentationsgesellschaft fur Chemie)   572
IDC Inorganic Data Base   572
IDC-KTHB (Information and Documentation Center of the Royal Institute of Technology Library)   930
IDC Organic Chemistry File   572
IDC Patent Data Bank   572
IDC Polymer File   572
Idea Bank   631
IDIS (Institut fur Dokumentation und Information uber Sozialmedizin und Offentliches Gesundheitswesen)   539
IDIS-SOMED-A   539
IDOL   965
IDRC (International Development Research Centre)   31
IDRC (International Development Research Centre)   34
IDRC (International Development Research Centre)   576
IDRC (International Development Research Centre)   596
IDRC (International Development Research Centre)   644
IDRC (International Development Research Centre)   794
IDRC (International Development Research Centre)   889
IDRC (International Development Research Centre)   1005
IDRC (International Development Research Centre)   1006
IDS (Institut fur Deutsche Sprache)   541
IEA (International Association for the Evaluation of Educational Achievement)   557
IEA (International Energy Agency)   782
IEA (International Energy Agency)   783
IEA (International Energy Agency)   784
IEA Coal Research - International Energy Agency   782
IEA Coal Research - International Energy Agency   783
IEA Data Bank Bulletin   557
IEC (Information Exchange Centre for Federally Supported Research in Canadian Universities)   152
IEE (Institution of Electrical Engineers)   549
IEE (Institution of Electrical Engineers)   550
IEE-Energy Data Bank (Institute of Energy Economics)   753
IEPRC (International Electronic Publishing Research Centre)   577
IFDO (International Federation of Data Organizations for the Social

Sciences) 581
IFE (Institut Francais de l'Energie) 386
IFIC (International Ferrocement Information Center) 32
IFIP (International Federation for Information Processing) 580
IFIP (International Federation for Information Processing) 597
IFIP Information Bulletin 580
IFIS (International Food Information Service) 583
IFIS (International Food Information Service) 584
IFIS (International Food Information Service) 585
IFIS Newsletter 583
IFLA (International Federation of Library Associations and Institutions) 582
IFLA (International Federation of Library Associations and Institutions) 644
IFLA Annual 582
IFLA Directory 582
IFLA Journal 582
IFO Data Base (I.P. Sharp Associates) 871
IFO-Institut fur Wirtschaftsforschung 501
IFO-Institute for Economic Research 501
IFO Time Series Data Bank 501
IFP (Institut Francais des Petroles) 387
IFP (Institut Francais des Petroles) 723
IFP-TH 387
IFS Data Base (I.P. Sharp Associates) 871
IGIS (International Group of Users of Information Systems) 586
IGIS Newsletter 586
IGL 237
IGODOC 593
IHS (Information Handling Services) 958
III (Institute for Information Industry) 542
IINTE (Instytut Informacji Naukowej, Technicznej i Ekonomicznej) - Poland 815
IIR (International Institute of Refrigeration) 590
IIS (Institute of Information Scientists) 544
IIS (International Information Service Ltd.) 588
IIS Monograph Series 544
IIS Sourcefinder Series 544
ILCS (Interlibrary Loan and Communication System) - Central Ontario Regional Library System 195
ILO (International Labour Organisation) 591
ILO (International Labour Organisation) 592
ILO (International Labour Organisation) 593
ILO (International Labour Organisation) 594
ILO (International Labour Organisation) 595
ILO Thesaurus 593
ILODOC 593
ILV (Fraunhofer-Institut fur Lebensmitteltechnologie und Verpackung) 584
IMAG (Instituut voor Mechanisatie, Arbeid en Gebouwen) 543
IMAG Dataservice 543
Image Base Videotex Design Inc. 502
IMCA (Information Management and Consulting Association) 526
IMCA Newsletter 526
IMCG (Information Management and Consulting Group) 526
IME (Indice Medico Espanol) 1082
IME (Information Management & Engineering Ltd.) 527
IME Newsletter 527
IMIA (International Medical Informatics Association) 597
IMIC (International Medical Information Center) 598
IMIC Journal 598
IML (Institute for Medical Literature) - South African Medical Research Council 888
IMM (Institution of Mining and Metallurgy) 551
IMM Abstracts 551
IMM Index to Mining and Metallurgy 1894-1949 551
IMMAGE Data Base 551
IMO Module 320
Impact of Demographic Change on Education Systems in the European Community 215
Imperial Chemical Industries Ltd. 503
Imperial College of Science and Technology - University of London 1056
Import/Export Microtables 780
IMPORTS Data Base (I.P. Sharp Associates) 871
IMS A.G. 504
IMS MIDAS Databank 504
IMSPACT Data Base 504
IMTC (International MARC Technical Centre) 582
In Search of a Sunrise 520
Incompatex 693
Indeks IoD 767
Independent Broadcasting Authority 779
Independent Chemical Information Services Ltd. 505
Independent Television Companies Association Ltd. 779
Index Analytique du Journal "Le Monde Diplomatique" 704
Index de la Litterature des Sports et des Loisirs 210
Index de l'Actualite Vue a Travers la Presse Ecrite 704
Index de Periodiques Canadiens 174

Index et Catalogues URBAMET 1091
Index of Articles (Aviation Informaiton Services Ltd.) 68
Index of Current Research on Pigs 229
Index of Fungi 229
Index of Indonesian Learned Periodicals 512
Index of Indonesian Survey and Research 512
Index of Publications Owned by Computing Services (Library) 1033
Index of Software Supported by Computing Services (PROGRAMLIST) 1033
Index to 19th Century Eretz-Israel Newspapers 1051
Index to 6500 Published Reports and Maps, Mineral Resources Group 778
Index to Conference Proceedings Received (British Library) 442
Index to Current Awareness in Particle Technology 676
Index to Geoscience Data in 8500 Exploration Reports 778
Index to Hebrew Periodicals Data Base 1051
Index to Literature on Atomic Collision Data (CIAMDA) 561
Index to Swedish Newspapers 116
Index to Swedish Periodicals 116
Index to The Alberta Gazette 11
Index to the Financial Times 328
Index to Theses Accepted for Higher Degrees by the Universities of Great Britain and Ireland 35
Index Veterinarius 229
Indexing and Abstracting Society of Canada 506
India - Council of Scientific and Industrial Research 507
India - Council of Scientific and Industrial Research 509
India - National Institute of Health and Family Welfare 508
India - National Institute of Oceanography 509
Indian Council of Agricultural Research 510
Indian Council of Social Science Research 511
Indian Education Index 511
Indian National Directory of Marine Research Projects 509
Indian National Directory of Marine Scientists 509
Indian National Directory of Training and Education in Marine Science 509
Indian National Oceanographic Data Centre 509
Indian National Scientific Documentation Centre 507
Indian Science Abstracts 507
Indicators of Industrial Activity 780
Indice Cientifico Valenciano 1082
Indice de Proyectos en Desarrollo en Ecologia de Zonas Aridas 702
Indice de Proyectos en Desarrollo en Ecologia Tropical 702
Indice Espanol de Ciencia y Tecnologia 890
Indice Espanol de Ciencias Sociales 891
Indice Espanol de Humanidades 891
Indice Medico Espanol 1082
Indices de Cours de la Compagnie des Agent de Change 389
Indonesia - National Scientific Documentation Center 512
Indonesian Institute of Sciences 512
Industrial Abstracts for Tanzania 955
Industrial Aerodynamics Abstracts 86
Industrial and Technological Information Bank 1027
Industrial Bank of Japan, Ltd. 498
Industrial Bank of Japan, Ltd. 754
Industrial Case Reports (Eurolex) 314
Industrial Data Bank Department - Gulf Organization for Industrial Consulting 471
Industrial Development Abstracts 1027
Industrial Development Department - Alberta Research Council 15
Industrial Documentation Service - Pont-a-Mousson Research Center 820
Industrial Economy Abstracts 801
Industrial Information - Industrial Development Department - Alberta Research Council 15
Industrial Information Section - United Nations Industrial Development Organization 1027
Industrial-Life Insurance Company 513
Industrial Life-Technical Services Inc. 513
Industrial Life-Technical Services Inc. 619
Industrial News Publishing Company 252
Industrial News Publishing Company 514
Industrial Performance Analysis 499
Industrial Research Division - Overseas Data Service, Company, Ltd. 789
Industrial Technical Information Service - Singapore Institute of Standards and Industrial Research 877
Industrielle-Services Techniques Inc. 513
Industrielle-Services Techniques Inc. 619
Industries Agro-Alimentaires Bibliographie Internationale 39
Industry and Environment Data Base - Industry and Environment Office - United Nations Environment Programme 1024
Industry and Environment Office - United Nations Environment Programme 1024
Industry Profile Series (Information Research Ltd.) 530
Industry Surveys 251
INED (International Network of Educational Information) 1021
iNet 2000 972
INF (Teknillinen Informaatiopalvelulaitos) - Valtion Teknillinen

Tutkimuskeskus   330
Infant Feeding Bibliography   47
INFIC (International Network of Feed Information Centers)   487
Info Globe   430
INFO-LINE - Australian Financial Review   55
Info-Marketing/Dialogsysteme - Gruner & Jahr AG & Co.   468
INFOBANK - Network Services Division - Computer Sciences of Australia Pty. Ltd.   237
INFOCLIMA (World Climate Data Information Referral Service)   1118
Infocom   515
Infocon Information Services, Ltd.   516
INFODATA Data Base   880
INFODIAL   385
INFOFISH   1011
INFOFISH Marketing Digest   1011
INFOFISH Trade News   1011
INFOIL II   769
Infolex Newsletter   517
Infolex Services Ltd.   517
InfoLine   802
InfoLine UPDATE   802
InfoLine Users Guide   802
INFOMAGIC   871
Infomart   518
Infomart   519
Infomart Telidon System Software - Version Two   518
INFOMEDIA   361
Infoquest   520
INFORCIEN   102
INFORM (Institute of Information Scientists)   544
Informacio-Elektronika   493
Informatech   619
INFORMATECH (Standards Council of Canada)   898
Informatheque Inc.   619
Informatheque-PRAUS - Universite de Sherbrooke   1071
Informatics and Scientometrics   492
Informatics Biblio Service - Paris District Informatics Administration   797
Informatics Engineering Ltd.   527
Informatie Lopend Onderzoek Sociale Wetenschappen   847
Informatik   395
Informatika   1121
Information and Advisory Department - Timber Research and Development Association   983
Information and Computer   542
Information and Documentation Center - Federal Research Center for Fisheries - Germany   421
Information and Documentation Center - French Stockbrokers Society   389
Information and Documentation Center - Royal Institute of Technology Library - Sweden   930
Information and Documentation Centre for Occupational Safety - Federal Institute for Occupational Safety - Germany   419
Information and Documentation Department - Institute for Employment Research - Federal Employment Institute - Germany   410
Information and Documentation Department - Swedish Center for Working Life   935
Information and Documentation Section - Delft Hydraulics Laboratory   268
Information and Documentation Section - National Road and Traffic Research Institute - Sweden   925
Information and Documentation Service - Glass Institute   429
Information and Documentation Services - German Plastics Institute   402
Information and Documentation Systems Department - Office of Study and Research - Electricite de France   295
Information and Library Service - Celltech Ltd.   181
Information and Library Services - Leatherhead Food Research Association   655
Information and Management   586
Information Bildungsforschung Schweiz   945
Information Bulletin of Australian Criminology   56
Information Bulletin on Radioactive Waste   434
Information Bulletin on the Survey of Chemicals Being Tested for Carcinogenicity   1113
Information Bulletin on the Survey of Chemicals Being Tested for Carcinogenicity Data Base   1113
Information Center - Asbestos Research Program - University of Sherbrooke   1071
Information Center Applied to Construction   610
Information Center for Building and Physical Planning   373
Information Center for Building and Physical Planning   374
Information Center for Building and Physical Planning   375
Information Center for Building and Physical Planning   376
Information Center for Building and Physical Planning   377
Information Center for Building and Physical Planning   378
Information Center for Building and Physical Planning   379
Information Center for Building and Physical Planning   380
Information Center for Building and Physical Planning Data Bases   373

Information Center for Energy, Physics, Mathematics   521
Information Center for Energy, Physics, Mathematics   901
Information Center for Information Science and Practice - Society for Information and Documentation   880
Information Center for Materials   522
Information Center for Spectroscopic and Physicochemical Analysis   466
Information Center for Tropical Plant Protection   409
Information Center on Medicaments   893
Information Centre - Research and Information Branch - Ontario Ministry of Education   777
Information Centre - Sports Council   896
Information Centre for Building - Ministry for Building and Urban Development - Hungary   494
Information Consultants, Freelancers and Brokers Directory   526
Information Department - BNF Metals Technology Centre   92
Information Department - British Standards Institution   111
Information Department - Finnish Foreign Trade Association   332
Information Department - Paint Research Association   792
Information Dissemination Office - National Institute for Research in Informatics and Automation - France   361
Information Dokumentation   395
Information Eaux   391
Information-Electronics   493
Information Exchange Centre for Federally Supported Research in Canadian Universities   152
Information for Research Libraries   269
Information Handling Services   958
Information India   523
Information Industries Ltd.   266
Information Industries Ltd.   524
Information Industry   1
Information London   525
Information Management and Consulting Association   526
Information Management and Consulting Group   526
Information Management & Engineering Ltd.   527
Information Management Associates Ltd.   527
Information Network for Official Statistics   749
Information on Current Social Science Research   847
Information on Educational Research and Development in Switzerland (SWINFED) Data Base   945
Information Plus Inc. (Toronto)   528
Information Processing Society of Japan   529
Information Provider System 3   764
Information Relayed Instantly from the Source   169
Information Research and Development Unit - National Foundation for Educational Research in England and Wales   724
Information Research Ltd.   530
Information Researchers, Inc.   531
Information Resources   532
Information Resources Annual   533
Information Resources Guide: Britain   432
Information Resources Ltd.   432
Information Resources Research   533
Information Retrieval Service - European Space Agency   317
Information Retrieval System for the Sociology of Leisure and Sport   1085
Information Service - British Universities Film & Video Council Ltd.   112
Information Service - Finnish Standards Association   334
Information Service and Development Department - Nomura Research Institute   760
Information Service on Toxicity and Biodegradability   463
Information Services - BHRA, The Fluid Engineering Centre   86
Information Services - Canadian Plains Research Center   1066
Information Services - Charities Aid Foundation   198
Information Services - Eastern Mediterranean Regional Office - World Health Organization   1112
Information Services - Helsinki School of Economics Library   481
Information Services - Production Engineering Research Association of Great Britain   826
Information Services - Royal Society of Chemistry   851
Information Services - Royal Society of Chemistry   852
Information Services - Royal Society of Chemistry   853
Information Services - Royal Society of Chemistry   854
Information Services - Royal Society of Chemistry   855
Information Services - Royal Society of Chemistry   856
Information Services - Society of Metaphysicians Ltd.   882
Information Services - The Welding Institute   1106
Information Services Division - Alberta Research Council   1033
Information Services Division - Canadian Engineering Publications Ltd.   171
Information Services Division - National Computing Centre Ltd.   721
Information Services for the Physics and Engineering Communities (INSPEC)   549
Information Services for the Physics and Engineering Communities (INSPEC)   550
Information Services Group - Greater London Council   465
Information System for Environmental Chemicals, Chemical Plants, and

Accidents (INFUCHS)   411
Information System for the Economy - National Institute of Statistics and Economic Studies - France   364
Information System on Production Plants for Iron & Steel   398
Information Systems and Data Banks Department - German Society for Chemical Equipment   403
Information Systems and Data Banks Department - German Society for Chemical Equipment   404
Information Systems and Data Banks Department - German Society for Chemical Equipment   405
Information Systems and Data Banks Department - German Society for Chemical Equipment   406
Information Systems Design   534
Information Systems Group - Computing Services - University of Alberta   1033
Information Systems Programme - Social Science Computing Laboratory - University of Western Ontario   1087
Information Technology & People   180
Information Technology Centre - Polytechnic of Central London   818
Information Technology Division - Department of Industry - Great Britain   450
Information Technology in Industrial Information Services   1054
Information Technology, Policy Decision Making in the U.K.   1054
Information Technology: Sources of Australian Information   520
Information Today   654
Information Trade Directory   654
Information Trade Directory Prestel File   69
Information uber Online-Zugriff   428
Information Unit - Brunel Institute for Bioengineering   114
Information Unit - English Tourist Board   297
Information Unlimited   535
Information World   258
Informations Internationales   251
Informations- och Dokumentationscentralen - Kungl. Tekniska Hogskolans Bibliotek   930
Informations-Technologie: Bibliographie der Nachschlagewerke   243
Informations- und Dokumentationsstelle - Bundesforschungsanstalt fur Fischerei - Germany   421
Informations- und Dokumentationsstelle - Institut fur Arbeitsmarkt- und Berufsforschung - Bundesanstalt fur Arbeit - Germany   410
Informations- und Dokumentationssystem Umwelt - Umweltbundesamt - Germany   411
Informations- und Dokumentationszentrum fur Arbeitsschutz - Bundesanstalt fur Arbeitsschutz - Germany   419
Informations- und Dokumentationszentrum fur Arbeitsschutz Data Base   419
Informationsdienst Krankenhauswesen   477
Informationsdienst Ubersetzungen   395
Informationsdienst Veranstaltungskalender   395
Informationsdienstkartei Tierische Produktion   487
Informationssystem Bezugsquellen - Deutsche Gesellschaft fur Chemisches Apparatewesen   406
Informationssystem Chemische Technik   403
Informationssystem Karlsruhe   521
Informationssystem Werkstoffe und Korrosion   405
Informationsvarden i Stockholm AB   260
Informationsvarden i Stockholm AB   990
Informationszentrum fur Schnittwerte - Laboratorium fur Werkzeugmaschinen und Betriebslehre - Technical University of Aachen   964
Informationszentrum Raum und Bau   373
Informationszentrum Raum und Bau   374
Informationszentrum Raum und Bau   375
Informationszentrum Raum und Bau   376
Informationszentrum Raum und Bau   377
Informationszentrum Raum und Bau   378
Informationszentrum Raum und Bau   379
Informationszentrum Raum und Bau   380
Informationszentrum Raum und Bau (IRB) Data Bases   373
InformationsZentrum Sozialwissenschaften - Arbeitsgemeinschaft Sozialwissenschaftlicher Institute   43
Informatique et Sciences Juridiques   355
Informativo SNI   212
Informatorium Medicamentorum   844
Informe Latinoamericano   651
Informes Especiales   651
Informetal   281
Informetrica Limited   536
INFOS (Information Network for Official Statistics)   749
INFOS (Informationszentrum fur Schnittwerte) - Laboratorium fur Werkzeugmaschinen und Betriebslehre - Technical University of Aachen   964
INFOS Newsletter   749
Infotecture Europe   1
Infotecture France   1
Infoterm (International Information Center for Terminology)   587
Infoterm Newsletter   587
INFOTERRA   1025
INFOTERRA Bulletin   1025
INFOTERRA International Directory of Sources   1025
INFSOC Data Base   591
INFUCHS (Information System for Environmental Chemicals, Chemical Plants, and Accidents)   411
Infytec, S.A.   537
Ingenieur-Wissenschaftliche Abteilung - Bayer AG   77
INID (Institutul National de Informare si Documentare) - Consiliul National pentru Stiinta si Tehnologie - Romania   843
INID (Romanian National Institute for Information and Documentation) Data Base   843
INIREB (Instituto Nacional de Investigaciones sobre Recursos Bioticos) - Mexico   702
INIREB Library - National Institute for Research on Biological Resources - Mexico   702
INIS (International Nuclear Information System)   560
INIS Atomindex   560
INIS Reference Series   560
INIS Today   560
INKA (Informationssystem Karlsruhe)   521
Inland Waters Directorate - Environment Canada   139
Inland Waters Directorate - Environment Canada   140
Inland Waters Directorate - Environment Canada   141
Inland Waters Directorate - Environment Canada   142
INNOVACQ   1094
Innovation & Produits Nouveaux   1
Innovation Awareness List   1021
INODC (Indian National Oceanographic Data Centre)   509
INODC Newsletter   509
Inorganic Chemistry Institute - University of Bonn   1042
Inorganic Crystal Structure Data Base   1042
Inorganic Data Base (IDC)   572
INPADOC (International Patent Documentation Center)   64
INPADOC (International Patent Documentation Center)   633
INPADOC Patent Gazette   64
Inpharma   5
INPI (Institut National de la Propriete Industrielle) - France   359
INPI (Institut National de la Propriete Industrielle) - France   360
INPI (Institut National de la Propriete Industrielle) - France   987
INPI-1   359
INPI-2   359
INPI-3   359
INPI-4   359
Inquiries into Empirical Social Research 1945-1982: Catalog of Holdings   1045
INRA (Institut National de la Recherche Agronomique) - France   362
INRIA (Institut National de Recherche en Informatique et en Automatique) - France   361
INRIATHEQUE   361
INS Data Base (I.P. Sharp Associates)   871
INSDOC (Indian National Scientific Documentation Centre)   507
Insearch Ltd.   538
Insearch Ltd./DIALOG   538
INSEE (Institut National de la Statistique et des Etudes Economiques) - France   363
INSEE (Institut National de la Statistique et des Etudes Economiques) - France   364
INSEE (Institut National de la Statistique et des Etudes Economiques) - France   365
INSEE (Institut National de la Statistique et des Etudes Economiques) - France   366
INSERM (Institut National de la Sante et de la Recherche Medicale) - France   358
INSERM Research Information Bank   358
INSIDER Service - Micromedia Ltd.   706
Insight Data Bases   163
Insight Data Bases   164
Insight Data Bases   165
Insight Data Bases   166
INSPEC (Information Services for the Physics and Engineering Communities)   549
INSPEC (Information Services for the Physics and Engineering Communities)   550
INSPEC Classification   549
INSPEC List of Journals and Other Serial Sources   549
INSPEC Matters   549
INSPEC Thesaurus   549
INSPEC User Manual   549
INSRE (Institut National de la Statistique et de la Recherche Economique) - Madagascar   681
INSTAB (Information Service on Toxicity and Biodegradability)   463
Institut Agronomique Mediterraneen   564
Institut d'Amenagement et d'Urbanisme de la Region d'Ile-de-France   1091
Institut de Recherche et Developpement d'Amiante   1071
Institut de Recherches sur les Fruits et Agrumes   547
Institut du Verre   429
Institut Francais de l'Energie   386
Institut Francais des Petroles   387
Institut Francais des Petroles   723

Institut Francais des Petroles Thermodynamique (IFP-TH) 387
Institut fur Angewandte Forschung GmbH 398
Institut fur Angewandte Forschung GmbH 399
Institut fur Arbeitsmarkt- und Berufsforschung - Bundesanstalt fur Arbeit - Germany 410
Institut fur Deutsche Sprache 541
Institut fur Dokumentation und Information uber Sozialmedizin und Offentliches Gesundheitswesen 539
Institut fur Ernahrungswissenschaft 545
Institut fur Krankenhausbau 477
Institut fur Wasserforschung GmbH Dortmund 284
Institut fur Weltforschung in Kiel 639
Institut Gustave-Roussy 357
Institut International du Froid 590
Institut National de la Propriete Industrielle - France 359
Institut National de la Propriete Industrielle - France 360
Institut National de la Recherche Agronomique - France 362
Institut National de la Sante et de la Recherche Medicale - France 358
Institut National de la Statistique et de la Recherche Economique - Madagascar 681
Institut National de la Statistique et des Etudes Economiques - France 363
Institut National de la Statistique et des Etudes Economiques - France 364
Institut National de la Statistique et des Etudes Economiques - France 365
Institut National de la Statistique et des Etudes Economiques - France 366
Institut National de Recherche en Informatique et en Automatique - France 361
Institut National de Statistique - Ministere des Affaires Economiques - Belgium 82
Institut National des Techniques de la Documentation 722
Institut Textile de France 390
Institut TNO voor Wiskunde, Informatieverwerking en Statistiek 741
Institut za Nuklearne Nauke Boris Kidric 96
Institute for Behavioural Research - York University 1120
Institute for Documentation and Information in Social Medicine and Public Health 539
Institute for Employment Research - Federal Employment Institute - Germany 410
Institute for Futures Studies 540
Institute for German Language 541
Institute for High Temperatures - Academy of Sciences of the U.S.S.R. 996
Institute for Information and Documentation in Science and Technology - Spain 890
Institute for Information and Documentation in the Social Sciences and Humanities - Spain 891
Institute for Information Industry 542
Institute for Information Retrieval and Computational Linguistics - Bar-Ilan University 74
Institute for Management and Planning in the Paris Region 1091
Institute for Marine Environmental Research - Natural Environment Research Council 729
Institute for Medical Information - Czechoslovakia 250
Institute for Medical Literature - South African Medical Research Council 888
Institute for Scientific, Technical and Economic Information - Poland 815
Institute for Study of Scientific Research & Documentation - National Research Council - Italy 624
Institute for Theoretical Astronomy - Academy of Sciences of the U.S.S.R. 997
Institute of African Studies 397
Institute of Agricultural Engineering 543
Institute of Asian Studies 397
Institute of Economics - Hungarian Academy of Sciences 491
Institute of Energy Economics (IEE) Energy Data Bank 753
Institute of Food Technologists 583
Institute of Hospital Building 477
Institute of Ibero-American Studies 397
Institute of Information Scientists 544
Institute of Law and Technology 656
Institute of Medical Microbiology, Infectious and Epidemic Medicine - Veterinary Faculty - Ludwig Maximilian's University 1114
Institute of Nutrition 545
Institute of Oceanographic Sciences - Natural Environment Research Council 730
Institute of Physics and Energy 546
Institute of Research on Fruits and Citrus Fruits 547
Institute of Scientific and Technical Information of China - China 801
Institute of Technical Information - China Building Technology Development Centre 203
Institute of Terrestrial Ecology - Great Britain 461
Institute TNO for Mathematics, Information Processing and Statistics 741
Institutet for Byggdokumentation 938
Institution of Chemical Engineers 548

Institution of Electrical Engineers 549
Institution of Electrical Engineers 550
Institution of Mining and Metallurgy 551
Instituto Brasileiro de Informacao em Ciencia e Tecnologia 103
Instituto Centro Americano de Investigacion y Tecnologia Industrial 193
Instituto de Informacion y Documentacion en Ciencia y Tecnologia - Spain 890
Instituto de Informacion y Documentacion en Ciencias Sociales y Humanidades - Spain 891
Instituto Nacional de Investigacao Cientifica - Portugal 821
Instituto Nacional de Investigaciones Nucleares - Mexico 703
Instituto Nacional de Investigaciones sobre Recursos Bioticos - Mexico 702
Instituto Nacional de Seguridad e Higiene en el Trabajo - Ministerio de Sanidad y Seguridad Social - Spain 892
Institutul National de Informare si Documentare - Consiliul National pentru Stiinta si Tehnologie - Romania 843
Instituut voor Mechanisatie, Arbeid en Gebouwen 543
Instrumentation and Techniques for Cardiology 114
Instruments of Testing and Research in Korea 645
Instytut Informacji Naukowej, Technicznej i Ekonomicznej - Poland 815
INTD (Institut National des Techniques de la Documentation) 722
INTDIS (International Drug Information System) Data Base 1115
Integrated Set of Information Systems (ISIS) 1017
Integrated System for the University of Lausanne Libraries 664
Intelegence Literature Searches 304
Intelmatique 552
INTER 257
Inter Company Comparisons 499
Inter-Corporate Ownership Data Base 165
Interactive Systems, Inc. 381
Interatomic Distances 125
Interceptor 527
INTERCIM Cement Data Base 188
InterCompany Comparisons 499
Intercontinental Marketing Corporation 635
INTERDOC (System of Documentary Reference of MINTER) 100
INTERFACT/SVP AB 553
Interfisc 715
Intergovernmental Bureau for Informatics 554
Intergovernmental Oceanographic Commission 1020
INTERLEGI (System of Legislative Reference of MINTER) 100
Interlending and Document Supply: Journal of the British Library Lending Division 442
Interlibrary Loan and Communication System - Central Ontario Regional Library System 195
Interlinked Computerized Storage and Processing System of Food and Agricultural Data 1014
Intermarc Group 555
Intermarc Information 555
Interministerial Documentation Service - National Telecommunications Research Center - France 367
Interministerial Mission for Scientific and Technical Information - France 344
International Abstracts of Biological Sciences 803
International Agency for Research on Cancer 1113
International Association for Statistical Computing 556
International Association for the Evaluation of Educational Achievement 557
International Association of Agricultural Librarians and Documentalists 558
International Association of Cancer Registries 1113
International Atomic Energy Agency 559
International Atomic Energy Agency 560
International Atomic Energy Agency 561
International Atomic Energy Agency 562
International Atomic Energy Agency (IAEA) Energy and Economic Data Bank 559
International Banking Service 690
International Bee Research Association 563
International Bibliography of Refugee Literature 602
International Bibliography of Standardized Vocabularies 587
International Bibliography of the Social Sciences 571
International Biodeterioration 229
International Biodeterioration Bulletin 1038
International Bonds Service 322
International Books in Print 863
International Building Services Abstracts 119
International Bureau - Universal Postal Union 1030
International Bureau of Education 1021
International Bureau of Education Documentation and Information Unit (IBEDOC) Data Base 1021
International Center for Higher Studies in Mediterranean Agronomy 564
International Centre for Scientific and Technical Information 565
International Children's Centre 566
International Civil Aviation Organization 567

International Civil Aviation Organization 568
International Civil Aviation Organization 569
International Civil Aviation Organization (ICAO) Air Transport Statistics Data Base 569
International Civil Aviation Organization (ICAO) Aircraft Accident Data Base 567
International Civil Aviation Organization (ICAO) Airport Characteristics Data Bank 568
International Civil Engineering Abstracts 208
International Co-operation in the Field of Transport Economics Documentation 309
International Coffee Organization 570
International Coffee Organization Library Monthly Entries 570
International Committee for Social Science Information and Documentation 571
International Committee on Alcohol, Drugs and Traffic Safety 936
International Commodities Clearing House Ltd. 672
International Company for Documentation in Chemistry 572
International Computer Archive of Modern English 768
International Computer, Ltd. 75
International Computing Education and Information Center - Central Statistical Office - Hungary 493
International Congress Series 296
International Cooperation in the Field of Transport Economics Documentation 309
International Council for Building Research, Studies and Documentation 373
International Council for Building Research, Studies and Documentation 573
International Council of Scientific Unions 574
International Council of Scientific Unions 575
International Council of Scientific Unions Abstracting Board 575
International Development Abstracts 393
International Development Information Network 781
International Development Research Centre 31
International Development Research Centre 34
International Development Research Centre 576
International Development Research Centre 596
International Development Research Centre 644
International Development Research Centre 794
International Development Research Centre 889
International Development Research Centre 1005
International Development Research Centre 1006
International Dictionary of Micrographics Terms 101
International Directory of Agencies for the Visually Disabled 115
International Directory of Marine Scientists 1008
International Directory of Refugee-Assisting Organizations 602
International Directory of Research Centres and Information Sources, Services and Systems in New and Renewable Energies 1018
International Documentation Center for Industries Using Agricultural Products 39
International Drug Information System (INTDIS) Data Base 1115
International Electronic Publishing Research Centre 577
International Embryological Institute 490
International Energy Agency 782
International Energy Agency 783
International Energy Agency 784
International Federation for Documentation 578
International Federation for Documentation 579
International Federation for Information Processing 580
International Federation for Information Processing 597
International Federation of Data Organizations for the Social Sciences 581
International Federation of Library Associations and Institutions 582
International Federation of Library Associations and Institutions 644
International Ferrocement Information Center 32
International Financial Securities Statistics Data Base (I.P. Sharp Associates) 871
International Food Information Service 583
International Food Information Service 584
International Food Information Service 585
International Forum on Information and Documentation 578
International Frequency List 606
International Frequency Register 606
International Geographical Bibliography 355
International Gravimetric Bureau 342
International Group of Users of Information Systems 586
International Guide to Microform Publishers 101
International Human Biometry and Ergonomics Data Bank 838
International I&D Committees with Memberships from the Federal Republic of Germany and West Berlin 880
International Information Center for Terminology 587
International Information Service Ltd. 588
International Information Services Company 207
International Information Services Company 589
International Information Services Company 860
International Information Services Company 987
International Information System for the Agricultural Sciences and Technology 1012
International Information System on Research in Documentation 579
International Institute of Refrigeration 590
International Institute of Refrigeration Bulletin 590
International Labour Documentation 593
International Labour Documentation Cumulative Catalogue 593
International Labour Office 591
International Labour Office 592
International Labour Office 593
International Labour Office 594
International Labour Office 595
International Labour Office Bureau of Statistics Data Base 592
International Labour Organisation 591
International Labour Organisation 592
International Labour Organisation 593
International Labour Organisation 594
International Labour Organisation 595
International List of Periodical Title Word Abbreviations 603
International Livestock Centre for Africa 596
International MARC Technical Centre 582
International Medical Informatics Association 597
International Medical Information Center 598
International Network for Communication Research and Policies 65
International Network of Educational Information 1021
International Network of Feed Information Centers 487
International Nuclear Information System 560
International Occupational Safety and Health Information Centre 595
International Office for the Universal Availability of Publications 582
International Office for Universal Bibliographic Control 582
International Oil Market Information System 784
International Online Information Meeting 654
International Online Retrieval Service Center - Institute of Scientific and Technical Information of China 801
International Organization for Standardization 599
International Packaging Abstracts 812
International Packet Switching Service 447
International Patent Documentation Center 64
International Patent Documentation Center 633
International Peace Research Association 800
International Petroleum Annual Data Base (I.P. Sharp Associates) 871
International Polymer Science and Technology 858
International Population Information Network (POPIN) 1003
International Railway Union 600
International Reference Center for Community Water Supply and Sanitation 601
International Reference Center for Community Water Supply and Sanitation 794
International Referral System for Sources of Environmental Information - United Nations Environment Programme 1025
International Refugee Integration Resource Centre 602
International Register of Potentially Toxic Chemicals 1026
International Register of Research on Visual Disability 115
International Relations Information System 337
International Reviews on Mathematical Education 521
International Road Research Documentation 786
International Science & Technology Information Service 588
International Serials Catalogue 575
International Serials Data System 603
International Social Science Council 311
International Social Security Association 595
International Society of Development Biologists 490
International Society of Ecological Modelling 604
International Statistical Institute 556
International Subscriptions Ltd. 432
International Survey of Aids for the Visually Disabled 115
International Technical Centre for Rubber and Plastics 858
International Technical Publications Ltd. 605
International Technical Thesaurus 382
International Telecommunication Union 606
International Telecommunications Users Group 607
International Thesaurus of Refugee Terminology 602
International Thomson Organisation 273
International Thomson Organisation 274
International Thomson Organisation 275
International Thomson Organisation 276
International Thomson Organisation 277
International Thomson Organisation 278
International Thomson Organisation 299
International Thomson Organisation 314
International Trade Data Bank (NEEDS-TS) 754
International Translations Centre 608
International Union of Building Centres 117
International Union of Geological Sciences 609
International Welding Thesaurus 1106
Internationale Dokumentationsgesellschaft fur Chemie 572
Internationale IuD-Gremien mit Beteiligung aus der Bundesrepublik Deutschland und Berlin (West) 880
Internationale Vereniging van Telecommunicatiegebruikers 607
Internationaler Eisenbahnverband 600
Internationales Bibliotheks-Handbuch 863

Internationales Patentdokumentations-Zentrum 64
Internationales Verzeichnis der Wirtschaftsverbande 863
Internationales Verzeichnis Wissenschaftlicher Verbande und Gesellschaften 863
InterPat Sweden 928
Interprofessional Technical Union of the National Federations of Buildings and Public Works 610
Interuniversity Documentation and Information Center for the Social Sciences 611
INTERVENTIONS 343
INTERVOC (Vocabulario Controlado do MINTER) 100
INTIB (Industrial and Technological Information Bank) 1027
INTROP (Information Center for Tropical Plant Protection) 409
INTUG (International Telecommunications Users Group) 607
INTUG Newsletter 607
Inventaire Canadien des Recherches Presentement en Vigueur en Nursing 1036
Inventaire des Centres Belges de Recherche Disposant d'une Bibliotheque ou d'un Service de Documentation 84
Inventory of Abstracting and Indexing Services Produced in the U.K. 1055
Inventory of Australian Surveys 61
Inventory of Belgian Scientific Units 84
Inventory of Canadian Agricultural Research 167
Inventory of Computer-aided Environmental Models 411
Inventory of Environmental Authorities 411
Inventory of Scientific Congresses 84
Inventory of the Scientific Clearinghouse and Documentation Services Division Holdings (Philippines) 808
Investdata System 975
Investment Markets 484
Investment Timing Monitor 1109
IOB (Inter-Organization Board for Information Systems) - United Nations 1001
IOC (Intergovernmental Oceanographic Commission) 1020
IPA Data Base (I.P. Sharp Associates) 871
Ipari es Epitoipari Statisztikai Ertesito 493
IPC Chemical Database 612
IPC Industrial Press Ltd. 612
IPSANET 871
IPSJ (Information Processing Society of Japan) 529
IPSS (International Packet Switching Service) 447
Iran - Ministry of Culture and Higher Education 613
IRANDOC (Iranian Documentation Centre) 613
IRANDOC Science Abstract Bulletin 613
IRANDOC Social Science Abstract Bulletin 613
IRANDOC Technical Bulletin 613
Iranian Documentation Centre 613
Iranian National Union List of Serials 613
IRB (Informationszentrum Raum und Bau) 373
IRB (Informationszentrum Raum und Bau) 374
IRB (Informationszentrum Raum und Bau) 375
IRB (Informationszentrum Raum und Bau) 376
IRB (Informationszentrum Raum und Bau) 377
IRB (Informationszentrum Raum und Bau) 378
IRB (Informationszentrum Raum und Bau) 379
IRB (Informationszentrum Raum und Bau) 380
IRB (Informationszentrum Raum und Bau) Data Bases 373
IRC (International Reference Center for Community Water Supply and Sanitation) 601
IRC (International Reference Center for Community Water Supply and Sanitation) 794
IRCS Journal of Medical Science 614
IRCS Medical Science 614
IRDA (Institut de Recherche et Developpement d'Amiante) 1071
Ireland Online Users' Group 776
IRFA (Institut de Recherches sur les Fruits et Agrumes) 547
IRI (Information Researchers, Inc.) 531
IRIRC (International Refugee Integration Resource Center) 602
IRIS (International Relations Information System) 337
IRIS Project Data Base 169
IRL (Information Research Ltd.) 530
IRL Press 181
Iron and Steel Documentation Service 192
Iron and Steel Research Institute, Dobra 281
IRPTC (International Register of Potentially Toxic Chemicals) 1026
IRPTC Bulletin 1026
Irradiation of Medical Products Abstract Bulletin 434
IRRD (International Road Research Documentation) 786
Irrigation and Drainage Abstracts 229
IRS (Information Retrieval Service) - European Space Agency 317
IRS-DIALTECH 615
IRS Info-Institute 36
ISDS (International Serials Data System) 603
ISDS Bulletin 603
ISDS Manual 603
ISDS Register 603
ISEM (International Society of Ecological Modelling) 604
ISIS (Integrated Set of Information Systems) 1017

ISO (International Organization for Standardization) 599
ISO Activities Report 599
ISO Bibliographies 599
ISO Bulletin 599
ISO Catalogue 599
ISO Information Network 599
ISO KWIC Index of International Standards 599
ISO Memento 599
ISO Standards Handbooks 599
ISOC (Instituto de Informacion y Documentacion en Ciencias Sociales y Humanidades) 891
ISONET (ISO Information Network) 599
ISORID (International Information System on Research in Documentation) 579
Ispra Establishment 221
Israel - Ministry of Energy and Infrastructure 616
Israel - Ministry of Energy and Infrastructure 617
Israel - National Center of Scientific and Technological Information 616
Israel - National Center of Scientific and Technological Information 617
Israel Atomic Energy Commission 618
ISRDS (Istituto di Studi sulla Ricerca e Documentazione Scientifica) - Consiglio Nazionale delle Ricerche - Italy 624
IST (Industrielle-Services Techniques Inc.) 513
IST (Industrielle-Services Techniques Inc.) 619
IST-Informatheque Inc. 619
ISTEI Reports 815
ISTIC (Institute of Scientific and Technical Information of China) - China 801
Istituto di Studi sulla Ricerca e Documentazione Scientifica - Consiglio Nazionale delle Ricerche - Italy 624
Istituto Superiore di Sociologia - Universita Degli Studi di Milano 1058
IT Focus 549
ItalCable 620
Italian Association for the Production and Distribution of Online Information 621
Italian Reference Center for Euronet DIANE 624
Italian Society for Telephone Use 622
Italy - National Library Service 811
Italy - National Research Council 623
Italy - National Research Council 624
Italy - National Research Council 625
ITC (International Translations Centre) 608
ITF (Institut Textile de France) 390
ITIS (Industrial Technical Information Service) - Singapore Institute of Standards and Industrial Research 877
ITIS Data Base 194
ITSS-V2 (Infomart Telidon System Software - Version 2) 518
ITU (International Telecommunication Union) 606
IuD-Termine 880
IUGS (International Union of Geological Sciences) 609
IWIS (Institut TNO voor Wiskunde, Informatieverwerking en Statistiek) 741
IZ (InformationsZentrum Sozialwissenschaften) - Arbeitsgemeinschaft Sozialwissenschaftlicher Institute 43
JAERI (Japan Atomic Energy Research Institute) 627
JAICI (Japan Association for International Chemical Information) 630
James R. LymBurner & Sons Ltd. 679
Japan - Environment Agency 626
Japan - Maritime Safety Agency 628
Japan - Ministry of Health and Welfare 634
Japan - National Diet Library 629
Japan - Prime Minister's Office 632
Japan - Science and Technology Agency 632
Japan Association for International Chemical Information 630
Japan Atomic Energy Research Institute 627
Japan Cancer Literature (JCL) Data Base 598
Japan Data Service Co., Ltd. 631
Japan Directory of Professional Associations 635
Japan Economic & Business Data Bank (NRI/E) 760
Japan English Books in Print 635
Japan English Magazine Directory 635
Japan Information Center of Science and Technology 632
Japan Information Center of Science and Technology (JICST) File on Medical Science in Japan 632
Japan Information Center of Science and Technology (JICST) File on Research in Progress in Japan 632
Japan Information Center of Science and Technology (JICST) File on Science and Technology 632
Japan Institute of Invention and Innovation 633
JAPAN/MARC 629
Japan National Diet Library Data Bases 629
Japan National Institute for Environmental Studies Data Bases 626
Japan Oceanographic Data Center 628
Japan Patent Information Center 633
Japan Patent Office 633
Japan Pharmaceutical Abstracts 634
Japan Pharmaceutical Information Center 634

Japan Publications Guide 635
Japan Publications Guide Service 635
Japanese National Bibliography 629
Japanese Non-priority Index 633
Japanese Overall Concordance 633
Japanese Patent Abstracts 633
Japanese Patent Index in English 633
Japanese Patent Indexes 633
Japanese Periodicals Index 629
Japanese Priority Index 633
JAPANFILE 712
JAPANPRINT 712
JAPANSCAN 712
JAPANSEARCH 712
JAPANTRANS 712
JAPATIC (Japan Patent Information Center) 633
JAPIC (Japan Pharmaceutical Information Center) 634
JAPIC Weekly Bulletin 634
JAPICDOC Data Base 634
JCL (Japan Cancer Literature) Data Base 598
JDPA (Japan Directory of Professional Associations) Database 635
JET Laboratory - Atomic Energy Authority - Great Britain 438
Jewish Law Service 74
JICST (Japan Information Center of Science and Technology) 632
JICST File on Medical Science in Japan 632
JICST File on Research in Progress in Japan 632
JICST File on Science and Technology 632
JICST On-line Information Service 632
JICST Thesaurus 632
JNN Data Bank 631
JODC (Japan Oceanographic Data Center) 628
JODC News 628
Johan van Halm & Associates 1095
John Fairfax Ltd. 55
John Fairfax Ltd. 908
Joho (JAPIC Weekly Bulletin) 634
Joho Shori/Information Processing 529
JOINT (Journal of Industrial Titles) Data Base 753
Joint Research Centre - Commission of the European Communities 221
Joint Research Centre - Commission of the European Communities 222
JOIS (JICST On-line Information Service) 632
Joongang Daily News 915
JORDAN 67
Jordan & Sons Ltd. 636
Jordan Line Services Data Base 636
Jordans Company Information 636
Jordans Surveys 636
Journal de Coupons 251
Journal of Documentation 35
Journal of Ferrocement 32
Journal of Geological Science 412
Journal of Industrial Titles (JOINT) Data Base 753
Journal of Information Processing 529
Journal of Information Processing and Management 632
Journal of Information Science 544
Journal of Planning Law (Eurolex) 314
Journal of Synthetic Methods 274
Journals in Translation 442
Journals in Translation 608
JPG Letter 635
JPGS (Japan Publications Guide Service) Database 635
JRC (Joint Research Centre) - Commission of the European Communities 221
JRC (Joint Research Centre) - Commission of the European Communities 222
JSCHEDULE Data Base (I.P. Sharp Associates) 871
JTW (C76 Journey-To-Work) Data Bases 237
Judicial Information System - Ministry of Justice - Germany 426
Jugoslovenski Centar za Tehnicku i Naucnu Dokumentaciju 1121
Juridical Databank 641
Juridische Databank 641
JURINNOV 336
JURINPI Data Base 360
JURIS (Juristisches Informationssystem) 426
JURIS-DATA 294
Jurisprudence Express 834
Juristisches Informationssystem 426
K.G. Saur Verlag 863
K-Konsult 637
Kagaku Shoho 630
KAIST (Korea Advanced Institute of Science and Technology) 644
Kalender (German Foundation for International Development) 397
Karlsruhe Informationssystem 521
Karolinska Institute Library and Information Center 921
Karolinska Institutets Bibliotek och Informationscentral 921
Katalog der Bauforschungsberichte 373
Katalog der Literaturhinweise 373

Katalog Over Svensk Standard 940
KATI Data Base 482
KBIA (Kent-Barlow Information Associates) 638
KBP (Kent-Barlow Publications Ltd.) 638
KC Information Systems Ltd. 642
Keio University Medical Library and Information Center 598
Kent-Barlow Information Associates 638
Kent-Barlow Publications Ltd. 638
KENTV Data Base (I.P. Sharp Associates) 871
Key Abstracts 549
Key British Enterprises 802
Key Note Publications 499
Key to Belgian Science 84
Key to Economic Science 733
Key-Word-Index of Wildlife Research 947
Keywords in Serial Titles (KIST) 442
KG Informatik Produktinform 825
KGST-CMEA Data Base 494
KIB (Karolinska Institutets Bibliotek) - Karolinska Institutets Bibliotek och Informationscentral 921
KIBIC (Karolinska Institutets Bibliotek och Informationscentral) 921
KIBIC-rapport 921
Kidric (Boris) Institute of Nuclear Sciences 96
Kidric (Boris) Laboratory for Information Systems Data Bases 96
KIEI (Korea International Economic Institute) 645
Kiel Institute for World Economics 639
Kieler Schrifttumskunden zu Wirtschaft und Gesellschaft 639
KIET (Korea Institute for Industrial Economics and Technology) 645
KINO MARC 640
Kinokuniya Company Ltd. 640
KIPS (Korea Information Processing System) 645
KKF (Kunstoffe Kautschuk Fasern) Data Base 402
Kluwer Publishing Company 641
Kluwer's Universeel Technisch Woordenboek 243
KMK (Konyvtartudomanyi es Modszertani Kozpont) - Orszagos Szechenyi Konyvtar - Hungary 495
KNMP (Koninklijke Nederlandse Maatschappij ter Bevordering der Pharmacie) 844
KNMP Drug Databank 844
Knowledge Source Index 152
Kokuritsu Kokkai Toshokan 629
Kommunikationszentrum fur Zukunfts- und Friedensforschung in Hannover 800
KOMPASS Data Base (DataArkiv AB) 260
Kompass Data Bases 642
Kompass Directories 642
KOMPASS EUROPE 94
KOMPASS-FRANCE 514
Kompass International Ltd. 642
KOMPASS SWEDEN 94
Koninklijk Instituut voor de Tropen 857
Koninklijk Museum voor Midden-Afrika 846
Koninklijke Nederlandse Akademie van Wetenschappen 847
Koninklijke Nederlandse Akademie van Wetenschappen 848
Koninklijke Nederlandse Maatschappij ter Bevordering der Pharmacie 844
Koninklijke Tijl 982
Koninklijke Vermande B.V. 643
Konyvtari es Dokumentacios Szakirodalom 495
Konyvtari Figyelo 495
Konyvtartudomanyi es Modszertani Kozpont - Orszagos Szechenyi Konyvtar - Hungary 495
Korea - Ministry of Commerce and Industry 645
Korea Advanced Institute of Science and Technology 644
Korea Information Processing System 645
Korea Institute for Industrial Economics and Technology 645
Korea International Economic Institute 645
Korea Scientific and Technological Information Center 645
Korean Medical Abstracts 645
Korean Patent Abstracts 645
Korean Periodicals Index 645
Korean Scientific Abstracts 645
KORSTIC (Korea Scientific and Technological Information Center) 645
Kort Geding 641
Kozgazdasagi Informacios Szolgalat - Kozgazdasagtudomanyi Intezete - Magyar Tudomanyos Akademia 491
Kozgazdasagtudomanyi Intezete - Magyar Tudomanyos Akademia 491
Kozponti Statisztikai Hivatal - Hungary 493
KTHB (Kungl. Tekniska Hogskolans Bibliotek) 930
KTS Information Systems 646
Kugler Publications 647
Kulfoldi Statisztikai Adatforrasok 493
Kungl. Biblioteket - Sweden 931
Kungl. Tekniska Hogskolans Bibliotek 930
Kunststoffe Kautschuk Fasern (KKF) Data Base 402
Kurchatov Atomic Energy Institute 999
KWIC Index to Rock Mechanics Literature 1056
Kyushu University 648
L.M. Warren, Inc. 1105

L.O.R. (Guernsey) Ltd. 505
La Documentation Francaise 384
La Fondation ADISQ/CIRPA 206
La Gazette du Palais 294
LABINFO 355
LABOR Data Base 591
LABOR Data Base 593
Laboratoire d'Anthropologie Appliquee - Universite Rene Descartes 838
Laboratoire de Physique des Gaz et des Plasmas - Universite de Paris-Sud 1063
Laboratoire de Science du Sol - Institut National de la Recherche Agronomique - France 362
Laboratorija za Informacijske Sisteme - Institut za Nuklearne Nauke Boris Kidric 96
Laboratorium fur Werkzeugmaschinen und Betriebslehre - Technical University of Aachen 964
Laboratory Equipment Index 958
Laboratory for Information Systems - Boris Kidric Institute of Nuclear Sciences 96
Laboratory Hazards Bulletin 855
Laboratory of Anthropology and Human Ecology - Rene Descartes University 838
Laboratory of Applied Anthropology - Rene Descartes University 838
Laboratory of Machine Tools and Production Engineering - Technical University of Aachen 964
LABORDOC 593
Labour Arbitration Cases 162
Labour Force Statistics 780
Labour Force Statistics Yearbook 780
Labour Information Database (LID) 591
LAN (Latin American Newsletters Ltd.) 651
Land Compensation Reports 162
Land of Israel Data Bank 1051
Landbouwdocumentatie/Agricultural Documentation 731
Landesanstalt fur Immissionsschutz des Landes Nordrhein-Westfalen 765
Lands Directorate - Environment Canada 143
LANDUP (Alberta Land Use Planning Data Bank) 10
Langton Electronic Publishing Systems Ltd. 649
Language Catalog 1033
Language Services Department - Siemens AG 876
L'Annee Boursiere 389
Larratt (Richard) and Associates Ltd. 650
LASER (London and South Eastern Library Region) 670
LASER Directory of Libraries 670
LASER Handbook 670
LASER ISBN & BNB Book Number and Location Finding List 670
LASER Union Catalogue 670
Latin America Commodities Report 651
Latin America Documentation Center - Institute of Ibero-American Studies 397
Latin America Weekly Report 651
Latin American Center for Economic and Social Documentation 1006
Latin American Demographic Center 1007
Latin American Newsletters Ltd. 651
Latin American Population Abstracts 1007
Latin American Population Documentation System 1007
Laval University Library 652
Law Databases 775
Law Library - University of Dundee 1047
Law School Library - Dalhousie University 254
LAWTERM 656
LDA (Lead Development Association) 1122
Lead Abstracts 1122
Lead Development Association 1122
Lead Monitor 228
Lead Quarterly 228
Lead, Zinc, Silver Mine Cost Model Databank 228
League of Arab States 653
League of Arab States Documentation and Information Center 653
League of Arab States Information System 653
Learned Information Ltd. 654
Learned Information Ltd. 970
Learned Societies, Journals and Collaboration with Publishers 1054
Leatherhead Food Research Association 655
L'Economie Francaise 773
LEDA (On-Line Earthnet Data Availability) Data Bank 317
Legal Data Processing Group - Court of Justice of the European Communities 214
Legal Technology Group 656
Legal Technology Ltd. 656
Leigh-Bell (Peter) & Associates Ltd. 657
Leistungs- und Konstruktions Datenbank (LKD) 716
Leisure, Recreation and Tourism Abstracts 229
Leisure Studies Data Bank 1084
Leisure Studies Data Bank Catalogue of Holdings 1084
Leitung und Planung von Wissenschaft und Technik 395
Lending Division - British Library 442

Lentil Abstracts 229
Les Rapports de la Cour Federale du Canada 828
Les Rapports de la Cour Supreme du Canada 828
Les Statuts Revises du Canada 828
Lettre de Transinove 987
Lettre du CEPII 185
Levantamentos Bibliograficos 99
LEX 977
LHB (Laboratory Hazards Bulletin) 855
LIBCAT (Harwell Central Information Service) 434
LIBCEPT 527
LIBRARIAN - Eurotec Consultants Ltd. 318
Library (Index of Publications Owned by Computing Services) 1033
Library - Australian National Gallery 58
Library - International Development Research Centre 576
Library and Abstracting Service - Zinc Development Association/Lead Development Association/Cadmium Association 1122
Library and Documentation Branch - Netherlands Foreign Trade Agency 733
Library and Documentation Literature 495
Library and Documentation Service - Central Statistical Office - Hungary 493
Library and Documentation System - Research Institute for International Politics and Security 337
Library and Documentation Systems Division - Food and Agriculture Organization 1013
Library & Information Centre - House of Lords - Great Britain 460
Library and Information Centre - Transport Canada 161
Library & Information Consultants Ltd. 658
Library and Information Research Group 659
Library and Information Research News 659
Library and Information Research Reports 444
Library and Information Science Abstracts 663
Library and Information Services - Institution of Mining and Metallurgy 551
Library and Information Services - Water Research Centre - Great Britain 464
Library and Information Services Unit - Australian Council for Educational Research 54
Library and Technical Information Department - Soreq Nuclear Research Center - Israel Atomic Energy Commission 618
Library Association of Australia 526
Library Association Publishing Ltd. 660
Library Association Publishing Ltd. 661
Library Association Publishing Ltd. 662
Library Association Publishing Ltd. 663
Library Automation System - National Diet Library - Japan 629
Library Bulletin (BSRIA) 119
LIBRARY Data Base (University of New Brunswick) 1059
Library Documentation Centre - National Library of Canada 149
Library Headquarters - Quebec Ministry of Education 831
Library Information On-line (LION) Data Base 562
Library Information System (LIBRIS) Data Base 931
Library Information System - Royal Library - Sweden 931
Library Instruction Materials Bank - Loughborough University of Technology Library 677
Library Instruction Materials Bank Index 677
Library Micromation News 818
Library Network of SIBIL Users 664
Library Network System - Data Processing Division - Siemens AG 875
Library of Parliament - Canada 157
Library Review 495
Library Service Ltd. 116
Library Services Branch - Environment Canada 144
Library Systems Seminar 555
LIBRIS (Library Information System) - Royal Library - Sweden 931
LIBRIS (Plasma Physics Library and Information Service) 438
LIBRIS Meddelanden 931
LID (Labour Information Database) 591
LID (Literaturdienst Medizin) - Osterreichisches Bundesinstitut fur Gesundheitswesen 66
LID Information Brochure 66
LIDAS Data Base 1104
Life Style Indicator 789
Lifestyles - Compusearch Market and Social Research Ltd. 236
LIFFE (The London International Financial Futures Exchange Ltd.) 672
LIMB (Library Instruction Materials Bank) - Loughborough University of Technology Library 677
LIMB Index 677
Limburg Industrial Development Fund 305
LINA (Literaturnachweise) 376
LINC (Library & Information Consultants Ltd.) 658
Linkedit 889
Linkoping University Library 665
Linkopings Universitetsbibliotek 665
L'Interrogation de la Banque des Donnees du Sous-sol 341
LION (Library Information On-line) Data Base 562
Lipman Management Resources, Ltd. 666
Liquified Petroleum Gas Report Data Base (I.P. Sharp Associates) 871

LIRG (Library and Information Research Group) 659
LIS (Library and Information Services) - Institution of Mining and Metallurgy 551
LISA (Library and Information Science Abstracts) 663
LISDOK (Literaturinformationssystem) - Landesanstalt fur Immissionsschutz des Landes Nordrhein-Westfalen 765
List Bio-med: Biomedical Serials in Scandinavian Libraries 921
List des Publications du Commissariat a l'Energie Atomique 339
List of Adverse Reactions to Drugs Reported in Japanese Clinical Journals 634
List of Archive Holdings (Central Archives for Empirical Social Research) 1045
List of Completed Research Projects on Agriculture and Animal Sciences 510
List of Information Science Journals 880
List of Ongoing Research Projects in Agriculture and Animal Sciences 510
List of Persons and Organizations Related to Asbestos Research and Technology 1071
List of Practicing Librarians and Doucmentalists in Tanzania 955
List of Services Accessible through Transpac 989
List of Ship Stations 606
List of Shipowners, Maritime Guide and Offshore Register 667
List of Telegraph Offices 606
List of Telegraph Offices Open for International Service 606
List of Thesauri 880
List of Theses for the Doctor's and Master's Degree in Korea 645
Liste de Congres Analyses (Electricite de France) 295
Liste de Revues Analysees (Electricite de France) 295
Liste des Normes Francaises Traduites 382
Liste Mondiale des Periodiques Specialises dans les Science Sociales 571
Listed Companies' Databank (NEEDS-TS) 754
Listing Ternisien 978
LITDOK (Literaturdokumentation) Data Base 419
Literatur-Schnelldienst Kunststoffe Kautschuk Fasern 402
Literaturdatenbank Elektrotechnik 960
Literaturdatenbank Maschinenbau 961
Literaturdienst Elektrotechnik 960
Literaturdienst Medizin - Osterreichisches Bundesinstitut fur Gesundheitswesen 66
Literaturdokumentation (LITDOK) Data Base 419
Literaturdokumentation zur Arbeitsmarkt- und Berufsforschung 410
Literature Compilations Data Base 376
Literature Documentation of the International Law of the Sea 413
Literature Information System - North Rhine-Westphalia Institute for Air Pollution Control 765
Literature of Outgassing Materials 316
Literature Service in Medicine - Austrian National Institute for Public Health 66
Literaturinformationssystem - Landesanstalt fur Immissionsschutz des Landes Nordrhein-Westfalen 765
Literaturnachweise (LINA) 376
Livestock Documentation Data Base 596
Living Philosophers Data Base 1048
LJUS 80
LKD (Leistungs- und Konstruktions Datenbank) 716
Lloyd's Casualty Files 667
Lloyd's List 667
Lloyd's New Construction File 667
Lloyd's of London Press Ltd. 667
Lloyd's Register Book File 667
Lloyd's Register of Shipping 667
Lloyd's Register of Ships 667
Lloyd's Shipowner and Parent Company File 667
Lloyd's Shipping Index 667
Lloyd's Shipping Information Services 667
Lloyd's Shipping Information Services Review 667
Lloyd's Shipping Movements - Voyage History File 667
Lloyd's Ships Latest Position File 667
Lloyd's Tanker Casualty Bulletin 667
LMR Information Systems 666
LOB Corpus 768
Local Area Data Bank (INSEE) 365
Local Catalogue Service - Bibliographic Services Division - British Library 440
LOCAS (Local Catalogue Service) - Bibliographic Services Division - British Library 440
LOCATE 237
Location Register of Twentieth Century English Literary Manuscripts and Letters 1065
Logica UK Ltd. 668
LOGIN 734
LOGOS 384
Lois Constitutionnelles du Canada 828
Lombard Interuniversity Consortium for Data Processing 669
London and South Eastern Library Region 670
London Community Services Data Base 525
London Community Services Directory 525

London Enterprise Agency 671
London Graduate School of Business Studies 481
London International Financial Futures Exchange Ltd. 672
London-Lund Corpus 768
London Over the Counter Market 673
London Researchers 674
LOR Newsletter 505
LOTC (London Over the Counter Market) 673
Loughborough University of Technology 675
Loughborough University of Technology 676
Loughborough University of Technology Library 677
Loughborough University of Technology Library 678
Lower Saxonia Serials Data Base 400
LPGAS Data Base (I.P. Sharp Associates) 871
LS-reports 618
LSIS (Lloyd's Shipping Information Services) 667
LTG (Legal Technology Group) 656
LTG Research Ltd. 656
Lubin (David) Memorial Library - Library and Documentation Systems Division - Food and Agriculture Organization 1013
Lucas Heights Research Laboratories Library - Australian Atomic Energy Commission 51
Ludwig Maximilian's University 1114
Lundberg Survey Retail Price Data Base (I.P. Sharp Associates) 871
Lundberg Survey Share of Market Data Base (I.P. Sharp Associates) 871
LymBurner (James R.) & Sons Ltd. 679
M & T (Agricultural Marketing and Trade) Database 126
M-G Videotex Services 714
Machine Readable Archives Division - Public Archives of Canada 158
MacLean-Hunter Ltd. 680
Macroeconomic Data Bank (INSEE) 366
MACTIS (Marine and Coastal Technology Information Service) 1008
Madagascar - Ministry of Finance and Economy 681
MADCAP 1088
Maghreb Data Base 186
MAGIC 871
MAGPIE 638
Magyar Konyvtari Szakirodalom Bibliografiaja 495
Magyar Tudomanyos Akademia 491
Magyar Tudomanyos Akademia Konyvtara 492
Mahasagar 509
Mahatma Gandhi Bibliography 511
MAILBOX (DIMDI) 428
MAILBOX - James R. LymBurner & Sons Ltd. 679
Mailbox - Prestel 448
Main Economic Indicators (OECD) 780
Main Library and Scientific Information Center - Technical University of Wroclaw 965
MAINS (Material Information System) for Iron & Steel 399
Maize Quality Protein Abstracts 229
Major Loss Record (Aviation Information Services Ltd.) 68
Major Projects File 536
Malaysian Serials: Non-government 1073
MALIMET (Master List of Medical Indexing Terms) 296
MANAGE 237
Management & Marketing Abstracts 812
Management College, Henley 484
Management Consultants International, Inc. 682
Management Information System of Science and Technology Resources (Republic of China) 726
Management Services Department - Agricultural Division - Imperial Chemical Industries Ltd. 503
Management System for Astronomical Data in Machine-Readable Form 995
Manitoba Decisions, Civil and Criminal Cases 1108
Manitoba Reports (National Reporter System) 828
Manitoba Statute Citator (SMC) 173
Manitoba Telephone System 519
Manpower Services Commission - Great Britain 462
Manual for the Development of National Documentation Units and Bibliographic Data Bases for Science and Technology Policy 1016
Manual on WESTPAC Data Management 628
Manufacturing and Materials Handling Index 958
Manufacturing and Retailing in the 80's 484
Manufacturing Technology Reviews 885
MANZ Datenbanken 683
MANZ Info Datenvermittlung GmbH 683
MANZsche Verlags- und Universitatsbuchhandlung 683
MARC Exchange Tape Service - Bibliographic Services Division - British Library 439
MARC Israel 1051
MARC Quebecois 833
MARC Records Distribution Service - National Library of Canada 150
Marcel van Dijk, SA; Bureau 122
MARCIS (MARC Israel) 1051
Marine Affairs Bibliography 254
Marine and Coastal Technology Information Service 1008
Marine Biological Association of the United Kingdom 684

MASTER INDEX

Marine Environmental Data Information Referral Catalogue 1020
Marine Environmental Data Information Referral System 1020
Marine Information and Advisory Service - Institute of Oceanographic Sciences - Natural Environment Research Council 730
Marine Information and Documentation System - Federal Institute for Geosciences and Natural Resources - Germany 413
Marine Pollution Information Centre 684
Marine Pollution Research Titles 684
Marine Research and Technology Data Base 413
Marine Science Contents Tables 1008
Maritime Information Centre/CMO 685
Maritime Law Book National Reporter System 828
Maritime Safety Agency - Japan 628
MARK II 296
Market and Statistics News 1083
Market Commentary 126
Market Data Reports on European Industries 499
Market Feasibility Studies - Compusearch Market and Social Research Ltd. 236
Market Information Bank 824
Market Location 686
Market Penetration Analysis - Compusearch Market and Social Research Ltd. 236
Market Research Abstracts 687
Market Research Society 687
Marketfax 326
Marketing and Economics Branch - Agriculture Canada 126
Marketing and Economics Branch - Agriculture Canada 127
Marketing Intelligence Corporation 688
Marketing Research Studies (Information Research Ltd.) 530
Marketscan 430
Marknadsbank 824
MARNA 685
MARNA Manual and Thesaurus 685
Marna-News 685
MARPIC (Marine Pollution Information Centre) 684
Martindale Newsletter 806
Martindale Online 806
Martindale Online User Guide 806
Martindale Thesaurus 806
Martins Printing Group 1089
MARUNET (Maruzen Online Network) 689
Maruzen Company, Ltd. 689
Maruzen Online Network 689
Maruzen Scientific Information Service (MASIS) Center 689
MASIS (Maruzen Scientific Information Service) Center 689
MASIS NEWS 689
Mass Spectra Data Base 856
Mass Spectral Data Sheets 856
Mass Spectrometry 856
Mass Spectrometry Bulletin 856
Mass Spectrometry Data Centre 856
MASSAGER 536
Master List of Medical Indexing Terms 296
Material Data Base (MDB) 399
Material Information System for Iron & Steel 399
Materials and Corrosion 405
Materials and Corrosion Information System 405
Materials Data Retrieval System - European Space Research and Technology Center 316
Materials Information Module 320
MATH (Mathematics Abstracts) 521
MATHDI 521
Mathematics Abstracts 521
Max Planck Society for the Advancement of Science 431
MAXIMS Data Base 504
MBANK Data Base (I.P. Sharp Associates) 871
McCarthy Information Ltd. 690
McGill University 691
McGill University 692
MCI (Management Consultants International, Inc.) 682
MDB (Material Data Base) 399
Measurement of Mechanical Quantities 415
Measurement of Mechanical Quantities Documentation 415
Mechanical Engineering 565
Mechanical Engineering (MechEn) Data Base 930
Mechanical Engineering Documentation 961
MechEn (Mechanical Engineering) Data Base 930
MEDI (Marine Environmental Data Information Referral System) 1020
MEDI Index 1020
MEDI Operations Manual 1020
Media Databank (NEEDS-TS) 754
Media P Data Bank 189
mediadoc 65
MEDIAFILE 823
MEDIAL 879
MEDIC Data Base 329
Medical Academy - Bulgaria 120
Medical and Dental Library - University of Leeds 1053

Medical Databases 775
Medical Information Center - Karolinska Institute Library and Information Center 921
Medical-Pharmaceutical Publishing Company 693
Medical Research Council - Great Britain 114
Medical Technology Documentation 962
Medical Textiles 873
MEDICINDATA 1049
Mediendokumentation zur Gesundheitserziehung 539
MEDINFO Congress 597
MEDINFO Congress Proceedings 597
MEDISTAT (Banque de Donnees Socio-economiques des Pays Mediterraneens) 564
MEDITEC (Dokumentation Medizinische Technik) 962
MEDTRAIN 440
MEDTRAIN Workbook 440
Meeting Agenda Data Base 339
MEF (Mideast File) 970
Memorial University of Newfoundland 694
MER Data Base (I.P. Sharp Associates) 871
MERCATIS 879
MERCATIS 881
Merilees Associates, Inc. 695
MERL-ECO 696
MERLIN GERIN Company 696
MERLIN GERIN Company 697
MERLIN-TECH 697
MeSH Workbook 440
Messtechnik, Regelungstechnik, Automatik 1098
METADEX (Metals Abstracts Index) 698
METAFORM 649
Metal Construction 1106
Metallurgical and Thermochemical Data Service 451
Metals Abstracts 698
Metals Abstracts Index (METADEX) 698
Metals Crystallographic (CRYSTMET) Data File 156
Metals Data Centre 156
Metals Datafile 698
Metals Information (London) 698
Metals Society 698
Methodological Materials and Documentation on Software Packages 565
Methods in Organic Synthesis 851
Metroline Computerized Bibliographic Search Service 699
Metropolitan Toronto Library Board 699
Mexican School of Public Health 700
Mexico - National Center for Health Information and Documentation 700
Mexico - National Council of Science and Technology 701
Mexico - National Institute for Research on Biological Resources 702
Mexico - National Institute of Nuclear Research 703
Mexico and Central America Report 651
Mezdunarodjyj Centr Nauchoj i Tehniceskoj Informacii 565
MIAS (Marine Information and Advisory Service) - Institute of Oceanographic Sciences - Natural Environment Research Council 730
MIAS Data Bank 730
MIAS News Bulletin 730
MIC (Medicinska Informationscentralen) - Karolinska Institutets Bibliotek och Informationscentral 921
MIC Nytt 921
Michael A. Dagg Associates 253
Micro-BIRD 836
Microelectronics Education Programme 485
MicroEXSTAT 323
Microfiche of Reports and Accounts 328
Microfiches Jurisprudence Express 834
Microfiches Novita 87
Microfilm in Information Systems 101
Microfor Inc. 704
Micrographics News 101
Microinfo, Ltd. 705
Microlog Index 706
Micromedia Ltd. 706
Micromedia Ltd. 707
Micromedia Ltd. 708
Micromedia Ltd. 910
Micronet 800 976
MicroNotes 175
MicroPOLYDOC 767
MicroQUERY 485
MIDAS 504
MIDAS (Multimode International Data Acquisition Service) 790
MIDAS Databank 504
MIDAS Operator's Manual 790
Middle East Documentation Center - German Orient Institute 397
Middle East Markets for Medical and Analytical Laboratory Equipment 515
Mideast File 970

MIDIST (Mission Interministerielle de l'Information Scientifique et Technique) - France 344
MIDIST Bulletin d'Information 344
Midland Marts Group 787
MIDORI Book Store Company 709
MIDS Newsletter 888
Mikro-Cerid 710
Mikros Enterprises 710
MILOR 589
Mine, Smelter, Refinery Databank 228
Mineral Briefs 727
Mineral Deposit Inventory 778
Mineral Development Division Library - Newfoundland Department of Mines & Energy 750
Mineral Dossiers 727
Mineral Information Section - Minerals Strategy and Economics Research Group - British Geological Survey - Natural Environment Research Council 727
Mineral Processing Technology (MINPROC) Data Base 131
Mineral Resources Group - Ontario Ministry of Natural Resources 778
Mineralogical Abstracts 711
Mineralogical Society of America 711
Mineralogical Society of Great Britain 711
Minerals Strategy and Economics Research Group - British Geological Survey - Natural Environment Research Council 727
MINERVA 790
Mini-Biblex 834
MINICS (Minimal-Input Cataloguing System) 678
Minimal-Input Cataloguing System 678
Mining, Minerals and Metals Monitor 394
Mining Technology Abstracts 131
MINIS 576
MINISIS 953
MINISIS-RM 953
Minister of Finance - Austria 64
Ministere Aupres de la Presidence de la Republique Charge des Finances et de l'Economie - Madagascar 681
Ministere de la Sante Publique - Belgium 83
Ministere de l'Education - France 346
Ministere de l'Education du Quebec 831
Ministere de l'Environnement du Quebec 832
Ministere de l'Industrie et de la Recherche - France 344
Ministere de l'Industrie et de la Recherche - France 981
Ministere des Affaires Economiques - Belgium 80
Ministere des Affaires Economiques - Belgium 81
Ministere des Affaires Economiques - Belgium 82
Ministerie van Buitenlandse Zaken 732
Ministerio da Agricultura - Brazil 99
Ministerio de Educacion Nacional - Colombia 212
Ministerio de Sanidad y Seguridad Social - Spain 892
Ministerio do Interior - Brazil 100
Ministry for Building and Urban Development - Hungary 494
Ministry for Food, Agriculture and Forestry - Germany 408
Ministry for Food, Agriculture and Forestry - Germany 421
Ministry for Research and Technology - Germany 43
Ministry for Research and Technology - Germany 399
Ministry for Research and Technology - Germany 401
Ministry for Research and Technology - Germany 424
Ministry for Research and Technology - Germany 880
Ministry for Research and Technology - Germany 1045
Ministry of Agriculture - Brazil 99
Ministry of Agriculture - France 39
Ministry of Agriculture and Fisheries - Netherlands 731
Ministry of Building - Germany 374
Ministry of Commerce and Industry - Korea 645
Ministry of Cultural Affairs - Denmark 269
Ministry of Culture and Higher Education - Iran 613
Ministry of Defense - France 345
Ministry of Economic Affairs - Belgium 80
Ministry of Economic Affairs - Belgium 81
Ministry of Economic Affairs - Belgium 82
Ministry of Economics - Germany 425
Ministry of Education - Finland 331
Ministry of Education - France 346
Ministry of Education - France 722
Ministry of Education - France 981
Ministry of Education and Sciences - Netherlands 608
Ministry of Education and Sciences - Netherlands 847
Ministry of Energy and Infrastructure - Israel 616
Ministry of Energy and Infrastructure - Israel 617
Ministry of Finance and Economy - Madagascar 681
Ministry of Finances and Customs - Norway 766
Ministry of Foreign Affairs - Netherlands 732
Ministry of Health - Belgium 83
Ministry of Health and Safety - Spain 892
Ministry of Health and Welfare - Japan 634
Ministry of Industry and Research - France 344
Ministry of Industry and Research - France 981
Ministry of Justice - Germany 426
Ministry of Posts and Telecommunications - France 989
Ministry of Posts and Telecommunications - Germany 427
Ministry of Science & Technology - Pakistan 793
Ministry of the Interior - Brazil 100
Ministry of Trade and Industry - Finland 330
Ministry of Urban and Rural Construction and Environmental Protection - China 203
Ministry of Youth, Family and Health - Germany 428
Minor Planets, Comets, and Satellites Department - Institute for Theoretical Astronomy - Academy of Sciences of the U.S.S.R. 997
MINPROC (Mineral Processing Technology) Data Base 131
MinSearch 727
MINSYS 394
MINTEC: Mining Technology Abstracts 131
MINTER (Ministerio do Interior) - Brazil 100
Minutes of the Council of the Corporation of the City of Toronto 985
MIRABILIS 1055
MIRAC (Microfiche of Reports and Accounts) 328
Mireille 71
MIS (Mineral Information Section) - Minerals Strategy and Economics Research Group - British Geological Survey - Natural Environment Research Council 727
MIS Bulletin 258
MISCA Microthesaurus 794
Mission Interministerielle de l'Information Scientifique et Technique - France 344
Mistel 69
MISTEL 767
MISTRAL 488
Mitaka 712
Mitteilungsblatt der AGB 374
MKV Interactive Videotex Terminal 764
MKV Teletext Decoder 764
MMA (Management & Marketing Abstracts) 812
MMI Data Base 1059
Modulad Data Base 361
Modulef Data Base 361
Molecular Structures and Dimensions 125
Money Market Rate Data Base (I.P. Sharp Associates) 871
Monitan Information Consultants Ltd. 713
Monitor 654
Monitoring Information Data Bank 606
Monthly Abstract of Statistics 749
Monthly Economic Review 536
Monthly Energy Review Data Base (I.P. Sharp Associates) 871
Monthly List of Foreign Scientific and Technical Publications 629
Monthly National Corporate Bankruptcy Report 969
Monthly Report of Heating Oil and Middle Distillates Data Base (I.P. Sharp Associates) 871
Monthly Statistics on the Paris Stock Exchange 389
Morgan-Grampian Plc. 714
Morgan Grenfell & Co. Ltd. 715
MORT (Mortgage Amortization) 828
Mortgage Amortization (MORT) 828
MOSAIC 536
MOST (Instruments of Testing and Research in Korea) 645
Motor Vehicle Documentation 716
Motor Vehicle Insurance Case Book 829
MRA (Machine Readable Archives Division) - Public Archives of Canada 158
MRA (Messtechnik, Regelungstechnik, Automatik) Data Base 1098
MRATE Data Base (I.P. Sharp Associates) 871
MRB International Ltd. 109
MRC Annual Report 888
MRDS (MARC Records Distribution Service) - National Library of Canada 150
MSB (Mass Spectrometry Bulletin) Data Base 856
MSDC (Mass Spectrometry Data Centre) 856
MTAK (Magyar Tudomanyos Akademia Konyvtara) 492
MTDS (Metallurgical and Thermochemical Data Service) 451
MTS (Manitoba Telephone System) 519
MULTI-3 895
Multilanguage Books on Deposit in the Public Libraries of Metropolitan Toronto 699
Multimode International Data Acquisition Service 790
Multinational Association of Producers and Retailers of Electricity-Documentation 717
Musee Royal de l'Afrique Centrale 846
Museum National d'Histoire Naturelle - France 349
Muszaki Gazdasagi Tajekoztato 496
Myer Emporium Ltd. 520
Nachrichten fur Aussenhandel 425
NADIR 361
Naerinfo-Indeks 767
NALJS (Nordic Atomic Libraries Joint Secretariat) 761
NAPLES 879
NAQUADAT (National Water Quality Data Bank) 141
NAQUADAT Dictionary of Parameter Codes 141
NAQUADAT Guide to Interactive Retrieval 141

NARD (Netherlands Agricultural Report Depository)   731
NASDATA Data Base   793
Nash Information Services Inc.   718
NASTOCK Data Base (I.P. Sharp Associates)   871
National Accounts of OECD Countries   780
National Advisory Council for Danish Research Libraries   269
National Agro-Industrial Union - Bulgaria   121
National and International Meetings on Science and Technology   991
National Association of the Pharmaceutical Industry   805
National Atomic Energy Commission - Argentina   27
National Autonomous University of Mexico   719
National Board of Health and Welfare - Sweden   922
National Board of Occupational Safety and Health - Sweden   923
National Bureau for Ocean Data - National Center for Ocean Utilization - France   347
National Bureau for Ocean Data - National Center for Ocean Utilization - France   348
National Bureau for Ocean Data - National Center for Ocean Utilization - France   349
National Bureau for Ocean Data - National Center for Ocean Utilization - France   350
National Bureau for Ocean Data - National Center for Ocean Utilization - France   351
National Bureau for Ocean Data - National Center for Ocean Utilization - France   352
National Bureau for Ocean Data - National Center for Ocean Utilization - France   353
National Bureau for Ocean Data - National Center for Ocean Utilization - France   354
National Catalogue of Scientific and Technical Periodicals of Bangladesh   70
National Center for Agricultural Documentary Information - Ministry of Agriculture - Brazil   99
National Center for Chemical Information   720
National Center for Health Information and Documentation - Mexico   700
National Center for Micrographic Development - Brazil   101
National Center for Ocean Utilization - France   347
National Center for Ocean Utilization - France   348
National Center for Ocean Utilization - France   349
National Center for Ocean Utilization - France   350
National Center for Ocean Utilization - France   351
National Center for Ocean Utilization - France   352
National Center for Ocean Utilization - France   353
National Center for Ocean Utilization - France   354
National Center for Pedagogical Documentation - France   346
National Center for Scientific and Technical Documentation - Royal Library of Belgium   84
National Center for Scientific Research - France   186
National Center for Scientific Research - France   355
National Center for Scientific Research - France   356
National Center for Scientific Research - France   357
National Center for Scientific Research - France   377
National Center for Scientific Research - France   412
National Center for Scientific Research - France   720
National Center for the Organization of Biological Oceanography - National Center for Ocean Utilization - France   349
National Center of Scientific and Technological Information - Israel   616
National Center of Scientific and Technological Information - Israel   617
National Central Bureau of Statistics - Sweden   932
National Central Library - Tanzania   955
National Chemical Emergency Centre - Atomic Energy Research Establishment, Harwell   435
National Coal Board   782
National Coal Board   783
National Commission for Nuclear Energy - Brazil   102
National Commission for Scientific and Technological Research - Chile   202
National Computing Centre Ltd.   721
National Conservatory of Arts and Crafts   722
National Council for Agricultural Research TNO   742
National Council for Science and Technology - Romania   843
National Council for Scientific and Technical Research - Argentina   28
National Council of Science and Technology - Mexico   701
National Council of Scientific and Technological Development - Brazil   103
National Diet Library - Japan   629
National Diet Library Catalog of Foreign Periodicals   629
National Diet Library Catalog of Japanese Periodicals   629
National Elf Aquitaine Company   723
National Emergency Equipment Locator System Data Base (I.P. Sharp Associates)   871
National Engineering Laboratory - Great Britain   548
National Engineering Laboratory's Thermophysical Properties Package   548
National Film Board of Canada   146
National Film Lending Collection Catalogue   48

National Forecast Service - Informetrica Limited   536
National Foundation for Educational Research in England and Wales   724
National Foundation for the Coordination of Maritime Research   685
National Geochemical Data Bank   728
National Geological Survey - France   340
National Geological Survey - France   341
National Geological Survey - France   342
National GEOSCAN Centre   135
National Hydrology Research Institute - Inland Waters Directorate - Environment Canada   139
National Income Forecasting Model of the Australian Economy Data Base (I.P. Sharp Associates)   871
National Index of Translations   507
National Information and Documentation Center - National Institute of Occupational Safety and Health - Ministry of Health and Safety - Spain   892
National Information System - Colombian Fund for Scientific Research   212
National Institute for Documentation Techniques   722
National Institute for Environmental Studies - Environment Agency - Japan   626
National Institute for Health and Medical Research - France   358
National Institute for Industrial Property - France   359
National Institute for Industrial Property - France   360
National Institute for Industrial Property - France   987
National Institute for Information and Documentation - National Council for Science and Technology - Romania   843
National Institute for Research in Informatics and Automation - France   361
National Institute for Research on Biological Resources - Mexico   702
National Institute for Scientific Research - Portugal   821
National Institute of Agronomic Research - France   362
National Institute of Health and Family Welfare - India   508
National Institute of Nuclear Research - Mexico   703
National Institute of Occupational Safety and Health - Ministry of Health and Safety - Spain   892
National Institute of Oceanography - India   509
National Institute of Science and Technology - Philippines   807
National Institute of Statistics and Economic Research - Ministry of Finance and Economy - Madagascar   681
National Institute of Statistics and Economic Studies - France   363
National Institute of Statistics and Economic Studies - France   364
National Institute of Statistics and Economic Studies - France   365
National Institute of Statistics and Economic Studies - France   366
National Library for Psychology and Education - Sweden   924
National Library for Science and Technology - Finland   483
National Library of Australia   48
National Library of Australia   49
National Library of Australia   50
National Library of Canada   147
National Library of Canada   148
National Library of Canada   149
National Library of Canada   150
National Library of Canada   151
National Library of Canada News   147
National Library of Canada Publications Catalogue   147
National Library of Canada Technical News   147
National Library of Economics - Kiel Institute for World Economics   639
National Library of Quebec   831
National Library of Quebec   833
National Library of Scotland   869
National Library Recent Acquisitions in the Field of Library Science   149
National Master Specification   242
National Medical Library - Czechoslovakia   250
National Mineral Inventory   134
National Ministry of Education - Colombia   212
National Online Meeting   654
National Physical Laboratory - Great Britain   451
National Physical Laboratory/Scientific Group Thermodata Europe (NPL/SGTE) Databank   451
National Planning Association Demographic Data Base (I.P. Sharp Associates)   871
National Planning Association Economic Data Base (I.P. Sharp Associates)   871
National Poison Control Center - Ministry of Health - Belgium   83
National Reporter System (NRS) Data Bases   828
National Reprographic Centre for Documentation   725
National Research Council - Italy   623
National Research Council - Italy   624
National Research Council - Italy   625
National Research Council of Canada   152
National Research Council of Canada   153
National Research Council of Canada   154
National Research Council of Canada   155
National Research Council of Canada   156
National Road and Traffic Research Institute - Sweden   925
National Science and Technology Authority - Philippines   808

National Science Council - Republic of China   726
National Scientific and Technical Information System (SINTO) - Poland   815
National Scientific and Technological Documentation Center - Bolivia   93
National Scientific and Technological Potential Survey Interviewer's Guide   1016
National Scientific Documentation Center - Indonesia   512
National Standards System (Canada)   898
National Statistical Institute - Ministry of Economic Affairs - Belgium   82
National Swedish Council for Building Research   938
National Swedish Environment Protection Board   926
National Swedish Road Administration   925
National Swedish Telecommunications Administration   927
National Szechenyi Library - Hungary   495
National Technical Information Centre and Library - Hungary   496
National Technological Library of Denmark   270
National Telecommunications Research Center - France   367
National Topographic Data Base of Canada   136
National Union Catalog of Scientific and Technical Books in Libraries of the Republic of China   726
National Union Catalogue (Netherlands)   240
National Union Catalogue of Library Materials for the Handicapped   48
National Union Catalogue of Serials   48
National Water Information Center - French Water Study Association   391
National Water Quality Data Bank   141
National Westminster Bank   671
Nationale Raad voor Landbouwkundig Onderzoek TNO   742
Natsionalen Agrarno-Promishlen Suyuz - Bulgaria   121
Natural Environment Data File   626
Natural Environment Research Council   727
Natural Environment Research Council   728
Natural Environment Research Council   729
Natural Environment Research Council   730
Natural Resources Survey & Exploration - Vasundhra   507
Nature Conservancy Council   461
Naval Annual   97
Naval Record   97
NAVF (Norges Almenvitenskapelige Forskningsrad)   768
NAVF (Norges Almenvitenskapelige Forskningsrad)   771
NAVFs EDB-Senter for Humanistisk Forskning   768
NCB (IEA Services) Ltd.   782
NCB (IEA Services) Ltd.   783
NCC (National Computing Centre Ltd.)   721
NCC/IBL (Nederlandse Centrale Catalogus/Interbibliothecair Leenverkeer System)   240
NCEC (National Chemical Emergency Centre) - Atomic Energy Research Establishment, Harwell   435
NCOM Data Base   763
NDT-Info   436
NDU Publishers-Elsevier   305
NEA (Nuclear Energy Agency) - Organisation for Economic Co-Operation and Development   785
NEA Data Bank   785
NEA Data Bank Newsletter   785
NEA-DB (Nuclear Energy Agency Data Bank)   785
Nederlands Genootschap voor Informatica   745
Nederlandsche Centrale Organisatie voor Toegepast-Natuurwetenschappelijk Onderzoek   739
Nederlandsche Centrale Organisatie voor Toegepast-Natuurwetenschappelijk Onderzoek   740
Nederlandsche Centrale Organisatie voor Toegepast-Natuurwetenschappelijk Onderzoek   741
Nederlandsche Centrale Organisatie voor Toegepast-Natuurwetenschappelijk Onderzoek   742
Nederlandsche Centrale Organisatie voor Toegepast-Natuurwetenschappelijk Onderzoek   743
Nederlandse Centrale Catalogus/Interbibliothecair Leenverkeer System   240
Nederlandse Jurisprudentie   641
Nederlandse Vereniging van Gebruikers van Online Informatie-systemen   734
NEEDS-IR (Nikkei Economic Electronic Databank System-Information Retrieval)   753
NEEDS-IR Information   753
NEEDS Portfolio System   754
NEEDS-TS (Nikkei Economic Electronic Databank System-Time Sharing)   754
NEEDS-TS Economy/Macro   754
NEEDS-TS Energy Review   754
NEEDS-TS Report   754
NEELS Data Base (I.P. Sharp Associates)   871
NEI (Nordic Energy Index)   761
NELPAC (National Engineering Laboratory's Thermophysical Properties Package)   548
Neometaphysical Digest   882
NEPHIS (Nested Phrase Indexing System) - School of Library and Information Science - University of Western Ontario   1086
Nested Phrase Indexing System - School of Library and Information Science - University of Western Ontario   1086
Netherlands - Ministry of Agriculture and Fisheries   731
Netherlands - Ministry of Education and Sciences   608
Netherlands - Ministry of Education and Sciences   847
Netherlands - Ministry of Foreign Affairs   732
Netherlands - Netherlands Foreign Trade Agency   733
Netherlands - Royal Library   239
Netherlands - Royal Library   240
Netherlands Agricultural Report Depository   731
Netherlands Association of Users of Online Information Systems   734
Netherlands Bibliographical and Documentary Committee   211
Netherlands Bibliographical and Documentary Committee   735
Netherlands Bureau for Information Provision   735
Netherlands Center for Information Policy   736
Netherlands Central Catalogue/Interlibrary Loan System   240
Netherlands Foreign Trade Agency   733
Netherlands Geological Survey   746
Netherlands Groundwater Survey Data Base   740
Netherlands in the Information Age   736
Netherlands Information Combine   737
Netherlands Office of Posts, Telegraphs, and Telephones   738
Netherlands Organization for Applied Scientific Research   739
Netherlands Organization for Applied Scientific Research   740
Netherlands Organization for Applied Scientific Research   741
Netherlands Organization for Applied Scientific Research   742
Netherlands Organization for Applied Scientific Research   743
Netherlands Organization for Information Policy   744
Netherlands Society for Informatics   745
Netherlands Soil Survey Institute   746
Netherlands Terminology and Documentation Section Data Bank   732
NETSDI   50
Network of Social Security Information Resources   145
Network Services Division - Computer Sciences of Australia Pty. Ltd.   237
Neue Bauforschungsberichte   373
Neue Literaturhinweise   373
Neutron Nuclear Data Evaluation Newsletter   785
New Brunswick Reports (National Reporter System)   828
New Opportunity Press Ltd.   747
New South Wales Institute of Technology   538
New South Wales Motor Vehicle 1982 Registrations Data Base   237
New Technologies: Impact on Employment and the Working Environment   591
New Zealand - Department of Scientific and Industrial Research   748
New Zealand - Department of Statistics   749
New Zealand Science Abstracts   748
New Zealand Scientific Literature Index   748
Newfoundland and Prince Edward Island Reports (National Reporter System)   828
Newfoundland Department of Development   751
Newfoundland Department of Mines & Energy   750
Newfoundland Mineral Development Data Bases   750
Newfoundland Telephone   751
News and Views   317
News Databases   775
News from NEA Data Bank   785
News in the Agricultural Practice   121
Newscheck   462
NEWSFILE   823
Newsidic   307
NEWSLaw (Eurolex)   314
Newsletter of the University of Sydney Sample Survey Centre   1072
NEWSLINE   335
Newstex (Canadian Press)   828
NFER (National Foundation for Educational Research in England and Wales)   724
NGB (Nippon Gijutsu Boeki Co., Ltd.)   758
NGDB (National Geochemical Data Bank)   728
NGI (Nederlands Genootschap voor Informatica)   745
NGI-Nieuws   745
NIC (Netherlands Information Combine)   737
Nichols Advanced Technologies Inc.   752
Nichols Applied Management   752
Nickel, Chrome, Molybdenum Monitor   228
NIF-10S Model Data Base   237
NIF10 Data Base (I.P. Sharp Associates)   871
Nihon Iyaku Joho Center   634
Nihon Keizai Shimbun (NKS) Article Information Data Base   753
Nihon Keizai Shimbun (NKS) Survey Databank   754
Nihon Keizai Shimbun, Inc.   753
Nihon Keizai Shimbun, Inc.   754
Nihon Keizai Shimbun, Inc.   755
NIKKEI (Nihon Keizai Shimbun, Inc.)   753
NIKKEI (Nihon Keizai Shimbun, Inc.)   754
NIKKEI (Nihon Keizai Shimbun, Inc.)   755
Nikkei Article Information Data Bank   753
Nikkei Commodity Prices   754

Nikkei Economic Electronic Databank System-Information Retrieval 753
Nikkei Economic Electronic Databank System-Time Sharing 754
Nikkei Economic Statistics 754
Nikkei Energy 754
Nikkei Household Survey 754
Nikkei Input/Output Tables 754
Nikkei News Recall Service 753
Nikkei Public and Corporate Bond Index 754
Nikkei Research, Inc. 754
Nikkei Stock and Bond Prices Databank 754
Nikkei SVP Co. Ltd. 756
NIMEXE 224
1981 Canadian Census Data Base (I.P. Sharp Associates) 871
1982 Survey of UK Online Users 775
Nineteenth Century Short Title Catalogue 757
Nineteenth Century Short Title Catalogue Newsletter 757
Nineteenth Century Short Title Catalogue Project 757
NIO (National Institute of Oceanography) - India 509
Nippon Gijutsu Boeki Co., Ltd. 758
Nippon Telegraph & Telephone Public Corporation 759
NIST (National Institute of Science and Technology) - Philippines 807
NKS (Nihon Keizai Shimbun) Article Information Data Base 753
NKS (Nihon Keizai Shimbun, Inc.) 753
NKS (Nihon Keizai Shimbun, Inc.) 754
NKS (Nihon Keizai Shimbun) Survey Databank 754
NLEX 643
NMS (National Master Specification) 242
NOBIN (Stichting Nederlands Orgaan voor de Bevordering van de Informatieverzorging) 744
NOGLI 1062
Noise Index 767
Nokia Electronics 480
Nomenclator 893
Nomura Research Institute 760
Nomura Research Institute (NRI/E) Japan Economic & Business Data Bank 760
Non-Destructive Testing Abstracts Journal 416
Non-Ferrous Metals Abstracts Data Base 92
Non-Listed Companies' Databank (NEEDS-TS) 754
Nondestructive Testing Centre - Atomic Energy Research Establishment, Harwell 436
Nondestructive Testing Centre (NTC) Data Base 436
Nondestructive Testing Documentation 416
NORDFORSK (Scandinavian Council for Applied Research) 864
Nordic Atomic Libraries Joint Secretariat 761
Nordic Council for Scientific Information and Research Libraries 762
Nordic Council for Scientific Information and Research Libraries 864
Nordic Council of Ministers 762
Nordic Documentation Center for Mass Communication Research 763
Nordic Energy Index 761
NORDICOM (Nordic Documentation Center for Mass Communication Research) 763
NORDICOM Newsletter 763
NORDINFO (Nordic Council for Scientific Information and Research Libraries) 762
NORDINFO (Nordic Council for Scientific Information and Research Libraries) 864
NORDINFO-NYTT 762
Nordisk databas i Pedagogik och Psykologi (PEPSY) 924
Nordisk Dokumentationscentral for Massekommunikationsforskning 763
NORDRUG 936
Norges Almenvitenskapelige Forskningsrad 768
Norges Almenvitenskapelige Forskningsrad 771
Norges Skipsforskningsinstituutt 872
Norges Standardiseringsforbund 772
Norges Tekniske Hogskole 1079
NORIANE (Normes et Reglements Informations Automatisees Accessibles en Ligne) 382
NORMARC (Norwegian MARC) System 1061
Normes et Reglements Informations Automatisees Accessibles en Ligne 382
NORPAK Corporation 764
NORSAR (Norwegian Seismic Array) 850
Norsk Bokfortegnelse 1061
Norsk Samfunnsvitenskapelig Datatjeneste 771
Norsk Senter for Informatikk 767
Norsk Termbank 1040
Norsk Tidsskriftartikler 1061
North America Imprints Publications Project 443
North American Company Service 690
North American Stock Market Data Base (I.P. Sharp Associates) 871
North American Travel Market 473
North Rhine-Westphalia Institute for Air Pollution Control 765
Northern Titles KWIC Index 95
Norway - Ministry of Finances and Customs 766
Norway's Official Statistics 766
Norwegian Building Research Institute 938

Norwegian Center for Informatics 767
Norwegian Computing Centre for the Humanities 768
Norwegian Institute of Technology 1079
Norwegian Language Council 1040
Norwegian MARC System 1061
Norwegian National Bibliography 1061
Norwegian Petroleum Directorate 769
Norwegian Petroleum Directorate 770
Norwegian Research Council for Science and the Humanities 768
Norwegian Research Council for Science and the Humanities 771
Norwegian Seismic Array 850
Norwegian Social Science Data Services 771
Norwegian Standards Association 772
Norwegian Standards Data Base 772
Norwegian Term Bank 1040
Norwegian University Press 1040
Notes of Recent Decisions Rendered by the Immigration Appeal Board 173
Noticiario Micrografico 101
Notiziario 624
Nouvelles du CRESM 186
Nova Scotia Reports (National Reporter System) 828
Novatex 974
NPADEMOG Data Base (I.P. Sharp Associates) 871
NPAECO Data Base (I.P. Sharp Associates) 871
NPL (National Physical Laboratory) - Great Britain 451
NPL/SGTE (National Physical Laboratory/Scientific Group Thermodata Europe) Databank 451
NRC Metals Crystallographic Data File 156
NRCd (National Reprographic Centre for Documentation) 725
NRI (Nomura Research Institute) 760
NRI Quarterly Economic Review 760
NRI/E Japan Economic & Business Data Bank 760
NRS (National Reporter System) Data Bases 828
NRS (Nikkei News Recall Service) 753
NSD (Norsk Samfunnsvitenskapelig Datatjeneste) 771
NSF (Norges Standardiseringsforbund) 772
NSI (Norsk Senter for Informatikk) 767
NSTA (National Science and Technology Authority) - Philippines 808
NSTC (Nineteenth Century Short Title Catalogue) Project 757
NSUB 643
NTC (Nondestructive Testing Centre) - Atomic Energy Research Establishment, Harwell 436
NTIS United Kingdom Service Center 705
Nuclear Data Center - Institute of Physics and Energy 546
Nuclear Data Section - International Atomic Energy Agency 561
Nuclear Development Corporation of South Africa 886
Nuclear Energy Agency - Organisation for Economic Co-Operation and Development 785
Nuclear Energy Agency Data Bank (NEA-DB) 785
Nuclear Information and Documentation Center - National Institute of Nuclear Research - Mexico 703
Nuclear Science Information of Japan 627
NUCOR (Nuclear Development Corporation of South Africa) 886
NUCOR Library and Information Services - Nuclear Development Corporation of South Africa 886
NUCOS (National Union Catalogue of Serials) 48
Numerical Data Base Service 64
Nutrition Abstracts and Reviews: Series A, Human and Experimental 229
Nutrition Abstracts and Reviews: Series B, Livestock Feeds and Feeding 229
Nutrition Index 767
NYTTFO 665
OAG Data Base (I.P. Sharp Associates) 871
OAND Data Base (I.P. Sharp Associates) 871
OAS (Organization of American States) 177
OAS (Organization of American States) 794
OBIG (Osterreichisches Bundesinstitut fur Gesundheitswesen) 66
Occupational Health and Safety Data Base (Spain) 892
Ocean Engineering Information Centre - Memorial Univeristy of Newfoundland 694
Oceanographic Data Base 509
Ocelot Library System 2
ODE (Online Data Entry) System 317
ODS (Overseas Data Service, Company, Ltd.) 789
ODS-LSI (Overseas Data Service, Life Style Indicator) 789
OECD (Organisation for Economic Co-Operation and Development) 309
OECD (Organisation for Economic Co-Operation and Development) 780
OECD (Organisation for Economic Co-Operation and Development) 781
OECD (Organisation for Economic Co-Operation and Development) 782
OECD (Organisation for Economic Co-Operation and Development) 783
OECD (Organisation for Economic Co-Operation and Development) 784

OECD (Organisation for Economic Co-Operation and Development) 785
OECD (Organisation for Economic Co-Operation and Development) 786
OECD (Organisation for Economic Co-Operation and Development) Economic Statistics and National Accounts Data Bases 780
OECD Liason Bulletin 781
OECD Magnetic Tape Subscription Service 780
OECD Quarterly Oil Statistics Data Base (I.P. Sharp Associates) 871
Oecumene 205
OEES Data Base (I.P. Sharp Associates) 871
OEIC (Ocean Engineering Information Centre) - Memorial University of Newfoundland 694
OEIC Information Bulletin 694
OEKON Data Base (I.P. Sharp Associates) 871
Office de la Langue Francaise - Quebec 830
Office for Official Publications - Commission of the European Communities 227
Office of Arid Lands Studies - College of Agriculture - University of Arizona 229
Office of Economic Information and Forecasting 773
Office of Legal and Technical Documentation - National Institute for Industrial Property - France 360
Office of Scientific Evaluation - National Institute for Health and Medical Research - France 358
Office of Study and Research - Electricite de France 295
Office of Tourism - Department of Industry, Trade & Commerce - Canada 137
Official Airline Guide Data Base (I.P. Sharp Associates) 871
Official Statistics of Sweden 932
Offshore Geological Bibliography 113
OIL Data Base 767
OIL Data Base 770
Oil Index 767
Oil Index 770
Oil Sands Researchers and Research Projects 13
OIN (Osrodek Informacji Naukowej) - Polska Akademia Nauk 816
OIN Catalogue of Microfilms 816
OIN Works 816
OLIS 897
Olje-Indeks 767
Olje-Indeks 770
Oljedirektoratet 769
Oljedirektoratet 770
OMIKK (Orszagos Muszaki Informacios Kozpont es Konyvtar) 496
OMKDK (Orszagos Muszaki Konyvtar es Dokumentacios Kozpont) 496
Omnibus 119
OMNISYS 394
OMPI (Organisation Mondiale de la Propriete Intellectuelle) 1116
ON (Osterreichisches Normungsinstitut) 587
On-Going Research Projects (Republic of China) 726
On-Line Earthnet Data Availability (LEDA) Data Bank 317
Oncology Information Service - Medical and Dental Library - University of Leeds 1053
Oncology Information Service Bulletins 1053
Oncology Information Service Data Base 1053
Onderzoek naar Milieu en Natuur in Nederland 743
Ongoing Research Project Data Bank - Ministry for Research and Technology - Germany 424
Online Authority Control System 1094
Online Data Entry System 317
Online Databases Prestel File 69
Online-GKS (German Union List of Conference Proceedings) 400
ONLINE GmbH 774
Online Information Centers in Denmark 256
Online Information Centre 775
Online Notes 775
Online-NZN (Lower Saxonia Serials Data Base) 400
Online Review 654
Online to Textile Literature 873
Online Users' Group / Ireland 776
Online-ZDB (German Union Catalog of Serials) 400
Ontario Appeal Cases (National Reporter System) 828
Ontario Decisions, Criminal Cases 1108
Ontario Education Resources Information System 777
Ontario Geological Survey 778
Ontario Geological Survey General Index 778
Ontario Geoscience Data Index 778
Ontario Mineral Deposit Inventory Database 778
Ontario Ministry of Colleges and Universities 777
Ontario Ministry of Education 777
Ontario Ministry of Natural Resources 778
Ontario Municipal Board Reports 162
Ontario Reports 162
ONTERIS (Ontario Education Resources Information System) 777
OON Data Base 152
OONL Data Base 148
OOT Data Base 161
Operational Hydrology Programme - Commission for Hydrology - World Meteorological Organization 1117
Operational Services Division - Central Research Establishment - Home Office Forensic Science Service - Great Britain 458
Opinionmeter Co., Ltd. 631
Optional Reception of Announcements by Coded Line Electronics (ORACLE) 779
ORACLE 779
ORACLE Teletext Ltd. 779
Oral Health Unit - Division of Noncommunicable Diseases - World Health Organization 1111
ORATEUR 384
ORBI 80
Organic Chemistry File (IDC) 572
Organisation for Economic Co-Operation and Development 309
Organisation for Economic Co-Operation and Development 780
Organisation for Economic Co-Operation and Development 781
Organisation for Economic Co-Operation and Development 782
Organisation for Economic Co-Operation and Development 783
Organisation for Economic Co-Operation and Development 784
Organisation for Economic Co-Operation and Development 785
Organisation for Economic Co-Operation and Development 786
Organisation for Economic Co-Operation and Development (OECD) Economic Statistics and National Accounts Data Bases 780
Organisation Mondiale de la Propriete Intellectuelle 1116
Organization of American States 177
Organization of American States 794
Organon International 804
Oriel Computer Services Limited 787
Orientering om Fremtidsforskning 540
Origin-Destination Data Base (I.P. Sharp Associates) 871
Original Equipment Suppliers to Vehicle Manufacturers Directory 67
ORL-Literaturinformationssystem (ORLIS) 379
ORLIS (ORL-Literaturinformationssystem) 379
Orna/Stevens Consultancy 788
Ornamental Horticulture 229
Orszagos Muszaki Informacios Kozpont es Konyvtar 496
Orszagos Muszaki Konyvtar es Dokumentacios Kozpont 496
Orszagos Szechenyi Konyvtar - Hungary 495
OSCHEDULE Data Base (I.P. Sharp Associates) 871
Osrodek Informacji Naukowej - Polska Akademia Nauk 816
Osterreichisches Bundesinstitut fur Gesundheitswesen 66
Osterreichisches Dokumentationszentrum fur Medien- und Kommunikationsforschung 65
Osterreichisches Normungsinstitut 587
Ostsprachige Fachliteratur 1031
OSzK (Orszagos Szechenyi Konyvtar) - Hungary 495
OTA-kirjasto 483
Outline of the JODC 628
Outlook Database 126
Overall Trade by Country (OECD) 780
Overseas Data Service, Company, Ltd. 631
Overseas Data Service, Company, Ltd. 789
Overseas Institute 397
Overseas Telecommunications Commission (Australia) 790
Oxford Microform Publications Ltd. 791
Oy Keskuslaboratorio - Centrallaboratorium Ab 333
PA (Press Association Ltd.) 823
Pacific Subscription Service 635
Packaging Science and Technology Abstracts 584
Packet SwitchStream 447
Packet SwitchStream, A Basic Guide and Directory 447
PACTI Data Base 893
PADIS (Pan-African Documentation and Information System) 1005
PADIS-ADMIN Data Base 1005
PADIS-COM Data Bases 1005
PADIS-DEV Data Base 1005
PADIS-NET 1005
PADIS-PROM Data Base 1005
PADIS-STAT Data Bases 1005
PADOC Data Base 935
PAGEMAKER 369
PAGETAKER 369
PAHO (Pan American Health Organization) 794
Paint Research Association 792
Paint Titles 792
Pakistan - Ministry of Science & Technology 793
Pakistan Current Contents 793
Pakistan Science Abstracts 793
Pakistan Science Foundation 793
Pakistan Scientific and Technological Information Centre 793
PAKLEGIS 812
PAKLEGIS: A Guide to Packaging Legislation 812
PAM (Patents Abstracts on Microfiche) 275
PAN (Polska Akademia Nauk) 816
Pan-African Documentation and Information System 1005
Pan American Centre for Sanitary Engineering & Environmental Sciences 794
Pan American Health Organization 794
Pan American Information & Documentation Network on Sanitary

Engineering & Environmental Sciences 794
Pan European Survey 839
Paper & Board Abstracts 812
Paper and Board, Printing and Packaging Industries Research Association 812
Papers in Historical Statistics 493
PAPRICAN (Pulp and Paper Research Institute of Canada) 827
PAPYRUS 384
Paralog 795
Paris Chamber of Commerce and Industry 796
Paris Chamber of Commerce and Industry 797
Paris District Gestion Informatique 797
Paris District Informatics Administration 797
Paris Office of Urbanization 798
Paris Stock Exchange Charts 389
Parkes Catalogue of Radio Sources 59
PARLEMENT 343
Parliament of Canada 157
Parliamentary Documentation and Information Printing Service - France 343
Parliamentary On-Line Information System 459
Parpinelli TECNON 799
PARTHES (Thesaurus for Parliamentary Materials) 422
Particle Science and Technology Information Service 676
PASCAL (Programme Applique a la Selection et a la Compilation Automatiques de la Litterature) 356
PASCAL Batiment Travaux Publics (PASCALBAT) Data Base 377
PASCAL EXPLORE 356
PASCAL FOLIO 356
PASCAL-GEODE 340
PASCAL M 356
PASCAL-Oceanologie 351
PASCAL S 356
PASCAL SIGMA 356
PASCAL THEMA 356
PASCALBAT (PASCAL Batiment Travaux Publics) Data Base 377
PASSAT 874
PASTIC (Pakistan Scientific and Technological Information Centre) 793
Patent and Registration Office - Sweden 928
Patent Applicant Service 64
Patent Applicant Service to Priorities 64
Patent Classification Service 64
Patent Data Bank (IDC) 572
Patent Family Service 64
Patent Inventor Service 64
Patent- och Registreringsverket - Sweden 928
Patent On-Line Information System 633
Patent Register Service 64
Patentdatenbank (PDB) 572
PATENTE 521
Patents Abstracts on Microfiche 275
Patents Databases 775
Patents Documentation Services - Derwent Publications Ltd. 275
Pathfinder 862
PATOLIS (Patent On-Line Information System) 633
PATSDI 521
PATSDI-TEST 521
PCODES (Postcode Locality Data Base) 237
PCPI (Permanent Committee on Patent Information) 1116
PDB (Patentdatenbank) 572
PDC (Population Documentation Center) - Human Resources, Institutions and Agrarian Reform Division - Food and Agriculture Organization 1010
PDR (Pharma-Dokumentationsring) 804
PDS (Pharma-Dokumentations-Service) 805
Peace Research Abstracts Journal 800
Peace Research Institute-Dundas 800
Peace Research Reviews 800
PEPSY Data Base 924
PERA (Production Engineering Research Association of Great Britain) 826
PERA Bulletin 826
Perennial Snow and Ice Section - National Hydrology Research Institute - Inland Waters Directorate - Environment Canada 139
Pergamon/BPCC Group 791
Pergamon Group 97
Pergamon Group 98
Pergamon InfoLine Ltd. 802
Pergamon Press 802
Pergamon Press 803
Pergamon Press 1056
Pergamon Press Canada Ltd. 802
PERIODEX 831
Periodica: Indice de Revistas Latinoamericanas en Ciencias 719
Periodicals in Southern African Libraries 885
Periodicals in the Library of the Norwegian Institute of Technology 1079
Periodicals Parade 847

Periodicos Brasileiros de Ciencia e Tecnologia 103
Periodiekenparade 847
PERLINE - Blackwell Technical Services Ltd. 90
Permanent Committee on Patent Information 1116
Permanent Inventory of Agricultural Research Projects in the European Communities Data Base 213
Permanent Inventory of Belgian Scientific Publications 84
Personal Statistical Analyses Service 317
Pest Control Literature Documentation 276
PESTDOC (Pest Control Literature Documentation) 276
Pesticide Research Information System - Scientific Information Retrieval Section - Agriculture Canada 128
Pesticide Use Index 128
Peter Leigh-Bell & Associates Ltd. 657
PETROCH (Rock Chemical Database) 778
Petrochemical Manufacturing and Market Trends 199
Petroflash Crude and Produce Reports Data Base (I.P. Sharp Associates) 871
Petroleum and Petrochemical Economics in Europe 199
Petroleum Argus Daily Market Report Data Base (I.P. Sharp Associates) 871
Petroleum Argus Prices Data Base (I.P. Sharp Associates) 871
Petroleum Engineering Division - Department of Energy - Great Britain 769
Petroleum Fractions Package 548
Petroleum Intelligence Weekly Data Base (I.P. Sharp Associates) 871
PFS (Private File Service) - Infomart 518
PGD 773
PGI (Paris District Gestion Informatique) 797
Pharma Documentation Ring 804
Pharma Documentation Service 805
Pharma-Dokumentations-Service 805
Pharma-Dokumentationsring 804
Pharmaceutical Literature Documentation (RINGDOC) 277
Pharmaceutical New Product Listing Service 907
Pharmaceutical Society of Great Britain 806
Pharmaceuticals and Toiletries Bulletin 712
Pharmline 285
PHI (Philosophie Informationsdienst) - Forschungsabteilung fur Philosophische Information und Dokumentation - Universitat Dusseldorf 1048
Philippine Ethnographic Series 1073
Philippine Men of Science 808
Philippine Patents Data Base 967
Philippine Presidential Documents Data Base 967
Philippine Science and Technology Abstracts 808
Philippines - National Institute of Science and Technology 807
Philippines - National Science and Technology Authority 808
Philips Information Systems and Automation 809
Philosophie Informationsdienst - Forschungsabteilung fur Philosophische Information und Dokumentation - Universitat Dusseldorf 1048
Philosophische Dokumentation 1048
Philosophy Information Service - Research Division for Philosophy Information and Documentation - University of Dusseldorf 1048
Phippard & Associates Strategic & Technological Consulting, Inc. 810
PHOENIX 1059
Photochemical Smog Data File 626
PHYS (Physics Briefs) 521
PHYSCOMP (Data Compilations in Physics) 521
Physical Properties Data Bank, CHEMCO 327
Physical Properties Package 548
Physical Property Data Service 548
Physics Abstracts 549
Physics Briefs 521
Physics Data 521
Physik Daten 521
Physikalische Berichte 521
Phytomedicine Data Base 409
Piaf 977
PICA (Project for Integrated Catalogue Automation) 239
PICA (Project for Integrated Catalogue Automation) 240
PICA (Property Services Agency Information on Construction and Architecture) Data Base 378
Piedmont Consortium for Information Systems 811
Pig News and Information 229
PIII 649
PINCCA (Price Index Numbers for Current Cost Accounting) Data Bank 454
Pipelines Abstracts 86
PIPS (Science and Technology Policies Information Exchange Programme) 1016
Pira Abstracts 812
Pira: Research Association for the Paper and Board, Printing and Packaging Industries 577
Pira: Research Association for the Paper and Board, Printing and Packaging Industries 812
Pira: Research Association for the Paper and Board, Printing and Packaging Industries 813
Pira Thesaurus 812

PISAL (Periodicals in Southern African Libraries) 885
PIT (Printing and Information Technology) Division - Pira: Research Association for the Paper and Board, Printing and Packaging Industries 813
PIW Data Base (I.P. Sharp Associates) 871
PKSCAT (Parkes Catalogue of Radio Sources) 59
Plain Man's Guide to the T.G.I. 109
Planck (Max) Society for the Advancement of Science 431
PLANINDEX 1006
PLANLaw (Eurolex) 314
Planning Consumer Markets 484
Planning Department - Royal University Library - University of Oslo 1061
Planning for Social Change 484
Plans and Projects Monitor Data Base 264
Plant Breeding Abstracts 229
Plant Growth Regulator Abstracts 229
PLANTFACTS 398
Plants and Processes Information System for Iron & Steel 398
Plasma Physics Library and Information Service - Culham Laboratory - Atomic Energy Authority - Great Britain 438
Plastics Research Society 402
PLIDOS 959
Pluridata System Data Bases 38
PMB Print Measurement Bureau 814
POETRI (Programme on Exchange and Transfer of Information on Community Water Supply and Sanitation) 601
POETRI Newsletter 601
Point de Repere 831
Point de Repere: Index Analytique d'Articles de Periodiques Quebecois et Etrangers 831
Poison Management Manual 1043
Poisoning Perspectives Newsletter 1043
Poland - Institute for Scientific, Technical and Economic Information 815
Poland - Polish Academy of Sciences 816
Police Science Abstracts 647
Policy, Planning and Information Branch - Health and Welfare Canada 145
POLIS (Parliamentary On-Line Information System) 459
Polish Academy of Sciences 816
Polish Committee of Standardization, Measures, and Quality 817
Politechnika Wroclawska 965
Political and Current Events Information Bank 384
Polska Akademia Nauk 816
Polski Komitet Normalizacji i Mair i Jakosci 817
POLUMAT 353
POLYDOC 767
Polymer File (IDC) 572
Polytechnic of Central London 818
Polytechnical School of Montreal 819
Pont-a-Mousson Industrial Information Bank 820
Pont-a-Mousson Research Center 820
POPFILE/ESCAP Bibliographic Information System 1003
POPIN (International Population Information Network) 1003
POPTIO 1010
Population and Social Statistics Branch - Central Statistics Bureau - British Columbia Ministry of Industry and Small Business Development 106
Population Clearing-house and Information Section - Population Division - Economic and Social Commission for Asia and the Pacific - United Nations 1003
Population Division - Economic and Social Commission for Asia and the Pacific - United Nations 1003
Population Documentation Center - Human Resources, Institutions and Agrarian Reform Division - Food and Agriculture Organization 1010
Population File 1010
Population File/ESCAP Bibliographic Information System 1003
Population Headliners 1003
Population Research Laboratory - Department of Sociology - University of Alberta 1035
Porritt and Dawson Library 858
Portugal - National Institute for Scientific Research 821
Portuguese Radio Marconi Company 822
Postcode Locality Data Base 237
Posts and Telegraphs - Denmark 271
Potato Abstracts 229
Potato Markets 8
Poultry Abstracts 229
PPDS (Physical Property Data Service) 548
PPDS-PPDATA 548
PPDS-VLE 548
PPR (Alberta Government Periodicals Publishing Record) Data Base 11
Prace IINTE 815
Prairie Forum 1066
Praktijkgids 641
PRAUS (Programme de Recherche sur l'Amiante de l'Universite de Sherbrooke) 1071
Praxis Juridique et Religion 205

PRECIS (Preserved Context Index System) 441
PRECIS (Preserved Context Index System) Thesaurus 441
PRECIS: A Manual of Concept Analysis and Subject Indexing 441
PRECIS Vocabulary Fiche 441
Precision Prospect Analysis - Compusearch Market and Social Research Ltd. 236
Predecessor and Defunct Companies Data Base 680
Presentation of Information 788
Preserved Context Index System (PRECIS) 441
Preserved Context Index System (PRECIS) Thesaurus 441
Preserved Milk 8
Press Association Ltd. 823
Press Information Bank (Gruner & Jahr) 468
Pressurklipp 824
Prestel 448
Prestel Gateway Cost Effectiveness 1100
Prestel User 448
PREVIEW 649
Prevision et Analyse Economique 1062
Previsions Glissantes Detaillees 773
Price Index Numbers for Current Cost Accounting (PINCCA) Data Bank 454
PRICEDATA 878
Primary Communications: An Annotated Review of the Literature Since 1970 1054
Primary Communications Research Centre 1054
Primary Computing 485
Prime Minister's Office - Japan 632
Primer for Agricultural Libraries 558
PRIMORDIAL 317
Principal Offshore Oil-Spill Accidents and Tanker Casualties Data Bank 387
Print Measurement Bureau (PMB) 814
Printing Abstracts 812
Printing and Information Technology Division - Pira: Research Association for the Paper and Board, Printing and Packaging Industries 813
PRIS (Pesticide Research Information System) - Scientific Information Retrieval System - Agriculture Canada 128
Prism Microproducts 976
Private File Service - Infomart 518
Probleme de Documentare si Informare 843
Problems of Economic, Scientific and Technical Cooperation of CMEA Member Countries 565
Problems of Information Systems 565
Problems of Scientific Information 816
Proceedings of the Annual Meeting on Information Science and Technology 632
Process Economics Research Planning 199
Process Engineering Index 958
Prodinform Technical Consulting Co. 825
Production Engineering Research Association of Great Britain 826
PROFILE: The Excerpta Medica Newsletter 296
Program: News of Computers in Libraries 35
PROGRAMLIST (Index of Software Supported by Computing Services) 1033
Programme Applique a la Selection et a la Compilation Automatiques de la Litterature (PASCAL) 356
Programme de Recherche sur l'Amiante de l'Universite de Sherbrooke 1071
Programme on Exchange and Transfer of Information on Community Water Supply and Sanitation 601
Programs Department - Atomic Energy Commission - France 338
Project FAIR (Fast Access Information Retrieval) 114
Project for Integrated Catalogue Automation 239
Project for Integrated Catalogue Automation 240
Project HERMES 450
Project Ida 519
Project IRIS 169
Projet Europeen d'Information sur la Biotechnologie 446
PROMEXPORT/PROMIMPORT 796
Promis Newsletter 871
Property & Compensation Reports (Eurolex) 314
Property Service 690
Property Services Agency Information on Construction and Architecture (PICA) Data Base 378
Property Services Agency Library Service - Department of the Environment - Great Britain 378
Propriete Industrielle Bulletin Documentaire 360
PROTEC 1062
Protozoological Abstracts 229
Provincial Construction Forecast Service - Informetrica Limited 536
Provincial Forecast Service - Informetrica Limited 536
Provisional Atlas of the Amphibians and Reptiles of the British Isles 461
Provisional Atlas of the Arachnida of the British Isles 461
Provisional Atlas of the Bryophytes of the British Isles 461
Provisional Atlas of the Crustacea of the British Isles 461
Provisional Atlas of the Insects of the British Isles 461

Provisional Atlas of the Mammals of the British Isles 461
Provisional Atlas of the Marine Dinoflagellates of the British Isles 461
Provisional Atlas of the Nematodes of the British Isles 461
Przeglad Dokumentacyjny Informacji Naukowej 815
PSS (Packet SwitchStream) 447
PSS, The Public Data Service Directory 447
PSS-The Technical Users Guide 447
PSTA (Packaging Science and Technology Abstracts) 584
Psychologischer Index 1078
PSYNDEX 1078
PTI (Publicacoes Tecnicas Internacionais Ltda.) 605
PTT Central Directorate - Netherlands Office of Posts, Telegraphs, and Telephones 738
Public Archives of Canada 158
Public Relations Division - Calgary Public Information Department 124
Public Services Branch - National Library of Canada 151
Publicacoes Tecnicas Internacionais Ltda. 605
Publication Services Branch - Alberta Public Affairs Bureau 11
Publications of the National Research Council of Canada 152
Publishers in English in Japan 635
Publishers' International Directory 863
Pudoc (Centrum voor Landbouwpublikaties en Landbouwdocumentatie) 583
Pudoc (Centrum voor Landbouwpublikaties en Landbouwdocumentatie) 731
Pudoc Bulletin 731
PUFFIN 638
Pulp and Paper Research Institute of Canada 827
Pulse Radiolysis 44
Pumps and Other Fluids Machinery Abstracts 86
Pusat Dokumentasi Ilmiah Nasional 512
QBANK Data Base (I.P. Sharp Associates) 871
QHBARK Data Base 920
QHGRVN Data Base 920
QL/MAIL 828
QL/NEWS 828
QL/SEARCH 828
QL/SEARCH User's Manual 828
QL Systems Limited 828
QL/TEXT 828
QL Update 828
QN System 755
QOS Data Base (I.P. Sharp Associates) 871
QT Handbook 436
QT News 436
Quaere Law Letter 829
Quaere Legal Resources Ltd. 829
QUALIS Data Base 594
Quality Technology Information Service 436
QUALTIS (Quality Technology Information Service) 436
QUANTUM 183
Quarterly Bulletin of IAALD 558
Quarterly Bulletin of Statistics for Asia and the Pacific 1004
Quarterly Labour Force Statistics (OECD) 780
Quarterly National Accounts Bulletin 780
Quarterly Petrochemical Business Analysis 199
Quarterly Survey of Consumer Buying Intentions Data Base 238
Que 3
Quebec - French Language Board 830
Quebec-Actualite Data Base 704
Quebec Information Bank on the Environment of Quebec 832
Quebec Ministry of Education 831
Quebec Ministry of the Environment 832
Quebec National Library 831
Quebec National Library 833
Quebec Society for Legal Information 834
Queen's University Interrogation of Legal Literature (QUILL) 836
Queen's University of Belfast 835
Queen's University of Belfast 836
Queen's University On-line Bibliographic Information Retrieval and Dissemination (QUOBIRD) 836
QUEST 485
QUEST - European Space Agency 317
Questel 977
QUESTIONS 343
Quetelet Library Data Base 81
QUICK (Quotation Information Center K.K.) 754
QUICK (Quotation Information Center K.K.) 755
QUICK Board 755
QUICK CB Board 755
QUICK Home Printer 755
QUICK Index Board 755
QUICK MT-I 755
QUICK News System 755
QUICK Video-Bond Money 755
QUICK Video-I 755
QUICK Video-II 755
QUICK Video-X300 755
QUILL (Queen's University Interrogation of Legal Literature) 836

QUOBIRD (Queen's University On-line Bibliographic Information Retrieval and Dissemination) 836
QUODAMP 835
QUORUM 157
Quotation Information Center K.K. 755
QUOTEL Insurance Services Ltd. 837
QZ (Stockholm University Computing Center) 904
R & D Index 767
R & D Philippines 808
R & D Projects in Documentation and Librarianship 579
RADAR (Repertoire Analytique d'Articles de Revues du Quebec) 831
RADIALS (Research and Development - Library and Information Science) Bulletin 661
Radio Guide 475
Radio Suisse Ltd. 266
Radiographie du Capital: Les Liaisons Financieres 251
Rail International 600
RAINSS (Regional Arab Information Network for Social Sciences) 1015
Rakennuskirja Oy 118
RAMA 71
RAMPI (Raw Materials Price Index) 878
RAPPORT 668
Rapport Annuel sur la Situation des Services Postaux 1030
Rapports de la Cour Federale du Canada 828
Rapports de la Cour Supreme du Canada 828
RAPRA (Rubber and Plastics Research Association of Great Britain) 858
RAPRA Abstracts 858
RAPRA Information Centre 858
RAPRA Online Users Manual 858
Raumordnung, Stadtebau, Wohnungswesen, Bauwesen (RSWB) 379
Raw Materials Price Index (RAMPI) 878
RCE (Repertoire Canadien sur l'Education) Data Base 170
RDS (Reperimento Documentazione Siderurgica) 192
RDZ (Ringier Dokumentationszentrum) 841
Reactions 5
REBUS (Reseau des Bibliotheques Utilisant SIBIL) 664
RECAP 434
Recent Trends in Wind Energy 507
Rechtspraak van de Week 641
Rechtsstands Lexicon 234
RECODEX (Report Collection Index) 906
Red Panamericana de Informacion y Documentacion en Ingenieria Sanitaria y Ciencias Ambientales 794
REDOSI 190
REFABS Data Base 602
REFCATSS 1094
Referatedienst Verpackung 584
Referateorgan Schweissen und Verwandte Verfahren 418
Referateorgan Zerstorungsfreie Prufung 416
Referativnyi Zhurnal 998
Referatove Vybery 250
Reference Bulletin 355
Reference Data Series No. 1: Energy, Electricity and Power Estimates for the Period up to 2000 559
Reference Department - University of Saskatchewan Library 1067
Reference Division - British Library 443
Reference Ile de France 1091
Reference Manual for Machine-Readable Bibliographic Descriptions 1023
Reference Manual for Machine-Readable Descriptions of Research Projects and Institutions 1023
Referral Service System - United Nations University 1028
Refugee Abstracts 602
Regio-Indeks 767
Regional Arab Information Network for Social Sciences 1015
Regional Bibliographic Products Department - Metropolitan Toronto Library Board 699
Regional Documentation Center - Asian Institute of Technology 30
Regional Documentation Center - Asian Institute of Technology 31
Regional Documentation Center - Asian Institute of Technology 32
Regional Documentation Center - Asian Institute of Technology 33
Regional Geochemical Atlases of the United Kingdom 728
Regional-Industrial Model (RIM) 536
Regional Planning, City Planning, Housing, Building Construction Data Base 379
Regional Planning, City Planning, Housing Research Projects Data Base 380
Regional Statistics 493
Regional Statistics Data Base (RSDB), Statistics Sweden 932
REGIS 940
REGIS 1062
Register of Current Community Legal Instruments 489
Register of Educational Research in the United Kingdom 724
Register of Exporters - Information Department - Finnish Foreign Trade Association 332
Register of Keyterms (World Textile Abstracts) 873
Register of Legal Documentation in the World 571

Register of Parliamentary Processes in the German Federal Diet and Federal Council   422
Register of Periodicals in the ILO Library   593
Register of Social Science Research   847
Register of United Nations Serials Publications   1001
Register zu den Verhandlungen des Deutschen Bundestages und des Bundesrates   422
Registered Corporate Income Report   969
Registry of Tropical and Arid Land Current Research   702
Regression Package   548
Regulations of Ontario   828
Regulatory Reporter   173
REHVA (Representatives of European Heating and Ventilation Associations)   119
Remote Sensing On-Line Retrieval System   132
Rene Descartes University   838
Renewable Energy Experts Directory   230
Renewable Energy Products Directory   230
Renewable Energy Resources Information Center   33
Renewable Energy Review Journal   33
Reperimento Documentazione Siderurgica   192
Repertoire Analytique d'Articles de Revues du Quebec   831
Repertoire Bibliographique des Institutions Chretiennes   205
Repertoire Bibliographique d'Histoire du Quebec et du Canada   704
Repertoire Canadien sur l'Education   170
Repertoire CATED   610
Repertoire d'Art et Archeologie   355
Repertoire des Theses de Maitrise Completees en Nursing   1037
Repertory of Art and Archaeology   355
REPIDISCA (Red Panamericana de Informacion y Documentacion en Ingenieria Sanitaria y Ciencias Ambientales)   794
REPIDISCA Newsletter   794
REPINDEX   794
Report Collection Index   906
Report of Policy Development in Science and Technology   726
Reports and Papers in the Social Sciences   1022
Reports in the Fields of Science and Technology   521
Reports of Patent Cases (Eurolex)   314
Representatives of European Heating and Ventilation Associations   119
Reprographics Quarterly   725
Republic of China - National Science Council   726
RERIC (Renewable Energy Resources Information Center)   33
RERIC Holdings List   33
RERIC News   33
Research and Development - Library and Information Science Bulletin   661
Research and Development Department - British Library   444
Research and Development Department - British Library   677
Research and Development Department - British Library   818
Research and Development Department - British Library   1039
Research and Development Index   767
Research and Development Projects in the Areas of Information Science and Practice   880
Research and Information Branch - Ontario Ministry of Education   777
Research Association for the Paper and Board, Printing and Packaging Industries   577
Research Association for the Paper and Board, Printing and Packaging Industries   812
Research Association for the Paper and Board, Printing and Packaging Industries   813
Research Center for the Stratigraphy and Petrography of the Central Alps   625
Research Division for Philosophy Information and Documentation - University of Dusseldorf   1048
Research Institute for Computing Applications - Central Statistical Office - Hungary   493
Research Institute for International Politics and Security   337
Research Institute of Fundamental Information Science - Kyushu University   648
Research Institute of National Defense - Sweden   929
Research on Environment and Nature in the Netherlands   743
Research on Transport Economics   309
Research Referral Service - International Federation for Documentation   579
Research Register of VTT   330
Research Report from the NIES   626
Research School of Social Sciences - Australian National University   60
Research School of Social Sciences - Australian National University   61
Research Services Ltd.   839
Research Unit for the Blind - Brunel University   115
Researching Heritage Buildings   138
Reseau des Bibliotheques Utilisant SIBIL   664
Reseau Documentaire en Sciences Humaines de la Sante   355
Reseau URBAMET   1091
RESHUS   355
Reso Data Bank   251
RESORS (Remote Sensing On-Line Retrieval System)   132
Resources   840
Responsa Project   74

Responsible National Oceanographic Data Center   628
Responsible National Oceanographic Data Center   730
RETAIL Data Base (I.P. Sharp Associates)   871
Retrospective Cumulative Index of Indian Social Science Journals   511
Reuters News Agency   321
Reuters News Agency   755
Review of Applied Entomology: Series A, Agricultural   229
Review of Applied Entomology: Series B, Medical and Veterinary   229
Review of Medical and Veterinary Mycology   229
Review of Plant Pathology   229
Reviews on Thermophysical Properties of Substances   996
Revised Statutes of Canada   828
Revista Espanola de Documentacion Cientifica   890
Revue Canadienne des Sciences de l'Information   168
Revue des Inventions Horlogeres   944
Revue Generale de Thermique   386
REVUMER   347
REWARD   371
Rheology and Tribology Documentation Center   417
Rheology Data Base   417
RIBA (Royal Institute of British Architects)   845
RIC (Repertoire Bibliographique des Institutions Chretiennes) Data Base   205
Rice Abstracts   229
Richard Larratt and Associates Ltd.   650
Rijks Universiteit Utrecht Bibliotheek   899
RIM (Regional-Industrial Model)   536
RINGDOC (Pharmaceutical Literature Documentation)   277
Ringier & Co.   841
Ringier Documentation Center   841
Ringier Dokumentationszentrum   841
RISE (Ruling Information System-Excise)   828
Risk Measurement Service   1060
Riso Library   842
Riso National Laboratory   842
RNODC (Responsible National Oceanographic Data Center)   628
RNODC (Responsible National Oceanographic Data Center)   730
Road Data Bank - Technical Division - Swedish National Road Administration   933
Road Research Documentation Center - Federal Research and Testing Establishment Arsenal - Federal Ministry of Buildings and Technology - Austria   63
Road Traffic Reports (Eurolex)   314
Road Transport Research Programme - Organisation for Economic Co-Operation and Development   786
Roadlit   62
Robert Debre Information Base   566
Robertson (T.L.) Library - Western Australian Institute of Technology   1107
ROC Information Industry Handbook   542
Rock Chemical Database (PETROCH)   778
Rock Mechanics Information Service   1056
Romania - National Council for Science and Technology   843
Romanian National Institute for Information and Documentation (INID) Data Base   843
Ronalds-Federated Limited   20
ROOMSERVICE - Control Data Australia Pty. Ltd.   245
Roomservice - Prestel   448
ROSCOP   354
Royal Dutch Society for Advancement of Pharmacy   844
Royal Institute of British Architects   845
Royal Institute of Chemistry   851
Royal Institute of Technology Library - Sweden   930
Royal Library - Netherlands   239
Royal Library - Netherlands   240
Royal Library - Sweden   931
Royal Library of Belgium   84
Royal Museum of Central Africa   846
Royal Netherlands Academy of Arts and Sciences   847
Royal Netherlands Academy of Arts and Sciences   848
Royal Netherlands Academy of Arts and Sciences Library   849
Royal Norwegian Council for Scientific and Industrial Research   850
Royal Society of Chemistry   851
Royal Society of Chemistry   852
Royal Society of Chemistry   853
Royal Society of Chemistry   854
Royal Society of Chemistry   855
Royal Society of Chemistry   856
Royal Society of Chemistry Information Services Newsletter   851
Royal Tropical Institute   857
Royal University Library - University of Oslo   1061
RRS (Research Referral Service) - International Federation for Documentation   579
RSC (Royal Society of Chemistry)   851
RSC (Royal Society of Chemistry)   852
RSC (Royal Society of Chemistry)   853
RSC (Royal Society of Chemistry)   854
RSC (Royal Society of Chemistry)   855
RSC (Royal Society of Chemistry)   856

RSDB (Regional Statistics Data Base), Statistics Sweden   932
RSL (Research Services Ltd.)   839
RSWB (Raumordnung, Stadtebau, Wohnungswesen, Bauwesen)   379
Rubber and Plastics Research Association of Great Britain   858
Rudolf Wolff & Co. Ltd.   1109
Ruling Information System-Excise (RISE)   828
Rural Development: A Selected Bibliography   1002
Rural Development Abstracts   229
Rural Extension, Education & Training Abstracts   229
RUSI/Brassey's Defence Yearbook   97
Russian Scientific & Technical Publications - An Accession List   507
Russian Space Exploration   432
RWK Ltd.   859
S.A. Waterabstracts   887
S.E.M.P. (Societe d'Editions Medico-Pharmaceutiques)   693
S.I.S. (Supplier Identification System)   671
S.J. Rundt World Risk Analysis Package Data Base (I.P. Sharp Associates)   871
Sabadell Computing Center   860
SABD (Servico de Acesso a Bancos de Dados) - Companhia Portuguesa Radio Marconi   822
SABE 2000 (Sistema de Alerta Bibliografico Especializado) Data Base   605
SABI/OC   965
SABI/OZ   965
SACDA (Systems Analysis, Control and Design Activity) - University of Western Ontario   1088
Sachem-Energy   185
Sachem-West   185
Saclay Nuclear Research Center   339
SAFE (Software Abstracts for Engineers)   208
SAILS (Swets Automated Independent Library System)   942
SALOMON   384
SALUS Data Base   576
Samenwerkingsverband voor Opleiding en Vorming op het Terrein van de Informatieverzorging via Netwerken   211
SAMKATPER (Union Catalog for Periodicals in Norwegian Libraries)   1061
Sample Survey Centre - University of Sydney   1072
Samsom Data Systems   861
Samsom Datanet   861
SANI Data Base   194
Sanoma Publishing Company   480
SANP Data Base   194
SARIS (South African Retrospective Information System)   885
SASC (Subject Analysis Systems Collection) - Faculty of Library and Information Science Library - University of Toronto   1077
SASDI (South African Selective Dissemination of Information)   885
SASK TEL (Saskatchewan Telecommunications)   862
Saskatchewan Decisions, Civil and Criminal Cases   1108
Saskatchewan Reports (National Reporter System)   828
Saskatchewan Telecommunications   862
SATELDATA   317
SATLINE (Science and Technology Library Network, Republic of China)   726
Satz Rechen Zentrum   401
Satz Rechen Zentrum   476
Saur (K.G.) Verlag   863
SAWIC (South African Water Information Centre)   887
SB-I (Biblio Service Informatique) - Paris District Gestion Informatique   797
SB-I CAS   797
SB-I Expertises   797
SBL (Serials in the British Library) Data Base   439
SBN (Servizio Biblioteca Nazionale) - Italy   811
SBS (Swedish Behavioural Sciences) Data Base   924
Scandinavian Council for Applied Research   864
Scandinavian Information Retrieval Service   123
Scandinavian Periodicals Index in Economics and Business   481
Scandinavian Technology Libraries' Congress Lists   1079
SCANINFO (Scandinavian Information Retrieval Service)   123
Scannet Foundation   864
Scannet Today   864
SCANP (Scandinavian Periodicals Index in Economics and Business)   481
SCB (Statistiska Centralbyran)   932
SCDSD (Scientific Clearinghouse and Documentation Services Division) - National Science and Technology Authority - Philippines   808
Scheduled Intra-European Passenger and Cargo Traffic of AEA Member Airlines   41
Schick Information Systems Ltd.   752
Schimmelpfeng GmbH   865
Schimmelpfeng GmbH   866
Schimmelpfeng Information Broker Service   866
Schimmelpfeng Informationsbroker   866
Schip & Schade   641
School of Library and Information Science - University of Western Ontario   1086
Schrifttum Bauwesen   373

Schrifttum Raumordnung Stadtebau Wohnungswesen   373
Schulbibliothek Aktuell   400
Schweizerische Koordinationsstelle fur Bildungsforschung   945
SCI Data Base   688
Scicon Ltd.   450
Scicon Ltd.   459
Scicon Ltd.   867
SCIDOC   885
Science. Technology. Industry.   965
Science Abstracts   549
Science and Technology Agency - Prime Minister's Office - Japan   632
Science and Technology Briefs   726
Science and Technology Collections in Canadian Government Libraries   152
Science & Technology Data Bank (SCITECH)   1033
Science and Technology Experts in ROC Data Base (Republic of China)   726
Science and Technology Information Center - National Science Council - Republic of China   726
Science and Technology Information Service   629
Science and Technology Library Network, Republic of China   726
Science and Technology Policies Information Exchange Programme   1016
Science Information Processing Center - University of Tsukuba   1080
Science Information Services in India   507
Science Reference Library - British Library   445
Science Reference Library - British Library   446
Scientific and Professional Meetings in Yugoslavia and Foreign Countries.   1121
Scientific and Technical Documentation Center - National Center for Scientific Research - France   356
Scientific and Technical Documentation Center - National Center for Scientific Research - France   377
Scientific and Technical Documentation Center - National Institute for Scientific Research - Portugal   821
Scientific and Technical Information   496
Scientific & Technical Information Network   901
Scientific and Technical Periodicals of Bangladesh   70
Scientific and Technical Research Centres in Australia   47
Scientific and Technical Research Council of Turkey   991
Scientific and Technical Societies of Canada   152
Scientific Clearinghouse and Documentation Services Division - National Science and Technology Authority - Philippines   808
Scientific Documentation Center in Oncology - National Center for Scientific Research - France   357
Scientific Documentation Centre Ltd.   868
Scientific Group Thermodata Europe   451
Scientific Group Thermodata Europe   981
Scientific Information Center - Polish Academy of Sciences   816
Scientific Information Retrieval Section - Agriculture Canada   128
Scientific Meetings in ROC (Republic of China)   726
Scientific Numeric Databases - Canada Institute for Scientific and Technical Information   155
Scientific Personnel in CSIR Laboratories Data Base   507
Scientific Policy, Research and Development in Canada   152
Scientific Research Abstracts in Republic of China   726
Scientific Serials in Australian Libraries   47
Scientists' Profile (Philippines)   808
Scientometrics   492
SCIMP (European Index of Management Periodicals)   481
SCIMP/SCANP Thesaurus   481
SCITECH (Science & Technology Data Bank)   1033
SCMO (Studie- en Informatiecentrum TNO voor Milieu-Onderzoek) - Nederlandsche Centrale Organisatie voor Toegepast-Natuurwetenschappelijk Onderzoek   743
SCOLCAP (Scottish Libraries Co-operative Automation Project)   869
SCOLCAT   869
Scotland - National Library of Scotland   869
Scotland's Top 500 Companies   636
Scots Law Times (Eurolex)   314
Scottish Libraries Co-operative Automation Project   869
SCPI (Small Computer Program Index)   17
SDC (Scientific Documentation Centre Ltd.)   868
SDC (System Development Corporation)   951
SDC (System Development Corporation)   952
SDC Bulletin   868
SDC Information Services   951
SDC Information Services - Europe   951
SDF (Standard Drug File)   277
SDI (Service de Documentation Interministerielle) - Centre National d'Etudes des Telecommunications - France   367
SDI/Laval & Telereference Service - Laval University Library   652
SDIM (System Dokumentation Information Metallurgie)   522
SDOE Data Base   194
SDOI Data Base   194
SDPA (STATUS Data Preparation Aid)   433
SDSB (Sub-area Statistical Data Base), Statistics Sweden   932
SEA Abstracts   808
Sea Beam Data Bank   347

SEANCE 343
SEARCA (Southeast Asian Regional Center for Graduate Study and Research in Agriculture) 889
Search/J - System Development Corporation of Japan, Ltd. 952
Search Program for Infrared Spectra (SPIR) 155
Searching in Free Text (SIFT) 768
Searching the Eighteenth Century 443
Seat-Belt Defense Cases 829
SEBAN Data Base 965
SECOBI (Servicio de Consulta a Bancos de Informacion) - Consejo Nacional de Ciencia y Tecnologia - Mexico 701
Secretariat d'Etat aux PTT - France 367
Secretariat General du Gouvernement - France 384
Secretary of State for Posts and Telecommunications - France 367
Securities Data Base (Financial Post) 680
SEDES (Societe d'Etudes pour le Developpement Economique et Social) 881
Sediment Data for Canadian Rivers 142
Sediment Data Reference Index 142
SEDIS (Service Information-Diffusion) - Institut National de Recherche en Informatique et en Automatique - France 361
SEDS Data Base (I.P. Sharp Associates) 871
SEED (Soviet and East European Data) 1033
Seed Abstracts 229
SEF Notices 251
Seguridad e Higiene en el Trabajo (SEHIT) Data Base 892
SEHIT (Seguridad e Higiene en el Trabajo) Data Base 892
Seismic Crew Count Data Base (I.P. Sharp Associates) 871
Seismological Central Observatory GRF 414
Seismologisches Zentralobservatorium GRF 414
SELDOM (Selective Dissemination of MARC) 1068
SELECT MAIL - Compusearch Market and Social Research Ltd. 236
Selected Bibliography of Hungarian Economic Books and Articles 491
Selected Journals on Water 887
Selecting Equipment for Online Information Retrieval 775
Selection of International Railway Documentation 600
Selective Cooperative Indexing of Management Periodicals (SCIMP) 481
Selective Design Data Collection 494
Selective Dissemination of MARC 1068
Selective Inventory of Information Services 1022
Selective Record Service - Bibliographic Services Division - British Library 439
SELECVAL Data Bank 251
Selskostopanska Akademiya - Bulgaria 121
SEMP (Societe d'Editions Medico-Pharmaceutiques) 693
Sempex 693
Senior Update 1099
Sentrum vir Wetenskaplike en Tegniese Inligting - Wetenskaplike en Nywerheidnavorsingsraad - South Africa 885
Serials in the British Library 439
SERIE 625
Serie Informacion y Documentacion 202
Series of Philippine Scientific Bibliographies 808
SERIX (Swedish Environmental Research Index) 926
Servi-Tech 870
Service Annuaire Electronique 552
Service Bases de Donnes - Association Francaise de Normalisation 382
Service Calvados 22
Service de Documentation - Centre d'Etudes Nucleaires de Saclay 339
Service de Documentation Industrielle - Centre de Recherches de Pont-a-Mousson 820
Service des Impressions de la Documentation Parlementaire et de l'Informatique 343
Service d'Etude des Sols - Laboratoire de Science du Sol - Institut National de la Recherche Agronomique - France 362
Service d'Information Documentaire - Societe Nationale Elf Aquitaine 723
Service Directory 1099
Service Documentation - Centre de Creation Industrielle 184
Service Documentation - Societe MERLIN GERIN 696
Service Documentation - Societe MERLIN GERIN 697
Service Dossiers 834
Service Geologique National - France 340
Service Geologique National - France 341
Service Information-Diffusion - Institut National de Recherche en Informatique et en Automatique - France 361
Service Information-Diffusion (SEDIS) Data Bases 361
Service Information et Documentation - Institut du Verre 429
Service National Geologique - France 342
Service Technique de l'Urbanisme Centre de Documentation sur l'Urbanisme 1091
Servicio de Consulta a Bancos de Informacion - Consejo Nacional de Ciencia y Tecnologia - Mexico 701
Servico de Acesso a Bancos de Dados - Companhia Portuguesa Radio Marconi 822
SERVIR 102
Servizio Biblioteca Nazionale - Italy 811

SEVENTEL 245
SFS (Suomen Standardisoimisliitto) 334
SFS Catalogue 334
SGB (Societe Generale de Banque) 73
SGN (Service Geologique National) - France 340
SGTE (Scientific Group Thermodata Europe) 451
SGTE (Scientific Group Thermodata Europe) 981
SGU (Sveriges Geologiska Undersokning) 920
Share Price Record 1060
Sharp (I.P.) Associates Limited 871
Sharp (I.P.) Newsletter 871
SHARP APL 871
Shiloah Research Center for Middle Eastern and African Studies 970
Ship Abstracts 872
Ship Abstracts Data Base 767
Ship Abstracts Data Base 872
Ship Research Institute of Norway 872
SHIPDES 685
SHIPDES Manual 685
Shirley Institute 873
SHL (Systemhouse Ltd.) 953
SIA Computer Services 207
SIBB Data Base 194
SIBIL (Systeme Informatise pour Bibliotheques) 664
SIC (Systeme Informatique pour la Conjoncture) 364
Sicherheitstechnische Dokumentation (SIDOK) Data Base 419
SIDOK (Sicherheitstechnische Dokumentation) Data Base 419
Siemens AG 874
Siemens AG 875
Siemens AG 876
SIEN Data Base 102
SIENA Data Bank 224
SIFT (Searching in Free Text) 768
SIGEDA 611
SIGLE (System for Information on Grey Literature in Europe) 226
SIGMA 356
Signposts Prestel Data Base 462
Silver Trends 228
SIMBAD 905
SIMSYS (Simulation System) 536
Simulation System (SIMSYS) 536
SINFDOK (Statens Rad for Vetenskaplig Information och Dokumentation) 937
Singapore Corporate Statistics Data Base (I.P. Sharp Associates) 871
Singapore Industrial Technical Information Service (ITIS) Data Base 877
Singapore Institute of Standards and Industrial Research 877
Singapore/Malaysia Conferences on Health and Related Sciences 1073
Singapore Stock Exchange Data Base (I.P. Sharp Associates) 871
SINGCORP Data Base (I.P. Sharp Associates) 871
SINGSTOCK Data Base (I.P. Sharp Associates) 871
SINT/NB 965
SINT/SD 965
SINTO (National Scientific and Technical Information System) - Poland 815
SIP (Societa Italiana per l'Esercizio Telefonico) 622
SIPO (Swiss Intellectual Property Office) - Switzerland 948
SIRC (Sport Information Resource Centre) - Coaching Association of Canada 210
SIRIS (Department of Scientific and Industrial Research Indexing System) 748
SIRLS (Information Retrieval System for the Sociology of Leisure and Sport) 1085
SIRLS Descriptor List & Thesaurus 1085
SIRLS User's Manual 1085
SIROCAT 47
SIS (Standards Information Service) - Standards Council of Canada 898
SIS (Supplier Identification System) 671
SIS (Swedish Standards Institution) 940
SISDATA (Statistical Information System) Data Banks 878
Sistema de Alerta Bibliografico Especializado (SABE) Data Base 605
Sistema de Documentacion sobre Poblacion en America Latina 1007
Sistema Nacional de Informacao e Documentacao Agricola 99
Sistema Nacional de Informacion - Fondo Colombiano de Investigaciones Cientificas 212
Sistemi Telematici srl 950
SITC Data Base (I.P. Sharp Associates) 871
SITI (Swiss Institute for Technical Information) 948
Situation Economique 681
16mm Films Available from the Public Libraries of Metropolitan Toronto 699
SJRUNDS Data Base (I.P. Sharp Associates) 871
SKBF (Schweizerische Koordinationsstelle fur Bildungsforschung) 945
SkyGuide 23
Skytrack - Prestel 448
SLAMARK International 878
Slavic Philology (SLAVICA) 1033

MASTER INDEX

SLAVICA (Slavic Philology) 1033
SLC (Special Libraries Cataloguing, Inc.) 894
SLIGOS 879
SLIGOS 881
SLUG (STATUS in Libraries Group) 900
Small Animal Abstracts 229
Small Computer Program Index 17
SMART (University of Saskatchewan Libraries Machine-Assisted Reference Teleservices) 1067
Smart Card System 552
SMC (Manitoba Statute Citator) 173
SMS (Survey Management System) 1072
SNEA (Societe Nationale Elf Aquitaine) 723
SNEI (Societe Nouvelle d'Editions Industrielles) 252
SNEI (Societe Nouvelle d'Editions Industrielles) 514
SNG (Service National Geologique) - France 342
SNI (Sistema Nacional de Informacion) - Fondo Colombiano de Investigaciones Cientificas 212
SNIDA (Sistema Nacional de Informacao e Documentacao Agricola) 99
SNV (Statens Naturvardsverk) 926
SOC Data Base 949
Sociaal-Wetenschappelijk Informatie- en Documentatiecentrum 847
Sociaal-Wetenschappelijk Informatie- en Documentatiecentrum 848
Social and Human Science Documentation Centre - United Nations Educational, Scientific and Cultural Organization 1022
Social and Human Science Documentation Centre Information Note 1022
Social and Labour Bulletin 591
Social Science Computing Laboratory - University of Western Ontario 1087
Social Science Data Archives - Department of Sociology and Anthropology - Carleton University. 178
Social Science Data Archives - Research School of Social Sciences - Australian National University 61
Social Science Documentation Centre - Indian Council of Social Science Research 511
Social Science Information and Documentation Center - Royal Netherlands Academy of Arts and Sciences 847
Social Science Information and Documentation Center - Royal Netherlands Academy of Arts and Sciences 848
Social Science Information System - Institute for Behavioural Research - York University 1120
Social Science Journal File 1120
Social Science Research Council 291
Social Sciences Information Center - Association of Social Sciences Institutes 43
Sociedade Brasileira de Cultura Inglesa 24
Societa Finanziaria Telefonica 620
Societa Italiana per l'Esercizio Telefonico 622
Societe d'Editions Medico-Pharmaceutiques 693
Societe d'Etudes pour le Developpement Economique et Social 881
Societe Francaise d'Etudes et de Realisations d'Equipements de Radiodiffusion et de Television 383
Societe France-Aquaculture 348
Societe Generale de Banque 73
Societe MERLIN GERIN 696
Societe MERLIN GERIN 697
Societe Nationale Elf Aquitaine 723
Societe Nouvelle d'Editions Industrielles 252
Societe Nouvelle d'Editions Industrielles 514
Societe pour l'Informatique 233
Societe Quebecoise d'Information Juridique 834
Society for Information and Documentation 583
Society for Information and Documentation 880
Society for the Study of Economic and Social Development 881
Society of Metaphysicians Ltd. 882
Socioeconomic Data Bank on the Mediterranean Countries 564
Sociology of Leisure & Sport Abstracts 1085
Socioscope Inc. 883
SOFRATEV (Societe Francaise d'Etudes et de Realisations d'Equipements de Radiodiffusion et de Television) 383
SOF'SPOT Microcomputer Software Directory 67
Software Abstracts for Engineers 208
Soil Information System - Netherlands Soil Survey Institute 746
Soil Science Laboratory - National Institute of Agronomic Research - France 362
Soil Studies Service - Soil Science Laboratory - National Institute of Agronomic Research - France 362
Soils and Fertilizers 229
SOL (INRIA) 361
SOL (Solid Waste Management) Data Base 140
Solar and Wind Energy Research Program Index 16
Solar and Wind Energy Research Program Information Centre - Alberta Research Council 16
Solid-Liquid Flow Abstracts 86
Solid Waste 767
Solid Waste Management (SOL) Data Base 140
Solid Waste Management Data Bank (AWIDAT) 411
Solid Waste Management in Developing Countries 507
SOLIS (Sozialwissenschaftliches Literaturinformationssystem) 43
SOM Data Base (I.P. Sharp Associates) 871
SOMED-A 539
SONAR 102
Sonoptic Communications Inc. 884
Sonoptic Media & Communications Corporation 884
SOQUIJ (Societe Quebecoise d'Information Juridique) 834
Soreq Nuclear Research Center - Israel Atomic Energy Commission 618
Sorghum and Millets Abstracts 229
SOS (Official Statistics of Sweden) 932
Sources of Australian Economic Information 520
Sources of Australian Financial Information 520
Sources of Australian Rural Information 520
Sources of Foreign Statistical Data 493
South Africa - Atomic Energy Board 886
South Africa - Council for Scientific and Industrial Research 885
South Africa - Nuclear Development Corporation of South Africa 886
South Africa - South African Water Information Centre 887
South African Medical Research Council 888
South African Retrospective Information System 885
South African Selective Dissemination of Information 885
South African Water Abstracts 887
South African Water Information Centre 887
Southam Inc. 67
Southam Inc. 518
Southeast Asian Regional Center for Graduate Study and Research in Agriculture 889
Southern Cone Report 651
Soviet and East European Data (SEED) 1033
SOVIN (Samenwerkingsverband voor Opleiding en Vorming op het Terrein van de Informatieverzorging via Netwerken) 211
Sowietische Wissenschaftlich-Technische Institutionen und Ihre Veroffentlichungen 1031
Soyabean Abstracts 229
Sozialwissenschaftliches Literaturinformationssystem (SOLIS) 43
Space Components (SPACECOMPS) Data Bank 317
SPACECOMPS (Space Components) Data Bank 317
Spain - Higher Council for Scientific Research 890
Spain - Higher Council for Scientific Research 891
Spain - Higher Council for Scientific Research 1082
Spain - Ministry of Health and Safety 892
Spanish Drug Information Center 893
Spanish Medical Index 1082
Spanish Pharmaceutical Specialities Data Bank 893
SPARTAK 995
Special Libraries Cataloguing, Inc. 894
Special Programme of Informatics for Development 554
Special Reports (Latin American Newsletters Ltd.) 651
Specialist Newsletters 53
Specialist Software Ltd. 895
Specialized Department for Terminology and Computer Applications - Commission of the European Communities 223
SPHINX Data Base 363
SPI (Societe pour l'Informatique) 233
SPIDEL 233
SPIN (Strategies and Policies for Informatics) 554
SPINDE (Special Programme of Informatics for Development) 554
SPINES (Science and Technology Policies Information Exchange System) 1016
SPINES Feasibility Study 1016
SPINES Subject Categories 1016
SPINES Thesaurus 1016
SPIR (Search Program for Infrared Spectra) 155
SPIRES Data Base Management 1033
SPIRES Reference to Data Library and Programlist 1033
SPIRES Searching of ERIC Data Bases 1033
SPOLIT (Sportliteratur) Data Base 420
Sport and Recreation for the Disabled 210
Sport and Recreation Index 210
Sport and Sports-Scientific Information System 420
Sport Bibliography 210
SPORT Data Base 210
Sport Information Resource Centre - Coaching Association of Canada 210
Sport Thesaurus 210
Sport und Sportwissenschaftliche Informationssystem 420
Sportdokumentation: Literatur der Sportwissenschaft 420
Sportliteratur (SPOLIT) Data Base 420
Sports Council 896
Sports Medicine 5
SPPB (Statens Psykologisk-Pedagogiska Bibliotek) 924
SPPE (Syndicat Professionel des Publications Electroniques) 1
SRDA (Systeme de Renseignements sur les Decisions de l'Accise) 828
SRZ (Satz Rechen Zentrum) 401
SRZ (Satz Rechen Zentrum) 476
SRZ Berlin 401
SRZ Berlin 476
SSC (Sample Survey Centre) - University of Sydney 1072

SSCL (Social Science Computing Laboratory) - University of Western Ontario 1087
SSCL Newsletter 1087
SSDA (Social Science Data Archives) - Department of Sociology and Anthropology - Carleton University 178
SSDA (Social Science Data Archives) - Research School of Social Sciences - Australian National University 61
SSDA Data Catalogue 61
SSDC (Social Science Documentation Centre) - Indian Council of Social Science Research 511
SSIS (Social Science Information System) - Institute for Behavioural Research - York University 1120
SSIS (Social Science Information System) Data Base 1120
SSRC (Social Science Research Council) 291
SSVA Data Base 623
Staatsbedrijf der Posterijen, Telegrafie, en Telefonie 738
Stacs Information Systems Ltd. 897
Stacs Record Centre Ltd. 897
Stadt- und Universitatsbibliothek Frankfurt 368
STALUS (Statute Law Updating Service) Data Base 517
Stand der Gesetzgebung des Bundes 422
STANDARD - Norwegian Standards Association 772
Standard Drug File (SDF) 277
Standard-Profildienst Schweisstechnik 418
Standards Council of Canada 898
Standards Information Service - Standards Council of Canada 898
State Deposit and Consignment Bank 71
State Energy Data System Data Base (I.P. Sharp Associates) 871
State-of-the-Art Reports (German Foundation for International Development) 397
State University of Utrecht Library 899
Statens Naturvardsverk 926
Statens Psykologisk-Pedagogiska Bibliotek 924
Statens Rad for Vetenskaplig Information och Dokumentation 937
Statens Vag- och Trafikinstitut - Sweden 925
Statens Vagverk - Sweden 933
STATEX Data Base (I.P. Sharp Associates) 871
STATISBUND Data Base (I.P. Sharp Associates) 871
Statistical Data Bases Unit - Statistics Sweden 932
Statistical Economic Documentation 425
Statistical Indicators for Asia and the Pacific 1004
Statistical Information System (SISDATA) Data Banks 878
Statistical Methods 493
Statistical Office of the European Communities 224
Statistical Office of the European Communities 225
Statistical Review 493
Statistical Services and Integration Branch - Central Statistics Bureau - British Columbia Ministry of Industry and Small Business Development 106
Statistics Canada 159
Statistics Canada 160
Statistics Division - Economic and Social Commission for Asia and the Pacific - United Nations 1004
Statistics Division - Food and Agriculture Organization 1014
Statistics of Foreign Trade (OECD) 780
Statistics of Foreign Trade, Monthly Bulletin 780
Statistics of Individual Railways 600
Statistics of Postal Services 1030
Statistics Section - Air Transport Bureau - International Civil Aviation Organization 569
Statistics Sweden 932
Statistique des Services Postaux 1030
Statistiques Mensuelles de la Bourse de Paris 389
Statistische Wirtschaftsdokumentation 425
Statistisk Sentralbyra 766
Statistiska Centralbyran 932
Statisztikai Modszerek Temadokumentacio 493
Statisztikai Szemle 493
Statni Lekarska Knihovna - Czechoslovakia 250
STATSID 723
STATUS 433
STATUS Data Preparation Aid 433
STATUS in Libraries Group 900
Status of Federal Legislation 422
STATUS Report Generator 433
STATUS Thesaurus 433
STATUS Users Group 900
STATUS Users Group Newsletter 900
Statute Law Updating Service (STALUS) Data Base 517
Statutes of Alberta 828
Statutes of British Columbia 828
Statutes of Manitoba 828
Statutes of New Brunswick 828
Statutes of Ontario 828
Statutes of Saskatchewan 828
Statutory Orders and Regulations 828
Statuts Revises du Canada 828
Steam Package 548
Steel Analysis 89

Steel and Iron Materials Data 399
Steel Information System - German Iron and Steel Engineers Association 399
Steel Monitor 228
Steel Products Database 238
STEELDOC Data Base 979
STEELFACTS/S 399
STEELFACTS/T 399
Steinmetz Archives 848
Steinmetz Archives Catalogue and Guide 848
Stellar Data Center - Strasbourg Observatory 905
Stellar Data Center - Strasbourg Observatory 995
Stellar Data Center Bulletin 905
STERIC Data Base 1076
STIBOKA (Stichting voor Bodemkartering) 746
STIC (Science and Technology Information Center) - National Science Council - Republic of China 726
Stichting Eurodata 303
Stichting Nederlands Orgaan voor de Bevordering van de Informatieverzorging 744
Stichting Nederlandse Informatie Combinatie 737
Stichting voor Bodemkartering 746
Stiftung Wissenschaft und Politik 337
STIPA (Systeme de Transfert de l'Information Pedologique et Agronomique) Data Bank 362
STN International 901
Stock Exchange, The 902
Stock Exchange TOPIC Data Base 902
STOCKBROKER 318
Stockholm School of Economics 903
Stockholm University Computing Center, QZ 904
Stockholms Datamaskincentral 904
Stockmarket Indices, Interest and Exchange Rates, and Commodities Data Base (Datastream) 267
Stoy-Indeks 767
Strasbourg Observatory 905
Strasbourg Observatory 995
Strasbourg Observatory Stellar Data Center Data Bases 905
Strategies and Policies for Informatics 554
STRC (Scientific and Technical Research Centres in Australia) 47
Streamline 267
String Indexing: NEPHIS 1086
STRIX 638
Studie- en Informatiecentrum TNO voor Milieu-Onderzoek - Nederlandsche Centrale Organisatie voor Toegepast-Natuurwetenschappelijk Onderzoek 743
Studsvik Energiteknik AB 906
Sub-area Statistical Data Base (SDSB), Statistics Sweden 932
Subject Analysis Systems Collection - Faculty of Library and Information Science Library - University of Toronto 1077
Subject Authority Fiche 441
Subject Authority of Community Information Subject Headings 525
Subject Index on Marine and Estuarine Pollution 684
Subject Systems Office - Bibliographic Services Division - British Library 441
Subscriber's Supplement to the Quarterly Canadian Forecast 238
Subsoil Data Bank 341
Summaries of Cases to be Heard by the Supreme Court of Canada 173
Summaries of Foreign-Language Articles 873
Summary of Monitoring Information Received by the IFRB 606
Summer Fun/Winter Fun 1099
Sunrise Update 520
Suomen Kirjallisuus 482
Suomen Standardisoimisliitto 334
Suplemento Internacional del Indice Medico Espanol 1082
Supplier Identification System (SIS) 671
Supply Sources Information System - Information Systems and Data Banks Department - German Society for Chemical Equipment 406
Supreme Court of Canada Decisions 1108
Supreme Court of Canada Reports 828
SUPRIR 102
Surface Coatings Abstracts 792
Surface Water Data 142
Surface Water Data Reference Index 142
Survey Force Ltd. 907
Survey Management System (SMS) 1072
Survey of Consumer Buying Intentions (AERIC) 238
Survey of Futures Studies 540
Survey of Large Scale Stores Databank 754
Survey of Scientists and Engineers in Republic of China 726
Survey of the Science of Science Information 816
Survey of UK Online Users 775
SUSIS (Sport und Sportwissenschaftliche Informationssystem) 420
Svensk Bokforteckning 931
Svensk Byggjanst 934
Svenska Dagbladet 553
Svenska Kommunforbundet 116
Svenska Tidningsartiklar 116

Svenska Tidskriftsartiklar 116
Sveriges Allmanna Biblioteksforening 116
Sveriges Geologiska Undersokning 920
Sveriges Lantbruksuniversitet 941
Sveriges Mekanforbund 939
SVIPA (Swiss Viewdata Information Providers Association) 946
SVIPA Newsletter 946
SVP Australia 908
SVP Benelux 909
SVP Canada 910
SVP Conseil 911
SVP Espana 912
SVP France 913
SVP/INTERFACT 553
SVP Italia 914
SVP Korea 915
SVP Network 553
SVP Network 756
SVP Network 908
SVP Network 909
SVP Network 910
SVP Network 911
SVP Network 912
SVP Network 913
SVP Network 914
SVP Network 915
SVP Network 916
SVP Network 917
SVP Network 918
SVP Sijthoff 916
SVP South Africa Ltd. 917
SVP United Kingdom 918
SWEDAGRI 941
Sweden - Geological Survey of Sweden 920
Sweden - Karolinska Institute Library and Information Center 921
Sweden - National Board of Health and Welfare 922
Sweden - National Board of Occupational Safety and Health 923
Sweden - National Central Bureau of Statistics 932
Sweden - National Library for Psychology and Education 924
Sweden - National Road and Traffic Research Institute 925
Sweden - National Swedish Environment Protection Board 926
Sweden - National Swedish Telecommunications Administration 927
Sweden - Patent and Registration Office 928
Sweden - Research Institute of National Defense 929
Sweden - Royal Institute of Technology Library 930
Sweden - Royal Library 931
Sweden - Swedish National Road Administration 925
Sweden - Swedish National Road Administration 933
SWEDIS (Swedish Drug Information System) 922
SWEDIS (Swedish Drug Information System) Data Bases 922
Swedish Behavioural Science Research Reports 924
Swedish Behavioural Sciences (SBS) Data Base 924
Swedish Building Center 934
Swedish Center for Technical Terminology 979
Swedish Center for Working Life 935
Swedish Council for Information on Alcohol and Other Drugs 936
Swedish Council for Scientific Information and Documentation 937
Swedish Council of Environmental Information 926
Swedish Delegation for Scientific and Technical Information 937
Swedish Drug Information System 922
Swedish Environmental Research Index 926
Swedish Geotechnical Institute 925
Swedish Institute of Building Documentation 938
Swedish Ironmasters Association 979
Swedish Library Association 116
Swedish Market Information Bank 824
Swedish Mechanical and Electrical Engineering Trade Association 939
Swedish National Bibliography 931
Swedish National Road Administration 933
Swedish Standards Institution 940
Swedish Standards Listed in Subject Groups 940
Swedish Union of Municipal Authorities 116
Swedish University of Agricultural Sciences 941
SWEMARC 931
SWERP (Solar and Wind Energy Research Program) Information Centre - Alberta Research Council 16
Swets & Zeitlinger 942
Swets Automated Independent Library System 942
Swets Catalogue of Serial Titles 942
Swets Info Bulletin 942
Swets Serials Title Database 942
Swets Subscription Service 942
SWIDOC (Sociaal-Wetenschappelijk Informatie- en Documentatiecentrum) 847
SWIDOC (Sociaal-Wetenschappelijk Informatie- en Documentatiecentrum) 848
SWIFT 638
SWINFED (Information on Educational Research and Development in Switzerland) Data Base 945

SWIS (Swiss Wildlife Information Service) 947
Swiss Academy of Medical Sciences 943
Swiss Center of Documentation in Microtechnology 944
Swiss Coordination Center for Research in Education 945
Swiss Institute for Technical Information 948
Swiss Intellectual Property Office - Switzerland 948
Swiss Viewdata Information Providers Association 946
Swiss Wildlife Information Service 947
Switzerland - Swiss Intellectual Property Office 948
SWP (Stiftung Wissenschaft und Politik) 337
SWP Thesaurus 337
SYD Data Base 949
Sydney Development Corporation 289
Sydney Stock Exchange Share Prices Data Base (I.P. Sharp Associates) 871
Sydney Stock Exchange Statex Prices Data Base (I.P. Sharp Associates) 871
SYDONI S.A. 949
SYDSTOCK Data Base (I.P. Sharp Associates) 871
SYGAL (System-Gaphyor-Language) 1063
Syndicat Professionel des Publications Electroniques 1
SYSTEL (Sistemi Telematici srl) 950
System Development Corporation 951
System Development Corporation 952
System Development Corporation of Japan, Ltd. 952
System Dokumentation Information Metallurgie 522
System for Documentation and Information in Metallurgy 522
System for Information on Grey Literature in Europe 226
System-Gaphyor-Language (SYGAL) 1063
System of Computerized Processing of Scientific Information 965
System of Documentary Reference of MINTER (INTERDOC) 100
System of Legislative Reference of MINTER (INTERLEGI) 100
Systeme de Renseignements sur les Decisions de l'Accise (SRDA) 828
Systeme de Transfert de l'Information Pedologique et Agronomique (STIPA) Data Bank 362
Systeme Informatique pour la Conjoncture 364
Systeme Informatise pour Bibliotheques 664
Systeme Integre pour les Bibliotheques Universitaires de Lausanne 664
Systemhouse Ltd. 953
Systems Analysis, Control and Design Activity - University of Western Ontario 1088
Systems and Planning Unit - University of Saskatchewan Library 1068
Szakirodalmi Tajekoztatok 496
Szamitastechnika 493
SZAMOK (International Computing Education and Information Center) - Central Statistical Office - Hungary 493
Szelektiv Tervezesi Adatgyujtemeny 494
SZISZ-EMIMAT Data Base 494
T.C. Library Services Ltd. 954
T.L. Robertson Library - Western Australian Institute of Technology 1107
T6 Data Base (I.P. Sharp Associates) 871
T9S Data Base (I.P. Sharp Associates) 871
TABCONT/CEPIS 794
TABL (Table Batch Retrieval System) 159
Table Batch Retrieval System (TABL) 159
Table des Codes Sources EDF (Electricite de France) 295
Table of Alberta Legislation 11
TAC-G GILTS 249
TALI (Tekniikan Aikakauslehti Indeksi) 483
Talking Books Catalog 699
TANDOC (Tanzania National Documentation Centre) 955
Tanzania - National Central Library 955
Tanzania National Documentation Centre 955
TAP (CANSIM Table Analysis Package) 159
TAR Paper 13
Tarex 693
Target Group Index - British Market Research Bureau Ltd. 109
Task Force Pro Libra 674
Taux de Rendement des Valeurs Francaises et des Valeurs des Autres Pays de la Zone Franc a Revenue Variable 389
Tax Advance Rulings 828
Tax and Charities 198
Tax Case Materials (Eurolex) 314
Taxen 844
Tayson Information Technology Inc. 956
Tayson Personal Videotex System 956
TBS (Tokyo Broadcasting System) 631
TC Library Services Ltd. 954
TCIC (Textile and Clothing Information Centre) 980
TEAM (Terminologie-Erfassungs- und Auswertungs- Methode) 876
TEARS (The Exeter Abstract Reference System) 319
Tech News (Greater London Council) 465
Technical Abstracts Journal 496
Technical and Economic Information on Building 494
Technical Center for Mechanical Industries 957
Technical Chemistry Laboratory - Federal Technical University 327

MASTER INDEX

Technical Division - Swedish National Road Administration 933
Technical Economic Information 496
Technical Export News 111
Technical Guide to the Australian Demographic Data Bank 60
Technical Help to Exporters - British Standards Institution 111
Technical Indexes Ltd. 958
Technical Information and Library Services - Transport and Road Research Laboratory - Departments of the Environment and Transport - Great Britain 455
Technical Information Branch - Chalk River Nuclear Laboratories 44
Technical Information Center 959
Technical Information Center 960
Technical Information Center 961
Technical Information Center 962
Technical Information-Documentation Consultants Ltd. 963
Technical Information Library 1031
Technical Information on Patents - Swiss Intellectual Property Office - Switzerland 948
Technical Information Section - Pulp and Paper Research Institute of Canada 827
Technical Information Service - Caribbean Industrial Research Institute 177
Technical Information Service - Finnish Pulp and Paper Research Institute 333
Technical Information Service - IEA Coal Research - International Energy Agency 782
Technical Information Service - Technical Research Centre of Finland 330
Technical Information Services - Whiteshell Nuclear Research Establishment 45
Technical Publications by JAERI Staff 627
Technical Research Centre of Finland 330
Technical Research Centre of Finland 938
Technical Services Automation - University of Saskatchewan Library 1068
Technical Services Department - The Stock Exchange 902
Technical Specifications for Using the Transpac Network 989
Technical Traders Bulletin 1109
Technical Union Catalogue (Netherlands) 240
Technical University of Aachen 964
Technical University of Wroclaw 965
Technisch-Chemisches Laboratorium - Eidgenossische Technische Hochschule 327
Technische Informationsbibliothek 1031
Technische Universitat Berlin 477
Technobank Program 967
Technocom 877
Technoinform 496
Technological Information Exchange System 1027
Technological Information System - Dutch State Mines 286
Technologie-Informationszentrum Gottingen GmbH 966
Technology Digest 34
Technology Highlights 632
Technology Information Center Gottingen 966
Technology Information Division - Canada Centre for Mineral and Energy Technology 131
Technology Resource Center 967
TECHNONET ASIA (Asian Network for Industrial Technology Information and Extension) 34
TECHNONET ASIA Newsletter 34
TECHSEARCH 615
TECLEARN 959
Tecnomedia 968
TECNON Consulting Group 799
TED (Tenders Electronic Daily) 227
Teikoku Bank and Company Yearbook 969
Teikoku Data Bank, Ltd. 969
Teikoku Ginko Kaisha Nenkan 969
Teikoku Information 969
Teikoku Joho 969
Teikoku Times 969
Tekniikan Aikakauslehti Indeksi 483
Teknillinen Informaatiopalvelulaitos - Valtion Teknillinen Tutkimuskeskus 330
Tel-Aviv University 970
Tele-Direct (Publications) Inc. 973
Telecom Canada 971
Telecom Canada 972
Telecommunication Journal 606
Telecommunications Annals 367
Teledata System 272
Teledoc 1064
TELEDOC Data Base 367
Teleglobe Canada 974
Teleguide 518
Telekurs Ag 975
Telekurs Investdata System Data Base 975
Telemap Ltd. 976
Telematique Program - Directorate of Telecommunications - France 552
Telepak 927
Telesat Canada 971
Telesat Canada 972
Telesystemes 977
TELETEL 552
Teletext Encoding System 764
Teletext Output of Price Information by Computer (TOPIC) 902
TeleWhich? 244
Telex Link - Prestel 448
TELEXPORT 796
Telichart 160
Telidon and Its Applications 883
Telidon Program - Canada Department of Communications 130
Telidon System Software (Infomart) 518
Telidon Technology Development Center - Polytechnical School of Montreal 819
Telset 480
Tenders Electronic Daily 227
TENTTU Data Base 483
Teratology Lookout 921
TERMDOK Data Base 979
Terminals Guide (ECHO) 219
Terminological Data Banks 587
Terminologie-Erfassungs- und Auswertungs- Methode (TEAM) 876
Terminology and Documentation Section - Translations Branch - Ministry of Foreign Affairs - Netherlands 732
Terminology Bank of Quebec 830
Terminology Evaluation and Acquisition Method (TEAM) 876
TERMINOQ 830
TermNet 587
TermNet News 587
Ternisien Listing 978
Teruleti Statisztika 493
TESA (Technical Services Automation) - University of Saskatchewan Library 1068
Tesauro de Informacion Industrial 193
TESS Search Service 979
TESS Sokservice 979
Text Query System (TQS) 657
Textile and Clothing Information Centre 980
Textile Digest 873
Textile Information and Documentation Center 390
Textile Information Services - Shirley Institute 873
Textile Information Treatment Users' Service 390
Textiles 873
TEXTLINE 335
TGI (Target Group Index) - British Market Research Bureau Ltd. 109
THE (Technical Help to Exporters) - British Standards Institution 111
The Birmingham Post & Mail 1102
The British Council 24
The British Council 108
The Economist Data Base (Datasolve World Reporter) 265
The Exeter Abstract Reference System 319
The Globe and Mail 430
The Globe and Mail Online 430
The Guardian Data Base (Datasolve World Reporter) 265
The Information Navigator 527
The Informetrica Model (TIM) 536
The London International Financial Futures Exchange Ltd. 672
The Metals Society 698
The Myer Emporium Ltd. 520
The Stock Exchange 902
The Welding Institute 1106
Theilheimer's Synthetic Methods of Organic Chemistry 274
THEMA 356
Themendienst (German Foundation for International Development) 397
Thermdoc Data Bank 981
Thermfact Ltd./Ltee. 691
Thermodata Association 981
Thermodata-Thermdoc Data Bank 981
Thermodynamic Data Banks 451
Thermodynamique (Institut Francais des Petroles) 387
Thermophysical Properties Center - Institute for High Temperatures - Academy of Sciences of the U.S.S.R. 996
Thermophysical Property Data Bank (DECHEMA) 404
THES Data Base 481
Thesaurus de SPHINX 363
Thesaurus des Liants Hydrauliques 188
Thesaurus EDF 295
Thesaurus for Information Processing in Sociology 571
Thesaurus for Parliamentary Materials (PARTHES) 422
Thesaurus Krankenhauswesen 477
Thesaurus Oceanologie 350
Thesaurus of Pulp and Paper Terms 827
Thesaurus of Rock and Soil Mechanics Terms 1056
Thesaurus Zerstorungsfreie Prufung 416
Theses Canadiennes 148

Theses Canadiennes sur Microfiches: Catalogue   148
Theses in Home Economics (THESIS)   1033
THESIS   481
THESIS (Theses in Home Economics)   1033
THORN EMI   264
THORN EMI   265
3RIP   795
ti (Technical Indexes Ltd.)   958
TI-Technical Information for Industry   885
TIB (Technische Informationsbibliothek)   1031
TIBORDER   1031
TID (Technology Information Division) - Canada Centre for Mineral and Energy Technology   131
Tidningarnas Telegrambyra   990
Tidningsdatabasen   94
TIES (Technological Information Exchange System)   1027
TIES Newsletter   1027
Tieteellisen Informoinnin Neuvosto   331
TII (European Association for the Transfer of Technologies, Innovation and Industrial Information)   306
Tijl Datapress   982
TIM (The Informetrica Model)   536
Timber Information Keyword Retrieval   983
Timber Pallet and Packaging Digest   983
Timber Research and Development Association   983
Time Series Data Base (TSDB), Statistics Sweden   932
Times Law Reports (Eurolex)   314
TIN (The Information Navigator)   527
Tin and Antimony Monitor   228
TINFO (Tieteellisen Informoinnin Neuvosto)   331
TINKER (Timber Information Keyword Retrieval)   983
TIPAT (Technical Information on Patents) - Swiss Intellectual Property Office - Switzerland   948
TIS (Technical Information Service) - Caribbean Industrial Research Institute   177
TIS (Technological Information System) - Dutch State Mines   286
TISDATA   286
TISFLO   286
Titels van Sociaalwetenschappelijk Onderzoek   847
Title List of ILO Publications and Documents   593
Titles of Social Science Research   847
TITUS (Textile Information Treatment Users' Service)   390
TMRK (Trade Marks Data Base)   166
TNO (Nederlandse Centrale Organisatie voor Toegepast-Natuurwetenschappelijk Onderzoek)   739
TNO (Nederlandsche Centrale Organisatie voor Toegepast-Natuurwetenschappelijk Onderzoek)   740
TNO (Nederlandsche Centrale Organisatie voor Toegepast-Natuurwetenschappelijk Onderzoek)   741
TNO (Nederlandsche Centrale Organisatie voor Toegepast-Natuurwetenschappelijk Onderzoek)   742
TNO (Nederlandsche Centrale Organisatie voor Toegepast-Natuurwetenschappelijk Onderzoek)   743
TNO Study and Information Center on Environmental Research - Netherlands Organization for Applied Scientific Research   743
Tokyo Broadcasting System   631
Tokyo Shoko Research, Ltd.   984
TOOL-IR (University of Tokyo On-Line Information Retrieval) System   1075
TOOL-IR Software   1075
TOPIC   902
Topics in Combustible Energy   386
Topographic Mapping Program of Canada   136
Topographical Survey Division - Department of Energy, Mines and Resources - Canada   136
Toronto Department of the City Clerk   985
Toronto Globe and Mail   430
Toronto Stock Exchange   986
Toronto Stock Exchange 300 Index and Stock Statistics   986
Torstar Corporation   518
Torteneti Statisztikai Fuzetek   493
Torteneti Statisztikai Kotetek   493
Tourism Division - Newfoundland Department of Development   751
Tourism Newfoundland   751
Tourism Research and Data Centre - Canada   137
Tourtel   297
TOX-INFO (Toxicological Information Service) - Karolinska Institute Library and Information Center   921
Tox-notiser   921
Toxicological Information Service - Karolinska Institute Library and Information Center   921
TQS (Text Query System)   657
TRACS (Transport and Road Abstracting and Cataloging System) Data Base   455
TRADA (Timber Research and Development Association)   983
Trade Descriptions Law Data Base   656
Trade Marks Data Base   166
Traded Options Data Base (Datastream)   267
Trademark Availability Searches   234

TRADSTAT (World Trade Statistics Database)   994
Traffic and Operating Data of AEA Airlines   41
TRAMIT Data Base   893
Transactions of Information Processing Society of Japan   529
TransCanada Telephone System   971
TransCanada Telephone System   972
TRANSDOC   309
TRANSIN   987
Transinove International   987
Translated Books Available from the BLLD   442
Translations Branch - Ministry of Foreign Affairs - Netherlands   732
Transnational Data Report   988
Transnational Data Reporting Service, Inc. (European Office)   988
Transpac   989
Transport and Road Abstracting and Cataloging System (TRACS) Data Base   455
Transport and Road Research Laboratory - Departments of the Environment and Transport - Great Britain   455
Transport Canada   161
TRAP   361
TRC (Technology Resource Center)   967
TRDC (Tourism Research and Data Centre) - Canada   137
Trends in Foreign Science and Technology   801
Tribology Index   417
Tribos: Tribology Abstracts   86
TRIBUN   343
Trivialnamenkartei   201
TROPAG Data Base   857
Tropical Geography   355
Tropical Oil Seeds Abstracts   229
TRRL (Transport and Road Research Laboratory) - Departments of the Environment and Transport - Great Britain   455
TSDB (Time Series Data Base), Statistics Sweden   932
TSE300 (Toronto Stock Exchange 300 Index and Stock Statistics)   986
Tsentar za Nauchno-Meditsinska Informatsiia - Bulgaria   120
Tsentur za Naouchno-Technicheska i Ikonomicheska Infomatsiya - Bulgaria   121
TSR (Tokyo Shoko Research, Ltd.)   984
Tsukuba University Library Information Processing System   1080
TT (Tidningarnas Telegrambyra)   990
TT Kalendern   260
TT Newsbank   990
TT Nyhetsbanken   990
Tudomanyos es Muszaki Tajekoztatas   496
TULIPS (Tsukuba University Library Information Processing System)   1080
Turbine Airliner Fleet Survey   68
TURDOK (Turkish Scientific and Technical Documentation Center)   991
Turkey - Scientific and Technical Research Council of Turkey   991
Turkish Dissertation Index   991
Turkish Scientific and Technical Documentation Center   991
Twenty Years of Indonesian Fiction 1940-1960: A Bibliography Selected from the IDC Collection   1073
UAP (International Office for the Universal Availability of Publications)   582
UB/TIB (Universitatsbibliothek Hannover und Technische Informationsbibliothek)   1031
UBC (International Office for Universal Bibliographic Control)   582
Ubersetzungszeitschriften   1031
UBO:BOK   1061
UCSL (Unilever Computer Services Ltd.)   993
UCSL (Unilever Computer Services Ltd.)   994
UDAC (Uppsala University Data Center)   922
UDC (Universal Decimal Classification)   578
UFORDAT (Data Bank for Environmental Research)   411
Uhde GmbH   992
Uhde Thermophysical Properties Program Package   992
UIC (Union des Industries Chimiques)   720
UIC (Union Internationale des Chemins de Fer)   600
UK Leisure Markets   484
UK MARC   439
UK Mineral Statistics   727
UK National Oceanographic Data Bank   730
UK Online Search Services   775
UKCIS (United Kingdom Chemical Information Service)   851
UKCSO Data Base (I.P. Sharp Associates)   871
UKCTRAIN   440
UKCTRAIN Workbook   440
UKOLUG (United Kingdom Online User Group)   1000
ULIDAT (Data Bank for Environmental Literature)   411
ULISYS (Universal Library Systems Ltd.)   1029
Ultuna Library   941
Ultunabiblioteket   941
Umea Universitet   1081
Umfragen aus der Empirischen Sozialforschung 1945-1982: Datenbestandskatalog   1045
UMPLIS (Informations- und Dokumentationssystem Umwelt) - Umweltbundesamt - Germany   411

Umweltbundesamt - Germany 411
UN/ESCAP Statistical Information Services - Statistics Division - Economic and Social Commission for Asia and the Pacific - United Nations 1004
Unde Thermophysical Properties Program Package 992
UNDP (United Nations Development Programme) 653
UNEP (United Nations Environment Programme) 1024
UNEP (United Nations Environment Programme) 1025
UNEP (United Nations Environment Programme) 1026
UNESCO (United Nations Educational, Scientific and Cultural Organization) 65
UNESCO (United Nations Educational, Scientific and Cultural Organization) 579
UNESCO (United Nations Educational, Scientific and Cultural Organization) 580
UNESCO (United Nations Educational, Scientific and Cultural Organization) 603
UNESCO (United Nations Educational, Scientific and Cultural Organization) 653
UNESCO (United Nations Educational, Scientific and Cultural Organization) 794
UNESCO (United Nations Educational, Scientific and Cultural Organization) 1015
UNESCO (United Nations Educational, Scientific and Cultural Organization) 1016
UNESCO (United Nations Educational, Scientific and Cultural Organization) 1017
UNESCO (United Nations Educational, Scientific and Cultural Organization) 1018
UNESCO (United Nations Educational, Scientific and Cultural Organization) 1019
UNESCO (United Nations Educational, Scientific and Cultural Organization) 1020
UNESCO (United Nations Educational, Scientific and Cultural Organization) 1021
UNESCO (United Nations Educational, Scientific and Cultural Organization) 1022
UNESCO (United Nations Educational, Scientific and Cultural Organization) 1023
UNESCO (United Nations Educational, Scientific and Cultural Organization) 1028
UNESCO/IBE Education Thesaurus 1021
UNESCO Journal of Information Science, Librarianship and Archives Administration 1019
UNESCO Social and Human Science Documentation Centre Data Base 1022
UNFPA (United Nations Fund for Population Activities) 1010
UNIBID (UNISIST International Centre for Bibliographic Descriptions) 1023
UNIDO (United Nations Industrial Development Organization) 1027
UNIDO Guides to Information Sources 1027
UNIDO Industrial Inquiry Service 1027
UNIDO Newsletter 1027
Unilever Computer Services Ltd. 993
Unilever Computer Services Ltd. 994
Unilever Holdings Ltd. 671
Unilever Ltd. 993
Unilever Ltd. 994
Unimedia Inc. 292
UNION (Union List of Scientific Serials in Canadian Libraries) 152
Union Catalog for Periodicals in Norwegian Libraries (SAMKATPER) 1061
Union Catalog of Foreign Acquisitions by Major Swedish Public Libraries 116
Union Catalog of Machine Readable Catalog Data of German Libraries 400
Union Catalog of Periodicals Held by Portuguese Libraries 821
Union Catalog of Scientific Periodicals in the Libraries of ROC (Republic of China) 726
Union Catalog of Scientific Periodicals in the Libraries of ROC (Republic of China) 726
Union Catalogue of Foreign Books in Swedish Research Libraries 931
Union Catalogue of Libraries in India 507
Union Catalogue of Scientific and Technical Periodicals in Libraries of Pakistan 793
Union Catalogue of Serials Division - Public Services Branch - National Library of Canada 151
Union Catalogue of Social Science Serials 511
Union Catalogues of Scientific and Technical Periodicals of the Libraries in Ankara, Izmir, and Istanbul 991
Union des Industries Chimiques 720
Union Internationale des Chemins de Fer 600
Union List of Abstracting and Indexing Services Received in Leading Libraries 616
Union List of Current Scientific Serials in India 507
Union List of Higher Degree Theses in Australian Libraries 1074
Union List of Periodicals in Tanzania 955
Union List of Scientific Periodicals in Libraries of the Republic of China 726

Union List of Scientific Serials in Canadian Libraries 152
Union List of Serials in Israel Libraries 478
Union List of Serials in the Social Sciences and Humanities Held by Canadian Libraries 151
Union List of Serials of NSTA Complex Libraries (Philippines) 808
Union List of Social Science Periodicals 511
Union List of Technion Recent Acquisitions 1051
Union of Soviet Socialist Republics - Academy of Sciences of the U.S.S.R. 995
Union of Soviet Socialist Republics - Academy of Sciences of the U.S.S.R. 996
Union of Soviet Socialist Republics - Academy of Sciences of the U.S.S.R. 997
Union of Soviet Socialist Republics - All-Union Institute of Scientific and Technical Information 998
Union of Soviet Socialist Republics - U.S.S.R. State Committee for Science and Technology 998
Union of Soviet Socialist Republics - U.S.S.R. State Committee on the Utilization of Atomic Energy 999
U.S.S.R. Center for Nuclear Structure and Reaction Data 999
U.S.S.R. State Committee for Science and Technology 998
U.S.S.R. State Committee on the Utilization of Atomic Energy 999
Union Postale Universelle 1030
Union Technique Interprofessionnelle des Federations Nationales du Batiment et des Travaux Publics 610
UNISIST (Universal System for Information in Science and Technology) 587
UNISIST (Universal System for Information in Science and Technology) 603
UNISIST (Universal System for Information in Science and Technology) 1019
UNISIST (Universal System for Information in Science and Technology) 1023
UNISIST International Centre for Bibliographic Descriptions 1023
UNISIST Newsletter (General Information Programme) 1019
United Kingdom Central Statistical Office Data Base (I.P. Sharp Associates) 871
United Kingdom Chemical Information Service 851
United Kingdom Macro-Economic Data Bank 449
United Kingdom Marine Biological Association 684
United Kingdom National Oceanographic Data Bank 730
United Kingdom National Oceanographic Data Centre 730
United Kingdom National Serials Data Centre 439
United Kingdom Online User Group 1000
U.K. Quoted Company Service 690
U.K. Trade Marks Journal 235
U.K. Treasury Databank 456
U.K. Treasury Macroeconomic Forecasting Model and Databank 456
U.K. Unquoted Company Service 690
United Nations 591
United Nations 592
United Nations 593
United Nations 595
United Nations 606
United Nations 1001
United Nations 1002
United Nations 1003
United Nations 1004
United Nations 1005
United Nations 1006
United Nations 1007
United Nations 1008
United Nations 1009
United Nations 1010
United Nations 1011
United Nations 1012
United Nations 1013
United Nations 1014
United Nations 1030
United Nations 1110
United Nations 1111
United Nations 1112
United Nations 1113
United Nations 1114
United Nations 1115
United Nations Administrative Committtee on Co-ordination 1001
United Nations Commodity Trade Statistics Data Base (I.P. Sharp Associates) 871
United Nations Development Programme 653
United Nations Development Programme 1005
United Nations Educational, Scientific and Cultural Organization 65
United Nations Educational, Scientific and Cultural Organization 579
United Nations Educational, Scientific and Cultural Organization 580
United Nations Educational, Scientific and Cultural Organization 603
United Nations Educational, Scientific and Cultural Organization 653
United Nations Educational, Scientific and Cultural Organization 794
United Nations Educational, Scientific and Cultural Organization 1015
United Nations Educational, Scientific and Cultural Organization 1016
United Nations Educational, Scientific and Cultural Organization 1017

United Nations Educational, Scientific and Cultural Organization   1018
United Nations Educational, Scientific and Cultural Organization   1019
United Nations Educational, Scientific and Cultural Organization   1020
United Nations Educational, Scientific and Cultural Organization   1021
United Nations Educational, Scientific and Cultural Organization   1022
United Nations Educational, Scientific and Cultural Organization   1023
United Nations Educational, Scientific and Cultural Organization   1028
United Nations Environment Programme   1024
United Nations Environment Programme   1025
United Nations Environment Programme   1026
United Nations Fund for Population Activities   1010
United Nations High Commissioner for Refugees   602
United Nations Industrial Development Organization   1027
United Nations Inter-Organization Board for Information Systems   1001
United Nations University   1028
United Nations University Referral Service System Data Base   1028
U.S. and European Crudes and Products Reports   505
U.S.-Asiatic Co., Ltd.   1092
United States Banks Data Base (I.P. Sharp Associates)   871
United States Bonds Data Base (I.P. Sharp Associates)   871
U.S.-BONDSPEC   895
United States Consumer Price Index Data Base (I.P. Sharp Associates)   871
United States Department of Energy Data Base (I.P. Sharp Associates)   871
United States Flow of Funds, Quarterly Data Base (I.P. Sharp Associates)   871
U.S. International Air Travel Statistics Data Base (I.P. Sharp Associates)   871
U.S. LPG Report   505
U.S. Patent Concordance   633
U.S. Patent Index   633
United States Petroleum Imports Data Base (I.P. Sharp Associates)   871
United States Producer Price Index Data Base (I.P. Sharp Associates)   871
United States Stock Market Data Base (I.P. Sharp Associates)   871
United States Stock Options Data Base (I.P. Sharp Associates)   871
United Way   525
Universal Decimal Classification   578
Universal Library Systems Ltd.   1029
Universal Postal Union   1030
Universal System for Information in Science and Technology   587
Universal System for Information in Science and Technology   603
Universal System for Information in Science and Technology   1019
Universal System for Information in Science and Technology   1023
Universidad de Valencia   1082
Universidad Mayor de San Andres   93
Universidad Nacional Autonoma de Mexico   719
Universita Degli Studi di Milano   1058
Universitat Bonn   1042
Universitat Dortmund   1046
Universitat Dusseldorf   1048
Universitat Hannover   1031
Universitat Hohenheim   487
Universitat Trier   1078
Universitat zu Koln   1045
Universitatsbibliothek Hannover und Technische Informationsbibliothek   1031
Universite Catholique de Louvain   611
Universite de Paris-Sud   1063
Universite de Sherbrooke   1071
Universite des Sciences Humaines de Strasbourg   205
Universite du Quebec   1064
Universite Laval Bibliotheque   652
Universite Libre de Bruxelles   611
Universite Rene Descartes   838
Universitetet i Trondheim   1079
Universitetsbiblioteket - Norges Tekniske Hogskole - Universitetet i Trondheim   1079
University Chemical Laboratory - Cambridge University   125
University Library - Norwegian Institute of Technology - University of Trondheim   1079
University Library/National Library for Science and Technology - Helsinki University of Technology   483
University Library of Hannover and Technical Information Library   1031
University of Aberdeen   1032
University of Aix-Marseille III   186
University of Alberta   1033
University of Alberta   1034
University of Alberta   1035
University of Alberta   1036
University of Alberta   1037
University of Arizona   229
University of Aston   1038
University of Bath   1039
University of Bergen   768

University of Bergen   1040
University of Birmingham   1041
University of Bonn   1042
University of British Columbia   1043
University of British Columbia   1044
University of British Columbia Data Library Catalogue   1044
University of Cologne   1045
University of Dortmund   1046
University of Dundee   1047
University of Dusseldorf   1048
University of Essex   291
University of Gothenburg   1049
University of Guelph Library   1050
University of Haifa Library   1051
University of Haifa Periodical Holdings   1051
University of Hannover   1031
University of Lausanne Libraries   664
University of Leeds   1052
University of Leeds   1053
University of Leicester   1054
University of London   1055
University of London   1056
University of Melbourne   1057
University of Milan   1058
University of New Brunswick Libraries   1059
University of New South Wales   1060
University of Oslo   1061
University of Paris-Nanterre   1062
University of Paris-South   1063
University of Provence   186
University of Quebec   1064
University of Reading Library   1065
University of Regina   1066
University of San Andres   93
University of Saskatchewan Libraries Machine-Assisted Reference Teleservices   1067
University of Saskatchewan Library   1067
University of Saskatchewan Library   1068
University of Saskatchewan Library Data Base   1068
University of Sheffield   1069
University of Sheffield   1070
University of Sherbrooke   1071
University of Sydney   1072
University of Sydney Library   1073
University of Tasmania Library   1074
University of the Humanities and Social Sciences of Strasbourg   205
University of Tokyo   1075
University of Tokyo   1076
University of Tokyo On-Line Information Retrieval System   1075
University of Toronto   1077
University of Toronto   1094
University of Toronto Library Automation Systems   1094
University of Trier   1078
University of Trondheim   1079
University of Tsukuba   1080
University of Tsukuba Online Processing of Information   1080
University of Umea   1081
University of Valencia   1082
University of Warwick Library   1083
University of Waterloo   1084
University of Waterloo   1085
University of Western Ontario   1086
University of Western Ontario   1087
University of Western Ontario   1088
University of Zurich   947
Unwin Brothers Ltd.   1089
Update AB   1090
Uppsala University Data Center   922
UPU (Union Postale Universelle)   1030
URBALINE   465
URBAMET (Urbanisme, Amenagement, Environnement et Transports) Data Base   1091
URBAMET Network   1091
Urban Abstracts   465
Urban Data Bank of Paris and the Paris Region   798
Urbanisme, Amenagement, Environnement et Transports (URBAMET) Data Base   1091
USACO Corporation   1092
USBANKS Data Base (I.P. Sharp Associates)   871
USBOND Data Base (I.P. Sharp Associates)   871
USCPI Data Base (I.P. Sharp Associates)   871
USDOE Data Base (I.P. Sharp Associates)   871
User Education Resources Data Base   204
User Manual to DC Host Centre   497
User News (Chisholm Institute of Technology Library)   204
Userlink Systems Ltd.   1093
USFLOW Data Base (I.P. Sharp Associates)   871
USOPT Data Base (I.P. Sharp Associates)   871
USPPI Data Base (I.P. Sharp Associates)   871

USSR Center for Nuclear Structure and Reaction Data 999
USSR State Committee for Science and Technology 998
USSR State Committee on the Utilization of Atomic Energy 999
USSTOCK Data Base (I.P. Sharp Associates) 871
Ustav Vedeckych Lekarskych Informaci - Czechoslovakia 250
Utlandska Nyforvarv 116
UTLAS Inc. 1094
UTLAS Newsletter 1094
UTOPIA (University of Tsukuba Online Processing of Information) 1080
UTOPIA User's Guide 1080
UVLI (Ustav Vedeckych Lekarskych Informaci) - Czechoslovakia 250
VA-NYTT 637
Vaccine Data Bank 1114
Vagdatabank - Technical Division - Swedish National Road Administration 933
Valencian Scientific Index 1082
Valtion Teknillinen Tutkimuskeskus 330
van Dijk (Marcel), SA; Bureau 122
van Halm (Johan) & Associates 1095
Vapor-Liquid Equilibrium Data Collection 1046
Vapour-Liquid-Equilibrium Package 548
VAT Tribunal Reports (Eurolex) 314
VCA (Virtual City Associates Ltd.) 1103
VDE (Verband Deutscher Elektrotechniker) 960
VDEh (Verein Deutscher Eisenhuttenleute) 398
VDEh (Verein Deutscher Eisenhuttenleute) 399
VDI (Verein Deutscher Ingenieure) 961
VDI (Verein Deutscher Ingenieure) 1096
VDI-Nachrichten 1096
VDI News Data Base 1096
VDI-Verlag GmbH 1096
VDMA (Verein Deutscher Maschinenbau-Anstalten) 961
Veaner (Allen B.) Associates 1097
Veckans Affarers Borsinformation 94
Vehicle Data Bank System 1104
Vengherskaya Literatura po Bibliotekovedeniu i Informatike - Referativny Zhurnal 495
VERA 939
Verband Deutscher Elektrotechniker 960
Verband Schweizerischer Bildschirmtext-Informationslieferanten 946
Verbundkatalog 400
Verein Deutscher Eisenhuttenleute 398
Verein Deutscher Eisenhuttenleute 399
Verein Deutscher Ingenieure 961
Verein Deutscher Ingenieure 1096
Verein Deutscher Maschinenbau-Anstalten 961
Verfahrenstechnische Berichte 77
Verlag Dokumentation Saur KG 863
Verlag Hoppenstedt & Co. 1098
Verres et Refractaires 429
Verzeichnis Deutscher Informations- und Dokumentationsstellen, Bundesrepublik Deutschland und Berlin (West) 880
Verzeichnis Informationswissenschaftlicher Zeitschriften 880
VETDOC (Veterinary Literature Documentation) 278
Veterinary Bulletin 229
Veterinary Faculty - Ludwig Maximilian's University 1114
Veterinary Literature Documentation 278
VIC (Vienna International Centre) Library - International Atomic Energy Agency 562
Victorian Motor Vehicle 1982 Registrations Data Base 237
Video Access 1099
Video-Gold 755
VideoAccess 1099
Videodisque 1
Videoinfo 705
Videomaster 755
Videorecordings Available in the Public Libraries of Metropolitan Toronto 699
Videotel 622
Videotex 1
Videotex: A Working Paper on the Study of Social Impact 883
Videotex America 518
Videotex Canada 973
Videotex Guide/Magazine 1
Videotex Industry Association Ltd. 1100
Videotex Information Service Providers Association of Canada 1101
Videotex International 1
Videotex Services Unit - Council for Educational Technology 247
Vidibord 738
Vidibus 738
Vidipoort 738
Viditel 738
Vienna International Centre Library - International Atomic Energy Agency 562
Vietnamese Collection of the ANU Library 1073
Viewdata Documentation Service Data Base 946
Viewdata Services - Communication Services Ltd. 231
Viewdata Services - Guinness Superlatives Limited 470

Viewdata Services - Hanover Press 473
Viewtel 202 Data Base 1102
Viewtel Services Ltd. 1102
VINE 818
VINITI (Vsesoyuznyy Institut Nauchnoy i Tekhnicheskoy Informatsii) 998
Virtual City Associates Ltd. 1103
VISDATA 479
VISPAC (Videotex Information Service Providers Association of Canada) 1101
VISPAC Newsletter 1101
VISTA 518
VITIS 585
VITIS-VEA (VITIS-Viticulture and Enology Abstracts) 585
VITIS-Viticulture and Enology Abstracts 585
Vocabulario Controlado do MINTER 100
Vocabulario Internacional de Termos Micrograficos 101
VOGIN (Nederlandse Vereniging van Gebruikers van Online Informatie-systemen) 734
Volkswagenwerk AG 1104
Volkswagenwerk Bibliographic Data Base 1104
Volkswagenwerk Referatedienst 1104
Vorschriften Informationssystem (VISDATA) Data Base 479
Vrije Universiteit Brussel 381
Vsesoyuznyy Institut Nauchnoy i Tekhnicheskoy Informatsii 998
VtB (Verfahrenstechnische Berichte) 77
VTI (Statens Vag- och Trafikinstitut) - Sweden 925
VTI Aktuellt 925
VTT (Valtion Teknillinen Tutkimuskeskus) 330
VTT Publications 330
VTT Research Notes 330
VTT Research Reports 330
VTT Symposium 330
VUB (Vrije Universiteit Brussel) 381
VUBIS 381
VUHZ (Vyzkumny Ustav Hutnictvi Zeleza, Dobra) 281
Vyzkumny Ustav Hutnictvi Zeleza, Dobra 281
Wage Rounds Data Bank 1032
WAIT (Western Australian Institute of Technology) 1107
WAIT Index to Newspapers 1107
Warren (L.M.), Inc. 1105
Warwick Statistics Service 1083
Washington Letter on Latin America 651
WASIRS (Women and Sports Information Retrieval System) Data Base 1033
Waste Management Information Bulletin 437
Waste Management Information Bureau - Waste Research Unit - Atomic Energy Research Establishment, Harwell 437
Waste Materials Biodegradation Research Titles 1038
Waste Research Unit - Atomic Energy Research Establishment, Harwell 437
WATCHDOG 810
WATDOC - Inland Waters Directorate - Environment Canada 140
WATDOC Database Descriptions 140
WATDOC Newsletter 140
Water Quality Branch - Inland Waters Directorate - Environment Canada 141
Water Quality Data File 626
Water Research Centre - Great Britain 463
Water Research Centre - Great Britain 464
Water Resources Branch - Inland Waters Directorate - Environment Canada 142
Water Supply & Sewage Engineering 203
Water Survey of Canada 142
WATERLIT 887
Waterloo Systems Specialists Ltd. 369
Waterloopkundig Laboratorium 268
WBANK Data Base (I.P. Sharp Associates) 871
WCL Data Base 1059
WDB (Werkstoffdatenbank) 399
WDEBT Data Base (I.P. Sharp Associates) 871
Weed Abstracts 229
Weekly Criminal Bulletin 162
Weekly Eurobond Guide 267
Weekly Law Reports (Eurolex) 314
Weekly Statistical Bulletin Data Base (I.P. Sharp Associates) 871
Weekly Survey of Periodicals (Finnish Pulp and Paper Research Institute) 333
Weekly Temperatures Data Base (I.P. Sharp Associates) 871
Weldasearch Abstracts 1106
Welding and Allied Processes Abstracts Journal 418
Welding Documentation 418
Welding Institute 1106
Welding Standard Profile Service 418
Werkstoffdaten Stahl-Eisen 399
Werkstoffdatenbank (WDB) 399
Werkstoffe und Korrosion 405
WEST Data Base 1107
West German Economic Outlook Survey Data Base (I.P. Sharp

Associates) 871
West German Statistical Data Base (I.P. Sharp Associates) 871
Western Australian Institute of Technology 1107
Western Legal Publications Ltd. 1108
Western Pacific Ocean Cooperative Study 628
Western Weekly Reports (WWR) 173
WESTPAC (Western Pacific Ocean Cooperative Study) 628
WESTPAC Newsletter 628
Wetenskaplike en Nywerheidnavorsingsraad - South Africa 885
Wharton Econometric Forecasting Associates Ltd. 207
Wheat, Barley and Triticale Abstracts 229
Whessoe Group 320
Which? 244
Whiteshell Nuclear Research Establishment 45
WHO (World Health Organization) 595
WHO (World Health Organization) 601
WHO (World Health Organization) 794
WHO (World Health Organization) 1110
WHO (World Health Organization) 1111
WHO (World Health Organization) 1112
WHO (World Health Organization) 1113
WHO (World Health Organization) 1114
WHO (World Health Organization) 1115
WHO Collaborating Centre for Collection and Evaluation of Data on Comparative Virology 1114
WHO Collaborating Centre for International Drug Monitoring 1115
Who is Doing What in Belguim 84
Who's Who in Europe 870
Who's Who Japan Data Base 969
WHOLESALE Data Base (I.P. Sharp Associates) 871
WHS (World Health Statistics) Data Base 1110
WI (The Welding Institute) 1106
WIIW Data Base (I.P. Sharp Associates) 871
Wildlife Research Database 947
Williams and Nevin 1093
Winged Bean Bibliography 889
Winged Bean Flyer 889
WIPO (World Intellectual Property Organization) 64
WIPO (World Intellectual Property Organization) 1116
Wira (Wool Industries Research Association) 873
WLP (Western Legal Publications) Data Base 1108
WMIB (Waste Management Information Bureau) - Waste Research Unit - Atomic Energy Research Establishment, Harwell 437
WMIB (Waste Management Information Bureau) Databank 437
WMO (World Meteorological Organization) 1117
WMO (World Meteorological Organization) 1118
WMO (World Meteorological Organization) 1119
WNNR (Wetenskaplike en Nywerheidnavorsingsraad) - South Africa 885
WNRE (Whiteshell Nuclear Research Establishment) 45
Wolff (Rudolf) & Co. Ltd. 1109
Wolff Charts Comprehensive Chart Service 1109
Wolff Research 1109
Women and Sports Information Retrieval System (WASIRS) Data Base 1033
Words and Phrases Used in the Pharmaceutical Industry 432
World Agricultural Economics and Rural Sociology Abstracts 229
World Bank Debt Tables Data Base (I.P. Sharp Associates) 871
World Climate Data Information Referral Service 1118
World Climate Programme Department - World Meteorological Organization 1118
World Coal Resources and Reserves Data Bank 783
World Coal Resources and Reserves Data Bank Service 783
World Conference on Transborder Data Flow Policies 554
World Congress of Agricultural Librarians and Documentalists: Proceedings 558
World Directory of National Science and Technology Policy-Making Bodies 1016
World Directory of Research Projects, Studies and Courses in Science and Technology Policy 1016
World Directory of Social Science Institutions 1022
World Economic Prospects 89
World Energy Information 753
World Exporter 264
World Glacier Inventory 139
World Gravimetric Data Bank 342
World Guide to Libraries 863
World Guide to Scientific Associations 863
World Guide to Terminological Activities 587
World Guide to Trade Associations 863
World Health Organization 595
World Health Organization 601
World Health Organization 794
World Health Organization 1110
World Health Organization 1111
World Health Organization 1112
World Health Organization 1113
World Health Organization 1114
World Health Organization 1115
World Health Statistics Annual 1110
World Health Statistics Data Base 1110
World Health Statistics Quarterly 1110
World Intellectual Property Organization 64
World Intellectual Property Organization 1116
World Inventory of Social Science Data Services 571
World List of Serial Titles in Aquatic Sciences and Fisheries 1008
World List of Social Science Periodicals 571
World List of Social Science Periodicals 1022
World Meteorological Organization 1117
World Meteorological Organization 1118
World Meteorological Organization 1119
World Mineral Statistics 727
World News about Building and Urban Development 494
World Patents Abstracts 275
World Patents Index 275
World Petrochemical Industry Data Bank 799
World Ports and Harbours Abstracts 86
World Reporter 265
World Request List for Neutron Data (WRENDA) 561
World Request List for Neutron Data (WRENDA) 785
World Surface Coatings Abstracts 792
World Textile Abstracts 873
World Textile Abstracts Printout Subject Indexes 873
World Textiles Database 873
World Trade Statistics Database 994
World Trademark Journal 234
World Transindex 608
World Viewdata Services 473
World Watch Service 234
World Weather Watch 1119
Worldwide Chemical Directory 612
Worldwide List of Published Standards 111
WPI (World Patents Index) 275
WRC (Water Research Centre) - Great Britain 463
WRC (Water Research Centre) - Great Britain 464
WRC Information 464
WRENDA (World Request List for Neutron Data) 561
WRENDA (World Request List for Neutron Data) 785
WSB Data Base (I.P. Sharp Associates) 871
WSCA (World Surface Coatings Abstracts) 792
WTA (World Textile Abstracts) 873
WTI (World Transindex) Data Base 608
WWR (Western Weekly Reports) 173
WWW (World Weather Watch) 1119
YBANK Data Base (I.P. Sharp Associates) 871
Year Book of Labour Statistics 592
Yearbook of North Africa 186
Yearbook of Regional Statistics (EUROSTAT) 225
Yearbook of the Research Register 330
Yield Stress of Steel and Iron 399
Yissum 478
YKB (Yukon Bibliography) 95
York University 1120
Yorkshire Regional Cancer Organisation 1053
YSCHEDULE Data Base (I.P. Sharp Associates) 871
Yugoslav Center for Technical and Scientific Documentation 1121
Yukon Bibliography (YKB) 95
Yukon Bibliography Updates 95
Z.A.R. (Zentralarchiv Retrieval) System 1045
ZA (Zentralarchiv fur Empirische Sozialforschung) - Universitat zu Koln 1045
ZA-Information 1045
ZADI (Zentralstelle fur Agrardokumentation und -Information) - Bundesministerium fur Ernahrung, Landwirtschaft und Forsten - Germany 408
ZDA (Zinc Development Association) 1122
ZDB (Zeitschriftendatenbank) 400
ZDE (Zentralstelle Dokumentation Elektrotechnik) 960
Zeitschriftendatenbank 400
Zeitschriftendatenbank (ZDB) 400
Zenkoku Kigyo Tosan Shukei 969
Zenkoku Kigyo Zaimu Shohyo Bunseki Tokei 969
Zentralarchiv fur Empirische Sozialforschung - Universitat zu Koln 1045
Zentralarchiv Retrieval System 1045
Zentralbibliothek der Wirtschaftswissenschaften - Institut fur Weltwirtschaft in Kiel 639
Zentralblatt fur Didaktik der Mathematik 521
Zentralblatt fur Mathematik und Ihre Grenzgebiete 521
Zentrale Dokumentation - Deutsche Stiftung fur Internationale Entwicklung 397
Zentralinstitut fur Information und Dokumentation - German Democratic Republic 395
Zentralstelle Dokumentation Elektrotechnik 960
Zentralstelle Dokumentation Elektrotechnik (ZDE) Data Base 960
Zentralstelle fur Agrardokumentation und -Information - Bundesministerium fur Ernahrung, Landwirtschaft und Forsten - Germany 408

Zentralstelle fur Psychologische Information und Dokumentation   1078
Zentralstelle fur Textildokumentation und -Information   390
Zentralverband der Elektronischen Industrie   960
Zentrum fur Historische Sozialforschung   183
ZfP (Dokumentation Zerstorungsfreie Prufung)   416
ZIID (Zentralinstitut fur Information und Dokumentation) - German Democratic Republic   395
ZIID-Schriftenreihe   395
Zinc Abstracts   1122
Zinc Development Association   1122
Zinc, Lead & Cadmium Abstracts (ZLC) Database   1122
Zinc Monitor   228
Zinc Quarterly   228
ZLC (Zinc, Lead & Cadmium Abstracts) Database   1122
Zoological Record   88
Zoological Record Search Guide   88
Zoological Society of London   88
ZooScene   88
ZPID (Zentralstelle fur Psychologische Information und Dokumentation)   1078
ZR (Zoological Record)   88
ZR (Zoological Record) Online   88
ZTDI (Zentralstelle fur Textildokumentation und -Information)   390
ZVEI (Zentralverband der Elektronischen Industrie)   960

DATA BASES INDEX

Machine-readable files produced by the organizations described in this book, including bibliographic, referral, full-text, numeric, statistical, online, videotex, offline, and other types of data bases. References in this index are generally made to the producing organization rather than to organizations providing online access or tape copies. In addition to actively maintained files, the index includes data bases that are no longer updated as well as those files in the process of being computerized for the first time. Data bases known by variant names and acronyms are entered under all approaches, including the names of corresponding publications if different. When there is no distinctive name for a file, it is listed under the name of the producing organization.

The Data Bases Index in this International Volume contains approximately 2,600 name and acronym listings for about 1,600 distinct data bases.

DATA BASES INDEX

A Computerized London Information System (ACOMPLIS) Data Base   465
A Network of Social Security Information Resources (ANSSIR) Data Base   145
AA (Apicultural Abstracts)   563
AARTI (Australian Art Index) Data Base   58
ABC (Abstracts in BioCommerce)   181
ABDA-Arzneistoffe (ABDA-STOFF) Data Base   428
ABDA-FAM (ABDA-Fertigarzneimittel) Data Base   428
ABDA-Fertigarzneimittel (ABDA-FAM) Data Base   428
ABDA-INTER (ABDA-Interaktionen) Data Base   428
ABDA-Interaktionen (ABDA-INTER) Data Base   428
ABDA-STOFF (ABDA-Arzneistoffe) Data Base   428
ABIS (Anglo-Brazilian Information Service) Data Base   24
ABIX   53
ABN (Australian Bibliographic Network) Data Base   49
ABOA (Australian Bibliography of Agriculture)   47
ABS (Australian Bureau of Statistics) Data Base   52
ABS (Australian Bureau of Statistics) Time Series Data Base   237
ABSDATA (I.P. Sharp Associates)   871
Abstracts in BioCommerce (ABC)   181
Abstracts on Tropical Agriculture (ATA) Data Base   857
ACDB (Airport Characteristics Data Bank)   568
ACOMDAILY Data Base (I.P. Sharp Associates)   871
ACOMPLINE   465
ACOMPLIS (A Computerized London Information System) Data Base   465
ACROPOL   384
ACT Data Base (I.P. Sharp Associates)   871
Actuarial Data Base (I.P. Sharp Associates)   871
ACUL   652
ADB (Anlagendatenbank)   398
ADDIMS Data Base   504
Adfacts   6
ADIGE (Archive of Italian Data of Geology) Data Bases   625
ADIGE2   625
ADMAC (Austrian Documentation Centre for Media and Communication Research) Data Base   65
Administration Laboratory Project (ALP) File   1034
ADO (Animal Disease Occurrence) Data Base   428
ADOC (AGORA-DOCUMENTAIRE)   388
ADREP (Aircraft Accident/Incident Reporting System) Data Base   567
AEA (Association of European Airlines) Data Base   41
AECC Data Base (I.P. Sharp Associates)   871
AECL Document Data Base   44
AECO (AGORA-ECONOMIE)   388
AEI (Australian Education Index) Data Base   54
AERIC National Database   238
AERIC Provincial Database   238
Aerospace Daily (ESA/IRS)   317
AES Data Base (I.P. Sharp Associates)   871
AESIS (Australian Earth Sciences Information System) Data Base   57
AFEE (Association Francaise pour l'Etude des Eaux) Data Base   391
AffarsDok   260
AFP-AGORA Data Bases   388
AFRE (Australian Financial Review) Data Base   55
AGC File   127
AGDATA (Agricultural Commodities Data Base)   9
AGE (Asian Information Center for Geotechnical Engineering) Data Base   30
AGE Digest Data Base   30
AGI (Alberta Gazette Index)   11
AgInfo   8
AGINSPEC   8
AGINTEL   8
AGNEWS   8
AGORA-DOCUMENTAIRE (ADOC)   388
AGORA-ECONOMIE (AECO)   388
AGORA-GENERAL (AGRA)   388
AGORA-SPORTS (ASPO)   388
AGRA (AGORA-GENERAL)   388
Agra Europe Data Bases   8
AGREP (Agricultural Research Projects) Data Base   213
AGRIASIA   889
Agricultural Commodities Data Base (AGDATA)   9
Agricultural Data Bank (NEEDS-TS)   754
Agricultural Data Bases (Australian Bureau of Statistics)   237
Agricultural Engineering Abstracts   229
Agricultural Information Bank for Asia (AIBA)   889
Agricultural Marketing and Trade (M & T) Database   126
Agricultural Research Personnel Inventory File   510
Agricultural Research Project Information System Data Base   510
Agricultural Research Projects (AGREP) Data Base   213
AGRIS (International Information System for the Agricultural Sciences and Technology) Data Base   1012
Agroclimatology Data Bank   846
AGSM Data Base (I.P. Sharp Associates)   871
AIBA (Agricultural Information Bank for Asia)   889
AID (Artikkel-Indeks)   767

AID Data Base   935
AIDIMS Data Base   504
AIDS (Automated Informatics Documentation System) Data Base   554
AIM (Arbeitsgemeinschaft Information Meeresforschung und Meerestechnik) Data Base   413
Air Charter Data Base (I.P. Sharp Associates)   871
Air Quality Data File   626
Air Transport Statistical Program Data Base (ICAO)   569
Aircraft Accident Data Base   68
Aircraft Accident/Incident Reporting System (ADREP) Data Base   567
Aircraft Histories Data Base   68
Airport Characteristics Data Bank (ACDB)   568
AISL (Aviation Information Services Ltd.) Aircraft Data Bases   68
Alberta Gazette Index (AGI)   11
Alberta Government Periodicals Publishing Record (PPR) Data Base   11
Alberta Land Use Planning Data Bank (LANDUP)   10
Alberta Legislation Information (ALI) Data Base   11
Alberta Oil Sands Index (AOSI)   13
Alberta Reports (National Reporter System)   828
ALCONARC   936
ALDOC (League of Arab States Documentation and Information Center) Data Base   653
ALI (Alberta Legislation Information) Data Base   11
ALICE (Archivio Libri Italiani su Calcolatore Elettronico)   87
ALIS (Automated Library Information System) Data Base   270
All-Canada Weekly Summaries Data Base   162
ALLOYDATA   451
ALPFILE   1034
Alpha 460 Prestel Data Base   18
American Viewdata Services   473
AMES Data Base (I.P. Sharp Associates)   871
AMIS (Australian Municipal Information System)   237
AMPEREDOC Data Base   717
ANAIS Data Bank   1062
ANB (Australian National Bibliography)   48
Anglo-Brazilian Information Service (ABIS) Data Base   24
Animal Breeding Abstracts   229
Animal Disease Occurrence   229
Animal Disease Occurrence (ADO) Data Base   428
Animal Production Information Card Service Data Base   487
Anlagendatenbank (ADB)   398
Annuaire d'Etudes en Education au Canada Data Base   170
Annual Bibliography of Austrian Mass Communication Literature   65
Annual Labour Force Statistics (OECD)   780
Annual National Accounts (OECD)   780
Annual Report Record   1060
ANSSIR (A Network of Social Security Information Resources) Data Base   145
Anthony Bird Associates Data Base   89
AOPUS (Australian Opinion Polls User Service) Data Base   1072
AOSI (Alberta Oil Sands Index)   13
AP (Associated Press) Data Base (Datasolve World Reporter)   265
APAIS (Australian Public Affairs Information Service) Data Base   48
Apercu Technique-Technisch Overzicht (ATO)   187
API (Architectural Periodicals Index)   845
Apicultural Abstracts (AA)   563
APIDIST Data Base (I.P. Sharp Associates)   871
APIN (System of Computerized Processing of Scientific Information) Data Bases   965
APR (Atlantic Provinces Reports)   173
AQUADOC   348
AQUALINE   464
Aquatic Sciences and Fisheries Abstracts (ASFA) Data Base   1008
ARATE Data Base (I.P. Sharp Associates)   871
Arbeitsgemeinschaft Information Meeresforschung und Meerestechnik Data Base   413
Architectural Periodicals Index (API)   845
Archive of Italian Data of Geology (ADIGE) Data Bases   625
Archivio Libri Italiani su Calcolatore Elettronico (ALICE)   87
Arctic Science and Technology Information System (ASTIS) Data Base   26
Area, Population & Household Databank (NEEDS-TS)   754
ARGREP Data Base (I.P. Sharp Associates)   871
ARGUS Data Base (I.P. Sharp Associates)   871
ARI (Australian Road Index)   62
ARIANE (Arrangement Reticule des Informations en vue de l'Approche des Notions par leur Environnement) Data Bank   610
Arid Lands Development Abstracts   229
Arrangement Reticule des Informations en vue de l'Approche des Notions par leur Environnement (ARIANE) Data Bank   610
ARRD (Australian Road Research Documentation)   62
ARRIP (Australian Road Research in Progress) Data Base   62
Art Sales Index (ASI) Data Bank   29
Article Index   767
Artikel-Sok   116
Artikkel-Indeks (AID)   767
ASBEST Data Base   1071
Asbestos Information   1071
Asbestos Manufacturers Catalog   1071

ASE Data Base (I.P. Sharp Associates)   871
ASFA (Aquatic Sciences and Fisheries Abstracts) Data Base   1008
ASFIS Register of Experts and Institutions   1008
ASI (Art Sales Index) Data Bank   29
ASI (Australian Science Index)   47
Asian Geotechnology Data Base   30
Asian Information Center for Geotechnical Engineering (AGE) Data Base   30
ASPO (AGORA-SPORTS)   388
Associated Press (AP) Data Base (Datasolve World Reporter)   265
Association Francaise pour l'Etude des Eaux (AFEE) Data Base   391
Association of European Airlines (AEA) Data Base   41
ASTIS (Arctic Science and Technology Information System) Data Base   26
ATA (Abstracts on Tropical Agriculture) Data Base   857
ATID (Australian Transport Information Directory)   46
Atlantic Provinces Reports (APR)   173
ATLIS (Australian Transport Literature Information System)   46
ATO (Apercu Technique-Technisch Overzicht)   187
Atomindex   560
ATRIP (Australian Transport Research in Progress)   46
AUCBE (Chiltern Advisory Unit for Computer Based Education) Data Bases   485
Audio-Visual Materials for Higher Education Catalogue   112
Australian Art Index (AARTI) Data Base   58
Australian Bibliographic Network (ABN) Data Base   49
Australian Bibliography of Agriculture (ABOA)   47
Australian Bureau of Statistics (ABS) Data Base   52
Australian Bureau of Statistics (ABS) Time Series Data Base   237
Australian Business Index   53
Australian Commodities Data Base (I.P. Sharp Associates)   871
Australian Demographic Data Bank   60
Australian Earth Sciences Information System (AESIS) Data Base   57
Australian Economic Statistics Data Base (I.P. Sharp Associates)   871
Australian Education Index (AEI) Data Base   54
Australian Energy Consumption Statistics Data Base (I.P. Sharp Associates)   871
Australian Export Statistics Data Base (I.P. Sharp Associates)   871
Australian Financial Data Base (I.P. Sharp Associates)   871
Australian Financial Markets Data Base (I.P. Sharp Associates)   871
Australian Financial Review (AFRE) Data Base   55
Australian Funds Market Data Base (I.P. Sharp Associates)   871
Australian Graduate School of Management, Corporate Data Base (I.P. Sharp Associates)   871
Australian Major Energy Statistics Data Base (I.P. Sharp Associates)   871
Australian Medical Index   50
Australian Municipal Information System   237
Australian National Bibliography (ANB)   48
Australian Opinion Polls User Service (AOPUS) Data Base   1072
Australian Public Affairs Information Service (APAIS) Data Base   48
Australian Road Index (ARI)   62
Australian Road Research Documentation (ARRD)   62
Australian Road Research in Progress (ARRIP) Data Base   62
Australian Science Index (ASI)   47
Australian Sector Cash Flow Data Base (I.P. Sharp Associates)   871
Australian Stock Exchange Indices Data Base (I.P. Sharp Associates)   871
Australian Transport Information Directory (ATID)   46
Australian Transport Literature Information System (ATLIS)   46
Australian Transport Research in Progress (ATRIP)   46
Austrian Documentation Centre for Media and Communication Research (ADMAC) Data Base   65
Austrian Economic Outlook Poll Data Base (I.P. Sharp Associates)   871
Automated Informatics Documentation System (AIDS) Data Base   554
Automated Inventory of Canadian Machine Readable Data Files   158
Automated Library Information System (ALIS) Data Base   270
Automated Standards and Regulations Information Online Data Base   382
Automatical System of Standards and Metrological Information Data Base   817
Automotive Parts Aftermarket Companies Directory   67
Aviation Information Services Ltd. (AISL) Aircraft Data Bases   68
AVMARC   439
AVS Intext Prestel Data Bases   69
AWIDAT (Solid Waste Management Data Bank)   411
AXESS   879
BADADUQ (Banque de Donnees a Acces Direct de l'Universite du Quebec)   1064
BALIS (Bayerisches Landwirtschaftliches Informationssystem) Data Banks   76
Bank Financials Databank (NEEDS-TS)   754
Bank for International Settlements, Quarterly Data Base (I.P. Sharp Associates)   871
Bank for International Settlements, Semi-Annual Data Base (I.P. Sharp Associates)   871
Bank of Canada Weekly Financial Statistics Data Base (I.P. Sharp Associates)   871
Bank of England Financial Statistics Data Base   72

Bank Society Data Base   73
Banking and Finance Data Bank (NEEDS-TS)   754
Banque de Donnees a Acces Direct de l'Universite du Quebec (BADADUQ)   1064
Banque de Donnees Agroclimatologie   846
Banque de Donnees du Service Annuaire Electronique   552
Banque de Donnees Internationales de Biometrie Humaine et d'Ergonomie   838
Banque de Donnees Locales (INSEE)   365
Banque de Donnees Macroeconomiques (INSEE)   366
Banque de Donnees Socio-economiques des Pays Mediterraneens   564
Banque de Donnees Urbaines de Paris et de la Region d'Ile-de-France (BDU)   798
Banque de l'Information Industrielle Pont-a-Mousson (BIIPAM)   820
Banque de Terminologie du Quebec (BTQ)   830
Banque des Donnees du Sous-sol   341
Banque d'Information sur les Recherches INSERM (BIR)   358
Banque d'Informations Automatisees sur les Medicaments (BIAM) Data Bank   257
Banque d'Informations Politiques et d'Actualites (BIPA)   384
Banque Mondiale des Donnees Gravimetriques   342
Banque Quebecoise d'Information sur l'Environnement Quebecois   832
Banques de Donnees Associees (BDA)   251
Banques de Donnees Associees (BDA)   252
Banques de Donnees Associees (BDA)   514
Baric Viewdata Data Base   75
BAS (Bibliographic Automated System) Data Base   731
Base de Donnees Cimentieres   188
Base d'Information Robert Debre (BIRD)   566
BASELINE   950
BATHEDA Thermophysical Data Bank   996
BATREGIO   773
BAUFO (Bauforschungsprojekte)   374
Bauforschungsprojekte (BAUFO)   374
Bauobjektdokumentation (BODO)   375
Bavarian Agricultural Information System Data Banks   76
Bayerisches Landwirtschaftliches Informationssystem (BALIS) Data Banks   76
BBC External Services News Data Base   104
BBC Summary of World Broadcasts   104
BCAVM (British Catalogue of Audiovisual Materials) Data Base   439
BCM (British Catalogue of Music) Data Base   439
BDA (Banques de Donnees Associees)   251
BDA (Banques de Donnees Associees)   252
BDA (Banques de Donnees Associees)   514
BDD (British Defence Directory)   98
BDL (Banque de Donnees Locales - INSEE)   365
BDM (Banque de Donnees Macroeconomiques - INSEE)   366
BDU (Banque de Donnees Urbaines de Paris et de la Region d'Ile-de-France)   798
BECAN (Biomedical Engineering Current Awareness Notification)   114
BEFO   959
BEI (British Education Index)   439
Belgian National Statistical Institute Data Bases   82
BfAi (Bundesstelle fur Aussenhandelsinformation) Data Base   425
BHI (British Humanities Index)   660
BHRA FLUIDEX   86
BIAM (Banque d'Informations Automatisees sur les Medicaments) Data Bank   257
BIB (Brunel Institute for Bioengineering) Data Base   114
BIBLINRIA   361
BIBLIO-DATA   423
Biblio Service Informatique (SB-I) Data Base   797
Bibliocentre Data Base   182
BIBLIOCOM   619
BiblioFem   209
Bibliographia Medica Cechoslovaca Data Base   250
Bibliographic Automated System (BAS) Data Base   731
Bibliographic Index of Library Documents (BILD)   481
Bibliographic Information on Southeast Asia (BISA)   1073
Bibliographic Star Index (BSI)   905
Bibliographical Repertory of Christian Institutions Data Base   205
Bibliographie der Pflanzenschutzliteratur Data Base   409
Bibliographie Linguistischer Literatur Data Base   368
Bibliography of Canadian Glaciology   139
Bibliography of Linguistic Literature (BLL) Data Base   368
Bibliography of Plant Protection Data Base   409
Bibliography of Quebec   833
BIBLIOL Data Base   576
BIBLIOS   384
Bibliotekstjanst (BTJ) Bibliographic Data Base   116
BIBSYS Data Base   1079
BIFORECAST Data Base (I.P. Sharp Associates)   871
BIHIST Data Base (I.P. Sharp Associates)   871
BIIPAM (Banque de l'Information Industrielle Pont-a-Mousson)   820
BIIPAM-CTIF Data Base   820
BILD (Bibliographic Index of Library Documents)   481
Bildschirmtext (Btx) Data Bases   427
BIOCEAN   349

DATA BASES INDEX

Biocontrol News and Information 229
BIODOC 870
Biological Records Centre (BRC) Data Bank 461
Biomedical Engineering Current Awareness Notification (BECAN) 114
Biotechnology Abstracts 273
Biotel 446
BIPA (Banque d'Informations Politiques et d'Actualites) 384
BIR (Banque d'Information sur les Recherches INSERM) 358
Bird (Anthony) Associates Data Base 89
BIRD (Base d'Information Robert Debre) 566
BISA (Bibliographic Information on Southeast Asia) 1073
BISQ Data Base (I.P. Sharp Associates) 871
BISS Data Base (I.P. Sharp Associates) 871
BJUS Data Base 282
Black (Prof. John B.) Communications Information Data Base 232
Blackwell BOOKFILE 90
BLAISE (British Library Automated Information Service) Data Bases 440
BLCMP (Library Services) Ltd. Data Base 91
BLEX Data Base 282
BLIS 959
BLL (Bibliography of Linguistic Literature) Data Base 368
BMA Press Cuttings Database (BMAP) 110
BMAP (BMA Press Cuttings Database) 110
BMFT (Bundesministerium fur Forschung und Technologie) Data Bank 424
BML (Bulgarian Medical Literature) Data Base 120
BNB (British National Bibliography) Data Base 439
BNDO (Bureau National des Donnees Oceaniques) Data Banks 347
BNF Abstracts Data Base 92
BNR (Brassey's Naval Record) 97
BNT (Boreal Northern Titles) 95
BODIL Data Base 938
BODO (Bauobjektdokumentation) 375
Bok-Sok 116
BOOKFILE 90
Boreal Library Catalogue 95
Boreal Northern Titles (BNT) 95
Boris Kidric Laboratory for Information Systems Data Bases 96
Bottin Data Bases 280
Brassey's Naval Record (BNR) 97
Brazil Ministry of the Interior Data Bases 100
Brazilian Bibliography in Science and Technology 103
Brazilian Union Catalog for Scientific and Technological Serials 103
BRC (Biological Records Centre) Data Bank 461
British Catalogue of Audiovisual Materials (BCAVM) Data Base 439
British Catalogue of Music (BCM) Data Base 439
British Columbia Manpower Survey Data Base 106
British Columbia Regulations 828
British Council Prestel File 108
British Defence Directory (BDD) 98
British Education Index (BEI) 439
British Humanities Index (BHI) 660
British Hydromechanics Research Association (BHRA) Data Base 86
British Library Automated Information Service (BLAISE) Data Bases 440
British Library Conference Proceedings Index 442
British Library Department of Printed Books (DPB) Data Base 440
British National Bibliography Data Base 439
British Standards Institution (BSI) Data Base 111
British Technology Index (BTI) 662
British Universities Film & Video Council (BUFVC) Catalogue 112
BRIX Data Base 453
Brown Corpus 768
Brunel Institute for Bioengineering (BIB) Data Base 114
BRWE (Business Review Weekly) Data Base 55
BSI (Bibliographic Star Index) 905
BSI (British Standards Institution) Data Base 111
BTE Information Systems 46
BTI (British Technology Index) 662
BTJ (Bibliotekstjanst) Bibliographic Data Base 116
BTQ (Banque de Terminologie du Quebec) 830
Btx (Bildschirmtext) Data Bases 427
BUFVC (British Universities Film & Video Council) Catalogue 112
Building Center Data Base 117
Building Commodity File 934
Building Product File 118
Building Research Projects Data Base 374
Buildings Documentation Data Base 375
Bulgarian Medical Literature (BML) Data Base 120
BULLETIN (Harwell Central Information Service) 434
Bulletin Bibliographique INTD Data Base 722
Bulletin de la Construction Mecanique Data Base 957
Bulletin Signaletique Data Bases 355
Bulletin Signaletique Data Bases 356
Bulletin Signaletique des Telecommunications 367
BUMS Data Base 116
BUNDESBANK Data Base (I.P. Sharp Associates) 871
Bundesstelle fur Aussenhandelsinformation (BfAi) Data Base 425

Bureau National des Donnees Oceaniques (BNDO) Data Banks 347
Bureau of Statistics Data Base (International Labour Office) 592
BUSINESS Data Base (ONLINE GmbH) 774
Business In View 473
Business International Economic Forecasts Data Base (I.P. Sharp Associates) 871
Business International Historical Data Base (I.P. Sharp Associates) 871
Business Review Weekly (BRWE) Data Base 55
BVR (Byggvaruregistret) 934
BYGGDOK (Swedish Institute of Building Documentation) Data Base 938
Byggvaruregistret 934
C-13 Nuclear Magnetic Resonance (BASF) 521
C76 Journey-To-Work Data Bases 237
C76 LGA Descriptor Data Base 237
C76 LGA File Zero Data Bases 237
C76 Postcode Data Bases 237
C81 Geographic Descriptor Data Base 237
C81 LGA Data Base 237
C81 Postcode Data Base 237
CAB (Commonwealth Agricultural Bureaux) Abstracts 229
CAB Abstracts/Animal (DIMDI) 428
CAB Abstracts/Plant (DIMDI) 428
CABIS (Computer Aided Bibliographic Information Service) Data Base 509
CABS (Current Awareness in Biological Sciences) Data Base 803
CAC (Compagnie des Agents de Change) Data Base 389
CADIS (Computer Aided Directory Information Service) Data Base 509
Cadmium Abstracts 1122
CAIRS (Computer Assisted Information Retrieval System) Data Base 655
CALDOC (Calgary Public Library Government Documents) 1033
Calgary Public Information Department Data Base 124
Calgary Public Library Government Documents (CALDOC) 1033
Calvados Service Data Bases 22
Cambridge Structural Database (CSD) 125
CAMN (Canadian Directory of Completed Master's Theses in Nursing) Data Base 1037
CAN (Centralforbundet for Alkohol- och Narkotikaupplysning) Data Bases 936
CAN/LAW 162
CAN/MARC 148
CAN/MARC 150
Canada-Histoire Data Base 704
Canada Institute for Scientific and Technical Information (CISTI) Data Bases 152
Canada Library of Parliament Data Bases 157
Canadian Art Auction Records Data Base 300
Canadian Bonds Data Base (I.P. Sharp Associates) 871
Canadian Business and Current Affairs 707
Canadian Business and Current Affairs 708
Canadian Business Index 707
Canadian Chartered Banks, Annual Data Base (I.P. Sharp Associates) 871
Canadian Chartered Banks, Monthly Data Base (I.P. Sharp Associates) 871
Canadian Chartered Banks Monthly Statement of Assets and Liabilities Data Base (I.P. Sharp Associates) 871
Canadian Chartered Banks, Quarterly Data Base (I.P. Sharp Associates) 871
Canadian Chartered Banks Quarterly Income Statement Data Base (I.P. Sharp Associates) 871
Canadian Chartered Banks, Yearly Data Base (I.P. Sharp Associates) 871
Canadian Clearinghouse for Ongoing Research in Nursing (CORN) Data Base 1036
Canadian Corporate Data Bank 680
Canadian Criminal Cases Data Base 162
Canadian Department of Insurance Data Base (I.P. Sharp Associates) 871
Canadian Department of Insurance Property and Casualty Insurance Data Base (I.P. Sharp Associates) 871
Canadian Directory of Completed Master's Theses in Nursing (CAMN) Data Base 1037
Canadian Education Index (CEI) Data Base 170
Canadian Energy Information System Data Bases 133
Canadian Environment (CENV) Data Base 140
Canadian Exchequer Reports 828
Canadian Federal Corporations and Directors Data Base (CFCD) 163
Canadian Financial Database 430
Canadian Geographic Information System (CGIS) Data Sets 143
Canadian Hydrological Operational Multipurpose Subprogramme (CHOMS) Data Base 140
Canadian Index to Geoscience Data 135
Canadian Inventory of Historic Building (CIHB) Data Base 138
Canadian Law Information Council (CLIC) Data Bases 173
Canadian MARC 148

DATA BASES INDEX

Canadian MARC 150
Canadian Mineral Occurrence Index (CANMINDEX) 134
Canadian News Index 708
Canadian On-line Record Database (CORD) 206
Canadian Operating Statistics Data Base (I.P. Sharp Associates) 871
Canadian Periodical Index (CPI) 174
Canadian Plains Research Center (CPRC) Data Base 1066
Canadian Press Extra (CPX) 828
Canadian Press Newstex (CPN) 828
Canadian Register of Research and Researchers in the Social Sciences 1087
Canadian Renewable Energy Database (ENERCAN) 16
Canadian Renewable Energy Database (ENERCAN) 152
Canadian Retail Gasoline Volume Data Base (I.P. Sharp Associates) 871
Canadian Social Science Abstracts 1120
Canadian Socio-Economic Information Management System (CANSIM) Data Bases 159
Canadian Standards Information Service Data Base 898
Canadian Stock Options (CDNOPT) Data Base 986
Canadian Transportation Documentation System Data Base 161
Canadian Women of Note Archive (CWONC) 1120
Canadiana 148
CANCERNET Data Base 357
CANMINDEX (Canadian Mineral Occurrence Index) 134
CANOM 720
CANPLAINS Data Base 1066
CANREGISTER 1087
CANSIM (Canadian Socio-Economic Information Management System) Cross-Classified Base 159
CANSIM (Canadian Socio-Economic Information Management System) Main Base 159
CANSIM (Canadian Socio-Economic Information Management System) Mini Base 159
CANSIM Summary Data System 159
Cantel 518
CANUCS (Union List of Serials in the Social Sciences and Humanities Held by Canadian Libraries) Data Base 151
CAP Databank 214
CAPA 80
Capital Market Indicators (NEEDS-TS) 754
CAPRI (Computerized Administration of Patent Documents Reclassified According to the IPC) Data Base 64
CAPTAIN (Character and Pattern Telephone Access Information Network) Data Base 759
Careerdata Data Base 747
Careers and Occupational Information Centre (COIC) Data Base 462
CARIS (Current Agricultural Research Information System) Data Base 1009
Carleton University Library Data Base 179
CARS Vehicle Data Bank System 1104
Case Law Report Updating Service (CLARUS) Data Base 517
Catalog of Patents Related to Asbestos 1071
Catalog of Stellar Groups (CSG) 905
Catalog of Stellar Indentifications (CSI) 905
Catalogo Italiano Riviste su Calcolatore Elettronico (CIRCE) 87
Catalogue Support System (CATSS) Data Base 1094
CATSS (Catalogue Support System) Data Base 1094
Cawkell Information & Technology Services Ltd. (CITECH) Data Base 180
CBA (Current Biotechnology Abstracts) 854
CBI (Canadian Business Index) 707
CBST (Current Bibliography on Science and Technology) Data Base 632
CDNBOND Data Base (I.P. Sharp Associates) 871
CDNOPT (Canadian Stock Options) Data Base 986
CDOIP Data Base (I.P. Sharp Associates) 871
CDS (Centre de Donnees Stellaires) Data Bases 905
CDS (Chemical Data Services) Chemical Database 612
CEA (Chemical Engineering Abstracts) 852
CEAS (Chemical Emergency Agency Service) Data Base 435
CECILE Data Base 184
CEDATAH (Collection des Etudes Documentaires Appliquees a la Traduction Automatique et Humaine) Data Base 191
CEDOCAR (Centre de Documentation de l'Armement) Data Base 345
CEEFAX Data Base 105
CEI (Canadian Education Index) Data Base 170
CELEX (Communitatis Europeae Lex) Data Bases 489
Cement Data Base 188
CENAGRI (Centro Nacional de Informacao Documental Agricola) Data Bases 99
Census of Commerce Databank (NEEDS-TS) 754
CENSUS81 Data Base (I.P. Sharp Associates) 871
Centennial College Bibliocentre Data Base 182
Center for Agricultural Documentation and Information Data Base 408
Center for Psychological Information and Documentation Data Base 1078
Center for Research and Studies on Mediterranean Societies Data Base 186

Center for the Study of Advertising Support Data Base 189
Center for Translation Documentation Data Base 191
Central American National and Regional Standards Data Base 193
Central American Patents Data Base 193
Central Patents Index (CPI) 275
Central Regional Databank (NEEDS-TS) 754
Central Statistical Office (CSO) Macro-Economic Data Bank 449
Centralforbundet for Alkohol- och Narkotikaupplysning (CAN) Data Bases 936
Centre de Documentation de l'Armement (CEDOCAR) Data Base 345
Centre de Donnees Stellaires Data Bases 905
Centre de Preparation Documentaire a la Traduction (CPDT) Data Base 191
Centre de Recherche Documentaire (CREDOC) Data Bases 282
Centre de Recherche et d'Etudes sur les Societes Mediterraneennes (CRESM) Data Base 186
Centre de Recherches Scientifiques et Techniques de l'Industrie des Fabrications Metalliques (CRIF) Data Base 187
Centre d'Etude des Supports de Publicite (CESP) Data Base 189
Centre International d'Informations de Securite et d'Hygiene du Travail (CIS) Data Base 595
Centre of Information Resource & Technology, Singapore (CIRTS) Biotechnology Data Base 197
Centre Technique des Industries Mecaniques (CETIM) Data Base 957
CENTREX Data Base 484
Centro Edile Data Base 117
Centro Latinoamericano de Documentacion Economica y Social (CLADES) Data Bases 1006
Centro Nacional de Informacao Documental Agricola (CENAGRI) Data Bases 99
CENV (Canadian Environment) Data Base 140
Cereal Data Base 583
CERVED (Centri Elettronici Reteconnessi Valutazione Elaborazione Dati) Data Bases 194
CESP (Centre d'Etude des Supports de Publicite) Data Base 189
CET Prestel Educational Umbrella Service Data Base 247
CETIM (Centre Technique des Industries Mecaniques) Data Base 957
CFCD (Canadian Federal Corporations and Directors Data Base) 163
CGIS (Canadian Geographic Information System) Data Sets 143
Character and Pattern Telephone Access Information Network (CAPTAIN) Data Base 759
Charging for Library Services Data Base 692
Charities Aid Foundation Data Bank 198
CHELEM (Comptes Harmonises sur les Echanges et l'Economie Mondiale) 185
Chem Systems International Data Base 199
CHEMCO Physical Properties Data Bank 327
CHEMDATA 435
Chemical Age Project File 200
Chemical and Process Engineering Abstracts Data Base 77
Chemical Data Services (CDS) Chemical Database 612
Chemical Emergency Agency Service (CEAS) Data Base 435
Chemical Engineering Abstracts (CEA) 852
Chemical Engineering and Biotechnology Abstracts Data Bank (DECHEMA) 403
Chemical Equipment Suppliers Data Base (DECHEMA) 406
Chemical Hazards in Industry (CHI) Data Base 853
Chemical Plant and Product Database 612
Chemical Reactions Documentation Service (CRDS) Data Base 274
CHEMSAFE 435
CHI (Chemical Hazards in Industry) Data Base 853
Chiltern Advisory Unit for Computer Based Education (AUCBE) Data Bases 485
Chinese Pharmacy Abstracts 801
CHOMS (Canadian Hydrological Operational Multipurpose Subprogramme) Data Base 140
Christmas Crafts 1099
CHRONOLOGIE 384
CIAMDA (Index to Literature on Atomic Collision Data) 561
CIBDOC Data Bases 373
CIHB (Canadian Inventory of Historic Building) Data Base 138
CIIS (Corporate Integrated Information System) Data Base 129
CIM Data Base 188
CIMPP (Comprehensive Industrial Materials Property Package) Data Bank 1088
CINCH (Computerised Information from National Criminological Holdings) 56
CINDA (Computer Index of Neutron Data) 785
CIRCE (Catalogo Italiano Riviste su Calcolatore Elettronico) 87
CIRCUL 652
CIRTS (Centre of Information Resource & Technology, Singapore) Biotechnology Data Base 197
CIS (Centre International d'Informations de Securite et d'Hygiene du Travail) Data Base 595
CIS Abstracts Data Base 595
CISTI (Canada Institute for Scientific and Technical Information) Data Bases 152
CISTI Catalogue 152
CITECH (Cawkell Information & Technology Services Ltd.) Data

Base 180
CITEX Data Base 980
CITH Data Bank 980
Citibank Economic Data Base (I.P. Sharp Associates) 871
Citibank Economic Forecast Data Base (I.P. Sharp Associates) 871
CITIBASE Data Base (I.P. Sharp Associates) 871
CITIFORECAST Data Base (I.P. Sharp Associates) 871
CitiService 500
Civil Engineering Hydraulics Abstracts 86
CJUS (Court of Justice of the European Communities) Data Bank 214
CLADBIB Data Base 1006
CLADES (Centro Latinoamericano de Documentacion Economica y Social) Data Bases 1006
CLADIR Data Base 1006
CLAIR (Computerised Library of Analysed Igneous Rocks) 1057
CLAPLAN Data Base 1006
CLARUS (Case Law Report Updating Service) Data Base 517
Classified List of Manufacturing Businesses Data Base 454
CLEO Data Base 1059
CLIC (Canadian Law Information Council) Data Bases 173
CLIN Data Base 1006
Clinical Literature Information Bases 296
Clothes and Textiles Bibliography (CLTXBIB) 1033
CLRA (Inter-Corporate Ownership Data Base) 165
CLRP (Coal Research Projects) Data Base 782
CLTXBIB (Clothes and Textiles Bibliography) 1033
CME 773
CNAM (Corporate Names Data Base) 164
CNEXO-BNDO Data Base 350
CNI (Canadian News Index) 708
CNRSLAB 355
COAL-ABS 14
Coal Data Base 782
Coal Research Projects Data Base 782
COALPRO 782
COALRIP 782
COAND Data Base (I.P. Sharp Associates) 871
Coast Frequency Reference File 606
CODOC (Cooperative Documents Network Project) Data Base 1050
COFFEELINE 570
COIC (Careers and Occupational Information Centre) Data Base 462
COIN (Computerized Information in Canada) Data Base 15
COINS Data Base 127
Collection des Etudes Documentaires Appliquees a la Traduction Automatique et Humaine (CEDATAH) Data Base 191
Collection District Data Bases 237
Combined T9/Service Segment Data Base (I.P. Sharp Associates) 871
COMERT1 Data Base (I.P. Sharp Associates) 871
COMERT2 Data Base (I.P. Sharp Associates) 871
COMERT3 Data Base (I.P. Sharp Associates) 871
COMEXT Data Bank 224
COMMBOND Data Base (I.P. Sharp Associates) 871
Commercial Laws of Europe (Eurolex) 314
Commodities Data Base (Wolff Research) 1109
Common Market Law Reports (Eurolex) 314
Commonwealth Agricultural Bureaux (CAB) Abstracts 229
Commonwealth Bank Bond Index Data Base (I.P. Sharp Associates) 871
Commonwealth Environmental Laws Data Base 656
Commonwealth Regional Renewable Energy Resources Information System (CRRERIS) Data Base 230
Commonwealth Scientific and Industrial Research Organization (CSIRO) Index 47
Communications Information Data Base 232
Communitatis Europeae Lex (CELEX) Data Bases 489
Commuter Online Origin-Destination Data Base (I.P. Sharp Associates) 871
Compagnie des Agents de Change (CAC) Data Base 389
Companies Registration Office Directory of Companies 802
Company Accounts Data Base (Datastream) 267
Comprehensive Industrial Materials Property Package (CIMPP) Data Bank 1088
Comptes Harmonises sur les Echanges et l'Economie Mondiale (CHELEM) 185
Compu-Mark (UK) Ltd. Data Base 235
Compu-Mark Data Base 234
Compusearch Market and Social Research Data Base 236
Computer Aided Bibliographic Information Service (CABIS) Data Base 509
Computer Aided Directory Information Service (CADIS) Data Base 509
Computer and Business Equipment Companies Directory 67
Computer and Control Abstracts 549
Computer Assisted Information Retrieval System (CAIRS) Data Base 655
Computer Directory of India Data Base 241
Computer Index of Neutron Data (CINDA) 785
Computerised Information from National Criminological Holdings (CINCH) 56
Computerised Library of Analysed Igneous Rocks (CLAIR) 1057
Computerized Administration of Patent Documents Reclassified According to the IPC (CAPRI) Data Base 64
Computerized ASFIS Register of Experts and Institutions 1008
Computerized Information in Canada (COIN) Data Base 15
Computerized London Information System Data Base 465
Computerized Text Processing and Retrieval System for Toronto City Council Information 985
COMPUTERPAT 802
Computing Journal Abstracts 721
CONF 521
Conference Proceedings Index (British Library) 442
CONSEILS DES MINISTRES 384
Constitutional Acts of Canada 828
Construction Data Bank (NEEDS-TS) 754
CONSUM 773
CONTEL Data Base 983
CONTEXT Data Base 983
Continuous Plankton Recorder Survey 729
Continuum Astronomical Data Files 59
Controlled Vocabulary of MINTER 100
Cooperative Documents Network Project (CODOC) Data Base 1050
Cooperative Group for Marine Research and Marine Technology Information Data Base 413
COPS Data Base (I.P. Sharp Associates) 871
CORALIE Data Base 282
CORD (Canadian On-line Record Database) 206
CORN (Canadian Clearinghouse for Ongoing Research in Nursing) Data Base 1036
CORP (Corporate Authorities) 521
Corporate Authorities (CORP) 521
Corporate Data Bank (Financial Post) 680
Corporate Integrated Information System (CIIS) Data Base 129
Corporate Names Data Base (CNAM) 164
Corrosion Data Base (DECHEMA) 405
COSMOS I 969
COSMOS II 969
Cotton and Tropical Fibres Abstracts 229
Council for Educational Technology Prestel Educational Umbrella Service Data Base 247
Council for Information on Alcohol and Other Drugs Data Bases 936
Council of Europe Conventions and Agreements (Eurolex) 314
Country Profiles Data Base 264
Court of Justice of the European Communities (CJUS) Data Bank 214
CPDT (Centre de Preparation Documentaire a la Traduction) Data Base 191
CPI (Canadian Periodical Index) 174
CPI (Central Patents Index) 275
CPN (Canadian Press Newstex) 828
CPRC (Canadian Plains Research Center) Data Base 1066
CPX (Canadian Press Extra) 828
CRDS (Chemical Reactions Documentation Service) Data Base 274
CREDOC (Centre de Recherche Documentaire) Data Bases 282
CRESM (Centre de Recherche et d'Etudes sur les Societes Mediterraneennes) Data Base 186
CREW Data Base (I.P. Sharp Associates) 871
CRIF (Centre de Recherches Scientifiques et Techniques de l'Industrie des Fabrications Metalliques) Data Base 187
Criminal Appeal Office Index (Eurolex) 314
Criminal Appeal Reports (Eurolex) 314
Criminology & Penology Abstracts 647
CRONOS Data Bank 225
Crop Physiology Abstracts 229
CRR (Regulatory Reporter) 173
CRRERIS (Commonwealth Regional Renewable Energy Resources Information System) Data Base 230
CRYST Data Base 125
Crystallographic Data Centre Data Base 125
CRYSTMET (Metals Crystallographic) Data File 156
CSD (Cambridge Structural Database) 125
CSG (Catalog of Stellar Groups) 905
CSI (Catalog of Stellar Identifications) 905
CSIRO (Commonwealth Scientific and Industrial Research Organization) Index 47
CSO Library and Documentation Service Data Base 493
CSO Macro-Economic Data Bank 449
CSO Statistical Data Base System 493
CTI (Current Technology Index) 662
CTIF-BIIPAM Data Base 820
Culham Laboratory Library Data Base 438
Currency and Share Index Databank 328
Currency Exchange Rates Data Base (I.P. Sharp Associates) 871
Current Agricultural Research Information System (CARIS) Data Base 1009
Current Awareness in Biological Sciences (CABS) Data Base 803
Current Awareness in Particle Technology Data Base 676
Current Bibliography on Science and Technology (CBST) Data Base 632

Current Biotechnology Abstracts (CBA) 854
Current Law (Eurolex) 314
CURRENT RESEARCH in Library & Information Science 661
Current Research Projects in CSIR Laboratories Data Base 507
Current Technology Index (CTI) 662
Cutting Data Information Center Data Bank 964
CWONC (Canadian Women of Note Archive) 1120
CYBERTEL Videotex Data Bases 245
Czechoslovak Medical Literature Data Base 250
DABAWAS (Datenbank fur Wassergefahrdende Stoffe) 284
DAFSA Data Bases 251
Daily Intelligence Bulletin Data Base 465
Dairy Science Abstracts 229
DAISY Data Base 1114
DAKOR Data Base 424
DALCTRAF 936
Danish Veterinary and Agricultural Library Catalogue (DVJB) Data Base 497
DARC Pluridata System (DPDS) Data Bases 38
DARE Data Base 1022
Data Bank for Environmental Literature (ULIDAT) 411
Data Bank for Environmental Research (UFORDAT) 411
Data Bank for Medicaments 257
Data Bank of European Doctoral Theses in Management (DISSERT 1) 313
Data Bank on Substances Harmful to Water (DABAWAS) 284
Data Base on Contemporary German 541
Data Compilations in Physics (PHYSCOMP) 521
Data Library 1033
Data Library and Archives Directory (DATALIB Resources) 1033
Data Library Catalogue 1033
Data on Occupations Retrieval System (DOORS) 462
Data Reference (DREF) Data Base (WATDOC) 140
Data-Star News-File 266
Database of Databases (University of Tsukuba) 1080
Database of Wildlife Research 947
Database on Atomic and Molecular Physics 835
Database Phytomedizin 409
DATALIB Resources (Data Library and Archives Directory) 1033
Dataline Data Bases 262
Datastream International Data Bases 267
Datenbank fur Forderungsvorhaben (DAVOR) Data Base 424
Datenbank fur Futtermittel 487
Datenbank fur Wassergefahrdende Stoffe (DABAWAS) 284
DATIMS Data Base 504
DAVID Data Base 504
DAVOR (Datenbank fur Forderungsvorhaben) Data Base 424
DBDB (University of Tsukuba Database of Databases) 1080
DDB (Dortmund Data Bank) 1046
DDB Data Base 504
DECHEMA Chemical Engineering and Biotechnology Abstracts Data Bank 403
DECHEMA Chemical Equipment Suppliers Data Base (DEQUIP) 406
DECHEMA Corrosion Data Base (DECOR) 405
DECHEMA Thermophysical Property Data Bank (DETHERM) 404
DECLARATIONS 384
DECNAT Databank 214
DECOR (DECHEMA Corrosion Data Base) 405
DEFOTEL 977
Delft Hydro Database 268
Delft Hydroscience Abstracts 268
Demografiska Databasen (Umea Universitet) 1081
Demographic Data Base (University of Umea) 1081
Department of Printed Books Data Base 440
DEQUIP (DECHEMA Chemical Equipment Suppliers Data Base) 406
Derwent Patents Documentation Services Data Bases 275
DESY (Deutsches Elektronen-Synchrotron) Documentation and Information Data Base 396
DESY-HEP 396
Detailed Foreign Trade Statistics (OECD) 780
DETHERM (DECHEMA Thermophysical Property Data Bank) 404
Deutsche Bibliographie Data Base 423
Deutsche Bundesbank Data Base (I.P. Sharp Associates) 871
Deutsche Stiftung fur Internationale Entwicklung Data Bank 397
Deutsches Elektronen-Synchrotron (DESY) Documentation and Information Data Base 396
Deutsches Informationszentrum fur Technische Regeln (DITR) Data Bank 407
Deutsches Patent- und Fachinformationssystem Data Base 401
Devindex Data Base 576
DEVSIS Data Base 576
DeWitt Petrochemical Newsletters Data Base (I.P. Sharp Associates) 871
DIANE Guide Data Base 654
DIB (Daily Intelligence Bulletin) Data Base 465
Didot-Bottin Data Bases 280
Dienst Grondwaterverkenning Data Base 740
DIF Data Base 949
Dining Guide 1099

DIP (Documentation and Information System for German Parliamentary Materials) Data Base 422
Direct Access Data Bank at the University of Quebec 1064
DIRECT Data Bases 809
Directory of Companies (Pergamon InfoLine Ltd.) 802
Directory of Companies Data Base (ICC Information Group Ltd.) 499
Directory of Completed Master's Theses in Nursing (Canadian) 1037
Directory of Computing Hardware 721
Directory of Computing Software 721
Directory of Computing Suppliers 721
Directory of CSIRO Research Programs 47
Directory of Education Studies in Canada Data Base 170
Directory of Federally Supported Research in Universities 152
Directory of On-going Research in Cancer Epidemiology Data Base 1113
Directory of On-going Research in Korea 645
Directory of On-line Databases in Sweden (DOLDIS) 930
Directory of Researchers in Korean Studies 645
Directory of United Nations Information Systems (DUNIS) Data Base 1001
Directory of Water and Sanitation Institutions in Latin America and the Caribbean 794
DIRSLEARN 521
Disclosure II Corporate Information Data Base (I.P. Sharp Associates) 871
DISSERT 1 (Data Bank of European Doctoral Theses in Management) 313
DITR (Deutsches Informationszentrum fur Technische Regeln) Data Bank 407
DKF (Dokumentation Kraftfahrwesen) Data Base 716
DKI-Dokumentation Kunststoffe Kautschuk Fasern 402
DOC-EXPORT 796
DOCOCEAN 351
DOCPAL (Sistema de Documentacion sobre Poblacion en America Latina) 1007
Documentary Information Bank 996
Documentation and Information System for German Parliamentary Materials (DIP) Data Base 422
Documentation and Information System on Developmental Biology 490
Documentation Rheology Data Base 417
Documentation Tribology Data Base 417
Documents, Ordres et Reglements Statutaires 828
DOIDB Data Base (I.P. Sharp Associates) 871
Dokumentation Kraftfahrwesen (DKF) Data Base 716
Dokumentation Maschinenbau (DOMA) Data Base 961
Dokumentation Medizinische Technik (MEDITEC) Data Base 962
Dokumentation Messen Mechanischer Grossen Data Base 415
Dokumentation Schweisstechnik (DS) 418
Dokumentation Zerstorungsfreie Prufung (ZfP) Data Base 416
Dokumentationsring Elektrotechnik (DRE) Data Base 960
DOLDIS (Directory of On-Line Databases in Sweden) 930
DOMA (Dokumentation Maschinenbau) Data Base 961
Dominion Law Reports Data Base 162
Dominion Reports Service 828
DOORS (Data on Occupations Retrieval System) 462
Dortmund Data Bank (DDB) 1046
DPB (British Library Department of Printed Books) Data Base 440
DPDS (DARC Pluridata System) Data Bases 38
DPFID Data Base (I.P. Sharp Associates) 871
DPIC Data Base (Drug and Poison Information Centre, University of British Columbia) 1043
DRE (Dokumentationsring Elektrotechnik) Data Base 960
DREF (Data Reference) Data Base (WATDOC) 140
Drug and Poison Information Centre Data Base (University of British Columbia) 1043
Drug Consumption Data Base 893
Drug Information Reference Data Base 1043
DRUGDOC 296
Drugs Data Base 634
DS (Dokumentation Schweisstechnik) 418
Duff and Phelps Fixed Income Data Base (I.P. Sharp Associates) 871
Dun & Bradstreet's Key British Enterprises 802
DUNIS (Directory of United Nations Information Systems) Data Base 1001
DVJB (Danish Veterinary and Agricultural Library Catalogue) Data Base 497
EABS (Euro Abstracts) Data Base 218
EAI (Economics Abstracts International) 733
Earning Estimates Data Bank (NEEDS-TS) 754
Eastel Database 287
Eastern Bloc Countries Economic Data Base (I.P. Sharp Associates) 871
EBIP (European Biotechnology Information Program) Data Base 446
EBIS (ESCAP Bibliographic Information System) 1002
EBIS/POPFILE (ESCAP Bibliographic Information System/Population File) 1003
EC Index 305
ECDIN (Environmental Chemicals Data and Information Network) Data

Bank 221
ECO Data Base 949
Ecological Abstracts 393
ECOM Data Base 893
ECOMP 521
Econintel Monitor Data Base 290
Econometric Data Bank (University of Melbourne) 237
Economic and Social Commission for Asia and the Pacific (ESCAP) Bibliographic Information System Data Base 1002
Economics Abstracts International (EAI) 733
Economics Series Data Base (Datastream) 267
Economist Data Base (Datasolve World Reporter) 265
Economist's Statistics Data Base 679
EDCKEY Data Base 1047
EDE (Environmental Data and Ecological Parameters Data Base) 604
EDF-DOC Data Base (Electricite de France) 295
Edimedia Inc. Data Base 292
EDIN (Education on INIS) 317
Education Information Network in the European Community (EURYDICE) Data Base 215
Education Management Information Exchange Data Bases 724
Education on INIS (EDIN) 317
EEC Official Journal (Eurolex) 314
Eight Peak Index of Mass Spectra 856
Eighteenth Century Short Title Catalogue (ESTC) 443
EK-MRA Data Base 1098
Eksport Indeks 767
ELECNUC Databank 338
Electric Utilities Reports Data Base (I.P. Sharp Associates) 871
Electrical and Electronics Abstracts 549
Electrical Engineering Documentation Center Data Base 960
Electrical Patents Index (EPI) 275
Electricite de France (EDF) Data Base 295
Electronic Directory Service Data Base 552
Electronic Materials Information Service (EMIS) 550
Electronic Publishing Abstracts (EPA) 812
ELIAS (Environment Libraries Automated System) Data Base 144
ELIPA (Experienced Librarians and Information Personnel in the Developing Countries of Asia and Oceania) Data Base 644
ELLIS (European Legal Literature Information Service) 305
EMBASE (Excerpta Medica Data Base) 296
EMCANCER 296
EMCLAS Classification System 296
EMDRUGS 296
EMFORENSIC 296
EMHEALTH 296
EMIE (Education Management Information Exchange) Data Bases 724
EMIS (Electronic Materials Information Service) 550
EMPIRES (Excerpta Medica Physicians Information Referral and Education Service) 296
EMTOX 296
EMTRAIN (DIMDI) 428
ENDOC (Environmental Information and Documentation Centers) Data Base 216
ENERCAN (Canadian Renewable Energy Database) 16
ENERCAN (Canadian Renewable Energy Database) 152
ENERDATA 878
ENERGI 339
ENERGIRAP 339
Energy and Economic Data Bank, IAEA 559
Energy Programs Data Base 133
Energy Projects Data Base 133
ENLIST Data Base 1059
ENREP (Environmental Research Projects) Data Base 217
ENSDF-MEDLIST 521
ENSIC (Environmental Sanitation Information Center) Data Base 31
ENV (Environnement) Data Base 140
Envirodoq 832
Environment Libraries Automated System (ELIAS) Data Base 144
Environment-related Hydrological Data Bank (HYDABA) 411
Environmental Chemicals Data and Information Network (ECDIN) Data Bank 221
Environmental Data and Ecological Parameters Data Base (EDE) 604
Environmental Information and Documentation Centers (ENDOC) Data Base 216
Environmental Numerical Data File 626
Environmental Research in the Netherlands Data Base 743
Environmental Research Projects (ENREP) Data Base 217
Environmental Sanitation Information Center (ENSIC) Data Base 31
Environnement (ENV) Data Base 140
EPA (Electronic Publishing Abstracts) 812
EPASYS (European Patent Administrative System) 315
EPCA (European Petrochemical Association) Trade Statistics Database 993
Ephemerides of Minor Planets Data Base 997
EPI (Electrical Patents Index) 275
EPICS (European Petrochemical Industry Computerized System) Data Base 799
EPO (European Patent Office) Data Banks 315

Equity Stocks Data Base (Datastream) 267
ER586 Service Segment Data Base (I.P. Sharp Associates) 871
ERGODATA Data Base 838
EROICA Data Base 1076
ESCAP (Economic and Social Commission for Asia and the Pacific) Bibliographic Information System Data Base 1002
ESCAP Bibliographic Information System/Population File 1003
Especialidades Farmaceuticas Espanolas Data Bank (ESPES) 893
ESPES (Especialidades Farmaceuticas Espanolas Data Bank) 893
Esselte Info 260
ESSOR 977
ESTC (Eighteenth Century Short Title Catalogue) 443
EUCAS 720
EUDISED (European Documentation and Information System for Education) R&D Data Base 248
EURECAS 720
EURECHA Chemical Data Bank 327
Euro Abstracts (EABS) Data Base 218
EURODICAUTOM 223
Eurolex Data Bases 314
European Biotechnology Information Program (EBIP) Data Base 446
European Community Law Data Bases 489
European Court Reports (Eurolex) 314
European Documentation and Information System for Education (EUDISED) R&D Data Base 248
European Human Rights Reports (Eurolex) 314
European Index of Management Periodicals (SCIMP) 481
European Law Centre Ltd. Data Base 314
European Law Digest (Eurolex) 314
European Legal Literature Information Service 305
European Patent Administrative System (EPASYS) 315
European Patent Register 315
European Patent Search Documentation System 315
European Petrochemical Association (EPCA) Trade Statistics Database 993
European Petrochemical Industry Computerized System (EPICS) Data Base 799
EURYDICE (Education Information Network in the European Community) Data Base 215
EVOC (Excerpta Medica Vocabulary) Data Base 296
EXBOND 322
Excerpta Medica Data Base (EMBASE) 296
Excerpta Medica Physicians Information Referral and Education Service (EMPIRES) 296
Excerpta Medica Vocabulary (EVOC) Data Base 296
Exchequer Reports 828
Exeter Abstract Reference System 319
EXFOR Files 561
EXFOR Files 785
EXIS (Expert Information Systems Ltd.) Data Bases 320
Experienced Librarians and Information Personnel in the Developing Countries of Asia and Oceania (ELIPA) Data Base 644
Expert Information Systems Ltd. (EXIS) Data Bases 320
Export Index 767
EXSHARE 321
EXSTAT 323
Extel International Bonds Database 322
EXTEMPLO 1049
Extra Pharmacopoeia Data Bank 806
Faba Bean Abstracts 229
Fabrimetal Data Base 187
Facility for the Analysis of Chemical Thermodynamics (Fact) Data Base 691
Fact (Facility for the Analysis of Chemical Thermodynamics) Data Base 691
Fahrzeug-Datenbank-System 1104
FAIREC (Fruits Agro-Industrie Regions Chaudes) Data Base 547
Fairplay International Research Services (FIRS) Data Base 324
FALI 80
FAO Documentation Data Base 1013
FAO Library Catalogue of Monographs Data Base 1013
FAO Statistics Data Bases 1014
Farm Bank (AERIC) 238
FARMODEX Drug Data Bank 325
Fast Avfall 767
Federal Court of Canada Reports 828
Federal Reserve Board Weekly Data Base (I.P. Sharp Associates) 871
Feed Composition Data Bank 487
FEES Data Base 692
Fiches Techniques (FITEK) Data Bank 252
Fichier MARC Quebecois (FMQ) 833
Field Crop Abstracts 229
Film Canadiana 146
Financial Data File (ICC Information Group Ltd.) 499
Financial Futures Data Base (Datastream) 267
Financial Post Canadian Corporate Data Base (I.P. Sharp Associates) 871
Financial Post Investment Data Bank 680
Financial Post Securities Data Base (I.P. Sharp Associates) 871

Financial Times Actuaries Share Indices Data Base (I.P. Sharp Associates) 871
Financial Times Commercial Law Reports (Eurolex) 314
Financial Times Company Information 328
Financial Times Currency and Share Index Databank 328
Financial Times Index 328
Financial Times Share Information Data Base (I.P. Sharp Associates) 871
FINDATA 903
Fine Chemicals Directory 372
FINMED Data Base 329
Finnish National Bibliography 482
Finnish Periodicals Index in Economics and Business (FINP) 481
Finnish Register of Exporters Data Base 332
Finnish Standards Association Data Base 334
FINP (Finnish Periodicals Index in Economics and Business) 481
Fire Research Library Automated Information Retrieval (FLAIR) Data Base 452
Fire Science Abstracts (FSA) 452
FIRMEXPORT 796
FIRMKAT Data Base 1079
FIRS (Fairplay International Research Services) Data Base 324
FITEK (Fiches Techniques) Data Bank 252
Fixed Interest Instruments Data Base (Datastream) 267
FLAIR (Fire Research Library Automated Information Retrieval) Data Base 452
Fleet Street Reports (Eurolex) 314
Fluid Flow Measurements Abstracts 86
Fluid Power Abstracts 86
Fluid Sealing Abstracts 86
FLUIDEX 86
FMQ (Fichier MARC Quebecois) 833
FOCUS 321
FODOK (Forschungsprojektdokumentation) Data Base 419
Fonds Quetelet Library Data Base 81
FONTE Data Base 102
Food Research Association Computerized Information Services (FRANCIS) Data Base 655
Food Science and Technology Abstracts (FSTA) 583
Foreign Trade Abstracts 733
Foreign Trade Statistics for Asia and the Pacific Data Base 1004
Forest Products Abstracts 229
Forestry Abstracts 229
FORIS (Forschungsinformationssystem Sozialwissenschaften) 43
Form 41 Data Base (I.P. Sharp Associates) 871
FORMAT 146
FORS (Forschungsprojekte Raumordnung Stadtebau Wohnungswesen) 380
Forschungsinformationssystem Sozialwissenschaften (FORIS) 43
Forschungsprojektdokumentation (FODOK) Data Base 419
Forschungsprojekte Raumordnung Stadtebau Wohnungswesen (FORS) 380
FoU-Indeks 767
FPCORP Data Base (I.P. Sharp Associates) 871
FPSTOCK Data Base (I.P. Sharp Associates) 871
FRANCIS (Food Research Association Computerized Information Services) Data Base 655
FRANCIS (French Retrieval Automated Network for Current Information in Social and Human Sciences) Data Bases 355
FRBW Data Base (I.P. Sharp Associates) 871
French Retrieval Automated Network for Current Information in Social and Human Sciences (FRANCIS) Data Bases 355
French Senate Data Bases 343
French Stockbrokers Society Data Base 389
FRIGINTER Data Base 590
Fruits Agro-Industrie Regions Chaudes (FAIREC) Data Base 547
FSA (Fire Science Asbtracts) 452
FSTA (Food Science and Technology Abstracts) 583
FTACT Data Base (I.P. Sharp Associates) 871
FTSTOCK Data Base (I.P. Sharp Associates) 871
Fund Monitor Unit Trusts and Insurance Bonds Data Base (I.P. Sharp Associates) 871
FUNDMONITOR Data Base (I.P. Sharp Associates) 871
FUTU (Futures Information Service) Data Base 540
Futures Information Service (FUTU) Data Base 540
G & J (Gruner & Jahr) Press Information Bank 468
GAP (Government of Alberta Publications) Data Base 11
GAPHYOR (Gaz-Physique-Orsay) Data Base 1063
Garden Guide 1099
Gas Physics Orsay (GAPHYOR) Data Base 1063
GATT (General Agreement on Tariffs and Trade) Data Base/Denmark 497
Gaz-Physique-Orsay (GAPHYOR) Data Base 1063
GDoc Data Base 1050
General Agreement on Tariffs and Trade (GATT) Data Base/Denmark 497
General Index to the Debates of the National Diet (Japan) 629
Geo Abstracts 393
GeoArchive 394

GEOBIB 625
Geochemical Analysis Data Base 387
GEODE 340
GEODIAL (Geoscience Data Index for Alberta) 12
geoIPOD 352
GEOLINE 412
Geological Bibliography of France 340
Geological Survey of Sweden Data Bases 920
Geomechanics Abstracts 1056
Geophysics and Tectonics Abstracts 393
GEOROAD Data Base 925
GEOSCAN Database 135
Geoscience Data Index for Alberta (GEODIAL) 12
Geoscience Literature Information Service Data Base 412
Geosources 394
Geowissenschaftlicher Literaturinformationsdienst Data Base 412
German Bibliography Data Base 423
German Federal Diet Data Base 422
German Foreign Trade Information Office Data Base 425
German Foundation for International Development Data Bank 397
German Information Center for Technical Rules Data Bank 407
German Information System for High Energy Physics Data Base 396
German Patent Information System Data Base 401
German Plastics Institute Data Base 402
German Psychological Literature Data Base (PSYNDEX) 1078
German Union Catalog of Serials 400
German Union List of Conference Proceedings 400
Glacier Inventory of Canada Data Base 139
Glass Institute Information and Documentation Data Base 429
Global Oral Data Bank 1111
Globe and Mail Online, The 430
Gmelin Handbook of Inorganic Chemistry Index 431
GOIC (Gulf Organization for Industrial Consulting) Data Bases 471
Government of Alberta Publications (GAP) Data Base 11
GRACE Data Base 1076
Graduate Theses in the Philippines Data Base 808
Grammatico-Lexicographical Data Base on Contemporary German 541
GRAPPE 977
Grassroots Data Bases 519
GRIPS Training Database (GRIPSLEARN) 428
GRIPSLEARN (GRIPS Training Database) 428
Groundwater Survey Data Base (Netherlands) 740
Grouped Enterprises Data Base 237
Gruner & Jahr Press Information Bank 468
Guardian Data Base (Datasolve World Reporter) 265
Guinness Superlatives Data Base 470
Gulf Organization for Industrial Consulting (GOIC) Data Bases 471
Handbuch der Grossunternehmen Data Base 1098
Hansard Oral Questions 828
Hansard Written Questions 828
Harmonized Trade and World Economy Accounts Data Banks 185
Harwell Central Information Service Data Bases 434
Hazfile 435
HDEG (Union List of Higher Degree Theses in Australian Libraries) Data Base 1074
Health and Medical Libraries Online Catalog (HEMLOC) 50
Health and Safety Executive (HSE) Data Base 457
Health Care Information Service Data Base 477
Health Care Literature Information Network (HECLINET) Data Base 477
HEATW Data Base (I.P. Sharp Associates) 871
Heavy Oil/Enhanced Recovery Index (HERI) 13
Hebrew University of Jerusalem Data Bases 478
HECLINET (Health Care Literature Information Network) Data Base 477
Helecon Data Bases 481
HELIOS 384
Helminthological Abstracts: Series A, Animal Helminthology 229
Helminthological Abstracts: Series B, Plant Nematology 229
HELPIS (Higher Education Learning Programmes Information Service Catalogue) 112
HEMLOC (Health and Medical Libraries Online Catalog) 50
Henley Centre for Forecasting Data Base 484
Henrik Ibsen Concordance 768
Herbage Abstracts 229
HERI (Heavy Oil/Enhanced Recovery Index) 13
Hertfordshire Business and Community Information Service 486
Hertfordshire Business Data Bank 486
High Energy Physics Index Data Base 396
High Temperature Materials Data Bank (HTM-DB) 222
Higher Education Learning Programmes Information Service Catalogue (HELPIS) 112
HISCABEQ 704
HKEP&BP (Hong Kong English Periodicals and Book Publishers) Data Base 635
HKSTOCK Data Base (I.P. Sharp Associates) 871
HMSO Statutes in Force (Eurolex) 314
Home Computing Guide 1099
Home Improvement Guide 1099

Home Office Forensic Science Service Data Base 458
HOMS (Hydrological Operational Multipurpose Subprogramme) Data Base 1117
Hong Kong English Periodicals and Book Publishers (HKEP&BP) Data Base 635
Hong Kong Stock Exchange Data Base (I.P. Sharp Associates) 871
Hoppenstedt Data Bases 1098
Horticultural Abstracts 229
House of Lords Library Data Bases 460
HSE (Health and Safety Executive) Data Base 457
HSELiNE Data Base 457
HTM-DB (High Temperature Materials Data Bank) 222
Hughes Rotary Drilling Rig Report Data Base (I.P. Sharp Associates) 871
Human Nutrition Database 545
Hungarian Academy of Sciences Publication Data Bank 492
HYDABA (Environment-related Hydrological Data Bank) 411
Hydrogene dans les Metaux 981
Hydrogene Information 981
HYDROLINE 412
Hydrological Operational Multipurpose Subprogramme (HOMS) Data Base 1117
IAB (Institut fur Arbeitsmarkt- und Berufsforschung) Data Bases 410
IAEA (International Atomic Energy Agency) Energy and Economic Data Bank 559
IALINE-Pascal 39
IATA North Atlantic Traffic Data Base (I.P. Sharp Associates) 871
IBECENT 1021
IBEDOC (International Bureau of Education Documentation and Information Unit) Data Base 1021
IBETERM 1021
IBI (Intergovernmental Bureau for Informatics) Documentation Data Base 554
IBIP (International Books in Print) Data Base 863
IBIS Data Base 194
IBJ Financial Data File 498
IBJDATA 498
IBR (Institute for Behavioural Research) Data Bases 1120
IBSEDEX Data Base 119
Ibsen (Henrik) Concordance 768
ICAO (International Civil Aviation Organization) Air Transport Statistics Data Base 569
ICAO (International Civil Aviation Organization) Aircraft Accident Data Base 567
ICAO (International Civil Aviation Organization) Airport Characteristics Data Bank 568
ICAO Regulations Module 320
ICAO Traffic Statistics Data Base (I.P. Sharp Associates) 871
ICAR (Inventory of Canadian Agricultural Research) 167
ICC Information Group Ltd. Data Bases 499
ICEREF 139
ICIS (Independent Chemical Information Services Ltd.) Data Base 505
ICONOS 384
ICS Data Bases (Interlinked Computerized Storage and Processing System of Food and Agricultural Data) 1014
ICSD (Inorganic Crystal Structure Data Base) 1042
ICV (Indice Cientifico Valenciano) 1082
ICYT (Instituto de Informacion y Documentacion en Ciencia y Tecnologia) Data Bank 890
IDA (Industrial Development Abstracts) 1027
IDB (INPADOC Data Base) 64
IDC Inorganic Data Base 572
IDC Organic Chemistry File 572
IDC Patent Data Bank 572
IDC Polymer File 572
IDIS (Institut fur Dokumentation und Information uber Sozialmedizin und Offentliches Gesundheitswesen) Data Bases 539
IDS (Institut fur Deutsche Sprache) Data Base 541
IEA (International Association for the Evaluation of Educational Achievement) Data Bank 557
IEC (Information Exchange Centre for Federally Supported Research in Canadian Universities) Data Base 152
IEE-Energy Data Bank (Institute of Energy Economics) 753
IFIC (International Ferrocement Information Center) Data Base 32
IFO Time Series Data Bank 501
IFP-TH 387
IFS Data Base (I.P. Sharp Associates) 871
IGODOC 593
ILCS (Interlibrary Loan and Communication System) Data Bases 195
ILODOC 593
IMAG Dataservice Data Bases 543
IME (Indice Medico Espanol) 1082
IMM Abstracts Data Base 551
IMMAGE Data Base 551
IMO Module 320
IMPORTS Data Base (I.P. Sharp Associates) 871
IMS MIDAS Databank 504
IMSPACT Data Base 504

Indeks IoD 767
Independent Chemical Information Services Ltd. (ICIS) Data Base 505
Index de la Litterature des Sports et des Loisirs 210
Index de Periodiques Canadiens 174
Index of Publications Owned by Computing Services (Library) 1033
Index of Software Supported by Computing Services (PROGRAMLIST) 1033
Index to Conference Proceedings Received (British Library) 442
Index to Hebrew Periodicals Data Base 1051
Index to Literature on Atomic Collision Data (CIAMDA) 561
Index to 19th Century Eretz-Israel Newspapers 1051
Index to Swedish Newspapers 116
Index to Swedish Periodicals 116
Index to the Financial Times 328
Index Veterinarius 229
Indian National Scientific Documentation Centre (INSDOC) Data Bases 507
Indicators of Industrial Activity (OECD) 780
Indice Cientifico Valenciano (ICV) 1082
Indice Espanol de Ciencia y Tecnologia 890
Indice Espanol de Ciencias Sociales 891
Indice Espanol de Humanidades 891
Indice Medico Espanol (IME) 1082
Industrial Aerodynamics Abstracts 86
Industrial Case Reports (Eurolex) 314
Industrial Data Banks (Gulf Organization for Industrial Consulting) 471
Industrial Development Abstracts (IDA) 1027
Industrial Technical Information Service (ITIS) Data Base, Singapore 877
Industries Agro-Alimentaires Bibliographie Internationale 39
Industry and Environment Data Base 1024
Infant Feeding Bibliography 47
Info Globe Data Bases 430
INFODATA Data Base 880
INFOFISH Data Base 1011
INFOIL II 769
Infolex Data Bases 517
INFOMEDIA 361
Informatics Biblio Service Data Base 797
Information and Documentation Centre for Occupational Safety Data Base 419
Information Bulletin on the Survey of Chemicals Being Tested for Carcinogenicity Data Base 1113
Information Center for Building and Physical Planning Data Bases 373
Information Eaux Data Base 391
Information Exchange Centre for Federally Supported Research in Canadian Universities (IEC) Data Base 152
Information London Data Base 525
Information Network for Official Statistics (INFOS) Data Base 749
Information on Educational Research and Development in Switzerland (SWINFED) Data Base 945
Information Retrieval System for the Sociology of Leisure and Sport (SIRLS) 1085
Information Services for the Physics and Engineering Communities (INSPEC) 549
Information System for Environmental Chemicals, Chemical Plants, and Accidents (INFUCHS) 411
Information System for the Economy Data Bank 364
Information System on Production Plants for Iron & Steel Data Base 398
Information Trade Directory Prestel File 69
Informations- und Dokumentationszentrum fur Arbeitsschutz Data Base 419
Informationsdienst Krankenhauswesen Data Base 477
Informationsdienstkartei Tierische Produktion Data Base 487
Informationssystem Karlsruhe (INKA) Data Bases 521
Informationszentrum fur Schnittwerte (INFOS) Data Bank 964
Informationszentrum Raum und Bau (IRB) Data Bases 373
InformationsZentrum Sozialwissenschaften (IZ) Data Bases 43
Informetal Data Base 281
Informetrica Limited Data Bases 536
INFOS (Information Network for Official Statistics) Data Base 749
INFOS (Informationszentrum fur Schnittwerte) Data Bank 964
Infoterm Data Bases 587
INFOTERRA Data Base 1025
INFSOC Data Base 591
INFUCHS (Information System for Environmental Chemicals, Chemical Plants, and Accidents) 411
INID (Romanian National Institute for Information and Documentation) Data Base 843
INIS (International Nuclear Information System) Data Base 560
Inorganic Crystal Structure Data Base (ICSD) 1042
Inorganic Data Base (IDC) 572
INPADOC (International Patent Documentation Center) Data Base 64
INPI-1 359
INPI-2 359
INPI-3 359
INPI-4 359

INS Data Base (I.P. Sharp Associates) 871
INSDOC (Indian National Scientific Documentation Centre) Data Bases 507
INSERM Research Information Bank 358
Insight Data Bases 163
Insight Data Bases 164
Insight Data Bases 165
Insight Data Bases 166
INSPEC (Information Services for the Physics and Engineering Communities) 549
Institut de Recherches sur les Fruits et Agrumes (IRFA) Data Base 547
Institut Francais des Petroles (IFP) Thermodynamique 387
Institut fur Deutsche Sprache (IDS) Data Base 541
Institut fur Dokumentation und Information uber Sozialmedizin und Offentliches Gesundheitswesen (IDIS) Data Bases 539
Institut fur Ernahrungswissenschaft Data Base 545
Institut National de la Propriete Industrielle (INPI) Data Bases 359
Institute for Behavioural Research (IBR) Data Bases 1120
Institute for Documentation and Information in Social Medicine and Public Health (IDIS) Data Bases 539
Institute for Employment Research (IAB) Data Bases 410
Institute for German Language Data Base 541
Institute of Energy Economics (IEE) Energy Data Bank 753
Institute of Nutrition Data Base 545
Institute of Research on Fruits and Citrus Fruits Data Base 547
Instituto de Informacion y Documentacion en Ciencia y Tecnologia (ICYT) Data Bank 890
Instruments of Testing and Research in Korea 645
INTDIS (International Drug Information System) Data Base 1115
Inter-Corporate Ownership Data Base (CLRA) 165
INTERCIM Cement Data Base 188
INTERDOC (System of Documentary Reference of MINTER) 100
Interfisc 715
Intergovernmental Bureau for Informatics (IBI) Documentation Data Base 554
INTERLEGI (System of Legislative Reference of MINTER) 100
Interlibrary Loan and Communication System (ICLS) Data Bases 195
Interlinked Computerized Storage and Processing System of Food and Agricultural Data (ICS) Data Bases 1014
International Association for the Evaluation of Educational Achievement (IEA) Data Bank 557
International Atomic Energy Agency (IAEA) Energy and Economic Data Bank 559
International Bibliography of the Social Sciences 571
International Biodeterioration 229
International Books in Print (IBIP) Data Base 863
International Building Services Abstracts Data Base 119
International Bureau of Education Documentation and Information Unit (IBEDOC) Data Base 1021
International Civil Aviation Organization (ICAO) Air Transport Statistics Data Base 569
International Civil Aviation Organization (ICAO) Aircraft Accident Data Base 567
International Civil Aviation Organization (ICAO) Airport Characteristics Data Bank 568
International Civil Engineering Abstracts 208
International Company for Documentation in Chemistry Data Bases 572
International Development Abstracts 393
International Development Information Network Data Bases 781
International Directory of Research Centres and Information Sources, Services and Systems in New and Renewable Energies 1018
International Drug Information System (INTDIS) Data Base 1115
International Ferrocement Information Center (IFIC) Data Base 32
International Financial Securities Statistics Data Base (I.P. Sharp Associates) 871
International Frequency Register 606
International Human Biometry and Ergonomics Data Bank 838
International Information System for the Agricultural Sciences and Technology (AGRIS) Data Base 1012
International Labour Documentation Data Base 593
International Labour Office Bureau of Statistics Data Base 592
International Livestock Centre for Africa Documentation Data Base 596
International Nuclear Information System (INIS) Data Base 560
International Occupational Safety and Health Information Centre Data Base 595
International Patent Documentation Center (INPADOC) Data Base 64
International Petroleum Annual Data Base (I.P. Sharp Associates) 871
International Railway Union Data Base 600
International Register of Potentially Toxic Chemicals (IRPTC) 1026
International Register of Research on Visual Disability 115
International Relations Information System (IRIS) Data Base 337
International Reviews on Mathematical Education 521
International Road Research Documentation (IRRD) Data Base 786
International Serials Data System (ISDS) Register 603
International Telecommunication Union (ITU) Data Bases 606
International Trade Data Bank (NEEDS-TS) 754

Internationale Dokumentationsgesellschaft fur Chemie (IDC) Data Bases 572
INTERVENTIONS 343
INTERVOC (Vocabulario Controlado do MINTER) 100
Inventaire Canadien des Recherches Presentement en Vigueur en Nursing 1036
Inventory of Abstracting and Indexing Services Produced in the U.K. 1055
Inventory of Canadian Agricultural Research (ICAR) 167
Inventory of the Scientific Clearinghouse and Documentation Services Division Holdings (Philippines) 808
Investdata System Data Base 975
IPA Data Base (I.P. Sharp Associates) 871
IPC Chemical Database 612
IRB (Informationszentrum Raum und Bau) Data Bases 373
IRCS Medical Science Database 614
IRFA (Institut de Recherches sur les Fruits et Agrumes) Data Base 547
IRIS (International Relations Information System) Data Base 337
IRIS Project Data Base 169
Iron and Steel Documentation Service Data Base 192
IRPTC (International Register of Potentially Toxic Chemicals) 1026
IRRD (International Road Research Documentation) Data Base 786
Irrigation and Drainage Abstracts 229
ISDS (International Serials Data System) Register 603
IT Focus Data Base 549
ITIS (Industrial Technical Information Service) Data Base, Singapore 877
ITIS Data Base 194
ITU (International Telecommunication Union) Data Bases 606
IZ (InformationsZentrum Sozialwissenschaften) Data Bases 43
James R. LymBurner & Sons Ltd. Data Base 679
Japan Cancer Literature (JCL) Data Base 598
Japan Directory of Professional Associations (JDPA) Database 635
Japan Economic & Business Data Bank (NRI/E) 760
Japan Information Center of Science and Technology (JICST) File on Medical Science in Japan 632
Japan Information Center of Science and Technology (JICST) File on Research in Progress in Japan 632
Japan Information Center of Science and Technology (JICST) File on Science and Technology 632
JAPAN/MARC 629
Japan National Diet Library Data Bases 629
Japan National Institute for Environmental Studies Data Bases 626
Japan Oceanographic Data Center (JODC) Data Base 628
Japan Patent Information Center (JAPATIC) Data Base 633
Japan Pharmaceutical Abstracts 634
Japan Publications Guide Service (JPGS) Database 635
Japanese National Bibliography 629
Japanese Periodicals Index 629
JAPANSCAN Data Base 712
JAPATIC (Japan Patent Information Center) Data Base 633
JAPICDOC Data Base 634
JCL (Japan Cancer Literature) Data Base 598
JDPA (Japan Directory of Professional Associations) Database 635
JICST (Japan Information Center of Science and Technology) File on Medical Science in Japan 632
JICST (Japan Information Center of Science and Technology) File on Research in Progress in Japan 632
JICST (Japan Information Center of Science and Technology) File on Science and Technology 632
JODC (Japan Oceanographic Data Center) Data Base 628
JOINT (Journal of Industrial Titles) Data Base 753
Jordan Line Services Data Base 636
Journal of Industrial Titles (JOINT) Data Base 753
Journal of Planning Law (Eurolex) 314
Journal of Synthetic Methods 274
JPGS (Japan Publications Guide Service) Database 635
JSCHEDULE Data Base (I.P. Sharp Associates) 871
JTW (C76 Journey-To-Work) Data Bases 237
Judicial Information System (JURIS) Data Base 426
Juridical Databank 641
Juridische Databank 641
JURINPI Data Base 360
JURIS (Juristisches Informationssystem) Data Base 426
JURIS-DATA 294
Juristisches Informationssystem (JURIS) Data Base 426
KATI Data Base 482
KENTV Data Base (I.P. Sharp Associates) 871
Key British Enterprises 802
KGST-CMEA Data Base 494
Kidric (Boris) Laboratory for Information Systems Data Bases 96
KKF (Kunstoffe Kautschuk Fasern) Data Base 402
KNMP (Koninklijke Nederlandse Maatschappij ter Bevordering der Pharmacie) Drug Databank 844
KOMPASS Data Base (DataArkiv AB) 260
Kompass Data Bases 642
KOMPASS EUROPE 94
KOMPASS-FRANCE 514

KOMPASS SWEDEN   94
Koninklijke Nederlandse Maatschappij ter Bevordering der Pharmacie (KNMP) Drug Databank   844
Korean Periodicals Index   645
Kunststoffe Kautschuk Fasern (KKF) Data Base   402
LABINFO   355
LABOR Data Base   591
LABOR Data Base   593
Laboratory Hazards Bulletin (LHB)   855
LABORDOC   593
Labour Information Database (LID)   591
LAN (Latin American Newsletters Ltd.) Data Base   651
Land of Israel Data Bank   1051
LANDUP (Alberta Land Use Planning Data Bank)   10
Language Catalog   1033
LASER (London and South Eastern Library Region) Data Base   670
Latin American Center for Economic and Social Documentation Data Bases   1006
Latin American Newsletters Ltd. (LAN) Data Base   651
Latin American Population Documentation System (DOCPAL)   1007
Lead Abstracts   1122
Lead, Zinc, Silver Mine Cost Model Databank   228
League of Arab States Documentation and Information Center (ALDOC) Data Base   653
LEDA (On-Line Earthnet Data Availability) Data Bank   317
Leistungs- und Konstruktions Datenbank (LKD)   716
Leisure, Recreation and Tourism Abstracts   229
Leisure Studies Data Bank   1084
Lentil Abstracts   229
Les Rapports de la Cour Federale du Canada   828
Les Rapports de la Cour Supreme du Canada   828
Les Statuts Revises du Canada   828
LEX   977
LHB (Laboratory Hazards Bulletin)   855
LIBCAT (Harwell Central Information Service)   434
Library (Index of Publications Owned by Computing Services)   1033
Library and Information Science Abstracts (LISA)   663
LIBRARY Data Base (University of New Brunswick)   1059
Library Information On-line (LION) Data Base   562
Library Information System (LIBRIS) Data Base   931
Library Instruction Materials Bank Index   677
Library Network of SIBIL Users Data Base   664
LIBRIS (Library Information System) Data Base   931
LIBRIS (Plasma Physics Library and Information Service)   438
LID (Labour Information Database)   591
LIDAS Data Base   1104
LIFFE (London International Financial Futures Exchange Ltd.) Data Base   672
LIMB Index   677
LINA (Literaturnachweise)   376
LION (Library Information On-line) Data Base   562
Liquified Petroleum Gas Report Data Base (I.P. Sharp Associates)   871
LISA (Library and Information Science Abstracts)   663
LISA Data Base   562
LISDOK (Literaturinformationssystem) Data Base   765
List of Persons and Organizations Related to Asbestos Research and Technology   1071
List of Ship Stations   606
List of Telegraph Offices   606
List of Theses for the Doctor's and Master's Degree in Korea   645
Listed Companies' Databank (NEEDS-TS)   754
LITDOK (Literaturdokumentation) Data Base   419
Literaturdatenbank Elektrotechnik   960
Literaturdatenbank Maschinenbau   961
Literaturdokumentation (LITDOK) Data Base   419
Literature Compilations Data Base   376
Literaturinformationssystem (LISDOK) Data Base   765
Literaturnachweise (LINA)   376
Livestock Documentation Data Base   596
Living Philosophers Data Base   1048
LJUS   80
LKD (Leistungs- und Konstruktions Datenbank)   716
Lloyd's Casualty Files   667
Lloyd's New Construction File   667
Lloyd's Register Book File   667
Lloyd's Shipowner and Parent Company File   667
Lloyd's Shipping Information Services (LSIS) Data Bases   667
Lloyd's Shipping Movements - Voyage History File   667
Lloyd's Ships Latest Position File   667
LOB Corpus   768
Local Area Data Bank (INSEE)   365
Location Register of Twentieth Century English Literary Manuscripts and Letters   1065
LOGOS   384
Lois Constitutionnelles du Canada   828
London and South Eastern Library Region (LASER) Data Base   670
London Community Services Data Base   525
London International Financial Futures Exchange Ltd. (LIFFE) Data Base   672

London-Lund Corpus   768
London Over the Counter Market (LOTC) Data Base   673
LOTC (London Over the Counter Market) Data Base   673
Lower Saxonia Serials Data Base   400
LPGAS Data Base (I.P. Sharp Associates)   871
LSIS (Lloyd's Shipping Information Services) Data Bases   667
Lundberg Survey Retail Price Data Base (I.P. Sharp Associates)   871
Lundberg Survey Share of Market Data Base (I.P. Sharp Associates)   871
LymBurner (James R.) & Sons Ltd. Data Base   679
M & T (Agricultural Marketing and Trade) Database   126
Macroeconomic Data Bank (INSEE)   366
MADCAP Data Bank   1088
Maghreb Data Base   186
Main Economic Indicators (OECD)   780
MAINS (Material Information System) for Iron & Steel   399
Maize Quality Protein Abstracts   229
MALIMET (Master List of Medical Indexing Terms)   296
Management & Marketing Abstracts (MMA)   812
Management Information System of Science and Technology Resources (Republic of China)   726
Management System for Astronomical Data in Machine-Readable Form Data Base   995
Manitoba Reports (National Reporter System)   828
Manitoba Statute Citator (SMC)   173
MARC Quebecois   833
Marine Affairs Bibliography   254
Marine Environmental Data Information Referral System (MEDI) Data Base   1020
Marine Information and Advisory Service (MIAS) Data Bank   730
Marine Research and Technology Data Base   413
Maritime Law Book National Reporter System   828
Market Information Bank   824
Market Location Data Bases   686
Market Research Abstracts   687
Marketfax Data Base   326
Marketscan   430
Marknadsbank   824
MARNA   685
Martindale Online   806
Mass Spectra Data Base   856
Mass Spectrometry Bulletin (MSB) Data Base   856
Master List of Medical Indexing Terms (MALIMET)   296
Material Data Base (MDB)   399
Material Information System (MAINS) for Iron & Steel   399
Materials Data Retrieval System Data Base   316
Materials Information Module   320
MATH (Mathematics Abstracts)   521
MATHDI   521
Mathematics Abstracts (MATH)   521
MAXIMS Data Base   504
MBANK Data Base (I.P. Sharp Associates)   871
MDB (Material Data Base)   399
Measurement of Mechanical Quantities Documentation Data Base   415
Mechanical Engineering (MechEn) Data Base   930
Mechanical Engineering Documentation Data Base   961
MechEn (Mechanical Engineering) Data Base   930
MEDI (Marine Environmental Data Information Referral System) Data Base   1020
Media Databank (NEEDS-TS)   754
Media P Data Bank   189
MEDIAFILE   823
MEDIAL   879
MEDIC Data Base   329
Medical-Pharmaceutical Publishing Company Data Base   693
Medical Technology Documentation Data Base   962
MEDISTAT (Banque de Donnees Socio-economiques des Pays Mediterraneens)   564
MEDITEC (Dokumentation Medizinische Technik) Data Base   962
MEDTRAIN   440
Meeting Agenda Data Base   339
MEF (Mideast File)   970
MER Data Base (I.P. Sharp Associates)   871
MERCATIS   879
MERCATIS   881
MERL-ECO   696
MERLIN-TECH   697
Messtechnik, Regelungstechnik, Automatik (MRA) Data Base   1098
METADEX (Metals Abstracts Index)   698
Metals Abstracts Index (METADEX)   698
Metals Crystallographic (CRYSTMET) Data File   156
Metals Datafile   698
Metropolitan Toronto Library Board Data Bases   699
MIAS (Marine Information and Advisory Service) Data Bank   730
MicroEXSTAT   323
Microlog Index   706
Micronet 800 Data Base   976
MIDAS Databank   504
Mideast File (MEF)   970

Mine, Smelter, Refinery Databank 228
Mineral Processing Technology (MINPROC) Data Base 131
Mineralogical Abstracts 711
Mining Technology Abstracts (MINTEC) Data Base 131
Minor Planets, Comets, and Satellites Data Base 997
MINPROC (Mineral Processing Technology) Data Base 131
MinSearch 727
MINSYS 394
MINTEC (Mining Technology Abstracts) Data Base 131
MISCA Microthesaurus 794
MMA (Management & Marketing Abstracts) 812
MMI Data Base 1059
Modulad Data Base 361
Modulef Data Base 361
Money Market Rate Data Base (I.P. Sharp Associates) 871
Monitoring Information Data Bank 606
Monthly Energy Review Data Base (I.P. Sharp Associates) 871
Monthly Report of Heating Oil and Middle Distillates Data Base (I.P. Sharp Associates) 871
MOST (Instruments of Testing and Research in Korea) 645
Motor Vehicle Documentation Data Base 716
MRA (Messtechnik, Regelungstechnik, Automatik) Data Base 1098
MRATE Data Base (I.P. Sharp Associates) 871
MSB (Mass Spectrometry Bulletin) Data Base 856
Naerinfo-Indeks 767
NAPLES 879
NAQUADAT (National Water Quality Data Bank) 141
NASDATA Data Base 793
NASTOCK Data Base (I.P. Sharp Associates) 871
National Computing Centre Data Bases 721
National Diet Library Data Bases 629
National Emergency Equipment Locator System Data Base (I.P. Sharp Associates) 871
National Engineering Laboratory's Thermophysical Properties Package 548
National Geochemical Data Bank (NGDB) 728
National Income Forecasting Model of the Australian Economy Data Base (I.P. Sharp Associates) 871
National Master Specification (NMS) Data Bank 242
National Physical Laboratory/Scientific Group Thermodata Europe (NPL/SGTE) Databank 451
National Planning Association Demographic Data Base (I.P. Sharp Associates) 871
National Planning Association Economic Data Base (I.P. Sharp Associates) 871
National Reporter System (NRS) Data Bases 828
National Science and Technology Authority Data Bases (Philippines) 808
National Topographic Data Base of Canada 136
National Union Catalogue of Serials (NUCOS) 48
National Water Quality Data Bank (NAQUADAT) 141
Natural Environment Data File 626
Naval Record 97
NAVFs EDB-Senter for Humanistisk Forskning Data Bases 768
NCC (National Computing Centre) Data Bases 721
NCC/IBL (Nederlandse Centrale Catalogus/Interbibliothecair Leenverkeer System) Data Base 240
NCOM Data Base 763
NDT-Info 436
NEA-DB (Nuclear Energy Agency Data Bank) 785
Nederlandse Centrale Catalogus/Interbibliothecair Leenverkeer System (NCC/IBL) Data Base 240
NEEDS-IR (Nikkei Economic Electronic Databank System-Information Retrieval) Data Bases 753
NEEDS Portfolio System 754
NEEDS-TS (Nikkei Economic Electronic Databank System-Time Sharing) Data Files 754
NEELS Data Base (I.P. Sharp Associates) 871
NEI (Nordic Energy Index) 761
NELPAC (National Engineering Laboratory's Thermophysical Properties Package) 548
Netherlands Central Catalogue/Interlibrary Loan System Data Base 240
Netherlands Groundwater Survey Data Base 740
Netherlands Terminology and Documentation Section Data Bank 732
Network of Social Security Information Resources Data Base 145
New Brunswick Reports (National Reporter System) 828
New South Wales Motor Vehicle 1982 Registrations Data Base 237
New Zealand Department of Statistics Data Base 749
New Zealand Science Abstracts 748
Newfoundland and Prince Edward Island Reports (National Reporter System) 828
Newfoundland Mineral Development Data Bases 750
NEWSFILE 823
NEWSLaw (Eurolex) 314
NEWSLINE 335
Newstex (Canadian Press) 828
NGDB (National Geochemical Data Bank) 728
NIF-10S Model Data Base 237

NIF10 Data Base (I.P. Sharp Associates) 871
Nihon Keizai Shimbun (NKS) Article Information Data Base 753
Nihon Keizai Shimbun (NKS) Survey Databank 754
Nikkei Article Information Data Bank 753
Nikkei Commodity Prices 754
Nikkei Economic Electronic Databank System-Information Retrieval (NEEDS-IR) Data Bases 753
Nikkei Economic Statistics 754
Nikkei Energy 754
Nikkei Household Survey 754
Nikkei Input/Output Tables 754
Nikkei Public and Corporate Bond Index 754
Nikkei Stock and Bond Prices Databank 754
1981 Canadian Census Data Base (I.P. Sharp Associates) 871
Nineteenth Century Short Title Catalogue (NTSC) 757
NKS (Nihon Keizai Shimbun) Article Information Data Base 753
NKS (Nihon Keizai Shimbun) Survey Databank 754
NLEX 643
NMS (National Master Specification) Data Bank 242
Noise Index 767
Nomura Research Institute (NRI/E) Japan Economic & Business Data Bank 760
Non-Ferrous Metals Abstracts Data Base 92
Non-Listed Companies' Databank (NEEDS-TS) 754
Nondestructive Testing Centre (NTC) Data Base 436
Nondestructive Testing Documentation Data Base 416
Nordic Documentation Center for Mass Communication Research (NORDICOM) Data Base 763
Nordic Energy Index (NEI) 761
NORDICOM (Nordic Documentation Center for Mass Communication Research) Data Base 763
Nordisk databas i Pedagogik och Psykologi (PEPSY) 924
NORDRUG 936
NORIANE (Normes et Reglements Informations Automatisees Accessibles en Ligne) 382
NORMARC (Norwegian MARC) System Data Base 1061
Normes et Reglements Informations Automatisees Accessibles en Ligne (NORIANE) 382
NORSAR (Norwegian Seismic Array) Data Base 850
Norsk Termbank 1040
North American Stock Market Data Base (I.P. Sharp Associates) 871
Norwegian Computing Centre for the Humanities Data Bases 768
Norwegian MARC (NORMARC) System Data Base 1061
Norwegian Seismic Array (NORSAR) Data Base 850
Norwegian Social Science Data Services Data Banks 771
Norwegian Standards Data Base 772
Norwegian Term Bank 1040
Nova Scotia Reports (National Reporter System) 828
NPADEMOG Data Base (I.P. Sharp Associates) 871
NPAECO Data Base (I.P. Sharp Associates) 871
NPL/SGTE (National Physical Laboratory/Scientific Group Thermodata Europe) Databank 451
NRC Metals Crystallographic Data File 156
NRI/E Japan Economic & Business Data Bank 760
NRS (National Reporter System) Data Bases 828
NSTA (Philippines National Science and Technology Authority) Data Bases 808
NSTC (Nineteenth Century Short Title Catalogue) 757
NSUB 643
NTC (Nondestructive Testing Centre) Data Base 436
Nuclear Energy Agency Data Bank (NEA-DB) 785
NUCOS (National Union Catalogue of Serials) 48
Nutrition Abstracts and Reviews: Series A, Human and Experimental 229
Nutrition Abstracts and Reviews: Series B, Livestock Feeds and Feeding 229
Nutrition Index 767
NYTTFO 665
OAG Data Base (I.P. Sharp Associates) 871
OAND Data Base (I.P. Sharp Associates) 871
Occupational Health and Safety Data Base (Spain) 892
Ocean Engineering Information Centre (OEIC) Data Base 694
Oceanographic Data Base 509
ODS (Overseas Data Service, Company, Ltd.) Data Bases 789
OECD (Organisation for Economic Co-Operation and Development) Economic Statistics and National Accounts Data Bases 780
OECD Quarterly Oil Statistics Data Base (I.P. Sharp Associates) 871
OEES Data Base (I.P. Sharp Associates) 871
OEIC (Ocean Engineering Information Centre) Data Base 694
OEKON Data Base (I.P. Sharp Associates) 871
Official Airline Guide Data Base (I.P. Sharp Associates) 871
OIL Data Base 767
OIL Data Base 770
Oil Index 767
Oil Index 770
Oil Sands Researchers and Research Projects 13
Olje-Indeks 767
Olje-Indeks 770
On-Line Earthnet Data Availability (LEDA) Data Bank 317

Oncology Information Service Data Base 1053
Ongoing Research Project Data Bank (German Ministry for Research and Technology) 424
Online Databases Prestel File 69
Online-GKS (German Union List of Conference Proceedings) 400
Online-NZN (Lower Saxonia Serials Data Base) 400
Online-ZDB (German Union Catalog of Serials) 400
Ontario Appeal Cases (National Reporter System) 828
Ontario Education Resources Information System (ONTERIS) Data Base 777
Ontario Geoscience Data Index 778
Ontario Mineral Deposit Inventory Database 778
ONTERIS (Ontario Education Resources Information System) Data Base 777
OON Data Base 152
OONL Data Base 148
OOT Data Base 161
Optional Reception of Announcements by Coded Line Electronics (ORACLE) Data Base 779
ORACLE Data Base 779
ORATEUR 384
ORBI 80
Organic Chemistry File (IDC) 572
Organisation for Economic Co-Operation and Development (OECD) Economic Statistics and National Accounts Data Bases 780
Oriel Computer Services Limited Data Base 787
Origin-Destination Data Base (I.P. Sharp Associates) 871
Original Equipment Suppliers to Vehicle Manufacturers Directory 67
ORL-Literaturinformationssystem (ORLIS) 379
ORLIS (ORL-Literaturinformationssystem) 379
Ornamental Horticulture 229
OSCHEDULE Data Base (I.P. Sharp Associates) 871
Outlook Database 126
Overall Trade by Country (OECD) 780
Overseas Data Service, Company, Ltd. (ODS) Data Bases 789
Packaging Science and Technology Abstracts (PSTA) 584
PACTI Data Base 893
PADIS-ADMIN Data Base 1005
PADIS-COM Data Bases 1005
PADIS-DEV Data Base 1005
PADIS-PROM Data Base 1005
PADIS-STAT Data Bases 1005
PADOC Data Base 935
PAKLEGIS 812
Pan European Survey 839
PAPRICAN (Pulp and Paper Research Institute of Canada) Data Base 827
PAPYRUS 384
Parkes Catalogue of Radio Sources (PKSCAT) 59
PARLEMENT 343
Parliamentary On-Line Information System (POLIS) Data Base 459
PARTHES (Thesaurus for Parliamentary Materials) 422
Particle Science and Technology Information Service Data Base 676
PASCAL (Programme Applique a la Selection et a la Compilation Automatiques de la Litterature) Data Bases 356
PASCAL Batiment Travaux Publics (PASCALBAT) Data Base 377
PASCAL-GEODE 340
PASCAL M 356
PASCAL-Oceanologie 351
PASCAL S 356
PASCALBAT (PASCAL Batiment Travaux Publics) Data Base 377
Patent Data Bank (IDC) 572
Patent On-Line Information System (PATOLIS) Data Bases 633
Patentdatenbank (PDB) 572
PATENTE 521
Patents Documentation Services Data Bases 275
PATOLIS (Patent On-Line Information System) Data Bases 633
PATSDI 521
PATSDI-TEST 521
PCODES (Postcode Locality Data Base) 237
PDB (Patentdatenbank) 572
Peace Research Abstracts Journal Data Base 800
PEPSY Data Base 924
Periodicals in Southern African Libraries (PISAL) 885
Permanent Inventory of Agricultural Research Projects in the European Communities Data Base 213
Pest Control Literature Documentation (PESTDOC) 276
PESTDOC (Pest Control Literature Documentation) 276
Pesticide Research Information System (PRIS) 128
PETROCH (Rock Chemical Database) 778
Petroflash Crude and Produce Reports Data Base (I.P. Sharp Associates) 871
Petroleum Argus Daily Market Report Data Base (I.P. Sharp Associates) 871
Petroleum Argus Prices Data Base (I.P. Sharp Associates) 871
Petroleum Intelligence Weekly Data Base (I.P. Sharp Associates) 871
PGD 773
Pharmaceutical Literature Documentation (RINGDOC) 277
Pharmline 285

Philippine Patents Data Base 967
Philippine Presidential Documents Data Base 967
Philippines National Science and Technology Authority (NSTA) Data Bases 808
Philips Information Systems Data Bases 809
Philosophische Dokumentation Data Base 1048
PHOENIX Data Bases 1059
Photochemical Smog Data File 626
PHYS (Physics Briefs) 521
PHYSCOMP (Data Compilations in Physics) 521
Physical Property Data Service (PPDS) Data Banks 548
Physics Abstracts 549
Physics Briefs (PHYS) 521
Phytomedicine Data Base 409
PICA (Project for Integrated Catalogue Automation) Data Base 239
PICA (Property Services Agency Information on Construction and Architecture) Data Base 378
Pig News and Information 229
PINCCA (Price Index Numbers for Current Cost Accounting) Data Bank 454
Pipelines Abstracts 86
PIPS (Science and Technology Policies Information Exchange Programme) Data Bases 1016
Pira Abstracts 812
PISAL (Periodicals in Southern African Libraries) 885
PIW Data Base (I.P. Sharp Associates) 871
PKSCAT (Parkes Catalogue of Radio Sources) 59
PLANLaw (Eurolex) 314
Plans and Projects Monitor Data Base 264
Plant Breeding Abstracts 229
Plant Growth Regulator Abstracts 229
PLANTFACTS 398
Plasma Physics Library and Information Service Data Base 438
Pluridata System Data Bases 38
PMB Print Measurement Bureau Data Base 814
Point de Repere 831
Poison Management Manual Data Base 1043
Police Science Abstracts 647
POLIS (Parliamentary On-Line Information System) Data Base 459
Political and Current Events Information Bank (BIPA) 384
POLUMAT 353
Polymer File (IDC) 572
Pont-a-Mousson Industrial Information Bank 820
POPFILE/ESCAP Bibliographic Information System 1003
POPTIO 1010
Population File 1010
Population File/ESCAP Bibliographic Information System 1003
Postcode Locality Data Base 237
Potato Abstracts 229
Poultry Abstracts 229
PPDS (Physical Property Data Service) Data Banks 548
PPDS-PPDATA 548
PPDS-VLE 548
PPR (Alberta Government Periodicals Publishing Record) Data Base 11
PRECIS (Preserved Context Index System) Thesaurus 441
Predecessor and Defunct Companies Data Base 680
Preserved Context Index System (PRECIS) Thesaurus 441
Press Information Bank (Gruner & Jahr) 468
Prestel Data Bases 448
Price Index Numbers for Current Cost Accounting (PINCCA) Data Bank 454
PRICEDATA 878
Principal Offshore Oil-Spill Accidents and Tanker Casualties Data Bank 387
Print Measurement Bureau (PMB) Data Base 814
PRIS (Pesticide Research Information System) 128
PROGRAMLIST (Index of Software Supported by Computing Services) 1033
Programme Applique a la Selection et a la Compilation Automatiques de la Litterature (PASCAL) Data Bases 356
Project for Integrated Catalogue Automation (PICA) Data Base 239
Project IRIS Data Base 169
PROMEXPORT/PROMIMPORT 796
Property & Compensation Reports (Eurolex) 314
Property Services Agency Information on Construction and Architecture (PICA) Data Base 378
Protozoological Abstracts 229
PSTA (Packaging Science and Technology Abstracts) 584
PSYNDEX 1078
Publishers' International Directory Data Base 863
Pulp and Paper Research Institute of Canada (PAPRICAN) Data Base 827
Pumps and Other Fluids Machinery Abstracts 86
QBANK Data Base (I.P. Sharp Associates) 871
QHBARK Data Base 920
QHGRVN Data Base 920
QOS Data Base (I.P. Sharp Associates) 871
QUALIS Data Base 594
Quarterly Labour Force Statistics (OECD) 780

Quarterly National Accounts (OECD) 780
Quarterly Survey of Consumer Buying Intentions Data Base 238
Quebec-Actualite Data Base 704
Quebec Information Bank on the Environment of Quebec 832
Quebec Society for Legal Information Data Base 834
Queen's University Interrogation of Legal Literature (QUILL) Data Bases 836
QUESTIONS 343
Quetelet Library Data Base 81
QUILL (Queen's University Interrogation of Legal Literature) Data Bases 836
QUODAMP 835
QUOTEL Data Base 837
R & D Index 767
RADAR (Repertoire Analytique d'Articles de Revues du Quebec) 831
RAMA 71
RAMPI (Raw Materials Price Index) 878
Rapports de la Cour Federale du Canada 828
Rapports de la Cour Supreme du Canada 828
RAPRA (Rubber and Plastics Research Association of Great Britain) Abstracts 858
Raumordnung, Stadtebau, Wohnungswesen, Bauwesen (RSWB) 379
Raw Materials Price Index (RAMPI) 878
RCE (Repertoire Canadien sur l'Education) Data Base 170
RDS (Reperimento Documentazione Siderurgica) Data Base 192
RDZ (Ringier Dokumentationszentrum) Data Base 841
REBUS (Reseau des Bibliotheques Utilisant SIBIL) Data Base 664
RECAP 434
RECODEX (Report Collection Index) 906
REDOSI 190
REFABS Data Base 602
Referatedienst Verpackung 584
Referativnyi Zhurnal 998
Refugee Abstracts 602
Regio-Indeks 767
Regional-Industrial Model (RIM) Data Bases 536
Regional Planning, City Planning, Housing, Building Construction Data Base 379
Regional Planning, City Planning, Housing Research Projects Data Base 380
Regional Statistics Data Base (RSDB), Statistics Sweden 932
REGIS 940
Registry of Tropical and Arid Land Current Research 702
Regulations of Ontario 828
Regulatory Reporter (CRR) 173
Remote Sensing On-Line Retrieval System (RESORS) 132
Renewable Energy Resources Information Center (RERIC) Data Base 33
Reperimento Documentazione Siderurgica (RDS) Data Base 192
Repertoire Analytique d'Articles de Revues du Quebec (RADAR) 831
Repertoire Bibliographique des Institutions Chretiennes (RIC) Data Base 205
Repertoire Canadien sur l'Education (RCE) Data Base 170
Repertoire des Theses de Maitrise Completees en Nursing 1037
REPINDEX Data Base 794
Report Collection Index (RECODEX) 906
Reports of Patent Cases (Eurolex) 314
RERIC (Renewable Energy Resources Information Center) Data Base 33
Research Institute for International Politics and Security Data Base 337
Research on Transport Economics Data Base 309
Research Register of VTT 330
Reseau des Bibliotheques Utilisant SIBIL (REBUS) Data Base 664
Reso Data Bank 251
RESORS (Remote Sensing On-Line Retrieval System) 132
Resources Data Base 840
Responsa Data Base 74
RETAIL Data Base (I.P. Sharp Associates) 871
Review of Applied Entomology: Series A, Agricultural 229
Review of Applied Entomology: Series B, Medical and Veterinary 229
Review of Medical and Veterinary Mycology 229
Review of Plant Pathology 229
Revised Statutes of Canada 828
REVUMER 347
Rheology Data Base 417
RIC (Repertoire Bibliographique des Institutions Chretiennes) Data Base 205
Rice Abstracts 229
RIM (Regional-Industrial Model) Data Bases 536
RINGDOC (Pharmaceutical Literature Documentation) 277
Ringier Dokumentationszentrum (RDZ) Data Base 841
RISE (Ruling Information System-Excise) 828
Road Data Bank (Swedish National Road Administration) 933
Road Traffic Reports (Eurolex) 314
Robert Debre Information Base 566
Rock Chemical Database (PETROCH) 778
Rock Mechanics Information Service Data Base 1056
Romanian National Institute for Information and Documentation (INID) Data Base 843
ROSCOP 354
Royal Dutch Society for Advancement of Pharmacy Databank 844
RSDB (Regional Statistics Data Base), Statistics Sweden 932
RSWB (Raumordnung, Stadtebau, Wohnungswesen, Bauwesen) 379
Rubber and Plastics Research Association of Great Britain (RAPRA) Abstracts 858
Ruling Information System-Excise (RISE) 828
Rural Development Abstracts 229
Rural Extension, Education & Training Abstracts 229
S.E.M.P. (Societe d'Editions Medico-Pharmaceutiques) Data Base 693
S.I.S. (Supplier Identification System) 671
S.J. Rundt World Risk Analysis Package Data Base (I.P. Sharp Associates) 871
SABE 2000 (Sistema de Alerta Bibliografico Especializado) Data Base 605
SAFE (Software Abstracts for Engineers) 208
SALOMON 384
SALUS Data Base 576
SAMKATPER (Union Catalog for Periodicals in Norwegian Libraries) 1061
SANI Data Base 194
SANP Data Base 194
SASC (Subject Analysis Systems Collection) Data Base 1077
Saskatchewan Reports (National Reporter System) 828
SATELDATA 317
SAWIC (South African Water Information Centre) Data Base 887
SB-I (Biblio Service Informatique) Data Base 797
SB-I CAS 797
SB-I Expertises 797
SBL (Serials in the British Library) Data Base 439
SBS (Swedish Behavioural Sciences) Data Base 924
Scandinavian Periodicals Index in Economics and Business (SCANP) 481
SCANP (Scandinavian Periodicals Index in Economics and Business) 481
SCI Data Base 688
SCIDOC 885
Science and Technology Briefs 726
Science & Technology Data Bank (SCITECH) 1033
Science and Technology Experts in ROC Data Base (Republic of China) 726
Science and Technology Policies Information Exchange Programme (PIPS) Data Bases 1016
Scientific and Technical Research Centres in Australia (STRC) 47
Scientific Meetings in ROC (Republic of China) 726
Scientific Personnel in CSIR Laboratories Data Base 507
Scientific Research Abstracts in Republic of China 726
Scientists' Profile (Philippines) 808
SCIMP (European Index of Management Periodicals) 481
SCITECH (Science & Technology Data Bank) 1033
SCOLCAP (Scottish Libraries Co-operative Automation Project) Data Base 869
Scots Law Times (Eurolex) 314
Scottish Libraries Co-operative Automation Project (SCOLCAP) Data Base 869
SCPI (Small Computer Program Index) Data Base 17
SDF (Standard Drug File) 277
SDIM (System Dokumentation Information Metallurgie) Data Base 522
SDOE Data Base 194
SDOI Data Base 194
SDSB (Sub-area Statistical Data Base), Statistics Sweden 932
Sea Beam Data Bank 347
SEANCE 343
Search Program for Infrared Spectra (SPIR) Data Base 155
SEBAN Data Base 965
Securities Data Base (Financial Post) 680
SEDIS (Service Information-Diffusion) Data Bases 361
SEDS Data Base (I.P. Sharp Associates) 871
SEED (Soviet and East European Data) 1033
Seed Abstracts 229
Seguridad e Higiene en el Trabajo (SEHIT) Data Base 892
SEHIT (Seguridad e Higiene en el Trabajo) Data Base 892
Seismic Crew Count Data Base (I.P. Sharp Associates) 871
Selective Cooperative Indexing of Management Periodicals (SCIMP) 481
SELECVAL Data Bank 251
Senior Update 1099
Serials in the British Library (SBL) Data Base 439
SERIE 625
SERIX (Swedish Environmental Research Index) Data Base 926
Service Annuaire Electronique Data Base 552
Service Directory 1099
Service Information-Diffusion (SEDIS) Data Bases 361
SFS (Suomen Standardisoimisliitto) Data Base 334
SGB (Societe Generale de Banque) Data Base 73
SGU (Sveriges Geologiska Undersokning) Data Bases 920
Share Price Record 1060
Ship Abstracts Data Base 767

DATA BASES INDEX

Ship Abstracts Data Base 872
SHIPDES 685
SIBB Data Base 194
SIC (Systeme Informatique pour la Conjoncture) Data Bank 364
Sicherheitstechnische Dokumentation (SIDOK) Data Base 419
SIDOK (Sicherheitstechnische Dokumentation) Data Base 419
SIEN Data Base 102
SIENA Data Bank 224
SIGEDA 611
SIGLE (System for Information on Grey Literature in Europe) Data Base 226
Signposts Prestel Data Base 462
SIMBAD 905
Singapore Corporate Statistics Data Base (I.P. Sharp Associates) 871
Singapore Industrial Technical Information Service (ITIS) Data Base 877
Singapore Stock Exchange Data Base (I.P. Sharp Associates) 871
SINGCORP Data Base (I.P. Sharp Associates) 871
SINGSTOCK Data Base (I.P. Sharp Associates) 871
SIRC (Sport Information Resource Centre) Data Base 210
SIRIS (Department of Scientific and Industrial Research Indexing System) 748
SIRLS (Information Retrieval System for the Sociology of Leisure and Sport) 1085
SIROCAT 47
SIS (Supplier Identification System) 671
SISDATA (Statistical Information System) Data Banks 878
Sistema de Alerta Bibliografico Especializado (SABE) Data Base 605
Sistema de Documentacion sobre Poblacion en America Latina (DOCPAL) 1007
SITC Data Base (I.P. Sharp Associates) 871
SJRUNDS Data Base (I.P. Sharp Associates) 871
SkyGuide 23
Slavic Philology (SLAVICA) 1033
SLAVICA (Slavic Philology) 1033
Small Animal Abstracts 229
Small Computer Program Index (SCPI) Data Base 17
SMC (Manitoba Statute Citator) 173
SOC Data Base 949
Social Science Information System (SSIS) Data Base 1120
Social Science Journal File 1120
Social Sciences Information Center (IZ) Data Bases 43
Societe d'Editions Medico-Pharmaceutiques (S.E.M.P.) Data Base 693
Societe Generale de Banque (SGB) Data Base 73
Societe Quebecoise d'Information Juridique (SOQUIJ) Data Base 834
Society of Metaphysicians Ltd. Data Base 882
Socioeconomic Data Bank on the Mediterranean Countries 564
Sociology of Leisure & Sport Abstracts 1085
SOF'SPOT Microcomputer Software Directory 67
Software Abstracts for Engineers (SAFE) 208
Soil Information System Data Base 746
Soils and Fertilizers 229
SOL (Solid Waste Management) Data Base 140
Solar and Wind Energy Research Program (SWERP) Information Centre Data Base 16
Solid-Liquid Flow Abstracts 86
Solid Waste 767
Solid Waste Management (SOL) Data Base 140
Solid Waste Management Data Bank (AWIDAT) 411
SOLIS (Sozialwissenschaftliches Literaturinformationssystem) 43
SOM Data Base (I.P. Sharp Associates) 871
SOQUIJ (Societe Quebecoise d'Information Juridique) Data Base 834
Sorghum and Millets Abstracts 229
South African Water Information Centre (SAWIC) Data Base 887
Soviet and East European Data (SEED) 1033
Soyabean Abstracts 229
Sozialwissenschaftliches Literaturinformationssystem (SOLIS) 43
Space Components (SPACECOMPS) Data Bank 317
SPACECOMPS (Space Components) Data Bank 317
Spanish Medical Index 1082
Spanish Pharmaceutical Specialities Data Bank 893
SPHINX Data Base 363
SPIR (Search Program for Infrared Spectra) Data Base 155
SPOLIT (Sportliteratur) Data Base 420
Sport and Recreation Index 210
Sport and Sports-Scientific Information System Data Base 420
SPORT Data Base 210
Sport Information Resource Centre (SIRC) Data Base 210
Sportliteratur (SPOLIT) Data Base 420
Sports Council Data Base 896
SRDA (Systeme de Renseignements sur les Decisions de l'Accise) 828
SSIS (Social Science Information System) Data Base 1120
SSVA Data Base 623
STALUS (Statute Law Updating Service) Data Base 517
STANDARD Data Base 772
Standard Drug File (SDF) 277
Standards Council of Canada Data Base 898
State Energy Data System Data Base (I.P. Sharp Associates) 871
STATEX Data Base (I.P. Sharp Associates) 871

STATISBUND Data Base (I.P. Sharp Associates) 871
Statistical Information System (SISDATA) Data Banks 878
Statistics of Foreign Trade (OECD) 780
Statistics of Postal Services Data Base 1030
Statistics Sweden Data Bases 932
STATSID 723
Statute Law Updating Service (STALUS) Data Base 517
Statutes of Alberta 828
Statutes of British Columbia 828
Statutes of Manitoba 828
Statutes of New Brunswick 828
Statutes of Ontario 828
Statutes of Saskatchewan 828
Statutory Orders and Regulations 828
Statuts Revises du Canada 828
Steel Information System Data Bases 399
Steel Products Database 238
STEELDOC Data Base 979
STEELFACTS/S 399
STEELFACTS/T 399
Stellar Data Center Data Bases 905
STERIC Data Base 1076
STIPA (Systeme de Transfert de l'Information Pedologique et Agronomique) Data Bank 362
Stock Exchange TOPIC Data Base 902
Stockmarket Indices, Interest and Exchange Rates, and Commodities Data Base (Datastream) 267
Stoy-Indeks 767
Strasbourg Observatory Stellar Data Center Data Bases 905
STRC (Scientific and Technical Research Centres in Australia) 47
Sub-area Statistical Data Base (SDSB), Statistics Sweden 932
Subject Analysis Systems Collection Data Base 1077
Subsoil Data Bank 341
Summer Fun/Winter Fun 1099
Suomen Standardisoimisliitto (SFS) Data Base 334
Supplier Identification System (SIS) 671
Supreme Court of Canada Reports 828
Surface Coatings Abstracts 792
Survey of Large Scale Stores Databank 754
SUSIS (Sport und Sportwissenschaftliche Informationssystem) Data Base 420
Svenska Tidningsartiklar 116
Svenska Tidskriftsartiklar 116
Sveriges Geologiska Undersokning (SGU) Data Bases 920
SWEDAGRI 941
SWEDIS (Swedish Drug Information System) Data Bases 922
Swedish Behavioural Sciences (SBS) Data Base 924
Swedish Drug Information System (SWEDIS) Data Bases 922
Swedish Environmental Research Index (SERIX) Data Base 926
Swedish Institute of Building Documentation (BYGGDOK) Data Base 938
Swedish Market Information Bank 824
Swedish National Bibliography 931
SWEMARC 931
SWERP (Solar and Wind Energy Research Program) Information Centre Data Base 16
Swets Serials Title Database 942
SWINFED (Information on Educational Research and Development in Switzerland) Data Base 945
SWIS (Swiss Wildlife Information Service) Data Base 947
Swiss Wildlife Information Service (SWIS) Data Base 947
SYD Data Base 949
Sydney Stock Exchange Share Prices Data Base (I.P. Sharp Associates) 871
Sydney Stock Exchange Statex Prices Data Base (I.P. Sharp Associates) 871
SYDONI Data Bases 949
SYDSTOCK Data Base (I.P. Sharp Associates) 871
System Dokumentation Information Metallurgie (SDIM) Data Base 522
System for Documentation and Information in Metallurgy Data Base 522
System for Information on Grey Literature in Europe (SIGLE) Data Base 226
System of Computerized Processing of Scientific Information (APIN) Data Bases 965
System of Documentary Reference of MINTER (INTERDOC) 100
System of Legislative Reference of MINTER (INTERLEGI) 100
Systeme de Renseignements sur les Decisions de l'Accise (SRDA) 828
Systeme de Transfert de l'Information Pedologique et Agronomique (STIPA) Data Bank 362
Systeme Informatique pour la Conjoncture (SIC) Data Bank 364
SZISZ-EMIMAT Data Base 494
T6 Data Base (I.P. Sharp Associates) 871
T9S Data Base (I.P. Sharp Associates) 871
TAC-G GILTS 249
TALI (Tekniikan Aikakauslehti Indeksi) Data Base 483
Target Group Index (TGI) Data Base 109
Tax Advance Rulings 828
Tax Case Materials (Eurolex) 314

TEAM (Terminologie-Erfassungs- und Auswertungs- Methode) Data Base 876
TEARS (The Exeter Abstract Reference System) 319
TECLEARN 959
TED (Tenders Electronic Daily) 227
Tekniikan Aikakauslehti Indeksi (TALI) Data Base 483
TELEDOC Data Base 367
Teleguide 518
Telekurs Investdata System Data Base 975
TELETEL Data Bases 552
Teletext Output of Price Information by Computer (TOPIC) Data Base 902
TeleWhich? Data Base 244
TELEXPORT 796
Telset Data Bases 480
Tenders Electronic Daily (TED) 227
TENTTU Data Base 483
TERMDOK Data Base 979
Terminals Guide (ECHO) 219
Terminologie-Erfassungs- und Auswertungs- Methode (TEAM) Data Base 876
Terminology Bank of Quebec 830
Terminology Evaluation and Acquisition Method (TEAM) Data Base 876
TERMINOQ 830
Ternisien Listing 978
Textile Information Treatment Users' Service (TITUS) 390
TEXTLINE 335
TGI (Target Group Index) Data Base 109
The Economist Data Base (Datasolve World Reporter) 265
The Exeter Abstract Reference System (TEARS) 319
The Globe and Mail Online 430
The Guardian Data Base (Datasolve World Reporter) 265
The Informetrica Model (TIM) Data Bases 536
Thermdoc Data Bank 981
Thermodata-Thermdoc Data Bank 981
Thermodynamic Data Banks 451
Thermodynamique (Institut Francais des Petroles) 387
Thermophysical Property Data Bank (DECHEMA) 404
THES Data Base 481
Thesaurus for Parliamentary Materials (PARTHES) 422
Thesaurus of Pulp and Paper Terms 827
Theses in Home Economics (THESIS) 1033
THESIS (Theses in Home Economics) 1033
THESIS Data Base 481
Tidningsdatabasen 94
Tijl Datapress Data Bases 982
TIM (The Informetrica Model) Data Bases 536
Timber Information Keyword Retrieval (TINKER) Data Base 983
Time Series Data Base (TSDB), Statistics Sweden 932
Times Law Reports (Eurolex) 314
TINKER (Timber Information Keyword Retrieval) Data Base 983
TISDATA 286
TITUS (Textile Information Treatment Users' Service) 390
TMRK (Trade Marks Data Base) 166
Tokyo Shoko Research, Ltd. (TSR) Data Base 984
TOPIC Data Base 902
Toronto Department of the City Clerk Data Bases 985
Toronto Globe and Mail 430
Toronto Stock Exchange 300 Index and Stock Statistics 986
Tourism Research and Data Centre (TRDC) Data Base 137
Tourtel 297
TRACS (Transport and Road Abstracting and Cataloging System) Data Base 455
TRADAREA Data Base 236
Trade Descriptions Law Data Base 656
Trade Marks Data Base (TMRK) 166
Traded Options Data Base (Datastream) 267
TRADSTAT (World Trade Statistics Database) 994
TRAMIT Data Base 893
TRANSDOC 309
TRANSIN 987
Transinove International Data Base 987
Transport and Road Abstracting and Cataloging System (TRACS) Data Base 455
TRAP 361
TRDC (Tourism Research and Data Centre) Data Base 137
Tribology Index 417
Tribos: Tribology Abstracts 86
TRIBUN 343
TROPAG Data Base 857
Tropical Oil Seeds Abstracts 229
TSDB (Time Series Data Base), Statistics Sweden 932
TSE300 (Toronto Stock Exchange 300 Index and Stock Statistics) 986
TSR (Tokyo Shoko Research, Ltd.) Data Base 984
TT Kalendern 260
TT Newsbank 990
TT Nyhetsbanken 990

UBO:BOK 1061
UFORDAT (Data Bank for Environmental Research) 411
Uhde Thermophysical Properties Program Package Data Base 992
UIC (Union Internationale des Chemins de Fer) Data Base 600
UK MARC 439
UK National Oceanographic Data Bank 730
UKCSO Data Base (I.P. Sharp Associates) 871
UKCTRAIN 440
ULIDAT (Data Bank for Environmental Literature) 411
UMPLIS Data Bases 411
UN/ESCAP Statistical Information Services Data Base 1004
UNESCO Social and Human Science Documentation Centre Data Base 1022
UNION (Union List of Scientific Serials in Canadian Libraries) 152
Union Catalog for Periodicals in Norwegian Libraries (SAMKATPER) 1061
Union Catalog of Periodicals Held by Portuguese Libraries 821
Union Catalog of Scientific Periodicals in the Libraries of ROC (Republic of China) 726
Union Catalogue of Foreign Books in Swedish Research Libraries 931
Union Catalogue of Libraries in India 507
Union Internationale des Chemins de Fer (UIC) Data Base 600
Union List of Higher Degree Theses in Australian Libraries (HDEG) Data Base 1074
Union List of Scientific Serials in Canadian Libraries 152
Union List of Serials in Israel Libraries 478
Union List of Serials in the Social Sciences and Humanities Held by Canadian Libraries (CANUCS) Data Base 151
Union List of Serials of NSTA Complex Libraries (Philippines) 808
United Kingdom Central Statistical Office Data Base (I.P. Sharp Associates) 871
United Kingdom Macro-Economic Data Bank 449
United Kingdom National Oceanographic Data Bank 730
U.K. Treasury Databank 456
United Nations Commodity Trade Statistics Data Base (I.P. Sharp Associates) 871
United Nations University Referral Service System Data Base 1028
United States Banks Data Base (I.P. Sharp Associates) 871
United States Bonds Data Base (I.P. Sharp Associates) 871
United States Consumer Price Index Data Base (I.P. Sharp Associates) 871
United States Department of Energy Data Base (I.P. Sharp Associates) 871
United States Flow of Funds, Quarterly Data Base (I.P. Sharp Associates) 871
U.S. International Air Travel Statistics Data Base (I.P. Sharp Associates) 871
United States Petroleum Imports Data Base (I.P. Sharp Associates) 871
United States Producer Price Index Data Base (I.P. Sharp Associates) 871
United States Stock Market Data Base (I.P. Sharp Associates) 871
United States Stock Options Data Base (I.P. Sharp Associates) 871
Universal Postal Union (UPU) Data Base 1030
University of Saskatchewan Library Data Base 1068
UPU (Universal Postal Union) Data Base 1030
URBALINE 465
URBAMET (Urbanisme, Amenagement, Environnement et Transports) Data Base 1091
Urban Data Bank of Paris and the Paris Region 798
Urbanisme, Amenagement, Environnement et Transports (URBAMET) Data Base 1091
USBANKS Data Base (I.P. Sharp Associates) 871
USBOND Data Base (I.P. Sharp Associates) 871
USCPI Data Base (I.P. Sharp Associates) 871
USDOE Data Base (I.P. Sharp Associates) 871
User Education Resources Data Base 204
USFLOW Data Base (I.P. Sharp Associates) 871
USOPT Data Base (I.P. Sharp Associates) 871
USPPI Data Base (I.P. Sharp Associates) 871
USSTOCK Data Base (I.P. Sharp Associates) 871
UTLAS Data Base 1094
VA-NYTT Data Base 637
Vaccine Data Bank 1114
Vagdatabank (Swedish National Road Administration) 933
Valencian Scientific Index 1082
Vapor-Liquid Equilibrium Data Collection 1046
VAT Tribunal Reports (Eurolex) 314
VDI News Data Base 1096
Veckans Affarers Borsinformation 94
Vehicle Data Bank System 1104
VERA 939
Verein Deutscher Ingenieure (VDI) News Data Base 1096
Verfahrenstechnische Berichte (VtB) Data Base 77
VETDOC (Veterinary Literature Documentation) 278
Veterinary Bulletin 229
Veterinary Literature Documentation (VETDOC) 278
Victorian Motor Vehicle 1982 Registrations Data Base 237
VideoAccess Data Bases 1099

Videotel Data Bases 622
Viditel Data Bases 738
Viewdata Documentation Service Data Base 946
Viewtel 202 Data Base 1102
VINITI (Vsesoyuznyy Institut Nauchnoy i Tekhnicheskoy Informatsii) Data Bases 998
VISDATA Data Base 479
VISTA 518
VITIS-VEA (VITIS-Viticulture and Enology Abstracts) 585
VITIS-Viticulture and Enology Abstracts (VITIS-VEA) 585
Vocabulario Controlado do MINTER (INTERVOC) 100
Volkswagenwerk Bibliographic Data Base 1104
Vorschriften Informationssystem (VISDATA) Data Base 479
VtB (Verfahrenstechnische Berichte) Data Base 77
Wage Rounds Data Bank 1032
WAIT Index to Newspapers 1107
WASIRS (Women and Sports Information Retrieval System) Data Base 1033
Waste Management Information Bureau (WMIB) Databank 437
WATDOC Data Bases 140
Water Quality Data File 626
Water Survey of Canada Data Base 142
WATERLIT 887
WBANK Data Base (I.P. Sharp Associates) 871
WCL Data Base 1059
WDB (Werkstoffdatenbank) 399
WDEBT Data Base (I.P. Sharp Associates) 871
Weed Abstracts 229
Weekly Criminal Bulletin Data Base 162
Weekly Law Reports (Eurolex) 314
Weekly Statistical Bulletin Data Base (I.P. Sharp Associates) 871
Weekly Temperatures Data Base (I.P. Sharp Associates) 871
Weldasearch Data Base 1106
Welding Documentation 418
Werkstoffdatenbank (WDB) 399
WEST Data Base 1107
West German Economic Outlook Survey Data Base (I.P. Sharp Associates) 871
West German Statistical Data Base (I.P. Sharp Associates) 871
Western Legal Publications (WLP) Data Base 1108
Western Weekly Reports (WWR) 173
Wheat, Barley and Triticale Abstracts 229
Which? Data Base 244
WHO Collaborating Centre for Collection and Evaluation of Data on Comparative Virology Data Base 1114
Who's Who in Europe Data Base 870
Who's Who Japan Data Base 969
WHOLESALE Data Base (I.P. Sharp Associates) 871
WHS (World Health Statistics) Data Base 1110
WIIW Data Base (I.P. Sharp Associates) 871
Wildlife Research Database 947
Winged Bean Data Base 889
WLP (Western Legal Publications) Data Base 1108
WMIB (Waste Management Information Bureau) Databank 437
Wolff Research Data Base 1109
Women and Sports Information Retrieval System (WASIRS) Data Base 1033
World Agricultural Economics and Rural Sociology Abstracts 229
World Bank Debt Tables Data Base (I.P. Sharp Associates) 871
World Coal Resources and Reserves Data Bank 783
World Directory of National Science and Technology Policy-Making Bodies 1016
World Directory of Research Projects, Studies and Courses in Science and Technology Policy 1016
World Exporter Data Bases 264
World Gravimetric Data Bank 342
World Guide to Libraries Data Base 863
World Guide to Scientific Associations Data Base 863
World Guide to Terminological Activities 587
World Guide to Trade Associations Data Base 863
World Health Statistics (WHS) Data Base 1110
World Patents Index (WPI) 275
World Petrochemical Industry Data Bank 799
World Ports and Harbours Abstracts 86
World Request List for Neutron Data (WRENDA) 785
World Surface Coatings Abstracts (WSCA) 792
World Textile Abstracts (WTA) 873
World Textiles Database 873
World Trade Statistics Database (TRADSTAT) 994
World Transindex (WTI) Data Base 608
World Viewdata Services 473
World Weather Watch Data Base 1119
WPI (World Patents Index) 275
WRENDA (World Request List for Neutron Data) 785
WSB Data Base (I.P. Sharp Associates) 871
WSCA (World Surface Coatings Abstracts) 792
WTA (World Textile Abstracts) 873
WTI (World Transindex) Data Base 608
WWR (Western Weekly Reports) 173

YBANK Data Base (I.P. Sharp Associates) 871
YKB (Yukon Bibliography) 95
YSCHEDULE Data Base (I.P. Sharp Associates) 871
Yukon Bibliography (YKB) 95
ZADI (Zentralstelle fur Agrardokumentation und -Information) Data Base 408
ZDB (Zeitschriftendatenbank) 400
ZDE (Zentralstelle Dokumentation Elektrotechnik) Data Base 960
Zeitschriftendatenbank (ZDB) 400
Zentralstelle Dokumentation Elektrotechnik (ZDE) Data Base 960
Zentralstelle fur Agrardokumentation und -Information (ZADI) Data Base 408
Zentralstelle fur Psychologische Information und Dokumentation (ZPID) Data Base 1078
ZfP (Dokumentation Zerstorungsfreie Prufung) Data Base 416
Zinc Abstracts 1122
Zinc, Lead & Cadmium Abstracts (ZLC) Database 1122
ZLC (Zinc, Lead & Cadmium Abstracts) Database 1122
Zoological Record (ZR) Online 88
ZPID (Zentralstelle fur Psychologische Information und Dokumentation) Data Base 1078
ZR (Zoological Record) Online 88

PUBLICATIONS INDEX

A listing of periodicals and other print and microform publications issued by the organizations described in this book. Among these are publications produced from computer-readable data bases (these are also listed in the Data Bases Index); user guides, search aids, and similar documentation; and newsletters, journals, and directories concerned with the information field.

More than 2,000 titles are listed in this index.

PUBLICATIONS INDEX

ABN: A Bibliography 49
ABN News 49
ABS Catalogue of Publications 52
Abstract of Scientific Periodicals and Monographs 726
Abstracts in BioCommerce 181
Abstracts of AIT Reports and Publications 33
Abstracts of Bulgarian Scientific Literature: Series A. Plant Breeding 121
Abstracts of Bulgarian Scientific Literature: Series B. Animal Breeding and Veterinary Medicine 121
Abstracts of Romanian Scientific and Technical Literature 843
Abstracts of Science and Technology in Japan 632
Abstracts on Tropical Agriculture 857
Academic Book Price Index 675
Accessoirex 693
ACCIS Newsletter 1001
Achievements and Perspectives 565
Acronyms Related to International Development 576
ACSPRI Newsletter 61
Actualidades 93
Actualite Combustible Energie 386
Administratiefrechtelijve Beslissingen 641
Administrative Information Sources 7
ADOPT: Asian and Worldwide Documents on Population Topics 1003
ADP Member's Handbook 40
Adverse Reaction Newsletter 1115
Adverse Reactions Titles 296
Advocates' Quarterly 162
AERIC Historical Supplements 238
AERIC Information and Documentation 238
Aerospace and Aviation Documents 958
AESIS Cumulation 57
AESIS Quarterly 57
African Administrative Abstracts 7
AGE Current Awareness Services 30
AGE Digest 30
AGE Holdings Lists 30
AGE News 30
Agora, Informatics in a Changing World 554
Agra Europe 8
AGREP-Permanent Inventory of Agricultural Research Projects in the European Communities 213
AGRIASIA 889
Agricultural Abstracts for Tanzania 955
Agricultural Documentation/Landbouwdocumentatie 731
Agricultural Engineering Abstracts 229
Agricultural Sciences - Kalpataru 507
AGRINDEX 1012
AGRITROP 467
AIBD International Bond Manual 267
Aids to Library Administration Series 675
Aircraft Accident Statistics 567
Aircraft Price Guide 68
Airport Characteristics 568
AISL Information Digest 68
AKB-bok 931
AKB-mikro 931
Alberta Decisions, Civil and Criminal Cases 1108
Alberta Government Publications Catalogue 11
Alberta Oil Sands Index 13
Alberta/Saskatchewan/Manitoba Criminal Conviction Cases 1108
Alcohol, Drugs and Traffic Safety: Current Research Literature 936
ALIF Index 653
All-Canada Weekly Summaries 162
All-Japan Statistical Analysis of Corporate Financial Statements 969
ALLC Bulletin 37
ALLC Journal 37
Allgemeine Wirtschaftsdokumentation 425
Alphabetical and Phonetic Directory of International Trademarks 234
Alphabetical Directory of Benelux Trademarks 234
Alphabetical Directory of French Trademarks 234
Alphabetical List of French Applications 234
Alphabetical Subject Guide to the INSPEC Classification 549
Alphaphonetic Directory of International Trademarks 234
Aluminium Monitor 228
Aluminium Quarterly 228
Aluminum Analysis 89
Aluminum Annual Review 89
Aluminum Production Costs 89
Analytical Abstracts 851
Analytical Instrument Industry Report 515
ANB Catalogue 48
Andean Group Report 651
Animal Breeding Abstracts 229
Animal Disease Occurrence 229
Annales des Telecommunications 367
Annals of Library Science and Documentation 507
Annotated Bibliography on Carbon Technology 507
Annotated Bibliography on the Child 1015

Annuaire CNRS 355
Annuaire de Banques de Donnees 385
Annuaire de l'Afrique du Nord 186
Annuaire des Pays Mediterraneens 564
Annuaire d'Etudes en Education au Canada 170
Annual Bibliography of Austrian Mass Communication Literature 65
Annual Index to Geo Abstracts 393
Annual Index to Hebrew Periodicals 1051
Annual Index to New Products (Rubber and Plastics Research Association of Great Britain 858
Annual of Czechoslovak Medical Literature 250
Annual Report of the NIES 626
Annual Report on the French Stock Exchange 389
Apicultural Abstracts 563
AQUA Data Bank 548
Aquaculture Abstracts (ASFA) 1008
AQUALINE Online User Guide 464
Aquatic Sciences and Fisheries Abstracts 1008
Arab Social Science Index 1015
Architectural Keywords 845
Architectural Periodicals Index 845
ARCSS Newsletter 1015
Arid Lands Development Abstracts 229
Art Sales Index 29
Article Index 767
Artificial Rainfall Newsletter 616
Artikkel-Indeks 767
ASFA Aquaculture Abstracts 1008
ASI Decade Publications 29
Asian Agricultural Research and Development: A Bibliography 1073
Asian and Worldwide Documents on Population Topics (ADOPT) 1003
Asian Bibliography 1002
Asian Geotechnical Engineering Abstracts 30
Asian-Pacific Population Programme News 1003
Aslib Information 35
Aslib Proceedings 35
ASTIS Bibliography 26
ASTIS Current Awareness Bulletin 26
ATID Bulletin 46
Atlas of Ferns of the British Isles 461
Atlas of the British Flora 461
Atlas of the Bumblebees of the British Isles 461
Atlas of the Lichens of the British Isles 461
Atlas of the Non-marine Mollusca of the British Isles 461
ATLIS Bulletin 46
Atomindex 560
ATRIP Bulletin 46
Auction Prices of American Artists 29
Australian Art Index 58
Australian Books: A Select List of Recent Publications and Standard Works in Print 48
Australian Business Index 53
Australian Company Service 690
Australian Demographic Data Bank 60
Australian Education Index 54
Australian Federal Government Profile 520
Australian Government Publications 48
Australian Journal of Management 1060
Australian Maps 48
Australian MARC Record Service 48
Australian MEDLINER 50
Australian National Bibliography 48
Australian National Gallery Library Catalogue 58
Australian National Gallery Library Class N Expansion Tables 58
Australian National Gallery Library List of Periodicals 58
Australian Opinion Polls 1072
Australian Public Affairs Information Service 48
Australian Road Index 62
Australian Road Research in Progress 62
Australian Science Index 47
Australian Scientific and Technological Reports 48
Australian Social Surveys: Journal Extracts 1974-1978 61
Australian Thesaurus of Earth Sciences and Related Terms 57
Austrian National Institute for Public Health Review 66
Austrian National Institute for Public Health Yearbook 66
Authority System Proposal for BISA 1073
Automated Informatics Documentation System, A Thesaurus for Informatics 554
Automated Informatics Documentation System Trilingual Dictionary 554
Aviation Newsletter (I.P. Sharp Associates) 871
Bangladesh Science and Technology Index 70
Bank of England Quarterly Bulletin 72
Basic Statistics of the Community 225
Battlefield Weapons Systems and Technology 97
BBC Summary of World Broadcasts 104
Beilstein Handbook of Organic Chemistry 79
Belgian Environmental Research Index 84
Beslissingen in Belastingzaken Nederlandse Belastingrechtspraak 641

Bestandsverzeichnis Thesauri 880
BFI-Informationsdienst Huttenwerksanlagen 398
Biblio Service Informatique 797
Bibliografia Brasileira de Agricultura 99
Bibliografia Brasileira de Energia Nuclear 102
Bibliografia Latinoamericana 719
Bibliografias Agricolas 99
Bibliographia Medica Cechoslovaca 250
Bibliographic Bulletin of the Clearinghouse at IINTE 815
Bibliographical Repertory of Christian Institutions 205
Bibliographie der Pflanzenschutzliteratur 409
Bibliographie der Wirtschaftswissenschaften 639
Bibliographie Deutschsprachiger Psychologischer Dissertationen 1078
Bibliographie du Quebec 833
Bibliographie du Sport 210
Bibliographie Linguistischer Literatur 368
Bibliographies of Regional Geology 394
Bibliographique Geographique Internationale 355
Bibliography, Machine-Readable Cataloguing and the ESTC 443
Bibliography of Afro-Asian-Australasian Geology 394
Bibliography of American Geology 394
Bibliography of Bibliographies in Social Sciences 1015
Bibliography of Canadian Glaciology 139
Bibliography of Canadian Law 173
Bibliography of Economic Geology 394
Bibliography of Education Theses: A List of Theses in Education Accepted for Higher Degrees at Australian Universities and Colleges 54
Bibliography of Engineering Geology 394
Bibliography of European Geology 394
Bibliography of Foreign S&T Collections in ISTIC 801
Bibliography of German Research on Developing Countries 397
Bibliography of Infant Foods and Nutrition, 1938-1977 47
Bibliography of Internal Migrations 100
Bibliography of Linguistic Literature 368
Bibliography of Nordic Mass Communication Literature 763
Bibliography of Plant Protection 409
Bibliography of Quebec 833
Bibliography of Scientific Research Reports Sponsored by National Science Council, Republic of China 726
Bibliography of Systematic Mycology 229
Bibliography of the Mediterranean Area 412
Bibliography of Urban Development 100
Bibliography on Automatic Data Processing 1121
Bibliography on Foreign Literature of Science and Technology 203
Bibliography on Marine and Estuarine Oil Pollution 684
Bibliography on Marine and Estuarine Pesticide Pollution 684
Bibliography on Petroleum and Social Values 1015
Bibliotheksdienst 400
Bildschirmtext Magazin fur Teleleser 427
BINS Bibliographic Series 95
Bio-Industry Bulletin 712
Biocontrol News and Information 229
Biodeterioration Research Titles 1038
Biomechanics and Orthopaedics 114
Biomedical Engineering Current Awareness Notification 114
Biotechnology Abstracts 273
Biotica 702
BISA Catalogue on Microfiche 1073
BLAISE-LINE Mini Manual 440
BLAISE-LINE User Manual 440
BLAISE-LINK Mini Manual 440
BLAISE-LINK User Manual 440
BLAISE Newsletter 440
BMFT Forderungskatalog 424
BNF Abstracts 92
BNR Monthly 97
Boletin Bibliografico 892
Boletin de Traducciones 890
Book Catalog of NSTA and Agencies (Philippines) 808
Book Catalogue of Tourism Research Studies 137
BOOKALERT 605
Boroughs Intelligence Newsletter 465
Brassey's Multi-Lingual Military Dictionary 97
Brazil Report 651
BRISES 355
Britain's Top 1000 Foreign Owned Companies 636
Britain's Top 2000 Private Companies 636
British Catalogue of Audiovisual Materials 439
British Catalogue of Music 439
British Columbia Decisions, Civil Cases 1108
British Columbia Decisions, Criminal Cases 1108
British Columbia Decisions, Labour Arbitration in B.C. 1108
British Columbia Decisions, Labour Relations Board Decisions 1108
British Columbia Economic Accounts 106
British Defence Directory 98
British Education Index 439
British Educational Reference Books 108
British Humanities Index 660

British Library Research and Development Newsletter 444
British Library Research Reviews 444
British National Bibliography 439
British Reports, Translations, and Theses 442
British Standards 958
British Technology Index 662
Brown's Geological Information Bulletin 113
Brukermeldinger 771
BSC Newsletter 107
BSRIA Statistics Bulletin 119
BUFVC Catalogue 112
Builders' and Repairers' Lien Case Book 829
Building Articles in Hungarian Publications 494
Building Commodity Index 934
Building/Construction/Architecture Databases 775
Building in China - Selected Papers 203
Building Research and Practice 573
Building Structures 203
Buildings of Canada 138
Bulk Ferro-Alloys Monitor 228
Bulletin Analytique du Centre de Documentation du CERILH 188
Bulletin Bibliographique Fonderie 820
Bulletin Bibliographique INTD 722
Bulletin Calvados 22
Bulletin CIS 595
Bulletin de Documentation Electricite de France 295
Bulletin de la Construction Mecanique 957
Bulletin de Liaison de la Recherche en Informatique et en Automatique 361
Bulletin inter Villes Nouvelles 1091
Bulletin Mensuel d'Information du Centre de Creation Industrielle CCI 184
Bulletin of Chinese Conference Proceedings and Papers 801
Bulletin of Documentation 1121
Bulletin of Entomological Research 229
Bulletin of Industry and Construction 493
Bulletin of Labour Statistics 592
Bulletin of Marine Ecology 729
Bulletin of Zoological Nomenclature 229
Bulletin Officiel de la Propriete Industrielle 359
Bulletin Scientifique de l'Institut Textile de France 390
Bulletin Signaletique 355
Bulletin Signaletique 356
Bulletin Signaletique des Telecommunications 367
Bulletin Signaletique Hebdomadaire 339
BUMS Manual 116
Bureau Gravimetrique International Bulletin d'Information 342
Business In View 473
Business Information Australia 55
Business Monitor Series 454
Byggreferat 938
Byggvaruforteckning 934
C.A.P. Monitor 8
CA Selects 851
CAB Abstracts Online Newsletter 229
CAB Serials Checklist 229
CAB Thesaurus 229
Cable 1
Cadmium Abstracts 1122
Cahiers de Documentation 1091
Cahiers Financiers 251
CAIS/ACSI Newsletter 168
Calendar of Forthcoming Scientific and Technological Meetings to be Held in Israel 616
Calendar of I&D Activities 880
CAMN User's Manual 1037
CAN/OLE Bulletin 153
CAN/OLE Database Manual 153
CAN/OLE User's Manual 153
CAN/SDI Profile Design Manual 154
Canada Corporations Bulletin 129
Canadian Art Auctions: Sales and Prices 300
Canadian Business Index 707
Canadian Business Law Journal 162
Canadian Catalog Service 171
Canadian Charter of Rights Decisions 1108
Canadian Contributions to Rock Mechanics 131
Canadian Criminal Cases 162
Canadian Directory of Public Legal Education and Information 173
Canadian Education Index 170
Canadian Education Subject Headings 170
Canadian Journal of Information Science 168
Canadian Library Handbook 706
Canadian Library/Information Science Research Projects: A List 149
Canadian Locations of Journals Indexed for MEDLINE 152
Canadian MARC Communication Format Specifications Series 150
Canadian Mineral Occurrence Index of the Geological Survey of Canada 134
Canadian Network Papers 147

Canadian News Index 708
Canadian Patent Reporter 162
Canadian Periodical Index 174
Canadian Plains Bulletin 1066
Canadian Press NewsFile 708
Canadian Record Catalogue 206
Canadian Social Science Data Archive Catalogue 1120
Canadian Studies in Population 1035
Canadian Subject Headings 148
Canadian Technical and Scientific Information News Journal 963
Canadian Theses 148
Canadian Theses on Microfiche: Catalogue 148
Canadiana 148
CANCERNET Thesaurus 357
CANCERNET User's Manual 357
Cancerologie/Oncology - Bulletin Signaletique 357
CANMET Review 131
CANSIM Main Base Series Directory 159
CANSIM Mini Base Series Directory 159
Caribbean Report 651
CAS Industrial Engineering Index 885
Catalog of Periodical Titles Abstracted in SPHINX 363
Catalogo Coletivo de Publicacoes Periodicas 103
Catalogo dei Libri in Commercio 87
Catalogo dei Periodici Italiani 87
Catalogue des Disques Canadiens 206
Catalogue des Normes Francaises 382
Catalogue des Normes ISO 382
Catalogue des Publications de la Documentation Francaise 384
Catalogue des Titres de Periodiques Depouilles dans SPHINX 363
Catalogue on English Translations of German Standards 407
Catchword and Trade Name Index 662
CATSS News 1094
CDS/ISIS Newsletter 1017
CENELEC Electronic Components Committee 958
Central Information Services News (University of London) 1055
Central Patents Index 275
Central Statistical Office Macro-Economic Data Bank Index 449
Centre for Catalogue Research Newsletter 1039
CENTREDOC Bulletin 944
Charitable Deeds of Covenant 198
Charity 198
Charity Statistics 198
Charts: The Stockholm Stock Market 903
CHEMCO Physical Properties Data Bank Manual 327
Chemfacts 612
Chemical Age Project File 200
Chemical and Process Engineering Abstracts 77
Chemical Company Profiles: The Americas 612
Chemical Company Profiles: Western Europe 612
Chemical Data Service Databooks 612
Chemical Data Services Plant and Product Data 612
Chemical Engineering Abstracts 852
Chemical Engineering and Biotechnology Abstracts 403
Chemical Group 1 505
Chemical Group 2 505
Chemical Hazards in Industry 853
Chemical Industry of Eastern Europe 1975-80 612
Chemical Industry Year Book 612
Chemical Plant Contractor Profiles 612
Chemical Process Economics 199
ChemInform 201
Chemischer Informationsdienst 201
Chiltern Computing 485
China Foreign Trade Information Monthly 588
China Medical Abstracts 588
China Science & Tecnology Abstracts 588
Chinese Kungfu Stories in Indonesian: A Bibliography Selected from the IDC Collection 1073
Ciencia da Informacao 103
CIIA Newsletter 172
CINDA, An Index to the Literature on Microscopic Neutron Data 785
CINFORM 102
CIS Abstracts 595
CIS List of Periodicals Abstracted 595
CIS Thesaurus 595
CIS User's Guide 595
CISTI News 152
CITH INFO 980
CitiService Update 500
Civil Aviation Statistics of the World 569
Civil Engineering Hydraulics Abstracts 86
CLAIM Research Reports 675
CLARUS Index 517
CLASE: Citas Latinoamericanas en Sociologia, Economia y Humanidades 719
Clinical Pharmacokinetics 5
CNEA Reports 27
Coal Abstracts 782

Coal Abstracts Serial Title Abbreviations 782
Coal Calendar 782
Coal Data Base Guide 782
Coal Data Base Thesaurus 782
Coal Research Projects 782
CODATA Bulletin 574
CODATA Directory of Data Sources for Science and Technology 574
CODATA Newsletter 574
CODOC Manual 1050
COFFEELINE Thesaurus 570
COGEODATA Newsletter 609
COIN: Computerized Information in Canada 15
COINS Bulletin 127
Collective Bargaining: A Response to the Recession in Industrialised Market Economy Countries 591
Commerce Exterieure 681
Commonwealth Regional Renewable Energy Resources Index 230
Company Management 355
Comprehensive Bibliography of Reference Works on Information Technology 243
Compulsory Schooling in the E.C. 215
Computer and Communications Technology Documents 958
Computer and Control Abstracts 549
Computer Bulletin 107
Computer Directory of India 241
Computer Hardware Record 721
Computer Installation Record 721
Computer Journal 107
Computer Market Statistics 721
Computer Newsletter 119
Computer Processing and Legal Sciences 355
Computers in Industry 580
Computing 107
Computing Journal Abstracts 721
Computing News Roundup 721
Computing Technics 493
Conditions of Work: A Cumulative Digest 594
Conditions of Work and Quality of Working Life: A Directory of Institutions 594
Congres, Colloques et Conferences, Salons et Expositions 339
Construction and Civil Enginering Index 958
Construction Cost Information Bulletin 177
Construction Technique 203
Contents (Japan Pharmaceutical Information Center) 634
Contents List of Soviet Scientific Periodicals 507
Copper Monitor 228
Copper Quarterly 228
Copper Studies 228
CORN User's Guide 1036
Corrosion Data Sheets 405
Costs and Prices (Henley Centre for Forecasting) 484
Cotton and Tropical Fibres Abstracts 229
CRE Reports 458
CRESM Newsletter 186
Criminal Law Quarterly 162
Criminology & Penology Abstracts 647
CRONOS System for the Management of Time Series 225
Crop Physiology Abstracts 229
CRRERIS Newsletter 230
Crude Oil & Oil Products Monitor 228
CRUS News 1070
CSIR Publications 885
CSIRO Index 47
CSIRO List of Publications 47
Cuadernos de Documentacion e Informatica Biomedica 1082
Culham Laboratory Library Bulletin 438
Cumulated Index to Hebrew Periodicals 1051
Cumulated ISDS Register/Bulletin Indexes 603
Currency Profiles 484
Current Advances in Biochemistry 803
Current Advances in Cell & Developmental Biology 803
Current Advances in Ecological Sciences 803
Current Advances in Endocrinology 803
Current Advances in Genetics & Molecular Biology 803
Current Advances in Immunology 803
Current Advances in Microbiology 803
Current Advances in Neuroscience 803
Current Advances in Pharmacology & Toxicology 803
Current Advances in Physiology 803
Current Advances in Plant Science 803
Current Agricultural Serials: A World List 558
Current Awareness Bulletin (Aslib) 35
Current Awareness in Biological Sciences 803
Current Awareness in Particle Technology 676
Current Bibliographies on Science and Technology 645
Current Bibliography on Science and Technology 632
Current Biotechnology Abstracts 854
Current Contents (Philippines) 808
Current Contents of Selected Scientific Periodicals 726

Current Information in the Construction Industry 378
Current Listing of Articles in Science and Technology Journals 645
Current Listing of Articles in Social Science Journals 645
Current Papers in Electrical and Electronics Engineering 549
Current Papers in Physics 549
Current Papers on Computers and Control 549
CURRENT RESEARCH in Library & Information Science 661
Current Science and Technology Research in Japan 632
Current Scientific and Technological Research Projects in the Universities and Research Institutions of Bangladesh 70
Current Serials Received (British Library) 442
Current Technology Index 662
Current Titles in Turkish Science 991
Daily Eurobond Prices 267
Daily Intelligence Bulletin 465
Daily Official List 902
Dairy Science Abstracts 229
Data Archive Bulletin 291
Data Communications in Europe, 1983-1991 303
Data Juridica 641
Databooks (Chemical Data Service) 612
Datacrown Client Letter 261
Datasolve World Reporter Newsletter 265
DBI-Materialien 400
DECHEMA Chemistry Data Series 404
DECHEMA Thesaurus fur die Chemische Technik 403
DECHEMA Werkstoff Tabelle 405
Defence Documents 958
Delft Hydroscience Abstracts 268
Demografia 493
Demography 493
Desalination Abstracts 616
Desenvolvimento de Sistemas Microgtaficos Avancados 101
Desfasses SEF Directory 251
Deutsche Bibliographie 423
Deutsche DIN Normen 958
Deutsche Soziologie 1945-1977 43
Development of Advanced Micrographics Systems 101
Devindex 576
Devindex Africa 1005
Diagnostic Marketing Research Service 907
Diagnostic New Product Listing Service 907
Dictionary of Active Principles and Excipients 893
Diffusion Hebdomadaire Systematique 820
DIMDI-News 428
DIN-Anzeiger fur Technische Regeln 407
DIN Catalogue 407
Directories of Charitable Needs 198
Director's Guide to the EEC Economies 484
Directory and Index of Standards 898
Directory of Agricultural Personnel in India 510
Directory of Agricultural Research Stations in India 510
Directory of Associations in Canada 706
Directory of Computing Hardware 721
Directory of Computing Software 721
Directory of Computing Suppliers 721
Directory of CSIRO Research Programs 47
Directory of Data Base Producers 385
Directory of Documentation and Information Services in Adult Education 1021
Directory of Education Studies in Canada 170
Directory of Educational Documentation and Information Services 1021
Directory of Educational Research Institutions 1021
Directory of Federally Supported Research in Universities 152
Directory of Grant-Making Trusts 198
Directory of Indian Scientific & Technical Translators 507
Directory of Industrial Information Services and Systems in Developing Countries 1027
Directory of Information Sources in Turkey 991
Directory of Non-Governmental Organisations in OECD Member Countries Active in Development Co-operation 781
Directory of On-going Research in Cancer Epidemiology 1113
Directory of Professional Organisations in India 511
Directory of Regional Demographic Research and Teaching Institutions 1003
Directory of Research Institutes and Industrial Laboratories in Israel 616
Directory of Scientific and Technical Associations in Israel 616
Directory of Scientific Periodicals of Pakistan 793
Directory of Scientific Research Institutions in India 507
Directory of Scientists and Technologists of Bangladesh 70
Directory of Social Science Research and Documentation Institutions in the Arab Region 1015
Directory of Social Science Research Institutions (India) 511
Directory of Special Libraries in Indonesia 512
Directory of Special Libraries in Israel 616
Directory of Specialized Information Centers and Agencies in the Federal Republic of Germany and West Berlin 880
Directory of Standards and Specifications Issued by Departments and Agencies of the Government of Canada 898
Directory of Standards Referenced in Canadian Federal Legislation 898
Directory of Training, Research and Information-Producing Centers in Iran 613
Directory of United Nations Information Systems 1001
DISPLAY 256
DKI-Thesaurus 402
DOCPAL Latin American Population Abstracts 1007
DOCPAL Resumenes sobre Poblacion en America Latina 1007
Doctoral Dissertations in the Social Sciences 847
Documentation and Information Problems 843
Documentation Occupational Health 419
Documentation Occupational Health 539
Documentation Review on Information Problems 815
Documentation Rheology 417
Documentation Tribology 417
Dokumentation Arbeitsmedizin 419
Dokumentation Arbeitsmedizin 539
Dokumentation der Forschungsvorhaben in der Okologischen Medizin in der Bundesrepublik Deutschland 539
Dokumentation Gefahrdung durch Alkohol, Rauchen, Drogen, Arzneimittel 539
Dokumentation Impfschaden-Impferfolge 539
Dokumentation Medizin im Umweltschutz 539
Dokumentation Rheologie 417
Dokumentation Sozialmedizin, Offentlicher Gesundheitsdienst, Arbeitsmedizin 539
Dokumentation Verfahrenstechnik 77
DOMA Referatedienst 961
Dominion Law Reports 162
DPS Newsletter 258
Driftmeddelanden 931
Drug Abuse: Research on the Treatment of Alcohol and Drug Dependence 936
Drug Information Perspectives Newsletter 1043
Drug Information Reference 1043
Drug Information Sources 432
Drug Literature Index 296
Drug Use in Australia: A Directory of Survey Research Projects 61
Drugs 5
Drugs in Japan 634
DSIR Documentation 748
E.A.O. 1
East Europe Agriculture 8
Eastern European Mineral Technolgy - Current Contents 131
EBIP Newsletter 446
EC Index 305
ECHO Newsletter 219
Ecological Abstracts 393
Economic Titles/Abstracts 733
Economie de l'Energie 355
Economie Generale 355
Economie Prospective Internationale 185
Economy Bulletins (Biomedical Information Service) 1069
ECSSID Bulletin 311
EDE System Manual 604
Educational Abstracts for Tanzania 955
Educational Documentation and Information: the IBE Bulletin 1021
Educational Research 724
Educational Research News 724
Eight Peak Index of Mass Spectra 856
Eighteenth Century Short Title Catalogue 443
Electrical and Electronics Abstracts 549
Electrical Patents Index 275
Electrodes for Medicine and Biology 114
Electronic Components of Assessed Quality 958
Electronic Engineering Index 958
Electronic Funds Transfer: A Comprehensive Bibliography 883
Electronic Library 654
Electronic Publishing Abstracts 812
Electronic Publishing Review 654
Empirical Social Research 1045
Empirische Sozialforschung 1045
Emploi et Formation 355
Employment and Training 355
ENDOC Directory 216
Energia-Bibliografia Seletiva 102
Energy Economics 355
Energy Newsletter (I.P. Sharp Associates) 871
Energy Service 690
Energy Storage 44
Enfo 31
Engineering Components and Materials Index 958
Enitesugyi es Varosfeileszteşi Vilaghirado 494
ENSIC Holdings List 31
Environmental Literature Information Service 411
Environmental Research Catalogue 411
Environmental Sanitation Abstracts - Low Cost Options 31

Environmental Sanitation Reviews   31
Ephemerides of Minor Planets   997
Epitesugyi Cikkek a Magyar Idoszaki Kiadvanyokban   494
Epitesugyi Muszaki es Gazdasagi Tajekoztato   494
Epoch News Japan   298
Equipment for the Disabled Poplation   114
Ergonomics Abstracts   1041
Ergonomics and the Electronic Office   520
ESA/IRS User Manual   317
ESCAP Documents and Publications   1002
ESCAP Statistical Yearbook for Asia and the Pacific   1004
Espial Data Base Directory   300
Estates and Trusts Quarterly   162
ESTC Cataloguing Rules   443
Estudio de Usarios de Informacion Industrial   193
Estudos Sobre o Desenvolvimento Agricola   99
Etat et Religion, State and Religion, Staat und Religion   205
Ethylene Cracker Report   505
EUDISED Multilingual Thesaurus   248
EUDISED R&D Bulletin   248
Euro Abstracts   218
Eurodata Foundation Yearbook   303
EURODICAUTOM Bulletin   223
Eurofish Report   8
Euronet DIANE Directory of Services   220
Euronet DIANE News   220
European Bioengineering Research Inventory   114
European Communities Publications: a Guide to British Library
  Resources   442
European Company Service   690
European Court of Justice Reporter   305
European Digest   465
European Index of Management Periodicals   481
European Legal Literature Information Service   305
European LPG Report   505
European Paint & Resin News Monthly   530
European Patent Bulletin   315
European Political Data Newsletter   310
EUROSTAT News   225
EUROSTAT Review   225
Eurostatistics   225
Eusidic Database Guide   307
Eusidic Database Guide   654
Evaluated Kinetic Data for High-Temperature Reactions   1052
Evaluation of Historic Buildings   138
Ex Libris   576
Excerpta Medica   296
Excerpta Medica Core Journals   296
Excerpta Medica Newsletters   296
Exchange Rate Movements Yearbook   484
EXPLORE   356
Express Bulletins (Biomedical Information Service)   1069
EXSHARE Focal Points   321
Extel Cards   323
Extensions and Corrections to the UDC   578
Extra Pharmacopoeia   806
Fact User's Guide   691
Fact's Listing of Compounds in Main Data Base   691
Faba Bean Abstracts   229
Fabrimetal   187
Facsimilia Scientia et Technica Norwegica   1079
Factotum   443
FAO Documentation - Current Bibliography   1013
FAO Fertilizer Yearbook   1014
FAO Library Catalogue of Monographs   1013
FAO Library List of Serials   1013
FAO Monthly Bulletin of Statistics   1014
FAO Production Yearbook   1014
FAO Trade Yearbook   1014
FAO Yearbook of Forest Products and Trade   1014
Far Eastern Economic Review Index on Microfiche   1073
FARMODEX Bulletin   325
Federal Court of Appeal Decisions   1108
Fennica   482
Feuille d'Information (Institut Francais des Petroles)   387
Fiches Banques   251
Fiches de Documentation (Institut Francais des Petroles)   387
Fiches FAN   251
Fiches Profils: Transformation des Matieres Plastiques   251
Fiches Synthetiques   251
FID Directory   578
FID News Bulletin   578
Field Crop Abstracts   229
Fil d'Ariane   223
Film and Video Acquisition   48
Film Canadiana   146
Financial and Economic Newsletter (I.P. Sharp Associates)   871
Finding Patents   520
Fine Chemicals Directory   372

Fine Chemicals Directory Handbook   372
FINMED   329
Finnish National Bibliography   482
Finnish Periodicals Index in Economics and Business   481
FINP/BILD Thesaurus   481
Fire Science Abstracts   452
FIRS Sale and Purchase Report   324
FIRS Weekly Newbuilding Report   324
Flora de Vercruz   702
Fluid Flow Measurements Abstracts   86
Fluid Power Abstracts   86
Fluid Sealing Abstracts   86
FOLIO   356
Food Annotated Bibliographies   583
Food Balance Sheets   1014
Food Industry Bulletin   712
Food Industry Update   520
Food Patents   655
Food Science and Technology Abstracts   583
Food Topics   655
Forecasts for the Forecasts' Users Group   1062
Forecasts of Exchange Rate Movements   484
Foreign Chemical Patent News   632
Foreign Exchange Outlook   484
Foreign Exchange Yearbook   290
Foreign Patents Information Bulletin   645
Foreign Trade News   425
Foreign Trade Statistics for Asia and the Pacific   1004
Forest Products Abstracts   229
Forestry Abstracts   229
Formanderungsfestigkeit Stahl-Eisen   399
Forschungs- und Entwicklungsprojekte in Informationswissenschaft und
  -Praxis   880
Forschungsarbeiten in den Sozialwissenschaften: Dokumentation   43
Forschungsberichte aus Technik und Naturwissenschaften   521
Forschungsdokumentation zur Arbeitsmarkt- und Berufsforschung   410
Forthcoming Bioengineering Conferences   114
Forthcoming International Scientific and Technical Conferences   35
Fortschrittsberichte Technik/Naturwissenschaften   1031
Forum Musikbibliothek   400
Fossilium Catalogus   647
FoU-Indeks   767
Framework Forecasts for the ECC Economies   484
Framework Forecasts for the UK Economy   484
French Shares Price Indexes   389
French Shares Yield   389
Freshwater and Aquaculture Contents Tables   1008
Fruits   547
FSTA Thesaurus   583
GAPHYOR Bulletin   1063
General Documentation on Trade and Economics   425
General Economy   355
General Index to the Debates of the National Diet (Japan)   629
General Information Programme: UNISIST Newsletter   1019
General Review of Heat   386
Geo Abstracts   393
GeoArchive Users' Guide   394
Geographie Tropicale   355
Geological Newsletter   609
Geomechanics Abstracts   1056
Geophysics and Tectonics Abstracts   393
Geoprofile - Vertebrate Paleontology   394
Geosaurus   394
Geoscience Documentation   394
Geosources   394
Geotitles Repertorium   394
Geotitles Weekly   394
Gerencia de Informacao/Information Management   605
German Books in Print   863
German DIN Standards   958
German Partners of Developing Countries   397
Gestion des Entreprises   355
Giornale della Libreria   87
Glacier Inventory Notes   139
Gmelin Handbook of Inorganic Chemistry   431
Going Online   775
Government Financing of Research and Development
  (EUROSTAT)   225
Graphiques de la Bourse de Paris   389
Greater London Council Intelligence Bulletins   465
Green Europe   8
Group Surveys   251
Guia Brasileiro de Instituicoes de Pesquisa em Agricultura   99
Guia Brasileiro de Pesquisadores em Agricultura   99
Guia Internacional dos Micropublicadores   101
Guida alle Banche Dati   950
Guide des Bibliotheques Canadiennes   706
Guide to BISA   1073
Guide to Choosing Viewdata Systems   1100

Guide to CSK Data 628
Guide to Data Banks 950
Guide to Norwegian Statistics 766
Guide to Overseas Qualifications 108
Guide to Periodicals and Newspapers in the Public Libraries of Metropolitan Toronto 699
Guide to Provincial Library Agencies in Canada 149
Guide to Research and Development 515
Guidelines for Space Materials Selection 316
Guides for Managers Series (Eurodata Foundation) 303
HAMKA: A Bibliography of the Works of Prof. Dr. Haji Abdul Malik Karim Amrullah 1073
Handbook of Environmental Data and Ecological Parameters 604
Handbook of Library Holdings on Commonwealth Literature 442
Handbook on Agricultural Statistics for Asia and the Pacific 1004
Handbuch der Grossunternehmen 1098
Harnessing the Information Resource 533
Harwell Information Bulletin 434
Hazards of Alcohol, Smoking, Drugs, Medicine 539
Health Care Information Service 477
Health Sciences Information in Canada: Libraries 152
Heating, Ventilating, & Air Conditioning 203
Heavy Oil/Enhanced Recovery Index 13
Helminthological Abstracts: Series A, Animal Helminthology 229
Helminthological Abstracts: Series B, Plant Nematology 229
Helppacks 1054
Herbage Abstracts 229
Hertfordshire Industrial and Commercial Register 486
HERTIS News 486
High Capacity Transport Register 68
High Energy Physics Index 396
High-Performance Textiles 873
Higher Education in the United Kingdom 108
Historical Sediment Data Summary 142
Historical Social Research 183
Historical Statistics 493
Historical Streamflow Summary 142
Historical Water Levels Summary 142
Historisch-Sozialwissenschaftliche Forschungen 183
Hochenergiephysik-Index 396
Hojin Shinkoku Shotoku 969
Holiday USA & Canada 473
HOMS Newsletter 1117
HOMS Reference Manual 1117
Horticultural Abstracts 229
House of Commons Library Thesaurus 459
House of Commons Weekly Information Bulletin 459
House of Lords Library Bulletin 460
Human Sciences of Health 355
Humanistiske Data 768
Hungarian Building Bulletin 494
Hungarian Library and Information Science Abstracts 495
Hungarian Library Literature 495
Hungarian Technical Abstracts 496
Hydromechanics and Hydraulic Engineering Abstracts 268
I.C.E. Abstracts 208
I.P. Sharp Newsletter 871
IA Reports 618
IAALD News 558
IAALD Quarterly Bulletin 558
IASC Newsletter 556
IASC/SCAD Newsletter 506
IBEDOC Information 1021
IBI Newsletter 554
ICAME News 768
ICAO/ADREP Reports Summary 567
ICAO Digests of Statistics 569
ICC Business Ratio Reports 499
ICC Database Newsletter 499
ICC/DIALOG User Manual 499
ICC Financial Surveys 499
ICC Viewdata User Manual 499
IDIS-SOMED-A 539
IEA Data Bank Bulletin 557
IFIP Information Bulletin 580
IFIS Newsletter 583
IFLA Annual 582
IFLA Directory 582
IFLA Journal 582
IGIS Newsletter 586
IIS Monograph Series 544
IIS Sourcefinder Series 544
ILO Thesaurus 593
IMCA Newsletter 526
IME Newsletter 527
IMIC Journal 598
IMM Abstracts 551
IMM Index to Mining and Metallurgy 1894-1949 551
Impact of Demographic Change on Education Systems in the European Community 215
Import/Export Microtables 780
In Search of a Sunrise 520
Incompatex 693
Index Analytique du Journal "Le Monde Diplomatique" 704
Index de la Litterature des Sports et des Loisirs 210
Index de l'Actualite Vue a Travers la Presse Ecrite 704
Index de Periodiques Canadiens 174
Index et Catalogues URBAMET 1091
Index of Articles (Aviation Information Services Ltd.) 68
Index of Current Research on Pigs 229
Index of Fungi 229
Index of Indonesian Learned Periodicals 512
Index of Indonesian Survey and Research 512
Index to Conference Proceedings Received (British Library) 442
Index to Current Awareness in Particle Technology 676
Index to Geoscience Data in 8500 Exploration Reports 778
Index to 6500 Published Reports and Maps, Mineral Resources Group 778
Index to Swedish Newspapers 116
Index to Swedish Periodicals 116
Index to The Alberta Gazette 11
Index to the Financial Times 328
Index to Theses Accepted for Higher Degrees by the Universities of Great Britain and Ireland 35
Index Veterinarius 229
Indian Education Index 511
Indian National Directory of Marine Research Projects 509
Indian National Directory of Marine Scientists 509
Indian National Directory of Training and Education in Marine Science 509
Indian Science Abstracts 507
Indicators of Industrial Activity 780
Indice Cientifico Valenciano 1082
Indice de Proyectos en Desarrollo en Ecologia de Zonas Aridas 702
Indice de Proyectos en Desarrollo en Ecologia Tropical 702
Indice Espanol de Ciencia y Tecnologia 890
Indice Espanol de Ciencias Sociales 891
Indice Espanol de Humanidades 891
Indice Medico Espanol 1082
Indices de Cours de la Compagnie des Agent de Change 389
Industrial Abstracts for Tanzania 955
Industrial Aerodynamics Abstracts 86
Industrial Development Abstracts 1027
Industrial Economy Abstracts 801
Industrial Performance Analysis 499
Industries Agro-Alimentaires Bibliographie Internationale 39
Industry Profile Series (Information Research Ltd.) 530
Industry Surveys 251
INFOFISH Marketing Digest 1011
INFOFISH Trade News 1011
Infolex Newsletter 517
InfoLine UPDATE 802
InfoLine Users Guide 802
INFORM (Institute of Information Scientists) 544
Informacio-Elektronika 493
INFORMATECH (Standards Council of Canada) 898
Informatics and Scientometrics 492
Informatie Lopend Onderzoek Sociale Wetenschappen 847
Informatik 395
Informatika 1121
Information and Computer 542
Information and Management 586
Information Bildungsforschung Schweiz 945
Information Bulletin of Australian Criminology 56
Information Bulletin on Radioactive Waste 434
Information Bulletin on the Survey of Chemicals Being Tested for Carcinogenicity 1113
Information Consultants, Freelancers and Brokers Directory 526
Information Dokumentation 395
Information Eaux 391
Information-Electronics 493
Information for Research Libraries 269
Information Industry 1
Information on Current Social Science Research 847
Information Resources Annual 533
Information Resources Guide: Britain 432
Information Technology & People 180
Information Technology in Industrial Information Services 1054
Information Technology, Policy Decision Making in the U.K. 1054
Information Technology: Sources of Australian Information 520
Information Today 654
Information Trade Directory 654
Information uber Online-Zugriff 428
Information World 258
Informations Internationales 251
Informations-Technologie: Bibliographie der Nachschlagewerke 243
Informationsdienst Krankenhauswesen 477
Informationsdienst Ubersetzungen 395

PUBLICATIONS INDEX

Informationsdienst Veranstaltungskalender 395
Informationsdienstkartei Tierische Produktion 487
Informatique et Sciences Juridiques 355
Informativo SNI 212
Informatorium Medicamentorum 844
Informe Latinoamericano 651
Informes Especiales 651
INFOS Newsletter 749
Infotecture Europe 1
Infotecture France 1
Infoterm Newsletter 587
INFOTERRA Bulletin 1025
INFOTERRA International Directory of Sources 1025
INIS Atomindex 560
INIS Reference Series 560
INIS Today 560
Innovation & Produits Nouveaux 1
Innovation Awareness List 1021
INODC Newsletter 509
INPADOC Patent Gazette 64
Inpharma 5
Inquiries into Empirical Social Research 1945-1982: Catalog of Holdings 1045
INRIATHEQUE 361
INSPEC Classification 549
INSPEC List of Journals and Other Serial Sources 549
INSPEC Matters 549
INSPEC Thesaurus 549
INSPEC User Manual 549
Instrumentation and Techniques for Cardiology 114
Interatomic Distances 125
Interlending and Document Supply: Journal of the British Library Lending Division 442
Intermarc Information 555
International Abstracts of Biological Sciences 803
International Banking Service 690
International Bibliography of Refugee Literature 602
International Bibliography of Standardized Vocabularies 587
International Bibliography of the Social Sciences 571
International Biodeterioration 229
International Biodeterioration Bulletin 1038
International Bonds Service 322
International Books in Print 863
International Building Services Abstracts 119
International Civil Engineering Abstracts 208
International Coffee Organization Library Monthly Entries 570
International Congress Series 296
International Development Abstracts 393
International Dictionary of Micrographics Terms 101
International Directory of Agencies for the Visually Disabled 115
International Directory of Marine Scientists 1008
International Directory of Refugee-Assisting Organizations 602
International Directory of Research Centres and Information Sources, Services and Systems in New and Renewable Energies 1018
International Forum on Information and Documentation 578
International Frequency List 606
International Geographical Bibliography 355
International Guide to Microform Publishers 101
International I&D Committees with Memberships from the Federal Republic of Germany and West Berlin 880
International Institute of Refrigeration Bulletin 590
International Labour Documentation 593
International Labour Documentation Cumulative Catalogue 593
International List of Periodical Title Word Abbreviations 603
International Packaging Abstracts 812
International Polymer Science and Technology 858
International Register of Potentially Toxic Chemicals 1026
International Register of Research on Visual Disability 115
International Reviews on Mathematical Education 521
International Road Research Documentation 786
International Serials Catalogue 575
International Survey of Aids for the Visually Disabled 115
International Technical Thesaurus 382
International Thesaurus of Refugee Terminology 602
International Welding Thesaurus 1106
Internationale IuD-Gremien mit Beteiligung aus der Bundesrepublik Deutschland und Berlin (West) 880
Internationales Bibliotheks-Handbuch 863
Internationales Verzeichnis der Wirtschaftsverbande 863
Internationales Verzeichnis Wissenschaftlicher Verbande und Gesellschaften 863
INTUG Newsletter 607
Inventaire des Centres Belges de Recherche Disposant d'une Bibliotheque ou d'un Service de Documentation 84
Inventory of Australian Surveys 61
Inventory of Belgian Scientific Units 84
Inventory of Computer-aided Environmental Models 411
Inventory of Environmental Authorities 411
Inventory of Scientific Congresses 84

Investment Markets 484
Investment Timing Monitor 1109
Ipari es Epitoipari Statisztikai Ertesito 493
IRANDOC Science Abstract Bulletin 613
IRANDOC Social Science Abstract Bulletin 613
IRANDOC Technical Bulletin 613
Iranian National Union List of Serials 613
IRCS Journal of Medical Science 614
IRCS Medical Science 614
IRPTC Bulletin 1026
Irradiation of Medical Products Abstract Bulletin 434
Irrigation and Drainage Abstracts 229
ISDS Bulletin 603
ISDS Manual 603
ISDS Register 603
ISO Activities Report 599
ISO Bibliographies 599
ISO Bulletin 599
ISO Catalogue 599
ISO KWIC Index of International Standards 599
ISO Memento 599
ISO Standards Handbooks 599
ISTEI Reports 815
IT Focus 549
IuD-Termine 880
Japan Directory of Professional Associations 635
Japan English Books in Print 635
Japan English Magazine Directory 635
Japan Pharmaceutical Abstracts 634
Japan Publications Guide Service 635
Japanese National Bibliography 629
Japanese Non-priority Index 633
Japanese Overall Concordance 633
Japanese Patent Abstracts 633
Japanese Patent Index in English 633
Japanese Patent Indexes 633
Japanese Periodicals Index 629
Japanese Priority Index 633
JAPIC Weekly Bulletin 634
JICST Thesaurus 632
JNN Data Bank 631
JODC News 628
Joho (JAPIC Weekly Bulletin) 634
Joho Shori/Information Processing 529
Jordans Surveys 636
Journal de Coupons 251
Journal of Documentation 35
Journal of Ferrocement 32
Journal of Geological Science 412
Journal of Information Processing 529
Journal of Information Processing and Management 632
Journal of Information Science 544
Journal of Synthetic Methods 274
Journals in Translation 442
Journals in Translation 608
JPG Letter 635
JURINNOV 336
Jurisprudence Express 834
Kagaku Shoho 630
Kalender (German Foundation for International Development) 397
Katalog der Bauforschungsberichte 373
Katalog der Literaturhinweise 373
Katalog Over Svensk Standard 940
Key Abstracts 549
Key Note Publications 499
Key to Belgian Science 84
Key to Economic Science 733
Key-Word-Index of Wildlife Research 947
Keywords in Serial Titles (KIST) 442
KIBIC-rapport 921
Kieler Schrifttumskunden zu Wirtschaft und Gesellschaft 639
Kluwer's Universeel Technisch Woordenboek 243
Kompass Directories 642
Konyvtari es Dokumentacios Szakirodalom 495
Konyvtari Figyelo 495
Korean Medical Abstracts 645
Korean Patent Abstracts 645
Korean Scientific Abstracts 645
Kort Geding 641
Kulfoldi Statisztikai Adatforrasok 493
KWIC Index to Rock Mechanics Literature 1056
Laboratory Equipment Index 958
Laboratory Hazards Bulletin 855
Labour Arbitration Cases 162
Labour Force Statistics 780
Labour Force Statistics Yearbook 780
Land Compensation Reports 162
Landbouwdocumentatie/Agricultural Documentation 731
L'Annee Boursiere 389

LASER Directory of Libraries 670
LASER Handbook 670
LASER ISBN & BNB Book Number and Location Finding List 670
LASER Union Catalogue 670
Latin America Commodities Report 651
Latin America Weekly Report 651
Latin American Newsletters 651
Latin American Population Abstracts 1007
Law Databases 775
Lead Abstracts 1122
Lead Monitor 228
Lead Quarterly 228
Learned Societies, Journals and Collaboration with Publishers 1054
L'Economie Francaise 773
Legal Technology 656
Leisure, Recreation and Tourism Abstracts 229
Leisure Studies Data Bank Catalogue of Holdings 1084
Leitung und Planung von Wissenschaft und Technik 395
Lentil Abstracts 229
Lettre de Transinove 987
Lettre du CEPII 185
Levantamentos Bibliograficos 99
Library and Documentation Literature 495
Library and Information Research News 659
Library and Information Research Reports 444
Library and Information Science Abstracts 663
Library Bulletin (BSRIA) 119
Library Micromation News 818
Library Review 495
Library Systems Seminar 555
LIBRIS Meddelanden 931
LID Information Brochure 66
Life Style Indicator 789
LIMB Index 677
Linkedit 889
L'Interrogation de la Banque des Donnees du Sous-sol 341
List Bio-med: Biomedical Serials in Scandinavian Libraries 921
List des Publications du Commissariat a l'Energie Atomique 339
List of Adverse Reactions to Drugs Reported in Japanese Clinical Journals 634
List of Archive Holdings (Central Archives for Empirical Social Research) 1045
List of Completed Research Projects on Agriculture and Animal Sciences 510
List of Information Science Journals 880
List of Ongoing Research Projects in Agriculture and Animal Sciences 510
List of Practicing Librarians and Doucmentalists in Tanzania 955
List of Services Accessible through Transpac 989
List of Ship Stations 606
List of Shipowners, Maritime Guide and Offshore Register 667
List of Telegraph Offices Open for International Service 606
List of Thesauri 880
Liste de Congres Analyses (Electricite de France) 295
Liste de Revues Analysees (Electricite de France) 295
Liste des Normes Francaises Traduites 382
Liste Mondiale des Periodiques Specialises dans les Science Sociales 571
Literatur-Schnelldienst Kunststoffe Kautschuk Fasern 402
Literaturdienst Elektrotechnik 960
Literaturdokumentation zur Arbeitsmarkt- und Berufsforschung 410
Literature Documentation of the International Law of the Sea 413
Literature of Outgassing Materials 316
Lloyd's List 667
Lloyd's Register of Ships 667
Lloyd's Shipping Index 667
Lloyd's Shipping Information Services Review 667
Lloyd's Tanker Casualty Bulletin 667
LOGIN 734
London Community Services Directory 525
LOR Newsletter 505
LS-reports 618
Magyar Konyvtari Szakirodalom Bibliografiaja 495
Mahasagar 509
Mahatma Gandhi Bibliography 511
Main Economic Indicators 780
Maize Quality Protein Abstracts 229
Major Loss Record (Aviation Information Services Ltd.) 68
Major Projects File 536
Malaysian Serials: Non-government 1073
Management & Marketing Abstracts 812
Manitoba Decisions, Civil and Criminal Cases 1108
Manual for the Development of National Documentation Units and Bibliographic Data Bases for Science and Technology Policy 1016
Manual on WESTPAC Data Management 628
Manufacturing and Materials Handling Index 958
Manufacturing and Retailing in the 80's 484
Manufacturing Technology Reviews 885
Marine Affairs Bibliography 254

Marine Environmental Data Information Referral Catalogue 1020
Marine Pollution Research Titles 684
Marine Science Contents Tables 1008
Market and Statistics News 1083
Market Commentary 126
Market Data Reports on European Industries 499
Market Research Abstracts 687
Marketing Research Studies (Information Research Ltd.) 530
MARNA Manual and Thesaurus 685
Marna-News 685
Martindale Newsletter 806
Martindale Online User Guide 806
Martindale Thesaurus 806
MASIS NEWS 689
Mass Spectral Data Sheets 856
Mass Spectrometry 856
Mass Spectrometry Bulletin 856
Master List of Medical Indexing Terms 296
Materials and Corrosion 405
Mathematics Abstracts 521
Measurement of Mechanical Quantities 415
Mechanical Engineering 565
MEDI Index 1020
MEDI Operations Manual 1020
mediadoc 65
Medical Databases 775
Medical Textiles 873
Mediendokumentation zur Gesundheitserziehung 539
MEDINFO Congress Proceedings 597
MEDTRAIN Workbook 440
MeSH Workbook 440
Messtechnik, Regelungstechnik, Automatik 1098
Metal Construction 1106
Metals Abstracts 698
Methodological Materials and Documentation on Software Packages 565
Methods in Organic Synthesis 851
Mexico and Central America Report 651
MIAS News Bulletin 730
MIC Nytt 921
Microfiches Jurisprudence Express 834
Microfiches Novita 87
Microfilm in Information Systems 101
Micrographics News 101
Microinfo 705
Microlog Index 706
MicroNotes 175
MIDAS Operator's Manual 790
Middle East Markets for Medical and Analytical Laboratory Equipment 515
Mideast File 970
MIDIST Bulletin d'Information 344
MIDS Newsletter 888
Mineral Briefs 727
Mineral Deposit Inventory 778
Mineral Dossiers 727
Mineralogical Abstracts 711
Mini-Biblex 834
Mining, Minerals and Metals Monitor 394
Mining Technology Abstracts 131
MINTEC: Mining Technology Abstracts 131
Minutes of the Council of the Corporation of the City of Toronto 985
MIS Bulletin 258
MISCA Microthesaurus 794
Mitteilungsblatt der AGB 374
Molecular Structures and Dimensions 125
Monitor 654
Monthly Abstract of Statistics 749
Monthly Economic Review 536
Monthly List of Foreign Scientific and Technical Publications 629
Monthly National Corporate Bankruptcy Report 969
Monthly Statistics on the Paris Stock Exchange 389
Motor Vehicle Insurance Case Book 829
MRC Annual Report 888
Multilanguage Books on Deposit in the Public Libraries of Metropolitan Toronto 699
Muszaki Gazdasagi Tajekoztato 496
Nachrichten fur Aussenhandel 425
NAQUADAT Dictionary of Parameter Codes 141
NAQUADAT Guide to Interactive Retrieval 141
National Accounts of OECD Countries 780
National and International Meetings on Science and Technology 991
National Catalogue of Scientific and Technical Periodicals of Bangladesh 70
National Diet Library Catalog of Foreign Periodicals 629
National Diet Library Catalog of Japanese Periodicals 629
National Film Lending Collection Catalogue 48
National Index of Translations 507
National Library of Canada News 147

National Library of Canada Publications Catalogue   147
National Library of Canada Technical News   147
National Library Recent Acquisitions in the Field of Library Science   149
National Master Specification   242
National Scientific and Technological Potential Survey Interviewer's Guide   1016
National Union Catalog of Scientific and Technical Books in Libraries of the Republic of China   726
National Union Catalogue of Library Materials for the Handicapped   48
National Union Catalogue of Serials   48
Natural Resources Survey & Exploration - Vasundhra   507
Naval Annual   97
NDT-Info   436
NEA Data Bank Newsletter   785
Nederlandse Jurisprudentie   641
NEEDS-IR Information   753
NEEDS-TS Economy/Macro   754
NEEDS-TS Energy Review   754
NEEDS-TS Report   754
Neometaphysical Digest   882
Netherlands in the Information Age   736
Neue Bauforschungsberichte   373
Neue Literaturhinweise   373
Neutron Nuclear Data Evaluation Newsletter   785
New Technologies: Impact on Employment and the Working Environment   591
New Zealand Science Abstracts   748
New Zealand Scientific Literature Index   748
News and Views   317
News Databases   775
News from NEA Data Bank   785
News in the Agricultural Practice   121
Newscheck   462
Newsidic   307
Newsletter of the University of Sydney Sample Survey Centre   1072
NGI-Nieuws   745
Nickel, Chrome, Molybdenum Monitor   228
1982 Survey of UK Online Users   775
Nineteenth Century Short Title Catalogue   757
Nineteenth Century Short Title Catalogue Newsletter   757
Nomenclator   893
Non-Destructive Testing Abstracts Journal   416
Nordic Energy Index   761
NORDICOM Newsletter   763
NORDINFO-NYTT   762
Norsk Bokfortegnelse   1061
Norsk Tidsskriftartikler   1061
North American Company Service   690
North American Travel Market   473
Northern Titles KWIC Index   95
Norway's Official Statistics   766
Norwegian National Bibliography   1061
Notes of Recent Decisions Rendered by the Immigration Appeal Board   173
Noticiario Micrografico   101
Notiziario   624
Nouvelles du CRESM   186
NRI Quarterly Economic Review   760
Nuclear Science Information of Japan   627
Numerical Data Base Service   64
Nutrition Abstracts and Reviews: Series A, Human and Experimental   229
Nutrition Abstracts and Reviews: Series B, Livestock Feeds and Feeding   229
ODS-LSI (Overseas Data Service, Life Style Indicator)   789
OECD Liason Bulletin   781
Oecumene   205
OEIC Information Bulletin   694
Official Statistics of Sweden   932
Offshore Geological Bibliography   113
Oil Index   770
Oil Sands Researchers and Research Projects   13
OIN Catalogue of Microfilms   816
OIN Works   816
Olje-Indeks   770
Omnibus   119
On-Going Research Projects (Republic of China)   726
Oncology Information Service Bulletins   1053
Onderzoek naar Milieu en Natuur in Nederland   743
Online Information Centers in Denmark   256
Online Notes   775
Online Review   654
Online to Textile Literature   873
Ontario Decisions, Criminal Cases   1108
Ontario Geological Survey General Index   778
Ontario Municipal Board Reports   162
Ontario Reports   162
Orientering om Fremtidsforskning   540
Ornamental Horticulture   229

Ostsprachige Fachliteratur   1031
OTA-kirjasto   483
Outline of the JODC   628
Packaging Science and Technology Abstracts   584
Packet SwitchStream, A Basic Guide and Directory   447
Paint Titles   792
Pakistan Current Contents   793
Pakistan Science Abstracts   793
PAKLEGIS: A Guide to Packaging Legislation   812
Pan European Survey   839
Paper & Board Abstracts   812
Papers in Historical Statistics   493
Paris Stock Exchange Charts   389
PASCAL EXPLORE   356
PASCAL FOLIO   356
PASCAL SIGMA   356
PASCAL THEMA   356
Patent Applicant Service   64
Patent Applicant Service to Priorities   64
Patent Classification Service   64
Patent Family Service   64
Patent Inventor Service   64
Patent Register Service   64
Patents Databases   775
Peace Research Abstracts Journal   800
Peace Research Reviews   800
PERA Bulletin   826
PERIODEX   831
Periodica: Indice de Revistas Latinoamericanas en Ciencias   719
Periodicals in Southern African Libraries   885
Periodicals in the Library of the Norwegian Institute of Technology   1079
Periodicals Parade   847
Periodicos Brasileiros de Ciencia e Tecnologia   103
Periodiekenparade   847
Permanent Inventory of Belgian Scientific Publications   84
Pesticide Use Index   128
Petrochemical Manufacturing and Market Trends   199
Petroleum and Petrochemical Economics in Europe   199
Pharmaceutical New Product Listing Service   907
Pharmaceuticals and Toiletries Bulletin   712
Pharmline   285
Philippine Ethnographic Series   1073
Philippine Men of Science   808
Philippine Science and Technology Abstracts   808
Philosophische Dokumentation   1048
Physics Abstracts   549
Physics Briefs   521
Physics Data   521
Physik Daten   521
Physikalische Berichte   521
Pig News and Information   229
Pipelines Abstracts   86
Pira Thesaurus   812
Plain Man's Guide to the T.G.I.   109
PLANINDEX   1006
Planning Consumer Markets   484
Planning for Social Change   484
Plant Breeding Abstracts   229
Plant Growth Regulator Abstracts   229
POETRI Newsletter   601
Point de Repere: Index Analytique d'Articles de Periodiques Quebecois et Etrangers   831
Poison Management Manual   1043
Poisoning Perspectives Newsletter   1043
Police Science Abstracts   647
Population Headliners   1003
Potato Abstracts   229
Potato Markets   8
Poultry Abstracts   229
Prace IINTE   815
Prairie Forum   1066
Praktijkgids   641
Praxis Juridique et Religion   205
PRECIS: A Manual of Concept Analysis and Subject Indexing   441
PRECIS Vocabulary Fiche   441
Presentation of Information   788
Preserved Milk   8
Prestel Gateway Cost Effectiveness   1100
Prestel User   448
Prevision et Analyse Economique   1062
Previsions Glissantes Detaillees   773
Primary Communications: An Annotated Review of the Literature Since 1970   1054
Primary Computing   485
Primer for Agricultural Libraries   558
Printing Abstracts   812
Probleme de Documentare si Informare   843
Problems of Economic, Scientific and Technical Cooperation of CMEA

Member Countries 565
Problems of Information Systems 565
Problems of Scientific Information 816
Proceedings of the Annual Meeting on Information Science and Technology 632
Process Economics Research Planning 199
Process Engineering Index 958
PROFILE: The Excerpta Medica Newsletter 296
Program: News of Computers in Libraries 35
Promis Newsletter 871
Property Service 690
Propriete Industrielle Bulletin Documentaire 360
Protozoological Abstracts 229
Provisional Atlas of the Amphibians and Reptiles of the British Isles 461
Provisional Atlas of the Arachnida of the British Isles 461
Provisional Atlas of the Bryophytes of the British Isles 461
Provisional Atlas of the Crustacea of the British Isles 461
Provisional Atlas of the Insects of the British Isles 461
Provisional Atlas of the Mammals of the British Isles 461
Provisional Atlas of the Marine Dinoflagellates of the British Isles 461
Provisional Atlas of the Nematodes of the British Isles 461
Przeglad Dokumentacyjny Informacji Naukowej 815
PSS, The Public Data Service Directory 447
PSS-The Technical Users Guide 447
Psychologischer Index 1078
Publications of the National Research Council of Canada 152
Publishers in English in Japan 635
Publishers' International Directory 863
Pudoc Bulletin 731
Pulse Radiolysis 44
Pumps and Other Fluids Machinery Abstracts 86
QL/SEARCH User's Manual 828
QL Update 828
QT Handbook 436
QT News 436
Quaere Law Letter 829
Quarterly Bulletin of IAALD 558
Quarterly Bulletin of Statistics for Asia and the Pacific 1004
Quarterly National Accounts Bulletin 780
Quarterly Petrochemical Business Analysis 199
QUORUM 157
R & D Philippines 808
R & D Projects in Documentation and Librarianship 579
RADAR (Repertoire Analytique d'Articles de Revues du Quebec) 831
RADIALS (Research and Development - Library and Information Science) Bulletin 661
Radio Guide 475
Radiographie du Capital: Les Liaisons Financieres 251
Rail International 600
Rapport Annuel sur la Situation des Services Postaux 1030
RAPRA Abstracts 858
RAPRA Online Users Manual 858
Reactions 5
Recent Trends in Wind Energy 507
Rechtspraak van de Week 641
Rechtsstands Lexicon 234
RECODEX 906
Referatedienst Verpackung 584
Referateorgan Schweissen und Verwandte Verfahren 418
Referateorgan Zerstorungsfreie Prufung 416
Referativnyi Zhurnal 998
Referatove Vybery 250
Reference Bulletin 355
Reference Data Series No. 1: Energy, Electricity and Power Estimates for the Period up to 2000 559
Reference Ile de France 1091
Reference Manual for Machine-Readable Bibliographic Descriptions 1023
Reference Manual for Machine-Readable Descriptions of Research Projects and Institutions 1023
Refugee Abstracts 602
Regional Geochemical Atlases of the United Kingdom 728
Regional Statistics 493
Register of Current Community Legal Instruments 489
Register of Educational Research in the United Kingdom 724
Register of Keyterms (World Textile Abstracts) 873
Register of Legal Documentation in the World 571
Register of Parliamentary Processes in the German Federal Diet and Federal Council 422
Register of Periodicals in the ILO Library 593
Register of Social Science Research 847
Register of United Nations Serials Publications 1001
Register zu den Verhandlungen des Deutschen Bundestages und des Bundesrates 422
Registered Corporate Income Report 969
Regulatory Reporter 173
Renewable Energy Experts Directory 230
Renewable Energy Products Directory 230

Renewable Energy Review Journal 33
Repertoire Analytique d'Articles de Revues du Quebec 831
Repertoire Bibliographique des Institutions Chretiennes 205
Repertoire Bibliographique d'Histoire du Quebec et du Canada 704
Repertoire Canadien sur l'Education 170
Repertoire CATED 610
Repertoire d'Art et Archeologie 355
Repertory of Art and Archaeology 355
REPIDISCA Newsletter 794
REPINDEX 794
Report of Policy Development in Science and Technology 726
Reports and Papers in the Social Sciences 1022
Reports in the Fields of Science and Technology 521
Reprographics Quarterly 725
RERIC Holdings List 33
RERIC News 33
Research and Development - Library and Information Science Bulletin 661
Research and Development Index 767
Research and Development Projects in the Areas of Information Science and Practice 880
Research on Environment and Nature in the Netherlands 743
Research on Transport Economics 309
Research Report from the NIES 626
Researching Heritage Buildings 138
Reseau Documentaire en Sciences Humaines de la Sante 355
RESHUS 355
Resources 840
Retrospective Cumulative Index of Indian Social Science Journals 511
Review of Applied Entomology: Series A, Agricultural 229
Review of Applied Entomology: Series B, Medical and Veterinary 229
Review of Medical and Veterinary Mycology 229
Review of Plant Pathology 229
Reviews on Thermophysical Properties of Substances 996
Revista Espanola de Documentacion Cientifica 890
Revue Canadienne des Sciences de l'Information 168
Revue des Inventions Horlogeres 944
Revue Generale de Thermique 386
Rice Abstracts 229
Risk Measurement Service 1060
Roadlit 62
ROC Information Industry Handbook 542
Royal Society of Chemistry Information Services Newsletter 851
Rural Development: A Selected Bibliography 1002
Rural Development Abstracts 229
Rural Extension, Education & Training Abstracts 229
RUSI/Brassey's Defence Yearbook 97
Russian Scientific & Technical Publications - An Accession List 507
Russian Space Exploration 432
S.A. Waterabstracts 887
SAMKATPER (Union Catalog for Periodicals in Norwegian Libraries) 1061
Saskatchewan Decisions, Civil and Criminal Cases 1108
Scandinavian Periodicals Index in Economics and Business 481
Scandinavian Technology Libraries' Congress Lists 1079
Scannet Today 864
Scheduled Intra-European Passenger and Cargo Traffic of AEA Member Airlines 41
Schip & Schade 641
Schrifttum Bauwesen 373
Schrifttum Raumordnung Stadtebau Wohnungswesen 373
Schulbibliothek Aktuell 400
Science. Technology. Industry. 965
Science and Technology Briefs 726
Science and Technology Collections in Canadian Government Libraries 152
Science and Technology Information Service 629
Science Information Services in India 507
Scientific and Professional Meetings in Yugoslavia and Foreign Countries. 1121
Scientific and Technical Information 496
Scientific and Technical Periodicals of Bangladesh 70
Scientific and Technical Research Centres in Australia 47
Scientific and Technical Societies of Canada 152
Scientific Policy, Research and Development in Canada 152
Scientific Research Abstracts in Republic of China 726
Scientific Serials in Australian Libraries 47
Scientometrics 492
SCIMP/SCANP Thesaurus 481
SCOLCAT 869
Scotland's Top 500 Companies 636
SDC Bulletin 868
SEA Abstracts 808
Searching the Eighteenth Century 443
Seat-Belt Defense Cases 829
Sediment Data for Canadian Rivers 142
Sediment Data Reference Index 142
Seed Abstracts 229
SEF Notices 251

Selected Bibliography of Hungarian Economic Books and Articles 491
Selected Journals on Water 887
Selecting Equipment for Online Information Retrieval 775
Selection of International Railway Documentation 600
Selective Design Data Collection 494
Selective Inventory of Information Services 1022
Sempex 693
Serials in the British Library 439
Serie Informacion y Documentacion 202
Series of Philippine Scientific Bibliographies 808
SFS Catalogue 334
Sharp (I.P.) Newsletter 871
Ship Abstracts 872
SHIPDES Manual 685
SIGMA 356
Silver Trends 228
Singapore/Malaysia Conferences on Health and Related Sciences 1073
SIRLS Descriptor List & Thesaurus 1085
SIRLS User's Manual 1085
Situation Economique 681
16mm Films Available from the Public Libraries of Metropolitan Toronto 699
Small Animal Abstracts 229
Small Computer Program Index 17
Social and Human Science Documentation Centre Information Note 1022
Social and Labour Bulletin 591
Sociology of Leisure & Sport Abstracts 1085
Software Abstracts for Engineers 208
Soils and Fertilizers 229
Solar and Wind Energy Research Program Index 16
Solid-Liquid Flow Abstracts 86
Solid Waste Management in Developing Countries 507
SOMED-A 539
Sorghum and Millets Abstracts 229
SOS (Official Statistics of Sweden) 932
Sources of Australian Economic Information 520
Sources of Australian Financial Information 520
Sources of Australian Rural Information 520
Sources of Foreign Statistical Data 493
South African Water Abstracts 887
Southern Cone Report 651
Sowietische Wissenschaftlich-Technische Institutionen und Ihre Veroffentlichungen 1031
Soyabean Abstracts 229
Special Reports (Latin American Newsletters Ltd.) 651
SPINES Feasibility Study 1016
SPINES Subject Categories 1016
SPINES Thesaurus 1016
SPIRES Data Base Management 1033
SPIRES Reference to Data Library and Programlist 1033
SPIRES Searching of ERIC Data Bases 1033
Sport and Recreation for the Disabled 210
Sport and Recreation Index 210
Sport Bibliography 210
Sport Thesaurus 210
Sportdokumentation: Literatur der Sportwissenschaft 420
Sports Medicine 5
SSCL Newsletter 1087
SSDA Data Catalogue 61
Stand der Gesetzgebung des Bundes 422
Standard-Profildienst Schweisstechnik 418
State-of-the-Art Reports (German Foundation for International Development) 397
Statistical Economic Documentation 425
Statistical Indicators for Asia and the Pacific 1004
Statistical Methods 493
Statistical Review 493
Statistics of Foreign Trade, Monthly Bulletin 780
Statistics of Individual Railways 600
Statistique des Services Postaux 1030
Statistiques Mensuelles de la Bourse de Paris 389
Statistische Wirtschaftsdokumentation 425
Statisztikai Modszerek Temadokumentacio 493
Statisztikai Szemle 493
Status of Federal Legislation 422
STATUS Users Group Newsletter 900
Steel Analysis 89
Steel and Iron Materials Data 399
Steel Monitor 228
Steinmetz Archives Catalogue and Guide 848
Stellar Data Center Bulletin 905
Streamline 267
String Indexing: NEPHIS 1086
Subject Authority Fiche 441
Subject Authority of Community Information Subject Headings 525
Subject Index on Marine and Estuarine Pollution 684
Subscriber's Supplement to the Quarterly Canadian Forecast 238

Summaries of Cases to be Heard by the Supreme Court of Canada 173
Summaries of Foreign-Language Articles 873
Summary of Monitoring Information Received by the IFRB 606
Sunrise Update 520
Suomen Kirjallisuus 482
Suplemento Internacional del Indice Medico Espanol 1082
Supreme Court of Canada Decisions 1108
Surface Water Data 142
Surface Water Data Reference Index 142
Survey of Consumer Buying Intentions (AERIC) 238
Survey of Futures Studies 540
Survey of Scientists and Engineers in Republic of China 726
Survey of the Science of Science Information 816
Survey of UK Online Users 775
Svensk Bokforteckning 931
Svenska Tidningsartiklar 116
Svenska Tidskriftsartiklar 116
SVIPA Newsletter 946
Swedish Behavioural Science Research Reports 924
Swedish National Bibliography 931
Swedish Standards Listed in Subject Groups 940
Swets Catalogue of Serial Titles 942
Swets Info Bulletin 942
SWP Thesaurus 337
Szakirodalmi Tajekoztatok 496
Szamitastechnika 493
Szelektiv Tervezesi Adatgyujtemeny 494
TABCONT/CEPIS 794
Table des Codes Sources EDF (Electricite de France) 295
Table of Alberta Legislation 11
TALI (Tekniikan Aikakauslehti Indeksi) 483
Talking Books Catalog 699
TAR Paper 13
Tarex 693
Target Group Index 109
Taux de Rendement des Valeurs Francaises et des Valeurs des Autres Pays de la Zone Franc a Revenue Variable 389
Tax and Charities 198
Taxen 844
Tech News (Greater London Council) 465
Technical Abstracts Journal 496
Technical and Economic Information on Building 494
Technical Economic Information 496
Technical Export News 111
Technical Guide to the Australian Demographic Data Bank 60
Technical Publications by JAERI Staff 627
Technical Specifications for Using the Transpac Network 989
Technical Traders Bulletin 1109
Technocom 877
Technology Digest 34
Technology Highlights 632
TECHNONET ASIA Newsletter 34
Teikoku Bank and Company Yearbook 969
Teikoku Ginko Kaisha Nenkan 969
Teikoku Information 969
Teikoku Joho 969
Teikoku Times 969
Tekniikan Aikakauslehti Indeksi 483
Telecommunication Journal 606
Telecommunications Annals 367
Teledoc 1064
Telidon and Its Applications 883
Teratology Lookout 921
Terminological Data Banks 587
TermNet News 587
Ternisien Listing 978
Teruleti Statisztika 493
Tesauro de Informacion Industrial 193
Textile Digest 873
Textiles 873
The Globe and Mail 430
THEMA 356
Themendienst (German Foundation for International Development) 397
Thesaurus de SPHINX 363
Thesaurus des Liants Hydrauliques 188
Thesaurus EDF 295
Thesaurus for Information Processing in Sociology 571
Thesaurus Krankenhauswesen 477
Thesaurus Oceanologie 350
Thesaurus of Pulp and Paper Terms 827
Thesaurus of Rock and Soil Mechanics Terms 1056
Thesaurus Zerstorungsfreie Prufung 416
Theses Canadiennes 148
Theses Canadiennes sur Microfiches: Catalogue 148
THESIS 481
TI-Technical Information for Industry 885
TIES Newsletter 1027

Timber Pallet and Packaging Digest 983
Tin and Antimony Monitor 228
Titels van Sociaalwetenschappelijk Onderzoek 847
Title List of ILO Publications and Documents 593
Titles of Social Science Research 847
Topics in Combustible Energy 386
Torteneti Statisztikai Fuzetek 493
Torteneti Statisztikai Kotetek 493
Tox-notiser 921
Traffic and Operating Data of AEA Airlines 41
Transactions of Information Processing Society of Japan 529
Translated Books Available from the BLLD 442
Transnational Data Report 988
Trends in Foreign Science and Technology 801
Tribos: Tribology Abstracts 86
Trivialnamenkartei 201
Tropical Geography 355
Tropical Oil Seeds Abstracts 229
Tudomanyos es Muszaki Tajekoztatas 496
Turbine Airliner Fleet Survey 68
Turkish Dissertation Index 991
Twenty Years of Indonesian Fiction 1940-1960: A Bibliography Selected from the IDC Collection 1073
Ubersetzungszeitschriften 1031
UK Leisure Markets 484
UK Mineral Statistics 727
UK Online Search Services 775
UKCTRAIN Workbook 440
Umfragen aus der Empirischen Sozialforschung 1945-1982: Datenbestandskatalog 1045
UNESCO/IBE Education Thesaurus 1021
UNESCO Journal of Information Science, Librarianship and Archives Administration 1019
UNIDO Guides to Information Sources 1027
UNIDO Newsletter 1027
Union Catalog for Periodicals in Norwegian Libraries (SAMKATPER) 1061
Union Catalog of Foreign Acquisitions by Major Swedish Public Libraries 116
Union Catalog of Machine Readable Catalog Data of German Libraries 400
Union Catalog of Periodicals Held by Portuguese Libraries 821
Union Catalogue of Foreign Books in Swedish Research Libraries 931
Union Catalogue of Scientific and Technical Periodicals in Libraries of Pakistan 793
Union Catalogue of Social Science Serials 511
Union Catalogues of Scientific and Technical Periodicals of the Libraries in Ankara, Izmir, and Istanbul 991
Union List of Abstracting and Indexing Services Received in Leading Libraries 616
Union List of Current Scientific Serials in India 507
Union List of Higher Degree Theses in Australian Libraries 1074
Union List of Periodicals in Tanzania 955
Union List of Scientific Periodicals in Libraries of the Republic of China 726
Union List of Scientific Serials in Canadian Libraries 152
Union List of Serials in the Social Sciences and Humanities Held by Canadian Libraries 151
Union List of Social Science Periodicals 511
Union List of Technion Recent Acquisitions 1051
UNISIST Newsletter (General Information Programme) 1019
U.K. Quoted Company Service 690
U.K. Trade Marks Journal 235
U.K. Unquoted Company Service 690
U.S. and European Crudes and Products Reports 505
U.S. LPG Report 505
U.S. Patent Concordance 633
U.S. Patent Index 633
University of British Columbia Data Library Catalogue 1044
University of Haifa Periodical Holdings 1051
Urban Abstracts 465
User Manual to DC Host Centre 497
User News (Chisholm Institute of Technology Library) 204
Utlandska Nyforvarv 116
UTLAS Newsletter 1094
UTOPIA User's Guide 1080
VA-NYTT 637
Vapor-Liquid Equilibrium Data Collection 1046
VDI-Nachrichten 1096
Vengherskaya Literatura po Bibliotekovedeniu i Informatike - Referativny Zhurnal 495
Verbundkatalog 400
Verres et Refractaires 429
Verzeichnis Deutscher Informations- und Dokumentationsstellen, Bundesrepublik Deutschland und Berlin (West) 880
Verzeichnis Informationswissenschaftlicher Zeitschriften 880
Veterinary Bulletin 229
Videodisque 1
Videoinfo 705

Videorecordings Available in the Public Libraries of Metropolitan Toronto 699
Videotex 1
Videotex: A Working Paper on the Study of Social Impact 883
Videotex Canada 973
Videotex Guide/Magazine 1
Videotex International 1
Vietnamese Collection of the ANU Library 1073
VINE 818
VISPAC Newsletter 1101
VITIS 585
VITIS-Viticulture and Enology Abstracts 585
Vocabulario Controlado do MINTER 100
Vocabulario Internacional de Termos Microgrraficos 101
Volkswagenwerk Referatedienst 1104
VTI Aktuellt 925
VTT Publications 330
VTT Research Notes 330
VTT Research Reports 330
VTT Symposium 330
Washington Letter on Latin America 651
Waste Management Information Bulletin 437
Waste Materials Biodegradation Research Titles 1038
WATDOC Database Descriptions 140
WATDOC Newsletter 140
Water Supply & Sewage Engineering 203
Weed Abstracts 229
Weekly Criminal Bulletin 162
Weekly Eurobond Guide 267
Weekly Survey of Periodicals (Finnish Pulp and Paper Research Institute) 333
Weldasearch Abstracts 1106
Welding and Allied Processes Abstracts Journal 418
Welding Standard Profile Service 418
Werkstoffdaten Stahl-Eisen 399
Werkstoffe und Korrosion 405
WESTPAC Newsletter 628
Wheat, Barley and Triticale Abstracts 229
Which? 244
Who is Doing What in Belguim 84
Who's Who in Europe 870
Winged Bean Bibliography 889
Winged Bean Flyer 889
Wolff Charts Comprehensive Chart Service 1109
Words and Phrases Used in the Pharmaceutical Industry 432
World Agricultural Economics and Rural Sociology Abstracts 229
World Congress of Agricultural Librarians and Documentalists: Proceedings 558
World Directory of National Science and Technology Policy-Making Bodies 1016
World Directory of Research Projects, Studies and Courses in Science and Technology Policy 1016
World Directory of Social Science Institutions 1022
World Economic Prospects 89
World Energy Information 753
World Guide to Libraries 863
World Guide to Scientific Associations 863
World Guide to Terminological Activities 587
World Guide to Trade Associations 863
World Health Statistics Annual 1110
World Health Statistics Quarterly 1110
World Inventory of Social Science Data Services 571
World List of Serial Titles in Aquatic Sciences and Fisheries 1008
World List of Social Science Periodicals 571
World List of Social Science Periodicals 1022
World Mineral Statistics 727
World News about Building and Urban Development 494
World Patents Abstracts 275
World Patents Index 275
World Ports and Harbours Abstracts 86
World Request List for Nuclear Data (WRENDA) 561
World Surface Coatings Abstracts 792
World Textile Abstracts 873
World Textile Abstracts Printout Subject Indexes 873
World Trademark Journal 234
World Transindex 608
Worldwide Chemical Directory 612
Worldwide List of Published Standards 111
WRC Information 464
WRENDA (World Request List for Nuclear Data) 561
Year Book of Labour Statistics 592
Yearbook of North Africa 186
Yearbook of Regional Statistics (EUROSTAT) 225
Yearbook of the Research Register 330
Yield Stress of Steel and Iron 399
Yukon Bibliography Updates 95
ZA-Information 1045
Zeitschriftendatenbank 400
Zenkoku Kigyo Tosan Shukei 969

Zenkoku Kigyo Zaimu Shohyo Bunseki Tokei   969
Zentralblatt fur Didaktik der Mathematik   521
Zentralblatt fur Mathematik und Ihre Grenzgebiete   521
ZIID-Schriftenreihe   395
Zinc Abstracts   1122
Zinc Monitor   228
Zinc Quarterly   228
Zoological Record   88
Zoological Record Search Guide   88
ZooScene   88

SOFTWARE INDEX

Software produced or provided by organizations listed in this book. Generally they are for such applications as information retrieval, automatic indexing, library automation, data base management, photocomposition, statistical data base analysis, and other information work. Listed under both full name and acronym.

SOFTWARE INDEX

Adaptive Information Management System (ADMIN) 666
Adaptive Library Management System (ADLIB) 666
ADLIB (Adaptive Library Management System) 666
ADMIN (Adaptive Information Management System) 666
Agricultural System for the Storage and Subsequent Selection of Information (ASSASSIN) 503
ANAIS 1062
AQUARIUS-STAIRS 80
AQUEST 1055
AQUILA 638
ARTEMIS 370
ARTWORK MANAGER 649
ASSASSIN (Agricultural System for the Storage and Subsequent Selection of Information) 503
ASSIST 1093
ATHESA 589
Automated Storage and Retrieval of Biomedical Information 296
Auxiliary System for Interactive Statistics (AXIS) 932
AXIS (Auxiliary System for Interactive Statistics) 932
BONDBOOK 895
BONDSPEC 895
BONTRAN 895
Brigitte 71
CANSIM Interactive System (CIS) 159
CANSIM Table Analysis Package (TAP) 159
Carleton Library System (CLS) 179
CDS/ISIS (Computerized Documentation Service/Integrated Set of Information Systems) 1017
CHEMLIST Package 370
CIMPP (Comprehensive Industrial Materials Property Package) 1088
CIS (CANSIM Interactive System) 159
CLAIR Data System 1057
CLS (Carleton Library System) 179
COM/PortaCOM 904
Comprehensive Industrial Materials Property Package (CIMPP) 1088
COMPUSET 649
Computer Oriented Reference System for Automatic Information Retrieval (CORSAIR) 929
Computer Retrieval of Organic Sub-structures Based on Wiswesser (CROSSBOW) 370
Computerized Documentation Service/Integrated Set of Information Systems (CDS/ISIS) 1017
CONFER 527
Connect 654
CORMORANT 638
CORSAIR (Computer Oriented Reference System for Automatic Information Retrieval) 929
Crocus 71
CRONOS 225
CROSSBOW (Computer Retrieval of Organic Sub-structures Based on Wiswesser) 370
DARC 977
DARC (Description, Acquisition, Retrieval, and Conception) 38
DARING 371
DARIUS 741
DATABANK 536
DATAFRANCE 469
DECO 994
DEPICT 237
Description, Acquisition, Retrieval, and Conception (DARC) 38
Development of Minicomputers in an Environment of Scientific and Technical Information Centers (DOMESTIC) 617
DIRECT 809
DISTAT 237
DOBIS (Dortmunder Bibliothekssystem) 147
DOMESTIC 617
DOMLIB 617
DOMPRINT 617
Dortmunder Bibliothekssystem (DOBIS) 147
EAGLE 638
Electronic Slide Presentation System (ESP) 369
EPOS-VIRA 930
Equation of State Package 548
ESA-QUEST 317
ESP (Electronic Slide Presentation) System 369
Estimation/Prediction Package 548
Eurobond System 249
FABIUS (Fabrication Automatique de Bibliographies et d'Index Utilisant des Syntagmes) 547
Fabrication Automatique de Bibliographies et d'Index Utilisant des Syntagmes (FABIUS) 547
Facility for the Analysis of Chemical Thermodynamics (Fact) 691
Fact (Facility for the Analysis of Chemical Thermodynamics) 691
FATES 527
FIBER 90
FICHE BUILDER 649
Filetab 721
FINLIST 903
FINPLAN 903
FINSORT 903
FINSTA 903
FINSUM 903
FIRST-1 Infrared Search Program 155
FIXIT 527
FLARES 237
FORMAT 649
FUZZIE 741
GC-20 71
GEISHA 341
General Relation Based Information Processing System (GRIPS) 428
GOLEM 874
GRIPS (General Relation Based Information Processing System) 428
GRIPS-Compact 428
Haifa On-Line Bibliographic Text System (HOBITS) 1051
HOBITS (Haifa On-line Bibliographic Text System) 1051
IGL 237
INFOMAGIC 871
Infomart Telidon System Software - Version Two (ITSS-V2) 518
INTER 257
Interceptor 527
ITSS-V2 (Infomart Telidon System Software - Version Two) 518
JORDAN 67
LAWTERM 656
LIBCEPT 527
LOCATE 237
MADCAP 1088
MAGPIE 638
MANAGE 237
MARK II 296
MASSAGER 536
Micro-BIRD 836
MicroPOLYDOC 767
MicroQUERY 485
MILOR 589
MINISIS 576
MINISIS 953
MINISIS-RM 953
MIRABILIS 1055
Mireille 71
Mistel 69
MISTEL 767
MISTRAL 488
MORT (Mortgage Amortization) 828
Mortgage Amortization (MORT) 828
MOSAIC 536
NEPHIS (Nested Phrase Indexing System) 1086
Nested Phrase Indexing System (NEPHIS) 1086
NETSDI 50
NOGLI 1062
Ocelot Library System 2
OMNISYS 394
PAGEMAKER 369
PAGETAKER 369
PASSAT 874
Petroleum Fractions Package 548
Physical Properties Package 548
Piaf 977
PIII 649
PLIDOS 959
POLYDOC 767
PREVIEW 649
PROTEC 1062
PUFFIN 638
QL/NEWS 828
QL/SEARCH 828
QL/TEXT 828
Queen's University Interrogation of Legal Literature (QUILL) 836
Queen's University On-line Bibliographic Information Retrieval and Dissemination (QUOBIRD) 836
QUEST 485
QUILL (Queen's University Interrogation of Legal Literature) 836
QUOBIRD (Queen's University On-line Bibliographic Information Retrieval and Dissemination) 836
RAPPORT 668
Regional-Industrial Model (RIM) 536
REGIS 1062
Regression Package 548
REWARD 371
RIM (Regional-Industrial Model) 536
Sachem-Energy 185
Sachem-West 185
SAILS (Swets Automated Independent Library System) 942
SDPA (STATUS Data Preparation Aid) 433
Search Program for Infrared Spectra (SPIR) 155
Searching in Free Text (SIFT) 768
SHARP APL 871
SIBIL (Systeme Informatise pour Bibliotheques) 664
SIFT (Searching in Free Text) 768

SIMSYS (Simulation System)   536
Simulation System (SIMSYS)   536
SMS (Survey Management System)   1072
SPIR (Search Program for Infrared Spectra)   155
STATUS   433
STATUS Data Preparation Aid (SDPA)   433
STATUS Report Generator   433
STATUS Thesaurus   433
Steam Package   548
STRIX   638
Survey Management System (SMS)   1072
Swets Automated Independent Library System (SAILS)   942
SWIFT   638
SYGAL (System-Gaphyor-Language)   1063
System-Gaphyor-Language (SYGAL)   1063
Systeme Informatise pour Bibliotheques (SIBIL)   664
Systeme Integre pour les Bibliotheques Universitaires de Lausanne   664
TABL (Table Batch Retrieval System)   159
Table Batch Retrieval System (TABL)   159
TAP (CANSIM Table Analysis Package)   159
TEAM (Terminologie-Erfassungs- und Auswertungs- Methode)   876
Telidon System Software (Infomart)   518
Terminologie-Erfassungs- und Auswertungs- Methode (TEAM)   876
Terminology Evaluation and Acquisition Method (TEAM)   876
Text Query System (TQS)   657
The Information Navigator (TIN)   527
The Informetrica Model (TIM)   536
3RIP   795
TIM (The Informetrica Model)   536
TIN (The Information Navigator)   527
TISFLO   286
TOOL-IR Software   1075
TQS (Text Query System)   657
ULISYS (Universal Library Systems Ltd.)   1029
Unde Thermophysical Properties Program Package   992
U.S.-BONDSPEC   895
University of Tsukuba Online Processing of Information (UTOPIA)   1080
UTOPIA (University of Tsukuba Online Processing of Information)   1080
Vapour-Liquid-Equilibrium Package   548

FUNCTION/SERVICE CLASSIFICATIONS

A consolidation of the separate indexes 6-20 in the fifth edition, with the addition of several new categories. Classifies organizations, systems, and services into 20 main categories according to their chief functions or types of services provided. Entries appear alphabetically in all applicable categories. The classifications can be cross-checked against each other or against terms in the Subject Index to produce more specific groupings. For example, firms that both produce data bases and operate online host services may be located by comparing the Data Base Producers and Publishers group against the Online Host Services category. Similarly, bibliographic data bases in the field of agriculture can be located by comparing the Abstracting and Indexing category against the appropriate subject headings in the Subject Index. Following are descriptions of the function/service classifications used. (New with this edition are Electronic Mail Applications, Magnetic Tape Providers, Personal Computer Oriented Services, and Software Producers.)

Abstracting and Indexing. Organizations whose activities include indexing, abstracting, or both. Emphasis is on organizations issuing computer-produced publications and bibliographic data bases that are publicly available.

Associations. Professional and trade associations and other membership groups with interests and programs in the information, electronic publishing, library automation, and related fields.

Community Information and Referral. Organizations using computer and micrographic technology to support the provision of referrals to human services agencies in their communities. Applications can include computer-generated microform or hardcopy directories of agencies, online searching in response to inquiries, demographic data collection and analysis, etc.

Computerized Searching. Organizations that conduct online or batch-mode current or retrospective retrieval from computer-readable data bases. Includes organizations using publicly available data bases as well as organizations providing services from their own files only.

Consultants. Organizations and services that provide consultation, and systems analysis and design in the fields of information provision and access.

Data Base Producers and Publishers. Organizations that create (or employ a contractor to create) computer-readable files of bibliographic or nonbibliographic information for internal use or public access. Data bases produced by these organizations are listed in the separate Data Bases Index.

Data Collection and Analysis. Organizations that collect, analyze, process, evaluate, and disseminate raw numeric data in such fields as social science, science and technology, economics, and medicine. Includes standard data reference centers, social science data archives, commercial demographic and marketing firms, government agencies, research institutes, and other organizations.

Document Delivery. Organizations that, on a demand basis, locate, retrieve, and deliver the full text of periodical articles, government documents, conference proceedings, patents, reports, and other materials required by the client. Includes organizations providing services only from their own collections as well as organizations using publicly available sources. In addition to the document suppliers, organizations offering electronic ordering facilities through which suppliers can be contacted are also listed here.

Electronic Mail Applications. Organizations whose information systems and services include capabilities allowing clients to electronically send and receive messages. (Organizations offering pure electronic mail services without providing information services fall outside the scope of this directory.)

Information on Demand. Organizations providing fee-based custom information services in client-specified subject areas using publicly available print and computerized information sources. Services provided usually include online searching; document delivery; literature compilations; library research; preparation of bibliographies, abstracts, or indexes; establishment of current awareness services; etc.

Library and Information Networks. Networks, consortia, and systems that represent cooperative efforts to share resources or provide information to a specific membership. Individual network members are not listed or referenced here.

Library Management Systems. Systems and software available for installation in a library or information center to support the management of circulation, acquisitions, catalog inquiry, administration, and similar library functions. Includes systems that are marketed by commercial firms as well as systems developed internally and maintained by libraries.

Magnetic Tape Providers. Organizations that make available proprietary or public information on computer tapes or diskettes for installation and use on the client's own facilities. Includes information producers that license copies of their data bases as well as service firms that package census and other public data in computer-readable form for use by clients.

Micrographic Applications. Organizations whose computerized information storage and retrieval systems include micrographic applications and products. Excluded from this directory are companies solely concerned with micropublication or the manufacture and distribution of micrographic equipment.

Online Host Services. Organizations that maintain data bases and software on their computer facilities and permit clients at multiple remote locations to retrieve needed information using online terminals. Includes commercial online search services, government systems, time-sharing companies that carry data bases, videotex/teletext information systems, online cataloging support services, and similar operations. Also listed in this index are the major international telecommunications networks through which computers and terminals communicate.

Personal Computer Oriented Services. Online services, software, library management systems, data bases, and other systems and products that are specifically designed for or actively marketed to personal computer users (often, end users).

Research and Research Projects. Institutes, libraries, centers, government units, and market research firms that conduct research in the information field on a continuing basis.

SDI/Current Awareness. Lists organizations that report selective dissemination of information (SDI) or current awareness programs, including those based on an organization's own information resources and those that cover all available sources.

Software Producers. Organizations that produce software and make it available for use on client facilities or through time-sharing. Software applications covered by this book include information storage and retrieval, cataloging and indexing, library automation, photocomposition, statistical analysis, and other information work. The individual software programs made available by organizations appearing here are separately listed in the Software Index.

Videotex/Teletext Information Services. Organizations that provide or operate videotex/teletext information systems or services, as well as other organizations involved in the field, including consulting firms, videotex data base producers, associations, research operations, etc. Organizations listed here are also entered in other categories for which they qualify; e.g., a videotex consultant appears here and in the Consultants catgory.

FUNCTION/SERVICE CLASSIFICATIONS

Abstracting and Indexing

ADIS Press Australasia Pty Ltd. — ADIS Drug Information Retrieval System 5
Admedia — Adfacts 6
African Training and Research Centre in Administration for Development — African Network of Administrative Information 7
Alberta Public Affairs Bureau — Publication Services Branch 11
Alberta Research Council — Alberta Geological Survey — Geoscience Data Index for Alberta 12
Alberta Research Council — Alberta Oil Sands Information Centre 13
Alberta Research Council — Coal Technology Information Centre 14
Alberta Research Council — Solar and Wind Energy Research Program Information Centre 16
ALLM Books — Small Computer Program Index 17
Arctic Institute of North America — Arctic Science and Technology Information System 26
Art Sales Index Ltd. 29
Asian Institute of Technology — Regional Documentation Center — Asian Information Center for Geotechnical Engineering 30
Asian Institute of Technology — Regional Documentation Center — Environmental Sanitation Information Center 31
Asian Institute of Technology —Regional Documentation Center — International Ferrocement Information Center 32
Asian Institute of Technology — Regional Documentation Center — Renewable Energy Resources Information Center 33
Aslib, The Association for Information Management 35
Association forthe Promotion of Industry-Agriculture — International Documentation Centerfor Industries Using Agricultural Products 39
Association of Social Sciences Institutes — Social Sciences Information Center 43
Atomic Energy of Canada, Ltd. — Chalk River Nuclear Laboratories — Technical Information Branch 44
Atomic Energy of Canada, Ltd. — Whiteshell Nuclear Research Establishment — Technical Information Services 45
Australia — Bureau of Transport Economics — BTE Information Systems 46
Australia — Commonwealth Scientific and Industrial Research Organization — Central Information, Library and Editorial Section 47
Australia — National Library of Australia 48
Australian Atomic Energy Commission — Lucas Heights Research Laboratories Library 51
Australian Business Index 53
Australian Council for Educational Research — Library and Information ServicesUnit 54
Australian Financial Review — INFO-LINE 55
Australian Institute of Criminology Library — Computerised Information from National Criminological Holdings 56
Australian Mineral Foundation — Australian Earth Sciences Information System 57
Australian National Gallery — Library 58
Australian Road Research Board — Australian Road Research Documentation 62
Austria — Federal Ministry of Buildings and Technology — Federal Researchand Testing Establishment Arsenal — Road Research Documentation Center 63
Austrian Documentation Centre for Media and Communication Research 65
Aviation Information Services Ltd. 68
Bangladesh National Scientific and Technical Documentation Centre 70
Bank Society — General Documentation — SGB Data Base 73
Bayer AG — Engineering Science Division — Chemical and Process Engineering Abstracts 77
Beilstein Institute for Literature in Organic Chemistry 79
Belgium — Royal Library of Belgium — NationalCenter for Scientific and Technical Documentation 84
BHRA, TheFluid Engineering Centre — Information Services 86
Bibliographic Publishing Co. 87
BIOSIS, U.K. Ltd. — Zoological Record 88
BNF Metals Technology Centre — Information Department 92
Bolivia — National Scientific and Technological Documentation Center 93
Boreal Institute for Northern Studies — Library Services 95
Brazil — Ministry of Agriculture — NationalCenter for Agricultural Documentary Information 99
Brazil —Ministryof the Interior — Documentation Coordination Unit 100
Brazil — National Commission for Nuclear Energy — Center for Nuclear Information 102
British Medical Association — BMA Press Cuttings Database 110
British Standards Institution — InformationDepartment 111
British Universities Film & Video Council Ltd. — Information Service 112
Brunel Univeristy — Brunel Institute for Bioengineering — Information Unit 114
BTJ 116
Building Center 117
Building Services Research andInformation Association — BSRIA Information Centre 119
Bulgaria — Medical Academy — Center for Scientific Information in Medicine andHealth 120
Bulgaria — National Agro-Industrial Union — Agricultural Academy — Center for Scientific, Technical and Economic Information 121
Cambridge University — University Chemical Laboratory— Cambridge Crystallographic Data Centre 125
Canada — Agriculture Canada — Marketing and Economics Branch — Cooperatives Unit —COINS 127
Canada — Department of Energy, Mines and Resources — Canada Centre for Mineral and Energy Technology — Technology Information Division 131
Canada — Department of Energy, Mines and Resources — Canada Centre for Remote Sensing — Remote Sensing On-Line Retrieval System 132
Canada — Department of Energy, Mines and Resources — Geological Survey of Canada — National GEOSCAN Centre 135
Canada— Department of Industry, Trade & Commerce — Office of Tourism — Tourism Research and Data Centre 137
Canada — Environment Canada — Inland Waters Directorate — National Hydrology Research Institute — Perennial Snow and Ice Section — Glacier Inventory of Canada 139
Canada — Environment Canada — Inland Waters Directorate — WATDOC 140
Canada — National Film Board of Canada — FORMAT 146
Canada — National Library of Canada — Cataloguing Branch — Canadiana Editorial Division 148
Canada — Parliament of Canada — Library of Parliament 157
Canadian Education Association — Canadian Education Index Data Base 170
Canadian Law Information Council 173
Canadian Library Association — Canadian Periodical Index 174
Celltech Ltd. — Information and Library Service 181
Center for Industrial Creation — Documentation Service 184
Center for Research and Studies on Mediterranean Societies 186
Center for Scientific and TechnicalResearch for the Metal Manufacturing Industry — Fabrimetal 187
Center for Study and Research of the Hydraulic Binders Industry — Documentation Center — INTERCIM Cement Data Base 188
Center for theStudy on Information Systems in Government 190
Center of Experimental Metallurgy — Iron and Steel Documentation Service 192
Chemical Information Center 201
China Building Technology Development Centre — Institute of Technical Information 203
Chisholm Institute of Technology Library — User Education Resources Data Base 204
Christian Institutions Research and Documentation Center 205
The CIRPA/ADISQ Foundation 206
CITIS Ltd. 208
City of London Polytechnic — Fawcett Library — BiblioFem 209
Coaching Association of Canada — Sport Information Resource Centre 210
Commission of the European Communities — Court of Justice of the European Communities — Legal Data Processing Group — CJUS Data Bank 214
Commission of the European Communities — Euro Abstracts 218
Commission of the European Communities — System for Information on Grey Literature in Europe 226
Commonwealth Agricultural Bureaux — CAB Abstracts 229
Commonwealth Regional Renewable Energy Resources Information System 230
Council of Europe — European Documentation and Information System for Education 248
Czechoslovakia — Institute for Medical Information 250
Dalhousie University — Law School Library — Marine Affairs Bibliography 254
Data Bank for Medicaments 257
Delft HydraulicsLaboratory — Information and Documentation Section 268
Derwent Publications Ltd. — Biotechnology Abstracts 273
Derwent Publications Ltd. — Chemical Reactions Documentation Service 274
Derwent Publications Ltd. — Patents Documentation Services 275
Derwent Publications Ltd. — Pest Control Literature Documentation 276
Derwent Publications Ltd. — Pharmaceutical Literature Documentation 277
Derwent Publications Ltd. — Veterinary Literature Documentation 278
Dobra Iron and Steel Research Institute — Informetal 281
Documentary Research Center 282
Drug Information Pharmacists Group — Pharmline 285
Editions Techniques — JURIS-DATA 294
Electricite de France — Office of Study and Research — Information and Documentation Systems Department — EDF-DOC Data

Abstracting and Indexing (Continued)

Base 295
Elsevier Science Publishers B.V. — Biomedical Division — Excerpta Medica 296
Esselte Group of Booksellers — Esselte Documentation System 302
Europe Data 305
European Conference of Ministers of Transport — International Co-operation in the Field of Transport Economics Documentation 309
European Space Agency — European Space Research and Technology Center — Materials Data Retrieval System 316
European Space Agency — Information Retrieval Service 317
Exeter University Teaching Services — The Exeter Abstract Reference System 319
Financial Times Business Information Ltd. — Business Information Service 328
Finland — Central Medical Library — MEDICData Base 329
Finnish Pulp and Paper Research Institute — Technical Information Service 333
Finnish Standards Association — Information Service 334
Finsbury Data Services Ltd. — TEXTLINE 335
Foundation for Science and Politics — Research Institute for International Politics and Security — Library and Documentation System 337
France — Bureau of Geological and Mining Research— National Geological Survey — Geological Information and Documentation Department 340
France — French Senate — Parliamentary Documentation and Information Printing Service 343
France — Ministry of Defense — General Office for Ordnance — Center for Documentation on Ordnance 345
France — National Center for Ocean Utilization — National Bureau for Ocean Data 347
France — National Center for Ocean Utilization — National Bureau for Ocean Data — CNEXO-BNDOData Base 350
France — National Center for Scientific Research — Documentation Center for Human Sciences 355
France — National Center for Scientific Research — Scientific and Technical Documentation Center 356
France — National Center for Scientific Research — Scientific Documentation Center in Oncology — CANCERNET 357
France — National Institute for Industrial Property — Division of Publications Documentation and Information — INPI Data Bases 359
France —National Institute for Industrial Property — Office of Legal and Technical Documentation — JURINPI Data Base 360
France — National Institute for Research in Informatics and Automation — Information Dissemination Office 361
France — National Institute of Statistics and Economic Studies — Documentation Division — SPHINX Data Base 363
France — National Telecommunications Research Center — Interministerial Documentation Service — TELEDOC 367
Frankfurt City and University Library — Bibliography of Linguistic Literature 368
Fraser Williams Ltd. — Fine Chemicals Directory 372
Fraunhofer Society — Information Center for Building and Physical Planning 373
Fraunhofer Society — Information Center for Building and Physical Planning — Buildings Documentation Data Base 375
Fraunhofer Society — Information Center for Building and Physical Planning — Literature Compilations Data Base 376
Fraunhofer Society — Information Center for Building and Physical Planning — PASCALBAT Data Base 377
Fraunhofer Society — Information Center for Building and Physical Planning — Property Services Agency Information on Construction and Architecture Data Base 378
Fraunhofer Society —Information Center for Building and Physical Planning — Regional Planning, City Planning, Housing, Building Construction Data Base 379
French Association for Standardization — Data Bases Service — Automated Standards and Regulations Information Online 382
French Documentation— Political and Current Events Information Bank 384
French Institute of Energy — Energy Studies and Information Center 386
French Petroleum Institute — Documentation Center 387
French Textile Institute— Textile Information Treatment Users' Service 390
French Water Study Association — National Water Information Center 391
Geo Abstracts Ltd. 393
Geosystems 394
German Democratic Republic — Central Institute for Information and Documentation 395
German Electron-Synchrotron — DESY Scientific Documentation and Information Service 396
German Foundation for International Development — Documentation Center 397

German Patent Information System 401
German Plastics Institute — Information and Documentation Services 402
German Society for Chemical Equipment — Information Systems and Data Banks Department — Chemical Technology Information System 403
German Society for Chemical Equipment — Information Systems and Data Banks Department — DECHEMA Substance Data Service 404
German Society for Chemical Equipment — Information Systems and Data Banks Department — Materials and Corrosion Information System 405
German Standards Institute — German Information Center for Technical Rules 407
Germany — Center for Agricultural Documentation and Information 408
Germany — Federal Biological Research Center for Agriculture and Forestry — Documentation Center for Phytomedicine 409
Germany — Federal Employment Institute — Institute for Employment Research — Information and Documentation Department 410
Germany — Federal Environmental Agency — Environmental Information and Documentation System 411
Germany — Federal Institute for Geosciences and Natural Resources — Geoscience Literature Information Service 412
Germany — Federal Institute for Geosciences and Natural Resources — Marine Information and Documentation System 413
Germany — Federal Institute for Materials Testing — Measurement of Mechanical Quantities Documentation 415
Germany —Federal Institute for Materials Testing — Nondestructive Testing Documentation 416
Germany — Federal Institute forMaterials Testing —Rheology and Tribology Documentation Center 417
Germany — Federal Institute for Materials Testing — Welding Documentation 418
Germany — Federal Institute for Occupational Safety — Information and Documentation Centre for Occupational Safety 419
Germany — Federal Institute for Sports Science — Documentationand Information Division — Sport and Sports-Scientific Information System 420
Germany — Federal Research Center for Fisheries — Information and DocumentationCenter 421
Germany — German FederalDiet — Division of Scientific Documentation — Documentation and Information System for Parliamentary Materials 422
Germany — Ministryof Economics — German Foreign Trade Information Office 425
Germany — Ministry of Justice — Judicial Information System 426
Glass Institute — Information and Documentation Service 429
The Globe and Mail — Info Globe 430
Gmelin Institute for Inorganic Chemistry and Related Fields 431
Great Britain — Atomic Energy Authority— Atomic Energy Research Establishment, Harwell — Harwell Central Information Service 434
Great Britain — Atomic Energy Authority — Atomic Energy Research Establishment, Harwell — Nondestructive Testing Centre — Quality Technology Information Service 436
Great Britain — Atomic Energy Authority — Atomic Energy Research Establishment, Harwell — Waste Management Information Bureau 437
Great Britain — Atomic Energy Authority — Culham Laboratory —Plasma Physics Library andInformation Service 438
Great Britain — British Library — Bibliographic Services Division 439
Great Britain — British Library — Bibliographic Services Division — Subject Systems Office — Preserved Context Index System 441
Great Britain — British Library — Lending Division 442
Great Britain — British Library — Reference Division — Eighteenth Century Short Title Catalogue 443
Great Britain — British Library — Science Reference Library — European Biotechnology Information Program 446
Great Britain — Department of the Environment — BuildingResearch Establishment —Fire Research Station Library — Fire Science Abstracts 452
Great Britain — Department of the Environment — Building Research Establishment Library — BRIX 453
Great Britain — Departments of the Environment and Transport — Transport and RoadResearch Laboratory — Technical Information and Library Services 455
Great Britain — Health and Safety Executive — HSE Library and Information Services 457
Great Britain — Home Office Forensic Science Service — Central Research Establishment — Operational Services Division 458
Great Britain — House of Commons Library — Parliamentary On-Line Information System 459
Great Britain — House of Lords — Library & Information Centre 460
Great Britain — Water Research Centre — Information Service on Toxicity and Biodegradability 463
Great Britain — Water Research Centre — Library and Information Services 464

Abstracting and Indexing (Continued)

Greater London Council — Information Services Group 465
Group for the Study and Research of Tropical Agronomy — AGRITROP 467
Health Care Literature Information Network 477
Heinze GmbH — VISDATA 479
Helsinki School of Economics Library — Information Services 481
Helsinki University Library — Finnish National Bibliography 482
Helsinki University of Technology — University Library/National Library for Science and Technology 483
Hohenheim University — Documentation Center on Animal Production 487
Honeywell Bull — Euris Host Service — European Community Law 489
Hubrecht Laboratory — Central Embryological Library — Documentation and InformationSystem on Developmental Biology 490
Hungarian Academy of Sciences — Institute of Economics — Economic Information Unit 491
Hungary — Ministry for Building and Urban Development — Information Centre for Building 494
Hungary — National Szechenyi Library — Centre for Library Scienceand Methodology 495
Hungary —National Technical InformationCentre and Library 496
India — Council of Scientific and Industrial Research — Indian National ScientificDocumentation Centre 507
India — National Institute of Health and Family Welfare — Documentation Centre 508
Indian Council of Agricultural Research — Agricultural Research Information Centre 510
Indian Council of Social Science Research — Social Science Documentation Centre 511
Indonesia — National Scientific Documentation Center 512
Infolex Services Ltd. 517
Information Center for Energy, Physics, Mathematics 521
Information Center for Materials — System for Documentation and Information in Metallurgy 522
Information Resources Research 533
Institute for Documentation and Information in Social Medicine and Public Health 539
Institute for Futures Studies — Futures Information Service 540
Institute of Nutrition — Documentation Department 545
Institute of Research on Fruits and Citrus Fruits — Documentation Center 547
Institution of Electrical Engineers — INSPEC 549
Institution of Electrical Engineers — INSPEC — Electronic Materials Information Service 550
Institution of Mining and Metallurgy — Library and Information Services 551
International Atomic Energy Agency — International Nuclear Information System 560
International Bee Research Association — Apicultural Abstracts 563
International Centre for Scientific and Technical Information 565
International Children's Centre — Documentation Service — Robert Debre Information Base 566
International Coffee Organization — COFFEELINE 570
International Committee for Social Science Information andDocumentation 571
International Company for Documentation in Chemistry 572
International Development Research Centre — Library 576
International Electronic Publishing Research Centre 577
International Food Information Service — Food Science and Technology Abstracts 583
International Food Information Service— Packaging Science and Technology Abstracts 584
International Food Information Service — VITIS-Viticulture and Enology Abstracts 585
International Information ServiceLtd. 588
International Institute of Refrigeration — Documentary Service 590
International Labour Office — Bureau for Labour Problems Analysis — LabourInformation Database 591
International Labour Office — Central Library and Documentation Branch 593
International Labour Office — International Occupational Safety and Health Information Centre 595
International Livestock Centrefor Africa — Documentation Centre 596
International MedicalInformation Center 598
International Organization for Standardization — ISO Information Network 599
International Refugee Integration Resource Centre 602
International Society of Ecological Modelling — Environmental Data and Ecological Parameters Data Base 604
International Translations Centre 608
Interuniversity Documentation and InformationCenter for the Social Sciences 611
Iran — Ministry of Culture and Higher Education — Iranian Documentation Centre 613
Israel — National Center of Scientific andTechnological Information 616
Israel Atomic Energy Commission — Soreq Nuclear Research Center — Library and Technical Information Department 618
Italy — National Research Council — Research Center for the Stratigraphy and Petrography of the Central Alps — Archive of Italian Data of Geology 625
Japan — Japan Atomic Energy Research Institute — Department of Technical Information 627
Japan — National Diet Library — Library Automation System 629
Japan Association for International Chemical Information 630
Japan Information Center of Science and Technology 632
Japan Patent Information Center 633
Japan Pharmaceutical Information Center 634
K-Konsult —VA-NYTT 637
Kiel Institute for World Economics — National Library of Economics 639
Korea Institute for Industrial Economics and Technology 645
Kugler Publications 647
League of Arab States — League of Arab States Documentation and Information Center 653
Leatherhead Food Research Association — Informationand Library Services 655
Library Association Publishing Ltd. — British Humanities Index 660
Library Association PublishingLtd. — Current Technology Index 662
Library Association Publishing Ltd. — Library and Information Science Abstracts 663
Loughborough University of Technology —Chemical Engineering Department — Particle Science and Technology Information Service 676
Loughborough University of Technology Library — Library Instruction Materials Bank 677
Marine Biological Association of the United Kingdom — Marine Pollution Information Centre 684
Maritime Information Centre/CMO 685
Market ResearchSociety — Market Research Abstracts 687
McCarthy Information Ltd. 690
McGill University — Graduate School of Library Science — FEES Data Base 692
Memorial University of Newfoundland — Ocean Engineering Information Centre 694
MERLIN GERIN Company — Documentation Department — MERL-ECO 696
MERLIN GERIN Company — Documentation Department — MERLIN-TECH 697
Mexico — National Institute for Research on Biological Resources — INIREBLibrary 702
Microfor Inc. 704
Micromedia Ltd. 706
Micromedia Ltd. — Canadian Business Index 707
Mineralogical Society of Great Britain — Mineralogical Abstracts 711
Mitaka — JAPANSCAN 712
Motor Vehicle Documentation 716
Multinational Association of Producers and Retailers of Electricity- Documentation 717
National Autonomous University of Mexico — Center for Scientific and Humanistic Information 719
National Computing Centre Ltd. — Information Services Division 721
National Conservatory of Arts and Crafts — National Institute for Documentation Techniques 722
National Reprographic Centre for Documentation 725
National Science Council — Science and Technology Information Center 726
Natural Environment Research Council — British Geological Survey — Minerals Strategy and Economics Research Group — Mineral Information Section 727
Netherlands — Ministry of Agriculture and Fisheries — Agricultural Research Division —Centre for Agricultural Publishing and Documentation 731
Netherlands — Netherlands Foreign Trade Agency — Library and Documentation Branch — Foreign Trade Abstracts 733
Netherlands Organization for Applied Scientific Research — TNO Study and Information Center on Environmental Research — Environmental Research in the Netherlands 743
New Zealand — Department of Scientific and Industrial Research — DSIR Central Library 748
Nihon Keizai Shimbun, Inc. — Databank Bureau — Nikkei Economic Electronic Databank System-Information Retrieval 753
Nineteenth Century Short Title Catalogue Project 757
Nippon Gijutsu Boeki Co., Ltd. 758
Nordic Atomic Libraries Joint Secretariat — Nordic Energy Index 761
Nordic Documentation Center for Mass Communication Research 763
North Rhine-Westphalia Institute for Air Pollution Control — Literature Information System 765
Norwegian Center for Informatics 767
Norwegian Petroleum Directorate — Oil Index 770

Abstracting and Indexing (Continued)

Norwegian Standards Association — STANDARD 772
Ontario Ministry of Education — Research and Information Branch — Information Centre — Ontario Education Resources Information System 777
Ontario Ministry of NaturalResources — Mineral Resources Group — Ontario Geological Survey — Geoscience Data Centre 778
Organisation for Economic Co-Operation and Development — International Energy Agency — IEA Coal Research — Technical Information Service 782
Organisation for Economic Co-Operation and Development — Nuclear Energy Agency — NEA Data Bank 785
Organisation for Economic Co-Operation and Development — Road Transport Research Programme — International Road Research Documentation 786
Oxford Microform Publications Ltd. 791
Paint Research Association — Information Department — World Surface Coatings Abstracts 792
Pakistan Scientific and Technological Information Centre 793
Pan American Health Organization — Pan American Centre forSanitary Engineering & Environmental Sciences — Pan American Information & Documentation Network on Sanitary Engineering& Environmental Sciences 794
Paris District Informatics Administration — Informatics Biblio Service 797
Peace Research Institute-Dundas — Peace Research Abstracts Journal 800
People's Republic of China — Institute of Scientific and Technical Information of China 801
Pergamon Press — Current Awareness in Biological Sciences 803
Pharmaceutical Society of Great Britain — Martindale Online 806
Philippines — National Institute of Science and Technology — Division of Information and Documentation 807
Philippines — National Science and Technology Authority — Scientific Clearinghouse and Documentation ServicesDivision 808
Philips Information Systems and Automation — DIRECT 809
Pira: Research Association for the Paper and Board, Printing and Packaging Industries — Comprehensive Information Services 812
Poland — Institute for Scientific, Technical and Economic Information 815
Pont-a-Mousson Research Center — Industrial Documentation Service — BIIPAM-CTIF Data Base 820
Pressurklipp — Swedish Market Information Bank 824
Quebec — French Language Board — Terminology Bank of Quebec 830
Quebec Ministry of Education — Library Headquarters — Point de Repere 831
Quebec Ministry of the Environment — Documentation Center — Envirodoq 832
Resources 840
Ringier & Co. — Ringier Documentation Center 841
Romania — National Council for Science and Technology — National Institute for Information and Documentation 843
Royal Institute of British Architects — British Architectural Library — Architectural Periodicals Index 845
Royal Netherlands Academy of Arts and Sciences — Social Science Information and DocumentationCenter 847
Royal Society of Chemistry — Information Services 851
Royal Society of Chemistry — Information Services —Chemical Engineering Abstracts 852
Royal Society of Chemistry — Information Services — Chemical Hazardsin Industry 853
Royal Society of Chemistry — Information Services — Current BiotechnologyAbstracts 854
Royal Society ofChemistry — Information Services — Laboratory Hazards Bulletin 855
Royal Society of Chemistry — Information Services — Mass Spectrometry Data Centre 856
Royal Tropical Institute — Agricultural Information & Documentation Section 857
Rubber and Plastics Research Association of Great Britain — RAPRA Information Centre 858
Scientific Documentation Centre Ltd. 868
Ship ResearchInstitute of Norway — Ship Abstracts 872
Shirley Institute — Textile Information Services 873
Singapore Institute of Standards and Industrial Research — Industrial Technical Information Service 877
Society for Information and Documentation — GID Information Center for Information Scienceand Practice 880
Society of Metaphysicians Ltd. — Information Services 882
South Africa — Council for Scientific and Industrial Research — Centre for Scientific and Technical Information 885
South Africa — Nuclear DevelopmentCorporation of South Africa — NUCOR Library and Information Services 886
South Africa —South African Water Information Centre 887
Southeast Asian Regional Center for Graduate Study and Research in Agriculture — Agricultural Information Bank for Asia 889
Spain— Higher Council for Scientific Research — Institute for Information and Documentation in Science and Technology 890
Spain — Higher Council for Scientific Research— Institute for Information and Documentation in the Social Sciences and Humanities 891
Spain — Ministry ofHealth and Safety — National Institute of Occupational Safety and Health — National Information and Documentation Center 892
Standards Council of Canada — Standards Information Service 898
Strasbourg Observatory — Stellar Data Center 905
Studsvik Energiteknik AB — Report CollectionIndex 906
Sweden — National Board of Occupational Safety and Health — CIS Centre 923
Sweden— National Library for Psychology and Education 924
Sweden — National Road and Traffic Research Institute — Information and Documentation Section 925
Sweden — National Swedish Environment Protection Board — Swedish Environmental Research Index 926
Sweden — Royal Institute of Technology Library — Information and Documentation Center 930
Swedish Building Centre — Building Commodity File 934
Swedish Council for Information on Alcohol and Other Drugs 936
Swedish Institute of Building Documentation 938
Swedish Mechanical and Electrical Engineering Trade Association — VERA 939
Swedish Standards Institution — REGIS 940
Swedish University of Agricultural Sciences — Ultuna Library — Documentation Section 941
Swiss Viewdata Information Providers Association 946
Swiss Wildlife Information Service 947
SYDONI S.A. 949
Tanzania — National Central Library — Tanzania National Documentation Centre 955
Technical Center for Mechanical Industries — Documentation Center for Mechanics 957
Technical Indexes Ltd. 958
Technical Information Center —Electrical Engineering Documentation Center 960
Technical Information Center — Mechanical Engineering Documentation 961
Technical Information Center — Medical Technology Documentation 962
Technical Information-Documentation Consultants Ltd. 963
Technical University of Wroclaw — Main Library and Scientific Information Center — System of Computerized Processing of Scientific Information 965
Technology Resource Center — Technobank Program 967
Tel-Aviv University — Shiloah Research Center for Middle Eastern and African Studies — DocumentationSystem — Mideast File 970
TimberResearch and Development Association — Information and Advisory Department — Timber Information Keyword Retrieval 983
TT Newsbank 990
Turkey — Scientific and Technical Research Council of Turkey — Turkish Scientific and Technical Documentation Center 991
Union of Soviet Socialist Republics — Academy of Sciences of the U.S.S.R. —Institute for High Temperatures — Thermophysical Properties Center 996
Union of SovietSocialist Republics — All-Union Institute of Scientific and Technical Information 998
United Nations — Economic and Social Commission for Asia and the Pacific — ESCAP Library — ESCAP Bibliographic Information System 1002
United Nations — Economic and Social Commission for Asia and the Pacific — Population Division — Population Clearing-house and Information Section 1003
United Nations — Economic Commission for Africa — Pan-African Documentation and Information System 1005
United Nations — Economic Commission for Latin America — Latin American Center for Economic and Social Documentation 1006
United Nations — Economic Commission for Latin America — Latin American Demographic Center — Latin American Population Documentation System 1007
United Nations — Food and Agriculture Organization — Aquatic Sciences and Fisheries Information System 1008
United Nations — Food and Agriculture Organization — Economic and Social Department — HumanResources, Institutions and Agrarian Reform Division — Population Documentation Center 1010
United Nations — Food and Agriculture Organization — International Information System for the Agricultural Sciences and Technology 1012
United Nations — Food and Agriculture Organization — Library and Documentation Systems Division — David Lubin Memorial Library 1013
United Nations Educational, Scientific and Cultural Organization — Center for Social Science Research and Documentation for theArab Region 1015

FUNCTION/SERVICE CLASSIFICATIONS

Abstracting and Indexing (Continued)

United Nations Educational, Scientific and Cultural Organization — International Bureau of Education — Documentation and Information Unit   1021
United Nations Environment Programme — Industry and Environment Office — Industry and Environment Data Base   1024
United Nations Industrial Development Organization — Industrial Information Section — Industrial and Technological Information Bank   1027
University Library of Hannover and Technical Information Library   1031
University of Alberta — Department of Educational Administration — Administration Laboratory Project File   1034
University of Birmingham — Department of Engineering Production — ErgonomicsInformation Analysis Centre   1041
University of Bonn — Inorganic Chemistry Institute — Inorganic Crystal StructureData Base   1042
University of Dundee — Law Library — European Documentation Centre   1047
University of Dusseldorf — Research Division for Philosophy Information and Documentation — Philosophy Information Service   1048
University of Haifa Library — Haifa On-line Bibliographic Text System   1051
University of Leeds — Medical and Dental Library — Oncology Information Service   1053
University of London — Imperial College of Science and Technology — Department of Mineral Resources Engineering — Rock Mechanics Information Service   1056
University of Paris-South — Gases and Plasmas Physics Laboratory — GAPHYOR   1063
University of Reading Library — Location Register of Twentieth Century English Literary Manuscripts and Letters   1065
University of Sheffield — Biomedical Information Service   1069
University of Sherbrooke — Asbestos Research Program — Information Center   1071
University of Sydney Library — Bibliographic Information on Southeast Asia   1073
University of Trier — Center for Psychological Information and Documentation   1078
University of Valencia — Biomedical Documentation and Information Center   1082
University of Waterloo — Faculty of Human Kinetics and Leisure Studies — Information Retrieval System for the Sociology of Leisure and Sport   1085
University of Western Ontario — School of Library and InformationScience — Nested Phrase Indexing System   1086
URBAMET Network   1091
Volkswagenwerk AG — Documentation Section   1104
The Welding Institute — Information Services   1106
Western Australian Institute of Technology — T.L. Robertson Library — WAIT Index to Newspapers   1107
Western Legal Publications Ltd.   1108
York University — Institute for Behavioural Research   1120
Yugoslav Center for Technical and Scientific Documentation   1121
Zinc Development Association/Lead Development Association/Cadmium Association — Library and Abstracting Service   1122

Associations

Aslib, The Association for Information Management   35
Association for Literary and Linguistic Computing   37
Association of Database Producers   40
Association of European Host Operators Group   42
British Computer Society   107
Canadian Association for Information Science/Association Canadienne des Sciences de l'Information   168
Canadian Information Industry Association   172
Canadian Law Information Council   173
Canadian Micrographic Society   175
Eurodata Foundation   303
European Association for the Transfer of Technologies, Innovation and Industrial Information   306
European Association of Information Services   307
European Information Providers Association   312
French Federation of Data Base Producers   385
Indexing and Abstracting Society of Canada   506
Information Management and Consulting Association   526
Information Processing Society of Japan   529
Institute of Information Scientists   544
Intergovernmental Bureau for Informatics   554
International Association for Statistical Computing   556
International Association of Agricultural Librarians and Documentalists   558
International Committee for Social Science Information and Documentation   571

Associations (Continued)

International Council for Building Research, Studies and Documentation   573
International Council of Scientific Unions — Committeeon Data for Science and Technology   574
International Council of Scientific Unions Abstracting Board   575
International Federation for Documentation   578
International Federation for Documentation — Research Referral Service   579
International Federation for Information Processing   580
International Federation of Data Organizations for the Social Sciences   581
International Federation of Library Associations and Institutions   582
International Group of Users of Information Systems   586
International Medical Informatics Association   597
International Telecommunication Union   606
International Telecommunications Users Group   607
International Union of Geological Sciences — Commission on Storage, Automatic Processing and Retrieval of Geological Data   609
Italian Association for the Production and Distribution of Online Information   621
Library and Information Research Group   659
Netherlands Association of Users of Online Information Systems   734
Netherlands Information Combine   737
Netherlands Society forInformatics   745
Online Users' Group/Ireland   776
Society for Information and Documentation — GID Information Center for Information Science and Practice   880
STATUS Users Group   900
Swiss Viewdata Information Providers Association   946
United Kingdom Online User Group   1000
Videotex Industry Association Ltd.   1100
Videotex Information ServiceProviders Association of Canada   1101

Community Information and Referral

Information London   525

Computerized Searching

A.JOUR   1
Alberta Municipal Affairs — Central Services Branch — Alberta Land Use Planning Data Bank   10
Alberta Research Council— Alberta Geological Survey — Geoscience Data Index for Alberta   12
Alberta Research Council — Alberta Oil Sands Information Centre   13
Alberta Research Council — Coal TechnologyInformation Centre   14
Alberta Research Council — IndustrialDevelopment Department — Industrial Information   15
Alberta Research Council — Solar and Wind Energy Research Program Information Centre   16
Alpha 460 Television Ltd.   18
Alpine ScienceInformation Service   21
Argentina — National Atomic Energy Commission — Division of Technical Information   27
Argentina — National Council for Scientific and Technical Research — Argentine Centerfor Scientific and Technological Information   28
Asian Institute of Technology — Regional Documentation Center — Asian Information Centerfor GeotechnicalEngineering   30
Asian Institute of Technology — Regional Documentation Center — Environmental Sanitation Information Center   31
Asian Institute of Technology — Regional DocumentationCenter — International Ferrocement Information Center   32
Asian Institute ofTechnology — Regional Documentation Center — Renewable Energy Resources Information Center   33
Asian Network for Industrial Technology Information and Extension   34
Aslib, The Association for Information Management   35
Association for Information Brokerage and Technological Consultancy — IRS Info-Institute   36
Association for Research and Development of Chemical Informatics — DARC Pluridata System   38
Association for the Promotion of Industry-Agriculture — International Documentation Center for Industries Using AgriculturalProducts   39
Association of Social Sciences Institutes — Social Sciences Information Center   43
Atomic Energy of Canada, Ltd. — Chalk River Nuclear Laboratories — Technical Information Branch   44
Atomic Energy of Canada, Ltd. — Whiteshell Nuclear Research Establishment —Technical Information Services   45
Australia —Bureau of Transport Economics — BTE Information Systems   46
Australia —Commonwealth Scientific and Industrial Research Organization — Central Information, Library and Editorial Section   47

Computerized Searching (Continued)

Australia— National Library of Australia 48
Australian Atomic EnergyCommission — Lucas Heights Research Laboratories Library 51
Australian Financial Review — INFO-LINE 55
Australian Institute of Criminology Library — Computerised Information from National Criminological Holdings 56
Australian Mineral Foundation — Australian Earth Sciences Information System 57
Australian National Gallery — Library 58
Australian Road Research Board — Australian Road Research Documentation 62
Austria — Federal Ministry of Buildings and Technology — Federal Research and Testing Establishment Arsenal — Road Research Documentation Center 63
Austria — Minister of Finance — International Patent Documentation Center 64
Austrian Documentation Centre for Media and Communication Research 65
Austrian National Institute for Public Health — Literature Service in Medicine 66
Bar-Ilan University — Institute for Information Retrieval and Computational Linguistics — Responsa Project 74
Belgium — Royal Library of Belgium — National Center for Scientific and Technical Documentation 84
BNF Metals Technology Centre — Information Department 92
Boris Kidric Institute of NuclearSciences — Laboratory for Information Systems 96
Brassey's Publishers Ltd. — Brassey's Naval Record 97
Brazil — Ministry of Agriculture — National Center for Agricultural Documentary Information 99
Brazil — Ministry of the Interior — Documentation Coordination Unit 100
Brazil — National Commission for NuclearEnergy — Center for Nuclear Information 102
Brazil — National Councilof Scientific and Technological Development — Brazilian Institute for Information in Science and Technology 103
British Broadcasting Corporation — BBC Data 104
British Columbia Ministry of Industry and Small Business Development — Central Statistics Bureau 106
British Computer Society 107
Brown's Geological Information Service Ltd. 113
Brunel Univeristy — Brunel Institute for Bioengineering — Information Unit 114
Building Center 117
Building Services Research and Information Association — BSRIA Information Centre 119
Bulgaria — Medical Academy — Center for Scientific Information in Medicine and Health 120
Bulgaria — National Agro-Industrial Union — Agricultural Academy — Center for Scientific, Technical and Economic Information 121
Bureau Marcel van Dijk, SA 122
Business Information International 123
Cambridge University — University Chemical Laboratory — Cambridge Crystallographic Data Centre 125
Canada — Agriculture Canada — Marketing and Economics Branch — Cooperatives Unit — COINS 127
Canada — Agriculture Canada — Scientific Information Retrieval Section — Pesticide Research Information System 128
Canada — Consumer and Corporate Affairs Canada — Corporations Branch — Corporate Integrated Information System 129
Canada — Department of Energy, Mines and Resources — Canada Centre for Mineral and Energy Technology — Technology Information Division 131
Canada — Department of Energy, Mines and Resources — Canada Centre for Remote Sensing — Remote Sensing On-Line Retrieval System 132
Canada — Department of Energy, Mines and Resources — Geological Survey of Canada — Economic Geology Division — Canadian Mineral Occurrence Index 134
Canada — Department of Energy, Mines and Resources — Geological Survey of Canada — National GEOSCAN Centre 135
Canada — Department of Industry, Trade & Commerce — Office of Tourism — Tourism Research and DataCentre 137
Canada — Environment Canada — Canadian Inventory of Historic Building 138
Canada — EnvironmentCanada — Inland Waters Directorate — National Hydrology Research Institute — Perennial Snow and Ice Section — Glacier Inventory of Canada 139
Canada — Environment Canada — Inland Waters Directorate — Water Quality Branch — National Water Quality Data Bank 141
Canada — Environment Canada — Lands Directorate — Canada Land Data Systems Division— Canada Geographic Information System 143
Canada— National Film Board of Canada — FORMAT 146
Canada —National Library of Canada 147
Canada — National Library ofCanada — MARC Records Distribution Service 150
Canada — National Research Council of Canada — Canada Institute for Scientific and Technical Information 152
Canada — National Research Council ofCanada — Canada Institute for Scientific and Technical Information — Scientific Numeric Databases 155
Canada — Parliament of Canada — Library of Parliament 157
Canada — Statistics Canada — CanadianSocio-Economic Information Management System 159
Canada — Transport Canada — Library and Information Centre 161
Canadian Agricultural Research Council — Inventory of Canadian AgriculturalResearch 167
Canadian Law Information Council 173
Caribbean Industrial Research Institute — Technical Information Service 177
Carleton University — Department of Sociology and Anthropology — Social Science Data Archives 178
Centennial College — Bibliocentre 182
Center for Industrial Creation — DocumentationService 184
Center for Research and Studies on Mediterranean Societies 186
Center for Scientific and Technical Research for the Metal Manufacturing Industry — Fabrimetal 187
Center for Study and Research of the Hydraulic Binders Industry — Documentation Center — INTERCIM Cement Data Base 188
Center of ExperimentalMetallurgy — Iron and Steel Documentation Service 192
Central American Research Institute for Industry — Division of Documentation and Information 193
Centre of Information Resource & Technology, Singapore 197
Charities Aid Foundation — Information Services 198
Chem Systems International Ltd. 199
Chemical Age — Chemical Age Project File 200
Chemical Information Center 201
China Building Technology Development Centre — Institute of Technical Information 203
The CIRPA/ADISQ Foundation 206
Coaching Association of Canada — Sport Information Resource Centre 210
Commission of the European Communities — EuroAbstracts 218
Commonwealth Regional Renewable Energy ResourcesInformation System 230
Compu-Mark 234
Compu-Mark Ltd. 235
Compusearch Market and Social Research Ltd. 236
Constellate Consultants Ltd. 241
Czechoslovakia — Institute for Medical Information 250
DAFSA 251
Datasearch Business Information Ltd. 263
Derwent Publications Ltd. — Chemical Reactions Documentation Service 274
Derwent Publications Ltd. — Veterinary Literature Documentation 278
Dobra Iron and Steel Research Institute — Informetal 281
Documentary Research Center 282
Dortmund Institute for WaterResearch — Data Bank on Substances Harmful to Water 284
Drug Information Pharmacists Group — Pharmline 285
Editec 293
Electricite de France — Office of Study and Research — Information and Documentation Systems Department — EDF-DOC Data Base 295
Elsevier Science Publishers B.V. — Biomedical Division — Excerpta Medica 296
Epoch Research Corporation 298
Euroline Inc. 304
European Association for the Transfer of Technologies,Innovation and Industrial Information 306
European Conference of Ministers of Transport — International Co-operation in the Field of Transport Economics Documentation 309
European Space Agency — European Space Research and Technology Center — Materials Data Retrieval System 316
Exeter University Teaching Services — The Exeter AbstractReference System 319
Fairplay Publications Ltd. — Fairplay International Research Services 324
FARMODEX Foundation — FARMODEX Drug Data Bank 325
Financial Times Business Information Ltd. — Business Information Service 328
Finland — CentralMedical Library — MEDIC Data Base 329
Finland — Technical Research Centre of Finland — Technical Information Service 330
Finnish Pulp and Paper Research Institute — Technical Information Service 333
FLA Groupe La Creatique 336
Foundation for Science and Politics — Research Institute for International Politics and Security — Library and Documentation System 337

Computerized Searching (Continued)

France — Atomic Energy Commission — Saclay Nuclear Research Center — Documentation Center 339
France — Bureau of Geological and Mining Research — National Geological Survey — Geological Information and Documentation Department 340
France — Bureau of Geological and Mining Research — National Geological Survey — Subsoil Data Bank 341
France — Bureau of Geological and Mining Research — National GeologicalSurvey — World Gravimetric Data Bank 342
France — National Center for Ocean Utilization — National Bureau for Ocean Data 347
France — National Center for Scientific Research — Documentation Center for Human Sciences 355
France — National Center for Scientific Research — Scientific and Technical Documentation Center 356
France — National Center for Scientific Research — Scientific Documentation Center in Oncology — CANCERNET 357
France — National Institute for Health and Medical Research — Office of Scientific Evaluation — INSERM Research Information Bank 358
France — National Institute for Industrial Property — Office of Legal and Technical Documentation — JURINPI Data Base 360
France — National Institute for Research in Informatics and Automation — Information Dissemination Office 361
France — National Institute of Statistics and Economic Studies — Local Area Data Bank 365
France — National Institute of Statistics and Economic Studies — Macroeconomic Data Bank 366
France — National Telecommunications Research Center — Interministerial Documentation Service — TELEDOC 367
Fraunhofer Society — Information Center for Building and Physical Planning 373
Fraunhofer Society — Information Center for Building and Physical Planning — Building Research Projects Data Base 374
Fraunhofer Society — Information Center for Building and Physical Planning — Buildings Documentation Data Base 375
Fraunhofer Society — InformationCenter for Building and Physical Planning — Literature Compilations Data Base 376
Fraunhofer Society — Information Center for Building and Physical Planning — PASCALBAT Data Base 377
FraunhoferSociety — Information Center for Building and Physical Planning — Property Services Agency Information on Construction and Architecture Data Base 378
Fraunhofer Society — Information Center for Building and Physical Planning — Regional Planning, City Planning, Housing, Building Construction Data Base 379
Fraunhofer Society — Information Center for Building and Physical Planning — Regional Planning, City Planning, Housing Research Projects Data Base 380
French Institute of Energy — Energy Studies and Information Center 386
French Petroleum Institute — Documentation Center 387
French Textile Institute — Textile Information Treatment Users' Service 390
Geosystems 394
German Electron-Synchrotron — DESY Scientific Documentation and Information Service 396
German Iron and Steel Engineers Association — Information System on Production Plants for Iron & Steel — PLANTFACTS 398
German Iron and Steel Engineers Association — Steel Information System 399
German Plastics Institute — Information and Documentation Services 402
German Society for Chemical Equipment — Information Systems and Data Banks Department — Chemical Technology Information System 403
German Society for Chemical Equipment — Information Systems and Data Banks Department — DECHEMA Substance Data Service 404
German Society for Chemical Equipment — Information Systems and Data Banks Department — Supply Sources Information System 406
German Standards Institute — German Information Centerfor Technical Rules 407
Germany — Federal Biological Research Center for Agriculture and Forestry — Documentation Center for Phytomedicine 409
Germany — Federal Employment Institute — Institutefor Employment Research — Information and Documentation Department 410
Germany — Federal Environmental Agency — Environmental Information and Documentation System 411
Germany — Federal Institute for Geosciences and Natural Resources — Geoscience Literature Information Service 412
Germany — Federal Institute for Geosciences and Natural Resources — Marine Information and Documentation System 413
Germany — Federal Institute for Materials Testing — Measurement ofMechanical Quantities Documentation 415
Germany — Federal Institute for Materials Testing — Nondestructive Testing Documentation 416
Germany — Federal Institute for Materials Testing — Rheologyand Tribology Documentation Center 417
Germany — Federal Institute for Materials Testing — Welding Documentation 418
Germany — Federal Institute for Occupational Safety — Information and Documentation Centre for Occupational Safety 419
Germany — FederalInstitute for Sports Science — Documentation and Information Division — Sport and Sports-Scientific Information System 420
Germany — Federal Research Center for Fisheries — Information and Documentation Center 421
Germany — German Federal Diet — Division of ScientificDocumentation — Documentation and Information System for Parliamentary Materials 422
Germany — Ministry for Research and Technology —Ongoing Research Project Data Bank 424
Germany — Ministry ofEconomics — German Foreign Trade Information Office 425
Germany — Ministry of Youth, Family and Health — German Institute for MedicalDocumentation and Information 428
Glass Institute — Information and Documentation Service 429
The Globe and Mail — InfoGlobe 430
Great Britain — Atomic Energy Authority — Atomic Energy Research Establishment, Harwell — Harwell Central Information Service 434
Great Britain — Atomic Energy Authority — Atomic Energy Research Establishment, Harwell — National Chemical Emergency Centre — CHEMSAFE 435
Great Britain — Atomic Energy Authority —Atomic Energy Research Establishment, Harwell — Nondestructive Testing Centre — Quality Technology Information Service 436
Great Britain— Atomic Energy Authority — Atomic Energy Research Establishment, Harwell— Waste Management Information Bureau 437
Great Britain — Atomic Energy Authority — Culham Laboratory — Plasma Physics Library andInformation Service 438
Great Britain — British Library — Bibliographic Services Division — BLAISE 440
Great Britain— British Library — Lending Division 442
Great Britain — British Library — Science Reference Library — Computer Search Service 445
Great Britain — British Library — Science Reference Library — European Biotechnology Information Program 446
GreatBritain — Department of the Environment — Building Research Establishment— Fire Research Station Library — Fire Science Abstracts 452
Great Britain — Department of the Environment — Building Research Establishment Library — BRIX 453
Great Britain — Departmentsof the Environment and Transport — Transport and Road Research Laboratory — Technical Information and Library Services 455
Great Britain— Health and Safety Executive — HSE Library and Information Services 457
Great Britain — Home Office Forensic Science Service — Central Research Establishment — Operational Services Division 458
Great Britain — House of Commons Library — Parliamentary On-Line Information System 459
Great Britain — House of Lords — Library & Information Centre 460
Great Britain — Institute of Terrestrial Ecology — Biological Records Centre 461
Great Britain — Water Research Centre — Information Service on Toxicity and Biodegradability 463
Great Britain — Water Research Centre — Library and Information Services 464
Greater London Council — Information Services Group 465
Group for the Advancement of Spectroscopic Methods and Physicochemical Analysis — Information Center for Spectroscopic and Physicochemical Analysis 466
Gruner & Jahr AG & Co. — G&J Press Information Bank 468
Gulf Organization for Industrial Consulting — Industrial Data Bank Department 471
Hands-On Ltd. 472
Harker's Specialist Book Importers — Harker'sInformation Retrieval Systems 474
Health Care Literature Information Network 477
Helsinki School of Economics Library — Information Services 481
Helsinki University of Technology — University Library/National Library for Science and Technology 483
Hertfordshire County Council — Chiltern Advisory Unit for Computer Based Education 485
Hohenheim University — Documentation Center on Animal Production 487
Hubrecht Laboratory — Central Embryological Library — Documentation and Information System on Developmental Biology 490
Hungarian Academy of Sciences Library — Department for Informatics and Science Analysis 492
Hungary — Central Statistical Office 493

Computerized Searching (Continued)

Hungary — Ministry for Building and Urban Development — Information Centre for Building 494
Hungary — National Technical Information Centre and Library 496
ICC Information Group Ltd. 499
IMS A.G. — MIDAS 504
India — Council of Scientific and Industrial Research — Indian NationalScientific Documentation Centre 507
India — National Institute of Oceanography — Indian National Oceanographic Data Centre 509
Indian Council of Agricultural Research — Agricultural Research Information Centre 510
Infocom 515
Infocon Information Services, Ltd. 516
Infoquest 520
Information Center for Energy, Physics, Mathematics 521
Information India 523
Information Researchers, Inc. 531
InformationResources 532
Information Systems Design 534
Information Unlimited 535
Informetrica Limited 536
Infytec, S.A. 537
Institute for Documentation and Information in Social Medicine and Public Health 539
Institute of Nutrition — Documentation Department 545
Institution of Electrical Engineers — INSPEC 549
INTERFACT/SVP AB 553
International Atomic Energy Agency — Energy and Economic Data Bank 559
International Atomic Energy Agency — Nuclear Data Section 561
International Atomic Energy Agency — Vienna International Centre Library 562
International Center for Higher Studies inMediterranean Agronomy — Socioeconomic Data Bank on the Mediterranean Countries 564
International Centre for Scientific and Technical Information 565
International Civil Aviation Organization — Air Navigation Bureau — Accident Investigation and Prevention Section — Aircraft Accident/Incident Reporting System 567
International Civil AviationOrganization — Air Navigation Bureau — Aerodromes Section — Airport Characteristics Data Bank 568
International Coffee Organization — COFFEELINE 570
International Committee for Social Science Information and Documentation 571
International Company for Documentation in Chemistry 572
International Development Research Centre — Library 576
International Food Information Service — Food Science and Technology Abstracts 583
International Institute of Refrigeration — Documentary Service 590
International Labour Office — Bureau for Labour Problems Analysis — Labour Information Database 591
International Labour Office — Central Library and Documentation Branch 593
International Labour Office —Conditions of Work and Welfare Facilities Branch — Clearing-house on Conditions of Work 594
International Labour Office — International Occupational Safety and Health Information Centre 595
International Livestock Centre for Africa — Documentation Centre 596
International Medical Information Center 598
International Refugee Integration Resource Centre 602
International Technical Publications Ltd. 605
Interprofessional Technical Union of the National Federations of Buildings and Public Works — Center for Technical Assistance and Documentation — ARIANE Data Bank 610
Interuniversity Documentation and Information Center for the Social Sciences 611
IPC Industrial Press Ltd. — Chemical Data Services 612
IRS-DIALTECH 615
Israel — National Center of Scientificand Technological Information 616
Israel Atomic Energy Commission — Soreq Nuclear Research Center — Library and Technical Information Department 618
Italy — National Research Council — ResearchCenter for the Stratigraphy and Petrography of the Central Alps — Archive ofItalian Data of Geology 625
Japan — Environment Agency —National Institute for Environmental Studies — Environmental Information Division 626
Japan — Japan Atomic Energy Research Institute — Department of Technical Information 627
Japan Association forInternational Chemical Information 630
Japan Information Center of Science and Technology 632
Japan Patent Information Center 633
Japan Pharmaceutical Information Center 634
Japan Publications Guide 635
Kinokuniya Company Ltd. — ASK Information Retrieval Services 640
Kompass International Ltd. 642
Korea Advanced Institute of Science and Technology — Experienced Librarians and Information Personnel in the Developing Countries of Asia and Oceania 644
Korea Institute for Industrial Economics andTechnology 645
Kugler Publications 647
Laval University Library — SDI/Laval & Telereference Service 652
Leatherhead Food Research Association — Information and Library Services 655
Legal Technology Group 656
Lloyd's Shipping Information Services 667
London Enterprise Agency — Supplier Identification System 671
London Researchers 674
Loughborough University of Technology — Chemical Engineering Department —Particle Science and Technology Information Service 676
Loughborough University of Technology Library — Library Instruction Materials Bank 677
Market Location 686
Maruzen Company, Ltd. — Maruzen Scientific Information Service Center 689
MemorialUniversity of Newfoundland — Ocean Engineering Information Centre 694
Mexico — National Center for Health Information and Documentation 700
Mexico — National Council of Science and Technology —Data Base Consultation Service 701
Mexico — National Institute for Research on Biological Resources — INIREB Library 702
Mexico — National Institute of Nuclear Research — Nuclear Information and Documentation Center 703
Microinfo, Ltd. 705
Mikro-Cerid 710
Monitan Information Consultants Ltd. 713
Nash Information Services Inc. 718
National Autonomous University ofMexico — Center for Scientific and Humanistic Information 719
National Center for Chemical Information 720
National Computing Centre Ltd. — Information Services Division 721
NationalFoundation for Educational Research in England and Wales — Information Research and Development Unit 724
National Science Council — Science and Technology Information Center 726
Natural Environment Research Council — British Geological Survey — Minerals Strategy and Economics Research Group — Mineral Information Section 727
NaturalEnvironment Research Council — British Geological Survey — National Geochemical Data Bank 728
Netherlands — Ministryof Agriculture and Fisheries — Agricultural Research Division — Centre for Agricultural Publishing and Documentation 731
Netherlands — Ministry of Foreign Affairs — Translations Branch — Terminology and Documentation Section 732
Netherlands Organization for Applied Scientific Research — Center for Information and Documentation 739
Netherlands Organization for Applied Scientific Research — Groundwater Survey 740
Netherlands Organization for Applied Scientific Research — National Council for Agricultural Research TNO — Central Project Administration for Current Agricultural Research in the Netherlands 742
Netherlands Organization for Applied Scientific Research — TNO Study and Information Centeron Environmental Research — Environmental Research in the Netherlands 743
Netherlands Soil Survey Institute — Soil Information System 746
New Zealand — Department of Scientific and Industrial Research — DSIR Central Library 748
Newfoundland Department of Mines & Energy — Mineral Development Division Library — Computerized Retrieval Services 750
Nichols Applied Management 752
Nihon Keizai Shimbun, Inc. — Databank Bureau — Nikkei Economic Electronic Databank System-Information Retrieval 753
Nippon Gijutsu Boeki Co., Ltd. 758
North Rhine-Westphalia Institute for Air Pollution Control — Literature Information System 765
Norwegian Center for Informatics 767
Norwegian Petroleum Directorate — INFOIL II 769
Office of Economic Information and Forecasting 773
ONLINE GmbH 774
Ontario Ministry of Natural Resources — Mineral Resources Group — Ontario Geological Survey — Geoscience Data Centre 778
Organisation for Economic Co-Operation andDevelopment — International Development Information Network 781
Organisation for Economic Co-Operation and Development — International Energy Agency — IEA Coal Research — Technical InformationService 782
Organisation for Economic Co-Operation and Development — Nuclear Energy Agency — NEA Data Bank 785

Computerized Searching (Continued)

Organisation for Economic Co-Operation and Development — Road Transport Research Programme — International Road Research Documentation   786
OxfordMicroform Publications Ltd.   791
Paint Research Association — Information Department — World Surface Coatings Abstracts   792
Pan American Health Organization — Pan American Centre for Sanitary Engineering & Environmental Sciences — Pan American Information & Documentation Network on Sanitary Engineering & Environmental Sciences   794
Paris Office of Urbanization — Urban Data Bank of Paris and the Paris Region   798
Peace Research Institute-Dundas — Peace Research Abstracts Journal   800
People's Republic of China — Institute of Scientific and Technical Information of China   801
Pergamon Press — Current Awareness inBiological Sciences   803
Pharma Documentation Ring   804
Pharma Documentation Service   805
Philips Information Systems and Automation — DIRECT   809
Piedmont Consortium for Information Systems   811
Pira: Research Association for the Paperand Board, Printing and Packaging Industries — Comprehensive Information Services   812
Pira: Research Association for the Paper and Board, Printing and Packaging Industries — Printing and Information Technology Division   813
Polish Committee of Standardization,Measures, and Quality — Centre for Information on Standardization and Metrology   817
Portugal — National Institute for Scientific Research — Scientific andTechnical Documentation Center   821
Production Engineering Research Association of Great Britain — Information Services   826
Pulp and Paper Research Institute of Canada — TechnicalInformation Section   827
Quaere Legal Resources Ltd.   829
Quebec — French Language Board — Terminology Bank of Quebec   830
Quebec Society for Legal Information   834
Queen's University of Belfast — Department of Computer Science — Database on Atomic and Molecular Physics   835
Ringier & Co. — Ringier Documentation Center   841
Riso National Laboratory — Riso Library   842
Romania — National Council for Science and Technology — National Institute for Information and Documentation   843
Royal Museum of Central Africa — Center for Informatics Applied to Development and Tropical Agriculture— Agroclimatology Data Bank   846
Royal Netherlands Academy of Arts and Sciences — Social Science Information and Documentation Center   847
Royal Netherlands Academy of Arts and Sciences — Social Science Information and Documentation Center — SteinmetzArchives   848
Royal Netherlands Academy of Arts and Sciences Library   849
Royal Society of Chemistry — Information Services   851
Royal Society of Chemistry — Information Services — Mass Spectrometry Data Centre   856
Royal Tropical Institute — Agricultural Information & Documentation Section   857
Rubber andPlastics Research Association of Great Britain — RAPRA Information Centre   858
RWK Ltd.   859
Schimmelpfeng GmbH — Schimmelpfeng Information Broker Service   866
Shirley Institute — Textile Information Services   873
Siemens AG — Language Services Department — Terminology Evaluation and Acquisition Method   876
Singapore Institute of Standards and Industrial Research — Industrial Technical Information Service   877
SLAMARK International   878
Society for Information and Documentation — GID Information Center for Information Science and Practice   880
South Africa — Council for Scientific and Industrial Research — Centre for Scientific and Technical Information   885
South Africa — Nuclear Development Corporation of South Africa — NUCOR Library and Information Services   886
South African Medical Research Council — Institute for Medical Literature   888
Southeast Asian Regional Center for Graduate Study and Research in Agriculture — Agricultural Information Bank for Asia   889
Spain — Higher Council for Scientific Research — Institute forInformation and Documentation in Science and Technology   890
Spain — Higher Council forScientific Research — Institute for Information and Documentation in the Social Sciences and Humanities   891
State University of Utrecht Library — Biomedical Information Department   899
Stockholm University Computing Center, QZ   904
Strasbourg Observatory — Stellar Data Center   905
SVP Canada   910
SVP Espana   912
SVP United Kingdom   918
Sweden — Geological Survey of Sweden — Groundwater Documentation Section   920
Sweden — Karolinska Institute Library and Information Center   921
Sweden — National Board of Health and Welfare — Department of Drugs — Swedish Drug Information System   922
Sweden — National Board of Occupational Safety and Health — CIS Centre   923
Sweden — National Library for Psychology and Education   924
Sweden— National Road and Traffic Research Institute — Information and Documentation Section   925
Sweden — Patent and Registration Office — InterPat Sweden   928
Sweden — Research Institute of National Defense — FOA Index Group   929
Sweden — Royal Instituteof Technology Library — Information and Documentation Center   930
Sweden — Swedish National Road Administration — Technical Division — Road Data Bank   933
Swedish Center for Working Life — Information and Documentation Department   935
Swedish Institute of Building Documentation   938
Swedish Mechanical and Electrical Engineering Trade Association — VERA   939
Swedish Standards Institution — REGIS   940
Swedish University of Agricultural Sciences — Ultuna Library — Documentation Section   941
Swiss Academy of Medical Sciences — Documentation Service   943
SwissCenter of Documentation in Microtechnology   944
Swiss Coordination Center for Research in Education   945
Swiss Wildlife Information Service   947
Switzerland — Swiss Intellectual Property Office — Technical Information on Patents   948
SYSTEL   950
Technical Information Center   959
Technical Information Center — Electrical Engineering Documentation Center   960
Technical Information Center — Mechanical Engineering Documentation   961
Technical University of Aachen — Laboratory of Machine Tools and Production Engineering — Cutting Data Information Center   964
Technical University of Wroclaw — Main Libraryand Scientific Information Center — System of Computerized Processing of Scientific Information   965
Technology Information Center Gottingen   966
Technology Resource Center — Technobank Program   967
Tecnomedia   968
Teikoku Data Bank, Ltd.   969
Textile and Clothing Information Centre   980
Thermodata Association — Thermodata-Thermdoc Data Bank   981
Timber Research and Development Association — Information and Advisory Department —Timber Information Keyword Retrieval   983
Toronto Department ofthe City Clerk — Computerized Text Processing and Retrieval System for City Council Information   985
Unilever Computer Services Ltd. — European Petrochemical AssociationTrade Statistics Database   993
Unilever Computer Services Ltd. — World Trade Statistics Database   994
Union of Soviet Socialist Republics — Academy of Sciences of the U.S.S.R. — Astronomical CouncilData Center — Management System for Astronomical Data in Machine-Readable Form   995
Union of Soviet Socialist Republics — Academy of Sciences of the U.S.S.R. — Institute for High Temperatures — Thermophysical Properties Center   996
Union of Soviet Socialist Republics — All-Union Institute of Scientific and Technical Information   998
Union of Soviet Socialist Republics — U.S.S.R.State Committee on the Utilization of Atomic Energy — Center for Nuclear Structure and Reaction Data   999
United Nations — Economic and Social Commission for Asia and thePacific — ESCAP Library — ESCAP Bibliographic Information System   1002
United Nations — Economic and Social Commission for Asia and the Pacific — Population Division — Population Clearing-house and Information Section   1003
United Nations — Economic and Social Commission for Asia and the Pacific — Statistics Division — UN/ESCAP Statistical Information Services   1004
United Nations — Economic Commission for Latin America — Latin American Center for Economic and Social Documentation   1006
United Nations — Economic Commission for Latin America — Latin American Demographic Center — Latin American Population Documentation System   1007
United Nations — Food and Agriculture Organization — Current Agricultural Research Information System   1009

Computerized Searching (Continued)

United Nations — Food and Agriculture Organization — Economic and Social Department — Human Resources, Institutions and Agrarian Reform Division — Population Documentation Center 1010
United Nations —Food and Agriculture Organization — Libraryand Documentation Systems Division — David Lubin Memorial Library 1013
United Nations — Food and Agriculture Organization — Statistics Division — Interlinked Computerized Storage and Processing System of Food and Agricultural Data 1014
United Nations Educational, Scientific and Cultural Organization — Intergovernmental Oceanographic Commission —Marine Environmental Data Information Referral System 1020
United Nations Educational, Scientificand Cultural Organization — InternationalBureau of Education — Documentation and Information Unit 1021
United Nations Educational, Scientific and Cultural Organization — Social and Human Science Documentation Centre 1022
United Nations Environment Programme — Industry and Environment Office — Industry and Environment Data Base 1024
United Nations Environment Programme — INFOTERRA 1025
United Nations Industrial Development Organization — Industrial Information Section — Industrial and Technological Information Bank 1027
United Nations University — Referral Service System
University Library of Hannover and Technical Information Library 1031
University of Alberta — Department of Sociology — Population Research Laboratory 1035
University of Bonn — Inorganic Chemistry Institute — Inorganic Crystal Structure Data Base 1042
University of British Columbia — B.C. Hospital Programs Branch — Drug and Poison Information Centre 1043
University of Cologne — Central Archives for Empirical Social Rèsearch 1045
University of Dusseldorf — Research Division for Philosophy Information and Documentation — Philosophy Information Service 1048
University of Leeds — Medical and Dental Library — Oncology Information Service 1053
University of London — Central Information Service 1055
University of London — Imperial College of Science and Technology — Department of MineralResources Engineering — Rock Mechanics Information Service 1056
University of Oslo — Royal University Library — Planning Department 1061
University of Paris-South — Gases and Plasmas Physics Laboratory — GAPHYOR 1063
University of Regina — Canadian Plains Research Center — Information Services 1066
Universityof Saskatchewan Library — Reference Department — University of Saskatchewan Libraries Machine-Assisted Reference Teleservices 1067
University of Sheffield — Biomedical Information Service 1069
University of Sherbrooke — Asbestos Research Program — Information Center 1071
University of Tokyo —Computer Center — University of Tokyo On-Line Information Retrieval System 1075
University of Trier — Center for Psychological Information and Documentation 1078
University of Trondheim — Norwegian Institute of Technology — University Library 1079
University of Umea — Demographic Data Base 1081
University of Valencia — Biomedical Documentation and Information Center 1082
University of Warwick Library — Warwick Statistics Service 1083
University of Waterloo — Department of Recreation — Leisure Studies DataBank 1084
University of Waterloo — Faculty of Human Kinetics and Leisure Studies — Information Retrieval System for the Sociology of Leisure and Sport 1085
University of Western Ontario — Social Science Computing Laboratory — Information Systems Programme 1087
Update AB 1090
USACO Corporation 1092
Volkswagenwerk AG — Documentation Section 1104
Warren, Inc. 1105
The Welding Institute — Information Services 1106
World Health Organization —Division of Noncommunicable Diseases — Oral Health Unit — Global Oral Data Bank 1111
World Health Organization — Eastern Mediterranean Regional Office — Information Services 1112
World Health Organization — International Agency for Research on Cancer — Clearing-Housefor On-going Research in Cancer Epidemiology 1113
World HealthOrganization — WHO Collaborating Centre for Collection and Evaluation of Data on Comparative Virology 1114
World Health Organization — WHO Collaborating Centre for International Drug Monitoring 1115
York University — Institute for Behavioural Research 1120
Zinc Development Association/Lead Development Association/Cadmium Association —Library and Abstracting Service 1122

Consultants

Aball Software Inc. 2
Acton Information Resources Management Ltd. 4
Alpha 460 Television Ltd. 18
Arabian Gulf Information Consulting Bureau 25
Association for Information Brokerage and Technological Consultancy —IRS Info-Institute 36
Australia — Commonwealth Scientific and Industrial Research Organization — Central Information, Library and Editorial Section 47
AVCOR 67
AVS Intext Ltd. 69
Baric Computing Services Ltd. — Baric Viewdata 75
Bureau Marcel van Dijk, SA 122
Business Information International 123
Capital Planning Information Ltd. 176
Cawkell Information & Technology Services Ltd. 180
Chile — National Commission for Scientific and Technological Research — Directoratefor Information and Documentation 202
Colombian Fund for Scientific Research — National Information System 212
Communication Services Ltd. — Viewdata Services 231
Constellate Consultants Ltd. 241
CONSULTEXT 243
Consumers' Association — TeleWhich? 244
Council for Educational Technology — Videotex Services Unit 247
Dagg Associates 253
Danish DIANE Center 256
Data Processing Services Company — DPS Information Centre 258
Denmark — Ministry of CulturalAffairs — National Advisory Council forDanish Research Libraries 269
Eastern Counties Newspapers —Eastel 287
ElsevierScience Publishers B.V. — Biomedical Division — Excerpta Medica 296
Epoch Research Corporation 298
Espial Productions 300
Euroline Inc. 304
European Business Associates On-Line 308
Eurotec Consultants Ltd. — LIBRARIAN 318
FLA Groupe La Creatique 336
France — Interministerial Mission for Scientific and TechnicalInformation 344
France — National Institute for Research inInformatics and Automation — Information Dissemination Office 361
Fraser Williams Ltd. — CROSSBOW 370
Geosystems 394
Hands-On Ltd. 472
Hanover Press — Viewdata Services 473
Hertfordshire County Council — Chiltern Advisory Unit for Computer Based Education 485
Hertfordshire Technical Library and Information Service — HERTIS Industrial Services 486
Hungary — National Szechenyi Library — Centre for Library Science and Methodology 495
Image Base Videotex Design Inc. 502
Infocom 515
Infomart 518
Information Management & Engineering Ltd. 527
Information Resources 532
Information Systems Design 534
Infytec, S.A. 537
Institute for Information Industry 542
Intelmatique 552
International Electronic Publishing Research Centre 577
Iran — Ministry of Culture and Higher Education — IranianDocumentation Centre 613
Israel — National Center of Scientific and Technological Information 616
Italy — National Research Council — Institute for Study of Scientific Research & Documentation — Italian Reference Center for Euronet DIANE 624
Kinokuniya Company Ltd. — ASK Information Retrieval Services 640
KTS Information Systems 646
Larratt and Associates Ltd. 650
League of Arab States — League of Arab States Documentation and Information Center 653
Learned Information Ltd. 654

Consultants (Continued)

Legal Technology Group 656
Leigh-Bell & Associates Ltd. 657
Library & Information Consultants Ltd. 658
Logica UK Ltd. 668
Loughborough University of Technology — Centre for Library and Information Management 675
Management Consultants International, Inc. 682
MANZ Info Datenvermittlung GmbH — MANZ Datenbanken 683
Market Location 686
Mexico — National Council of Science and Technology — Data Base Consultation Service 701
Microfor Inc. 704
Nash Information Services Inc. 718
National Center for Chemical Information 720
National Computing Centre Ltd. — Information Services Division 721
National Reprographic Centre for Documentation 725
Netherlands Center for Information Policy 736
Netherlands Organization for Applied Scientific Research — Center for Information and Documentation 739
Netherlands Organization for Applied Scientific Research — Institute TNO for Mathematics, Information Processing and Statistics 741
Nichols Applied Management 752
Norwegian Center for Informatics 767
Norwegian Research Council for Science and the Humanities — Norwegian Social Science Data Services 771
Online Information Centre 775
Oriel Computer Services Limited 787
Orna/Stevens Consultancy 788
Overseas Data Service, Company, Ltd. 789
Phippard & Associates Strategic & Technological Consulting, Inc. 810
Piedmont Consortium for Information Systems 811
Pira: Research Association for the Paper and Board, Printing and Packaging Industries — Printing and Information Technology Division 813
Poland — Institute for Scientific, Technical and Economic Information 815
Polytechnical School of Montreal — Telidon Technology Development Center 819
Prodinform Technical Consulting Co. 825
QL Systems Limited 828
Quaere Legal Resources Ltd. 829
Research Services Ltd. — Pan European Survey 839
Scannet Foundation 864
Sharp Associates Limited 871
SLAMARK International 878
Socioscope Inc. 883
Sonoptic Communications Inc. 884
Specialist Software Ltd. 895
Stacs Information Systems Ltd. 897
Sweden — Research Institute of National Defense — FOA Index Group 929
SYSTEL 950
Technical Information-Documentation Consultants Ltd. 963
Tele-Direct Inc. 973
United Nations — Advisory Committee for the Co-ordination of Information Systems 1001
United Nations — Economic Commission for Africa — Pan-African Documentation and Information System 1005
United Nations Educational, Scientific and Cultural Organization — Division of Science and Technology Policies — Science and Technology Policies Information Exchange Programme 1016
United Nations Educational, Scientific and Cultural Organization — General Information Programme 1019
United Nations Educational, Scientific and Cultural Organization — Universal System for Information in Science and Technology — UNISIST International Centre for Bibliographic Descriptions 1023
University of Bath — Centre for Catalogue Research 1039
University of London — Central Information Service 1055
University of Sheffield — Centre for Research on User Studies 1070
University of Waterloo — Department of Recreation — Leisure Studies Data Bank 1084
Update AB 1090
USACO Corporation 1092
Userlink Systems Ltd. 1093
UTLAS Inc. 1094
Van Halm & Associates 1095
Veaner Associates 1097
VideoAccess 1099
Viewtel Services Ltd. 1102
Virtual City Associates Ltd. 1103
Warren, Inc. 1105
York University — Institute for Behavioural Research 1120
Yugoslav Center for Technical and Scientific Documentation 1121

Data Base Producers and Publishers

Admedia — Adfacts 6
Agra Europe 8
Alberta Department of Agriculture — Economic Services Division — Agricultural Commodities Data Base 9
Alberta Municipal Affairs — Central Services Branch — Alberta Land Use Planning Data Bank 10
Alberta Public Affairs Bureau — Publication Services Branch 11
Alberta Research Council — Alberta Geological Survey — Geoscience Data Index for Alberta 12
Alberta Research Council — Alberta Oil Sands Information Centre 13
Alberta Research Council — Coal Technology Information Centre 14
Alberta Research Council — Industrial Development Department — Industrial Information 15
Alberta Research Council — Solar and Wind Energy Research Program Information Centre 16
ALLM Books — Small Computer Program Index 17
Alpha 460 Television Ltd. 18
American College in Paris — Service Calvados 22
American Express Europe Ltd. — SkyGuide 23
Arctic Institute of North America — Arctic Science and Technology Information System 26
Art Sales Index Ltd. 29
Asian Institute of Technology — Regional Documentation Center — Asian Information Center for Geotechnical Engineering 30
Asian Institute of Technology — Regional Documentation Center — Environmental Sanitation Information Center 31
Asian Institute of Technology — Regional Documentation Center — International Ferrocement Information Center 32
Asian Institute of Technology — Regional Documentation Center — Renewable Energy Resources Information Center 33
Association for Research and Development of Chemical Informatics — DARC Pluridata System 38
Association for the Promotion of Industry-Agriculture — International Documentation Center for Industries Using Agricultural Products 39
Association of European Airlines — AEA Data Base 41
Association of Social Sciences Institutes — Social Sciences Information Center 43
Australia — Bureau of Transport Economics — BTE Information Systems 46
Australia — Commonwealth Scientific and Industrial Research Organization — Central Information, Library and Editorial Section 47
Australia — National Library of Australia 48
Australia — National Library of Australia — Australian MEDLINE Network 50
Australian Bureau of Statistics 52
Australian Business Index 53
Australian Council for Educational Research — Library and Information Services Unit 54
Australian Financial Review — INFO-LINE 55
Australian Institute of Criminology Library — Computerised Information from National Criminological Holdings 56
Australian Mineral Foundation — Australian Earth Sciences Information System 57
Australian National Gallery — Library 58
Australian National Radio Astronomy Observatory — Parkes Catalogue of Radio Sources 59
Australian National University — Research School of Social Sciences — Australian Demographic Data Bank 60
Australian Road Research Board — Australian Road Research Documentation 62
Austria — Minister of Finance — International Patent Documentation Center 64
Austrian Documentation Centre for Media and Communication Research 65
AVCOR 67
Aviation Information Services Ltd. 68
AVS Intext Ltd. 69
Bank of England — Financial Statistics Division 72
Bank Society — General Documentation — SGB Data Base 73
Bar-Ilan University — Institute for Information Retrieval and Computational Linguistics — Responsa Project 74
Baric Computing Services Ltd. — Baric Viewdata 75
Bavarian Ministry for Food, Agriculture and Forestry — Bavarian Agricultural Information System 76
Bayer AG — Engineering Science Division — Chemical and Process Engineering Abstracts 77
BBM Bureau of Measurement 78
Belgium — Ministry of Economic Affairs — Fonds Quetelet Library Data Base 81
Belgium — Ministry of Economic Affairs — National Statistical Institute 82
Belgium — Ministry of Health — National Poison Control Center 83
BHRA, The Fluid Engineering Centre — Information Services 86
Bibliographic Publishing Co. 87
BIOSIS, U.K. Ltd. — Zoological Record 88

Data Base Producers and Publishers (Continued)

Bird Associates 89
Blackwell Technical Services Ltd. 90
BLCMP Ltd. 91
BNF Metals Technology Centre — Information Department 92
Boreal Institute for Northern Studies —Library Services 95
Boris Kidric Institute of Nuclear Sciences— Laboratory for Information Systems 96
Brassey's Publishers Ltd. — Brassey's Naval Record 97
Brassey's Publishers Ltd.— British Defence Directory 98
Brazil — Ministry of Agriculture — National Center for Agricultural Documentary Information 99
Brazil — Ministry of the Interior — Documentation Coordination Unit 100
Brazil — National Commission for Nuclear Energy —Center for Nuclear Information 102
Brazil — National Council of Scientific and Technological Development — BrazilianInstitute for Information in Science and Technology 103
British Broadcasting Corporation — BBC Data 104
British Broadcasting Corporation — CEEFAX 105
British Columbia Ministry of Industry and Small Business Development — Central Statistics Bureau 106
The BritishCouncil — Central Information Service 108
British Market Research Bureau Ltd. — Target Group Index 109
British Medical Association — BMA Press Cuttings Database 110
British Standards Institution — Information Department 111
British Universities Film & Video Council Ltd. — Information Service 112
Brunel Univeristy — Brunel Institute for Bioengineering —Information Unit 114
Brunel University — Research Unit for the Blind — International Register of Research on Visual Disability 115
BTJ 116
Building Center 117
Building Information Institute 118
Building Services Research and Information Association — BSRIA Information Centre 119
Bulgaria— Medical Academy — Center for Scientific Information in Medicine and Health 120
Calgary Public Information Department — Public Relations Division — Civichannel 124
Cambridge University — University Chemical Laboratory — Cambridge Crystallographic Data Centre 125
Canada — Agriculture Canada — Marketing and Economics Branch— Agricultural Marketing and Trade Database 126
Canada —Agriculture Canada— Marketing and Economics Branch — Cooperatives Unit — COINS 127
Canada — Agriculture Canada — Scientific Information RetrievalSection — Pesticide Research Information System 128
Canada — Consumer and Corporate Affairs Canada — Corporations Branch — Corporate Integrated Information System 129
Canada — Department of Energy, Mines and Resources — Canada Centre for Mineral and Energy Technology— Technology Information Division 131
Canada — Department of Energy, Mines and Resources — Canada Centre for Remote Sensing — Remote Sensing On-Line Retrieval System 132
Canada — Department of Energy, Mines and Resources — Conservation and Renewable Energy Branch — Canadian Energy Information System 133
Canada— Departmentof Energy, Mines and Resources — Geological Survey of Canada — Economic Geology Division — Canadian Mineral Occurrence Index 134
Canada — Department of Energy, Mines and Resources — GeologicalSurvey of Canada — National GEOSCAN Centre 135
Canada — Department of Energy, Mines and Resources — Topographical Survey Division — Digital Mapping System 136
Canada — Department of Industry, Trade & Commerce — Office of Tourism — Tourism Research and Data Centre 137
Canada — Environment Canada — Canadian Inventory of Historic Building 138
Canada — Environment Canada — InlandWaters Directorate — National Hydrology Research Institute — Perennial Snow and Ice Section — Glacier Inventory of Canada 139
Canada — Environment Canada — Inland Waters Directorate — WATDOC 140
Canada — Environment Canada — Inland Waters Directorate — WaterQuality Branch— National Water Quality Data Bank 141
Canada— Environment Canada — Inland Waters Directorate — Water Resources Branch — WaterSurvey of Canada 142
Canada — Environment Canada — LandsDirectorate — Canada Land Data Systems Division — Canada Geographic Information System 143
Canada — Environment Canada — Library Services Branch — Environment Libraries Automated System 144
Canada — Health and Welfare Canada — Policy, Planning and Information Branch — A Network of Social Security Information Resources 145
Canada — National Film Board of Canada — FORMAT 146
Canada — National Library of Canada 147
Canada — National Library of Canada — Cataloguing Branch — Canadiana Editorial Division 148
Canada — National Library of Canada — Public Services Branch — Union Catalogue of Serials Division 151
Canada— National Research Council of Canada — Canada Institute for Scientific and TechnicalInformation 152
Canada — National Research Council of Canada — Canada Institute for Scientific and Technical Information —ScientificNumeric Databases 155
Canada — National Research Council ofCanada — Chemistry Division — Metals Data Centre 156
Canada — Public Archives of Canada — Machine Readable Archives Division 158
Canada — Statistics Canada — Canadian Socio-Economic Information Management System 159
Canada — Transport Canada — Library and Information Centre 161
Canada Law Book Ltd. 162
Canada Systems Group — Federal Systems Division — Canadian Federal Corporations and Directors Data Base 163
CanadaSystems Group — Federal Systems Division — Corporate Names Data Base 164
Canada Systems Group — Federal Systems Division — Inter-Corporate Ownership Data Base 165
Canada Systems Group — Federal Systems Division — Trade Marks Data Base 166
Canadian Agricultural Research Council — Inventory of Canadian Agricultural Research 167
Canadian Broadcasting Corporation — Project IRIS 169
Canadian Education Association — Canadian Education Index Data Base 170
Canadian Law Information Council 173
Canadian Library Association — Canadian Periodical Index 174
Carleton University Library — Carleton Library System 179
Cawkell Information & Technology Services Ltd. 180
Celltech Ltd. — Information and Library Service 181
Center for Industrial Creation — Documentation Service 184
Center for International Prospective Studies 185
Center for Research and Studies on MediterraneanSocieties 186
Center for Scientific and Technical Research forthe Metal Manufacturing Industry — Fabrimetal 187
Center for Study and Research of the Hydraulic Binders Industry — DocumentationCenter— INTERCIM Cement Data Base 188
Center for the Study of Advertising Support 189
Center for the Study on Information Systems in Government 190
Center for Translation Documentation 191
Center of Experimental Metallurgy — Iron and Steel Documentation Service 192
Central American Research Institute for Industry— Division of Documentation and Information 193
Central Electronic Network for Data Processing and Analysis 194
Central Ontario Regional Library System — Interlibrary Loan and Communication System 195
Centre of Information Resource & Technology, Singapore 197
Charities Aid Foundation — Information Services 198
Chem Systems International Ltd. 199
Chemical Age — Chemical Age Project File 200
Chisholm Institute of Technology Library — User Education Resources Data Base 204
Christian Institutions Research and Documentation Center 205
The CIRPA/ADISQFoundation 206
CITIS Ltd. 208
City of London Polytechnic — Fawcett Library — BiblioFem 209
Coaching Association of Canada — Sport Information Resource Centre 210
Commission of the European Communities — Agricultural Research Projects Data Base 213
Commission of the European Communities — Court of Justice of the European Communities — Legal Data Processing Group — CJUS Data Bank 214
Commission of the European Communities — Education Information Network in the European Community 215
Commissionof the European Communities — Environmental Information and DocumentationCenters Data Base 216
Commission of the European Communities —Environmental Research Projects Data Base 217
Commission of the European Communities — Euro Abstracts 218
Commission of the European Communities — Joint Research Centre — Environmental ChemicalsData and Information Network 221
Commission of the European Communities — Joint Research Centre — High Temperature Materials Data Bank 222
Commission of the European Communities — Specialized Department for Terminology and Computer Applications — EURODICAUTOM 223

Data Base Producers and Publishers (Continued)

Commission of the European Communities — Statistical Office of the European Communities — COMEXT Data Bank 224
Commission of the European Communities — Statistical Office of the European Communities — CRONOS Data Bank 225
Commission of the European Communities — System for Information on Grey Literature in Europe 226
Commission of the European Communities — Tenders Electronic Daily 227
Commodities Research Unit Ltd. 228
Commonwealth Agricultural Bureaux — CAB Abstracts 229
Commonwealth Regional Renewable Energy Resources Information System 230
Communication Services Ltd. — Viewdata Services 231
Compu-Mark 234
Compu-Mark Ltd. 235
Compusearch Market and Social Research Ltd. 236
Computer Sciences of Australia Pty. Ltd. — Network Services Division — INFOBANK 237
Conference Board of Canada — Applied Economic Research and Information Centre — AERIC System 238
Consortium of Royal Library and University Libraries — Project for Integrated Catalogue Automation 239
Consortium of Royal Library and University Libraries — Project for Integrated Catalogue Automation — Netherlands Central Catalogue/Interlibrary Loan System 240
Constellate Consultants Ltd. 241
Construction Specifications Canada — National Master Specification 242
Consumers' Association — TeleWhich? 244
Council for Educational Technology — Videotex Services Unit 247
Council of Europe — European Documentation and Information System for Education 248
Cumulus Systems Ltd. 249
Czechoslovakia — Institute for Medical Information 250
DAFSA 251
DAFSA-SNEI S.A. — FITEK 252
Dalhousie University — Law School Library — Marine Affairs Bibliography 254
Data Bank for Medicaments 257
DataArkiv AB 260
Datasolve Ltd. — World Exporter 264
Datastream International Ltd. 267
Delft Hydraulics Laboratory — Information and Documentation Section 268
Denmark — National Technological Library of Denmark — Automated Library Information System 270
Denmark Telecommunications Administration — Danish Teledata System 272
Derwent Publications Ltd. — Biotechnology Abstracts 273
Derwent Publications Ltd. — Chemical Reactions Documentation Service 274
Derwent Publications Ltd. — Patents Documentation Services 275
Derwent Publications Ltd. — Pest Control Literature Documentation 276
Derwent Publications Ltd. — Pharmaceutical Literature Documentation 277
Derwent Publications Ltd. — Veterinary Literature Documentation 278
Didot-Bottin — Bottin Data Bases 280
Dobra Iron and Steel Research Institute — Informetal 281
Documentary Research Center 282
Dortmund Institute for Water Research — Data Bank on Substances Harmful to Water 284
Drug Information Pharmacists Group — Pharmline 285
Dutch State Mines — TISDATA 286
Eastern Counties Newspapers — Fastel 287
Econintel Information Services Ltd. — Econintel Monitor 290
Edimedia Inc. 292
Editions Techniques — JURIS-DATA 294
Electricite de France — Office of Study and Research — Information and Documentation Systems Department — EDF-DOC Data Base 295
Elsevier Science Publishers B.V. — Biomedical Division — Excerpta Medica 296
English Tourist Board — Information Unit — Tourtel 297
Espial Productions 300
Europe Data 305
European Association of Information Services 307
European Conference of Ministers of Transport — International Co-operation in the Field of Transport Economics Documentation 309
European Law Centre Ltd. — Eurolex 314
European Patent Office — EDP Department — EPO Data Banks 315
European Space Agency — European Space Research and Technology Center — Materials Data Retrieval System 316
European Space Agency — Information Retrieval Service 317
Exeter University Teaching Services — The Exeter Abstract Reference System 319
Expert Information Systems Ltd. — EXIS 1 320
Extel Computing Ltd. — EXSHARE 321
Extel Statistical Services Ltd. — EXBOND 322
Extel Statistical Services Ltd. — EXSTAT 323
Fairplay Publications Ltd. — Fairplay International Research Services 324
FARMODEX Foundation — FARMODEX Drug Data Bank 325
Faxtel Information Systems Ltd. — Marketfax 326
Federal Technical University — Technical Chemistry Laboratory — CHEMCO Physical Properties Data Bank 327
Financial Times Business Information Ltd. — Business Information Service 328
Finland — Central Medical Library — MEDIC DataBase 329
Finland — Technical Research Centre of Finland — Technical Information Service 330
Finnish Foreign Trade Association — Information Department — Register of Exporters 332
Finnish Standards Association — Information Service 334
Finsbury Data Services Ltd. — TEXTLINE 335
Foundation for Science and Politics — Research Institute for International Politics and Security — Library and Documentation System 337
France — Atomic Energy Commission — Programs Department — ELECNUC Databank 338
France — Atomic Energy Commission — Saclay Nuclear Research Center — Documentation Center 339
France — Bureau of Geological and Mining Research — National Geological Survey — Geological Information and Documentation Department 340
France — Bureau of Geological and Mining Research — National Geological Survey — Subsoil Data Bank 341
France — Bureau of Geological and Mining Research — National Geological Survey — World Gravimetric Data Bank 342
France — French Senate — Parliamentary Documentation and Information Printing Service 343
France — Ministry of Defense — General Office for Ordnance — Center for Documentation on Ordnance 345
France — National Center for Ocean Utilization — National Bureau for Ocean Data 347
France — National Center for Ocean Utilization — National Bureau for Ocean Data — AQUADOC 348
France — National Center for Ocean Utilization — National Bureau for Ocean Data — BIOCEAN 349
France — National Center for Ocean Utilization — National Bureau for Ocean Data — CNEXO-BNDO Data Base 350
France — National Center for Ocean Utilization — National Bureau for Ocean Data — DOCOCEAN 351
France — National Center for Ocean Utilization — National Bureau for Ocean Data — geoIPOD 352
France — National Center for Ocean Utilization — National Bureau for Ocean Data — POLUMAT 353
France — National Center for Ocean Utilization — National Bureau for Ocean Data — ROSCOP 354
France — National Center for Scientific Research — Documentation Center for Human Sciences 355
France — National Center for Scientific Research — Scientific and Technical Documentation Center 356
France — National Center for Scientific Research — Scientific Documentation Center in Oncology — CANCERNET 357
France — National Institute for Health and Medical Research — Office of Scientific Evaluation — INSERM Research Information Bank 358
France — National Institute for Industrial Property — Division of Publications Documentation and Information — INPI Data Bases 359
France — National Institute for Industrial Property — Office of Legal and Technical Documentation — JURINPI Data Base 360
France — National Institute for Research in Informatics and Automation — Information Dissemination Office 361
France — National Institute of Agronomic Research — Soil Science Laboratory — Soil Studies Service 362
France — National Institute of Statistics and Economic Studies — Documentation Division — SPHINX Data Base 363
France — National Institute of Statistics and Economic Studies — Information System for the Economy 364
France — National Institute of Statistics and Economic Studies — Local Area Data Bank 365
France — National Institute of Statistics and Economic Studies — Macroeconomic Data Bank 366
France — National Telecommunications Research Center — Interministerial Documentation Service — TELEDOC 367
Frankfurt City and University Library — Bibliography of Linguistic Literature 368
Fraser Williams Ltd. — Fine Chemicals Directory 372
Fraunhofer Society — Information Center for Building and Physical Planning 373

Data Base Producers and Publishers (Continued)

Fraunhofer Society — Information Center for Building and Physical Planning— Building Research Projects Data Base 374
Fraunhofer Society — Information Center for Building and Physical Planning — Buildings Documentation Data Base 375
Fraunhofer Society — Information Center forBuilding and Physical Planning — Literature Compilations Data Base 376
Fraunhofer Society — Information Center for Building and PhysicalPlanning — PASCALBAT Data Base 377
Fraunhofer Society — Information Center for Building and Physical Planning — Property Services Agency Information on Construction and Architecture Data Base 378
Fraunhofer Society — Information Center for Building and Physical Planning — Regional Planning, City Planning, Housing, Building Construction DataBase 379
Fraunhofer Society — Information Center for Building and Physical Planning — Regional Planning, City Planning, Housing ResearchProjects Data Base 380
Free University of Brussels — Central Library — VUBIS 381
French Association for Standardization— Data Bases Service — Automated Standards and Regulations Information Online 382
French Documentation — Political and Current EventsInformationBank 384
French Institute of Energy — Energy Studies and Information Center 386
French Petroleum Institute — Documentation Center 387
French Press Agency — Telematics Department — AGORA 388
French Stockbrokers Society — Information and Documentation Center 389
French Textile Institute — Textile Information Treatment Users' Service 390
French Water Study Association — National Water Information Center 391
Geo Abstracts Ltd. 393
Geosystems 394
German Electron-Synchrotron — DESY Scientific Documentation and Information Service 396
German Foundation for International Development — Documentation Center 397
German Iron and Steel Engineers Association — Information System on Production Plants for Iron & Steel — PLANTFACTS 398
German Iron and Steel Engineers Association — Steel Information System 399
German Library Institute 400
German Patent Information System 401
German Plastics Institute — Information and Documentation Services 402
German Society for ChemicalEquipment — Information Systems and Data Banks Department — Chemical Technology Information System 403
German Society for Chemical Equipment — Information Systems and Data Banks Department — DECHEMASubstance Data Service 404
German Society for Chemical Equipment — Information Systems and Data Banks Department — Materials and Corrosion Information System 405
German Society for Chemical Equipment— Information Systems and Data Banks Department — Supply Sources Information System 406
German Standards Institute — German Information Center for Technical Rules 407
Germany — Center for Agricultural Documentation and Information 408
Germany — Federal Biological Research Center for Agriculture and Forestry — Documentation Center for Phytomedicine 409
Germany — Federal Employment Institute — Institute for Employment Research — Information and Documentation Department 410
Germany — Federal Environmental Agency — Environmental Information and Documentation System 411
Germany —Federal Institute for Geosciences and Natural Resources — Geoscience Literature InformationService 412
Germany — Federal Institute for Geosciences andNatural Resources — Marine Information and Documentation System 413
Germany — Federal Institute for Geosciences and Natural Resources — Seismological Central Observatory GRF 414
Germany — Federal Institute for Materials Testing — Measurement of MechanicalQuantities Documentation 415
Germany — Federal Institute for Materials Testing — Nondestructive Testing Documentation 416
Germany — Federal Institute for Materials Testing — Rheology and Tribology Documentation Center 417
Germany — Federal Institute forMaterials Testing — Welding Documentation 418
Germany — Federal Institutefor Occupational Safety — Information and Documentation Centre for Occupational Safety 419
Germany — Federal Institute for Sports Science — Documentation and Information Division — Sport and Sports-Scientific Information System 420

Germany — German Federal Diet — Division of Scientific Documentation — Documentation and Information System for Parliamentary Materials 422
Germany — German National Library — BIBLIO-DATA 423
Germany — Ministry for Research and Technology — Ongoing Research Project Data Bank 424
Germany — Ministry of Economics — German Foreign Trade InformationOffice 425
Germany — Ministry of Justice — Judicial Information System 426
Germany — Ministry of Youth, Family and Health — German Institute for Medical Documentation and Information 428
Glass Institute — Information and Documentation Service 429
The Globe and Mail — Info Globe 430
Gmelin Institute for Inorganic Chemistry and Related Fields 431
Great Britain — Atomic Energy Authority — Atomic Energy Research Establishment, Harwell — Harwell Central Information Service 434
Great Britain — Atomic Energy Authority — Atomic Energy Research Establishment, Harwell — National Chemical Emergency Centre — CHEMSAFE 435
Great Britain — AtomicEnergy Authority — Atomic Energy Research Establishment, Harwell — Nondestructive Testing Centre — Quality Technology Information Service 436
Great Britain — Atomic Energy Authority — Atomic Energy Research Establishment, Harwell — Waste Management Information Bureau 437
Great Britain — Atomic Energy Authority — Culham Laboratory — Plasma Physics Library and Information Service 438
Great Britain — British Library — Bibliographic Services Division 439
Great Britain — British Library — Bibliographic Services Division — Subject Systems Office — Preserved Context Index System 441
Great Britain — British Library — Lending Division 442
Great Britain — British Library — Reference Division — Eighteenth Century ShortTitle Catalogue 443
Great Britain — British Library — Science Reference Library — European Biotechnology Information Program 446
Great Britain — British Telecommunications — Prestel 448
Great Britain — Central Statistical Office — CSO Macro-Economic Data Bank 449
Great Britain — Department of Industry —National Physical Laboratory — Division of Materials Applications — Metallurgical and Thermochemical Data Service 451
Great Britain —Department of the Environment — Building Research Establishment — Fire Research Station Library — Fire Science Abstracts 452
Great Britain — Department of the Environment — Building Research Establishment Library — BRIX 453
Great Britain — Department of Trade and Industry — Business Statistics Office 454
Great Britain —Departments of the Environment and Transport — Transport and Road Research Laboratory — Technical Information and Library Services 455
Great Britain — H.M. Treasury — U.K. Treasury Macroeconomic Forecasting Model and Databank 456
Great Britain — Healthand Safety Executive — HSE Library and Information Services 457
Great Britain — Home Office Forensic Science Service — Central Research Establishment — Operational Services Division 458
Great Britain — House of Commons Library — Parliamentary On-Line Information System 459
Great Britain — House of Lords — Library & Information Centre 460
Great Britain — Institute of Terrestrial Ecology — Biological Records Centre 461
Great Britain — Manpower Services Commission — Careers and Occupational Information Centre 462
Great Britain — Water Research Centre — Library and Information Services 464
Greater London Council — Information Services Group 465
Gruner & Jahr AG & Co. — G&J Press InformationBank 468
Gulf Organization for Industrial Consulting — Industrial Data Bank Department 471
Hanover Press — Viewdata Services 473
Health Care Literature Information Network 477
Hebrew University of Jerusalem — Automated Library Expandable Program Hebrew University of Jerusalem 478
Heinze GmbH — VISDATA 479
Helsinki School of Economics Library — Information Services 481
Helsinki University Library — Finnish National Bibliography 482
Helsinki University of Technology — University Library/National Library for Science and Technology 483
Henley Centre for Forecasting 484
Hertfordshire County Council — Chiltern Advisory Unit for Computer Based Education 485
Hertfordshire Technical Library and Information Service — HERTIS Industrial Services 486
Hohenheim University — Documentation Center on Animal Production 487

Data Base Producers and Publishers (Continued)

Honeywell Bull — Euris Host Service — European Community Law 489
Hubrecht Laboratory — Central Embryological Library — Documentation and Information System on Developmental Biology 490
Hungarian Academy of Sciences Library — Department for Informatics and ScienceAnalysis 492
Hungary — Central Statistical Office 493
Hungary — Ministry for Building and Urban Development — Information Centre for Building 494
IBJ Data Service Co. 498
ICC Information Group Ltd. 499
ICV Information SystemsLtd. — CitiService 500
IFO-Institute for Economic Research — Department of Econometrics and Data Processing — IFO Time Series Data Bank 501
IMS A.G. — MIDAS 504
Independent Chemical Information Services Ltd. 505
India — Council of Scientific and Industrial Research — Indian National Scientific Documentation Centre 507
India — National Institute of Oceanography — Indian National Oceanographic Data Centre 509
Indian Council of Agricultural Research — Agricultural Research Information Centre 510
Industrial News Publishing Company — KOMPASS-FRANCE 514
Infolex Services Ltd. 517
Infomart 518
Infomart — Grassroots 519
Information Center for Energy, Physics, Mathematics 521
Information Center for Materials — System forDocumentation and Information in Metallurgy 522
Information London 525
Informetrica Limited 536
Institute for Documentation and Information in Social Medicine and Public Health 539
Institute for Futures Studies — Futures Information Service 540
Institute for German Language 541
Institute of Agricultural Engineering — IMAG Dataservice 543
Institute of Nutrition — Documentation Department 545
Institute of Physicsand Energy — Nuclear Data Center 546
Institute of Research on Fruits and Citrus Fruits — Documentation Center 547
Institution of Chemical Engineers — Physical Property Data Service 548
Institution of Electrical Engineers — INSPEC 549
Institution of Electrical Engineers — INSPEC — ElectronicMaterials Information Service 550
Institution of Mining and Metallurgy — Library and Information Services 551
Intergovernmental Bureau for Informatics 554
International Association for the Evaluation of Educational Achievement — IEA Data Bank 557
International Atomic Energy Agency — Energy and Economic Data Bank 559
International Atomic Energy Agency — International Nuclear Information System 560
International Atomic Energy Agency — Nuclear Data Section 561
International Atomic Energy Agency — Vienna International Centre Library 562
International Bee ResearchAssociation — Apicultural Abstracts 563
International Center for Higher Studies in Mediterranean Agronomy — Socioeconomic Data Bank on the Mediterranean Countries 564
International Centre for Scientific and Technical Information 565
International Children's Centre — Documentation Service — Robert Debre Information Base 566
International Civil Aviation Organization — Air Navigation Bureau — Accident Investigation and Prevention Section — Aircraft Accident/Incident Reporting System 567
International Civil Aviation Organization — Air Navigation Bureau — Aerodromes Section — Airport Characteristics Data Bank 568
International Civil Aviation Organization — Air Transport Bureau — Statistics Section — Air Transport Statistical Program 569
International Coffee Organization — COFFEELINE 570
International Committee for Social Science Information and Documentation 571
International Company for Documentation in Chemistry 572
International Development Research Centre — Library 576
International Electronic Publishing Research Centre 577
International Food Information Service — Food Science and TechnologyAbstracts 583
International Food Information Service — Packaging Science and Technology Abstracts 584
International Food Information Service — VITIS-Viticulture and Enology Abstracts 585
International Information Center for Terminology 587
International Institute of Refrigeration — Documentary Service 590
International Labour Office — Bureau for Labour Problems Analysis — Labour Information Database 591
International Labour Office — Bureau of Statistics 592
International Labour Office — CentralLibrary and DocumentationBranch 593
International Labour Office — Conditions of Workand Welfare Facilities Branch — Clearing-house on Conditions of Work 594
International Labour Office — International Occupational Safetyand Health Information Centre 595
International Livestock Centre for Africa — Documentation Centre 596
International Medical Information Center 598
International Refugee Integration Resource Centre 602
International Serials Data System 603
International Society of Ecological Modelling— Environmental Data and Ecological Parameters Data Base 604
International Technical Publications Ltd. 605
International Telecommunication Union 606
International Translations Centre 608
Interprofessional Technical Union of the National Federationsof Buildings and Public Works — Center for Technical Assistance and Documentation — ARIANE Data Bank 610
Interuniversity Documentation and Information Center for the Social Sciences 611
IPC Industrial Press Ltd. — Chemical Data Services 612
IRCS Medical Science — IRCS Medical ScienceDatabase 614
Israel — National Center of Scientific and Technological Information 616
Italy — National Research Council— Research Center for the Stratigraphy and Petrography of the Central Alps — Archive of Italian Data of Geology 625
Japan — Environment Agency — National Institute for Environmental Studies — Environmental Information Division 626
Japan — Maritime Safety Agency — Hydrographic Department — Japan Oceanographic Data Center 628
Japan — National Diet Library — Library Automation System 629
Japan Information Center of Science and Technology 632
Japan Patent Information Center 633
Japan Pharmaceutical Information Center 634
Japan Publications Guide 635
Jordan & Sons Ltd. — Jordans Company Information 636
K-Konsult — VA-NYTT 637
Kluwer Publishing Company — Juridical Databank 641
Kompass International Ltd. 642
Koninklijke Vermande B.V. 643
Korea Advanced Institute of Science and Technology — Experienced Librarians and Information Personnel in the Developing Countries of Asia and Oceania 644
Korea Institute for Industrial Economics and Technology 645
Kugler Publications 647
Latin American Newsletters Ltd. 651
Laval University Library — SDI/Laval & Telereference Service 652
League of Arab States — League of Arab States Documentation and Information Center 653
Learned Information Ltd. 654
Leatherhead Food Research Association — Information and Library Services 655
Legal Technology Group 656
Library Association Publishing Ltd. — British Humanities Index 660
Library Association Publishing Ltd. — CURRENT RESEARCH in Library & Information Science 661
Library Association Publishing Ltd. — Current Technology Index 662
Library Association Publishing Ltd. —Library and Information Science Abstracts 663
Library Network of SIBIL Users 664
Linkoping University Library — NYTTFO 665
Lloyd's Shipping Information Services 667
London and South Eastern LibraryRegion 670
London Enterprise Agency — Supplier Identification System 671
The London International Financial Futures Exchange Ltd. 672
London Over the Counter Market 673
Loughborough University of Technology — Chemical Engineering Department —Particle Science and Technology Information Service 676
Loughborough University of Technology Library — Library Instruction Materials Bank 677
LymBurner & Sons Ltd. — Economist's Statistics 679
MacLean-Hunter Ltd. — Financial PostDivision — Financial Post Investment Data Bank 680
MaritimeInformation Centre/CMO 685
Market Location 686
Market Research Society — Market Research Abstracts 687
Marketing Intelligence Corporation 688
McGill University — Faculty of Engineering — Department of Mining and Metallurgical Engineering —Facility for the Analysis of Chemical Thermodynamics 691
McGill University — Graduate School of Library Science — FEES Data Base 692

Data Base Producers and Publishers (Continued)

Medical-Pharmaceutical Publishing Company 693
Memorial University of Newfoundland— Ocean Engineering Information Centre 694
MERLIN GERIN Company — Documentation Department — MERLECO 696
MERLIN GERIN Company — Documentation Department — MERLIN-TECH 697
Metropolitan Toronto Library Board — Regional Bibliographic Products Department 699
Mexico — National Institute for Research on Biological Resources — INIREB Library 702
Microfor Inc. 704
Micromedia Ltd. 706
Micromedia Ltd. — Canadian Business Index 707
Micromedia Ltd. — Canadian News Index 708
Mineralogical Society of Great Britain — Mineralogical Abstracts 711
Mitaka — JAPANSCAN 712
Morgan Grenfell &Co. Ltd. — Interfisc 715
Motor Vehicle Documentation 716
Multinational Association of Producers and Retailers of Electricity-Documentation 717
National Autonomous University of Mexico — Center for Scientific and Humanistic Information 719
National Center for Chemical Information 720
National Computing Centre Ltd. — Information Services Division 721
National Conservatory of Arts and Crafts — National Institutefor Documentation Techniques 722
National Elf Aquitaine Company — Documentary Information Service — STATSID 723
National Foundation for Educational Research in England and Wales — Information Research and Development Unit 724
National Science Council — Science and Technology Information Center 726
Natural Environment Research Council — British Geological Survey — Minerals Strategy and Economics Research Group — Mineral Information Section 727
Natural Environment Research Council — British Geological Survey — National Geochemical Data Bank 728
Natural Environment Research Council —Institute for Marine EnvironmentalResearch — Continuous Plankton Recorder Survey 729
Natural Environment Research Council — Institute of Oceanographic Sciences — Marine Information and Advisory Service 730
Netherlands — Ministry of Agriculture and Fisheries — Agricultural Research Division — Centre for Agricultural Publishing and Documentation 731
Netherlands — Ministry of Foreign Affairs — Translations Branch — Terminology and Documentation Section 732
Netherlands — Netherlands Foreign Trade Agency — Library and Documentation Branch — Foreign Trade Abstracts 733
Netherlands Organization for Applied Scientific Research — Groundwater Survey 740
Netherlands Organization for Applied Scientific Research — TNO Study and Information Center on Environmental Research— Environmental Research in the Netherlands 743
NetherlandsSoil Survey Institute — Soil Information System 746
New Opportunity Press Ltd. — Careerdata 747
New Zealand — Department of Scientific and Industrial Research — DSIR Central Library 748
New Zealand — Department of Statistics — Information Network forOfficial Statistics 749
Newfoundland Department of Mines & Energy — Mineral Development Division Library— Computerized Retrieval Services 750
Newfoundland Telephone — Tourism Newfoundland 751
Nihon Keizai Shimbun, Inc. —Databank Bureau — Nikkei EconomicElectronic Databank System-Information Retrieval 753
Nihon Keizai Shimbun, Inc. — Databank Bureau —Nikkei Economic Electronic Databank System-Time Sharing 754
Nihon Keizai Shimbun, Inc. — Quotation Information Center K.K. 755
Nineteenth Century Short Title Catalogue Project 757
Nomura Research Institute — Information Service and Development Department — NRI/E Japan Economic & Business Data Bank 760
Nordic Atomic Libraries Joint Secretariat — Nordic Energy Index 761
Nordic Documentation Center for Mass Communication Research 763
North Rhine-Westphalia Institute for Air Pollution Control — Literature Information System 765
Norwegian Center for Informatics 767
Norwegian Computing Centre for the Humanities 768
Norwegian Petroleum Directorate — INFOIL II 769
Norwegian Petroleum Directorate — Oil Index 770
Norwegian Standards Association — STANDARD 772
Office ofEconomic Information and Forecasting 773
ONLINE GmbH 774
Ontario Ministry of Education — Research and Information Branch — Information Centre — Ontario Education Resources Information System 777
Ontario Ministry of Natural Resources — Mineral Resources Group — Ontario Geological Survey — Geoscience Data Centre 778
ORACLE Teletext Ltd. 779
Organisation for Economic Co-Operation and Development — Economic Statistics and National Accounts Division —OECD Magnetic Tape Subscription Service 780
Organisation for Economic Co-Operation and Development — International Development Information Network 781
Organisation for Economic Co-Operation and Development — International Energy Agency — IEA Coal Research — Technical Information Service 782
Organisation for Economic Co-Operation and Development — International Energy Agency — IEA Coal Research — World Coal Resources and Reserves Data Bank Service 783
Organisation for Economic Co-Operation and Development — Nuclear Energy Agency — NEA DataBank 785
Organisation for Economic Co-Operation and Development — Road Transport Research Programme — International Road Research Documentation 786
Oriel Computer Services Limited 787
Overseas Data Service, Company, Ltd. 789
Oxford Microform Publications Ltd. 791
Paint Research Association — Information Department — World Surface Coatings Abstracts 792
Pan American Health Organization — Pan American Centre for Sanitary Engineering & Environmental Sciences — Pan American Information & Documentation Network on Sanitary Engineering & Environmental Sciences 794
Paris Chamber of Commerce and Industry — Department of International Relations — TELEXPORT 796
Paris District Informatics Administration — Informatics Biblio Service 797
Paris Office of Urbanization — Urban Data Bank of Paris and the Paris Region 798
Parpinelli TECNON — World Petrochemical Industry Data Bank 799
Peace Research Institute-Dundas — Peace Research Abstracts Journal 800
People's Republic of China — Institute of Scientific and Technical Information of China 801
Pergamon Press — Current Awareness in Biological Sciences 803
Pharma Documentation Ring 804
Pharmaceutical Society of Great Britain — Martindale Online 806
Philippines — National Science and Technology Authority — Scientific Clearinghouse and Documentation Services Division 808
Philips InformationSystems and Automation — DIRECT 809
Pira: Research Association for the Paper and Board, Printing and Packaging Industries — Comprehensive Information Services 812
PMB Print Measurement Bureau 814
Polish Committee of Standardization, Measures, and Quality — Centre for Information on Standardization and Metrology 817
Pont-a-Mousson Research Center — Industrial Documentation Service — BIIPAM-CTIFData Base 820
Portugal — National Institute for Scientific Research — Scientific and Technical Documentation Center 821
Press Association Ltd. — NEWSFILE 823
Pressurklipp — Swedish Market Information Bank 824
Pulp and Paper Research Institute of Canada — Technical Information Section 827
Quebec — French Language Board — Terminology Bank of Quebec 830
Quebec Ministry of Education — Library Headquarters — Point de Repere 831
Quebec Ministry of the Environment — Documentation Center — Envirodoq 832
Quebec National Library — FMQ 833
Quebec Society for Legal Information 834
Queen's University of Belfast — Department of Computer Science — Database on Atomic and Molecular Physics 835
Queen's University of Belfast — Department of Computer Science — Queen's University Interrogation of Legal Literature 836
QUOTEL Insurance Services Ltd. 837
Rene Descartes University — Laboratory of Applied Anthropology — ERGODATA 838
Research Services Ltd. — Pan European Survey 839
Resources 840
Ringier & Co. — Ringier Documentation Center 841
Romania — National Council for Science and Technology — National Institute for Information and Documentation 843
Royal Dutch Society for Advancement of Pharmacy — KNMP Drug Databank 844
Royal Institute of British Architects — British Architectural Library — Architectural Periodicals Index 845
Royal Museum of Central Africa — Center for Informatics Applied to Development and Tropical Agriculture — Agroclimatology Data Bank 846
Royal Netherlands Academy of Arts and Sciences — Social Science Information and Documentation Center 847

Data Base Producers and Publishers (Continued)

Royal Netherlands Academy of Arts and Sciences Library 849
Royal Norwegian Council for Scientific and Industrial Research — Norwegian Seismic Array 850
Royal Society of Chemistry — Information Services 851
Royal Society of Chemistry — Information Services — Chemical Engineering Abstracts 852
Royal Society of Chemistry — Information Services — Chemical Hazards in Industry 853
Royal Society of Chemistry — Information Services — Current Biotechnology Abstracts 854
Royal Society of Chemistry — Information Services — Laboratory Hazards Bulletin 855
Royal Society of Chemistry — Information Services — Mass Spectrometry Data Centre 856
Royal Tropical Institute — Agricultural Information & Documentation Section 857
Rubber and Plastics Research Association of Great Britain — RAPRA Information Centre 858
Saur Verlag 863
Schimmelpfeng GmbH 865
Scotland — National Library of Scotland — Scottish Libraries Co-operative Automation Project 869
Servi-Tech — BIODOC 870
Sharp Associates Limited 871
Ship Research Institute of Norway — Ship Abstracts 872
Shirley Institute — Textile Information Services 873
Siemens AG — Language Services Department — Terminology Evaluation and Acquisition Method 876
Singapore Institute of Standards and Industrial Research — Industrial Technical Information Service 877
SLAMARK International 878
SLIGOS 879
Society for Information and Documentation — GID Information Center for Information Science and Practice 880
Society for the Study of Economic and Social Development — MERCATIS 881
Society of Metaphysicians Ltd. — Information Services 882
South Africa — Council for Scientific and Industrial Research — Centre for Scientific and Technical Information 885
South Africa — South African Water Information Centre 887
Southeast Asian Regional Center for Graduate Study and Research in Agriculture — Agricultural Information Bank for Asia 889
Spain — Higher Council for Scientific Research — Institute for Information and Documentation in Science and Technology 890
Spain — Higher Council for Scientific Research — Institute for Information and Documentation in the Social Sciences and Humanities 891
Spain — Ministry of Health and Safety — National Institute of Occupational Safety and Health — National Information and Documentation Center 892
Spanish Drug Information Center — Spanish Pharmaceutical Specialities Data Bank 893
Sports Council — Information Centre 896
Standards Council of Canada — Standards Information Service 898
The Stock Exchange — Technical Services Department — TOPIC 902
Stockholm School of Economics — Economics Research Institute — FINDATA 903
Strasbourg Observatory — Stellar Data Center 905
Studsvik Energiteknik AB — Report Collection Index 906
Sweden — Geological Survey of Sweden — Groundwater Documentation Section 920
Sweden — National Board of Health and Welfare — Department of Drugs — Swedish Drug Information System 922
Sweden — National Library for Psychology and Education 924
Sweden — National Road and Traffic Research Institute — Information and Documentation Section 925
Sweden — National Swedish Environment Protection Board — Swedish Environmental Research Index 926
Sweden — Royal Institute of Technology Library — Information and Documentation Center 930
Sweden — Royal Library — Library Information System 931
Sweden — Statistics Sweden — Statistical Data Bases Unit 932
Sweden — Swedish National Road Administration — Technical Division — Road Data Bank 933
Swedish Building Centre — Building Commodity File 934
Swedish Center for Working Life — Information and Documentation Department 935
Swedish Council for Information on Alcohol and Other Drugs 936
Swedish Institute of Building Documentation 938
Swedish Mechanical and Electrical Engineering Trade Association — VERA 939
Swedish Standards Institution — REGIS 940
Swets Subscription Service 942
Swiss Coordination Center for Research in Education 945
Swiss Viewdata Information Providers Association 946
Swiss Wildlife Information Service 947

SYDONI S.A. 949
SYSTEL 950
Technical Center for Mechanical Industries — Documentation Center for Mechanics 957
Technical Information Center 959
Technical Information Center — Electrical Engineering Documentation Center 960
Technical Information Center — Mechanical Engineering Documentation 961
Technical Information Center — Medical Technology Documentation 962
Technical University of Aachen — Laboratory of Machine Tools and Production Engineering — Cutting Data Information Center 964
Technical University of Wroclaw — Main Library and Scientific Information Center — System of Computerized Processing of Scientific Information 965
Technology Resource Center — Technobank Program 967
Teikoku Data Bank, Ltd. 969
Tel-Aviv University — Shiloah Research Center for Middle Eastern and African Studies — Documentation System — Mideast File 970
Telekurs Ag — Investdata System 975
Telemap Ltd. — Micronet 800 976
TernisienListing 978
Textile and Clothing Information Centre 980
Thermodata Association — Thermodata-Thermdoc Data Bank 981
Tijl Datapress 982
Timber Research and Development Association — Information and Advisory Department — Timber Information Keyword Retrieval 983
Tokyo Shoko Research, Ltd. — Data Bank Service 984
Toronto Department of the City Clerk — Computerized Text Processing and Retrieval System for City Council Information 985
Toronto Stock Exchange — Data Products 986
Transinove International 987
TT Newsbank 990
Uhde GmbH — Uhde Thermophysical Properties Program Package 992
Unilever Computer Services Ltd. — European Petrochemical Association Trade Statistics Database 993
Unilever Computer Services Ltd. — World Trade Statistics Database 994
Union of Soviet Socialist Republics — Academy of Sciences of the U.S.S.R. — Astronomical Council Data Center — Management System for Astronomical Data in Machine-Readable Form 995
Union of Soviet Socialist Republics — Academy of Sciences of the U.S.S.R. — Institute for High Temperatures — Thermophysical Properties Center 996
Union of Soviet Socialist Republics — Academy of Sciences of the U.S.S.R. — Institute for Theoretical Astronomy — Minor Planets, Comets, and Satellites Department 997
Union of Soviet Socialist Republics — All-Union Institute of Scientific and Technical Information 998
Union of Soviet Socialist Republics — U.S.S.R. State Committee on the Utilization of Atomic Energy — Center for Nuclear Structure and Reaction Data 999
United Nations — Advisory Committee for the Co-ordination of Information Systems 1001
United Nations — Economic and Social Commission for Asia and the Pacific — ESCAP Library — ESCAP Bibliographic Information System 1002
United Nations — Economic and Social Commission for Asia and the Pacific — Population Division — Population Clearing-house and Information Section 1003
United Nations — Economic and Social Commission for Asia and the Pacific — Statistics Division — UN/ESCAP Statistical Information Services 1004
United Nations — Economic Commission for Africa — Pan-African Documentation and Information System 1005
United Nations — Economic Commission for Latin America — Latin American Center for Economic and Social Documentation 1006
United Nations — Economic Commission for Latin America — Latin American Demographic Center — Latin American Population Documentation System 1007
United Nations — Food and Agriculture Organization — Aquatic Sciences and Fisheries Information System 1008
United Nations — Food and Agriculture Organization — Current Agricultural Research Information System 1009
United Nations — Food and Agriculture Organization — Economic and Social Department — Human Resources, Institutions and Agrarian Reform Division — Population Documentation Center 1010
United Nations — Food and Agriculture Organization — INFOFISH 1011
United Nations — Food and Agriculture Organization — International Information System for the Agricultural Sciences and Technology 1012
United Nations — Food and Agriculture Organization — Library and Documentation Systems Division — David Lubin Memorial Library 1013

Data Base Producers and Publishers (Continued)

United Nations — Food and Agriculture Organization — Statistics Division — Interlinked Computerized Storage and Processing System of Food and Agricultural Data   1014
United Nations Educational, Scientific and Cultural Organization — Division of Science and Technology Policies — Science and Technology Policies Information Exchange Programme   1016
United Nations Educational, Scientific and Cultural Organization — Energy Information Section   1018
United Nations Educational, Scientific and Cultural Organization — Intergovernmental Oceanographic Commission — Marine Environmental Data Information Referral System   1020
United Nations Educational, Scientific and Cultural Organization — International Bureau of Education — Documentation and Information Unit   1021
United Nations Educational, Scientific and Cultural Organization — Social and Human Science Documentation Centre   1022
United Nations Environment Programme — Industry and Environment Office — Industry and Environment Data Base   1024
United Nations Environment Programme — INFOTERRA   1025
United Nations Environment Programme — International Register of Potentially Toxic Chemicals   1026
United Nations Industrial Development Organization — Industrial Information Section — Industrial and Technological Information Bank   1027
United Nations University — Referral Service System   1028
Universal Postal Union — International Bureau — Statistics of Postal Services   1030
University of Aberdeen — Department of Political Economy — Wage Rounds DataBank   1032
University of Alberta — Computing Services — Information Systems Group   1033
University of Alberta — Department of Educational Administration — Administration Laboratory Project File   1034
University of Alberta — Department of Sociology — Population Research Laboratory   1035
University of Alberta — Faculty of Nursing — Canadian Clearinghouse for Ongoing Research in Nursing   1036
University of Alberta — Faculty of Nursing — Canadian Directory of Completed Master's Theses in Nursing   1037
University of Bergen — Department of Scandinavian Languages and Literature — Norwegian Term Bank   1040
University of Bonn — Inorganic Chemistry Institute — Inorganic Crystal Structure Data Base   1042
University of British Columbia — B.C. Hospital Programs Branch — Drug and Poison Information Centre   1043
University of Dortmund — Dortmund Data Bank   1046
University of Dundee — Law Library — European Documentation Centre   1047
University of Dusseldorf — Research Division for Philosophy Information and Documentation — Philosophy Information Service   1048
University of Guelph Library — Cooperative Documents Network Project   1050
University of Haifa Library — Haifa On-line Bibliographic Text System   1051
University of Leeds — Medical and Dental Library — Oncology Information Service   1053
University of London — Central Information Service   1055
University of London — Imperial College of Science and Technology — Department of Mineral Resources Engineering — Rock Mechanics Information Service   1056
University of Melbourne — Department of Geology — Computerised Library of Analysed Igneous Rocks   1057
University of Milan — Higher Institute of Sociology — Data and Program Archive for the Social Sciences   1058
University of New Brunswick Libraries — PHOENIX   1059
University of New South Wales — Australian Graduate School of Management — Centre for Research in Finance   1060
University of Oslo — Royal University Library — Planning Department   1061
University of Paris-Nanterre — Group for Applied Macroeconomic Analysis   1062
University of Paris-South — Gases and Plasmas Physics Laboratory — GAPHYOR   1063
University of Quebec — Direct Access Data Bank at the University of Quebec   1064
University of Reading Library — Location Register of Twentieth Century English Literary Manuscripts and Letters   1065
University of Regina — Canadian Plains Research Center — Information Services   1066
University of Sherbrooke — Asbestos Research Program — Information Center   1071
University of Sydney — Sample Survey Centre   1072
University of Sydney Library — Bibliographic Information on Southeast Asia   1073
University of Tasmania Library — Union List of Higher Degree Theses in Australian Libraries   1074
University of Tokyo — Faculty of Engineering — Department of Synthetic Chemistry — EROICA System for Basic Properties of Organic Compounds   1076
University of Toronto — Faculty of Library and Information Science Library — Subject Analysis Systems Collection   1077
University of Trier — Center for Psychological Information and Documentation   1078
University of Trondheim — Norwegian Institute of Technology — University Library   1079
University of Tsukuba — Science Information Processing Center   1080
University of Umea — Demographic Data Base   1081
University of Valencia — Biomedical Documentation and Information Center   1082
University of Waterloo — Department of Recreation— Leisure Studies Data Bank   1084
University of Waterloo — Faculty of Human Kinetics and Leisure Studies — Information Retrieval System for the Sociology of Leisure and Sport   1085
University of Western Ontario — Social Science Computing Laboratory — Information Systems Programme   1087
University of Western Ontario — Systems Analysis, Control and Design Activity   1088
URBAMET Network   1091
UTLAS Inc.   1094
VDI-Verlag GmbH — VDI News Data Base   1096
Verlag Hoppenstedt & Co. — EK-MRA Data Base   1098
VideoAccess   1099
ViewtelServices Ltd.   1102
Volkswagenwerk AG — Documentation Section   1104
The Welding Institute — Information Services   1106
Western Australian Institute of Technology — T.L. Robertson Library — WAIT Index to Newspapers   1107
Western Legal Publications Ltd.   1108
Wolff & Co. Ltd. — Wolff Research   1109
World Health Organization — Division of Health Statistics — World Health Statistics Data Base   1110
World Health Organization — Division of Noncommunicable Diseases — Oral Health Unit — Global Oral Data Bank   1111
World Health Organization — International Agency for Research on Cancer — Clearing-House for On-going Research in Cancer Epidemiology   1113
World Health Organization — WHO Collaborating Centre for Collection and Evaluation of Data on Comparative Virology   1114
World Health Organization — WHO Collaborating Centre for International Drug Monitoring   1115
World Meteorological Organization — Commission for Hydrology — Operational Hydrology Programme — Hydrological Operational Multipurpose Subprogramme   1117
World Meteorological Organization — World Weather Watch   1119
York University — Institute for Behavioural Research   1120
Zinc Development Association/Lead Development Association/Cadmium Association — Library and Abstracting Service   1122

Data Collection and Analysis

Agra Europe   8
Alberta Department of Agriculture — Economic Services Division — Agricultural Commodities Data Base   9
Alberta Municipal Affairs — Central Services Branch — Alberta Land Use Planning Data Bank   10
Alberta Research Council — Alberta Geological Survey — Geoscience Data Index for Alberta   12
Alberta Research Council — Solar and Wind Energy Research Program Information Centre   16
Association for Research and Development of Chemical Informatics — DARC Pluridata System   38
Association of European Airlines — AEA Data Base   41
Australian Bureau of Statistics   52
Australian National Radio Astronomy Observatory — Parkes Catalogue of Radio Sources   59
Australian National University — Research School of Social Sciences — Australian Demographic Data Bank   60
Australian National University — Research School of Social Sciences — Social Science Data Archives   61
Aviation Information Services Ltd.   68
Bank of England — Financial Statistics Division   72
Bavarian Ministry for Food, Agriculture and Forestry — Bavarian Agricultural Information System   76
BBM Bureau of Measurement   78
Beilstein Institute for Literature in Organic Chemistry   79
Belgium — Ministry of Economic Affairs — National Statistical Institute   82
Belgium — Ministry of Health — National Poison Control Center   83

Data Collection and Analysis (Continued)

Bird Associates 89
British Columbia Ministry of Industry and Small Business Development — Central Statistics Bureau 106
British Market Research Bureau Ltd. — Target Group Index 109
British Standards Institution — Information Department 111
Bulgaria — Medical Academy — Center for Scientific Information in Medicine and Health 120
CambridgeUniversity — University Chemical Laboratory — Cambridge Crystallographic Data Centre 125
Canada — Agriculture Canada — Marketing and Economics Branch — Agricultural Marketing and Trade Database 126
Canada — Agriculture Canada — Scientific Information Retrieval Section — Pesticide Research Information System 128
Canada — Consumer and Corporate Affairs Canada — Corporations Branch — Corporate Integrated Information System 129
Canada — Department of Energy, Mines and Resources — Geological Survey of Canada — Economic Geology Division — Canadian Mineral Occurrence Index 134
Canada — Department of Energy, Mines and Resources — Topographical Survey Division — Digital Mapping System 136
Canada — Environment Canada — Canadian Inventoryof Historic Building 138
Canada — Environment Canada — Inland Waters Directorate — National Hydrology Research Institute — Perennial Snow and Ice Section — Glacier Inventory of Canada 139
Canada — Environment Canada — Inland Waters Directorate — Water Quality Branch — National Water Quality Data Bank 141
Canada — Environment Canada — Inland Waters Directorate — Water Resources Branch — Water Survey of Canada 142
Canada — Environment Canada — Lands Directorate — Canada Land Data Systems Division — Canada Geographic Information System 143
Canada — Health and Welfare Canada — Policy, Planning and Information Branch — A Network of Social Security Information Resources 145
Canada — National Research Council ofCanada — Canada Institute for Scientific and Technical Information — Canadian Service for the Selective Dissemination of Information 154
Canada — National Research Council of Canada — Canada Institute for Scientific and Technical Information — Scientific Numeric Databases 155
Canada — National Research Council of Canada — Chemistry Division — Metals Data Centre 156
Canada — PublicArchives of Canada — Machine Readable Archives Division 158
Canada — Statistics Canada — Canadian Socio-Economic Information Management System 159
Canada Law Book Ltd. 162
Canadian Engineering Publications Ltd. — Information Services Division 171
Carleton University — Department of Sociology and Anthropology — Social Science DataArchives 178
Center for Historical Social Research 183
Center for International Prospective Studies 185
Center for the Study of Advertising Support 189
Centre for the Study of Developing Societies — Data Unit 196
Charities Aid Foundation — Information Services 198
Commission of the EuropeanCommunities — Joint Research Centre — Environmental Chemicals Data and Information Network 221
Commission of the European Communities — Joint Research Centre — High Temperature Materials Data Bank 222
Commission of the European Communities — Statistical Office of the European Communities — COMEXT Data Bank 224
Commission of the European Communities — Statistical Office of the European Communities — CRONOS Data Bank 225
Commodities Research Unit Ltd. 228
Compusearch Market and Social Research Ltd. 236
Computer Sciences of Australia Pty. Ltd. — Network Services Division — INFOBANK 237
Conference Board of Canada — Applied Economic Research and Information Centre — AERIC System 238
Cumulus Systems Ltd. 249
DAFSA 251
DAFSA-SNEI S.A. — FITEK 252
Data Bank for Medicaments 257
Datastream International Ltd. 267
Dortmund Institute for Water Research — Data Bank on Substances Harmful to Water 284
DutchState Mines — TISDATA 286
Econintel Information Services Ltd. — Econintel Monitor 290
Economic and Social Research Council — Data Archive 291
ESDU International Limited 299
European Space Agency — European Space Research and Technology Center — Materials Data Retrieval System 316
European Space Agency — Information Retrieval Service 317
Expert Information Systems Ltd. — EXIS 1 320

Extel Computing Ltd. — EXSHARE 321
Extel Statistical Services Ltd. — EXBOND 322
Extel Statistical Services Ltd. — EXSTAT 323
Fairplay Publications Ltd. — Fairplay International Research Services 324
FARMODEX Foundation — FARMODEX Drug Data Bank 325
FaxtelInformation Systems Ltd. — Marketfax 326
Federal Technical University — Technical Chemistry Laboratory — CHEMCO Physical Properties Data Bank 327
Financial Times Business Information Ltd. — Business Information Service 328
France — Atomic Energy Commission — Programs Department — ELECNUC Databank 338
France — Bureau of Geological and Mining Research — National Geological Survey — Subsoil Data Bank 341
France — Bureau of Geological and Mining Research — National Geological Survey — World Gravimetric Data Bank 342
France — National Center for Ocean Utilization — National Bureau for Ocean Data 347
France — National Center for Ocean Utilization — National Bureau for Ocean Data — BIOCEAN 349
France — National Center for Ocean Utilization — National Bureau forOcean Data — geoIPOD 352
France — National Center for Ocean Utilization — National Bureau for Ocean Data — ROSCOP 354
France — National Institute of Agronomic Research — Soil Science Laboratory — Soil Studies Service 362
France — National Institute of Statistics and Economic Studies — Information System for the Economy 364
France — National Institute of Statistics and Economic Studies — Local Area Data Bank 365
France — National Institute of Statistics and Economic Studies — Macroeconomic Data Bank 366
French Petroleum Institute — Documentation Center 387
French Stockbrokers Society — Information and Documentation Center 389
FRI Information Services Ltd. 392
German Iron and Steel Engineers Association — Information System on Production Plants for Iron & Steel — PLANTFACTS 398
German Iron and Steel EngineersAssociation — Steel Information System 399
German Society for Chemical Equipment — Information Systems and Data Banks Department — DECHEMA Substance Data Service 404
Germany — Federal Environmental Agency — Environmental Information and Documentation System 411
Germany — Federal Institute for Geosciences and Natural Resources — Seismological Central Observatory GRF 414
Germany — Federal Institute for Sports Science — Documentation and Information Division — Sport and Sports-Scientific Information System 420
Germany — Ministry of Economics — German Foreign Trade Information Office 425
Great Britain — Atomic Energy Authority — Atomic Energy ResearchEstablishment, Harwell — National Chemical Emergency Centre — CHEMSAFE 435
Great Britain — Central Statistical Office — CSO Macro-Economic Data Bank 449
Great Britain — Department of Industry — National Physical Laboratory — Division of Materials Applications — Metallurgicaland Thermochemical Data Service 451
Great Britain— Department of Trade and Industry — Business Statistics Office 454
Great Britain — H.M. Treasury — U.K. Treasury Macroeconomic Forecasting Model and Databank 456
Great Britain — Home OfficeForensic Science Service — Central Research Establishment — Operational Services Division 458
Great Britain — Institute of Terrestrial Ecology — Biological Records Centre 461
Great Britain — Water Research Centre — Information Service on Toxicity and Biodegradability 463
Group for the Advancement of Spectroscopic Methods and Physicochemical Analysis — Information Center for Spectroscopic and Physicochemical Analysis 466
GSI-ECO 469
Gulf Organizationfor Industrial Consulting — Industrial Data Bank Department 471
Henley Centre for Forecasting 484
Hohenheim University — Documentation Center on Animal Production 487
Hungary — Central Statistical Office 493
IBJ Data Service Co. 498
ICC Information Group Ltd. 499
ICV Information Systems Ltd. — CitiService 500
IFO-Institute for Economic Research — Department of Econometrics and Data Processing — IFO Time Series Data Bank 501
IMS A.G. — MIDAS 504

Data Collection and Analysis (Continued)

Independent Chemical Information Services Ltd. 505
India — National Institute of Oceanography — Indian National Oceanographic Data Centre 509
Information Center for Energy, Physics, Mathematics 521
Informetrica Limited 536
Institute for Documentation and Information in Social Medicine and Public Health 539
Institute of Agricultural Engineering — IMAG Dataservice 543
Institute of Physics and Energy — Nuclear Data Center 546
Institution of Chemical Engineers — Physical Property Data Service 548
Institution of Electrical Engineers — INSPEC — Electronic Materials Information Service 550
International Association for the Evaluation of Educational Achievement — IEA Data Bank 557
International AtomicEnergy Agency — Energy and Economic Data Bank 559
International Atomic Energy Agency — Nuclear Data Section 561
International Centerfor Higher Studies in Mediterranean Agronomy — Socioeconomic Data Bank on the Mediterranean Countries 564
International Civil Aviation Organization — Air Transport Bureau — Statistics Section — Air Transport Statistical Program 569
International Labour Office — Bureau of Statistics 592
International Railway Union — DocumentationBureau 600
International Society of Ecological Modelling — Environmental Data and Ecological Parameters Data Base 604
International Technical Publications Ltd. 605
International Telecommunication Union 606
International Union of Geological Sciences — Commission on Storage, Automatic Processing and Retrieval of Geological Data 609
Interprofessional Technical Union of the National Federations of Buildings and Public Works — Center for Technical Assistance and Documentation — ARIANE Data Bank 610
Interuniversity Documentation and Information Center for the Social Sciences 611
IPC Industrial Press Ltd. — Chemical Data Services 612
Italy — National Research Council — Research Center for the Stratigraphy and Petrography of the Central Alps — Archive of Italian Data of Geology 625
Japan — Environment Agency — National Institute for Environmental Studies — Environmental Information Division 626
Japan — Maritime Safety Agency — Hydrographic Department — Japan Oceanographic Data Center 628
Japan Data Service Co., Ltd. 631
Jordan & Sons Ltd. — Jordans Company Information 636
Lloyd's Shipping Information Services 667
The London International Financial Futures Exchange Ltd. 672
LymBurner & Sons Ltd. — Economist's Statistics 679
MacLean-Hunter Ltd. — FinancialPost Division — Financial Post Investment Data Bank 680
Madagascar — Ministry of Finance and Economy — National Institute of Statistics and Economic Research 681
Market Location 686
Marketing Intelligence Corporation 688
McGill University — Faculty of Engineering — Department of Mining and Metallurgical Engineering — Facility for the Analysis of Chemical Thermodynamics 691
Medical-Pharmaceutical Publishing Company 693
National Elf Aquitaine Company — Documentary Information Service — STATSID 723
Natural Environment Research Council — British Geological Survey — National Geochemical Data Bank 728
Natural Environment Research Council — Institute for Marine Environmental Research — Continuous PlanktonRecorder Survey 729
Natural Environment Research Council — Institute of Oceanographic Sciences — Marine Information and Advisory Service 730
Netherlands Organization for Applied Scientific Research — Groundwater Survey 740
Netherlands Soil Survey Institute — Soil Information System 746
New Zealand — Department of Statistics — Information Network for Official Statistics 749
Nihon Keizai Shimbun, Inc. — Databank Bureau — Nikkei Economic Electronic Databank System-Time Sharing 754
Nihon Keizai Shimbun, Inc. — Quotation Information Center K.K. 755
Nomura Research Institute — Information Service and Development Department — NRI/E Japan Economic& Business Data Bank 760
Norway — Ministry of Finances and Customs — Central Bureau of Statistics 766
Norwegian Research Council for Science and the Humanities — Norwegian Social Science Data Services 771
Office of Economic Information and Forecasting 773
Ontario Ministry of Natural Resources — Mineral Resources Group — Ontario Geological Survey — Geoscience Data Centre 778
Organisation for Economic Co-Operation and Development — Economic Statisticsand National Accounts Division — OECD Magnetic Tape Subscription Service 780
Organisation for Economic Co-Operation and Development — International Energy Agency — IEA Coal Research — World Coal Resources and Reserves Data Bank Service 783
Organisation for Economic Co-Operation and Development — International Energy Agency — International Oil Market Information System 784
Organisation for Economic Co-Operation and Development — Nuclear Energy Agency — NEA Data Bank 785
Overseas Data Service, Company, Ltd. 789
Paris Office ofUrbanization — Urban Data Bank of Paris and the Paris Region 798
Parpinelli TECNON — World Petrochemical Industry Data Bank 799
People's Republic of China — Institute of Scientific and Technical Informationof China 801
PMB Print Measurement Bureau 814
Queen's University of Belfast — Department of Computer Science — Databaseon Atomic and Molecular Physics 835
QUOTEL Insurance Services Ltd. 837
Rene Descartes University — Laboratory of Applied Anthropology — ERGODATA 838
Research Services Ltd. — Pan European Survey 839
Royal Dutch Society for Advancement of Pharmacy — KNMP Drug Databank 844
Royal Museum of CentralAfrica — Center for Informatics Applied to Development and Tropical Agriculture — Agroclimatology Data Bank 846
Royal Netherlands Academyof Arts and Sciences — Social Science Information and Documentation Center — Steinmetz Archives 848
Royal Norwegian Council for Scientific and Industrial Research — Norwegian Seismic Array 850
Royal Society of Chemistry — Information Services — Mass Spectrometry Data Centre 856
Schimmelpfeng GmbH 865
SLAMARK International 878
SLIGOS 879
Society for the Study ofEconomic and Social Development — MERCATIS 881
Spanish DrugInformation Center — Spanish Pharmaceutical Specialities Data Bank 893
The Stock Exchange — Technical Services Department — TOPIC 902
Stockholm School of Economics — Economics Research Institute — FINDATA 903
Strasbourg Observatory — Stellar Data Center 905
Survey Force Ltd. 907
Sweden — GeologicalSurvey of Sweden — Groundwater Documentation Section 920
Sweden — National Board of Health and Welfare — Department of Drugs — Swedish Drug Information System 922
Sweden — Statistics Sweden — Statistical Data Bases Unit 932
Sweden — Swedish National Road Administration — Technical Division — Road Data Bank 933
Technical University of Aachen — Laboratory of Machine Tools and Production Engineering — Cutting Data Information Center 964
Teikoku Data Bank, Ltd. 969
Telekurs Ag — Investdata System 975
Textile and Clothing Information Centre 980
Thermodata Association — Thermodata-Thermdoc Data Bank 981
Tijl Datapress 982
Toronto Stock Exchange — Data Products 986
Turkey — Scientific and Technical Research Council of Turkey — Turkish Scientific and Technical Documentation Center 991
Uhde GmbH — Uhde Thermophysical Properties Program Package 992
Unilever Computer Services Ltd. — European Petrochemical Association Trade Statistics Database 993
Unilever Computer Services Ltd. — World Trade Statistics Database 994
Union of Soviet Socialist Republics — Academy of Sciences of the U.S.S.R. — Astronomical Council DataCenter — Management System for Astronomical Data in Machine-Readable Form 995
Union of Soviet Socialist Republics — Academy of Sciences of the U.S.S.R. — Institute for High Temperatures — Thermophysical Properties Center 996
Union of Soviet Socialist Republics — Academyof Sciences of the U.S.S.R. — Institute for Theoretical Astronomy — MinorPlanets, Comets, and Satellites Department 997
Union of SovietSocialist Republics — U.S.S.R. State Committee on the Utilization of Atomic Energy — Center for Nuclear Structure and Reaction Data 999
United Nations — Economic and Social Commission for Asia and the Pacific — Statistics Division — UN/ESCAP Statistical Information Services 1004
United Nations — Food and Agriculture Organization — Statistics Division — Interlinked Computerized Storage and Processing System of Food andAgricultural Data 1014
United Nations Environment Programme — International Register of Potentially Toxic Chemicals 1026

Data Collection and Analysis (Continued)

Universal Postal Union — International Bureau — Statistics of Postal Services 1030
University of Alberta — Department of Sociology —Population Research Laboratory 1035
University of Bonn — Inorganic Chemistry Institute — Inorganic Crystal Structure Data Base 1042
University of British Columbia — B.C. Hospital Programs Branch — Drug and Poison Information Centre 1043
University of British Columbia — Data Library 1044
University of Cologne — Central Archives for Empirical Social Research 1045
University of Dortmund — Dortmund Data Bank 1046
University of Leeds — Department of Physical Chemistry — High Temperature Reaction Rate Data Centre 1052
University of Melbourne — Department of Geology —Computerised Library of Analysed Igneous Rocks 1057
Universityof Milan — Higher Institute of Sociology — Data and Program Archive for the Social Sciences 1058
University of New South Wales — AustralianGraduate School of Management — Centre for Research in Finance 1060
University of Paris-Nanterre — Group for Applied MacroeconomicAnalysis 1062
University of Paris-South — Gases and PlasmasPhysicsLaboratory — GAPHYOR 1063
University of Sydney —Sample Survey Centre 1072
University of Tokyo — Faculty of Engineering — Department of Synthetic Chemistry — EROICA System for Basic Properties of Organic Compounds 1076
University of Umea — DemographicData Base 1081
University of Warwick Library — Warwick Statistics Service 1083
University of Waterloo — Department of Recreation — Leisure Studies Data Bank 1084
University of Western Ontario — Social Science Computing Laboratory — Information Systems Programme 1087
University of Western Ontario — Systems Analysis, Control and Design Activity 1088
Volkswagenwerk AG— Documentation Section 1104
Wolff & Co. Ltd. — Wolff Research 1109
World Health Organization — Division of Health Statistics — World Health Statistics Data Base 1110
World Health Organization — Division of Noncommunicable Diseases — Oral Health Unit— Global Oral Data Bank 1111
World Health Organization —WHO Collaborating Centre for Collection and Evaluation of Data on Comparative Virology 1114
World Health Organization — WHO Collaborating Centre for International Drug Monitoring 1115
World Meteorological Organization — World Climate Programme Department — World Climate Data Information Referral Service 1118
World Meteorological Organization — World Weather Watch 1119
York University — Institute for Behavioural Research 1120

Document Delivery

Alberta PublicAffairs Bureau — Publication Services Branch 11
Alberta Research Council — Industrial Development Department — IndustrialInformation 15
Alpine Science Information Service 21
AsianInstitute of Technology — Regional Documentation Center — Asian Information Center for Geotechnical Engineering 30
Asian Institute of Technology — Regional Documentation Center — Environmental Sanitation Information Center 31
Asian Institute of Technology —Regional Documentation Center — International Ferrocement Information Center 32
Asian Institute of Technology — Regional Documentation Center — Renewable Energy Resources Information Center 33
Association for Information Brokerage and Technological Consultancy — IRS Info-Institute 36
Association for the Promotion of Industry-Agriculture — International Documentation Center for Industries Using Agricultural Products 39
Australia — National Library of Australia — Australian MEDLINE Network 50
Australian Financial Review — INFO-LINE 55
Austria — Minister of Finance — International Patent Documentation Center 64
Bangladesh National Scientific andTechnical Documentation Centre 70
Bank Society — General Documentation —SGB Data Base 73
BHRA, The Fluid Engineering Centre — Information Services 86
BNF Metals Technology Centre— InformationDepartment 92
Brazil — Ministry of Agriculture — National Center for Agricultural Documentary Information 99
Brazil — National Commission for Nuclear Energy — Center for Nuclear Information 102
Brunel Univeristy — Brunel Institute for Bioengineering — Information Unit 114

Document Delivery (Continued)

Building Services Research and Information Association — BSRIA Information Centre 119
Business Information International 123
Canada — National Library of Canada 147
Canada — National Library of Canada — Cataloguing Branch — Canadiana Editorial Division 148
Canada — NationalResearch Council of Canada — Canada Institute for Scientific and Technical Information 152
Canada — National Research Council of Canada — Canada Institute for Scientific and Technical Information — Canadian Online Enquiry System 153
Canada — Parliament of Canada — Library of Parliament 157
Canadian Law Information Council 173
Center for Scientific and Technical Research forthe Metal Manufacturing Industry — Fabrimetal 187
Center for Study and Research of the Hydraulic Binders Industry — Documentation Center— INTERCIM Cement Data Base 188
Center for the Study on Information Systems inGovernment 190
China Building Technology Development Centre — Institute of Technical Information 203
CITIS Ltd. 208
Coaching Association of Canada — Sport Information Resource Centre 210
Commission of the European Communities — System for Information on Grey Literature in Europe 226
Commonwealth Agricultural Bureaux — CAB Abstracts 229
Commonwealth Regional Renewable Energy Resources Information System 230
Datasearch Business Information Ltd. 263
Denmark — NationalTechnological Library of Denmark — Automated Library Information System 270
Derwent Publications Ltd. — Biotechnology Abstracts 273
DerwentPublications Ltd. — Patents Documentation Services 275
Epoch Research Corporation 298
Europe Data 305
European Space Agency — Information Retrieval Service 317
Finland — Technical Research Centre of Finland — Technical Information Service 330
France — Atomic Energy Commission — Saclay Nuclear Research Center — Documentation Center 339
France — National Center for Ocean Utilization — National Bureau for Ocean Data 347
France — National Center for Scientific Research — Documentation Center for Human Sciences 355
France — National Center for Scientific Research — Scientific and Technical Documentation Center 356
France — National Center for Scientific Research — Scientific Documentation Center in Oncology — CANCERNET 357
France — National Institute for Industrial Property — Division of Publications Documentation and Information — INPI Data Bases 359
France — National Institute for Research in Informatics and Automation — Information Dissemination Office 361
France — National Telecommunications Research Center — Interministerial Documentation Service — TELEDOC 367
Fraunhofer Society — Information Center for Building and Physical Planning 373
French Association for Standardization — Data Bases Service — Automated Standards and Regulations Information Online 382
French Documentation — Political and Current Events InformationBank 384
French Stockbrokers Society — Information and Documentation Center 389
French Water Study Association — National Water Information Center 391
Geosystems 394
German Plastics Institute — Information and Documentation Services 402
Germany — Federal Institute for Materials Testing — Measurement of Mechanical Quantities Documentation 415
Germany — Federal Institute for Materials Testing — Nondestructive Testing Documentation 416
Germany — Federal Institute for Materials Testing — Welding Documentation 418
Germany — Federal Institute for Occupational Safety — Information and Documentation Centre for Occupational Safety 419
Germany — Ministry of Youth, Family and Health — German Institute for Medical Documentation and Information 428
Glass Institute — Information and Documentation Service 429
Great Britain — Atomic Energy Authority — Atomic Energy Research Establishment, Harwell — Waste Management Information Bureau 437
Great Britain — British Library — Lending Division 442
Great Britain — British Library — Science Reference Library —European Biotechnology Information Program 446
Great Britain — Department of Industry — Information Technology Division — HERMES 450

Document Delivery (Continued)

Great Britain — Department of the Environment — Building Research Establishment — Fire Research Station Library — Fire Science Abstracts 452
Great Britain — Water Research Centre — Libraryand Information Services 464
Hands-On Ltd. 472
Harker's Specialist Book Importers — Harker's Information Retrieval Systems 474
Health Care Literature Information Network 477
Helsinki School of Economics Library — Information Services 481
Helsinki University of Technology — University Library/National Library for Science and Technology 483
Hubrecht Laboratory — Central Embryological Library — Documentation and Information System on Developmental Biology 490
I/S Datacentralen 497
ICC Information Group Ltd. 499
Indian Council of Social Science Research — Social Science Documentation Centre 511
Infocon Information Services, Ltd. 516
Infoquest 520
Information India 523
Information Researchers, Inc. 531
Information Unlimited 535
Institute for Futures Studies — Futures Information Service 540
International Atomic Energy Agency — International Nuclear Information System 560
International Children's Centre — Documentation Service — Robert Debre Information Base 566
International Company for Documentation in Chemistry 572
International Food Information Service — Food Science and Technology Abstracts 583
International Food Information Service — Packaging Science and Technology Abstracts 584
International Food Information Service — VITIS-Viticulture and Enology Abstracts 585
International Information Service Ltd. 588
International Institute ofRefrigeration — Documentary Service 590
International Labour Office — International Occupational Safety and Health Information Centre 595
International Livestock Centre for Africa — Documentation Centre 596
International Medical Information Center 598
International Translations Centre 608
IRCS Medical Science — IRCS Medical Science Database 614
IST-Informatheque Inc. 619
Japan — National Diet Library — Library Automation System 629
Japan Information Center of Science and Technology 632
Japan Pharmaceutical Information Center 634
Jordan & Sons Ltd. — Jordans Company Information 636
K-Konsult — VA-NYTT 637
Library & Information Consultants Ltd. 658
London Researchers 674
Loughborough University of Technology — Chemical Engineering Department — Particle Science and Technology Information Service 676
Marine Biological Association of the United Kingdom — Marine Pollution Information Centre 684
Maritime Information Centre/CMO 685
Market Research Society — Market Research Abstracts 687
Maruzen Company, Ltd. — Maruzen Scientific Information Service Center 689
Mexico — National Center for Health Information and Documentation 700
Mexico — National Council of Science and Technology — Data Base Consultation Service 701
Microinfo, Ltd. 705
MicromediaLtd. 706
Mikro-Cerid 710
Mitaka — JAPANSCAN 712
Nash Information Services Inc. 718
National Autonomous University of Mexico — Center for Scientific and Humanistic Information 719
National Center for Chemical Information 720
National Computing Centre Ltd. — Information Services Division 721
National Science Council — Science and Technology Information Center 726
Netherlands — Netherlands Foreign Trade Agency — Library and Documentation Branch — Foreign Trade Abstracts 733
Nichols Applied Management 752
Nihon Keizai Shimbun,Inc. — Databank Bureau — Nikkei Economic Electronic Databank System-Information Retrieval 753
Nordic Atomic Libraries Joint Secretariat — Nordic Energy Index 761
Norwegian Petroleum Directorate — Oil Index 770
ONLINE GmbH 774
Pan American Health Organization — Pan American Centre for Sanitary Engineering & Environmental Sciences — Pan American Information & Documentation Network on SanitaryEngineering & Environmental Sciences 794
Pergamon Press — Current Awareness in Biological Sciences 803
Philippines — National Institute of Science and Technology — Divisionof Information and Documentation 807
Philippines — NationalScience and Technology Authority — Scientific Clearinghouse and Documentation Services Division 808
Pira: Research Association for the Paper and Board, Printing and Packaging Industries — Comprehensive Information Services 812
Pont-a-Mousson Research Center — Industrial Documentation Service — BIIPAM-CTIF Data Base 820
Portugal — National Institute for Scientific Research — Scientific and Technical Documentation Center 821
Pressurklipp — Swedish Market Information Bank 824
Quebec Society for Legal Information 834
Ringier & Co. — Ringier Documentation Center 841
Romania — National Council for Science and Technology — National Institute for Information and Documentation 843
Royal Institute of British Architects — British Architectural Library — Architectural Periodicals Index 845
Royal Museum of Central Africa — Center for Informatics Applied to Development and Tropical Agriculture — Agroclimatology Data Bank 846
Royal Netherlands Academy of Arts and Sciences Library 849
Royal Society of Chemistry — Information Services — Mass Spectrometry Data Centre 856
Royal Tropical Institute — Agricultural Information & Documentation Section 857
Rubber and Plastics Research Association ofGreat Britain — RAPRA Information Centre 858
Schimmelpfeng GmbH — Schimmelpfeng Information Broker Service 866
Ship Research Institute of Norway — Ship Abstracts 872
Shirley Institute — Textile Information Services 873
Singapore Institute of Standards and Industrial Research — Industrial Technical Information Service 877
Society for Information and Documentation — GID Information Center for Information Science and Practice 880
South Africa — Council for Scientific and Industrial Research — Centre for Scientific and Technical Information 885
South African Medical Research Council — Institute for Medical Literature 888
Southeast Asian Regional Center for Graduate Study and Research in Agriculture — Agricultural Information Bank for Asia 889
Spain — Higher Council for Scientific Research — Institute for Information and Documentation in the Social Sciences and Humanities 891
Studsvik Energiteknik AB —Report Collection Index 906
SVP Australia 908
SVP Canada 910
SVP South Africa Ltd. 917
Sweden — Karolinska Institute Library and Information Center 921
Sweden — National Library for Psychology and Education 924
Swedish Mechanical and Electrical Engineering Trade Association — VERA 939
Swiss Center of Documentation in Microtechnology 944
Swiss Wildlife Information Service 947
Switzerland — Swiss Intellectual Property Office — Technical Information on Patents 948
Tanzania — National Central Library — Tanzania National Documentation Centre 955
Technical Center for Mechanical Industries — Documentation Center for Mechanics 957
Technical InformationCenter 959
Technical Information Center — Electrical Engineering Documentation Center 960
Technical Information Center — Mechanical Engineering Documentation 961
Technical Information Center — Medical Technology Documentation 962
Technology Information Center Gottingen 966
United Nations — Economic Commission for Africa — Pan-African Documentation and Information System 1005
United Nations — Economic Commission for Latin America — Latin American Demographic Center — Latin American Population Documentation System 1007
United Nations — Food and Agriculture Organization— Library and Documentation Systems Division —David Lubin Memorial Library 1013
United Nations Educational, Scientific and Cultural Organization — International Bureau of Education —Documentation and Information Unit 1021
University Library of Hannover and Technical Information Library 1031
University of Birmingham — Department of Engineering Production — Ergonomics Information Analysis Centre 1041
University of Saskatchewan Library — Reference Department — University of Saskatchewan Libraries Machine-Assisted Reference

Document Delivery (Continued)

Teleservices 1067
University of Trondheim — Norwegian Institute of Technology — University Library 1079
University of Waterloo — Faculty of Human Kinetics and Leisure Studies — Information Retrieval System for the Sociology of Leisure and Sport 1085
Update AB 1090
URBAMET Network 1091
Warren, Inc. 1105
The Welding Institute — Information Services 1106
Western Legal Publications Ltd. 1108
Zinc Development Association/Lead Development Association/Cadmium Association — Library and Abstracting Service 1122

Electronic Mail Applications

American College in Paris — Service Calvados 22
Blackwell Technical Services Ltd. 90
Central Ontario Regional Library System — Interlibrary Loan and Communication System 195
Communication Services Ltd. — Viewdata Services 231
Data-Star 266
Denmark Telecommunications Administration — Danish Teledata System 272
European Association of Information Services 307
European Space Agency — Information Retrieval Service 317
Germany — Ministry of Posts and Telecommunications — German Federal Postal Service —Bildschirmtext 427
Germany — Ministry of Youth, Family and Health — German Institute for Medical Documentation and Information 428
Great Britain — British Telecommunications — Prestel 448
Great Britain — Department of Industry — Information Technology Division — HERMES 450
Infomart — Grassroots 519
Italian Society for Telephone Use — Videotel 622
Jordan & Sons Ltd. — Jordans Company Information 636
LymBurner & Sons Ltd. — Economist's Statistics 679
Netherlands Office of Posts, Telegraphs, and Telephones — PTT Central Directorate — Viditel 738
Overseas Telecommunications Commission — Multimode International Data Acquisition Service 790
QL Systems Limited 828
Scotland — National Library of Scotland — Scottish Libraries Co-operative Automation Project 869
Stockholm University Computing Center, QZ 904
Telemap Ltd.— Micronet 800 976
Transpac 989
UTLAS Inc. 1094
Warren, Inc. 1105

Information on Demand

Alberta Research Council — Industrial Development Department — Industrial Information 15
Alpine Science Information Service 21
Association for Information Brokerage and Technological Consultancy — IRS Info-Institute 36
Australian Financial Review — INFO-LINE 55
Austrian National Institute for Public Health — Literature Service in Medicine 66
Bureau Marcel van Dijk, SA 122
Business Information International 123
Capital Planning Information Ltd. 176
Centre of Information Resource & Technology, Singapore 197
Dagg Associates 253
Datasearch Business Information Ltd. 263
Editec 293
Epoch Research Corporation 298
Euroline Inc. 304
FLA Groupe La Creatique 336
Gothard House Groupof Companies, Ltd. 432
Hands-On Ltd. 472
Harker's Specialist Book Importers — Harker's Information Retrieval Systems 474
Infocon Information Services, Ltd. 516
Infoquest 520
Information India 523
Information Plus Inc. 528
Information Research Ltd. 530
Information Researchers, Inc. 531
Information Resources 532
Information Systems Design 534

Information on Demand (Continued)

Information Unlimited 535
Infytec, S.A. 537
INTERFACT/SVP AB 553
Israel — National Center of Scientific and Technological Information 616
Library & Information Consultants Ltd. 658
London Researchers 674
MANZ Info Datenvermittlung GmbH — MANZ Datenbanken 683
Mikro-Cerid 710
Monitan Information Consultants Ltd. 713
Nash Information Services Inc. 718
Netherlands Organization for Applied Scientific Research — Center for Information and Documentation 739
Nikkei SVP Co. Ltd. 756
ONLINE GmbH 774
Piedmont Consortium for Information Systems 811
Quaere Legal Resources Ltd. 829
RWK Ltd. 859
Schimmelpfeng GmbH — SchimmelpfengInformation Broker Service 866
State University of Utrecht Library — Biomedical Information Department 899
SVP Australia 908
SVP Benelux 909
SVP Canada 910
SVP Conseil 911
SVP Espana 912
SVP France 913
SVP Italia 914
SVP Korea 915
SVP Sijthoff 916
SVP South Africa Ltd. 917
SVP United Kingdom 918
Technical Information-Documentation Consultants Ltd. 963
Technology Information Center Gottingen 966
Tecnomedia 968
Update AB 1090
Warren, Inc. 1105

Library and Information Networks

Asian Network for Industrial Technology Information and Extension 34
Australia — National Library of Australia — Australian BibliographicNetwork 49
BLCMP Ltd. 91
Commission of the European Communities — Education Information Network in the European Community 215
Commonwealth Regional Renewable Energy Resources Information System 230
Consortium of Royal Library and University Libraries — Project for Integrated Catalogue Automation 239
Consortium of Royal Library and University Libraries — Project for Integrated Catalogue Automation — Netherlands Central Catalogue/Interlibrary Loan System 240
Cooperative Automation Group 246
Council of Europe — European Documentation and Information System for Education 248
European Conference of Ministers of Transport — International Co-operation in the Field of Transport Economics Documentation 309
German Library Institute 400
Health Care Literature Information Network 477
Intermarc Group 555
International Atomic Energy Agency — International Nuclear Information System 560
International Information Center for Terminology 587
International Labour Office — Conditions of Work and Welfare Facilities Branch — Clearing-house on Conditions of Work 594
International Organization for Standardization — ISO Information Network 599
International Reference Center for Community Water Supply and Sanitation — Programme on Exchange and Transfer of Information on Community Water Supply and Sanitation 601
LibraryNetwork of SIBIL Users 664
London and South Eastern Library Region 670
Multinational Association of Producers and Retailers of Electricity-Documentation 717
Organisation for Economic Co-Operation and Development — Road TransportResearch Programme — InternationalRoad Research Documentation 786
Piedmont Consortium for Information Systems 811
Scotland — National Library of Scotland — Scottish Libraries Co-operative Automation Project 869
Southeast Asian Regional Center for Graduate Study and Research in Agriculture — Agricultural Information Bank for Asia 889

Library and Information Networks (Continued)

SWALCAP 919
United Nations — Economic and Social Commission for Asia and the Pacific — Population Division — Population Clearing-house and Information Section 1003
United Nations — Food and Agriculture Organization — Aquatic Sciences and Fisheries Information System 1008
United Nations — Food and Agriculture Organization — International Information System for the Agricultural Sciences andTechnology 1012
United Nations Educational, Scientific and Cultural Organization — Center for Social Science Research and Documentation forthe Arab Region 1015
United Nations Educational, Scientific and Cultural Organization — International Bureau of Education — Documentation and Information Unit 1021
United Nations Environment Programme — INFOTERRA 1025
United Nations Industrial Development Organization — Industrial Information Section — Industrial and Technological Information Bank 1027
URBAMET Network 1091
UTLAS Inc. 1094
World Health Organization — Eastern Mediterranean Regional Office — Information Services 1112

Library Management Systems

Aball Software Inc. 2
Atomic Energy of Canada, Ltd. — Chalk River Nuclear Laboratories — Technical Information Branch 44
Blackwell Technical Services Ltd. 90
BTJ 116
Carleton University Library — Carleton Library System 179
Easy Data Systems Ltd. — Easy Data Integrated Library System 289
Eurotec Consultants Ltd. — LIBRARIAN 318
Free University of Brussels — Central Library — VUBIS 381
Great Britain — Departments of the Environment and Transport — Transport and Road Research Laboratory —Technical Information and Library Services 455
Hebrew University of Jerusalem — Automated Library Expandable Program Hebrew University of Jerusalem 478
Israel — National Center of Scientific and Technological Information — DOMESTIC 617
KTS Information Systems 646
Library Network of SIBIL Users 664
LipmanManagement Resources, Ltd. — LMR Information Systems — Adaptive Library Management System 666
Loughborough University of Technology Library — Minimal-Input Cataloguing System 678
Siemens AG — Data Processing Division — Library Network System 875
SWALCAP 919
Swets Subscription Service 942
Systemhouse Ltd. — MINISIS 953
Universal Library Systems Ltd. 1029
University of Saskatchewan Library — Systems and Planning Unit 1068

Magnetic Tape Providers

ALLM Books — Small Computer Program Index 17
Asian Institute of Technology — Regional Documentation Center — Asian Information Center for Geotechnical Engineering 30
Association for the Promotion of Industry-Agriculture — International Documentation Center for Industries Using Agricultural Products 39
Association of Social Sciences Institutes — Social Sciences Information Center 43
Australia — National Library of Australia — Australian Bibliographic Network 49
Australian Bureau of Statistics 52
Australian Business Index 53
Australian National Radio Astronomy Observatory — Parkes Catalogue of Radio Sources 59
Australian National University — Research School of Social Sciences — Australian Demographic Data Bank 60
Australian National University — Research School of Social Sciences — Social Science Data Archives 61
Austria — Minister of Finance — International Patent Documentation Center 64
Bank of England — Financial Statistics Division 72
Bayer AG — Engineering Science Division — Chemical and Process Engineering Abstracts 77
BIOSIS, U.K. Ltd. — Zoological Record 88

Magnetic Tape Providers (Continued)

BNF Metals Technology Centre — Information Department 92
Brassey's Publishers Ltd. — Brassey's Naval Record 97
Brazil — Ministry of the Interior — Documentation Coordination Unit 100
British Market Research Bureau Ltd. — Target Group Index 109
Brunel Univeristy — Brunel Institute forBioengineering — Information Unit 114
Building Services Research and Information Association — BSRIA Information Centre 119
Bulgaria — National Agro-IndustrialUnion — Agricultural Academy —Center for Scientific, Technical and Economic Information 121
Cambridge University — University Chemical Laboratory — Cambridge Crystallographic Data Centre 125
Canada — Consumer and Corporate Affairs Canada — Corporations Branch — Corporate Integrated Information System 129
Canada — Environment Canada — Inland Waters Directorate — Water Resources Branch — Water Survey of Canada 142
Canada — National Film Board of Canada — FORMAT 146
Canada — National Library of Canada — Cataloguing Branch — Canadiana Editorial Division 148
Canada — National Library of Canada — MARC Records Distribution Service 150
Canada — National Research Council of Canada — Canada Institute for Scientific and Technical Information — Scientific Numeric Databases 155
Canada — Public Archives of Canada — Machine Readable Archives Division 158
Canada — Statistics Canada — Canadian Socio-Economic Information ManagementSystem 159
Centennial College — Bibliocentre 182
Center for the Study of Advertising Support 189
ChemicalInformation Center 201
Christian Institutions Research and Documentation Center 205
Commission of the European Communities — Agricultural Research Projects Data Base 213
Commission of the European Communities — Environmental Research Projects Data Base 217
Commission of the European Communities — Euro Abstracts 218
Commission of the European Communities — Statistical Office of the European Communities — COMEXT Data Bank 224
Commodities Research Unit Ltd. 228
Commonwealth Agricultural Bureaux — CABAbstracts 229
Compu-Mark 234
Construction Specifications Canada — National Master Specification 242
Council of Europe — European Documentation and Information System for Education 248
DAFSA 251
Derwent Publications Ltd. — Chemical Reactions Documentation Service 274
Derwent Publications Ltd. — Patents Documentation Services 275
Derwent Publications Ltd. — Pest Control Literature Documentation 276
Derwent Publications Ltd. — Pharmaceutical Literature Documentation 277
Derwent Publications Ltd. — Veterinary Literature Documentation 278
Docupro 283
Economic and Social Research Council — Data Archive 291
Elsevier Science Publishers B.V. — Biomedical Division — Excerpta Medica 296
European Conference of Ministers of Transport — International Co-operation in the Field of TransportEconomics Documentation 309
European Patent Office — EDP Department — EPO Data Banks 315
Expert Information Systems Ltd. — EXIS 1 320
Extel Computing Ltd. — EXSHARE 321
Extel Statistical Services Ltd. — EXBOND 322
ExtelStatistical Services Ltd. — EXSTAT 323
Fairplay Publications Ltd. — Fairplay International Research Services 324
FARMODEX Foundation — FARMODEX Drug Data Bank 325
Federal Technical University — Technical Chemistry Laboratory — CHEMCO Physical PropertiesData Bank 327
Financial Times Business Information Ltd. — Business Information Service 328
Foundation for Science and Politics — Research Institute for International Politics and Security — Library and Documentation System 337
France — Bureau of Geologicaland Mining Research — National Geological Survey — Subsoil Data Bank 341
France — Bureau of Geological and Mining Research — National Geological Survey — World Gravimetric Data Bank 342
France — National Center for Ocean Utilization — National Bureau for Ocean Data 347
France — National Center for Scientific Research — Scientific and Technical Documentation Center 356

Magnetic Tape Providers (Continued)

France — National Center for Scientific Research — Scientific Documentation Center in Oncology — CANCERNET 357
Fraser Williams Ltd. — Fine Chemicals Directory 372
Fraunhofer Society — Information Center for Building and Physical Planning 373
Fraunhofer Society — Information Center for Building and Physical Planning — Building Research Projects Data Base 374
Fraunhofer Society — Information Center for Building and Physical Planning — Buildings Documentation Data Base 375
Fraunhofer Society — Information Center for Building and Physical Planning — Literature Compilations Data Base 376
Fraunhofer Society — Information Center for Building and Physical Planning — Regional Planning, City Planning, Housing, Building Construction Data Base 379
Fraunhofer Society — Information Center for Building and Physical Planning — Regional Planning, City Planning, Housing Research Projects Data Base 380
French Association for Standardization — Data Bases Service — Automated Standards and Regulations Information Online 382
French Stockbrokers Society — Information and Documentation Center 389
French Textile Institute — Textile Information Treatment Users' Service 390
Geosystems 394
German Electron-Synchrotron — DESY Scientific Documentation and Information Service 396
German Patent Information System 401
German Plastics Institute — Information and Documentation Services 402
German Society for Chemical Equipment — Information Systems and Data Banks Department — Chemical Technology Information System 403
German Society for Chemical Equipment — Information Systems and Data Banks Department — DECHEMA Substance Data Service 404
German Standards Institute — German Information Center for Technical Rules 407
Germany — Federal Institute for Sports Science — Documentation and Information Division — Sport and Sports-Scientific Information System 420
Germany — German National Library — BIBLIO-DATA 423
Great Britain — Atomic Energy Authority — Atomic Energy Research Establishment, Harwell — Harwell Central Information Service 434
Great Britain — Atomic Energy Authority — Atomic Energy Research Establishment, Harwell — National Chemical Emergency Centre — CHEMSAFE 435
Great Britain — British Library — Bibliographic Services Division 439
Great Britain — British Library — Bibliographic Services Division — Subject Systems Office — Preserved Context Index System 441
Great Britain — Central Statistical Office — CSO Macro-Economic Data Bank 449
Great Britain— Department of Trade and Industry — Business Statistics Office 454
Great Britain — House of Commons Library — Parliamentary On-Line Information System 459
Hohenheim University — Documentation Center on Animal Production 487
IBJ Data Service Co. 498
ICC Information Group Ltd. 499
Independent Chemical Information Services Ltd. 505
India — National Institute of Oceanography — Indian National Oceanographic Data Centre 509
Information Center for Energy, Physics, Mathematics 521
Informetrica Limited 536
Institution of Chemical Engineers — Physical Property Data Service 548
Institution of Electrical Engineers — INSPEC 549
Institution of Mining and Metallurgy — Library and Information Services 551
International Atomic Energy Agency — Nuclear Data Section 561
International Civil Aviation Organization — Air Navigation Bureau — Aerodromes Section — Airport Characteristics Data Bank 568
International Civil Aviation Organization — Air Transport Bureau — Statistics Section — Air Transport Statistical Program 569
International Company for Documentation in Chemistry 572
International Food Information Service — Food Science and Technology Abstracts 583
International Food Information Service — Packaging Science and Technology Abstracts 584
International Food Information Service — VITIS-Viticulture and Enology Abstracts 585
International Labour Office — Conditions of Work and Welfare Facilities Branch — Clearing-house on Conditions of Work 594
International Serials Data System 603
Japan — Maritime Safety Agency — Hydrographic Department — Japan Oceanographic Data Center 628
Japan — National Diet Library — Library Automation System 629
Jordan & Sons Ltd. — Jordans Company Information 636
Learned Information Ltd. 654
Library Association Publishing Ltd. — CURRENT RESEARCH in Library & Information Science 661
Library Association Publishing Ltd. — Current Technology Index 662
Library Association Publishing Ltd. — Library and Information Science Abstracts 663
Lloyd's Shipping Information Services 667
London and South Eastern Library Region 670
LymBurner & Sons Ltd. — Economist's Statistics 679
MacLean-Hunter Ltd. — Financial Post Division — Financial Post Investment Data Bank 680
Market Location 686
Motor Vehicle Documentation 716
National Elf Aquitaine Company — Documentary Information Service — STATSID 723
Netherlands — Netherlands Foreign Trade Agency — Library and Documentation Branch — Foreign Trade Abstracts 733
Netherlands Soil Survey Institute — Soil Information System 746
New Zealand — Department of Statistics — Information Network for Official Statistics 749
Nihon Keizai Shimbun, Inc. — Databank Bureau — Nikkei Economic Electronic Databank System-Time Sharing 754
Nihon Keizai Shimbun, Inc. — Quotation Information Center K.K. 755
Norwegian Center for Informatics 767
Norwegian Computing Centre for the Humanities 768
Ontario Ministry of Natural Resources — Mineral Resources Group — Ontario Geological Survey — Geoscience Data Centre 778
Organisation for Economic Co-Operation and Development — Economic Statistics and National Accounts Division — OECD Magnetic Tape Subscription Service 780
Organisation for Economic Co-Operation and Development — Nuclear Energy Agency — NEA Data Bank 785
Organisation for Economic Co-Operation and Development — Road Transport Research Programme — International Road Research Documentation 786
Pan American Health Organization — Pan American Centre for Sanitary Engineering & Environmental Sciences — Pan American Information & Documentation Network on Sanitary Engineering & Environmental Sciences 794
Philips Information Systems and Automation — DIRECT 809
Pira: Research Association for the Paper and Board, Printing and Packaging Industries — Comprehensive Information Services 812
Pulp and Paper Research Institute of Canada — Technical Information Section 827
Quebec National Library — FMQ 833
Romania — National Council for Science and Technology — National Institute for Information and Documentation 843
Royal Dutch Society for Advancement of Pharmacy — KNMP Drug Databank 844
Royal Institute of British Architects — British Architectural Library — Architectural Periodicals Index 845
Royal Netherlands Academy of Arts and Sciences — Social Science Information and Documentation Center — Steinmetz Archives 848
Royal Norwegian Council for Scientific and Industrial Research — Norwegian Seismic Array 850
Royal Society of Chemistry — Information Services 851
Royal Society of Chemistry — Information Services — Chemical Engineering Abstracts 852
Royal Society of Chemistry — Information Services — Chemical Hazards in Industry 853
Royal Society of Chemistry — Information Services — Current Biotechnology Abstracts 854
Royal Society of Chemistry — Information Services — Laboratory Hazards Bulletin 855
Royal Society of Chemistry — Information Services — Mass Spectrometry Data Centre 856
Royal Tropical Institute — Agricultural Information & Documentation Section 857
Rubber and Plastics Research Association of Great Britain — RAPRA Information Centre 858
Scotland — National Library of Scotland — Scottish Libraries Co-operative Automation Project 869
Ship Research Institute of Norway — Ship Abstracts 872
Shirley Institute — Textile Information Services 873
Siemens AG — Language Services Department — Terminology Evaluation and Acquisition Method 876
Society of Metaphysicians Ltd. — Information Services 882
Special Libraries Cataloguing, Inc. 894
Strasbourg Observatory — Stellar Data Center 905
Sweden — Geological Survey of Sweden — Groundwater Documentation Section 920
Sweden — National Road and Traffic Research Institute — Information and Documentation Section 925
Sweden — Royal Library — Library Information System 931
Sweden — Statistics Sweden — Statistical DataBases Unit 932

Magnetic Tape Providers (Continued)

Sweden — Swedish National Road Administration — Technical Division — Road Data Bank   933
Swets Subscription Service   942
Technical Information Center — Electrical Engineering Documentation Center   960
Technical Information Center — Mechanical Engineering Documentation   961
Teikoku Data Bank, Ltd.   969
Tel-Aviv University — Shiloah Research Center for Middle Eastern and African Studies — Documentation System — Mideast File   970
Telekurs Ag — Investdata System   975
Textile and Clothing Information Centre   980
Tokyo Shoko Research, Ltd. — Data Bank Service   984
Toronto StockExchange — Data Products   986
Union of Soviet Socialist Republics — U.S.S.R. State Committee on the Utilization of Atomic Energy — Center for NuclearStructure and Reaction Data   999
United Nations — Economic and Social Commission for Asia and the Pacific — ESCAP Library — ESCAP Bibliographic Information System   1002
United Nations — Food and Agriculture Organization — Aquatic Sciences and Fisheries Information System   1008
United Nations — Food and Agriculture Organization — International Information System for the Agricultural Sciences andTechnology   1012
United Nations — Food and Agriculture Organization — Library and Documentation Systems Division — David Lubin Memorial Library   1013
United Nations — Food and Agriculture Organization — Statistics Division — Interlinked Computerized Storage and Processing System ofFood and Agricultural Data   1014
United Nations Educational, Scientific and Cultural Organization — Division of Science and Technology Policies — Science and Technology Policies Information Exchange Programme   1016
United Nations Educational, Scientific and Cultural Organization — Energy Information Section   1018
United Nations Educational,Scientific and Cultural Organization — International Bureau of Education — Documentation and Information Unit   1021
United Nations Educational, Scientific and Cultural Organization — Social and Human Science Documentation Centre   1022
United Nations Environment Programme — INFOTERRA   1025
University of Aberdeen — Departmentof Political Economy — Wage Rounds Data Bank   1032
University of Alberta — Department of Sociology — Population Research Laboratory   1035
University of Bergen — Department of Scandinavian Languages and Literature — Norwegian Term Bank   1040
University of Bonn — Inorganic Chemistry Institute — Inorganic Crystal Structure Data Base   1042
University of British Columbia — Data Library   1044
University of Dortmund — Dortmund Data Bank   1046
University of Milan — Higher Institute of Sociology — Data and ProgramArchive for the Social Sciences   1058
University of New South Wales — Australian Graduate School of Management — Centre for Research in Finance   1060
University of Sydney Library — Bibliographic Information onSoutheast Asia   1073
University of Umea — Demographic Data Base   1081
University of Waterloo — Department of Recreation — Leisure Studies Data Bank   1084
UTLAS Inc.   1094
The Welding Institute — Information Services   1106
WorldHealth Organization — Division of Health Statistics — World Health Statistics Data Base   1110
World Health Organization — WHOCollaborating Centre for Collection and Evaluation of Data on Comparative Virology   1114
World Health Organization — WHO Collaborating Centre for International Drug Monitoring   1115
World Meteorological Organization — Commission for Hydrology — Operational Hydrology Programme — Hydrological Operational Multipurpose Subprogramme   1117
World Meteorological Organization — World Weather Watch   1119
York University — Institute for Behavioural Research   1120
ZincDevelopment Association/Lead Development Association/Cadmium Association — Library and Abstracting Service   1122

Micrographic Applications

African Training and Research Centre in Administration for Development — African Network of Administrative Information   7
Arctic Institute ofNorth America — Arctic Science and Technology Information System   26
Art Sales Index Ltd.   29

Micrographic Applications (Continued)

Asian Institute of Technology — Regional Documentation Center — Asian Information Center for Geotechnical Engineering   30
Asian Institute of Technology — Regional Documentation Center — Environmental Sanitation Information Center   31
Asian Institute of Technology — Regional Documentation Center— International Ferrocement Information Center   32
Asian Institute of Technology — Regional Documentation Center — Renewable Energy Resources Information Center   33
Association for the Promotion of Industry-Agriculture — International Documentation Center for Industries Using Agricultural Products   39
Atomic Energy of Canada, Ltd. — Chalk River Nuclear Laboratories — Technical Information Branch   44
Australia — Bureau of Transport Economics — BTE Information Systems   46
Australia — Commonwealth Scientific and Industrial Research Organization — Central Information, Library and Editorial Section   47
Australia — National Library of Australia   48
Australia — National Library of Australia — Australian Bibliographic Network   49
Australian Atomic Energy Commission — Lucas Heights Research Laboratories Library   51
Australian Bureau of Statistics   52
Australian Business Index   53
Australian Financial Review — INFO-LINE   55
Australian Mineral Foundation —Australian Earth Sciences Information System   57
Australian National Gallery — Library   58
Australian National University — Research School of Social Sciences — Social Science Data Archives   61
Australian Road Research Board — Australian Road Research Documentation   62
Austria — Minister of Finance — International Patent Documentation Center   64
Bangladesh National Scientific and Technical Documentation Centre   70
Bank of England — Financial Statistics Division   72
Bar-Ilan University — Institute for Information Retrieval and Computational Linguistics — Responsa Project   74
Bayer AG — Engineering Science Division — Chemical and Process Engineering Abstracts   77
Belgium — Ministry of Economic Affairs — Fonds Quetelet Library Data Base   81
Belgium —Royal Library of Belgium — National Center for Scientific and Technical Documentation   84
Bemrose Printing   85
BHRA, The Fluid Engineering Centre — Information Services   86
Bibliographic Publishing Co.   87
BIOSIS, U.K. Ltd. — Zoological Record   88
BLCMP Ltd.   91
BNF Metals Technology Centre — Information Department   92
Boreal Institute for Northern Studies —Library Services   95
Brazil — Ministry of Agriculture— National Center for Agricultural Documentary Information   99
Brazil — National Council of Scientific and Technological Development —Brazilian Institute for Information in Science and Technology   103
British Universities Film & Video Council Ltd. — Information Service   112
Brunel Univeristy — Brunel Institute for Bioengineering —Information Unit   114
BTJ   116
Bulgaria — National Agro-Industrial Union — Agricultural Academy — Center for Scientific, Technical and Economic Information   121
Canada — Consumer and Corporate Affairs Canada — Corporations Branch — Corporate Integrated Information System   129
Canada — Department of Energy, Mines and Resources — Geological Survey of Canada — National GEOSCAN Centre   135
Canada — Environment Canada — Inland Waters Directorate — Water Resources Branch — Water Survey of Canada   142
Canada —National Film Board of Canada — FORMAT   146
Canada — National Library of Canada   147
Canada — National Library of Canada — Cataloguing Branch — Canadiana Editorial Division   148
Canada — National Library of Canada — MARC Records Distribution Service   150
Canada — National Library of Canada — Public ServicesBranch — Union Catalogue of Serials Division   151
Canada — National Research Council of Canada — Canada Institute for Scientific and Technical Information   152
Canada — Public Archives of Canada — Machine Readable Archives Division   158
Canada — Transport Canada — Library and Information Centre   161
CanadianEngineering Publications Ltd. — Information Services Division   171
Canadian Micrographic Society   175
Carleton University Library— Carleton Library System   179

Micrographic Applications (Continued)

Centennial College — Bibliocentre   182
Center for Translation Documentation   191
Chemical Information Center   201
Chile — National Commission for Scientific and Technological Research — Directorate for Information and Documentation   202
Chisholm Institute of Technology Library — User Education Resources Data Base   204
The CIRPA/ADISQ Foundation   206
City of London Polytechnic — Fawcett Library — BiblioFem   209
Coaching Association of Canada — SportInformation Resource Centre   210
Commission of the European Communities — Euro Abstracts   218
Commission of the European Communities — Statistical Office of the European Communities — COMEXT Data Bank   224
Commonwealth Agricultural Bureaux — CAB Abstracts   229
Commonwealth Regional Renewable Energy Resources Information System   230
Compu-Mark Ltd.   235
Constellate Consultants Ltd.   241
Czechoslovakia — Institute for Medical Information   250
Datacrown Inc.   261
Datasearch BusinessInformation Ltd.   263
Denmark — National Technological Library of Denmark — Automated Library Information System   270
Derwent Publications Ltd. — Chemical Reactions Documentation Service   274
Derwent Publications Ltd. — Patents Documentation Services   275
Derwent Publications Ltd. — Pest Control Literature Documentation   276
Derwent Publications Ltd. — Pharmaceutical Literature Documentation   277
Derwent Publications Ltd. — Veterinary Literature Documentation   278
Documentary Research Center   282
Docupro   283
Drug Information Pharmacists Group — Pharmline   285
Elsevier Science Publishers B.V. — BiomedicalDivision — Excerpta Medica   296
European Conference of Ministers of Transport — International Co-operation in the Field of Transport Economics Documentation   309
European Patent Office — EDP Department — EPO Data Banks   315
European Space Agency — Information Retrieval Service   317
FARMODEX Foundation — FARMODEX Drug Data Bank   325
Financial Times Business Information Ltd. —Business Information Service   328
Finland — Technical Research Centre of Finland — Technical Information Service   330
France — Atomic Energy Commission — Saclay Nuclear Research Center — Documentation Center   339
France — Bureau of Geological and MiningResearch — National Geological Survey — Geological Information and Documentation Department   340
France — National Center for Scientific Research — Documentation Center for Human Sciences   355
France — National Institute for Research in Informatics and Automation — Information Dissemination Office   361
France — National Telecommunications Research Center — Interministerial Documentation Service — TELEDOC   367
Fraser Williams Ltd. — Fine Chemicals Directory   372
Fraunhofer Society — Information Center for Building and Physical Planning — Regional Planning, City Planning, Housing Research Projects Data Base   380
Free University of Brussels — Central Library — VUBIS   381
French Documentation — Political and Current Events Information Bank   384
French Water Study Association —National Water Information Center   391
Geosystems   394
German Democratic Republic — Central Institute for Information and Documentation   395
German Library Institute   400
German Plastics Institute — Information and Documentation Services   402
German Standards Institute — German Information Center for TechnicalRules   407
Germany — Federal Institute for Occupational Safety — Information and Documentation Centre for Occupational Safety   419
Great Britain — British Library — Bibliographic Services Division   439
Great Britain — British Library — Bibliographic Services Division — BLAISE   440
Great Britain — British Library — Bibliographic Services Division — Subject Systems Office — Preserved Context Index System   441
Great Britain — British Library — Lending Division   442
Great Britain — British Library — Reference Division — Eighteenth Century Short Title Catalogue   443
Great Britain — Home Office Forensic Science Service — Central Research Establishment — Operational Services Division   458
Great Britain — Water Research Centre — Library and Information Services   464
Greater London Council — Information Services Group   465
Gruner & Jahr AG & Co. — G&J Press Information Bank   468
Health Care Literature Information Network   477
Helsinki University Library — Finnish National Bibliography   482
Helsinki University of Technology — University Library/National Library for Science and Technology   483
Hungary — National Technical Information Centre and Library   496
ICC Information Group Ltd.   499
India — Council of Scientific and Industrial Research — IndianNational Scientific Documentation Centre   507
Indian Council ofSocial Science Research — Social Science Documentation Centre   511
Indonesia — National Scientific Documentation Center   512
Information Center for Materials — System for Documentation and Informationin Metallurgy   522
Information Resources Research   533
Infytec, S.A.   537
Institute for Documentation and Information in Social Medicine and Public Health   539
Institution of Electrical Engineers — INSPEC   549
Institution of Mining and Metallurgy — Library and Information Services   551
International Atomic Energy Agency — International Nuclear Information System   560
International Atomic Energy Agency — Vienna International Centre Library   562
International Bee Research Association — Apicultural Abstracts   563
International Center for Higher Studies inMediterranean Agronomy — Socioeconomic Data Bank on the Mediterranean Countries   564
International Company for Documentation in Chemistry   572
International Development Research Centre — Library   576
International Labour Office — Bureau for Labour Problems Analysis — Labour Information Database   591
International Labour Office — Central Library and Documentation Branch   593
International Labour Office — International Occupational Safety and Health Information Centre   595
International Livestock Centre for Africa — Documentation Centre   596
International Serials Data System   603
Japan Information Center of Science and Technology   632
Japan Patent Information Center   633
Jordan & Sons Ltd. —Jordans Company Information   636
Library Association PublishingLtd. — British Humanities Index   660
Library Association Publishing Ltd. — Current Technology Index   662
Library Association Publishing Ltd. — Library and Information Science Abstracts   663
Lloyd's Shipping Information Services   667
London andSouth Eastern Library Region   670
Loughborough University of Technology — Chemical Engineering Department — Particle Science and Technology Information Service   676
Loughborough University of Technology Library — Library Instruction Materials Bank   677
Loughborough University of Technology Library — Minimal-Input Cataloguing System   678
Maruzen Company, Ltd. — Maruzen Scientific Information Service Center   689
McCarthy Information Ltd.   690
Medical-Pharmaceutical Publishing Company   693
Memorial University of Newfoundland — Ocean Engineering Information Centre   694
Microinfo, Ltd.   705
Micromedia Ltd.   706
Motor Vehicle Documentation   716
Nash Information Services Inc.   718
National Computing Centre Ltd. — Information Services Division   721
National Foundation for Educational Research in England andWales — Information Research and Development Unit   724
National Reprographic Centre for Documentation   725
National Science Council — Science and Technology Information Center   726
Natural Environment Research Council — British Geological Survey — National Geochemical Data Bank   728
Netherlands — Ministry of Agriculture andFisheries — Agricultural Research Division — Centre for AgriculturalPublishing and Documentation   731
Netherlands — Netherlands Foreign Trade Agency — Library and Documentation Branch — Foreign Trade Abstracts   733
New Zealand — Department of Scientific and Industrial Research — DSIR Central Library   748
Nineteenth CenturyShort Title Catalogue Project   757
Nippon Gijutsu Boeki Co., Ltd.   758
Nordic Atomic Libraries Joint Secretariat — Nordic Energy Index   761

Micrographic Applications (Continued)

Norwegian Computing Centre for the Humanities 768
Ontario Ministry of Natural Resources — Mineral Resources Group — Ontario Geological Survey — Geoscience Data Centre 778
Organisation for Economic Co-Operation and Development — Economic Statistics and National Accounts Division — OECD Magnetic Tape Subscription Service 780
Organisation for Economic Co-Operation and Development — International Energy Agency — IEA Coal Research — Technical InformationService 782
Organisation for Economic Co-Operation and Development — Road Transport Research Programme — International Road Research Documentation 786
Oriel Computer Services Limited 787
Oxford Microform Publications Ltd. 791
Pakistan Scientificand Technological Information Centre 793
Pan American Health Organization — Pan American Centre for Sanitary Engineering & Environmental Sciences — Pan American Information & Documentation Network on Sanitary Engineering & Environmental Sciences 794
Pergamon Press — Current Awareness in Biological Sciences 803
Philips Information Systemsand Automation — DIRECT 809
Poland — Polish Academy of Sciences — Scientific Information Center 816
Pressurklipp — Swedish Market Information Bank 824
Pulp and Paper Research Institute of Canada — Technical Information Section 827
Quebec Ministryof Education — Library Headquarters — Point de Repere 831
Quebec Society for Legal Information 834
Ringier & Co. — Ringier Documentation Center 841
Riso National Laboratory — Riso Library 842
Romania — National Council for Science and Technology — National Institute for Information and Documentation 843
Royal Dutch Society for Advancement of Pharmacy — KNMP Drug Databank 844
Royal Institute of British Architects — British Architectural Library — Architectural Periodicals Index 845
Royal Netherlands Academy of Arts and Sciences — Social Science Information and Documentation Center 847
Royal Netherlands Academy of Arts and Sciences — Social Science Information and Documentation Center — Steinmetz Archives 848
Royal Society of Chemistry — InformationServices 851
Scientific Documentation Centre Ltd. 868
Scotland — National Library of Scotland — Scottish Libraries Co-operative Automation Project 869
Servi-Tech — BIODOC 870
Shirley Institute — Textile Information Services 873
Siemens AG — Language Services Department — Terminology Evaluation and Acquisition Method 876
Society for Information and Documentation — GID Information Center for Information Science and Practice 880
South Africa — Council for Scientific and Industrial Research —Centre for Scientific and Technical Information 885
Southeast Asian Regional Center for Graduate Study and Research in Agriculture — Agricultural Information Bank for Asia 889
Special Libraries Cataloguing, Inc. 894
The Stock Exchange — Technical Services Department — TOPIC 902
Strasbourg Observatory — Stellar Data Center 905
Studsvik Energiteknik AB — Report Collection Index 906
Sweden — Karolinska Institute Library and Information Center 921
Sweden — Royal Library — Library Information System 931
Sweden — Swedish National Road Administration — Technical Division — Road Data Bank 933
Swets Subscription Service 942
SYDONI S.A. 949
Technical Indexes Ltd. 958
Technology Resource Center — Technobank Program 967
Tel-Aviv University — Shiloah Research Center for Middle Eastern and African Studies — Documentation System — Mideast File 970
Union of Soviet Socialist Republics — All-Union Institute of Scientific and Technical Information 998
United Nations — Economic and Social Commission for Asia and the Pacific — Population Division — Population Clearing-house and Information Section 1003
United Nations — Economic Commission for Africa — Pan-African Documentation and Information System 1005
United Nations — Food and Agriculture Organization — Library and Documentation Systems Division — David Lubin Memorial Library 1013
United Nations Educational, Scientific and Cultural Organization — Center for Social Science Research and Documentation forthe Arab Region 1015
United Nations Educational, Scientific and Cultural Organization — International Bureau of Education — Documentation and Information Unit 1021
University Library of Hannover and Technical Information Library 1031

University of Bergen — Department of Scandinavian Languages and Literature — Norwegian Term Bank 1040
University of British Columbia — Data Library 1044
University of Guelph Library — Cooperative Documents Network Project 1050
University of New South Wales — Australian Graduate School of Management — Centre for Research in Finance 1060
University of Oslo — Royal University Library — Planning Department 1061
University of Quebec — Direct Access Data Bank at the University of Quebec 1064
University of Reading Library — Location Register of Twentieth Century English Literary Manuscripts and Letters 1065
University of Saskatchewan Library — Systems and Planning Unit 1068
University of Sydney — Sample Survey Centre 1072
University of Sydney Library — Bibliographic Information on Southeast Asia 1073
University of Trondheim — Norwegian Institute of Technology —University Library 1079
University of Tsukuba — Science Information Processing Center 1080
University of Waterloo — Faculty of Human Kinetics and Leisure Studies — Information Retrieval System forthe Sociology of Leisure and Sport 1085
URBAMET Network 1091
UTLAS Inc. 1094
The Welding Institute — Information Services 1106
World Health Organization — WHO Collaborating Centre for Collection and Evaluation of Data on ComparativeVirology 1114
World Health Organization — WHO CollaboratingCentre for International Drug Monitoring 1115
World Meteorological Organization — World Weather Watch 1119
York University— Institute for Behavioural Research 1120
Yugoslav Center for Technical andScientific Documentation 1121

Online Host Services

ACI Computer Services 3
Alpha 460 Television Ltd. 18
American College in Paris — Service Calvados 22
Art Sales Index Ltd. 29
Association for Research and Development of Chemical Informatics — DARC Pluridata System 38
Australia — Commonwealth Scientific and Industrial Research Organization — Central Information, Library and Editorial Section 47
Australia — National Library of Australia — Australian Bibliographic Network 49
Australia — National Library of Australia — Australian MEDLINE Network 50
Australian Atomic Energy Commission — Lucas Heights Research Laboratories Library 51
Austria — Minister of Finance — International Patent Documentation Center 64
Bank Group for Automation in Management 71
Bar-Ilan University — Institute for Information Retrieval and Computational Linguistics — Responsa Project 74
Bavarian Ministry for Food, Agriculture and Forestry — Bavarian Agricultural Information System 76
Belgium — Ministry ofEconomic Affairs — Data Processing Center — Belgian Information and Dissemination Service 80
Blackwell Technical Services Ltd. 90
BLCMP Ltd. 91
Bonnier Business Publishing Group —AffarsData 94
British Broadcasting Corporation— CEEFAX 105
BTJ 116
Building Services Research and Information Association — BSRIA Information Centre 119
Calgary Public Information Department — Public Relations Division — Civichannel 124
Canada — Agriculture Canada — Scientific Information Retrieval Section — Pesticide Research Information System 128
Canada — Department of Energy, Mines and Resources — Canada Centre for Remote Sensing — Remote Sensing On-Line Retrieval System 132
Canada— Environment Canada — Inland Waters Directorate — Water Quality Branch — National Water Quality Data Bank 141
Canada — Environment Canada — Lands Directorate — Canada Land Data Systems Division — Canada Geographic Information System 143
Canada— National Research Council of Canada — Canada Institute for Scientific and Technical Information — Canadian Online Enquiry System 153

Online Host Services (Continued)

Canada — National Research Council of Canada — Canada Institute for Scientific and Technical Information — Scientific Numeric Databases 155
Canada — Statistics Canada — Canadian Socio-Economic Information Management System — Telichart 160
Canada Systems Group — Federal Systems Division — Canadian Federal Corporations and Directors Data Base 163
Canadian Broadcasting Corporation — Project IRIS 169
Carleton University Library — Carleton Library System 179
Centennial College — Bibliocentre 182
Central Electronic Network for Data Processing and Analysis 194
Central Ontario Regional Library System — Interlibrary Loan and Communication System 195
The CIRPA/ADISQ Foundation 206
CISI-Wharton Econometric Forecasting Associates Ltd. 207
Commission of the European Communities — European Commission Host Organization 219
Commission of the European Communities — European On-Line Information Network — Direct Information Access Network for Europe 220
Communication Services Ltd. — Viewdata Services 231
Compusearch Market and Social Research Ltd. 236
Computer Sciences of Australia Pty. Ltd. — Network Services Division — INFOBANK 237
Conference Board of Canada — Applied Economic Research and Information Centre — AERIC System 238
Consortium of Royal Library and University Libraries — Project for Integrated Catalogue Automation 239
Consortium of Royal Library and University Libraries — Project for Integrated Catalogue Automation — Netherlands Central Catalogue/Interlibrary Loan System 240
Control Data Australia Pty. Ltd. — CYBERTEL Videotex Service 245
Cumulus Systems Ltd. 249
Data Bank for Medicaments 257
DataArkiv AB 260
Datacrown Inc. 261
Dataline Inc. 262
Datasolve Ltd. — World Exporter 264
Datasolve Ltd. — World Reporter 265
Data-Star 266
Datastream International Ltd. 267
Denmark — Posts and Telegraphs Denmark — Central Telecommunications Services — DATAPAK 271
Denmark Telecommunications Administration — Danish Teledata System 272
Dutch State Mines — TISDATA 286
Eastern Telecommunications Philippines, Inc. — Database Access Service 288
Esselte Business Information 301
European Patent Office — EDP Department — EPO Data Banks 315
European Space Agency — Information Retrieval Service 317
Expert Information Systems Ltd. — EXIS 1 320
Faxtel Information Systems Ltd. — Marketfax 326
Finland — Central Medical Library — MEDIC Data Base 329
Finsbury Data Services Ltd. — TEXTLINE 335
Foundation for Science and Politics — Research Institute for International Politics and Security — Library and Documentation System 337
France — Ministry of Defense — General Office for Ordnance — Center for Documentation on Ordnance 345
France — National Center for Ocean Utilization — National Bureau for Ocean Data 347
FRI Information Services Ltd. 392
German Iron and Steel Engineers Association — Steel Information System 399
German Library Institute 400
German Standards Institute — German Information Center for Technical Rules 407
Germany — Ministry of Justice — Judicial Information System 426
Germany — Ministry of Posts and Telecommunications — German Federal Postal Service — Bildschirmtext 427
Germany — Ministry of Youth, Family and Health — German Institute for Medical Documentation and Information 428
The Globe and Mail — Info Globe 430
Great Britain — British Library — Bibliographic Services Division — BLAISE 440
Great Britain — British Telecommunications — Packet SwitchStream 447
Great Britain — British Telecommunications — Prestel 448
GSI-ECO 469
Harris Media Systems Ltd. 475
Hartmann & Heenemann — Computer Composition Center 476
Hebrew University of Jerusalem — Automated Library Expandable Program Hebrew University of Jerusalem 478
Helsingin Telset Oy — Telset 480
Helsinki School of Economics Library — Information Services 481

Helsinki University of Technology — University Library/National Library for Science and Technology 483
Honeywell Bull — Euris Host Service 488
Hungarian Academy of Sciences Library — Department for Informatics and Science Analysis 492
I/S Datacentralen 497
ICC Information Group Ltd. 499
IFO-Institute for Economic Research — Department of Econometrics and Data Processing — IFO Time Series Data Bank 501
Imperial Chemical Industries Ltd. — Agricultural Division — Management Services Department — ASSASSIN 503
IMSA.G. — MIDAS 504
Industrial Life-Technical Services Inc. 513
Infomart 518
Infomart — Grassroots 519
Information Center for Energy, Physics, Mathematics 521
International Atomic Energy Agency — International Nuclear Information System 560
International Centre for Scientific and Technical Information 565
International Development Research Centre — Library 576
International Information Services Company 589
Interprofessional Technical Union of the National Federations of Buildings and Public Works — Center for Technical Assistance and Documentation — ARIANE Data Bank 610
IST-Informatheque Inc. 619
ItalCable — Direct Access to Remote Data Bases Overseas 620
Italian Society for Telephone Use — Videotel 622
Italy — National Research Council — CNUCE Institute 623
Japan Information Center of Science and Technology 632
Japan Patent Information Center 633
Jordan & Sons Ltd. — Jordans Company Information 636
K-Konsult — VA-NYTT 637
Kluwer Publishing Company — Juridical Databank 641
Leigh-Bell & Associates Ltd. 657
Linkoping University Library — NYTTFO 665
Lloyd's Shipping Information Services 667
Lombard Interuniversity Consortium for Data Processing 669
London and South Eastern Library Region 670
LymBurner & Sons Ltd. — Economist's Statistics 679
Marketing Intelligence Corporation 688
Maruzen Company, Ltd. — Maruzen Scientific Information Service Center 689
Metropolitan Toronto Library Board — Regional Bibliographic Products Department 699
Netherlands Office of Posts, Telegraphs, and Telephones — PTT Central Directorate — Viditel 738
New Zealand — Department of Statistics — Information Network for Official Statistics 749
Nihon Keizai Shimbun, Inc. — Databank Bureau — Nikkei Economic Electronic Databank System-Information Retrieval 753
Nihon Keizai Shimbun, Inc. — Databank Bureau — Nikkei Economic Electronic Databank System-Time Sharing 754
Nihon Keizai Shimbun, Inc. — Quotation Information Center K.K. 755
Nippon Telegraph & Telephone Public Corporation — CAPTAIN 759
Norwegian Center for Informatics 767
Norwegian Standards Association — STANDARD 772
ORACLE Teletext Ltd. 779
Overseas Telecommunications Commission — Multimode International Data Acquisition Service 790
Pergamon InfoLine Ltd. 802
Polytechnical School of Montreal — Telidon Technology Development Center 819
Portuguese Radio Marconi Company — Data Bank Access Service 822
Press Association Ltd. — NEWSFILE 823
QL Systems Limited 828
Quebec — French Language Board — Terminology Bank of Quebec 830
Quebec Ministry of Education — Library Headquarters — Point de Repere 831
Quebec Society for Legal Information 834
QUOTEL Insurance Services Ltd. 837
Rene Descartes University — Laboratory of Applied Anthropology — ERGODATA 838
Royal Norwegian Council for Scientific and Industrial Research — Norwegian Seismic Array 850
Sabadell Computing Center 860
Saskatchewan Telecommunications — Agritex 862
Scicon Ltd. 867
Scotland — National Library of Scotland — Scottish Libraries Co-operative Automation Project 869
Sharp Associates Limited 871
SLIGOS 879
Society for Information and Documentation — GID Information Center for Information Science and Practice 880
Society for the Study of Economic and Social Development — MERCATIS 881

Online Host Services (Continued)

SouthAfrica — Council for Scientific and Industrial Research — Centre for Scientific and Technical Information 885
South African Medical Research Council — Institute for Medical Literature 888
Spanish Drug Information Center — Spanish Pharmaceutical Specialities Data Bank 893
STN International 901
The Stock Exchange — Technical Services Department — TOPIC 902
Stockholm School ofEconomics — Economics Research Institute — FINDATA 903
Stockholm University Computing Center, QZ 904
Studsvik Energiteknik AB — Report Collection Index 906
SWALCAP 919
Sweden — Karolinska Institute Library and Information Center 921
Sweden — National Board of Health and Welfare — Department of Drugs — Swedish Drug Information System 922
Sweden — National Board of Occupational Safety and Health — CISCentre 923
Sweden — National Swedish Telecommunications Administration — Datapak 927
Sweden — Royal Institute of Technology Library — Information and Documentation Center 930
Sweden — Royal Library —Library Information System 931
Swedish Building Centre — Building Commodity File 934
Swedish Center for Working Life — Information and Documentation Department 935
Swedish Institute of Building Documentation 938
System Development Corporation ofJapan, Ltd. — Search/J 952
Technical Information Center 959
Technical University of Wroclaw — Main Library and Scientific Information Center — System of Computerized Processing of Scientific Information 965
Telecom Canada — Datapac 971
Telecom Canada — iNet 2000 972
Telekurs Ag — Investdata System 975
Telemap Ltd. — Micronet 800 976
Telesystemes — Questel 977
TESS Search Service 979
Thermodata Association — Thermodata-ThermdocData Bank 981
Transpac 989
TT Newsbank 990
Unilever Computer Services Ltd. — European Petrochemical Association Trade Statistics Database 993
Unilever Computer ServicesLtd. — World Trade Statistics Database 994
United Nations — Economic Commission for Africa — Pan-African Documentation and Information System 1005
United Nations — Food and Agriculture Organization — INFOFISH 1011
University of Alberta — Computing Services — Information SystemsGroup 1033
University of Gothenburg — MEDICINDATA 1049
University of New Brunswick Libraries — PHOENIX 1059
University of Oslo — Royal University Library — Planning Department 1061
University of Quebec — Direct Access Data Bank at the University of Quebec 1064
University of Tokyo — Computer Center — University of Tokyo On-Line Information Retrieval System 1075
University of Tsukuba — Science Information Processing Center 1080
University of Umea — DemographicData Base 1081
University of Waterloo — Faculty of Human Kinetics and Leisure Studies — Information Retrieval System for the Sociology of Leisure and Sport 1085
University of Western Ontario — Systems Analysis, Control and Design Activity 1088
UTLAS Inc. 1094
World Health Organization — WHO Collaborating Centre for International Drug Monitoring 1115

Personal Computer Oriented Services

Aball Software Inc. 2
ALLM Books — Small Computer Program Index 17
American College in Paris — Service Calvados 22
AVCOR 67
Canada — Statistics Canada — Canadian Socio-EconomicInformation Management System — Telichart 160
The CIRPA/ADISQ Foundation 206
CommunicationServices Ltd. — Viewdata Services 231
Eurotec Consultants Ltd. — LIBRARIAN 318
Extel Computing Ltd. — EXSHARE 321
Extel Statistical Services Ltd. — EXSTAT 323

Personal Computer Oriented Services (Continued)

Fraser Videotex Services 369
Great Britain — Atomic Energy Authority — Atomic Energy Research Establishment, Harwell — National Chemical Emergency Centre — CHEMSAFE 435
Information Management & Engineering Ltd. 527
Polytechnic of Central London — Information Technology Centre 818
Queen's University of Belfast — Department of Computer Science — Queen's University Interrogation of Legal Literature 836
Tayson Information Technology Inc. 956
Telemap Ltd. — Micronet 800 976
University of London — Central Information Service 1055
Userlink Systems Ltd. 1093
UTLAS Inc. 1094

Research and Research Projects

Aslib, The Associationfor Information Management 35
Belgium — Royal Library of Belgium — National Center for Scientific and Technical Documentation 84
Cambridge University — University Chemical Laboratory — Cambridge Crystallographic Data Centre 125
Canadian Law Information Council 173
Colombian Fund for Scientific Research — National Information System 212
Council for Educational Technology — Videotex Services Unit 247
Denmark — Ministry of Cultural Affairs — National Advisory Council for Danish Research Libraries 269
Finnish Council for Scientific Information and Research Libraries 331
France — Interministerial Mission for Scientific and Technical Information 344
France — National Center for Scientific Research — Scientific and Technical Documentation Center 356
France — National Institute for Research in Informatics and Automation — Information Dissemination Office 361
German Library Institute 400
Great Britain — British Library — Research and DevelopmentDepartment 444
Hertfordshire County Council — Chiltern Advisory Unit for Computer Based Education 485
Hungary — Ministry for Building and Urban Development — Information Centre for Building 494
Hungary — National Szechenyi Library — Centre for Library Science and Methodology 495
Information Resources Research 533
International Electronic Publishing Research Centre 577
Iran — Ministry of Culture and Higher Education — Iranian Documentation Centre 613
Italy — National Research Council — CNUCE Institute 623
Kyushu University — Research Institute of Fundamental Information Science 648
Library and Information Research Group 659
Logica UK Ltd. 668
LoughboroughUniversity of Technology — Centre for Library and Information Management 675
Netherlands Organization for Applied Scientific Research — Institute TNO for Mathematics, Information Processing and Statistics 741
People's Republic of China — Institute of Scientific and Technical Information of China 801
Pira:Research Association for the Paper and Board, Printing and Packaging Industries— Printing and Information Technology Division 813
Poland — Institute for Scientific, Technical and Economic Information 815
Poland — Polish Academy ofSciences — Scientific Information Center 816
Socioscope Inc. 883
Survey Force Ltd. 907
Sweden — Research Institute of National Defense — FOA Index Group 929
Sweden — Royal Institute of Technology Library — Information and Documentation Center 930
Union of Soviet Socialist Republics — All-Union Institute of Scientific and Technical Information 998
Universityof Bath — Centre for Catalogue Research 1039
University of Leicester — Primary Communications Research Centre 1054
University of Sheffield — Centre for Research on User Studies 1070
Van Halm & Associates 1095
Yugoslav Center for Technical andScientific Documentation 1121

SDI/Current Awareness

ADIS Press Australasia Pty Ltd. — ADIS Drug Information Retrieval System 5
Admedia — Adfacts 6
Alberta Research Council — Industrial Development Department — Industrial Information 15
Alpine Science Information Service 21
Argentina — National Council for Scientific and Technical Research — Argentine Center for Scientific and Technological Information 28
Asian Institute of Technology — Regional Documentation Center — Asian Information Center for Geotechnical Engineering 30
Asian Institute of Technology — Regional Documentation Center — Environmental Sanitation Information Center 31
Asian Institute of Technology — Regional Documentation Center — International Ferrocement Information Center 32
Asian Institute of Technology — Regional Documentation Center — Renewable Energy Resources Information Center 33
Asian Network for Industrial Technology Information and Extension 34
Association for Information Brokerage and Technological Consultancy — IRS Info-Institute 36
Association for the Promotion of Industry-Agriculture — International Documentation Center for Industries Using Agricultural Products 39
Association of Social Sciences Institutes — Social Sciences Information Center 43
Atomic Energy of Canada, Ltd. — Chalk River Nuclear Laboratories — Technical Information Branch 44
Atomic Energy of Canada, Ltd. — Whiteshell Nuclear Research Establishment — Technical Information Services 45
Australia — Commonwealth Scientific and Industrial Research Organization — Central Information, Library and Editorial Section 47
Australia — National Library of Australia — Australian MEDLINE Network 50
Australian Atomic Energy Commission — Lucas Heights Research Laboratories Library 51
Australian Road Research Board — Australian Road Research Documentation 62
Austria — Federal Ministry of Buildings and Technology — Federal Research and Testing Establishment Arsenal — Road Research Documentation Center 63
Austrian Documentation Centre for Media and Communication Research 65
Austrian National Institute for Public Health — Literature Service in Medicine 66
Belgium — Ministry of Economic Affairs — Data Processing Center — Belgian Information and Dissemination Service 80
Belgium — Royal Library of Belgium — National Center for Scientific and Technical Documentation 84
Boris Kidric Institute of Nuclear Sciences — Laboratory for Information Systems 96
Brassey's Publishers Ltd. — Brassey's Naval Record 97
Brazil — Ministry of Agriculture — National Center for Agricultural Documentary Information 99
Brazil — National Commission for Nuclear Energy — Center for Nuclear Information 102
Brown's Geological Information Service Ltd. 113
Brunel Univeristy — Brunel Institute for Bioengineering — Information Unit 114
Building Center 117
Bulgaria — Medical Academy — Center for Scientific Information in Medicine and Health 120
Bulgaria — National Agro-Industrial Union — Agricultural Academy — Center for Scientific, Technical and Economic Information 121
Bureau Marcel van Dijk, SA 122
Business Information International 123
Cambridge University — University Chemical Laboratory — Cambridge Crystallographic Data Centre 125
Canada — Department of Energy, Mines and Resources — Canada Centre for Mineral and Energy Technology — Technology Information Division 131
Canada — National Library of Canada 147
Canada — National Research Council of Canada — Canada Institute for Scientific and Technical Information 152
Canada — National Research Council of Canada — Canada Institute for Scientific and Technical Information — Canadian Service for the Selective Dissemination of Information 154
Canada — Parliament of Canada — Library of Parliament 157
Canada — Transport Canada — Library and Information Centre 161
Caribbean Industrial Research Institute — Technical Information Service 177
Center for Scientific and Technical Research for the Metal Manufacturing Industry — Fabrimetal 187
Centre of Information Resource & Technology, Singapore 197
Chemical Information Center 201
Christian Institutions Research and Documentation Center 205
Coaching Association of Canada — Sport Information Resource Centre 210

Commission of the European Communities — Tenders Electronic Daily 227
Compu-Mark 234
Constellate Consultants Ltd. 241
Czechoslovakia — Institute for Medical Information 250
Data Processing Services Company — DPS Information Centre 258
Dataline Inc. 262
Data-Star 266
Dobra Iron and Steel Research Institute — Informetal 281
Editec 293
Editions Techniques — JURIS-DATA 294
Electricite de France — Office of Study and Research — Information and Documentation Systems Department — EDF-DOC Data Base 295
Elsevier Science Publishers B.V. — Biomedical Division — Excerpta Medica 296
Espial Productions 300
European Conference of Ministers of Transport — International Co-operation in the Field of Transport Economics Documentation 309
European Space Agency — Information Retrieval Service 317
Financial Times Business Information Ltd. — Business Information Service 328
Finland — Technical Research Centre of Finland — Technical Information Service 330
France — Atomic Energy Commission — Saclay Nuclear Research Center — Documentation Center 339
France — Bureau of Geological and Mining Research — National Geological Survey — Geological Information and Documentation Department 340
France — National Center for Ocean Utilization — National Bureau for Ocean Data 347
France — National Center for Scientific Research — Documentation Center for Human Sciences 355
France — National Center for Scientific Research — Scientific and Technical Documentation Center 356
France — National Center for Scientific Research — Scientific Documentation Center in Oncology — CANCERNET 357
France — National Telecommunications Research Center — Interministerial Documentation Service — TELEDOC 367
Fraunhofer Society — Information Center for Building and Physical Planning 373
Fraunhofer Society — Information Center for Building and Physical Planning — Building Research Projects Data Base 374
Fraunhofer Society — Information Center for Building and Physical Planning — Buildings Documentation Data Base 375
Fraunhofer Society — Information Center for Building and Physical Planning — Literature Compilations Data Base 376
Fraunhofer Society — Information Center for Building and Physical Planning — PASCALBAT Data Base 377
Fraunhofer Society — Information Center for Building and Physical Planning — Property Services Agency Information on Construction and Architecture Data Base 378
Fraunhofer Society — Information Center for Building and Physical Planning — Regional Planning, City Planning, Housing, Building Construction Data Base 379
Fraunhofer Society — Information Center for Building and Physical Planning — Regional Planning, City Planning, Housing Research Projects Data Base 380
Free University of Brussels — Central Library — VUBIS 381
French Institute of Energy — Energy Studies and Information Center 386
French Petroleum Institute — Documentation Center 387
French Textile Institute — Textile Information Treatment Users' Service 390
French Water Study Association — National Water Information Center 391
Geosystems 394
German Electron-Synchrotron — DESY Scientific Documentation and Information Service 396
German Patent Information System 401
German Plastics Institute — Information and Documentation Services 402
German Society for Chemical Equipment — Information Systems and Data Banks Department — Chemical Technology Information System 403
German Society for Chemical Equipment — Information Systems and Data Banks Department — Materials and Corrosion Information System 405
German Standards Institute — German Information Center for Technical Rules 407
Germany — Federal Employment Institute — Institute for Employment Research — Information and Documentation Department 410
Germany — Federal Environmental Agency — Environmental Information and Documentation System 411
Germany — Federal Institute for Geosciences and Natural Resources — Geoscience Literature Information Service 412

SDI/Current Awareness (Continued)

Germany — Federal Institute for Geosciences and Natural Resources — Marine Information and Documentation System 413
Germany — Federal Institute for Materials Testing — Nondestructive Testing Documentation 416
Germany — Federal Institute for Materials Testing — Rheology and Tribology Documentation Center 417
Germany — Federal Institute for Occupational Safety — Information and Documentation Centre for Occupational Safety 419
Germany — Federal Research Center for Fisheries — Information and Documentation Center 421
Germany — Ministry of Youth, Family and Health — German Institute for Medical Documentation and Information 428
Glass Institute — Information and Documentation Service 429
Gothard House Group of Companies, Ltd. 432
Great Britain — Atomic Energy Authority — Atomic Energy Research Establishment, Harwell — Harwell Central Information Service 434
Great Britain — Atomic Energy Authority — Atomic Energy Research Establishment, Harwell — Nondestructive Testing Centre — Quality Technology Information Service 436
Great Britain — Atomic Energy Authority — Culham Laboratory — Plasma Physics Library and Information Service 438
Great Britain — British Library — Bibliographic Services Division 439
Great Britain — British Library — Bibliographic Services Division — BLAISE 440
Great Britain — British Library — Science Reference Library — Computer Search Service 445
Great Britain — Departments of the Environment and Transport — Transport and Road Research Laboratory — Technical Information and Library Services 455
Great Britain — House of Lords — Library & Information Centre 460
Great Britain — Water Research Centre — Library and Information Services 464
Harker's Specialist Book Importers — Harker's Information Retrieval Systems 474
Health Care Literature Information Network 477
Helsinki School of Economics Library — Information Services 481
Helsinki University of Technology — University Library/National Library for Science and Technology 483
Hohenheim University — Documentation Center on Animal Production 487
Hungarian Academy of Sciences Library — Department for Informatics and Science Analysis 492
Hungary — Ministry for Building and Urban Development — Information Centre for Building 494
Hungary — National Szechenyi Library — Centre for Library Science and Methodology 495
I/S Datacentralen 497
ICC Information Group Ltd. 499
India — Council of Scientific and Industrial Research — Indian National Scientific Documentation Centre 507
Indian Council of Agricultural Research — Agricultural Research Information Centre 510
Infoquest 520
Information Center for Energy, Physics, Mathematics 521
Information Researchers, Inc. 531
Information Systems Design 534
Information Unlimited 535
Institute of Nutrition — Documentation Department 545
Institution of Electrical Engineers — INSPEC 549
Institution of Mining and Metallurgy — Library and Information Services 551
INTERFACT/SVP AB 553
International Atomic Energy Agency — Vienna International Centre Library 562
International Centre for Scientific and Technical Information 565
International Coffee Organization — COFFEELINE 570
International Company for Documentation in Chemistry 572
International Development Research Centre — Library 576
International Food Information Service — Food Science and Technology Abstracts 583
International Food Information Service — Packaging Science and Technology Abstracts 584
International Food Information Service — VITIS-Viticulture and Enology Abstracts 585
International Labour Office — Central Library and Documentation Branch 593
International Livestock Centre for Africa — Documentation Centre 596
International Medical Information Center 598
International Reference Center for Community Water Supply and Sanitation — Programme on Exchange and Transfer of Information on Community Water Supply and Sanitation 601
Interprofessional Technical Union of the National Federations of Buildings and Public Works — Center for Technical Assistance and Documentation — ARIANE Data Bank 610
Interuniversity Documentation and Information Center for the Social Sciences 611

Israel — National Center of Scientific and Technological Information 616
Israel Atomic Energy Commission — Soreq Nuclear Research Center — Library and Technical Information Department 618
IST-Informatheque Inc. 619
Japan Association for International Chemical Information 630
Japan Information Center of Science and Technology 632
Japan Patent Information Center 633
Jordan & Sons Ltd. — Jordans Company Information 636
Kiel Institute for World Economics — National Library of Economics 639
Kinokuniya Company Ltd. — ASK Information Retrieval Services 640
Korea Institute for Industrial Economics and Technology 645
Laval University Library — SDI/Laval & Telereference Service 652
Leatherhead Food Research Association — Information and Library Services 655
Loughborough University of Technology — Chemical Engineering Department — Particle Science and Technology Information Service 676
Loughborough University of Technology Library — Library Instruction Materials Bank 677
Marine Biological Association of the United Kingdom — Marine Pollution Information Centre 684
Maruzen Company, Ltd. — Maruzen Scientific Information Service Center 689
McCarthy Information Ltd. 690
Mexico — National Center for Health Information and Documentation 700
Mexico — National Council of Science and Technology — Data Base Consultation Service 701
Mexico — National Institute of Nuclear Research — Nuclear Information and Documentation Center 703
Mikro-Cerid 710
Mitaka — JAPANSCAN 712
Motor Vehicle Documentation 716
National Autonomous University of Mexico — Center for Scientific and Humanistic Information 719
National Center for Chemical Information 720
National Foundation for Educational Research in England and Wales — Information Research and Development Unit 724
National Science Council — Science and Technology Information Center 726
Natural Environment Research Council — British Geological Survey — Minerals Strategy and Economics Research Group — Mineral Information Section 727
Netherlands — Ministry of Agriculture and Fisheries — Agricultural Research Division — Centre for Agricultural Publishing and Documentation 731
Netherlands Organization for Applied Scientific Research — Center for Information and Documentation 739
Newfoundland Department of Mines & Energy — Mineral Development Division Library — Computerized Retrieval Services 750
Nihon Keizai Shimbun, Inc. — Databank Bureau — Nikkei Economic Electronic Databank System-Information Retrieval 753
Nippon Gijutsu Boeki Co., Ltd. 758
North Rhine-Westphalia Institute for Air Pollution Control — Literature Information System 765
ONLINE GmbH 774
Organisation for Economic Co-Operation and Development — International Energy Agency — IEA Coal Research — Technical Information Service 782
Organisation for Economic Co-Operation and Development — Road Transport Research Programme — International Road Research Documentation 786
Paint Research Association — Information Department — World Surface Coatings Abstracts 792
Pan American Health Organization — Pan American Centre for Sanitary Engineering & Environmental Sciences — Pan American Information & Documentation Network on Sanitary Engineering & Environmental Sciences 794
People's Republic of China — Institute of Scientific and Technical Information of China 801
Pergamon InfoLine Ltd. 802
Pergamon Press — Current Awareness in Biological Sciences 803
Philippines — National Science and Technology Authority — Scientific Clearinghouse and Documentation Services Division 808
Philips Information Systems and Automation — DIRECT 809
Pira: Research Association for the Paper and Board, Printing and Packaging Industries — Comprehensive Information Services 812
Portugal — National Institute for Scientific Research — Scientific and Technical Documentation Center 821
Production Engineering Research Association of Great Britain — Information Services 826
Pulp and Paper Research Institute of Canada — Technical Information Section 827
Riso National Laboratory — Riso Library 842

SDI/Current Awareness (Continued)

Romania— National Council for Science and Technology — National Institute for Information and Documentation 843
Royal Museum of Central Africa — Center for Informatics Applied to Development and Tropical Agriculture —Agroclimatology Data Bank 846
Royal Netherlands Academy of Arts and Sciences Library 849
Royal Society of Chemistry — Information Services 851
Royal Tropical Institute — AgriculturalInformation & Documentation Section 857
Schimmelpfeng GmbH — Schimmelpfeng Information Broker Service 866
Scientific Documentation Centre Ltd. 868
Shirley Institute — Textile Information Services 873
Singapore Institute of Standards and Industrial Research — Industrial Technical Information Service 877
SLAMARK International 878
Society for Information and Documentation — GID InformationCenter for Information Science and Practice 880
Society of Metaphysicians Ltd. — Information Services 882
South Africa — Council for Scientific and Industrial Research — Centre for Scientific and Technical Information 885
South Africa — Nuclear DevelopmentCorporation of South Africa — NUCOR Library and Information Services 886
South Africa — South African Water Information Centre 887
South African Medical Research Council — Institute for Medical Literature 888
Southeast Asian Regional Center for Graduate Studyand Research in Agriculture — Agricultural Information Bank for Asia 889
Spain — Higher Council for Scientific Research — Institute for Information and Documentation in the Social Sciences andHumanities 891
State University of Utrecht Library — Biomedical Information Department 899
SVP South Africa Ltd. 917
Sweden — Karolinska Institute Library and Information Center 921
Sweden — National Board of Occupational Safety and Health — CIS Centre 923
Sweden — National Library for Psychology and Education 924
Sweden — National Road and Traffic ResearchInstitute — Information and Documentation Section 925
Sweden — Research Institute of National Defense — FOA Index Group 929
Sweden — Royal Institute of Technology Library — Information and Documentation Center 930
Swedish Center for Working Life — Information and Documentation Department 935
Swedish Institute ofBuilding Documentation 938
Swedish University of Agricultural Sciences — Ultuna Library — Documentation Section 941
Swiss Academy of MedicalSciences — Documentation Service 943
Swiss Center of Documentation in Microtechnology 944
SYSTEL 950
Technical Information Center 959
Technical Information Center — Electrical Engineering Documentation Center 960
Technical Information Center — Mechanical Engineering Documentation 961
Technical Information-Documentation Consultants Ltd. 963
TechnicalUniversity of Wroclaw — Main Library and Scientific Information Center — System of Computerized Processing of Scientific Information 965
Timber Research and Development Association — Informationand Advisory Department — Timber Information Keyword Retrieval 983
Turkey —Scientific and Technical Research Council of Turkey — Turkish Scientific andTechnical Documentation Center 991
Union of Soviet Socialist Republics — All-Union Institute of Scientific and Technical Information 998
United Nations — Economic and Social Commission for Asia and the Pacific — ESCAP Library — ESCAP Bibliographic Information System 1002
United Nations — Food and Agriculture Organization — Aquatic Sciences and Fisheries Information System 1008
United Nations — Food and Agriculture Organization — Library and Documentation Systems Division — David Lubin Memorial Library 1013
United Nations Educational, Scientific and Cultural Organization — Center for Social ScienceResearch and Documentation for the Arab Region 1015
United Nations Educational, Scientific and Cultural Organization — International Bureauof Education — Documentation and Information Unit 1021
United Nations Educational, Scientific and Cultural Organization —Social and Human Science Documentation Centre 1022
United Nations Industrial Development Organization — Industrial Information Section —Industrial andTechnological Information Bank 1027

University Library of Hannover and Technical Information Library 1031
University of Dusseldorf — Research Division for Philosophy Information and Documentation — Philosophy Information Service 1048
University of Haifa Library — Haifa On-line Bibliographic Text System 1051
University ofLeeds — Medical and Dental Library — Oncology Information Service 1053
University of London — Central Information Service 1055
University of Paris-South — Gases and Plasmas PhysicsLaboratory — GAPHYOR 1063
University of Saskatchewan Library — Reference Department — University of Saskatchewan Libraries Machine-Assisted Reference Teleservices 1067
University of Saskatchewan Library — Systems and Planning Unit 1068
University of Sheffield — Biomedical Information Service 1069
University of Tokyo — Computer Center — University of Tokyo On-Line Information Retrieval System 1075
University of Trier — Center for Psychological Information and Documentation 1078
University of Trondheim — Norwegian Institute of Technology — University Library 1079
Update AB 1090
URBAMET Network 1091
USACO Corporation 1092
Warren, Inc. 1105
The Welding Institute — Information Services 1106
Yugoslav Center for Technical and Scientific Documentation 1121
Zinc Development Association/Lead Development Association/Cadmium Association — Library and AbstractingService 1122

Software Producers

Aball Software Inc. 2
Association for Research and Development of Chemical Informatics — DARC Pluridata System 38
AVCOR 67
AVSIntext Ltd. 69
Blackwell Technical Services Ltd. 90
Cambridge University — University Chemical Laboratory — Cambridge Crystallographic Data Centre 125
Canada — National Research Council of Canada — Canada Institute for Scientific and Technical Information — Scientific Numeric Databases 155
Canada — Statistics Canada — Canadian Socio-Economic Information Management System 159
Carleton University Library — Carleton Library System 179
Center for International Prospective Studies 185
Commission of the European Communities — Statistical Office of the European Communities — CRONOS Data Bank 225
Cumulus Systems Ltd. 249
Dataline Inc. 262
Dutch State Mines — TISDATA 286
Elsevier Science Publishers B.V. — Biomedical Division — Excerpta Medica 296
France — Bureau of Geological and Mining Research — National Geological Survey — Subsoil Data Bank 341
Fraser Videotex Services 369
Fraser Williams Ltd. — CROSSBOW 370
Fraser Williams Ltd. — DARING 371
Geosystems 394
Germany — Ministry of Youth, Family and Health — German Institute for Medical Documentation and Information 428
Great Britain — Atomic Energy Authority — Atomic Energy Research Establishment, Harwell — Computer Science and Systems Division — STATUS 433
GSI-ECO 469
Hertfordshire County Council — Chiltern Advisory Unit for Computer Based Education 485
Honeywell Bull — Euris Host Service 488
IFO-Institute for Economic Research — Department of Econometrics and Data Processing — IFO Time Series Data Bank 501
Imperial Chemical Industries Ltd. — AgriculturalDivision — Management Services Department — ASSASSIN 503
Infomart 518
Information Management & Engineering Ltd. 527
Informetrica Limited 536
Institution of Chemical Engineers — Physical Property Data Service 548
InternationalCentre forScientific and Technical Information 565
International Development Research Centre — Library 576
International InformationServices Company 589

Software Producers (Continued)

Israel — National Center of Scientific and Technological Information 616
Israel — National Center of Scientific and Technological Information — DOMESTIC 617
Italy — National Research Council — CNUCE Institute 623
Kent-Barlow Publications Ltd. 638
Langton Electronic Publishing Systems Ltd. 649
Learned Information Ltd. 654
Legal Technology Group 656
Leigh-Bell & Associates Ltd. 657
Library Network of SIBIL Users 664
Lipman Management Resources, Ltd. — LMR Information Systems — Adaptive Library Management System 666
Logica UK Ltd. 668
McGill University — Faculty of Engineering — Department of Mining and Metallurgical Engineering — Facility for the Analysis of Chemical Thermodynamics 691
Microfor Inc. 704
National Computing Centre Ltd. — Information Services Division 721
Netherlands Organization for Applied Scientific Research — Institute TNO for Mathematics, Information Processing and Statistics 741
Norwegian Center for Informatics 767
Norwegian Computing Centre for the Humanities 768
Office of Economic Information and Forecasting 773
Paralog — 3RIP 795
Philips Information Systems and Automation — DIRECT 809
Press Association Ltd. — NEWSFILE 823
QL Systems Limited 828
Queen's University of Belfast — Department of Computer Science — Queen's University Interrogation of Legal Literature 836
Sharp Associates Limited 871
Siemens AG — Data Processing Division — GOLEM 874
Siemens AG — Language Services Department — Terminology Evaluation and Acquisition Method 876
Specialist Software Ltd. 895
Stacs Information Systems Ltd. 897
Stockholm School of Economics — Economics Research Institute — FINDATA 903
Stockholm University Computing Center, QZ 904
Sweden — Research Institute of National Defense — FOA Index Group 929
Sweden — Royal Institute of Technology Library — Information and Documentation Center 930
Sweden — Statistics Sweden — Statistical Data Bases Unit 932
Swets Subscription Service 942
Systemhouse Ltd. — MINISIS 953
Technical Information Center 959
Technical University of Aachen — Laboratory of Machine Tools and Production Engineering — Cutting Data Information Center 964
Telesystemes — Questel 977
Uhde GmbH — Uhde Thermophysical Properties Program Package 992
United Nations Educational, Scientific and Cultural Organization — Division of the UNESCO Library, Archives and Documentation Services — Computerized Documentation Service/Integrated Set of Information Systems 1017
United Nations Educational, Scientific and Cultural Organization — Universal System for Information in Science and Technology — UNISIST International Centre for Bibliographic Descriptions 1023
Universal Library Systems Ltd. 1029
University of Haifa Library — Haifa On-line Bibliographic Text System 1051
University of London — Central Information Service 1055
University of Melbourne — Department of Geology — Computerised Library of Analysed Igneous Rocks 1057
University of Paris-South — Gases and Plasmas Physics Laboratory — GAPHYOR 1063
University of Sydney — Sample Survey Centre 1072
University of Tsukuba — Science Information Processing Center 1080
University of Western Ontario — School of Library and Information Science — Nested Phrase Indexing System 1086
University of Western Ontario — Systems Analysis, Control and Design Activity 1088
Userlink Systems Ltd. 1093

Videotex/Teletext Information Services

A.JOUR 1
Agra Europe 8
Alpha 460 Television Ltd. 18
Alphatel Systems Ltd. 19
American Express Europe Ltd. — SkyGuide 23
AVCOR 67
AVS Intext Ltd. 69
Baric Computing Services Ltd. — Baric Viewdata 75

Videotex/Teletext Information Services (Continued)

Bird Associates 89
British Broadcasting Corporation — CEEFAX 105
The British Council — Central Information Service 108
Calgary Public Information Department — Public Relations Division — Civichannel 124
Canada — Department of Communications — Telidon Program 130
Canada — Statistics Canada — Canadian Socio-Economic Information Management System — Telichart 160
Canadian Broadcasting Corporation — Project IRIS 169
The CIRPA/ADISQ Foundation 206
Communication Services Ltd. — Viewdata Services 231
Consumers' Association — TeleWhich? 244
Control Data Australia Pty. Ltd. — CYBERTEL Videotex Service 245
Council for Educational Technology — Videotex Services Unit 247
Cumulus Systems Ltd. 249
Dagg Associates 253
Data Bank for Medicaments 257
Datastream International Ltd. 267
Denmark Telecommunications Administration — Danish Teledata System 272
Eastern Counties Newspapers — Eastel 287
Edimedia Inc. 292
English Tourist Board — Information Unit — Tourtel 297
Esselte Business Information 301
FLA Groupe La Creatique 336
France — Ministry of Education — National Center for Pedagogical Documentation 346
Fraser Videotex Services 369
French Company for the Design & Implementation of Radio & Television Broadcasting Equipment — Antiope Teletext System 383
Germany — Ministry of Posts and Telecommunications — German Federal Postal Service — Bildschirmtext 427
Great Britain — British Library — Science Reference Library — European Biotechnology Information Program 446
Great Britain — British Telecommunications — Prestel 448
Great Britain — Manpower Services Commission — Careers and Occupational Information Centre 462
Hanover Press — Viewdata Services 473
Hartmann & Heenemann — Computer Composition Center 476
Helsingin Telset Oy — Telset 480
Hertfordshire County Council — Chiltern Advisory Unit for Computer Based Education 485
Hertfordshire Technical Library and Information Service — HERTIS Industrial Services 486
ICC Information Group Ltd. 499
ICV Information Systems Ltd. — CitiService 500
Image Base Videotex Design Inc. 502
Infolex Services Ltd. 517
Infomart 518
Infomart — Grassroots 519
Intelmatique 552
Italian Society for Telephone Use — Videotel 622
Langton Electronic Publishing Systems Ltd. 649
Larratt and Associates Ltd. 650
Legal Technology Group 656
Lloyd's Shipping Information Services 667
Logica UK Ltd. 668
London and South Eastern Library Region 670
Management Consultants International, Inc. 682
Morgan-Grampian Plc. — M-G Videotex Services 714
National Reprographic Centre for Documentation 725
Netherlands Office of Posts, Telegraphs, and Telephones — PTT Central Directorate — Viditel 738
New Opportunity Press Ltd. — Careerdata 747
Newfoundland Telephone — Tourism Newfoundland 751
Nippon Telegraph & Telephone Public Corporation — CAPTAIN 759
NORPAK Corporation 764
Norwegian Center for Informatics 767
ORACLE Teletext Ltd. 779
Phippard & Associates Strategic & Technological Consulting, Inc. 810
Polytechnical School of Montreal — Telidon Technology Development Center 819
Press Association Ltd. — NEWSFILE 823
Saskatchewan Telecommunications — Agritex 862
Society for the Study of Economic and Social Development — MERCATIS 881
Sonoptic Communications Inc. 884
Sports Council — Information Centre 896
The Stock Exchange — Technical Services Department — TOPIC 902
Swiss Viewdata Information Providers Association 946
Tayson Information Technology Inc. 956
Tele-Direct Inc. 973
Telemap Ltd. — Micronet 800 976
Tijl Datapress 982
Timber Research and Development Association — Information and Advisory Department — Timber Information Keyword Retrieval 983

Videotex/Teletext Information Services (Continued)

VideoAccess 1099
Videotex Information Service Providers Association of Canada 1101
Viewtel Services Ltd. 1102

PERSONAL NAME INDEX

An alphabetical listing of approximately 1,400 personal names appearing in entries in the main body of this book. Includes persons who are directors of organizations and systems as well as persons who serve as contact points for information about the operations. Personal and organizational titles are generally not included here.

A

Aarniala, Marjatta
  Finnish Standards Association — Information Service (334)
Abati, Mr. A.
  Central Electronic Network for Data Processing and Analysis (194)
Acevedo-Alvarez, Mr. J.
  Fraunhofer Society — Information Center for Building and Physical Planning (373)
Acevedo-Alvarez, Mr. J.
  Fraunhofer Society — Information Center for Building andPhysical Planning — Building Research Projects Data Base (374)
Acevedo-Alvarez, Mr. J.
  Fraunhofer Society — Information Center for Building and Physical Planning — Buildings Documentation Data Base (375)
Acevedo-Alvarez, Mr. J.
  Fraunhofer Society — Information Center for Building and Physical Planning — Literature Compilations Data Base (376)
Acevedo-Alvarez, Mr. J.
  Fraunhofer Society — Information Center for Building and Physical Planning — PASCALBAT Data Base (377)
Acevedo-Alvarez, Mr. J.
  Fraunhofer Society — Information Center for Building and Physical Planning — Property Services Agency Information on Construction and Architecture Data Base (378)
Acevedo-Alvarez, Mr. J.
  Fraunhofer Society — Information Center for Building and Physical Planning — Regional Planning, City Planning, Housing, Building Construction Data Base (379)
Acevedo-Alvarez, Mr. J.
  Fraunhofer Society — Information Center for Building and Physical Planning — Regional Planning, City Planning, Housing Research Projects Data Base (380)
Acton, Patricia
  Acton Information Resources Management Ltd. (4)
Addie, Kathryn E.
  QL Systems Limited (828)
Adey, Margaret
  International Bee Research Association — Apicultural Abstracts (563)
Adler, Elhanan
  University of Haifa Library — Haifa On-line Bibliographic Text System (1051)
Adolfsson, Bo
  Sweden — National Swedish Telecommunications Administration — Datapak (927)
Affleck, Jennifer L.
  Insearch Ltd./DIALOG (538)
Agoston, Mihaly
  Hungary — National Technical Information Centre and Library (496)
Agrawal, Shri S.P.
  Indian Council of Social Science Research — Social Science Documentation Centre (511)
Aguilar Caceres, Alma
  Mexico — National Institute for Research on Biological Resources — INIREB Library (702)
Aichele, Dr. Helmut
  Germany — Federal Institute for Geosciences and Natural Resources — Seismological Central Observatory GRF (414)
Aitchison, T.M.
  Institution of Electrical Engineers — INSPEC (549)
Aitchison, T.M.
  Institution ofElectrical Engineers — INSPEC — Electronic Materials Information Service (550)
Akeda, Yoshiaki
  Nomura Research Institute — Information Service and Development Department — NRI/E Japan Economic & Business Data Bank (760)
Akyuz, E.F.
  United Nations — Food and Agriculture Organization — Aquatic Sciences and Fisheries Information System (1008)
Alenius-Santaoja, Maarit
  FinnishStandards Association — Information Service (334)
Alewaeters, Dr. Gerrit
  Free University of Brussels — Central Library — VUBIS (381)
Allaya, Prof. M.
  International Center for Higher Studies in Mediterranean Agronomy — Socioeconomic Data Bank on the Mediterranean Countries (564)
Allcorn, R.T.
  Timber Research and Development Association — Information and Advisory Department — Timber Information Keyword Retrieval (983)
Almadhi, Jaffer
  Arabian Gulf Information Consulting Bureau (25)
Alonso, C.
  Sabadell Computing Center (860)
Alston, R.C.
  Great Britain — British Library — Reference Division — Eighteenth Century Short Title Catalogue (443)
Alves Forjaz, Alberto Augusto
  Brazil — Ministry of Agriculture — National Center for Agricultural Documentary Information (99)
Amano, Yoshio
  International Medical Information Center (598)
Ammundsen, Peter
  Commission of the European Communities — Specialized Department for Terminology and Computer Applications — EURODICAUTOM (223)
Amores, Dr. Irene D.
  Philippines — National Science and Technology Authority — Scientific Clearinghouse and Documentation ServicesDivision (808)
Anderegg, Rolf
  Swiss Wildlife Information Service (947)
Anderson, Dr. Beryl L.
  Canada — National Library of Canada — Library Documentation Centre (149)
Anderson, June M.
  Infoquest (520)
Anderton, Monica
  Monitan Information Consultants Ltd. (713)
Ando, K.
  International Federation for Information Processing (580)
Andrew, Geoff
  Videotex Industry Association Ltd. (1100)
Andrews, Mr. Vian
  Quaere Legal Resources Ltd. (829)
Angel, Mr. G.W.
  Eurotec Consultants Ltd. —LIBRARIAN (318)
Antoine, J.
  Center for the Study of Advertising Support (189)
Apostolov, Prof. N.
  Bulgaria — National Agro-Industrial Union — Agricultural Academy — Center for Scientific, Technical and Economic Information (121)
Appelgren, Gunilla
  Sweden — National Library for Psychology and Education (924)
Arboleda, Orlando
  Pan American Health Organization — Pan American Centre for Sanitary Engineering & Environmental Sciences — Pan American Information & Documentation Network on Sanitary Engineering & Environmental Sciences (794)
Arnaud, Raymond
  MERLIN GERIN Company — Documentation Department — MERL-ECO (696)
Arnaud, Raymond
  MERLIN GERIN Company — Documentation Department — MERLIN-TECH (697)
Arondel, Olivier
  Transinove International (987)
Asano, Chooichiro
  Kyushu University — Research Institute of Fundamental Information Science (648)
Ash, Mr. R.
  Great Britain — Department of Trade and Industry — Business Statistics Office (454)
Asiedu, E.S.
  African Training and Research Centre in Administration for Development — African Network of Administrative Information (7)
Assal, William
  University of Paris-South — Gases and Plasmas Physics Laboratory — GAPHYOR (1063)
Aston, Mike
  HertfordshireCounty Council — Chiltern Advisory Unit for Computer Based Education (485)
Atlani, Ch.
  Association for Research and Developmentof Chemical Informatics — DARC Pluridata System (38)
Audet, Paul A.
  Edimedia Inc. (292)
Aufiero, Joan I.
  Quaere Legal Resources Ltd. (829)
Auger, Marie Claude
  Mikro-Cerid (710)
Aulo, Dr. Thea
  HelsinkiUniversity Library — Finnish National Bibliography (482)
Auracher, Dr. Otto
  Austria — Minister of Finance — InternationalPatent Documentation Center (64)
Austin, Derek
  Great Britain — British Library — Bibliographic Services Division — Subject Systems Office — Preserved Context Index System (441)
Avedon, Dr. E.M.
  University of Waterloo — Department of Recreation — Leisure Studies Data Bank (1084)
Averdal, Jan
  Sweden — Patent and Registration Office — InterPat Sweden (928)

Avery, G.S.
  ADIS Press Australasia Pty Ltd. — ADIS Drug Information Retrieval System (5)

B

Bachelin, Robert
  Swiss Center of Documentation in Microtechnology (944)
Bachmann, Prof. Dr. Peter A.
  World Health Organization — WHO Collaborating Centre for Collection and Evaluation of Data on Comparative Virology (1114)
Baibuz, Dr. Victor F.
  Union of Soviet Socialist Republics — Academy of Sciences of the U.S.S.R. — Institute for High Temperatures — Thermophysical Properties Center (996)
Baker, Mr. A.
  Organisation for Economic Co-Operation and Development — International Energy Agency — IEA Coal Research — Technical Information Service (782)
Bakker, Raymond M.G.P.B.
  CONSULTEXT (243)
Balck, Gun-Britt
  TT Newsbank (990)
Ball, A.J.S.
  Aball Software Inc. (2)
Ball, Ray J.
  University of New South Wales — Australian Graduate School of Management — Centre for Research in Finance (1060)
Ball, Warren E.
  Japan Publications Guide (635)
Ballantyne, James
  British Universities Film & Video Council Ltd. — Information Service (112)
Baltais, Helen
  Metropolitan Toronto Library Board — Regional Bibliographic Products Department (699)
Bandinelli, Dr. Rolando
  Italy — National Research Council — CNUCE Institute (623)
Bankowski, Prof. Dr. Jacek
  Poland — Institute for Scientific, Technical and Economic Information (815)
Barkla, Mr. J.K.
  University of Sheffield — Biomedical Information Service (1069)
Barkshire, R.R. St. J.
  The London International Financial Futures Exchange Ltd. (672)
Barlow, D.H.
  European Information Providers Association (312)
Barlow, Derek H.
  Kent-Barlow Publications Ltd. (638)
Barnes, Colin I.
  United Nations — Food and Agriculture Organization — Library and Documentation Systems Division — David Lubin Memorial Library (1013)
Barnholdt, Bent
  Denmark — National Technological Library of Denmark — Automated Library Information System (270)
Barreiro, Selma Chi
  Brazil — National Commission for Nuclear Energy — Center for Nuclear Information (102)
Barrett, W.F.
  Council of Europe — European Documentation and Information System for Education (248)
Barry, Dr. T.I.
  Great Britain — Department of Industry — National Physical Laboratory — Division of Materials Applications — Metallurgical and Thermochemical Data Service (451)
Barthelmess, Helmut
  Germany — Federal Institute for Materials Testing — Welding Documentation (418)
Baskin, Judith A.
  Australia — National Libraryof Australia — Australian Bibliographic Network (49)
Bathurst, David
  Jordan & Sons Ltd. — Jordans Company Information (636)
Batrakov, Prof. Yu. V.
  Union of Soviet Socialist Republics — Academy of Sciences of the U.S.S.R. — Institute for Theoretical Astronomy — Minor Planets, Comets, and Satellites Department (997)
Baude, Dr. Hans
  Sweden — Karolinska Institute Library and Information Center (921)
Bauer, C.
  United Nations Educational, Scientific and Cultural Organization — Social and Human Science Documentation Centre (1022)
Baulch, Dr. D.L.
  University of Leeds — Department of Physical Chemistry — High Temperature Reaction Rate Data Centre (1052)

Baum, Robert
  AVCOR (67)
Bauske, Franz
  University of Cologne — Central Archives for Empirical Social Research (1045)
Bavin, Jeanne
  Belgium — Ministry of Economic Affairs — National Statistical Institute (82)
Bayne, B.L.
  Natural Environment Research Council — Institute for Marine Environmental Research — Continuous PlanktonRecorder Survey (729)
Becker, K.
  United Nations — Food and Agriculture Organization — Statistics Division — Interlinked Computerized Storage and Processing System of Food and Agricultural Data (1014)
Bednar, Dr. Kurt
  MANZ Info Datenvermittlung GmbH — MANZ Datenbanken (683)
Beed, Dr. Terence W.
  University of Sydney — Sample Survey Centre (1072)
Begley, R.
  New Opportunity Press Ltd. — Careerdata (747)
Bekisz, Stanislaw
  Technical University of Wroclaw — Main Library and Scientific Information Center — System of Computerized Processing of Scientific Information (965)
Beling, Jurgen
  University of Trier — Center for Psychological Information and Documentation (1078)
Beliveau, Karen D.
  Alberta Research Council — Solar and Wind Energy Research Program Information Centre (16)
Bell, D.
  University of Aberdeen — Department of Political Economy — Wage Rounds Data Bank (1032)
Bellard, Dr. S.
  Cambridge University — University Chemical Laboratory — Cambridge Crystallographic Data Centre (125)
Belleudy, Francois
  Center for the Study on Information Systems in Government (190)
Bennett, JohnB.C.
  Charities Aid Foundation — Information Services (198)
Bergerhoff, Dr. G.
  University of Bonn — Inorganic Chemistry Institute — Inorganic Crystal Structure Data Base (1042)
Bernas, Walter J.
  ItalCable — Direct Access to Remote Data Bases Overseas (620)
Bernasconi, Prof. Fermin A.
  Intergovernmental Bureau for Informatics (554)
Berndt, Dr. H.
  International Food Information Service — VITIS-Viticulture and Enology Abstracts (585)
Berthelot, Yves
  Center for International Prospective Studies (185)
Beyersdorff, Prof. Gunter
  German Library Institute (400)
Bhargava, Mr. R.M.S.
  India — National Institute of Oceanography — Indian National Oceanographic Data Centre (509)
Bialas, Peter
  Germany — Federal Environmental Agency — Environmental Information and Documentation System (411)
Bidd, Donald
  Canada — National FilmBoard of Canada — FORMAT (146)
Biggs, Mrs. P.T.
  Library Association Publishing Ltd. — CURRENT RESEARCH in Library & Information Science (661)
Bilboul, Roger
  Learned Information Ltd. (654)
Billib, Andreas
  Germany — Federal Institute for Geosciences and Natural Resources — Marine Information and Documentation System (413)
Bird, Tony
  Bird Associates (89)
Birkenshaw, John W.
  International Electronic Publishing Research Centre (577)
Bisogno, Prof. Paolo
  Italy — National Research Council — Institute for Study of Scientific Research & Documentation — Italian Reference Center for Euronet DIANE (624)
Bisson, M.
  France — National Telecommunications Research Center — Interministerial Documentation Service — TELEDOC (367)
Biswas, Ahsan A.
  Bangladesh National Scientific and Technical Documentation Centre (70)
Black, Leslie
  Alberta Research Council — Coal Technology Information Centre (14)

Black, Neil
  Image Base Videotex Design Inc.   (502)
Blain, Mrs. Gillian
  University of Tasmania Library — Union List of Higher Degree Theses in Australian Libraries   (1074)
Blease, J. Graham
  Finsbury Data Services Ltd. — TEXTLINE   (335)
Blegvad, Annette
  Institute for Futures Studies — Futures Information Service   (540)
Blekastad, Tor
  University of Oslo — Royal University Library — Planning Department   (1061)
Bligh, Dr. Donald A.
  Exeter University Teaching Services — The Exeter Abstract Reference System   (319)
Blum, Mr. C.
  Textile and Clothing Information Centre   (980)
Blunden, Brian W.
  International Electronic Publishing Research Centre   (577)
Blunden, Brian W.
  Pira: Research Association for the Paper and Board, Printing and Packaging Industries — Comprehensive Information Services   (812)
Blunden, Brian W.
  Pira: Research Association for the Paper and Board, Printing and Packaging Industries — Printing and Information Technology Division   (813)
Boals, Russell G.
  Canada — Environment Canada — Inland Waters Directorate — Water Resources Branch — Water Survey of Canada   (142)
Bodard, Francoise
  Group for the Study and Research of Tropical Agronomy —AGRITROP   (467)
Bohm, Dr. Peter
  Germany — Ministry of Economics — German Foreign Trade Information Office   (425)
Bon, Frederic
  International Federation of Data Organizations for the Social Sciences   (581)
Boni, Dr. M.
  Commission of the European Communities — Joint Research Centre — Environmental Chemicals Data and Information Network   (221)
Book, Mr. A.
  American Express Europe Ltd. — SkyGuide   (23)
Borchardt, Peter
  German Library Institute   (400)
Bornes, M.
  France — National Institute for Research in Informatics and Automation — Information Dissemination Office   (361)
Bose, Mr. P.C.
  Indian Council of Agricultural Research — Agricultural Research Information Centre   (510)
Bose, Shankar
  Centre for the Study of Developing Societies — Data Unit   (196)
Bossers, A.
  Consortium of Royal Library and University Libraries — Project for Integrated Catalogue Automation   (239)
Boudard, Anne-Marie
  Center for International Prospective Studies   (185)
Bouvier, Dominique
  Company for Informatics — SPIDEL   (233)
Bowness, Mr. Cuyler
  MacLean-Hunter Ltd. — Financial Post Division — Financial Post Investment Data Bank   (680)
Boychuk, Robert R.
  University of Saskatchewan Library — Reference Department — University of Saskatchewan Libraries Machine-Assisted Reference Teleservices   (1067)
Boyle, Dr. L.
  Fraser Williams Ltd. — CROSSBOW   (370)
Boyle, Dr. L.
  Fraser Williams Ltd. — Fine Chemicals Directory   (372)
Bradford, Rae
  Canada — Department of Industry, Trade & Commerce — Office of Tourism — Tourism Research and Data Centre   (137)
Braham, Dr. Mark
  International Refugee Integration Resource Centre   (602)
Braithwaite, Stanley
  Faxtel Information Systems Ltd. — Marketfax   (326)
Brak, Dr. J.A.W.
  Royal Netherlands Academy of Arts and Sciences Library   (849)
Branse, Jody
  University of Haifa Library — Haifa On-line Bibliographic Text System   (1051)
Braun, Dietrich
  German Plastics Institute — Information and Documentation Services   (402)

Braun, Prof. T.
  Hungarian Academy of Sciences Library — Department for Informatics and Science Analysis   (492)
Bregt, A.K.
  Netherlands Soil Survey Institute — Soil Information System   (746)
Breniere, Francine
  French Institute of Energy — Energy Studies and Information Center   (386)
Brewin, Mr. P.
  Bemrose Printing   (85)
Brewis, Dr. M.
  Pergamon Press — Current Awareness in Biological Sciences   (803)
Briere, Gerard
  IndustrialLife-Technical Services Inc.   (513)
Briere, Gerard
  IST-Informatheque Inc.   (619)
Brindley, Lynne J.
  Cooperative Automation Group   (246)
Broad, Charles F.
  Canadian Engineering Publications Ltd. — Information Services Division   (171)
Brodmeier, Dr. Beate
  German Foundation for International Development — Documentation Center   (397)
Broms, Henri
  Helsinki School of Economics Library — Information Services   (481)
Brown, G.H.
  Brown's Geological Information Service Ltd.   (113)
Brown-Tourigny, J.
  Tele-Direct Inc.   (973)
Bru, Alfonso
  SVP Espana   (912)
Brunka, Victor V.
  SVP Canada   (910)
Bruyere, Mr. B.
  Textile and Clothing Information Centre   (980)
Bryan, Harrison
  Australia — National Library of Australia   (48)
Bryant, Philip
  University of Bath — Centre for Catalogue Research   (1039)
Bryant, Rodney T.
  The Welding Institute — Information Services   (1106)
Buchbinder, Dr. Reinhard
  Germany — German National Library — BIBLIO-DATA   (423)
Buckingham, M.C.S.
  IRCS Medical Science — IRCS Medical Science Database   (614)
Bud, Mari
  Sweden — Royal Library — Library Information System   (931)
Budinger, Dr. Peter
  Society for Information and Documentation — GID Information Center for Information Science and Practice   (880)
Bullens, O.
  European Patent Office — EDP Department — EPO Data Banks   (315)
Bullock, Bonnie
  Canada — National Research Council of Canada — Canada Institute for Scientific and Technical Information — Canadian Online Enquiry System   (153)
Bullock, Bonnie
  Canada — National Research Council of Canada — Canada Institute for Scientific and Technical Information — Canadian Service for the Selective Dissemination of Information   (154)
Bunbury, Michael R.
  GreatBritain — House of Commons Library — Parliamentary On-Line Information System   (459)
Bunbury, Michael R.
  Scicon Ltd.   (867)
Bungum, Hilmar
  Royal Norwegian Council for Scientific and Industrial Research — Norwegian Seismic Array   (850)
Burgess, Ken
  Expert Information Systems Ltd. — EXIS 1   (320)
Burk, Alan C.
  University of New Brunswick Libraries — PHOENIX   (1059)
Burshtyn, Hyman
  Carleton University — Department of Sociology and Anthropology — Social Science Data Archives   (178)
Burslem, Peter
  University of Saskatchewan Library — Systems and Planning Unit   (1068)
Bushnell, I.W.
  Great Britain — Department of Trade and Industry — Business Statistics Office   (454)
Butler, Bruce
  Nichols Applied Management   (752)
Butler, R.E.
  International Telecommunication Union   (606)

Buttner, Peter
　Information Center for Materials — System for Documentation and Information in Metallurgy   (522)
Bystram, Mrs. A.M.
　Canada — Environment Canada — Library Services Branch — Environment Libraries Automated System   (144)

C

Caldwell, Prof. J.C.
　Australian National University — Research School of Social Sciences — Australian Demographic Data Bank   (60)
Calvert, Dr. L.D.
　Canada — National Research Council of Canada — Chemistry Division — Metals Data Centre   (156)
Cameron, C.
　Canada — Environment Canada — Canadian Inventory of Historic Building   (138)
Cameron, Mr. R.J.
　Australian Bureau of Statistics   (52)
Campbell, Evangeline
　Canada — Environment Canada — Inland Waters Directorate — WATDOC   (140)
Campbell, Harry
　Espial Productions   (300)
Campbell, Helen
　Information Management and Consulting Association   (526)
Campion, Serge G.
　Canada — Transport Canada — Library and Information Centre   (161)
Cancelier, Gerard
　Society for the Study of Economic and SocialDevelopment — MERCATIS   (881)
Cantrill, Paul
　Rubber and Plastics Research Association of Great Britain — RAPRA Information Centre   (858)
Caplin, Edward B.
　Specialist Software Ltd.   (895)
Cardiga, Carlos
　Portuguese Radio Marconi Company — Data Bank Access Service   (822)
Carosella, Maria Pia
　Italy — National Research Council — Institute for Study of Scientific Research & Documentation — Italian Reference Center for Euronet DIANE   (624)
Carra, Gisele
　Association for the Promotionof Industry-Agriculture — International Documentation Center for Industries Using Agricultural Products   (39)
Carruthers, Dr. J.F.
　NORPAK Corporation   (764)
Caruso, Guy
　Organisation for Economic Co-Operation and Development — International Energy Agency — International Oil Market Information System   (784)
Carvalho de Souza, Altair
　Brazil — National Commission for Nuclear Energy — Center for Nuclear Information   (102)
Cassen, M.
　France — Interministerial Mission for Scientific and Technical Information   (344)
Castell, Dr. Stephen
　Infolex Services Ltd.   (517)
Castle, John A.
　ESDU International Limited   (299)
Castro, Aureo P.
　Technology Resource Center — Technobank Program   (967)
Cathro, W.S.
　Australia — National Library of Australia — Australian Bibliographic Network   (49)
Cattapan, Paolo
　Tecnomedia   (968)
Cavallaro, Umberto
　SYSTEL   (950)
Cawkell, Mr. A.E.
　Cawkell Information & Technology Services Ltd.   (180)
Chafe, H. David
　Metals Information   (698)
Champagne, Michelle
　Canada — Agriculture Canada — Marketing and Economics Branch — Cooperatives Unit — COINS   (127)
Chang, Jean
　Institute for Information Industry   (542)
Chaplin, John
　PMB Print Measurement Bureau   (814)

Chapman, B.A.
　Fraser Williams Ltd. — CROSSBOW   (370)
Chapman, B.A.
　Fraser Williams Ltd. — DARING   (371)
Chapuis, Bernard
　Swiss Center of Documentation in Microtechnology   (944)
Chauveinc, M.
　Intermarc Group   (555)
Chesnais, Robert
　France — Ministry of Education — National Center for Pedagogical Documentation   (346)
Chevalier, Mr.
　France — National Institute of Statistics and Economic Studies — Documentation Division — SPHINX Data Base   (363)
Cheynet, Dr. Bertrand
　Thermodata Association — Thermodata-Thermdoc Data Bank   (981)
Chiasson, Gilles
　Coaching Association of Canada — Sport Information Resource Centre   (210)
Chico, Dr. Leon V.
　Asian Network for Industrial Technology Information and Extension   (34)
Chihara, Dr. Hideaki
　Japan Association for International Chemical Information   (630)
Chomicz, Pam
　Royal Society of Chemistry — Information Services — Chemical Engineering Abstracts   (852)
Chomicz, Pam
　Royal Society of Chemistry — Information Services — Chemical Hazards in Industry   (853)
Chomicz, Pam
　Royal Society of Chemistry — Information Services — Current Biotechnology Abstracts   (854)
Chomicz, Pam
　Royal Society of Chemistry — Information Services — Laboratory Hazards Bulletin   (855)
Chomicz, Pam
　Royal Society of Chemistry — Information Services — Mass Spectrometry Data Centre   (856)
Choplin, Miss D.
　International Railway Union — Documentation Bureau   (600)
Choueka, Prof. Yaacov
　Bar-Ilan University — Institute for Information Retrieval and Computational Linguistics — Responsa Project   (74)
Chow, William
　Communication Services Ltd. — Viewdata Services   (231)
Chukreev, Dr. F.E.
　Union of Soviet Socialist Republics — U.S.S.R. State Committee on the Utilization of Atomic Energy — Center for Nuclear Structure and Reaction Data   (999)
Chung, In-sup
　SVP Korea   (915)
Citroen, Charles L.
　Netherlands Information Combine   (737)
Citroen, Charles L.
　Netherlands Organization for AppliedScientific Research — Center for Information and Documentation   (739)
Claassen, Mr. W.
　Technical Information Center — Electrical Engineering Documentation Center   (960)
Claridge, Dr. P.N.
　Natural Environment Research Council — Institute for Marine Environmental Research — Continuous Plankton Recorder Survey   (729)
Clark, Mary
　European Business Associates On-Line   (308)
Clark, Mike
　Market Location   (686)
Claus, Paul
　World Intellectual Property Organization — Permanent Committee onPatent Information   (1116)
Clavel, Jean-Pierre
　Library Network of SIBIL Users   (664)
Clayton, Graham
　British Broadcasting Corporation — CEEFAX   (105)
Clayton, Prof. Keith M.
　Geo Abstracts Ltd.   (393)
Clemens, Mme. I.
　Belgium — Royal Library of Belgium — National Center for Scientific and Technical Documentation   (84)
Clowes, Myra
　Canada — National Library of Canada — Public Services Branch — Union Catalogue of Serials Division   (151)
Cobb, Mr. P.G.W.
　Great Britain — Home Office Forensic Science Service — Central Research Establishment — Operational Services Division   (458)

Coblentz, Prof. A.
 Rene Descartes University — Laboratory of Applied Anthropology — ERGODATA (838)
Cockx, Dr. A.
 Belgium — Royal Library of Belgium — National Center for Scientific and Technical Documentation (84)
Cohen, Mrs. E.Z.R.
 Royal Netherlands Academy of Arts and Sciences — Social Science Information and Documentation Center (847)
Collins, Elaine
 Canada — Consumer and Corporate Affairs Canada — Corporations Branch — Corporate Integrated Information System (129)
Colyer, Mary Ann
 LondonResearchers (674)
Conning, Dr. Arthur M.
 United Nations — Economic Commission for Latin America — Latin American DemographicCenter — Latin American Population Documentation System (1007)
Conway, Mr. M.J.
 Zinc Development Association/Lead Development Association/Cadmium Association — Library and Abstracting Service (1122)
Cook, Elaine
 Commonwealth Agricultural Bureaux — CAB Abstracts (229)
Cook, Mr. K.J.
 Bank of England — Financial Statistics Division (72)
Cook, Michael
 Overseas Telecommunications Commission — Multimode International Data Acquisition Service (790)
Cooke, Mrs. G.A.
 Boreal Institutefor Northern Studies — Library Services (95)
Cooper, Phyllis M.
 T.C. Library Services Ltd. (954)
Coquand, P.
 European Conference of Ministers of Transport — International Co-operation in the Field of Transport Economics Documentation (309)
Cornelius, Peter
 Schimmelpfeng GmbH — Schimmelpfeng InformationBroker Service (866)
Cornish, Barry
 Great Britain — Manpower Services Commission — Careers and Occupational Information Centre (462)
Corns, Dr. Thomas N.
 Association for Literary and Linguistic Computing (37)
Costa, Mr. Michele
 Bibliographic Publishing Co. (87)
Costers, L.
 Consortium of Royal Library and University Libraries — Project for Integrated Catalogue Automation (239)
Costers, L.
 Consortium of Royal Library and University Libraries — Project for Integrated Catalogue Automation — Netherlands Central Catalogue/Interlibrary Loan System (240)
Cote, J.R.
 United Nations Industrial Development Organization — Industrial Information Section — Industrial and Technological Information Bank (1027)
Cotter, Nancy
 Western Legal Publications Ltd. (1108)
Courbis, Prof. Raymond
 University of Paris-Nanterre — Group for Applied Macroeconomic Analysis (1062)
Cox, Annette
 Admedia — Adfacts (6)
Crafts-Lighty, Dr. Anita
 Celltech Ltd. — Information and Library Service (181)
Crain, Ian K.
 Canada — Environment Canada — Lands Directorate — Canada Land Data Systems Division — CanadaGeographic Information System (143)
Crainey, M.
 Standards Council of Canada — Standards Information Service (898)
Craven, Timothy C.
 University of Western Ontario — School of Library and Information Science — Nested Phrase Indexing System (1086)
Crespo Queiroz Neves, Angela Maria
 Brazil — Ministry of the Interior — Documentation Coordination Unit (100)
Crofts, Mrs. B.A.
 Great Britain — Departments of the Environment and Transport — Transport and Road Research Laboratory — Technical Information and Library Services (455)
Cross, Nergida
 University of Sydney Library — Bibliographic Information on Southeast Asia (1073)
Crowe, D.S.
 Australian Mineral Foundation — Australian Earth Sciences Information System (57)
Crump, M.J.
 Great Britain — British Library — Reference Division — Eighteenth Century Short Title Catalogue (443)
Csahok, Dr. Istvan
 Hungary — Central Statistical Office (493)
Csepan, Dr. Robert
 Austrian National Institute for Public Health — Literature Service in Medicine (66)
Cumberbirch, R.J.E.
 Shirley Institute — Textile Information Services (873)
Cumberland, Robert F.
 Great Britain — Atomic Energy Authority — Atomic Energy Research Establishment, Harwell — National Chemical Emergency Centre — CHEMSAFE (435)
Cummins, N. Peter
 United Nations — Economic and Social Commission for Asia and the Pacific — ESCAP Library — ESCAP Bibliographic Information System (1002)

D

Dacong, Aurelia C.
 University of Alberta — Department of EducationalAdministration — Administration Laboratory Project File (1034)
Dadd, Michael N.
 BIOSIS, U.K. Ltd. — Zoological Record (88)
Dagallier, M. Xavier
 French Water Study Association — National Water Information Center (391)
Dagg, Michael A.
 Canadian Information Industry Association (172)
Dagg, Michael A.
 Dagg Associates (253)
Dahl, Brad
 Alphatel Systems Ltd. (19)
Daina, Dr. L.
 Italian Association for the Production and Distribution of Online Information (621)
Dam, Benny
 Denmark Telecommunications Administration — Danish Teledata System (272)
Danckwortt, Dieter
 German Foundation for International Development — Documentation Center (397)
Dancoisne, Michel
 Telesystemes — Questel (977)
Danell, Christina
 University of Umea — Demographic Data Base (1081)
Daniel, Tony
 The Stock Exchange — Technical Services Department — TOPIC (902)
Danke, Eric
 Germany — Ministry of Posts and Telecommunications — German Federal Postal Service — Bildschirmtext (427)
Dare, Miss G.A.
 Blackwell Technical Services Ltd. (90)
Darroch, Prof. Gordon
 York University — Institute for Behavioural Research (1120)
Dasgupta, D.
 Paint Research Association — Information Department — World Surface Coatings Abstracts (792)
D'Ath, R.H.
 New Zealand — Department of Statistics — Information Network for Official Statistics (749)
Dathe, Gert
 German Iron and Steel Engineers Association — Steel Information System (399)
Dauphin, Dr. J.
 European Space Agency — European Space Research and Technology Center — Materials Data Retrieval System (316)
Davidson, Robert M.
 Organisation for Economic Co-Operation and Development — International Energy Agency — IEA Coal Research — Technical Information Service (782)
Davis, Maureen
 Canadian Education Association — Canadian Education Index Data Base (170)
Davis, Michael H.
 Alpha 460 Television Ltd. (18)
Davison, P.S.
 Scientific Documentation Centre Ltd. (868)
Dawe, Peter H.
 Australia — Commonwealth Scientific and Industrial Research Organization — Central Information, Library and Editorial Section (47)

Dawson, Dr. J.
    British Medical Association — BMA Press Cuttings Database   (110)
Dean, Peter
    IPC Industrial Press Ltd. — Chemical Data Services   (612)
de Billy, Marie Claude
    Microfor Inc.   (704)
De Castro, Rosario B.
    Philippines — National Institute of Science and Technology — Division of Information and Documentation   (807)
de Gastines, Brigitte
    SVP France   (913)
De Geujer, Francois
    Commission of the European Communities — Statistical Office of the European Communities — CRONOS Data Bank   (225)
de Guchteneire, Dr. Paul F.A.
    International Federation of Data Organizations for the Social Sciences   (581)
de Guchteneire, Dr. Paul F.A.
    Royal Netherlands Academy of Arts and Sciences — Social Science Information and Documentation Center — Steinmetz Archives   (848)
de Heer, Dr. T.
    Netherlands Organization for Applied Scientific Research — Institute TNO for Mathematics, Information Processing and Statistics   (741)
de Hemptinne, Yvan
    United Nations Educational, Scientific and Cultural Organization — Division of Science and Technology Policies — Science and Technology Policies Information Exchange Programme   (1016)
de Jaeger, Herman-Karel
    Information Resources Research   (533)
de la Bruslerie, Bernard
    Society for the Study of Economic and Social Development — MERCATIS   (881)
De la Garza, Maria Luisa
    Mexico — National Institute for Research on Biological Resources — INIREB Library   (702)
de la Viesca, Rosa
    Spain — Higher Council for Scientific Research — Institute for Information and Documentation in Science and Technology   (890)
de Lavieter, L.
    Netherlands Organization for Applied Scientific Research — TNO Study and Information Centeron Environmental Research — Environmental Research in the Netherlands   (743)
Delcroix, Prof. Jean-Loup
    University of Paris-South — Gases and Plasmas Physics Laboratory — GAPHYOR   (1063)
Delmas, Bruno
    National Conservatory of Arts and Crafts — NationalInstitute for Documentation Techniques   (722)
De Lotto, Prof.Ivo
    Lombard Interuniversity Consortium for Data Processing   (669)
de Mes, W.W.
    Delft Hydraulics Laboratory — Information and Documentation Section   (268)
Deniel, Yves
    Thermodata Association — Thermodata-Thermdoc Data Bank   (981)
Denolf, Henri
    Canada — Consumer and Corporate Affairs Canada — Corporations Branch — Corporate Integrated Information System   (129)
de Padirac, Bruno
    United Nations Educational, Scientific and Cultural Organization — Division of Science and Technology Policies — Science and Technology Policies Information Exchange Programme   (1016)
De SaedePeer, G.
    Belgium — Ministry of Economic Affairs — Fonds Quetelet Library Data Base   (81)
Despiegeleer, R.
    Bank Society — General Documentation — SGB Data Base   (73)
Deunette, Jacky
    Online Information Centre   (775)
de Valence, Francois
    A.JOUR   (1)
Devoge, Mr. J.
    Interprofessional Technical Union of the National Federations of Buildings and Public Works — Center for Technical Assistance and Documentation —ARIANE Data Bank   (610)
Diaz, J.A.
    Sabadell Computing Center   (860)
Dietvorst, C.H.
    International Reference Center for Community Water Supply and Sanitation — Programme on Exchangeand Transfer of Information on Community Water Supply and Sanitation   (601)
Dijkens, Drs. K.
    Philips Information Systems and Automation — DIRECT   (809)
Dolan, Paul
    Datasearch Business Information Ltd.   (263)

Douezy, Marc
    French Stockbrokers Society — Information and Documentation Center   (389)
Doughan, David
    City of London Polytechnic — Fawcett Library — BiblioFem   (209)
Down, Stephen
    Royal Society of Chemistry — Information Services — Mass Spectrometry Data Centre   (856)
Draghi, Stefano
    University of Milan — Higher Institute of Sociology — Data and Program Archive for the Social Sciences   (1058)
Dravnieks, Gunnar
    K-Konsult — VA-NYTT   (637)
Drbalek, Dr. Jiri
    Czechoslovakia — Institute for MedicalInformation   (250)
Drube, Keld
    Danish DIANE Center   (256)
Duax, Dr. W.
    Cambridge University — University Chemical Laboratory — Cambridge Crystallographic Data Centre   (125)
Dubois, Mr. C.P.R.
    International Coffee Organization — COFFEELINE   (570)
Dubois, Jacques-Emile
    Association for Research and Development of Chemical Informatics — DARC Pluridata System   (38)
Du Breuil, Laval
    University of Quebec — Direct Access Data Bank at the University of Quebec   (1064)
Ducker, J.M.
    Datasolve Ltd. — World Exporter   (264)
Ducker, J.M.
    Datasolve Ltd. — World Reporter   (265)
Duckett, John
    ESDU International Limited   (299)
Ducrot, Dr. H.
    Data Bank for Medicaments   (257)
Ducrot, Jean-Marie
    French Textile Institute — Textile Information Treatment Users' Service   (390)
Duffus, Lyn
    Library Association Publishing Ltd. — British Humanities Index   (660)
Dufour, Doris
    Laval University Library — SDI/Laval & Telereference Service   (652)
Dunn, Sarah
    Pergamon InfoLine Ltd.   (802)
Durieux, Philippe
    Editions Techniques — JURIS-DATA   (294)
Dyer, Lois
    Canadian Law Information Council   (173)

E

Eaves, A.R.
    Building Services Research and Information Association — BSRIA Information Centre   (119)
Ebata, Tsuneo
    Teikoku Data Bank, Ltd.   (969)
Ebel, Sandra
    Toronto Department of the City Clerk — Computerized Text Processing and Retrieval System for City Council Information   (985)
Eckermann, Dr. Reiner
    German Society for Chemical Equipment — Information Systems and Data Banks Department — Chemical Technology Information System   (403)
Eckermann, Dr. Reiner
    German Society for Chemical Equipment — Information Systems and Data Banks Department — DECHEMA Substance Data Service   (404)
Eckermann, Dr.Reiner
    German Society for Chemical Equipment — Information Systemsand Data Banks Department — Materials and Corrosion Information System   (405)
Eckermann, Dr. Reiner
    German Society for Chemical Equipment — Information Systems and Data Banks Department — Supply SourcesInformation System   (406)
Eddie, Mr. P.
    Norwegian Standards Association — STANDARD   (772)
Edmonds, Dr. Beryl
    Institution of Chemical Engineers — Physical Property Data Service   (548)
Edstrom, Malin
    Scannet Foundation   (864)

Edvardson, Lars
  Studsvik Energiteknik AB — Report Collection Index   (906)
Edwards, Tom
  Library AssociationPublishing Ltd. — Current Technology Index   (662)
Egli, Mr. R.
  Switzerland — Swiss Intellectual Property Office — Technical Information on Patents   (948)
Eklof, Jan
  Sweden — Statistics Sweden — Statistical Data Bases Unit   (932)
Eklund, Erik
  Stockholm School of Economics — Economics Research Institute — FINDATA   (903)
Ekman, Elin
  Sweden — National Library for Psychology and Education   (924)
Eldred, Pauline
  Expert Information Systems Ltd. — EXIS 1   (320)
Eldridge, Cyril
  Alphatext, Inc.   (20)
Elena, Ms.
  International Serials Data System   (603)
Elliott, R.F.
  University of Aberdeen — Department of Political Economy — Wage Rounds Data Bank   (1032)
Elrod, J. McRee
  SpecialLibraries Cataloguing, Inc.   (894)
El Shooky, Mrs. Effat
  Data Processing Services Company — DPS Information Centre   (258)
Elvin, P.J.
  Great Britain — Department of the Environment — Building Research Establishment Library — BRIX   (453)
El-Zanati, A.G.
  International Telecommunication Union   (606)
Eresund, Mr. Bergt
  Swedish Institute of Building Documentation   (938)
Ergo, Ing. A.B.
  Royal Museum of Central Africa — Center for Informatics Applied to Development and Tropical Agriculture — Agroclimatology Data Bank   (846)
Eriksson, Lars-Erik
  Esselte Group of Booksellers — Esselte Documentation System   (302)
Escorcia Saldarriaga, German
  Colombian Fund for Scientific Research — National Information System   (212)
Ettel, Dr. Wolfgang H.
  Society for Information and Documentation — GID Information Center for Information Science and Practice   (880)
Evangelista, Claudionor
  United Nations — Economic Commission for Latin America — Latin American Center for Economic and Social Documentation   (1006)
Evans, Prof. A.J.
  Loughborough University of Technology Library — Minimal-Input Cataloguing System   (678)
Evans, Gwynneth
  Canada — National Library of Canada   (147)
Evett, Ian W.
  Great Britain — Home Office Forensic Science Service — Central Research Establishment — Operational Services Division   (458)
Ewers, Rudolf
  German Iron and Steel Engineers Association — Information System on Production Plants for Iron & Steel — PLANTFACTS   (398)
Exton, Valerie
  Logica UK Ltd.   (668)

F

Faber, Dr. J.
  Hubrecht Laboratory — Central Embryological Library — Documentation and Information System on Developmental Biology   (490)
Fabo, I.
  Hungarian Academy of Sciences — Institute of Economics — Economic Information Unit   (491)
Falkenberg, Dr. Goran
  Sweden — Karolinska InstituteLibrary and Information Center   (921)
Farley, Christopher
  Latin American Newsletters Ltd.   (651)
Farrell, Peter J.
  Computer Sciences of Australia Pty. Ltd. — Network Services Division — INFOBANK   (237)
Fawcett, Margaret J.
  Financial Times Business Information Ltd. — Business Information Service   (328)

Feeney, Mary
  University of Leicester — Primary Communications Research Centre   (1054)
Felber, Prof. Helmut
  International Information Center for Terminology   (587)
Feldhaus, Erich
  Motor Vehicle Documentation   (716)
Ferraiuolo, Angelo
  Italian Society for Telephone Use — Videotel   (622)
Findlay, Margaret A.
  Australian Council for Educational Research — Library and Information Services Unit   (54)
Fish, Janet
  Australian Financial Review — INFO-LINE   (55)
Fish, Janet
  SVP Australia   (908)
Flain, Rita M.
  Great Britain — Water Research Centre — Information Serviceon Toxicity and Biodegradability   (463)
Flemming, Dr. N.C.
  Natural Environment Research Council — Institute of Oceanographic Sciences — Marine Information and Advisory Service   (730)
Fluck, Dr. H.C. Ekkehard
  Gmelin Institute for Inorganic Chemistry and Related Fields   (431)
Fock, Hans W.
  German Patent Information System   (401)
Fock, Hans W.
  Hartmann & Heenemann — Computer Composition Center   (476)
Foldi, Tamas
  Hungarian Academy of Sciences — Institute of Economics — Economic Information Unit   (491)
Fontaine, Marcel
  Quebec NationalLibrary — FMQ   (833)
Forster, William A.
  Hertfordshire Technical Library and Information Service — HERTIS Industrial Services   (486)
Forsyth, D.H.
  Infomart — Grassroots   (519)
Fortin, Jean-Marie
  Quebec — French Language Board — Terminology Bank of Quebec   (830)
Fortin, Mr. P.
  Transpac   (989)
Foss, Martin
  Carleton University Library — Carleton Library System   (179)
Foster, Leslie A.
  Dalhousie University — Law School Library — Marine Affairs Bibliography   (254)
Foster, M. Anne
  Canada Law Book Ltd.   (162)
Foster, Ruth
  Telecom Canada — Datapac   (971)
Foster, Ruth
  Telecom Canada — iNet 2000   (972)
Fowler, Mrs. J.
  Lipman Management Resources, Ltd. — LMR Information Systems — Adaptive Library Management System   (666)
Foxton, John V.
  Viewtel Services Ltd.   (1102)
Fraser, Niall M.
  Fraser Videotex Services   (369)
Freeman, Robert R.
  United Nations — Food and Agriculture Organization — Aquatic Sciences and Fisheries Information System   (1008)
French, Mr. E.J.
  International Organization for Standardization — ISO Information Network   (599)
Frisina, Nick
  University of New South Wales — Australian Graduate School of Management — Centre for Research in Finance   (1060)
Fritz, Dr. Rolf
  Germany — Ministry of Youth, Family and Health — German Institute for Medical Documentation and Information   (428)
Fukami, Takeshi
  Japan — Japan Atomic Energy Research Institute — Department of Technical Information   (627)
Fuller, Cvetka
  Information Research Ltd.   (530)
Furtado, Aida M.
  United Nations Educational, Scientific and Cultural Organization — International Bureauof Education — Documentation and Information Unit   (1021)
Fux, Norbert
  Austria — Minister of Finance — International Patent Documentation Center   (64)

G

Gac, Andre
  International Institute of Refrigeration — Documentary Service (590)
Gagne, Frank X.
  Micromedia Ltd. (706)
Gagne, Frank X.
  Micromedia Ltd. — Canadian Business Index (707)
Gagne, Frank X.
  Micromedia Ltd. — Canadian News Index (708)
Galhardo, Christina
  International Technical Publications Ltd. (605)
Gallivan, Bernard
  Scotland — National Library of Scotland — Scottish Libraries Co-operative Automation Project (869)
Gama de Queiroz, Gilda
  Brazil — National Commission for Nuclear Energy — Center for Nuclear Information (102)
Garber, Nathan
  Information London (525)
Garcia Inesta, Antonio
  Spanish Drug Information Center — Spanish Pharmaceutical Specialities Data Bank (893)
Garlot, Christian
  Medical-Pharmaceutical Publishing Company (693)
Garnett, Anthony
  McCarthy Information Ltd. (690)
Garrow, Clyde
  Australia — Commonwealth Scientific and Industrial Research Organization — Central Information, Library and Editorial Section (47)
Garson, D.F.
  Canada — Department of Energy, Mines and Resources — Geological Survey of Canada — Economic Geology Division — Canadian Mineral Occurrence Index (134)
Geldart, Peter D.
  Euroline Inc. (304)
Genberg, Per
  Sweden — Swedish National Road Administration — Technical Division — RoadData Bank (933)
Genest, Helene
  Laval University Library — SDI/Laval & Telereference Service (652)
George, Phil
  Western Legal Publications Ltd. (1108)
Gerhards, Albert
  Germany — Ministry of Economics — German Foreign Trade Information Office (425)
Gero, Vera
  Hungary — National Szechenyi Library — Centre for Library Science and Methodology (495)
Geronimo, Jose E.
  Eastern Telecommunications Philippines, Inc. — Database Access Service (288)
Gerrese, Ir. J.
  Netherlands Office of Posts, Telegraphs, and Telephones — PTT Central Directorate — Viditel (738)
Gevers, Florent
  Compu-Mark (234)
Gevers, Florent
  Compu-Mark Ltd. (235)
Ghani, MD. Osman
  Bangladesh National Scientific and Technical Documentation Centre (70)
Ghenna, Kebour
  United Nations — Economic Commission for Africa — Pan-African Documentation and Information System (1005)
Gheorghe, Mr. Anghel
  Romania — National Council for Science and Technology — National Institute for Information and Documentation (843)
Ghirardi, Dr. L.
  France — National Center for Scientific Research — Scientific Documentation Center in Oncology — CANCERNET (357)
Gibb, Mr. J.M.
  Commission of the European Communities — System for Information on Grey Literature in Europe (226)
Gibbons, Rex
  Newfoundland Department of Mines & Energy — Mineral Development Division Library — Computerized Retrieval Services (750)
Gibson, Robert
  Micromedia Ltd. (706)
Gibson, Robert
  Micromedia Ltd. — Canadian Business Index (707)
Gibson, Robert
  Micromedia Ltd. — Canadian News Index (708)
Giel, Karel
  Europe Data (305)
Gifford, Mrs. Elli
  Wolff & Co. Ltd. — Wolff Research (1109)
Gilat, Mrs. G.
  Israel — National Center of Scientific and Technological Information (616)
Gilbert, M.
  United Nations Environment Programme — International Register of Potentially Toxic Chemicals (1026)
Gilbert, Nicole
  Quebec Ministry of Education — Library Headquarters — Point de Repere (831)
Gilham, Anton
  FRI Information Services Ltd. (392)
Gill, Dr. J.M.
  Brunel University — Research Unit for the Blind — International Register of Research on Visual Disability (115)
Gillham, Virginia
  University of Guelph Library — Cooperative Documents Network Project (1050)
Gladman, Peter
  Great Britain — British Telecommunications — Packet SwitchStream (447)
Glaeser, Phyllis
  International Council of Scientific Unions — Committee on Data for Science and Technology (574)
Glockner, Christian
  European Association for the Transfer of Technologies, Innovation and Industrial Information (306)
Goetschalckx, Mr. J.
  Commission of the European Communities — Specialized Department for Terminology and Computer Applications — EURODICAUTOM (223)
Golden, Linda
  ORACLE Teletext Ltd. (779)
Goldrian, Georg
  IFO-Institute for Economic Research — Department of Econometrics and Data Processing — IFO Time Series Data Bank (501)
Goldstein, Mr. R.B.
  Commodities Research Unit Ltd. (228)
Gomersall, Alan
  Greater London Council — Information Services Group (465)
Goodhart, Rear Admiral H.C.N.
  Brassey's Publishers Ltd. — Brassey's Naval Record (97)
Goodhart, Rear Admiral H.C.N.
  Brassey's Publishers Ltd. — British Defence Directory (98)
Goodwin, Ross
  Arctic Institute of North America — Arctic Science and Technology Information System (26)
Gorski, Alex
  Business Information International (123)
Gothard, Richard S.
  Gothard House Group of Companies, Ltd. (432)
Gotto, Anthea
  Geosystems (394)
Gottschalk, C.M.
  United Nations Educational, Scientific and Cultural Organization — Energy Information Section (1018)
Goudet, M.
  Universal Postal Union — International Bureau — Statistics of Postal Services (1030)
Gourdin, Jean-Luc
  National Conservatory of Arts and Crafts — National Institute for Documentation Techniques (722)
Govaerts-Lepicard, Dr. Monique
  Belgium — Ministry of Health — National Poison Control Center (83)
Grau, Xavier
  SVP Espana (912)
Gravesteijn, J.
  France — Bureau of Geological and Mining Research — National Geological Survey — Geological Information and Documentation Department (340)
Greenshields, Harry
  Atomic Energy of Canada, Ltd. — Chalk River Nuclear Laboratories — Technical Information Branch (44)
Greensmith, David
  Great Britain — Manpower Services Commission — Careers and Occupational Information Centre (462)
Greenwood, Derek
  Great Britain — British Library — Science Reference Library — Computer Search Service (445)
Gregoire, Lise
  Industrial Life-Technical Services Inc. (513)
Grenon, Philip
  Microfor Inc. (704)

Gretler, Armin
 Swiss Coordination Center for Research in Education (945)
Grimm, Andrea
 Informetrica Limited (536)
Grimshaw, Anne
 National Reprographic Centre for Documentation (725)
Groen, H.A.
 Ontario Ministry of Natural Resources — Mineral Resources Group — Ontario Geological Survey — Geoscience Data Centre (778)
Grosse, Dr. Ulrich
 Association for Information Brokerage and Technological Consultancy — IRS Info-Institute (36)
Grossmann, Pierre
 International Technical Publications Ltd. (605)
Guerette, Jacques
 Canada — Department of Energy, Mines and Resources — Canada Centre for Remote Sensing — Remote Sensing On-Line Retrieval System (132)
Guillot, Mlle.
 France — National Telecommunications Research Center — Interministerial Documentation Service — TELEDOC (367)
Guirguis, G.A.
 World Health Organization — Eastern Mediterranean Regional Office — Information Services (1112)
Gumbs, Barbara
 Caribbean Industrial Research Institute — Technical Information Service (177)
Gumpert, Jan
 BTJ (116)
Gundersen, Arvid
 International Group of Users of Information Systems (586)
Gundersen, Arvid
 International Medical Informatics Association (597)
Gurstein, Michael
 Socioscope Inc. (883)
Gutierrez, Elsa
 Argentina — National Atomic Energy Commission — Division of Technical Information (27)
Guy, Claude
 Pont-a-Mousson Research Center — Industrial Documentation Service — BIIPAM-CTIF Data Base (820)
Gwilliam, Anthony B.
 National Foundation for Educational Research in England and Wales — Information Research and Development Unit (724)
Gyozo, Gabriel
 Prodinform Technical Consulting Co. (825)

H

Haber, Roland
 Association of European Host Operators Group (42)
Haber, Roland
 Commission of the European Communities — European Commission Host Organization (219)
Haber, Roland
 Commission of the European Communities — Tenders Electronic Daily (227)
Haendler, Dr. Harald
 Hohenheim University — Documentation Center on Animal Production (487)
Hagenaar, K.E.
 Royal Dutch Society for Advancement of Pharmacy — KNMP Drug Databank (844)
Hagting, A.
 Institute of Agricultural Engineering — IMAG Dataservice (543)
Haibara, Kazuhiko
 Tokyo Shoko Research, Ltd. — Data Bank Service (984)
Hailu, Michael
 International Livestock Centre for Africa — Documentation Centre (596)
Haimerl, Dr. Hans
 Bavarian Ministry for Food, Agriculture and Forestry — Bavarian Agricultural Information System (76)
Hakkinen, Ms. Merja
 Building Information Institute (118)
Hakone, Hiroshi
 Marketing Intelligence Corporation (688)
Hakulinen, Erkki
 Sweden — Karolinska Institute Library and Information Center (921)
Haldea, Prithvi
 Constellate Consultants Ltd. (241)
Haley, Prof. K.B.
 University of Birmingham — Department of Engineering Production — Ergonomics Information Analysis Centre (1041)

Hall, A.R.
 BLCMP Ltd. (91)
Hall, J.L.
 Great Britain — Atomic Energy Authority — Culham Laboratory — Plasma Physics Library and Information Service (438)
Hamrefors, Sven
 INTERFACT/SVP AB (553)
Hamvay, Peter
 Hungary — Ministry for Building and Urban Development — Information Centre for Building (494)
Hanis, Dr. Edward H.
 University of Western Ontario — Social Science Computing Laboratory — Information Systems Programme (1087)
Hansen, Claus Kragh
 Nordic Documentation Center for Mass Communication Research (763)
Hansen, Hans-Erik
 Danish Committee for Scientific and Technical Information and Documentation (255)
Hansluwka, Dr. H.
 World Health Organization — Division of Health Statistics — World Health Statistics Data Base (1110)
Harding, D.W.
 British Computer Society (107)
Harding, Paul T.
 Great Britain — Institute of Terrestrial Ecology — Biological Records Centre (461)
Harker-Mortlock, James
 Harker's Specialist Book Importers — Harker's Information Retrieval Systems (474)
Harper, Gregory
 FrenchCompany for the Design & Implementation of Radio & Television Broadcasting Equipment — Antiope Teletext System (383)
Harris, Colin
 University of Sheffield — Centre for Research on User Studies (1070)
Harris, Robert E.
 Harris Media Systems Ltd. (475)
Harrison, Mr. C.
 Bemrose Printing (85)
Harrison, Michael A.
 Management Consultants International, Inc. (682)
Hart, David R.
 University of Dundee — Law Library — European Documentation Centre (1047)
Hart, Mary E.
 Alberta Research Council — Industrial Development Department — Industrial Information (15)
Hartel, Dr.
 InternationalCompany for Documentation in Chemistry (572)
Hartmann, Genevieve
 Group for the Study and Research of Tropical Agronomy — AGRITROP (467)
Hartmann, K.
 Gruner & Jahr AG & Co. — G&J Press Information Bank (468)
Harvey, Susan
 Commonwealth Regional Renewable Energy Resources Information System (230)
Hauchecorne, Jean
 Office of Economic Information and Forecasting (773)
Hauge, Jostein H.
 Norwegian Computing Centre for the Humanities (768)
Haworth, S.C.
 Paint Research Association — Information Department — World Surface Coatings Abstracts (792)
Hayes, Paul A.
 Aviation Information Services Ltd. (68)
Hayter, G.A.
 The Stock Exchange — Technical Services Department — TOPIC (902)
Head, Peter
 Morgan-Grampian Plc. — M-G Videotex Services (714)
Heaslip, Lloyd
 Canada — Parliament of Canada — Library of Parliament (157)
Heggstad, Kolbjorn
 University of Bergen — Department of Scandinavian Languages and Literature — Norwegian Term Bank (1040)
Heidemann, Dr. Erwin
 Kiel Institute for World Economics — National Library of Economics (639)
Heidrich, Anne
 Kompass International Ltd. (642)
Heijnen, J.H.M.
 Netherlands Bibliographical and Documentary Committee (735)
Heinrich, Hans-Peter
 Germany — Ministry for Research and Technology — Ongoing Research Project Data Bank (424)

Hellner, Barbro
  Sweden — National Swedish Environment ProtectionBoard —
  Swedish Environmental Research Index   (926)
Helman, A.L.
  Datastream International Ltd.   (267)
Helmchen, Dr. Michael G.
  Chemical Information Center   (201)
Hempel, Erik
  United Nations — Food and Agriculture Organization —
  INFOFISH   (1011)
Henderson, Diane
  University of Toronto — Faculty of Library and Information Science
  Library — Subject Analysis Systems Collection   (1077)
Henderson, Helen
  European Association of Information Services   (307)
Henderson, Roy V.
  Toronto Department of the City Clerk — Computerized Text
  Processing and Retrieval System for City Council Information   (985)
Henderson, Sandra
  Australia — National Library of Australia — Australian MEDLINE
  Network   (50)
Henrichs, Dr. Norbert
  University of Dusseldorf — Research Division for Philosophy
  Information and Documentation — Philosophy Information
  Service   (1048)
Henrichsen, Bjorn
  Norwegian Research Council for Science and the Humanities —
  Norwegian Social Science Data Services   (771)
Henry, M.
  French Federation of Data Base Producers   (385)
Henry, Michel
  URBAMET Network   (1091)
Heritier, Serge
  France — Ministry of Education — National Center for Pedagogical
  Documentation   (346)
Herman, S.A.
  Datastream International Ltd.   (267)
Hernandez, Vicente
  Eastern Telecommunications Philippines, Inc. — Database Access
  Service   (288)
Hewlett, Richard
  British Broadcasting Corporation — BBC Data   (104)
Hibbs, Genevieve M.
  Resources   (840)
Hilf, Mlle.
  Commission of the European Communities — Statistical Office of the
  European Communities — COMEXT Data Bank   (224)
Hilgartner, Romana
  Fraser Videotex Services   (369)
Hinshelwood, Mr. H.
  Independent Chemical Information Services Ltd.   (505)
Hirosaki, Dr. Shota
  Japan — Environment Agency — National Institute for Environmental
  Studies — Environmental Information Division   (626)
Hislop, Richard
  Art SalesIndex Ltd.   (29)
Hizette, Denise
  Commission of the European Communities — Education Information
  Network in the European Community   (215)
Hodgson, Paul
  Australia — National Library of Australia — Australian MEDLINE
  Network   (50)
Hoekstra, Dr. W.
  Philips Information Systems and Automation — DIRECT   (809)
Holm, Birgitta
  Finnish Pulp and Paper Research Institute — Technical Information
  Service   (333)
Holmes, Dr. Philip L.
  Blackwell Technical Services Ltd.   (90)
Hooper, Richard
  Great Britain — British Telecommunications — Prestel   (448)
Horn, B.
  Organisation for Economic Co-Operation and Development — Road
  Transport Research Programme — International Road Research
  Documentation   (786)
Hosking, J.E.
  Agra Europe   (8)
Houle, J.L.
  Polytechnical School of Montreal — Telidon Technology Development
  Center   (819)
Howard, Dr. John P.
  Information Research Ltd.   (530)
Howell, Dr. T.F.
  European Space Agency — Information Retrieval Service   (317)
Howells, Bernard J.
  Communication Services Ltd.— Viewdata Services   (231)
Howie, Professor R. A.
  Mineralogical Society of Great Britain — Mineralogical
  Abstracts   (711)

Hubbard, Paul S.J.
  Fairplay Publications Ltd. — Fairplay International Research
  Services   (324)
Huber, Wolfgang
  Commission of the European Communities — European On-Line
  InformationNetwork — Direct Information Access Network for
  Europe   (220)
Hudson, Richard F.B.
  SWALCAP   (919)
Hughes, Geoffrey
  ORACLE Teletext Ltd.   (779)
Hughes, Dr. J.G.
  Queen's University of Belfast — Department of Computer Science —
  Database on Atomic and Molecular Physics   (835)
Hughes, J.R.
  Lloyd's Shipping Information Services   (667)
Huismans, Jan W.
  United Nations Environment Programme — International Register of
  Potentially Toxic Chemicals   (1026)
Hulshoff, Mr. J. Sander E.
  Kluwer Publishing Company — Juridical Databank   (641)
Humphrey, Robert D.
  Extel Statistical Services Ltd. — EXBOND   (322)
Humphrey, Robert D.
  Extel Statistical Services Ltd. — EXSTAT   (323)
Hunter, David
  Commonwealth Agricultural Bureaux — CAB Abstracts   (229)
Hurt, C.D.
  McGill University — Graduate School of Library Science — FEESData
  Base   (692)
Hurter, Diana
  The British Council — Central Information Service   (108)
Husson, Michel
  France — National Center for Ocean Utilization — National Bureau for
  Ocean Data   (347)
Husson, Michel
  France — National Center for Ocean Utilization — National Bureau for
  Ocean Data — AQUADOC   (348)
Husson, Michel
  France — National Center for Ocean Utilization — National Bureau for
  Ocean Data — BIOCEAN   (349)
Husson, Michel
  France — National Center for Ocean Utilization — National Bureau for
  Ocean Data — CNEXO-BNDO Data Base   (350)
Husson, Michel
  France — National Center for Ocean Utilization — National Bureau for
  Ocean Data — DOCOCEAN   (351)
Husson, Michel
  France — National Center for Ocean Utilization — National Bureau for
  Ocean Data — geoIPOD   (352)
Husson, Michel
  France — National Center for Ocean Utilization — National Bureau for
  Ocean Data — POLUMAT   (353)
Husson, Michel
  France — National Center for Ocean Utilization — National Bureau for
  Ocean Data — ROSCOP   (354)
Hyland, Barbara
  The Globe and Mail — Info Globe   (430)
Hyun, Ki-woong
  SVP Korea   (915)

I

Ifshin, Steve
  ElsevierScience Publishers B.V. — Biomedical Division — Excerpta
  Medica   (296)
Ignazi, Dr. G.
  Rene Descartes University — Laboratory of Applied Anthropology —
  ERGODATA   (838)
Imagawa, Mr. Koichi
  Japan — National Diet Library — Library Automation System   (629)
Immonen, S.T.
  Association of European Airlines — AEA Data Base   (41)
Inglis, Susan
  System Development Corporation — SDC Information Services -
  Europe   (951)
Isgaard, Shirley
  International Association for the Evaluation of Educational
  Achievement — IEA Data Bank   (557)
Istvan, Kovacs
  Prodinform Technical Consulting Co.   (825)
Ito, Yo
  Tokyo Shoko Research, Ltd. — Data Bank Service   (984)
Iwabuchi, Dr. Yoshio
  Japan — Maritime Safety Agency — Hydrographic Department —
  Japan Oceanographic Data Center   (628)

J

Jamieson, Dr. D.T.
　Institution of Chemical Engineers — Physical Property Data Service　(548)
Janelle, A.
　Polytechnical School of Montreal — Telidon Technology Development Center　(819)
Jansen, Arnold A.J.
　Elsevier Science Publishers B.V. — Biomedical Division — Excerpta Medica　(296)
Janson, Florentia
　Canada — National Research Council of Canada — Canada Institute for Scientific and Technical Information　(152)
Jarvis, Helen
　University of Sydney Library — Bibliographic Information on Southeast Asia　(1073)
Jaschek, Prof. C.
　Strasbourg Observatory — Stellar Data Center　(905)
Javitch, Ronald A.
　Technical Information-Documentation Consultants Ltd.　(963)
Jenkins, Roy J.
　Information Unlimited　(535)
Jenschke, Dr. B.
　Information Center for Energy, Physics, Mathematics　(521)
Jensen, Vagn D.
　Denmark — Posts and Telegraphs Denmark — Central Telecommunications Services — DATAPAK　(271)
Jewitt, Mr. A.J.
　ICC Information Group Ltd.　(499)
Jimenez C., Alejandro
　Editec　(293)
Joergensen, Dr. Sven Erik
　International Society of Ecological Modelling — Environmental Data and Ecological Parameters Data Base　(604)
Johnson, Betty
　United Nations — Economic Commission for Latin America — Latin American Demographic Center — Latin American Population Documentation System　(1007)
Johnson, Kevin
　British Broadcasting Corporation — BBC Data　(104)
Johnston, Jill
　Great Britain — Department of the Environment — Building Research Establishment — Fire Research Station Library — Fire Science Abstracts　(452)
Jollet, P.
　European Space Agency — European Space Research and Technology Center — Materials Data Retrieval System　(316)
Jones, Hywel G.
　Henley Centre for Forecasting　(484)
Jones, N.G.
　Commonwealth Agricultural Bureaux — CAB Abstracts　(229)
Jones, Mr. P.J.
　Great Britain — Atomic Energy Authority — Atomic Energy Research Establishment, Harwell — Harwell Central Information Service　(434)
Jones, Roger
　Australian National University — Research School of Social Sciences — Social Science Data Archives　(61)
Jonescu, Dr. M. Evelyn
　University of Regina — Canadian Plains Research Center — Information Services　(1066)
Joseph, Mr. R.
　Unwin Brothers Ltd.　(1089)
Judge, Peter J.
　Australia — Commonwealth Scientific and Industrial Research Organization — Central Information, Library and Editorial Section　(47)
Jungskar, Marianne
　Sweden — National Library for Psychology and Education　(924)

K

Kahl, Raymond W., Jr.
　RWK Ltd.　(859)
Kallioja, Tapio
　Helsingin Telset Oy — Telset　(480)
Kamijo, Toshiaki
　Nomura Research Institute — Information Service and Development Department — NRI/E Japan Economic & Business Data Bank　(760)
Kanasy, Dr. James E.
　Canada — Department of Energy, Mines and Resources — Canada Centre for Mineral and Energy Technology — Technology Information Division　(131)
Kanda, Kenzo
　Overseas Data Service, Company, Ltd.　(789)
Kars, A.W.
　Samsom Data Systems — Samsom Datanet　(861)
Katagiri, Fumio
　Marketing Intelligence Corporation　(688)
Katcs, Michael W.
　SVP South Africa Ltd.　(917)
Katoh, Katsuhiro
　IBJ Data Service Co.　(498)
Kaungamno, Mr. E.E.
　Tanzania — National Central Library — Tanzania National Documentation Centre　(955)
Kavanagh, Rosemary
　Central Ontario Regional Library System — Interlibrary Loan and Communication System　(195)
Keenan, Stella
　International Federation for Documentation　(578)
Keenan, Stella
　International Federation for Documentation — Research Referral Service　(579)
Kelman, Bryan
　Western Australian Institute of Technology — T.L. Robertson Library — WAIT Index to Newspapers　(1107)
Kennard, Dr. Olga
　Cambridge University — University Chemical Laboratory — Cambridge Crystallographic Data Centre　(125)
Kennedy, Ilona
　Library & Information Consultants Ltd.　(658)
Kennedy, L.W.
　University of Alberta — Department of Sociology — Population Research Laboratory　(1035)
Kennington, Don
　Capital Planning Information Ltd.　(176)
Kent, Dr. Anthony K.
　Kent-Barlow Publications Ltd.　(638)
Kester, Nicholas
　Press Association Ltd. — NEWSFILE　(823)
Khalifa, Dr. Ahmad M.
　United Nations Educational, Scientific and Cultural Organization — Center for Social Science Research and Documentation for the Arab Region　(1015)
Khan, Ghulam Hamid
　Pakistan Scientific and Technological Information Centre　(793)
Kidd, H.
　Royal Society of Chemistry — Information Services — Current Biotechnology Abstracts　(854)
Kieran, Brian Laurence
　Morgan Grenfell & Co. Ltd. — Interfisc　(715)
Kingsmill, Brian
　IRS-DIALTECH　(615)
Kinzel, Cliff
　University of Alberta — Department of Sociology — Population Research Laboratory　(1035)
Kirchner, Dr. Wulf P.
　Germany — Federal Research Center for Fisheries — Information and Documentation Center　(421)
Kirk, Douglas W.
　Canada — Environment Canada — Inland Waters Directorate — Water Resources Branch — Water Survey of Canada　(142)
Klement, Susan P.
　Information Resources　(532)
Klimowicz, Dr. A.A.
　Eurotec Consultants Ltd. — LIBRARIAN　(318)
Kling, Gunnel
　Sweden — National Swedish Telecommunications Administration — Datapak　(927)
Klop, Kristina
　Australian Institute of Criminology Library — Computerised Information from National Criminological Holdings　(56)
Knight, Dr. R.M.
　Brown's Geological Information Service Ltd.　(113)
Knopf, Peter
　Swiss Coordination Center for Research in Education　(945)
Kochhar, Ved Bhushan
　India — National Institute of Health and Family Welfare — Documentation Centre　(508)
Kockar, Rezan
　Turkey — Scientific and Technical Research Council of Turkey — Turkish Scientific and Technical Documentation Center　(991)
Koelling, Juergen
　German Standards Institute — German Information Center for Technical Rules　(407)
Koenig, Wilfried
　Technical University of Aachen — Laboratory of Machine Tools and Production Engineering — Cutting Data Information Center　(964)
Kok, G.S.
　Maritime Information Centre/CMO　(685)
Kolarova, Dr. M.
　Bulgaria — National Agro-Industrial Union — Agricultural Academy — Center for Scientific, Technical and Economic Information　(121)

Kolb, Dr.
International Company for Documentation in Chemistry (572)
Kolbe, Helen K.
United Nations — Economic and Social Commission for Asia and the Pacific — Population Division — Population Clearing-house and Information Section (1003)
Komatsu, Masakata
Nihon Keizai Shimbun, Inc. — Databank Bureau — Nikkei Economic Electronic Databank System-Information Retrieval (753)
Korkie, S.P.
South Africa — Nuclear Development Corporation of South Africa — NUCOR Library and Information Services (886)
Korsberg, Ronny
Update AB (1090)
Koshino, Mr. H.
Nippon Gijutsu Boeki Co., Ltd. (758)
Kotzias, Klaus
Siemens AG — Data Processing Division — GOLEM (874)
Kotzias, Klaus
Siemens AG — Data Processing Division — Library Network System (875)
Krishnamoorthy, Dr. S.
Australian National University — Research School of Social Sciences — Australian Demographic Data Bank (60)
Krockel, H.
Commission of the European Communities — Joint Research Centre — High Temperature Materials Data Bank (222)
Kroese, J.J.
Netherlands Organization for Information Policy (744)
Krog, Hans K.
Norwegian Center for Informatics (767)
Krommer-Benz, Magdalena
International Information Center for Terminology (587)
Krutz, Dr. Michael
Dortmund Institute for Water Research — Data Bank on Substances Harmful to Water (284)
Kruythof, Ms. O.
Hubrecht Laboratory — Central Embryological Library — Documentation and Information System on Developmental Biology (490)
Krywolt, Susan
Alberta Public Affairs Bureau — Publication Services Branch (11)
Kubo, Fuminae
Japan Pharmaceutical Information Center (634)
Kuczek, Elaine
United Nations — Advisory Committee for the Co-ordination of Information Systems (1001)
Kugler, Simon
Kugler Publications (647)
Kuhnle, Stein
European Consortium for Political Research — Data Information Service (310)
Kukkola, Mr. Seppo
Finnish Foreign Trade Association — Information Department — Register of Exporters (332)
Kurzwelly, Mr. H.-E.
Germany — Ministry of Youth, Family and Health — German Institute for Medical Documentation and Information (428)

L

Lacasse, Mireille
Quebec — French Language Board — Terminology Bank of Quebec (830)
Lachenicht, Siegfried
Germany — Federal Institute for Sports Science — Documentation andInformation Division — Sport and Sports-Scientific Information System (420)
Lafay, Gerard
Center for International Prospective Studies (185)
Laidlaw, Sheila
University of New Brunswick Libraries — PHOENIX (1059)
Laing, Cameron D.
Canadian Agricultural Research Council — Inventory of Canadian Agricultural Research (167)
Lainton, Keith F.
Survey Force Ltd. (907)
Laitinen, Sauli
Finland — Technical Research Centre of Finland — Technical Information Service (330)
Lamont, Mrs. Yana M.
University of Alberta — Computing Services— Information Systems Group (1033)
Landon, Gordon K.
FRI Information Services Ltd. (392)

Langille, Delphine
Alberta Municipal Affairs — Central Services Branch — Alberta Land Use Planning Data Bank (10)
Langton, Barry
Blackwell Technical Services Ltd. (90)
Larratt, Richard
Larratt and Associates Ltd. (650)
Larsson, Ingemar
Pressurklipp — Swedish Market Information Bank (824)
Larsson, Monica
Stockholm University Computing Center, QZ (904)
Larsson, Dr. Sune
Sweden — Karolinska Institute Library andInformation Center (921)
Lau, Anna
Ontario Ministry of Education — Research and Information Branch — Information Centre —Ontario Education Resources Information System (777)
Laughton, Mary Frances
Canadian Association for Information Science/Association Canadienne des Sciences de l'Information (168)
Laurent, Philippe
Interuniversity Documentation and Information Center for the Social Sciences (611)
Lauwerys, Jacques
Belgium — Ministry of Economic Affairs — Data Processing Center — Belgian Information and Dissemination Service (80)
Laux, Prof. Wolfrudolf
Germany — Federal Biological Research Center for Agriculture and Forestry — Documentation Center for Phytomedicine (409)
Lawford, Hugh
QL Systems Limited (828)
Lay, Mrs. J.O.
STATUS Users Group (900)
Lea, Graham
Association of Database Producers (40)
Lea, Graham
Geosystems (394)
Leake, Ralph D.S.
Jordan & Sons Ltd. — Jordans Company Information (636)
Leblanc, N.A.
French Federation of Data Base Producers (385)
Lebowitz, A.
United Nations — Food and Agriculture Organization — International Information System for the Agricultural Sciences and Technology (1012)
Lee, Michael
Technical Indexes Ltd. (958)
Lee, Rossanne
Infomart (518)
Lee, Woyen
United Nations Environment Programme — INFOTERRA (1025)
Legros, Jean Paul
France — National Institute of Agronomic Research —Soil Science Laboratory — Soil Studies Service (362)
Lehmann, Klaus-Dieter
Frankfurt City and University Library — Bibliography of Linguistic Literature (368)
Lehti, Mr. Esko
Building Information Institute (118)
Leigh, John A.
Great Britain — British Library — Science Reference Library — EuropeanBiotechnology Information Program (446)
Leigh-Bell, Peter
Leigh-Bell & Associates Ltd. (657)
Leitch, Robert
Sonoptic Communications Inc. (884)
Lemaire, Anne
Paris District Informatics Administration — Informatics Biblio Service (797)
LeMaitre, Mlle.
Paris Chamber of Commerce and Industry — Department of International Relations — TELEXPORT (796)
Le Moal, Monique
Didot-Bottin — Bottin Data Bases (280)
Le Mottais, Mme.
France — Atomic Energy Commission — Programs Department — ELECNUC Databank (338)
Lepretre, Jean-Pierre
France — Bureau of Geological and Mining Research— National Geological Survey — Subsoil Data Bank (341)
Lepretre, Jean-Pierre
France — Bureau of Geological and Mining Research — National Geological Survey — World Gravimetric Data Bank (342)
Leps, Bruno
Infomart — Grassroots (519)
Le Sourd, Beatrice
Center for the Study of Advertising Support (189)

Levencrown, Leonard
  Videotex Information Service Providers Association of Canada (1101)
Levi, Judith
  Hebrew University of Jerusalem — Automated Library Expandable Program Hebrew University of Jerusalem (478)
Levy, Mrs. Zeeva
  Israel — National Center of Scientific and Technological Information (616)
Levy, Mrs. Zeeva
  Israel — National Center of Scientific and Technological Information — DOMESTIC (617)
Lewis, Dennis A.
  Aslib, The Association for Information Management (35)
Lewis, P.R.
  Great Britain — British Library — Bibliographic Services Division (439)
Libmann, Francois
  FLA Groupe La Creatique (336)
Lichtensteiger, B.
  Telekurs Ag — Investdata System (975)
Lidman, Olov
  Sweden — Research Institute of National Defense — FOA Index Group (929)
Lienau, Hans-Joachim
  Gruner & Jahr AG & Co. — G&J Press Information Bank (468)
Lilly, Megan
  Chisholm Institute of Technology Library — User Education Resources Data Base (204)
Lin, Zixin
  People's Republic of China — Institute of Scientific and Technical Information of China (801)
Lincoln, Sue
  Eastern Counties Newspapers — Eastel (287)
Lindinger, Mrs. Lore
  Austrian National Institute for Public Health — Literature Service in Medicine (66)
Line, Dr. M.B.
  Great Britain — British Library — LendingDivision (442)
Lingre, Gerard
  K-Konsult — VA-NYTT (637)
Lippert, Dr. Walter
  Gmelin Institute for Inorganic Chemistry and Related Fields (431)
Littlejohn, David. A.
  Lloyd's Shipping Information Services (667)
Liu, Chung-Ling
  National Science Council — Science and Technology Information Center (726)
Liverani, Prof. Antonio
  Lombard Interuniversity Consortium for Data Processing (669)
Lloyd, Mr. P.J.
  Loughborough University of Technology — Chemical Engineering Department — Particle Science and Technology Information Service (676)
Loaiza-Teran, Hugo
  Bolivia — National Scientific and Technological Documentation Center (93)
Lobb, Miss J.
  ADIS Press Australasia Pty Ltd. — ADIS Drug Information Retrieval System (5)
Lofrese, Elena
  Italy — National Research Council — CNUCE Institute (623)
Lohner, Wolfgang
  United Nations Educational, Scientific and Cultural Organization — UniversalSystem for Information in Science and Technology — UNISIST International Centre for Bibliographic Descriptions (1023)
Loomis, Barbara
  Universal Library Systems Ltd. (1029)
Lopes da Silva, Gabriela
  Portugal — National Institute for Scientific Research —Scientific and Technical Documentation Center (821)
Lorenz, A.
  International Atomic Energy Agency — Nuclear Data Section (561)
Losseau, Ms. I.
  United Nations — Food and Agriculture Organization — Economic and Social Department — Human Resources, Institutions and Agrarian Reform Division — Population Documentation Center (1010)
Lossois, Pierre
  Institute of Research on Fruits and Citrus Fruits — Documentation Center (547)
Lowe, David
  International Bee Research Association — Apicultural Abstracts (563)
Lowenberg, Emilie
  Canada — National Library of Canada — Public Services Branch — Union Catalogue of Serials Division (151)
Lucas, Barbara
  English Tourist Board — Information Unit — Tourtel (297)
Lucas, G.
  Datacrown Inc. (261)
Lucas, Ms. R.
  Netherlands Society for Informatics (745)
Luckenbach, Dr. Reiner
  Beilstein Institute for Literature in Organic Chemistry (79)
Lugowski, Dr. Bronislaw
  Poland — Polish Academy of Sciences — Scientific Information Center (816)
Luke, M.O.
  Atomic Energy of Canada, Ltd. — Whiteshell Nuclear Research Establishment — Technical Information Services (45)
Lund, Miss M.A.
  Great Britain — Atomic Energy Authority — Atomic Energy Research Establishment, Harwell — Waste Management Information Bureau (437)
Lunde, Svein
  Ship Research Institute of Norway — Ship Abstracts (872)
Lunenberg, E.
  International Association for Statistical Computing (556)
Lynham, V.H.P.
  Agra Europe (8)
Lyons, Rick
  Calgary Public Information Department — Public Relations Division — Civichannel (124)

M

MacDonald, Carol
  University of Regina — Canadian Plains Research Center — Information Services (1066)
MacGillivray, Joseph R.
  Alberta Research Council — Alberta Geological Survey — Geoscience DataIndex for Alberta (12)
Macias-Chapula, Dr. Cesar A.
  Mexico — National Center for Health Information and Documentation (700)
Magill, Brian P.
  Control Data Australia Pty. Ltd. —CYBERTEL Videotex Service (245)
Magnan, J.P.
  Organisation for Economic Co-Operation and Development — Road Transport Research Programme — International Road Research Documentation (786)
Magnusson, Mik
  United Nations Environment Programme — INFOTERRA (1025)
Mahdavi, M.N.
  Iran — Ministry of Culture and Higher Education — Iranian Documentation Centre (613)
Malley, Ian
  Loughborough University of Technology Library — Library Instruction Materials Bank (677)
Manell, Per
  Sweden — National Board of Health and Welfare — Department of Drugs — Swedish Drug Information System (922)
Mann, Ernest J.
  International Food Information Service — Food Science and Technology Abstracts (583)
Mann, Ernest J.
  International Food Information Service — Packaging Science and Technology Abstracts (584)
Mann, Ernest J.
  International Food Information Service — VITIS-Viticulture and Enology Abstracts (585)
Mann, Peter H.
  Loughborough University of Technology — Centre for Library and Information Management (675)
Manojlovich, Slavko
  University of Western Ontario — Social Science Computing Laboratory — Information Systems Programme (1087)
Mansa, Helge
  Denmark Telecommunications Administration — Danish Teledata System (272)
Mapp, Leslie
  Council for Educational Technology — Videotex Services Unit (247)
Marban, Ms. Rocio M.
  Central American Research Institute for Industry — Division of Documentation and Information (193)
Marce, Denis
  French Textile Institute — Textile Information Treatment Users' Service (390)
Marks, Dr. A.F.
  Royal Netherlands Academy of Arts and Sciences — Social Science Information and Documentation Center (847)
Marsh, Roy
  Canada — Department of Communications — Telidon Program (130)

Martin, David
  Great Britain — British Library — BibliographicServices Division — BLAISE (440)
Martin, Peter
  Information Industries Ltd. (524)
Marzolo, Mr. G.
  SVP Italia (914)
Mathieu, Pierre
  Edimedia Inc. (292)
Matkin, Derek I.
  Great Britain — Atomic Energy Authority — Atomic Energy Research Establishment, Harwell — Computer Science and Systems Division — STATUS (433)
Maughan, T.J.
  The British Council — Central Information Service (108)
Maunier, Miss C.
  International Institute of Refrigeration — Documentary Service (590)
Maurice, Marcel M.
  Commissionof the European Communities — System for Information on Grey Literature in Europe (226)
Maxwell, Kevin
  Brassey's Publishers Ltd. — Brassey's Naval Record (97)
Maxwell, Kevin
  Brassey's Publishers Ltd. — British Defence Directory (98)
Mayer, Marie-Claire
  Center for Industrial Creation — Documentation Service (184)
McConnell, Robert
  Infomart (518)
McDowell, Liz
  Library and Information Research Group (659)
McGarr, Michael
  Institution of Mining and Metallurgy — Library and Information Services (551)
McIntosh, Lord
  SVP United Kingdom (918)
McLauchlan, John
  Faxtel Information Systems Ltd. — Marketfax (326)
McLean, Neil
  Polytechnic of Central London — Information Technology Centre (818)
McNeil, C.S.L.
  Canada — Department ofEnergy, Mines and Resources — Conservation and Renewable Energy Branch — Canadian Energy Information System (133)
McReynolds, Dr. W.P.
  British Columbia Ministry of Industry and Small Business Development — Central Statistics Bureau (106)
Meadows, Prof. A.J.
  University of Leicester — Primary Communications Research Centre (1054)
Mealing, Miss P.K.
  Great Britain — Department of the Environment — Building Research Establishment — Fire Research Station Library — Fire Science Abstracts (452)
Mears, G.
  Institution of Electrical Engineers — INSPEC (549)
Mears, G.
  Institution of Electrical Engineers — INSPEC — Electronic Materials Information Service (550)
Meijburg, R.C.
  Netherlands Office of Posts, Telegraphs, and Telephones — PTT Central Directorate — Viditel (738)
Melguen, Dr. Marthe
  France — National Center for Ocean Utilization — National Bureau for Ocean Data (347)
Menden, Prof. Dr. Erich
  Institute of Nutrition— Documentation Department (545)
Mendez, Aida
  Spain — Higher Council for Scientific Research — Institute for Information and Documentation in the Social Sciences and Humanities (891)
Mengarduque, J.R.
  Netherlands — Ministry of Foreign Affairs — Translations Branch — Terminology and Documentation Section (732)
Menzel, Reinhard
  International Civil Aviation Organization —Air Navigation Bureau — Accident Investigation and Prevention Section — Aircraft Accident/Incident Reporting System (567)
Mertzweiller, Anne-Marie
  Pont-a-Mousson Research Center — Industrial Documentation Service — BIIPAM-CTIF Data Base (820)
Metcalfe, Mr. C.L.
  International Telecommunications Users Group (607)
Meyriat, Jean
  International Committee for Social Science Information and Documentation (571)

Michel, Andre J.
  Intergovernmental Bureau for Informatics (554)
Michel, M.
  France — National Center for Scientific Research — Scientific and TechnicalDocumentation Center (356)
Michel, V.
  Center for Research and Studies on Mediterranean Societies (186)
Middleton, Dr. Robert
  European Information Providers Association (312)
Midgley, Sue
  Brassey's Publishers Ltd. — Brassey's Naval Record (97)
Midgley, Sue
  Brassey's Publishers Ltd. — British Defence Directory (98)
Mikkelsen, Jon
  I/S Datacentralen (497)
Miller, Dr. G.M.
  Nineteenth Century Short Title Catalogue Project (757)
Miller, Maureen A.
  Hanover Press — Viewdata Services (473)
Ming, Mr. Lee
  International Information Service Ltd. (588)
Minian, Robin
  Boreal Institute for Northern Studies — Library Services (95)
Minowa, Shigeo
  United Nations University — Referral Service System (1028)
Miodrag, Alexsic
  Yugoslav Center for Technical and Scientific Documentation (1121)
Mitchell, Philip
  British Market Research Bureau Ltd. — Target Group Index (109)
Mittag, Ulla-Britt
  Swedish Standards Institution — REGIS (940)
Mittag, Ulla-Britt
  TESS Search Service (979)
Miura, Isao
  Kinokuniya Company Ltd. — ASK Information Retrieval Services (640)
Miura, Yasuhide
  Overseas Data Service, Company, Ltd. (789)
Miwa, Makiko
  Epoch Research Corporation (298)
Miwa, Masahito
  Epoch Research Corporation (298)
Mochmann, Ekkehard
  University of Cologne — Central Archives for Empirical Social Research (1045)
Moglestue, Idar
  Norway — Ministry of Finances and Customs — Central Bureau of Statistics (766)
Mohajir, Dr. A.R.
  Pakistan Scientific and Technological Information Centre (793)
Mohr, Curt
  German Standards Institute — German Information Center for Technical Rules (407)
Mok, Youn Kyun
  Korea Institute for Industrial Economics and Technology (645)
Mommertz, Prof. Karl Heinz
  German Iron and Steel Engineers Association — Information System on ProductionPlants for Iron & Steel — PLANTFACTS (398)
Mommertz, Prof. Karl Heinz
  German Iron and Steel Engineers Association — Steel Information System (399)
Montada, Leo
  University of Trier — Center for Psychological Information and Documentation (1078)
Montague, P. McC.
  Viewtel Services Ltd. (1102)
Montier, Bruno
  French Stockbrokers Society — Information andDocumentation Center (389)
Moon, Hiwhoa
  Korea Institute for Industrial Economics and Technology (645)
Moore, Nicholas L.
  Library Association Publishing Ltd. — Library and Information Science Abstracts (663)
Moos, J.U.
  I/S Datacentralen (497)
Morais, Marius
  Canadian Broadcasting Corporation — Project IRIS (169)
Morgan, Roger
  Great Britain — House of Lords — Library & Information Centre (460)
Morin, Marie-France
  France — Interministerial Mission for Scientific and Technical Information (344)
Morley, Heather
  CISI-Wharton Econometric Forecasting Associates Ltd. (207)
Morrison, Sylvia
  Canadian Library Association — Canadian Periodical Index (174)

Morse, Dr. Janice
 University of Alberta — Faculty of Nursing — Canadian Clearinghouse for Ongoing Research in Nursing (1036)
Morse, Dr. Janice
 University of Alberta — Faculty of Nursing — Canadian Directory of Completed Master's Theses in Nursing (1037)
Mort, David
 University of Warwick Library — Warwick Statistics Service (1083)
Moulder, David S.
 Marine Biological Association of the United Kingdom — Marine Pollution Information Centre (684)
Muir, Dr. C.S.
 World Health Organization — International Agency for Research on Cancer — Clearing-House for On-going Research in Cancer Epidemiology (1113)
Mukaida, Mrs. Keiko
 Kyushu University — Research Institute of Fundamental Information Science (648)
Mulder, R.M.M.
 Koninklijke Vermande B.V. (643)
Muller, Dr. E.
 Germany — Center for Agricultural Documentation and Information (408)
Muller, Dr. E.A.
 Lloyd's Shipping Information Services (667)
Muller, W.
 Technical Information Center — Mechanical Engineering Documentation (961)
Muraszkiewicz, Dr. M.
 Poland — Institute for Scientific, Technical and Economic Information (815)
Murphy, Donal P.
 CITIS Ltd. (208)
Muylle, C.A.
 Servi-Tech — BIODOC (870)
Mwinyimvua, Mr. E.A.
 Tanzania — National Central Library — Tanzania National Documentation Centre (955)

N

Nagayama, Taisuke
 Japan Pharmaceutical Information Center (634)
Nahon, Georges
 Intelmatique (552)
Nail, C.
 France — Bureau of Geological and Mining Research — National Geological Survey — Geological Information and Documentation Department (340)
Nakayama, Kazuhiko
 University of Tsukuba — Science Information Processing Center (1080)
Namekawa, Masao
 System Development Corporation of Japan, Ltd. — Search/J (952)
Nash, Dr. John C.
 Nash Information Services Inc. (718)
Nash, Mary M.
 Nash Information Services Inc. (718)
Natvig, Kristin
 Norwegian Computing Centre for the Humanities (768)
Naugler, Harold A.
 Canada — Public Archives of Canada — Machine Readable Archives Division (158)
Navin, Avner
 Hebrew University of Jerusalem — Automated LibraryExpandable Program Hebrew University of Jerusalem (478)
Neale, Wilson H.
 Australian Atomic Energy Commission — Lucas Heights Research Laboratories Library (51)
Neale, Wilson H.
 International Atomic Energy Agency — Vienna International Centre Library (562)
Nectoux, Philippe
 Editions Techniques — JURIS-DATA (294)
Neligan, Agnes
 Online Users' Group/Ireland (776)
Nelson, Mary
 University of British Columbia — B.C. Hospital Programs Branch — Drug and Poison Information Centre (1043)
Nemec, Prof. J.
 World Meteorological Organization — Commission for Hydrology — Operational Hydrology Programme — Hydrological Operational Multipurpose Subprogramme (1117)
Nemeth, Mrs. Aranka
 Hungary — Ministry for Building and Urban Development — Information Centre for Building (494)

Neuenschwander, Max E.
 Kompass International Ltd. (642)
Neumann, Dr. Klaus
 Uhde GmbH — Uhde Thermophysical Properties Program Package (992)
Neumeister, Mr. K-H.
 Association of European Airlines — AEA Data Base (41)
Newbold, Richard
 Loughborough University of Technology — Chemical Engineering Department — Particle Science and Technology Information Service (676)
Newby, Prof. Howard
 Economic and Social Research Council — Data Archive (291)
Newcombe, Dr. Alan G.
 Peace Research Institute-Dundas — Peace Research Abstracts Journal (800)
Newcombe, Dr. Hanna
 Peace Research Institute-Dundas — Peace Research AbstractsJournal (800)
Newell, Robert A.
 Newfoundland Telephone — Tourism Newfoundland (751)
Newman, Lorna E.
 Great Britain — Water Research Centre — Library and Information Services (464)
Nichols, Peter
 Nichols Applied Management (752)
Nigg, Erwin A.
 Swiss Viewdata Information Providers Association (946)
Nilsson, Goran
 University of Gothenburg — MEDICINDATA (1049)
Nishio, Shigehisa
 Kinokuniya Company Ltd. — ASK Information Retrieval Services (640)
Nissen, Line
 Nordic Atomic Libraries Joint Secretariat — Nordic Energy Index (761)
Niwa, Masayuki
 MIDORI Book Store Company (709)
Nobrega, Gerard
 Quebec Ministry of the Environment — Documentation Center — Envirodoq (832)
Noerr, Kathleen Bivins
 Information Management & EngineeringLtd. (527)
Nols, Mr.
 Commission of the European Communities — Statistical Office of the European Communities — CRONOS Data Bank (225)
Noonan, Richard
 International Associationfor the Evaluation of Educational Achievement — IEA Data Bank (557)
Nordstrand, Staffan
 Esselte Business Information (301)
Norevik, Bjarne
 University of Bergen — Department ofScandinavian Languages and Literature — Norwegian Term Bank (1040)
Northeast, Anthony J.
 Financial Times Business Information Ltd. — Business Information Service (328)
Nouwen, J.J.
 Swets Subscription Service (942)
Nowak, J.
 Germany — Federal Institute for Geosciences and Natural Resources — Geoscience Literature Information Service (412)
Nozaki, Margaret
 LymBurner & Sons Ltd. — Economist's Statistics (679)
Nunes Pereira, Renata
 Brazil — Ministry of Agriculture — National Center for Agricultural Documentary Information (99)
Nunn, Hilary
 Chem Systems International Ltd. (199)

O

Oberg, Irja-Liisa
 Finland — Central Medical Library — MEDIC Data Base (329)
Och, Mr. H.
 German Democratic Republic — Central Institute for Information and Documentation (395)
Ochsner, Heinz
 Data-Star (266)
Oda, Shigeake
 Japan Patent Information Center (633)
Odelycke, Per
 Sweden — National Board of Occupational Safety and Health — CIS Centre (923)
Oien, Arne
 Norway — Ministry ofFinances and Customs — Central Bureau of Statistics (766)

Oker-Blom, Teodora
 Nordic Council for Scientific Information and Research Libraries (762)
Olsen, Bengt
 Stockholm University Computing Center, QZ (904)
Olsen, Torkil
 Denmark — Ministry of Cultural Affairs — National Advisory Council for Danish Research Libraries (269)
Olsson, Sten
 World Health Organization — WHO Collaborating Centre for International Drug Monitoring (1115)
Olsson, Tommy
 Sweden — Geological Survey of Sweden — Groundwater Documentation Section (920)
Olthuis, Margaret
 Construction Specifications Canada — National Master Specification (242)
Ommanney, C. Simon L.
 Canada — Environment Canada — Inland Waters Directorate — National Hydrology Research Institute — Perennial Snow and Ice Section — Glacier Inventory of Canada (139)
Onken, Prof. Dr.U.
 University of Dortmund — Dortmund Data Bank (1046)
Oram, Anne
 York University — Institute for Behavioural Research (1120)
O'Reilly, James C.
 Multinational Association of Producers and Retailers of Electricity-Documentation (717)
O'Reilly, R.
 Canadian Broadcasting Corporation — Project IRIS (169)
Orfus, Marthe
 International Council of Scientific Unions Abstracting Board (575)
Orna, Elizabeth
 Orna/Stevens Consultancy (788)
Orr, David F.
 Toronto Stock Exchange — Data Products (986)
Ostermann, J.N.
 Technical Center for Mechanical Industries — Documentation Center for Mechanics (957)
Ottesen, Mr. O.B.
 Norwegian Standards Association — STANDARD (772)
Oudit, Nirupa
 Caribbean Industrial Research Institute — Technical Information Service (177)
Oudshoorn, J.H.
 Collective for Training and Education in Connection with Information Provision via Networks (211)
Ozawa, Dr. Hiroshi
 University of Tokyo — Computer Center — University of Tokyo On-Line Information Retrieval System (1075)
Ozimek, J.A.
 Learned Information Ltd. (654)

P

Pagliucci, Dr. Carlo
 Center of Experimental Metallurgy — Iron and Steel Documentation Service (192)
Pantry, Sheila
 Great Britain — Health and Safety Executive — HSE Library and Information Services (457)
Paradi, Dr. Joseph C.
 Dataline Inc. (262)
Pariboni, F.
 United Nations — Food and Agriculture Organization — Statistics Division — Interlinked Computerized Storage and Processing System of Food and Agricultural Data (1014)
Parise, Denise
 International Children's Centre — Documentation Service — Robert Debre Information Base (566)
Park, Mr. Ke Hong
 Korea Advanced Institute of Science and Technology — Experienced Librarians and Information Personnel in the Developing Countries of Asia and Oceania (644)
Parker, Arthur D.
 UTLAS Inc. (1094)
Parker, Chris
 United Kingdom Online User Group (1000)
Passey, David A.
 Henley Centre for Forecasting (484)
Payne, Elizabeth
 Canada — Health and Welfare Canada — Policy, Planning and Information Branch — A Network of Social Security Information Resources (145)
Peare, Trevor
 Online Users' Group/Ireland (776)

Pedersen, Birgit
 Nordic Atomic Libraries Joint Secretariat — Nordic Energy Index (761)
Pedersen, Eva
 Nordic Atomic Libraries Joint Secretariat — Nordic Energy Index (761)
Pedersen, Eva
 Riso National Laboratory — Riso Library (842)
Peinemann, Isolde
 Technology Information Center Gottingen (966)
Pelissier, D.
 France — National Center for Scientific Research — Scientific and Technical Documentation Center (356)
Pernsteiner, R.
 Technical Information Center (959)
Perry, Mr. B.J.
 Great Britain — British Library — Research and Development Department (444)
Persson, Doris
 Sweden — Statistics Sweden — Statistical Data Bases Unit (932)
Persson, Dr. Gosta
 Sweden — Geological Survey of Sweden — Groundwater Documentation Section (920)
Peska, Dr. Jan
 Czechoslovakia — Institute for Medical Information (250)
Peters, Gerd
 Germany — Federal Employment Institute — Institute for Employment Research — Information and Documentation Department (410)
Petrovic, Dr. Miodrag
 Boris Kidric Institute of Nuclear Sciences — Laboratory for Information Systems (96)
Pettelat, Andre
 International Railway Union — Documentation Bureau (600)
Pettit, Dominique
 French Press Agency — Telematics Department — AGORA (388)
Philipson, Lotte
 Denmark — Ministry of Cultural Affairs — National Advisory Council for Danish Research Libraries (269)
Phippard, Gary
 Phippard & Associates Strategic & Technological Consulting, Inc. (810)
Pierson, Gerard
 Center for Translation Documentation (191)
Pieters, Dr. Th.W.J.
 Netherlands Association of Users of Online Information Systems (734)
Pieters, Dr.Th. W.J.
 Royal Netherlands Academy of Arts and Sciences Library (849)
Pike, Ross T.
 Finsbury Data Services Ltd. — TEXTLINE (335)
Pinner, S.J.
 Extel Statistical Services Ltd. — EXBOND (322)
Pinner, S.J.
 Extel Statistical Services Ltd. — EXSTAT (323)
Pioch, Jean
 Mikro-Cerid (710)
Pisters, Mr. M.
 Association of European Airlines — AEA Data Base (41)
Plaister, Miss J.M.
 London and South Eastern Library Region (670)
Plaistowe, Alan D.
 Chem Systems International Ltd. (199)
Planer-Gorska, Danuta
 Polish Committee of Standardization, Measures, and Quality — Centre for Information on Standardization and Metrology (817)
Plass, Dietrich
 North Rhine-Westphalia Institute for Air Pollution Control — Literature Information System (765)
Plummer, Stephen
 American College in Paris — Service Calvados (22)
Podehl, W.M.
 Canada — Statistics Canada — Canadian Socio-Economic Information Management System (159)
Podehl, W.M.
 Canada — Statistics Canada — Canadian Socio-Economic Information Management System — Telichart (160)
Poliart, M.
 Commission of the European Communities — Statistical Office of the European Communities — COMEXT Data Bank (224)
Polushkin, V.A.
 International Centre for Scientific and Technical Information (565)
Porter, Linda M.
 Eurodata Foundation (303)
Porto Carreiro, Jayme
 International Atomic Energy Agency — Energy and Economic Data Bank (559)

PERSONAL NAME INDEX

Potenza, Dr. Roberto
  Italy — National Research Council — Research Center for the Stratigraphy and Petrography of the Central Alps — Archive of Italian Data of Geology (625)
Potter, Dr. Thomas D.
  World Meteorological Organization — World Climate Programme Department — World Climate Data Information Referral Service (1118)
Powell, Wyley L.
  UTLAS Inc. (1094)
Powilleit, Mrs. Ortrud
  Institute of Nutrition — Documentation Department (545)
Press, Zal
  AVCOR (67)
Price, Mrs. J.
  Pergamon Press— Current Awareness in Biological Sciences (803)
Prime, John
  Fairplay Publications Ltd. — Fairplay International Research Services (324)
Pringgoadisurjo, Miss Luwarsih
  Indonesia — National Scientific Documentation Center (512)
Pringle, Bill
  Calgary Public Information Department — Public Relations Division — Civichannel (124)
Pritchard, Alan
  ALLM Books — Small Computer Program Index (17)
Probst, Hans R.
  Data-Star (266)
Proca, Dr. Georges A.
  European Space Agency — Information Retrieval Service (317)
Pulido, Carlos
  Portugal — National Institute for Scientific Research— Scientific and Technical Documentation Center (821)
Pummell, Eric
  Eastern Counties Newspapers — Eastel (287)
Purmalis, Ilze
  Ontario Ministry of Education — Research and Information Branch — Information Centre — Ontario Education Resources Information System (777)
Puschmann, Herbert
  German Society for Chemical Equipment — Information Systems and Data Banks Department — Materials and Corrosion Information System (405)

Q

Quenot, Mr. J.
  Honeywell Bull — Euris Host Service (488)
Quenot, Mr. J.
  Honeywell Bull — Euris Host Service — European Community Law (489)
Queren, Wolfgang
  Information Center for Materials — System for Documentation and Information in Metallurgy (522)
Quinney, John
  Unwin Brothers Ltd. (1089)
Quirino-Lanhounmey, Dr. J.K.
  United Nations — Economic Commission for Africa — Pan-African Documentation and Information System (1005)

R

Radvanyi, Helga
  Alberta Research Council — Alberta Oil Sands Information Centre (13)
Rahard, Maryse
  France — National Center for Scientific Research — Documentation Center for Human Sciences (355)
Rajagopalan, T.S.
  India — Council of Scientific and Industrial Research — Indian National Scientific Documentation Centre (507)
Ramanana-Rahary, Raphael
  Madagascar — Ministry of Finance and Economy — National Institute of Statistics and Economic Research (681)
Rambaud-Chanoz, M.
  Commission of the European Communities — Statistical Office of the European Communities — COMEXT Data Bank (224)
Ramsden, Anne
  Natural Environment Research Council — BritishGeological Survey — Minerals Strategy and Economics Research Group — Mineral Information Section (727)
Rand, Eric
  Tele-Direct Inc. (973)

Rasmussen, Nancy
  Information Systems Design (534)
Ravinet, J.M.
  Interprofessional Technical Union of the National Federations of Buildings and Public Works — Center for Technical Assistance and Documentation — ARIANE Data Bank (610)
Rayment, Stephen
  Finsbury Data Services Ltd. — TEXTLINE (335)
Reade, David S.
  Canada — Department of Energy, Mines and Resources — Geological Survey of Canada — National GEOSCAN Centre (135)
Reed, Bernard
  The London International Financial Futures Exchange Ltd. (672)
Regnier, Jean-Jacques
  Center for Research and Studies on Mediterranean Societies (186)
Reinhold, Gisela
  Admedia — Adfacts (6)
Reinke, Dr. Herbert
  Center for Historical Social Research (183)
Remmelts, J.
  Netherlands Organization for Applied Scientific Research — Institute TNO for Mathematics, Information Processing and Statistics (741)
Renaud, Patrick
  Center for Industrial Creation — Documentation Service (184)
Rennie, Dr. J.C.
  Canadian Agricultural Research Council — Inventory of Canadian Agricultural Research (167)
Retlev, Ulla
  Danish DIANE Center (256)
Reynolds, J.E.F.
  Pharmaceutical Society of Great Britain — Martindale Online (806)
Rhodes, G.T.
  Cumulus Systems Ltd. (249)
Richardson, J.
  Commission of the European Communities — Education Information Network in the European Community (215)
Richardson, Peter
  TaysonInformation Technology Inc. (956)
Richmond, Mr. R.A.
  Canadian Micrographic Society (175)
Richter, Silvia
  IFO-Institute for Economic Research — Department of Econometrics and DataProcessing — IFO Time Series Data Bank (501)
Rickard, AnnC.
  Brunel Univeristy — Brunel Institute for Bioengineering — Information Unit (114)
Rietveld, Dr. H.M.
  NetherlandsAssociation of Users of Online Information Systems (734)
Ringdal, Frode
  Royal Norwegian Council for Scientific and Industrial Research — Norwegian Seismic Array (850)
Rippin, Prof. D.W.T.
  Federal Technical University — Technical Chemistry Laboratory — CHEMCO Physical Properties Data Bank (327)
Risseeuw, Mrs. M.
  International Translations Centre (608)
Rittberger, Dr. Werner
  Information Center for Energy, Physics, Mathematics (521)
Roberts, Daphne
  University of Leeds — Medical and Dental Library — Oncology Information Service (1053)
Roberts, G.
  International Federation for Information Processing (580)
Robertson, Carolyn
  Canada — National Library of Canada — Library Documentation Centre (149)
Robinson, Dr. F.J.G.
  Nineteenth Century Short Title Catalogue Project (757)
Robinson, G.A.
  Natural Environment Research Council — Institute for Marine Environmental Research — Continuous Plankton Recorder Survey (729)
Robson, Jack H.
  Canadian Micrographic Society (175)
Rodden, Ms. B.
  Memorial University of Newfoundland — Ocean Engineering Information Centre (694)
Rogers, Michael L.
  Drug Information Pharmacists Group — Pharmline (285)
Rolim, Flavio
  Anglo-Brazilian Information Service (24)
Roman, Adelaida
  Spain — Higher Council for Scientific Research — Institute for Information and Documentation in the SocialSciences and Humanities (891)
Romanenko, Arkady G.
  International Atomic Energy Agency — International Nuclear Information System (560)

Romberg, Fredrik
  Esselte Business Information (301)
Roof, J.
  Swets Subscription Service (942)
Rose, Dr. L.M.
  Federal Technical University — Technical Chemistry Laboratory — CHEMCO Physical Properties Data Bank (327)
Rosen, Earl
  The CIRPA/ADISQ Foundation (206)
Rosenbaum, Mrs. M.
  International Serials Data System (603)
Rosenbrand, P.J.C.
  Collective for Training and Education in Connection with Information Provision via Networks (211)
Rosselle, E.
  Belgium — Ministry of Economic Affairs — National Statistical Institute (82)
Rossouw, Dr. Steve F.
  South African Medical Research Council — Institute for Medical Literature (888)
Rothlauf, Walter
  Center for Study and Research of the Hydraulic BindersIndustry — Documentation Center — INTERCIM Cement Data Base (188)
Rovaris, Renzo
  Piedmont Consortium for Information Systems (811)
Rowbottom, Mary
  Polytechnic of Central London — Information Technology Centre (818)
Rowland, Colin
  Logica UK Ltd. (668)
Rudolph, Edith
  Germany — Federal Institute for Materials Testing — Rheology and Tribology Documentation Center (417)
Ruegg, Max
  Telekurs Ag — Investdata System (975)
Rufelt, Brita
  Swedish University of Agricultural Sciences — Ultuna Library — Documentation Section (941)
Rumble, Mona
  Market Research Society — Market Research Abstracts (687)
Ruscoe, Carol
  Alphatext, Inc. (20)
Rusyn, Richard J.
  Datacrown Inc. (261)
Ruus, Ms. Laine
  University of British Columbia — Data Library (1044)
Ryttarson, Mr. Magnus
  Swedish Institute of Building Documentation (938)

S

Sabat, Dennis
  SaskatchewanTelecommunications — Agritex (862)
Sabatini, Ing. Alessandro
  Center of Experimental Metallurgy — Iron and Steel Documentation Service (192)
Sagnert, Britt
  Sweden — Royal Library — Library Information System (931)
Sahib, Mr. M.A.
  United Nations — Economic and Social Commission for Asia and the Pacific — Statistics Division — UN/ESCAP Statistical Information Services (1004)
Saint-Maurice, Mr. S.
  France — National Institute of Statistics and Economic Studies — Documentation Division — SPHINXData Base (363)
Saito, Hideo
  Japan Patent Information Center (633)
Sakamoto, Masumi
  Information Processing Society of Japan (529)
Sakamoto, Yukihiko
  Japan Data Service Co., Ltd. (631)
Saksida, Marino
  Association of European Host Operators Group (42)
Salant, Ami
  Tel-Aviv University — Shiloah Research Center for Middle Eastern and African Studies — Documentation System — Mideast File (970)
Salmona, Jean
  Center for the Study on Information Systems in Government (190)
Salter, John
  Anglo-Brazilian Information Service (24)
Samaha, E.K.
  United Nations — Food and Agriculture Organization — Current Agricultural Research Information System (1009)
Sandino, Madame D.
  Group for the Advancement of Spectroscopic Methods and Physicochemical Analysis — Information Center for Spectroscopic and Physicochemical Analysis (466)
Sandoval, Dr. Armando M.
  National Autonomous University of Mexico — Center for Scientific and Humanistic Information (719)
Sarfati, Mrs. H.
  International Labour Office — Bureau for Labour Problems Analysis — Labour Information Database (591)
Sasamura, Mikio
  Teikoku Data Bank, Ltd. (969)
Sassen, Dr. Gerhard
  Institute for Documentation and Information in Social Medicine and Public Health (539)
Sattler, Mr. M.J.
  Australian Bureau of Statistics (52)
Saur, Klaus G.
  Saur Verlag (863)
Saveant, Renee
  Office of Economic Information and Forecasting (773)
Savignon, Irene
  France — National Institute for Industrial Property — Division of Publications Documentation and Information — INPI Data Bases (359)
Sawyer, Deborah C.
  Information Plus Inc. (528)
Scarfe, David
  Sports Council — Information Centre (896)
Schabas, Ann H.
  Indexing and Abstracting Society of Canada (506)
Schael, Fritz
  Volkswagenwerk AG — Documentation Section (1104)
Schanche, Grete
  Norwegian Petroleum Directorate — INFOIL II (769)
Schanche, Grete
  Norwegian Petroleum Directorate — Oil Index (770)
Schepers, Dr. H.
  Germany — German Federal Diet — Division of Scientific Documentation — Documentation and Information System for Parliamentary Materials (422)
Scherff, H.L.
  Commission of the European Communities — Euro Abstracts (218)
Scheuch, Prof. Dr. Erwin K.
  University of Cologne — Central Archives for Empirical Social Research (1045)
Schippers, J.M.
  Netherlands — Ministry of Agriculture and Fisheries — Agricultural Research Division — Centre for Agricultural Publishing and Documentation (731)
Schlick, Jean
  Christian Institutions Research and Documentation Center (205)
Schlitt, Dr. Gerhard
  University Library of Hannover and TechnicalInformation Library (1031)
Schmidt, Dipl.-Phys. Dietmar
  German Electron-Synchrotron — DESY Scientific Documentation and Information Service (396)
Schmidt, Dr. Ernst O.
  Bayer AG — Engineering Science Division — Chemical and Process Engineering Abstracts (77)
Schmidt, Joseph J.
  International Atomic Energy Agency — Nuclear Data Section (561)
Schmidt, Dr. KarlHeinz
  Dortmund Institute for Water Research — Data Bank on Substances Harmful to Water (284)
Schmolke, Prof. Dr. Michael
  Austrian Documentation Centre for Media and Communication Research (65)
Schneemann, Rudiger
  Health Care Literature Information Network (477)
Schneider, Dr. Thomas
  Siemens AG — Language Services Department — Terminology Evaluation and Acquisition Method (876)
Schnellenberg, John W.
  Hands-On Ltd. (472)
Schoenmakers, Pauline
  Europe Data (305)
Schoonmaker, Timothy R.
  Telemap Ltd. — Micronet 800 (976)
Schulze, Dr. Lothar
  Peace Research Institute-Dundas — Peace Research Abstracts Journal (800)
Schulze, Wilfried
  Germany — Federal Institute for Materials Testing — Measurement of Mechanical Quantities Documentation (415)
Schumacher, Dr. Dieter
  ONLINE GmbH (774)
Schurmann, Wolfram
  Motor Vehicle Documentation (716)

PERSONAL NAME INDEX

Schutzsack, Dr. Udo
 International Food Information Service — Food Science and Technology Abstracts (583)
Schutzsack, Dr. Udo
 International Food Information Service — Packaging Science and Technology Abstracts (584)
Schutzsack, Dr. Udo
 International Food Information Service — VITIS-Viticulture and Enology Abstracts (585)
Scott, Marianne
 Canada — National Library of Canada (147)
Scurr, Erica
 International Labour Office — International Occupational Safety and Health Information Centre (595)
Seelbach, H.E.
 KTS Information Systems (646)
Seelos, Dr. Jurgen
 Health Care Literature Information Network (477)
Seggelke, Prof. Juergen
 Germany — Federal Environmental Agency — Environmental Information and Documentation System (411)
Segre, Giuseppe
 Piedmont Consortium for Information Systems (811)
Sellin, Miss A.
 Glass Institute — Information and Documentation Service (429)
Selva, Carmen
 Spanish Drug Information Center — Spanish Pharmaceutical Specialities Data Bank (893)
Selwyn, R.B.
 Microinfo, Ltd. (705)
Senda, Ron
 University of Alberta — Computing Services — Information Systems Group (1033)
Sereda, Lloyd
 Alberta Department of Agriculture — Economic Services Division — Agricultural Commodities Data Base (9)
Sexsmith, Michele
 Compusearch Market and Social Research Ltd. (236)
Seydel, Dietrich
 Foundation for Science and Politics — Research Institute for International Politics and Security — Library and Documentation System (337)
Shaked, Haim
 Tel-Aviv University — Shiloah Research Center for Middle Eastern and African Studies — Documentation System — Mideast File (970)
Shapcott, John B.
 Extel Computing Ltd. — EXSHARE (321)
Sharma, Savita
 Information India (523)
Sharp, I.P.
 Sharp Associates Limited (871)
Sharpe, Mr. R.S.
 Great Britain — Atomic Energy Authority — Atomic Energy Research Establishment, Harwell — Nondestructive Testing Centre — Quality Technology Information Service (436)
Shaw, David
 Sonoptic Communications Inc. (884)
Shaw, Margaret
 Australian National Gallery — Library (58)
Shearer, Jan
 Great Britain — British Telecommunications — Prestel (448)
Sheen, Brian
 Canada — Health and Welfare Canada — Policy, Planning and Information Branch — A Network of Social Security Information Resources (145)
Sheppard, David
 Compu-Mark Ltd. (235)
Sherif, R.H.
 United Nations — Economic and Social Commission for Asia and the Pacific — Statistics Division — UN/ESCAP Statistical Information Services (1004)
Shewchuk, Cecil F.
 University of Western Ontario — Systems Analysis, Control and Design Activity (1088)
Shiba, Mr. Kitokuro
 Nihon Keizai Shimbun, Inc. — Quotation Information Center K.K. (755)
Shimada, Mr. M.
 Nippon Gijutsu Boeki Co., Ltd. (758)
Shimizu, Shigeru
 Nihon Keizai Shimbun, Inc. — Databank Bureau — Nikkei Economic Electronic Databank System-Time Sharing (754)
Shimokawa, Dr. Junichi
 Japan — Japan Atomic Energy Research Institute — Department of Technical Information (627)
Shirai, Mr. Kunihiko
 Japan — Environment Agency — National Institute for Environmental Studies — Environmental Information Division (626)

Shor, Dr. V.A.
 Union of Soviet Socialist Republics — Academy of Sciences of the U.S.S.R. — Institute for Theoretical Astronomy — Minor Planets, Comets, and Satellites Department (997)
Shum, C.N.
 International Information Service Ltd. (588)
Sidwell, A.J.
 Market Location (686)
Siefkes, Dr. Frauke
 Kiel Institute for World Economics — National Library of Economics (639)
Siegel, Herbert
 International Labour Office — International Occupational Safety and Health Information Centre (595)
Sievanen-Allen, Ritva
 Finland — Central Medical Library — MEDIC Data Base (329)
Sigurdson, Leigh
 Infomart — Grassroots (519)
Silva, Antonio Paulo A.
 Brazil — National Center for Micrographic Development (101)
Sim, Mary F.
 Asian Network for Industrial Technology Information and Extension (34)
Simon, Bernard
 Transpac (989)
Singh, D.C.
 International Civil Aviation Organization — Air Transport Bureau — Statistics Section — Air Transport Statistical Program (569)
Singh, Dr. V.B.
 Centre for the Study of Developing Societies — Data Unit (196)
Sison, Josephine C.
 Southeast Asian Regional Center for Graduate Study and Research in Agriculture — Agricultural Information Bank for Asia (889)
Sjostrom, Erik
 Swedish Standards Institution — REGIS (940)
Skandera, Boris
 Dobra Iron and Steel Research Institute — Informetal (281)
Slade, Stuart
 Chemical Age — Chemical Age Project File (200)
Sloane, Douglas
 Telecom Canada — Datapac (971)
Sloane, Douglas
 Telecom Canada — iNet 2000 (972)
Sloggett, Tony
 Oxford Microform Publications Ltd. (791)
Smith, A.M.
 University of London — Imperial College of Science and Technology — Department of Mineral Resources Engineering — Rock Mechanics Information Service (1056)
Smith, Alan E.
 Aviation Information Services Ltd. (68)
Smith, Betty
 University of Waterloo — Faculty of Human Kinetics and Leisure Studies — Information Retrieval System for the Sociology of Leisure and Sport (1085)
Smith, Caroline
 ICC Information Group Ltd. (499)
Smith, Clive A.
 Mitaka — JAPANSCAN (712)
Smith, Elmer V.
 Canada — National Research Council of Canada — Canada Institute for Scientific and Technical Information (152)
Smith, Prof. F.J.
 Queen's University of Belfast — Department of Computer Science — Database on Atomic and Molecular Physics (835)
Smith, Prof. F.J.
 Queen's University of Belfast — Department of Computer Science — Queen's University Interrogation of Legal Literature (836)
Smith, Prof. H.
 Pergamon Press — Current Awareness in Biological Sciences (803)
Smith, Malcolm G.
 AVS Intext Ltd. (69)
Smith, Peter
 Logica UK Ltd. (668)
Smith, Peter
 London and South Eastern Library Region (670)
Smith, Sandra
 Image Base Videotex Design Inc. (502)
Smits, G.B.R.
 Tijl Datapress (982)
Smurthwaite, Jennie
 European Law Centre Ltd. — Eurolex (314)
Smythe-Wright, Dr. Denise
 Natural Environment Research Council — Institute of Oceanographic Sciences — Marine Information and Advisory Service (730)
Soares, Helena
 Portuguese Radio Marconi Company — Data Bank Access Service (822)

Sobhi, Mohamed Ibrahim
 Universal Postal Union — International Bureau —Statistics of Postal Services (1030)
Soisalon-Soininen, Marjatta
 Helsinki University Library — Finnish National Bibliography (482)
Sokov, Mrs. Asta
 University of Sherbrooke — Asbestos Research Program — Information Center (1071)
Soloviev, Georgy
 European Coordination Centre for Research and Documentation in Social Sciences (311)
Sommer, Peter
 London Over the Counter Market (673)
Sommer, Peter
 Virtual City Associates Ltd. (1103)
Sondergaard, Klaus
 Danish DIANE Center (256)
Soule, Richard M.
 Financial Times Business Information Ltd. — Business Information Service (328)
Spaan, Ben
 Admedia — Adfacts (6)
Spannagel, Dr. Wolfgang
 Schimmelpfeng GmbH (865)
Spear, Michael
 Infocon Information Services, Ltd. (516)
Speight, J.A.
 Universal Library Systems Ltd. (1029)
Speirs, Neil
 Australian Business Index (53)
Spencer, G.V.
 Great Britain — British Telecommunications — Packet SwitchStream (447)
Spicer, E.J.
 Canada — Parliament of Canada — Library of Parliament (157)
Spinola, Catherine
 Telesystemes — Questel (977)
Springe, Dr. Wolfgang
 Bayer AG — Engineering Science Division — Chemical and Process Engineering Abstracts (77)
Stahl, Mrs. Hella
 Pulp and Paper Research Institute of Canada — Technical Information Section (827)
Stanko, Orest
 Image Base Videotex Design Inc. (502)
Stantcheva, Borjana
 Bulgaria — Medical Academy — Center for Scientific Information in Medicine and Health (120)
Stanzel, Gertraud
 Pharma Documentation Service (805)
Stapleton, Miss C.
 University of Birmingham — Department of Engineering Production — Ergonomics Information Analysis Centre (1041)
Steck, Mr. R.
 Rene Descartes University — Laboratory of Applied Anthropology — ERGODATA (838)
Steidle, Volker
 Foundation for Science and Politics — Research Institute for International Politics and Security — Library and Documentation System (337)
Stein, Prof. Dimitri R.
 Gmelin Institute for Inorganic Chemistry and Related Fields (431)
Steinberg, Eric
 Quebec Society for Legal Information (834)
Stern, Adolf
 Swedish Institute of Building Documentation (938)
Stevens, G.
 Langton Electronic Publishing Systems Ltd. (649)
Stevens, Graham
 Orna/Stevens Consultancy (788)
Stewart, Margaret
 Canada — National Library of Canada — MARC Records Distribution Service (150)
Stewart, Mr. Terry
 University of Waterloo — Department of Recreation — Leisure Studies Data Bank (1084)
Stewen, Werner
 Germany — Ministry of Justice — Judicial Information System (426)
Stickel, Dr. Gerhard
 Institute for German Language (541)
Stoddart, Linda
 International Labour Office — Conditions of Work and Welfare Facilities Branch — Clearing-house on Conditions of Work (594)
Stow, Philip C.
 Technical Indexes Ltd. (958)
Streatfield, David R.
 National Foundation for Educational Research in England and Wales — Information Research and Development Unit (724)

Streil, Jochen
 Commission of the European Communities — Court of Justice of the European Communities — Legal Data Processing Group — CJUS Data Bank (214)
Stroemfelt, Ralph
 Swedish Mechanical and Electrical Engineering Trade Association — VERA (939)
Stroetmann, Dr. Karl A.
 Association of Social Sciences Institutes — Social Sciences Information Center (43)
Stroud, Paul
 Technical Indexes Ltd. (958)
Sturen, Mr. Olle
 International Organization for Standardization — ISO Information Network (599)
Su, Ms. Yuanyuan
 China Building Technology Development Centre — Institute of Technical Information (203)
Suchan, Dr. Elke
 Frankfurt City and University Library — Bibliography of Linguistic Literature (368)
Sumarokov, Leonid N.
 International Centre for Scientific and Technical Information (565)
Sundin, Prof. Jan
 University of Umea — Demographic Data Base (1081)
Sundvall, Eva
 Bonnier Business Publishing Group — AffarsData (94)
Suter, Tito
 Argentina — National Atomic Energy Commission — Division of Technical Information (27)
Sutton, Dr. David C.
 University of Reading Library — Location Register of Twentieth Century English Literary Manuscripts and Letters (1065)
Suzuki, Takashi
 Nihon Keizai Shimbun, Inc. — Databank Bureau — Nikkei Economic Electronic Databank System-Time Sharing (754)
Swee, Mrs. Tan Kim
 Singapore Institute of Standards and Industrial Research — Industrial Technical Information Service (877)
Szente, Ferenc
 Hungary — National Szechenyi Library — Centre for Library Science and Methodology (495)
Szentirmay, Paul
 New Zealand — Department of Scientific and Industrial Research — DSIR Central Library (748)

T

Tabata, Shintaro
 Japan Information Center of Science and Technology (632)
Tagg, Dr. W.
 Hertfordshire County Council — Chiltern Advisory Unit for Computer Based Education (485)
Tahara, Reiji
 Japan Data Service Co., Ltd. (631)
Takeya, Shun-ichi
 Kyushu University — Research Institute of Fundamental Information Science (648)
Taky, Jacques
 Canada — Agriculture Canada — Scientific Information Retrieval Section — Pesticide Research Information System (128)
Talarczyk, Lucja
 Technical University of Wroclaw — Main Library and Scientific Information Center — System of Computerized Processing of Scientific Information (965)
Tamm, Goran
 DataArkiv AB (260)
Tan, Ernest Kwan-Boon
 Centre of InformationResource & Technology, Singapore (197)
Taylor, Mr. D.A.
 ICV Information Systems Ltd. — CitiService (500)
Taylor, Elizabeth
 Polytechnic of Central London — Information Technology Centre (818)
Taylor, F. John
 Royal Society of Chemistry — Information Services — Chemical Engineering Abstracts (852)
Taylor, James
 Universal Library Systems Ltd. (1029)
Taylor, Marcia
 Economic and Social Research Council — Data Archive (291)
Teague, Cheryl
 Royal Society of Chemistry — Information Services (851)
Tehnzen, Jobst
 University Library of Hannover and Technical Information Library (1031)

Tellis, D.A.
  Australian Mineral Foundation — Australian Earth Sciences Information System (57)
Temple, Dr. D.A.
  Zinc Development Association/Lead Development Association/Cadmium Association — Library and Abstracting Service (1122)
Templer, Sheila
  Royal Society of Chemistry — Information Services — Chemical Hazards in Industry (853)
Templer, Sheila
  Royal Society of Chemistry — Information Services — Laboratory Hazards Bulletin (855)
Teramura, Ken I.
  Maruzen Company, Ltd. — Maruzen Scientific Information Service Center (689)
Terlouw, Jan C.
  European Conference of Ministers of Transport — International Co-operation in the Field of Transport Economics Documentation (309)
Ternisien, Dr. Jean A.
  Ternisien Listing (978)
Terrada Ferrandis, Prof. Maria-Luz
  University of Valencia — Biomedical Documentation and Information Center (1082)
Terragno, Mr. P.J.
  Pergamon InfoLine Ltd. (802)
Terragno, Rodolfo H.
  Latin American Newsletters Ltd. (651)
Terris, Mrs. Olwen
  British Universities Film & Video Council Ltd. — Information Service (112)
Terry, A.R.
  Baric Computing Services Ltd. — Baric Viewdata (75)
Tetrault, J.-M.
  Quebec Society for Legal Information (834)
Thackwray, P.
  London Enterprise Agency — Supplier Identification System (671)
Thalberg, Knut
  University of Trondheim — Norwegian Institute of Technology — University Library (1079)
Thomas, Mr. P.
  Overseas Telecommunications Commission — Multimode International Data Acquisition Service (790)
Thomasson, Bjorn
  Nordic Council for Scientific Information and Research Libraries (762)
Thomasson, Bjorn
  Swedish Delegation for Scientificand Technical Information (937)
Thome, Karita
  Swedish Mechanical and Electrical Engineering Trade Association — VERA (939)
Thompson, D.
  Standards Council of Canada — StandardsInformation Service (898)
Thompson, George
  United Nations — Advisory Committee for the Co-ordination of Information Systems (1001)
Thompson, Margaret
  Australia — Bureau of Transport Economics — BTE Information Systems (46)
Thorgeirson, Gordon
  NORPAK Corporation (764)
Thunqvist, Lars
  Swedish Building Centre — Building Commodity File (934)
Tibbitt, Steven J.
  United Nations Educational, Scientific and Cultural Organization — Intergovernmental Oceanographic Commission — Marine Environmental Data Information Referral System (1020)
Tibert, John
  York University — Institute for Behavioural Research (1120)
Tischer, Harald
  Germany — Federal Institute forMaterials Testing — Rheology and Tribology Documentation Center (417)
Tokizane, Soichi
  Japan Association for International Chemical Information (630)
Toller, Michael H.
  Stacs Information Systems Ltd. (897)
Tollet, Mr. C.G.
  Finnish Foreign Trade Association — Information Department — Register of Exporters (332)
Tomlinson, Dr. N.R.
  London Enterprise Agency — Supplier Identification System (671)
Tomlinson, N.R.
  Unilever Computer Services Ltd. — World Trade Statistics Database (994)
Tornudd, Elin
  Helsinki University of Technology — University Library/National Library for Science and Technology (483)

Torres, Luis
  Infytec, S.A. (537)
Tothfalusi, Andras
  Hungarian Academy of Sciences — Institute of Economics — Economic Information Unit (491)
Tournesac, Denis
  IST-Informatheque Inc. (619)
Townsend, Colin
  Systemhouse Ltd. — MINISIS (953)
Trachtenherts, Dr. Michail S.
  Union of Soviet Socialist Republics — Academy of Sciences of the U.S.S.R. — Institute for High Temperatures — Thermophysical PropertiesCenter (996)
Trevisan, Giorgio
  Commission of the European Communities — Agricultural Research Projects Data Base (213)
Trew, Andrew J.M.
  Legal Technology Group (656)
Truchet, M.
  France — National Telecommunications Research Center — Interministerial Documentation Service — TELEDOC (367)
Trumpy, Dr. Ing. Stefano
  Italy — National Research Council — CNUCE Institute (623)
Tsui, Josephine
  Metropolitan Toronto Library Board — Regional Bibliographic Products Department (699)
Turuguet Mayol, Domenec
  Spain — Ministry of Health and Safety — National Institute of Occupational Safety and Health — National Information and Documentation Center (892)
Turvey, Dr. R.
  International Labour Office — Bureau of Statistics (592)

U

Urbanek, Dr. Zdenek
  Swiss Academy of Medical Sciences — Documentation Service (943)
Ushiba, Daizo
  International Medical Information Center (598)
Utzinger, Dr. Robert
  Alpine Science Information Service (21)

V

Valentin, Thomas
  France — Ministry of Education — National Center for Pedagogical Documentation (346)
Valiant, S.J.
  Eurodata Foundation (303)
Valls, Dr. Jacques
  Asian Institute of Technology — Regional Documentation Center — Asian Information Center for Geotechnical Engineering (30)
Valls, Dr. Jacques
  Asian Institute of Technology — Regional Documentation Center — Environmental Sanitation Information Center (31)
Valls, Dr. Jacques
  Asian Institute of Technology — Regional Documentation Center — International Ferrocement Information Center (32)
Valls, Dr. Jacques
  Asian Institute of Technology — Regional Documentation Center — Renewable Energy Resources Information Center (33)
Valtchev, Prof. Alexi
  Bulgaria — Medical Academy— Center for Scientific Information in Medicine and Health (120)
Valverius, Sonja
  Swedish Council for Information on Alcohol and Other Drugs (936)
van Bergeijk, D.
  International Translations Centre (608)
van Dam, Mr. Toon A.
  International Reference Center for Community Water Supply and Sanitation — Programme on Exchange and Transfer of Information on Community Water Supply and Sanitation (601)
van den Abeele, R.
  Belgium — Ministryof Economic Affairs — Data Processing Center — Belgian Information and Dissemination Service (80)
van den Berg, A.
  Netherlands Organization for Applied Scientific Research — National Council for Agricultural Research TNO — Central Project Administration for Current AgriculturalResearch in the Netherlands (742)
Vander Elst, Mr. A.
  SVP Benelux (909)

van der Wateren, Jan
  Royal Institute of British Architects — British Architectural Library — Architectural Periodicals Index (845)
Van der Weyden, W.G.A.
  Koninklijke Vermande B.V. (643)
van de Werken, G.
  Institute of Agricultural Engineering — IMAG Dataservice (543)
van Dijk, J.E.
  Netherlands Bibliographical and Documentary Committee (735)
van Dijk, Marcel
  Bureau Marcel van Dijk, SA (122)
van Halm, Johan
  Van Halm & Associates (1095)
van Houten, Dr. Rob
  South Africa — Council for Scientific and Industrial Research — Centre for Scientific and Technical Information (885)
van Leeuwen, J.K.W.
  Netherlands Center for Information Policy (736)
van Nuland, J.B.P.
  Dutch State Mines — TISDATA (286)
van Putte, Dr. N.W.
  Pharma Documentation Ring (804)
van Slype, Georges
  Bureau Marcel van Dijk, SA (122)
Varadachari, Dr. V.V.R.
  India — National Institute of Oceanography — Indian National Oceanographic Data Centre (509)
Veaner, Allen B.
  Veaner Associates (1097)
Velazquez, Harriet
  UTLAS Inc. (1094)
Vellacott, Mr. E.R.
  Australia — National Library of Australia (48)
Veretenicoff, Serge
  Group for the Study and Research of Tropical Agronomy — AGRITROP (467)
Verheijen-Voogd, Dr. Christina
  State University of Utrecht Library — Biomedical Information Department (899)
Verrel, Barbara
  Saur Verlag (863)
Vickery, Mrs. Alina
  University of London — Central Information Service (1055)
Vilain, Michel
  France — French Senate — Parliamentary Documentation and Information Printing Service (343)
Villard, Hubert A.
  Library Network of SIBIL Users (664)
Villarreal, Milagros
  Spain — Higher Council for Scientific Research — Institute for Information and Documentation in Science and Technology (890)
Vincent, Mme.
  French Water Study Association — National Water Information Center (391)
Visakorpi, J.K.
  Finnish Council for Scientific Information and Research Libraries (331)
Vogel, Dr. Oskar
  European Coordination Centre for Research and Documentation in Social Sciences (311)
Volkel, Dr. Uta
  Germany — Federal Institute for Materials Testing — Nondestructive Testing Documentation (416)
von Lossow, Wilfried
  Association of Social Sciences Institutes — Social Sciences Information Center (43)
von Selle, Dr. K.O.
  Germany — Center for Agricultural Documentation and Information (408)
Vowinckel, Kathleen
  Larratt and Associates Ltd. (650)

W

Wainwright, Jane
  Great Britain — House of Commons Library — Parliamentary On-Line Information System (459)
Wakao, Mr. N.
  Nihon Keizai Shimbun, Inc. — Quotation Information Center K.K. (755)
Walby, Basil J.
  Australia — Commonwealth Scientific and Industrial Research Organization — Central Information, Library and Editorial Section (47)
Walker, John
  Australian Institute of Criminology Library — Computerised Information from National Criminological Holdings (56)
Walker, Dr. Nigel
  Unilever Computer Services Ltd. — European Petrochemical Association Trade Statistics Database (993)
Walker, Dr. Nigel
  Unilever Computer Services Ltd. — World Trade Statistics Database (994)
Wall, Maria Vahlgren
  Update AB (1090)
Wall, Dr. R.A.
  Loughborough University of Technology Library — Minimal-Input Cataloguing System (678)
Wallace, Graham
  Datastream International Ltd. (267)
Wallin, Kristian
  Linkoping University Library — NYTTFO (665)
Wallin, Marie
  Sweden — Royal Institute of Technology Library — Information and Documentation Center (930)
Wang, C.M.
  Institute for Information Industry (542)
Wang, Xiaochu
  People's Republic of China — Institute of Scientific and Technical Information of China (801)
Wanklyn, Margaret
  Information Management and Consulting Association (526)
Warmuth, C.H.
  Austria — Federal Ministry of Buildings and Technology — Federal Research and Testing Establishment Arsenal — Road Research Documentation Center (63)
Warren, Lois M.
  Warren , Inc. (1105)
Watkins, Wendy
  Carleton University — Department of Sociology and Anthropology — Social Science Data Archives (178)
Watson, Peter G.
  VideoAccess (1099)
Watts, Mr. G.A.
  BHRA, The Fluid Engineering Centre — Information Services (86)
Watts, V.C.
  Production Engineering Research Association of Great Britain — Information Services (826)
Waugh, John
  SVP Australia (908)
Weckert, H.-K.
  Schimmelpfeng GmbH (865)
Weil, Mrs. S.
  Israel Atomic Energy Commission — Soreq Nuclear Research Center — Library and Technical Information Department (618)
Weir, Gary
  British Columbia Ministry of Industry and Small Business Development — Central Statistics Bureau (106)
Weiske, Dr. Christian
  Chemical Information Center (201)
Weiss, E.O.
  International Telecommunications Users Group (607)
Weitzman, Didier
  GSI-ECO (469)
Welham, Robert
  Royal Society of Chemistry — Information Services (851)
Wentzel, Doug
  Centennial College — Bibliocentre (182)
Wheeler, Jean V.
  Indexing and Abstracting Society of Canada (506)
White, Brenda
  Capital Planning Information Ltd. (176)
White, S.
  Great Britain — Department of Industry — Information Technology Division — HERMES (450)
White, Susan M.
  Pira: Research Association for the Paper and Board, Printing and Packaging Industries — Comprehensive Information Services (812)
Whitlow, S.
  Canada — Environment Canada — Inland Waters Directorate — Water Quality Branch — National Water Quality Data Bank (141)
Whittick, Ms. J.A.
  Memorial University of Newfoundland — Ocean Engineering Information Centre (694)
Widdowson, John S.
  British Standards Institution — Information Department (111)
Widstrand, Ninna
  BTJ (116)
Wiebe, Victor G.
  University of Saskatchewan Library — Reference Department — University of Saskatchewan Libraries Machine-Assisted Reference Teleservices (1067)
Wierer, Jutta
  German Plastics Institute — Information and Documentation Services (402)

Wijnstroom, Dr. Margreet
International Federation of Library Associations and Institutions (582)
Wiktor, Christian L.
Dalhousie University — Law School Library — Marine Affairs Bibliography (254)
Wild, Kate
International Labour Office — Central Library and Documentation Branch (593)
Wild, Rosanne
Sharp Associates Limited (871)
Wilde, Kenneth K.
International Civil Aviation Organization — Air Navigation Bureau — Aerodromes Section — Airport Characteristics Data Bank (568)
Wilkinson, Dr. Gordon
Docupro (283)
Wilkinson, Dr. Gordon
Infocom (515)
Willetts, Mr. G.K.
Bank of England — Financial Statistics Division (72)
Williams, Bernard J.S.
National Reprographic Centre for Documentation (725)
Williams, G.P.L.
Atomic Energy of Canada, Ltd. — Chalk River Nuclear Laboratories — Technical Information Branch (44)
Williams, Helen B.
Userlink Systems Ltd. (1093)
Williams, Karan
Phippard & Associates Strategic & Technological Consulting, Inc. (810)
Williams, Dr. Philip W.
Userlink Systems Ltd. (1093)
Williamson, Dr. John J.
Society of Metaphysicians Ltd. — Information Services (882)
Wilmot, A.H.
Canada — Agriculture Canada — Marketing and Economics Branch — Agricultural Marketing and Trade Database (126)
Wilson, Richard M.
Royal Tropical Institute — Agricultural Information & Documentation Section (857)
Wilson, W.X.
Langton Electronic Publishing Systems Ltd. (649)
Wimmer, Dr. Rainer
Institute for German Language (541)
Winkel, P.
Netherlands Organization for Applied Scientific Research — TNO Study and Information Center on Environmental Research — Environmental Research in the Netherlands (743)
Wissmann, Dr.-Ing. Wilhelm
Fraunhofer Society — Information Center for Building and Physical Planning (373)
Wissmann, Dr.-Ing. Wilhelm
Fraunhofer Society — Information Center for Building and Physical Planning — Building Research Projects Data Base (374)
Wissmann, Dr.-Ing. Wilhelm
Fraunhofer Society — Information Center for Building and Physical Planning — Buildings Documentation DataBase (375)
Wissmann, Dr.-Ing. Wilhelm
Fraunhofer Society — Information Center for Building and Physical Planning — Literature Compilations Data Base (376)
Wissmann, Dr.-Ing. Wilhelm
Fraunhofer Society — Information Center for Building and Physical Planning — PASCALBAT Data Base (377)
Wissmann, Dr.-Ing. Wilhelm
Fraunhofer Society — Information Center for Building and PhysicalPlanning — Property Services Agency Information on Construction and Architecture Data Base (378)
Wissmann, Dr.-Ing. Wilhelm
Fraunhofer Society — Information Center for Building and Physical Planning — Regional Planning, City Planning, Housing, Building Construction Data Base (379)
Wissmann, Dr.-Ing. Wilhelm
Fraunhofer Society —Information Center for Building and Physical Planning — Regional Planning, City Planning, Housing Research Projects Data Base (380)
Withers, Hastings
PMB Print Measurement Bureau (814)
Witt, Barbara
Canada — Transport Canada — Library and Information Centre (161)
Wolff-Terroine, M.
France — NationalCenter for Scientific Research — Scientific Documentation Center in Oncology— CANCERNET (357)
Wolodarski, Jurek
Stockholm University Computing Center, QZ (904)
Woloshyn, Bohdan
Dataline Inc. (262)

Wood, D.S.
Aslib, The Association for Information Management (35)
Wood, Dr. G.H.
Canada — National Research Council of Canada — Canada Institute for Scientific and Technical Information — Scientific Numeric Databases (155)
Wood, Dr. G.H.
Canada — National Research Council of Canada — Chemistry Division — Metals Data Centre (156)
Woods, Ian B.
Geo Abstracts Ltd. (393)
Worlock, David R.
European Law Centre Ltd. — Eurolex (314)
Wortley, Miss P.J.
International Association of Agricultural Librarians and Documentalists (558)
Wright, Dr. Alan E.
Australian National Radio Astronomy Observatory — Parkes Catalogue of Radio Sources (59)
Wyatt, John F.
Parpinelli TECNON — World Petrochemical Industry Data Bank (799)

X

Xi, Mr. Ruilin
China Building Technology Development Centre — Institute of Technical Information (203)
Xu, Mr. Ronglie
China Building Technology Development Centre — Institute of Technical Information (203)

Y

Yamaguchi, Akihisa
Japan Data Service Co., Ltd. (631)
Yamakawa, Mr. Takashi
USACO Corporation (1092)
Yano, Miss Fumi
Mitaka — JAPANSCAN (712)
Yashiro, Akira
Information Researchers, Inc. (531)
Young, M.E.H.
Canada — Department of Energy, Mines and Resources — Topographical Survey Division — Digital Mapping System (136)
Ypma, J.H.
Netherlands — Netherlands Foreign Trade Agency — Library and Documentation Branch — Foreign Trade Abstracts (733)
Yrjola, Hellevi
Finnish Council for Scientific Information and Research Libraries (331)

Z

Zahawi, Mrs. Faria
League of Arab States — League of Arab States Documentation and Information Center (653)
Zamora Rodriguez, Prof. Pedro
Mexico — National Institute of Nuclear Research — Nuclear Information and Documentation Center (703)
Zimmermann, Marie
Christian Institutions Research and Documentation Center (205)

GEOGRAPHIC INDEX BY COUNTRY

Arranges organizations, systems, and services described in the International Volume according to countries in which they are located. Some 65 countries are listed in alphabetical order, from Argentina to Yugoslavia. Within each country, entries are subarranged alphabetically by city. Entries in this index include English-language organization and system name, full address, telephone number, director name, and main section entry number.

GEOGRAPHIC INDEX

ARGENTINA

ARGENTINA — NATIONAL ATOMIC ENERGY COMMISSION — DIVISION OF TECHNICAL INFORMATION   (27)
Av. del Libertador 8250
1429 Buenos Aires, Argentina
Phone: 70 7711
Tito Suter

ARGENTINA — NATIONAL COUNCIL FOR SCIENTIFIC AND TECHNICAL RESEARCH — ARGENTINE CENTER FOR SCIENTIFIC AND TECHNOLOGICAL INFORMATION   (28)
Moreno 431
1091 Buenos Aires, Argentina
Phone: 341777

AUSTRALIA

AUSTRALIAN BUREAU OF STATISTICS   (52)
P.O. Box 10
Belconnen, A.C.T. 2616, Australia
Phone: 062 526627
Mr. R.J. Cameron

AUSTRALIA — BUREAU OF TRANSPORT ECONOMICS — BTE INFORMATION SYSTEMS   (46)
P.O. Box 501 Civic Square
Canberra, A.C.T. 2608, Australia
Phone: 062 469616

AUSTRALIA — NATIONAL LIBRARY OF AUSTRALIA   (48)
Parkes Place
Canberra, A.C.T. 2600, Australia
Phone: 062 621111
Harrison Bryan

AUSTRALIA — NATIONAL LIBRARY OF AUSTRALIA — AUSTRALIAN BIBLIOGRAPHIC NETWORK   (49)
Parkes Place
Canberra, A.C.T. 2600, Australia
Phone: 062 621111
Judith A. Baskin

AUSTRALIA — NATIONAL LIBRARY OF AUSTRALIA — AUSTRALIAN MEDLINE NETWORK   (50)
Parkes Place
Canberra, A.C.T. 2600, Australia
Phone: 062 621523
Paul Hodgson

AUSTRALIAN NATIONAL GALLERY — LIBRARY   (58)
G.P.O. Box 1150
Canberra, A.C.T. 2601, Australia
Phone: 062 712530
Margaret Shaw

AUSTRALIAN NATIONAL UNIVERSITY — RESEARCH SCHOOL OF SOCIAL SCIENCES — AUSTRALIAN DEMOGRAPHIC DATA BANK   (60)
G.P.O. Box 4
Canberra, A.C.T. 2601, Australia
Prof. J.C. Caldwell

AUSTRALIAN NATIONAL UNIVERSITY — RESEARCH SCHOOL OF SOCIAL SCIENCES — SOCIAL SCIENCE DATA ARCHIVES   (61)
G.P.O. Box 4
Canberra, A.C.T. 2601, Australia
Phone: 062 494400
Roger Jones

CHISHOLM INSTITUTE OF TECHNOLOGY LIBRARY — USER EDUCATION RESOURCES DATA BASE   (204)
900 Dandenong Rd.
Caulfield East, Vic. 3145, Australia
Phone: 03 5732523
Megan Lilly

ACI COMPUTER SERVICES   (3)
P.O. Box 42
Clayton, Vic. 3168, Australia
Phone: 03 5448433

AUSTRALIA — COMMONWEALTH SCIENTIFIC AND INDUSTRIAL RESEARCH ORGANIZATION — CENTRAL INFORMATION, LIBRARY AND EDITORIAL SECTION   (47)
314 Albert St.
P.O. Box 89
East Melbourne, Vic. 3002, Australia
Phone: 03 4187333
Peter J. Judge

COMMONWEALTH REGIONAL RENEWABLE ENERGY RESOURCES INFORMATION SYSTEM   (230)
CSIRO, P.O. Box 89
314 Albert St.
East Melbourne, Vic. 3002, Australia
Phone: 03 4187333
Susan Harvey

HARKER'S SPECIALIST BOOK IMPORTERS — HARKER'S INFORMATION RETRIEVAL SYSTEMS   (474)
74 Glebe Point Rd.
Glebe, N.S.W. 2037, Australia
Phone: 02 6607666
James Harker-Mortlock

AUSTRALIAN MINERAL FOUNDATION — AUSTRALIAN EARTH SCIENCES INFORMATION SYSTEM   (57)
P.O. Box 97
Glenside, S.A. 5065, Australia
Phone: 08 797821
D.S. Crowe

AUSTRALIAN BUSINESS INDEX   (53)
1 Leslie St.
Hawthorn, Vic. 3122, Australia
Phone: 03 8194672
Neil Speirs

AUSTRALIAN COUNCIL FOR EDUCATIONAL RESEARCH — LIBRARY AND INFORMATION SERVICES UNIT   (54)
P.O. Box 210
Hawthorn, Vic. 3122, Australia
Phone: 03 8181271
Margaret A. Findlay

INSEARCH LTD./DIALOG   (538)
P.O. Box K16
Haymarket, N.S.W. 2000, Australia
Phone: 02 2646344
Jennifer L. Affleck

UNIVERSITY OF TASMANIA LIBRARY — UNION LIST OF HIGHER DEGREE THESES IN AUSTRALIAN LIBRARIES   (1074)
Box 252C, G.P.O.
Hobart, Tasmania 7001, Australia
Phone: 002 202219
Mrs. Gillian Blain

UNIVERSITY OF NEW SOUTH WALES — AUSTRALIAN GRADUATE SCHOOL OF MANAGEMENT — CENTRE FOR RESEARCH IN FINANCE   (1060)
P.O. Box 1
Kensington, N.S.W. 2033, Australia
Phone: 662 0300
Ray J. Ball

CONTROL DATA AUSTRALIA PTY. LTD. — CYBERTEL VIDEOTEX SERVICE   (245)
493 St. Kilda Rd.
Melbourne, Vic. 3004, Australia
Phone: 03 2689500
Brian P. Magill

INFOQUEST   (520)
123 Lonsdale St.
Melbourne, Vic. 3000, Australia
Phone: 03 662 3566
June M. Anderson

INFORMATION MANAGEMENT AND CONSULTING ASSOCIATION   (526)
G.P.O Box 2128T
Melbourne Vic., 3001, Australia
Phone: 03 8198231
Helen Campbell

AUSTRALIAN NATIONAL RADIO ASTRONOMY OBSERVATORY — PARKES CATALOGUE OF RADIO SOURCES   (59)
P.O. Box 276
Parkes, N.S.W. 2870, Australia
Phone: 068 633131
Dr. Alan E. Wright

UNIVERSITY OF MELBOURNE — DEPARTMENT OF GEOLOGY — COMPUTERISED LIBRARY OF ANALYSED IGNEOUS ROCKS   (1057)
Parkville, Vic. 3052, Australia
Phone: 345 1844

AUSTRALIAN INSTITUTE OF CRIMINOLOGY LIBRARY — COMPUTERISED INFORMATION FROM NATIONAL CRIMINOLOGICAL HOLDINGS   (56)
10-18 Colbee Court
Phillip, A.C.T. 2606, Australia
Phone: 062 822111
John Walker

COMPUTER SCIENCES OF AUSTRALIA PTY. LTD. — NETWORK SERVICES DIVISION — INFOBANK   (237)
460 Pacific Hwy.
St. Leonards, N.S.W. 2065, Australia
Phone: 02 4390033
Peter J. Farrell

WESTERN AUSTRALIAN INSTITUTE OF TECHNOLOGY — T.L. ROBERTSON LIBRARY — WAIT INDEX TO NEWSPAPERS   (1107)
Kent St.
South Bentley, W.A. 6102, Australia
Phone: 09 3507203
Bryan Kelman

AUSTRALIAN ATOMIC ENERGY COMMISSION — LUCAS HEIGHTS RESEARCH LABORATORIES LIBRARY   (51)
Private Mail Bag
Sutherland, N.S.W. 2232, Australia
Phone: 02 5430111
Wilson H. Neale

AUSTRALIAN FINANCIAL REVIEW — INFO-LINE   (55)
Box 506, GPO
Sydney, N.S.W. 2001, Australia
Phone: 02 2822822
Janet Fish

OVERSEAS TELECOMMUNICATIONS COMMISSION — MULTIMODE INTERNATIONAL DATA ACQUISITION SERVICE   (790)
G.P.O. Box 7000
Sydney, N.S.W. 2001, Australia
Phone: 02 2305000
Mr. P. Thomas

SVP AUSTRALIA   (908)
Australian Financial Review
Box 506, GPO
Sydney, N.S.W. 2001, Australia
Phone: 02 2822822
John Waugh

UNIVERSITY OF SYDNEY — SAMPLE SURVEY CENTRE   (1072)
City Rd.
Sydney, N.S.W. 2006, Australia
Phone: 02 6923624
Dr. Terence W. Beed

UNIVERSITY OF SYDNEY LIBRARY — BIBLIOGRAPHIC INFORMATION ON SOUTHEAST ASIA   (1073)
Sydney, N.S.W. 2006, Australia
Phone: 02 6923738
Helen Jarvis

AUSTRALIAN ROAD RESEARCH BOARD — AUSTRALIAN ROAD RESEARCH DOCUMENTATION   (62)
500 Burwood Hwy.
Vermont South, Vic. 3133, Australia
Phone: 03 2331211

AUSTRIA

AUSTRIA — FEDERAL MINISTRY OF BUILDINGS AND TECHNOLOGY — FEDERAL RESEARCH AND TESTING ESTABLISHMENT ARSENAL — ROAD RESEARCH DOCUMENTATION CENTER   (63)
Geotechnisches Institut
Franz-Grill-Str. 9, P.O. Box 8
A-1031 Vienna 3, Austria
Phone: 0222 782531
C.H. Warmuth

AUSTRIA — MINISTER OF FINANCE — INTERNATIONAL PATENT DOCUMENTATION CENTER   (64)
Mollwaldplatz 4
A-1040 Vienna, Austria
Phone: 0222 658784
Dr. Otto Auracher

AUSTRIAN DOCUMENTATION CENTRE FOR MEDIA AND COMMUNICATION RESEARCH   (65)
Universitatsstr. 7
A-1010 Vienna, Austria
Phone: 0222 43002640
Prof. Dr. Michael Schmolke

AUSTRIAN NATIONAL INSTITUTE FOR PUBLIC HEALTH — LITERATURE SERVICE IN MEDICINE   (66)
Stubenring 6
A-1010 Vienna, Austria
Phone: 0222 52966154
Dr. Robert Csepan

EUROPEAN COORDINATION CENTRE FOR RESEARCH AND DOCUMENTATION IN SOCIAL SCIENCES   (311)
P.O. Box 974
Grunangergasse 2
A-1011 Vienna, Austria
Phone: 524333
Dr. Oskar Vogel

INTERNATIONAL ATOMIC ENERGY AGENCY — ENERGY AND ECONOMIC DATA BANK   (559)
P.O. Box 100
Wagramerstr. 5
A-1400 Vienna, Austria
Phone: 0222 2360
Jayme Porto Carreiro

INTERNATIONAL ATOMIC ENERGY AGENCY — INTERNATIONAL NUCLEAR INFORMATION SYSTEM   (560)
P.O. Box 100
Wagramerstr. 5
A-1400 Vienna, Austria
Phone: 0222 2360
Arkady G. Romanenko

INTERNATIONAL ATOMIC ENERGY AGENCY — NUCLEAR DATA SECTION   (561)
P.O. Box 100
Wagramerstr. 5
A-1400 Vienna, Austria
Phone: 0222 2360
Joseph J. Schmidt

INTERNATIONAL ATOMIC ENERGY AGENCY — VIENNA INTERNATIONAL CENTRE LIBRARY   (562)
P.O. Box 100
Wagramerstr. 5
A-1400 Vienna, Austria
Phone: 0222 2360
Wilson H. Neale

INTERNATIONAL INFORMATION CENTER FOR TERMINOLOGY   (587)
P.O. Box 130
A-1021 Vienna, Austria
Phone: 0222 267535
Prof. Helmut Felber

MANZ INFO DATENVERMITTLUNG GmbH — MANZ DATENBANKEN   (683)
Wiedner Hauptstr. 18
A-1040 Vienna, Austria
Phone: 573620
Dr. Kurt Bednar

UNITED NATIONS INDUSTRIAL DEVELOPMENT ORGANIZATION — INDUSTRIAL INFORMATION SECTION — INDUSTRIAL AND TECHNOLOGICAL INFORMATION BANK   (1027)
Vienna International Centre
P.O. Box 300
A-1400 Vienna, Austria
Phone: 0222 26310

BAHRAIN

ARABIAN GULF INFORMATION CONSULTING BUREAU   (25)
P.O. Box 922
Manama, Bahrain
Phone: 681276
Jaffer Almadhi

BANGLADESH

BANGLADESH NATIONAL SCIENTIFIC AND TECHNICAL DOCUMENTATION CENTRE   (70)
Science Laboratories
Dacca 5, Bangladesh
Phone: 507196
Ahsan A. Biswas

BELGIUM

ASSOCIATION OF EUROPEAN AIRLINES — AEA DATA BASE   (41)
Bte. 4
350, ave. Louise
B-1050 Brussels, Belgium
Phone: 02 6403175
Mr. K-H. Neumeister

BANK SOCIETY — GENERAL DOCUMENTATION — SGB DATA BASE   (73)
Montagne du Parc 3
B-1000 Brussels, Belgium
Phone: 02 5136600

BELGIUM — MINISTRY OF ECONOMIC AFFAIRS — DATA PROCESSING CENTER — BELGIAN INFORMATION AND DISSEMINATION SERVICE   (80)
30, rue J.A. de Mot
B-1040 Brussels, Belgium
Phone: 02 2336737
R. van den Abeele

BELGIUM — MINISTRY OF ECONOMIC AFFAIRS — FONDS QUETELET LIBRARY DATA BASE   (81)
6, rue de l'Industrie
B-1040 Brussels, Belgium
Phone: 02 5127950
G. De SaedePeer

BELGIUM — MINISTRY OF ECONOMIC AFFAIRS — NATIONAL STATISTICAL INSTITUTE   (82)
44, rue de Louvain
B-1000 Brussels, Belgium
Phone: 02 5139650
E. Rosselle

BELGIUM — MINISTRY OF HEALTH — NATIONAL POISON CONTROL CENTER   (83)
15 rue Joseph Stallaert
B-1060 Brussels, Belgium
Phone: 02 3441515
Dr. Monique Govaerts-Lepicard

BELGIUM — ROYAL LIBRARY OF BELGIUM — NATIONAL CENTER FOR SCIENTIFIC AND TECHNICAL DOCUMENTATION   (84)
4, blvd. de l'Empereur
B-1000 Brussels, Belgium
Phone: 02 5136180
Dr. A. Cockx

BUREAU MARCEL VAN DIJK, SA   (122)
Ave. Louise 409
Box 1
B-1050 Brussels, Belgium
Phone: 02 6486697
Marcel van Dijk

CENTER FOR SCIENTIFIC AND TECHNICAL RESEARCH FOR THE METAL MANUFACTURING INDUSTRY — FABRIMETAL   (187)
21, rue des Drapiers
B-1050 Brussels, Belgium
Phone: 02 5112370

COMMISSION OF THE EUROPEAN COMMUNITIES — EDUCATION INFORMATION NETWORK IN THE EUROPEAN COMMUNITY   (215)
Central Unit of EURYDICE
17, rue Archimede
B-1040 Brussels, Belgium
Phone: 02 2300398
J. Richardson

DOCUMENTARY RESEARCH CENTER   (282)
P.O. Box 11
Rue de la Montagne, 34
B-1000 Brussels, Belgium
Phone: 02 5139213

FREE UNIVERSITY OF BRUSSELS — CENTRAL LIBRARY — VUBIS   (381)
Pleinlaan 2
B-1050 Brussels, Belgium
Phone: 02 6401260
Dr. Gerrit Alewaeters

HONEYWELL BULL — EURIS HOST SERVICE   (488)
Square de Meeus 5
B-1040 Brussels, Belgium
Phone: 02 5138238
Mr. J. Quenot

HONEYWELL BULL — EURIS HOST SERVICE — EUROPEAN
COMMUNITY LAW (489)
Square de Meeus 5   Phone: 02 5138238
B-1040 Brussels, Belgium   Mr. J. Quenot

INFORMATION RESOURCES RESEARCH (533)
Bibliotheque Royale/CNDST   Phone: 02 5136180
4, blvd. de l'Empereur   Herman-Karel de Jaeger
B-1000 Brussels, Belgium

SVP BENELUX (909)
World Trade Center   Phone: 02 2194000
Bd. Emile Jacqmain, 126 - Box 12   Mr. A. Vander Elst
B-1000 Brussels, Belgium

TEXTILE AND CLOTHING INFORMATION CENTRE (980)
24, rue Montoyer   Phone: 02 2307629
B-1040 Brussels, Belgium   Mr. C. Blum

INTERUNIVERSITY DOCUMENTATION AND INFORMATION CENTER
FOR THE SOCIAL SCIENCES (611)
1, Place Montesquieu   Phone: 010 418181
P.O. Box 18   Philippe Laurent
B-1348 Louvain-la-Neuve, Belgium

COMPU-MARK (234)
P.O. Box 61   Phone: 031 499840
B-2510 Mortsel, Belgium   Florent Gevers

ROYAL MUSEUM OF CENTRAL AFRICA — CENTER FOR INFORMATICS
APPLIED TO DEVELOPMENT AND TROPICAL AGRICULTURE —
AGROCLIMATOLOGY DATA BANK (846)
13, chaussee de Louvain   Phone: 02 7675401
B-1980 Tervuren, Belgium

SERVI-TECH — BIODOC (870)
Ave. de l'Automne 32   Phone: 02 3548249
B-1410 Waterloo, Belgium   C.A. Muylle

BOLIVIA

BOLIVIA — NATIONAL SCIENTIFIC AND TECHNOLOGICAL
DOCUMENTATION CENTER (93)
P.O. Box 3283   Phone: 359587
La Paz, Bolivia   Hugo Loaiza-Teran

BRAZIL

BRAZIL — MINISTRY OF AGRICULTURE — NATIONAL CENTER FOR
AGRICULTURAL DOCUMENTARY INFORMATION (99)
Caixa Postal 10.2432   Phone: 061 2251101
Anexo I, Bloco H, Ala Oeste   Alberto Augusto Alves Forjaz
70043 Brasilia DF, Brazil

BRAZIL — MINISTRY OF THE INTERIOR — DOCUMENTATION
COORDINATION UNIT (100)
Esplanada dos Ministerios   Phone: 061 2257802
Bldg. A, 2nd Floor   Angela Maria Crespo Queiroz Neves
70054 Brasilia DF, Brazil

BRAZIL — NATIONAL COUNCIL OF SCIENTIFIC AND
TECHNOLOGICAL DEVELOPMENT — BRAZILIAN INSTITUTE FOR
INFORMATION IN SCIENCE AND TECHNOLOGY (103)
Bloco A, Ed. Bittar Lote 1
70750 Brasilia, Brazil

BRAZIL — NATIONAL COMMISSION FOR NUCLEAR ENERGY —
CENTER FOR NUCLEAR INFORMATION (102)
Rua General Severiano, 90   Phone: 021 2958545
22294 Rio de Janeiro RJ, Brazil   Altair Carvalho de Souza

RWK LTD. (859)
Ave. Rio Branco 245, Gr. 1003   Phone: 021 2208549
20040 Rio de Janeiro RJ, Brazil   Raymond W. Kahl, Jr.

ANGLO-BRAZILIAN INFORMATION SERVICE (24)
Rua Deputado Lacerda Franco, 333   Phone: 011 8144155
05418 Sao Paulo SP, Brazil   John Salter

BRAZIL — NATIONAL CENTER FOR MICROGRAPHIC
DEVELOPMENT (101)
Rua Haddock Lobo, 585-5   Phone: 011 2820319
01414 Sao Paulo SP, Brazil   Antonio Paulo A. Silva

INTERNATIONAL TECHNICAL PUBLICATIONS LTD. (605)
Rua Peixoto Gomide, 209   Phone: 011 2588442
01409 Sao Paulo SP, Brazil   Pierre Grossmann

BULGARIA

BULGARIA — MEDICAL ACADEMY — CENTER FOR SCIENTIFIC
INFORMATION IN MEDICINE AND HEALTH (120)
1, Georgi Sofijsky St.   Phone: 522342
Sofia, 1431, Bulgaria   Prof. Alexi Valtchev

BULGARIA — NATIONAL AGRO-INDUSTRIAL UNION —
AGRICULTURAL ACADEMY — CENTER FOR SCIENTIFIC, TECHNICAL
AND ECONOMIC INFORMATION (121)
125, Lenin Blvd., Block No. 1   Phone: 74371
1113 Sofia, Bulgaria   Prof. N. Apostolov

CANADA

CANADA LAW BOOK LTD. (162)
240 Edward St.   Phone: (416) 773-6300
Aurora, ON, Canada L4G 3S9

LEIGH-BELL & ASSOCIATES LTD. (657)
1302 Dunbar Rd.   Phone: (416) 634-0012
Burlington, ON, Canada L7P 2J9   Peter Leigh-Bell

ARCTIC INSTITUTE OF NORTH AMERICA — ARCTIC SCIENCE AND
TECHNOLOGY INFORMATION SYSTEM (26)
University of Calgary   Phone: (403) 284-7515
2500 University Dr., N.W.   Ross Goodwin
Calgary, AB, Canada T2N 1N4

CALGARY PUBLIC INFORMATION DEPARTMENT — PUBLIC
RELATIONS DIVISION — CIVICHANNEL (124)
P.O. Box 2100, Station M   Phone: (403) 268-4774
Calgary, AB, Canada T2P 2M5   Rick Lyons

INFOCON INFORMATION SERVICES, LTD. (516)
P.O. Box 774   Phone: (403) 264-9477
Station G   Michael Spear
Calgary, AB, Canada T3A 0E0

STACS INFORMATION SYSTEMS LTD. (897)
3651 23rd St., N.E.   Phone: (403) 276-8501
Calgary, AB, Canada T2E 6T2   Michael H. Toller

ATOMIC ENERGY OF CANADA, LTD. — CHALK RIVER NUCLEAR
LABORATORIES — TECHNICAL INFORMATION BRANCH (44)
                                            Phone: (613) 687-5581
Chalk River, ON, Canada K0J 1J0   G.P.L. Williams

LARRATT AND ASSOCIATES LTD. (650)
R.R. 1   Phone: (613) 476-5309
Demorestville, ON, Canada K0K 1W0   Richard Larratt

BBM BUREAU OF MEASUREMENT (78)
1500 Don Mills Rd.   Phone: (416) 445-9800
Don Mills, ON, Canada M3B 3L7

YORK UNIVERSITY — INSTITUTE FOR BEHAVIOURAL
RESEARCH (1120)
Administrative Studies Bldg.   Phone: (416) 667-3026
4700 Keele St.   Prof. Gordon Darroch
Downsview, ON, Canada M3J 2R6

PEACE RESEARCH INSTITUTE-DUNDAS — PEACE RESEARCH
ABSTRACTS JOURNAL (800)
25 Dundana Ave.   Phone: (416) 628-2356
Dundas, ON, Canada L9H 4E5   Dr. Alan G. Newcombe

ALBERTA DEPARTMENT OF AGRICULTURE — ECONOMIC SERVICES
DIVISION — AGRICULTURAL COMMODITIES DATA BASE (9)
7000 - 113 St., 3rd Floor   Phone: (403) 427-8239
Edmonton, AB, Canada T6H 5T6   Lloyd Sereda

GEOGRAPHIC INDEX

ALBERTA MUNICIPAL AFFAIRS — CENTRAL SERVICES BRANCH — ALBERTA LAND USE PLANNING DATA BANK (10)
Jarvis Bldg., 10th Floor
9925 107 St.
Edmonton, AB, Canada T5K 2H9
Phone: (403) 427-0652
Delphine Langille

ALBERTA PUBLIC AFFAIRS BUREAU — PUBLICATION SERVICES BRANCH (11)
11510 Kingsway Ave.
Edmonton, AB, Canada T5G 2Y5
Phone: (403) 427-4387
Susan Krywolt

ALBERTA RESEARCH COUNCIL — ALBERTA GEOLOGICAL SURVEY — GEOSCIENCE DATA INDEX FOR ALBERTA (12)
Terrace Plaza, 3rd Floor
4445 Calgary Trail South
Edmonton, AB, Canada T6H 5R7
Phone: (403) 438-0555
Joseph R. MacGillivray

ALBERTA RESEARCH COUNCIL — ALBERTA OIL SANDS INFORMATION CENTRE (13)
10010 - 106th St., 6th Floor
Edmonton, AB, Canada T5J 3L8
Phone: (403) 427-8382
Helga Radvanyi

ALBERTA RESEARCH COUNCIL — COAL TECHNOLOGY INFORMATION CENTRE (14)
11315 - 87th Ave.
Edmonton, AB, Canada T6G 2C2
Phone: (403) 439-5916
Leslie Black

ALBERTA RESEARCH COUNCIL — INDUSTRIAL DEVELOPMENT DEPARTMENT — INDUSTRIAL INFORMATION (15)
Terrace Plaza, 4th Floor
4445 Calgary Trail South
Edmonton, AB, Canada T6H 5R7
Phone: (403) 438-1555
Mary E. Hart

ALBERTA RESEARCH COUNCIL — SOLAR AND WIND ENERGY RESEARCH PROGRAM INFORMATION CENTRE (16)
Terrace Plaza, 5th Floor
4445 Calgary Trail South
Edmonton, AB, Canada T6H 5R7
Phone: (403) 438-1666
Karen D. Beliveau

ALPHATEL SYSTEMS LTD. (19)
11430 168 St.
Edmonton, AB, Canada T5M 3T9
Phone: (403) 452-6555

BOREAL INSTITUTE FOR NORTHERN STUDIES — LIBRARY SERVICES (95)
Rm. CW401, Biological Science Bldg.
University of Alberta
Edmonton, AB, Canada T6G 2E9
Phone: (403) 432-4409
Mrs. G.A. Cooke

LIBRARY & INFORMATION CONSULTANTS LTD. (658)
9747 93rd Ave.
Edmonton, AB, Canada T6E 2V8
Phone: (403) 433-4867
Ilona Kennedy

NICHOLS APPLIED MANAGEMENT (752)
10180 102nd St.
400 Bentall Bldg.
Edmonton, AB, Canada T5J 0W5
Phone: (403) 424-0091
Peter Nichols

UNIVERSITY OF ALBERTA — COMPUTING SERVICES — INFORMATION SYSTEMS GROUP (1033)
352 General Services Bldg.
Edmonton, AB, Canada T6G 2H1
Phone: (403) 432-3884
Ron Senda

UNIVERSITY OF ALBERTA — DEPARTMENT OF EDUCATIONAL ADMINISTRATION — ADMINISTRATION LABORATORY PROJECT FILE (1034)
Edmonton, AB, Canada T6G 2H4
Phone: (403) 432-3792
Aurelia C. Dacong

UNIVERSITY OF ALBERTA — DEPARTMENT OF SOCIOLOGY — POPULATION RESEARCH LABORATORY (1035)
Edmonton, AB, Canada T6G 2H4
Phone: (403) 432-4659
L.W. Kennedy

UNIVERSITY OF ALBERTA — FACULTY OF NURSING — CANADIAN CLEARINGHOUSE FOR ONGOING RESEARCH IN NURSING (1036)
3-103-H Clinical Sciences Bldg.
Edmonton, AB, Canada T6G 2G3
Phone: (403) 432-6250
Dr. Janice Morse

UNIVERSITY OF ALBERTA — FACULTY OF NURSING — CANADIAN DIRECTORY OF COMPLETED MASTER'S THESES IN NURSING (1037)
3-103-H Clinical Sciences Bldg.
Edmonton, AB, Canada T6G 2G3
Phone: (403) 432-6250
Dr. Janice Morse

UNIVERSITY OF NEW BRUNSWICK LIBRARIES — PHOENIX (1059)
Box 7500
Fredericton, NB, Canada E3B 5H5
Phone: (506) 453-4740
Sheila Laidlaw

UNIVERSITY OF GUELPH LIBRARY — COOPERATIVE DOCUMENTS NETWORK PROJECT (1050)
Library Administration Office
Guelph, ON, Canada N1G 2W1
Phone: (519) 824-4120
Virginia Gillham

DALHOUSIE UNIVERSITY — LAW SCHOOL LIBRARY — MARINE AFFAIRS BIBLIOGRAPHY (254)
6061 University Ave.
Halifax, NS, Canada B3H 4H9
Phone: (902) 424-2124
Christian L. Wiktor

CANADA — CONSUMER AND CORPORATE AFFAIRS CANADA — CORPORATIONS BRANCH — CORPORATE INTEGRATED INFORMATION SYSTEM (129)
Place du Portage, Phase II, 4th Fl.
50 Victoria St.
Hull, PQ, Canada K1A 0C9
Phone: (819) 997-1071
Henri Denolf

NORPAK CORPORATION (764)
10 Hearst Way
Kanata, ON, Canada K2L 2P4
Phone: (613) 592-4164
Dr. J.F. Carruthers

QL SYSTEMS LIMITED (828)
797 Princess St.
Kingston, ON, Canada K7L 1G1
Phone: (613) 549-4611
Hugh Lawford

INFORMATION LONDON (525)
388 Dundas St.
London, ON, Canada N6B 1V8
Phone: (519) 432-2211
Nathan Garber

UNIVERSITY OF WESTERN ONTARIO — SCHOOL OF LIBRARY AND INFORMATION SCIENCE — NESTED PHRASE INDEXING SYSTEM (1086)
London, ON, Canada N6G 1H1
Phone: (519) 679-3542
Timothy C. Craven

UNIVERSITY OF WESTERN ONTARIO — SOCIAL SCIENCE COMPUTING LABORATORY — INFORMATION SYSTEMS PROGRAMME (1087)
London, ON, Canada N6A 5C2
Phone: (519) 679-6378
Dr. Edward H. Hanis

UNIVERSITY OF WESTERN ONTARIO — SYSTEMS ANALYSIS, CONTROL AND DESIGN ACTIVITY (1088)
Engineering Science Bldg.
London, ON, Canada N6A 5B9
Phone: (519) 679-6570
Cecil F. Shewchuk

VIDEOACCESS (1099)
24 Erie Ave.
London, ON, Canada N6J 1J1
Phone: (519) 672-2432
Peter G. Watson

CANADA — AGRICULTURE CANADA — MARKETING AND ECONOMICS BRANCH — COOPERATIVES UNIT — COINS (127)
Ecole des Hautes Etudes
Commerciales, 5525, ave. Decelles
Montreal, PQ, Canada H3T 1U6
Michelle Champagne

CANADA — NATIONAL FILM BOARD OF CANADA — FORMAT (146)
P.O. Box 6100, Station A
Montreal, PQ, Canada H3C 3H5
Phone: (514) 333-4524
Donald Bidd

FRI INFORMATION SERVICES LTD. (392)
1801 McGill College Ave., Suite 600
Montreal, PQ, Canada H3A 2N4
Phone: (514) 842-5091
Gordon K. Landon

INDUSTRIAL LIFE-TECHNICAL SERVICES INC. (513)
2, complexe Desjardins
Montreal, PQ, Canada H5B 1B3
Phone: (514) 284-1111

INTERNATIONAL CIVIL AVIATION ORGANIZATION — AIR NAVIGATION BUREAU — ACCIDENT INVESTIGATION AND PREVENTION SECTION — AIRCRAFT ACCIDENT/INCIDENT REPORTING SYSTEM (567)
1000 Sherbrooke St. W., Suite 400
Montreal, PQ, Canada H3A 2R2
Phone: (514) 285-8160

INTERNATIONAL CIVIL AVIATION ORGANIZATION — AIR NAVIGATION BUREAU — AERODROMES SECTION — AIRPORT CHARACTERISTICS DATA BANK (568)
1000 Sherbrooke St. W., Suite 400
Montreal, PQ, Canada H3A 2R2
Phone: (514) 285-8179
Kenneth K. Wilde

GEOGRAPHIC INDEX

INTERNATIONAL CIVIL AVIATION ORGANIZATION — AIR TRANSPORT BUREAU — STATISTICS SECTION — AIR TRANSPORT STATISTICAL PROGRAM (569)
1000 Sherbrooke St. W., Suite 400 Phone: (514) 285-8064
Montreal, PQ, Canada H3A 2R2 D.C. Singh

IST-INFORMATHEQUE INC. (619)
2, complexe Desjardins Phone: (514) 284-1111
Suite 1317 Gerard Briere
Montreal, PQ, Canada H5B 1B3

McGILL UNIVERSITY — FACULTY OF ENGINEERING — DEPARTMENT OF MINING AND METALLURGICAL ENGINEERING — FACILITY FOR THE ANALYSIS OF CHEMICAL THERMODYNAMICS (691)
3480 University St. Phone: (514) 392-5426
Montreal, PQ, Canada H3A 2A7

McGILL UNIVERSITY — GRADUATE SCHOOL OF LIBRARY SCIENCE — FEES DATA BASE (692)
McLennan Library Bldg. Phone: (514) 392-5945
3459 McTavish St. C.D. Hurt
Montreal, PQ, Canada H3A 1Y1

POLYTECHNICAL SCHOOL OF MONTREAL — TELIDON TECHNOLOGY DEVELOPMENT CENTER (819)
C.P. 6079, Succursale A Phone: (514) 344-4753
Montreal, PQ, Canada H3C 3A7 J.L. Houle

QUEBEC MINISTRY OF EDUCATION — LIBRARY HEADQUARTERS — POINT DE REPERE (831)
1685, rue Fleury est Phone: (514) 382-0895
Montreal, PQ, Canada H2C 1T1 Nicole Gilbert

QUEBEC NATIONAL LIBRARY — FMQ (833)
1700, rue Saint-Denis Phone: (514) 873-2783
Montreal, PQ, Canada H2X 3K6 Marcel Fontaine

QUEBEC SOCIETY FOR LEGAL INFORMATION (834)
276, rue St-Jacques, Suite 310 Phone: (514) 842-8741
Montreal, PQ, Canada H2Y 1N3 J.-M. Tetrault

TECHNICAL INFORMATION-DOCUMENTATION CONSULTANTS LTD. (963)
4650 St. Catherine St. W. Phone: (514) 937-0000
Montreal, PQ, Canada H3Z 1S5 Ronald A. Javitch

PHIPPARD & ASSOCIATES STRATEGIC & TECHNOLOGICAL CONSULTING, INC. (810)
94 Knollsbrook Dr. Phone: (613) 825-1893
Nepean, ON, Canada K2J 1L8 Gary Phippard

SPECIAL LIBRARIES CATALOGUING, INC. (894)
2012 Dollarton Hwy. Phone: (604) 929-3966
North Vancouver, BC, Canada V7H 1A4 J. McRee Elrod

ALPHATEXT, INC. (20)
240 Catherine St. Phone: (613) 238-5333
Ottawa, ON, Canada K2P 2G8 Cyril Eldridge

CANADA — AGRICULTURE CANADA — MARKETING AND ECONOMICS BRANCH — AGRICULTURAL MARKETING AND TRADE DATABASE (126)
Sir John Carling Bldg. Phone: (613) 995-9554
Ottawa, ON, Canada K1A 0C5 A.H. Wilmot

CANADA — AGRICULTURE CANADA — SCIENTIFIC INFORMATION RETRIEVAL SECTION — PESTICIDE RESEARCH INFORMATION SYSTEM (128)
Central Experimental Farm Phone: (613) 995-9073
K.W. Neatby Bldg., Room 1133 Jacques Taky
Ottawa, ON, Canada K1A 0C6

CANADA — DEPARTMENT OF COMMUNICATIONS — TELIDON PROGRAM (130)
365 Laurier Ave. W. Phone: (613) 995-4743
Journal Tower S., Room 1706 Roy Marsh
Ottawa, ON, Canada K1A 0C8

CANADA — DEPARTMENT OF ENERGY, MINES AND RESOURCES — CANADA CENTRE FOR MINERAL AND ENERGY TECHNOLOGY — TECHNOLOGY INFORMATION DIVISION (131)
555 Booth St. Phone: (613) 995-4029
Ottawa, ON, Canada K1A 0G1 Dr. James E. Kanasy

CANADA — DEPARTMENT OF ENERGY, MINES AND RESOURCES — CANADA CENTRE FOR REMOTE SENSING — REMOTE SENSING ON-LINE RETRIEVAL SYSTEM (132)
240 Bank St., 5th Floor Phone: (613) 995-5645
Ottawa, ON, Canada K1A 0Y7 Jacques Guerette

CANADA — DEPARTMENT OF ENERGY, MINES AND RESOURCES — CONSERVATION AND RENEWABLE ENERGY BRANCH — CANADIAN ENERGY INFORMATION SYSTEM (133)
580 Booth St. Phone: (613) 995-9447
Ottawa, ON, Canada K1A 0E4 C.S.L. McNeil

CANADA — DEPARTMENT OF ENERGY, MINES AND RESOURCES — GEOLOGICAL SURVEY OF CANADA — ECONOMIC GEOLOGY DIVISION — CANADIAN MINERAL OCCURRENCE INDEX (134)
601 Booth St.
Ottawa, ON, Canada K1A 0E8 D.F. Garson

CANADA — DEPARTMENT OF ENERGY, MINES AND RESOURCES — GEOLOGICAL SURVEY OF CANADA — NATIONAL GEOSCAN CENTRE (135)
601 Booth St., Room 180 Phone: (613) 992-9550
Ottawa, ON, Canada K1A 0E8 David S. Reade

CANADA — DEPARTMENT OF ENERGY, MINES AND RESOURCES — TOPOGRAPHICAL SURVEY DIVISION — DIGITAL MAPPING SYSTEM (136)
615 Booth St. Phone: (613) 995-4637
Ottawa, ON, Canada K1A 0E9 M.E.H. Young

CANADA — DEPARTMENT OF INDUSTRY, TRADE & COMMERCE — OFFICE OF TOURISM — TOURISM RESEARCH AND DATA CENTRE (137)
235 Queen St., 4th Floor, E. Phone: (613) 995-2754
Ottawa, ON, Canada K1A 0H6 Rae Bradford

CANADA — ENVIRONMENT CANADA — CANADIAN INVENTORY OF HISTORIC BUILDING (138)
Les Terrasses de la Chaudiere Phone: (819) 994-2866
Ottawa, ON, Canada K1A 1G2 C. Cameron

CANADA — ENVIRONMENT CANADA — INLAND WATERS DIRECTORATE — NATIONAL HYDROLOGY RESEARCH INSTITUTE — PERENNIAL SNOW AND ICE SECTION — GLACIER INVENTORY OF CANADA (139)
  Phone: (819) 997-2385
Ottawa, ON, Canada K1A 0E7 C. Simon L. Ommanney

CANADA — ENVIRONMENT CANADA — INLAND WATERS DIRECTORATE — WATDOC (140)
  Phone: (819) 997-1238
Ottawa, ON, Canada K1A 0E7 Evangeline Campbell

CANADA — ENVIRONMENT CANADA — INLAND WATERS DIRECTORATE — WATER QUALITY BRANCH — NATIONAL WATER QUALITY DATA BANK (141)
Place Vincent Massey Phone: (819) 997-3422
Ottawa, ON, Canada K1A 0E7 S. Whitlow

CANADA — ENVIRONMENT CANADA — INLAND WATERS DIRECTORATE — WATER RESOURCES BRANCH — WATER SURVEY OF CANADA (142)
  Phone: (819) 997-2098
Ottawa, ON, Canada K1A 0E7 Russell G. Boals

CANADA — ENVIRONMENT CANADA — LANDS DIRECTORATE — CANADA LAND DATA SYSTEMS DIVISION — CANADA GEOGRAPHIC INFORMATION SYSTEM (143)
  Phone: (819) 997-2510
Ottawa, ON, Canada K1A 0E7 Ian K. Crain

CANADA — ENVIRONMENT CANADA — LIBRARY SERVICES BRANCH — ENVIRONMENT LIBRARIES AUTOMATED SYSTEM (144)
  Phone: (613) 997-1767
Ottawa, ON, Canada K1A 1C7 Mrs. A.M. Bystram

CANADA — HEALTH AND WELFARE CANADA — POLICY, PLANNING AND INFORMATION BRANCH — A NETWORK OF SOCIAL SECURITY INFORMATION RESOURCES (145)
Brooke-Claxton Bldg. Phone: (613) 995-2891
Tunney's Pasture Elizabeth Payne
Ottawa, ON, Canada K1A 0K9

CANADA — NATIONAL LIBRARY OF CANADA (147)
395 Wellington St. Phone: (613) 995-9481
Ottawa, ON, Canada K1A 0N4 Marianne Scott

CANADA — NATIONAL LIBRARY OF CANADA — CATALOGUING
BRANCH — CANADIANA EDITORIAL DIVISION   (148)
395 Wellington St.   Phone: (819) 977-6200
Ottawa, ON, Canada K1A 0N4

CANADA — NATIONAL LIBRARY OF CANADA — LIBRARY
DOCUMENTATION CENTRE   (149)
395 Wellington St.   Phone: (613) 995-8717
Ottawa, ON, Canada K1A 0N4   Dr. Beryl L. Anderson

CANADA — NATIONAL LIBRARY OF CANADA — MARC RECORDS
DISTRIBUTION SERVICE   (150)
395 Wellington St.   Phone: (819) 997-6200
Ottawa, ON, Canada K1A 0N4   Margaret Stewart

CANADA — NATIONAL LIBRARY OF CANADA — PUBLIC SERVICES
BRANCH — UNION CATALOGUE OF SERIALS DIVISION   (151)
395 Wellington St.   Phone: (613) 993-6128
Ottawa, ON, Canada K1A 0N4   Myra Clowes

CANADA — NATIONAL RESEARCH COUNCIL OF CANADA — CANADA
INSTITUTE FOR SCIENTIFIC AND TECHNICAL INFORMATION   (152)
Montreal Rd.   Phone: (613) 993-1600
Ottawa, ON, Canada K1A 0S2   Elmer V. Smith

CANADA — NATIONAL RESEARCH COUNCIL OF CANADA — CANADA
INSTITUTE FOR SCIENTIFIC AND TECHNICAL INFORMATION —
CANADIAN ONLINE ENQUIRY SYSTEM   (153)
Montreal Rd.   Phone: (613) 993-1210
Ottawa, ON, Canada K1A 0S2   Bonnie Bullock

CANADA — NATIONAL RESEARCH COUNCIL OF CANADA — CANADA
INSTITUTE FOR SCIENTIFIC AND TECHNICAL INFORMATION —
CANADIAN SERVICE FOR THE SELECTIVE DISSEMINATION OF
INFORMATION   (154)
Montreal Rd.   Phone: (613) 993-1210
Ottawa, ON, Canada K1A 0S2   Bonnie Bullock

CANADA — NATIONAL RESEARCH COUNCIL OF CANADA — CANADA
INSTITUTE FOR SCIENTIFIC AND TECHNICAL INFORMATION —
SCIENTIFIC NUMERIC DATABASES   (155)
Montreal Rd.   Phone: (613) 993-3294
Ottawa, ON, Canada K1A 0S2   Dr. G.H. Wood

CANADA — NATIONAL RESEARCH COUNCIL OF CANADA —
CHEMISTRY DIVISION — METALS DATA CENTRE   (156)
Montreal Rd.   Phone: (613) 993-2527
Ottawa, ON, Canada K1A 0R6   Dr. L.D. Calvert

CANADA — PARLIAMENT OF CANADA — LIBRARY OF
PARLIAMENT   (157)
Centre Block, Parliament Bldgs.   Phone: (613) 992-3122
Ottawa, ON, Canada K1A 0A9   E.J. Spicer

CANADA — PUBLIC ARCHIVES OF CANADA — MACHINE READABLE
ARCHIVES DIVISION   (158)
395 Wellington St.   Phone: (613) 593-7772
Ottawa, ON, Canada K1A 0N3   Harold A. Naugler

CANADA — STATISTICS CANADA — CANADIAN SOCIO-ECONOMIC
INFORMATION MANAGEMENT SYSTEM   (159)
R.H. Coats Bldg., 9th Floor   Phone: (613) 995-7406
Tunney's Pasture   W.M. Podehl
Ottawa, ON, Canada K1A 0T6

CANADA — STATISTICS CANADA — CANADIAN SOCIO-ECONOMIC
INFORMATION MANAGEMENT SYSTEM — TELICHART   (160)
R.H. Coats Bldg., 9th Floor   Phone: (613) 995-0575
Tunney's Pasture   W.M. Podehl
Ottawa, ON, Canada K1A 0T6

CANADA — TRANSPORT CANADA — LIBRARY AND INFORMATION
CENTRE   (161)
2nd Floor, Tower C   Phone: (613) 992-4529
Place de Ville   Serge G. Campion
Ottawa, ON, Canada K1A 0N5

CANADA SYSTEMS GROUP — FEDERAL SYSTEMS DIVISION —
CANADIAN FEDERAL CORPORATIONS AND DIRECTORS DATA
BASE   (163)
Products Sales Directorate   Phone: (613) 563-4444
90 Sparks St., Suite 704
Ottawa, ON, Canada K1P 5B4

CANADA SYSTEMS GROUP — FEDERAL SYSTEMS DIVISION —
CORPORATE NAMES DATA BASE   (164)
Product Sales Directorate   Phone: (613) 563-4444
90 Sparks St., Suite 704
Ottawa, ON, Canada K1P 5B4

CANADA SYSTEMS GROUP — FEDERAL SYSTEMS DIVISION —
INTER-CORPORATE OWNERSHIP DATA BASE   (165)
Product Sales Directorate   Phone: (613) 563-4444
90 Sparks St., Suite 704
Ottawa, ON, Canada K1P 5B4

CANADA SYSTEMS GROUP — FEDERAL SYSTEMS DIVISION —
TRADE MARKS DATA BASE   (166)
Product Sales Directorate   Phone: (613) 563-4444
90 Sparks St., Suite 704
Ottawa, ON, Canada K1P 5B4

CANADIAN AGRICULTURAL RESEARCH COUNCIL — INVENTORY OF
CANADIAN AGRICULTURAL RESEARCH   (167)
Central Experimental Farm   Phone: (613) 995-9073
K.W. Neatby Bldg., Room 1133   Dr. J.C. Rennie
Ottawa, ON, Canada K1A 0C6

CANADIAN ASSOCIATION FOR INFORMATION SCIENCE/
ASSOCIATION CANADIENNE DES SCIENCES DE
L'INFORMATION   (168)
44 Bayswater Ave., Suite 100   Phone: (613) 725-0332
Ottawa, ON, Canada K1Y 4K3   Mary Frances Laughton

CANADIAN BROADCASTING CORPORATION — PROJECT IRIS   (169)
Box 8478   Phone: (613) 731-3111
Ottawa, ON, Canada K1G 3J5   R. O'Reilly

CANADIAN INFORMATION INDUSTRY ASSOCIATION   (172)
P.O. Box 9211   Phone: (613) 741-5274
Ottawa, ON, Canada K1G 3T9   Michael A. Dagg

CANADIAN LAW INFORMATION COUNCIL   (173)
161 Laurier West   Phone: (613) 236-9766
Ottawa, ON, Canada K1P 5J2   Lois Dyer

CANADIAN LIBRARY ASSOCIATION — CANADIAN PERIODICAL
INDEX   (174)
151 Sparks St.   Phone: (613) 232-9625
Ottawa, ON, Canada K1P 5E3   Sylvia Morrison

CARLETON UNIVERSITY — DEPARTMENT OF SOCIOLOGY AND
ANTHROPOLOGY — SOCIAL SCIENCE DATA ARCHIVES   (178)
Loeb Bldg., Rooms A711 & A713   Phone: (613) 231-7426
Colonel By Dr.   Hyman Burshtyn
Ottawa, ON, Canada K1S 5B6

CARLETON UNIVERSITY LIBRARY — CARLETON LIBRARY
SYSTEM   (179)
Colonel By Drive   Phone: (613) 231-6350
Ottawa, ON, Canada K1S 5J7   Martin Foss

COACHING ASSOCIATION OF CANADA — SPORT INFORMATION
RESOURCE CENTRE   (210)
333 River Rd.   Phone: (613) 746-5357
Ottawa, ON, Canada K1L 8B9   Gilles Chiasson

CONFERENCE BOARD OF CANADA — APPLIED ECONOMIC RESEARCH
AND INFORMATION CENTRE — AERIC SYSTEM   (238)
25 McArthur Rd., Suite 100   Phone: (613) 746-1261
Ottawa, ON, Canada K1L 6R3

DAGG ASSOCIATES   (253)
P.O. Box 9211   Phone: (613) 741-5274
Ottawa, ON, Canada K1G 3T9   Michael A. Dagg

EUROLINE INC.   (304)
P.O. Box 3121, Station D   Phone: (613) 236-3434
Ottawa, ON, Canada K1P 6H7   Peter D. Geldart

INFORMETRICA LIMITED   (536)
P.O. Box 828, Station B   Phone: (613) 238-4831
Ottawa, ON, Canada K1P 5P9   Andrea Grimm

INTERNATIONAL DEVELOPMENT RESEARCH CENTRE —
LIBRARY   (576)
P.O. Box 8500   Phone: (613) 236-6163
60 Queen St.
Ottawa, ON, Canada K1G 3H9

GEOGRAPHIC INDEX

NASH INFORMATION SERVICES INC. (718)
1975 Bel Air Dr.
Ottawa, ON, Canada K2C 0X1
Phone: (613) 225-3781
Dr. John C. Nash

SOCIOSCOPE INC. (883)
529 Clarence St.
Ottawa, ON, Canada K1N 5S4
Phone: (613) 235-7120
Michael Gurstein

SONOPTIC COMMUNICATIONS INC. (884)
44 Bayswater Ave., Suite 100
Ottawa, ON, Canada K1Y 4K3
Phone: (613) 725-0332
Robert Leitch

STANDARDS COUNCIL OF CANADA — STANDARDS INFORMATION SERVICE (898)
350 Sparks St., Room 1203
Ottawa, ON, Canada K1R 7S8
Phone: (613) 238-3222
M. Crainey

SYSTEMHOUSE LTD. — MINISIS (953)
2827 Riverside Dr.
Ottawa, ON, Canada K1V 0C4
Phone: (613) 526-0670
Colin Townsend

TELECOM CANADA — DATAPAC (971)
410 Laurier Ave. W., Room 770
Ottawa, ON, Canada K1P 6H5
Phone: (613) 560-3030
Douglas Sloane

TELECOM CANADA — INET 2000 (972)
410 Laurier Ave. W., Room 770
Ottawa, ON, Canada K1P 6H5
Phone: (613) 560-3030
Douglas Sloane

VIDEOTEX INFORMATION SERVICE PROVIDERS ASSOCIATION OF CANADA (1101)
130 Albert St., Suite 1007
Ottawa, ON, Canada K1P 5G4
Phone: (613) 236-4756

ATOMIC ENERGY OF CANADA, LTD. — WHITESHELL NUCLEAR RESEARCH ESTABLISHMENT — TECHNICAL INFORMATION SERVICES (45)
Pinawa, MB, Canada R0E 1L0
Phone: (204) 753-2311
M.O. Luke

PULP AND PAPER RESEARCH INSTITUTE OF CANADA — TECHNICAL INFORMATION SECTION (827)
570 St. John's Blvd.
Pointe Claire, PQ, Canada H9R 3J9
Phone: (514) 697-4110
Mrs. Hella Stahl

LAVAL UNIVERSITY LIBRARY — SDI/LAVAL & TELEREFERENCE SERVICE (652)
Cite Universitaire
Quebec, PQ, Canada G1K 7P4
Phone: (418) 656-3969

MICROFOR INC. (704)
800, place d'Youville
Bureau 1805
Quebec, PQ, Canada G1R 3P4
Phone: (418) 692-4369

QUEBEC — FRENCH LANGUAGE BOARD — TERMINOLOGY BANK OF QUEBEC (830)
700, blvd. Saint-Cyrille Est
Quebec, PQ, Canada G1R 5G7
Phone: (418) 643-1802
Jean-Marie Fortin

EDIMEDIA INC. (292)
390, rue St. Vallierest
Quebec City, PQ, Canada G1K 7J6
Phone: (418) 657-3551
Paul A. Audet

ABALL SOFTWARE INC. (2)
2268 Osler St.
Regina, SK, Canada S4P 1W8
Phone: (306) 569-2180
A.J.S. Ball

SASKATCHEWAN TELECOMMUNICATIONS — AGRITEX (862)
2121 Saskatchewan Dr.
Regina, SK, Canada S4P 3Y2
Phone: (306) 347-2112
Dennis Sabat

UNIVERSITY OF REGINA — CANADIAN PLAINS RESEARCH CENTER — INFORMATION SERVICES (1066)
Regina, SK, Canada S4S 0A2
Phone: (306) 584-4758
Dr. M. Evelyn Jonescu

CENTRAL ONTARIO REGIONAL LIBRARY SYSTEM — INTERLIBRARY LOAN AND COMMUNICATION SYSTEM (195)
129 Church St., S.
Richmond Hill, ON, Canada L4C 1W4
Phone: (416) 884-4395
Rosemary Kavanagh

MEMORIAL UNIVERSITY OF NEWFOUNDLAND — OCEAN ENGINEERING INFORMATION CENTRE (694)
Bartlett Bldg., K-122
St. John's, NF, Canada A1B 3X5
Phone: (709) 737-8377
Ms. J.A. Whittick

NEWFOUNDLAND DEPARTMENT OF MINES & ENERGY — MINERAL DEVELOPMENT DIVISION LIBRARY — COMPUTERIZED RETRIEVAL SERVICES (750)
P.O. Box 4750
St. John's, NF, Canada A1C 5T7
Phone: (709) 737-3159
Rex Gibbons

NEWFOUNDLAND TELEPHONE — TOURISM NEWFOUNDLAND (751)
Fort William Bldg.
P.O. Box 2110
St. Johns, NF, Canada A1C 5H6
Phone: (709) 739-2005
Robert A. Newell

QUEBEC MINISTRY OF THE ENVIRONMENT — DOCUMENTATION CENTER — ENVIRODOQ (832)
2360, Chemin Ste-Foy
Sainte-Foy, PQ, Canada G1V 4H2
Phone: (418) 643-5363
Gerard Nobrega

UNIVERSITY OF QUEBEC — DIRECT ACCESS DATA BANK AT THE UNIVERSITY OF QUEBEC (1064)
2875, blvd. Laurier
Sainte-Foy, PQ, Canada G1V 2M3
Phone: (418) 657-2450
Laval Du Breuil

UNIVERSITY OF SASKATCHEWAN LIBRARY — REFERENCE DEPARTMENT — UNIVERSITY OF SASKATCHEWAN LIBRARIES MACHINE-ASSISTED REFERENCE TELESERVICES (1067)
Saskatoon, SK, Canada S7N 0W0
Phone: (306) 343-4295
Victor G. Wiebe

UNIVERSITY OF SASKATCHEWAN LIBRARY — SYSTEMS AND PLANNING UNIT (1068)
Saskatoon, SK, Canada S7N 0W0
Phone: (306) 343-4216
Peter Burslem

CENTENNIAL COLLEGE — BIBLIOCENTRE (182)
80 Cowdray Court
Scarborough, ON, Canada M1S 4N1
Phone: (416) 299-1515
Doug Wentzel

TELE-DIRECT INC. (973)
55 Town Centre Ct., 5th Floor
Scarborough, ON, Canada M1P 4X5
Phone: (416) 296-4435
Eric Rand

UNIVERSITY OF SHERBROOKE — ASBESTOS RESEARCH PROGRAM — INFORMATION CENTER (1071)
Sherbrooke, PQ, Canada J1K 2R1
Phone: (819) 565-3616
Mrs. Asta Sokov

AVCOR (67)
512 King St. E., Suite 303
Toronto, ON, Canada M5A 1M1
Phone: (416) 864-9240
Robert Baum

CANADIAN EDUCATION ASSOCIATION — CANADIAN EDUCATION INDEX DATA BASE (170)
252 Bloor St. W., Suite 8-200
Toronto, ON, Canada M5S 1V5
Phone: (416) 924-7721
Maureen Davis

CANADIAN ENGINEERING PUBLICATIONS LTD. — INFORMATION SERVICES DIVISION (171)
111 Peter St., Suite 411
Toronto, ON, Canada M5V 2W2
Phone: (416) 596-1624
Charles F. Broad

THE CIRPA/ADISQ FOUNDATION (206)
144 Front St. W., Suite 330
Toronto, ON, Canada M5J 2L7
Phone: (416) 593-4545
Earl Rosen

COMPUSEARCH MARKET AND SOCIAL RESEARCH LTD. (236)
16 Madison Ave.
Toronto, ON, Canada M5R 2S1
Phone: (416) 967-5881
Michele Sexsmith

CONSTRUCTION SPECIFICATIONS CANADA — NATIONAL MASTER SPECIFICATION (242)
1 St. Clair Ave. W., Suite 1206
Toronto, ON, Canada M4V 1K6
Phone: (416) 922-3159

DATALINE INC. (262)
175 Bedford Rd.
Toronto, ON, Canada M5R 2L2
Phone: (416) 964-9515
Dr. Joseph C. Paradi

ESPIAL PRODUCTIONS (300)
P.O. Box 624, Station K
Toronto, ON, Canada M4P 2H1
Phone: (416) 485-8063
Harry Campbell

FAXTEL INFORMATION SYSTEMS LTD. — MARKETFAX (326)
12 Sheppard St., Suite 500
Toronto, ON, Canada M5H 3A1
Phone: (416) 365-1899
John McLauchlan

THE GLOBE AND MAIL — INFO GLOBE (430)
444 Front St., W.
Phone: (416) 585-5250
Toronto, ON, Canada M5V 2S9
Barbara Hyland

HARRIS MEDIA SYSTEMS LTD. (475)
20 Holly St., Suite 208
Phone: (416) 487-2111
Toronto, ON, Canada M4S 3B1
Robert E. Harris

IMAGE BASE VIDEOTEX DESIGN INC. (502)
1011 Pape Ave., Suite 2
Phone: (416) 421-1958
Toronto, ON, Canada M4K 3V9
Neil Black

INDEXING AND ABSTRACTING SOCIETY OF CANADA (506)
P.O. Box 744, Station F
Toronto, ON, Canada M4Y 2N6
Ann H. Schabas

INFOMART (518)
164 Merton St.
Phone: (416) 489-6640
Toronto, ON, Canada M4S 3A8
Robert McConnell

INFORMATION PLUS INC. (528)
2 Bloor St. E., Suite 2612
Phone: (416) 968-1062
Toronto, ON, Canada M4W 1A8
Deborah C. Sawyer

INFORMATION RESOURCES (532)
45 Inglewood Dr.
Phone: (416) 486-0239
Toronto, ON, Canada M4T 1G9
Susan P. Klement

LYMBURNER & SONS LTD. — ECONOMIST'S STATISTICS (679)
20 Victoria St.
Phone: (416) 862-0595
Toronto, ON, Canada M5C 2N8
Margaret Nozaki

MacLEAN-HUNTER LTD. — FINANCIAL POST DIVISION — FINANCIAL POST INVESTMENT DATA BANK (680)
481 University Ave.
Phone: (416) 596-5693
Toronto, ON, Canada M5W 1A7
Mr. Cuyler Bowness

MANAGEMENT CONSULTANTS INTERNATIONAL, INC. (682)
56 The Esplanade, Suite 303
Phone: (416) 364-0299
Toronto, ON, Canada M5E 1A7
Michael A. Harrison

METROPOLITAN TORONTO LIBRARY BOARD — REGIONAL BIBLIOGRAPHIC PRODUCTS DEPARTMENT (699)
789 Yonge St.
Phone: (416) 928-5333
Toronto, ON, Canada M4W 2G8
Josephine Tsui

MICROMEDIA LTD. (706)
144 Front St. W.
Phone: (416) 593-5211
Toronto, ON, Canada M5J 2L7
Robert Gibson

MICROMEDIA LTD. — CANADIAN BUSINESS INDEX (707)
144 Front St. W.
Phone: (416) 593-5211
Toronto, ON, Canada M5J 2L7
Robert Gibson

MICROMEDIA LTD. — CANADIAN NEWS INDEX (708)
144 Front St. W.
Phone: (416) 593-5211
Toronto, ON, Canada M5J 2L7
Robert Gibson

ONTARIO MINISTRY OF EDUCATION — RESEARCH AND INFORMATION BRANCH — INFORMATION CENTRE — ONTARIO EDUCATION RESOURCES INFORMATION SYSTEM (777)
Mowat Block, 13th Floor
Phone: (416) 965-4110
Queen's Park
Anna Lau
Toronto, ON, Canada M7A 1L2

ONTARIO MINISTRY OF NATURAL RESOURCES — MINERAL RESOURCES GROUP — ONTARIO GEOLOGICAL SURVEY — GEOSCIENCE DATA CENTRE (778)
77 Grenville St., 8th Fl.
Phone: (416) 965-4641
Toronto, ON, Canada M5S 1B3
H.A. Groen

PMB PRINT MEASUREMENT BUREAU (814)
11 Yorkville Ave.
Phone: (416) 961-3205
Toronto, ON, Canada M4W 1L3
John Chaplin

SHARP ASSOCIATES LIMITED (871)
P.O. Box 418, Exchange Tower
Phone: (416) 364-5361
2 First Canadian Place, Suite 1900
I.P. Sharp
Toronto, ON, Canada M5X 1E3

SVP CANADA (910)
Micromedia Ltd.
Phone: (416) 593-5211
144 Front St. W.
Victor V. Brunka
Toronto, ON, Canada M5J 2L7

TAYSON INFORMATION TECHNOLOGY INC. (956)
275 Comstock Rd.
Phone: (416) 288-0550
Toronto, ON, Canada M1L 2H2
Peter Richardson

TORONTO DEPARTMENT OF THE CITY CLERK — COMPUTERIZED TEXT PROCESSING AND RETRIEVAL SYSTEM FOR CITY COUNCIL INFORMATION (985)
Toronto City Hall
Phone: (416) 947-7020
100 Queen St. W.
Roy V. Henderson
Toronto, ON, Canada M5H 2N2

TORONTO STOCK EXCHANGE — DATA PRODUCTS (986)
The Exchange Tower
Phone: (416) 947-4700
2 First Canadian Place
David F. Orr
Toronto, ON, Canada M5X 1J2

UNIVERSITY OF TORONTO — FACULTY OF LIBRARY AND INFORMATION SCIENCE LIBRARY — SUBJECT ANALYSIS SYSTEMS COLLECTION (1077)
140 St. George St.
Phone: (416) 978-7060
Toronto, ON, Canada M5S 1A1
Diane Henderson

UTLAS INC. (1094)
80 Bloor St. W., 2nd Floor
Phone: (416) 923-0890
Toronto, ON, Canada M5S 2V1
Arthur D. Parker

VEANER ASSOCIATES (1097)
45 Inglewood Dr.
Phone: (416) 486-0239
Toronto, ON, Canada M4T 1G9
Allen B. Veaner

EASY DATA SYSTEMS LTD. — EASY DATA INTEGRATED LIBRARY SYSTEM (289)
1385 W. 8th Ave.
Phone: (604) 734-8822
Vancouver, BC, Canada V6H 3V9

QUAERE LEGAL RESOURCES LTD. (829)
1140 W. 7th Ave.
Phone: (604) 736-7284
Vancouver, BC, Canada V6H 1B5
Mr. Vian Andrews

UNIVERSITY OF BRITISH COLUMBIA — B.C. HOSPITAL PROGRAMS BRANCH — DRUG AND POISON INFORMATION CENTRE (1043)
St. Paul's Hospital
Phone: (604) 682-2344
1081 Burrard St.
Mary Nelson
Vancouver, BC, Canada V6Z 1Y6

UNIVERSITY OF BRITISH COLUMBIA — DATA LIBRARY (1044)
Computing Centre
Phone: (604) 228-5587
2075 Wesbrook Mall
Ms. Laine Ruus
Vancouver, BC, Canada V6T 1W5

WARREN, INC. (1105)
2000 W. 12th Ave.
Phone: (604) 734-0755
Vancouver, BC, Canada V6J 2G2
Lois M. Warren

WESTERN LEGAL PUBLICATIONS LTD. (1108)
301 One Alexander St.
Phone: (604) 687-5671
Vancouver, BC, Canada V6A 1B2
Phil George

ACTON INFORMATION RESOURCES MANAGEMENT LTD. (4)
884 Darwin Ave.
Phone: (604) 384-2444
Victoria, BC, Canada V8X 2X6
Patricia Acton

BRITISH COLUMBIA MINISTRY OF INDUSTRY AND SMALL BUSINESS DEVELOPMENT — CENTRAL STATISTICS BUREAU (106)
1405 Douglas St.
Phone: (604) 387-4521
Victoria, BC, Canada V8W 3C1
Dr. W.P. McReynolds

FRASER VIDEOTEX SERVICES (369)
43 Bridgeport Rd. E.
Phone: (519) 884-0840
Waterloo, ON, Canada N2J 2J4
Niall M. Fraser

UNIVERSITY OF WATERLOO — DEPARTMENT OF RECREATION — LEISURE STUDIES DATA BANK (1084)
2026 Administrative Services Bldg.
Phone: (519) 885-1211
Waterloo, ON, Canada N2L 3G1
Dr. E.M. Avedon

UNIVERSITY OF WATERLOO — FACULTY OF HUMAN KINETICS AND LEISURE STUDIES — INFORMATION RETRIEVAL SYSTEM FOR THE SOCIOLOGY OF LEISURE AND SPORT (1085)
Phone: (519) 885-1211
Waterloo, ON, Canada N2L 3G1
Betty Smith

UNIVERSAL LIBRARY SYSTEMS LTD. (1029)
205-1571 Bellevue Ave.
Phone: (604) 926-7421
West Vancouver, BC, Canada V7V 1A6
J.A. Speight

CANADIAN MICROGRAPHIC SOCIETY (175)
2175 Sheppard Ave. E., Suite 309
Phone: (416) 499-6552
Willowdale, ON, Canada M2J 1W8
Mr. R.A. Richmond

DATACROWN INC. (261)
650 McNicoll Ave.
Phone: (416) 499-1012
Willowdale, ON, Canada M2H 2E1
G. Lucas

INFOMART — GRASSROOTS (519)
1661 Portage Ave., Suite 511
Phone: (204) 772-9453
Winnipeg, MB, Canada R3J 3T7
Bruno Leps

CHILE

CHILE — NATIONAL COMMISSION FOR SCIENTIFIC AND TECHNOLOGICAL RESEARCH — DIRECTORATE FOR INFORMATION AND DOCUMENTATION (202)
Casilla 297-V
Phone: 744537
Canada 308
Santiago, Chile

UNITED NATIONS — ECONOMIC COMMISSION FOR LATIN AMERICA — LATIN AMERICAN CENTER FOR ECONOMIC AND SOCIAL DOCUMENTATION (1006)
Avda. Dag Hammarskjold s/n
Phone: 485051
Casilla 179-D
Claudionor Evangelista
Santiago, Chile

UNITED NATIONS — ECONOMIC COMMISSION FOR LATIN AMERICA — LATIN AMERICAN DEMOGRAPHIC CENTER — LATIN AMERICAN POPULATION DOCUMENTATION SYSTEM (1007)
Alonso de Cordova 3107
Phone: 2283206
Casilla 91
Betty Johnson
Santiago, Chile

CHINA, PEOPLE'S REPUBLIC OF

CHINA BUILDING TECHNOLOGY DEVELOPMENT CENTRE — INSTITUTE OF TECHNICAL INFORMATION (203)
19 Che Gong Zhuang St.
Phone: 8992613
Beijing, People's Republic of China
Mr. Xu Ronglie

PEOPLE'S REPUBLIC OF CHINA — INSTITUTE OF SCIENTIFIC AND TECHNICAL INFORMATION OF CHINA (801)
P.O. Box 640
Phone: 464746
Beijing, People's Republic of China
Lin Zixin

COLOMBIA

COLOMBIAN FUND FOR SCIENTIFIC RESEARCH — NATIONAL INFORMATION SYSTEM (212)
Trv 9A No. 133-28
Phone: 2740468
Apdo. Aereo 051580
German Escorcia Saldarriaga
Bogota, Colombia

EDITEC (293)
Calle 22 N., No. 3N-20
Phone: 686359
Cali, Valle, Colombia
Alejandro Jimenez C.

CZECHOSLOVAKIA

DOBRA IRON AND STEEL RESEARCH INSTITUTE — INFORMETAL (281)
Phone: 54215
73951 Dobra, Czechoslovakia
Boris Skandera

CZECHOSLOVAKIA — INSTITUTE FOR MEDICAL INFORMATION (250)
Vitezneho unora 31
Phone: 299956
12132 Prague 2, Czechoslovakia
Dr. Jan Peska

DENMARK

NORDIC DOCUMENTATION CENTER FOR MASS COMMUNICATION RESEARCH (763)
State and University Library
Phone: 06 122022
Universitetsparken
Claus Kragh Hansen
DK-8000 Aarhus C, Denmark

BUSINESS INFORMATION INTERNATIONAL (123)
34, Kompagnistr.
Phone: 01 152348
DK-1208 Copenhagen, Denmark
Alex Gorski

DANISH COMMITTEE FOR SCIENTIFIC AND TECHNICAL INFORMATION AND DOCUMENTATION (255)
Industriradet, Teknisk afd.
H.C. Andersens Blvd. 18
Hans-Erik Hansen
DK-1596 Copenhagen, Denmark

DENMARK — MINISTRY OF CULTURAL AFFAIRS — NATIONAL ADVISORY COUNCIL FOR DANISH RESEARCH LIBRARIES (269)
8, Christians Brygge
Phone: 01 150111
DK-1219 Copenhagen, Denmark
Torkil Olsen

DENMARK — POSTS AND TELEGRAPHS DENMARK — CENTRAL TELECOMMUNICATIONS SERVICES — DATAPAK (271)
Dept. TFT-MA/dt
Phone: 01 124844
Farvergade 17
DK-1007 Copenhagen, Denmark

DENMARK TELECOMMUNICATIONS ADMINISTRATION — DANISH TELEDATA SYSTEM (272)
KTAS, Norregade 21
Phone: 01 993008
DK-1199 Copenhagen, Denmark
Helge Mansa

INSTITUTE FOR FUTURES STUDIES — FUTURES INFORMATION SERVICE (540)
Vesterbrogade 4A
Phone: 01 117176
DK-1620 Copenhagen V, Denmark
Annette Blegvad

DANISH DIANE CENTER (256)
Danmarks Tekniske Hojskole
Phone: 02886666
Bygning 101
DK-2800 Lyngby, Denmark

DENMARK — NATIONAL TECHNOLOGICAL LIBRARY OF DENMARK — AUTOMATED LIBRARY INFORMATION SYSTEM (270)
Anker Engelunds Vej 1
Phone: 02 883088
DK-2800 Lyngby, Denmark
Bent Barnholdt

NORDIC ATOMIC LIBRARIES JOINT SECRETARIAT — NORDIC ENERGY INDEX (761)
Riso Library
Phone: 02 371212
P.O. Box 49
Eva Pedersen
DK-4000 Roskilde, Denmark

RISO NATIONAL LABORATORY — RISO LIBRARY (842)
P.O. Box 49
Phone: 02 371212
DK-4000 Roskilde, Denmark
Eva Pedersen

INTERNATIONAL SOCIETY OF ECOLOGICAL MODELLING — ENVIRONMENTAL DATA AND ECOLOGICAL PARAMETERS DATA BASE (604)
Langkaer Vaenge 9
Phone: 02 480600
DK-3500 Vaerloese, Denmark
Dr. Sven Erik Joergensen

I/S DATACENTRALEN (497)
Retortvej 6-8
Phone: 1 468122
DK-2500 Valby, Denmark
J.U. Moos

EGYPT

WORLD HEALTH ORGANIZATION — EASTERN MEDITERRANEAN REGIONAL OFFICE — INFORMATION SERVICES (1112)
P.O. Box 1517
Phone: 30090
Alexandria, Egypt

DATA PROCESSING SERVICES COMPANY — DPS INFORMATION CENTRE (258)
87, Street 9, Maadi
Phone: 507475
Cairo, Egypt
Mrs. Effat El Shooky

UNITED NATIONS EDUCATIONAL, SCIENTIFIC AND CULTURAL ORGANIZATION — CENTER FOR SOCIAL SCIENCE RESEARCH AND DOCUMENTATION FOR THE ARAB REGION (1015)
Zamalek P.O. Phone: 650159
Cairo, Egypt Dr. Ahmad M. Khalifa

ENGLAND

GREAT BRITAIN — ATOMIC ENERGY AUTHORITY — CULHAM LABORATORY — PLASMA PHYSICS LIBRARY AND INFORMATION SERVICE (438)
Phone: 0235 21840
Abingdon, Oxon. OX14 3DB, England J.L. Hall

DOCUPRO (283)
Microinfo, Ltd.
P.O. Box 3, Newman Lane Phone: 0420 86848
Alton, Hamps. GU34 2PG, England

MICROINFO, LTD. (705)
P.O. Box 3, Newman Lane Phone: 0420 86848
Alton, Hampshire GU34 2PG, England R.B. Selwyn

DATASEARCH BUSINESS INFORMATION LTD. (263)
11 Kingsmead Square Phone: 0225 60526
Bath, Avon BA1 2AB, England Paul Dolan

UNIVERSITY OF BATH — CENTRE FOR CATALOGUE RESEARCH (1039)
Claverton Down Phone: 0225 61244
Bath BA2 7AY, England Philip Bryant

BHRA, THE FLUID ENGINEERING CENTRE — INFORMATION SERVICES (86)
Cranfield Phone: 0234 750422
Bedford MK43 0AJ, England Mr. G.A. Watts

BLCMP LTD. (91)
University of Birmingham Library
P.O. Box 353 Phone: 021 4711179
Birmingham B15 2TT, England A.R. Hall

UNIVERSITY OF BIRMINGHAM — DEPARTMENT OF ENGINEERING PRODUCTION — ERGONOMICS INFORMATION ANALYSIS CENTRE (1041)
P.O. Box 363 Phone: 021 4721301
Birmingham B15 2TT, England Prof. K.B. Haley

VIEWTEL SERVICES LTD. (1102)
28 Colmore Circus Phone: 021 2363366
Birmingham B4 6AX, England P. McC. Montague

GREAT BRITAIN — DEPARTMENT OF THE ENVIRONMENT — BUILDING RESEARCH ESTABLISHMENT — FIRE RESEARCH STATION LIBRARY — FIRE SCIENCE ABSTRACTS (452)
Melrose Ave. Phone: 953 6177
Borehamwood, Herts. WD6 2BL, England Jill Johnston

BUILDING SERVICES RESEARCH AND INFORMATION ASSOCIATION — BSRIA INFORMATION CENTRE (119)
Old Bracknell Lane West Phone: 0344 426511
Bracknell, Berks. RG12 4AH, England A.R. Eaves

INFORMATION INDUSTRIES LTD. (524)
Willougby Rd.
Bracknell, Berks., England Peter Martin

TECHNICAL INDEXES LTD. (958)
Willoughby Rd. Phone: 0344 426311
Bracknell, Berks. RG12 4DW, England Michael Lee

INFORMATION UNLIMITED (535)
114 Harrogate St. Phone: 0274 638877
Bradford, West Yorks. BD3 0LE, England Roy J. Jenkins

AMERICAN EXPRESS EUROPE LTD. — SKYGUIDE (23)
P.O. Box 68 Phone: 0273 693555
Amex House, Edward St. Mr. A. Book
Brighton, East Sussex BN2 2LP, England

ALPHA 460 TELEVISION LTD. (18)
Scarletts, Manor Lane Phone: 027581 3549
Abbots Leigh Michael H. Davis
Bristol BS8 3RU, England

SWALCAP (919)
14 Portland Sq. Phone: 0272 277603
Bristol BS2, England Richard F.B. Hudson

CAMBRIDGE UNIVERSITY — UNIVERSITY CHEMICAL LABORATORY — CAMBRIDGE CRYSTALLOGRAPHIC DATA CENTRE (125)
Lensfield Rd. Phone: 0223 66499
Cambridge CB2 1EW, England Dr. Olga Kennard

THE WELDING INSTITUTE — INFORMATION SERVICES (1106)
Abington Hall Phone: 0223 891162
Cambridge CB1 6AL, England Rodney T. Bryant

ORIEL COMPUTER SERVICES LIMITED (787)
1-5 West St. Phone: 0608 41351
Chipping Norton, Oxon. OX7 5LY, England

IMPERIAL CHEMICAL INDUSTRIES LTD. — AGRICULTURAL DIVISION — MANAGEMENT SERVICES DEPARTMENT — ASSASSIN (503)
P.O. Box 1, Billingham Phone: 0642 553601
Cleveland TS23 1LB, England

ECONOMIC AND SOCIAL RESEARCH COUNCIL — DATA ARCHIVE (291)
University of Essex Phone: 0206 860570
Wivenhoe Park Prof. Howard Newby
Colchester, Essex CO4 3SQ, England

EUROTEC CONSULTANTS LTD. — LIBRARIAN (318)
143 Hythe Hill Phone: 0206 72538
Colchester, Essex CO1 2NF, England Dr. A.A. Klimowicz

MONITAN INFORMATION CONSULTANTS LTD. (713)
Berry Edge Rd. Phone: 0207 500957
Consett, Durham DH8 5EU, England Monica Anderton

UNIVERSITY OF WARWICK LIBRARY — WARWICK STATISTICS SERVICE (1083)
Gibbet Hill Rd. Phone: 0203 418938
Coventry CV4 7AL, England David Mort

INFOCOM (515)
P.O. Box 61 Phone: 0342 713296
Crawley, West Sussex RH10 4FA, England Dr. Gordon Wilkinson

GREAT BRITAIN — DEPARTMENTS OF THE ENVIRONMENT AND TRANSPORT — TRANSPORT AND ROAD RESEARCH LABORATORY — TECHNICAL INFORMATION AND LIBRARY SERVICES (455)
Old Wokingham Rd. Phone: 03446 3131
Crowthorne, Berks. RG11 6AU, England Mrs. B.A. Crofts

BEMROSE PRINTING (85)
P.O. Box 32 Phone: 0332 31242
Wayzgoose Dr. Mr. P. Brewin
Derby, Derbyshire DE2 6XH, England

GREAT BRITAIN — ATOMIC ENERGY AUTHORITY — ATOMIC ENERGY RESEARCH ESTABLISHMENT, HARWELL — COMPUTER SCIENCE AND SYSTEMS DIVISION — STATUS (433)
Harwell Laboratory Phone: 0235 24141
Didcot, Oxon. OX11 0RA, England Derek I. Matkin

GREAT BRITAIN — ATOMIC ENERGY AUTHORITY — ATOMIC ENERGY RESEARCH ESTABLISHMENT, HARWELL — HARWELL CENTRAL INFORMATION SERVICE (434)
Bldg. 465, Harwell Laboratory Phone: 0235 24141
Didcot, Oxon. OX11 0RB, England Mr. P.J. Jones

GREAT BRITAIN — ATOMIC ENERGY AUTHORITY — ATOMIC ENERGY RESEARCH ESTABLISHMENT, HARWELL — NATIONAL CHEMICAL EMERGENCY CENTRE — CHEMSAFE (435)
Bldg. 7.22, Harwell Laboratory Phone: 0235 24141
Didcot, Oxon. OX11 0RA, England Robert F. Cumberland

GREAT BRITAIN — ATOMIC ENERGY AUTHORITY — ATOMIC ENERGY RESEARCH ESTABLISHMENT, HARWELL — NONDESTRUCTIVE TESTING CENTRE — QUALITY TECHNOLOGY INFORMATION SERVICE (436)
Harwell Laboratory Phone: 0235 24141
Didcot, Oxon. OX11 0RA, England Mr. R.S. Sharpe

GREAT BRITAIN — ATOMIC ENERGY AUTHORITY — ATOMIC ENERGY RESEARCH ESTABLISHMENT, HARWELL — WASTE MANAGEMENT INFORMATION BUREAU (437)
Environmental Safety Group Phone: 0235 24141
Bldg. 7.12, Harwell Laboratory Miss M.A. Lund
Didcot, Oxon. OX11 0RA, England

GEOGRAPHIC INDEX

STATUS USERS GROUP (900)
SERC, Rutherford Appleton Lab.   Phone: 0235 445666
Chilton   Mrs. J.O. Lay
Didcot, Oxon. OX11 0QY, England

EXETER UNIVERSITY TEACHING SERVICES — THE EXETER
ABSTRACT REFERENCE SYSTEM (319)
Streatham Court, Rennes Dr.   Phone: 0392 77911
Exeter, Devon. EX4 4PU, England   Dr. Donald A. Bligh

BARIC COMPUTING SERVICES LTD. — BARIC VIEWDATA (75)
Forest Rd.   Phone: 1890 1414
Feltham, Middlesex TW13 7EJ, England   A.R. Terry

INTERNATIONAL BEE RESEARCH ASSOCIATION — APICULTURAL
ABSTRACTS (563)
Hill House, Chalfont St. Peter   Phone: 0753 885011
Gerrards Cross, Bucks. SL9 0NR, England   Margaret Adey

NATURAL ENVIRONMENT RESEARCH COUNCIL — INSTITUTE OF
OCEANOGRAPHIC SCIENCES — MARINE INFORMATION AND
ADVISORY SERVICE (730)
Brook Rd., Wormley   Phone: 042 8794141
Godalming, Surrey GU8 5UB, England   Dr. N.C. Flemming

INDEPENDENT CHEMICAL INFORMATION SERVICES LTD. (505)
La Tour Gand House
Pollet, St. Peter Port   Mr. H. Hinshelwood
Guernsey, England

SOCIETY OF METAPHYSICIANS LTD. — INFORMATION
SERVICES (882)
Archers' Court   Phone: 0424 751577
Stonestile Lane, The Ridge   Dr. John J. Williamson
Hastings, Sussex TN35 4PG, England

HERTFORDSHIRE COUNTY COUNCIL — CHILTERN ADVISORY UNIT
FOR COMPUTER BASED EDUCATION (485)
Endymion Rd.   Phone: 07072 65443
Hatfield, Herts. AL10 8AU, England   Dr. W. Tagg

HERTFORDSHIRE TECHNICAL LIBRARY AND INFORMATION SERVICE
— HERTIS INDUSTRIAL SERVICES (486)
Hatfield Polytechnic Library   Phone: 07072 68100
P.O. Box 110   William A. Forster
Hatfield, Herts. AL10 9AD, England

GOTHARD HOUSE GROUP OF COMPANIES, LTD. (432)
Gothard House   Phone: 0491 573602
Henley-on-Thames, Oxon. RG9 1AJ,   Richard S. Gothard
England

NATIONAL REPROGRAPHIC CENTRE FOR DOCUMENTATION (725)
The Hatfield Polytechnic   Phone: 0992 552341
Bayfordbury   Bernard J.S. Williams
Hertford, Herts. SG13 8LD, England

TIMBER RESEARCH AND DEVELOPMENT ASSOCIATION —
INFORMATION AND ADVISORY DEPARTMENT — TIMBER
INFORMATION KEYWORD RETRIEVAL (983)
Stocking Lane   Phone: 0240 243091
Hughenden Valley   R.T. Allcorn
High Wycombe, Bucks. HP14 4ND,
England

INSTITUTION OF ELECTRICAL ENGINEERS — INSPEC (549)
Station House   Phone: 0462 53331
Nightingale Rd.   T.M. Aitchison
Hitchin, Herts. SG5 1RJ, England

INSTITUTION OF ELECTRICAL ENGINEERS — INSPEC —
ELECTRONIC MATERIALS INFORMATION SERVICE (550)
Station House   Phone: 0462 53331
Nightingale Rd.   T.M. Aitchison
Hitchin, Herts. SG5 1RJ, England

AVIATION INFORMATION SERVICES LTD. (68)
208 Epsom Square   Phone: 01-897 1066
London Heathrow Airport   Alan E. Smith
Hounslow, Middlesex TW6 2BO, England

GREAT BRITAIN — INSTITUTE OF TERRESTRIAL ECOLOGY —
BIOLOGICAL RECORDS CENTRE (461)
Monks Wood Experimental Station   Phone: 04873 381
Abbots Ripton   Paul T. Harding
Huntingdon, Cambs. PE17 2LS, England

RESOURCES (840)
465 Twickenham Rd.
Isleworth, Middlesex TW7 7DZ, England   Genevieve M. Hibbs

NATURAL ENVIRONMENT RESEARCH COUNCIL — BRITISH
GEOLOGICAL SURVEY — MINERALS STRATEGY AND ECONOMICS
RESEARCH GROUP — MINERAL INFORMATION SECTION (727)
    Phone: 06077 6111
Keyworth, Notts. NG12 5GG, England   Anne Ramsden

BIRD ASSOCIATES (89)
193 Richmond Rd.
Kingston, Surrey KT2 5DD, England   Tony Bird

INFORMATION MANAGEMENT & ENGINEERING LTD. (527)
Gough House, 57 Eden St.   Phone: 01-546 7968
Kingston on Thames KT1 1DA, England   Kathleen Bivins Noerr

IRCS MEDICAL SCIENCE — IRCS MEDICAL SCIENCE
DATABASE (614)
St. Leonard's House   Phone: 0524 68116
St. Leonardgate   M.C.S. Buckingham
Lancaster LA1 1PF, England

MARKET LOCATION (686)
17 Waterloo Place   Phone: 0926 34235
Warwick St.   A.J. Sidwell
Leamington Spa, Warwicks. CV32 5LA,
England

MITAKA — JAPANSCAN (712)
3-5 Tavistock St.   Phone: 0926 311126
Leamington Spa, Warwicks. CV32 5PJ,   Clive A. Smith
England

INTERNATIONAL ELECTRONIC PUBLISHING RESEARCH
CENTRE (577)
Pira House   Phone: 0372 376161
Randalls Rd.   Brian W. Blunden
Leatherhead, Surrey KT22 7RU, England

LEATHERHEAD FOOD RESEARCH ASSOCIATION — INFORMATION
AND LIBRARY SERVICES (655)
Randalls Rd.   Phone: 76761
Leatherhead, Surrey KT22 7RY, England

PIRA: RESEARCH ASSOCIATION FOR THE PAPER AND BOARD,
PRINTING AND PACKAGING INDUSTRIES — COMPREHENSIVE
INFORMATION SERVICES (812)
Randalls Rd.   Phone: 0372 376161
Leatherhead, Surrey KT22 7RU, England   Brian W. Blunden

PIRA: RESEARCH ASSOCIATION FOR THE PAPER AND BOARD,
PRINTING AND PACKAGING INDUSTRIES — PRINTING AND
INFORMATION TECHNOLOGY DIVISION (813)
Randalls Rd.   Phone: 0372 376161
Leatherhead, Surrey KT22 7RU, England   Brian W. Blunden

UNIVERSITY OF LEEDS — DEPARTMENT OF PHYSICAL CHEMISTRY
— HIGH TEMPERATURE REACTION RATE DATA CENTRE (1052)
    Phone: 0532 31751
Leeds, Yorkshire LS2 9JT, England   Dr. D.L. Baulch

UNIVERSITY OF LEEDS — MEDICAL AND DENTAL LIBRARY —
ONCOLOGY INFORMATION SERVICE (1053)
    Phone: 0532 450059
Leeds, W. Yorks. LS2 9JT, England   Daphne Roberts

UNIVERSITY OF LEICESTER — PRIMARY COMMUNICATIONS
RESEARCH CENTRE (1054)
University Rd.   Phone: 0533 556223
Leicester LE1 7RH, England   Prof. A.J. Meadows

ASLIB, THE ASSOCIATION FOR INFORMATION MANAGEMENT (35)
Information House   Phone: 01-430 2671
26/27 Boswell St.   Dennis A. Lewis
London WC1N 3JZ, England

ASSOCIATION OF DATABASE PRODUCERS (40)
Geosystems   Phone: 01-222 7305
P.O. Box 1024, Westminster   Graham Lea
London SW1P 2JL, England

AVS INTEXT LTD. (69)
145 Oxford St.   Phone: 01-434 2034
London W1R 1TB, England   Malcolm G. Smith

BANK OF ENGLAND — FINANCIAL STATISTICS DIVISION (72)
Threadneedle St.   Phone: 01-601 4918
London EC2R 8AH, England   Mr. G.K. Willetts

BRITISH BROADCASTING CORPORATION — BBC DATA (104)
The Langham, Room 3   Phone: 01-580 4468
Portland Place   Richard Hewlett
London W1A 1AA, England

BRITISH BROADCASTING CORPORATION — CEEFAX (105)
BBC Television Centre   Phone: 01-743 8000
Wood Lane   Graham Clayton
London W12 7RJ, England

BRITISH COMPUTER SOCIETY (107)
13 Mansfield St.   Phone: 01-637 0471
London W1M 0BP, England   D.W. Harding

THE BRITISH COUNCIL — CENTRAL INFORMATION SERVICE (108)
10 Spring Gardens   Phone: 01-930 8466
London SW1A 2BN, England   T.J. Maughan

BRITISH MARKET RESEARCH BUREAU LTD. — TARGET GROUP INDEX (109)
Saunders House   Phone: 01-567 3060
53 The Mall, Ealing   Philip Mitchell
London W5 3TE, England

BRITISH MEDICAL ASSOCIATION — BMA PRESS CUTTINGS DATABASE (110)
Tavistock Square   Phone: 01-387 4499
London WC1H 9JP, England   Dr. J. Dawson

BRITISH UNIVERSITIES FILM & VIDEO COUNCIL LTD. — INFORMATION SERVICE (112)
55 Greek St.   Phone: 01-734 3687
London W1V 5LR, England   James Ballantyne

BROWN'S GEOLOGICAL INFORMATION SERVICE LTD. (113)
134 Great Portland St.   Phone: 01-580 4701
London W1N 5PH, England   G.H. Brown

CHEM SYSTEMS INTERNATIONAL LTD. (199)
28 St. James's Square   Phone: 01-839 4652
London SW1Y 4JH, England   Alan D. Plaistowe

CHEMICAL AGE — CHEMICAL AGE PROJECT FILE (200)
12 Vandy St.   Phone: 01-370 4600
London EC2 2DE, England   Stuart Slade

CISI-WHARTON ECONOMETRIC FORECASTING ASSOCIATES LTD. (207)
23 Lower Belgrave St.
London SW1W 0NW, England

CITY OF LONDON POLYTECHNIC — FAWCETT LIBRARY — BIBLIOFEM (209)
Old Castle St.   Phone: 01-283 1030
London E1 7NT, England   David Doughan

COMMODITIES RESEARCH UNIT LTD. (228)
31 Mount Pleasant   Phone: 01-278 0414
London WC1X 0AD, England   Mr. R.B. Goldstein

COMPU-MARK LTD. (235)
93 Chancery Lane   Phone: 01-405 1305
London WC2A 1DT, England   Florent Gevers

CONSUMERS' ASSOCIATION — TELEWHICH? (244)
14 Buckingham St.   Phone: 01-839 1222
London WC2N 6DS, England

COOPERATIVE AUTOMATION GROUP (246)
British Library Bibliographic
Services Division, 2 Sheraton St.   Lynne J. Brindley
London W1V 4BH, England

COUNCIL FOR EDUCATIONAL TECHNOLOGY — VIDEOTEX SERVICES UNIT (247)
3 Devonshire St.   Phone: 01-580 7553
London W1N 2BA, England   Leslie Mapp

DATASTREAM INTERNATIONAL LTD. (267)
Monmouth House   Phone: 01-250 3000
58-64 City Rd.   A.L. Helman
London EC1Y 2AL, England

DERWENT PUBLICATIONS LTD. — BIOTECHNOLOGY ABSTRACTS (273)
Rochdale House   Phone: 01-242 5823
128 Theobalds Rd.
London WC1X 8RP, England

DERWENT PUBLICATIONS LTD. — CHEMICAL REACTIONS DOCUMENTATION SERVICE (274)
Rochdale House   Phone: 01-242 5823
128 Theobalds Rd.
London WC1X 8RP, England

DERWENT PUBLICATIONS LTD. — PATENTS DOCUMENTATION SERVICES (275)
Rochdale House   Phone: 01-242 5823
128 Theobalds Rd.
London WC1X 8RP, England

DERWENT PUBLICATIONS LTD. — PEST CONTROL LITERATURE DOCUMENTATION (276)
Rochdale House   Phone: 01-242 5823
128 Theobalds Rd.
London WC1X 8RP, England

DERWENT PUBLICATIONS LTD. — PHARMACEUTICAL LITERATURE DOCUMENTATION (277)
Rochdale House   Phone: 01-242 5823
128 Theobalds Rd.
London WC1X 8RP, England

DERWENT PUBLICATIONS LTD. — VETERINARY LITERATURE DOCUMENTATION (278)
Rochdale House   Phone: 01-242 5823
128 Theobalds Rd.
London WC1X 8RP, England

DRUG INFORMATION PHARMACISTS GROUP — PHARMLINE (285)
The London Hospital   Phone: 01-247 5454
Whitechapel Rd.   Michael L. Rogers
London E1 1BB, England

ECONINTEL INFORMATION SERVICES LTD. — ECONINTEL MONITOR (290)
37 Ludgate Hill   Phone: 01-248 4958
London EC4M 7JN, England

ENGLISH TOURIST BOARD — INFORMATION UNIT — TOURTEL (297)
4 Grosvenor Gardens   Phone: 01-730 3400
London SW1W 0DU, England

ESDU INTERNATIONAL LIMITED (299)
251/9 Regent St.   Phone: 01-437 4894
London W1R 7AD, England   John A. Castle

EURODATA FOUNDATION (303)
Broad Street House   Phone: 01-638 3702
55 Old Broad St.   S.J. Valiant
London EC2M 1RX, England

EUROPEAN ASSOCIATION OF INFORMATION SERVICES (307)
P.O. Box 429   Phone: 01-546 7968
London W4 1UJ, England   Helen Henderson

EUROPEAN INFORMATION PROVIDERS ASSOCIATION (312)
Kingsmead House   Phone: 01-351 2776
250 Kings Rd.   Dr. Robert Middleton
London SW3, England

EUROPEAN LAW CENTRE LTD. — EUROLEX (314)
4 Bloomsbury Square   Phone: 01-404 4300
London WC1A 2RL, England   David R. Worlock

EXPERT INFORMATION SYSTEMS LTD. — EXIS 1 (320)
38 Tavistock St.   Phone: 01-240 0837
London WC2E 7PB, England   Ken Burgess

EXTEL COMPUTING LTD. — EXSHARE (321)
Lowndes House   Phone: 01-638 5544
1-9 City Rd.   John B. Shapcott
London EC1Y 1AA, England

EXTEL STATISTICAL SERVICES LTD. — EXBOND (322)
37-45 Paul St.   Phone: 01-253 3400
London EC2A 4PB, England   S.J. Pinner

EXTEL STATISTICAL SERVICES LTD. — EXSTAT   (323)
37-45 Paul St.   Phone: 01-253 3400
London EC2A 4PB, England   S.J. Pinner

FAIRPLAY PUBLICATIONS LTD. — FAIRPLAY INTERNATIONAL
RESEARCH SERVICES   (324)
52-54 Southwark St.   Phone: 01-403 3437
London SE1 1UJ, England   John Prime

FINANCIAL TIMES BUSINESS INFORMATION LTD. — BUSINESS
INFORMATION SERVICE   (328)
Bracken House   Phone: 01-248 8000
10 Cannon St.   Richard M. Soule
London EC4P 4BY, England

FINSBURY DATA SERVICES LTD. — TEXTLINE   (335)
68-74 Carter Lane   Phone: 01-248 9828
London EC4V 5EA, England   J. Graham Blease

GEOSYSTEMS   (394)
P.O. Box 1024, Westminster   Phone: 01-222 7305
London SW1P 2JL, England   Graham Lea

GREAT BRITAIN — BRITISH LIBRARY — BIBLIOGRAPHIC SERVICES
DIVISION   (439)
2 Sheraton St.   Phone: 01-636 1544
London W1V 4BH, England   P.R. Lewis

GREAT BRITAIN — BRITISH LIBRARY — BIBLIOGRAPHIC SERVICES
DIVISION — BLAISE   (440)
2 Sheraton St.   Phone: 01-636 1544
London W1V 4BH, England   David Martin

GREAT BRITAIN — BRITISH LIBRARY — BIBLIOGRAPHIC SERVICES
DIVISION — SUBJECT SYSTEMS OFFICE — PRESERVED CONTEXT
INDEX SYSTEM   (441)
2 Sheraton St.   Phone: 01-636 1544
London W1V 4BH, England   Derek Austin

GREAT BRITAIN — BRITISH LIBRARY — REFERENCE DIVISION —
EIGHTEENTH CENTURY SHORT TITLE CATALOGUE   (443)
Great Russell St.   Phone: 01-636 8983
London WC1B 3DG, England   R.C. Alston

GREAT BRITAIN — BRITISH LIBRARY — RESEARCH AND
DEVELOPMENT DEPARTMENT   (444)
2 Sheraton St.   Phone: 01-636 1544
London W1V 4BH, England   Mr. B.J. Perry

GREAT BRITAIN — BRITISH LIBRARY — SCIENCE REFERENCE
LIBRARY — COMPUTER SEARCH SERVICE   (445)
25 Southampton Bldgs.   Phone: 01-405 8721
Chancery Lane   Derek Greenwood
London WC2A 1AW, England

GREAT BRITAIN — BRITISH LIBRARY — SCIENCE REFERENCE
LIBRARY — EUROPEAN BIOTECHNOLOGY INFORMATION
PROGRAM   (446)
Aldwych Reading Room   Phone: 01-379 6488
9 Kean St.   John A. Leigh
London WC2B 4AT, England

GREAT BRITAIN — BRITISH TELECOMMUNICATIONS — PACKET
SWITCHSTREAM   (447)
G07 Lutyens House   Phone: 01-920 0661
1-6 Finsbury Circus   G.V. Spencer
London EC2M 7LY, England

GREAT BRITAIN — BRITISH TELECOMMUNICATIONS —
PRESTEL   (448)
Telephone House   Phone: 01-583 9811
Temple Ave.   Richard Hooper
London EC4Y 0HL, England

GREAT BRITAIN — CENTRAL STATISTICAL OFFICE — CSO MACRO-
ECONOMIC DATA BANK   (449)
Great George St.   Phone: 01-233 6135
London SW1P 4AQ, England

GREAT BRITAIN — DEPARTMENT OF INDUSTRY — INFORMATION
TECHNOLOGY DIVISION — HERMES   (450)
29 Bressenden Place   Phone: 01-213 6533
London SW1E 5DT, England

GREAT BRITAIN — H.M. TREASURY — U.K. TREASURY
MACROECONOMIC FORECASTING MODEL AND DATABANK   (456)
Treasury Chambers   Phone: 01-233 3000
Parliament St.
London SW1, England

GREAT BRITAIN — HOUSE OF COMMONS LIBRARY —
PARLIAMENTARY ON-LINE INFORMATION SYSTEM   (459)
                                                  Phone: 01-219 5714
London SW1A 0AA, England   Jane Wainwright

GREAT BRITAIN — HOUSE OF LORDS — LIBRARY & INFORMATION
CENTRE   (460)
                                                  Phone: 01-219 5242
London SW1A 0PW, England   Roger Morgan

GREATER LONDON COUNCIL — INFORMATION SERVICES
GROUP   (465)
Director General's Dept.   Phone: 01-633 7149
County Hall   Alan Gomersall
London SE1 7PB, England

HANOVER PRESS — VIEWDATA SERVICES   (473)
80 Highgate Rd.   Phone: 01-267 9521
London NW5, England   Maureen A. Miller

HENLEY CENTRE FOR FORECASTING   (484)
2 Tudor St., Blackfriars   Phone: 01-353 9961
London EC4Y 0AA, England   Hywel G. Jones

ICC INFORMATION GROUP LTD.   (499)
28-42 Banner St.   Phone: 01-253 6131
London EC1Y 8QE, England   Mr. A.J. Jewitt

INFOLEX SERVICES LTD.   (517)
Hambleton House   Phone: 01-499 2410
17B Curzon St.   Dr. Stephen Castell
London W1, England

INFORMATION RESEARCH LTD.   (530)
40-42 Oxford St.   Phone: 01-580 3914
London W1N 9FJ, England   Dr. John P. Howard

INSTITUTION OF MINING AND METALLURGY — LIBRARY AND
INFORMATION SERVICES   (551)
44 Portland Place   Phone: 01-580 3802
London W1N 4BR, England   Michael McGarr

INTERNATIONAL ASSOCIATION OF AGRICULTURAL LIBRARIANS AND
DOCUMENTALISTS   (558)
TDRI, College House
Wrights Lane   Miss P.J. Wortley
London W8 5SJ, England

INTERNATIONAL COFFEE ORGANIZATION — COFFEELINE   (570)
22 Berners St.   Phone: 01-580 8591
London W1P 4DD, England   Mr. C.P.R. Dubois

IRS-DIALTECH   (615)
Ebury Bridge House   Phone: 01-730 9678
2-18 Ebury Bridge Rd.
London SW1W 8QD, England

JORDAN & SONS LTD. — JORDANS COMPANY INFORMATION   (636)
Jordan House   Phone: 01-253 3030
47 Brunswick Place   Ralph D.S. Leake
London N1 6EE, England

KENT-BARLOW PUBLICATIONS LTD.   (638)
Kingsmead House   Phone: 01-351 2776
250 Kings Rd., Chelsea   Derek H. Barlow
London SW3 5UE, England

LANGTON ELECTRONIC PUBLISHING SYSTEMS LTD.   (649)
133 Oxford St.   Phone: 01-434 1031
London W1R 1TD, England   W.X. Wilson

LATIN AMERICAN NEWSLETTERS LTD.   (651)
Boundary House   Phone: 01-251 0012
91-93 Charterhouse St.   Rodolfo H. Terragno
London BEC1M 6LN, England

LEGAL TECHNOLOGY GROUP   (656)
58 S. Eaton Place   Phone: 01-730 8040
London SW1W 9JJ, England   Andrew J.M. Trew

LIBRARY ASSOCIATION PUBLISHING LTD. — BRITISH HUMANITIES INDEX   (660)
7 Ridgmount St.
London WC1E 7AE, England
Phone: 01-636 7543
Lyn Duffus

LIBRARY ASSOCIATION PUBLISHING LTD. — CURRENT RESEARCH IN LIBRARY & INFORMATION SCIENCE   (661)
7 Ridgmount St.
London WC1E 7AE, England
Phone: 01-636 7543
Mrs. P.T. Biggs

LIBRARY ASSOCIATION PUBLISHING LTD. — CURRENT TECHNOLOGY INDEX   (662)
7 Ridgmount St.
London WC1E 7AE, England
Phone: 01-636 7543
Tom Edwards

LIBRARY ASSOCIATION PUBLISHING LTD. — LIBRARY AND INFORMATION SCIENCE ABSTRACTS   (663)
7 Ridgmount St.
London WC1E 7AE, England
Phone: 01-636 7543
Nicholas L. Moore

LLOYD'S SHIPPING INFORMATION SERVICES   (667)
4 Lloyds Ave.
London EC3N 3ED, England
Phone: 01-709 9166
J.R. Hughes

LOGICA UK LTD.   (668)
64 Newman St.
London W1A 4SE, England
Phone: 01-637 9111
Colin Rowland

LONDON AND SOUTH EASTERN LIBRARY REGION   (670)
33/34 Alfred Place
London WC1E 7DP, England
Phone: 01-636 9537
Miss J.M. Plaister

LONDON ENTERPRISE AGENCY — SUPPLIER IDENTIFICATION SYSTEM   (671)
69 Cannon St.
London EC4N 5AB, England
Phone: 01-248 9383
P. Thackwray

THE LONDON INTERNATIONAL FINANCIAL FUTURES EXCHANGE LTD.   (672)
Royal Exchange
London EC3V 3PJ, England
Phone: 01-623 0444
R.R. St. J. Barkshire

LONDON OVER THE COUNTER MARKET   (673)
21 Upper Brook St.
London W1, England
Phone: 01-629 5983
Peter Sommer

LONDON RESEARCHERS   (674)
76 Park Rd.
London NW1 4SH, England
Phone: 01-723 8530
Mary Ann Colyer

MARKET RESEARCH SOCIETY — MARKET RESEARCH ABSTRACTS   (687)
15 Belgrave Square
London SW1X 8PF, England
Phone: 01-235 4709

METALS INFORMATION   (698)
The Metals Society
1 Carlton House Terrace
London SW1Y 5DB, England
Phone: 01-839 4071
H. David Chafe

MINERALOGICAL SOCIETY OF GREAT BRITAIN — MINERALOGICAL ABSTRACTS   (711)
41 Queen's Gate
London SW7 5HR, England
Phone: 01-584 7516
Professor R. A. Howie

MORGAN-GRAMPIAN PLC. — M-G VIDEOTEX SERVICES   (714)
30 Calderwood St.
London SE18 6QH, England
Phone: 01-855 7777
Peter Head

MORGAN GRENFELL & CO. LTD. — INTERFISC   (715)
23 Great Winchester St.
London EC2P 2AX, England
Phone: 01-588 4545
Brian Laurence Kieran

NATURAL ENVIRONMENT RESEARCH COUNCIL — BRITISH GEOLOGICAL SURVEY — NATIONAL GEOCHEMICAL DATA BANK   (728)
London EC1R 5DU, England

NEW OPPORTUNITY PRESS LTD. — CAREERDATA   (747)
76 St. James Lane
London N10 3RD, England
Phone: 01-444 7281
R. Begley

ONLINE INFORMATION CENTRE   (775)
Information House
26/27 Boswell St.
London WC1N 3JZ, England
Phone: 01-430 2502
Jacky Deunette

ORACLE TELETEXT LTD.   (779)
Craven House, 25-32 Marshall St.
London W1, England
Phone: 01-434 3121
Geoffrey Hughes

ORGANISATION FOR ECONOMIC CO-OPERATION AND DEVELOPMENT — INTERNATIONAL ENERGY AGENCY — IEA COAL RESEARCH — TECHNICAL INFORMATION SERVICE   (782)
14/15 Lower Grosvenor Place
London SW1W 0EX, England
Phone: 01-828 4661
Mr. A. Baker

ORGANISATION FOR ECONOMIC CO-OPERATION AND DEVELOPMENT — INTERNATIONAL ENERGY AGENCY — IEA COAL RESEARCH — WORLD COAL RESOURCES AND RESERVES DATA BANK SERVICE   (783)
14/15 Lower Grosvenor Place
London SW1W 0EX, England
Phone: 01-828 4661

PERGAMON INFOLINE LTD.   (802)
12 Vandy St.
London EC2A 2DE, England
Phone: 01-377 4650
Sarah Dunn

PHARMACEUTICAL SOCIETY OF GREAT BRITAIN — MARTINDALE ONLINE   (806)
1 Lambeth High St.
London SE1 7JN, England
Phone: 01-735 9141
J.E.F. Reynolds

POLYTECHNIC OF CENTRAL LONDON — INFORMATION TECHNOLOGY CENTRE   (818)
309 Regent St.
London W1R 8AL, England
Phone: 01-636 2383
Neil McLean

PRESS ASSOCIATION LTD. — NEWSFILE   (823)
85 Fleet St.
London EC4P 4BE, England
Phone: 01-353 7440
Nicholas Kester

QUOTEL INSURANCE SERVICES LTD.   (837)
83 Clerkenwell Rd.
London EC1, England
Phone: 01-242 0747

ROYAL INSTITUTE OF BRITISH ARCHITECTS — BRITISH ARCHITECTURAL LIBRARY — ARCHITECTURAL PERIODICALS INDEX   (845)
66 Portland Place
London W1N 4AD, England
Phone: 01-580 5533
Jan van der Wateren

SCICON LTD.   (867)
Sanderson House
49 Berners St.
London W1P 4AQ, England
Phone: 01-580 5599

SPECIALIST SOFTWARE LTD.   (895)
4 London Wall Bldgs.
London EC2, England
Phone: 01-920 0522
Edward B. Caplin

SPORTS COUNCIL — INFORMATION CENTRE   (896)
16 Upper Woburn Place
London WC1H 0QP, England
Phone: 01-388 1277
David Scarfe

THE STOCK EXCHANGE — TECHNICAL SERVICES DEPARTMENT — TOPIC   (902)
London EC2N 1HP, England
Phone: 01-588 2355
G.A. Hayter

SVP UNITED KINGDOM   (918)
12 Argyll St.
London W1V 1AB, England
Phone: 01-734 9272
Lord McIntosh

TELEMAP LTD. — MICRONET 800   (976)
Scriptor Court
155 Farringdon Rd.
London EC1B 1PA, England
Phone: 01-278 3143
Timothy R. Schoonmaker

UNIVERSITY OF LONDON — CENTRAL INFORMATION SERVICE   (1055)
Senate House, Malet St.
London WC1 7HU, England
Phone: 01 6368000
Mrs. Alina Vickery

UNIVERSITY OF LONDON — IMPERIAL COLLEGE OF SCIENCE AND TECHNOLOGY — DEPARTMENT OF MINERAL RESOURCES ENGINEERING — ROCK MECHANICS INFORMATION SERVICE   (1056)
Royal School of Mines
Prince Consort Rd.
London SW7 2BP, England
Phone: 01-589 5111
A.M. Smith

VIDEOTEX INDUSTRY ASSOCIATION LTD. (1100)
Borough High St.
London SE1 1HH, England

VIRTUAL CITY ASSOCIATES LTD. (1103)
21 Upper Brook St. Phone: 01-491 2775
London W1, England Peter Sommer

WOLFF & CO. LTD. — WOLFF RESEARCH (1109)
Plantation House, 2nd Floor Phone: 01-626 8765
10-15 Mincing Lane Mrs. Elli Gifford
London EC3M 3DB, England

ZINC DEVELOPMENT ASSOCIATION/LEAD DEVELOPMENT
ASSOCIATION/CADMIUM ASSOCIATION — LIBRARY AND
ABSTRACTING SERVICE (1122)
34 Berkeley Square Phone: 01-499 6636
London W1X 6AJ, England Dr. D.A. Temple

LOUGHBOROUGH UNIVERSITY OF TECHNOLOGY — CENTRE FOR
LIBRARY AND INFORMATION MANAGEMENT (675)
Phone: 0509 213176
Loughborough, Leics. LE11 3TU, England Peter H. Mann

LOUGHBOROUGH UNIVERSITY OF TECHNOLOGY — CHEMICAL
ENGINEERING DEPARTMENT — PARTICLE SCIENCE AND
TECHNOLOGY INFORMATION SERVICE (676)
Ashby Rd. Phone: 0509 263171
Loughborough, Leics. LE11 3TU, England Mr. P.J. Lloyd

LOUGHBOROUGH UNIVERSITY OF TECHNOLOGY LIBRARY — LIBRARY
INSTRUCTION MATERIALS BANK (677)
Ashby Rd. Phone: 0509 263171
Loughborough, Leics. LE11 3TU, England Ian Malley

LOUGHBOROUGH UNIVERSITY OF TECHNOLOGY LIBRARY —
MINIMAL-INPUT CATALOGUING SYSTEM (678)
Ashby Rd. Phone: 0509 263171
Loughborough, Leics. LE11 3TU, England Dr. R.A. Wall

LIPMAN MANAGEMENT RESOURCES, LTD. — LMR INFORMATION
SYSTEMS — ADAPTIVE LIBRARY MANAGEMENT SYSTEM (666)
54-70 Moorbridge Rd. Phone: 0628 37123
Maidenhead, Berks. SL6 8BN, England

NATIONAL COMPUTING CENTRE LTD. — INFORMATION SERVICES
DIVISION (721)
Oxford Rd. Phone: 061 2286333
Manchester M1 7ED, England

SHIRLEY INSTITUTE — TEXTILE INFORMATION SERVICES (873)
Didsbury Phone: 061 4458141
Manchester M20 8RX, England R.J.E. Cumberbirch

PRODUCTION ENGINEERING RESEARCH ASSOCIATION OF GREAT
BRITAIN — INFORMATION SERVICES (826)
Phone: 0664 64133
Melton Mowbray, Leics., England V.C. Watts

BRITISH STANDARDS INSTITUTION — INFORMATION
DEPARTMENT (111)
Linford Wood Phone: 0908 320033
Milton Keynes, Bucks. MK14 6LE, England John S. Widdowson

LIBRARY AND INFORMATION RESEARCH GROUP (659)
The Library Phone: 0632 326002
Newcastle upon Tyne Polytechnic Liz McDowell
Newcastle upon Tyne NE1 8ST, England

NINETEENTH CENTURY SHORT TITLE CATALOGUE PROJECT (757)
Avero Publications Ltd. Phone: 0632 615790
20 Great North Rd. Dr. F.J.G. Robinson
Newcastle upon Tyne NE2 4PS, England

EASTERN COUNTIES NEWSPAPERS — EASTEL (287)
Prospect House Phone: 0603 28311
Rouen Rd. Eric Pummell
Norwich, Norfolk NR1 1RE, England

GEO ABSTRACTS LTD. (393)
Regency House Phone: 0603 26327
34 Duke St. Prof. Keith M. Clayton
Norwich NR3 3AP, England

ORNA/STEVENS CONSULTANCY (788)
55 Telegraph Lane E. Phone: 0603 611795
Norwich, Norfolk NR1 4AR, England Elizabeth Orna

ROYAL SOCIETY OF CHEMISTRY — INFORMATION SERVICES (851)
The University Phone: 0602 57411
Nottingham NG7 2RD, England Robert Welham

ROYAL SOCIETY OF CHEMISTRY — INFORMATION SERVICES —
CHEMICAL ENGINEERING ABSTRACTS (852)
The University Phone: 0602 57411
Nottingham NG7 2RD, England F. John Taylor

ROYAL SOCIETY OF CHEMISTRY — INFORMATION SERVICES —
CHEMICAL HAZARDS IN INDUSTRY (853)
The University Phone: 0602 57411
Nottingham NG7 2RD, England Sheila Templer

ROYAL SOCIETY OF CHEMISTRY — INFORMATION SERVICES —
CURRENT BIOTECHNOLOGY ABSTRACTS (854)
The University Phone: 0602 57411
Nottingham NG7 2RD, England H. Kidd

ROYAL SOCIETY OF CHEMISTRY — INFORMATION SERVICES —
LABORATORY HAZARDS BULLETIN (855)
The University Phone: 0602 57411
Nottingham NG7 2RD, England Sheila Templer

ROYAL SOCIETY OF CHEMISTRY — INFORMATION SERVICES —
MASS SPECTROMETRY DATA CENTRE (856)
The University Phone: 0602 57411
Nottingham NG7 2RD, England Stephen Down

UNWIN BROTHERS LTD. (1089)
Gresham Press
Old Woking, Surrey, England John Quinney

INTERNATIONAL TELECOMMUNICATIONS USERS GROUP (607)
Beechy Lees Lodge, Pilgrims' Way Phone: 0959 23784
Otford, Kent TN14 5SA, England E.O. Weiss

BLACKWELL TECHNICAL SERVICES LTD. (90)
Beaver House Phone: 0865 244944
Hythe Bridge St. Dr. Philip L. Holmes
Oxford OX1 2ET, England

BRASSEY'S PUBLISHERS LTD. — BRASSEY'S NAVAL RECORD (97)
Headington Hill Hall Phone: 0865 64881
Oxford OX3 0BW, England Rear Admiral H.C.N. Goodhart

BRASSEY'S PUBLISHERS LTD. — BRITISH DEFENCE
DIRECTORY (98)
Headington Hill Hall Phone: 0865 64881
Oxford OX3 0BW, England Rear Admiral H.C.N. Goodhart

LEARNED INFORMATION LTD. (654)
Besselsleigh Rd. Phone: 0865 730275
Abingdon Roger Bilboul
Oxford OX13 6LG, England

OXFORD MICROFORM PUBLICATIONS LTD. (791)
Headington Hill Hall Phone: 0865 64881
Oxford OX3 0BW, England Tony Sloggett

PERGAMON PRESS — CURRENT AWARENESS IN BIOLOGICAL
SCIENCES (803)
Headington Hill Hall Phone: 0865 64881
Oxford OX3 0BW, England Prof. H. Smith

MARINE BIOLOGICAL ASSOCIATION OF THE UNITED KINGDOM —
MARINE POLLUTION INFORMATION CENTRE (684)
The Laboratory, Citadel Hill Phone: 0752 21761
Plymouth PL1 2PB, England David S. Moulder

NATURAL ENVIRONMENT RESEARCH COUNCIL — INSTITUTE FOR
MARINE ENVIRONMENTAL RESEARCH — CONTINUOUS PLANKTON
RECORDER SURVEY (729)
Prospect Place, The Hoe Phone: 0752 21371
Plymouth, Devon. PL1 3DH, England B.L. Bayne

FRASER WILLIAMS LTD. — CROSSBOW (370)
London House Phone: 0625 871126
London Rd. S. B.A. Chapman
Poynton, Ches. SK12 1YP, England

FRASER WILLIAMS LTD. — DARING (371)
London House
London Rd. S.
Poynton, Ches. SK12 1YP, England
Phone: 0625 871126
B.A. Chapman

FRASER WILLIAMS LTD. — FINE CHEMICALS DIRECTORY (372)
London House
London Rd. S.
Poynton, Ches. SK12 1YP, England
Phone: 0625 871126
Dr. L. Boyle

GREAT BRITAIN — HOME OFFICE FORENSIC SCIENCE SERVICE — CENTRAL RESEARCH ESTABLISHMENT — OPERATIONAL SERVICES DIVISION (458)
Aldermaston
Reading, Berks. RG7 4PN, England
Phone: 07356 4100
Mr. P.G.W. Cobb

INSTITUTE OF INFORMATION SCIENTISTS (544)
Harvest House
62 London Rd.
Reading, Berks. RG1 5AS, England
Phone: 0734 861345

UNITED KINGDOM ONLINE USER GROUP (1000)
Institute of Information Scientists
Harvest House, 62 London Rd.
Reading, Berks. RG1 5AS, England
Phone: 0734 861345
Chris Parker

UNIVERSITY OF READING LIBRARY — LOCATION REGISTER OF TWENTIETH CENTURY ENGLISH LITERARY MANUSCRIPTS AND LETTERS (1065)
Whiteknights
Reading RG6 2AE, England
Phone: 0734 751364
Dr. David C. Sutton

CUMULUS SYSTEMS LTD. (249)
1 High St.
Rickmansworth, Herts. WD3 1ET, England
Phone: 0923 720477
G.T. Rhodes

INSTITUTION OF CHEMICAL ENGINEERS — PHYSICAL PROPERTY DATA SERVICE (548)
George E. Davis Bldg.
165-171 Railway Terrace
Rugby, Warw. CV21 3HQ, England
Phone: 0788 78214
Dr. Beryl Edmonds

GREAT BRITAIN — HEALTH AND SAFETY EXECUTIVE — HSE LIBRARY AND INFORMATION SERVICES (457)
Red Hill
Sheffield S3 7HQ, England
Phone: 0742 78141
Sheila Pantry

GREAT BRITAIN — MANPOWER SERVICES COMMISSION — CAREERS AND OCCUPATIONAL INFORMATION CENTRE (462)
Moorfoot
Sheffield S1 4PQ, England
Phone: 0742 704575
Barry Cornish

UNIVERSITY OF SHEFFIELD — BIOMEDICAL INFORMATION SERVICE (1069)
Sheffield S10 2TN, England
Phone: 0742 78555
Mr. J.K. Barkla

UNIVERSITY OF SHEFFIELD — CENTRE FOR RESEARCH ON USER STUDIES (1070)
Western Bank
Sheffield S10 2TN, England
Phone: 0742 738608
Colin Harris

RUBBER AND PLASTICS RESEARCH ASSOCIATION OF GREAT BRITAIN — RAPRA INFORMATION CENTRE (858)
Shawbury
Shrewsbury, Shrops. SY4 4NR, England
Phone: 0939 250383
Paul Cantrill

SURVEY FORCE LTD. (907)
Algarve House
140 Borden Lane
Sittingbourne, Kent ME9 8HR, England
Phone: 0795 23778
Keith F. Lainton

CELLTECH LTD. — INFORMATION AND LIBRARY SERVICE (181)
244-250 Bath Rd.
Slough SL1 4DY, England
Phone: 0753 36162
Dr. Anita Crafts-Lighty

COMMONWEALTH AGRICULTURAL BUREAUX — CAB ABSTRACTS (229)
Farnham House, Farnham Royal
Slough SL2 3BN, England
Phone: 02814 2281
N.G. Jones

NATIONAL FOUNDATION FOR EDUCATIONAL RESEARCH IN ENGLAND AND WALES — INFORMATION RESEARCH AND DEVELOPMENT UNIT (724)
The Mere
Upton Park
Slough, Berks. SL1 2DQ, England
Phone: 74123
David R. Streatfield

GREAT BRITAIN — WATER RESEARCH CENTRE — INFORMATION SERVICE ON TOXICITY AND BIODEGRADABILITY (463)
Stevenage Laboratory
Elder Way
Stevenage, Herts. SG1 1TH, England
Phone: 0438 312444
Rita M. Flain

GREAT BRITAIN — WATER RESEARCH CENTRE — LIBRARY AND INFORMATION SERVICES (464)
Stevenage Laboratory
Elder Way
Stevenage, Herts. SG1 1TH, England
Phone: 0438 312444
Lorna E. Newman

USERLINK SYSTEMS LTD. (1093)
Mansion House Chambers
22A High St.
Stockport, Ches. SK1 1EG, England
Phone: 061 4298232
Dr. Philip W. Williams

DATASOLVE LTD. — WORLD EXPORTER (264)
99 Staines Rd. W.
Sunbury-on-Thames, Middlesex TW16 7AH, England
Phone: 09327 85566
J.M. Ducker

DATASOLVE LTD. — WORLD REPORTER (265)
99 Staines Rd. W.
Sunbury-on-Thames, Middlesex TW16 7AH, England
Phone: 09327 85566
J.M. Ducker

T.C. LIBRARY SERVICES LTD. (954)
London Rd.
Sunningdale, Berks. SL5 0EP, England
Phone: 0990 22009
Phyllis M. Cooper

IPC INDUSTRIAL PRESS LTD. — CHEMICAL DATA SERVICES (612)
Quadrant House
The Quadrant
Sutton, Surrey SM2 5AS, England
Phone: 01-661 3500
Peter Dean

GREAT BRITAIN — DEPARTMENT OF INDUSTRY — NATIONAL PHYSICAL LABORATORY — DIVISION OF MATERIALS APPLICATIONS — METALLURGICAL AND THERMOCHEMICAL DATA SERVICE (451)
Teddington, Middlesex TW11 0LW, England
Phone: 01-977 3622
Dr. T.I. Barry

PAINT RESEARCH ASSOCIATION — INFORMATION DEPARTMENT — WORLD SURFACE COATINGS ABSTRACTS (792)
Waldegrave Rd.
Teddington, Middlesex TW11 8LD, England
Phone: 01 977 4427
D. Dasgupta

CHARITIES AID FOUNDATION — INFORMATION SERVICES (198)
48 Pembury Rd.
Tonbridge, Kent TN9 2JD, England
Phone: 0732 356323
John B.C. Bennett

AGRA EUROPE (8)
16 Lonsdale Gardens
Tunbridge Wells, Kent TN1 1PD, England
Phone: 0892 33813
V.H.P. Lynham

BRUNEL UNIVERISTY — BRUNEL INSTITUTE FOR BIOENGINEERING — INFORMATION UNIT (114)
Uxbridge, Middlesex UB8 3PH, England
Phone: 0895 71206
Ann C. Rickard

BRUNEL UNIVERSITY — RESEARCH UNIT FOR THE BLIND — INTERNATIONAL REGISTER OF RESEARCH ON VISUAL DISABILITY (115)
Uxbridge, Middlesex UB8 3PH, England
Phone: 0895 71206
Dr. J.M. Gill

CAWKELL INFORMATION & TECHNOLOGY SERVICES LTD. (180)
P.O. Box 5, Ickenham
Uxbridge, Middlesex UB10 8AF, England
Phone: 0895 34327
Mr. A.E. Cawkell

SYSTEM DEVELOPMENT CORPORATION — SDC INFORMATION SERVICES - EUROPE (951)
Bakers Court
Bakers Rd.
Uxbridge, Middlesex UB8 1RG, England
Susan Inglis

BNF METALS TECHNOLOGY CENTRE — INFORMATION DEPARTMENT (92)
Grove Laboratories
Denchworth Rd.
Wantage, Oxon. OX12 9BJ, England
Phone: 023 57 2992

McCARTHY INFORMATION LTD. (690)
Manor House
Ash Walk   Phone: 0985 215151
Warminster, Wilts. BA12 8PY, England   Anthony Garnett

ALLM BOOKS — SMALL COMPUTER PROGRAM INDEX (17)
21 Beechcroft Rd., Bushey   Phone: 0923 30150
Watford, Herts. WD2 2JU, England   Alan Pritchard

GREAT BRITAIN — DEPARTMENT OF THE ENVIRONMENT —
BUILDING RESEARCH ESTABLISHMENT LIBRARY — BRIX (453)
Bucknall's Lane, Garston   Phone: 0923 674040
Watford, Herts. WD2 7JR, England   P.J. Elvin

UNILEVER COMPUTER SERVICES LTD. — EUROPEAN
PETROCHEMICAL ASSOCIATION TRADE STATISTICS
DATABASE (993)
55/57 Clarendon Rd.   Phone: 0923 47911
Watford, Herts. WD1 1SA, England   Dr. Nigel Walker

UNILEVER COMPUTER SERVICES LTD. — WORLD TRADE STATISTICS
DATABASE (994)
55/57 Clarendon Rd.   Phone: 0923 47911
Watford, Herts. WD1 1SA, England   Dr. Nigel Walker

RESEARCH SERVICES LTD. — PAN EUROPEAN SURVEY (839)
Station House, Harrow Rd.   Phone: 01-903 8511
Stonebridge Park
Wembley, Middlesex HA9 6DE, England

GREAT BRITAIN — BRITISH LIBRARY — LENDING DIVISION (442)
Boston Spa   Phone: 0937 843434
Wetherby, West Yorks. LS23 7BQ,   Dr. M.B. Line
England

ART SALES INDEX LTD. (29)
Pond House   Phone: 42678
Weybridge, Surrey KT13 8SQ, England   Richard Hislop

ICV INFORMATION SYSTEMS LTD. — CITISERVICE (500)
72 Chertsey Rd.   Phone: 04862 27431
Woking, Surrey, England   Mr. D.A. Taylor

BIOSIS, U.K. LTD. — ZOOLOGICAL RECORD (88)
54 Mickelgate   Phone: 0904 642816
York YO1 1L7, England   Michael N. Dadd

ETHIOPIA

INTERNATIONAL LIVESTOCK CENTRE FOR AFRICA —
DOCUMENTATION CENTRE (596)
P.O. Box 5689   Phone: 183215
Addis Ababa, Ethiopia   Michael Hailu

UNITED NATIONS — ECONOMIC COMMISSION FOR AFRICA — PAN-
AFRICAN DOCUMENTATION AND INFORMATION SYSTEM (1005)
P.O. Box 3001   Phone: 447200
Addis Ababa, Ethiopia   Dr. J.K. Quirino-Lanhounmey

FINLAND

FINLAND — TECHNICAL RESEARCH CENTRE OF FINLAND —
TECHNICAL INFORMATION SERVICE (330)
Vuorimiehentie 5   Phone: 90 4561
SF-02150 Espoo 15, Finland   Sauli Laitinen

HELSINKI UNIVERSITY OF TECHNOLOGY — UNIVERSITY LIBRARY/
NATIONAL LIBRARY FOR SCIENCE AND TECHNOLOGY (483)
Otaniementie 9   Phone: 90 4512812
SF-02150 Espoo 15, Finland   Elin Tornudd

NORDIC COUNCIL FOR SCIENTIFIC INFORMATION AND RESEARCH
LIBRARIES (762)
Helsinki University of Technology   Phone: 445 2633
Library, Otnasvagen 9   Bjorn Thomasson
SF-02150 Espoo 15, Finland

BUILDING INFORMATION INSTITUTE (118)
Lonnrotinkatu 20 B   Phone: 90 645615
SF-00120 Helsinki 12, Finland   Mr. Esko Lehti

FINLAND — CENTRAL MEDICAL LIBRARY — MEDIC DATA
BASE (329)
Haartmaninkatu 4   Phone: 90 418544
SF-00290 Helsinki 29, Finland   Ritva Sievanen-Allen

FINNISH COUNCIL FOR SCIENTIFIC INFORMATION AND RESEARCH
LIBRARIES (331)
P.O. Box 504   Phone: 90 1734233
SF-00101 Helsinki 10, Finland   J.K. Visakorpi

FINNISH FOREIGN TRADE ASSOCIATION — INFORMATION
DEPARTMENT — REGISTER OF EXPORTERS (332)
Arkadiankatu 4-6 B   Phone: 90 6941122
P.O. Box 908   Mr. C.G. Tollet
SF-00101 Helsinki 10, Finland

FINNISH PULP AND PAPER RESEARCH INSTITUTE — TECHNICAL
INFORMATION SERVICE (333)
P.O. Box 136   Phone: 90 460411
SF-00101 Helsinki 10, Finland   Birgitta Holm

FINNISH STANDARDS ASSOCIATION — INFORMATION
SERVICE (334)
P.O. Box 205   Phone: 0645601
SF-00121 Helsinki 12, Finland   Marjatta Aarniala

HELSINGIN TELSET OY — TELSET (480)
Keskuskatu 4B   Phone: 0171681
SF-00101 Helsinki 10, Finland   Tapio Kallioja

HELSINKI SCHOOL OF ECONOMICS LIBRARY — INFORMATION
SERVICES (481)
Runeberginkatu 22-24   Phone: 90 43131
SF-00100 Helsinki 10, Finland   Henri Broms

HELSINKI UNIVERSITY LIBRARY — FINNISH NATIONAL
BIBLIOGRAPHY (482)
Tukholmankatu 2   Phone: 0410566
SF-00250 Helsinki 25, Finland   Marjatta Soisalon-Soininen

FRANCE

CENTER FOR RESEARCH AND STUDIES ON MEDITERRANEAN
SOCIETIES (186)
Maison de la Mediterranee   Phone: 42 230386
5, ave. Pasteur
F-13100 Aix en Provence, France

FRENCH TEXTILE INSTITUTE — TEXTILE INFORMATION
TREATMENT USERS' SERVICE (390)
B.P. 79   Phone: 1 8251890
35, rue des Abondances   Denis Marce
F-92105 Boulogne-Billancourt Cedex,
France

MIKRO-CERID (710)
134 bis, rue du Vieux Pont   Phone: 01 6099414
de Sevres   Jean Pioch
F-92100 Boulogne sur Seine, France

FRANCE — NATIONAL CENTER FOR OCEAN UTILIZATION —
NATIONAL BUREAU FOR OCEAN DATA (347)
Centre Oceanologique de Bretagne   Phone: 98 458055
B.P. 337   Dr. Marthe Melguen
F-29273 Brest Cedex, France

FRANCE — NATIONAL CENTER FOR OCEAN UTILIZATION —
NATIONAL BUREAU FOR OCEAN DATA — AQUADOC (348)
Centre Oceanologique de Bretagne   Phone: 98 458055
B.P. 337
F-29273 Brest Cedex, France

FRANCE — NATIONAL CENTER FOR OCEAN UTILIZATION —
NATIONAL BUREAU FOR OCEAN DATA — BIOCEAN (349)
Centre Oceanologique de Bretagne   Phone: 98 458055
B.P. 337
F-29273 Brest Cedex, France

FRANCE — NATIONAL CENTER FOR OCEAN UTILIZATION —
NATIONAL BUREAU FOR OCEAN DATA — CNEXO-BNDO DATA
BASE (350)
Centre Oceanologie de Bretagne   Phone: 98 458055
B.P. 337
F-29273 Brest Cedex, France

GEOGRAPHIC INDEX

FRANCE — NATIONAL CENTER FOR OCEAN UTILIZATION —
NATIONAL BUREAU FOR OCEAN DATA — DOCOCEAN   (351)
Centre Oceanologique de Bretagne   Phone: 98 458055
B.P. 337
F-29273 Brest Cedex, France

FRANCE — NATIONAL CENTER FOR OCEAN UTILIZATION —
NATIONAL BUREAU FOR OCEAN DATA — GEOIPOD   (352)
Centre Oceanologique de Bretagne   Phone: 98 458055
B.P. 337
F-29273 Brest Cedex, France

FRANCE — NATIONAL CENTER FOR OCEAN UTILIZATION —
NATIONAL BUREAU FOR OCEAN DATA — POLUMAT   (353)
Centre Oceanologie de Bretagne   Phone: 98 458055
B.P. 337
F-29273 Brest Cedex, France

FRANCE — NATIONAL CENTER FOR OCEAN UTILIZATION —
NATIONAL BUREAU FOR OCEAN DATA — ROSCOP   (354)
Centre Oceanologique de Bretagne   Phone: 98 458055
B.P. 337
F-29273 Brest Cedex, France

ELECTRICITE DE FRANCE — OFFICE OF STUDY AND RESEARCH —
INFORMATION AND DOCUMENTATION SYSTEMS DEPARTMENT —
EDF-DOC DATA BASE   (295)
B.P. 408   Phone: 01 7654321
1, ave. du General de Gaulle
F-92141 Clamart Cedex, France

COMPANY FOR INFORMATICS — SPIDEL   (233)
98, blvd. Victor Hugo   Phone: 7311191
F-92115 Clichy, France

PARIS DISTRICT INFORMATICS ADMINISTRATION — INFORMATICS
BIBLIO SERVICE   (797)
8, place Salvador Allende   Phone: 01 8989102
B.P. 98   Anne Lemaire
F-94003 Creteil Cedex, France

FRANCE — ATOMIC ENERGY COMMISSION — SACLAY NUCLEAR
RESEARCH CENTER — DOCUMENTATION CENTER   (339)
F-91191 Gif-sur-Yvette Cedex, France   Phone: 6 9082208

ORGANISATION FOR ECONOMIC CO-OPERATION AND DEVELOPMENT
— NUCLEAR ENERGY AGENCY — NEA DATA BANK   (785)
B.P. 9   Phone: 9084912
F-91190 Gif-sur-Yvette, France

MERLIN GERIN COMPANY — DOCUMENTATION DEPARTMENT —
MERL-ECO   (696)
   Phone: 76 579460
F-38050 Grenoble Cedex, France   Raymond Arnaud

MERLIN GERIN COMPANY — DOCUMENTATION DEPARTMENT —
MERLIN-TECH   (697)
   Phone: 76 579460
F-38050 Grenoble Cedex, France   Raymond Arnaud

FRANCE — NATIONAL TELECOMMUNICATIONS RESEARCH CENTER
— INTERMINISTERIAL DOCUMENTATION SERVICE —
TELEDOC   (367)
38-40, rue du General Leclerc   Phone: 1 6384444
F-92131 Issy les Moulineaux, France   M. Truchet

FRANCE — NATIONAL INSTITUTE FOR RESEARCH IN INFORMATICS
AND AUTOMATION — INFORMATION DISSEMINATION
OFFICE   (361)
B.P. 105   Phone: 3 9549020
F-78153 Le Chesnay Cedex, France   M. Bornes

TERNISIEN LISTING   (978)
60, Allee de la Meute   Phone: 9521745
F-78110 Le Vesinet, France   Dr. Jean A. Ternisien

WORLD HEALTH ORGANIZATION — INTERNATIONAL AGENCY FOR
RESEARCH ON CANCER — CLEARING-HOUSE FOR ON-GOING
RESEARCH IN CANCER EPIDEMIOLOGY   (1113)
150, cours Albert Thomas   Phone: 7 8758181
F-69372 Lyon Cedex 08, France   Dr. C.S. Muir

CENTER FOR THE STUDY ON INFORMATION SYSTEMS IN
GOVERNMENT   (190)
122, ave. de Hambourg   Phone: 91 739018
F-13008 Marseille, France   Jean Salmona

ASSOCIATION FOR THE PROMOTION OF INDUSTRY-AGRICULTURE —
INTERNATIONAL DOCUMENTATION CENTER FOR INDUSTRIES USING
AGRICULTURAL PRODUCTS   (39)
Ave. des Olympiades   Phone: 6 9209738
F-91305 Massy Cedex, France   Gisele Carra

FRANCE — NATIONAL INSTITUTE OF AGRONOMIC RESEARCH —
SOIL SCIENCE LABORATORY — SOIL STUDIES SERVICE   (362)
Place Viala   Phone: 67 630013
F-34060 Montpellier, France

INTERNATIONAL CENTER FOR HIGHER STUDIES IN MEDITERRANEAN
AGRONOMY — SOCIOECONOMIC DATA BANK ON THE
MEDITERRANEAN COUNTRIES   (564)
Institut Agronomique Mediterraneen   Phone: 67 632880
B.P. 1239   Prof. M. Allaya
F-34060 Montpellier Cedex, France

FRENCH COMPANY FOR THE DESIGN & IMPLEMENTATION OF RADIO
& TELEVISION BROADCASTING EQUIPMENT — ANTIOPE TELETEXT
SYSTEM   (383)
21-23, rue de la Vanne   Phone: 331 657133
F-92120 Montrouge, France

UNIVERSITY OF PARIS-NANTERRE — GROUP FOR APPLIED
MACROECONOMIC ANALYSIS   (1062)
2, rue de Rouen   Phone: 01 7259234
F-92001 Nanterre, France   Prof. Raymond Courbis

OFFICE OF ECONOMIC INFORMATION AND FORECASTING   (773)
122, ave. Charles de Gaulle   Phone: 01 7471166
F-92522 Neuilly, France   Jean Hauchecorne

FRANCE — BUREAU OF GEOLOGICAL AND MINING RESEARCH —
NATIONAL GEOLOGICAL SURVEY — GEOLOGICAL INFORMATION AND
DOCUMENTATION DEPARTMENT   (340)
B.P. 6009   Phone: 38 638001
F-45060 Orleans Cedex, France   J. Gravesteijn

FRANCE — BUREAU OF GEOLOGICAL AND MINING RESEARCH —
NATIONAL GEOLOGICAL SURVEY — SUBSOIL DATA BANK   (341)
B.P. 6009   Phone: 38 638001
F-45060 Orleans Cedex, France   Jean-Pierre Lepretre

FRANCE — BUREAU OF GEOLOGICAL AND MINING RESEARCH —
NATIONAL GEOLOGICAL SURVEY — WORLD GRAVIMETRIC DATA
BANK   (342)
B.P. 6009   Phone: 38 638001
F-45060 Orleans Cedex, France   Jean-Pierre Lepretre

UNIVERSITY OF PARIS-SOUTH — GASES AND PLASMAS PHYSICS
LABORATORY — GAPHYOR   (1063)
Bldg. 212   Phone: 6 9417250
F-91405 Orsay Cedex, France   Prof. Jean-Loup Delcroix

A.JOUR   (1)
11, rue du Marche Saint Honore   Phone: 01 2614517
F-75001 Paris, France   Francois de Valence

AMERICAN COLLEGE IN PARIS — SERVICE CALVADOS   (22)
B.P. 21-07   Phone: 01 7050904
31, ave. Bosquet   Stephen Plummer
F-75007 Paris, France

ASSOCIATION FOR RESEARCH AND DEVELOPMENT OF CHEMICAL
INFORMATICS — DARC PLURIDATA SYSTEM   (38)
25, rue Jussieu   Phone: 01 6332370
F-75005 Paris, France   Jacques-Emile Dubois

BANK GROUP FOR AUTOMATION IN MANAGEMENT   (71)
Tour Maine-Montparnasse   Phone: 01 5381030
33, ave. du Maine
F-75755 Paris Cedex 15, France

CENTER FOR INDUSTRIAL CREATION — DOCUMENTATION
SERVICE   (184)
Centre Georges Pompidou   Phone: 01 2771233
F-75191 Paris Cedex 4, France   Marie-Claire Mayer

CENTER FOR INTERNATIONAL PROSPECTIVE STUDIES   (185)
9, rue Georges Pitard   Phone: 01 8426800
F-75015 Paris, France   Yves Berthelot

CENTER FOR STUDY AND RESEARCH OF THE HYDRAULIC BINDERS
INDUSTRY — DOCUMENTATION CENTER — INTERCIM CEMENT
DATA BASE   (188)
23, rue de Cronstadt   Phone: 01 5311810
F-75015 Paris, France   Walter Rothlauf

GEOGRAPHIC INDEX

CENTER FOR THE STUDY OF ADVERTISING SUPPORT   (189)
32, ave. Georges-Mandel   Phone: 01 5532210
F-75116 Paris, France   J. Antoine

CENTER FOR TRANSLATION DOCUMENTATION   (191)
16, rue Beaurepaire   Phone: 01 2088632
F-75010 Paris, France   Gerard Pierson

DAFSA   (251)
125, rue Montmartre   Phone: 01 2332123
F-75081 Paris Cedex 02, France

DAFSA-SNEI S.A. — FITEK   (252)
16, rue de la Banque   Phone: 01 2615124
F-75002 Paris, France

DATA BANK FOR MEDICAMENTS   (257)
156, rue de Vaugirard   Phone: 01 5559280
F-75015 Paris, France   Dr. H. Ducrot

DIDOT-BOTTIN — BOTTIN DATA BASES   (280)
28, rue du Docteur-Finlay   Phone: 01 5786166
F-75738 Paris Cedex 15, France

EDITIONS TECHNIQUES — JURIS-DATA   (294)
123, rue d'Alesia   Phone: 01 5392291
F-75678 Paris Cedex 14, France   Philippe Durieux

EUROPEAN CONFERENCE OF MINISTERS OF TRANSPORT —
INTERNATIONAL CO-OPERATION IN THE FIELD OF TRANSPORT
ECONOMICS DOCUMENTATION   (309)
19, rue de Franqueville   Phone: 01 5249722
F-75775 Paris Cedex 16, France   Jan C. Terlouw

FLA GROUPE LA CREATIQUE   (336)
31 blvd. Lefebvre   Phone: 01 5436811
F-75015 Paris, France   Francois Libmann

FRANCE — ATOMIC ENERGY COMMISSION — PROGRAMS
DEPARTMENT — ELECNUC DATABANK   (338)
B.P. 510   Phone: 01 5458418
F-75752 Paris Cedex 15, France

FRANCE — FRENCH SENATE — PARLIAMENTARY DOCUMENTATION
AND INFORMATION PRINTING SERVICE   (343)
5, rue de Vaugirard   Phone: 01 3291262
F-75291 Paris Cedex 6, France   Michel Vilain

FRANCE — INTERMINISTERIAL MISSION FOR SCIENTIFIC AND
TECHNICAL INFORMATION   (344)
9, rue Georges Pitard   Phone: 01 8426464
F-75015 Paris, France   M. Cassen

FRANCE — MINISTRY OF EDUCATION — NATIONAL CENTER FOR
PEDAGOGICAL DOCUMENTATION   (346)
29, rue d'Ulm   Phone: 01 3292164
F-75230 Paris Cedex 5, France   Serge Heritier

FRANCE — NATIONAL CENTER FOR SCIENTIFIC RESEARCH —
DOCUMENTATION CENTER FOR HUMAN SCIENCES   (355)
54, blvd. Raspail   Phone: 01 5443849
F-75270 Paris Cedex 6, France

FRANCE — NATIONAL CENTER FOR SCIENTIFIC RESEARCH —
SCIENTIFIC AND TECHNICAL DOCUMENTATION CENTER   (356)
26, rue Boyer   Phone: 01 3583559
F-75971 Paris Cedex 20, France   M. Michel

FRANCE — NATIONAL INSTITUTE FOR HEALTH AND MEDICAL
RESEARCH — OFFICE OF SCIENTIFIC EVALUATION — INSERM
RESEARCH INFORMATION BANK   (358)
101, rue de Tolbiac   Phone: 01 5841441
F-75654 Paris Cedex 13, France

FRANCE — NATIONAL INSTITUTE FOR INDUSTRIAL PROPERTY —
DIVISION OF PUBLICATIONS DOCUMENTATION AND INFORMATION
— INPI DATA BASES   (359)
26 bis, rue de Leningrad   Phone: 01 5225371
F-75800 Paris Cedex 8, France

FRANCE — NATIONAL INSTITUTE FOR INDUSTRIAL PROPERTY —
OFFICE OF LEGAL AND TECHNICAL DOCUMENTATION — JURINPI
DATA BASE   (360)
26 bis, rue de Leningrad   Phone: 01 2932120
F-75800 Paris Cedex 8, France

FRANCE — NATIONAL INSTITUTE OF STATISTICS AND ECONOMIC
STUDIES — DOCUMENTATION DIVISION — SPHINX DATA
BASE   (363)
18, blvd. Adolphe Pinard   Phone: 01 5401212
F-75675 Paris Cedex 14, France   Mr. Chevalier

FRANCE — NATIONAL INSTITUTE OF STATISTICS AND ECONOMIC
STUDIES — INFORMATION SYSTEM FOR THE ECONOMY   (364)
18, blvd. Adolphe Pinard   Phone: 01 5400113
F-75675 Paris Cedex 14, France

FRANCE — NATIONAL INSTITUTE OF STATISTICS AND ECONOMIC
STUDIES — LOCAL AREA DATA BANK   (365)
F-75675 Paris Cedex 14, France

FRANCE — NATIONAL INSTITUTE OF STATISTICS AND ECONOMIC
STUDIES — MACROECONOMIC DATA BANK   (366)
F-75675 Paris Cedex 14, France

FRENCH DOCUMENTATION — POLITICAL AND CURRENT EVENTS
INFORMATION BANK   (384)
8, ave. de l'Opera   Phone: 01 2961422
F-75001 Paris, France

FRENCH FEDERATION OF DATA BASE PRODUCERS   (385)
103, rue de Lille   Phone: 01 5518078
F-75007 Paris, France   M. Henry

FRENCH INSTITUTE OF ENERGY — ENERGY STUDIES AND
INFORMATION CENTER   (386)
3, rue Henri Heine   Phone: 01 5244614
F-75016 Paris, France   Francine Breniere

FRENCH PRESS AGENCY — TELEMATICS DEPARTMENT —
AGORA   (388)
11, place de la Bourse   Phone: 01 2334466
B.P. 20   Dominique Pettit
F-75061 Paris Cedex 2, France

FRENCH STOCKBROKERS SOCIETY — INFORMATION AND
DOCUMENTATION CENTER   (389)
4, place de la Bourse   Phone: 01 2618590
F-75080 Paris Cedex 2, France   Bruno Montier

FRENCH WATER STUDY ASSOCIATION — NATIONAL WATER
INFORMATION CENTER   (391)
21, rue Madrid   Phone: 01 5221467
F-75008 Paris, France   M. Xavier Dagallier

GLASS INSTITUTE — INFORMATION AND DOCUMENTATION
SERVICE   (429)
34, rue Michel-Ange   Phone: 01 6514568
F-75016 Paris, France   Miss A. Sellin

GROUP FOR THE ADVANCEMENT OF SPECTROSCOPIC METHODS AND
PHYSICOCHEMICAL ANALYSIS — INFORMATION CENTER FOR
SPECTROSCOPIC AND PHYSICOCHEMICAL ANALYSIS   (466)
88, blvd. Malesherbes   Phone: 01 5639304
F-75008 Paris, France   Madame D. Sandino

GROUP FOR THE STUDY AND RESEARCH OF TROPICAL AGRONOMY —
AGRITROP   (467)
42, rue Scheffer   Phone: 01 7043215
F-75116 Paris, France   Genevieve Hartmann

GSI-ECO   (469)
25, blvd. de l'Amiral Bruix   Phone: 01 5021220
F-75782 Paris Cedex 16, France

INDUSTRIAL NEWS PUBLISHING COMPANY — KOMPASS-
FRANCE   (514)
22, ave. F.D. Roosevelt   Phone: 01 3593759
F-75008 Paris, France

INSTITUTE OF RESEARCH ON FRUITS AND CITRUS FRUITS —
DOCUMENTATION CENTER   (547)
6, rue de General Clergerie   Phone: 01 5531692
F-75116 Paris, France   Pierre Lossois

INTELMATIQUE   (552)
98, rue de Sevres   Phone: 01 3061636
F-75007 Paris, France   Georges Nahon

INTERMARC GROUP   (555)
61, rue de Richelieu   Phone: 01 2618283
F-75002 Paris, France   M. Chauveinc

INTERNATIONAL CHILDREN'S CENTRE — DOCUMENTATION
SERVICE — ROBERT DEBRE INFORMATION BASE (566)
Chateau de Longchamp
Bois de Boulogne
F-75016 Paris, France
Phone: 01 5067992
Denise Parise

INTERNATIONAL COMMITTEE FOR SOCIAL SCIENCE INFORMATION
AND DOCUMENTATION (571)
27, rue Saint-Guillaume
F-75341 Paris Cedex 7, France
Phone: 01 2603960
Jean Meyriat

INTERNATIONAL COUNCIL OF SCIENTIFIC UNIONS — COMMITTEE
ON DATA FOR SCIENCE AND TECHNOLOGY (574)
51, blvd. de Montmorency
F-75016 Paris, France
Phone: 01 5250496
Phyllis Glaeser

INTERNATIONAL COUNCIL OF SCIENTIFIC UNIONS ABSTRACTING
BOARD (575)
51, blvd. de Montmorency
F-75016 Paris, France
Phone: 01 5256592
Marthe Orfus

INTERNATIONAL INFORMATION SERVICES COMPANY (589)
35, blvd. Brune
F-75680 Paris Cedex 14, France
Phone: 01 5458000

INTERNATIONAL INSTITUTE OF REFRIGERATION — DOCUMENTARY
SERVICE (590)
177, blvd. Malesherbes
F-75017 Paris, France
Phone: 01 2273235
Andre Gac

INTERNATIONAL RAILWAY UNION — DOCUMENTATION
BUREAU (600)
14-15, rue Jean Rey
F-75015 Paris, France
Phone: 01 2730120
Andre Pettelat

INTERNATIONAL SERIALS DATA SYSTEM (603)
20, rue Bachaumont
F-75002 Paris, France
Phone: 01 2367381
Mrs. M. Rosenbaum

INTERNATIONAL UNION OF GEOLOGICAL SCIENCES — COMMISSION
ON STORAGE, AUTOMATIC PROCESSING AND RETRIEVAL OF
GEOLOGICAL DATA (609)
IUGS Secretariat
77, rue Claude Bernard
F-75005 Paris, France
Phone: 01 7079196

INTERPROFESSIONAL TECHNICAL UNION OF THE NATIONAL
FEDERATIONS OF BUILDINGS AND PUBLIC WORKS — CENTER FOR
TECHNICAL ASSISTANCE AND DOCUMENTATION — ARIANE DATA
BANK (610)
9, rue La Perouse
F-75784 Paris Cedex 16, France
Phone: 01 7208800
Mr. J. Devoge

MEDICAL-PHARMACEUTICAL PUBLISHING COMPANY (693)
26, rue Le Brun
F-75013 Paris, France
Phone: 01 3378350
Christian Garlot

NATIONAL CENTER FOR CHEMICAL INFORMATION (720)
28 ter, rue Saint Dominique
F-75007 Paris, France

NATIONAL CONSERVATORY OF ARTS AND CRAFTS — NATIONAL
INSTITUTE FOR DOCUMENTATION TECHNIQUES (722)
292, rue Saint-Martin
F-75141 Paris Cedex 3, France
Phone: 01 2712414
Bruno Delmas

NATIONAL ELF AQUITAINE COMPANY — DOCUMENTARY
INFORMATION SERVICE — STATSID (723)
F-75739 Paris Cedex 15, France

ORGANISATION FOR ECONOMIC CO-OPERATION AND DEVELOPMENT
— ECONOMIC STATISTICS AND NATIONAL ACCOUNTS DIVISION —
OECD MAGNETIC TAPE SUBSCRIPTION SERVICE (780)
2, rue Andre Pascal
F-75775 Paris Cedex 16, France
Phone: 01 5248200

ORGANISATION FOR ECONOMIC CO-OPERATION AND DEVELOPMENT
— INTERNATIONAL DEVELOPMENT INFORMATION
NETWORK (781)
Development Center
94, rue Chardon-Lagache
F-75016 Paris, France
Phone: 01 5248200

ORGANISATION FOR ECONOMIC CO-OPERATION AND DEVELOPMENT
— INTERNATIONAL ENERGY AGENCY — INTERNATIONAL OIL
MARKET INFORMATION SYSTEM (784)
2, rue Andre Pascal
F-75775 Paris Cedex 16, France
Phone: 01 5249887
Guy Caruso

ORGANISATION FOR ECONOMIC CO-OPERATION AND DEVELOPMENT
— ROAD TRANSPORT RESEARCH PROGRAMME — INTERNATIONAL
ROAD RESEARCH DOCUMENTATION (786)
2, rue Andre Pascal
F-75775 Paris Cedex 16, France
Phone: 01 5248200
J.P. Magnan

PARIS CHAMBER OF COMMERCE AND INDUSTRY — DEPARTMENT OF
INTERNATIONAL RELATIONS — TELEXPORT (796)
Bourse de Commerce
2, rue de Viarmes
F-75001 Paris, France
Phone: 01 5083643
Mlle. LeMaitre

PARIS OFFICE OF URBANIZATION — URBAN DATA BANK OF PARIS
AND THE PARIS REGION (798)
17, blvd. Morland
F-75004 Paris, France
Phone: 01 2712814

RENE DESCARTES UNIVERSITY — LABORATORY OF APPLIED
ANTHROPOLOGY — ERGODATA (838)
45, rue des Saints-Peres
F-75270 Paris Cedex 06, France
Phone: 01 2603720
Prof. A. Coblentz

SOCIETY FOR THE STUDY OF ECONOMIC AND SOCIAL DEVELOPMENT
— MERCATIS (881)
15, rue Bleue
F-75009 Paris, France
Phone: 01 7706161
Gerard Cancelier

SVP FRANCE (913)
54, rue de Monceau
F-75384 Paris Cedex 8, France
Phone: 01 7871111
Brigitte de Gastines

SYDONI S.A. (949)
1, rue du Boccador
F-75008 Paris, France
Phone: 01 7208834

TELESYSTEMES — QUESTEL (977)
83-85, blvd. Vincent Auriol
F-75013 Paris, France
Phone: 01 5826464
Michel Dancoisne

TRANSINOVE INTERNATIONAL (987)
INPI
26 bis, rue de Leningrad
F-75800 Paris Cedex 8, France
Phone: 01 2932120
Olivier Arondel

TRANSPAC (989)
33, ave. du Maine, B.P. 145
F-75755 Paris Cedex 15, France
Phone: 01 5385211
Mr. P. Fortin

UNITED NATIONS EDUCATIONAL, SCIENTIFIC AND CULTURAL
ORGANIZATION — DIVISION OF SCIENCE AND TECHNOLOGY
POLICIES — SCIENCE AND TECHNOLOGY POLICIES INFORMATION
EXCHANGE PROGRAMME (1016)
7, place de Fontenoy
F-75700 Paris, France
Phone: 01 5681000
Yvan de Hemptinne

UNITED NATIONS EDUCATIONAL, SCIENTIFIC AND CULTURAL
ORGANIZATION — DIVISION OF THE UNESCO LIBRARY, ARCHIVES
AND DOCUMENTATION SERVICES — COMPUTERIZED
DOCUMENTATION SERVICE/INTEGRATED SET OF INFORMATION
SYSTEMS (1017)
7, Place de Fontenoy
F-75700 Paris, France
Phone: 01 5771610

UNITED NATIONS EDUCATIONAL, SCIENTIFIC AND CULTURAL
ORGANIZATION — ENERGY INFORMATION SECTION (1018)
7, Place de Fontenoy
F-75700 Paris, France
Phone: 01 5683903
C.M. Gottschalk

UNITED NATIONS EDUCATIONAL, SCIENTIFIC AND CULTURAL
ORGANIZATION — GENERAL INFORMATION PROGRAMME (1019)
7, Place de Fontenoy
F-75700 Paris, France
Phone: 01 5771610

UNITED NATIONS EDUCATIONAL, SCIENTIFIC AND CULTURAL
ORGANIZATION — INTERGOVERNMENTAL OCEANOGRAPHIC
COMMISSION — MARINE ENVIRONMENTAL DATA INFORMATION
REFERRAL SYSTEM (1020)
7, place de Fontenoy
F-75700 Paris, France
Phone: 01 5771610

UNITED NATIONS EDUCATIONAL, SCIENTIFIC AND CULTURAL ORGANIZATION — SOCIAL AND HUMAN SCIENCE DOCUMENTATION CENTRE (1022)
7, place de Fontenoy
F-75700 Paris, France
Phone: 01 5681000

UNITED NATIONS EDUCATIONAL, SCIENTIFIC AND CULTURAL ORGANIZATION — UNIVERSAL SYSTEM FOR INFORMATION IN SCIENCE AND TECHNOLOGY — UNISIST INTERNATIONAL CENTRE FOR BIBLIOGRAPHIC DESCRIPTIONS (1023)
7, Place de Fontenoy
F-75700 Paris, France
Wolfgang Lohner

UNITED NATIONS ENVIRONMENT PROGRAMME — INDUSTRY AND ENVIRONMENT OFFICE — INDUSTRY AND ENVIRONMENT DATA BASE (1024)
17, rue Margueritte
F-75017 Paris, France
Phone: 01 7661640

URBAMET NETWORK (1091)
IAURIF
21-23, rue Miollis
F-75732 Paris Cedex 15, France
Phone: 01 5675503

FRANCE — MINISTRY OF DEFENSE — GENERAL OFFICE FOR ORDNANCE — CENTER FOR DOCUMENTATION ON ORDNANCE (345)
F-75996 Paris-Armees, France

FRENCH ASSOCIATION FOR STANDARDIZATION — DATA BASES SERVICE — AUTOMATED STANDARDS AND REGULATIONS INFORMATION ONLINE (382)
Tour Europe, Cedex 7
F-92080 Paris la Defense, France
Phone: 01 7781326

PONT-A-MOUSSON RESEARCH CENTER — INDUSTRIAL DOCUMENTATION SERVICE — BIIPAM-CTIF DATA BASE (820)
B.P. 28
F-54703 Pont-a-Mousson Cedex, France
Phone: 8 3816029
Claude Guy

SLIGOS (879)
91, rue Jean-Jaures
F-92807 Puteaux Cedex, France
Phone: 01 7764242

FRENCH PETROLEUM INSTITUTE — DOCUMENTATION CENTER (387)
1-4, ave. de Bois-Preau
F-92506 Rueil-Malmaison, France
Phone: 01 7490214

THERMODATA ASSOCIATION — THERMODATA-THERMDOC DATA BANK (981)
Domaine Universitaire
P.O. Box 66
F-38402 St-Martin-d'Heres Cedex, France
Phone: 76 427690
Yves Deniel

TECHNICAL CENTER FOR MECHANICAL INDUSTRIES — DOCUMENTATION CENTER FOR MECHANICS (957)
P.O. Box 67
F-60304 Senlis, France
Phone: 4 4533266
J.N. Ostermann

CHRISTIAN INSTITUTIONS RESEARCH AND DOCUMENTATION CENTER (205)
9, Place de l'Universite
F-67084 Strasbourg Cedex, France
Phone: 88 355539
Jean Schlick

COUNCIL OF EUROPE — EUROPEAN DOCUMENTATION AND INFORMATION SYSTEM FOR EDUCATION (248)
B.P. 431 R6
F-67006 Strasbourg Cedex, France
Phone: 88 614961
W.F. Barrett

STRASBOURG OBSERVATORY — STELLAR DATA CENTER (905)
11, rue de l'Universite
F-67000 Strasbourg, France
Phone: 88 354300
Prof. C. Jaschek

FRANCE — NATIONAL CENTER FOR SCIENTIFIC RESEARCH — SCIENTIFIC DOCUMENTATION CENTER IN ONCOLOGY — CANCERNET (357)
3, rue Guy Moquet
F-94800 Villejuif, France
Phone: 01 6771616
M. Wolff-Terroine

GERMAN DEMOCRATIC REPUBLIC

GERMAN DEMOCRATIC REPUBLIC — CENTRAL INSTITUTE FOR INFORMATION AND DOCUMENTATION (395)
Kopenicker Str. 80-82
DDR-1020 Berlin, German Democratic Republic
Phone: 2391280
Mr. H. Och

GERMANY, FEDERAL REPUBLIC OF

TECHNICAL UNIVERSITY OF AACHEN — LABORATORY OF MACHINE TOOLS AND PRODUCTION ENGINEERING — CUTTING DATA INFORMATION CENTER (964)
Werkzeugmaschinenlabor, RWTH
Steinbachstr. 53B
D-5100 Aachen, Fed. Rep. of Germany
Phone: 0241 807402
Wilfried Koenig

CHEMICAL INFORMATION CENTER (201)
2 Steinplatz
D-1000 Berlin 12, Fed. Rep. of Germany
Phone: 030 3190030
Dr. Michael G. Helmchen

GERMAN LIBRARY INSTITUTE (400)
Bundesallee 184-185
D-1000 Berlin 31, Fed. Rep. of Germany
Phone: 030 85050
Prof. Gunter Beyersdorff

GERMAN PATENT INFORMATION SYSTEM (401)
SRZ Berlin
Lutzowstr. 105
D-1000 Berlin 30, Fed. Rep. of Germany
Phone: 030 2621081
Hans W. Fock

GERMAN STANDARDS INSTITUTE — GERMAN INFORMATION CENTER FOR TECHNICAL RULES (407)
Postfach 1107
Burggrafenstr. 4-10
D-1000 Berlin 30, Fed. Rep. of Germany
Phone: 030 2601600
Curt Mohr

GERMANY — FEDERAL BIOLOGICAL RESEARCH CENTER FOR AGRICULTURE AND FORESTRY — DOCUMENTATION CENTER FOR PHYTOMEDICINE (409)
Konigin Luise Str. 19
D-1000 Berlin 33, Fed. Rep. of Germany
Phone: 030 8304215
Prof. Wolfrudolf Laux

GERMANY — FEDERAL ENVIRONMENTAL AGENCY — ENVIRONMENTAL INFORMATION AND DOCUMENTATION SYSTEM (411)
Bismarckplatz 1
D-1000 Berlin 33, Fed. Rep. of Germany
Phone: 030 8903291
Prof. Juergen Seggelke

GERMANY — FEDERAL INSTITUTE FOR MATERIALS TESTING — MEASUREMENT OF MECHANICAL QUANTITIES DOCUMENTATION (415)
Unter den Eichen 87
D-1000 Berlin 45, Fed. Rep. of Germany
Phone: 030 81046101
Wilfried Schulze

GERMANY — FEDERAL INSTITUTE FOR MATERIALS TESTING — NONDESTRUCTIVE TESTING DOCUMENTATION (416)
Unter den Eichen 87
D-1000 Berlin 45, Fed. Rep. of Germany
Phone: 030 81046201
Dr. Uta Volkel

GERMANY — FEDERAL INSTITUTE FOR MATERIALS TESTING — RHEOLOGY AND TRIBOLOGY DOCUMENTATION CENTER (417)
Unter den Eichen 87
D-1000 Berlin 45, Fed. Rep. of Germany
Phone: 030 81045201

GERMANY — FEDERAL INSTITUTE FOR MATERIALS TESTING — WELDING DOCUMENTATION (418)
Unter den Eichen 87
D-1000 Berlin 45, Fed. Rep. of Germany
Phone: 030 81046401
Helmut Barthelmess

HARTMANN & HEENEMANN — COMPUTER COMPOSITION CENTER (476)
Lutzowstr. 105
D-1000 Berlin 30, Fed. Rep. of Germany
Phone: 030 2621081
Hans W. Fock

HEALTH CARE LITERATURE INFORMATION NETWORK (477)
Institut fur Krankenhausbau
Strasse des 17. Juni 135
D-1000 Berlin 12, Fed. Rep. of Germany
Phone: 030 3143905
Rudiger Schneemann

INFORMATION CENTER FOR MATERIALS — SYSTEM FOR DOCUMENTATION AND INFORMATION IN METALLURGY (522)
Unter den Eichen 87
D-1000 Berlin 45, Fed. Rep. of Germany
Phone: 030 81040051
Peter Buttner

INSTITUTE FOR DOCUMENTATION AND INFORMATION IN SOCIAL
MEDICINE AND PUBLIC HEALTH   (539)
Postfach 20 10 12   Phone: 0521 86033
Westerfeldstr. 15   Dr. Gerhard Sassen
D-4800 Bielefeld 1, Fed. Rep. of Germany

ASSOCIATION OF SOCIAL SCIENCES INSTITUTES — SOCIAL
SCIENCES INFORMATION CENTER   (43)
Lennestr. 30   Phone: 0228 22810
D-5300 Bonn 1, Fed. Rep. of Germany   Dr. Karl A. Stroetmann

GERMAN FOUNDATION FOR INTERNATIONAL DEVELOPMENT —
DOCUMENTATION CENTER   (397)
Hans-Bockler-Str. 5   Phone: 0228 40010
D-5300 Bonn 3, Fed. Rep. of Germany   Dieter Danckwortt

GERMANY — CENTER FOR AGRICULTURAL DOCUMENTATION AND
INFORMATION   (408)
Villichgasse 17   Phone: 0228 357097
D-5300 Bonn 2, Fed. Rep. of Germany   Dr. E. Muller

GERMANY — GERMAN FEDERAL DIET — DIVISION OF SCIENTIFIC
DOCUMENTATION — DOCUMENTATION AND INFORMATION SYSTEM
FOR PARLIAMENTARY MATERIALS   (422)
Bundeshaus   Phone: 0228 161
D-5300 Bonn, Fed. Rep. of Germany

GERMANY — MINISTRY FOR RESEARCH AND TECHNOLOGY —
ONGOING RESEARCH PROJECT DATA BANK   (424)
Heinemannstr. 2   Phone: 0228 593375
D-5300 Bonn 2, Fed. Rep. of Germany   Hans-Peter Heinrich

GERMANY — MINISTRY OF JUSTICE — JUDICIAL INFORMATION
SYSTEM   (426)
Heinemannstr. 6   Phone: 0228 5814715
Postfach 20 06 50   Werner Stewen
D-5300 Bonn 2, Fed. Rep. of Germany

GERMANY — MINISTRY OF POSTS AND TELECOMMUNICATIONS —
GERMAN FEDERAL POSTAL SERVICE — BILDSCHIRMTEXT   (427)
Referat 251   Phone: 0228 142510
Postfach 8001   Eric Danke
D-5300 Bonn, Fed. Rep. of Germany

UNIVERSITY OF BONN — INORGANIC CHEMISTRY INSTITUTE —
INORGANIC CRYSTAL STRUCTURE DATA BASE   (1042)
Gerhard-Domagk-Str. 1   Phone: 0228 732657
D-5300 Bonn 1, Fed. Rep. of Germany   Dr. G. Bergerhoff

HEINZE GmbH — VISDATA   (479)
Postfach 505   Phone: 05141 500
Bremerweg 184
D-3100 Celle, Fed. Rep. of Germany

CENTER FOR HISTORICAL SOCIAL RESEARCH   (183)
Greinstr. 2   Phone: 0221 4704404
D-5000 Cologne 41, Fed. Rep. of Germany

GERMANY — FEDERAL INSTITUTE FOR SPORTS SCIENCE —
DOCUMENTATION AND INFORMATION DIVISION — SPORT AND
SPORTS-SCIENTIFIC INFORMATION SYSTEM   (420)
Hertzstr. 1   Phone: 02234 76011
D-5000 Cologne 40, Fed. Rep. of Germany Siegfried Lachenicht

GERMANY — MINISTRY OF ECONOMICS — GERMAN FOREIGN
TRADE INFORMATION OFFICE   (425)
Postfach 108007   Phone: 0221 20571
Blaubach 13   Dr. Peter Bohm
D-5000 Cologne, Fed. Rep. of Germany

GERMANY — MINISTRY OF YOUTH, FAMILY AND HEALTH — GERMAN
INSTITUTE FOR MEDICAL DOCUMENTATION AND
INFORMATION   (428)
Weisshausstr. 27   Phone: 0221 47241
Postfach 420580   Dr. Rolf Fritz
D-5000 Cologne 41, Fed. Rep. of Germany

UNIVERSITY OF COLOGNE — CENTRAL ARCHIVES FOR EMPIRICAL
SOCIAL RESEARCH   (1045)
Bachemer Str. 40   Phone: 0221 444086
D-5000 Cologne 41, Fed. Rep. of Germany Prof. Dr. Erwin K. Scheuch

GERMAN PLASTICS INSTITUTE — INFORMATION AND
DOCUMENTATION SERVICES   (402)
Schlossgartenstr. 6 R   Phone: 06151 162206
D-6100 Darmstadt, Fed. Rep. of Germany Dietrich Braun

VERLAG HOPPENSTEDT & CO. — EK-MRA DATA BASE   (1098)
Havelstr. 9   Phone: 06151 3801
D-6100 Darmstadt 1, Fed. Rep. of Germany

GERMANY — FEDERAL INSTITUTE FOR OCCUPATIONAL SAFETY —
INFORMATION AND DOCUMENTATION CENTRE FOR OCCUPATIONAL
SAFETY   (419)
Vogelpothsweg 50-52   Phone: 0231 17631
Postfach 17 02 02
**D-4600 Dortmund 17 (Dorstfeld), Fed.
Rep. of Germany**

UHDE GmbH — UHDE THERMOPHYSICAL PROPERTIES PROGRAM
PACKAGE   (992)
Postfach 262   Phone: 0231 5472710
Friedrich-Uhde-Str.   Dr. Klaus Neumann
**D-4600 Dortmund 1, Fed. Rep. of
Germany**

UNIVERSITY OF DORTMUND — DORTMUND DATA BANK   (1046)
Lehrstuhl Technische Chemie B   Phone: 0231 7552696
P.O. Box 500500   Prof. Dr.U. Onken
**D-4600 Dortmund 50, Fed. Rep. of
Germany**

GERMAN IRON AND STEEL ENGINEERS ASSOCIATION —
INFORMATION SYSTEM ON PRODUCTION PLANTS FOR IRON & STEEL
— PLANTFACTS   (398)
Betriebsforschungsinst. - Inst. fur   Phone: 0211 67071
Angewandte Forschung, Sohnstr. 65   Prof. Karl Heinz Mommertz
**D-4000 Dusseldorf 1, Fed. Rep. of
Germany**

GERMAN IRON AND STEEL ENGINEERS ASSOCIATION — STEEL
INFORMATION SYSTEM   (399)
Betriebsforschungsinst. - Inst. fur   Phone: 0211 67071
Angewandte Forschung, Sohnstr. 65   Prof. Karl Heinz Mommertz
**D-4000 Dusseldorf 1, Fed. Rep. of
Germany**

UNIVERSITY OF DUSSELDORF — RESEARCH DIVISION FOR
PHILOSOPHY INFORMATION AND DOCUMENTATION — PHILOSOPHY
INFORMATION SERVICE   (1048)
Universitatsstr. 1   Phone: 0611 3112913
**D-4000 Dusseldorf 1, Fed. Rep. of   Dr. Norbert Henrichs
Germany**

VDI-VERLAG GMBH — VDI NEWS DATA BASE   (1096)
Graf-Recke-Str. 84   Phone: 0211 62141
**D-4000 Dusseldorf 1, Fed. Rep. of
Germany**

FOUNDATION FOR SCIENCE AND POLITICS — RESEARCH INSTITUTE
FOR INTERNATIONAL POLITICS AND SECURITY — LIBRARY AND
DOCUMENTATION SYSTEM   (337)
Haus Eggenberg   Phone: 08178 701
**D-8026 Ebenhausen, Fed. Rep. of   Dietrich Seydel
Germany**

INFORMATION CENTER FOR ENERGY, PHYSICS,
MATHEMATICS   (521)
                                            Phone: 07247 824500
**D7514 Eggenstein-Leopoldshafen 2, Fed.   Dr. Werner Rittberger
Rep. of Germany**

GERMANY — FEDERAL INSTITUTE FOR GEOSCIENCES AND NATURAL
RESOURCES — SEISMOLOGICAL CENTRAL OBSERVATORY
GRF   (414)
Krankenhausstr. 1-3   Phone: 09131 25900
D-8520 Erlangen, Fed. Rep. of Germany   Dr. Helmut Aichele

NORTH RHINE-WESTPHALIA INSTITUTE FOR AIR POLLUTION
CONTROL — LITERATURE INFORMATION SYSTEM   (765)
Wallneyer Str. 6   Phone: 0201 79951
D-4300 Essen 1, Fed. Rep. of Germany   Dietrich Plass

BEILSTEIN INSTITUTE FOR LITERATURE IN ORGANIC
CHEMISTRY   (79)
Varrentrappstr. 40-42   Phone: 069 7917251
**D-6000 Frankfurt am Main 90, Fed. Rep.   Dr. Reiner Luckenbach
of Germany**

FRANKFURT CITY AND UNIVERSITY LIBRARY — BIBLIOGRAPHY OF
LINGUISTIC LITERATURE   (368)
Bockenheimer Landstr. 134-138   Phone: 069 7907235
**D-6000 Frankfurt am Main, Fed. Rep. of   Klaus-Dieter Lehmann
Germany**

GERMAN SOCIETY FOR CHEMICAL EQUIPMENT — INFORMATION SYSTEMS AND DATA BANKS DEPARTMENT — CHEMICAL TECHNOLOGY INFORMATION SYSTEM   (403)
Theodor-Heuss-Allee 25
D-6000 Frankfurt am Main 97, Fed. Rep. of Germany
Phone: 069 7564244
Dr. Reiner Eckermann

GERMAN SOCIETY FOR CHEMICAL EQUIPMENT — INFORMATION SYSTEMS AND DATA BANKS DEPARTMENT — DECHEMA SUBSTANCE DATA SERVICE   (404)
Theodor-Heuss-Allee 25
D-6000 Frankfurt am Main 97, Fed. Rep. of Germany
Phone: 069 7564244
Dr. Reiner Eckermann

GERMAN SOCIETY FOR CHEMICAL EQUIPMENT — INFORMATION SYSTEMS AND DATA BANKS DEPARTMENT — MATERIALS AND CORROSION INFORMATION SYSTEM   (405)
Theodor-Heuss-Allee 25
D-6000 Frankfurt am Main 97, Fed. Rep. of Germany
Phone: 069 7564244
Dr. Reiner Eckermann

GERMAN SOCIETY FOR CHEMICAL EQUIPMENT — INFORMATION SYSTEMS AND DATA BANKS DEPARTMENT — SUPPLY SOURCES INFORMATION SYSTEM   (406)
Theodor-Heuss-Allee 25
D-6000 Frankfurt am Main 97, Fed. Rep. of Germany
Phone: 069 7564244
Dr. Reiner Eckermann

GERMANY — GERMAN NATIONAL LIBRARY — BIBLIO-DATA   (423)
Zeppelinallee 4-8
D-6000 Frankfurt am Main 1, Fed. Rep. of Germany
Phone: 069 75661
Dr. Reinhard Buchbinder

GMELIN INSTITUTE FOR INORGANIC CHEMISTRY AND RELATED FIELDS   (431)
Varrentrappstr. 40/42
Carl-Bosch-Haus
D-6000 Frankfurt am Main 90, Fed. Rep. of Germany
Phone: 069 79171
Dr. H.C. Ekkehard Fluck

INTERNATIONAL COMPANY FOR DOCUMENTATION IN CHEMISTRY   (572)
Hamburger Allee 26-28
D-6000 Frankfurt am Main 90, Fed. Rep. of Germany
Phone: 069 79171

INTERNATIONAL FOOD INFORMATION SERVICE — FOOD SCIENCE AND TECHNOLOGY ABSTRACTS   (583)
Lyoner Str. 44-48
D-6000 Frankfurt am Main 71, Fed. Rep. of Germany
Phone: 069 6687338
Dr. Udo Schutzsack

INTERNATIONAL FOOD INFORMATION SERVICE — PACKAGING SCIENCE AND TECHNOLOGY ABSTRACTS   (584)
Lyoner Str. 44-48
D-6000 Frankfurt am Main 71, Fed. Rep. of Germany
Phone: 069 6687338
Dr. Udo Schutzsack

INTERNATIONAL FOOD INFORMATION SERVICE — VITIS-VITICULTURE AND ENOLOGY ABSTRACTS   (585)
Lyoner Str. 44-48
D-6000 Frankfurt am Main 71, Fed. Rep. of Germany
Phone: 069 6687338
Dr. H. Berndt

PHARMA DOCUMENTATION SERVICE   (805)
Karlstr. 21
D-6000 Frankfurt am Main, Fed. Rep. of Germany
Phone: 069 2556268
Gertraud Stanzel

SCHIMMELPFENG GmbH   (865)
Postfach 16720
Am Hauptbahnhof 6
D-6000 Frankfurt am Main 1, Fed. Rep. of Germany
Phone: 069 26851
H.-K. Weckert

SCHIMMELPFENG GmbH — SCHIMMELPFENG INFORMATION BROKER SERVICE   (866)
Postfach 16720
Am Hauptbahnhof 6
D-6000 Frankfurt am Main 1, Fed. Rep. of Germany
Phone: 069 2685314
Peter Cornelius

SOCIETY FOR INFORMATION AND DOCUMENTATION — GID INFORMATION CENTER FOR INFORMATION SCIENCE AND PRACTICE   (880)
P.O. Box 710370
Lyoner Strasse 44-48
D-6000 Frankfurt am Main 71, Fed. Rep. of Germany
Phone: 069 66871
Dr. Peter Budinger

TECHNICAL INFORMATION CENTER   (959)
Postfach 600547
D-6000 Frankfurt am Main 60, Fed. Rep. of Germany
Phone: 069 43081

TECHNICAL INFORMATION CENTER — ELECTRICAL ENGINEERING DOCUMENTATION CENTER   (960)
Postfach 600547
D-6000 Frankfurt am Main 60, Fed. Rep. of Germany
Phone: 069 4308255
Mr. W. Claassen

TECHNICAL INFORMATION CENTER — MECHANICAL ENGINEERING DOCUMENTATION   (961)
Postfach 600547
D-6000 Frankfurt am Main 60, Fed. Rep. of Germany
Phone: 069 4308227
W. Muller

TECHNICAL INFORMATION CENTER — MEDICAL TECHNOLOGY DOCUMENTATION   (962)
Postfach 600547
D-6000 Frankfurt am Main 60, Fed. Rep. of Germany
Phone: 069 4308250

INSTITUTE OF NUTRITION — DOCUMENTATION DEPARTMENT   (545)
Goethestr. 55
D-6300 Giessen, Fed. Rep. of Germany
Phone: 0641 7026022
Prof. Dr. Erich Menden

TECHNOLOGY INFORMATION CENTER GOTTINGEN   (966)
Postfach 3522
Zindelstr. 3/5
D-3400 Gottingen, Fed. Rep. of Germany
Phone: 0551 44982
Isolde Peinemann

GERMAN ELECTRON-SYNCHROTRON — DESY SCIENTIFIC DOCUMENTATION AND INFORMATION SERVICE   (396)
Notkestr. 85
D-2000 Hamburg 52, Fed. Rep. of Germany
Phone: 040 89983602
Dipl.-Phys. Dietmar Schmidt

GERMANY — FEDERAL RESEARCH CENTER FOR FISHERIES — INFORMATION AND DOCUMENTATION CENTER   (421)
Palmaille 9
D-2000 Hamburg 50, Fed. Rep. of Germany
Phone: 040 38905113
Dr. Wulf P. Kirchner

GRUNER & JAHR AG & CO. — G&J PRESS INFORMATION BANK   (468)
Warburgstr. 50
D-2000 Hamburg 36, Fed. Rep. of Germany
Phone: 040 41182051
Hans-Joachim Lienau

GERMANY — FEDERAL INSTITUTE FOR GEOSCIENCES AND NATURAL RESOURCES — GEOSCIENCE LITERATURE INFORMATION SERVICE   (412)
Stilleweg 2, Postfach 510 153
D-3000 Hannover 51, Fed. Rep. of Germany
Phone: 0511 6430
J. Nowak

GERMANY — FEDERAL INSTITUTE FOR GEOSCIENCES AND NATURAL RESOURCES — MARINE INFORMATION AND DOCUMENTATION SYSTEM   (413)
Am Klagesmarkt 14-17
D-3000 Hannover 1, Fed. Rep. of Germany
Phone: 0511 1064398
Andreas Billib

UNIVERSITY LIBRARY OF HANNOVER AND TECHNICAL INFORMATION LIBRARY   (1031)
Welfengarten 1B
D-3000 Hannover 1, Fed. Rep. of Germany
Phone: 0511 7622268
Dr. Gerhard Schlitt

ONLINE GmbH   (774)
Poststr. 42
D-6900 Heidelberg 1, Fed. Rep. of Germany
Phone: 6221 21536
Dr. Dieter Schumacher

STN INTERNATIONAL   (901)
STN-Karlsruhe
Postfach 2465
D-7500 Karlsruhe 1, Fed. Rep. of Germany
Phone: 07247 824566

KIEL INSTITUTE FOR WORLD ECONOMICS — NATIONAL LIBRARY OF ECONOMICS   (639)
Dusternbrooker Weg 120
Postfach 4309
D-2300 Kiel 1, Fed. Rep. of Germany
Phone: 0431 8841
Dr. Erwin Heidemann

BAYER AG — ENGINEERING SCIENCE DIVISION — CHEMICAL AND PROCESS ENGINEERING ABSTRACTS   (77)
Bayerwerk
D-5090 Leverkusen, Fed. Rep. of Germany
Phone: 0214 3071763
Dr. Wolfgang Springe

MOTOR VEHICLE DOCUMENTATION   (716)
Gronerstr. 5
D-7140 Ludwigsburg, Fed. Rep. of Germany
Phone: 07141 44084

INSTITUTE FOR GERMAN LANGUAGE   (541)
Friedrich-Karl-Str. 12
D-6800 Mannheim 1, Fed. Rep. of Germany
Phone: 0621 44011

ASSOCIATION FOR INFORMATION BROKERAGE AND TECHNOLOGICAL CONSULTANCY — IRS INFO-INSTITUTE   (36)
Blumenstr. 1
D-8000 Munich 2, Fed. Rep. of Germany
Phone: 089 263060
Dr. Ulrich Grosse

BAVARIAN MINISTRY FOR FOOD, AGRICULTURE AND FORESTRY — BAVARIAN AGRICULTURAL INFORMATION SYSTEM   (76)
Ludwigstr. 2
D-8000 Munich 22, Fed. Rep. of Germany
Phone: 089 21820
Dr. Hans Haimerl

IFO-INSTITUTE FOR ECONOMIC RESEARCH — DEPARTMENT OF ECONOMETRICS AND DATA PROCESSING — IFO TIME SERIES DATA BANK   (501)
Poschingerstr. 5
D-8000 Munich 86, Fed. Rep. of Germany
Phone: 089 92241
Georg Goldrian

KTS INFORMATION SYSTEMS   (646)
Leopoldstr. 87
D-8000 Munich 40, Fed. Rep. of Germany
Phone: 089 398057
H.E. Seelbach

SAUR VERLAG   (863)
Possenbacherstr. 2b
D-8000 Munich 71, Fed. Rep. of Germany
Phone: 089 798901
Klaus G. Saur

SIEMENS AG — DATA PROCESSING DIVISION — GOLEM   (874)
Otto-Hahn-Ring 6
D-8000 Munich 83, Fed. Rep. of Germany
Phone: 089 63646184

SIEMENS AG — DATA PROCESSING DIVISION — LIBRARY NETWORK SYSTEM   (875)
Otto-Hahn-Ring 6
D-8000 Munich 83, Fed. Rep. of Germany
Phone: 089 6362763

SIEMENS AG — LANGUAGE SERVICES DEPARTMENT — TERMINOLOGY EVALUATION AND ACQUISITION METHOD   (876)
Hofmannstr. 51
D-8000 Munich 70, Fed. Rep. of Germany
Phone: 089 72241373
Dr. Thomas Schneider

WORLD HEALTH ORGANIZATION — WHO COLLABORATING CENTRE FOR COLLECTION AND EVALUATION OF DATA ON COMPARATIVE VIROLOGY   (1114)
Veterinarstr. 13
D-8000 Munich 22, Fed. Rep. of Germany
Phone: 089 21802155
Prof. Dr. Peter A. Bachmann

GERMANY — FEDERAL EMPLOYMENT INSTITUTE — INSTITUTE FOR EMPLOYMENT RESEARCH — INFORMATION AND DOCUMENTATION DEPARTMENT   (410)
Regensburger Str. 104
D-8500 Nuremberg, Fed. Rep. of Germany
Phone: 0911 173016
Gerd Peters

DORTMUND INSTITUTE FOR WATER RESEARCH — DATA BANK ON SUBSTANCES HARMFUL TO WATER   (284)
Zum Kellerbach
D-5840 Schwerte-Geisecke, Fed. Rep. of Germany
Phone: 02304 107350
Dr. KarlHeinz Schmidt

FRAUNHOFER SOCIETY — INFORMATION CENTER FOR BUILDING AND PHYSICAL PLANNING   (373)
Nobelstr. 12
D-7000 Stuttgart 80, Fed. Rep. of Germany
Phone: 0711 6868500
Dr.-Ing. Wilhelm Wissmann

FRAUNHOFER SOCIETY — INFORMATION CENTER FOR BUILDING AND PHYSICAL PLANNING — BUILDING RESEARCH PROJECTS DATA BASE   (374)
Nobelstr. 12
D-7000 Stuttgart 80, Fed. Rep. of Germany
Phone: 0711 6868500
Dr.-Ing. Wilhelm Wissmann

FRAUNHOFER SOCIETY — INFORMATION CENTER FOR BUILDING AND PHYSICAL PLANNING — BUILDINGS DOCUMENTATION DATA BASE   (375)
Nobelstr. 12
D-7000 Stuttgart 80, Fed. Rep. of Germany
Phone: 0711 6868500
Dr.-Ing. Wilhelm Wissmann

FRAUNHOFER SOCIETY — INFORMATION CENTER FOR BUILDING AND PHYSICAL PLANNING — LITERATURE COMPILATIONS DATA BASE   (376)
Nobelstr. 12
D-7000 Stuttgart 80, Fed. Rep. of Germany
Phone: 0711 6868500
Dr.-Ing. Wilhelm Wissmann

FRAUNHOFER SOCIETY — INFORMATION CENTER FOR BUILDING AND PHYSICAL PLANNING — PASCALBAT DATA BASE   (377)
Nobelstr. 12
D-7000 Stuttgart 80, Fed. Rep. of Germany
Phone: 0711 6868500
Dr.-Ing. Wilhelm Wissmann

FRAUNHOFER SOCIETY — INFORMATION CENTER FOR BUILDING AND PHYSICAL PLANNING — PROPERTY SERVICES AGENCY INFORMATION ON CONSTRUCTION AND ARCHITECTURE DATA BASE   (378)
Nobelstr. 12
D-7000 Stuttgart 80, Fed. Rep. of Germany
Phone: 0711 6868500
Dr.-Ing. Wilhelm Wissmann

FRAUNHOFER SOCIETY — INFORMATION CENTER FOR BUILDING AND PHYSICAL PLANNING — REGIONAL PLANNING, CITY PLANNING, HOUSING, BUILDING CONSTRUCTION DATA BASE   (379)
Nobelstr. 12
D-7000 Stuttgart 80, Fed. Rep. of Germany
Phone: 0711 6868500
Dr.-Ing. Wilhelm Wissmann

FRAUNHOFER SOCIETY — INFORMATION CENTER FOR BUILDING AND PHYSICAL PLANNING — REGIONAL PLANNING, CITY PLANNING, HOUSING RESEARCH PROJECTS DATA BASE   (380)
Nobelstr. 12
D-7000 Stuttgart 80, Fed. Rep. of Germany
Phone: 0711 6868500
Dr.-Ing. Wilhelm Wissmann

HOHENHEIM UNIVERSITY — DOCUMENTATION CENTER ON ANIMAL PRODUCTION   (487)
Postfach 700562
Paracelsusstr. 2
D-7000 Stuttgart 70, Fed. Rep. of Germany
Phone: 0711 45012110
Dr. Harald Haendler

UNIVERSITY OF TRIER — CENTER FOR PSYCHOLOGICAL INFORMATION AND DOCUMENTATION   (1078)
Postfach 3825
Schneidershof
D-5500 Trier, Fed. Rep. of Germany
Phone: 0651 716221
Leo Montada

VOLKSWAGENWERK AG — DOCUMENTATION SECTION   (1104)
Postfach
D-3180 Wolfsburg 1, Fed. Rep. of Germany
Phone: 05361 924639
Fritz Schael

GUATEMALA

CENTRAL AMERICAN RESEARCH INSTITUTE FOR INDUSTRY — DIVISION OF DOCUMENTATION AND INFORMATION   (193)
Apdo. Postal 1552
Avenida la Reforma 4-47, Zona 10
Guatemala, Guatemala
Phone: 310631/5
Ms. Rocio M. Marban

HONG KONG

INTERNATIONAL INFORMATION SERVICE LTD.   (588)
Reliance Manufactory Bldg., 6th Fl.
24 Wong Chuk Hang Rd.
Aberdeen, Hong Kong
Phone: 5 520196
C.N. Shum

COMMUNICATION SERVICES LTD. — VIEWDATA SERVICES   (231)
G.P.O. Box 9872
Hong Kong
Phone: 05 8288220
Bernard J. Howells

GEOGRAPHIC INDEX

HUNGARY

HUNGARIAN ACADEMY OF SCIENCES — INSTITUTE OF ECONOMICS — ECONOMIC INFORMATION UNIT   (491)
Budaorsi ut 45
H-1112 Budapest, Hungary
Phone: 850 878
Tamas Foldi

HUNGARIAN ACADEMY OF SCIENCES LIBRARY — DEPARTMENT FOR INFORMATICS AND SCIENCE ANALYSIS   (492)
Akademia u.2
H-1361 Budapest, Hungary
Phone: 113400
Prof. T. Braun

HUNGARY — CENTRAL STATISTICAL OFFICE   (493)
Keleti Karoly utca 5
H-1525 Budapest Pf. 51, Hungary
Phone: 358 530

HUNGARY — MINISTRY FOR BUILDING AND URBAN DEVELOPMENT — INFORMATION CENTRE FOR BUILDING   (494)
P.O. Box 83
Harsfa u. 21
H-1400 Budapest VII, Hungary
Phone: 117 317
Peter Hamvay

HUNGARY — NATIONAL SZECHENYI LIBRARY — CENTRE FOR LIBRARY SCIENCE AND METHODOLOGY   (495)
Budapest VIII, Muzeum utca 3
H-1827 Budapest Pf. 486, Hungary
Phone: 335 590
Ferenc Szente

HUNGARY — NATIONAL TECHNICAL INFORMATION CENTRE AND LIBRARY   (496)
P.O. Box 12
Reviczky u. 6
H-1428 Budapest, Hungary
Phone: 336 300
Mihaly Agoston

PRODINFORM TECHNICAL CONSULTING CO.   (825)
P.O. Box 453
H-1372 Budapest, Hungary
Phone: 317 960
Kovacs Istvan

INDIA

CENTRE FOR THE STUDY OF DEVELOPING SOCIETIES — DATA UNIT   (196)
29 Rajpur Rd.
Delhi 110054, India
Phone: 231190
Dr. V.B. Singh

INDIA — NATIONAL INSTITUTE OF OCEANOGRAPHY — INDIAN NATIONAL OCEANOGRAPHIC DATA CENTRE   (509)
NIO Information, Publication and
Data Division
Dona Paula 403004, Goa, India
Phone: 3291
Dr. V.V.R. Varadachari

CONSTELLATE CONSULTANTS LTD.   (241)
505 Vishal Bhavan
95 Nehru Place
New Delhi 110019, India
Phone: 6417015
Prithvi Haldea

INDIA — COUNCIL OF SCIENTIFIC AND INDUSTRIAL RESEARCH — INDIAN NATIONAL SCIENTIFIC DOCUMENTATION CENTRE   (507)
14, Satsang Vihar Marg
New Delhi 110067, India
Phone: 665837
T.S. Rajagopalan

INDIA — NATIONAL INSTITUTE OF HEALTH AND FAMILY WELFARE — DOCUMENTATION CENTRE   (508)
New Mehrauli Rd.
Munirka
New Delhi 110067, India
Phone: 666059
Ved Bhushan Kochhar

INDIAN COUNCIL OF AGRICULTURAL RESEARCH — AGRICULTURAL RESEARCH INFORMATION CENTRE   (510)
ICAR Bhavan, Dr. K.S. Krishnau Rd.
New Delhi 110012, India
Phone: 587121
Mr. P.C. Bose

INDIAN COUNCIL OF SOCIAL SCIENCE RESEARCH — SOCIAL SCIENCE DOCUMENTATION CENTRE   (511)
35, Ferozshah Rd.
New Delhi 110001, India
Phone: 381571
Shri S.P. Agrawal

INFORMATION INDIA   (523)
Madhya Pradesh Bhawan
2 Kautilya Lane, Chanakyapuri
New Delhi, India
Phone: 375545
Savita Sharma

INDONESIA

INDONESIA — NATIONAL SCIENTIFIC DOCUMENTATION CENTER   (512)
Jalan Jenderal Gatot Subroto
P.O. Box 3065/Jkt.
Jakarta, Indonesia
Phone: 583467
Miss Luwarsih Pringgoadisurjo

IRAN

IRAN — MINISTRY OF CULTURE AND HIGHER EDUCATION — IRANIAN DOCUMENTATION CENTRE   (613)
1188, Enqelab Ave.
P.O. Box 51-1387
Tehran, Iran
Phone: 662223
M.N. Mahdavi

IRELAND

CITIS LTD.   (208)
2 Rosemount Terrace
Blackrock
Dublin, Ireland
Phone: 01 885971
Donal P. Murphy

MULTINATIONAL ASSOCIATION OF PRODUCERS AND RETAILERS OF ELECTRICITY-DOCUMENTATION   (717)
Electricity Supply Board
Lower Fitzwilliam St.
Dublin 2, Ireland
Phone: 01 771821
James C. O'Reilly

ONLINE USERS' GROUP/IRELAND   (776)
The Library
Trinity College
Dublin 2, Ireland
Phone: 01 772941
Trevor Peare

IRELAND, NORTHERN

QUEEN'S UNIVERSITY OF BELFAST — DEPARTMENT OF COMPUTER SCIENCE — DATABASE ON ATOMIC AND MOLECULAR PHYSICS   (835)
Belfast BT7 1NN, Northern Ireland
Phone: 0232 245133
Prof. F.J. Smith

QUEEN'S UNIVERSITY OF BELFAST — DEPARTMENT OF COMPUTER SCIENCE — QUEEN'S UNIVERSITY INTERROGATION OF LEGAL LITERATURE   (836)
Belfast BT7 1NN, Northern Ireland
Phone: 0232 245133
Prof. F.J. Smith

ISRAEL

UNIVERSITY OF HAIFA LIBRARY — HAIFA ON-LINE BIBLIOGRAPHIC TEXT SYSTEM   (1051)
Mount Carmel
Haifa 31999, Israel
Phone: 04 240288
Elhanan Adler

HEBREW UNIVERSITY OF JERUSALEM — AUTOMATED LIBRARY EXPANDABLE PROGRAM HEBREW UNIVERSITY OF JERUSALEM   (478)
Yissum, P.O. Box 4279
Jerusalem 91042, Israel
Phone: 02 584266
Avner Navin

BAR-ILAN UNIVERSITY — INSTITUTE FOR INFORMATION RETRIEVAL AND COMPUTATIONAL LINGUISTICS — RESPONSA PROJECT   (74)
Ramat-gan 52100, Israel
Phone: 03 718410
Prof. Yaacov Choueka

ISRAEL — NATIONAL CENTER OF SCIENTIFIC AND TECHNOLOGICAL INFORMATION   (616)
P.O. Box 20125
84 Hachashmonaim St.
Tel-Aviv 61201, Israel
Phone: 03 297781
Mrs. Zeeva Levy

ISRAEL — NATIONAL CENTER OF SCIENTIFIC AND TECHNOLOGICAL INFORMATION — DOMESTIC   (617)
P.O. Box 20125   Phone: 03 297781
84 Hachashmonaim St.   Mrs. Zeeva Levy
Tel-Aviv 61201, Israel

TEL-AVIV UNIVERSITY — SHILOAH RESEARCH CENTER FOR MIDDLE EASTERN AND AFRICAN STUDIES — DOCUMENTATION SYSTEM — MIDEAST FILE   (970)
Ramat-Aviv   Phone: 03 420993
Tel-Aviv, Israel   Haim Shaked

ISRAEL ATOMIC ENERGY COMMISSION — SOREQ NUCLEAR RESEARCH CENTER — LIBRARY AND TECHNICAL INFORMATION DEPARTMENT   (618)
                                                  Phone: 054 84380
Yavne 70600, Israel   Mrs. S. Weil

ITALY

COMMISSION OF THE EUROPEAN COMMUNITIES — JOINT RESEARCH CENTRE — ENVIRONMENTAL CHEMICALS DATA AND INFORMATION NETWORK   (221)
Ispra Establishment   Phone: 0332 789880
I-21020 Ispra (Varese), Italy   Dr. M. Boni

BIBLIOGRAPHIC PUBLISHING CO.   (87)
Viale Vittorio Veneto 24   Phone: 02 6597950
I-20124 Milan, Italy   Mr. Michele Costa

ITALY — NATIONAL RESEARCH COUNCIL — RESEARCH CENTER FOR THE STRATIGRAPHY AND PETROGRAPHY OF THE CENTRAL ALPS — ARCHIVE OF ITALIAN DATA OF GEOLOGY   (625)
Dipartimento di Scienze della Terra   Phone: 02 293994
Via Mangiagalli 34   Dr. Roberto Potenza
I-20135 Milan, Italy

PARPINELLI TECNON — WORLD PETROCHEMICAL INDUSTRY DATA BANK   (799)
Via Egadi 7   Phone: 02 4980141
I-20144 Milan, Italy   John F. Wyatt

SVP ITALIA   (914)
Via Piccinni 3   Phone: 02 2043451
I-20131 Milan, Italy

UNIVERSITY OF MILAN — HIGHER INSTITUTE OF SOCIOLOGY — DATA AND PROGRAM ARCHIVE FOR THE SOCIAL SCIENCES   (1058)
via G. Cantoni 4   Phone: 02 4986187
I-20144 Milan, Italy   Stefano Draghi

CENTRAL ELECTRONIC NETWORK FOR DATA PROCESSING AND ANALYSIS   (194)
Corso Stati Uniti, 14   Phone: 49 760733
I-35100 Padova, Italy

ITALY — NATIONAL RESEARCH COUNCIL — CNUCE INSTITUTE   (623)
Via S. Maria 36   Phone: 050 593111
I-56100 Pisa, Italy   Dr. Ing. Stefano Trumpy

CENTER OF EXPERIMENTAL METALLURGY — IRON AND STEEL DOCUMENTATION SERVICE   (192)
Via di Castel Romano   Phone: 06 6495223
I-00100 Rome, Italy   Dr. Carlo Pagliucci

EUROPEAN SPACE AGENCY — INFORMATION RETRIEVAL SERVICE   (317)
ESRIN, Via Galileo Galilei, C.P. 64   Phone: 39 694011
I-00044 Frascati (Rome), Italy   Dr. T.F. Howell

INTERGOVERNMENTAL BUREAU FOR INFORMATICS   (554)
P.O. Box 10253   Phone: 5916041
23, viale Civilta del Lavoro   Prof. Fermin A. Bernasconi
I-00144 Rome, Italy

ITALCABLE — DIRECT ACCESS TO REMOTE DATA BASES OVERSEAS   (620)
Via Calabria 46-48   Phone: 396 47701
I-00187 Rome, Italy

ITALIAN ASSOCIATION FOR THE PRODUCTION AND DISTRIBUTION OF ONLINE INFORMATION   (621)
via G. Trevis, 88
I-00147 Rome, Italy   Dr. L. Daina

ITALIAN SOCIETY FOR TELEPHONE USE — VIDEOTEL   (622)
Via Flaminia, 189   Phone: 06 36881
I-00196 Rome, Italy   Angelo Ferraiuolo

ITALY — NATIONAL RESEARCH COUNCIL — INSTITUTE FOR STUDY OF SCIENTIFIC RESEARCH & DOCUMENTATION — ITALIAN REFERENCE CENTER FOR EURONET DIANE   (624)
Via Cesare de Lollis 12   Phone: 06 4952351
I-00185 Rome, Italy   Prof. Paolo Bisogno

SLAMARK INTERNATIONAL   (878)
Via Ignazio Guido, 4   Phone: 06 5140176 476
I-00147 Rome, Italy

UNITED NATIONS — FOOD AND AGRICULTURE ORGANIZATION — AQUATIC SCIENCES AND FISHERIES INFORMATION SYSTEM   (1008)
Via delle Terme di Caracalla   Phone: 06 5797
I-00100 Rome, Italy   E.F. Akyuz

UNITED NATIONS — FOOD AND AGRICULTURE ORGANIZATION — CURRENT AGRICULTURAL RESEARCH INFORMATION SYSTEM   (1009)
CARIS Coordinating Center   Phone: 06 57971
Via delle Terme di Caracalla
I-00100 Rome, Italy

UNITED NATIONS — FOOD AND AGRICULTURE ORGANIZATION — ECONOMIC AND SOCIAL DEPARTMENT — HUMAN RESOURCES, INSTITUTIONS AND AGRARIAN REFORM DIVISION — POPULATION DOCUMENTATION CENTER   (1010)
Via delle Terme di Caracalla   Phone: 06 57973628
I-00100 Rome, Italy   Ms. I. Losseau

UNITED NATIONS — FOOD AND AGRICULTURE ORGANIZATION — INTERNATIONAL INFORMATION SYSTEM FOR THE AGRICULTURAL SCIENCES AND TECHNOLOGY   (1012)
AGRIS Coordinating Center   Phone: 06 5797
Via delle Terme di Caracalla   A. Lebowitz
I-00100 Rome, Italy

UNITED NATIONS — FOOD AND AGRICULTURE ORGANIZATION — LIBRARY AND DOCUMENTATION SYSTEMS DIVISION — DAVID LUBIN MEMORIAL LIBRARY   (1013)
Via delle Terme di Caracalla   Phone: 06 57971
I-00100 Rome, Italy

UNITED NATIONS — FOOD AND AGRICULTURE ORGANIZATION — STATISTICS DIVISION — INTERLINKED COMPUTERIZED STORAGE AND PROCESSING SYSTEM OF FOOD AND AGRICULTURAL DATA   (1014)
Via delle Terme di Caracalla   Phone: 06 5797
I-00100 Rome, Italy   K. Becker

BUILDING CENTER   (117)
Via Rivoltana 8   Phone: 02 7530951
I-20090 Segrate/Milan, Italy

LOMBARD INTERUNIVERSITY CONSORTIUM FOR DATA PROCESSING   (669)
Via R. Sanzio 4   Phone: 02 2132541
I-20090 Segrate/Milan, Italy   Prof. Ivo De Lotto

SYSTEL   (950)
Via Cibrario 27   Phone: 011 7492225
I-10143 Torino, Italy   Umberto Cavallaro

PIEDMONT CONSORTIUM FOR INFORMATION SYSTEMS   (811)
Corso Unione Sovietica 216   Phone: 011 33071
I-10134 Turin, Italy   Renzo Rovaris

TECNOMEDIA   (968)
Via Antonio Caccia, n. 32   Phone: 0432 43341
I-33100 Udine, Italy   Paolo Cattapan

JAPAN

KYUSHU UNIVERSITY — RESEARCH INSTITUTE OF FUNDAMENTAL INFORMATION SCIENCE   (648)
10-1, Hakozaki 6-Chome
Higashi-ku, Fukuoka-shi
Fukuoka City 812, Japan
Phone: 092 6411101
Chooichiro Asano

JAPAN — ENVIRONMENT AGENCY — NATIONAL INSTITUTE FOR ENVIRONMENTAL STUDIES — ENVIRONMENTAL INFORMATION DIVISION   (626)
16-2 Onogawa
Yatabe-machi, Tsukuba-gun
Ibaraki 305, Japan
Phone: 0298 516111
Dr. Shota Hirosaki

UNIVERSITY OF TSUKUBA — SCIENCE INFORMATION PROCESSING CENTER   (1080)
1-1-1 Tennodai
Sakura-mura, Niihari-gun
Ibaraki-ken, Japan 305
Phone: 0298 532451
Kazuhiko Nakayama

MIDORI BOOK STORE COMPANY   (709)
Nishi Hankyu Bldg.
Shibata 2-Chome, 1-18 Kitaku
Osaka, Japan
Phone: 06 3715395
Masayuki Niwa

EPOCH RESEARCH CORPORATION   (298)
2-7-12-106 Nakano
Nakano-ku
Tokyo 164, Japan
Phone: 03 3821384
Masahito Miwa

IBJ DATA SERVICE CO.   (498)
3-3, 1-Chome
Marunouchi Chiyoda-ku
Tokyo 100, Japan
Phone: 214-1111
Katsuhiro Katoh

INFORMATION PROCESSING SOCIETY OF JAPAN   (529)
Kikai Shinko Bldg.
3-5-8 Shiba-Koen, Minato-ku
Tokyo 105, Japan
Phone: 03 4312808
Masumi Sakamoto

INFORMATION RESEARCHERS, INC.   (531)
No. 59-3, Yoyogi 4-chome
Shibuya-ku
Tokyo 151, Japan
Phone: 03 3704475
Akira Yashiro

INTERNATIONAL MEDICAL INFORMATION CENTER   (598)
30, Daikyo-cho
Shinjuku-ku
Tokyo 160, Japan
Phone: 03 3579002
Daizo Ushiba

JAPAN — JAPAN ATOMIC ENERGY RESEARCH INSTITUTE — DEPARTMENT OF TECHNICAL INFORMATION   (627)
2-2-2 Uchisaiwai-cho, Chiyoda-ku
Tokyo 100, Japan
Phone: 03 5036111
Dr. Junichi Shimokawa

JAPAN — MARITIME SAFETY AGENCY — HYDROGRAPHIC DEPARTMENT — JAPAN OCEANOGRAPHIC DATA CENTER   (628)
No. 3-1, Tsukiji 5-Chome
Chuo-ku
Tokyo 104, Japan
Phone: 03 5413811
Dr. Yoshio Iwabuchi

JAPAN — NATIONAL DIET LIBRARY — LIBRARY AUTOMATION SYSTEM   (629)
10-1, 1-Chome
Nagato-cho, Chiyoda-ku
Tokyo 100, Japan
Phone: 03 5812331
Mr. Koichi Imagawa

JAPAN ASSOCIATION FOR INTERNATIONAL CHEMICAL INFORMATION   (630)
Gakkai Center Bldg.
2-4-16 Yayoi, Bunkyo-ku
Tokyo 113, Japan
Phone: 03 8163462
Soichi Tokizane

JAPAN DATA SERVICE CO., LTD.   (631)
Shugetsu Bldg.
3-12-7 Kita-Aoyama, Minato-ku
Tokyo 107, Japan
Phone: 03 4007507
Akihisa Yamaguchi

JAPAN INFORMATION CENTER OF SCIENCE AND TECHNOLOGY   (632)
5-2, Nagatacho, 2-Chome, Chiyoda-ku
C.P.O. Box 1478
Tokyo, Japan
Phone: 03 5816411
Shintaro Tabata

JAPAN PATENT INFORMATION CENTER   (633)
Bansui Bldg.
1-5-16, Toranomon, Minato-ku
Tokyo 105, Japan
Phone: 03 5036181
Hideo Saito

JAPAN PHARMACEUTICAL INFORMATION CENTER   (634)
12-15-601, Shibuya 2-Chome
Shibuya-ku, Yakugakukaikan
Tokyo 150, Japan
Phone: 03 4061811
Fuminae Kubo

JAPAN PUBLICATIONS GUIDE   (635)
CPO Box 971
Tokyo 100-91, Japan
Phone: 03 6618373
Warren E. Ball

KINOKUNIYA COMPANY LTD. — ASK INFORMATION RETRIEVAL SERVICES   (640)
Kakoh Sakuragaoka Bldg.
3-24, Sakuragaoka-cho, Shibuyaku
Tokyo 150, Japan
Phone: 03 4634391
Isao Miura

MARKETING INTELLIGENCE CORPORATION   (688)
14-11, Yato-cho 2-Chome
Tanashi-shi
Tokyo 188, Japan
Phone: 0424 231111
Hiroshi Hakone

NIHON KEIZAI SHIMBUN, INC. — DATABANK BUREAU — NIKKEI ECONOMIC ELECTRONIC DATABANK SYSTEM-INFORMATION RETRIEVAL   (753)
9-5, Ohtemachi, 1-Chome, Chiyoda-ku
Tokyo 100, Japan
Phone: 03 2700251

NIHON KEIZAI SHIMBUN, INC. — DATABANK BUREAU — NIKKEI ECONOMIC ELECTRONIC DATABANK SYSTEM-TIME SHARING   (754)
9-5 Ohtemachi, 1-Chome, Chiyoda-ku
Tokyo 100, Japan
Phone: 03 2700251
Takashi Suzuki

NIHON KEIZAI SHIMBUN, INC. — QUOTATION INFORMATION CENTER K.K.   (755)
828 Otemachi Bldg.
1-6-1 Otemachi, Chiyoda-ku
Tokyo 100, Japan
Phone: 03 2165911
Mr. Kitokuro Shiba

NIKKEI SVP CO. LTD.   (756)
1-9-5 Ohtemachi, Chiyoda-Ku
Tokyo 100, Japan

NIPPON GIJUTSU BOEKI CO., LTD.   (758)
Kasumigaseki Bldg., 32-F, No. 2-5
Kasumigaseki 3-Chome, Chiyoda-ku
Tokyo 100, Japan
Phone: 03 5817711
Mr. M. Shimada

NIPPON TELEGRAPH & TELEPHONE PUBLIC CORPORATION — CAPTAIN   (759)
1-1-6, Uchisaiwai-cho
Chiyoda-ku
Tokyo 100, Japan
Phone: 03 5095913

NOMURA RESEARCH INSTITUTE — INFORMATION SERVICE AND DEVELOPMENT DEPARTMENT — NRI/E JAPAN ECONOMIC & BUSINESS DATA BANK   (760)
Edobashi Bldg.
1-11-1 Nihonbashi, Chuo-ku
Tokyo 103, Japan
Phone: 03 2764768
Toshiaki Kamijo

OVERSEAS DATA SERVICE, COMPANY, LTD.   (789)
Shugetsu Bldg.
3-12-7 Kita-Aoyama, Minato-Ku
Tokyo 107, Japan
Phone: 03 4007090
Yasuhide Miura

SYSTEM DEVELOPMENT CORPORATION OF JAPAN, LTD. — SEARCH/J   (952)
Nishi-Shinjuku-Showa Bldg.
1-13-12 Nishi-Shinjuku, Shinjuku-ku
Tokyo 160, Japan
Phone: 03 3498521
Masao Namekawa

TEIKOKU DATA BANK, LTD.   (969)
5-20, Minami-Aoyama 2-Chome
Minato-ku
Tokyo 107, Japan
Phone: 03 4044311
Tsuneo Ebata

TOKYO SHOKO RESEARCH, LTD. — DATA BANK SERVICE   (984)
Shinichi Bldg., 9-6, 1-Chome
Shinbashi, Minato-ku
Tokyo 105, Japan
Phone: 03 574 2219
Yo Ito

UNITED NATIONS UNIVERSITY — REFERRAL SERVICE
SYSTEM   (1028)
Toho Seimei Bldg.　　　　　　　　　　　　Phone: 03 4992811
15-1 Shibuya, 2-Chome, Shibuya-ku　　　　　　Shigeo Minowa
Tokyo 150, Japan

UNIVERSITY OF TOKYO — COMPUTER CENTER — UNIVERSITY OF
TOKYO ON-LINE INFORMATION RETRIEVAL SYSTEM   (1075)
2-11-16 Yayoi, Bunkyo-ku　　　　　　　　Phone: 03 8122111
Tokyo 113, Japan　　　　　　　　　　　Dr. Hiroshi Ozawa

UNIVERSITY OF TOKYO — FACULTY OF ENGINEERING —
DEPARTMENT OF SYNTHETIC CHEMISTRY — EROICA SYSTEM FOR
BASIC PROPERTIES OF ORGANIC COMPOUNDS   (1076)
7-3-1 Hongo, Bunkyo-ku　　　　　　　　　Phone: 03 8122111
Tokyo 113, Japan

USACO CORPORATION   (1092)
13-12 Shimbashi　　　　　　　　　　　　Phone: 03 5026471
1-Chome, Minato-ku　　　　　　　　　Mr. Takashi Yamakawa
Tokyo 105, Japan

MARUZEN COMPANY, LTD. — MARUZEN SCIENTIFIC INFORMATION
SERVICE CENTER   (689)
P.O. Box 5335　　　　　　　　　　　　　Phone: 03 2716068
Tokyo International 100-31, Japan　　　　　Ken I. Teramura

KENYA

UNITED NATIONS ENVIRONMENT PROGRAMME —
INFOTERRA   (1025)
P.O. Box 30552　　　　　　　　　　　　　Phone: 333930
Nairobi, Kenya　　　　　　　　　　　　　Woyen Lee

KOREA, REPUBLIC OF

KOREA ADVANCED INSTITUTE OF SCIENCE AND TECHNOLOGY —
EXPERIENCED LIBRARIANS AND INFORMATION PERSONNEL IN THE
DEVELOPING COUNTRIES OF ASIA AND OCEANIA   (644)
KAIST Library　　　　　　　　　　　　　Phone: 02 9673692
P.O. Box 131, Dong Dae Mun　　　　　　　Mr. Ke Hong Park
Seoul 133-00, Korea

KOREA INSTITUTE FOR INDUSTRIAL ECONOMICS AND
TECHNOLOGY   (645)
P.O. Box 205　　　　　　　　　　　　　　Phone: 9656211
Cheong Ryang　　　　　　　　　　　　　Hiwhoa Moon
Seoul 131, Korea

SVP KOREA   (915)
Joongang Daily News　　　　　　　　　　Phone: 02 7527741
58-9 Seosomun-dong, Joong-ku　　　　　　　In-sup Chung
Seoul, Korea

LUXEMBOURG

EUROPEAN BUSINESS ASSOCIATES ON-LINE   (308)
69, rue de la Petrusse　　　　　　　　　　Phone: 352 318884
L-8084 Bertrange, Luxembourg　　　　　　　Mary Clark

COMMISSION OF THE EUROPEAN COMMUNITIES — AGRICULTURAL
RESEARCH PROJECTS DATA BASE   (213)
Batiment Jean Monnet, B.P. 1907　　　　　　Phone: 352 43011
Rue Alcide de Gasperi　　　　　　　　　　Giorgio Trevisan
Kirchberg, Luxembourg

COMMISSION OF THE EUROPEAN COMMUNITIES — COURT OF
JUSTICE OF THE EUROPEAN COMMUNITIES — LEGAL DATA
PROCESSING GROUP — CJUS DATA BANK   (214)
B.P. 1406　　　　　　　　　　　　　　　Phone: 352 43031
Kirchberg, Luxembourg　　　　　　　　　Jochen Streil

COMMISSION OF THE EUROPEAN COMMUNITIES —
ENVIRONMENTAL INFORMATION AND DOCUMENTATION CENTERS
DATA BASE   (216)
Batiment Jean Monnet, B.P. 1907　　　　　Phone: 352 43012875
Rue Alcide de Gasperi
Kirchberg, Luxembourg

COMMISSION OF THE EUROPEAN COMMUNITIES —
ENVIRONMENTAL RESEARCH PROJECTS DATA BASE   (217)
Batiment Jean Monnet, B.P. 1907　　　　　Phone: 352 43012875
Rue Alcide de Gasperi
Kirchberg, Luxembourg

COMMISSION OF THE EUROPEAN COMMUNITIES — EURO
ABSTRACTS   (218)
Batiment Jean Monnet, B.P. 1907　　　　　Phone: 352 43012948
Rue Alcide de Gasperi　　　　　　　　　　H.L. Scherff
Kirchberg, Luxembourg

COMMISSION OF THE EUROPEAN COMMUNITIES — EUROPEAN ON-
LINE INFORMATION NETWORK — DIRECT INFORMATION ACCESS
NETWORK FOR EUROPE   (220)
Batiment Jean Monnet, B.P. 1907　　　　　Phone: 352 43012879
Rue Alcide de Gasperi　　　　　　　　　　Wolfgang Huber
Kirchberg, Luxembourg

COMMISSION OF THE EUROPEAN COMMUNITIES — SPECIALIZED
DEPARTMENT FOR TERMINOLOGY AND COMPUTER APPLICATIONS
— EURODICAUTOM   (223)
Batiment Jean Monnet A2/101　　　　　　Phone: 352 43012389
B.P. 1907, Rue Alcide de Gasperi　　　　　Mr. J. Goetschalckx
Kirchberg, Luxembourg

COMMISSION OF THE EUROPEAN COMMUNITIES — STATISTICAL
OFFICE OF THE EUROPEAN COMMUNITIES — COMEXT DATA
BANK   (224)
Batiment Jean Monnet, B.P. 1907　　　　　Phone: 352 43013530
Rue Alcide de Gasperi　　　　　　　　　　Mlle. Hilf
Kirchberg, Luxembourg

COMMISSION OF THE EUROPEAN COMMUNITIES — STATISTICAL
OFFICE OF THE EUROPEAN COMMUNITIES — CRONOS DATA
BANK   (225)
Batiment Jean Monnet, B.P. 1907　　　　　Phone: 352 43011
Rue Alcide de Gasperi　　　　　　　　　　Mr. Nols
Kirchberg, Luxembourg

COMMISSION OF THE EUROPEAN COMMUNITIES — SYSTEM FOR
INFORMATION ON GREY LITERATURE IN EUROPE   (226)
Batiment Jean Monnet, B.P. 1907　　　　　Phone: 4301 2908
Rue Alcide de Gasperi　　　　　　　　Marcel M. Maurice
Kirchberg, Luxembourg

EUROPEAN ASSOCIATION FOR THE TRANSFER OF TECHNOLOGIES,
INNOVATION AND INDUSTRIAL INFORMATION   (306)
7, rue Alcide de Gasperi　　　　　　　　Phone: 352 438096
B.P. 1704　　　　　　　　　　　　　　Christian Glockner
L-1017 Kirchberg, Luxembourg

ASSOCIATION OF EUROPEAN HOST OPERATORS GROUP   (42)
ECHO, 15 ave. de la Faiencerie　　　　　　Phone: 352 20764
L-1510 Luxembourg, Luxembourg　　　　　Marino Saksida

COMMISSION OF THE EUROPEAN COMMUNITIES — EUROPEAN
COMMISSION HOST ORGANIZATION   (219)
15, ave. de la Faiencerie　　　　　　　　　Phone: 352 20764
Luxembourg　　　　　　　　　　　　　Roland Haber

COMMISSION OF THE EUROPEAN COMMUNITIES — TENDERS
ELECTRONIC DAILY   (227)
ECHO　　　　　　　　　　　　　　　　Phone: 352 20764
15, ave. de la Faiencerie
Luxembourg

MADAGASCAR

MADAGASCAR — MINISTRY OF FINANCE AND ECONOMY —
NATIONAL INSTITUTE OF STATISTICS AND ECONOMIC
RESEARCH   (681)
B.P. 485　　　　　　　　　　　　　　　Phone: 20081
Antananarivo, Madagascar　　　Raphael Ramanana-Rahary

MALAYSIA

UNITED NATIONS — FOOD AND AGRICULTURE ORGANIZATION —
INFOFISH   (1011)
P.O. Box 10899　　　　　　　　　　　　Phone: 914466
Kuala Lumpur 01-02, Malaysia　　　　　　　Erik Hempel

MEXICO

INFYTEC, S.A. (537)
Apdo. Postal No. 32-0360
Mexico City 06470 D.F., Mexico
Phone: (905) 535-9939
Luis Torres

MEXICO — NATIONAL CENTER FOR HEALTH INFORMATION AND DOCUMENTATION (700)
Rio Mixcoac 36, 9 Piso
Col. del Valle
Mexico City 03100, D.F., Mexico
Phone: (905) 534-4820
Dr. Cesar A. Macias-Chapula

MEXICO — NATIONAL COUNCIL OF SCIENCE AND TECHNOLOGY — DATA BASE CONSULTATION SERVICE (701)
Circuito Cultural Universitario
Ciudad Universitaria
Mexico City 04515 D.F., Mexico
Phone: 652 4000

MEXICO — NATIONAL INSTITUTE OF NUCLEAR RESEARCH — NUCLEAR INFORMATION AND DOCUMENTATION CENTER (703)
Apdo. Postal No. 27-190
Mexico City, Mexico 18, D.F.
Phone: 563 7100
Prof. Pedro Zamora Rodriguez

NATIONAL AUTONOMOUS UNIVERSITY OF MEXICO — CENTER FOR SCIENTIFIC AND HUMANISTIC INFORMATION (719)
Apdo. Postal 70-392
Ciudad Universitaria
Mexico City 04510 D.F., Mexico
Phone: 5480858
Dr. Armando M. Sandoval

MEXICO — NATIONAL INSTITUTE FOR RESEARCH ON BIOLOGICAL RESOURCES — INIREB LIBRARY (702)
Km. 2.5 Antigua Carretera a
Coatepec, Apartado Postal 63
Xalapa 91000, Veracruz, Mexico
Phone: 281 79274
Alma Aguilar Caceres

MOROCCO

AFRICAN TRAINING AND RESEARCH CENTRE IN ADMINISTRATION FOR DEVELOPMENT — AFRICAN NETWORK OF ADMINISTRATIVE INFORMATION (7)
P.O Box 310
19, Abou-Al-Alae Al-Maari
Tangier, Morocco
Phone: 36430
E.S. Asiedu

NETHERLANDS

INTERNATIONAL GROUP OF USERS OF INFORMATION SYSTEMS (586)
Enschedepad 41
NL-1324 GB Almere-Stad, Netherlands
Phone: 03240 31341
Arvid Gundersen

INTERNATIONAL MEDICAL INFORMATICS ASSOCIATION (597)
Enschedepad 41
NL-1324 GB Almere-Stad, Netherlands
Phone: 03240 31341
Arvid Gundersen

SAMSOM DATA SYSTEMS — SAMSOM DATANET (861)
Postbus 180
Wilhelminalaan 1
NL-2400 AD Alphen aan den Rijn, Netherlands
Phone: 1720 66633

VAN HALM & ASSOCIATES (1095)
P.O. Box 688
NL-3800 AR Amersfoort, Netherlands
Phone: 033 18024
Johan van Halm

KUGLER PUBLICATIONS (647)
P.O. Box 516
NL-1180 AM Amstelveen, Netherlands
Phone: 020 278070
Simon Kugler

ADMEDIA — ADFACTS (6)
Postbus 7902
NL-1008 AC Amsterdam, Netherlands
Phone: 020 5411345
Ben Spaan

COLLECTIVE FOR TRAINING AND EDUCATION IN CONNECTION WITH INFORMATION PROVISION VIA NETWORKS (211)
St. Antoniesbreestr. 16
P.O. Box 16601
NL-1001 RC Amsterdam, Netherlands
Phone: 020 223955
J.H. Oudshoorn

ELSEVIER SCIENCE PUBLISHERS B.V. — BIOMEDICAL DIVISION — EXCERPTA MEDICA (296)
P.O. Box 1527
Molenwerf 1
NL-1000 BM Amsterdam, Netherlands
Phone: 020 5803535
Arnold A.J. Jansen

INTERNATIONAL FEDERATION OF DATA ORGANIZATIONS FOR THE SOCIAL SCIENCES (581)
Steinmetz Archives
410 Herengracht
NL-1017 BX Amsterdam, Netherlands
Phone: 020 225061
Frederic Bon

NETHERLANDS ASSOCIATION OF USERS OF ONLINE INFORMATION SYSTEMS (734)
Library KNAW
Kloveniersburgwal 29
NL-1011 JV Amsterdam, Netherlands
Phone: 020 222902
Dr. H.M. Rietveld

NETHERLANDS BIBLIOGRAPHICAL AND DOCUMENTARY COMMITTEE (735)
St. Antoniesbreestr. 16
P.O. Box 16601
NL-1001 RC Amsterdam, Netherlands
Phone: 020 223955
J.H.M. Heijnen

NETHERLANDS SOCIETY FOR INFORMATICS (745)
Paulus Potterstr. 40
NL-1071 DB Amsterdam, Netherlands
Phone: 020 728222
Ms. R. Lucas

ROYAL NETHERLANDS ACADEMY OF ARTS AND SCIENCES — SOCIAL SCIENCE INFORMATION AND DOCUMENTATION CENTER (847)
410 Herengracht
NL-1017 BX Amsterdam, Netherlands
Phone: 020 225061
Dr. A.F. Marks

ROYAL NETHERLANDS ACADEMY OF ARTS AND SCIENCES — SOCIAL SCIENCE INFORMATION AND DOCUMENTATION CENTER — STEINMETZ ARCHIVES (848)
410 Herengracht
NL-1017 BX Amsterdam, Netherlands
Phone: 020 225061
Dr. Paul F.A. de Guchteneire

ROYAL NETHERLANDS ACADEMY OF ARTS AND SCIENCES LIBRARY (849)
Kloveniersburgwal 29
P.O. Box 19121
NL-1000 GC Amsterdam, Netherlands
Phone: 020 222902
Dr. J.A.W. Brak

ROYAL TROPICAL INSTITUTE — AGRICULTURAL INFORMATION & DOCUMENTATION SECTION (857)
Mauritskade 63
NL-1092 AD Amsterdam, Netherlands
Phone: 020 924949
Richard M. Wilson

TRANSNATIONAL DATA REPORTING SERVICE, INC. (988)
P.O. Box 6152
NL-1005 ED Amsterdam, Netherlands
Phone: 3120 737311

DELFT HYDRAULICS LABORATORY — INFORMATION AND DOCUMENTATION SECTION (268)
P.O. Box 177
NL-2600 MH Delft, Netherlands
Phone: 015 569353
W.W. de Mes

INTERNATIONAL TRANSLATIONS CENTRE (608)
101 Doelenstr.
NL-2611 NS Delft, Netherlands
Phone: 015 142242
D. van Bergeijk

NETHERLANDS INFORMATION COMBINE (737)
P.O. Box 36
NL-2600 AA Delft, Netherlands
Phone: 015 569330

NETHERLANDS ORGANIZATION FOR APPLIED SCIENTIFIC RESEARCH — CENTER FOR INFORMATION AND DOCUMENTATION (739)
P.O. Box 36
Schoemakerstr. 97
NL-2600 AA Delft, Netherlands
Phone: 015 569330
Charles L. Citroen

NETHERLANDS ORGANIZATION FOR APPLIED SCIENTIFIC RESEARCH — GROUNDWATER SURVEY (740)
Schoemakerstr. 97
P.O. Box 285
NL-2600 AG Delft, Netherlands
Phone: 015 569330

NETHERLANDS ORGANIZATION FOR APPLIED SCIENTIFIC RESEARCH — TNO STUDY AND INFORMATION CENTER ON ENVIRONMENTAL RESEARCH — ENVIRONMENTAL RESEARCH IN THE NETHERLANDS (743)
P.O. Box 186
NL-2600 AD Delft, Netherlands
Phone: 015 569330
P. Winkel

KLUWER PUBLISHING COMPANY — JURIDICAL DATABANK (641)
P.O. Box 23　　　　　　　　　　　　　　Phone: 05700 91180
NL-7400 GA Deventer, Netherlands　　Mr. J. Sander E. Hulshoff

PHILIPS INFORMATION SYSTEMS AND AUTOMATION — DIRECT (809)
Philips International B.V.　　　　　　　　Phone: 040 784034
Bldg. VN 304, Boschdijk　　　　　　　　　Drs. K. Dijkens
Eindhoven, Netherlands

DUTCH STATE MINES — TISDATA (286)
P.O. Box 18　　　　　　　　　　　　　　Phone: 04494 65393
NL-6160 MD Geleen, Netherlands　　　J.B.P. van Nuland

KONINKLIJKE VERMANDE B.V. (643)
Postbus 20　　　　　　　　　　　　　　Phone: 02550 19013
Platinastr. 33　　　　　　　　　　　　　W.G.A. Van der Weyden
NL-5200 AA Lelystad, Netherlands

SWETS SUBSCRIPTION SERVICE (942)
347b Heereweg　　　　　　　　　　　　Phone: 2521 19113
NL-2161 CA Lisse, Netherlands　　　　J. Roof

EUROPE DATA (305)
Bredestr. 24　　　　　　　　　　　　　Phone: 043 54751
NL-6211 HC Maastricht, Netherlands　Karel Giel

FARMODEX FOUNDATION — FARMODEX DRUG DATA BANK (325)
Geert Grooteplein Zuid 10　　　　　　　Phone: 080 516887
NL-6525 GA Nijmegen, Netherlands

EUROPEAN SPACE AGENCY — EUROPEAN SPACE RESEARCH AND TECHNOLOGY CENTER — MATERIALS DATA RETRIEVAL SYSTEM (316)
Postbus 299　　　　　　　　　　　　　Phone: 01719 82118
NL-8200 AG Noordwijk ZH, Netherlands　Dr. J. Dauphin

PHARMA DOCUMENTATION RING (804)
Organon International　　　　　　　　　Phone: 04120 62409
P.O. Box 20　　　　　　　　　　　　　　Dr. N.W. van Putte
NL-5340 BH Oss, Netherlands

COMMISSION OF THE EUROPEAN COMMUNITIES — JOINT RESEARCH CENTRE — HIGH TEMPERATURE MATERIALS DATA BANK (222)
P.O. Box 2　　　　　　　　　　　　　　Phone: 02246 5208
NL-1755 ZG Petten, Netherlands　　　H. Krockel

EUROPEAN PATENT OFFICE — EDP DEPARTMENT — EPO DATA BANKS (315)
P.B. 5818, Patentlaan 2　　　　　　　　Phone: 070 906789
NL-2280 HV Rijswijk ZH, Netherlands　O. Bullens

INTERNATIONAL REFERENCE CENTER FOR COMMUNITY WATER SUPPLY AND SANITATION — PROGRAMME ON EXCHANGE AND TRANSFER OF INFORMATION ON COMMUNITY WATER SUPPLY AND SANITATION (601)
P.O. Box 5500　　　　　　　　　　　　Phone: 070 949322
NL-2280 HM Rijswijk, Netherlands　　Mr. Toon A. van Dam

SVP SIJTHOFF (916)
NL-2288 BC Rijswijk, Netherlands

CONSULTEXT (243)
Kadyk 4　　　　　　　　　　　　　　　Phone: 05137 1530
NL-8463 VC Rotsterhaule, Netherlands　Raymond M.G.P.B. Bakker

INTERNATIONAL COUNCIL FOR BUILDING RESEARCH, STUDIES AND DOCUMENTATION (573)
Weena 704　　　　　　　　　　　　　Phone: 10 110240
P.O. Box 20704
NL-3001 JA Rotterdam, Netherlands

MARITIME INFORMATION CENTRE/CMO (685)
P.O. Box 21873　　　　　　　　　　　Phone: 010 130960
NL-3001 AW Rotterdam, Netherlands　G.S. Kok

CONSORTIUM OF ROYAL LIBRARY AND UNIVERSITY LIBRARIES — PROJECT FOR INTEGRATED CATALOGUE AUTOMATION (239)
Prins Willem Alexanderhof 5　　　　　　Phone: 070 140460
NL-2595 BE The Hague, Netherlands　L. Costers

CONSORTIUM OF ROYAL LIBRARY AND UNIVERSITY LIBRARIES — PROJECT FOR INTEGRATED CATALOGUE AUTOMATION — NETHERLANDS CENTRAL CATALOGUE/INTERLIBRARY LOAN SYSTEM (240)
Prins Willem Alexanderhof 5　　　　　　Phone: 070 140460
NL-2595 BE The Hague, Netherlands　L. Costers

INTERNATIONAL FEDERATION FOR DOCUMENTATION (578)
P.O. Box 90402　　　　　　　　　　　　Phone: 070 606915
NL-2509 LK The Hague, Netherlands　Stella Keenan

INTERNATIONAL FEDERATION FOR DOCUMENTATION — RESEARCH REFERRAL SERVICE (579)
P.O. Box 90402　　　　　　　　　　　　Phone: 070 606915
NL-2509 LK The Hague, Netherlands　Stella Keenan

INTERNATIONAL FEDERATION OF LIBRARY ASSOCIATIONS AND INSTITUTIONS (582)
P.O. Box 95312　　　　　　　　　　　　Phone: 070 140884
NL-2509 CH The Hague, Netherlands　Dr. Margreet Wijnstroom

NETHERLANDS — MINISTRY OF FOREIGN AFFAIRS — TRANSLATIONS BRANCH — TERMINOLOGY AND DOCUMENTATION SECTION (732)
P.O. Box 20061　　　　　　　　　　　　Phone: 070 209270
Casuariestr. 16　　　　　　　　　　　　J.R. Mengarduque
NL-2500 EB The Hague, Netherlands

NETHERLANDS — NETHERLANDS FOREIGN TRADE AGENCY — LIBRARY AND DOCUMENTATION BRANCH — FOREIGN TRADE ABSTRACTS (733)
Bezuidenhoutseweg 151　　　　　　　　Phone: 070 797221
NL-2594 AH The Hague, Netherlands　J.H. Ypma

NETHERLANDS CENTER FOR INFORMATION POLICY (736)
Prinses Beatrixlaan 5　　　　　　　　　　Phone: 070 476161
NL-2595 AK The Hague, Netherlands　J.K.W. van Leeuwen

NETHERLANDS OFFICE OF POSTS, TELEGRAPHS, AND TELEPHONES — PTT CENTRAL DIRECTORATE — VIDITEL (738)
P.O. Box 30000　　　　　　　　　　　　Phone: 70754074
NL-2500 GA The Hague, Netherlands　R.C. Meijburg

NETHERLANDS ORGANIZATION FOR APPLIED SCIENTIFIC RESEARCH — INSTITUTE TNO FOR MATHEMATICS, INFORMATION PROCESSING AND STATISTICS (741)
P.O. Box 297　　　　　　　　　　　　　Phone: 070 824161
Koningin Marialaan 21　　　　　　　　　J. Remmelts
NL-2501 BD The Hague, Netherlands

NETHERLANDS ORGANIZATION FOR APPLIED SCIENTIFIC RESEARCH — NATIONAL COUNCIL FOR AGRICULTURAL RESEARCH TNO — CENTRAL PROJECT ADMINISTRATION FOR CURRENT AGRICULTURAL RESEARCH IN THE NETHERLANDS (742)
Adelheidstr. 84　　　　　　　　　　　　Phone: 070 471021
P.O. Box 297　　　　　　　　　　　　　A. van den Berg
NL-2501 BD The Hague, Netherlands

NETHERLANDS ORGANIZATION FOR INFORMATION POLICY (744)
19 Burgemeester van Karnebeeklaan　　　Phone: 070 607833
NL-2585 BA The Hague, Netherlands　J.J. Kroese

ROYAL DUTCH SOCIETY FOR ADVANCEMENT OF PHARMACY — KNMP DRUG DATABANK (844)
P.O. Box 30460　　　　　　　　　　　　Phone: 070 655922
Alexanderstr. 11　　　　　　　　　　　　K.E. Hagenaar
NL-2514 JL The Hague, Netherlands

HUBRECHT LABORATORY — CENTRAL EMBRYOLOGICAL LIBRARY — DOCUMENTATION AND INFORMATION SYSTEM ON DEVELOPMENTAL BIOLOGY (490)
Uppsalalaan 8　　　　　　　　　　　　Phone: 030 510211
NL-3584 CT Utrecht, Netherlands　　Dr. J. Faber

STATE UNIVERSITY OF UTRECHT LIBRARY — BIOMEDICAL INFORMATION DEPARTMENT (899)
Yalelaan 1, P.O. Box 80159　　　　　　Phone: 030 534637
NL-3508 TD Utrecht, Netherlands　　Dr. Christina Verheijen-Voogd

INTERNATIONAL ASSOCIATION FOR STATISTICAL COMPUTING (556)
428 Prinses Beatrixlaan　　　　　　　　Phone: 070 694341
NL-2270 AZ Voorburg, Netherlands　E. Lunenberg

INSTITUTE OF AGRICULTURAL ENGINEERING — IMAG DATASERVICE (543)
Mansholtlaan 10-12　　　　　　　　　Phone: 08370 19119
NL-6708 PA Wageningen, Netherlands　A. Hagting

NETHERLANDS — MINISTRY OF AGRICULTURE AND FISHERIES — AGRICULTURAL RESEARCH DIVISION — CENTRE FOR AGRICULTURAL PUBLISHING AND DOCUMENTATION (731)
P.O. Box 4　　　　　　　　　　　　　Phone: 08370 89222
Gen. Foulkesweg 19　　　　　　　　　J.M. Schippers
NL-6700 AA Wageningen, Netherlands

NETHERLANDS SOIL SURVEY INSTITUTE — SOIL INFORMATION SYSTEM (746)
P.O. Box 98
Prinses Marijkeweg 11
NL-6700 AB Wageningen, Netherlands
Phone: 08370 19100
A.K. Bregt

TIJL DATAPRESS (982)
Blaloweg 20
NL-8041 AH Zwolle, Netherlands
Phone: 05200 10801
G.B.R. Smits

NEW ZEALAND

ADIS PRESS AUSTRALASIA PTY LTD. — ADIS DRUG INFORMATION RETRIEVAL SYSTEM (5)
P.O. Box 34-030, Birkenhead
Auckland 10, New Zealand
Phone: 486-125
G.S. Avery

HANDS-ON LTD. (472)
35-37 Victoria St.
Wellington, New Zealand
Phone: 725224
John W. Schnellenberg

NEW ZEALAND — DEPARTMENT OF SCIENTIFIC AND INDUSTRIAL RESEARCH — DSIR CENTRAL LIBRARY (748)
P.O. Box 9741
Wellington, New Zealand
Phone: 858939
Paul Szentirmay

NEW ZEALAND — DEPARTMENT OF STATISTICS — INFORMATION NETWORK FOR OFFICIAL STATISTICS (749)
Private Bag
Wellington, New Zealand
Phone: 04 729119
R.H. D'Ath

NORWAY

EUROPEAN CONSORTIUM FOR POLITICAL RESEARCH — DATA INFORMATION SERVICE (310)
Hans Holmboesgate 22
N-5000 Bergen, Norway
Phone: 05 212117
Stein Kuhnle

NORWEGIAN RESEARCH COUNCIL FOR SCIENCE AND THE HUMANITIES — NORWEGIAN SOCIAL SCIENCE DATA SERVICES (771)
Hans Holmboesgate 22
N-5000 Bergen, Norway
Phone: 05 212117
Bjorn Henrichsen

UNIVERSITY OF BERGEN — DEPARTMENT OF SCANDINAVIAN LANGUAGES AND LITERATURE — NORWEGIAN TERM BANK (1040)
Stromgaten 53
N-5000 Bergen, Norway
Phone: 05 320040
Kolbjorn Heggstad

NORWEGIAN COMPUTING CENTRE FOR THE HUMANITIES (768)
Harald Harfagresgate 31
P.O. Box 53
N-5014 Bergen-Universitetet, Norway
Phone: 05 320040
Jostein H. Hauge

ROYAL NORWEGIAN COUNCIL FOR SCIENTIFIC AND INDUSTRIAL RESEARCH — NORWEGIAN SEISMIC ARRAY (850)
P.O. Box 51
N-2007 Kjeller, Norway
Phone: 02 716915
Frode Ringdal

NORWAY — MINISTRY OF FINANCES AND CUSTOMS — CENTRAL BUREAU OF STATISTICS (766)
Skippergt. 15
P.O. Box 4131 DEP
Oslo 1, Norway
Phone: 02 413820
Arne Oien

NORWEGIAN CENTER FOR INFORMATICS (767)
Forskningsveien 1
Oslo 3, Norway
Phone: 02 452010
Hans K. Krog

NORWEGIAN STANDARDS ASSOCIATION — STANDARD (772)
P.O. Box 7072 Homansbyen
N-0306 Oslo 3, Norway
Phone: 02 466094
Mr. O.B. Ottesen

SHIP RESEARCH INSTITUTE OF NORWAY — SHIP ABSTRACTS (872)
P.O. Box 6099
Etterstad
Oslo 6, Norway
Phone: 02 689280
Svein Lunde

UNIVERSITY OF OSLO — ROYAL UNIVERSITY LIBRARY — PLANNING DEPARTMENT (1061)
Drammensvegen 42
Oslo 2, Norway
Phone: 02 564980
Tor Blekastad

NORWEGIAN PETROLEUM DIRECTORATE — INFOIL II (769)
P.O. Box 600
Lagardsveien 80
N-4001 Stavanger, Norway
Phone: 04 533160
Grete Schanche

NORWEGIAN PETROLEUM DIRECTORATE — OIL INDEX (770)
P.O. Box 600
Lagardsveien 80
N-4001 Stavanger, Norway
Phone: 04 533160
Grete Schanche

UNIVERSITY OF TRONDHEIM — NORWEGIAN INSTITUTE OF TECHNOLOGY — UNIVERSITY LIBRARY (1079)
N-7034 Trondheim NTH, Norway
Phone: 7 595110
Knut Thalberg

PAKISTAN

PAKISTAN SCIENTIFIC AND TECHNOLOGICAL INFORMATION CENTRE (793)
P-13, El-Markaz Square
Sector F-7/2, P.O. Box 1217
Islamabad, Pakistan
Phone: 24161
Dr. A.R. Mohajir

PERU

PAN AMERICAN HEALTH ORGANIZATION — PAN AMERICAN CENTRE FOR SANITARY ENGINEERING & ENVIRONMENTAL SCIENCES — PAN AMERICAN INFORMATION & DOCUMENTATION NETWORK ON SANITARY ENGINEERING & ENVIRONMENTAL SCIENCES (794)
Los Pinos 259, Camacho
Casilla 4337
Lima 100, Peru
Phone: 35 4135
Orlando Arboleda

PHILIPPINES

SOUTHEAST ASIAN REGIONAL CENTER FOR GRADUATE STUDY AND RESEARCH IN AGRICULTURE — AGRICULTURAL INFORMATION BANK FOR ASIA (889)
College
Laguna 3720, Philippines
Phone: 6735007
Josephine C. Sison

EASTERN TELECOMMUNICATIONS PHILIPPINES, INC. — DATABASE ACCESS SERVICE (288)
Telecoms Plaza
316 Sen. Gil J. Puyat Ave., Makati
Manila, Philippines
Phone: 856011
Vicente Hernandez

PHILIPPINES — NATIONAL INSTITUTE OF SCIENCE AND TECHNOLOGY — DIVISION OF INFORMATION AND DOCUMENTATION (807)
P.O. Box 774
Manila, Philippines
Phone: 503041
Rosario B. De Castro

PHILIPPINES — NATIONAL SCIENCE AND TECHNOLOGY AUTHORITY — SCIENTIFIC CLEARINGHOUSE AND DOCUMENTATION SERVICES DIVISION (808)
Bicutan, Taguig, Metro Manila
P.O. Box 3596
Manila, Philippines
Phone: 8450960
Dr. Irene D. Amores

TECHNOLOGY RESOURCE CENTER — TECHNOBANK PROGRAM (967)
University of Life
Bonifacio Bldg., 3rd Floor
Pasig Metro Manila, Philippines
Phone: 6735162
Aureo P. Castro

POLAND

POLAND — INSTITUTE FOR SCIENTIFIC, TECHNICAL AND ECONOMIC INFORMATION (815)
ul. Zurawia 3/5
00-926 Warsaw, Poland
Phone: 252809
Prof. Dr. Jacek Bankowski

POLAND — POLISH ACADEMY OF SCIENCES — SCIENTIFIC INFORMATION CENTER (816)
Nowy Swiat 72
00-330 Warsaw, Poland
Phone: 268410
Dr. Bronislaw Lugowski

POLISH COMMITTEE OF STANDARDIZATION, MEASURES, AND QUALITY — CENTRE FOR INFORMATION ON STANDARDIZATION AND METROLOGY (817)
Plac Dzierzynskiego 1
00-139 Warsaw, Poland
Phone: 209606
Danuta Planer-Gorska

TECHNICAL UNIVERSITY OF WROCLAW — MAIN LIBRARY AND SCIENTIFIC INFORMATION CENTER — SYSTEM OF COMPUTERIZED PROCESSING OF SCIENTIFIC INFORMATION (965)
Wybrzeze Wyspianskiego 27
50-370 Wroclaw, Poland
Phone: 202305
Stanislaw Bekisz

PORTUGAL

PORTUGAL — NATIONAL INSTITUTE FOR SCIENTIFIC RESEARCH — SCIENTIFIC AND TECHNICAL DOCUMENTATION CENTER (821)
Av. Prof. Gama Pinto 2
1699 Lisbon codex, Portugal
Phone: 11 762891
Carlos Pulido

PORTUGUESE RADIO MARCONI COMPANY — DATA BANK ACCESS SERVICE (822)
Praca Marques de Pombal, 15
1200 Lisbon, Portugal
Phone: 534191
Helena Soares

QATAR

GULF ORGANIZATION FOR INDUSTRIAL CONSULTING — INDUSTRIAL DATA BANK DEPARTMENT (471)
P.O. Box 5114
Doha, Qatar
Phone: 321461

ROMANIA

ROMANIA — NATIONAL COUNCIL FOR SCIENCE AND TECHNOLOGY — NATIONAL INSTITUTE FOR INFORMATION AND DOCUMENTATION (843)
Str. Cosmonautilor, no. 27-29
Sector 1
Bucharest 70141, Romania
Phone: 90 134010
Mr. Anghel Gheorghe

SCOTLAND

UNIVERSITY OF ABERDEEN — DEPARTMENT OF POLITICAL ECONOMY — WAGE ROUNDS DATA BANK (1032)
Aberdeen AB9 2TY, Scotland
Phone: 0224 40241
R.F. Elliott

UNIVERSITY OF DUNDEE — LAW LIBRARY — EUROPEAN DOCUMENTATION CENTRE (1047)
Perth Rd.
Dundee DD1 4HN, Scotland
Phone: 0382 23181
David R. Hart

SCIENTIFIC DOCUMENTATION CENTRE LTD. (868)
Halbeath House
Dunfermline, Fife KY12 0TZ, Scotland
Phone: 0383 23535

CAPITAL PLANNING INFORMATION LTD. (176)
6 Castle St.
Edinburgh, Scotland
Phone: 031 2264367
Brenda White

SCOTLAND — NATIONAL LIBRARY OF SCOTLAND — SCOTTISH LIBRARIES CO-OPERATIVE AUTOMATION PROJECT (869)
George IV Bridge
Edinburgh EH1 1EW, Scotland
Phone: 031 2264531
Bernard Gallivan

SINGAPORE

ASIAN NETWORK FOR INDUSTRIAL TECHNOLOGY INFORMATION AND EXTENSION (34)
RELC International House, Rm. 803
30 Orange Grove Rd.
Singapore 1025, Republic of Singapore
Phone: 7343331
Dr. Leon V. Chico

CENTRE OF INFORMATION RESOURCE & TECHNOLOGY, SINGAPORE (197)
170, Upper Bukit Timah Rd.
No. 05-08
Singapore 2158, Republic of Singapore
Phone: 4684192
Ernest Kwan-Boon Tan

INFORMATION SYSTEMS DESIGN (534)
3 Greenleaf Place
Singapore 1027, Republic of Singapore
Phone: 4689555
Nancy Rasmussen

SINGAPORE INSTITUTE OF STANDARDS AND INDUSTRIAL RESEARCH — INDUSTRIAL TECHNICAL INFORMATION SERVICE (877)
P.O. Box 2611
179 River Valley Rd.
Singapore 0617, Republic of Singapore
Phone: 3360933
Mrs. Tan Kim Swee

SOUTH AFRICA

SVP SOUTH AFRICA LTD. (917)
P.O. Box 92400
Norwood 2117
Johannesburg, South Africa
Phone: 728 7410
Michael W. Katcs

SOUTH AFRICA — COUNCIL FOR SCIENTIFIC AND INDUSTRIAL RESEARCH — CENTRE FOR SCIENTIFIC AND TECHNICAL INFORMATION (885)
P.O. Box 395
Pretoria 0001, South Africa
Phone: 012 869211
Dr. Rob van Houten

SOUTH AFRICA — NUCLEAR DEVELOPMENT CORPORATION OF SOUTH AFRICA — NUCOR LIBRARY AND INFORMATION SERVICES (886)
Private Mail Bag X256
Pretoria 0001, South Africa
Phone: 012 213311
S.P. Korkie

SOUTH AFRICA — SOUTH AFRICAN WATER INFORMATION CENTRE (887)
P.O. Box 395
Pretoria 0001, South Africa
Phone: 012 869211

SOUTH AFRICAN MEDICAL RESEARCH COUNCIL — INSTITUTE FOR MEDICAL LITERATURE (888)
P.O. Box 70
Tygerberg 7505, South Africa
Phone: 21 9312151
Dr. Steve F. Rossouw

SPAIN

SABADELL COMPUTING CENTER (860)
Carretera Ripollet a Santiga
Km. 2'750, Barbera del Valles
Barcelona, Spain
Phone: 3 7181699
J.A. Diaz

SPAIN — MINISTRY OF HEALTH AND SAFETY — NATIONAL INSTITUTE OF OCCUPATIONAL SAFETY AND HEALTH — NATIONAL INFORMATION AND DOCUMENTATION CENTER (892)
Calle Dulcet, s/n
Barcelona 08034, Spain
Phone: 932044500
Domenec Turuguet Mayol

SVP ESPANA (912)
Diagonal, 508 4a
Barcelona 08006, Spain
Phone: 93 2176463
Xavier Grau

SPAIN — HIGHER COUNCIL FOR SCIENTIFIC RESEARCH — INSTITUTE FOR INFORMATION AND DOCUMENTATION IN SCIENCE AND TECHNOLOGY   (890)
Joaquin Costa, 22
Madrid 6, Spain
Phone: 91 2614808
Rosa de la Viesca

SPAIN — HIGHER COUNCIL FOR SCIENTIFIC RESEARCH — INSTITUTE FOR INFORMATION AND DOCUMENTATION IN THE SOCIAL SCIENCES AND HUMANITIES   (891)
Vitrubio 4, 6a
Madrid 6, Spain
Phone: 2627755
Aida Mendez

SPANISH DRUG INFORMATION CENTER — SPANISH PHARMACEUTICAL SPECIALITIES DATA BANK   (893)
Calle Valenzuela 5 - 2 Izqda.
Madrid 14, Spain
Phone: 91 2324300
Antonio Garcia Inesta

UNIVERSITY OF VALENCIA — BIOMEDICAL DOCUMENTATION AND INFORMATION CENTER   (1082)
Avda. Blasco Ibanez, 17
Valencia 10, Spain
Phone: 96 3610373
Prof. Maria-Luz Terrada Ferrandis

SWEDEN

SWEDEN — SWEDISH NATIONAL ROAD ADMINISTRATION — TECHNICAL DIVISION — ROAD DATA BANK   (933)
S-781 87 Borlange, Sweden
Phone: 0243 75000
Per Genberg

UNIVERSITY OF GOTHENBURG — MEDICINDATA   (1049)
P.O. Box 33031
S-400 33 Gothenburg, Sweden
Phone: 031 411110

UPDATE AB   (1090)
P.O. Box 53120
S-400 15 Gothenburg, Sweden
Phone: 031 178390
Ronny Korsberg

LINKOPING UNIVERSITY LIBRARY — NYTTFO   (665)
S-581 83 Linkoping, Sweden
Phone: 13 281000

SWEDEN — NATIONAL ROAD AND TRAFFIC RESEARCH INSTITUTE — INFORMATION AND DOCUMENTATION SECTION   (925)
S-581 01 Linkoping, Sweden
Phone: 013 115200

BTJ   (116)
Tornavagen 9, Box 1706
S-221 01 Lund, Sweden
Phone: 046 140480
Jan Gumpert

STUDSVIK ENERGITEKNIK AB — REPORT COLLECTION INDEX   (906)
Studsvik Library
S-611 82 Nykoping, Sweden
Phone: 155 80000

ESSELTE BUSINESS INFORMATION   (301)
Box 1391
S-171 27 Solna, Sweden
Phone: 08 7343400
Staffan Nordstrand

SWEDEN — NATIONAL BOARD OF OCCUPATIONAL SAFETY AND HEALTH — CIS CENTRE   (923)
S-171 84 Solna, Sweden
Phone: 08 7309585
Per Odelycke

SWEDEN — NATIONAL SWEDISH ENVIRONMENT PROTECTION BOARD — SWEDISH ENVIRONMENTAL RESEARCH INDEX   (926)
Box 1302
S-171 25 Solna, Sweden
Phone: 08 981800

BONNIER BUSINESS PUBLISHING GROUP — AFFARSDATA   (94)
P.O. Box 3188
S-103 63 Stockholm, Sweden
Phone: 08 7364000

DATAARKIV AB   (260)
P.O. Box 12079
S-102 22 Stockholm, Sweden
Phone: 08 165220
Goran Tamm

ESSELTE GROUP OF BOOKSELLERS — ESSELTE DOCUMENTATION SYSTEM   (302)
P.O. Box 62
S-101 20 Stockholm, Sweden
Phone: 08 237990
Lars-Erik Eriksson

INTERFACT/SVP AB   (553)
Kungsgatan 29
P.O. Box 7037
S-10386 Stockholm, Sweden
Phone: 08 145545
Sven Hamrefors

INTERNATIONAL ASSOCIATION FOR THE EVALUATION OF EDUCATIONAL ACHIEVEMENT — IEA DATA BANK   (557)
Inst. of International Education
University of Stockholm
S-106 91 Stockholm, Sweden
Phone: 08 156656
Richard Noonan

K-KONSULT — VA-NYTT   (637)
Library
Liljeholmstorget 7
S-117 80 Stockholm, Sweden
Phone: 08 7440000
Gunnar Dravnieks

PARALOG — 3RIP   (795)
P.O. Box 2284
S-103 17 Stockholm, Sweden
Phone: 08 144190

PRESSURKLIPP — SWEDISH MARKET INFORMATION BANK   (824)
S-112 85 Stockholm, Sweden
Phone: 08 541420
Ingemar Larsson

SCANNET FOUNDATION   (864)
Halsingegatan 47
S-113 31 Stockholm, Sweden
Phone: 08 305940
Malin Edstrom

STOCKHOLM SCHOOL OF ECONOMICS — ECONOMICS RESEARCH INSTITUTE — FINDATA   (903)
Skeppsbron 22
S-111 30 Stockholm, Sweden
Phone: 08 238230
Erik Eklund

STOCKHOLM UNIVERSITY COMPUTING CENTER, QZ   (904)
P.O. Box 27322
S-102 54 Stockholm, Sweden
Phone: 08 679280
Bengt Olsen

SWEDEN — KAROLINSKA INSTITUTE LIBRARY AND INFORMATION CENTER   (921)
P.O. Box 60201
1 Solnavagen
S-104 01 Stockholm, Sweden
Phone: 08 340560
Dr. Hans Baude

SWEDEN — NATIONAL LIBRARY FOR PSYCHOLOGY AND EDUCATION   (924)
P.O. Box 50063
Frescati Hagvag 10
S-104 05 Stockholm, Sweden
Phone: 08 151820
Elin Ekman

SWEDEN — NATIONAL SWEDISH TELECOMMUNICATIONS ADMINISTRATION — DATAPAK   (927)
P.O. Box 7294
S-103 90 Stockholm, Sweden
Phone: 08 7808750
Bo Adolfsson

SWEDEN — PATENT AND REGISTRATION OFFICE — INTERPAT SWEDEN   (928)
P.O. Box 5055
S-102 42 Stockholm, Sweden
Phone: 08 7822885
Jan Averdal

SWEDEN — RESEARCH INSTITUTE OF NATIONAL DEFENSE — FOA INDEX GROUP   (929)
Box 27322
S-102 54 Stockholm, Sweden
Phone: 08 631500
Olov Lidman

SWEDEN — ROYAL INSTITUTE OF TECHNOLOGY LIBRARY — INFORMATION AND DOCUMENTATION CENTER   (930)
S-100 44 Stockholm, Sweden
Phone: 08 7878950
Marie Wallin

SWEDEN — ROYAL LIBRARY — LIBRARY INFORMATION SYSTEM   (931)
P.O. Box 5039
S-102 41 Stockholm, Sweden
Phone: 08 241040
Mari Bud

SWEDEN — STATISTICS SWEDEN — STATISTICAL DATA BASES UNIT   (932)
S-115 81 Stockholm, Sweden
Phone: 08 140560
Jan Eklof

SWEDISH BUILDING CENTRE — BUILDING COMMODITY FILE   (934)
P.O. Box 7853
S-103 99 Stockholm, Sweden
Phone: 08 7305100

SWEDISH CENTER FOR WORKING LIFE — INFORMATION AND DOCUMENTATION DEPARTMENT   (935)
P.O. Box 5606
S-114 86 Stockholm, Sweden
Phone: 08 229980

SWEDISH COUNCIL FOR INFORMATION ON ALCOHOL AND OTHER DRUGS (936)
S-102 54 Stockholm, Sweden

SWEDISH DELEGATION FOR SCIENTIFIC AND TECHNICAL INFORMATION (937)
P.O. Box 43033
Liljeholmstorget 7
S-100 72 Stockholm, Sweden
Phone: 08 7442840
Bjorn Thomasson

SWEDISH INSTITUTE OF BUILDING DOCUMENTATION (938)
Halsingegatan 49
S-113 31 Stockholm, Sweden
Phone: 08 340170
Adolf Stern

SWEDISH MECHANICAL AND ELECTRICAL ENGINEERING TRADE ASSOCIATION — VERA (939)
P.O. Box 5506
S-114 85 Stockholm, Sweden
Phone: 08 7838000
Ralph Stroemfelt

SWEDISH STANDARDS INSTITUTION — REGIS (940)
P.O. Box 3295
S-103 66 Stockholm, Sweden
Phone: 08 230400
Erik Sjostrom

TESS SEARCH SERVICE (979)
P.O. Box 3295
S-103 66 Stockholm, Sweden
Phone: 08 230400

TT NEWSBANK (990)
Kungsholmstorg 5
S-105 12 Stockholm, Sweden
Phone: 08 132600
Gun-Britt Balck

UNIVERSITY OF UMEA — DEMOGRAPHIC DATA BASE (1081)
Phone: 090 165723
S-901 87 Umea, Sweden
Prof. Jan Sundin

SWEDEN — GEOLOGICAL SURVEY OF SWEDEN — GROUNDWATER DOCUMENTATION SECTION (920)
Box 670
S-751 28 Uppsala, Sweden
Phone: 018 179000
Tommy Olsson

SWEDEN — NATIONAL BOARD OF HEALTH AND WELFARE — DEPARTMENT OF DRUGS — SWEDISH DRUG INFORMATION SYSTEM (922)
P.O. Box 607
S-751 25 Uppsala, Sweden
Phone: 018 174600
Per Manell

SWEDISH UNIVERSITY OF AGRICULTURAL SCIENCES — ULTUNA LIBRARY — DOCUMENTATION SECTION (941)
Phone: 018 171000
S-750 07 Uppsala, Sweden
Brita Rufelt

WORLD HEALTH ORGANIZATION — WHO COLLABORATING CENTRE FOR INTERNATIONAL DRUG MONITORING (1115)
P.O. Box 607
S-751 25 Uppsala, Sweden
Phone: 018 155880

SWITZERLAND

SWISS COORDINATION CENTER FOR RESEARCH IN EDUCATION (945)
Entfelderstr. 61
CH-5000 Aarau, Switzerland
Phone: 064 211916
Armin Gretler

SVP CONSEIL (911)
Kaufhausgasse 7
CH-4001 Basel, Switzerland
Phone: 061 238470

DATA-STAR (266)
Radio Suisse Ltd.
Schwarztorstr. 61
CH-3000 Berne 14, Switzerland
Phone: 031 659111
Hans R. Probst

SWISS ACADEMY OF MEDICAL SCIENCES — DOCUMENTATION SERVICE (943)
Waldheimstr. 20
CH-3012 Berne, Switzerland
Phone: 031 232572
Dr. Zdenek Urbanek

SWITZERLAND — SWISS INTELLECTUAL PROPERTY OFFICE — TECHNICAL INFORMATION ON PATENTS (948)
Einsteinstr. 2
CH-3003 Berne, Switzerland
Phone: 031 614806
Mr. R. Egli

UNIVERSAL POSTAL UNION — INTERNATIONAL BUREAU — STATISTICS OF POSTAL SERVICES (1030)
Weltpoststr. 4
CH-3000 Berne 15, Switzerland
Phone: 031 432211
Mohamed Ibrahim Sobhi

INTERNATIONAL FEDERATION FOR INFORMATION PROCESSING (580)
3, rue de Marche
CH-1204 Geneva, Switzerland
Phone: 022 282649
K. Ando

INTERNATIONAL LABOUR OFFICE — BUREAU FOR LABOUR PROBLEMS ANALYSIS — LABOUR INFORMATION DATABASE (591)
4, route des Morillons
CH-1211 Geneva 22, Switzerland
Phone: 022 996759
Mrs. H. Sarfati

INTERNATIONAL LABOUR OFFICE — BUREAU OF STATISTICS (592)
4, route des Morillons
CH-1211 Geneva 22, Switzerland
Phone: 022 996111
Dr. R. Turvey

INTERNATIONAL LABOUR OFFICE — CENTRAL LIBRARY AND DOCUMENTATION BRANCH (593)
4, route des Morillons
CH-1211 Geneva 22, Switzerland
Phone: 022 998676
Kate Wild

INTERNATIONAL LABOUR OFFICE — CONDITIONS OF WORK AND WELFARE FACILITIES BRANCH — CLEARING-HOUSE ON CONDITIONS OF WORK (594)
Phone: 022 997078
CH-1211 Geneva 22, Switzerland
Linda Stoddart

INTERNATIONAL LABOUR OFFICE — INTERNATIONAL OCCUPATIONAL SAFETY AND HEALTH INFORMATION CENTRE (595)
Phone: 022 996740
CH-1211 Geneva 22, Switzerland
Herbert Siegel

INTERNATIONAL ORGANIZATION FOR STANDARDIZATION — ISO INFORMATION NETWORK (599)
ISO Central Secretariat
1, rue de Varembe
CH-1211 Geneva 20, Switzerland
Phone: 022 341240
Mr. Olle Sturen

INTERNATIONAL REFUGEE INTEGRATION RESOURCE CENTRE (602)
5-7, ave. de la Paix
CH-1202, Geneva, Switzerland
Phone: 022 310261
Dr. Mark Braham

INTERNATIONAL TELECOMMUNICATION UNION (606)
Place des Nations
CH-1211 Geneva 20, Switzerland
Phone: 022 995511
R.E. Butler

UNITED NATIONS — ADVISORY COMMITTEE FOR THE CO-ORDINATION OF INFORMATION SYSTEMS (1001)
Pavillons du Petit-Saconnex
16, ave. Jean-Trembley
CH-1209 Geneva, Switzerland
Phone: 022 346011
George Thompson

UNITED NATIONS EDUCATIONAL, SCIENTIFIC AND CULTURAL ORGANIZATION — INTERNATIONAL BUREAU OF EDUCATION — DOCUMENTATION AND INFORMATION UNIT (1021)
P.O. Box 199
CH-1211 Geneva 20, Switzerland
Phone: 022 981455
Aida M. Furtado

UNITED NATIONS ENVIRONMENT PROGRAMME — INTERNATIONAL REGISTER OF POTENTIALLY TOXIC CHEMICALS (1026)
Palais des Nations
CH-1211 Geneva 10, Switzerland
Phone: 022 985850
Jan W. Huismans

WORLD HEALTH ORGANIZATION — DIVISION OF HEALTH STATISTICS — WORLD HEALTH STATISTICS DATA BASE (1110)
20, ave. Appia
CH-1211 Geneva 27, Switzerland
Phone: 022 912111

WORLD HEALTH ORGANIZATION — DIVISION OF NONCOMMUNICABLE DISEASES — ORAL HEALTH UNIT — GLOBAL ORAL DATA BANK (1111)
CH-1211 Geneva 27, Switzerland

WORLD INTELLECTUAL PROPERTY ORGANIZATION — PERMANENT COMMITTEE ON PATENT INFORMATION (1116)
34, chemin des Colombettes
CH-1211 Geneva 20, Switzerland
Phone: 022 999111
Paul Claus

WORLD METEOROLOGICAL ORGANIZATION — COMMISSION FOR HYDROLOGY — OPERATIONAL HYDROLOGY PROGRAMME — HYDROLOGICAL OPERATIONAL MULTIPURPOSE SUBPROGRAMME   (1117)
Case Postale No. 5
41, avenue Giuseppe Motta
CH-1211 Geneva 20, Switzerland
Phone: 022 346400
Prof. J. Nemec

WORLD METEOROLOGICAL ORGANIZATION — WORLD CLIMATE PROGRAMME DEPARTMENT — WORLD CLIMATE DATA INFORMATION REFERRAL SERVICE   (1118)
Case Postale No. 5
41, ave. Giuseppe Motta
CH-1211 Geneva 20, Switzerland
Phone: 022 346400
Dr. Thomas D. Potter

WORLD METEOROLOGICAL ORGANIZATION — WORLD WEATHER WATCH   (1119)
Case Postale No. 5
41, ave. Giuseppe Motta
CH-1211 Geneva 20, Switzerland
Phone: 022 346400

LIBRARY NETWORK OF SIBIL USERS   (664)
University of Lausanne Libraries
6, place de la Riponne
CH-1005 Lausanne, Switzerland
Phone: 021 228831
Jean-Pierre Clavel

SWISS CENTER OF DOCUMENTATION IN MICROTECHNOLOGY   (944)
Rue Breguet 2
CH-2000 Neuchatel 7, Switzerland
Phone: 038 254181
Bernard Chapuis

ALPINE SCIENCE INFORMATION SERVICE   (21)
CH-3813 Saxeten, Switzerland
Phone: 036 231041
Dr. Robert Utzinger

IMS A.G. — MIDAS   (504)
Gartenstr. 2
CH-6300 Zug, Switzerland
Phone: 42 215323

FEDERAL TECHNICAL UNIVERSITY — TECHNICAL CHEMISTRY LABORATORY — CHEMCO PHYSICAL PROPERTIES DATA BANK   (327)
ETH-Zentrum
Universitatstr. 6
CH-8092 Zurich, Switzerland
Phone: 01 2562211
Prof. D.W.T. Rippin

KOMPASS INTERNATIONAL LTD.   (642)
Neuhausstr. 4
CH-8044 Zurich, Switzerland
Phone: 01 478009
Max E. Neuenschwander

RINGIER & CO. — RINGIER DOCUMENTATION CENTER   (841)
Pressehaus, Dufourstr. 23
CH-8008 Zurich, Switzerland
Phone: 01 2596111

SWISS VIEWDATA INFORMATION PROVIDERS ASSOCIATION   (946)
P.O. Box 184
CH-8021 Zurich, Switzerland
Phone: 01 2213187
Erwin A. Nigg

SWISS WILDLIFE INFORMATION SERVICE   (947)
Strickhofstr. 39
CH-8057 Zurich, Switzerland
Phone: 01 3627728
Rolf Anderegg

TELEKURS AG — INVESTDATA SYSTEM   (975)
Neugasse 247
CH-8021 Zurich, Switzerland
Phone: 01 2752111
Max Ruegg

TAIWAN

INSTITUTE FOR INFORMATION INDUSTRY   (542)
116 Nanking E Rd.
Sec. 2, 10th Floor
Taipei, Republic of China
Phone: 02 5422540
C.M. Wang

NATIONAL SCIENCE COUNCIL — SCIENCE AND TECHNOLOGY INFORMATION CENTER   (726)
P.O. Box 4, Nankang
Taipei, Republic of China
Phone: 02 7822183
Chung-Ling Liu

TANZANIA

TANZANIA — NATIONAL CENTRAL LIBRARY — TANZANIA NATIONAL DOCUMENTATION CENTRE   (955)
P.O. Box 9283
Dar es Salaam, Tanzania
Phone: 26121
Mr. E.A. Mwinyimvua

THAILAND

ASIAN INSTITUTE OF TECHNOLOGY — REGIONAL DOCUMENTATION CENTER — ASIAN INFORMATION CENTER FOR GEOTECHNICAL ENGINEERING   (30)
P.O. Box 2754
Bangkok 10501, Thailand
Phone: 523 9300
Dr. Jacques Valls

ASIAN INSTITUTE OF TECHNOLOGY — REGIONAL DOCUMENTATION CENTER — ENVIRONMENTAL SANITATION INFORMATION CENTER   (31)
P.O. Box 2754
Bangkok 10501, Thailand
Phone: 523 9300
Dr. Jacques Valls

ASIAN INSTITUTE OF TECHNOLOGY — REGIONAL DOCUMENTATION CENTER — INTERNATIONAL FERROCEMENT INFORMATION CENTER   (32)
P.O. Box 2754
Bangkok 10501, Thailand
Phone: 523 9300
Dr. Jacques Valls

ASIAN INSTITUTE OF TECHNOLOGY — REGIONAL DOCUMENTATION CENTER — RENEWABLE ENERGY RESOURCES INFORMATION CENTER   (33)
P.O. Box 2754
Bangkok 10501, Thailand
Phone: 523 9300
Dr. Jacques Valls

UNITED NATIONS — ECONOMIC AND SOCIAL COMMISSION FOR ASIA AND THE PACIFIC — ESCAP LIBRARY — ESCAP BIBLIOGRAPHIC INFORMATION SYSTEM   (1002)
United Nations Bldg.
Rajadamnern Ave.
Bangkok 10200, Thailand
Phone: 282 9161
N. Peter Cummins

UNITED NATIONS — ECONOMIC AND SOCIAL COMMISSION FOR ASIA AND THE PACIFIC — POPULATION DIVISION — POPULATION CLEARING-HOUSE AND INFORMATION SECTION   (1003)
United Nations Bldg.
Rajadamnern Ave.
Bangkok 10200, Thailand
Phone: 282 9161
Helen K. Kolbe

UNITED NATIONS — ECONOMIC AND SOCIAL COMMISSION FOR ASIA AND THE PACIFIC — STATISTICS DIVISION — UN/ESCAP STATISTICAL INFORMATION SERVICES   (1004)
United Nations Bldg.
Rajadamnern Ave.
Bangkok 10200, Thailand
Phone: 282 9161
Mr. M.A. Sahib

TRINIDAD AND TOBAGO

CARIBBEAN INDUSTRIAL RESEARCH INSTITUTE — TECHNICAL INFORMATION SERVICE   (177)
Tunapuna Post Office
Trinidad, Rep. of Trinidad and Tobago
Phone: 663 4171
Barbara Gumbs

TUNISIA

LEAGUE OF ARAB STATES — LEAGUE OF ARAB STATES DOCUMENTATION AND INFORMATION CENTER   (653)
37, Khereddine Pacha St.
Tunis, Tunisia
Phone: 890100
Mrs. Faria Zahawi

TURKEY

TURKEY — SCIENTIFIC AND TECHNICAL RESEARCH COUNCIL OF TURKEY — TURKISH SCIENTIFIC AND TECHNICAL DOCUMENTATION CENTER   (991)
Ataturk Bulvari 221
Kavaklidere
Ankara, Turkey
Phone: 262770

UNION OF SOVIET SOCIALIST REPUBLICS

UNION OF SOVIET SOCIALIST REPUBLICS — ACADEMY OF SCIENCES OF THE U.S.S.R. — INSTITUTE FOR THEORETICAL ASTRONOMY — MINOR PLANETS, COMETS, AND SATELLITES DEPARTMENT (997)
Naberezhnaya Kutuzova 10
191187 Leningrad, U.S.S.R.
Phone: 272 9083
Prof. Yu. V. Batrakov

INTERNATIONAL CENTRE FOR SCIENTIFIC AND TECHNICAL INFORMATION (565)
Kuusinena 21-b
125252 Moscow, U.S.S.R.
Phone: 198 7230
Leonid N. Sumarokov

UNION OF SOVIET SOCIALIST REPUBLICS — ACADEMY OF SCIENCES OF THE U.S.S.R. — ASTRONOMICAL COUNCIL DATA CENTER — MANAGEMENT SYSTEM FOR ASTRONOMICAL DATA IN MACHINE-READABLE FORM (995)
Pyatnitskaya 48
109017 Moscow, U.S.S.R.
Phone: 233 1702

UNION OF SOVIET SOCIALIST REPUBLICS — ACADEMY OF SCIENCES OF THE U.S.S.R. — INSTITUTE FOR HIGH TEMPERATURES — THERMOPHYSICAL PROPERTIES CENTER (996)
Korovinskoje r., IVTAN
127412, Moscow I-412, U.S.S.R.
Phone: 4859572
Dr. Victor F. Baibuz

UNION OF SOVIET SOCIALIST REPUBLICS — ALL-UNION INSTITUTE OF SCIENTIFIC AND TECHNICAL INFORMATION (998)
Baltiyskaya Ulitsa 14
Moscow A-219, U.S.S.R.
Phone: 151 5501

UNION OF SOVIET SOCIALIST REPUBLICS — U.S.S.R. STATE COMMITTEE ON THE UTILIZATION OF ATOMIC ENERGY — CENTER FOR NUCLEAR STRUCTURE AND REACTION DATA (999)
Kurchatov Atomic Energy Institute
196182 Moscow, U.S.S.R.
Phone: 1961557
Dr. F.E. Chukreev

INSTITUTE OF PHYSICS AND ENERGY — NUCLEAR DATA CENTER (546)
Obninsk, U.S.S.R.

WALES

ASSOCIATION FOR LITERARY AND LINGUISTIC COMPUTING (37)
University College of North Wales
Department of English
Bangor, Gwynedd LL57 2DG, Wales
Phone: 0248 351151
Dr. Thomas N. Corns

GREAT BRITAIN — DEPARTMENT OF TRADE AND INDUSTRY — BUSINESS STATISTICS OFFICE (454)
Government Bldgs.
Cardiff Rd.
Newport, Gwent NPT 1XG, Wales
Phone: 0633 56111
Mr. R. Ash

YUGOSLAVIA

BORIS KIDRIC INSTITUTE OF NUCLEAR SCIENCES — LABORATORY FOR INFORMATION SYSTEMS (96)
P.O. Box 522
YU-11000 Belgrade, Yugoslavia
Phone: 011 444961
Dr. Miodrag Petrovic

YUGOSLAV CENTER FOR TECHNICAL AND SCIENTIFIC DOCUMENTATION (1121)
Slobodana Penezica-Krcuna 29/31
P.O. Box 724
YU-11000 Belgrade, Yugoslavia
Phone: 644184
Alexsic Miodrag

SUBJECT INDEX

An index to the general and specific subject interests reported by the organizations described in this book. Emphasis is on thorough indexing of subjects covered by computer-readable data bases and their print counterparts, although selected information industry service activities are also indexed here. Terms used are based on a modified Library of Congress subject heading list, including "see" and "see also" references. Entries in this index now include organization and service name, followed by the entry number in parentheses.

SUBJECT INDEX

Abstracting (See also Indexing)
   Indexing and Abstracting Society of Canada   (506)
   International Council of Scientific Unions Abstracting Board   (575)
   University of London — Central Information Service   (1055)

Academic dissertations SEE: Dissertations, academic

Accounting
   Great Britain — Department of Trade and Industry — Business Statistics Office   (454)

Acoustics
   France — National Telecommunications Research Center — Interministerial Documentation Service — TELEDOC   (367)

Acquisitions, automated library SEE: Automated library acquisitions

Administration, business SEE: Business and business administration

Administration, educational SEE: Educational administration

Administration, hospital SEE: Hospital administration

Administration, personnel SEE: Personnel administration

Administration, public SEE: Public administration

Adult education SEE: Education, adult

Advertising and marketing
   Admedia — Adfacts   (6)
   British Market Research Bureau Ltd. — Target Group Index   (109)
   Center for the Study of Advertising Support   (189)
   Compusearch Market and Social Research Ltd.   (236)
   DataArkiv AB   (260)
   Eastern Counties Newspapers — Eastel   (287)
   Harris Media Systems Ltd.   (475)
   Japan Data Service Co., Ltd.   (631)
   Market Research Society — Market Research Abstracts   (687)
   Marketing Intelligence Corporation   (688)
   Nihon Keizai Shimbun, Inc. — Databank Bureau — Nikkei Economic Electronic Databank System-Time Sharing   (754)
   Overseas Data Service, Company, Ltd.   (789)
   Pira: Research Association for the Paper and Board, Printing and Packaging Industries — Comprehensive Information Services   (812)
   PMB Print Measurement Bureau   (814)
   Pressurklipp — Swedish Market Information Bank   (824)

Aerodynamics
   BHRA, The Fluid Engineering Centre — Information Services   (86)
   ESDU International Limited   (299)

Aeronautical safety SEE: Flight safety

Aeronautics
   European Space Agency — Information Retrieval Service   (317)
   Information Center for Energy, Physics, Mathematics   (521)

Aerospace SEE: Aeronautics; Astronautics; Space technology

Africa
   African Training and Research Centre in Administration for Development — African Network of Administrative Information   (7)
   Center for Research and Studies on Mediterranean Societies   (186)
   German Foundation for International Development — Documentation Center   (397)
   Royal Museum of Central Africa — Center for Informatics Applied to Development and Tropical Agriculture — Agroclimatology Data Bank   (846)
   United Nations — Economic Commission for Africa — Pan-African Documentation and Information System   (1005)
   York University — Institute for Behavioural Research   (1120)

Agricultural chemistry (See also Fertilizers; Pesticides)
   Derwent Publications Ltd. — Patents Documentation Services   (275)
   Derwent Publications Ltd. — Pest Control Literature Documentation   (276)

Agricultural economics
   Alberta Department of Agriculture — Economic Services Division — Agricultural Commodities Data Base   (9)
   Association for the Promotion of Industry-Agriculture — International Documentation Center for Industries Using Agricultural Products   (39)
   Bavarian Ministry for Food, Agriculture and Forestry — Bavarian Agricultural Information System   (76)
   Canada — Agriculture Canada — Marketing and Economics Branch — Agricultural Marketing and Trade Database   (126)
   Commonwealth Agricultural Bureaux — CAB Abstracts   (229)
   Germany — Center for Agricultural Documentation and Information   (408)
   International Center for Higher Studies in Mediterranean Agronomy — Socioeconomic Data Bank on the Mediterranean Countries   (564)
   United Nations — Food and Agriculture Organization — Library and Documentation Systems Division — David Lubin Memorial Library   (1013)
   United Nations — Food and Agriculture Organization — Statistics Division — Interlinked Computerized Storage and Processing System of Food and Agricultural Data   (1014)

Agricultural engineering
   Institute of Agricultural Engineering — IMAG Dataservice   (543)
   VDI-Verlag GmbH — VDI News Data Base   (1096)

Agricultural libraries
   Brazil — Ministry of Agriculture — National Center for Agricultural Documentary Information   (99)
   International Association of Agricultural Librarians and Documentalists   (558)

Agricultural research
   Canada — Agriculture Canada — Scientific Information Retrieval Section — Pesticide Research Information System   (128)
   Canadian Agricultural Research Council — Inventory of Canadian Agricultural Research   (167)
   Commission of the European Communities — Agricultural Research Projects Data Base   (213)
   Commission of the European Communities — Euro Abstracts   (218)
   Germany — Center for Agricultural Documentation and Information   (408)
   Indian Council of Agricultural Research — Agricultural Research Information Centre   (510)
   Netherlands Organization for Applied Scientific Research — National Council for Agricultural Research TNO — Central Project Administration for Current Agricultural Research in the Netherlands   (742)
   United Nations — Food and Agriculture Organization — Current Agricultural Research Information System   (1009)

Agriculture
   Agra Europe   (8)
   Australia — Commonwealth Scientific and Industrial Research Organization — Central Information, Library and Editorial Section   (47)
   Bavarian Ministry for Food, Agriculture and Forestry — Bavarian Agricultural Information System   (76)
   Brazil — Ministry of Agriculture — National Center for Agricultural Documentary Information   (99)
   Bulgaria — National Agro-Industrial Union — Agricultural Academy — Center for Scientific, Technical and Economic Information   (121)
   Canada — Statistics Canada — Canadian Socio-Economic Information Management System   (159)
   Commission of the European Communities — Agricultural Research Projects Data Base   (213)
   Commission of the European Communities — Statistical Office of the European Communities — CRONOS Data Bank   (225)
   Commonwealth Agricultural Bureaux — CAB Abstracts   (229)
   Computer Sciences of Australia Pty. Ltd. — Network Services Division — INFOBANK   (237)
   Conference Board of Canada — Applied Economic Research and Information Centre — AERIC System   (238)
   France — National Center for Scientific Research — Scientific and Technical Documentation Center   (356)
   France — National Institute of Statistics and Economic Studies — Information System for the Economy   (364)
   Germany — Center for Agricultural Documentation and Information   (408)
   Group for the Study and Research of Tropical Agronomy — AGRITROP   (467)
   Indian Council of Agricultural Research — Agricultural Research Information Centre   (510)
   Infomart — Grassroots   (519)
   Institute of Agricultural Engineering — IMAG Dataservice   (543)
   Institute of Research on Fruits and Citrus Fruits — Documentation Center   (547)
   International Association of Agricultural Librarians and Documentalists   (558)
   International Center for Higher Studies in Mediterranean Agronomy — Socioeconomic Data Bank on the Mediterranean Countries   (564)
   Netherlands — Ministry of Agriculture and Fisheries — Agricultural Research Division — Centre for Agricultural Publishing and Documentation   (731)
   Nihon Keizai Shimbun, Inc. — Databank Bureau — Nikkei Economic Electronic Databank System-Time Sharing   (754)

SUBJECT INDEX

Royal Museum of Central Africa — Center for Informatics Applied to Development and Tropical Agriculture — Agroclimatology Data Bank (846)
Royal Tropical Institute — Agricultural Information & Documentation Section (857)
Saskatchewan Telecommunications — Agritex (862)
Southeast Asian Regional Center for Graduate Study and Research in Agriculture — Agricultural Information Bank for Asia (889)
Swedish University of Agricultural Sciences — Ultuna Library — Documentation Section (941)
United Nations — Food and Agriculture Organization — International Information System for the Agricultural Sciences and Technology (1012)
United Nations — Food and Agriculture Organization — Library and Documentation Systems Division — David Lubin Memorial Library (1013)
United Nations — Food and Agriculture Organization — Statistics Division — Interlinked Computerized Storage and Processing System of Food and Agricultural Data (1014)

Agronomy SEE: Agriculture

Air pollution SEE: Pollution, air

Air transportation (See also Flight safety)
American Express Europe Ltd. — SkyGuide (23)
Association of European Airlines — AEA Data Base (41)
Aviation Information Services Ltd. (68)
Canada — Transport Canada — Library and Information Centre (161)
International Civil Aviation Organization — Air Navigation Bureau — Accident Investigation and Prevention Section — Aircraft Accident/Incident Reporting System (567)
International Civil Aviation Organization — Air Navigation Bureau — Aerodromes Section — Airport Characteristics Data Bank (568)
International Civil Aviation Organization — Air Transport Bureau — Statistics Section — Air Transport Statistical Program (569)
Sharp Associates Limited (871)

Aircraft
Aviation Information Services Ltd. (68)
ESDU International Limited (299)
International Civil Aviation Organization — Air Navigation Bureau — Accident Investigation and Prevention Section — Aircraft Accident/Incident Reporting System (567)

Alaska
Boreal Institute for Northern Studies — Library Services (95)

Alberta, Canada
Alberta Municipal Affairs — Central Services Branch — Alberta Land Use Planning Data Bank (10)
Alberta Public Affairs Bureau — Publication Services Branch (11)
Alberta Research Council — Alberta Geological Survey — Geoscience Data Index for Alberta (12)
Calgary Public Information Department — Public Relations Division — Civichannel (124)
University of Alberta — Department of Sociology — Population Research Laboratory (1035)

Alcohol and alcoholism
Institute for Documentation and Information in Social Medicine and Public Health (539)
Swedish Council for Information on Alcohol and Other Drugs (936)

Algeria
Center for Research and Studies on Mediterranean Societies (186)

Alloys
Great Britain — Department of Industry — National Physical Laboratory — Division of Materials Applications — Metallurgical and Thermochemical Data Service (451)
Zinc Development Association/Lead Development Association/Cadmium Association — Library and Abstracting Service (1122)

Aluminum
Bird Associates (89)
Commodities Research Unit Ltd. (228)

Animal diseases SEE: Veterinary medicine

Animal feed
Commonwealth Agricultural Bureaux — CAB Abstracts (229)
Hohenheim University — Documentation Center on Animal Production (487)

Animal husbandry (See also Veterinary medicine)
Bavarian Ministry for Food, Agriculture and Forestry — Bavarian Agricultural Information System (76)
Commonwealth Agricultural Bureaux — CAB Abstracts (229)
Germany — Center for Agricultural Documentation and Information (408)
Hohenheim University — Documentation Center on Animal Production (487)
International Livestock Centre for Africa — Documentation Centre (596)
Netherlands — Ministry of Agriculture and Fisheries — Agricultural Research Division — Centre for Agricultural Publishing and Documentation (731)
United Nations — Food and Agriculture Organization — International Information System for the Agricultural Sciences and Technology (1012)
United Nations — Food and Agriculture Organization — Statistics Division — Interlinked Computerized Storage and Processing System of Food and Agricultural Data (1014)

Antarctic SEE: Polar regions

Anthropology (See also Ethnology)
International Committee for Social Science Information and Documentation (571)

Apiculture
International Bee Research Association — Apicultural Abstracts (563)

Apparel SEE: Clothing

Aquaculture
France — National Center for Ocean Utilization — National Bureau for Ocean Data (347)
France — National Center for Ocean Utilization — National Bureau for Ocean Data — AQUADOC (348)
France — National Center for Ocean Utilization — National Bureau for Ocean Data — DOCOCEAN (351)
United Nations — Food and Agriculture Organization — Aquatic Sciences and Fisheries Information System (1008)

Aquatic biology (See also Marine biology)
United Nations — Food and Agriculture Organization — Aquatic Sciences and Fisheries Information System (1008)

Aquatic pollution SEE: Pollution, water

Arab countries (See also Middle East)
Gulf Organization for Industrial Consulting — Industrial Data Bank Department (471)
League of Arab States — League of Arab States Documentation and Information Center (653)
United Nations Educational, Scientific and Cultural Organization — Center for Social Science Research and Documentation for the Arab Region (1015)

Architecture (See also Building construction)
Canada — Environment Canada — Canadian Inventory of Historic Building (138)
Center for Industrial Creation — Documentation Service (184)
Fraunhofer Society — Information Center for Building and Physical Planning (373)
Fraunhofer Society — Information Center for Building and Physical Planning — Property Services Agency Information on Construction and Architecture Data Base (378)
International Council for Building Research, Studies and Documentation (573)
Royal Institute of British Architects — British Architectural Library — Architectural Periodicals Index (845)

Architecture, naval SEE: Naval architecture

Archives (See also Public records)
International Federation for Documentation — Research Referral Service (579)
Library Association Publishing Ltd. — CURRENT RESEARCH in Library & Information Science (661)

Arctic SEE: Polar regions

Arid regions
Mexico — National Institute for Research on Biological Resources — INIREB Library (702)

Art and art history
Art Sales Index Ltd. (29)
Australian National Gallery — Library (58)
Espial Productions (300)
France — National Center for Scientific Research — Documentation Center for Human Sciences (355)

Artificial rainfall
Israel — National Center of Scientific and Technological Information (616)

Asbestos
University of Sherbrooke — Asbestos Research Program — Information Center (1071)

Asia
German Foundation for International Development — Documentation Center (397)
Korea Advanced Institute of Science and Technology — Experienced Librarians and Information Personnel in the Developing Countries of Asia and Oceania (644)
United Nations — Economic and Social Commission for Asia and the Pacific — ESCAP Library — ESCAP Bibliographic Information System (1002)
United Nations — Economic and Social Commission for Asia and the Pacific — Population Division — Population Clearing-house and Information Section (1003)
United Nations — Economic and Social Commission for Asia and the Pacific — Statistics Division — UN/ESCAP Statistical Information Services (1004)
United Nations — Food and Agriculture Organization — INFOFISH (1011)

Asia, Southeast SEE: Southeast Asia

Associations
Israel — National Center of Scientific and Technological Information (616)
Japan Publications Guide (635)
Saur Verlag (863)
University of Leicester — Primary Communications Research Centre (1054)

Astronautics (See also Space technology; Rockets and missiles; Satellites)
European Space Agency — Information Retrieval Service (317)
Information Center for Energy, Physics, Mathematics (521)

Astronomy (See also Planets; Stars)
Australian National Radio Astronomy Observatory — Parkes Catalogue of Radio Sources (59)
Information Center for Energy, Physics, Mathematics (521)
Strasbourg Observatory — Stellar Data Center (905)
Union of Soviet Socialist Republics — Academy of Sciences of the U.S.S.R. — Astronomical Council Data Center — Management System for Astronomical Data in Machine-Readable Form (995)

Astrophysics
Information Center for Energy, Physics, Mathematics (521)

Atlases SEE: Maps

Atmospheric sciences (See also Meteorology)
United Nations Environment Programme — INFOTERRA (1025)

Atomic cross sections SEE: Cross sections (nuclear physics)

Atomic energy SEE: Nuclear energy

Atomic power plants SEE: Nuclear power plants

Atomic weapons SEE: Weapons, nuclear

Audiovisual material (See also Motion pictures)
British Universities Film & Video Council Ltd. — Information Service (112)
Canada — National Film Board of Canada — FORMAT (146)
Great Britain — British Library — Bibliographic Services Division (439)
University of Alberta — Department of Educational Administration — Administration Laboratory Project File (1034)

Auditing SEE: Accounting

Australia
Australia — Bureau of Transport Economics — BTE Information Systems (46)
Australia — National Library of Australia (48)
Australian Bureau of Statistics (52)
Australian Business Index (53)
Australian Financial Review — INFO-LINE (55)
Australian National University — Research School of Social Sciences — Australian Demographic Data Bank (60)
Australian National University — Research School of Social Sciences — Social Science Data Archives (61)
Computer Sciences of Australia Pty. Ltd. — Network Services Division — INFOBANK (237)
Control Data Australia Pty. Ltd. — CYBERTEL Videotex Service (245)
Sharp Associates Limited (871)
University of Sydney — Sample Survey Centre (1072)
Western Australian Institute of Technology — T.L. Robertson Library — WAIT Index to Newspapers (1107)

Automated library acquisitions (See also Library automation)
Blackwell Technical Services Ltd. (90)
BLCMP Ltd. (91)
Swets Subscription Service (942)
University of London — Central Information Service (1055)
UTLAS Inc. (1094)

Automated library cataloging SEE: Machine-readable cataloging

Automated library circulation (See also Library automation)
BLCMP Ltd. (91)
BTJ (116)
SWALCAP (919)
Universal Library Systems Ltd. (1029)

Automatic control (See also Instrumentation)
Institution of Electrical Engineers — INSPEC (549)
Technical Information Center — Electrical Engineering Documentation Center (960)
Verlag Hoppenstedt & Co. — EK-MRA Data Base (1098)

Automatic indexing
Great Britain — British Library — Bibliographic Services Division — Subject Systems Office — Preserved Context Index System (441)
Langton Electronic Publishing Systems Ltd. (649)
University of Western Ontario — School of Library and Information Science — Nested Phrase Indexing System (1086)

Automatic information retrieval systems SEE: Information storage and retrieval systems

Automation, library SEE: Library automation

Automation, office SEE: Office automation

Automotive engineering
Motor Vehicle Documentation (716)
VDI-Verlag GmbH — VDI News Data Base (1096)
Volkswagenwerk AG — Documentation Section (1104)

Automotive industry
AVCOR (67)
Motor Vehicle Documentation (716)
Volkswagenwerk AG — Documentation Section (1104)

Aviation SEE: Aeronautics

Aviation safety SEE: Flight safety

Bahrain
Tel-Aviv University — Shiloah Research Center for Middle Eastern and African Studies — Documentation System — Mideast File (970)

Ballistic missiles SEE: Rockets and missiles

Banking and finance (See also Stocks and Bonds)
Australian Financial Review — INFO-LINE (55)
Bank of England — Financial Statistics Division (72)
Bank Society — General Documentation — SGB Data Base (73)
Computer Sciences of Australia Pty. Ltd. — Network Services Division — INFOBANK (237)
Control Data Australia Pty. Ltd. — CYBERTEL Videotex Service (245)
Cumulus Systems Ltd. (249)
Datacrown Inc. (261)
Dataline Inc. (262)
Datastream International Ltd. (267)
Econintel Information Services Ltd. — Econintel Monitor (290)
Faxtel Information Systems Ltd. — Marketfax (326)
Financial Times Business Information Ltd. — Business Information Service (328)
FRI Information Services Ltd. (392)
GSI-ECO (469)
IBJ Data Service Co. (498)
ICV Information Systems Ltd. — CitiService (500)
The London International Financial Futures Exchange Ltd. (672)
LymBurner & Sons Ltd. — Economist's Statistics (679)

McCarthy Information Ltd. (690)
MERLIN GERIN Company — Documentation Department — MERL-ECO (696)
Nihon Keizai Shimbun, Inc. — Databank Bureau — Nikkei Economic Electronic Databank System-Information Retrieval (753)
Nihon Keizai Shimbun, Inc. — Databank Bureau — Nikkei Economic Electronic Databank System-Time Sharing (754)
Nihon Keizai Shimbun, Inc. — Quotation Information Center K.K. (755)
Sharp Associates Limited (871)
SLIGOS (879)
Teikoku Data Bank, Ltd. (969)
Tijl Datapress (982)
University of New South Wales — Australian Graduate School of Management — Centre for Research in Finance (1060)

Batteries
Zinc Development Association/Lead Development Association/Cadmium Association — Library and Abstracting Service (1122)

Bees SEE: Apiculture

Behavioral sciences (See also Psychology; Social science)
Sweden — National Library for Psychology and Education (924)

Belgium
Belgium — Ministry of Economic Affairs — National Statistical Institute (82)
Documentary Research Center (282)
Interuniversity Documentation and Information Center for the Social Sciences (611)

Beverage industry
International Coffee Organization — COFFEELINE (570)

Bible
Bar-Ilan University — Institute for Information Retrieval and Computational Linguistics — Responsa Project (74)

Bibliography (See also Cataloging; Indexing; Library science)
Australia — National Library of Australia (48)
Australia — National Library of Australia — Australian Bibliographic Network (49)
Brazil — National Council of Scientific and Technological Development — Brazilian Institute for Information in Science and Technology (103)
Canada — National Library of Canada (147)
Canada — National Library of Canada — Cataloguing Branch — Canadiana Editorial Division (148)
Germany — German National Library — BIBLIO-DATA (423)
Great Britain — British Library — Bibliographic Services Division (439)
Helsinki University Library — Finnish National Bibliography (482)
Japan Publications Guide (635)
Sweden — Royal Library — Library Information System (931)
United Nations Educational, Scientific and Cultural Organization — Universal System for Information in Science and Technology — UNISIST International Centre for Bibliographic Descriptions (1023)

Biochemistry (See also Chemistry, organic)
Pergamon Press — Current Awareness in Biological Sciences (803)
Royal Society of Chemistry — Information Services (851)
Royal Society of Chemistry — Information Services — Current Biotechnology Abstracts (854)

Biodegradation
Commonwealth Agricultural Bureaux — CAB Abstracts (229)
Great Britain — Water Research Centre — Information Service on Toxicity and Biodegradability (463)

Bioengineering
Bayer AG — Engineering Science Division — Chemical and Process Engineering Abstracts (77)
Brunel Univeristy — Brunel Institute for Bioengineering — Information Unit (114)
Celltech Ltd. — Information and Library Service (181)
Centre of Information Resource & Technology, Singapore (197)
Derwent Publications Ltd. — Biotechnology Abstracts (273)
France — National Center for Scientific Research — Scientific and Technical Documentation Center (356)
German Society for Chemical Equipment — Information Systems and Data Banks Department — Chemical Technology Information System (403)
Gothard House Group of Companies, Ltd. (432)
Great Britain — British Library — Science Reference Library — European Biotechnology Information Program (446)
Mitaka — JAPANSCAN (712)
Royal Society of Chemistry — Information Services — Current Biotechnology Abstracts (854)
Survey Force Ltd. (907)
Technical Information Center — Medical Technology Documentation (962)

Bioethics SEE: Medical ethics

Biography
Brassey's Publishers Ltd. — British Defence Directory (98)
Servi-Tech — BIODOC (870)
Teikoku Data Bank, Ltd. (969)

Biological engineering SEE: Bioengineering

Biology (See also Botany; Zoology)
Commonwealth Agricultural Bureaux — CAB Abstracts (229)
France — National Center for Scientific Research — Scientific and Technical Documentation Center (356)
Pergamon Press — Current Awareness in Biological Sciences (803)
Royal Society of Chemistry — Information Services (851)
South African Medical Research Council — Institute for Medical Literature (888)

Biology, aquatic SEE: Aquatic biology

Biology, developmental SEE: Developmental biology

Biology, marine SEE: Marine biology

Biomedical engineering SEE: Bioengineering

Biomedical sciences
Australia — National Library of Australia — Australian MEDLINE Network (50)
Czechoslovakia — Institute for Medical Information (250)
Elsevier Science Publishers B.V. — Biomedical Division — Excerpta Medica (296)
Germany — Ministry of Youth, Family and Health — German Institute for Medical Documentation and Information (428)
International Medical Information Center (598)
IRCS Medical Science — IRCS Medical Science Database (614)
Mexico — National Center for Health Information and Documentation (700)
Sweden — Karolinska Institute Library and Information Center (921)
University of Sheffield — Biomedical Information Service (1069)
University of Valencia — Biomedical Documentation and Information Center (1082)

Biotechnology SEE: Bioengineering

Birth control SEE: Family planning

Birth defects SEE: Teratology

Blind
Brunel University — Research Unit for the Blind — International Register of Research on Visual Disability (115)

Bonds SEE: Stocks and bonds

Books
Bibliographic Publishing Co. (87)
Blackwell Technical Services Ltd. (90)
Canada — National Library of Canada (147)
Canada — National Library of Canada — Cataloguing Branch — Canadiana Editorial Division (148)
Canada — National Library of Canada — MARC Records Distribution Service (150)
Esselte Group of Booksellers — Esselte Documentation System (302)
Germany — German National Library — BIBLIO-DATA (423)
Great Britain — British Library — Bibliographic Services Division (439)
Great Britain — British Library — Reference Division — Eighteenth Century Short Title Catalogue (443)
Helsinki University Library — Finnish National Bibliography (482)
International Technical Publications Ltd. (605)
Japan — National Diet Library — Library Automation System (629)
Japan Publications Guide (635)
Nineteenth Century Short Title Catalogue Project (757)
Quebec National Library — FMQ (833)
Saur Verlag (863)
Sweden — Royal Library — Library Information System (931)
University of Oslo — Royal University Library — Planning Department (1061)

SUBJECT INDEX

Books, union catalogs of SEE: **Union catalogs and lists**

Botany (See also Horticulture; Plant pathology)
    Commonwealth Agricultural Bureaux — CAB Abstracts (229)
    Germany — Federal Biological Research Center for Agriculture and Forestry — Documentation Center for Phytomedicine (409)
    Great Britain — Institute of Terrestrial Ecology — Biological Records Centre (461)
    Mexico — National Institute for Research on Biological Resources — INIREB Library (702)
    Pergamon Press — Current Awareness in Biological Sciences (803)

Brand names SEE: **Trademarks**

Brazil
    Brazil — Ministry of the Interior — Documentation Coordination Unit (100)
    Latin American Newsletters Ltd. (651)

Bridge construction
    Sweden — Swedish National Road Administration — Technical Division — Road Data Bank (933)

Britain SEE: **Great Britain**

Broadcasting SEE: **Communication arts; Radio broadcasting; Television Broadcasting**

Building construction (See also Architecture; Construction industry)
    Building Center (117)
    Building Services Research and Information Association — BSRIA Information Centre (119)
    China Building Technology Development Centre — Institute of Technical Information (203)
    Construction Specifications Canada — National Master Specification (242)
    France — National Center for Scientific Research — Scientific and Technical Documentation Center (356)
    Fraunhofer Society — Information Center for Building and Physical Planning (373)
    Fraunhofer Society — Information Center for Building and Physical Planning — Building Research Projects Data Base (374)
    Fraunhofer Society — Information Center for Building and Physical Planning — Buildings Documentation Data Base (375)
    Fraunhofer Society — Information Center for Building and Physical Planning — Literature Compilations Data Base (376)
    Fraunhofer Society — Information Center for Building and Physical Planning — PASCALBAT Data Base (377)
    Fraunhofer Society — Information Center for Building and Physical Planning — Property Services Agency Information on Construction and Architecture Data Base (378)
    Fraunhofer Society — Information Center for Building and Physical Planning — Regional Planning, City Planning, Housing, Building Construction Data Base (379)
    Great Britain — Department of the Environment — Building Research Establishment Library — BRIX (453)
    Health Care Literature Information Network (477)
    Heinze GmbH — VISDATA (479)
    Hungary — Ministry for Building and Urban Development — Information Centre for Building (494)
    International Council for Building Research, Studies and Documentation (573)
    Interprofessional Technical Union of the National Federations of Buildings and Public Works — Center for Technical Assistance and Documentation — ARIANE Data Bank (610)
    Royal Institute of British Architects — British Architectural Library — Architectural Periodicals Index (845)
    Swedish Building Centre — Building Commodity File (934)
    Swedish Institute of Building Documentation (938)

Buildings (See also Architecture)
    Canada — Environment Canada — Canadian Inventory of Historic Building (138)
    Fraunhofer Society — Information Center for Building and Physical Planning — Buildings Documentation Data Base (375)

Business and business administration (See also Commerce and trade; Management)
    Australian Business Index (53)
    Australian Financial Review — INFO-LINE (55)
    Bonnier Business Publishing Group — AffarsData (94)
    Control Data Australia Pty. Ltd. — CYBERTEL Videotex Service (245)
    DataArkiv AB (260)
    Esselte Business Information (301)
    Financial Times Business Information Ltd. — Business Information Service (328)
    Finsbury Data Services Ltd. — TEXTLINE (335)
    The Globe and Mail — Info Globe (430)
    Great Britain — Department of Trade and Industry — Business Statistics Office (454)
    Helsingin Telset Oy — Telset (480)
    Helsinki School of Economics Library — Information Services (481)
    MERLIN GERIN Company — Documentation Department — MERL-ECO (696)
    Micromedia Ltd. — Canadian Business Index (707)
    Nihon Keizai Shimbun, Inc. — Databank Bureau — Nikkei Economic Electronic Databank System-Information Retrieval (753)

Business corporations SEE: **Corporations**

Business executives SEE: **Executives**

Business forecasting
    Henley Centre for Forecasting (484)

Business, international (See also Foreign trade)
    Center for International Prospective Studies (185)
    Commission of the European Communities — Tenders Electronic Daily (227)
    Datasolve Ltd. — World Exporter (264)
    Datasolve Ltd. — World Reporter (265)
    Germany — Ministry of Economics — German Foreign Trade Information Office (425)
    Henley Centre for Forecasting (484)
    Netherlands — Netherlands Foreign Trade Agency — Library and Documentation Branch — Foreign Trade Abstracts (733)
    Norwegian Center for Informatics (767)
    ONLINE GmbH (774)
    Paris Chamber of Commerce and Industry — Department of International Relations — TELEXPORT (796)
    Sharp Associates Limited (871)

Cadmium
    Zinc Development Association/Lead Development Association/Cadmium Association — Library and Abstracting Service (1122)

Canada
    Boreal Institute for Northern Studies — Library Services (95)
    British Columbia Ministry of Industry and Small Business Development — Central Statistics Bureau (106)
    Canada — Agriculture Canada — Marketing and Economics Branch — Agricultural Marketing and Trade Database (126)
    Canada — Consumer and Corporate Affairs Canada — Corporations Branch — Corporate Integrated Information System (129)
    Canada — Environment Canada — Lands Directorate — Canada Land Data Systems Division — Canada Geographic Information System (143)
    Canada — National Film Board of Canada — FORMAT (146)
    Canada — Statistics Canada — Canadian Socio-Economic Information Management System (159)
    Canada — Statistics Canada — Canadian Socio-Economic Information Management System — Telichart (160)
    Canada Law Book Ltd. (162)
    Canada Systems Group — Federal Systems Division — Canadian Federal Corporations and Directors Data Base (163)
    Canada Systems Group — Federal Systems Division — Corporate Names Data Base (164)
    Canada Systems Group — Federal Systems Division — Inter-Corporate Ownership Data Base (165)
    Canadian Broadcasting Corporation — Project IRIS (169)
    Carleton University — Department of Sociology and Anthropology — Social Science Data Archives (178)
    Compusearch Market and Social Research Ltd. (236)
    Conference Board of Canada — Applied Economic Research and Information Centre — AERIC System (238)
    The Globe and Mail — Info Globe (430)
    Informetrica Limited (536)
    Microfor Inc. (704)
    Micromedia Ltd. (706)
    Micromedia Ltd. — Canadian Business Index (707)
    Micromedia Ltd. — Canadian News Index (708)
    QL Systems Limited (828)
    Sharp Associates Limited (871)
    University of Alberta — Department of Sociology — Population Research Laboratory (1035)
    University of Regina — Canadian Plains Research Center — Information Services (1066)
    Western Legal Publications Ltd. (1108)
    York University — Institute for Behavioural Research (1120)

Canadian history
    Canada — Environment Canada — Canadian Inventory of Historic Building (138)
    Microfor Inc. (704)
    University of Regina — Canadian Plains Research Center — Information Services (1066)

SUBJECT INDEX

Canadiana
   Canada — National Library of Canada (147)
   Canada — National Library of Canada — Cataloguing Branch — Canadiana Editorial Division (148)
   Canada — Parliament of Canada — Library of Parliament (157)
   Canada — Public Archives of Canada — Machine Readable Archives Division (158)
   Canadian Library Association — Canadian Periodical Index (174)
   Microfor Inc. (704)
   QL Systems Limited (828)

Cancer
   Elsevier Science Publishers B.V. — Biomedical Division — Excerpta Medica (296)
   France — National Center for Scientific Research — Scientific and Technical Documentation Center (356)
   France — National Center for Scientific Research — Scientific Documentation Center in Oncology — CANCERNET (357)
   International Medical Information Center (598)
   University of Leeds — Medical and Dental Library — Oncology Information Service (1053)
   World Health Organization — Division of Health Statistics — World Health Statistics Data Base (1110)
   World Health Organization — International Agency for Research on Cancer — Clearing-House for On-going Research in Cancer Epidemiology (1113)

Carcinogenesis SEE: Cancer

Cardiac diseases SEE: Heart

Career education SEE: Education, vocational

Career placement
   Great Britain — Manpower Services Commission — Careers and Occupational Information Centre (462)
   New Opportunity Press Ltd. — Careerdata (747)

Caribbean area
   Latin American Newsletters Ltd. (651)
   United Nations — Economic Commission for Latin America — Latin American Demographic Center — Latin American Population Documentation System (1007)

Cartography (See also Maps)
   Canada — Department of Energy, Mines and Resources — Topographical Survey Division — Digital Mapping System (136)
   Geo Abstracts Ltd. (393)

Cataloging (See also Indexing)
   Great Britain — British Library — Bibliographic Services Division (439)
   University of Bath — Centre for Catalogue Research (1039)
   University of Toronto — Faculty of Library and Information Science Library — Subject Analysis Systems Collection (1077)

Cataloging, machine-readable SEE: Machine-readable cataloging

Cataloging, subject SEE: Subject cataloging

Catalogs, union SEE: Union catalogs and lists

Cement SEE: Concrete and cement

Census (See also Population)
   Australian Bureau of Statistics (52)
   Belgium — Ministry of Economic Affairs — National Statistical Institute (82)
   Canada — Statistics Canada — Canadian Socio-Economic Information Management System (159)
   Compusearch Market and Social Research Ltd. (236)
   Computer Sciences of Australia Pty. Ltd. — Network Services Division — INFOBANK (237)
   Madagascar — Ministry of Finance and Economy — National Institute of Statistics and Economic Research (681)
   New Zealand — Department of Statistics — Information Network for Official Statistics (749)
   Norway — Ministry of Finances and Customs — Central Bureau of Statistics (766)
   Sweden — Statistics Sweden — Statistical Data Bases Unit (932)
   York University — Institute for Behavioural Research (1120)

Ceramics
   Thermodata Association — Thermodata-Thermdoc Data Bank (981)
   Zinc Development Association/Lead Development Association/Cadmium Association — Library and Abstracting Service (1122)

Cereals SEE: Grain

Charitable trusts and foundations SEE: Foundations (philanthropic)

Chemical engineering
   Bayer AG — Engineering Science Division — Chemical and Process Engineering Abstracts (77)
   Chem Systems International Ltd. (199)
   Dutch State Mines — TISDATA (286)
   ESDU International Limited (299)
   Federal Technical University — Technical Chemistry Laboratory — CHEMCO Physical Properties Data Bank (327)
   German Society for Chemical Equipment — Information Systems and Data Banks Department — Chemical Technology Information System (403)
   German Society for Chemical Equipment — Information Systems and Data Banks Department — DECHEMA Substance Data Service (404)
   Institution of Chemical Engineers — Physical Property Data Service (548)
   Norwegian Center for Informatics (767)
   Royal Society of Chemistry — Information Services (851)
   Royal Society of Chemistry — Information Services — Chemical Engineering Abstracts (852)

Chemical geology SEE: Geochemistry

Chemical industry
   Chem Systems International Ltd. (199)
   Chemical Age — Chemical Age Project File (200)
   Commission of the European Communities — Joint Research Centre — Environmental Chemicals Data and Information Network (221)
   Fraser Williams Ltd. — Fine Chemicals Directory (372)
   German Society for Chemical Equipment — Information Systems and Data Banks Department — Supply Sources Information System (406)
   Independent Chemical Information Services Ltd. (505)
   IPC Industrial Press Ltd. — Chemical Data Services (612)
   Parpinelli TECNON — World Petrochemical Industry Data Bank (799)
   Royal Society of Chemistry — Information Services (851)
   Royal Society of Chemistry — Information Services — Chemical Hazards in Industry (853)
   Royal Society of Chemistry — Information Services — Laboratory Hazards Bulletin (855)

Chemical reactions
   Derwent Publications Ltd. — Chemical Reactions Documentation Service (274)
   University of Leeds — Department of Physical Chemistry — High Temperature Reaction Rate Data Centre (1052)

Chemical structure (See also Molecular structure)
   Association for Research and Development of Chemical Informatics — DARC Pluridata System (38)
   Cambridge University — University Chemical Laboratory — Cambridge Crystallographic Data Centre (125)
   Fraser Williams Ltd. — CROSSBOW (370)
   Fraser Williams Ltd. — DARING (371)
   International Company for Documentation in Chemistry (572)
   National Center for Chemical Information (720)
   University of Paris-South — Gases and Plasmas Physics Laboratory — GAPHYOR (1063)

Chemicals (See also Petrochemicals)
   Association for Research and Development of Chemical Informatics — DARC Pluridata System (38)
   Commission of the European Communities — Joint Research Centre — Environmental Chemicals Data and Information Network (221)
   Dortmund Institute for Water Research — Data Bank on Substances Harmful to Water (284)
   Expert Information Systems Ltd. — EXIS 1 (320)
   Fraser Williams Ltd. — Fine Chemicals Directory (372)
   German Society for Chemical Equipment — Information Systems and Data Banks Department — DECHEMA Substance Data Service (404)
   Germany — Federal Environmental Agency — Environmental Information and Documentation System (411)
   Great Britain — Atomic Energy Authority — Atomic Energy Research Establishment, Harwell — National Chemical Emergency Centre — CHEMSAFE (435)
   Great Britain — Water Research Centre — Information Service on Toxicity and Biodegradability (463)
   Institution of Chemical Engineers — Physical Property Data Service (548)
   International Society of Ecological Modelling — Environmental Data and Ecological Parameters Data Base (604)

IPC Industrial Press Ltd. — Chemical Data Services (612)
National Center for Chemical Information (720)
Uhde GmbH — Uhde Thermophysical Properties Program Package (992)
Unilever Computer Services Ltd. — European Petrochemical Association Trade Statistics Database (993)
United Nations Environment Programme — International Register of Potentially Toxic Chemicals (1026)
University of Western Ontario — Systems Analysis, Control and Design Activity (1088)
World Health Organization — International Agency for Research on Cancer — Clearing-House for On-going Research in Cancer Epidemiology (1113)

Chemicals, hazardous SEE: Hazardous substances

Chemistry
Association for Research and Development of Chemical Informatics — DARC Pluridata System (38)
Chemical Information Center (201)
Derwent Publications Ltd. — Patents Documentation Services (275)
France — National Center for Scientific Research — Scientific and Technical Documentation Center (356)
Gmelin Institute for Inorganic Chemistry and Related Fields (431)
Great Britain — Department of Industry — National Physical Laboratory — Division of Materials Applications — Metallurgical and Thermochemical Data Service (451)
International Company for Documentation in Chemistry (572)
Japan Association for International Chemical Information (630)
Japan Information Center of Science and Technology (632)
National Center for Chemical Information (720)
Royal Society of Chemistry — Information Services (851)
Royal Society of Chemistry — Information Services — Mass Spectrometry Data Centre (856)
Thermodata Association — Thermodata-Thermdoc Data Bank (981)
University of Bonn — Inorganic Chemistry Institute — Inorganic Crystal Structure Data Base (1042)
University of Dortmund — Dortmund Data Bank (1046)
University of Tokyo — Faculty of Engineering — Department of Synthetic Chemistry — EROICA System for Basic Properties of Organic Compounds (1076)

Chemistry, agricultural SEE: Agricultural chemistry

Chemistry, biological SEE: Biochemistry

Chemistry, food SEE: Food chemistry

Chemistry, organic (See also Biochemistry)
Beilstein Institute for Literature in Organic Chemistry (79)
Cambridge University — University Chemical Laboratory — Cambridge Crystallographic Data Centre (125)
Derwent Publications Ltd. — Chemical Reactions Documentation Service (274)
Institution of Chemical Engineers — Physical Property Data Service (548)
International Company for Documentation in Chemistry (572)
Royal Society of Chemistry — Information Services (851)
University of Tokyo — Faculty of Engineering — Department of Synthetic Chemistry — EROICA System for Basic Properties of Organic Compounds (1076)

Children
International Children's Centre — Documentation Service — Robert Debre Information Base (566)

Circulation, automated library SEE: Automated library circulation

City planning (See also Land use; Regional planning)
Fraunhofer Society — Information Center for Building and Physical Planning (373)
Fraunhofer Society — Information Center for Building and Physical Planning — Literature Compilations Data Base (376)
Fraunhofer Society — Information Center for Building and Physical Planning — PASCALBAT Data Base (377)
Fraunhofer Society — Information Center for Building and Physical Planning — Regional Planning, City Planning, Housing, Building Construction Data Base (379)
Fraunhofer Society — Information Center for Building and Physical Planning — Regional Planning, City Planning, Housing Research Projects Data Base (380)
Greater London Council — Information Services Group (465)
International Council for Building Research, Studies and Documentation (573)
Paris Office of Urbanization — Urban Data Bank of Paris and the Paris Region (798)
Royal Institute of British Architects — British Architectural Library — Architectural Periodicals Index (845)
Swedish Institute of Building Documentation (938)
URBAMET Network (1091)

Civil engineering
BHRA, The Fluid Engineering Centre — Information Services (86)
CITIS Ltd. (208)
Fraunhofer Society — Information Center for Building and Physical Planning (373)
Fraunhofer Society — Information Center for Building and Physical Planning — Building Research Projects Data Base (374)
Fraunhofer Society — Information Center for Building and Physical Planning — Literature Compilations Data Base (376)
Fraunhofer Society — Information Center for Building and Physical Planning — Regional Planning, City Planning, Housing, Building Construction Data Base (379)
International Council for Building Research, Studies and Documentation (573)
Swedish Institute of Building Documentation (938)
University of London — Imperial College of Science and Technology — Department of Mineral Resources Engineering — Rock Mechanics Information Service (1056)

Climatology SEE: Meteorology

Clothing
Textile and Clothing Information Centre (980)
University of Alberta — Computing Services — Information Systems Group (1033)

Coal
Alberta Research Council — Coal Technology Information Centre (14)
Canada — Department of Energy, Mines and Resources — Canada Centre for Mineral and Energy Technology — Technology Information Division (131)
Commission of the European Communities — Euro Abstracts (218)
Organisation for Economic Co-Operation and Development — International Energy Agency — IEA Coal Research — Technical Information Service (782)
Organisation for Economic Co-Operation and Development — International Energy Agency — IEA Coal Research — World Coal Resources and Reserves Data Bank Service (783)

Coasts
France — National Center for Ocean Utilization — National Bureau for Ocean Data (347)
France — National Center for Ocean Utilization — National Bureau for Ocean Data — CNEXO-BNDO Data Base (350)

Coatings, protective SEE: Protective coatings

Coffee
International Coffee Organization — COFFEELINE (570)

Cold regions SEE: Polar regions

Collective bargaining agreements SEE: Labor agreements

College education SEE: Education, higher

Combustion
Alberta Research Council — Coal Technology Information Centre (14)
Great Britain — Department of the Environment — Building Research Establishment — Fire Research Station Library — Fire Science Abstracts (452)
University of Leeds — Department of Physical Chemistry — High Temperature Reaction Rate Data Centre (1052)

Commerce and trade (See also Foreign trade; Retail trade)
Canada — Statistics Canada — Canadian Socio-Economic Information Management System (159)
Central Electronic Network for Data Processing and Analysis (194)
Commission of the European Communities — Statistical Office of the European Communities — CRONOS Data Bank (225)
France — National Institute of Statistics and Economic Studies — Information System for the Economy (364)
Netherlands — Netherlands Foreign Trade Agency — Library and Documentation Branch — Foreign Trade Abstracts (733)
Nihon Keizai Shimbun, Inc. — Databank Bureau — Nikkei Economic Electronic Databank System-Time Sharing (754)
Overseas Data Service, Company, Ltd. (789)
Unilever Computer Services Ltd. — World Trade Statistics Database (994)
University of Trondheim — Norwegian Institute of Technology — University Library (1079)

University of Warwick Library — Warwick Statistics Service   (1083)

Commodity futures
Alberta Department of Agriculture — Economic Services Division — Agricultural Commodities Data Base   (9)
Commodities Research Unit Ltd.   (228)
Cumulus Systems Ltd.   (249)
Datastream International Ltd.   (267)
Faxtel Information Systems Ltd. — Marketfax   (326)
ICV Information Systems Ltd. — CitiService   (500)
Infomart — Grassroots   (519)
The London International Financial Futures Exchange Ltd.   (672)
LymBurner & Sons Ltd. — Economist's Statistics   (679)
Nihon Keizai Shimbun, Inc. — Databank Bureau — Nikkei Economic Electronic Databank System-Time Sharing   (754)
Nihon Keizai Shimbun, Inc. — Quotation Information Center K.K.   (755)
Sharp Associates Limited   (871)
The Stock Exchange — Technical Services Department — TOPIC   (902)
Telekurs Ag — Investdata System   (975)
Wolff & Co. Ltd. — Wolff Research   (1109)

Communicable diseases SEE: Public health

Communication arts (See also Mass media; Radio broadcasting; Television broadcasting)
Austrian Documentation Centre for Media and Communication Research   (65)

Communication, science SEE: Science communication

Communications (See also Electronics; Telecommunications)
Management Consultants International, Inc.   (682)
Society for Information and Documentation — GID Information Center for Information Science and Practice   (880)
Technical Information Center — Electrical Engineering Documentation Center   (960)
University of Leicester — Primary Communications Research Centre   (1054)

Communications, data SEE: Data communications

Companies SEE: Corporations

Components, technical SEE: Technical components

Computer-assisted instruction
Hertfordshire County Council — Chiltern Advisory Unit for Computer Based Education   (485)

Computer graphics
Canada — Statistics Canada — Canadian Socio-Economic Information Management System — Telichart   (160)
Fraser Videotex Services   (369)
Langton Electronic Publishing Systems Ltd.   (649)

Computer installations
Constellate Consultants Ltd.   (241)
National Computing Centre Ltd. — Information Services Division   (721)
Paris District Informatics Administration — Informatics Biblio Service   (797)

Computer programs
ALLM Books — Small Computer Program Index   (17)
AVCOR   (67)
CITIS Ltd.   (208)
National Computing Centre Ltd. — Information Services Division   (721)
Telemap Ltd. — Micronet 800   (976)

Computerized information services SEE: Information services

Computerized information storage and retrieval systems SEE: Information storage and retrieval systems

Computerized searching (See also Information retrieval)
Collective for Training and Education in Connection with Information Provision via Networks   (211)
Danish DIANE Center   (256)
European Association of Information Services   (307)
Italy — National Research Council — Institute for Study of Scientific Research & Documentation — Italian Reference Center for Euronet DIANE   (624)
Kinokuniya Company Ltd. — ASK Information Retrieval Services   (640)
Learned Information Ltd.   (654)
Netherlands Association of Users of Online Information Systems   (734)
Online Information Centre   (775)
Online Users' Group/Ireland   (776)
Piedmont Consortium for Information Systems   (811)
United Kingdom Online User Group   (1000)
Userlink Systems Ltd.   (1093)

Computerized typesetting (See also Photocomposition)
Bemrose Printing   (85)
Langton Electronic Publishing Systems Ltd.   (649)
Oriel Computer Services Limited   (787)
Pira: Research Association for the Paper and Board, Printing and Packaging Industries — Printing and Information Technology Division   (813)
QL Systems Limited   (828)
Siemens AG — Language Services Department — Terminology Evaluation and Acquisition Method   (876)
Unwin Brothers Ltd.   (1089)

Computers (See also Electronic data processing; Microcomputers)
AVCOR   (67)
British Computer Society   (107)
Constellate Consultants Ltd.   (241)
Data Processing Services Company — DPS Information Centre   (258)
France — National Telecommunications Research Center — Interministerial Documentation Service — TELEDOC   (367)
Information Processing Society of Japan   (529)
Institute for Information Industry   (542)
Institution of Electrical Engineers — INSPEC   (549)
Intergovernmental Bureau for Informatics   (554)
International Federation for Information Processing   (580)
National Computing Centre Ltd. — Information Services Division   (721)
Society for Information and Documentation — GID Information Center for Information Science and Practice   (880)

Concrete and cement
Asian Institute of Technology — Regional Documentation Center — International Ferrocement Information Center   (32)
Center for Study and Research of the Hydraulic Binders Industry — Documentation Center — INTERCIM Cement Data Base   (188)

Conferences and conventions
Aslib, The Association for Information Management   (35)
France — Atomic Energy Commission — Saclay Nuclear Research Center — Documentation Center   (339)
German Library Institute   (400)
Great Britain — British Library — Lending Division   (442)
Information Center for Energy, Physics, Mathematics   (521)

Congresses SEE: Conferences and conventions

Conservation of natural resources (See also Natural resources)
Canada — Environment Canada — Library Services Branch — Environment Libraries Automated System   (144)

Construction, bridge SEE: Bridge construction

Construction, building SEE: Building construction

Construction industry
Building Center   (117)
Building Information Institute   (118)
Chemical Age — Chemical Age Project File   (200)
Datasolve Ltd. — World Exporter   (264)
Hungary — Ministry for Building and Urban Development — Information Centre for Building   (494)
Informetrica Limited   (536)
Nihon Keizai Shimbun, Inc. — Databank Bureau — Nikkei Economic Electronic Databank System-Time Sharing   (754)
Office of Economic Information and Forecasting   (773)
Swedish Building Centre — Building Commodity File   (934)

Consultants
Korea Advanced Institute of Science and Technology — Experienced Librarians and Information Personnel in the Developing Countries of Asia and Oceania   (644)

Consumer goods
Admedia — Adfacts   (6)
British Market Research Bureau Ltd. — Target Group Index   (109)
Japan Data Service Co., Ltd.   (631)
Office of Economic Information and Forecasting   (773)

SUBJECT INDEX

Consumer protection
  Consumers' Association — TeleWhich? (244)

Containers SEE: Packaging

Continuing education SEE: Education, adult

Contraceptives SEE: Family planning

Contracts, government SEE: Government contracts

Control, automatic SEE: Automatic control

Conventions SEE: Conferences and conventions

Cooperatives
  Canada — Agriculture Canada — Marketing and Economics Branch — Cooperatives Unit — COINS (127)

Copper
  Bird Associates (89)
  Commodities Research Unit Ltd. (228)

Copying and duplicating
  National Reprographic Centre for Documentation (725)
  Society for Information and Documentation — GID Information Center for Information Science and Practice (880)

Corporate executives SEE: Executives

Corporations
  Bonnier Business Publishing Group — AffarsData (94)
  Canada — Consumer and Corporate Affairs Canada — Corporations Branch — Corporate Integrated Information System (129)
  Canada Systems Group — Federal Systems Division — Canadian Federal Corporations and Directors Data Base (163)
  Canada Systems Group — Federal Systems Division — Corporate Names Data Base (164)
  Canada Systems Group — Federal Systems Division — Inter-Corporate Ownership Data Base (165)
  Central Electronic Network for Data Processing and Analysis (194)
  Compusearch Market and Social Research Ltd. (236)
  DAFSA (251)
  DAFSA-SNEI S.A. — FITEK (252)
  DataArkiv AB (260)
  Datasearch Business Information Ltd. (263)
  Datastream International Ltd. (267)
  Didot-Bottin — Bottin Data Bases (280)
  Extel Statistical Services Ltd. — EXSTAT (323)
  Financial Times Business Information Ltd. — Business Information Service (328)
  Finsbury Data Services Ltd. — TEXTLINE (335)
  French Stockbrokers Society — Information and Documentation Center (389)
  Great Britain — Department of Trade and Industry — Business Statistics Office (454)
  Hertfordshire Technical Library and Information Service — HERTIS Industrial Services (486)
  IBJ Data Service Co. (498)
  ICC Information Group Ltd. (499)
  Industrial News Publishing Company — KOMPASS-FRANCE (514)
  Jordan & Sons Ltd. — Jordans Company Information (636)
  Kompass International Ltd. (642)
  MacLean-Hunter Ltd. — Financial Post Division — Financial Post Investment Data Bank (680)
  Market Location (686)
  McCarthy Information Ltd. (690)
  Micromedia Ltd. — Canadian Business Index (707)
  Morgan Grenfell & Co. Ltd. — Interfisc (715)
  Nihon Keizai Shimbun, Inc. — Databank Bureau — Nikkei Economic Electronic Databank System-Information Retrieval (753)
  Nihon Keizai Shimbun, Inc. — Databank Bureau — Nikkei Economic Electronic Databank System-Time Sharing (754)
  Pergamon InfoLine Ltd. (802)
  Schimmelpfeng GmbH (865)
  Sharp Associates Limited (871)
  SLIGOS (879)
  Stockholm School of Economics — Economics Research Institute — FINDATA (903)
  Teikoku Data Bank, Ltd. (969)
  Tijl Datapress (982)
  Tokyo Shoko Research, Ltd. — Data Bank Service (984)
  University of New South Wales — Australian Graduate School of Management — Centre for Research in Finance (1060)
  University of Warwick Library — Warwick Statistics Service (1083)
  Verlag Hoppenstedt & Co. — EK-MRA Data Base (1098)

Corrosion and anti-corrosives
  BNF Metals Technology Centre — Information Department (92)
  German Society for Chemical Equipment — Information Systems and Data Banks Department — Materials and Corrosion Information System (405)
  Paint Research Association — Information Department — World Surface Coatings Abstracts (792)
  Pont-a-Mousson Research Center — Industrial Documentation Service — BIIPAM-CTIF Data Base (820)
  The Welding Institute — Information Services (1106)
  Zinc Development Association/Lead Development Association/Cadmium Association — Library and Abstracting Service (1122)

Cosmetics
  Medical-Pharmaceutical Publishing Company (693)

Credit rating
  Central Electronic Network for Data Processing and Analysis (194)
  Schimmelpfeng GmbH (865)
  Teikoku Data Bank, Ltd. (969)

Crime and criminals (See also Law enforcement)
  Australian Institute of Criminology Library — Computerised Information from National Criminological Holdings (56)
  Kugler Publications (647)

Criminology SEE: Crime and criminals

Crops, field SEE: Field crops

Cross sections (nuclear physics)
  Union of Soviet Socialist Republics — U.S.S.R. State Committee on the Utilization of Atomic Energy — Center for Nuclear Structure and Reaction Data (999)

Cryogenics
  International Institute of Refrigeration — Documentary Service (590)

Crystallography
  Association for Research and Development of Chemical Informatics — DARC Pluridata System (38)
  Cambridge University — University Chemical Laboratory — Cambridge Crystallographic Data Centre (125)
  Canada — National Research Council of Canada — Canada Institute for Scientific and Technical Information — Scientific Numeric Databases (155)
  Canada — National Research Council of Canada — Chemistry Division — Metals Data Centre (156)
  University of Bonn — Inorganic Chemistry Institute — Inorganic Crystal Structure Data Base (1042)
  University of Gothenburg — MEDICINDATA (1049)

Current events SEE: News and newspapers

Cybernetics
  Philips Information Systems and Automation — DIRECT (809)

Dairy products
  Agra Europe (8)
  Commonwealth Agricultural Bureaux — CAB Abstracts (229)

Data base management (See also Information storage and retrieval systems)
  Commission of the European Communities — Statistical Office of the European Communities — CRONOS Data Bank (225)
  Great Britain — Atomic Energy Authority — Atomic Energy Research Establishment, Harwell — Computer Science and Systems Division — STATUS (433)
  International Information Services Company (589)
  Logica UK Ltd. (668)
  Paralog — 3RIP (795)
  Siemens AG — Data Processing Division — GOLEM (874)
  Siemens AG — Data Processing Division — Library Network System (875)

Data base production
  Association of Database Producers (40)
  French Federation of Data Base Producers (385)

Data base services SEE: Information services

Data communications
  Eurodata Foundation (303)
  France — National Telecommunications Research Center — Interministerial Documentation Service — TELEDOC (367)
  Logica UK Ltd. (668)

Data processing SEE: Electronic data processing

Data, scientific and technical SEE: Scientific and technical data

Data storage and retrieval systems SEE: Information storage and retrieval systems

Defense, national SEE: National defense

Defense research and development
France — Ministry of Defense — General Office for Ordnance — Center for Documentation on Ordnance (345)

Deformaties SEE: Teratology

Demography SEE: Population

Dentistry
World Health Organization — Division of Noncommunicable Diseases — Oral Health Unit — Global Oral Data Bank (1111)

Desalination SEE: Saline water conversion

Design
Center for Industrial Creation — Documentation Service (184)
Royal Institute of British Architects — British Architectural Library — Architectural Periodicals Index (845)

Developing nations (See also Economic development; Industrial development; International development)
Centre for the Study of Developing Societies — Data Unit (196)
Commission of the European Communities — Statistical Office of the European Communities — CRONOS Data Bank (225)
German Foundation for International Development — Documentation Center (397)
International Development Research Centre — Library (576)
International Reference Center for Community Water Supply and Sanitation — Programme on Exchange and Transfer of Information on Community Water Supply and Sanitation (601)
Organisation for Economic Co-Operation and Development — International Development Information Network (781)
United Nations — Food and Agriculture Organization — Current Agricultural Research Information System (1009)
United Nations — Food and Agriculture Organization — Economic and Social Department — Human Resources, Institutions and Agrarian Reform Division — Population Documentation Center (1010)
United Nations Industrial Development Organization — Industrial Information Section — Industrial and Technological Information Bank (1027)

Development, economic SEE: Economic development

Development, industrial SEE: Industrial development

Development, international SEE: International development

Development, rural SEE: Rural development

Developmental biology
Hubrecht Laboratory — Central Embryological Library — Documentation and Information System on Developmental Biology (490)
Pergamon Press — Current Awareness in Biological Sciences (803)

Dictionaries
Quebec — French Language Board — Terminology Bank of Quebec (830)
Siemens AG — Language Services Department — Terminology Evaluation and Acquisition Method (876)

Diffraction data
Cambridge University — University Chemical Laboratory — Cambridge Crystallographic Data Centre (125)
Canada — National Research Council of Canada — Chemistry Division — Metals Data Centre (156)

Disabled SEE: Handicapped

Dissertations, academic
Aslib, The Association for Information Management (35)
Australian Council for Educational Research — Library and Information Services Unit (54)
Canada — National Library of Canada — Cataloguing Branch — Canadiana Editorial Division (148)
Germany — German National Library — BIBLIO-DATA (423)
Helsinki School of Economics Library — Information Services (481)
Philippines — National Science and Technology Authority — Scientific Clearinghouse and Documentation Services Division (808)
University of Alberta — Faculty of Nursing — Canadian Directory of Completed Master's Theses in Nursing (1037)
University of Tasmania Library — Union List of Higher Degree Theses in Australian Libraries (1074)

Documentation (See also Information science)
Aslib, The Association for Information Management (35)
Danish Committee for Scientific and Technical Information and Documentation (255)
India — Council of Scientific and Industrial Research — Indian National Scientific Documentation Centre (507)
International Federation for Documentation (578)
International Federation for Documentation — Research Referral Service (579)
Library Association Publishing Ltd. — CURRENT RESEARCH in Library & Information Science (661)
National Conservatory of Arts and Crafts — National Institute for Documentation Techniques (722)
National Reprographic Centre for Documentation (725)
Nordic Council for Scientific Information and Research Libraries (762)
Norwegian Center for Informatics (767)
Saur Verlag (863)
Society for Information and Documentation — GID Information Center for Information Science and Practice (880)
Yugoslav Center for Technical and Scientific Documentation (1121)

Documents, government SEE: Government publications

Drug abuse
Institute for Documentation and Information in Social Medicine and Public Health (539)
Swedish Council for Information on Alcohol and Other Drugs (936)
World Health Organization — WHO Collaborating Centre for International Drug Monitoring (1115)

Drugs (See also Pharmacy and pharmacology)
ADIS Press Australasia Pty Ltd. — ADIS Drug Information Retrieval System (5)
Data Bank for Medicaments (257)
Derwent Publications Ltd. — Pharmaceutical Literature Documentation (277)
Drug Information Pharmacists Group — Pharmline (285)
Elsevier Science Publishers B.V. — Biomedical Division — Excerpta Medica (296)
FARMODEX Foundation — FARMODEX Drug Data Bank (325)
Germany — Ministry of Youth, Family and Health — German Institute for Medical Documentation and Information (428)
Japan Pharmaceutical Information Center (634)
Medical-Pharmaceutical Publishing Company (693)
Pharmaceutical Society of Great Britain — Martindale Online (806)
Royal Dutch Society for Advancement of Pharmacy — KNMP Drug Databank (844)
Spanish Drug Information Center — Spanish Pharmaceutical Specialities Data Bank (893)
Sweden — National Board of Health and Welfare — Department of Drugs — Swedish Drug Information System (922)
University of British Columbia — B.C. Hospital Programs Branch — Drug and Poison Information Centre (1043)
World Health Organization — WHO Collaborating Centre for International Drug Monitoring (1115)

Duplicating SEE: Copying and duplicating

Earth science SEE: Geology

Earthquakes
Asian Institute of Technology — Regional Documentation Center — Asian Information Center for Geotechnical Engineering (30)
Royal Norwegian Council for Scientific and Industrial Research — Norwegian Seismic Array (850)

Ecology (See also Environment)
Geo Abstracts Ltd. (393)
Great Britain — Institute of Terrestrial Ecology — Biological Records Centre (461)
International Society of Ecological Modelling — Environmental Data and Ecological Parameters Data Base (604)
Marine Biological Association of the United Kingdom — Marine Pollution Information Centre (684)
Mexico — National Institute for Research on Biological Resources — INIREB Library (702)
Netherlands — Ministry of Agriculture and Fisheries — Agricultural Research Division — Centre for Agricultural Publishing and Documentation (731)
Pergamon Press — Current Awareness in Biological Sciences (803)
Royal Museum of Central Africa — Center for Informatics Applied to Development and Tropical Agriculture — Agroclimatology Data Bank (846)

Swiss Wildlife Information Service   (947)

Econometrics
British Columbia Ministry of Industry and Small Business Development — Central Statistics Bureau   (106)
CISI-Wharton Econometric Forecasting Associates Ltd.   (207)
Computer Sciences of Australia Pty. Ltd. — Network Services Division — INFOBANK   (237)
France — National Institute of Statistics and Economic Studies — Macroeconomic Data Bank   (366)
Great Britain — H.M. Treasury — U.K. Treasury Macroeconomic Forecasting Model and Databank   (456)
Informetrica Limited   (536)
Nomura Research Institute — Information Service and Development Department — NRI/E Japan Economic & Business Data Bank   (760)
SLAMARK International   (878)

Economic development (See also Developing nations)
International Development Research Centre — Library   (576)
Latin American Newsletters Ltd.   (651)
Organisation for Economic Co-Operation and Development — International Development Information Network   (781)
Southeast Asian Regional Center for Graduate Study and Research in Agriculture — Agricultural Information Bank for Asia   (889)
Technology Resource Center — Technobank Program   (967)
United Nations — Advisory Committee for the Co-ordination of Information Systems   (1001)
United Nations — Economic and Social Commission for Asia and the Pacific — ESCAP Library — ESCAP Bibliographic Information System   (1002)
United Nations — Economic Commission for Africa — Pan-African Documentation and Information System   (1005)
United Nations — Economic Commission for Latin America — Latin American Center for Economic and Social Documentation   (1006)

Economic forecasting (See also Business forecasting)
Bird Associates   (89)
CISI-Wharton Econometric Forecasting Associates Ltd.   (207)
Henley Centre for Forecasting   (484)
IFO-Institute for Economic Research — Department of Econometrics and Data Processing — IFO Time Series Data Bank   (501)
Informetrica Limited   (536)
Nomura Research Institute — Information Service and Development Department — NRI/E Japan Economic & Business Data Bank   (760)
Office of Economic Information and Forecasting   (773)
Sharp Associates Limited   (871)
University of Paris-Nanterre — Group for Applied Macroeconomic Analysis   (1062)

Economic statistics SEE: Econometrics

Economics (See also Prices)
Admedia — Adfacts   (6)
Australian Bureau of Statistics   (52)
Bank Society — General Documentation — SGB Data Base   (73)
Belgium — Ministry of Economic Affairs — Fonds Quetelet Library Data Base   (81)
Belgium — Ministry of Economic Affairs — National Statistical Institute   (82)
Bonnier Business Publishing Group — AffarsData   (94)
British Columbia Ministry of Industry and Small Business Development — Central Statistics Bureau   (106)
Canada — Statistics Canada — Canadian Socio-Economic Information Management System   (159)
Center for International Prospective Studies   (185)
Central Electronic Network for Data Processing and Analysis   (194)
CISI-Wharton Econometric Forecasting Associates Ltd.   (207)
Commission of the European Communities — Statistical Office of the European Communities — CRONOS Data Bank   (225)
Compusearch Market and Social Research Ltd.   (236)
Computer Sciences of Australia Pty. Ltd. — Network Services Division — INFOBANK   (237)
Conference Board of Canada — Applied Economic Research and Information Centre — AERIC System   (238)
Datacrown Inc.   (261)
Datasolve Ltd. — World Reporter   (265)
Datastream International Ltd.   (267)
Economic and Social Research Council — Data Archive   (291)
Financial Times Business Information Ltd. — Business Information Service   (328)
Finsbury Data Services Ltd. — TEXTLINE   (335)
France — National Center for Scientific Research — Documentation Center for Human Sciences   (355)
France — National Institute of Statistics and Economic Studies — Documentation Division — SPHINX Data Base   (363)
France — National Institute of Statistics and Economic Studies — Information System for the Economy   (364)
France — National Institute of Statistics and Economic Studies — Macroeconomic Data Bank   (366)
French Press Agency — Telematics Department — AGORA   (388)
French Stockbrokers Society — Information and Documentation Center   (389)
Great Britain — Central Statistical Office — CSO Macro-Economic Data Bank   (449)
Great Britain — Department of Trade and Industry — Business Statistics Office   (454)
GSI-ECO   (469)
Helsinki School of Economics Library — Information Services   (481)
Hungarian Academy of Sciences — Institute of Economics — Economic Information Unit   (491)
Hungary — Central Statistical Office   (493)
IFO-Institute for Economic Research — Department of Econometrics and Data Processing — IFO Time Series Data Bank   (501)
Industrial Life-Technical Services Inc.   (513)
Informetrica Limited   (536)
International Committee for Social Science Information and Documentation   (571)
International Information Services Company   (589)
Interuniversity Documentation and Information Center for the Social Sciences   (611)
Kiel Institute for World Economics — National Library of Economics   (639)
Kompass International Ltd.   (642)
LymBurner & Sons Ltd. — Economist's Statistics   (679)
Madagascar — Ministry of Finance and Economy — National Institute of Statistics and Economic Research   (681)
MERLIN GERIN Company — Documentation Department — MERL-ECO   (696)
Micromedia Ltd. — Canadian Business Index   (707)
Netherlands — Netherlands Foreign Trade Agency — Library and Documentation Branch — Foreign Trade Abstracts   (733)
New Zealand — Department of Statistics — Information Network for Official Statistics   (749)
Nihon Keizai Shimbun, Inc. — Databank Bureau — Nikkei Economic Electronic Databank System-Information Retrieval   (753)
Nihon Keizai Shimbun, Inc. — Databank Bureau — Nikkei Economic Electronic Databank System-Time Sharing   (754)
Nomura Research Institute — Information Service and Development Department — NRI/E Japan Economic & Business Data Bank   (760)
Norway — Ministry of Finances and Customs — Central Bureau of Statistics   (766)
Organisation for Economic Co-Operation and Development — Economic Statistics and National Accounts Division — OECD Magnetic Tape Subscription Service   (780)
People's Republic of China — Institute of Scientific and Technical Information of China   (801)
Sharp Associates Limited   (871)
SLAMARK International   (878)
SLIGOS   (879)
Society for the Study of Economic and Social Development — MERCATIS   (881)
Sweden — Statistics Sweden — Statistical Data Bases Unit   (932)
United Nations — Economic and Social Commission for Asia and the Pacific — Statistics Division — UN/ESCAP Statistical Information Services   (1004)
University of Sydney Library — Bibliographic Information on Southeast Asia   (1073)
University of Warwick Library — Warwick Statistics Service   (1083)

Economics, agricultural SEE: Agricultural economics

Economics, home SEE: Home economics

Education
Australian Council for Educational Research — Library and Information Services Unit   (54)
The British Council — Central Information Service   (108)
Canadian Education Association — Canadian Education Index Data Base   (170)
Commission of the European Communities — Education Information Network in the European Community   (215)
Council for Educational Technology — Videotex Services Unit   (247)
Council of Europe — European Documentation and Information System for Education   (248)
France — Ministry of Education — National Center for Pedagogical Documentation   (346)
France — National Center for Scientific Research — Documentation Center for Human Sciences   (355)
Great Britain — British Library — Bibliographic Services Division   (439)
Hertfordshire County Council — Chiltern Advisory Unit for Computer Based Education   (485)
International Association for the Evaluation of Educational Achievement — IEA Data Bank   (557)

Norwegian Center for Informatics (767)
Ontario Ministry of Education — Research and Information Branch — Information Centre — Ontario Education Resources Information System (777)
Sweden — National Library for Psychology and Education (924)
United Nations Educational, Scientific and Cultural Organization — International Bureau of Education — Documentation and Information Unit (1021)
York University — Institute for Behavioural Research (1120)

Education, adult
United Nations Educational, Scientific and Cultural Organization — International Bureau of Education — Documentation and Information Unit (1021)

Education, career SEE: Education, vocational

Education, health SEE: Health education

Education, higher
British Universities Film & Video Council Ltd. — Information Service (112)
Exeter University Teaching Services — The Exeter Abstract Reference System (319)

Education, physical
Coaching Association of Canada — Sport Information Resource Centre (210)

Education, rural
Commonwealth Agricultural Bureaux — CAB Abstracts (229)

Education, teacher
Hertfordshire County Council — Chiltern Advisory Unit for Computer Based Education (485)

Education, vocational
Great Britain — Manpower Services Commission — Careers and Occupational Information Centre (462)
International Labour Office — Central Library and Documentation Branch (593)

Educational administration
University of Alberta — Department of Educational Administration — Administration Laboratory Project File (1034)

Educational research
Council of Europe — European Documentation and Information System for Education (248)
Exeter University Teaching Services — The Exeter Abstract Reference System (319)
National Foundation for Educational Research in England and Wales — Information Research and Development Unit (724)
Ontario Ministry of Education — Research and Information Branch — Information Centre — Ontario Education Resources Information System (777)
Swiss Coordination Center for Research in Education (945)
United Nations Educational, Scientific and Cultural Organization — International Bureau of Education — Documentation and Information Unit (1021)

Educational testing
International Association for the Evaluation of Educational Achievement — IEA Data Bank (557)

Egypt
Tel-Aviv University — Shiloah Research Center for Middle Eastern and African Studies — Documentation System — Mideast File (970)

Electric batteries SEE: Batteries

Electric lighting SEE: Lighting

Electric power
MERLIN GERIN Company — Documentation Department — MERLIN-TECH (697)
Multinational Association of Producers and Retailers of Electricity-Documentation (717)
Technical Information Center — Electrical Engineering Documentation Center (960)

Electric vehicles
Zinc Development Association/Lead Development Association/Cadmium Association — Library and Abstracting Service (1122)

Electrical engineering
Building Services Research and Information Association — BSRIA Information Centre (119)
Derwent Publications Ltd. — Patents Documentation Services (275)
Institution of Electrical Engineers — INSPEC (549)
MERLIN GERIN Company — Documentation Department — MERLIN-TECH (697)
Swedish Mechanical and Electrical Engineering Trade Association — VERA (939)
Technical Information Center — Electrical Engineering Documentation Center (960)
VDI-Verlag GmbH — VDI News Data Base (1096)

Electricity
Electricite de France — Office of Study and Research — Information and Documentation Systems Department — EDF-DOC Data Base (295)
MERLIN GERIN Company — Documentation Department — MERLIN-TECH (697)
Multinational Association of Producers and Retailers of Electricity-Documentation (717)

Electronic data processing (See also Computers)
Association for Literary and Linguistic Computing (37)
British Computer Society (107)
Center for the Study on Information Systems in Government (190)
France — National Institute for Research in Informatics and Automation — Information Dissemination Office (361)
I/S Datacentralen (497)
Information Processing Society of Japan (529)
Institute for Information Industry (542)
Institution of Electrical Engineers — INSPEC (549)
Intergovernmental Bureau for Informatics (554)
International Association for Statistical Computing (556)
International Federation for Information Processing (580)
International Group of Users of Information Systems (586)
International Medical Informatics Association (597)
Legal Technology Group (656)
MERLIN GERIN Company — Documentation Department — MERLIN-TECH (697)
National Computing Centre Ltd. — Information Services Division (721)
Netherlands Organization for Applied Scientific Research — Institute TNO for Mathematics, Information Processing and Statistics (741)
Netherlands Society for Informatics (745)
Norwegian Computing Centre for the Humanities (768)
Paris District Informatics Administration — Informatics Biblio Service (797)
Philips Information Systems and Automation — DIRECT (809)
Piedmont Consortium for Information Systems (811)
Technical Information Center — Electrical Engineering Documentation Center (960)

Electronic mail
Great Britain — Department of Industry — Information Technology Division — HERMES (450)

Electronic publishing SEE: Publishing; Computerized typesetting

Electronics (See also Communications; Electrical engineering)
DAFSA-SNEI S.A. — FITEK (252)
Derwent Publications Ltd. — Patents Documentation Services (275)
Electricite de France — Office of Study and Research — Information and Documentation Systems Department — EDF-DOC Data Base (295)
European Space Agency — Information Retrieval Service (317)
France — National Telecommunications Research Center — Interministerial Documentation Service — TELEDOC (367)
Institution of Electrical Engineers — INSPEC (549)
Institution of Electrical Engineers — INSPEC — Electronic Materials Information Service (550)
MERLIN GERIN Company — Documentation Department — MERLIN-TECH (697)
Office of Economic Information and Forecasting (773)
Overseas Data Service, Company, Ltd. (789)
Philips Information Systems and Automation — DIRECT (809)
Technical Information Center — Electrical Engineering Documentation Center (960)

Electronics, medical SEE: Medical electronics

Electrotechnology (See also Electrical engineering)
Institution of Electrical Engineers — INSPEC (549)
Technical Information Center — Electrical Engineering Documentation Center (960)

Embryology
Hubrecht Laboratory — Central Embryological Library — Documentation and Information System on Developmental

Biology (490)

Employment SEE: Career placement; Labor

Endocrinology
   Pergamon Press — Current Awareness in Biological Sciences (803)

Energy conversion
   Alberta Research Council — Coal Technology Information Centre (14)

Energy, geothermal SEE: Geothermal energy

Energy, nuclear SEE: Nuclear energy

Energy research
   Canada — Department of Energy, Mines and Resources — Conservation and Renewable Energy Branch — Canadian Energy Information System (133)
   Commission of the European Communities — Euro Abstracts (218)
   Information Center for Energy, Physics, Mathematics (521)
   Nordic Atomic Libraries Joint Secretariat — Nordic Energy Index (761)

Energy resources (See also Fuels; Solar energy; etc.)
   Asian Institute of Technology — Regional Documentation Center — Renewable Energy Resources Information Center (33)
   Brazil — National Commission for Nuclear Energy — Center for Nuclear Information (102)
   Canada — Department of Energy, Mines and Resources — Conservation and Renewable Energy Branch — Canadian Energy Information System (133)
   Canada — Department of Energy, Mines and Resources — Geological Survey of Canada — National GEOSCAN Centre (135)
   Commonwealth Regional Renewable Energy Resources Information System (230)
   Dataline Inc. (262)
   Electricite de France — Office of Study and Research — Information and Documentation Systems Department — EDF-DOC Data Base (295)
   France — Atomic Energy Commission — Saclay Nuclear Research Center — Documentation Center (339)
   France — National Center for Scientific Research — Documentation Center for Human Sciences (355)
   France — National Center for Scientific Research — Scientific and Technical Documentation Center (356)
   French Institute of Energy — Energy Studies and Information Center (386)
   French Petroleum Institute — Documentation Center (387)
   Helsinki University of Technology — University Library/National Library for Science and Technology (483)
   Information Center for Energy, Physics, Mathematics (521)
   International Atomic Energy Agency — Energy and Economic Data Bank (559)
   Japan Information Center of Science and Technology (632)
   Multinational Association of Producers and Retailers of Electricity- Documentation (717)
   Nihon Keizai Shimbun, Inc. — Databank Bureau — Nikkei Economic Electronic Databank System-Information Retrieval (753)
   Nihon Keizai Shimbun, Inc. — Databank Bureau — Nikkei Economic Electronic Databank System-Time Sharing (754)
   Nordic Atomic Libraries Joint Secretariat — Nordic Energy Index (761)
   Riso National Laboratory — Riso Library (842)
   Sharp Associates Limited (871)
   SLAMARK International (878)
   Studsvik Energiteknik AB — Report Collection Index (906)
   United Nations Educational, Scientific and Cultural Organization — Energy Information Section (1018)
   University of Alberta — Computing Services — Information Systems Group (1033)

Energy, solar SEE: Solar energy

Energy, thermal SEE: Thermal energy

Energy, wind SEE: Wind energy

Engineering (See also Science and technology)
   Asian Institute of Technology — Regional Documentation Center — Asian Information Center for Geotechnical Engineering (30)
   Canada — National Research Council of Canada — Canada Institute for Scientific and Technical Information (152)
   CITIS Ltd. (208)
   ESDU International Limited (299)
   European Space Agency — Information Retrieval Service (317)
   France — National Center for Scientific Research — Scientific and Technical Documentation Center (356)
   Helsinki University of Technology — University Library/National Library for Science and Technology (483)
   Japan Information Center of Science and Technology (632)
   Library Association Publishing Ltd. — Current Technology Index (662)
   London Enterprise Agency — Supplier Identification System (671)
   Pont-a-Mousson Research Center — Industrial Documentation Service — BIIPAM-CTIF Data Base (820)
   Singapore Institute of Standards and Industrial Research — Industrial Technical Information Service (877)
   South Africa — Council for Scientific and Industrial Research — Centre for Scientific and Technical Information (885)
   Technical Indexes Ltd. (958)
   Technical Information Center (959)
   Union of Soviet Socialist Republics — All-Union Institute of Scientific and Technical Information (998)
   University of New Brunswick Libraries — PHOENIX (1059)
   VDI-Verlag GmbH — VDI News Data Base (1096)

Engineering, aeronautical SEE: Aeronautics

Engineering, agricultural SEE: Agricultural engineering

Engineering, automotive SEE: Automotive engineering

Engineering, biological SEE: Bioengineering

Engineering, chemical SEE: Chemical engineering

Engineering, civil SEE: Civil engineering

Engineering, coastal SEE: Coasts

Engineering, electrical SEE: Electrical engineering

Engineering, environmental SEE: Environmental engineering

Engineering, foundation SEE: Foundation engineering

Engineering, highway SEE: Highway engineering

Engineering, human SEE: Human engineering

Engineering, mechanical SEE: Mechanical engineering

Engineering, nuclear SEE: Nuclear engineering

Engineering, production SEE: Production engineering

Engineering, sanitary SEE: Sanitary engineering

Engineering, structural SEE: Structural engineering

Engineering, traffic SEE: Traffic engineering

England SEE: Great Britain

Enology SEE: Wine and wine making

Entomology (See also Pesticides)
   Commonwealth Agricultural Bureaux — CAB Abstracts (229)

Environment (See also Conservation of natural resources; Ecology; Pollution)
   Asian Institute of Technology — Regional Documentation Center — Environmental Sanitation Information Center (31)
   Canada — Environment Canada — Inland Waters Directorate — WATDOC (140)
   Canada — Environment Canada — Library Services Branch — Environment Libraries Automated System (144)
   Commission of the European Communities — Environmental Information and Documentation Centers Data Base (216)
   Commission of the European Communities — Environmental Research Projects Data Base (217)
   Commission of the European Communities — Euro Abstracts (218)
   Commission of the European Communities — Joint Research Centre — Environmental Chemicals Data and Information Network (221)
   Dortmund Institute for Water Research — Data Bank on Substances Harmful to Water (284)
   Germany — Federal Environmental Agency — Environmental Information and Documentation System (411)
   International Society of Ecological Modelling — Environmental Data and Ecological Parameters Data Base (604)
   Japan — Environment Agency — National Institute for Environmental Studies — Environmental Information Division (626)
   K-Konsult — VA-NYTT (637)
   Netherlands Organization for Applied Scientific Research — TNO Study and Information Center on Environmental Research —

Environmental Research in the Netherlands (743)
Norwegian Center for Informatics (767)
QL Systems Limited (828)
Quebec Ministry of the Environment — Documentation Center — Envirodoq (832)
Riso National Laboratory — Riso Library (842)
Sweden — National Swedish Environment Protection Board — Swedish Environmental Research Index (926)
United Nations — Food and Agriculture Organization — International Information System for the Agricultural Sciences and Technology (1012)
United Nations Educational, Scientific and Cultural Organization — Intergovernmental Oceanographic Commission — Marine Environmental Data Information Referral System (1020)
United Nations Environment Programme — Industry and Environment Office — Industry and Environment Data Base (1024)
United Nations Environment Programme — INFOTERRA (1025)
URBAMET Network (1091)
World Meteorological Organization — World Weather Watch (1119)

Environmental engineering
Pan American Health Organization — Pan American Centre for Sanitary Engineering & Environmental Sciences — Pan American Information & Documentation Network on Sanitary Engineering & Environmental Sciences (794)

Environmental health
Elsevier Science Publishers B.V. — Biomedical Division — Excerpta Medica (296)
Great Britain — Water Research Centre — Information Service on Toxicity and Biodegradability (463)
Institute for Documentation and Information in Social Medicine and Public Health (539)
International Labour Office — International Occupational Safety and Health Information Centre (595)
Royal Society of Chemistry — Information Services — Chemical Hazards in Industry (853)

Environmental impact statements
Quebec Ministry of the Environment — Documentation Center — Envirodoq (832)

Environmental law
Legal Technology Group (656)

Environmental sciences SEE: Environment

Ephemeral literature SEE: Fugitive literature

Ephemerides
Union of Soviet Socialist Republics — Academy of Sciences of the U.S.S.R. — Institute for Theoretical Astronomy — Minor Planets, Comets, and Satellites Department (997)

Ergonomics SEE: Human engineering

Ethics, medical SEE: Medical ethics

Ethnology
France — National Center for Scientific Research — Documentation Center for Human Sciences (355)

Europe
Association of European Airlines — AEA Data Base (41)
Europe Data (305)
European Law Centre Ltd. — Eurolex (314)
Finsbury Data Services Ltd. — TEXTLINE (335)
International Center for Higher Studies in Mediterranean Agronomy — Socioeconomic Data Bank on the Mediterranean Countries (564)
Research Services Ltd. — Pan European Survey (839)
Servi-Tech — BIODOC (870)
Sharp Associates Limited (871)
University of Alberta — Computing Services — Information Systems Group (1033)

European Economic Community
Agra Europe (8)
Bank Society — General Documentation — SGB Data Base (73)
Commission of the European Communities — Court of Justice of the European Communities — Legal Data Processing Group — CJUS Data Bank (214)
Commission of the European Communities — Education Information Network in the European Community (215)
Commission of the European Communities — Statistical Office of the European Communities — COMEXT Data Bank (224)
Commission of the European Communities — Statistical Office of the European Communities — CRONOS Data Bank (225)
European Law Centre Ltd. — Eurolex (314)
Finsbury Data Services Ltd. — TEXTLINE (335)
Honeywell Bull — Euris Host Service (488)
Honeywell Bull — Euris Host Service — European Community Law (489)
University of Dundee — Law Library — European Documentation Centre (1047)

Executives
Canada — Consumer and Corporate Affairs Canada — Corporations Branch — Corporate Integrated Information System (129)
Canada Systems Group — Federal Systems Division — Canadian Federal Corporations and Directors Data Base (163)
ICC Information Group Ltd. (499)

Family planning
India — National Institute of Health and Family Welfare — Documentation Centre (508)
United Nations — Economic and Social Commission for Asia and the Pacific — Population Division — Population Clearing-house and Information Section (1003)

Federal government (See also Government contracts; Government publications)
France — French Senate — Parliamentary Documentation and Information Printing Service (343)
Great Britain — House of Commons Library — Parliamentary On-Line Information System (459)
Great Britain — House of Lords — Library & Information Centre (460)

Federal records SEE: Public records

Feed SEE: Animal feed

Ferrocement
Asian Institute of Technology — Regional Documentation Center — International Ferrocement Information Center (32)

Fertilizers
Commonwealth Agricultural Bureaux — CAB Abstracts (229)
United Nations — Food and Agriculture Organization — Statistics Division — Interlinked Computerized Storage and Processing System of Food and Agricultural Data (1014)

Fibers, textile SEE: Textiles

Field crops
Commonwealth Agricultural Bureaux — CAB Abstracts (229)
Royal Tropical Institute — Agricultural Information & Documentation Section (857)
United Nations — Food and Agriculture Organization — Statistics Division — Interlinked Computerized Storage and Processing System of Food and Agricultural Data (1014)

Field theory, quantum SEE: Quantum field theory

Films SEE: Audiovisual material; Motion pictures

Finance SEE: Banking and finance

Finland
Helsinki University Library — Finnish National Bibliography (482)

Fires and fire prevention
Building Services Research and Information Association — BSRIA Information Centre (119)
Great Britain — Atomic Energy Authority — Atomic Energy Research Establishment, Harwell — National Chemical Emergency Centre — CHEMSAFE (435)
Great Britain — Department of the Environment — Building Research Establishment — Fire Research Station Library — Fire Science Abstracts (452)

Fisheries (See also Marine biology)
Agra Europe (8)
Canada — Environment Canada — Inland Waters Directorate — WATDOC (140)
Commission of the European Communities — Agricultural Research Projects Data Base (213)
France — National Center for Ocean Utilization — National Bureau for Ocean Data — DOCOCEAN (351)
Germany — Federal Research Center for Fisheries — Information and Documentation Center (421)
Maritime Information Centre/CMO (685)
United Nations — Food and Agriculture Organization — Aquatic Sciences and Fisheries Information System (1008)
United Nations — Food and Agriculture Organization — INFOFISH (1011)

United Nations — Food and Agriculture Organization — International Information System for the Agricultural Sciences and Technology (1012)
United Nations — Food and Agriculture Organization — Library and Documentation Systems Division — David Lubin Memorial Library (1013)
United Nations — Food and Agriculture Organization — Statistics Division — Interlinked Computerized Storage and Processing System of Food and Agricultural Data (1014)
United Nations Educational, Scientific and Cultural Organization — Intergovernmental Oceanographic Commission — Marine Environmental Data Information Referral System (1020)

Flight safety
Aviation Information Services Ltd. (68)
International Civil Aviation Organization — Air Navigation Bureau — Accident Investigation and Prevention Section — Aircraft Accident/Incident Reporting System (567)

Fluid mechanics (See also Hydraulics)
BHRA, The Fluid Engineering Centre — Information Services (86)
Delft Hydraulics Laboratory — Information and Documentation Section (268)
ESDU International Limited (299)

Fluids
BHRA, The Fluid Engineering Centre — Information Services (86)

Food chemistry
International Food Information Service — Food Science and Technology Abstracts (583)
Leatherhead Food Research Association — Information and Library Services (655)

Food industry (See also Beverage industry)
Agra Europe (8)
Association for the Promotion of Industry-Agriculture — International Documentation Center for Industries Using Agricultural Products (39)
France — National Center for Scientific Research — Scientific and Technical Documentation Center (356)
International Food Information Service — Food Science and Technology Abstracts (583)
Leatherhead Food Research Association — Information and Library Services (655)
United Nations — Food and Agriculture Organization — Statistics Division — Interlinked Computerized Storage and Processing System of Food and Agricultural Data (1014)

Food science and technology
Association for the Promotion of Industry-Agriculture — International Documentation Center for Industries Using Agricultural Products (39)
Commission of the European Communities — Agricultural Research Projects Data Base (213)
Documentary Research Center (282)
Germany — Center for Agricultural Documentation and Information (408)
Institute of Nutrition — Documentation Department (545)
International Food Information Service — Food Science and Technology Abstracts (583)
Leatherhead Food Research Association — Information and Library Services (655)
Mitaka — JAPANSCAN (712)
Norwegian Center for Informatics (767)
Southeast Asian Regional Center for Graduate Study and Research in Agriculture — Agricultural Information Bank for Asia (889)
United Nations — Food and Agriculture Organization — International Information System for the Agricultural Sciences and Technology (1012)
United Nations — Food and Agriculture Organization — Library and Documentation Systems Division — David Lubin Memorial Library (1013)

Forecasting
Institute for Futures Studies — Futures Information Service (540)

Forecasting, business SEE: Business forecasting

Forecasting, economic SEE: Economic forecasting

Foreign affairs SEE: International relations

Foreign aid SEE: Developing nations

Foreign policy SEE: International relations

Foreign relations SEE: International relations

Foreign trade (See also Business, international)
AVCOR (67)
Center for International Prospective Studies (185)
Central Electronic Network for Data Processing and Analysis (194)
Commission of the European Communities — Statistical Office of the European Communities — COMEXT Data Bank (224)
Commission of the European Communities — Statistical Office of the European Communities — CRONOS Data Bank (225)
Datasolve Ltd. — World Exporter (264)
Finnish Foreign Trade Association — Information Department — Register of Exporters (332)
Germany — Ministry of Economics — German Foreign Trade Information Office (425)
GSI-ECO (469)
Hungarian Academy of Sciences — Institute of Economics — Economic Information Unit (491)
International Center for Higher Studies in Mediterranean Agronomy — Socioeconomic Data Bank on the Mediterranean Countries (564)
Netherlands — Netherlands Foreign Trade Agency — Library and Documentation Branch — Foreign Trade Abstracts (733)
Nihon Keizai Shimbun, Inc. — Databank Bureau — Nikkei Economic Electronic Databank System-Time Sharing (754)
Organisation for Economic Co-Operation and Development — Economic Statistics and National Accounts Division — OECD Magnetic Tape Subscription Service (780)
Paris Chamber of Commerce and Industry — Department of International Relations — TELEXPORT (796)
Sharp Associates Limited (871)
Unilever Computer Services Ltd. — European Petrochemical Association Trade Statistics Database (993)
Unilever Computer Services Ltd. — World Trade Statistics Database (994)
United Nations — Economic and Social Commission for Asia and the Pacific — Statistics Division — UN/ESCAP Statistical Information Services (1004)
United Nations — Food and Agriculture Organization — Statistics Division — Interlinked Computerized Storage and Processing System of Food and Agricultural Data (1014)

Forensic medicine SEE: Medicine, legal

Forensic sciences
Elsevier Science Publishers B.V. — Biomedical Division — Excerpta Medica (296)
Great Britain — Home Office Forensic Science Service — Central Research Establishment — Operational Services Division (458)
Kugler Publications (647)

Forest products
Commonwealth Agricultural Bureaux — CAB Abstracts (229)
Timber Research and Development Association — Information and Advisory Department — Timber Information Keyword Retrieval (983)
United Nations — Food and Agriculture Organization — Statistics Division — Interlinked Computerized Storage and Processing System of Food and Agricultural Data (1014)

Forestry
Canada — Environment Canada — Library Services Branch — Environment Libraries Automated System (144)
Commission of the European Communities — Agricultural Research Projects Data Base (213)
Commonwealth Agricultural Bureaux — CAB Abstracts (229)
Germany — Center for Agricultural Documentation and Information (408)
Netherlands — Ministry of Agriculture and Fisheries — Agricultural Research Division — Centre for Agricultural Publishing and Documentation (731)
United Nations — Food and Agriculture Organization — International Information System for the Agricultural Sciences and Technology (1012)
United Nations — Food and Agriculture Organization — Library and Documentation Systems Division — David Lubin Memorial Library (1013)
United Nations — Food and Agriculture Organization — Statistics Division — Interlinked Computerized Storage and Processing System of Food and Agricultural Data (1014)

Fossil fuels SEE: Fuels

Foundation engineering
Asian Institute of Technology — Regional Documentation Center — Asian Information Center for Geotechnical Engineering (30)
CITIS Ltd. (208)

Foundations (philanthropic)
Charities Aid Foundation — Information Services (198)

Foundries SEE: Metalworking industry

France
Center for the Study of Advertising Support (189)
DAFSA (251)
Didot-Bottin — Bottin Data Bases (280)
Editions Techniques — JURIS-DATA (294)
France — French Senate — Parliamentary Documentation and Information Printing Service (343)
France — Ministry of Education — National Center for Pedagogical Documentation (346)
France — National Institute of Statistics and Economic Studies — Documentation Division — SPHINX Data Base (363)
France — National Institute of Statistics and Economic Studies — Information System for the Economy (364)
France — National Institute of Statistics and Economic Studies — Local Area Data Bank (365)
France — National Institute of Statistics and Economic Studies — Macroeconomic Data Bank (366)
French Documentation — Political and Current Events Information Bank (384)
French Press Agency — Telematics Department — AGORA (388)
French Stockbrokers Society — Information and Documentation Center (389)
Industrial News Publishing Company — KOMPASS-FRANCE (514)
International Information Services Company (589)
Microfor Inc. (704)
Office of Economic Information and Forecasting (773)
Paris Office of Urbanization — Urban Data Bank of Paris and the Paris Region (798)
Quebec Ministry of Education — Library Headquarters — Point de Repere (831)
SLIGOS (879)
Society for the Study of Economic and Social Development — MERCATIS (881)
SYDONI S.A. (949)
University of Paris-Nanterre — Group for Applied Macroeconomic Analysis (1062)

Freshwater biology SEE: Aquatic biology

Fruits and vegetables
Institute of Research on Fruits and Citrus Fruits — Documentation Center (547)

Fuels (See also Coal; Natural gas; Petroleum and petroleum technology)
Asian Institute of Technology — Regional Documentation Center — Renewable Energy Resources Information Center (33)
French Petroleum Institute — Documentation Center (387)

Fugitive literature
Commission of the European Communities — System for Information on Grey Literature in Europe (226)

Fungi SEE: Mycology

Futures, commodity SEE: Commodity futures

Futurology
Institute for Futures Studies — Futures Information Service (540)

Galvanizing
Zinc Development Association/Lead Development Association/Cadmium Association — Library and Abstracting Service (1122)

Gardening SEE: Horticulture

Gas dynamics
University of Leeds — Department of Physical Chemistry — High Temperature Reaction Rate Data Centre (1052)

Gas, natural SEE: Natural gas

Genetics
Celltech Ltd. — Information and Library Service (181)
Hubrecht Laboratory — Central Embryological Library — Documentation and Information System on Developmental Biology (490)
Pergamon Press — Current Awareness in Biological Sciences (803)
Royal Society of Chemistry — Information Services — Current Biotechnology Abstracts (854)

Geochemistry
Australian Mineral Foundation — Australian Earth Sciences Information System (57)
France — Bureau of Geological and Mining Research — National Geological Survey — Geological Information and Documentation Department (340)
Geosystems (394)
Germany — Federal Institute for Geosciences and Natural Resources — Geoscience Literature Information Service (412)
Mineralogical Society of Great Britain — Mineralogical Abstracts (711)
Natural Environment Research Council — British Geological Survey — National Geochemical Data Bank (728)

Geochronology
Geosystems (394)

Geography (See also Maps)
Canada — Environment Canada — Lands Directorate — Canada Land Data Systems Division — Canada Geographic Information System (143)
France — National Center for Scientific Research — Documentation Center for Human Sciences (355)
Geo Abstracts Ltd. (393)

Geological physics SEE: Geophysics

Geological time SEE: Geochronology

Geology (See also Mineral resources; Mineralogy; Paleontology; Sedimentology)
Alberta Research Council — Alberta Geological Survey — Geoscience Data Index for Alberta (12)
Asian Institute of Technology — Regional Documentation Center — Asian Information Center for Geotechnical Engineering (30)
Australian Mineral Foundation — Australian Earth Sciences Information System (57)
Brown's Geological Information Service Ltd. (113)
Canada — Department of Energy, Mines and Resources — Geological Survey of Canada — Economic Geology Division — Canadian Mineral Occurrence Index (134)
Canada — Department of Energy, Mines and Resources — Geological Survey of Canada — National GEOSCAN Centre (135)
France — Bureau of Geological and Mining Research — National Geological Survey — Geological Information and Documentation Department (340)
France — Bureau of Geological and Mining Research — National Geological Survey — Subsoil Data Bank (341)
France — National Center for Scientific Research — Scientific and Technical Documentation Center (356)
French Petroleum Institute — Documentation Center (387)
Geo Abstracts Ltd. (393)
Geosystems (394)
Germany — Federal Institute for Geosciences and Natural Resources — Geoscience Literature Information Service (412)
Institution of Mining and Metallurgy — Library and Information Services (551)
International Union of Geological Sciences — Commission on Storage, Automatic Processing and Retrieval of Geological Data (609)
Italy — National Research Council — Research Center for the Stratigraphy and Petrography of the Central Alps — Archive of Italian Data of Geology (625)
Natural Environment Research Council — British Geological Survey — National Geochemical Data Bank (728)
Netherlands Soil Survey Institute — Soil Information System (746)

Geology, marine SEE: Marine geology

Geomorphology
Geo Abstracts Ltd. (393)
Geosystems (394)

Geophysics
Australian Mineral Foundation — Australian Earth Sciences Information System (57)
Geo Abstracts Ltd. (393)
Geosystems (394)
Germany — Federal Institute for Geosciences and Natural Resources — Geoscience Literature Information Service (412)
University of London — Imperial College of Science and Technology — Department of Mineral Resources Engineering — Rock Mechanics Information Service (1056)

Geothermal energy
Commonwealth Regional Renewable Energy Resources Information System (230)
France — Bureau of Geological and Mining Research — National Geological Survey — Subsoil Data Bank (341)
Riso National Laboratory — Riso Library (842)

Germany
Germany — German Federal Diet — Division of Scientific Documentation — Documentation and Information System for Parliamentary Materials   (422)
Germany — German National Library — BIBLIO-DATA   (423)
Germany — Ministry of Justice — Judicial Information System   (426)
IFO-Institute for Economic Research — Department of Econometrics and Data Processing — IFO Time Series Data Bank   (501)
Institute for German Language   (541)
Sharp Associates Limited   (871)

Glaciology
Canada — Environment Canada — Inland Waters Directorate — National Hydrology Research Institute — Perennial Snow and Ice Section — Glacier Inventory of Canada   (139)

Glass
Glass Institute — Information and Documentation Service   (429)

Government SEE: Federal government; Municipal government; Political science; Public administration

Government contracts
Commission of the European Communities — Tenders Electronic Daily   (227)

Government publications
Alberta Public Affairs Bureau — Publication Services Branch   (11)
Canada — National Library of Canada — Cataloguing Branch — Canadiana Editorial Division   (148)
Great Britain — House of Commons Library — Parliamentary On-Line Information System   (459)
Great Britain — House of Lords — Library & Information Centre   (460)
Microinfo, Ltd.   (705)
Micromedia Ltd.   (706)
Quebec National Library — FMQ   (833)
University of Dundee — Law Library — European Documentation Centre   (1047)
University of Guelph Library — Cooperative Documents Network Project   (1050)

Government records SEE: Public records

Grain
International Food Information Service — Food Science and Technology Abstracts   (583)

Grapes
International Food Information Service — VITIS-Viticulture and Enology Abstracts   (585)

Graphics, computer SEE: Computer graphics

Grasses
Commonwealth Agricultural Bureaux — CAB Abstracts   (229)

Gravity
France — Bureau of Geological and Mining Research — National Geological Survey — World Gravimetric Data Bank   (342)

Gray literature SEE: Fugitive literature

Great Britain
Anglo-Brazilian Information Service   (24)
Bank of England — Financial Statistics Division   (72)
Brassey's Publishers Ltd. — British Defence Directory   (98)
The British Council — Central Information Service   (108)
British Market Research Bureau Ltd. — Target Group Index   (109)
Economic and Social Research Council — Data Archive   (291)
European Law Centre Ltd. — Eurolex   (314)
Financial Times Business Information Ltd. — Business Information Service   (328)
Great Britain — British Library — Bibliographic Services Division   (439)
Great Britain — British Library — Reference Division — Eighteenth Century Short Title Catalogue   (443)
Great Britain — Central Statistical Office — CSO Macro-Economic Data Bank   (449)
Great Britain — Department of Trade and Industry — Business Statistics Office   (454)
Great Britain — H.M. Treasury — U.K. Treasury Macroeconomic Forecasting Model and Databank   (456)
Great Britain — House of Commons Library — Parliamentary On-Line Information System   (459)
Great Britain — House of Lords — Library & Information Centre   (460)
ICC Information Group Ltd.   (499)
Jordan & Sons Ltd. — Jordans Company Information   (636)
Market Location   (686)
Nineteenth Century Short Title Catalogue Project   (757)
Pergamon InfoLine Ltd.   (802)
Press Association Ltd. — NEWSFILE   (823)
Sharp Associates Limited   (871)

Great Plains
University of Regina — Canadian Plains Research Center — Information Services   (1066)

Guided missiles SEE: Rockets and missiles

Handicapped
Brunel Univeristy — Brunel Institute for Bioengineering — Information Unit   (114)

Hazardous substances
Commission of the European Communities — Joint Research Centre — Environmental Chemicals Data and Information Network   (221)
Dortmund Institute for Water Research — Data Bank on Substances Harmful to Water   (284)
Expert Information Systems Ltd. — EXIS 1   (320)
Germany — Federal Environmental Agency — Environmental Information and Documentation System   (411)
Great Britain — Atomic Energy Authority — Atomic Energy Research Establishment, Harwell — National Chemical Emergency Centre — CHEMSAFE   (435)
Great Britain — Health and Safety Executive — HSE Library and Information Services   (457)
Great Britain — Water Research Centre — Information Service on Toxicity and Biodegradability   (463)
Royal Society of Chemistry — Information Services — Chemical Hazards in Industry   (853)
Royal Society of Chemistry — Information Services — Laboratory Hazards Bulletin   (855)
United Nations Environment Programme — International Register of Potentially Toxic Chemicals   (1026)

Health care
Australia — National Library of Australia — Australian MEDLINE Network   (50)
Austrian National Institute for Public Health — Literature Service in Medicine   (66)
France — National Center for Scientific Research — Documentation Center for Human Sciences   (355)
Health Care Literature Information Network   (477)
International Development Research Centre — Library   (576)
International Medical Informatics Association   (597)
International Medical Information Center   (598)
South African Medical Research Council — Institute for Medical Literature   (888)
World Health Organization — Eastern Mediterranean Regional Office — Information Services   (1112)

Health economics SEE: Medical economics

Health education
Institute for Documentation and Information in Social Medicine and Public Health   (539)

Health, environmental SEE: Environmental health

Health, industrial SEE: Industrial hygiene

Health manpower
World Health Organization — Division of Health Statistics — World Health Statistics Data Base   (1110)

Health, public SEE: Public health

Heart
Brunel Univeristy — Brunel Institute for Bioengineering — Information Unit   (114)

Heat SEE: High temperatures; Thermodynamics

Heating
Building Services Research and Information Association — BSRIA Information Centre   (119)

Hebraica SEE: Jewish studies

Helminthology
Commonwealth Agricultural Bureaux — CAB Abstracts   (229)

SUBJECT INDEX

High energy physics SEE: Physics, high energy

High temperatures
Commission of the European Communities — Joint Research Centre — High Temperature Materials Data Bank (222)
University of Leeds — Department of Physical Chemistry — High Temperature Reaction Rate Data Centre (1052)

Higher education SEE: Education, higher

Highway engineering (See also Traffic engineering; Transportation)
Australian Road Research Board — Australian Road Research Documentation (62)
Austria — Federal Ministry of Buildings and Technology — Federal Research and Testing Establishment Arsenal — Road Research Documentation Center (63)
CITIS Ltd. (208)
Great Britain — Departments of the Environment and Transport — Transport and Road Research Laboratory — Technical Information and Library Services (455)
Organisation for Economic Co-Operation and Development — Road Transport Research Programme — International Road Research Documentation (786)
Sweden — National Road and Traffic Research Institute — Information and Documentation Section (925)
Sweden — Swedish National Road Administration — Technical Division — Road Data Bank (933)

Highway safety SEE: Traffic safety

Hispanic America SEE: Latin America

History
France — National Center for Scientific Research — Documentation Center for Human Sciences (355)
Great Britain — British Library — Reference Division — Eighteenth Century Short Title Catalogue (443)
Nineteenth Century Short Title Catalogue Project (757)

History, art SEE: Art and art history

History, Canadian SEE: Canadian history

Holland SEE: Netherlands

Home economics
University of Alberta — Computing Services — Information Systems Group (1033)

Horticulture (See also Botany)
Commonwealth Agricultural Bureaux — CAB Abstracts (229)
Netherlands — Ministry of Agriculture and Fisheries — Agricultural Research Division — Centre for Agricultural Publishing and Documentation (731)

Hospital administration
Elsevier Science Publishers B.V. — Biomedical Division — Excerpta Medica (296)
Health Care Literature Information Network (477)

Hospitals
Health Care Literature Information Network (477)
World Health Organization — Division of Health Statistics — World Health Statistics Data Base (1110)

House construction SEE: Building construction

Housing
Computer Sciences of Australia Pty. Ltd. — Network Services Division — INFOBANK (237)
Fraunhofer Society — Information Center for Building and Physical Planning (373)
Fraunhofer Society — Information Center for Building and Physical Planning — Literature Compilations Data Base (376)
Fraunhofer Society — Information Center for Building and Physical Planning — Regional Planning, City Planning, Housing, Building Construction Data Base (379)
Fraunhofer Society — Information Center for Building and Physical Planning — Regional Planning, City Planning, Housing Research Projects Data Base (380)
International Council for Building Research, Studies and Documentation (573)
Swedish Institute of Building Documentation (938)
URBAMET Network (1091)

Human engineering
Germany — Federal Institute for Occupational Safety — Information and Documentation Centre for Occupational Safety (419)
International Labour Office — International Occupational Safety and Health Information Centre (595)
Rene Descartes University — Laboratory of Applied Anthropology — ERGODATA (838)
Socioscope Inc. (883)
University of Birmingham — Department of Engineering Production — Ergonomics Information Analysis Centre (1041)

Humanities (See also Art and art history; Literature; Music and music industry; etc.)
Association for Literary and Linguistic Computing (37)
Australia — National Library of Australia (48)
Canada — National Library of Canada (147)
France — National Center for Scientific Research — Documentation Center for Human Sciences (355)
Library Association Publishing Ltd. — British Humanities Index (660)
National Autonomous University of Mexico — Center for Scientific and Humanistic Information (719)
Norwegian Computing Centre for the Humanities (768)
Spain — Higher Council for Scientific Research — Institute for Information and Documentation in the Social Sciences and Humanities (891)

Hungary
Hungary — Central Statistical Office (493)

Hydraulics
BHRA, The Fluid Engineering Centre — Information Services (86)
Canada — Environment Canada — Inland Waters Directorate — WATDOC (140)
CITIS Ltd. (208)
Delft Hydraulics Laboratory — Information and Documentation Section (268)

Hydrobiology SEE: Aquatic biology

Hydroelectric power
Asian Institute of Technology — Regional Documentation Center — Renewable Energy Resources Information Center (33)

Hydrology (See also Water resources)
Canada — Environment Canada — Inland Waters Directorate — WATDOC (140)
France — National Center for Ocean Utilization — National Bureau for Ocean Data (347)
French Water Study Association — National Water Information Center (391)
Geo Abstracts Ltd. (393)
Germany — Federal Institute for Geosciences and Natural Resources — Geoscience Literature Information Service (412)
South Africa — South African Water Information Centre (887)
Sweden — Geological Survey of Sweden — Groundwater Documentation Section (920)
World Meteorological Organization — Commission for Hydrology — Operational Hydrology Programme — Hydrological Operational Multipurpose Subprogramme (1117)

Hydromechanics SEE: Fluid mechanics

Hygiene, industrial SEE: Industrial hygiene

Hygiene, public SEE: Public health

Immunology (See also Public health)
France — National Center for Scientific Research — Scientific Documentation Center in Oncology — CANCERNET (357)
Pergamon Press — Current Awareness in Biological Sciences (803)
Royal Society of Chemistry — Information Services — Current Biotechnology Abstracts (854)

Indexing (See also Automatic indexing)
Great Britain — British Library — Bibliographic Services Division — Subject Systems Office — Preserved Context Index System (441)
Indexing and Abstracting Society of Canada (506)
International Council of Scientific Unions Abstracting Board (575)
University of London — Central Information Service (1055)

Indexing, automatic SEE: Automatic indexing

India
Centre for the Study of Developing Societies — Data Unit (196)

Indonesia
University of Sydney Library — Bibliographic Information on Southeast Asia (1073)

Industrial development
  Asian Network for Industrial Technology Information and Extension (34)
  Central American Research Institute for Industry — Division of Documentation and Information (193)
  European Association for the Transfer of Technologies, Innovation and Industrial Information (306)
  Gulf Organization for Industrial Consulting — Industrial Data Bank Department (471)
  International Atomic Energy Agency — Vienna International Centre Library (562)
  Korea Institute for Industrial Economics and Technology (645)
  Tanzania — National Central Library — Tanzania National Documentation Centre (955)
  United Nations Industrial Development Organization — Industrial Information Section — Industrial and Technological Information Bank (1027)

Industrial hygiene
  Elsevier Science Publishers B.V. — Biomedical Division — Excerpta Medica (296)
  Germany — Federal Institute for Occupational Safety — Information and Documentation Centre for Occupational Safety (419)
  Great Britain — Health and Safety Executive — HSE Library and Information Services (457)
  Institute for Documentation and Information in Social Medicine and Public Health (539)
  International Labour Office — Conditions of Work and Welfare Facilities Branch — Clearing-house on Conditions of Work (594)
  International Labour Office — International Occupational Safety and Health Information Centre (595)
  Resources (840)
  Spain — Ministry of Health and Safety — National Institute of Occupational Safety and Health — National Information and Documentation Center (892)
  Sweden — National Board of Occupational Safety and Health — CIS Centre (923)

Industrial medicine SEE: Medicine, industrial

Industrial relations (See also Labor; Management)
  International Labour Office — Bureau for Labour Problems Analysis — Labour Information Database (591)
  International Labour Office — Central Library and Documentation Branch (593)
  Swedish Center for Working Life — Information and Documentation Department (935)

Industrial research
  Caribbean Industrial Research Institute — Technical Information Service (177)
  Korea Institute for Industrial Economics and Technology (645)
  Singapore Institute of Standards and Industrial Research — Industrial Technical Information Service (877)
  South Africa — Council for Scientific and Industrial Research — Centre for Scientific and Technical Information (885)
  Sweden — Royal Institute of Technology Library — Information and Documentation Center (930)

Industrial safety
  Germany — Federal Institute for Occupational Safety — Information and Documentation Centre for Occupational Safety (419)
  Great Britain — Health and Safety Executive — HSE Library and Information Services (457)
  International Labour Office — Conditions of Work and Welfare Facilities Branch — Clearing-house on Conditions of Work (594)
  International Labour Office — International Occupational Safety and Health Information Centre (595)
  Resources (840)
  Royal Society of Chemistry — Information Services — Chemical Hazards in Industry (853)
  Royal Society of Chemistry — Information Services — Laboratory Hazards Bulletin (855)
  Spain — Ministry of Health and Safety — National Institute of Occupational Safety and Health — National Information and Documentation Center (892)
  Sweden — National Board of Occupational Safety and Health — CIS Centre (923)

Industry
  Bonnier Business Publishing Group — AffarsData (94)
  Canada — Statistics Canada — Canadian Socio-Economic Information Management System (159)
  CISI-Wharton Econometric Forecasting Associates Ltd. (207)
  Computer Sciences of Australia Pty. Ltd. — Network Services Division — INFOBANK (237)
  DAFSA-SNEI S.A. — FITEK (252)
  Didot-Bottin — Bottin Data Bases (280)
  European Association for the Transfer of Technologies, Innovation and Industrial Information (306)
  Financial Times Business Information Ltd. — Business Information Service (328)
  Great Britain — Central Statistical Office — CSO Macro-Economic Data Bank (449)
  Great Britain — Department of Trade and Industry — Business Statistics Office (454)
  ICC Information Group Ltd. (499)
  Kompass International Ltd. (642)
  Market Location (686)
  McCarthy Information Ltd. (690)
  Micromedia Ltd. — Canadian Business Index (707)
  Nihon Keizai Shimbun, Inc. — Databank Bureau — Nikkei Economic Electronic Databank System-Time Sharing (754)
  Nomura Research Institute — Information Service and Development Department — NRI/E Japan Economic & Business Data Bank (760)
  Norwegian Center for Informatics (767)
  Office of Economic Information and Forecasting (773)
  Overseas Data Service, Company, Ltd. (789)
  People's Republic of China — Institute of Scientific and Technical Information of China (801)
  SLIGOS (879)
  Tijl Datapress (982)
  United Nations Environment Programme — Industry and Environment Office — Industry and Environment Data Base (1024)

Information centers SEE: Information services

Information industry
  A.JOUR (1)
  Association of European Host Operators Group (42)
  Canadian Information Industry Association (172)
  Commission of the European Communities — European On-Line Information Network — Direct Information Access Network for Europe (220)
  Epoch Research Corporation (298)
  European Association of Information Services (307)
  European Business Associates On-Line (308)
  European Information Providers Association (312)
  Information Management and Consulting Association (526)
  Learned Information Ltd. (654)
  Management Consultants International, Inc. (682)
  Van Halm & Associates (1095)

Information networks SEE: Library and information networks

Information retrieval (See also Computerized searching; Information storage and retrieval systems)
  Aslib, The Association for Information Management (35)
  Sweden — Research Institute of National Defense — FOA Index Group (929)
  University of Tsukuba — Science Information Processing Center (1080)

Information science (See also Documentation; Library science)
  Aslib, The Association for Information Management (35)
  Belgium — Royal Library of Belgium — National Center for Scientific and Technical Documentation (84)
  Brazil — National Council of Scientific and Technological Development — Brazilian Institute for Information in Science and Technology (103)
  Canada — National Library of Canada — Library Documentation Centre (149)
  Canadian Association for Information Science/Association Canadienne des Sciences de l'Information (168)
  Cawkell Information & Technology Services Ltd. (180)
  CONSULTEXT (243)
  France — Interministerial Mission for Scientific and Technical Information (344)
  France — National Center for Scientific Research — Scientific and Technical Documentation Center (356)
  France — National Institute for Research in Informatics and Automation — Information Dissemination Office (361)
  German Democratic Republic — Central Institute for Information and Documentation (395)
  Great Britain — British Library — Research and Development Department (444)
  Hungarian Academy of Sciences Library — Department for Informatics and Science Analysis (492)
  Hungary — National Szechenyi Library — Centre for Library Science and Methodology (495)
  India — Council of Scientific and Industrial Research — Indian National Scientific Documentation Centre (507)
  Information Processing Society of Japan (529)
  Information Resources Research (533)
  Institute of Information Scientists (544)

Institution of Electrical Engineers — INSPEC (549)
Intergovernmental Bureau for Informatics (554)
International Centre for Scientific and Technical Information (565)
International Federation for Documentation (578)
International Federation for Documentation — Research Referral Service (579)
International Group of Users of Information Systems (586)
Israel — National Center of Scientific and Technological Information (616)
Kyushu University — Research Institute of Fundamental Information Science (648)
Library and Information Research Group (659)
Library Association Publishing Ltd. — CURRENT RESEARCH in Library & Information Science (661)
Library Association Publishing Ltd. — Library and Information Science Abstracts (663)
National Conservatory of Arts and Crafts — National Institute for Documentation Techniques (722)
Netherlands Society for Informatics (745)
Norwegian Center for Informatics (767)
Poland — Institute for Scientific, Technical and Economic Information (815)
Poland — Polish Academy of Sciences — Scientific Information Center (816)
Romania — National Council for Science and Technology — National Institute for Information and Documentation (843)
Society for Information and Documentation — GID Information Center for Information Science and Practice (880)
South Africa — Council for Scientific and Industrial Research — Centre for Scientific and Technical Information (885)
Turkey — Scientific and Technical Research Council of Turkey — Turkish Scientific and Technical Documentation Center (991)
Union of Soviet Socialist Republics — All-Union Institute of Scientific and Technical Information (998)
United Nations — Economic Commission for Latin America — Latin American Center for Economic and Social Documentation (1006)
United Nations Educational, Scientific and Cultural Organization — General Information Programme (1019)
University of Gothenburg — MEDICINDATA (1049)
University of Leicester — Primary Communications Research Centre (1054)
University of Sheffield — Centre for Research on User Studies (1070)
University of Western Ontario — School of Library and Information Science — Nested Phrase Indexing System (1086)

Information services
A.JOUR (1)
Alberta Research Council — Industrial Development Department — Industrial Information (15)
Association of Database Producers (40)
Association of European Host Operators Group (42)
Australia — Bureau of Transport Economics — BTE Information Systems (46)
AVS Intext Ltd. (69)
Baric Computing Services Ltd. — Baric Viewdata (75)
Bureau Marcel van Dijk, SA (122)
Business Information International (123)
Canadian Law Information Council (173)
Cawkell Information & Technology Services Ltd. (180)
Colombian Fund for Scientific Research — National Information System (212)
Commission of the European Communities — Environmental Information and Documentation Centers Data Base (216)
Commission of the European Communities — European Commission Host Organization (219)
Constellate Consultants Ltd. (241)
Danish DIANE Center (256)
Data Processing Services Company — DPS Information Centre (258)
Epoch Research Corporation (298)
Espial Productions (300)
European Association of Information Services (307)
European Information Providers Association (312)
Finnish Council for Scientific Information and Research Libraries (331)
FLA Groupe La Creatique (336)
France — Interministerial Mission for Scientific and Technical Information (344)
French Federation of Data Base Producers (385)
Gothard House Group of Companies, Ltd. (432)
Great Britain — British Library — Science Reference Library — European Biotechnology Information Program (446)
I/S Datacentralen (497)
Infoquest (520)
Information Management and Consulting Association (526)
International Centre for Scientific and Technical Information (565)
International Committee for Social Science Information and Documentation (571)

International Council of Scientific Unions — Committee on Data for Science and Technology (574)
International Council of Scientific Unions Abstracting Board (575)
International Electronic Publishing Research Centre (577)
International Federation of Library Associations and Institutions (582)
International Information Center for Terminology (587)
International Union of Geological Sciences — Commission on Storage, Automatic Processing and Retrieval of Geological Data (609)
Israel — National Center of Scientific and Technological Information (616)
Italian Association for the Production and Distribution of Online Information (621)
Langton Electronic Publishing Systems Ltd. (649)
Learned Information Ltd. (654)
Legal Technology Group (656)
Maruzen Company, Ltd. — Maruzen Scientific Information Service Center (689)
MIDORI Book Store Company (709)
Netherlands — Ministry of Agriculture and Fisheries — Agricultural Research Division — Centre for Agricultural Publishing and Documentation (731)
Netherlands Bibliographical and Documentary Committee (735)
Netherlands Center for Information Policy (736)
Netherlands Information Combine (737)
Netherlands Organization for Information Policy (744)
Nordic Council for Scientific Information and Research Libraries (762)
Norwegian Center for Informatics (767)
Online Information Centre (775)
Pira: Research Association for the Paper and Board, Printing and Packaging Industries — Comprehensive Information Services (812)
Poland — Institute for Scientific, Technical and Economic Information (815)
Scannet Foundation (864)
Society for Information and Documentation — GID Information Center for Information Science and Practice (880)
Sweden — Royal Institute of Technology Library — Information and Documentation Center (930)
Swedish Delegation for Scientific and Technical Information (937)
SYSTEL (950)
Tele-Direct Inc. (973)
United Kingdom Online User Group (1000)
United Nations — Advisory Committee for the Co-ordination of Information Systems (1001)
United Nations — Economic Commission for Latin America — Latin American Center for Economic and Social Documentation (1006)
United Nations Educational, Scientific and Cultural Organization — Energy Information Section (1018)
United Nations Educational, Scientific and Cultural Organization — General Information Programme (1019)
United Nations Educational, Scientific and Cultural Organization — Intergovernmental Oceanographic Commission — Marine Environmental Data Information Referral System (1020)
United Nations Educational, Scientific and Cultural Organization — Social and Human Science Documentation Centre (1022)
United Nations Environment Programme — INFOTERRA (1025)
University of London — Central Information Service (1055)
University of Tsukuba — Science Information Processing Center (1080)
USACO Corporation (1092)
Van Halm & Associates (1095)
Videotex Industry Association Ltd. (1100)
World Meteorological Organization — World Climate Programme Department — World Climate Data Information Referral Service (1118)

Information storage and retrieval systems (See also Automatic indexing; Data base management; Machine-readable cataloging; Management information systems)
Alphatext, Inc. (20)
Association for Research and Development of Chemical Informatics — DARC Pluridata System (38)
AVCOR (67)
Bank Group for Automation in Management (71)
Canada — Department of Communications — Telidon Program (130)
Center for the Study on Information Systems in Government (190)
Eurotec Consultants Ltd. — LIBRARIAN (318)
Fraser Williams Ltd. — CROSSBOW (370)
Fraser Williams Ltd. — DARING (371)
French Company for the Design & Implementation of Radio & Television Broadcasting Equipment — Antiope Teletext System (383)
Great Britain — Atomic Energy Authority — Atomic Energy Research Establishment, Harwell — Computer Science and Systems Division — STATUS (433)

Honeywell Bull — Euris Host Service (488)
Imperial Chemical Industries Ltd. — Agricultural Division — Management Services Department — ASSASSIN (503)
Information Management & Engineering Ltd. (527)
International Centre for Scientific and Technical Information (565)
Israel — National Center of Scientific and Technological Information (616)
Israel — National Center of Scientific and Technological Information — DOMESTIC (617)
Kent-Barlow Publications Ltd. (638)
KTS Information Systems (646)
Langton Electronic Publishing Systems Ltd. (649)
Leigh-Bell & Associates Ltd. (657)
Logica UK Ltd. (668)
National Reprographic Centre for Documentation (725)
Netherlands Organization for Applied Scientific Research — Institute TNO for Mathematics, Information Processing and Statistics (741)
Norwegian Center for Informatics (767)
Paralog — 3RIP (795)
Philips Information Systems and Automation — DIRECT (809)
Queen's University of Belfast — Department of Computer Science — Queen's University Interrogation of Legal Literature (836)
Siemens AG — Data Processing Division — GOLEM (874)
Siemens AG — Data Processing Division — Library Network System (875)
Siemens AG — Language Services Department — Terminology Evaluation and Acquisition Method (876)
Stacs Information Systems Ltd. (897)
STATUS Users Group (900)
Sweden — Research Institute of National Defense — FOA Index Group (929)
Sweden — Statistics Sweden — Statistical Data Bases Unit (932)
Systemhouse Ltd. — MINISIS (953)
Telesystemes — Questel (977)
United Nations Educational, Scientific and Cultural Organization — Division of the UNESCO Library, Archives and Documentation Services — Computerized Documentation Service/Integrated Set of Information Systems (1017)
United Nations Educational, Scientific and Cultural Organization — Universal System for Information in Science and Technology — UNISIST International Centre for Bibliographic Descriptions (1023)
University of Haifa Library — Haifa On-line Bibliographic Text System (1051)
University of London — Central Information Service (1055)
University of Tokyo — Computer Center — University of Tokyo On-Line Information Retrieval System (1075)
University of Tsukuba — Science Information Processing Center (1080)

Information systems SEE: Information services; Information storage and retrieval systems; Library and information networks

Infrared spectroscopy
Canada — National Research Council of Canada — Canada Institute for Scientific and Technical Information — Scientific Numeric Databases (155)
Group for the Advancement of Spectroscopic Methods and Physicochemical Analysis — Information Center for Spectroscopic and Physicochemical Analysis (466)

Insecticides SEE: Pesticides

Insects SEE: Entomology

Installations, computer SEE: Computer installations

Instrumentation (See also Automatic control)
Brunel Univeristy — Brunel Institute for Bioengineering — Information Unit (114)
Germany — Federal Institute for Materials Testing — Measurement of Mechanical Quantities Documentation (415)
Verlag Hoppenstedt & Co. — EK-MRA Data Base (1098)

Insurance
QUOTEL Insurance Services Ltd. (837)
Sharp Associates Limited (871)

Insurance, social SEE: Social security

Interactive searching SEE: Computerized searching

International affairs SEE: International relations

International business SEE: Business, international

International development (See also Developing nations)
Geo Abstracts Ltd. (393)
German Foundation for International Development — Documentation Center (397)
United Nations Educational, Scientific and Cultural Organization — Center for Social Science Research and Documentation for the Arab Region (1015)

International relations
British Broadcasting Corporation — BBC Data (104)
Datasolve Ltd. — World Reporter (265)
Foundation for Science and Politics — Research Institute for International Politics and Security — Library and Documentation System (337)
Microfor Inc. (704)
Peace Research Institute-Dundas — Peace Research Abstracts Journal (800)

International Standard Serial Number (ISSN)
International Serials Data System (603)

International trade SEE: Foreign trade

Inventions (See also Patents; Technology transfer)
Transinove International (987)

Investments (See also Money market; Stocks and bonds)
Faxtel Information Systems Ltd. — Marketfax (326)
FRI Information Services Ltd. (392)
Henley Centre for Forecasting (484)
Netherlands — Netherlands Foreign Trade Agency — Library and Documentation Branch — Foreign Trade Abstracts (733)

Iran
Tel-Aviv University — Shiloah Research Center for Middle Eastern and African Studies — Documentation System — Mideast File (970)

Iraq
Tel-Aviv University — Shiloah Research Center for Middle Eastern and African Studies — Documentation System — Mideast File (970)

Iron (See also Metallurgy; Steel)
Center of Experimental Metallurgy — Iron and Steel Documentation Service (192)
German Iron and Steel Engineers Association — Steel Information System (399)
Pont-a-Mousson Research Center — Industrial Documentation Service — BIIPAM-CTIF Data Base (820)
TESS Search Service (979)

Israel
Tel-Aviv University — Shiloah Research Center for Middle Eastern and African Studies — Documentation System — Mideast File (970)
University of Haifa Library — Haifa On-line Bibliographic Text System (1051)

ISSN SEE: International Standard Serial Number

Italy
Bibliographic Publishing Co. (87)
Central Electronic Network for Data Processing and Analysis (194)
SLAMARK International (878)
University of Milan — Higher Institute of Sociology — Data and Program Archive for the Social Sciences (1058)

Japan
IBJ Data Service Co. (498)
Japan — National Diet Library — Library Automation System (629)
Japan Data Service Co., Ltd. (631)
Japan Publications Guide (635)
Marketing Intelligence Corporation (688)
Mitaka — JAPANSCAN (712)
Nihon Keizai Shimbun, Inc. — Databank Bureau — Nikkei Economic Electronic Databank System-Information Retrieval (753)
Nihon Keizai Shimbun, Inc. — Databank Bureau — Nikkei Economic Electronic Databank System-Time Sharing (754)
Nomura Research Institute — Information Service and Development Department — NRI/E Japan Economic & Business Data Bank (760)
Overseas Data Service, Company, Ltd. (789)
Teikoku Data Bank, Ltd. (969)
Tokyo Shoko Research, Ltd. — Data Bank Service (984)

Jewish studies
Bar-Ilan University — Institute for Information Retrieval and Computational Linguistics — Responsa Project (74)

University of Haifa Library — Haifa On-line Bibliographic Text System (1051)

Job vacancies SEE: Career placement

Jordan
Tel-Aviv University — Shiloah Research Center for Middle Eastern and African Studies — Documentation System — Mideast File (970)

Judaica SEE: Jewish studies

Kuwait
Tel-Aviv University — Shiloah Research Center for Middle Eastern and African Studies — Documentation System — Mideast File (970)

Labor (See also Industrial relations; Management)
Canada — Statistics Canada — Canadian Socio-Economic Information Management System (159)
DataArkiv AB (260)
France — National Center for Scientific Research — Documentation Center for Human Sciences (355)
Germany — Federal Employment Institute — Institute for Employment Research — Information and Documentation Department (410)
Great Britain — Central Statistical Office — CSO Macro-Economic Data Bank (449)
International Labour Office — Bureau for Labour Problems Analysis — Labour Information Database (591)
International Labour Office — Bureau of Statistics (592)
International Labour Office — Central Library and Documentation Branch (593)
International Labour Office — Conditions of Work and Welfare Facilities Branch — Clearing-house on Conditions of Work (594)
International Labour Office — International Occupational Safety and Health Information Centre (595)
Interuniversity Documentation and Information Center for the Social Sciences (611)
Organisation for Economic Co-Operation and Development — Economic Statistics and National Accounts Division — OECD Magnetic Tape Subscription Service (780)
Swedish Center for Working Life — Information and Documentation Department (935)

Labor agreements
University of Aberdeen — Department of Political Economy — Wage Rounds Data Bank (1032)

Labor relations SEE: Industrial relations

Land use (See also City planning; Regional planning)
Alberta Municipal Affairs — Central Services Branch — Alberta Land Use Planning Data Bank (10)
Canada — Environment Canada — Lands Directorate — Canada Land Data Systems Division — Canada Geographic Information System (143)
Canada — Environment Canada — Library Services Branch — Environment Libraries Automated System (144)
United Nations — Food and Agriculture Organization — Statistics Division — Interlinked Computerized Storage and Processing System of Food and Agricultural Data (1014)
United Nations Environment Programme — INFOTERRA (1025)

Language and languages (See also Linguistics; Translation)
Frankfurt City and University Library — Bibliography of Linguistic Literature (368)
Institute for German Language (541)
University of Alberta — Computing Services — Information Systems Group (1033)

Latin America
Brazil — Ministry of the Interior — Documentation Coordination Unit (100)
German Foundation for International Development — Documentation Center (397)
Latin American Newsletters Ltd. (651)
National Autonomous University of Mexico — Center for Scientific and Humanistic Information (719)
United Nations — Economic Commission for Latin America — Latin American Center for Economic and Social Documentation (1006)
United Nations — Economic Commission for Latin America — Latin American Demographic Center — Latin American Population Documentation System (1007)

Law (See also Legislation)
Canada — Parliament of Canada — Library of Parliament (157)
Canada Law Book Ltd. (162)
Canadian Law Information Council (173)
Commission of the European Communities — Court of Justice of the European Communities — Legal Data Processing Group — CJUS Data Bank (214)
Documentary Research Center (282)
Editions Techniques — JURIS-DATA (294)
Europe Data (305)
European Law Centre Ltd. — Eurolex (314)
FLA Groupe La Creatique (336)
France — National Center for Scientific Research — Documentation Center for Human Sciences (355)
France — National Institute for Industrial Property — Office of Legal and Technical Documentation — JURINPI Data Base (360)
Germany — Ministry of Justice — Judicial Information System (426)
Infolex Services Ltd. (517)
Kluwer Publishing Company — Juridical Databank (641)
Koninklijke Vermande B.V. (643)
Legal Technology Group (656)
QL Systems Limited (828)
Quaere Legal Resources Ltd. (829)
Quebec Society for Legal Information (834)
Queen's University of Belfast — Department of Computer Science — Queen's University Interrogation of Legal Literature (836)
SYDONI S.A. (949)
University of New Brunswick Libraries — PHOENIX (1059)
Western Legal Publications Ltd. (1108)

Law enforcement
Kugler Publications (647)

Law, environmental SEE: Environmental law

Law, international
European Law Centre Ltd. — Eurolex (314)
Honeywell Bull — Euris Host Service — European Community Law (489)

Law libraries
Quaere Legal Resources Ltd. (829)

Law, maritime SEE: Maritime law

Law, nuclear SEE: Nuclear law

Law of the sea SEE: Maritime law

Lead
Commodities Research Unit Ltd. (228)
Zinc Development Association/Lead Development Association/Cadmium Association — Library and Abstracting Service (1122)

Lebanon
Tel-Aviv University — Shiloah Research Center for Middle Eastern and African Studies — Documentation System — Mideast File (970)

Legal medicine SEE: Medicine, legal

Legislation
Alberta Public Affairs Bureau — Publication Services Branch (11)
Brazil — Ministry of the Interior — Documentation Coordination Unit (100)
Canada — Parliament of Canada — Library of Parliament (157)
Documentary Research Center (282)
European Law Centre Ltd. — Eurolex (314)
France — French Senate — Parliamentary Documentation and Information Printing Service (343)
Germany — German Federal Diet — Division of Scientific Documentation — Documentation and Information System for Parliamentary Materials (422)
Great Britain — House of Commons Library — Parliamentary On-Line Information System (459)
Honeywell Bull — Euris Host Service — European Community Law (489)
Japan — National Diet Library — Library Automation System (629)
Kluwer Publishing Company — Juridical Databank (641)
Koninklijke Vermande B.V. (643)
Pira: Research Association for the Paper and Board, Printing and Packaging Industries — Comprehensive Information Services (812)
QL Systems Limited (828)

Leisure
Coaching Association of Canada — Sport Information Resource Centre (210)
University of Waterloo — Department of Recreation — Leisure Studies Data Bank (1084)

SUBJECT INDEX

University of Waterloo — Faculty of Human Kinetics and Leisure Studies — Information Retrieval System for the Sociology of Leisure and Sport (1085)

Less developed nations SEE: Developing nations

Libraries, agricultural SEE: Agricultural libraries

Libraries, law SEE: Law libraries

Libraries, research SEE: Research libraries

Library and information networks
Canada — National Library of Canada — Library Documentation Centre (149)

Library automation (See also Automated library acquisitions; Automated library circulation; Computerized searching; Machine-readable cataloging)
Aball Software Inc. (2)
Aslib, The Association for Information Management (35)
Belgium — Royal Library of Belgium — National Center for Scientific and Technical Documentation (84)
Blackwell Technical Services Ltd. (90)
Canada — National Library of Canada (147)
Canada — National Library of Canada — Library Documentation Centre (149)
Carleton University Library — Carleton Library System (179)
Centennial College — Bibliocentre (182)
Central Ontario Regional Library System — Interlibrary Loan and Communication System (195)
Consortium of Royal Library and University Libraries — Project for Integrated Catalogue Automation (239)
Consortium of Royal Library and University Libraries — Project for Integrated Catalogue Automation — Netherlands Central Catalogue/Interlibrary Loan System (240)
Denmark — Ministry of Cultural Affairs — National Advisory Council for Danish Research Libraries (269)
Easy Data Systems Ltd. — Easy Data Integrated Library System (289)
Eurotec Consultants Ltd. — LIBRARIAN (318)
Free University of Brussels — Central Library — VUBIS (381)
Hebrew University of Jerusalem — Automated Library Expandable Program Hebrew University of Jerusalem (478)
Infocon Information Services, Ltd. (516)
Information Management & Engineering Ltd. (527)
Israel — National Center of Scientific and Technological Information (616)
Israel — National Center of Scientific and Technological Information — DOMESTIC (617)
Japan — National Diet Library — Library Automation System (629)
KTS Information Systems (646)
Laval University Library — SDI/Laval & Telereference Service (652)
Library Network of SIBIL Users (664)
Lipman Management Resources, Ltd. — LMR Information Systems — Adaptive Library Management System (666)
Mikro-Cerid (710)
National Autonomous University of Mexico — Center for Scientific and Humanistic Information (719)
Nichols Applied Management (752)
Oriel Computer Services Limited (787)
Piedmont Consortium for Information Systems (811)
Polytechnic of Central London — Information Technology Centre (818)
Scotland — National Library of Scotland — Scottish Libraries Co-operative Automation Project (869)
Siemens AG — Data Processing Division — Library Network System (875)
South Africa — Council for Scientific and Industrial Research — Centre for Scientific and Technical Information (885)
Swets Subscription Service (942)
Systemhouse Ltd. — MINISIS (953)
Technical University of Wroclaw — Main Library and Scientific Information Center — System of Computerized Processing of Scientific Information (965)
Universal Library Systems Ltd. (1029)
University of Saskatchewan Library — Systems and Planning Unit (1068)
University of Tsukuba — Science Information Processing Center (1080)
UTLAS Inc. (1094)

Library holdings SEE: Union catalogs and lists

Library orientation
Loughborough University of Technology Library — Library Instruction Materials Bank (677)

Library science (See also Bibliography; Cataloging)
Aslib, The Association for Information Management (35)
Canada — National Library of Canada — Library Documentation Centre (149)
Chisholm Institute of Technology Library — User Education Resources Data Base (204)
German Library Institute (400)
Great Britain — British Library — Research and Development Department (444)
Hungary — National Szechenyi Library — Centre for Library Science and Methodology (495)
International Association of Agricultural Librarians and Documentalists (558)
International Federation for Documentation — Research Referral Service (579)
International Federation of Library Associations and Institutions (582)
Israel — National Center of Scientific and Technological Information (616)
Korea Advanced Institute of Science and Technology — Experienced Librarians and Information Personnel in the Developing Countries of Asia and Oceania (644)
Library and Information Research Group (659)
Library Association Publishing Ltd. — CURRENT RESEARCH in Library & Information Science (661)
Library Association Publishing Ltd. — Library and Information Science Abstracts (663)
Loughborough University of Technology — Centre for Library and Information Management (675)
McGill University — Graduate School of Library Science — FEES Data Base (692)
National Conservatory of Arts and Crafts — National Institute for Documentation Techniques (722)
Nordic Council for Scientific Information and Research Libraries (762)
Saur Verlag (863)
Society for Information and Documentation — GID Information Center for Information Science and Practice (880)
University of Sheffield — Centre for Research on User Studies (1070)

Library union catalogs SEE: Union catalogs and lists

Libya
Center for Research and Studies on Mediterranean Societies (186)
Tel-Aviv University — Shiloah Research Center for Middle Eastern and African Studies — Documentation System — Mideast File (970)

Lighting
Building Services Research and Information Association — BSRIA Information Centre (119)
Philips Information Systems and Automation — DIRECT (809)

Linguistics (See also Language and languages)
Association for Literary and Linguistic Computing (37)
Frankfurt City and University Library — Bibliography of Linguistic Literature (368)
Norwegian Computing Centre for the Humanities (768)
Siemens AG — Language Services Department — Terminology Evaluation and Acquisition Method (876)

Literature
Association for Literary and Linguistic Computing (37)
France — National Center for Scientific Research — Documentation Center for Human Sciences (355)
Norwegian Computing Centre for the Humanities (768)
University of Reading Library — Location Register of Twentieth Century English Literary Manuscripts and Letters (1065)

Literature, fugitive SEE: Fugitive literature

Livestock
International Livestock Centre for Africa — Documentation Centre (596)

Local government SEE: Municipal government

Local transit SEE: Urban transportation

London, England
Greater London Council — Information Services Group (465)

Machine-readable cataloging (See also Library automation)
Australia — National Library of Australia (48)
Australia — National Library of Australia — Australian Bibliographic Network (49)
Blackwell Technical Services Ltd. (90)

BLCMP Ltd. (91)
BTJ (116)
Canada — National Library of Canada — Cataloguing Branch — Canadiana Editorial Division (148)
Canada — National Library of Canada — MARC Records Distribution Service (150)
Carleton University Library — Carleton Library System (179)
Consortium of Royal Library and University Libraries — Project for Integrated Catalogue Automation (239)
Consortium of Royal Library and University Libraries — Project for Integrated Catalogue Automation — Netherlands Central Catalogue/Interlibrary Loan System (240)
Cooperative Automation Group (246)
Denmark — National Technological Library of Denmark — Automated Library Information System (270)
Free University of Brussels — Central Library — VUBIS (381)
Germany — German National Library — BIBLIO-DATA (423)
Great Britain — British Library — Bibliographic Services Division (439)
Great Britain — British Library — Bibliographic Services Division — BLAISE (440)
Helsinki University of Technology — University Library/National Library for Science and Technology (483)
Intermarc Group (555)
Japan — National Diet Library — Library Automation System (629)
Kinokuniya Company Ltd. — ASK Information Retrieval Services (640)
Library Network of SIBIL Users (664)
London and South Eastern Library Region (670)
Loughborough University of Technology Library — Minimal-Input Cataloguing System (678)
Metropolitan Toronto Library Board — Regional Bibliographic Products Department (699)
Quebec National Library — FMQ (833)
Scotland — National Library of Scotland — Scottish Libraries Co-operative Automation Project (869)
Special Libraries Cataloguing, Inc. (894)
SWALCAP (919)
Sweden — Royal Library — Library Information System (931)
Technical University of Wroclaw — Main Library and Scientific Information Center — System of Computerized Processing of Scientific Information (965)
United Nations Educational, Scientific and Cultural Organization — Universal System for Information in Science and Technology — UNISIST International Centre for Bibliographic Descriptions (1023)
University of Bath — Centre for Catalogue Research (1039)
University of Haifa Library — Haifa On-line Bibliographic Text System (1051)
University of New Brunswick Libraries — PHOENIX (1059)
University of Oslo — Royal University Library — Planning Department (1061)
University of Quebec — Direct Access Data Bank at the University of Quebec (1064)
University of Saskatchewan Library — Systems and Planning Unit (1068)
UTLAS Inc. (1094)

Machine tools
Technical Center for Mechanical Industries — Documentation Center for Mechanics (957)
Technical Information Center — Mechanical Engineering Documentation (961)
Technical University of Aachen — Laboratory of Machine Tools and Production Engineering — Cutting Data Information Center (964)

Macromolecules
German Plastics Institute — Information and Documentation Services (402)

Madagascar
Madagascar — Ministry of Finance and Economy — National Institute of Statistics and Economic Research (681)

Magazines SEE: Periodicals

Mail, electronic SEE: Electronic mail

Mail service SEE: Postal service

Mailing lists
Didot-Bottin — Bottin Data Bases (280)

Malagasy SEE: Madagascar

Malaysia
University of Sydney Library — Bibliographic Information on Southeast Asia (1073)

Management (See also Business and business administration; Industrial relations; Labor)
African Training and Research Centre in Administration for Development — African Network of Administrative Information (7)
France — National Center for Scientific Research — Documentation Center for Human Sciences (355)
Helsinki School of Economics Library — Information Services (481)
International Labour Office — International Occupational Safety and Health Information Centre (595)
MERLIN GERIN Company — Documentation Department — MERL-ECO (696)
Pira: Research Association for the Paper and Board, Printing and Packaging Industries — Comprehensive Information Services (812)
Technical Information Center (959)

Management, data base SEE: Data base management

Management information systems
Data Processing Services Company — DPS Information Centre (258)

Manpower SEE: Labor

Manpower, health SEE: Health manpower

Manufacturing
Canada — Statistics Canada — Canadian Socio-Economic Information Management System (159)
Great Britain — Department of Trade and Industry — Business Statistics Office (454)
London Enterprise Agency — Supplier Identification System (671)
Market Location (686)
Production Engineering Research Association of Great Britain — Information Services (826)

Manufacturing engineering SEE: Production engineering

Maps (See also Cartography; Geography)
Canada — Department of Energy, Mines and Resources — Topographical Survey Division — Digital Mapping System (136)
Canada — Environment Canada — Lands Directorate — Canada Land Data Systems Division — Canada Geographic Information System (143)
Geosystems (394)
Netherlands Soil Survey Institute — Soil Information System (746)
Quebec National Library — FMQ (833)

Marine biology (See also Oceanography; Fisheries)
France — National Center for Ocean Utilization — National Bureau for Ocean Data (347)
France — National Center for Ocean Utilization — National Bureau for Ocean Data — BIOCEAN (349)
France — National Center for Ocean Utilization — National Bureau for Ocean Data — DOCOCEAN (351)
Germany — Federal Research Center for Fisheries — Information and Documentation Center (421)
India — National Institute of Oceanography — Indian National Oceanographic Data Centre (509)
Marine Biological Association of the United Kingdom — Marine Pollution Information Centre (684)
Natural Environment Research Council — Institute for Marine Environmental Research — Continuous Plankton Recorder Survey (729)
United Nations — Food and Agriculture Organization — Aquatic Sciences and Fisheries Information System (1008)
United Nations Educational, Scientific and Cultural Organization — Intergovernmental Oceanographic Commission — Marine Environmental Data Information Referral System (1020)

Marine geology
France — Bureau of Geological and Mining Research — National Geological Survey — Geological Information and Documentation Department (340)
France — National Center for Ocean Utilization — National Bureau for Ocean Data (347)
France — National Center for Ocean Utilization — National Bureau for Ocean Data — geoIPOD (352)
India — National Institute of Oceanography — Indian National Oceanographic Data Centre (509)
Japan — Maritime Safety Agency — Hydrographic Department — Japan Oceanographic Data Center (628)
Natural Environment Research Council — Institute of Oceanographic Sciences — Marine Information and Advisory Service (730)
United Nations Educational, Scientific and Cultural Organization — Intergovernmental Oceanographic Commission — Marine Environmental Data Information Referral System (1020)

SUBJECT INDEX

Marine pollution SEE: Pollution, marine

Marine transportation (See also Ships and shipping)
   Canada — Transport Canada — Library and Information Centre   (161)
   Fairplay Publications Ltd. — Fairplay International Research Services   (324)
   Lloyd's Shipping Information Services   (667)

Maritime law
   Dalhousie University — Law School Library — Marine Affairs Bibliography   (254)
   Germany — Federal Institute for Geosciences and Natural Resources — Marine Information and Documentation System   (413)
   Maritime Information Centre/CMO   (685)

Marketing SEE: Advertising and marketing

Mass media (See also News and newspapers; Radio broadcasting; Television broadcasting)
   Austrian Documentation Centre for Media and Communication Research   (65)
   British Market Research Bureau Ltd. — Target Group Index   (109)
   Center for the Study of Advertising Support   (189)
   Harris Media Systems Ltd.   (475)
   Japan Data Service Co., Ltd.   (631)
   Nihon Keizai Shimbun, Inc. — Databank Bureau — Nikkei Economic Electronic Databank System-Time Sharing   (754)
   Nordic Documentation Center for Mass Communication Research   (763)
   PMB Print Measurement Bureau   (814)
   Research Services Ltd. — Pan European Survey   (839)

Mass spectrometry
   Association for Research and Development of Chemical Informatics — DARC Pluridata System   (38)
   Group for the Advancement of Spectroscopic Methods and Physicochemical Analysis — Information Center for Spectroscopic and Physicochemical Analysis   (466)
   Royal Society of Chemistry — Information Services — Mass Spectrometry Data Centre   (856)
   University of Gothenburg — MEDICINDATA   (1049)

Mass transit SEE: Urban transportation

Materials science
   Center for Scientific and Technical Research for the Metal Manufacturing Industry — Fabrimetal   (187)
   Commission of the European Communities — Joint Research Centre — High Temperature Materials Data Bank   (222)
   German Iron and Steel Engineers Association — Steel Information System   (399)
   German Society for Chemical Equipment — Information Systems and Data Banks Department — Materials and Corrosion Information System   (405)
   Germany — Federal Institute for Materials Testing — Measurement of Mechanical Quantities Documentation   (415)
   Germany — Federal Institute for Materials Testing — Nondestructive Testing Documentation   (416)
   Germany — Federal Institute for Materials Testing — Rheology and Tribology Documentation Center   (417)
   Institution of Electrical Engineers — INSPEC — Electronic Materials Information Service   (550)
   Technical Information Center — Mechanical Engineering Documentation   (961)

Mathematics (See also Statistics)
   France — National Center for Scientific Research — Scientific and Technical Documentation Center   (356)
   Information Center for Energy, Physics, Mathematics   (521)
   Netherlands Organization for Applied Scientific Research — Institute TNO for Mathematics, Information Processing and Statistics   (741)

Mechanical engineering
   Derwent Publications Ltd. — Patents Documentation Services   (275)
   ESDU International Limited   (299)
   Germany — Federal Institute for Materials Testing — Measurement of Mechanical Quantities Documentation   (415)
   Pont-a-Mousson Research Center — Industrial Documentation Service — BIIPAM-CTIF Data Base   (820)
   Sweden — Royal Institute of Technology Library — Information and Documentation Center   (930)
   Swedish Mechanical and Electrical Engineering Trade Association — VERA   (939)
   Technical Center for Mechanical Industries — Documentation Center for Mechanics   (957)
   Technical Information Center — Mechanical Engineering Documentation   (961)
   VDI-Verlag GmbH — VDI News Data Base   (1096)

Mechanics, fluid SEE: Fluid mechanics

Mechanized information storage and retrieval systems SEE: Information storage and retrieval systems

Media, mass SEE: Mass media

Medical care SEE: Health care

Medical economics
   Elsevier Science Publishers B.V. — Biomedical Division — Excerpta Medica   (296)
   Health Care Literature Information Network   (477)

Medical electronics
   Brunel Univeristy — Brunel Institute for Bioengineering — Information Unit   (114)

Medical engineering SEE: Bioengineering

Medical ethics
   British Medical Association — BMA Press Cuttings Database   (110)

Medical jurisprudence SEE: Medicine, legal

Medical records
   Institute for Documentation and Information in Social Medicine and Public Health   (539)

Medical research
   Brunel Univeristy — Brunel Institute for Bioengineering — Information Unit   (114)
   France — National Institute for Health and Medical Research — Office of Scientific Evaluation — INSERM Research Information Bank   (358)
   IRCS Medical Science — IRCS Medical Science Database   (614)
   University of Alberta — Faculty of Nursing — Canadian Clearinghouse for Ongoing Research in Nursing   (1036)

Medical sociology
   British Medical Association — BMA Press Cuttings Database   (110)
   Institute for Documentation and Information in Social Medicine and Public Health   (539)

Medical specialties
   Elsevier Science Publishers B.V. — Biomedical Division — Excerpta Medica   (296)

Medical technology SEE: Bioengineering

Medicine (See also Biomedical sciences; Health care; Public health; and specific areas of medicine such as Nursing and Dentistry)
   Australia — National Library of Australia   (48)
   Australia — National Library of Australia — Australian MEDLINE Network   (50)
   Austrian National Institute for Public Health — Literature Service in Medicine   (66)
   British Medical Association — BMA Press Cuttings Database   (110)
   Brunel Univeristy — Brunel Institute for Bioengineering — Information Unit   (114)
   Bulgaria — Medical Academy — Center for Scientific Information in Medicine and Health   (120)
   Canada — National Research Council of Canada — Canada Institute for Scientific and Technical Information   (152)
   Czechoslovakia — Institute for Medical Information   (250)
   Elsevier Science Publishers B.V. — Biomedical Division — Excerpta Medica   (296)
   Finland — Central Medical Library — MEDIC Data Base   (329)
   France — National Center for Scientific Research — Scientific and Technical Documentation Center   (356)
   Germany — Ministry of Youth, Family and Health — German Institute for Medical Documentation and Information   (428)
   Gothard House Group of Companies, Ltd.   (432)
   Institute for Documentation and Information in Social Medicine and Public Health   (539)
   International Medical Information Center   (598)
   IRCS Medical Science — IRCS Medical Science Database   (614)
   Japan Information Center of Science and Technology   (632)
   Royal Netherlands Academy of Arts and Sciences Library   (849)
   South African Medical Research Council — Institute for Medical Literature   (888)
   Sweden — Karolinska Institute Library and Information Center   (921)
   University of Valencia — Biomedical Documentation and Information Center   (1082)

Medicine, environmental SEE: **Environmental health**

Medicine, industrial (See also Industrial hygiene)
  Institute for Documentation and Information in Social Medicine and Public Health   (539)

Medicine, legal
  Institute for Documentation and Information in Social Medicine and Public Health   (539)

Medicine, veterinary SEE: **Veterinary medicine**

Mediterranean countries
  Center for Research and Studies on Mediterranean Societies   (186)
  International Center for Higher Studies in Mediterranean Agronomy — Socioeconomic Data Bank on the Mediterranean Countries   (564)

Meetings SEE: **Conferences and conventions**

Mental testing SEE: **Educational testing**

Merchandising SEE: **Advertising and marketing**

Metallurgy (See also Aluminum; Iron; Metals; Steel; etc.)
  Australian Mineral Foundation — Australian Earth Sciences Information System   (57)
  BNF Metals Technology Centre — Information Department   (92)
  Canada — Department of Energy, Mines and Resources — Canada Centre for Mineral and Energy Technology — Technology Information Division   (131)
  Center for Scientific and Technical Research for the Metal Manufacturing Industry — Fabrimetal   (187)
  Dobra Iron and Steel Research Institute — Informetal   (281)
  France — National Center for Scientific Research — Scientific and Technical Documentation Center   (356)
  Information Center for Materials — System for Documentation and Information in Metallurgy   (522)
  Institution of Mining and Metallurgy — Library and Information Services   (551)
  Japan Information Center of Science and Technology   (632)
  Pont-a-Mousson Research Center — Industrial Documentation Service — BIIPAM-CTIF Data Base   (820)
  Ternisien Listing   (978)
  Thermodata Association — Thermodata-Thermdoc Data Bank   (981)
  The Welding Institute — Information Services   (1106)

Metals (See also Metallurgy)
  Bird Associates   (89)
  BNF Metals Technology Centre — Information Department   (92)
  Canada — National Research Council of Canada — Chemistry Division — Metals Data Centre   (156)
  Commodities Research Unit Ltd.   (228)
  Dobra Iron and Steel Research Institute — Informetal   (281)
  Information Center for Materials — System for Documentation and Information in Metallurgy   (522)
  Metals Information   (698)
  Technical Center for Mechanical Industries — Documentation Center for Mechanics   (957)
  Zinc Development Association/Lead Development Association/Cadmium Association — Library and Abstracting Service   (1122)

Metalworking industry
  DAFSA-SNEI S.A. — FITEK   (252)
  Pont-a-Mousson Research Center — Industrial Documentation Service — BIIPAM-CTIF Data Base   (820)
  Prodinform Technical Consulting Co.   (825)
  Technical Center for Mechanical Industries — Documentation Center for Mechanics   (957)
  Technical Information Center — Mechanical Engineering Documentation   (961)

Meteorology (See also Atmospheric sciences)
  Geo Abstracts Ltd.   (393)
  Royal Museum of Central Africa — Center for Informatics Applied to Development and Tropical Agriculture — Agroclimatology Data Bank   (846)
  World Meteorological Organization — World Climate Programme Department — World Climate Data Information Referral Service   (1118)
  World Meteorological Organization — World Weather Watch   (1119)

Metrology
  Polish Committee of Standardization, Measures, and Quality — Centre for Information on Standardization and Metrology   (817)

Microbiology
  Celltech Ltd. — Information and Library Service   (181)
  Derwent Publications Ltd. — Biotechnology Abstracts   (273)
  International Food Information Service — Food Science and Technology Abstracts   (583)
  Pergamon Press — Current Awareness in Biological Sciences   (803)
  Royal Society of Chemistry — Information Services — Current Biotechnology Abstracts   (854)

Microcomputers
  ALLM Books — Small Computer Program Index   (17)
  American College in Paris — Service Calvados   (22)
  Cawkell Information & Technology Services Ltd.   (180)
  Hertfordshire County Council — Chiltern Advisory Unit for Computer Based Education   (485)
  Polytechnic of Central London — Information Technology Centre   (818)

Microforms SEE: **Micrographics**

Micrographics
  Brazil — National Center for Micrographic Development   (101)
  Canadian Micrographic Society   (175)
  Langton Electronic Publishing Systems Ltd.   (649)
  Library Association Publishing Ltd. — Library and Information Science Abstracts   (663)
  Microinfo, Ltd.   (705)
  National Reprographic Centre for Documentation   (725)

Microprocessors SEE: **Microcomputers**

Micropublishing SEE: **Micrographics**

Middle East (See also Arab countries)
  German Foundation for International Development — Documentation Center   (397)
  Tel-Aviv University — Shiloah Research Center for Middle Eastern and African Studies — Documentation System — Mideast File   (970)

Military ordnance SEE: **Ordnance**

Military research SEE: **Defense research and development**

Military science (See also Defense research and development; National defense)
  Brassey's Publishers Ltd. — Brassey's Naval Record   (97)
  Brassey's Publishers Ltd. — British Defence Directory   (98)

Milk SEE: **Dairy products**

Mineral industries
  Institution of Mining and Metallurgy — Library and Information Services   (551)
  Natural Environment Research Council — British Geological Survey — Minerals Strategy and Economics Research Group — Mineral Information Section   (727)

Mineral resources (See also Geology; Mines and mining)
  Alberta Research Council — Alberta Geological Survey — Geoscience Data Index for Alberta   (12)
  Australian Mineral Foundation — Australian Earth Sciences Information System   (57)
  Canada — Department of Energy, Mines and Resources — Canada Centre for Mineral and Energy Technology — Technology Information Division   (131)
  Canada — Department of Energy, Mines and Resources — Geological Survey of Canada — Economic Geology Division — Canadian Mineral Occurrence Index   (134)
  Canada — Department of Energy, Mines and Resources — Geological Survey of Canada — National GEOSCAN Centre   (135)
  France — Bureau of Geological and Mining Research — National Geological Survey — Geological Information and Documentation Department   (340)
  Geosystems   (394)
  Institution of Mining and Metallurgy — Library and Information Services   (551)
  Natural Environment Research Council — British Geological Survey — Minerals Strategy and Economics Research Group — Mineral Information Section   (727)
  Newfoundland Department of Mines & Energy — Mineral Development Division Library — Computerized Retrieval Services   (750)
  Ontario Ministry of Natural Resources — Mineral Resources Group — Ontario Geological Survey — Geoscience Data Centre   (778)

Mineralogy
  Brown's Geological Information Service Ltd.   (113)

France — Bureau of Geological and Mining Research — National Geological Survey — Geological Information and Documentation Department (340)
Germany — Federal Institute for Geosciences and Natural Resources — Geoscience Literature Information Service (412)
Mineralogical Society of Great Britain — Mineralogical Abstracts (711)

Mines and mining
Alberta Research Council — Coal Technology Information Centre (14)
Australian Mineral Foundation — Australian Earth Sciences Information System (57)
Canada — Department of Energy, Mines and Resources — Canada Centre for Mineral and Energy Technology — Technology Information Division (131)
Commodities Research Unit Ltd. (228)
Geosystems (394)
Helsinki University of Technology — University Library/National Library for Science and Technology (483)
Institution of Mining and Metallurgy — Library and Information Services (551)
Natural Environment Research Council — British Geological Survey — Minerals Strategy and Economics Research Group — Mineral Information Section (727)
Newfoundland Department of Mines & Energy — Mineral Development Division Library — Computerized Retrieval Services (750)
Norwegian Center for Informatics (767)
Ontario Ministry of Natural Resources — Mineral Resources Group — Ontario Geological Survey — Geoscience Data Centre (778)
Organisation for Economic Co-Operation and Development — International Energy Agency — IEA Coal Research — Technical Information Service (782)
Organisation for Economic Co-Operation and Development — International Energy Agency — IEA Coal Research — World Coal Resources and Reserves Data Bank Service (783)
University of London — Imperial College of Science and Technology — Department of Mineral Resources Engineering — Rock Mechanics Information Service (1056)

Molecular structure (See also Chemical structure)
Cambridge University — University Chemical Laboratory — Cambridge Crystallographic Data Centre (125)
Fraser Williams Ltd. — CROSSBOW (370)
Fraser Williams Ltd. — DARING (371)
University of Paris-South — Gases and Plasmas Physics Laboratory — GAPHYOR (1063)

Money market (See also Banking and finance)
Cumulus Systems Ltd. (249)
Datastream International Ltd. (267)
Econintel Information Services Ltd. — Econintel Monitor (290)
Financial Times Business Information Ltd. — Business Information Service (328)
Henley Centre for Forecasting (484)
ICV Information Systems Ltd. — CitiService (500)
The London International Financial Futures Exchange Ltd. (672)
LymBurner & Sons Ltd. — Economist's Statistics (679)
Nihon Keizai Shimbun, Inc. — Databank Bureau — Nikkei Economic Electronic Databank System-Time Sharing (754)
Nihon Keizai Shimbun, Inc. — Quotation Information Center K.K. (755)
Sharp Associates Limited (871)
The Stock Exchange — Technical Services Department — TOPIC (902)
Telekurs Ag — Investdata System (975)

Morocco
Center for Research and Studies on Mediterranean Societies (186)

Motion pictures
British Universities Film & Video Council Ltd. — Information Service (112)
Canada — National Film Board of Canada — FORMAT (146)
Metropolitan Toronto Library Board — Regional Bibliographic Products Department (699)

Municipal government (See also Public administration)
Calgary Public Information Department — Public Relations Division — Civichannel (124)
Greater London Council — Information Services Group (465)
Toronto Department of the City Clerk — Computerized Text Processing and Retrieval System for City Council Information (985)

Music and music industry
The CIRPA/ADISQ Foundation (206)

Great Britain — British Library — Bibliographic Services Division (439)

Mycology
Commonwealth Agricultural Bureaux — CAB Abstracts (229)

Names SEE: Terminology

Names, brand SEE: Trademarks

Narcotics abuse SEE: Drug abuse

National archives SEE: Public records

National defense (See also Defense research and development)
France — Ministry of Defense — General Office for Ordnance — Center for Documentation on Ordnance (345)

Natural gas
Canada — Department of Energy, Mines and Resources — Canada Centre for Mineral and Energy Technology — Technology Information Division (131)
French Petroleum Institute — Documentation Center (387)
National Elf Aquitaine Company — Documentary Information Service — STATSID (723)

Natural resources (See also Conservation of natural resources; Mineral resources; Water resources; etc.)
Canada — Environment Canada — Lands Directorate — Canada Land Data Systems Division — Canada Geographic Information System (143)
Swiss Wildlife Information Service (947)
United Nations — Food and Agriculture Organization — International Information System for the Agricultural Sciences and Technology (1012)
United Nations Environment Programme — INFOTERRA (1025)

Naval architecture (See also Ships and shipping)
Brassey's Publishers Ltd. — Brassey's Naval Record (97)
Ship Research Institute of Norway — Ship Abstracts (872)

Naval weapons SEE: Weapons, naval

Near East SEE: Middle East

Nematology
Commonwealth Agricultural Bureaux — CAB Abstracts (229)

Netherlands
Admedia — Adfacts (6)
Kluwer Publishing Company — Juridical Databank (641)
Koninklijke Vermande B.V. (643)
Netherlands Office of Posts, Telegraphs, and Telephones — PTT Central Directorate — Viditel (738)
Royal Netherlands Academy of Arts and Sciences — Social Science Information and Documentation Center (847)
Royal Netherlands Academy of Arts and Sciences — Social Science Information and Documentation Center — Steinmetz Archives (848)
Tijl Datapress (982)

Networks, library and information SEE: Library and information networks

Neurology
Pergamon Press — Current Awareness in Biological Sciences (803)

Neutrons
Institute of Physics and Energy — Nuclear Data Center (546)
International Atomic Energy Agency — Nuclear Data Section (561)
Organisation for Economic Co-Operation and Development — Nuclear Energy Agency — NEA Data Bank (785)

New products
Transinove International (987)

New Zealand
New Zealand — Department of Statistics — Information Network for Official Statistics (749)

News and newspapers
Alberta Public Affairs Bureau — Publication Services Branch (11)
British Broadcasting Corporation — BBC Data (104)
British Broadcasting Corporation — CEEFAX (105)
British Market Research Bureau Ltd. — Target Group Index (109)
British Medical Association — BMA Press Cuttings Database (110)
BTJ (116)
Canadian Broadcasting Corporation — Project IRIS (169)

Communication Services Ltd. — Viewdata Services (231)
Datasolve Ltd. — World Reporter (265)
Denmark Telecommunications Administration — Danish Teledata System (272)
Eastern Counties Newspapers — Eastel (287)
Edimedia Inc. (292)
Finsbury Data Services Ltd. — TEXTLINE (335)
French Documentation — Political and Current Events Information Bank (384)
French Press Agency — Telematics Department — AGORA (388)
The Globe and Mail — Info Globe (430)
Gruner & Jahr AG & Co. — G&J Press Information Bank (468)
Helsingin Telset Oy — Telset (480)
Infomart — Grassroots (519)
Microfor Inc. (704)
Micromedia Ltd. — Canadian News Index (708)
Netherlands Office of Posts, Telegraphs, and Telephones — PTT Central Directorate — Viditel (738)
Nihon Keizai Shimbun, Inc. — Databank Bureau — Nikkei Economic Electronic Databank System-Information Retrieval (753)
ORACLE Teletext Ltd. (779)
Press Association Ltd. — NEWSFILE (823)
Pressurklipp — Swedish Market Information Bank (824)
QL Systems Limited (828)
Ringier & Co. — Ringier Documentation Center (841)
TT Newsbank (990)
Viewtel Services Ltd. (1102)
Western Australian Institute of Technology — T.L. Robertson Library — WAIT Index to Newspapers (1107)

Newspapers SEE: News and newspapers

Noise pollution SEE: Pollution, noise

Non-destructive testing
Germany — Federal Institute for Materials Testing — Nondestructive Testing Documentation (416)
Great Britain — Atomic Energy Authority — Atomic Energy Research Establishment, Harwell — Nondestructive Testing Centre — Quality Technology Information Service (436)

Northern regions SEE: Polar regions

Norway
Norway — Ministry of Finances and Customs — Central Bureau of Statistics (766)
Norwegian Research Council for Science and the Humanities — Norwegian Social Science Data Services (771)
University of Bergen — Department of Scandinavian Languages and Literature — Norwegian Term Bank (1040)
University of Oslo — Royal University Library — Planning Department (1061)

Nuclear cross sections SEE: Cross sections (nuclear physics)

Nuclear energy
Argentina — National Atomic Energy Commission — Division of Technical Information (27)
International Atomic Energy Agency — Energy and Economic Data Bank (559)
International Atomic Energy Agency — International Nuclear Information System (560)
International Atomic Energy Agency — Vienna International Centre Library (562)
Mexico — National Institute of Nuclear Research — Nuclear Information and Documentation Center (703)
Riso National Laboratory — Riso Library (842)
South Africa — Nuclear Development Corporation of South Africa — NUCOR Library and Information Services (886)
Studsvik Energiteknik AB — Report Collection Index (906)

Nuclear engineering (See also Nuclear science)
Atomic Energy of Canada, Ltd. — Chalk River Nuclear Laboratories — Technical Information Branch (44)
Atomic Energy of Canada, Ltd. — Whiteshell Nuclear Research Establishment — Technical Information Services (45)
International Atomic Energy Agency — International Nuclear Information System (560)

Nuclear explosions (See also Weapons, nuclear)
Royal Norwegian Council for Scientific and Industrial Research — Norwegian Seismic Array (850)

Nuclear law
International Atomic Energy Agency — International Nuclear Information System (560)

Nuclear magnetic resonance
Association for Research and Development of Chemical Informatics — DARC Pluridata System (38)
Group for the Advancement of Spectroscopic Methods and Physicochemical Analysis — Information Center for Spectroscopic and Physicochemical Analysis (466)

Nuclear power plants
Electricite de France — Office of Study and Research — Information and Documentation Systems Department — EDF-DOC Data Base (295)
France — Atomic Energy Commission — Programs Department — ELECNUC Databank (338)

Nuclear reactors
Great Britain — Atomic Energy Authority — Culham Laboratory — Plasma Physics Library and Information Service (438)

Nuclear research
Commission of the European Communities — Euro Abstracts (218)
Great Britain — Atomic Energy Authority — Atomic Energy Research Establishment, Harwell — Harwell Central Information Service (434)
Information Center for Energy, Physics, Mathematics (521)
International Atomic Energy Agency — International Nuclear Information System (560)

Nuclear safety
International Atomic Energy Agency — International Nuclear Information System (560)

Nuclear science (See also Nuclear engineering)
Atomic Energy of Canada, Ltd. — Chalk River Nuclear Laboratories — Technical Information Branch (44)
Atomic Energy of Canada, Ltd. — Whiteshell Nuclear Research Establishment — Technical Information Services (45)
Australian Atomic Energy Commission — Lucas Heights Research Laboratories Library (51)
Boris Kidric Institute of Nuclear Sciences — Laboratory for Information Systems (96)
Brazil — National Commission for Nuclear Energy — Center for Nuclear Information (102)
France — Atomic Energy Commission — Saclay Nuclear Research Center — Documentation Center (339)
Great Britain — Atomic Energy Authority — Atomic Energy Research Establishment, Harwell — Harwell Central Information Service (434)
Helsinki University of Technology — University Library/National Library for Science and Technology (483)
Information Center for Energy, Physics, Mathematics (521)
International Atomic Energy Agency — International Nuclear Information System (560)
International Atomic Energy Agency — Nuclear Data Section (561)
Israel Atomic Energy Commission — Soreq Nuclear Research Center — Library and Technical Information Department (618)
Japan — Japan Atomic Energy Research Institute — Department of Technical Information (627)
Organisation for Economic Co-Operation and Development — Nuclear Energy Agency — NEA Data Bank (785)
Royal Netherlands Academy of Arts and Sciences Library (849)
South Africa — Nuclear Development Corporation of South Africa — NUCOR Library and Information Services (886)
Union of Soviet Socialist Republics — U.S.S.R. State Committee on the Utilization of Atomic Energy — Center for Nuclear Structure and Reaction Data (999)

Nuclear structure
International Atomic Energy Agency — Nuclear Data Section (561)
Organisation for Economic Co-Operation and Development — Nuclear Energy Agency — NEA Data Bank (785)
Union of Soviet Socialist Republics — U.S.S.R. State Committee on the Utilization of Atomic Energy — Center for Nuclear Structure and Reaction Data (999)

Nuclear wastes SEE: Radioactive wastes

Nuclear weapons SEE: Weapons, nuclear

Numerical data, scientific and technical SEE: Scientific and technical data

Nursing
University of Alberta — Faculty of Nursing — Canadian Clearinghouse for Ongoing Research in Nursing (1036)
University of Alberta — Faculty of Nursing — Canadian Directory of Completed Master's Theses in Nursing (1037)

Nutrition (See also Food science and technology)
Australia — Commonwealth Scientific and Industrial Research Organization — Central Information, Library and Editorial Section (47)
Commonwealth Agricultural Bureaux — CAB Abstracts (229)
Hohenheim University — Documentation Center on Animal Production (487)
Institute of Nutrition — Documentation Department (545)
Leatherhead Food Research Association — Information and Library Services (655)
Netherlands — Ministry of Agriculture and Fisheries — Agricultural Research Division — Centre for Agricultural Publishing and Documentation (731)
Norwegian Center for Informatics (767)
United Nations — Food and Agriculture Organization — International Information System for the Agricultural Sciences and Technology (1012)

Occupational health SEE: Industrial hygiene

Occupational placement SEE: Career placement

Occupational safety SEE: Industrial safety

Ocean law SEE: Maritime law

Oceanography (See also Coasts; Marine biology)
France — National Center for Ocean Utilization — National Bureau for Ocean Data (347)
France — National Center for Ocean Utilization — National Bureau for Ocean Data — CNEXO-BNDO Data Base (350)
France — National Center for Ocean Utilization — National Bureau for Ocean Data — DOCOCEAN (351)
France — National Center for Ocean Utilization — National Bureau for Ocean Data — geoIPOD (352)
France — National Center for Ocean Utilization — National Bureau for Ocean Data — ROSCOP (354)
Germany — Federal Institute for Geosciences and Natural Resources — Marine Information and Documentation System (413)
India — National Institute of Oceanography — Indian National Oceanographic Data Centre (509)
Japan — Maritime Safety Agency — Hydrographic Department — Japan Oceanographic Data Center (628)
Memorial University of Newfoundland — Ocean Engineering Information Centre (694)
Natural Environment Research Council — Institute of Oceanographic Sciences — Marine Information and Advisory Service (730)
United Nations Educational, Scientific and Cultural Organization — Intergovernmental Oceanographic Commission — Marine Environmental Data Information Referral System (1020)
World Meteorological Organization — World Climate Programme Department — World Climate Data Information Referral Service (1118)
World Meteorological Organization — World Weather Watch (1119)

Office automation
Cawkell Information & Technology Services Ltd. (180)
Data Processing Services Company — DPS Information Centre (258)
France — National Telecommunications Research Center — Interministerial Documentation Service — TELEDOC (367)
Institution of Electrical Engineers — INSPEC (549)
Overseas Data Service, Company, Ltd. (789)
Paris District Informatics Administration — Informatics Biblio Service (797)

Oil (petroleum) SEE: Petroleum and petroleum technology

Oil spills
France — National Center for Ocean Utilization — National Bureau for Ocean Data — POLUMAT (353)
French Petroleum Institute — Documentation Center (387)
Marine Biological Association of the United Kingdom — Marine Pollution Information Centre (684)

Oman
Tel-Aviv University — Shiloah Research Center for Middle Eastern and African Studies — Documentation System — Mideast File (970)

Online data bases SEE: Information services

Online industry SEE: Information industry

Online searching SEE: Computerized searching

Ordnance
Brassey's Publishers Ltd. — Brassey's Naval Record (97)

Organic chemistry SEE: Chemistry, organic

Pacemakers SEE: Medical electronics

Pacific Islands
Australian Financial Review — INFO-LINE (55)
United Nations — Economic and Social Commission for Asia and the Pacific — ESCAP Library — ESCAP Bibliographic Information System (1002)
United Nations — Economic and Social Commission for Asia and the Pacific — Population Division — Population Clearing-house and Information Section (1003)
United Nations — Economic and Social Commission for Asia and the Pacific — Statistics Division — UN/ESCAP Statistical Information Services (1004)
United Nations — Food and Agriculture Organization — INFOFISH (1011)

Packaging
International Food Information Service — Packaging Science and Technology Abstracts (584)
Pira: Research Association for the Paper and Board, Printing and Packaging Industries — Comprehensive Information Services (812)

Paint
Paint Research Association — Information Department — World Surface Coatings Abstracts (792)
Zinc Development Association/Lead Development Association/Cadmium Association — Library and Abstracting Service (1122)

Painting SEE: Art and art history

Paleontology
Geosystems (394)
Germany — Federal Institute for Geosciences and Natural Resources — Geoscience Literature Information Service (412)

Paper and paper technology
Finnish Pulp and Paper Research Institute — Technical Information Service (333)
Pira: Research Association for the Paper and Board, Printing and Packaging Industries — Comprehensive Information Services (812)
Pulp and Paper Research Institute of Canada — Technical Information Section (827)

Paris, France
Paris Office of Urbanization — Urban Data Bank of Paris and the Paris Region (798)

Parliaments
Canada — Parliament of Canada — Library of Parliament (157)
France — French Senate — Parliamentary Documentation and Information Printing Service (343)
Germany — German Federal Diet — Division of Scientific Documentation — Documentation and Information System for Parliamentary Materials (422)
Great Britain — House of Commons Library — Parliamentary On-Line Information System (459)
Great Britain — House of Lords — Library & Information Centre (460)
Honeywell Bull — Euris Host Service — European Community Law (489)

Particle technology
Loughborough University of Technology — Chemical Engineering Department — Particle Science and Technology Information Service (676)

Patents (See also Trademarks)
Austria — Minister of Finance — International Patent Documentation Center (64)
Central American Research Institute for Industry — Division of Documentation and Information (193)
Derwent Publications Ltd. — Patents Documentation Services (275)
European Patent Office — EDP Department — EPO Data Banks (315)
France — National Institute for Industrial Property — Division of Publications Documentation and Information — INPI Data Bases (359)
France — National Institute for Industrial Property — Office of Legal and Technical Documentation — JURINPI Data Base (360)
German Patent Information System (401)

International Company for Documentation in Chemistry (572)
Japan Information Center of Science and Technology (632)
Japan Patent Information Center (633)
Netherlands Organization for Applied Scientific Research — Center for Information and Documentation (739)
Nippon Gijutsu Boeki Co., Ltd. (758)
Sweden — Patent and Registration Office — InterPat Sweden (928)
Technology Resource Center — Technobank Program (967)
Transinove International (987)
World Intellectual Property Organization — Permanent Committee on Patent Information (1116)

Pathology, plant SEE: Plant pathology

Peace
Peace Research Institute-Dundas — Peace Research Abstracts Journal (800)

Perfumes SEE: Cosmetics

Periodicals (See also News and newspapers)
Bibliographic Publishing Co. (87)
Blackwell Technical Services Ltd. (90)
BTJ (116)
Canada — National Library of Canada — Cataloguing Branch — Canadiana Editorial Division (148)
Canada — National Library of Canada — MARC Records Distribution Service (150)
Canada — National Library of Canada — Public Services Branch — Union Catalogue of Serials Division (151)
Esselte Group of Booksellers — Esselte Documentation System (302)
German Library Institute (400)
Germany — German National Library — BIBLIO-DATA (423)
Great Britain — British Library — Bibliographic Services Division (439)
Great Britain — British Library — Lending Division (442)
Helsinki University Library — Finnish National Bibliography (482)
International Committee for Social Science Information and Documentation (571)
International Council of Scientific Unions Abstracting Board (575)
International Serials Data System (603)
International Technical Publications Ltd. (605)
Japan — National Diet Library — Library Automation System (629)
Japan Publications Guide (635)
Quebec National Library — FMQ (833)
Swets Subscription Service (942)
University of Haifa Library — Haifa On-line Bibliographic Text System (1051)
University of Oslo — Royal University Library — Planning Department (1061)

Periodicals, union lists of SEE: Union catalogs and lists

Personal computers SEE: Microcomputers

Personnel administration
International Labour Office — Bureau for Labour Problems Analysis — Labour Information Database (591)
Swedish Center for Working Life — Information and Documentation Department (935)

Pesticides
Canada — Agriculture Canada — Scientific Information Retrieval Section — Pesticide Research Information System (128)
Derwent Publications Ltd. — Pest Control Literature Documentation (276)

Petrochemicals
Chem Systems International Ltd. (199)
French Petroleum Institute — Documentation Center (387)
Independent Chemical Information Services Ltd. (505)
Parpinelli TECNON — World Petrochemical Industry Data Bank (799)
University of Western Ontario — Systems Analysis, Control and Design Activity (1088)

Petroleum and petroleum technology
Alberta Research Council — Alberta Oil Sands Information Centre (13)
Brown's Geological Information Service Ltd. (113)
Canada — Department of Energy, Mines and Resources — Canada Centre for Mineral and Energy Technology — Technology Information Division (131)
French Petroleum Institute — Documentation Center (387)
Independent Chemical Information Services Ltd. (505)
National Elf Aquitaine Company — Documentary Information Service — STATSID (723)
Norwegian Center for Informatics (767)
Norwegian Petroleum Directorate — INFOIL II (769)
Norwegian Petroleum Directorate — Oil Index (770)
Organisation for Economic Co-Operation and Development — International Energy Agency — International Oil Market Information System (784)
Sharp Associates Limited (871)

Petroleum spills SEE: Oil spills

Petrology SEE: Rocks

Pharmacology SEE: Pharmacy and pharmacology

Pharmacy and pharmacology (See also Drugs)
ADIS Press Australasia Pty Ltd. — ADIS Drug Information Retrieval System (5)
Data Bank for Medicaments (257)
Derwent Publications Ltd. — Patents Documentation Services (275)
Derwent Publications Ltd. — Pharmaceutical Literature Documentation (277)
Derwent Publications Ltd. — Veterinary Literature Documentation (278)
Drug Information Pharmacists Group — Pharmline (285)
Elsevier Science Publishers B.V. — Biomedical Division — Excerpta Medica (296)
Germany — Ministry of Youth, Family and Health — German Institute for Medical Documentation and Information (428)
Gothard House Group of Companies, Ltd. (432)
IMS A.G. — MIDAS (504)
Japan Pharmaceutical Information Center (634)
Medical-Pharmaceutical Publishing Company (693)
Mitaka — JAPANSCAN (712)
People's Republic of China — Institute of Scientific and Technical Information of China (801)
Pergamon Press — Current Awareness in Biological Sciences (803)
Pharma Documentation Ring (804)
Pharma Documentation Service (805)
Pharmaceutical Society of Great Britain — Martindale Online (806)
Royal Society of Chemistry — Information Services — Current Biotechnology Abstracts (854)
Survey Force Ltd. (907)

Philosophy
France — National Center for Scientific Research — Documentation Center for Human Sciences (355)
Society of Metaphysicians Ltd. — Information Services (882)
University of Dusseldorf — Research Division for Philosophy Information and Documentation — Philosophy Information Service (1048)

Phonograph records SEE: Music and music industry

Photocomposition (See also Computerized typesetting)
Alphatext, Inc. (20)
Hartmann & Heenemann — Computer Composition Center (476)

Photocopying SEE: Copying and duplicating

Physically handicapped SEE: Handicapped

Physics (See also Nuclear science)
France — National Center for Scientific Research — Scientific and Technical Documentation Center (356)
Information Center for Energy, Physics, Mathematics (521)
Institute of Physics and Energy — Nuclear Data Center (546)
Institution of Electrical Engineers — INSPEC (549)
Japan Information Center of Science and Technology (632)
Organisation for Economic Co-Operation and Development — Nuclear Energy Agency — NEA Data Bank (785)
Queen's University of Belfast — Department of Computer Science — Database on Atomic and Molecular Physics (835)

Physics, astronomical SEE: Astrophysics

Physics, geological SEE: Geophysics

Physics, high energy
France — Atomic Energy Commission — Saclay Nuclear Research Center — Documentation Center (339)
German Electron-Synchrotron — DESY Scientific Documentation and Information Service (396)
Information Center for Energy, Physics, Mathematics (521)

Physics, plasma
France — Atomic Energy Commission — Saclay Nuclear Research Center — Documentation Center (339)

Great Britain — Atomic Energy Authority — Culham Laboratory — Plasma Physics Library and Information Service   (438)
University of Paris-South — Gases and Plasmas Physics Laboratory — GAPHYOR   (1063)

Physics, solid state (See also Semiconductors)
Institution of Electrical Engineers — INSPEC — Electronic Materials Information Service   (550)

Physics, terrestrial SEE: Geophysics

Physiography SEE: Geomorphology

Physiology
Pergamon Press — Current Awareness in Biological Sciences   (803)

Phytopathology SEE: Plant pathology

Pipelines
BHRA, The Fluid Engineering Centre — Information Services   (86)
Pont-a-Mousson Research Center — Industrial Documentation Service — BIIPAM-CTIF Data Base   (820)
The Welding Institute — Information Services   (1106)

Placement, career SEE: Career placement

Plains, Great SEE: Great Plains

Planets
Union of Soviet Socialist Republics — Academy of Sciences of the U.S.S.R. — Institute for Theoretical Astronomy — Minor Planets, Comets, and Satellites Department   (997)

Planning, city SEE: City planning

Planning, regional SEE: Regional planning

Planning, urban SEE: City planning

Plant pathology
Commonwealth Agricultural Bureaux — CAB Abstracts   (229)
Germany — Federal Biological Research Center for Agriculture and Forestry — Documentation Center for Phytomedicine   (409)

Plant science SEE: Botany

Plasma physics SEE: Physics, plasma

Plastics
Center for Scientific and Technical Research for the Metal Manufacturing Industry — Fabrimetal   (187)
Derwent Publications Ltd. — Patents Documentation Services   (275)
German Plastics Institute — Information and Documentation Services   (402)
Rubber and Plastics Research Association of Great Britain — RAPRA Information Centre   (858)

Plumbing (See also Sanitary engineering)
Building Services Research and Information Association — BSRIA Information Centre   (119)

Poisons SEE: Toxicology

Polar regions
Arctic Institute of North America — Arctic Science and Technology Information System   (26)
Boreal Institute for Northern Studies — Library Services   (95)
Memorial University of Newfoundland — Ocean Engineering Information Centre   (694)

Police science SEE: Crime and criminals; Law enforcement

Political science
Association of Social Sciences Institutes — Social Sciences Information Center   (43)
British Broadcasting Corporation — BBC Data   (104)
Datasolve Ltd. — World Reporter   (265)
European Consortium for Political Research — Data Information Service   (310)
Foundation for Science and Politics — Research Institute for International Politics and Security — Library and Documentation System   (337)
French Documentation — Political and Current Events Information Bank   (384)
Great Britain — House of Commons Library — Parliamentary On-Line Information System   (459)
International Committee for Social Science Information and Documentation   (571)
University of Milan — Higher Institute of Sociology — Data and Program Archive for the Social Sciences   (1058)
York University — Institute for Behavioural Research   (1120)

Pollution (See also Environment)
Electricite de France — Office of Study and Research — Information and Documentation Systems Department — EDF-DOC Data Base   (295)
Japan — Environment Agency — National Institute for Environmental Studies — Environmental Information Division   (626)
United Nations Environment Programme — Industry and Environment Office — Industry and Environment Data Base   (1024)
United Nations Environment Programme — INFOTERRA   (1025)

Pollution, air
Germany — Federal Environmental Agency — Environmental Information and Documentation System   (411)
K-Konsult — VA-NYTT   (637)
North Rhine-Westphalia Institute for Air Pollution Control — Literature Information System   (765)
Quebec Ministry of the Environment — Documentation Center — Envirodoq   (832)

Pollution, marine
France — National Center for Ocean Utilization — National Bureau for Ocean Data   (347)
France — National Center for Ocean Utilization — National Bureau for Ocean Data — CNEXO-BNDO Data Base   (350)
France — National Center for Ocean Utilization — National Bureau for Ocean Data — POLUMAT   (353)
Japan — Maritime Safety Agency — Hydrographic Department — Japan Oceanographic Data Center   (628)
Marine Biological Association of the United Kingdom — Marine Pollution Information Centre   (684)
Maritime Information Centre/CMO   (685)
Ship Research Institute of Norway — Ship Abstracts   (872)
United Nations Educational, Scientific and Cultural Organization — Intergovernmental Oceanographic Commission — Marine Environmental Data Information Referral System   (1020)

Pollution, noise
Germany — Federal Environmental Agency — Environmental Information and Documentation System   (411)
K-Konsult — VA-NYTT   (637)
North Rhine-Westphalia Institute for Air Pollution Control — Literature Information System   (765)
Norwegian Center for Informatics   (767)

Pollution, oil SEE: Oil spills

Pollution, water (See also Pollution, marine)
Asian Institute of Technology — Regional Documentation Center — Environmental Sanitation Information Center   (31)
Canada — Environment Canada — Inland Waters Directorate — WATDOC   (140)
Canada — Environment Canada — Inland Waters Directorate — Water Quality Branch — National Water Quality Data Bank   (141)
Dortmund Institute for Water Research — Data Bank on Substances Harmful to Water   (284)
French Water Study Association — National Water Information Center   (391)
Germany — Federal Environmental Agency — Environmental Information and Documentation System   (411)
Great Britain — Water Research Centre — Information Service on Toxicity and Biodegradability   (463)
Great Britain — Water Research Centre — Library and Information Services   (464)
K-Konsult — VA-NYTT   (637)
Quebec Ministry of the Environment — Documentation Center — Envirodoq   (832)
South Africa — South African Water Information Centre   (887)

Polymers and polymerization (See also Macromolecules)
Derwent Publications Ltd. — Patents Documentation Services   (275)
German Plastics Institute — Information and Documentation Services   (402)
International Company for Documentation in Chemistry   (572)
Rubber and Plastics Research Association of Great Britain — RAPRA Information Centre   (858)

Population (See also Census; Family planning; Vital statistics)
Australian National University — Research School of Social Sciences — Australian Demographic Data Bank   (60)
Bank Society — General Documentation — SGB Data Base   (73)
British Columbia Ministry of Industry and Small Business Development — Central Statistics Bureau   (106)
Canada — Statistics Canada — Canadian Socio-Economic Information Management System   (159)

Compusearch Market and Social Research Ltd. (236)
Computer Sciences of Australia Pty. Ltd. — Network Services Division — INFOBANK (237)
France — National Institute of Statistics and Economic Studies — Documentation Division — SPHINX Data Base (363)
France — National Institute of Statistics and Economic Studies — Local Area Data Bank (365)
Great Britain — Central Statistical Office — CSO Macro-Economic Data Bank (449)
Hungary — Central Statistical Office (493)
International Center for Higher Studies in Mediterranean Agronomy — Socioeconomic Data Bank on the Mediterranean Countries (564)
Nihon Keizai Shimbun, Inc. — Databank Bureau — Nikkei Economic Electronic Databank System-Time Sharing (754)
Sharp Associates Limited (871)
SLAMARK International (878)
United Nations — Economic and Social Commission for Asia and the Pacific — Population Division — Population Clearing-house and Information Section (1003)
United Nations — Economic and Social Commission for Asia and the Pacific — Statistics Division — UN/ESCAP Statistical Information Services (1004)
United Nations — Economic Commission for Latin America — Latin American Demographic Center — Latin American Population Documentation System (1007)
United Nations — Food and Agriculture Organization — Economic and Social Department — Human Resources, Institutions and Agrarian Reform Division — Population Documentation Center (1010)
United Nations — Food and Agriculture Organization — Statistics Division — Interlinked Computerized Storage and Processing System of Food and Agricultural Data (1014)
University of Alberta — Department of Sociology — Population Research Laboratory (1035)
University of Umea — Demographic Data Base (1081)
World Health Organization — Division of Health Statistics — World Health Statistics Data Base (1110)

Postal service
Universal Postal Union — International Bureau — Statistics of Postal Services (1030)

Power, electric SEE: Electric power

Power, hydroelectric SEE: Hydroelectric power

Power plants
Technical Information Center — Electrical Engineering Documentation Center (960)

Power plants, nuclear SEE: Nuclear power plants

Power resources SEE: Energy resources

Predictions SEE: Forecasting

Press SEE: News and newspapers

Prices (See also Economics)
Canada — Statistics Canada — Canadian Socio-Economic Information Management System (159)
France — National Institute of Statistics and Economic Studies — Information System for the Economy (364)
Great Britain — Department of Trade and Industry — Business Statistics Office (454)
Nihon Keizai Shimbun, Inc. — Databank Bureau — Nikkei Economic Electronic Databank System-Time Sharing (754)
SLAMARK International (878)

Printing
Great Britain — British Library — Reference Division — Eighteenth Century Short Title Catalogue (443)
Nineteenth Century Short Title Catalogue Project (757)
Pira: Research Association for the Paper and Board, Printing and Packaging Industries — Comprehensive Information Services (812)
Pira: Research Association for the Paper and Board, Printing and Packaging Industries — Printing and Information Technology Division (813)

Production engineering
Production Engineering Research Association of Great Britain — Information Services (826)
Technical Information Center — Mechanical Engineering Documentation (961)
VDI-Verlag GmbH — VDI News Data Base (1096)

Programs, computer SEE: Computer programs

Properties, thermodynamic SEE: Thermodynamic properties

Properties, thermophysical SEE: Thermophysical properties

Protection, consumer SEE: Consumer protection

Protective coatings
Paint Research Association — Information Department — World Surface Coatings Abstracts (792)
Pont-a-Mousson Research Center — Industrial Documentation Service — BIIPAM-CTIF Data Base (820)
Technical Center for Mechanical Industries — Documentation Center for Mechanics (957)

Psychiatry and psychoanalysis
University of Trier — Center for Psychological Information and Documentation (1078)

Psychology
Sweden — National Library for Psychology and Education (924)
University of Trier — Center for Psychological Information and Documentation (1078)

Public administration (See also Federal government; Municipal government)
African Training and Research Centre in Administration for Development — African Network of Administrative Information (7)
Center for the Study on Information Systems in Government (190)
I/S Datacentralen (497)

Public contracts SEE: Government contracts

Public health (See also Health care; Immunology)
Bulgaria — Medical Academy — Center for Scientific Information in Medicine and Health (120)
Czechoslovakia — Institute for Medical Information (250)
Elsevier Science Publishers B.V. — Biomedical Division — Excerpta Medica (296)
India — National Institute of Health and Family Welfare — Documentation Centre (508)
Institute for Documentation and Information in Social Medicine and Public Health (539)
World Health Organization — Division of Health Statistics — World Health Statistics Data Base (1110)

Public housing SEE: Housing

Public hygiene SEE: Public health

Public opinion polls (See also Social surveys)
Carleton University — Department of Sociology and Anthropology — Social Science Data Archives (178)
University of Sydney — Sample Survey Centre (1072)
York University — Institute for Behavioural Research (1120)

Public records
Canada — Public Archives of Canada — Machine Readable Archives Division (158)

Public welfare (See also Social service)
Canada — Health and Welfare Canada — Policy, Planning and Information Branch — A Network of Social Security Information Resources (145)

Publishing
Bibliographic Publishing Co. (87)
Esselte Group of Booksellers — Esselte Documentation System (302)
International Electronic Publishing Research Centre (577)
Library Association Publishing Ltd. — Library and Information Science Abstracts (663)
Orna/Stevens Consultancy (788)
Pira: Research Association for the Paper and Board, Printing and Packaging Industries — Comprehensive Information Services (812)
Saur Verlag (863)
University of Leicester — Primary Communications Research Centre (1054)

Pulpwood SEE: Paper and paper technology

Pumping machinery
BHRA, The Fluid Engineering Centre — Information Services (86)

Qatar
Tel-Aviv University — Shiloah Research Center for Middle Eastern and African Studies — Documentation System — Mideast File (970)

Quantum field theory
German Electron-Synchrotron — DESY Scientific Documentation and Information Service (396)

Quebec
IST-Informatheque Inc. (619)
Microfor Inc. (704)
Quebec Ministry of Education — Library Headquarters — Point de Repere (831)
Quebec Ministry of the Environment — Documentation Center — Envirodoq (832)
Quebec National Library — FMQ (833)

Radio broadcasting
BBM Bureau of Measurement (78)
France — National Telecommunications Research Center — Interministerial Documentation Service — TELEDOC (367)
International Telecommunication Union (606)

Radioactive wastes
Great Britain — Atomic Energy Authority — Atomic Energy Research Establishment, Harwell — Harwell Central Information Service (434)

Railroads
International Railway Union — Documentation Bureau (600)

Rain-making
Israel — National Center of Scientific and Technological Information (616)

Rapid transit SEE: Urban transportation

Reactions, chemical SEE: Chemical reactions

Reactors, nuclear SEE: Nuclear reactors

Recordings, phonograph SEE: Music and music industry

Records management
Nichols Applied Management (752)
Stacs Information Systems Ltd. (897)
Systemhouse Ltd. — MINISIS (953)

Records, medical SEE: Medical records

Records, public SEE: Public records

Refrigeration and air conditioning
Building Services Research and Information Association — BSRIA Information Centre (119)
International Institute of Refrigeration — Documentary Service (590)

Refugees
International Refugee Integration Resource Centre (602)

Regional planning (See also City planning; Land use)
Brazil — Ministry of the Interior — Documentation Coordination Unit (100)
Fraunhofer Society — Information Center for Building and Physical Planning (373)
Fraunhofer Society — Information Center for Building and Physical Planning — Literature Compilations Data Base (376)
Fraunhofer Society — Information Center for Building and Physical Planning — PASCALBAT Data Base (377)
Fraunhofer Society — Information Center for Building and Physical Planning — Regional Planning, City Planning, Housing, Building Construction Data Base (379)
Fraunhofer Society — Information Center for Building and Physical Planning — Regional Planning, City Planning, Housing Research Projects Data Base (380)
Geo Abstracts Ltd. (393)
Greater London Council — Information Services Group (465)
International Council for Building Research, Studies and Documentation (573)
Norwegian Center for Informatics (767)
Piedmont Consortium for Information Systems (811)
Swedish Institute of Building Documentation (938)
URBAMET Network (1091)

Rehabilitation (See also Handicapped)
Institute for Documentation and Information in Social Medicine and Public Health (539)

Religion and theology (See also Bible)
Bar-Ilan University — Institute for Information Retrieval and Computational Linguistics — Responsa Project (74)
Christian Institutions Research and Documentation Center (205)
France — National Center for Scientific Research — Documentation Center for Human Sciences (355)

Remote sensing
Canada — Department of Energy, Mines and Resources — Canada Centre for Remote Sensing — Remote Sensing On-Line Retrieval System (132)
European Space Agency — Information Retrieval Service (317)
Geo Abstracts Ltd. (393)

Reports, technical SEE: Technical reports

Reprography SEE: Copying and duplicating

Research
Association of Social Sciences Institutes — Social Sciences Information Center (43)
Australia — Bureau of Transport Economics — BTE Information Systems (46)
Australia — Commonwealth Scientific and Industrial Research Organization — Central Information, Library and Editorial Section (47)
Australian Road Research Board — Australian Road Research Documentation (62)
Boris Kidric Institute of Nuclear Sciences — Laboratory for Information Systems (96)
Brunel University — Research Unit for the Blind — International Register of Research on Visual Disability (115)
Canada — National Research Council of Canada — Canada Institute for Scientific and Technical Information (152)
Commission of the European Communities — Environmental Research Projects Data Base (217)
Commission of the European Communities — Euro Abstracts (218)
European Conference of Ministers of Transport — International Co-operation in the Field of Transport Economics Documentation (309)
Finland — Technical Research Centre of Finland — Technical Information Service (330)
France — National Center for Scientific Research — Documentation Center for Human Sciences (355)
Fraunhofer Society — Information Center for Building and Physical Planning — Building Research Projects Data Base (374)
Fraunhofer Society — Information Center for Building and Physical Planning — Regional Planning, City Planning, Housing Research Projects Data Base (380)
Germany — Federal Environmental Agency — Environmental Information and Documentation System (411)
Germany — Ministry for Research and Technology — Ongoing Research Project Data Bank (424)
Great Britain — British Library — Research and Development Department (444)
India — Council of Scientific and Industrial Research — Indian National Scientific Documentation Centre (507)
International Centre for Scientific and Technical Information (565)
International Federation for Documentation — Research Referral Service (579)
Israel — National Center of Scientific and Technological Information (616)
Japan Information Center of Science and Technology (632)
Library Association Publishing Ltd. — CURRENT RESEARCH in Library & Information Science (661)
Linkoping University Library — NYTTFO (665)
National Science Council — Science and Technology Information Center (726)
Netherlands Organization for Applied Scientific Research — TNO Study and Information Center on Environmental Research — Environmental Research in the Netherlands (743)
Norwegian Center for Informatics (767)
Norwegian Computing Centre for the Humanities (768)
Norwegian Petroleum Directorate — INFOIL II (769)
Organisation for Economic Co-Operation and Development — International Development Information Network (781)
Organisation for Economic Co-Operation and Development — International Energy Agency — IEA Coal Research — Technical Information Service (782)
Philippines — National Science and Technology Authority — Scientific Clearinghouse and Documentation Services Division (808)
Royal Netherlands Academy of Arts and Sciences — Social Science Information and Documentation Center (847)
Sweden — National Swedish Environment Protection Board — Swedish Environmental Research Index (926)
Technical University of Wroclaw — Main Library and Scientific Information Center — System of Computerized Processing of Scientific Information (965)
University of Leicester — Primary Communications Research Centre (1054)
University of Regina — Canadian Plains Research Center — Information Services (1066)

University of Western Ontario — Social Science Computing Laboratory — Information Systems Programme (1087)

Research, agricultural SEE: Agricultural research

Research, defense SEE: Defense research and development

Research, educational SEE: Educational research

Research, industrial SEE: Industrial research

Research libraries
Denmark — Ministry of Cultural Affairs — National Advisory Council for Danish Research Libraries (269)
Finnish Council for Scientific Information and Research Libraries (331)
Nordic Council for Scientific Information and Research Libraries (762)
Sweden — Royal Library — Library Information System (931)

Research, medical SEE: Medical research

Research, nuclear SEE: Nuclear research

Research reports SEE: Technical reports

Resources, energy SEE: Energy resources

Resources, mineral SEE: Mineral resources

Resources, natural SEE: Natural resources

Resources, water SEE: Water resources

Retail trade
Admedia — Adfacts (6)
AVCOR (67)
Great Britain — Department of Trade and Industry — Business Statistics Office (454)
Market Location (686)
Society for the Study of Economic and Social Development — MERCATIS (881)

Retrieval, information SEE: Information retrieval

Retrieval systems, information storage and SEE: Information storage and retrieval systems

Rheology
Germany — Federal Institute for Materials Testing — Rheology and Tribology Documentation Center (417)

Road engineering SEE: Highway engineering

Rock mechanics
Asian Institute of Technology — Regional Documentation Center — Asian Information Center for Geotechnical Engineering (30)
Canada — Department of Energy, Mines and Resources — Canada Centre for Mineral and Energy Technology — Technology Information Division (131)
University of London — Imperial College of Science and Technology — Department of Mineral Resources Engineering — Rock Mechanics Information Service (1056)

Rockets and missiles (See also Satellites)
European Space Agency — European Space Research and Technology Center — Materials Data Retrieval System (316)

Rocks (See also Rock mechanics)
France — Bureau of Geological and Mining Research — National Geological Survey — Geological Information and Documentation Department (340)
Natural Environment Research Council — British Geological Survey — National Geochemical Data Bank (728)
University of Melbourne — Department of Geology — Computerised Library of Analysed Igneous Rocks (1057)

Rubber
German Plastics Institute — Information and Documentation Services (402)
Rubber and Plastics Research Association of Great Britain — RAPRA Information Centre (858)

Rural development
International Development Research Centre — Library (576)
United Nations — Economic and Social Commission for Asia and the Pacific — ESCAP Library — ESCAP Bibliographic Information System (1002)
United Nations — Food and Agriculture Organization — Economic and Social Department — Human Resources, Institutions and Agrarian Reform Division — Population Documentation Center (1010)
United Nations — Food and Agriculture Organization — Library and Documentation Systems Division — David Lubin Memorial Library (1013)

Rural education SEE: Education, rural

Russia SEE: Soviet Union

Rust SEE: Corrosion and anti-corrosives

Safety, flight SEE: Flight safety

Safety, industrial SEE: Industrial safety

Safety, nuclear SEE: Nuclear safety

Safety, occupational SEE: Industrial safety

Safety, traffic SEE: Traffic safety

Sales promotion SEE: Advertising and marketing

Saline water conversion
Germany — Federal Institute for Geosciences and Natural Resources — Marine Information and Documentation System (413)
Israel — National Center of Scientific and Technological Information (616)

Sanitary engineering
Asian Institute of Technology — Regional Documentation Center — Environmental Sanitation Information Center (31)
Pan American Health Organization — Pan American Centre for Sanitary Engineering & Environmental Sciences — Pan American Information & Documentation Network on Sanitary Engineering & Environmental Sciences (794)

Satellites (See also Rockets and missiles)
European Space Agency — Information Retrieval Service (317)
France — National Telecommunications Research Center — Interministerial Documentation Service — TELEDOC (367)

Saudi Arabia
Tel-Aviv University — Shiloah Research Center for Middle Eastern and African Studies — Documentation System — Mideast File (970)

Science and technology (See also Engineering; Research; and specific sciences such as Biology)
Argentina — National Council for Scientific and Technical Research — Argentine Center for Scientific and Technological Information (28)
Australia — Commonwealth Scientific and Industrial Research Organization — Central Information, Library and Editorial Section (47)
Australia — National Library of Australia (48)
Bangladesh National Scientific and Technical Documentation Centre (70)
Belgium — Royal Library of Belgium — National Center for Scientific and Technical Documentation (84)
Bolivia — National Scientific and Technological Documentation Center (93)
Brazil — National Council of Scientific and Technological Development — Brazilian Institute for Information in Science and Technology (103)
Canada — National Research Council of Canada — Canada Institute for Scientific and Technical Information (152)
Canada — National Research Council of Canada — Canada Institute for Scientific and Technical Information — Scientific Numeric Databases (155)
Chile — National Commission for Scientific and Technological Research — Directorate for Information and Documentation (202)
Finland — Technical Research Centre of Finland — Technical Information Service (330)
Finnish Council for Scientific Information and Research Libraries (331)
France — Interministerial Mission for Scientific and Technical Information (344)
France — National Center for Scientific Research — Scientific and Technical Documentation Center (356)
German Democratic Republic — Central Institute for Information and Documentation (395)
Helsinki University of Technology — University Library/National Library for Science and Technology (483)
Hungarian Academy of Sciences Library — Department for Informatics and Science Analysis (492)

Hungary — National Technical Information Centre and Library   (496)
India — Council of Scientific and Industrial Research — Indian National Scientific Documentation Centre   (507)
Indonesia — National Scientific Documentation Center   (512)
International Centre for Scientific and Technical Information   (565)
International Council of Scientific Unions — Committee on Data for Science and Technology   (574)
International Council of Scientific Unions Abstracting Board   (575)
International Information Service Ltd.   (588)
International Translations Centre   (608)
Iran — Ministry of Culture and Higher Education — Iranian Documentation Centre   (613)
Israel — National Center of Scientific and Technological Information   (616)
Japan Information Center of Science and Technology   (632)
Korea Institute for Industrial Economics and Technology   (645)
Library Association Publishing Ltd. — Current Technology Index   (662)
MIDORI Book Store Company   (709)
National Autonomous University of Mexico — Center for Scientific and Humanistic Information   (719)
National Science Council — Science and Technology Information Center   (726)
Netherlands Organization for Applied Scientific Research — Center for Information and Documentation   (739)
New Zealand — Department of Scientific and Industrial Research — DSIR Central Library   (748)
Norwegian Center for Informatics   (767)
Pakistan Scientific and Technological Information Centre   (793)
People's Republic of China — Institute of Scientific and Technical Information of China   (801)
Philippines — National Institute of Science and Technology — Division of Information and Documentation   (807)
Philippines — National Science and Technology Authority — Scientific Clearinghouse and Documentation Services Division   (808)
Poland — Institute for Scientific, Technical and Economic Information   (815)
Poland — Polish Academy of Sciences — Scientific Information Center   (816)
Portugal — National Institute for Scientific Research — Scientific and Technical Documentation Center   (821)
Romania — National Council for Science and Technology — National Institute for Information and Documentation   (843)
Royal Netherlands Academy of Arts and Sciences Library   (849)
South Africa — Council for Scientific and Industrial Research — Centre for Scientific and Technical Information   (885)
Spain — Higher Council for Scientific Research — Institute for Information and Documentation in Science and Technology   (890)
Swedish Delegation for Scientific and Technical Information   (937)
Tanzania — National Central Library — Tanzania National Documentation Centre   (955)
Technical Information-Documentation Consultants Ltd.   (963)
Technical University of Wroclaw — Main Library and Scientific Information Center — System of Computerized Processing of Scientific Information   (965)
Turkey — Scientific and Technical Research Council of Turkey — Turkish Scientific and Technical Documentation Center   (991)
Union of Soviet Socialist Republics — All-Union Institute of Scientific and Technical Information   (998)
University Library of Hannover and Technical Information Library   (1031)
University of Trondheim — Norwegian Institute of Technology — University Library   (1079)
University of Valencia — Biomedical Documentation and Information Center   (1082)
Yugoslav Center for Technical and Scientific Documentation   (1121)

Science communication
University of Leicester — Primary Communications Research Centre   (1054)

Science policy
United Nations Educational, Scientific and Cultural Organization — Division of Science and Technology Policies — Science and Technology Policies Information Exchange Programme   (1016)

Science research SEE: Research

Scientific and technical data
Canada — National Research Council of Canada — Canada Institute for Scientific and Technical Information — Scientific Numeric Databases   (155)
International Council of Scientific Unions — Committee on Data for Science and Technology   (574)
International Union of Geological Sciences — Commission on Storage, Automatic Processing and Retrieval of Geological Data   (609)
World Meteorological Organization — World Climate Programme Department — World Climate Data Information Referral Service   (1118)

Searching, computerized SEE: Computerized searching

Securities SEE: Stocks and bonds

Sedimentology
Canada — Environment Canada — Inland Waters Directorate — Water Resources Branch — Water Survey of Canada   (142)
France — Bureau of Geological and Mining Research — National Geological Survey — Geological Information and Documentation Department   (340)
Geo Abstracts Ltd.   (393)
Germany — Federal Institute for Geosciences and Natural Resources — Geoscience Literature Information Service   (412)

Seismology (See also Earthquakes)
Germany — Federal Institute for Geosciences and Natural Resources — Seismological Central Observatory GRF   (414)
Royal Norwegian Council for Scientific and Industrial Research — Norwegian Seismic Array   (850)

Semiconductors (See also Physics, solid state)
Zinc Development Association/Lead Development Association/Cadmium Association — Library and Abstracting Service   (1122)

Serials SEE: Periodicals

Ships and shipping (See also Marine transportation; Naval architecture)
Brassey's Publishers Ltd. — Brassey's Naval Record   (97)
Fairplay Publications Ltd. — Fairplay International Research Services   (324)
Kluwer Publishing Company — Juridical Databank   (641)
Lloyd's Shipping Information Services   (667)
Maritime Information Centre/CMO   (685)
Norwegian Center for Informatics   (767)
Ship Research Institute of Norway — Ship Abstracts   (872)

Shores and beaches SEE: Coasts

Silver
Commodities Research Unit Ltd.   (228)

Singapore
Sharp Associates Limited   (871)
University of Sydney Library — Bibliographic Information on Southeast Asia   (1073)

Social medicine SEE: Medical sociology

Social science
Association of Social Sciences Institutes — Social Sciences Information Center   (43)
Australia — National Library of Australia   (48)
Australian National University — Research School of Social Sciences — Social Science Data Archives   (61)
Belgium — Ministry of Economic Affairs — Fonds Quetelet Library Data Base   (81)
Canada — National Library of Canada   (147)
Carleton University — Department of Sociology and Anthropology — Social Science Data Archives   (178)
Center for Historical Social Research   (183)
Economic and Social Research Council — Data Archive   (291)
European Coordination Centre for Research and Documentation in Social Sciences   (311)
France — National Center for Scientific Research — Documentation Center for Human Sciences   (355)
France — National Institute of Statistics and Economic Studies — Documentation Division — SPHINX Data Base   (363)
Indian Council of Social Science Research — Social Science Documentation Centre   (511)
International Committee for Social Science Information and Documentation   (571)
Interuniversity Documentation and Information Center for the Social Sciences   (611)
Iran — Ministry of Culture and Higher Education — Iranian Documentation Centre   (613)
National Autonomous University of Mexico — Center for Scientific and Humanistic Information   (719)
Norwegian Research Council for Science and the Humanities — Norwegian Social Science Data Services   (771)
Royal Netherlands Academy of Arts and Sciences — Social Science Information and Documentation Center   (847)
Royal Netherlands Academy of Arts and Sciences — Social Science Information and Documentation Center — Steinmetz Archives   (848)
Spain — Higher Council for Scientific Research — Institute for Information and Documentation in the Social Sciences and Humanities   (891)

United Nations Educational, Scientific and Cultural Organization — Center for Social Science Research and Documentation for the Arab Region   (1015)
United Nations Educational, Scientific and Cultural Organization — Social and Human Science Documentation Centre   (1022)
University of British Columbia — Data Library   (1044)
University of Cologne — Central Archives for Empirical Social Research   (1045)
University of Milan — Higher Institute of Sociology — Data and Program Archive for the Social Sciences   (1058)
University of Sydney — Sample Survey Centre   (1072)
University of Waterloo — Faculty of Human Kinetics and Leisure Studies — Information Retrieval System for the Sociology of Leisure and Sport   (1085)
University of Western Ontario — Social Science Computing Laboratory — Information Systems Programme   (1087)
York University — Institute for Behavioural Research   (1120)

Social science data centers
European Consortium for Political Research — Data Information Service   (310)
International Federation of Data Organizations for the Social Sciences   (581)

Social security
Canada — Health and Welfare Canada — Policy, Planning and Information Branch — A Network of Social Security Information Resources   (145)

Social service (See also Public welfare)
Information London   (525)

Social surveys (See also Public opinion polls; Social science)
Australian National University — Research School of Social Sciences — Social Science Data Archives   (61)
Centre for the Study of Developing Societies — Data Unit   (196)
Economic and Social Research Council — Data Archive   (291)
Market Research Society — Market Research Abstracts   (687)
Overseas Data Service, Company, Ltd.   (789)
Research Services Ltd. — Pan European Survey   (839)
University of Cologne — Central Archives for Empirical Social Research   (1045)
University of Sydney — Sample Survey Centre   (1072)

Social welfare SEE: Public welfare

Social work SEE: Social service

Societies SEE: Associations

Sociology (See also Social service)
Association of Social Sciences Institutes — Social Sciences Information Center   (43)
University of Alberta — Department of Sociology — Population Research Laboratory   (1035)
University of Trier — Center for Psychological Information and Documentation   (1078)
York University — Institute for Behavioural Research   (1120)

Sociology, medical SEE: Medical sociology

Software SEE: Computer programs

Soil mechanics
Asian Institute of Technology — Regional Documentation Center — Asian Information Center for Geotechnical Engineering   (30)
CITIS Ltd.   (208)
University of London — Imperial College of Science and Technology — Department of Mineral Resources Engineering — Rock Mechanics Information Service   (1056)

Soil sciences
Bavarian Ministry for Food, Agriculture and Forestry — Bavarian Agricultural Information System   (76)
Commonwealth Agricultural Bureaux — CAB Abstracts   (229)
France — Bureau of Geological and Mining Research — National Geological Survey — Geological Information and Documentation Department   (340)
France — Bureau of Geological and Mining Research — National Geological Survey — Subsoil Data Bank   (341)
France — National Institute of Agronomic Research — Soil Science Laboratory — Soil Studies Service   (362)
Germany — Center for Agricultural Documentation and Information   (408)
Natural Environment Research Council — British Geological Survey — National Geochemical Data Bank   (728)
Netherlands Soil Survey Institute — Soil Information System   (746)

Solar energy
Alberta Research Council — Solar and Wind Energy Research Program Information Centre   (16)
Asian Institute of Technology — Regional Documentation Center — Renewable Energy Resources Information Center   (33)
Commonwealth Regional Renewable Energy Resources Information System   (230)
Riso National Laboratory — Riso Library   (842)

Solid state physics SEE: Physics, solid state

Solid wastes SEE: Wastes, solid

South America SEE: Latin America

Southeast Asia
University of Sydney Library — Bibliographic Information on Southeast Asia   (1073)

Soviet Union
University of Alberta — Computing Services — Information Systems Group   (1033)

Space flight SEE: Astronautics

Space technology (See also Astronautics; Rockets and missiles; Satellites)
European Space Agency — European Space Research and Technology Center — Materials Data Retrieval System   (316)
European Space Agency — Information Retrieval Service   (317)
Information Center for Energy, Physics, Mathematics   (521)

Spacecraft SEE: Rockets and missiles; Satellites

Spanish America SEE: Latin America

Specialties, medical SEE: Medical specialties

Specifications (See also Standards)
Construction Specifications Canada — National Master Specification   (242)
European Space Agency — Information Retrieval Service   (317)
French Association for Standardization — Data Bases Service — Automated Standards and Regulations Information Online   (382)
German Standards Institute — German Information Center for Technical Rules   (407)

Spectrometry, mass SEE: Mass spectrometry

Spectroscopy
Group for the Advancement of Spectroscopic Methods and Physicochemical Analysis — Information Center for Spectroscopic and Physicochemical Analysis   (466)
Union of Soviet Socialist Republics — Academy of Sciences of the U.S.S.R. — Astronomical Council Data Center — Management System for Astronomical Data in Machine-Readable Form   (995)

Spectroscopy, infrared SEE: Infrared spectroscopy

Spills, oil SEE: Oil spills

Sports
Coaching Association of Canada — Sport Information Resource Centre   (210)
French Press Agency — Telematics Department — AGORA   (388)
Germany — Federal Institute for Sports Science — Documentation and Information Division — Sport and Sports-Scientific Information System   (420)
Sports Council — Information Centre   (896)
University of Alberta — Computing Services — Information Systems Group   (1033)
University of Waterloo — Department of Recreation — Leisure Studies Data Bank   (1084)
University of Waterloo — Faculty of Human Kinetics and Leisure Studies — Information Retrieval System for the Sociology of Leisure and Sport   (1085)

Standards
British Standards Institution — Information Department   (111)
Central American Research Institute for Industry — Division of Documentation and Information   (193)
Finnish Standards Association — Information Service   (334)
French Association for Standardization — Data Bases Service — Automated Standards and Regulations Information Online   (382)
German Standards Institute — German Information Center for Technical Rules   (407)
International Information Center for Terminology   (587)
International Organization for Standardization — ISO Information Network   (599)

Norwegian Standards Association — STANDARD (772)
Polish Committee of Standardization, Measures, and Quality — Centre for Information on Standardization and Metrology (817)
Standards Council of Canada — Standards Information Service (898)
Swedish Standards Institution — REGIS (940)
Technical Indexes Ltd. (958)

Stars
Strasbourg Observatory — Stellar Data Center (905)

Statistics (See also Census; Econometrics; Mathematics)
Australian Bureau of Statistics (52)
Belgium — Ministry of Economic Affairs — National Statistical Institute (82)
British Columbia Ministry of Industry and Small Business Development — Central Statistics Bureau (106)
Canada — Statistics Canada — Canadian Socio-Economic Information Management System (159)
Canada — Statistics Canada — Canadian Socio-Economic Information Management System — Telichart (160)
Commission of the European Communities — Statistical Office of the European Communities — CRONOS Data Bank (225)
Computer Sciences of Australia Pty. Ltd. — Network Services Division — INFOBANK (237)
Hungary — Central Statistical Office (493)
International Association for Statistical Computing (556)
Madagascar — Ministry of Finance and Economy — National Institute of Statistics and Economic Research (681)
Netherlands Organization for Applied Scientific Research — Institute TNO for Mathematics, Information Processing and Statistics (741)
New Zealand — Department of Statistics — Information Network for Official Statistics (749)
Norway — Ministry of Finances and Customs — Central Bureau of Statistics (766)
Sharp Associates Limited (871)
SLAMARK International (878)
Sweden — Statistics Sweden — Statistical Data Bases Unit (932)
United Nations — Food and Agriculture Organization — Statistics Division — Interlinked Computerized Storage and Processing System of Food and Agricultural Data (1014)
University of Warwick Library — Warwick Statistics Service (1083)

Statistics, economic SEE: Econometrics

Statistics, vital SEE: Vital statistics

Steel (See also Iron; Metallurgy)
Center of Experimental Metallurgy — Iron and Steel Documentation Service (192)
Commission of the European Communities — Euro Abstracts (218)
Commodities Research Unit Ltd. (228)
Conference Board of Canada — Applied Economic Research and Information Centre — AERIC System (238)
Dobra Iron and Steel Research Institute — Informetal (281)
German Iron and Steel Engineers Association — Information System on Production Plants for Iron & Steel — PLANTFACTS (398)
German Iron and Steel Engineers Association — Steel Information System (399)
TESS Search Service (979)

Steel industry
Bird Associates (89)
German Iron and Steel Engineers Association — Information System on Production Plants for Iron & Steel — PLANTFACTS (398)

Stocks and bonds (See also Investments)
American College in Paris — Service Calvados (22)
Bonnier Business Publishing Group — AffarsData (94)
Communication Services Ltd. — Viewdata Services (231)
Cumulus Systems Ltd. (249)
DAFSA (251)
Dataline Inc. (262)
Datastream International Ltd. (267)
Extel Computing Ltd. — EXSHARE (321)
Extel Statistical Services Ltd. — EXBOND (322)
Faxtel Information Systems Ltd. — Marketfax (326)
Financial Times Business Information Ltd. — Business Information Service (328)
French Stockbrokers Society — Information and Documentation Center (389)
FRI Information Services Ltd. (392)
The Globe and Mail — Info Globe (430)
ICV Information Systems Ltd. — CitiService (500)
The London International Financial Futures Exchange Ltd. (672)
London Over the Counter Market (673)
LymBurner & Sons Ltd. — Economist's Statistics (679)
MacLean-Hunter Ltd. — Financial Post Division — Financial Post Investment Data Bank (680)
McCarthy Information Ltd. (690)
Nihon Keizai Shimbun, Inc. — Databank Bureau — Nikkei Economic Electronic Databank System-Time Sharing (754)
Nihon Keizai Shimbun, Inc. — Quotation Information Center K.K. (755)
Nomura Research Institute — Information Service and Development Department — NRI/E Japan Economic & Business Data Bank (760)
Sharp Associates Limited (871)
Specialist Software Ltd. (895)
The Stock Exchange — Technical Services Department — TOPIC (902)
Stockholm School of Economics — Economics Research Institute — FINDATA (903)
Telekurs Ag — Investdata System (975)
Tijl Datapress (982)
Toronto Stock Exchange — Data Products (986)
University of New South Wales — Australian Graduate School of Management — Centre for Research in Finance (1060)

Storage and retrieval systems, information SEE: Information storage and retrieval systems

Storage batteries SEE: Batteries

Structural engineering
CITIS Ltd. (208)
ESDU International Limited (299)

Structure, chemical SEE: Chemical structure

Structure, molecular SEE: Molecular structure

Structure, nuclear SEE: Nuclear structure

Students
International Association for the Evaluation of Educational Achievement — IEA Data Bank (557)

Subject cataloging
Great Britain — British Library — Bibliographic Services Division — Subject Systems Office — Preserved Context Index System (441)
University of Toronto — Faculty of Library and Information Science Library — Subject Analysis Systems Collection (1077)

Sudan
Tel-Aviv University — Shiloah Research Center for Middle Eastern and African Studies — Documentation System — Mideast File (970)

Surgery SEE: Medicine

Surveys, social SEE: Social surveys

Sweden
Bonnier Business Publishing Group — AffarsData (94)
BTJ (116)
DataArkiv AB (260)
Pressurklipp — Swedish Market Information Bank (824)
Stockholm School of Economics — Economics Research Institute — FINDATA (903)
Sweden — Royal Library — Library Information System (931)
Sweden — Statistics Sweden — Statistical Data Bases Unit (932)
Sweden — Swedish National Road Administration — Technical Division — Road Data Bank (933)
TT Newsbank (990)
University of Umea — Demographic Data Base (1081)

Syria
Tel-Aviv University — Shiloah Research Center for Middle Eastern and African Studies — Documentation System — Mideast File (970)

Systems, communications SEE: Communications

Systems, information storage and retrieval SEE: Information storage and retrieval systems

Taxation
DataArkiv AB (260)
Morgan Grenfell & Co. Ltd. — Interfisc (715)
SYDONI S.A. (949)

SUBJECT INDEX

Taxonomy
   BIOSIS, U.K. Ltd. — Zoological Record (88)

Teacher education SEE: Education, teacher

Teaching aids SEE: Audiovisual material

Technical components
   European Space Agency — Information Retrieval Service (317)
   Technical Indexes Ltd. (958)
   Technical Information Center — Electrical Engineering Documentation Center (960)

Technical reports
   Studsvik Energiteknik AB — Report Collection Index (906)

Technology SEE: Engineering; Science and technology; Technology transfer

Technology transfer (See also New products)
   Constellate Consultants Ltd. (241)
   European Association for the Transfer of Technologies, Innovation and Industrial Information (306)
   FLA Groupe La Creatique (336)
   Technology Resource Center — Technobank Program (967)
   Tecnomedia (968)
   Transinove International (987)
   World Meteorological Organization — Commission for Hydrology — Operational Hydrology Programme — Hydrological Operational Multipurpose Subprogramme (1117)

Telecommunications (See also Communications)
   Cawkell Information & Technology Services Ltd. (180)
   Electricite de France — Office of Study and Research — Information and Documentation Systems Department — EDF-DOC Data Base (295)
   Eurodata Foundation (303)
   France — National Telecommunications Research Center — Interministerial Documentation Service — TELEDOC (367)
   Intelmatique (552)
   International Telecommunication Union (606)
   International Telecommunications Users Group (607)
   Overseas Data Service, Company, Ltd. (789)

Telephony
   France — National Telecommunications Research Center — Interministerial Documentation Service — TELEDOC (367)
   International Telecommunication Union (606)

Teletext SEE: Videotex/Teletext

Television broadcasting
   BBM Bureau of Measurement (78)
   France — National Telecommunications Research Center — Interministerial Documentation Service — TELEDOC (367)

Teratology
   Sweden — Karolinska Institute Library and Information Center (921)

Terminology
   Commission of the European Communities — Specialized Department for Terminology and Computer Applications — EURODICAUTOM (223)
   International Information Center for Terminology (587)
   Netherlands — Ministry of Foreign Affairs — Translations Branch — Terminology and Documentation Section (732)
   Quebec — French Language Board — Terminology Bank of Quebec (830)
   Siemens AG — Language Services Department — Terminology Evaluation and Acquisition Method (876)
   TESS Search Service (979)
   University of Bergen — Department of Scandinavian Languages and Literature — Norwegian Term Bank (1040)

Terrestrial physics SEE: Geophysics

Testing, educational SEE: Educational testing

Testing, non-destructive SEE: Non-destructive testing

Text editing
   Alphatext, Inc. (20)
   Langton Electronic Publishing Systems Ltd. (649)
   QL Systems Limited (828)
   Siemens AG — Data Processing Division — GOLEM (874)

Textiles
   French Textile Institute — Textile Information Treatment Users' Service (390)
   Shirley Institute — Textile Information Services (873)
   Textile and Clothing Information Centre (980)
   University of Alberta — Computing Services — Information Systems Group (1033)

Theology SEE: Religion and theology

Thermal energy (See also Geothermal energy; Solar energy)
   French Institute of Energy — Energy Studies and Information Center (386)
   Riso National Laboratory — Riso Library (842)

Thermochemistry
   McGill University — Faculty of Engineering — Department of Mining and Metallurgical Engineering — Facility for the Analysis of Chemical Thermodynamics (691)
   Thermodata Association — Thermodata-Thermdoc Data Bank (981)

Thermodynamic properties
   Great Britain — Department of Industry — National Physical Laboratory — Division of Materials Applications — Metallurgical and Thermochemical Data Service (451)
   University of Western Ontario — Systems Analysis, Control and Design Activity (1088)

Thermodynamics
   French Petroleum Institute — Documentation Center (387)
   Great Britain — Department of Industry — National Physical Laboratory — Division of Materials Applications — Metallurgical and Thermochemical Data Service (451)
   Institution of Chemical Engineers — Physical Property Data Service (548)
   International Institute of Refrigeration — Documentary Service (590)
   McGill University — Faculty of Engineering — Department of Mining and Metallurgical Engineering — Facility for the Analysis of Chemical Thermodynamics (691)
   Thermodata Association — Thermodata-Thermdoc Data Bank (981)

Thermophysical properties
   Dutch State Mines — TISDATA (286)
   German Society for Chemical Equipment — Information Systems and Data Banks Department — DECHEMA Substance Data Service (404)
   Institution of Chemical Engineers — Physical Property Data Service (548)
   Uhde GmbH — Uhde Thermophysical Properties Program Package (992)
   Union of Soviet Socialist Republics — Academy of Sciences of the U.S.S.R. — Institute for High Temperatures — Thermophysical Properties Center (996)

Thesauri (See also Indexing)
   University of Toronto — Faculty of Library and Information Science Library — Subject Analysis Systems Collection (1077)

Theses SEE: Dissertations, academic

Third World SEE: Developing nations

Timber SEE: Forest products

Topography (See also Maps)
   Natural Environment Research Council — British Geological Survey — National Geochemical Data Bank (728)

Toronto, Ontario
   Toronto Department of the City Clerk — Computerized Text Processing and Retrieval System for City Council Information (985)

Tourist trade
   Canada — Department of Industry, Trade & Commerce — Office of Tourism — Tourism Research and Data Centre (137)
   English Tourist Board — Information Unit — Tourtel (297)
   Hanover Press — Viewdata Services (473)
   Newfoundland Telephone — Tourism Newfoundland (751)

Town planning SEE: City planning

Toxicology
   Belgium — Ministry of Health — National Poison Control Center (83)

Derwent Publications Ltd. — Pest Control Literature Documentation   (276)
Elsevier Science Publishers B.V. — Biomedical Division — Excerpta Medica   (296)
Pergamon Press — Current Awareness in Biological Sciences   (803)
Royal Society of Chemistry — Information Services   (851)
Royal Society of Chemistry — Information Services — Chemical Hazards in Industry   (853)
Royal Society of Chemistry — Information Services — Laboratory Hazards Bulletin   (855)
Sweden — Karolinska Institute Library and Information Center   (921)
University of British Columbia — B.C. Hospital Programs Branch — Drug and Poison Information Centre   (1043)

Trade SEE: Commerce and trade; Foreign trade; Retail trade

Trade unions SEE: Labor

Trademarks
Canada Systems Group — Federal Systems Division — Trade Marks Data Base   (166)
Compu-Mark   (234)
Compu-Mark Ltd.   (235)
France — National Institute for Industrial Property — Office of Legal and Technical Documentation — JURINPI Data Base   (360)
Japan Patent Information Center   (633)

Traffic engineering (See also Highway engineering)
Great Britain — Departments of the Environment and Transport — Transport and Road Research Laboratory — Technical Information and Library Services   (455)
Sweden — National Road and Traffic Research Institute — Information and Documentation Section   (925)
Sweden — Swedish National Road Administration — Technical Division — Road Data Bank   (933)

Traffic safety
Great Britain — Departments of the Environment and Transport — Transport and Road Research Laboratory — Technical Information and Library Services   (455)
Organisation for Economic Co-Operation and Development — Road Transport Research Programme — International Road Research Documentation   (786)
Sweden — National Road and Traffic Research Institute — Information and Documentation Section   (925)
Sweden — Swedish National Road Administration — Technical Division — Road Data Bank   (933)
Swedish Council for Information on Alcohol and Other Drugs   (936)

Transfer of technology SEE: Technology transfer

Translation
Belgium — Royal Library of Belgium — National Center for Scientific and Technical Documentation   (84)
Canada — National Research Council of Canada — Canada Institute for Scientific and Technical Information   (152)
Center for Translation Documentation   (191)
Commission of the European Communities — Specialized Department for Terminology and Computer Applications — EURODICAUTOM   (223)
International Information Center for Terminology   (587)
International Translations Centre   (608)
Quebec — French Language Board — Terminology Bank of Quebec   (830)

Transportation (See also Highway engineering; Railroads)
Australia — Bureau of Transport Economics — BTE Information Systems   (46)
Austria — Federal Ministry of Buildings and Technology — Federal Research and Testing Establishment Arsenal — Road Research Documentation Center   (63)
Canada — Transport Canada — Library and Information Centre   (161)
European Conference of Ministers of Transport — International Co-operation in the Field of Transport Economics Documentation   (309)
Great Britain — Departments of the Environment and Transport — Transport and Road Research Laboratory — Technical Information and Library Services   (455)
Organisation for Economic Co-Operation and Development — Road Transport Research Programme — International Road Research Documentation   (786)
URBAMET Network   (1091)

Transportation, air SEE: Air transportation

Transportation, marine SEE: Marine transportation

Transportation, urban SEE: Urban transportation

Travel (See also Tourist trade)
Denmark Telecommunications Administration — Danish Teledata System   (272)
English Tourist Board — Information Unit — Tourtel   (297)
Great Britain — British Telecommunications — Prestel   (448)
Hanover Press — Viewdata Services   (473)
ItalCable — Direct Access to Remote Data Bases Overseas   (620)
Morgan-Grampian Plc. — M-G Videotex Services   (714)
University of Waterloo — Department of Recreation — Leisure Studies Data Bank   (1084)

Treaties
European Law Centre Ltd. — Eurolex   (314)
Morgan Grenfell & Co. Ltd. — Interfisc   (715)

Treatment, water SEE: Water treatment

Tribology
BHRA, The Fluid Engineering Centre — Information Services   (86)
ESDU International Limited   (299)
Germany — Federal Institute for Materials Testing — Rheology and Tribology Documentation Center   (417)

Tropics
Asian Institute of Technology — Regional Documentation Center — Renewable Energy Resources Information Center   (33)
France — National Center for Scientific Research — Documentation Center for Human Sciences   (355)
Group for the Study and Research of Tropical Agronomy — AGRITROP   (467)
Institute of Research on Fruits and Citrus Fruits — Documentation Center   (547)
Mexico — National Institute for Research on Biological Resources — INIREB Library   (702)
Royal Museum of Central Africa — Center for Informatics Applied to Development and Tropical Agriculture — Agroclimatology Data Bank   (846)
Royal Tropical Institute — Agricultural Information & Documentation Section   (857)

Tunisia
Center for Research and Studies on Mediterranean Societies   (186)

Turkey
Tel-Aviv University — Shiloah Research Center for Middle Eastern and African Studies — Documentation System — Mideast File   (970)

Typesetting, computerized SEE: Computerized typesetting

Underdeveloped countries SEE: Developing nations

Unemployment SEE: Labor

Union catalogs and lists
Argentina — National Council for Scientific and Technical Research — Argentine Center for Scientific and Technological Information   (28)
Australia — Commonwealth Scientific and Industrial Research Organization — Central Information, Library and Editorial Section   (47)
Australia — National Library of Australia   (48)
Australia — National Library of Australia — Australian Bibliographic Network   (49)
Australia — National Library of Australia — Australian MEDLINE Network   (50)
Belgium — Royal Library of Belgium — National Center for Scientific and Technical Documentation   (84)
Brazil — National Council of Scientific and Technological Development — Brazilian Institute for Information in Science and Technology   (103)
BTJ   (116)
Canada — Environment Canada — Library Services Branch — Environment Libraries Automated System   (144)
Canada — National Library of Canada   (147)
Canada — National Library of Canada — Public Services Branch — Union Catalogue of Serials Division   (151)
Canada — National Research Council of Canada — Canada Institute for Scientific and Technical Information   (152)
Centennial College — Bibliocentre   (182)
Central American Research Institute for Industry — Division of Documentation and Information   (193)
Consortium of Royal Library and University Libraries — Project for Integrated Catalogue Automation   (239)

Consortium of Royal Library and University Libraries — Project for Integrated Catalogue Automation — Netherlands Central Catalogue/Interlibrary Loan System (240)
Denmark — National Technological Library of Denmark — Automated Library Information System (270)
German Library Institute (400)
Hebrew University of Jerusalem — Automated Library Expandable Program Hebrew University of Jerusalem (478)
India — Council of Scientific and Industrial Research — Indian National Scientific Documentation Centre (507)
Indian Council of Social Science Research — Social Science Documentation Centre (511)
Indonesia — National Scientific Documentation Center (512)
Iran — Ministry of Culture and Higher Education — Iranian Documentation Centre (613)
Israel — National Center of Scientific and Technological Information (616)
London and South Eastern Library Region (670)
Metropolitan Toronto Library Board — Regional Bibliographic Products Department (699)
National Science Council — Science and Technology Information Center (726)
Pakistan Scientific and Technological Information Centre (793)
Philippines — National Science and Technology Authority — Scientific Clearinghouse and Documentation Services Division (808)
Portugal — National Institute for Scientific Research — Scientific and Technical Documentation Center (821)
Scotland — National Library of Scotland — Scottish Libraries Co-operative Automation Project (869)
South Africa — Council for Scientific and Industrial Research — Centre for Scientific and Technical Information (885)
SWALCAP (919)
Sweden — Royal Library — Library Information System (931)
Tanzania — National Central Library — Tanzania National Documentation Centre (955)
Turkey — Scientific and Technical Research Council of Turkey — Turkish Scientific and Technical Documentation Center (991)
University of Guelph Library — Cooperative Documents Network Project (1050)
University of Haifa Library — Haifa On-line Bibliographic Text System (1051)
University of New Brunswick Libraries — PHOENIX (1059)
University of Oslo — Royal University Library — Planning Department (1061)
University of Tasmania Library — Union List of Higher Degree Theses in Australian Libraries (1074)
UTLAS Inc. (1094)

Union of Soviet Socialist Republics SEE: Soviet Union

Unions SEE: Labor

United Arab Emirates
Tel-Aviv University — Shiloah Research Center for Middle Eastern and African Studies — Documentation System — Mideast File (970)

United Kingdom SEE: Great Britain

United Nations
United Nations — Advisory Committee for the Co-ordination of Information Systems (1001)
United Nations University — Referral Service System (1028)

United States
Sharp Associates Limited (871)

University education SEE: Education, higher

Uranium
Riso National Laboratory — Riso Library (842)

Urban planning SEE: City planning

Urban renewal (See also City planning)
Fraunhofer Society — Information Center for Building and Physical Planning (373)

Urban studies
Greater London Council — Information Services Group (465)

Urban transportation
European Conference of Ministers of Transport — International Co-operation in the Field of Transport Economics Documentation (309)

Vegetables SEE: Fruits and vegetables

Vehicles, electric SEE: Electric vehicles

Veterinary medicine
Commonwealth Agricultural Bureaux — CAB Abstracts (229)
Derwent Publications Ltd. — Veterinary Literature Documentation (278)
United Nations — Food and Agriculture Organization — International Information System for the Agricultural Sciences and Technology (1012)

Videotex/teletext
A.JOUR (1)
Alpha 460 Television Ltd. (18)
AVCOR (67)
AVS Intext Ltd. (69)
Baric Computing Services Ltd. — Baric Viewdata (75)
Canada — Department of Communications — Telidon Program (130)
Cawkell Information & Technology Services Ltd. (180)
Communication Services Ltd. — Viewdata Services (231)
Council for Educational Technology — Videotex Services Unit (247)
Dagg Associates (253)
Eastern Counties Newspapers — Eastel (287)
FLA Groupe La Creatique (336)
France — National Telecommunications Research Center — Interministerial Documentation Service — TELEDOC (367)
Fraser Videotex Services (369)
French Federation of Data Base Producers (385)
Image Base Videotex Design Inc. (502)
Infomart (518)
Intelmatique (552)
Langton Electronic Publishing Systems Ltd. (649)
Larratt and Associates Ltd. (650)
Learned Information Ltd. (654)
Legal Technology Group (656)
Library Association Publishing Ltd. — Library and Information Science Abstracts (663)
Logica UK Ltd. (668)
Management Consultants International, Inc. (682)
National Reprographic Centre for Documentation (725)
Nippon Telegraph & Telephone Public Corporation — CAPTAIN (759)
NORPAK Corporation (764)
ORACLE Teletext Ltd. (779)
Phippard & Associates Strategic & Technological Consulting, Inc. (810)
Polytechnical School of Montreal — Telidon Technology Development Center (819)
Socioscope Inc. (883)
Swiss Viewdata Information Providers Association (946)
Tayson Information Technology Inc. (956)
Tele-Direct Inc. (973)
VideoAccess (1099)
Videotex Industry Association Ltd. (1100)
Videotex Information Service Providers Association of Canada (1101)
Viewtel Services Ltd. (1102)

Viewdata SEE: Videotex/teletext

Virology
France — National Center for Scientific Research — Scientific Documentation Center in Oncology — CANCERNET (357)
World Health Organization — WHO Collaborating Centre for Collection and Evaluation of Data on Comparative Virology (1114)

Vital statistics (See also Census)
Australian Bureau of Statistics (52)
Australian National University — Research School of Social Sciences — Australian Demographic Data Bank (60)

Viticulture SEE: Grapes

Vocational education SEE: Education, vocational

Waste management
Asian Institute of Technology — Regional Documentation Center — Environmental Sanitation Information Center (31)
Canada — Environment Canada — Inland Waters Directorate — WATDOC (140)
Great Britain — Atomic Energy Authority — Atomic Energy Research Establishment, Harwell — Waste Management Information Bureau (437)
Great Britain — Water Research Centre — Information Service on Toxicity and Biodegradability (463)
Great Britain — Water Research Centre — Library and Information Services (464)
International Reference Center for Community Water Supply and Sanitation — Programme on Exchange and Transfer of Information

on Community Water Supply and Sanitation (601)
K-Konsult — VA-NYTT (637)

Wastes, radioactive SEE: Radioactive wastes

Wastes, solid (See also Waste management)
Germany — Federal Environmental Agency — Environmental Information and Documentation System (411)
K-Konsult — VA-NYTT (637)
Norwegian Center for Informatics (767)

Water desalination SEE: Saline water conversion

Water pollution SEE: Pollution, water

Water resources (See also Hydrology)
Canada — Environment Canada — Inland Waters Directorate — WATDOC (140)
Canada — Environment Canada — Inland Waters Directorate — Water Quality Branch — National Water Quality Data Bank (141)
Canada — Environment Canada — Inland Waters Directorate — Water Resources Branch — Water Survey of Canada (142)
Delft Hydraulics Laboratory — Information and Documentation Section (268)
France — National Center for Ocean Utilization — National Bureau for Ocean Data — DOCOCEAN (351)
French Water Study Association — National Water Information Center (391)
Germany — Federal Institute for Geosciences and Natural Resources — Geoscience Literature Information Service (412)
Great Britain — Water Research Centre — Library and Information Services (464)
International Reference Center for Community Water Supply and Sanitation — Programme on Exchange and Transfer of Information on Community Water Supply and Sanitation (601)
Netherlands Organization for Applied Scientific Research — Groundwater Survey (740)
Pan American Health Organization — Pan American Centre for Sanitary Engineering & Environmental Sciences — Pan American Information & Documentation Network on Sanitary Engineering & Environmental Sciences (794)
South Africa — South African Water Information Centre (887)
Sweden — Geological Survey of Sweden — Groundwater Documentation Section (920)

Water treatment
Asian Institute of Technology — Regional Documentation Center — Environmental Sanitation Information Center (31)
French Water Study Association — National Water Information Center (391)
Great Britain — Water Research Centre — Library and Information Services (464)
International Reference Center for Community Water Supply and Sanitation — Programme on Exchange and Transfer of Information on Community Water Supply and Sanitation (601)
K-Konsult — VA-NYTT (637)

Weapons, naval
Brassey's Publishers Ltd. — Brassey's Naval Record (97)

Weapons, nuclear
Royal Norwegian Council for Scientific and Industrial Research — Norwegian Seismic Array (850)

Weapons technology
Brassey's Publishers Ltd. — Brassey's Naval Record (97)

Weather SEE: Meteorology

Weeds
Commonwealth Agricultural Bureaux — CAB Abstracts (229)

Welding
Center for Scientific and Technical Research for the Metal Manufacturing Industry — Fabrimetal (187)
France — National Center for Scientific Research — Scientific and Technical Documentation Center (356)
Germany — Federal Institute for Materials Testing — Welding Documentation (418)
Technical Center for Mechanical Industries — Documentation Center for Mechanics (957)
The Welding Institute — Information Services (1106)

Welfare, public SEE: Public welfare

Wildlife (See also Zoology)
Canada — Environment Canada — Library Services Branch — Environment Libraries Automated System (144)

Great Britain — Institute of Terrestrial Ecology — Biological Records Centre (461)
Swiss Wildlife Information Service (947)
United Nations Environment Programme — INFOTERRA (1025)

Wind energy
Alberta Research Council — Solar and Wind Energy Research Program Information Centre (16)
Asian Institute of Technology — Regional Documentation Center — Renewable Energy Resources Information Center (33)
Commonwealth Regional Renewable Energy Resources Information System (230)
Riso National Laboratory — Riso Library (842)

Wine and wine making
International Food Information Service — VITIS-Viticulture and Enology Abstracts (585)

Women
City of London Polytechnic — Fawcett Library — BiblioFem (209)
University of Alberta — Computing Services — Information Systems Group (1033)
York University — Institute for Behavioural Research (1120)

Wood products SEE: Forest products

Wood pulp SEE: Paper and paper technology

Word processing
Langton Electronic Publishing Systems Ltd. (649)
Library Association Publishing Ltd. — Library and Information Science Abstracts (663)
National Reprographic Centre for Documentation (725)

Work SEE: Labor

World politics SEE: International relations

World trade SEE: Foreign trade

Xerography SEE: Copying and duplicating

Yemen
Tel-Aviv University — Shiloah Research Center for Middle Eastern and African Studies — Documentation System — Mideast File (970)

Zinc
Commodities Research Unit Ltd. (228)
Zinc Development Association/Lead Development Association/Cadmium Association — Library and Abstracting Service (1122)

Zoology (See also Wildlife)
BIOSIS, U.K. Ltd. — Zoological Record (88)
France — National Center for Scientific Research — Scientific and Technical Documentation Center (356)
Great Britain — Institute of Terrestrial Ecology — Biological Records Centre (461)
Mexico — National Institute for Research on Biological Resources — INIREB Library (702)